OFFICIAL

SCRABBLE
BRAND Crossword Game

LISTS

HarperCollins Publishers
Westerhill Road
Bishopbriggs
Glasgow
G64 2QT

Third edition 2011

Reprint 10 9 8 7 6 5 4 3 2 1 0

© HarperCollins Publishers 2004, 2005, 2006, 2008, 2011

ISBN 978-0-00-742563-1

www.collinslanguage.com

A catalogue record for this book is available from the British Library

Typeset by
Davidson Publishing Solutions, Glasgow

Printed in Great Britain by
Clays Ltd, St Ives plc

Scrabble Consultants
Darryl Francis
Allan Simmons

For the Publisher
Lucy Cooper
Kerry Ferguson
Elaine Higgleton

Computing Support
Thomas Callan

Contents

Introduction

Collins Scrabble Lists is the companion volume to Collins Official ScrabbleWords, the official word list for Scrabble. While Words contains the complete list of words that are valid in Scrabble, Scrabble Lists provides strategies for memorizing the most useful of these words. With over 270,000 words eligible for play in Scrabble, it is virtually impossible for anyone to learn them all. What this book does is present the words that are most useful in the game in a manner in which they can be easily learned and remembered for Scrabble situations. Essentially, Collins Scrabble Lists is a collection of lists, each of which groups together words for exploiting a particular tactic or learning method. The lists allow for learning different groups of words and spotting opportunities to play them during a game.

In various parts of the book, you will come across specific terminology – power tiles, benjamins, stems, hooks, blockers, awkward combinations, multiplets, alphagrams, and the like. If you're not familiar with these terms, each is explained in the appropriate text prior to the associated lists of words.

Here is just a flavour of some of the lists presented in this book. You will find straightforward lists of all the two-, three- and four-letter words. There are lists of words using the power tiles, JQXZ, sorted by the individual letter and word length. There are lists of words beginning with particular prefixes, and ending with particular suffixes, encouraging the player to consider these prefixes and suffixes when searching for bonus plays. There are lists of words which will be helpful in offloading excessive vowels from your rack and offloading awkward combinations of consonants. There are extensive lists of hook words, whereby you can add a single letter at the front or end of a word, allowing you to play another word by hooking an existing word. And then there are blockers, the opposite of hooks, words which cannot have a letter added at the front or end.

There are extensive lists of six-letter stems, groups of six letters which are particularly productive in combining with a seventh letter to form valid seven-letter words. And beyond that, there are the seven-letter stems which are most productive when combining with an eighth letter.

There are lists of variant spellings – which should help you with recalling whether, for example, a particular word is spelled COSEY, COSIE, COSY, COZEY, COZIE or COZY (All six are valid!). And what about those -ISE and -IZE endings? Are they always interchangeable?

And, occupying about 400 pages, you can check to see whether any particular set of seven- or eight-letters forms one or more valid words.

You'll be introduced to word families, word from varieties of English around the world, words which are placenames. And many more.

The lists in this book bring to the fore a great many words that will be unfamiliar to most people, and even to most Scrabble players. By adding these words to their vocabulary, players are equipping themselves with a powerful arsenal that they can deploy on the Scrabble board. These words, and the varied approaches to word-learning in this book, should enable any player to improve his or her game, no matter at what level the game is played.

Foreword

In this age of online and computer resources, it's good that Collins is still producing their *Official Scrabble Lists* in print. To me at least, it's still much easier to work with type than a computer screen: all of the hard work is done for you.

This book provides all of the essential information you need to enhance your playing ability – hooks, unusual words with J, Q, X, Z, vowel-heavy words, anagrams etc, etc.

I particularly like Chapter 9: *Miscellaneous Lists*. It includes lists of the most frequently played words, which are particularly useful for those who want to improve our Scrabble playing vocabulary, but don't have a clue where to start. Also, it's a lot easier to remember a word if you already know it as someone's name e.g. ABIGAIL, or as a location like SOMERSET. It's excellent that a lot of the words in this section are defined, as that reassures you that you're playing a proper game based on the English language, rather than just remembering letter strings.

Chapter 4, *Beginnings and Endings*, is also extremely helpful, particularly the 'Endings' which are not easily obtained from just reviewing the dictionary. I was surprised to find out that there are 89 seven- and eight-letter words ending in –ETTE. Pretty much all of these are worth knowing; some particularly high probability words include PIANETTE and GRISETTE. I also had a little laugh when I found out that BIMBETTE and CHAVETTE were allowable.

Not many of us are going to become National or World Champions but we can all increase our scores with this book.

Philip Nelkon

Scrabble Resources

Associations

World English-Language Scrabble Players Association (WESPA) –
www.wespa.org

Details of UK Scrabble Clubs – www.absp.org.uk./Publcations/clublist.xls,
email scrabbleuk@mattel.com
or call 01628 500283

UK Scrabble Tournaments – www.absp.org.uk

Schools Scrabble contact – youthscrabble@absp.org.uk

Facebook

Scrabble Facebook Fan Page – www.facebook.com/scrabble

Play Online Scrabble on Facebook – search for Scrabble Worldwide

Interactive Scrabble games

Mobile phone – Real Networks

Sky Interactive – Sky TV platform

iTouch/iPhone/iPad – Electronic Arts (EA)

CHAPTER 1
SHORT WORDS

While long words may yield spectacular scores in Scrabble – and words of up to 15 letters in length can be formed – the chances to achieve such coups are few and far between. A Scrabble player's best chance of consistently high scores comes not from long words but from remembering the short, useful words that can ensure a good play in even the most difficult situations. Short words are easy to squeeze onto the board when there is little or no room for longer words and can still score well if they contain one of the higher-scoring letters. They can also serve to open up the board easily if that is required. The short words containing only or mostly vowels also serve to help resolve a vowel-heavy rack (eg AI, OU, EAU, AIA, ILIA, UNAU).

Two-letter words

Two-letter words are vital to the serious Scrabble player. While very few two-letter words afford big scores in their own right, they are crucial linking elements in the game. Essentially, two-letter words are the nuts and bolts of the game, allowing longer words to be played parallel to each other or for slotting in a high-scoring letter on a premium square to form words in two directions. There are 124 valid two-letter words in Scrabble, all of which are listed in this section.

AA	DO	IF	NY	SO
AB	EA	IN	OB	ST
AD	ED	IO	OD	TA
AE	EE	IS	OE	TE
AG	EF	IT	OF	TI
AH	EH	JA	OH	TO
AI	EL	JO	OI	UG
AL	EM	KA	OM	UH
AM	EN	KI	ON	UM
AN	ER	KO	OO	UN
AR	ES	KY	OP	UP
AS	ET	LA	OR	UR
AT	EX	LI	OS	US
AW	FA	LO	OU	UT
AX	FE	MA	OW	WE
AY	FY	ME	OX	WO
BA	GI	MI	OY	XI
BE	GO	MM	PA	XU
BI	GU	MO	PE	YA
BO	HA	MU	PI	YE
BY	HE	MY	PO	YO
CH	HI	NA	QI	YU
DA	HM	NE	RE	ZA
DE	HO	NO	SH	ZO
DI	ID	NU	SI	

Three-letter words

Three-letter words aren't quite as important as two-letter words, but they are still an essential weapon in every Scrabble player's armoury. It's especially worth noting those three-letter words that are one-letter extensions (hooks) of two-letter words (before or after). You should at least be familiar with those that are -S plurals of two-letter words.

There are 1,310 valid three-letter words in Scrabble, all of which are listed in this section. Not all are valuable in Scrabble but are all listed here for completeness.

AAH	APO	BEY	CHE	DID
AAL	APP	BEZ	CHI	DIE
AAS	APT	BIB	CID	DIF
ABA	ARB	BID	CIG	DIG
ABB	ARC	BIG	CIS	DIM
ABO	ARD	BIN	CIT	DIN
ABS	ARE	BIO	CLY	DIP
ABY	ARF	BIS	COB	DIS
ACE	ARK	BIT	COD	DIT
ACH	ARM	BIZ	COG	DIV
ACT	ARS	BOA	COL	DOB
ADD	ART	BOB	CON	DOC
ADO	ARY	BOD	COO	DOD
ADS	ASH	BOG	COP	DOE
ADZ	ASK	BOH	COR	DOF
AFF	ASP	BOI	COS	DOG
AFT	ASS	BOK	COT	DOH
AGA	ATE	BON	COW	DOL
AGE	ATS	BOO	COX	DOM
AGO	ATT	BOP	COY	DON
AGS	AUA	BOR	COZ	DOO
AHA	AUE	BOS	CRU	DOP
AHI	AUF	BOT	CRY	DOR
AHS	AUK	BOW	CUB	DOS
AIA	AVA	BOX	CUD	DOT
AID	AVE	BOY	CUE	DOW
AIL	AVO	BRA	CUM	DOY
AIM	AWA	BRO	CUP	DRY
AIN	AWE	BRR	CUR	DSO
AIR	AWK	BRU	CUT	DUB
AIS	AWL	BUB	CUZ	DUD
AIT	AWN	BUD	CWM	DUE
AKA	AXE	BUG	DAB	DUG
AKE	AYE	BUM	DAD	DUH
ALA	AYS	BUN	DAE	DUI
ALB	AYU	BUR	DAG	DUN
ALE	AZO	BUS	DAH	DUO
ALF	BAA	BUT	DAK	DUP
ALL	BAC	BUY	DAL	DUX
ALP	BAD	BYE	DAM	DYE
ALS	BAG	BYS	DAN	DZO
ALT	BAH	CAA	DAP	EAN
ALU	BAL	CAB	DAS	EAR
AMA	BAM	CAD	DAW	EAS
AME	BAN	CAG	DAY	EAT
AMI	BAP	CAM	DEB	EAU
AMP	BAR	CAN	DEE	EBB
AMU	BAS	CAP	DEF	ECH
ANA	BAT	CAR	DEG	ECO
AND	BAY	CAT	DEI	ECU
ANE	BED	CAW	DEL	EDH
ANI	BEE	CAY	DEN	EDS
ANN	BEG	CAZ	DEV	EEK
ANS	BEL	CEE	DEW	EEL
ANT	BEN	CEL	DEX	EEN
ANY	BES	CEP	DEY	EFF
APE	BET	CHA	DIB	EFS

EFT	FEH	GEN	HER	IOS
EGG	FEM	GEO	HES	IRE
EGO	FEN	GER	HET	IRK
EHS	FER	GET	HEW	ISH
EIK	FES	GEY	HEX	ISM
EKE	FET	GHI	HEY	ISO
ELD	FEU	GIB	HIC	ITA
ELF	FEW	GID	HID	ITS
ELK	FEY	GIE	HIE	IVY
ELL	FEZ	GIF	HIM	IWI
ELM	FIB	GIG	HIN	JAB
ELS	FID	GIN	HIP	JAG
ELT	FIE	GIO	HIS	JAI
EME	FIG	GIP	HIT	JAK
EMO	FIL	GIS	HMM	JAM
EMS	FIN	GIT	HOA	JAP
EMU	FIR	GJU	HOB	JAR
END	FIT	GNU	HOC	JAW
ENE	FIX	GOA	HOD	JAY
ENG	FIZ	GOB	HOE	JEE
ENS	FLU	GOD	HOG	JET
EON	FLY	GOE	HOH	JEU
ERA	FOB	GON	HOI	JEW
ERE	FOE	GOO	HOM	JIB
ERF	FOG	GOR	HON	JIG
ERG	FOH	GOS	HOO	JIN
ERK	FON	GOT	HOP	JIZ
ERM	FOP	GOV	HOS	JOB
ERN	FOR	GOX	HOT	JOE
ERR	FOU	GOY	HOW	JOG
ERS	FOX	GUB	HOX	JOL
ESS	FOY	GUE	HOY	JOR
EST	FRA	GUL	HUB	JOT
ETA	FRO	GUM	HUE	JOW
ETH	FRY	GUN	HUG	JOY
EUK	FUB	GUP	HUH	JUD
EVE	FUD	GUR	HUI	JUG
EVO	FUG	GUS	HUM	JUN
EWE	FUM	GUT	HUN	JUS
EWK	FUN	GUV	HUP	JUT
EWT	FUR	GUY	HUT	KAB
EXO	GAB	GYM	HYE	KAE
EYE	GAD	GYP	HYP	KAF
FAA	GAE	HAD	ICE	KAI
FAB	GAG	HAE	ICH	KAK
FAD	GAK	HAG	ICK	KAM
FAE	GAL	HAH	ICY	KAS
FAG	GAM	HAJ	IDE	KAT
FAH	GAN	HAM	IDS	KAW
FAN	GAP	HAN	IFF	KAY
FAP	GAR	HAO	IFS	KEA
FAR	GAS	HAP	IGG	KEB
FAS	GAT	HAS	ILK	KED
FAT	GAU	HAT	ILL	KEF
FAW	GAW	HAW	IMP	KEG
FAX	GAY	HAY	ING	KEN
FAY	GED	HEH	INK	KEP
FED	GEE	HEM	INN	KET
FEE	GEL	HEN	INS	KEX
FEG	GEM	HEP	ION	KEY

KHI	LOP	MOE	NOS	ORC
KID	LOR	MOG	NOT	ORD
KIF	LOS	MOI	NOW	ORE
KIN	LOT	MOL	NOX	ORF
KIP	LOU	MOM	NOY	ORS
KIR	LOW	MON	NTH	ORT
KIS	LOX	MOO	NUB	OSE
KIT	LOY	MOP	NUN	OUD
KOA	LUD	MOR	NUR	OUK
KOB	LUG	MOS	NUS	OUP
KOI	LUM	MOT	NUT	OUR
KON	LUR	MOU	NYE	OUS
KOP	LUV	MOW	NYS	OUT
KOR	LUX	MOY	OAF	OVA
KOS	LUZ	MOZ	OAK	OWE
KOW	LYE	MUD	OAR	OWL
KUE	LYM	MUG	OAT	OWN
KYE	MAA	MUM	OBA	OWT
KYU	MAC	MUN	OBE	OXO
LAB	MAD	MUS	OBI	OXY
LAC	MAE	MUT	OBO	OYE
LAD	MAG	MUX	OBS	OYS
LAG	MAK	MYC	OCA	PAC
LAH	MAL	NAB	OCH	PAD
LAM	MAM	NAE	ODA	PAH
LAP	MAN	NAG	ODD	PAL
LAR	MAP	NAH	ODE	PAM
LAS	MAR	NAM	ODS	PAN
LAT	MAS	NAN	OES	PAP
LAV	MAT	NAP	OFF	PAR
LAW	MAW	NAS	OFT	PAS
LAX	MAX	NAT	OHM	PAT
LAY	MAY	NAW	OHO	PAV
LEA	MED	NAY	OHS	PAW
LED	MEE	NEB	OIK	PAX
LEE	MEG	NED	OIL	PAY
LEG	MEH	NEE	OIS	PEA
LEI	MEL	NEF	OKA	PEC
LEK	MEM	NEG	OKE	PED
LEP	MEN	NEK	OLD	PEE
LES	MES	NEP	OLE	PEG
LET	MET	NET	OLM	PEH
LEU	MEU	NEW	OMS	PEL
LEV	MEW	NIB	ONE	PEN
LEW	MHO	NID	ONO	PEP
LEX	MIB	NIE	ONS	PER
LEY	MIC	NIL	ONY	PES
LEZ	MID	NIM	OOF	PET
LIB	MIG	NIP	OOH	PEW
LID	MIL	NIS	OOM	PHI
LIE	MIM	NIT	OON	PHO
LIG	MIR	NIX	OOP	PHT
LIN	MIS	NOB	OOR	PIA
LIP	MIX	NOD	OOS	PIC
LIS	MIZ	NOG	OOT	PIE
LIT	MNA	NOH	OPE	PIG
LOB	MOA	NOM	OPS	PIN
LOD	MOB	NON	OPT	PIP
LOG	MOC	NOO	ORA	PIR
LOO	MOD	NOR	ORB	PIS

PIT	REG	SAY	SUE	TOE
PIU	REH	SAZ	SUG	TOG
PIX	REI	SEA	SUI	TOM
PLU	REM	SEC	SUK	TON
PLY	REN	SED	SUM	TOO
POA	REO	SEE	SUN	TOP
POD	REP	SEG	SUP	TOR
POH	RES	SEI	SUQ	TOT
POI	RET	SEL	SUR	TOW
POL	REV	SEN	SUS	TOY
POM	REW	SER	SWY	TRY
POO	REX	SET	SYE	TSK
POP	REZ	SEW	SYN	TUB
POS	RHO	SEX	TAB	TUG
POT	RHY	SEY	TAD	TUI
POW	RIA	SEZ	TAE	TUM
POX	RIB	SHA	TAG	TUN
POZ	RID	SHE	TAI	TUP
PRE	RIF	SHH	TAJ	TUT
PRO	RIG	SHY	TAK	TUX
PRY	RIM	SIB	TAM	TWA
PSI	RIN	SIC	TAN	TWO
PST	RIP	SIF	TAO	TWP
PUB	RIT	SIK	TAP	TYE
PUD	RIZ	SIM	TAR	TYG
PUG	ROB	SIN	TAS	UDO
PUH	ROC	SIP	TAT	UDS
PUL	ROD	SIR	TAU	UEY
PUN	ROE	SIS	TAV	UFO
PUP	ROK	SIT	TAW	UGH
PUR	ROM	SIX	TAX	UGS
PUS	ROO	SKA	TAY	UKE
PUT	ROT	SKI	TEA	ULE
PUY	ROW	SKY	TEC	ULU
PYA	RUB	SLY	TED	UMM
PYE	RUC	SMA	TEE	UMP
PYX	RUD	SNY	TEF	UMS
QAT	RUE	SOB	TEG	UMU
QIN	RUG	SOC	TEL	UNI
QIS	RUM	SOD	TEN	UNS
QUA	RUN	SOG	TES	UPO
RAD	RUT	SOH	TET	UPS
RAG	RYA	SOL	TEW	URB
RAH	RYE	SOM	TEX	URD
RAI	SAB	SON	THE	URE
RAJ	SAC	SOP	THO	URN
RAM	SAD	SOS	THY	URP
RAN	SAE	SOT	TIC	USE
RAP	SAG	SOU	TID	UTA
RAS	SAI	SOV	TIE	UTE
RAT	SAL	SOW	TIG	UTS
RAV	SAM	SOX	TIK	UTU
RAW	SAN	SOY	TIL	UVA
RAX	SAP	SOZ	TIN	VAC
RAY	SAR	SPA	TIP	VAE
REB	SAT	SPY	TIS	VAG
REC	SAU	SRI	TIT	VAN
RED	SAV	STY	TIX	VAR
REE	SAW	SUB	TOC	VAS
REF	SAX	SUD	TOD	VAT

VAU	WAG	WIZ	YAR	YUP
VAV	WAI	WOE	YAW	YUS
VAW	WAN	WOF	YAY	ZAG
VEE	WAP	WOG	YEA	ZAP
VEG	WAR	WOK	YEH	ZAS
VET	WAS	WON	YEN	ZAX
VEX	WAT	WOO	YEP	ZEA
VIA	WAW	WOP	YES	ZED
VID	WAX	WOS	YET	ZEE
VIE	WAY	WOT	YEW	ZEK
VIG	WEB	WOW	YEX	ZEL
VIM	WED	WOX	YGO	ZEP
VIN	WEE	WRY	YID	ZEX
VIS	WEM	WUD	YIN	ZHO
VLY	WEN	WUS	YIP	ZIG
VOE	WET	WYE	YOB	ZIN
VOL	WEX	WYN	YOD	ZIP
VOR	WEY	XIS	YOK	ZIT
VOW	WHA	YAD	YOM	ZIZ
VOX	WHO	YAE	YON	ZOA
VUG	WHY	YAG	YOU	ZOL
VUM	WIG	YAH	YOW	ZOO
WAB	WIN	YAK	YUG	ZOS
WAD	WIS	YAM	YUK	ZUZ
WAE	WIT	YAP	YUM	ZZZ

Four-letter words

Four-letter words are generally even less valuable than three-letter words. The ones that are most useful during play tend to be those that can be formed by hooking three-letter words before or after (eg ALOW, LOWE), those that contain awkward combinations of letters (eg VEHM) or three vowels (eg HIOI) that help to resolve problems, or those that contain a power tile (eg ROJI). All the 5,525 four-letter words are listed here for completeness.

AAHS	ACRE	AGIO	AJEE	ALKY
AALS	ACTA	AGLU	AKAS	ALLS
ABAC	ACTS	AGLY	AKED	ALLY
ABAS	ACYL	AGMA	AKEE	ALMA
ABBA	ADAW	AGOG	AKES	ALME
ABBE	ADDS	AGON	AKIN	ALMS
ABBS	ADDY	AGUE	ALAE	ALOD
ABED	ADIT	AHED	ALAN	ALOE
ABET	ADOS	AHEM	ALAP	ALOO
ABID	ADRY	AHIS	ALAR	ALOW
ABLE	ADZE	AHOY	ALAS	ALPS
ABLY	AEON	AIAS	ALAY	ALSO
ABOS	AERO	AIDA	ALBA	ALTO
ABRI	AERY	AIDE	ALBE	ALTS
ABUT	AESC	AIDS	ALBS	ALUM
ABYE	AFAR	AIGA	ALCO	ALUS
ABYS	AFFY	AILS	ALEC	AMAH
ACAI	AFRO	AIMS	ALEE	AMAS
ACCA	AGAR	AINE	ALEF	AMBO
ACED	AGAS	AINS	ALES	AMEN
ACER	AGED	AIRN	ALEW	AMES
ACES	AGEE	AIRS	ALFA	AMIA
ACHE	AGEN	AIRT	ALFS	AMID
ACHY	AGER	AIRY	ALGA	AMIE
ACID	AGES	AITS	ALIF	AMIN
ACME	AGHA	AITU	ALIT	AMIR
ACNE	AGIN	AJAR	ALKO	AMIS

AMLA	ARIS	AXED	BARM	BETH
AMMO	ARKS	AXEL	BARN	BETS
AMOK	ARLE	AXES	BARP	BEVY
AMPS	ARMS	AXIL	BARS	BEYS
AMUS	ARMY	AXIS	BASE	BHAI
AMYL	ARNA	AXLE	BASH	BHAT
ANAL	AROW	AXON	BASK	BHEL
ANAN	ARPA	AYAH	BASS	BHUT
ANAS	ARSE	AYES	BAST	BIAS
ANCE	ARSY	AYIN	BATE	BIBB
ANDS	ARTI	AYRE	BATH	BIBS
ANES	ARTS	AYUS	BATS	BICE
ANEW	ARTY	AZAN	BATT	BIDE
ANGA	ARUM	AZON	BAUD	BIDI
ANIL	ARVO	AZYM	BAUK	BIDS
ANIS	ARYL	BAAL	BAUR	BIEN
ANKH	ASAR	BAAS	BAWD	BIER
ANNA	ASCI	BABA	BAWL	BIFF
ANNO	ASEA	BABE	BAWN	BIGA
ANNS	ASHY	BABU	BAWR	BIGG
ANOA	ASKS	BABY	BAYE	BIGS
ANON	ASPS	BACH	BAYS	BIKE
ANOW	ATAP	BACK	BAYT	BILE
ANSA	ATES	BACS	BEAD	BILK
ANTA	ATMA	BADE	BEAK	BILL
ANTE	ATOC	BADS	BEAM	BIMA
ANTI	ATOK	BAEL	BEAN	BIND
ANTS	ATOM	BAFF	BEAR	BINE
ANUS	ATOP	BAFT	BEAT	BING
APAY	ATUA	BAGH	BEAU	BINK
APED	AUAS	BAGS	BECK	BINS
APER	AUFS	BAHT	BEDE	BINT
APES	AUKS	BAHU	BEDS	BIOG
APEX	AULA	BAIL	BEDU	BIOS
APOD	AULD	BAIT	BEEF	BIRD
APOS	AUNE	BAJU	BEEN	BIRK
APPS	AUNT	BAKE	BEEP	BIRL
APSE	AURA	BALD	BEER	BIRO
APSO	AUTO	BALE	BEES	BIRR
APTS	AVAL	BALK	BEET	BISE
AQUA	AVAS	BALL	BEGO	BISH
ARAK	AVEL	BALM	BEGS	BISK
ARAR	AVER	BALS	BEIN	BIST
ARBA	AVES	BALU	BELL	BITE
ARBS	AVID	BAMS	BELS	BITO
ARCH	AVOS	BANC	BELT	BITS
ARCO	AVOW	BAND	BEMA	BITT
ARCS	AWAY	BANE	BEND	BIZE
ARDS	AWDL	BANG	BENE	BLAB
AREA	AWED	BANI	BENI	BLAD
ARED	AWEE	BANK	BENJ	BLAE
AREG	AWES	BANS	BENS	BLAG
ARES	AWFY	BANT	BENT	BLAH
ARET	AWKS	BAPS	BERE	BLAM
AREW	AWLS	BAPU	BERG	BLAT
ARFS	AWNS	BARB	BERK	BLAW
ARGH	AWNY	BARD	BERM	BLAY
ARIA	AWOL	BARE	BEST	BLEB
ARID	AWRY	BARF	BETA	BLED
ARIL	AXAL	BARK	BETE	BLEE

BLET	BOPS	BRUT	CAAS	CAUL
BLEW	BORA	BRUX	CABA	CAUM
BLEY	BORD	BUAT	CABS	CAUP
BLIN	BORE	BUBA	CACA	CAVA
BLIP	BORK	BUBO	CACK	CAVE
BLIT	BORM	BUBS	CADE	CAVY
BLOB	BORN	BUBU	CADI	CAWK
BLOC	BORS	BUCK	CADS	CAWS
BLOG	BORT	BUDA	CAFE	CAYS
BLOT	BOSH	BUDI	CAFF	CEAS
BLOW	BOSK	BUDO	CAGE	CECA
BLUB	BOSS	BUDS	CAGS	CEDE
BLUE	BOTA	BUFF	CAGY	CEDI
BLUR	BOTE	BUFO	CAID	CEES
BOAB	BOTH	BUGS	CAIN	CEIL
BOAK	BOTS	BUHL	CAKE	CELL
BOAR	BOTT	BUHR	CAKY	CELS
BOAS	BOUK	BUIK	CALF	CELT
BOAT	BOUN	BUKE	CALK	CENS
BOBA	BOUT	BULB	CALL	CENT
BOBS	BOWL	BULK	CALM	CEPE
BOCK	BOWR	BULL	CALO	CEPS
BODE	BOWS	BUMF	CALP	CERE
BODS	BOXY	BUMP	CALX	CERO
BODY	BOYF	BUMS	CAMA	CERT
BOEP	BOYG	BUNA	CAME	CESS
BOET	BOYO	BUND	CAMO	CETE
BOFF	BOYS	BUNG	CAMP	CHAD
BOGS	BOZO	BUNK	CAMS	CHAI
BOGY	BRAD	BUNN	CANE	CHAL
BOHO	BRAE	BUNS	CANG	CHAM
BOHS	BRAG	BUNT	CANN	CHAO
BOIL	BRAK	BUOY	CANS	CHAP
BOIS	BRAN	BURA	CANT	CHAR
BOKE	BRAS	BURB	CANY	CHAS
BOKO	BRAT	BURD	CAPA	CHAT
BOKS	BRAW	BURG	CAPE	CHAV
BOLA	BRAY	BURK	CAPH	CHAW
BOLD	BRED	BURL	CAPI	CHAY
BOLE	BREE	BURN	CAPO	CHEF
BOLL	BREI	BURP	CAPS	CHER
BOLO	BREN	BURR	CARB	CHEW
BOLT	BRER	BURS	CARD	CHEZ
BOMA	BREW	BURY	CARE	CHIA
BOMB	BREY	BUSH	CARK	CHIB
BONA	BRIE	BUSK	CARL	CHIC
BOND	BRIG	BUSS	CARN	CHID
BONE	BRIK	BUST	CARP	CHIK
BONG	BRIM	BUSY	CARR	CHIN
BONK	BRIN	BUTE	CARS	CHIP
BONY	BRIO	BUTS	CART	CHIS
BOOB	BRIS	BUTT	CASA	CHIT
BOOH	BRIT	BUYS	CASE	CHIV
BOOK	BROD	BUZZ	CASH	CHIZ
BOOL	BROG	BYDE	CASK	CHOC
BOOM	BROO	BYES	CAST	CHOG
BOON	BROS	BYKE	CATE	CHON
BOOR	BROW	BYRE	CATS	CHOP
BOOS	BRRR	BYRL	CAUF	CHOU
BOOT	BRUS	BYTE	CAUK	CHOW

CHUB	COGS	COVE	CUSK	DAWS
CHUG	COHO	COWK	CUSP	DAWT
CHUM	COIF	COWL	CUSS	DAYS
CHUR	COIL	COWP	CUTE	DAZE
CHUT	COIN	COWS	CUTS	DEAD
CIAO	COIR	COWY	CWMS	DEAF
CIDE	COIT	COXA	CYAN	DEAL
CIDS	COKE	COXY	CYMA	DEAN
CIEL	COKY	COYS	CYME	DEAR
CIGS	COLA	COZE	CYST	DEAW
CILL	COLD	COZY	CYTE	DEBE
CINE	COLE	CRAB	CZAR	DEBS
CION	COLL	CRAG	DAAL	DEBT
CIRE	COLS	CRAM	DABS	DECK
CIRL	COLT	CRAN	DACE	DECO
CIST	COLY	CRAP	DACK	DEED
CITE	COMA	CRAW	DADA	DEEK
CITO	COMB	CRAY	DADO	DEEM
CITS	COME	CRED	DADS	DEEN
CITY	COMM	CREE	DAES	DEEP
CIVE	COMP	CREM	DAFF	DEER
CLAD	COMS	CREW	DAFT	DEES
CLAG	COND	CRIA	DAGO	DEET
CLAM	CONE	CRIB	DAGS	DEEV
CLAN	CONF	CRIM	DAHL	DEFI
CLAP	CONI	CRIS	DAHS	DEFO
CLAT	CONK	CRIT	DAIS	DEFT
CLAW	CONN	CROC	DAKS	DEFY
CLAY	CONS	CROG	DALE	DEGS
CLEF	CONY	CROP	DALI	DEGU
CLEG	COOF	CROW	DALS	DEID
CLEM	COOK	CRUD	DALT	DEIF
CLEW	COOL	CRUE	DAME	DEIL
CLIP	COOM	CRUS	DAMN	DEKE
CLIT	COON	CRUX	DAMP	DELE
CLOD	COOP	CUBE	DAMS	DELF
CLOG	COOS	CUBS	DANG	DELI
CLON	COOT	CUDS	DANK	DELL
CLOP	COPE	CUED	DANS	DELO
CLOT	COPS	CUES	DANT	DELS
CLOU	COPY	CUFF	DAPS	DELT
CLOW	CORD	CUIF	DARB	DEME
CLOY	CORE	CUIT	DARE	DEMO
CLUB	CORF	CUKE	DARG	DEMY
CLUE	CORK	CULL	DARI	DENE
COAL	CORM	CULM	DARK	DENI
COAT	CORN	CULT	DARN	DENS
COAX	CORS	CUMS	DART	DENT
COBB	CORY	CUNT	DASH	DENY
COBS	COSE	CUPS	DATA	DERE
COCA	COSH	CURB	DATE	DERM
COCH	COSS	CURD	DATO	DERN
COCK	COST	CURE	DAUB	DERO
COCO	COSY	CURF	DAUD	DERV
CODA	COTE	CURL	DAUR	DESI
CODE	COTH	CURN	DAUT	DESK
CODS	COTS	CURR	DAVY	DEUS
COED	COTT	CURS	DAWD	DEVA
COFF	COUP	CURT	DAWK	DEVS
COFT	COUR	CUSH	DAWN	DEWS

DEWY	DJIN	DOUC	DUIT	ECRU
DEXY	DOAB	DOUK	DUKA	ECUS
DEYS	DOAT	DOUM	DUKE	EDDO
DHAK	DOBS	DOUN	DULE	EDDY
DHAL	DOBY	DOUP	DULL	EDGE
DHOL	DOCK	DOUR	DULY	EDGY
DHOW	DOCO	DOUT	DUMA	EDHS
DIAL	DOCS	DOUX	DUMB	EDIT
DIBS	DODO	DOVE	DUMP	EECH
DICE	DODS	DOWD	DUNE	EELS
DICH	DOEK	DOWF	DUNG	EELY
DICK	DOEN	DOWL	DUNK	EERY
DICT	DOER	DOWN	DUNS	EEVN
DIDO	DOES	DOWP	DUNT	EFFS
DIDY	DOFF	DOWS	DUOS	EFTS
DIEB	DOGE	DOWT	DUPE	EGAD
DIED	DOGS	DOXY	DUPS	EGAL
DIEL	DOGY	DOYS	DURA	EGER
DIES	DOHS	DOZE	DURE	EGGS
DIET	DOIT	DOZY	DURN	EGGY
DIFF	DOJO	DRAB	DURO	EGIS
DIFS	DOLE	DRAC	DURR	EGMA
DIGS	DOLL	DRAD	DUSH	EGOS
DIKA	DOLS	DRAG	DUSK	EHED
DIKE	DOLT	DRAM	DUST	EIDE
DILL	DOME	DRAP	DUTY	EIKS
DIME	DOMS	DRAT	DWAM	EILD
DIMP	DOMY	DRAW	DYAD	EINA
DIMS	DONA	DRAY	DYED	EINE
DINE	DONE	DREE	DYER	EISH
DING	DONG	DREG	DYES	EKED
DINK	DONS	DREK	DYKE	EKES
DINO	DOOB	DREW	DYNE	EKKA
DINS	DOOK	DREY	DZHO	ELAN
DINT	DOOL	DRIB	DZOS	ELDS
DIOL	DOOM	DRIP	EACH	ELFS
DIPS	DOON	DROP	EALE	ELHI
DIPT	DOOR	DROW	EANS	ELKS
DIRE	DOOS	DRUB	EARD	ELLS
DIRK	DOPA	DRUG	EARL	ELMS
DIRL	DOPE	DRUM	EARN	ELMY
DIRT	DOPS	DRYS	EARS	ELSE
DISA	DOPY	DSOS	EASE	ELTS
DISC	DORB	DUAD	EAST	EMES
DISH	DORE	DUAL	EASY	EMEU
DISK	DORK	DUAN	EATH	EMIC
DISS	DORM	DUAR	EATS	EMIR
DITA	DORP	DUBS	EAUS	EMIT
DITE	DORR	DUCI	EAUX	EMMA
DITS	DORS	DUCE	EAVE	EMMY
DITT	DORT	DUCK	EBBS	EMOS
DITZ	DORY	DUCT	EBON	EMPT
DIVA	DOSE	DUDE	ECAD	EMUS
DIVE	DOSH	DUDS	ECCE	EMYD
DIVI	DOSS	DUED	ECCO	EMYS
DIVO	DOST	DUEL	ECHE	ENDS
DIVS	DOTE	DUES	ECHO	ENES
DIXI	DOTH	DUET	ECHT	ENEW
DIXY	DOTS	DUFF	ECOD	ENGS
DIYA	DOTY	DUGS	ECOS	ENOL

ENOW	EXIT	FAYS	FIND	FOEN
ENUF	EXON	FAZE	FINE	FOES
ENVY	EXPO	FEAL	FINI	FOGS
EOAN	EXUL	FEAR	FINK	FOGY
EONS	EYAS	FEAT	FINO	FOHN
EORL	EYED	FECK	FINS	FOID
EPEE	EYEN	FEDS	FIQH	FOIL
EPHA	EYER	FEEB	FIRE	FOIN
EPIC	EYES	FEED	FIRK	FOLD
EPOS	EYNE	FEEL	FIRM	FOLK
ERAS	EYOT	FEEN	FIRN	FOND
ERED	EYRA	FEER	FIRS	FONE
ERES	EYRE	FEES	FISC	FONS
EREV	EYRY	FEET	FISH	FONT
ERGO	FAAN	FEGS	FISK	FOOD
ERGS	FAAS	FEHM	FIST	FOOL
ERHU	FABS	FEHS	FITS	FOOT
ERIC	FACE	FEIS	FITT	FOPS
ERKS	FACT	FELL	FIVE	FORA
ERNE	FADE	FELT	FIXT	FORB
ERNS	FADO	FEME	FIZZ	FORD
EROS	FADS	FEMS	FLAB	FORE
ERRS	FADY	FEND	FLAG	FORK
ERST	FAFF	FENI	FLAK	FORM
ERUV	FAGS	FENS	FLAM	FORT
ESES	FAHS	FENT	FLAN	FOSS
ESKY	FAIK	FEOD	FLAP	FOUD
ESNE	FAIL	FERE	FLAT	FOUL
ESPY	FAIN	FERM	FLAW	FOUR
ESSE	FAIR	FERN	FLAX	FOUS
ESTS	FAIX	FESS	FLAY	FOWL
ETAS	FAKE	FEST	FLEA	FOXY
ETAT	FALL	FETA	FLED	FOYS
ETCH	FALX	FETE	FLEE	FOZY
ETEN	FAME	FETS	FLEG	FRAB
ETHE	FAND	FETT	FLEW	FRAE
ETHS	FANE	FEUD	FLEX	FRAG
ETIC	FANG	FEUS	FLEY	FRAP
ETNA	FANK	FEWS	FLIC	FRAS
ETUI	FANO	FEYS	FLIM	FRAT
EUGE	FANS	FIAR	FLIP	FRAU
EUGH	FARD	FIAT	FLIR	FRAY
EUKS	FARE	FIBS	FLIT	FREE
EUOI	FARL	FICE	FLIX	FRET
EURO	FARM	FICO	FLOB	FRIB
EVEN	FARO	FIDO	FLOC	FRIG
EVER	FARS	FIDS	FLOE	FRIS
EVES	FART	FIEF	FLOG	FRIT
EVET	FASH	FIER	FLOP	FRIZ
EVIL	FAST	FIFE	FLOR	FROE
EVOE	FATE	FIGO	FLOW	FROG
EVOS	FATS	FIGS	FLOX	FROM
EWER	FAUN	FIKE	FLUB	FROS
EWES	FAUR	FIKY	FLUE	FROW
EWKS	FAUT	FILA	FLUS	FRUG
EWTS	FAUX	FILE	FLUX	FUBS
EXAM	FAVA	FILL	FOAL	FUCI
EXEC	FAVE	FILM	FOAM	FUCK
EXED	FAWN	FILO	FOBS	FUDS
EXES	FAWS	FILS	FOCI	FUEL

FUFF	GAPE	GHEE	GNUS	GREE
FUGS	GAPO	GHIS	GOAD	GREN
FUGU	GAPS	GIBE	GOAF	GREW
FUJI	GAPY	GIBS	GOAL	GREX
FULL	GARB	GIDS	GOAS	GREY
FUME	GARE	GIED	GOAT	GRID
FUMS	GARI	GIEN	GOBI	GRIG
FUMY	GARS	GIES	GOBO	GRIM
FUND	GART	GIFT	GOBS	GRIN
FUNG	GASH	GIGA	GOBY	GRIP
FUNK	GASP	GIGS	GODS	GRIS
FUNS	GAST	GILA	GOEL	GRIT
FURL	GATE	GILD	GOER	GROG
FURR	GATH	GILL	GOES	GROK
FURS	GATS	GILT	GOEY	GROT
FURY	GAUD	GIMP	GOFF	GROW
FUSC	GAUM	GING	GOGO	GRRL
FUSE	GAUN	GINK	GOJI	GRUB
FUSS	GAUP	GINN	GOLD	GRUE
FUST	GAUR	GINS	GOLE	GRUM
FUTZ	GAUS	GIOS	GOLF	GUAN
FUZE	GAVE	GIPS	GOLP	GUAR
FUZZ	GAWD	GIRD	GONE	GUBS
FYCE	GAWK	GIRL	GONG	GUCK
FYKE	GAWP	GIRN	GONK	GUDE
FYLE	GAWS	GIRO	GONS	GUES
FYRD	GAYS	GIRR	GOOD	GUFF
GABS	GAZE	GIRT	GOOF	GUGA
GABY	GAZY	GISM	GOOG	GUID
GADE	GEAL	GIST	GOOK	GULA
GADI	GEAN	GITE	GOOL	GULE
GADS	GEAR	GITS	GOON	GULF
GAED	GEAT	GIVE	GOOP	GULL
GAEN	GECK	GIZZ	GOOR	GULP
GAES	GEDS	GJUS	GOOS	GULS
GAFF	GEED	GLAD	GORA	GULY
GAGA	GEEK	GLAM	GORE	GUMP
GAGE	GEEP	GLED	GORI	GUMS
GAGS	GEES	GLEE	GORM	GUNG
GAID	GEEZ	GLEG	GORP	GUNK
GAIN	GEIT	GLEI	GORY	GUNS
GAIR	GELD	GLEN	GOSH	GUPS
GAIT	GELS	GLEY	GOSS	GURL
GAJO	GELT	GLIA	GOTH	GURN
GAKS	GEMS	GLIB	GOUK	GURS
GALA	GENA	GLID	GOUT	GURU
GALE	GENE	GLIM	GOVS	GUSH
GALL	GENS	GLIT	GOWD	GUST
GALS	GENT	GLOB	GOWF	GUTS
GAMA	GENU	GLOM	GOWK	GUVS
GAMB	GEOS	GLOP	GOWL	GUYS
GAME	GERE	GLOW	GOWN	GYAL
GAMP	GERM	GLUE	GOYS	GYBE
GAMS	GERS	GLUG	GRAB	GYMP
GAMY	GERT	GLUM	GRAD	GYMS
GANE	GEST	GLUT	GRAM	GYNY
GANG	GETA	GNAR	GRAN	GYPS
GANS	GETS	GNAT	GRAT	GYRE
GANT	GEUM	GNAW	GRAV	GYRI
GAOL	GHAT	GNOW	GRAY	GYRO

GYTE	HATS	HIED	HONG	HURL
GYVE	HAUD	HIES	HONK	HURT
HAAF	HAUF	HIGH	HONS	HUSH
HAAR	HAUL	HIKE	HOOD	HUSK
HABU	HAUT	HILA	HOOF	HUSO
HACK	HAVE	HILD	HOOK	HUSS
HADE	HAWK	HILI	HOON	HUTS
HADJ	HAWM	HILL	HOOP	HWAN
HADS	HAWS	HILT	HOOR	HWYL
HAED	HAYS	HIMS	HOOT	HYED
HAEM	HAZE	HIND	HOPE	HYEN
HAEN	HAZY	HING	HOPS	HYES
HAES	HEAD	HINS	HORA	HYKE
HAET	HEAL	HINT	HORE	HYLA
HAFF	HEAP	HIOI	HORI	HYLE
HAFT	HEAR	HIPS	HORN	HYMN
HAGG	HEAT	HIPT	HORS	HYPE
HAGS	HEBE	HIRE	HOSE	HYPO
HAHA	HECH	HISH	HOSS	HYPS
HAHS	HECK	HISN	HOST	HYTE
HAIK	HEED	HISS	HOTE	IAMB
HAIL	HEEL	HIST	HOTS	IBEX
HAIN	HEFT	HITS	HOUF	IBIS
HAIR	HEHS	HIVE	HOUR	ICED
HAJI	HEID	HIYA	HOUT	ICER
HAJJ	HEIL	HIZZ	HOVE	ICES
HAKA	HEIR	HOAR	HOWE	ICHS
HAKE	HELD	HOAS	HOWF	ICKY
HAKU	HELE	HOAX	HOWK	ICON
HALE	HELL	HOBO	HOWL	IDEA
HALF	HELM	HOBS	HOWS	IDEE
HALL	HELO	HOCK	HOYA	IDEM
HALM	HELP	HODS	HOYS	IDES
HALO	HEME	HOED	HUBS	IDLE
HALT	HEMP	HOER	HUCK	IDLY
HAME	HEMS	HOES	HUED	IDOL
HAMS	HEND	HOGG	HUER	IDYL
HAND	HENS	HOGH	HUES	IFFY
HANG	HENT	HOGS	HUFF	IGAD
HANK	HEPS	HOHA	HUGE	IGGS
HANT	HEPT	HOHS	HUGS	IGLU
HAOS	HERB	HOIK	HUGY	IKAN
HAPS	HERD	HOKA	HUHU	IKAT
HAPU	HERE	HOKE	HUIA	IKON
HARD	HERL	HOKI	HUIC	ILEA
HARE	HERM	HOLD	HUIS	ILEX
HARK	HERN	HOLE	HULA	ILIA
HARL	HERO	HOLK	HULE	ILKA
HARM	HERS	HOLM	HULK	ILKS
HARN	HERY	HOLP	HULL	ILLS
HARO	HESP	HOLS	HUMA	ILLY
HARP	HEST	HOLT	HUMF	IMAM
HART	HETE	HOLY	HUMP	IMID
HASH	HETH	HOMA	HUMS	IMMY
HASK	HETS	HOME	HUNG	IMPI
HASP	HEWN	HOMO	HUNH	IMPS
HASS	HEWS	HOMS	HUNK	INBY
HAST	HEYS	HOMY	HUNS	INCH
HATE	HICK	HOND	HUNT	INFO
HATH	HIDE	HONE	HUPS	INGO

INGS	JAYS	JORS	KANE	KHAN
INIA	JAZY	JOSH	KANG	KHAT
INKS	JAZZ	JOSS	KANS	KHET
INKY	JEAN	JOTA	KANT	KHIS
INLY	JEAT	JOTS	KAON	KHOR
INNS	JEDI	JOUK	KAPA	KHUD
INRO	JEED	JOUR	KAPH	KIBE
INTI	JEEL	JOWL	KARA	KICK
INTO	JEEP	JOWS	KARK	KIDS
IONS	JEER	JOYS	KARN	KIEF
IOTA	JEES	JUBA	KARO	KIER
IRED	JEEZ	JUBE	KART	KIEV
IRES	JEFE	JUCO	KATA	KIFF
IRID	JEFF	JUDO	KATI	KIFS
IRIS	JEHU	JUDS	KATS	KIKE
IRKS	JELL	JUDY	KAVA	KILD
IRON	JEON	JUGA	KAWA	KILL
ISBA	JERK	JUGS	KAWS	KILN
ISIT	JESS	JUJU	KAYO	KILO
ISLE	JEST	JUKE	KAYS	KILP
ISMS	JETE	JUKU	KAZI	KILT
ISNA	JETS	JUMP	KBAR	KINA
ISOS	JEUX	JUNK	KEAS	KIND
ITAS	JEWS	JUPE	KEBS	KINE
ITCH	JIAO	JURA	KECK	KING
ITEM	JIBB	JURE	KEDS	KINK
IURE	JIBE	JURY	KEEF	KINO
IWIS	JIBS	JUST	KEEK	KINS
IXIA	JIFF	JUTE	KEEL	KIPE
IZAR	JIGS	JUTS	KEEN	KIPP
JAAP	JILL	JUVE	KEEP	KIPS
JABS	JILT	JYNX	KEET	KIRK
JACK	JIMP	KAAL	KEFS	KIRN
JADE	JINK	KAAS	KEGS	KIRS
JAFA	JINN	KABS	KEIR	KISH
JAGA	JINS	KACK	KEKS	KISS
JAGG	JINX	KADE	KELL	KIST
JAGS	JIRD	KADI	KELP	KITE
JAIL	JISM	KAED	KELT	KITH
JAKE	JIVE	KAES	KEMB	KITS
JAKS	JIVY	KAFS	KEMP	KIVA
JAMB	JIZZ	KAGO	KENO	KIWI
JAMS	JOBE	KAGU	KENS	KLAP
JANE	JOBS	KAID	KENT	KLIK
JANN	JOCK	KAIE	KEPI	KNAG
JAPE	JOCO	KAIF	KEPS	KNAP
JAPS	JOES	KAIK	KEPT	KNAR
JARK	JOEY	KAIL	KERB	KNEE
JARL	JOGS	KAIM	KERF	KNEW
JARP	JOHN	KAIN	KERN	KNIT
JARS	JOIN	KAIS	KERO	KNOB
JASP	JOKE	KAKA	KESH	KNOP
JASS	JOKY	KAKI	KEST	KNOT
JASY	JOLE	KAKS	KETA	KNOW
JATO	JOLL	KALE	KETE	KNUB
JAUK	JOLS	KALI	KETO	KNUR
JAUP	JOLT	KAMA	KETS	KNUT
JAVA	JOMO	KAME	KEWL	KOAN
JAWS	JONG	KAMI	KEYS	KOAP
JAXY	JOOK	KANA	KHAF	KOAS

KOBO	LACY	LEAM	LILL	LOLL
KOBS	LADE	LEAN	LILT	LOMA
KOEL	LADS	LEAP	LILY	LOME
KOFF	LADY	LEAR	LIMA	LONE
KOHA	LAER	LEAS	LIMB	LONG
KOHL	LAGS	LEAT	LIME	LOOF
KOIS	LAHS	LECH	LIMN	LOOK
KOJI	LAIC	LEED	LIMO	LOOM
KOKA	LAID	LEEK	LIMP	LOON
KOLA	LAIK	LEEP	LIMY	LOOP
KOLO	LAIN	LEER	LIND	LOOR
KOND	LAIR	LEES	LINE	LOOS
KONK	LAKE	LEET	LING	LOOT
KONS	LAKH	LEFT	LINK	LOPE
KOOK	LAKY	LEGS	LINN	LOPS
KOPH	LALL	LEHR	LINO	LORD
KOPS	LAMA	LEIR	LINS	LORE
KORA	LAMB	LEIS	LINT	LORN
KORE	LAME	LEKE	LINY	LORY
KORO	LAMP	LEKS	LION	LOSE
KORS	LAMS	LEKU	LIPA	LOSH
KORU	LANA	LEME	LIPE	LOSS
KOSS	LAND	LEND	LIPO	LOST
KOTO	LANE	LENG	LIPS	LOTA
KOWS	LANG	LENO	LIRA	LOTE
KRAB	LANK	LENS	LIRE	LOTH
KRIS	LANT	LENT	LIRI	LOTI
KSAR	LANX	LEPS	LIRK	LOTO
KUDO	LAPS	LEPT	LISK	LOTS
KUDU	LARD	LERE	LISP	LOUD
KUEH	LARE	LERP	LIST	LOUN
KUES	LARI	LESS	LITE	LOUP
KUFI	LARK	LEST	LITH	LOUR
KUIA	LARN	LETS	LITS	LOUS
KUKU	LARS	LEUD	LITU	LOUT
KULA	LASE	LEVA	LIVE	LOVE
KUNA	LASH	LEVE	LOAD	LOWE
KUNE	LASS	LEVO	LOAF	LOWN
KURI	LAST	LEVY	LOAM	LOWP
KURU	LATE	LEWD	LOAN	LOWS
KUTA	LATH	LEYS	LOBE	LOWT
KUTI	LATI	LEZZ	LOBI	LOYS
KUTU	LATS	LIAR	LOBO	LUAU
KUZU	LATU	LIAS	LOBS	LUBE
KVAS	LAUD	LIBS	LOCA	LUCE
KYAK	LAUF	LICE	LOCH	LUCK
KYAR	LAVA	LICH	LOCI	LUDE
KYAT	LAVE	LICK	LOCK	LUDO
KYBO	LAVS	LIDO	LOCO	LUDS
KYES	LAWK	LIDS	LODE	LUES
KYLE	LAWN	LIED	LODS	LUFF
KYND	LAWS	LIEF	LOFT	LUGE
KYNE	LAYS	LIEN	LOGE	LUGS
KYPE	LAZE	LIER	LOGO	LUIT
KYTE	LAZO	LIES	LOGS	LUKE
KYUS	LAZY	LIEU	LOGY	LULL
LABS	LEAD	LIFE	LOID	LULU
LACE	LEAF	LIFT	LOIN	LUMA
LACK	LEAK	LIGS	LOIR	LUMP
LACS	LEAL	LIKE	LOKE	LUMS

LUNA	MAMA	MEGA	MILO	MOLL
LUNE	MAMS	MEGS	MILS	MOLS
LUNG	MANA	MEIN	MILT	MOLT
LUNK	MAND	MELA	MIME	MOLY
LUNT	MANE	MELD	MINA	MOME
LUNY	MANG	MELL	MIND	MOMI
LURE	MANI	MELS	MINE	MOMS
LURK	MANO	MELT	MING	MONA
LURS	MANS	MEME	MINI	MONG
LUSH	MANY	MEMO	MINK	MONK
LUSK	MAPS	MEMS	MINO	MONO
LUST	MARA	MEND	MINT	MONS
LUTE	MARC	MENE	MINX	MONY
LUTZ	MARD	MENG	MINY	MOOD
LUVS	MARE	MENO	MIPS	MOOI
LUXE	MARG	MENT	MIRE	MOOK
LWEI	MARK	MENU	MIRI	MOOL
LYAM	MARL	MEOU	MIRK	MOON
LYCH	MARM	MEOW	MIRO	MOOP
LYES	MARS	MERC	MIRS	MOOR
LYME	MART	MERE	MIRV	MOOS
LYMS	MARY	MERI	MIRY	MOOT
LYNE	MASA	MERK	MISE	MOPE
LYNX	MASE	MERL	MISO	MOPS
LYRA	MASH	MESA	MISS	MOPY
LYRE	MASK	MESE	MIST	MORA
LYSE	MASS	MESH	MITE	MORE
LYTE	MAST	MESS	MITT	MORN
MAAR	MASU	META	MITY	MORS
MAAS	MATE	METE	MIXT	MORT
MABE	MATH	METH	MIXY	MOSE
MACE	MATS	METS	MIZZ	MOSH
MACH	MATT	MEUS	MNAS	MOSK
MACK	MATY	MEVE	MOAI	MOSS
MACS	MAUD	MEWL	MOAN	MOST
MADE	MAUL	MEWS	MOAS	MOTE
MADS	MAUN	MEZE	MOAT	MOTH
MAES	MAUT	MEZZ	MOBE	MOTI
MAGE	MAWK	MHOS	MOBS	MOTS
MAGG	MAWN	MIBS	MOBY	MOTT
MAGI	MAWR	MICA	MOCH	MOTU
MAGS	MAWS	MICE	MOCK	MOUE
MAHA	MAXI	MICH	MOCS	MOUP
MAID	MAYA	MICK	MODE	MOUS
MAIK	MAYO	MICO	MODI	MOVE
MAIL	MAYS	MICS	MODS	MOWA
MAIM	MAZE	MIDI	MOER	MOWN
MAIN	MAZY	MIDS	MOES	MOWS
MAIR	MEAD	MIEN	MOFO	MOXA
MAKE	MEAL	MIFF	MOGS	MOYA
MAKI	MEAN	MIGG	MOHR	MOYL
MAKO	MEAT	MIGS	MOIL	MOYS
MAKS	MECK	MIHA	MOIT	MOZE
MALA	MEDS	MIHI	MOJO	MOZO
MALE	MEED	MIKE	MOKE	MOZZ
MALI	MEEK	MILD	MOKI	MUCH
MALL	MEER	MILE	MOKO	MUCK
MALM	MEES	MILF	MOLA	MUDS
MALS	MEET	MILK	MOLD	MUFF
MALT	MEFF	MILL	MOLE	MUGG

MUGS	NANS	NIES	NOWL	OHED
MUID	NAOI	NIFE	NOWN	OHIA
MUIL	NAOS	NIFF	NOWS	OHMS
MUIR	NAPA	NIGH	NOWT	OIKS
MULE	NAPE	NILL	NOWY	OILS
MULL	NAPS	NILS	NOYS	OILY
MUMM	NARC	NIMB	NUBS	OINK
MUMP	NARD	NIMS	NUDE	OINT
MUMS	NARE	NINE	NUFF	OKAS
MUMU	NARK	NIPA	NUKE	OKAY
MUNG	NARY	NIPS	NULL	OKEH
MUNI	NATS	NIRL	NUMB	OKES
MUNS	NAVE	NISH	NUNS	OKRA
MUNT	NAVY	NISI	NURD	OKTA
MUON	NAYS	NITE	NURL	OLDE
MURA	NAZE	NITS	NURR	OLDS
MURE	NAZI	NIXE	NURS	OLDY
MURK	NEAL	NIXY	NUTS	OLEA
MURL	NEAP	NOAH	NYAS	OLEO
MURR	NEAR	NOBS	NYED	OLES
MUSE	NEAT	NOCK	NYES	OLID
MUSH	NEBS	NODE	OAFS	OLIO
MUSK	NECK	NODI	OAKS	OLLA
MUSO	NEDS	NODS	OAKY	OLMS
MUSS	NEED	NOEL	OARS	OLPE
MUST	NEEM	NOES	OARY	OMBU
MUTE	NEEP	NOGG	OAST	OMEN
MUTI	NEFS	NOGS	OATH	OMER
MUTS	NEGS	NOIL	OATS	OMIT
MUTT	NEIF	NOIR	OATY	OMOV
MUZZ	NEKS	NOLE	OBAS	ONCE
MWAH	NEMA	NOLL	OBES	ONER
MYAL	NEMN	NOLO	OBEY	ONES
MYCS	NENE	NOMA	OBIA	ONIE
MYNA	NEON	NOME	OBIS	ONLY
MYTH	NEPS	NOMS	OBIT	ONOS
MYXO	NERD	NONA	OBOE	ONST
MZEE	NERK	NONE	OBOL	ONTO
NAAM	NESH	NONG	OBOS	ONUS
NAAN	NESS	NONI	OCAS	ONYX
NABE	NEST	NOOB	OCCY	OOFS
NABK	NETE	NOOK	OCHE	OOFY
NABS	NETS	NOON	OCTA	OOHS
NACH	NETT	NOOP	ODAH	OOMS
NADA	NEUK	NOPE	ODAL	OONS
NADS	NEUM	NORI	ODAS	OONT
NAFF	NEVE	NORK	ODDS	OOPS
NAGA	NEVI	NORM	ODEA	OOSE
NAGS	NEWS	NOSE	ODES	OOSY
NAIF	NEWT	NOSH	ODIC	OOTS
NAIK	NEXT	NOSY	ODOR	OOZE
NAIL	NGAI	NOTA	ODSO	OOZY
NAIN	NIBS	NOTE	ODYL	OPAH
NALA	NICE	NOTT	OFAY	OPAL
NAME	NICK	NOUL	OFFS	OPED
NAMS	NIDE	NOUN	OFFY	OPEN
NAMU	NIDI	NOUP	OGAM	OPES
NANA	NIDS	NOUS	OGEE	OPPO
NANE	NIED	NOUT	OGLE	OPTS
NANG	NIEF	NOVA	OGRE	OPUS

ORAD	PACA	PEAK	PHUT	PLIE
ORAL	PACE	PEAL	PIAL	PLIM
ORBS	PACK	PEAN	PIAN	PLOD
ORBY	PACO	PEAR	PIAS	PLOP
ORCA	PACS	PEAS	PICA	PLOT
ORCS	PACT	PEAT	PICE	PLOW
ORDO	PACY	PEBA	PICK	PLOY
ORDS	PADI	PECH	PICS	PLUE
ORES	PADS	PECK	PIED	PLUG
ORFE	PAGE	PECS	PIER	PLUM
ORFS	PAHS	PEDS	PIES	PLUS
ORGY	PAID	PEED	PIET	POAS
ORLE	PAIK	PEEK	PIGS	POCK
ORRA	PAIL	PEEL	PIKA	POCO
ORTS	PAIN	PEEN	PIKE	PODS
ORYX	PAIR	PEEP	PIKI	POEM
ORZO	PAIS	PEER	PILA	POEP
OSAR	PALE	PEES	PILE	POET
OSES	PALL	PEGH	PILI	POGO
OSSA	PALM	PEGS	PILL	POGY
OTIC	PALP	PEHS	PILY	POIS
OTTO	PALS	PEIN	PIMA	POKE
OUCH	PALY	PEKE	PIMP	POKY
OUDS	PAMS	PELA	PINA	POLE
OUKS	PAND	PELE	PINE	POLK
OULD	PANE	PELF	PING	POLL
OULK	PANG	PELL	PINK	POLO
OUMA	PANS	PELS	PINS	POLS
OUPA	PANT	PELT	PINT	POLT
OUPH	PAPA	PEND	PINY	POLY
OUPS	PAPE	PENE	PION	POME
OURN	PAPS	PENI	PIOY	POMO
OURS	PARA	PENK	PIPA	POMP
OUST	PARD	PENS	PIPE	POMS
OUTS	PARE	PENT	PIPI	POND
OUZO	PARK	PEON	PIPS	PONE
OVAL	PARP	PEPO	PIPY	PONG
OVEL	PARR	PEPS	PIRL	PONK
OVEN	PARS	PERE	PIRN	PONS
OVER	PART	PERI	PIRS	PONT
OVUM	PASE	PERK	PISE	PONY
OWED	PASH	PERM	PISH	POOD
OWER	PASS	PERN	PISO	POOF
OWES	PAST	PERP	PISS	POOH
OWLS	PATE	PERT	PITA	POOK
OWLY	PATH	PERV	PITH	POOL
OWNS	PATS	PESO	PITS	POON
OWRE	PATU	PEST	PITY	POOP
OWSE	PATY	PETS	PIUM	POOR
OWTS	PAUA	PEWS	PIXY	POOS
OXEN	PAUL	PFFT	PIZE	POOT
OXER	PAVE	PFUI	PLAN	POPE
OXES	PAVS	PHAT	PLAP	POPS
OXID	PAWA	PHEW	PLAT	PORE
OXIM	PAWK	PHIS	PLAY	PORK
OYER	PAWL	PHIZ	PLEA	PORN
OYES	PAWN	PHOH	PLEB	PORT
OYEZ	PAWS	PHON	PLED	PORY
PAAL	PAYS	PHOS	PLEW	POSE
PAAN	PEAG	PHOT	PLEX	POSH

POSS	PULA	QUOD	RAYA	RICH
POST	PULE	QUOP	RAYS	RICK
POSY	PULI	RABI	RAZE	RICY
POTE	PULK	RACA	RAZZ	RIDE
POTS	PULL	RACE	READ	RIDS
POTT	PULP	RACH	REAK	RIEL
POUF	PULS	RACK	REAL	RIEM
POUK	PULU	RACY	REAM	RIFE
POUR	PULY	RADE	REAN	RIFF
POUT	PUMA	RADS	REAP	RIFS
POWN	PUMP	RAFF	REAR	RIFT
POWS	PUMY	RAFT	REBS	RIGG
POXY	PUNA	RAGA	RECK	RIGS
POZZ	PUNG	RAGE	RECS	RILE
PRAD	PUNK	RAGG	REDD	RILL
PRAM	PUNS	RAGI	REDE	RIMA
PRAO	PUNT	RAGS	REDO	RIME
PRAT	PUNY	RAGU	REDS	RIMS
PRAU	PUPA	RAHS	REED	RIMU
PRAY	PUPS	RAIA	REEF	RIMY
PREE	PUPU	RAID	REEK	RIND
PREM	PURE	RAIK	REEL	RINE
PREP	PURI	RAIL	REEN	RING
PREX	PURL	RAIN	REES	RINK
PREY	PURR	RAIS	REFS	RINS
PREZ	PURS	RAIT	REFT	RIOT
PRIG	PUSH	RAJA	REGO	RIPE
PRIM	PUSS	RAKE	REGS	RIPP
PROA	PUTS	RAKI	REHS	RIPS
PROB	PUTT	RAKU	REIF	RIPT
PROD	PUTZ	RALE	REIK	RISE
PROF	PUYS	RAMI	REIN	RISK
PROG	PYAS	RAMP	REIS	RISP
PROM	PYAT	RAMS	REKE	RITE
PROO	PYES	RANA	RELY	RITS
PROP	PYET	RAND	REMS	RITT
PROS	PYIC	RANG	REND	RITZ
PROW	PYIN	RANI	RENK	RIVA
PRUH	PYNE	RANK	RENS	RIVE
PRYS	PYOT	RANT	RENT	RIVO
PSIS	PYRE	RAPE	RENY	RIZA
PSST	PYRO	RAPS	REOS	ROAD
PTUI	QADI	RAPT	REPO	ROAM
PUBE	QAID	RARE	REPP	ROAN
PUBS	QATS	RARK	REPS	ROAR
PUCE	QINS	RASE	RESH	ROBE
PUCK	QOPH	RASH	REST	ROBS
PUDS	QUAD	RASP	RETE	ROCH
PUDU	QUAG	RAST	RETS	ROCK
PUER	QUAI	RATA	REVS	ROCS
PUFF	QUAT	RATE	REWS	RODE
PUGH	QUAY	RATH	RHEA	RODS
PUGS	QUEP	RATO	RHOS	ROED
PUHA	QUEY	RATS	RHUS	ROES
PUIR	QUID	RATU	RIAD	ROIL
PUJA	QUIM	RAUN	RIAL	ROIN
PUKA	QUIN	RAVE	RIAS	ROJI
PUKE	QUIP	RAVS	RIBA	ROKE
PUKU	QUIT	RAWN	RIBS	ROKS
PUKY	QUIZ	RAWS	RICE	ROKY

ROLE	RUMP	SANG	SEGO	SHOE
ROLF	RUMS	SANK	SEGS	SHOG
ROLL	RUND	SANS	SEIF	SHOO
ROMA	RUNE	SANT	SEIK	SHOP
ROMP	RUNG	SAPS	SEIL	SHOT
ROMS	RUNS	SARD	SEIR	SHOW
RONE	RUNT	SARI	SEIS	SHRI
RONG	RURP	SARK	SEKT	SHUL
RONT	RURU	SARS	SELD	SHUN
RONZ	RUSA	SASH	SELE	SHUT
ROOD	RUSE	SASS	SELF	SHWA
ROOF	RUSH	SATE	SELL	SIAL
ROOK	RUSK	SATI	SELS	SIBB
ROOM	RUST	SAUL	SEME	SIBS
ROON	RUTH	SAUT	SEMI	SICE
ROOP	RUTS	SAVE	SENA	SICH
ROOS	RYAL	SAVS	SEND	SICK
ROOT	RYAS	SAWN	SENE	SICS
ROPE	RYES	SAWS	SENS	SIDA
ROPY	RYFE	SAXE	SENT	SIDE
RORE	RYKE	SAYS	SEPS	SIDH
RORT	RYND	SCAB	SEPT	SIEN
RORY	RYOT	SCAD	SERA	SIES
ROSE	RYPE	SCAG	SERE	SIFT
ROST	SAAG	SCAM	SERF	SIGH
ROSY	SABE	SCAN	SERK	SIGN
ROTA	SABS	SCAR	SERR	SIJO
ROTE	SACK	SCAT	SERS	SIKA
ROTI	SACS	SCAW	SESE	SIKE
ROTL	SADE	SCOG	SESH	SILD
ROTO	SADI	SCOP	SESS	SILE
ROTS	SADO	SCOT	SETA	SILK
ROUE	SADS	SCOW	SETS	SILL
ROUL	SAFE	SCRY	SETT	SILO
ROUM	SAFT	SCUD	SEWN	SILT
ROUP	SAGA	SCUG	SEWS	SIMA
ROUT	SAGE	SCUL	SEXT	SIMI
ROUX	SAGO	SCUM	SEXY	SIMP
ROVE	SAGS	SCUP	SEYS	SIMS
ROWS	SAGY	SCUR	SHAD	SIND
ROWT	SAIC	SCUT	SHAG	SINE
RUBE	SAID	SCYE	SHAH	SING
RUBS	SAIL	SEAL	SHAM	SINH
RUBY	SAIM	SEAM	SHAN	SINK
RUCK	SAIN	SEAN	SHAT	SINS
RUCS	SAIR	SEAR	SHAW	SIPE
RUDD	SAIS	SEAS	SHAY	SIPS
RUDE	SAKE	SEAT	SHEA	SIRE
RUDS	SAKI	SECH	SHED	SIRI
RUED	SALE	SECO	SHES	SIRS
RUER	SALL	SECS	SHET	SISS
RUES	SALP	SECT	SHEW	SIST
RUFF	SALS	SEED	SHIM	SITE
RUGA	SALT	SEEK	SHIN	SITH
RUGS	SAMA	SEEL	SHIP	SITS
RUIN	SAME	SEEM	SHIR	SITZ
RUKH	SAMP	SEEN	SHIT	SIZE
RULE	SAMS	SEEP	SHIV	SIZY
RULY	SAND	SEER	SHMO	SJOE
RUME	SANE	SEES	SHOD	SKAG

SKAS	SMUT	SORA	STAP	SUSS
SKAT	SNAB	SORB	STAR	SUSU
SKAW	SNAG	SORD	STAT	SWAB
SKEE	SNAP	SORE	STAW	SWAD
SKEG	SNAR	SORI	STAY	SWAG
SKEN	SNAW	SORN	STED	SWAM
SKEO	SNEB	SORT	STEM	SWAN
SKEP	SNED	SOSS	STEN	SWAP
SKER	SNEE	SOTH	STEP	SWAT
SKET	SNIB	SOTS	STET	SWAY
SKEW	SNIG	SOUK	STEW	SWEE
SKID	SNIP	SOUL	STEY	SWEY
SKIM	SNIT	SOUM	STIE	SWIG
SKIN	SNOB	SOUP	STIM	SWIM
SKIO	SNOD	SOUR	STIR	SWIZ
SKIP	SNOG	SOUS	STOA	SWOB
SKIS	SNOT	SOUT	STOB	SWOP
SKIT	SNOW	SOVS	STOP	SWOT
SKOL	SNUB	SOWF	STOT	SWUM
SKRY	SNUG	SOWL	STOW	SYBO
SKUA	SNYE	SOWM	STUB	SYCE
SKUG	SOAK	SOWN	STUD	SYED
SKYF	SOAP	SOWP	STUM	SYEN
SKYR	SOAR	SOWS	STUN	SYES
SLAB	SOBA	SOYA	STYE	SYKE
SLAE	SOBS	SOYS	SUBA	SYLI
SLAG	SOCA	SPAE	SUBS	SYNC
SLAM	SOCK	SPAG	SUCH	SYND
SLAP	SOCS	SPAM	SUCK	SYNE
SLAT	SODA	SPAN	SUDD	SYPE
SLAW	SODS	SPAR	SUDS	SYPH
SLAY	SOFA	SPAS	SUED	TAAL
SLEB	SOFT	SPAT	SUER	TABI
SLED	SOGS	SPAW	SUES	TABS
SLEE	SOHO	SPAY	SUET	TABU
SLEW	SOHS	SPAZ	SUGH	TACE
SLEY	SOIL	SPEC	SUGO	TACH
SLID	SOJA	SPED	SUGS	TACK
SLIM	SOKE	SPEK	SUID	TACO
SLIP	SOLA	SPET	SUIT	TACT
SLIT	SOLD	SPEW	SUKH	TADS
SLOB	SOLE	SPIC	SUKS	TAED
SLOE	SOLI	SPIE	SULK	TAEL
SLOG	SOLO	SPIF	SULU	TAES
SLOP	SOLS	SPIK	SUMO	TAGS
SLOT	SOMA	SPIM	SUMP	TAHA
SLOW	SOME	SPIN	SUMS	TAHR
SLUB	SOMS	SPIT	SUMY	TAIG
SLUE	SOMY	SPIV	SUNG	TAIL
SLUG	SONE	SPOD	SUNI	TAIN
SLUM	SONG	SPOT	SUNK	TAIS
SLUR	SONS	SPRY	SUNN	TAIT
SLUT	SOOK	SPUD	SUNS	TAKA
SMEE	SOOL	SPUE	SUPE	TAKE
SMEW	SOOM	SPUG	SUPS	TAKI
SMIR	SOON	SPUN	SUQS	TAKS
SMIT	SOOP	SPUR	SURA	TAKY
SMOG	SOOT	SRIS	SURD	TALA
SMUG	SOPH	STAB	SURE	TALC
SMUR	SOPS	STAG	SURF	TALE

TALI	TEFF	TIDS	TOLA	TREK
TALK	TEFS	TIDY	TOLD	TRES
TALL	TEGG	TIED	TOLE	TRET
TAME	TEGS	TIER	TOLL	TREW
TAMP	TEGU	TIES	TOLT	TREY
TAMS	TEHR	TIFF	TOLU	TREZ
TANA	TEIL	TIFT	TOMB	TRIE
TANE	TEIN	TIGE	TOME	TRIG
TANG	TELA	TIGS	TOMO	TRIM
TANH	TELD	TIKA	TOMS	TRIN
TANK	TELE	TIKE	TONE	TRIO
TANS	TELL	TIKI	TONG	TRIP
TAOS	TELS	TIKS	TONK	TROD
TAPA	TELT	TILE	TONS	TROG
TAPE	TEME	TILL	TONY	TRON
TAPS	TEMP	TILS	TOOK	TROP
TAPU	TEMS	TILT	TOOL	TROT
TARA	TEND	TIME	TOOM	TROW
TARE	TENE	TINA	TOON	TROY
TARN	TENS	TIND	TOOT	TRUE
TARO	TENT	TINE	TOPE	TRUG
TARP	TEPA	TING	TOPH	TRYE
TARS	TERF	TINK	TOPI	TRYP
TART	TERM	TINS	TOPO	TSAR
TASH	TERN	TINT	TOPS	TSKS
TASK	TEST	TINY	TORA	TUAN
TASS	TETE	TIPI	TORC	TUBA
TATE	TETH	TIPS	TORE	TUBE
TATH	TETS	TIPT	TORI	TUBS
TATS	TEWS	TIRE	TORN	TUCK
TATT	TEXT	TIRL	TORO	TUFA
TATU	THAE	TIRO	TORR	TUFF
TAUS	THAN	TIRR	TORS	TUFT
TAUT	THAR	TITE	TORT	TUGS
TAVA	THAT	TITI	TORY	TUIS
TAVS	THAW	TITS	TOSA	TULE
TAWA	THEE	TIVY	TOSE	TUMP
TAWS	THEM	TIZZ	TOSH	TUMS
TAWT	THEN	TOAD	TOSS	TUNA
TAXA	THEW	TOBY	TOST	TUND
TAXI	THEY	TOCK	TOTE	TUNE
TAYS	THIG	TOCO	TOTS	TUNG
TEAD	THIN	TOCS	TOUK	TUNS
TEAK	THIO	TODS	TOUN	TUNY
TEAL	THIR	TODY	TOUR	TUPS
TEAM	THIS	TOEA	TOUT	TURD
TEAR	THON	TOED	TOWN	TURF
TEAS	THOU	TOES	TOWS	TURK
TEAT	THRO	TOEY	TOWT	TURM
TECH	THRU	TOFF	TOWY	TURN
TECS	THUD	TOFT	TOYO	TUSH
TEDS	THUG	TOFU	TOYS	TUSK
TEDY	THUS	TOGA	TOZE	TUTS
TEED	TIAN	TOGE	TRAD	TUTU
TEEK	TIAR	TOGS	TRAM	TUZZ
TEEL	TICE	TOHO	TRAP	TWAE
TEEM	TICH	TOIL	TRAT	TWAL
TEEN	TICK	TOIT	TRAY	TWAS
TEER	TICS	TOKE	TREE	TWAT
TEES	TIDE	TOKO	TREF	TWAY

TWEE	UPGO	VEGA	VOES	WARB
TWIG	UPON	VEGO	VOID	WARD
TWIN	UPSY	VEHM	VOIP	WARE
TWIT	UPTA	VEIL	VOLA	WARK
TWOS	URAO	VEIN	VOLE	WARM
TYDE	URBS	VELA	VOLK	WARN
TYED	URDE	VELD	VOLS	WARP
TYEE	URDS	VELE	VOLT	WARS
TYER	URDY	VELL	VORS	WART
TYES	UREA	VENA	VOTE	WARY
TYGS	URES	VEND	VOWS	WASE
TYIN	URGE	VENT	VRIL	WASH
TYKE	URIC	VERA	VROT	WASP
TYMP	URNS	VERB	VROU	WAST
TYND	URPS	VERD	VROW	WATE
TYNE	URSA	VERS	VUGG	WATS
TYPE	URUS	VERT	VUGH	WATT
TYPO	URVA	VERY	VUGS	WAUK
TYPP	USED	VEST	VULN	WAUL
TYPY	USER	VETO	VUMS	WAUR
TYRE	USES	VETS	WAAC	WAVE
TYRO	UTAS	VEXT	WABS	WAVY
TYTE	UTES	VIAE	WACK	WAWA
TZAR	UTIS	VIAL	WADD	WAWE
UDAL	UTUS	VIAS	WADE	WAWL
UDON	UVAE	VIBE	WADI	WAWS
UDOS	UVAS	VIBS	WADS	WAXY
UEYS	UVEA	VICE	WADT	WAYS
UFOS	VACS	VIDE	WADY	WEAK
UGHS	VADE	VIDS	WAES	WEAL
UGLY	VAES	VIED	WAFF	WEAN
UKES	VAGI	VIER	WAFT	WEAR
ULAN	VAGS	VIES	WAGE	WEBS
ULES	VAIL	VIEW	WAGS	WEDS
ULEX	VAIN	VIGA	WAID	WEED
ULNA	VAIR	VIGS	WAIF	WEEK
ULUS	VALE	VILD	WAIL	WEEL
ULVA	VALI	VILE	WAIN	WEEM
UMBO	VAMP	VILL	WAIR	WEEN
UMMA	VANE	VIMS	WAIS	WEEP
UMPH	VANG	VINA	WAIT	WEER
UMPS	VANS	VINE	WAKA	WEES
UMPY	VANT	VINO	WAKE	WEET
UMRA	VARA	VINS	WAKF	WEFT
UMUS	VARE	VINT	WALD	WEID
UNAI	VARS	VINY	WALE	WEIL
UNAU	VARY	VIOL	WALI	WEIR
UNBE	VASA	VIRE	WALK	WEKA
UNCE	VASE	VIRL	WALL	WELD
UNCI	VAST	VISA	WALY	WELK
UNCO	VATS	VISE	WAME	WELL
UNDE	VATU	VITA	WAND	WELS
UNDO	VAUS	VITE	WANE	WELT
UNDY	VAUT	VIVA	WANG	WEMB
UNIS	VAVS	VIVE	WANK	WEMS
UNIT	VAWS	VIVO	WANS	WENA
UNTO	VEAL	VIZY	WANT	WEND
UPAS	VEEP	VLEI	WANY	WENS
UPBY	VEER	VLOG	WAPS	WENT
UPDO	VEES	VOAR	WAQF	WEPT

WERE	WIRY	YABA	YIDS	YUZU
WERO	WISE	YACK	YIKE	YWIS
WERT	WISH	YADS	YILL	ZACK
WEST	WISP	YAFF	YINS	ZAGS
WETA	WISS	YAGI	YIPE	ZANY
WETS	WIST	YAGS	YIPS	ZAPS
WEXE	WITE	YAHS	YIRD	ZARF
WEYS	WITH	YAKS	YIRK	ZARI
WHAE	WITS	YALD	YIRR	ZATI
WHAM	WIVE	YALE	YITE	ZEAL
WHAP	WOAD	YAMS	YLEM	ZEAS
WHAT	WOCK	YANG	YLKE	ZEBU
WHEE	WOES	YANK	YMPE	ZEDS
WHEN	WOFS	YAPP	YMPT	ZEES
WHET	WOGS	YAPS	YOBS	ZEIN
WHEW	WOKE	YARD	YOCK	ZEKS
WHEY	WOKS	YARE	YODE	ZELS
WHID	WOLD	YARK	YODH	ZEPS
WHIG	WOLF	YARN	YODS	ZERK
WHIM	WOMB	YARR	YOGA	ZERO
WHIN	WONK	YATE	YOGH	ZEST
WHIO	WONS	YAUD	YOGI	ZETA
WHIP	WONT	YAUP	YOKE	ZEZE
WHIR	WOOD	YAWL	YOKS	ZHOS
WHIT	WOOF	YAWN	YOLD	ZIFF
WHIZ	WOOL	YAWP	YOLK	ZIGS
WHOA	WOON	YAWS	YOMP	ZILA
WHOM	WOOS	YAWY	YOND	ZILL
WHOP	WOOT	YAYS	YONI	ZIMB
WHOT	WOPS	YBET	YONT	ZINC
WHOW	WORD	YEAD	YOOF	ZINE
WHUP	WORE	YEAH	YOOP	ZING
WHYS	WORK	YEAN	YORE	ZINS
WICE	WORM	YEAR	YORK	ZIPS
WICH	WORN	YEAS	YORP	ZITE
WICK	WORT	YEBO	YOUK	ZITI
WIDE	WOST	YECH	YOUR	ZITS
WIEL	WOTS	YEDE	YOUS	ZIZZ
WIFE	WOVE	YEED	YOWE	ZOBO
WIGS	WOWF	YEGG	YOWL	ZOBU
WIKI	WOWS	YELD	YOWS	ZOEA
WILD	WRAP	YELK	YUAN	ZOIC
WILE	WREN	YELL	YUCA	ZOLS
WILI	WRIT	YELM	YUCH	ZONA
WILL	WUDS	YELP	YUCK	ZONE
WILT	WUDU	YELT	YUFT	ZONK
WILY	WULL	YENS	YUGA	ZOOM
WIMP	WUSS	YEPS	YUGS	ZOON
WIND	WYCH	YERD	YUKE	ZOOS
WINE	WYES	YERK	YUKO	ZOOT
WING	WYLE	YESK	YUKS	ZORI
WINK	WYND	YEST	YUKY	ZOUK
WINN	WYNN	YETI	YULE	ZULU
WINO	WYNS	YETT	YUMP	ZUPA
WINS	WYTE	YEUK	YUNX	ZURF
WINY	XRAY	YEVE	YUPS	ZYGA
WIPE	XYST	YEWS	YURT	ZYME
WIRE	YAAR	YGOE	YUTZ	ZZZS

CHAPTER 2
POWER TILES

The highest-scoring tiles in the game are J, Q, X, and Z, with J and X scoring eight points each, while Q and Z are worth ten. These 'power tiles' are the most potent weapons in the Scrabble player's arsenal, but need to be carefully deployed. This isn't always a matter of using them in a long word – a carefully positioned short word can be just as good a move. You should also remember that, on average, in a two-player game you are only likely to get each one every other game so it isn't worth concentrating just on these words at the expense of learning new short words or bonus-scoring words.

This section lists all of the power-tile words of two and three letters, with a brief definition for each. It's worth learning all of these words as they can be tremendously useful, combining the assets of all short words with the high scores afforded by the power tiles. Knowing the definitions of these words will help you commit them to memory.

The subsequent lists include all of the power-tile words from four to eight letters. While there may be too many of these to remember, studying the list will provide you with a range of useful options for game situations where you have one of these valuable tiles on your rack. You should initially focus on four or five letter words that begin or end in a power tile because that is a standard length between a double or triple letter square and a double or triple word square.

Using J

There is only one J tile in Scrabble, so for any word with two Js (eg HAJJ or JUJU) a blank is required. When you are trying to use a word with J for parallel play, remember that there are only two two-letter words with J – JA and JO. The J can be as awkward as the Q and is not as flexible as the X and Z so it is wise to try and use it as soon as it arrives on your rack rather than hold onto it hoping for a better score later. Don't forget unusual combinations like the FJ in FJELD and FJORD, or the DJ in DJIN, DJINN and their plurals. An examination of the following lists will also reveal a number of words that contain a JR combination, including BAJRA, BAJRI, and HIJRA. Learning some of these more unusual JR words will give you greater ammunition to make the best use of the J if more common words are unplayable. If there is a Z on the board or on your rack when you have a J, there are several words that could impress your opponent (eg JIZ, JAZY).

Two-letter words

JA	yes
JO	Scots word for sweetheart

Three-letter words

GJU	type of violin used in Shetland
HAJ	pilgrimage a Muslim makes to Mecca
JAB	poke sharply
JAG	period of uncontrolled indulgence in an activity
JAI	victory (to)
JAK	device for raising a motor vehicle or other heavy object
JAM	pack tightly into a place
JAP	splash
JAR	wide-mouthed container, usu round and made of glass
JAW	one of the bones in which the teeth are set
JAY	bird with a pinkish body and blue-and-black wings
JEE	to move aside
JET	aircraft driven by jet propulsion
JEU	game
JEW	obsolete offensive word for haggle
JIB	taunt or jeer
JIG	type of lively dance
JIN	Chinese unit of weight

JIZ	wig	JUG	container for liquids, with a handle
JOB	occupation or paid employment		and small spout
JOE	Scots word for sweetheart	JUN	North and South Korean monetary
JOG	run at a gentle pace, esp for exercise		unit worth one hundredth of a won
JOL	party	JUS	right, power, or authority
JOR	movement in Indian music	JUT	project or stick out
JOT	write briefly	RAJ	(in India) government
JOW	ring (a bell)	TAJ	tall conical cap worn as a mark of
JOY	feeling of great delight or pleasure		distinction by Muslims
JUD	large block of coal		

Four-letter words	JEAT	JOLE	**Five-letter words**	JADES
AJAR	JEDI	JOLL		JAFAS
AJEE	JEED	JOLS	AFLAJ	JAFFA
BAJU	JEEL	JOLT	AJIVA	JAGAS
BENJ	JEEP	JOMO	AJUGA	JAGER
DJIN	JEER	JONG	AJWAN	JAGGS
DOJO	JEES	JOOK	BAJAN	JAGGY
FUJI	JEEZ	JORS	BAJRA	JAGIR
GAJO	JEFE	JOSH	BAJRI	JAGRA
GJUS	JEFF	JOSS	BAJUS	JAILS
GOJI	JEHU	JOTA	BANJO	JAKES
HADJ	JELL	JOTS	BASIJ	JAKEY
HAJI	JEON	JOUK	BHAJI	JALAP
HAJJ	JERK	JOUR	BIJOU	JALOP
JAAP	JESS	JOWL	BUNJE	JAMBE
JABS	JEST	JOWS	BUNJY	JAMBO
JACK	JETE	JOYS	CAJON	JAMBS
JADE	JETS	JUBA	CAJUN	JAMBU
JAFA	JEUX	JUBE	DJINN	JAMES
JAGA	JEWS	JUCO	DJINS	JAMMY
JAGG	JIAO	JUDO	DOJOS	JAMON
JAGS	JIBB	JUDS	EEJIT	JANES
JAIL	JIBE	JUDY	EJECT	JANNS
JAKE	JIBS	JUGA	ENJOY	JANNY
JAKS	JIFF	JUGS	FALAJ	JANTY
JAMB	JIGS	JUJU	FJELD	JAPAN
JAMS	JILL	JUKE	FJORD	JAPED
JANE	JILT	JUKU	FUJIS	JAPER
JANN	JIMP	JUMP	GADJE	JAPES
JAPE	JINK	JUNK	GADJO	JARKS
JAPS	JINN	JUPE	GAJOS	JARLS
JARK	JINS	JURA	GANJA	JARPS
JARL	JINX	JURE	GAUJE	JARTA
JARP	JIRD	JURY	GOJIS	JARUL
JARS	JISM	JUST	HADJI	JASEY
JASP	JIVE	JUTE	HAJES	JASPE
JASS	JIVY	JUTS	HAJIS	JASPS
JASY	JIZZ	JUVE	HAJJI	JATOS
JATO	JOBE	JYNX	HEJAB	JAUKS
JAUK	JOBS	KOJI	HEJRA	JAUNT
JAUP	JOCK	MOJO	HIJAB	JAUPS
JAVA	JOCO	PUJA	HIJRA	JAVAS
JAWS	JOES	RAJA	HODJA	JAVEL
JAXY	JOEY	ROJI	JAAPS	JAWAN
JAYS	JOGS	SIJO	JABOT	JAWED
JAZY	JOHN	SJOE	JACAL	JAXIE
JAZZ	JOIN	SOJA	JACKS	JAZZY
JEAN	JOKE		JACKY	JEANS
	JOKY		JADED	JEATS

			Six-letter	FRIJOL
JEBEL	JNANA	JUMBO	**words**	GADJES
JEDIS	JOBED	JUMBY	ABJECT	GAIJIN
JEELS	JOBES	JUMPS	ABJURE	GANJAH
JEELY	JOCKO	JUMPY	ACAJOU	GANJAS
JEEPS	JOCKS	JUNCO	ADJIGO	GARJAN
JEERS	JODEL	JUNKS	ADJOIN	GAUJES
JEFES	JOEYS	JUNKY	ADJURE	GIDJEE
JEFFS	JOHNS	JUNTA	ADJUST	GOUJON
JEHAD	JOINS	JUNTO	AJIVAS	GURJUN
JEHUS	JOINT	JUPES	AJOWAN	GYTTJA
JELAB	JOIST	JUPON	AJUGAS	HADJEE
JELLO	JOKED	JURAL	AJWANS	HADJES
JELLS	JOKER	JURAT	BAJADA	HADJIS
JELLY	JOKES	JUREL	BAJANS	HAJJAH
JEMBE	JOKEY	JUROR	BAJRAS	HAJJES
JEMMY	JOKOL	JUSTS	BAJREE	HAJJIS
JENNY	JOLED	JUTES	BAJRIS	HANJAR
JERID	JOLES	JUTTY	BANJAX	HEJABS
JERKS	JOLLS	JUVES	BANJOS	HEJIRA
JERKY	JOLLY	JUVIE	BASEEJ	HEJRAS
JERRY	JOLTS	KANJI	BEJADE	HIJABS
JESSE	JOLTY	KHOJA	BEJANT	HIJACK
JESTS	JOMON	KOJIS	BENJES	HIJRAH
JESUS	JOMOS	KOPJE	BHAJAN	HIJRAS
JETES	JONES	LAPJE	BHAJEE	HOBJOB
JETON	JONGS	MAJOR	BHAJIA	HODJAS
JETTY	JONTY	MOJOS	BHAJIS	INJECT
JEUNE	JOOKS	MUJIK	BIJOUS	INJERA
JEWED	JORAM	NINJA	BIJOUX	INJURE
JEWEL	JORUM	OBJET	BOOJUM	INJURY
JEWIE	JOTAS	OJIME	BUNJEE	INKJET
JHALA	JOTTY	OUIJA	BUNJES	JABBED
JIAOS	JOTUN	POLJE	BUNJIE	JABBER
JIBBA	JOUAL	POOJA	CAJOLE	JABBLE
JIBBS	JOUGS	PUJAH	COJOIN	JABERS
JIBED	JOUKS	PUJAS	CONJEE	JABIRU
JIBER	JOULE	PUNJI	CROJIK	JABOTS
JIBES	JOURS	RAJAH	DEEJAY	JACALS
JIFFS	JOUST	RAJAS	DEJECT	JACANA
JIFFY	JOWAR	RAJES	DJEBEL	JACARE
JIGGY	JOWED	REJIG	DJEMBE	JACENT
JIGOT	JOWLS	REJON	DJINNI	JACKAL
JIHAD	JOWLY	RIOJA	DJINNS	JACKED
JILLS	JOYED	ROJAK	DJINNY	JACKER
JILTS	JUBAS	ROJIS	DONJON	JACKET
JIMMY	JUBES	SAJOU	EEJITS	JACKSY
JIMPY	JUCOS	SHOJI	EJECTA	JADERY
JINGO	JUDAS	SIJOS	EJECTS	JADING
JINKS	JUDGE	SLOJD	ENJAMB	JADISH
JINNE	JUDOS	SOJAS	ENJOIN	JAEGER
JINNI	JUGAL	SUJEE	ENJOYS	JAFFAS
JINNS	JUGUM	TAJES	EVEJAR	JAGAED
JIRDS	JUICE	THUJA	FAJITA	JAGERS
JIRGA	JUICY	UNJAM	FANJET	JAGGED
JIRRE	JUJUS	UPJET	FEIJOA	JAGGER
JISMS	JUKED	WILJA	FIGJAM	JAGHIR
JIVED	JUKES	YOJAN	FINJAN	JAGIRS
JIVER	JUKUS	ZANJA	FJELDS	JAGRAS
JIVES	JULEP		FJORDS	JAGUAR
JIVEY	JUMAR			

JAILED	JAWING	JIBBAH	JOHNNY	JUDIES
JAILER	JAXIES	JIBBAS	JOINED	JUDOGI
JAILOR	JAYCEE	JIBBED	JOINER	JUDOKA
JAKEYS	JAYGEE	JIBBER	JOINTS	JUGALS
JALAPS	JAYVEE	JIBERS	JOISTS	JUGATE
JALOPS	JAZIES	JIBING	JOJOBA	JUGFUL
JALOPY	JAZZBO	JICAMA	JOKERS	JUGGED
JAMAAT	JAZZED	JIGGED	JOKIER	JUGGLE
JAMBED	JAZZER	JIGGER	JOKILY	JUGLET
JAMBEE	JAZZES	JIGGLE	JOKING	JUGULA
JAMBER	JEANED	JIGGLY	JOLING	JUGUMS
JAMBES	JEBELS	JIGJIG	JOLLED	JUICED
JAMBOK	JEEING	JIGOTS	JOLLER	JUICER
JAMBUL	JEELED	JIGSAW	JOLLEY	JUICES
JAMBUS	JEELIE	JIHADI	JOLLOP	JUJUBE
JAMJAR	JEEPED	JIHADS	JOLTED	JUKING
JAMMED	JEERED	JILBAB	JOLTER	JULEPS
JAMMER	JEERER	JILGIE	JOOKED	JULIET
JAMPAN	JEFFED	JILLET	JORAMS	JUMARS
JAMPOT	JEHADI	JILTED	JORDAN	JUMART
JANGLE	JEHADS	JILTER	JORUMS	JUMBAL
JANGLY	JEJUNA	JIMINY	JOSEPH	JUMBIE
JANKER	JEJUNE	JIMJAM	JOSHED	JUMBLE
JANSKY	JELABS	JIMMIE	JOSHER	JUMBLY
JANTEE	JELLED	JIMPER	JOSHES	JUMBOS
JAPANS	JELLOS	JIMPLY	JOSKIN	JUMPED
JAPERS	JEMBES	JIMSON	JOSSER	JUMPER
JAPERY	JEMIMA	JINGAL	JOSSES	JUNCOS
JAPING	JENNET	JINGKO	JOSTLE	JUNCUS
JAPPED	JERBIL	JINGLE	JOTTED	JUNGLE
JARFUL	JERBOA	JINGLY	JOTTER	JUNGLI
JARGON	JEREED	JINKED	JOTUNN	JUNGLY
JARINA	JERIDS	JINKER	JOTUNS	JUNIOR
JAROOL	JERKED	JINNEE	JOUALS	JUNKED
JARPED	JERKER	JINNIS	JOUKED	JUNKER
JARRAH	JERKIN	JINXED	JOULED	JUNKET
JARRED	JERQUE	JINXES	JOULES	JUNKIE
JARTAS	JERRID	JIRBLE	JOUNCE	JUNTAS
JARULS	JERSEY	JIRGAS	JOUNCY	JUNTOS
JARVEY	JESSED	JISSOM	JOURNO	JUPATI
JARVIE	JESSES	JITNEY	JOUSTS	JUPONS
JASEYS	JESSIE	JITTER	JOVIAL	JURANT
JASIES	JESTED	JIVERS	JOWARI	JURATS
JASMIN	JESTEE	JIVIER	JOWARS	JURELS
JASPER	JESTER	JIVING	JOWING	JURIED
JASPES	JESUIT	JIZZES	JOWLED	JURIES
JASPIS	JETLAG	JNANAS	JOWLER	JURIST
JASSES	JETONS	JOANNA	JOYFUL	JURORS
JASSID	JETSAM	JOBBED	JOYING	JUSTED
JATAKA	JETSOM	JOBBER	JOYOUS	JUSTER
JAUKED	JETSON	JOBBIE	JOYPAD	JUSTLE
JAUNCE	JETTED	JOBING	JOYPOP	JUSTLY
JAUNSE	JETTON	JOCKEY	JUBATE	JUTTED
JAUNTS	JETWAY	JOCKOS	JUBBAH	JUVIES
JAUNTY	JEWELS	JOCOSE	JUBHAH	JYMOLD
JAUPED	JEWIES	JOCUND	JUBILE	JYNXES
JAVELS	JEWING	JODELS	JUDDER	KANJIS
JAWANS	JEZAIL	JOGGED	JUDGED	KHODJA
JAWARI	JHALAS	JOGGER	JUDGER	KHOJAS
JAWBOX	JHATKA	JOGGLE	JUDGES	KOPJES

LAPJES	UNJAMS	CARJACK	INJURED	JAMBERS
LOGJAM	UNJUST	CATJANG	INJURER	JAMBEUX
MAJLIS	UPJETS	COJOINS	INJURES	JAMBIER
MAJORS	VEEJAY	COJONES	JABBERS	JAMBING
MASJID	WILJAS	CONJECT	JABBING	JAMBIYA
MATJES	WILTJA	CONJEED	JABBLED	JAMBOKS
MEJLIS	YOJANA	CONJEES	JABBLES	JAMBONE
MOJITO	YOJANS	CONJOIN	JABIRUS	JAMBOOL
MOJOES	ZANJAS	CONJURE	JACALES	JAMBULS
MOUJIK		CONJURY	JACAMAR	JAMDANI
MUJIKS	**Seven-letter**	CROJIKS	JACANAS	JAMESES
MUSJID	**words**	DEEJAYS	JACARES	JAMJARS
MUZJIK	ABJECTS	DEJECTA	JACCHUS	JAMLIKE
NINJAS	ABJOINT	DEJECTS	JACINTH	JAMMERS
NUTJOB	ABJURED	DEJEUNE	JACKALS	JAMMIER
OBJECT	ABJURER	DISJECT	JACKASS	JAMMIES
OBJETS	ABJURES	DISJOIN	JACKDAW	JAMMING
OBJURE	ACAJOUS	DISJUNE	JACKEEN	JAMPANI
OJIMES	ADJIGOS	DJEBELS	JACKERS	JAMPANS
OUIJAS	ADJOINS	DJEMBES	JACKETS	JAMPOTS
OUTJET	ADJOINT	DJIBBAH	JACKIES	JANGLED
OUTJUT	ADJOURN	DONJONS	JACKING	JANGLER
PAJAMA	ADJUDGE	EJECTED	JACKLEG	JANGLES
PAJOCK	ADJUNCT	EJECTOR	JACKMAN	JANITOR
POLJES	ADJURED	ENJAMBS	JACKMEN	JANIZAR
POOJAH	ADJURER	ENJOINS	JACKPOT	JANKERS
POOJAS	ADJURES	ENJOYED	JACKSIE	JANNIES
POPJOY	ADJUROR	ENJOYER	JACOBIN	JANNOCK
POTJIE	ADJUSTS	EVEJARS	JACOBUS	JANSKYS
PRAJNA	AJOWANS	FAJITAS	JACONET	JANTIER
PROJET	AJUTAGE	FANJETS	JACUZZI	JANTIES
PUJAHS	ALFORJA	FEIJOAS	JADEDLY	JAPINGS
PUJARI	ANTIJAM	FIGJAMS	JADEITE	JAPPING
PUNJIS	APAREJO	FINJANS	JADITIC	JARFULS
PYJAMA	AZULEJO	FJORDIC	JAEGERS	JARGONS
RAJAHS	BAJADAS	FRIJOLE	JAGAING	JARGONY
RAKIJA	BAJREES	GANJAHS	JAGGARY	JARGOON
RAMJET	BANJOES	GARJANS	JAGGERS	JARHEAD
REJECT	BASENJI	GIDJEES	JAGGERY	JARINAS
REJIGS	BEJADED	GJETOST	JAGGIER	JARKMAN
REJOIN	BEJADES	GOUJONS	JAGGIES	JARKMEN
RHANJA	BEJANTS	GURJUNS	JAGGING	JARLDOM
RIOJAS	BEJESUS	GYTTJAS	JAGHIRE	JAROOLS
ROJAKS	BEJEWEL	HADJEES	JAGHIRS	JARPING
ROMAJI	BHAJANS	HAJJAHS	JAGLESS	JARRAHS
SAJOUS	BHAJEES	HANDJAR	JAGUARS	JARRING
SANJAK	BLOWJOB	HANDJOB	JAILERS	JARSFUL
SEJANT	BLUEJAY	HANJARS	JAILING	JARVEYS
SHINJU	BONJOUR	HARIJAN	JAILORS	JARVIES
SHOJIS	BOOJUMS	HEJIRAS	JAKESES	JASMINE
SLOJDS	BRINJAL	HIJACKS	JALABIB	JASMINS
SOOJEY	BUNJEES	HIJINKS	JALAPIC	JASPERS
SUJEES	BUNJIES	HIJRAHS	JALAPIN	JASPERY
SVARAJ	CAJAPUT	HOBJOBS	JALOPPY	JASSIDS
SWARAJ	CAJEPUT	IJTIHAD	JALOUSE	JATAKAS
TAJINE	CAJOLED	INJECTS	JAMAATS	JAUKING
THUJAS	CAJOLER	INJELLY	JAMADAR	JAUNCED
TINAJA	CAJOLES	INJERAS	JAMBART	JAUNCES
TRIJET	CAJONES	INJOINT	JAMBEAU	JAUNSED
UJAMAA	CAJUPUT	INJUNCT	JAMBEES	JAUNSES

JAUNTED	JERKING	JILBABS	JOISTED	JUBILEE
JAUNTEE	JERKINS	JILGIES	JOJOBAS	JUBILES
JAUNTIE	JERQUED	JILLETS	JOKIEST	JUDASES
JAUPING	JERQUER	JILLION	JOLLERS	JUDDERS
JAVELIN	JERQUES	JILTERS	JOLLEYS	JUDDERY
JAWARIS	JERREED	JILTING	JOLLIED	JUDGERS
JAWBONE	JERRIDS	JIMJAMS	JOLLIER	JUDGING
JAWFALL	JERRIES	JIMMIED	JOLLIES	JUDOGIS
JAWHOLE	JERSEYS	JIMMIES	JOLLIFY	JUDOIST
JAWINGS	JESSAMY	JIMMINY	JOLLILY	JUDOKAS
JAWLESS	JESSANT	JIMPEST	JOLLING	JUGFULS
JAWLIKE	JESSIES	JIMPIER	JOLLITY	JUGGING
JAWLINE	JESSING	JIMPSON	JOLLOPS	JUGGINS
JAYBIRD	JESTEES	JINGALL	JOLLYER	JUGGLED
JAYCEES	JESTERS	JINGALS	JOLTERS	JUGGLER
JAYGEES	JESTFUL	JINGLED	JOLTIER	JUGGLES
JAYVEES	JESTING	JINGLER	JOLTILY	JUGHEAD
JAYWALK	JESUITS	JINGLES	JOLTING	JUGLETS
JAZZBOS	JETBEAD	JINGLET	JONESED	JUGSFUL
JAZZERS	JETFOIL	JINGOES	JONESES	JUGULAR
JAZZIER	JETLAGS	JINJILI	JONNOCK	JUGULUM
JAZZILY	JETLIKE	JINKERS	JONQUIL	JUICERS
JAZZING	JETPORT	JINKING	JONTIES	JUICIER
JAZZMAN	JETSAMS	JINXING	JOOKERY	JUICILY
JAZZMEN	JETSOMS	JIPYAPA	JOOKING	JUICING
JEALOUS	JETSONS	JIRBLED	JORDANS	JUJITSU
JEELIED	JETTIED	JIRBLES	JOSEPHS	JUJUBES
JEELIES	JETTIER	JISSOMS	JOSHERS	JUJUISM
JEELING	JETTIES	JITNEYS	JOSHING	JUJUIST
JEEPERS	JETTING	JITTERS	JOSKINS	JUJUTSU
JEEPING	JETTONS	JITTERY	JOSSERS	JUKEBOX
JEEPNEY	JETWAYS	JIVEASS	JOSTLED	JUKSKEI
JEERERS	JEWELED	JIVIEST	JOSTLER	JULIETS
JEERING	JEWELER	JOANNAS	JOSTLES	JUMARED
JEFFING	JEWELRY	JOANNES	JOTTERS	JUMARTS
JEHADIS	JEWFISH	JOBBERS	JOTTIER	JUMBALS
JEJUNAL	JEZAILS	JOBBERY	JOTTING	JUMBIES
JEJUNUM	JEZEBEL	JOBBIES	JOTUNNS	JUMBLED
JELLABA	JHATKAS	JOBBING	JOUKERY	JUMBLER
JELLIED	JIBBAHS	JOBLESS	JOUKING	JUMBLES
JELLIES	JIBBERS	JOBNAME	JOULING	JUMBUCK
JELLIFY	JIBBING	JOCKEYS	JOUNCED	JUMELLE
JELLING	JIBBONS	JOCKISH	JOUNCES	JUMPERS
JEMADAR	JIBBOOM	JOCULAR	JOURNAL	JUMPIER
JEMIDAR	JICAMAS	JODHPUR	JOURNEY	JUMPILY
JEMIMAS	JIFFIES	JOGGERS	JOURNOS	JUMPING
JEMMIED	JIGABOO	JOGGING	JOUSTED	JUMPOFF
JEMMIER	JIGAJIG	JOGGLED	JOUSTER	JUNCATE
JEMMIES	JIGAJOG	JOGGLER	JOWARIS	JUNCOES
JENNETS	JIGGERS	JOGGLES	JOWLERS	JUNGLED
JENNIES	JIGGIER	JOGTROT	JOWLIER	JUNGLES
JEOFAIL	JIGGING	JOHNNIE	JOWLING	JUNGLIS
JEOPARD	JIGGISH	JOHNSON	JOYANCE	JUNIORS
JERBILS	JIGGLED	JOINDER	JOYLESS	JUNIPER
JERBOAS	JIGGLES	JOINERS	JOYPADS	JUNKERS
JEREEDS	JIGJIGS	JOINERY	JOYPOPS	JUNKETS
JERKERS	JIGLIKE	JOINING	JOYRIDE	JUNKIER
JERKIER	JIGSAWN	JOINTED	JOYRODE	JUNKIES
JERKIES	JIGSAWS	JOINTER	JUBBAHS	JUNKING
JERKILY	JIHADIS	JOINTLY	JUBHAHS	JUNKMAN

JUNKMEN	OVERJOY	**Eight-letter**	CONJOINT	JACKBOOT
JUPATIS	PAJAMAS	**words**	CONJUGAL	JACKDAWS
JURALLY	PAJOCKE	ABJECTED	CONJUNCT	JACKEENS
JURANTS	PAJOCKS	ABJECTLY	CONJUNTO	JACKEROO
JURIDIC	PERJINK	ABJOINTS	CONJURED	JACKETED
JURISTS	PERJURE	ABJURERS	CONJURER	JACKFISH
JURYING	PERJURY	ABJURING	CONJURES	JACKINGS
JURYMAN	PIROJKI	ADJACENT	CONJUROR	JACKLEGS
JURYMEN	POOJAHS	ADJOINED	CRACKJAW	JACKPOTS
JUSSIVE	POPJOYS	ADJOINTS	CUNJEVOI	JACKROLL
JUSTERS	POTJIES	ADJOURNS	DEEJAYED	JACKSIES
JUSTEST	PRAJNAS	ADJUDGED	DEJECTED	JACKSTAY
JUSTICE	PREJINK	ADJUDGES	DEJEUNER	JACOBINS
JUSTIFY	PROJECT	ADJUNCTS	DEJEUNES	JACONETS
JUSTING	PROJETS	ADJURERS	DEMIJOHN	JACQUARD
JUSTLED	PROPJET	ADJURING	DISJECTS	JACULATE
JUSTLES	PUJARIS	ADJURORS	DISJOINS	JACUZZIS
JUTTIED	PYJAMAS	ADJUSTED	DISJOINT	JADEITES
JUTTIES	RAKIJAS	ADJUSTER	DISJUNCT	JADELIKE
JUTTING	RAMJETS	ADJUSTOR	DISJUNES	JADERIES
JUVENAL	REEJECT	ADJUTAGE	DJELLABA	JADISHLY
KAJAWAH	REENJOY	ADJUTANT	DJIBBAHS	JAGGEDER
KAJEPUT	REJECTS	ADJUVANT	DOORJAMB	JAGGEDLY
KHANJAR	REJOICE	AJUTAGES	EJECTING	JAGGHERY
KHODJAS	REJOINS	ALFORJAS	EJECTION	JAGGIEST
KILLJOY	REJONEO	APAREJOS	EJECTIVE	JAGHIRES
KIPUNJI	REJONES	AZULEJOS	EJECTORS	JAILABLE
KUNJOOS	REJOURN	BANJAXED	ENJAMBED	JAILBAIT
LOCKJAW	REJUDGE	BANJAXES	ENJOINED	JAILBIRD
LOGJAMS	RESOJET	BANJOIST	ENJOINER	JAILLESS
MAATJES	RHANJAS	BASENJIS	ENJOYERS	JAKFRUIT
MAHJONG	ROMAJIS	BEJABERS	ENJOYING	JALAPENO
MAJAGUA	SANJAKS	BEJADING	FEIJOADA	JALAPINS
MAJESTY	SAPAJOU	BEJEEZUS	FLAPJACK	JALFREZI
MAJORAT	SEJEANT	BEJESUIT	FORJUDGE	JALOPIES
MAJORED	SHINJUS	BEJEWELS	FRABJOUS	JALOUSED
MAJORLY	SJAMBOK	BEJUMBLE	FRIJOLES	JALOUSES
MANJACK	SKYJACK	BENJAMIN	GJETOSTS	JALOUSIE
MASJIDS	SOJOURN	BIJUGATE	GOUJEERS	JAMADARS
MISJOIN	SOOJEYS	BIJUGOUS	HANDJARS	JAMBARTS
MOJARRA	SUBJECT	BIJWONER	HANDJOBS	JAMBEAUX
MOJITOS	SUBJOIN	BLOWJOBS	HARIJANS	JAMBIERS
MOUJIKS	TAJINES	BLUEJACK	HIGHJACK	JAMBIYAH
MUDEJAR	TINAJAS	BLUEJAYS	HIJACKED	JAMBIYAS
MUNTJAC	TOLARJI	BOERTJIE	HIJACKER	JAMBOLAN
MUNTJAK	TRAJECT	BOOTJACK	IJTIHADS	JAMBONES
MUSJIDS	TRIJETS	BRINJALS	INJECTED	JAMBOOLS
MUZJIKS	TWINJET	CAJAPUTS	INJECTOR	JAMBOREE
NAARTJE	UJAMAAS	CAJEPUTS	INJOINTS	JAMDANIS
NARTJIE	UNJADED	CAJOLERS	INJUNCTS	JAMMABLE
NONJURY	UNJOINT	CAJOLERY	INJURERS	JAMMIEST
NUTJOBS	VEEJAYS	CAJOLING	INJURIES	JAMMINGS
OBJECTS	WILTJAS	CAJUPUTS	INJURING	JAMPANEE
OBJURED	WUDJULA	CARCAJOU	JABBERED	JAMPANIS
OBJURES	YOJANAS	CARJACKS	JABBERER	JANGLERS
OUTJEST	ZANJERO	CARJACOU	JABBLING	JANGLIER
OUTJETS		CATJANGS	JACAMARS	JANGLING
OUTJINX		COJOINED	JACINTHE	JANIFORM
OUTJUMP		CONJECTS	JACINTHS	JANISARY
OUTJUTS		CONJOINS	JACKAROO	JANITORS

JANITRIX	JELLYING	JINGBANG	JORDELOO	JUNGLIST
JANIZARS	JELUTONG	JINGKOES	JOSTLERS	JUNIPERS
JANIZARY	JEMADARS	JINGLERS	JOSTLING	JUNKANOO
JANNOCKS	JEMIDARS	JINGLETS	JOTTIEST	JUNKETED
JANTIEST	JEMMIEST	JINGLIER	JOTTINGS	JUNKETER
JAPANISE	JEMMYING	JINGLING	JOUNCIER	JUNKIEST
JAPANIZE	JEOFAILS	JINGOISH	JOUNCING	JUNKYARD
JAPANNED	JEOPARDS	JINGOISM	JOURNALS	JURASSIC
JAPANNER	JEOPARDY	JINGOIST	JOURNEYS	JURATORY
JAPERIES	JEREMIAD	JINJILIS	JOUSTERS	JURISTIC
JAPINGLY	JEREPIGO	JINKERED	JOUSTING	JURYLESS
JAPONICA	JERKIEST	JIPIJAPA	JOVIALLY	JURYMAST
JARARACA	JERKINGS	JIPYAPAS	JOVIALTY	JUSSIVES
JARARAKA	JEROBOAM	JIRBLING	JOWLIEST	JUSTICER
JARGONED	JERQUERS	JIRKINET	JOYANCES	JUSTICES
JARGONEL	JERQUING	JITTERED	JOYFULLY	JUSTLING
JARGOONS	JERREEDS	JIUJITSU	JOYOUSLY	JUSTNESS
JARHEADS	JERRICAN	JIUJUTSU	JOYRIDER	JUTELIKE
JARLDOMS	JERRYCAN	JOBATION	JOYRIDES	JUTTYING
JAROSITE	JERSEYED	JOBBINGS	JOYSTICK	JUVENALS
JAROVISE	JESTBOOK	JOBNAMES	JUBILANT	JUVENILE
JAROVIZE	JESTINGS	JOBSHARE	JUBILATE	KABELJOU
JARRINGS	JESUITIC	JOCKETTE	JUBILEES	KAJAWAHS
JASMINES	JESUITRY	JOCKEYED	JUDDERED	KAJEPUTS
JASPISES	JETBEADS	JOCOSELY	JUDGMENT	KHANJARS
JATROPHA	JETFOILS	JOCOSITY	JUDICIAL	KILLJOYS
JAUNCING	JETLINER	JOCUNDLY	JUDOISTS	KINKAJOU
JAUNDICE	JETPORTS	JODELLED	JUGGINGS	KIPUNJIS
JAUNSING	JETTIEST	JODHPURS	JUGGLERS	KNEEJERK
JAUNTIER	JETTISON	JOGGINGS	JUGGLERY	KOMITAJI
JAUNTIES	JETTYING	JOGGLERS	JUGGLING	LOCKJAWS
JAUNTILY	JEWELERS	JOGGLING	JUGHEADS	LOGJUICE
JAUNTING	JEWELING	JOGPANTS	JUGULARS	LONGJUMP
JAVELINA	JEWELLED	JOGTROTS	JUGULATE	MAHARAJA
JAVELINS	JEWELLER	JOHANNES	JUICIEST	MAHJONGG
JAWBONED	JEZEBELS	JOHNBOAT	JUJITSUS	MAHJONGS
JAWBONER	JIBBERED	JOHNNIES	JUJUISMS	MAJAGUAS
JAWBONES	JIBBINGS	JOHNSONS	JUJUISTS	MAJESTIC
JAWBOXES	JIBBOOMS	JOINABLE	JUJUTSUS	MAJLISES
JAWFALLS	JIBINGLY	JOINDERS	JUKSKEIS	MAJOLICA
JAWHOLES	JICKAJOG	JOININGS	JULIENNE	MAJORATS
JAWLINES	JIGABOOS	JOINTERS	JUMARING	MAJORING
JAYBIRDS	JIGAJIGS	JOINTING	JUMARRED	MAJORITY
JAYWALKS	JIGAJOGS	JOINTURE	JUMBLERS	MANJACKS
JAZERANT	JIGGERED	JOISTING	JUMBLIER	MARJORAM
JAZZIEST	JIGGIEST	JOKESOME	JUMBLING	MARYJANE
JAZZLIKE	JIGGINGS	JOKESTER	JUMBOISE	MEJLISES
JEALOUSE	JIGGLIER	JOKINESS	JUMBOIZE	MICROJET
JEALOUSY	JIGGLING	JOKINGLY	JUMBUCKS	MIJNHEER
JEANETTE	JIGSAWED	JOLLEYER	JUMELLES	MISJOINS
JEELYING	JIHADEEN	JOLLIERS	JUMPABLE	MISJUDGE
JEEPNEYS	JIHADISM	JOLLIEST	JUMPIEST	MOJARRAS
JEERINGS	JIHADIST	JOLLYERS	JUMPINGS	MULTIJET
JEHADEEN	JILLAROO	JOLLYING	JUMPOFFS	MUNTJACS
JEHADISM	JILLIONS	JOLTHEAD	JUMPSUIT	MUNTJAKS
JEHADIST	JIMCRACK	JOLTIEST	JUNCATES	NAARTJES
JEJUNELY	JIMMYING	JONCANOE	JUNCTION	NAARTJIE
JEJUNITY	JIMPIEST	JONESING	JUNCTURE	NARTJIES
JELLABAH	JIMPNESS	JONGLEUR	JUNCUSES	NIGHTJAR
JELLABAS	JINGALLS	JONQUILS	JUNGLIER	NINJITSU

NINJUTSU	POPJOYED	REJECTER	SHOWJUMP	TWINJETS
NONJUROR	PREJUDGE	REJECTOR	SJAMBOKS	UNDERJAW
NONMAJOR	PROJECTS	REJIGGED	SKIJORER	UNJAMMED
OBJECTED	PROPJETS	REJIGGER	SKIPJACK	UNJOINED
OBJECTOR	PULSEJET	REJOICED	SKYJACKS	UNJOINTS
OBJURING	PULSOJET	REJOICER	SLAPJACK	UNJOYFUL
OUTJESTS	PYJAMAED	REJOICES	SOJOURNS	UNJOYOUS
OUTJUMPS	QUILLAJA	REJOINED	STICKJAW	UNJUDGED
OVERJOYS	RAJASHIP	REJONEOS	SUBJECTS	UNJUSTER
OVERJUMP	READJUST	REJOURNS	SUBJOINS	UNJUSTLY
OVERJUST	REEJECTS	REJUDGED	SUCURUJU	UPJETTED
PAJAMAED	REENJOYS	REJUDGES	SUPERJET	VERJUICE
PAJOCKES	REINJECT	REJUGGLE	SVARAJES	WATERJET
PEJORATE	REINJURE	REOBJECT	SWARAJES	WHIPJACK
PERJURED	REINJURY	RESOJETS	TJANTING	WUDJULAS
PERJURER	REJACKET	SAPAJOUS	TOLARJEV	ZABAJONE
PERJURES	REJECTED	SCRAMJET	TRAJECTS	ZANJEROS
POPINJAY	REJECTEE	SERJEANT	TURBOJET	

Using Q

Along with Z, Q is the highest-scoring letter in Scrabble. Unlike Z, Q can be tricky to use because the majority of words that contain Q also require a U. You shouldn't unnecessarily hold onto the Q and hope for a U to go with it. It is better being played as soon as possible and there are a number of words that contain Q but no U which can help. A complete list of these follows in this section. It's easy enough to learn all of these, especially the more likely shorter ones. There's only one two-letter word with Q, QI, which is very useful as you are either likely to have an I on your rack or one available on the board. It's also worth committing the few three-letter Q words to memory. If you are lucky enough to have a Q and U on your rack, or a U is available on the board then the four or five-letter Q words are more likely to get you the best scores. It can help to remember some of them in sets such as (QUAD, QUID, QUOD) and (QUINA, QUINE, QUINO).

Two-letter words

QI — (in Chinese medicine) a person's life-force

QIN — Chinese plucked stringed instrument related to the zither

QIS — plural of qi

QUA — in the capacity of

SUQ — (in Muslim countries) a marketplace

narcotic properties

Three-letter words

QAT — white-flowered evergreen shrub of Africa and Arabia whose leaves have

Four-letter words

AQUA	QUIN	FIQHS	QUAIS	QUEEN
FIQH	QUIP	FIQUE	QUAKE	QUEER
QADI	QUIT	GUQIN	QUAKY	QUELL
QAID	QUIZ	MAQUI	QUALE	QUEME
QATS	QUOD	NIQAB	QUALM	QUENA
QINS	QUOP	PIQUE	QUANT	QUERN
QOPH	SUQS	QADIS	QUARE	QUERY
QUAD	WAQF	QAIDS	QUARK	QUEST
QUAG		QANAT	QUART	QUEUE
QUAI	**Five-letter words**	QIBLA	QUASH	QUEYN
QUAT		QOPHS	QUASI	QUEYS
QUAY	AQUAE	QORMA	QUASS	QUICH
QUEP	AQUAS	QUACK	QUATE	QUICK
QUEY	BURQA	QUADS	QUATS	QUIDS
QUID	EQUAL	QUAFF	QUAYD	QUIET
QUIM	EQUID	QUAGS	QUAYS	QUIFF
	EQUIP	QUAIL	QUBIT	QUILL
	FAQIR	QUAIR	QUEAN	QUILT

QUIMS	CHEQUE	QUAIGH	QUILLS	SQUABS
QUINA	CHEQUY	QUAILS	QUILTS	SQUADS
QUINE	CINQUE	QUAINT	QUINAS	SQUAIL
QUINO	CIRQUE	QUAIRS	QUINCE	SQUALL
QUINS	CLAQUE	QUAKED	QUINES	SQUAMA
QUINT	CLIQUE	QUAKER	QUINIC	SQUAME
QUIPO	CLIQUY	QUAKES	QUINIE	SQUARE
QUIPS	CLOQUE	QUALIA	QUININ	SQUARK
QUIPU	COQUET	QUALMS	QUINOA	SQUASH
QUIRE	DIQUAT	QUALMY	QUINOL	SQUATS
QUIRK	EQUALI	QUANGO	QUINOS	SQUAWK
QUIRT	EQUALS	QUANTA	QUINSY	SQUAWS
QUIST	EQUANT	QUANTS	QUINTA	SQUEAK
QUITE	EQUATE	QUARER	QUINTE	SQUEAL
QUITS	EQUIDS	QUARKS	QUINTS	SQUEGS
QUOAD	EQUINE	QUARRY	QUINZE	SQUIBS
QUODS	EQUIPE	QUARTE	QUIPOS	SQUIDS
QUOIF	EQUIPS	QUARTO	QUIPPU	SQUIER
QUOIN	EQUITY	QUARTS	QUIPPY	SQUIFF
QUOIT	EXEQUY	QUARTZ	QUIPUS	SQUILL
QUOLL	FAQIRS	QUASAR	QUIRED	SQUINT
QUONK	FAQUIR	QUATCH	QUIRES	SQUINY
QUOPS	FIQUES	QUATRE	QUIRKS	SQUIRE
QUOTA	GUQINS	QUAVER	QUIRKY	SQUIRM
QUOTE	HAIQUE	QUAZZY	QUIRTS	SQUIRR
QUOTH	JERQUE	QUBITS	QUISTS	SQUIRT
QURSH	LASQUE	QUBYTE	QUITCH	SQUISH
QUYTE	LIQUID	QUEACH	QUITED	SQUITS
ROQUE	LIQUOR	QUEANS	QUITES	SQUUSH
SQUAB	LOQUAT	QUEASY	QUIVER	TALAQS
SQUAD	MANQUE	QUEAZY	QUOHOG	TOQUES
SQUAT	MAQUIS	QUEBEC	QUOIFS	TOQUET
SQUAW	MARQUE	QUEENS	QUOINS	TORQUE
SQUEG	MASQUE	QUEENY	QUOIST	TRANQS
SQUIB	MOSQUE	QUEERS	QUOITS	TUQUES
SQUID	NIQABS	QUEEST	QUOKKA	UBIQUE
SQUIT	OPAQUE	QUEINT	QUOLLS	UMIAQS
SQUIZ	PIQUED	QUELCH	QUONKS	UNIQUE
TALAQ	PIQUES	QUELEA	QUOOKE	USQUES
TOQUE	PIQUET	QUELLS	QUORUM	YANQUI
TRANQ	PLAQUE	QUEMED	QUOTAS	YAQONA
TUQUE	PULQUE	QUEMES	QUOTED	
UMIAQ	QABALA	QUENAS	QUOTER	**Seven-letter**
USQUE	QANATS	QUENCH	QUOTES	**words**
WAQFS	QASIDA	QUERNS	QUOTHA	ACEQUIA
	QAWWAL	QUESTS	QUOTUM	ACQUEST
Six-letter	QIBLAS	QUETCH	QURUSH	ACQUIRE
words	QIGONG	QUETHE	QUYTED	ACQUIST
ACQUIS	QINDAR	QUEUED	QUYTES	ACQUITE
ACQUIT	QINTAR	QUEUER	QWERTY	ACQUITS
ASQUAT	QIVIUT	QUEUES	REQUIN	ALFAQUI
BARQUE	QORMAS	QUEYNS	REQUIT	ALIQUOT
BASQUE	QUACKS	QUEZAL	RISQUE	ANTIQUE
BISQUE	QUACKY	QUICHE	ROQUES	AQUAFER
BOSQUE	QUAERE	QUICKS	ROQUET	AQUAFIT
BUQSHA	QUAFFS	QUICKY	SACQUE	AQUARIA
BURQAS	QUAGGA	QUIDAM	SAIQUE	AQUATIC
CAIQUE	QUAGGY	QUIETS	SEQUEL	AQUAVIT
CALQUE	QUAHOG	QUIFFS	SEQUIN	AQUEOUS
CASQUE	QUAICH	QUIGHT	SHEQEL	AQUIFER

AQUILON	EQUERRY	PIROQUE	QUATRES	QUINCES
AQUIVER	EQUINAL	PLAQUES	QUAVERS	QUINCHE
ASQUINT	EQUINES	PREQUEL	QUAVERY	QUINELA
BANQUET	EQUINIA	PULQUES	QUAYAGE	QUINIES
BAROQUE	EQUINOX	QABALAH	QUBYTES	QUININA
BARQUES	EQUIPES	QABALAS	QUEACHY	QUININE
BASQUED	EQUITES	QASIDAS	QUEBECS	QUININS
BASQUES	ESQUIRE	QAWWALI	QUEECHY	QUINNAT
BEQUEST	FAQUIRS	QAWWALS	QUEENED	QUINOAS
BEZIQUE	GRECQUE	QIGONGS	QUEENIE	QUINOID
BISQUES	HAIQUES	QINDARS	QUEENLY	QUINOLS
BOSQUES	INQILAB	QINTARS	QUEERED	QUINONE
BOSQUET	INQUERE	QIVIUTS	QUEERER	QUINTAL
BOUQUET	INQUEST	QUACKED	QUEERLY	QUINTAN
BRIQUET	INQUIET	QUACKER	QUEESTS	QUINTAR
BRUSQUE	INQUIRE	QUACKLE	QUELEAS	QUINTAS
BUQSHAS	INQUIRY	QUADDED	QUELLED	QUINTES
CACIQUE	JERQUED	QUADRAT	QUELLER	QUINTET
CAIQUES	JERQUER	QUADRIC	QUEMING	QUINTIC
CALQUED	JERQUES	QUAERED	QUERIDA	QUINTIN
CALQUES	JONQUIL	QUAERES	QUERIED	QUINZES
CASQUED	KUMQUAT	QUAFFED	QUERIER	QUIPPED
CASQUES	LACQUER	QUAFFER	QUERIES	QUIPPER
CAZIQUE	LACQUEY	QUAGGAS	QUERIST	QUIPPUS
CHARQUI	LALIQUE	QUAHAUG	QUESTED	QUIRING
CHEQUER	LASQUES	QUAHOGS	QUESTER	QUIRKED
CHEQUES	LEQUEAR	QUAICHS	QUESTOR	QUIRTED
CINQUES	LIQUATE	QUAIGHS	QUETHES	QUITING
CIRQUES	LIQUEFY	QUAILED	QUETSCH	QUITTAL
CLAQUER	LIQUEUR	QUAKERS	QUETZAL	QUITTED
CLAQUES	LIQUIDS	QUAKIER	QUEUERS	QUITTER
CLIQUED	LIQUIFY	QUAKILY	QUEUING	QUITTOR
CLIQUES	LIQUORS	QUAKING	QUEYNIE	QUIVERS
CLIQUEY	LOQUATS	QUALIFY	QUEZALS	QUIVERY
CLOQUES	MACAQUE	QUALITY	QUIBBLE	QUIXOTE
COEQUAL	MADOQUA	QUAMASH	QUIBLIN	QUIZZED
COMIQUE	MAQUILA	QUANGOS	QUICHED	QUIZZER
CONQUER	MARQUEE	QUANNET	QUICHES	QUIZZES
COQUETS	MARQUES	QUANTAL	QUICKEN	QUODDED
COQUINA	MARQUIS	QUANTED	QUICKER	QUODLIN
COQUITO	MASQUER	QUANTIC	QUICKIE	QUOHOGS
CROQUET	MASQUES	QUANTUM	QUICKLY	QUOIFED
CROQUIS	MESQUIN	QUAREST	QUIDAMS	QUOINED
CUMQUAT	MESQUIT	QUARREL	QUIDDIT	QUOISTS
DAQUIRI	MEZQUIT	QUARTAN	QUIDDLE	QUOITED
DEQUEUE	MOSQUES	QUARTER	QUIESCE	QUOITER
DIQUARK	OBLIQUE	QUARTES	QUIETED	QUOKKAS
DIQUATS	OBLOQUY	QUARTET	QUIETEN	QUOMODO
DOCQUET	OBSEQUY	QUARTIC	QUIETER	QUONDAM
ENQUEUE	OPAQUED	QUARTOS	QUIETLY	QUONKED
ENQUIRE	OPAQUER	QUARTZY	QUIETUS	QUOPPED
ENQUIRY	OPAQUES	QUASARS	QUIGHTS	QUORATE
EQUABLE	OQUASSA	QUASHED	QUILLAI	QUORUMS
EQUABLY	PARQUET	QUASHEE	QUILLED	QUOTERS
EQUALED	PASQUIL	QUASHER	QUILLET	QUOTING
EQUALLY	PERIQUE	QUASHES	QUILLON	QUOTUMS
EQUANTS	PICQUET	QUASHIE	QUILTED	QURSHES
EQUATED	PIQUANT	QUASSES	QUILTER	QUYTING
EQUATES	PIQUETS	QUASSIA	QUINARY	QWERTYS
EQUATOR	PIQUING	QUASSIN	QUINATE	RACQUET

REEQUIP	SQUIRED	AQUARIST	COTQUEAN	INQUIETS
RELIQUE	SQUIRES	AQUARIUM	CRITIQUE	INQUIRED
REPIQUE	SQUIRMS	AQUASHOW	CROQUETS	INQUIRER
REQUERE	SQUIRMY	AQUATICS	CUMQUATS	INQUIRES
REQUEST	SQUIRRS	AQUATINT	DAIQUIRI	JACQUARD
REQUIEM	SQUIRTS	AQUATONE	DAQUIRIS	JERQUERS
REQUINS	SQUISHY	AQUAVITS	DEQUEUED	JERQUING
REQUIRE	SQUITCH	AQUEDUCT	DEQUEUES	JONQUILS
REQUITE	SQUOOSH	AQUIFERS	DETRAQUE	KUMQUATS
REQUITS	SUBAQUA	AQUILINE	DIQUARKS	LACQUERS
REQUOTE	TEQUILA	AQUILONS	DISQUIET	LACQUEYS
RISQUES	TOQUETS	ARQUEBUS	DOCQUETS	LALIQUES
ROCQUET	TORQUED	BANQUETS	ELOQUENT	LEQUEARS
ROQUETS	TORQUER	BARBEQUE	EMBUSQUE	LIQUABLE
RORQUAL	TORQUES	BAROQUES	ENQUEUED	LIQUATED
SACQUES	TSADDIQ	BASQUINE	ENQUEUES	LIQUATES
SAIQUES	TZADDIQ	BEDQUILT	ENQUIRED	LIQUESCE
SEQUELA	UNEQUAL	BELIQUOR	ENQUIRER	LIQUEURS
SEQUELS	UNIQUER	BEQUEATH	ENQUIRES	LIQUIDLY
SEQUENT	UNIQUES	BEQUESTS	EQUALING	LIQUIDUS
SEQUINS	UNQUEEN	BEZIQUES	EQUALISE	LIQUORED
SEQUOIA	UNQUIET	BIUNIQUE	EQUALITY	LOQUITUR
SHEQELS	UNQUOTE	BLANQUET	EQUALIZE	LUSTIQUE
SILIQUA	VAQUERO	BOSQUETS	EQUALLED	MACAQUES
SILIQUE	YANQUIS	BOUQUETS	EQUATING	MADOQUAS
SQUABBY	YAQONAS	BOUTIQUE	EQUATION	MAQUETTE
SQUACCO		BRELOQUE	EQUATIVE	MAQUILAS
SQUADDY	**Eight-letter**	BRIQUETS	EQUATORS	MAROQUIN
SQUAILS	**words**	BRUSQUER	EQUINELY	MARQUEES
SQUALID	ACEQUIAS	CACIQUES	EQUINIAS	MARQUESS
SQUALLS	ACQUAINT	CALQUING	EQUINITY	MARQUISE
SQUALLY	ACQUESTS	CAZIQUES	EQUIPAGE	MASQUERS
SQUALOR	ACQUIGHT	CHAQUETA	EQUIPPED	MBAQANGA
SQUAMAE	ACQUIRAL	CHARQUID	EQUIPPER	MESQUINE
SQUAMES	ACQUIRED	CHARQUIS	EQUISETA	MESQUITE
SQUARED	ACQUIREE	CHEQUERS	EQUITANT	MESQUITS
SQUARER	ACQUIRER	CHEQUIER	EQUITIES	MEZQUITE
SQUARES	ACQUIRES	CHEQUING	EQUIVOKE	MEZQUITS
SQUARKS	ACQUISTS	CINQUAIN	ESQUIRED	MIQUELET
SQUASHY	ACQUITES	CLAQUERS	ESQUIRES	MISQUOTE
SQUATLY	ADEQUACY	CLAQUEUR	ESQUISSE	MOQUETTE
SQUATTY	ADEQUATE	CLINIQUE	EXEQUIAL	MORESQUE
SQUAWKS	AEQUORIN	CLIQUIER	EXEQUIES	MOSQUITO
SQUAWKY	ALFAQUIN	CLIQUING	FILIOQUE	MUQADDAM
SQUEAKS	ALFAQUIS	CLIQUISH	FREQUENT	MUSQUASH
SQUEAKY	ALIQUANT	CLIQUISM	GODSQUAD	MYSTIQUE
SQUEALS	ALIQUOTS	COEQUALS	GRECQUES	NARQUOIS
SQUEEZE	ANTIQUED	COEQUATE	HAQUETON	NONEQUAL
SQUEEZY	ANTIQUER	COLLOQUE	HENEQUEN	NONQUOTA
SQUELCH	ANTIQUES	COLLOQUY	HENEQUIN	OBLIQUED
SQUIDGE	ANTIQUEY	COMIQUES	HENIQUEN	OBLIQUER
SQUIDGY	APPLIQUE	CONQUERS	HENIQUIN	OBLIQUES
SQUIERS	AQUACADE	CONQUEST	HUAQUERO	OBLIQUID
SQUIFFY	AQUAFARM	CONQUIAN	ILLIQUID	OBSEQUIE
SQUILLA	AQUAFERS	COQUETRY	INEQUITY	ODALIQUE
SQUILLS	AQUAFITS	COQUETTE	INIQUITY	OLDSQUAW
SQUINCH	AQUALUNG	COQUILLA	INQILABS	OPAQUELY
SQUINNY	AQUANAUT	COQUILLE	INQUERED	OPAQUEST
SQUINTS	AQUARIAL	COQUINAS	INQUERES	OPAQUING
SQUINTY	AQUARIAN	COQUITOS	INQUESTS	OQUASSAS

OUTQUOTE	QUALMIER	QUEERISH	QUILLMAN	QUOITING
PARAQUAT	QUALMING	QUEERITY	QUILLMEN	QUOMODOS
PARAQUET	QUALMISH	QUELCHED	QUILLONS	QUONKING
PAROQUET	QUANDANG	QUELCHES	QUILTERS	QUOPPING
PARQUETS	QUANDARY	QUELLERS	QUILTING	QUOTABLE
PASQUILS	QUANDONG	QUELLING	QUINCHED	QUOTABLY
PEQUISTE	QUANNETS	QUENCHED	QUINCHES	QUOTIENT
PERIQUES	QUANTICS	QUENCHER	QUINCUNX	QURUSHES
PERRUQUE	QUANTIFY	QUENCHES	QUINELAS	QWERTIES
PETANQUE	QUANTILE	QUENELLE	QUINELLA	RACQUETS
PHYSIQUE	QUANTING	QUERCINE	QUINIELA	RAMEQUIN
PICQUETS	QUANTISE	QUERIDAS	QUININAS	REEQUIPS
PIQUANCE	QUANTITY	QUERIERS	QUININES	RELIQUES
PIQUANCY	QUANTIZE	QUERISTS	QUINNATS	REMARQUE
PIQUETED	QUANTONG	QUERYING	QUINOIDS	REPIQUED
PIQUILLO	QUANTUMS	QUESTANT	QUINOLIN	REPIQUES
PIROQUES	QUARRELS	QUESTERS	QUINONES	REQUERED
POSTIQUE	QUARRIAN	QUESTING	QUINSIED	REQUERES
PRATIQUE	QUARRIED	QUESTION	QUINSIES	REQUESTS
PREQUELS	QUARRIER	QUESTORS	QUINTAIN	REQUIEMS
QABALAHS	QUARRIES	QUETCHED	QUINTALS	REQUIGHT
QABALISM	QUARRION	QUETCHES	QUINTANS	REQUIRED
QABALIST	QUARTANS	QUETHING	QUINTARS	REQUIRER
QAIMAQAM	QUARTERN	QUETZALS	QUINTETS	REQUIRES
QALAMDAN	QUARTERS	QUEUEING	QUINTETT	REQUITAL
QAWWALIS	QUARTETS	QUEUINGS	QUINTICS	REQUITED
QINDARKA	QUARTETT	QUEYNIES	QUINTILE	REQUITER
QINTARKA	QUARTICS	QUEZALES	QUINTINS	REQUITES
QUAALUDE	QUARTIER	QUIBBLED	QUIPPERS	REQUOTED
QUACKERS	QUARTILE	QUIBBLER	QUIPPIER	REQUOTES
QUACKERY	QUARTZES	QUIBBLES	QUIPPING	REQUOYLE
QUACKIER	QUASHEES	QUIBLINS	QUIPPISH	ROCQUETS
QUACKING	QUASHERS	QUICHING	QUIPSTER	ROQUETED
QUACKISH	QUASHIES	QUICKENS	QUIRKIER	ROQUETTE
QUACKISM	QUASHING	QUICKEST	QUIRKILY	RORQUALS
QUACKLED	QUASSIAS	QUICKIES	QUIRKING	SEAQUAKE
QUACKLES	QUASSINS	QUICKSET	QUIRKISH	SEQUELAE
QUADDING	QUATCHED	QUIDDANY	QUIRTING	SEQUENCE
QUADPLAY	QUATCHES	QUIDDITS	QUISLING	SEQUENCY
QUADPLEX	QUATORZE	QUIDDITY	QUITCHED	SEQUENTS
QUADRANS	QUATRAIN	QUIDDLED	QUITCHES	SEQUINED
QUADRANT	QUAVERED	QUIDDLER	QUITRENT	SEQUITUR
QUADRATE	QUAVERER	QUIDDLES	QUITTALS	SEQUOIAS
QUADRATS	QUAYAGES	QUIDNUNC	QUITTERS	SERVQUAL
QUADRICS	QUAYLIKE	QUIESCED	QUITTING	SHEQALIM
QUADRIGA	QUAYSIDE	QUIESCES	QUITTORS	SILIQUAE
QUADROON	QUAZZIER	QUIETENS	QUIVERED	SILIQUAS
QUAESTOR	QUEACHES	QUIETERS	QUIVERER	SILIQUES
QUAFFERS	QUEASIER	QUIETEST	QUIXOTES	SOLIQUID
QUAFFING	QUEASILY	QUIETING	QUIXOTIC	SQUABASH
QUAGGIER	QUEAZIER	QUIETISM	QUIXOTRY	SQUABBED
QUAGMIRE	QUEENDOM	QUIETIST	QUIZZERS	SQUABBER
QUAGMIRY	QUEENIER	QUIETIVE	QUIZZERY	SQUABBLE
QUAHAUGS	QUEENIES	QUIGHTED	QUIZZIFY	SQUACCOS
QUAICHES	QUEENING	QUILLAIA	QUIZZING	SQUADDED
QUAILING	QUEENITE	QUILLAIS	QUODDING	SQUADDIE
QUAINTER	QUEENLET	QUILLAJA	QUODLINS	SQUADRON
QUAINTLY	QUEERDOM	QUILLETS	QUOIFING	SQUAILED
QUAKIEST	QUEEREST	QUILLING	QUOINING	SQUAILER
QUAKINGS	QUEERING		QUOITERS	SQUALENE

SQUALLED	SQUATTER	SQUIFFED	SQUIRTED	TURQUOIS
SQUALLER	SQUATTLE	SQUIFFER	SQUIRTER	TZADDIQS
SQUALOID	SQUAWKED	SQUIGGLE	SQUISHED	UBIQUITY
SQUALORS	SQUAWKER	SQUIGGLY	SQUISHES	UMQUHILE
SQUAMATE	SQUAWMAN	SQUILGEE	SQUIZZES	UNEQUALS
SQUAMOSE	SQUAWMEN	SQUILLAE	SQUOOSHY	UNIQUELY
SQUAMOUS	SQUEAKED	SQUILLAS	SQUUSHED	UNIQUEST
SQUAMULA	SQUEAKER	SQUINIED	SQUUSHES	UNQUEENS
SQUAMULE	SQUEALED	SQUINIES	SUBEQUAL	UNQUIETS
SQUANDER	SQUEALER	SQUINTED	SURQUEDY	UNQUOTED
SQUARELY	SQUEEGEE	SQUINTER	TAQUERIA	UNQUOTES
SQUARERS	SQUEEZED	SQUIRAGE	TEQUILAS	USQUABAE
SQUAREST	SQUEEZER	SQUIREEN	TEQUILLA	USQUEBAE
SQUARIAL	SQUEEZES	SQUIRELY	TOQUILLA	VANQUISH
SQUARING	SQUEGGED	SQUIRESS	TORQUATE	VAQUEROS
SQUARISH	SQUEGGER	SQUIRING	TORQUERS	VEHMIQUE
SQUARSON	SQUELCHY	SQUIRISH	TORQUING	VERQUERE
SQUASHED	SQUIBBED	SQUIRMED	TRANQUIL	VERQUIRE
SQUASHER	SQUIDDED	SQUIRMER	TRUQUAGE	
SQUASHES	SQUIDGED	SQUIRRED	TRUQUEUR	
SQUATTED	SQUIDGES	SQUIRREL	TSADDIQS	

Q but not U

There are few things more infuriating in Scrabble than having a Q on your rack but no U with which to play it! But this situation needn't be disastrous: there are a surprisingly high number of words that have a Q but not U. A complete list of these words is included here. These have short definitions to help you remember them; it is well worth learning them all, as they can be extremely useful. Note that the A is a key vowel in quite a few of these words.

FAQIR	FAQIRS		QAWWALIS	QAWWALS	
FIQH	FIQHS		QI	QIS	
INQILAB	INQILABS		QIBLA	QIBLAS	
MBAQANGA	MBAQANGAS		QIGONG	QIGONGS	
NIQAB	NIQABS		QIN	QINS	
QABALA			QINDAR	QINDARKA	QINDARS
QABALAH	QABALAHS	QABALAS	QINTAR	QINTARKA	QINTARS
QABALISM	QABALISMS		QOPH	QOPHS	
QABALIST	QABALISTIC	QABALISTS	QORMA	QORMAS	
QADI	QADIS		QWERTY	QWERTIES	QWERTYS
QAID	QAIDS		SHEQEL	SHEQALIM	SHEQELS
QAIMAQAM			TALAQ	TALAQS	
QAIMAQAMS	QALAMDAN	QALAMDANS	TRANQ	TRANQS	
QANAT	QANATS		TSADDIQ	TSADDIQIM	TSADDIQS
QASIDA	QASIDAS		TZADDIQ	TZADDIQIM	TZADDIQS
QAT	QATS		WAQF	WAQFS	
QAWWAL	QAWWALI		YAQONA	YAQONAS	

Q and K

Looking at the words that contain Q but not U, you may well notice that many are of Arabic or Hebrew origin. Of course, these languages aren't written using the Roman alphabet, so these words are transliterations from a different script. It's an interesting – and helpful – fact that the Arabic consonant that is represented as a Q in Roman script can also be transliterated as a K, which means that many of the Q-but-no-U words can also be spelt with a K. This is useful for two reasons. Firstly, looking at the list of K alternatives will help you remember the Q-only words. Secondly, K is a sort of 'semi-power' tile, scoring five points and being the most valuable letter after the power tiles. Thus it's quite useful to know these unusual words using K for their own sake.

FAQIR	FAKIR	QAIMAQAMS	KAIMAKAMS	SHEQEL	SHEKEL
FAQIRS	FAKIRS	QALAMDAN	KALAMDAN	SHEQELS	SHEKELS
NIQAB	NIKAB	QALAMDANS	KALAMDANS	TALAQ	TALAK
NIQABS	NIKABS	QAT	KAT	TALAQS	TALAKS
QABALA	KABALA	QATS	KATS	TRANQ	TRANK
QABALAS	KABALAS	QI	KI	TRANQS	TRANKS
QABALISM	KABALISM	QIBLA	KIBLA	TSADDIQ	TSADDIK
QABALISMS	KABALISMS	QIBLAS	KIBLAS	TSADDIQIM	TSADDIKIM
QABALIST	KABALIST	QIN	KIN	TSADDIQS	TSADDIKS
QABALISTIC	KABALISTIC	QINS	KINS	TZADDIQ	TZADDIK
QABALISTS	KABALISTS	QIS	KIS	TZADDIQIM	TZADDIKIM
QADI	KADI	QOPH	KOPH	TZADDIQS	TZADDIKS
QADIS	KADIS	QOPHS	KOPHS	WAQF	WAKF
QAID	KAID	QORMA	KORMA	WAQFS	WAKFS
QAIDS	KAIDS	QORMAS	KORMAS		
QAIMAQAM	KAIMAKAM	SHEQALIM	SHEKALIM		

Using X

X is perhaps the most versatile of the power tiles, simply because of the extensive number of two and three-letter words that contain it. It can reap many points through parallel play, especially if the X falls on a premium square, because there is a two-letter word for every vowel. It is fairly easy to spot words that end in X so it's worth learning a few words that begin with X when a board may not favour X-ending words (eg XENIA, XYST). Of all the power tiles, the X is the only one that it can be worthwhile holding back in the hope of a better score later, providing you can score reasonably well with your other tiles meanwhile.

Two-letter words

AX	tool with a sharp blade for felling trees or chopping wood
EX	not including
OX	castrated bull
XI	14th letter in the Greek alphabet
XU	Vietnamese currency unit

Three-letter words

AXE	tool with a sharp blade for felling trees or chopping wood
BOX	container with a firm flat base and sides
COX	coxswain
DEX	dextroamphetamine
DUX	(in Scottish and certain other schools) the top pupil in a class or school
EXO	excellent
FAX	electronic system for sending facsimiles of documents by telephone
FIX	make or become firm, stable, or secure
FOX	reddish-brown bushy-tailed animal of the dog family
GOX	gaseous oxygen
HEX	to put a spell on (someone)
HOX	hamstring
KEX	any of several large hollow-stemmed umbelliferous plants, such as cow parsnip and chervil

LAX	not strict
LEX	system or body of laws
LOX	liquid oxygen
LUX	unit of illumination
MAX	reach the full extent
MIX	combine or blend into one mass
MUX	spoil
NIX	be careful! watch out!
NOX	nitrogen oxide
OXO	acid that contains oxygen
OXY	analgesic drug
PAX	kiss of peace
PIX	any receptacle for the Eucharistic Host
POX	disease in which skin pustules form
PYX	any receptacle for the Eucharistic Host
RAX	stretch or extend
REX	king
SAX	saxophone
SEX	state of being male or female
SIX	one more than five
SOX	informal spelling of 'socks'
TAX	compulsory payment levied by a government on income, property, etc to raise revenue
TEX	unit of weight used to measure yarn density
TIX	tickets
TUX	short for tuxedo
VEX	frustrate, annoy
VOX	voice or sound

WAX	solid shiny fatty or oily substance		alphabet
	used for sealing, making candles, etc	YEX	hiccup
WEX	wax	ZAX	tool used for cutting slate
WOX	waxed	ZEX	same as ZAX
XIS	plural, 14th letter in the Greek		

Four-letter words

	MAXI	AXMEN	EXIES	LAXES
	MINX	AXOID	EXILE	LAXLY
APEX	MIXT	AXONE	EXINE	LEXES
AXAL	MIXY	AXONS	EXING	LEXIS
AXED	MOXA	BEAUX	EXIST	LIMAX
AXEL	MYXO	BEMIX	EXITS	LINUX
AXES	NEXT	BOLIX	EXODE	LOXED
AXIL	NIXE	BORAX	EXONS	LOXES
AXIS	NIXY	BOXED	EXPAT	LUREX
AXLE	ONYX	BOXEN	EXPEL	LUXES
AXON	ORYX	BOXER	EXPOS	MALAX
BOXY	OXEN	BOXES	EXTOL	MAXED
BRUX	OXER	BOXTY	EXTRA	MAXES
CALX	OXES	BRAXY	EXUDE	MAXIM
COAX	OXID	BUXOM	EXULS	MAXIS
COXA	OXIM	CALIX	EXULT	MIREX
COXY	PIXY	CALYX	EXURB	MIXED
CRUX	PLEX	CAPEX	FAXED	MIXEN
DEXY	POXY	CAREX	FAXES	MIXER
DIXI	PREX	CAXON	FEDEX	MIXES
DIXY	ROUX	CHOUX	FIXED	MIXTE
DOUX	SAXE	CIMEX	FIXER	MIXUP
DOXY	SEXT	CODEX	FIXES	MOXAS
EAUX	SEXY	COMIX	FIXIT	MOXIE
EXAM	TAXA	COXAE	FLAXY	MUREX
EXEC	TAXI	COXAL	FLEXO	MUXED
EXED	TEXT	COXED	FOREX	MUXES
EXES	ULEX	COXES	FOXED	MYXOS
EXIT	VEXT	COXIB	FOXES	NEXTS
EXON	WAXY	CULEX	FOXIE	NEXUS
EXPO	WEXE	CYLIX	GALAX	NIXED
EXUL	XRAY	DEOXY	GOXES	NIXER
FAIX	XYST	DESEX	HAPAX	NIXES
FALX	YUNX	DETOX	HELIX	NIXIE
FAUX		DEWAX	HEXAD	NOXAL
FIXT	**Five-letter**	DEXES	HEXED	NOXES
FLAX	**words**	DEXIE	HEXER	ORIXA
FLEX	ADDAX	DIXIE	HEXES	OXBOW
FLIX	ADMIX	DIXIT	HEXYL	OXERS
FLOX	AFFIX	DOXIE	HOXED	OXEYE
FLUX	ANNEX	DRUXY	HOXES	OXIDE
FOXY	ATAXY	DUXES	HYRAX	OXIDS
GREX	AUXIN	EMBOX	IMMIX	OXIES
HOAX	AXELS	ENFIX	INBOX	OXIME
IBEX	AXIAL	EPOXY	INDEX	OXIMS
ILEX	AXILE	EXACT	INFIX	OXLIP
IXIA	AXILS	EXALT	IXIAS	OXTER
JAXY	AXING	EXAMS	IXORA	PANAX
JEUX	AXIOM	EXCEL	IXTLE	PAXES
JINX	AXION	EXEAT	JAXIE	PHLOX
JYNX	AXITE	EXECS	KEXES	PIXEL
LANX	AXLED	EXEEM	KYLIX	PIXES
LUXE	AXLES	EXEME	LATEX	PIXIE
LYNX	AXMAN	EXERT	LAXER	PODEX

POXED	VEXIL	AXISES	DEXIES	EXONIC
POXES	VIBEX	AXITES	DEXTER	EXONYM
PREXY	VITEX	AXLIKE	DEXTRO	EXOPOD
PROXY	VIXEN	AXOIDS	DIAXIN	EXOTIC
PYREX	VOXEL	AXONAL	DIOXAN	EXPAND
PYXED	WAXED	AXONES	DIOXID	EXPATS
PYXES	WAXEN	AXONIC	DIOXIN	EXPECT
PYXIE	WAXER	AXSEED	DIPLEX	EXPELS
PYXIS	WAXES	BANJAX	DIXIES	EXPEND
RADIX	WEXED	BAXTER	DIXITS	EXPERT
RAXED	WEXES	BEMBEX	DOGFOX	EXPIRE
RAXES	WOXEN	BEMBIX	DOXIES	EXPIRY
REDOX	WUXIA	BEMIXT	DUPLEX	EXPORT
REDUX	XEBEC	BIAXAL	EARWAX	EXPOSE
REFIX	XENIA	BIFLEX	EFFLUX	EXPUGN
RELAX	XENIC	BIJOUX	ELIXIR	EXSECT
REMEX	XENON	BOLLIX	ETHOXY	EXSERT
REMIX	XERIC	BOLLOX	EUTAXY	EXTANT
RETAX	XEROX	BOMBAX	EXACTA	EXTASY
REWAX	XERUS	BOMBYX	EXACTS	EXTEND
REXES	XOANA	BONXIE	EXACUM	EXTENT
SALIX	XRAYS	BOXCAR	EXALTS	EXTERN
SAXES	XYLAN	BOXERS	EXAMEN	EXTINE
SEXED	XYLEM	BOXFUL	EXARCH	EXTIRP
SEXER	XYLIC	BOXIER	EXCAMB	EXTOLD
SEXES	XYLOL	BOXILY	EXCEED	EXTOLL
SEXTO	XYLYL	BOXING	EXCELS	EXTOLS
SEXTS	XYSTI	BOYAUX	EXCEPT	EXTORT
SILEX	XYSTS	BRUXED	EXCESS	EXTRAS
SIXER	YEXED	BRUXES	EXCIDE	EXUDED
SIXES	YEXES	CALXES	EXCISE	EXUDES
SIXMO	ZAXES	CARFAX	EXCITE	EXULTS
SIXTE	ZEXES	CARFOX	EXCUSE	EXURBS
SIXTH		CARNYX	EXEATS	EXUVIA
SIXTY	**Six-letter**	CAUDEX	EXEDRA	FAXING
SOREX	**words**	CAXONS	EXEEMS	FIXATE
TAXED	ADIEUX	CERVIX	EXEMED	FIXERS
TAXER	ADMIXT	CHENIX	EXEMES	FIXING
TAXES	ADNEXA	CLAXON	EXEMPT	FIXITY
TAXIS	AFFLUX	CLIMAX	EXEQUY	FIXIVE
TAXON	ALEXIA	COAXAL	EXERGY	FIXURE
TAXOR	ALEXIC	COAXED	EXERTS	FLAXEN
TAXUS	ALEXIN	COAXER	EXEUNT	FLAXES
TELEX	ALKOXY	COAXES	EXHALE	FLEXED
TEXAS	ANNEXE	COCCYX	EXHORT	FLEXES
TEXES	ANOXIA	COMMIX	EXHUME	FLEXOR
TEXTS	ANOXIC	CONFIX	EXILED	FLEXOS
TOXIC	APEXES	CONVEX	EXILER	FLIXED
TOXIN	ATAXIA	CORTEX	EXILES	FLIXES
TUXES	ATAXIC	COWPOX	EXILIC	FLUXED
TWIXT	ATWIXT	COXIBS	EXINES	FLUXES
UNBOX	AUSPEX	COXIER	EXISTS	FORFEX
UNFIX	AUXINS	COXING	EXITED	FORNIX
UNMIX	AXEMAN	CRUXES	EXODES	FOXIER
UNSEX	AXEMEN	DEFLEX	EXODIC	FOXIES
UNTAX	AXENIC	DEIXES	EXODOI	FOXILY
VARIX	AXILLA	DEIXIS	EXODOS	FOXING
VEXED	AXIOMS	DELUXE	EXODUS	FRUTEX
VEXER	AXIONS	DENTEX	EXOGEN	GALAXY
VEXES	AXISED	DESOXY	EXOMIS	GREXES

GUANXI	MIXIER	PRAXES	TAXMEN	YUNXES
HALLUX	MIXING	PRAXIS	TAXONS	
HANDAX	MIXUPS	PREFIX	TAXORS	**Seven-letter**
HATBOX	MOXIES	PREMIX	TEABOX	**words**
HAYBOX	MUSKOX	PRETAX	TETTIX	ABAXIAL
HEXACT	MUXING	PREXES	TEXTED	ABAXILE
HEXADE	MYXOID	PROLIX	TEXTER	ABRASAX
HEXADS	MYXOMA	PTYXES	THORAX	ABRAXAS
HEXANE	NEXTLY	PTYXIS	TOXICS	ADAXIAL
HEXENE	NITROX	PYXIES	TOXINE	ADDAXES
HEXERS	NIXERS	PYXING	TOXINS	ADMIXED
HEXING	NIXIES	RAXING	TOXOID	ADMIXES
HEXONE	NIXING	REFLEX	TRIMIX	ADNEXAL
HEXOSE	NONTAX	REFLUX	TUTRIX	AFFIXAL
HEXYLS	ONYXES	REMIXT	TUXEDO	AFFIXED
HOAXED	OREXIN	REXINE	ULEXES	AFFIXER
HOAXER	OREXIS	RHEXES	UNAXED	AFFIXES
HOAXES	ORIFEX	RHEXIS	UNFIXT	AIRPROX
HOTBOX	ORIXAS	SAXAUL	UNISEX	ALEXIAS
HOXING	ORYXES	SAXONY	UNMIXT	ALEXINE
IBEXES	OUTBOX	SCOLEX	UNSEXY	ALEXINS
ICEBOX	OUTFOX	SEXERS	UNVEXT	ALLOXAN
ILEXES	OXALIC	SEXFID	URTEXT	ANAXIAL
IMBREX	OXALIS	SEXIER	VERNIX	ANNEXED
IMPLEX	OXBOWS	SEXILY	VERTEX	ANNEXES
INFLUX	OXCART	SEXING	VEXERS	ANOREXY
ISOLEX	OXEYES	SEXISM	VEXILS	ANOXIAS
IXODID	OXFORD	SEXIST	VEXING	ANTEFIX
IXORAS	OXGANG	SEXPOT	VIXENS	ANTHRAX
IXTLES	OXGATE	SEXTAN	VOLVOX	ANTISEX
JAWBOX	OXHEAD	SEXTET	VORTEX	ANTITAX
JAXIES	OXHIDE	SEXTON	VOXELS	ANXIETY
JINXED	OXIDES	SEXTOS	WAXERS	ANXIOUS
JINXES	OXIDIC	SEXUAL	WAXEYE	APOPLEX
JYNXES	OXIMES	SILVEX	WAXIER	APRAXIA
KLAXON	OXLAND	SIXAIN	WAXILY	APRAXIC
LARNAX	OXLIKE	SIXERS	WAXING	APTERYX
LARYNX	OXLIPS	SIXMOS	WEXING	ARUSPEX
LAXEST	OXSLIP	SIXTES	WRAXLE	ASEXUAL
LAXISM	OXTAIL	SIXTHS	WUXIAS	ASPHYXY
LAXIST	OXTERS	SKYBOX	XEBECS	ATARAXY
LAXITY	OXYGEN	SMILAX	XENIAL	ATAXIAS
LEXEME	OXYMEL	SPADIX	XENIAS	ATAXICS
LEXICA	PAXWAX	SPHINX	XENIUM	ATAXIES
LOXING	PEGBOX	SPHYNX	XENONS	AUXESES
LUMMOX	PEROXO	STORAX	XEROMA	AUXESIS
LUXATE	PEROXY	STYRAX	XOANON	AUXETIC
LUXURY	PHENIX	SUBFIX	XYLANS	AUXINIC
LYNXES	PICKAX	SUFFIX	XYLEMS	AXEBIRD
MAGNOX	PINXIT	SUPLEX	XYLENE	AXIALLY
MASTIX	PIXELS	SURTAX	XYLOID	AXILLAE
MATRIX	PIXIES	SYNTAX	XYLOLS	AXILLAR
MAXIMA	PLEXAL	SYRINX	XYLOMA	AXILLAS
MAXIMS	PLEXES	TAXEME	XYLOSE	AXINITE
MAXING	PLEXOR	TAXERS	XYLYLS	AXOLOTL
MAXIXE	PLEXUS	TAXIED	XYSTER	AXONEME
MENINX	POLEAX	TAXIES	XYSTOI	AXSEEDS
MINXES	POLLEX	TAXING	XYSTOS	BANDBOX
MIXENS	POXIER	TAXITE	XYSTUS	BATEAUX
MIXERS	POXING	TAXMAN	YEXING	BAUXITE

BAXTERS	COXITIS	EXCHEAT	EXOTICS	FEDEXES
BEATBOX	COXLESS	EXCIDED	EXOTISM	FEEDBOX
BEESWAX	CULEXES	EXCIDES	EXPANDS	FIREBOX
BEMIXED	CURTAXE	EXCIMER	EXPANSE	FIXABLE
BEMIXES	DEINDEX	EXCIPLE	EXPECTS	FIXATED
BETAXED	DESEXED	EXCISED	EXPENDS	FIXATES
BETWIXT	DESEXES	EXCISES	EXPENSE	FIXATIF
BIAXIAL	DETOXED	EXCITED	EXPERTS	FIXEDLY
BOLIXED	DETOXES	EXCITER	EXPIATE	FIXINGS
BOLIXES	DEWAXED	EXCITES	EXPIRED	FIXTURE
BONXIES	DEWAXES	EXCITON	EXPIRER	FIXURES
BOOMBOX	DEXTERS	EXCITOR	EXPIRES	FLAXIER
BORAXES	DEXTRAL	EXCLAIM	EXPLAIN	FLEXILE
BOSTRYX	DEXTRAN	EXCLAVE	EXPLANT	FLEXING
BOXBALL	DEXTRIN	EXCLUDE	EXPLODE	FLEXION
BOXCARS	DIAXONS	EXCRETA	EXPLOIT	FLEXORS
BOXFISH	DIGOXIN	EXCRETE	EXPLORE	FLEXURE
BOXFULS	DIOXANE	EXCUDIT	EXPORTS	FLIXING
BOXHAUL	DIOXANS	EXCURSE	EXPOSAL	FLUMMOX
BOXIEST	DIOXIDE	EXCUSAL	EXPOSED	FLUXING
BOXINGS	DIOXIDS	EXCUSED	EXPOSER	FLUXION
BOXLIKE	DIOXINS	EXCUSER	EXPOSES	FLUXIVE
BOXPLOT	DISTRIX	EXCUSES	EXPOSIT	FOREXES
BOXROOM	DRUXIER	EXECUTE	EXPOUND	FOWLPOX
BOXTIES	EDITRIX	EXEDRAE	EXPRESS	FOXFIRE
BOXWOOD	ELIXIRS	EXEEMED	EXPUGNS	FOXFISH
BRAXIES	EMBOXED	EXEGETE	EXPULSE	FOXHOLE
BROADAX	EMBOXES	EXEMING	EXPUNCT	FOXHUNT
BRUXING	ENFIXED	EXEMPLA	EXPUNGE	FOXIEST
BRUXISM	ENFIXES	EXEMPLE	EXPURGE	FOXINGS
BUREAUX	EPAXIAL	EXEMPTS	EXSCIND	FOXLIKE
BUXOMER	EPITAXY	EXERGUE	EXSECTS	FOXSHIP
BUXOMLY	EPOXIDE	EXERTED	EXSERTS	FOXSKIN
CACHEXY	EPOXIED	EXHALED	EXTATIC	FOXTAIL
CADEAUX	EPOXIES	EXHALES	EXTENDS	FOXTROT
CALYXES	EPOXYED	EXHAUST	EXTENSE	FUNPLEX
CAPEXES	EQUINOX	EXHEDRA	EXTENTS	FUZZBOX
CARAPAX	ETHOXYL	EXHIBIT	EXTERNE	GALAXES
CASEMIX	EUTAXIA	EXHORTS	EXTERNS	GATEAUX
CASHBOX	EUTEXIA	EXHUMED	EXTINCT	GEARBOX
CELOTEX	EXABYTE	EXHUMER	EXTINES	GRAVLAX
CHAMOIX	EXACTAS	EXHUMES	EXTIRPS	GUANXIS
CHOENIX	EXACTED	EXIGENT	EXTOLLS	HAPAXES
CLAXONS	EXACTER	EXILERS	EXTORTS	HELIXES
COALBOX	EXACTLY	EXILIAN	EXTRACT	HELLBOX
COANNEX	EXACTOR	EXILING	EXTRAIT	HEXACTS
COAXERS	EXACUMS	EXILITY	EXTREAT	HEXADES
COAXIAL	EXALTED	EXISTED	EXTREMA	HEXADIC
COAXING	EXALTER	EXITING	EXTREME	HEXAGON
COEXERT	EXAMENS	EXOCARP	EXTRUDE	HEXANES
COEXIST	EXAMINE	EXODERM	EXUDATE	HEXAPLA
COMMIXT	EXAMPLE	EXODIST	EXUDING	HEXAPOD
COMPLEX	EXAPTED	EXOGAMY	EXULTED	HEXARCH
CONFLUX	EXARATE	EXOGENS	EXURBAN	HEXENES
CONTEXT	EXARCHS	EXOMION	EXURBIA	HEXEREI
CORIXID	EXARCHY	EXONYMS	EXUVIAE	HEXINGS
COTEAUX	EXCAMBS	EXOPODS	EXUVIAL	HEXONES
COXALGY	EXCEEDS	EXORDIA	EXUVIUM	HEXOSAN
COXCOMB	EXCEPTS	EXOSMIC	FAREBOX	HEXOSES
COXIEST	EXCERPT	EXOTICA	FEDEXED	HEXYLIC

HOAXERS	MINXISH	PHARYNX	SEXINGS	TOOLBOX
HOAXING	MIREXES	PHENOXY	SEXISMS	TORTRIX
HOMOSEX	MIXABLE	PHLOXES	SEXISTS	TOXEMIA
HUMIDEX	MIXDOWN	PHOENIX	SEXLESS	TOXEMIC
HYDROXY	MIXEDLY	PICKAXE	SEXPERT	TOXICAL
HYPOXIA	MIXIBLE	PILLBOX	SEXPOTS	TOXINES
HYPOXIC	MIXIEST	PIXYISH	SEXTAIN	TOXOIDS
HYRAXES	MIXTION	PLANXTY	SEXTANS	TREEWAX
IMMIXED	MIXTURE	PLEXORS	SEXTANT	TRIAXON
IMMIXES	MONAXON	PLEXURE	SEXTETS	TRIOXID
IMPOSEX	MUREXES	PODEXES	SEXTETT	TRIPLEX
INBOXES	MYXOMAS	POLEAXE	SEXTILE	TUBIFEX
INDEXAL	NARTHEX	POLLAXE	SEXTONS	TUXEDOS
INDEXED	NEXUSES	POSTBOX	SEXTUOR	ULEXITE
INDEXER	NOXIOUS	POSTFIX	SHOEBOX	UNBOXED
INDEXES	ORATRIX	POSTTAX	SHOWBOX	UNBOXES
INDOXYL	OREXINS	POXIEST	SILEXES	UNFIXED
INEXACT	OUTJINX	PREMIXT	SIMPLEX	UNFIXES
INFIXED	OVERLAX	PRETEXT	SIXAINE	UNMIXED
INFIXES	OVERMIX	PREXIES	SIXAINS	UNMIXES
INVEXED	OVERTAX	PRINCOX	SIXFOLD	UNSEXED
IXODIDS	OXALATE	PROXIES	SIXTEEN	UNSEXES
JAMBEUX	OXAZINE	PROXIMO	SIXTHLY	UNTAXED
JINXING	OXBLOOD	PYREXES	SIXTIES	UNTAXES
JUKEBOX	OXCARTS	PYREXIA	SOAPBOX	UNVEXED
KICKBOX	OXFORDS	PYREXIC	SONOVOX	UNWAXED
KLAXONS	OXGANGS	PYXIDES	SOREXES	URTEXTS
KLEENEX	OXGATES	PYXIDIA	SPANDEX	UXORIAL
LATEXES	OXHEADS	QUIXOTE	SUBTAXA	VAUDOUX
LAXATOR	OXHEART	RADIXES	SUBTEXT	VEXEDLY
LAXISMS	OXHIDES	REAFFIX	SYNAXES	VEXILLA
LAXISTS	OXIDANT	REANNEX	SYNAXIS	VEXINGS
LAXNESS	OXIDASE	RECTRIX	TALKBOX	VICTRIX
LEXEMES	OXIDATE	REDOXES	TAXABLE	VITEXES
LEXEMIC	OXIDISE	REEXPEL	TAXABLY	VITRAUX
LEXICAL	OXIDIZE	REFIXED	TAXEMES	VIXENLY
LEXICON	OXLANDS	REFIXES	TAXEMIC	WAXABLE
LEXISES	OXONIUM	REINDEX	TAXICAB	WAXBILL
LINUXES	OXSLIPS	RELAXED	TAXIING	WAXEYES
LIXIVIA	OXTAILS	RELAXER	TAXIMAN	WAXIEST
LOCKBOX	OXTERED	RELAXES	TAXIMEN	WAXINGS
LOXYGEN	OXYACID	RELAXIN	TAXINGS	WAXLIKE
LUREXES	OXYGENS	REMIXED	TAXITES	WAXWEED
LUXATED	OXYMELS	REMIXES	TAXITIC	WAXWING
LUXATES	OXYMORA	RESEAUX	TAXIWAY	WAXWORK
MAILBOX	OXYNTIC	RETAXED	TAXLESS	WAXWORM
MALAXED	OXYPHIL	RETAXES	TAXPAID	WOADWAX
MALAXES	OXYSALT	REWAXED	TAXWISE	WOODBOX
MARTEXT	OXYSOME	REWAXES	TAXYING	WOODWAX
MAXILLA	OXYTONE	REXINES	TECTRIX	WORKBOX
MAXIMAL	PACKWAX	SALPINX	TELEFAX	WRAXLED
MAXIMIN	PANAXES	SALTBOX	TELETEX	WRAXLES
MAXIMUM	PANCHAX	SANDBOX	TELEXED	XANTHAM
MAXIMUS	PARADOX	SAXAULS	TELEXES	XANTHAN
MAXIXES	PAXIUBA	SAXHORN	TEXASES	XANTHIC
MAXWELL	PEMPHIX	SAXTUBA	TEXTERS	XANTHIN
MEATAXE	PEROXID	SEALWAX	TEXTILE	XENOPUS
METHOXY	PERPLEX	SEEDBOX	TEXTING	XERAFIN
MILIEUX	PERSPEX	SEXFOIL	TEXTUAL	XERARCH
MINIMAX	PHALANX	SEXIEST	TEXTURE	XERASIA

XEROMAS	AUXOCYTE	CARFAXES	DIOXANES	EXCAMBED
XEROSES	AVIATRIX	CARFOXES	DIOXIDES	EXCAVATE
XEROSIS	AXEBIRDS	CARNIFEX	DIPLEXER	EXCEEDED
XEROTES	AXIALITY	CARNYXES	DISANNEX	EXCEEDER
XEROTIC	AXILEMMA	CATHEXES	DOGFOXES	EXCELLED
XEROXED	AXILLARS	CATHEXIS	DOXAPRAM	EXCEPTED
XEROXES	AXILLARY	CAUDEXES	DOXASTIC	EXCEPTOR
XERUSES	AXINITES	CERVIXES	DOXOLOGY	EXCERPTA
XIPHOID	AXIOLOGY	CHAPEAUX	DRUXIEST	EXCERPTS
XYLENES	AXLETREE	CHATEAUX	DUPLEXED	EXCESSED
XYLENOL	AXOLEMMA	CHENIXES	DUPLEXER	EXCESSES
XYLIDIN	AXOLOTLS	CHRONAXY	DUPLEXES	EXCHANGE
XYLITOL	AXONEMAL	CICATRIX	DUXELLES	EXCHEATS
XYLOGEN	AXONEMES	CINEPLEX	DYSLEXIA	EXCIDING
XYLOMAS	AXOPLASM	CLACKBOX	DYSLEXIC	EXCIMERS
XYLONIC	BANDEAUX	CLANGBOX	DYSTAXIA	EXCIPLES
XYLOSES	BANJAXED	CLIMAXED	EARTHWAX	EXCISING
XYSTERS	BANJAXES	CLIMAXES	EARWAXES	EXCISION
ZEUXITE	BANXRING	COCCYXES	ECONOBOX	EXCITANT
ZOOTAXY	BATTEAUX	COEXERTS	ECOTOXIC	EXCITERS
	BATTLEAX	COEXISTS	EFFLUXES	EXCITING
Eight-letter	BAUXITES	COEXTEND	EKTEXINE	EXCITONS
words	BAUXITIC	COMMIXED	EMBOXING	EXCITORS
ACETOXYL	BEAUXITE	COMMIXES	ENDEIXES	EXCLAIMS
ADMIXING	BEMBEXES	CONFIXED	ENDEIXIS	EXCLAVES
AFFIXERS	BEMBIXES	CONFIXES	ENDEXINE	EXCLUDED
AFFIXIAL	BEMIXING	CONTEXTS	ENFIXING	EXCLUDEE
AFFIXING	BERCEAUX	CONVEXED	EPICALYX	EXCLUDER
AFFLUXES	BICONVEX	CONVEXES	EPITAXES	EXCLUDES
AFTERTAX	BIOTOXIN	CONVEXLY	EPITAXIC	EXCRETAL
ALDOXIME	BISEXUAL	CORIXIDS	EPITAXIS	EXCRETED
ALEXINES	BOBBYSOX	CORTEXES	EPOXIDES	EXCRETER
ALEXINIC	BOLIXING	COTURNIX	EPOXYING	EXCRETES
ALKOXIDE	BOLLIXED	COUTEAUX	ETHOXIDE	EXCUBANT
ALLOXANS	BOLLIXES	COWPOXES	ETHOXIES	EXCURSED
AMPHIOXI	BOLLOXED	COXALGIA	ETHOXYLS	EXCURSES
AMPLEXUS	BOLLOXES	COXALGIC	EUTAXIAS	EXCURSUS
ANATEXES	BOMBAXES	COXCOMBS	EUTAXIES	EXCUSALS
ANATEXIS	BOMBYXES	COXINESS	EUTAXITE	EXCUSERS
ANATOXIN	BORDEAUX	COXSWAIN	EUTEXIAS	EXCUSING
ANNEXING	BOXBALLS	CREATRIX	EUXENITE	EXCUSIVE
ANNEXION	BOXBERRY	CRUCIFIX	EXABYTES	EXECRATE
ANNEXURE	BOXBOARD	CURATRIX	EXACTERS	EXECUTED
ANOREXIA	BOXHAULS	CURTALAX	EXACTEST	EXECUTER
ANOREXIC	BOXINESS	CURTAXES	EXACTING	EXECUTES
ANOXEMIA	BOXPLOTS	CYBERSEX	EXACTION	EXECUTOR
ANOXEMIC	BOXROOMS	DEFLEXED	EXACTORS	EXECUTRY
ANTEFIXA	BOXTHORN	DEFLEXES	EXAHERTZ	EXEEMING
ANTHELIX	BOXWOODS	DEIXISES	EXALTERS	EXEGESES
APOMIXES	BRAINBOX	DENTEXES	EXALTING	EXEGESIS
APOMIXIS	BREADBOX	DESEXING	EXAMINED	EXEGETES
APOPLEXY	BROADAXE	DETOXIFY	EXAMINEE	EXEGETIC
APPENDIX	BRUXISMS	DETOXING	EXAMINER	EXEMPLAR
APRAXIAS	BUXOMEST	DEWAXING	EXAMINES	EXEMPLES
APYREXIA	CACHEXIA	DEXTRANS	EXAMPLAR	EXEMPLUM
ASPHYXIA	CACHEXIC	DEXTRINE	EXAMPLED	EXEMPTED
ATARAXIA	CACODOXY	DEXTRINS	EXAMPLES	EXEQUIAL
ATARAXIC	CACOMIXL	DEXTROSE	EXANTHEM	EXEQUIES
AUXETICS	CAMAIEUX	DEXTROUS	EXAPTIVE	EXERCISE
AUXILIAR	CARBOXYL	DIGOXINS	EXARCHAL	EXERGIES

EXERGUAL	EXPECTER	EXTINCTS	FOXTROTS	LIXIVIAL
EXERGUES	EXPEDITE	EXTIRPED	GALAXIES	LIXIVIUM
EXERTING	EXPELLED	EXTOLLED	GENETRIX	LOOSEBOX
EXERTION	EXPELLEE	EXTOLLER	GENITRIX	LOXYGENS
EXERTIVE	EXPELLER	EXTORTED	GEOTAXES	LUMMOXES
EXHALANT	EXPENDED	EXTORTER	GEOTAXIS	LUNCHBOX
EXHALENT	EXPENDER	EXTRACTS	GIAMBEUX	LUXATING
EXHALING	EXPENSED	EXTRADOS	GLOXINIA	LUXATION
EXHAUSTS	EXPENSES	EXTRAITS	HANDAXES	LUXMETER
EXHEDRAE	EXPERTED	EXTRANET	HARUSPEX	LUXURIES
EXHIBITS	EXPERTLY	EXTREATS	HATBOXES	LUXURIST
EXHORTED	EXPIABLE	EXTREMAL	HAYBOXES	LYNXLIKE
EXHORTER	EXPIATED	EXTREMER	HERETRIX	MAGNOXES
EXHUMATE	EXPIATES	EXTREMES	HERITRIX	MALAXAGE
EXHUMERS	EXPIATOR	EXTREMUM	HEXAFOIL	MALAXATE
EXHUMING	EXPIRANT	EXTRORSE	HEXAGONS	MALAXING
EXIGEANT	EXPIRERS	EXTRUDED	HEXAGRAM	MANTEAUX
EXIGENCE	EXPIRIES	EXTRUDER	HEXAMINE	MARTEXTS
EXIGENCY	EXPIRING	EXTRUDES	HEXANOIC	MASTIXES
EXIGENTS	EXPLAINS	EXTUBATE	HEXAPLAR	MATCHBOX
EXIGIBLE	EXPLANTS	EXUDATES	HEXAPLAS	MATRIXES
EXIGUITY	EXPLICIT	EXULTANT	HEXAPODS	MAXICOAT
EXIGUOUS	EXPLODED	EXULTING	HEXAPODY	MAXILLAE
EXILABLE	EXPLODER	EXURBIAS	HEXARCHY	MAXILLAR
EXIMIOUS	EXPLODES	EXUVIATE	HEXEREIS	MAXILLAS
EXISTENT	EXPLOITS	FABLIAUX	HEXOSANS	MAXIMALS
EXISTING	EXPLORED	FEDEXING	HEXYLENE	MAXIMINS
EXITANCE	EXPLORER	FIXATIFS	HOMEOBOX	MAXIMISE
EXITLESS	EXPLORES	FIXATING	HORSEBOX	MAXIMIST
EXOCARPS	EXPONENT	FIXATION	HORSEPOX	MAXIMITE
EXOCRINE	EXPORTED	FIXATIVE	HOTBOXES	MAXIMIZE
EXOCYTIC	EXPORTER	FIXATURE	HYDROXYL	MAXIMUMS
EXODERMS	EXPOSALS	FIXITIES	HYPOXIAS	MAXWELLS
EXODISTS	EXPOSERS	FIXTURES	ICEBOXES	MEATAXES
EXODUSES	EXPOSING	FLAXIEST	IMMIXING	MEGAPLEX
EXOERGIC	EXPOSITS	FLAXSEED	IMPLEXES	METHOXYL
EXOGAMIC	EXPOSURE	FLEXAGON	INDEXERS	MICROLUX
EXOMIONS	EXPOUNDS	FLEXIBLE	INDEXING	MILLILUX
EXOMISES	EXPRESSO	FLEXIBLY	INDOXYLS	MIREPOIX
EXONUMIA	EXPUGNED	FLEXIONS	INEXPERT	MIXDOWNS
EXOPHAGY	EXPULSED	FLEXTIME	INFIXING	MIXOLOGY
EXOPLASM	EXPULSES	FLEXUOSE	INFIXION	MIXTIONS
EXORABLE	EXPUNCTS	FLEXUOUS	INFLEXED	MIXTURES
EXORCISE	EXPUNGED	FLEXURAL	INFLUXES	MONAXIAL
EXORCISM	EXPUNGER	FLEXURES	INTERMIX	MONAXONS
EXORCIST	EXPUNGES	FLUXGATE	INTERREX	MONOXIDE
EXORCIZE	EXPURGED	FLUXIONS	INTERSEX	MORCEAUX
EXORDIAL	EXPURGES	FORFEXES	ISOLEXES	MUSKOXEN
EXORDIUM	EXSCINDS	FOURPLEX	JAMBEAUX	MYXAMEBA
EXOSMOSE	EXSECANT	FOXBERRY	JANITRIX	MYXEDEMA
EXOSPORE	EXSECTED	FOXFIRES	JAWBOXES	MYXOCYTE
EXOTERIC	EXSERTED	FOXGLOVE	KETOXIME	MYXOMATA
EXOTISMS	EXTASIES	FOXHOLES	KLAXONED	NALOXONE
EXOTOXIC	EXTENDED	FOXHOUND	LARYNXES	NAPROXEN
EXOTOXIN	EXTENDER	FOXHUNTS	LAXATION	NEOTOXIN
EXPANDED	EXTENSOR	FOXINESS	LAXATIVE	NEURAXON
EXPANDER	EXTERIOR	FOXSHARK	LAXATORS	NEXTDOOR
EXPANDOR	EXTERNAL	FOXSHIPS	LAXITIES	NEXTNESS
EXPANSES	EXTERNAT	FOXSKINS	LEXICONS	NITROXES
EXPECTED	EXTERNES	FOXTAILS	LEXIGRAM	NITROXYL

NONTAXES	PEROXIDE	REWAXING	SUPERFIX	UNDERTAX
NONTOXIC	PEROXIDS	RHEXISES	SUPERMAX	UNEXOTIC
NOUVEAUX	PHENIXES	RONDEAUX	SUPERSEX	UNEXPERT
OCTUPLEX	PHORMINX	ROULEAUX	SUPERTAX	UNFIXING
OPOPANAX	PHYLAXIS	SARDONYX	SUPLEXES	UNFIXITY
OREXISES	PICKAXED	SAUCEBOX	SURTAXED	UNFLEXED
ORIFEXES	PICKAXES	SAXATILE	SURTAXES	UNIAXIAL
ORTHODOX	PIXIEISH	SAXHORNS	SWEATBOX	UNISEXES
OTOTOXIC	PIXINESS	SAXICOLE	SWINEPOX	UNMIXING
OUTBOXED	PLATEAUX	SAXONIES	SYNTAXES	UNSEXING
OUTBOXES	PLEXURES	SAXONITE	SYNTEXIS	UNSEXIST
OUTFOXED	PLEXUSES	SAXTUBAS	SYRINXES	UNSEXUAL
OUTFOXES	POLEAXED	SCRUMPOX	TABLEAUX	UNTAXING
OXALATED	POLEAXES	SEXFOILS	TAXABLES	UXORIOUS
OXALATES	POLLAXED	SEXINESS	TAXATION	VERNIXES
OXALISES	POLLAXES	SEXOLOGY	TAXATIVE	VERTEXES
OXAZEPAM	POLYAXON	SEXPERTS	TAXIARCH	VEXATION
OXAZINES	PONCEAUX	SEXTAINS	TAXICABS	VEXATORY
OXBLOODS	PONTIFEX	SEXTANTS	TAXINGLY	VEXILLAR
OXHEARTS	POXVIRUS	SEXTARII	TAXIWAYS	VEXILLUM
OXIDABLE	PRAXISES	SEXTETTE	TAXONOMY	VEXINGLY
OXIDANTS	PREAXIAL	SEXTETTS	TAXPAYER	VIDEOTEX
OXIDASES	PRECIEUX	SEXTILES	TEABOXES	VIXENISH
OXIDASIC	PREEXIST	SEXTOLET	TEGUEXIN	VOLVOXES
OXIDATED	PREFIXAL	SEXTUORS	TELETEXT	VORTEXES
OXIDATES	PREFIXED	SEXTUPLE	TELEXING	WATCHBOX
OXIDISED	PREFIXES	SEXTUPLY	TETRAXON	WATERPOX
OXIDISER	PREMIXED	SEXUALLY	TETROXID	WAXBERRY
OXIDISES	PREMIXES	SILOXANE	TETTIXES	WAXBILLS
OXIDIZED	PRETEXTS	SILVEXES	TEXTBOOK	WAXCLOTH
OXIDIZER	PROLIXLY	SIXAINES	TEXTILES	WAXINESS
OXIDIZES	PROTOXID	SIXPENCE	TEXTINGS	WAXPLANT
OXIMETER	PROXEMIC	SIXPENNY	TEXTLESS	WAXWEEDS
OXIMETRY	PROXIMAL	SIXSCORE	TEXTUARY	WAXWINGS
OXONIUMS	PTYXISES	SIXTEENS	TEXTURAL	WAXWORKS
OXPECKER	PYREXIAL	SIXTIETH	TEXTURED	WAXWORMS
OXTERING	PYREXIAS	SIXTYISH	TEXTURES	WRAXLING
OXTONGUE	PYROXENE	SKYBOXES	THORAXES	XANTHAMS
OXYACIDS	PYROXYLE	SMALLPOX	THYROXIN	XANTHANS
OXYGENIC	PYXIDIUM	SMILAXES	TOADFLAX	XANTHATE
OXYMORON	QUADPLEX	SMOKEBOX	TONNEAUX	XANTHEIN
OXYPHILE	QUINCUNX	SNUFFBOX	TOXAEMIA	XANTHENE
OXYPHILS	QUIXOTES	SOUNDBOX	TOXAEMIC	XANTHINE
OXYSALTS	QUIXOTIC	SPADIXES	TOXEMIAS	XANTHINS
OXYSOMES	QUIXOTRY	SPARAXIS	TOXICANT	XANTHISM
OXYTOCIC	REEXPELS	SPHINXES	TOXICITY	XANTHOMA
OXYTOCIN	REEXPORT	SPHYNXES	TOXOCARA	XANTHONE
OXYTONES	REEXPOSE	SPINIFEX	TRACTRIX	XANTHOUS
OXYTONIC	REFIXING	SPINTEXT	TRANSFIX	XENOGAMY
PAINTBOX	REFLEXED	STORAXES	TRIAXIAL	XENOGENY
PANMIXES	REFLEXES	STYRAXES	TRIAXONS	XENOLITH
PANMIXIA	REFLEXLY	SUBAXIAL	TRIMIXES	XENOPHYA
PANMIXIS	REFLUXED	SUBFIXES	TRIOXIDE	XENOTIME
PARADOXY	REFLUXES	SUBINDEX	TRIOXIDS	XENURINE
PARALLAX	RELAXANT	SUBOXIDE	TRUMEAUX	XERAFINS
PARAXIAL	RELAXERS	SUBTAXON	TUTRIXES	XERANSES
PAROXYSM	RELAXING	SUBTEXTS	TUXEDOED	XERANSIS
PAXIUBAS	RELAXINS	SUFFIXAL	TUXEDOES	XERANTIC
PAXWAXES	REMIXING	SUFFIXED	ULEXITES	XERAPHIN
PEGBOXES	RETAXING	SUFFIXES	UNBOXING	XERASIAS

XEROMATA	XYLENOLS	XYLOCARP	XYLOMATA	ZEUXITES
XEROSERE	XYLIDINE	XYLOGENS	XYLONITE	ZOOTOXIC
XEROXING	XYLIDINS	XYLOIDIN	XYLOTOMY	ZOOTOXIN
XIPHOIDS	XYLITOLS	XYLOLOGY	ZELATRIX	

Using Z

Z scores the same as Q: ten points. But is an easier letter to use primarily because of the two two-letter words (ZA, ZO). Occasionally it may be worth considering holding the Z back if no great scores are immediately available but generally you should try to play it sooner rather than later. It is worth familiarizing yourself with some unusual three four and five-letter words with the Z, especially those with low-scoring other letters (eg ZEA, ZOA, ZEIN, ZILA, ZONAE, ZANTE). There are a few Z words that also contain another power tile (JIZ, JAZY, ZAX, ZEX, QUIZ). Although these appear to very useful, in practice if you have two power tiles on your rack, it can be wiser to play them separately over two turns. There are also quite a few words with a double Z (BUZZ and FUZZ), for example); while these may appear useless for Scrabble, as there is only one Z in the game so you would need to use a blank as the second Z.

Two-letter words

ZA	pizza
ZO	Tibetan breed of cattle, developed by crossing the yak with common cattle

Three-letter words

ADZ	tool with an arched blade at right angles to the handle
AZO	of, consisting of, or containing the divalent group -N:N-
BEZ	part of deer's horn
BIZ	business
CAZ	casual
COZ	cousin
CUZ	cousin
DZO	Tibetan breed of cattle, developed by crossing the yak with common cattle
FEZ	brimless tasselled cap, orig. from Turkey
FIZ	make a hissing or bubbling noise
JIZ	wig
LEZ	lesbian (offensive)
LUZ	supposedly indestructible bone of the human body
MIZ	misery
MOZ	hex
POZ	positive
REZ	informal word for an instance of reserving; reservation
RIZ	(in some dialects) past form of rise
SAZ	Middle Eastern stringed instrument

SEZ	informal spelling of 'says'
SOZ	informal variant of 'sorry'
WIZ	wizard
ZAG	change direction sharply
ZAP	kill (by shooting)
ZAS	pizzas
ZAX	saxophone
ZEA	corn silk
ZED	British and New Zealand spoken form of the letter z
ZEE	zed
ZEK	Soviet prisoner
ZEL	Turkish cymbal
ZEP	type of long sandwich
ZEX	tool for cutting roofing slate
ZHO	Tibetan breed of cattle, developed by crossing the yak with common cattle
ZIG	change direction sharply
ZIN	zinfandel
ZIP	zipper
ZIT	spot or pimple
ZIZ	short sleep
ZOA	plural of zoon
ZOL	South African slang for a cannabis cigarette
ZOO	place where live animals are kept for show
ZOS	plural of zo
ZUZ	ancient Hebrew silver coin
ZZZ	informal word for sleep

Four-letter words

ADZE	BUZZ	DOZE	FUTZ	HAZY
AZAN	CHEZ	DOZY	FUZE	HIZZ
AZON	CHIZ	DZHO	FUZZ	IZAR
AZYM	COZE	DZOS	GAZE	JAZY
BIZE	COZY	FAZE	GAZY	JAZZ
BOZO	CZAR	FIZZ	GEEZ	JEEZ
	DAZE	FOZY	GIZZ	JIZZ
	DITZ	FRIZ	HAZE	KAZI

KUZU	ZEIN	AZINE	DITZY	HERTZ
LAZE	ZEKS	AZLON	DIZEN	HIZEN
LAZO	ZELS	AZOIC	DIZZY	HUZZA
LAZY	ZEPS	AZOLE	DOOZY	HUZZY
LEZZ	ZERK	AZONS	DOZED	IZARD
LUTZ	ZERO	AZOTE	DOZEN	IZARS
MAZE	ZEST	AZOTH	DOZER	IZZAT
MAZY	ZETA	AZUKI	DOZES	JAZZY
MEZE	ZEZE	AZURE	DURZI	KANZU
MEZZ	ZHOS	AZURN	DZHOS	KARZY
MIZZ	ZIFF	AZURY	ENZYM	KAZIS
MOZE	ZIGS	AZYGY	FAZED	KAZOO
MOZO	ZILA	AZYME	FAZES	KHAZI
MOZZ	ZILL	AZYMS	FEAZE	KLUTZ
MUZZ	ZIMB	BAIZA	FEEZE	KRANZ
MZEE	ZINC	BAIZE	FEZES	KUDZU
NAZE	ZINE	BAZAR	FEZZY	KUZUS
NAZI	ZING	BAZOO	FIZZY	LAZAR
OOZE	ZINS	BEZEL	FORZA	LAZED
OOZY	ZIPS	BEZES	FORZE	LAZES
ORZO	ZITE	BEZIL	FRITZ	LAZOS
OUZO	ZITI	BIZES	FRIZE	LAZZI
OYEZ	ZITS	BIZZO	FRIZZ	LAZZO
PHIZ	ZIZZ	BLAZE	FROZE	LEAZE
PIZE	ZOBO	BLITZ	FURZE	LEEZE
POZZ	ZOBU	BONZA	FURZY	LEZES
PREZ	ZOEA	BONZE	FUZED	LEZZA
PUTZ	ZOIC	BOOZE	FUZEE	LEZZY
QUIZ	ZOLS	BOOZY	FUZES	LOZEN
RAZE	ZONA	BORTZ	FUZIL	MAIZE
RAZZ	ZONE	BOZOS	FUZZY	MATZA
RITZ	ZONK	BRAZA	GAUZE	MATZO
RIZA	ZOOM	BRAZE	GAUZY	MAZED
RONZ	ZOON	BRIZE	GAZAL	MAZER
SITZ	ZOOS	BUAZE	GAZAR	MAZES
SIZE	ZOOT	BUZZY	GAZED	MAZEY
SIZY	ZORI	BWAZI	GAZER	MAZUT
SPAZ	ZOUK	CAPIZ	GAZES	MEZES
SWIZ	ZULU	CEAZE	GAZON	MEZZE
TIZZ	ZUPA	CEZVE	GAZOO	MEZZO
TOZE	ZURF	CHIZZ	GHAZI	MILTZ
TREZ	ZYGA	CLOZE	GINZO	MIRZA
TUZZ	ZYME	COBZA	GIZMO	MIZEN
TZAR	ZZZS	COLZA	GLAZE	MIZZY
VIZY		COOZE	GLAZY	MOTZA
WHIZ	**Five-letter**	COZED	GLITZ	MOZED
YUTZ	**words**	COZEN	GLOZE	MOZES
YUZU	ABUZZ	COZES	GONZO	MOZOS
ZACK	ADOZE	COZEY	GRAZE	MUZZY
ZAGS	ADZED	COZIE	GRIZE	MZEES
ZANY	ADZES	CRAZE	GROSZ	NAZES
ZAPS	AGAZE	CRAZY	GYOZA	NAZIR
ZARF	AIZLE	CROZE	HAFIZ	NAZIS
ZARI	AMAZE	CZARS	HAMZA	NEEZE
ZATI	ASSEZ	DARZI	HAZAN	NERTZ
ZEAL	AVIZE	DAZED	HAZED	NIZAM
ZEAS	AVYZE	DAZER	HAZEL	NUDZH
ZEBU	AZANS	DAZES	HAZER	OOZED
ZEDS	AZIDE	DIAZO	HAZES	OOZES
ZEES	AZIDO		HEEZE	ORZOS

OUZEL	TROOZ	ZILLS	**Six-letter**	BEZILS
OUZOS	TZARS	ZIMBI	**words**	BEZOAR
OZEKI	ULZIE	ZIMBS	ABLAZE	BEZZLE
OZONE	UNZIP	ZINCO	ABRAZO	BIZAZZ
OZZIE	VEZIR	ZINCS	ADZING	BIZONE
PEAZE	VIZIR	ZINCY	ADZUKI	BIZZES
PEIZE	VIZOR	ZINEB	AGAZED	BIZZOS
PIEZO	VOZHD	ZINES	AGNIZE	BLAIZE
PIZED	WALTZ	ZINGS	AGRIZE	BLAZAR
PIZES	WANZE	ZINGY	AGRYZE	BLAZED
PIZZA	WAREZ	ZINKE	AGUIZE	BLAZER
PLAZA	WAZIR	ZINKY	AIZLES	BLAZES
PLOTZ	WAZOO	ZIPPO	ALTEZA	BLAZON
PONZU	WEIZE	ZIPPY	AMAZED	BLINTZ
POZZY	WHIZZ	ZIRAM	AMAZES	BLOWZE
PRIZE	WINZE	ZITIS	AMAZON	BLOWZY
PUZEL	WIZEN	ZIZEL	APOZEM	BONZER
PZAZZ	WIZES	ZIZIT	ASSIZE	BONZES
RAZED	WOOTZ	ZLOTE	AVIZED	BOOZED
RAZEE	WOOZY	ZLOTY	AVIZES	BOOZER
RAZER	YUZUS	ZOAEA	AVYZED	BOOZES
RAZES	ZABRA	ZOBOS	AVYZES	BOOZEY
RAZOO	ZACKS	ZOBUS	AZALEA	BORZOI
RAZOR	ZAIRE	ZOCCO	AZERTY	BRAIZE
RITZY	ZAKAT	ZOEAE	AZIDES	BRAZAS
RIZAS	ZAMAN	ZOEAL	AZINES	BRAZED
ROZET	ZAMBO	ZOEAS	AZIONE	BRAZEN
ROZIT	ZAMIA	ZOISM	AZLONS	BRAZER
SADZA	ZANJA	ZOIST	AZOLES	BRAZES
SAZES	ZANTE	ZOMBI	AZOLLA	BRAZIL
SCUZZ	ZANZA	ZONAE	AZONAL	BREEZE
SEAZE	ZANZE	ZONAL	AZONIC	BREEZY
SEIZE	ZAPPY	ZONDA	AZOTED	BRIZES
SENZA	ZARFS	ZONED	AZOTES	BRONZE
SIZAR	ZARIS	ZONER	AZOTHS	BRONZY
SIZED	ZATIS	ZONES	AZOTIC	BROUZE
SIZEL	ZAXES	ZONKS	AZUKIS	BUAZES
SIZER	ZAYIN	ZOOEA	AZURES	BUZUKI
SIZES	ZAZEN	ZOOEY	AZYGOS	BUZZED
SMAZE	ZEALS	ZOOID	AZYMES	BUZZER
SOYUZ	ZEBEC	ZOOKS	BAIZAS	BUZZES
SOZIN	ZEBRA	ZOOMS	BAIZED	BWAZIS
SPAZA	ZEBUB	ZOONS	BAIZES	BYZANT
SPAZZ	ZEBUS	ZOOTY	BANZAI	CEAZED
SPITZ	ZEINS	ZOPPA	BARAZA	CEAZES
SQUIZ	ZERDA	ZOPPO	BAZAAR	CEZVES
SWIZZ	ZERKS	ZORIL	BAZARS	CHAZAN
TAZZA	ZEROS	ZORIS	BAZAZZ	CHINTZ
TAZZE	ZESTS	ZORRO	BAZOOS	CIZERS
TEAZE	ZESTY	ZOUKS	BEDAZE	CLOZES
TIZZY	ZETAS	ZOWIE	BEEZER	COBZAS
TOAZE	ZEXES	ZULUS	BEGAZE	COLZAS
TOPAZ	ZEZES	ZUPAN	BENZAL	COOZES
TOUZE	ZHOMO	ZUPAS	BENZIL	COROZO
TOUZY	ZIBET	ZURFS	BENZIN	CORYZA
TOWZE	ZIFFS	ZUZIM	BENZOL	COUZIN
TOWZY	ZIGAN	ZYGAL	BENZYL	COZENS
TOZED	ZILAS	ZYGON	BEZANT	COZEYS
TOZES	ZILCH	ZYMES	BEZAZZ	COZIED
TOZIE	ZILLA	ZYMIC	BEZELS	COZIER

COZIES	FRANZY	HAMZAH	LEZZAS	NUZZER
COZILY	FRAZIL	HAMZAS	LEZZES	NUZZLE
COZING	FREEZE	HAZANS	LEZZIE	NYANZA
COZZES	FRENZY	HAZARD	LIZARD	OOZIER
CRAZED	FRIEZE	HAZELS	LIZZIE	OOZILY
CRAZES	FRIZED	HAZERS	LOZELL	OOZING
CROZER	FRIZER	HAZIER	LOZENS	OUZELS
CROZES	FRIZES	HAZILY	LUTZES	OYEZES
CRUZIE	FRIZZY	HAZING	LUZERN	OZAENA
CUZZES	FROUZY	HAZMAT	LUZZES	OZALID
CUZZIE	FROWZY	HAZZAN	MAHZOR	OZEKIS
CZAPKA	FROZEN	HEEZED	MAIZES	OZONES
DARZIS	FURZES	HEEZES	MAMZER	OZONIC
DAZERS	FUTZED	HEEZIE	MATZAH	OZZIES
DAZING	FUTZES	HIZENS	MATZAS	PANZER
DAZZLE	FUZEES	HIZZED	MATZOH	PATZER
DEFUZE	FUZILS	HIZZES	MATZOS	PAZAZZ
DEZINC	FUZING	HOWZAT	MATZOT	PEAZED
DIAZIN	FUZZED	HOWZIT	MAZARD	PEAZES
DIAZOS	FUZZES	HUTZPA	MAZERS	PEIZED
DITZES	FUZZLE	HUZOOR	MAZHBI	PEIZES
DIZAIN	GAUZES	HUZZAH	MAZIER	PEZANT
DIZENS	GAZABO	HUZZAS	MAZILY	PHEEZE
DONZEL	GAZALS	IMBIZO	MAZING	PHIZES
DOOZER	GAZARS	IODIZE	MAZOUT	PHIZOG
DOOZIE	GAZEBO	IONIZE	MAZUMA	PIAZZA
DORIZE	GAZERS	IZARDS	MAZUTS	PIAZZE
DOZENS	GAZIER	IZZARD	MEAZEL	PIZAZZ
DOZERS	GAZING	IZZATS	MEZAIL	PIZING
DOZIER	GAZONS	JAZIES	MEZCAL	PIZZAS
DOZILY	GAZOON	JAZZBO	MEZUZA	PIZZAZ
DOZING	GAZOOS	JAZZED	MEZZES	PIZZLE
DRAZEL	GAZUMP	JAZZER	MEZZOS	PLAZAS
DURZIS	GEEZAH	JAZZES	MIRZAS	PODZOL
DZEREN	GEEZER	JEZAIL	MIZENS	PONZUS
ECZEMA	GHAZAL	JIZZES	MIZUNA	POTZER
ENTREZ	GHAZEL	KAIZEN	MIZZEN	POZOLE
ENZIAN	GHAZIS	KAMEEZ	MIZZES	PREZES
ENZONE	GIZMOS	KANZUS	MIZZLE	PRIZED
ENZYME	GIZZEN	KAZOOS	MIZZLY	PRIZER
ENZYMS	GIZZES	KHAZEN	MOMZER	PRIZES
EPIZOA	GLAZED	KHAZIS	MOTZAS	PUTZED
ERSATZ	GLAZEN	KIBITZ	MOZING	PUTZES
EVZONE	GLAZER	KLUTZY	MOZZES	PUZELS
FAZING	GLAZES	KOLHOZ	MOZZIE	PUZZEL
FEAZED	GLITZY	KOLKOZ	MOZZLE	PUZZLE
FEAZES	GLOZED	KRANTZ	MUZAKY	QUARTZ
FEEZED	GLOZES	KUDZUS	MUZHIK	QUAZZY
FEEZES	GOZZAN	KUVASZ	MUZJIK	QUEAZY
FEZZED	GRAZED	KWANZA	MUZZED	QUEZAL
FEZZES	GRAZER	LAZARS	MUZZES	QUINZE
FIZGIG	GRAZES	LAZIED	MUZZLE	RANZEL
FIZZED	GRIZES	LAZIER	MZUNGU	RAZEED
FIZZEN	GROSZE	LAZIES	NAZIFY	RAZEES
FIZZER	GROSZY	LAZILY	NAZIRS	RAZERS
FIZZES	GUIZER	LAZING	NEEZED	RAZING
FIZZLE	GUTZER	LAZOED	NEEZES	RAZOOS
FLOOZY	GUZZLE	LAZOES	NIZAMS	RAZORS
FOOZLE	GYOZAS	LAZULI	NOZZER	RAZURE
FOZIER	HALUTZ	LEAZES	NOZZLE	RAZZED

RAZZES	SPRITZ	WINZES	ZEREBA	ZONOID
RAZZIA	STANZA	WIZARD	ZERIBA	ZONULA
RAZZLE	STANZE	WIZENS	ZEROED	ZONULE
REBOZO	STANZO	WIZIER	ZEROES	ZONURE
RESIZE	STOOZE	WIZZEN	ZEROTH	ZOOEAE
REZERO	SUIVEZ	WIZZES	ZESTED	ZOOEAL
REZONE	SYZYGY	WURZEL	ZESTER	ZOOEAS
REZZES	TARZAN	WUZZLE	ZEUGMA	ZOOIDS
RHIZIC	TAZZAS	YAKUZA	ZHOMOS	ZOOIER
RITZES	TEAZED	YUTZES	ZIBETH	ZOOMED
RIZARD	TEAZEL	ZABETA	ZIBETS	ZOONAL
RIZZAR	TEAZES	ZABRAS	ZIGANS	ZOONED
RIZZER	TEAZLE	ZADDIK	ZIGGED	ZOONIC
RIZZOR	TENZON	ZAFFAR	ZIGZAG	ZOOZOO
RONZER	TIZWAS	ZAFFER	ZILLAH	ZORILS
ROZETS	TIZZES	ZAFFIR	ZILLAS	ZORINO
ROZITS	TOAZED	ZAFFRE	ZIMBIS	ZORROS
ROZZER	TOAZES	ZAFTIG	ZINCED	ZOSTER
SADZAS	TOLZEY	ZAGGED	ZINCIC	ZOUAVE
SAZHEN	TOUZED	ZAIKAI	ZINCKY	ZOUNDS
SAZZES	TOUZES	ZAIRES	ZINCOS	ZOYSIA
SCAZON	TOUZLE	ZAKATS	ZINEBS	ZUFOLI
SCHIZO	TOWZED	ZAMANG	ZINGED	ZUFOLO
SCHIZY	TOWZES	ZAMANS	ZINGEL	ZUPANS
SCHNOZ	TOZIES	ZAMBOS	ZINGER	ZUZZIM
SCOZZA	TOZING	ZAMBUK	ZINKED	ZYDECO
SCRUZE	TREZES	ZAMIAS	ZINKES	ZYGOID
SCUZZY	TUZZES	ZANANA	ZINNIA	ZYGOMA
SEAZED	TWEEZE	ZANDER	ZIPPED	ZYGOSE
SEAZES	TZADDI	ZANIED	ZIPPER	ZYGOTE
SEIZED	TZETSE	ZANIER	ZIPPOS	ZYMASE
SEIZER	TZETZE	ZANIES	ZIPTOP	ZYMITE
SEIZES	TZURIS	ZANILY	ZIRAMS	ZYMOID
SEIZIN	ULZIES	ZANJAS	ZIRCON	ZYMOME
SEIZOR	UMFAZI	ZANTES	ZITHER	ZYTHUM
SHAZAM	UNZIPS	ZANZAS	ZIZELS	
SHITZU	UPGAZE	ZANZES	ZIZITH	**Seven-letter**
SIZARS	UPSIZE	ZAPATA	ZIZZED	**words**
SIZELS	VEZIRS	ZAPPED	ZIZZES	ABRAZOS
SIZERS	VIZARD	ZAPPER	ZIZZLE	ADONIZE
SIZIER	VIZIED	ZARAPE	ZLOTYS	ADZUKIS
SIZING	VIZIER	ZAREBA	ZOAEAE	AGATIZE
SIZISM	VIZIES	ZARIBA	ZOAEAS	AGENIZE
SIZIST	VIZIRS	ZARNEC	ZOARIA	AGNIZED
SIZZLE	VIZORS	ZAYINS	ZOCALO	AGNIZES
SLEAZE	VIZSLA	ZAZENS	ZOCCOS	AGONIZE
SLEAZO	VIZZIE	ZEALOT	ZODIAC	AGRIZED
SLEAZY	VOZHDS	ZEATIN	ZOECIA	AGRIZES
SLEEZY	WANZED	ZEBECK	ZOETIC	AGRYZED
SMAZES	WANZES	ZEBECS	ZOFTIG	AGRYZES
SNAZZY	WAZIRS	ZEBRAS	ZOISMS	AGUIZED
SNEEZE	WAZOOS	ZEBUBS	ZOISTS	AGUIZES
SNEEZY	WEAZEN	ZECHIN	ZOMBIE	ALBIZIA
SNOOZE	WEIZED	ZELANT	ZOMBIS	ALCAZAR
SNOOZY	WEIZES	ZELOSO	ZONARY	ALCORZA
SOZINE	WEZAND	ZENANA	ZONATE	ALFEREZ
SOZINS	WHEEZE	ZENDIK	ZONDAS	ALIZARI
SOZZLE	WHEEZY	ZENITH	ZONERS	ALTEZAS
SOZZLY	WHIZZO	ZEPHYR	ZONING	ALTEZZA
SPELTZ	WHIZZY	ZERDAS	ZONKED	AMAZING

AMAZONS	BEZZANT	CANZONI	DEZINCS	FIZGIGS
ANALYZE	BEZZAZZ	CAPIZES	DIALYZE	FIZZENS
ANODIZE	BEZZLED	CAPSIZE	DIARIZE	FIZZERS
ANZIANI	BEZZLES	CAZIQUE	DIAZINE	FIZZGIG
APIEZON	BIZARRE	CEAZING	DIAZINS	FIZZIER
APOZEMS	BIZARRO	CERVEZA	DIAZOES	FIZZING
APPRIZE	BIZNAGA	CHALAZA	DIAZOLE	FIZZLED
ARABIZE	BIZONAL	CHALUTZ	DITZIER	FIZZLES
ASSIZED	BIZONES	CHAMETZ	DIZAINS	FLOOZIE
ASSIZER	BIZZIES	CHAZANS	DIZENED	FOOZLED
ASSIZES	BLAZARS	CHAZZAN	DIZZARD	FOOZLER
ATHEIZE	BLAZERS	CHAZZEN	DIZZIED	FOOZLES
ATOMIZE	BLAZING	CHINTZY	DIZZIER	FORZATI
AVIZING	BLAZONS	CHIZZED	DIZZIES	FORZATO
AVYZING	BLINTZE	CHIZZES	DIZZILY	FOZIEST
AZALEAS	BLITZED	CHOMETZ	DOCKIZE	FRAWZEY
AZIMUTH	BLITZER	CHORIZO	DONZELS	FRAZILS
AZIONES	BLITZES	CHUTZPA	DOOZERS	FRAZZLE
AZOLLAS	BLOWZED	CITIZEN	DOOZIES	FREEZER
AZOTISE	BLOWZES	COALIZE	DOPIAZA	FREEZES
AZOTIZE	BONANZA	COGNIZE	DORIZED	FRIEZED
AZOTOUS	BOOZERS	COROZOS	DORIZES	FRIEZES
AZULEJO	BOOZIER	CORYZAL	DOZENED	FRITZES
AZUREAN	BOOZILY	CORYZAS	DOZENTH	FRIZERS
AZURINE	BOOZING	COUZINS	DOZIEST	FRIZING
AZURITE	BORAZON	COZENED	DOZINGS	FRIZZED
AZYGIES	BORTZES	COZENER	DRAZELS	FRIZZER
AZYGOUS	BORZOIS	COZIERS	DRIZZLE	FRIZZES
AZYMITE	BRAIZES	COZIEST	DRIZZLY	FRIZZLE
AZYMOUS	BRAZENS	COZYING	DUALIZE	FRIZZLY
BAIZING	BRAZERS	CRAZIER	DZERENS	FURZIER
BANZAIS	BRAZIER	CRAZIES	EBONIZE	FUTZING
BAPTIZE	BRAZILS	CRAZILY	ECHOIZE	FUZZBOX
BARAZAS	BRAZING	CRAZING	ECTOZOA	FUZZIER
BAZAARS	BREEZED	CROZERS	ECZEMAS	FUZZILY
BAZOOKA	BREEZES	CROZIER	EGOTIZE	FUZZING
BAZOOMS	BRITZKA	CRUIZIE	ELEGIZE	FUZZLED
BAZOUKI	BROMIZE	CRUZADO	EMBLAZE	FUZZLES
BAZZAZZ	BRONZED	CRUZIES	EMPRIZE	GALLIZE
BEDAZED	BRONZEN	CUZZIES	ENDOZOA	GAUZIER
BEDAZES	BRONZER	CYANIZE	ENDOZONE	GAUZILY
BEDIZEN	BRONZES	CYCLIZE	ENFROZE	GAZABOS
BEEZERS	BROUZES	CZAPKAS	ENTOZOA	GAZANIA
BEGAZED	BRULZIE	CZARDAS	ENZIANS	GAZEBOS
BEGAZES	BUMBAZE	CZARDOM	ENZONED	GAZEFUL
BEMAZED	BUZUKIA	CZARINA	ENZONES	GAZELLE
BENZALS	BUZUKIS	CZARISM	ENZYMES	GAZETTE
BENZENE	BUZZARD	CZARIST	ENZYMIC	GAZIEST
BENZILS	BUZZCUT	DAMOZEL	EPAZOTE	GAZINGS
BENZINE	BUZZERS	DANAZOL	EPIZOAN	GAZOOKA
BENZINS	BUZZIER	DAZEDLY	EPIZOIC	GAZOONS
BENZOIC	BUZZING	DAZZLED	EPIZOON	GAZUMPS
BENZOIN	BUZZWIG	DAZZLER	EROTIZE	GEEZAHS
BENZOLE	BYZANTS	DAZZLES	EVZONES	GEEZERS
BENZOLS	CABEZON	DEFROZE	FAHLERZ	GENIZAH
BENZOYL	CADENZA	DEFUZED	FANZINE	GENIZOT
BENZYLS	CALZONE	DEFUZES	FAZENDA	GHAZALS
BEZANTS	CALZONI	DEGLAZE	FEAZING	GHAZELS
BEZIQUE	CANZONA	DENIZEN	FEEZING	GHAZIES
BEZOARS	CANZONE	DEUTZIA	FILAZER	GINZOES

GIZZARD	ISOZYME	MAZIEST	OUTSIZE	RAZURES
GIZZENS	ITEMIZE	MAZOUTS	OXAZINE	RAZZIAS
GLAZERS	IZZARDS	MAZUMAS	OXIDIZE	RAZZING
GLAZIER	JACUZZI	MAZURKA	OZAENAS	RAZZLES
GLAZILY	JANIZAR	MAZZARD	OZALIDS	REALIZE
GLAZING	JAZZBOS	MEAZELS	OZONATE	REBOZOS
GLITZED	JAZZERS	MENAZON	OZONIDE	REFROZE
GLITZES	JAZZIER	MESTIZA	OZONISE	REGLAZE
GLOZING	JAZZILY	MESTIZO	OZONIZE	REPRIZE
GOZZANS	JAZZING	METAZOA	OZONOUS	RESEIZE
GRAZERS	JAZZMAN	MEZAILS	PALAZZI	RESIZED
GRAZIER	JAZZMEN	MEZCALS	PALAZZO	RESIZES
GRAZING	JEZAILS	MEZQUIT	PANZERS	REZEROS
GRECIZE	JEZEBEL	MEZUZAH	PARAZOA	REZONED
GRIZZLE	KAIZENS	MEZUZAS	PATZERS	REZONES
GRIZZLY	KARZIES	MEZUZOT	PAZZAZZ	RHIZINE
GROZING	KHAZENS	MIDSIZE	PEAZING	RHIZOID
GUEREZA	KIBBITZ	MILTZES	PECTIZE	RHIZOMA
GUIZERS	KIBBUTZ	MITZVAH	PEIZING	RHIZOME
GUTZERS	KLEZMER	MIZMAZE	PEPTIZE	RHIZOPI
GUZZLED	KLUTZES	MIZUNAS	PEZANTS	RIOTIZE
GUZZLER	KOLHOZY	MIZZENS	PHEAZAR	RITZIER
GUZZLES	KOLKHOZ	MIZZLED	PHEEZED	RITZILY
HAFIZES	KOLKOZY	MIZZLES	PHEEZES	RIZARDS
HAMZAHS	KRANZES	MOMZERS	PHIZOGS	RIZZARS
HAZANIM	KREUZER	MOZETTA	PHIZZES	RIZZART
HAZARDS	KUNZITE	MOZETTE	PIAZZAS	RIZZERS
HAZELLY	KWANZAS	MOZZIES	PIZAZZY	RIZZORS
HAZIEST	KYANIZE	MOZZLES	PIZZAZZ	ROMANZA
HAZINGS	LAICIZE	MUEZZIN	PIZZLES	RONZERS
HAZMATS	LAIRIZE	MUZHIKS	PLOTZED	ROZELLE
HAZZANS	LAYDEEZ	MUZJIKS	PLOTZES	ROZETED
HEEZIES	LAZARET	MUZZIER	PODZOLS	ROZITED
HEEZING	LAZIEST	MUZZILY	POETIZE	ROZZERS
HEROIZE	LAZOING	MUZZING	POLYZOA	SAZERAC
HERTZES	LAZULIS	MUZZLED	POTZERS	SAZHENS
HIZZING	LAZYING	MUZZLER	POZOLES	SCAZONS
HOATZIN	LAZYISH	MUZZLES	POZZIES	SCHANZE
HORIZON	LEZZIES	MYTHIZE	PRENZIE	SCHERZI
HUMBUZZ	LIONIZE	MZUNGUS	PRETZEL	SCHERZO
HUTZPAH	LIZARDS	NEEZING	PREZZIE	SCHIZOS
HUTZPAS	LIZZIES	NETIZEN	PRIZERS	SCHIZZY
HUZOORS	LOZELLS	NONZERO	PRIZING	SCHMALZ
HUZZAED	LOZENGE	NOZZERS	PUTZING	SCHMELZ
HUZZAHS	LOZENGY	NOZZLES	PUZZELS	SCHMOOZ
HUZZIES	LUZERNS	NUDZHED	PUZZLED	SCHNOZZ
ICONIZE	MACHZOR	NUDZHES	PUZZLER	SCOZZAS
IDOLIZE	MADZOON	NUZZERS	PUZZLES	SCRUZED
IMBIZOS	MAHZORS	NUZZLED	PZAZZES	SCRUZES
IMBLAZE	MAMZERS	NUZZLER	QUARTZY	SCUZZES
IODIZED	MATZAHS	NUZZLES	QUETZAL	SEAZING
IODIZER	MATZOHS	NYANZAS	QUEZALS	SEIZERS
IODIZES	MATZOON	OBELIZE	QUINZES	SEIZING
IONIZED	MATZOTH	ODORIZE	QUIZZED	SEIZINS
IONIZER	MAZARDS	ODZOOKS	QUIZZER	SEIZORS
IONIZES	MAZEDLY	OOZIEST	QUIZZES	SEIZURE
IRIDIZE	MAZEFUL	ORGANZA	RANZELS	SELTZER
IRONIZE	MAZHBIS	OUTGAZE	RAZORED	SHEGETZ

SHIATZU	TARZANS	VIZORED	ZANDERS	ZEUGMAS
SHITZUS	TEAZELS	VIZSLAS	ZANELLA	ZEUXITE
SHMALTZ	TEAZING	VIZYING	ZANIEST	ZIBETHS
SHMOOZE	TEAZLED	VIZZIED	ZANJERO	ZIFFIUS
SHMOOZY	TEAZLES	VIZZIES	ZANYING	ZIGANKA
SHOWBIZ	TENDENZ	WALTZED	ZANYISH	ZIGGING
SIAMEZE	TENZONS	WALTZER	ZANYISM	ZIGZAGS
SIZABLE	THIAZIN	WALTZES	ZAPATEO	ZIKURAT
SIZABLY	THIAZOL	WANZING	ZAPPERS	ZILCHES
SIZEISM	TIZZIES	WARZONE	ZAPPIER	ZILLAHS
SIZEIST	TOAZING	WAZZOCK	ZAPPING	ZILLION
SIZIEST	TOLZEYS	WEAZAND	ZAPTIAH	ZIMOCCA
SIZINGS	TOPAZES	WEAZENS	ZAPTIEH	ZINCATE
SIZISMS	TOUZIER	WEBZINE	ZARAPES	ZINCIER
SIZISTS	TOUZING	WEIZING	ZAREBAS	ZINCIFY
SIZZLED	TOUZLED	WEZANDS	ZAREEBA	ZINCING
SIZZLER	TOUZLES	WHAIZLE	ZARIBAS	ZINCITE
SIZZLES	TOWZIER	WHEEZED	ZARNECS	ZINCKED
SLEAZES	TOWZING	WHEEZER	ZARNICH	ZINCODE
SNEEZED	TRAPEZE	WHEEZES	ZEALANT	ZINCOID
SNEEZER	TRIAZIN	WHEEZLE	ZEALFUL	ZINCOUS
SNEEZES	TRIZONE	WHIZZED	ZEALOTS	ZINGANI
SNOOZED	TUILZIE	WHIZZER	ZEALOUS	ZINGANO
SNOOZER	TWEEZED	WHIZZES	ZEATINS	ZINGARA
SNOOZES	TWEEZER	WIZARDS	ZEBECKS	ZINGARE
SNOOZLE	TWEEZES	WIZENED	ZEBRAIC	ZINGARI
SNUZZLE	TWIZZLE	WIZIERS	ZEBRANO	ZINGARO
SOVKHOZ	TZADDIK	WIZZENS	ZEBRASS	ZINGELS
SOYUZES	TZADDIQ	WOOTZES	ZEBRINA	ZINGERS
SOZINES	TZADDIS	WOOZIER	ZEBRINE	ZINGIER
SOZZLED	TZARDOM	WOOZILY	ZEBROID	ZINGING
SOZZLES	TZARINA	WRIZLED	ZEBRULA	ZINKIER
SPATZLE	TZARISM	WURZELS	ZEBRULE	ZINKIFY
SPAZZED	TZARIST	WUZZLED	ZECCHIN	ZINKING
SPAZZES	TZETSES	WUZZLES	ZECHINS	ZINNIAS
SPITZES	TZETZES	ZABETAS	ZEDOARY	ZIPLESS
SPREAZE	TZIGANE	ZABTIEH	ZELANTS	ZIPLOCK
SPREEZE	TZIGANY	ZACATON	ZELATOR	ZIPPERS
SPULZIE	TZIMMES	ZADDICK	ZELKOVA	ZIPPIER
SQUEEZE	TZITZIS	ZADDIKS	ZEMSTVA	ZIPPING
SQUEEZY	TZITZIT	ZAFFARS	ZEMSTVO	ZIRCONS
STANZAS	UMFAZIS	ZAFFERS	ZENAIDA	ZITHERN
STANZES	UNCRAZY	ZAFFIRS	ZENANAS	ZITHERS
STANZOS	UNFAZED	ZAFFRES	ZENDIKS	ZIZANIA
STARETZ	UNFROZE	ZAGGING	ZENITHS	ZIZZING
STOOZED	UNGAZED	ZAIKAIS	ZEOLITE	ZIZZLED
STOOZER	UNISIZE	ZAITECH	ZEPHYRS	ZIZZLES
STOOZES	UNITIZE	ZAKUSKA	ZEPPOLE	ZLOTIES
STYLIZE	UNRAZED	ZAKUSKI	ZEPPOLI	ZLOTYCH
SUBZERO	UNSIZED	ZAMANGS	ZEREBAS	ZOARIAL
SUBZONE	UNZONED	ZAMARRA	ZERIBAS	ZOARIUM
SWAZZLE	UPGAZED	ZAMARRO	ZEROING	ZOCALOS
SWIZZED	UPGAZES	ZAMBUCK	ZESTERS	ZOCCOLO
SWIZZES	UPSIZED	ZAMBUKS	ZESTFUL	ZODIACS
SWIZZLE	UPSIZES	ZAMOUSE	ZESTIER	ZOECIUM
SWOZZLE	UTILIZE	ZAMPONE	ZESTILY	ZOEFORM
SYZYGAL	VIZARDS	ZAMPONI	ZESTING	ZOISITE
TAILZIE	VIZIERS	ZANANAS	ZETETIC	ZOMBIES

ZOMBIFY	ZYZZYVA	ATOMIZES	BLITZING	CAPONIZE
ZONALLY		ATRAZINE	BLIZZARD	CAPSIZAL
ZONATED	**Eight-letter**	ATTICIZE	BLOWZIER	CAPSIZED
ZONINGS	**words**	AUTOLYZE	BLOWZILY	CAPSIZES
ZONKING	ACTIVIZE	AVIANIZE	BONANZAS	CATALYZE
ZONULAE	ADONIZED	AZIMUTHS	BOOZIEST	CAZIQUES
ZONULAR	ADONIZES	AZOTEMIA	BOOZINGS	CENOZOIC
ZONULAS	AGATIZED	AZOTEMIC	BORAZONS	CERVEZAS
ZONULES	AGATIZES	AZOTISED	BOTANIZE	CHALAZAE
ZONULET	AGENIZED	AZOTISES	BOUZOUKI	CHALAZAL
ZONURES	AGENIZES	AZOTIZED	BOZZETTI	CHALAZAS
ZOOECIA	AGNIZING	AZOTIZES	BOZZETTO	CHALAZIA
ZOOGAMY	AGONIZED	AZOTURIA	BRAZENED	CHAZANIM
ZOOGENY	AGONIZES	AZULEJOS	BRAZENLY	CHAZZANS
ZOOGLEA	AGRIZING	AZURINES	BRAZENRY	CHAZZENS
ZOOGONY	AGRYZING	AZURITES	BRAZIERS	CHINTZES
ZOOIDAL	AGUIZING	AZYGOSES	BRAZIERY	CHIZZING
ZOOIEST	ALBITIZE	AZYMITES	BRAZILIN	CHORIZOS
ZOOLITE	ALBIZIAS	BANALIZE	BREEZIER	CHROMIZE
ZOOLITH	ALBIZZIA	BAPTIZED	BREEZILY	CHUTZPAH
ZOOLOGY	ALCAZARS	BAPTIZER	BREEZING	CHUTZPAS
ZOOMING	ALCORZAS	BAPTIZES	BRITZKAS	CITIZENS
ZOONING	ALGUAZIL	BAROMETZ	BRITZSKA	CIVILIZE
ZOONITE	ALIZARIN	BARTIZAN	BROMIZED	COALIZED
ZOONOMY	ALIZARIS	BAZAZZES	BROMIZES	COALIZES
ZOOPERY	ALKALIZE	BAZOOKAS	BRONZERS	COENZYME
ZOOTAXY	ALLOZYME	BAZOUKIS	BRONZIER	COGNIZED
ZOOTIER	ALTEZZAS	BEDAZING	BRONZIFY	COGNIZER
ZOOTOMY	AMAZEDLY	BEDAZZLE	BRONZING	COGNIZES
ZOOTYPE	AMORTIZE	BEDIZENS	BRONZITE	COLONIZE
ZOOZOOS	ANALYZED	BEGAZING	BRUILZIE	COLORIZE
ZORBING	ANALYZER	BEJEEZUS	BRULZIES	COMPRIZE
ZORGITE	ANALYZES	BEMUZZLE	BRUNIZEM	COZENAGE
ZORILLA	ANNALIZE	BENZENES	BRYOZOAN	COZENERS
ZORILLE	ANODIZED	BENZIDIN	BULLDOZE	COZENING
ZORILLO	ANODIZES	BENZINES	BUMBAZED	COZINESS
ZORINOS	ANTICIZE	BENZOATE	BUMBAZES	CRAZIEST
ZOSTERS	APHETIZE	BENZOINS	BURDIZZO	CREDENZA
ZOUAVES	APHORIZE	BENZOLES	BUZKASHI	CREOLIZE
ZOYSIAS	APPETIZE	BENZOYLS	BUZZARDS	CREUTZER
ZUFFOLI	APPRIZED	BENZYLIC	BUZZBAIT	CROZIERS
ZUFFOLO	APPRIZER	BEZAZZES	BUZZCUTS	CROZZLED
ZYDECOS	APPRIZES	BEZIQUES	BUZZIEST	CRUIZIES
ZYGOMAS	ARABIZED	BEZONIAN	BUZZINGS	CRUZADOS
ZYGOSES	ARABIZES	BEZZANTS	BUZZKILL	CRUZEIRO
ZYGOSIS	ARBORIZE	BEZZLING	BUZZWIGS	CURARIZE
ZYGOTES	ARCHAIZE	BITESIZE	BUZZWORD	CUTINIZE
ZYGOTIC	ARMOZEEN	BIZARRES	CABEZONE	CYANIZED
ZYMASES	ARMOZINE	BIZARROS	CABEZONS	CYANIZES
ZYMITES	ARRHIZAL	BIZAZZES	CADENZAS	CYCLIZED
ZYMOGEN	ASSIZERS	BIZCACHA	CALABAZA	CYCLIZES
ZYMOMES	ASSIZING	BIZNAGAS	CALORIZE	CZARDOMS
ZYMOSAN	ATHEIZED	BLAZERED	CALZONES	CZAREVNA
ZYMOSES	ATHEIZES	BLAZONED	CANALIZE	CZARINAS
ZYMOSIS	ATHETIZE	BLAZONER	CANONIZE	CZARISMS
ZYMOTIC	ATMOLYZE	BLAZONRY	CANZONAS	CZARISTS
ZYMURGY	ATOMIZED	BLINTZES	CANZONES	CZARITSA
ZYTHUMS	ATOMIZER	BLITZERS	CANZONET	CZARITZA

DAIDZEIN	ECHOIZES	FLOOZIES	GIZZENED	IMBLAZES
DAMOZELS	ECTOZOAN	FLUIDIZE	GLAZIERS	IMMUNIZE
DANAZOLS	ECTOZOIC	FOCALIZE	GLAZIERY	INFAMIZE
DAZZLERS	ECTOZOON	FOOZLERS	GLAZIEST	IODIZERS
DAZZLING	EGOTIZED	FOOZLING	GLAZINGS	IODIZING
DEFREEZE	EGOTIZES	FORZANDI	GLITZIER	IONIZERS
DEFROZEN	ELEGIZED	FORZANDO	GLITZILY	IONIZING
DEFUZING	ELEGIZES	FORZATOS	GLITZING	IRIDIZED
DEGLAZED	EMBEZZLE	FOZINESS	GLOZINGS	IRIDIZES
DEGLAZES	EMBLAZED	FRANCIZE	GOHONZON	IRONIZED
DEIONIZE	EMBLAZER	FRANZIER	GOLDSIZE	IRONIZES
DEMONIZE	EMBLAZES	FRAWZEYS	GRAECIZE	ISOZYMES
DENAZIFY	EMBLAZON	FRAZZLED	GRAZABLE	ISOZYMIC
DENIZENS	EMBOLIZE	FRAZZLES	GRAZIERS	ITEMIZED
DEPUTIZE	EMPERIZE	FREEZERS	GRAZINGS	ITEMIZER
DEUTZIAS	EMPRIZES	FREEZING	GRAZIOSO	ITEMIZES
DEZINCED	ENDOZOIC	FRENZIED	GRECIZED	IZVESTIA
DIALYZED	ENDOZOON	FRENZIES	GRECIZES	JACUZZIS
DIALYZER	ENDZONES	FRENZILY	GRIZZLED	JALFREZI
DIALYZES	ENERGIZE	FRIEZING	GRIZZLER	JANIZARS
DIARIZED	ENFREEZE	FRIZETTE	GRIZZLES	JANIZARY
DIARIZES	ENFROZEN	FRIZZERS	GUEREZAS	JAPANIZE
DIAZEPAM	ENTOZOAL	FRIZZIER	GUZZLERS	JAROVIZE
DIAZINES	ENTOZOAN	FRIZZIES	GUZZLING	JAZERANT
DIAZINON	ENTOZOIC	FRIZZILY	HALAZONE	JAZZIEST
DIAZOLES	ENTOZOON	FRIZZING	HALUTZIM	JAZZLIKE
DIGITIZE	ENZONING	FRIZZLED	HAZARDED	JEZEBELS
DIMERIZE	ENZOOTIC	FRIZZLER	HAZARDER	JUMBOIZE
DIPLOZOA	EPAZOTES	FRIZZLES	HAZARDRY	KAMEEZES
DISPRIZE	EPIZOANS	FROUZIER	HAZELHEN	KAMIKAZE
DISSEIZE	EPIZOISM	FROWZIER	HAZELNUT	KAZACHKI
DITZIEST	EPIZOITE	FROWZILY	HAZINESS	KAZACHOC
DIVINIZE	EPIZOOTY	FROZENLY	HAZZANIM	KAZACHOK
DIZENING	EQUALIZE	FURZIEST	HEBRAIZE	KAZATSKI
DIZYGOUS	ERGOTIZE	FUZZIEST	HEMOLYZE	KAZATSKY
DIZZARDS	EROTIZED	FUZZLING	HEPATIZE	KAZATZKA
DIZZIEST	EROTIZES	FUZZTONE	HEROIZED	KHAZENIM
DIZZYING	ERSATZES	GADZOOKS	HEROIZES	KIBITZED
DOCKIZED	ETERNIZE	GALLIZED	HIZZONER	KIBITZER
DOCKIZES	ETHERIZE	GALLIZES	HOACTZIN	KIBITZES
DOPIAZAS	ETHICIZE	GARBANZO	HOATZINS	KLEZMERS
DORIZING	EULOGIZE	GAUZIEST	HOLOZOIC	KLUTZIER
DOUZEPER	EUPHUIZE	GAZABOES	HOMINIZE	KOLHOZES
DOWNSIZE	EXAHERTZ	GAZANIAS	HORIZONS	KOLKHOZY
DOWNZONE	EXORCIZE	GAZEBOES	HOWITZER	KOLKOZES
DOZENING	FABULIZE	GAZELLES	HUMANIZE	KRANTZES
DOZENTHS	FANZINES	GAZEMENT	HUTZPAHS	KREUTZER
DOZINESS	FARADIZE	GAZETTED	HUZZAHED	KREUZERS
DRIZZLED	FAZENDAS	GAZETTES	HUZZAING	KUNZITES
DRIZZLES	FEMINAZI	GAZOGENE	HYDROZOA	KUVASZOK
DUALIZED	FEMINIZE	GAZOOKAS	HYLOZOIC	KYANIZED
DUALIZES	FIBERIZE	GAZPACHO	ICONIZED	KYANIZES
DYNAMIZE	FILAZERS	GAZUMPED	ICONIZES	LAICIZED
EBENEZER	FINALIZE	GAZUMPER	IDEALIZE	LAICIZES
EBIONIZE	FIZZGIGS	GAZUNDER	IDOLIZED	LAIRIZED
EBONIZED	FIZZIEST	GENIZAHS	IDOLIZER	LAIRIZES
EBONIZES	FIZZINGS	GENIZOTH	IDOLIZES	LATERIZE
ECHOIZED	FIZZLING	GIZZARDS	IMBLAZED	LATINIZE

LAZARETS	MISPRIZE	OZONATES	PUZZLING	ROZELLES
LAZINESS	MITZVAHS	OZONIDES	PYRAZOLE	ROZETING
LAZULITE	MITZVOTH	OZONISED	PYRITIZE	ROZITING
LAZURITE	MIZMAZES	OZONISER	PYROLIZE	RURALIZE
LEGALIZE	MIZZLIER	OZONISES	PYROLYZE	SALINIZE
LIONIZED	MIZZLING	OZONIZED	QUANTIZE	SAMIZDAT
LIONIZER	MOBILIZE	OZONIZER	QUARTZES	SANITIZE
LIONIZES	MOMZERIM	OZONIZES	QUATORZE	SARRAZIN
LOCALIZE	MONAZITE	PAGANIZE	QUAZZIER	SATIRIZE
LOGICIZE	MONETIZE	PALAZZOS	QUEAZIER	SAZERACS
LOZENGED	MORALIZE	PAPALIZE	QUETZALS	SCHANTZE
LOZENGES	MOTORIZE	PARALYZE	QUEZALES	SCHANZES
LYRICIZE	MOZETTAS	PARAZOAN	QUIZZERS	SCHERZOS
LYSOZYME	MOZZETTA	PARAZOON	QUIZZERY	SCHIZIER
MACARIZE	MOZZETTE	PARTIZAN	QUIZZIFY	SCHIZOID
MACHZORS	MUEZZINS	PATINIZE	QUIZZING	SCHIZONT
MADERIZE	MUZZIEST	PAZAZZES	RACEMIZE	SCHMALTZ
MADZOONS	MUZZLERS	PECTIZED	RAZEEING	SCHMALZY
MAGAZINE	MUZZLING	PECTIZES	RAZMATAZ	SCHMELZE
MAHZORIM	MYTHIZED	PENALIZE	RAZORING	SCHMOOZE
MAMZERIM	MYTHIZES	PEPTIZED	REALIZED	SCHMOOZY
MANZELLO	NASALIZE	PEPTIZER	REALIZER	SCHNOZES
MARZIPAN	NAZIFIED	PEPTIZES	REALIZES	SCRUZING
MATZOONS	NAZIFIES	PETUNTZE	REFREEZE	SCUZZBAG
MAXIMIZE	NEBULIZE	PEZIZOID	REFROZEN	SCUZZIER
MAZAEDIA	NETIZENS	PHEAZARS	REGLAZED	SEIZABLE
MAZARINE	NIZAMATE	PHEEZING	REGLAZES	SEIZINGS
MAZELIKE	NODALIZE	PHENAZIN	REGULIZE	SEIZURES
MAZELTOV	NOMADIZE	PIAZZIAN	RENDZINA	SELTZERS
MAZEMENT	NOTARIZE	PINTSIZE	REPRIZED	SFORZATI
MAZINESS	NOVELIZE	PIROZHKI	REPRIZES	SFORZATO
MAZOURKA	NUDZHING	PIROZHOK	RESEIZED	SHIATZUS
MAZURKAS	NUZZLERS	PIZAZZES	RESEIZES	SHKOTZIM
MAZZARDS	NUZZLING	PIZZAZES	RESINIZE	SHMALTZY
MECHITZA	OBELIZED	PIZZAZZY	RESIZING	SHMOOZED
MELANIZE	OBELIZES	PIZZELLE	REZEROED	SHMOOZER
MELODIZE	ODORIZED	PIZZERIA	REZEROES	SHMOOZES
MEMORIZE	ODORIZES	PLOTZING	REZONING	SHVARTZE
MENAZONS	OOZINESS	PODZOLIC	RHIZINES	SIAMEZED
MESOZOAN	OPALIZED	POETIZED	RHIZOBIA	SIAMEZES
MESOZOIC	OPSONIZE	POETIZER	RHIZOIDS	SIEROZEM
MESPRIZE	OPTIMIZE	POETIZES	RHIZOMES	SIMAZINE
MESTIZAS	ORGANIZE	POLARIZE	RHIZOMIC	SIMILIZE
MESTIZOS	ORGANZAS	POLEMIZE	RHIZOPOD	SIMONIZE
METALIZE	OUTBLAZE	POLONIZE	RHIZOPUS	SINICIZE
METAZOAL	OUTGAZED	POLYZOAN	RIBOZYME	SIRENIZE
METAZOAN	OUTGAZES	POLYZOIC	RIGIDIZE	SIRONIZE
METAZOIC	OUTPRIZE	POLYZOON	RIOTIZES	SITZMARK
METAZOON	OUTSIZED	POZZOLAN	RITZIEST	SIZEABLE
METRAZOL	OUTSIZES	PREFROZE	RIVALIZE	SIZEABLY
MEZEREON	OVERSIZE	PRETZELS	RIZZARED	SIZEISMS
MEZEREUM	OVERZEAL	PREZZIES	RIZZARTS	SIZEISTS
MEZQUITE	OXAZEPAM	PRIZABLE	RIZZERED	SIZINESS
MEZQUITS	OXAZINES	PRIZEMAN	RIZZORED	SIZZLERS
MEZUZAHS	OXIDIZED	PRIZEMEN	ROBOTIZE	SIZZLING
MEZUZOTH	OXIDIZER	PROTOZOA	ROMANIZE	SLEAZIER
MIDSIZED	OXIDIZES	PTYALIZE	ROMANZAS	SLEAZILY
MINIMIZE	OZONATED	PUZZLERS	ROYALIZE	SLEAZOID

SLEEZIER	SUBZONAL	TZARITZA	WHIZZERS	ZELKOVAS
SMORZATO	SUBZONES	TZATZIKI	WHIZZIER	ZEMINDAR
SNAZZIER	SUNGAZER	TZIGANES	WHIZZING	ZEMSTVOS
SNAZZILY	SURPRIZE	TZITZITH	WIZARDLY	ZENAIDAS
SNEEZERS	SUZERAIN	UNAMAZED	WIZARDRY	ZENITHAL
SNEEZIER	SWAZZLES	UNDAZZLE	WIZENING	ZEOLITES
SNEEZING	SWIZZING	UNFREEZE	WOMANIZE	ZEOLITIC
SNOOZERS	SWIZZLED	UNFROZEN	WOOZIEST	ZEPPELIN
SNOOZIER	SWIZZLER	UNGAZING	WURTZITE	ZEPPOLES
SNOOZING	SWIZZLES	UNGLAZED	WUZZLING	ZERUMBET
SNOOZLED	SWOZZLES	UNGRAZED	YAHRZEIT	ZESTIEST
SNOOZLES	SYZYGIAL	UNIONIZE	YOKOZUNA	ZESTLESS
SNUZZLED	SYZYGIES	UNITIZED	ZABAIONE	ZETETICS
SNUZZLES	TAILZIES	UNITIZER	ZABAJONE	ZEUXITES
SOBERIZE	TEAZELED	UNITIZES	ZABTIEHS	ZIBELINE
SODOMIZE	TEAZLING	UNMUZZLE	ZACATONS	ZIGANKAS
SOLARIZE	TERRAZZO	UNPRIZED	ZADDIKIM	ZIGGURAT
SOLECIZE	TERZETTA	UNPUZZLE	ZAIBATSU	ZIGZAGGY
SOLONETZ	TERZETTI	UNSEIZED	ZAITECHS	ZIKKURAT
SORORIZE	TERZETTO	UNVIZARD	ZAKOUSKA	ZIKURATS
SOVKHOZY	TETANIZE	UNZIPPED	ZAKOUSKI	ZILLIONS
SOZZLIER	THEORIZE	UPGAZING	ZAMARRAS	ZIMOCCAS
SOZZLING	THIAZIDE	UPSIZING	ZAMARROS	ZINCATES
SPAETZLE	THIAZINE	URBANIZE	ZAMBOMBA	ZINCIEST
SPATZLES	THIAZINS	UTILIZED	ZAMBUCKS	ZINCITES
SPAZZING	THIAZOLE	UTILIZER	ZAMINDAR	ZINCKIER
SPELTZES	THIAZOLS	UTILIZES	ZAMOUSES	ZINCKIFY
SPETSNAZ	TIZWASES	VALORIZE	ZAMPOGNA	ZINCKING
SPETZNAZ	TOPAZINE	VAPORIZE	ZAMZAWED	ZINCODES
SPOROZOA	TOTALIZE	VELARIZE	ZANELLAS	ZINDABAD
SPREAZED	TOUZIEST	VIRILIZE	ZANINESS	ZINGIBER
SPREAZES	TOUZLING	VITALIZE	ZANJEROS	ZINGIEST
SPREEZED	TOWZIEST	VIZAMENT	ZANYISMS	ZINKIEST
SPREEZES	TRAPEZED	VIZARDED	ZAPATEOS	ZIPLOCKS
SPRITZED	TRAPEZES	VIZCACHA	ZAPPIEST	ZIPPERED
SPRITZER	TRAPEZIA	VIZIRATE	ZAPTIAHS	ZIPPIEST
SPRITZES	TRAPEZII	VIZIRIAL	ZAPTIEHS	ZIRCALOY
SPRITZIG	TRIAZINE	VIZORING	ZARATITE	ZIRCONIA
SPUILZIE	TRIAZINS	VOCALIZE	ZAREEBAS	ZIRCONIC
SPULZIED	TRIAZOLE	VOLUMIZE	ZARNICHS	ZITHERNS
SPULZIES	TRISTEZA	VOWELIZE	ZARZUELA	ZIZANIAS
SQUEEZED	TRIZONAL	VUVUZELA	ZASTRUGA	ZIZYPHUS
SQUEEZER	TRIZONES	WALTZERS	ZASTRUGI	ZIZZLING
SQUEEZES	TSARITZA	WALTZING	ZEALANTS	ZOCCOLOS
SQUIZZES	TUILZIED	WARZONES	ZEALLESS	ZODIACAL
STANZAED	TUILZIES	WAZZOCKS	ZEALOTRY	ZOETROPE
STANZAIC	TUTORIZE	WEAZANDS	ZEBRANOS	ZOIATRIA
STANZOES	TWEEZERS	WEAZENED	ZEBRINAS	ZOISITES
STARGAZE	TWEEZING	WEBZINES	ZEBRINES	ZOLPIDEM
STOOZERS	TWIZZLED	WHAIZLED	ZEBRINNY	ZOMBIISM
STOOZING	TWIZZLES	WHAIZLES	ZEBRULAS	ZOMBORUK
STRELITZ	TZADDIKS	WHEEZERS	ZEBRULES	ZONATION
STYLIZED	TZADDIQS	WHEEZIER	ZECCHINE	ZONELESS
STYLIZER	TZARDOMS	WHEEZILY	ZECCHINI	ZONETIME
STYLIZES	TZAREVNA	WHEEZING	ZECCHINO	ZONULETS
SUBERIZE	TZARINAS	WHEEZLED	ZECCHINS	ZOOBLAST
SUBITIZE	TZARISMS	WHEEZLES	ZELATORS	ZOOCHORE
SUBSIZAR	TZARISTS	WHIZBANG	ZELATRIX	ZOOCHORY

ZOOCYTIA	ZOOMANCY	ZOOPHILE	ZOOTYPES	ZYGANTRA
ZOOECIUM	ZOOMANIA	ZOOPHILY	ZOOTYPIC	ZYGODONT
ZOOGENIC	ZOOMETRY	ZOOPHOBE	ZOPILOTE	ZYGOMATA
ZOOGLEAE	ZOOMORPH	ZOOPHORI	ZORBINGS	ZYGOSITY
ZOOGLEAL	ZOONITES	ZOOPHYTE	ZORGITES	ZYGOTENE
ZOOGLEAS	ZOONITIC	ZOOSCOPY	ZORILLAS	ZYLONITE
ZOOGLOEA	ZOONOMIA	ZOOSPERM	ZORILLES	ZYMOGENE
ZOOGRAFT	ZOONOMIC	ZOOSPORE	ZORILLOS	ZYMOGENS
ZOOLATER	ZOONOSES	ZOOTHOME	ZUCCHINI	ZYMOGRAM
ZOOLATRY	ZOONOSIS	ZOOTIEST	ZUCHETTA	ZYMOLOGY
ZOOLITES	ZOONOTIC	ZOOTOMIC	ZUCHETTO	ZYMOSANS
ZOOLITHS	ZOOPATHY	ZOOTOXIC	ZUGZWANG	ZYMOTICS
ZOOLITIC	ZOOPERAL	ZOOTOXIN	ZWIEBACK	ZYZZYVAS
ZOOLOGIC	ZOOPHAGY	ZOOTROPE	ZYGAENID	

CHAPTER 3
WORD FAMILIES

by Allan Simmons

You wouldn't be reading this book if you weren't interested in learning some useful words for Scrabble! But not everyone finds it easy nor has the patience to learn tedious lists of words. I have always found it ideal to learn words in small manageable sets that are going to have a high yield on the Scrabble board. To be manageable a list has to be fairly short and restricted to a single page. To have a high yield the list has to focus on words that are more likely to crop up during play.

It was with these criteria in mind that I first created the concept of word families – a sort of mind-map of words centred around a short root word. Two- and three-letter words regularly appear on the board so showing how those words can be developed is very relevant. And because all the words in the 'family' contain the embedded root word, clumps of words with similar patterns naturally occur and these can be grouped together for convenient learning. Through careful arrangement of family members with shorter words near the centre and longer words further away, it is also possible to reflect the natural extension of the shorter words into longer words (hooks). Generally, I try to show the words that start with the root word flowing to the right of each diagram and those that contain the root word flowing to the left, but this will always depend on the number of words in the family that start or end with the root word. The overall aim is to provide an aesthetically pleasing and useful arrangement of words of relevance to the game.

In selecting the best words to use as root words I have analysed the two letter words to ascertain those that produce the more useful and pleasing families. For example, there is little point in using the two-letter word IT because it will generate far too many words, and the 'IT' within longer words will not be a significant component of most of those words. Whereas a root word with a higher-scoring tile or an unusual combination of two-letters (eg KO, ZO, IO) generate shorter lists where the two-letter sequence for the most part remains a key component of the family members.

The maximum length of words selected for each family is mostly five, or sometimes six depending on the volume of words generated in each case. In order to keep the families uncluttered all -S plurals of words have been excluded. However, so that the reader can easily identify those that do and do not take an -S extension, an asterisk (*) follows every word that can NOT be extended by -S. That does not mean that such words cannot be pluralized because in some cases the plural may be something other than an -S. Inflections of verbs and plurals of words that take the form -ES have been included, providing they are within the length criteria.

I trust you find the word families of great use and interest to improve your Scrabble vocabulary. They've also been fun to compile and I'm sure I've learned one or two new words in the process as well. You might like to try and create further families yourself, making use of the extensive lists in this book to find the appropriate words.

Happy Families!

This is an original idea by Allan Simmons, reproduced here with kind permission. These word families first appeared in ONWORDS Scrabble magazine (now defunct) from 1995.

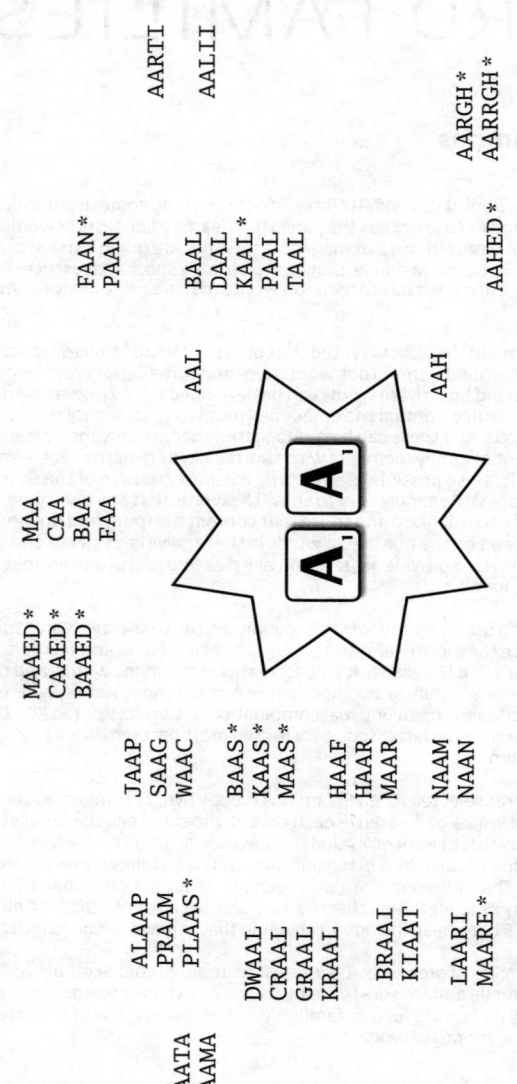

AARTI
AALII

AARGH *
AARRGH *

AAHED *

FAAN *
PAAN

BAAL
DAAL
KAAL *
PAAL
TAAL

AAL

AAH

MAA
CAA
BAA
FAA

MAAED *
CAAED *
BAAED *

JAAP
SAAG
WAAC

BAAS *
KAAS *
MAAS *

HAAF
HAAR
MAAR

NAAM
NAAN

ALAAP
PRAAM
PLAAS *

DWAAL
CRAAL
GRAAL
KRAAL

BRAAI
KIAAT

LAARI
MAARE *

TAATA
KAAMA

* = word does not take an -s extension

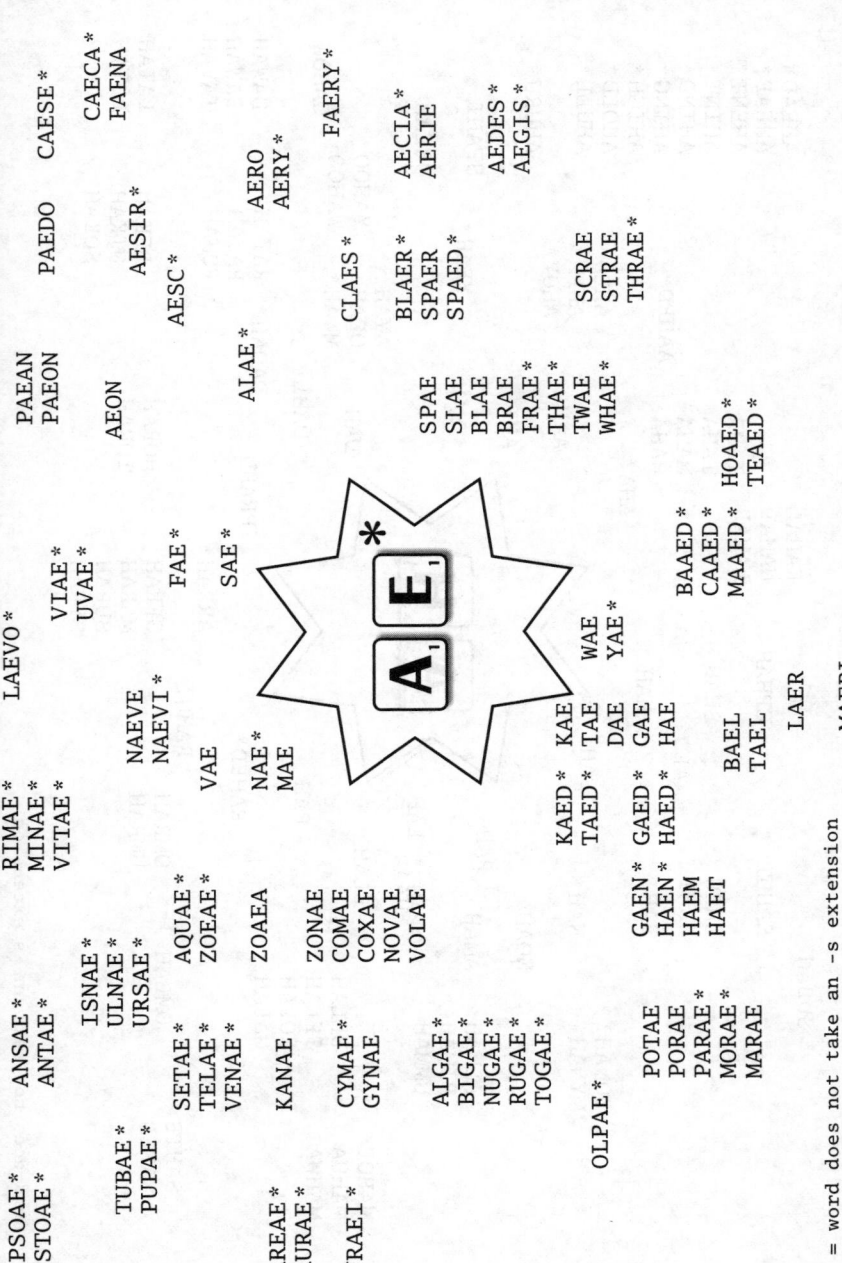

PSOAE *
STOAE *

ANSAE *
ANTAE *

RIMAE *
MINAE *
VITAE *

LAEVO *

PAEAN
PAEON

PAEDO

CAESE *

CAECA *
FAENA

TUBAE *
PUPAE *

ISNAE *
ULNAE *
URSAE *

AEON

AESIR *

AESC *

VIAE *
UVAE *

AERO
AERY *

AREAE *
AURAE *

SETAE *
TELAE *
VENAE *

AQUAE *
ZOEAE *

NAEVE
NAEVI *

FAE *

ALAE *

CLAES *

FAERY *

URAEI *

KANAE

ZOAEA

VAE

SAE *

BLAER *
SPAER
SPAED *

AECIA *
AERIE

CYMAE *
GYNAE

ZONAE
COMAE
COXAE
NOVAE
VOLAE

NAE *
MAE

SPAE
SLAE
BLAE
BRAE
FRAE *
THAE *
TWAE
WHAE *

SCRAE
STRAE
THRAE *

AEDES *
AEGIS *

ALGAE *
BIGAE *
NUGAE *
RUGAE *
TOGAE *

KAED *
TAED *

GAED *
HAED *

KAE
TAE
DAE
GAE
HAE

WAE
YAE *

BAAED *
CAAED *
MAAED *

HOAED *
TEAED *

OLPAE *

GAEN *
HAEN *
HAEM
HAET

BAEL
TAEL

LAER

MAERL

POTAE
PORAE
PARAE *
MORAE *
MARAE

* = word does not take an -s extension

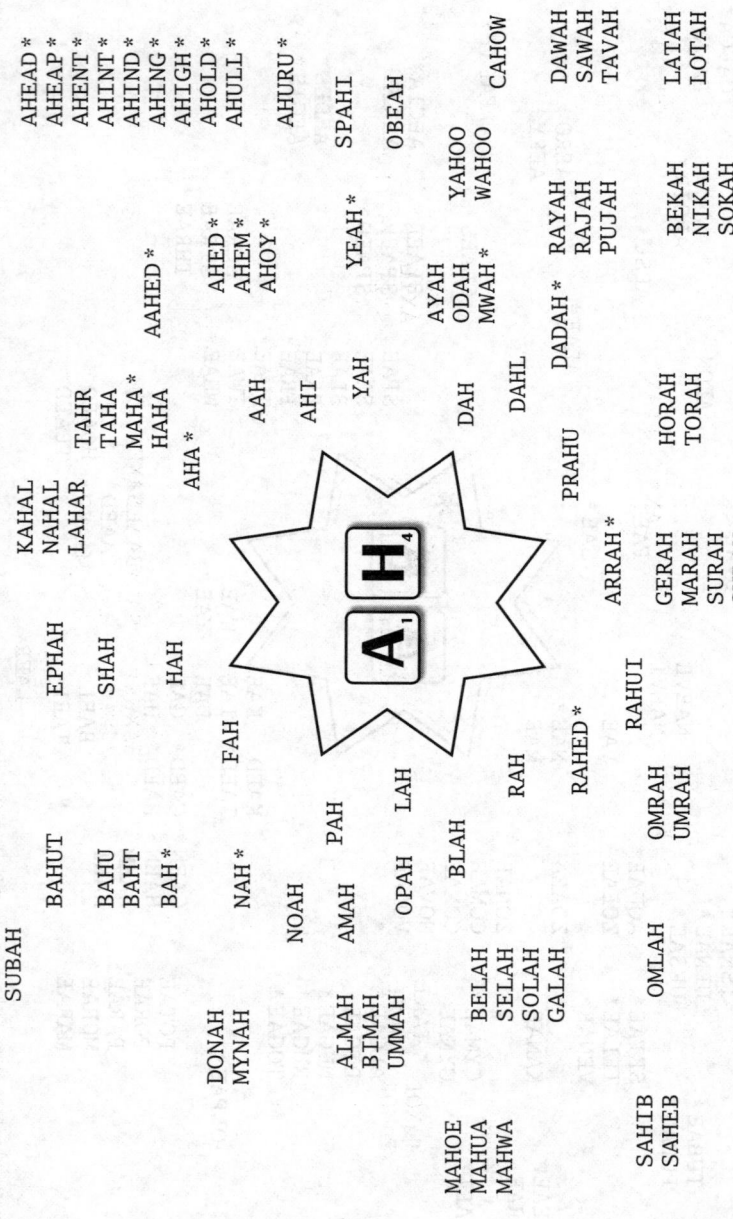

SUBAH

AHEAD *
AHEAP *
AHENT *
AHINT *
AHIND *
AHING *
AHIGH *
AHOLD *
AHULL *

AHURU *

SPAHI

OBEAH

CAHOW

DAWAH
SAWAH
TAVAH

LATAH
LOTAH

BAHUT

BAHU
BAHT

BAH *

EPHAH

SHAH

HAH

KAHAL
NAHAL
LAHAR

TAHR
TAHA
MAHA *
HAHA

AHA *

AAHED *

AHED *
AHEM *
AHOY *

YEAH *

AYAH
ODAH
MWAH *

YAH

DAH

DAHL

AAH

AHI

DADAH *

RAYAH
RAJAH
PUJAH

BEKAH
NIKAH
SOKAH

YAHOO
WAHOO

HORAH
TORAH

GERAH
MARAH
SURAH
SYRAH

PRAHU

ARRAH *

DONAH
MYNAH

NAH *

FAH

NOAH

AMAH

OPAH

PAH

LAH

BLAH

RAH

RAHED *

RAHUI

OMRAH
UMRAH

RAHED *

ALMAH
BIMAH
UMMAH

BELAH
SELAH
SOLAH
GALAH

MAHOE
MAHUA
MAHWA

OMLAH

SAHIB
SAHEB

* = word does not take an -s extension

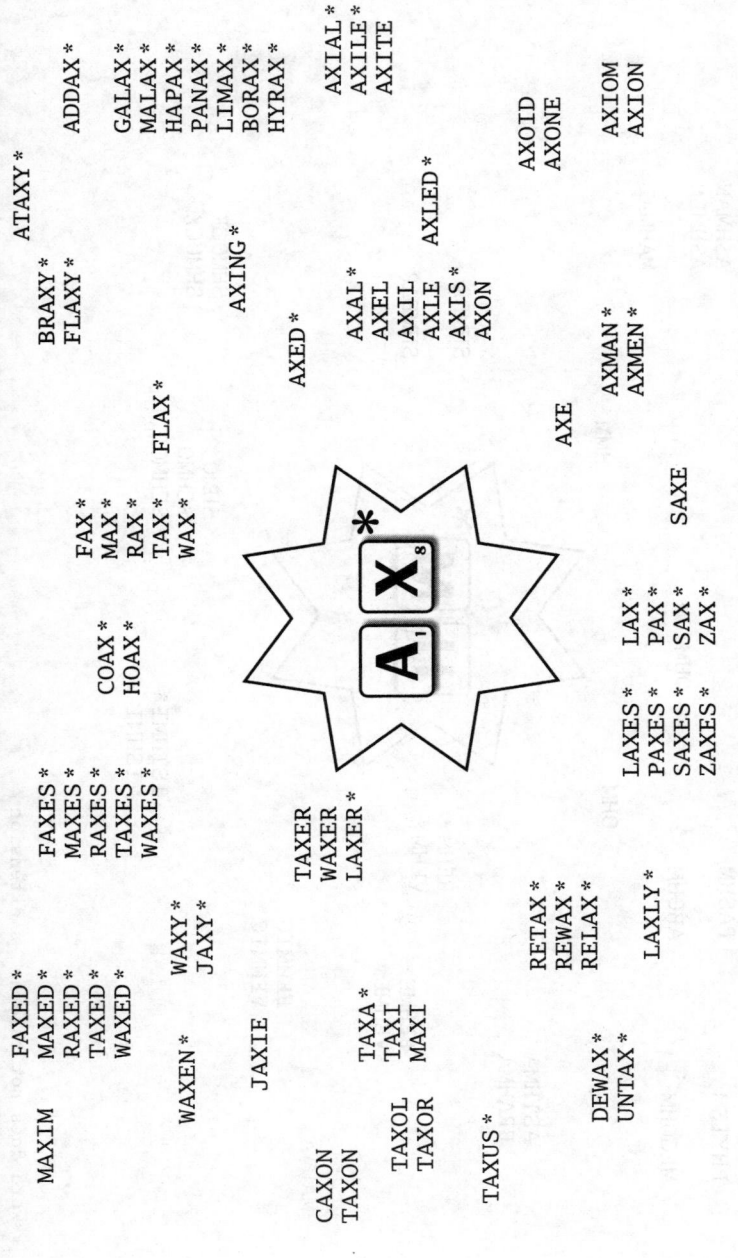

MAXIM

FAXED *
MAXED *
RAXED *
TAXED *
WAXED *

WAXEN *
JAXY *

JAXIE

CAXON
TAXON

TAXOL
TAXOR

TAXUS *

WAXY *

TAXA *
TAXI
MAXI

RETAX *
REWAX *
RELAX *

DEWAX *
UNTAX *

LAXLY *

TAXER
WAXER
LAXER *

LAXES *
PAXES *
SAXES *
ZAXES *

FAXES *
MAXES *
RAXES *
TAXES *
WAXES *

COAX *
HOAX *

LAX *
PAX *
SAX *
ZAX *

FAX *
MAX *
RAX *
TAX *
WAX *

SAXE

FLAX *

AXE

AXMAN *
AXMEN *

AXED *

AXAL *
AXEL
AXIL
AXLE
AXIS *
AXON

AXING *

AXLED *

AXIOM
AXION

AXOID
AXONE

BRAXY *
FLAXY *

ATAXY *

AXIAL *
AXILE *
AXITE

ADDAX *

GALAX *
MALAX *
HAPAX *
PANAX *
LIMAX *
BORAX *
HYRAX *

* = word does not take an -s extension

DRACHM

RHYTHM

MEGOHM

OHMAGE

PASHM

ABOHM

ASHMAN *
ASHMEN *

MAHMAL

OHMIC *

SHMEK

SHMEAR

HMM *

OHM

SHMOCK
SHMUCK

SHMO *
SCHMO
SCHMOE

FEHM *
VEHM *

ISTHMI *
MISHMI

FEHME *
VEHME *

FEHMIC *
VEHMIC *

ASTHMA
BRAHMA

* = word does not take an -s extension

FIORD
KIOSK
RIOJA

KIORE

AIOLI

PIONY *
PIOYE

ADDIO
AMNIO

ARIOT *
GRIOT

DANIO

BIOME
BIONT

RADIO
RATIO
PATIO

AGIO
OLIO

HIOI

BIO
GIO

NGAIO

FOLIO
POLIO
HELIO

FUGIO
CURIO
AUDIO

DIODE

VIOLA
VIOLD *

CION
LION

DIOL
VIOL

PIOUS *

PION
PIOY

RIOT

BIOG

BIOTA
DIOTA

IOTA

ION

IODIC *
IODID
IODIN
IONIC

ADIOS *
APIOL
AVION
AXIOM
AXION

CRIOS *
SCION
PSION
PRION
PRIOR
TRIOR
TRIOL
THIOL

ANION
INION
ONION
UNION

IDIOM
IDIOT

BRIO
SKIO
TRIO
THIO *
WHIO

* = word does not take an -s extension

JODEL
JOCKO
JOKOL *
JOKER
JOKEY *

JOCK
JOCO *
JOKE
JOKY *

JOULE
JOUAL
JOUGS *
JONES *

JOMON *

JOSH *
JOSS *

JONTY *
JOTTY *

JOLTY *
JOLLY *
JOWLY *

JOEY

JOOK
JOUK

JOUR

JOMO
JOIN
JOHN
JONG

JOBE
JOLE
JOLT
JOLL
JOWL

JOE

SJOE *

JOY

JOB
JOG

JOL
JOW

JORAM
JORUM

JOTUN

JOR

JOT

JOTA

J₈ **O**₁ *

ENJOY

JOYED *
JOBED *
JOKED *
JOLED *
JOWED *

JOWAR

BANJO
GADJO *

BIJOU
SAJOU

DOJO
GAJO
SIJO
MOJO

FJORD

MAJOR

CAJON *
REJON *

JOINT
JOIST
JOUST

* = word does not take an -s extension

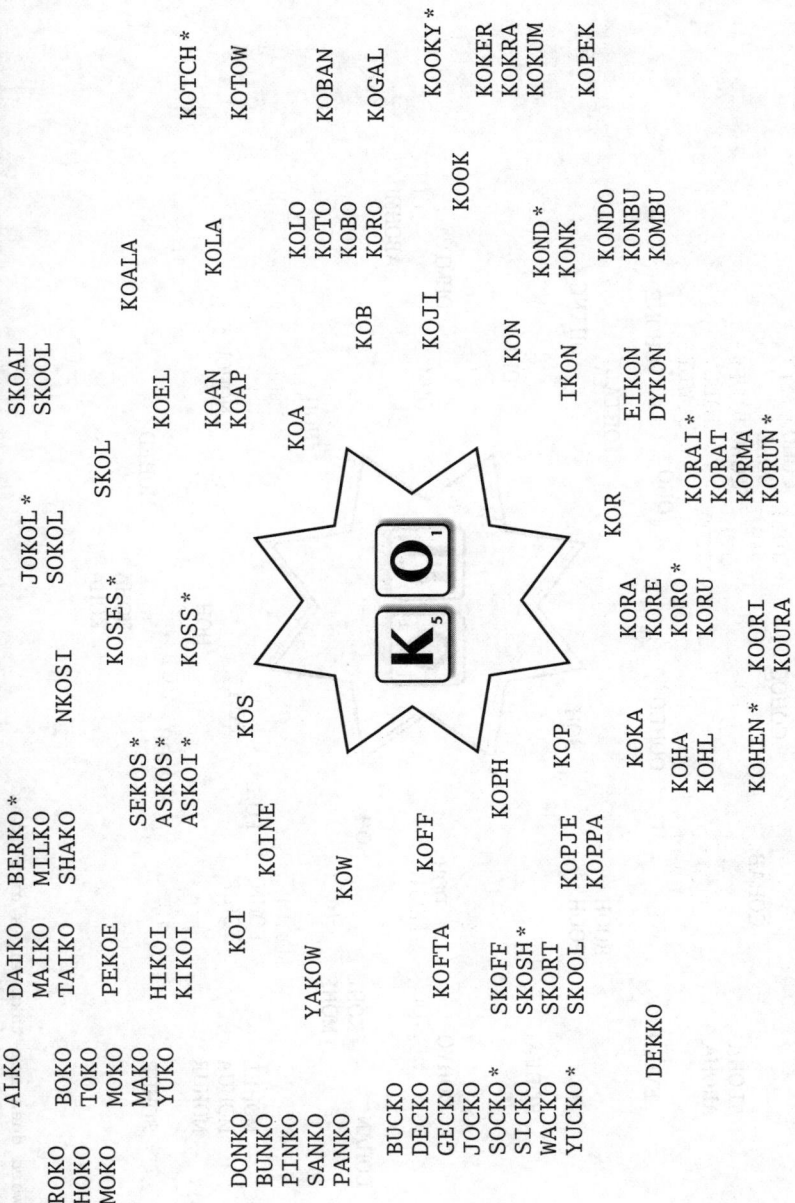

IROKO
CHOKO
SMOKO

ALKO
BOKO
TOKO
MOKO
MAKO
YUKO

DAIKO
MAIKO
TAIKO
PEKOE

BERKO *
MILKO
SHAKO

JOKOL *
SOKOL
SKOL

SKOAL
SKOOL

KOTCH *
KOTOW

SEKOS *
ASKOS *
ASKOI *

KOSES *

KOSS *

NKOSI

KOALA

KOEL

KOAN
KOAP

KOLA

KOBAN

KOGAL

KOOKY *

KOKER
KOKRA
KOKUM

KOPEK

DONKO
BUNKO
PINKO
SANKO
PANKO

KOI

KOINE

KOS

KOA

KOB

KOJI

KON

IKON

KOLO
KOTO
KOBO
KORO

KOOK

KOND *
KONK

KONDO
KONBU
KOMBU

EIKON
DYKON

KORAI *
KORAT
KORMA
KORUN *

YAKOW

KOW

KOFF

KOPH

KOP

KOR

BUCKO
DECKO
GECKO
JOCKO
SOCKO *
SICKO
WACKO
YUCKO *

KOFTA

SKOFF
SKOSH *
SKORT
SKOOL

KOPJE
KOPPA

KOKA

KORA
KORE
KORO *
KORU

DEKKO

KOHA
KOHL

KOHEN *

KOORI
KOURA

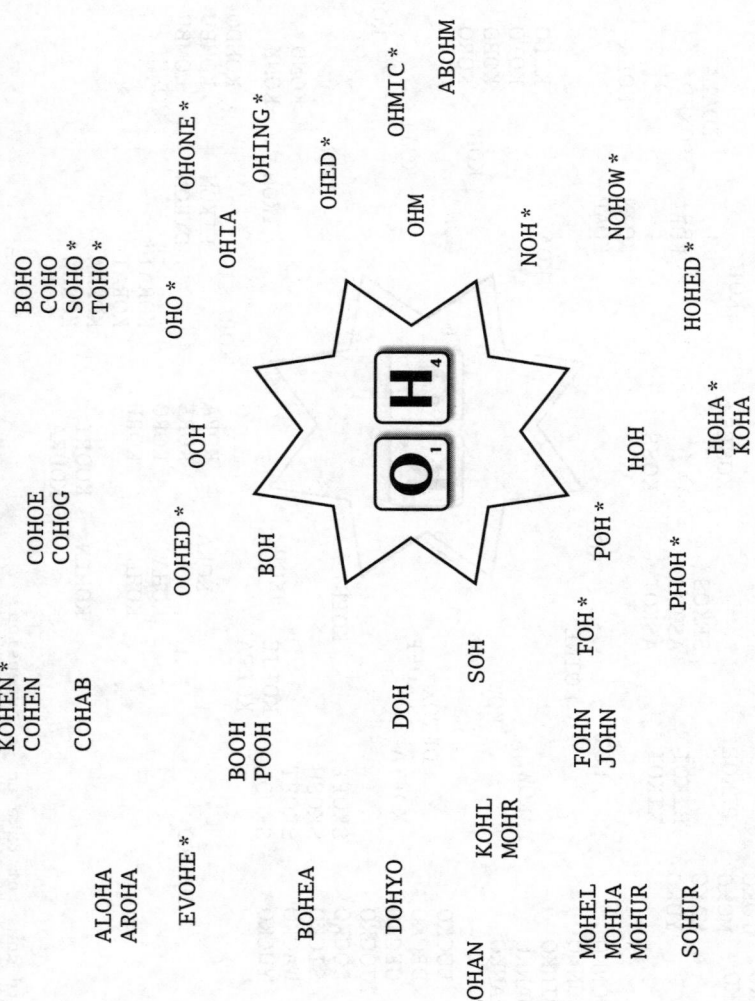

KOHEN *
COHEN

COHAB

BOHO
COHO
SOHO *
TOHO *

OHO *

OHONE *

OHIA

OHING *

OHED *

OHMIC *

ABOHM

OHM

NOH *

NOHOW *

HOHED *

COHOE
COHOG

OOHED *

OOH

BOH

HOH

HOHA *
KOHA

POH *

PHOH *

O₁ H₄

SOH

FOH *

DOH

BOOH
POOH

EVOHE *

ALOHA
AROHA

BOHEA

DOHYO

KOHL
MOHR

FOHN
JOHN

MOHEL
MOHUA
MOHUR

SOHUR

LOHAN

COXIB

COXAE *
COXAL *
DOXIE
MOXIE
FOXIE

COXA *
MOXA

WOXEN *
BOXEN *

BOXER

BOXTY *

BOXY *
COXY *
DOXY *
FOXY *
POXY *

WOX *
BOX *
COX *
LOX *
FOX *
HOX *
POX *

BOXES *
COXES *
LOXES *
FOXES *
HOXES *
POXES *

BOXED *
COXED *
LOXED *
FOXED *
HOXED *
POXED *

FLOX *

EPOXY *

PROXY *

NOXES *
GOXES *

NOXAL *

OXID
OXIM
OXEN *
OXER
OXES *

OXIDE
OXIME

OXBOW
OXEYE
OXLIP
OXTER

O_1 X_8 *

NOX *
GOX *

OXIES *

SOX *
VOX *

VOXEL

PHLOX *

OXO *

OXY *

DETOX *
REDOX *
XEROX *

EMBOX *
INBOX *
UNBOX *

DEOXY *

TOXIC
TOXIN

* = word does not take an -s extension

QUAKED *
QUAKER
QUAVER

QUASAR

QUARTE
QUARTO
QUARTZ *

QUARK
QUAKE
QUAKY *
QUACK

QUAINT *
QUATCH *
QUAICH
QUAIGH

QUATRE

QUASH *
QUASI *
QUASS *

QUAFF

QUANTA *
QUARRY *
QUAERE
QUARER *

QUALIA *
QUALMY *

QUAZZY *
QUAGGY *

QUAGGA
QUAHOG

QUANGO

QUANT
QUART
QUAIL
QUAIR
QUALM

QUARE *
QUATE *
QUALE *

QUAYD *

EQUANT
EQUATE

EQUALI *

EQUAL

QUAT
QUAD
QUAG

QUAI
QUAY

AQUA

AQUAE *

SQUARE

SQUAIL
SQUALL

SQUAMA *
SQUAME

ASQUAT *

DIQUAT
LOQUAT

SQUASH *
SQUAWK
SQUARK

SQUAB
SQUAD
SQUAT
SQUAW

Central tiles: Q₁₀ U₁ A₁ *

* = word does not take an -s extension

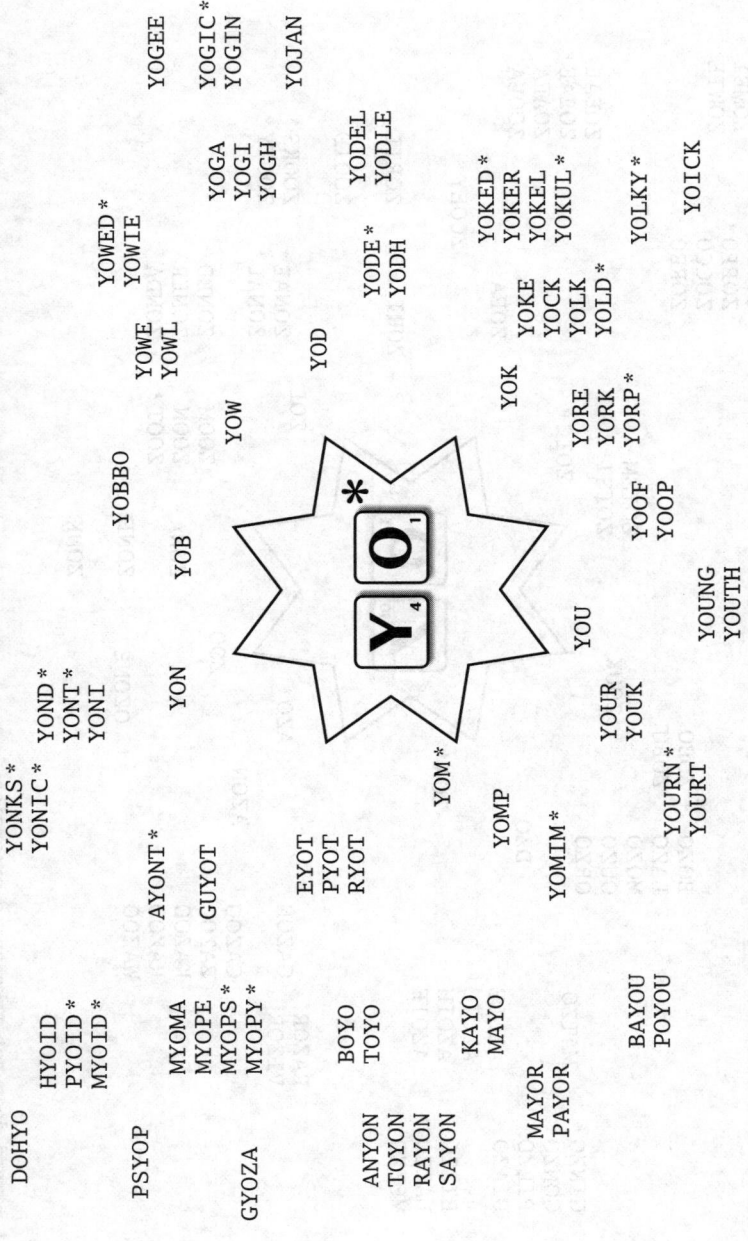

DOHYO

HYOID
PYOID *
MYOID *

PSYOP

MYOMA
MYOPE
MYOPS *
MYOPY *

GYOZA

BOYO
TOYO

ANYON
TOYON
RAYON
SAYON

KAYO
MAYO

MAYOR
PAYOR

BAYOU
POYOU

YONKS *
YONIC *

YOND *
YONT *
YONI

YON

AYONT *

GUYOT

EYOT
PYOT
RYOT

YOM *

YOMP

YOMIM *

YOURN *
YOURT

YOU

YOUR
YOUK

YOBBO

YOB

YOW

YOWE
YOWL

YOWED *
YOWIE

YOD

YODE *
YODH

YOK

YOKE
YOCK
YOLK
YOLD *

YOKED *
YOKER
YOKEL
YOKUL *

YORE
YORK
YORP *

YOOF
YOOP

YOUNG
YOUTH
YOUSE *

YOGA
YOGI
YOGH

YOGEE

YOGIC *
YOGIN

YOJAN

YODEL
YODLE

YOLKY *

YOICK

* = word does not take an -s extension

ZOMBI
ZOWIE *

ZOEAL *
ZOEAE *
ZOAEA
ZOOEA

ZOPPA *
ZOPPO *
ZOCCO
ZORRO

ZOOEY *

ZORIL

ZOOID

ZOOKS *
ZOOTY *

ZOEA

ZORI

ZONAE *
ZONAL *

ZONED *
ZONER
ZONDA

ZOIC *

ZOISM
ZOIST

ZOL

ZOOM
ZOON
ZOOT *

Z O

ZONA *

ZONE

ZONK

ZOO

OZONE

ZOUK

ZOBO
ZOBU

BOZO
LAZO
MOZO
OUZO
ORZO

DZO

ZOA *

AZO *

AZON

GAZON

RAZOR
VIZOR

GAZOO
BAZOO
KAZOO
RAZOO
WAZOO

MATZO

AZOLE
AZOIC *
AZOTH
AZOTE

GINZO *
GONZO *
PIEZO *
DIAZO

BIZZO
LAZZO *
MEZZO

* = word does not take an -s extension

CHAPTER 4
BEGINNINGS AND ENDINGS

Prefixes

It's very useful to be aware of the common prefixes in English, as these provide a wealth of opportunities for building on words that are already on the board. Moreover, they can help players find bonus words on their rack by forming prefixes and seeing if the remaining letters, maybe using a letter on the board, fit with it to make a valid seven or eight-letter word . The following lists show the most common prefixes in English, along with the valid words of seven and eight letters that they form from other existing words. Only those words which can be formed from a word already on the board are shown. In some cases, the words shown are not strictly examples of the prefix in question: ABALONE (AB-ALONE), for instance. These are still included, however, because they work in the same way on the Scrabble board, and are useful in encouraging a little lateral thinking when trying to build on words already in play.

Also included is a list of three-letter extensions to five-letter words – these are the so-called 'benjamins' (named after French champion, Benjamin Hannuna, who was a great exponent of such plays). The value of these words for Scrabble comes from the fact that the first play on a board is often a five-letter play in order to use a double-letter square in conjunction with the central double-word square. If such a word is played to the left then it may be possible to later reap the benefits of the triple word square by adding three-letters before it. Some are straightforward prefixes (eg MOUNT becoming DISMOUNT) but others are more interesting because the form of the word changes (eg CHANT becoming PENCHANT or GLAND becoming GANGLAND). To be most relevant to the game only those five letter words that begin with a letter worth two or more points have been included because a player is more likely to play that letter on the double-letter square. The equivalent suffix extensions to extend a word to the right triple word square have not been listed because they are more straightforward to spot with many of them being simple -ING extensions.

Words that begin with AB-

Seven-letter words				
ABACTOR	ABLUTED	ABSORBS	ABAPICAL	ABORALLY
ABALONE	ABOLLAS	ABSTAIN	ABASHING	ABORIGIN
ABASHED	ABOMASA	ABSURDS	ABDUCTED	ABRAIDED
ABASHES	ABOUGHT	ABTHANE	ABEARING	ABRAYING
ABAXIAL	ABRAIDS	ABUSAGE	ABEGGING	ABREACTS
ABAXILE	ABRAYED	ABUSERS	ABERRANT	ABRIDGED
ABDUCES	ABREACT	ABUSING	ABESSIVE	ABRIDGER
ABDUCTS	ABREAST	ABUTTER	ABFARADS	ABRIDGES
ABFARAD	ABREGES	ABVOLTS	ABHENRYS	ABROOKED
ABHENRY	ABRIDGE	ABWATTS	ABJOINTS	ABSEILED
ABJOINT	ABROACH		ABLEGATE	ABSENTED
ABLATED	ABROADS	**Eight-letter**	ABNEGATE	ABSOLUTE
ABLINGS	ABSEILS	**words**	ABNORMAL	ABSOLVED
	ABSENTS	ABACTORS	ABOMASAL	ABSOLVER
	ABSOLVE	ABAMPERE	ABOMASUM	ABSOLVES

| ABSONANT | ABSTAINS | ABTHANES | ABUSAGES |
| ABSORBED | ABSTRICT | ABUSABLE | ABUTTERS |

Words that begin with AD-

Seven-letter	ADJOINT	ADVERBS	ADDICTED	ADMIXING
words	ADJUDGE	ADVERSE	ADDOOMED	ADMONISH
ADAGIOS	ADJUROR	ADVERTS	ADDUCTED	ADNATION
ADAPTED	ADJUSTS	ADVICES	ADENOSES	ADOPTERS
ADAPTER	ADLANDS	ADVISED	ADENOSIS	ADOPTING
ADAWING	ADMIRED	ADVISES	ADEQUATE	ADOPTION
ADAXIAL	ADMIRES	ADVISOR	ADESSIVE	ADSCRIPT
ADDEEMS	ADMIXED	ADWARDS	ADJACENT	ADSORBED
ADDICTS	ADMIXES	ADWARES	ADJOINED	ADUMBRAL
ADDINGS	ADNOUNS	ADWOMAN	ADJOINTS	ADUNCATE
ADDOOMS	ADOPTED	ADWOMEN	ADJUDGED	ADVERSER
ADDRESS	ADOPTER		ADJUDGES	ADVERTED
ADDREST	ADPRESS	**Eight-letter**	ADJURORS	ADVISING
ADDUCES	ADREADS	**words**	ADJUSTED	ADVISORS
ADDUCTS	ADRENAL	ADAPTING	ADJUSTER	ADWARDED
ADHERES	ADSORBS	ADDEBTED	ADMASSES	
ADJOINS	ADVENTS	ADDEEMED	ADMIRING	

Words that begin with AIR-

Seven-letter	AIRLINE	**Eight-letter**	AIRFLOWS	AIRSHAFT
words	AIRLOCK	**words**	AIRFOILS	AIRSHEDS
AIRBAGS	AIRMAIL	AIRBASES	AIRFRAME	AIRSHIPS
AIRBASE	AIRPARK	AIRBOARD	AIRGLOWS	AIRSHOTS
AIRBOAT	AIRPLAY	AIRBOATS	AIRGRAPH	AIRSHOWS
AIRCONS	AIRPORT	AIRBORNE	AIRHEADS	AIRSIDES
AIRCREW	AIRPOST	AIRBOUND	AIRHOLES	AIRSPACE
AIRDATE	AIRSHED	AIRBRICK	AIRLIFTS	AIRSPEED
AIRDROP	AIRSHIP	AIRBRUSH	AIRLINER	AIRSTOPS
AIRFARE	AIRSHOT	AIRBURST	AIRLINES	AIRSTRIP
AIRFLOW	AIRSHOW	AIRBUSES	AIRLOCKS	AIRTHING
AIRFOIL	AIRSICK	AIRCHECK	AIRMAILS	AIRTIGHT
AIRGAPS	AIRSIDE	AIRCOACH	AIRPARKS	AIRTIMES
AIRGLOW	AIRSTOP	AIRCRAFT	AIRPLANE	AIRWARDS
AIRGUNS	AIRTIME	AIRCREWS	AIRPLAYS	AIRWAVES
AIRHEAD	AIRTING	AIRDATES	AIRPORTS	AIRWOMAN
AIRHOLE	AIRWARD	AIRDRAWN	AIRPOSTS	AIRWOMEN
AIRINGS	AIRWAVE	AIRDROME	AIRPOWER	
AIRLESS	AIRWAYS	AIRDROPS	AIRPROOF	
AIRLIFT	AIRWISE	AIRFARES	AIRSCAPE	
AIRLIKE		AIRFIELD	AIRSCREW	

Words that begin with BE-

Seven-letter	BEBLOOD	BECLOAK	BECRUST	BEDECKS
words	BEBUNGS	BECLOGS	BECURLS	BEDELLS
BEACHED	BECALLS	BECLOUD	BECURSE	BEDEMAN
BEACHES	BECALMS	BECLOWN	BECURST	BEDEVIL
BEADMAN	BECAUSE	BECOMES	BEDAMNS	BEDEWED
BEADMEN	BECHALK	BECRAWL	BEDAUBS	BEDIGHT
BEARISH	BECHARM	BECRIME	BEDAZED	BEDIRTY
BEAVERS	BECLASP	BECROWD	BEDAZES	BEDIZEN

BEDRAIL	BELACES	BESHONE	BETWEEN	BEDEWING
BEDRAPE	BELATED	BESHOUT	BETWIXT	BEDIAPER
BEDROLL	BELAUDS	BESHREW	BEVOMIT	BEDIGHTS
BEDROPS	BELAYED	BESIDES	BEWAILS	BEDIMMED
BEDROPT	BELAYER	BESIEGE	BEWARED	BEDIMPLE
BEDRUGS	BELEAPS	BESIGHS	BEWARES	BEDIZENS
BEDUCKS	BELEAPT	BESINGS	BEWEARY	BEDOTTED
BEDUMBS	BELIEFS	BESLAVE	BEWEEPS	BEDRAILS
BEDUNCE	BELIERS	BESLIME	BEWHORE	BEDRAPED
BEDUNGS	BELIEVE	BESMEAR	BEWITCH	BEDRAPES
BEDUSTS	BELONGS	BESMILE	BEWORMS	BEDRENCH
BEDWARF	BELOVED	BESMOKE	BEWORRY	BEDRIVEL
BEECHES	BELOVES	BESMUTS	BEWRAPS	BEDROLLS
BEFALLS	BELYING	BESNOWS	BEWRAPT	BEDUCKED
BEFLAGS	BEMADAM	BESORTS		BEDUMBED
BEFLEAS	BEMAULS	BESPAKE	**Eight-letter**	BEDUNCES
BEFLECK	BEMAZED	BESPATE	**words**	BEDUNGED
BEFOAMS	BEMEANS	BESPEAK	BEACHIER	BEDUSTED
BEFOOLS	BEMEANT	BESPEED	BEACHING	BEDWARFS
BEFOULS	BEMEDAL	BESPICE	BEARABLE	BEDYEING
BEFRETS	BEMETED	BESPITS	BEBLOODS	BEFALLEN
BEGALLS	BEMETES	BESPOKE	BEBOPPED	BEFINGER
BEGAZED	BEMIRED	BESPORT	BEBOPPER	BEFINNED
BEGAZES	BEMIRES	BESPOTS	BECALLED	BEFITTED
BEGIFTS	BEMISTS	BESPOUT	BECALMED	BEFLECKS
BEGILDS	BEMIXED	BESTAIN	BECAPPED	BEFLOWER
BEGIRDS	BEMIXES	BESTARS	BECARPET	BEFOAMED
BEGLADS	BEMOANS	BESTEAD	BECHALKS	BEFOGGED
BEGLOOM	BEMOCKS	BESTICK	BECHANCE	BEFOOLED
BEGNAWS	BEMOILS	BESTILL	BECHARMS	BEFOULED
BEGOING	BEMOUTH	BESTING	BECLAMOR	BEFOULER
BEGONIA	BEMUSED	BESTIRS	BECLASPS	BEFRIEND
BEGORED	BEMUSES	BESTORM	BECLOAKS	BEFRINGE
BEGRIME	BENAMED	BESTOWS	BECLOTHE	BEFUDDLE
BEGROAN	BENAMES	BESTREW	BECLOUDS	BEGALLED
BEGUILE	BENEATH	BESTROW	BECLOWNS	BEGAZING
BEGULFS	BENEMPT	BESTUCK	BECOMING	BEGEMMED
BEGUNKS	BENIGHT	BESTUDS	BECOWARD	BEGETTER
BEHAVER	BENUMBS	BESWARM	BECRAWLS	BEGIFTED
BEHAVES	BEPAINT	BETAKEN	BECRIMED	BEGILDED
BEHEADS	BEPEARL	BETAKES	BECRIMES	BEGINNER
BEHESTS	BEPELTS	BETAXED	BECROWDS	BEGIRDED
BEHIGHT	BEPROSE	BETEEMS	BECRUSTS	BEGIRDLE
BEHINDS	BEPUFFS	BETHANK	BECUDGEL	BEGLAMOR
BEHOLDS	BEQUEST	BETHINK	BECURLED	BEGLOOMS
BEHOOFS	BERAKED	BETHORN	BECURSED	BEGNAWED
BEHOOVE	BERAKES	BETHUMB	BECURSES	BEGOTTEN
BEHOVED	BERATED	BETHUMP	BEDABBLE	BEGRIMED
BEHOVES	BERATES	BETIDED	BEDAGGLE	BEGRIMES
BEHOWLS	BERAYED	BETIDES	BEDAMNED	BEGROANS
BEINKED	BEREAVE	BETIGHT	BEDARKEN	BEGRUDGE
BEJADED	BERHYME	BETIMED	BEDASHED	BEGUILED
BEJADES	BERIMED	BETIMES	BEDASHES	BEGUILER
BEJESUS	BERIMES	BETITLE	BEDAUBED	BEGUILES
BEJEWEL	BEROBED	BETOILS	BEDAZING	BEGULFED
BEKNAVE	BESAINT	BETOKEN	BEDAZZLE	BEHALVES
BEKNOTS	BESCOUR	BETRAYS	BEDEAFEN	BEHAPPEN
BEKNOWN	BESEEMS	BETREAD	BEDECKED	BEHATTED
BELABOR	BESHAME	BETRIMS	BEDESMAN	BEHAVERS
BELACED	BESHINE	BETROTH	BEDEVILS	BEHAVING

BEHAVIOR	BEMEANED	BERAKING	BESMEARS	BESUITED
BEHEADED	BEMEDALS	BERASCAL	BESMILED	BESWARMS
BEHEADER	BEMETING	BERATING	BESMILES	BETAKING
BEHIGHTS	BEMINGLE	BERAYING	BESMIRCH	BETATTER
BEHOLDEN	BEMIRING	BEREAVED	BESMOKED	BETEEMED
BEHOLDER	BEMISTED	BEREAVER	BESMOKES	BETHANKS
BEHOOVED	BEMIXING	BEREAVES	BESMOOTH	BETHINKS
BEHOOVES	BEMOANED	BERHYMED	BESMUDGE	BETHORNS
BEHOVING	BEMOANER	BERHYMES	BESMUTCH	BETHRALL
BEHOWLED	BEMOCKED	BERIMING	BESNOWED	BETHUMBS
BEJABERS	BEMOILED	BERINGED	BESOOTHE	BETHUMPS
BEJADING	BEMOUTHS	BEROBBED	BESORTED	BETHWACK
BEJESUIT	BEMUDDED	BEROUGED	BESOTTED	BETIDING
BEJEWELS	BEMUDDLE	BESAINTS	BESOUGHT	BETIMING
BEJUMBLE	BEMUFFLE	BESCORCH	BESOULED	BETITLED
BEKISSED	BEMURMUR	BESCOURS	BESPEAKS	BETITLES
BEKISSES	BEMUSING	BESCRAWL	BESPEEDS	BETOILED
BEKNAVES	BEMUZZLE	BESCREEN	BESPICED	BETOKENS
BEKNIGHT	BENAMING	BESEEING	BESPICES	BETONIES
BELABORS	BENETTED	BESEEMED	BESPOKEN	BETOSSED
BELABOUR	BENIGHTS	BESEEMLY	BESPORTS	BETOSSES
BELACING	BENUMBED	BESETTER	BESPOUSE	BETREADS
BELADIES	BEPAINTS	BESHADOW	BESPOUTS	BETROTHS
BELAUDED	BEPATTED	BESHAMED	BESPREAD	BETWEENS
BELAYERS	BEPEARLS	BESHAMES	BESPRENT	BEUNCLED
BELAYING	BEPELTED	BESHINES	BESTAINS	BEVOMITS
BELEAPED	BEPEPPER	BESHIVER	BESTEADS	BEWAILED
BELEEING	BEPESTER	BESHOUTS	BESTICKS	BEWAILER
BELIEVER	BEPIMPLE	BESHREWS	BESTILLS	BEWARING
BELIEVES	BEPITIED	BESHROUD	BESTORMS	BEWETTED
BELIQUOR	BEPITIES	BESIEGED	BESTOWED	BEWHORED
BELITTLE	BEPLUMED	BESIEGER	BESTOWER	BEWHORES
BELONGED	BEPOMMEL	BESIEGES	BESTREAK	BEWIGGED
BELONGER	BEPOWDER	BESIGHED	BESTREWN	BEWILDER
BELOVING	BEPRAISE	BESLAVED	BESTREWS	BEWINGED
BEMADAMS	BEPROSED	BESLAVER	BESTRIDE	BEWORMED
BEMADDED	BEPROSES	BESLAVES	BESTRODE	
BEMADDEN	BEPUFFED	BESLIMED	BESTROWN	
BEMAULED	BEQUESTS	BESLIMES	BESTROWS	

Words that begin with BI-

Seven-letter words	BIFOCAL	BIPOLAR	BICAUDAL	BIJUGATE
	BIKINGS	BIPRISM	BICHROME	BILABIAL
BIACHES	BILAYER	BISECTS	BICOLORS	BILANDER
BIASSES	BILEVEL	BISHOPS	BICOLOUR	BILAYERS
BIAXIAL	BILIMBI	BISTATE	BICONVEX	BILEVELS
BIBASIC	BILOBAR	BITABLE	BICUSPID	BILINEAR
BIBLESS	BILOBED	BITINGS	BICYCLED	BILOBATE
BIBLIST	BIMETAL	BITONAL	BICYCLER	BIMANUAL
BICARBS	BIMODAL	BIVALVE	BICYCLES	BIMENSAL
BICHORD	BIMORPH	BIVINYL	BICYCLIC	BIMESTER
BICOLOR	BIOLOGY	BIZONAL	BIDENTAL	BIMETALS
BICORNS	BIONTIC	BIZONES	BIELDING	BIMETHYL
BICYCLE	BIOPTIC		BIFACIAL	BIMORPHS
BIDENTS	BIPACKS	**Eight-letter**	BIFORKED	BIOBLAST
BIDINGS	BIPARTY	**words**	BIFORMED	BIOTITIC
BIFACES	BIPEDAL	BIACETYL	BIGEMINY	BIOVULAR
BIFILAR	BIPLANE	BIANNUAL	BIHOURLY	BIPAROUS

BIPARTED	BIRACIAL	BISERIAL	BITINGLY	BIWEEKLY
BIPHASIC	BIRADIAL	BISEXUAL	BIUNIQUE	BIYEARLY
BIPHENYL	BIRAMOSE	BISTABLE	BIVALVED	
BIPLANES	BIRAMOUS	BISTOURY	BIVALVES	
BIPRISMS	BISECTOR	BITEWING	BIVINYLS	

Words that begin with COM-

Seven-letter words	COMMONS	COMPORT	COMMERES	COMPENDS
COMAKES	COMMOTE	COMPOSE	COMMERGE	COMPERES
COMARBS	COMMOTS	COMPOST	COMMIXED	COMPILED
COMARTS	COMMOVE	COMPOTE	COMMIXES	COMPILER
COMATES	COMMUTE	COMPOTS	COMMODES	COMPILES
COMBATS	COMPACT	COMRADE	COMMONER	COMPLAIN
COMBIER	COMPAGE	COMUSES	COMMONEY	COMPLEAT
COMBINE	COMPAND		COMMOTES	COMPLIED
COMBING	COMPARE	**Eight-letter**	COMMOVED	COMPLIER
COMBUST	COMPART	**words**	COMMOVES	COMPLIES
COMETIC	COMPASS	COMAKING	COMMUTED	COMPLOTS
COMFIER	COMPAST	COMBATED	COMMUTER	COMPORTS
COMFITS	COMPEAR	COMBINER	COMMUTES	COMPOSED
COMFORT	COMPEER	COMBINES	COMPACTS	COMPOSER
COMICES	COMPELS	COMBINGS	COMPADRE	COMPOSES
COMINGS	COMPEND	COMBLESS	COMPAGES	COMPOSTS
COMMAND	COMPERE	COMBUSTS	COMPANDS	COMPOTES
COMMEND	COMPILE	COMEMBER	COMPARED	COMPOUND
COMMENT	COMPING	COMETHER	COMPARER	COMPRESS
COMMERE	COMPLEX	COMFIEST	COMPARES	COMPRINT
COMMIXT	COMPLOT	COMFORTS	COMPARTS	COMPRISE
COMMODE	COMPONE	COMINGLE	COMPEARS	COMPRIZE
	COMPONY	COMMENDS	COMPEERS	COMPULSE

Words that begin with CON-

Seven-letter words	CONFESS	CONNIES	**Eight-letter words**	CONDUITS
CONACRE	CONFEST	CONNOTE		CONFIDES
CONARIA	CONFINE	CONSEIL	CONACRED	CONFINED
CONCAVE	CONFIRM	CONSENT	CONACRES	CONFINER
CONCEDE	CONFITS	CONSIGN	CONCAUSE	CONFINES
CONCENT	CONFLUX	CONSIST	CONCAVED	CONFIRMS
CONCERT	CONFORM	CONSOLE	CONCAVES	CONFIXED
CONCHAL	CONFUSE	CONSOLS	CONCEDED	CONFIXES
CONCHAS	CONGAED	CONSORT	CONCEDER	CONFOCAL
CONCORD	CONGEAL	CONSPUE	CONCEDES	CONFORMS
CONCREW	CONGEED	CONTACT	CONCENTS	CONFOUND
CONCURS	CONGEES	CONTAIN	CONCERTS	CONFRERE
CONCUSS	CONGERS	CONTEND	CONCLAVE	CONFRONT
CONDIES	CONGEST	CONTENT	CONCOLOR	CONFUSED
CONDOES	CONGOES	CONTEST	CONCORDS	CONFUSES
CONDOLE	CONGREE	CONTEXT	CONCOURS	CONGEALS
CONDOMS	CONGRUE	CONTORT	CONCREWS	CONGENIC
CONDONE	CONJEED	CONTOUR	CONDENSE	CONGESTS
CONDORS	CONJEES	CONTRAT	CONDOLED	CONGLOBE
CONDUCE	CONJOIN	CONTUND	CONDOLES	CONGREED
CONDUCT	CONJURE	CONURES	CONDONER	CONGREES
CONDUIT	CONJURY	CONVENT	CONDORES	CONGREET
CONFABS	CONKIER	CONVERT	CONDUCES	CONGRUED
	CONKING	CONVIVE	CONDUCTS	CONGRUES

CONJOINS	CONSERVE	CONSPUES	CONTEXTS	CONURBIA
CONJOINT	CONSIDER	CONSTATE	CONTORTS	CONVENTS
CONJUGAL	CONSIGNS	CONTACTS	CONTOURS	CONVERGE
CONJUNTO	CONSISTS	CONTAINS	CONTRACT	CONVERSE
CONJUROR	CONSOLED	CONTANGO	CONTRAIL	CONVERSO
CONNOTED	CONSOLER	CONTEMPO	CONTRATS	CONVERTS
CONNOTES	CONSOLES	CONTEMPT	CONTRIST	CONVEXED
CONQUEST	CONSORTS	CONTENDS	CONTRITE	CONVEXES
CONSEILS	CONSPIRE	CONTENTS	CONTUNDS	CONVIVES
CONSENTS	CONSPUED	CONTESTS	CONURBAN	CONVOLVE

Words that begin with DE-

Seven-letter words

	DECOLOR	DEFUSED	DEMESNE	DESCENT
	DECOYED	DEFUSES	DEMISES	DESEEDS
DEADMAN	DECOYER	DEFUZED	DEMISTS	DESERVE
DEADMEN	DECREED	DEFUZES	DEMOSES	DESEXED
DEAIRED	DECREES	DEGAMES	DEMOTED	DESEXES
DEALATE	DECREWS	DEGASES	DEMOTES	DESIGNS
DEASHED	DECRIED	DEGAUSS	DEMOUNT	DESINED
DEASHES	DECRIER	DEGERMS	DEMURED	DESINES
DEBARKS	DECRIES	DEGLAZE	DEMURES	DESIRED
DEBASED	DECROWN	DEGOUTS	DENOTED	DESIRER
DEBASER	DECRYPT	DEGRADE	DENOTES	DESIRES
DEBASES	DECURIA	DEGREED	DENUDER	DESISTS
DEBATED	DECURVE	DEGREES	DENUDES	DESKILL
DEBATES	DEDUCES	DEGUSTS	DENYING	DESNOOD
DEBEAKS	DEDUCTS	DEHORNS	DEONTIC	DESORBS
DEBEARD	DEFACED	DEICERS	DEORBIT	DESPITE
DEBONED	DEFACER	DEICING	DEPAINT	DESPOIL
DEBONER	DEFACES	DEICTIC	DEPARTS	DESPOTS
DEBONES	DEFAMED	DEINDEX	DEPENDS	DESTAIN
DEBRIDE	DEFAMES	DEJEUNE	DEPERMS	DESTOCK
DEBRIEF	DEFANGS	DELAPSE	DEPLANE	DESTROY
DEBUNKS	DEFAULT	DELATED	DEPLOYS	DESUGAR
DEBURRS	DEFEATS	DELAYED	DEPLUME	DESYNED
DEBUSED	DEFENCE	DELAYER	DEPONES	DESYNES
DEBUSES	DEFENDS	DELEADS	DEPORTS	DETAILS
DECADES	DEFIERS	DELEAVE	DEPOSED	DETAINS
DECAFFS	DEFILED	DELIGHT	DEPOSER	DETENTS
DECAMPS	DEFILER	DELIMED	DEPOSES	DETENUE
DECANAL	DEFILES	DELIMES	DEPOSIT	DETESTS
DECANES	DEFINED	DELIMIT	DEPRESS	DETICKS
DECANTS	DEFINER	DELISTS	DEQUEUE	DETORTS
DECARBS	DEFINES	DELIVER	DERAILS	DETOURS
DECARES	DEFLEAS	DELOPED	DERANGE	DETRACT
DECEASE	DEFOAMS	DELOPES	DERATED	DETRAIN
DECIDED	DEFOCUS	DELOUSE	DERATES	DETUNED
DECIDER	DEFORCE	DELUDES	DERAYED	DETUNES
DECIDES	DEFORMS	DELUGED	DERIDER	DEVALUE
DECLAIM	DEFOULS	DELUGES	DERIDES	DEVEINS
DECLASS	DEFRAGS	DEMAINS	DERIVED	DEVESTS
DECLAWS	DEFRAUD	DEMARKS	DERIVER	DEVICES
DECLINE	DEFRAYS	DEMASTS	DERIVES	DEVISED
DECODED	DEFROCK	DEMEANE	DESALTS	DEVISES
DECODER	DEFROST	DEMEANS	DESANDS	DEVISOR
DECODES	DEFROZE	DEMERGE	DESCALE	DEVOICE
DECOKED	DEFUELS	DEMERIT	DESCANT	DEVOLVE
DECOKES	DEFUNDS	DEMERSE	DESCEND	DEVOTED
				DEVOTES

DEWATER	DECLUTCH	DEFUNDED	DEMURING	DESERVES
DEWAXED	DECODERS	DEFUSING	DENATURE	DESEXING
DEWAXES	DECODING	DEFUZING	DENAZIFY	DESIGNED
DEWOOLS	DECOKING	DEGASSED	DENETTED	DESIGNEE
DEWORMS	DECOLORS	DEGASSER	DENOTATE	DESIGNER
DEZINCS	DECOLOUR	DEGASSES	DENOTING	DESILVER
	DECOMMIT	DEGENDER	DEORBITS	DESINING
Eight-letter	DECOUPLE	DEGERMED	DEPAINTS	DESIRING
words	DECOYING	DEGLAZED	DEPARTED	DESISTED
DEAERATE	DECREASE	DEGLAZES	DEPARTER	DESKILLS
DEAIRING	DECREWED	DEGRADED	DEPEINCT	DESNOODS
DEALATED	DECRIERS	DEGRADER	DEPENDED	DESOLATE
DEALATES	DECROWNS	DEGRADES	DEPEOPLE	DESORBED
DEARLING	DECRYING	DEGREASE	DEPERMED	DESPIGHT
DEASHING	DECRYPTS	DEGUMMED	DEPLANED	DESPITED
DEBAGGED	DECUBITI	DEGUSTED	DEPLANES	DESPITES
DEBARKED	DECURIAS	DEHORNED	DEPLOYED	DESPOILS
DEBARKER	DECURIES	DEHORNER	DEPLUMED	DESTAINS
DEBARRED	DECURVED	DEIONISE	DEPLUMES	DESTOCKS
DEBASING	DECURVES	DEIONIZE	DEPOLISH	DESTROYS
DEBATING	DEDUCTED	DELAPSED	DEPONENT	DESUGARS
DEBEAKED	DEFACERS	DELAPSES	DEPORTED	DESULFUR
DEBEARDS	DEFACING	DELAYERS	DEPORTER	DESYNING
DEBELLED	DEFAMING	DELAYING	DEPOSERS	DETACHES
DEBITING	DEFANGED	DELEADED	DEPOSING	DETAILED
DEBONERS	DEFATTED	DELEAVED	DEPOSITS	DETAILER
DEBONING	DEFAULTS	DELEAVES	DEQUEUED	DETANGLE
DEBOSHES	DEFEATED	DELEGACY	DEQUEUES	DETASSEL
DEBOSSED	DEFEATER	DELEGATE	DERAILED	DETENUES
DEBOSSES	DEFENCED	DELIBATE	DERAILER	DETESTED
DEBOUCHE	DEFENCES	DELIGHTS	DERANGED	DETESTER
DEBRIDED	DEFENDED	DELIMING	DERANGER	DETHATCH
DEBRIDES	DEFENDER	DELIMITS	DERANGES	DETHRONE
DEBRIEFS	DEFIANCE	DELISTED	DERATING	DETICKED
DEBRUISE	DEFILERS	DELIVERS	DERATION	DETICKER
DEBUDDED	DEFILING	DELIVERY	DERATTED	DETOURED
DEBUGGED	DEFINERS	DELOPING	DERAYING	DETRACTS
DEBUGGER	DEFINING	DELOUSED	DERELICT	DETRAINS
DEBUNKED	DEFINITE	DELOUSER	DERIDERS	DETUNING
DEBUNKER	DEFLEXED	DELOUSES	DERIDING	DEVALUED
DEBURRED	DEFLEXES	DELUGING	DERIGGED	DEVALUES
DEBUSING	DEFLOWER	DELUSTER	DERINGER	DEVEINED
DEBUSSED	DEFLUENT	DEMANNED	DERIVERS	DEVERBAL
DEBUSSES	DEFOAMED	DEMARKED	DERIVING	DEVESTED
DECADENT	DEFOAMER	DEMARKET	DESALTED	DEVIATOR
DECALLED	DEFOGGED	DEMASTED	DESALTER	DEVISING
DECAMPED	DEFOGGER	DEMEANED	DESANDED	DEVISORS
DECANTED	DEFORCED	DEMEANES	DESCALED	DEVOICED
DECANTER	DEFORCER	DEMERGED	DESCALES	DEVOICES
DECEASED	DEFORCES	DEMERGER	DESCANTS	DEVOLVED
DECEASES	DEFOREST	DEMERGES	DESCENDS	DEVOLVES
DECENTER	DEFORMED	DEMERITS	DESCENTS	DEVOTING
DECENTRE	DEFORMER	DEMERSES	DESCHOOL	DEWATERS
DECERNED	DEFOULED	DEMESNES	DESCRIBE	DEWAXING
DECIDERS	DEFRAUDS	DEMISTED	DESCRIED	DEWITTED
DECIDING	DEFRAYED	DEMISTER	DESCRIES	DEWOOLED
DECIPHER	DEFREEZE	DEMOBBED	DESCRIVE	DEWORMED
DECLAIMS	DEFROCKS	DEMONISM	DESEEDED	DEWORMER
DECLAWED	DEFROSTS	DEMONIST	DESELECT	DEZINCED
DECLINAL	DEFROZEN	DEMOTION	DESERVED	
DECLINES	DEFUELED	DEMOUNTS	DESERVER	

Words that begin with DIS-

Seven-letter words

DISABLE
DISALLY
DISARMS
DISAVOW
DISBAND
DISBARK
DISBARS
DISBUDS
DISCAGE
DISCANT
DISCARD
DISCASE
DISCIDE
DISCOED
DISCORD
DISCURE
DISCUSS
DISEASE
DISEDGE
DISFAME
DISFORM
DISGEST
DISGOWN
DISGUST
DISHELM
DISHING
DISHOME
DISHORN
DISJOIN
DISKING
DISLEAF
DISLEAL
DISLIKE
DISLIMB
DISLIMN
DISLINK
DISLOAD
DISMALS
DISMANS
DISMASK
DISMAST
DISMAYS
DISMISS
DISNEST
DISOBEY
DISOWNS
DISPACE
DISPARK

DISPART
DISPELS
DISPEND
DISPLAY
DISPLED
DISPONE
DISPORT
DISPOSE
DISPOST
DISPRAD
DISRANK
DISRATE
DISROBE
DISROOT
DISSAVE
DISSEAT
DISSECT
DISSENT
DISSING
DISTAIN
DISTEND
DISTENT
DISTICH
DISTILL
DISTILS
DISTOME
DISTORT
DISTUNE
DISUSED
DISUSES
DISYOKE

Eight-letter words

DISABLED
DISABLER
DISABLES
DISABUSE
DISADORN
DISAGREE
DISALLOW
DISANNEX
DISANNUL
DISAPPLY
DISARMED
DISARMER
DISARRAY
DISASTER
DISAVOWS
DISBANDS

DISBARKS
DISBENCH
DISBOSOM
DISBOUND
DISBOWEL
DISBURSE
DISCAGED
DISCAGES
DISCANDY
DISCANTS
DISCARDS
DISCASED
DISCASES
DISCIDED
DISCIDES
DISCINCT
DISCLAIM
DISCLOSE
DISCOLOR
DISCORDS
DISCOUNT
DISCOURE
DISCOVER
DISCROWN
DISCURED
DISCURES
DISEASED
DISEASES
DISEDGED
DISEDGES
DISENDOW
DISENROL
DISFAMES
DISFAVOR
DISFLESH
DISFORMS
DISFROCK
DISGAVEL
DISGESTS
DISGORGE
DISGOWNS
DISGRACE
DISGRADE
DISGUISE
DISGUSTS
DISHABIT
DISHABLE
DISHELMS
DISHINGS
DISHOMED

DISHOMES
DISHONOR
DISHORNS
DISHORSE
DISHOUSE
DISINTER
DISINURE
DISJOINS
DISJOINT
DISLEAFS
DISLEAVE
DISLIKED
DISLIKEN
DISLIKER
DISLIKES
DISLIMBS
DISLIMNS
DISLINKS
DISLOADS
DISLODGE
DISLOYAL
DISMASKS
DISMASTS
DISMAYED
DISMOUNT
DISNESTS
DISOBEYS
DISODIUM
DISORBED
DISORDER
DISOWNED
DISOWNER
DISPACED
DISPACES
DISPARKS
DISPARTS
DISPATCH
DISPEACE
DISPENCE
DISPENDS
DISPERSE
DISPLACE
DISPLANT
DISPLAYS
DISPLING
DISPLUME
DISPONES
DISPORTS
DISPOSED
DISPOSER

DISPOSES
DISPOSTS
DISPRIZE
DISPROOF
DISPROVE
DISPURSE
DISQUIET
DISRANKS
DISRATED
DISRATES
DISROBED
DISROBES
DISROOTS
DISSAVED
DISSAVES
DISSEATS
DISSECTS
DISSEISE
DISSEIZE
DISSENTS
DISSERVE
DISSEVER
DISSIGHT
DISSOLVE
DISTAINS
DISTALLY
DISTASTE
DISTENDS
DISTILLS
DISTINCT
DISTOMES
DISTORTS
DISTRACT
DISTRAIL
DISTRAIN
DISTRAIT
DISTRESS
DISTRUST
DISTUNED
DISTUNES
DISUNION
DISUNITE
DISUNITY
DISUSAGE
DISUSING
DISVALUE
DISVOUCH
DISYOKED
DISYOKES

Words that begin with EM-

Seven-letter words

EMAILED
EMBAILS

EMBALED
EMBALES
EMBALLS
EMBALMS

EMBANKS
EMBARKS
EMBASED
EMBASES

EMBASSY
EMBASTE
EMBATHE
EMBAYED

EMBLAZE
EMBLOOM
EMBOILS
EMBOLUS

EMBOSKS	EMPARES	EMBATTLE	EMBRAVED	EMPATHIC
EMBOSOM	EMPARTS	EMBAYING	EMBRAVES	EMPATRON
EMBOUND	EMPEACH	EMBEDDED	EMBREADS	EMPEOPLE
EMBOWED	EMPERCE	EMBEZZLE	EMBROILS	EMPERCED
EMBOWEL	EMPIGHT	EMBITTER	EMBROWNS	EMPERCES
EMBOWER	EMPLACE	EMBLAZED	EMBRUTED	EMPERISH
EMBOXED	EMPLANE	EMBLAZER	EMBRUTES	EMPHASES
EMBOXES	EMPLOYS	EMBLAZES	EMBUSIED	EMPHASIS
EMBRACE	EMPLUME	EMBLAZON	EMBUSIES	EMPHATIC
EMBRAID	EMPOWER	EMBLOOMS	EMBUSING	EMPIERCE
EMBRAVE	EMPRESS	EMBODIED	EMBUSSED	EMPLACED
EMBREAD	EMPRISE	EMBODIES	EMBUSSES	EMPLACES
EMBROIL	EMPRIZE	EMBOGGED	EMDASHES	EMPLANED
EMBROWN	EMPUSES	EMBOILED	EMENDERS	EMPLANES
EMBRUTE		EMBOLDEN	EMENDING	EMPLEACH
EMBUSED	**Eight-letter**	EMBORDER	EMMARBLE	EMPLONGE
EMBUSES	**words**	EMBOSOMS	EMMESHED	EMPLOYED
EMENDED	EMAILING	EMBOSSED	EMMESHES	EMPLUMED
EMENDER	EMBAILED	EMBOSSER	EMMEWING	EMPLUMES
EMIRATE	EMBALING	EMBOSSES	EMMOVING	EMPOISON
EMMEWED	EMBALLED	EMBOUNDS	EMPACKET	EMPOLDER
EMMOVED	EMBALMED	EMBOWELS	EMPAIRED	EMPOWERS
EMMOVES	EMBANKED	EMBOWERS	EMPAIRES	EMPRISES
EMPAIRE	EMBANKER	EMBOWING	EMPALING	EMPRIZES
EMPALED	EMBARKED	EMBOXING	EMPANADA	EMPURPLE
EMPALER	EMBARRED	EMBRACED	EMPANELS	EMPYEMIC
EMPALES	EMBASING	EMBRACER	EMPARING	
EMPANEL	EMBATHED	EMBRACES	EMPARLED	
EMPARED	EMBATHES	EMBRAIDS	EMPARTED	

Words that begin with EN-

Seven-letter	ENCLOUD	ENFEOFF	ENGORGE	ENLIVEN
words	ENCODED	ENFEVER	ENGRACE	ENLOCKS
ENABLED	ENCODER	ENFILED	ENGRAFF	ENMEWED
ENABLER	ENCODES	ENFIRED	ENGRAFT	ENMOVED
ENABLES	ENCORED	ENFIRES	ENGRAIL	ENMOVES
ENACTED	ENCORES	ENFIXED	ENGRAIN	ENNOBLE
ENACTOR	ENCRUST	ENFIXES	ENGRAMS	ENOLOGY
ENAMINE	ENCRYPT	ENFLAME	ENGRASP	ENOUNCE
ENAMOUR	ENCYSTS	ENFLESH	ENGRAVE	ENPLANE
ENARMED	ENDARTS	ENFOLDS	ENGROSS	ENPRINT
ENCAGED	ENDEARS	ENFORCE	ENGUARD	ENQUEUE
ENCAGES	ENDEMIC	ENFORMS	ENGULFS	ENQUIRE
ENCALMS	ENDEWED	ENFRAME	ENGULPH	ENRACED
ENCAMPS	ENDINGS	ENFREED	ENHALOS	ENRACES
ENCASED	ENDITED	ENFREES	ENHANCE	ENRAGED
ENCASES	ENDITES	ENFROZE	ENISLED	ENRAGES
ENCAVED	ENDIVES	ENGAGED	ENISLES	ENRANGE
ENCAVES	ENDORSE	ENGAGER	ENJAMBS	ENRANKS
ENCHAFE	ENDOWED	ENGAGES	ENJOINS	ENRHEUM
ENCHAIN	ENDOWER	ENGAOLS	ENJOYED	ENRINGS
ENCHANT	ENDUING	ENGILDS	ENLACED	ENRIVEN
ENCHARM	ENDURED	ENGIRDS	ENLACES	ENROBED
ENCHASE	ENDURES	ENGLOBE	ENLARDS	ENROBES
ENCHEER	ENDUROS	ENGLOOM	ENLARGE	ENROLLS
ENCLASP	ENFACED	ENGLUTS	ENLIGHT	ENROOTS
ENCLAVE	ENFACES	ENGORED	ENLINKS	ENROUGH
ENCLOSE	ENFELON	ENGORES	ENLISTS	ENROUND

ENSEALS	ENZYMIC	ENDASHES	ENGRAVEN	ENRIDGED
ENSEAMS		ENDEARED	ENGRAVER	ENRINGED
ENSEARS	**Eight-letter**	ENDEIXES	ENGRAVES	ENROBING
ENSERFS	**words**	ENDEIXIS	ENGRIEVE	ENROLLED
ENSEWED	ENABLING	ENDERMIC	ENGROOVE	ENROLLER
ENSHELL	ENACTING	ENDEWING	ENGUARDS	ENROOTED
ENSIGNS	ENACTION	ENDITING	ENGULFED	ENROUGHS
ENSILED	ENACTIVE	ENDORSER	ENGULPHS	ENROUNDS
ENSILES	ENACTORS	ENDOSSED	ENHALOED	ENSAMPLE
ENSKIED	ENACTURE	ENDOSSES	ENHALOES	ENSCONCE
ENSKIES	ENAMINES	ENDOWERS	ENHANCES	ENSCROLL
ENSKYED	ENAMOURS	ENDOWING	ENHEARSE	ENSEALED
ENSLAVE	ENARCHED	ENDURING	ENHUNGER	ENSEAMED
ENSNARE	ENARCHES	ENFACING	ENHYDROS	ENSEARED
ENSNARL	ENARMING	ENFEEBLE	ENISLING	ENSEMBLE
ENSOULS	ENAUNTER	ENFELONS	ENJAMBED	ENSEWING
ENSTAMP	ENCAGING	ENFEOFFS	ENJOINED	ENSHEATH
ENSTEEP	ENCALMED	ENFETTER	ENJOINER	ENSHELLS
ENSTYLE	ENCAMPED	ENFEVERS	ENJOYING	ENSHIELD
ENSUING	ENCARPUS	ENFIERCE	ENKERNEL	ENSHRINE
ENSURED	ENCASHED	ENFIRING	ENKINDLE	ENSHROUD
ENSURER	ENCASHES	ENFIXING	ENLACING	ENSIGNED
ENSURES	ENCASING	ENFLAMED	ENLARDED	ENSILAGE
ENSWEEP	ENCAVING	ENFLAMES	ENLARGEN	ENSILING
ENSWEPT	ENCHAFED	ENFLOWER	ENLARGER	ENSKYING
ENTAILS	ENCHAFES	ENFOLDED	ENLARGES	ENSLAVED
ENTAMED	ENCHAINS	ENFOLDER	ENLIGHTS	ENSLAVER
ENTAMES	ENCHANTS	ENFORCED	ENLINKED	ENSLAVES
ENTICED	ENCHARGE	ENFORCER	ENLISTED	ENSNARED
ENTICES	ENCHARMS	ENFORCES	ENLISTEE	ENSNARER
ENTIRES	ENCHASED	ENFOREST	ENLISTER	ENSNARES
ENTITLE	ENCHASER	ENFORMED	ENLIVENS	ENSNARLS
ENTOILS	ENCHASES	ENFRAMED	ENLOCKED	ENSOULED
ENTOMBS	ENCHEERS	ENFRAMES	ENLUMINE	ENSPHERE
ENTOPIC	ENCHORIC	ENFREEZE	ENMESHED	ENSTAMPS
ENTRAIL	ENCIPHER	ENFROZEN	ENMESHES	ENSTEEPS
ENTRAIN	ENCIRCLE	ENGAGERS	ENMEWING	ENSTYLED
ENTRANT	ENCLASPS	ENGAGING	ENMOSSED	ENSTYLES
ENTRAPS	ENCLAVES	ENGAOLED	ENMOVING	ENSURING
ENTREAT	ENCLITIC	ENGENDER	ENNOBLER	ENSWATHE
ENTREES	ENCLOSED	ENGILDED	ENNOBLES	ENSWEEPS
ENTRIES	ENCLOSER	ENGIRDED	ENOUNCES	ENTAILED
ENTRIST	ENCLOSES	ENGIRDLE	ENPLANED	ENTAILER
ENTRUST	ENCLOTHE	ENGLOBED	ENPLANES	ENTAMING
ENTWINE	ENCLOUDS	ENGLOBES	ENPRINTS	ENTANGLE
ENTWIST	ENCODERS	ENGLOOMS	ENQUEUED	ENTELLUS
ENURNED	ENCODING	ENGORGED	ENQUEUES	ENTENDER
ENVAULT	ENCOLOUR	ENGORGES	ENQUIRED	ENTHETIC
ENVENOM	ENCOLURE	ENGORING	ENQUIRES	ENTHRALL
ENVIERS	ENCORING	ENGRACED	ENRACING	ENTHRONE
ENVYING	ENCRADLE	ENGRACES	ENRAGING	ENTHUSES
ENWALLS	ENCREASE	ENGRAFFS	ENRANGED	ENTICING
ENWHEEL	ENCRINAL	ENGRAFTS	ENRANGES	ENTITLED
ENWINDS	ENCRUSTS	ENGRAILS	ENRANKED	ENTITLES
ENWOMBS	ENCRYPTS	ENGRAINS	ENRAUNGE	ENTOILED
ENWOUND	ENCUMBER	ENGRAMMA	ENRAVISH	ENTOMBED
ENWRAPS	ENCYCLIC	ENGRAMME	ENRHEUMS	ENTRAILS
ENZONED	ENDAMAGE	ENGRASPS	ENRICHED	ENTRAINS
ENZONES	ENDANGER	ENGRAVED	ENRICHER	ENTRANCE
ENZYMES	ENDARTED	ENGRAVED	ENRICHES	ENTRANTS

ENTREATS	ENTWINES	ENVASSAL	ENVISION	ENWREATH
ENTREATY	ENTWISTS	ENVAULTS	ENVYINGS	ENZONING
ENTRENCH	ENURESES	ENVENOMS	ENWALLED	
ENTROPIC	ENURESIS	ENVIABLE	ENWALLOW	
ENTRUSTS	ENURETIC	ENVIABLY	ENWHEELS	
ENTWINED	ENURNING	ENVISAGE	ENWOMBED	

Words that begin with EX-

Seven-letter words	EXPANDS	EXTORTS	EXCITING	EXPOUNDS
EXACTED	EXPENDS	EXTRACT	EXCLAIMS	EXPULSED
EXACTOR	EXPERTS	EXTRAIT	EXCLAVES	EXPULSES
EXALTER	EXPLAIN	EXTREAT	EXCURSED	EXPURGED
EXAMENS	EXPLANT	EXTREMA	EXCURSES	EXPURGES
EXAMINE	EXPORTS	EXURBAN	EXCURSUS	EXSECANT
EXAMPLE	EXPOSED	EXURBIA	EXEMPTED	EXTENDED
EXAPTED	EXPOSER		EXHALING	EXTENDER
EXCHEAT	EXPOSES	**Eight-letter words**	EXHUMATE	EXTENSOR
EXCIDED	EXPOSIT	EXACTING	EXODISTS	EXTERNAL
EXCIDES	EXPOUND	EXACTION	EXOGAMIC	EXTERNES
EXCITED	EXPRESS	EXACTORS	EXOSMOSE	EXTINCTS
EXCITER	EXPULSE	EXALTERS	EXPANDER	EXTOLLED
EXCITES	EXPURGE	EXAMINES	EXPENDED	EXTOLLER
EXCLAIM	EXSECTS	EXANTHEM	EXPERTLY	EXTRACTS
EXCLAVE	EXTENDS	EXCELLED	EXPLAINS	EXTRAITS
EXCURSE	EXTENSE	EXCESSED	EXPLANTS	EXTREATS
EXEMPTS	EXTENTS	EXCESSES	EXPONENT	EXTUBATE
EXHALED	EXTERNE	EXCHANGE	EXPORTED	EXURBIAS
EXHALES	EXTERNS	EXCHEATS	EXPORTER	
EXODIST	EXTINCT	EXCIDING	EXPOSERS	
EXOSMIC	EXTINES	EXCITERS	EXPOSING	
	EXTOLLS		EXPOSITS	

Words that begin with FOOT-

Seven-letter words	FOOTPAD	FOOTERED	FOOTPACE	FOOTSORE
FOOTAGE	FOOTRAS	FOOTFALL	FOOTPADS	FOOTSTEP
FOOTBAG	FOOTWAY	FOOTGEAR	FOOTPAGE	FOOTWALL
FOOTBAR		FOOTHILL	FOOTPATH	FOOTWAYS
FOOTBOY	**Eight-letter words**	FOOTHOLD	FOOTPOST	FOOTWEAR
FOOTERS	FOOTAGES	FOOTINGS	FOOTPUMP	FOOTWELL
FOOTING	FOOTBAGS	FOOTLESS	FOOTRACE	FOOTWORK
FOOTLED	FOOTBALL	FOOTLIKE	FOOTREST	FOOTWORN
FOOTLES	FOOTBARS	FOOTLING	FOOTROPE	
FOOTMAN	FOOTBATH	FOOTMARK	FOOTRULE	
FOOTMEN	FOOTBOYS	FOOTMUFF	FOOTSIES	
		FOOTNOTE	FOOTSLOG	

Words that begin with FOR-

Seven-letter words	FORBARE	FORDING	FORFEND	FORGOES
FORAGED	FORBEAR	FORDOES	FORGAVE	FORGONE
FORAGER	FORBIDS	FORDONE	FORGERS	FORHENT
FORAGES	FORBODE	FORESTS	FORGETS	FORHOWS
FORAMEN	FORBORE	FOREVER	FORGING	FORKIER
FORBADE	FORCATS	FOREXES	FORGIVE	FORKING
	FORCEPS	FORFAIR	FORGOER	FORLANA

FORLEND	FORSLOW	FORBODED	FORGOING	FORSOOTH
FORLENT	FORSOOK	FORBODES	FORHENTS	FORSPEAK
FORLORN	FORTIES	FORBORNE	FORJUDGE	FORSPEND
FORMALS	FORTING	FORDOING	FORLANAS	FORSPENT
FORMATE	FORTUNE	FORDONNE	FORLENDS	FORSPOKE
FORMATS	FORWARD	FOREKING	FORMATED	FORSWEAR
FORMICA	FORWARN	FORELAIN	FORMATES	FORSWINK
FORMING	FORWENT	FORELAND	FORMICAS	FORSWORE
FORMOLS	FORWORN	FORESTER	FORMINGS	FORSWORN
FORPETS	FORZATI	FORFAIRS	FORPINED	FORTHINK
FORPINE		FORFAULT	FORPINES	FORTRESS
FORPITS	**Eight-letter**	FORFENDS	FORRAYED	FORTUNED
FORRAYS	**words**	FORGINGS	FORSAKER	FORTUNES
FORSAID	FORAGERS	FORGIVEN	FORSAKES	FORWARDS
FORSAKE	FORAGING	FORGIVER	FORSLACK	FORWARNS
FORSAYS	FORAMENS	FORGIVES	FORSLOES	FORWASTE
FORSLOE	FORBEARS	FORGOERS	FORSLOWS	FORWEARY

Words that begin with IM-

Seven-letter	IMPALES	IMPULSE	IMMERSES	IMPLEADS
words	IMPANEL	IMPURER	IMMESHED	IMPLEDGE
IMAGERS	IMPARKS		IMMESHES	IMPLEXES
IMAGING	IMPARTS	**Eight-letter**	IMMEWING	IMPLUNGE
IMAGISM	IMPASSE	**words**	IMMINGLE	IMPLYING
IMAGIST	IMPASTE	IMAGINGS	IMMINUTE	IMPOCKET
IMAMATE	IMPAVED	IMAGISMS	IMMIXING	IMPOLDER
IMARETS	IMPAVES	IMAGISTS	IMMOBILE	IMPOLICY
IMBALMS	IMPAVID	IMAMATES	IMMODEST	IMPOLITE
IMBARKS	IMPAWNS	IMBALMED	IMMOMENT	IMPONENT
IMBASED	IMPEACH	IMBARKED	IMMORTAL	IMPOROUS
IMBASES	IMPEARL	IMBARRED	IMMOTILE	IMPORTED
IMBATHE	IMPEDES	IMBASING	IMMURING	IMPORTER
IMBLAZE	IMPENDS	IMBATHED	IMPAINTS	IMPOSERS
IMBOSKS	IMPERIL	IMBATHES	IMPAIRED	IMPOSING
IMBOSOM	IMPIETY	IMBEDDED	IMPAIRER	IMPOSTED
IMBOWER	IMPINGS	IMBITTER	IMPALING	IMPOSTER
IMBRAST	IMPIOUS	IMBLAZED	IMPANELS	IMPOTENT
IMBROWN	IMPLANT	IMBLAZES	IMPARITY	IMPOUNDS
IMBRUTE	IMPLATE	IMBODIED	IMPARKED	IMPOWERS
IMBURSE	IMPLEAD	IMBODIES	IMPARLED	IMPRESES
IMMASKS	IMPLIED	IMBOLDEN	IMPARTED	IMPRESTS
IMMENSE	IMPLIES	IMBORDER	IMPARTER	IMPRINTS
IMMERGE	IMPONES	IMBOSOMS	IMPASSES	IMPRISON
IMMERSE	IMPORTS	IMBOSSED	IMPASTED	IMPROPER
IMMEWED	IMPOSED	IMBOSSES	IMPASTES	IMPROVED
IMMIXED	IMPOSER	IMBOWERS	IMPAVING	IMPROVER
IMMIXES	IMPOSES	IMBROWNS	IMPAWNED	IMPROVES
IMMORAL	IMPOSTS	IMBRUTED	IMPEARLS	IMPUDENT
IMMURED	IMPOUND	IMBRUTES	IMPENDED	IMPULSED
IMMURES	IMPOWER	IMBURSES	IMPERILS	IMPULSES
IMPACTS	IMPRESA	IMMANENT	IMPINGED	IMPURELY
IMPAINT	IMPRESE	IMMANTLE	IMPINGER	IMPUREST
IMPAIRS	IMPRESS	IMMASKED	IMPLANTS	IMPURITY
IMPALAS	IMPREST	IMMATURE	IMPLATED	IMPURPLE
IMPALED	IMPRINT	IMMERGED	IMPLATES	
IMPALER	IMPROVE	IMMERGES	IMPLEACH	

Words that begin with IN-

Seven-letter words

INANGAS
INAPTLY
INARMED
INBEING
INBOARD
INBOUND
INBOXES
INBREAK
INBREDS
INBREED
INBRING
INBUILT
INBURST
INCAGED
INCAGES
INCANTS
INCASED
INCASES
INCAVED
INCAVES
INCEDED
INCEDES
INCENSE
INCENTS
INCHASE
INCITED
INCITER
INCITES
INCIVIL
INCLASP
INCLINE
INCLIPS
INCLOSE
INCOMER
INCOMES
INCROSS
INCRUST
INCURVE
INDARTS
INDENES
INDENTS
INDEWED
INDEXES
INDICES
INDICTS
INDITED
INDITES
INDOLES
INDOORS
INDORSE
INDOWED
INDRAFT
INDRAWN
INDUCES
INDUCTS
INDUING

INDWELL
INDWELT
INEARTH
INEXACT
INFALLS
INFAMED
INFAMES
INFANCY
INFARES
INFAUNA
INFEOFF
INFESTS
INFIELD
INFIGHT
INFILLS
INFIRMS
INFIXED
INFIXES
INFLAME
INFLOWS
INFOLDS
INFORCE
INFORMS
INFRACT
INFUSED
INFUSES
INGATES
INGENUS
INGESTS
INGLOBE
INGOING
INGRAFT
INGRAIN
INGRATE
INGROSS
INGROUP
INGROWN
INGULFS
INGULPH
INHABIT
INHALED
INHALER
INHALES
INHAULS
INHERES
INHOOPS
INHUMAN
INISLED
INISLES
INJELLY
INJOINT
INLACED
INLACES
INLANDS
INLAYER
INLIERS
INLOCKS
INLYING

INMATES
INNARDS
INNERVE
INORBED
INPHASE
INPOURS
INQUEST
INQUIET
INQUIRE
INROADS
INSANER
INSCAPE
INSCULP
INSEAMS
INSECTS
INSEEMS
INSHELL
INSHIPS
INSHORE
INSIDER
INSIDES
INSIGHT
INSINEW
INSISTS
INSNARE
INSOFAR
INSOLES
INSOOTH
INSOULS
INSPANS
INSPIRE
INSTALL
INSTARS
INSTATE
INSTEAD
INSTEPS
INSTILL
INSURED
INSURER
INSURES
INSWEPT
INSWING
INTAKES
INTENDS
INTENSE
INTENTS
INTERNE
INTERNS
INTINES
INTITLE
INTOMBS
INTONED
INTONER
INTONES
INTORTS
INTRANT
INTREAT
INTRONS

INTRUST
INTURNS
INTWINE
INTWIST
INURNED
INUTILE
INVADED
INVADES
INVALID
INVENTS
INVERSE
INVERTS
INVESTS
INVEXED
INVITAL
INVOICE
INVOLVE
INWALLS
INWARDS
INWEAVE
INWICKS
INWINDS
INWORKS
INWOUND
INWOVEN
INWRAPS

Eight-letter words

INACTION
INACTIVE
INARABLE
INARCHED
INARCHES
INARMING
INAURATE
INBEINGS
INBOARDS
INBOUNDS
INBREAKS
INBREEDS
INBRINGS
INBURSTS
INCAGING
INCANTED
INCASING
INCAVING
INCEDING
INCENSED
INCENSER
INCENSES
INCENSOR
INCENTER
INCENTRE
INCHASED
INCHASES
INCITERS
INCITING

INCIVISM
INCLASPS
INCLINES
INCLOSED
INCLOSER
INCLOSES
INCOMERS
INCOMING
INCORPSE
INCREASE
INCREATE
INCRUSTS
INCUMBER
INCURRED
INCURVED
INCURVES
INDARTED
INDEBTED
INDECENT
INDENTED
INDEVOUT
INDEWING
INDICTED
INDIGEST
INDIRECT
INDITING
INDOCILE
INDOLENT
INDORSER
INDORSES
INDOWING
INDRAFTS
INDRENCH
INDUCTED
INDWELLS
INEARTHS
INEDIBLE
INEDITED
INEQUITY
INERRANT
INESSIVE
INEXPERT
INFAMING
INFAMOUS
INFAUNAE
INFAUNAL
INFAUNAS
INFECUND
INFEOFFS
INFERIAE
INFESTER
INFIELDS
INFIGHTS
INFILLED
INFINITE
INFIRMED
INFIRMER
INFIRMLY

INFIXING	INGULPHS	INRUSHES	INSTABLE	INTURNED
INFLAMED	INHABITS	INSANELY	INSTALLS	INTWINED
INFLAMER	INHALERS	INSANEST	INSTANCE	INTWINES
INFLAMES	INHALING	INSANIES	INSTATED	INTWISTS
INFLATUS	INHAULER	INSANITY	INSTATES	INUNDATE
INFLEXED	INHEARSE	INSCAPES	INSTILLS	INURBANE
INFLIGHT	INHOLDER	INSCIENT	INSTRESS	INURNING
INFLUENT	INHOOPED	INSCONCE	INSTROKE	INUSTION
INFLUXES	INHUMANE	INSCRIBE	INSUCKEN	INVADING
INFOLDED	INHUMATE	INSCROLL	INSURING	INVENTED
INFOLDER	INISLING	INSCULPS	INSWATHE	INVENTER
INFORCED	INJOINTS	INSCULPT	INSWINGS	INVERITY
INFORCES	INJURIES	INSEAMED	INTARSIA	INVERSED
INFORMAL	INLACING	INSECURE	INTENDED	INVERSES
INFORMED	INLANDER	INSEEMED	INTENDER	INVERTED
INFORMER	INLAYERS	INSETTER	INTENSER	INVESTED
INFOUGHT	INLAYING	INSHEATH	INTERNAL	INVIABLE
INFRACTS	INLOCKED	INSHELLS	INTERNED	INVIABLY
INFRINGE	INMESHED	INSHRINE	INTERNES	INVIRILE
INFRUGAL	INMESHES	INSIDERS	INTHRALL	INVISCID
INFUSING	INNATIVE	INSIGHTS	INTHRONE	INVOICED
INFUSION	INNERVED	INSINEWS	INTIMIST	INVOICES
INGATHER	INNERVES	INSISTED	INTITLED	INVOLUTE
INGLOBED	INNOCENT	INSISTER	INTITLES	INVOLVED
INGLOBES	INNOVATE	INSNARED	INTITULE	INVOLVES
INGOINGS	INORBING	INSNARER	INTOMBED	INWALLED
INGRAFTS	INORNATE	INSNARES	INTONERS	INWEAVED
INGRAINS	INPOURED	INSOLATE	INTONING	INWEAVES
INGRATES	INPUTTED	INSOULED	INTRANTS	INWICKED
INGROOVE	INPUTTER	INSOURCE	INTREATS	INWORKED
INGROUND	INQUESTS	INSPHERE	INTRENCH	
INGROUPS	INQUIETS	INSPIRED	INTREPID	
INGROWTH	INQUIRED	INSPIRES	INTRUSTS	
INGULFED	INQUIRES	INSPIRIT	INTUBATE	

Words that begin with ISO-

Seven-letter words	ISOLEAD	**Eight-letter words**	ISOGAMIC	ISOPHONE
	ISOLINE		ISOGENIC	ISOSPINS
ISOAMYL	ISOLOGS	ISOAMYLS	ISOGLOSS	ISOTACHS
ISOBARE	ISOMERE	ISOBARES	ISOGRAFT	ISOTHERE
ISOBARS	ISONOME	ISOBARIC	ISOGRAMS	ISOTHERM
ISOBASE	ISOPODS	ISOBASES	ISOGRAPH	ISOTONES
ISOBATH	ISOSPIN	ISOBATHS	ISOLATED	ISOTONIC
ISODOSE	ISOTACH	ISOBUTYL	ISOLEADS	ISOTOPES
ISOFORM	ISOTONE	ISOCHASM	ISOLEXES	ISOTOPIC
ISOGAMY	ISOTOPE	ISOCHIME	ISOLINES	ISOTRONS
ISOGONE	ISOTRON	ISOCHORE	ISOMERES	ISOTYPES
ISOGONS	ISOTYPE	ISOCLINE	ISOMORPH	ISOTYPIC
ISOGRAM	ISOZYME	ISODOSES	ISONOMES	ISOZYMES
ISOLATE		ISOFORMS	ISONOMIC	ISOZYMIC

Words that begin with MAN-

Seven-letter words	MANAGES	MANDATE	MANGELS	MANGOES
	MANAIAS	MANDOMS	MANGERS	MANGOLD
MANAGED	MANAKIN	MANGABY	MANGING	MANHOLE
MANAGER	MANANAS	MANGALS	MANGLED	MANHOOD

MANHUNT	MANNOSE	MANTRAP	MANDRILL	MANPOWER
MANJACK	MANPACK	MANURES	MANFULLY	MANRENTS
MANKIER	MANREDS	MANWARD	MANGOLDS	MANRIDER
MANKIND	MANRENT	MANWISE	MANGROVE	MANROPES
MANLESS	MANROPE		MANHOLES	MANSARDS
MANLIER	MANSARD	**Eight-letter**	MANHOODS	MANSHIFT
MANLIKE	MANTEEL	**words**	MANHUNTS	MANSWORN
MANLILY	MANTELS	MANAGERS	MANJACKS	MANTEELS
MANMADE	MANTIDS	MANAGING	MANKINDS	MANTRAMS
MANNANS	MANTIES	MANDATED	MANNITES	MANTRAPS
MANNISH	MANTOES	MANDATES	MANNOSES	MANURIAL
MANNITE	MANTRAM	MANDRAKE	MANPACKS	MANWARDS

Words that begin with MIS-

Seven-letter	MISGAVE	MISSALS	**Eight-letter**	MISDATED
words	MISGIVE	MISSAYS	**words**	MISDATES
MISACTS	MISGOES	MISSEAT	MISACTED	MISDEALS
MISADDS	MISGONE	MISSEEM	MISADAPT	MISDEALT
MISAIMS	MISGREW	MISSEEN	MISADDED	MISDEEDS
MISALLY	MISGROW	MISSEES	MISAGENT	MISDEEMS
MISAVER	MISHAPS	MISSELL	MISAIMED	MISDEMPT
MISBIAS	MISHEAR	MISSELS	MISALIGN	MISDIALS
MISBILL	MISHITS	MISSEND	MISALLOT	MISDIETS
MISBIND	MISJOIN	MISSENT	MISALTER	MISDIGHT
MISBORN	MISKEEP	MISSETS	MISAPPLY	MISDOERS
MISCALL	MISKENS	MISSHOD	MISARRAY	MISDOING
MISCAST	MISKENT	MISSIES	MISASSAY	MISDONNE
MISCITE	MISKEPT	MISSILE	MISATONE	MISDOUBT
MISCODE	MISKEYS	MISSING	MISAVERS	MISDRAWN
MISCOIN	MISKICK	MISSOLD	MISAWARD	MISDRAWS
MISCOOK	MISKNEW	MISSORT	MISBEGAN	MISDREAD
MISCOPY	MISKNOW	MISSOUT	MISBEGIN	MISDRIVE
MISCUED	MISLAID	MISSTEP	MISBEGOT	MISDROVE
MISCUES	MISLAIN	MISSTOP	MISBEGUN	MISEASES
MISCUTS	MISLAYS	MISSUIT	MISBILLS	MISEATEN
MISDATE	MISLEAD	MISTAKE	MISBINDS	MISEDITS
MISDEAL	MISLIES	MISTELL	MISBIRTH	MISENROL
MISDEED	MISLIKE	MISTEND	MISBOUND	MISENTER
MISDEEM	MISLIVE	MISTERM	MISBRAND	MISENTRY
MISDIAL	MISLUCK	MISTIER	MISBUILD	MISEVENT
MISDIET	MISMADE	MISTIME	MISBUILT	MISFAITH
MISDOER	MISMAKE	MISTING	MISCALLS	MISFALLS
MISDOES	MISMARK	MISTOLD	MISCARRY	MISFARED
MISDONE	MISMATE	MISTOOK	MISCASTS	MISFARES
MISDRAW	MISMEET	MISTUNE	MISCHIEF	MISFEEDS
MISDREW	MISMOVE	MISTYPE	MISCHOSE	MISFEIGN
MISEASE	MISNAME	MISUSED	MISCITED	MISFIELD
MISEATS	MISPAGE	MISUSER	MISCITES	MISFILED
MISEDIT	MISPART	MISUSES	MISCLAIM	MISFILES
MISERES	MISPENS	MISWEEN	MISCLASS	MISFIRED
MISFALL	MISPLAN	MISWEND	MISCODED	MISFIRES
MISFARE	MISPLAY	MISWENT	MISCODES	MISFOCUS
MISFEED	MISPLED	MISWORD	MISCOINS	MISFORMS
MISFELL	MISRATE	MISWRIT	MISCOLOR	MISFRAME
MISFILE	MISREAD	MISYOKE	MISCOOKS	MISGAUGE
MISFIRE	MISRELY		MISCOUNT	MISGIVEN
MISFITS	MISRULE		MISCREED	MISGIVES
MISFORM	MISSAID		MISCUING	MISGOING

MISGRADE	MISLODGE	MISPOISE	MISSPELL	MISTRACE
MISGRAFF	MISLUCKS	MISPRICE	MISSPELT	MISTRAIN
MISGRAFT	MISLYING	MISPRINT	MISSPEND	MISTREAT
MISGROWN	MISMAKES	MISPRISE	MISSPENT	MISTRESS
MISGROWS	MISMARKS	MISPRIZE	MISSPOKE	MISTRIAL
MISGUESS	MISMARRY	MISPROUD	MISSTAMP	MISTRUST
MISGUIDE	MISMATCH	MISQUOTE	MISSTART	MISTRUTH
MISHEARD	MISMATED	MISRAISE	MISSTATE	MISTRYST
MISHEARS	MISMATES	MISRATED	MISSTEER	MISTUNED
MISINFER	MISMEETS	MISRATES	MISSTEPS	MISTUNES
MISINTER	MISMETRE	MISREADS	MISSTOPS	MISTUTOR
MISJOINS	MISMOVED	MISREFER	MISSTYLE	MISTYPED
MISJUDGE	MISMOVES	MISROUTE	MISSUITS	MISTYPES
MISKEEPS	MISNAMED	MISRULED	MISSUSES	MISUNION
MISKEYED	MISNAMES	MISRULES	MISTAKEN	MISUSAGE
MISKICKS	MISOLOGY	MISSABLE	MISTAKER	MISUSERS
MISKNOWN	MISORDER	MISSEATS	MISTAKES	MISUSING
MISKNOWS	MISPAGED	MISSEEMS	MISTEACH	MISVALUE
MISLABEL	MISPAGES	MISSELLS	MISTELLS	MISWEENS
MISLABOR	MISPAINT	MISSENDS	MISTENDS	MISWENDS
MISLAYER	MISPARSE	MISSENSE	MISTERMS	MISWORDS
MISLEADS	MISPARTS	MISSHAPE	MISTHINK	MISWRITE
MISLEARN	MISPATCH	MISSILES	MISTHREW	MISWROTE
MISLIGHT	MISPLACE	MISSISES	MISTHROW	MISYOKED
MISLIKED	MISPLANS	MISSORTS	MISTIMED	MISYOKES
MISLIKER	MISPLANT	MISSOUND	MISTIMES	
MISLIKES	MISPLAYS	MISSOUTS	MISTINGS	
MISLIVED	MISPLEAD	MISSPACE	MISTITLE	
MISLIVES	MISPOINT	MISSPEAK	MISTOUCH	

Words that begin with NON-

Seven-letter words	NONHOME	NONWORD	NONEQUAL	NONLYRIC
NONACID	NONIRON	NONWORK	NONEVENT	NONMAJOR
NONAGED	NONJURY	NONZERO	NONFACTS	NONMETAL
NONAGES	NONLIFE		NONFATAL	NONMETRO
NONAGON	NONMEAT	**Eight-letter words**	NONFATTY	NONMODAL
NONANES	NONNEWS		NONFINAL	NONMONEY
NONARTS	NONNIES	NONACIDS	NONFLUID	NONMORAL
NONBANK	NONOILY	NONACTOR	NONFOCAL	NONMUSIC
NONBODY	NONORAL	NONADULT	NONGLARE	NONNASAL
NONBOOK	NONPAID	NONAGONS	NONGREEN	NONNAVAL
NONCASH	NONPAST	NONBANKS	NONGUEST	NONNOBLE
NONCOLA	NONPEAK	NONBASIC	NONGUILT	NONNOVEL
NONCOMS	NONPLAY	NONBEING	NONHARDY	NONOBESE
NONCORE	NONPLUS	NONBLACK	NONHUMAN	NONOHMIC
NONDRIP	NONPOOR	NONBOOKS	NONIDEAL	NONOWNER
NONDRUG	NONPROS	NONBRAND	NONIMAGE	NONPAGAN
NONEGOS	NONSELF	NONCLASS	NONINERT	NONPAPAL
NONFACT	NONSKID	NONCLING	NONIONIC	NONPARTY
NONFANS	NONSLIP	NONCOLAS	NONISSUE	NONPASTS
NONFARM	NONSTOP	NONCOLOR	NONJUROR	NONPLAYS
NONFOOD	NONSUCH	NONCRIME	NONLABOR	NONPOINT
NONFUEL	NONSUIT	NONDAIRY	NONLEAFY	NONPOLAR
NONGAME	NONUSER	NONDANCE	NONLEGAL	NONPRINT
NONGAYS	NONUSES	NONELECT	NONLEVEL	NONQUOTA
NONHEME	NONWAGE	NONELITE	NONLIVES	NONRATED
NONHERO	NONWOOL	NONEMPTY	NONLOCAL	NONRIGID
		NONENTRY	NONLOYAL	NONRIVAL

NONROYAL	NONSTOPS	NONTITLE	NONURBAN	NONVOTER
NONRURAL	NONSTORY	NONTONAL	NONUSERS	NONWHITE
NONSENSE	NONSTYLE	NONTONIC	NONUSING	NONWOODY
NONSKIER	NONSUGAR	NONTOXIC	NONVALID	NONWORDS
NONSOLAR	NONSUITS	NONTRUMP	NONVIRAL	NONWOVEN
NONSOLID	NONTAXES	NONTRUTH	NONVITAL	
NONSTICK	NONTIDAL	NONUNION	NONVOCAL	

Words that begin with OUT-

Seven-letter words	OUTFIND	OUTLETS	OUTROPE	OUTWEAR
	OUTFIRE	OUTLIED	OUTROWS	OUTWEED
OUTACTS	OUTFISH	OUTLIER	OUTRUNG	OUTWEEP
OUTADDS	OUTFITS	OUTLIES	OUTRUNS	OUTWELL
OUTAGES	OUTFLEW	OUTLINE	OUTRUSH	OUTWENT
OUTASKS	OUTFLOW	OUTLIVE	OUTSAID	OUTWEPT
OUTBACK	OUTFOOL	OUTLOOK	OUTSAIL	OUTWICK
OUTBAKE	OUTFOOT	OUTLOVE	OUTSANG	OUTWILE
OUTBARK	OUTGAIN	OUTMANS	OUTSAYS	OUTWILL
OUTBARS	OUTGATE	OUTMODE	OUTSEEN	OUTWIND
OUTBAWL	OUTGAVE	OUTMOST	OUTSEES	OUTWING
OUTBEAM	OUTGAZE	OUTMOVE	OUTSELL	OUTWINS
OUTBEGS	OUTGIVE	OUTNAME	OUTSETS	OUTWISH
OUTBIDS	OUTGLOW	OUTNESS	OUTSHOT	OUTWITH
OUTBRAG	OUTGNAW	OUTPACE	OUTSIDE	OUTWITS
OUTBRED	OUTGOER	OUTPART	OUTSING	OUTWORE
OUTBULK	OUTGOES	OUTPASS	OUTSINS	OUTWORK
OUTBURN	OUTGONE	OUTPEEP	OUTSITS	OUTWORN
OUTBUYS	OUTGREW	OUTPEER	OUTSIZE	OUTWRIT
OUTCALL	OUTGRIN	OUTPITY	OUTSOAR	OUTYELL
OUTCAST	OUTGROW	OUTPLAN	OUTSOLD	OUTYELP
OUTCHID	OUTGUNS	OUTPLAY	OUTSOLE	
OUTCITY	OUTGUSH	OUTPLOD	OUTSPAN	**Eight-letter**
OUTCOME	OUTHAUL	OUTPLOT	OUTSPED	**words**
OUTCOOK	OUTHEAR	OUTPOLL	OUTSTAY	OUTACTED
OUTCROP	OUTHIRE	OUTPORT	OUTSTEP	OUTADDED
OUTCROW	OUTHITS	OUTPOST	OUTSULK	OUTARGUE
OUTDARE	OUTHOWL	OUTPOUR	OUTSUMS	OUTASKED
OUTDATE	OUTHUNT	OUTPRAY	OUTSUNG	OUTBACKS
OUTDOER	OUTINGS	OUTPULL	OUTSWAM	OUTBAKED
OUTDOES	OUTJEST	OUTPUSH	OUTSWIM	OUTBAKES
OUTDONE	OUTJETS	OUTPUTS	OUTSWUM	OUTBARKS
OUTDOOR	OUTJINX	OUTRACE	OUTTAKE	OUTBAWLS
OUTDRAG	OUTJUMP	OUTRAGE	OUTTALK	OUTBEAMS
OUTDRAW	OUTJUTS	OUTRANG	OUTTASK	OUTBITCH
OUTDREW	OUTKEEP	OUTRANK	OUTTELL	OUTBLAZE
OUTDROP	OUTKEPT	OUTRATE	OUTTOLD	OUTBLEAT
OUTDUEL	OUTKICK	OUTRAVE	OUTTOOK	OUTBLESS
OUTDURE	OUTKILL	OUTREAD	OUTTOPS	OUTBLOOM
OUTEARN	OUTKISS	OUTREDS	OUTTROT	OUTBLUFF
OUTEATS	OUTLAID	OUTRIDE	OUTTURN	OUTBLUSH
OUTECHO	OUTLAIN	OUTRIGS	OUTVIED	OUTBOARD
OUTEDGE	OUTLAND	OUTRING	OUTVIES	OUTBOAST
OUTFACE	OUTLASH	OUTROAR	OUTVOTE	OUTBOUND
OUTFALL	OUTLAST	OUTROCK	OUTWAIT	OUTBOXED
OUTFAST	OUTLAWS	OUTRODE	OUTWALK	OUTBOXES
OUTFAWN	OUTLAYS	OUTROLL	OUTWARD	OUTBRAGS
OUTFEEL	OUTLEAD	OUTROOP	OUTWARS	OUTBRAVE
OUTFELT	OUTLEAP	OUTROOT	OUTWASH	OUTBRAWL

OUTBREAK	OUTDWELL	OUTHOMER	OUTPULLS	OUTSMILE
OUTBREED	OUTDWELT	OUTHOUSE	OUTPUNCH	OUTSMOKE
OUTBRIBE	OUTEARNS	OUTHOWLS	OUTPUPIL	OUTSNORE
OUTBROKE	OUTEATEN	OUTHUMOR	OUTQUOTE	OUTSOARS
OUTBUILD	OUTEDGES	OUTHUNTS	OUTRACED	OUTSOLES
OUTBUILT	OUTFABLE	OUTJESTS	OUTRACES	OUTSPANS
OUTBULGE	OUTFACED	OUTJUMPS	OUTRAGED	OUTSPEAK
OUTBULKS	OUTFACES	OUTKEEPS	OUTRAGES	OUTSPEED
OUTBULLY	OUTFALLS	OUTKICKS	OUTRAISE	OUTSPELL
OUTBURNS	OUTFASTS	OUTKILLS	OUTRANCE	OUTSPELT
OUTBURNT	OUTFAWNS	OUTLANDS	OUTRANGE	OUTSPEND
OUTBURST	OUTFEAST	OUTLASTS	OUTRANKS	OUTSPENT
OUTCALLS	OUTFEELS	OUTLAUGH	OUTRATED	OUTSPOKE
OUTCAPER	OUTFENCE	OUTLAWED	OUTRATES	OUTSPORT
OUTCASTE	OUTFIELD	OUTLEADS	OUTRAVED	OUTSTAND
OUTCASTS	OUTFIGHT	OUTLEAPS	OUTRAVES	OUTSTARE
OUTCATCH	OUTFINDS	OUTLEAPT	OUTREACH	OUTSTART
OUTCAVIL	OUTFIRED	OUTLEARN	OUTREADS	OUTSTATE
OUTCHARM	OUTFIRES	OUTLIERS	OUTREIGN	OUTSTAYS
OUTCHEAT	OUTFLANK	OUTLINED	OUTRIDER	OUTSTEER
OUTCHIDE	OUTFLASH	OUTLINER	OUTRIDES	OUTSTEPS
OUTCLASS	OUTFLIES	OUTLINES	OUTRIGHT	OUTSTOOD
OUTCLIMB	OUTFLING	OUTLIVED	OUTRINGS	OUTSTRIP
OUTCLOMB	OUTFLOAT	OUTLIVER	OUTRIVAL	OUTSTUDY
OUTCOACH	OUTFLOWN	OUTLIVES	OUTROARS	OUTSTUNT
OUTCOMES	OUTFLOWS	OUTLOOKS	OUTROCKS	OUTSULKS
OUTCOOKS	OUTFLUSH	OUTLOVED	OUTROLLS	OUTSWARE
OUTCOUNT	OUTFOOLS	OUTLOVES	OUTROOPS	OUTSWEAR
OUTCRAWL	OUTFOOTS	OUTLYING	OUTROOTS	OUTSWEEP
OUTCRIED	OUTFOUND	OUTMARCH	OUTROPER	OUTSWELL
OUTCRIES	OUTFOXED	OUTMATCH	OUTROPES	OUTSWEPT
OUTCROPS	OUTFOXES	OUTMODES	OUTROWED	OUTSWIMS
OUTCROSS	OUTFROWN	OUTMOVED	OUTSAILS	OUTSWING
OUTCROWD	OUTGAINS	OUTMOVES	OUTSAVOR	OUTSWORE
OUTCROWS	OUTGASES	OUTNAMED	OUTSCOLD	OUTSWORN
OUTCURSE	OUTGATES	OUTNAMES	OUTSCOOP	OUTSWUNG
OUTCURVE	OUTGAZED	OUTNIGHT	OUTSCORE	OUTTAKEN
OUTDANCE	OUTGAZES	OUTPACED	OUTSCORN	OUTTAKES
OUTDARED	OUTGIVEN	OUTPACES	OUTSELLS	OUTTALKS
OUTDARES	OUTGIVES	OUTPAINT	OUTSERVE	OUTTASKS
OUTDATED	OUTGLARE	OUTPARTS	OUTSHAME	OUTTELLS
OUTDATES	OUTGLEAM	OUTPEEPS	OUTSHINE	OUTTHANK
OUTDODGE	OUTGLOWS	OUTPEERS	OUTSHONE	OUTTHINK
OUTDOERS	OUTGNAWN	OUTPITCH	OUTSHOOT	OUTTHREW
OUTDOING	OUTGNAWS	OUTPLACE	OUTSHOTS	OUTTHROB
OUTDOORS	OUTGOERS	OUTPLANS	OUTSHOUT	OUTTHROW
OUTDRAGS	OUTGOING	OUTPLAYS	OUTSIDER	OUTTOWER
OUTDRANK	OUTGRINS	OUTPLODS	OUTSIDES	OUTTRADE
OUTDRAWN	OUTGROSS	OUTPLOTS	OUTSIGHT	OUTTRICK
OUTDRAWS	OUTGROUP	OUTPOINT	OUTSINGS	OUTTROTS
OUTDREAM	OUTGROWN	OUTPOLLS	OUTSIZED	OUTTRUMP
OUTDRESS	OUTGROWS	OUTPORTS	OUTSIZES	OUTTURNS
OUTDRINK	OUTGUARD	OUTPOSTS	OUTSKATE	OUTVALUE
OUTDRIVE	OUTGUESS	OUTPOURS	OUTSKIRT	OUTVAUNT
OUTDROPS	OUTGUIDE	OUTPOWER	OUTSLEEP	OUTVENOM
OUTDROVE	OUTHAULS	OUTPRAYS	OUTSLEPT	OUTVOICE
OUTDRUNK	OUTHEARD	OUTPREEN	OUTSLICK	OUTVOTED
OUTDUELS	OUTHEARS	OUTPRESS	OUTSMART	OUTVOTER
OUTDURED	OUTHIRED	OUTPRICE	OUTSMELL	OUTVOTES
OUTDURES	OUTHIRES	OUTPRIZE	OUTSMELT	OUTVYING

OUTWAITS	OUTWEARY	OUTWICKS	OUTWORKS	OUTYELLS
OUTWALKS	OUTWEEDS	OUTWILED	OUTWORTH	OUTYELPS
OUTWARDS	OUTWEEPS	OUTWILES	OUTWOUND	OUTYIELD
OUTWASTE	OUTWEIGH	OUTWILLS	OUTWREST	
OUTWATCH	OUTWELLS	OUTWINDS	OUTWRITE	
OUTWEARS	OUTWHIRL	OUTWINGS	OUTWROTE	

Words that begin with OVER-

Seven-letter words	OVERRED	OVERBUYS	OVERFOND	OVERKILL
OVERACT	OVERREN	OVERCALL	OVERFOUL	OVERKIND
OVERAGE	OVERRUN	OVERCAME	OVERFREE	OVERKING
OVERALL	OVERSAD	OVERCAST	OVERFULL	OVERKNEE
OVERAPT	OVERSAW	OVERCLAD	OVERFUND	OVERLADE
OVERARM	OVERSEA	OVERCLOY	OVERGALL	OVERLAID
OVERATE	OVERSEE	OVERCLUB	OVERGANG	OVERLAIN
OVERAWE	OVERSET	OVERCOAT	OVERGAVE	OVERLAND
OVERBED	OVERSEW	OVERCOLD	OVERGEAR	OVERLAPS
OVERBET	OVERSOW	OVERCOME	OVERGETS	OVERLARD
OVERBID	OVERSUP	OVERCOOK	OVERGILD	OVERLATE
OVERBIG	OVERTAX	OVERCOOL	OVERGILT	OVERLAYS
OVERBUY	OVERTIP	OVERCRAM	OVERGIRD	OVERLEAF
OVERCOY	OVERTOP	OVERCRAW	OVERGIRT	OVERLEAP
OVERCUT	OVERUSE	OVERCROP	OVERGIVE	OVERLEND
OVERDID	OVERWET	OVERCROW	OVERGLAD	OVERLENT
OVERDOG		OVERCURE	OVERGOAD	OVERLETS
OVERDRY	**Eight-letter words**	OVERCUTS	OVERGOES	OVERLEWD
OVERDUB		OVERDARE	OVERGONE	OVERLIER
OVERDUE	OVERABLE	OVERDEAR	OVERGREW	OVERLIES
OVERDYE	OVERACTS	OVERDECK	OVERGROW	OVERLIVE
OVEREAT	OVERAGED	OVERDOER	OVERHAIR	OVERLOAD
OVEREGG	OVERAGES	OVERDOES	OVERHALE	OVERLOCK
OVEREYE	OVERALLS	OVERDOGS	OVERHAND	OVERLONG
OVERFAR	OVERARCH	OVERDONE	OVERHANG	OVERLOOK
OVERFAT	OVERARMS	OVERDOSE	OVERHARD	OVERLORD
OVERFED	OVERAWED	OVERDRAW	OVERHATE	OVERLOUD
OVERFIT	OVERAWES	OVERDREW	OVERHAUL	OVERLOVE
OVERFLY	OVERBAKE	OVERDUBS	OVERHEAD	OVERLUSH
OVERGET	OVERBANK	OVERDUST	OVERHEAP	OVERMANS
OVERGOT	OVERBEAR	OVERDYED	OVERHEAR	OVERMANY
OVERHIT	OVERBEAT	OVERDYER	OVERHEAT	OVERMAST
OVERHOT	OVERBETS	OVERDYES	OVERHELD	OVERMEEK
OVERING	OVERBIDS	OVEREASY	OVERHENT	OVERMELT
OVERJOY	OVERBILL	OVEREATS	OVERHIGH	OVERMILD
OVERLAP	OVERBITE	OVEREDIT	OVERHITS	OVERMILK
OVERLAX	OVERBLEW	OVEREGGS	OVERHOLD	OVERMINE
OVERLAY	OVERBLOW	OVEREYED	OVERHOLY	OVERMUCH
OVERLET	OVERBOIL	OVEREYES	OVERHOPE	OVERNAME
OVERLIE	OVERBOLD	OVERFALL	OVERHUNG	OVERNEAR
OVERLIT	OVERBOOK	OVERFAST	OVERHUNT	OVERNEAT
OVERMAN	OVERBOOT	OVERFEAR	OVERHYPE	OVERNETS
OVERMEN	OVERBORE	OVERFEED	OVERIDLE	OVERNICE
OVERMIX	OVERBORN	OVERFELL	OVERJOYS	OVERPACK
OVERNET	OVERBRED	OVERFILL	OVERJUMP	OVERPAGE
OVERNEW	OVERBRIM	OVERFINE	OVERJUST	OVERPAID
OVERPAY	OVERBROW	OVERFISH	OVERKEEN	OVERPART
OVERPLY	OVERBULK	OVERFLEW	OVERKEEP	OVERPASS
OVERRAN	OVERBURN	OVERFLOW	OVERKEPT	OVERPAST
	OVERBUSY	OVERFOLD	OVERKEST	OVERPAYS

OVERPEER	OVERRUFF	OVERSLIP	OVERTAME	OVERWARM
OVERPERT	OVERRULE	OVERSLOW	OVERTART	OVERWARY
OVERPLAN	OVERRUNS	OVERSOAK	OVERTASK	OVERWASH
OVERPLAY	OVERSAIL	OVERSOFT	OVERTEEM	OVERWEAK
OVERPLOT	OVERSALE	OVERSOLD	OVERTHIN	OVERWEAR
OVERPLUS	OVERSALT	OVERSOON	OVERTIME	OVERWEEN
OVERPOST	OVERSAVE	OVERSOUL	OVERTIPS	OVERWENT
OVERPUMP	OVERSEAS	OVERSOWN	OVERTIRE	OVERWETS
OVERRACK	OVERSEED	OVERSOWS	OVERTOIL	OVERWIDE
OVERRAKE	OVERSEEN	OVERSPIN	OVERTONE	OVERWILY
OVERRANK	OVERSEER	OVERSTAY	OVERTOOK	OVERWIND
OVERRASH	OVERSEES	OVERSTEP	OVERTOPS	OVERWING
OVERRATE	OVERSELL	OVERSTIR	OVERTRIM	OVERWISE
OVERREAD	OVERSETS	OVERSUDS	OVERTRIP	OVERWORD
OVERREDS	OVERSEWN	OVERSUPS	OVERTURN	OVERWORE
OVERRENS	OVERSEWS	OVERSURE	OVERTYPE	OVERWORK
OVERRICH	OVERSHOE	OVERSWAM	OVERURGE	OVERWORN
OVERRIDE	OVERSHOT	OVERSWAY	OVERUSED	OVERWRAP
OVERRIFE	OVERSICK	OVERSWIM	OVERUSES	OVERYEAR
OVERRIPE	OVERSIDE	OVERSWUM	OVERVEIL	OVERZEAL
OVERRODE	OVERSIZE	OVERTAKE	OVERVIEW	
OVERRUDE	OVERSKIP	OVERTALK	OVERVOTE	

Words that begin with PER-

Seven-letter words	PERJURE	PERSONS	PERCOLIN	PEROXIDS
PERACID	PERJURY	PERSUED	PERDURED	PERPENDS
PERAEON	PERKIER	PERSUES	PERDURES	PERPENTS
PERCASE	PERKING	PERTAIN	PERFORCE	PERRADII
PERCENT	PERKINS	PERTAKE	PERFORMS	PERSALTS
PERCHER	PERKISH	PERTEST	PERFUMED	PERSAUNT
PERCINE	PERLITE	PERTOOK	PERFUMER	PERSEITY
PERCUSS	PERLOUS	PERUKES	PERFUMES	PERSISTS
PERDUES	PERMING	PERUSED	PERFUSED	PERSPIRE
PERDURE	PERMUTE	PERUSER	PERFUSES	PERSPIRY
PEREGAL	PERNODS	PERUSES	PERIODIC	PERSUING
PEREONS	PERORAL	PERVADE	PERIODID	PERTAINS
PERFINS	PEROXID	PERVERT	PERISHES	PERTAKEN
PERFORM	PERPEND	PERVIER	PERLITES	PERTAKES
PERFUME	PERPENT		PERMEANT	PERUSERS
PERFUMY	PERPLEX	**Eight-letter words**	PERMEASE	PERUSING
PERFUSE	PERSALT	PERACIDS	PERMUTED	PERVADED
PERHAPS	PERSANT	PERACUTE	PERMUTES	PERVADES
PERICON	PERSING	PERAEONS	PERNANCY	PERVERSE
PERJINK	PERSIST	PERCENTS	PERORATE	PERVERTS
			PEROXIDE	

Words that begin with PRE-

Seven-letter words	PREARMS	PREBOOK	PRECODE	PREDICT
PREACED	PREAVER	PREBOOM	PRECOOK	PREDIED
PREACES	PREBADE	PREBORN	PRECOOL	PREDIES
PREACHY	PREBAKE	PREBUYS	PRECOUP	PREDIVE
PREACTS	PREBEND	PRECAST	PRECURE	PREDOOM
PREAGED	PREBIDS	PRECAVA	PRECUTS	PREDUSK
PREAMPS	PREBILL	PRECEDE	PREDATE	PREEDIT
PREANAL	PREBIND	PRECENT	PREDAWN	PREEMPT
	PREBOIL	PRECESS	PREDIAL	PREEVES

PREFABS	PRESTED	PREBUILT	PREGUIDE	PRESCUTA
PREFACE	PRETAPE	PRECASTS	PREHEATS	PRESELLS
PREFADE	PRETEEN	PRECEDED	PREHENDS	PRESENTS
PREFARD	PRETELL	PRECEDES	PREHUMAN	PRESERVE
PREFILE	PRETEND	PRECENTS	PREJUDGE	PRESHAPE
PREFIRE	PRETERM	PRECHECK	PRELEGAL	PRESHIPS
PREFORM	PRETEST	PRECHILL	PRELIMIT	PRESHOWN
PREFUND	PRETEXT	PRECHOSE	PRELIVES	PRESHOWS
PREGAME	PRETOLD	PRECINCT	PRELOADS	PRESIDED
PREHEAT	PRETORS	PRECITED	PRELOVED	PRESIDER
PREHEND	PRETRIM	PRECLEAN	PRELUDES	PRESIDES
PREJINK	PRETYPE	PRECLEAR	PRELUNCH	PRESIFTS
PRELACY	PREVAIL	PRECODED	PREMEDIC	PRESLEEP
PRELATE	PREVENT	PRECODES	PREMISES	PRESLICE
PRELIFE	PREVERB	PRECOOKS	PREMIXED	PRESOAKS
PRELOAD	PREVIEW	PRECOOLS	PREMIXES	PRESOLVE
PRELUDE	PREVISE	PRECRASH	PREMOLAR	PRESORTS
PREMADE	PREWARM	PRECURED	PREMOLDS	PRESPLIT
PREMEAL	PREWARN	PRECURES	PREMORAL	PRESTAMP
PREMEDS	PREWASH	PRECURSE	PREMORSE	PRESTING
PREMEET	PREWIRE	PREDATED	PREMOVED	PRESTORE
PREMISE	PREWORK	PREDATES	PREMOVES	PRETAPED
PREMISS	PREWORN	PREDAWNS	PRENAMES	PRETAPES
PREMIXT	PREWRAP	PREDEATH	PRENASAL	PRETASTE
PREMOLD	PREWYNS	PREDIALS	PRENATAL	PRETEENS
PREMOLT		PREDICTS	PRENOMEN	PRETELLS
PREMOVE	**Eight-letter**	PREDOOMS	PREORDER	PRETENDS
PRENAME	**words**	PREDRAFT	PREOWNED	PRETENSE
PRENEED	PREACHED	PREDRIED	PREPACKS	PRETERMS
PRENOON	PREACHES	PREDRIES	PREPARED	PRETESTS
PREORAL	PREACING	PREDRILL	PREPARER	PRETEXTS
PREPACK	PREACTED	PREDUSKS	PREPARES	PRETONIC
PREPAID	PREADAPT	PREDYING	PREPASTE	PRETRAIN
PREPARE	PREADMIT	PREEDITS	PREPAVED	PRETREAT
PREPAVE	PREADOPT	PREELECT	PREPAVES	PRETRIAL
PREPAYS	PREADULT	PREEMPTS	PREPLACE	PRETRIMS
PREPILL	PREALLOT	PREENACT	PREPLANS	PRETYPED
PREPLAN	PREALTER	PREERECT	PREPLANT	PRETYPES
PREPONE	PREAMBLE	PREEXIST	PREPONES	PREUNION
PREPOSE	PREAPPLY	PREFACED	PREPOSED	PREUNITE
PREPUCE	PREARMED	PREFACER	PREPOSES	PREVAILS
PREPUPA	PREASSES	PREFACES	PREPRESS	PREVALUE
PRERACE	PREAUDIT	PREFADED	PREPRICE	PREVENTS
PRERIOT	PREAVERS	PREFADES	PREPRINT	PREVERBS
PREROCK	PREAXIAL	PREFIGHT	PREPUBES	PREVIEWS
PRESAGE	PREBAKED	PREFILED	PREPUBIS	PREVISED
PRESALE	PREBAKES	PREFILES	PREPUCES	PREVISES
PRESELL	PREBASAL	PREFIRED	PREPUNCH	PREVISIT
PRESENT	PREBENDS	PREFIRES	PREPUPAE	PREVISOR
PRESETS	PREBILLS	PREFIXED	PREPUPAL	PREWARMS
PRESHIP	PREBINDS	PREFIXES	PREPUPAS	PREWARNS
PRESHOW	PREBIRTH	PREFLAME	PRERADIO	PREWEIGH
PRESIDE	PREBLESS	PREFOCUS	PRERENAL	PREWIRED
PRESIFT	PREBOARD	PREFORMS	PRERINSE	PREWIRES
PRESOAK	PREBOILS	PREFRANK	PRESAGER	PREWORKS
PRESOLD	PREBOOKS	PREFROZE	PRESAGES	PREWRAPS
PRESONG	PREBOUND	PREFUNDS	PRESALES	
PRESORT	PREBUILD	PREGAMES	PRESCORE	

Words that begin with PRO-

Seven-letter words

PROBALL
PROBAND
PROBANG
PROBATE
PROBING
PROBITS
PROCARP
PROCESS
PROCURE
PRODRUG
PRODUCE
PRODUCT
PROFACE
PROFANE
PROFESS
PROFILE
PROFITS
PROFUSE
PROGRAM
PROJETS
PROKING
PROLATE
PROLEGS
PROLINE
PROLING
PROLOGS
PROLONG
PROMINE
PROMISE
PROMOTE

PRONAOI
PRONAOS
PRONEST
PRONOTA
PRONOUN
PROOTIC
PROPAGE
PROPALE
PROPANE
PROPELS
PROPEND
PROPENE
PROPINE
PROPONE
PROPOSE
PRORATE
PROSAIC
PROSECT
PROSERS
PROSING
PROSOMA
PROSTIE
PROTEAS
PROTEIN
PROTEND
PROTEST
PROTONS
PROTORE
PROVANT
PROVEND
PROVERB
PROVERS

PROVIDE
PROVINE
PROWEST

Eight-letter words

PROBANDS
PROBANGS
PROBATED
PROBATES
PROCARPS
PROCHAIN
PROCINCT
PROCLAIM
PROCURED
PROCURER
PROCURES
PRODROME
PRODRUGS
PRODUCES
PRODUCTS
PROFANES
PROFILED
PROFILER
PROFILES
PROFOUND
PROGRADE
PROGRAMS
PROLABOR
PROLAPSE
PROLATED
PROLINES

PROLONGE
PROLONGS
PROMETAL
PROMINES
PROMISER
PROMISES
PROMOTED
PROMOTES
PROMOTOR
PRONATES
PRONOTAL
PRONOTUM
PRONOUNS
PROPAGED
PROPAGES
PROPALED
PROPALES
PROPANES
PROPENAL
PROPENDS
PROPENES
PROPHAGE
PROPHASE
PROPINED
PROPINES
PROPOLIS
PROPONES
PROPOSED
PROPOSER
PROPOSES
PROPOUND
PROPYLON

PRORATED
PRORATES
PROROGUE
PROSAIST
PROSECCO
PROSECTS
PROSEMEN
PROSINGS
PROSODIC
PROSOMAS
PROSTATE
PROSTIES
PROSTYLE
PROTAMIN
PROTEASE
PROTEINS
PROTENDS
PROTENSE
PROTESTS
PROTONIC
PROTORES
PROTRACT
PROTRADE
PROUNION
PROVENDS
PROVERBS
PROVINED
PROVINES
PROVIRAL
PROVIRUS
PROVISOR

Words that begin with RE-

Seven-letter words

REACHED
REACHES
REACTED
REACTOR
READAPT
READDED
READMIT
READOPT
READORN
REAFFIX
REAGENT
REAKING
REALIGN
REALIST
REALLOT
REALTER
REAMEND
REANNEX
REAPERS
REAPING

REAPPLY
REARGUE
REARISE
REARMED
REAROSE
REAVAIL
REAVERS
REAVOWS
REAWAKE
REAWOKE
REBACKS
REBADGE
REBAITS
REBATED
REBATES
REBECKS
REBEGAN
REBEGIN
REBEGUN
REBILLS
REBINDS
REBIRTH

REBITES
REBLEND
REBLENT
REBLOOM
REBOARD
REBOILS
REBOOKS
REBOOTS
REBORED
REBORES
REBOUND
REBOZOS
REBRACE
REBRAND
REBREED
REBUFFS
REBUILD
REBUILT
REBUKES
REBUSES
RECALLS
RECANED

RECANES
RECANTS
RECARRY
RECASTS
RECATCH
RECEDED
RECEDES
RECENSE
RECHART
RECHEAT
RECHECK
RECHEWS
RECHIPS
RECHOSE
RECITAL
RECITED
RECITER
RECITES
RECLADS
RECLAIM
RECLAME
RECLASP

RECLEAN
RECLIMB
RECLINE
RECLOSE
RECOALS
RECOATS
RECOCKS
RECODED
RECODES
RECOILS
RECOINS
RECOLOR
RECOMBS
RECOOKS
RECORDS
RECORKS
RECOUNT
RECOUPE
RECOUPS
RECOURE
RECOVER
RECOWER

RECRATE	REFINDS	REHANGS	REMATCH	REPLIED
RECROSS	REFINED	REHEARD	REMATED	REPLIER
RECROWN	REFINER	REHEARS	REMATES	REPLIES
RECURED	REFINES	REHEATS	REMEADS	REPLOTS
RECURES	REFIRED	REHEELS	REMEETS	REPLOWS
RECURVE	REFIRES	REHINGE	REMELTS	REPLUMB
RECYCLE	REFIXED	REHIRED	REMENDS	REPOINT
REDATED	REFIXES	REHIRES	REMERCY	REPOLLS
REDATES	REFLAGS	REHOMED	REMERGE	REPONES
REDEALS	REFLIES	REHOMES	REMINDS	REPORTS
REDEALT	REFLOAT	REHOUSE	REMINTS	REPOSED
REDEARS	REFLOOD	REIMAGE	REMISES	REPOSER
REDEEMS	REFLOWN	REINCUR	REMIXED	REPOSES
REDIALS	REFLOWS	REINDEX	REMIXES	REPOSIT
REDOCKS	REFOCUS	REINKED	REMODEL	REPOSTS
REDOING	REFOLDS	REINTER	REMOLDS	REPOURS
REDOUBT	REFOOTS	REISSUE	REMORAS	REPOWER
REDOUTS	REFORGE	REJOINS	REMORSE	REPRESS
REDRAFT	REFORMS	REJONES	REMOTES	REPRICE
REDRAWN	REFOUND	REJUDGE	REMOULD	REPRIME
REDRAWS	REFRACT	REKEYED	REMOUNT	REPRINT
REDREAM	REFRAME	REKNITS	REMOVED	REPRISE
REDRESS	REFRESH	REKNOTS	REMOVER	REPRIZE
REDRIED	REFRIED	RELABEL	REMOVES	REPROBE
REDRIES	REFRIES	RELACED	RENAILS	REPROOF
REDRILL	REFRONT	RELACES	RENAMED	REPROVE
REDRIVE	REFROZE	RELANDS	RENAMES	REPULPS
REDROVE	REFUELS	RELAPSE	RENESTS	REPULSE
REDUCES	REFUNDS	RELATED	RENEWED	REPUMPS
REDUITS	REFUSED	RELATER	RENEWER	REPURED
REEARNS	REFUSES	RELAXER	RENYING	REPURES
REECHED	REGAINS	RELAXES	REOCCUR	REQUEST
REECHES	REGALES	RELAYED	REOFFER	REQUINS
REEDIFY	REGALLY	RELEARN	REOILED	REQUIRE
REEDITS	REGAUGE	RELEASE	REOPENS	REQUITE
REEJECT	REGEARS	RELENDS	REORDER	REQUITS
REEKING	REGENTS	RELEVES	REPACKS	REQUOTE
REELECT	REGESTS	RELIEFS	REPAINT	RERACKS
REELMEN	REGIFTS	RELIERS	REPAIRS	RERAILS
REEMITS	REGILDS	RELIEVE	REPANEL	RERAISE
REENACT	REGIVEN	RELIGHT	REPAPER	REREADS
REENDOW	REGIVES	RELINED	REPARKS	REREDOS
REENJOY	REGLAZE	RELINES	REPASTS	RERENTS
REENTER	REGLOSS	RELINKS	REPATCH	RERISEN
REENTRY	REGLOWS	RELISTS	REPAVED	RERISES
REEQUIP	REGLUED	RELIVED	REPAVES	REROLLS
REERECT	REGLUES	RELIVER	REPEALS	REROOFS
REEVOKE	REGORGE	RELIVES	REPEATS	REROUTE
REEXPEL	REGRADE	RELOADS	REPENTS	RESAILS
REFACED	REGRAFT	RELOANS	REPERKS	RESALES
REFACES	REGRANT	RELOCKS	REPINED	RESAWED
REFALLS	REGRATE	RELOOKS	REPINES	RESCALE
REFEEDS	REGREEN	RELYING	REPIQUE	RESCORE
REFEELS	REGREET	REMAILS	REPLACE	RESEALS
REFENCE	REGRIND	REMAINS	REPLANS	RESEATS
REFIGHT	REGROOM	REMAKER	REPLANT	RESECTS
REFILED	REGROUP	REMAKES	REPLATE	RESEEDS
REFILES	REGROWN	REMANET	REPLAYS	RESEEKS
REFILLS	REGROWS	REMARKS	REPLEAD	RESEIZE
REFILMS	REGULAR	REMARRY	REPLICA	RESELLS

RESENDS	RESTING	RETURFS	REWRITE	REAWAKED
RESENTS	RESTIVE	RETURNS	REWROTE	REAWAKEN
RESERVE	RESTOCK	RETWIST	REZEROS	REAWAKES
RESEWED	RESTOKE	RETYING	REZONED	REAWOKEN
RESHAPE	RESTORE	RETYPED	REZONES	REBACKED
RESHAVE	RESTUDY	RETYPES		REBADGED
RESHINE	RESTUFF	REUNIFY	**Eight-letter**	REBADGES
RESHIPS	RESTUMP	REUNION	**words**	REBAITED
RESHOED	RESTYLE	REUNITE	REABSORB	REBATING
RESHOES	RESURGE	REURGED	REACCEDE	REBEGINS
RESHONE	RETABLE	REURGES	REACCENT	REBELLED
RESHOOT	RETACKS	REUSING	REACCEPT	REBELLOW
RESHOWN	RETAILS	REUTTER	REACCUSE	REBIDDEN
RESHOWS	RETAINS	REVALUE	REACHING	REBILLED
RESIDED	RETAKEN	REVAMPS	REACTANT	REBIRTHS
RESIDER	RETAKER	REVEALS	REACTING	REBITING
RESIDES	RETAKES	REVENGE	REACTION	REBITTEN
RESIFTS	RETALLY	REVENUE	REACTIVE	REBLENDS
RESIGHT	RETAPED	REVERBS	REACTORS	REBLOOMS
RESIGNS	RETAPES	REVERSE	READAPTS	REBOARDS
RESILED	RETASTE	REVERSO	READDICT	REBODIED
RESILES	RETAXED	REVERTS	READDING	REBODIES
RESINED	RETAXES	REVESTS	READJUST	REBOILED
RESISTS	RETEACH	REVIEWS	READMITS	REBOOKED
RESITED	RETEAMS	REVILER	READOPTS	REBOOTED
RESITES	RETEARS	REVISED	READORNS	REBORING
RESIZED	RETELLS	REVISES	READVISE	REBORROW
RESIZES	RETENES	REVISIT	REAFFIRM	REBOTTLE
RESKEWS	RETESTS	REVISOR	REAGENCY	REBOUGHT
RESKILL	RETHINK	REVIVER	REAGENTS	REBOUNDS
RESLATE	RETILED	REVIVES	REALIGNS	REBRACED
RESMELT	RETILES	REVOICE	REALLIED	REBRACES
RESOAKS	RETIMED	REVOLTS	REALLIES	REBRANCH
RESOLED	RETIMES	REVOLVE	REALLOTS	REBRANDS
RESOLES	RETINAS	REVOTED	REALTERS	REBREEDS
RESOLVE	RETINES	REVOTES	REAMENDS	REBUFFED
RESORBS	RETINTS	REVYING	REANOINT	REBUILDS
RESORTS	RETIRED	REWAKED	REANSWER	REBURIAL
RESOUND	RETIRES	REWAKEN	REAPPEAR	REBURIED
RESOWED	RETITLE	REWAKES	REARGUED	REBURIES
RESPACE	RETOOLS	REWARDS	REARGUES	REBUTTED
RESPADE	RETORTS	REWARMS	REARISEN	REBUTTER
RESPEAK	RETOTAL	REWATER	REARISES	REBUTTON
RESPELL	RETOUCH	REWAXED	REARMING	REBUYING
RESPELT	RETOURS	REWAXES	REAROUSE	RECALLED
RESPIRE	RETRACE	REWEARS	REARREST	RECALLER
RESPITE	RETRACK	REWEAVE	REASCEND	RECANING
RESPLIT	RETRACT	REWEIGH	REASCENT	RECANTED
RESPOKE	RETRAIN	REWELDS	REASSAIL	RECANTER
RESPOOL	RETRAIT	REWIDEN	REASSERT	RECAPPED
RESPOTS	RETREAD	REWINDS	REASSESS	RECAPTOR
RESPRAY	RETREAT	REWIRED	REASSIGN	RECARPET
RESTACK	RETREES	REWIRES	REASSORT	RECAUGHT
RESTAFF	RETRIAL	REWOKEN	REASSUME	RECEDING
RESTAGE	RETRIED	REWORDS	REASSURE	RECEMENT
RESTAMP	RETRIES	REWORKS	REATTACH	RECENSED
RESTART	RETRIMS	REWOUND	REATTACK	RECENSES
RESTATE	RETUNDS	REWOVEN	REATTAIN	RECENSOR
RESTEMS	RETUNED	REWRAPS	REAVAILS	RECENTER
RESTIFF	RETUNES	REWRAPT	REAVOWED	RECENTRE

RECESSED	RECURVES	REEVOKES	REGAUGES	REINJURY
RECESSES	RECYCLED	REEXPELS	REGEARED	REINKING
RECHANGE	RECYCLER	REEXPORT	REGELATE	REINSERT
RECHARGE	RECYCLES	REEXPOSE	REGIFTED	REINSTAL
RECHARTS	REDAMAGE	REFACING	REGILDED	REINSURE
RECHEATS	REDATING	REFALLEN	REGIVING	REINTERS
RECHECKS	REDECIDE	REFASTEN	REGLAZED	REINVADE
RECHEWED	REDEEMED	REFELLED	REGLAZES	REINVENT
RECHOOSE	REDEFEAT	REFENCED	REGLOWED	REINVEST
RECHOSEN	REDEFECT	REFENCES	REGLUING	REINVITE
RECIRCLE	REDEFIED	REFIGHTS	REGORGED	REINVOKE
RECITALS	REDEFIES	REFIGURE	REGORGES	REISSUED
RECITERS	REDEFINE	REFILING	REGRADED	REISSUER
RECITING	REDEMAND	REFILLED	REGRADES	REISSUES
RECLAIMS	REDENIED	REFILMED	REGRAFTS	REJACKET
RECLAMES	REDENIES	REFILTER	REGRANTS	REJIGGED
RECLASPS	REDEPLOY	REFINERS	REGRATED	REJIGGER
RECLEANS	REDESIGN	REFINERY	REGRATER	REJOINED
RECLIMBS	REDIALED	REFINING	REGRATES	REJUDGED
RECLINES	REDIGEST	REFINISH	REGREENS	REJUDGES
RECLOSED	REDIPPED	REFIRING	REGREETS	REJUGGLE
RECLOSES	REDIRECT	REFITTED	REGRINDS	REKEYING
RECLOTHE	REDISTIL	REFIXING	REGROOMS	REKINDLE
RECOALED	REDIVIDE	REFLEXED	REGROOVE	RELABELS
RECOATED	REDOCKED	REFLEXES	REGROUND	RELACHES
RECOCKED	REDOLENT	REFLOATS	REGROUPS	RELACING
RECODIFY	REDONNED	REFLOODS	REGROWTH	RELANDED
RECODING	REDOUBLE	REFLOWED	REHAMMER	RELAPSED
RECOILED	REDOUBTS	REFLOWER	REHANDLE	RELAPSER
RECOILER	REDRAFTS	REFLUENT	REHANGED	RELAPSES
RECOINED	REDRAWER	REFLUXED	REHARDEN	RELAUNCH
RECOLLET	REDREAMS	REFLUXES	REHASHED	RELAYING
RECOLORS	REDREAMT	REFLYING	REHASHES	RELEARNS
RECOMBED	REDRILLS	REFOLDED	REHEARSE	RELEARNT
RECOMMIT	REDRIVEN	REFOOTED	REHEATED	RELEASED
RECONFER	REDRIVES	REFOREST	REHEATER	RELEASER
RECONNED	REDRYING	REFORGED	REHEELED	RELEASES
RECONVEY	REDUBBED	REFORGES	REHEMMED	RELEGATE
RECOOKED	REDYEING	REFORMAT	REHINGED	RELETTER
RECOPIED	REEARNED	REFORMED	REHINGES	RELEVANT
RECOPIES	REECHING	REFORMER	REHIRING	RELIABLE
RECORDED	REECHOED	REFOUGHT	REHOMING	RELIEVER
RECORDER	REECHOES	REFOUNDS	REHOUSED	RELIEVES
RECORKED	REEDITED	REFRACTS	REHOUSES	RELIGHTS
RECOUNTS	REEJECTS	REFRAMED	REIGNITE	RELINING
RECOUPED	REELECTS	REFRAMES	REILLUME	RELINKED
RECOUPLE	REEMBARK	REFREEZE	REIMAGED	RELISTED
RECOURED	REEMBODY	REFRINGE	REIMAGES	RELIVERS
RECOURES	REEMERGE	REFRONTS	REIMPORT	RELIVING
RECOURSE	REEMPLOY	REFROZEN	REIMPOSE	RELOADED
RECOVERS	REENACTS	REFRYING	REINCITE	RELOADER
RECOWERS	REENDOWS	REFUELED	REINCURS	RELOANED
RECRATED	REENGAGE	REFUNDED	REINDICT	RELOCATE
RECRATES	REENJOYS	REFUNDER	REINDUCE	RELOCKED
RECREANT	REENLIST	REFUSING	REINDUCT	RELOOKED
RECREATE	REENROLL	REFUSION	REINFECT	RELUCENT
RECROWNS	REENTERS	REGAINED	REINFORM	RELUMINE
RECURING	REEQUIPS	REGAINER	REINFUSE	REMAILED
RECURRED	REERECTS	REGATHER	REINJECT	REMAINED
RECURVED	REEVOKED	REGAUGED	REINJURE	REMAKERS

REMAKING	REPAPERS	REPROVER	RESELECT	RESPADED
REMANENT	REPARKED	REPROVES	RESELLER	RESPADES
REMANIES	REPASSED	REPUBLIC	RESEMBLE	RESPEAKS
REMANNED	REPASSES	REPULPED	RESENTED	RESPELLS
REMAPPED	REPASTED	REPULSED	RESERVED	RESPIRED
REMARKED	REPAVING	REPULSER	RESERVER	RESPIRES
REMARKER	REPAYING	REPULSES	RESERVES	RESPITED
REMARKET	REPEALED	REPUMPED	RESETTER	RESPITES
REMARQUE	REPEGGED	REPURIFY	RESETTLE	RESPLICE
REMASTER	REPEOPLE	REPURING	RESEWING	RESPLITS
REMATING	REPERKED	REPURSUE	RESHAPED	RESPOKEN
REMEDIAL	REPERUSE	REQUESTS	RESHAPER	RESPOOLS
REMELTED	REPHRASE	REQUIGHT	RESHAPES	RESPRANG
REMEMBER	REPINING	REQUIRED	RESHAVED	RESPRAYS
REMENDED	REPINNED	REQUIRES	RESHAVEN	RESPREAD
REMERGED	REPIQUED	REQUITED	RESHAVES	RESPRING
REMERGES	REPIQUES	REQUITES	RESHINED	RESPROUT
REMINDED	REPLACED	REQUOTED	RESHINES	RESPRUNG
REMINDER	REPLACER	REQUOTES	RESHOOTS	RESTABLE
REMINTED	REPLACES	RERACKED	RESHOWED	RESTACKS
REMIXING	REPLANTS	RERAILED	RESHOWER	RESTAFFS
REMODELS	REPLATED	RERAISED	RESIDERS	RESTAGED
REMODIFY	REPLATES	RERAISES	RESIDING	RESTAGES
REMOLDED	REPLAYED	RERECORD	RESIFTED	RESTAMPS
REMORSES	REPLEADS	REREMIND	RESIGHTS	RESTARTS
REMOTION	REPLEDGE	RERENTED	RESIGNED	RESTATED
REMOULDS	REPLIERS	REREPEAT	RESIGNER	RESTATES
REMOUNTS	REPLOWED	REREVIEW	RESILING	RESTINGS
REMOVERS	REPLUMBS	REREVISE	RESILVER	RESTITCH
REMOVING	REPLUNGE	REREWARD	RESINING	RESTOCKS
REMURMUR	REPLYING	RERIGGED	RESISTED	RESTOKED
RENAILED	REPOINTS	RERISING	RESISTER	RESTOKES
RENAMING	REPOLISH	REROLLED	RESITING	RESTORED
RENATURE	REPOLLED	REROLLER	RESIZING	RESTORER
RENEGATE	REPORTED	REROOFED	RESKETCH	RESTORES
RENESTED	REPORTER	REROUTED	RESKEWED	RESTRAIN
RENEWING	REPOSERS	REROUTES	RESKILLS	RESTRESS
RENOTIFY	REPOSING	RESADDLE	RESLATED	RESTRICT
RENOVATE	REPOSITS	RESAILED	RESLATES	RESTRIKE
RENUMBER	REPOSTED	RESALUTE	RESMELTS	RESTRING
REOBJECT	REPOTTED	RESAMPLE	RESMOOTH	RESTRIVE
REOBTAIN	REPOURED	RESAWING	RESOAKED	RESTROVE
REOCCUPY	REPOUSSE	RESAYING	RESODDED	RESTRUCK
REOCCURS	REPOWERS	RESCALED	RESOFTEN	RESTRUNG
REOFFEND	REPREEVE	RESCALES	RESOLDER	RESTUFFS
REOFFERS	REPRICED	RESCHOOL	RESOLING	RESTUMPS
REOILING	REPRICES	RESCORED	RESOLUTE	RESTYLED
REOPENED	REPRIEFE	RESCORES	RESOLVED	RESTYLES
REOPENER	REPRIEVE	RESCREEN	RESOLVER	RESUBMIT
REOPPOSE	REPRIMED	RESCRIPT	RESOLVES	RESUMMON
REORDAIN	REPRIMES	RESCULPT	RESONANT	RESUPINE
REORDERS	REPRINTS	RESEALED	RESORBED	RESUPPLY
REORIENT	REPRISED	RESEARCH	RESORTED	RESURGED
REOUTFIT	REPRISES	RESEASON	RESORTER	RESURGES
REPACIFY	REPRIZED	RESEATED	RESOUGHT	RESURVEY
REPACKED	REPRIZES	RESECURE	RESOUNDS	RETABLES
REPAINTS	REPROBED	RESEEDED	RESOURCE	RETACKED
REPAIRED	REPROBES	RESEEING	RESOWING	RETACKLE
REPAIRER	REPROOFS	RESEIZED	RESPACED	RETAGGED
REPANELS	REPROVED	RESEIZES	RESPACES	RETAILED

RETAILER	RETOOLED	REUNITED	REVERSOS	REWARDER
RETAILOR	RETOTALS	REUNITER	REVERTED	REWARMED
RETAKERS	RETOURED	REUNITES	REVESTED	REWASHED
RETAKING	RETRACED	REUPTAKE	REVESTRY	REWASHES
RETAPING	RETRACER	REURGING	REVETTED	REWATERS
RETARGET	RETRACES	REUSABLE	REVIEWED	REWAXING
RETASTED	RETRACKS	REUTTERS	REVIEWER	REWEAVED
RETASTES	RETRACTS	REVALUED	REVISING	REWEAVES
RETAUGHT	RETRAINS	REVALUES	REVISION	REWEDDED
RETAXING	RETRAITS	REVAMPED	REVISITS	REWEIGHS
RETEAMED	RETREADS	REVAMPER	REVISORS	REWELDED
RETELLER	RETREATS	REVEALED	REVIVERS	REWETTED
RETEMPER	RETRENCH	REVEALER	REVIVIFY	REWIDENS
RETESTED	RETRIALS	REVENGED	REVOICED	REWINDED
RETHINKS	RETRYING	REVENGER	REVOICES	REWINDER
RETHREAD	RETUNDED	REVENGES	REVOLTED	REWIRING
RETIEING	RETUNING	REVENUES	REVOLUTE	REWORDED
RETILING	RETURFED	REVERIFY	REVOLVED	REWORKED
RETIMING	RETURNED	REVERIST	REVOLVES	REWRITER
RETINTED	RETURNER	REVERSAL	REVOTING	REWRITES
RETIRING	RETWISTS	REVERSED	REWAKENS	REZEROED
RETITLED	RETYPING	REVERSER	REWAKING	REZEROES
RETITLES	REUNIONS	REVERSES	REWARDED	REZONING

Words that begin with RED-

Seven-letter words	REDFINS	REDROVE	REDBONES	REDRIVEN
REDACTS	REDFISH	REDSEAR	REDBRICK	REDRIVES
REDATES	REDFOOT	REDSKIN	REDCOATS	REDROOTS
REDBACK	REDHEAD	REDTAIL	REDDINGS	REDSHANK
REDBAIT	REDLEGS	REDTOPS	REDFOOTS	REDSHARE
REDBAYS	REDLINE	REDWARE	REDHEADS	REDSHIFT
REDBIRD	REDNECK	REDWING	REDHORSE	REDSHIRE
REDBONE	REDNESS	REDWOOD	REDLINED	REDSHIRT
REDBUDS	REDOUTS		REDLINER	REDSHORT
REDBUGS	REDOXES	**Eight-letter**	REDLINES	REDSKINS
REDCAPS	REDPOLL	**words**	REDNECKS	REDSTART
REDCOAT	REDRAFT	REDACTED	REDOLENT	REDTAILS
REDDENS	REDRAWN	REDACTOR	REDONNED	REDWARES
REDDING	REDRAWS	REDARGUE	REDPOLLS	REDWATER
REDDISH	REDREAM	REDBACKS	REDRAFTS	REDWINGS
REDEARS	REDRILL	REDBAITS	REDRAWER	REDWOODS
REDEYES	REDRIVE	REDBELLY	REDREAMS	
	REDROOT	REDBIRDS	REDRILLS	

Words that begin with SEA-

Seven-letter words	SEAFOWL	SEAMARK	SEATING	Eight-letter words
SEABAGS	SEAGIRT	SEAMING	SEAWALL	SEABANKS
SEABANK	SEAGULL	SEAPORT	SEAWANS	SEABEACH
SEABEDS	SEAHAWK	SEARATS	SEAWANT	SEABIRDS
SEABIRD	SEAHOGS	SEAREST	SEAWARD	SEABLITE
SEABOOT	SEAKALE	SEARING	SEAWARE	SEABOARD
SEACOCK	SEALANT	SEASICK	SEAWAYS	SEABOOTS
SEADOGS	SEALIFT	SEASIDE	SEAWEED	SEABORNE
SEAFOLK	SEALINE	SEASING	SEAWIFE	SEACOAST
SEAFOOD	SEALING	SEASONS	SEAWORM	SEACOCKS
	SEAMAID	SEASURE	SEAZING	

SEACRAFT	SEAHAWKS	SEAMARKS	SEASCOUT	SEAWANTS
SEADROME	SEAHORSE	SEAMINGS	SEASHELL	SEAWARDS
SEAFARER	SEAHOUND	SEAMOUNT	SEASHORE	SEAWARES
SEAFLOOR	SEAKALES	SEAPIECE	SEASIDES	SEAWATER
SEAFOLKS	SEALANTS	SEAPLANE	SEASPEAK	SEAWEEDS
SEAFOODS	SEALIFTS	SEAPORTS	SEASURES	SEAWIVES
SEAFOWLS	SEALINES	SEAQUAKE	SEATINGS	SEAWOMAN
SEAFRONT	SEALINGS	SEARINGS	SEATRAIN	SEAWOMEN
SEAGOING	SEAMAIDS	SEAROBIN	SEATROUT	SEAWORMS
SEAGULLS	SEAMANLY	SEASCAPE	SEAWALLS	

Words that begin with SUB-

Seven-letter words	SUBOVAL	SUBBASAL	SUBGENUS	SUBSALES
	SUBPART	SUBBASES	SUBGOALS	SUBSCALE
SUBACID	SUBPLOT	SUBBASIN	SUBGRADE	SUBSECTS
SUBACTS	SUBRACE	SUBBINGS	SUBGRAPH	SUBSENSE
SUBALAR	SUBRENT	SUBBLOCK	SUBGROUP	SUBSERES
SUBAQUA	SUBRING	SUBBREED	SUBHEADS	SUBSERVE
SUBAREA	SUBRULE	SUBCASTE	SUBHUMAN	SUBSHAFT
SUBARID	SUBSALE	SUBCAUSE	SUBHUMID	SUBSHELL
SUBATOM	SUBSECT	SUBCELLS	SUBIDEAS	SUBSHRUB
SUBBASE	SUBSERE	SUBCHIEF	SUBIMAGO	SUBSIDED
SUBBASS	SUBSETS	SUBCHORD	SUBINDEX	SUBSIDER
SUBBING	SUBSIDE	SUBCLAIM	SUBITEMS	SUBSIDES
SUBCELL	SUBSIST	SUBCLANS	SUBJOINS	SUBSISTS
SUBCLAN	SUBSITE	SUBCLASS	SUBLATED	SUBSITES
SUBCODE	SUBSOIL	SUBCLERK	SUBLEASE	SUBSIZAR
SUBCOOL	SUBSONG	SUBCODES	SUBLEVEL	SUBSKILL
SUBCULT	SUBTACK	SUBCOOLS	SUBLIMED	SUBSOILS
SUBDEAN	SUBTASK	SUBCOSTA	SUBLIMES	SUBSOLAR
SUBDEBS	SUBTAXA	SUBCRUST	SUBLIMIT	SUBSONGS
SUBDEWS	SUBTEEN	SUBCULTS	SUBLINES	SUBSONIC
SUBDUAL	SUBTEND	SUBCUTES	SUBLUNAR	SUBSPACE
SUBDUCE	SUBTEST	SUBCUTIS	SUBMENTA	SUBSTAGE
SUBDUCT	SUBTEXT	SUBDEANS	SUBMENUS	SUBSTATE
SUBDUED	SUBTILE	SUBDEPOT	SUBMERGE	SUBSTYLE
SUBDUES	SUBTONE	SUBDEWED	SUBMERSE	SUBTACKS
SUBECHO	SUBTYPE	SUBDUALS	SUBNASAL	SUBTALAR
SUBEDIT	SUBUNIT	SUBDUCES	SUBNICHE	SUBTASKS
SUBERIC	SUBURBS	SUBDUCTS	SUBNODAL	SUBTAXON
SUBFEUS	SUBVERT	SUBDUING	SUBOCEAN	SUBTEENS
SUBFILE	SUBWAYS	SUBDUPLE	SUBOPTIC	SUBTENDS
SUBFUSC	SUBZERO	SUBDURAL	SUBORDER	SUBTENSE
SUBGOAL	SUBZONE	SUBDWARF	SUBOVATE	SUBTESTS
SUBGUMS		SUBEDITS	SUBOXIDE	SUBTEXTS
SUBHEAD	**Eight-letter words**	SUBENTRY	SUBPANEL	SUBTHEME
SUBIDEA		SUBEPOCH	SUBPARTS	SUBTIDAL
SUBITEM	SUBABBOT	SUBEQUAL	SUBPHASE	SUBTILER
SUBJOIN	SUBACRID	SUBERECT	SUBPHYLA	SUBTITLE
SUBLATE	SUBACTED	SUBEROSE	SUBPLOTS	SUBTONES
SUBLETS	SUBACUTE	SUBFEUED	SUBPOLAR	SUBTONIC
SUBLIME	SUBADULT	SUBFIELD	SUBPRIME	SUBTOPIC
SUBLINE	SUBAGENT	SUBFILES	SUBPRIOR	SUBTOTAL
SUBLOTS	SUBAREAS	SUBFIXES	SUBPUBIC	SUBTRACT
SUBMENU	SUBATOMS	SUBFLOOR	SUBRACES	SUBTREND
SUBMISS	SUBAUDIO	SUBFLUID	SUBRENTS	SUBTRIBE
SUBNETS	SUBAURAL	SUBFRAME	SUBRINGS	SUBTRIST
SUBORAL	SUBAXIAL	SUBGENRE	SUBRULES	SUBTUNIC

SUBTYPES	SUBURBIA	SUBVERTS	SUBVIRUS	SUBWORLD
SUBUNITS	SUBVERSE	SUBVICAR	SUBVOCAL	SUBZONAL
SUBURBAN	SUBVERST	SUBVIRAL	SUBWAYED	SUBZONES

Words that begin with SUN-

Seven-letter words	SUNFAST	SUNTANS	SUNBURNT	SUNPORCH
SUNBACK	SUNFISH	SUNTRAP	SUNBURST	SUNPROOF
SUNBAKE	SUNGARS	SUNWARD	SUNCHOKE	SUNRISES
SUNBATH	SUNGLOW	SUNWISE	SUNDARIS	SUNROOFS
SUNBEAM	SUNHATS		SUNDECKS	SUNROOMS
SUNBEAT	SUNKETS	**Eight-letter words**	SUNDERED	SUNSCALD
SUNBEDS	SUNLAMP		SUNDIALS	SUNSHADE
SUNBELT	SUNLAND	SUNBAKED	SUNDOWNS	SUNSHINE
SUNBIRD	SUNLESS	SUNBAKES	SUNDRESS	SUNSHINY
SUNBOWS	SUNLIKE	SUNBATHE	SUNDRIES	SUNSPOTS
SUNBURN	SUNNIES	SUNBATHS	SUNDRILY	SUNSTARS
SUNDAES	SUNRAYS	SUNBEAMS	SUNDROPS	SUNSTONE
SUNDARI	SUNRISE	SUNBEAMY	SUNGAZER	SUNSUITS
SUNDECK	SUNROOF	SUNBELTS	SUNGLASS	SUNTRAPS
SUNDEWS	SUNROOM	SUNBERRY	SUNGLOWS	SUNWARDS
SUNDIAL	SUNSETS	SUNBIRDS	SUNGREBE	
SUNDOGS	SUNSPOT	SUNBLIND	SUNLAMPS	
SUNDOWN	SUNSTAR	SUNBLOCK	SUNLANDS	
	SUNSUIT	SUNBURNS	SUNLIGHT	

Words that begin with TRI-

Seven-letter words	TRIGONS	TRITONE	TRICOLOR	TRIPHASE
TRIABLE	TRIGRAM	TRITONS	TRICORNS	TRIPHONE
TRIACID	TRIJETS	TRIUMPH	TRICYCLE	TRIPLANE
TRIAGED	TRILITH	TRIVETS	TRIDARNS	TRIPLIED
TRIAGES	TRILOBE	TRIVIAL	TRIDENTS	TRIPLIES
TRIARCH	TRILOGY	TRIZONE	TRIETHYL	TRIPLING
TRIAXON	TRINARY		TRIFLING	TRIPODAL
TRIBADE	TRIODES	**Eight-letter words**	TRIFOCAL	TRIPOLIS
TRIBALS	TRIONES		TRIGLYPH	TRIPOSES
TRIBLET	TRIOSES	TRIACIDS	TRIGRAMS	TRISECTS
TRIBUTE	TRIOXID	TRIAGING	TRIGRAPH	TRISEMES
TRICARS	TRIPACK	TRIALIST	TRILEMMA	TRISHAWS
TRICEPS	TRIPART	TRIANGLE	TRILITHS	TRISTATE
TRICLAD	TRIPIER	TRIAXIAL	TRILOBED	TRISTICH
TRICORN	TRIPLED	TRIAXONS	TRILOBES	TRITHING
TRICOTS	TRIPLEX	TRIAZINE	TRIMETER	TRITICAL
TRIDARN	TRIPODS	TRIAZOLE	TRIMIXES	TRITIDES
TRIDENT	TRIPSIS	TRIBALLY	TRIMORPH	TRITONES
TRIDUAN	TRISECT	TRIBASIC	TRIMOTOR	TRIUNITY
TRIENES	TRISEME	TRIBLETS	TRINODAL	TRIVALVE
TRIFLED	TRISHAW	TRIBRACH	TRIOLEIN	TRIZONAL
TRIFOLD	TRISOME	TRIBUTES	TRIOXIDE	TRIZONES
TRIFORM	TRISOMY	TRICHINA	TRIOXIDS	
TRIGAMY	TRITEST	TRICHORD	TRIPACKS	
	TRITIDE	TRICLADS	TRIPEDAL	

Words that begin with UN-

Seven-letter words

UNACTED	UNBUILT	UNCURSE	UNGATED	UNLACED
UNADDED	UNBULKY	UNDATED	UNGAZED	UNLACES
UNADEPT	UNBURNT	UNDEALT	UNGEARS	UNLADED
UNADULT	UNCAGED	UNDECKS	UNGILDS	UNLADEN
UNAGILE	UNCAGES	UNDEIFY	UNGIRDS	UNLADES
UNAGING	UNCAKED	UNDERNS	UNGIRTH	UNLATCH
UNAIDED	UNCAKES	UNDIGHT	UNGLOVE	UNLAWED
UNAIMED	UNCANNY	UNDINES	UNGLUED	UNLEADS
UNAIRED	UNCAPED	UNDOCKS	UNGLUES	UNLEARN
UNAKING	UNCAPES	UNDOERS	UNGODLY	UNLEASH
UNALIKE	UNCARED	UNDOING	UNGORED	UNLEVEL
UNALIST	UNCARTS	UNDRAPE	UNGOWNS	UNLIKED
UNALIVE	UNCASED	UNDRAWN	UNGREEN	UNLIKES
UNAPTLY	UNCASES	UNDRAWS	UNGROWN	UNLIMED
UNARMED	UNCEDED	UNDRESS	UNGUARD	UNLIMES
UNASKED	UNCHAIN	UNDREST	UNGULAR	UNLINED
UNAWAKE	UNCHAIR	UNDRIED	UNGYVED	UNLINES
UNAWARE	UNCHARM	UNDRUNK	UNGYVES	UNLINKS
UNBAKED	UNCHARY	UNDYING	UNHABLE	UNLIVED
UNBALED	UNCHECK	UNEAGER	UNHAIRS	UNLIVES
UNBALES	UNCHILD	UNEARED	UNHANDS	UNLOADS
UNBARED	UNCHOKE	UNEARTH	UNHANDY	UNLOBED
UNBARES	UNCITED	UNEASES	UNHANGS	UNLOCKS
UNBARKS	UNCIVIL	UNEATEN	UNHAPPY	UNLOOSE
UNBASED	UNCLAMP	UNEDGED	UNHARDY	UNLORDS
UNBATED	UNCLASP	UNEDGES	UNHASPS	UNLOVED
UNBEARS	UNCLEAN	UNENDED	UNHASTY	UNLOVES
UNBEGET	UNCLEAR	UNEQUAL	UNHEADS	UNLUCKY
UNBEGOT	UNCLEFT	UNFACTS	UNHEALS	UNMACHO
UNBEGUN	UNCLEWS	UNFADED	UNHEARD	UNMAKER
UNBEING	UNCLING	UNFAIRS	UNHEART	UNMAKES
UNBELTS	UNCLIPS	UNFAITH	UNHEEDY	UNMANLY
UNBENDS	UNCLIPT	UNFAKED	UNHELED	UNMARRY
UNBINDS	UNCLOAK	UNFAMED	UNHELES	UNMASKS
UNBITTS	UNCLOGS	UNFANCY	UNHELMS	UNMATED
UNBLENT	UNCLOSE	UNFAZED	UNHINGE	UNMEANT
UNBLESS	UNCLOUD	UNFENCE	UNHIRED	UNMERRY
UNBLEST	UNCOCKS	UNFEUED	UNHITCH	UNMETED
UNBLIND	UNCODED	UNFILED	UNHIVED	UNMEWED
UNBLOCK	UNCOILS	UNFIRED	UNHIVES	UNMINED
UNBLOWN	UNCOLTS	UNFITLY	UNHOARD	UNMITER
UNBOLTS	UNCOMFY	UNFIXED	UNHOODS	UNMITRE
UNBONED	UNCOMIC	UNFIXES	UNHOOKS	UNMIXED
UNBONES	UNCOPED	UNFLESH	UNHOOPS	UNMIXES
UNBOOTS	UNCOPES	UNFLUSH	UNHOPED	UNMOLDS
UNBORNE	UNCORDS	UNFOLDS	UNHORSE	UNMOORS
UNBOSOM	UNCORKS	UNFOOLS	UNHOUSE	UNMORAL
UNBOUND	UNCOUTH	UNFORMS	UNHUMAN	UNMOULD
UNBOWED	UNCOVER	UNFOUND	UNHUSKS	UNMOUNT
UNBOXED	UNCOWLS	UNFREED	UNIDEAL	UNMOVED
UNBOXES	UNCRATE	UNFREES	UNJADED	UNNAILS
UNBRACE	UNCRAZY	UNFROCK	UNJOINT	UNNAMED
UNBRAID	UNCROSS	UNFROZE	UNKEMPT	UNNEATH
UNBRAKE	UNCROWN	UNFUMED	UNKINGS	UNNERVE
UNBROKE	UNCUFFS	UNFUNNY	UNKINKS	UNNESTS
UNBUILD	UNCURBS	UNFURLS	UNKNITS	UNNOBLE
	UNCURED	UNFUSED	UNKNOTS	UNNOISY
	UNCURLS	UNFUSSY	UNKNOWN	UNNOTED

UNOAKED	UNRUFFE	UNSPENT	UNTUNES	UNAGEING
UNOFTEN	UNRULED	UNSPIDE	UNTURFS	UNAGREED
UNOILED	UNRULES	UNSPIED	UNTURNS	UNALLIED
UNORDER	UNSAFER	UNSPILT	UNTWINE	UNAMAZED
UNOWNED	UNSAINT	UNSPLIT	UNTWIST	UNAMUSED
UNPACED	UNSATED	UNSPOKE	UNTYING	UNANCHOR
UNPACKS	UNSAVED	UNSPOOL	UNURGED	UNANELED
UNPAGED	UNSAWED	UNSTACK	UNUSUAL	UNARCHED
UNPAINT	UNSCALE	UNSTAID	UNVAILS	UNARGUED
UNPANEL	UNSCARY	UNSTATE	UNVEILS	UNARISEN
UNPAPER	UNSCREW	UNSTEEL	UNVEXED	UNARMING
UNPARED	UNSEALS	UNSTEPS	UNVISOR	UNARTFUL
UNPAVED	UNSEAMS	UNSTICK	UNVITAL	UNATONED
UNPERCH	UNSEATS	UNSTOCK	UNVOCAL	UNAVOWED
UNPICKS	UNSEELS	UNSTOPS	UNVOICE	UNAWAKED
UNPILED	UNSELFS	UNSTOWS	UNWAGED	UNBACKED
UNPILES	UNSELLS	UNSTRAP	UNWAKED	UNBAGGED
UNPLACE	UNSENSE	UNSTRIP	UNWARES	UNBAITED
UNPLAIT	UNSEWED	UNSTUCK	UNWATER	UNBALING
UNPLUGS	UNSEXED	UNSTUNG	UNWAXED	UNBANDED
UNPLUMB	UNSEXES	UNSUITS	UNWAYED	UNBANKED
UNPLUME	UNSHALE	UNSUNNY	UNWEALS	UNBANNED
UNPOPES	UNSHAPE	UNSURED	UNWEARY	UNBARBED
UNPOSED	UNSHARP	UNSURER	UNWEAVE	UNBARING
UNPRAYS	UNSHELL	UNSWEAR	UNWHIPT	UNBARKED
UNPROPS	UNSHENT	UNSWEET	UNWHITE	UNBARRED
UNPURSE	UNSHEWN	UNSWEPT	UNWILLS	UNBASTED
UNQUEEN	UNSHIFT	UNSWORE	UNWINDS	UNBATHED
UNQUIET	UNSHIPS	UNSWORN	UNWIPED	UNBEARED
UNQUOTE	UNSHOED	UNTACKS	UNWIRED	UNBEATEN
UNRACED	UNSHOES	UNTAKEN	UNWIRES	UNBEDDED
UNRAKED	UNSHOOT	UNTAMED	UNWISER	UNBEGETS
UNRAKES	UNSHORN	UNTAMES	UNWITCH	UNBEGGED
UNRATED	UNSHOUT	UNTAXED	UNWITTY	UNBEINGS
UNRAVEL	UNSHOWN	UNTAXES	UNWIVED	UNBELIEF
UNRAZED	UNSHOWY	UNTEACH	UNWIVES	UNBELTED
UNREADY	UNSHUTS	UNTEAMS	UNWOMAN	UNBENDED
UNREAVE	UNSIGHT	UNTENTS	UNWOOED	UNBENIGN
UNREELS	UNSINEW	UNTENTY	UNWORKS	UNBEREFT
UNREEVE	UNSIZED	UNTHAWS	UNWORTH	UNBESEEM
UNREINS	UNSLAIN	UNTHINK	UNWOUND	UNBIASED
UNRESTS	UNSLICK	UNTILED	UNWOVEN	UNBIASES
UNRIGHT	UNSLING	UNTILES	UNWRAPS	UNBIDDEN
UNRIMED	UNSLUNG	UNTIMED	UNWRITE	UNBILLED
UNRIPER	UNSMART	UNTIRED	UNWROTE	UNBISHOP
UNRISEN	UNSMOTE	UNTOMBS	UNWRUNG	UNBITTED
UNRIVEN	UNSNAGS	UNTONED	UNYOKED	UNBITTEN
UNRIVET	UNSNAPS	UNTRACE	UNYOKES	UNBITTER
UNROBED	UNSNARL	UNTRACK	UNYOUNG	UNBLAMED
UNROBES	UNSNECK	UNTREAD	UNZONED	UNBLINDS
UNROLLS	UNSOBER	UNTRIDE		UNBLOCKS
UNROOFS	UNSOLID	UNTRIED	**Eight-letter**	UNBLOODY
UNROOST	UNSONSY	UNTRIMS	**words**	UNBLOWED
UNROOTS	UNSOOTE	UNTRUER	UNABATED	UNBOBBED
UNROPED	UNSOULS	UNTRULY	UNABUSED	UNBODIED
UNROPES	UNSOUND	UNTRUSS	UNACHING	UNBODING
UNROUGH	UNSOWED	UNTRUST	UNACIDIC	UNBOILED
UNROUND	UNSPARS	UNTRUTH	UNACTIVE	UNBOLTED
UNROVEN	UNSPEAK	UNTUCKS	UNADORED	UNBONDED
UNROYAL	UNSPELL	UNTUNED	UNAFRAID	UNBONING

UNBONNET	UNCIPHER	UNDERATE	UNFILIAL	UNGREEDY
UNBOOKED	UNCLAMPS	UNDESERT	UNFILLED	UNGROUND
UNBOOTED	UNCLASPS	UNDEVOUT	UNFILMED	UNGUARDS
UNBOSOMS	UNCLASSY	UNDIGHTS	UNFINISHED	UNGUIDED
UNBOTTLE	UNCLAWED	UNDIMMED	UNFITTED	UNGUILTY
UNBOUGHT	UNCLENCH	UNDINTED	UNFITTER	UNGUMMED
UNBOUNCY	UNCLEWED	UNDIPPED	UNFIXING	UNGYVING
UNBOWING	UNCLINCH	UNDIVINE	UNFIXITY	UNHACKED
UNBOXING	UNCLOAKS	UNDOABLE	UNFLASHY	UNHAILED
UNBRACED	UNCLOSED	UNDOCILE	UNFLAWED	UNHAIRED
UNBRACES	UNCLOSES	UNDOCKED	UNFLEXED	UNHALLOW
UNBRAIDS	UNCLOTHE	UNDOINGS	UNFLUTED	UNHALSED
UNBRAKED	UNCLOUDS	UNDOOMED	UNFOILED	UNHALVED
UNBRAKES	UNCLOUDY	UNDOTTED	UNFOLDED	UNHANDED
UNBREECH	UNCLOVEN	UNDOUBLE	UNFOLDER	UNHANGED
UNBRIDLE	UNCLOYED	UNDRAPED	UNFOOLED	UNHARMED
UNBRIGHT	UNCLUTCH	UNDRAPES	UNFOOTED	UNHASPED
UNBROKEN	UNCOATED	UNDREAMT	UNFORBID	UNHATTED
UNBUCKLE	UNCOCKED	UNDRIVEN	UNFORCED	UNHEADED
UNBUDDED	UNCOFFIN	UNDROSSY	UNFORGED	UNHEALED
UNBUILDS	UNCOILED	UNDUBBED	UNFORGOT	UNHEALTH
UNBUNDLE	UNCOINED	UNDULLED	UNFORKED	UNHEARSE
UNBURDEN	UNCOLTED	UNEARNED	UNFORMAL	UNHEARTS
UNBURIED	UNCOMBED	UNEARTHS	UNFORMED	UNHEATED
UNBURIES	UNCOMELY	UNEASIER	UNFOUGHT	UNHEDGED
UNBURNED	UNCOMMON	UNEASILY	UNFRAMED	UNHEEDED
UNBURROW	UNCOOKED	UNEDGING	UNFREEZE	UNHELING
UNBUSTED	UNCOOLED	UNEDIBLE	UNFRIEND	UNHELMED
UNBUTTON	UNCOPING	UNEDITED	UNFROCKS	UNHELPED
UNCAGING	UNCORDED	UNELATED	UNFROZEN	UNHEROIC
UNCAKING	UNCORKED	UNENDING	UNFUNDED	UNHIDDEN
UNCALLED	UNCOSTLY	UNENVIED	UNFURLED	UNHINGED
UNCANDID	UNCOUPLE	UNEQUALS	UNFURRED	UNHINGES
UNCANNED	UNCOVERS	UNERASED	UNGAGGED	UNHIPPER
UNCAPING	UNCOWLED	UNEROTIC	UNGAINLY	UNHIVING
UNCAPPED	UNCRATED	UNERRING	UNGALLED	UNHOARDS
UNCARDED	UNCRATES	UNESPIED	UNGARBED	UNHOLIER
UNCARING	UNCREATE	UNEVADED	UNGAUGED	UNHOLILY
UNCARTED	UNCREWED	UNEVENER	UNGAZING	UNHOLPEN
UNCARVED	UNCROWNS	UNEVENLY	UNGEARED	UNHOMELY
UNCASHED	UNCUFFED	UNEXOTIC	UNGELDED	UNHONEST
UNCASING	UNCULLED	UNEXPERT	UNGENIAL	UNHOODED
UNCASKED	UNCURBED	UNFABLED	UNGENTLE	UNHOOKED
UNCATCHY	UNCURLED	UNFADING	UNGENTLY	UNHOOPED
UNCAUGHT	UNCURSED	UNFAIRED	UNGIFTED	UNHORSED
UNCAUSED	UNCURSES	UNFAIRER	UNGILDED	UNHORSES
UNCHAINS	UNCURVED	UNFAIRLY	UNGIRDED	UNHOUSED
UNCHAIRS	UNDAMMED	UNFAITHS	UNGIRTHS	UNHOUSES
UNCHANCY	UNDAMNED	UNFALLEN	UNGIVING	UNHUNTED
UNCHARGE	UNDAMPED	UNFAMOUS	UNGLAZED	UNHUSKED
UNCHARMS	UNDARING	UNFANNED	UNGLOVED	UNIDEAED
UNCHASTE	UNDASHED	UNFASTEN	UNGLOVES	UNIMBUED
UNCHECKS	UNDAZZLE	UNFAULTY	UNGLUING	UNINURED
UNCHEWED	UNDECENT	UNFEARED	UNGODDED	UNIONISE
UNCHICLY	UNDECKED	UNFELLED	UNGORGED	UNIONIZE
UNCHILDS	UNDEEDED	UNFELTED	UNGOTTEN	UNIRONED
UNCHOKED	UNDEFIED	UNFENCED	UNGOWNED	UNIRONIC
UNCHOKES	UNDELETE	UNFENCES	UNGRACED	UNISSUED
UNCHOSEN	UNDENIED	UNFETTER	UNGRADED	UNJAMMED
UNCHURCH	UNDENTED	UNFEUDAL	UNGRAZED	UNJOINED

UNJOINTS	UNMAKING	UNPAYING	UNREALLY	UNSCREWS
UNJOYFUL	UNMANFUL	UNPEELED	UNREAPED	UNSEALED
UNJOYOUS	UNMANNED	UNPEERED	UNREASON	UNSEAMED
UNJUDGED	UNMANTLE	UNPEGGED	UNREAVED	UNSEARED
UNJUSTER	UNMAPPED	UNPENNED	UNREAVES	UNSEASON
UNJUSTLY	UNMARKED	UNPEOPLE	UNRECKED	UNSEATED
UNKEELED	UNMARRED	UNPERSON	UNREELED	UNSECRET
UNKENNED	UNMASKED	UNPICKED	UNREELER	UNSEEDED
UNKENNEL	UNMASKER	UNPILING	UNREEVED	UNSEEING
UNKINDER	UNMATTED	UNPINKED	UNREEVES	UNSEELED
UNKINDLY	UNMEETLY	UNPINNED	UNREINED	UNSEELIE
UNKINGED	UNMELLOW	UNPITIED	UNRENTED	UNSEEMLY
UNKINGLY	UNMELTED	UNPITTED	UNREPAID	UNSEIZED
UNKINKED	UNMENDED	UNPLACED	UNREPAIR	UNSELDOM
UNKISSED	UNMESHED	UNPLACES	UNRESTED	UNSELFED
UNKISSES	UNMESHES	UNPLAITS	UNRETIRE	UNSELVES
UNKNIGHT	UNMEWING	UNPLAYED	UNRHYMED	UNSENSED
UNKNOWNS	UNMILKED	UNPLIANT	UNRIBBED	UNSENSES
UNKOSHER	UNMILLED	UNPLOWED	UNRIDDEN	UNSERVED
UNLACING	UNMINDED	UNPLUMBS	UNRIDDLE	UNSETTLE
UNLADING	UNMINGLE	UNPLUMED	UNRIFLED	UNSEWING
UNLASHED	UNMISSED	UNPLUMES	UNRIGGED	UNSEXING
UNLASHES	UNMITERS	UNPOETIC	UNRIGHTS	UNSEXIST
UNLAWFUL	UNMITRED	UNPOISED	UNRINGED	UNSEXUAL
UNLAWING	UNMITRES	UNPOISON	UNRINSED	UNSHADED
UNLAYING	UNMIXING	UNPOLISH	UNRIPELY	UNSHADOW
UNLEADED	UNMOANED	UNPOLITE	UNRIPEST	UNSHAKED
UNLEARNS	UNMODISH	UNPOLLED	UNRIPPED	UNSHAKEN
UNLEARNT	UNMOLDED	UNPOSTED	UNRIVETS	UNSHALED
UNLEASED	UNMOLTEN	UNPOTTED	UNROBING	UNSHALES
UNLETHAL	UNMONIED	UNPRAISE	UNROLLED	UNSHAMED
UNLETTED	UNMOORED	UNPRAYED	UNROOFED	UNSHAPED
UNLEVELS	UNMOULDS	UNPREACH	UNROOSTS	UNSHAPEN
UNLEVIED	UNMOUNTS	UNPRETTY	UNROOTED	UNSHAPES
UNLICKED	UNMOVING	UNPRICED	UNROPING	UNSHARED
UNLIDDED	UNMUFFLE	UNPRIEST	UNROTTED	UNSHAVED
UNLIKELY	UNMUZZLE	UNPRIMED	UNROTTEN	UNSHAVEN
UNLIMBER	UNNAILED	UNPRISON	UNROUGED	UNSHELLS
UNLIMING	UNNATIVE	UNPRIZED	UNROUNDS	UNSHIFTS
UNLINEAL	UNNEEDED	UNPROBED	UNROUSED	UNSHOOTS
UNLINING	UNNERVED	UNPROPER	UNRUBBED	UNSHOUTS
UNLINKED	UNNERVES	UNPROVED	UNRUFFLE	UNSHROUD
UNLISTED	UNNESTED	UNPROVEN	UNRULIER	UNSHRUNK
UNLIVELY	UNNETTED	UNPRUNED	UNRUSHED	UNSICKER
UNLIVING	UNNOBLES	UNPUCKER	UNRUSTED	UNSIFTED
UNLOADED	UNOBEYED	UNPULLED	UNSADDLE	UNSIGHTS
UNLOADER	UNOPENED	UNPURELY	UNSAFELY	UNSIGNED
UNLOCKED	UNORDERS	UNPURGED	UNSAFEST	UNSILENT
UNLOOKED	UNORNATE	UNPURSED	UNSAFETY	UNSINEWS
UNLOOSED	UNPACKED	UNPURSES	UNSAILED	UNSINFUL
UNLOOSEN	UNPACKER	UNPUZZLE	UNSAINED	UNSLAKED
UNLOOSES	UNPADDED	UNQUEENS	UNSAINTS	UNSLICED
UNLOPPED	UNPAINED	UNQUIETS	UNSALTED	UNSLINGS
UNLORDED	UNPAINTS	UNQUOTED	UNSAPPED	UNSLUICE
UNLORDLY	UNPAIRED	UNQUOTES	UNSASHED	UNSMOKED
UNLOVELY	UNPANELS	UNRACKED	UNSATING	UNSMOOTH
UNLOVING	UNPANGED	UNRAISED	UNSAVORY	UNSNARLS
UNMAILED	UNPAPERS	UNRAKING	UNSAYING	UNSNECKS
UNMAIMED	UNPARTED	UNRANKED	UNSCALED	UNSOAKED
UNMAKERS	UNPATHED	UNRAVELS	UNSCALES	UNSOAPED

UNSOCIAL	UNSTRIPS	UNTHINKS	UNTWINES	UNWEANED
UNSOCKET	UNSTRUCK	UNTHREAD	UNTWISTS	UNWEAPON
UNSODDEN	UNSTRUNG	UNTHRIFT	UNUNITED	UNWEAVES
UNSOILED	UNSTUFFY	UNTHRONE	UNUSABLE	UNWEBBED
UNSOLDER	UNSUBTLE	UNTIDIED	UNUSABLY	UNWEDDED
UNSOLEMN	UNSUBTLY	UNTIDIER	UNUSEFUL	UNWEEDED
UNSOLVED	UNSUCKED	UNTIDIES	UNVAILED	UNWEENED
UNSONSIE	UNSUITED	UNTIDILY	UNVALUED	UNWEIGHT
UNSORTED	UNSUMMED	UNTIEING	UNVARIED	UNWELDED
UNSOUGHT	UNSUNNED	UNTILING	UNVEILED	UNWETTED
UNSOULED	UNSUPPLE	UNTILLED	UNVEILER	UNWIELDY
UNSOURED	UNSURELY	UNTILTED	UNVEINED	UNWIFELY
UNSPARED	UNSUREST	UNTIMELY	UNVENTED	UNWIGGED
UNSPEAKS	UNSWATHE	UNTINGED	UNVERSED	UNWILFUL
UNSPELLS	UNSWAYED	UNTINNED	UNVESTED	UNWILLED
UNSPHERE	UNSWEARS	UNTIPPED	UNVETTED	UNWINDER
UNSPOILT	UNTACKED	UNTIRING	UNVIABLE	UNWINGED
UNSPOKEN	UNTACKLE	UNTITLED	UNVIEWED	UNWIRING
UNSPOOLS	UNTAGGED	UNTOMBED	UNVIRTUE	UNWISDOM
UNSPRUNG	UNTAILED	UNTOWARD	UNVISORS	UNWISELY
UNSTABLE	UNTAMING	UNTRACED	UNVIZARD	UNWISEST
UNSTABLY	UNTANGLE	UNTRACES	UNVOICED	UNWISHED
UNSTACKS	UNTANNED	UNTRACKS	UNVOICES	UNWISHES
UNSTARCH	UNTAPPED	UNTRADED	UNVULGAR	UNWITTED
UNSTARRY	UNTARRED	UNTREADS	UNWALLED	UNWIVING
UNSTATED	UNTASTED	UNTRENDY	UNWANING	UNWOMANS
UNSTATES	UNTAUGHT	UNTRUEST	UNWANTED	UNWONTED
UNSTAYED	UNTAXING	UNTRUISM	UNWARDED	UNWOODED
UNSTEADY	UNTEAMED	UNTRUSTS	UNWARIER	UNWORDED
UNSTEELS	UNTEMPER	UNTRUSTY	UNWARILY	UNWORKED
UNSTICKS	UNTENANT	UNTRUTHS	UNWARMED	UNWORMED
UNSTITCH	UNTENDED	UNTUCKED	UNWARNED	UNWORTHS
UNSTOCKS	UNTENDER	UNTUFTED	UNWARPED	UNWORTHY
UNSTONED	UNTENTED	UNTUNING	UNWASHED	UNWRITES
UNSTOWED	UNTESTED	UNTURBID	UNWASHEN	UNYEANED
UNSTRAPS	UNTETHER	UNTURFED	UNWASTED	UNYOKING
UNSTRESS	UNTHATCH	UNTURNED	UNWATERS	UNZIPPED
UNSTRING	UNTHAWED	UNTWINED	UNWATERY	

Words that begin with UP-

Seven-letter words	UPCASTS	UPDRAGS	UPGRADE	UPLEAPS
	UPCATCH	UPDRAWN	UPGROWN	UPLEAPT
UPBEARS	UPCHEER	UPDRAWS	UPGROWS	UPLIFTS
UPBEATS	UPCHUCK	UPDRIED	UPHANGS	UPLIGHT
UPBINDS	UPCLIMB	UPDRIES	UPHAUDS	UPLINKS
UPBLOWN	UPCLOSE	UPENDED	UPHEAPS	UPLOADS
UPBLOWS	UPCOAST	UPFIELD	UPHEAVE	UPLOCKS
UPBOILS	UPCOILS	UPFILLS	UPHILLS	UPLOOKS
UPBORNE	UPCOMES	UPFLING	UPHOARD	UPLYING
UPBOUND	UPCOURT	UPFLOWS	UPHOIST	UPMAKER
UPBRAID	UPCURLS	UPFLUNG	UPHOLDS	UPMAKES
UPBRAST	UPCURVE	UPFOLDS	UPHOORD	UPPILED
UPBRAYS	UPDARTS	UPFRONT	UPHURLS	UPPILES
UPBREAK	UPDATED	UPFURLS	UPKEEPS	UPPINGS
UPBRING	UPDATER	UPGANGS	UPKNITS	UPPROPS
UPBROKE	UPDATES	UPGAZED	UPLANDS	UPRAISE
UPBUILD	UPDIVED	UPGAZES	UPLEADS	UPRATED
UPBUILT	UPDIVES	UPGIRDS	UPLEANS	UPRATES
UPBURST	UPDRAFT	UPGOING	UPLEANT	UPREACH

UPREARS	UPSWING	UPCLOSED	UPLAYING	UPSPRANG
UPRESTS	UPSWUNG	UPCLOSES	UPLEANED	UPSPRING
UPRIGHT	UPTAKEN	UPCOILED	UPLEAPED	UPSPRUNG
UPRISEN	UPTAKES	UPCOMING	UPLIFTED	UPSTAGED
UPRISER	UPTALKS	UPCURLED	UPLIFTER	UPSTAGER
UPRISES	UPTEARS	UPCURVED	UPLIGHTS	UPSTAGES
UPRIVER	UPTEMPO	UPCURVES	UPLINKED	UPSTAIRS
UPROARS	UPTHREW	UPDARTED	UPLOADED	UPSTANDS
UPROLLS	UPTHROW	UPDATERS	UPLOCKED	UPSTARED
UPROOTS	UPTICKS	UPDATING	UPLOOKED	UPSTARES
UPROUSE	UPTIGHT	UPDIVING	UPMAKERS	UPSTARTS
UPSCALE	UPTILTS	UPDRAFTS	UPMAKING	UPSTATER
UPSELLS	UPTIMES	UPDRYING	UPMARKET	UPSTATES
UPSENDS	UPTOWNS	UPENDING	UPPILING	UPSTAYED
UPSHIFT	UPTRAIN	UPFILLED	UPRAISED	UPSTREAM
UPSHOOT	UPTREND	UPFLINGS	UPRAISER	UPSTROKE
UPSHOTS	UPTURNS	UPFLOWED	UPRAISES	UPSURGED
UPSIDES	UPTYING	UPFOLDED	UPRATING	UPSURGES
UPSIZED	UPVALUE	UPFOLLOW	UPREARED	UPSWAYED
UPSIZES	UPWAFTS	UPFURLED	UPRIGHTS	UPSWEEPS
UPSKILL	UPWARDS	UPGATHER	UPRISERS	UPSWELLS
UPSLOPE	UPWELLS	UPGAZING	UPRISING	UPSWINGS
UPSOARS	UPWHIRL	UPGIRDED	UPRIVERS	UPTAKING
UPSPAKE	UPWINDS	UPGOINGS	UPROARED	UPTALKED
UPSPEAK	UPWOUND	UPGRADED	UPROLLED	UPTEMPOS
UPSPEAR	UPWRAPS	UPGRADER	UPROOTED	UPTHROWN
UPSPOKE		UPGRADES	UPROOTER	UPTHROWS
UPSTAGE	**Eight-letter**	UPGROWTH	UPROUSED	UPTHRUST
UPSTAIR	**words**	UPGUSHED	UPROUSES	UPTILTED
UPSTAND	UPBEARER	UPGUSHES	UPRUSHED	UPTOSSED
UPSTARE	UPBOILED	UPHEAPED	UPRUSHES	UPTOSSES
UPSTART	UPBRAIDS	UPHEAVED	UPSCALED	UPTRAINS
UPSTATE	UPBRAYED	UPHEAVER	UPSCALES	UPTRENDS
UPSTAYS	UPBREAKS	UPHEAVES	UPSETTER	UPTURNED
UPSTEPS	UPBRINGS	UPHOARDS	UPSHIFTS	UPVALUED
UPSTIRS	UPBROKEN	UPHOISTS	UPSHOOTS	UPVALUES
UPSTOOD	UPBUILDS	UPHOLDER	UPSIZING	UPWAFTED
UPSURGE	UPBURSTS	UPHOORDS	UPSKILLS	UPWELLED
UPSWAYS	UPCAUGHT	UPHUDDEN	UPSOARED	UPWHIRLS
UPSWEEP	UPCHEERS	UPHURLED	UPSPEAKS	
UPSWELL	UPCHUCKS	UPJETTED	UPSPEARS	
UPSWEPT	UPCLIMBS	UPLANDER	UPSPOKEN	

Words that begin with WAR-

Seven-letter	WARLING	WARTIER	WARDROPS	WARPINGS
words	WARLOCK	WARTIME	WARFARED	WARPLANE
WARBIER	WARLORD	WARWOLF	WARFARER	WARPOWER
WARBIRD	WARMING	WARWORK	WARFARES	WARRANDS
WARBLED	WARPAGE	WARWORN	WARHABLE	WARRANTS
WARDENS	WARPATH	WARZONE	WARHEADS	WARRAYED
WARDING	WARPING		WARHORSE	WARSHIPS
WARDOGS	WARRAND	**Eight-letter**	WARLINGS	WARSLING
WARDROP	WARRANT	**words**	WARLOCKS	WARTIMES
WARFARE	WARRAYS	WARBIRDS	WARLORDS	WARTWEED
WARHEAD	WARRENS	WARBLING	WARMAKER	WARWORKS
WARKING	WARRING	WARCRAFT	WARMINGS	WARZONES
WARLESS	WARSAWS	WARDERED	WARMOUTH	
WARLIKE	WARSHIP	WARDINGS	WARPAGES	
	WARSLED	WARDRESS	WARPATHS	

Benjamins

RUBBABOO	SALBANDS	SURBATED	BAYBERRY	RUBBINGS
BUYBACKS	TURBANDS	UNABATED	BILBERRY	SABBINGS
CUTBACKS	TURBANED	NIOBATES	BOXBERRY	SOBBINGS
DIEBACKS	BUGBANES	PROBATES	COWBERRY	SUBBINGS
FATBACKS	COWBANES	SORBATES	DEWBERRY	TUBBINGS
FINBACKS	DOGBANES	SURBATES	DOGBERRY	VERBINGS
FLYBACKS	FLYBANES	SUNBATHE	FOXBERRY	WEBBINGS
HOGBACKS	HENBANES	BEDBATHS	HAGBERRY	ZORBINGS
LAYBACKS	MIRBANES	EYEBATHS	INKBERRY	SYMBIONT
OUTBACKS	MYRBANES	ISOBATHS	MULBERRY	ANTBIRDS
PAYBACKS	LUMBANGS	MUDBATHS	NISBERRY	AWLBIRDS
REDBACKS	PROBANGS	SABBATHS	PEABERRY	AXEBIRDS
RUNBACKS	SHEBANGS	SUNBATHS	SUNBERRY	BOOBIRDS
SETBACKS	BIOBANKS	CIABATTA	TAYBERRY	CATBIRDS
SOWBACKS	CANBANKS	OUTBAWLS	TEABERRY	COWBIRDS
TIEBACKS	CUTBANKS	SEABEACH	WAXBERRY	FATBIRDS
TOMBACKS	EYEBANKS	JETBEADS	GIBBETED	JAYBIRDS
WETBACKS	NONBANKS	EYEBEAMS	RABBETED	MAYBIRDS
REDBAITS	SEABANKS	OUTBEAMS	DIABETES	OILBIRDS
OUTBAKED	TURBANTS	SUNBEAMS	TURBETHS	REDBIRDS
PARBAKED	RHUBARBS	SUNBEAMY	GAMBETTA	SEABIRDS
PREBAKED	RHUBARBY	BOGBEANS	MORBIDER	SUNBIRDS
SUNBAKED	BOMBARDE	SHEBEANS	CARBIDES	WARBIRDS
DAWBAKES	BOMBARDS	SOYBEANS	GAMBIERS	WOSBIRDS
OUTBAKES	GABBARDS	ANTBEARS	JAMBIERS	MISBIRTH
PARBAKES	LIBBARDS	BUGBEARS	STABILES	PREBIRTH
PREBAKES	LUBBARDS	CUDBEARS	VERBILES	ARABISES
SUNBAKES	ISOBARES	FORBEARS	MISBILLS	SOUBISES
CABBALAS	BARBARIC	DRYBEATS	PREBILLS	TABBISES
FALBALAS	ISOBARIC	OFFBEATS	SAWBILLS	OUTBITCH
KABBALAS	DISBARKS	CORBEAUS	TWIBILLS	RABBITER
TAMBALAS	OUTBARKS	JAMBEAUX	WAXBILLS	NIOBITES
PIEBALDS	TANBARKS	LIMBECKS	WAYBILLS	SORBITES
PYEBALDS	CARBARNS	MISBEGAN	WRYBILLS	RABBITOS
GIMBALED	PREBASAL	MISBEGIN	TURBINAL	BABBITTS
CYMBALER	SUBBASAL	MISBEGOT	COWBINDS	BOBBITTS
TIMBALES	SURBASED	MISBEGUN	HOPBINDS	ARABIZES
BOXBALLS	AIRBASES	NONBEING	MISBINDS	EYEBLACK
EARBALLS	ANABASES	BARBELLS	PREBINDS	NONBLACK
EYEBALLS	DIABASES	COWBELLS	COMBINER	SAWBLADE
FUSBALLS	FANBASES	GORBELLY	CARBINES	CLUBLAND
GUMBALLS	ISOBASES	POTBELLY	COMBINES	SCABLAND
ICEBALLS	SUBBASES	REDBELLY	HOPBINES	SLOBLAND
LOWBALLS	SURBASES	SOWBELLY	STIBINES	BIOBLAST
NETBALLS	DIABASIC	TUNBELLY	TURBINES	EPIBLAST
ODDBALLS	NONBASIC	FURBELOW	BOMBINGS	MYOBLAST
PATBALLS	TRIBASIC	RUMBELOW	COMBINGS	NEOBLAST
PINBALLS	SUBBASIN	FLYBELTS	CUBBINGS	ZOOBLAST
GLOBALLY	ANABASIS	SUNBELTS	CURBINGS	OUTBLAZE
TRIBALLY	KOLBASIS	ALEBENCH	DAUBINGS	OUTBLEAT
VERBALLY	KOLBASSI	DISBENCH	DUBBINGS	BARBLESS
ARMBANDS	LAMBASTE	PREBENDS	JIBBINGS	COMBLESS
DISBANDS	BOMBASTS	CARBENES	JOBBINGS	CURBLESS
HATBANDS	LAMBASTS	SORBENTS	KERBINGS	GARBLESS
HAYBANDS	BARBATED	BERBERES	LAMBINGS	HERBLESS
HUSBANDS	COMBATED	ICEBERGS	MOBBINGS	LIMBLESS
PROBANDS	GLOBATED	HAUBERKS	PUBBINGS	OUTBLESS
RIBBANDS	PROBATED	BARBERRY	RIBBINGS	PREBLESS

TOM**BLESS**	WAM**BLING**	PAR**BOILS**	MIS**BOUND**	CLU**BROOM**
VER**BLESS**	WAR**BLING**	POT**BOILS**	OUT**BOUND**	CRI**BROSE**
FEE**BLEST**	WIB**BLING**	PRE**BOILS**	POT**BOUND**	NUT**BROWN**
HUM**BLEST**	WIM**BLING**	KEM**BOING**	PRE**BOUND**	EYE**BROWS**
NIM**BLEST**	WOB**BLING**	KIM**BOING**	FAU**BOURG**	LOW**BROWS**
STA**BLEST**	EYE**BLINK**	MAM**BOING**	DIS**BOWEL**	UNI**BROWS**
BOM**BLETS**	ICE**BLINK**	BAR**BOLAS**	TEA**BOWLS**	AIR**BRUSH**
BUL**BLETS**	QUI**BLINS**	TOM**BOLAS**	OUT**BOXED**	CLU**BRUSH**
DOU**BLETS**	SEA**BLITE**	SYM**BOLES**	HAT**BOXES**	HAT**BRUSH**
DRI**BLETS**	WIT**BLITS**	DIA**BOLOS**	HAY**BOXES**	HAW**BUCKS**
HER**BLETS**	SUB**BLOCK**	TOM**BOLOS**	HOT**BOXES**	JUM**BUCKS**
TRI**BLETS**	SUN**BLOCK**	DOG**BOLTS**	ICE**BOXES**	KEB**BUCKS**
GOR**BLIMY**	HOT**BLOOD**	EYE**BOLTS**	JAW**BOXES**	ROE**BUCKS**
PUR**BLIND**	OUT**BLOOM**	HAG**BOLTS**	OUT**BOXES**	SAW**BUCKS**
SUN**BLIND**	INK**BLOTS**	RAG**BOLTS**	PEG**BOXES**	ZAM**BUCKS**
BAB**BLING**	FLY**BLOWN**	TUR**BONDS**	SKY**BOXES**	KEY**BUGLE**
BAU**BLING**	FLY**BLOWS**	HAM**BONED**	TEA**BOXES**	MIS**BUILD**
BOB**BLING**	OUT**BLUFF**	JAW**BONED**	CAR**BOYED**	OUT**BUILD**
BUB**BLING**	OUT**BLUSH**	RAW**BONED**	COW**BOYED**	PRE**BUILD**
BUM**BLING**	AIR**BOARD**	RIB**BONED**	VAM**BRACE**	MIS**BUILT**
BUR**BLING**	BED**BOARD**	JAW**BONER**	TRI**BRACH**	OUT**BUILT**
COB**BLING**	BOX**BOARD**	HAM**BONES**	SHA**BRACK**	PRE**BUILT**
CYM**BLING**	CUP**BOARD**	HIP**BONES**	OUT**BRAGS**	SAM**BUKES**
DAB**BLING**	DAM**BOARD**	JAM**BONES**	END**BRAIN**	OUT**BULGE**
DIB**BLING**	FUN**BOARD**	JAW**BONES**	MAD**BRAIN**	OUT**BULKS**
DOU**BLING**	GAR**BOARD**	PIN**BONES**	MID**BRAIN**	OUT**BULLY**
ENA**BLING**	KEY**BOARD**	RED**BONES**	MIS**BRAND**	GEE**BUNGS**
FEE**BLING**	LAP**BOARD**	SAW**BONES**	NON**BRAND**	TAM**BURAS**
FUM**BLING**	LAR**BOARD**	BOO**BOOKS**	MEM**BRANE**	CAR**BURET**
GAB**BLING**	LEE**BOARD**	DAY**BOOKS**	OUT**BRAVE**	HAM**BURGS**
GAM**BLING**	LOG**BOARD**	FLY**BOOKS**	OUT**BRAWL**	HOM**BURGS**
GAR**BLING**	MOP**BOARD**	LAW**BOOKS**	BEE**BREAD**	TAM**BURIN**
GOB**BLING**	OUT**BOARD**	LOG**BOOKS**	FRY**BREAD**	MOW**BURNS**
HAM**BLING**	PEG**BOARD**	NON**BOOKS**	RYE**BREAD**	OUT**BURNS**
HOB**BLING**	PIN**BOARD**	PRE**BOOKS**	SOW**BREAD**	SUN**BURNS**
HUM**BLING**	PRE**BOARD**	JAM**BOOLS**	TEA**BREAD**	MOW**BURNT**
JAB**BLING**	RUB**BOARD**	JIB**BOOMS**	WAY**BREAD**	OUT**BURNT**
JIR**BLING**	SEA**BOARD**	CAM**BOOSE**	DAY**BREAK**	SUN**BURNT**
JUM**BLING**	SKY**BOARD**	TOL**BOOTH**	OUT**BREAK**	DIS**BURSE**
KIB**BLING**	TAG**BOARD**	GUM**BOOTS**	PAR**BREAK**	AIR**BURST**
LAM**BLING**	TEA**BOARD**	SEA**BOOTS**	TIE**BREAK**	OUT**BURST**
MAR**BLING**	WAY**BOARD**	SLY**BOOTS**	OUT**BREED**	SUN**BURST**
MOB**BLING**	OUT**BOAST**	BOM**BORAS**	SUB**BREED**	NIM**BUSED**
MUM**BLING**	AIR**BOATS**	CAR**BORAS**	DOO**BREYS**	UNA**BUSED**
NIB**BLING**	BUM**BOATS**	RAS**BORAS**	OUT**BRIBE**	AIR**BUSES**
NOB**BLING**	CAT**BOATS**	HAR**BORED**	AIR**BRICK**	IAM**BUSES**
NUB**BLING**	DAY**BOATS**	JAM**BOREE**	RED**BRICK**	LIM**BUSES**
PEB**BLING**	FLY**BOATS**	HAR**BORER**	CAT**BRIER**	MOR**BUSES**
RAB**BLING**	FOY**BOATS**	AIR**BORNE**	AUM**BRIES**	NIM**BUSES**
RAM**BLING**	GUN**BOATS**	FOR**BORNE**	DAU**BRIES**	SOR**BUSES**
REM**BLING**	ICE**BOATS**	SEA**BORNE**	DAW**BRIES**	COM**BUSTS**
RUB**BLING**	PIG**BOATS**	SKY**BORNE**	DOO**BRIES**	TRI**BUTES**
RUM**BLING**	ROW**BOATS**	DIS**BOSOM**	ATA**BRINE**	ISO**BUTYL**
SAI**BLING**	TOW**BOATS**	CHA**BOUKS**	SOM**BRING**	EXA**BYTES**
SEM**BLING**	TUG**BOATS**	CHI**BOUKS**	ATA**BRINS**	AMI**CABLE**
SNO**BLING**	KEB**BOCKS**	AIR**BOUND**	ATE**BRINS**	CAS**CABLE**
STA**BLING**	FOR**BODED**	DIS**BOUND**	DAM**BRODS**	EDU**CABLE**
TRE**BLING**	FOR**BODES**	FOG**BOUND**	PAN**BROIL**	EVO**CABLE**
TUM**BLING**	GAR**BOILS**	ICE**BOUND**	OUT**BROKE**	PEC**CABLE**
WAB**BLING**	GUM**BOILS**	MAW**BOUND**	PEM**BROKE**	PLA**CABLE**

BRO**CADES**	URI**CASES**	COU**CHANT**	ZOO**CHORE**	SUB**CLERK**
CAS**CADES**	OUT**CASTE**	MER**CHANT**	MIS**CHOSE**	OUT**CLIMB**
FAL**CADES**	SUB**CASTE**	PEN**CHANT**	PRE**CHOSE**	ISO**CLINE**
SAC**CADES**	MET**CASTS**	CLO**CHARD**	PIT**CHOUT**	SYN**CLINE**
SUC**CADES**	MIS**CASTS**	MOU**CHARD**	WAT**CHOUT**	CIR**CLING**
MUS**CADET**	MOB**CASTS**	PIL**CHARD**	SAL**CHOWS**	MUS**CLING**
DIS**CAGED**	OFF**CASTS**	OUT**CHARM**	NUM**CHUCK**	NON**CLING**
BOS**CAGES**	OUT**CASTS**	TRO**CHARS**	DIS**CIDED**	ORA**CLING**
BRO**CAGES**	POD**CASTS**	PET**CHARY**	SUI**CIDED**	CIR**CLIPS**
DIS**CAGES**	PRE**CASTS**	PUR**CHASE**	PLA**CIDER**	GEM**CLIPS**
RIB**CAGES**	VOD**CASTS**	ISO**CHASM**	RAN**CIDER**	TOE**CLIPS**
SOC**CAGES**	WEB**CASTS**	TEU**CHATS**	BIO**CIDES**	OUT**CLOMB**
TRU**CAGES**	OUT**CATCH**	OUT**CHEAT**	DEI**CIDES**	DIS**CLOSE**
PAN**CAKED**	SEE**CATCH**	AIR**CHECK**	DIS**CIDES**	PAR**CLOSE**
ASH**CAKES**	PLA**CATER**	HAT**CHECK**	ECO**CIDES**	OIL**CLOTH**
CAR**CAKES**	EDU**CATES**	PAY**CHECK**	OVI**CIDES**	WAX**CLOTH**
CUP**CAKES**	EMI**CATES**	PIN**CHECK**	SUI**CIDES**	AIR**COACH**
HOE**CAKES**	EVO**CATES**	PRE**CHECK**	DIS**CINCT**	OUT**COACH**
HOT**CAKES**	FUR**CATES**	CUR**CHEFS**	PRE**CINCT**	SEA**COAST**
OAT**CAKES**	JUN**CATES**	TOR**CHERE**	PRO**CINCT**	PEA**COATS**
PAN**CAKES**	PLA**CATES**	BUT**CHEST**	SUC**CINCT**	RED**COATS**
TEA**CAKES**	PLI**CATES**	GAU**CHEST**	BRU**CINES**	SUR**COATS**
CAT**CALLS**	ZIN**CATES**	LOU**CHEST**	CAL**CINES**	TOP**COATS**
MIS**CALLS**	CON**CAUSE**	TEU**CHEST**	DOU**CINES**	BAW**COCKS**
OUT**CALLS**	SUB**CAUSE**	FIT**CHEWS**	FAS**CINES**	BIB**COCKS**
EPI**CALYX**	CON**CAVED**	CHE**CHIAS**	GLY**CINES**	DAW**COCKS**
OIL**CAMPS**	CON**CAVES**	ONY**CHIAS**	HYA**CINES**	GOR**COCKS**
DIS**CANDY**	OUT**CAVIL**	COL**CHICA**	LEU**CINES**	HAY**COCKS**
CHI**CANED**	SUR**CEASE**	BOY**CHICK**	PIS**CINES**	MEA**COCKS**
CHI**CANER**	CON**CEDED**	DAB**CHICK**	VAC**CINES**	PEA**COCKS**
CHI**CANES**	PRE**CEDED**	DIP**CHICK**	EPI**CISTS**	PET**COCKS**
JON**CANOE**	CON**CEDER**	DOB**CHICK**	FAS**CISTS**	SEA**COCKS**
ALI**CANTS**	CON**CEDES**	PSY**CHICS**	NAR**CISTS**	PEA**COCKY**
DES**CANTS**	EPI**CEDES**	OUT**CHIDE**	ELI**CITED**	BAR**CODED**
DIS**CANTS**	PRE**CEDES**	KER**CHIEF**	MIS**CITED**	MIS**CODED**
OUT**CAPER**	BRU**CELLA**	MIS**CHIEF**	PRE**CITED**	PRE**CODED**
INS**CAPES**	MAR**CELLA**	SUB**CHIEF**	CIR**CITER**	BAR**CODES**
BAC**CARAT**	CAN**CELLI**	BOY**CHIKS**	BRU**CITES**	MIS**CODES**
BRO**CARDS**	SUB**CELLS**	GOD**CHILD**	CAL**CITES**	PRE**CODES**
DIS**CARDS**	DUE**CENTO**	MER**CHILD**	DUL**CITES**	SAR**CODES**
KEY**CARDS**	SEI**CENTO**	TWI**CHILD**	LEU**CITES**	SUB**CODES**
PLA**CARDS**	TRE**CENTO**	TRO**CHILI**	MIS**CITES**	ZIN**CODES**
DAY**CARES**	CON**CENTS**	PRE**CHILL**	ZIN**CITES**	MIS**COINS**
MAS**CARON**	DES**CENTS**	ISO**CHIME**	TRI**CLADS**	NON**COLAS**
APO**CARPS**	PER**CENTS**	KAT**CHINA**	DIS**CLAIM**	BRI**COLES**
EPI**CARPS**	PRE**CENTS**	TRI**CHINA**	MIS**CLAIM**	GLY**COLIC**
EXO**CARPS**	CAN**CERED**	ZEC**CHINE**	PRO**CLAIM**	PER**COLIN**
PRO**CARPS**	PIN**CERED**	ZEC**CHINO**	SUB**CLAIM**	CON**COLOR**
SYN**CARPS**	GLY**CERIA**	KIN**CHINS**	SUB**CLANS**	DIS**COLOR**
MIS**CARRY**	GLY**CERIC**	SCU**CHINS**	TIE**CLASP**	MIS**COLOR**
DOG**CARTS**	BRA**CEROS**	ZEC**CHINS**	MIS**CLASS**	NON**COLOR**
TEA**CARTS**	CON**CERTS**	BIO**CHIPS**	NON**CLASS**	TRI**COLOR**
TIP**CARTS**	BIA**CETYL**	PUT**CHOCK**	OUT**CLASS**	UNI**COLOR**
CAR**CASED**	DIA**CETYL**	MOU**CHOIR**	SUB**CLASS**	LEU**COMAS**
DIS**CASED**	PRO**CHAIN**	SUN**CHOKE**	CON**CLAVE**	NAR**COMAS**
CAR**CASES**	ARM**CHAIR**	SUB**CHORD**	CAT**CLAWS**	SAR**COMAS**
DIS**CASES**	BED**CHAIR**	TRI**CHORD**	DEW**CLAWS**	BUN**COMBE**
FRA**CASES**	PAS**CHALS**	URO**CHORD**	BIO**CLEAN**	COX**COMBS**
NUT**CASES**	BRE**CHAMS**	ISO**CHORE**	PRE**CLEAN**	NEW**COMER**
PIN**CASES**	BAC**CHANT**	POE**CHORE**	PRE**CLEAR**	WEL**COMER**

OUTCOMES	DISCOVER	SUBCUTIS	MANDATES	WEDDERED
WELCOMES	GIMCRACK	BIOCYCLE	MISDATES	WILDERED
BEACONED	JIMCRACK	EPICYCLE	OUTDATES	WONDERED
DEACONED	AIRCRAFT	TRICYCLE	OXIDATES	PYODERMA
DRACONES	PENCRAFT	UNICYCLE	PREDATES	EPIDERMS
MUSCONES	SEACRAFT	OTOCYSTS	PREDAWNS	EXODERMS
ZIRCONIA	WARCRAFT	VENDACES	MISDEALS	MILDEWED
ANICONIC	PRECRASH	SOLDADOS	MISDEALT	SUBDEWED
DRACONIC	EXECRATE	FREDAINE	SUBDEANS	CAUDEXES
GLYCONIC	FULCRATE	MONDAINE	PREDEATH	FEEDHOLE
ITACONIC	BESCRAWL	NONDAIRY	SUNDECKS	WOODHOLE
ZIRCONIC	OUTCRAWL	UPADAISY	MISDEEDS	CORDIALS
CHACONNE	MISCREED	SANDALED	MISDEEMS	MISDIALS
MISCOOKS	AIRCREWS	PARDALES	GONDELAY	PREDIALS
OLICOOKS	CONCREWS	RUNDALES	URODELES	STADIALS
OLYCOOKS	UNSCREWS	PARDALIS	SONDELIS	SUNDIALS
OUTCOOKS	DESCRIED	ANODALLY	BRIDEMAN	CADDICES
PRECOOKS	OUTCRIED	BRIDALLY	SPADEMAN	CAUDICES
PRECOOLS	DESCRIER	CAUDALLY	ACADEMES	SPADICES
SUBCOOLS	DESCRIES	FEUDALLY	ACADEMIC	NIDDICKS
PUCCOONS	OUTCRIES	BELDAMES	EPIDEMIC	PREDICTS
RACCOONS	NONCRIME	MESDAMES	PANDEMIC	VERDICTS
HENCOOPS	APOCRINE	GODDAMNS	MISDEMPT	MISDIETS
SYNCOPAL	CANCRINE	ABIDANCE	CONDENSE	MISDIGHT
APOCOPES	EXOCRINE	GUIDANCE	ERODENTS	SARDINED
SYNCOPES	OUTCROPS	NONDANCE	EVIDENTS	CORDINER
CONCORDS	OUTCROSS	OUTDANCE	MORDENTS	AMIDINES
DISCORDS	TOPCROSS	RIDDANCE	PENDENTS	GRADINES
RIPCORDS	OUTCROWD	TENDANCE	STUDENTS	NANDINES
RANCORED	DISCROWN	VOIDANCE	TRIDENTS	NUNDINES
RESCORED	GORCROWS	MORDANCY	SUBDEPOT	SARDINES
SUCCORED	OUTCROWS	VERDANCY	BORDERED	SORDINES
SUCCORER	PILCROWS	MRIDANGS	CINDERED	UREDINES
RESCORES	PIECRUST	SLADANGS	DANDERED	URIDINES
PILCORNS	SUBCRUST	YARDANGS	DIDDERED	ABIDINGS
POPCORNS	MISCUING	FONDANTS	DODDERED	BANDINGS
TRICORNS	RESCUING	GARDANTS	DONDERED	BEADINGS
UNICORNS	BISCUITS	MORDANTS	FENDERED	BEDDINGS
DULCOSES	CIRCUITS	OXIDANTS	FODDERED	BENDINGS
GLUCOSES	MIDCULTS	PENDANTS	GANDERED	BIDDINGS
GLYCOSES	SUBCULTS	OUTDARED	GENDERED	BINDINGS
NARCOSES	CURCUMIN	PANDARED	HINDERED	BIRDINGS
SACCOSES	DISCURED	OUTDARES	JUDDERED	BLADINGS
VISCOSES	OBSCURED	BANDARIS	LADDERED	BONDINGS
SUBCOSTA	PRECURED	PINDARIS	MOIDERED	BUDDINGS
ALECOSTS	PROCURED	SUNDARIS	MOLDERED	CARDINGS
BOYCOTTS	OBSCURER	GOLDARNS	MURDERED	CHIDINGS
HICCOUGH	PROCURER	TRIDARNS	PANDERED	CORDINGS
DISCOUNT	DISCURES	CAUDATED	POLDERED	EILDINGS
MISCOUNT	EPICURES	GRADATED	PONDERED	FARDINGS
OUTCOUNT	OBSCURES	MANDATED	POWDERED	FEEDINGS
VISCOUNT	PRECURES	MISDATED	PUDDERED	FEUDINGS
DISCOURE	PROCURES	OUTDATED	RENDERED	FINDINGS
BESCOURS	OUTCURSE	OXIDATED	SAWDERED	FOLDINGS
CONCOURS	PRECURSE	PREDATED	SOLDERED	FUNDINGS
RANCOURS	OUTCURVE	AIRDATES	SUNDERED	GELDINGS
SUCCOURS	EXECUTER	CAUDATES	TEDDERED	GILDINGS
LAWCOURT	ELOCUTES	DEODATES	TENDERED	GIRDINGS
SELCOUTH	EXECUTES	EXUDATES	WANDERED	GLIDINGS
BEDCOVER	SUBCUTES	GRADATES	WARDERED	GRADINGS

GUIDINGS	SKYDIVER	LETDOWNS	MISDROVE	MARDYING
HEADINGS	KHEDIVES	LOWDOWNS	OUTDROVE	MOODYING
HILDINGS	SKYDIVES	MIXDOWNS	WINDROWS	MUDDYING
HOLDINGS	BURDOCKS	PINDOWNS	PRODRUGS	PANDYING
HYLDINGS	CANDOCKS	PUTDOWNS	DOLDRUMS	PREDYING
LANDINGS	DADDOCKS	RUBDOWNS	EARDRUMS	READYING
LEADINGS	HADDOCKS	RUNDOWNS	HUMDRUMS	RUDDYING
LENDINGS	HORDOCKS	SUNDOWNS	OUTDRUNK	STUDYING
LOADINGS	MADDOCKS	PREDRAFT	GRADUALS	TARDYING
LORDINGS	PADDOCKS	OUTDRAGS	SUBDUALS	TOADYING
MENDINGS	PIDDOCKS	HANDRAIL	OVIDUCAL	WADDYING
MINDINGS	PUDDOCKS	HEADRAIL	CONDUCES	VANDYKED
MODDINGS	RUDDOCKS	LANDRAIL	PRODUCES	VANDYKES
MOLDINGS	WINDOCKS	MANDRAKE	SUBDUCES	ANODYNES
NODDINGS	OUTDODGE	FINDRAMS	TRADUCES	BUFFABLE
PADDINGS	MISDOERS	OUTDRANK	GEODUCKS	OUTFABLE
PUDDINGS	OUTDOERS	QUADRANT	GWEDUCKS	REEFABLE
RAIDINGS	HANDOFFS	QUADRATS	HEYDUCKS	SURFABLE
READINGS	LEADOFFS	WOODRATS	CONDUCTS	OUTFACED
REDDINGS	SENDOFFS	AIRDRAWN	OVIDUCTS	PREFACED
REEDINGS	FORDOING	MISDRAWN	PRODUCTS	SURFACED
ROADINGS	MISDOING	OUTDRAWN	SUBDUCTS	PREFACER
RODDINGS	OUTDOING	MISDRAWS	VIADUCTS	SURFACER
SANDINGS	CONDOLED	OUTDRAWS	OUTDUELS	CATFACES
SEEDINGS	CONDOLES	MISDREAD	FONDUING	DOGFACES
SENDINGS	CONDONER	DAYDREAM	SUBDUING	OUTFACES
SHADINGS	PARDONER	OUTDREAM	CONDUITS	PIGFACES
SINDINGS	FORDONNE	OUTDRESS	PENDULES	PREFACES
SLIDINGS	MISDONNE	SUNDRESS	SCEDULES	SURFACES
SYNDINGS	PUNDONOR	WARDRESS	SUBDUPLE	UNIFACES
TRADINGS	BANDOOKS	HEADREST	EPIDURAL	BIOFACTS
VENDINGS	BUNDOOKS	PREDRIED	SUBDURAL	GEOFACTS
VOIDINGS	PREDOOMS	TAWDRIER	BANDURAS	NONFACTS
WADDINGS	OUTDOORS	BAWDRIES	PANDURAS	PREFADED
WARDINGS	PANDOORS	FOUDRIES	OUTDURED	PREFADES
WEDDINGS	TANDOORS	PREDRIES	PERDURED	JEOFAILS
WEEDINGS	BANDORES	SUNDRIES	VERDURED	FORFAIRS
WELDINGS	CONDORES	TAWDRIES	BORDURES	FUNFAIRS
WILDINGS	MOIDORES	MANDRILL	OUTDURES	FURFAIRS
WINDINGS	PANDORES	PREDRILL	PERDURES	MISFAITH
WORDINGS	WINDORES	SUNDRILY	RONDURES	ASHFALLS
YARDINGS	ACIDOSES	TAWDRILY	VERDURES	CATFALLS
PUDDINGY	APODOSES	OUTDRINK	GOLDURNS	DEWFALLS
RONDINOS	ISODOSES	MISDRIVE	CORDUROY	ICEFALLS
TONDINOS	LORDOSES	OUTDRIVE	PREDUSKS	JAWFALLS
GORDITAS	EPIDOTES	DENDROID	SAWDUSTS	MISFALLS
COEDITED	MISDOUBT	BEADROLL	SAWDUSTY	OUTFALLS
CREDITED	FOLDOUTS	HANDROLL	WOODWALE	PINFALLS
INEDITED	HANDOUTS	AIRDROME	SUBDWARF	PITFALLS
REEDITED	HOLDOUTS	PRODROME	OUTDWELL	DISFAMES
UNEDITED	READOUTS	SEADROME	OUTDWELT	PROFANES
CHEDITES	HANDOVER	SYNDROME	BANDYING	GONFANON
CORDITES	HOLDOVER	AIRDROPS	BOODYING	FANFARED
CRUDITES	PANDOWDY	DEWDROPS	BUDDYING	MISFARED
ERUDITES	SHADOWED	EARDROPS	BUNDYING	WARFARED
LYDDITES	WINDOWED	EYEDROPS	CADDYING	WAYFARED
VERDITES	SHADOWER	GUMDROPS	CANDYING	SEAFARER
KHEDIVAS	CUTDOWNS	OUTDROPS	CANDYING	WARFARER
SKYDIVED	HAGDOWNS	SUNDROPS	GIDDYING	WAYFARER
SANDIVER	HOEDOWNS	WARDROPS	HOWDYING	AIRFARES
			KIDDYING	

CAR**FARES**	BUF**FIEST**	PRE**FIXED**	CON**FOCAL**	AIR**FRAME**
EEL**FARES**	COM**FIEST**	SUF**FIXED**	EPI**FOCAL**	BED**FRAME**
FAN**FARES**	DAF**FIEST**	CON**FIXES**	NON**FOCAL**	MIS**FRAME**
LAW**FARES**	FUF**FIEST**	PRE**FIXES**	PAR**FOCAL**	SUB**FRAME**
MIS**FARES**	GOO**FIEST**	SUB**FIXES**	TRI**FOCAL**	PRE**FRANK**
WAR**FARES**	GUL**FIEST**	SUF**FIXES**	MIS**FOCUS**	ECO**FREAK**
WAY**FARES**	HUF**FIEST**	PRE**FLAME**	PRE**FOCUS**	CON**FRERE**
WEL**FARES**	LEA**FIEST**	OUT**FLANK**	AIR**FOILS**	COF**FRETS**
OUT**FASTS**	MIF**FIEST**	CAT**FLAPS**	JET**FOILS**	POM**FRETS**
SIT**FASTS**	NIF**FIEST**	COW**FLAPS**	MIL**FOILS**	BEL**FRIED**
TUB**FASTS**	POO**FIEST**	EAR**FLAPS**	SEX**FOILS**	PAN**FRIED**
NON**FATAL**	PUF**FIEST**	MUD**FLAPS**	TIN**FOILS**	BEL**FRIES**
SUL**FATED**	REE**FIEST**	OUT**FLASH**	TRE**FOILS**	PAN**FRIES**
SUL**FATES**	ROO**FIEST**	MUD**FLATS**	EYE**FOLDS**	DIS**FROCK**
NON**FATTY**	SUR**FIEST**	RUN**FLATS**	FAN**FOLDS**	SAF**FRONS**
FOR**FAULT**	TOF**FIEST**	DIS**FLESH**	PEN**FOLDS**	BOW**FRONT**
AVI**FAUNA**	TUR**FIEST**	PAR**FLESH**	PIN**FOLDS**	CON**FRONT**
EPI**FAUNA**	WOO**FIEST**	CALF**LICK**	TEN**FOLDS**	SEA**FRONT**
DIS**FAVOR**	BUN**FIGHT**	RUF**FLIER**	TWO**FOLDS**	SHO**FROTH**
OUT**FAWNS**	CAT**FIGHT**	WAF**FLIER**	KIN**FOLKS**	OUT**FROWN**
CAR**FAXES**	DOG**FIGHT**	BAR**FLIES**	MEN**FOLKS**	PRE**FROZE**
OUT**FEAST**	GUN**FIGHT**	BOT**FLIES**	MER**FOLKS**	EGG**FRUIT**
MIS**FEEDS**	OUT**FIGHT**	DAY**FLIES**	SEA**FOLKS**	FOG**FRUIT**
PIG**FEEDS**	PRE**FIGHT**	GAD**FLIES**	PLA**FONDS**	JAK**FRUIT**
OUT**FEELS**	UNI**FILAR**	MAY**FLIES**	SEA**FOODS**	BUM**FUCKS**
MIS**FEIGN**	MIS**FILED**	MED**FLIES**	OUT**FOOLS**	BIO**FUELS**
MAT**FELON**	PRE**FILED**	OUT**FLIES**	TOM**FOOLS**	SYN**FUELS**
OUT**FENCE**	PRO**FILED**	SAW**FLIES**	BIG**FOOTS**	AIM**FULLY**
FOR**FENDS**	PRO**FILER**	BAF**FLING**	FIN**FOOTS**	ART**FULLY**
PIL**FERER**	MIS**FILES**	COF**FLING**	HOT**FOOTS**	FIT**FULLY**
SUF**FERER**	PRE**FILES**	CUF**FLING**	OUT**FOOTS**	IRE**FULLY**
SAL**FERNS**	PRO**FILES**	HAL**FLING**	RED**FOOTS**	JOY**FULLY**
FUN**FESTS**	SUB**FILES**	MAF**FLING**	PER**FORCE**	LAW**FULLY**
GAB**FESTS**	FUL**FILLS**	MUF**FLING**	REN**FORCE**	MAN**FULLY**
TAF**FETAS**	BIO**FILMS**	OUT**FLING**	TEL**FORDS**	RUE**FULLY**
BUF**FETED**	NON**FINAL**	PIF**FLING**	HAY**FORKS**	SIN**FULLY**
SUF**FETES**	HAW**FINCH**	PUR**FLING**	AUS**FORMS**	USE**FULLY**
SUB**FEUED**	OUT**FINDS**	RAF**FLING**	CON**FORMS**	WIL**FULLY**
EDI**FICES**	COF**FINED**	RIF**FLING**	DIS**FORMS**	WOE**FULLY**
ORI**FICES**	CON**FINED**	RUF**FLING**	ISO**FORMS**	PER**FUMED**
SUF**FICES**	TIF**FINED**	SIF**FLING**	MIS**FORMS**	PER**FUMER**
CON**FIDES**	CON**FINER**	STI**FLING**	PER**FORMS**	PER**FUMES**
SUL**FIDES**	CON**FINES**	TRI**FLING**	PRE**FORMS**	PRE**FUNDS**
AIR**FIELD**	OLE**FINES**	WAF**FLING**	UNI**FORMS**	FUR**FURAL**
CAN**FIELD**	RAT**FINKS**	WOL**FLING**	COM**FORTS**	FUR**FURAN**
GAS**FIELD**	MIS**FIRED**	GUN**FLINT**	PIE**FORTS**	FUR**FUROL**
HAY**FIELD**	OIL**FIRED**	BOB**FLOAT**	CON**FOUND**	CON**FUSED**
ICE**FIELD**	OUT**FIRED**	OUT**FLOAT**	DUM**FOUND**	DIF**FUSED**
MID**FIELD**	PRE**FIRED**	SEA**FLOOR**	NEW**FOUND**	PER**FUSED**
MIS**FIELD**	BON**FIRES**	SUB**FLOOR**	OUT**FOUND**	SUF**FUSED**
OIL**FIELD**	FOX**FIRES**	COW**FLOPS**	PRO**FOUND**	CON**FUSES**
OUT**FIELD**	GUN**FIRES**	RYE**FLOUR**	BAT**FOWLS**	DIF**FUSES**
SUB**FIELD**	MIS**FIRES**	OUT**FLOWN**	PEA**FOWLS**	DOO**FUSES**
URN**FIELD**	OUT**FIRES**	AIR**FLOWS**	SEA**FOWLS**	PER**FUSES**
DEI**FIERS**	PRE**FIRES**	MUD**FLOWS**	OUT**FOXED**	SUF**FUSES**
EDI**FIERS**	RIM**FIRES**	OUT**FLOWS**	CAR**FOXES**	DIG**GABLE**
REI**FIERS**	CON**FIRMS**	BUM**FLUFF**	DOG**FOXES**	HAN**GABLE**
UNI**FIERS**	LUT**FISKS**	NON**FLUID**	OUT**FOXES**	HUG**GABLE**
BEE**FIEST**	SEL**FISTS**	SUB**FLUID**	DIF**FRACT**	LUG**GABLE**
BOO**FIEST**	CON**FIXED**	OUT**FLUSH**	TAF**FRAIL**	SIN**GABLE**

BRIGADES	SYNGENIC	RAGGINGS	CONGLOBE	PANGRAMS
FOUGADES	ZOOGENIC	RANGINGS	ISOGLOSS	PROGRAMS
RHAGADES	SUBGENRE	RIDGINGS	FOXGLOVE	TANGRAMS
BAGGAGES	COAGENTS	RIGGINGS	KIDGLOVE	TRIGRAMS
BURGAGES	EXIGENTS	RINGINGS	AIRGLOWS	EMIGRANT
FOGGAGES	MARGENTS	RUGGINGS	DAYGLOWS	FLAGRANT
LUGGAGES	REAGENTS	SAGGINGS	OUTGLOWS	FRAGRANT
BARGAINS	TANGENTS	SERGINGS	SUNGLOWS	AIRGRAPH
OUTGAINS	SUBGENUS	SINGINGS	ANAGLYPH	APOGRAPH
GREGALES	BERGERES	SOGGINGS	DIAGLYPH	BIOGRAPH
CUPGALLS	ETAGERES	STAGINGS	TRIGLYPH	DIAGRAPH
GINGALLS	GOUGERES	SUGGINGS	OUTGNAWN	EPIGRAPH
JINGALLS	LARGESSE	SURGINGS	OUTGNAWS	ISOGRAPH
NUTGALLS	BARGESTS	TAGGINGS	SUBGOALS	MYOGRAPH
FRUGALLY	CONGESTS	TUGGINGS	FORGOERS	ODOGRAPH
BERGAMAS	DISGESTS	WEDGINGS	OUTGOERS	SUBGRAPH
ENDGAMES	SUGGESTS	WIGGINGS	CARGOING	SYNGRAPH
PREGAMES	SANGHATS	BATGIRLS	DINGOING	TRIGRAPH
APOGAMIC	BARGHEST	BUSGIRLS	FORGOING	COWGRASS
EPIGAMIC	LAIGHEST	COWGIRLS	MISGOING	CUTGRASS
EXOGAMIC	ROUGHEST	DAYGIRLS	OUTGOING	EELGRASS
ISOGAMIC	TEUGHEST	IMAGISMS	SEAGOING	LOPGRASS
PANGAMIC	TOUGHEST	LEGGISMS	TANGOING	MATGRASS
SYNGAMIC	ZINGIBER	ELEGISTS	WAYGOING	NUTGRASS
SIRGANGS	WERGILDS	ELOGISTS	MANGOLDS	PINGRASS
TAGGANTS	BAGGINGS	IMAGISTS	OLIGOMER	RAYGRASS
BIOGASES	BEGGINGS	OLIGISTS	DOGGONER	RIBGRASS
OILGASES	BIGGINGS	OLOGISTS	WAGGONER	ROTGRASS
OUTGASES	BUGGINGS	TERGITES	BARGOONS	RYEGRASS
SYNGASES	COGGINGS	TURGITES	DRAGOONS	SAWGRASS
ENDGATES	DAGGINGS	ZORGITES	JARGOONS	EMIGRATE
FRIGATES	DIGGINGS	FORGIVEN	BARGOOSE	BURGRAVE
OUTGATES	DODGINGS	MISGIVEN	CARGOOSE	MARGRAVE
VIRGATES	DOGGINGS	OUTGIVEN	MONGOOSE	SUNGREBE
VULGATES	FAGGINGS	FORGIVER	MUNGOOSE	CONGREED
AVIGATOR	FORGINGS	LAWGIVER	WAYGOOSE	UNAGREED
MISGAUGE	GANGINGS	FORGIVES	DISGORGE	NONGREEN
ARMGAUNT	GAUGINGS	MISGIVES	BURGOUTS	SENGREEN
DISGAVEL	HANGINGS	OUTGIVES	HANGOUTS	SHAGREEN
OUTGAZED	HEDGINGS	GANGLAND	BEDGOWNS	CONGREES
SUNGAZER	HOGGINGS	NONGLARE	DISGOWNS	PUGGREES
OUTGAZES	IMAGINGS	OUTGLARE	GARGOYLE	CONGREET
CONGEALS	JIGGINGS	BURGLARY	GURGOYLE	DIAGRIDS
BARGEESE	JOGGINGS	CUTGLASS	BONGRACE	CHAGRINS
CARGEESE	JUGGINGS	EYEGLASS	DISGRACE	OUTGRINS
MONGEESE	LAGGINGS	SPYGLASS	DISGRADE	DRAGROPE
WERGELDS	LEGGINGS	SUNGLASS	MISGRADE	OUTGROSS
GINGELLY	LIGGINGS	OUTGLEAM	PAYGRADE	OUTGROUP
WERGELTS	LODGINGS	LANGLEYS	PROGRADE	SUBGROUP
PANGENES	LOGGINGS	GANGLIAL	SUBGRADE	MANGROVE
BIOGENIC	LONGINGS	SCAGLIAS	MISGRAFF	MISGROWN
CONGENIC	MERGINGS	FANGLIKE	ISOGRAFT	OUTGROWN
DYSGENIC	MUGGINGS	FROGLIKE	MISGRAFT	MISGROWS
EPIGENIC	NAGGINGS	GONGLIKE	ZOOGRAFT	OUTGROWS
EROGENIC	NOGGINGS	KINGLIKE	ANAGRAMS	CONGRUED
ISOGENIC	PARGINGS	RINGLIKE	DIAGRAMS	CONGRUES
MYOGENIC	PEGGINGS	SNAGLIKE	EPIGRAMS	HATGUARD
OROGENIC	PIGGINGS	SONGLIKE	GROGRAMS	MUDGUARD
OXYGENIC	PUGGINGS	TWIGLIKE	ISOGRAMS	OUTGUARD
PYOGENIC	PURGINGS	WINGLIKE	MYOGRAMS	VANGUARD

COU**GUARS**	UN**CHASTE**	CEP**HEIDS**	NOT**HINGS**	HOG**HOODS**
MIS**GUESS**	DET**HATCH**	DIT**HEIST**	RU**CHINGS**	LAD**HOODS**
OUT**GUESS**	NUT**HATCH**	BUS**HELED**	RUS**HINGS**	MAN**HOODS**
BAR**GUEST**	UNT**HATCH**	NO**CHELED**	TIT**HINGS**	NUN**HOODS**
NON**GUEST**	LIT**HATES**	ANT**HELIX**	VIS**HINGS**	SON**HOODS**
MIS**GUIDE**	RE**CHATES**	EN**SHELLS**	WAS**HINGS**	EYE**HOOKS**
OUT**GUIDE**	BOX**HAULS**	IN**SHELLS**	WIS**HINGS**	MUD**HOOKS**
PRE**GUIDE**	OUT**HAULS**	MO**CHELLS**	OUT**HIRED**	POT**HOOKS**
NON**GUILT**	RES**HAVEN**	MU**CHELLS**	JAG**HIRES**	SKY**HOOKS**
DIS**GUISE**	UNS**HAVEN**	UN**SHELLS**	OUT**HIRES**	TYP**HOONS**
CIN**GULAR**	RES**HAVES**	DIS**HELMS**	MYT**HISTS**	RES**HOOTS**
LIN**GULAR**	HEE**HAWED**	AL**CHEMIC**	SOP**HISTS**	UNS**HOOTS**
SIN**GULAR**	UNT**HAWED**	ANT**HEMIC**	TA**CHISTS**	UPS**HOOTS**
ARU**GULAS**	DOR**HAWKS**	IS**CHEMIC**	AR**CHIVED**	BIS**HOPED**
LIN**GULAS**	GOS**HAWKS**	LIT**HEMIC**	BES**HIVER**	WAN**HOPES**
TRA**GULES**	SEA**HAWKS**	SA**CHEMIC**	AR**CHIVES**	AMP**HORAL**
VIR**GULES**	SAS**HAYED**	NOW**HENCE**	BEE**HIVES**	AMP**HORAS**
SEA**GULLS**	AIR**HEADS**	SIT**HENCE**	PAT**HOGEN**	SEN**HORAS**
BUR**GUNDY**	BED**HEADS**	PRE**HENDS**	LIT**HOING**	ALP**HORNS**
DIS**GUSTS**	BIG**HEADS**	FOR**HENTS**	UN**CHOKED**	ALT**HORNS**
DAL**GYTES**	BOW**HEADS**	PS**CHENTS**	UN**CHOKES**	BET**HORNS**
DIS**HABIT**	CAT**HEADS**	COW**HERBS**	TOE**HOLDS**	BIG**HORNS**
CAS**HABLE**	CUP**HEADS**	POT**HERBS**	POT**HOLED**	COE**HORNS**
DIS**HABLE**	EGG**HEADS**	COW**HERDS**	AIR**HOLES**	DIS**HORNS**
FIS**HABLE**	FAT**HEADS**	HOU**HERES**	ARM**HOLES**	FOG**HORNS**
OAT**HABLE**	GOD**HEADS**	NOW**HERES**	ASS**HOLES**	INK**HORNS**
TIT**HABLE**	HOP**HEADS**	BIO**HERMS**	BOT**HOLES**	LEG**HORNS**
WAR**HABLE**	HOT**HEADS**	CIT**HERNS**	CAT**HOLES**	SAX**HORNS**
WAS**HABLE**	JAR**HEADS**	LUT**HERNS**	DOG**HOLES**	TIN**HORNS**
UNS**HADED**	JUG**HEADS**	ZIT**HERNS**	EYE**HOLES**	BAT**HORSE**
BRU**HAHAS**	MOP**HEADS**	EXA**HERTZ**	FOX**HOLES**	DIS**HORSE**
EN**CHAINS**	NET**HEADS**	EST**HETES**	JAW**HOLES**	RED**HORSE**
UN**CHAINS**	PIN**HEADS**	MA**CHETES**	KEY**HOLES**	SAW**HORSE**
CO**CHAIRS**	PIT**HEADS**	ES**CHEWED**	LUG**HOLES**	SEA**HORSE**
MA**CHAIRS**	POT**HEADS**	RE**CHEWED**	MAN**HOLES**	WAR**HORSE**
UN**CHAIRS**	RAG**HEADS**	UN**CHEWED**	MUD**HOLES**	RE**CHOSEN**
UNS**HALED**	RAW**HEADS**	ES**CHEWER**	OIL**HOLES**	UN**CHOSEN**
UNS**HALES**	RED**HEADS**	CAT**HEXES**	PIE**HOLES**	BAT**HOSES**
OMP**HALOS**	SAP**HEADS**	COW**HIDED**	PIN**HOLES**	KYP**HOSES**
ASP**HALTS**	SUB**HEADS**	RAW**HIDED**	POT**HOLES**	ORT**HOSES**
BES**HAMED**	TOW**HEADS**	COW**HIDES**	RAT**HOLES**	PAT**HOSES**
UNS**HAMED**	WAR**HEADS**	RA**CHIDES**	SPY**HOLES**	ALT**HOUGH**
BES**HAMES**	WEB**HEADS**	RAP**HIDES**	TAP**HOLES**	ELK**HOUND**
BE**CHANCE**	ALL**HEALS**	RAW**HIDES**	DIS**HOMED**	FOX**HOUND**
COW**HANDS**	COW**HEARD**	ANT**HILLS**	FAT**HOMED**	SEA**HOUND**
FLY**HANDS**	MIS**HEARD**	AR**CHINGS**	FAT**HOMER**	ALE**HOUSE**
BET**HANKS**	OUT**HEARD**	BAS**HINGS**	OUT**HOMER**	ART**HOUSE**
EN**CHANTS**	MIS**HEARS**	BUS**HINGS**	DIS**HOMES**	BAG**HOUSE**
ET**CHANTS**	OUT**HEARS**	DIS**HINGS**	SKY**HOMES**	BUG**HOUSE**
BEG**HARDS**	EN**SHEATH**	ET**CHINGS**	BON**HOMIE**	CAT**HOUSE**
DIE**HARDS**	IN**SHEATH**	FIS**HINGS**	SIP**HONED**	COW**HOUSE**
OR**CHARDS**	ES**CHEATS**	HAS**HINGS**	SYP**HONED**	DIS**HOUSE**
PO**CHARDS**	EX**CHEATS**	IT**CHINGS**	DIP**HONES**	DOG**HOUSE**
NON**HARDY**	PRE**HEATS**	LAS**HINGS**	DIS**HONOR**	FUN**HOUSE**
UNS**HARED**	RE**CHEATS**	LAT**HINGS**	APE**HOODS**	GAS**HOUSE**
FUT**HARKS**	RE**CHECKS**	MAS**HINGS**	BOY**HOODS**	GIN**HOUSE**
BE**CHARMS**	UN**CHECKS**	MES**HINGS**	CAT**HOODS**	GUN**HOUSE**
EN**CHARMS**	SHA**HEEDS**	MI**CHINGS**	CUB**HOODS**	HEN**HOUSE**
UN**CHARMS**	COW**HEELS**	MOS**HINGS**	ELF**HOODS**	HOT**HOUSE**
RE**CHARTS**	EN**WHEELS**	NIT**HINGS**	GOD**HOODS**	ICE**HOUSE**

MADHOUSE	BUCKAROO	JACKINGS	GRIMACER	DISMASKS
NUTHOUSE	JACKAROO	JERKINGS	GRIMACES	DISMASTS
OUTHOUSE	BLOKARTS	KIRKINGS	STOMACHS	DURMASTS
POTHOUSE	FLOKATIS	LEKKINGS	CROMACKS	TOPMASTS
RATHOUSE	TASKBARS	LICKINGS	STOMACKS	ABOMASUS
TAPHOUSE	BUCKEENS	LOCKINGS	FROMAGES	MISMATCH
TEAHOUSE	JACKEENS	LURKINGS	PLUMAGES	OUTMATCH
BESHOUTS	NANKEENS	MARKINGS	PRIMAGES	ANIMATED
UNSHOUTS	BARKEEPS	MASKINGS	REIMAGES	BROMATED
WASHOUTS	MISKEEPS	MILKINGS	RUMMAGES	CLIMATED
WITHOUTS	OUTKEEPS	MOCKINGS	BARMAIDS	CREMATED
PUSHOVER	SHEKELIM	NECKINGS	MERMAIDS	FORMATED
OUTHOWLS	COCKEREL	PACKINGS	SEAMAIDS	GEMMATED
UPCHUCKS	MACKEREL	PARKINGS	AIRMAILS	MISMATED
NONHUMAN	PICKEREL	PECKINGS	WEBMAILS	PALMATED
PANHUMAN	RESKETCH	PICKINGS	CREMAINS	SIGMATED
PREHUMAN	COCKEYED	PINKINGS	GERMAINS	SUMMATED
SUBHUMAN	HAWKEYED	QUAKINGS	PTOMAINS	ANIMATER
SUBHUMID	JOCKEYED	RACKINGS	NONMAJOR	AGEMATES
OUTHUMOR	LACKEYED	RANKINGS	BEDMAKER	ANIMATES
BETHUMPS	MICKEYED	ROCKINGS	CAPMAKER	BEDMATES
FOXHUNTS	MISKEYED	SACKINGS	CARMAKER	BROMATES
MANHUNTS	MONKEYED	SARKINGS	DIEMAKER	CLIMATES
OUTHUNTS	BARKHANS	SHAKINGS	FLYMAKER	CREMATES
YOGHURTS	SABKHATS	SINKINGS	GUNMAKER	FORMATES
METHYLIC	CHIKHORS	SMOKINGS	HATMAKER	GEMMATES
BOTHYMEN	MARKHORS	SOAKINGS	HAYMAKER	IMAMATES
OMOHYOID	MISKICKS	SUCKINGS	ICEMAKER	MISMATES
CARJACKS	OUTKICKS	TACKINGS	LAWMAKER	PRIMATES
MANJACKS	TOPKICKS	TALKINGS	MAPMAKER	SIGMATES
SKYJACKS	ROCKIERS	TANKINGS	REGMAKER	STOMATES
GOUJEERS	DESKILLS	TASKINGS	TEAMAKER	SUMMATES
OUTJESTS	OUTKILLS	TICKINGS	TOPMAKER	HAEMATIN
CONJOINS	RESKILLS	TUSKINGS	WARMAKER	SCHMATTE
DISJOINS	UPSKILLS	WALKINGS	WIGMAKER	CLIMAXED
MISJOINS	MANKINDS	WICKINGS	MISMAKES	CLIMAXES
SUBJOINS	ARCKINGS	WINKINGS	HARMALAS	DISMAYED
CONJOINT	AWAKINGS	WORKINGS	SHEMALES	UNAMAZED
DISJOINT	BACKINGS	CHEKISTS	ANIMALIC	MIZMAZES
BANJOIST	BALKINGS	LOOKISTS	HOGMANES	NUTMEALS
FRIJOLES	BANKINGS	BURKITES	SIAMANGS	OATMEALS
MAHJONGS	BONKINGS	UNAKITES	APIMANIA	PERMEANT
MARJORAM	BOOKINGS	WEEKLONG	EGOMANIA	PERMEASE
POPJOYED	BROKINGS	NICKNACK	ZOOMANIA	NUTMEATS
FORJUDGE	BUCKINGS	PENKNIFE	GERMANIC	PIGMEATS
MISJUDGE	BULKINGS	BOWKNOTS	SHAMANIC	SCHMECKS
PREJUDGE	BUSKINGS	TOPKNOTS	SEAMANLY	PREMEDIC
CONJUGAL	CALKINGS	MISKNOWN	YEOMANLY	SCHMEERS
LOGJUICE	COOKINGS	MISKNOWS	OUTMARCH	MISMEETS
VERJUICE	DECKINGS	LOCKNUTS	DAYMARES	DYSMELIC
OUTJUMPS	DESKINGS	COOKOFFS	DAYMARKS	TRAMELLS
CONJUNTO	DICKINGS	FUCKOFFS	EARMARKS	VERMELLS
CONJUROR	DOCKINGS	KICKOFFS	FINMARKS	RESMELTS
NONJUROR	DUCKINGS	PICKOFFS	MISMARKS	TAGMEMES
COCKADES	ERLKINGS	LEUKOSES	OSTMARKS	COMMENDS
PARKADES	FUCKINGS	SAKKOSES	PUGMARKS	REAMENDS
POLKAING	GASKINGS	SHAKUDOS	SEAMARKS	STAMENED
SEAKALES	HACKINGS	VALKYRIE	WAYMARKS	SARMENTA
SERKALIS	HAWKINGS	WALKYRIE	MISMARRY	SUBMENTA
CHIKARAS	HUSKINGS	GRIMACED	FOUMARTS	TEGMENTA

TORMENTA	FULMINED	CHAMISES	COMMONEY	ANIMUSES
SUBMENUS	VERMINED	CHEMISES	NONMONEY	CORMUSES
GEMMEOUS	EXAMINER	DERMISES	OKIMONOS	HOUMUSES
GRAMERCY	TERMINER	EXOMISES	MIDMONTH	HUMMUSES
DORMERED	ALUMINES	ITEMISES	SCHMOOSE	LACMUSES
HAMMERED	BROMINES	KERMISES	BALMORAL	LITMUSES
MAMMERED	CARMINES	KOUMISES	NONMORAL	PRIMUSES
SIMMERED	COSMINES	PREMISES	PREMORAL	SHAMUSES
SUMMERED	DESMINES	PROMISES	CREMORNE	THYMUSES
YAMMERED	DIAMINES	SURMISES	CROMORNE	WAMMUSES
DUMMERER	ENAMINES	CHAMISOS	OXYMORON	NONMUSIC
HAMMERER	ETAMINES	ANIMISTS	BIOMORPH	BESMUTCH
YAMMERER	EXAMINES	ATOMISTS	ISOMORPH	COMMUTED
CHIMERES	FLAMINES	CHEMISTS	NEOMORPH	PERMUTED
COMMERES	FULMINES	CHYMISTS	TRIMORPH	COMMUTER
EPIMERES	HARMINES	COSMISTS	ZOOMORPH	COMMUTES
ISOMERES	JASMINES	GNOMISTS	PREMORSE	PERMUTES
UROMERES	PRIMINES	PALMISTS	ANEMOSES	GEOMYOID
COMMERGE	PROMINES	PLUMISTS	COSMOSES	DISPACED
REEMERGE	THYMINES	RHYMISTS	GUMMOSES	MYSPACED
SUBMERGE	BEAMINGS	SUMMISTS	HOMMOSES	OUTPACED
SUBMERSE	BOOMINGS	SCIMITER	KOSMOSES	RESPACED
COSMESES	BRIMINGS	AZYMITES	MARMOSES	DISPACES
HORMESES	CALMINGS	EREMITES	PHIMOSES	MYSPACES
SIAMESES	COAMINGS	GUMMITES	HARMOSTS	OUTPACES
GUNMETAL	DIMMINGS	MARMITES	MIDMOSTS	RESPACES
NONMETAL	FARMINGS	TERMITES	PROMOTED	CALPACKS
PROMETAL	FOAMINGS	MAMMITIS	COMMOTES	DAYPACKS
HELMETED	FORMINGS	COMMIXED	PROMOTES	ICEPACKS
BIOMETER	FRAMINGS	PREMIXED	MAMMOTHS	MANPACKS
DIAMETER	GUMMINGS	APOMIXES	PROMOTOR	MUDPACKS
GEOMETER	HUMMINGS	COMMIXES	PULMOTOR	PREPACKS
LUXMETER	JAMMINGS	PANMIXES	TRIMOTOR	RATPACKS
ODOMETER	LAMMINGS	PREMIXES	DISMOUNT	TRIPACKS
OHMMETER	LEMMINGS	TRIMIXES	SEAMOUNT	COMPACTS
OROMETER	MAIMINGS	BUMMOCKS	SURMOUNT	COMPADRE
OXIMETER	MUMMINGS	GAMMOCKS	DORMOUSE	NEOPAGAN
TRIMETER	PRIMINGS	HAMMOCKS	TITMOUSE	NONPAGAN
UDOMETER	RIMMINGS	HOMMOCKS	BADMOUTH	MISPAGED
VIAMETER	ROAMINGS	HUMMOCKS	BIGMOUTH	PROPAGED
YAWMETER	ROUMINGS	MAMMOCKS	DRYMOUTH	RAMPAGED
AGAMETES	SEAMINGS	MUMMOCKS	VERMOUTH	RAMPAGER
COSMETIC	SEEMINGS	SCHMOCKS	WARMOUTH	COMPAGES
HERMETIC	SOUMINGS	NONMODAL	COMMOVED	KIPPAGES
HORMETIC	SUMMINGS	ALAMODES	MISMOVED	MISPAGES
KISMETIC	TEAMINGS	COMMODES	OUTMOVED	PROPAGES
MISMETRE	WARMINGS	OUTMODES	PREMOVED	RAMPAGES
NONMETRO	CREMINIS	TURMOILS	COMMOVES	SEEPAGES
SIAMEZES	CRIMINIS	GRIMOIRE	MISMOVES	WARPAGES
FORMICAS	TROMINOS	WAGMOIRE	OUTMOVES	WEBPAGES
GIMMICKS	CATMINTS	BESMOKES	PREMOVES	CALPAINS
MIMMICKS	VARMINTS	PREMOLAR	ATEMOYAS	MISPAINT
GIMMICKY	TERMINUS	PREMOLDS	SCHMUCKS	OUTPAINT
BESMILES	PISMIRES	WADMOLLS	BESMUDGE	DESPAIRS
SOYMILKS	ATOMISER	HORMONAL	EARMUFFS	TAMPALAS
SAWMILLS	ITEMISER	CREMONAS	GEMMULES	PROPALED
ALUMINAS	PROMISER	COMMONER	PLUMULES	CARPALES
SHAMINAS	SURMISER	GAMMONER	MULMULLS	PROPALES
STAMINAS	ATOMISES	SERMONER	MURMURED	PULPALLY
EXAMINED	BROMISES	SUMMONER	UNAMUSED	OPOPANAX

CREPANCE	TAXPAYER	SUBPHASE	DUMPINGS	OUTPLACE
COMPANDS	DISPEACE	TRIPHASE	GAPPINGS	PREPLACE
SUBPANEL	BESPEAKS	CAMPHENE	GASPINGS	CHAPLAIN
PARPANES	RESPEAKS	GRAPHENE	HARPINGS	COMPLAIN
PROPANES	UNSPEAKS	CAMPHONE	HELPINGS	AIRPLANE
TREPANGS	UPSPEAKS	CARPHONE	HIPPINGS	SEAPLANE
TYMPANIC	PAMPEANS	DIAPHONE	HOPPINGS	SKIPLANE
JOGPANTS	COMPEARS	EARPHONE	JUMPINGS	SPYPLANE
NONPAPAL	UPSPEARS	GEOPHONE	KEEPINGS	TOWPLANE
KAUPAPAS	HENPECKS	ISOPHONE	KEMPINGS	TRIPLANE
ENDPAPER	RYEPECKS	PAYPHONE	LAMPINGS	VOLPLANE
FLYPAPER	TRIPEDAL	SULPHONE	LAPPINGS	WARPLANE
GUNPAPER	STAPEDES	TRIPHONE	LIMPINGS	MISPLANS
OILPAPER	OUTPEEPS	GRYPHONS	LIPPINGS	OUTPLANS
TARPAPER	COMPEERS	APOPHONY	LISPINGS	PREPLANS
MAMPARAS	OUTPEERS	DIAPHONY	LOOPINGS	ASHPLANT
HIPPARCH	RESPELLS	SYMPHONY	LOPPINGS	DISPLANT
JEOPARDS	UNSPELLS	SUBPHYLA	MAPPINGS	EGGPLANT
LEOPARDS	PROPENAL	SALPIANS	PIMPINGS	MISPLANT
JEOPARDY	DISPENCE	UTOPIANS	PUMPINGS	PIEPLANT
COMPARED	FIPPENCE	ABAPICAL	RAMPINGS	PREPLANT
PREPARED	SIXPENCE	ATYPICAL	RAPPINGS	SUPPLANT
UNSPARED	SUSPENCE	ETYPICAL	RASPINGS	WAXPLANT
COMPARER	TENPENCE	TROPICAL	REPPINGS	SHIPLAPS
PREPARER	TUPPENCE	EARPICKS	RIPPINGS	SUIPLAPS
COMPARES	TWOPENCE	NITPICKS	RISPINGS	WHIPLASH
PREPARES	COMPENDS	NUTPICKS	SHAPINGS	AXOPLASM
AIRPARKS	DISPENDS	RAMPICKS	SNIPINGS	BIOPLASM
DISPARKS	PARPENDS	NITPICKY	SOOPINGS	EXOPLASM
MISPARSE	PERPENDS	CODPIECE	SOPPINGS	NEOPLASM
CLIPARTS	PROPENDS	EARPIECE	STOPINGS	APOPLAST
COMPARTS	STIPENDS	EYEPIECE	TAMPINGS	BIOPLAST
DISPARTS	SUSPENDS	SEAPIECE	TAPPINGS	SYMPLAST
MISPARTS	DAMPENED	TOEPIECE	TIPPINGS	BEDPLATE
OUTPARTS	DEEPENED	DRAPIERS	TOPPINGS	ENDPLATE
RAMPARTS	HAPPENED	RIPPIERS	VAMPINGS	HOTPLATE
SUBPARTS	LIPPENED	DESPIGHT	WARPINGS	OMOPLATE
NONPARTY	REOPENED	GARPIKES	WEEPINGS	TEMPLATE
CASPASES	UNOPENED	MUSPIKES	YAWPINGS	TINPLATE
DIAPASES	PROPENES	RAMPIKES	YELPINGS	TOEPLATE
LAMPASES	TERPENES	RANPIKES	CAMPIONS	VAMPLATE
PAMPASES	SIXPENNY	COMPILED	LAMPIONS	AIRPLAYS
LAMPASSE	TENPENNY	COMPILER	POMPIONS	DISPLAYS
PREPASTE	TUPPENNY	COMPILES	PUMPIONS	ENDPLAYS
FLYPASTS	TWOPENNY	HUIPILES	RAMPIONS	GUNPLAYS
NONPASTS	PARPENTS	FORPINED	TAMPIONS	MISPLAYS
DESPATCH	PERPENTS	PROPINED	TOMPIONS	NONPLAYS
DISPATCH	SERPENTS	ALEPINES	BAGPIPED	OUTPLAYS
MISPATCH	COMPERES	CHOPINES	BAGPIPER	MISPLEAD
CUSPATED	OOSPERMS	FORPINES	BAGPIPES	COMPLEAT
PALPATED	LAMPERNS	PROPINES	DESPISES	COMPLIED
PALPATES	DISPERSE	TROPINES	JASPISES	SUPPLIED
TOWPATHS	SEXPERTS	BUMPINGS	KALPISES	TRIPLIED
WARPATHS	ANAPESTS	CAMPINGS	FLYPITCH	COMPLIER
CHUPATTY	TEMPESTS	CAPPINGS	OUTPITCH	DIMPLIER
RAUPATUS	RISPETTI	CARPINGS	ANTPITTA	PIMPLIER
DIAPAUSE	RISPETTO	CUPPINGS	ANYPLACE	POPPLIER
PREPAVED	PROPHAGE	DAMPINGS	DISPLACE	PURPLIER
PREPAVES	ANAPHASE	DIPPINGS	MISPLACE	RIPPLIER
SUPPAWNS	PROPHASE	DOPPINGS		RUMPLIER

SUP**PLIER**	COW**POKES**	PUR**POSES**	MIS**PRIZE**	CON**QUEST**
COM**PLIES**	NON**POLAR**	SUP**POSES**	OUT**PRIZE**	OPA**QUEST**
SUP**PLIES**	SUB**POLAR**	TRI**POSES**	SUR**PRIZE**	UNI**QUEST**
TRI**PLIES**	UNI**POLAR**	OVI**POSIT**	GEO**PROBE**	LAC**QUEYS**
CAM**PLING**	MAY**POLES**	AIR**POSTS**	AIR**PROOF**	DIS**QUIET**
COU**PLING**	RAM**POLES**	BED**POSTS**	DIS**PROOF**	BED**QUILT**
DAP**PLING**	TAD**POLES**	COM**POSTS**	OIL**PROOF**	BAS**QUINE**
DIM**PLING**	ZEP**POLES**	DIS**POSTS**	RAT**PROOF**	MES**QUINE**
DIS**PLING**	PRO**POLIS**	OUT**POSTS**	SUN**PROOF**	REE**QUIPS**
DUM**PLING**	TRI**POLIS**	WAY**POSTS**	WET**PROOF**	VER**QUIRE**
HIR**PLING**	OUT**POLLS**	COM**POTES**	PIT**PROPS**	MES**QUITE**
HOP**PLING**	RED**POLLS**	COM**POUND**	MIS**PROUD**	MEZ**QUITE**
NIP**PLING**	DES**PONDS**	GEE**POUND**	DIS**PROVE**	MES**QUITS**
PEO**PLING**	RES**PONDS**	LIS**POUND**	PRE**PUBES**	MEZ**QUITS**
POP**PLING**	DIS**PONES**	PRO**POUND**	SUB**PUBIC**	NON**QUOTA**
PUR**PLING**	PRE**PONES**	OUT**POURS**	PRE**PUBIS**	MIS**QUOTE**
RIM**PLING**	PRO**PONES**	BES**POUTS**	PRE**PUCES**	OUT**QUOTE**
RIP**PLING**	ARA**PONGA**	CAM**POUTS**	LAM**PUKAS**	PER**VADED**
RUM**PLING**	CAM**PONGS**	DRO**POUTS**	SEP**PUKUS**	UNE**VADED**
SAM**PLING**	KAM**PONGS**	EEL**POUTS**	SCA**PULAS**	COU**VADES**
SAP**PLING**	CAR**POOLS**	SLI**POUTS**	SCO**PULAS**	PER**VADES**
SIM**PLING**	RES**POOLS**	AIR**POWER**	STI**PULED**	PRE**VAILS**
SIP**PLING**	UNS**POOLS**	MAN**POWER**	STI**PULES**	REA**VAILS**
SOU**PLING**	VAN**POOLS**	OUT**POWER**	OUT**PULLS**	TRA**VAILS**
STA**PLING**	HAR**POONS**	WAR**POWER**	COM**PULSE**	CHE**VALET**
SUP**PLING**	LAM**POONS**	COW**POXES**	KEY**PUNCH**	NON**VALID**
TIP**PLING**	POM**POONS**	RES**PRANG**	OUT**PUNCH**	DIS**VALUE**
TOP**PLING**	COR**PORAL**	UPS**PRANG**	PRE**PUNCH**	MIS**VALUE**
TRI**PLING**	TEM**PORAL**	STU**PRATE**	ARA**PUNGA**	OUT**VALUE**
WIM**PLING**	SUN**PORCH**	OUT**PRAYS**	TRA**PUNTO**	PRE**VALUE**
SNA**PLINK**	OOS**PORES**	RES**PRAYS**	PRE**PUPAE**	TRI**VALVE**
OUT**PLODS**	AIR**PORTS**	WHI**PRAYS**	PRE**PUPAL**	UNI**VALVE**
COW**PLOPS**	BES**PORTS**	OUT**PREEN**	PRE**PUPAS**	DOG**VANES**
BOX**PLOTS**	CAR**PORTS**	BES**PRENT**	OUT**PUPIL**	SER**VANTS**
COM**PLOTS**	COM**PORTS**	COM**PRESS**	MUD**PUPPY**	CAL**VARIA**
MAR**PLOTS**	DIS**PORTS**	HOT**PRESS**	COU**PURES**	CAN**VASES**
OUT**PLOTS**	GOS**PORTS**	OUT**PRESS**	GUI**PURES**	SIL**VATIC**
SUB**PLOTS**	GUN**PORTS**	PRE**PRESS**	PUR**PURES**	SYL**VATIC**
EAR**PLUGS**	JET**PORTS**	SUP**PRESS**	PUR**PURIN**	OUT**VAUNT**
DIS**PLUME**	OUT**PORTS**	KOU**PREYS**	CUT**PURSE**	SUR**VEILS**
KER**PLUNK**	PUR**PORTS**	LAM**PREYS**	DIS**PURSE**	MAU**VEINS**
TRI**PODAL**	RAP**PORTS**	MIS**PRICE**	CAM**PUSES**	LOW**VELDS**
URO**PODAL**	SEA**PORTS**	OUT**PRICE**	COR**PUSES**	KNE**VELLS**
SYM**PODIA**	SUP**PORTS**	PRE**PRICE**	GAU**PUSES**	PRO**VENDS**
ACU**POINT**	COM**POSED**	PIN**PRICK**	GAW**PUSES**	SCA**VENGE**
DEW**POINT**	DIS**POSED**	SUB**PRIME**	HIP**PUSES**	OUT**VENOM**
DRY**POINT**	MAL**POSED**	COM**PRINT**	MAW**PUSES**	CON**VENTS**
END**POINT**	PRE**POSED**	MIS**PRINT**	PAP**PUSES**	PRE**VENTS**
EYE**POINT**	PRO**POSED**	NON**PRINT**	RUM**PUSES**	SOL**VENTS**
GUN**POINT**	PUR**POSED**	OFF**PRINT**	WAM**PUSES**	PAR**VENUS**
MID**POINT**	SUP**POSED**	PRE**PRINT**	PRO**PYLON**	PRE**VERBS**
MIS**POINT**	COM**POSER**	SUR**PRINT**	SEA**QUAKE**	PRO**VERBS**
NON**POINT**	DIS**POSER**	SUB**PRIOR**	ALI**QUANT**	CON**VERGE**
OUT**POINT**	PRO**POSER**	COM**PRISE**	MUS**QUASH**	CON**VERSE**
PAR**POINT**	SUP**POSER**	MES**PRISE**	ADE**QUATE**	PER**VERSE**
PEN**POINT**	ADI**POSES**	MIS**PRISE**	COE**QUATE**	REN**VERSE**
PIN**POINT**	COM**POSES**	SUR**PRISE**	TOR**QUATE**	SUB**VERSE**
WAY**POINT**	DIS**POSES**	COM**PRIZE**	CUM**QUATS**	TRA**VERSE**
MIS**POISE**	PRE**POSES**	DIS**PRIZE**	KUM**QUATS**	UNI**VERSE**
POR**POISE**	PRO**POSES**	MES**PRIZE**	COT**QUEAN**	

CONVERSO	SURVIVER	NORWARDS	PIGWEEDS	KNOWINGS
RENVERST	CONVIVES	OUTWARDS	PINWEEDS	LAPWINGS
SUBVERST	SURVIVES	SEAWARDS	RAGWEEDS	OUTWINGS
CONVERTS	NONVOCAL	SKYWARDS	SEAWEEDS	REDWINGS
COUVERTS	SUBVOCAL	STEWARDS	TARWEEDS	SHOWINGS
CULVERTS	UNIVOCAL	SUNWARDS	WAXWEEDS	SLOWINGS
PERVERTS	OUTVOICE	BADWARES	MIDWEEKS	STEWINGS
SIEVERTS	FRIVOLED	BARWARES	BETWEENS	STOWINGS
SUBVERTS	COEVOLVE	MALWARES	MISWEENS	THAWINGS
HARVESTS	CONVOLVE	REDWARES	ENSWEEPS	UPSWINGS
CONVEXED	OUTVOTED	SEAWARES	OUTWEEPS	VIEWINGS
CONVEXES	NONVOTER	SPYWARES	UPSWEEPS	WAXWINGS
SILVEXES	OUTVOTER	TEAWARES	OUTWEIGH	CHEWINKS
PLUVIALS	OUTVOTES	TINWARES	PREWEIGH	EYEWINKS
SUBVICAR	DISVOUCH	UNAWARES	DRYWELLS	PREWIRED
CREVICED	REAVOWED	WETWARES	INDWELLS	HAYWIRES
SERVICED	UNAVOWED	BULWARKS	INKWELLS	PREWIRES
CERVICES	BEVVYING	BESWARMS	MAXWELLS	WAYWISER
CREVICES	BIVVYING	PREWARMS	OUTWELLS	BREWISES
SERVICES	CHEVYING	FORWARNS	UPSWELLS	ENTWISTS
BOUVIERS	CHIVVYING	PREWARNS	MISWENDS	INTWISTS
BREVIERS	DIVVYING	BLEWARTS	NARWHALE	RETWISTS
CLAVIERS	NAVVYING	TISWASES	BOBWHEEL	UNTWISTS
KLAVIERS	OUTVYING	TIZWASES	COGWHEEL	MIDWIVED
PREVIEWS	SAVVYING	FORWASTE	FLYWHEEL	ALEWIVES
PURVIEWS	BULWADDY	OUTWASTE	PINWHEEL	HUSWIVES
SURVIEWS	ASSWAGED	RADWASTE	RAGWHEEL	MIDWIVES
PULVILLI	ASSWAGES	DOGWATCH	WEBWHEEL	OLDWIVES
DREVILLS	BREWAGES	MIDWATCH	ANYWHERE	SEAWIVES
CORVINAS	FLOWAGES	OUTWATCH	EREWHILE	REAWOKEN
PROVINED	STOWAGES	CUTWATER	TARWHINE	AIRWOMAN
SPAVINED	OUTWAITS	EYEWATER	OUTWHIRL	BATWOMAN
FLAVINES	REAWAKED	POMWATER	EGGWHISK	LAYWOMAN
MAUVINES	UNAWAKED	REDWATER	BOBWHITE	MADWOMAN
NERVINES	REAWAKEN	SEAWATER	NONWHITE	PENWOMAN
OLIVINES	REAWAKES	NEWWAVER	BLOWHOLE	SEAWOMAN
PROVINES	GUNWALES	AIRWAVES	OUTWICKS	TOYWOMAN
SYLVINES	PINWALES	EARWAXES	MIDWIFED	AIRWOMEN
OLIVINIC	QAWWALIS	PAXWAXES	HUSWIFES	BATWOMEN
NONVIRAL	CATWALKS	SUBWAYED	MIDWIFES	LAYWOMEN
PROVIRAL	JAYWALKS	UNSWAYED	EARWIGGY	MADWOMEN
SUBVIRAL	OUTWALKS	UPSWAYED	OUTWILED	PENWOMEN
POXVIRUS	SKYWALKS	DAYWEARS	OUTWILES	SEAWOMEN
PROVIRUS	DRYWALLS	EYEWEARS	OUTWILLS	TOYWOMEN
REOVIRUS	GADWALLS	LEGWEARS	OUTWINDS	BARWOODS
SUBVIRUS	SEAWALLS	OUTWEARS	ENTWINED	BAYWOODS
PREVISED	SETWALLS	UNSWEARS	INTWINED	BOGWOODS
BREVISES	WITWALLS	FORWEARY	UNTWINED	BOXWOODS
CLEVISES	ELLWANDS	OUTWEARY	ENTWINES	CAMWOODS
PARVISES	SEAWANTS	COBWEBBY	ICEWINES	DAGWOODS
PELVISES	AIRWARDS	BURWEEDS	INTWINES	DOGWOODS
PREVISES	BEDWARDS	CUDWEEDS	LAUWINES	DYEWOODS
TRAVISES	FORWARDS	DYEWEEDS	UNTWINES	ELMWOODS
TREVISES	FROWARDS	GUMWEEDS	BLOWINGS	FATWOODS
PREVISIT	GODWARDS	HOGWEEDS	BREWINGS	FIRWOODS
PREVISOR	HAYWARDS	MATWEEDS	DRAWINGS	GUMWOODS
PROVISOR	HOGWARDS	MAYWEEDS	GAYWINGS	INKWOODS
CURVITAL	LEEWARDS	OARWEEDS	GNAWINGS	LOGWOODS
NONVITAL	MANWARDS	OREWEEDS	GROWINGS	NUTWOODS
GRAVITAS	NAYWARDS	OUTWEEDS	INSWINGS	PLYWOODS

RED**WOODS**	WEB**WORKS**	RAG**WORTS**	RE**CYCLED**	BUZZ**INGS**
SAP**WOODS**	SUB**WORLD**	RIB**WORTS**	MID**YEARS**	FIZZ**INGS**
NON**WOODY**	BAG**WORMS**	OUT**WOUND**	OUT**YELLS**	GLAZ**INGS**
KEY**WORDS**	BUD**WORMS**	NON**WOVEN**	OUT**YELPS**	GLOZ**INGS**
MIS**WORDS**	CAT**WORMS**	BOW**WOWED**	EMP**YESES**	GRAZ**INGS**
NAY**WORDS**	CUT**WORMS**	POW**WOWED**	OUT**YIELD**	SEIZ**INGS**
NON**WORDS**	EAR**WORMS**	EEL**WRACK**	CLAY**LIKE**	EPI**ZOISM**
WAN**WORDY**	EEL**WORMS**	PRE**WRAPS**	LADY**LIKE**	SUB**ZONAL**
ART**WORKS**	LOB**WORMS**	OUT**WREST**	LILY**LIKE**	TRI**ZONAL**
CAT**WORKS**	LUG**WORMS**	AVO**WRIES**	PLAY**LIKE**	BLA**ZONED**
CUT**WORKS**	PIN**WORMS**	CHO**WRIES**	QUAY**LIKE**	BLA**ZONER**
DAY**WORKS**	RAG**WORMS**	SCO**WRIES**	RUBY**LIKE**	HIZ**ZONER**
GAS**WORKS**	SEA**WORMS**	SHOW**RING**	WHEY**LIKE**	CAL**ZONES**
LAP**WORKS**	WAX**WORMS**	MIS**WRITE**	DIS**YOKED**	CAN**ZONES**
LEG**WORKS**	WEB**WORMS**	OUT**WRITE**	MIS**YOKED**	END**ZONES**
NET**WORKS**	OUT**WORTH**	SKY**WRITE**	DIS**YOKES**	SUB**ZONES**
OUT**WORKS**	TAM**WORTH**	MIS**WROTE**	MIS**YOKES**	TRI**ZONES**
PIN**WORKS**	WAN**WORTH**	OUT**WROTE**	BAR**YONIC**	WAR**ZONES**
PRE**WORKS**	AWL**WORTS**	SKY**WROTE**	GUA**YULES**	GAD**ZOOKS**
RAG**WORKS**	BLA**WORTS**	BOW**YANGS**	ALI**ZARIS**	MAD**ZOONS**
RIB**WORKS**	BUG**WORTS**	BEE**YARDS**	BEN**ZINES**	MAT**ZOONS**
TIN**WORKS**	FAN**WORTS**	HAL**YARDS**	DIA**ZINES**	EPI**ZOOTY**
TOP**WORKS**	FEL**WORTS**	INN**YARDS**	FAN**ZINES**	ISO**ZYMES**
TRY**WORKS**	FIG**WORTS**	LAN**YARDS**	OXA**ZINES**	ISO**ZYMIC**
TUT**WORKS**	MAD**WORTS**	TAN**YARDS**	RHI**ZINES**	
WAR**WORKS**	MUD**WORTS**	BI**CYCLED**	WEB**ZINES**	
WAX**WORKS**	MUG**WORTS**	CAL**YCLED**	BOO**ZINGS**	

Suffixes

Suffixes are just as useful as prefixes for the same reasons, but it can be less easy to spot opportunities to employ them. Therefore, it's a good idea to study the lists of the most commonly available suffixes to help you find those elusive bonus words. This list is also useful for remembering which adjective stems also form adverbs, as a glance at the -LY list demonstrates. As with the prefixes list, words which end in the suffix letters by coincidence rather than etymology are included, as they are useful in exactly the same way, and may be less obvious. Unlike prefixes though, the root part of the word may not always be a stand-alone word because often the root is modified when the suffix is added (eg DUTIFUL, EQUABLE).

Words that end with -ABLE

Seven-letter	DOW**ABLE**	GET**ABLE**	NAM**ABLE**	SAL**ABLE**
words	DRY**ABLE**	GIV**ABLE**	NOT**ABLE**	SAV**ABLE**
ACC**ABLE**	DUP**ABLE**	HAT**ABLE**	OWN**ABLE**	SAY**ABLE**
ACT**ABLE**	DUR**ABLE**	HEW**ABLE**	PAC**ABLE**	SEE**ABLE**
ADD**ABLE**	DYE**ABLE**	HID**ABLE**	PAP**ABLE**	SEW**ABLE**
AFF**ABLE**	EAT**ABLE**	HIR**ABLE**	PAR**ABLE**	SIZ**ABLE**
AMI**ABLE**	EFF**ABLE**	LIK**ABLE**	PAY**ABLE**	SKI**ABLE**
AST**ABLE**	EQU**ABLE**	LIN**ABLE**	PLI**ABLE**	SOW**ABLE**
BAT**ABLE**	ERR**ABLE**	LIV**ABLE**	POK**ABLE**	SUE**ABLE**
BIT**ABLE**	EYE**ABLE**	LOS**ABLE**	POS**ABLE**	TAK**ABLE**
BUY**ABLE**	FAD**ABLE**	LOV**ABLE**	POT**ABLE**	TAM**ABLE**
CAP**ABLE**	FIN**ABLE**	MAK**ABLE**	RAT**ABLE**	TAX**ABLE**
CIT**ABLE**	FIX**ABLE**	MIN**ABLE**	RET**ABLE**	TEN**ABLE**
COD**ABLE**	FLY**ABLE**	MIR**ABLE**	RID**ABLE**	TOT**ABLE**
CUR**ABLE**	FRI**ABLE**	MIX**ABLE**	ROP**ABLE**	TOW**ABLE**
DAT**ABLE**	FRY**ABLE**	MOV**ABLE**	ROW**ABLE**	TRI**ABLE**
DIS**ABLE**	GEL**ABLE**	MUT**ABLE**	RUL**ABLE**	TUN**ABLE**

TYPABLE	CULPABLE	HEALABLE	OBEYABLE	SAVEABLE
UNHABLE	CURBABLE	HEARABLE	OBVIABLE	SCALABLE
USEABLE	CUTTABLE	HEATABLE	OPENABLE	SEALABLE
VATABLE	DAMNABLE	HELPABLE	OPERABLE	SEISABLE
VOCABLE	DATEABLE	HIREABLE	OPINABLE	SEIZABLE
VOLABLE	DENIABLE	HITTABLE	OUTFABLE	SELLABLE
VOTABLE	DIGGABLE	HOLDABLE	OVENABLE	SENDABLE
WADABLE	DIMMABLE	HUGGABLE	OVERABLE	SERVABLE
WAXABLE	DIPPABLE	HUMMABLE	OXIDABLE	SHAKABLE
WIRABLE	DISHABLE	HUNTABLE	PACKABLE	SHAMABLE
	DRAPABLE	IMITABLE	PALPABLE	SHAPABLE
Eight-letter	DRAWABLE	INARABLE	PANTABLE	SHARABLE
words	DRIVABLE	INSTABLE	PARSABLE	SHAVABLE
ABATABLE	DUTIABLE	INVIABLE	PASSABLE	SHEDABLE
ABUSABLE	EDITABLE	ISOLABLE	PAWNABLE	SHOWABLE
ADORABLE	EDUCABLE	ISSUABLE	PECCABLE	SIGNABLE
AGITABLE	ENVIABLE	JAILABLE	PEELABLE	SINGABLE
ALLIABLE	ERASABLE	JAMMABLE	PETTABLE	SINKABLE
AMENABLE	ERODABLE	JOINABLE	PICKABLE	SIZEABLE
AMICABLE	EVADABLE	JUMPABLE	PINTABLE	SLAKABLE
AMUSABLE	EVITABLE	KEEPABLE	PITIABLE	SLAYABLE
ARGUABLE	EVOCABLE	KICKABLE	PLACABLE	SLIDABLE
ATONABLE	EXILABLE	KILLABLE	PLAYABLE	SMOKABLE
AVOWABLE	EXORABLE	KISSABLE	PLOWABLE	SOCIABLE
BAILABLE	EXPIABLE	KNOWABLE	PORTABLE	SOLVABLE
BANKABLE	FACEABLE	LAPSABLE	POSEABLE	SORBABLE
BANNABLE	FARMABLE	LAUDABLE	POTTABLE	SORTABLE
BARRABLE	FEEDABLE	LEASABLE	POURABLE	SPARABLE
BEARABLE	FELLABLE	LENDABLE	PRIZABLE	STATABLE
BEATABLE	FILEABLE	LETTABLE	PROBABLE	STEWABLE
BEDDABLE	FILLABLE	LEVIABLE	PROVABLE	STONABLE
BENDABLE	FILMABLE	LIENABLE	PRUNABLE	STORABLE
BIDDABLE	FINDABLE	LIFTABLE	QUOTABLE	STOWABLE
BILLABLE	FINEABLE	LIKEABLE	RACEABLE	SUITABLE
BINDABLE	FIREABLE	LINEABLE	RADIABLE	SUMMABLE
BISTABLE	FISHABLE	LINKABLE	RAISABLE	SURFABLE
BITEABLE	FITTABLE	LIQUABLE	RATEABLE	SWAYABLE
BLAMABLE	FOAMABLE	LISTABLE	READABLE	SYLLABLE
BOATABLE	FOILABLE	LIVEABLE	REAPABLE	TAKEABLE
BOILABLE	FOLDABLE	LOANABLE	REEFABLE	TALKABLE
BOMBABLE	FORDABLE	LOCKABLE	REELABLE	TAMEABLE
BONDABLE	FORMABLE	LOVEABLE	RELIABLE	TANNABLE
BOOKABLE	FRAMABLE	LUGGABLE	RENTABLE	TAPEABLE
BOOTABLE	FUNDABLE	MAILABLE	RESTABLE	TAPPABLE
BRIBABLE	FURLABLE	MAKEABLE	REUSABLE	TASTABLE
BUFFABLE	GAGEABLE	MAPPABLE	RIDEABLE	TEARABLE
BURNABLE	GAINABLE	MASKABLE	RINSABLE	TEASABLE
CALLABLE	GETTABLE	MELTABLE	RIPPABLE	TELLABLE
CARTABLE	GIFTABLE	MENDABLE	ROCKABLE	TESTABLE
CASCABLE	GIVEABLE	MILLABLE	ROLLABLE	TILLABLE
CASHABLE	GNAWABLE	MINEABLE	ROPEABLE	TILTABLE
CASTABLE	GRADABLE	MISSABLE	RUINABLE	TIPPABLE
CAUSABLE	GRAZABLE	MOCKABLE	RUNNABLE	TITHABLE
CHEWABLE	GROWABLE	MOLDABLE	RUSTABLE	TITRABLE
CITEABLE	GUIDABLE	MOOTABLE	SACKABLE	TOLLABLE
CLOSABLE	GULLABLE	MOVEABLE	SAILABLE	TOTEABLE
CLUBABLE	GUSTABLE	NAMEABLE	SALEABLE	TRADABLE
COINABLE	HACKABLE	NESTABLE	SALVABLE	TUBBABLE
COOKABLE	HANGABLE	NETTABLE	SANDABLE	TUNEABLE
COPYABLE	HATEABLE	OATHABLE	SATIABLE	TURNABLE

TYPEABLE	VARIABLE	VOTEABLE	WEARABLE	WIPEABLE
UNDOABLE	VENDABLE	WADEABLE	WELDABLE	WORKABLE
UNSTABLE	VIEWABLE	WALKABLE	WETTABLE	WRITABLE
UNUSABLE	VIOLABLE	WARHABLE	WILLABLE	
UNVIABLE	VITIABLE	WASHABLE	WINDABLE	
VALUABLE	VOIDABLE	WASTABLE	WINNABLE	

Words that end with -AGE

Seven-letter words	FLOTAGE	PIERAGE	THENAGE	BROCKAGE
	FLOWAGE	PILLAGE	TILLAGE	CABOTAGE
ABUSAGE	FOGGAGE	PIPEAGE	TOLLAGE	CARRIAGE
ACREAGE	FOLIAGE	PLUMAGE	TONNAGE	CARUCAGE
AJUTAGE	FOOTAGE	PLUSAGE	TRUCAGE	CHANTAGE
AMENAGE	FROMAGE	PONDAGE	TUNNAGE	CHUMMAGE
APANAGE	FULLAGE	PONTAGE	UMBRAGE	CLEARAGE
ARRIAGE	GARBAGE	PORTAGE	UNITAGE	CLEAVAGE
ASSUAGE	GUIDAGE	POSTAGE	UPSTAGE	CLOUDAGE
ASSWAGE	GUNNAGE	POTTAGE	VANTAGE	COMANAGE
AULNAGE	HAULAGE	PRESAGE	VENDAGE	COVERAGE
AVERAGE	HAYLAGE	PRIMAGE	VENTAGE	COZENAGE
BAGGAGE	HEADAGE	PRISAGE	VIDUAGE	CREEPAGE
BANDAGE	HERBAGE	PROPAGE	VILLAGE	CRIBBAGE
BARRAGE	HIREAGE	QUAYAGE	VINTAGE	DIALLAGE
BEERAGE	HOSTAGE	RAILAGE	VITRAGE	DISUSAGE
BONDAGE	KEELAGE	RAMPAGE	VOLTAGE	DRAINAGE
BOSCAGE	KIPPAGE	REIMAGE	VORLAGE	DRESSAGE
BOSKAGE	LAIRAGE	REMUAGE	WAFTAGE	DRIFTAGE
BREWAGE	LASTAGE	RESTAGE	WAINAGE	ENALLAGE
BROCAGE	LEAFAGE	RIBCAGE	WANTAGE	ENDAMAGE
BROKAGE	LEAKAGE	RIFFAGE	WARPAGE	ENSILAGE
BULKAGE	LIGNAGE	ROOTAGE	WASTAGE	ENVISAGE
BUOYAGE	LINEAGE	RUMMAGE	WATTAGE	EQUIPAGE
BURGAGE	LINKAGE	SACKAGE	WEBPAGE	FERRIAGE
CABBAGE	LOCKAGE	SALVAGE	WEFTAGE	FLOATAGE
CARNAGE	LUGGAGE	SAUSAGE	WINDAGE	FLOORAGE
CARTAGE	MASSAGE	SCALAGE	WORDAGE	FOOTPAGE
CENTAGE	MELTAGE	SCAVAGE	YARDAGE	FRAUTAGE
COINAGE	MESSAGE	SCUTAGE		FRONDAGE
COLLAGE	MILEAGE	SEEPAGE	Eight-letter words	FRONTAGE
COMPAGE	MILLAGE	SELVAGE		FROTTAGE
CORDAGE	MINTAGE	SEPTAGE	ACCORAGE	FRUITAGE
CORKAGE	MISPAGE	SERFAGE	ACIERAGE	FUSELAGE
CORNAGE	MOCKAGE	SIGNAGE	ADJUTAGE	GRAFTAGE
CORSAGE	MONTAGE	SINKAGE	AGIOTAGE	GRAINAGE
COTTAGE	MOORAGE	SOAKAGE	ALIENAGE	GRAMMAGE
COURAGE	MOULAGE	SOCCAGE	ALTARAGE	GRILLAGE
COWHAGE	NONWAGE	SOILAGE	AMPERAGE	GROUPAGE
CRANAGE	ONSTAGE	SONDAGE	APPANAGE	GUARDAGE
CUTTAGE	OUTRAGE	SPINAGE	BADINAGE	HELOTAGE
DISCAGE	OUVRAGE	STORAGE	BARONAGE	HERITAGE
DOCKAGE	OVERAGE	STOWAGE	BERTHAGE	HOMEPAGE
DRAYAGE	PACKAGE	SULLAGE	BEVERAGE	INTERAGE
DUNNAGE	PANNAGE	TALLAGE	BIRDCAGE	LANGRAGE
ECOTAGE	PASSAGE	TANKAGE	BLINDAGE	LANGUAGE
ESCUAGE	PAWNAGE	TANNAGE	BLOCKAGE	LAYERAGE
ETALAGE	PAYSAGE	TEENAGE	BRAKEAGE	LEVERAGE
FALDAGE	PEERAGE	TENTAGE	BRASSAGE	LITREAGE
FARDAGE	PEONAGE	THANAGE	BREAKAGE	MALAXAGE

MARITAGE	PLANTAGE	SMALLAGE	STRAVAGE	VAULTAGE
MARRIAGE	PLOTTAGE	SPILLAGE	STREWAGE	VAUNTAGE
MESSUAGE	PLUSSAGE	SPOILAGE	STUMPAGE	VERBIAGE
METAYAGE	POUNDAGE	SPOUSAGE	SUBSTAGE	VICARAGE
METERAGE	PROPHAGE	SQUIRAGE	SUFFRAGE	VICINAGE
MISUSAGE	PUCELAGE	STAFFAGE	THIRLAGE	WAGONAGE
MORTGAGE	PUPILAGE	STALLAGE	TRACKAGE	WATERAGE
MUCILAGE	REDAMAGE	STEALAGE	TRUCKAGE	WEIGHAGE
MULTIAGE	REENGAGE	STEARAGE	TRUQUAGE	WHARFAGE
NONIMAGE	ROUGHAGE	STEERAGE	TUTELAGE	WRAPPAGE
OFFSTAGE	SABOTAGE	STERNAGE	TUTORAGE	WRECKAGE
OVERPAGE	SEWERAGE	STILLAGE	TWEENAGE	
PILOTAGE	SHORTAGE	STOCKAGE	UMPIRAGE	
PINOTAGE	SLIPPAGE	STOPPAGE	UNDERAGE	

Words that end with -ANCE

Seven-letter	ROMANCE	ALLIANCE	FEASANCE	PIQUANCE
words	SONANCE	AMBIANCE	GUIDANCE	PITTANCE
ADVANCE	SURANCE	AMORANCE	INSTANCE	PORTANCE
AIDANCE	VACANCE	BECHANCE	ISSUANCE	RADIANCE
ASKANCE	VALANCE	BRISANCE	ITERANCE	RELIANCE
BALANCE		BUOYANCE	LAITANCE	RESIANCE
CREANCE	**Eight-letter**	CREPANCE	NONDANCE	RIDDANCE
DURANCE	**words**	DEFIANCE	NUISANCE	SORTANCE
ENHANCE	ABEYANCE	DEVIANCE	ORDNANCE	TENDANCE
FINANCE	ABIDANCE	DISTANCE	OUTDANCE	VALIANCE
JOYANCE	ACUTANCE	ELEGANCE	OUTRANCE	VARIANCE
NOYANCE	ADAMANCE	ENTRANCE	PARLANCE	VIBRANCE
PENANCE	AFFIANCE	EXITANCE	PASTANCE	VOIDANCE

Words that end with -ANCY

Seven-letter	UNFANCY	BUOYANCY	MORDANCY	UNCHANCY
words	VACANCY	CLAMANCY	MYOMANCY	VAGRANCY
ERRANCY		DEVIANCY	PECCANCY	VALIANCY
INFANCY	**Eight-letter**	DORMANCY	PERNANCY	VERDANCY
PLIANCY	**words**	ELEGANCY	PIQUANCY	VIBRANCY
SONANCY	ABEYANCY	GEOMANCY	RADIANCY	ZOOMANCY
TENANCY	ADAMANCY	IMITANCY	RAMPANCY	
TRUANCY	BLATANCY	INSTANCY	REGNANCY	

Words that end with -ARCH

Seven-letter	MONARCH	**Eight-letter**	OLIGARCH	POLYARCH
words	NAVARCH	**words**	OMNIARCH	RESEARCH
AUTARCH	NOMARCH	ETHNARCH	OUTMARCH	TAXIARCH
ENDARCH	TOPARCH	HEPTARCH	OVERARCH	TETRARCH
HEXARCH	TRIARCH	HIERARCH	PENTARCH	UNSTARCH
MESARCH	XERARCH	HIPPARCH	PHYLARCH	

Words that end with -BACK

Seven-letter words	SETBACK	CLAWBACK	HARDBACK	SCATBACK
BUYBACK	SOWBACK	COMEBACK	HOLDBACK	SEATBACK
CUTBACK	SUNBACK	DRAWBACK	HOWLBACK	SKEWBACK
DIEBACK	TIEBACK	FALLBACK	HUMPBACK	SLOTBACK
FATBACK	TOMBACK	FASTBACK	KICKBACK	SLOWBACK
FINBACK	WETBACK	FEEDBACK	LIFTBACK	SNAPBACK
FLYBACK		FIREBACK	LOANBACK	SOFTBACK
HOGBACK	**Eight-letter words**	FLATBACK	MOSSBACK	SWAYBACK
LAYBACK		FOLDBACK	PICKBACK	TAILBACK
OUTBACK	BAREBACK	FULLBACK	PLAYBACK	TALKBACK
PAYBACK	BLOWBACK	GIVEBACK	PLOWBACK	TURNBACK
REDBACK	BLUEBACK	GRAYBACK	PULLBACK	WINGBACK
RUNBACK	CALLBACK	GREYBACK	ROLLBACK	ZWIEBACK
	CASHBACK	HALFBACK	ROORBACK	

Words that end with -BALL

Seven-letter words	PATBALL	CORNBALL	GOOFBALL	PUFFBALL
BOXBALL	PINBALL	FASTBALL	HAIRBALL	PUSHBALL
EARBALL	PROBALL	FIREBALL	HANDBALL	SNOWBALL
EYEBALL		FISHBALL	HARDBALL	SOFTBALL
FUSBALL	**Eight-letter words**	FOOSBALL	HEELBALL	SOURBALL
GUMBALL		FOOTBALL	HIGHBALL	SPITBALL
ICEBALL	BASEBALL	FORKBALL	KICKBALL	TRAPBALL
LOWBALL	BEANBALL	FOURBALL	KORFBALL	WASHBALL
NETBALL	BLOWBALL	FUSSBALL	MEATBALL	
ODDBALL	BLUEBALL	GLUEBALL	MOTHBALL	
	COALBALL	GOALBALL	PITHBALL	

Words that end with -BAND

Seven-letter words	HUSBAND	Eight-letter words	HAIRBAND	RAINBAND
ARMBAND	MIDBAND		HEADBAND	SARABAND
DISBAND	PROBAND	BACKBAND	NECKBAND	SIDEBAND
HATBAND	RIBBAND	BASEBAND	NOSEBAND	WAVEBAND
HAYBAND	SALBAND	BROWBAND	PASSBAND	WIDEBAND
	TURBAND	FAHLBAND	PLATBAND	

Words that end with -BIRD

Seven-letter words	JAYBIRD	Eight-letter words	JAILBIRD	REEDBIRD
ANTBIRD	MAYBIRD		KINGBIRD	RICEBIRD
AWLBIRD	OILBIRD	BELLBIRD	LADYBIRD	SNOWBIRD
AXEBIRD	REDBIRD	BLUEBIRD	LOVEBIRD	SONGBIRD
BOOBIRD	SEABIRD	COCKBIRD	LYREBIRD	SURFBIRD
CATBIRD	SUNBIRD	FERNBIRD	OVENBIRD	WHIPBIRD
COWBIRD	WARBIRD	FIREBIRD	PUFFBIRD	YARDBIRD
FATBIRD	WOSBIRD	GAOLBIRD	RAILBIRD	
		HANGBIRD	RAINBIRD	

Words that end with -DOM

Seven-letter words	GEEKDOM	TZARDOM	GYPSYDOM	QUEERDOM
BABUDOM	GURUDOM	WIFEDOM	HIPPYDOM	REBELDOM
BOREDOM	HALIDOM		HOTELDOM	SAINTDOM
BOSSDOM	HEIRDOM	**Eight-letter**	LEECHDOM	SHEIKDOM
CHEFDOM	HOBODOM	**words**	LIEGEDOM	SWELLDOM
CZARDOM	JARLDOM	BABELDOM	MOTORDOM	THANEDOM
DOGEDOM	KINGDOM	BIRTHDOM	MOVIEDOM	THRALDOM
DOLLDOM	PAPADOM	BLOKEDOM	NOVELDOM	UNSELDOM
DUKEDOM	POPEDOM	CHIEFDOM	PACHADOM	UNWISDOM
EARLDOM	RHABDOM	CLERKDOM	PAGANDOM	VILLADOM
FIEFDOM	SELFDOM	DEVILDOM	PAPPADOM	WHOREDOM
FILMDOM	SERFDOM	DUNCEDOM	PASHADOM	
FOGYDOM	SHAHDOM	FAIRYDOM	POPPADOM	
FREEDOM	STARDOM	FOGEYDOM	PUPPYDOM	
	TSARDOM	GIPSYDOM	QUEENDOM	

Words that end with -EAUX

Seven-letter words	GATEAUX	BATTEAUX	JAMBEAUX	RONDEAUX
	RESEAUX	BERCEAUX	MANTEAUX	ROULEAUX
BATEAUX		BORDEAUX	MORCEAUX	TABLEAUX
BUREAUX	**Eight-letter**	CHAPEAUX	NOUVEAUX	TONNEAUX
CADEAUX	**words**	CHATEAUX	PLATEAUX	TRUMEAUX
COTEAUX	BANDEAUX	COUTEAUX	PONCEAUX	

Words that end with -ENCE

Seven-letter words	OFFENCE	**Eight-letter**	LENIENCE	SENTENCE
	POTENCE	**words**	MERGENCE	SEQUENCE
ABSENCE	REFENCE	AMBIENCE	NASCENCE	SITHENCE
CADENCE	REGENCE	AUDIENCE	NOWHENCE	SIXPENCE
COGENCE	SCIENCE	CLARENCE	OPULENCE	SUSPENCE
DEFENCE	SILENCE	COMMENCE	OUTFENCE	TANGENCE
ESSENCE	UNFENCE	CREDENCE	PATIENCE	TENDENCE
FAIENCE	URGENCE	DISPENCE	PRESENCE	TENPENCE
FAYENCE	VALENCE	EMINENCE	PRETENCE	TUPPENCE
FLUENCE		EVIDENCE	PRUDENCE	TWOPENCE
LATENCE		EXIGENCE	PUNGENCE	VERGENCE
LICENCE		FIPPENCE	SALIENCE	VIOLENCE
LUCENCE		FLORENCE	SAPIENCE	

Words that end with -ENCY

Seven-letter words	ORIENCY	**Eight-letter**	LAMBENCY	SEQUENCY
	PATENCY	**words**	LENIENCY	SOLVENCY
ARDENCY	POTENCY	CLEMENCY	NASCENCY	TANGENCY
CADENCY	PUDENCY	COAGENCY	OPULENCY	TENDENCY
COGENCY	RECENCY	CURRENCY	PENDENCY	TURGENCY
DECENCY	REGENCY	EMINENCY	PUNGENCY	VERGENCY
FLUENCY	URGENCY	EXIGENCY	REAGENCY	
LATENCY	VALENCY	FERVENCY	SALIENCY	
LUCENCY	VIVENCY	FULGENCY	SAPIENCY	

Words that end with -EST

Seven-letter words			
ACHIEST	CRUDEST	FIKIEST	LAZIEST	OORIEST
ACIDEST	CURTEST	FIRMEST	LEALEST	OOSIEST
ACQUEST	DAFTEST	FITTEST	LEANEST	OOZIEST
ACUTEST	DAMPEST	FLUIEST	LEFTEST	OPENEST
ADDREST	DANKEST	FONDEST	LENGEST	ORBIEST
AERIEST	DARKEST	FOULEST	LEWDEST	OULDEST
AGILEST	DEADEST	FOXIEST	LIEFEST	OURIEST
AIRIEST	DEAFEST	FOZIEST	LIEVEST	OUTJEST
AMPLEST	DEAREST	FULLEST	LIMIEST	OWLIEST
ANAPEST	DEEDEST	FUMIEST	LIMPEST	OWRIEST
ARCHEST	DEEPEST	FUNFEST	LINIEST	PACIEST
ARIDEST	DEFFEST	FUNNEST	LITHEST	PAIREST
ARMREST	DEFTEST	GABFEST	LOGIEST	PALIEST
ARSIEST	DEIDEST	GAINEST	LONGEST	PERTEST
ARTIEST	DEIFEST	GAMIEST	LOOSEST	PINIEST
ASHIEST	DENSEST	GAPIEST	LOTHEST	PINKEST
AULDEST	DEWIEST	GASHEST	LOUDEST	PIPIEST
AVIDEST	DICIEST	GAZIEST	LOWSEST	POKIEST
AWAREST	DIKIEST	GLUIEST	LUNIEST	POOREST
AWNIEST	DIMMEST	GOLDEST	LUSHEST	PORIEST
BABIEST	DINKEST	GOOIEST	MADDEST	POSHEST
BADDEST	DISGEST	GORIEST	MAINEST	POSIEST
BALDEST	DISNEST	GOWDEST	MATIEST	POXIEST
BARGEST	DOMIEST	GRAVEST	MAUVEST	PRETEST
BASSEST	DOPIEST	GRAYEST	MAZIEST	PRONEST
BEQUEST	DOTIEST	GREYEST	MEANEST	PROTEST
BIGGEST	DOUCEST	HADDEST	MEEKEST	PROWEST
BLATEST	DOVIEST	HARDEST	MEETEST	PUIREST
BLUIEST	DOWIEST	HARVEST	MIDDEST	PUKIEST
BOLDEST	DOZIEST	HAYIEST	MILDEST	PULIEST
BONIEST	DROLEST	HAZIEST	MIMMEST	PUNIEST
BOSSEST	DUFFEST	HEPPEST	MINIEST	PUNKEST
BOXIEST	DULLEST	HIGHEST	MIRIEST	QUAREST
BRAVEST	DUMBEST	HIPPEST	MIRKEST	RACIEST
BRAWEST	DUNNEST	HOKIEST	MITIEST	RADDEST
BUFFEST	DUSKEST	HOLIEST	MIXIEST	RADGEST
BUMMEST	DYKIEST	HOMIEST	MOOTEST	RANKEST
BUSIEST	EARNEST	HOTTEST	MOPIEST	RASHEST
CAGIEST	EASIEST	ICKIEST	MOSTEST	RATHEST
CAKIEST	EDGIEST	ICKLEST	MOTIEST	REALEST
CALMEST	EELIEST	IFFIEST	MURKEST	REDDEST
CAMPEST	EERIEST	IMPREST	NAFFEST	RENKEST
CANIEST	EGGIEST	INANEST	NAIFEST	REQUEST
CANTEST	ELMIEST	INKIEST	NAIVEST	RICHEST
CHICEST	EVENEST	INQUEST	NEAREST	RICIEST
CLOSEST	EVILEST	IRATEST	NEATEST	RILIEST
COKIEST	FABBEST	JIMPEST	NESHEST	RIMIEST
COLDEST	FADIEST	JIVIEST	NIGHEST	ROKIEST
CONFEST	FAINEST	JOKIEST	NOBLEST	ROPIEST
CONGEST	FAIREST	JUSTEST	NOSIEST	RORIEST
CONTEST	FAKIEST	KEENEST	NUMBEST	ROSIEST
COOLEST	FALSEST	KEWLEST	OAKIEST	RUBIEST
COSIEST	FASTEST	KINDEST	OARIEST	RULIEST
COWIEST	FATTEST	LACIEST	OATIEST	RUMMEST
COXIEST	FAUREST	LAKIEST	OBESEST	SADDEST
COZIEST	FEATEST	LANGEST	OILIEST	SAFTEST
	FELLEST	LANKEST	ONLIEST	SAGIEST
		LARGEST	OOFIEST	SAIDEST

SAIREST
SALTEST
SAMIEST
SEAREST
SEIKEST
SEXIEST
SICKEST
SIZIEST
SKEWEST
SKYIEST
SLOWEST
SNIDEST
SOFTEST
SOONEST
SOUREST
SPAREST
SPRIEST
SPRYEST
STALEST
STEYEST
SUAVEST
SUBTEST
SUGGEST
TAKIEST
TALLEST
TANNEST
TARTEST
TAUTEST
TAWIEST
TEDIEST
TEMPEST
TENSEST
TERSEST
TIDIEST
TINIEST
TOEIEST
TONIEST
TOOMEST
TOWIEST
TRITEST
TUNIEST
TYPIEST
UGLIEST
UNBLEST
UNCOEST
UNDREST
VAGUEST
VAINEST
VASTEST
VERIEST
VIBIEST
VINIEST
VOGIEST
WACKEST
WALIEST
WANIEST
WANNEST
WARIEST
WARMEST
WATTEST

WAVIEST
WAXIEST
WEAKEST
WEETEST
WETTEST
WHITEST
WILDEST
WILIEST
WILLEST
WINIEST
WIRIEST
WOTTEST
WOWFEST
YUKIEST
ZANIEST
ZOOIEST

Eight-letter words
ACERBEST
ACIDIEST
ACRIDEST
ADEPTEST
AFFOREST
ALCAHEST
ALERTEST
ALKAHEST
ALMAGEST
ANAPAEST
ANGRIEST
ANTSIEST
ARBALEST
ARBELEST
ARTSIEST
ASTUTEST
AUTOTEST
BACKREST
BAGGIEST
BALDIEST
BALKIEST
BALMIEST
BANALEST
BANDIEST
BARDIEST
BARGHEST
BARGUEST
BARKIEST
BARMIEST
BARNIEST
BARRIEST
BASSIEST
BATTIEST
BAWDIEST
BEADIEST
BEAKIEST
BEAMIEST
BEATIEST
BEEFIEST
BEERIEST
BEIGIEST

BENDIEST
BENTIEST
BILGIEST
BIRKIEST
BIRSIEST
BITSIEST
BITTIEST
BLACKEST
BLADIEST
BLANDEST
BLANKEST
BLEAKEST
BLEAREST
BLINDEST
BLINGEST
BLITHEST
BLOKIEST
BLONDEST
BLOWIEST
BLUDIEST
BLUFFEST
BLUNTEST
BODGIEST
BOGGIEST
BONEYEST
BONNIEST
BOOFIEST
BOOKIEST
BOOKREST
BOOMIEST
BOOZIEST
BORTIEST
BOSKIEST
BOSSIEST
BOUSIEST
BOYSIEST
BRAGGEST
BRAIDEST
BRAKIEST
BRASHEST
BRENTEST
BRIEFEST
BRILLEST
BRINIEST
BRISKEST
BROADEST
BROSIEST
BRUSKEST
BUDDIEST
BUFFIEST
BUGGIEST
BULGIEST
BULKIEST
BULLIEST
BUMPIEST
BUNTIEST
BURLIEST
BURRIEST
BUSHIEST

BUSTIEST
BUTCHEST
BUXOMEST
BUZZIEST
CACKIEST
CADGIEST
CALMIEST
CAMPIEST
CANNIEST
CANTIEST
CARNIEST
CASKIEST
CATTIEST
CAULDEST
CHARIEST
CHASTEST
CHEAPEST
CHEWIEST
CHIEFEST
CHILLEST
CHIRKEST
CHOICEST
CHOKIEST
CHUFFEST
CISSIEST
CLAYIEST
CLEANEST
CLEAREST
COALIEST
COARSEST
COATTEST
COBBIEST
COCKIEST
COMBIEST
COMFIEST
CONKIEST
CONQUEST
COOMIEST
COPSIEST
CORKIEST
CORNIEST
COULDEST
COUTHEST
CRANKEST
CRAPIEST
CRASSEST
CRAZIEST
CREPIEST
CRISPEST
CRONKEST
CROOKEST
CROSSEST
CRUELEST
CRUMPEST
CUBBIEST
CUPPIEST
CURDIEST
CURLIEST
CURNIEST

CURVIEST
CUSHIEST
CUSPIEST
CUTTIEST
DAFFIEST
DAGGIEST
DAMNDEST
DAMPIEST
DANCIEST
DANDIEST
DARNDEST
DASHIEST
DAUBIEST
DEBBIEST
DEEDIEST
DEFOREST
DEMUREST
DICKIEST
DICTIEST
DIDDIEST
DILLIEST
DINGIEST
DINKIEST
DIPPIEST
DIRTIEST
DISHIEST
DITSIEST
DITZIEST
DIVINEST
DIVVIEST
DIZZIEST
DOCILEST
DODDIEST
DODGIEST
DOGGIEST
DOILTEST
DONSIEST
DOOMIEST
DORKIEST
DORTIEST
DOTTIEST
DOTTLEST
DOWDIEST
DOWLIEST
DOWNIEST
DRABBEST
DRAPIEST
DREAREST
DROLLEST
DRONIEST
DRUNKEST
DRUSIEST
DRUXIEST
DUCKIEST
DUDDIEST
DULLIEST
DUMMIEST
DUMPIEST
DUNGIEST
DUNNIEST

DURGIEST	FORKIEST	GOOPIEST	HORNIEST	LEARIEST
DURNDEST	FRAILEST	GOOSIEST	HORSIEST	LEAVIEST
DUSKIEST	FRANKEST	GORMIEST	HOUSIEST	LEDGIEST
DUSTIEST	FRESHEST	GORSIEST	HUFFIEST	LEERIEST
DWARFEST	FROWIEST	GOUTIEST	HUGGIEST	LEGGIEST
EAGEREST	FUBBIEST	GRANDEST	HULKIEST	LEISHEST
EARLIEST	FUBSIEST	GRAPIEST	HULLIEST	LICHTEST
ECHOIEST	FUFFIEST	GREATEST	HUMANEST	LIGHTEST
EMONGEST	FUGGIEST	GREENEST	HUMBLEST	LIMBIEST
EMPTIEST	FUGLIEST	GRIMIEST	HUMIDEST	LINGIEST
ENFOREST	FUNKIEST	GRIMMEST	HUMPIEST	LINKIEST
EVILLEST	FUNNIEST	GRIPIEST	HUNKIEST	LINTIEST
EXACTEST	FURRIEST	GRITTEST	HUSHIEST	LIPPIEST
FABBIEST	FURTHEST	GRODIEST	HUSKIEST	LITTLEST
FADDIEST	FURZIEST	GROSSEST	IMMODEST	LIVIDEST
FAGGIEST	FUSSIEST	GROUSEST	IMPUREST	LOAMIEST
FAINTEST	FUSTIEST	GRUFFEST	INDIGEST	LOATHEST
FANCIEST	FUTILEST	GRUMMEST	INEPTEST	LOFTIEST
FARTHEST	FUZZIEST	GUCKIEST	INERTEST	LOGGIEST
FATTIEST	GABBIEST	GULFIEST	INSANEST	LOOBIEST
FAWNIEST	GAMMIEST	GULPIEST	INTEREST	LOONIEST
FEEBLEST	GAPPIEST	GUMMIEST	IRONIEST	LOOPIEST
FEINTEST	GASPIEST	GUNGIEST	ITCHIEST	LOPPIEST
FEIRIEST	GASSIEST	GUNKIEST	JAGGIEST	LOSSIEST
FELTIEST	GAUCHEST	GURLIEST	JAMMIEST	LOUCHEST
FEMMIEST	GAUCIEST	GUSHIEST	JANTIEST	LOURIEST
FENDIEST	GAUDIEST	GUSTIEST	JAZZIEST	LOUSIEST
FENNIEST	GAUMIEST	GUTSIEST	JEMMIEST	LOVEFEST
FERLIEST	GAUNTEST	GUTTIEST	JERKIEST	LOWLIEST
FERNIEST	GAUZIEST	HAILIEST	JETTIEST	LOYALEST
FESTIEST	GAWCIEST	HAIRIEST	JIGGIEST	LUCIDEST
FETIDEST	GAWKIEST	HAMMIEST	JIMPIEST	LUCKIEST
FICKLEST	GAWSIEST	HANDIEST	JOLLIEST	LUMMIEST
FIERCEST	GEEKIEST	HANGNEST	JOLTIEST	LUMPIEST
FIERIEST	GELIDEST	HAPPIEST	JOTTIEST	LURIDEST
FILMIEST	GEMMIEST	HARDIEST	JOWLIEST	LUSHIEST
FINNIEST	GENTIEST	HARSHEST	JUICIEST	LUSTIEST
FIRRIEST	GENTLEST	HASHIEST	JUMPIEST	MALMIEST
FISHIEST	GERMIEST	HASTIEST	JUNKIEST	MALTIEST
FISTIEST	GIDDIEST	HEADIEST	KEDGIEST	MANGIEST
FITLIEST	GIMPIEST	HEADREST	KEMPIEST	MANIFEST
FIZZIEST	GINNIEST	HEAPIEST	KERKIEST	MANKIEST
FLAKIEST	GIRLIEST	HEAVIEST	KICKIEST	MANLIEST
FLAMIEST	GIRNIEST	HEDGIEST	KIDGIEST	MARDIEST
FLARIEST	GLADDEST	HEFTIEST	KINKIEST	MARLIEST
FLASHEST	GLADIEST	HEMPIEST	KISSIEST	MARVIEST
FLATTEST	GLARIEST	HENNIEST	KITTLEST	MASHIEST
FLAWIEST	GLAZIEST	HERBIEST	KOOKIEST	MASSIEST
FLAXIEST	GLEBIEST	HILLIEST	LAIGHEST	MASTIEST
FLEETEST	GLEGGEST	HINKIEST	LAIRIEST	MATUREST
FLIPPEST	GLIBBEST	HIPPIEST	LAMBIEST	MAWKIEST
FLORIEST	GLIDDEST	HISSIEST	LANKIEST	MEAGREST
FLUKIEST	GLUMMEST	HOARIEST	LARDIEST	MEALIEST
FLUSHEST	GOATIEST	HOARSEST	LARKIEST	MEATIEST
FLUTIEST	GOBBIEST	HOLEYEST	LARNIEST	MELTIEST
FOAMIEST	GODLIEST	HOODIEST	LATHIEST	MERRIEST
FOGGIEST	GOLDIEST	HOOKIEST	LAWNIEST	MESHIEST
FOLKIEST	GOODIEST	HOOLIEST	LEADIEST	MESSIEST
FOOTIEST	GOOFIEST	HOOTIEST	LEAFIEST	MICKLEST
FOOTREST	GOONIEST	HOPPIEST	LEAKIEST	MIDGIEST

MIFFIEST	NONGUEST	POTTIEST	ROOPIEST	SLICKEST
MIGHTEST	NOOKIEST	POUTIEST	ROOTIEST	SLIMIEST
MILKIEST	NOUNIEST	PRICIEST	RORTIEST	SLIMMEST
MILTIEST	NOWTIEST	PRIMMEST	ROUGHEST	SLOPIEST
MIMSIEST	NUBBIEST	PRIVIEST	ROUNDEST	SLUGFEST
MINCIEST	NURDIEST	PROSIEST	ROUPIEST	SMALLEST
MINGIEST	NUTSIEST	PROUDEST	ROWDIEST	SMARTEST
MINTIEST	NUTTIEST	PUDGIEST	RUDDIEST	SMILIEST
MINUTEST	OBTUSEST	PUDSIEST	RUGGIEST	SMOKIEST
MIRKIEST	OFTENEST	PUFFIEST	RUMMIEST	SMUGGEST
MIRLIEST	ONERIEST	PUGGIEST	RUNNIEST	SNAKIEST
MISSIEST	OPAQUEST	PULPIEST	RUNTIEST	SNARIEST
MISTIEST	ORANGEST	PUNKIEST	RUSHIEST	SNELLEST
MOCHIEST	ORNATEST	PUNNIEST	RUSTIEST	SNIDIEST
MOISTEST	OUTWREST	PURPLEST	RUTTIEST	SNIPIEST
MOLDIEST	OVERKEST	PURSIEST	SAGGIEST	SNODDEST
MOODIEST	PALLIEST	PURTIEST	SALTIEST	SNOWIEST
MOONIEST	PALMIEST	PUSHIEST	SANDIEST	SNUGGEST
MOORIEST	PALSIEST	PUSSIEST	SAPPIEST	SOAPIEST
MOPPIEST	PAPPIEST	QUAKIEST	SARKIEST	SOBEREST
MOROSEST	PARKIEST	QUEEREST	SASSIEST	SODDIEST
MOSSIEST	PASTIEST	QUICKEST	SAUCIEST	SOGGIEST
MOTHIEST	PAWKIEST	QUIETEST	SAVAGEST	SOILIEST
MOTLIEST	PEAKIEST	RABIDEST	SAVVIEST	SOLIDEST
MOTTIEST	PEARTEST	RAGGIEST	SCALIEST	SOMBREST
MOUSIEST	PEATIEST	RAINIEST	SCANTEST	SONGFEST
MUCKIEST	PECKIEST	RAMMIEST	SCARCEST	SONSIEST
MUDDIEST	PEERIEST	RANDIEST	SCARIEST	SOOTHEST
MUGGIEST	PEPPIEST	RANGIEST	SCODIEST	SOOTIEST
MUMSIEST	PERKIEST	RAPIDEST	SEAMIEST	SOPPIEST
MURKIEST	PERVIEST	RASPIEST	SECUREST	SORRIEST
MURLIEST	PESKIEST	RATTIEST	SEDATEST	SOUNDEST
MUSHIEST	PESTIEST	RAUCLEST	SEDGIEST	SOUPIEST
MUSKIEST	PETTIEST	READIEST	SEEDIEST	SPACIEST
MUSSIEST	PHATTEST	REAMIEST	SEELIEST	SPARSEST
MUSTIEST	PHONIEST	REARREST	SEEPIEST	SPEWIEST
MUZZIEST	PICKIEST	REDDIEST	SEMPLEST	SPICIEST
MYTHIEST	PIGGIEST	REDIGEST	SERENEST	SPICKEST
NAGGIEST	PINKIEST	REEDIEST	SEVEREST	SPIKIEST
NAKEDEST	PIPPIEST	REEFIEST	SHADIEST	SPINIEST
NAPPIEST	PITHIEST	REEKIEST	SHAKIEST	SPIRIEST
NARKIEST	PLAINEST	REFOREST	SHALIEST	SPRUCEST
NASTIEST	PLATIEST	REINVEST	SHARPEST	SPUMIEST
NATTIEST	PLUMIEST	REMOTEST	SHEEREST	SQUAREST
NEDDIEST	PLUMMEST	RESTIEST	SHINIEST	STABLEST
NEEDIEST	PLUMPEST	RIBBIEST	SHOALEST	STAGIEST
NERDIEST	PLUSHEST	RICHTEST	SHORTEST	STAIDEST
NERVIEST	POCKIEST	RIDGIEST	SHOWIEST	STARKEST
NETTIEST	PODDIEST	RIFTIEST	SILKIEST	STEEPEST
NEWSIEST	PODGIEST	RIGHTEST	SILLIEST	STEEVEST
NIFFIEST	POLITEST	RIGIDEST	SILTIEST	STERNEST
NIFTIEST	PONCIEST	RINDIEST	SIMPLEST	STEWIEST
NIMBLEST	PONGIEST	RISKIEST	SINKIEST	STIEVEST
NIPPIEST	POOFIEST	RITZIEST	SISSIEST	STIFFEST
NIRLIEST	POOVIEST	ROARIEST	SKIEYEST	STILLEST
NITTIEST	POPPIEST	ROCKIEST	SKINTEST	STIVIEST
NOBBIEST	PORKIEST	ROILIEST	SKIVIEST	STONIEST
NODDIEST	PORNIEST	ROOFIEST	SLACKEST	STOUTEST
NOILIEST	PORTIEST	ROOKIEST	SLATIEST	STYLIEST
NOISIEST	POSTTEST	ROOMIEST	SLEEKEST	SUBTLEST

SUCKIEST
SUDSIEST
SUETIEST
SULKIEST
SUNNIEST
SUPPLEST
SURFIEST
SURGIEST
SURLIEST
SVELTEST
SWALIEST
SWANKEST
SWEETEST
SWEIREST
SWELLEST
SWIFTEST
SWIPIEST
SWISHEST
TACKIEST
TAGGIEST
TALCIEST
TALKFEST
TALKIEST
TANGIEST
TARDIEST
TARRIEST
TARTIEST
TASTIEST
TATTIEST
TAWNIEST
TAWTIEST
TEARIEST
TECHIEST
TEENIEST
TENTIEST
TEPIDEST
TESTIEST
TEUCHEST
TEUGHEST
THAWIEST
THEWIEST
THICKEST
THINNEST
THYMIEST
TICHIEST
TIDDIEST
TIGHTEST
TILLIEST
TIMIDEST
TINNIEST
TINTIEST
TIPPIEST
TIPSIEST
TIREDEST
TOCKIEST
TOFFIEST
TOPPIEST
TOSHIEST
TOSSIEST
TOTTIEST
TOUGHEST
TOUSIEST
TOUTIEST
TOUZIEST
TOWNIEST
TOWSIEST
TOWZIEST
TRAPNEST
TRIFFEST
TRIGGEST
TRIMMEST
TRIPIEST
TUBBIEST
TUFTIEST
TUMPIEST
TURFIEST
TUSKIEST
TWINIEST
UNHONEST
UNIQUEST
UNPRIEST
UNRIPEST
UNSAFEST
UNSUREST
UNTRUEST
UNWISEST
URBANEST
UTTEREST
VAIRIEST
VALIDEST
VAMPIEST
VAPIDEST
VASTIEST
VEALIEST
VEILIEST
VEINIEST
VIEWIEST
VIVIDEST
VOGUIEST
VUGGIEST
VUGHIEST
VUTTIEST
WACKIEST
WALLIEST
WALTIEST
WANKIEST
WARBIEST
WARTIEST
WASHIEST
WASPIEST
WASPNEST
WEARIEST
WEBBIEST
WEDGIEST
WEEDIEST
WEENIEST
WEEPIEST
WEIRDEST
WENNIEST
WERSHEST
WHEYIEST
WHINIEST
WHITIEST
WIFTIEST
WIGGIEST
WIMPIEST
WINDIEST
WINGIEST
WISPIEST
WITHIEST
WITTIEST
WOMBIEST
WONKIEST
WOODIEST
WOOFIEST
WOOLIEST
WOOZIEST
WORDIEST
WORMIEST
WOULDEST
WRONGEST
WUSSIEST
YAPPIEST
YAWNIEST
YECHIEST
YEUKIEST
YOLKIEST
YOUNGEST
YUCKIEST
YUKKIEST
YUMMIEST
ZAPPIEST
ZESTIEST
ZINCIEST
ZINGIEST
ZINKIEST
ZIPPIEST
ZOOTIEST

Words that end with -ETTE

Seven-letter words

AILETTE
ARIETTE
AVIETTE
BLUETTE
BURETTE
BUVETTE
CASETTE
CUNETTE
CURETTE
CUVETTE
DINETTE
FOUETTE
FUMETTE
GALETTE
GAZETTE
GENETTE
LADETTE
LAYETTE
LORETTE
LUNETTE
MINETTE
MOFETTE
MOZETTE
MUSETTE
NAVETTE
NEDETTE
NONETTE
OCTETTE
PALETTE
PIPETTE
POPETTE
PROETTE
ROSETTE
STRETTE
SYRETTE
TONETTE
VEDETTE
VIDETTE

Eight-letter words

AIGRETTE
AMUSETTE
ANISETTE
BAGNETTE
BAGUETTE
BARBETTE
BARRETTE
BIMBETTE
BRUNETTE
CASSETTE
CHAVETTE
COQUETTE
CORVETTE
CREVETTE
DANCETTE
DISKETTE
DRABETTE
FAUVETTE
FLATETTE
FOSSETTE
FRISETTE
FRIZETTE
GRISETTE
HACKETTE
JEANETTE
JOCKETTE
MAQUETTE
MOFFETTE
MOQUETTE
MOZZETTE
NOISETTE
OMELETTE
PALLETTE
PALMETTE
PARKETTE
PIANETTE
POCHETTE
RACLETTE
REINETTE
RINGETTE
ROOMETTE
ROQUETTE
ROULETTE
SEPTETTE
SESTETTE
SEXTETTE
SOCKETTE
SPINETTE
STAGETTE
SUEDETTE
TOILETTE
UMBRETTE
VIGNETTE

Words that end with -EUR

Seven-letter words	LIQUEUR	Eight-letter words	FROIDEUR	SEIGNEUR
AMATEUR	MASSEUR		FRONDEUR	SIFFLEUR
DANSEUR	MINCEUR	BATELEUR	FROTTEUR	SIGNIEUR
DOUCEUR	PRIMEUR	BLAGUEUR	GRANDEUR	TAILLEUR
FARCEUR	PRONEUR	CHASSEUR	JONGLEUR	TROUVEUR
FLANEUR	REMUEUR	CISELEUR	LONGUEUR	TRUQUEUR
FRISEUR	SABREUR	CLAQUEUR	MONSIEUR	VOYAGEUR
HAUTEUR	SIGNEUR	COIFFEUR	SABOTEUR	
	TRACEUR	ECRASEUR	SECATEUR	

Words that end with -FISH

Seven-letter words	OARFISH	Eight-letter words	FOOLFISH	ROSEFISH
BATFISH	OUTFISH		FROGFISH	SAILFISH
BOXFISH	PANFISH	BAITFISH	GOATFISH	SALTFISH
CATFISH	PIGFISH	BANDFISH	GOLDFISH	SANDFISH
CODFISH	PINFISH	BILLFISH	GRAYFISH	SCARFISH
COWFISH	PUPFISH	BLOWFISH	GRUFFISH	SCOMFISH
DEAFISH	RAFFISH	BLUEFISH	HEADFISH	SCUMFISH
DOGFISH	RATFISH	BOARFISH	JACKFISH	SNIFFISH
FINFISH	REDFISH	BONEFISH	KINGFISH	SPOFFISH
FOXFISH	SAWFISH	CAVEFISH	LADYFISH	STARFISH
GARFISH	SELFISH	COALFISH	LIONFISH	STIFFISH
GEMFISH	SERFISH	CRAWFISH	LUMPFISH	STUDFISH
HAGFISH	SUNFISH	CRAYFISH	LUNGFISH	SUCKFISH
HOGFISH	TOFFISH	DEALFISH	MILKFISH	SURFFISH
HUFFISH	TUBFISH	DRAFFISH	MONKFISH	TILEFISH
JEWFISH	WAIFISH	DRUMFISH	MOONFISH	TOADFISH
LUBFISH	WOLFISH	DWARFISH	NUMBFISH	WALLFISH
MUDFISH		FALLFISH	OVERFISH	WEAKFISH
MUFFISH		FILEFISH	PIPEFISH	WOLFFISH
		FLATFISH	ROCKFISH	

Words that end with -FORM

Seven-letter words	PREFORM	ENSIFORM	NATIFORM	RAMIFORM
ACIFORM	TRIFORM	FILIFORM	NUBIFORM	RANIFORM
ALIFORM	UNIFORM	FREEFORM	OMNIFORM	REINFORM
AUSFORM	ZOEFORM	FUSIFORM	PALIFORM	RENIFORM
AVIFORM		GASIFORM	PARAFORM	RETIFORM
CONFORM	Eight-letter words	GRUIFORM	PEDIFORM	ROTIFORM
DEIFORM		IODOFORM	PICIFORM	SETIFORM
DIFFORM	AERIFORM	JANIFORM	PILIFORM	SLIPFORM
DISFORM	ARCIFORM	LANDFORM	PIRIFORM	TUBIFORM
ISOFORM	AURIFORM	LAVAFORM	PISIFORM	UNCIFORM
MISFORM	COLIFORM	LYRIFORM	PLANFORM	URSIFORM
OVIFORM	CONIFORM	MANIFORM	PLATFORM	VARIFORM
PERFORM	CUBIFORM	MURIFORM	POSTFORM	VASIFORM
	CUNIFORM	NAPIFORM	PYRIFORM	WAVEFORM

Words that end with -FUL

Seven-letter words

ARMSFUL
BAGSFUL
BALEFUL
BANEFUL
BASHFUL
BOATFUL
BODEFUL
BOOKFUL
BOWLFUL
BRIMFUL
CAGEFUL
CANSFUL
CAREFUL
CARTFUL
CROPFUL
CUPSFUL
DAREFUL
DEEDFUL
DERNFUL
DIREFUL
DISHFUL
DOLEFUL
DOOMFUL
DUREFUL
DUTIFUL
EASEFUL
FACTFUL
FATEFUL
FEARFUL
FISHFUL
FISTFUL
FOODFUL
FORKFUL
FORMFUL
FRETFUL
GAINFUL
GASHFUL
GAZEFUL
GLADFUL
GLEEFUL
GUSTFUL
GUTSFUL
HANDFUL
HARMFUL
HATEFUL
HATSFUL
HEADFUL
HEEDFUL
HELPFUL
HOPEFUL
HORNFUL
HURTFUL

HUSHFUL
JARSFUL
JESTFUL
JUGSFUL
KISTFUL
LIFEFUL
LISTFUL
LOCKFUL
LOOFFUL
LUNGFUL
LUSTFUL
MASTFUL
MAZEFUL
MINDFUL
MISTFUL
MOANFUL
MUSEFUL
NEEDFUL
NESTFUL
ODORFUL
PAGEFUL
PAILFUL
PAINFUL
PALMFUL
PESTFUL
PIPEFUL
PITHFUL
PITIFUL
PLAYFUL
PLOTFUL
POKEFUL
POUTFUL
PREYFUL
PUSHFUL
RACKFUL
RAGEFUL
RESTFUL
RISKFUL
ROOMFUL
RUTHFUL
SACKFUL
SHEDFUL
SHIPFUL
SHOPFUL
SIGHFUL
SKEPFUL
SKILFUL
SKINFUL
SONGFUL
SOULFUL
SWAYFUL
TACTFUL
TALEFUL
TANKFUL

TEARFUL
TEEMFUL
TEENFUL
TENTFUL
TOILFUL
TRAYFUL
TUBEFUL
TUNEFUL
VIALFUL
WAILFUL
WAKEFUL
WAMEFUL
WILEFUL
WILLFUL
WISHFUL
WISTFUL
WORKFUL
ZEALFUL
ZESTFUL

Eight-letter words

APRONFUL
AVAILFUL
BASINFUL
BELLYFUL
BLAMEFUL
BLISSFUL
BLUSHFUL
BOASTFUL
CHARMFUL
CHEEKFUL
CHEERFUL
CHESTFUL
CHOCKFUL
COLORFUL
CRATEFUL
CRIMEFUL
DEARNFUL
DEATHFUL
DIRGEFUL
DOUBTFUL
DREADFUL
DREAMFUL
EVENTFUL
FAITHFUL
FANCIFUL
FAULTFUL
FEASTFUL
FORCEFUL
FORKSFUL
FOUNTFUL
FRAUDFUL
FREAKFUL

FRISKFUL
FRUITFUL
GHASTFUL
GLASSFUL
GLOOMFUL
GRACEFUL
GRATEFUL
GRIEFFUL
GROANFUL
GUILEFUL
HANDSFUL
HASTEFUL
HONEYFUL
HOUSEFUL
HUMORFUL
LADLEFUL
LAUGHFUL
LIGHTFUL
LOATHFUL
MENSEFUL
MERCIFUL
MIGHTFUL
MIRTHFUL
MOISTFUL
MOURNFUL
MOUTHFUL
NIEVEFUL
NOISEFUL
ODOURFUL
PAILSFUL
PAUSEFUL
PEACEFUL
PLAINFUL
PLATEFUL
POUCHFUL
POWERFUL
PRANKFUL
PRESSFUL
PRIDEFUL
PROUDFUL
PURSEFUL
RIGHTFUL
SACKSFUL
SCENTFUL
SCOOPFUL
SCORNFUL
SENSEFUL
SHAMEFUL
SHEENFUL
SHELFFUL
SHELLFUL
SKILLFUL
SLOTHFUL
SMILEFUL

SNEERFUL
SNOOTFUL
SOOTHFUL
SPADEFUL
SPEEDFUL
SPELLFUL
SPITEFUL
SPOILFUL
SPOONFUL
SPORTFUL
STAGEFUL
STARTFUL
STICKFUL
STORMFUL
SURGEFUL
TABLEFUL
TASTEFUL
THANKFUL
TOOTHFUL
TRADEFUL
TRAINFUL
TRISTFUL
TROTHFUL
TROUTFUL
TRUCKFUL
TRUNKFUL
TRUSTFUL
TRUTHFUL
UDDERFUL
UNARTFUL
UNJOYFUL
UNLAWFUL
UNMANFUL
UNSINFUL
UNUSEFUL
UNWILFUL
VAUNTFUL
VENGEFUL
VOICEFUL
WAGONFUL
WASTEFUL
WATCHFUL
WEARIFUL
WORTHFUL
WRACKFUL
WRATHFUL
WREAKFUL
WRECKFUL
WRONGFUL
WROTHFUL
YOUTHFUL

Words that end with -GEN

Seven-letter words	KEROGEN	SMIDGEN	AMYLOGEN	HYALOGEN
	LOXYGEN	TRUDGEN	ANDROGEN	HYDROGEN
ACROGEN	LUCIGEN	TWIGGEN	COLLAGEN	MISCEGEN
ANLAGEN	LYSOGEN	XYLOGEN	CULTIGEN	NITROGEN
ANTIGEN	MITOGEN	ZYMOGEN	CYANOGEN	OSTEOGEN
CRYOGEN	MUCIGEN		DIPLOGEN	PATHOGEN
ENDOGEN	MUTAGEN	**Eight-letter**	ENLARGEN	PHOTOGEN
HALOGEN	ONCOGEN	**words**	ESTROGEN	ROENTGEN
HUMOGEN	PIROGEN	ABORIGEN	FLORIGEN	STARAGEN
INDIGEN	PYROGEN	ALLERGEN	GLYCOGEN	
IONOGEN	RONTGEN	AMIDOGEN	HISTOGEN	

Words that end with -GRAM

Seven-letter words	TANGRAM	DEKAGRAM	KYMOGRAM	PARAGRAM
	TRIGRAM	ECHOGRAM	LEXIGRAM	PICOGRAM
ANAGRAM		ERGOGRAM	LIPOGRAM	RENOGRAM
DIAGRAM	**Eight-letter**	ETHOGRAM	LOGOGRAM	SKIAGRAM
EPIGRAM	**words**	GENOGRAM	MAILGRAM	SONOGRAM
GROGRAM	AEROGRAM	HEXAGRAM	MARIGRAM	TELEGRAM
ISOGRAM	BAROGRAM	HOLOGRAM	MONOGRAM	TOMOGRAM
MYOGRAM	DATAGRAM	IDEOGRAM	NANOGRAM	VENOGRAM
PANGRAM	DECAGRAM	IDIOGRAM	NOMOGRAM	ZYMOGRAM
PROGRAM	DECIGRAM	KILOGRAM	ONDOGRAM	

Words that end with -HOLE

Seven-letter words	KEYHOLE	**Eight-letter**	FUNKHOLE	POSTHOLE
	LUGHOLE	**words**	GUNKHOLE	SHITHOLE
AIRHOLE	MANHOLE	ANETHOLE	HELLHOLE	SHOTHOLE
ARMHOLE	MUDHOLE	ARSEHOLE	KNEEHOLE	SINKHOLE
ASSHOLE	OILHOLE	BLOWHOLE	KNOTHOLE	SUCKHOLE
BOTHOLE	PIEHOLE	BOLTHOLE	LAMPHOLE	WEEPHOLE
CATHOLE	PINHOLE	BOREHOLE	LOOPHOLE	WELLHOLE
DOGHOLE	POTHOLE	BUNGHOLE	PEEPHOLE	WOODHOLE
EYEHOLE	RATHOLE	COALHOLE	PESTHOLE	WORMHOLE
FOXHOLE	SPYHOLE	DOWNHOLE	PLUGHOLE	
JAWHOLE	TAPHOLE	FEEDHOLE	PORTHOLE	

Words that end with -HOOD

Seven-letter words	GODHOOD	**Eight-letter**	KINGHOOD	PUMPHOOD
	HOGHOOD	**words**	LADYHOOD	SELFHOOD
APEHOOD	LADHOOD	AUNTHOOD	MAIDHOOD	SERFHOOD
BOYHOOD	MANHOOD	BABYHOOD	MISSHOOD	WIFEHOOD
CATHOOD	NUNHOOD	DOLLHOOD	MONKHOOD	WIVEHOOD
CUBHOOD	SONHOOD	GIRLHOOD	PAGEHOOD	
ELFHOOD		IDLEHOOD	POPEHOOD	

Words that end with -HORN

Seven-letter words	DISHORN	UNSHORN	CRUMHORN	SHOEHORN
	ELKHORN		GEMSHORN	SLUGHORN
ALPHORN	FOGHORN	**Eight-letter words**	HAWTHORN	STAGHORN
ALTHORN	INKHORN		KRUMHORN	WALDHORN
BETHORN	LEGHORN	BOXTHORN	LANTHORN	
BIGHORN	SAXHORN	BUCKHORN	LONGHORN	
COEHORN	TINHORN	BULLHORN	RAMSHORN	

Words that end with -IBLE

Seven-letter words	RISIBLE	ERODIBLE	GULLIBLE	RUNCIBLE
	VISIBLE	EROSIBLE	HORRIBLE	SENSIBLE
ADDIBLE		EVADIBLE	INEDIBLE	SUASIBLE
AUDIBLE	**Eight-letter words**	EVASIBLE	LAPSIBLE	TANGIBLE
DELIBLE		EXIGIBLE	MANDIBLE	TENSIBLE
DOCIBLE	CREDIBLE	FALLIBLE	MISCIBLE	TERRIBLE
FUSIBLE	CRUCIBLE	FEASIBLE	PARTIBLE	THURIBLE
LEGIBLE	EDUCIBLE	FENCIBLE	PASSIBLE	UNEDIBLE
MIXIBLE	ELIDIBLE	FLEXIBLE	POSSIBLE	VENDIBLE
PATIBLE	ELIGIBLE	FORCIBLE	RENDIBLE	VINCIBLE
RIBIBLE	ELUDIBLE	FUNGIBLE	RINSIBLE	

Words that end with -IFY

Seven-letter words	FRUTIFY	PROSIFY	**Eight-letter words**	QUIZZIFY
	GLORIFY	PULPIFY		REAEDIFY
ACETIFY	GRATIFY	QUALIFY	ALKALIFY	RECODIFY
ACIDIFY	HORRIFY	RECTIFY	AMMONIFY	REMODIFY
AMPLIFY	ICONIFY	REEDIFY	BEAUTIFY	RENOTIFY
ANGLIFY	JELLIFY	REUNIFY		
BEATIFY	JOLLI			
BRUTIFY	JUSTI			
CALCIFY	LIGNI			
CAPRIFY	LIQUI			
CARNIFY	LITHI			
CERTIFY	MAGNI			
CHYLIFY	MATTI			
CHYMIFY	MERCI			
CLARIFY	METRI			
COALIFY	MICRI			
CORNIFY	MOLLI			
CRUCIFY	MORTI			
DAMNIFY	MUMMI			
DANDIFY	MUNDI			
DENSIFY	MYSTI			
DIGNIFY	NIGRI			
DULCIFY	NITRI			
FALSIFY	NULLI			
FANCIFY	OPACI			
FARCIFY	PETRI			
FISHIFY	PLEBI			
FORTIFY	PONTI			

COOIN...
COM...
COM...
COOINGS
COPINGS
COVINGS
COVINGS
CRYINGS
CUEINGS
DARINGS
DATINGS
DICINGS
DIVINGS
DONINGS
DOPINGS
DOTINGS
DOZINGS
DRYINGS
DYEINGS
EARINGS
EASINGS
EATINGS
EDGINGS
EFFINGS
ELDINGS
ENDINGS

LIV...
LOBINGS
LORINGS
LOSINGS
LOVINGS
LOWINGS
LOWTINGS
LUGINGS
LURINGS
LUTINGS
MAKINGS
MATINGS
MAYINGS
MERINGS
MININGS
MOWINGS

S...
TAK...
TAMINGS
TAMINGS
TARINGS
TAWINGS
TAXINGS
TIDINGS
TILINGS

Words that end with -INGS

Seven-letter words	ENRINGS	MUSINGS	TIMINGS	BELLINGS
	ERRINGS	NAMINGS	TIRINGS	BELTINGS
ABLINGS	FACINGS	NIDINGS	TOLINGS	BENDINGS
ACHINGS	FADINGS	NOSINGS	TONINGS	BETTINGS
ACTINGS	FILINGS	OFFINGS	TOWINGS	BIASINGS
ADDINGS	FININGS	OGLINGS	TOYINGS	BIDDINGS
AGEINGS	FIRINGS	ONDINGS	TRYINGS	BIGGINGS
AIRINGS	FIXINGS	OUTINGS	TUBINGS	BILLINGS
ANTINGS	FLYINGS	PAGINGS	TUNINGS	BINDINGS
ARCINGS	FOXINGS	PALINGS	TYPINGS	BIRDINGS
ARMINGS	FROINGS	PARINGS	ULLINGS	BIRLINGS
ASKINGS	FRYINGS	PAVINGS	UNKINGS	BITTINGS
AUDINGS	GAMINGS	PAYINGS	UPPINGS	BLADINGS
AWNINGS	GAPINGS	PIKINGS	URGINGS	BLOWINGS
BAAINGS	GATINGS	PILINGS	URNINGS	BLUEINGS
BAKINGS	GAZINGS	PIPINGS	VEXINGS	BOATINGS
BESINGS	GIVINGS	POLINGS	VIKINGS	BOILINGS
BIDINGS	GORINGS	POSINGS	VOTINGS	BOLTINGS
BIKINGS	HAVINGS	PRYINGS	WADINGS	BOMBINGS
BITINGS	HAYINGS	PULINGS	WAKINGS	BONDINGS
BLUINGS	HAZINGS	RACINGS	WANINGS	BONKINGS
BODINGS	HEWINGS	RAGINGS	WAVINGS	BOOKINGS
BONINGS	HEXINGS	RAKINGS	WAXINGS	BOOMINGS
BORINGS	HIDINGS	RATINGS	WIPINGS	BOOZINGS
BOWINGS	HIRINGS	RAVINGS	WIRINGS	BOSSINGS
BOXINGS	HOLINGS	RAWINGS	WONINGS	BOWLINGS
BUSINGS	HOMINGS	RIDINGS	WOOINGS	BRACINGS
BUYINGS	HYPINGS	RISINGS	YOKINGS	BREWINGS
CAKINGS	IMPINGS	ROBINGS	ZONINGS	BRIMINGS
CANINGS	INNINGS	RODINGS		BROKINGS
CARINGS	JAPINGS	ROPINGS	**Eight-letter words**	BRUTINGS
CASINGS	JAWINGS	ROVINGS		BUCKINGS
CAVINGS	KEYINGS	ROWINGS	ABIDINGS	BUDDINGS
CAWINGS	KITINGS	RUEINGS	AISLINGS	BUFFINGS
⬛DINGS	LACINGS	RULINGS	AMBLINGS	BUGGINGS
⬛NGS	LADINGS	SAVINGS	ANGLINGS	BULKINGS
⬛S	LAKINGS	SAWINGS	ARCHINGS	BULLINGS
	LASINGS	SAYINGS	ARCKINGS	BUMPINGS
	LAWINGS	SEEINGS	AWAKINGS	BUNTINGS
	LAYINGS	SEWINGS	BACKINGS	BURNINGS
	LIKINGS	SEXINGS	BAGGINGS	BUSHINGS
	⬛LIMINGS	SIDINGS	BAITINGS	BUSKINGS
	⬛NINGS	SIRINGS	BALKINGS	BUSSINGS
	⬛NGS	SIZINGS	BALLINGS	BUSTINGS
	⬛GS	SKIINGS	BANDINGS	BUZZINGS
		SORINGS	BANKINGS	CABLINGS
		SOWINGS	BANTINGS	CALKINGS
		SPAINGS	BARRINGS	CALLINGS
		SPRINGS	BASHINGS	CALMINGS
		SPYINGS	BASTINGS	CAMPINGS
		⬛RINGS	BATTINGS	CANNINGS
		⬛NGS	BAWLINGS	CANTINGS
		⬛S	BEADINGS	CAPPINGS
			BEAMINGS	CARDINGS
			BEARINGS	CARLINGS
			BEATINGS	CARPINGS
			BEDDINGS	CARVINGS
			BEGGINGS	CASTINGS

CATLINGS	DROVINGS	FRAYINGS	HERRINGS	KILTINGS
CEASINGS	DUBBINGS	FUCKINGS	HIDLINGS	KIRKINGS
CEILINGS	DUCKINGS	FUNDINGS	HILDINGS	KISSINGS
CHASINGS	DUCTINGS	FURRINGS	HILLINGS	KITLINGS
CHIDINGS	DUFFINGS	GADLINGS	HINTINGS	KNIFINGS
CIELINGS	DUMPINGS	GAFFINGS	HIPPINGS	KNOWINGS
CISSINGS	DUNNINGS	GAININGS	HIRLINGS	LAGGINGS
CLONINGS	DUSTINGS	GANGINGS	HISSINGS	LALLINGS
CLOSINGS	EANLINGS	GAPPINGS	HOGGINGS	LAMBINGS
COAMINGS	EARNINGS	GASKINGS	HOLDINGS	LAMMINGS
COATINGS	EARRINGS	GASPINGS	HOPPINGS	LAMPINGS
CODLINGS	EASTINGS	GASSINGS	HORNINGS	LANDINGS
COGGINGS	EBAYINGS	GAUGINGS	HORSINGS	LAPPINGS
COININGS	EDITINGS	GAYWINGS	HOSTINGS	LAPWINGS
COLLINGS	EEVNINGS	GEARINGS	HOTTINGS	LASHINGS
COMBINGS	EILDINGS	GELDINGS	HOUSINGS	LASTINGS
CONNINGS	EMPTINGS	GETTINGS	HOUTINGS	LATHINGS
COOKINGS	ENVYINGS	GILDINGS	HOWLINGS	LEADINGS
COOLINGS	ERLKINGS	GINNINGS	HUFFINGS	LEANINGS
CORDINGS	ETCHINGS	GIRDINGS	HUMMINGS	LEASINGS
COSTINGS	EVENINGS	GLAZINGS	HUNTINGS	LEAVINGS
COWLINGS	FABLINGS	GLEYINGS	HURLINGS	LEERINGS
CRAVINGS	FAGGINGS	GLIDINGS	HUSKINGS	LEGGINGS
CUBBINGS	FAILINGS	GLOVINGS	HUSTINGS	LEKKINGS
CULLINGS	FAIRINGS	GLOZINGS	HUTTINGS	LEMMINGS
CUNNINGS	FALLINGS	GNAWINGS	HYLDINGS	LENDINGS
CUPPINGS	FANNINGS	GODLINGS	IMAGINGS	LETTINGS
CURBINGS	FARCINGS	GOLFINGS	INBEINGS	LICKINGS
CURLINGS	FARDINGS	GOSLINGS	INBRINGS	LIGGINGS
CURSINGS	FARMINGS	GRADINGS	INGOINGS	LIMPINGS
CUTTINGS	FASTINGS	GRATINGS	INKLINGS	LIPPINGS
CYCLINGS	FATLINGS	GRAVINGS	INSWINGS	LISPINGS
CYMLINGS	FAWNINGS	GRAZINGS	IRONINGS	LISTINGS
DAFFINGS	FEEDINGS	GREYINGS	ITCHINGS	LOADINGS
DAGGINGS	FEELINGS	GRICINGS	JACKINGS	LOAFINGS
DAMPINGS	FEERINGS	GROWINGS	JAMMINGS	LOANINGS
DANCINGS	FELLINGS	GUIDINGS	JARRINGS	LOCKINGS
DARLINGS	FELTINGS	GUISINGS	JEERINGS	LODGINGS
DARNINGS	FENCINGS	GUMMINGS	JERKINGS	LOGGINGS
DAUBINGS	FERNINGS	GUNNINGS	JESTINGS	LONGINGS
DAWNINGS	FEUDINGS	HACKINGS	JIBBINGS	LOONINGS
DEALINGS	FILLINGS	HAININGS	JIGGINGS	LOOPINGS
DECKINGS	FINDINGS	HALLINGS	JOBBINGS	LOOSINGS
DESKINGS	FIRRINGS	HALTINGS	JOGGINGS	LOOTINGS
DEVLINGS	FISHINGS	HANGINGS	JOININGS	LOPPINGS
DIALINGS	FITTINGS	HARLINGS	JOTTINGS	LORDINGS
DIETINGS	FIZZINGS	HARPINGS	JUGGINGS	LOURINGS
DIGGINGS	FLUTINGS	HASHINGS	JUMPINGS	LUGEINGS
DILLINGS	FLYTINGS	HASTINGS	KARTINGS	LURKINGS
DIMMINGS	FOAMINGS	HATTINGS	KAYOINGS	MADLINGS
DIPPINGS	FOILINGS	HAWKINGS	KEELINGS	MAILINGS
DISHINGS	FOLDINGS	HEADINGS	KEENINGS	MAIMINGS
DOATINGS	FOOLINGS	HEALINGS	KEEPINGS	MALLINGS
DOCKINGS	FOOTINGS	HEATINGS	KEGLINGS	MALTINGS
DODGINGS	FOPLINGS	HEAVINGS	KEMPINGS	MAPPINGS
DOGGINGS	FORGINGS	HEDGINGS	KENNINGS	MARKINGS
DOPPINGS	FORMINGS	HEELINGS	KERBINGS	MARLINGS
DRAWINGS	FOULINGS	HELPINGS	KERNINGS	MASHINGS
DRIVINGS	FOWLINGS	HERLINGS	KIDLINGS	MASKINGS
	FRAMINGS		KILLINGS	MATTINGS

MEANINGS	PEELINGS	REEFINGS	SELFINGS	SUBRINGS
MEETINGS	PEGGINGS	REELINGS	SELLINGS	SUCKINGS
MELTINGS	PELTINGS	RENNINGS	SENDINGS	SUGGINGS
MENDINGS	PERFINGS	RENTINGS	SENSINGS	SUITINGS
MERGINGS	PETTINGS	REPPINGS	SERGINGS	SUMMINGS
MERLINGS	PHASINGS	RESTINGS	SERVINGS	SURFINGS
MESHINGS	PICKINGS	RIBBINGS	SETTINGS	SURGINGS
MICHINGS	PIECINGS	RIDGINGS	SHADINGS	SWALINGS
MILKINGS	PIGGINGS	RIFLINGS	SHAKINGS	SWAYINGS
MILLINGS	PIGLINGS	RIGGINGS	SHAPINGS	SYNDINGS
MINDINGS	PILLINGS	RIGLINGS	SHARINGS	TABLINGS
MISTINGS	PIMPINGS	RIMMINGS	SHAVINGS	TACKINGS
MOANINGS	PINKINGS	RINGINGS	SHOEINGS	TAGGINGS
MOBBINGS	PINNINGS	RINSINGS	SHORINGS	TAILINGS
MOCKINGS	PIONINGS	RIOTINGS	SHOVINGS	TALKINGS
MODDINGS	PITTINGS	RIPPINGS	SHOWINGS	TAMPINGS
MOLDINGS	PLACINGS	RISPINGS	SIBLINGS	TANKINGS
MOORINGS	PLATINGS	ROADINGS	SIFTINGS	TANLINGS
MOOTINGS	POLLINGS	ROAMINGS	SIGNINGS	TANNINGS
MORLINGS	POSTINGS	ROARINGS	SINDINGS	TAPPINGS
MORNINGS	POURINGS	ROCKINGS	SINGINGS	TARRINGS
MOSHINGS	POUTINGS	RODDINGS	SINKINGS	TASKINGS
MOSLINGS	PRATINGS	ROLFINGS	SITTINGS	TASTINGS
MOUSINGS	PRAYINGS	ROLLINGS	SKATINGS	TATTINGS
MUGGINGS	PRICINGS	ROOFINGS	SKIVINGS	TEAMINGS
MUMMINGS	PRIMINGS	ROOTINGS	SLATINGS	TEASINGS
MUNTINGS	PROSINGS	RORTINGS	SLICINGS	TELLINGS
NAGGINGS	PROVINGS	ROUMINGS	SLIDINGS	TENTINGS
NAILINGS	PRUNINGS	ROUTINGS	SLOWINGS	TESTINGS
NECKINGS	PUBBINGS	RUBBINGS	SMILINGS	TEXTINGS
NERVINGS	PUDDINGS	RUCHINGS	SMOKINGS	THAWINGS
NESTINGS	PUFFINGS	RUGGINGS	SNARINGS	TICKINGS
NETTINGS	PUGGINGS	RUININGS	SNIPINGS	TIFFINGS
NITHINGS	PUMPINGS	RUNNINGS	SNORINGS	TILLINGS
NODDINGS	PUNNINGS	RUSHINGS	SOAKINGS	TILTINGS
NOGGINGS	PURGINGS	RUSTINGS	SOARINGS	TINNINGS
NOONINGS	PURLINGS	RUTTINGS	SOBBINGS	TINTINGS
NOTHINGS	PURRINGS	SABBINGS	SOGGINGS	TIPPINGS
NULLINGS	PUTTINGS	SACKINGS	SOILINGS	TITHINGS
NURSINGS	PYONINGS	SACRINGS	SOOPINGS	TITLINGS
NUTTINGS	QUAKINGS	SAGGINGS	SOPPINGS	TOILINGS
OAKLINGS	QUEUINGS	SAILINGS	SORNINGS	TOLLINGS
ONGOINGS	RACKINGS	SALTINGS	SORTINGS	TOOLINGS
OPENINGS	RAFTINGS	SALVINGS	SOSSINGS	TOPPINGS
OUTRINGS	RAGGINGS	SANDINGS	SOTTINGS	TOSSINGS
OUTSINGS	RAIDINGS	SAPLINGS	SOUMINGS	TOTTINGS
OUTWINGS	RAILINGS	SARKINGS	SOURINGS	TOURINGS
PACKINGS	RAISINGS	SCALINGS	SOUSINGS	TOUSINGS
PADDINGS	RAMPINGS	SCORINGS	SPACINGS	TRACINGS
PAIRINGS	RANGINGS	SCRYINGS	SPAEINGS	TRADINGS
PANNINGS	RANKINGS	SEALINGS	SPILINGS	TUBBINGS
PANTINGS	RANTINGS	SEAMINGS	STAGINGS	TUFTINGS
PARGINGS	RAPPINGS	SEARINGS	STARINGS	TUGGINGS
PARKINGS	RASPINGS	SEATINGS	STEWINGS	TUNNINGS
PARSINGS	RATLINGS	SEEDINGS	STONINGS	TURFINGS
PARTINGS	RATTINGS	SEELINGS	STOPINGS	TURNINGS
PASSINGS	READINGS	SEEMINGS	STOVINGS	TUSKINGS
PASTINGS	REDDINGS	SEININGS	STOWINGS	TUTTINGS
PAUSINGS	REDWINGS	SEISINGS	STYLINGS	TWININGS
PECKINGS	REEDINGS	SEIZINGS	SUBBINGS	UNBEINGS

UNDOINGS	VERSINGS	WARNINGS	WELLINGS	WOLFINGS
UNITINGS	VESTINGS	WARPINGS	WELTINGS	WOLVINGS
UNSLINGS	VETTINGS	WASHINGS	WESTINGS	WONNINGS
UNTYINGS	VIEWINGS	WASTINGS	WETTINGS	WORDINGS
UPBRINGS	VISHINGS	WAULINGS	WHALINGS	WORKINGS
UPFLINGS	VOGUINGS	WAWLINGS	WHININGS	WRITINGS
UPGOINGS	VOICINGS	WAXWINGS	WHITINGS	YARDINGS
UPSWINGS	VOIDINGS	WEANINGS	WICKINGS	YAWNINGS
VAMPINGS	WADDINGS	WEARINGS	WIGGINGS	YAWPINGS
VANNINGS	WAFTINGS	WEAVINGS	WILDINGS	YEALINGS
VARYINGS	WAILINGS	WEBBINGS	WINCINGS	YELLINGS
VEERINGS	WAITINGS	WEBRINGS	WINDINGS	YELPINGS
VEILINGS	WALKINGS	WEDDINGS	WINKINGS	YORLINGS
VEININGS	WALLINGS	WEDGINGS	WINNINGS	YOWLINGS
VENDINGS	WARDINGS	WEEDINGS	WISHINGS	ZORBINGS
VENTINGS	WARLINGS	WEEPINGS	WITLINGS	
VERBINGS	WARMINGS	WELDINGS	WITTINGS	

Words that end with -ISE

Seven-letter words	GENOISE	SUNRISE	COLONISE	FESSWISE
ABSCISE	GRECISE	SUNWISE	COLORISE	FIBERISE
ADONISE	HEROISE	SURMISE	COMBWISE	FINALISE
AGATISE	ICONISE	TAXWISE	COMPRISE	FLATWISE
AGENISE	IDOLISE	TRENISE	COVETISE	FLUIDISE
AGONISE	IRIDISE	UNITISE	CRABWISE	FOCALISE
AIRWISE	IRONISE	UPRAISE	CREOLISE	FRANCISE
ANODISE	ITEMISE	UTILISE	CURARISE	GRAECISE
ANYWISE	KYANISE		CUTINISE	HEBRAISE
APPRISE	LAICISE	**Eight-letter words**	DEBRUISE	HEPATISE
ARABISE	LAIRISE	ACTIVISE	DEIONISE	HIGHRISE
ATHEISE	LIONISE	ALBITISE	DEMONISE	HOMINISE
ATOMISE	MALAISE	ALKALISE	DEPUTISE	HUMANISE
AZOTISE	MANWISE	AMORTISE	DIGITISE	IDEALISE
BAPTISE	MAPWISE	ANNALISE	DIMERISE	IMMUNISE
BROMISE	MORTISE	ANTICISE	DISGUISE	INFAMISE
CHAMISE	MYTHISE	APHETISE	DISSEISE	JAPANISE
CHEMISE	NICOISE	APHORISE	DIVINISE	JAROVISE
COALISE	OBELISE	APPETISE	DROPWISE	JUMBOISE
COGNISE	ODORISE	APPRAISE	DYNAMISE	LATERISE
CONCISE	OXIDISE	ARBORISE	EBIONISE	LATINISE
COTTISE	OZONISE	ARCHAISE	EDGEWISE	LEGALISE
CYANISE	PARVISE	ARCHWISE	EGLOMISE	LIKEWISE
CYCLISE	PECTISE	ATHETISE	ELSEWISE	LOCALISE
DESPISE	PENTISE	ATTICISE	EMBOLISE	LOGICISE
DIARISE	PEPTISE	AVIANISE	EMPERISE	LONGWISE
DOCKISE	POETISE	BANALISE	ENERGISE	LYRICISE
DUALISE	PRECISE	BENDWISE	EQUALISE	MACARISE
EBONISE	PREMISE	BEPRAISE	ERGOTISE	MADERISE
ECHOISE	PREVISE	BOTANISE	ETERNISE	MARQUISE
EGOTISE	PROMISE	BRANDISE	ETHERISE	MAUVAISE
ELEGISE	REALISE	CALORISE	ETHICISE	MAXIMISE
EMPRISE	REARISE	CANALISE	EULOGISE	MELANISE
ENDWISE	REPRISE	CANONISE	EUPHUISE	MELODISE
EROTISE	RERAISE	CAPONISE	EXERCISE	MEMORISE
FADAISE	RIOTISE	CHASTISE	EXORCISE	MESPRISE
FANWISE	SOUBISE	CHROMISE	FABULISE	METALISE
GALLISE	STYLISE	CIVILISE	FARADISE	MINIMISE
	SUCCISE		FEMINISE	MISPOISE

MISPRISE	PAIRWISE	REREVISE	SODOMISE	TREATISE
MISRAISE	PALEWISE	RESINISE	SOLARISE	TUTORISE
MOBILISE	PAPALISE	RIGIDISE	SOLECISE	UNIONISE
MONETISE	PARADISE	RINGWISE	SOMEWISE	UNPRAISE
MOONRISE	PATINISE	RIVALISE	SORORISE	URBANISE
MORALISE	PENALISE	ROBOTISE	STEPWISE	VALORISE
MOTORISE	POLARISE	ROMANISE	SUBERISE	VAPORISE
NASALISE	POLEMISE	ROYALISE	SUBITISE	VELARISE
NEBULISE	POLONISE	RURALISE	SUCHWISE	VIRILISE
NODALISE	PORPOISE	SALINISE	SURPRISE	VITALISE
NOMADISE	PORTOISE	SANITISE	TEAMWISE	VOCALISE
NOTARISE	PRACTISE	SATIRISE	TELEVISE	VOLUMISE
NOVELISE	PTYALISE	SIDEWISE	TENTWISE	VOWELISE
OPSONISE	PYRITISE	SIMILISE	TETANISE	WARPWISE
OPTIMISE	PYROLISE	SIMONISE	THEORISE	WEFTWISE
ORGANISE	QUANTISE	SINICISE	THUSWISE	WOMANISE
OUTRAISE	RACEMISE	SIRENISE	TORTOISE	
OVERWISE	READVISE	SIRONISE	TOTALISE	
PAGANISE	REGULISE	SOBERISE	TRAVOISE	

Words that end with -ISH

Seven-letter words

ABOLISH	COLDISH	FINFISH	HOGFISH	MOREISH
ALUMISH	COLTISH	FLEMISH	HOGGISH	MUDFISH
ANGUISH	COOLISH	FOGYISH	HORNISH	MUFFISH
BABYISH	COWFISH	FOLKISH	HOTTISH	MUGGISH
BADDISH	CRONISH	FOOLISH	HUFFISH	MUMPISH
BALDISH	CUBBISH	FOPPISH	HUNNISH	MURKISH
BATFISH	CULTISH	FOXFISH	JEWFISH	NEBBISH
BEAMISH	CURRISH	FULLISH	JIGGISH	NEDDISH
BEARISH	DAMPISH	FURBISH	JOCKISH	NERDISH
BEAUISH	DANKISH	FURNISH	KADDISH	NICEISH
BIGGISH	DARKISH	GAMPISH	KERNISH	NOIRISH
BLEMISH	DEAFISH	GARFISH	KIDDISH	NOURISH
BLOKISH	DERVISH	GARNISH	KNAVISH	NUNNISH
BLUEISH	DIMMISH	GAWKISH	LADDISH	NURDISH
BOARISH	DOGFISH	GEMFISH	LADYISH	OARFISH
BOBBISH	DOGGISH	GIRLISH	LARGISH	OGREISH
BOGGISH	DOLLISH	GNOMISH	LARKISH	OOFTISH
BOOBISH	DOLTISH	GOATISH	LAZYISH	OUTFISH
BOOKISH	DONNISH	GOLDISH	LEFTISH	OUTWISH
BOORISH	DORKISH	GOODISH	LOGGISH	PANFISH
BOXFISH	DOVEISH	GRAYISH	LOMPISH	PARKISH
BRINISH	DRONISH	GREYISH	LONGISH	PEAKISH
BRUTISH	DULLISH	GUARISH	LOUDISH	PECKISH
BUCKISH	DUMPISH	GULLISH	LOUTISH	PEEVISH
BULLISH	DUNCISH	HAGFISH	LUBFISH	PERKISH
BURNISH	DUNNISH	HAGGISH	LUMPISH	PETTISH
CADDISH	DUSKISH	HAIMISH	LUSKISH	PIEDISH
CARLISH	ENGLISH	HARDISH	MADDISH	PIGFISH
CATFISH	EVANISH	HASHISH	MAIDISH	PIGGISH
CATTISH	FADDISH	HAWKISH	MANNISH	PINFISH
CHAVISH	FAIRISH	HEIMISH	MAWKISH	PINKISH
CHERISH	FALSISH	HELLISH	MINXISH	PIXYISH
CLAYISH	FASTISH	HENNISH	MISSISH	PLANISH
COCKISH	FATTISH	HICKISH	MOBBISH	PLENISH
CODFISH	FENNISH	HIGHISH	MONKISH	POORISH
	FILMISH	HIPPISH	MOONISH	POPPISH
	FINEISH	HOBBISH	MOORISH	PRUDISH

PUBLISH
PUCKISH
PUGGISH
PUNKISH
PUPFISH
RAFFISH
RAMMISH
RANKISH
RASPISH
RATFISH
RATTISH
REDDISH
REDFISH
RELLISH
RIGGISH
ROGUISH
ROINISH
ROMPISH
ROOKISH
ROYNISH
RUBBISH
RUMMISH
RUNTISH
RUTTISH
SADDISH
SALTISH
SAWFISH
SELFISH
SERFISH
SICKISH
SLAVISH
SLOWISH
SNAKISH
SNOWISH
SOFTISH
SOTTISH
SOURISH
STONISH
STYLISH
SUNFISH
SWINISH
TALLISH
TANNISH
TARNISH
TARTISH
TIGRISH
TITTISH
TOADISH
TOFFISH
TONNISH
TOWNISH
TUBBISH
TUBFISH
TUNDISH
VAMPISH
VARNISH
VOGUISH
WAGGISH
WAIFISH
WAMPISH

WANNISH
WARMISH
WASPISH
WEAKISH
WEARISH
WEBLISH
WENNISH
WETTISH
WHEYISH
WHITISH
WHORISH
WILDISH
WIMPISH
WISPISH
WOGGISH
WOLFISH
WOLVISH
WORDISH
WORMISH
YOBBISH
ZANYISH

Eight-letter words
ACTORISH
ADMONISH
ASTONISH
BABELISH
BAIRNISH
BAITFISH
BAKSHISH
BANDFISH
BILLFISH
BLACKISH
BLANDISH
BLEAKISH
BLIMPISH
BLOCKISH
BLOKEISH
BLONDISH
BLOWFISH
BLUEFISH
BLUNTISH
BOARFISH
BONEFISH
BOOBYISH
BRACKISH
BRAINISH
BRANDISH
BRASSISH
BRATTISH
BRISKISH
BROADISH
BROGUISH
BROWNISH
CAMELISH
CAVEFISH
CEORLISH
CHEAPISH
CHILDISH

CHURLISH
CLANNISH
CLAPDISH
CLERKISH
CLIQUISH
CLODDISH
CLOTTISH
CLOWNISH
CLUBBISH
CLUMPISH
COALFISH
COARSISH
COMPLISH
CRANKISH
CRAWFISH
CRAYFISH
CROSSISH
DANDYISH
DEALFISH
DEMOLISH
DEPOLISH
DEVILISH
DIMINISH
DOWDYISH
DRABBISH
DRAFFISH
DREGGISH
DROLLISH
DROOGISH
DRUMFISH
DWARFISH
DWEEBISH
EMPERISH
ENRAVISH
ESSAYISH
ETHERISH
FAINTISH
FALLFISH
FEEBLISH
FEVERISH
FIENDISH
FIFTYISH
FILEFISH
FLATFISH
FLATTISH
FLIRTISH
FLOURISH
FOGEYISH
FOOLFISH
FORTYISH
FRAILISH
FREAKISH
FRESHISH
FROGFISH
FRUMPISH
GHOULISH
GIPSYISH
GLUMPISH
GOATFISH
GOLDFISH

GRAYFISH
GREENISH
GRUFFISH
GRUMPISH
GYPSYISH
HEADFISH
IDIOTISH
JACKFISH
JINGOISH
KINGFISH
KNACKISH
LADYFISH
LANGUISH
LEMONISH
LIGHTISH
LIONFISH
LITTLISH
LIVERISH
LUMPFISH
LUNGFISH
MILKFISH
MINIDISH
MONKFISH
MOONFISH
NABOBISH
NANNYISH
NINNYISH
NOHOWISH
NOVELISH
NUMBFISH
NYMPHISH
ORANGISH
OVERFISH
PAGANISH
PIPEFISH
PIXIEISH
PLAINISH
PLUMPISH
POKERISH
POSERISH
PRANKISH
PRIGGISH
PROUDISH
PSEUDISH
PUPPYISH
PURPLISH
PYGMYISH
QUACKISH
QUALMISH
QUEERISH
QUIPPISH
QUIRKISH
RAWMAISH
REFINISH
REPOLISH
RIGHTISH
ROCKFISH
ROSEFISH
ROUGHISH
ROUNDISH

ROWDYISH
SAILFISH
SAINTISH
SALTFISH
SANDFISH
SANDYISH
SCAMPISH
SCARFISH
SCOMFISH
SCUMFISH
SHARPISH
SHEEPISH
SHORTISH
SHREWISH
SISSYISH
SIXTYISH
SKIRMISH
SKITTISH
SLANGISH
SLIMMISH
SLOBBISH
SLUGGISH
SLUTTISH
SMALLISH
SMARTISH
SNAPPISH
SNEAKISH
SNIFFISH
SNOBBISH
SNOUTISH
SNUBBISH
SOLIDISH
SORRYISH
SPARKISH
SPOFFISH
SPOOKISH
SQUARISH
SQUIRISH
STABLISH
STANDISH
STARFISH
STARTISH
STEEPISH
STIFFISH
STILTISH
STOCKISH
STOUTISH
STUDFISH
SUCKFISH
SUMPHISH
SURFFISH
SWAINISH
SWAMPISH
SWEETISH
SWELLISH
SYLPHISH
THICKISH
THIEVISH
THINNISH
THUGGISH

TICKLISH	TOADYISH	UNMODISH	VIPERISH	WOMANISH
TIGERISH	TOLLDISH	UNPOLISH	VIXENISH	YOKELISH
TIGHTISH	TOUGHISH	VAGARISH	WALLFISH	YOUNGISH
TILEFISH	TOVARISH	VANQUISH	WATERISH	
TINGLISH	TRAMPISH	VAPORISH	WEAKFISH	
TOADFISH	TRICKISH	VIGORISH	WOLFFISH	

Words that end with -ISM

Seven-letter words

ABLEISM	FOGYISM	TROPISM	CRONYISM	INTIMISM
AMORISM	FOODISM	TSARISM	CULLYISM	IOTACISM
ANIMISM	GURUISM	TYCHISM	CYNICISM	JEHADISM
ASTEISM	HANDISM	TZARISM	DANDYISM	JIHADISM
ATAVISM	HEROISM	URANISM	DEMONISM	JINGOISM
ATHEISM	HEURISM	UTOPISM	DEVILISM	KABALISM
ATOMISM	HOBOISM	WHOLISM	DIMERISM	LABORISM
BAALISM	IDOLISM	YOBBISM	DIOECISM	LACONISM
BABUISM	IMAGISM	ZANYISM	DIRIGISM	LEGALISM
BAPTISM	ITACISM		DITHEISM	LOBBYISM
BARDISM	JUJUISM	**Eight-letter words**	DONATISM	LOCALISM
BIPRISM	KARAISM		DOWDYISM	LOGICISM
BOGYISM	LADDISM	ACOSMISM	DRUDGISM	LOOKSISM
BOSSISM	LADYISM	ACROTISM	DRUIDISM	LOYALISM
BROMISM	LAICISM	ACTINISM	DWARFISM	LUMINISM
BRUTISM	LEFTISM	ACTIVISM	DYNAMISM	LYRICISM
BRUXISM	LEGGISM	ALARMISM	EBIONISM	MACARISM
CAMBISM	LIONISM	ALBINISM	EMBOLISM	MACHOISM
CHARISM	LOCOISM	ALGORISM	ENDEMISM	MELANISM
CHEMISM	LOOKISM	ALIENISM	ENTRYISM	MERYCISM
CHORISM	MAIDISM	ALLELISM	EPIZOISM	METOPISM
CLADISM	MOBBISM	ALPINISM	ERETHISM	MINIMISM
CLONISM	MYALISM	ALTRUISM	ERGOTISM	MODALISM
COPYISM	MYTHISM	ANEURISM	ESCAPISM	MONADISM
COSMISM	NARCISM	APHORISM	ETHERISM	MORALISM
CRETISM	NEURISM	APTERISM	ETHICISM	MORONISM
CULTISM	OBELISM	ARCHAISM	EUGENISM	NABOBISM
CZARISM	ODYLISM	ASTERISM	EUMERISM	NASALISM
DADAISM	OGREISM	ATROPISM	EUPHUISM	NATIVISM
DIORISM	ONANISM	ATTICISM	EXORCISM	NATURISM
DODOISM	ORALISM	AUTECISM	FAIRYISM	NAVALISM
DONNISM	ORPHISM	BABELISM	FAKIRISM	NEGROISM
DUALISM	PEONISM	BATHMISM	FAMILISM	NEPHRISM
ECHOISM	PHAEISM	BETACISM	FARADISM	NEPOTISM
EGOTISM	PHOBISM	BINARISM	FATALISM	NIHILISM
ELITISM	PHOTISM	BOGEYISM	FEMINISM	NIMBYISM
ENTRISM	PIANISM	BOOBYISM	FINALISM	NOMADISM
EPICISM	PIETISM	BOTULISM	FINITISM	NOVELISM
EROTISM	PLENISM	BOYARISM	FOGEYISM	OBEAHISM
ETACISM	RANKISM	BULLYISM	FUTURISM	OCKERISM
ETATISM	REALISM	CABALISM	GIANTISM	OPIUMISM
EXOTISM	SELFISM	CAFFEISM	GYPSYISM	OPTIMISM
FADDISM	SENSISM	CASTEISM	HEDONISM	ORGANISM
FALSISM	SIZEISM	CENTRISM	HELOTISM	PACIFISM
FASCISM	SLUMISM	CHARTISM	HOBBYISM	PAEANISM
FATTISM	SOPHISM	CIVICISM	HUMANISM	PAGANISM
FAUVISM	STATISM	CLASSISM	HYLICISM	PALUDISM
FIDEISM	TACHISM	CLIQUISM	IDEALISM	PAPALISM
	TACTISM	CLUBBISM	IDIOTISM	PARECISM
	TOURISM	COLORISM	INCIVISM	PARTYISM

PELORISM	PUGILISM	SAPPHISM	SWINGISM	ULTRAISM
PETALISM	PUPPYISM	SATANISM	SYBOTISM	UNDINISM
PEYOTISM	PYGMYISM	SAVAGISM	TANTRISM	UNIONISM
PHALLISM	QABALISM	SCIOLISM	TERATISM	UNTRUISM
PHRENISM	QUACKISM	SCRIBISM	THUGGISM	URBANISM
PLUMBISM	QUIETISM	SEISMISM	TIGERISM	VEGANISM
POLONISM	RACEMISM	SIMPLISM	TITANISM	VIRILISM
POPULISM	REGALISM	SINAPISM	TOADYISM	VITALISM
PRIAPISM	RIGHTISM	SNOBBISM	TOKENISM	VOCALISM
PRIGGISM	RIGORISM	SOLARISM	TOTALISM	VOLTAISM
PROSAISM	ROBOTISM	SOLECISM	TOTEMISM	WOMANISM
PSELLISM	ROWDYISM	SOLIDISM	TRIADISM	XANTHISM
PSEPHISM	ROYALISM	SOMATISM	TRIALISM	YAHOOISM
PSYCHISM	RURALISM	STOICISM	TROILISM	ZOMBIISM
PTYALISM	SAINTISM	STRABISM	TUTORISM	

Words that end with -IST

	DUALIST	JUDOIST	STYLIST	AVIARIST
Seven-letter	DUELIST	JUJUIST	SUBSIST	BACKLIST
words	DUMAIST	LEFTIST	SUMMIST	BANJOIST
ABLEIST	EBONIST	LOOKIST	SUMOIST	BIGAMIST
ACQUIST	ECHOIST	MAPPIST	TACHIST	BLURBIST
AGONIST	EGOTIST	METRIST	TENNIST	BONGOIST
ALTOIST	ELEGIST	MIDLIST	TITLIST	BOTANIST
AMORIST	ELITIST	MYALIST	TOURIST	BURINIST
ANGLIST	ELOGIST	MYTHIST	TROPIST	CABALIST
ANIMIST	ENTRIST	NAIVIST	TSARIST	CALORIST
ATAVIST	ENTWIST	NARCIST	TUBAIST	CANOEIST
ATHEIST	EPEEIST	OCULIST	TZARIST	CANONIST
ATOMIST	EPICIST	OLIGIST	UNALIST	CENTOIST
ATTRIST	ETATIST	OLOGIST	UNTWIST	CENTRIST
BAPTIST	EXODIST	ONANIST	UPHOIST	CERAMIST
BASSIST	FADDIST	ORALIST	UTOPIST	CHARTIST
BIBLIST	FASCIST	PALMIST	VACUIST	CIVILIST
BUNDIST	FATTIST	PAYLIST	VIOLIST	CLASSIST
CAMBIST	FAUNIST	PERSIST	WHOLIST	CLUBBIST
CASUIST	FAUVIST	PHOBIST		COASSIST
CELLIST	FEUDIST	PIANIST	**Eight-letter**	COLONIST
CHEKIST	FIDEIST	PIARIST	**words**	COLORIST
CHEMIST	FLORIST	PIETIST	ACOSMIST	CONTRIST
CHORIST	FLUTIST	PLENIST	ACTIVIST	CREOLIST
CHUTIST	FUGUIST	PLUMIST	ALARMIST	DEMONIST
CHYMIST	GAMBIST	POLLIST	ALIENIST	DEMOTIST
CLADIST	GNOMIST	POLOIST	ALPINIST	DIALLIST
COEXIST	HARPIST	PROTIST	ALTRUIST	DIGAMIST
CONSIST	HERBIST	QUERIST	ANNALIST	DITHEIST
COPYIST	HORNIST	REALIST	APHORIST	DRUGGIST
CORNIST	HYGEIST	RETWIST	APIARIST	DUELLIST
COSMIST	HYLOIST	REVUIST	AQUARIST	DUETTIST
CULTIST	HYMNIST	RHYMIST	ARBALIST	DYNAMIST
CYCLIST	IAMBIST	SACRIST	ARBORIST	ENTRYIST
CZARIST	IDOLIST	SELFIST	ARCANIST	ERRORIST
DADAIST	IDYLIST	SENSIST	ARCHAIST	ESCAPIST
DENTIST	IMAGIST	SIZEIST	ARMORIST	ESSAYIST
DIALIST	INTWIST	SOLOIST	ARSONIST	ETHERIST
DIARIST	IRONIST	SOPHIST	ATTICIST	ETHICIST
DIETIST	IVORIST	STATIST	AVANTIST	EUGENIST

EULOGIST	JEHADIST	MODELIST	PROSAIST	SODALIST
EUPHUIST	JIHADIST	MONODIST	PSALMIST	SODOMIST
EXORCIST	JINGOIST	MORALIST	PSYCHIST	SOLARIST
FABULIST	JUNGLIST	MOTORIST	PUCKFIST	SOLECIST
FATALIST	KABALIST	MURALIST	PUGILIST	SOLIDIST
FEMINIST	LABORIST	NATIVIST	QABALIST	SOMATIST
FIGURIST	LAPIDIST	NATURIST	QUIETIST	STOCKIST
FINALIST	LEGALIST	NEPOTIST	RALLYIST	SUBTRIST
FLAUTIST	LIBELIST	NIELLIST	REENLIST	TANGOIST
FUTURIST	LINGUIST	NIHILIST	REGALIST	TENORIST
GARAGIST	LOBBYIST	NOVELIST	REVERIST	THEORIST
GLOSSIST	LOCALIST	ODONTIST	RIGHTIST	TOTALIST
GREYLIST	LOGICIST	OGHAMIST	RIGORIST	TOTEMIST
GROUPIST	LONGLIST	OOLOGIST	ROYALIST	TRIADIST
HAGADIST	LOYALIST	OPTICIST	RURALIST	TRIALIST
HALAKIST	LUMINIST	OPTIMIST	SAFARIST	TROILIST
HANDLIST	LUNARIST	ORGANIST	SAPPHIST	ULTRAIST
HEDONIST	LUTANIST	PACIFIST	SARODIST	UNIONIST
HOBBYIST	LUTENIST	PAGANIST	SATANIST	UNSEXIST
HOMILIST	LUXURIST	PANELIST	SATIRIST	URBANIST
HUMANIST	LYRICIST	PAPALIST	SCIOLIST	VEGETIST
HUMORIST	MAXIMIST	PARODIST	SEMITIST	VISAGIST
HYGIEIST	MEDALIST	PEYOTIST	SHITLIST	VITALIST
HYLICIST	MELANIST	PHALLIST	SHOOTIST	VOCALIST
HYPOCIST	MELODIST	PLAYLIST	SILURIST	VOLUMIST
IDEALIST	METALIST	POLEMIST	SIMONIST	VOTARIST
IDYLLIST	METALIST	POPULIST	SIMPLIST	WAITLIST
INTIMIST	MODALIST	PREEXIST	SITARIST	WOMANIST

Words that end with -ITY

Seven-letter words	FALSITY	SPIRITY	AURALITY	EQUINITY
	FATUITY	SUAVITY	AXIALITY	ETERNITY
ABILITY	FURMITY	SURDITY	BANALITY	EXIGUITY
ACIDITY	GASEITY	TENSITY	BASICITY	FACILITY
AGILITY	GRAVITY	TENUITY	BIFIDITY	FATALITY
AMENITY	INANITY	TRINITY	BISCUITY	FELICITY
AMINITY	JOLLITY	UNICITY	BOVINITY	FELINITY
ANALITY	LAICITY	UTILITY	CADUCITY	FEMALITY
ANILITY	NULLITY	VACUITY	CALAMITY	FEMINITY
ANNUITY	OBESITY	VARSITY	CALIDITY	FERACITY
ARIDITY	OMNEITY	VASTITY	CANINITY	FEROCITY
AUREITY	OPACITY	VIDUITY	CAPACITY	FETIDITY
AVIDITY	ORALITY		CELERITY	FIDELITY
BIGGITY	OUTCITY	**Eight-letter words**	CHASTITY	FINALITY
BREVITY	OUTPITY		CIRCUITY	FLUIDITY
CHARITY	OVALITY	ACERBITY	CIVILITY	FORTUITY
CLARITY	PANEITY	ACRIDITY	CONCEITY	FUGACITY
CRUDITY	PAUCITY	ACTIVITY	CONICITY	FUMOSITY
CURVITY	PIOSITY	ADUNCITY	CUBICITY	FURACITY
DABBITY	PRAVITY	AFFINITY	CUPIDITY	FUTILITY
DACOITY	PRIVITY	ALACRITY	DEBILITY	FUTURITY
DAKOITY	PROBITY	ALGIDITY	DICACITY	GELIDITY
DENSITY	QUALITY	ALTERITY	DISUNITY	GRATUITY
DIGNITY	RABBITY	ANTICITY	DIVINITY	GULOSITY
DUALITY	RAUCITY	ASPERITY	DOCILITY	HELICITY
EDACITY	REALITY	ASTUCITY	DUMOSITY	HEREDITY
EGALITY	RUBBITY	ATROCITY	ENORMITY	HILARITY
EXILITY	SICCITY	AUDACITY	EQUALITY	HUMANITY

HUMIDITY	LUCIDITY	OBTUSITY	SANCTITY	TOXICITY
HUMILITY	MAJORITY	ORGANITY	SAPIDITY	TRIALITY
IDEALITY	MATURITY	OTIOSITY	SATANITY	TRIUNITY
IDENTITY	MEGACITY	PENALITY	SCANTITY	TUMIDITY
IDONEITY	MINACITY	PERSEITY	SCARCITY	UBIQUITY
IMMANITY	MINORITY	PILOSITY	SECURITY	UNFIXITY
IMMUNITY	MOBILITY	POLARITY	SEDULITY	URBANITY
IMPARITY	MODALITY	POROSITY	SENILITY	VAGILITY
IMPUNITY	MOLALITY	PRIORITY	SERENITY	VALIDITY
IMPURITY	MOLARITY	PUDICITY	SEROSITY	VAPIDITY
INEQUITY	MORALITY	QUANTITY	SEVERITY	VELLEITY
INFINITY	MORONITY	QUEERITY	SODALITY	VELOCITY
INIQUITY	MOROSITY	QUIDDITY	SODICITY	VENALITY
INSANITY	MOTILITY	RABIDITY	SOLICITY	VENOSITY
INTIMITY	MOTIVITY	RAMOSITY	SOLIDITY	VERACITY
INVERITY	MUCIDITY	RAPACITY	SONORITY	VICINITY
IONICITY	MUCOSITY	RAPIDITY	SORORITY	VINOSITY
JEJUNITY	MULTEITY	REGALITY	SPARSITY	VIRIDITY
JOCOSITY	NASALITY	RIGIDITY	TEMERITY	VIRILITY
LABILITY	NATALITY	RIMOSITY	TENACITY	VITALITY
LANOSITY	NATIVITY	RIVALITY	TEPIDITY	VIVACITY
LATINITY	NIHILITY	RUGOSITY	TIMIDITY	VIVIDITY
LEGALITY	NOBILITY	RURALITY	TONALITY	VOCALITY
LEGERITY	NODALITY	SAGACITY	TONICITY	VORACITY
LIVIDITY	NODOSITY	SALACITY	TOROSITY	ZYGOSITY
LOCALITY	NUBILITY	SALINITY	TOTALITY	

Words that end with -IUM

Seven-letter words	PALLIUM	ALLODIUM	EULOGIUM	ORDALIUM
ALODIUM	PLAGIUM	ALLUVIUM	EUROPIUM	OSSARIUM
ALUMIUM	PREMIUM	AMMONIUM	EXORDIUM	PATAGIUM
BALLIUM	PROTIUM	APTERIUM	FRANCIUM	PECULIUM
BOHRIUM	PYTHIUM	AQUARIUM	FUSARIUM	PEPONIUM
CADMIUM	RHENIUM	ASCIDIUM	GERANIUM	PERIDIUM
CAESIUM	RHODIUM	ASPIDIUM	GONIDIUM	PHORMIUM
CALCIUM	SPODIUM	BASIDIUM	GRAPHIUM	POLONIUM
CAMBIUM	STADIUM	BDELLIUM	GYNECIUM	PROPRIUM
CRANIUM	STIBIUM	BIENNIUM	HELENIUM	PSYLLIUM
DUBNIUM	STOMIUM	BOTHRIUM	HYMENIUM	PUPARIUM
ELOGIUM	TAEDIUM	BRACHIUM	ILLINIUM	PYGIDIUM
ELUVIUM	TERBIUM	CALADIUM	ILLUVIUM	PYXIDIUM
ERODIUM	TERTIUM	CHROMIUM	IMPERIUM	RANARIUM
EXUVIUM	THORIUM	CIBORIUM	INDICIUM	REFUGIUM
FERMIUM	THULIUM	CONARIUM	INDUSIUM	ROSARIUM
GALLIUM	TRITIUM	CONIDIUM	INGENIUM	RUBIDIUM
HAFNIUM	TRIVIUM	COREMIUM	LIXIVIUM	SAMARIUM
HAHNIUM	URANIUM	CORONIUM	LUTECIUM	SCANDIUM
HASSIUM	UREDIUM	CYATHIUM	LUTETIUM	SCHOLIUM
HOLMIUM	YTTRIUM	CYMATIUM	MASURIUM	SEDILIUM
IRIDIUM	ZOARIUM	DELIRIUM	MECONIUM	SELENIUM
ISCHIUM	ZOECIUM	DIDYMIUM	MOTORIUM	SILICIUM
LITHIUM		DILUVIUM	MYCELIUM	SILPHIUM
MUONIUM	**Eight-letter words**	DISODIUM	NEBULIUM	SIMULIUM
NATRIUM		DOMATIUM	NOBELIUM	SOLARIUM
NIOBIUM	ACHENIUM	DOMINIUM	ONCIDIUM	SOLATIUM
ORARIUM	ACTINIUM	EMPORIUM	ONYCHIUM	SOREDIUM
OXONIUM	AECIDIUM	ENCOMIUM	OOGONIUM	SPLENIUM
	AEROBIUM	ERYNGIUM	OPSONIUM	SUDARIUM

SYCONIUM	TITANIUM	UNUNBIUM	VELARIUM	VIVARIUM
THALLIUM	TRILLIUM	VANADIUM	VENIDIUM	ZOOECIUM

Words that end with -KIN

Seven-letter words	FOXSKIN	RAMAKIN	CAPESKIN	MOUSEKIN
	GHERKIN	RAMEKIN	CIDERKIN	MUNCHKIN
BARMKIN	GRISKIN	REDSKIN	COONSKIN	MUTCHKIN
BAWDKIN	HUFFKIN	SHINKIN	COOTIKIN	PANNIKIN
BODIKIN	KIDSKIN	SIMPKIN	CUITIKIN	PONYSKIN
BOOMKIN	KIPSKIN	WOLFKIN	DAMASKIN	SEALSKIN
BRODKIN	LADYKIN		DEERSKIN	SPILIKIN
BUMPKIN	LAMBKIN	Eight-letter	DEVILKIN	SWANSKIN
CANAKIN	LIMPKIN	words	DUNNAKIN	THUMBKIN
CANIKIN	LORDKIN	BAUDEKIN	FINICKIN	TURNSKIN
CATSKIN	LUMPKIN	BEARSKIN	FISHSKIN	WINESKIN
COWSKIN	MANAKIN	BOOTIKIN	FORESKIN	WOLFSKIN
CUTIKIN	MANIKIN	BRODEKIN	GOATSKIN	WOODSKIN
DOESKIN	MINIKIN	BUCKSKIN	LAMBSKIN	WOOLSKIN
DOGSKIN	OILSKIN	BYRLAKIN	LARRIKIN	
DOITKIN	PIGSKIN	CALFSKIN	MANNIKIN	
FINIKIN	PUMPKIN	CANNIKIN	MOLESKIN	

Words that end with -LAND

Seven-letter words	LAWLAND	BOOKLAND	GANGLAND	PLOWLAND
	LOWLAND	BUSHLAND	HEADLAND	PORTLAND
BADLAND	MIDLAND	CLUBLAND	HIGHLAND	SCABLAND
BOGLAND	NORLAND	CORNLAND	HOMELAND	SHETLAND
COTLAND	OUTLAND	CROPLAND	LACKLAND	SLOBLAND
DRYLAND	RIMLAND	DOCKLAND	LAKELAND	SNOWLAND
ELFLAND	SUNLAND	DOWNLAND	MAINLAND	SOAPLAND
FENLAND	TROLAND	DUNELAND	MOORLAND	TIDELAND
GARLAND	WETLAND	EASTLAND	MOSSLAND	TOWNLAND
GOLLAND		FARMLAND	OVERLAND	WASHLAND
GOWLAND	Eight-letter	FILMLAND	PARKLAND	WILDLAND
HIELAND	words	FLATLAND	PEATLAND	WOODLAND
HOLLAND	BACKLAND	FOLKLAND	PINELAND	YARDLAND
LALLAND	BARELAND	FORELAND	PLAYLAND	

Words that end with -LESS

Seven-letter words	BITLESS	FATLESS	HITLESS	LIPLESS
	BOWLESS	FEELESS	HUELESS	MANLESS
AGELESS	BRALESS	FINLESS	ICELESS	MAPLESS
AIDLESS	BUDLESS	FLYLESS	INKLESS	MATLESS
AIMLESS	CAPLESS	FOGLESS	INNLESS	NAPLESS
AIRLESS	CARLESS	FURLESS	IRELESS	NETLESS
ARMLESS	COXLESS	GAPLESS	JAGLESS	OARLESS
ARTLESS	CUBLESS	GASLESS	JAWLESS	ORBLESS
ASHLESS	DEWLESS	GODLESS	JOBLESS	PEGLESS
AWELESS	EARLESS	GUMLESS	JOYLESS	PIPLESS
AWNLESS	EBBLESS	GUNLESS	KEYLESS	RAYLESS
BAGLESS	EGGLESS	GUTLESS	KINLESS	RIBLESS
BARLESS	EGOLESS	HAPLESS	LAWLESS	RIMLESS
BEDLESS	ENDLESS	HATLESS	LEGLESS	RODLESS
BIBLESS	EYELESS	HIPLESS	LIDLESS	RUNLESS

SACLESS	CLUELESS	GEARLESS	LOSSLESS	RESTLESS
SAPLESS	COALLESS	GIFTLESS	LOVELESS	RIFTLESS
SEXLESS	COATLESS	GOALLESS	LUCKLESS	RIMELESS
SINLESS	CODELESS	GOLDLESS	LUNGLESS	RINDLESS
SKYLESS	COMBLESS	GORMLESS	LUSTLESS	RINGLESS
SONLESS	COOKLESS	GRITLESS	MAIDLESS	RISKLESS
SUMLESS	CORDLESS	GUSTLESS	MAILLESS	RITELESS
SUNLESS	CORELESS	HAIRLESS	MAKELESS	RIVALESS
TAGLESS	COSTLESS	HALTLESS	MANELESS	ROADLESS
TAXLESS	CREWLESS	HANDLESS	MASSLESS	ROCKLESS
TIELESS	CROPLESS	HARMLESS	MASTLESS	ROOFLESS
TIPLESS	CUFFLESS	HATELESS	MATELESS	ROOTLESS
TOELESS	CURBLESS	HEADLESS	MEALLESS	ROSELESS
TOPLESS	CURELESS	HEATLESS	MEATLESS	RULELESS
TOYLESS	DATELESS	HEEDLESS	MILKLESS	RUMPLESS
TUGLESS	DEBTLESS	HEELLESS	MINDLESS	RUNGLESS
UNBLESS	DEEDLESS	HEIRLESS	MOONLESS	RUSTLESS
USELESS	DEVILESS	HELMLESS	MOVELESS	RUTHLESS
VOWLESS	DINTLESS	HELPLESS	NAILLESS	SACKLESS
WARLESS	DISKLESS	HERBLESS	NAMELESS	SAIKLESS
WAYLESS	DOORLESS	HIDELESS	NATHLESS	SAILLESS
WEBLESS	DOWNLESS	HILTLESS	NECKLESS	SALTLESS
WIGLESS	DRIPLESS	HIVELESS	NEEDLESS	SANDLESS
WINLESS	DUCTLESS	HOLELESS	NEWSLESS	SASHLESS
WITLESS	DUSTLESS	HOMELESS	NORMLESS	SATELESS
ZIPLESS	EASELESS	HOODLESS	NOSELESS	SCARLESS
	ECHOLESS	HOOFLESS	NOTELESS	SCUMLESS
Eight-letter	EDGELESS	HOOKLESS	NOUNLESS	SEAMLESS
words	EXITLESS	HOOPLESS	ODORLESS	SEATLESS
BACKLESS	FACELESS	HOPELESS	OUTBLESS	SEEDLESS
BARBLESS	FADELESS	HORNLESS	PAINLESS	SEEMLESS
BARKLESS	FAMELESS	HUMPLESS	PANELESS	SELFLESS
BASELESS	FANGLESS	HURTLESS	PANGLESS	SHIPLESS
BASHLESS	FEARLESS	HYMNLESS	PASSLESS	SHITLESS
BATELESS	FECKLESS	IDEALESS	PASTLESS	SHOELESS
BATHLESS	FEETLESS	IRONLESS	PATHLESS	SHUNLESS
BEAKLESS	FERNLESS	ISLELESS	PEAKLESS	SIGHLESS
BEAMLESS	FILMLESS	JAILLESS	PEERLESS	SIGNLESS
BEATLESS	FINELESS	JURYLESS	PELTLESS	SKILLESS
BEEFLESS	FIRELESS	KEELLESS	PILELESS	SKINLESS
BELTLESS	FIRMLESS	KINDLESS	PIPELESS	SLIPLESS
BLOTLESS	FISHLESS	KINGLESS	PITHLESS	SLITLESS
BODILESS	FLAGLESS	KNOTLESS	PITILESS	SMOGLESS
BOLTLESS	FLAPLESS	LACELESS	PLANLESS	SNAPLESS
BONDLESS	FLAWLESS	LANDLESS	PLAYLESS	SNOWLESS
BONELESS	FOAMLESS	LEADLESS	PLOTLESS	SOAPLESS
BOOKLESS	FOODLESS	LEAFLESS	PLUGLESS	SOCKLESS
BOONLESS	FOOTLESS	LEAKLESS	POETLESS	SODALESS
BOOTLESS	FORDLESS	LENSLESS	POLELESS	SOILLESS
BRIMLESS	FORKLESS	LIFELESS	POPELESS	SOLELESS
BROWLESS	FORMLESS	LIMBLESS	PORTLESS	SONGLESS
BUSHLESS	FRETLESS	LIMELESS	PREBLESS	SOOTLESS
CALFLESS	FUMELESS	LINELESS	PULPLESS	SOULLESS
CARELESS	FUNDLESS	LINTLESS	PUMPLESS	SOUPLESS
CASHLESS	FUSELESS	LISTLESS	RAILLESS	SPANLESS
CHADLESS	GAINLESS	LOAMLESS	RAINLESS	SPINLESS
CHAPLESS	GAOLLESS	LOBELESS	RANKLESS	SPOTLESS
CHINLESS	GARBLESS	LOCKLESS	RECKLESS	SPURLESS
CLAWLESS	GATELESS	LOFTLESS	REDELESS	STARLESS
CLOYLESS	GAUMLESS	LORDLESS	REINLESS	STAYLESS

STEMLESS	TEXTLESS	TUBELESS	VOTELESS	WINGLESS
STIRLESS	THAWLESS	TUNELESS	WAGELESS	WIRELESS
STOPLESS	THEWLESS	TURFLESS	WAKELESS	WISHLESS
SUCKLESS	THOWLESS	TUSKLESS	WARDLESS	WITELESS
SUDSLESS	TIDELESS	TWIGLESS	WARELESS	WONTLESS
TACKLESS	TIMELESS	TYRELESS	WARTLESS	WOODLESS
TACTLESS	TINTLESS	VANELESS	WATTLESS	WORDLESS
TAILLESS	TIRELESS	VEILLESS	WAVELESS	WORKLESS
TAMELESS	TOADLESS	VEINLESS	WEEDLESS	YOKELESS
TANKLESS	TOILLESS	VENTLESS	WEETLESS	YOLKLESS
TAPELESS	TOMBLESS	VERBLESS	WELDLESS	ZEALLESS
TASKLESS	TONELESS	VESTLESS	WHIPLESS	ZESTLESS
TEARLESS	TOOLLESS	VETOLESS	WICKLESS	ZONELESS
TEEMLESS	TOWNLESS	VICELESS	WIFELESS	
TENTLESS	TRAMLESS	VIEWLESS	WINDLESS	
TERMLESS	TREELESS	VINELESS	WINELESS	

Words that end with -LET

Seven-letter words	FORTLET	RIVULET	BRACELET	NONUPLET
	FROGLET	ROOTLET	BRACTLET	OCTUPLET
ANNULET	GANTLET	ROYALET	BROOKLET	PAMPHLET
ARCHLET	GURGLET	RUNDLET	CAPELLET	PANTALET
BEAMLET	HACKLET	SCARLET	CHAINLET	PISTOLET
BENDLET	HARSLET	SERVLET	CHEVALET	PLANTLET
BOMBLET	HERBLET	SINGLET	CLOUDLET	PLATELET
BOOKLET	HOOKLET	SKILLET	CORSELET	PLUMELET
BOOMLET	HORNLET	SNIGLET	COURTLET	QUEENLET
BULBLET	JINGLET	STARLET	COVERLET	RECOLLET
CACOLET	KINGLET	STEMLET	CROSSLET	RONDELET
CANTLET	LAKELET	STERLET	CROWNLET	ROUNDLET
CAPELET	LEAFLET	SWALLET	DRIBBLET	SEXTOLET
CHAMLET	MANTLET	TARTLET	DRUPELET	SPANGLET
CHAPLET	MARTLET	TEMPLET	FLAMELET	SPARKLET
CIRCLET	MEDALET	TOWNLET	FOVEOLET	SPIKELET
CORSLET	MOONLET	TRIBLET	FRONTLET	SPIRELET
COUPLET	NECKLET	TRIOLET	FRUITLET	STATELET
COVELET	NOTELET	TRIPLET	GAUNTLET	SWIFTLET
CUMULET	OSSELET	TWIGLET	GLOBULET	TERCELET
DEERLET	OVERLET	VEINLET	GREENLET	TRICKLET
DEVILET	PARTLET	WAVELET	GROUPLET	TROUTLET
DOUBLET	PICULET	WINGLET	HEARTLET	UMBELLET
DOVELET	PIKELET	ZONULET	HERBELET	UNDERLET
DRIBLET	PLAYLET		LANCELET	VALVELET
DROPLET	QUILLET	**Eight-letter words**	MANTELET	VEINULET
EPAULET	RINGLET	BANDELET	MIQUELET	VERSELET
FLATLET	RIPPLET	BARRULET	MURRELET	WRISTLET
FONTLET			NERVELET	

Words that end with -LIKE

Seven-letter words	BAGLIKE	BUDLIKE	ELFLIKE	GEMLIKE
	BATLIKE	CATLIKE	EYELIKE	GODLIKE
AIRLIKE	BEDLIKE	CUPLIKE	FADLIKE	GUMLIKE
ANTLIKE	BEELIKE	DISLIKE	FANLIKE	GUTLIKE
APELIKE	BIBLIKE	DOGLIKE	FATLIKE	HAGLIKE
ARMLIKE	BOWLIKE	EARLIKE	FINLIKE	HATLIKE
ASSLIKE	BOXLIKE	EELLIKE	FOXLIKE	HENLIKE

HIPLIKE	WIGLIKE	FROGLIKE	LORDLIKE	SLITLIKE
HOBLIKE		FUMELIKE	LYNXLIKE	SNAGLIKE
HOELIKE	**Eight-letter**	FUSELIKE	MASKLIKE	SNOWLIKE
HOGLIKE	**words**	GAMELIKE	MASTLIKE	SOAPLIKE
HUTLIKE	AGUELIKE	GATELIKE	MAZELIKE	SONGLIKE
ICELIKE	AUNTLIKE	GERMLIKE	MILKLIKE	SOULLIKE
INKLIKE	BALMLIKE	GLENLIKE	MOATLIKE	SOUPLIKE
IVYLIKE	BARNLIKE	GLUELIKE	MOONLIKE	SPARLIKE
JAMLIKE	BEADLIKE	GNATLIKE	MOSSLIKE	STARLIKE
JAWLIKE	BEAKLIKE	GOADLIKE	MOTHLIKE	STEMLIKE
JETLIKE	BEAMLIKE	GOATLIKE	NECKLIKE	STEPLIKE
JIGLIKE	BEANLIKE	GONGLIKE	NESTLIKE	SUCHLIKE
KIDLIKE	BEARLIKE	GULFLIKE	NOOKLIKE	SUITLIKE
LAWLIKE	BIRDLIKE	HAIRLIKE	NOSELIKE	SURFLIKE
LEGLIKE	BOATLIKE	HALOLIKE	NOVALIKE	SWANLIKE
LIPLIKE	BOLTLIKE	HANDLIKE	OVENLIKE	TAILLIKE
MANLIKE	BOWLLIKE	HARELIKE	PALMLIKE	TANKLIKE
MAPLIKE	BUSHLIKE	HAWKLIKE	PARKLIKE	TAPELIKE
MISLIKE	CAGELIKE	HEADLIKE	PEAKLIKE	TENTLIKE
NETLIKE	CALFLIKE	HEMPLIKE	PINELIKE	TIDELIKE
NIBLIKE	CAVELIKE	HERBLIKE	PIPELIKE	TILELIKE
NUNLIKE	CLAMLIKE	HERDLIKE	PITHLIKE	TOADLIKE
NUTLIKE	CLAWLIKE	HIVELIKE	PLAYLIKE	TOMBLIKE
OAKLIKE	CLAYLIKE	HOMELIKE	PLUMLIKE	TRAPLIKE
OARLIKE	COCKLIKE	HOODLIKE	POETLIKE	TREELIKE
OATLIKE	COKELIKE	HOOFLIKE	POPELIKE	TUBELIKE
OWLLIKE	COMBLIKE	HOOKLIKE	PUMPLIKE	TURFLIKE
PEALIKE	CORDLIKE	HOOPLIKE	PUSSLIKE	TUSKLIKE
PEGLIKE	CORKLIKE	HORNLIKE	QUAYLIKE	TWIGLIKE
PIGLIKE	CORMLIKE	HOSELIKE	RASHLIKE	VASELIKE
PODLIKE	CRABLIKE	HUMPLIKE	REEDLIKE	VEILLIKE
POTLIKE	CULTLIKE	HUSKLIKE	RINGLIKE	VEINLIKE
PUSLIKE	DAWNLIKE	HYMNLIKE	ROCKLIKE	VESTLIKE
RATLIKE	DEERLIKE	IRONLIKE	ROOFLIKE	VICELIKE
RAYLIKE	DISCLIKE	JADELIKE	ROOTLIKE	VINELIKE
RIBLIKE	DISHLIKE	JAZZLIKE	ROPELIKE	VISELIKE
RODLIKE	DISKLIKE	JUTELIKE	ROSELIKE	WAIFLIKE
RUGLIKE	DOMELIKE	KILTLIKE	RUBYLIKE	WANDLIKE
SACLIKE	DOVELIKE	KINGLIKE	RUFFLIKE	WARTLIKE
SAWLIKE	DOWNLIKE	KITELIKE	RUNELIKE	WASPLIKE
SICLIKE	DRUMLIKE	KNOBLIKE	RUSHLIKE	WAVELIKE
SKYLIKE	DUNELIKE	KNOTLIKE	SACKLIKE	WEEDLIKE
SONLIKE	DUSTLIKE	LACELIKE	SALTLIKE	WHEYLIKE
SUNLIKE	EPICLIKE	LADYLIKE	SANDLIKE	WHIPLIKE
TAGLIKE	FANGLIKE	LAKELIKE	SCABLIKE	WIFELIKE
TEALIKE	FAUNLIKE	LAMBLIKE	SCUMLIKE	WINGLIKE
TINLIKE	FAWNLIKE	LARDLIKE	SEALLIKE	WIRELIKE
TOELIKE	FELTLIKE	LATHLIKE	SEAMLIKE	WISPLIKE
TOYLIKE	FERNLIKE	LAVALIKE	SEEDLIKE	WOLFLIKE
TUBLIKE	FILMLIKE	LEAFLIKE	SERFLIKE	WOMBLIKE
UNALIKE	FISHLIKE	LIFELIKE	SHEDLIKE	WOOLLIKE
URNLIKE	FOAMLIKE	LILYLIKE	SIGHLIKE	WORMLIKE
WARLIKE	FOLKLIKE	LINELIKE	SILKLIKE	
WAXLIKE	FOOTLIKE	LIONLIKE	SKINLIKE	
WEBLIKE	FORKLIKE	LOFTLIKE	SLABLIKE	

Words that end with -LOGY

Seven-letter words	Eight-letter words			
ANALOGY	AEROLOGY	CYTOLOGY	MYCOLOGY	PYROLOGY
APOLOGY	AGROLOGY	DEKALOGY	NOMOLOGY	RHEOLOGY
BIOLOGY	ALGOLOGY	DEMOLOGY	NOSOLOGY	SEROLOGY
DYSLOGY	ANTILOGY	DOSOLOGY	OECOLOGY	SEXOLOGY
ECOLOGY	APIOLOGY	DOXOLOGY	OENOLOGY	SINOLOGY
ENOLOGY	ARCOLOGY	ETHOLOGY	OINOLOGY	SITOLOGY
GEOLOGY	AREOLOGY	ETIOLOGY	ONCOLOGY	THEOLOGY
MYOLOGY	ATMOLOGY	FETOLOGY	ONTOLOGY	TOCOLOGY
NEOLOGY	AUTOLOGY	GEMOLOGY	OPTOLOGY	TOKOLOGY
NOOLOGY	AXIOLOGY	HOMOLOGY	OREOLOGY	TOPOLOGY
OROLOGY	BATOLOGY	HOROLOGY	OUROLOGY	TYPOLOGY
OTOLOGY	BRYOLOGY	IDEALOGY	PARALOGY	VENOLOGY
TRILOGY	CACOLOGY	IDEOLOGY	PEDOLOGY	VINOLOGY
UFOLOGY	CETOLOGY	KIDOLOGY	PELOLOGY	VIROLOGY
UROLOGY	CHAOLOGY	MENOLOGY	PENOLOGY	XYLOLOGY
ZOOLOGY	CODOLOGY	MISOLOGY	PODOLOGY	ZYMOLOGY
		MIXOLOGY	POMOLOGY	
		MONOLOGY	POSOLOGY	

Words that end with -LY

Seven-letter words				
ACRIDLY	BEASTLY	CAPABLY	DAFFILY	EQUALLY
ACTORLY	BEEFILY	CATTILY	DANDILY	ERECTLY
ACUTELY	BEERILY	CAVALLY	DATEDLY	EROSELY
ADDEDLY	BEETFLY	CECALLY	DAYLILY	EXACTLY
ADEPTLY	BIFIDLY	CHARILY	DAZEDLY	FADEDLY
ADULTLY	BLACKLY	CHEAPLY	DEARNLY	FAINTLY
AFFABLY	BLANDLY	CHEERLY	DEATHLY	FAIRILY
AGILELY	BLANKLY	CHIEFLY	DEEDILY	FALSELY
ALERTLY	BLEAKLY	CHILDLY	DEERFLY	FANCILY
ALIENLY	BLINDLY	CHIMBLY	DENSELY	FATALLY
ALONELY	BLOWFLY	CIVILLY	DICYCLY	FATTILY
ALOOFLY	BLUFFLY	CLEANLY	DINGILY	FETIDLY
AMIABLY	BLUNTLY	CLEARLY	DIRTILY	FIERILY
ANGERLY	BOGUSLY	CLERKLY	DISALLY	FIFTHLY
ANGRILY	BONNILY	CLOSELY	DIZZILY	FILMILY
ANOMALY	BOOZILY	COCKILY	DOOMILY	FINALLY
ANTICLY	BOSSILY	CORNFLY	DOTTILY	FIREFLY
APETALY	BRAMBLY	CORNILY	DOUCELY	FIRSTLY
APHYLLY	BRASHLY	COURTLY	DOWDILY	FISHILY
APISHLY	BRAVELY	COWEDLY	DREADLY	FIXEDLY
AREALLY	BRIEFLY	CRACKLY	DRIBBLY	FLAKILY
AUDIBLY	BRISKLY	CRANKLY	DRIZZLY	FLEETLY
AURALLY	BRISTLY	CRASSLY	DROPFLY	FLESHLY
AWFULLY	BRITTLY	CRAZILY	DUCALLY	FLUIDLY
AXIALLY	BROADLY	CRINKLY	DUMPILY	FLUKILY
BAGGILY	BRUTELY	CRISPLY	DUOPOLY	FOAMILY
BAIRNLY	BUIRDLY	CROSSLY	DURABLY	FOCALLY
BALKILY	BULKILY	CRUDELY	DUSKILY	FOGGILY
BALMILY	BUMPILY	CRUELLY	DUSTILY	FRAILLY
BANALLY	BURLILY	CRUMBLY	DYINGLY	FRANKLY
BASALLY	BUSHFLY	CRUMPLY	EAGERLY	FRECKLY
BAWDILY	BUSHILY	CRUSILY	EARTHLY	FRESHLY
BEADILY	BUXOMLY	CUBICLY	ELDERLY	FRIARLY
BEAMILY	CAMPILY	CURABLY	EMPTILY	FRITFLY
	CANNILY	CURLILY	EPIBOLY	FRIZZLY
	CANTILY	CUSHILY	EQUABLY	FUGALLY

FUGGILY	HOARILY	LUCKILY	NOTEDLY	REEDILY
FUNKILY	HORNILY	LUMPILY	NOVELLY	REGALLY
FUNNILY	HORSILY	LURIDLY	NUTTILY	RETALLY
FURRILY	HUFFILY	LUSTILY	NYMPHLY	RIANTLY
FUSIBLY	HUMANLY	LYINGLY	OBESELY	RIGHTLY
FUSSILY	HUMIDLY	MAJORLY	OCTUPLY	RIGIDLY
FUSTILY	HUSKILY	MANGILY	ORDERLY	RISIBLY
FUZZILY	IDEALLY	MANLILY	OVATELY	RISKILY
GALLFLY	IGNOBLY	MASCULY	OVERFLY	RITZILY
GASSILY	INANELY	MAZEDLY	OVERPLY	ROCKILY
GAUDILY	INAPTLY	MEATILY	OVERTLY	ROOMILY
GAUNTLY	INEPTLY	MERRILY	PANOPLY	ROUGHLY
GAUZILY	INERTLY	MESALLY	PAPALLY	ROUNDLY
GAWKILY	INJELLY	MESSILY	PASTILY	ROUPILY
GELIDLY	INNERLY	METALLY	PAWKILY	ROWDILY
GEMMILY	IRATELY	MIFFILY	PAYABLY	ROYALLY
GHASTLY	ITCHILY	MILKILY	PEARTLY	RUDDILY
GHOSTLY	JADEDLY	MIRKILY	PENALLY	RUMMILY
GIANTLY	JAZZILY	MISALLY	PEPPILY	RURALLY
GIDDILY	JERKILY	MISERLY	PERKILY	RUSTILY
GINGELY	JOINTLY	MISRELY	PESKILY	RUTTILY
GLAZILY	JOLLILY	MISTILY	PETTILY	SAINTLY
GLOWFLY	JOLTILY	MIXEDLY	PHONILY	SALABLY
GODLILY	JUICILY	MODALLY	PICKILY	SALTILY
GOOFILY	JUMPILY	MOISTLY	PIOUSLY	SANDFLY
GOUTFLY	JURALLY	MONTHLY	PITHILY	SAPPILY
GOUTILY	KINKILY	MOODILY	PLAINLY	SARKILY
GRADELY	KNOBBLY	MOONILY	PLIABLY	SASSILY
GRANDLY	KNUBBLY	MORALLY	PLUMPLY	SAUCILY
GRAVELY	KNUCKLY	MOUSILY	PLUSHLY	SAVVILY
GRAYFLY	KOOKILY	MOVABLY	POCKILY	SCANTLY
GREATLY	LADYFLY	MUCKILY	PODGILY	SCARILY
GREENLY	LAIRDLY	MUDDILY	PRICILY	SCHELLY
GREISLY	LAITHLY	MUGGILY	PRICKLY	SCRAWLY
GRIESLY	LANKILY	MURKILY	PRIMELY	SEEDILY
GRIMILY	LARGELY	MUSHILY	PRIORLY	SHADFLY
GRISELY	LEAKILY	MUSKILY	PRIVILY	SHADILY
GRISTLY	LEERILY	MUSSILY	PRONELY	SHAKILY
GRIZZLY	LEGALLY	MUSTILY	PROSILY	SHAMBLY
GROSSLY	LEGIBLY	MUTABLY	PROUDLY	SHAPELY
GRUFFLY	LEVELLY	MUTEDLY	PUDGILY	SHARPLY
GRUMBLY	LICHTLY	MUZZILY	PUFFILY	SHEERLY
GRYSELY	LICITLY	NAIVELY	PULPILY	SHINGLY
GUMMILY	LIGHTLY	NAKEDLY	PURSILY	SHINILY
GUSHILY	LIKABLY	NARGILY	PUSHILY	SHOGGLY
GUSTILY	LITHELY	NASALLY	QUAKILY	SHOOFLY
GUTSILY	LIVIDLY	NASTILY	QUEENLY	SHOOGLY
GYRALLY	LOATHLY	NATTILY	QUEERLY	SHORTLY
HAMMILY	LOCALLY	NAVALLY	QUICKLY	SHOWILY
HANDILY	LOFTILY	NEEDILY	QUIETLY	SHRILLY
HAPPILY	LOOBILY	NERVILY	RABIDLY	SIGHTLY
HARDILY	LOONILY	NIFTILY	RAINILY	SILKILY
HARSHLY	LOOPILY	NIGHTLY	RANDILY	SILLILY
HARTELY	LOOSELY	NINTHLY	RANGILY	SIXTHLY
HASTILY	LOUSILY	NIPPILY	RAPIDLY	SIZABLY
HAZELLY	LOVABLY	NOBBILY	RATABLY	SLACKLY
HEADILY	LOVERLY	NODALLY	RATTILY	SLANTLY
HEARTLY	LOWLILY	NOISILY	RAVELLY	SLEEKLY
HEAVILY	LOYALLY	NONOILY	READILY	SLICKLY
HEFTILY	LUCIDLY	NOTABLY	REAPPLY	SLIMILY

SMARTLY	TENTHLY	WASPILY	ASSEMBLY	CATCHFLY
SMICKLY	TEPIDLY	WEARILY	ASTRALLY	CAUDALLY
SMOKILY	TERSELY	WEASELY	ASTUTELY	CAUSALLY
SNAKILY	TESTILY	WEEDILY	ATONALLY	CHANCILY
SNIDELY	TEUGHLY	WEEPILY	AUGUSTLY	CHASTELY
SNIFFLY	THEGNLY	WEEVILY	AVERSELY	CHATTILY
SNOWILY	THICKLY	WEIRDLY	AVOWABLY	CHEEKILY
SNUFFLY	THIRDLY	WHITELY	AVOWEDLY	CHEERILY
SOAPILY	THISTLY	WIGHTLY	BADGERLY	CHEESILY
SOBERLY	THRILLY	WINDILY	BANKERLY	CHESTILY
SOGGILY	TIDALLY	WISPILY	BARRENLY	CHILLILY
SOLIDLY	TIGERLY	WITTILY	BAULKILY	CHIRPILY
SOLUBLY	TIGHTLY	WOFULLY	BEARABLY	CHOICELY
SOOTHLY	TIMIDLY	WOMANLY	BEASTILY	CHOPPILY
SOOTILY	TINNILY	WOOZILY	BEGGARLY	CHORALLY
SOPPILY	TIPSILY	WORDILY	BEHOVELY	CHUBBILY
SORRILY	TIREDLY	WORLDLY	BENIGNLY	CHUMMILY
SOUNDLY	TONALLY	WORMFLY	BESEEMLY	CHUNKILY
SPANGLY	TOSSILY	WRIGGLY	BIASEDLY	CHURCHLY
SPARELY	TOTALLY	WRINKLY	BIDDABLY	CLAMMILY
SPARKLY	TOUGHLY	WRONGLY	BIHOURLY	CLASSILY
SPICILY	TREACLY	YOUNGLY	BINATELY	CLEVERLY
SPIKILY	TREMBLY	YOUTHLY	BITCHILY	CLINALLY
SPINDLY	TRICKLY	ZESTILY	BITINGLY	CLOGGILY
SPRAWLY	TRIFOLY	ZONALLY	BITTERLY	CLONALLY
SQUALLY	TRITELY		BIWEEKLY	CLOUDILY
SQUATLY	TUFTILY	**Eight-letter**	BIYEARLY	CLUBBILY
STAGILY	TUMIDLY	**words**	BLACKFLY	CLUMSILY
STAIDLY	TUNABLY	ABASEDLY	BLAMABLY	COARSELY
STALELY	TWADDLY	ABJECTLY	BLEARILY	COEVALLY
STARKLY	TWIDDLY	ABORALLY	BLITHELY	COGENTLY
STARTLY	TWINKLY	ABRUPTLY	BLOODILY	COITALLY
STATELY	UNAPTLY	ABSENTLY	BLOUSILY	COMELILY
STEEPLY	UNFITLY	ABSURDLY	BLOWSILY	COMMONLY
STERNLY	UNGODLY	ACHINGLY	BLOWZILY	CONVEXLY
STIFFLY	UNMANLY	ACTIVELY	BLURRILY	COOINGLY
STONILY	UNTRULY	ACTUALLY	BODINGLY	COSTALLY
STOUTLY	USEABLY	ADORABLY	BORINGLY	COUSINLY
STUBBLY	USUALLY	ADROITLY	BOTCHILY	COVERTLY
STUMBLY	UTTERLY	AERIALLY	BOUNCILY	COWARDLY
SUAVELY	VAGALLY	AFFINELY	BOVINELY	COYISHLY
SULKILY	VAGUELY	AGUISHLY	BOWINGLY	CRABBILY
SUNNILY	VALIDLY	AIMFULLY	BOYISHLY	CRAFTILY
SURLILY	VAPIDLY	ALDERFLY	BRAINILY	CRAGGILY
SWEETLY	VENALLY	ALPINELY	BRASSILY	CRANEFLY
SWIFTLY	VERMILY	AMAZEDLY	BRAWNILY	CRANKILY
SWITHLY	VEXEDLY	AMENABLY	BRAZENLY	CRAVENLY
TACITLY	VICARLY	AMICABLY	BREEZILY	CREAKILY
TACKILY	VIRALLY	AMORALLY	BRIDALLY	CREAMILY
TAILFLY	VISIBLY	AMUSEDLY	BRIGHTLY	CREDIBLY
TARDILY	VITALLY	ANIMALLY	BROKENLY	CREEPILY
TARTILY	VIVIDLY	ANNUALLY	BROODILY	CRISPILY
TASTILY	VIXENLY	ANODALLY	BRUTALLY	CROAKILY
TATTILY	VOCABLY	APICALLY	BUCCALLY	CROUPILY
TAWNILY	VOCALLY	ARCANELY	BUNCHILY	CROUSELY
TAXABLY	VOLUBLY	ARDENTLY	CAECALLY	CRUSTILY
TEARILY	VOWELLY	ARGUABLY	CANDIDLY	CRYINGLY
TECHILY	VYINGLY	ARGUTELY	CARINGLY	CULPABLY
TENABLY	WACKILY	ARRANTLY	CARNALLY	CURSEDLY
TENSELY	WASHILY	ARTFULLY	CASUALLY	CURVEDLY

CUSSEDLY	FAUNALLY	GINGERLY	INTENTLY	MANNERLY
CYCLICLY	FEASIBLY	GLASSILY	INVIABLY	MANUALLY
CYMOSELY	FEISTILY	GLITZILY	INWARDLY	MARKEDLY
DAINTILY	FELINELY	GLOBALLY	IREFULLY	MARTYRLY
DAMNABLY	FELLOWLY	GLOOMILY	ISSUABLY	MASSEDLY
DAPPERLY	FERNALLY	GLOSSILY	JADISHLY	MASTERLY
DARINGLY	FERVIDLY	GLUMPILY	JAGGEDLY	MATRONLY
DATIVELY	FESTALLY	GOLDENLY	JAPINGLY	MATTEDLY
DECENTLY	FEUDALLY	GORBELLY	JAUNTILY	MATURELY
DEMISSLY	FIERCELY	GORGEDLY	JEJUNELY	MEAGERLY
DEMURELY	FILIALLY	GOSPELLY	JIBINGLY	MEAGRELY
DENIABLY	FILTHILY	GRAITHLY	JOCOSELY	MEDIALLY
DENTALLY	FINITELY	GRASSILY	JOCUNDLY	MEDIANLY
DEUCEDLY	FISCALLY	GRAVELLY	JOKINGLY	MELLOWLY
DEVOUTLY	FITFULLY	GRAVIDLY	JOVIALLY	MENIALLY
DIRECTLY	FLABBILY	GREASILY	JOYFULLY	MENTALLY
DISAPPLY	FLASHILY	GREEDILY	JOYOUSLY	MESIALLY
DISMALLY	FLEECILY	GREENFLY	KERNELLY	METABOLY
DISTALLY	FLESHILY	GRITTILY	KINDLILY	MIGHTILY
DIVERSLY	FLEXIBLY	GROGGILY	KISSABLY	MINUTELY
DIVINELY	FLIMSILY	GROOVILY	KNIGHTLY	MISAPPLY
DOCILELY	FLINTILY	GRUBBILY	KNOTTILY	MODERNLY
DOCTORLY	FLOPPILY	GRUFFILY	LABIALLY	MODESTLY
DOGGEDLY	FLORALLY	GRUMPILY	LAICALLY	MODISHLY
DOOLALLY	FLORIDLY	GUILTILY	LATENTLY	MOLTENLY
DORSALLY	FLOSSILY	GULLABLY	LATTERLY	MOMENTLY
DOTARDLY	FLUENTLY	GULLIBLY	LAUDABLY	MONOPOLY
DOTINGLY	FLUFFILY	HEARTILY	LAVISHLY	MOPINGLY
DRAFTILY	FOETIDLY	HEATEDLY	LAWFULLY	MOPISHLY
DREAMILY	FOLKSILY	HEAVENLY	LAWYERLY	MORBIDLY
DREARILY	FORCEDLY	HECTICLY	LEADENLY	MOROSELY
DRESSILY	FORCIBLY	HECTORLY	LETHALLY	MORTALLY
DRIPPILY	FORKEDLY	HEROICLY	LIKEABLY	MOTHERLY
DROOPILY	FORMABLY	HIDDENLY	LIMBERLY	MOUTHILY
DROWSILY	FORMALLY	HITCHILY	LIMPIDLY	MOVEABLY
DUDISHLY	FORMERLY	HOARSELY	LINEALLY	MOVINGLY
DULCETLY	FOURTHLY	HOLLOWLY	LINEARLY	MULISHLY
EARTHILY	FREAKILY	HOMELILY	LIQUIDLY	MULTIPLY
EASTERLY	FRENZILY	HONESTLY	LISSOMLY	MUSINGLY
EFFETELY	FRIENDLY	HONIEDLY	LITHERLY	MUTUALLY
EIGHTHLY	FRIGIDLY	HOPINGLY	LIVELILY	MYOPHILY
ELATEDLY	FRISKILY	HORRIBLY	LIVINGLY	MYSTICLY
ELFISHLY	FRIZZILY	HORRIDLY	LOBATELY	NARGHILY
ELIGIBLY	FROSTILY	HORSEFLY	LOBLOLLY	NARROWLY
ELVISHLY	FROTHILY	HOUSEFLY	LONELILY	NATANTLY
ENTIRELY	FROWZILY	HOVERFLY	LOSINGLY	NATIVELY
ENVIABLY	FROZENLY	HUMANELY	LOUCHELY	NEURALLY
EPICALLY	FRUGALLY	HUNGERLY	LOVEABLY	NEWISHLY
EQUINELY	FRUITILY	HUNGRILY	LOVELILY	NOCENTLY
ERRANTLY	FRUMPILY	HUNTEDLY	LOVINGLY	NORMALLY
ERRINGLY	FUMINGLY	HUSHEDLY	LUBBERLY	NOUNALLY
EVANGELY	FUTILELY	IMMANELY	LUCENTLY	OAFISHLY
EXPERTLY	GAGEABLY	IMPISHLY	LUMBERLY	OBLATELY
FACETELY	GAPINGLY	IMPURELY	LUMPENLY	OBLONGLY
FACIALLY	GARISHLY	INDIGNLY	LUNATELY	OBTUSELY
FACILELY	GAUCHELY	INEDIBLY	LURINGLY	OCCULTLY
FALLIBLY	GENIALLY	INFIRMLY	LYRATELY	OCULARLY
FAMOUSLY	GIBINGLY	INNATELY	MAIDENLY	ODIOUSLY
FATHERLY	GIFTEDLY	INSANELY	MALIGNLY	OFFISHLY
FAULTILY	GINGELLY	INTACTLY	MANFULLY	OGRISHLY

ONWARDLY	PULPALLY	SCRIBBLY	SNIFFILY	STURDILY
OPAQUELY	PUNCHILY	SCRIGGLY	SNIPPILY	SUDDENLY
OPERABLY	PUTRIDLY	SCRIMPLY	SNIVELLY	SUITABLY
ORNATELY	QUAINTLY	SCUMMILY	SNOBBILY	SULLENLY
OTIOSELY	QUEASILY	SCURVILY	SNOOPILY	SULTRILY
OUTBULLY	QUIRKILY	SEAMANLY	SNOOTILY	SUMMERLY
OVERHOLY	QUOTABLY	SECANTLY	SNOTTILY	SUNDRILY
OVERWILY	RACIALLY	SECONDLY	SNUFFILY	SUPERBLY
OWLISHLY	RADIALLY	SECRETLY	SOCIABLY	SUPINELY
PALLIDLY	RAGGEDLY	SECUNDLY	SOCIALLY	SUPPLELY
PALPABLY	RAGINGLY	SECURELY	SODDENLY	SVELTELY
PALTRILY	RAKISHLY	SEDATELY	SOLEMNLY	SWANKILY
PANDERLY	RAMOSELY	SELDOMLY	SOMBERLY	SWEATILY
PASSABLY	RAMOUSLY	SELECTLY	SOMBRELY	SWIMMILY
PASSIBLY	RANCIDLY	SENILELY	SORDIDLY	SYMPHILY
PASTORLY	RANDOMLY	SENSIBLY	SORTABLY	TAKINGLY
PATCHILY	RASCALLY	SERENELY	SOTTEDLY	TANGIBLY
PATENTLY	RATEABLY	SERIALLY	SOUTERLY	TARNALLY
PATRONLY	RAVINGLY	SEVERELY	SOVRANLY	TARTARLY
PEACHILY	READABLY	SEXTUPLY	SOWBELLY	TASSELLY
PEDATELY	READERLY	SEXUALLY	SPARKILY	TAWDRILY
PETTEDLY	RECENTLY	SHABBILY	SPARSELY	TAXINGLY
PIPINGLY	RECTALLY	SHAGGILY	SPEEDILY	TENDERLY
PITCHILY	REDBELLY	SHAMABLY	SPIFFILY	TENSIBLY
PITIABLY	REFLEXLY	SHAUCHLY	SPINALLY	TERRIBLY
PLACABLY	RELIABLY	SHIFTILY	SPIRALLY	TETCHILY
PLACIDLY	REMISSLY	SHIRTILY	SPONGILY	THORNILY
PLAGUILY	REMOTELY	SHITTILY	SPOOKILY	THRAWNLY
PLIANTLY	REPANDLY	SHODDILY	SPOONILY	THWARTLY
PLUCKILY	RESUPPLY	SHREWDLY	SPORTILY	TIMOUSLY
PLUGUGLY	RETRALLY	SICKERLY	SPOTTILY	TINSELLY
PLURALLY	RIBALDLY	SICKLILY	SPRITELY	TONISHLY
PLUSHILY	RIMOSELY	SIGNALLY	SPRUCELY	TOOTHILY
PLYINGLY	RITUALLY	SILENTLY	SPUNKILY	TORPIDLY
POLITELY	ROBUSTLY	SILVERLY	SQUARELY	TORRIDLY
POPISHLY	ROOTEDLY	SINFULLY	SQUIGGLY	TOUCHILY
POROUSLY	ROTTENLY	SISTERLY	SQUIRELY	TOWARDLY
PORTABLY	ROTUNDLY	SIZEABLY	STALKILY	TOYISHLY
PORTERLY	ROVINGLY	SKIMPILY	STANCHLY	TRASHILY
POSINGLY	RUEFULLY	SLANGILY	STARRILY	TRENDILY
POSSIBLY	RUGGEDLY	SLEAZILY	STATEDLY	TREVALLY
POSTALLY	RUGOSELY	SLEEPILY	STEADILY	TRIBALLY
POTBELLY	RUSTICLY	SLIGHTLY	STEAMILY	TRICKILY
POTENTLY	SACREDLY	SLINKILY	STEEVELY	TRUANTLY
PREAPPLY	SAILORLY	SLIPPILY	STICKILY	TRUSTILY
PREPPILY	SALEABLY	SLOPPILY	STIEVELY	TRYINGLY
PRETTILY	SALLOWLY	SLOVENLY	STINGILY	TUNBELLY
PRIESTLY	SALVABLY	SLUSHILY	STOCKILY	TUNEABLY
PRIMALLY	SATIABLY	SLUTTILY	STODGILY	TURBIDLY
PRINCELY	SAVAGELY	SMALMILY	STOLIDLY	TURGIDLY
PRISSILY	SAVINGLY	SMARMILY	STONEFLY	TWEEDILY
PROBABLY	SAVORILY	SMEARILY	STORMILY	UNCHICLY
PROLIXLY	SAVOURLY	SMIRKILY	STRAGGLY	UNCIALLY
PROMPTLY	SCABBILY	SMOOTHLY	STRAITLY	UNCOMELY
PROPERLY	SCALABLY	SMUDGILY	STRICTLY	UNCOSTLY
PROVABLY	SCANTILY	SMUTTILY	STRONGLY	UNEASILY
PROVENLY	SCARCELY	SNAPPILY	STUBBILY	UNEVENLY
PRYINGLY	SCATTILY	SNARKILY	STUFFILY	UNFAIRLY
PUBLICLY	SCRABBLY	SNAZZILY	STUMPILY	UNGAINLY
PULINGLY	SCRAGGLY	SNEAKILY	STUPIDLY	UNGENTLY

UNHOLILY	UNSTABLY	VACANTLY	VISCIDLY	WITTOLLY
UNHOMELY	UNSUBTLY	VALUABLY	VISUALLY	WIZARDLY
UNIQUELY	UNSURELY	VARIABLY	VOTIVELY	WOEFULLY
UNITEDLY	UNTIDILY	VARIEDLY	VULGARLY	WONTEDLY
UNJUSTLY	UNTIMELY	VEILEDLY	WANTONLY	WOODENLY
UNKINDLY	UNUSABLY	VENDIBLY	WATERILY	WOOINGLY
UNKINGLY	UNWARELY	VENIALLY	WEASELLY	WOOLLILY
UNLIKELY	UNWARILY	VENOUSLY	WEEVILLY	WORKABLY
UNLIVELY	UNWIFELY	VERBALLY	WESTERLY	WORTHILY
UNLORDLY	UNWISELY	VERNALLY	WHEEZILY	WOUNDILY
UNLOVELY	UPPISHLY	VESTALLY	WHIMSILY	WRATHILY
UNMEETLY	UPWARDLY	VEXINGLY	WHITEFLY	WRITERLY
UNPURELY	URBANELY	VINCIBLY	WICKEDLY	YEASTILY
UNREALLY	URGENTLY	VINOUSLY	WILFULLY	YELLOWLY
UNRIPELY	URGINGLY	VIOLABLY	WINGEDLY	YEOMANLY
UNSAFELY	USEFULLY	VIRGINLY	WINTERLY	YONDERLY
UNSEEMLY	UVULARLY	VIRILELY	WINTRILY	ZOOPHILY

Words that end with -MAN

Seven-letter words	FOOTMAN	LOCOMAN	SANDMAN	BANDYMAN
ADWOMAN	FOREMAN	MAGSMAN	SEEDMAN	BANKSMAN
ALMSMAN	FREEMAN	MAILMAN	SHIPMAN	BARGEMAN
ANATMAN	FROGMAN	MALTMAN	SHOPMAN	BATWOMAN
ANTIMAN	GADSMAN	MARKMAN	SHOWMAN	BEADSMAN
ARTSMAN	GATEMAN	MASHMAN	SIDEMAN	BEDESMAN
AUTOMAN	GLEEMAN	MEATMAN	SNOWMAN	BLUESMAN
BASEMAN	GOODMAN	MESSMAN	SOCKMAN	BOARDMAN
BATSMAN	GOWNMAN	MILKMAN	SOKEMAN	BOATSMAN
BEADMAN	GRIPMAN	MOBSMAN	SONGMAN	BOGEYMAN
BEDEMAN	GUDEMAN	MOORMAN	SPAEMAN	BONDSMAN
BELLMAN	HACKMAN	MOOTMAN	SURFMAN	BOOGYMAN
BELTMAN	HANGMAN	NEWSMAN	SWAGMAN	BOTHYMAN
BILLMAN	HANUMAN	OARSMAN	TAPSMAN	BRAKEMAN
BIRDMAN	HARDMAN	ODDSMAN	TAXIMAN	BRIDEMAN
BOATMAN	HEADMAN	ORRAMAN	TELEMAN	BRINKMAN
BOGYMAN	HELIMAN	OTTOMAN	TOLLMAN	BUTTYMAN
BONDMAN	HERDMAN	OVERMAN	TONGMAN	CANDYMAN
BOOKMAN	HIGHMAN	PACEMAN	TOOLMAN	CHAINMAN
BRAHMAN	HOODMAN	PACKMAN	TOPSMAN	CHAIRMAN
BUSHMAN	HOSEMAN	PASSMAN	TRUEMAN	CHESSMAN
BYREMAN	INHUMAN	PEATMAN	TURFMAN	CHINAMAN
CASEMAN	IRONMAN	PIKEMAN	UNHUMAN	CHOIRMAN
CAVEMAN	ISLEMAN	PLOWMAN	UNWOMAN	CHOREMAN
CHAPMAN	JACKMAN	POLLMAN	WAKEMAN	CLANSMAN
CLUBMAN	JARKMAN	PORTMAN	WINGMAN	CLASSMAN
COALMAN	JAZZMAN	POSTMAN	WIREMAN	COACHMAN
CREWMAN	JUNKMAN	PROPMAN	WOODMAN	COLORMAN
DAYSMAN	JURYMAN	PULLMAN	WOOLMAN	CORPSMAN
DEADMAN	KEELMAN	RAFTMAN	WORKMAN	CRAGSMAN
DECUMAN	KINSMAN	RAILMAN	YARDMAN	DAIRYMAN
DESKMAN	KIRKMAN	REEDMAN	YEGGMAN	DALESMAN
DOORMAN	LANDMAN	REELMAN		DOOMSMAN
DRAYMAN	LEADMAN	REPOMAN	**Eight-letter words**	DOORSMAN
DUSTMAN	LENSMAN	RINGMAN		DRAGOMAN
FACEMAN	LIFTMAN	ROADMAN	AIRWOMAN	DRAGSMAN
FIREMAN	LINEMAN	RODSMAN	ALDERMAN	DUTCHMAN
FLAGMAN	LINKMAN	RUCKMAN	BAILSMAN	EARTHMAN
	LOCKMAN	SAGAMAN	BANDSMAN	EVERYMAN

FERRYMAN	HUNTSMAN	PITCHMAN	SHEARMAN	TALESMAN
FOILSMAN	ISLESMAN	PIVOTMAN	SHEEPMAN	TALISMAN
FORGEMAN	KNIFEMAN	PLACEMAN	SHIREMAN	TALLYMAN
FREEDMAN	LANDSMAN	PLAIDMAN	SHOREMAN	TIDESMAN
FRESHMAN	LAYWOMAN	PLATEMAN	SIDESMAN	TOWNSMAN
FRONTMAN	LEADSMAN	POINTMAN	SONARMAN	TOYWOMAN
FUGLEMAN	LIEGEMAN	PREHUMAN	SOUNDMAN	TRACKMAN
FUNNYMAN	LINESMAN	PRESSMAN	SPACEMAN	TRAINMAN
GAMESMAN	LINKSMAN	PRIZEMAN	SPADEMAN	TRASHMAN
GANGSMAN	LOCKSMAN	PROSEMAN	SPEARMAN	TREWSMAN
GAVELMAN	LODESMAN	PUNTSMAN	SQUAWMAN	TRUCHMAN
GILDSMAN	LOFTSMAN	QUILLMAN	STAFFMAN	TRUCKMAN
GLASSMAN	MADWOMAN	RADIOMAN	STALLMAN	UNDERMAN
GOADSMAN	MARCHMAN	RAFTSMAN	STEELMAN	VERSEMAN
GOWNSMAN	MARKSMAN	RAMPSMAN	STICKMAN	WATCHMAN
HANDYMAN	MERESMAN	RANCHMAN	STILLMAN	WATERMAN
HEADSMAN	MERRYMAN	REINSMAN	STOCKMAN	WEALSMAN
HELMSMAN	MONEYMAN	RIFLEMAN	STOREMAN	WEIGHMAN
HENCHMAN	MOTORMAN	RIVERMAN	STUNTMAN	WHALEMAN
HERDSMAN	NOBLEMAN	ROADSMAN	SUBHUMAN	WHEELMAN
HIELAMAN	NONHUMAN	ROUTEMAN	SUPERMAN	WIDOWMAN
HOASTMAN	OVERSMAN	SALESMAN	SWAGSMAN	WINCHMAN
HOISTMAN	PANHUMAN	SCENEMAN	SWEETMAN	WOODSMAN
HORSEMAN	PENWOMAN	SEAWOMAN	SWINGMAN	YACHTMAN
HOTELMAN	PETERMAN	SEEDSMAN	SWORDMAN	YARRAMAN
HOUSEMAN	PILOTMAN	SHAREMAN	TACKSMAN	

Words that end with -MEN

Seven-letter words	COALMEN	HELIMEN	MESSMEN	RODSMEN
	CREWMEN	HERDMEN	MILKMEN	RUCKMEN
ABDOMEN	DAYSMEN	HIGHMEN	MOBSMEN	SAGAMEN
ADWOMEN	DEADMEN	HILLMEN	MOLIMEN	SANDMEN
AGNOMEN	DESKMEN	HOODMEN	MOORMEN	SEEDMEN
ALBUMEN	DOORMEN	HOSEMEN	MOOTMEN	SHIPMEN
ALMSMEN	DRAYMEN	IRONMEN	NEWSMEN	SHOPMEN
ARTSMEN	DURAMEN	ISLEMEN	OARSMEN	SHOWMEN
AUTOMEN	DUSTMEN	JACKMEN	ODDSMEN	SIDEMEN
BASEMEN	FACEMEN	JARKMEN	ORRAMEN	SNOWMEN
BATSMEN	FIREMEN	JAZZMEN	OVERMEN	SOCKMEN
BEADMEN	FLAGMEN	JUNKMEN	PACEMEN	SOKEMEN
BEDEMEN	FLEHMEN	JURYMEN	PACKMEN	SONGMEN
BELLMEN	FOOTMEN	KEELMEN	PASSMEN	SPAEMEN
BELTMEN	FORAMEN	KINSMEN	PEATMEN	SUDAMEN
BILLMEN	FOREMEN	KIRKMEN	PIKEMEN	SURFMEN
BIRDMEN	FREEMEN	LANDMEN	PLOWMEN	SWAGMEN
BITUMEN	FROGMEN	LEADMEN	POLLMEN	TAPSMEN
BOATMEN	GADSMEN	LENSMEN	PORTMEN	TAXIMEN
BOGYMEN	GATEMEN	LIFTMEN	POSTMEN	TEGUMEN
BONDMEN	GLEEMEN	LINEMEN	PROPMEN	TELEMEN
BOOKMEN	GOODMEN	LINKMEN	PUTAMEN	TOLLMEN
BUSHMEN	GOWNMEN	LOCKMEN	RAFTMEN	TONGMEN
BYREMEN	GRIPMEN	LOCOMEN	RAILMEN	TOOLMEN
CACUMEN	GUDEMEN	MAGSMEN	REEDMEN	TOPSMEN
CASEMEN	HACKMEN	MAILMEN	REELMEN	TRUEMEN
CAVEMEN	HANGMEN	MALTMEN	REGIMEN	TURFMEN
CERUMEN	HARDMEN	MARKMEN	REPOMEN	VELAMEN
CHAPMEN	HEADMEN	MASHMEN	RINGMEN	WAKEMEN
CLUBMEN	HEGUMEN	MEATMEN	ROADMEN	WINGMEN

WIREMEN	CLANSMEN	HENCHMEN	PRENOMEN	STOCKMEN
WOODMEN	CLASSMEN	HERDSMEN	PRESSMEN	STOREMEN
WOOLMEN	CLINAMEN	HOASTMEN	PRIZEMEN	STUNTMEN
WORKMEN	COACHMEN	HOISTMEN	PROSEMEN	SUPERMEN
YARDMEN	COGNOMEN	HORSEMEN	PUNTSMEN	SWAGSMEN
YEGGMEN	COLORMEN	HOTELMEN	QUILLMEN	SWEETMEN
	CORPSMEN	HOUSEMEN	RADIOMEN	SWINGMEN
Eight-letter	CRAGSMEN	HUNTSMEN	RAFTSMEN	SWORDMEN
words	CYCLAMEN	ISLESMEN	RAMPSMEN	TACKSMEN
AIRWOMEN	DAIRYMEN	KNIFEMEN	RANCHMEN	TALESMEN
ALDERMEN	DALESMEN	LANDSMEN	REINSMEN	TALLYMEN
BAILSMEN	DOOMSMEN	LAYWOMEN	RIFLEMEN	TIDESMEN
BANDSMEN	DOORSMEN	LEADSMEN	RIVERMEN	TOWNSMEN
BANDYMEN	DRAGOMEN	LIEGEMEN	ROADSMEN	TOYWOMEN
BANKSMEN	DRAGSMEN	LINESMEN	ROUTEMEN	TRACKMEN
BARGEMEN	DUTCHMEN	LINKSMEN	SALESMEN	TRAINMEN
BATWOMEN	EARTHMEN	LOCKSMEN	SCENEMEN	TRASHMEN
BEADSMEN	EVERYMEN	LODESMEN	SEAWOMEN	TREWSMEN
BEDESMEN	FERRYMEN	LOFTSMEN	SEEDSMEN	TRUCHMEN
BLUESMEN	FOILSMEN	MADWOMEN	SHAREMEN	TRUCKMEN
BOARDMEN	FORGEMEN	MARCHMEN	SHEARMEN	UNDERMEN
BOATSMEN	FREEDMEN	MARKSMEN	SHEEPMEN	VERSEMEN
BOGEYMEN	FRESHMEN	MERESMEN	SHIREMEN	WATCHMEN
BONDSMEN	FRONTMEN	MERRYMEN	SHOREMEN	WATERMEN
BOOGYMEN	FUGLEMEN	MONEYMEN	SIDESMEN	WEALSMEN
BOTHYMEN	FUNNYMEN	MOTORMEN	SONARMEN	WEIGHMEN
BRAKEMEN	GAMESMEN	NOBLEMEN	SOUNDMEN	WHALEMEN
BRIDEMEN	GANGSMEN	OVERSMEN	SPACEMEN	WHEELMEN
BRINKMEN	GAVELMEN	PENWOMEN	SPADEMEN	WIDOWMEN
BUTTYMEN	GILDSMEN	PETERMEN	SPEARMEN	WINCHMEN
CANDYMEN	GLASSMEN	PILOTMEN	SPECIMEN	WOODSMEN
CHAINMEN	GOADSMEN	PITCHMEN	SQUAWMEN	YACHTMEN
CHAIRMEN	GOWNSMEN	PIVOTMEN	STAFFMEN	YARRAMEN
CHESSMEN	GRAVAMEN	PLACEMEN	STALLMEN	
CHINAMEN	HANDYMEN	PLAIDMEN	STEELMEN	
CHOIRMEN	HEADSMEN	PLATEMEN	STICKMEN	
CHOREMEN	HELMSMEN	POINTMEN	STILLMEN	

Words that end with -NESS

Seven-letter words	HARNESS	SADNESS	ALBINESS	BUSYNESS
ALLNESS	HIPNESS	SETNESS	ARCHNESS	CAGINESS
APTNESS	HOTNESS	SHINESS	ARIDNESS	CAGYNESS
BADNESS	ICINESS	SHYNESS	ARTINESS	CAKINESS
BIGNESS	ILLNESS	SLYNESS	ASHINESS	CALMNESS
COYNESS	LAXNESS	TWONESS	AVIDNESS	CAMPNESS
DIMNESS	LIONESS	WAENESS	AWAYNESS	CANONESS
DRYNESS	LOWNESS	WANNESS	BALDNESS	CHICNESS
DUENESS	MADNESS	WETNESS	BARENESS	COLDNESS
DULNESS	NEWNESS	WITNESS	BARONESS	COOLNESS
DUNNESS	NOWNESS	WOENESS	BASENESS	COSINESS
FARNESS	ODDNESS	WRYNESS	BASSNESS	COXINESS
FATNESS	OLDNESS		BEINNESS	COZINESS
FEWNESS	ONENESS	**Eight-letter words**	BIASNESS	CURTNESS
FEYNESS	OUTNESS		BLUENESS	CUTENESS
FITNESS	PATNESS	ACHINESS	BOLDNESS	DAFTNESS
FULNESS	RAWNESS	ACIDNESS	BONINESS	DAMPNESS
GAYNESS	REDNESS	AGEDNESS	BOXINESS	DANKNESS
	RUMNESS	AIRINESS	BUSINESS	DARKNESS

DEADNESS	GLUINESS	LONENESS	PIPINESS	SPRYNESS
DEAFNESS	GLUMNESS	LONGNESS	PIXINESS	SUCHNESS
DEARNESS	GONENESS	LORNNESS	POKINESS	SURENESS
DEEPNESS	GOODNESS	LOSTNESS	POORNESS	TALLNESS
DEFTNESS	GOOINESS	LOTHNESS	PORINESS	TAMENESS
DEMONESS	GORINESS	LOUDNESS	POSHNESS	TARTNESS
DEWINESS	GRAYNESS	LUNINESS	PRIMNESS	TAUTNESS
DIRENESS	GREYNESS	LUSHNESS	PUNINESS	THATNESS
DONENESS	GRIMNESS	MALENESS	PURENESS	THINNESS
DOPINESS	GRUMNESS	MATINESS	RACINESS	THISNESS
DOURNESS	HALENESS	MAZINESS	RANKNESS	THUSNESS
DOWFNESS	HALFNESS	MEANNESS	RAPTNESS	TIDINESS
DOZINESS	HARDNESS	MEEKNESS	RARENESS	TININESS
DRABNESS	HAZINESS	MEETNESS	RASHNESS	TITANESS
DULLNESS	HERENESS	MILDNESS	REALNESS	TRIGNESS
DUMBNESS	HIGHNESS	MIRINESS	RICHNESS	TRIMNESS
DUSKNESS	HOKINESS	MOOTNESS	RIFENESS	TRUENESS
EASINESS	HOLINESS	MOPINESS	RIMINESS	TWEENESS
EDGINESS	HOMINESS	MORENESS	RIPENESS	UGLINESS
EERINESS	HUGENESS	MUCHNESS	ROPINESS	VAINNESS
EVENNESS	ICKINESS	MUTENESS	ROSINESS	VASTNESS
EVILNESS	IDLENESS	NAFFNESS	RUDENESS	VILDNESS
EYEDNESS	IFFINESS	NAIFNESS	SAFENESS	VILENESS
FAINNESS	INKINESS	NEARNESS	SAGENESS	VOIDNESS
FAIRNESS	IRONNESS	NEATNESS	SALTNESS	WARINESS
FASTNESS	JIMPNESS	NESHNESS	SAMENESS	WARMNESS
FELLNESS	JOKINESS	NEXTNESS	SANENESS	WASTNESS
FINENESS	JUSTNESS	NICENESS	SEARNESS	WAVINESS
FIRMNESS	KEENNESS	NIGHNESS	SEEDNESS	WAXINESS
FLATNESS	KINDNESS	NOSINESS	SELFNESS	WEAKNESS
FONDNESS	LACINESS	NUDENESS	SEXINESS	WELLNESS
FOULNESS	LAMENESS	NULLNESS	SICKNESS	WHATNESS
FOXINESS	LANKNESS	NUMBNESS	SIZINESS	WIDENESS
FOZINESS	LATENESS	OILINESS	SKEWNESS	WILDNESS
FREENESS	LAZINESS	OOZINESS	SLIMNESS	WILINESS
FULLNESS	LEANNESS	OPENNESS	SLOWNESS	WIRINESS
GAMENESS	LEWDNESS	OVALNESS	SMUGNESS	WISENESS
GAMINESS	LIKENESS	PACKNESS	SNUBNESS	WOODNESS
GAMYNESS	LIMINESS	PALENESS	SNUGNESS	WORNNESS
GASTNESS	LIMPNESS	PASTNESS	SOFTNESS	ZANINESS
GLADNESS	LITENESS	PERTNESS	SOLENESS	
GLEGNESS	LIVENESS	PIEDNESS	SORENESS	
GLIBNESS	LOGINESS	PINKNESS	SOURNESS	

Words that end with -OID

Seven-letter words	ASTROID	CRICOID	ETHMOID	HYDROID
ACAROID	BYSSOID	CRINOID	EUPLOID	HYENOID
ADENOID	CACTOID	CTENOID	FACTOID	HYPNOID
AGAMOID	CESTOID	CYCLOID	FIBROID	LABROID
AGATOID	CHELOID	CYSTOID	FUNGOID	LENTOID
AMBROID	CHOROID	DELTOID	GLENOID	LIANOID
AMEBOID	CIRSOID	DENTOID	GLOBOID	LITHOID
AMYLOID	CISSOID	DERMOID	GOBIOID	MASTOID
ANDROID	COCCOID	DESMOID	HAEMOID	MATTOID
ANEROID	COLLOID	DIPLOID	HAPLOID	MUSCOID
ANTHOID	CORMOID	DISCOID	HELCOID	MYELOID
ARCTOID	COSMOID	EMEROID	HISTOID	NAEVOID
	COTTOID	ERICOID	HYALOID	NEGROID

NEUROID	XIPHOID	DENDROID	NEMATOID	SEPALOID
OBOVOID	ZEBROID	DORIDOID	NEPHROID	SESAMOID
OCELOID	ZINCOID	ECHINOID	NOCTUOID	SILUROID
OCHROID		ELYTROID	NUCLEOID	SINUSOID
OIDIOID	**Eight-letter**	EMBRYOID	OCTOPOID	SISTROID
OSTEOID	**words**	EMULSOID	ODONTOID	SLEAZOID
PERCOID	ACTINOID	ERGATOID	OMOHYOID	SOLENOID
PHACOID	ALKALOID	GABBROID	ONISCOID	SORICOID
PHYTOID	AMBEROID	GALENOID	PARANOID	SPHENOID
PIGMOID	AMMONOID	GEOMYOID	PAROTOID	SPHEROID
PLACOID	AMOEBOID	GROUPOID	PETALOID	SPONGOID
PYGMOID	ANCONOID	GYNECOID	PEZIZOID	SQUALOID
QUINOID	ARILLOID	HELICOID	PHALLOID	STURNOID
RHIZOID	ASTEROID	HEMATOID	PHELLOID	TAENIOID
SARCOID	ATHETOID	HISTIOID	PHYLLOID	TAPIROID
SAUROID	AUTACOID	HOMALOID	PINACOID	TARSIOID
SIALOID	AUTOCOID	HOMINOID	PINAKOID	TERATOID
SIGMOID	BLASTOID	HUMANOID	PITYROID	TETANOID
SIMIOID	BOTRYOID	HYDATOID	PLASMOID	THALLOID
SPAROID	CALYCOID	HYRACOID	POLYPOID	THYREOID
SPIROID	CAMELOID	INDIGOID	PRISMOID	THYRSOID
SPOROID	CANCROID	ISTHMOID	PSYCHOID	TRENDOID
STEROID	CARDIOID	KERATOID	PYRANOID	TRICHOID
STYLOID	CATENOID	LAMBDOID	PYRENOID	TRIPLOID
TABLOID	CENTROID	LEMUROID	RACEMOID	TROCHOID
TENIOID	CERATOID	LIGULOID	RESINOID	TUBEROID
THEROID	CHOREOID	LIMULOID	RETINOID	VARICOID
THYROID	CHORIOID	LYMPHOID	RHABDOID	VIBRIOID
TIGROID	CICHLOID	MANATOID	RHOMBOID	VIRUSOID
TURDOID	CLUPEOID	MEDUSOID	SCAPHOID	VOLUTOID
TYPHOID	CONCHOID	MELANOID	SCHIZOID	YPSILOID
VALGOID	CORACOID	MUCINOID	SCINCOID	
VESPOID	CORONOID	MYCELOID	SCIUROID	
VISCOID	COTYLOID	MYTILOID	SCLEROID	

Words that end with -OR

Seven-letter	CHANTOR	ERECTOR	MACHZOR	QUESTOR
words	CHIKHOR	EVERTOR	MALODOR	QUITTOR
ABACTOR	CITATOR	EVICTOR	MAORMOR	REACTOR
ABETTOR	CLANGOR	EXACTOR	MARKHOR	REALTOR
ABLATOR	COACTOR	EXCITOR	MATADOR	RECOLOR
ADAPTOR	CREATOR	FEOFFOR	MIRADOR	RELATOR
ADJUROR	CURATOR	FUNCTOR	MONITOR	REVISOR
ADVISOR	DEBITOR	GENITOR	MORMAOR	REVIVOR
AERATOR	DECOLOR	GRANTOR	NEGATOR	ROTATOR
AGISTOR	DELATOR	GYRATOR	NONPOOR	SANTOOR
ALASTOR	DEVISOR	HERITOR	OBLIGOR	SCISSOR
ALIENOR	DILATOR	HUMIDOR	OFFEROR	SENATOR
ANAPHOR	DILUTOR	IGNITOR	OUTDOOR	SEPTUOR
ASSUROR	DIVISOR	IMPEDOR	PANDOOR	SETTLOR
ATHANOR	DONATOR	INCISOR	PARADOR	SEXTUOR
AUDITOR	EDUCTOR	ISOCHOR	PARITOR	SIGNIOR
AVIATOR	EJECTOR	JANITOR	PICADOR	SIMILOR
BELABOR	ELECTOR	LANGUOR	PLEDGOR	SPONSOR
BICOLOR	EMPEROR	LAXATOR	PLESSOR	SQUALOR
BIOPHOR	EMULSOR	LEGATOR	PRAETOR	STENTOR
CAMPHOR	ENACTOR	LEVATOR	PRESSOR	STERTOR
CHADDOR	EQUATOR	LOCATOR	PROCTOR	STRIDOR

TANDOOR	CANEPHOR	EVOCATOR	MISTUTOR	RELEASOR
TEMBLOR	CATAPHOR	EXCEPTOR	NARRATOR	REMITTOR
TRACTOR	CAVEATOR	EXECUTOR	NEIGHBOR	RESISTOR
TRAITOR	CHELATOR	EXPANDOR	NEXTDOOR	RETAILOR
TRUSTOR	COANCHOR	EXPIATOR	NITRATOR	RONCADOR
TWISTOR	COAUTHOR	EXTENSOR	NONACTOR	SCULPTOR
UNVISOR	CODEBTOR	EXTERIOR	NONCOLOR	SEAFLOOR
VAVASOR	COEDITOR	FELLATOR	NONJUROR	SECRETOR
VENATOR	COENAMOR	GILLYVOR	NONLABOR	SECTATOR
VISITOR	COFACTOR	GOVERNOR	NONMAJOR	SEDUCTOR
WARRIOR	COLESSOR	HELIODOR	OBJECTOR	SEIGNIOR
ZELATOR	COLLATOR	HYDRATOR	OBSESSOR	SELECTOR
	CONCOLOR	IDOLATOR	OBVIATOR	SERVITOR
Eight-letter	CONJUROR	IMITATOR	OCCLUSOR	SPLENDOR
words	CONVENOR	IMPACTOR	OPERATOR	STRESSOR
ABDUCTOR	CONVEYOR	IMPELLOR	OUTHUMOR	SUBFLOOR
ACCENTOR	COPASTOR	IMPOSTOR	OUTSAVOR	SUBPRIOR
ACCEPTOR	CORRIDOR	INCENSOR	PALPATOR	SUPERIOR
ACTUATOR	CREDITOR	INCEPTOR	PARACHOR	SURVEYOR
ADDUCTOR	CREMATOR	INDENTOR	PATENTOR	SURVIVOR
ADJUSTOR	CURSITOR	INDICTOR	PHOSPHOR	TESTATOR
ADULATOR	CUSPIDOR	INDORSOR	PISCATOR	THEREFOR
AGITATOR	DEFECTOR	INDUCTOR	PLEDGEOR	THRUSTOR
ALACHLOR	DEFLATOR	INFECTOR	PREDATOR	TITRATOR
ANCESTOR	DEMEANOR	INFERIOR	PREVISOR	TOREADOR
ANIMATOR	DEPICTOR	INFLATOR	PRODITOR	TRADITOR
ANTERIOR	DETECTOR	INJECTOR	PROLABOR	TRAPDOOR
APPELLOR	DETRUSOR	INTERIOR	PROMISOR	TRICOLOR
ARRESTOR	DEVIATOR	INVENTOR	PROMOTOR	TRIMOTOR
ASPERSOR	DICTATOR	INVERTOR	PRONATOR	ULTERIOR
ASSENTOR	DIFFUSOR	INVESTOR	PROVEDOR	UNANCHOR
ASSERTOR	DIGESTOR	IODOPHOR	PROVIDOR	UNICOLOR
ASSESSOR	DIRECTOR	ISOLATOR	PROVISOR	URINATOR
ASSIGNOR	DISCOLOR	KOMONDOR	PULMOTOR	UTILIDOR
ASSISTOR	DISFAVOR	KURVEYOR	PULSATOR	VALUATOR
ATTESTOR	DISHONOR	LABRADOR	PUNDONOR	VARACTOR
AVIGATOR	EDUCATOR	LAUDATOR	PURVEYOR	VARISTOR
BACHELOR	EFFECTOR	LICENSOR	QUAESTOR	VAVASSOR
BACKDOOR	ELEVATOR	MAINDOOR	RADIATOR	VERDEROR
BARRATOR	ELICITOR	MANDATOR	RECAPTOR	VIBRATOR
BARRETOR	EMANATOR	MARKHOOR	RECENSOR	VIOLATOR
BECLAMOR	EMBRASOR	MEDIATOR	RECEPTOR	VITIATOR
BEGLAMOR	EMULATOR	METAPHOR	REDACTOR	WHEREFOR
BEHAVIOR	ENDEAVOR	MIGRATOR	REDUCTOR	
BELIQUOR	ENDORSOR	MISCOLOR	REGRATOR	
BISECTOR	EPILATOR	MISLABOR	REJECTOR	

Words that end with -OUS

Seven-letter	AMOROUS	AZYGOUS	BURNOUS	CITROUS
words	ANUROUS	AZYMOUS	CACHOUS	COCCOUS
ACAJOUS	ANXIOUS	BADIOUS	CALLOUS	CONGOUS
ACEROUS	APODOUS	BILIOUS	CARIOUS	COPIOUS
ACETOUS	AQUEOUS	BINIOUS	CASEOUS	CORIOUS
ACINOUS	ARDUOUS	BIVIOUS	CEREOUS	CORMOUS
ADIPOUS	ARENOUS	BOUBOUS	CESIOUS	COYPOUS
AENEOUS	ATHEOUS	BRUMOUS	CHYLOUS	CUPROUS
AGAMOUS	ATOKOUS	BULBOUS	CHYMOUS	CURIOUS
AMADOUS	AZOTOUS	BULLOUS	CIRROUS	DEVIOUS

DUBIOUS	PICEOUS	ANTICOUS	EUROKOUS	NODULOUS
DUTEOUS	PILEOUS	APHONOUS	EXIGUOUS	NUBILOUS
EMULOUS	PISTOUS	APHTHOUS	EXIMIOUS	NUMEROUS
ENVIOUS	PITEOUS	APTEROUS	FABULOUS	NUMINOUS
ESTROUS	PLUMOUS	ARACEOUS	FACTIOUS	OCHEROUS
FATUOUS	POMPOUS	ARANEOUS	FASHIOUS	OCHREOUS
FEATOUS	PORTOUS	ARBOROUS	FASTUOUS	OESTROUS
FERROUS	PULPOUS	ARSENOUS	FEATEOUS	OOGAMOUS
FIBROUS	RAMEOUS	ARSONOUS	FEATUOUS	ORAGIOUS
FOLIOUS	RAUCOUS	ASPEROUS	FELONOUS	ORDUROUS
FULVOUS	RHODOUS	ASTOMOUS	FERREOUS	ORGULOUS
FUNGOUS	RIOTOUS	ATROPOUS	FEVEROUS	OVARIOUS
FURIOUS	ROUCOUS	BIBULOUS	FIDDIOUS	PABULOUS
FUSCOUS	ROUTOUS	BIGAMOUS	FLATUOUS	PALUDOUS
GALLOUS	RUBIOUS	BIJUGOUS	FLEXUOUS	PAPULOUS
GASEOUS	RUINOUS	BIMANOUS	FRABJOUS	PATULOUS
GEALOUS	SANIOUS	BIPAROUS	FRONDOUS	PERILOUS
GIBBOUS	SARCOUS	BIRAMOUS	GEMINOUS	PERVIOUS
GLEBOUS	SERIOUS	BUTYROUS	GEMMEOUS	PETALOUS
GLOBOUS	SIMIOUS	CADUCOUS	GENEROUS	PLUMBOUS
GRUMOUS	SINUOUS	CAESIOUS	GLABROUS	PLUVIOUS
GUMMOUS	SOUKOUS	CANOROUS	GLAREOUS	POACEOUS
HEINOUS	SPINOUS	CAPTIOUS	GLAUCOUS	POLYPOUS
HERBOUS	SPUMOUS	CARIBOUS	GLORIOUS	POPULOUS
HIDEOUS	SUCCOUS	CARNEOUS	GOITROUS	PORTEOUS
HOUMOUS	TALCOUS	CAUTIOUS	GORGEOUS	PRECIOUS
HUGEOUS	TAUHOUS	CERNUOUS	GRACIOUS	PREVIOUS
HYDROUS	TEDIOUS	CHLOROUS	GRIEVOUS	PYRITOUS
IGNEOUS	TENUOUS	CHROMOUS	GRISEOUS	PYRRHOUS
IMPIOUS	TIMEOUS	CITREOUS	GYPSEOUS	RACEMOUS
INVIOUS	TYPHOUS	CORNEOUS	HALITOUS	RAMULOUS
JEALOUS	UBEROUS	COUSCOUS	HAMULOUS	RAVENOUS
LENTOUS	UMBROUS	COVETOUS	HUMOROUS	RESINOUS
LEPROUS	URANOUS	COVINOUS	ICHOROUS	RIGOROUS
LIMBOUS	URINOUS	CRANKOUS	IDONEOUS	ROSINOUS
LUTEOUS	USUROUS	CRIBROUS	IMPOROUS	RUCTIOUS
MEVROUS	VACUOUS	CROCEOUS	INCUBOUS	RUMOROUS
NACROUS	VALGOUS	CROUPOUS	INERMOUS	SABULOUS
NERVOUS	VARIOUS	CUMBROUS	INFAMOUS	SAPAJOUS
NIMIOUS	VEINOUS	CUMULOUS	KOUSKOUS	SAPOROUS
NIOBOUS	VICIOUS	CUPREOUS	LACTEOUS	SAVOROUS
NITROUS	VIDUOUS	DARTROUS	LAMINOUS	SCABIOUS
NIVEOUS	VILLOUS	DECOROUS	LEAPROUS	SCABROUS
NOCUOUS	VISCOUS	DESIROUS	LIBELOUS	SCARIOUS
NOXIOUS	VITIOUS	DEXTROUS	LIGNEOUS	SCIOLOUS
OBVIOUS	VOUDOUS	DIDYMOUS	LUMINOUS	SCLEROUS
OCHROUS	ZEALOUS	DIECIOUS	LUSCIOUS	SCORIOUS
ODOROUS	ZINCOUS	DIGAMOUS	LUSTROUS	SEDULOUS
OMINOUS		DIGYNOUS	MANITOUS	SELENOUS
ONEROUS	**Eight-letter**	DIMEROUS	MARABOUS	SENSUOUS
ONYMOUS	**words**	DIOICOUS	MELANOUS	SEPALOUS
OPACOUS	ACARPOUS	DIPNOOUS	MIASMOUS	SETULOUS
ORIHOUS	ACAULOUS	DITOKOUS	MUCINOUS	SIBILOUS
OSMIOUS	ACOELOUS	DIZYGOUS	MUTICOUS	SOMBROUS
OSSEOUS	ADUNCOUS	DOLOROUS	MUTINOUS	SONOROUS
OZONOUS	AMBEROUS	EDACIOUS	NACREOUS	SOPOROUS
PAPPOUS	ANGINOUS	ELYTROUS	NAUSEOUS	SPACIOUS
PARLOUS	ANGULOUS	ENGINOUS	NEBULOUS	SPECIOUS
PERLOUS	ANOUROUS	ENORMOUS	NEMOROUS	SPERMOUS
PETROUS	ANSEROUS	EPIGEOUS	NIDOROUS	SPURIOUS

SQUAMOUS	TENUIOUS	TUMOROUS	VALOROUS	VITREOUS
STANNOUS	THALLOUS	TUMULOUS	VANADOUS	VOMITOUS
STOCIOUS	TIMOROUS	TURACOUS	VAPOROUS	WAMEFOUS
STOTIOUS	TINAMOUS	ULCEROUS	VENOMOUS	WAREHOUS
STRATOUS	TITANOUS	UNCTUOUS	VENTROUS	WAVEROUS
STRUMOUS	TORTIOUS	UNDULOUS	VENULOUS	WONDROUS
STUDIOUS	TORTUOUS	UNFAMOUS	VERTUOUS	WRONGOUS
SUBEROUS	TRAPPOUS	UNJOYOUS	VIGOROUS	XANTHOUS
SUDOROUS	TUBEROUS	USURIOUS	VIPEROUS	YTTRIOUS
TEMEROUS	TUBULOUS	UXORIOUS	VIRTUOUS	

Words that end with -OUT

Seven-letter words	HANDOUT	SPINOUT	BULLPOUT	RUNABOUT
	HANGOUT	SURTOUT	CARRYOUT	SEASCOUT
ASPROUT	HIDEOUT	TAKEOUT	CHECKOUT	SEATROUT
BACKOUT	HOLDOUT	TIMEOUT	CLOSEOUT	SHAKEOUT
BAILOUT	KICKOUT	TURNOUT	FLAMEOUT	SHOOTOUT
BESHOUT	LOCKOUT	UNSHOUT	FREAKOUT	SLEEPOUT
BESPOUT	LOOKOUT	WALKOUT	GADABOUT	SPEAKOUT
BLOWOUT	MISSOUT	WASHOUT	HORNPOUT	STAKEOUT
BURGOUT	PASSOUT	WIDEOUT	INDEVOUT	STANDOUT
BURNOUT	PUCKOUT	WIPEOUT	KNOCKOUT	STICKOUT
CAMPOUT	PULLOUT	WITHOUT	LAYABOUT	TACAHOUT
COOKOUT	RAINOUT	WORKOUT	MARABOUT	THEREOUT
DROPOUT	READOUT		OUTSHOUT	UNDEVOUT
EELPOUT	ROLLOUT	**Eight-letter words**	PHASEOUT	WATCHOUT
FADEOUT	SELLOUT		PITCHOUT	WHEREOUT
FALLOUT	SHUTOUT	BLACKOUT	PRINTOUT	WHITEOUT
FOLDOUT	SICKOUT	BREAKOUT	RACAHOUT	
GRAYOUT	SLIPOUT	BROWNOUT	RESPROUT	

Words that end with -SET

Seven-letter words	HANDSET	NAILSET	**Eight-letter words**	SOMERSET
	HARDSET	OVERSET		THICKSET
BACKSET	HAROSET	SEAMSET	CHAROSET	THORNSET
BONESET	HEADSET	SIROSET	EARTHSET	UNDERSET
BRASSET	KNESSET	TOOLSET	HEAVYSET	
CHIPSET	LOCKSET	TWINSET	MARMOSET	
CRESSET	MINDSET	TYPESET	PHOTOSET	
FILMSET	MOONSET		QUICKSET	

Words that end with -SHIP

Seven-letter words	MIDSHIP	ANTISHIP	GURUSHIP	POETSHIP
	NUNSHIP	BARDSHIP	HARDSHIP	POPESHIP
AIRSHIP	PALSHIP	CHUMSHIP	HEADSHIP	RAJASHIP
DOGSHIP	PRESHIP	CLANSHIP	HEIRSHIP	SERFSHIP
DONSHIP	SIBSHIP	DEANSHIP	HEROSHIP	STARSHIP
ENDSHIP	SONSHIP	DEMYSHIP	KINGSHIP	TANKSHIP
FOXSHIP	WARSHIP	DOGESHIP	LADYSHIP	TOWNSHIP
GODSHIP	WORSHIP	DUKESHIP	LONGSHIP	TRANSHIP
GUNSHIP		EARLSHIP	LORDSHIP	TREESHIP
HERSHIP	**Eight-letter words**	FIRESHIP	MAGESHIP	TWINSHIP
KINSHIP		FLAGSHIP	MATESHIP	WARDSHIP
LUDSHIP	AMIDSHIP	FORESHIP	PEATSHIP	WINDSHIP

Words that end with -SKIN

Seven-letter words		Eight-letter words		
CATSKIN	KIDSKIN		DEERSKIN	SWANSKIN
COWSKIN	KIPSKIN	BEARSKIN	FISHSKIN	TURNSKIN
DOESKIN	OILSKIN	BUCKSKIN	FORESKIN	WINESKIN
DOGSKIN	PIGSKIN	CALFSKIN	GOATSKIN	WOLFSKIN
FOXSKIN	REDSKIN	CAPESKIN	LAMBSKIN	WOODSKIN
GRISKIN		COONSKIN	MOLESKIN	WOOLSKIN
		DAMASKIN	PONYSKIN	
			SEALSKIN	

Words that end with -SMAN

Seven-letter words	RODSMAN	CLASSMAN	HERDSMAN	RAMPSMAN
ALMSMAN	TAPSMAN	CORPSMAN	HUNTSMAN	REINSMAN
ARTSMAN	TOPSMAN	CRAGSMAN	ISLESMAN	ROADSMAN
BATSMAN		DALESMAN	LANDSMAN	SALESMAN
DAYSMAN	**Eight-letter**	DOOMSMAN	LEADSMAN	SEEDSMAN
GADSMAN	**words**	DOORSMAN	LINESMAN	SIDESMAN
KINSMAN	BAILSMAN	DRAGSMAN	LINKSMAN	SWAGSMAN
LENSMAN	BANDSMAN	FOILSMAN	LOCKSMAN	TACKSMAN
MAGSMAN	BANKSMAN	GAMESMAN	LODESMAN	TALESMAN
MESSMAN	BEADSMAN	GANGSMAN	LOFTSMAN	TALISMAN
MOBSMAN	BEDESMAN	GILDSMAN	MARKSMAN	TIDESMAN
NEWSMAN	BLUESMAN	GLASSMAN	MERESMAN	TOWNSMAN
OARSMAN	BOATSMAN	GOADSMAN	OVERSMAN	TREWSMAN
ODDSMAN	BONDSMAN	GOWNSMAN	PRESSMAN	WEALSMAN
PASSMAN	CHESSMAN	HEADSMAN	PUNTSMAN	WOODSMAN
	CLANSMAN	HELMSMAN	RAFTSMAN	

Words that end with -SMEN

Seven-letter words	RODSMEN	CLASSMEN	HERDSMEN	RAMPSMEN
ALMSMEN	TAPSMEN	CORPSMEN	HUNTSMEN	REINSMEN
ARTSMEN	TOPSMEN	CRAGSMEN	ISLESMEN	ROADSMEN
BATSMEN		DALESMEN	LANDSMEN	SALESMEN
DAYSMEN	**Eight-letter**	DOOMSMEN	LEADSMEN	SEEDSMEN
GADSMEN	**words**	DOORSMEN	LINESMEN	SIDESMEN
KINSMEN	BAILSMEN	DRAGSMEN	LINKSMEN	SWAGSMEN
LENSMEN	BANDSMEN	FOILSMEN	LOCKSMEN	TACKSMEN
MAGSMEN	BANKSMEN	GAMESMEN	LODESMEN	TALESMEN
MESSMEN	BEADSMEN	GANGSMEN	LOFTSMEN	TIDESMEN
MOBSMEN	BEDESMEN	GILDSMEN	MARKSMEN	TOWNSMEN
NEWSMEN	BLUESMEN	GLASSMEN	MERESMEN	TREWSMEN
OARSMEN	BOATSMEN	GOADSMEN	OVERSMEN	WEALSMEN
ODDSMEN	BONDSMEN	GOWNSMEN	PRESSMEN	WOODSMEN
PASSMEN	CHESSMEN	HEADSMEN	PUNTSMEN	
	CLANSMEN	HELMSMEN	RAFTSMEN	

Words that end with -SOME

Seven-letter words	FULSOME	OXYSOME	WAESOME	Eight-letter words
AWESOME	GAYSOME	TOYSOME	WAGSOME	ACROSOME
BEESOME	IRKSOME	TRISOME	WINSOME	AUTOSOME
EPISOME	LISSOME	TWASOME	WOESOME	BORESOME
EYESOME	NOISOME	TWOSOME		CLOYSOME
	NOYSOME	UROSOME		

CYTOSOME	FRETSOME	HOLESOME	LYSOSOME	ROOMSOME
DARKSOME	GAMESOME	JOKESOME	MEROSOME	TEDISOME
DOLESOME	GLADSOME	LARKSOME	MESOSOME	TIRESOME
DUELSOME	GLEESOME	LIFESOME	MONOSOME	TOILSOME
ENDOSOME	GONOSOME	LIPOSOME	MURKSOME	TWIGSOME
FEARSOME	GREWSOME	LONESOME	PLAYSOME	WAILSOME
FLAYSOME	GRUESOME	LONGSOME	POLYSOME	WORKSOME
FLEASOME	HANDSOME	LOTHSOME	PYROSOME	YAWNSOME
FOURSOME	HEALSOME	LOVESOME	RIBOSOME	

Words that end with -TIME

Seven-letter words	MISTIME	Eight-letter words	LIFETIME	SEEDTIME
	ONETIME		LONGTIME	SHOWTIME
AIRTIME	PASTIME	CALLTIME	MARITIME	SOMETIME
ANYTIME	RAGTIME	CHOWTIME	MEALTIME	TALKTIME
BEDTIME	SEPTIME	DOWNTIME	MEANTIME	TERMTIME
BIGTIME	TEATIME	FLEXTIME	NOONTIME	XENOTIME
CENTIME	WARTIME	FORETIME	OVERTIME	ZONETIME
DAYTIME		GOODTIME	PLAYTIME	
LAYTIME		HALFTIME	REALTIME	

Words that end with -TION

Seven-letter words	STATION	DEVOTION	IGNITION	OBLATION
	SUCTION	DILATION	ILLATION	PACATION
ALATION	TACTION	DILUTION	INACTION	PETITION
AMATION	TUITION	DONATION	INUSTION	POSITION
AMOTION	UNCTION	DOTATION	IODATION	POTATION
AUCTION	UNITION	DURATION	JOBATION	PUNITION
BASTION		EDUCTION	JUNCTION	PUPATION
CANTION	Eight-letter words	EGESTION	LAVATION	QUESTION
CAPTION		EJECTION	LAXATION	REACTION
CAUTION	ABLATION	ELECTION	LEGATION	RELATION
COCTION	ABLUTION	EMICTION	LENITION	REMOTION
COITION	ABORTION	ENACTION	LIBATION	ROGATION
DICTION	ADAPTION	EQUATION	LIGATION	ROTATION
EDITION	ADDITION	ERECTION	LIMATION	SANCTION
ELATION	ADNATION	ERUPTION	LOBATION	SCONTION
ELUTION	ADOPTION	EVECTION	LOCATION	SEDATION
EMOTION	AERATION	EVICTION	LOCUTION	SEDITION
EMPTION	AGNATION	EXACTION	LUNATION	SOLATION
ENATION	AMBITION	EXERTION	LUXATION	SOLUTION
FACTION	AUDITION	FETATION	MONITION	SORPTION
FICTION	AVIATION	FIXATION	MUNITION	STICTION
LECTION	BIBATION	FLECTION	MUTATION	SUDATION
MENTION	CIBATION	FRACTION	NATATION	SWAPTION
MICTION	CITATION	FRICTION	NEGATION	TAXATION
MIXTION	COACTION	FRUITION	NIDATION	TRACTION
ORATION	CONATION	FUNCTION	NIVATION	VACATION
OVATION	COOPTION	GELATION	NODATION	VENATION
PACTION	CREATION	GUMPTION	NOLITION	VEXATION
PORTION	DELATION	GYRATION	NOTATION	VOCATION
RECTION	DELETION	HALATION	NOVATION	VOLITION
RUCTION	DEMOTION	HIMATION	NUDATION	VOLUTION
SECTION	DERATION	IDEATION	NUTATION	ZONATION

Words that end with -URE

Seven-letter words				
	GESTURE	RECOURE	CISELURE	OSSATURE
	GRAVURE	RONDURE	COCKSURE	OVERCURE
ABATURE	GUIPURE	RUPTURE	COENDURE	OVERSURE
BORDURE	GYPLURE	SEASURE	COIFFURE	OVERTURE
BRAVURE	HACHURE	SEISURE	COINSURE	PAINTURE
BRISURE	LEASURE	SEIZURE	CREATURE	PEDICURE
CAPTURE	LECTURE	SEYSURE	CUBATURE	PLEASURE
CENSURE	LEISURE	SOILURE	CYNOSURE	PRESSURE
CLOSURE	MEASURE	STATURE	DENATURE	PUNCTURE
CLOTURE	MIXTURE	TEXTURE	DISCOURE	REASSURE
COENURE	MONTURE	TONSURE	DISINURE	REFIGURE
CONJURE	MORSURE	TORTURE	DOUBLURE	REINJURE
COUPURE	MULTURE	VENTURE	ENACTURE	REINSURE
COUTURE	NERVURE	VERDURE	ENCOLURE	RENATURE
CULTURE	NURTURE	VESTURE	EXPOSURE	REPOSURE
DASYURE	OBSCURE	VOITURE	FILATURE	RESECURE
DENTURE	OUTDURE	VULTURE	FIXATURE	ROUNDURE
DISCURE	PARTURE	WAFTURE	FRACTURE	SCISSURE
EPICURE	PASTURE		GENITURE	SCRIMURE
ERASURE	PERDURE	**Eight-letter words**	HUMITURE	SINECURE
FACTURE	PERJURE		IMMATURE	TAINTURE
FAILURE	PICTURE	ANNEXURE	INCISURE	TINCTURE
FEATURE	PLEXURE	APERTURE	INSECURE	TOURNURE
FISSURE	POSTURE	ARCATURE	JOINTURE	TREASURE
FIXTURE	PRECURE	ARMATURE	JUNCTURE	TRESSURE
FLEXURE	PROCURE	AVENTURE	LIGATURE	TUBULURE
FRISURE	PULTURE	BROCHURE	LINCTURE	
FRITURE	PURPURE	CEINTURE	MANICURE	
GARBURE	RAPTURE	CINCTURE	MOISTURE	

Words that end with -WARD

Seven-letter words		Eight-letter words	HELLWARD	REARWARD
	MANWARD		HINDWARD	REREWARD
	NAYWARD		HIVEWARD	SELFWARD
AIRWARD	NORWARD	BACKWARD	HOMEWARD	SIDEWARD
AWKWARD	OUTWARD	BEARWARD	KIRKWARD	THRAWARD
BEDWARD	SEAWARD	BECOWARD	LANDWARD	UNTOWARD
FORWARD	SKYWARD	CITYWARD	LEFTWARD	WESTWARD
FROWARD	STEWARD	DOWNWARD	MISAWARD	WINDWARD
GODWARD	SUNWARD	EASTWARD	MOONWARD	WOODWARD
HAYWARD	VANWARD	FOREWARD	PARKWARD	WOOLWARD
HOGWARD	WAYWARD	GOALWARD	POLEWARD	
LEEWARD	WEYWARD	HEADWARD		

Words that end with -WARDS

Seven-letter words		Eight-letter words	GODWARDS	NORWARDS
	REWARDS		HAYWARDS	OUTWARDS
	TOWARDS		HOGWARDS	SEAWARDS
ADWARDS	UPWARDS	AIRWARDS	LEEWARDS	SKYWARDS
COWARDS	USWARDS	BEDWARDS	MANWARDS	STEWARDS
INWARDS	VAWARDS	FORWARDS	NAYWARDS	SUNWARDS
ONWARDS		FROWARDS		

Words that end with -WAY

Seven-letter words

ARCHWAY	LANEWAY	TIDEWAY	ENTRYWAY	SOAKAWAY
AREAWAY	LAYAWAY	TOLLWAY	EVERYWAY	SOARAWAY
BELTWAY	LICHWAY	TOWAWAY	FADEAWAY	SPEEDWAY
BIKEWAY	LIFEWAY	TRAMWAY	FALLAWAY	SPILLWAY
CARAWAY	PACEWAY	WALKWAY	FLOODWAY	STAIRWAY
CARTWAY	PACKWAY	WELAWAY	FOLDAWAY	STAYAWAY
CUTAWAY	PARKWAY	WINDWAY	GIVEAWAY	STERNWAY
DOORWAY	PARTWAY	WIREWAY	GREENWAY	STOWAWAY
FAIRWAY	PATHWAY		GUIDEWAY	TAKEAWAY
FARAWAY	RACEWAY	**Eight-letter words**	HATCHWAY	TEARAWAY
FISHWAY	RAILWAY		HEREAWAY	THATAWAY
FLYAWAY	RINGWAY	AISLEWAY	HIDEAWAY	THISAWAY
FOLKWAY	ROADWAY	ALLEYWAY	HOISTWAY	TRACKWAY
FOOTWAY	RODEWAY	BROADWAY	HORSEWAY	TRAINWAY
FREEWAY	ROLLWAY	CABLEWAY	HUNTAWAY	UNDERWAY
GANGWAY	ROPEWAY	CARRAWAY	LOCKAWAY	WALKAWAY
GATEWAY	RUNAWAY	CASTAWAY	MOTORWAY	WANTAWAY
GETAWAY	SHIPWAY	CAUSEWAY	MULLOWAY	WASHAWAY
HADAWAY	SIDEWAY	CLEARWAY	OVERSWAY	WASTEWAY
HALFWAY	SKIDWAY	COLORWAY	RIDGEWAY	WATERWAY
HALLWAY	SLIPWAY	CRAWLWAY	RIVERWAY	WELLAWAY
HEADWAY	SOMEWAY	CROSSWAY	ROCKAWAY	WIDTHWAY
HIGHWAY	SPURWAY	CYCLEWAY	ROLLAWAY	
	TAXIWAY	DRANGWAY	ROUTEWAY	
	THRUWAY	DRIVEWAY	SLIDEWAY	

Words that end with -WISE

Seven-letter words

AIRWISE	SUNWISE	CRABWISE	OVERWISE	TEAMWISE
ANYWISE	TAXWISE	DROPWISE	PAIRWISE	TENTWISE
ENDWISE		EDGEWISE	PALEWISE	THUSWISE
FANWISE	**Eight-letter words**	ELSEWISE	RINGWISE	WARPWISE
MANWISE		FESSWISE	SIDEWISE	WEFTWISE
MAPWISE	ARCHWISE	FLATWISE	SOMEWISE	
	BENDWISE	LIKEWISE	STEPWISE	
	COMBWISE	LONGWISE	SUCHWISE	

Words that end with -WOOD

Seven-letter words

BARWOOD	FIRWOOD	BACKWOOD	FUELWOOD	PORKWOOD
BAYWOOD	GUMWOOD	BASSWOOD	GILTWOOD	PULPWOOD
BOGWOOD	INKWOOD	BEARWOOD	HARDWOOD	ROSEWOOD
BOXWOOD	LOGWOOD	BEEFWOOD	HAREWOOD	SASSWOOD
CAMWOOD	NUTWOOD	BENTWOOD	IRONWOOD	SOFTWOOD
DAGWOOD	PLYWOOD	BLUEWOOD	KINGWOOD	SOURWOOD
DOGWOOD	REDWOOD	COLTWOOD	LACEWOOD	TEAKWOOD
DYEWOOD	SAPWOOD	CORDWOOD	LATEWOOD	WILDWOOD
ELMWOOD		CORKWOOD	MILKWOOD	WORMWOOD
FATWOOD	**Eight-letter words**	CRABWOOD	OVENWOOD	
	AGALWOOD	DEADWOOD	PEARWOOD	
		FIREWOOD	PINEWOOD	

Words that end with -WORK

Seven-letter words	WARWORK	FARMWORK	LACEWORK	SALTWORK
ARTWORK	WAXWORK	FIREWORK	LATHWORK	SCUTWORK
CUTWORK	WEBWORK	FLATWORK	LEADWORK	SEATWORK
DAYWORK		FLUEWORK	LIFEWORK	SLOPWORK
LAPWORK	**Eight-letter**	FOOTWORK	LINKWORK	STUDWORK
LEGWORK	**words**	FORMWORK	MESHWORK	TASKWORK
NETWORK	BACKWORK	FRETWORK	MILLWORK	TEAMWORK
NONWORK	BEADWORK	GOLDWORK	OPENWORK	TELEWORK
OUTWORK	BODYWORK	HACKWORK	OVERWORK	TIMEWORK
PINWORK	BOOKWORK	HAIRWORK	PARTWORK	TUBEWORK
PREWORK	BUHLWORK	HANDWORK	PILEWORK	WIREWORK
RAGWORK	BUSYWORK	HEADWORK	PIPEWORK	WOODWORK
RIBWORK	CAGEWORK	HOMEWORK	RACKWORK	WOOLWORK
TINWORK	CAPEWORK	HORNWORK	RINGWORK	YARDWORK
TOPWORK	CASEWORK	IRONWORK	ROADWORK	
TUTWORK	CRIBWORK	KNOTWORK	ROCKWORK	
	DUCTWORK	KOFTWORK	ROPEWORK	

Words that end with -WORM

Seven-letter words	RAGWORM	CLAMWORM	INCHWORM	SANDWORM
BAGWORM	SEAWORM	CORNWORM	LEAFWORM	SHIPWORM
BUDWORM	WAXWORM	FIREWORM	LINDWORM	SILKWORM
CATWORM	WEBWORM	FISHWORM	LONGWORM	SLOWWORM
CUTWORM		FLATWORM	LUNGWORM	SPANWORM
EARWORM	**Eight-letter**	GAPEWORM	MALTWORM	TAPEWORM
EELWORM	**words**	GLOWWORM	MEALWORM	TUBEWORM
LOBWORM	ARMYWORM	GRUBWORM	MUCKWORM	WHIPWORM
LUGWORM	BOLLWORM	HAIRWORM	PILLWORM	WIREWORM
PINWORM	BOOKWORM	HOOKWORM	RINGWORM	WOODWORM
	CASEWORM	HORNWORM	ROOTWORM	

Words that end with -WORT

Seven-letter words	MUDWORT	DAMEWORT	MILKWORT	SOAPWORT
AWLWORT	MUGWORT	DANEWORT	MODIWORT	STARWORT
BLAWORT	RAGWORT	DROPWORT	MOONWORT	WALLWORT
BUGWORT	RIBWORT	FLEAWORT	MOORWORT	WARTWORT
FANWORT		GOUTWORT	PILEWORT	
FELWORT	**Eight-letter**	HONEWORT	PILLWORT	
FIGWORT	**words**	HORNWORT	PIPEWORT	
MADWORT	BELLWORT	LEADWORT	SALTWORT	
	COLEWORT	LUNGWORT	SANDWORT	

Words that end with -YARD

Seven-letter words	**Eight-letter words**	DEERYARD	KAILYARD	SHIPYARD
BEEYARD	BACKYARD	DOCKYARD	KALEYARD	SHOWYARD
HALYARD	BALLYARD	DOORYARD	KIRKYARD	TILTYARD
INNYARD	BARNYARD	FARMYARD	MAINYARD	VINEYARD
LANYARD	BOATYARD	FEEDYARD	METEYARD	WHINYARD
TANYARD	BONEYARD	FOREYARD	RICKYARD	WILLYARD
	COALYARD	HAULYARD	SALEYARD	WOODYARD
		JUNKYARD	SAVOYYARD	

Vowel endings

E aside, it can be difficult to think of words that end in the vowels. But these words can be very useful. A, I, O and U represent almost a third of the tiles in the game, and there are a great many two-letter words that begin or end with vowels other than E. Words that end in vowels give you great opportunities for tagging your main word onto an exist word making a two-letter word with the vowel in the process. Or it may be that the vowel you need to end with for a double- or triple-word score is already on the board. The lists in this section detail all words from two letters to eight in length, ending in A, I, O or U. Definitions are provided for the two-letter and three-letter words.

Words that end with -A

Two-letter words

AA	volcanic rock consisting of angular blocks of lava with a very rough surface
BA	symbol for the soul in Ancient Egyptian religion
DA	Burmese knife
EA	river
FA	musical note
HA	exclamation expressing triumph, surprise, or scorn
JA	yes
KA	(in ancient Egypt) attendant spirit supposedly dwelling as a vital force in a man or statue
LA	musical note
MA	mother
NA	not
PA	father
TA	a thank you
YA	you
ZA	pizza

Three-letter words

ABA	type of cloth from Syria, made of goat hair or camel hair
AGA	title of respect, often used with the title of a senior position
AHA	exclamation expressing triumph, surprise, etc, according to the intonation of the speaker
AIA	female servant in East
AKA	vine, *Metrosideros scandens*, found in New Zealand
ALA	wing or flat winglike process or structure, such as a part of some bones and cartilages
AMA	vessel for water
ANA	(of ingredients in a prescription) in equal quantities
AUA	yellow-eye mullet
AVA	at all
AWA	away
BAA	make the characteristic bleating sound of a sheep
BOA	large nonvenomous snake

BRA	brassiere
CAA	to call
CHA	tea
ERA	period of time
ETA	seventh letter in the Greek alphabet
FAA	to fall
FRA	brother: a title given to an Italian monk or friar
GOA	type of gazelle
HOA	to cause to stop
ITA	type of palm
KEA	large brownish-green parrot of NZ
KOA	Hawaiian leguminous tree
LEA	meadow
MAA	(of goats) to bleat
MNA	Greek weight
MOA	large extinct flightless New Zealand bird
OBA	(in W Africa) a Yoruba chief or ruler
OCA	any of various South American herbaceous plants
ODA	room in a harem
OKA	unit of weight used in Turkey
ORA	plural of os, bone
OVA	plural of ovum, egg
PEA	plant with seeds growing in pods
PIA	membrane that covers the brain and spinal cord
POA	type of grass
PYA	monetary unit of Myanmar worth one hundredth of a kyat
QUA	in the capacity of
RIA	long narrow inlet of the seacoast, being a former valley that was submerged by a rise in the level of the sea. Rias are found esp on the coasts of SW Ireland and NW Spain
RYA	type of rug originating in Scandinavia
SEA	mass of salt water covering three quarters of the earth's surface
SHA	be quiet
SKA	type of West Indian pop music of the 1960s
SMA	small
SPA	resort with a mineral-water spring

TEA	drink made from infusing the dried leaves of an Asian bush in boiling water		VIA	a roadway
			WHA	who
			YEA	yes
TWA	two		ZEA	a maize extract
UTA	side-blotched lizard		ZOA	plural of zoon, creature
UVA	grape or fruit resembling this			

Four-letter words

	CHIA	HUIA	MALA	PIKA
	COCA	HULA	MAMA	PILA
ABBA	CODA	HUMA	MANA	PIMA
ACCA	COLA	HYLA	MARA	PINA
ACTA	COMA	IDEA	MASA	PIPA
AGHA	COXA	ILEA	MAYA	PITA
AGMA	CRIA	ILIA	MEGA	PLEA
AIDA	CYMA	ILKA	MELA	PROA
AIGA	DADA	INIA	MESA	PUHA
ALBA	DATA	IOTA	META	PUJA
ALFA	DEVA	ISBA	MICA	PUKA
ALGA	DIKA	ISNA	MIHA	PULA
ALMA	DISA	IXIA	MINA	PUMA
AMIA	DITA	JAFA	MOLA	PUNA
AMLA	DIVA	JAGA	MONA	PUPA
ANGA	DIYA	JAVA	MORA	RACA
ANNA	DONA	JOTA	MOWA	RAGA
ANOA	DOPA	JUBA	MOXA	RAIA
ANSA	DUKA	JUGA	MOYA	RAJA
ANTA	DUMA	JURA	MURA	RANA
AQUA	DURA	KAKA	MYNA	RATA
ARBA	EGMA	KAMA	NADA	RAYA
AREA	EINA	KANA	NAGA	RHEA
ARIA	EKKA	KAPA	NALA	RIBA
ARNA	EMMA	KARA	NANA	RIMA
ARPA	EPHA	KATA	NAPA	RIVA
ASEA	ETNA	KAVA	NEMA	RIZA
ATMA	EYRA	KAWA	NIPA	ROMA
ATUA	FAVA	KETA	NOMA	ROTA
AULA	FETA	KINA	NONA	RUGA
AURA	FILA	KIVA	NOTA	RUSA
BABA	FLEA	KOHA	NOVA	SAGA
BEMA	FORA	KOKA	OBIA	SAMA
BETA	GAGA	KOLA	OCTA	SENA
BIGA	GALA	KORA	ODEA	SERA
BIMA	GAMA	KUIA	OHIA	SETA
BOBA	GENA	KULA	OKRA	SHEA
BOLA	GETA	KUNA	OKTA	SHWA
BOMA	GIGA	KUTA	OLEA	SIDA
BONA	GILA	LAMA	OLLA	SIKA
BORA	GLIA	LANA	ORCA	SIMA
BOTA	GORA	LAVA	ORRA	SKUA
BUBA	GUGA	LEVA	OSSA	SOBA
BUDA	GULA	LIMA	OUMA	SOCA
BUNA	HAHA	LIPA	OUPA	SODA
BURA	HAKA	LIRA	PACA	SOFA
CABA	HILA	LOCA	PAPA	SOJA
CACA	HIYA	LOMA	PARA	SOLA
CAMA	HOHA	LOTA	PAUA	SOMA
CAPA	HOKA	LUMA	PAWA	SORA
CASA	HOMA	LUNA	PEBA	SOYA
CAVA	HORA	LYRA	PELA	STOA
CECA	HOYA	MAHA	PICA	SUBA

SURA	**Five-letter**	BATTA	COTTA	FORZA
TAHA	**words**	BELGA	COUTA	FOSSA
TAKA	ABACA	BENGA	CRENA	FOVEA
TALA	ABAKA	BETTA	CRURA	FRENA
TANA	ABAYA	BHUNA	CULPA	FURCA
TAPA	ABOMA	BIGHA	CUPPA	GABBA
TARA	ABUNA	BIOTA	CURIA	GAITA
TAVA	ACETA	BIVIA	DABBA	GALEA
TAWA	ADYTA	BOCCA	DACHA	GAMBA
TAXA	AECIA	BOHEA	DAGGA	GAMMA
TELA	AFARA	BONZA	DARGA	GANJA
TEPA	AGAMA	BORNA	DELTA	GARDA
TIKA	AGILA	BOYLA	DERMA	GEMMA
TINA	AGITA	BRAVA	DICTA	GENOA
TOEA	AGORA	BRAZA	DINNA	GENUA
TOGA	AGRIA	BUBBA	DIOTA	GLEBA
TOLA	AGUNA	BUFFA	DIVNA	GOGGA
TORA	AINGA	BULLA	DOBLA	GOMPA
TOSA	AJIVA	BUNIA	DOBRA	GONIA
TUBA	AJUGA	BUNYA	DOGMA	GONNA
TUFA	AKELA	BURKA	DOLIA	GOTTA
TUNA	AKITA	BURQA	DOLMA	GOURA
ULNA	ALAPA	BURSA	DONGA	GRAMA
ULVA	ALDEA	BWANA	DONNA	GRANA
UMMA	ALIYA	CAECA	DOONA	GROMA
UMRA	ALOHA	CALLA	DORBA	GUANA
UPTA	ALPHA	CALPA	DORSA	GUAVA
UREA	ALULA	CANNA	DOULA	GUMMA
URSA	AMEBA	CARTA	DOUMA	GUSLA
URVA	AMIGA	CAUDA	DOURA	GUTTA
UVEA	AMNIA	CAUSA	DOWNA	GYOZA
VARA	ANANA	CEIBA	DRAMA	HAIKA
VASA	ANATA	CELLA	DUKKA	HAKEA
VEGA	ANIMA	CERIA	DULIA	HALFA
VELA	ANTRA	CESTA	DUMKA	HALMA
VENA	AORTA	CHANA	DURRA	HALVA
VERA	APNEA	CHARA	EDEMA	HAMBA
VIGA	ARABA	CHAYA	ENEMA	HAMZA
VINA	ARECA	CHEKA	ENTIA	HANSA
VISA	ARENA	CHELA	ERBIA	HAOMA
VITA	AREPA	CHICA	ERICA	HASTA
VIVA	AROBA	CHINA	ETYMA	HATHA
VOLA	AROHA	CHOLA	EXTRA	HEJRA
WAKA	AROMA	CHOTA	FACIA	HENNA
WAWA	ASANA	CHUFA	FAENA	HERMA
WEKA	ASYLA	CILIA	FANGA	HEVEA
WENA	ATRIA	CIRCA	FATWA	HIJRA
WETA	BABKA	CNIDA	FAUNA	HODJA
WHOA	BACCA	COALA	FELLA	HOLLA
YABA	BACHA	COBIA	FERIA	HONDA
YOGA	BAIZA	COBRA	FESTA	HOOKA
YUCA	BAJRA	COBZA	FETTA	HOSTA
YUGA	BAKRA	COCOA	FETWA	HOVEA
ZETA	BALSA	COLZA	FINCA	HUDNA
ZILA	BANDA	COMMA	FITNA	HURRA
ZOEA	BANIA	CONGA	FLAVA	HUTIA
ZONA	BANYA	CONIA	FLORA	HUZZA
ZUPA	BARCA	COPRA	FLOTA	HYDRA
ZYGA	BARRA	CORIA	FOLIA	HYENA
	BASTA	COSTA	FONDA	HYPHA

IDOLA	LLAMA	MUTHA	PLAYA	SANGA
INDIA	LOGIA	MYOMA	PLAZA	SANSA
INFRA	LONGA	NABLA	PLENA	SAOLA
INTRA	LOOFA	NAIRA	PLICA	SAUBA
INULA	LOUMA	NAKFA	POAKA	SAUNA
IXORA	LUBRA	NALLA	PODIA	SCALA
JAFFA	LUFFA	NAMMA	POLKA	SCAPA
JAGRA	LUTEA	NANNA	PONGA	SCENA
JARTA	LYCEA	NANUA	POOJA	SCHWA
JHALA	LYCRA	NAPPA	POOKA	SCOPA
JIBBA	LYSSA	NERKA	POPPA	SCUBA
JIRGA	LYTTA	NGANA	PORTA	SCUTA
JNANA	MAFIA	NGOMA	PRANA	SELLA
JUNTA	MAGMA	NINJA	PRESA	SELVA
KAAMA	MAHUA	NORIA	PRIMA	SENNA
KACHA	MAHWA	NORMA	PRUTA	SENSA
KAIKA	MALVA	NUBIA	PSORA	SENZA
KALPA	MALWA	NUCHA	PUCKA	SEPIA
KANGA	MAMBA	NULLA	PUKKA	SEPTA
KAPPA	MAMMA	NYALA	PULKA	SERRA
KARMA	MANGA	NYSSA	PUNGA	SESSA
KASHA	MANIA	OCREA	PUNKA	SHAMA
KEEMA	MANNA	OIDIA	PURDA	SHAYA
KEHUA	MANTA	OMASA	QIBLA	SHEVA
KERMA	MARIA	OMEGA	QORMA	SHIVA
KHAYA	MARKA	OPERA	QUENA	SHOLA
KHEDA	MASSA	ORGIA	QUINA	SHURA
KHOJA	MATZA	ORIXA	QUOTA	SIDHA
KIBLA	MBIRA	OSSIA	RAGGA	SIGLA
KINDA	MECCA	OSTIA	RAITA	SIGMA
KIPPA	MEDIA	OUIJA	RAKIA	SIGNA
KOALA	MEKKA	PACHA	RANGA	SILVA
KOFTA	MELBA	PACTA	RASTA	SIMBA
KOKRA	MENSA	PADMA	RATHA	SIRRA
KOPPA	MENTA	PAISA	REATA	SITKA
KORMA	MICRA	PAKKA	RECTA	SOFTA
KOURA	MIKRA	PALEA	REDIA	SOPRA
KRONA	MILIA	PALLA	REGMA	SORDA
KURTA	MILPA	PAMPA	REGNA	SORRA
KWELA	MIRZA	PANDA	RENGA	SORTA
LABDA	MISSA	PANGA	REPLA	SPAZA
LABIA	MOCHA	PARKA	RETIA	SPICA
LABRA	MOHUA	PARRA	RHYTA	SPINA
LAIKA	MOIRA	PASHA	RIATA	SPUTA
LAKSA	MOLLA	PASTA	RIOJA	STELA
LAMIA	MOMMA	PATKA	ROOSA	STIPA
LARVA	MOOLA	PELMA	RUANA	STOMA
LAURA	MORIA	PELTA	RUEDA	STRIA
LAVRA	MORRA	PENNA	RUMBA	STUPA
LEHUA	MOTZA	PEPLA	RUPIA	SUBHA
LEMMA	MOWRA	PEREA	RUSMA	SULFA
LEPRA	MUDRA	PHOCA	SABHA	SUMMA
LEPTA	MUGGA	PHYLA	SABRA	SUNNA
LEZZA	MULGA	PICRA	SACRA	SUPRA
LIANA	MULLA	PIETA	SADZA	SURRA
LIBRA	MUNGA	PILEA	SAIGA	SUTRA
LIMBA	MURRA	PINNA	SAKIA	SUTTA
LIMMA	MURVA	PINTA	SALPA	SYLVA
LIMPA	MUSCA	PITTA	SALSA	TAATA
LINGA	MUSHA	PIZZA	SAMBA	TABLA

TAFIA	VERRA	ABOLLA	ATAXIA	CANCHA
TAGMA	VESPA	ABULIA	ATOCIA	CANOLA
TAIGA	VESTA	ACACIA	ATONIA	CANULA
TAIRA	VIFDA	ACEDIA	AUCUBA	CAPITA
TALEA	VIGIA	ADNEXA	AURORA	CARDIA
TALMA	VILLA	AFTOSA	AVRUGA	CARINA
TALPA	VINCA	AGENDA	AXILLA	CASABA
TANGA	VIOLA	AGGADA	AZALEA	CASAVA
TANKA	VIRGA	AGOUTA	AZOLLA	CASITA
TANNA	VISTA	AHIMSA	BACKRA	CASSIA
TAPPA	VITTA	AIKONA	BACULA	CATENA
TARGA	VIVDA	AKATEA	BAHADA	CEDULA
TAYRA	VODKA	AKHARA	BAJADA	CEMBRA
TAZZA	VOEMA	ALALIA	BALATA	CENTRA
TECTA	VOILA	ALASKA	BALBOA	CESURA
TEGUA	VOLTA	ALBATA	BANANA	CHACMA
TELIA	VOLVA	ALEXIA	BARAZA	CHAETA
TENIA	VULVA	ALISMA	BARYTA	CHAKRA
TERGA	WAGGA	ALODIA	BATATA	CHALLA
TERRA	WALLA	ALOGIA	BAUERA	CHANGA
TESLA	WANNA	ALPACA	BEFANA	CHAPKA
TESTA	WHATA	ALTEZA	BEFLEA	CHARKA
TETRA	WICCA	ALTHEA	BELUGA	CHARTA
THANA	WIGGA	ALUMNA	BEMATA	CHATTA
THECA	WILGA	AMARNA	BERTHA	CHICHA
THEMA	WILJA	AMELIA	BETCHA	CHIGGA
THETA	WINNA	AMENTA	BHAJIA	CHIMLA
THUJA	WIRRA	AMOEBA	BHAKTA	CHOANA
THUYA	WISHA	AMRITA	BHOONA	CHOKRA
TIARA	WOKKA	AMUSIA	BILBOA	CHOLLA
TIBIA	WONGA	ANATTA	BOCCIA	CHORDA
TICCA	WUXIA	ANCORA	BODEGA	CHOREA
TIKKA	XENIA	ANEMIA	BONITA	CHORIA
TINEA	XOANA	ANGINA	BOONGA	CHROMA
TOMIA	YABBA	ANGOLA	BOORKA	CHUKKA
TONGA	YACCA	ANGORA	BOSHTA	CHUPPA
TONKA	YACKA	ANICCA	BRAATA	CICADA
TORTA	YAKKA	ANNONA	BRAHMA	CICALA
TREFA	YARFA	ANOPIA	BREGMA	CICUTA
TREMA	YARTA	ANOXIA	BROLGA	CINEMA
TRONA	YENTA	ANTARA	BUCKRA	CITOLA
TRYMA	YERBA	ANTLIA	BUDDHA	CLIVIA
TSUBA	YUCCA	ANURIA	BUGSHA	CLOACA
TUGRA	YURTA	APHTHA	BUNNIA	CLUSIA
TUINA	ZABRA	APNOEA	BUQSHA	COAITA
TULPA	ZAMIA	APORIA	BURKHA	COBAEA
ULAMA	ZANJA	ARAARA	BUSERA	CODEIA
ULEMA	ZANZA	ARALIA	BUSHWA	CONCHA
ULTRA	ZEBRA	ARCANA	CABALA	CONIMA
UMBRA	ZERDA	AREOLA	CABANA	CONTRA
UNCIA	ZILLA	ARGALA	CADAGA	COPITA
URBIA	ZOAEA	ARISTA	CAEOMA	COPPRA
URENA	ZONDA	ARMADA	CAFILA	COPULA
USNEA	ZOOEA	ARNICA	CALESA	CORNEA
UVULA	ZOPPA	AROLLA	CALIMA	CORNUA
VACUA		ARRIBA	CALTHA	CORONA
VANDA	**Six-letter**	ARROBA	CAMBIA	CORREA
VARIA	**words**	ASRAMA	CAMERA	CORYZA
VARNA	ABASIA	ASTHMA	CAMISA	COSMEA
VEENA	ABELIA	ATAATA	CANADA	COWPEA

CRACKA	FAVELA	HRYVNA	KIRANA	MEDAKA
CRANIA	FECULA	HULLOA	KISHKA	MEDINA
CRESTA	FEDORA	HUTZPA	KOCHIA	MEDUSA
CRISSA	FEIJOA	HYAENA	KORORA	MEGARA
CRISTA	FEMORA	HYDRIA	KORUNA	MELENA
CROWEA	FERULA	IDEATA	KUCCHA	MESETA
CRUSTA	FIBULA	IGUANA	KUMARA	METEPA
CUBICA	FIESTA	IMPALA	KUMERA	MEZUZA
CUESTA	FLAUTA	INANGA	KUTCHA	MGANGA
CUMBIA	FOOTRA	INDABA	KWACHA	MIASMA
CUPOLA	FOUSSA	INDUNA	KWANZA	MIBUNA
CUPULA	FOUTRA	INFIMA	LABARA	MIMOSA
CURARA	FRAENA	INFULA	LACUNA	MINIMA
CUTCHA	FRISKA	INJERA	LAGENA	MIZUNA
CZAPKA	FRUSTA	INSULA	LAGUNA	MODENA
DAGABA	FULCRA	INTIMA	LAMBDA	MODICA
DAGOBA	FUNKIA	INYALA	LAMINA	MOKSHA
DAHLIA	FUSUMA	ISCHIA	LATINA	MONERA
DATCHA	GALENA	ISTANA	LATRIA	MOORVA
DATURA	GAMBIA	JACANA	LEIPOA	MORCHA
DEFLEA	GARRYA	JARINA	LEXICA	MORULA
DHAMMA	GARUDA	JATAKA	LIGULA	MOTUCA
DHARMA	GEISHA	JEJUNA	LIKUTA	MUCOSA
DHARNA	GELADA	JEMIMA	LIMINA	MULETA
DHOORA	GENERA	JERBOA	LINGUA	MUMMIA
DHURNA	GENEVA	JHATKA	LIPOMA	MURENA
DHURRA	GITANA	JICAMA	LITHIA	MURRHA
DOLINA	GLIOMA	JOANNA	LOBOLA	MUTUCA
DOOSRA	GLORIA	JOJOBA	LOCHIA	MYOPIA
DUENNA	GLOSSA	JUDOKA	LOGGIA	MYRICA
DUHKHA	GNAMMA	JUGULA	LOMATA	MYXOMA
DUKKHA	GOANNA	KABAKA	LORCHA	NAGANA
DUMELA	GOONDA	KABALA	LORICA	NATURA
ECZEMA	GOPURA	KABAYA	LUCUMA	NAUSEA
EGESTA	GORGIA	KACCHA	LUMINA	NEBULA
EIDOLA	GOTCHA	KAFILA	LUNULA	NEPETA
EJECTA	GRAMMA	KAHUNA	LUSTRA	NOCTUA
ELODEA	GRAMPA	KAINGA	MABELA	NOMINA
ELUVIA	GRAPPA	KALMIA	MACOYA	NOVENA
ELYTRA	GRINGA	KAMALA	MACULA	NUMINA
EMPUSA	GUINEA	KAMELA	MAFFIA	NUTRIA
ENCINA	GYTTJA	KAMILA	MAKUTA	NYANZA
ENIGMA	HALALA	KANAKA	MALTHA	NYMPHA
ENTERA	HALLOA	KANGHA	MANAIA	OBELIA
EPEIRA	HAMADA	KANTHA	MANANA	OCHREA
EPIZOA	HANIWA	KANUKA	MANAWA	OEDEMA
EPOCHA	HAPUKA	KAPUKA	MANILA	OMENTA
ERRATA	HARIRA	KARAKA	MANTRA	OMERTA
ESPADA	HAWALA	KATANA	MANTUA	ONYCHA
EUPNEA	HEBONA	KEMBLA	MANUKA	OPTIMA
EUREKA	HEDERA	KENTIA	MARACA	ORARIA
EXACTA	HEGIRA	KERRIA	MARINA	ORBITA
EXEDRA	HEJIRA	KETMIA	MARKKA	ORGANA
EXUVIA	HEMINA	KGOTLA	MASALA	ORISHA
FACULA	HERNIA	KHANDA	MASHUA	OSCULA
FAJITA	HILLOA	KHANGA	MASULA	OSETRA
FANEGA	HOLLOA	KHODJA	MATATA	OTTAVA
FARINA	HOLMIA	KHURTA	MAUNNA	OZAENA
FASCIA	HOODIA	KINARA	MAXIMA	PAELLA
FATSIA	HOOPLA	KINEMA	MAZUMA	PAGODA

PAJAMA	QASIDA	SCROTA	TANKIA	WOMERA
PAKEHA	QUAGGA	SEMEIA	TANTRA	WOTCHA
PAKORA	QUALIA	SEMINA	TAONGA	XEROMA
PALAMA	QUANTA	SENECA	TAPETA	XYLOMA
PALAPA	QUELEA	SENEGA	TARAMA	YAKUZA
PALLIA	QUINOA	SENORA	TARSIA	YANTRA
PANADA	QUINTA	SEROSA	TEGULA	YAQONA
PANAMA	QUOKKA	SHAMBA	TELEGA	YARPHA
PAPAYA	QUOTHA	SHARIA	TEPHRA	YAUTIA
PAPULA	RADULA	SHEILA	TERATA	YOJANA
PARERA	RAFFIA	SHELTA	TERBIA	YTTRIA
PARURA	RAKIJA	SHERIA	TEREFA	YUKATA
PASELA	RAMADA	SHERPA	TERTIA	ZABETA
PASHKA	RAMBLA	SHIKSA	THANNA	ZANANA
PATACA	RAMONA	SHIRRA	THORIA	ZAPATA
PATAKA	RANULA	SHISHA	THULIA	ZAREBA
PATERA	RAPHIA	SHOORA	TINAJA	ZARIBA
PATINA	RAZZIA	SIDDHA	TIPULA	ZENANA
PAYOLA	REALIA	SIENNA	TIPUNA	ZEREBA
PELOTA	REDOWA	SIERRA	TORANA	ZERIBA
PENNIA	REGINA	SIESTA	TORULA	ZEUGMA
PERAEA	REGULA	SIFAKA	TOTARA	ZINNIA
PEREIA	RELATA	SILICA	TRAUMA	ZOARIA
PESETA	REMORA	SISTRA	TREIFA	ZOECIA
PESEWA	REMUDA	SITULA	TRIVIA	ZONULA
PESHWA	RESEDA	SKOLIA	TROIKA	ZOYSIA
PETARA	RETAMA	SMEGMA	TSAMBA	ZYGOMA
PHARMA	RETINA	SOLERA	TUATUA	
PHOBIA	RHANJA	SOMATA	TUGHRA	**Seven-letter**
PIAZZA	RHUMBA	SONATA	TUNDRA	**words**
PICARA	RISTRA	SPIREA	TUNICA	ABOMASA
PILULA	ROSTRA	SQUAMA	TUPUNA	ABOULIA
PINATA	ROSULA	SRADHA	UJAMAA	ABROSIA
PINETA	ROTULA	STADDA	ULTIMA	ACANTHA
PIRANA	RUCOLA	STADIA	UNGULA	ACAPNIA
PIRAYA	RUGOLA	STANZA	URANIA	ACCIDIA
PITARA	RUGOSA	STATUA	UREDIA	ACEQUIA
PITAYA	RUMINA	STELLA	UREMIA	ACEROLA
PLANTA	RUSSIA	STEMMA	URTICA	ACHARYA
PLASMA	SABKHA	STERNA	UTOPIA	ACHENIA
PLEURA	SAHIBA	STIGMA	VAGINA	ACHOLIA
PNEUMA	SALINA	STIRRA	VAHANA	ACICULA
POISHA	SALIVA	STOMIA	VALETA	ACRASIA
POPERA	SALVIA	STRATA	VALUTA	ACROMIA
PORINA	SAMARA	STRIGA	VARROA	ACTINIA
POSADA	SAMOSA	STROMA	VEDUTA	ACUSHLA
PRAJNA	SANCTA	STRUMA	VELETA	ADDENDA
PREMIA	SANGHA	SUBSEA	VESICA	ADENOMA
PROTEA	SAPOTA	SULPHA	VICUNA	ADHARMA
PRUINA	SASTRA	SUNDRA	VIENNA	ADIPSIA
PSYLLA	SATARA	SYLVIA	VIHARA	AECIDIA
PTERIA	SATYRA	SYNURA	VIMANA	AEROBIA
PULKHA	SCARPA	TABULA	VIMINA	AGEUSIA
PUNCTA	SCHEMA	TAENIA	VIZSLA	AGNOSIA
PURANA	SCILLA	TAFFIA	VOMICA	AGRAPHA
PYEMIA	SCLERA	TAHINA	WAIATA	AKRASIA
PYJAMA	SCOLIA	TAIAHA	WAIRUA	ALAMEDA
PYROLA	SCORIA	TAIHOA	WHATNA	ALBIZIA
PYURIA	SCOTIA	TALUKA	WHENUA	ALCHERA
QABALA	SCOZZA	TAMARA	WILTJA	ALCORZA

ALFALFA	ASHRAMA	BRITZKA	CHIASMA	DEUTZIA
ALFORJA	ASPIDIA	BRUHAHA	CHICANA	DHOURRA
ALGEBRA	ASTASIA	BUBINGA	CHIKARA	DIANOIA
ALGESIA	ASTERIA	BUCCINA	CHIMERA	DIASCIA
ALLODIA	ATALAYA	BULIMIA	CHOLERA	DICAMBA
ALLUVIA	ATEMOYA	BULLOSA	CHRISMA	DIGAMMA
ALPACCA	ATHLETA	BUMELIA	CHUTZPA	DIHEDRA
ALTEZZA	ATRESIA	BURSERA	CIBORIA	DILEMMA
ALTHAEA	ATROPIA	BUZUKIA	CIMELIA	DILUVIA
ALUMINA	AURELIA	CABBALA	CINEREA	DIORAMA
AMADODA	AUREOLA	CABOMBA	CINGULA	DIPLOMA
AMANDLA	BABESIA	CACHACA	CITHARA	DIPTERA
AMANITA	BACCARA	CADENZA	CLARKIA	DIPTYCA
AMBOINA	BACHCHA	CAESURA	COAGULA	DOGMATA
AMBOYNA	BACLAVA	CAFFILA	COCHLEA	DOMATIA
AMENTIA	BAKLAVA	CALDERA	CODEINA	DONGOLA
AMMONIA	BAKLAWA	CALLUNA	CODETTA	DOPATTA
AMNESIA	BALISTA	CALUMBA	CODILLA	DOPIAZA
AMOKURA	BANDANA	CAMELIA	COMITIA	DOULEIA
AMOROSA	BANDORA	CAMISIA	COMMATA	DRACENA
AMPHORA	BANDURA	CAMORRA	CONARIA	DRACHMA
AMPULLA	BANKSIA	CAMPANA	CONIDIA	DROSERA
AMREETA	BANSELA	CANASTA	COPAIBA	DUODENA
ANAEMIA	BARBOLA	CANDELA	COPAIVA	DUPATTA
ANALGIA	BARILLA	CANDIDA	COQUINA	DVANDVA
ANALOGA	BARISTA	CANELLA	CORALLA	DYSPNEA
ANCHUSA	BARTSIA	CANNULA	CORBINA	DYSURIA
ANCILIA	BASIDIA	CANTALA	CORDOBA	ECHIDNA
ANCILLA	BATAVIA	CANTATA	CORELLA	ECTASIA
ANERGIA	BATTUTA	CANTINA	COREMIA	ECTHYMA
ANESTRA	BAZOOKA	CANZONA	COROLLA	ECTOPIA
ANGARIA	BEFFANA	CAPUERA	CORPORA	ECTOZOA
ANGIOMA	BEGONIA	CARAMBA	CORRIDA	EDEMATA
ANHINGA	BEGORRA	CARANNA	CORTINA	EMBLEMA
ANNATTA	BERETTA	CARAUNA	CORVINA	EMERITA
ANONYMA	BERGAMA	CARBORA	COTINGA	EMPORIA
ANOPSIA	BHANGRA	CARIAMA	CRAPOLA	EMPYEMA
ANOSMIA	BIDARKA	CARIOCA	CREMONA	ENCOMIA
ANTENNA	BIENNIA	CASCARA	CRIMINA	ENDOZOA
APADANA	BIODATA	CASSABA	CROTALA	ENEMATA
APEPSIA	BIRETTA	CASSATA	CULMINA	ENTASIA
APHAGIA	BISNAGA	CASSAVA	CURACOA	ENTOZOA
APHAKIA	BIZNAGA	CASSENA	CURCUMA	EPHEDRA
APHASIA	BOFFOLA	CASSINA	CURIOSA	EPISCIA
APHELIA	BOHEMIA	CATALPA	CURTANA	EPYLLIA
APHONIA	BOLIVIA	CATASTA	CYATHIA	EQUINIA
APLASIA	BOLOGNA	CATAWBA	CYMATIA	EROTEMA
APRAXIA	BOMBORA	CAVALLA	CYPSELA	EROTICA
APTERIA	BONAMIA	CEDILLA	CZARINA	EUGENIA
AQUARIA	BONANZA	CELESTA	DAMIANA	EUGLENA
ARABICA	BONSELA	CELOSIA	DAPHNIA	EULOGIA
ARAROBA	BORONIA	CEMENTA	DAROGHA	EUPNOEA
ARCADIA	BOTHRIA	CEREBRA	DATARIA	EUTAXIA
ARCHAEA	BOTTEGA	CERVEZA	DAVIDIA	EUTEXIA
ARGYRIA	BOURKHA	CHACHKA	DECIDUA	EXCRETA
ARIETTA	BRACCIA	CHALAZA	DECURIA	EXEMPLA
ARMILLA	BRACHIA	CHALUPA	DEJECTA	EXHEDRA
ARUGOLA	BRAVURA	CHAMISA	DELENDA	EXORDIA
ARUGULA	BRECCIA	CHARKHA	DELIRIA	EXOTICA
ASCIDIA	BRITSKA	CHECHIA	DEODARA	EXTREMA

EXURBIA	GRANOLA	KARAKIA	MANCALA	NARCOMA
FALBALA	GRAVIDA	KARANGA	MANDALA	NEMESIA
FALCULA	GUARANA	KATCINA	MANDIRA	NEUROMA
FARINHA	GUEREZA	KATORGA	MANDOLA	NEURULA
FARRUCA	GUMMATA	KATSURA	MANDORA	NGARARA
FAUNULA	GUNNERA	KAUPAPA	MANILLA	NIGELLA
FAVELLA	GYNECIA	KEITLOA	MANIOCA	NIHONGA
FAZENDA	HAFTARA	KERBAYA	MANUMEA	NIRVANA
FELICIA	HAGGADA	KERYGMA	MANYATA	NONCOLA
FELUCCA	HALACHA	KHALIFA	MAQUILA	NORTENA
FERMATA	HALAKHA	KHEDIVA	MARANTA	NOTANDA
FIBROMA	HAMMADA	KIBITKA	MARASCA	NOTITIA
FILARIA	HARAMDA	KITHARA	MAREMMA	NOUMENA
FIMBRIA	HARIANA	KOEKOEA	MARGOSA	NOVALIA
FISTULA	HARISSA	KOPIYKA	MARIMBA	NOVELLA
FLORULA	HARMALA	KUCHCHA	MARKKAA	OCARINA
FLUTINA	HELLOVA	KULBASA	MARSALA	OCTAPLA
FONTINA	HELLUVA	LABELLA	MASCARA	OLEARIA
FORLANA	HEMIOLA	LACINIA	MASTABA	OLESTRA
FORMICA	HETAERA	LAMBADA	MATILDA	OMMATEA
FORMULA	HETAIRA	LAMELLA	MAXILLA	OMNIANA
FOSSULA	HEUREKA	LAMPUKA	MAZURKA	ONDATRA
FOVEOLA	HEXAPLA	LANGAHA	MEDACCA	ONYCHIA
FREESIA	HIDALGA	LANTANA	MEDRESA	OOGONIA
FRENULA	HIMATIA	LASAGNA	MEDULLA	OOTHECA
FUCHSIA	HOROEKA	LATAKIA	MEGILLA	OPHIURA
FUNCKIA	HOSANNA	LATILLA	MELISMA	OPUNTIA
FURCULA	HRYVNIA	LAVOLTA	MELODIA	OQUASSA
FURLANA	HRYVNYA	LEMMATA	MEROPIA	ORGANZA
FUSARIA	HYDROMA	LEMPIRA	MESHUGA	OROPESA
GALABEA	HYGROMA	LEUCOMA	MESTIZA	OSMUNDA
GALABIA	HYMENIA	LEUKOMA	METAZOA	OSSETRA
GALANGA	HYPOGEA	LEWISIA	MICELLA	OSTEOMA
GALATEA	HYPONEA	LINGULA	MILITIA	OSTRACA
GALLETA	HYPOXIA	LIPEMIA	MINEOLA	OSTRAKA
GALLICA	IGNATIA	LIPURIA	MINORCA	OTALGIA
GANGLIA	IKEBANA	LIXIVIA	MINUTIA	OUGUIYA
GANGSTA	ILLUVIA	LOBELIA	MITUMBA	OVERSEA
GAROUPA	IMPERIA	LOCUSTA	MOCHILA	OVIPARA
GASTREA	IMPRESA	LOGANIA	MOJARRA	OXYMORA
GAZANIA	INDICIA	LOMENTA	MOMENTA	PADELLA
GAZOOKA	INDUSIA	LORDOMA	MONARDA	PAENULA
GENISTA	INEDITA	MACCHIA	MONILIA	PAISANA
GERBERA	INERTIA	MACUMBA	MORPHIA	PALABRA
GERMINA	INFANTA	MADEIRA	MORRHUA	PALINKA
GERTCHA	INFAUNA	MADONNA	MOUSAKA	PALMYRA
GIARDIA	INGESTA	MADOQUA	MOVIOLA	PALOOKA
GINGIVA	INOCULA	MADRASA	MOZETTA	PANACEA
GLOMERA	INTRADA	MADRONA	MUDIRIA	PANDORA
GLUCINA	IPOMOEA	MAGENTA	MULATTA	PANDURA
GOBURRA	ISODICA	MAGMATA	MURAENA	PANOCHA
GODETIA	ISODOMA	MAHATMA	MUTANDA	PAPAUMA
GONDOLA	JAMBIYA	MAHONIA	MYALGIA	PAPILLA
GONIDIA	JELLABA	MAJAGUA	MYCELIA	PAPRICA
GORDITA	JIPYAPA	MALACCA	MYCELLA	PAPRIKA
GORILLA	KABBALA	MALACIA	MYELOMA	PARATHA
GOSPODA	KACHCHA	MALANGA	MYOMATA	PARAZOA
GRANDMA	KACHINA	MALARIA	MYRINGA	PAREIRA
GRANDPA	KALIMBA	MAMILLA	NANDINA	PARELLA
GRANITA	KANTELA	MAMPARA	NAPHTHA	PARERGA

PARGANA	PUNALUA	SANGRIA	STOMATA	TRYMATA
PARTITA	PUPARIA	SANTERA	STRETTA	TSANTSA
PASSATA	PUPUNHA	SAPHENA	STRIATA	TSARINA
PASTINA	PURPURA	SARCINA	SUBAQUA	TUATARA
PATAGIA	PYAEMIA	SARCOMA	SUBAREA	TUATERA
PATELLA	PYGIDIA	SARDANA	SUBIDEA	TURISTA
PAVLOVA	PYREXIA	SATSUMA	SUBPENA	TUTANIA
PAXIUBA	PYXIDIA	SAVANNA	SUBTAXA	TYMPANA
PECULIA	QUASSIA	SAXTUBA	SUCCUBA	TZARINA
PEISHWA	QUERIDA	SCAGLIA	SUDARIA	ULNARIA
PELORIA	QUINELA	SCANDIA	SULTANA	URAEMIA
PEMBINA	QUININA	SCAPULA	SUMATRA	URETHRA
PENTHIA	RABANNA	SCHISMA	SUPREMA	VACCINA
PEREIRA	RADIATA	SCHOLIA	SYCONIA	VALONEA
PERGOLA	RAMENTA	SCOPULA	SYNOVIA	VALONIA
PERIDIA	RAOULIA	SCOTOMA	SYRINGA	VALVULA
PERILLA	RASBORA	SCYBALA	TACHINA	VANESSA
PERINEA	RATAFIA	SECRETA	TAFFETA	VANILLA
PERSONA	REFUGIA	SEDILIA	TAGMATA	VARIOLA
PESSIMA	REGALIA	SELECTA	TALARIA	VASCULA
PETUNIA	REGATTA	SENHORA	TALOOKA	VEDALIA
PHILTRA	REGMATA	SENOPIA	TAMASHA	VELARIA
PIASABA	REPLICA	SEQUELA	TAMBALA	VENTANA
PIASAVA	RESIDUA	SEQUOIA	TAMBURA	VERANDA
PICCATA	RETSINA	SERIEMA	TAMPALA	VERBENA
PIGNORA	RHIZOMA	SERINGA	TANAGRA	VERRUCA
PINNULA	RHODORA	SESTINA	TANIWHA	VERRUGA
PINTADA	RHYTINA	SEVRUGA	TANTARA	VETTURA
PIRAGUA	RICKSHA	SHAHADA	TAPIOCA	VEXILLA
PIRANHA	RICOTTA	SHAMINA	TARAMEA	VIATICA
PISCINA	RIFFOLA	SHASTRA	TARTANA	VICUGNA
PITUITA	RIKISHA	SHEESHA	TAUPATA	VIDENDA
PLACITA	RIVIERA	SHEHITA	TAVERNA	VIHUELA
PLANULA	ROBINIA	SHEIKHA	TEGMINA	VINCULA
PLATINA	ROBUSTA	SHICKSA	TEMPERA	VIRANDA
PLECTRA	ROMAIKA	SHORTIA	TEMPURA	VIREMIA
PLEROMA	ROMANZA	SIGNORA	TEQUILA	VISCERA
PLUGOLA	ROMNEYA	SILESIA	TEREBRA	VIVARIA
PLUMULA	ROSACEA	SILIQUA	TESSERA	VIVERRA
PODAGRA	ROSALIA	SILPHIA	THANGKA	VOLUSPA
PODESTA	ROSARIA	SINOPIA	THEMATA	WAKANDA
POGONIA	ROSELLA	SITELLA	THRIMSA	WALLABA
POLACCA	ROSEOLA	SKIMMIA	THRYMSA	WANKSTA
POLENTA	ROTUNDA	SOKAIYA	TIKANGA	WEIGELA
POLYNIA	RUBELLA	SOLARIA	TILAPIA	WHOOPLA
POLYNYA	RUBEOLA	SOLATIA	TIMPANA	WIRILDA
POLYOMA	RUELLIA	SOREDIA	TITANIA	WOMMERA
POLYZOA	RUFIYAA	SPATULA	TOCCATA	WOODSIA
POTASSA	RUNANGA	SPECTRA	TOHEROA	WOOMERA
POUSADA	RUSALKA	SPECULA	TOHUNGA	WOORARA
PRECAVA	RUSSULA	SPICULA	TOMBOLA	WUDJULA
PREPUPA	SABELLA	SPINULA	TOMENTA	XERASIA
PRIMULA	SABURRA	SPIRAEA	TORMINA	YAMALKA
PRONOTA	SACELLA	SPIRULA	TOSTADA	YAMULKA
PROPRIA	SADHANA	SPLENIA	TOXEMIA	YESHIVA
PROPYLA	SAGITTA	SQUILLA	TRACHEA	ZAKUSKA
PROSOMA	SAGRADA	SRADDHA	TREHALA	ZAMARRA
PTERYLA	SAMBUCA	STAMINA	TRIELLA	ZANELLA
PUDENDA	SAMSARA	STASIMA	TRISULA	ZAREEBA
PUKATEA	SANGOMA	STHENIA	TRITOMA	ZEBRINA

ZEBRULA	ANTHODIA	BLASTULA	CHATCHKA	DIASPORA
ZELKOVA	ANTIDORA	BOLTONIA	CHICKPEA	DIASTEMA
ZEMSTVA	ANTISERA	BONSELLA	CHILLADA	DIATRETA
ZENAIDA	ANTPITTA	BORRELIA	CHIMAERA	DICENTRA
ZIGANKA	APIMANIA	BOTANICA	CHIMINEA	DICHASIA
ZIMOCCA	APOLOGIA	BOTTARGA	CHINAMPA	DIELYTRA
ZINGARA	APOSITIA	BRACIOLA	CHINKARA	DIPLEGIA
ZIZANIA	APYREXIA	BRANCHIA	CHIRAGRA	DIPLOPIA
ZOOECIA	ARAPAIMA	BRASSICA	CHLOASMA	DIPLOZOA
ZOOGLEA	ARAPONGA	BREGMATA	CHOLEMIA	DJELLABA
ZORILLA	ARAPUNGA	BRESAOLA	CHURINGA	DRACAENA
ZYZZYVA	ARBORETA	BRITZSKA	CHYLURIA	DULCIANA
	ARETHUSA	BROMELIA	CIABATTA	DULCINEA
Eight-letter	ARMONICA	BRONCHIA	CINCHONA	DYSCHROA
words	ARYTHMIA	BROUGHTA	CISTERNA	DYSLALIA
ABDOMINA	ASHTANGA	BROUHAHA	CLAUSTRA	DYSLEXIA
ABRACHIA	ASPERMIA	BRUCELLA	CLAUSULA	DYSMELIA
ABSCISSA	ASPHYXIA	BUDDLEIA	CLITELLA	DYSPNOEA
ACADEMIA	ASPIRATA	BURLETTA	COCCIDIA	DYSTAXIA
ACELDAMA	ASTHENIA	CAATINGA	COCINERA	DYSTOCIA
ACHAENIA	ASTIGMIA	CABRESTA	COCOBOLA	DYSTONIA
ACHILLEA	ASYNDETA	CABRETTA	COENOBIA	DYSTOPIA
ACIDEMIA	ATARAXIA	CABRILLA	COLCHICA	EARTHPEA
ACIDURIA	ATHEROMA	CACHEXIA	COLLEGIA	ECCLESIA
ADESPOTA	ATROPHIA	CACHUCHA	COLLUVIA	EFFLUVIA
ADULARIA	AUBRETIA	CACUMINA	COLLYRIA	EGOMANIA
ADYNAMIA	AUBRIETA	CALABAZA	COLOBOMA	EMPANADA
AGENESIA	AURICULA	CALAMATA	COLUMNEA	ENCAENIA
AGLOSSIA	AUTOMATA	CALATHEA	COMATULA	ENDAMEBA
AGNOMINA	AUTOPSIA	CALCANEA	CONFERVA	ENDOSTEA
AGRAPHIA	AVIFAUNA	CALCARIA	CONSULTA	ENGRAMMA
AGRYPNIA	AXILEMMA	CALCTUFA	CONTAGIA	ENIGMATA
AKINESIA	AXOLEMMA	CALDARIA	CONTESSA	ENTAMEBA
ALBIZZIA	AYURVEDA	CALISAYA	CONTINUA	EPENDYMA
ALGAROBA	AZOTEMIA	CALVARIA	CONURBIA	EPHEMERA
ALIGARTA	AZOTURIA	CALYPTRA	COPREMIA	EPICEDIA
ALLELUIA	BABIRUSA	CAMBOGIA	COPROSMA	EPIFAUNA
ALOCASIA	BABUSHKA	CAMELLIA	COQUILLA	EPIMYSIA
ALOPECIA	BACTERIA	CAMPAGNA	CORMIDIA	EPITHECA
AMBERINA	BAIDARKA	CAPITULA	COXALGIA	EPITHEMA
AMBROSIA	BALLISTA	CAPOEIRA	CREDENDA	EPOPOEIA
AMPHIBIA	BANDANNA	CAPONATA	CREDENZA	EQUISETA
AMYGDALA	BANDEIRA	CAPYBARA	CRIBELLA	ERYTHEMA
ANABAENA	BAPTISIA	CARACARA	CRITERIA	ESTANCIA
ANACONDA	BARATHEA	CARAGANA	CROMORNA	ESTHESIA
ANALECTA	BARRANCA	CARNAUBA	CTENIDIA	ETCETERA
ANALEMMA	BASILICA	CARPALIA	CUBICULA	EUPEPSIA
ANAPHORA	BATTALIA	CASTELLA	CUNABULA	EUPHOBIA
ANASARCA	BAUHINIA	CATHEDRA	CUTICULA	EUPHONIA
ANATHEMA	BEDSONIA	CATHISMA	CYMBIDIA	EUPHORIA
ANECDOTA	BERGENIA	CATTLEYA	CZAREVNA	EUTHYMIA
ANGELICA	BERRETTA	CAVATINA	CZARITSA	EXCERPTA
ANIRIDIA	BERYLLIA	CECROPIA	CZARITZA	EXONUMIA
ANOESTRA	BETHESDA	CELOMATA	DAHABIYA	FALDETTA
ANOOPSIA	BIGNONIA	CERCARIA	DECENNIA	FANEGADA
ANOREXIA	BIRRETTA	CHALAZIA	DEMENTIA	FANTASIA
ANOXEMIA	BISCACHA	CHAMPACA	DEMERARA	FASCIOLA
ANTEFIXA	BIZCACHA	CHAQUETA	DENTALIA	FASCISTA
ANTHELIA	BLASTEMA	CHARANGA	DENTARIA	FEIJOADA
ANTHEMIA	BLASTOMA	CHARISMA	DIARRHEA	FENESTRA

FETERITA	HEPATICA	LINGUISA	MUCHACHA	PIGNOLIA
FIBRILLA	HEPATOMA	LIPAEMIA	MYCETOMA	PITAHAYA
FISTIANA	HERBARIA	LIPOMATA	MYOTONIA	PIZZERIA
FLABELLA	HETAIRIA	LISTERIA	MYXAMEBA	PLACENTA
FLAGELLA	HEUCHERA	LITHEMIA	MYXEDEMA	PLANARIA
FLOTILLA	HINAHINA	LODICULA	MYXOMATA	PLANURIA
FOCACCIA	HIRAGANA	LONICERA	NASSELLA	PLATANNA
FORAMINA	HORDEOLA	LYMPHOMA	NAVICULA	PLATYSMA
FRITTATA	HOROKAKA	MACAHUBA	NOCTURIA	PLETHORA
FUGHETTA	HOSPITIA	MADRASSA	NONQUOTA	PLUMERIA
FURCRAEA	HYDREMIA	MAGNESIA	NUBECULA	POLLINIA
GALABIYA	HYDRILLA	MAGNOLIA	NYMPHAEA	POLYGALA
GALLABEA	HYDROZOA	MAHARAJA	OCCIPITA	POLYPNEA
GALLABIA	HYPALGIA	MAIOLICA	ODONTOMA	POLYURIA
GALLERIA	HYPHEMIA	MAJOLICA	OEDEMATA	POSTCAVA
GALTONIA	HYPOGAEA	MALAROMA	OITICICA	PREDELLA
GAMBETTA	HYPONOIA	MALVASIA	OLIGEMIA	PRESCUTA
GAMBUSIA	HYPOPNEA	MAMALIGA	OLIGURIA	PRESIDIA
GAMMADIA	HYSTERIA	MAMMILLA	OMBRELLA	PROFORMA
GAMMATIA	ICEKHANA	MANDIOCA	OMNIVORA	PROGERIA
GARCINIA	IMPLUVIA	MANDORLA	ONGAONGA	PROTOZOA
GARDENIA	INSIGNIA	MANTILLA	OPERCULA	PRUNELLA
GASTRAEA	INSOMNIA	MANTISSA	OPERETTA	PRYTANEA
GASTRULA	INTARSIA	MANUBRIA	OPUSCULA	PSORALEA
GELSEMIA	INTIFADA	MANYATTA	ORCHELLA	PTERYGIA
GEMATRIA	ISABELLA	MARCELLA	ORCHILLA	PUERPERA
GERARDIA	ISCHEMIA	MARCHESA	PAHAUTEA	PUTAMINA
GEROPIGA	ISCHURIA	MARINARA	PALESTRA	PYCNIDIA
GESNERIA	IZVESTIA	MARINERA	PALLADIA	PYODERMA
GLABELLA	JAPONICA	MARIPOSA	PALPEBRA	PYORRHEA
GLADIOLA	JARARACA	MARSUPIA	PANATELA	QINDARKA
GLAUCOMA	JARARAKA	MARTYRIA	PANCETTA	QINTARKA
GLIOMATA	JATROPHA	MASSOOLA	PANDEMIA	QUADRIGA
GLORIOSA	JAVELINA	MATADORA	PANETELA	QUILLAIA
GLOSSINA	JIPIJAPA	MATAMATA	PANMIXIA	QUILLAJA
GLOXINIA	KALAMATA	MAUSOLEA	PANORAMA	QUINELLA
GLUMELLA	KALYPTRA	MAZAEDIA	PARABEMA	QUINIELA
GLYCEMIA	KAMAAINA	MAZOURKA	PARABOLA	RACHILLA
GLYCERIA	KARATEKA	MBAQANGA	PARANOEA	RADIALIA
GOLCONDA	KAREAREA	MECHITZA	PARANOIA	RAKSHASA
GOLFIANA	KATAKANA	MELANOMA	PARAPARA	RAMTILLA
GOLGOTHA	KATCHINA	MELODICA	PARHELIA	RANGIORA
GUERILLA	KAUMATUA	MENSTRUA	PAROEMIA	RAPHANIA
GURDWARA	KAVAKAVA	MESHUGGA	PAROSMIA	REDDENDA
GYMKHANA	KAWAKAWA	MESOGLEA	PAROUSIA	RENDZINA
GYMNASIA	KAZATZKA	METADATA	PASHMINA	REPTILIA
GYNAECEA	KERATOMA	METANOIA	PELLAGRA	RESINATA
GYNAECIA	KHANSAMA	METASOMA	PENUMBRA	RESPONSA
GYNOECIA	KIELBASA	MIASMATA	PEPONIDA	RETICULA
HABANERA	KINAKINA	MILIARIA	PERFECTA	RETINULA
HACIENDA	KRAMERIA	MILTONIA	PERIAGUA	REWAREWA
HAMARTIA	LABRUSCA	MINNEOLA	PETECHIA	RHIZOBIA
HAPHTARA	LAVALAVA	MOKOPUNA	PHACELIA	ROSTELLA
HAPLOPIA	LAVATERA	MOLLUSCA	PHELONIA	RUTABAGA
HATTERIA	LECANORA	MONSTERA	PHOTINIA	SACRARIA
HEARTPEA	LEKGOTLA	MONTARIA	PHOTOPIA	SALICETA
HEKETARA	LEUCEMIA	MOUSSAKA	PHRYGANA	SALSILLA
HEMATOMA	LEUKEMIA	MOVIEOLA	PHYSALIA	SANTERIA
HEMIOLIA	LEVODOPA	MOZZETTA	PIASSABA	SAPREMIA
HEMIOPIA	LINGUICA	MRIDANGA	PIASSAVA	SAPUCAIA

SARMENTA	SONATINA	SYNEDRIA	TRIENNIA	VIRAEMIA
SASARARA	SORBARIA	SYNERGIA	TRIFECTA	VIRGINIA
SASTRUGA	SPARTINA	SYNKARYA	TRIFORIA	VIRTUOSA
SAYONARA	SPIRILLA	SYNTAGMA	TRIHEDRA	VISCACHA
SCABIOSA	SPORIDIA	SYSSITIA	TRILEMMA	VISCARIA
SCHAPSKA	SPOROZOA	TAKAMAKA	TRIPTYCA	VITICETA
SCHEMATA	SQUAMULA	TAMANDUA	TRIPUDIA	VIVIPARA
SCIATICA	STALAGMA	TAMBOURA	TRISTEZA	VIZCACHA
SCLEREMA	STAPELIA	TAPADERA	TRITONIA	VULSELLA
SCLEROMA	STAROSTA	TAQUERIA	TROCHLEA	VUVUZELA
SCOLIOMA	STEATOMA	TEGMENTA	TROPARIA	WAHCONDA
SCOTOMIA	STEMMATA	TEGUMINA	TSAREVNA	WEIGELIA
SCOTOPIA	STERIGMA	TENACULA	TSARITSA	WISTARIA
SCROFULA	STICHERA	TENTORIA	TSARITZA	WISTERIA
SCUTELLA	STIGMATA	TEQUILLA	TZAREVNA	XANTHOMA
SEMANTRA	STOCCATA	TERATOMA	TZARITSA	XENOPHYA
SEMICOMA	STOKESIA	TERRARIA	TZARITZA	XEROMATA
SEMIGALA	STOMODEA	TERRELLA	ULTIMATA	XYLOMATA
SEMINOMA	STOTINKA	TERZETTA	UMBRELLA	YARMULKA
SEMOLINA	STROBILA	TESSELLA	UNDERSEA	YERSINIA
SEMUNCIA	STROMATA	TETRAPLA	UNGUENTA	YOKOZUNA
SENORITA	STRONTIA	THERIACA	UREDINIA	YTTERBIA
SENSILLA	SUBCOSTA	THIOTEPA	URINEMIA	ZAKOUSKA
SENSORIA	SUBMENTA	THIOUREA	UROPYGIA	ZAMBOMBA
SEPARATA	SUBPHYLA	TIGRIDIA	VACCINIA	ZAMPOGNA
SEPTARIA	SUBPOENA	TITHONIA	VAGINULA	ZARZUELA
SEPTLEVA	SUBTOPIA	TOKONOMA	VALENCIA	ZASTRUGA
SERENATA	SUBUCULA	TOPALGIA	VALLONIA	ZIRCONIA
SHAMIANA	SUBURBIA	TOQUILLA	VELAMINA	ZOIATRIA
SHECHITA	SUDAMINA	TORMENTA	VELATURA	ZOOCYTIA
SHIGELLA	SVASTIKA	TORTILLA	VENDETTA	ZOOGLOEA
SHILLALA	SWASTICA	TOURISTA	VERATRIA	ZOOMANIA
SHRADDHA	SWASTIKA	TOXAEMIA	VERONICA	ZOONOMIA
SIDALCEA	SYMPODIA	TOXOCARA	VERTEBRA	ZUCHETTA
SIGNORIA	SYMPOSIA	TRACHOMA	VESICULA	ZYGANTRA
SILICULA	SYNANGIA	TRAPEZIA	VESTIGIA	ZYGOMATA
SIMARUBA	SYNAPHEA	TRAUMATA	VIBRISSA	
SINFONIA	SYNCYTIA	TRICHINA	VICTORIA	
SITTELLA	SYNECHIA	TRIDACNA	VIEWDATA	
			VINIFERA	

Words that end with -I

Two-letter words

AI	three-toed sloth of South America
BI	bisexual person
DI	a plural of deus, god
GI	loose-fitting white martial-art suit
HI	hello
KI	Japanese martial art
LI	Chinese measurement of distance
MI	(in tonic sol-fa) the third degree of any major scale
OI	shout to attract attention
PI	sixteenth letter in the Greek alphabet
QI	(Chinese medicine) life force
SI	musical note
TI	musical note
XI	14th letter in the Greek alphabet

Three-letter words

AHI	yellowfin tuna
AMI	male friend
ANI	American bird with black plumage, long square-tipped tail, and heavily hooked bill
BOI	lesbian who dresses like a boy
CHI	22nd letter of the Greek alphabet
DEI	a plural of deus, god
DUI	a plural of duo, duet
GHI	clarified butter
HOI	interjection
HUI	meeting of Māori people
IWI	any Māori tribe
JAI	victory (to)
KAI	food
KHI	letter of the Greek alphabet

KOI	any of various ornamental forms of the common carp		SAI	South American monkey
			SEI	type of rorqual
LEI	garland of flowers		SKI	one of a pair of long runners fastened to boots for gliding over snow or water
MOI	me, used in mock affectation		
OBI	broad sash tied in a large flat bow at the back, worn by Japanese women and children		SRI	title of respect used when addressing a Hindu
			SUI	of itself
PHI	21st letter in the Greek alphabet		TAI	Chinese system of callisthenics characterized by coördinated and rhythmic movements
POI	ball of woven flax swung rhythmically by Māori women during poi dances		
PSI	23rd letter of the Greek alphabet		TUI	New Zealand honeyeater that mimics human speech and the songs of other birds
RAI	type of Algerian popular music based on traditional Algerian music influenced by modern Western pop		
			UNI	(in informal English) university
REI	name for a former Portuguese coin, more properly called a real		WAI	in New Zealand, water

Four-letter words	HILI	MUTI	TALI	ARIKI
ABRI	HIOI	NAOI	TAXI	ASKOI
ACAI	HOKI	NAZI	TIKI	ASSAI
ANTI	HORI	NEVI	TIPI	ATIGI
ARTI	IMPI	NGAI	TITI	AULOI
ASCI	INTI	NIDI	TOPI	AUREI
BANI	JEDI	NISI	TORI	AZUKI
BENI	KADI	NODI	UNAI	BAJRI
BHAI	KAKI	NONI	UNCI	BALTI
BIDI	KALI	NORI	VAGI	BAMBI
BREI	KAMI	PADI	VALI	BASSI
BUDI	KATI	PENI	VLEI	BASTI
CADI	KAZI	PERI	WADI	BEEDI
CAPI	KEPI	PFUI	WALI	BENNI
CEDI	KIWI	PIKI	WIKI	BESTI
CHAI	KOJI	PILI	WILI	BHAJI
CONI	KUFI	PIPI	YAGI	BIALI
DALI	KURI	PTUI	YETI	BINDI
DARI	KUTI	PULI	YOGI	BLINI
DEFI	LARI	PURI	YONI	BOCCI
DELI	LATI	QADI	ZARI	BODHI
DENI	LIRI	QUAI	ZATI	BOOAI
DESI	LOBI	RABI	ZITI	BRAAI
DIVI	LOCI	RAGI	ZORI	BRAVI
DIXI	LOTI	RAKI		BRIKI
DUCI	LWEI	RAMI	**Five-letter words**	BUFFI
ELHI	MAGI	RANI		BUSTI
ETUI	MAKI	ROJI	AALII	BWAZI
EUOI	MALI	ROTI	AARTI	BYSSI
FENI	MANI	SADI	ABACI	CACTI
FINI	MAXI	SAKI	ACARI	CAMPI
FOCI	MERI	SARI	ACINI	CARDI
FUCI	MIDI	SATI	ADUKI	CARPI
FUJI	MIHI	SEMI	AGAMI	CEILI
GADI	MINI	SHRI	AGGRI	CELLI
GARI	MIRI	SIMI	AGUTI	CERCI
GLEI	MOAI	SIRI	AIDOI	CESTI
GOBI	MODI	SOLI	AIOLI	CHILI
GOJI	MOKI	SORI	ALIBI	CHOLI
GORI	MOMI	SUNI	AMICI	CIPPI
GYRI	MOOI	SYLI	ANIMI	CIRRI
HAJI	MOTI	TABI	APPUI	CLAVI
	MUNI	TAKI	ARDRI	COATI

COCCI	KHAZI	PERAI	THYMI	CALAMI
COMBI	KIBBI	PETRI	TONDI	CANTHI
CORGI	KIBEI	PETTI	TOPHI	CAROLI
CORNI	KIKOI	PIANI	TOPOI	CASINI
CROCI	KIRRI	PILEI	TORII	CENTAI
CULTI	KOORI	PIRAI	TORSI	CESTOI
CUNEI	KORAI	POORI	TRAGI	CESTUI
CURLI	KRUBI	PRIMI	TSADI	CHADRI
CURSI	KUKRI	PSOAI	TUTTI	CHATTI
DARZI	KULFI	PULLI	UGALI	CHICHI
DASHI	LAARI	PUNJI	UMAMI	CHILLI
DESHI	LANAI	PUTTI	URAEI	CHOKRI
DHOBI	LASSI	QUASI	URALI	CHOWRI
DHOTI	LATHI	RABBI	URARI	CLYPEI
DHUTI	LAZZI	RADII	UTERI	COLOBI
DILLI	LENTI	RAHUI	VILLI	COLONI
DISCI	LIBRI	RANGI	VOLTI	CONGII
DOLCI	LICHI	RECTI	WONGI	CUBITI
DUOMI	LIMBI	REIKI	XYSTI	CUMULI
DURZI	LITAI	RISHI	ZIMBI	CURARI
ELCHI	LOGOI	ROSHI	ZOMBI	CYATHI
ELEMI	LUNGI	ROSTI		CYTISI
ENNUI	LURGI	RUBAI	**Six-letter**	DALASI
ENOKI	MACHI	SAKAI	**words**	DECANI
ENVOI	MANDI	SALMI	ACULEI	DEGAMI
FARCI	MAQUI	SAMPI	ADSUKI	DENARI
FASCI	MARRI	SATAI	ADZUKI	DEWANI
FASTI	MATAI	SCAPI	AGAPAI	DHIMMI
FERMI	MAURI	SCUDI	AGOUTI	DHOOTI
FILII	MEDII	SEGNI	ALFAKI	DJINNI
FILMI	MODII	SEHRI	ALKALI	DROMOI
FRATI	MOOLI	SENGI	ALUMNI	DUELLI
FUNDI	MUFTI	SENSI	AMBARI	DUETTI
FUNGI	MURRI	SENTI	ANELLI	ECHINI
GADDI	MURTI	SERAI	ANNULI	ELTCHI
GARNI	MYTHI	SHCHI	ARCHEI	EMBOLI
GENII	NAEVI	SHIAI	ARGALI	EPHEBI
GHAZI	NASHI	SHOGI	ARGULI	EPHORI
GIBLI	NGATI	SHOJI	ARILLI	EQUALI
GLOBI	NIMBI	SOLDI	ARIOSI	EURIPI
GOBBI	NISEI	SOLEI	ASKARI	EXODOI
GUSLI	NKOSI	SPAHI	AVANTI	FAMULI
HADJI	NOMOI	STOAI	BAILLI	FLOCCI
HAJJI	OBELI	STYLI	BANZAI	FRACTI
HANGI	OBOLI	SUCCI	BHAKTI	FUMULI
HIKOI	OCULI	SULCI	BHINDI	GARDAI
HONGI	OKAPI	SUSHI	BHISTI	GELATI
HOURI	ORIBI	SWAMI	BIKINI	GEMINI
IAMBI	OVOLI	TAKHI	BINDHI	GHARRI
IMARI	OZEKI	TANGI	BINGHI	GHIBLI
IMSHI	PADRI	TANTI	BOLETI	GILGAI
INDRI	PAGRI	TARSI	BONACI	GLUTEI
ISSEI	PALKI	TAWAI	BONSAI	GOMUTI
JINNI	PALPI	TELOI	BOOHAI	GRIGRI
KANJI	PAOLI	TEMPI	BORZOI	GUANXI
KARRI	PAPPI	TERAI	BUIBUI	GURAMI
KATTI	PARDI	TETRI	BUKSHI	HAIKAI
KAURI	PARKI	THAGI	BURITI	HAKARI
KHADI	PARTI	THALI	BUZUKI	HAMULI
KHAKI	PENNI	THOLI	CADAGI	HEGARI

HEISHI	NEROLI	SCYPHI	YOGINI	COENURI
HERMAI	NIELLI	SENITI	ZAIKAI	COLIBRI
HUMERI	NIGIRI	SENSEI	ZUFOLI	COLOSSI
ILLUPI	NILGAI	SESELI		CORTILI
INCAVI	NOSTOI	SHALLI	**Seven-letter**	CREMINI
INCUBI	NUCLEI	SHANTI	**words**	CRIMINI
INKOSI	OCELLI	SHTCHI	ABOMASI	DACTYLI
ISTHMI	OCTOPI	SHUFTI	ACANTHI	DAKOITI
JAWARI	OCTROI	SIDDHI	ACOUCHI	DAQUIRI
JEHADI	ONAGRI	SIFREI	AFGHANI	DASHEKI
JIHADI	OORALI	SIGLOI	ALFAQUI	DASHIKI
JOWARI	OURALI	SILENI	ALIZARI	DEMENTI
JUDOGI	OURARI	SIMPAI	ALVEOLI	DENARII
JUNGLI	OUREBI	SMALTI	AMAKOSI	DIDAKAI
JUPATI	PAKAHI	SMRITI	AMORINI	DIDAKEI
KABIKI	PAKIHI	SOLIDI	ANESTRI	DIDICOI
KABUKI	PALAGI	SOMONI	ANZIANI	DOCHMII
KAIKAI	PANINI	SONERI	APICULI	EFFENDI
KALUKI	PAPYRI	SOUARI	APPALTI	ELENCHI
KAMAHI	PATIKI	STELAI	ARCHAEI	EMERITI
KIMCHI	PERITI	STRATI	ASSAGAI	EPHEBOI
KOKIRI	PEROGI	SUNDRI	ASSEGAI	EPIGONI
KONAKI	PETSAI	SURIMI	ASTATKI	EPINAOI
KONINI	PHALLI	TABULI	BACCHII	EREMURI
KORARI	PIROGI	TAHINI	BACILLI	ETOURDI
KOUROI	PITHOI	TAMARI	BAMBINI	FAGOTTI
KOWHAI	PITURI	TANUKI	BANDARI	FIASCHI
KROONI	PLUTEI	TAPETI	BANOFFI	FLOKATI
KULAKI	POHIRI	TATAMI	BASENJI	FORZATI
KUMARI	POLYPI	TATSOI	BASMATI	FUMETTI
LAOGAI	PRIAPI	TAUIWI	BAZOUKI	FUSILLI
LAZULI	PROTEI	TAWHAI	BHISHTI	GHILGAI
LIMULI	PUJARI	TENUTI	BILIMBI	GINGELI
LITCHI	PUNANI	THALLI	BIRIANI	GINGILI
LOBULI	PURIRI	THOLOI	BIRYANI	GLUTAEI
LOCULI	PUTELI	THYRSI	BOUILLI	GNOCCHI
LUNGYI	PYLORI	TIFOSI	BREWSKI	GOURAMI
MALLEI	RAGINI	TIRITI	BROCOLI	GRADINI
MALOTI	RAMULI	TITOKI	BRONCHI	GUARANI
MANATI	RAPINI	TITULI	BUSUUTI	HALLALI
MARABI	REGULI	TOITOI	CADUCEI	HALOUMI
MARARI	RENVOI	TORULI	CALATHI	HARAMDI
MAULVI	RHOMBI	TROCHI	CALCULI	HAVARTI
MAZHBI	ROESTI	TROPHI	CALZONI	HEITIKI
MEHNDI	ROMAJI	TSOTSI	CAMOODI	HELLERI
MEISHI	RUBATI	TUFOLI	CANNOLI	HEXEREI
MILADI	RUMAKI	TULADI	CANZONI	HIBACHI
MIRCHI	SACCOI	TUMULI	CAVETTI	HOKONUI
MIRITI	SAFARI	TZADDI	CEMBALI	INKHOSI
MISHMI	SAIKEI	UAKARI	CHAPATI	INTAGLI
MODULI	SAKKOI	UMFAZI	CHARPAI	JACUZZI
MOIRAI	SALAMI	UNCINI	CHARQUI	JAMDANI
MOKIHI	SALUKI	URACHI	CHIANTI	JAMPANI
MOOLVI	SAMITI	WAKIKI	CHIASMI	JINJILI
MOPANI	SANCAI	WAPITI	CHIVARI	JUKSKEI
MUESLI	SANDHI	WARAGI	CHONDRI	KABADDI
MUNSHI	SANSEI	WASABI	CHORAGI	KACHERI
MYTHOI	SATORI	XYSTOI	CHOREGI	KAHAWAI
NAGARI	SBIRRI	YANQUI	CHUPATI	KALOOKI
NEINEI	SCAMPI	YIDAKI	CLARINI	KAMICHI

KAROSHI	PRONAOI	TAWHIRI	CALYCULI	KIELBASI
KIPUNJI	PULVINI	TERMINI	CANCELLI	KIRIGAMI
KOKOWAI	PUNAANI	THALAMI	CANTHARI	KOFTGARI
KOLBASI	QAWWALI	THROMBI	CAPITANI	KOHLRABI
KONGONI	QUILLAI	TIMPANI	CAPRICCI	KOLBASSI
KOROWAI	RABBONI	TOFUTTI	CASTRATI	KOLINSKI
LAMPUKI	RANGOLI	TOLARJI	CHAPATTI	KOMITAJI
LAPILLI	RAPPINI	TONDINI	CHAPPATI	KUMBALOI
LECYTHI	RAURIKI	TORTONI	CHIGETAI	KUMIKUMI
LEKYTHI	RAVIOLI	TRIPOLI	CHUPATTI	LEKYTHOI
MACRAMI	REMBLAI	TSUNAMI	CICERONI	LEMNISCI
MAESTRI	REREMAI	TURFSKI	CICISBEI	LEYLANDI
MAFIOSI	REVERSI	TYMPANI	CLAFOUTI	LIBRETTI
MAMMATI	RHIZOPI	URCEOLI	CONCEPTI	LINGUINI
MANKINI	RHOMBOI	VENTURI	CONCERTI	LITERATI
MARCONI	RHONCHI	VIRELAI	CONCETTI	LUMBRICI
MARTINI	RHYTHMI	VITELLI	CONDUCTI	MACARONI
MATSURI	RIKISHI	VOLVULI	CONFETTI	MAHARANI
MELTEMI	RILIEVI	WISTITI	CORNETTI	MAHIMAHI
MENISCI	RIPIENI	WOORALI	COTHURNI	MALIHINI
MERANTI	RISORII	WOORARI	CROSTINI	MALLEOLI
MINISKI	SACCULI	WOURALI	CUMBUNGI	MANUHIRI
MODELLI	SAIMIRI	ZAKUSKI	CUNJEVOI	MARAVEDI
MODIOLI	SAMADHI	ZAMPONI	DAIQUIRI	MARCHESI
MOLOSSI	SAMITHI	ZEPPOLI	DAISHIKI	MARIACHI
MONOSKI	SAMURAI	ZINGANI	DECUBITI	MENOMINI
NAUPLII	SANTIMI	ZINGARI	DIADOCHI	MONOKINI
NAUTILI	SANYASI	ZUFFOLI	DIGERATI	MORBILLI
NEGRONI	SAOUARI		DIPTEROI	NANNYGAI
NILGHAI	SARANGI	**Eight-letter**	DIVIDIVI	NARCISSI
NONETTI	SASHIMI	**words**	DOUPIONI	NENNIGAI
NUCELLI	SCALENI	ACERVULI	DRACHMAI	NIRAMIAI
NURAGHI	SCHERZI	ACOEMETI	DUPONDII	NOTTURNI
NYLGHAI	SCIRRHI	ALBERGHI	DURUKULI	NUCLEOLI
OBLASTI	SECONDI	AMARETTI	DUUMVIRI	OBLIGATI
OMPHALI	SENARII	AMORETTI	ESOPHAGI	OSTINATI
ORIGAMI	SERKALI	AMPHIOXI	FASCISMI	OUISTITI
OUAKARI	SERRATI	ANOESTRI	FASCISTI	PACHOULI
OUSTITI	SHIKARI	ANTENATI	FEDELINI	PARCHESI
PACHISI	SHIVITI	ASSEGAAI	FEMINAZI	PARCHISI
PADRONI	SIGNORI	BANDITTI	FLOCCULI	PASTICCI
PAESANI	SKYPHOI	BERIBERI	FORZANDI	PASTRAMI
PAHLAVI	SLOUGHI	BHELPURI	FRASCATI	PASTROMI
PALAZZI	SONDELI	BIMBASHI	FUNICULI	PATUTUKI
PANDANI	SOPRANI	BIRIYANI	GINGELLI	PECORINI
PARODOI	SORDINI	BISCOTTI	GINGILLI	PEDICULI
PECCAVI	SPINONI	BONAMANI	GINGLYMI	PEPERONI
PENTITI	SPLENII	BORLOTTI	GLADIOLI	PERFECTI
PENUCHI	SPUMONI	BOSTANGI	GRAFFITI	PERIBOLI
PIEROGI	STAMNOI	BOUSOUKI	GRISSINI	PERRADII
PIGNOLI	STICHOI	BOUZOUKI	HAEREMAI	PIHOIHOI
PINDARI	STIMULI	BOZZETTI	HALLOUMI	PIROSHKI
PIROGHI	STRETTI	BRAHMANI	HETAIRAI	PIROZHKI
PIROJKI	SUCCUBI	BRINDISI	HYDROSKI	POPLITEI
PLATYPI	SUFFARI	BROCCOLI	IGNORAMI	POSTNATI
POLYNYI	SUNDARI	BUCATINI	JALFREZI	PRINCIPI
PORANGI	SURCULI	BUMALOTI	KACHAHRI	PRODROMI
PORCINI	SYLLABI	BUZKASHI	KAKARIKI	PULVILLI
POWHIRI	TABOULI	CALAMARI	KAZACHKI	RASMALAI
PRELUDI	TANKINI	CALCANEI	KAZATSKI	RENMINBI

RETIARII	SHANGHAI	STOTINKI	TERIYAKI	VIRTUOSI
RIGATONI	SHERWANI	STROBILI	TERZETTI	WATERSKI
RISPETTI	SHILINGI	SUKIYAKI	THESAURI	WHARENUI
RYOTWARI	SIGISBEI	SUMOTORI	TORTELLI	YAKITORI
SANNYASI	SIGNIORI	TABBOULI	TRAPEZII	ZAKOUSKI
SARTORII	SOFFIONI	TAGLIONI	TROCHILI	ZASTRUGI
SASTRUGI	SOLFEGGI	TANDOORI	TZATZIKI	ZECCHINI
SCALDINI	SOUVLAKI	TARAKIHI	UMBILICI	ZOOPHORI
SEXTARII	STACCATI	TEOCALLI	URANISCI	ZUCCHINI
SFORZATI	STAPEDII	TERAKIHI	UTRICULI	

Words that end with -O

Two-letter words

BO	exclamation uttered to startle or surprise someone, esp a child in a game
DO	perform or complete (a deed or action)
GO	move to or from a place
HO	derogatory term for a woman
IO	interjection expressing joy
JO	Scots word for sweetheart
KO	(in New Zealand) traditional digging tool
LO	look!
MO	moment
NO	denial, disagreement, or refusal
OO	(Scots) wool
PO	chamber pot
SO	such an extent
TO	indicating movement towards
WO	archaic spelling of woe, grief
YO	expression used as a greeting or to attract someone's attention
ZO	Tibetan breed of cattle, developed by crossing the yak with common cattle

Three-letter words

ABO	an offensive term for an aborigine
ADO	fuss, trouble
AGO	in the past
APO	type of protein
AVO	Macao currency unit
AZO	of, consisting of, or containing the divalent nitrogen group -N:N-
BIO	biography
BOO	to shout disapproval
BRO	brother or close friend
COO	(of a dove or pigeon) to make a soft murmuring sound
DOO	dove
DSO	Tibetan breed of cattle
DUO	duet
DZO	Tibetan breed of cattle
ECO	short for ecology
EGO	conscious mind of an individual
EMO	type of music combining hard rock with emotional lyrics
EVO	informal Australian word for evening
EXO	informal Australian word for excellent
FRO	away
GEO	gully, creek
GIO	gully, creek
GOO	sticky substance
HAO	monetary unit of Vietnam, worth one tenth of a dõng
HOO	interjection of boisterous emotion
ISO	short segment of film that can be replayed easily
LOO	lavatory
MHO	unit of electrical conductance
MOO	(of a cow) to make a long deep cry
NOO	now
OBO	ship carrying oil and ore
OHO	exclamation expressing surprise, exultation, or derision
ONO	Hawaiian fish
OXO	acid that contains oxygen
PHO	Vietnamese noodle soup
POO	defecate
PRO	in favour of
REO	language
RHO	17th letter in the Greek alphabet, a consonant transliterated as R or RH
ROO	kangaroo
TAO	(in Confucian philosophy) path of virtuous conduct
THO	though
TOO	also, as well
TWO	one more than one
UDO	stout perennial plant of Japan and China with berry-like black fruits and young shoots that are edible when blanched
UFO	flying saucer
UPO	upon
WHO	which person
WOO	to seek the love or affection of
YGO	obsolete past tense of go
ZHO	Tibetan breed of cattle
ZOO	place where live animals are kept for show

Four-letter words

AERO	EXPO	MANO	THIO	BANJO
AFRO	FADO	MAYO	THRO	BARDO
AGIO	FANO	MEMO	TIRO	BARRO
ALCO	FARO	MENO	TOCO	BASHO
ALKO	FICO	MICO	TOHO	BASSO
ALOO	FIDO	MILO	TOKO	BASTO
ALSO	FIGO	MINO	TOMO	BAZOO
ALTO	FILO	MIRO	TOPO	BEANO
AMBO	FINO	MISO	TORO	BENTO
AMMO	GAJO	MOFO	TOYO	BERKO
ANNO	GAPO	MOJO	TRIO	BIFFO
APSO	GIRO	MOKO	TYPO	BILBO
ARCO	GOBO	MONO	TYRO	BIMBO
ARVO	GOGO	MOZO	UMBO	BINGO
AUTO	GYRO	MUSO	UNCO	BIZZO
BEGO	HALO	MYXO	UNDO	BOFFO
BIRO	HARO	NOLO	UNTO	BOMBO
BITO	HELO	ODSO	UPDO	BONGO
BOHO	HERO	OLEO	UPGO	BORGO
BOKO	HOBO	OLIO	URAO	BRAVO
BOLO	HOMO	ONTO	VEGO	BROMO
BOYO	HUSO	OPPO	VETO	BUCKO
BOZO	HYPO	ORDO	VINO	BUFFO
BRIO	INFO	ORZO	VIVO	BUMBO
BROO	INGO	OTTO	WERO	BUNCO
BUBO	INRO	OUZO	WHIO	BUNKO
BUDO	INTO	PACO	WINO	BUROO
BUFO	JATO	PEPO	YEBO	BURRO
CALO	JIAO	PESO	YUKO	BUTEO
CAMO	JOCO	PISO	ZERO	CACAO
CAPO	JOMO	POCO	ZOBO	CAMEO
CERO	JUCO	POGO		CAMPO
CHAO	JUDO	POLO	**Five-letter words**	CANSO
CIAO	KAGO	POMO		CANTO
CITO	KARO	PRAO	ABMHO	CARBO
COCO	KAYO	PROO	ACHOO	CARGO
COHO	KENO	PYRO	ADDIO	CASCO
DADO	KERO	RATO	ADOBO	CELLO
DAGO	KETO	REDO	AGGRO	CENTO
DATO	KILO	REGO	AGLOO	CHACO
DECO	KINO	REPO	ALAMO	CHADO
DEFO	KOBO	RIVO	ALTHO	CHEMO
DELO	KOLO	ROTO	AMIDO	CHIAO
DEMO	KORO	SADO	AMIGO	CHICO
DERO	KOTO	SAGO	AMINO	CHIMO
DIDO	KUDO	SECO	AMNIO	CHINO
DINO	KYBO	SEGO	ANCHO	CHIRO
DIVO	LAZO	SHMO	ANDRO	CHOCO
DOCO	LENO	SHOO	ANGLO	CHOKO
DODO	LEVO	SIJO	APPRO	CHOLO
DOJO	LIDO	SILO	ASPRO	CISCO
DURO	LIMO	SKEO	AUDIO	CLARO
DZHO	LINO	SKIO	AVISO	COCCO
ECCO	LIPO	SOHO	AWATO	COMBO
ECHO	LOBO	SOLO	AWETO	COMMO
EDDO	LOCO	SUGO	AZIDO	COMPO
ERGO	LOGO	SUMO	BABOO	CONDO
EURO	LOTO	SYBO	BACCO	CONGO
	LUDO	TACO	BALOO	CONTO
	MAKO	TARO	BANCO	CONVO

CORNO	GODSO	MANGO	POSHO	STENO
CORSO	GOMBO	MANTO	POTOO	STYLO
CREDO	GONZO	MATLO	POTTO	SULFO
CUFFO	GREBO	MATZO	PRIMO	TABOO
CURIO	GREGO	MENTO	PROMO	TACHO
CUSSO	GUACO	MESTO	PROSO	TAIKO
CUTTO	GUANO	METHO	PROTO	TANGO
CYANO	GUIRO	METRO	PUBCO	TANTO
CYCLO	GUMBO	MEZZO	PULAO	TARDO
DAIKO	GUSTO	MICRO	PULMO	TELCO
DANIO	GYPPO	MILKO	PUNTO	TEMPO
DATTO	HALLO	MIMEO	PUTTO	TENNO
DECKO	HELIO	MISDO	QUINO	THORO
DEFFO	HELLO	MISGO	QUIPO	TIMBO
DEKKO	HILLO	MOLTO	RADIO	TONDO
DERRO	HIMBO	MONDO	RATIO	TORSO
DIAZO	HIPPO	MONGO	RATOO	TRIGO
DILDO	HOLLO	MORRO	RAUPO	TRUGO
DINGO	HOWSO	MOSSO	RAZOO	TURBO
DIPSO	HULLO	MOTTO	REALO	TYPTO
DISCO	HYDRO	MUCHO	RECCO	UREDO
DITTO	IGAPO	MUCRO	RECTO	VERSO
DOBRO	IGLOO	MUNGO	REFFO	VIDEO
DOGGO	IMAGO	NACHO	REGGO	VIREO
DOHYO	IMIDO	NAPOO	REPRO	VISTO
DONKO	IMINO	NARCO	RESTO	VULGO
DRACO	INTRO	NEGRO	RETRO	WACKO
DSOBO	IROKO	NGAIO	RHINO	WAHOO
DSOMO	JAMBO	NITRO	RODEO	WALDO
DUBBO	JELLO	NUTSO	ROMEO	WAZOO
DUMBO	JINGO	ORTHO	RONDO	WHAMO
DUNNO	JOCKO	OUTDO	RONEO	WHOSO
DUOMO	JUMBO	OUTGO	RUMBO	WILCO
ERUGO	JUNCO	OUTRO	RUMPO	YAHOO
ESTRO	JUNTO	OVOLO	SADDO	YARCO
FANGO	KAROO	PAEDO	SALTO	YARTO
FATSO	KAZOO	PANKO	SALVO	YOBBO
FIBRO	KEENO	PANTO	SAMBO	YUCKO
FILLO	KEMBO	PAOLO	SANGO	YUMMO
FLEXO	KENDO	PAREO	SANKO	ZAMBO
FOLIO	KIDDO	PARGO	SANTO	ZHOMO
FORDO	KIMBO	PARVO	SARGO	ZINCO
FORGO	KONDO	PASEO	SCHMO	ZIPPO
FUERO	KUSSO	PATIO	SCUDO	ZOCCO
FUGIO	LAEVO	PEDRO	SECCO	ZOPPO
FUNGO	LARGO	PENGO	SEGNO	ZORRO
GADJO	LASSO	PESTO	SERVO	
GADSO	LAZZO	PETTO	SEXTO	**Six-letter**
GALVO	LENTO	PHONO	SHAKO	**words**
GAMBO	LESBO	PHOTO	SHISO	ABRAZO
GARBO	LEUCO	PIANO	SICKO	ADAGIO
GAZOO	LIMBO	PIEZO	SIXMO	ADJIGO
GECKO	LINGO	PILAO	SKIMO	AERUGO
GENRO	LITHO	PINGO	SMOKO	AHCHOO
GESSO	LLANO	PINKO	SOCKO	AIKIDO
GINZO	LOTTO	PINTO	SOLDO	AKIMBO
GIPPO	MACHO	PISCO	SORBO	ALBEDO
GISMO	MACRO	POLIO	SORDO	ALBINO
GIZMO	MAIKO	PONGO	SORGO	ALBUGO
GOBBO	MAMBO	PORNO	SPADO	ALNICO

AMMINO	CONCHO	GUANGO	MOJITO	RUBIGO
AMMONO	COOCOO	HAIRDO	MOKORO	SAMFOO
ANATTO	COROZO	HALLOO	MONOAO	SANCHO
ANGICO	CRAMBO	HERETO	MOOLOO	SANPRO
APOLLO	CRYPTO	HETERO	MORPHO	SAPEGO
ARIOSO	CUATRO	HOLLOO	NANDOO	SBIRRO
ARISTO	CUCKOO	HONCHO	NARDOO	SCAMTO
ARROYO	DAIMIO	HOODOO	NIELLO	SCHIZO
ARSENO	DAIMYO	HOOPOO	NONEGO	SCRUTO
ARSINO	DAYGLO	HOOROO	NOSTRO	SHACKO
ASIAGO	DEXTRO	HULLOO	NUNCIO	SHEEPO
AUSUBO	DINERO	HUPIRO	NYMPHO	SHIPPO
AWHATO	DOMINO	IGNARO	OBENTO	SHIVOO
AWHETO	DOODOO	IMBIZO	OCTAVO	SHYPOO
BABACO	DOPPIO	INCAVO	OLINGO	SISSOO
BAGNIO	DORADO	INDIGO	OVERDO	SKIDOO
BAGUIO	DRONGO	JAZZBO	OVERGO	SLEAZO
BAMBOO	DUELLO	JINGKO	PAKOKO	SMALTO
BAROLO	DUETTO	JOURNO	PALOLO	SOLANO
BARRIO	DYNAMO	KAKAPO	PANINO	SOLITO
BASUCO	EMBRYO	KAKURO	PARAMO	SORGHO
BAYAMO	ENDURO	KARORO	PEDALO	SPEEDO
BEENTO	ENHALO	KARROO	PEPINO	SPINTO
BILLYO	ENVIRO	KATIPO	PERNIO	STALKO
BISTRO	ERINGO	KEKENO	PEROXO	STANZO
BLANCO	ERYNGO	KIMONO	PHYLLO	STATTO
BLOTTO	ESCUDO	KLEPTO	PHYSIO	STEREO
BOLERO	FASCIO	KOKAKO	PICARO	STINGO
BONITO	FIASCO	KOODOO	PIOPIO	STINKO
BONOBO	FINITO	KORERO	PLONKO	STUCCO
BOOBOO	FINSKO	KOUSSO	POMATO	STUDIO
BOOCOO	FOREDO	KWAITO	POMELO	SUBITO
BOOHOO	FOREGO	LADINO	PONCHO	TAPALO
BOOKOO	FORHOO	LANUGO	POTATO	TATTOO
BRASCO	FRANCO	LATIGO	PRESTO	TECHNO
BRILLO	FRESCO	LATINO	PRONTO	TENUTO
BROCHO	FUGATO	LAVABO	PSEUDO	TERCIO
BRONCO	FUMADO	LEGATO	PSYCHO	TEREDO
BUMALO	GABBRO	LIBERO	PUEBLO	THICKO
BURGOO	GALAGO	LIBIDO	PUKEKO	THUGGO
CABRIO	GAUCHO	LIVEDO	PUMELO	TIFOSO
CALICO	GAZABO	LOBOLO	PUNCTO	TOLEDO
CALIGO	GAZEBO	LOLIGO	QUANGO	TOMATO
CAMSHO	GELATO	LUCUMO	QUARTO	TORERO
CARDIO	GENTOO	MACACO	RABATO	TRILLO
CASHOO	GHERAO	MADURO	RACINO	TROPPO
CASINO	GHETTO	MAMAKO	RANCHO	TUKTOO
CATALO	GIGOLO	MANITO	REBATO	TUPELO
CHARRO	GINGKO	MANOAO	REBOZO	TURACO
CHEAPO	GINKGO	MAOMAO	REECHO	TUXEDO
CHEERO	GITANO	MARERO	REGULO	ULTIMO
CHOCHO	GIUSTO	MATICO	REZERO	VAUDOO
CHOCKO	GOMBRO	MATIPO	RIALTO	VELCRO
CHROMO	GOMUTO	MEDICO	RIGHTO	VIBRIO
CHURRO	GONGYO	MELANO	ROADEO	VIGORO
CICERO	GOOROO	MENUDO	ROBALO	VIRAGO
COGITO	GORGIO	MERINO	ROCOCO	VIRINO
COLUGO	GREEBO	MIKADO	ROMANO	VOMITO
COMEDO	GRINGO	MIOMBO	ROTOLO	VOODOO
COMODO	GROTTO	MODULO	RUBATO	VORAGO

VOSTRO	BUSHIDO	LLANERO	PLENIPO	SYNCHRO
WANDOO	CABILDO	LUMBAGO	POBLANO	TALLYHO
WEIRDO	CALALOO	MADRONO	POINADO	TAMARAO
WHACKO	CALANDO	MAESTRO	POMPANO	TANGELO
WHAMMO	CALYPSO	MAFIOSO	POMPELO	TARTUFO
WHATSO	CANTICO	MAGNETO	PORCINO	TENTIGO
WHIZZO	CARABAO	MALICHO	PORRIGO	TESTUDO
WHOMSO	CASSINO	MANGEAO	PORTICO	THEORBO
WOOHOO	CATTALO	MARCATO	POTOROO	THERETO
ZELOSO	CAVETTO	MARENGO	PRIMERO	TIMPANO
ZOCALO	CEMBALO	MARRANO	PRIVADO	TOBACCO
ZOOZOO	CENTAVO	MEMENTO	PROVISO	TOMBOLO
ZORINO	CENTIMO	MENDIGO	PROXIMO	TONDINO
ZUFOLO	CERRADO	MESTESO	PRURIGO	TORNADO
ZYDECO	CHAMISO	MESTINO	PUMMELO	TORPEDO
	CHANOYO	MESTIZO	QUOMODO	TOSTADO
Seven-letter	CHEERIO	MISTICO	RABBITO	TOURACO
words	CHICANO	MOCKADO	REJONEO	TREMOLO
AGITATO	CHORIZO	MODELLO	RELIEVO	TROMINO
AILANTO	CLARINO	MOMENTO	RELLENO	TWIGLOO
AKIRAHO	COMMODO	MONTERO	REVERSO	TYMPANO
ALBERGO	CONCEDO	MORELLO	RIDOTTO	UNDERDO
ALFREDO	COQUITO	MORENDO	RILIEVO	UNDERGO
ALLEGRO	CORANTO	MORISCO	RIPIENO	UNMACHO
AMORINO	CORNUTO	MOROCCO	RISOTTO	UPTEMPO
AMOROSO	CRIOLLO	MULATTO	ROGALLO	VAQUERO
ANIMATO	CRUSADO	NATHEMO	RONDINO	VERISMO
ANNATTO	CRUZADO	NAVARHO	ROSOLIO	VERTIGO
APAREJO	CURACAO	NELUMBO	RUBABOO	VIBRATO
APPALTO	CYMBALO	NITROSO	SAGUARO	VILIACO
ARBORIO	DIABOLO	NONETTO	SAHUARO	VILIAGO
ARNATTO	DINITRO	NONHERO	SALTATO	VIRANDO
ARNOTTO	EIGHTVO	NONZERO	SAMSHOO	VOLCANO
ARRIERO	ELECTRO	NORTENO	SANTERO	VOLPINO
ASINICO	EMBARGO	OKIMONO	SAPSAGO	WENDIGO
ATISHOO	ESPARTO	OLOROSO	SCALADO	WHERESO
AVOCADO	ETAERIO	OREGANO	SCHERZO	WHERETO
AZULEJO	FAGOTTO	OUTECHO	SCIOLTO	WINDIGO
BACALAO	FARRAGO	PACHUCO	SCREAMO	ZAMARRO
BAMBINO	FERRUGO	PAESANO	SECONDO	ZANJERO
BANDITO	FINNSKO	PAISANO	SEMIPRO	ZAPATEO
BAROCCO	FORZATO	PAKAPOO	SENECIO	ZEBRANO
BARRICO	FUMETTO	PALAZZO	SENTIMO	ZEMSTVO
BATTERO	FURIOSO	PAMPERO	SERPIGO	ZINGANO
BATTUTO	GAMBADO	PAPILIO	SERRANO	ZINGARO
BEEFALO	GESTAPO	PASSADO	SFUMATO	ZOCCOLO
BIZARRO	GIOCOSO	PATRICO	SHAKUDO	ZORILLO
BONIATO	GRADINO	PEDRERO	SHAMPOO	ZUFFOLO
BOTARGO	GUANACO	PEEKABO	SIROCCO	
BRACCIO	HAPKIDO	PEKEPOO	SKIDDOO	**Eight-letter**
BRACERO	HIDALGO	PENTITO	SMOKEHO	**words**
BRASERO	HISTRIO	PERSICO	SOLDADO	ALFRESCO
BRAVADO	HORNITO	PIANINO	SOPRANO	AMARETTO
BRONCHO	HUANACO	PICACHO	SORDINO	AMORETTO
BUCARDO	IMPASTO	PICCOLO	SQUACCO	ANTIHERO
BUDGERO	INFERNO	PIFFERO	STELLIO	ARMIGERO
BUFFALO	JIGABOO	PIMENTO	STRETTO	ARPEGGIO
BUGABOO	KARENGO	PINTADO	SUBECHO	ASSIENTO
BUMMALO	KERCHOO	PINTANO	SUBZERO	ATAMASCO
BURRITO	LENTIGO	PLACEBO	SUPREMO	AUTOGIRO

AUTOGYRO	COROCORO	JACKAROO	OTTAVINO	SOLIDAGO
BALLYHOO	COURANTO	JACKEROO	PACHINKO	SOMBRERO
BARBASCO	CROSTINO	JALAPENO	PADERERO	SPADILLO
BARGELLO	CRUZEIRO	JEREPIGO	PALAMINO	SPICCATO
BARRANCO	CURCULIO	JILLAROO	PALISADO	STACCATO
BESOGNIO	DOLCETTO	JORDELOO	PALMETTO	STAMPEDO
BISCOTTO	DOLOROSO	JUNKANOO	PALOMINO	STICCADO
BOCACCIO	DUECENTO	KAKEMONO	PARLANDO	STICCATO
BONAMANO	DUETTINO	KAMOKAMO	PASTITSO	STILETTO
BOOGALOO	ELDORADO	KANGAROO	PATERERO	STOCCADO
BORACHIO	ENCIERRO	KORIMAKO	PECORINO	SUBAUDIO
BORDELLO	ESCALADO	KOROMIKO	PEDERERO	SUBIMAGO
BOZZETTO	ESCAPADO	LARGANDO	PEEKABOO	SUPEREGO
BUCKAROO	ESPRESSO	LEGGIERO	PEEKAPOO	SUPERLOO
BUCKAYRO	ESPUMOSO	LENTANDO	PEPERINO	SUPERPRO
BUCKEROO	EXPRESSO	LIBECCIO	PERDENDO	SUPPEAGO
BURDIZZO	FALSETTO	LIBRETTO	PERFECTO	TALEGGIO
CABESTRO	FANDANGO	LITERATO	PIMIENTO	TAPACOLO
CABRESTO	FAROLITO	LOCOFOCO	PIQUILLO	TAPACULO
CACAFOGO	FASCISMO	LOTHARIO	PLUMBAGO	TAPADERO
CALLALOO	FELLATIO	MACHISMO	POIGNADO	TENEBRIO
CAMISADO	FINNESKO	MAESTOSO	POLITICO	TERRAZZO
CAPITANO	FINOCHIO	MAKIMONO	PRELUDIO	TERZETTO
CAPUCCIO	FLAMENCO	MALGRADO	PRERADIO	TOKOTOKO
CASTRATO	FLAMINGO	MALLECHO	PRESIDIO	TORNILLO
CAUDILLO	FORZANDO	MAMELUCO	PROSECCO	TRAPUNTO
CAVALERO	FRICANDO	MANCANDO	PRUNELLO	TRECENTO
CHARANGO	GALAPAGO	MANZELLO	PULVILIO	TUCOTUCO
CHARNECO	GARBANZO	MARTELLO	PYINKADO	TUCUTUCO
CHECHAKO	GARDYLOO	MERCAPTO	RANCHERO	TWELVEMO
CHUBASCO	GAZPACHO	MICROMHO	REDDENDO	UMBRELLO
CICISBEO	GERONIMO	MILESIMO	RENEGADO	VARGUENO
CILANTRO	GILLAROO	MILLIMHO	RIRORIRO	VARLETTO
CIOPPINO	GRACIOSO	MINIMOTO	RISOLUTO	VERDELHO
CLASSICO	GRAFFITO	MIROMIRO	RISPETTO	VIGOROSO
COCKAPOO	GRAZIOSO	MODERATO	RITENUTO	VILLAGIO
COCKATOO	GRISSINO	MOKOMOKO	ROSOGLIO	VILLIACO
COCOBOLO	GUACHARO	MONTANTO	RUBBABOO	VILLIAGO
COLORADO	HABANERO	MOSQUITO	SALTANDO	VINDALOO
COMMANDO	HALLALOO	MUCHACHO	SARGASSO	VIRTUOSO
CONCERTO	HEREINTO	MUNDUNGO	SCALDINO	VITILIGO
CONCETTO	HEREUNTO	NEUTRINO	SCENARIO	WALLAROO
CONFETTO	HITHERTO	NOCTILIO	SCIROCCO	WANDEROO
CONJUNTO	HOROPITO	NONMETRO	SCORDATO	WATERLOO
CONTANGO	HUAQUERO	NOPALITO	SEICENTO	WAYLEGGO
CONTEMPO	HUARACHO	NOTTURNO	SEMIHOBO	WHAKAIRO
CONTINUO	HUBBUBOO	OBLIGATO	SERAGLIO	YAKIMONO
CONTORNO	IMPETIGO	OCOTILLO	SESTETTO	ZECCHINO
CONVERSO	INNUENDO	ORATORIO	SFORZATO	ZUCHETTO
CORAGGIO	INTAGLIO	OSSOBUCO	SIGISBEO	
CORNETTO	INTONACO	OSTINATO	SMORZATO	

Words that end with -U

Two-letter words

GU	type of violin used in Shetland
MU	12th letter in the Greek alphabet, a consonant, transliterated as *m*
NU	13th letter in the Greek alphabet
OU	man, bloke, or chap
XU	Vietnamese currency unit
YU	jade

Three-letter words

ALU	(in Indian cookery) potato
AMU	unit of mass
AYU	small Japanese fish
BRU	(South African) informal word for a friend
CRU	(in France) a vineyard
EAU	river
ECU	any of various former French gold or silver coins
EMU	large Australian flightless bird with long legs
FEU	(in Scotland) right of use of land in return for a fixed annual payment
FLU	any of various viral infections, esp a respiratory or intestinal infection
FOU	full
GAU	district set up by the Nazi Party during the Third Reich
GJU	type of violin used in Shetland
GNU	ox-like S African antelope
JEU	game
KYU	(in judo) one of the five student grades for inexperienced competitors
LEU	standard monetary unit of Romania and Moldova
LOU	(Scots) to love
MEU	European plant
MOU	Scots form of mouth
PIU	more (quickly, softly, etc)
PLU	beaver skin used as a unit of value in the fur trade
SAU	Vietnamese currency unit
SOU	former French coin
TAU	19th letter in the Greek alphabet
ULU	type of knife
UMU	type of oven
UTU	reward
VAU	obsolete letter of Greek alphabet
YOU	person or people addressed

Four-letter words

AGLU	KUDU	TAPU	CHIRU	POYOU
AITU	KUKU	TATU	CORNU	PRAHU
BABU	KURU	TEGU	COYPU	QUIPU
BAHU	KUTU	THOU	FICHU	SADHU
BAJU	KUZU	THRU	FOGOU	SAJOU
BALU	LATU	TOFU	FONDU	SAMFU
BAPU	LEKU	TOLU	HAIKU	SHOYU
BEAU	LIEU	TUTU	HINAU	SNAFU
BEDU	LITU	UNAU	HOKKU	TATOU
BUBU	LUAU	VATU	JAMBU	TENDU
CHOU	LULU	VROU	KANZU	TUKTU
CLOU	MASU	WUDU	KAURU	UHURU
DEGU	MENU	YUZU	KAWAU	URUBU
ECRU	MEOU	ZEBU	KOMBU	VERTU
EMEU	MOTU	ZOBU	KONBU	VIRTU
ERHU	MUMU	ZULU	KUDZU	VODOU
FRAU	NAMU		LASSU	VOULU
FUGU	OMBU	**Five-letter words**	MAPAU	WAGYU
GENU	PATU	ADIEU	MIAOU	WUSHU
GURU	PRAU	AHURU	MUNTU	
HABU	PUDU	BANTU	NAIRU	**Six-letter words**
HAKU	PUKU	BATTU	NANDU	ABATTU
HAPU	PULU	BAYOU	NIKAU	ACAJOU
HUHU	PUPU	BIJOU	NOYAU	ALLYOU
IGLU	RAGU	BITOU	OTAKU	AMADOU
JEHU	RAKU	BOYAU	PAREU	APERCU
JUJU	RATU	BUCHU	PENDU	BATEAU
JUKU	RIMU	BUCKU	PERDU	BHIKHU
KAGU	RURU	BUNDU	PIKAU	BINIOU
KORU	SULU	BUSSU	PILAU	BOUBOU
	SUSU	CENTU	POILU	BUREAU
	TABU		PONZU	

CACHOU	MUUMUU	BANDEAU	PARVENU	CARCAJOU
CADEAU	MZUNGU	BATTEAU	PLATEAU	CARIACOU
CALALU	NHANDU	BEBEERU	PONCEAU	CARJACOU
CONGOU	NILGAU	BERCEAU	PURLIEU	COUMAROU
COTEAU	NOGAKU	BUNRAKU	RAUPATU	FELDGRAU
COYPOU	ORIHOU	CAMAIEU	ROKKAKU	FLAMBEAU
DETENU	ORMOLU	CANDIRU	RONDEAU	FROUFROU
EPERDU	PILLAU	CARDECU	ROULEAU	HAUSFRAU
GAGAKU	PISTOU	CARIBOU	SANTIMU	JIUJITSU
GATEAU	PIUPIU	CATECHU	SAPAJOU	JIUJUTSU
GOMOKU	QUIPPU	CATTABU	SEPPUKU	KABELJOU
GRUGRU	RAWARU	CHANOYU	SHIATSU	KEIRETSU
HALERU	RESEAU	CHAPEAU	SHIATZU	KINKAJOU
HAPUKU	ROUCOU	CHATEAU	SUBMENU	MAIREHAU
INGENU	SADDHU	CORBEAU	TABLEAU	MINSHUKU
JABIRU	SAMSHU	COUTEAU	TAMANDU	NINJITSU
KARAMU	SENRYU	DAIMOKU	TAMARAU	NINJUTSU
KERERU	SHINJU	FABLIAU	TAUHINU	NUNCHAKU
KIKUYU	SHITZU	INCONNU	TIMARAU	PIRARUCU
KOKOPU	SUBFEU	JAMBEAU	TINAMOU	PRIEDIEU
KOTUKU	TAMANU	JUJITSU	TONNEAU	PYENGADU
LANDAU	TAUHOU	JUJUTSU	TRUMEAU	ROUSSEAU
MADAFU	TELEDU	MAMAKAU	TURACOU	SUCURUJU
MAHEWU	UBUNTU	MANITOU	UMLUNGU	SURUCUCU
MAKUTU	VOUDOU	MANTEAU	WAMEFOU	THANKYOU
MALIBU	WHANAU	MARABOU	WAREHOU	TIRAMISU
MAMAKU	YNAMBU	MOINEAU		TSUTSUMU
MANATU		MORCEAU	**Eight-letter**	TUCUTUCU
MANITU	**Seven-letter**	MWALIMU	**words**	VERMOULU
MATATU	**words**	NILGHAU	ABOIDEAU	WILLIWAU
MEVROU	ANTIFLU	NOUVEAU	ABOITEAU	ZAIBATSU
MILIEU	BABASSU	NYLGHAU	BERIMBAU	

CHAPTER 5
VOWEL AND CONSONANT THEMES

Awkward vowel combinations

A problem every Scrabble player faces is an unpromising combination of letters. With the exception of E, drawing duplicates of any vowel can be awkward. In this respect duplicate As and Os are bad enough, but duplicate Is and Us are even worse. If you find yourself with three or more of a particular vowel on your rack, it's a good idea to try and offload the excess ones. With three Is on your rack, you should try to play a word with two of them. And because I is one of the most common letters in the game, if you don't get rid of both Is in a single turn, you are highly likely to end up with the same problem in the next round. It's a very good idea, therefore, to have a cache of words that uses duplicate vowels so that you can deal with the problem as soon as it arises, allowing you to clear out the excess vowels on your rack without falling behind on the score.

The lists in this section provide three- and four-letter words with two of each vowel (except E), and five and six-letter words with three or more Os or Us.

Using As

Three-letter words with two As

AAH	AGA	ALA	AVA	FAA
AAL	AHA	AMA	AWA	MAA
AAS	AIA	ANA	BAA	
ABA	AKA	AUA	CAA	

Four-letter words with two As

AAHS	AIAS	ALMA	AQUA	AULA
AALS	AIDA	AMAH	ARAK	AURA
ABAC	AIGA	AMAS	ARAR	AVAL
ABAS	AJAR	AMIA	ARBA	AVAS
ABBA	AKAS	AMLA	AREA	AWAY
ACAI	ALAE	ANAL	ARIA	AXAL
ACCA	ALAN	ANAN	ARNA	AYAH
ACTA	ALAP	ANAS	ARPA	AZAN
ADAW	ALAR	ANGA	ASAR	BAAL
AFAR	ALAS	ANNA	ASEA	BAAS
AGAR	ALAY	ANOA	ATAP	BABA
AGAS	ALBA	ANSA	ATMA	CAAS
AGHA	ALFA	ANTA	ATUA	CABA
AGMA	ALGA	APAY	AUAS	CACA

CAMA	JAAP	MAAR	PAAN	TAHA
CAPA	JAFA	MAAS	PACA	TAKA
CASA	JAGA	MAHA	PAPA	TALA
CAVA	JAVA	MALA	PARA	TANA
DAAL	KAAL	MAMA	PAUA	TAPA
DADA	KAAS	MANA	PAWA	TARA
DATA	KAKA	MARA	RACA	TAVA
FAAN	KAMA	MASA	RAGA	TAWA
FAAS	KANA	MAYA	RAIA	TAXA
FAVA	KAPA	NAAM	RAJA	VARA
GAGA	KARA	NAAN	RANA	VASA
GALA	KATA	NADA	RATA	WAAC
GAMA	KAVA	NAGA	RAYA	WAKA
HAAF	KAWA	NALA	SAAG	WAWA
HAAR	LAMA	NANA	SAGA	YAAR
HAHA	LANA	NAPA	SAMA	YABA
HAKA	LAVA	PAAL	TAAL	

Five-letter words with three As

ABACA	AFARA	ALAPA	ARABA	TAATA
ABAKA	AGAMA	ANANA	ASANA	
ABAYA	ALAAP	ANATA	KAAMA	

Six-letter words with three As

ABACAS	ANANAS	BARAZA	KABAYA	PATAKA
ABAKAS	ANATAS	BATATA	KAMALA	QABALA
ABASIA	ANATTA	BAZAAR	KANAKA	RAMADA
ABAYAS	ANTARA	BRAATA	KARAKA	SALAAM
ACACIA	ARABAS	CABALA	KATANA	SAMAAN
AFARAS	ARALIA	CABANA	LABARA	SAMARA
AGAMAS	ARCANA	CADAGA	MANAIA	SATARA
AGAPAE	ARGALA	CANADA	MANANA	TAATAS
AGAPAI	ARMADA	CASABA	MANAWA	TAIAHA
AGGADA	ASANAS	CASAVA	MARACA	TAMARA
AKATEA	ASRAMA	DAGABA	MASALA	TARAMA
AKHARA	ATABAL	HALALA	MATATA	UJAMAA
ALAAPS	ATAMAN	HAMADA	NAGANA	VAHANA
ALALIA	ATAXIA	HAWALA	PAJAMA	WAIATA
ALAPAS	AVATAR	JACANA	PALAMA	ZANANA
ALASKA	AZALEA	JAMAAT	PALAPA	ZAPATA
ALBATA	BAHADA	JATAKA	PANADA	
ALPACA	BAJADA	KAAMAS	PANAMA	
AMARNA	BALATA	KABAKA	PAPAYA	
ANABAS	BANANA	KABALA	PATACA	

Using Es

Four-letter words with three Es
EPEE

Five-letter words with three Es

BELEE	EMEER	GELEE	NEESE	RESEE
BESEE	EPEES	HEEZE	NEEZE	SEMEE
DEERE	ETWEE	KEEVE	PEECE	TEENE
DEEVE	EXEEM	LEESE	PEEPE	TEPEE
EERIE	EXEME	LEEZE	PEEVE	WEEKE
EEVEN	FEESE	LEVEE	PEWEE	WEETE
ELPEE	FEEZE	MELEE	REEDE	
EMCEE	GEESE	NEELE	REEVE	

Six-letter words with four Es

BEEBEE	PEEWEE	TEEPEE	VEEPEE	WEEWEE

Using Is

Four-letter words with two Is

BIDI	IMID	IXIA	NISI	TITI
DIVI	IMPI	KIWI	PIKI	WIKI
DIXI	INIA	LIRI	PILI	WILI
FINI	INTI	MIDI	PIPI	ZITI
HILI	IRID	MIHI	SIMI	
HIOI	IRIS	MINI	SIRI	
IBIS	ISIT	MIRI	TIKI	
ILIA	IWIS	NIDI	TIPI	

Five-letter words with two Is

AALII	DIXIT	INDIE	LIPID	REIKI
ACINI	FICIN	INDRI	LIPIN	RICIN
AIDOI	FILMI	INFIX	LITAI	RIGID
AIOLI	FINIS	INION	LIVID	RISHI
ALIBI	FIRIE	INNIT	MEDII	SHIAI
AMICI	FIXIT	INTIL	MIDIS	SIGIL
ANIMI	GENII	INTIS	MIHIS	SIMIS
ARIKI	GIBLI	INWIT	MILIA	SIRIH
ATIGI	HIKOI	IODIC	MIMIC	SIRIS
BIALI	HIOIS	IODID	MINIM	TEIID
BIDIS	IAMBI	IODIN	MINIS	TIBIA
BIFID	IBRIK	IONIC	MIRIN	TIKIS
BIKIE	ICIER	IRIDS	MITIS	TIMID
BINDI	ICILY	IRING	MODII	TIPIS
BINIT	ICING	ISSEI	NIHIL	TITIS
BIVIA	ICTIC	IVIED	NIMBI	TIYIN
BLINI	IDIOM	IVIES	NISEI	TORII
BRIKI	IDIOT	IXIAS	NITID	VIGIA
CEILI	ILIAC	JINNI	NIXIE	VIGIL
CHILI	ILIAD	KIBBI	OBIIT	VILLI
CILIA	ILIAL	KIBEI	OIDIA	VINIC
CIPPI	ILIUM	KIKOI	ORIBI	VIRID
CIRRI	IMARI	KILIM	PIANI	VISIE
CIVIC	IMIDE	KININ	PIING	VISIT
CIVIE	IMIDO	KIRRI	PIKIS	VIVID
CIVIL	IMIDS	KIWIS	PILEI	VIZIR
DIDIE	IMINE	LIBRI	PILIS	WIFIE
DIGIT	IMINO	LICHI	PIPIS	WIKIS
DILLI	IMMIT	LICIT	PIPIT	WILIS
DINIC	IMMIX	LIKIN	PIRAI	YITIE
DISCI	IMPIS	LIMBI	PIXIE	ZIMBI
DIVIS	IMSHI	LIMIT	PRIMI	ZITIS
DIXIE	INDIA	LININ	RADII	ZIZIT

Six-letter words with three Is

BIKINI	IRIDIC	IRITIS	NIGIRI
IMIDIC	IRITIC	MIRITI	TIRITI

Using Os

Five-letter words with three Os

OVOLO	POTOO

Six-letter words with three Os

BONOBO	COOCOO	GOOROO	LOBOLO	POTOOS
BOOBOO	COROZO	HOLLOO	MOKORO	ROCOCO
BOOCOO	DOOCOT	HOODOO	MONOAO	ROTOLO
BOOHOO	DOODOO	HOOPOE	MOOLOO	VOODOO
BOOKOO	DOOWOP	HOOPOO	OOLOGY	WOOHOO
COCOON	FORHOO	HOOROO	OOLONG	ZOOZOO
COMODO	GOOGOL	KOODOO	OVOLOS	

Using Us

Three-letter words with two Us

ULU	UMU	UTU

Four-letter words with two Us

BUBU	KUDU	LULU	RURU	UNAU
FUGU	KUKU	MUMU	SULU	URUS
GURU	KURU	PUDU	SUSU	UTUS
HUHU	KUTU	PUKU	TUTU	WUDU
JUJU	KUZU	PULU	ULUS	YUZU
JUKU	LUAU	PUPU	UMUS	ZULU

Five-letter words with two Us

AHURU	FUGUS	LUAUS	SUHUR	UPRUN
AUGUR	GURUS	LULUS	SUKUK	URUBU
AURUM	HUDUD	LUPUS	SULUS	USQUE
BUBUS	HUHUS	LUSUS	SUNUP	USUAL
BUCHU	HUMUS	MUCUS	SUSUS	USURE
BUCKU	JUGUM	MUMUS	TUKTU	USURP
BUNDU	JUJUS	MUNTU	TUQUE	USURY
BUSSU	JUKUS	PUDUS	TUTUS	UVULA
BUTUT	KAURU	PUKUS	UHURU	VOULU
CUSUM	KUDUS	PULUS	UNAUS	WUDUS
CUTUP	KUDZU	PUPUS	UNCUS	WUSHU
DUFUS	KUKUS	QUEUE	UNCUT	YUZUS
DURUM	KURUS	QUIPU	UNDUE	ZULUS
FUCUS	KUTUS	RUBUS	UNDUG	
FUGUE	KUZUS	RURUS	UNGUM	

Six-letter words with three Us

MUTUUM	UBUNTU	UHURUS	URUBUS

Light words

While duplicate vowels on your rack can be a real pain, having too many vowels in general can be frustrating. For this reason, it's helpful to have a number of 'light' words up your sleeve – words that contain a high proportion of vowels. The lists of light words include words from two to eight letters, of which more than half are vowels. Words of four or more letters are listed alphabetically according to the vowels they contain.

Two-letter words (two vowels)

AA	AI	EE	OE	OO
AE	EA	IO	OI	OU

Three-letter words (three vowels)

AIA	AUA	AUE	EAU

Four-letter words (three vowels or more)

AAE	ALAE	**AEI**	AIDE		INIA		IDEE
	AREA		AINE		IXIA	**EEO**	EVOE
	ASEA		AMIE	**AIO**	AGIO		OGEE
AAI	ACAI		EINA		CIAO	**EEU**	EMEU
	AIAS		IDEA		IOTA		EUGE
	AIDA		ILEA		JIAO	**EIO**	ONIE
	AIGA		KAIE		MOAI	**EIOU**	EUOI
	AMIA		VIAE		NAOI	**EIU**	ETUI
	ARIA	**AEO**	AEON		OBIA		IURE
	RAIA		AERO		OHIA		LIEU
AAO	ANOA		ALOE	**AIU**	AITU	**EOO**	OBOE
AAU	AQUA		EOAN		HUIA		OLEO
	ATUA		ODEA		KUIA		OOSE
	AUAS		OLEA		QUAI		OOZE
	AULA		TOEA		UNAI	**EOU**	EURO
	AURA		ZOEA	**AOO**	ALOO		MEOU
	PAUA	**AEU**	AGUE	**AOU**	AUTO		MOUE
AEE	AGEE		AUNE		OUMA		ROUE
	AJEE		BEAU		OUPA	**IIO**	HIOI
	AKEE		EAUS		URAO	**IOO**	MOOI
	ALEE		EAUX	**AUU**	LUAU		OLIO
	AWEE		UREA		UNAU	**OOU**	OUZO
	EALE		UVAE	**EEE**	EPEE		
	EASE		UVEA	**EEI**	EIDE		
	EAVE	**AII**	ILIA		EINE		

Five-letter words (four vowels)

AAEE	AREAE		AINEE		AIOLI	**EEEI**	EERIE
AAEI	AECIA	**AEEO**	ZOEAE		OIDIA	**EEOO**	COOEE
AAEO	ZOAEA	**AEIU**	ADIEU	**AIOO**	BOOAI	**EEUU**	QUEUE
AAEU	AQUAE		AUREI	**AIOU**	AUDIO	**EIOO**	LOOIE
	AURAE		URAEI		AULOI		OORIE
AAII	AALII	**AEOO**	ZOOEA		MIAOU	**EIOU**	LOUIE
AEEI	AERIE	**AIIO**	AIDOI		OUIJA		OURIE

Six-letter words (four vowels or more)

AAAA	ARAARA		AKEAKE		AVAILE		ZOAEAS
	ATAATA		AMEBAE		AVIATE	**AAEU**	ACUATE
AAAE	AGAPAE		EATAGE		FACIAE		ALULAE
	AKATEA		GALEAE		IDEATA		AUBADE
	AZALEA		PALEAE		LAMIAE		AURATE
AAAI	ABASIA		PERAEA		REALIA		BATEAU
	ACACIA		TALEAE		TAENIA		BAUERA
	AGAPAI	**AAEEO**	ZOAEAE	**AAEO**	AGORAE		CADEAU
	ALALIA	**AAEI**	ABELIA		AMOEBA		CAUDAE
	ARALIA		ACEDIA		AORTAE		CAUSAE
	ATAXIA		AECIAL		APNOEA		FAUNAE
	MANAIA		AERIAL		AREOLA		GATEAU
	TAIAHA		ALEXIA		CAEOMA		LAURAE
	WAIATA		AMELIA		COBAEA		NAUSEA
AAAU	UJAMAA		ANEMIA		OARAGE	**AAII**	AALIIS
AAEE	AERATE		ARAISE		OZAENA		HAIKAI

	KAIKAI		LAESIE		OAKIES	**AIOO**	ARIOSO
	ZAIKAI		MEALIE		OARIER		BOOAIS
AAIO	ADAGIO		MEANIE		OATIER		BOOHAI
	AIKONA		MEDIAE		OBELIA		HOODIA
	ALODIA		PEREIA		OPIATE		OOIDAL
	ALOGIA		REDIAE		ROADIE		OOMIAC
	ANOPIA		SEMEIA		ROARIE		OOMIAK
	ANOXIA		TENIAE		SOAPIE		OORALI
	APORIA	**AEEO**	AEROBE		ZOECIA		OORIAL
	ASIAGO		APOGEE	**AEIU**	ACULEI	**AIOU**	AGOUTI
	ATOCIA		AREOLE		ADIEUS		AUDIOS
	ATONIA		COATEE		ADIEUX		BAGUIO
	COAITA		ELODEA		AECIUM		GIAOUR
	LAOGAI		EVOVAE		AGUISE		MIAOUS
	ORARIA		FOVEAE		AGUIZE		OUIJAS
	TAIHOA		GOATEE		AUDILE		OURALI
	ZOARIA		LOANEE		AUGITE		OURARI
AAIU	ABULIA		OCREAE		AUNTIE		QUINOA
	AMUSIA		OEDEMA		CAIQUE		SOUARI
	ANURIA		OLEATE		CURIAE		UTOPIA
	AUDIAL	**AEEOO**	ZOOEAE		DAUTIE	**AOOO**	MONOAO
	AUMAIL	**AEEOUU**	EUOUAE		ELUVIA	**AOOU**	VAUDOO
	GUAIAC	**AEEU**	AEMULE		EQUALI	**AOUU**	AUROUS
	IGUANA		AENEUS		EUCAIN		AUSUBO
	QUALIA		AVENUE		EXUVIA		TAUHOU
	UAKARI		BAUBEE		GAUCIE	**EEEE**	BEEBEE
	URANIA		ELUATE		GUINEA		PEEWEE
	WAIRUA		EPAULE		HAIQUE		TEEPEE
	YAUTIA		EQUATE		SAIQUE		VEEPEE
AAOO	MANOAO		EUPNEA		SAULIE		WEEWEE
	MAOMAO		EUREKA		TAUPIE	**EEEI**	BEEDIE
AAOU	ACAJOU		FEAGUE		UNCIAE		DEEPIE
	AGOUTA		HEAUME		UREDIA		EELIER
	AMADOU		LEAGUE		UREMIA		EERIER
	AOUDAD		QUAERE	**AEOO**	AMOOVE		FEERIE
	AURORA		QUELEA		ROADEO		HEEZIE
	OUBAAS		RESEAU		ZOOEAL		JEELIE
AAUU	AUCUBA		UNEASE		ZOOEAS		KEELIE
	TUATUA		UREASE	**AEOU**	AERUGO		MEEMIE
AEEE	HEALEE	**AEII**	AIRIER		AROUSE		PEERIE
AEEI	AEDILE		BAILIE		AUTOED		REEKIE
	AEDINE		LIAISE		AVOURE		SEELIE
	AERIED		SAIKEI		COTEAU		WEENIE
	AERIER		TIBIAE		DOUANE		WEEPIE
	AERIES	**AEIO**	AEONIC		OPAQUE	**EEEO**	EOCENE
	APIECE		ANOMIE		OUTAGE		EPOPEE
	BAILEE		ARIOSE		OUTATE	**EEEU**	EKUELE
	BEANIE		AZIONE		OUTEAT		EMEUTE
	DEARIE		BOATIE		ZOUAVE	**EEII**	FEIRIE
	DEAWIE		CODEIA	**AEUU**	AUREUS		HEINIE
	EASIED		EIDOLA		AUTEUR		KIEKIE
	EASIER		EOLIAN		BUREAU		KIERIE
	EASIES		EONIAN		URAEUS		MEINIE
	EPEIRA		EPIZOA		UVULAE		MIELIE
	FAERIE		FEIJOA	**AIIO**	AIKIDO		NEINEI
	FERIAE		GOALIE		AIOLIS		WIENIE
	HEARIE		HOAGIE		ARIOSI	**EEIO**	EOSINE
	IDEAED		IODATE		DAIMIO		ETOILE
	IDEATE		LEIPOA		MOIRAI		LOERIE
	KEAVIE		OAKIER	**AIIU**	TAUIWI		OLEINE

	OREIDE		MILIEU		OORIER	EOOU	QUOOKE
	SOIREE		QUINIE		OOSIER	EOUU	UVEOUS
	TOEBIE	EIOO	BLOOIE		OOZIER	IIOO	OPIOID
	TOEIER		BOOBIE		ORIOLE		PIOPIO
	VOIDEE		BOODIE		OROIDE		TOITOI
EEIU	ECURIE		BOOGIE		OTIOSE	IIOU	BINIOU
	EPUISE		BOOKIE		ROOFIE		IONIUM
	EQUINE		BOOTIE		ROOKIE		OIDIUM
	EQUIPE		COOKIE		ROOMIE	IIUU	BUIBUI
	UREIDE		COOLIE		SOOGIE		PIUPIU
EEOO	BOOTEE		COORIE		TOOLIE	IOOU	IODOUS
	COOEED		COOTIE		TOONIE		KOUROI
	COOEES		DOOBIE		TOORIE		ODIOUS
	DOOLEE		DOOLIE		WOODIE		ORIHOU
	SOOGEE		DOOZIE		WOOLIE	OOOO	BOOBOO
	TOETOE		EXODOI		WOOPIE		BOOCOO
EEOU	COULEE		FLOOIE		ZOOIER		BOOHOO
	COUPEE		FOODIE	EIOU	BOUGIE		BOOKOO
	EVOLUE		FOOTIE		COURIE		COOCOO
	MEOUED		GOODIE		FOULIE		DOODOO
	OEUVRE		GOOIER		LOUIES		GOOROO
	OUTSEE		GOOLIE		LOURIE		HOODOO
	TOUPEE		GOONIE		MOUSIE		HOOPOO
EEUU	QUEUED		GOORIE		OUGLIE		HOOROO
	QUEUER		HOODIE		OUREBI		KOODOO
	QUEUES		HOOLIE		OURIER		MOOLOO
EIIO	IODIDE		IONONE		OUTLIE		VOODOO
	IODINE		KOOKIE		OUTVIE		WOOHOO
	IODISE		LOOIES		POURIE		ZOOZOO
	IODIZE		LOONIE		SOUTIE	OOUU	BOUBOU
	IOLITE		LOOSIE		TOURIE		ROUCOU
	IONISE		NOOGIE		TOUTIE		VOUDOU
	IONIZE		NOOKIE	EIUU	UBIQUE	UUUU	MUUMUU
	OILIER		OOFIER		UNIQUE		
EIIU	EURIPI		OOLITE	EOOO	HOOPOE		

Seven-letter words (five vowels or more)

AAAEI	ANAEMIA		URAEMIA		EUGARIE		MOINEAU
AAAIU	AQUARIA	AAEOU	AUREOLA		EUGENIA		SEQUOIA
AAEEI	TAENIAE		AURORAE		EUTEXIA	AEOUU	AQUEOUS
AAEEO	AMOEBAE	AAIIO	DIANOIA		EXUVIAE		AUTOCUE
	AREOLAE	AAIOU	ABOULIA	AEEOO	KOEKOEA		COUTEAU
AAEEU	AUREATE		OUABAIN	AEEOU	AENEOUS		NOUVEAU
AAEII	AECIDIA		OUAKARI		AUREOLE		ROULEAU
AAEIO	AEOLIAN		RAOULIA	AEEOUU	EUOUAES	AIOOO	OOGONIA
	AEONIAN		SAOUARI	AEIIO	EPINAOI	AIOUU	OUGUIYA
	AEROBIA	AEEEI	ALIENEE	AEIIU	EQUINIA	EEEIU	EPUISEE
	OLEARIA		EATERIE	AEIOO	IPOMOEA		QUEENIE
AAEIU	ACEQUIA	AEEEU	EVACUEE		ZOOECIA	EEEUU	DEQUEUE
	AGEUSIA	AEEII	AIERIES	AEIOU	DOULEIA		ENQUEUE
	AURELIA	AEEIO	ETAERIO		EULOGIA	IIIOO	OIDIOID
	CAMAIEU	AEEIU	AUDITEE		MIAOUED		
	EUTAXIA		EUCAINE				

Eight-letter words (five vowels or more)

AAAAE	ANABAENA		LAUREATE		ANALOGUE		SEQUELAE
AAAAI	ARAPAIMA		NAUSEATE		AQUATONE	**AEEII**	AEGIRINE
	ATARAXIA		PAENULAE		ARACEOUS		AEGIRITE
	KAMAAINA		SEAQUAKE		ARANEOUS		AERIFIED
AAAEE	KAREAREA	**AAEII**	ACIDEMIA		AUREOLAS		AERIFIES
AAAEI	ACADEMIA		ACTINIAE		AUROREAN		ASEITIES
	ACHAENIA		AECIDIAL		AUTOCADE		EPICEDIA
	ANAEMIAS		AKINESIA		AUTOMATE		GAIETIES
	ASSEGAAI		APIARIES		AUTOSAVE		IDEALISE
	MAZAEDIA		AVIANISE		MAUSOLEA		IDEALIZE
AAAEO	PARANOEA		AVIANIZE		OCEANAUT		IDEATIVE
AAAEU	ACAUDATE		AVIARIES		OUBAASES		INERTIAE
	AGUACATE		CAVIARIE	**AAEUU**	FAUNULAE		INFERIAE
	AQUACADE		FILARIAE		QUAALUDE		METAIRIE
	PAHAUTEA		HETAIRAI		USQUABAE		WEIGELIA
AAAII	APIARIAN		HETAIRIA	**AAIII**	ANIRIDIA	**AEEIO**	ACOEMETI
	APIMANIA		LACINIAE		MILIARIA		AEROLITE
	RADIALIA		LIPAEMIA		NIRAMIAI		AMEIOSES
AAAIO	ALOCASIA		VIRAEMIA	**AAIIO**	APOSITIA		ETAERIOS
	PARANOIA	**AAEIO**	AERATION		AVIATION		ETIOLATE
AAAIU	ADULARIA		AGIOTAGE		DIANOIAS		FOEDARIE
	AQUARIAL		ALOPECIA		MAIOLICA		OEDIPEAN
	AQUARIAN		ANOREXIA		ZOIATRIA		OEILLADE
	AULARIAN		ANOXEMIA	**AAIIU**	ACIDURIA		PAEONIES
	AVIFAUNA		APOGAEIC		AUXILIAR	**AEEIOO**	EPOPOEIA
	MAIASAUR		AZOTEMIA		BAUHINIA	**AEEIOU**	EULOGIAE
	SAPUCAIA		CAPOEIRA		IGUANIAN	**AEEIU**	ACQUIREE
AAAOU	AUTOMATA		EGOMANIA		QUILLAIA		AEDICULE
AAAUU	AQUANAUT		FEIJOADA		UNIAXIAL		AGUELIKE
	KAUMATUA		METANOIA	**AAIOO**	ANOOPSIA		AUDIENCE
AAEEE	AMEERATE		OLEARIAS		APOLOGIA		AUDITEES
	DEAERATE		PAROEMIA		ZOOMANIA		BANLIEUE
	HETAERAE		TOXAEMIA	**AAIOU**	ABOULIAS		BEAUTIED
AAEEI	ACIERAGE		ZABAIONE		AUTACOID		BEAUTIES
	ACIERATE	**AAEIOU**	ABOIDEAU		AUTOPSIA		BEAUXITE
	AGACERIE		ABOITEAU		AZOTURIA		CAUSERIE
	AGENESIA	**AAEIU**	ACAULINE		CARIACOU		DECIDUAE
	ALIENAGE		ACEQUIAS		GUAIACOL		ELUVIATE
	ALIENATE		ACICULAE		OUABAINS		EQUALISE
	AWEARIED		AGEUSIAS		OUAKARIS		EQUALIZE
	EMACIATE		ALLELUIA		PAROUSIA		EQUATIVE
	ENCAENIA		AUBRETIA		RAOULIAS		EQUIPAGE
	EPIGAEAL		AUBRIETA		SAOUARIS		EQUISETA
	EPIGAEAN		AUMAILED	**AAIUU**	AQUARIUM		EUCAINES
	ERADIATE		AURELIAN		AURICULA		EUGARIES
	FACETIAE		AURELIAS		GUAIACUM		EUGENIAS
	HAEREMAI		CAMAIEUX	**AAOUU**	ACAULOUS		EUPEPSIA
	TAENIATE		DIAPAUSE	**AEEEE**	EMEERATE		EUTAXIES
AAEEO	AMOEBEAN		EPIFAUNA		RELEASEE		EUTAXITE
	ANAEROBE		EUTAXIAS	**AEEEI**	ALIENEES		EUTEXIAS
	AREOLATE		INAURATE		DETAINEE		EXEQUIAL
	OEDEMATA		INFAUNAE		EARPIECE		EXUVIATE
AAEEOU	AUREOLAE		MAIREHAU		EATERIES		LEUCEMIA
AAEEU	ACULEATE		MAUVAISE		EMERITAE		LEUKEMIA
	ADEQUATE		PERIAGUA		EXAMINEE		MAUVEINE
	CAESURAE		TAQUERIA		SEAPIECE		QUEASIER
	ECAUDATE		URAEMIAS	**AEEEU**	AGUEWEED		QUEAZIER
	EVACUATE	**AAEOU**	ACAULOSE		EMERAUDE		UNEASIER
	EVALUATE		AERONAUT		EVACUEES		UNIDEAED

AEEOO AEROTONE
FOVEOLAE
KOEKOEAS
OOGAMETE
OOTHECAE
PAHOEHOE
PEEKABOO
PEEKAPOO
ZOOGLEAE
AEEOU AEGLOGUE
ALEHOUSE
ALEURONE
AUREOLED
AUREOLES
COEQUATE
EUDAEMON
EUPNOEAS
FEATEOUS
JEALOUSE
OUTEATEN
REAROUSE
TEAHOUSE
AEEUU NEURULAE
URAEUSES
USQUEBAE
AEIII INITIATE
RETIARII
AEIIO AMEIOSIS
HEMIOLIA
HEMIOPIA
IBOGAINE
IDEATION
IODINATE
NOTITIAE
OLIGEMIA
TAENIOID
AEIIU ACUITIES
AECIDIUM
AIGUILLE
AQUILINE
AUDITIVE
AURIFIED
AURIFIES
EQUINIAS
INDUCIAE
INDUVIAE
MAIEUTIC
MINUTIAE
QUINIELA
SILIQUAE
UINTAITE
UREDINIA
URINEMIA
AEIOO AEROFOIL
AMOEBOID
COENOBIA
IPOMOEAS

KALOOKIE
MOVIEOLA
OOGAMIES
OVARIOLE
PATOOTIE
AEIOU AEQUORIN
AEROBIUM
AGOUTIES
CAESIOUS
DIALOGUE
DOUANIER
DOULEIAS
EDACIOUS
EQUATION
EUDAIMON
EULOGIAS
EUPHOBIA
EUPHONIA
EUPHORIA
EUSOCIAL
EXONUMIA
JALOUSIE
MOINEAUS
ODALIQUE
OUTRAISE
POULAINE
SAUTOIRE
SEQUOIAS
THIOUREA
AEIUU AUGURIES
AUTUNITE
FAUTEUIL
AEOOO ZOOGLOEA
AEOOU ACOELOUS
APOLOGUE
AUTOSOME
POACEOUS
AEOUU AUTOCUES
AUTOTUNE
BEAUCOUP
COUTEAUX
FEATUOUS
HUAQUERO
NAUSEOUS
NOUVEAUX
OUTARGUE
OUTVALUE
ROULEAUS
ROULEAUX
ROUSSEAU
AIIIO OITICICA
AIIIU DAIQUIRI
AIIOO AVOISION
IODATION
IOPANOIC
AIIOU AUDITION
MIAOUING

OLIGURIA
AIOOO OOGONIAL
ORATORIO
ZOONOMIA
AIOOU AUTOCOID
AUTOGIRO
ORAGIOUS
OVARIOUS
AIOUU CAUTIOUS
GUAIOCUM
OUGUIYAS
SUBAUDIO
AOOOO BOOGALOO
AOOOU OOGAMOUS
AOOUU ANOUROUS
COUMAROU
EEEEI EYEPIECE
EEEEU SQUEEGEE
EEEIO EOLIENNE
TOEPIECE
EEEIU EUXENITE
EXEQUIES
MEUNIERE
QUEENIER
QUEENIES
QUEENITE
UNSEELIE
EEEOU ETOUFFEE
EEEUU DEQUEUED
DEQUEUES
ENQUEUED
ENQUEUES
EEIIO BOISERIE
DEIONISE
DEIONIZE
DIOECIES
EBIONISE
EBIONIZE
EGOITIES
EOLIPILE
EPIZOITE
ERIONITE
MEIONITE
MOIETIES
OILERIES
OSIERIES
EEIIU EQUITIES
PRIEDIEU
QUIETIVE
UBIETIES
EEIOO COOEEING
EOLOPILE
MOVIEOKE
OOGENIES
OPTIONEE
EEIOU BOUDERIE
EPIGEOUS

EPILOGUE
EQUIVOKE
ETOURDIE
EULOGIES
EULOGISE
EULOGIZE
EUPNOEIC
EUROKIES
ICEHOUSE
OBSEQUIE
OUVRIERE
EEIUU EUPHUISE
EUPHUIZE
QUEUEING
QUIETUDE
EEOOU EURONOTE
HONOUREE
EIIIO IDIOCIES
EIIOO ONIONIER
EIIOU DIECIOUS
EXIMIOUS
FILIOQUE
UNIONISE
UNIONIZE
EIIUU BIUNIQUE
EIOOO FORHOOIE
OOLOGIES
EIOOU IDONEOUS
ISOLOGUE
OUTVOICE
ZOOECIUM
EIOUU BOUTIQUE
EULOGIUM
EUROPIUM
EXIGUOUS
OUTGUIDE
TENUIOUS
EOOOO BOOHOOED
HOODOOED
VOODOOED
EOOUU DUOLOGUE
EUROKOUS
OUTHOUSE
OUTQUOTE
VOUDOUND
IIIOO PIHOIHOI
IIIOU OUISTITI
IIOOU DIOICOUS
DOUPIONI
IOOOU OOGONIUM
IOOUU BOUSOUKI
BOUZOUKI
UXORIOUS
IOUUU USURIOUS

Awkward consonant combinations

Certain consonants can be just as awkward as vowels when they show up more than one at a time on your rack. The following lists provide words of three to five letters with doubles of B, C, F, H, V, W and Y (where such words exist; but note that there are no three-letter words with two Cs).

Using Bs

Three-letter words with two Bs

ABB	BIB	BOB	BUB	EBB

Four-letter words with two Bs

ABBA	BABY	BLUB	BUBA	COBB
ABBE	BARB	BOAB	BUBO	EBBS
ABBS	BIBS	BOBA	BUBS	JIBB
BABA	BLAB	BOBS	BUBU	SIBB
BABE	BLEB	BOMB	BULB	
BABU	BLOB	BOOB	BURB	

Five-letter words with two or more Bs

ABBAS	BILBO	BUBAL	EBBED	MOBBY
ABBED	BILBY	BUBAS	EBBET	NABOB
ABBES	BIMBO	BUBBA	FABBY	NOBBY
ABBEY	BLABS	BUBBY	FUBBY	NUBBY
ABBOT	BLEBS	BUBUS	GABBA	RABBI
BABAS	BLOBS	BULBS	GABBY	REBBE
BABEL	BLUBS	BUMBO	GOBBI	RIBBY
BABES	BLURB	BURBS	GOBBO	RUBBY
BABKA	BOABS	BUSBY	GOBBY	SIBBS
BABOO	BOBAC	CABBY	HOBBY	SLUBB
BABUL	BOBAK	CABOB	HUBBY	SUBBY
BABUS	BOBAS	COBBS	JIBBA	SYBBE
BAMBI	BOBBY	COBBY	JIBBS	TABBY
BARBE	BOBOL	CUBBY	KABAB	TUBBY
BARBS	BOMBE	CUBEB	KABOB	WEBBY
BARBY	BOMBO	DABBA	KEBAB	YABBA
BEBOP	BOMBS	DEBBY	KEBOB	YABBY
BEROB	BOOBS	DIBBS	KIBBE	YOBBO
BIBBS	BOOBY	DOBBY	KIBBI	ZEBUB
BIBLE	BRIBE	DUBBO	LOBBY	

Using Cs

Four-letter words with two Cs

ACCA	CECA	COCA	COCO	ECCO
CACA	CHIC	COCH	CROC	OCCY
CACK	CHOC	COCK	ECCE	

Five-letter words with two or more Cs

ACCAS	BOCCA	CACKY	CERIC	CHICO
ACCOY	BOCCE	CACTI	CHACE	CHICS
ACMIC	BOCCI	CAECA	CHACK	CHOCK
ACOCK	CABOC	CASCO	CHACO	CHOCO
BACCA	CACAO	CATCH	CHECK	CHOCS
BACCO	CACAS	CECAL	CHICA	CHUCK
BACCY	CACHE	CECUM	CHICH	CINCH
BICCY	CACKS	CERCI	CHICK	CINCT

CIRCA	COCCI	COUCH	CUTCH	PICCY
CIRCS	COCCO	CRACK	CWTCH	RECCE
CISCO	COCKS	CRAIC	CYCAD	RECCO
CIVIC	COCKY	CRICK	CYCAS	RECCY
CLACH	COCOA	CROCI	CYCLE	SECCO
CLACK	COCOS	CROCK	CYCLO	SUCCI
CLECK	CODEC	CROCS	CYNIC	TICCA
CLICK	COLIC	CRUCK	ICTIC	WICCA
CLOCK	COMIC	CUBIC	LECCY	YACCA
CLUCK	CONCH	CULCH	MECCA	YECCH
COACH	CONIC	CUMEC	MUCIC	YUCCA
COACT	COOCH	CURCH	OCCAM	YUCCH
COCAS	COSEC	CUSEC	OCCUR	ZOCCO

Using Fs

Three-letter words with two Fs

AFF	EFF	IFF	OFF

Four-letter words with two or more Fs

AFFY	DOFF	HAFF	MUFF	RUFF
BAFF	DUFF	HUFF	NAFF	TEFF
BIFF	EFFS	IFFY	NIFF	TIFF
BOFF	FAFF	JEFF	NUFF	TOFF
BUFF	FIEF	JIFF	OFFS	TUFF
CAFF	FIFE	KIFF	OFFY	WAFF
COFF	FUFF	KOFF	PFFT	YAFF
CUFF	GAFF	LUFF	PUFF	ZIFF
DAFF	GOFF	MEFF	RAFF	
DIFF	GUFF	MIFF	RIFF	

Five-letter words with two or more Fs

AFFIX	CUFFS	GLIFF	NIFFS	SKOFF
BAFFS	DAFFS	GOFFS	NIFFY	SLUFF
BAFFY	DAFFY	GRAFF	NUFFS	SNIFF
BIFFO	DEFFO	GRIFF	NYAFF	SNUFF
BIFFS	DIFFS	GRUFF	OFFAL	SOWFF
BIFFY	DOFFS	GUFFS	OFFED	SPIFF
BLAFF	DRAFF	HAFFS	OFFER	STAFF
BLUFF	DUFFS	HOUFF	OFFIE	STIFF
BOFFO	EFFED	HOWFF	PLUFF	STUFF
BOFFS	FAFFS	HUFFS	POUFF	TAFFY
BUFFA	FEOFF	HUFFY	PUFFS	TEFFS
BUFFE	FIEFS	JAFFA	PUFFY	TIFFS
BUFFI	FIFED	JEFFS	QUAFF	TOFFS
BUFFO	FIFER	JIFFS	QUIFF	TOFFY
BUFFS	FIFES	JIFFY	RAFFS	TRIFF
BUFFY	FIFTH	KOFFS	REFFO	TUFFE
CAFFS	FIFTY	LUFFA	RIFFS	TUFFS
CHAFF	FLAFF	LUFFS	RUFFE	WAFFS
CHUFF	FLUFF	MEFFS	RUFFS	WAUFF
CLIFF	FUFFS	MIFFS	SCAFF	WHIFF
CLOFF	FUFFY	MIFFY	SCOFF	YAFFS
COFFS	GAFFE	MUFFS	SCUFF	ZIFFS
CUFFO	GAFFS	NAFFS	SKIFF	

Using Hs

Three-letter words with two Hs

HAH	HEH	HOH	HUH	SHH

Four-letter words with two Hs

HAHA	HECH	HISH	HUHU	SHAH
HAHS	HEHS	HOGH	HUNH	
HASH	HETH	HOHA	HUSH	
HATH	HIGH	HOHS	PHOH	

Five-letter words with two Hs

AHIGH	HATHA	HIGHT	HOUGH	KHETH
CHETH	HAUGH	HILCH	HUHUS	PHPHT
CHICH	HEATH	HITCH	HUMPH	SHAHS
EPHAH	HECHT	HITHE	HUNCH	SHASH
HAHAS	HEIGH	HOGHS	HUSHY	SHCHI
HAITH	HETHS	HOHED	HUTCH	SHISH
HANCH	HEUCH	HOOCH	HYPHA	SHUSH
HARSH	HEUGH	HOOSH	HYPHY	THIGH
HASHY	HEWGH	HORAH	HYTHE	WHICH
HATCH	HIGHS	HOTCH	KHAPH	WHISH

Using Vs

Four-letter words with two Vs

VAVS	VIVA	VIVE	VIVO

Five-letter words with two Vs

BEVVY	LAVVY	VALVE	VIVAT	VIVID
BIVVY	LUVVY	VARVE	VIVDA	VOLVA
CIVVY	NAVVY	VERVE	VIVER	VOLVE
DIVVY	SAVVY	VIVAS	VIVES	VULVA

Using Ws

Three-letter words with two Ws

WAW	WOW

Four-letter words with two Ws

WAWA	WAWL	WHEW	WOWF
WAWE	WAWS	WHOW	WOWS

Five-letter words with two Ws

EWHOW	WAWAS	WAWLS	WIDOW	WOWEE
PAWAW	WAWES	WHEWS	WOWED	WRAWL

Using Ys

Four-letter words with two Ys

EYRY	TYPY	YAYS
GYNY	YAWY	YUKY

Five-letter words with two Ys

AZYGY	GAYLY	SHYLY	YABBY	YOLKY
BOYSY	GYNNY	SKYEY	YAMPY	YUCKY
BYWAY	GYPPY	SLYLY	YAPPY	YUKKY
COYLY	GYPSY	STYMY	YAWEY	YUMMY
DOYLY	HAYEY	THYMY	YAWNY	YUPPY
DRYLY	HYPHY	TYIYN	YECHY	
DYKEY	MYOPY	TYPEY	YESTY	
FEYLY	MYTHY	WRYLY	YEUKY	
FLYBY	PYGMY	XYLYL	YIPPY	

Heavy words

In contrast to light words, 'heavy' words have a high proportion of consonants. (Y is used as a vowel in many words, but counts as a consonant here for our purposes.) These lists contain words with no vowels (apart from Y), of two to five letters, and words of six letters that contain either no vowels or only one. Noun plurals ending in S have not been included in these lists.

Two-letter words (no vowels except Y)

BY	FY	KY	MY	SH
CH	HM	MM	NY	ST

Three-letter words (no vowels except Y)

BRR	GYP	PRY	SNY	TWP
CLY	HMM	PST	SPY	TYG
CRY	HYP	PYX	STY	VLY
CWM	LYM	RHY	SWY	WHY
DRY	MYC	SHH	SYN	WRY
FLY	NTH	SHY	THY	WYN
FRY	PHT	SKY	TRY	ZZZ
GYM	PLY	SLY	TSK	

Four-letter words (no vowels except Y)

BRRR	HWYL	PFFT	SPRY	TYPP
BYRL	HYMN	PSST	SYNC	TYPY
CYST	JYNX	RYND	SYND	WYCH
FYRD	KYND	SCRY	SYPH	WYND
GRRL	LYCH	SKRY	TRYP	WYNN
GYMP	LYNX	SKYF	TYMP	XYST
GYNY	MYTH	SKYR	TYND	YMPT

Five-letter words (no vowels except Y)

CHYND	GLYPH	KYDST	PSYCH	SYNTH
CRWTH	GRRRL	LYMPH	PYGMY	THYMY
CRYPT	GRYPT	LYNCH	SHYLY	TRYST
CWTCH	GYNNY	MYRRH	SLYLY	WRYLY
DRYLY	GYPPY	MYTHY	STYMY	XYLYL
FLYBY	GYPSY	NYMPH	SYLPH	
GHYLL	HYPHY	PHPHT	SYNCH	

Six-letter words (one vowel)

BLANCH	BRICHT	CHRISM	CRANCH	DRACHM
BLENCH	BRIGHT	CHURCH	CRANTS	DRENCH
BLIGHT	BROWST	CLASPT	CRATCH	DROWND
BLINTZ	BRUNCH	CLATCH	CROTCH	FLANCH
BLOTCH	CATCHT	CLENCH	CRUNCH	FLENCH
BORSCH	CHINCH	CLINCH	CRUTCH	FLETCH
BORSHT	CHINTS	CLUNCH	CULTCH	FLIGHT
BRANCH	CHINTZ	CLUTCH	DIRNDL	FLINCH

FLITCH	SCHELM	SHREWD	SPLIFF	STRONG
FLYSCH	SCHISM	SHRIFT	SPLINT	STROWN
FRATCH	SCHIST	SHRILL	SPLISH	STRUCK
FRENCH	SCHLEP	SHRIMP	SPLOSH	STRUNG
FRICHT	SCHLUB	SHRINK	SPRACK	STRUNT
FRIGHT	SCHNOZ	SHROFF	SPRANG	SWARTH
FROWST	SCHORL	SHROWD	SPRAWL	SWATCH
GLITCH	SCHRIK	SHRUNK	SPREDD	SWITCH
GLUMPS	SCHROD	SHTCHI	SPRENT	SWOWND
GLUNCH	SCHTIK	SHTETL	SPRING	TCHICK
GRINCH	SCHTUM	SHTICK	SPRINT	THATCH
GROWTH	SCHULN	SHTUCK	SPRITZ	THETCH
GRUMPH	SCHUSS	SHTUMM	SPRONG	THIRST
GRUTCH	SCLAFF	SKARTH	SPRUNG	THRALL
HIGHTH	SCLIFF	SKETCH	SPRUSH	THRANG
KIRSCH	SCORCH	SKITCH	STANCH	THRASH
KITSCH	SCOTCH	SKLENT	STANCK	THRAWN
KLATCH	SCOWTH	SKLIFF	STARCH	THRESH
KLEPHT	SCRAMB	SKRIMP	STENCH	THRIFT
KNICKS	SCRAWL	SKRONK	STITCH	THRILL
KNIGHT	SCRAWM	SKRUMP	STOWND	THRIST
KNITCH	SCRAWP	SLATCH	STRACK	THRONG
KRANTZ	SCRIMP	SLIGHT	STRAFF	THROWN
KVETCH	SCRIPT	SLUTCH	STRAMP	THRUSH
LENGTH	SCROLL	SMATCH	STRAND	THRUST
MENSCH	SCRORP	SMIGHT	STRANG	THWACK
MONGST	SCROWL	SMIRCH	STRASS	THWART
PHLEGM	SCRUFF	SMUTCH	STRATH	TRENCH
PLANCH	SCRUMP	SNATCH	STRAWN	TROGGS
PLENCH	SCRUNT	SNITCH	STRESS	TROWTH
PLIGHT	SCULCH	SPARTH	STREWN	TSKING
PLINTH	SCULPT	SPELTZ	STRICH	TSKTSK
PLONGD	SCUTCH	SPERST	STRICK	TWIGHT
PRANCK	SHLEPP	SPETCH	STRICT	TWITCH
PROMPT	SHLOCK	SPHINX	STRIFT	WARMTH
PUTSCH	SHLUMP	SPHYNX	STRING	WHILST
RHYTHM	SHMOCK	SPIGHT	STRIPT	WHISHT
SCARPH	SHMUCK	SPILTH	STROLL	WRENCH
SCARTH	SHNAPS	SPLASH	STROMB	WRETCH
SCATCH	SHRANK	SPLENT	STROND	WRIGHT

CHAPTER 6
BONUS WORDS

No matter what letters you have on your rack, using all of them in a single turn is usually the best way to score points. The 50-point bonus that you get for using all the letters on your rack is likely to exceed any other score except that from an exceptionally high-scoring word that lands on a triple-word square. For this reason, any serious Scrabble player should devote serious effort to mastering 'bonus words' – words of seven or eight letters that will allow you to empty your rack in one go. This section contains a number of different methods of memorizing words that will help you to scoop up those 50-point bonuses.

Stems and mnemonics

Knowing whether the letters on your rack can be used to form a word that will use up all your tiles gives you a great advantage in a game. If you know that there is a seven- or eight-letter word that fits your letters, then it's simply a matter of finding the right word from the letters. If, on the other hand, you know that there isn't a valid word that you can fit on the board, you won't need to waste time looking for one. One invaluable way of knowing whether your rack can furnish you with a bonus word is to be aware of 'stems'. Stems are groups of six and seven letters which combine with one more letter to form a valid word. This can be a daunting task, but it's made much easier if you concentrate only on the stems that are both likely and rewarding (ie those that are most common, and which will combine with many letters). In the following lists, the best stems have been determined for you, based on an algorithm of likelihood applied to the words in *Collins Official Scrabble Words*.

Another way to help remember which letters combine with which stems is through the use of 'mnemonics'. To create a mnemonic, identify the letters that combine with a given stem, and arrange those letters into a short phrase or sentence. It doesn't matter if you have to repeat some of the letters. Then find a common or easy-to-spot word that can be made from the letters of the stem that could possibly be connected to the phrase or sentence. In other words, establish a link between the stem and the phrase. For example, the six-letter stem **AEINRT** goes with B C D E F G H I J K L M N O P R S T U W. So for the sentence, you might come up with: Keep light brown ducks from Jim. A common word that can be made from the letters of the AEINRT stem is RETAIN. So you would then up with:

    RETAIN - Keep light brown ducks from Jim

Similarly, for seven-letter stems:

    EINORST goes with A B C D E G H I J K L N O P R S T U V Y Z
    ORIENTS: Eastern helpers buy good jazzy stock every time

Alternatively, form a mnemonic from the stem letters and the letters that don't work with it. For example:

    AEINST goes with A B C D E F G H I J K L M N O P R S T U V W X Z

So, with reference to James Bond, you could ask:

    Y Q **is neat**

This is easy to remember, and it's obvious that Y and Q are the letters in question, and that **IS NEAT** is the stem.

Many veteran Scrabble players will have their own mnemonics, but if you are new to the game, try devising some for yourself from the stems and combining sets listed here. The key is getting a memorable phrase with a strong association with the stem word. This is a great test of your skill with anagrams, and your creativity generally; if you can come up with some good mnemonics, you will be honing your Scrabble skills in the process!

Six-letter stems

The 250 stems given here are derived from an algorithm which was developed by Mike Barron to assess the usefulness of each stem for Scrabble play. The first list here shows the rankings of usefulness: the most useful stem is AEINRT, followed by AEINST, then AEIRST, and so on. Against each stem is shown a word that can be made from the letters of the stem, the most common word being used where there are several. In cases where the stem does not make a valid word on its own, an invented word has been supplied as a mnemonic device. These invented words are set within brackets and are **not** valid Scrabble words.

The subsequent lists show each of the six-letter stems in alphabetical order, along with their ranking of usefulness, a common word which can be made from the stem's letters, the letters which can be added to the stem, and the seven-letter words which can be formed.

Six-letter stems in order of usefulness

1:	AEINRT	-	RETINA	46:	ADEIST	-	[SAITED]	91:	ADERST	-	TREADS
2:	AEINST	-	TISANE	47:	EINRTU	-	UNITER	92:	EILNST	-	TINSEL
3:	AEIRST	-	TERAIS	48:	AEILOR	-	[ARIOLE]	93:	AEEIRS	-	EASIER
4:	EIORST	-	TRIOSE	49:	AEILNO	-	EOLIAN	94:	AEIORS	-	ARIOSE
5:	AEEIRT	-	[EATIER]	50:	ADEORS	-	SOARED	95:	ADINOR	-	ORDAIN
6:	ADEINR	-	RANDIE	51:	AEEINT	-	TENIAE	96:	EIORTU	-	TOURIE
7:	AEILNR	-	RENAIL	52:	AELORT	-	LORATE	97:	DEINRS	-	SNIDER
8:	EINORS	-	SONERI	53:	ADEINT	-	NIDATE	98:	AINRST	-	TRAINS
9:	AEORST	-	ROATES	54:	AELORS	-	SOLERA	99:	DEEIRS	-	RESIDE
10:	AENORT	-	ORNATE	55:	ADENOR	-	[ROANED]	100:	ELORST	-	TORSEL
11:	AEINRS	-	SARNIE	56:	DEIORT	-	TRIODE	101:	DEORST	-	TRODES
12:	EEINRT	-	TRIENE	57:	AELRST	-	TARSEL	102:	AEGNOR	-	ORANGE
13:	EINORT	-	TONIER	58:	AEIRTT	-	TERTIA	103:	ADENRT	-	RANTED
14:	EINOST	-	TONIES	59:	AENRTU	-	NATURE	104:	AEIMRT	-	MATIER
15:	AENRST	-	TRANSE	60:	ADENOT	-	DONATE	105:	EEORST	-	STEREO
16:	AEILRT	-	TAILER	61:	AELNRT	-	TERNAL	106:	AELNOT	-	TOLANE
17:	AEGINR	-	REGINA	62:	AEGNRT	-	GARNET	107:	EIINST	-	TINIES
18:	AEILNT	-	TINEAL	63:	AEENRT	-	RATEEN	108:	EEILRS	-	RESILE
19:	ADEIRS	-	SAIRED	64:	ADEORT	-	TROADE	109:	AEIMNR	-	REMAIN
20:	AEIORT	-	OATIER	65:	DEINST	-	TEINDS	110:	AEGILN	-	LINAGE
21:	ADEIRT	-	TIRADE	66:	EIINRT	-	TINIER	111:	AEINTU	-	AUNTIE
22:	AEIOST	-	[OATIES]	67:	AEIMNT	-	TAMINE	112:	ACEINR	-	CARNIE
23:	EILNOR	-	NEROLI	68:	AEIRRT	-	IRATER	113:	AEELRT	-	RELATE
24:	AEINOT	-	[ATONIE]	69:	EEINST	-	SEITEN	114:	AEENRS	-	RANEES
25:	ENORST	-	TRONES	70:	DEEINR	-	RENIED	115:	INORST	-	NITROS
26:	AENORS	-	SENORA	71:	AELNRS	-	RANSEL	116:	DEIRST	-	STRIDE
27:	DEINOR	-	ROINED	72:	AEGORT	-	TOERAG	117:	ANORST	-	TRONAS
28:	AEILRS	-	SERIAL	73:	ADEILS	-	SAILED	118:	DEILOR	-	ROILED
29:	ADEILR	-	RELAID	74:	AELOST	-	SOLATE	119:	AEENST	-	STEANE
30:	EINRST	-	TRINES	75:	EEINRS	-	SERINE	120:	AGINRT	-	TARING
31:	EILORT	-	TOILER	76:	AELNST	-	LATENS	121:	EIRSTU	-	URITES
32:	AINORT	-	RATION	77:	EGINOR	-	REGION	122:	AEEINR	-	[EANIER]
33:	ADEINS	-	SDAINE	78:	AIORST	-	SATORI	123:	AAERST	-	SEARAT
34:	AEINOS	-	[ANOISE]	79:	EENRST	-	TREENS	124:	ADENRS	-	SNARED
35:	EEIRST	-	RETIES	80:	DEIOST	-	TODIES	125:	AEMNOR	-	MONERA
36:	AEINOR	-	[ARIONE]	81:	EILRST	-	TILERS	126:	DEINOT	-	OINTED
37:	AEERST	-	TEASER	82:	ADENST	-	STANED	127:	AEEORT	-	[OREATE]
38:	EILOST	-	TOILES	83:	AEGINS	-	EASING	128:	ADEERT	-	TEARED
39:	AEILNS	-	SILANE	84:	AINOST	-	[SAINTO]	129:	AAEIRT	-	[ARIATE]
40:	EILNOT	-	LIONET	85:	DEINOS	-	ONSIDE	130:	AEIPRT	-	PTERIA
41:	EILNOS	-	SOLEIN	86:	AELNOS	-	LANOSE	131:	ADEINO	-	[ADONIE]
42:	AENOST	-	ATONES	87:	AEEILN	-	[LEANIE]	132:	AEEORS	-	[AREOSE]
43:	DEIORS	-	ROSIED	88:	EGINRT	-	ENGIRT	133:	ADENRU	-	UNREAD
44:	AEILST	-	STELAI	89:	AEEILR	-	[EALIER]	134:	AEORTU	-	[AROUTE]
45:	EILORS	-	REOILS	90:	DEINRU	-	URINED	135:	EEGINR	-	[EERING]

136:	AEELRS	- SEALER	175:	DENORS	- SORNED	214: EEIOST - [ETIOSE]
137:	EGINOS	- SOIGNE	176:	EINSTU	- UNTIES	215: AINRTU - NUTRIA
138:	AELNOR	- RELOAN	177:	EILNRS	- LINERS	216: EEILNR - RELINE
139:	ADEIOR	- ROADIE	178:	ADINRT	- INDART	217: AEGLNR - REGNAL
140:	EGINRS	- SINGER	179:	AEINPT	- PINETA	218: AGINOR - ORIGAN
141:	CEIORT	- TERCIO	180:	AEGIRT	- TRIAGE	219: AEEGNR - GENERA
142:	ENOSTU	- [OUTENS]	181:	ADEEIR	- REDIAE	220: ENORTU - TENOUR
143:	DENORT	- RODENT	182:	EEILNT	- LENITE	221: AEINNT - TANNIE
144:	DEILOS	- SOILED	183:	AEINRR	- [RAINER]	222: ADENTU - UNDATE
145:	DEINRT	- TRINED	184:	ENORSU	- ROUENS	223: EIMNOT - [MONTIE]
146:	EILNRT	- LINTER	185:	AILOST	- OSTIAL	224: AENSTU - UNSEAT
147:	ABEINT	- BINATE	186:	ADNORT	- [TANDOR]	225: DEORTU - TOURED
148:	EIOSTT	- [OTTIES]	187:	AEINPR	- RAPINE	226: AERSTT - TREATS
149:	ABEORT	- REBATO	188:	ACEINT	- ENATIC	227: AENRRT - RANTER
150:	DENOST	- STONED	189:	AINORS	- NORIAS	228: ACENRT - TRANCE
151:	AEGINT	- TEAING	190:	AEISTT	- TATIES	229: GINORT - TRIGON
152:	ACENOT	- OCTANE	191:	AEIIRS	- [AIRIES]	230: AEILRR - RERAIL
153:	ADELRT	- DARTLE	192:	EEILST	- LISTEE	231: ACEIRT - [CARTIE]
154:	EGILNT	- TINGLE	193:	DEEIST	- [ESTIDE]	232: AEIRTV - TAIVER
155:	DEILRT	- TIRLED	194:	ENRSTU	- UNREST	233: ABEIRT - TERBIA
156:	AILNOT	- TALION	195:	DEGINR	- RINGED	234: DEENRS - SENDER
157:	ADEERS	- SEARED	196:	AEIINR	- [RAINIE]	235: AEIMNS - SEMINA
158:	EEILRT	- RETILE	197:	AAEINT	- TAENIA	236: ACEORS - ROSACE
159:	DEEINT	- ENDITE	198:	AEGIST	- AGEIST	237: DEIINT - TINEID
160:	AEELNR	- LEANER	199:	AEEILT	- [ILEATE]	238: AEGNST - AGENTS
161:	AEGRST	- TARGES	200:	AEEIST	- [EASTIE]	239: AAENST - ANSATE
162:	AENRTT	- RATTEN	201:	ADELRS	- SARDEL	240: AEOPRT - PROTEA
163:	EINOPR	- PROINE	202:	AEILOT	- [OLIATE]	241: DELORT - RETOLD
164:	AELORU	- [ALOURE]	203:	AEELNT	- LATEEN	242: AEILNU - [ALUNIE]
165:	ADELOR	- RELOAD	204:	ADELOT	- [ALOTED]	243: CEINOT - NOTICE
166:	ADEIOS	- [ADIOSE]	205:	AEGNRS	- SERANG	244: EGIORT - GOITRE
167:	AEIPRS	- SPIREA	206:	EIOOST	- OTIOSE	245: EENORS - [NEROSE]
168:	ADEILN	- NAILED	207:	BEINOT	- [BONITE]	246: EEILNS - SILENE
169:	DEENOR	- REDONE	208:	EINORR	- IRONER	247: ADEEST - TEASED
170:	ADELNR	- RELAND	209:	AEILOS	- [ALIOSE]	248: EIOPST - SOPITE
171:	EEIORT	- TOEIER	210:	AERSTU	- URATES	249: AEIMST - TAMISE
172:	EEIORS	- SOIREE	211:	ACEORT	- RECOAT	250: ADEGOT - TOGAED
173:	ADEOST	- [OASTED]	212:	DENORU	- UNDOER	
174:	EINRTT	- TINTER	213:	ADELOS	- ALDOSE	

aaeint 197 - taenia

E	TAENIAE	M AMENTIA	P PATINAE	TAENIAS
L	ANTLIAE	ANIMATE	S ENTASIA	

aaeirt 129 - [ariate]

D	AIRDATE	H HETAIRA	R TARAIRE	ATRESIA	W AWAITER
	RADIATE	M AMIRATE	S ARISTAE	T ARIETTA	
	TIARAED	P APTERIA	ASTERIA	V VARIATE	

aaenst 239 - ansate

A	ANATASE	G AGNATES	L SEALANT	P ANAPEST	SANTERA
C	CATENAS	I ENTASIA	M NAMASTE	PEASANT	V SAVANTE
D	ANSATED	TAENIAS	N ANNATES	R ANESTRA	W SEAWANT

aaerst 123 - searat

B	ABATERS	G AGRASTE	ATRESIA	N ANESTRA	S SEARATS
	ABREAST	GASTREA	K KARATES	SANTERA	U AURATES
C	ACATERS	TEARGAS	L TARSEAL	O AEROSAT	W AWAREST
	CARATES	I ARISTAE	M AMEARST	P PETARAS	
E	AERATES	ASTERIA	RETAMAS	R ERRATAS	

abeint 147 - binate

C	CABINET	I	BAINITE	O	NIOBATE	S	BANTIES
E	BETAINE	K	BEATNIK	P	BEPAINT		BASINET
G	BEATING	M	AMBIENT	R	ATEBRIN		BESAINT

	BESTAIN
T	TABINET

abeirt 233 - terbia

D	REDBAIT	F	BAREFIT		TRIABLE	S	BAITERS
	TRIBADE		FIBRATE	N	ATEBRIN		BARITES
E	BEATIER	L	LIBRATE	R	ARBITER		REBAITS
	EBRIATE		TABLIER		RAREBIT		TERBIAS

T	BATTIER
	BIRETTA
	RATBITE
V	VIBRATE

abeort 149 - rebato

A	AEROBAT	L	BLOATER	P	PROBATE		BOATERS
D	ABORTED	M	BROMATE	R	ABORTER		BORATES
	BORATED	N	BARONET		ARBORET		REBATOS
	TABORED		REBOANT		TABORER		SORBATE
E	ABORTEE	O	AEROBOT	S	BOASTER	T	ABETTOR

	BATTERO
	TABORET

aceinr 112 - carnie

A	ACARINE	E	CINEREA	M	CARMINE		ARSENIC
	CARINAE	F	FANCIER	N	CANNIER		CARNIES
B	CARBINE	G	ANERGIC		NARCEIN		CERASIN
D	CAIRNED		GRECIAN	P	CAPRINE	T	CANTIER
	CARNIED	H	ARCHINE	R	CARNIER		CERATIN
	DANCIER	L	CARLINE	S	ARCSINE		CERTAIN

	CREATIN
	CRINATE
	NACRITE
	TACRINE

aceint 188 - enatic

B	CABINET	O	ACONITE		CREATIN		CINEAST
H	CHANTIE		ANOETIC		CRINATE	T	NICTATE
K	ANTICKE	P	PICANTE		NACRITE		TETANIC
M	EMICANT	R	CANTIER		TACRINE	U	TUNICAE
	NEMATIC		CERATIN	S	ACETINS	V	VENATIC
N	ANCIENT		CERTAIN		CANIEST	X	INEXACT

Y	CYANITE
Z	ZINCATE

aceirt 231 - [cartie]

C	CREATIC		TALCIER		CRINATE	R	CIRRATE
G	CIGARET	M	MATRICE		NACRITE		ERRATIC
H	THERIAC	N	CANTIER		TACRINE	S	ATRESIC
K	TACKIER		CERATIN	O	EROTICA		CRISTAE
L	ARTICLE		CERTAIN	P	PARETIC		RACIEST
	RECITAL		CREATIN		PICRATE		STEARIC

T	ATRETIC
	CATTIER
	CITRATE

acenot 152 - octane

C	COENACT		COGNATE	L	LACTONE	S	COSTEAN
D	TACNODE	I	ACONITE	N	CONNATE		OCTANES
E	ACETONE		ANOETIC	P	PATONCE	T	ATTONCE
G	COAGENT	J	JACONET	R	ENACTOR	V	CENTAVO

acenrt 228 - trance

A	CATERAN	H	CHANTER		NACRITE		NECTARS
D	CANTRED		TRANCHE		TACRINE		RECANTS
	TRANCED	I	CANTIER	L	CENTRAL		SCANTER
E	CENTARE		CERATIN	M	CREMANT		TANRECS
	CRENATE		CERTAIN	O	ENACTOR		TRANCES
	REENACT		CREATIN	S	CANTERS	T	TRANECT
F	CANTREF		CRINATE		CARNETS	U	CENTAUR

	UNCRATE
	UNTRACE
Y	ENCRATY
	NECTARY
	TRANCEY

aceors 236 - rosace

A	ROSACEA		ORACHES		ORACLES		CORNEAS		RECOATS
B	BORACES		ROACHES		RECOALS		EARCONS	U	ACEROUS
D	SARCODE	I	CARIOSE		SOLACER		NARCOSE		CAROUSE
E	ACEROSE		ORACIES	M	AMORCES	R	COARSER	W	CROWEAS
G	CARGOES		SCORIAE		SCREAMO		CORREAS	X	COAXERS
	CORSAGE	L	CLAROES	N	CANOERS	S	ROSACES		
	SOCAGER		COALERS		CARNOSE	T	COASTER		
H	CHOREAS		ESCOLAR		COARSEN		COATERS		

aceort 211 - recoat

D	CORDATE	I	EROTICA	R	ACROTER	S	COASTER	U	OUTRACE
	REDCOAT	L	LOCATER		CREATOR		COATERS	V	OVERACT
E	OCREATE	N	ENACTOR		REACTOR		RECOATS	X	EXACTOR

adeeir 181 - rediae

B	BEADIER	D	DEAIRED		FEDARIE	R	READIER	W	WEARIED
	BEARDIE		READIED	H	HEADIER	S	DEARIES		
C	DECIARE	F	AREFIED	L	LEADIER		READIES		

adeers 157 - seared

B	BEADERS		HEADERS		REDEALS		SPEARED		REASTED
	DEBASER		HEARSED	M	MEDRESA	R	DREARES		REDATES
	SABERED		HEDERAS		REMADES		READERS		SEDATER
C	CREASED		SHEARED		REMEADS		REDEARS		STEARED
	DECARES	I	DEARIES		SMEARED		REDSEAR		TASERED
	SEARCED		READIES	N	DEANERS		REREADS	V	ADVERSE
D	DEADERS	K	DEKARES		ENDEARS	S	RESEDAS		EVADERS
G	DRAGEES		SKEARED	O	OREADES	T	DEAREST	W	DRAWEES
	GREASED	L	DEALERS	P	PREASED		DERATES		RESAWED
H	ADHERES		LEADERS		RESPADE		ESTRADE		

adeert 128 - teared

A	AERATED		CREATED		ALTERED	R	RETREAD		TASERED
B	BERATED		REACTED		REDEALT		TREADER	T	ARETTED
	BETREAD	D	DERATED		RELATED	S	DEAREST		TREATED
	DEBATER		REDATED		TREADLE		DERATES	V	AVERTED
	REBATED		TREADED	M	REMATED		ESTRADE		TAVERED
	TABERED	F	DRAFTEE	P	ADEPTER		REASTED	W	DEWATER
C	CATERED	H	EARTHED		PREDATE		REDATES		TARWEED
	CEDRATE		HEARTED		RETAPED		SEDATER		WATERED
	CERATED	L	ALERTED		TAPERED		STEARED	X	RETAXED

adeest 247 - teased

B	BEASTED	F	DEAFEST	L	DELATES		DERATES		TASERED
	BESTEAD		DEFASTE		STEALED		ESTRADE	S	SEDATES
	DEBATES		DEFEATS	M	STEAMED		REASTED	T	ESTATED
D	DEADEST		FEASTED	N	STANDEE		REDATES	U	SAUTEED
	SEDATED	H	HEADSET		STEANED		SEDATER	W	SWEATED
	STEADED	I	IDEATES	R	DEAREST		STEARED	Y	YEASTED

adegot 250 - togaed

E	DOGEATE	F	FAGOTED	L	GLOATED	R	GAROTED		DOTAGES
	GOATEED	I	GODETIA	N	TANGOED	S	DOGATES	T	TOGATED

adeiln 168 - nailed

C	INLACED	DEALING	K KNAIDEL	S DENIALS	V ANDVILE
E	ALIENED	LEADING	N ANNELID	SNAILED	ANVILED
	DELAINE	H HIELAND	LINDANE	U ALIUNDE	X INDEXAL
G	ALIGNED	INHALED	P PLAINED	UNIDEAL	

adeilr 29 - relaid

A	RADIALE	RADICEL	IRIDEAL	R LARDIER	U UREDIAL
B	BALDIER	RADICLE	L DALLIER	S DERAILS	V RIVALED
	BEDRAIL	D DIEDRAL	DIALLER	DIALERS	VALIDER
	BLADIER	DRAILED	RALLIED	REDIALS	Y READILY
	BRAILED	E LEADIER	O DARIOLE	SIDERAL	
	RAILBED	G GLADIER	P LIPREAD	T DILATER	
	RIDABLE	GLAIRED	PEDRAIL	REDTAIL	
C	DECRIAL	I DELIRIA	PREDIAL	TRAILED	

adeils 73 - sailed

B	BALDIES	H HALIDES	MEDIALS	LAPIDES	T DETAILS
	DIABLES	I DAILIES	MISDEAL	PAIDLES	DILATES
	DISABLE	LIAISED	MISLEAD	PALSIED	U AUDILES
C	SCAILED	SEDILIA	N DENIALS	PLEIADS	DEASIUL
D	DAIDLES	K SKAILED	SNAILED	R DERAILS	DUALISE
	LADDIES	L DALLIES	O DEASOIL	DIALERS	V DEVISAL
E	AEDILES	DISLEAL	ISOLEAD	REDIALS	Y DIALYSE
	DEISEAL	LALDIES	P ALIPEDS	SIDERAL	EYLIADS
F	DISLEAF	SALLIED	ELAPIDS	S AIDLESS	
G	SILAGED	M MAELIDS	LAIPSED	DEASILS	

adeino 131 - [adonie]

C	CODEINA	M AMIDONE	S ADONISE	V NAEVOID	ANODIZE
	OCEANID	DOMAINE	ANODISE	X DIOXANE	
D	ADENOID	R ANEROID	SODAINE	Z ADONIZE	

adeinr 6 - randie

A	ARANEID	DRAINED	GRAINED	O ANEROID	T ANTIRED
B	BANDIER	F FRIANDE	READING	P PARDINE	DETRAIN
	BRAINED	G AREDING	H HANDIER	R DRAINER	TRAINED
C	CAIRNED	DEARING	I DENARII	RANDIER	U UNAIRED
	CARNIED	DERAIGN	M ADERMIN	S RANDIES	URANIDE
	DANCIER	EARDING	INARMED	SANDIER	V INVADER
D	DANDIER	GRADINE	N NARDINE	SARDINE	RAVINED

adeins 33 - sdaine

A	NAIADES	F FADEINS	MEDINAS	SPAINED	NIDATES
B	BANDIES	G AGNISED	SIDEMAN	R RANDIES	SAINTED
	BASINED	K KANDIES	N DANNIES	SANDIER	SATINED
C	CANDIES	L DENIALS	O ADONISE	SARDINE	STAINED
	INCASED	SNAILED	ANODISE	S SDAINES	V INVADES
D	DANDIES	M DEMAINS	SODAINE	T DESTAIN	W DEWANIS
	SDAINED	MAIDENS	P PANDIES	DETAINS	
E	ANISEED	MEDIANS	PANSIED	INSTEAD	

adeint 53 - nidate

D	NIDATED	P DEPAINT	TRAINED	SAINTED	V DEVIANT
F	DEFIANT	PAINTED	S DESTAIN	SATINED	
	FAINTED	PATINED	DETAINS	STAINED	
I	INEDITA	R ANTIRED	INSTEAD	T TAINTED	
M	MEDIANT	DETRAIN	NIDATES	U AUDIENT	

adeior 139 - roadie

D RADIOED	N ANEROID	SOREDIA	AVOIDER
L DARIOLE	S ROADIES	V AVODIRE	X EXORDIA

adeios 166 - [adiose]

C CODEIAS	N ADONISE	P ADIPOSE	T IODATES	Z DIAZOES
L DEASOIL	ANODISE	R ROADIES	TOADIES	
ISOLEAD	SODAINE	SOREDIA	X OXIDASE	

adeirs 19 - saired

A ARAISED	READIES	K DAIKERS	SANDIER	ASTRIDE
B ABIDERS	F FARSIDE	DARKIES	SARDINE	DIASTER
BARDIES	FRAISED	L DERAILS	O ROADIES	DISRATE
BRAISED	G AGRISED	DIALERS	SOREDIA	STAIDER
DARBIES	H AIRSHED	REDIALS	P ASPIRED	STAIRED
SEABIRD	DASHIER	SIDERAL	DESPAIR	TARDIES
SIDEBAR	HARDIES	M ADMIRES	DIAPERS	TIRADES
C CARDIES	SHADIER	MARDIES	PRAISED	U RESIDUA
DARCIES	I AIRSIDE	MISREAD	R ARRIDES	V ADVISER
RADICES	DAIRIES	SEDARIM	RAIDERS	VARDIES
SIDECAR	DIARIES	SIDEARM	T ARIDEST	X RADIXES
E DEARIES	DIARISE	N RANDIES	ASTERID	

adeirt 21 - tirade

A AIRDATE	H AIRTHED	DETRAIN	S ARIDEST	TARDIES
RADIATE	K TRAIKED	TRAINED	ASTERID	TIRADES
TIARAED	L DILATER	P DIPTERA	ASTRIDE	T ATTIRED
B REDBAIT	REDTAIL	PARTIED	DIASTER	V TARDIVE
TRIBADE	TRAILED	PIRATED	DISRATE	Y DIETARY
D TARDIED	M READMIT	R TARDIER	STAIDER	
G TRIAGED	N ANTIRED	TARRIED	STAIRED	

adeist 46 - [saited]

B BASTIDE	L DETAILS	SAINTED	DIASTER	U DAUTIES
C ACIDEST	DILATES	SATINED	DISRATE	V AVIDEST
DACITES	M DIASTEM	STAINED	STAIDER	DATIVES
D TADDIES	MISDATE	O IODATES	STAIRED	VISTAED
E IDEATES	N DESTAIN	TOADIES	TARDIES	W DAWTIES
F DAFTIES	DETAINS	R ARIDEST	TIRADES	WAISTED
FADIEST	INSTEAD	ASTERID	S DISSEAT	
G AGISTED	NIDATES	ASTRIDE	SAIDEST	

adelnr 170 - reland

A ADRENAL	G DANGLER	M MANDREL	RELANDS	RUNDALE
B BLANDER	GNARLED	O LADRONE	SLANDER	Y DEARNLY
C CANDLER	H HANDLER	S DARNELS	SNARLED	
D DANDLER	K RANKLED	ENLARDS	U LAUNDER	
E LEARNED	L LANDLER	LANDERS	LURDANE	

adelor 165 - reload

B LABORED	I DARIOLE	P LEOPARD	ORDEALS	U ROULADE
C CAROLED	L ODALLER	PAROLED	RELOADS	
ORACLED	M EARLDOM	PRELOAD	T DELATOR	
F ALFREDO	N LADRONE	S LOADERS	LEOTARD	

adelos 213 - aldose

B	ALBEDOS	I	DEASOIL	P	DEPOSAL	S	ALDOSES	W	WALDOES
C	COLEADS		ISOLEAD		PEDALOS		LASSOED		
	SOLACED	K	SKOALED	R	LOADERS	T	SALTOED		
E	ELODEAS	M	DAMOSEL		ORDEALS		SOLATED		
H	SHOALED	N	LOADENS		RELOADS	V	SALVOED		

adelot 204 - [aloted]

B	BLOATED	F	FLOATED	N	TALONED	R	DELATOR		SOLATED
	LOBATED	G	GLOATED	P	PLOATED		LEOTARD	T	TOTALED
C	LOCATED	H	LOATHED		TADPOLE	S	SALTOED	U	OUTLEAD

adelrs 201 - sardel

B	BEDRALS	E	DEALERS		DIALERS		LANDERS	R	LARDERS
	BLADERS		LEADERS		REDIALS		RELANDS	S	RASSLED
C	CRADLES		REDEALS		SIDERAL		SLANDER		SARDELS
	RECLADS	F	FARDELS	K	DARKLES		SNARLED	T	DARTLES
	SCALDER	G	DARGLES	L	LADLERS	O	LOADERS		SLARTED
D	LADDERS	H	HARELDS	M	MEDLARS		ORDEALS	U	LAUDERS
	RADDLES		HERALDS	N	DARNELS		RELOADS	W	WARSLED
	SADDLER	I	DERAILS		ENLARDS	P	PEDLARS	Z	DRAZELS

adelrt 153 - dartle

A	LATERAD	E	ALERTED		TREADLE	O	DELATOR	T	RATTLED
B	BLARTED		ALTERED	I	DILATER		LEOTARD	W	TRAWLED
C	CLARTED		REDEALT		REDTAIL	S	DARTLES	X	DEXTRAL
D	DARTLED		RELATED		TRAILED		SLARTED	Y	LYRATED

adenor 55 - [roaned]

B	BANDORE	D	ADORNED	M	MADRONE		PADRONE	T	TORNADE
	BROADEN	G	GROANED		ROADMEN		PANDORE	U	RONDEAU
C	ACORNED	I	ANEROID	P	APRONED	R	ADORNER		
	DRACONE	L	LADRONE		OPERAND		READORN		

adenot 60 - donate

B	BATONED	G	TANGOED		TONEPAD		ONSTEAD	Z	ZONATED
C	TACNODE	L	TALONED	R	TORNADE	T	ATTONED		
D	DONATED	O	ODONATE	S	ASTONED		NOTATED		
	NODATED	P	NOTEPAD		DONATES	V	NOVATED		

adenrs 124 - snared

B	BANDERS		GARDENS		LANDERS	R	DARNERS		DANSEUR
C	DANCERS	H	HANDERS		RELANDS		ERRANDS		DAUNERS
D	DANDERS		HARDENS		SLANDER		SNARRED	W	DAWNERS
E	DEANERS	I	RANDIES		SNARLED	S	SANDERS		WANDERS
	ENDEARS		SANDIER	M	DAMNERS		SARSDEN		WARDENS
F	FARDENS		SARDINE		MANREDS	T	ENDARTS	Z	ZANDERS
	SNARFED	K	DARKENS		RANDEMS		STANDER		
G	DANGERS	L	DARNELS		REMANDS		STARNED		
	GANDERS		ENLARDS	P	PANDERS	U	ASUNDER		

adenrt 103 - ranted

B	BARTEND		GRANTED	O	TORNADE	U	DAUNTER	X	DEXTRAN
C	CANTRED	I	ANTIRED	S	ENDARTS		NATURED	Y	DENTARY
	TRANCED		DETRAIN		STANDER		UNRATED		TRAYNED
D	DRANTED		TRAINED		STARNED		UNTREAD		TYRANED
G	DRAGNET	K	DARKNET	T	TRANTED	V	VERDANT		

adenru 133 - unread

B	UNBARED		RAUNGED		RUNDALE		UNPARED		UNTREAD
C	DURANCE	H	UNHEARD	M	DURAMEN	S	ASUNDER	Y	UNREADY
	UNCARED	I	UNAIRED		MANURED		DANSEUR	Z	UNRAZED
	UNRACED		URANIDE		MAUNDER		DAUNERS		
D	DAUNDER	K	UNRAKED		UNARMED	T	DAUNTER		
E	UNEARED	L	LAUNDER	O	RONDEAU		NATURED		
G	ENGUARD		LURDANE	P	UNDRAPE		UNRATED		

adenst 82 - staned

A	ANSATED	H	HANDSET		STAINED	O	ASTONED		STARNED
C	DECANTS	I	DESTAIN	K	DANKEST		DONATES	T	ATTENDS
	DESCANT		DETAINS		STANKED		ONSTEAD	U	SAUNTED
	SCANTED		INSTEAD	L	DENTALS	P	PEDANTS		UNSATED
E	STANDEE		NIDATES		SLANTED		PENTADS	V	ADVENTS
	STEANED		SAINTED	M	TANDEMS	R	ENDARTS	Y	STAYNED
G	STANGED		SATINED	N	STANDEN		STANDER		

adentu 222 - undate

B	UNBATED	H	HAUNTED		UNTAMED		UNTREAD	V	VAUNTED
C	UNACTED	I	AUDIENT	P	UNADEPT	S	SAUNTED	X	UNTAXED
D	DAUNTED	J	JAUNTED	Q	QUANTED		UNSATED		
	UNDATED	L	LUNATED	R	DAUNTER	T	ATTUNED		
G	GAUNTED		UNDEALT		NATURED		NUTATED		
	UNGATED	M	UNMATED		UNRATED		TAUNTED		

adeors 50 - soared

C	SARCODE	I	ROADIES	M	RADOMES	T	DOATERS	V	OVERSAD
D	DEODARS		SOREDIA	O	ROADEOS		ROASTED		SAVORED
E	OREADES	L	LOADERS	R	ADORERS		TORSADE	W	REDOWAS
F	FEDORAS		ORDEALS		DROSERA		TROADES		
G	DOGEARS		RELOADS	S	SARODES	U	AROUSED		

adeort 64 - troade

B	ABORTED	G	GAROTED	O	ODORATE		TORSADE		OUTREAD
	BORATED	K	TROAKED	P	ADOPTER		TROADES		READOUT
	TABORED	L	DELATOR		READOPT	T	ROTATED		
C	CORDATE		LEOTARD	S	DOATERS		TROATED		
	REDCOAT	N	TORNADE		ROASTED	U	OUTDARE		

adeost 173 - [oasted]

B	BOASTED	H	HOASTED		SOLATED	P	PODESTA		TROADES
C	COASTED	I	IODATES	N	ASTONED	R	DOATERS	T	TOASTED
G	DOGATES		TOADIES		DONATES		ROASTED		
	DOTAGES	L	SALTOED		ONSTEAD		TORSADE		

aderst 91 - treads

B	DABSTER		STEARED		ASTRIDE	M	SMARTED		DARTRES
	TABERDS		TASERED		DIASTER	N	ENDARTS		RETARDS
C	REDACTS	F	STRAFED		DISRATE		STANDER		STARRED
	SCARTED	G	RADGEST		STAIDER		STARNED		TRADERS
D	ADDREST	H	DEARTHS		STAIRED	O	DOATERS	T	STARTED
	RADDEST		HARDEST		TARDIES		ROASTED		TETRADS
E	DEAREST		HARDSET		TIRADES		TORSADE	V	ADVERTS
	DERATES		HATREDS	K	DARKEST		TROADES		STARVED
	ESTRADE		THREADS		STARKED	P	DEPARTS	W	STEWARD
	REASTED		TRASHED		STRAKED		DRAPETS		STRAWED
	REDATES	I	ARIDEST	L	DARTLES		PETARDS		WRASTED
	SEDATER		ASTERID		SLARTED	R	DARTERS	Y	STRAYED

adinor 95 - ordain

B	INBOARD		GRADINO	P	PADRONI		ORDAINS
D	ANDROID		ROADING		PONIARD		SADIRON
E	ANEROID	L	ORDINAL	R	ORDINAR	T	DIATRON
G	ADORING	N	ANDIRON	S	INROADS	V	VIRANDO

adinrt 178 - indart

A	INTRADA	E	ANTIRED	F	INDRAFT	O	DIATRON	U	TRIDUAN
	RADIANT		DETRAIN	G	DARTING	R	TRIDARN		UNITARD
B	ANTBIRD		TRAINED		TRADING	S	INDARTS		

adnort 186 - [tandor]

A	ONDATRA	L	TROLAND	N	DONNART		TANDOOR	Y	TARDYON
E	TORNADE	M	DORMANT	O	DONATOR		TORNADO		
I	DIATRON		MORDANT		ODORANT	U	ROTUNDA		

aeegnr 219 - genera

B	REBEGAN		GRANDEE	L	ENLARGE	S	ENRAGES	U	RENAGUE
C	ENGRACE		GRENADE		GENERAL	T	GRANTEE		UNEAGER
D	ANGERED	F	FREEGAN		GLEANER		GREATEN	V	AVENGER
	DERANGE	G	ENGAGER	M	GERMANE		NEGATER		ENGRAVE
	ENRAGED	I	REGINAE	N	ENRANGE		REAGENT		

aeeiln 87 - [leanie]

D	ALIENED	E	ALIENEE	P	ALEPINE	R	ALIENER	T	LINEATE
	DELAINE	G	LINEAGE		ELAPINE	S	SEALINE	X	ALEXINE

aeeilr 89 - [ealier]

D	LEADIER		LEAKIER	N	ALIENER		REALISE		VEALIER
F	FILAREE	L	REALLIE	R	EARLIER	T	ATELIER	Z	REALIZE
	LEAFIER	M	EMAILER		LEARIER		REALTIE		
K	EARLIKE		MEALIER	S	EARLIES	V	LEAVIER		

aeeilt 199 - [ileate]

G	EGALITE	N	LINEATE		PILEATE		REALTIE	V	ELATIVE
K	TEALIKE	P	EPILATE	R	ATELIER	T	AILETTE		

aeeinr 122 - [eanier]

C	CINEREA	H	HERNIAE	M	REMANIE	T	ARENITE		TRAINEE
G	REGINAE	L	ALIENER	P	PERINEA		RETINAE		

aeeint 51 - teniae

A	TAENIAE	L	LINEATE		MATINEE		RETINAE	S	ETESIAN
B	BETAINE	M	ETAMINE	R	ARENITE		TRAINEE	V	NAIVETE

aeeirs 93 - easier

D	DEARIES		FREESIA	M	SEAMIER	R	REARISE	W	WEARIES
	READIES	I	AIERIES		SERIEMA		RERAISE		
F	AREFIES	L	EARLIES	P	APERIES	T	AERIEST		
	FAERIES		REALISE		EPEIRAS		SERIATE		

aeeirt 5 - [eatier]

B	BEATIER		REALTIE	N	ARENITE	P	PEATIER	T	ARIETTE
	EBRIATE	M	EMERITA		RETINAE	R	TEARIER		ITERATE
E	EATERIE		EMIRATE		TRAINEE	S	AERIEST		
L	ATELIER		MEATIER	O	ETAERIO		SERIATE	V	EVIRATE

aeeist 200 - [eastie]
B	BEASTIE	H	ATHEISE	N	ETESIAN		SERIATE
D	IDEATES	M	STEAMIE	R	AERIEST	S	EASIEST

aeelnr 160 - leaner
B	ENABLER	G	ENLARGE	M	REELMAN	S	LEANERS		TELERAN
C	CLEANER		GENERAL	P	REPANEL	T	ALTERNE	W	RENEWAL
	RECLEAN		GLEANER	R	LEARNER		ENTERAL		
D	LEARNED	I	ALIENER		RELEARN		ETERNAL		

aeelnt 203 - lateen
B	TENABLE	G	ELEGANT	M	MANTEEL		ETERNAL		LEANEST
C	LATENCE	H	LETHEAN		TELEMAN		TELERAN	Y	ENTAYLE
D	EDENTAL	I	LINEATE	R	ALTERNE	S	ELANETS		
	LATENED	K	KANTELE		ENTERAL		LATEENS		

aeelrs 136 - sealer
C	ALERCES	G	GALERES	P	LEAPERS		SEALERS		REVEALS
	CEREALS		REGALES		PLEASER	T	ELATERS		SEVERAL
	RELACES	H	HEALERS		PRESALE		REALEST		VEALERS
	RESCALE	I	EARLIES		RELAPSE		RELATES	X	RELAXES
	SCLERAE		REALISE		REPEALS		RESLATE	Y	SEALERY
D	DEALERS	K	LEAKERS	S	EARLESS		STEALER		
	LEADERS	M	MEALERS		LEASERS	U	LEASURE		
	REDEALS	N	LEANERS		RESALES	V	LAVEERS		
E	RELEASE	O	AREOLES		RESEALS		LEAVERS		

aeelrt 113 - relate
A	LAETARE		RELATED	M	LAMETER		PRELATE		REALEST
B	BLEATER		TREADLE	N	ALTERNE		REPLATE		RELATES
	RETABLE	F	REFLATE		ENTERAL	R	ALERTER		RESLATE
C	TREACLE	H	HALTERE		ETERNAL		ALTERER		STEALER
D	ALERTED		LEATHER		TELERAN		REALTER	X	EXALTER
	ALTERED	I	ATELIER	P	PETRALE		RELATER		
	REDEALT		REALTIE		PLEATER	S	ELATERS		

aeenrs 114 - ranees
C	CAREENS		ENDEARS	M	MEANERS	P	PANEERS		EASTERN
	CASERNE	G	ENRAGES		RENAMES	R	EARNERS		NEAREST
	ENRACES	H	ARSHEEN	N	ENSNARE		REEARNS		RATEENS
	RECANES	K	SNEAKER		RENNASE	S	ENSEARS	W	WEANERS
D	DEANERS	L	LEANERS	O	ARENOSE	T	EARNEST		

aeenrt 63 - rateen
C	CENTARE		REAGENT	K	RETAKEN	R	TERRANE		RATTEEN
	CRENATE	H	EARTHEN	L	ALTERNE	S	EARNEST		TERNATE
	REENACT		HEARTEN		ENTERAL		EASTERN	V	AVENTRE
G	GRANTEE	I	ARENITE		ETERNAL		NEAREST		NERVATE
	GREATEN		RETINAE		TELERAN		RATEENS		VETERAN
	NEGATER		TRAINEE	M	REMANET	T	ENTREAT		

aeenst 119 - steane
C	CETANES	H	ETHANES	M	ENTAMES	R	EARNEST		SENATES
	TENACES	I	ETESIAN		MEANEST		EASTERN		SENSATE
D	STANDEE	J	SEJEANT	N	NEATENS		NEAREST		STEANES
	STEANED	L	ELANETS	P	NEPETAS		RATEENS	T	NEATEST
G	NEGATES		LATEENS		PENATES	S	ENTASES		
	SANGEET		LEANEST		PESANTE		SATEENS		

aeeors 132 - [areose]

B AEROBES	D OREADES	N ARENOSE	S SEROSAE	V OVERSEA
C ACEROSE	L AREOLES	R REAROSE	T ROSEATE	

aeeort 127 - [oreate]

B ABORTEE	I ETAERIO	P OPERATE	V OVERATE
C OCREATE	M EROTEMA	S ROSEATE	OVEREAT

aeerst 37 - teaser

A AERATES	REDATES	SERIATE	N EARNEST	SAETERS
B BEATERS	SEDATER	K RETAKES	EASTERN	SEAREST
BERATES	STEARED	SAKERET	NEAREST	SEATERS
REBATES	TASERED	L ELATERS	RATEENS	STEARES
C CERATES	F AFREETS	REALEST	O ROSEATE	TEASERS
CREATES	FEASTER	RELATES	P REPEATS	TESSERA
ECARTES	G ERGATES	RESLATE	RETAPES	T ESTREAT
SECRETA	RESTAGE	STEALER	R RETEARS	RESTATE
D DEAREST	H AETHERS	M REMATES	SERRATE	RETASTE
DERATES	HEATERS	RETEAMS	TEARERS	U AUSTERE
ESTRADE	REHEATS	STEAMER	S EASTERS	W SWEATER
REASTED	I AERIEST	TEAMERS	RESEATS	X RETAXES

aegiln 110 - linage

C ANGELIC	G EAGLING	MEALING	LAERING	GELATIN
ANGLICE	GEALING	N ANELING	LEARING	GENITAL
GALENIC	LIGNAGE	EANLING	NARGILE	TAGLINE
D ALIGNED	H HEALING	LEANING	REALIGN	U LINGUAE
DEALING	K LEAKING	NEALING	REGINAL	UNAGILE
LEADING	LINKAGE	P LEAPING	S LEASING	V LEAVING
E LINEAGE	L GALLEIN	PEALING	LINAGES	VEALING
F FEALING	NIGELLA	PLEAING	SEALING	Y ALEYING
FINAGLE	M GEMINAL	R ALIGNER	T ATINGLE	YEALING
LEAFING	LEAMING	ENGRAIL	ELATING	

aeginr 17 - regina

A ANERGIA	F FEARING	M GERMAIN	R ANGRIER	REGINAS
B BEARING	G GEARING	GERMINA	EARRING	SEARING
C ANERGIC	NAGGIER	MANGIER	GRAINER	SERINGA
GRECIAN	H HEARING	MEARING	RANGIER	T GRANITE
D AREDING	K REAKING	REAMING	REARING	GRATINE
DEARING	L ALIGNER	N AGINNER	S ANGRIES	INGRATE
DERAIGN	ENGRAIL	EARNING	EARINGS	TANGIER
EARDING	LAERING	ENGRAIN	ERASING	TEARING
GRADINE	LEARING	GRANNIE	GAINERS	V REAVING
GRAINED	NARGILE	NEARING	GRAINES	VINEGAR
READING	REALIGN	O ORIGANE	REAGINS	W WEARING
E REGINAE	REGINAL	P REAPING	REGAINS	Z ZINGARE

aegins 83 - easing

B SABEING	SEALING	SPINAGE	S AGNISES	TANGIES
C CEASING	M ENIGMAS	R ANGRIES	EASINGS	TEASING
INCAGES	GAMINES	EARINGS	SEASING	TSIGANE
D AGNISED	MEASING	ERASING	T EASTING	U GUINEAS
E AGENISE	SEAMING	GAINERS	EATINGS	Y EASYING
F FEASING	N INNAGES	GRAINES	GAINEST	Z AGNIZES
G AGEINGS	SEANING	REAGINS	GENISTA	SEAZING
SIGNAGE	O AGONIES	REGAINS	INGATES	
K SINKAGE	AGONISE	REGINAS	INGESTA	
L LEASING	P PEASING	SEARING	SEATING	
LINAGES	SPAEING	SERINGA	TAGINES	

aegint 151 - teaing

B BEATING	GENITAL	GENTIAN	EATINGS	TANGIES
F FEATING	TAGLINE	R GRANITE	GAINEST	TEASING
H GAHNITE	M MINTAGE	GRATINE	GENISTA	TSIGANE
HEATING	TEAMING	INGRATE	INGATES	U UNITAGE
L ATINGLE	TEGMINA	TANGIER	INGESTA	V VINTAGE
ELATING	N ANTEING	TEARING	SEATING	Z TEAZING
GELATIN	ANTIGEN	S EASTING	TAGINES	TZIGANE

aegirt 180 - triage

C CIGARET	RAGTIME	TEARING	SEAGIRT	V VIRGATE
D TRIAGED	N GRANITE	O GOATIER	STAGIER	VITRAGE
F FRIGATE	GRATINE	S AGISTER	STRIGAE	
G TAGGIER	INGRATE	AIGRETS	TIRAGES	
M MIGRATE	TANGIER	GAITERS	TRIAGES	

aegist 198 - ageist

A AGATISE	TAIGLES	INGESTA	AIGRETS	SAGIEST
C CAGIEST	M GAMIEST	SEATING	GAITERS	U AUGITES
D AGISTED	SIGMATE	TAGINES	SEAGIRT	Y GASEITY
G STAGGIE	N EASTING	TANGIES	STAGIER	Z GAZIEST
L AGILEST	EATINGS	TEASING	STRIGAE	
AIGLETS	GAINEST	TSIGANE	TIRAGES	
GELATIS	GENISTA	P GAPIEST	TRIAGES	
LIGATES	INGATES	R AGISTER	S AGEISTS	

aeglnr 217 - regnal

A ALNAGER	GENERAL	LEARING	P GRAPNEL	TRANGLE
B BRANGLE	GLEANER	NARGILE	S ANGLERS	U GRANULE
C CLANGER	F FLANGER	REALIGN	ERLANGS	W WANGLER
GLANCER	G GANGREL	REGINAL	LANGERS	WRANGLE
D DANGLER	I ALIGNER	J JANGLER	LARGENS	Y ANGERLY
GNARLED	ENGRAIL	L LANGREL	LARGENS	
E ENLARGE	LAERING	M MANGLER	SLANGER	
			T TANGLER	

aegnor 102 - orange

B BEGROAN	I ORIGANE	O OREGANO	ORANGES	
C ACROGEN	K KARENGO	R GROANER	T NEGATOR	
CORNAGE	M MARENGO	ORANGER	W WAGONER	
D GROANED	MEGARON	S ONAGERS	Y ORANGEY	

aegnrs 205 - serang

B BANGERS	H GNASHER	REAGINS	LARGENS	RANGERS
GRABENS	HANGERS	REGAINS	SLANGER	S SANGERS
D DANGERS	REHANGS	REGINAS	M ENGRAMS	SERANGS
GANDERS	SHERANG	SEARING	GERMANS	T ARGENTS
GARDENS	I ANGRIES	SERINGA	MANGERS	GARNETS
E ENRAGES	EARINGS	K SKANGER	O ONAGERS	STRANGE
G GANGERS	ERASING	L ANGLERS	ORANGES	U RAUNGES
GRANGES	GAINERS	ERLANGS	P ENGRASP	UNGEARS
NAGGERS	GRAINES	LANGERS	R GARNERS	W GNAWERS

aegnrt 62 - garnet

A TANAGER	REAGENT	TEARING	N REGNANT	GARNETS
D DRAGNET	F ENGRAFT	L TANGLER	O NEGATOR	STRANGE
GRANTED	I GRANITE	TRANGLE	P TREPANG	U GAUNTER
E GRANTEE	GRATINE	M GARMENT	R GRANTER	W TWANGER
GREATEN	INGRATE	MARGENT	REGRANT	Y AGENTRY
NEGATER	TANGIER	RAGMENT	S ARGENTS	

aegnst 238 - agents

A	AGNATES	EATINGS	TAGINES	TANGLES		STRANGE
D	STANGED	GAINEST	TANGIES	M	MAGNETS	T	GESTANT
E	NEGATES	GENISTA	TEASING	N	GANNETS	
	SANGEET	INGATES	TSIGANE	O	ONSTAGE	
H	STENGAH	INGESTA	L	GELANTS	R	ARGENTS
I	EASTING	SEATING	LANGEST		GARNETS

aegort 72 - toerag

D	GAROTED		LEGATOR		POTAGER		STORAGE
F	FAGOTER	N	NEGATOR	R	GARROTE		TOERAGS
I	GOATIER	O	ROOTAGE	S	GAROTES	T	GAROTTE
L	GLOATER	P	PORTAGE		ORGEATS	U	OUTRAGE

aegrst 161 - targes

A	AGRASTE	GARGETS	STAGIER	O	GAROTES	S	GASTERS
	GASTREA	STAGGER	STRIGAE		ORGEATS		STAGERS
	TEARGAS	TAGGERS	TIRAGES		STORAGE	T	TARGETS
B	BARGEST	H	GATHERS	TRIAGES		TOERAGS	V	GRAVEST
D	RADGEST	I	AGISTER	L	LARGEST	P	PARGETS	Y	GRAYEST
E	ERGATES	AIGRETS	N	ARGENTS	R	GARRETS		GYRATES
	RESTAGE	GAITERS	GARNETS		GARTERS		STAGERY
G	GAGSTER	SEAGIRT	STRANGE		GRATERS

aeiinr 196 - [rainie]

D	DENARII	L	AIRLINE	R	RAINIER	S	SENARII	T	INERTIA

aeiirs 191 - [airies]

D	AIRSIDE		DIARISE	L	LAIRISE		IRISATE
	DAIRIES	E	AIERIES	N	SENARII	W	AIRWISE
	DIARIES	F	FAIRIES	T	AIRIEST

aeilno 49 - eolian

A	AEOLIAN	M	MINEOLA	R	AILERON		ALIENOR	T	ELATION
K	KAOLINE	P	OPALINE		ALERION	S	ANISOLE		TOENAIL

aeilnr 7 - renail

C	CARLINE		REGINAL		MINERAL	R	LARNIER		RETINAL
E	ALIENER	H	HERNIAL		RAILMEN	S	ALINERS		TRENAIL
G	ALIGNER		INHALER	O	AILERON		NAILERS	V	RAVELIN
	ENGRAIL	I	AIRLINE		ALERION		RENAILS	W	LAWNIER
	LAERING	K	LANKIER		ALIENOR	T	ENTRAIL	X	RELAXIN
	LEARING	L	RALLINE	P	PEARLIN		LATRINE	Y	INLAYER
	NARGILE	M	MANLIER		PLAINER		RATLINE		NAILERY
	REALIGN		MARLINE		PRALINE		RELIANT

aeilns 39 - silane

B	LESBIAN		LINAGES	O	ANISOLE		SILANES		TENAILS
C	INLACES		SEALING	P	ALPINES	T	EASTLIN	U	INSULAE
	SANICLE	H	INHALES		PINEALS		ELASTIN		INULASE
	SCALENI	K	ALKINES		SPANIEL		ENTAILS	V	ALEVINS
D	DENIALS	L	AINSELL		SPLENIA		NAILSET		VALINES
	SNAILED	M	ISLEMAN	R	ALINERS		SALIENT	W	LAWINES
E	SEALINE		MALINES		NAILERS		SALTINE	X	ALEXINS
F	FINALES		MENIALS		RENAILS		SLAINTE	Y	ELYSIAN
G	LEASING		SEMINAL	S	SALINES		STANIEL

aeilnt 18 - tineal

A	ANTLIAE		TAGLINE	R	ENTRAIL		ELASTIN		TENAILS
E	LINEATE	K	ANTLIKE		LATRINE		ENTAILS	U	ALUNITE
F	INFLATE	M	AILMENT		RATLINE		NAILSET	V	VENTAIL
G	ATINGLE		ALIMENT		RELIANT		SALIENT		
	ELATING	O	ELATION		RETINAL		SALTINE		
	GELATIN		TOENAIL		TRENAIL		SLAINTE		
	GENITAL	P	PANTILE	S	EASTLIN		STANIEL		

aeilnu 242 - [alunie]

C	CAULINE	G	LINGUAE	M	ALUMINE		INULASE	W	LAUWINE
D	ALIUNDE		UNAGILE	Q	EQUINAL	T	ALUNITE		
	UNIDEAL				QUINELA	V	UNALIVE		
F	INFULAE	L	UILLEAN	S	INSULAE		UNVAILE		
		K	UNALIKE						

aeilor 48 - [ariole]

A	OLEARIA		COALIER	H	AIRHOLE	N	AILERON	P	PELORIA
C	CALORIE		LORICAE	K	OARLIKE		ALERION	V	VARIOLE
	CARIOLE	D	DARIOLE	M	LOAMIER		ALIENOR		

aeilos 209 - [aliose]

B	OBELIAS		COALISE		ISOLEAD		SOILAGE	P	LEIPOAS
C	CELOSIA	D	DEASOIL	G	GOALIES	N	ANISOLE	T	ISOLATE

aeilot 202 - [oliate]

C	ALOETIC	K	KEITLOA	N	ELATION	S	ISOLATE
F	FOLIATE		OATLIKE		TOENAIL	V	VIOLATE

aeilrr 230 - rerail

C	CERRIAL	F	FLARIER	K	LARKIER	N	LARNIER		RETRIAL
D	LARDIER		FRAILER	L	RALLIER	S	RAILERS		TRAILER
E	EARLIER	G	GLARIER	M	LARMIER		RERAILS		
	LEARIER	I	LAIRIER		MARLIER	T	RETIRAL		

aeilrs 28 - serial

A	AERIALS	E	EARLIES		SERKALI	P	PALSIER	T	REALIST
B	BAILERS		REALISE	L	RALLIES		PARLIES		RETAILS
C	CLARIES	G	GLAIRES		SALLIER	R	RAILERS		SALTIER
	ECLAIRS		GRAILES	M	MAILERS		RERAILS		SALTIRE
	SCALIER	H	HAILERS		REALISM	S	AIRLESS		SLATIER
D	DERAILS		SHALIER		REMAILS		RESAILS		TAILERS
	DIALERS	I	LAIRISE	N	ALINERS		SAILERS	V	REVISAL
	REDIALS	J	JAILERS		NAILERS		SERAILS	W	SWALIER
	SIDERAL	K	LAIKERS		RENAILS		SERIALS		WAILERS

aeilrt 16 - tailer

B	LIBRATE	E	ATELIER		MALTIER		PLATIER		TAILERS
	TABLIER		REALTIE		MARLITE	R	RETIRAL	T	TERTIAL
	TRIABLE						RETRIAL	U	URALITE
C	ARTICLE	H	LATHIER	N	ENTRAIL				
	RECITAL	K	RATLIKE		LATRINE		TRAILER	W	WALTIER
	TALCIER		TALKIER		RATLINE	S	REALIST	Y	IRATELY
D	DILATER	L	LITERAL		RELIANT		RETAILS		REALITY
	REDTAIL		TALLIER		RETINAL		SALTIER		TEARILY
	TRAILED		TRIELLA		TRENAIL		SALTIRE		
		M	LAMITER	P	PLAITER		SLATIER		

aeilst 44 - stelai

B	ABLEIST		SALICET	I	LAITIES		SLAINTE		SLATIER
	ALBITES	D	DETAILS	K	LAKIEST		STANIEL		TAILERS
	ASTILBE		DILATES		TALKIES		TENAILS	S	SALTIES
	BASTILE	F	FETIALS	L	SITELLA	O	ISOLATE	U	SITULAE
	BESTIAL		SEALIFT		TAILLES	P	APLITES	V	ESTIVAL
	BLASTIE	G	AGILEST		TALLIES		PALIEST	W	WALIEST
	LIBATES		AIGLETS	N	EASTLIN		PLATIES	Y	TAILYES
	STABILE		GELATIS		ELASTIN		TALIPES	Z	LAZIEST
C	ASTELIC		LIGATES		ENTAILS	R	REALIST		
	ELASTIC		TAIGLES		NAILSET		RETAILS		
	LACIEST	H	HALITES		SALIENT		SALTIER		
	LATICES		HELIAST		SALTINE		SALTIRE		

aeimnr 109 - remain

B	MIRBANE		GERMINA	L	MANLIER	R	MARINER		RAIMENT
C	CARMINE		MANGIER		MARLINE	S	MARINES	V	VERMIAN
D	ADERMIN		MEARING		MINERAL		REMAINS	W	WIREMAN
	INARMED		REAMING		RAILMEN		SEMINAR		
E	REMANIE	H	HARMINE	O	MORAINE		SIRNAME		
F	FIREMAN	K	MANKIER		ROMAINE	T	MERANTI		
G	GERMAIN		RAMEKIN	P	PERMIAN		MINARET		

aeimns 235 - semina

A	AMNESIA	E	MEANIES		HEMINAS	O	ANOMIES		MAINEST
	ANEMIAS		NEMESIA	J	JASMINE	R	MARINES		MANTIES
C	AMNESIC	F	FAMINES	K	KINEMAS		REMAINS		TAMEINS
	CINEMAS		INFAMES	L	ISLEMAN		SEMINAR		TAMINES
D	DEMAINS	G	ENIGMAS		MALINES		SIRNAME	W	MANWISE
	MAIDENS		GAMINES		MENIALS	S	INSEAMS		
	MEDIANS		MEASING		SEMINAL		SAMISEN		
	MEDINAS		SEAMING	M	AMMINES	T	ETAMINS		
	SIDEMAN	H	HAEMINS		MISNAME		INMATES		

aeimnt 67 - tamine

A	AMENTIA	E	ETAMINE	I	INTIMAE	R	MERANTI		MANTIES
	ANIMATE		MATINEE		MINIATE		MINARET		TAMEINS
B	AMBIENT	G	MINTAGE	L	AILMENT		RAIMENT		TAMINES
C	EMICANT		TEAMING		ALIMENT	S	ETAMINS	X	TAXIMEN
	NEMATIC		TEGMINA	N	MANNITE		INMATES	Y	AMENITY
D	MEDIANT	H	HEMATIN	O	AMNIOTE		MAINEST		ANYTIME

aeimrt 104 - matier

A	AMIRATE	G	MIGRATE	M	MARMITE	S	IMARETS		SMARTIE
C	MATRICE		RAGTIME		TRAMMIE		MAESTRI	U	MURIATE
D	READMIT	I	AIRTIME	N	MERANTI		MAISTER	V	VITAMER
E	EMERITA	L	LAMITER		MINARET		MASTIER	W	WARTIME
	EMIRATE		MALTIER		RAIMENT		MISRATE		
	MEATIER		MARLITE	P	PRIMATE		SEMITAR		

aeimst 249 - tamise

C	ACMITES	I	AMITIES		MANTIES		MAESTRI		SAMITES
	ETACISM		ATIMIES		TAMEINS		MAISTER		TAMISES
	MICATES	K	KETMIAS		TAMINES		MASTIER	T	ETATISM
	SEMATIC		MISTAKE	O	AMOSITE		MISRATE		MATIEST
D	DIASTEM	M	MISMATE		ATOMIES		SEMITAR		MATTIES
	MISDATE		SEMIMAT		ATOMISE		SMARTIE	Z	MAZIEST
E	STEAMIE		TAMMIES		OSMIATE	S	ASTEISM		MESTIZA
G	GAMIEST	N	ETAMINS	P	IMPASTE		MISEATS		
	SIGMATE		INMATES		PASTIME		MISSEAT		
H	ATHEISM		MAINEST	R	IMARETS		SAMIEST		

aeinnt 221 - tannie

C	ANCIENT		GENTIAN	P	PANTINE	S	INANEST	T	ANTIENT
F	INFANTE	K	NEATNIK		PINNATE		NANITES		
G	ANTEING	M	MANNITE	R	ENTRAIN		STANINE		
	ANTIGEN	O	ENATION		TRANNIE		TANNIES		

aeinor 36 - [arione]

D	ANEROID	L	AILERON		ALIENOR		ROMAINE	T	NOTAIRE
G	ORIGANE		ALERION	M	MORAINE	S	ERASION		OTARINE

aeinos 34 - [anoise]

C	ACINOSE		SODAINE	L	ANISOLE		SENOPIA	T	ATONIES
D	ADONISE	G	AGONIES	M	ANOMIES	R	ERASION	V	EVASION
	ANODISE		AGONISE	P	EPINAOS	S	ANOESIS	Z	AZIONES

aeinot 24 - [atonie]

B	NIOBATE		ANOETIC		TOENAIL	N	ENATION		OTARINE
C	ACONITE	L	ELATION	M	AMNIOTE	R	NOTAIRE	S	ATONIES

aeinpr 187 - rapine

C	CAPRINE	G	REAPING		PLAINER	P	NAPPIER		PERTAIN
D	PARDINE	H	HEPARIN		PRALINE	S	PANIERS		REPAINT
E	PERINEA	K	RANPIKE	M	PERMIAN		RAPINES		
F	FIREPAN	L	PEARLIN	N	PANNIER	T	PAINTER		

aeinpt 179 - pineta

A	PATINAE		PAINTED	N	PANTINE		REPAINT		SPINATE
B	BEPAINT		PATINED		PINNATE	S	PANTIES	T	PATIENT
C	PICANTE	H	PENTHIA	R	PAINTER		PATINES	U	PETUNIA
D	DEPAINT	L	PANTILE		PERTAIN		SAPIENT	Y	PANEITY

aeinrr 183 - [rainer]

B	BARNIER	F	REFRAIN		RANGIER	L	LARNIER	T	RETRAIN
C	CARNIER	G	ANGRIER		REARING	M	MARINER		TERRAIN
D	DRAINER		EARRING	I	RAINIER	S	SIERRAN		TRAINER
	RANDIER		GRAINER	K	NARKIER		SNARIER		

aeinrs 11 - sarnie

C	ARCSINE		ERASING	J	INJERAS	O	ERASION		RESIANT
	ARSENIC		GAINERS	K	SNAKIER	P	PANIERS		RETAINS
	CARNIES		GRAINES	L	ALINERS		RAPINES		RETINAS
	CERASIN		REAGINS		NAILERS	R	SIERRAN		RETSINA
D	RANDIES		REGAINS		RENAILS		SNARIER		STAINER
	SANDIER		REGINAS	M	MARINES	S	ARSINES		STARNIE
	SARDINE		SEARING		REMAINS		SARNIES		STEARIN
F	INFARES		SERINGA		SEMINAR	T	ANESTRI	V	AVENIRS
	SERAFIN	H	ARSHINE		SIRNAME		ANTSIER		RAVINES
G	ANGRIES		HERNIAS	N	INSANER		NASTIER		
	EARINGS	I	SENARII		INSNARE		RATINES		

aeinrt 1 - retina

B	ATEBRIN		DETRAIN		INGRATE	K	KERATIN		RAIMENT
C	CANTIER		TRAINED		TANGIER	L	ENTRAIL	N	ENTRAIN
	CERATIN	E	ARENITE		TEARING		LATRINE		TRANNIE
	CERTAIN		RETINAE	H	HAIRNET		RATLINE	O	NOTAIRE
	CREATIN		TRAINEE		INEARTH		RELIANT		OTARINE
	CRINATE	F	FAINTER		THERIAN		RETINAL	P	PAINTER
	NACRITE		FENITAR	I	INERTIA		TRENAIL		PERTAIN
	TACRINE		GRANITE	J	JANTIER	M	MERANTI		REPAINT
D	ANTIRED	G	GRATINE		NARTJIE		MINARET	R	RETRAIN

	TERRAIN		RATINES		STAINER		NATTIER		TAURINE
	TRAINER		RESIANT		STARNIE		NITRATE		URANITE
S	ANESTRI		RETAINS		STEARIN		TARTINE		URINATE
	ANTSIER		RETINAS	T	INTREAT		TERTIAN	W	TAWNIER
	NASTIER		RETSINA		ITERANT	U	RUINATE		TINWARE

aeinst 2 - tisane

A	ENTASIA		NAIFEST		TANKIES		TANNIES		SEITANS
	TAENIAS	G	EASTING	L	EASTLIN	O	ATONIES		SESTINA
B	BANTIES		EATINGS		ELASTIN	P	PANTIES		TANSIES
	BASINET		GAINEST		ENTAILS		PATINES		TISANES
	BESAINT		GENISTA		NAILSET		SAPIENT	T	INSTATE
	BESTAIN		INGATES		SALIENT		SPINATE		SATINET
C	ACETINS		INGESTA		SALTINE	R	ANESTRI	U	AUNTIES
	CANIEST		SEATING		SLAINTE		ANTSIER		SINUATE
	CINEAST		TAGINES		STANIEL		NASTIER	V	NAIVEST
D	DESTAIN		TANGIES		TENAILS		RATINES		NATIVES
	DETAINS		TEASING	M	ETAMINS		RESIANT		VAINEST
	INSTEAD		TSIGANE		INMATES		RETAINS	W	AWNIEST
	NIDATES	H	SHEITAN		MAINSET		RETINAS		TAWNIES
	SAINTED		STHENIA		MANTIES		RETSINA		WANIEST
	SATINED	I	ISATINE		TAMEINS		STAINER		WANTIES
	STAINED	J	JANTIES		TAMINES		STARNIE	X	ANTISEX
E	ETESIAN		TAJINES	N	INANEST		STEARIN		SEXTAIN
F	FAINEST	K	INTAKES		NANITES	S	ENTASIS	Z	ZANIEST
	FANSITE		KENTIAS		STANINE		NASTIES		ZEATINS

aeintu 111 - auntie

C	TUNICAE	K	UNAKITE		QUINATE		URINATE
D	AUDIENT	L	ALUNITE	R	RUINATE	S	AUNTIES
G	UNITAGE	P	PETUNIA		TAURINE		SINUATE
J	JAUNTIE	Q	ANTIQUE		URANITE	V	VAUNTIE

aeiors 94 - ariose

B	ISOBARE				SCORIAE	N	ERASION		OTARIES
C	CARIOSE	D	ROADIES	P	SOAPIER	V	OVARIES
	ORACIES		SOREDIA	T	OARIEST		

aeiort 20 - oatier

C	EROTICA	G	GOATIER		OTARINE		OTARIES
E	ETAERIO	N	NOTAIRE	S	OARIEST		

aeiost 22 - [oaties]

B	BOATIES	K	OAKIEST		ATOMISE		OPIATES	T	OATIEST
C	SOCIATE	L	ISOLATE		OSMIATE	R	OARIEST		OSTIATE
D	IODATES	M	AMOSITE	N	ATONIES		OTARIES		TOASTIE
	TOADIES		ATOMIES	P	ATOPIES	S	SOSATIE	Z	AZOTISE

aeiprs 167 - spirea

A	SPIRAEA	G	GASPIER		SAMPIRE		RASPIER		PIASTER
C	EPACRIS		PRISAGE	N	PANIERS		REPAIRS		PIASTRE
	SCRAPIE		SPAIRGE		RAPINES	S	ASPIRES		PIRATES
	SPACIER	H	HARPIES	O	SOAPIER		PARESIS		PRATIES
D	ASPIRED		SHARPIE	P	APPRISE		PARISES		TRAIPSE
	DESPAIR	K	PARKIES		SAPPIER		PRAISES	U	SPURIAE
	DIAPERS		SPARKIE	R	ASPIRER		SPIREAS		UPRAISE
	PRAISED	L	PALSIER		PARRIES	T	PAIREST	V	PARVISE
E	APERIES		PARLIES		PRAISER		PARTIES		PAVISER
	EPEIRAS	M	IMPRESA		RAPIERS		PASTIER	W	WASPIER

aeiprt 130 - pteria

A APTERIA	E PEATIER	REPAINT	PIASTER	V PRIVATE
C PARETIC	L PLAITER	P PERIAPT	PIASTRE	W WIRETAP
PICRATE	PLATIER	R PARTIER	PIRATES	
D DIPTERA	M PRIMATE	S PAIREST	PRATIES	
PARTIED	N PAINTER	PARTIES	TRAIPSE	
PIRATED	PERTAIN	PASTIER	T PARTITE	

aeirrt 68 - irater

A TARAIRE	D TARDIER	TRAILER	R TARRIER	T RATTIER
B ARBITER	TARRIED	N RETRAIN	S ARTSIER	RETRAIT
RAREBIT	E TEARIER	TERRAIN	SERRATI	TARTIER
C CIRRATE	L RETIRAL	TRAINER	TARRIES	W WARTIER
ERRATIC	RETRIAL	P PARTIER	TARSIER	Y RETIARY

aeirst 3 - terais

A ARISTAE	TIRADES	RETAILS	RETSINA	ARTSIES
ASTERIA	E AERIEST	SALTIER	STAINER	SAIREST
ATRESIA	SERIATE	SALTIRE	STARNIE	SATIRES
B BAITERS	F FAIREST	SLATIER	STEARIN	TIRASSE
BARITES	G AGISTER	TAILERS	O OARIEST	T ARTIEST
REBAITS	AIGRETS	M IMARETS	OTARIES	ARTISTE
TERBIAS	GAITERS	MAESTRI	P PAIREST	ATTIRES
C ATRESIC	SEAGIRT	MAISTER	PARTIES	IRATEST
CRISTAE	STAGIER	MASTIER	PASTIER	RATITES
RACIEST	STRIGAE	MISRATE	PIASTER	STRIATE
STEARIC	TIRAGES	SEMITAR	PIASTRE	TASTIER
D ARIDEST	TRIAGES	SMARTIE	PIRATES	TERTIAS
ASTERID	H HASTIER	N ANESTRI	PRATIES	V TAIVERS
ASTRIDE	SHERIAT	ANTSIER	TRAIPSE	VASTIER
DIASTER	I AIRIEST	NASTIER	R ARTSIER	VERITAS
DISRATE	IRISATE	RATINES	SERRATI	W WAISTER
STAIDER	K ARKITES	RESIANT	TARRIES	WAITERS
STAIRED	KARITES	RETAINS	TARSIER	WARIEST
TARDIES	L REALIST	RETINAS	S ARSIEST	WASTRIE

aeirtt 58 - tertia

A ARIETTA	E ARIETTE	TARTINE	ATTIRES	TITRATE
B BATTIER	ITERATE	TERTIAN	IRATEST	V TAIVERT
BIRETTA	F FATTIER	P PARTITE	RATITES	W TAWTIER
RATBITE	L TERTIAL	R RATTIER	STRIATE	X EXTRAIT
C ATRETIC	N INTREAT	RETRAIT	TASTIER	
CATTIER	ITERANT	TARTIER	TERTIAS	
CITRATE	NATTIER	S ARTIEST	T ATTRITE	
D ATTIRED	NITRATE	ARTISTE	TATTIER	

aeirtv 232 - taiver

A VARIATE	E EVIRATE	M VITAMER	VASTIER	Y VARIETY
B VIBRATE	G VIRGATE	P PRIVATE	VERITAS	
D TARDIVE	VITRAGE	S TAIVERS	T TAIVERT	

aeistt 190 - taties

A SATIATE	H ATHEIST	O OATIEST	IRATEST	V STATIVE
B BATISTE	STAITHE	OSTIATE	RATITES	W TAWIEST
BATTIES	K TAKIEST	TOASTIE	STRIATE	TWAITES
BISTATE	M ETATISM	P PATTIES	TASTIER	X TAXITES
C CATTIES	MATIEST	TAPETIS	TERTIAS	Y SATIETY
STATICE	MATTIES	R ARTIEST	T ETATIST	
TIETACS	N INSTATE	ARTISTE	TATTIES	
F FATTIES	SATINET	ATTIRES	U SITUATE	

aelnor 138 - reloan

C CORNEAL	ALERION	M ALMONER	ORLEANS	V VERONAL
D LADRONE	ALIENOR	NEMORAL	RELOANS	
I AILERON	L LLANERO	S LOANERS	U ALEURON	

aelnos 86 - lanose

B BONSELA	LOANEES	M MELANOS	R LOANERS	TOLANES
C SECONAL	G ENGAOLS	O ALSOONE	ORLEANS	
D LOADENS	H ENHALOS	P ESPANOL	RELOANS	
E ENOLASE	I ANISOLE	NOPALES	T ETALONS	

aelnot 106 - tolane

B NOTABLE	H ANETHOL	M LOMENTA	S ETALONS	
C LACTONE	ETHANOL	OMENTAL	TOLANES	
D TALONED	I ELATION	TELAMON	V VOLANTE	
G TANGELO	TOENAIL	P POLENTA	Y ANOLYTE	

aelnrs 71 - ransel

A ARSENAL	RELANDS	LARGENS	LANNERS	T ANTLERS
B BRANLES	SLANDER	SLANGER	O LOANERS	RENTALS
BRANSLE	SNARLED	I ALINERS	ORLEANS	SALTERN
C LANCERS	E LEANERS	NAILERS	RELOANS	SLANTER
RANCELS	F SALFERN	RENAILS	P PLANERS	STERNAL
D DARNELS	G ANGLERS	K RANKLES	REPLANS	V VERLANS
ENLARDS	ERLANGS	M ALMNERS	R SNARLER	Y LARNEYS
LANDERS	LANGERS	N ENSNARL	S RANSELS	Z RANZELS

aelnrt 61 - ternal

B BRANTLE	G TANGLER	RELIANT	PLANTER	STERNAL
C CENTRAL	TRANGLE	RETINAL	REPLANT	T TRENTAL
E ALTERNE	H ENTHRAL	TRENAIL	S ANTLERS	U NEUTRAL
ENTERAL	I ENTRAIL	L ENTRALL	RENTALS	V VENTRAL
ETERNAL	LATRINE	N LANTERN	SALTERN	
TELERAN	RATLINE	P PANTLER	SLANTER	

aelnst 76 - latens

A SEALANT	G GELANTS	SLAINTE	O ETALONS	LATTENS
C CANTLES	LANGEST	STANIEL	TOLANES	TALENTS
CENTALS	TANGLES	TENAILS	P PLANETS	U ELUANTS
LANCETS	H HANTLES	K ANKLETS	PLATENS	LUNATES
SCANTLE	I EASTLIN	ASKLENT	R ANTLERS	UNLASTE
D DENTALS	ELASTIN	LANKEST	RENTALS	V LEVANTS
SLANTED	ENTAILS	M LAMENTS	SALTERN	Y STANYEL
E ELANETS	NAILSET	MANTELS	SLANTER	Z ZELANTS
LATEENS	SALIENT	MANTLES	STERNAL	
LEANEST	SALTINE	N STANNEL	T LATENTS	

aelors 54 - solera

A AREOLAS	SOLACER	G GALORES	RELOANS	SEROSAL
B LABROSE	D LOADERS	GAOLERS	O AEROSOL	SOLERAS
C CLAROES	ORDEALS	H SHOALER	ROSEOLA	T OESTRAL
COALERS	RELOADS	L ROSELLA	P PAROLES	OLESTRA
ESCOLAR	E AREOLES	M MORALES	REPOSAL	
ORACLES	F LOAFERS	N LOANERS	S LASSOER	
RECOALS	SAFROLE	ORLEANS	OARLESS	

aelort 52 - lorate

B	BLOATER		FLOREAT		RATHOLE	S	OESTRAL	V	LEVATOR
C	LOCATER		REFLOAT	L	REALLOT		OLESTRA	Y	ROYALET
D	DELATOR	G	GLOATER	P	PROLATE	T	RETOTAL	Z	ZELATOR
	LEOTARD		LEGATOR	R	REALTOR	U	ROTULAE		
F	FLOATER	H	LOATHER		RELATOR		TORULAE		

aeloru 164 - [aloure]

A	AUREOLA	D	ROULADE	M	MORULAE	T	ROTULAE	U	ROULEAU
B	RUBEOLA	E	AUREOLE	N	ALEURON		TORULAE		

aelost 74 - solate

B	BOATELS		TALCOSE		LEGATOS		TOLANES	S	SOLATES
	OBLATES	D	SALTOED	H	LOATHES	P	APOSTLE	V	SOLVATE
C	ALECOST		SOLATED	I	ISOLATE		PELOTAS	Z	ZEALOTS
	LACTOSE	E	OLEATES	K	SKATOLE		POTALES		
	LOCATES	F	FOLATES	M	MALTOSE	R	OESTRAL		
	SCATOLE	G	GELATOS	N	ETALONS		OLESTRA		

aelrst 57 - tarsel

A	TARSEAL		RELATES		TAILERS		OLESTRA		STARTLE
B	ALBERTS		RESLATE	K	STALKER	P	PALTERS		TATLERS
	BATLERS		STEALER		TALKERS		PERSALT	U	ESTRUAL
	BLASTER	F	FALTERS	L	STELLAR		PLASTER		SALUTER
	LABRETS	G	LARGEST		TELLARS		PLATERS	V	TRAVELS
	STABLER	H	HALTERS	M	ARMLETS		PSALTER		VARLETS
C	CARTELS		HARSLET		LAMSTER		STAPLER		VESTRAL
	CLARETS		LATHERS		MARTELS	S	ARTLESS	W	WARSTLE
	CRESTAL		SLATHER		TRAMELS		LASTERS		WASTREL
	SCARLET		THALERS	N	ANTLERS		SALTERS		WRASTLE
	TARCELS	I	REALIST		RENTALS		SLATERS	Y	RAYLETS
D	DARTLES		RETAILS		SALTERN		TARSELS		
	SLARTED		SALTIER		SLANTER	T	RATTLES		
E	ELATERS		SALTIRE		STERNAL		SLATTER		
	REALEST		SLATIER	O	OESTRAL		STARLET		

aemnor 125 - monera

A	AMARONE		FOREMAN	L	ALMONER	S	ENAMORS	V	OVERMAN
C	CREMONA	G	MARENGO		NEMORAL		MOANERS	Y	ANYMORE
	ROMANCE		MEGARON	N	MONERAN		OARSMEN		ROMNEYA
D	MADRONE	H	MENORAH	P	MANROPE	T	TONEARM		
	ROADMEN	I	MORAINE		REPOMAN	U	ENAMOUR		
F	FORAMEN		ROMAINE	R	ORRAMEN		NEUROMA		

aenors 26 - senora

B	BORANES		NARCOSE	I	ERASION		OARSMEN		SANTERO
C	CANOERS	E	ARENOSE	L	LOANERS	P	PERSONA		SENATOR
	CARNOSE	G	ONAGERS		ORLEANS	R	SERRANO		TREASON
	COARSEN		ORANGES		RELOANS	S	REASONS	U	ARENOUS
	CORNEAS	H	HOARSEN	M	ENAMORS		SENORAS		
	EARCONS		SENHORA		MOANERS	T	ATONERS		

aenort 10 - ornate

B	BARONET	G	NEGATOR	M	TONEARM		PROTEAN		SENATOR
	REBOANT	H	ANOTHER	N	NORTENA	R	ORNATER		TREASON
C	ENACTOR	I	NOTAIRE	P	OPERANT	S	ATONERS	U	OUTEARN
D	TORNADE		OTARINE		PRONATE		SANTERO	V	VENATOR

aenost 42 - atones

B	ONBEATS		ONSTEAD	M	MANTOES		TREASON	V	NOVATES
C	COSTEAN	G	ONSTAGE	P	TEOPANS	S	ASTONES		
	OCTANES	I	ATONIES	R	ATONERS	T	ATTONES		
D	ASTONED	L	ETALONS		SANTERO		NOTATES		
	DONATES		TOLANES		SENATOR	U	SOUTANE		

aenrrt 227 - ranter

A	NARRATE		REGRANT		TRAINER	S	ERRANTS	Y	TERNARY
E	TERRANE	I	RETRAIN	O	ORNATER		RANTERS		
G	GRANTER		TERRAIN	P	PARTNER	T	TRANTER		

aenrst 15 - transe

A	ANESTRA	EASTERN	RETINAS	SARMENT	RANTERS
	SANTERA	NEAREST	RETSINA	SMARTEN	S SARSNET
B	BANTERS	RATEENS	STAINER	N TANNERS	TRANSES
	BARNETS	G ARGENTS	STARNIE	O ATONERS	T NATTERS
C	CANTERS	GARNETS	STEARIN	SANTERO	RATTENS
	CARNETS	STRANGE	K RANKEST	SENATOR	U AUNTERS
	NECTARS	H ANTHERS	STARKEN	TREASON	NATURES
	RECANTS	HARTENS	TANKERS	P ARPENTS	SAUNTER
	SCANTER	THENARS	L ANTLERS	ENTRAPS	V SERVANT
	TANRECS	I ANESTRI	RENTALS	PANTERS	TAVERNS
	TRANCES	ANTSIER	SALTERN	PARENTS	VERSANT
D	ENDARTS	NASTIER	SLANTER	PASTERN	W STRAWEN
	STANDER	RATINES	STERNAL	PERSANT	WANTERS
	STARNED	RESIANT	M ARTSMEN	TREPANS	Y TRAYNES
E	EARNEST	RETAINS	MARTENS	R ERRANTS	

aenrtt 162 - ratten

A	TARTANE	TERNATE	TARTINE	REPTANT	Y NATTERY
C	TRANECT	I INTREAT	TERTIAN	R TRANTER	
D	TRANTED	ITERANT	L TRENTAL	S NATTERS	
E	ENTREAT	NATTIER	N ENTRANT	RATTENS	
	RATTEEN	NITRATE	P PATTERN	U TAUNTER	

aenrtu 59 - nature

A	NATURAE	NATURED	UNHEART	L NEUTRAL	T TAUNTER
	TAUREAN	UNRATED	URETHAN	M TRUEMAN	V VAUNTER
C	CENTAUR	UNTREAD	I RUINATE	O OUTEARN	W UNWATER
	UNCRATE	G GAUNTER	TAURINE	S AUNTERS	
	UNTRACE	H HAUNTER	URANITE	NATURES	
D	DAUNTER	UNEARTH	URINATE	SAUNTER	

aenstu 224 - unseat

B	BUTANES	SINUATE	O SOUTANE	SAUNTER	TETANUS
	SUNBEAT	L ELUANTS	P PEANUTS	S NASUTES	UNSTATE
C	NUTCASE	LUNATES	PESAUNT	UNSEATS	X UNTAXES
D	SAUNTED	UNLASTE	Q EQUANTS	T ATTUNES	
	UNSATED	M UNTAMES	R AUNTERS	NUTATES	
I	AUNTIES	UNTEAMS	NATURES	TAUTENS	

aeoprt 240 - protea

B	PROBATE	G PORTAGE	N OPERANT	PRORATE	T PORTATE
D	ADOPTER	POTAGER	PRONATE	S ESPARTO	V OVERAPT
	READOPT	H PHORATE	PROTEAN	PROTEAS	
E	OPERATE	L PROLATE	R PRAETOR	SEAPORT	

aeorst 9 - roates

A AEROSAT
B BOASTER BOATERS BORATES REBATOS SORBATE
C COASTER COATERS RECOATS
D DOATERS ROASTED TORSADE TROADES
E ROSEATE
G GAROTES ORGEATS STORAGE TOERAGS
H ASTHORE EARSHOT HAROSET
I OARIEST OTARIES
K KOTARES
L OESTRAL OLESTRA
M AMORETS MAESTRO OMERTAS
N ATONERS SANTERO SENATOR TREASON
P ESPARTO PROTEAS SEAPORT
R ROASTER
S OSETRAS OSSETRA
T ROTATES TOASTER

aeortu 134 - [aroute]

C OUTRACE
D OUTDARE OUTREAD READOUT
G OUTRAGE
H OUTHEAR
L ROTULAE TORULAE
N OUTEARN
Q EQUATOR QUORATE
T OUTRATE
V OUTRAVE
W OUTWEAR

aerstt 226 - treats

B BATTERS TABRETS
C SCATTER
D STARTED TETRADS
E ESTREAT RESTATE RETASTE
G TARGETS
H HATTERS RATHEST SHATTER THREATS
I ARTIEST ARTISTE ATTIRES IRATEST RATITES STRIATE TASTIER TERTIAS
L RATTLES SLATTER STARLET STARTLE TATLERS
M MATTERS SMATTER
N NATTERS RATTENS
O ROTATES TOASTER
P PATTERS SPATTER TAPSTER
R RATTERS RESTART STARTER
S ASTERTS STARETS STATERS TASTERS
T STRETTA TARTEST TATTERS
U ASTUTER STATURE
V VATTERS
W SWATTER TEWARTS
Y YATTERS
Z STARETZ

aerstu 210 - urates

A AURATES
B ARBUTES BURSATE SURBATE
C ACTURES CAUTERS CRUSTAE CURATES
E AUSTERE
F FAUREST
L ESTRUAL SALUTER
M MATURES STRUMAE
N AUNTERS NATURES SAUNTER
P PASTURE UPRATES UPSTARE UPTEARS
Q QUAREST QUARTES QUATRES
T ASTUTER STATURE
U AUTEURS
Y ESTUARY

aginor 218 - origan

C ORGANIC
D ADORING GRADINO ROADING
E ORIGANE
H HOARING
L RANGOLI
M ROAMING
P PIGNORA PORANGI
R ROARING
S IGNAROS ORIGANS SIGNORA SOARING
T ORATING ROATING
Z ZINGARO

aginrt 120 - taring

A GRANITA
C CARTING CRATING TRACING
D DARTING TRADING
E GRANITE GRATINE INGRATE TANGIER TEARING
F FARTING INGRAFT RAFTING
G GRATING TARGING
I AIRTING RAITING
K KARTING
L RATLING
M MARTING MIGRANT
N RANTING
O ORATING ROATING
P PARTING PRATING TRAPING
R TARRING
S GASTRIN GRATINS RATINGS STARING TARINGS
T RATTING TARTING
W RINGTAW
Y GIANTRY

ailnot 156 - talion

A AILANTO ALATION
B BITONAL TOENAIL
E ELATION
G ANTILOG
N ANTLION
S LATINOS TALIONS
U OUTLAIN

ailost 185 - ostial

A	SOLATIA	E	ISOLATE	M	SOMITAL		TOPSAIL		TAILORS
B	OBLASTI	G	GALIOTS	N	LATINOS	R	ORALIST	T	ALTOIST
C	CITOLAS		LATIGOS		TALIONS		RIALTOS	U	OUTSAIL
	STOICAL		SALIGOT	P	APOSTIL		SLIOTAR	X	OXTAILS

ainors 189 - norias

C	AIRCONS		ORDAINS	G	IGNAROS	M	MAINORS	T	AROINTS
	RACINOS		SADIRON		ORIGANS	P	PARISON		RATIONS
	SARONIC	E	ERASION		SIGNORA		PORINAS	W	WARISON
D	INROADS	F	INSOFAR		SOARING		SOPRANI		

ainort 32 - ration

B	TABORIN	E	NOTAIRE	H	ORTHIAN	P	ATROPIN	W	WAITRON
C	CAROTIN		OTARINE	J	JANITOR	S	AROINTS	X	TRIAXON
	CORTINA	G	ORATING	M	TORMINA		RATIONS		
D	DIATRON		ROATING	O	ORATION	U	RAINOUT		

ainost 84 - [sainto]

A	ATONIAS		ATONICS	K	KATIONS	N	ANOINTS	T	STATION
B	BASTION		CATIONS	L	LATINOS		NATIONS		
	BONITAS	E	ATONIES		TALIONS		ONANIST		
	OBTAINS	G	AGONIST	M	MANITOS	R	AROINTS		
C	ACTIONS		GITANOS		STAMNOI		RATIONS		

ainrst 98 - trains

A	ANTIARS		NASTIER		STEARIN	L	RATLINS		SANTIRS
	ARTISAN		RATINES	G	GASTRIN	M	MARTINS		STRAINS
	TSARINA		RESIANT		GRATINS	O	AROINTS	T	STRAINT
B	BRISANT		RETAINS		RATINGS		RATIONS		TRANSIT
C	NARCIST		RETINAS		STARING	P	SPIRANT	U	NUTRIAS
D	INDARTS		RETSINA		TARINGS		SPRAINT		
E	ANESTRI		STAINER	H	TARNISH	Q	QINTARS		
	ANTSIER		STARNIE	K	KIRTANS	S	INSTARS		

ainrtu 215 - nutria

C	CURTAIN	E	RUINATE	F	ANTIFUR	P	PURITAN	Y	UNITARY
	TURACIN		TAURINE	M	NATRIUM		UPTRAIN		
D	TRIDUAN		URANITE	N	URINANT	Q	QUINTAR		
	UNITARD		URINATE	O	RAINOUT	S	NUTRIAS		

aiorst 78 - satori

B	ORBITAS		ORGIAST		RIALTOS	P	AIRPOST	U	SAUTOIR
D	ASTROID	H	AIRSHOT		SLIOTAR		AIRSTOP	V	TRAVOIS
E	OARIEST		SHORTIA		TAILORS		PAROTIS		VIATORS
	OTARIES		THORIAS	M	AMORIST	S	AORISTS	Y	OSTIARY
F	FAITORS	K	TROIKAS	N	AROINTS		ARISTOS		
G	AGISTOR	L	ORALIST		RATIONS		SATORIS		

anorst 117 - tronas

A	TORANAS	E	ATONERS		RATIONS	O	RATOONS		RATTONS
B	BARTONS		SANTERO	L	LATRONS		SANTOOR		ROTTANS
C	CANTORS		SENATOR	M	MATRONS	P	PARTONS	U	ROUSANT
	CARTONS		TREASON		TRANSOM		PATRONS		SANTOUR
	CONTRAS	G	SNOTRAG	N	NATRONS		TARPONS	Y	AROYNTS
	CRATONS	I	AROINTS		NONARTS	T	ATTORNS		

beinot 207 - [bonite]

A	NIOBATE	I	NIOBITE	R	BORNITE		EBONIST
E	EBONITE	O	EOBIONT	S	BONIEST	T	BOTTINE

ceinot 243 - notice

A	ACONITE		NOTICED	M	CENTIMO		NEPOTIC		SECTION
	ANOETIC	H	HENOTIC		ENTOMIC	R	COINTER	T	ENTOTIC
C	CONCEIT	K	KENOTIC		TONEMIC		NOTICER		TONETIC
D	CTENOID		KETONIC	O	COONTIE		RECTION	X	EXCITON
	DEONTIC	L	LECTION	P	ENTOPIC	S	NOTICES		

ceiort 141 - tercio

A	EROTICA	G	ERGOTIC	M	MORTICE	S	EROTICS	X	EXCITOR
C	CEROTIC	H	ROTCHIE	N	COINTER		TERCIOS		XEROTIC
	ORECTIC		THEORIC		NOTICER	T	COTTIER		
D	CORDITE	K	TOCKIER		RECTION	V	EVICTOR		
E	COTERIE	L	CORTILE	P	PTEROIC	W	COWRITE		

deeinr 70 - renied

B	BENDIER		FENDIER	H	INHERED		RIPENED	W	REWIDEN
	INBREED		REFINED	K	REINKED	R	DERNIER		WIDENER
C	CEDRINE	G	DREEING	L	REDLINE		NERDIER	X	INDEXER
D	NEDDIER		ENERGID		RELINED	S	DENIERS		REINDEX
E	NEEDIER		GREINED	M	ERMINED		NEREIDS		
F	DEFINER		REEDING	O	ORDINEE		RESINED		
	ENFIRED		REIGNED	P	REPINED	U	UREDINE		

deeint 159 - endite

C	ENTICED	F	FEINTED	M	DEMENTI		ENDITES	U	DETINUE
D	ENDITED	I	DIETINE	N	DENTINE		STEINED	V	EVIDENT
	TEINDED	L	LENITED	S	DESTINE	T	DINETTE		

deeirs 99 - reside

A	DEARIES	E	SEEDIER	O	OREIDES		SERRIED	V	DERIVES
	READIES	F	DEFIERS		OSIERED	S	DESIRES		DEVISER
B	BREDIES		SERIFED	P	PREDIES		RESIDES		DIVERSE
	DERBIES	G	SEDGIER		PRESIDE	T	DIESTER		REVISED
C	DECRIES	L	RESILED		SPEIRED		DIETERS	W	SWEIRED
	DEICERS	M	REMEIDS		SPIERED		REEDITS	Z	RESIZED
D	DERIDES		REMISED	R	DERRIES		REISTED		
	DESIRED	N	DENIERS		DESIRER		RESISTED		
	DIEDRES		NEREIDS		REDRIES	U	RESIDUE		
	RESIDED		RESINED		RESIDER		UREIDES		

deeist 193 - [estide]

A	IDEATES	F	DEIFEST	N	DESTINE		DIETERS	W	DEWIEST
B	BETIDES	G	EDGIEST		ENDITES		REEDITS	X	EXISTED
C	DECEITS	H	HEISTED		STEINED		REISTED		
D	DEIDEST	I	DEITIES	P	DESPITE		RESITED		
	TEDDIES	L	ISLETED	R	DIESTER	T	TEDIEST		

deenor 169 - redone

B	DEBONER		ENCORED	N	ENDERON	T	ERODENT
	ENROBED	G	ENGORED	O	RONEOED	W	ENDOWER
	REDBONE	I	ORDINEE	P	REPONED		REENDOW
C	ENCODER	M	MODERNE	S	ENDORSE	Z	REZONED

deenrs 234 - sender

A	DEANERS		SERENED		RESINED	P	SPENDER		TENDRES
	ENDEARS		SNEERED	L	LENDERS	R	RENDERS	U	ENDURES
B	BENDERS	F	FENDERS		RELENDS	S	REDNESS		ENSURED
C	DECERNS	G	GENDERS		SLENDER		RESENDS	V	VENDERS
	SCERNED	H	HERDENS	M	MENDERS		SENDERS	Z	DZERENS
D	REDDENS	I	DENIERS		REMENDS	T	STERNED
E	NEEDERS		NEREIDS	O	ENDORSE		TENDERS

deginr 195 - ringed

A	AREDING	B	BREDING		REEDING	O	ERODING	S	DINGERS
	DEARING	C	CRINGED		REIGNED		GROINED		ENGIRDS
	DERAIGN	D	GRINDED	F	FRINGED		IGNORED	U	DUNGIER
	EARDING		REDDING	H	HERDING		NEGROID	W	REDWING
	GRADINE	E	DREEING	I	DINGIER		REDOING		WRINGED
	GRAINED		ENERGID	N	GRINNED	R	GRINDER	Y	YERDING
	READING		GREINED		RENDING		REGRIND

deiint 237 - tineid

A	INEDITA	D	INDITED		EDITING		TENIOID	S	INDITES
C	IDENTIC	E	DIETINE		IGNITED	R	INDITER		TINEIDS
	INCITED	G	DIETING	O	EDITION		NITRIDE	V	INVITED

deilor 118 - roiled

A	DARIOLE	E	REOILED	K	RODLIKE	S	SOLDIER
B	BROILED	G	GLORIED	L	DOLLIER		SOLIDER
C	DOCILER		GODLIER	M	MOLDIER	T	DOILTER
D	DROILED		GOLDIER	P	LEPORID	W	DOWLIER

deilos 144 - soiled

A	DEASOIL	I	DOILIES		SMOILED		DIPLOES		SOLIDER
	ISOLEAD		IDOLISE	N	DOLINES		DIPOLES	V	LIVEDOS
B	BOLIDES	K	KELOIDS		INDOLES		PELOIDS	Y	DOYLIES
C	COLDIES	L	DOLLIES		SONDELI		SOLIPED
D	DILDOES	M	MELOIDS	O	DOOLIES		SPOILED
E	OILSEED		MIDSOLE	P	DESPOIL	R	SOLDIER

deilrt 155 - tirled

A	DILATER	D	TIDDLER	H	THIRLED		TRINDLE	W	TWIRLED
	REDTAIL	E	RETILED	K	KIRTLED	O	DOILTER	Y	TIREDLY
	TRAILED	F	FLIRTED	L	TRILLED	P	TRIPLED
B	DRIBLET		TRIFLED	N	TENDRIL	U	DILUTER

deinor 27 - roined

A	ANEROID		IGNORED	N	ENDIRON		INDORSE	W	DOWNIER
B	INORBED		NEGROID	P	POINDER		ORDINES		WINDORE
D	NODDIER		REDOING		PROINED		ROSINED
E	ORDINEE	H	HORDEIN	R	DRONIER		SORDINE
G	ERODING	J	JOINDER	S	DINEROS	U	DOURINE
	GROINED	M	MINORED		DONSIER		NEUROID

deinos 85 - onside

A	ADONISE	G	DINGOES		SONDELI		SPINODE	S	ONSIDES
	ANODISE	H	HOIDENS	M	DOMINES	R	DINEROS	T	DITONES
	SODAINE	I	IODINES		EMODINS		DONSIER		STONIED
C	CODEINS		IONISED		MISDONE		INDORSE
	CONDIES	K	DOESKIN	N	DONNIES		ORDINES
	SECONDI	L	DOLINES		ONDINES		ROSINED
D	NODDIES		INDOLES	P	DISPONE		SORDINE

deinot 126 - ointed

C	CTENOID	D	DENTOID	TENIOID	N	INTONED	S DITONES
	DEONTIC	G	INGOTED	J JOINTED		NOINTED	STONIED
	NOTICED	I	EDITION	L LENTOID	P	POINTED	

deinrs 97 - snider

A	RANDIES		RESCIND	ENGIRDS	M	MINDERS	SORDINE
	SANDIER	E	DENIERS	H HINDERS		REMINDS	P PINDERS
	SARDINE		NEREIDS	NERDISH	N	DINNERS	T TINDERS
B	BINDERS		RESINED	SHRINED		ENDRINS	U INSURED
	INBREDS	F	FINDERS	I INSIDER	O	DINEROS	V VERDINS
	REBINDS		FRIENDS	SNIDIER		DONSIER	W REWINDS
C	CINDERS		REDFINS	K KINDERS		INDORSE	WINDERS
	DISCERN		REFINDS	KINREDS		ORDINES	
	NERDICS	G	DINGERS	REDSKIN		ROSINED	

deinrt 145 - trined

A	ANTIRED		NITRIDE	S TINDERS		UNTIRED	Y TINDERY
	DETRAIN	L	TENDRIL	T TRIDENT		UNTRIDE	
	TRAINED		TRINDLE	U INTRUDE		UNTIRED	
I	INDITER	P	PRINTED	TURDINE	X	DEXTRIN	

deinru 90 - urined

A	UNAIRED	F	UNFIRED	M UNRIMED	R	NURDIER	UNTRIDE
	URANIDE	G	DUNGIER	N DUNNIER	S	INSURED	UNTRIED
C	INDUCER	H	UNHIRED	INURNED	T	INTRUDE	W UNWIRED
D	UNDRIED	I	URIDINE	O DOURINE		TURDINE	
E	UREDINE	J	INJURED	NEUROID		UNTIRED	

deinst 65 - teinds

A	DESTAIN	E	DESTINE	K DINKEST		STONIED	STINTED
	DETAINS		ENDITES	KINDEST	P	DIPNETS	U DISTUNE
	INSTEAD		STEINED	L DENTILS		STIPEND	DUNITES
	NIDATES	F	SNIFTED	M MINDSET	R	TINDERS	Y DENSITY
	SAINTED	G	NIDGETS	MISTEND	S	DISNEST	DESTINY
	SATINED		STEDING	N DENTINS		DISSENT	
	STAINED		STINGED	INDENTS		SNIDEST	
B	BIDENTS	I	INDITES	INTENDS	T	DENTIST	
D	DISTEND		TINEIDS	O DITONES		DISTENT	

deiors 43 - rosied

A	ROADIES		OSIERED	INDORSE	T	EDITORS	VISORED
	SOREDIA	H	RHODIES	ORDINES		ROISTED	VOIDERS
B	BORIDES	I	IODISER	ROSINED		ROSITED	W DOWRIES
	DISROBE	L	SOLDIER	SORDINE		SORTIED	ROWDIES
C	DISCOER		SOLIDER	O ODORISE		STEROID	WEIRDOS
	SCODIER	M	MISDOER	OROIDES		STORIED	Z DORIZES
D	DORISED		MOIDERS	P PERIODS		TRIODES	
	SODDIER	N	DINEROS	S DORISES	V	DEVISOR	
E	OREIDES		DONSIER	DOSSIER		DEVOIRS	

deiort 56 - triode

B	DEBITOR	H	THEROID	PERIDOT		ROSITED	T DOTTIER
	DEORBIT	I	DIORITE	PROTEID		SORTIED	U ETOURDI
	ORBITED	L	DOILTER	R DORTIER		STEROID	IODURET
C	CORDITE	P	DIOPTER	S EDITORS		STORIED	OUTRIDE
G	GOITRED		DIOPTRE	ROISTED		TRIODES	Z ROZITED

deiost 80 - todies

A	IODATES	J	JOISTED	P	DEPOSIT		ROSITED		TEDIOUS
	TOADIES	M	DISTOME		DOPIEST		SORTIED	V	DOVIEST
C	CESTOID		DOMIEST		PODITES		STEROID	W	DOWIEST
	COEDITS		MODISTE		POSITED		STORIED	X	EXODIST
	COTISED		MOISTED		SOPITED		TRIODES	Z	DOZIEST
D	TODDIES	N	DITONES		TOPSIDE	T	DOTIEST		
F	FOISTED		STONIED	R	EDITORS		STOITED		
H	HOISTED	O	OSTEOID		ROISTED	U	OUTSIDE		

deirst 116 - stride

A	ARIDEST	B	BESTRID	F	FRISTED		ROISTED		STRIDER
	ASTERID		BISTRED	H	DITHERS		ROSITED	S	DISSERT
	ASTRIDE	C	CREDITS		SHIRTED		SORTIED		STRIDES
	DIASTER		DIRECTS	I	DIRTIES		STEROID	U	DUSTIER
	DISRATE	E	DIESTER		DITSIER		STORIED		REDUITS
	STAIDER		DIETERS		TIDIERS		TRIODES		STUDIER
	STAIRED		REEDITS	K	SKIRTED	P	SPIRTED	V	DIVERTS
	TARDIES		REISTED	N	TINDERS		STRIPED		STRIVED
	TIRADES		RESITED	O	EDITORS	R	STIRRED		VERDITS

delort 241 - retold

A	DELATOR	I	DOILTER	P	DROPLET		STRODLE
	LEOTARD	L	TROLLED		PRETOLD	T	DOTTLER
D	TODDLER	N	ENTROLD	S	DROLEST		DOTTREL
F	TELFORD	O	ROOTLED		OLDSTER	U	TROULED

denors 175 - sorned

B	BONDERS	E	ENDORSE		SORDINE	R	DRONERS		UNDOERS
C	CONDERS	H	DEHORNS	L	RONDELS	S	SONDERS	V	VENDORS
	CORSNED	I	DINEROS	M	MODERNS	T	RODENTS	W	DOWNERS
	SCORNED		DONSIER		RODSMEN		SNORTED		WONDERS
D	DONDERS		INDORSE	P	PERNODS	U	ENDUROS	Y	YONDERS
	NODDERS		ORDINES		PONDERS		RESOUND		
	SNODDER		ROSINED		RESPOND		SOUNDER		

denort 143 - rodent

A	TORNADE	H	NORTHED	L	ENTROLD	P	PORTEND
D	TRODDEN		THONDER	M	MORDENT		PROTEND
E	ERODENT		THORNED	N	DONNERT	S	RODENTS
F	FRONTED		THRONED		TENDRON		SNORTED

denoru 212 - undoer

A	RONDEAU		UNDERDO	I	DOURINE	P	POUNDER		SOUNDER
B	BOUNDER	F	FOUNDER		NEUROID		UNROPED		UNDOERS
	REBOUND		REFOUND	L	LOUNDER	R	RONDURE	W	REWOUND
	UNROBED	G	GUERDON		ROUNDEL		ROUNDER		WOUNDER
C	CRUNODE		UNDERGO		ROUNDLE		UNORDER		
D	REDOUND		UNGORED	M	MOURNED	S	ENDUROS		
	ROUNDED	H	HOUNDER	N	ENROUND		RESOUND		

denost 150 - stoned

A	ASTONED	C	DOCENTS		STONIED		TENDONS		SNORTED
	DONATES	E	DENOTES	K	STONKED	O	SNOOTED	T	SNOTTED
	ONSTEAD	F	FONDEST	M	ENDMOST		STOODEN	U	DEUTONS
B	OBTENDS	I	DITONES	N	STONNED	R	RODENTS		SNOUTED

deorst 101 - trodes

A	DOATERS		FROSTED		STORIED	P	DEPORTS		OUTREDS
	ROASTED	G	STODGER		TRIODES		REDTOPS		REDOUTS
	TORSADE		TODGERS	K	STROKED		SPORTED		ROUSTED
	TROADES	H	DEHORTS	L	DROLEST	R	DORTERS	W	STROWED
B	DEBTORS		SHORTED		OLDSTER		RODSTER		WORSTED
	STROBED	I	EDITORS		STRODLE	T	DETORTS	Y	DESTROY
E	OERSTED		ROISTED	M	STORMED		DOTTERS		ROYSTED
	ROSETED		ROSITED	N	RODENTS	U	DETOURS		STROYED
	TEREDOS		SORTIED		SNORTED		DOUREST		
F	DEFROST		STEROID	O	ROOSTED		DOUTERS		

deortu 225 - toured

A	OUTDARE		REDOUBT	I	ETOURDI	P	TROUPED		REDOUTS
	OUTREAD	C	COURTED		IODURET	Q	TORQUED		ROUSTED
	READOUT		EDUCTOR		OUTRIDE	S	DETOURS	T	TUTORED
B	DOUBTER	F	FOUTRED	L	TROULED		DOUREST	U	OUTDURE
	OBTRUDE	G	DROGUET	O	OUTDOER		DOUTERS	W	OUTDREW
	OUTBRED		GROUTED		OUTRODE		OUTREDS		

eeginr 135 - [eering]

A	REGINAE		ENERGID		REEFING		REGIMEN		TEERING
B	BIGENER		GREINED	G	GREEING	N	ENGINER		TREEING
	BREINGE		REEDING	H	REHINGE		INGENER	V	REEVING
	REBEGIN		REIGNED	J	JEERING	P	PEERING		REGIVEN
C	CREEING	E	GREENIE	K	REEKING		PREEING		VEERING
	ENERGIC	F	FEERING	L	LEERING	S	GREISEN		
	GENERIC		FEIGNER		REELING	T	GENTIER		
D	DREEING		FREEING	M	MEERING		INTEGER		

eeilnr 216 - reline

A	ALIENER	D	REDLINE		REELING	S	LIERNES
B	BERLINE		RELINED	M	ERMELIN		RELINES
C	RECLINE	G	LEERING	O	ELOINER	V	LIVENER

eeilns 246 - silene

A	SEALINE		LINSEED	O	OLEINES		SENILES		TENSILE
C	LICENSE	F	FELINES	P	PENSILE		SENSILE	Y	YEELINS
	SELENIC	G	LEESING	R	LIERNES		SILENES		
	SILENCE		SEELING		RELINES	T	LENITES		
D	ENISLED	L	NELLIES	S	ENISLES		LISENTE		
	ENSILED	M	ISLEMEN		ENSILES		SETLINE		

eeilnt 182 - lenite

A	LINEATE	D	LENITED	K	NETLIKE	S	LENITES		TENSILE
C	CENTILE	G	GENTILE	N	LENIENT		LISENTE	T	ENTITLE
	LICENTE	H	THEELIN	P	PENLITE		SETLINE	V	VEINLET

eeilrs 108 - resile

A	EARLIES		REFILES		RELLIES	S	IRELESS		RELIVES
	REALISE		REFLIES	N	LIERNES		RESILES		REVILES
B	BELIERS		RELIEFS		RELINES	T	LEISTER		SERVILE
C	CEILERS	G	LEIGERS	O	LOERIES		RETILES		VEILERS
D	RESILED		LIEGERS	P	REPLIES		STERILE	X	EXILERS
E	SEELIER	H	LEISHER		SPIELER	U	LEISURE		
F	FERLIES	L	LEISLER	R	RELIERS	V	LEVIERS		

eeilrt 158 - retile

A	ATELIER	D	RETILED	M	MELTIER	S	LEISTER	
	REALTIE	F	FELTIER	O	TROELIE		RETILES	
C	RETICLE		FERTILE	P	PERLITE		STERILE	
	TIERCEL	L	TREILLE		REPTILE	T	RETITLE	

eeilst 192 - listee

C	SECTILE	G	ELEGIST	N	LENITES		PELITES	V	EVILEST
D	ISLETED		ELEGITS		LISENTE	R	LEISTER		LEVITES
E	EELIEST	H	SHELTIE		SETLINE		RETILES		LIEVEST
	STEELIE	K	KELTIES		TENSILE		STERILE		VELITES
F	FELSITE		SLEEKIT	O	ESTOILE	S	LISTEES	X	SEXTILE
	LEFTIES	L	TELLIES		ETOILES		TELESIS		
	LIEFEST	M	ELMIEST	P	EPISTLE		TIELESS		

eeinrs 75 - serine

C	CERESIN		FINEERS	M	ERMINES	T	ENTIRES		VENIRES
	SCRIENE		REFINES	N	NERINES		ENTRIES		VERSINE
	SINCERE	G	GREISEN	P	EREPSIN		NERITES	W	NEWSIER
D	DENIERS	H	HENRIES		REPINES		RETINES		WEINERS
	NEREIDS		INHERES	R	RERISEN		TRENISE		WIENERS
	RESINED		RESHINE		RESINER		TRIENES	X	REXINES
E	ESERINE	K	KEIRENS	S	SEINERS	V	ENVIERS		
F	ENFIRES	L	LIERNES		SEREINS		INVERSE		
	FEERINS		RELINES		SERINES		VEINERS		

eeinrt 12 - triene

A	ARENITE	F	FEINTER	I	ERINITE		RENTIER		TRIENES
	RETINAE	G	GENTIER		NITERIE		TERRINE	T	NETTIER
	TRAINEE		INTEGER	K	KERNITE	S	ENTIRES		TENTIER
B	BENTIER		TEERING	N	INTERNE		ENTRIES	U	NEURITE
C	ENTERIC		TREEING	P	INEPTER		NERITES		RETINUE
	ENTICER	H	NEITHER	R	INERTER		RETINES		REUNITE
E	TEENIER		THEREIN		REINTER		TRENISE		UTERINE

eeinst 69 - seiten

A	ETESIAN	I	SIENITE	N	INTENSE		RETINES	V	TENSIVE
C	ENTICES	L	LENITES		TENNIES		TRENISE		VENITES
D	DESTINE		LISENTE	P	PENTISE		TRIENES	X	EXTINES
	ENDITES		SETLINE	R	ENTIRES	S	SEITENS		SIXTEEN
	STEINED		TENSILE		ENTRIES		SESTINE	Y	SYENITE
H	THEINES	M	EMETINS		NERITES	T	NETTIES		

eeiors 172 - soiree

B	EBRIOSE		OSIERED	L	LOERIES	R	ROSIERE	T	EROTISE
D	OREIDES	H	HEROISE	M	ISOMERE	S	SOIREES	V	EROSIVE

eeiort 171 - toeier

A	ETAERIO	C	COTERIE	L	TROELIE	S	EROTISE	Z	EROTIZE

eeiost 214 - [etiose]

B	TOEBIES	G	EGOTISE	L	ESTOILE	P	POETISE	S	ISOETES
C	COESITE		GOETIES		ETOILES	R	EROTISE	T	TOEIEST

eeirst 35 - reties

A AERIEST	RESITED	METIERS	TRIENES	S RESITES
SERIATE	E EERIEST	REEMITS	O EROTISE	T TESTIER
B REBITES	F FESTIER	RETIMES	P PESTIER	U SUETIER
C CERITES	H HEISTER	TREMIES	RESPITE	V RESTIVE
RECITES	K KEISTER	TRISEME	R ETRIERS	SIEVERT
TIERCES	KIESTER	N ENTIRES	REITERS	STIEVER
D DIESTER	L LEISTER	ENTRIES	RESTIER	VERIEST
DIETERS	RETILES	NERITES	RETIRES	VERITES
REEDITS	STERILE	RETINES	RETRIES	W STEWIER
REISTED	M MEISTER	TRENISE	TERRIES	Z ZESTIER

eenors 245 - [nerose]

A ARENOSE	D ENDORSE	M MOREENS	REPONES	Z REZONES
B BOREENS	G ENGORES	P OPENERS	S SENORES	
ENROBES	NEGROES	PEREONS	T ESTRONE	
C ENCORES	H RESHONE	PERONES	Y ONEYERS	
NECROSE	J REJONES	REOPENS	ONEYRES	

eenrst 79 - treens

A EARNEST	RETENES	K RENKEST	R RENTERS	RETUNES
EASTERN	TEENERS	L NESTLER	RERENTS	TENURES
NEAREST	G GERENTS	RELENTS	STERNER	TUREENS
RATEENS	REGENTS	SLENTER	S NESTERS	V VENTERS
C CENTERS	H THRENES	N RENNETS	RENESTS	VENTRES
CENTRES	I ENTIRES	TENNERS	RESENTS	W WESTERN
TENRECS	ENTRIES	O ESTRONE	STRENES	X EXTERNS
D STERNED	NERITES	P PENSTER	T NETTERS	Y STYRENE
TENDERS	RETINES	PRESENT	TENTERS	YESTERN
TENDRES	TRENISE	REPENTS	TESTERN	
E ENTREES	TRIENES	SERPENT	U NEUTERS	

eeorst 105 - stereo

A ROSEATE	I EROTISE	METEORS	STEREOS	VETOERS
D OERSTED	J RESOJET	REMOTES	T ROSETTE	X XEROTES
ROSETED	K RESTOKE	N ESTRONE	V ESTOVER	Y ESOTERY
TEREDOS	L SOLERET	R RESTORE	OVERSET	
H HETEROS	M EMOTERS	S OSSETER	REVOTES	

egilnt 154 - tingle

A ATINGLE	TINGLED	K KINGLET	TINGLER	T ETTLING
ELATING	E GENTILE	L GILLNET	TRINGLE	LETTING
GELATIN	F FELTING	TELLING	S GLISTEN	U ELUTING
GENITAL	H ENLIGHT	M MELTING	LESTING	W WELTING
TAGLINE	LIGHTEN	O LENTIGO	SINGLET	WINGLET
B BELTING	I LIGNITE	P PELTING	SNIGLET	
D GLINTED	J JINGLET	R RINGLET	TINGLES	

eginor 77 - region

A ORIGANE	NEGROID	O GOONIER	S ERINGOS	V OVERING
C COREIGN	REDOING	P PERIGON	IGNORES	Z ZEROING
D ERODING	F FOREIGN	PIROGEN	REGIONS	
GROINED	M MOERING	PONGIER	SIGNORE	
IGNORED	N NEGRONI	R IGNORER	T GENITOR	

eginos 137 - soigne

A	AGONIES	E	GENOISE	LIGNOSE
	AGONISE		SOIGNEE	LINGOES
B	BINGOES	H	HONGIES	LONGIES
	BIOGENS		SHOEING	M MISGONE
C	COGNISE	J	JINGOES	O GOONIES
	COIGNES	L	ELOIGNS	ISOGONE
D	DINGOES		LEGIONS	NOOGIES

P EPIGONS	U IGNEOUS
PIGEONS	W WIGEONS
PINGOES	Y ISOGENY
R ERINGOS	Z GINZOES
IGNORES	
REGIONS	
SIGNORE	

eginrs 140 - singer

A	ANGRIES	D DINGERS	SLINGER
	EARINGS	ENGIRDS	M GERMINS
	ERASING	E GREISEN	MERINGS
	GAINERS	F FINGERS	MINGERS
	GRAINES	FRINGES	N ENRINGS
	REAGINS	G GINGERS	GINNERS
	REGAINS	NIGGERS	O ERINGOS
	REGINAS	SERGING	IGNORES
	SEARING	SNIGGER	REGIONS
	SERINGA	H HINGERS	SIGNORE
B	BINGERS	L GIRNELS	P PERSING
C	CRINGES	LINGERS	PINGERS

SPRINGE	RUEINGS
R ERRINGS	SIGNEUR
GIRNERS	V SERVING
RINGERS	VERSING
SERRING	W SWINGER
S INGRESS	WINGERS
RESIGNS	Y SYRINGE
SIGNERS	Z ZINGERS
SINGERS	
T RESTING	
STINGER	
U REUSING	

eginrt 88 - engirt

A	GRANITE	INTEGER	TIGRINE
	GRATINE	TEERING	L RINGLET
	INGRATE	TREEING	TINGLER
	TANGIER	H RIGHTEN	TRINGLE
	TEARING	I IGNITER	M METRING
E	GENTIER	TIERING	TERMING

N RENTING	T GITTERN
RINGENT	RETTING
TERNING	U TRUEING
O GENITOR	V VERTING
S RESTING	Y RETYING
STINGER	

egiort 244 - goitre

A GOATIER	D GOITRED	S GOITERS	GORIEST
C ERGOTIC	N GENITOR	GOITRES	U GOUTIER

V VERTIGO
Z ZORGITE

eiinrt 66 - tinier

A	INERTIA	NITRIDE	TIGRINE
C	CITRINE	E ERINITE	H INHERIT
	CRINITE	NITERIE	L LINTIER
	INCITER	F NIFTIER	NITRILE
	NERITIC	G IGNITER	M INTERIM
D	INDITER	TIERING .	MINTIER

TERMINI	VITRINE
N TINNIER	W TWINIER
T NITRITE	
NITTIER	
TINTIER	
V INVITER	

eiinst 107 - tinies

A	ISATINE	F FINITES	M MINIEST
B	STIBINE	NIFTIES	N INTINES
C	INCITES	G IGNITES	TINNIES
D	INDITES	K INKIEST	O INOSITE
	TINEIDS	L LINIEST	P PINIEST
E	SIENITE	LINTIES	PINITES

TIEPINS	VINIEST
T SITTINE	W WINIEST
TINIEST	
U UNITIES	
UNITISE	
V INVITES	

eilnor 23 - neroli

A	AILERON	E ELOINER	O LOONIER
	ALERION	I NOILIER	P PLERION
	ALIENOR	N ONLINER	PROLINE

R LORINER
S NEROLIS
T RETINOL

eilnos 41 - solein

A ANISOLE	SONDELI	LONGIES	M LOMEINS	INSOLES
B BOLINES	E OLEINES	I ELISION	MOLINES	LESIONS
C CINEOLS	F OLEFINS	ISOLINE	O LOONIES	LIONESS
CONSEIL	G ELOIGNS	LIONISE	P EPSILON	T ENTOILS
INCLOSE	LEGIONS	K SONLIKE	PINOLES	LIONETS
D DOLINES	LIGNOSE	L LIONELS	R NEROLIS	ONLIEST
INDOLES	LINGOES	NIELLOS	S ESLOINS	U ELUSION

eilnot 40 - lionet

A ELATION	H HOTLINE	PONTILE	LIONETS	W TOWLINE
TOENAIL	NEOLITH	POTLINE	ONLIEST	
C LECTION	I ETIOLIN	TOPLINE	U ELUTION	
D LENTOID	M MOLINET	R RETINOL	OUTLINE	
G LENTIGO	P POINTEL	S ENTOILS	V VIOLENT	

eilnrs 177 - liners

A ALINERS	RELINES	RESILIN	MERLINS	SNIRTLE
NAILERS	G GIRNELS	K LINKERS	O NEROLIS	V SILVERN
RENAILS	LINGERS	RELINKS	P PILSNER	
B BERLINS	SLINGER	SLINKER	T LINTERS	
E LIERNES	I INLIERS	M LIMNERS	SLINTER	

eilnrt 146 - linter

A ENTRAIL	RETINAL	G RINGLET	NITRILE	SLINTER
LATRINE	TRENAIL	TINGLER	K TINKLER	SNIRTLE
RATLINE	D TENDRIL	TRINGLE	O RETINOL	Y INERTLY
RELIANT	TRINDLE	I LINTIER	S LINTERS	

eilnst 92 - tinsel

A EASTLIN	LENTISC	TINGLES	ONLIEST	U LUNIEST
ELASTIN	STENCIL	I LINIEST	P LEPTINS	LUTEINS
ENTAILS	D DENTILS	LINTIES	PINTLES	UNTILES
NAILSET	E LENITES	K LENTISK	PLENIST	UTENSIL
SALIENT	LISENTE	TINKLES	R LINTERS	V VENTILS
SALTINE	SETLINE	L LENTILS	SLINTER	W WESTLIN
SLAINTE	TENSILE	LINTELS	SNIRTLE	WINTLES
STANIEL	G GLISTEN	TELLINS	S ENLISTS	
TENAILS	LESTING	N LINNETS	LISTENS	
C CLIENTS	SINGLET	O ENTOILS	SILENTS	
LECTINS	SNIGLET	LIONETS	TINSELS	

eilors 45 - reoils

B BOILERS	SOLIDER	N NEROLIS	LOSSIER	LOUSIER
LIBEROS	E LOERIES	O ORIOLES	RISSOLE	SOILURE
REBOILS	G GLOIRES	P SLOPIER	T ESTRIOL	V OLIVERS
C COILERS	GLORIES	SPOILER	LOITERS	VIOLERS
RECOILS	I SOILIER	R LORRIES	TOILERS	W LOWRIES
D SOLDIER	M MOILERS	S LORISES	U LOURIES	

eilort 31 - toiler

B TRILOBE	F LOFTIER	N RETINOL	S ESTRIOL	TRIOLET
C CORTILE	TREFOIL	O TROOLIE	LOITERS	U OUTLIER
D DOILTER	J JOLTIER	P POITREL	TOILERS	V OVERLIT
E TROELIE	M MOTLIER	POLITER	T TORTILE	

eilost 38 - toiles

A	ISOLATE	H	EOLITHS		TOLLIES		STOOLIE	T	LITOTES
B	BETOILS		HOLIEST	M	MOTILES		TOOLIES		TOILETS
C	CITOLES		HOSTILE	N	ENTOILS	P	PIOLETS	U	OUTLIES
E	ESTOILE	I	IOLITES		LIONETS		PISTOLE	V	OLIVETS
	ETOILES		OILIEST		ONLIEST	R	ESTRIOL		VIOLETS
G	ELOGIST	L	OILLETS	O	OOLITES		LOITERS	W	OWLIEST
	LOGIEST		STELLIO		OSTIOLE		TOILERS	Z	ZLOTIES

eilrst 81 - tilers

A	REALIST		RETILES	J	JILTERS		SNIRTLE		STILTER
	RETAILS		STERILE	K	KILTERS	O	ESTRIOL		TESTRIL
	SALTIER	F	FILTERS		KIRTLES		LOITERS		TILTERS
	SALTIRE		LIFTERS		KLISTER		TOILERS		TITLERS
	SLATIER		STIFLER	L	RILLETS	P	RESPLIT	U	LUSTIER
	TAILERS		TRIFLES		STILLER		SPIRTLE		RULIEST
B	BLISTER	G	GLISTER		TILLERS		TRIPLES		RUTILES
	BRISTLE		GRISTLE		TRELLIS	S	LISTERS	Y	STYLIER
	RIBLETS	H	SLITHER	M	MILTERS		RELISTS		
C	RELICTS	I	RILIEST	N	LINTERS	T	LITTERS		
E	LEISTER		SILTIER		SLINTER		SLITTER		

eimnot 223 - [montie]

A	AMNIOTE	E	ONETIME	N	MENTION	S	MESTINO	Y	OMNEITY
C	CENTIMO	G	EMOTING	O	EMOTION		MOISTEN		OMNIETY
	ENTOMIC		MITOGEN	P	EMPTION		MONTIES		
	TONEMIC	L	MOLINET		PIMENTO		SENTIMO		

einopr 163 - proine

C	PERICON		PIONEER	I	RIPIENO	R	PORNIER		PTERION
	PONCIER	F	FORPINE	L	PLERION	S	ORPINES		REPOINT
	PORCINE	G	PERIGON		PROLINE		PIONERS		TROPINE
D	POINDER		PIROGEN	M	PROMINE		PROINES	V	PROVINE
	PROINED		PONGIER	P	POPERIN	T	POINTER		
E	PEREION	H	PHONIER		PROPINE		PROTEIN		

einorr 208 - ironer

C	CORNIER	E	ONERIER	H	HORNIER	L	LORINER	S	IRONERS
D	DRONIER	G	IGNORER	I	IRONIER	P	PORNIER		ROSINER

einors 8 - soneri

A	ERASION		ORDINES		IRONISE		PROINES		TERSION
C	COINERS		ROSINED		NOISIER	R	IRONERS		TRIONES
	CRINOSE		SORDINE	J	JOINERS		ROSINER	U	URINOSE
	CRONIES	G	ERINGOS		REJOINS	S	ORNISES	V	ENVIROS
	ORCEINS		IGNORES	L	NEROLIS		SENIORS		RENVOIS
	ORCINES		REGIONS	M	MERINOS		SONERIS		VERSION
	RECOINS		SIGNORE		MERSION		SONSIER	W	SNOWIER
	SERICON	H	HEROINS	N	RONNIES	T	NORITES	X	OREXINS
D	DINEROS		INSHORE	O	EROSION		OESTRIN		
	DONSIER	I	IONISER	P	ORPINES		ORIENTS		
	INDORSE		IRONIES		PIONERS		STONIER		

einort 13 - tonier

A	NOTAIRE	G	GENITOR	P	POINTER		OESTRIN	U	ROUTINE
	OTARINE	J	JOINTER		PROTEIN		ORIENTS	W	NOWTIER
B	BORNITE	L	RETINOL		PTERION		STONIER		TOWNIER
C	COINTER	N	INTONER		REPOINT		TERSION	Z	TRIZONE
	NOTICER		NOINTER		TROPINE		TRIONES		
	RECTION		TERNION	S	NORITES	T	TRITONE		

einost 14 - tonies

A	ATONIES		HISTONE		MONTIES		PONTIES		SONTIES
B	BONIEST	I	INOSITE		SENTIMO	R	NORITES		STONIES
	EBONIST	J	JONTIES	N	INTONES		OESTRIN	T	SNOTTIE
C	NOTICES	L	ENTOILS		TENSION		ORIENTS		TONIEST
	SECTION		LIONETS	O	ISOTONE		STONIER		TONITES
D	DITONES		ONLIEST		TOONIES		TERSION	W	TOWNIES
	STONIED	M	MESTINO	P	PINTOES		TRIONES		TWONIES
H	ETHIONS		MOISTEN		POINTES	S	NOSIEST	X	TOXINES

einrst 30 - trines

A	ANESTRI	D	TINDERS		SKINTER		OESTRIN		TINTERS
	ANTSIER	E	ENTIRES		STINKER		ORIENTS	U	NUTSIER
	NASTIER		ENTRIES		TINKERS		STONIER		TRIUNES
	RATINES		NERITES	L	LINTERS		TERSION		UNITERS
	RESIANT		RETINES		SLINTER		TRIONES	V	INVERTS
	RETAINS		TRENISE		SNIRTLE	P	NIPTERS		STRIVEN
	RETINAS		TRIENES	M	ENTRISM		PTERINS	W	TWINERS
	RETSINA	F	SNIFTER		MINSTER	S	ESTRINS		WINTERS
	STAINER	G	RESTING		MINTERS		INSERTS	Y	SINTERY
	STARNIE		STINGER		REMINTS		SINTERS		
	STEARIN	H	HINTERS	N	INTERNS	T	ENTRIST		
C	CISTERN		NITHERS		TINNERS		RETINTS		
	CRETINS	K	REKNITS	O	NORITES		STINTER		

einrtt 174 - tinter

A	INTREAT	B	BITTERN		RETTING	O	TRITONE	W	TWINTER
	ITERANT	C	CITTERN	I	NITRITE	S	ENTRIST		WRITTEN
	NATTIER	D	TRIDENT		NITTIER		RETINTS		
	NITRATE	E	NETTIER		TINTIER		STINTER		
	TARTINE		TENTIER	K	KNITTER		TINTERS		
	TERTIAN	G	GITTERN		TRINKET	U	NUTTIER		

einrtu 47 - uniter

A	RUINATE	D	INTRUDE		REUNITE	O	ROUTINE	V	UNRIVET
	TAURINE		TURDINE		UTERINE	P	REPUNIT		VENTURI
	URANITE		UNTIRED	G	TRUEING	R	RUNTIER	W	UNWRITE
	URINATE		UNTRIDE	M	MINUTER	S	NUTSIER		
B	BUNTIER		UNTRIED		MUNTRIE		TRIUNES		
	TRIBUNE	E	NEURITE		UNMITER		UNITERS		
	TURBINE		RETINUE		UNMITRE	T	NUTTIER		

einstu 176 - unties

A	AUNTIES	I	UNITIES	M	MINUETS	P	PUNIEST		UNITERS
	SINUATE		UNITISE		MINUTES		PUNTIES	S	INTUSES
C	NEUSTIC	L	LUNIEST		MISTUNE	Q	INQUEST	T	TUNIEST
D	DISTUNE		LUTEINS		MUNITES		QUINTES		
	DUNITES		UNTILES		MUTINES	R	NUTSIER		
G	GUNITES		UTENSIL	N	TUNNIES		TRIUNES		

eioost 206 - otiose

B	BOOTIES		OOFIEST		OSTIOLE	P	ISOTOPE	S	OOSIEST
C	COOTIES	G	GOOIEST		STOOLIE	R	OORIEST	T	TOOTSIE
D	OSTEOID	H	TOOSHIE		TOOLIES		ROOTIES	Z	OOZIEST
F	FOOTIES	K	STOOKIE	N	ISOTONE		SOOTIER		ZOOIEST
	FOOTSIE	L	OOLITES		TOONIES		TOORIES		

eiopst 248 - sopite

A	ATOPIES	E	POETISE		STOMPIE		REPOSIT		SPOTTIE
	OPIATES	H	ETHIOPS	N	PINTOES		RIPOSTE		TIPTOES
C	POETICS		OPHITES		POINTES		ROPIEST	U	PITEOUS
D	DEPOSIT	J	POTJIES		PONTIES	S	POSIEST	X	EXPOSIT
	DOPIEST	K	POKIEST	O	ISOTOPE		POSTIES		POXIEST
	PODITES	L	PIOLETS	P	POTPIES		POTSIES	Y	ISOTYPE
	POSITED		PISTOLE	R	PERIOST		SEPIOST		
	SOPITED	M	MOPIEST		PORIEST		SOPITES		
	TOPSIDE		OPTIMES		PROSTIE	T	POTTIES		

eiorst 4 - triose

A	OARIEST	F	FOISTER	M	EROTISM	P	PERIOST		STORIES
	OTARIES		FORTIES		MOISTER		PORIEST		TOSSIER
B	ORBIEST	G	GOITERS		MORTISE		PROSTIE		TRIOSES
	SORBITE		GOITRES		TRISOME		REPOSIT	T	STOITER
C	EROTICS		GORIEST	N	NORITES		RIPOSTE	U	OURIEST
	TERCIOS	H	HERIOTS		OESTRIN		ROPIEST		STOURIE
D	EDITORS		HOISTER		ORIENTS	R	RIOTERS		TOURIES
	ROISTED		SHORTIE		STONIER		ROISTER		TOUSIER
	ROSITED		TOSHIER		TERSION		RORIEST	V	TORSIVE
	SORTIED	I	RIOTISE		TRIONES	S	ROESTIS	W	OWRIEST
	STEROID	K	ROKIEST	O	OORIEST		ROSIEST		TOWSIER
	STORIED	L	ESTRIOL		ROOTIES		SIROSET		
	TRIODES		LOITERS		SOOTIER		SORITES		
E	EROTISE		TOILERS		TOORIES		SORTIES		

eiortu 96 - tourie

D	ETOURDI	G	GOUTIER	N	ROUTINE		STOURIE	V	VOITURE
	IODURET	H	OUTHIRE	P	POUTIER		TOURIES	Z	TOUZIER
	OUTRIDE		ROUTHIE	Q	QUOITER		TOUSIER		
F	OUTFIRE	L	OUTLIER	S	OURIEST	T	TOUTIER		

eiostt 148 - [otties]

A	OATIEST	D	DOTIEST		TOILETS		TONITES	T	STOTTIE
	OSTIATE		STOITED	M	MOTIEST	O	TOOTSIE		TOTTIES
	TOASTIE	E	TOEIEST		MOTTIES	P	POTTIES	U	TOUSTIE
B	BOTTIES	G	EGOTIST		TITMOSE		SPOTTIE	W	TOWIEST
C	COTTISE	H	HOTTIES	N	SNOTTIE		TIPTOES		
	SCOTTIE	L	LITOTES		TONIEST	R	STOITER		

eirstu 121 - urites

B	BUSTIER		STUDIER		TUSKIER	O	OURIEST	R	RUSTIER
	RUBIEST	E	SUETIER	L	LUSTIER		STOURIE	S	SUITERS
C	CUITERS	F	FUSTIER		RULIEST		TOURIES	T	TERTIUS
	CURIETS		SURFEIT		RUTILES		TOUSIER	V	REVUIST
	CURITES	G	GUSTIER	M	MUSTIER	P	PERITUS		STUIVER
	ICTERUS		GUTSIER	N	NUTSIER		PUIREST		VIRTUES
D	DUSTIER	H	HIRSUTE		TRIUNES	Q	QUERIST		
	REDUITS	K	TURKIES		UNITERS		REQUITS		

elorst 100 - torsel

A	OESTRAL	D	DROLEST		LOITERS		RETOOLS		SETTLOR
	OLESTRA		OLDSTER		TOILERS		ROOTLES		SLOTTER
B	BOLSTER		STRODLE	J	JOLTERS		TOOLERS		TOLTERS
	BOLTERS	E	SOLERET		JOSTLER	P	PETROLS	U	ELUTORS
	LOBSTER	F	FLORETS	L	TOLLERS		REPLOTS		OUTLERS
C	COLTERS		LOFTERS	M	MERLOTS	S	OSTLERS		TROULES
	CORSLET	H	HOLSTER		MOLTERS		STEROLS	V	REVOLTS
	COSTREL		HOSTLER	N	LENTORS		TORSELS	W	TROWELS
	LECTORS	I	ESTRIOL	O	LOOTERS	T	LOTTERS		WORTLES

enorst 25 - trones

A	ATONERS		CRONETS	I	NORITES	L	LENTORS	S	NESTORS
	SANTERO	D	RODENTS		OESTRIN	M	MENTORS		STONERS
	SENATOR		SNORTED		ORIENTS		MONSTER		TENSORS
	TREASON	E	ESTRONE		STONIER		MONTRES	T	ROTTENS
B	BRETONS	F	FRONTES		TERSION	N	STONERN		SNOTTER
	SORBENT	G	TONGERS		TRIONES		TONNERS		STENTOR
C	CONSTER	H	HORNETS	K	REKNOTS	O	ENROOTS	U	TENOURS
	CORNETS		SHORTEN		STONKER	P	POSTERN		TONSURE
	CRESTON		THRENOS		STROKEN		PRONEST	Y	TYRONES
	CRETONS		THRONES		TONKERS	R	SNORTER		

enorsu 184 - rouens

A	ARENOUS		ROUNCES	G	SURGEON		NONUSER	V	NERVOUS
B	BOURNES	D	ENDUROS	H	UNHORSE	O	ONEROUS	W	UNSWORE
	UNROBES		RESOUND	I	URINOSE	P	UNROPES	Z	ZONURES
	UNSOBER		SOUNDER	L	NOURSLE	T	TENOURS		
C	CONURES		UNDOERS	N	NEURONS		TONSURE		

enortu 220 - tenour

A	OUTEARN		RECOUNT	I	ROUTINE		REMOUNT		TONSURE
C	CORNUTE		TROUNCE	M	MONTURE	N	NEUTRON	W	UNWROTE
	COUNTER	F	FORTUNE		MOUNTER	S	TENOURS	Y	TOURNEY

enostu 142 - [outens]

A	SOUTANE		UNCOEST	G	TONGUES	O	UNSOOTE		TONUSES
B	SUBTONE	D	DEUTONS	L	LENTOUS	R	TENOURS	T	STOUTEN
C	CONTUSE		SNOUTED	M	UNSMOTE		TONSURE		TENUTOS
	ECONUTS	E	OUTSEEN	N	NEUSTON	S	OUTNESS	U	TENUOUS

enrstu 194 - unrest

A	AUNTERS	C	ENCRUST	G	GUNTERS		UNITERS		TONSURE
	NATURES	D	RETUNDS		GURNETS	L	RUNLETS	P	PUNSTER
	SAUNTER		UNDREST		SURGENT	M	MUNSTER		PUNTERS
B	BRUNETS	E	NEUTERS	H	HUNTERS		MUNTERS	R	RETURNS
	BUNTERS		RETUNES		SHUNTER		STERNUM		TURNERS
	BURNETS		TENURES		UNHERST	N	RUNNETS	S	UNRESTS
	BURSTEN		TUREENS	I	NUTSIER		STUNNER	T	ENTRUST
	SUBRENT	F	FUNSTER		TRIUNES	O	TENOURS		NUTTERS

ginort 229 - trigon

A	ORATING	I	IGNITOR		TROPING		TRIGONS		TOURING
	ROATING		RIOTING	R	RORTING	T	ROTTING	W	ROWTING
D	DORTING	K	TROKING	S	ROSTING	U	OUTGRIN		TROWING
E	GENITOR	O	ROOTING		SORTING		OUTRING		
F	FORTING	P	PORTING		STORING		ROUTING		

inorst 115 - nitros

A	AROINTS		CORTINS		TRIONES	H	HORNIST		TORSION
	RATIONS	E	NORITES	F	FORINTS	I	IRONIST	P	TROPINS
B	RIBSTON		OESTRIN	G	ROSTING	L	NOSTRIL	T	INTORTS
C	CISTRON		ORIENTS		SORTING	N	INTRONS		TRITONS
	CITRONS		STONIER		STORING	O	ISOTRON	U	NITROUS
	CORNIST		TERSION		TRIGONS		NITROSO		TURIONS

Seven-letter stems

Seven-letter stems in order of usefulness

As with the six-letter stems, the top 250 seven-letter stems are listed here in usefulness order. The most useful combination of tiles is AEINORT, followed by AEINRST, then EINORST, and so on. Underneath the list, the individual stems are shown in alphabetical order together with the words that can be formed by combining them with another letter. Once again, words with no valid anagram are followed by invented words, set within brackets. These invented words are not valid for play in Scrabble.

1:	AEINORT	-	OTARINE	
2:	AEINRST	-	STEARIN	
3:	EINORST	-	TRIONES	
4:	AEILORT	-	[OILTEAR]	
5:	AEIORST	-	OTARIES	
6:	AENORST	-	TREASON	
7:	ADEINRT	-	TRAINED	
8:	AEILNRT	-	TRENAIL	
9:	ADEINOT	-	[ANTIDOE]	
10:	ADEINRS	-	SARDINE	
11:	AEEIRST	-	SERIATE	
12:	AEEINRT	-	TRAINEE	
13:	EEINRST	-	TRIENES	
14:	AEILRST	-	TAILERS	
15:	AEEILRT	-	REALTIE	
16:	AEINORS	-	ERASION	
17:	ADEIRST	-	TIRADES	
18:	DEINORT	-	[INTERDO]	
19:	ADEIORT	-	[OARTIDE]	
20:	AEILNRS	-	RENAILS	
21:	AEINOST	-	ATONIES	
22:	AEENRST	-	RATEENS	
23:	ADEINST	-	STAINED	
24:	EEINORT	-	[ONETIRE]	
25:	AEILORS	-	[EARSOIL]	
26:	DEINORS	-	SORDINE	
27:	AEGILNR	-	REGINAL	
28:	EILNOST	-	ONLIEST	
29:	EILORST	-	TOILERS	
30:	AAEINRT	-	[ANTIEAR]	
31:	AEINRS	-	[NEARIES]	
32:	AEINRTU	-	URINATE	
33:	AEGINRT	-	TEARING	
34:	ADEINOR	-	ANEROID	
35:	DEIORST	-	TRIODES	
36:	AEILNOT	-	TOENAIL	
37:	AELORST	-	OLESTRA	
38:	ADEEIRT	-	[DIERATE]	
39:	AINORST	-	RATIONS	
40:	AEGINRS	-	SERINGA	
41:	ADENORT	-	TORNADE	
42:	AEELNRT	-	TELERAN	
43:	EILNORS	-	NEROLIS	
44:	ADEGINR	-	READING	
45:	ACEINRT	-	TACRINE	
46:	AEIINRT	-	INERTIA	
47:	EILNORT	-	RETINOL	
48:	DEEIRST	-	RESITED	
49:	AEILOST	-	ISOLATE	
50:	DEEINRT	-	[REDNITE]	
51:	AEGINST	-	TSIGANE	
52:	AEINPRT	-	REPAINT	
53:	ADEILNT	-	[LATINED]	
54:	EENORST	-	ESTRONE	
55:	DEEINST	-	STEINED	
56:	AEILNOR	-	ALIENOR	
57:	AEINRTT	-	TERTIAN	
58:	AEGILNT	-	TAGLINE	
59:	AEELRST	-	STEALER	
60:	AEILNST	-	TENAILS	
61:	ADEILRT	-	TRAILED	
62:	ADEINOS	-	SODAINE	
63:	ADEILRS	-	SIDERAL	
64:	AEELORT	-	[REALTOE]	
65:	EEIORST	-	EROTISE	
66:	DEINOST	-	STONIED	
67:	ADINORT	-	DIATRON	
68:	ADEEINT	-	[ANTIDEE]	
69:	EIINORT	-	[NOIRITE]	
70:	EGINORS	-	SIGNORE	
71:	EINRSTU	-	UNITERS	
72:	AELNORT	-	[ONLATER]	
73:	EIINRST	-	[TINRISE]	
74:	AEILNOS	-	ANISOLE	
75:	EIORSTU	-	TOUSIER	
76:	CEINORT	-	RECTION	
77:	AEIRRST	-	TARSIER	
78:	AILNORT	-	[LATINOR]	
79:	AEINRSU	-	[URANISE]	
80:	AENRSTU	-	SAUNTER	
81:	AEORSTU	-	[OUTEARS]	
82:	AEIRSTT	-	TERTIAS	
83:	AEEILRS	-	REALISE	
84:	AEINOTT	-	[ANTITOE]	
85:	AEEILNT	-	LINEATE	
86:	AEEGINR	-	REGINAE	
87:	DEEINRS	-	RESINED	
88:	ADENORS	-	[SANDORE]	
89:	AEEINST	-	ETESIAN	
90:	EEILRST	-	STERILE	
91:	AEIMRST	-	SMARTIE	
92:	DEINRTU	-	UNTRIED	
93:	EINORTT	-	TRITONE	
94:	DEINRST	-	TINDERS	
95:	AELNRST	-	STERNAL	
96:	EEILNST	-	TENSILE	
97:	AEEILNS	-	SEALINE	
98:	AEEILNR	-	ALIENER	
99:	AEINRRT	-	TRAINER	
100:	EINORRT	-	[NORTIER]	

101:	ADEORST	– TROADES
102:	DEILNOT	– LENTOID
103:	AAENRST	– SANTERA
104:	EILNRST	– SNIRTLE
105:	EEINOST	– [ETONISE]
106:	ACEINST	– CINEAST
107:	AEINNRS	– INSNARE
108:	AENORTU	– OUTEARN
109:	ENORSTU	– TONSURE
110:	ADEILOT	– [TOEDIAL]
111:	ADEEINR	– [EARDINE]
112:	AADEIRT	– TIARAED
113:	AAEILNT	– ANTLIAE
114:	AEILRTT	– TERTIAL
115:	AEINSTT	– SATINET
116:	AEEORST	– ROSEATE
117:	AEEGIRT	– [GREATIE]
118:	ADEINRU	– URANIDE
119:	ADEIORS	– SOREDIA
120:	EGINRST	– STINGER
121:	AEIIRST	– IRISATE
122:	AEIMNRT	– RAIMENT
123:	EEGINRS	– GREISEN
124:	EEGINRT	– TREEING
125:	ADENOST	– ONSTEAD
126:	EEINORS	– [ONERIES]
127:	ADINORS	– SADIRON
128:	AEEGNRT	– REAGENT
129:	AEINNOT	– ENATION
130:	DEILNOS	– SONDELI
131:	AEENORT	– [ONERATE]
132:	ADEGORT	– GAROTED
133:	EINORTU	– ROUTINE
134:	ADENRTU	– UNTREAD
135:	ABEINST	– BESTAIN
136:	AEIMNST	– TAMINES
137:	DEEIORT	– [DOETIRE]
138:	ADEERST	– TASERED
139:	AEIPRST	– TRAIPSE
140:	AEGNRST	– STRANGE
141:	ACENORT	– ENACTOR
142:	ADEEIST	– IDEATES
143:	ADEEIRS	– READIES
144:	AEORRST	– ROASTER
145:	AEINNRT	– TRANNIE
146:	AEHIRST	– SHERIAT
147:	ADEILNO	– [ONEDIAL]
148:	ADEIOST	– TOADIES
149:	EEILORT	– TROELIE
150:	AAEIRST	– ATRESIA
151:	ABEORST	– SORBATE
152:	ADIORST	– ASTROID
153:	AILORST	– TAILORS
154:	ACEINRS	– CERASIN
155:	AEGILNS	– SEALING
156:	EIORRST	– RORIEST
157:	ADEENRT	– [NETREAD]
158:	EEIINRT	– NITERIE
159:	AEEILST	– [TEALIES]
160:	ADEILST	– DILATES
161:	AEIINST	– ISATINE
162:	ACEINOT	– ANOETIC
163:	DEENORS	– ENDORSE
164:	AGINORT	– ROATING
165:	ADEEILR	– LEADIER
166:	ADEENRS	– ENDEARS
167:	ADEEGNR	– GRENADE
168:	ADEILOS	– ISOLEAD
169:	EIORSTT	– STOITER
170:	AEIMNRS	– SIRNAME
171:	EELORST	– SOLERET
172:	EEINRTT	– TENTIER
173:	AEEIMRT	– MEATIER
174:	EINNORT	– TERNION
175:	AENORTT	– [OATRENT]
176:	AEINSST	– TISANES
177:	AEGORST	– TOERAGS
178:	AILNOST	– TALIONS
179:	ADEIRTT	– ATTIRED
180:	AEIRSTW	– WASTRIE
181:	AEILPRT	– PLATIER
182:	AENORSU	– ARENOUS
183:	AELORSU	– [EARSOUL]
184:	AAEINST	– TAENIAS
185:	AEGINOR	– ORIGANE
186:	AEORSTT	– TOASTER
187:	EHINORT	– [THRONIE]
188:	ADEILNS	– SNAILED
189:	DEEORST	– TEREDOS
190:	EEILORS	– LOERIES
191:	ADEGIRT	– TRIAGED
192:	AEILRTU	– URALITE
193:	AEGINOS	– AGONISE
194:	AEIINRS	– SENARII
195:	ADEILNR	– [LANDIER]
196:	AEINSTV	– VAINEST
197:	CEINOST	– SECTION
198:	EIMORST	– TRISOME
199:	EEGINST	– [SEETING]
200:	AEILRRT	– TRAILER
201:	AGILNOT	– ANTILOG
202:	AEHINRT	– THERIAN
203:	DENORTU	– [OUTREND]
204:	EINOPRS	– PROINES
205:	AEILOTT	– [TEATOIL]
206:	AGINRST	– TARINGS
207:	AENOORT	– [OARNOTE]
208:	ADEIMNR	– INARMED
209:	EHIORST	– TOSHIER
210:	AEILNPT	– PANTILE
211:	EGILNOR	– [LONGIER]
212:	ADEILOR	– DARIOLE
213:	ACINORT	– CORTINA
214:	EGINORT	– GENITOR
215:	DEILOST	– [OLDISTE]
216:	DEEINOS	– [EONISED]
217:	DEENORT	– ERODENT
218:	CEINORS	– SERICON
219:	EILRSTU	– RUTILES
220:	DEILORT	– DOILTER

```
221: EEINSTT - NETTIES          236: EIOPRST - ROPIEST
222: AEIORTT - [TOATIER]        237: DEIORTU - OUTRIDE
223: AEEGINS - AGENISE          238: ADEGNOR - GROANED
224: AEINPST - SPINATE          239: DEILORS - SOLIDER
225: AEGILRS - GRAILES          240: BEINOST - EBONIST
226: ADENRST - STARNED          241: AELNORU - ALEURON
227: AEILRSU - [LAURIES]        242: DEINSTU - DUNITES
228: EIILRST - SILTIER          243: AEMNORS - OARSMEN
229: AEINSTU - SINUATE          244: ADIINOT - [TOINDIA]
230: AGINORS - SOARING          245: AEENRTU - [EARTUNE]
231: ADEIINT - INEDITA          246: ADEEINS - ANISEED
232: AEIMNOT - AMNIOTE          247: AEINPRS - RAPINES
233: AEENORS - ARENOSE          248: ACDEIRT - [CATRIDE]
234: EEINRSU - [NEURIES]        249: ADINRST - INDARTS
235: AEEGINT - [ANTIGEE]        250: ACEILRT - TALCIER
```

aadeirt 112 - tiaraed

C RADICATE	L LARIATED	S AIRDATES	T DIATRETA	
D RADIATED	N DENTARIA	DATARIES	V VARIATED	
E ERADIATE	RAINDATE	RADIATES		

aaeilnt 113 - antliae

C ANALCITE	E ALIENATE	H ANTHELIA	M ALAIMENT	P PALATINE
LAITANCE	G AGENTIAL	K ANTILEAK	ANTIMALE	T ANTLIATE
D DENTALIA	ALGINATE	L ALLANITE	LAMINATE	V AVENTAIL

aaeinrt 30 - [antiear]

B ATABRINE	RAINDATE	O AERATION	RESINATA	U INAURATE
RABATINE	G AERATING	P ANTIRAPE	SANTERIA	W ANTIWEAR
C CARINATE	J NAARTJIE	S ANTISERA	SEATRAIN	Z ATRAZINE
CRANIATE	M ANIMATER	ARTESIAN	T ATTAINER	
D DENTARIA	MARINATE	RATANIES	REATTAIN	

aaeinst 184 - taenias

B BASANITE	H ASTHENIA	ARTESIAN	SEATRAIN	V SANATIVE
C ESTANCIA	M AMENTIAS	RATANIES	S ENTASIAS	X ANATEXIS
F FANTASIE	ANIMATES	RESINATA	T ASTATINE	
G SAGINATE	R ANTISERA	SANTERIA	SANITATE	

aaeirst 150 - atresia

D AIRDATES	N ANTISERA	SEATRAIN	S ASTERIAS	W AWAITERS
DATARIES	ARTESIAN	P ASPIRATE	ATRESIAS	
RADIATES	RATANIES	PARASITE	T ARIETTAS	
H HETAIRAS	RESINATA	SEPTARIA	ARISTATE	
M AMIRATES	SANTERIA	R TARAIRES	V VARIATES	

aaenrst 103 - santera

B ANTBEARS	SERENATA	RATANIES	L ASTERNAL	S SANTERAS
RATSBANE	G STARAGEN	RESINATA	M SARMENTA	T TARTANES
C CANASTER	TANAGERS	SANTERIA	SEMANTRA	V TAVERNAS
CATERANS	I ANTISERA	SEATRAIN	O ANOESTRA	TSAREVNA
E ARSENATE	ARTESIAN	J NAARTJES	R NARRATES	

abeinst 135 - bestain

A BASANITE	BEATINGS	M AMBIENTS	R ATEBRINS	BESTAINS
C BASCINET	H ABSINTHE	O BOTANIES	BANISTER	T TABINETS
CABINETS	I BAINITES	BOTANISE	BARNIEST	
D BANDIEST	K BEATNIKS	NIOBATES	S BASINETS	
E BETAINES	SNAKEBIT	OBEISANT	BASSINET	
G BEASTING	L INSTABLE	P BEPAINTS	BESAINTS	

abeorst 151 - sorbate

A	AEROBATS	E	ABORTEES		SORTABLE	P	PROBATES		SORBATES
	RABATOES		REBATOES		STORABLE	R	ABORTERS	T	ABETTORS
C	CABESTRO	H	BATHORSE	M	BROMATES		ARBORETS		BATTEROS
	CABRESTO	I	SABOTIER	N	BARONETS		TABORERS		TABORETS
D	BROADEST	L	BLOATERS	O	AEROBOTS	S	BOASTERS	U	SABOTEUR

acdeirt 248 - [catride]

A	RADICATE		TRACHEID	M	DERMATIC	O	CERATOID		TETRACID
C	ACCREDIT	I	RATICIDE		TIMECARD	P	PICRATED		TETRADIC
D	READDICT	L	ARTICLED	N	CRINATED	S	ACRIDEST		
H	THRIDACE		LACERTID		DICENTRA	T	CITRATED		

aceilrt 250 - talcier

A	TAILRACE	M	METRICAL	P	PARTICLE		ARTICLES	T	TRACTILE
D	ARTICLED	N	CLARINET		PRELATIC		RECITALS	U	RETICULA
	LACERTID						SELICTAR	V	VERTICAL
K	TALCKIER	O	EROTICAL	R	CLARTIER		STERICAL	Y	LITERACY
			LORICATE	S	ALTRICES				

aceinot 162 - anoetic

C	ACETONIC		INCHOATE		ANORETIC		CANOEIST		INVOCATE
D	ACTIONED	M	COINMATE		CREATION		SONICATE	X	EXACTION
	CATENOID	N	ENACTION		REACTION	T	TACONITE		
H	ETHANOIC	R	ACTIONER	S	ACONITES	V	CONATIVE		

aceinrs 154 - cerasin

A	ACARINES		RESIANCE	I	RIANCIES	O	SCENARIO		CISTERNA
	CANARIES	F	FANCIERS	K	SKINCARE	S	ARCSINES		CREATINS
	CESARIAN		FRANCISE	L	CARLINES		ARSENICS		NACRITES
	SARCINAE	G	CREASING		LANCIERS		CERASINS		SCANTIER
B	BRISANCE		GRECIANS	M	CARMINES		RACINESS		TACRINES
	CARBINES		SEARCING		CREMAINS	T	CANISTER		
E	CINEREAS	H	ARCHINES	N	CRANNIES		CARNIEST		
	INCREASE		INARCHES		NARCEINS		CERATINS		

aceinrt 45 - tacrine

A	CARINATE		CREATINE		REACTING	R	TRANCIER		SCANTIER
	CRANIATE		INCREATE	I	ARENITIC	S	CANISTER		TACRINES
B	BACTERIN		ITERANCE	L	CLARINET		CARNIEST	T	INTERACT
C	ACENTRIC	G	ARGENTIC	O	ACTIONER		CERATINS	U	ANURETIC
D	CRINATED		CATERING		ANORETIC		CISTERNA	V	NAVICERT
	DICENTRA		CITRANGE		CREATION		CREATINS	X	XERANTIC
E	CENTIARE		CREATING		REACTION		NACRITES		

aceinst 106 - cineast

A	ESTANCIA		CHANTIES		INSECTAN		CISTERNA		ENTASTIC
B	BASCINET	I	ANTICISE		INSTANCE		CREATINS		NICTATES
	CABINETS		CANITIES	O	ACONITES		NACRITES		TETANICS
D	DANCIEST	L	CANISTEL		CANOEIST		SCANTIER	V	CISTVAEN
	DISTANCE	M	AMNESTIC		SONICATE		TACRINES		VESICANT
E	CINEASTE		SEMANTIC	R	CANISTER	S	CINEASTS	Y	CYANITES
F	FANCIEST	N	ANCIENTS		CARNIEST		SCANTIES	Z	ZINCATES
H	ASTHENIC		CANNIEST		CERATINS	T	CANTIEST		

acenort 141 - enactor

C	ACCENTOR	H	ANCHORET		REACTION	S	ANCESTOR	T	CONTRATE
D	CARTONED	I	ACTIONER	O	CORONATE		ENACTORS	U	COURANTE
	NOTECARD		ANORETIC	P	COPARENT		SARCONET		OUTRANCE
E	CAROTENE		CREATION		PORTANCE		SORTANCE	Y	ENACTORY

acinort 213 - cortina

A	RAINCOAT		ANORETIC	K	ANTIROCK		CONTRAIR	U	NOCTURIA
C	CRATONIC		CREATION	L	CILANTRO	S	CANTORIS	Y	CARYOTIN
	NARCOTIC		REACTION		CONTRAIL		CAROTINS		
D	TORNADIC	F	FRACTION	M	ROMANTIC		CORTINAS		
E	ACTIONER	H	ANORTHIC	R	CARROTIN	T	TRACTION		

adeegnr 167 - grenade

A	GADARENE	E	RENEGADE	M	GENDARME		GARNERED		UNAGREED
C	ENGRACED	H	REHANGED	N	ENDANGER	S	DERANGES		UNDERAGE
D	DANGERED	I	REGAINED		ENRANGED		GRANDEES		UNGEARED
	DERANGED	L	ENLARGED	O	RENEGADO		GRENADES	V	ENGRAVED
	GANDERED		LANGERED	R	DERANGER	U	DUNGAREE		
	GARDENED		LARGENED		GARDENER		RENAGUED		

adeeilr 165 - leadier

B	RIDEABLE	L	REALLIED	P	PEDALIER		RESAILED		RETAILED
D	DEADLIER	M	REMAILED	R	DERAILER		SIDEREAL	Z	REALIZED
	DERAILED		REMEDIAL		RERAILED	T	DETAILER		
	REDIALED	N	RENAILED	S	REALISED		ELATERID		

adeeinr 111 - [eardine]

C	DERACINE	L	RENAILED	S	ARSENIDE		NEARSIDE	V	REINVADE
F	FREDAINE	M	REMAINED		DENARIES	T	DETAINER		
G	REGAINED	P	PINDAREE		DRAISENE		RETAINED		

adeeins 246 - aniseed

G	AGENISED		INSEAMED	R	ARSENIDE		NEARSIDE		
L	DELAINES	N	ADENINES		DENARIES	S	ANISEEDS		
M	DEMAINES		ANDESINE		DRAISENE	T	ANDESITE		

adeeint 68 - [antidee]

D	DETAINED		ENTAILED	P	DIAPENTE	S	ANDESITE		
E	DETAINEE		LINEATED	R	DETAINER	W	ANTIWEED		
L	DATELINE	M	DEMENTIA		RETAINED				

adeeirs 143 - readies

B	BEARDIES	L	REALISED		DENARIES		RERAISED	V	READVISE
C	DECIARES		RESAILED		DRAISENE	T	READIEST		
F	FEDARIES		SIDEREAL		NEARSIDE		SERIATED		
G	DISAGREE	M	MADERISE	P	AIRSPEED		SIDERATE		
J	JADERIES	N	ARSENIDE	R	DREARIES		STEADIER		

adeeirt 38 - [dierate]

A	ERADIATE	L	DETAILER	N	DETAINER		STEADIER	W	WAITERED
B	EBRIATED		ELATERID		RETAINED	T	ITERATED		
	REBAITED		RETAILED	S	READIEST	V	DERIVATE		
G	GAITERED	M	DIAMETER		SERIATED		EVIRATED		
H	DEATHIER		REMEDIAT		SIDERATE		TAIVERED		

adeeist 142 - ideates

B	BEADIEST	H	ATHEISED	M	MEDIATES		SIDERATE	V	DEVIATES
	DIABETES		HEADIEST	N	ANDESITE		STEADIER		SEDATIVE
D	STEADIED	J	JADEITES	R	READIEST	S	STEADIES		
F	SAFETIED	L	LEADIEST		SERIATED	U	AUDITEES		

adeenrs 166 - endears

C ASCENDER	GRANDEES	NEARSIDE	N ENSNARED	UNSEARED
REASCEND	GRENADES	K KNEADERS	O REASONED	W ANSWERED
E ENSEARED	I ARSENIDE	M AMENDERS	S DEARNESS	Y YEARENDS
SERENADE	DENARIES	MEANDERS	U UNDERSEA	
G DERANGES	DRAISENE	REAMENDS	UNERASED	

adeenrt 157 - [netread]

B BANTERED	RECANTED	THREADEN	T ATTENDER	UNDEREAT
C CANTERED	D ENDARTED	I DETAINER	NATTERED	V AVENTRED
CRENATED	H ADHERENT	RETAINED	RATTENED	
DECANTER	HARTENED	L ANTLERED	U DENATURE	
NECTARED	NEATHERD	P PARENTED	UNDERATE	

adeerst 138 - tasered

B BETREADS	I READIEST	M MASTERED	RASTERED	RESTATED
BREASTED	SERIATED	STREAMED	RETREADS	RETASTED
DEBATERS	SIDERATE	P PEDERAST	SERRATED	W DEWATERS
C CEDRATES	STEADIER	PREDATES	TREADERS	TARWEEDS
E RESEATED	K STREAKED	REPASTED	S ASSERTED	WASTERED
F DRAFTEES	L DESALTER	TRAPESED	DEAREST	Y ESTRAYED
G RESTAGED	RESLATED	R ARRESTED	ESTRADES	
H HEADREST	TREADLES	DREAREST	T ASTERTED	

adeginr 44 - reading

A AREADING	E REGAINED	DRAGLINE	S DERAIGNS	Y DERAYING
DRAINAGE	H ADHERING	M DREAMING	GRADINES	READYING
GARDENIA	HEADRING	MARGINED	READINGS	YEARDING
B BEARDING	I DEAIRING	MIDRANGE	T DERATING	
BREADING	K DAKERING	N GRANNIED	GRADIENT	
D DREADING	L DANGLIER	O ORGANDIE	REDATING	
READDING	DEARLING	R DREARING	TREADING	

adegirt 191 - triaged

E GAITERED	H GRAITHED	M MIGRATED	GRADIENT	TREADING
F DRIFTAGE	I DIGERATI	N DERATING	REDATING	O ERGATOID

adegnor 238 - groaned

B BONDAGER	F FRONDAGE	J JARGONED	N ANDROGEN	P DOGNAPER
E RENEGADO	I ORGANDIE	M DRAGOMEN	DRAGONNE	T DRAGONET

adegort 132 - garoted

B BOGARTED	I ERGATOID	R GARROTED	U OUTRAGED	
E DEROGATE	N DRAGONET	S GOADSTER	RAGOUTED	
H GOATHERD	P PORTAGED	T GAROTTED	W WATERDOG	

adeiint 231 - inedita

C ACTINIDE	INDICATE	O IDEATION	R DAINTIER	V VANITIED
CTENIDIA	G IDEATING	IODINATE	S ADENITIS	
DIACTINE	M MINIATED	TAENIOID	DAINTIES	

adeilno 147 - [onedial]

G GALENOID	M MELANOID	P PALINODE	T DELATION	
H LIONHEAD	N NONIDEAL	S NODALISE	Z NODALIZE	

adeilnr 195 - [landier]

B BILANDER	F FILANDER	DEARLING	H HARDLINE	S ISLANDER
E RENAILED	G DANGLIER	DRAGLINE	N INLANDER	

adeilns 188 - snailed

D	ISLANDED	G	DEALINGS	K	SANDLIKE	O	NODALISE	U	UNSAILED
	LANDSIDE		LEADINGS	N	ANNELIDS	P	SANDPILE	V	ANDVILES
E	DELAINES		SIGNALED		LINDANES	R	ISLANDER		

adeilnt 53 - [latined]

A	DENTALIA	E	DATELINE	F	INFLATED	O	DELATION	V	DIVALENT
B	BIDENTAL		ENTAILED	G	DELATING	P	PANTILED		
D	TIDELAND		LINEATED	N	DENTINAL	U	UNTAILED		

adeilor 212 - dariole

F	FORELAID	L	ARILLODE		SOLIDARE	T	IDOLATER	V	OVERLAID
G	DIALOGER	S	DARIOLES		SOREDIAL		TAILORED	X	EXORDIAL

adeilos 168 - isolead

C	COALISED	P	EPISODAL		SOREDIAL		ISOLATED		SLEAZOID
G	GOLIASED		OPALISED	S	ASSOILED		SODALITE		
M	DAMOISEL		SEPALOID		DEASOILS		SOLIDATE		
	MELODIAS	R	DARIOLES		ISOLEADS	U	DOULEIAS		
N	NODALISE		SOLIDARE	T	DIASTOLE	Z	DIAZOLES		

adeilot 110 - [toedial]

F	FOLIATED	P	PETALOID	S	DIASTOLE		SOLIDATE		VIOLATED
K	TOADLIKE	R	IDOLATER		ISOLATED	T	DATOLITE		
N	DELATION		TAILORED		SODALITE	V	DOVETAIL		

adeilrs 63 - sideral

A	SALARIED		RADICLES	I	LAIRISED		SOLIDARE		SPIRALED
B	BEDRAILS	D	DIEDRALS	L	DALLIERS		SOREDIAL	T	DILATERS
	DISABLER	E	REALISED		DIALLERS	P	LIPREADS		LARDIEST
	RAILBEDS		RESAILED	M	DISMALER		PARSLIED		REDTAILS
C	DECRIALS		SIDEREAL	N	ISLANDER		PEDRAILS	U	RESIDUAL
	RADICELS	G	SLAIRGED	O	DARIOLES		PREDIALS	Y	DIALYSER

adeilrt 61 - trailed

A	LARIATED	E	DETAILER	O	IDOLATER	S	DILATERS	Y	DIELYTRA
B	LIBRATED		ELATERID		TAILORED		LARDIEST		
C	ARTICLED		RETAILED	P	DIPTERAL		REDTAILS		
	LACERTID	L	TRIALLED		TRIPEDAL	T	DETRITAL		

adeilst 160 - dilates

B	BALDIEST	E	LEADIEST		MISDEALT		SOLIDATE		REDTAILS
	BLADIEST	G	GLADIEST	O	DIASTOLE	P	TALIPEDS	V	VALIDEST
C	CITADELS	I	IDEALIST		ISOLATED	R	DILATERS	Y	DIASTYLE
	DIALECTS	M	MEDALIST		SODALITE		LARDIEST		STEADILY

adeimnr 208 - inarmed

A	MARINADE	G	DREAMING	I	MERIDIAN	S	ADERMINS	Y	DAIRYMEN
B	BRIDEMAN		MARGINED	O	RADIOMEN		SIRNAMED	Z	ZEMINDAR
E	REMAINED		MIDRANGE	R	MANRIDER	U	MURAENID		

adeinor 34 - aneroid

B	DEBONAIR	M	RADIOMEN	S	ANEROIDS		DERATION	U	DOUANIER
D	ORDAINED	R	ORDAINER		DONARIES		ORDINATE		
G	ORGANDIE		REORDAIN	T	AROINTED		RATIONED		

adeinos 62 - sodaine

B BEDSONIA		ANODISED	DAIMONES	S ADENOSIS	Z ADONIZES
C CODEINAS	G AGONISED	DOMAINES	ADONISES	ANODIZES
DIOCESAN	DIAGNOSE	NOMADIES	ANODISES	
OCEANIDS	H ADHESION	NOMADISE	T ASTONIED	
D ADENOIDS	L NODALISE	R ANEROIDS	SEDATION	
ADONISED	M AMIDONES	DONARIES	X DIOXANES	

adeinot 9 - [antidoe]

B OBTAINED		TAENIOID	ANTINODE	RATIONED	V DONATIVE
C ACTIONED	L DELATION	P ANTIPODE	S ASTONIED	
CATENOID	M DOMINATE	R AROINTED	SEDATION	
I IDEATION	NEMATOID	DERATION	T ANTIDOTE	
IODINATE	N ANOINTED	ORDINATE	TETANOID	

adeinrs 10 - sardine

A ARANEIDS		NEARSIDE	M ADERMINS	SERRANID	UNRAISED
B BRANDIES	F FRIANDES	SIRNAMED	S ARIDNESS	URANIDES
BRANDISE	G DERAIGNS	N INSNARED	SARDINES	V INVADERS
D SARDINED	GRADINES	O ANEROIDS	T DETRAINS	SANDIVER
E ARSENIDE	READINGS	DONARIES	RANDIEST	Y SYNEDRIA
DENARIES	I DRAISINE	P SPRAINED	STRAINED	
DRAISENE	L ISLANDER	R DRAINERS	U DENARIUS	

adeinrt 7 - trained

A DENTARIA		RETAINED	I DAINTIER	S DETRAINS	RUINATED
RAINDATE	G DERATING	O AROINTED	RANDIEST	URINATED
C CRINATED	GRADIENT	DERATION	STRAINED	
DICENTRA	REDATING	ORDINATE	T NITRATED	
D INDARTED	TREADING	RATIONED	U DATURINE	
E DETAINER	H ANTHERID	P DIPTERAN	INDURATE	

adeinru 118 - uranide

F UNFAIRED	M MURAENID	UNREPAID	URANIDES	RUINATED
H UNHAIRED	O DOUANIER	S DENARIUS	T DATURINE	URINATED
I UREDINIA	P UNPAIRED	UNRAISED	INDURATE	V UNVARIED

adeinst 23 - stained

B BANDIEST	G SEDATING	M MEDIANTS	R DETRAINS	T INSTATED
C DANCIEST	STEADING	TIDESMAN	RANDIEST	U AUDIENTS
DISTANCE	H HANDIEST	O ASTONIED	STRAINED	SINUATED
D DANDIEST	I ADENITIS	SEDATION	S DESTAINS	V DEVIANTS
E ANDESITE	DAINTIES	P DEPAINTS	SANDIEST	Y DESYATIN

adeiors 119 - soredia

C IDOCRASE	F FORESAID	SOREDIAL	P DIASPORE	V AVODIRES
D ROADSIDE	L DARIOLES	N ANEROIDS	PARODIES	AVOIDERS
SIDEROAD	SOLIDARE	DONARIES	T ASTEROID	

adeiort 19 - [oartide]

C CERATOID	L IDOLATER	N AROINTED	RATIONED	T TERATOID
G ERGATOID	TAILORED	DERATION	R ADROITER	V DEVIATOR
K KERATOID	M MEDIATOR	ORDINATE	S ASTEROID	

adeiost 148 - toadies

G GODETIAS		SODALITE	N ASTONIED	R ASTEROID
L DIASTOLE		SOLIDATE	SEDATION	X OXIDATES
ISOLATED	M ATOMISED	P DIOPTASE	Z AZOTISED	

adeirst 17 - tirades

A	AIRDATES	D	DISRATED	L	DILATERS	O	ASTEROID		DISASTER
	DATARIES	E	READIEST		LARDIEST	P	DIPTERAS		DISRATES
	RADIATES		SERIATED		REDTAILS		DRAPIEST	T	STRAITED
B	BARDIEST		SIDERATE	M	MARDIEST		RAPIDEST		STRIATED
	BRAIDEST		STEADIER		MISRATED		SPIRATED		TARDIEST
	RABIDEST	H	HAIRSTED		READMITS		TARSIPED	W	TAWDRIES
	REDBAITS		HARDIEST	N	DETRAINS		TRAIPSED		
	TRIBADES	I	IRISATED		RANDIEST	S	ASTERIDS		
C	ACRIDEST	K	STRAIKED		STRAINED		DIASTERS		

adeirtt 179 - attired

A	DIATRETA		TETRADIC	M	ADMITTER	S	STRAITED	T	ATTRITED
C	CITRATED	E	ITERATED	N	NITRATED		STRIATED		TITRATED
	TETRACID	L	DETRITAL	O	TERATOID		TARDIEST		

adenors 88 - [sandore]

B	BANDORES	E	REASONED	L	LADRONES		ROADSMEN	R	ADORNERS
	BROADENS	H	HARDNOSE		SOLANDER	P	OPERANDS		READORNS
C	DRACONES	I	ANEROIDS	M	MADRONES		PADRONES	T	TORNADES
	ENDOSARC		DONARIES		RANSOMED		PANDORES		

adenort 41 - tornade

C	CARTONED	I	AROINTED		RATIONED	P	PRONATED	W	DANEWORT
	NOTECARD		DERATION	N	NONRATED	S	TORNADES		TEARDOWN
G	DRAGONET		ORDINATE	O	RATOONED	T	ATTORNED	Y	AROYNTED

adenost 125 - onstead

C	ENDOCAST	E	ENDOSTEA		SEDATION	P	NOTEPADS	R	TORNADES
	TACNODES	I	ASTONIED	O	ODONATES		TONEPADS	S	ONSTEADS

adenrst 226 - starned

B	BANDSTER		STRANDED		RANDIEST	R	STRANDER		UNTREADS
	BARTENDS	G	DRAGNETS		STRAINED	S	STANDERS	X	DEXTRANS
C	CANTREDS		GRANDEST	K	DARKNETS	U	DAUNTERS		
D	DARNDEST	I	DETRAINS	O	TORNADES		TRANSUDE		

adenrtu 134 - untread

B	BREADNUT	D	DRAUNTED	I	DATURINE	P	DEPURANT	T	TRUANTED
	TURBANED		UNTRADED		INDURATE		UNPARTED	X	UNDERTAX
C	UNCARTED	E	DENATURE		RUINATED	R	UNTARRED		
	UNCRATED		UNDERATE		URINATED	S	DAUNTERS		
	UNDERACT		UNDEREAT	L	DENTURAL		TRANSUDE		
	UNTRACED	H	UNTHREAD	M	UNDREAMT		UNTREADS		

adeorst 101 - troades

B	BROADEST	L	DELATORS	N	TORNADES		READOPTS	U	OUTDARES
C	REDCOATS		LEOTARDS	P	ADOPTERS	R	ROADSTER		OUTREADS
G	GOADSTER		LODESTAR		ASPORTED	S	ASSORTED		READOUTS
I	ASTEROID	M	STROAMED		PASTORED		TORSADES	X	EXTRADOS

adiinot 244 - [toindia]

C	ACTINOID	E	IDEATION	G	IODATING	O	IODATION
	DIATONIC		IODINATE	L	DILATION	U	AUDITION
D	ADDITION		TAENIOID	N	NIDATION		

adinors 127 - sadiron

B	INBOARDS	E	ANEROIDS	N	ANDIRONS	T	DIATRONS
C	SARDONIC		DONARIES	P	PONIARDS		INTRADOS
D	ANDROIDS	G	ROADINGS	R	ORDINARS	U	DINOSAUR
	DISADORN	L	ORDINALS	S	SADIRONS	V	VIRANDOS

adinort 67 - diatron

		E	AROINTED		RATIONED	O	TANDOORI	U	DURATION
A	ANTIDORA		DERATION	L	TRINODAL	S	DIATRONS
C	TORNADIC		ORDINATE	N	ORDINANT		INTRADOS

adinrst 249 - [indarts]

A	INTRADAS	E	DETRAINS	F	INDRAFTS	K	STINKARD	R	TRIDARNS
	RADIANTS		RANDIEST	G	TRADINGS	O	DIATRONS	U	UNITARDS
B	ANTBIRDS		STRAINED	I	DISTRAIN		INTRADOS

adiorst 152 - astroid

C	CAROTIDS	I	TARSIOID		INTRADOS	S	ASTROIDS	U	AUDITORS
E	ASTEROID	L	DILATORS	P	PARODIST		SARODIST
G	GORDITAS	N	DIATRONS		PAROTIDS	T	STRADIOT

aeeginr 86 - reginae

B	BAREGINE	G	AGREEING	M	GERMAINE	S	ANERGIES		GRATINEE
	BERGENIA	I	AEGIRINE	P	PERIGEAN		GESNERIA		INTERAGE
D	REGAINED	L	ALGERINE	R	REGAINER	T	ENARGITE	Z	RAZEEING

aeegins 223 - agenise

A	AGENESIA	L	ENSILAGE		GESNERIA		ASSIGNEE	V	ENVISAGE
C	AGENCIES		LINEAGES	S	AGENESIS	T	SAGENITE	Z	AGENIZES
D	AGENISED	R	ANERGIES		AGENISES	U	EUGENIAS

aeegint 235 - [antigee]

C	AGENETIC		LEGATINE	R	ENARGITE	S	SAGENITE	X	EXIGEANT
L	GALENITE	M	GEMINATE		GRATINEE	V	AGENTIVE
	GELATINE	N	ANTIGENE		INTERAGE		NEGATIVE

aeegirt 117 - [greatie]

D	GAITERED	I	AEGIRITE		REMIGATE		INTERAGE
F	FIGEATER	L	LITREAGE	N	ENARGITE	T	AIGRETTE
H	HERITAGE	M	EMIGRATE		GRATINEE	V	ERGATIVE

aeegnrt 128 - reagent

A	TAGAREEN	I	ENARGITE	M	AGREMENT		GRANTEES		SEGREANT
E	GENERATE		GRATINEE	N	GENERANT		GREATENS		SERGEANT
	RENEGATE		INTERAGE	R	ETRANGER		NEGATERS		STERNAGE
	TEENAGER	L	REGENTAL	S	ESTRANGE		REAGENTS	U	GAUNTREE

aeeilnr 98 - aliener

C	CARELINE	D	RENAILED	P	PERINEAL	T	ELATERIN
	CINEREAL	F	FLANERIE	R	NEARLIER		ENTAILER
	RELIANCE	G	ALGERINE	S	ALIENERS		TREENAIL

aeeilns 97 - sealine

B	BASELINE	E	ALIENEES	M	MELANISE		PENALISE	S	SEALINES
C	SALIENCE	G	ENSILAGE	N	SELENIAN		SEPALINE	V	VASELINE
D	DELAINES		LINEAGES	P	ALEPINES	R	ALIENERS	X	ALEXINES

aeeilnt 85 - lineate

A	ALIENATE	G	GALENITE	M	MELANITE	ENTAILER
D	DATELINE		GELATINE	P	PETALINE	TREENAIL
	ENTAILED		LEGATINE		TAPELINE	V ELVANITE
	LINEATED	L	TENAILLE	R	ELATERIN	VENTAILE

aeeilrs 83 - realise

C	ESCALIER	G	GASELIER	N	ALIENERS		EARLIEST	Z	REALIZES
D	REALISED	H	SHIRALEE	P	ESPALIER		LATERISE		SLEAZIER
	RESAILED	L	REALLIES		PEARLIES		LEARIEST		
	SIDEREAL	M	ALMERIES	R	REALISER		REALTIES		
F	FILAREES		EMAILERS	S	REALISES	V	VELARISE		
	SERAFILE		MEASLIER	T	ATELIERS	Y	YEARLIES		

aeeilrt 15 - realtie

B	LIBERATE	G	LITREAGE	N	ELATERIN	S	ATELIERS		LITERATE
D	DETAILER	H	ETHERIAL		ENTAILER		EARLIEST	V	LEVIRATE
	ELATERID	L	LAETRILE		TREENAIL		LATERISE		RELATIVE
	RETAILED	M	EREMITAL	O	AEROLITE		LEARIEST	Z	LATERIZE
F	FEATLIER		MATERIEL	P	PEARLITE		REALTIES		
	FRAILTEE		REALTIME	R	RETAILER	T	LATERITE		

aeeilst 159 - [tealies]

B	SEABLITE	G	EGALITES		METALISE		LEARIEST		LEAVIEST
D	LEADIEST		ELEGIAST	P	EPILATES		REALTIES		VEALIEST
F	FEALTIES	K	LEAKIEST	R	ATELIERS	S	ASTELIES		
	FETIALES	L	LEALTIES		EARLIEST	T	AILETTES		
	LEAFIEST	M	MEALIEST		LATERISE	V	ELATIVES		

aeeimrt 173 - meatier

B	AMBERITE	E	EMERITAE	L	EREMITAL	S	EMERITAS	V	VIAMETER
C	CEMITARE	G	EMIGRATE		MATERIEL		EMIRATES		
D	DIAMETER		REMIGATE		REALTIME		REAMIEST		
	REMEDIAT	I	METAIRIE	N	ANTIMERE		STEAMIER		

aeeinrs 31 - [nearies]

C	CINEREAS		DRAISENE	K	SNEAKIER	R	REARISEN		STEARINE
	INCREASE		NEARSIDE	L	ALIENERS	S	SENARIES		TRAINEES
	RESIANCE	G	ANERGIES	M	REMANIES	T	ARENITES	U	UNEASIER
D	ARSENIDE		GESNERIA	N	ANSERINE		ARSENITE		
	DENARIES	H	INHEARSE	P	NAPERIES		RESINATE		

aeeinrt 12 - trainee

C	CENTIARE		RETAINED		HERNIATE		ENTAILER	S	ARENITES
	CREATINE	G	ENARGITE	I	INERTIAE		TREENAIL		ARSENITE
	INCREATE		GRATINEE	K	ANKERITE	M	ANTIMERE		RESINATE
	ITERANCE		INTERAGE		KREATINE	P	APERIENT		STEARINE
D	DETAINER	H	ATHERINE	L	ELATERIN	R	RETAINER		TRAINEES

aeeinst 89 - etesian

B	BETAINES	M	ETAMINES	R	ARENITES		TRAINEES		TETANIES
C	CINEASTE		MATINEES		ARSENITE	S	ETESIANS		TETANISE
D	ANDESITE		MISEATEN		RESINATE		TENIASES	V	NAIVETES
G	SAGENITE		SEMINATE		STEARINE	T	ANISETTE		

aeeirst 11 - seriate

D	READIEST		LATERISE		ARSENITE		REASTIER	W SWEATIER
	SERIATED		LEARIEST		RESINATE	S	SERIATES	TAWERIES
	SIDERATE		REALTIES		STEARINE	T	ARIETTES	WASTERIE
	STEADIER	M	EMERITAS		TRAINEES		ITERATES	WEARIEST
E	EATERIES		EMIRATES	O	ETAERIOS		TEARIEST	Y YEASTIER
H	HEARTIES		REAMIEST	P	PARIETES		TREATIES	
L	ATELIERS		STEAMIER		PETARIES		TREATISE	
	EARLIEST	N	ARENITES	R	ARTERIES	V	EVIRATES	

aeelnrt 42 - teleran

B	RENTABLE	H LEATHERN	M	LAMENTER	S	ALTERNES		RELEVANT
D	ANTLERED	I ELATERIN	N	LANNERET		ETERNALS	W	TREELAWN
E	LATEENER	ENTAILER	O	REALTONE		TELERANS	X	EXTERNAL
G	REGENTAL	TREENAIL	R	RELEARNT	V	LEVANTER		

aeelort 64 - [realtoe]

A	AREOLATE		RELOCATE	N	REALTONE	T	TOLERATE		OVERLATE
C	CORELATE	I	AEROLITE	S	OLEASTER	V	ELEVATOR	W	TOLEWARE

aeelrst 59 - stealer

A	LAETARES	D DESALTER		LATERISE		PLEATERS		TESSERAL
B	ARBELEST		RESLATED		LEARIEST		PRELATES	T ALERTEST
	BLEAREST		TREADLES		REALTIES		REPLATES	U RESALUTE
	BLEATERS	E TEASELER	M	LAMETERS	R	ALTERERS	X EXALTERS
	RESTABLE	F REFLATES	N	ALTERNES		REALTERS	Y EASTERLY
	RETABLES	H HALTERES		ETERNALS		RELATERS	
C	CLEAREST		LEATHERS		TELERANS	S	RESLATES	
	SCELERAT	I ATELIERS	O	OLEASTER		STEALERS	
	TREACLES		EARLIEST	P	PETRALES		TEARLESS	

aeenors 233 - arenose

B	SEABORNE	P PERAEONS	R	REASONER		SEASONER		RESONATE
D	REASONED	PERSONAE	S	RESEASON	T	EARSTONE	

aeenort 131 - [onerate]

C	CAROTENE	O AEROTONE		RESONATE		RENOVATE
L	REALTONE	S EARSTONE	V	OVERNEAT	

aeenrst 22 - rateens

A	ARSENATE	F FASTENER		SERGEANT	J	SERJEANT		EARNESTS
	SERENATA	FENESTRA		STERNAGE	L	ALTERNES		SARSENET
B	ABSENTER	REFASTEN	H	HASTENER		ETERNALS	T	ENTREATS
C	CENTARES	G ESTRANGE		HEARTENS		TELERANS		RATTEENS
	ENCASTRE	GRANTEES	I	ARENITES	M	REMANETS	U	SAUTERNE
	REASCENT	GREATENS		ARSENITE	O	EARSTONE	V	AVENTRES
	REENACTS	NEGATERS		RESINATE		RESONATE		VETERANS
	SARCENET	REAGENTS		STEARINE	R	TERRANES	
E	SERENATE	SEGREANT		TRAINEES	S	ASSENTER	

aeenrtu 245 - [eartune]

C	ENACTURE		UNDERATE	H	URETHANE	R	RENATURE
	UNCREATE		UNDEREAT	M	NUMERATE	S	SAUTERNE
D	DENATURE	G GAUNTREE	N	ENAUNTER	V	AVENTURE

aeeorst 116 - roseate

B	ABORTEES	I ETAERIOS	L	OLEASTER		RESONATE	V OVEREATS
	REBATOES	K KERATOSE	M	EROTEMAS	P	OPERATES	
C	CREASOTE	KREASOTE	N	EARSTONE		PROTEASE	

aegilnr 27 - reginal

A GERANIAL	G GANGLIER	MALINGER	REALIGNS	TERAGLIN
REGALIAN	LAGERING	N LEARNING	SALERING	TRIANGLE
B BLEARING	REGALING	O GERANIOL	SANGLIER	V RAVELING
C CLEARING	H NARGHILE	REGIONAL	SIGNALER	X RELAXING
RELACING	NARGILEH	P GRAPLINE	SLANGIER	Y LAYERING
D DANGLIER	I GAINLIER	PEARLING	T ALERTING	RELAYING
DEARLING	J JANGLIER	R GNARLIER	ALTERING	YEARLING
DRAGLINE	L ALLERGIN	S ALIGNERS	INTEGRAL	
E ALGERINE	M GERMINAL	ENGRAILS	RELATING	
F FINAGLER	MALIGNER	NARGILES	TANGLIER	

aegilns 155 - sealing

B SIGNABLE	H HEALINGS	LEANINGS	SANGLIER	GENITALS
SINGABLE	LEASHING	O GASOLINE	SIGNALER	STEALING
D DEALINGS	SHEALING	P ELAPSING	SLANGIER	TAGLINES
LEADINGS	K LINKAGES	PLEASING	S GAINLESS	V LEAVINGS
SIGNALED	SNAGLIKE	R ALIGNERS	GLASSINE	SLEAVING
E ENSILAGE	L GALLEINS	ENGRAILS	LEASINGS	W SWEALING
LINEAGES	NIGELLAS	NARGILES	SEALINGS	Y YEALINGS
F FINAGLES	M MEASLING	REALIGNS	T EASTLING	
G LIGNAGES	N EANLINGS	SALERING	GELATINS	

aegilnt 58 - tagline

A AGENTIAL	GELATINE	METALING	ALTERING	GENITALS
ALGINATE	LEGATINE	TEGMINAL	INTEGRAL	STEALING
B BELATING	G GELATING	N GANTLINE	RELATING	TAGLINES
BLEATING	LEGATING	LATENING	TANGLIER	V VALETING
TANGIBLE	TEAGLING	O GELATION	TERAGLIN	X EXALTING
C CLEATING	H ATHELING	LEGATION	TRIANGLE	Z TEAZLING
D DELATING	K GNATLIKE	P PLEATING	S EASTLING	
E GALENITE	M LIGAMENT	R ALERTING	GELATINS	

aegilrs 225 - grailes

A GASALIER	D SLAIRGED	N ALIGNERS	SIGNALER	T GLARIEST
LAIRAGES	E GASELIER	ENGRAILS	SLANGIER	REGALIST
RAILAGES	G SLAGGIER	NARGILES	O GASOLIER	Y GREASILY
REGALIAS	M GREMIALS	REALIGNS	GIRASOLE	Z GLAZIERS
C GLACIERS	LAMIGERS	SALERING	SERAGLIO	
GRACILES	REGALISM	SANGLIER	S GLASSIER	

aeginor 185 - origane

B ABORIGEN	L GERANIOL	R ORANGIER	ORGANISE	Z ORGANIZE
D ORGANDIE	REGIONAL	S IGNAROES	ORIGANES	

aeginos 193 - agonise

B BEGONIAS	DIAGNOSE	N ANGINOSE	ORGANISE	Z AGONIZES
C COINAGES	G SEAGOING	GANOINES	ORIGANES	
D AGONISED	L GASOLINE	R IGNAROES	S AGONISES	

aeginrs 40 - seringa

A ANERGIAS	GRADINES	SHEARING	SLANGIER	ORIGANES
ANGARIES	READINGS	K SKEARING	M GERMAINS	P PREASING
ARGINASE	E ANERGIES	L ALIGNERS	SMEARING	SPEARING
B BEARINGS	GESNERIA	ENGRAILS	N AGINNERS	R EARRINGS
SABERING	G GEARINGS	NARGILES	EARNINGS	GRAINERS
C CREASING	GREASING	REALIGNS	ENGRAINS	S ASSIGNER
GRECIANS	SNAGGIER	SALERING	GRANNIES	REASSIGN
SEARCING	H HEARINGS	SANGLIER	O IGNAROES	SEARINGS
D DERAIGNS	HEARSING	SIGNALER	ORGANISE	SERINGAS

T	ANGRIEST		GANTRIES		REASTING	W	RESAWING		SYNERGIA
	ANGSTIER		GRANITES		STEARING		SWEARING		
	ASTRINGE		INGRATES		TASERING		WEARINGS		
	GANISTER		RANGIEST	V	VINEGARS	Y	RESAYING		

aeginrt 33 - tearing

A	AERATING		REDATING		INTEGRAL		ASTRINGE		TREATING
B	BERATING		TREADING		RELATING		GANISTER	V	AVERTING
	REBATING	E	ENARGITE		TANGLIER		GANTRIES		GRIEVANT
	TABERING		GRATINEE		TERAGLIN		GRANITES		TAVERING
C	ARGENTIC		INTERAGE		TRIANGLE		INGRATES		VINTAGER
	CATERING	H	EARTHING	M	EMIGRANT		RANGIEST	W	TWANGIER
	CITRANGE		HEARTING		REMATING		REASTING		WATERING
	CREATING		INGATHER	P	RETAPING		STEARING	X	RETAXING
	REACTING	K	RETAKING		TAPERING		TASERING		
D	DERATING	L	ALERTING	S	ANGRIEST	T	ARETTING		
	GRADIENT		ALTERING		ANGSTIER		GNATTIER		

aeginst 51 - tsigane

A	SAGINATE	L	EASTLING	N	ANTIGENS		RANGIEST	T	ESTATING
B	BEASTING		GELATINS		GENTIANS		REASTING		TANGIEST
	BEATINGS		GENITALS		STEANING		STEARING	U	SAUTEING
D	SEDATING		STEALING	R	ANGRIEST		TASERING		UNITAGES
	STEADING		TAGLINES		ANGSTIER	S	EASTINGS	V	VINTAGES
E	SAGENITE	M	MANGIEST		ASTRINGE		GENISTAS	W	SWEATING
F	FEASTING		MINTAGES		GANISTER		GIANTESS	Y	YEASTING
G	NAGGIEST		MISAGENT		GANTRIES		SEATINGS	Z	TZIGANES
H	GAHNITES		STEAMING		GRANITES		TEASINGS		
	HEATINGS		TEAMINGS		INGRATES		TSIGANES		

aegnrst 140 - strange

A	STARAGEN		REAGENTS		GANISTER		TANGLERS		STONERAG
	TANAGERS		SEGREANT		GANTRIES		TRANGLES	P	TREPANGS
B	BANGSTER		SERGEANT		GRANITES	M	GARMENTS	R	GRANTERS
D	DRAGNETS		STERNAGE		INGRATES		MARGENTS		REGRANTS
	GRANDEST	F	ENGRAFTS		RANGIEST		RAGMENTS		STRANGER
E	ESTRANGE	G	GANGSTER		REASTING	O	ESTRAGON	S	STRANGES
	GRANTEES	I	ANGRIEST		STEARING		NEGATORS	U	STRAUNGE
	GREATENS		ANGSTIER		TASERING		ORANGEST	W	TWANGERS
	NEGATERS		ASTRINGE	L	STRANGLE		RAGSTONE		

aegorst 177 - toerags

C	ESCARGOT	L	GLOATERS		ORANGEST	P	PORTAGES	T	GAROTTES
D	GOADSTER		LEGATORS		RAGSTONE		POTAGERS	U	OUTRAGES
F	FAGOTERS	N	ESTRAGON		STONERAG	R	GARROTES		
H	SHORTAGE		NEGATORS	O	ROOTAGES	S	STORAGES		

aehinrt 202 - therian

D	ANTHERID	G	EARTHING	O	ANTIHERO		INEARTHS	W	TARWHINE
E	ATHERINE		HEARTING	P	PERIANTH		THERIANS		
	HERNIATE		INGATHER	S	HAIRNETS	U	HAURIENT		

aehirst 146 - sheriat

A	HETAIRAS	D	HAIRSTED	I	HAIRIEST	O	HOARIEST	U	THESAURI
C	CHARIEST		HARDIEST	N	HAIRNETS	P	TRIPHASE	W	SWATHIER
	STICHERA	E	HEARTIES		INEARTHS	R	TRASHIER		WATERISH
	THERIACS	F	FAITHERS		THERIANS	S	SHERIATS	Y	HYSTERIA

aeiinrs 194 - senarii

B	BINARIES	K	KAISERIN	N	SIRENIAN		RAINIEST
C	RIANCIES	L	AIRLINES	S	AIRINESS	Y	YERSINIA
D	DRAISINE		SNAILIER	T	INERTIAS		

aeiinrt 46 - inertia

C	ARENITIC	E	INERTIAE	L	INERTIAL	P	PAINTIER		RAINIEST
D	DAINTIER	F	FAINTIER	N	TRIENNIA	S	INERTIAS	Z	TRIAZINE

aeiinst 161 - isatine

B	BAINITES	F	FAINITES	M	MINIATES	S	ISATINES	X	AXINITES
C	ANTICISE	K	KAINITES	P	PATINISE		SANITIES	Z	SANITIZE
	CANITIES	L	ALIENIST		PIANISTE		SANITISE		
D	ADENITIS		LATINISE	R	INERTIAS		TENIASIS		
	DAINTIES		LITANIES		RAINIEST	V	VANITIES		

aeiirst 121 - irisate

D	IRISATED		LISTERIA		RAINIEST		SATIRISE	Z	SATIRIZE
F	RATIFIES	M	AIRTIMES	P	PARITIES	V	VAIRIEST		
H	HAIRIEST		SERIATIM	R	RARITIES	W	WISTERIA		
L	LAIRIEST	N	INERTIAS	S	IRISATES	X	SEXTARII		

aeilnor 56 - alienor

C	ACROLEIN	F	FORELAIN	P	PELORIAN	T	ORIENTAL
	COLINEAR	G	GERANIOL	S	AILERONS		RELATION
	CREOLIAN		REGIONAL		ALERIONS		TAILERON
	LONICERA	L	ALLERION		ALIENORS	V	OVERLAIN

aeilnos 74 - anisole

D	NODALISE		MINEOLAS	R	AILERONS	T	ELATIONS
G	GASOLINE		SEMOLINA		ALERIONS		INSOLATE
K	KAOLINES	N	SOLANINE		ALIENORS		TOENAILS
M	LAMINOSE	P	OPALINES	S	ANISOLES	X	SILOXANE

aeilnot 36 - toenail

B	TAILBONE	G	GELATION	R	ORIENTAL	S	ELATIONS	T	TONALITE
D	DELATION		LEGATION		RELATION		INSOLATE		
F	OLEFIANT	P	ANTIPOLE		TAILERON		TOENAILS		

aeilnpt 210 - pantile

A	PALATINE	D	PANTILED	O	ANTIPOLE		TRIPLANE	T	TINPLATE
B	PINTABLE	E	PETALINE	P	PIEPLANT	S	PANELIST	Y	PENALITY
C	PECTINAL		TAPELINE	R	INTERLAP		PANTILES		
	PLANETIC	G	PLEATING		TRAPLINE		PLAINEST		

aeilnrs 20 - renails

B	RINSABLE		REALIGNS	M	MARLINES	R	SNARLIER		SLANTIER
C	CARLINES		SALERING		MINERALS	S	RAINLESS		TRENAILS
	LANCIERS		SANGLIER		MISLEARN	T	ENTRAILS	U	LUNARIES
D	ISLANDER		SIGNALER	O	AILERONS		LARNIEST	V	RAVELINS
E	ALIENERS		SLANGIER		ALERIONS		LATRINES	X	RELAXINS
G	ALIGNERS	H	INHALERS		ALIENORS		RATLINES	Y	INLAYERS
	ENGRAILS	I	AIRLINES	P	PEARLINS		REINSTAL		SNAILERY
	NARGILES		SNAILIER		PRALINES		RETINALS		

aeilnrt 8 - trenail

C	CLARINET		RELATING	O	ORIENTAL		LATRINES		RETINULA
E	ELATERIN		TANGLIER		RELATION		RATLINES		TENURIAL
	ENTAILER		TERAGLIN		TAILERON		REINSTAL	V	INTERVAL
	TREENAIL		TRIANGLE	P	INTERLAP		RETINALS	Y	INTERLAY
F	INFLATER	I	INERTIAL		TRAPLINE		SLANTIER		
G	ALERTING	M	TERMINAL		TRIPLANE		TRENAILS		
	ALTERING		TRAMLINE	S	ENTRAILS	T	RATTLINE		
	INTEGRAL	N	INTERNAL		LARNIEST	U	AUNTLIER		

aeilnst 60 - tenails

B	INSTABLE		LATINISE		INSOLATE		REINSTAL		STANIELS
C	CANISTEL		LITANIES		TOENAILS		RETINALS	U	ALUNITES
F	INFLATES	K	LANKIEST	P	PANELIST		SLANTIER		INSULATE
G	EASTLING	M	AILMENTS		PANTILES		TRENAILS	V	VENTAILS
	GELATINS		ALIMENTS		PLAINEST	S	EASTLINS	W	LAWNIEST
	GENITALS		MANLIEST	R	ENTRAILS		ELASTINS		
	STEALING		MELANIST		LARNIEST		NAILSETS		
	TAGLINES		SMALTINE		LATRINES		SALIENTS		
I	ALIENIST	O	ELATIONS		RATLINES		SALTINES		

aeilors 25 - [earsoil]

A	OLEARIAS		SOLIDARE	H	AIRHOLES	P	PELORIAS		VARIOLES
B	BOREALIS		SOREDIAL		SHOALIER		POLARISE		VOLARIES
C	CALORIES	F	FORESAIL	M	MORALISE	S	SOLARISE	Y	ROYALISE
	CALORISE	G	GASOLIER	N	AILERONS	T	SOTERIAL	Z	SOLARIZE
	CARIOLES		GIRASOLE		ALERIONS	V	OVERSAIL		
D	DARIOLES		SERAGLIO		ALIENORS		VALORISE		

aeilort 4 - [oiltear]

B	LABORITE		TAILORED	M	AMITROLE		TAILERON	S	SOTERIAL
C	EROTICAL	E	AEROLITE		ROLAMITE	P	EPILATOR	T	LITERATO
	LORICATE	F	FLOATIER	N	ORIENTAL		PETIOLAR	V	VIOLATER
D	IDOLATER	H	AEROLITH		RELATION	R	RETAILOR	Z	TRIAZOLE

aeilost 49 - isolate

C	ALOETICS		ISOLATED	G	LATIGOES	N	ELATIONS	R	SOTERIAL
	COALIEST		SODALITE		OTALGIES		INSOLATE	S	ISOLATES
	SOCIETAL		SOLIDATE	K	KEITLOAS		TOENAILS	T	TOTALISE
D	DIASTOLE	F	FOLIATES	M	LOAMIEST	P	SPOLIATE	V	VIOLATES

aeilott 205 - [teatoil]

D	DATOLITE	N	TONALITE	S	TOTALISE	Z	TOTALIZE
E	ETIOLATE	R	LITERATO	V	VOLITATE		

aeilprt 181 - platier

A	PARIETAL		TRIPEDAL	N	INTERLAP	R	PALTRIER	V	LIVETRAP
B	PARTIBLE	E	PEARLITE		TRAPLINE		PRETRIAL		
C	PARTICLE	I	LIPARITE		TRIPLANE	S	PILASTER		
	PRELATIC		REPTILIA	O	EPILATOR		PLAISTER		
D	DIPTERAL	K	TRAPLIKE		PETIOLAR		PLAITERS		

aeilrrt 200 - trailer

A	ARTERIAL	O	RETAILOR	S	RETIRALS	T	RATTLIER
C	CLARTIER	P	PALTRIER		RETRIALS	U	RURALITE
E	RETAILER		PRETRIAL		TRAILERS	Y	LITERARY

aeilrst 14 - tailers

B	BLASTIER	E	ATELIERS	K	LARKIEST	N	ENTRAILS		PLAITERS
	LIBRATES		EARLIEST		STALKIER		LARNIEST	R	RETIRALS
	TABLIERS		LATERISE		STARLIKE		LATRINES		RETRIALS
C	ALTRICES		LEARIEST	L	LITERALS		RATLINES		TRAILERS
	ARTICLES		REALTIES		TALLIERS		REINSTAL	S	REALISTS
	RECITALS	F	FLARIEST		TRIELLAS		RETINALS		SALTIERS
	SELICTAR		FRAILEST	M	LAMISTER		SLANTIER		SALTIRES
	STERICAL	G	GLARIEST		LAMITERS		TRENAILS		SLAISTER
D	DILATERS		REGALIST		MARLIEST	O	SOTERIAL	T	TERTIALS
	LARDIEST	I	LAIRIEST		MARLITES	P	PILASTER	U	URALITES
	REDTAILS		LISTERIA		MISALTER		PLAISTER		

aeilrsu 227 - [lauries]

A	AURELIAS	F	FAILURES	N	LUNARIES	R	RURALISE
C	AURICLES	H	HAULIERS	P	SPIRULAE	T	URALITES
D	RESIDUAL	L	RUELLIAS	Q	SQUAILER		

aeilrtt 114 - tertial

B	TITRABLE	E	LATERITE	G	AGLITTER	N	RATTLINE	S	TERTIALS
C	TRACTILE		LITERATE	I	LITERATI	O	LITERATO	Y	ALTERITY
D	DETRITAL	F	FILTRATE	M	REMITTAL	R	RATTLIER		

aeilrtu 192 - uralite

C	RETICULA	G	LIGATURE		RETINULA		REQUITAL	V	VAULTIER
F	FAULTIER	L	TAILLEUR		TENURIAL	R	RURALITE	Z	LAZURITE
	FILATURE	N	AUNTLIER	Q	QUARTILE	S	URALITES		

aeimnot 232 - amniote

A	METANOIA		NEMATOID		NOMINATE		MASONITE	Z	MONAZITE
C	COINMATE	M	AMMONITE	P	PTOMAINE		MISATONE		
D	DOMINATE	N	ANTINOME	S	AMNIOTES		SOMNIATE		

aeimnrs 170 - sirname

B	MIRBANES	G	GERMAINS		MINERALS	R	MARINERS	U	ANEURISM
C	CARMINES		SMEARING		MISLEARN	S	SEMINARS	Y	SEMINARY
	CREMAINS	H	HARMINES	N	REINSMAN		SIRNAMES		
D	ADERMINS		SHIREMAN	O	MORAINES	T	MERANTIS		
	SIRNAMED	K	RAMEKINS		ROMAINES		MINARETS		
E	REMANIES	L	MARLINES		ROMANISE		RAIMENTS		

aeimnrt 122 - raiment

A	ANIMATER		REMATING	S	MERANTIS		MARTINET
	MARINATE	L	TERMINAL		MINARETS	U	RUMINATE
E	ANTIMERE		TRAMLINE		RAIMENTS	W	WARIMENT
G	EMIGRANT	N	TRAINMEN	T	INTERMAT	Y	TYRAMINE

aeimnst 136 - tamines

A	AMENTIAS		MATINEES		TEAMINGS		MELANIST		MINARETS
	ANIMATES		MISEATEN	H	HEMATINS		SMALTINE		RAIMENTS
B	AMBIENTS		SEMINATE	I	MINIATES	N	MANNITES	S	MANTISES
C	AMNESTIC	F	MANIFEST	K	MANKIEST	O	AMNIOTES		MATINESS
	SEMANTIC	G	MANGIEST		MISTAKEN		MASONITE		
D	MEDIANTS		MINTAGES	L	AILMENTS		MISATONE		
	TIDESMAN		MISAGENT		ALIMENTS		SOMNIATE		
E	ETAMINES		STEAMING		MANLIEST	R	MERANTIS		

aeimrst 91 - smartie

A	AMIRATES		EMIRATES		SITKAMER		MINARETS		SMARTIES
B	BARMIEST		REAMIEST	L	LAMISTER		RAIMENTS	T	MISTREAT
C	CERAMIST		STEAMIER		LAMITERS	O	AMORTISE		TERATISM
	MATRICES	G	MAGISTER		MARLIEST		ATOMISER	U	MURIATES
	MISTRACE		MIGRATES		MARLITES	P	APTERISM		SEMITAUR
	SCIMETAR		RAGTIMES		MISALTER		PRIMATES	V	MARVIEST
D	MARDIEST		STERIGMA	M	MARMITES	S	ASTERISM		VITAMERS
	MISRATED	I	AIRTIMES		RAMMIEST		MAISTERS	W	WARTIMES
	READMITS		SERIATIM		TRAMMIES		MISRATES	X	MATRIXES
E	EMERITAS	K	MISTAKER	N	MERANTIS		SEMITARS	Y	SYMITARE

aeinnot 129 - enation

C	ENACTION	G	NEGATION	R	ANOINTER	S	ENATIONS	V	INNOVATE
D	ANOINTED	M	ANTINOME		INORNATE		SONATINE		VENATION
	ANTINODE		NOMINATE		REANOINT	T	INTONATE		

aeinnrs 107 - insnare

C	CRANNIES	G	AGINNERS	I	SIRENIAN	R	INSNARER	U	ANEURINS
	NARCEINS		EARNINGS	M	REINSMAN	S	INSNARES		UNARISEN
D	INSNARED		ENGRAINS	O	RAISONNE	T	ENTRAINS	W	SWANNIER
E	ANSERINE		GRANNIES	P	PANNIERS		TRANNIES		

aeinnrt 145 - trannie

I	TRIENNIA	M	TRAINMEN		INORNATE	R	INERRANT		TRANNIES
L	INTERNAL	O	ANOINTER		REANOINT	S	ENTRAINS	T	INTRANET

aeinors 16 - erasion

B	BARONIES	G	IGNAROES	M	MORAINES	T	ANOESTRI		SENORITA
	SEAROBIN		ORGANISE		ROMAINES		ARSONITE	V	AVERSION
C	SCENARIO		ORIGANES		ROMANISE		NOTAIRES		
D	ANEROIDS	L	AILERONS	N	RAISONNE		NOTARIES		
	DONARIES		ALERIONS	S	ERASIONS		NOTARISE		
F	FARINOSE		ALIENORS		SENSORIA		ROSINATE		

aeinort 1 - otarine

A	AERATION		CREATION	L	ORIENTAL	R	ANTERIOR		SENORITA
B	BARITONE		REACTION		RELATION	S	ANOESTRI	T	TENTORIA
	OBTAINER	D	AROINTED		TAILERON		ARSONITE	Z	NOTARIZE
	REOBTAIN		DERATION	N	ANOINTER		NOTAIRES		
	TABORINE		ORDINATE		INORNATE		NOTARIES		
C	ACTIONER		RATIONED		REANOINT		NOTARISE		
	ANORETIC	H	ANTIHERO	P	ATROPINE		ROSINATE		

aeinost 21 - atonies

B	BOTANIES		SONICATE	M	AMNIOTES	P	SAPONITE		ROSINATE
	BOTANISE	D	ASTONIED		MASONITE	R	ANOESTRI		SENORITA
	NIOBATES		SEDATION		MISATONE		ARSONITE	S	ASSIENTO
	OBEISANT	L	ELATIONS		SOMNIATE		NOTAIRES		ASTONIES
C	ACONITES		INSOLATE	N	ENATIONS		NOTARIES	V	STOVAINE
	CANOEIST		TOENAILS		SONATINE		NOTARISE	X	SAXONITE

aeinott 84 - [antitoe]

C	TACONITE		TETANOID	H	THIONATE	L	TONALITE	R	TENTORIA
D	ANTIDOTE	F	FETATION	I	NOTITIAE	N	INTONATE		

aeinprs 247 - rapines

A	PANARIES	G	PREASING	K	RANPIKES	T	PAINTERS		REPAINTS
D	SPRAINED		SPEARING	L	PEARLINS		PANTRIES	U	UNPRAISE
E	NAPERIES	H	HEPARINS		PRALINES		PERTAINS	W	SPAWNIER
F	FIREPANS		PARISHEN	N	PANNIERS		PINASTER		
	PANFRIES		SERAPHIN	P	SNAPPIER		PRISTANE		

aeinprt 52 - repaint

A	ANTIRAPE	H	PERIANTH	O	ATROPINE		PERTAINS	U	PAINTURE
D	DIPTERAN	I	PAINTIER	R	PRETRAIN		PINASTER	X	EXPIRANT
E	APERIENT	L	INTERLAP		TERRAPIN		PRISTANE		
G	RETAPING		TRAPLINE	S	PAINTERS		REPAINTS		
	TAPERING		TRIPLANE		PANTRIES	T	TRIPTANE		

aeinpst 224 - spinate

B	BEPAINTS		PIANISTE	N	PANTINES		PERTAINS		STEAPSIN
D	DEPAINTS	K	SNAKEPIT	O	SAPONITE		PINASTER	T	PATIENTS
H	PENTHIAS	L	PANELIST	P	NAPPIEST		PRISTANE	U	PETUNIAS
	THESPIAN		PANTILES	R	PAINTERS		REPAINTS		SUPINATE
I	PATINISE		PLAINEST		PANTRIES	S	SAPIENTS	Y	EPINASTY

aeinrrt 99 - trainer

C	TRANCIER	O	ANTERIOR	S	RESTRAIN		TERRAINS	T	RETIRANT
E	RETAINER	P	PRETRAIN		RETRAINS		TRAINERS	V	VERATRIN
N	INERRANT		TERRAPIN		STRAINER		TRANSIRE	W	INTERWAR

aeinrst 2 - stearin

A	ANTISERA		STRAINED	H	HAIRNETS	N	ENTRAINS		TRAINERS
	ARTESIAN	E	ARENITES		INEARTHS		TRANNIES		TRANSIRE
	RATANIES		ARSENITE		THERIANS	O	ANOESTRI	S	ARTINESS
	RESINATA		RESINATE	I	INERTIAS		ARSONITE		RESIANTS
	SANTERIA		STEARINE		RAINIEST		NOTAIRES		RETSINAS
	SEATRAIN		TRAINEES	J	NARTJIES		NOTARIES		SNARIEST
B	ATEBRINS	F	FAINTERS	K	KERATINS		NOTARISE		STAINERS
	BANISTER		FENITARS		NARKIEST		ROSINATE		STARNIES
	BARNIEST	G	ANGRIEST	L	ENTRAILS		SENORITA		STEARINS
C	CANISTER		ANGSTIER		LARNIEST	P	PAINTERS	T	INTREATS
	CARNIEST		ASTRINGE		LATRINES		PANTRIES		NITRATES
	CERATINS		GANISTER		RATLINES		PERTAINS		STRAITEN
	CISTERNA		GANTRIES		REINSTAL		PINASTER		TARTINES
	CREATINS		GRANITES		RETINALS		PRISTANE		TERTIANS
	NACRITES		INGRATES		SLANTIER		REPAINTS	U	RUINATES
	SCANTIER		RANGIEST		TRENAILS	R	RESTRAIN		TAURINES
	TACRINES		REASTING	M	MERANTIS		RETRAINS		URANITES
D	DETRAINS		STEARING		MINARETS		STRAINER		URINATES
	RANDIEST		TASERING		RAIMENTS		TERRAINS	W	TINWARES

aeinrsu 79 - [uranise]

B	ANBURIES		URANIDES	N	ANEURINS		SENARIUS		URINATES
	URBANISE	E	UNEASIER		UNARISEN	T	RUINATES	V	VAURIENS
D	DENARIUS	L	LUNARIES	P	UNPRAISE		TAURINES	Z	AZURINES
	UNRAISED	M	ANEURISM	S	ANURESIS		URANITES		SUZERAIN

aeinrtt 57 - tertian

A	ATTAINER	G	ARETTING	M	INTERMAT	P	TRIPTANE		STRAITEN
	REATTAIN		GNATTIER		MARTINET	R	RETIRANT		TARTINES
C	INTERACT		TREATING	N	INTRANET	S	INTREATS		TERTIANS
D	NITRATED	L	RATTLINE	O	TENTORIA		NITRATES	U	TAINTURE

aeinrtu 32 - urinate

A INAURATE	INDURATE	L AUNTLIER	Q ANTIQUER	URINATES
B BRAUNITE	RUINATED	RETINULA	QUAINTER	T TAINTURE
URBANITE	URINATED	TENURIAL	S RUINATES	V VAUNTIER
C ANURETIC	H HAURIENT	M RUMINATE	TAURINES	
D DATURINE	J JAUNTIER	P PAINTURE	URANITES	

aeinsst 176 - tisanes

A ENTASIAS	G EASTINGS	SANITISE	STANINES	S SAINTESS
B BASINETS	GENISTAS	TENIASIS	O ASSIENTO	SESTINAS
BASSINET	GIANTESS	K SNAKIEST	ASTONIES	T ANTSIEST
BESAINTS	SEATINGS	L EASTLINS	P SAPIENTS	INSTATES
BESTAINS	TEASINGS	ELASTINS	STEAPSIN	NASTIEST
C CINEASTS	TSIGANES	NAILSETS	R ARTINESS	SATINETS
SCANTIES	H ANTHESIS	SALIENTS	RESIANTS	TITANESS
D DESTAINS	SHANTIES	SALTINES	RETSINAS	U SINUATES
SANDIEST	SHEITANS	STANIELS	SNARIEST	X SEXTAINS
E ETESIANS	STHENIAS	M MANTISES	STAINERS	
TENIASES	I ISATINES	MATINESS	STARNIES	
F FANSITES	SANITIES	N INSANEST	STEARINS	

aeinstt 115 - satinet

A ASTATINE	D INSTATED	H HESITANT	STRAITEN	TITANESS
SANITATE	E ANISETTE	J JANTIEST	TARTINES	T NATTIEST
B TABINETS	TETANIES	N ANTIENTS	TERTIANS	V TASTEVIN
C CANTIEST	TETANISE	STANNITE	S ANTSIEST	W TAWNIEST
ENTASTIC	F FAINTEST	P PATIENTS	INSTATES	
NICTATES	G ESTATING	R INTREATS	NASTIEST	
TETANICS	TANGIEST	NITRATES	SATINETS	

aeinstu 229 - sinuate

D AUDIENTS	J JAUNTIES	P PETUNIAS	R RUINATES	S SINUATES
SINUATED	K UNAKITES	SUPINATE	TAURINES	V SUIVANTE
G SAUTEING	L ALUNITES	Q ANTIQUES	URANITES	
UNITAGES	INSULATE	QUANTISE	URINATES	

aeinstv 196 - vainest

A SANATIVE	D DEVIANTS	I VANITIES	O STOVAINE
C CISTVAEN	E NAIVETES	K KISTVAEN	T TASTEVIN
VESICANT	G VINTAGES	L VENTAILS	U SUIVANTE

aeiorst 5 - otaries

B SABOTIER	L SOTERIAL	NOTAIRES	R ROARIEST	V TRAVOISE
D ASTEROID	M AMORTISE	NOTARIES	ROTARIES	VIATORES
E ETAERIOS	ATOMISER	NOTARISE	T TOASTIER	VOTARIES
H HOARIEST	N ANOESTRI	ROSINATE	U OUTRAISE	
J JAROSITE	ARSONITE	SENORITA	SAUTOIRE	

aeiortt 222 - [toatier]

D TERATOID	M AMORETTI	S TOASTIER
L LITERATO	N TENTORIA	V ROTATIVE

aeiprst 139 - traipse

A	ASPIRATE	D	DIPTERAS	H	TRIPHASE

A	ASPIRATE	D DIPTERAS	H TRIPHASE	PANTRIES	PIASTRES
	PARASITE	DRAPIEST	I PARITIES	PERTAINS	RASPIEST
	SEPTARIA	RAPIDEST	K PARKIEST	PINASTER	TRAIPSES
B	BAPTISER	SPIRATED	L PILASTER	PRISTANE	V PRIVATES
C	CRAPIEST	TARSIPED	PLAISTER	REPAINTS	W WIRETAPS
	CRISPATE	TRAIPSED	PLAITERS	P PERIAPTS	Y ASPERITY
	PARETICS	E PARIETES	M APTERISM	R PARTIERS	
	PICRATES	PETARIES	PRIMATES	S PASTRIES	
	PRACTISE	G GRAPIEST	N PAINTERS	PIASTERS	

aeirrst 77 - tarsier

A	TARAIRES	REASTIER	TRAILERS	TRANSIRE	S TARSIERS
B	ARBITERS	F FRATRIES	N RESTRAIN	O ROARIEST	T RETRAITS
	BARRIEST	H TRASHIER	RETRAINS	ROTARIES	STRAITER
	RAREBITS	I RARITIES	STRAINER	P PARTIERS	TARRIEST
C	ERRATICS	L RETIRALS	TERRAINS	R STARRIER	W STRAWIER
E	ARTERIES	RETRIALS	TRAINERS	TARRIERS	

aeirstt 82 - tertias

A	ARIETTAS	TARDIEST	M MISTREAT	R RETRAITS	TARTIEST
	ARISTATE	E ARIETTES	TERATISM	STRAITER	TITRATES
B	BIRETTAS	ITERATES	N INTREATS	TARRIEST	TRISTATE
C	CITRATES	TEARIEST	NITRATES	S ARTISTES	W SWATTIER
	CRISTATE	TREATIES	STRAITEN	ARTSIEST	WARTIEST
	SCATTIER	TREATISE	TARTINES	STRIATES	X EXTRAITS
D	STRAITED	G STRIGATE	TERTIANS	T ATTRITES	Z TRISTEZA
	STRIATED	L TERTIALS	O TOASTIER	RATTIEST	

aeirstw 180 - wastrie

A	AWAITERS	WASTERIE	I WISTERIA	R STRAWIER	WARTIEST
B	WARBIEST	WEARIEST	K WATERSKI	S WAISTERS	
D	TAWDRIES	F WASTRIFE	M WARTIMES	WAITRESS	
E	SWEATIER	H SWATHIER	N TINWARES	WASTRIES	
	TAWERIES	WATERISH	P WIRETAPS	T SWATTIER	

aelnort 72 - [onlater]

E	REALTONE	I ORIENTAL	TAILERON	TOLERANT	Y ORNATELY
F	FLOREANT	RELATION	T TETRONAL	U OUTLEARN	

aelnoru 241 - aleuron

D	UNLOADER	E ALEURONE	S ALEURONS	T OUTLEARN	
	URODELAN	N NEURONAL	NEUROSAL		

aelnrst 95 - sternal

A	ASTERNAL	G STRANGLE	LATRINES	N LANTERNS	T SLATTERN
B	BRANTLES	TANGLERS	RATLINES	P PANTLERS	TRENTALS
C	CENTRALS	TRANGLES	REINSTAL	PLANTERS	U NEUTRALS
E	ALTERNES	H ENTHRALS	RETINALS	REPLANTS	V VENTRALS
	ETERNALS	I ENTRAILS	SLANTIER	S SALTERNS	
	TELERANS	LARNIEST	TRENAILS	SLANTERS	

aelorst 37 - olestra

B	BLOATERS	LODESTAR	H LOATHERS	PROLATES	V LEVATORS
	SORTABLE	E OLEASTER	RATHOLES	R REALTORS	OVERSALT
	STORABLE	F FLOATERS	I SOTERIAL	RELATORS	Y ROYALETS
C	LOCATERS	FORESTAL	L REALLOTS	RESTORAL	Z ZELATORS
	SECTORAL	REFLOATS	ROSTELLA	S OLESTRAS	
D	DELATORS	G GLOATERS	P PETROSAL	T RETOTALS	
	LEOTARDS	LEGATORS	POLESTAR	U ROSULATE	

aelorsu 183 - [earsoul]

A	AUREOLAS	D	ROULADES	G	GLAREOUS		NEUROSAL	U	ROULEAUS
B	RUBEOLAS	E	AUREOLES	M	RAMULOSE	P	LEAPROUS		
C	CAROUSEL	F	FUSAROLE	N	ALEURONS	T	ROSULATE		

aemnors 243 - oarsmen

A	AMARONES	F	FORAMENS	I	MORAINES	P	MANROPES		TONEARMS
C	CREMONAS	G	MEGARONS		ROMAINES		PROSEMAN	U	ENAMOURS
	ROMANCES	H	HORSEMAN		ROMANISE	R	RANSOMER		NEUROMAS
D	MADRONES		MENORAHS	L	ALMONERS	T	MONSTERA	V	OVERMANS
	RANSOMED		RHAMNOSE	N	MONERANS		ONSTREAM		OVERSMAN
	ROADSMEN		SHOREMAN		SONARMEN		STOREMAN	Y	ROMNEYAS

aenoort 207 - [oarnote]

C	CORONATE	D	RATOONED	E	AEROTONE	M	ANTEROOM	R	RATOONER

aenorst 6 - treason

A	ANOESTRA	F	SEAFRONT		NOTARIES		RESONANT		TREASONS
B	BARONETS	G	ESTRAGON		NOTARISE	P	OPERANTS	T	ORNATEST
C	ANCESTOR		NEGATORS		ROSINATE		PRONATES	U	OUTEARNS
	ENACTORS		ORANGEST		SENORITA		PROTEANS	V	VENATORS
	SARCONET		RAGSTONE	M	MONSTERA	R	ANTRORSE	W	STONERAW
	SORTANCE		STONERAG		ONSTREAM	S	ASSENTOR		
D	TORNADES	I	ANOESTRI		STOREMAN		SANTEROS		
E	EARSTONE		ARSONITE		TONEARMS		SENATORS		
	RESONATE		NOTAIRES	N	NORTENAS		STARNOSE		

aenorsu 182 - arenous

A	ARANEOUS	F	FURANOSE	M	ENAMOURS	S	ANSEROUS	V	RAVENOUS
C	CARNEOUS	L	ALEURONS		NEUROMAS		ARSENOUS		
	NACREOUS		NEUROSAL	N	UNREASON	T	OUTEARNS		

aenortt 175 - [oatrent]

B	BETATRON	G	TETRAGON		TOLERANT	S	ORNATEST	Y	ATTORNEY
C	CONTRATE	I	TENTORIA	M	TORMENTA	V	TEVATRON		
D	ATTORNED	L	TETRONAL	P	PATENTOR	X	TETRAXON		

aenortu 108 - outearn

A	AERONAUT		OUTRANCE	L	OUTLEARN	N	UNORNATE
C	COURANTE	G	OUTRANGE	M	ROUTEMAN	S	OUTEARNS

aenrstu 80 - saunter

B	UNBRASTE		TRANSUDE		UNHEARTS	M	ANESTRUM	T	TAUNTERS
	URBANEST		UNTREADS		URETHANS		MENSTRUA	V	VAUNTERS
C	CENTAURS	E	SAUTERNE	I	RUINATES		TRANSUME	W	UNWATERS
	RECUSANT	F	AFTERSUN		TAURINES	O	OUTEARNS		
	UNCRATES	G	STRAUNGE		URANITES	P	PERSAUNT		
	UNTRACES	H	HAUNTERS		URINATES	S	ANESTRUS		
D	DAUNTERS		UNEARTHS	L	NEUTRALS		SAUNTERS		

aeorrst 144 - roaster

A	AERATORS		REACTORS		RELATORS		PRORATES		ROASTERS
B	ABORTERS	D	ROADSTER		RESTORAL	R	ARRESTOR	T	ROSTRATE
	ARBORETS	G	GARROTES	M	REARMOST	S	ASSERTOR		
	TABORERS	I	ROARIEST	N	ANTRORSE		ASSORTER		
C	ACROTERS		ROTARIES	O	SORORATE		ORATRESS		
	CREATORS	L	REALTORS	P	PRAETORS		REASSORT		

aeorstt 186 - toaster

A	AEROSTAT	C	SECTATOR	L	RETOTALS	S	STRATOSE	U	OUTRATES
B	ABETTORS	G	GAROTTES	N	ORNATEST		TOASTERS		OUTSTARE
	BATTEROS	H	RHEOSTAT	P	PROSTATE	T	ATTESTOR		SEATROUT
	TABORETS	I	TOASTIER	R	ROSTRATE		TESTATOR		

aeorstu 81 - [outears]

B	SABOTEUR	G	OUTRAGES		SAUTOIRE		QUAESTOR	V	OUTRAVES
C	OUTRACES	H	ARTHOUSE	L	ROSULATE	S	OSSATURE	W	OUTSWARE
D	OUTDARES		OUTHEARS	N	OUTEARNS	T	OUTRATES		OUTSWEAR
	OUTREADS		RATHOUSE	P	APTEROUS		OUTSTARE		OUTWEARS
	READOUTS	I	OUTRAISE	Q	EQUATORS		SEATROUT		

agilnot 201 - antilog

A	GALTONIA	E	GELATION		GOATLING		TAGLIONI		SALTOING
B	BLOATING		LEGATION	H	LOATHING	P	PLOATING		SOLATING
	OBLIGANT	F	FLOATING	I	INTAGLIO	R	TRIGONAL	T	TOTALING
C	LOCATING	G	GLOATING		LIGATION	S	ANTILOGS	Y	ANTILOGY

aginors 230 - soaring

C	ORGANICS		ORIGANES	M	ORGANISM	S	ASSIGNOR		ROASTING
D	ROADINGS	H	ORANGISH		ROAMINGS		SIGNORAS	U	AROUSING
E	IGNAROES	I	SIGNORIA	R	GARRISON		SOARINGS	V	SAVORING
	ORGANISE	L	RANGOLIS		ROARINGS	T	ORGANIST		

aginort 164 - roating

B	ABORTING	I	RIGATONI	O	ROGATION		TROATING
	BORATING	K	TROAKING	S	ORGANIST	V	GRAVITON
	TABORING	L	TRIGONAL		ROASTING	Y	GYRATION
G	GAROTING	N	IGNORANT	T	ROTATING		ORGANITY

aginrst 206 - tarings

A	GRANITAS		GRANITES	H	TRASHING	O	ORGANIST	V	STARVING
B	BRASTING		INGRATES	K	KARTINGS		ROASTING	W	RINGTAWS
C	SCARTING		RANGIEST		STARKING	P	PARTINGS		STRAWING
	TRACINGS		REASTING	L	RATLINGS		PRATINGS		WRASTING
D	TRADINGS		STEARING		SLARTING	R	STARRING	Y	STINGRAY
E	ANGRIEST		TASERING		STARLING		TARRINGS		STRAYING
	ANGSTIER	F	INGRAFTS	M	MIGRANTS	S	GASTRINS		
	ASTRINGE		RAFTINGS		SMARTING		STARINGS		
	GANISTER		STRAFING	N	RANTINGS	T	RATTINGS		
	GANTRIES	G	GRATINGS		STARNING		STARTING		

ailnort 78 - [latinor]

A	NOTARIAL	D	TRINODAL	F	FLATIRON	L	ANTIROLL
	RATIONAL	E	ORIENTAL		INFLATOR	M	TORMINAL
C	CILANTRO		RELATION	G	TRIGONAL	S	TONSILAR
	CONTRAIL		TAILERON	H	HORNTAIL	Z	TRIZONAL

ailnost 178 - talions

A	AILANTOS		INSOLATE		SALTOING	N	ANTLIONS	Y	LANOSITY
	ALATIONS		TOENAILS		SOLATING	O	SOLATION		
E	ELATIONS	G	ANTILOGS	L	STALLION	R	TONSILAR		

ailorst 153 - tailors

B	LABORIST	D	DILATORS	O	ISOLATOR		SOLARIST		SOLITARY
	ORBITALS	E	SOTERIAL		OSTIOLAR	T	ORLISTAT		
	STROBILA	M	MORALIST	S	ORALISTS	U	SUTORIAL		
C	CALORIST	N	TONSILAR		SLIOTARS	Y	ROYALIST		

ainorst 39 - rations

B	TABORINS	E	ANOESTRI		SENORITA	L	TONSILAR		SUTORIAN
C	CANTORIS		ARSONITE	G	ORGANIST	O	ORATIONS	W	WAITRONS
	CAROTINS		NOTAIRES		ROASTING	P	ATROPINS	X	TRIAXONS
	CORTINAS		NOTARIES	H	TRAHISON	S	ARSONIST		
D	DIATRONS		NOTARISE	J	JANITORS	T	STRONTIA		
	INTRADOS		ROSINATE	K	SKIATRON	U	RAINOUTS		

beinost 240 - ebonist

A	BOTANIES	B	NOBBIEST	K	STEINBOK	R	BORNITES	U	BOUNTIES
	BOTANISE	E	BETONIES	N	BONNIEST		RIBSTONE		
	NIOBATES		EBONITES	O	BONITOES	S	EBONISTS		
	OBEISANT	I	NIOBITES		EOBIONTS	T	BOTTINES		

ceinors 218 - sericon

A	SCENARIO		FORENSIC	I	RECISION	P	CONSPIRE		RECTIONS
B	BICORNES		FORINSEC		SORICINE		INCORPSE	U	COINSURE
C	CONCISER		FORNICES	L	INCLOSER	R	RESORCIN		INSOURCE
	CORNICES		INFORCES		LICENSOR	S	NECROSIS		NOURICES
	CROCEINS	G	COGNISER	M	CREMOSIN		SERICONS		ROUNCIES
D	CONSIDER		COREIGNS		INCOMERS	T	COINTERS		
F	COINFERS		COSIGNER		SERMONIC		CORNIEST		
	CONIFERS	H	CHORINES	N	INCENSOR		NOTICERS		

ceinort 76 - rection

A	ACTIONER	D	CENTROID	H	NOTCHIER		PRETONIC	T	CONTRITE
	ANORETIC		DOCTRINE	I	RETINOIC	R	TRICORNE		CORNETTI
	CREATION			J	INJECTOR	S	COINTERS	U	NEUROTIC
	REACTION	E	ERECTION				CORNIEST		UNEROTIC
C	CONCERTI		NEOTERIC	M	INTERCOM		NOTICERS	V	CONTRIVE
	NECROTIC	F	INFECTOR	P	ENTROPIC		RECTIONS		
		G	GERONTIC		INCEPTOR				

ceinost 197 - section

A	ACONITES		SEICENTO	M	CENTIMOS		RECTIONS	X	EXCITONS
	CANOEIST	G	ESCOTING	O	COONTIES	S	SECTIONS	Y	CYTOSINE
	SONICATE	K	CONKIEST	P	PONCIEST	T	CENTOIST		
C	CONCEITS		KENOTICS	R	COINTERS		STENOTIC		
D	DEONTICS	L	LECTIONS		CORNIEST		TONETICS		
E	ICESTONE		TELSONIC		NOTICERS	U	COUNTIES		

deeinos 216 - [eonised]

B	EBONISED	L	ESLOINED		DOMINEES	R	INDORSEE	V	NOSEDIVE
C	CODEINES		LESIONED	P	DISPONEE		ORDINEES		
I	DEIONISE	M	DEMONISE		OPENSIDE	T	SIDENOTE		

deeinrs 87 - [resined]

A	ARSENIDE	F	DEFINERS		RESHINED	S	DIRENESS	V	INVERSED
	DENARIES	G	DESIGNER	K	DEERSKIN	T	INSERTED	W	REWIDENS
	DRAISENE		ENERGIDS	L	REDLINES		NERDIEST		WIDENERS
	NEARSIDE		REDESIGN	N	SINNERED		RESIDENT	X	INDEXERS
B	INBREEDS		REEDINGS	O	INDORSEE		SINTERED		
E	NEREIDES		RESIGNED		ORDINEES		TRENDIES		
	REDENIES	H	DRISHEEN	P	SPENDIER	U	UREDINES		

deeinrt 50 - [rednite]

A	DETAINER	K	TINKERED	O	ORIENTED		RESIDENT		REUNITED
	RETAINED	M	REMINTED	R	INTERRED		SINTERED	V	INVERTED
B	INTERBED	N	INDENTER		TRENDIER		TRENDIES	W	WINTERED
D	DENDRITE		INTENDER	S	INSERTED	T	RETINTED	X	DEXTRINE
H	NITHERED		INTERNED		NERDIEST	U	RETINUED		

deeinst 55 - steined

A ANDESITE	G INGESTED	LISTENED	O SIDENOTE	S DESTINES
B BENDIEST	SIGNETED	TINSELED	P PENTISED	T DINETTES
D DESTINED	STEEDING	M DEMENTIS	R INSERTED	INSETTED
NEDDIEST	H DISTHENE	SEDIMENT	NERDIEST	U DETINUES
E NEEDIEST	I DIETINES	TIDESMEN	RESIDENT	V EVIDENTS
F FENDIEST	L ENLISTED	N DENTINES	SINTERED	INVESTED
INFESTED	LINTSEED	DESINENT	TRENDIES	

deeiort 137 - [doetire]

F FOETIDER	LOITERED	PROTEIDE	V OVEREDIT
G GOITERED	N ORIENTED	S EROTISED	Z EROTIZED
L DOLERITE	P PERIDOTE	U ETOURDIE	

deeirst 48 - resited

A READIEST	DISCRETE	L RELISTED	TRENDIES	SISTERED
SERIATED	D REDDIEST	M DEMERITS	O EROTISED	T TIREDEST
SIDERATE	E REEDIEST	DEMISTER	P PREEDITS	U ERUDITES
STEADIER	F RESIFTED	DIMETERS	PRIESTED	SURETIED
B BEDRITES	G DIGESTER	MISTERED	RESPITED	V VERDITES
BESTRIDE	ESTRIDGE	N INSERTED	R DESTRIER	W WEIRDEST
BISTERED	REDIGEST	NERDIEST	S DIESTERS	
C DESERTIC	H DIETHERS	RESIDENT	EDITRESS	
DISCREET	I SIDERITE	SINTERED	RESISTED	

deenors 163 - endorse

A REASONED	ENCODERS	E ENDORSEE	SERMONED	T ERODENTS
B DEBONERS	NECROSED	I INDORSEE	N ENDERONS	W ENDOWERS
REDBONES	SECONDER	ORDINEES	R ENDORSER	REENDOWS
C CENSORED	D ENDORSED	M MODERNES	S ENDORSES	WORSENED

deenort 217 - erodent

C CENTRODE	I ORIENTED	M ENTODERM	S ERODENTS
H DETHRONE	L REDOLENT	MENTORED	U DEUTERON
THRENODE	RONDELET	O ENROOTED	

deeorst 189 - teredos

B BESORTED	F DEFOREST	M MODESTER	RESTORED	X DEXTROSE
BESTRODE	FORESTED	N ERODENTS	ROSTERED	Y OYSTERED
C CORSETED	FOSTERED	P DOPESTER	S DOSSERET	STOREYED
ESCORTED	G GOSTERED	POSTERED	OERSTEDS	
SECTORED	I EROTISED	REPOSTED	T ROSETTED	
E STEREOED	K RESTOKED	R RESORTED	TETRODES	

deilnos 130 - sondeli

A NODALISE	LESIONED	I LIONISED	R DISENROL	U DELUSION
C INCLOSED	G GLENOIDS	O EIDOLONS	S SONDELIS	INSOULED
E ESLOINED	SIDELONG	SOLENOID	T LENTOIDS	UNSOILED

deilnot 102 - lentoid

A DELATION	ENTOILED	N INDOLENT	S LENTOIDS
E DELETION	I TOLIDINE	P TOPLINED	U OUTLINED

deilors 239 - solider

A DARIOLES	C SCLEROID	N DISENROL	T STOLIDER
SOLIDARE	I IDOLISER	P LEPORIDS	U SOULDIER
SOREDIAL	L DOLLIERS	S SOLDIERS	Y SOLDIERY

deilort 220 - doilter

A	IDOLATER	B	TRILOBED	LOITERED	S	STOLIDER
	TAILORED	E	DOLERITE	L	TROLLIED	Y	ELYTROID

deilost 215 - [oldiste]

A	DIASTOLE	C	DOCILEST	M	MELODIST	P	PISTOLED	T	DOILTEST
	ISOLATED	D	DELTOIDS		MODELIST		POSTILED	U	SOLITUDE
	SODALITE	G	GODLIEST		MOLDIEST	R	STOLIDER		TOLUIDES
	SOLIDATE		GOLDIEST	N	LENTOIDS	S	SOLIDEST	W	DOWLIEST

deinors 26 - sordine

A	ANEROIDS	G	NEGROIDS	J	JOINDERS	R	INDORSER	W	DISOWNER
	DONARIES	H	HORDEINS	L	DISENROL	S	INDORSES		WINDORES
C	CONSIDER	I	DERISION	N	ENDIRONS		SORDINES		
D	INDORSED		IRONISED	P	DISPONER	T	DRONIEST		
E	INDORSEE		IRONSIDE		POINDERS	U	DOURINES		
	ORDINEES		RESINOID		PRISONED		SOURDINE		

deinort 18 - [interdo]

A	AROINTED		RATIONED	D	TRENDOID	M	DORMIENT	S	DRONIEST
	DERATION	C	CENTROID	E	ORIENTED	N	INDENTOR	T	INTORTED
	ORDINATE		DOCTRINE	I	RETINOID	P	DIPTERON		

deinost 66 - stonied

A	ASTONIED	D	NODDIEST	I	EDITIONS	M	DEMONIST	W	DOWNIEST
	SEDATION	E	SIDENOTE		SEDITION	R	DRONIEST		
C	DEONTICS	H	HEDONIST	L	LENTOIDS	S	DONSIEST		

deinrst 94 - tinders

A	DETRAINS		NERDIEST	I	DISINTER		TENDRILS		TRIDENTS
	RANDIEST		RESIDENT		INDITERS		TRINDLES	U	INTRUDES
	STRAINED		SINTERED		NITRIDES	O	DRONIEST		NURDIEST
D	STRIDDEN		TRENDIES		RINDIEST	P	SPRINTED	X	DEXTRINS
E	INSERTED	G	STRINGED	L	SNIRTLED	T	STRIDENT		

deinrtu 92 - untried

A	DATURINE	B	TURBINED	E	RETINUED	M	RUDIMENT	R	INTRUDER
	INDURATE		UNDERBIT		REUNITED		UNMITRED	S	INTRUDES
	RUINATED	C	REINDUCT	I	UNTIDIER	N	INTURNED		NURDIEST
	URINATED	D	INTRUDED	L	UNDERLIT	P	TURNIPED	W	UNDERWIT

deinstu 242 - dunites

A	AUDIENTS	G	DUNGIEST	L	DILUENTS		DUNNITES	U	UNSUITED
	SINUATED	I	DISUNITE		INSULTED	Q	SQUINTED		
D	DISTUNED		NUDITIES		UNLISTED	R	INTRUDES		
E	DETINUES		UNITISED	M	MISTUNED		NURDIEST		
F	UNSIFTED		UNTIDIES	N	DUNNIEST	S	DISTUNES		

deiorst 35 - triodes

A	ASTEROID		GRODIEST	N	DRONIEST		PROTEIDS		OUTRIDES
B	DEBITORS		STODGIER	P	DIOPTERS		RIPOSTED		OUTSIDER
	DEORBITS	I	DIORITES		DIOPTRES		TOPSIDER		SUITORED
C	CORDITES	K	DORKIEST		DIPTEROS	S	STEROIDS	W	ROWDIEST
E	EROTISED	L	STOLIDER		PERIDOTS	T	DORTIEST		WORDIEST
G	DIGESTOR	M	MORTISED		PORTSIDE	U	IODURETS		

deiortu 237 - outride

B	TUBEROID	F	OUTFIRED	S	IODURETS		SUITORED
C	OUTCRIED	H	OUTHIRED		OUTRIDES	V	OUTDRIVE
E	ETOURDIE	R	OUTRIDER		OUTSIDER		

denortu 203 - [outrend]

C	CORNUTED	E	DEUTERON	L	ROUNDLET	S	ROUNDEST	T	UNROTTED
	TROUNCED	F	FORTUNED	O	UNROOTED		TONSURED	W	UNDERTOW
D	ROTUNDED	G	TRUDGEON	R	ROTUNDER		UNSORTED		

eeginrs 123 - greisen

A	ANERGIES		READINGS	H	GREENISH		INGENERS		REESTING
	GESNERIA		RESIGNED		REHINGES		SERENING		STEERING
B	BIGENERS	E	ENERGIES		SHEERING		SNEERING		STREIGNE
	BREINGES		ENERGISE	J	JEERINGS	O	ERINGOES	U	SEIGNEUR
	REBEGINS		GREENIES	K	KREESING	P	SPEERING	V	SEVERING
C	CREESING		RESEEING		SKEERING		SPREEING		VEERINGS
	GENERICS	F	FEERINGS	L	LEERINGS	R	RESIGNER	W	RESEWING
D	DESIGNER		FEIGNERS		REELINGS	S	GREISENS		SEWERING
	ENERGIDS		REEFINGS	M	REGIMENS	T	GENTRIES		SWEERING
	REDESIGN	G	GREESING	N	ENGINERS		INTEGERS		

eeginrt 124 - treeing

A	ENARGITE	G	GREETING		REGIMENT		REESTING	V	EVERTING
	GRATINEE	I	REIGNITE	N	ENTERING		STEERING	W	TWEERING
	INTERAGE		RETIEING	P	PETERING		STREIGNE	X	EXERTING
C	ERECTING	L	GREENLIT	S	GENTRIES	T	RINGETTE		GENETRIX
	GENTRICE	M	METERING		INTEGERS	U	GENITURE		

eeginst 199 - [seeting]

A	SAGENITE	G	EGESTING		STEELING		INTEGERS		VENTIGES
B	BEESTING	H	SEETHING	M	MEETINGS		REESTING	W	SWEETING
	BEIGNETS		SHEETING		STEEMING		STEERING	X	EXIGENTS
C	GENETICS	K	KITENGES	N	STEENING		STREIGNE		
D	INGESTED		STEEKING	O	EGESTION	T	GENTIEST		
	SIGNETED	L	GENTILES	P	STEEPING	U	EUGENIST		
	STEEDING		SLEETING	R	GENTRIES	V	STEEVING		

eeiinrt 158 - niterie

A	INERTIAE		REINCITE	O	ERIONITE	T	INTERTIE
B	BENITIER	G	REIGNITE	S	ERINITES		RETINITE
C	ICTERINE		RETIEING		NITERIES	V	REINVITE

eeilnst 96 - tensile

B	STILBENE		TINSELED	H	THEELINS	P	PENLITES	S	LITENESS
	TENSIBLE	E	ENLISTEE	I	LENITIES		PLENTIES		SETLINES
C	CENTILES		SELENITE	K	NESTLIKE	R	ENLISTER	T	ENTITLES
D	ENLISTED	G	GENTILES	N	LENIENTS		LISTENER	V	VEINLETS
	LINTSEED		SLEETING		SENTINEL		REENLIST		
	LISTENED		STEELING	O	NOSELITE		SILENTER		

eeilors 190 - loeries

B	EROSIBLE	I	OILERIES	N	ELOINERS		TROELIES		VOLERIES
C	CREOLISE	K	ROSELIKE	P	PELORIES	V	OVERLIES	W	OWLERIES
F	FORELIES	L	ORSEILLE	T	LITEROSE		RELIEVOS		

eeilort 149 - troelie

A	AEROLITE		LOITERED	K	LORIKEET	R	LOITERER		TROELIES
D	DOLERITE	H	HOTELIER	M	MOTELIER	S	LITEROSE		

eeilrst 90 - sterile

A ATELIERS	TIERCELS	I TILERIES	SILENTER	SPIRELET
EARLIEST	TRISCELE	K TRISKELE	O LITEROSE	S LEISTERS
LATERISE	D RELISTED	L TREILLES	TROELIES	RITELESS
LEARIEST	E LEERIEST	M TERMLIES	P EPISTLER	TIRELESS
REALTIES	SLEETIER	N ENLISTER	PELTRIES	T RETITLES
C RETICLES	STEELIER	LISTENER	PERLITES	
SCLERITE	F FERLIEST	REENLIST	REPTILES	

eeinors 126 - [oneries]

D INDORSEE	H HEROINES	L ELOINERS	PEREIONS	T ONERIEST
ORDINEES	NOSHERIE	M EMERSION	PIONEERS	SEROTINE
G ERINGOES	K KEROSINE	P ISOPRENE	S ESSOINER	V EVERSION

eeinort 24 - [onetire]

B TENEBRIO	D ORIENTED	I ERIONITE	REORIENT	T TENORITE
C ERECTION	H ETHERION	M TIMONEER	S ONERIEST	X EXERTION
NEOTERIC	HEREINTO	R ORIENTER	SEROTINE	

eeinost 105 - [etonise]

B BETONIES	SEICENTO	L NOSELITE	R ONERIEST	T NOISETTE
EBONITES	D SIDENOTE	M MONETISE	SEROTINE	TEOSINTE
C ICESTONE	G EGESTION	SEMITONE	S ESSONITE	

eeinrst 13 - trienes

A ARENITES	RESIDENT	I ERINITES	R INSERTER	TRIENTES
ARSENITE	SINTERED	NITERIES	REINSERT	U ESURIENT
RESINATE	TRENDIES	K KERNITES	REINTERS	NEURITES
STEARINE	E ETERNISE	L ENLISTER	RENTIERS	RETINUES
TRAINEES	TEENSIER	LISTENER	TERRINES	REUNITES
C CENTRIES	F FERNIEST	REENLIST	S INTERESS	V NERVIEST
ENTERICS	INFESTER	SILENTER	SENTRIES	REINVEST
ENTICERS	G GENTRIES	M MISENTER	TRENISES	SERVIENT
SCIENTER	INTEGERS	N INTENSER	T INERTEST	SIRVENTE
SECRETIN	REESTING	INTERNES	INSETTER	X INTERSEX
D INSERTED	STEERING	O ONERIEST	INTEREST	Y SERENITY
NERDIEST	STREIGNE	SEROTINE	STERNITE	

eeinrsu 234 - [neuries]

A UNEASIER	F REINFUSE	RESUPINE	R REINSURE	NEURITES
C INSECURE	G SEIGNEUR	Q ENQUIRES	S ENURESIS	RETINUES
SINECURE	N NEURINES	INQUERES	ERINUSES	REUNITES
D UREDINES	P PENURIES	SQUIREEN	T ESURIENT	V UNIVERSE

eeinrtt 172 - tentier

B REBITTEN	TEENTIER	RETINITE	O TENORITE	STERNITE
C RETICENT	G RINGETTE	L NETTLIER	S INERTEST	TRIENTES
D RETINTED	H THIRTEEN	N INTERNET	INSETTER	Y ENTIRETY
E REINETTE	I INTERTIE	RENITENT	INTEREST	ETERNITY

eeinstt 221 - netties

A ANISETTE	E TEENIEST	N SENTIENT	INSETTER	W TENTWISE
TETANIES	F FEINTEST	O NOISETTE	INTEREST	TWENTIES
TETANISE	G GENTIEST	TEOSINTE	STERNITE	X EXISTENT
B BENTIEST	I ENTITIES	P INEPTEST	TRIENTES	
D DINETTES	L ENTITLES	SPINETTE	T NETTIEST	
INSETTED	M MINETTES	R INERTEST	TENTIEST	

eeiorst 65 - erotise

A	ETAERIOS	G	ERGOTISE	L	LITEROSE		SEROTINE		EROTISES
C	COTERIES	H	ISOTHERE		TROELIES	P	POETISER	Z	EROTIZES
	ESOTERIC		THEORIES	M	TIRESOME		POETRIES		
D	EROTISED		THEORISE	N	ONERIEST	S	EROTESIS		

eelorst 171 - soleret

A	OLEASTER		SELECTOR		TROELIES	S	SOLERETS
C	CORSELET	E	SLOETREE	L	SOLLERET	T	LORETTES
	ELECTORS	H	HOSTELER	M	MOLESTER	U	RESOLUTE
	ELECTROS	I	LITEROSE	N	ENTRESOL	V	OVERLETS

eenorst 54 - estrone

A	EARSTONE		SOFTENER	L	ENTRESOL	O	OESTRONE	V	OVERNETS
	RESONATE	G	ESTROGEN	M	SERMONET		ROESTONE	X	EXTENSOR
D	ERODENTS	H	HONESTER		STOREMEN	P	PROTENSE		
F	ENFOREST	I	ONERIEST	N	ENTERONS	S	ESTRONES		
	RESOFTEN		SEROTINE		TENONERS	T	ONSETTER		

egilnor 211 - [longier]

A	GERANIOL	E	ELOIGNER		RELIGION	U	LOUNGIER
	REGIONAL	F	FLORIGEN		REOILING	W	LOWERING
B	IGNOBLER	I	LIGROINE	S	RESOLING		ROWELING

eginors 70 - signore

A	IGNAROES		COREIGNS	L	RESOLING		SPONGIER		ROSETING
	ORGANISE		COSIGNER	M	NEGROISM	R	IGNORERS	W	RESOWING
	ORIGANES	D	NEGROIDS	N	NEGRONIS	S	GORINESS	Y	SEIGNORY
B	SOBERING	E	ERINGOES	P	PERIGONS		SIGNORES		
C	COGNISER	I	SEIGNIOR		REPOSING	T	GENITORS		

eginort 214 - genitor

C	GERONTIC		RINGTONE	T	OTTERING	V	REVOTING	Z	ROZETING
H	THROEING	S	GENITORS	U	OUTREIGN	W	TOWERING		
N	NITROGEN		ROSETING		ROUTEING	X	OXTERING		

eginrst 120 - stinger

A	ANGRIEST		TASERING		IGNITERS	N	RENTINGS		TRESSING
	ANGSTIER	C	CRESTING		REISTING		STERNING		TRIGNESS
	ASTRINGE	D	STRINGED		RESITING	O	GENITORS	T	GITTERNS
	GANISTER	E	GENTRIES		STINGIER		ROSETING	V	STERVING
	GANTRIES		INTEGERS		STRIGINE	P	PRESTING	W	STREWING
	GRANITES		REESTING	L	LINGSTER	R	RESTRING		WRESTING
	INGRATES		STEERING		RINGLETS		RINGSTER		
	RANGIEST		STREIGNE		STERLING		STRINGER		
	REASTING	H	RIGHTENS		TINGLERS	S	RESTINGS		
	STEARING	I	GIRNIEST		TRINGLES		STINGERS		

ehinort 187 - [thronie]

A	ANTIHERO		HEREINTO	N	INTHRONE	S	HORNIEST
C	NOTCHIER	G	THROEING	P	TRIPHONE		ORNITHES
E	ETHERION	M	THERMION	R	THORNIER	V	OVERTHIN

ehiorst 209 - toshier

A	HOARIEST		THEORISE		ORNITHES		HORSIEST	U	OUTHIRES
C	ROTCHIES	G	GHOSTIER	O	TOOSHIER		HOSTRIES		SHOUTIER
	THEORICS	M	ISOTHERM	P	TROPHIES		SHORTIES	V	OVERHITS
E	ISOTHERE		MOITHERS	R	HERITORS	T	THEORIST	W	WORTHIES
	THEORIES	N	HORNIEST	S	HOISTERS		THORITES		

eiilrst 228 - siltier

A	LAIRIEST	E	TILERIES	M	LIMITERS	O	ROILIEST	U	UTILISER
	LISTERIA	F	FILISTER		MIRLIEST	P	TRIPLIES		
B	TRILBIES	G	GIRLIEST	N	NIRLIEST	T	SLITTIER		
D	REDISTIL	L	STILLIER		NITRILES		STILTIER		

eiinort 69 - [noirite]

C	RETINOIC	E	ERIONITE	L	TRIOLEIN		POITRINE	S	IRONIEST
D	RETINOID	F	NOTIFIER	P	POINTIER	R	INTERIOR		

eiinrst 73 - [tinrise]

A	INERTIAS		NITRIDES		RESITING		MINISTER	U	NEURITIS
	RAINIEST		RINDIEST		STINGIER		MISINTER		UNITISER
B	BRINIEST	E	ERINITES		STRIGINE	O	IRONIEST	V	INVITERS
C	CITRINES		NITERIES	H	INHERITS	P	PRISTINE		VINTRIES
	CRINITES	F	SNIFTIER	K	STINKIER	S	INSISTER		VITRINES
	INCITERS	G	GIRNIEST	L	NIRLIEST		SINISTER		
D	DISINTER		IGNITERS		NITRILES	T	NITRITES		
	INDITERS		REISTING	M	INTERIMS		STINTIER		

eilnors 43 - nerolis

A	AILERONS		LICENSOR	I	LIONISER		PROLINES
	ALERIONS	D	DISENROL	M	MISENROL	R	LORINERS
	ALIENORS	E	ELOINERS	N	ONLINERS	S	IRONLESS
C	INCLOSER	G	RESOLING	P	PLERIONS	T	RETINOLS

eilnort 47 - retinol

A	ORIENTAL	I	TRIOLEIN	R	RITORNEL	U	OUTLINER
	RELATION	P	TERPINOL	S	RETINOLS	W	TOWNLIER
	TAILERON		TOPLINER	T	TROTLINE		

eilnost 28 - onliest

A	ELATIONS	E	NOSELITE	L	STELLION		PONTILES	V	NOVELIST
	INSOLATE	H	HOLSTEIN	M	MOLINETS		POTLINES		VIOLENTS
	TOENAILS		HOTLINES	N	INSOLENT		TOPLINES	W	TOWLINES
C	LECTIONS		NEOLITHS	O	LOONIEST	R	RETINOLS		
	TELSONIC	I	ETIOLINS		OILSTONE	U	ELUTIONS		
D	LENTOIDS		NOILIEST	P	POINTELS		OUTLINES		

eilnrst 104 - snirtle

A	ENTRAILS		TRENAILS		SILENTER		NITRILES	S	SLINTERS
	LARNIEST	D	SNIRTLED	G	LINGSTER	K	LINKSTER		SNIRTLES
	LATRINES		TENDRILS		RINGLETS		STRINKLE	U	INSULTER
	RATLINES		TRINDLES		STERLING		TINKLERS		LUSTRINE
	REINSTAL	E	ENLISTER		TINGLERS	M	MINSTREL	Y	TINSELRY
	RETINALS		LISTENER		TRINGLES	O	RETINOLS		
	SLANTIER		REENLIST	I	NIRLIEST	P	SPLINTER		

eilorst 29 - toilers

A	SOTERIAL		COSTLIER	F	FLORIEST	N	RETINOLS	T	TRIOLETS
B	STROBILE		CREOLIST		TREFOILS	O	OESTRIOL	U	LOURIEST
	TRILOBES	D	STOLIDER	I	ROILIEST		TROOLIES		OUTLIERS
C	CLOISTER	E	LITEROSE	L	TRILLOES	P	POITRELS		
	COISTREL		TROELIES		TROLLIES	S	ESTRIOLS		

eilrstu 219 - rutiles

A	URALITES	D	DILUTERS	I	UTILISER		OUTLIERS		SURTITLE
B	BURLIEST		LURIDEST	M	MURLIEST	Q	QUILTERS	V	RIVULETS
	SUBTILER		STUDLIER	N	INSULTER	R	SULTRIER		
C	CURLIEST	G	GURLIEST		LUSTRINE	S	SURLIEST		
	UTRICLES	H	LUTHIERS	O	LOURIEST	T	SLUTTIER		

eimorst 198 - trisome

A	AMORTISE	G	ERGOTISM		ROOMIEST		TRISOMES		WORMIEST
	ATOMISER		GORMIEST	P	IMPOSTER	T	OMITTERS	Y	ISOMETRY
C	MORTICES	H	ISOTHERM	R	MORTISER	U	MISROUTE		
D	MORTISED		MOITHERS		STORMIER		MOISTURE		
E	TIRESOME	O	MOORIEST	S	EROTISMS	V	VOMITERS		
F	SETIFORM		MOTORISE		MORTISES	W	MISWROTE		

einnort 174 - ternion

A	ANOINTER	D	INDENTOR	H	INTHRONE		NOINTERS	U	NEUTRINO
	INORNATE	G	NITROGEN	N	NONINERT		TERNIONS	V	INVENTOR
	REANOINT		RINGTONE	S	INTONERS	T	TONTINER		NOVERINT

einoprs 204 - proines

C	CONSPIRE		PIONEERS		PROLINES	R	PRISONER		REPOINTS
	INCORPSE	F	FORPINES	M	PROMINES	S	PORINESS		TROPINES
D	DISPONER	G	PERIGONS	O	POISONER		PRESSION	U	PRUINOSE
	POINDERS		REPOSING		SNOOPIER		ROPINESS	V	OVERSPIN
	PRISONED		SPONGIER		SPOONIER	T	POINTERS		PROVINES
E	ISOPRENE	I	RIPIENOS	P	POPERINS		PORNIEST		
	PEREIONS	L	PLERIONS		PROPINES		PROTEINS		

einorrt 100 - [nortier]

A	ANTERIOR		REORIENT	I	INTERIOR		SNORTIER		
C	TRICORNE	F	FRONTIER	L	RITORNEL	V	INVERTOR		
E	ORIENTER	H	THORNIER	S	INTRORSE	W	INTERROW		

einorst 3 - triones

A	ANOESTRI		CORNIEST	I	IRONIEST		PROTEINS	U	ROUTINES
	ARSONITE		NOTICERS	J	JOINTERS		REPOINTS		SNOUTIER
	NOTAIRES		RECTIONS	K	INSTROKE		TROPINES	V	INVESTOR
	NOTARIES	D	DRONIEST	L	RETINOLS	R	INTRORSE	X	NITROXES
	NOTARISE	E	ONERIEST	N	INTONERS		SNORTIER	Y	SEROTINY
	ROSINATE		SEROTINE		NOINTERS	S	OESTRINS		TYROSINE
	SENORITA	G	GENITORS		TERNIONS		TERSIONS	Z	TRIZONES
B	BORNITES		ROSETING	O	SNOOTIER	T	SNOTTIER		
	RIBSTONE	H	HORNIEST	P	POINTERS		TENORIST		
C	COINTERS		ORNITHES		PORNIEST		TRITONES		

einortt 93 - tritone

A	TENTORIA	D	INTORTED	K	KNOTTIER	S	SNOTTIER	U	RITENUTO
C	CONTRITE	E	TENORITE	L	TROTLINE		TENORIST		
	CORNETTI	G	OTTERING	N	TONTINER		TRITONES		

einortu 133 - routine

C	NEUROTIC		ROUTEING	N	NEUTRINO		SNOUTIER		
	UNEROTIC	J	JOINTURE	P	ERUPTION	T	RITENUTO		
G	OUTREIGN	L	OUTLINER	S	ROUTINES				

einrstu 71 - uniters

A	RUINATES	D	INTRUDES		UNITISER	N	RUNNIEST	Q	SQUINTER
	TAURINES		NURDIEST	L	INSULTER		STURNINE	T	RUNTIEST
	URANITES	E	ESURIENT		LUSTRINE	O	ROUTINES	V	UNRIVETS
	URINATES		NEURITES	M	MUNTRIES		SNOUTIER		VENTURIS
B	TRIBUNES		RETINUES		TERMINUS	P	REPUNITS	W	UNWRITES
	TURBINES		REUNITES		UNMITERS		UNPRIEST		
C	CURNIEST	I	NEURITIS		UNMITRES		UNRIPEST		

eioprst 236 - ropiest

C	PERSICOT	E	POETISER	N	POINTERS	S	PERIOSTS		SPOTTIER
D	DIOPTERS		POETRIES		PORNIEST		PROSIEST	U	ROUPIEST
	DIOPTRES	F	FIREPOTS		PROTEINS		PROSTIES		SPOUTIER
	DIPTEROS		PIEFORTS		REPOINTS		REPOSITS	V	OVERTIPS
	PERIDOTS		POSTFIRE		TROPINES		RIPOSTES		PIVOTERS
	PORTSIDE	H	TROPHIES	O	PORTOISE		SPORTIES		SORPTIVE
	PROTEIDS	K	PORKIEST		ROOPIEST		TRIPOSES		SPORTIVE
	RIPOSTED	L	POITRELS	R	PIERROTS	T	PORTIEST		
	TOPSIDER	M	IMPOSTER		SPORTIER		RISPETTO		

eiorrst 156 - roriest

A	ROARIEST	H	HERITORS		SNORTIER		TERROIRS	U	STOURIER
	ROTARIES	I	RIOTRIES	O	ROOTSIER	S	RESISTOR	V	OVERSTIR
B	ORBITERS	M	MORTISER	P	PIERROTS		ROISTERS		SERVITOR
F	FROSTIER		STORMIER		SPORTIER		SORRIEST		
	ROTIFERS	N	INTRORSE	R	ERRORIST	T	RORTIEST		

eiorstt 169 - stoiter

A	TOASTIER		THORITES		TRITONES		SPOTTIER	V	VIRETOTS
B	BORTIEST	L	TRIOLETS	O	ROOTIEST	R	RORTIEST	W	SWOTTIER
C	COTTIERS	M	OMITTERS		TORTOISE	S	STOITERS		
D	DORTIEST	N	SNOTTIER	P	PORTIEST	U	TOUSTIER		
H	THEORIST		TENORIST		RISPETTO		TUTORISE		

eiorstu 75 - tousier

A	OUTRAISE		OUTSIDER		SHOUTIER		SNOUTIER		TUTORISE
	SAUTOIRE		SUITORED	L	LOURIEST	P	ROUPIEST	V	VIRTUOSE
C	CITREOUS	F	FOUSTIER		OUTLIERS		SPOUTIER		VITREOUS
	OUTCRIES		OUTFIRES	M	MISROUTE	Q	QUOITERS		VOITURES
D	IODURETS	G	GOUSTIER		MOISTURE	R	STOURIER		
	OUTRIDES	H	OUTHIRES	N	ROUTINES	T	TOUSTIER		

enorstu 109 - tonsure

A	OUTEARNS		RECOUNTS	G	STURGEON		MOUNTERS	V	VENTROUS
B	BURSTONE		TROUNCES	H	SOUTHERN		REMOUNTS	Y	TOURNEYS
	RUBSTONE	D	ROUNDEST	I	ROUTINES	N	NEUTRONS		
C	CONSTRUE		TONSURED		SNOUTIER	O	OUTSNORE		
	CORNUTES		UNSORTED	L	TURNSOLE	S	TONSURES		
	COUNTERS	F	FORTUNES	M	MONTURES	T	STENTOUR		

AEIOU bonus words

These two short lists contain the very few seven and eight-letter words to contain one each of all five vowels. It's worth learning these words for occasions when you find yourself with a vowel-heavy rack. Definitions are provided for these words as an aide-memoire.

Seven-letter words

DOULEIA	inferior veneration accorded to saints and angels
EULOGIA	blessing
MIAOUED	made the crying sound of a cat
MOINEAU	small fortification
SEQUOIA	giant Californian tree

Eight-letter words

AEQUORIN	type of protein
AEROBIUM	organism that requires oxygen to live
AGOUTIES	small South American rodents
CAESIOUS	having a waxy bluish-grey coating
DIALOGUE	conversation between two people
DOUANIER	customs officer
DOULEIAS	inferior venerations accorded to saints and angels
EDACIOUS	devoted to eating
EQUATION	mathematical statement that two expressions are equal
EUDAIMON	good spirit
EULOGIAS	blessings
EUPHOBIA	fear of good news
EUPHONIA	agreeable sound
EUPHORIA	sense of elation
EUSOCIAL	using division of labour
EXONUMIA	numismatic objects that are not coins, such as medals and tokens
JALOUSIE	outside shutter with slats
MOINEAUS	small fortifications
ODALIQUE	female slave in a harem
OUTRAISE	to raise more money than
POULAINE	tapering toe of shoe
SAUTOIRE	heraldic design
SEQUOIAS	giant Californian trees
THIOUREA	white water-soluble crystalline substance with a bitter taste

Non-words

Six-letter words that do not combine with another letter

In addition to remembering some of the bonus-word sets listed in this chapter, it's a good idea to remember that sometimes you will draw a rack which cannot form a seven-letter bonus word. If you can recognize such combinations early on, it will save you valuable time, and allow you to look for other options. The first list on 'non-words' contains valid six-letter words, but which cannot be changed into any valid word with the addition of another letter. If you can form one of the six-letter words with the letters on your rack, you can tell straight away that there is no valid seven-letter word to be formed from them; the only possibility of making a bonus play is to find an eight-letter word utilizing a letter already on the board. The six-letter word list contains just over 200 words. Words with any of JKQXZ have been removed, words with more than three of the same letter have been removed (eg no words with three Es), words with more than two repeated letters have been removed (eg no words with 2 Es and 2 Ns). The 200-plus words are presented in alphabetic order. The first word on the six-letter list is ABUNAS - and just to reiterate, there is no seven-letter word which can be made containing these letters.

ABUNAS	FAUNAS	HORRID	PHWOAH	TYIYNS
ADAPTS	FAVEST	HOUSEY	PHWOAR	UNCUTE
ADIPIC	FAVOSE	HOVEAS	PIBALS	UNMIRY
ADOBOS	FAWNED	HUGEST	PIVOTS	UNSOFT
AERIFY	FAYEST	IBADAH	POLITY	UNTIDY
AFLAME	FAYNES	INBENT	POOVES	UNWONT
AFLOAT	FEALTY	INFIMA	PRUTAH	UPDOVE
AIMFUL	FENMAN	LARVAS	PUBCOS	UPGOES
ANBURY	FERVID	LAWMEN	PUNCTA	UPGONE
ARIOSI	FEVERS	LEGACY	PUNNED	VACANT
ASTOOP	FEYEST	LOOKED	PURITY	VAGROM
AUDIAL	FLANNY	LOOVES	RAGULY	VANMEN
AVIARY	FOEHNS	LOUCHE	RARELY	VANNED
AWEIGH	FOGIES	MAFTED	REMEDY	VATMAN
AWHATO	FOGOUS	MAPAUS	RIVERY	VATTED
AWHIRL	FOLEYS	MAUVER	ROOTSY	VAUNTY
BAVINS	FONNED	MAVENS	RUBATI	VAWTED
BEAUTY	FORGOT	MAWGER	SAFETY	VEDUTE
BEGETS	FOUNTS	MEETLY	SANIFY	VELDTS
BEWIGS	FOYNED	MERELY	SAYONS	VENERY
BIGOTS	FOYNES	MIAOUS	SNIFTY	VIBIER
BINMEN	FRANCO	MIAOWS	SNOTTY	VIENNA
BITTED	FRIARS	MIEVES	SNOUTY	VIFDAS
BOLLEN	FRIGID	MIHIED	STROWN	VINTRY
BOOAYS	FRONDS	MIRVED	SUETTY	VIOLAS
BOOHED	FUGIOS	MOATED	SUGARY	VISTAS
BRANDY	FUNNED	MONACT	SWATTY	VOGUED
BRAWNS	FUTONS	MOPILY	SWIPED	VORAGO
BUOYED	GAVOTS	MOULTS	SWIVED	WAGYUS
CABMEN	GAWPED	MOUPED	TAIHOA	WAIFED
CHAVVY	GLAURY	MUTINY	TAWDRY	WAIFTS
CLONAL	GLOVED	NINETY	THEMED	WAILED
CLOVEN	GOOFED	NOUNAL	THRAWN	WANNEL
DAWNED	GRAFTS	NOVITY	TIGLIC	WANNER
DEFOGS	GREEDY	NOWAYS	TINCTS	WAURED
DRAFTY	GRYDES	NULLED	TIYINS	WAVERY
DRIFTY	GUIDED	OBTECT	TODAYS	WEBIFY
DRILLS	GYLDEN	ODDITY	TOMBED	WEFTED
DROOLY	HALFEN	ODIOUS	TOWERY	WHINEY
DUVETS	HALVED	OIDIUM	TRIPLY	WHINGY
EGOITY	HENGES	ORIHOU	TRYPAN	WILIER
ETYMIC	HENNAS	OTALGY	TUFTED	WISPED
EULOGY	HERYED	OUBAAS	TURGID	WOADED
EURIPI	HOBOED	OVOIDS	TWEEDY	WRISTY
EVENLY	HOLONS	OWELTY	TWEENY	YBRENT
FAMULI	HOOVED	PANTRY	TWIRLS	YIRRED
FANALS	HOOVEN	PARODY	TWIRLY	YITIES
FAUNAE	HOPPUS	PENURY	TWIRPS	YOWIES

Seven-letter words that do not combine with another letter

The seven-letter word list is slightly different in concept. These are valid seven-letter words, and potentially playable on a board. However, if you find that the seven-letter word isn't playable, you may begin to consider whether an eight-letter can be played through a letter already on the board. None of these seven-letter words combines with an eighth letter, so you can save time wasted by searching for any. The criteria for inclusion in the seven-letter are the same as for the six-letter list. The seven-letter word list contains over 200 words. Words with any of JKQXZ have been removed, words with more than three of the same letter have been removed (eg no words with three Es), words with more than two repeated letters have been removed (eg no words with 2 Es and 2 Ns). The 200-plus words are presented in alphabetic order. The first word on the seven-letter list is ABEYANT - and just to be clear, although this is a valid seven-letter word, there is no valid eight-letter word which can be made containing these letters.

ABEYANT	CAEOMAS	GLADIUS	NOVENAS	TEUGHER
ABUSIVE	CANOLAS	GLOUTED	OBELION	THIEVED
ACAROID	COOMIER	GONADIC	OBOVATE	THINNED
ADIPOUS	DADOING	GOOFIER	OLDWIFE	THRIVED
ADOPTED	DAIKONS	GOVERNS	OLITORY	TIPTOED
AEFAULD	DAIMIOS	GOWDEST	ORGANDY	TOWNEES
AEOLIAN	DATURIC	GREYEST	ORIENCY	TRIFOLD
AEROBIA	DAWTING	GRITTED	OUTGAVE	TURDOID
AGATOID	DEFANGS	GROUPED	OUTGREW	TURTLED
AGELONG	DEVIOUS	HAVENED	OUTLAID	TUYERES
AGOUTAS	DILUTED	HOARILY	OUTWENT	TWINGED
ALIBIED	DITHIOL	HOGTIED	OVARIAN	UNNEATH
ALIYOTH	DITTANY	HONDLES	OVATELY	UNOFTEN
ALONELY	DOCIBLE	HONGIED	OVERBIG	UNROYAL
ALSOONE	DODGIER	HOODIAS	OVERGOT	UNSWEET
ALUMNAE	DOTARDS	HOSIERY	OVIPARA	UNWAGED
AMATIVE	DOVEISH	HURTLED	PAVONES	URINARY
AMOEBAS	DOWDIER	IMAGERY	PEAVIES	UVEITIS
AMOEBIC	EBRIETY	INNERLY	PENSIVE	VALGOID
ANNUITY	ENTROPY	INSWEPT	PERENTY	VANNERS
ANTIGAY	EPINAOI	INVADED	PLONGES	VAWNTIE
ARRIVED	EVINCES	INVIOUS	POOFIER	VESPINE
AUDITED	FADDIER	IRACUND	POOVIER	VOMICAE
AUREITY	FAGOTTI	IRONMAN	POYNTED	VUTTIER
AUTOMAN	FAITHED	IVORIED	RESTUDY	WAFERED
AVOIDED	FANEGAS	LAWNIER	REUNIFY	WAIRING
BEDIRTY	FANNERS	LEAFERY	RILIEVO	WAIRUAS
BESPATE	FEAGUED	LEAGUED	RORTING	WANIONS
BILGIER	FERVENT	LETHIED	RUINOUS	WANNEST
BINDERY	FESTIVE	LITHOID	SATIETY	WAREHOU
BIODATA	FOISTED	MEADOWS	SIALOID	WAURING
BIRDIES	FOLIOED	MIAOWED	SNAFUED	WAVIEST
BODGIER	FOODIES	MIDGIER	SNOTTED	WAYGONE
BOILERY	FOREDID	MILORDS	SOVIETS	WIFTIER
BONEYER	FORGAVE	MIOCENE	STALLED	WIREMEN
BOOFIER	FOSSATE	MISWENT	STIFLED	WURLIES
BOOGIED	FUNGOES	NAUPLII	SUDARIA	YAUTIAS
BOOSTED	GAUCIER	NAYSAID	SUDATES	YONNIES
BOUGIES	GAUDERY	NERVILY	SWINERY	
BOVINES	GAWCIER	NOISILY	TAGUANS	
BRACTED	GHASTED	NONWAGE	TAUIWIS	
BRAVOED	GHOSTED	NOTCHED	TEAPOYS	
BRIGUED	GIFTEES	NOVELTY	TENUITY	

Special eights

If you are landed with a 'non-word' rack, you needn't abandon all hope of playing a bonus word. Some racks that don't form seven-letter words will form eight-letter words with letters on the board. This is where 'special eights' come in handy. Special eights are eight-letter words that have no other eight-letter anagrams, and contain no seven-letter words. These are great words to know, as each of them is a solution to eight different problem racks. The top 250 special eights are listed below, in alphabetical order.

ABNEGATE	BIOMETER	FONTANEL	LITIGATE	RELOADED
ABOIDEAU	BOOGALOO	FOREHAND	LOBELESS	RELOADER
ABOITEAU	BOTTARGA	FOREREAD	LOOSENER	RETIARII
ABSENTEE	BOUDERIE	FRUITION	LOTHARIO	RISORIUS
ACUITIES	BOUNTREE	FUSIONAL	LOWERIER	ROTAVATE
ADDITION	BUCATINI	GAIETIES	LOWERING	ROTOVATE
AEDICULE	CANDYMEN	GEODETIC	METADATA	ROYALISE
AEGIRITE	CAPOEIRA	GLEETIER	METAFILE	SARTORII
AEQUORIN	CAREWARE	GOLDTONE	MEUNIERE	SEAMFREE
AEROBIUM	COENOBIA	GRAPHENE	MIRLITON	SEMIOVAL
AEROFOIL	COOEEING	GREENEYE	MONOTASK	SHATOOSH
AEROTONE	COROTATE	GROOLIER	MOONCAKE	SIALIDAN
AGIOTAGE	DANCICAL	GUILTIER	MOUTERED	SOLIDARY
AIRBOARD	DATAGRAM	HABANERO	NANOWIRE	STALAGMA
ALEHOUSE	DESEEDED	HAEREMAI	NAUSEATE	TABEFIED
ALOPECIA	DETAINEE	HANDKNIT	NEATENED	TALEGGIO
AMARETTO	DEVOTION	HAURIANT	NEONATAL	TALKTIME
ANAEROBE	DIGITATE	HEADWALL	NEOTENIC	TAPENADE
ANATEXES	DIGITULE	HEATWAVE	NODALITY	TAQUERIA
ANNEALED	DILATATE	HELOTAGE	NONGLARE	TELEWORK
ANNULOSE	DILATIVE	HORDEOLA	NOTATION	TENEBRAE
ANOREXIA	DOLOMITE	IANTHINE	NUTATION	THIONATE
ANOREXIC	DOTATION	IDEALITY	OCEANAUT	TOILETED
ANTIWEED	DROOLIER	IDEOGRAM	OEDIPEAN	TOLEWARE
AORTITIS	DUETTINO	IDONEOUS	OEILLADE	TRIBUNAL
APERITIF	DYSTONIA	ILLATION	OILFIRED	TRIZONAL
APOSITIA	EBENISTE	ILMENITE	OLIGEMIA	TROOPIAL
AQUATONE	ECLOGITE	INDAGATE	OLIGURIC	UINTAITE
ARTIFICE	ECOLODGE	INDUCIAE	ONIONIER	UNEASIER
ATENOLOL	EGOISTIC	INDUVIAE	OOGAMETE	UNHAIRER
ATHETOID	ELOINING	INFERIAE	OPIATING	UNPITIED
AUDITION	ENCAENIA	INFERNAL	OPTIONEE	UNSEELIE
AUDITIVE	ENVIABLE	INITIATE	OREODONT	UROBOROS
AURIFIED	EQUATIVE	INTOMBED	ORONASAL	VANITORY
AUTACOID	EUCARYON	INTUITED	OUTEATEN	VENEREAL
AUTODYNE	EUPHONIA	INVERTOR	OVERBANK	VENOSITY
AUTOGENY	EURONOTE	IODATION	OVERFINE	VESTIGIA
AUTOGIRO	EVECTION	IOPANOIC	OVERLOAD	VINIFERA
AUTOSAVE	EXERGIES	IRONLIKE	PARANOEA	VIOLATOR
AUTUNITE	EXERTION	IRONWARE	PATOOTIE	VOIDABLE
AVIANISE	EXPIATOR	IRRIGATE	PELERINE	WAGMOIRE
AVIARIES	EYELINER	JATROPHA	PETAFLOP	WAILSOME
AVIATION	EYESTONE	JEHADEEN	PITIKINS	WANDEROO
AVOIDANT	FACEBOOK	JETLINER	QINTARKA	WANTAWAY
BANNERET	FACETIAE	JIHADEEN	RACEABLE	WANTONED
BARONIAL	FAROLITO	KISSIEST	RADIATOR	WATERLOO
BEIGIEST	FEIJOADA	KUNEKUNE	RAILROAD	WEBIFIED
BEMOANER	FERNALLY	LATEWOOD	RAINWEAR	WEBIFIES
BETOILED	FETATION	LAVANDIN	REBOOTED	WEBISODE
BIENNALE	FLEABITE	LIGATIVE	RECOILER	WIPEABLE

Multiplets

Multiplets, a word borrowed from physics, are groups of letters with a given number of anagrams. So, a couplet is a set of two anagrams; a triplet is a set of three anagrams; a quadruplet is a set of four anagrams; and so on. The lists here contain seven-letter words. You'll see that the largest group in any of these lists contains 11 anagrams.

The benefit of studying these words is that if you get the requisite letters on your rack, you don't need to waste any time on looking for bonus words that aren't there. Also, multiplets can serve as memory-joggers for other anagrams in the same group. For example, remembering that there are 11 anagrams of RETAINS should enable you to recall the others. If you are interested in multiplet eight-letter anagrams, you could compile your own lists using the eight-letter anagrams section of this book.

Couplets

ABACTOR	ACARINE	ACHIRAL	ADERMIN	ADWOMEN
ACROBAT	CARINAE	RACHIAL	INARMED	WOMANED
ABATERS	ACATERS	ACIDEST	ADHARMA	AEDILES
ABREAST	CARATES	DACITES	HARAMDA	DEISEAL
ABATORS	ACATOUR	ACIFORM	ADHERED	AEGISES
RABATOS	AUTOCAR	FORMICA	REDHEAD	ASSIEGE
ABDUCES	ACCITES	ACNODAL	ADHERER	AERIEST
SCUBAED	ASCETIC	CALANDO	REHEARD	SERIATE
ABETTER	ACCOILS	ACNODES	ADIPSIA	AEROSOL
BERETTA	CALICOS	DEACONS	ASPIDIA	ROSEOLA
ABIDDEN	ACCOMPT	ACOLYTE	ADMIRAL	AFFAIRS
BANDIED	COMPACT	COTYLAE	AMILDAR	RAFFIAS
ABIOSES	ACCOYLD	ACONITE	ADMIRED	AFFIXER
ISOBASE	CACODYL	ANOETIC	MARDIED	REAFFIX
ABLATED	ACCRUAL	ACORNED	ADONIZE	AFFYING
DATABLE	CARACUL	DRACONE	ANODIZE	YAFFING
ABLATES	ACCRUED	ACQUIST	ADOPTER	AFREETS
ASTABLE	CARDECU	ACQUITS	READOPT	FEASTER
ABLINGS	ACCUSED	ACRIDER	ADORERS	AGAMETE
SABLING	SUCCADE	CARRIED	DROSERA	AGEMATE
ABLUENT	ACERBIC	ACROGEN	ADORNER	AGAROSE
TUNABLE	BRECCIA	CORNAGE	READORN	OARAGES
ABOUNDS	ACEROUS	ACTINGS	ADUSTED	AGEINGS
BAUSOND	CAROUSE	CASTING	SUDATED	SIGNAGE
ABRASAX	ACETALS	ACUTEST	ADVENED	AGEISTS
ABRAXAS	LACTASE	SCUTATE	DAVENED	SAGIEST
ABRIDGE	ACETOSE	ADAPTER	ADVERSE	AGELESS
BRIGADE	COATEES	READAPT	EVADERS	ALGESES
ABSENTS	ACETYLS	ADDICTS	ADVERTS	AGENDUM
BASNETS	SCYTALE	DIDACTS	STARVED	GUDEMAN
ABYEING	ACHARNE	ADDINGS	ADVISER	AGGADAH
EBAYING	ARCHEAN	SADDING	VARDIES	HAGGADA
ABYSMAL	ACHENES	ADDREST	ADVISES	AGGRADE
BALSAMY	ENCHASE	RADDEST	DISSAVE	GARAGED
ACANTHI	ACHIEST	ADDUCES	ADWARES	AGISTOR
TACHINA	AITCHES	SCAUDED	SEAWARD	ORGIAST

AGNAMED	ALCOVES	ALLONGE	AMBARIS	AMOOVES
MANAGED	COEVALS	GALLEON	MARABIS	VAMOOSE
AGNIZES	ALDOSES	ALLOVER	AMBOINA	AMORCES
SEAZING	LASSOED	OVERALL	BONAMIA	SCREAMO
AGNOMEN	ALEGARS	ALLUDED	AMBONES	AMPERES
NONGAME	LAAGERS	DUALLED	BEMOANS	EMPARES
AGNOSIC	ALEMBIC	ALLUDES	AMEARST	AMRITAS
ANGICOS	CEMBALI	ALUDELS	RETAMAS	TAMARIS
AGONIES	ALEPINE	ALLURED	AMELIAS	AMULETS
AGONISE	ELAPINE	UDALLER	MALAISE	MULETAS
AGONIST	ALETHIC	ALLURES	AMENDED	ANADEMS
GITANOS	ETHICAL	LAURELS	DEADMEN	MAENADS
AGRISES	ALEVINS	ALMANAC	AMENING	ANAPEST
GASSIER	VALINES	MANCALA	MEANING	PEASANT
AGUISED	ALEYING	ALMONDS	AMENITY	ANCILIA
GAUDIES	YEALING	DOLMANS	ANYTIME	LACINIA
AIBLINS	ALFAKIS	ALMONER	AMENTIA	ANCONES
BILIANS	KAFILAS	NEMORAL	ANIMATE	SONANCE
AIDLESS	ALIENED	ALMUCES	AMERCER	ANCRESS
DEASILS	DELAINE	MACULES	CREAMER	CASERNS
AILANTO	ALINING	ALMUDES	AMIDASE	ANDVILE
ALATION	NAILING	MEDUSAL	SEAMAID	ANVILED
AILMENT	ALISMAS	ALNICOS	AMIDINE	ANERGIC
ALIMENT	SALAMIS	OILCANS	DIAMINE	GRECIAN
AIRBASE	ALISONS	ALOGIAS	AMIDINS	ANESTRA
ARABISE	SIALONS	LAOGAIS	DIAMINS	SANTERA
AIRIEST	ALIUNDE	ALPEENS	AMIDONE	ANETHOL
IRISATE	UNIDEAL	SPELEAN	DOMAINE	ETHANOL
AIRPORT	ALKANET	ALSIKES	AMISSES	ANGINAS
PARITOR	KANTELA	ASSLIKE	MESSIAS	INANGAS
AIRTING	ALLAYER	ALYSSUM	AMITIES	ANGLIFY
RAITING	AREALLY	ASYLUMS	ATIMIES	FLAYING
ALANYLS	ALLEDGE	AMABILE	AMMETER	ANGUINE
NASALLY	ALLEGED	AMIABLE	METAMER	GUANINE
ALBUGOS	ALLICES	AMANDLA	AMMINES	ANGUISH
SUBGOAL	CAILLES	MANDALA	MISNAME	HAUSING
ALCADES	ALLISES	AMARANT	AMNESIA	ANICUTS
SCALADE	SALLIES	MARANTA	ANEMIAS	NAUTICS
ALCAICS	ALLODIA	AMATION	AMNESIC	ANKLING
CICALAS	ALODIAL	ANIMATO	CINEMAS	LANKING

ANNELID	APICALS	ARCADES	ARNOTTO	ASQUINT
LINDANE	SPACIAL	ASCARED	RATTOON	QUINTAS
ANNOYED	APIEZON	ARCHERS	AROINTS	ASSARTS
ANODYNE	EPIZOAN	CRASHER	RATIONS	SASTRAS
ANSWERS	APLENTY	ARCHILS	ARRIDES	ASSENTS
RAWNESS	PENALTY	CARLISH	RAIDERS	SNASTES
ANTHEMS	APNOEAS	ARCHLET	ARRIERO	ASSERTS
HETMANS	PAESANO	TRACHLE	ROARIER	TRASSES
ANTIBUG	APNOEIC	ARCMINS	ARRIVES	ASSIGNS
TABUING	PAEONIC	NARCISM	VARIERS	SASSING
ANTICLY	APOLLOS	ARCTOID	ARROBAS	ASSUAGE
CANTILY	PALOLOS	CAROTID	RASBORA	SAUSAGE
ANTIFLU	APOMICT	AREFIED	ARSHINE	ASSUMED
FLUTINA	POTAMIC	FEDARIE	HERNIAS	MEDUSAS
ANTINGS	APOSTIL	ARETTED	ARSHINS	ASSURED
STANING	TOPSAIL	TREATED	SHAIRNS	RUDASES
ANTIQUE	APPENDS	ARGALIS	ARSINES	ASSURER
QUINATE	SNAPPED	GARIALS	SARNIES	RASURES
ANTISEX	APPLIES	ARGHANS	ARTSMAN	ASSURES
SEXTAIN	LAPPIES	HANGARS	MANTRAS	SARUSES
ANTRUMS	APPOSED	ARGLING	ARUGULA	ASTARTS
UNSMART	PEAPODS	GLARING	AUGURAL	STRATAS
ANUROUS	APPOSER	ARGONON	ASCIDIA	ASTHENY
URANOUS	POPERAS	ORGANON	DIASCIA	SHANTEY
ANYMORE	APPRESS	ARGUERS	ASCITES	ASTHMAS
ROMNEYA	SAPPERS	SUGARER	ECTASIS	MATSAHS
APEDOMS	APPRISE	ARGYLES	ASCITIC	ASTRALS
POMADES	SAPPIER	GRAYLES	SCIATIC	TARSALS
APELIKE	APPRIZE	ARIETTE	ASEPSIS	ASTRAND
PEALIKE	ZAPPIER	ITERATE	ASPISES	TARANDS
APERCUS	APTOTES	ARISTAS	ASININE	ASTUTER
SCAUPER	TEAPOTS	TARSIAS	INSANIE	STATURE
APERIES	ARAYSED	ARKITES	ASKINGS	ASTYLAR
EPEIRAS	DARESAY	KARITES	GASKINS	SATYRAL
APHESES	ARAYSES	ARMINGS	ASPERGE	ATABEGS
SPAHEES	ASSAYER	MARGINS	PRESAGE	TEABAGS
APHETIC	ARBITER	ARMLOCK	ASPORTS	ATELIER
HEPATIC	RAREBIT	LOCKRAM	PASTORS	REALTIE
APHIDES	ARBORES	ARMREST	ASPREAD	ATHAMES
DIPHASE	BRASERO	SMARTER	PARADES	HAMATES

ATHEIST	AVENGER	BAGARRE	BANTAMS	BASALLY
STAITHE	ENGRAVE	BARRAGE	BATSMAN	SALABLY
ATLATLS	AVENGES	BAGASSE	BANTERS	BASHERS
TALLATS	GENEVAS	SEABAGS	BARNETS	BRASHES
ATOCIAS	AVENIRS	BAGFULS	BAPTISM	BASHLIK
COAITAS	RAVINES	BAGSFUL	BITMAPS	KIBLAHS
ATOPIES	AVERTED	BAGGERS	BARAZAS	BASSEST
OPIATES	TAVERED	BEGGARS	BAZAARS	BASSETS
ATRIUMS	AVGASES	BAGNIOS	BARBIES	BASTARD
MATSURI	SAVAGES	GABIONS	RABBIES	TABARDS
ATTONED	AVIATIC	BAGUETS	BARCODE	BASTLES
NOTATED	VIATICA	TUBAGES	BROCADE	STABLES
ATTONES	AVIETTE	BAKINGS	BARDING	BATBOYS
NOTATES	EVITATE	BASKING	BRIGAND	BOBSTAY
ATTRIST	AVISING	BALDING	BAREFIT	BATCHER
ATTRITS	VISAING	BLADING	FIBRATE	BRACHET
AUCTION	AVOCETS	BALEENS	BARGING	BATFISH
CAUTION	OCTAVES	ENABLES	GARBING	BIFTAHS
AUGMENT	AVODIRE	BALKILY	BARISTA	BATTERS
MUTAGEN	AVOIDER	LIKABLY	BARTSIA	TABRETS
AULDEST	AWELESS	BALLAST	BARKEEP	BATTLED
SALUTED	WEASELS	BALLATS	PREBAKE	BLATTED
AULNAGE	AWESOME	BALLUTE	BARKIER	BAUBLES
LEGUAAN	WAESOME	BULLATE	BRAKIER	BUBALES
AUNTIES	AWMRIES	BALSAMS	BARKING	BAUERAS
SINUATE	SEMIRAW	SAMBALS	BRAKING	SUBAREA
AUTOCUE	BABBLED	BAMPOTS	BARLESS	BAWBLES
COUTEAU	BLABBED	SPAMBOT	BRALESS	WABBLES
AUTOING	BABIEST	BANDARS	BAROLOS	BAWLERS
OUTGAIN	TABBIES	SANDBAR	ROBALOS	WARBLES
AUTOPSY	BABOOSH	BANDIER	BARONET	BAWLEYS
PAYOUTS	HABOOBS	BRAINED	REBOANT	BYELAWS
AVAILED	BACCIES	BANDIES	BARONGS	BAWLING
VEDALIA	SEBACIC	BASINED	BROGANS	BLAWING
AVALING	BACKERS	BANDORE	BARRETS	BEADIER
VAGINAL	REBACKS	BROADEN	BARTERS	BEARDIE
AVARICE	BACKOUT	BANGERS	BARRIES	BEAKERS
CAVIARE	OUTBACK	GRABENS	BRASIER	BERAKES
AVENGED	BAETYLS	BANKERS	BARYTES	BEARERS
VENDAGE	BEASTLY	BARKENS	BETRAYS	BREARES

BEATIER	BEEZERS	BERGAMA	BILOBED	BLETHER
EBRIATE	BREEZES	MEGABAR	LOBBIED	HERBLET
BECALMS	BEFANAS	BERRIED	BILTONG	BLINDER
SCAMBLE	FANBASE	BRIERED	BOLTING	BRINDLE
BECRUST	BEFLUMS	BERTHES	BIMBOES	BLOATED
BECURST	FUMBLES	SHERBET	MOBBIES	LOBATED
BEDERAL	BEGIRDS	BESCOUR	BINGOES	BLOBBED
BLEARED	BRIDGES	OBSCURE	BIOGENS	BOBBLED
BEDIGHT	BEGUINS	BESINGS	BIOGENY	BLOGGED
BIGHTED	BUNGIES	BIGNESS	OBEYING	BOGGLED
BEDLAMS	BELACED	BESLIME	BIOPICS	BLOGGER
BELDAMS	DEBACLE	BESMILE	BIOPSIC	BOGGLER
BEDLESS	BELATED	BESPAKE	BIPEDAL	BLONDES
BLESSED	BLEATED	BESPEAK	PIEBALD	BOLDENS
BEDRALS	BELAYED	BESTILL	BIPOLAR	BLOODED
BLADERS	DYEABLE	BILLETS	PARBOIL	BOODLED
BEDRAPE	BELGARD	BESTORM	BIRDIES	BLOOMER
PREBADE	GARBLED	MOBSTER	BRIDIES	REBLOOM
BEDROCK	BELTERS	BESTREW	BIRDING	BLOTTED
BROCKED	TREBLES	WEBSTER	BRIDING	BOTTLED
BEDSORE	BELTMAN	BESTRID	BIRSIER	BLOTTER
SOBERED	LAMBENT	BISTRED	RIBIERS	BOTTLER
BEDTIME	BELUGAS	BESTUCK	BIRSLED	BLOUSED
BETIMED	BLAGUES	BUCKETS	BRIDLES	DOUBLES
BEDUINS	BEMETES	BETIDED	BIRSLES	BLOUSES
BUNDIES	BETEEMS	DEBITED	RIBLESS	BOLUSES
BEDUSTS	BEMIRED	BHAKTAS	BISTORT	BLOWERS
BESTUDS	BERIMED	SABKHAT	BITTORS	BOWLERS
BEECHES	BEMUSED	BHINDIS	BITTURS	BLOWFLY
BESEECH	EMBUSED	BINDHIS	TURBITS	FLYBLOW
BEEFIER	BEMUSES	BICOLOR	BIZARRE	BLOWING
FREEBIE	EMBUSES	BROCOLI	BRAZIER	BOWLING
BEEGAHS	BENDIER	BICORNS	BLATHER	BLOWSES
BHAGEES	INBREED	BICRONS	HALBERT	BOWLESS
BEENTOS	BENISON	BIFTERS	BLEARER	BLOWUPS
BONESET	BONNIES	FIBSTER	ERRABLE	UPBLOWS
BEETING	BENTHIC	BILBOES	BLEATER	BLUBBED
BEIGNET	BITCHEN	LOBBIES	RETABLE	BUBBLED
BEEYARD	BERDASH	BILLERS	BLENDER	BLUBBER
BERAYED	BRASHED	REBILLS	REBLEND	BUBBLER

BLUDGER	BOOGERS	BOUGETS	BRAIZES	BROMINS
BURGLED	GOOBERS	OUTBEGS	ZERIBAS	MISBORN
BLUEING	BOOGIES	BOULDER	BRANDER	BROOSES
BULGINE	GOOBIES	DOUBLER	REBRAND	SORBOSE
BLUEISH	BOOHING	BOULTED	BRANLES	BROUZES
HELIBUS	HOBOING	DOUBLET	BRANSLE	SUBZERO
BLUIEST	BOOKERS	BOULTER	BRASHER	BRUCKLE
SUBTILE	REBOOKS	TROUBLE	HERBARS	BUCKLER
BLUNDER	BOOKIER	BOUNCED	BRASSED	BRUISED
BUNDLER	BROOKIE	BUNCOED	SERDABS	BURDIES
BLUNGED	BOOKIES	BOUNDEN	BRAWEST	BRUMOUS
BUNGLED	BOOKSIE	UNBONED	WABSTER	UMBROUS
BLUNGER	BOONGAS	BOUSIER	BRAWLED	BRUSHES
BUNGLER	GABOONS	OUREBIS	WARBLED	BUSHERS
BLUNGES	BOOSTER	BOUTONS	BRAWLER	BRUSKER
BUNGLES	REBOOTS	UNBOOTS	WARBLER	BURKERS
BLUSHER	BOOZERS	BOWELED	BRAWLIE	BRUTELY
BURHELS	REBOZOS	ELBOWED	WIRABLE	BUTLERY
BLUSHES	BORACIC	BOWINGS	BREAKUP	BRUTERS
BUSHELS	BRACCIO	BOWSING	UPBREAK	BURSTER
BOATELS	BORDURE	BOWLDER	BREDIES	BUCKSAW
OBLATES	BOURDER	LOWBRED	DERBIES	SAWBUCK
BOCAGES	BOREENS	BOWLEGS	BRETONS	BUDDERS
BOSCAGE	ENROBES	WEBLOGS	SORBENT	REDBUDS
BODICES	BORIDES	BOWSERS	BREWING	BUFFERS
CEBOIDS	DISROBE	BROWSES	WEBRING	REBUFFS
BOGLING	BORKING	BOXIEST	BRIBERS	BUFFEST
GLOBING	BROKING	BOXTIES	RIBBERS	BUFFETS
BOMBERS	BORSCHT	BOXWOOD	BRIBING	BUGLING
MOBBERS	BORTSCH	WOODBOX	RIBBING	BULGING
BOMBING	BORTIER	BOYARDS	BRICOLE	BUILDUP
MOBBING	ORBITER	BYROADS	CORBEIL	UPBUILD
BONDAGE	BOSHTER	BRADOON	BRIGUES	BUISTED
DOGBANE	BOTHERS	ONBOARD	RUGBIES	SUBEDIT
BONIEST	BOSSEST	BRAHMAS	BRINING	BULGHUR
EBONIST	BOSSETS	SAMBHAR	INBRING	BURGHUL
BONXIES	BOSSIER	BRAILLE	BRISTLY	BULKERS
INBOXES	RIBOSES	LIBERAL	TRILBYS	BURLESK
BOODIES	BOUCHES	BRAIRDS	BRISTOL	BULLOUS
DOOBIES	SUBECHO	BRIARDS	STROBIL	LOBULUS

BUMMLED	BUTENES	CALIPER	CANFULS	CAPOUCH
MUMBLED	SUBTEEN	REPLICA	CANSFUL	PACHUCO
BUNDIST	BUYOUTS	CALKING	CANGLES	CAPTION
DUSTBIN	OUTBUYS	LACKING	GLANCES	PACTION
BUNTALS	BYREMAN	CALLOPS	CANGUES	CARACKS
TULBANS	MYRBANE	SCALLOP	UNCAGES	CRACKAS
BURDASH	CACHETS	CALLOSE	CANKERS	CARBEEN
RHABDUS	CATCHES	LOCALES	SNACKER	CARBENE
BURIALS	CACHING	CALLUNA	CANKLES	CARBONS
RAILBUS	CHACING	LACUNAL	SLACKEN	CORBANS
BURKHAS	CACKLED	CALMANT	CANNERS	CARDERS
KURBASH	CLACKED	CLAMANT	SCANNER	SCARRED
BURLERS	CACTOID	CALMEST	CANNIER	CARDIOS
BURRELS	OCTADIC	CAMLETS	NARCEIN	SARCOID
BURNOUT	CADRANS	CALQUES	CANTRED	CAREERS
OUTBURN	CANARDS	CLAQUES	TRANCED	CREASER
BURPING	CAESTUS	CALTROP	CANULAE	CARGOED
UPBRING	CUESTAS	PROCTAL	LACUNAE	CORDAGE
BURSERA	CAIMANS	CALVARY	CANULAR	CARHOPS
SABREUR	MANIACS	CAVALRY	LACUNAR	COPRAHS
BURYING	CAITIVE	CALYCES	CANULAS	CARIOUS
RUBYING	VICIATE	CYCLASE	LACUNAS	CURIOSA
BUSBIES	CAKIEST	CALYCLE	CANYONS	CARNEYS
SUBBIES	TACKIES	CECALLY	SONANCY	SCENARY
BUSIEST	CALALUS	CAMARON	CAPABLE	CAROCHE
SUBSITE	CLAUSAL	NARCOMA	PACABLE	COACHER
BUSINGS	CALAMUS	CAMBREL	CAPERER	CAROLED
BUSSING	MACULAS	CLAMBER	PRERACE	ORACLED
BUSTICS	CALDERA	CAMOTES	CAPITAL	CAROMED
CUBISTS	CRAALED	COMATES	PLACITA	COMRADE
BUSTIER	CALENDS	CAMPERS	CAPITAN	CAROTIN
RUBIEST	CANDLES	SCAMPER	CAPTAIN	CORTINA
BUSTING	CALIBER	CAMPLED	CAPIZES	CARPING
TUBINGS	CALIBRE	CLAMPED	CAPSIZE	CRAPING
BUSTLES	CALICES	CANDIES	CAPLETS	CARRIES
SUBLETS	CELIACS	INCASED	PLACETS	SCARIER
BUSYING	CALICHE	CANDIRU	CAPLINS	CARROTS
BUYINGS	CHALICE	IRACUND	INCLASP	TROCARS
BUTANES	CALIMAS	CANDOUR	CAPORAL	CARSEYS
SUNBEAT	CAMAILS	CAUDRON	CRAPOLA	SCRAYES

CARTOON	CATSUPS	CEROTIC	CHANGES	CHEERED
CORANTO	UPCASTS	ORECTIC	GANCHES	REECHED
CARVERS	CATTILY	CERRADO	CHANSON	CHEERIO
CRAVERS	TACITLY	CORRADE	NONCASH	ECHOIER
CARVING	CAUDLES	CERTIFY	CHANTER	CHEERLY
CRAVING	CEDULAS	RECTIFY	TRANCHE	LECHERY
CASABAS	CAULOME	CERVIDS	CHAPKAS	CHELOID
CASSABA	LEUCOMA	SCRIVED	PACHAKS	HELCOID
CASAVAS	CAUSEYS	CESIUMS	CHARGES	CHELONE
CASSAVA	CAYUSES	MISCUES	CREAGHS	ECHELON
CASCADE	CAUSING	CESSERS	CHARIOT	CHEMISE
SACCADE	SAUCING	CRESSES	HARICOT	SCHEMIE
CASKIER	CAUSTIC	CESSPIT	CHARMED	CHEMIST
EIRACKS	CICUTAS	SEPTICS	MARCHED	MITCHES
CASQUES	CAUTELS	CESTODE	CHARMER	CHENARS
SACQUES	SULCATE	ESCOTED	MARCHER	RANCHES
CASSOCK	CAVEATS	CETANES	CHARNEL	CHENETS
COSSACK	VACATES	TENACES	LARCHEN	TENCHES
CASTLES	CAVERNS	CHACHKA	CHARPAI	CHERISH
SCLATES	CRAVENS	KACHCHA	HAIRCAP	SHRIECH
CASTOFF	CAWKERS	CHACOES	CHARTED	CHESILS
OFFCAST	WACKERS	COACHES	RATCHED	CHISELS
CASTORS	CEASING	CHAINED	CHARTER	CHETAHS
COSTARS	INCAGES	ECHIDNA	RECHART	HATCHES
CASUALS	CEILING	CHAINES	CHASTEN	CHEVETS
CAUSALS	CIELING	INCHASE	NATCHES	VETCHES
CATALOS	CELESTA	CHAKRAS	CHATTEL	CHEVIES
COASTAL	SELECTA	CHARKAS	LATCHET	SEVICHE
CATCHER	CELOSIA	CHALKED	CHATTER	CHEWERS
RECATCH	COALISE	HACKLED	RATCHET	RECHEWS
CATCHUP	CENSING	CHALLIE	CHAWING	CHIASMS
UPCATCH	SCENING	HELICAL	CHINWAG	SCHISMA
CATFLAP	CENTILE	CHAMISA	CHEAPED	CHICEST
FLATCAP	LICENTE	CHIASMA	PEACHED	HECTICS
CATHOLE	CENTRED	CHAMISO	CHEAPER	CHICLES
CHOLATE	CREDENT	CHAMOIS	PEACHER	CLICHES
CATLING	CERAMIC	CHANCER	CHECKER	CHICONS
TALCING	RACEMIC	CHANCRE	RECHECK	COCHINS
CATLINS	CERIUMS	CHANGED	CHEEPED	CHIDERS
TINCALS	MURICES	GANCHED	DEPECHE	HERDICS

CHIELDS	CHORIST	CITATOR	CLINGER	CNEMIAL
CHILDES	OSTRICH	RICOTTA	CRINGLE	MELANIC
CHIGRES	CHOROID	CITHERN	CLINKED	COAGENT
SCREIGH	OCHROID	CITHREN	NICKLED	COGNATE
CHIKORS	CHORTEN	CITIZEN	CLINKER	COARSER
CHOKRIS	NOTCHER	ZINCITE	CRINKLE	CORREAS
CHIMERS	CHOUSES	CITOLAS	CLIPPER	COATING
MICHERS	HOCUSES	STOICAL	CRIPPLE	COTINGA
CHIMING	CHOWDER	CLADDER	CLOBBER	COCAINE
MICHING	COWHERD	CRADLED	COBBLER	OCEANIC
CHIPSET	CHOWSED	CLANGER	CLOCKED	COCKERS
PITCHES	COWSHED	GLANCER	COCKLED	RECOCKS
CHIVIES	CHROMAS	CLAQUER	CLOCKER	COCKILY
VICHIES	MORCHAS	LACQUER	COCKLER	COLICKY
CHOICER	CHUNDER	CLARINO	CLODDED	CODDLES
CHOREIC	CHURNED	CLARION	CODDLED	SCOLDED
CHOKEYS	CHYLOUS	CLASHES	CLOGGED	CODEINA
HOCKEYS	SLOUCHY	SEALCHS	COGGLED	OCEANID
CHOKING	CHYMIST	CLASPED	CLOISON	CODLING
HOCKING	TYCHISM	SCALPED	SCOLION	LINGCOD
CHOLENT	CHYPRES	CLASSED	CLOKING	CODRIVE
NOTCHEL	CYPHERS	DECLASS	LOCKING	DIVORCE
CHOLERS	CIDARIS	CLASSES	CLONERS	CODROVE
ORCHELS	SCIARID	SACLESS	CORNELS	VOCODER
CHOLINE	CILICES	CLAVIES	CLOSEST	COENURI
HELICON	ICICLES	VESICAL	CLOSETS	NOURICE
CHOOSER	CINGULA	CLEANER	CLOSURE	COFFERS
SOROCHE	GLUCINA	RECLEAN	COLURES	SCOFFER
CHOPINE	CINQUES	CLEANUP	CLOTTER	COGENER
PHOCINE	QUINCES	UNPLACE	CROTTLE	CONGREE
CHOPINS	CIPOLIN	CLEFTED	CLOVERS	COGNISE
PHONICS	PICOLIN	DEFLECT	VELCROS	COIGNES
CHORDAE	CIRCARS	CLEUCHS	CLUEING	COHEIRS
ROACHED	RICRACS	CULCHES	LUCIGEN	HEROICS
CHORDAL	CIRCLES	CLEUGHS	CLUMBER	COIFFES
DORLACH	CLERICS	GULCHES	CRUMBLE	OFFICES
CHORING	CIRRATE	CLIMATE	CLUMPER	COILERS
OCHRING	ERRATIC	METICAL	CRUMPLE	RECOILS
CHORISM	CISTERN	CLIMBER	CLUNKER	COLEADS
CHRISOM	CRETINS	RECLIMB	CRUNKLE	SOLACED

COLITIS	CONGAED	COOPERS	COSIERS	CRANIUM
SOLICIT	DECAGON	SCOOPER	CRIOSES	CUMARIN
COLLOPS	CONGIUS	COOSERS	COSMIST	CRAPPIE
SCOLLOP	SOUCING	ROSCOES	SITCOMS	EPICARP
COLLUDE	CONICAL	COOTERS	COSTEAN	CRASHED
LOCULED	LACONIC	SCOOTER	OCTANES	ECHARDS
COLOBUS	CONIINE	COPITAS	COSTING	CREASES
SUBCOOL	INCONIE	PSOATIC	GNOSTIC	SEARCES
COLONES	CONINES	COPOUTS	COTTISE	CRECHES
CONSOLE	CONNIES	OCTOPUS	SCOTTIE	SCREECH
COLORER	CONKERS	COPTERS	COUGHED	CREDITS
RECOLOR	RECKONS	PROSECT	GOUCHED	DIRECTS
COMARBS	CONKING	COPULAR	COUNSEL	CREEPED
CRAMBOS	NOCKING	CUPOLAR	UNCLOSE	PRECEDE
COMBERS	CONSENT	CORCASS	COUPLET	CREMATE
RECOMBS	NOCENTS	CORSACS	OCTUPLE	MEERCAT
COMBIER	CONSIST	CORDATE	COUPONS	CREMONA
MICROBE	TOCSINS	REDCOAT	SOUPCON	ROMANCE
COMICES	CONSORT	CORDERS	COURIES	CREMSIN
MOCCIES	CROTONS	RECORDS	SCOURIE	MINCERS
COMPARE	CONSULT	CORELLA	COURTED	CREOLES
COMPEAR	UNCOLTS	OCELLAR	EDUCTOR	RECLOSE
COMPEER	CONSUME	CORKIER	COUTILS	CREPING
COMPERE	MUSCONE	ROCKIER	OCULIST	PERCING
COMPILE	CONURES	CORKING	COUZINS	CRETISM
POLEMIC	ROUNCES	ROCKING	ZINCOUS	METRICS
COMPOST	CONVEYS	CORNERS	COVERER	CRIMINA
COMPOTS	COVYNES	SCORNER	RECOVER	MINICAR
COMUSES	COOKERS	CORNILY	COWRIES	CRIMSON
MUSCOSE	RECOOKS	LYRICON	SCOWRIE	MICRONS
CONARIA	COOKOUT	CORNUAL	COYOTES	CRISPED
OCARINA	OUTCOOK	COURLAN	OOCYTES	DISCERP
CONCENT	COOLANT	CORONAS	CRAFTED	CRISPER
CONNECT	OCTANOL	RACOONS	FRACTED	PRICERS
CONDOES	COOLERS	CORONER	CRAFTER	CROQUET
SECONDO	CREOSOL	CROONER	REFRACT	ROCQUET
CONDORS	COOLEST	CORPSES	CRAMPIT	CROSSED
CORDONS	OCELOTS	PROCESS	PTARMIC	SCORSED
CONDUIT	COOLING	CORSIVE	CRANING	CROSSES
NOCTUID	LOCOING	VOICERS	RANCING	SCORSES

CROUPED	CUPELED	DABBLES	DARLING	DECANES
PRODUCE	DECUPLE	SLABBED	LARDING	ENCASED
CROUPER	CUPFULS	DABSTER	DARSHAN	DECERNS
PROCURE	CUPSFUL	TABERDS	DHARNAS	SCERNED
CROWERS	CUPPERS	DADDLES	DARTING	DECIDER
SCOWRER	SCUPPER	SADDLED	TRADING	DECRIED
CROWNED	CUPRITE	DAFTIES	DARTLES	DECILES
DECROWN	PICTURE	FADIEST	SLARTED	DELICES
CROWNER	CURACAO	DAGGLES	DASHERS	DECKELS
RECROWN	CURACOA	SLAGGED	SHADERS	DECKLES
CRUDEST	CURAGHS	DAIDLES	DASHING	DECKOED
CRUSTED	SCRAUGH	LADDIES	SHADING	DECOKED
CRUELTY	CURATED	DAIKERS	DATARIA	DECODER
CUTLERY	TRADUCE	DARKIES	RADIATA	RECODED
CRUISED	CURDIER	DALLIED	DAUNTED	DECREED
DISCURE	CURRIED	DIALLED	UNDATED	RECEDED
CRUIVES	CURDLES	DALTONS	DAWDING	DECREET
CURSIVE	SCUDLER	SANDLOT	WADDING	ERECTED
CRUNKED	CURNIER	DAMAGER	DAWDLED	DECREWS
DRUCKEN	REINCUR	MEGARAD	WADDLED	SCREWED
CRUSADE	CURPELS	DAMMERS	DAWTIES	DECRIES
SCAURED	SCRUPLE	SMARMED	WAISTED	DEICERS
CRUSTAL	CURTAIL	DAMPEST	DAYWORK	DECTETS
CURTALS	TRUCIAL	STAMPED	WORKDAY	DETECTS
CRYINGS	CURTAIN	DAMPISH	DEAIRED	DEDIMUS
SCRYING	TURACIN	PHASMID	READIED	MUDDIES
CUDDLES	CURTESY	DANDIER	DEANERS	DEDUCES
SCUDDLE	CURTSEY	DRAINED	ENDEARS	SEDUCED
CUFFLES	CUSPATE	DANDIES	DEARIES	DEEDEST
SCUFFLE	TEACUPS	SDAINED	READIES	STEEDED
CUISHES	CUSSING	DANGLED	DEASOIL	DEEDILY
CUSHIES	SCUSING	GLADDEN	ISOLEAD	YIELDED
CULTIER	CUTOFFS	DANGLER	DEAVING	DEEDING
UTRICLE	OFFCUTS	GNARLED	EVADING	DEIGNED
CUMBERS	CYCLISE	DANKEST	DEBASES	DEEPEST
SCUMBER	CYLICES	STANKED	SEABEDS	STEEPED
CUMMERS	CYSTEIN	DANTONS	DEBTORS	DEFACER
SCUMMER	CYSTINE	DONNATS	STROBED	REFACED
CUNNERS	CYTASES	DARINGS	DECAMPS	DEFAULT
SCUNNER	ECSTASY	GRADINS	SCAMPED	FAULTED

DEFIANT	DELIMIT	DEPICTS	DESNOOD	DHURRIE
FAINTED	LIMITED	DISCEPT	SNOODED	HURRIED
DEFIERS	DELIRIA	DEPLANE	DESPISE	DIALYSE
SERIFED	IRIDEAL	PANELED	PEDESIS	EYLIADS
DEFILED	DELVING	DEPLOYS	DESUGAR	DIASTEM
FIELDED	DEVLING	PODLEYS	SUGARED	MISDATE
DEFOCUS	DEMANDS	DEPONES	DESYNES	DIATOMS
FOCUSED	MADDENS	SPONDEE	ENDYSES	MASTOID
DEFORMS	DEMERGE	DEPOSAL	DETAILS	DIAXONS
SERFDOM	EMERGED	PEDALOS	DILATES	DIOXANS
DEFOULS	DEMESNE	DEPOSED	DETENTE	DIAZINS
FLOUSED	SEEDMEN	SEEDPOD	NEDETTE	DIZAINS
DEFROCK	DEMISED	DEPOSER	DETENTS	DIBBLER
FROCKED	MISDEED	REPOSED	STENTED	DRIBBLE
DEFROST	DEMOING	DEPOSES	DETENUS	DICHTED
FROSTED	MENDIGO	SPEEDOS	DETUNES	DITCHED
DEFUSER	DEMOUNT	DERAYED	DETERGE	DICINGS
REFUSED	MOUNTED	YEARDED	GREETED	DISCING
DEHORTS	DEMURES	DERNIER	DETICKS	DICKENS
SHORTED	RESUMED	NERDIER	STICKED	SNICKED
DEIDEST	DENDRON	DERVISH	DETORTS	DICKERS
TEDDIES	DONNERD	SHRIVED	DOTTERS	SCRIKED
DEIFIED	DENGUES	DESANDS	DETRACT	DICTIER
EDIFIED	UNEDGES	SADDENS	TRACTED	ICTERID
DEIFIES	DENIALS	DESCEND	DEUCING	DIDDLER
EDIFIES	SNAILED	SCENDED	EDUCING	RIDDLED
DEINDEX	DENNETS	DESCENT	DEUTONS	DIEDRAL
INDEXED	STENNED	SCENTED	SNOUTED	DRAILED
DEISTIC	DENSITY	DESERVE	DEVEINS	DIEHARD
DICIEST	DESTINY	SEVERED	ENDIVES	DIHEDRA
DEKARES	DENTALS	DESIGNS	DEVOLVE	DIEOFFS
SKEARED	SLANTED	SDEIGNS	EVOLVED	OFFSIDE
DELATES	DENTELS	DESIRES	DEWITTS	DIGESTS
STEALED	NESTLED	RESIDES	TWISTED	DISGEST
DELATOR	DENTING	DESKILL	DEWLAPS	DIGNITY
LEOTARD	TENDING	SKILLED	SPAWLED	TIDYING
DELENDA	DENUDER	DESMANS	DHANSAK	DIGONAL
LADENED	ENDURED	MADNESS	KHANDAS	LOADING
DELIGHT	DEPERMS	DESMINE	DHIMMIS	DILUENT
LIGHTED	PREMEDS	SIDEMEN	DIMMISH	UNTILED

DILUTES	DISEURS	DIVVIER	DOOKETS	DOWNIER
DUELIST	SUDSIER	VIVIDER	STOOKED	WINDORE
DIMNESS	DISGOWN	DOCKERS	DOOLANS	DRAFTER
MISSEND	DOWSING	REDOCKS	ONLOADS	REDRAFT
DINDLES	DISHORN	DODGERS	DOOMILY	DRAGEES
SLIDDEN	DRONISH	GORSEDD	MOODILY	GREASED
DINGERS	DISMAYD	DODGING	DOORMAN	DRAGNET
ENGIRDS	MIDDAYS	GODDING	MADRONO	GRANTED
DINGEYS	DISMAYL	DODMANS	DOORMEN	DRAGOON
DYEINGS	LADYISM	ODDSMAN	MORENDO	GADROON
DINKEST	DISPELS	DOGATES	DOPINGS	DRAINER
KINDEST	DISPLES	DOTAGES	PONGIDS	RANDIER
DINKEYS	DISPLED	DOGEATE	DORISED	DRAPERS
KIDNEYS	PIDDLES	GOATEED	SODDIER	SPARRED
DINKIES	DISPONE	DOGLEGS	DORISES	DRAPPIE
KINDIES	SPINODE	SLOGGED	DOSSIER	PREPAID
DINKING	DISROOT	DOGLIKE	DORMANT	DRAWEES
KINDING	TOROIDS	GODLIKE	MORDANT	RESAWED
DINNERS	DISSEAT	DOGSHIP	DORMINS	DRAWING
ENDRINS	SAIDEST	GODSHIP	NIMRODS	WARDING
DINNLES	DISSERT	DOILIES	DORTERS	DRAYAGE
LINDENS	STRIDES	IDOLISE	RODSTER	YARDAGE
DINTING	DISSING	DOLINAS	DOSAGES	DRAYING
TINDING	SIDINGS	LADINOS	SEADOGS	YARDING
DIOXIDS	DISTUNE	DONATED	DOSSERS	DRAYMAN
IXODIDS	DUNITES	NODATED	DROSSES	YARDMAN
DIPHONE	DITCHES	DONGLES	DOTCOMS	DRAYMEN
PHONIED	SICHTED	GOLDENS	TOMCODS	YARDMEN
DIPNETS	DITHERS	DONGOLA	DOTIEST	DREADED
STIPEND	SHIRTED	GONDOLA	STOITED	READDED
DIPNOAN	DITHIOL	DONINGS	DOTTLER	DREADLY
NONPAID	LITHOID	ONDINGS	DOTTREL	LADDERY
DIRHAMS	DITONES	DONNERT	DOURINE	DRESSER
MIDRASH	STONIED	TENDRON	NEUROID	REDRESS
DIRTIED	DIURONS	DONNIES	DOUSING	DRILLER
TIDDIER	DURIONS	ONDINES	GUIDONS	REDRILL
DISCOER	DIVERGE	DOODLER	DOWAGER	DROGUET
SCODIER	GRIEVED	DROOLED	WORDAGE	GROUTED
DISEASE	DIVISOR	DOOFERS	DOWNERS	DROICHS
SEASIDE	VIROIDS	FORDOES	WONDERS	ORCHIDS

DROOMES	DUKKAHS	DWINDLE	EEVNING	EMAILER
SMOORED	DUKKHAS	WINDLED	EVENING	MEALIER
DROPLET	DULCIAN	DWINING	EFTSOON	EMBLICS
PRETOLD	INCUDAL	WINDING	FESTOON	LIMBECS
DROPOUT	DULOSIS	DYELINE	EGGLERS	EMBRUED
OUTDROP	SOLIDUS	NEEDILY	LEGGERS	UMBERED
DROWSED	DUMAIST	EARFLAP	EGOISMS	EMENDER
SWORDED	STADIUM	PARAFLE	MISGOES	REEDMEN
DRUGGED	DUMMIER	EARLIER	EGOISTS	EMERGES
GRUDGED	IMMURED	LEARIER	STOGIES	MERGEES
DRUGGER	DUMMIES	EARLIES	EGOTISE	EMICANT
GRUDGER	MEDIUMS	REALISE	GOETIES	NEMATIC
DRUMBLE	DUMPIER	EARLIKE	EILDING	EMITTER
RUMBLED	UMPIRED	LEAKIER	ELIDING	TERMITE
DRUPELS	DUMPLES	EARNERS	EISWEIN	EMONGES
SLURPED	SLUMPED	REEARNS	WIENIES	GENOMES
DRUSIER	DUNGING	EARTHED	ELATION	EMOTING
DURRIES	NUDGING	HEARTED	TOENAIL	MITOGEN
DRYSUIT	DUNNEST	EARTHEN	ELCHEES	EMPALER
SURDITY	STUNNED	HEARTEN	LEECHES	PREMEAL
DUALINS	DUNNIER	EARWIGS	ELECTOR	EMPANEL
SUNDIAL	INURNED	GAWSIER	ELECTRO	EMPLANE
DUALIST	DUNNIES	EBAYERS	ELEGIES	EMPARED
TULADIS	UNDINES	EYEBARS	ELEGISE	PREMADE
DUCTILE	DUNSHES	EBONIES	ELEGIST	EMPORIA
DULCITE	SNUSHED	EBONISE	ELEGITS	MEROPIA
DUDDIER	DUNTING	ECHOIST	ELEMENT	EMPTIES
RUDDIED	TUNDING	TOISECH	TELEMEN	SEPTIME
DUELERS	DUOTONE	ECOMAPS	ELOGIST	EMPTINS
ELUDERS	OUTDONE	POMACES	LOGIEST	PIMENTS
DUETTOS	DUPIONS	ECONOMY	ELOPERS	EMPTION
TESTUDO	UNIPODS	MONOECY	LEPROSE	PIMENTO
DUFFEST	DURIANS	EDENTAL	ELUATES	EMULGES
STUFFED	SUNDARI	LATENED	SETUALE	LEGUMES
DUGITES	DURMAST	EDGINGS	ELUENTS	EMUNGED
GIUSTED	MUSTARD	SNIGGED	UNSTEEL	GUDEMEN
DUGONGS	DUSTERS	EDITION	ELUTION	ENAMELS
GUNDOGS	TRUSSED	TENIOID	OUTLINE	MELENAS
DUIKERS	DWARVES	EELIEST	EMAILED	ENAMOUR
DUSKIER	SWARVED	STEELIE	LIMEADE	NEUROMA

ENCAVED	ENGLISH	ENSOULS	EPIGRAM	ERYNGOS
VENDACE	SHINGLE	NOUSLES	PRIMAGE	GROYNES
ENCHARM	ENGLUTS	ENSTAMP	EPILATE	ESCROCS
MARCHEN	GLUTENS	TAPSMEN	PILEATE	SOCCERS
ENCLASP	ENGORES	ENSTEEP	EPIMERE	ESPADAS
SPANCEL	NEGROES	STEEPEN	PREEMIE	PASSADE
ENCLAVE	ENGUARD	ENSTYLE	EPINAOS	ESPANOL
VALENCE	RAUNGED	TENSELY	SENOPIA	NOPALES
ENCODER	ENJOYER	ENTAMES	EPISODE	ESPIERS
ENCORED	REENJOY	MEANEST	POESIED	PRESSIE
ENCODES	ENLIGHT	ENTASIA	EPISTLE	ESPOUSE
SECONDE	LIGHTEN	TAENIAS	PELITES	POSEUSE
ENCORES	ENLOCKS	ENTERIC	EPOXIDE	ESQUIRE
NECROSE	SLOCKEN	ENTICER	EPOXIED	QUERIES
ENDARCH	ENMOVED	ENTERON	EPSILON	ESSOYNE
RANCHED	VENOMED	TENONER	PINOLES	NOYESES
ENDINGS	ENOLASE	ENTOPIC	EQUATOR	ESTEEMS
SENDING	LOANEES	NEPOTIC	QUORATE	MESTEES
ENDITED	ENOLOGY	ENTOTIC	EQUINAL	ESTHETE
TEINDED	NEOLOGY	TONETIC	QUINELA	TEETHES
ENDNOTE	ENQUIRE	ENTOZOA	ERATHEM	ESTOILE
TENONED	INQUERE	OZONATE	THERMAE	ETOILES
ENDOWER	ENRACED	ENTRAIN	ERECTER	ESTREPE
REENDOW	RECANED	TRANNIE	REERECT	STEEPER
ENDURES	ENRINGS	ENTRUST	EREPSIN	ESTRUAL
ENSURED	GINNERS	NUTTERS	REPINES	SALUTER
ENDWISE	ENROUGH	ENTWIST	ERGATES	ETALAGE
SINEWED	ROUGHEN	TWINSET	RESTAGE	GALEATE
ENDZONE	ENSIGNS	ENWOUND	ERINITE	ETALONS
ENZONED	SENSING	UNOWNED	NITERIE	TOLANES
ENEWING	ENSKIED	EPACRID	ERISTIC	ETAMINE
WEENING	SKEINED	PERACID	RICIEST	MATINEE
ENFOLDS	ENSKIES	EPARCHS	EROTICS	ETATIST
FONDLES	KINESES	PARCHES	TERCIOS	TATTIES
ENFRAME	ENSLAVE	EPARCHY	ERRANTS	ETCHERS
FREEMAN	LEAVENS	PREACHY	RANTERS	RETCHES
ENGINED	ENSNARE	EPEIRIC	ERRATUM	ETHIONS
NEEDING	RENNASE	EPICIER	MATURER	HISTONE
ENGINER	ENSNARL	EPHEBOS	ERUPTED	ETHIOPS
INGENER	LANNERS	PHOEBES	REPUTED	OPHITES

ETHNICS	EYELIDS	FARCERS	FELCHES	FINITES
STHENIC	SEEDILY	SCARFER	FLECHES	NIFTIES
ETTLING	EYESPOT	FARCIES	FELLATE	FINKING
LETTING	PEYOTES	FIACRES	LEAFLET	KNIFING
EUMONGS	FACIEND	FARDENS	FELTIER	FIRELIT
MUNGOES	FANCIED	SNARFED	FERTILE	FITLIER
EVANISH	FACTORS	FARFELS	FEMINAL	FIREPOT
VAHINES	FORCATS	RAFFLES	INFLAME	PIEFORT
EVENTER	FACTURE	FARMERS	FEODARY	FIRLOTS
EVERNET	FURCATE	FRAMERS	FORAYED	FLORIST
EVOKERS	FAIENCE	FARMING	FERNIER	FIRMEST
REVOKES	FIANCEE	FRAMING	REFINER	FREMITS
EVOLUTE	FAINNES	FARMOST	FERROUS	FISTING
VELOUTE	FANNIES	FORMATS	FURORES	SIFTING
EVOLVER	FAINTER	FARSIDE	FETIALS	FITNESS
REVOLVE	FENITAR	FRAISED	SEALIFT	INFESTS
EXACTER	FAIRISH	FASTENS	FETICHE	FITTERS
EXCRETA	HAIRIFS	FATNESS	FITCHEE	TITFERS
EXAMPLE	FALCONS	FASTERS	FETTLES	FITTING
EXEMPLA	FLACONS	STRAFES	LEFTEST	TIFTING
EXCEPTS	FALLERS	FASTEST	FEUTRED	FIZZERS
EXPECTS	REFALLS	SAFTEST	REFUTED	FRIZZES
EXCIDES	FALLOUT	FATSOES	FEUTRES	FLARIER
EXCISED	OUTFALL	FOSSATE	REFUTES	FRAILER
EXCITOR	FALSERS	FAUTORS	FICKLED	FLASHED
XEROTIC	FLASERS	FOUTRAS	FLICKED	FLEADHS
EXCURSE	FALSIES	FAVORER	FICKLER	FLATCAR
EXCUSER	FILASSE	OVERFAR	FLICKER	FRACTAL
EXPANDS	FAMINES	FEATHER	FILAREE	FLECKER
SPANDEX	INFAMES	TEREFAH	LEAFIER	FRECKLE
EXPERTS	FANGLED	FECHTER	FILLERS	FLEMISH
SEXPERT	FLANGED	FETCHER	REFILLS	HIMSELF
EXPIRES	FANGLES	FEEDERS	FILMERS	FLENSER
PREXIES	FLANGES	REFEEDS	REFILMS	FRESNEL
EXPOSED	FANKLED	FEEDING	FILMSET	FLESHED
PODEXES	FLANKED	FEIGNED	LEFTISM	SHELFED
EXPOSIT	FANNELL	FEELERS	FINALIS	FLESHER
POXIEST	FLANNEL	REFEELS	FINIALS	HERSELF
EXTINES	FANTAIL	FEELING	FINGERS	FLETTON
SIXTEEN	TAILFAN	FLEEING	FRINGES	FONTLET

FLIRTED	FONDUED	FUGLING	GALLONS	GAUFERS
TRIFLED	FOUNDED	GULFING	GOLLANS	GAUFRES
FLIRTER	FORAMEN	FULNESS	GALORES	GAUNTED
TRIFLER	FOREMAN	UNSELFS	GAOLERS	UNGATED
FLITING	FORBARE	FUNDERS	GAMBIST	GEARING
LIFTING	FORBEAR	REFUNDS	GAMBITS	NAGGIER
FLOOSIE	FORESTS	FUNDIES	GAMBLER	GELATOS
FOLIOSE	FOSTERS	INFUSED	GAMBREL	LEGATOS
FLORETS	FORETOP	FUNFAIR	GAMETES	GELDING
LOFTERS	POOFTER	RUFFIAN	METAGES	NIGGLED
FLOURED	FORFEIT	FURANES	GAMIEST	GEMMATE
FOULDER	TOFFIER	UNSAFER	SIGMATE	TAGMEME
FLUATES	FORMERS	FUROLES	GAMMERS	GENOISE
SULFATE	REFORMS	OURSELF	GRAMMES	SOIGNEE
FLUERIC	FORRAYS	FUSIBLE	GAMONES	GENTLED
LUCIFER	ORFRAYS	SUBFILE	MANGOES	GLENTED
FLUIEST	FORWARD	FUSTIER	GANGING	GENTLES
SULFITE	FROWARD	SURFEIT	NAGGING	LENGEST
FLUSHED	FOUNDER	GABBLER	GANSEYS	GENUINE
SHEDFUL	REFOUND	GRABBLE	GAYNESS	INGENUE
FLUTIER	FOUTERS	GABELLE	GANTING	GENUSES
FUTILER	FOUTRES	GELABLE	TANGING	NEGUSES
FLUVIAL	FRANGER	GABNASH	GAOLING	GERENTS
VIALFUL	GRANFER	NASHGAB	GOALING	REGENTS
FLYOVER	FRENUMS	GADGETS	GARNERS	GERMING
OVERFLY	SURFMEN	STAGGED	RANGERS	MERGING
FOALING	FRESHER	GAHNITE	GASLESS	GESTATE
LOAFING	REFRESH	HEATING	GLASSES	TAGETES
FOCUSER	FRESHET	GALERES	GASPERS	GHRELIN
REFOCUS	HEFTERS	REGALES	SPARGES	HERLING
FOCUSES	FRESHIE	GALLEIN	GASSERS	GIBBONS
FUCOSES	HEIFERS	NIGELLA	GRASSES	SOBBING
FOISTER	FRETFUL	GALLICA	GASTERS	GILDING
FORTIES	TRUFFLE	GLACIAL	STAGERS	GLIDING
FOLDERS	FRETSAW	GALLIES	GASTRIC	GILLERS
REFOLDS	WAFTERS	GALLISE	TRAGICS	GRILLES
FOLDUPS	FRONTER	GALLING	GATEWAY	GILLNET
UPFOLDS	REFRONT	GINGALL	GETAWAY	TELLING
FONDLER	FUGLIER	GALLNUT	GAUDGIE	GIMMERS
FORLEND	GULFIER	NUTGALL	GUIDAGE	MEGRIMS

GINGALS	GLAIKET	GLUIEST	GRADING	GRINDER
LAGGINS	TAGLIKE	UGLIEST	NIGGARD	REGRIND
GINGELY	GLAIRES	GLUTTED	GRADINI	GRINNED
GLEYING	GRAILES	GUTTLED	RAIDING	RENDING
GINGKOS	GLEAVES	GNARRED	GRAFTER	GRIPMAN
GINKGOS	SELVAGE	GRANDER	REGRAFT	RAMPING
GINNELS	GLEEING	GNASHED	GRAHAMS	GROANER
LENSING	NEGLIGE	HAGDENS	GRAMASH	ORANGER
GINNERY	GLEEMAN	GOALIES	GRANDAM	GROOMER
RENYING	MELANGE	SOILAGE	GRANDMA	REGROOM
GINNIER	GLIBBER	GODDENS	GRANTER	GROOVED
REINING	GRIBBLE	GODSEND	REGRANT	OVERDOG
GINSHOP	GLIMPSE	GODLING	GRAPING	GROSERS
POSHING	MEGILPS	LODGING	PARGING	GROSSER
GIPPERS	GLINTED	GOLOSHE	GRAPLIN	GROSSED
GRIPPES	TINGLED	SHOOGLE	PARLING	SODGERS
GIRAFFE	GLISTER	GONGING	GRASPER	GROUPER
RIFFAGE	GRISTLE	NOGGING	SPARGER	REGROUP
GIRASOL	GLOATER	GONIFFS	GRATING	GROUPIE
GLORIAS	LEGATOR	OFFINGS	TARGING	PIROGUE
GIRDERS	GLOIRES	GOODIES	GRAVELS	GROUSER
RIDGERS	GLORIES	SOOGIED	VERGLAS	ROGUERS
GIRLOND	GLOMERA	GOOLIES	GRAVURE	GROWERS
LORDING	GOMERAL	OLOGIES	VERRUGA	REGROWS
GIRNING	GLONOIN	GOORIES	GREASER	GROWNUP
RINGING	LOONING	GOOSIER	REGEARS	UPGROWN
GIRONNY	GLOSSED	GOOSIES	GREATER	GRUEING
ROYNING	GODLESS	SOOGIES	REGRATE	GUNGIER
GIRSHES	GLOSSER	GORGETS	GREENED	GRUMOSE
SIGHERS	REGLOSS	TOGGERS	RENEGED	MORGUES
GIRTHED	GLOVERS	GORINGS	GREETER	GRUNGES
RIGHTED	GROVELS	GRINGOS	REGREET	SNUGGER
GIRTING	GLOWERS	GOSLING	GREMIAL	GRUNTED
RINGGIT	REGLOWS	OGLINGS	LAMIGER	TRUDGEN
GITTERN	GLOWING	GOWANED	GRIEVES	GRUSHIE
RETTING	GOWLING	WAGONED	REGIVES	GUSHIER
GLACIER	GLUEING	GRADDAN	GRIFFIN	GRUTTEN
GRACILE	LUGEING	GRANDAD	RIFFING	TURGENT
GLADIER	GLUGGED	GRADERS	GRINDED	GUBBINS
GLAIRED	GUGGLED	REGARDS	REDDING	SUBBING

GUDDLES	HACKLES	HAMMERS	HASSOCK	HEPTADS
SLUDGED	SHACKLE	SHAMMER	SHACKOS	SPATHED
GULLIES	HACKSAW	HANDERS	HASTIER	HERMITS
LIGULES	KWACHAS	HARDENS	SHERIAT	MITHERS
GULPERS	HADARIM	HANDLES	HASTING	HERNIAL
SPLURGE	HARAMDI	HANDSEL	TASHING	INHALER
GUNDIES	HAEMINS	HANDOFF	HATFULS	HEROINS
SUEDING	HEMINAS	OFFHAND	HATSFUL	INSHORE
GUNLESS	HAGBORN	HANGOUT	HATTING	HEROISM
GUNSELS	HORNBAG	TOHUNGA	TATHING	MOREISH
GUNSHIP	HAGDONS	HANGUPS	HAULING	HERRIED
PUSHING	SANDHOG	UPHANGS	NILGHAU	REHIRED
GURGING	HAGRIDE	HANJARS	HAVINGS	HERRIES
RUGGING	HEADRIG	RHANJAS	SHAVING	REHIRES
GURRIES	HAILERS	HANKERS	HAWKIES	HESPING
SURGIER	SHALIER	HARKENS	WEAKISH	PHESING
GURSHES	HAILING	HANTING	HAYRIDE	HEURISM
GUSHERS	NILGHAI	TANGHIN	HYDRIAE	MUSHIER
GUSHING	HAIQUES	HAPLESS	HAZMATS	HICATEE
SUGHING	QUASHIE	PLASHES	MATZAHS	TEACHIE
GUSTIER	HALAKAH	HAPLONT	HEADPIN	HIDLING
GUTSIER	HALAKHA	NAPHTOL	PINHEAD	HILDING
GUSTILY	HALITES	HARDASS	HEAVERS	HIELAND
GUTSILY	HELIAST	SRADHAS	RESHAVE	INHALED
GUSTING	HALITUS	HARDIER	HEEDING	HIGHTED
GUTSING	THULIAS	HARRIED	NEIGHED	THIGHED
GUTLESS	HALLANS	HARDMEN	HEELERS	HILLERS
TUGLESS	NALLAHS	HERDMAN	REHEELS	RELLISH
GUTROTS	HALLOED	HAREEMS	HEIRESS	HILLOES
ROTGUTS	HOLLAED	MAHSEER	HERISSE	HOLLIES
GUTTIER	HALLOOS	HARELDS	HELIMEN	HILTING
TURGITE	HOLLOAS	HERALDS	HEMLINE	LITHING
GUYLING	HALLOWS	HARISSA	HELLERI	HINDGUT
UGLYING	SHALLOW	SHARIAS	HELLIER	UNDIGHT
GYMNAST	HALTERE	HARPIES	HELLERS	HINGING
SYNTAGM	LEATHER	SHARPIE	SHELLER	NIGHING
GYMPIES	HALTING	HARVEST	HEMPIES	HINTERS
PYGMIES	LATHING	THRAVES	IMPHEES	NITHERS
GYRATED	HAMBLES	HASSLED	HEPCATS	HINTING
TRAGEDY	SHAMBLE	SLASHED	PATCHES	NITHING

HIPBONE	HOPPERS	HURTLES	IMBOWER	INAPTLY
HOPBINE	SHOPPER	HUSTLER	WOMBIER	PTYALIN
HIPPENS	HORMONE	HUSHERS	IMBRUTE	INCANTS
SHIPPEN	MOORHEN	SHUSHER	TERBIUM	STANNIC
HIPPIES	HORRENT	HYACINE	IMPAINT	INCESTS
SHIPPIE	NORTHER	HYAENIC	TIMPANI	INSECTS
HIRINGS	HORSING	HYALINS	IMPALED	INCISED
SHIRING	SHORING	LINHAYS	IMPLEAD	INDICES
HIRSELS	HORSTES	HYDRATE	IMPALES	INCLUDE
HIRSLES	TOSHERS	THREADY	PALMIES	NUCLIDE
HISSELF	HOSTING	HYDROUS	IMPANEL	INDEWED
SELFISH	TOSHING	SHROUDY	MANIPLE	WIDENED
HITLESS	HOTCHES	HYLISTS	IMPASSE	INDEXER
TEHSILS	SHOCHET	STYLISH	PESSIMA	REINDEX
HITTERS	HOTLINE	ICECAPS	IMPASTE	INDITER
TITHERS	NEOLITH	IPECACS	PASTIME	NITRIDE
HITTING	HOTTING	ICELESS	IMPASTO	INDITES
TITHING	TONIGHT	SIECLES	MATIPOS	TINEIDS
HOARSEN	HOUTING	ICHNITE	IMPEDES	INDOORS
SENHORA	THOUING	NITCHIE	SEMIPED	SORDINO
HODDENS	HOWEVER	ICINESS	IMPLATE	INDRAWN
SHODDEN	WHOEVER	INCISES	PALMIET	WINNARD
HOEDOWN	HOWLETS	IDEATUM	IMPONES	INDUSIA
WOODHEN	THOWELS	TAEDIUM	PEONISM	SUIDIAN
HOLDUPS	HUDDLER	IDENTIC	IMPORTS	INDWELT
UPHOLDS	HURDLED	INCITED	TROPISM	WINTLED
HOLINGS	HUMECTS	IGNITOR	IMPOSES	INFARES
LONGISH	MUTCHES	RIOTING	MOPSIES	SERAFIN
HOLSTER	HUMIDOR	IGNOBLE	IMPOSTS	INFEFTS
HOSTLER	RHODIUM	INGLOBE	MISSTOP	STIFFEN
HOMAGES	HUMITES	ILLAPSE	IMPRESA	INFIDEL
OHMAGES	TUMSHIE	PALLIES	SAMPIRE	INFIELD
HOMERED	HUNGANS	ILLICIT	IMPREST	INGESTS
REHOMED	UNHANGS	ILLITIC	PERMITS	SIGNETS
HONGIES	HURLIES	ILLIPES	IMPUGNS	INHUMER
SHOEING	LUSHIER	PILLIES	SPUMING	RHENIUM
HOODMAN	HURRIES	ILLUDES	IMPURER	INISLED
MANHOOD	RUSHIER	SULLIED	PRIMEUR	LINDIES
HOOPING	HURTFUL	IMBOSOM	IMPUTER	INKPOTS
POOHING	RUTHFUL	MIOMBOS	TUMPIER	INKSPOT

INLAYER	INTERNS	IONIZER	JAMBULS	KALMIAS
NAILERY	TINNERS	IRONIZE	JUMBALS	KAMILAS
INLIERS	INTIMAE	IONOMER	JAMMIES	KANGHAS
RESILIN	MINIATE	MOONIER	JEMIMAS	KHANGAS
INNAGES	INTINES	IRELESS	JANTIER	KANTING
SEANING	TINNIES	RESILES	NARTJIE	TANKING
INNINGS	INTONED	IRISING	JANTIES	KARAMUS
SINNING	NOINTED	NIGIRIS	TAJINES	KUMARAS
INQUEST	INTONES	IRKSOME	JARFULS	KARYONS
QUINTES	TENSION	SMOKIER	JARSFUL	RYOKANS
INSANER	INTORTS	IRONERS	JAWINGS	KASBAHS
INSNARE	TRITONS	ROSINER	JIGSAWN	SABKHAS
INSCAPE	INTRADA	IRONING	JAYVEES	KASHERS
PINCASE	RADIANT	ROINING	VEEJAYS	SHAKERS
INSEAMS	INTWIST	IRRUPTS	JERBILS	KASHMIR
SAMISEN	NITWITS	STIRRUP	JIRBLES	KHIMARS
INSIDER	INVADED	ISOSPIN	JERKINS	KAYOING
SNIDIER	VIDENDA	SINOPIS	JINKERS	OKAYING
INSTATE	INVADER	ISOTONE	JITTERS	KEELERS
SATINET	RAVINED	TOONIES	TRIJETS	SLEEKER
INSTEPS	INVERTS	ISSUANT	JOINERS	KEENEST
SPINETS	STRIVEN	SUSTAIN	REJOINS	KETENES
INSULAE	INVITER	ISSUERS	JOLLITY	KEENING
INULASE	VITRINE	RISUSES	JOLTILY	KNEEING
INSULAR	INVITES	ITCHIER	JOLTERS	KEEPING
URINALS	VINIEST	TICHIER	JOSTLER	PEEKING
INSULIN	INWRAPS	IVORIST	JOUNCES	KEESTER
INULINS	RIPSAWN	VISITOR	JUNCOES	SKEETER
INSULSE	IODATED	IVRESSE	JOURNOS	KEGGERS
SILENUS	TOADIED	REVISES	SOJOURN	SKEGGER
INSURER	IODATES	JACKIES	JOYPOPS	KEIRINS
RUINERS	TOADIES	JACKSIE	POPJOYS	SINKIER
INSURES	IODIDES	JACKMAN	JUGFULS	KEISTER
SUNRISE	IODISED	MANJACK	JUGSFUL	KIESTER
INTAGLI	IODINES	JALOUSE	JUJITSU	KEITLOA
TAILING	IONISED	JEALOUS	JUJUIST	OATLIKE
INTENSE	IOLITES	JAMBOKS	JUMARED	KEKENOS
TENNIES	OILIEST	SJAMBOK	MUDEJAR	KONEKES
INTENTS	IONIUMS	JAMBONE	KAISERS	KELLIES
TENNIST	NIMIOUS	JOBNAME	KARSIES	SKELLIE

KELSONS	KIRNING	LACINGS	LASINGS	LECHWES
SLOKENS	RINKING	SCALING	SIGNALS	WELCHES
KELTIES	KIRPANS	LADINGS	LASKETS	LEEPING
SLEEKIT	PARKINS	LIGANDS	SKLATES	PEELING
KENOTIC	KISSING	LADRONS	LASQUES	LEERING
KETONIC	SKIINGS	LARDONS	SQUEALS	REELING
KEPHIRS	KISTFUL	LADYISH	LATINOS	LEESING
PERKISH	LUTFISK	SHADILY	TALIONS	SEELING
KERRIAS	KITSCHY	LAGERED	LATTICE	LEEWAYS
SARKIER	SHTICKY	REGALED	TACTILE	WEASELY
KETMIAS	KNEADER	LAIKERS	LAUNCED	LEGGISM
MISTAKE	NAKEDER	SERKALI	UNLACED	MIGGLES
KEYINGS	KNEIDEL	LAISSES	LAVAGES	LEIGERS
YESKING	LIKENED	LASSIES	SALVAGE	LIEGERS
KEYRING	KNITTER	LAKIEST	LAWINGS	LEIRING
YERKING	TRINKET	TALKIES	SWALING	LINGIER
KICKOUT	KNURLED	LAKINGS	LAYINGS	LEISLER
OUTKICK	RUNKLED	SLAKING	SLAYING	RELLIES
KIDDERS	KOORIES	LAMINAL	LAYOUTS	LEMURES
SKIDDER	ROOKIES	MANILLA	OUTLAYS	RELUMES
KILLERS	KRAKENS	LAMINAR	LAYOVER	LENGTHY
RESKILL	SKANKER	RAILMAN	OVERLAY	THEGNLY
KILTING	KREESED	LAMMIES	LAYTIME	LENTISK
KITLING	SKEERED	MELISMA	MEATILY	TINKLES
KIMMERS	KUMARIS	LAMPING	LEACHER	LESSONS
SKIMMER	RUMAKIS	PALMING	RELACHE	SONLESS
KIMONOS	KUMITES	LANCERS	LEAGUER	LETTERN
MONOSKI	MISTEUK	RANCELS	REGULAE	NETTLER
KINARAS	KURSAAL	LANGARS	LEAKING	LEVERED
KIRANAS	RUSALKA	RAGLANS	LINKAGE	REVELED
KINDLES	KYANISE	LANGUID	LEARNER	LEWDEST
SLINKED	YANKIES	LAUDING	RELEARN	SWELTED
KINGCUP	KYLIKES	LANIARD	LEASHED	LEXISES
PUCKING	SKYLIKE	NADIRAL	SHEALED	SILEXES
KINGPIN	LABELER	LAPPING	LEAVIER	LIAISES
PINKING	RELABEL	PALPING	VEALIER	SILESIA
KINSHIP	LABOURS	LARIATS	LEAVING	LICHENS
PINKISH	SUBORAL	LATRIAS	VEALING	LINCHES
KIPPERS	LABRUMS	LARMIER	LECHAIM	LIERNES
SKIPPER	LUMBARS	MARLIER	MICHAEL	RELINES

LIGATED	LINIEST	LOCOMEN	LOUNDED	LURRIES
TAIGLED	LINTIES	MONOCLE	NODULED	SURLIER
LIGHTER	LINSEYS	LOCULES	LOUVARS	LUSHING
RELIGHT	LYSINES	OCELLUS	VALOURS	SHULING
LIGNANS	LINTIER	LOCUSTA	LOVABLE	LUSKING
LINSANG	NITRILE	TALCOUS	VOLABLE	SULKING
LIGNINS	LIONELS	LOESSIC	LOVINGS	LUTITES
LININGS	NIELLOS	OSSICLE	SOLVING	TITULES
LIGROIN	LIPPENS	LOFTIER	LOWERED	LYCHEES
ROILING	NIPPLES	TREFOIL	ROWELED	SLEECHY
LIGULAS	LIQUATE	LOGGERS	LOWPING	LYDDITE
LUGSAIL	TEQUILA	SLOGGER	PLOWING	TIDDLEY
LIKINGS	LISTERS	LOMEINS	LOWSEST	MACABER
SILKING	RELISTS	MOLINES	SLOWEST	MACABRE
LILTING	LITOTES	LOMENTS	LOXYGEN	MADRONE
TILLING	TOILETS	MELTONS	XYLOGEN	ROADMEN
LIMACEL	LITTERY	LOMPISH	LUCITES	MAGIANS
MICELLA	TRITELY	PHLOMIS	LUETICS	SIAMANG
LIMACES	LITTLIE	LOOKERS	LUCUMOS	MAGNONS
MALICES	TILLITE	RELOOKS	OSCULUM	SONGMAN
LIMACON	LIVINGS	LOOKOUT	LUDSHIP	MAGPIES
MALONIC	SLIVING	OUTLOOK	SULPHID	MISPAGE
LIMITER	LIVYERS	LOOKUPS	LUMINED	MAIMERS
MILTIER	SILVERY	UPLOOKS	UNLIMED	RAMMIES
LIMMERS	LOACHES	LOOMING	LUMPENS	MAISTRY
SLIMMER	OSCHEAL	MOOLING	PLENUMS	SYMITAR
LIMNERS	LOAFERS	LOOPING	LUMPERS	MAKEUPS
MERLINS	SAFROLE	POOLING	RUMPLES	UPMAKES
LIMPEST	LOATHER	LOOSEST	LUMPIER	MAKINGS
LIMPETS	RATHOLE	LOTOSES	PLUMIER	MASKING
LINCHET	LOATHLY	LOOTING	LUMPING	MALANGA
TINCHEL	TALLYHO	TOOLING	PLUMING	NAGMAAL
LINEMAN	LOBBERS	LOPPERS	LUNATED	MALICHO
MELANIN	SLOBBER	PROPELS	UNDEALT	MOCHILA
LINGAMS	LOCKERS	LORDOMA	LUNGIES	MANATIS
MALIGNS	RELOCKS	MALODOR	SLUEING	STAMINA
LINGUAE	LOCKETS	LOTHEST	LUNKERS	MANDOLA
UNAGILE	LOCKSET	SHOTTLE	RUNKLES	MONADAL
LINGUAL	LOCKUPS	LOTIONS	LURINGS	MANDRIL
LINGULA	UPLOCKS	SOLITON	RULINGS	RIMLAND

MANEGES	MARMITE	MATCHER	MEGASSE	MILDEST
MENAGES	TRAMMIE	REMATCH	MESSAGE	MISTLED
MANGELS	MAROONS	MATLESS	MEGILLA	MILLETS
MANGLES	ROMANOS	SAMLETS	MILLAGE	MISTELL
MANIHOC	MARQUES	MATRONS	MEINEYS	MIMESES
MOHICAN	MASQUER	TRANSOM	MENYIES	MISSEEM
MANIKIN	MARRANO	MATROSS	MELICKS	MINCEUR
MANKINI	ORRAMAN	STROAMS	MICKLES	NUMERIC
MANITOS	MARRIES	MATTERS	MELLAYS	MINDERS
STAMNOI	SIMARRE	SMATTER	MESALLY	REMINDS
MANITOU	MARRUMS	MATURES	MENDERS	MINDSET
TINAMOU	MURRAMS	STRUMAE	REMENDS	MISTEND
MANKIER	MARTIAN	MAUGRES	MERCERY	MINIMUS
RAMEKIN	TAMARIN	MURAGES	REMERCY	MINIUMS
MANPACK	MARTING	MAULERS	MERELLS	MINUEND
PACKMAN	MIGRANT	SERUMAL	SMELLER	UNMINED
MANRENT	MASALAS	MAUMETS	MERINOS	MIREXES
REMNANT	SALAAMS	SUMMATE	MERSION	REMIXES
MANROPE	MASCOTS	MAUVEIN	MERISIS	MISDOER
REPOMAN	SCAMTOS	MAUVINE	MISSIER	MOIDERS
MANTEEL	MASHIER	MAXIMIN	MERISMS	MISEASE
TELEMAN	MISHEAR	MINIMAX	SIMMERS	SIAMESE
MANTRAP	MASHIES	MAZIEST	MERLOTS	MISERLY
RAMPANT	MESSIAH	MESTIZA	MOLTERS	MISRELY
MAORMOR	MASHING	MEANERS	MESEEMS	MISHAPS
MORMAOR	SHAMING	RENAMES	SEMEMES	PASHIMS
MAPLESS	MASHUPS	MEANIES	MESETAS	MISPLAN
SAMPLES	SMASHUP	NEMESIA	SEAMSET	PLASMIN
MARBLED	MASONRY	MEDAKAS	MESTERS	MISSEES
RAMBLED	MORNAYS	SMAAKED	RESTEMS	SEMISES
MARBLER	MASQUES	MEDALET	METRING	MISSOUT
RAMBLER	SQUAMES	METALED	TERMING	SUMOIST
MARCONI	MASSIER	MEDICOS	METTLES	MISTERS
MINORCA	SARMIES	MISCODE	STEMLET	SMITERS
MARENGO	MASSIVE	MEDUSAN	MIDTERM	MISTERY
MEGARON	MAVISES	SUDAMEN	TRIMMED	SMYTRIE
MARITAL	MASTERS	MEERING	MIGRATE	MISTLES
MARTIAL	STREAMS	REGIMEN	RAGTIME	SMILETS
MARKERS	MASTICH	MEETING	MIKRONS	MISTRAL
REMARKS	TACHISM	TEEMING	MORKINS	RAMTILS

MITERER	MOONLET	MUCHELS	NANDINE	NEURONS
TRIREME	TOOLMEN	MULCHES	NANNIED	NONUSER
MITISES	MOORIER	MUCOIDS	NAPPIES	NEXUSES
STIMIES	ROOMIER	MUSCOID	PINESAP	UNSEXES
MITOSES	MOORING	MUDGERS	NARKING	NHANDUS
SOMITES	ROOMING	SMUDGER	RANKING	UNHANDS
MITTENS	MOORVAS	MUGGERS	NASTILY	NICKERS
SMITTEN	VAROOMS	SMUGGER	SAINTLY	SNICKER
MODELER	MOOTING	MUISTED	NASUTES	NICTATE
REMODEL	TOOMING	TEDIUMS	UNSEATS	TETANIC
MODERNS	MOPPIER	MUNDANE	NATRONS	NIFFERS
RODSMEN	POMPIER	UNNAMED	NONARTS	SNIFFER
MODULES	MORAINE	MURDERS	NATTERS	NIPPERS
MOUSLED	ROMAINE	SMURRED	RATTENS	SNIPPER
MOITHER	MORONIC	MURLAIN	NATURAE	NIPTERS
MOTHIER	OMICRON	RUMINAL	TAUREAN	PTERINS
MOLLAHS	MOROSER	MURREES	NAVARIN	NITROUS
OLLAMHS	ROOMERS	RESUMER	NIRVANA	TURIONS
MOMENTO	MORTALS	MUSIMON	NEAPING	NOIRISH
MOOTMEN	STROMAL	OMNIUMS	PEANING	ROINISH
MOMENTS	MOTIVED	MUSINGS	NEBULAS	NONETTI
MONTEMS	VOMITED	MUSSING	UNBALES	TONTINE
MOMUSES	MOTTIER	MUSKLES	NEGATES	NONPAST
MOUSMES	OMITTER	SKELUMS	SANGEET	PANTONS
MONARCH	MOULDER	MUSMONS	NEGATON	NONSTOP
NOMARCH	REMOULD	SUMMONS	TONNAGE	PONTONS
MONAULS	MOUSERS	MUSSELS	NEITHER	NOODLES
SOLANUM	SMOUSER	SUMLESS	THEREIN	SNOOLED
MONGERS	MOUSING	MUTANDA	NEOSOUL	NOOKIER
MORGENS	SOUMING	TAMANDU	UNLOOSE	ROOINEK
MONISMS	MOUSSED	MUTUALS	NERVIER	NORITIC
NOMISMS	SMOUSED	UMLAUTS	VERNIER	TIRONIC
MONITOR	MOUSSES	MUTUELS	NESTLES	NOSHERS
TROMINO	SMOUSES	MUTULES	NETLESS	SENHORS
MONOMER	MOUSTED	MUTULAR	NETTIER	NOSTOCS
MOORMEN	SMOUTED	TUMULAR	TENTIER	ONCOSTS
MONOSIS	MOUTERS	MYOSOTE	NETTING	NOTAIRE
SIMOONS	OESTRUM	TOYSOME	TENTING	OTARINE
MONTANE	MOWINGS	MYTHIER	NETTLES	NOTCHES
NONMEAT	SOWMING	THYMIER	TELNETS	TECHNOS

NOTEPAD	OFFENDS	OPPRESS	OUTDRAW	OUTTURN
TONEPAD	SENDOFF	PORPESS	OUTWARD	TURNOUT
NOTICES	OFFERER	OPPUGNS	OUTGUNS	OUTWALK
SECTION	REOFFER	POPGUNS	OUTSUNG	WALKOUT
NOUGATS	OFFPUTS	OPSONIC	OUTHIRE	OUTWASH
OUTSANG	PUTOFFS	POCOSIN	ROUTHIE	WASHOUT
NOUNIER	OFFSETS	OPUNTIA	OUTJEST	OUTWITH
REUNION	SETOFFS	UTOPIAN	OUTJETS	WITHOUT
NOVALIA	OFFTAKE	ORATING	OUTLIED	OUTWORK
VALONIA	TAKEOFF	ROATING	TOLUIDE	WORKOUT
NOWHERE	OGRISMS	ORBIEST	OUTNESS	OVARIAL
WHEREON	SIMORGS	SORBITE	TONUSES	VARIOLA
NOWTIER	OILCUPS	ORDERER	OUTPASS	OVERATE
TOWNIER	UPCOILS	REORDER	PASSOUT	OVEREAT
NUCLEUS	OILNUTS	OREIDES	OUTPOST	OVERLIE
NUCULES	ULTIONS	OSIERED	OUTTOPS	RELIEVO
NURDLED	OLIVERS	ORGONES	OUTPULL	OVERMEN
RUNDLED	VIOLERS	OROGENS	PULLOUT	VENOMER
NURSING	OLIVETS	ORPHISM	OUTPUTS	OVERNEW
URNINGS	VIOLETS	ROMPISH	PUTOUTS	REWOVEN
NURSLES	OMELETS	ORRISES	OUTRIGS	OVERPLY
RUNLESS	TELOMES	ROSIERS	RIGOUTS	PLOVERY
NURTURE	OMNEITY	OSETRAS	OUTROLL	OVERRED
UNTRUER	OMNIETY	OSSETRA	ROLLOUT	REDROVE
NUZZLES	ONAGERS	OSPREYS	OUTRUNS	OVERRUN
SNUZZLE	ORANGES	PYROSES	RUNOUTS	RUNOVER
OARIEST	ONEYERS	OSSELET	OUTSELL	OVERSAD
OTARIES	ONEYRES	TOELESS	SELLOUT	SAVORED
OARSMAN	OOMPAHS	OSSETER	OUTSETS	OVERTIP
RAMONAS	SHAMPOO	STEREOS	SETOUTS	PIVOTER
OBDURES	OORALIS	OSSUARY	OUTSIDE	OWRIEST
ROSEBUD	OORIALS	SUASORY	TEDIOUS	TOWSIER
ODDNESS	OOZIEST	OTTERED	OUTSINS	OYSTERS
SODDENS	ZOOIEST	TETRODE	USTIONS	STOREYS
ODORISE	OPCODES	OUGHTED	OUTSPED	PACKERS
OROIDES	SCOOPED	TOUGHED	SPOUTED	REPACKS
OESTRAL	OPERONS	OUTACTS	OUTSTEP	PADANGS
OLESTRA	SNOOPER	OUTCAST	TOUPETS	PADNAGS
OEUVRES	OPINING	OUTDOER	OUTTAKE	PADRONI
OVERUSE	PIONING	OUTRODE	TAKEOUT	PONIARD

PAINIMS	PARROTY	PATROON	PEERING	PERITUS
PIANISM	PORTRAY	PRONOTA	PREEING	PUIREST
PALETTE	PARSONS	PATTERN	PEEVERS	PERJINK
PELTATE	SANPROS	REPTANT	PREEVES	PREJINK
PALLIER	PARTERS	PATTIES	PEISING	PERKINS
PERILLA	PRATERS	TAPETIS	PIGSNIE	PINKERS
PALLONE	PARTIAL	PATTLES	PELORIC	PERLITE
PLEONAL	PATRIAL	PELTAST	POLICER	REPTILE
PALMARY	PARTURE	PAULINS	PENCILS	PERORAL
PALMYRA	RAPTURE	SPINULA	SPLENIC	PREORAL
PALSHIP	PARTYER	PAUNCES	PENNATE	PERSUES
SHIPLAP	PETRARY	UNCAPES	PENTANE	PERUSES
PALSIER	PARURES	PAUPERS	PENNIES	PERTUSE
PARLIES	UPREARS	UPSPEAR	PINENES	REPUTES
PANDITS	PARVISE	PAYINGS	PENSELS	PERUSAL
SANDPIT	PAVISER	SPAYING	SPLEENS	PLEURAS
PANGENS	PASEARS	PAYSLIP	PENSIVE	PERUSER
PENANGS	SARAPES	SAPPILY	VESPINE	REPURES
PANIERS	PASSADO	PEACODS	PEPPIER	PERVIER
RAPINES	POSADAS	PEASCOD	PREPPIE	REPRIVE
PANNERS	PASSELS	PEANUTS	PEPTISE	PERVING
SPANNER	SAPLESS	PESAUNT	TIPPEES	PREVING
PANTINE	PASSING	PEARTER	PERCALE	PESTERS
PINNATE	SPAINGS	TAPERER	REPLACE	PRESETS
PARETIC	PASSMAN	PECKIER	PERCENT	PESTIER
PICRATE	SAMPANS	PICKEER	PRECENT	RESPITE
PARIAHS	PASTELS	PEDALED	PERCEPT	PETALED
RAPHIAS	STAPLES	PLEADED	PRECEPT	PLEATED
PARIANS	PASTEUP	PEDANTS	PERCUSS	PETASOS
PIRANAS	PUPATES	PENTADS	SPRUCES	SAPOTES
PARKIES	PASTILS	PEDDERS	PERDURE	PETITES
SPARKIE	SPITALS	SPREDDE	REPURED	PETTIES
PARODIC	PASTILY	PEDDLES	PEREION	PETROLS
PICADOR	PAYLIST	SPELDED	PIONEER	REPLOTS
PAROLES	PATENTS	PEDICEL	PERFECT	PHAETON
REPOSAL	PATTENS	PEDICLE	PREFECT	PHONATE
PARPING	PATRICK	PEDLERS	PERFORM	PHENOMS
RAPPING	TRIPACK	SPELDER	PREFORM	SHOPMEN
PARROTS	PATROLS	PEERIES	PERILED	PHILTER
RAPTORS	PORTALS	SEEPIER	REPLIED	PHILTRE

PHRASED	PIPLESS	PLEROMA	POINDER	POSSERS
SHARPED	SIPPLES	RAMPOLE	PROINED	PROSSES
PHYTOID	PISHEOG	PLOATED	POISERS	POSTBOY
TYPHOID	PISHOGE	TADPOLE	PROSSIE	POTBOYS
PICAROS	PISMIRE	PLODDED	POISONS	POSTERN
PROSAIC	PRIMSIE	PODDLED	POISSON	PRONEST
PICENES	PISSANT	PLODGES	POITREL	POSTING
PIECENS	PTISANS	SPLODGE	POLITER	STOPING
PICKETS	PISSERS	PLOPPED	POLDERS	POSTMEN
SKEPTIC	PRISSES	POPPLED	PRESOLD	TOPSMEN
PICKLER	PISTOLS	PLOTFUL	POLINGS	POTASSA
PRICKLE	POSTILS	TOPFULL	SLOPING	SAPOTAS
PIGNORA	PITIERS	PLOUTER	POLLERS	POTLUCK
PORANGI	TIPSIER	POULTER	REPOLLS	PUTLOCK
PIGNUTS	PITSAWS	PLOWERS	POLOIST	POUDERS
STUPING	SAWPITS	REPLOWS	TOPSOIL	POUDRES
PILEUPS	PLACITS	PLUGGED	POODLES	POULPES
UPPILES	PLASTIC	PUGGLED	SPOOLED	UPSLOPE
PILLAUS	PLACOID	PLUMBER	POPERIN	POUNCED
PILULAS	PODALIC	REPLUMB	PROPINE	UNCOPED
PINANGS	PLAGUES	PLUMBIC	PORGIES	POUNDER
SPANING	PLUSAGE	UPCLIMB	SERPIGO	UNROPED
PINCHES	PLAICES	PLUMOSE	PORKERS	POURERS
SPHENIC	SPECIAL	PUMELOS	PROKERS	REPOURS
PINDARI	PLAITED	PLUNGED	PORKING	POURIES
PRIDIAN	TALIPED	PUNGLED	PROKING	SOUPIER
PINGLES	PLAITER	PLUNGES	PORTAGE	POURSUE
SPIGNEL	PLATIER	PUNGLES	POTAGER	UPROUSE
PINIONS	PLANERS	PLUSSES	PORTEND	POUSSES
SPINONI	REPLANS	PUSSELS	PROTEND	SPOUSES
PINNERS	PLANETS	PLUTEUS	PORTICO	POUSSIN
SPINNER	PLATENS	PUSTULE	PROOTIC	SPINOUS
PINOCLE	PLASHER	PLUTONS	PORTING	POWNIES
PLEONIC	SPHERAL	PULTONS	TROPING	WINESOP
PIOLETS	PLASMIC	POCOSEN	PORTOUS	POWTERS
PISTOLE	PSALMIC	POONCES	UPROOTS	PROWEST
PIONIES	PLECTRE	PODIUMS	POSINGS	PRAETOR
SINOPIE	PRELECT	SPODIUM	POSSING	PRORATE
PIPINGS	PLERION	POGONIP	POSNETS	PRAWNED
SIPPING	PROLINE	POOPING	STEPSON	PREDAWN

PRAWNER	PRISONS	PUNCHER	QUESTER	RATTING
PREWARN	SPINORS	UNPERCH	REQUEST	TARTING
PREARMS	PRISSED	PUNIEST	QUIETER	RAUNCHY
RAMPERS	SPIDERS	PUNTIES	REQUITE	UNCHARY
PREDOOM	PROETTE	PUNKIES	QUINNAT	RAUNGES
PROMOED	TREETOP	SPUNKIE	QUINTAN	UNGEARS
PREEDIT	PROGENY	PUNNETS	RABATTE	RAVAGES
TEPIDER	PYROGEN	UNSPENT	TABARET	SAVAGER
PREENED	PROLLED	PUNSTER	RACISTS	RAWHEAD
PRENEED	REDPOLL	PUNTERS	SACRIST	WARHEAD
PREFILE	PRONAOS	PURITAN	RACKERS	RAYLESS
PRELIFE	SOPRANO	UPTRAIN	RERACKS	SLAYERS
PREIFES	PROOFER	PURLERS	RAGGIES	REALTOR
PRIEFES	REPROOF	SLURPER	SAGGIER	RELATOR
PREMIER	PROPERS	PURSIER	RAGTAGS	REAMERS
REPRIME	PROSPER	UPRISER	TAGRAGS	SMEARER
PRENTED	PROTIST	PURSUED	RAGWEED	REAMIER
PRETEND	TROPIST	USURPED	WAGERED	REREMAI
PREPAYS	PROTORE	PURSUER	RAILERS	REAPERS
YAPPERS	TROOPER	USURPER	RERAILS	SPEARER
PREPONE	PRUNERS	PUTTERS	RAKINGS	REARISE
PROPENE	SPURNER	SPUTTER	SARKING	RERAISE
PRESHIP	PRUSIKS	PUTTIED	RALLIES	REASONS
SHIPPER	SPRUIKS	TITUPED	SALLIER	SENORAS
PRESONG	PSALMED	PUZZELS	RAMSONS	REAVAIL
SPONGER	SAMPLED	PUZZLES	RANSOMS	VELARIA
PRESSES	PSEUDOS	PYEMIAS	RAMSTAM	REAVING
SPERSES	SPOUSED	YAMPIES	TAMMARS	VINEGAR
PRESSOR	PUDDERS	PYRALID	RANDOMS	REBORES
PROSERS	SPUDDER	RAPIDLY	RODSMAN	SOBERER
PRESUME	PUDDLES	PYRITES	RASHERS	REBUSES
SUPREME	SPUDDLE	STRIPEY	SHARERS	SUBSERE
PRETEEN	PUISNES	QUEERER	RASSLED	RECITED
TERPENE	SUPINES	REQUERE	SARDELS	TIERCED
PREVISE	PULSANT	QUELEAS	RATLIKE	RECLUSE
PRIEVES	PULTANS	SEQUELA	TALKIER	RECULES
PREWRAP	PULSION	QUERIER	RATOONS	RECULED
WRAPPER	UPSILON	REQUIRE	SANTOOR	ULCERED
PRINTER	PUMPERS	QUERIST	RATTILY	RECURED
REPRINT	REPUMPS	REQUITS	TARTILY	REDUCER

REDACTS	REPEATS	RETELLS	REWINDS	RIVALED
SCARTED	RETAPES	TELLERS	WINDERS	VALIDER
REDBAIT	REPINED	RETHINK	REWIRED	RIVERET
TRIBADE	RIPENED	THINKER	WEIRDER	RIVETER
REDDEST	REPINER	RETICLE	REWIRES	RIVETED
TEDDERS	RIPENER	TIERCEL	SWEIRER	VERDITE
REDDLES	REPLIES	RETIRER	REWORDS	RIVIERA
SLEDDER	SPIELER	TERRIER	SWORDER	VAIRIER
REDLINE	RERISEN	RETRACK	REWORKS	ROADIES
RELINED	RESINER	TRACKER	WORKERS	SOREDIA
REDWING	REROLLS	RETREAD	REWOUND	RODENTS
WRINGED	ROLLERS	TREADER	WOUNDER	SNORTED
REEDILY	REROOFS	RETREES	REWRAPS	ROGUING
YIELDER	ROOFERS	STEERER	WARPERS	ROUGING
REESTED	RESEEDS	RETRIMS	RHUMBAS	ROLLTOP
STEERED	SEEDERS	TRIMERS	SAMBHUR	TROLLOP
REFUTAL	RESELLS	RETUNDS	RIBAUDS	ROOTLET
TEARFUL	SELLERS	UNDREST	SUBARID	TOOTLER
REGRESS	RESHOWS	RETURNS	RIBBONS	RORTERS
SERGERS	SHOWERS	TURNERS	ROBBINS	TERRORS
REGROWN	RESIDUE	REUTTER	RICKEYS	RORTIER
WRONGER	UREIDES	UTTERER	YICKERS	TERROIR
REISSUE	RESIGHT	REVAMPS	RIDGIER	ROSALIA
SEISURE	SIGHTER	VAMPERS	RIGIDER	SOLARIA
REIVING	RESISTS	REVENUE	RIKISHA	ROSYING
RIEVING	SISTERS	UNREEVE	SHIKARI	SIGNORY
RELEVES	RESIZES	REVIEWS	RILIEST	ROTATED
SLEEVER	SEIZERS	VIEWERS	SILTIER	TROATED
RELIVER	RESKEWS	REWAKED	RIMLESS	ROTATES
REVILER	SKEWERS	WREAKED	SMILERS	TOASTER
REMEIDS	RESTIFF	REWAKEN	RIPTIDE	ROTCHIE
REMISED	STIFFER	WAKENER	TIDERIP	THEORIC
REMORSE	RESTING	REWATER	RISINGS	ROTULAE
ROEMERS	STINGER	WATERER	SIRINGS	TORULAE
RENAGUE	RESTYLE	REWEIGH	RISTRAS	ROTULAS
UNEAGER	TERSELY	WEIGHER	STIRRAS	TORULAS
RENNETS	RESURGE	REWELDS	RITTERS	ROUSANT
TENNERS	REURGES	WELDERS	TERRITS	SANTOUR
RENOWNS	RETAKES	REWIDEN	RITUALS	ROUSING
WONNERS	SAKERET	WIDENER	TRISULA	SOURING

ROWDILY	SALINES	SAUCIER	SCRIEVE	SERVERS
WORDILY	SILANES	URICASE	SERVICE	VERSERS
ROWINGS	SALOONS	SAUNTED	SCULKED	SERVEWE
WORSING	SOLANOS	UNSATED	SUCKLED	WEEVERS
ROWTING	SALTANT	SAVINES	SDEIGNE	SERVING
TROWING	TALANTS	VINASSE	SEEDING	VERSING
ROYSTER	SALTISH	SAVIOUR	SEAMIER	SERVLET
STROYER	TAHSILS	VARIOUS	SERIEMA	SVELTER
RUBACES	SALTOED	SAVORER	SEAWORM	SESELIS
SUBRACE	SOLATED	SEROVAR	WOMERAS	SESSILE
RUBELLA	SALUTES	SAWDERS	SECKELS	SESTETS
RULABLE	TALUSES	SWEARDS	SECKLES	TSETSES
RUINOUS	SAMOYED	SAWLIKE	SEEKING	SETTEES
URINOUS	SOMEDAY	WALKIES	SKEEING	TESTEES
RUNDLET	SANDERS	SAWYERS	SEETHED	SETTING
TRUNDLE	SARSDEN	SWAYERS	SHEETED	TESTING
RUNNETS	SANGERS	SAXTUBA	SEETHER	SEWINGS
STUNNER	SERANGS	SUBTAXA	SHEETER	SWINGES
RUSTRES	SANIOUS	SCAMPIS	SEEWING	SHAITAN
TRUSSER	SUASION	SPASMIC	SWEEING	TAHINAS
SABELLA	SANNIES	SCAPING	SEITENS	SHAPEUP
SALABLE	SIENNAS	SPACING	SESTINE	UPHEAPS
SACBUTS	SANNUPS	SCEDULE	SELFIST	SHAWLIE
SUBACTS	UNSNAPS	SECLUDE	STIFLES	WHAISLE
SACHETS	SANSEIS	SCHOUTS	SELSYNS	SHEIKHS
SCATHES	SASINES	SCOUTHS	SLYNESS	SHIKSEH
SACKBUT	SANTOLS	SCHTICK	SEMMITS	SHEITAN
SUBTACK	STANOLS	TCHICKS	TSIMMES	STHENIA
SACKERS	SANTONS	SCHTIKS	SENNITS	SHEWELS
SCREAKS	SONANTS	SHTICKS	SINNETS	WELSHES
SACRIFY	SANTURS	SCOURGE	SENSUAL	SHIATSU
SCARIFY	SUNSTAR	SCROUGE	UNSEALS	THIASUS
SADDISH	SAPOURS	SCOWING	SEPHENS	SHICKER
SIDDHAS	UPSOARS	SOWCING	SPHENES	SKRIECH
SAGENES	SARCOUS	SCOWLER	SEPTATE	SHINERS
SENEGAS	SOUCARS	SCROWLE	SPATTEE	SHRINES
SAIMINS	SAROSES	SCREAKY	SERENER	SHIRKED
SIMIANS	SEROSAS	YACKERS	SNEERER	SHRIKED
SALADES	SARSNET	SCREICH	SERRANS	SHIRRAS
SALSAED	TRANSES	SCRIECH	SNARERS	SIRRAHS

SHIVERS	SITUSES	SNORING	STABBED	STIPELS
SHRIVES	TISSUES	SORNING	TEBBADS	TIPLESS
SHLOCKY	SIZEIST	SNOWING	STACKET	STIPPLE
SHYLOCK	SIZIEST	WONINGS	TACKETS	TIPPLES
SHOUTED	SKIVING	SOLANDS	STALKER	STIRING
SOUTHED	VIKINGS	SOLDANS	TALKERS	TIRINGS
SHOUTER	SKLATED	SOLDIER	STANDEE	STIRRED
SOUTHER	STALKED	SOLIDER	STEANED	STRIDER
SHOVERS	SKREIGH	SOLLERS	STARDOM	STODGER
SHROVES	SKRIEGH	SORELLS	TSARDOM	TODGERS
SHYSTER	SKRYING	SOMBERS	STARTED	STOKERS
THYRSES	SKYRING	SOMBRES	TETRADS	STROKES
SICKLED	SLAMMED	SOREXES	STARTUP	STOMPER
SLICKED	SMALMED	XEROSES	UPSTART	TROMPES
SIDEWAY	SLEEPRY	SOULDAN	STATELY	STONERN
WAYSIDE	YELPERS	UNLOADS	STYLATE	TONNERS
SIDLERS	SLEWING	SOVIETS	STATING	STONILY
SLIDERS	SWINGLE	STOVIES	TASTING	TYLOSIN
SIDLING	SLIPWAY	SOWARRY	STATINS	STONING
SLIDING	WASPILY	YARROWS	TANISTS	TONINGS
SIERRAN	SLITTED	SOWINGS	STATUTE	STONNED
SNARIER	STILTED	SOWSING	TAUTEST	TENDONS
SIESTAS	SLOPIER	SPALTED	STAYING	STOOKER
TASSIES	SPOILER	STAPLED	STYGIAN	STROOKE
SIEVING	SMOKILY	SPEEDER	STEEVES	STOOLED
VISEING	SOYMILK	SPEERED	VESTEES	TOLEDOS
SIGNARY	SMOODGE	SPINARS	STELLAR	STOPPLE
SYRINGA	SMOOGED	SPRAINS	TELLARS	TOPPLES
SIGNING	SNAFUED	SPIRANT	STEMING	STOTTIE
SINGING	UNDEAFS	SPRAINT	TEMSING	TOTTIES
SILOING	SNEAPED	SPIRITS	STERVED	STOUTEN
SOILING	SPEANED	TRIPSIS	VERDETS	TENUTOS
SILVERS	SNICKET	SPIRTED	STEWERS	STOVERS
SLIVERS	TICKENS	STRIPED	WESTERS	VOTRESS
SIPHONS	SNOOPED	SPURIAE	STICKUP	STOVING
SONSHIP	SPOONED	UPRAISE	UPTICKS	VOTINGS
SIPPLED	SNOOTED	SPUTNIK	STIDDIE	STOWAGE
SLIPPED	STOODEN	UPKNITS	TIDDIES	TOWAGES
SITTINE	SNORERS	SPYWARE	STINGOS	STRAINT
TINIEST	SORNERS	YAWPERS	TOSSING	TRANSIT

STRAWEN	SULLENS	SWAPPER	TACKLED	TEAZELS
WANTERS	UNSELLS	WAPPERS	TALCKED	TEAZLES
STREELS	SULPHUR	SWARDED	TACTICS	TEAZING
TRESSEL	UPHURLS	WADDERS	TICTACS	TZIGANE
STREETY	SUMATRA	SWATTED	TAKEUPS	TEETERS
SYRETTE	TRAUMAS	WADSETT	UPTAKES	TERETES
STRETTE	SUNDECK	SWATTER	TALLEST	TEMENOS
TETTERS	UNDECKS	TEWARTS	TALLETS	TONEMES
STREWED	SUNDERS	SWEEPER	TALLOWY	TEMPLAR
WRESTED	UNDRESS	WEEPERS	TOLLWAY	TRAMPLE
STREWER	SUNLIKE	SWIGGER	TAMARAS	TENDRIL
WRESTER	UNLIKES	WIGGERS	TARAMAS	TRINDLE
STROWED	SUNROOF	SWILLER	TAMPANS	TENOURS
WORSTED	UNROOFS	WILLERS	TAPSMAN	TONSURE
STUDDIE	SUNROOM	SWINDGE	TANGLER	TENSIVE
STUDIED	UNMOORS	SWINGED	TRANGLE	VENITES
STUDENT	SUNSPOT	SWINDLE	TANGRAM	THIRSTS
STUNTED	UNSTOPS	WINDLES	TRANGAM	THRISTS
STUDIES	SUNSUIT	SWINGER	TANNAHS	THIRSTY
TISSUED	UNSUITS	WINGERS	THANNAS	THRISTY
STUMBLE	SUNTRAP	SWINKER	TANNERY	THRAWED
TUMBLES	UNSTRAP	WINKERS	TYRANNE	WRATHED
STURNUS	SUNWARD	SWIPIER	TANNEST	TICKLER
UNTRUSS	UNDRAWS	WISPIER	TENANTS	TRICKLE
STURTED	SUPPING	SWIRLED	TANTARA	TILTING
TRUSTED	UPPINGS	WILDERS	TARTANA	TITLING
STUSHIE	SURAMIN	SWISHED	TARDIER	TITANIS
TUSHIES	URANISM	WHISSED	TARRIED	TITIANS
STYLITE	SURGING	SWISHER	TARTLET	TOOLSET
TESTILY	URGINGS	WISHERS	TATTLER	TOOTLES
STYLIZE	SWADDIE	SWISHES	TATUING	TOPWORK
ZESTILY	WADDIES	WHISSES	TAUTING	WORKTOP
STYRENE	SWAGGER	SWOONED	TAWIEST	TORPEDO
YESTERN	WAGGERS	WOODENS	TWAITES	TROOPED
SUBDEAN	SWALIER	SWOOPED	TAWNIER	TORTILE
UNBASED	WAILERS	WOOPSED	TINWARE	TRIOLET
SUEABLE	SWALLOW	SWOUNED	TAXWISE	TORTIVE
USEABLE	WALLOWS	UNSOWED	WAXIEST	VIRETOT
SUITORS	SWANKER	TABLEAU	TEABOWL	TORTURE
TSOURIS	WANKERS	TABULAE	TOWABLE	TROUTER

TOSSILY	TWINERS	UNNOTED	VALISES	WESTLIN
TYLOSIS	WINTERS	UNTONED	VESSAIL	WINTLES
TOWNIES	TWINTER	UNRAVEL	VAMPIER	WETHERS
TWONIES	WRITTEN	VENULAR	VAMPIRE	WRETHES
TOWTING	TWIRING	UNRIVET	VENTERS	WHEEDLE
WOTTING	WRITING	VENTURI	VENTRES	WHEELED
TRAVOIS	ULICONS	UNROOST	VENTOSE	WHITIER
VIATORS	UNCOILS	UNROOTS	VOTEENS	WITHIER
TREVETS	UNAIRED	UNSEENS	VIRGATE	WHITIES
VETTERS	URANIDE	UNSENSE	VITRAGE	WITHIES
TRIDUAN	UNALIVE	UNSPILT	VIRINOS	WHITING
UNITARD	UNVAILE	UNSPLIT	VIRIONS	WITHING
TRISHAW	UNBARES	UNSTACK	VIRTUAL	WHITRET
WRAITHS	UNBEARS	UNTACKS	VITULAR	WHITTER
TRIVIAL	UNCAPED	UNSTUCK	VODOUNS	WIGGLER
VITRAIL	UNPACED	UNTUCKS	VOUDONS	WRIGGLE
TROWELS	UNCASES	UNSWEAR	VOLATIC	WILLEST
WORTLES	USANCES	UNWARES	VOLTAIC	WILLETS
TUBULIN	UNDRAPE	UNTAMES	WANGLER	WILTING
UNBUILT	UNPARED	UNTEAMS	WRANGLE	WITLING
TUFTIER	UNFILDE	UNWIRES	WARNERS	WINKLER
TURFITE	UNFILED	UNWISER	WARRENS	WRINKLE
TUILZIE	UNFURLS	UPDATER	WASHIER	WISENTS
UTILIZE	URNFULS	UPRATED	WEARISH	WITNESS
TULCHAN	UNGLUED	UPDRAWS	WEIRING	ZAFFERS
UNLATCH	UNGULED	UPWARDS	WINGIER	ZAFFRES
TUMBLER	UNITIES	UPSPAKE	WELKINS	ZANIEST
TUMBREL	UNITISE	UPSPEAK	WINKLES	ZEATINS
TURKIES	UNLADES	UPSWELL	WELTING	
TUSKIER	UNLEADS	UPWELLS	WINGLET	
TURNIPS	UNLIVES	UPWINDS	WENCHES	
UNSTRIP	UNVEILS	WINDUPS	WHENCES	
TURNUPS	UNMATED	VAILING	WESANDS	
UPTURNS	UNTAMED	VIALING	WESSAND	
TWEEDLE	UNNAILS	VALETED	WESKITS	
TWEELED	UNSLAIN	VELATED	WISKETS	

Triplets

ABASING	ACROTER	AGNISES	ALTESSE	ANKLETS
BAAINGS	CREATOR	EASINGS	STEALES	ASKLENT
BISNAGA	REACTOR	SEASING	TEASELS	LANKEST
ABETTOR	ACTINAL	AGRASTE	AMBEERS	ANOINTS
BATTERO	ALICANT	GASTREA	BEAMERS	NATIONS
TABORET	ANTICAL	TEARGAS	BESMEAR	ONANIST
ABLEISM	ACTINON	AGREGES	AMBERED	ANOPIAS
EMBAILS	CANTION	RAGGEES	BREAMED	ANOPSIA
LAMBIES	CONTAIN	REGGAES	EMBREAD	PAISANO
ABORDED	ACTIONS	AILERON	AMENDES	ANTEING
BOARDED	ATONICS	ALERION	DEMEANS	ANTIGEN
ROADBED	CATIONS	ALIENOR	SEEDMAN	GENTIAN
ABORTED	ACTRESS	AIRCONS	AMERCED	ANTHERS
BORATED	CASTERS	RACINOS	CREAMED	HARTENS
TABORED	RECASTS	SARONIC	RACEMED	THENARS
ABORTER	ADMIRER	AIRDATE	AMERCES	ANTIARS
ARBORET	MARDIER	RADIATE	CAREMES	ARTISAN
TABORER	MARRIED	TIARAED	RACEMES	TSARINA
ABREACT	ADONISE	AIRNING	AMNIONS	ANTICKS
BEARCAT	ANODISE	INGRAIN	MANSION	CATKINS
CABARET	SODAINE	RAINING	ONANISM	CATSKIN
ABREGES	ADORING	AIRPOST	AMORETS	ANTIRED
BAREGES	GRADINO	AIRSTOP	MAESTRO	DETRAIN
BARGEES	ROADING	PAROTIS	OMERTAS	TRAINED
ABRUPTS	ADPRESS	AIRSHOT	AMOUNTS	ANURIAS
SUBPART	SPADERS	SHORTIA	MOUTANS	SAURIAN
UPBRAST	SPREADS	THORIAS	OUTMANS	URANIAS
ABSCISE	AETHERS	AISLING	AMTRACS	AORISTS
SCABIES	HEATERS	NILGAIS	RAMCATS	ARISTOS
SEBASIC	REHEATS	SAILING	TARMACS	SATORIS
ACARIDS	AFFRETS	ALBATAS	AMUSERS	APOSTLE
ASCARID	RESTAFF	ATABALS	ASSUMER	PELOTAS
CARDIAS	STAFFER	BALATAS	MASSEUR	POTALES
ACCRUES	AGELAST	ALERTLY	ANCHORS	APPERIL
ACCURSE	ALGATES	ELYTRAL	ARCHONS	APPLIER
ACCUSER	LASTAGE	RETALLY	RANCHOS	ARIPPLE
ACERBER	AGENTED	ALIBIES	ANGELED	APPLETS
CEREBRA	ENDGATE	BAILIES	GELANDE	LAPPETS
REBRACE	NEGATED	BIALIES	GLEANED	STAPPLE
ACETINS	AGGRESS	ALIGNED	ANGELIC	APPULSE
CANIEST	SAGGERS	DEALING	ANGLICE	PAPULES
CINEAST	SEGGARS	LEADING	GALENIC	UPLEAPS
ACHINGS	AGNAMES	ALINERS	ANIMIST	APTNESS
CASHING	MANAGES	NAILERS	INTIMAS	PATNESS
CHASING	SAGAMEN	RENAILS	SANTIMI	PESANTS

ARBUTES	ARTICLE	AUDILES	BASEMEN	BELLIED
BURSATE	RECITAL	DEASIUL	BEMEANS	DELIBLE
SURBATE	TALCIER	DUALISE	BENAMES	LIBELED
ARCHING	ASCENTS	AUNTERS	BASSIER	BEMIRES
CHAGRIN	SECANTS	NATURES	BRAISES	BERIMES
CHARING	STANCES	SAUNTER	BRASSIE	BIREMES
ARCTIID	ASCIANS	AUTOMEN	BASTION	BESORTS
TRIACID	CASSINA	NOTAEUM	BONITAS	SORBETS
TRIADIC	SANCAIS	OUTNAME	OBTAINS	STROBES
AREFIES	ASEPTIC	AVENTRE	BATHERS	BETRIMS
FAERIES	PACIEST	NERVATE	BERTHAS	TIMBERS
FREESIA	SPICATE	VETERAN	BREATHS	TIMBRES
ARENITE	ASPHALT	AVIDEST	BATISTE	BIGENER
RETINAE	SPATHAL	DATIVES	BATTIES	BREINGE
TRAINEE	TAPLASH	VISTAED	BISTATE	REBEGIN
ARGENTS	ASPINES	AVOWERS	BATTIER	BIMETAL
GARNETS	PANSIES	OVERSAW	BIRETTA	LIMBATE
STRANGE	SAPIENS	REAVOWS	RATBITE	TIMBALE
ARGUSES	ASRAMAS	AWNINGS	BATTLER	BINDERS
SAUGERS	SAMARAS	SNAWING	BLATTER	INBREDS
USAGERS	SAMSARA	WANINGS	BRATTLE	REBINDS
ARISHES	ASTHORE	BABBLER	BEADERS	BLISTER
RASHIES	EARSHOT	BLABBER	DEBASER	BRISTLE
SHERIAS	HAROSET	BRABBLE	SABERED	RIBLETS
ARISTAE	ASTONED	BACKETS	BEADMEN	BLITTER
ASTERIA	DONATES	BACKSET	BEDEMAN	BRITTLE
ATRESIA	ONSTEAD	SETBACK	BENAMED	TRIBLET
ARKOSES	ASUNDER	BAILOUT	BEARDED	BLUDIER
RESOAKS	DANSEUR	OBITUAL	BREADED	BUILDER
SOAKERS	DAUNERS	TABOULI	DEBEARD	REBUILD
ARMADAS	ATHIRST	BALDEST	BEASTED	BLURBED
MADRASA	RATTISH	BLASTED	BESTEAD	BURBLED
RAMADAS	TARTISH	STABLED	DEBATES	RUBBLED
ARMFULS	ATRETIC	BALDIES	BEATERS	BOILERS
ARMSFUL	CATTIER	DIABLES	BERATES	LIBEROS
FULMARS	CITRATE	DISABLE	REBATES	REBOILS
ARMPITS	ATTORNS	BANSHEE	BEDROOM	BOLSTER
IMPARTS	RATTONS	BEENAHS	BOREDOM	BOLTERS
MISPART	ROTTANS	SHEBEAN	BROOMED	LOBSTER
ARRESTS	ATTRITE	BARBELS	BEDRUGS	BORINGS
RASTERS	TATTIER	RABBLES	BUDGERS	ROBINGS
STARERS	TITRATE	SLABBER	REDBUGS	SORBING
ARRISES	ATTUNED	BARBETS	BELDAME	BOSSING
RAISERS	NUTATED	RABBETS	BEMEDAL	GIBSONS
SIERRAS	TAUNTED	STABBER	EMBALED	OBSIGNS

BOULLES	CAIRNED	CARGOES	CERESIN	CHORALS
LOBULES	CARNIED	CORSAGE	SCRIENE	LORCHAS
SOLUBLE	DANCIER	SOCAGER	SINCERE	SCHOLAR
BOUNDER	CAISSON	CARINAL	CERITES	CHORDEE
REBOUND	CASINOS	CLARAIN	RECITES	COHERED
UNROBED	CASSINO	CRANIAL	TIERCES	OCHERED
BOURNES	CAKINGS	CARIOSE	CESSION	CHOREAS
UNROBES	CASKING	ORACIES	COSINES	ORACHES
UNSOBER	SACKING	SCORIAE	OSCINES	ROACHES
BREEDER	CALKERS	CARLOTS	CESTOID	CHOREUS
BREERED	LACKERS	CROTALS	COEDITS	CHOUSER
REBREED	SLACKER	SCROTAL	COTISED	ROUCHES
BRIDALS	CALVERS	CARPERS	CESURAL	CHOUSED
LABRIDS	CARVELS	SCARPER	RECUSAL	DOUCHES
RIBALDS	CLAVERS	SCRAPER	SECULAR	HOCUSED
BRIEFED	CAMBERS	CARTERS	CHALETS	CIERGES
DEBRIEF	CEMBRAS	CRATERS	LATCHES	GRECISE
FIBERED	CRAMBES	TRACERS	SATCHEL	GRIECES
BRISURE	CANALED	CARTING	CHAPTER	CINEOLS
BRUISER	CANDELA	CRATING	PATCHER	CONSEIL
BURIERS	DECANAL	TRACING	REPATCH	INCLOSE
BUGLERS	CANDORS	CASEINS	CHARISM	CITHERS
BULGERS	CARDONS	CASSINE	CHIMARS	ESTRICH
BURGLES	DACRONS	INCASES	CHRISMA	RICHEST
BUMMELS	CANGLED	CASEMEN	CHASERS	CLARIES
BUMMLES	CLANGED	EMACSEN	CRASHES	ECLAIRS
MUMBLES	GLANCED	MENACES	ESCHARS	SCALIER
BUNTIER	CANINES	CATTIES	CHETNIK	CLASHER
TRIBUNE	ENCINAS	STATICE	KITCHEN	LARCHES
TURBINE	NANCIES	TIETACS	THICKEN	RASCHEL
BURNIES	CANTHUS	CATTISH	CHILDER	CLEANED
RUBINES	CHAUNTS	CHATTIS	CHIRLED	ELANCED
SUBERIN	STAUNCH	TACHIST	ELDRICH	ENLACED
CACKLER	CAPELIN	CENTARE	CHINING	CLOSERS
CLACKER	PANICLE	CRENATE	INCHING	CRESOLS
CRACKLE	PELICAN	REENACT	NICHING	ESCROLS
CAFILAS	CAPERED	CENTAUR	CHIRTED	CLOTURE
FACIALS	PEARCED	UNCRATE	DITCHER	CLOUTER
FASCIAL	PREACED	UNTRACE	RICHTED	COULTER
CAGANER	CAPOTES	CENTERS	CHOKERS	COASTER
CARNAGE	SCOPATE	CENTRES	HOCKERS	COATERS
CRANAGE	TOECAPS	TENRECS	SHOCKER	RECOATS
CAHIERS	CAPSTAN	CENTIMO	CHOLERA	CODEINS
CASHIER	CAPTANS	ENTOMIC	CHORALE	CONDIES
ERIACHS	CATNAPS	TONEMIC	CHOREAL	SECONDI

CODILLE	CORNICE	CREPIER	DANGERS	DEIFIER
COLLIDE	CROCEIN	PIERCER	GANDERS	EDIFIER
COLLIED	CROCINE	REPRICE	GARDENS	REIFIED
COEXIST	CORVETS	CRISPEN	DAPPLES	DELAYER
COXIEST	COVERTS	PINCERS	SAPPLED	LAYERED
EXOTICS	VECTORS	PRINCES	SLAPPED	RELAYED
COINFER	COSIEST	CRUDDLE	DARKEST	DELETES
CONIFER	COTISES	CUDDLER	STARKED	SLEETED
INFORCE	OECISTS	CURDLED	STRAKED	STEELED
COINTER	COSMINE	CRUELLS	DARNERS	DEMIREP
NOTICER	INCOMES	CULLERS	ERRANDS	EPIDERM
RECTION	MESONIC	SCULLER	SNARRED	IMPEDER
COMBATS	COUPERS	CRUISER	DARNING	DENIERS
MOBCAST	CROUPES	CURRIES	NARDING	NEREIDS
TOMBACS	RECOUPS	SUCRIER	RANDING	RESINED
CONATUS	COURSED	CRUISES	DAUBERS	DENTARY
NOCTUAS	SCOURED	CRUSIES	EARBUDS	TRAYNED
TOUCANS	SOURCED	CUISSER	SUBEDAR	TYRANED
CONDERS	COURSER	CTENOID	DAWDLER	DENTINS
CORSNED	CRUORES	DEONTIC	DRAWLED	INDENTS
SCORNED	SCOURER	NOTICED	WADDLER	INTENDS
CONSPUE	COUTERS	CUATROS	DAWDLES	DENTIST
POUNCES	CROUTES	SURCOAT	SWADDLE	DISTENT
UNCOPES	SCOUTER	TURACOS	WADDLES	STINTED
CONTOUR	COUTHER	CURTEST	DAWNERS	DENTURE
CORNUTO	RETOUCH	CUTTERS	WANDERS	RETUNED
CROUTON	TOUCHER	SCUTTER	WARDENS	TENURED
CONTUSE	COUVERT	CUTLETS	DEADEST	DENUDES
ECONUTS	CUTOVER	CUTTLES	SEDATED	DUDEENS
UNCOEST	OVERCUT	SCUTTLE	STEADED	DUENDES
COPERED	CRADLES	CUTLINE	DEALERS	DEPAINT
PRECODE	RECLADS	LINECUT	LEADERS	PAINTED
PROCEED	SCALDER	TUNICLE	REDEALS	PATINED
COPIERS	CRASSER	DABBLER	DEBITOR	DEPARTS
COPSIER	SCARERS	DRABBLE	DEORBIT	DRAPETS
PERSICO	SCARRES	RABBLED	ORBITED	PETARDS
COPULAS	CREASED	DAILIES	DEBONER	DEPORTS
CUPOLAS	DECARES	LIAISED	ENROBED	REDTOPS
SCOPULA	SEARCED	SEDILIA	REDBONE	SPORTED
COPYISM	CREEING	DAIMONS	DECANTS	DEPRAVE
MISCOPY	ENERGIC	DOMAINS	DESCANT	PERVADE
MYOPICS	GENERIC	MADISON	SCANTED	REPAVED
CORKERS	CREMINI	DALLIER	DECRIAL	DEPRESS
RECORKS	CRIMINE	DIALLER	RADICEL	PRESSED
ROCKERS	MINCIER	RALLIED	RADICLE	SPERSED

DEPRIVE	DIPTERA	DRAPIER	EARPLUG	EMPTING
PREDIVE	PARTIED	PARRIED	GRAUPEL	PIGMENT
PRIEVED	PIRATED	RAPIDER	PLAGUER	TEMPING
DERATED	DIRTIES	DRAUNTS	EATCHES	EMULING
REDATED	DITSIER	DURANTS	ESCHEAT	GUMLINE
TREADED	TIDIERS	TUNDRAS	TEACHES	LEGUMIN
DERIVER	DISHING	DREAMER	EIGHTHS	EMULSIN
REDRIVE	HIDINGS	REARMED	HEIGHTS	LUMINES
RIVERED	SHINDIG	REDREAM	HIGHEST	UNLIMES
DESERTS	DISNEST	DREIDLS	EKISTIC	ENAMORS
DESSERT	DISSENT	RIDDLES	ICKIEST	MOANERS
TRESSED	SNIDEST	SLIDDER	TICKIES	OARSMEN
DESINED	DISPORT	DROGUES	ELANETS	ENCRATY
NEDDIES	TORPIDS	GOURDES	LATEENS	NECTARY
SDEINED	TRIPODS	GROUSED	LEANEST	TRANCEY
DESTINE	DIVERTS	DROLEST	ELAPSES	ENDARTS
ENDITES	STRIVED	OLDSTER	PLEASES	STANDER
STEINED	VERDITS	STRODLE	SAPELES	STARNED
DESTOCK	DOLINES	DROWNED	ELICHES	ENDGAME
DOCKETS	INDOLES	ROWNDED	HELICES	MANEGED
STOCKED	SONDELI	WONDRED	LICHEES	MENAGED
DESTROY	DOMINES	DUELING	ELISION	ENERVES
ROYSTED	EMODINS	ELUDING	ISOLINE	EVENERS
STROYED	MISDONE	INDULGE	LIONISE	VENEERS
DEWATER	DONDERS	DUFFELS	ELITISM	ENGRAMS
TARWEED	NODDERS	DUFFLES	LIMIEST	GERMANS
WATERED	SNODDER	SLUFFED	LIMITES	MANGERS
DIALING	DOOMIER	DUNGERS	ELUANTS	ENISLED
GLIADIN	MOIDORE	GERUNDS	LUNATES	ENSILED
LAIDING	MOODIER	NUDGERS	UNLASTE	LINSEED
DIESELS	DORSELS	DURANCE	ELUTORS	ENLARGE
IDLESSE	RODLESS	UNCARED	OUTLERS	GENERAL
SEIDELS	SOLDERS	UNRACED	TROULES	GLEANER
DIETING	DOTTELS	DUSTIER	EMANATE	ENRIVEN
EDITING	DOTTLES	REDUITS	ENEMATA	INNERVE
IGNITED	SLOTTED	STUDIER	MANATEE	NERVINE
DIETIST	DOWRIES	DUSTPAN	EMERITA	ENSUING
DITTIES	ROWDIES	STANDUP	EMIRATE	GUNNIES
TIDIEST	WEIRDOS	UPSTAND	MEATIER	INGENUS
DILATER	DOWSERS	EAGLING	EMIGRES	ENTOILS
REDTAIL	DROWSES	GEALING	REGIMES	LIONETS
TRAILED	SOWDERS	LIGNAGE	REMIGES	ONLIEST
DIMPLES	DRAGGLE	EARFULS	EMOTERS	ENTREAT
MISPLED	GARGLED	FERULAS	METEORS	RATTEEN
SIMPLED	RAGGLED	REFUSAL	REMOTES	TERNATE

ENTREES	ESTRIOL	FERRIED	FORPITS	GAULTER
RETENES	LOITERS	REFIRED	PROFITS	TEGULAR
TEENERS	TOILERS	REFRIED	SPORTIF	TRAGULE
ENVIOUS	ESTRUMS	FERRIES	FRANTIC	GELANTS
NIVEOUS	MUSTERS	REFIRES	INFARCT	LANGEST
VEINOUS	STUMERS	REFRIES	INFRACT	TANGLES
ENVIROS	ETATISM	FERULES	FRATERS	GELATED
RENVOIS	MATIEST	FUELERS	RAFTERS	LEGATED
VERSION	MATTIES	REFUELS	STRAFER	TEAGLED
ENWRAPS	ETHYLIC	FIFTIES	FRITURE	GELIDER
PAWNERS	LECYTHI	IFFIEST	FRUITER	LEDGIER
SPAWNER	TECHILY	STIFFIE	TURFIER	LEIDGER
EOLITHS	ETOURDI	FIGHTER	GALIOTS	GEMINAL
HOLIEST	IODURET	FREIGHT	LATIGOS	LEAMING
HOSTILE	OUTRIDE	REFIGHT	SALIGOT	MEALING
EOSINIC	FAINEST	FISHERS	GALLATE	GEMMIER
ICONISE	FANSITE	SERFISH	GALLETA	GREMMIE
NICOISE	NAIFEST	SHERIFS	TALLAGE	IMMERGE
EPACRIS	FALSEST	FISSURE	GANGERS	GENESIS
SCRAPIE	FATLESS	FUSSIER	GRANGES	SEEINGS
SPACIER	FESTALS	SURFIES	NAGGERS	SIGNEES
EPIGONS	FANCIES	FLANEUR	GAPINGS	GERMINS
PIGEONS	FASCINE	FRENULA	GASPING	MERINGS
PINGOES	FIANCES	FUNERAL	PAGINGS	MINGERS
ERBIUMS	FARTING	FLOATER	GARGLES	GESTAPO
IMBRUES	INGRAFT	FLOREAT	LAGGERS	POSTAGE
IMBURSE	RAFTING	REFLOAT	RAGGLES	POTAGES
ESPARTO	FASTIES	FLOODER	GARMENT	GINGERY
PROTEAS	FIESTAS	FLOORED	MARGENT	GREYING
SEAPORT	FISSATE	REFLOOD	RAGMENT	NIGGERY
ESPYING	FATHERS	FLOWING	GARNISH	GIRDING
PEYSING	HAFTERS	FOWLING	RASHING	GRIDING
PIGSNEY	SHAFTER	WOLFING	SHARING	RIDGING
ESSOINS	FEALING	FLUENTS	GARRETS	GIRDLED
OSSEINS	FINAGLE	NESTFUL	GARTERS	GLIDDER
SESSION	LEAFING	NETFULS	GRATERS	GRIDDLE
ESTRAYS	FEIRIER	FLUSTER	GARVIES	GIRNELS
STAYERS	FIERIER	FLUTERS	GRAVIES	LINGERS
STAYRES	REIFIER	RESTFUL	RIVAGES	SLINGER
ESTREAT	FELSITE	FOETORS	GASPIER	GLAIRIN
RESTATE	LEFTIES	FOOTERS	PRISAGE	LAIRING
RETASTE	LIEFEST	REFOOTS	SPAIRGE	RAILING
ESTRINS	FELTERS	FOOTIES	GASTING	GLOBINS
INSERTS	REFLETS	FOOTSIE	GATINGS	GOBLINS
SINTERS	TELFERS	OOFIEST	STAGING	LOBINGS

GLORIED	GUERDON	HEEDERS	IGNITER	INTAKES
GODLIER	UNDERGO	HEREDES	TIERING	KENTIAS
GOLDIER	UNGORED	SHEERED	TIGRINE	TANKIES
GNOMISH	GUILERS	HEGARIS	IMMURES	INTERIM
HOMINGS	LIGURES	HEGIRAS	MUMSIER	MINTIER
MOSHING	LURGIES	HIRAGES	RUMMIES	TERMINI
GOGLETS	GUNTERS	HELIUMS	IMPETUS	INTONER
LOGGETS	GURNETS	HUMLIES	IMPUTES	NOINTER
TOGGLES	SURGENT	MUHLIES	UPTIMES	TERNION
GOITERS	GUSTFUL	HENRIES	IMPOSER	INURING
GOITRES	GUTFULS	INHERES	PROMISE	RUINING
GORIEST	GUTSFUL	RESHINE	SEMIPRO	URINING
GOONIES	HAIRNET	HEROONS	INCHERS	IRATELY
ISOGONE	INEARTH	ONSHORE	NICHERS	REALITY
NOOGIES	THERIAN	SOREHON	RICHENS	TEARILY
GORPING	HALSING	HEWINGS	INCISAL	IRENICS
GROPING	LASHING	SHEWING	SALICIN	SERICIN
PORGING	SHALING	WHINGES	SINICAL	SIRENIC
GOSTERS	HAMMALS	HIDDERS	INGINES	ISMATIC
GROSETS	MAHMALS	REDDISH	INSIGNE	ITACISM
STORGES	MASHLAM	SHIDDER	SEINING	SIMATIC
GRASPED	HAPTENE	HINDERS	INGROUP	ISOMERS
SPADGER	HEPTANE	NERDISH	POURING	MOISERS
SPARGED	PHENATE	SHRINED	ROUPING	MOSSIER
GRAYEST	HAPTICS	HOLIDAY	INKLESS	ISONOME
GYRATES	PATHICS	HYALOID	KINLESS	MOONIES
STAGERY	SPATHIC	HYOIDAL	SILKENS	NOISOME
GREENER	HARPERS	HOMERIC	INKLING	ISOTRON
REGREEN	PHRASER	MOCHIER	KILNING	NITROSO
RENEGER	SHARPER	MORICHE	LINKING	TORSION
GREISLY	HASLETS	HOTPOTS	INKPADS	KAROROS
GRIESLY	HATLESS	HOTSPOT	KIDNAPS	KARROOS
GRISELY	SHELTAS	POTSHOT	SKIDPAN	KORORAS
GREMLIN	HASTENS	HUNTERS	INLACES	KARTERS
MERLING	SNATHES	SHUNTER	SANICLE	KRATERS
MINGLER	SNEATHS	UNHERST	SCALENI	STARKER
GRINGAS	HAWSERS	HURTING	INROADS	KASHRUT
RAGINGS	SWASHER	UNGIRTH	ORDAINS	KHURTAS
SIRGANG	WASHERS	UNRIGHT	SADIRON	TUSHKAR
GRIPMEN	HAWSING	HUSTLES	INSCULP	KELTERS
IMPREGN	SHAWING	LUSHEST	SCULPIN	KESTREL
PERMING	WASHING	SLEUTHS	UNCLIPS	SKELTER
GRUELED	HEARERS	ICKLEST	INSTARS	KILTERS
GUELDER	REHEARS	STICKLE	SANTIRS	KIRTLES
REGLUED	SHEARER	TICKLES	STRAINS	KLISTER

KINDERS	LENDERS	LIPREAD	LUSTIER	MASTING
KINREDS	RELENDS	PEDRAIL	RULIEST	MATINGS
REDSKIN	SLENDER	PREDIAL	RUTILES	TAMINGS
KISTING	LENTILS	LISTEES	LUSTING	MEDLING
KITINGS	LINTELS	TELESIS	LUTINGS	MELDING
SKITING	TELLINS	TIELESS	SINGULT	MINGLED
KITTELS	LEOPARD	LISTETH	LUSTRED	MEETERS
KITTLES	PAROLED	LITHEST	RUSTLED	REMEETS
SKITTLE	PRELOAD	THISTLE	STRUDEL	TEEMERS
KREESES	LEPTINS	LITERAL	MAILERS	MELOIDS
RESEEKS	PINTLES	TALLIER	REALISM	MIDSOLE
SEEKERS	PLENIST	TRIELLA	REMAILS	SMOILED
LADDERS	LIBRATE	LOADERS	MALATES	MENTORS
RADDLES	TABLIER	ORDEALS	MALTASE	MONSTER
SADDLER	TRIABLE	RELOADS	TAMALES	MONTRES
LAIRAGE	LICENSE	LOANERS	MALISON	MERANTI
RAILAGE	SELENIC	ORLEANS	MONIALS	MINARET
REGALIA	SILENCE	RELOANS	SOMNIAL	RAIMENT
LAMENTS	LICKERS	LOMENTA	MANATUS	MERCHES
MANTELS	RICKLES	OMENTAL	MANTUAS	SCHEMER
MANTLES	SLICKER	TELAMON	TAMANUS	SCHMEER
LAMITER	LIMINGS	LORISES	MANITUS	MESSILY
MALTIER	SLIMING	LOSSIER	SANTIMU	MILSEYS
MARLITE	SMILING	RISSOLE	TSUNAMI	SMILEYS
LAPPERS	LIMOSES	LOTUSES	MANURES	MILADIS
RAPPELS	LISSOME	SOLUTES	MURENAS	MISDIAL
SLAPPER	SMOILES	TOUSLES	SURNAME	MISLAID
LAPSING	LINGOTS	LOUDENS	MAPPERS	MILREIS
PALINGS	TIGLONS	NODULES	PAMPERS	SLIMIER
SAPLING	TOLINGS	NOUSLED	PREAMPS	SMILIER
LATENTS	LINGUAS	LOUDEST	MARACAS	MINTAGE
LATTENS	NILGAUS	OULDEST	MARASCA	TEAMING
TALENTS	SALUING	TOUSLED	MASCARA	TEGMINA
LAUNDER	LINKERS	LOUNDER	MAREROS	MIOTICS
LURDANE	RELINKS	ROUNDEL	REMORAS	MISTICO
RUNDALE	SLINKER	ROUNDLE	ROAMERS	SOMITIC
LEAPING	LINKUPS	LOURIES	MASCLES	MIRIEST
PEALING	SKULPIN	LOUSIER	MESCALS	MISTIER
PLEAING	UPLINKS	SOILURE	SCAMELS	RIMIEST
LEASING	LINTERS	LOUVERS	MASTERY	MISDIET
LINAGES	SLINTER	LOUVRES	MAYSTER	MISEDIT
SEALING	SNIRTLE	VELOURS	STREAMY	STIMIED
LEISTER	LIPPERS	LUCARNE	MASTICS	MISLIES
RETILES	RIPPLES	NUCLEAR	MISACTS	MISSILE
STERILE	SLIPPER	UNCLEAR	MISCAST	SIMILES

MISMATE	NESTING	OERSTED	PAPERER	PENSION
SEMIMAT	SENTING	ROSETED	PREPARE	PINONES
TAMMIES	TENSING	TEREDOS	REPAPER	SPINONE
MISUSER	NESTLER	OILLETS	PARISON	PERICON
MUSSIER	RELENTS	STELLIO	PORINAS	PONCIER
SURMISE	SLENTER	TOLLIES	SOPRANI	PORCINE
MONTURE	NESTORS	OPERANT	PARKEES	PERIGON
MOUNTER	STONERS	PRONATE	RESPEAK	PIROGEN
REMOUNT	TENSORS	PROTEAN	SPEAKER	PONGIER
MOOTEST	NETTERS	OPPOSER	PARKERS	PERIQUE
MOTTOES	TENTERS	POOPERS	REPARKS	REEQUIP
TOOMEST	TESTERN	PROPOSE	SPARKER	REPIQUE
MOPIEST	NEWSIER	OPTIONS	PARTING	PERNODS
OPTIMES	WEINERS	POSITON	PRATING	PONDERS
STOMPIE	WIENERS	POTIONS	TRAPING	RESPOND
MOTHERS	NICKELS	ORIGINS	PARTLET	PERSING
SMOTHER	NICKLES	SIGNIOR	PLATTER	PINGERS
THERMOS	SLICKEN	SIGNORI	PRATTLE	SPRINGE
MOTIEST	NIDGETS	ORPINES	PARTONS	PERTEST
MOTTIES	STEDING	PIONERS	PATRONS	PETTERS
TITMOSE	STINGED	PROINES	TARPONS	PRETEST
MUNSTER	NIDINGS	OSTENTS	PARULIS	PHYTONS
MUNTERS	SINDING	STETSON	SPIRULA	PYTHONS
STERNUM	SNIDING	TESTONS	UPRISAL	TYPHONS
MUREINS	NITRITE	OSTLERS	PASCUAL	PICKERS
MURINES	NITTIER	STEROLS	PAUCALS	RIPECKS
NEURISM	TINTIER	TORSELS	SCAPULA	SPICKER
MUTISMS	NOOSERS	OUTDARE	PASTERS	PIERROT
SUMMIST	SEROONS	OUTREAD	REPASTS	PORTIER
SUMMITS	SOONERS	READOUT	SPAREST	PRERIOT
NAGARIS	NOSIEST	OUTSERT	PATTERS	PIGSKIN
SANGRIA	SONTIES	STOUTER	SPATTER	PIKINGS
SARANGI	STONIES	TOUTERS	TAPSTER	SPIKING
NAIVEST	NUPTIAL	PAINTER	PEARLIN	PINIEST
NATIVES	PATULIN	PERTAIN	PLAINER	PINITES
VAINEST	UNPLAIT	REPAINT	PRALINE	TIEPINS
NEEDERS	NUTSIER	PALASES	PEASING	PINNETS
SERENED	TRIUNES	PASELAS	SPAEING	SPINNET
SNEERED	UNITERS	PLAASES	SPINAGE	TENPINS
NEPETAS	OATIEST	PANDIES	PEELERS	PINTOES
PENATES	OSTIATE	PANSIED	SLEEPER	POINTES
PESANTE	TOASTIE	SPAINED	SPEELER	PONTIES
NEPHRIC	OBSERVE	PANTLER	PENSILS	PISHERS
PHRENIC	OBVERSE	PLANTER	SPINELS	RESHIPS
PINCHER	VERBOSE	REPLANT	SPLINES	SERIPHS

PISTONS	PRESELL	RASHEST	RESPLIT	RHETORS
POSTINS	RESPELL	SHASTER	SPIRTLE	ROTHERS
SPINTOS	SPELLER	TRASHES	TRIPLES	SHORTER
PITTERS	PRESSER	RATTANS	RESTOCK	RICKETS
SPITTER	REPRESS	TANTRAS	ROCKETS	STICKER
TIPSTER	SPERRES	TARTANS	STOCKER	TICKERS
PLANATE	PRISING	RATTERS	RESTUFF	RINGLET
PLANTAE	RISPING	RESTART	STUFFER	TINGLER
PLATANE	SPIRING	STARTER	TRUFFES	TRINGLE
PLANTAS	PROYNES	RATTIER	RESTUMP	RIOTERS
PLATANS	PYONERS	RETRAIT	STUMPER	ROISTER
SALTPAN	PYRONES	TARTIER	SUMPTER	RORIEST
PLESSOR	PRUDENT	REBATER	RETEARS	RIPPLET
SLOPERS	PRUNTED	TABRERE	SERRATE	TIPPLER
SPLORES	UPTREND	TEREBRA	TEARERS	TRIPPLE
POOREST	PRUINES	RECURES	RETIRAL	RISQUES
POOTERS	PURINES	RESCUER	RETRIAL	SQUIERS
STOOPER	UPRISEN	SECURER	TRAILER	SQUIRES
POPSTER	PRYINGS	REDCAPS	RETIRED	RONDURE
STOPPER	PRYSING	SCARPED	RETRIED	ROUNDER
TOPPERS	SPRINGY	SCRAPED	TIREDER	UNORDER
POSEURS	PUDSIER	REDNESS	RETRAIN	ROOSTER
SEROPUS	SIRUPED	RESENDS	TERRAIN	ROOTERS
SOUPERS	UPDRIES	SENDERS	TRAINER	TOREROS
POSTMAN	PULIEST	REDOUND	RETRATE	ROTTENS
TAMPONS	PUTELIS	ROUNDED	RETREAT	SNOTTER
TOPSMAN	STIPULE	UNDERDO	TREATER	STENTOR
POTHERS	PULSATE	REEVING	RETWIST	ROWDIER
STROPHE	PUTEALS	REGIVEN	TWISTER	WORDIER
THORPES	SPATULE	VEERING	WITTERS	WORRIED
POTTERS	PUSLEYS	RENTERS	REUSING	RUCKLES
PROTEST	PUSSLEY	RERENTS	RUEINGS	SCULKER
SPOTTER	SPULYES	STERNER	SIGNEUR	SUCKLER
POTTIES	PUSSIER	RENTING	REVISIT	RUMPIES
SPOTTIE	SUSPIRE	RINGENT	STIVIER	SPUMIER
TIPTOES	UPRISES	TERNING	VISITER	UMPIRES
POULDER	QUAREST	RERISES	REVUIST	RUSSETS
POULDRE	QUARTES	SERRIES	STUIVER	TRUSSES
PROULED	QUATRES	SIRREES	VIRTUES	TUSSERS
PRAYERS	RANDIES	RESEAUS	REWARMS	RUTTERS
RESPRAY	SANDIER	SEASURE	SWARMER	TRUSTER
SPRAYER	SARDINE	UREASES	WARMERS	TURRETS
PREASED	RANKEST	RESIFTS	REWEARS	SACHEMS
RESPADE	STARKEN	SIFTERS	SWEARER	SAMECHS
SPEARED	TANKERS	STRIFES	WEARERS	SCHEMAS

SALIVAS	SHREIKS	STERNED	SUNNIER	UNHEALS
SALVIAS	SHRIEKS	TENDERS	UNREINS	UNLEASH
VASSAIL	SHRIKES	TENDRES	UNRISEN	UNSHALE
SALLETS	SHUTING	STEWARD	SWATHER	UNIPEDS
STELLAS	TUSHING	STRAWED	THAWERS	UNSPIDE
TASSELL	UNSIGHT	WRASTED	WREATHS	UNSPIED
SALVETE	SISTRUM	STEWING	SWELTER	VERSUTE
VALETES	TRISMUS	TWINGES	WELTERS	VERTUES
VELETAS	TRUISMS	WESTING	WRESTLE	VESTURE
SALVING	SITELLA	STORMER	SWIPING	WARLESS
SLAVING	TAILLES	TERMORS	WIPINGS	WARSLES
VALSING	TALLIES	TREMORS	WISPING	WRASSLE
SEAGULL	SKIRRET	STOTTER	SWITHER	WARSTLE
SULLAGE	SKIRTER	STRETTO	WITHERS	WASTREL
ULLAGES	STRIKER	TOTTERS	WRITHES	WRASTLE
SEEDLIP	SNOTTIE	STOWING	TAIVERS	WEATHER
SPEILED	TONIEST	TOWINGS	VASTIER	WHEREAT
SPIELED	TONITES	TOWSING	VERITAS	WREATHE
SEINERS	SONNETS	STRETTA	TEWHITS	WENDIGO
SEREINS	STONNES	TARTEST	WETTISH	WIDGEON
SERINES	TENSONS	TATTERS	WHITEST	WONGIED
SENDUPS	SPARTHE	STRETTI	THAIRMS	WHERRIT
SUSPEND	TEPHRAS	TITTERS	THIRAMS	WHIRRET
UPSENDS	THREAPS	TRITEST	THRIMSA	WRITHER
SERVANT	SPELDIN	STRINGY	THEATER	
TAVERNS	SPINDLE	STYRING	THEATRE	
VERSANT	SPLINED	TRYINGS	THEREAT	
SETWALL	SPROUTS	SUNBELT	TRAVELS	
SWALLET	STROUPS	UNBELTS	VARLETS	
WALLETS	STUPORS	UNBLEST	VESTRAL	

Quadruplets

ABSEILS	ACTURES	AIRSHED	ALLERGY	AMBLING
BALISES	CAUTERS	DASHIER	GALLERY	BALMING
ISABELS	CRUSTAE	HARDIES	LARGELY	BLAMING
LABISES	CURATES	SHADIER	REGALLY	LAMBING
ABUSERS	ADEPTER	AIRSIDE	ALMAINS	AMOSITE
BUSERAS	PREDATE	DAIRIES	ANIMALS	ATOMIES
RUBASSE	RETAPED	DIARIES	LAMINAS	ATOMISE
SURBASE	TAPERED	DIARISE	MANILAS	OSMIATE
ACMITES	AGAINST	ALERTER	ALPINES	ANELING
ETACISM	AGITANS	ALTERER	PINEALS	EANLING
MICATES	ANTISAG	REALTER	SPANIEL	LEANING
SEMATIC	GITANAS	RELATER	SPLENIA	NEALING
ACRASIN	AIMLESS	ALGESIS	ALTERNE	ANGELUS
ARNICAS	MESAILS	GLASSIE	ENTERAL	LAGUNES
CARINAS	SAMIELS	LIGASES	ETERNAL	LANGUES
SARCINA	SEISMAL	SILAGES	TELERAN	LEGUANS

ANGRILY	ASHIEST	BARDIER	CAPITOL	CERIPHS
NARGILY	SAITHES	BRAIDER	COALPIT	CIPHERS
RANGILY	STASHIE	BRIARED	OPTICAL	RECHIPS
RAYLING	TAISHES	RABIDER	TOPICAL	SPHERIC
APLITES	ASHLERS	BASTERS	CAPSULE	CESTUIS
PALIEST	HALSERS	BESTARS	SCALEUP	CUEISTS
PLATIES	LASHERS	BRASSET	SPECULA	CUTISES
TALIPES	SLASHER	BREASTS	UPSCALE	ICTUSES
APRICOT	ASHLESS	BECHARM	CARDIES	CHEAPOS
APROTIC	HASSELS	BRECHAM	DARCIES	EPOCHAS
PAROTIC	HASSLES	CHAMBER	RADICES	POACHES
PATRICO	SLASHES	CHAMBRE	SIDECAR	SHOEPAC
APRONED	ASPIRED	BEMOILS	CAREENS	CINDERS
OPERAND	DESPAIR	EMBOILS	CASERNE	DISCERN
PADRONE	DIAPERS	MOBILES	ENRACES	NERDICS
PANDORE	PRAISED	OBELISM	RECANES	RESCIND
ARBORED	ASTERTS	BLUSTER	CARLESS	CIRROSE
BOARDER	STARETS	BUSTLER	CLASSER	CORRIES
BROADER	STATERS	BUTLERS	SCALERS	CROSIER
REBOARD	TASTERS	SUBTLER	SCLERAS	ORRICES
ARCKING	ATOMICS	BURBLES	CAROLUS	CISTRON
CARKING	MATICOS	LUBBERS	OCULARS	CITRONS
CRAKING	OSMATIC	RUBBLES	OSCULAR	CORNIST
RACKING	SOMATIC	SLUBBER	RUCOLAS	CORTINS
ARCSINE	ATONERS	CALLERS	CARPETS	CITADEL
ARSENIC	SANTERO	CELLARS	PREACTS	DELTAIC
CARNIES	SENATOR	RECALLS	PRECAST	DIALECT
CERASIN	TREASON	SCLERAL	SPECTRA	EDICTAL
ARMLETS	ATRESIC	CALMIER	CARVIES	CITRINE
LAMSTER	CRISTAE	CLAIMER	CAVIERS	CRINITE
MARTELS	RACIEST	MIRACLE	VARICES	INCITER
TRAMELS	STEARIC	RECLAIM	VISCERA	NERITIC
ARTISTS	AWNIEST	CALORIE	CASSENE	CLEANSE
SITTARS	TAWNIES	CARIOLE	ENCASES	ELANCES
STRAITS	WANIEST	COALIER	SEANCES	ENLACES
TSARIST	WANTIES	LORICAE	SENECAS	SCALENE
ARTSIER	BAITERS	CAMERAL	CATERER	CLEARED
SERRATI	BARITES	CARAMEL	RECRATE	CREEDAL
TARRIES	REBAITS	CERAMAL	RETRACE	DECLARE
TARSIER	TERBIAS	MACERAL	TERRACE	RELACED
ARTSMEN	BALMIER	CANTLES	CENSERS	CLIENTS
MARTENS	LAMBIER	CENTALS	SCERNES	LECTINS
SARMENT	MIRABLE	LANCETS	SCREENS	LENTISC
SMARTEN	REMBLAI	SCANTLE	SECERNS	STENCIL
ASCRIBE	BANTIES	CANTORS	CERATES	CLOSEUP
CABRIES	BASINET	CARTONS	CREATES	COUPLES
CARBIES	BESAINT	CONTRAS	ECARTES	OPUSCLE
CARIBES	BESTAIN	CRATONS	SECRETA	UPCLOSE

COLORED	DANGLES	DEVISOR	EMPARTS	ERRINGS
CROODLE	GLANDES	DEVOIRS	RESTAMP	GIRNERS
CROOLED	LAGENDS	VISORED	STAMPER	RINGERS
DECOLOR	SLANGED	VOIDERS	TAMPERS	SERRING
COLTERS	DAUNTER	DINGLES	ENDUROS	ESLOINS
CORSLET	NATURED	ELDINGS	RESOUND	INSOLES
COSTREL	UNRATED	ENGILDS	SOUNDER	LESIONS
LECTORS	UNTREAD	SINGLED	UNDOERS	LIONESS
COPINGS	DEAFEST	DIOPTER	ENFIRES	ESTOVER
COPSING	DEFASTE	DIOPTRE	FEERINS	OVERSET
PICONGS	DEFEATS	PERIDOT	FINEERS	REVOTES
SCOPING	FEASTED	PROTEID	REFINES	VETOERS
CORNUTE	DEANERY	DISTOME	ENGINES	EVILEST
COUNTER	RENAYED	DOMIEST	GENNIES	LEVITES
RECOUNT	YEAREND	MODISTE	NEESING	LIEVEST
TROUNCE	YEARNED	MOISTED	SNEEING	VELITES
CREESED	DEFILER	DOATERS	ENIGMAS	FAUNIST
DECREES	FERLIED	ROASTED	GAMINES	FIAUNTS
RECEDES	FIELDER	TORSADE	MEASING	FUSTIAN
SECEDER	REFILED	TROADES	SEAMING	INFAUST
CRESSET	DEFINER	DONATOR	ENLISTS	FEERING
RESECTS	ENFIRED	ODORANT	LISTENS	FEIGNER
SCREETS	FENDIER	TANDOOR	SILENTS	FREEING
SECRETS	REFINED	TORNADO	TINSELS	REEFING
CROSSER	DELAPSE	DOUBTER	ENTERER	FERLIES
RECROSS	ELAPSED	OBTRUDE	REENTER	REFILES
SCORERS	PLEASED	OUTBRED	TERREEN	REFLIES
SCORSER	SEPALED	REDOUBT	TERRENE	RELIEFS
CUITERS	DELIVER	DRAWERS	ENTRISM	FILTERS
CURIETS	LIVERED	REDRAWS	MINSTER	LIFTERS
CURITES	RELIVED	REWARDS	MINTERS	STIFLER
ICTERUS	REVILED	WARDERS	REMINTS	TRIFLES
CUNDIES	DERAILS	DURAMEN	ENTRIST	FINDERS
INCUDES	DIALERS	MANURED	RETINTS	FRIENDS
INCUSED	REDIALS	MAUNDER	STINTER	REDFINS
INDUCES	SIDERAL	UNARMED	TINTERS	REFINDS
CUSTODE	DERIDER	EARNEST	ERETHIC	FLOWERS
DOUCEST	REDDIER	EASTERN	ETHERIC	FOWLERS
DOUCETS	REDRIED	NEAREST	HERETIC	REFLOWS
SCOUTED	RIDERED	RATEENS	TECHIER	WOLFERS
DALLIES	DERIDES	EARTHLY	ERINGOS	FRISEUR
DISLEAL	DESIRED	HARTELY	IGNORES	FRISURE
LALDIES	DIEDRES	HEARTLY	REGIONS	FURRIES
SALLIED	RESIDED	LATHERY	SIGNORE	SURFIER
DAMNERS	DERIVES	EMPARLS	EROTISM	GAGSTER
MANREDS	DEVISER	LAMPERS	MOISTER	GARGETS
RANDEMS	DIVERSE	PALMERS	MORTISE	STAGGER
REMANDS	REVISED	SAMPLER	TRISOME	TAGGERS

GAROTES	GRISONS	IMPRESS	LATESTS	LUMBERS
ORGEATS	INGROSS	PREMISS	SALTEST	RUMBLES
STORAGE	SIGNORS	SIMPERS	STALEST	SLUMBER
TOERAGS	SORINGS	SPIREMS	TASLETS	UMBRELS
GATEMAN	GUNSHOT	INANEST	LEGLINS	LUNIEST
MAGENTA	HOGNUTS	NANITES	LINGELS	LUTEINS
MAGNATE	NOUGHTS	STANINE	LINGLES	UNTILES
NAMETAG	SHOTGUN	TANNIES	SELLING	UTENSIL
GELDERS	HASPING	INCEPTS	LENITES	LURDENS
LEDGERS	PASHING	INSPECT	LISENTE	NURDLES
REDLEGS	PHASING	PECTINS	SETLINE	NURSLED
SLEDGER	SHAPING	PEINCTS	TENSILE	RUNDLES
GENTIER	HATTERS	INERTER	LEPROUS	MACHERS
INTEGER	RATHEST	REINTER	PELORUS	MARCHES
TEERING	SHATTER	RENTIER	PERLOUS	MESARCH
TREEING	THREATS	TERRINE	SPORULE	SCHMEAR
GEOMANT	HAUNTER	INGRESS	LIMPERS	MADRONA
MAGNETO	UNEARTH	RESIGNS	PRELIMS	MANDORA
MEGATON	UNHEART	SIGNERS	RIMPLES	MONARDA
MONTAGE	URETHAN	SINGERS	SIMPLER	ROADMAN
GINGERS	HEAPERS	INSEEMS	LINEUPS	MAELIDS
NIGGERS	RESHAPE	MISSEEN	LUPINES	MEDIALS
SERGING	SPHAERE	NEMESIS	SPINULE	MISDEAL
SNIGGER	SPHEARE	SIEMENS	UNPILES	MISLEAD
GINGLES	HEPSTER	INSPIRE	LISPING	MAINTOP
LEGGINS	PETHERS	PIRNIES	PILINGS	PTOMAIN
NIGGLES	SPERTHE	SNIPIER	SLIPING	TAMPION
SNIGGLE	THREEPS	SPINIER	SPILING	TIMPANO
GIRKINS	HERIOTS	IONISER	LISTING	MANDIOC
GRISKIN	HOISTER	IRONIES	SILTING	MONACID
KRISING	SHORTIE	IRONISE	STILING	MONADIC
RISKING	TOSHIER	NOISIER	TILINGS	NOMADIC
GISARME	HISTING	ISLEMAN	LOOPERS	MANLIER
IMAGERS	INSIGHT	MALINES	POOLERS	MARLINE
MAIGRES	SHITING	MENIALS	RESPOOL	MINERAL
MIRAGES	SITHING	SEMINAL	SPOOLER	RAILMEN
GLURGES	HORNETS	LAMMERS	LOOTERS	MARINES
GURGLES	SHORTEN	RAMMELS	RETOOLS	REMAINS
LUGGERS	THRENOS	RAMMLES	ROOTLES	SEMINAR
SLUGGER	THRONES	SLAMMER	TOOLERS	SIRNAME
GNASHER	IGNAROS	LASCARS	LOTTERS	MEDRESA
HANGERS	ORIGANS	RASCALS	SETTLOR	REMADES
REHANGS	SIGNORA	SACRALS	SLOTTER	REMEADS
SHERANG	SOARING	SCALARS	TOLTERS	SMEARED
GRANTEE	IMPALER	LASSOER	LOWINGS	MELTERS
GREATEN	IMPEARL	OARLESS	LOWSING	REMELTS
NEGATER	LEMPIRA	SEROSAL	SLOWING	RESMELT
REAGENT	PALMIER	SOLERAS	SOWLING	SMELTER

MERISES	OOLITES	PASSIVE	PETRALE	REKNOTS
MESSIER	OSTIOLE	PAVISES	PLEATER	STONKER
MISERES	STOOLIE	PAVISSE	PRELATE	STROKEN
REMISES	TOOLIES	SPAVIES	REPLATE	TONKERS
MESTINO	OORIEST	PASTIES	PIECERS	REMATES
MOISTEN	ROOTIES	PATSIES	PIERCES	RETEAMS
MONTIES	SOOTIER	PETSAIS	PRECISE	STEAMER
SENTIMO	TOORIES	TAPISES	RECIPES	TEAMERS
MINUTED	OPENEST	PASTINA	PLUSING	RESERVE
MUNITED	PENTOSE	PATINAS	PULINGS	REVERES
MUTINED	POSTEEN	PINATAS	PULSING	REVERSE
UNTIMED	POTEENS	TAIPANS	PUSLING	SEVERER
MINUTER	ORALIST	PASTURE	POINTEL	RESEWED
MUNTRIE	RIALTOS	UPRATES	PONTILE	SEWERED
UNMITER	SLIOTAR	UPSTARE	POTLINE	SWEERED
UNMITRE	TAILORS	UPTEARS	TOPLINE	WEEDERS
MISTING	ORNISES	PEARLED	PREDIES	RESORTS
SMITING	SENIORS	PEDALER	PRESIDE	ROSTERS
STIMING	SONERIS	PLEADER	SPEIRED	SORTERS
TIMINGS	SONSIER	REPLEAD	SPIERED	STORERS
MOLDERS	OURIEST	PEARTLY	PROIGNS	RETORTS
REMOLDS	STOURIE	PEYTRAL	PROSING	ROTTERS
SLORMED	TOURIES	PRELATY	ROPINGS	STERTOR
SMOLDER	TOUSIER	PTERYLA	SPORING	TORRETS
NAPPERS	OUSTING	PELMETS	PULPERS	REVESTS
PARPENS	OUTINGS	STEMPEL	PURPLES	STERVES
PARSNEP	OUTSING	STEMPLE	REPULPS	VERSETS
SNAPPER	TOUSING	TEMPLES	SUPPLER	VERSTES
NESTERS	OUTGRIN	PELTERS	PURISTS	RILLETS
RENESTS	OUTRING	PETRELS	SPRUITS	STILLER
RESENTS	ROUTING	RESPELT	UPRISTS	TILLERS
STRENES	TOURING	SPELTER	UPSTIRS	TRELLIS
NEURITE	PANTIES	PENSTER	QUESTOR	ROSTING
RETINUE	PATINES	PRESENT	QUOTERS	SORTING
REUNITE	SAPIENT	REPENTS	ROQUETS	STORING
UTERINE	SPINATE	SERPENT	TORQUES	TRIGONS
NEUTERS	PARINGS	PERDUES	REIVERS	RUINATE
RETUNES	PARSING	PERSUED	REVERSI	TAURINE
TENURES	RASPING	PERUSED	REVISER	URANITE
TUREENS	SPARING	SUPERED	RIEVERS	URINATE
NORTHED	PARTANS	PERRIES	REKNITS	SALVERS
THONDER	SPARTAN	PRISERE	SKINTER	SERVALS
THORNED	TARPANS	REPRISE	STINKER	SLAVERS
THRONED	TRAPANS	RESPIRE	TINKERS	VERSALS

SKATERS	STAWING	SYSTOLE
STRAKES	TAWINGS	TOLSEYS
STREAKS	TAWSING	TOYLESS
TASKERS	WASTING	TYLOSES

SKATING	STIVERS	WAISTER
STAKING	STRIVES	WAITERS
TAKINGS	TREVISS	WARIEST
TASKING	VERISTS	WASTRIE

Quintuplets

ABORTUS	ALECOST	ANGRIER	ASPIRES	BRUNETS
OUTBARS	LACTOSE	EARRING	PARESIS	BUNTERS
ROBUSTA	LOCATES	GRAINER	PARISES	BURNETS
RUBATOS	SCATOLE	RANGIER	PRAISES	BURSTEN
TABOURS	TALCOSE	REARING	SPIREAS	SUBRENT

ADHERES	ALERCES	ANOSMIC	ASTELIC	CALIVER
HEADERS	CEREALS	CAMIONS	ELASTIC	CAVILER
HEARSED	RELACES	CONIMAS	LACIEST	CLAVIER
HEDERAS	RESCALE	MANIOCS	LATICES	VALERIC
SHEARED	SCLERAE	MASONIC	SALICET	VELARIC

ADMIRES	ALERTED	ANTLERS	ATINGLE	CARTELS
MARDIES	ALTERED	RENTALS	ELATING	CLARETS
MISREAD	REDEALT	SALTERN	GELATIN	CRESTAL
SEDARIM	RELATED	SLANTER	GENITAL	SCARLET
SIDEARM	TREADLE	STERNAL	TAGLINE	TARCELS

AGILEST	ALNAGES	ARCHEST	ATTUNES	CATERED
AIGLETS	ANLAGES	CHARETS	NUTATES	CEDRATE
GELATIS	GALENAS	CHASTER	TAUTENS	CERATED
LIGATES	LAGENAS	RACHETS	TETANUS	CREATED
TAIGLES	LASAGNE	RATCHES	UNSTATE	REACTED

AGINNER	AMBLERS	ARCINGS	BATLETS	CENSUAL
EARNING	BLAMERS	CARINGS	BATTELS	LACUNES
ENGRAIN	LAMBERS	RACINGS	BATTLES	LAUNCES
GRANNIE	MARBLES	SACRING	BLATEST	UNLACES
NEARING	RAMBLES	SCARING	TABLETS	UNSCALE

AIRINGS	ANGERED	ARCUSES	BERATED	CERUSES
ARISING	DERANGE	CAUSERS	BETREAD	CESURES
RAGINIS	ENRAGED	CESURAS	DEBATER	RECUSES
RAISING	GRANDEE	SAUCERS	REBATED	RESCUES
SAIRING	GRENADE	SUCRASE	TABERED	SECURES

AIRLESS	ANGLERS	ARSIEST	BESTIRS	CHEEROS
RESAILS	ERLANGS	ARTSIES	BISTERS	CHOREES
SAILERS	LANGERS	SAIREST	BISTRES	COHERES
SERAILS	LARGENS	SATIRES	BITSERS	ECHOERS
SERIALS	SLANGER	TIRASSE	BREISTS	RECHOSE

ALBERTS	ANGLIST	ARTLESS	BOASTER	CLUSTER
BATLERS	LASTING	LASTERS	BOATERS	CULTERS
BLASTER	SALTING	SALTERS	BORATES	CUSTREL
LABRETS	SLATING	SLATERS	REBATOS	CUTLERS
STABLER	STALING	TARSELS	SORBATE	RELUCTS

CONSTER	DREEING	ESPIALS	LETTERS	POSIEST
CORNETS	ENERGID	LAIPSES	LETTRES	POSTIES
CRESTON	GREINED	LAPISES	SETTLER	POTSIES
CRETONS	REEDING	LIPASES	STERLET	SEPIOST
CRONETS	REIGNED	PALSIES	TRESTLE	SOPITES
COURSES	EARLESS	GASTRIN	LEVIERS	RACKETS
SCOURSE	LEASERS	GRATINS	RELIVES	RESTACK
SCOUSER	RESALES	RATINGS	REVILES	RETACKS
SOURCES	RESEALS	STARING	SERVILE	STACKER
SUCROSE	SEALERS	TARINGS	VEILERS	TACKERS
DAEMONS	ELATERS	GERMAIN	LOGIONS	RATTLES
MASONED	REALEST	GERMINA	LOOSING	SLATTER
MODENAS	RELATES	MANGIER	OLINGOS	STARLET
MONADES	RESLATE	MEARING	SOLOING	STARTLE
NOMADES	STEALER	REAMING	SOOLING	TATLERS
DARTERS	ELOIGNS	GLISTEN	MARSHES	RECUSED
DARTRES	LEGIONS	LESTING	MASHERS	REDUCES
RETARDS	LIGNOSE	SINGLET	SHAMERS	RESCUED
STARRED	LINGOES	SNIGLET	SHMEARS	SECURED
TRADERS	LONGIES	TINGLES	SMASHER	SEDUCER
DEMAINS	ENISLES	GRANITE	MINUETS	RESTIVE
MAIDENS	ENSILES	GRATINE	MINUTES	SIEVERT
MEDIANS	SENILES	INGRATE	MISTUNE	STIEVER
MEDINAS	SENSILE	TANGIER	MUNITES	VERIEST
SIDEMAN	SILENES	TEARING	MUTINES	VERITES
DEMERIT	ENTASES	HALTERS	OPENERS	RETESTS
DIMETER	SATEENS	HARSLET	PEREONS	SETTERS
MERITED	SENATES	LATHERS	PERONES	STREETS
MITERED	SENSATE	SLATHER	REOPENS	TERSEST
RETIMED	STEANES	THALERS	REPONES	TESTERS
DEMERSE	ENVIERS	HOOTERS	PARLEYS	RETOURS
EMERSED	INVERSE	RESHOOT	PARSLEY	ROUSTER
MEDRESE	VEINERS	SHEROOT	PLAYERS	ROUTERS
REDEEMS	VENIRES	SHOOTER	REPLAYS	TOURERS
REMEDES	VERSINE	SOOTHER	SPARELY	TROUSER
DERRIES	ERODING	INTRUDE	PARSERS	SOWTERS
DESIRER	GROINED	TURDINE	RASPERS	STOWERS
REDRIES	IGNORED	UNTIRED	SPARERS	STOWRES
RESIDER	NEGROID	UNTRIDE	SPARRES	TOWSERS
SERRIED	REDOING	UNTRIED	SPARSER	WORSETS
DIESTER	ESCAPER	LAVEERS	POINTER	
DIETERS	PEARCES	LEAVERS	PROTEIN	
REEDITS	PERCASE	REVEALS	PTERION	
REISTED	PREACES	SEVERAL	REPOINT	
RESITED	RESPACE	VEALERS	TROPINE	
DREARES	ESCARPS	LEAPERS	PORTERS	
READERS	PARSECS	PLEASER	PRESORT	
REDEARS	SCRAPES	PRESALE	PRETORS	
REDSEAR	SECPARS	RELAPSE	REPORTS	
REREADS	SPACERS	REPEALS	SPORTER	

Sextuplets

ABIDERS	CANOERS	DESPOIL	ETAMINS	NORITES
BARDIES	CARNOSE	DIPLOES	INMATES	OESTRIN
BRAISED	COARSEN	DIPOLES	MAINEST	ORIENTS
DARBIES	CORNEAS	PELOIDS	MANTIES	STONIER
SEABIRD	EARCONS	SOLIPED	TAMEINS	TERSION
SIDEBAR	NARCOSE	SPOILED	TAMINES	TRIONES
AMENDER	CHEATER	DETOURS	ETRIERS	PALTERS
ENARMED	HECTARE	DOUREST	REITERS	PERSALT
MEANDER	RECHATE	DOUTERS	RESTIER	PLASTER
REAMEND	RECHEAT	OUTREDS	RETIRES	PLATERS
REEDMAN	RETEACH	REDOUTS	RETRIES	PSALTER
RENAMED	TEACHER	ROUSTED	TERRIES	STAPLER
ASPERSE	CLAROES	DINEROS	HECTORS	PERIOST
PARESES	COALERS	DONSIER	ROCHETS	PORIEST
PRAESES	ESCOLAR	INDORSE	ROTCHES	PROSTIE
PREASES	ORACLES	ORDINES	TOCHERS	REPOSIT
PREASSE	RECOALS	ROSINED	TORCHES	RIPOSTE
SERAPES	SOLACER	SORDINE	TROCHES	ROPIEST
ASPIRER	CORSETS	EAGLETS	INTREAT	PHRASES
PARRIES	COSTERS	GELATES	ITERANT	SERAPHS
PRAISER	ESCORTS	LEGATES	NATTIER	SHAPERS
RAPIERS	SCOTERS	SEGETAL	NITRATE	SHERPAS
RASPIER	SCROTES	TEAGLES	TARTINE	SPHAERS
REPAIRS	SECTORS	TELEGAS	TERTIAN	SPHEARS
ASTEISM	DARNELS	ENTASIS	LITTERS	PORTESS
MISEATS	ENLARDS	NASTIES	SLITTER	POSTERS
MISSEAT	LANDERS	SEITANS	STILTER	PRESTOS
SAMIEST	RELANDS	SESTINA	TESTRIL	REPOSTS
SAMITES	SLANDER	TANSIES	TILTERS	RESPOTS
TAMISES	SNARLED	TISANES	TITLERS	STOPERS
BALDIER	DEARTHS	ENTIRES	LUSTERS	REALIST
BEDRAIL	HARDEST	ENTRIES	LUSTRES	RETAILS
BLADIER	HARDSET	NERITES	RESULTS	SALTIER
BRAILED	HATREDS	RETINES	RUSTLES	SALTIRE
RAILBED	THREADS	TRENISE	SUTLERS	SLATIER
RIDABLE	TRASHED	TRIENES	ULSTERS	TAILERS
CAMELID	DEPOSIT	ENTRAIL	MEISTER	RECEPTS
CLAIMED	DOPIEST	LATRINE	METIERS	RESPECT
DECIMAL	PODITES	RATLINE	REEMITS	SCEPTER
DECLAIM	POSITED	RELIANT	RETIMES	SCEPTRE
MALICED	SOPITED	RETINAL	TREMIES	SPECTER
MEDICAL	TOPSIDE	TRENAIL	TRISEME	SPECTRE

Septuplets

ALIGNER	ARPENTS	CARPELS	EDITORS	PETROUS
ENGRAIL	ENTRAPS	CLASPER	ROISTED	POSTURE
LAERING	PANTERS	CRAPLES	ROSITED	POUTERS
LEARING	PARENTS	PARCELS	SORTIED	PROTEUS
NARGILE	PASTERN	PLACERS	STEROID	SEPTUOR
REALIGN	PERSANT	RECLASP	STORIED	SPOUTER
REGINAL	TREPANS	SCALPER	TRIODES	TROUPES
ALIPEDS	CANTERS	COINERS	GILDERS	
ELAPIDS	CARNETS	CRINOSE	GIRDLES	
LAIPSED	NECTARS	CRONIES	GLIDERS	
LAPIDES	RECANTS	ORCEINS	GRISLED	
PAIDLES	SCANTER	ORCINES	LIDGERS	
PALSIED	TANRECS	RECOINS	REGILDS	
PLEIADS	TRANCES	SERICON	RIDGELS	
AREDING	CANTIER	DESTAIN	IMARETS	
DEARING	CERATIN	DETAINS	MAESTRI	
DERAIGN	CERTAIN	INSTEAD	MAISTER	
EARDING	CREATIN	NIDATES	MASTIER	
GRADINE	CRINATE	SAINTED	MISRATE	
GRAINED	NACRITE	SATINED	SEMITAR	
READING	TACRINE	STAINED	SMARTIE	

Octuplets

ABLEIST	ARTIEST	EASTERS	PAIREST
ALBITES	ARTISTE	RESEATS	PARTIES
ASTILBE	ATTIRES	SAETERS	PASTIER
BASTILE	IRATEST	SEAREST	PIASTER
BESTIAL	RATITES	SEATERS	PIASTRE
BLASTIE	STRIATE	STEARES	PIRATES
LIBATES	TASTIER	TEASERS	PRATIES
STABILE	TERTIAS	TESSERA	TRAIPSE
AGISTER	DEAREST	EMPIRES	ROESTIS
AIGRETS	DERATES	EMPRISE	ROSIEST
GAITERS	ESTRADE	EPIMERS	SIROSET
SEAGIRT	REASTED	IMPRESE	SORITES
STAGIER	REDATES	PERMIES	SORTIES
STRIGAE	SEDATER	PREMIES	STORIES
TIRAGES	STEARED	PREMISE	TOSSIER
TRIAGES	TASERED	SPIREME	TRIOSES

Nontuplets

ARIDEST	EASTLIN	ESPRITS	ESTROUS
ASTERID	ELASTIN	PERSIST	OESTRUS
ASTRIDE	ENTAILS	PRIESTS	OUSTERS
DIASTER	NAILSET	SITREPS	SOUREST
DISRATE	SALIENT	SPRIEST	SOUTERS
STAIDER	SALTINE	SPRITES	STOURES
STAIRED	SLAINTE	STIRPES	TOUSERS
TARDIES	STANIEL	STRIPES	TROUSES
TIRADES	TENAILS	TRIPSES	TUSSORE

Decuplets

ANGRIES
EARINGS
ERASING
GAINERS
GRAINES
REAGINS
REGAINS
REGINAS
SEARING
SERINGA

Undecuplets

ANESTRI	EASTING
ANTSIER	EATINGS
NASTIER	GAINEST
RATINES	GENISTA
RESIANT	INGATES
RETAINS	INGESTA
RETINAS	SEATING
RETSINA	TAGINES
STAINER	TANGIES
STARNIE	TEASING
STEARIN	TSIGANE

CHAPTER 7
VARIANTS

One of the confusing things about the English language is the number of variant spellings that exist. But to a Scrabble player, variant spellings can be a great opportunity. If you know that a word can end in -EY as well as -Y, for example, then you have an extra possibility for playing it, maybe using up a surplus E. American spellings are one great source of variants – think of all the -RE words that are spelt -ER in the US, for example. But there are also many other variations, which you will find in the list below. This list contains most of the common variant spellings in English; the words are listed in alphabetical order. Excluded from this section are the most obvious set of variants - verbs that end in -IZE or -ISE. There are simply far too many of these to include; instead, you will find a list of all the verbs ending in -ISE that *don't* have a variant ending in -IZE where you might expect them to, and vice versa.

-ABLE/-IBLE

ADDABLE – ADDIBLE	GULLABLE – GULLIBLE	RINSABLE – RINSIBLE
EDUCABLE – EDUCIBLE	LAPSABLE – LAPSIBLE	VENDABLE – VENDIBLE
ERODABLE – ERODIBLE	MIXABLE – MIXIBLE	
EVADABLE – EVADIBLE	PASSABLE – PASSIBLE	

-AE/-E

ACHAENIA – ACHENIA	ANAPAEST – ANAPEST	DAEMONIC – DEMONIC
AEDILE – EDILE	APOGAEIC – APOGEIC	DAEMONS – DEMONS
AEDILES – EDILES	ARCHAEAN – ARCHEAN	DRACAENA – DRACENA
AEGIS – EGIS	ARCHAEI – ARCHEI	EPIGAEAL – EPIGEAL
AEGISES – EGISES	ARCHAEUS – ARCHEUS	EPIGAEAN – EPIGEAN
AEMULE – EMULE	AREOLAE – AREOLE	EUDAEMON – EUDEMON
AEMULED – EMULED	CAECA – CECA	FAECAL – FECAL
AEMULES – EMULES	CAECAL – CECAL	FAECES – FECES
AEMULING – EMULING	CAECALLY – CECALLY	FRAENA – FRENA
AEOLIAN – EOLIAN	CAECITIS – CECITIS	FRAENUM – FRENUM
AEON – EON	CAECUM – CECUM	FRAENUMS – FRENUMS
AEONIAN – EONIAN	CAERULE – CERULE	GASTRAEA – GASTREA
AEONS – EONS	CAESIOUS – CESIOUS	GLUTAEAL – GLUTEAL
AERUGO – ERUGO	CAESIUM – CESIUM	GLUTAEI – GLUTEI
AERUGOS – ERUGOS	CAESIUMS – CESIUMS	GLUTAEUS – GLUTEUS
AESTHETE – ESTHETE	CAESTUS – CESTUS	GRAECISE – GRECISE
AESTIVAL – ESTIVAL	CAESURA – CESURA	GRAECIZE – GRECIZE
AETHER – ETHER	CAESURAE – CESURAE	GYNAECIA – GYNECIA
AETHERIC – ETHERIC	CAESURAL – CESURAL	HAEMAL – HEMAL
AETHERS – ETHERS	CAESURAS – CESURAS	HAEMATAL – HEMATAL
AGAPAE – AGAPE	CESURAE – CESURE	HAEMATIC – HEMATIC
ALTHAEA – ALTHEA	CHIMAERA – CHIMERA	HAEMATIN – HEMATIN
ALTHAEAS – ALTHEAS	COAEVAL – COEVAL	HAEMIC – HEMIC
ANAEMIA – ANEMIA	COAEVALS – COEVALS	HAEMIN – HEMIN
ANAEMIAS – ANEMIAS	DAEDAL – DEDAL	HAEMINS – HEMINS
ANAEMIC – ANEMIC	DAEMON – DEMON	HAEMOID – HEMOID

HAEREDES - HEREDES	PAEON - PEON	SAECULUM - SECULUM
HAERES - HERES	PAEONIES - PEONIES	SPELAEAN - SPELEAN
HYAENA - HYENA	PAEONS - PEONS	SPHAERE - SPHERE
HYAENAS - HYENAS	PAEONY - PEONY	SPHAERES - SPHERES
HYAENIC - HYENIC	PERAEA - PEREA	SPIRAEA - SPIREA
HYPOGAEA - HYPOGEA	PERAEON - PEREON	SPIRAEAS - SPIREAS
KANAES - KANES	PERAEONS - PEREONS	TAEDIUM - TEDIUM
LAERED - LERED	PIGMAEAN - PIGMEAN	TAEDIUMS - TEDIUMS
LAERING - LERING	PINNULAE - PINNULE	TAENIA - TENIA
LAEVO - LEVO	PORAES - PORES	TAENIAE - TENIAE
LAEVULIN - LEVULIN	PRAECIPE - PRECIPE	TAENIAS - TENIAS
LERNAEAN - LERNEAN	PRAEDIAL - PREDIAL	TAENIOID - TENIOID
LIPAEMIA - LIPEMIA	PRAEFECT - PREFECT	TOXAEMIA - TOXEMIA
MAENAD - MENAD	PRAELECT - PRELECT	TOXAEMIC - TOXEMIC
MAENADS - MENADS	PRAESES - PRESES	URAEMIA - UREMIA
MAERL - MERL	PRAETOR - PRETOR	URAEMIAS - UREMIAS
MAERLS - MERLS	PRAETORS - PRETORS	URAEMIC - UREMIC
MURAENA - MURENA	PYAEMIA - PYEMIA	VALVULAE - VALVULE
MURAENAS - MURENAS	PYAEMIAS - PYEMIAS	VIRAEMIA - VIREMIA
NAEVE - NEVE	PYAEMIC - PYEMIC	VIRAEMIC - VIREMIC
NAEVES - NEVES	PYGMAEAN - PYGMEAN	ZOAEA - ZOEA
NAEVI - NEVI	QUAESTOR - QUESTOR	ZOAEAE - ZOEAE
NAEVOID - NEVOID	RAPHAE - RAPHE	ZOAEAS - ZOEAS
NAEVUS - NEVUS	READEDIFY - REEDIFY	
OLPAE - OLPE	RHAPHAE - RHAPHE	

-EI/-IE

BEIN - BIEN	LEIGER - LIEGER	SCREICH - SCRIECH
BREI - BRIE	LEIGERS - LIEGERS	SCREICHS - SCRIECHS
BREIS - BRIES	LEIR - LIER	SHEILING - SHIELING
CEIL - CIEL	LEIRS - LIERS	SHREIK - SHRIEK
CEILED - CIELED	MEIN - MIEN	SHREIKED - SHRIEKED
CEILING - CIELING	MEINS - MIENS	SHREIKS - SHRIEKS
CEILINGS - CIELINGS	NEIF - NIEF	SKREIGH - SKRIEGH
CEILS - CIELS	NEIFS - NIEFS	SKREIGHS - SKRIEGHS
DEIL - DIEL	NEIVE - NIEVE	SPEIL - SPIEL
DREIGH - DRIEGH	NEIVES - NIEVES	SPEILED - SPIELED
FEINT - FIENT	OMNEITY - OMNIETY	SPEILING - SPIELING
FEINTS - FIENTS	POLEIS - POLIES	SPEILS - SPIELS
FEIRIER - FIERIER	PREIF - PRIEF	SPEIR - SPIER
FEIRIEST - FIERIEST	PREIFE - PRIEFE	SPEIRED - SPIERED
FEIST - FIEST	PREIFES - PRIEFES	SPEIRING - SPIERING
GREISLY - GRIESLY	PREIFS - PRIEFS	SPEIRS - SPIERS
HEID - HIED	REIVE - RIEVE	VLEIS - VLIES
KEIR - KIER	REIVER - RIEVER	WEIL - WIEL
KEIRS - KIERS	REIVERS - RIEVERS	WEILS - WIELS
KEISTER - KIESTER	REIVES - RIEVES	WEINER - WIENER
KEISTERS - KIESTERS	REIVING - RIEVING	WEINERS - WIENERS

EN-/IN-

ENACTION - INACTION	ENARMED - INARMED	ENCAGING - INCAGING
ENACTIVE - INACTIVE	ENARMING - INARMING	ENCASE - INCASE
ENARCH - INARCH	ENARMS - INARMS	ENCASED - INCASED
ENARCHED - INARCHED	ENCAGE - INCAGE	ENCASES - INCASES
ENARCHES - INARCHES	ENCAGED - INCAGED	ENCASING - INCASING
ENARM - INARM	ENCAGES - INCAGES	ENCAVE - INCAVE

ENCAVED - INCAVED	ENFORCED - INFORCED	ENSOULED - INSOULED
ENCAVES - INCAVES	ENFORCES - INFORCES	ENSOULS - INSOULS
ENCAVING - INCAVING	ENFORM - INFORM	ENSPHERE - INSPHERE
ENCHASE - INCHASE	ENFORMED - INFORMED	ENSURE - INSURE
ENCHASED - INCHASED	ENFORMS - INFORMS	ENSURED - INSURED
ENCHASES - INCHASES	ENGINE - INGINE	ENSURER - INSURER
ENCLASP - INCLASP	ENGINES - INGINES	ENSURERS - INSURERS
ENCLASPS - INCLASPS	ENGLOBE - INGLOBE	ENSURES - INSURES
ENCLOSE - INCLOSE	ENGLOBED - INGLOBED	ENSURING - INSURING
ENCLOSED - INCLOSED	ENGLOBES - INGLOBES	ENSWATHE - INSWATHE
ENCLOSER - INCLOSER	ENGRAFT - INGRAFT	ENSWEPT - INSWEPT
ENCLOSES - INCLOSES	ENGRAFTS - INGRAFTS	ENTENDER - INTENDER
ENCREASE - INCREASE	ENGRAIN - INGRAIN	ENTERS - INTERS
ENCRUST - INCRUST	ENGRAINS - INGRAINS	ENTHRAL - INTHRAL
ENCRUSTS - INCRUSTS	ENGRAM - INGRAM	ENTHRALL - INTHRALL
ENCUMBER - INCUMBER	ENGROOVE - INGROOVE	ENTHRALS - INTHRALS
ENDART - INDART	ENGROSS - INGROSS	ENTHRONE - INTHRONE
ENDARTED - INDARTED	ENGULF - INGULF	ENTIRE - INTIRE
ENDARTS - INDARTS	ENGULFED - INGULFED	ENTITLE - INTITLE
ENDEW - INDEW	ENGULFS - INGULFS	ENTITLED - INTITLED
ENDEWED - INDEWED	ENGULPH - INGULPH	ENTITLES - INTITLES
ENDEWING - INDEWING	ENGULPHS - INGULPHS	ENTOMB - INTOMB
ENDEWS - INDEWS	ENHEARSE - INHEARSE	ENTOMBED - INTOMBED
ENDITE - INDITE	ENISLE - INISLE	ENTOMBS - INTOMBS
ENDITED - INDITED	ENISLED - INISLED	ENTRANT - INTRANT
ENDITES - INDITES	ENISLES - INISLES	ENTRANTS - INTRANTS
ENDITING - INDITING	ENISLING - INISLING	ENTREAT - INTREAT
ENDORSE - INDORSE	ENLACE - INLACE	ENTREATS - INTREATS
ENDORSED - INDORSED	ENLACED - INLACED	ENTRENCH - INTRENCH
ENDORSEE - INDORSEE	ENLACES - INLACES	ENTROLD - INTROLD
ENDORSER - INDORSER	ENLACING - INLACING	ENTRUST - INTRUST
ENDORSES - INDORSES	ENLOCK - INLOCK	ENTRUSTS - INTRUSTS
ENDORSOR - INDORSOR	ENLOCKED - INLOCKED	ENTWINE - INTWINE
ENDOW - INDOW	ENLOCKS - INLOCKS	ENTWINED - INTWINED
ENDOWED - INDOWED	ENMESH - INMESH	ENTWINES - INTWINES
ENDOWING - INDOWING	ENMESHED - INMESHED	ENTWIST - INTWIST
ENDOWS - INDOWS	ENMESHES - INMESHES	ENTWISTS - INTWISTS
ENDUE - INDUE	ENNAGE - INNAGE	ENURE - INURE
ENDUED - INDUED	ENNAGES - INNAGES	ENURED - INURED
ENDUES - INDUES	ENQUIRE - INQUIRE	ENURES - INURES
ENDUING - INDUING	ENQUIRED - INQUIRED	ENURING - INURING
ENFANT - INFANT	ENQUIRER - INQUIRER	ENURN - INURN
ENFANTS - INFANTS	ENQUIRES - INQUIRES	ENURNED - INURNED
ENFEOFF - INFEOFF	ENQUIRY - INQUIRY	ENURNING - INURNING
ENFEOFFS - INFEOFFS	ENSCONCE - INSCONCE	ENURNS - INURNS
ENFESTED - INFESTED	ENSCROLL - INSCROLL	ENVEIGLE - INVEIGLE
ENFIX - INFIX	ENSEAM - INSEAM	ENVIABLE - INVIABLE
ENFIXED - INFIXED	ENSEAMED - INSEAMED	ENVIABLY - INVIABLY
ENFIXES - INFIXES	ENSEAMS - INSEAMS	ENVIOUS - INVIOUS
ENFIXING - INFIXING	ENSHEATH - INSHEATH	ENWALL - INWALL
ENFLAME - INFLAME	ENSHELL - INSHELL	ENWALLED - INWALLED
ENFLAMED - INFLAMED	ENSHELLS - INSHELLS	ENWALLS - INWALLS
ENFLAMES - INFLAMES	ENSHRINE - INSHRINE	ENWIND - INWIND
ENFOLD - INFOLD	ENSNARE - INSNARE	ENWINDS - INWINDS
ENFOLDED - INFOLDED	ENSNARED - INSNARED	ENWOUND - INWOUND
ENFOLDER - INFOLDER	ENSNARER - INSNARER	ENWRAP - INWRAP
ENFOLDS - INFOLDS	ENSNARES - INSNARES	ENWRAPS - INWRAPS
ENFORCE - INFORCE	ENSOUL - INSOUL	

-ER/-OR

ABATER - ABATOR	EFFECTER - EFFECTOR	PROMOTER - PROMOTOR
ABETTER - ABETTOR	ENDORSER - ENDORSOR	PROVIDER - PROVIDOR
ACCEPTER - ACCEPTOR	ERECTER - ERECTOR	QUESTER - QUESTOR
ADAPTER - ADAPTOR	EXACTER - EXACTOR	QUITTER - QUITTOR
ADJURER - ADJUROR	EXCITER - EXCITOR	RAZER - RAZOR
ADJUSTER - ADJUSTOR	EXECUTER - EXECUTOR	REALTER - REALTOR
ADVISER - ADVISOR	EXPANDER - EXPANDOR	REGRATER - REGRATOR
AGISTER - AGISTOR	FEOFFER - FEOFFOR	REJECTER - REJECTOR
ALIENER - ALIENOR	GIMMER - GIMMOR	RELATER - RELATOR
ANIMATER - ANIMATOR	GRANTER - GRANTOR	RELEASER - RELEASOR
ARMER - ARMOR	HUMIDER - HUMIDOR	REMITTER - REMITTOR
ARRESTER - ARRESTOR	IDOLATER - IDOLATOR	RESISTER - RESISTOR
ASPERSER - ASPERSOR	IGNITER - IGNITOR	RETAILER - RETAILOR
ASSENTER - ASSENTOR	IMPACTER - IMPACTOR	REVISER - REVISOR
ASSERTER - ASSERTOR	IMPEDER - IMPEDOR	REVIVER - REVIVOR
ASSIGNER - ASSIGNOR	IMPELLER - IMPELLOR	RIZZER - RIZZOR
ASSISTER - ASSISTOR	IMPOSTER - IMPOSTOR	SAILER - SAILOR
ASSURER - ASSUROR	INCENSER - INCENSOR	SALVER - SALVOR
ATTESTER - ATTESTOR	INDENTER - INDENTOR	SECRETER - SECRETOR
BAILER - BAILOR	INDICTER - INDICTOR	SEISER - SEISOR
BARRATER - BARRATOR	INDORSER - INDORSOR	SEIZER - SEIZOR
BETTER - BETTOR	INFECTER - INFECTOR	SETTLER - SETTLOR
BEVER - BEVOR	INFLATER - INFLATOR	STATER - STATOR
BITTER - BITTOR	INVENTER - INVENTOR	STRIDER - STRIDOR
CANTER - CANTOR	INVERTER - INVERTOR	SUITER - SUITOR
CASTER - CASTOR	JAILER - JAILOR	SURVIVER - SURVIVOR
CENSER - CENSOR	KRONER - KRONOR	TABER - TABOR
CHANTER - CHANTOR	LESSER - LESSOR	TAILER - TAILOR
CLANGER - CLANGOR	LICENSER - LICENSOR	TAXER - TAXOR
XCONDER - CONDOR	LOCATER - LOCATOR	TENSER - TENSOR
CONJURER - CONJUROR	NARRATER - NARRATOR	TERMER - TERMOR
CONVENER - CONVENOR	NEGATER - NEGATOR	THRUSTER - THRUSTOR
CONVEYER - CONVEYOR	NESTER - NESTOR	TRIER - TRIOR
CURSER - CURSOR	OBLIGER - OBLIGOR	TRUSTER - TRUSTOR
DEFLATER - DEFLATOR	OFFERER - OFFEROR	TUSSER - TUSSOR
DEPICTER - DEPICTOR	OUTDOER - OUTDOOR	TWISTER - TWISTOR
DETECTER - DETECTOR	PARADER - PARADOR	VENDER - VENDOR
DEVISER - DEVISOR	PAWNER - PAWNOR	VERDERER - VERDEROR
DIFFUSER - DIFFUSOR	PAYER - PAYOR	VIOLATER - VIOLATOR
DIGESTER - DIGESTOR	PLEDGER - PLEDGEOR	VISITER - VISITOR
DILATER - DILATOR	- PLEDGOR	WELDER - WELDOR
DILUTER - DILUTOR	PRESSER - PRESSOR	
DIRECTER - DIRECTOR	PROMISER - PROMISOR	

-EY/-IE/-Y

AERIE - AERY	BAILEY - BAILIE	BIGGIE - BIGGY
AGLY - AGLEY	BARBIE - BARBY	BILLIE - BILLY
ALKIE - ALKY	BARDIE - BARDY	BITTIE - BITTY
ALLY - ALLEY	BARMIE - BARMY	BLASTIE - BLASTY
ANOMIE - ANOMY	BARNY - BARNEY	BLIMY - BLIMEY
APPLY - APPLEY	BARRIE - BARRY	BLOCKIE - BLOCKY
ARSY - ARSEY	BATTERIE - BATTERY	BLOOEY - BLOOIE
AUNTIE - AUNTY	BAWTIE - BAWTY	BLOWIE - BLOWY
AWMRIE - AWMRY	BEANIE - BEANY	BLUDIE - BLUDY
BADDIE - BADDY	BEARDIE - BEARDY	BOGEY - BOGIE -
BAGGIE - BAGGY	BHEESTIE - BHEESTY	BOGY

BOLSHIE - BOLSHY
BONEY - BONIE - BONY
BONNIE - BONNY
BOOBIE - BOOBY
BOODIE - BOODY
BOOGEY - BOOGIE - BOOGY
BOOKIE - BOOKY
BOOKSIE - BOOKSY
BOOTIE - BOOTY
BOOZY - BOOZEY
BOTHIE - BOTHY
BOWSEY - BOWSIE
BRASSIE - BRASSY
BRAWLIE - BRAWLY
BRICKIE - BRICKY
BROWNIE - BROWNY
BUFTY - BUFTIE
BUNGEY - BUNGIE - BUNGY
BUNJIE - BUNJY
BUPPIE - BUPPY
BURLY - BURLEY
BUSHIE - BUSHY
CABBAGY - CABBAGEY
CABBIE - CABBY
CADDIE - CADDY
CAGY - CAGEY
CAKY - CAKEY
CALORIE - CALORY
CANDIE - CANDY
CANNIE - CANNY
CARDIE - CARDY
CARNEY - CARNIE - CARNY
CATTIE - CATTY
CAVIE - CAVY
CERTY - CERTIE
CHALLIE - CHALLY
CHANCY - CHANCEY
CHANTEY - CHANTIE - CHANTY
CHAPPIE - CHAPPY
CHARLEY - CHARLIE
CHEAPIE - CHEAPY
CHEWIE - CHEWY
CHIMBLY - CHIMBLEY
CHINKIE - CHINKY
CHIPPIE - CHIPPY
CHOKY - CHOKEY
CHOOSY - CHOOSEY
CHRISTIE - CHRISTY
CHUCKIE - CHUCKY
CIGGIE - CIGGY
CLIQUY - CLIQUEY
COLLIE - COLLY
COLY - COLEY
COMMIE - COMMY
CONCHIE - CONCHY
CONY - CONEY

COOKEY - COOKIE - COOKY
COOLIE - COOLY
COONTIE - COONTY
CORBIE - CORBY
CORY - COREY
COSEY - COSIE - COSY
COUTHIE - COUTHY
COWRIE - COWRY
COZEY - COZIE - COZY
CRAPPIE - CRAPPY
CREEPIE - CREEPY
CREPY - CREPEY
CRICKY - CRICKEY
CROPPIE - CROPPY
CROWDIE - CROWDY
CRUMMIE - CRUMMY
CRUNCHIE - CRUNCHY
CRUSIE - CRUSY
CUDDIE - CUDDY
CURNY - CURNEY
CURRIE - CURRY
CURTSY - CURTSEY
CURVY - CURVEY
CUSHIE - CUSHY
CUTESIE - CUTESY
CUTEY - CUTIE
DANCY - DANCEY
DARKEY - DARKIE - DARKY
DEARIE - DEARY
DEAWIE - DEAWY
DEXIE - DEXY
DICKEY - DICKIE - DICKY
DIDDLY - DIDDLEY
DIDIE - DIDY
DINGY - DINGEY
DINKEY - DINKIE - DINKY
DIXIE - DIXY
DOBBIE - DOBBY
DOBIE - DOBY
DOGEY - DOGIE - DOGY
DOGGIE - DOGGY
DONSIE - DONSY
DOOBREY - DOOBRIE
DOOLIE - DOOLY
DOOZIE - DOOZY
DOPY - DOPEY
DORMIE - DORMY
DOVEKEY - DOVEKIE
DOXIE - DOXY
DOYLY - DOYLEY
DRAPPIE - DRAPPY
DRUGGIE - DRUGGY
DUCKIE - DUCKY
DUDDIE - DUDDY
DURRIE - DURRY
EATERIE - EATERY

EERIE - EERY
EYRIE - EYRY
FAERIE - FAERY
FANTASIE - FANTASY
FARCIE - FARCY
FERLIE - FERLY
FIDDLY - FIDDLEY
FLAKY - FLAKEY
FLANNY - FLANNIE
FLATTIE - FLATTY
FLEECIE - FLEECY
FLOOEY - FLOOIE
FLOOSIE - FLOOSY
FLOOZIE - FLOOZY
FLOSSIE - FLOSSY
FLUKY - FLUKEY
FLUNKEY - FLUNKIE - FLUNKY
FLUTY - FLUTEY
FOGEY - FOGIE - FOGY
FOLEY - FOLIE
FOLKIE - FOLKY
FOODIE - FOODY
FOOTIE - FOOTY
FOOTSIE - FOOTSY
FOXIE - FOXY
FROWIE - FROWY
FUNDIE - FUNDY
GALLY - GALLEY
GAMY - GAMEY
GARBAGY - GARBAGEY
GARVEY - GARVIE
GAUCIE - GAUCY
GAWSIE - GAWSY
GILLIE - GILLY
GILPY - GILPEY
GINGELY - GINGELEY
GIRLIE - GIRLY
GLASSIE - GLASSY
GOODIE - GOODY
GOOLEY - GOOLIE - GOOLY
GOONEY - GOONIE - GOONY
GOORIE - GOORY
GOOSY - GOOSEY
GRANNIE - GRANNY
GRAPY - GRAPEY
GREENIE - GREENY
GREMMIE - GREMMY
GRIESIE - GRIESY
GRIPY - GRIPEY
GROUPIE - GROUPY
GRUMPHIE - GRUMPHY
GRUNGY - GRUNGEY
GULLY - GULLEY
GUSSIE - GUSSY
GUSTIE - GUSTY
GYNIE - GYNY
GYNNY - GYNNEY

GYPPIE - GYPPY
HANKIE - HANKY
HAWKEY - HAWKIE
HEMPIE - HEMPY
HICKEY - HICKIE
HIPPIE - HIPPY
HOAGIE - HOAGY
HOLY - HOLEY
HOMEY - HOMIE - HOMY
HONKEY - HONKIE - HONKY
HOODIE - HOODY
HOOKY - HOOKEY
HOOLEY - HOOLIE - HOOLY
HORSY - HORSEY
HOTTIE - HOTTY
HOWDIE - HOWDY
HUNKEY - HUNKIE - HUNKY
HURLY - HURLEY
INCONIE - INCONY
JACKSIE - JACKSY
JARVEY - JARVIE
JASY - JASEY
JAUNTIE - JAUNTY
JAXIE - JAXY
JEELIE - JEELY
JIMMIE - JIMMY
JIVY - JIVEY
JOHNNIE - JOHNNY
JOKY - JOKEY
JOLLY - JOLLEY
JUMBIE - JUMBY
JUNKIE - JUNKY
KARSY - KARSEY
KELPIE - KELPY
KELTIE - KELTY
KIDDIE - KIDDY
KILTIE - KILTY
KINDIE - KINDY
KOOKIE - KOOKY
LACY - LACEY
LALDIE - LALDY
LAMBIE - LAMBY
LAMMIE - LAMMY
LEFTIE - LEFTY
LEZZIE - LEZZY
LIMPSY - LIMPSEY
LIMY - LIMEY
LINNY - LINNEY
LINTIE - LINTY
LINY - LINEY
LIPPIE - LIPPY
LOGGIE - LOGGY
LOGIE - LOGY
LOOEY - LOOIE
LOONEY - LOONIE - LOONY

LOUNGY - LOUNGEY
LOURIE - LOURY
LOWRIE - LOWRY
LUCKIE - LUCKY
LUVVIE - LUVVY
MALARKY - MALARKEY
MAMEY - MAMIE
MAMMEY - MAMMIE - MAMMY
MANGABY - MANGABEY
MANGY - MANGEY
MASHIE - MASHY
MATY - MATEY
MAZY - MAZEY
MEALIE - MEALY
MEANIE - MEANY
MEINEY - MEINIE - MEINY
MICKY - MICKEY
MIDDIE - MIDDY
MIDGIE - MIDGY
MIMSY - MIMSEY
MINNIE - MINNY
MOBBIE - MOBBY
MOBIE - MOBY - MOBEY
MOCHIE - MOCHY
MOGGIE - MOGGY
MOLLIE - MOLLY
MONEY - MONIE - MONY
MOOLY - MOOLEY
MOPY - MOPEY
MOSSIE - MOSSY
MOUSEY - MOUSIE - MOUSY
MURRY - MURREY
MUSKIE - MUSKY
NANNIE - NANNY
NAPPIE - NAPPY
NELLIE - NELLY
NETTIE - NETTY
NEWSIE - NEWSY
NIGHTIE - NIGHTY
NIRLIE - NIRLY
NITERIE - NITERY
NIXIE - NIXY
NOOKIE - NOOKY
NOSHERIE - NOSHERY
NOSY - NOSEY
OBSEQUIE - OBSEQUY
OCHRY - OCHREY
OFFY - OFFIE
OLDIE - OLDY
ONIE - ONY
ORANGY - ORANGEY
ORGANDIE - ORGANDY
OVERLIE - OVERLY
PACY - PACEY
PALMIE - PALMY
PANTIE - PANTY
PARDIE - PARDY

PARKIE - PARKY
PARLY - PARLEY
PASTIE - PASTY
PATTIE - PATTY
PEAVY - PEAVEY
PEERIE - PEERY
PERDIE - PERDY
PERENTIE - PERENTY
PHONY - PHONEY
PIGGIE - PIGGY
PIGSNEY - PIGSNIE - PIGSNY
PINKEY - PINKIE - PINKY
PINNIE - PINNY
PINY - PINEY
PIONY - PIONEY
PIXIE - PIXY
PLAGUY - PLAGUEY
PLISKIE - PLISKY
PLOOKIE - PLOOKY
PLOTTIE - PLOTTY
PLOUKIE - PLOUKY
PLUMPIE - PLUMPY
PODDIE - PODDY
POGY - POGEY
POKEY - POKIE - POKY
POLLICIE - POLLICY
POLONIE - POLONY
POLY - POLEY
POMMIE - POMMY
PONCY - PONCEY
PONTIE - PONTY
PONY - PONEY
POPSIE - POPSY
PORGIE - PORGY
POSY - POSEY
POTSIE - POTSY
POWNEY - POWNIE - POWNY
PRATIE - PRATY
PREMIE - PREMY
PREPPIE - PREPPY
PRICY - PRICEY
PUDSY - PUDSEY
PUGGIE - PUGGY
PUKY - PUKEY
PUMIE - PUMY
PUNKEY - PUNKIE - PUNKY
PURPIE - PURPY
PUSSLY - PUSSLEY
PUTTIE - PUTTY
QUEENIE - QUEENY
QUICKY - QUICKIE
RANDIE - RANDY
REALLIE - REALLY
REALTIE - REALTY
REECHIE - REECHY
REEKIE - REEKY

RELIE - RELY
RENY - RENEY
REVERIE - REVERY
RHODIE - RHODY
RICY - RICEY
ROARIE - ROARY
ROOFIE - ROOFY
ROOKIE - ROOKY
ROOMIE - ROOMY
ROPY - ROPEY
RORIE - RORY
ROUGHIE - ROUGHY
SALTIE - SALTY
SARNEY - SARNIE
SAVVY - SAVVEY
SCARY - SCAREY
SCROGGIE - SCROGGY
SCRUMMIE - SCRUMMY
SEELIE - SEELY
SHALY - SHALEY
SHANTY - SHANTEY
SHARPIE - SHARPY
SHAWLEY - SHAWLIE
SHEENEY - SHEENIE -
  SHEENY
SHELTIE - SHELTY
SHIMMY - SHIMMEY
SHINNY - SHINNEY
SHORTIE - SHORTY
SILKIE - SILKY
SKELLIE - SKELLY
SKIVIE - SKIVY
SKOLLIE - SKOLLY
SLATY - SLATEY
SMARTIE - SMARTY
SMOKY - SMOKEY
SMOOTHIE - SMOOTHY
SNAKY - SNAKEY
SNOTTIE - SNOTTY
SOAPIE - SOAPY
SOFTIE - SOFTY
SONSIE - SONSY
SPACY - SPACEY
SPAMMIE - SPAMMY
SPARKIE - SPARKY
SPICY - SPICEY
SPIE - SPY
SPIKY - SPIKEY
SPINNY - SPINNEY
SPOONY - SPOONEY
SPOTTIE - SPOTTY
SPUNKIE - SPUNKY

SPURRY - SPURREY
SQUADDIE - SQUADDY
STAGGIE - STAGGY
STAGY - STAGEY
STEAMIE - STEAMY
STEELIE - STEELY
STEY - STIE - STY
STIE - STY - STEY
STIFFIE - STIFFY
STIMIE - STIMY
STOGEY - STOGIE -
  STOGY
STONY - STONEY
STORY - STOREY
STOTTY - STOTTIE
STOURIE - STOURY
STRIPY - STRIPEY
STUBBIE - STUBBY
STY - STEY - STIE
STYMIE - STYMY
SUBBIE - SUBBY
SURFIE - SURFY
SWABBIE - SWABBY
SWADDIE - SWADDY
SWANKEY - SWANKIE -
  SWANKY
SWANNIE - SWANNY
SWEENY - SWEENEY
SWEETIE - SWEETY
SWIFTIE - SWIFTY
TACKY - TACKEY
TALKIE - TALKY
TAMMIE - TAMMY
TANGIE - TANGY
TATTIE - TATTY
TAWNY - TAWNEY
TECHIE - TECHY
TEDDIE - TEDDY
TENTIE - TENTY
THICKIE - THICKY
THY - THEY
THYMY - THYMEY
TICKY - TICKEY
TIDDLY - TIDDLEY
TINNIE - TINNY
TITTIE - TITTY
TOASTIE - TOASTY
TOLLIE - TOLLY -
  TOLLEY
TONY - TONEY
TOOTSIE - TOOTSY
TOTTIE - TOTTY

TOUGHIE - TOUGHY
TOWIE - TOWY
TOWNIE - TOWNY
TRANNIE - TRANNY
TREY - TRIE - TRY
TRICKIE - TRICKY
TRIPY - TRIPEY
TROELIE - TROELY
TROLLY - TROLLEY
TUSHIE - TUSHY
TWEENIE - TWEENY
TYPY - TYPEY
UMPIE - UMPY
UNSONSIE - UNSONSY
UNWARIE - UNWARY
UPSY - UPSEY
VAUNTIE - VAUNTY
VERRY - VERREY
VISNOMIE - VISNOMY
WADDIE - WADDY
WALLIE - WALLY
WANY - WANEY
WASPIE - WASPY
WASTERIE - WASTERY
WASTRIE - WASTRY
WAVY - WAVEY
WEBBIE - WEBBY
WEDGIE - WEDGY
WEENIE - WEENY
WEEPIE - WEEPY
WEIRDIE - WEIRDY
WELLIE - WELLY
WHEELIE - WHEELY
WHIMSY - WHIMSEY
WHINY - WHINEY
WHISKY - WHISKEY
WHITY - WHITEY
WIDDIE - WIDDY
WIFEY - WIFIE
WILLEY - WILLIE -
  WILLY
WINY - WINEY
WOODIE - WOODY
WOOLIE - WOOLY
WURLEY - WURLIE
YABBIE - YABBY
YAPPIE - YAPPY
YAWY - YAWEY
YIPPIE - YIPPY
YUPPIE - YUPPY

-LL/-L

ALLAY - ALAY	CAROLLED - CAROLED	EMBALLED - EMBALED
ALLAYED - ALAYED	CAROLLER - CAROLER	ENROLL - ENROL
ALLAYING - ALAYING	CARRELL - CARREL	ENROLLS - ENROLS
ALLAYS - ALAYS	CARRELLS - CARRELS	ENTHRALL - ENTHRAL
ALLEE - ALEE	CAVILLED - CAVILED	EQUALLED - EQUALED
ALLEGGE - ALEGGE	CAVILLER - CAVILER	ESCALLOP - ESCALOP
ALLEGGED - ALEGGED	CHALLAH - CHALAH	ESCROLL - ESCROL
ALLEGGES - ALEGGES	CHALLAHS - CHALAHS	ESCROLLS - ESCROLS
ALLERION - ALERION	CHALLAN - CHALAN	EVILLER - EVILER
ALLEYED - ALEYED	CHALLANS - CHALANS	EVILLEST - EVILEST
ALLOD - ALOD	CHALLOT - CHALOT	EXTOLL - EXTOL
ALLODIA - ALODIA	CHALLOTH - CHALOTH	EXTOLLS - EXTOLS
ALLODIAL - ALODIAL	CHILLI - CHILI	FANNELL - FANNEL
ALLODIUM - ALODIUM	CHILLIES - CHILIES	FANNELLS - FANNELS
ALLODS - ALODS	CHILLIS - CHILIS	FAVELL - FAVEL
ALLOW - ALOW	CHOLLA - CHOLA	FAVELLA - FAVELA
ALLURE - ALURE	CHOLLAS - CHOLAS	FAVELLAS - FAVELAS
ALLURES - ALURES	CHOLLERS - CHOLERS	FILLE - FILE
ANVILLED - ANVILED	COLL - COL	FILLES - FILES
APPALL - APPAL	COLLED - COLED	FILLET - FILET
APPALLS - APPALS	COLLIES - COLIES	FILLETED - FILETED
APPERILL - APPERIL	COLLINS - COLINS	FILLETS - FILETS
BAILLIE - BAILIE	COLLS - COLS	FILLIBEG - FILIBEG
BAILLIES - BAILIES	COLLY - COLY	FILLING - FILING
BALLADIN - BALADIN	XCOOLLY - COOLY	FILLINGS - FILINGS
BALLISTA - BALISTA	CROPFULL - CROPFUL	FILLO - FILO
BARBELL - BARBEL	CRUELLER - CRUELER	FILLOS - FILOS
BARBELLS - BARBELS	CRUELLS - CRUELS	FUELLED - FUELED
BASTILLE - BASTILE	CULLET - CULET	FUELLER - FUELER
BEDELL - BEDEL	CULLETS - CULETS	FUELLERS - FUELERS
BEDELLS - BEDELS	CUPELLED - CUPELED	FUELLING - FUELING
BELLYING - BELYING	CUPELLER - CUPELER	FULFILL - FULFIL
BEVELLED - BEVELED	DECALLED - DECALED	FULFILLS - FULFILS
BEVELLER - BEVELER	DEVELLED - DEVELED	FULLNESS - FULNESS
BOERBULL - BOERBUL	DEVILLED - DEVILED	GALLABEA - GALABEA
BOLLIX - BOLIX	DHOLL - DHOL	GALLABIA - GALABIA
BOLLIXED - BOLIXED	DHOLLS - DHOLS	GALLANT - GALANT
BOLLIXES - BOLIXES	DIALLED - DIALED	GALLIOT - GALIOT
BONSELLA - BONSELA	DIALLER - DIALER	GALLIOTS - GALIOTS
BORRELL - BORREL	DIALLERS - DIALERS	GALLIPOT - GALIPOT
BORSTALL - BORSTAL	DIALLING - DIALING	GALLOOT - GALOOT
BOULLE - BOULE	DIALLIST - DIALIST	GALLOOTS - GALOOTS
BOULLES - BOULES	DISTILL - DISTIL	GALLOP - GALOP
BOWELLED - BOWELED	DISTILLS - DISTILS	GALLOPED - GALOPED
BRAILLED - BRAILED	DOWELLED - DOWELED	GALLOPS - GALOPS
BRIMFULL - BRIMFUL	DROLLER - DROLER	GALLUMPH - GALUMPH
BULLBAR - BULBAR	DROLLEST - DROLEST	GAVELLED - GAVELED
BULLGINE - BULGINE	DUELLED - DUELED	GELLANT - GELANT
BULLRUSH - BULRUSH	DUELLER - DUELER	GELLANTS - GELANTS
BURRELL - BURREL	DUELLERS - DUELERS	GILLET - GILET
BURRELLS - BURRELS	DUELLING - DUELING	GILLETS - GILETS
CALLALOO - CALALOO	DUELLIST - DUELIST	GINGALL - GINGAL
CALLID - CALID	DULLNESS - DULNESS	GINGALLS - GINGALS
CALLIPEE - CALIPEE	DULLY - DULY	GINGELLI - GINGELI
CALLIPER - CALIPER	EISELL - EISEL	GINGELLY - GINGELY
CAMELLIA - CAMELIA	EISELLS - EISELS	GINGILLI - GINGILI
CANALLED - CANALED	ELLOPS - ELOPS	GRAVELLY - GRAVELY
CAPELLET - CAPELET	ELLOPSES - ELOPSES	GRUELLED - GRUELED

GRUELLER - GRUELER	MULLING - MULING	SALLETS - SALETS
HALLAL - HALAL	MULMULL - MULMUL	SCULL - SCUL
HALLALS - HALALS	MULMULLS - MULMULS	SCULLS - SCULS
HALLING - HALING	MURALLED - MURALED	SELLE - SELE
HALLOUMI - HALOUMI	MYALL - MYAL	SELLES - SELES
HOVELLED - HOVELED	NALLA - NALA	SEPALLED - SEPALED
IDYLL - IDYL	NALLAS - NALAS	SHALLOT - SHALOT
IDYLLIST - IDYLIST	NELLIES - NELIES	SHALLOTS - SHALOTS
IDYLLS - IDYLS	NEWELL - NEWEL	SIBYLLIC - SIBYLIC
ILLIAD - ILIAD	NEWELLS - NEWELS	SILLER - SILER
ILLIADS - ILIADS	NILL - NIL	SILLERS - SILERS
INSTALL - INSTAL	NILLS - NILS	SKELLUM - SKELUM
INSTALLS - INSTALS	PALLET - PALET	SKELLUMS - SKELUMS
INSTILL - INSTIL	PALLETS - PALETS	SKILLFUL - SKILFUL
INSTILLS - INSTILS	PALLETTE - PALETTE	SOLLAR - SOLAR
INTHRALL - INTHRAL	PANELLED - PANELED	SOLLARS - SOLARS
JEWELLED - JEWELED	PEDALLED - PEDALED	SOLLER - SOLER
JEWELLER - JEWELER	PEDALLER - PEDALER	SOLLERET - SOLERET
JINGALL - JINGAL	PERILLED - PERILED	SOLLERS - SOLERS
JINGALLS - JINGALS	PETALLED - PETALED	SORELL - SOREL
JOLL - JOL	PILLAR - PILAR	SORELLS - SORELS
JOLLED - JOLED	PILLAU - PILAU	SPALLE - SPALE
JOLLING - JOLING	PILLAUS - PILAUS	SPALLES - SPALES
JOLLS - JOLS	PLIMSOLL - PLIMSOL	SPILLED - SPILED
LABELLED - LABELED	POLLICES - POLICES	SPILLING - SPILING
LABELLER - LABELER	POLLICY - POLICY	STELLA - STELA
LAPELLED - LAPELED	POLLIES - POLIES	STELLAR - STELAR
LEVELLED - LEVELED	POLLING - POLING	SWILLER - SWILER
LEVELLER - LEVELER	POLLINGS - POLINGS	SWILLERS - SWILERS
LIBELLED - LIBELED	PROLLED - PROLED	TALLENT - TALENT
LIBELLEE - LIBELEE	PROLLER - PROLER	TALLENTS - TALENTS
LIBELLER - LIBELER	PROLLERS - PROLERS	TASSELL - TASSEL
LOYALLER - LOYALER	PROLLING - PROLING	TASSELLS - TASSELS
MALLAM - MALAM	PULLI - PULI	TEQUILLA - TEQUILA
MALLAMS - MALAMS	PULLUS - PULUS	TESTRILL - TESTRIL
MALLEATE - MALEATE	PUPILLAR - PUPILAR	THALLI - THALI
MANDRILL - MANDRIL	QUINELLA - QUINELA	TOPFULL - TOPFUL
MANILLA - MANILA	RAMILLIE - RAMILIE	TOTALLED - TOTALED
MANILLAS - MANILAS	RAVELLED - RAVELED	TOWELLED - TOWELED
MARSHALL - MARSHAL	RAVELLER - RAVELER	TRAMELL - TRAMEL
MEDALLED - MEDALED	RECALL - RECAL	TRAMELLS - TRAMELS
MELL - MEL	RECALLS - RECALS	TULLE - TULE
MELLS - MELS	REFELL - REFEL	TULLES - TULES
MERELL - MEREL	REFILLED - REFILED	TWIBILL - TWIBIL
MERELLS - MERELS	RELLIE - RELIE	TWIBILLS - TWIBILS
METALLED - METALED	RELLIES - RELIES	UMBELLED - UMBELED
MILLIARY - MILIARY	RELLISH - RELISH	VALLONIA - VALONIA
MISSEL - MISSELL	REPOSALL - REPOSAL	VELLUM - VELUM
MISSELS - MISSELLS	REVELLED - REVELED	VIALLED - VIALED
MODELLED - MODELED	REVELLER - REVELER	VIALLING - VIALING
MODELLER - MODELER	RIGOLL - RIGOL	VILLIACO - VILIACO
MOLLA - MOLA	RIGOLLS - RIGOLS	VILLIAGO - VILIAGO
MOLLAS - MOLAS	RIVALLED - RIVALED	WADMOLL - WADMOL
MORALL - MORAL	ROWELLED - ROWELED	WADMOLLS - WADMOLS
MORALLS - MORALS	SALL - SAL	WALLIER - WALIER
MUCHELL - MUCHEL	SALLAD - SALAD	WALLIES - WALIES
MUCHELLS - MUCHELS	SALLADS - SALADS	WALLIEST - WALIEST
MULLED - MULED	SALLAL - SALAL	WALLING - WALING
MULLEY - MULEY	SALLALS - SALALS	WALLY - WALY
MULLEYS - MULEYS	SALLET - SALET	WEASELLY - WEASELY

WEEVILLY - WEEVILY
WELLAWAY - WELAWAY
WILLFUL - WILFUL
WOOLLED - WOOLED
WOOLLEN - WOOLEN

WOOLLENS - WOOLENS
WOOLLIER - WOOLIER
WOOLLIES - WOOLIES
WOOLLY - WOOLY
WOOSELL - WOOSEL

WOOSELLS - WOOSELS
YODELLED - YODELED
YODELLER - YODELER
ZILLA - ZILA
ZILLAS - ZILAS

-OE/-E

AMOEBA - AMEBA
AMOEBAE - AMEBAE
AMOEBAN - AMEBAN
AMOEBAS - AMEBAS
AMOEBEAN - AMEBEAN
AMOEBIC - AMEBIC
AMOEBOID - AMEBOID
ANOESTRA - ANESTRA
ANOESTRI - ANESTRI
ANOETIC - ANETIC
APNOEA - APNEA
APNOEAL - APNEAL
APNOEAS - APNEAS
APNOEIC - APNEIC
CHOENIX - CHENIX
COELIAC - CELIAC
COELIACS - CELIACS
COELOM - CELOM
COELOMIC - CELOMIC
COELOMS - CELOMS

COENACLE - CENACLE
DYSPNOEA - DYSPNEA
EUPNOEA - EUPNEA
EUPNOEAS - EUPNEAS
EUPNOEIC - EUPNEIC
FOEDARIE - FEDARIE
FOETAL - FETAL
FOETID - FETID
FOETIDER - FETIDER
FOETIDLY - FETIDLY
FOETOR - FETOR
FOETORS - FETORS
FOETUS - FETUS
FOETUSES - FETUSES
GYNOECIA - GYNECIA
OECOLOGY - ECOLOGY
OEDEMA - EDEMA
OEDEMAS - EDEMAS
OEDEMATA - EDEMATA
OENOLOGY - ENOLOGY

OESTRAL - ESTRAL
OESTRIN - ESTRIN
OESTRINS - ESTRINS
OESTRIOL - ESTRIOL
OESTRONE - ESTRONE
OESTROUS - ESTROUS
OESTRUM - ESTRUM
OESTRUMS - ESTRUMS
OESTRUS - ESTRUS
PHOENIX - PHENIX
SUBPOENA - SUBPENA
ZOOEA - ZOEA
ZOOEAE - ZOEAE
ZOOEAL - ZOEAL
ZOOEAS - ZOEAS
ZOOECIA - ZOECIA
ZOOECIUM - ZOECIUM
ZOOGLOEA - ZOOGLEA

-OUR/-OR

ARBOUR - ARBOR
ARDOUR - ARDOR
ARMOUR - ARMOR
BELABOUR - BELABOR
BICOLOUR - BICOLOR
BITTOUR - BITTOR
CANDOUR - CANDOR
CLAMOUR - CLAMOR
CLANGOUR - CLANGOR
COLOUR - COLOR
DECOLOUR - DECOLOR
DOLOUR - DOLOR
ENAMOUR - ENAMOR
FAITOUR - FAITOR
FAVOUR - FAVOR

FERVOUR - FERVOR
FLAVOUR - FLAVOR
FULGOUR - FULGOR
GLAMOUR - GLAMOR
HARBOUR - HARBOR
HAVIOUR - HAVIOR
HONOUR - HONOR
HUMOUR - HUMOR
LABOUR - LABOR
MAINOUR - MAINOR
MALODOUR - MALODOR
ODOUR - ODOR
PARLOUR - PARLOR
PAVIOUR - PAVIOR
RANCOUR - RANCOR

RIGOUR - RIGOR
RUMOUR - RUMOR
SAPOUR - SAPOR
SAVIOUR - SAVIOR
SAVOUR - SAVOR
STENTOUR - STENTOR
SUCCOUR - SUCCOR
TABOUR - TABOR
TENOUR - TENOR
TUMOUR - TUMOR
VALOUR - VALOR
VAPOUR - VAPOR
VAVASOUR - VAVASOR
VIGOUR - VIGOR

-RE/-ER

BAYADERE - BAYADEER
BISTRE - BISTER
BRERE - BREER
CABRE - CABER
CADASTRE - CADASTER
CALIBRE - CALIBER
CENTRE - CENTER
CHAMBRE - CHAMBER

CHANCRE - CHANCER
COMPERE - COMPEER
DARTRE - DARTER
DECENTRE - DECENTER
DIOPTRE - DIOPTER
EAGRE - EAGER
FERE - FEER
FIBRE - FIBER

FILTRE - FILTER
FOUTRE - FOUTER
GAUFRE - GAUFER
GOITRE - GOITER
INCENTRE - INCENTER
LARE - LAER
LERE - LEER
LETTRE - LETTER

LITRE - LITER	OUTRE - OUTER	SPECTRE - SPECTER
LOUVRE - LOUVER	PHILTRE - PHILTER	TENDRE - TENDER
LUSTRE - LUSTER	PIASTRE - PIASTER	THEATRE - THEATER
MACABRE - MACABER	POUDRE - POUDER	TIMBRE - TIMBER
MAUGRE - MAUGER	POULDRE - POULDER	TITRE - TITER
MEAGRE - MEAGER	RECENTRE - RECENTER	TWIRE - TWIER
METRE - METER	SABRE - SABER	UMBRE - UMBER
MITRE - MITER	SALTIRE - SALTIER	UNMITRE - UNMITER
NITRE - NITER	SCEPTRE - SCEPTER	VENTRE - VENTER
OCHRE - OCHER	SEMPRE - SEMPER	ZAFFRE - ZAFFER
OMBRE - OMBER	SOMBRE - SOMBER	
ONEYRE - ONEYER	SPARRE - SPARER	

-SMAN/-MAN

BATSMAN - BATMAN	HERDSMAN - HERDMAN	RAFTSMAN - RAFTMAN
BEADSMAN - BEADMAN	ISLESMAN - ISLEMAN	ROADSMAN - ROADMAN
BEDESMAN - BEDEMAN	LANDSMAN - LANDMAN	RODSMAN - RODMAN
BOATSMAN - BOATMAN	LEADSMAN - LEADMAN	SEEDSMAN - SEEDMAN
BONDSMAN - BONDMAN	LINESMAN - LINEMAN	SIDESMAN - SIDEMAN
DESMAN - DEMAN	LINKSMAN - LINKMAN	SWAGSMAN - SWAGMAN
DOORSMAN - DOORMAN	LOCKSMAN - LOCKMAN	TOPSMAN - TOPMAN
GOWNSMAN - GOWNMAN	MARKSMAN - MARKMAN	WOODSMAN - WOODMAN
HEADSMAN - HEADMAN	OVERSMAN - OVERMAN	

-ISE not -IZE

ABSCISE	ENFRANCHISE	PREVISE
ADVISE	EXCISE	READVISE
AFFRANCHISE	EXERCISE	SEXERCISE
BALISE	FAINEANTISE	SUBINCISE
BRANDISE	FRANCHISE	SUCCISE
CHASTISE	GALLIARDISE	SUPERVISE
CIRCUMCISE	IMPARADISE	SURMISE
COTISE	IMPROVISE	TELEVISE
COTTISE	INCISE	TRAVOISE
COVETISE	MISADVISE	TREATISE
DISCOURTEISE	MORTISE	TRENISE
DISENFRANCHISE	OVEREXERCISE	UNMORTISE
DISFRANCHISE	PARVISE	UNPARADISE
DISGUISE	PENTISE	VALISE
DISPRAISE	POSTEXERCISE	VICHYSSOISE
EGLOMISE	PRACTISE	WALISE
EMPARADISE	PRESURMISE	WARRANTISE

-IZE not -ISE

ASSIZE	DISPRIZE	PREJUDIZE
CAPSIZE	HAZARDIZE	

CHAPTER 8
HOOKS AND BLOCKERS

Hooks are words that can be transformed into other valid words by the addition of a single letter at the beginning or the end. Such words are called hooks because they allow other words to be attached to them: if you wish to play a word which has a letter that will go with a hook already on the board, you can attach the new word on the hook by playing the new word perpendicular to it, forming a longer word in the process. Hooks that form valid words with a letter added to their beginning are known as front hooks; those that take a letter at the end are, naturally enough, end hooks. Many words are both front hooks and end hooks. As an example, the word HOOK itself is both a front hook and an end hook, as it can form SHOOK (or CHOOK) and HOOKS (or HOOKA or HOOKY). It may well be that the word RETAINS on your rack can only played on the board by utilising the front hook of HOOK, make SHOOK and RETAINS at the same time.

This section is organised by length of hook word, then alphabetical order of hook word within that. The hook word itself is shown in **bold** and the words formed by hooking shown after each hook word. Root words of 5-8 letters that only take an -S end hook are excluded.

Two-letter root words

AA	CAD	VAE	BAH	**AL**
BAA	DAD	WAE	DAH	AAL
CAA	FAD	YAE	FAH	BAL
FAA	GAD	**AG**	HAH	DAL
MAA	HAD	BAG	LAH	GAL
AAH	LAD	CAG	NAH	MAL
AAL	MAD	DAG	PAH	PAL
AAS	PAD	FAG	RAH	SAL
AB	RAD	GAG	YAH	ALA
CAB	SAD	HAG	AHA	ALB
DAB	TAD	JAG	AHI	ALE
FAB	WAD	LAG	AHS	ALF
GAB	YAD	MAG	**AI**	ALL
JAB	ADD	NAG	JAI	ALP
KAB	ADO	RAG	KAI	ALS
LAB	ADS	SAG	RAI	ALT
NAB	ADZ	TAG	SAI	ALU
SAB	**AE**	VAG	TAI	**AM**
TAB	DAE	WAG	WAI	BAM
WAB	FAE	YAG	AIA	CAM
ABA	GAE	ZAG	AID	DAM
ABB	HAE	AGA	AIL	GAM
ABO	KAE	AGE	AIM	HAM
ABS	MAE	AGO	AIN	JAM
ABY	NAE	AGS	AIR	KAM
AD	SAE	**AH**	AIS	LAM
BAD	TAE	AAH	AIT	MAM

NAM	ARY	VAW	BEG	DAS
PAM	**AS**	WAW	BEL	DAW
RAM	AAS	YAW	BEN	DAY
SAM	BAS	AWA	BES	**DE**
TAM	DAS	AWE	BET	IDE
YAM	EAS	AWK	BEY	ODE
AMA	FAS	AWL	BEZ	DEB
AME	GAS	AWN	**BI**	DEE
AMI	HAS	**AX**	OBI	DEF
AMP	KAS	FAX	BIB	DEG
AMU	LAS	LAX	BID	DEI
AN	MAS	MAX	BIG	DEL
BAN	NAS	PAX	BIN	DEN
CAN	PAS	RAX	BIO	DEV
DAN	RAS	SAX	BIS	DEW
EAN	TAS	TAX	BIT	DEX
FAN	VAS	WAX	BIZ	DEY
GAN	WAS	ZAX	**BO**	**DI**
HAN	ZAS	AXE	ABO	DIB
MAN	ASH	**AY**	OBO	DID
NAN	ASK	BAY	BOA	DIE
PAN	ASP	CAY	BOB	DIF
RAN	ASS	DAY	BOD	DIG
SAN	**AT**	FAY	BOG	DIM
TAN	BAT	GAY	BOH	DIN
VAN	CAT	HAY	BOI	DIP
WAN	EAT	JAY	BOK	DIS
ANA	FAT	KAY	BON	DIT
AND	GAT	LAY	BOO	DIV
ANE	HAT	MAY	BOP	**DO**
ANI	KAT	NAY	BOR	ADO
ANN	LAT	PAY	BOS	UDO
ANS	MAT	RAY	BOT	DOB
ANT	NAT	SAY	BOW	DOC
ANY	OAT	TAY	BOX	DOD
AR	PAT	WAY	BOY	DOE
BAR	QAT	YAY	**BY**	DOF
CAR	RAT	AYE	ABY	DOG
EAR	SAT	AYS	BYE	DOH
FAR	TAT	AYU	BYS	DOL
GAR	VAT	**BA**	**CH**	DOM
JAR	WAT	ABA	ACH	DON
LAR	ATE	OBA	ECH	DOO
MAR	ATS	BAA	ICH	DOP
OAR	ATT	BAC	OCH	DOR
PAR	**AW**	BAD	CHA	DOS
SAR	CAW	BAG	CHE	DOT
TAR	DAW	BAH	CHI	DOW
VAR	FAW	BAL	**DA**	DOY
WAR	GAW	BAM	ODA	**EA**
YAR	HAW	BAN	DAB	KEA
ARB	JAW	BAP	DAD	LEA
ARC	KAW	BAR	DAE	PEA
ARD	LAW	BAS	DAG	SEA
ARE	MAW	BAT	DAH	TEA
ARF	NAW	BAY	DAK	YEA
ARK	PAW	**BE**	DAL	ZEA
ARM	RAW	OBE	DAM	EAN
ARS	SAW	BED	DAN	EAR
ART	TAW	BEE	DAP	EAS

EAT	GEL	FES	FEE	HAJ
EAU	MEL	HES	FEG	HAM
ED	PEL	LES	FEH	HAN
BED	SEL	MES	FEM	HAO
FED	TEL	OES	FEN	HAP
GED	ZEL	PES	FER	HAS
KED	ELD	RES	FES	HAT
LED	ELF	TES	FET	HAW
MED	ELK	YES	FEU	HAY
NED	ELL	ESS	FEW	**HE**
PED	ELM	EST	FEY	CHE
RED	ELS	**ET**	FEZ	SHE
SED	ELT	BET	**GI**	THE
TED	**EM**	FET	GIB	HEH
WED	FEM	GET	GID	HEM
ZED	GEM	HET	GIE	HEN
EDH	HEM	JET	GIF	HEP
EDS	MEM	KET	GIG	HER
EE	REM	LET	GIN	HES
BEE	WEM	MET	GIO	HET
CEE	EME	NET	GIP	HEW
DEE	EMO	PET	GIS	HEX
FEE	EMS	RET	GIT	HEY
GEE	EMU	SET	**GO**	**HI**
JEE	**EN**	TET	AGO	AHI
LEE	BEN	VET	EGO	CHI
MEE	DEN	WET	YGO	GHI
NEE	EEN	YET	GOA	KHI
PEE	FEN	ETA	GOB	PHI
REE	GEN	ETH	GOD	HIC
SEE	HEN	**EX**	GOE	HID
TEE	KEN	DEX	GON	HIE
VEE	MEN	HEX	GOO	HIM
WEE	PEN	KEX	GOR	HIN
ZEE	REN	LEX	GOS	HIP
EEK	SEN	REX	GOT	HIS
EEL	TEN	SEX	GOV	HIT
EEN	WEN	TEX	GOX	**HM**
EF	YEN	VEX	GOY	OHM
DEF	END	WEX	**GU**	HMM
KEF	ENE	YEX	GUB	**HO**
NEF	ENG	ZEX	GUE	MHO
REF	ENS	EXO	GUL	OHO
TEF	**ER**	**FA**	GUM	PHO
EFF	FER	FAA	GUN	RHO
EFS	GER	FAB	GUP	THO
EFT	HER	FAD	GUR	WHO
EH	PER	FAE	GUS	ZHO
FEH	SER	FAG	GUT	HOA
HEH	ERA	FAH	GUV	HOB
MEH	ERE	FAN	GUY	HOC
PEH	ERF	FAP	**HA**	HOD
REH	ERG	FAR	AHA	HOE
YEH	ERK	FAS	CHA	HOG
EHS	ERM	FAT	SHA	HOH
EL	ERN	FAW	WHA	HOI
BEL	ERR	FAX	HAD	HOM
CEL	ERS	FAY	HAE	HON
DEL	**ES**	**FE**	HAG	HOO
EEL	BES	FED	HAH	HOP

HOS	AIS	AKA	**LO**	UMM
HOT	BIS	OKA	LOB	**MO**
HOW	CIS	SKA	LOD	EMO
HOX	DIS	KAB	LOG	MOA
HOY	GIS	KAE	LOO	MOB
ID	HIS	KAF	LOP	MOC
AID	KIS	KAI	LOR	MOD
BID	LIS	KAK	LOS	MOE
CID	MIS	KAM	LOT	MOG
DID	NIS	KAS	LOU	MOI
FID	OIS	KAT	LOW	MOL
GID	PIS	KAW	LOX	MOM
HID	QIS	KAY	LOY	MON
KID	SIS	**KI**	**MA**	MOO
LID	TIS	SKI	AMA	MOP
MID	VIS	KID	SMA	MOR
NID	WIS	KIF	MAA	MOS
RID	XIS	KIN	MAC	MOT
TID	ISH	KIP	MAD	MOU
VID	ISM	KIR	MAE	MOW
YID	ISO	KIS	MAG	MOY
IDE	**IT**	KIT	MAK	MOZ
IDS	AIT	**KO**	MAL	**MU**
IF	BIT	KOA	MAM	AMU
DIF	CIT	KOB	MAN	EMU
GIF	DIT	KOI	MAP	UMU
KIF	FIT	KON	MAR	MUD
RIF	GIT	KOP	MAS	MUG
SIF	HIT	KOR	MAT	MUM
IFF	KIT	KOS	MAW	MUN
IFS	LIT	KOW	MAX	MUS
IN	NIT	**KY**	MAY	MUT
AIN	PIT	SKY	**ME**	MUX
BIN	RIT	KYE	AME	**MY**
DIN	SIT	KYU	EME	MYC
FIN	TIT	**LA**	MED	**NA**
GIN	WIT	ALA	MEE	ANA
HIN	ZIT	LAB	MEG	MNA
JIN	ITA	LAC	MEH	NAB
KIN	ITS	LAD	MEL	NAE
LIN	**JA**	LAG	MEM	NAG
PIN	JAB	LAH	MEN	NAH
QIN	JAG	LAM	MES	NAM
RIN	JAI	LAP	MET	NAN
SIN	JAK	LAR	MEU	NAP
TIN	JAM	LAS	MEW	NAS
VIN	JAP	LAT	**MI**	NAT
WIN	JAR	LAV	AMI	NAW
YIN	JAW	LAW	MIB	NAY
ZIN	JAY	LAX	MIC	**NE**
ING	**JO**	LAY	MID	ANE
INK	JOB	**LI**	MIG	ENE
INN	JOE	LIB	MIL	ONE
INS	JOG	LID	MIM	NEB
IO	JOL	LIE	MIR	NED
BIO	JOR	LIG	MIS	NEE
GIO	JOT	LIN	MIX	NEF
ION	JOW	LIP	MIZ	NEG
IOS	JOY	LIS	**MM**	NEK
IS	**KA**	LIT	HMM	NEP

NET	ROD	BON	BOR	POW
NEW	SOD	CON	COR	ROW
NO	TOD	DON	DOR	SOW
ONO	YOD	EON	FOR	TOW
NOB	ODA	FON	GOR	VOW
NOD	ODD	GON	JOR	WOW
NOG	ODE	HON	KOR	YOW
NOH	ODS	ION	LOR	OWE
NOM	**OE**	KON	MOR	OWL
NON	DOE	MON	NOR	OWN
NOO	FOE	NON	OOR	OWT
NOR	GOE	OON	TOR	**OX**
NOS	HOE	SON	VOR	BOX
NOT	JOE	TON	ORA	COX
NOW	MOE	WON	ORB	FOX
NOX	ROE	YON	ORC	GOX
NOY	TOE	ONE	ORD	HOX
NU	VOE	ONO	ORE	LOX
GNU	WOE	ONS	ORF	NOX
NUB	OES	ONY	ORS	POX
NUN	**OF**	**OO**	ORT	SOX
NUR	DOF	BOO	**OS**	VOX
NUS	OOF	COO	BOS	WOX
NUT	WOF	DOO	COS	OXO
NY	OFF	GOO	DOS	OXY
ANY	OFT	HOO	GOS	**OY**
ONY	**OH**	LOO	HOS	BOY
SNY	BOH	MOO	IOS	COY
NYE	DOH	NOO	KOS	DOY
NYS	FOH	POO	LOS	FOY
OB	HOH	ROO	MOS	GOY
BOB	NOH	TOO	NOS	HOY
COB	OOH	WOO	OOS	JOY
DOB	POH	ZOO	POS	LOY
FOB	SOH	OOF	SOS	MOY
GOB	OHM	OOH	WOS	NOY
HOB	OHO	OOM	ZOS	SOY
JOB	OHS	OON	OSE	TOY
KOB	**OI**	OOP	**OU**	OYE
LOB	BOI	OOR	FOU	OYS
MOB	HOI	OOS	LOU	**PA**
NOB	KOI	OOT	MOU	SPA
ROB	MOI	**OP**	SOU	PAC
SOB	POI	BOP	YOU	PAD
YOB	OIK	COP	OUD	PAH
OBA	OIL	DOP	OUK	PAL
OBE	OIS	FOP	OUP	PAM
OBI	**OM**	HOP	OUR	PAN
OBO	DOM	KOP	OUS	PAP
OBS	HOM	LOP	OUT	PAR
OD	MOM	MOP	**OW**	PAS
BOD	NOM	OOP	BOW	PAT
COD	OOM	POP	COW	PAV
DOD	POM	SOP	DOW	PAW
GOD	ROM	TOP	HOW	PAX
HOD	SOM	WOP	JOW	PAY
LOD	TOM	OPE	KOW	**PE**
MOD	YOM	OPS	LOW	APE
NOD	OMS	OPT	MOW	OPE
POD	**ON**	**OR**	NOW	PEA

PEC	REO	TAI	JUG	BUR
PED	REP	TAJ	LUG	CUR
PEE	RES	TAK	MUG	FUR
PEG	RET	TAM	PUG	GUR
PEH	REV	TAN	RUG	LUR
PEL	REW	TAO	SUG	NUR
PEN	REX	TAP	TUG	OUR
PEP	REZ	TAR	VUG	PUR
PER	**SH**	TAS	YUG	SUR
PES	ASH	TAT	UGH	URB
PET	ISH	TAU	UGS	URD
PEW	SHA	TAV	**UH**	URE
PI	SHE	TAW	DUH	URN
PIA	SHH	TAX	HUH	URP
PIC	SHY	TAY	PUH	**US**
PIE	**SI**	**TE**	**UM**	BUS
PIG	PSI	ATE	BUM	GUS
PIN	SIB	UTE	CUM	JUS
PIP	SIC	TEA	FUM	MUS
PIR	SIF	TEC	GUM	NUS
PIS	SIK	TED	HUM	OUS
PIT	SIM	TEE	LUM	PUS
PIU	SIN	TEF	MUM	SUS
PIX	SIP	TEG	RUM	WUS
PO	SIR	TEL	SUM	YUS
APO	SIS	TEN	TUM	USE
UPO	SIT	TES	VUM	**UT**
POA	SIX	TET	YUM	BUT
POD	**SO**	TEW	UMM	CUT
POH	DSO	TEX	UMP	GUT
POI	ISO	**TI**	UMS	HUT
POL	SOB	TIC	UMU	JUT
POM	SOC	TID	**UN**	MUT
POO	SOD	TIE	BUN	NUT
POP	SOG	TIG	DUN	OUT
POS	SOH	TIK	FUN	PUT
POT	SOL	TIL	GUN	RUT
POW	SOM	TIN	HUN	TUT
POX	SON	TIP	JUN	UTA
POZ	SOP	TIS	MUN	UTE
QI	SOS	TIT	NUN	UTS
QIN	SOT	TIX	PUN	UTU
QIS	SOU	**TO**	RUN	**WE**
RE	SOV	TOC	SUN	AWE
ARE	SOW	TOD	TUN	EWE
ERE	SOX	TOE	UNI	OWE
IRE	SOY	TOG	UNS	WEB
ORE	SOZ	TOM	**UP**	WED
PRE	**ST**	TON	CUP	WEE
URE	EST	TOO	DUP	WEM
REB	PST	TOP	GUP	WEN
REC	STY	TOR	HUP	WET
RED	**TA**	TOT	OUP	WEX
REE	ETA	TOW	PUP	WEY
REF	ITA	TOY	SUP	**WO**
REG	UTA	**UG**	TUP	TWO
REH	TAB	BUG	YUP	WOE
REI	TAD	DUG	UPO	WOF
REM	TAE	FUG	UPS	WOG
REN	TAG	HUG	**UR**	WOK

WON	YAH	NYE	**YO**	YUS
WOO	YAK	OYE	YOB	**ZA**
WOP	YAM	PYE	YOD	ZAG
WOS	YAP	RYE	YOK	ZAP
WOT	YAR	SYE	YOM	ZAS
WOW	YAW	TYE	YON	ZAX
WOX	YAY	WYE	YOU	**ZO**
XI	**YE**	YEA	YOW	AZO
XIS	AYE	YEH	**YU**	DZO
YA	BYE	YEN	AYU	ZOA
PYA	DYE	YEP	KYU	ZOL
RYA	EYE	YES	YUG	ZOO
YAD	HYE	YET	YUK	ZOS
YAE	KYE	YEW	YUM	
YAG	LYE	YEX	YUP	

Three-letter root words

AAH	ABYS	LADS	RAGE	LAHS
AAHS	**ACE**	MADS	SAGE	PAHS
AAL	DACE	NADS	WAGE	RAHS
BAAL	FACE	PADS	AGED	YAHS
DAAL	LACE	RADS	AGEE	**AIA**
KAAL	MACE	SADS	AGEN	RAIA
PAAL	PACE	TADS	AGER	AIAS
TAAL	RACE	WADS	AGES	**AID**
AALS	TACE	YADS	**AGO**	CAID
AAS	ACED	**ADZ**	DAGO	GAID
BAAS	ACER	ADZE	KAGO	KAID
CAAS	ACES	**AFF**	SAGO	LAID
FAAS	**ACH**	BAFF	AGOG	MAID
KAAS	BACH	CAFF	AGON	PAID
MAAS	EACH	DAFF	**AGS**	QAID
ABA	MACH	FAFF	BAGS	RAID
BABA	NACH	GAFF	CAGS	SAID
CABA	RACH	HAFF	DAGS	WAID
YABA	TACH	NAFF	FAGS	AIDA
ABAC	ACHE	RAFF	GAGS	AIDE
ABAS	ACHY	WAFF	HAGS	AIDS
ABB	**ACT**	YAFF	JAGS	**AIL**
ABBA	FACT	AFFY	LAGS	BAIL
ABBE	PACT	**AFT**	MAGS	FAIL
ABBS	TACT	BAFT	NAGS	HAIL
ABO	ACTA	DAFT	RAGS	JAIL
ABOS	ACTS	HAFT	SAGS	KAIL
ABS	**ADD**	RAFT	TAGS	MAIL
CABS	WADD	SAFT	VAGS	NAIL
DABS	ADDS	WAFT	WAGS	PAIL
FABS	ADDY	**AGA**	YAGS	RAIL
GABS	**ADO**	GAGA	ZAGS	SAIL
JABS	DADO	JAGA	**AHA**	TAIL
KABS	FADO	NAGA	HAHA	VAIL
LABS	SADO	RAGA	MAHA	WAIL
NABS	ADOS	SAGA	TAHA	AILS
SABS	**ADS**	AGAR	**AHI**	**AIM**
TABS	BADS	AGAS	AHIS	KAIM
WABS	CADS	**AGE**	**AHS**	MAIM
ABY	DADS	CAGE	AAHS	SAIM
BABY	FADS	GAGE	DAHS	AIMS
GABY	GADS	MAGE	FAHS	**AIN**
ABYE	HADS	PAGE	HAHS	CAIN

FAIN	SAKE	**ALP**	GAMP	**ANS**
GAIN	TAKE	CALP	LAMP	BANS
HAIN	WAKE	PALP	RAMP	CANS
KAIN	AKED	SALP	SAMP	DANS
LAIN	AKEE	ALPS	TAMP	EANS
MAIN	AKES	**ALS**	VAMP	FANS
NAIN	**ALA**	AALS	AMPS	GANS
PAIN	GALA	BALS	**AMU**	KANS
RAIN	MALA	DALS	NAMU	MANS
SAIN	NALA	GALS	AMUS	NANS
TAIN	TALA	MALS	**ANA**	PANS
VAIN	ALAE	PALS	KANA	SANS
WAIN	ALAN	SALS	LANA	TANS
AINE	ALAP	ALSO	MANA	VANS
AINS	ALAR	**ALT**	NANA	WANS
AIR	ALAS	DALT	RANA	ANSA
FAIR	ALAY	HALT	TANA	**ANT**
GAIR	**ALB**	MALT	ANAL	BANT
HAIR	ALBA	SALT	ANAN	CANT
LAIR	ALBE	ALTO	ANAS	DANT
MAIR	ALBS	ALTS	**AND**	GANT
PAIR	**ALE**	**ALU**	BAND	HANT
SAIR	BALE	BALU	FAND	KANT
VAIR	DALE	ALUM	HAND	LANT
WAIR	EALE	ALUS	LAND	PANT
AIRN	GALE	**AMA**	MAND	RANT
AIRS	HALE	CAMA	PAND	SANT
AIRT	KALE	GAMA	RAND	VANT
AIRY	MALE	KAMA	SAND	WANT
AIS	PALE	LAMA	WAND	ANTA
DAIS	RALE	MAMA	ANDS	ANTE
KAIS	SALE	SAMA	**ANE**	ANTI
PAIS	TALE	AMAH	BANE	ANTS
RAIS	VALE	AMAS	CANE	**ANY**
SAIS	WALE	**AME**	FANE	CANY
TAIS	YALE	CAME	GANE	MANY
WAIS	ALEC	DAME	JANE	WANY
AIT	ALEE	FAME	KANE	ZANY
BAIT	ALEF	GAME	LANE	**APE**
GAIT	ALES	HAME	MANE	CAPE
RAIT	ALEW	KAME	NANE	GAPE
TAIT	**ALF**	LAME	PANE	JAPE
WAIT	CALF	NAME	SANE	NAPE
AITS	HALF	SAME	TANE	PAPE
AITU	ALFA	TAME	VANE	RAPE
AKA	ALFS	WAME	WANE	TAPE
HAKA	**ALL**	AMEN	ANES	APED
KAKA	BALL	AMES	ANEW	APER
TAKA	CALL	**AMI**	**ANI**	APES
WAKA	FALL	KAMI	BANI	APEX
AKAS	GALL	RAMI	MANI	**APO**
AKE	HALL	AMIA	RANI	CAPO
BAKE	LALL	AMID	ANIL	GAPO
CAKE	MALL	AMIE	ANIS	APOD
FAKE	PALL	AMIN	**ANN**	APOS
HAKE	SALL	AMIR	CANN	**APP**
JAKE	TALL	AMIS	JANN	YAPP
LAKE	WALL	**AMP**	ANNA	APPS
MAKE	ALLS	CAMP	ANNO	**APT**
RAKE	ALLY	DAMP	ANNS	RAPT

APTS	JARK	DASH	MATS	AWAY	
ARB	KARK	FASH	NATS	**AWE**	
BARB	LARK	GASH	OATS	WAWE	
CARB	MARK	HASH	PATS	AWED	
DARB	NARK	LASH	QATS	AWEE	
GARB	PARK	MASH	RATS	AWES	
WARB	RARK	PASH	TATS	**AWK**	
ARBA	SARK	RASH	VATS	CAWK	
ARBS	WARK	SASH	WATS	DAWK	
ARC	YARK	TASH	**ATT**	GAWK	
MARC	ARKS	WASH	BATT	HAWK	
NARC	**ARM**	ASHY	MATT	LAWK	
ARCH	BARM	**ASK**	TATT	MAWK	
ARCO	FARM	BASK	WATT	PAWK	
ARCS	HARM	CASK	**AUA**	AWKS	
ARD	MARM	HASK	PAUA	**AWL**	
BARD	WARM	MASK	AUAS	BAWL	
CARD	ARMS	TASK	**AUF**	PAWL	
EARD	ARMY	ASKS	CAUF	WAWL	
FARD	**ARS**	**ASP**	HAUF	YAWL	
HARD	BARS	GASP	LAUF	AWLS	
LARD	CARS	HASP	AUFS	**AWN**	
MARD	EARS	JASP	**AUK**	BAWN	
NARD	FARS	RASP	BAUK	DAWN	
PARD	GARS	WASP	CAUK	FAWN	
SARD	JARS	ASPS	JAUK	LAWN	
WARD	LARS	**ASS**	WAUK	MAWN	
YARD	MARS	BASS	AUKS	PAWN	
ARDS	OARS	HASS	**AVA**	RAWN	
ARE	PARS	JASS	CAVA	SAWN	
BARE	SARS	LASS	FAVA	YAWN	
CARE	TARS	MASS	JAVA	AWNS	
DARE	VARS	PASS	KAVA	AWNY	
FARE	WARS	SASS	LAVA	**AXE**	
GARE	ARSE	TASS	TAVA	SAXE	
HARE	ARSY	**ATE**	AVAL	AXED	
LARE	**ART**	BATE	AVAS	AXEL	
MARE	CART	CATE	**AVE**	AXES	
NARE	DART	DATE	CAVE	**AYE**	
PARE	FART	FATE	EAVE	BAYE	
RARE	GART	GATE	FAVE	AYES	
TARE	HART	HATE	GAVE	**AYS**	
VARE	KART	LATE	HAVE	BAYS	
WARE	MART	MATE	LAVE	CAYS	
YARE	PART	PATE	NAVE	DAYS	
AREA	TART	RATE	PAVE	FAYS	
ARED	WART	SATE	RAVE	GAYS	
AREG	ARTI	TATE	SAVE	HAYS	
ARES	ARTS	WATE	WAVE	JAYS	
ARET	ARTY	YATE	AVEL	KAYS	
AREW	**ARY**	ATES	AVER	LAYS	
ARF	MARY	**ATS**	AVES	MAYS	
BARF	NARY	BATS	**AVO**	NAYS	
ZARF	OARY	CATS	AVOS	PAYS	
ARFS	VARY	EATS	AVOW	RAYS	
ARK	WARY	FATS	**AWA**	SAYS	
BARK	ARYL	GATS	KAWA	TAYS	
CARK	**ASH**	HATS	PAWA	WAYS	
DARK	BASH	KATS	TAWA	YAYS	
HARK	CASH	LATS	WAWA	**AYU**	

AYUS	BASS	BIGG	BONY	BROW
AZO	BAST	BIGS	**BOO**	**BRR**
LAZO	**BAT**	**BIN**	BOOB	BRRR
AZON	BATE	BIND	BOOH	**BRU**
BAA	BATH	BINE	BOOK	BRUS
BAAL	BATS	BING	BOOL	BRUT
BAAS	BATT	BINK	BOOM	BRUX
BAC	**BAY**	BINS	BOON	**BUB**
ABAC	BAYE	BINT	BOOR	BUBA
BACH	BAYS	**BIO**	BOOS	BUBO
BACK	BAYT	BIOG	BOOT	BUBS
BACS	**BED**	BIOS	**BOP**	BUBU
BAD	ABED	**BIS**	BOPS	**BUD**
BADE	BEDE	IBIS	**BOR**	BUDA
BADS	BEDS	OBIS	BORA	BUDI
BAG	BEDU	BISE	BORD	BUDO
BAGH	**BEE**	BISH	BORE	BUDS
BAGS	BEEF	BISK	BORK	**BUG**
BAH	BEEN	BIST	BORM	BUGS
BAHT	BEEP	**BIT**	BORN	**BUM**
BAHU	BEER	OBIT	BORS	BUMF
BAL	BEES	BITE	BORT	BUMP
BALD	BEET	BITO	**BOS**	BUMS
BALE	**BEG**	BITS	ABOS	**BUN**
BALK	BEGO	BITT	OBOS	BUNA
BALL	BEGS	**BIZ**	BOSH	BUND
BALM	**BEL**	BIZE	BOSK	BUNG
BALS	BELL	**BOA**	BOSS	BUNK
BALU	BELS	BOAB	**BOT**	BUNN
BAM	BELT	BOAK	BOTA	BUNS
BAMS	**BEN**	BOAR	BOTE	BUNT
BAN	BEND	BOAS	BOTH	**BUR**
BANC	BENE	BOAT	BOTS	BURA
BAND	BENI	**BOB**	BOTT	BURB
BANE	BENJ	BOBA	**BOW**	BURD
BANG	BENS	BOBS	BOWL	BURG
BANI	BENT	**BOD**	BOWR	BURK
BANK	**BES**	BODE	BOWS	BURL
BANS	OBES	BODS	**BOX**	BURN
BANT	BEST	BODY	BOXY	BURP
BAP	**BET**	**BOG**	**BOY**	BURR
BAPS	ABET	BOGS	BOYF	BURS
BAPU	YBET	BOGY	BOYG	BURY
BAR	BETA	**BOH**	BOYO	**BUS**
KBAR	BETE	BOHO	BOYS	BUSH
BARB	BETH	BOHS	**BRA**	BUSK
BARD	BETS	**BOI**	BRAD	BUSS
BARE	**BEY**	BOIL	BRAE	BUST
BARF	OBEY	BOIS	BRAG	BUSY
BARK	BEYS	**BOK**	BRAK	**BUT**
BARM	**BIB**	BOKE	BRAN	ABUT
BARN	BIBB	BOKO	BRAS	BUTE
BARP	BIBS	BOKS	BRAT	BUTS
BARS	**BID**	**BON**	BRAW	BUTT
BAS	ABID	EBON	BRAY	**BUY**
ABAS	BIDE	BONA	**BRO**	BUYS
OBAS	BIDI	BOND	BROD	**BYE**
BASE	BIDS	BONE	BROG	ABYE
BASH	**BIG**	BONG	BROO	BYES
BASK	BIGA	BONK	BROS	**BYS**

ABYS	**CAY**	**COD**	COTS	DADA
CAA	CAYS	ECOD	COTT	DADO
CAAS	**CEE**	CODA	**COW**	DADS
CAB	CEES	CODE	SCOW	**DAE**
SCAB	**CEL**	CODS	COWK	DAES
CABA	CELL	**COG**	COWL	**DAG**
CABS	CELS	SCOG	COWP	DAGO
CAD	CELT	COGS	COWS	DAGS
ECAD	**CEP**	**COL**	COWY	**DAH**
SCAD	CEPE	COLA	**COX**	ODAH
CADE	CEPS	COLD	COXA	DAHL
CADI	**CHA**	COLE	COXY	DAHS
CADS	CHAD	COLL	**COY**	**DAK**
CAG	CHAI	COLS	COYS	DAKS
SCAG	CHAL	COLT	**COZ**	**DAL**
CAGE	CHAM	COLY	COZE	ODAL
CAGS	CHAO	**CON**	COZY	UDAL
CAGY	CHAP	ICON	**CRU**	DALE
CAM	CHAR	COND	ECRU	DALI
SCAM	CHAS	CONE	CRUD	DALS
CAMA	CHAT	CONF	CRUE	DALT
CAME	CHAV	CONI	CRUS	**DAM**
CAMO	CHAW	CONK	CRUX	DAME
CAMP	CHAY	CONN	**CRY**	DAMN
CAMS	**CHE**	CONS	SCRY	DAMP
CAN	ACHE	CONY	**CUB**	DAMS
SCAN	ECHE	**COO**	CUBE	**DAN**
CANE	OCHE	COOF	CUBS	DANG
CANG	CHEF	COOK	**CUD**	DANK
CANN	CHER	COOL	SCUD	DANS
CANS	CHEW	COOM	CUDS	DANT
CANT	CHEZ	COON	**CUE**	**DAP**
CANY	**CHI**	COOP	CUED	DAPS
CAP	CHIA	COOS	CUES	**DAS**
CAPA	CHIB	COOT	**CUM**	ODAS
CAPE	CHIC	**COP**	SCUM	DASH
CAPH	CHID	SCOP	CUMS	**DAW**
CAPI	CHIK	COPE	**CUP**	ADAW
CAPO	CHIN	COPS	SCUP	DAWD
CAPS	CHIP	COPY	CUPS	DAWK
CAR	CHIS	**COR**	**CUR**	DAWN
SCAR	CHIT	CORD	SCUR	DAWS
CARB	CHIV	CORE	CURB	DAWT
CARD	CHIZ	CORF	CURD	**DAY**
CARE	**CID**	CORK	CURE	DAYS
CARK	ACID	CORM	CURF	DEB
CARL	CIDE	CORN	CURL	DEBE
CARN	CIDS	CORS	CURN	DEBS
CARP	**CIG**	CORY	CURR	DEBT
CARR	CIGS	**COS**	CURS	**DEE**
CARS	**CIS**	ECOS	CURT	IDEE
CART	CIST	COSE	**CUT**	DEED
CAT	**CIT**	COSH	SCUT	DEEK
SCAT	CITE	COSS	CUTE	DEEM
CATE	CITO	COST	CUTS	DEEN
CATS	CITS	COSY	**CWM**	DEEP
CAW	CITY	**COT**	CWMS	DEER
SCAW	**COB**	SCOT	**DAB**	DEES
CAWK	COBB	COTE	DABS	DEET
CAWS	COBS	COTH	**DAD**	DEEV

DEF	DINO	UDON	DUDE	CEAS
DEFI	DINS	DONA	DUDS	KEAS
DEFO	DINT	DONE	**DUE**	LEAS
DEFT	**DIP**	DONG	DUED	PEAS
DEFY	DIPS	DONS	DUEL	SEAS
DEG	DIPT	**DOO**	DUES	TEAS
DEGS	**DIS**	DOOB	DUET	YEAS
DEGU	DISA	DOOK	**DUG**	ZEAS
DEI	DISC	DOOL	DUGS	EASE
DEID	DISH	DOOM	**DUI**	EAST
DEIF	DISK	DOON	DUIT	EASY
DEIL	DISS	DOOR	**DUN**	**EAT**
DEL	**DIT**	DOOS	DUNE	BEAT
DELE	ADIT	**DOP**	DUNG	FEAT
DELF	EDIT	DOPA	DUNK	GEAT
DELI	DITA	DOPE	DUNS	HEAT
DELL	DITE	DOPS	DUNT	JEAT
DELO	DITS	DOPY	**DUO**	LEAT
DELS	DITT	**DOR**	DUOS	MEAT
DELT	DITZ	ODOR	**DUP**	NEAT
DEN	**DIV**	DORB	DUPE	PEAT
DENE	DIVA	DORE	DUPS	SEAT
DENI	DIVE	DORK	**DYE**	TEAT
DENS	DIVI	DORM	DYED	EATH
DENT	DIVO	DORP	DYER	EATS
DENY	DIVS	DORR	DYES	**EAU**
DEV	**DOB**	DORS	**DZO**	BEAU
DEVA	DOBS	DORT	DZOS	EAUS
DEVS	DOBY	DORY	**EAN**	EAUX
DEW	**DOC**	**DOS**	BEAN	**EBB**
DEWS	DOCK	ADOS	DEAN	EBBS
DEWY	DOCO	UDOS	GEAN	**ECH**
DEX	DOCS	DOSE	JEAN	EECH
DEXY	**DOD**	DOSH	LEAN	HECH
DEY	DODO	DOSS	MEAN	LECH
DEYS	DODS	DOST	PEAN	PECH
DIB	DOE	DOT	REAN	SECH
DIBS	DOEK	DOTE	SEAN	TECH
DID	DOEN	DOTH	WEAN	YECH
DIDO	DOER	DOTS	YEAN	ECHE
DIDY	DOES	DOTY	EANS	ECHO
DIE	**DOF**	**DOW**	**EAR**	ECHT
DIEB	DOFF	DOWD	BEAR	**ECO**
DIED	**DOG**	DOWF	DEAR	DECO
DIEL	DOGE	DOWL	FEAR	SECO
DIES	DOGS	DOWN	GEAR	ECOD
DIET	DOGY	DOWP	HEAR	ECOS
DIF	**DOH**	DOWS	LEAR	**ECU**
DIFF	DOHS	DOWT	NEAR	ECUS
DIFS	**DOL**	**DOY**	PEAR	**EDH**
DIG	IDOL	DOYS	REAR	EDHS
DIGS	DOLE	**DRY**	SEAR	**EDS**
DIM	DOLL	ADRY	TEAR	BEDS
DIME	DOLS	DRYS	WEAR	FEDS
DIMP	DOLT	**DSO**	YEAR	GEDS
DIMS	**DOM**	ODSO	EARD	KEDS
DIN	DOME	DSOS	EARL	MEDS
DINE	DOMS	**DUB**	EARN	NEDS
DING	DOMY	DUBS	EARS	PEDS
DINK	**DON**	**DUD**	**EAS**	REDS

TEDS	REGO	**ELS**	VEND	SERF
WEDS	SEGO	BELS	WEND	TERF
ZEDS	VEGO	CELS	ENDS	**ERG**
EEK	EGOS	DELS	**ENE**	BERG
DEEK	**EHS**	EELS	BENE	ERGO
GEEK	FEHS	GELS	DENE	ERGS
KEEK	HEHS	MELS	GENE	**ERK**
LEEK	PEHS	PELS	MENE	BERK
MEEK	REHS	SELS	NENE	JERK
PEEK	**EIK**	TELS	PENE	MERK
REEK	REIK	WELS	SENE	NERK
SEEK	SEIK	ZELS	TENE	PERK
TEEK	EIKS	ELSE	ENES	SERK
WEEK	**EKE**	**ELT**	ENEW	YERK
EEL	DEKE	BELT	**ENG**	ZERK
FEEL	LEKE	CELT	LENG	ERKS
HEEL	PEKE	DELT	MENG	**ERM**
JEEL	REKE	FELT	ENGS	BERM
KEEL	EKED	GELT	**ENS**	DERM
PEEL	EKES	KELT	BENS	FERM
REEL	**ELD**	MELT	CENS	GERM
SEEL	GELD	PELT	DENS	HERM
TEEL	HELD	TELT	FENS	PERM
WEEL	MELD	WELT	GENS	TERM
EELS	SELD	YELT	HENS	**ERN**
EELY	TELD	ELTS	KENS	DERN
EEN	VELD	**EME**	LENS	FERN
BEEN	WELD	DEME	PENS	HERN
DEEN	YELD	FEME	RENS	KERN
FEEN	ELDS	HEME	SENS	PERN
KEEN	**ELF**	LEME	TENS	TERN
PEEN	DELF	MEME	WENS	ERNE
REEN	PELF	SEME	YENS	ERNS
SEEN	SELF	TEME	**EON**	**ERR**
TEEN	ELFS	EMES	AEON	SERR
WEEN	**ELK**	EMEU	JEON	ERRS
EFF	WELK	**EMO**	NEON	**ERS**
JEFF	YELK	DEMO	PEON	GERS
MEFF	ELKS	MEMO	EONS	HERS
TEFF	**ELL**	EMOS	**ERA**	SERS
EFFS	BELL	**EMS**	SERA	VERS
EFS	CELL	FEMS	VERA	ERST
KEFS	DELL	GEMS	ERAS	**ESS**
NEFS	FELL	HEMS	**ERE**	CESS
REFS	HELL	MEMS	BERE	FESS
TEFS	JELL	REMS	CERE	JESS
EFT	KELL	TEMS	DERE	LESS
DEFT	MELL	WEMS	FERE	MESS
HEFT	PELL	**EMU**	GERE	NESS
LEFT	SELL	EMUS	HERE	SESS
REFT	TELL	**END**	LERE	ESSE
WEFT	VELL	BEND	MERE	**EST**
EFTS	WELL	FEND	PERE	BEST
EGG	YELL	HEND	SERE	FEST
TEGG	ELLS	LEND	WERE	GEST
YEGG	**ELM**	MEND	ERED	HEST
EGGS	HELM	PEND	ERES	JEST
EGGY	YELM	REND	EREV	KEST
EGO	ELMS	SEND	**ERF**	LEST
BEGO	ELMY	TEND	KERF	NEST

PEST	FAAS	FENI	**FLU**	FUGS
REST	**FAB**	FENS	FLUB	FUGU
TEST	FABS	FENT	FLUE	**FUM**
VEST	**FAD**	**FER**	FLUS	FUME
WEST	FADE	FERE	FLUX	FUMS
YEST	FADO	FERM	**FOB**	FUMY
ZEST	FADS	FERN	FOBS	**FUN**
ESTS	FADY	**FES**	**FOE**	FUND
ETA	**FAG**	FESS	FOEN	FUNG
BETA	FAGS	FEST	FOES	FUNK
FETA	**FAH**	**FET**	**FOG**	FUNS
GETA	FAHS	FETA	FOGS	**FUR**
KETA	**FAN**	FETE	FOGY	FURL
META	FAND	FETS	**FOH**	FURR
SETA	FANE	FETT	FOHN	FURS
WETA	FANG	**FEU**	**FON**	FURY
ZETA	FANK	FEUD	FOND	**GAB**
ETAS	FANO	FEUS	FONE	GABS
ETAT	FANS	**FEW**	FONS	GABY
ETH	**FAR**	FEWS	FONT	**GAD**
BETH	AFAR	**FEY**	**FOP**	EGAD
HETH	FARD	FEYS	FOPS	IGAD
METH	FARE	**FIB**	**FOR**	GADE
TETH	FARL	FIBS	FORA	GADI
ETHE	FARM	**FID**	FORB	GADS
ETHS	FARO	FIDO	FORD	**GAE**
EUK	FARS	FIDS	FORE	GAED
NEUK	FART	**FIE**	FORK	GAEN
YEUK	**FAS**	FIEF	FORM	GAES
EUKS	FASH	FIER	FORT	**GAG**
EVE	FAST	**FIG**	**FOU**	GAGA
LEVE	**FAT**	FIGO	FOUD	GAGE
MEVE	FATE	FIGS	FOUL	GAGS
NEVE	FATS	**FIL**	FOUR	**GAK**
YEVE	**FAW**	FILA	FOUS	GAKS
EVEN	FAWN	FILE	**FOX**	**GAL**
EVER	FAWS	FILL	FOXY	EGAL
EVES	**FAY**	FILM	**FOY**	GALA
EVET	OFAY	FILO	FOYS	GALE
EVO	FAYS	FILS	**FRA**	GALL
LEVO	**FED**	**FIN**	FRAB	GALS
EVOE	FEDS	FIND	FRAE	**GAM**
EVOS	**FEE**	FINE	FRAG	OGAM
EWE	FEEB	FINI	FRAP	GAMA
EWER	FEED	FINK	FRAS	GAMB
EWES	FEEL	FINO	FRAT	GAME
EWK	FEEN	FINS	FRAU	GAMP
EWKS	FEER	**FIR**	FRAY	GAMS
EWT	FEES	FIRE	**FRO**	GAMY
NEWT	FEET	FIRK	AFRO	**GAN**
EWTS	**FEG**	FIRM	FROE	GANE
EXO	FEGS	FIRN	FROG	GANG
EXON	**FEH**	FIRS	FROM	GANS
EYE	FEHM	**FIT**	FROS	GANT
EYED	FEHS	FITS	FROW	**GAP**
EYEN	**FEM**	FITT	**FUB**	GAPE
EYER	FEME	**FIX**	FUBS	GAPO
EYES	FEMS	FIXT	**FUD**	GAPS
FAA	**FEN**	**FIZ**	FUDS	GAPY
FAAN	FEND	FIZZ	**FUG**	**GAR**

AGAR	GERS	GOES	GURS	WHAP
GARB	GERT	GOEY	GURU	HAPS
GARE	GET	GON	GUS	HAPU
GARI	GETA	AGON	GUSH	HAS
GARS	GETS	GONE	GUST	CHAS
GART	GHI	GONG	GUT	HASH
GAS	GHIS	GONK	GUTS	HASK
AGAS	GIB	GONS	GUV	HASP
GASH	GIBE	GOO	GUVS	HASS
GASP	GIBS	GOOD	GUY	HAST
GAST	GID	GOOF	GUYS	HAT
GAT	GIDS	GOOG	GYM	BHAT
GATE	GIE	GOOK	GYMP	CHAT
GATH	GIED	GOOL	GYMS	GHAT
GATS	GIEN	GOON	GYP	KHAT
GAU	GIES	GOOP	GYPS	PHAT
GAUD	GIF	GOOR	HAD	SHAT
GAUM	GIFT	GOOS	CHAD	THAT
GAUN	GIG	GOR	SHAD	WHAT
GAUP	GIGA	GORA	HADE	HATE
GAUR	GIGS	GORE	HADJ	HATH
GAUS	GIN	GORI	HADS	HATS
GAW	AGIN	GORM	HAE	HAW
GAWD	GING	GORP	THAE	CHAW
GAWK	GINK	GORY	WHAE	SHAW
GAWP	GINN	GOS	HAED	THAW
GAWS	GINS	EGOS	HAEM	HAWK
GAY	GIO	GOSH	HAEN	HAWM
GAYS	AGIO	GOSS	HAES	HAWS
GED	GIOS	GOT	HAET	HAY
AGED	GIP	GOTH	HAG	CHAY
GEDS	GIPS	GOV	SHAG	SHAY
GEE	GIS	GOVS	HAGG	HAYS
AGEE	EGIS	GOY	HAGS	HEH
OGEE	GISM	GOYS	HAH	HEHS
GEED	GIST	GUB	SHAH	HEM
GEEK	GIT	GUBS	HAHA	AHEM
GEEP	GITE	GUE	HAHS	THEM
GEES	GITS	AGUE	HAJ	HEME
GEEZ	GJU	GUES	HAJI	HEMP
GEL	GJUS	GUL	HAJJ	HEMS
GELD	GNU	GULA	HAM	HEN
GELS	GNUS	GULE	CHAM	THEN
GELT	GOA	GULF	SHAM	WHEN
GEM	GOAD	GULL	WHAM	HEND
GEMS	GOAF	GULP	HAME	HENS
GEN	GOAL	GULS	HAMS	HENT
AGEN	GOAS	GULY	HAN	HEP
GENA	GOAT	GUM	KHAN	HEPS
GENE	GOB	GUMP	SHAN	HEPT
GENS	GOBI	GUMS	THAN	HER
GENT	GOBO	GUN	HAND	CHER
GENU	GOBS	GUNG	HANG	HERB
GEO	GOBY	GUNK	HANK	HERD
GEOS	GOD	GUNS	HANT	HERE
GER	GODS	GUP	HAO	HERL
AGER	GOE	GUPS	CHAO	HERM
EGER	YGOE	GUR	HAOS	HERN
GERE	GOEL	GURL	HAP	HERO
GERM	GOER	GURN	CHAP	HERS

HERY	HISH	HOOK	HUMA	PICK
HES	HISN	HOON	HUMF	RICK
SHES	HISS	HOOP	HUMP	SICK
HESP	HIST	HOOR	HUMS	TICK
HEST	**HIT**	HOOT	**HUN**	WICK
HET	CHIT	**HOP**	HUNG	ICKY
KHET	SHIT	CHOP	HUNH	**ICY**
SHET	WHIT	SHOP	HUNK	RICY
WHET	HITS	WHOP	HUNS	**IDE**
HETE	**HOA**	HOPE	HUNT	AIDE
HETH	WHOA	HOPS	**HUP**	BIDE
HETS	HOAR	**HOS**	WHUP	CIDE
HEW	HOAS	MHOS	HUPS	EIDE
CHEW	HOAX	PHOS	**HUT**	HIDE
PHEW	**HOB**	RHOS	BHUT	NIDE
SHEW	HOBO	ZHOS	CHUT	RIDE
THEW	HOBS	HOSE	PHUT	SIDE
WHEW	**HOC**	HOSS	SHUT	TIDE
HEWN	CHOC	HOST	HUTS	VIDE
HEWS	HOCK	**HOT**	**HYE**	WIDE
HEY	**HOD**	PHOT	HYED	IDEA
THEY	SHOD	SHOT	HYEN	IDEE
WHEY	HODS	WHOT	HYES	IDEM
HEYS	**HOE**	HOTE	**HYP**	IDES
HIC	SHOE	HOTS	HYPE	**IDS**
CHIC	HOED	**HOW**	HYPO	AIDS
HICK	HOER	CHOW	HYPS	BIDS
HID	HOES	DHOW	**ICE**	CIDS
CHID	**HOG**	SHOW	BICE	FIDS
WHID	CHOG	WHOW	DICE	GIDS
HIDE	SHOG	HOWE	FICE	KIDS
HIE	HOGG	HOWF	LICE	LIDS
HIED	HOGH	HOWK	MICE	MIDS
HIES	HOGS	HOWL	NICE	NIDS
HIM	**HOH**	HOWS	PICE	RIDS
SHIM	PHOH	**HOY**	RICE	TIDS
WHIM	HOHA	AHOY	SICE	VIDS
HIMS	HOHS	HOYA	TICE	YIDS
HIN	**HOI**	HOYS	VICE	**IFF**
CHIN	HOIK	**HUB**	WICE	BIFF
SHIN	**HOM**	CHUB	ICED	DIFF
THIN	WHOM	HUBS	ICER	JIFF
WHIN	HOMA	**HUE**	ICES	KIFF
HIND	HOME	HUED	**ICH**	MIFF
HING	HOMO	HUER	DICH	NIFF
HINS	HOMS	HUES	LICH	RIFF
HINT	HOMY	**HUG**	MICH	TIFF
HIP	**HON**	CHUG	RICH	ZIFF
CHIP	CHON	THUG	SICH	IFFY
SHIP	PHON	HUGE	TICH	**IFS**
WHIP	THON	HUGS	WICH	DIFS
HIPS	HOND	HUGY	ICHS	KIFS
HIPT	HONE	**HUH**	**ICK**	RIFS
HIS	HONG	HUHU	DICK	**IGG**
AHIS	HONK	**HUI**	HICK	BIGG
CHIS	HONS	HUIA	KICK	MIGG
GHIS	**HOO**	HUIC	LICK	RIGG
KHIS	SHOO	HUIS	MICK	IGGS
PHIS	HOOD	**HUM**	MICK	**ILK**
THIS	HOOF	CHUM	NICK	BILK

MILK	MINK	LIRK	JAKS	**JOR**
SILK	OINK	MIRK	**JAM**	JORS
ILKA	PINK	YIRK	JAMB	**JOT**
ILKS	RINK	IRKS	JAMS	JOTA
ILL	SINK	**ISH**	**JAP**	JOTS
BILL	TINK	BISH	JAPE	**JOW**
CILL	WINK	DISH	JAPS	JOWL
DILL	INKS	EISH	**JAR**	JOWS
FILL	INKY	FISH	AJAR	**JOY**
GILL	**INN**	HISH	JARK	JOYS
HILL	GINN	KISH	JARL	**JUD**
JILL	JINN	NISH	JARP	JUDO
KILL	LINN	PISH	JARS	JUDS
LILL	WINN	WISH	**JAW**	JUDY
MILL	INNS	**ISM**	JAWS	**JUG**
NILL	**INS**	GISM	**JAY**	JUGA
PILL	AINS	JISM	JAYS	JUGS
RILL	BINS	ISMS	**JEE**	**JUN**
SILL	DINS	**ISO**	AJEE	JUNK
TILL	FINS	MISO	JEED	**JUS**
VILL	GINS	PISO	JEEL	GJUS
WILL	HINS	ISOS	JEEP	JUST
YILL	JINS	**ITA**	JEER	**JUT**
ZILL	KINS	DITA	JEES	JUTE
ILLS	LINS	PITA	JEEZ	JUTS
ILLY	PINS	VITA	**JET**	KAB
IMP	QINS	ITAS	JETE	KABS
DIMP	RINS	**ITS**	JETS	KAE
GIMP	SINS	AITS	**JEU**	KAED
JIMP	TINS	BITS	JEUX	KAES
LIMP	VINS	CITS	**JEW**	**KAF**
PIMP	WINS	DITS	JEWS	KAFS
SIMP	YINS	FITS	**JIB**	**KAI**
WIMP	ZINS	GITS	JIBB	KAID
IMPI	**ION**	HITS	JIBE	KAIE
IMPS	CION	KITS	JIBS	KAIF
ING	LION	LITS	**JIG**	KAIK
BING	PION	NITS	JIGS	KAIL
DING	IONS	PITS	**JIN**	KAIM
GING	**IOS**	RITS	DJIN	KAIN
HING	BIOS	SITS	JINK	KAIS
KING	GIOS	TITS	JINN	**KAK**
LING	**IRE**	WITS	JINS	KAKA
MING	CIRE	ZITS	JINX	KAKI
PING	DIRE	**IVY**	JIZ	KAKS
RING	FIRE	JIVY	JIZZ	**KAM**
SING	HIRE	TIVY	**JOB**	KAMA
TING	LIRE	**IWI**	JOBE	KAME
WING	MIRE	KIWI	JOBS	KAMI
ZING	SIRE	IWIS	**JOE**	**KAS**
INGO	TIRE	**JAB**	SJOE	AKAS
INGS	VIRE	JABS	JOES	OKAS
INK	WIRE	**JAG**	JOEY	SKAS
BINK	IRED	JAGA	**JOG**	**KAT**
DINK	IRES	JAGG	JOGS	IKAT
FINK	**IRK**	JAGS	**JOL**	SKAT
GINK	BIRK	**JAI**	JOLE	KATA
JINK	DIRK	JAIL	JOLL	KATI
KINK	FIRK	**JAK**	JOLS	KATS
LINK	KIRK	JAKE	JOLT	**KAW**

SKAW	KIPS	BLAD	LAVA	GLEI
KAWA	**KIR**	CLAD	LAVE	VLEI
KAWS	KIRK	GLAD	LAVS	LEIR
KAY	KIRN	LADE	**LAW**	LEIS
OKAY	KIRS	LADS	BLAW	**LEK**
KAYO	**KIS**	LADY	CLAW	LEKE
KAYS	SKIS	**LAG**	FLAW	LEKS
KEA	KISH	BLAG	SLAW	LEKU
KEAS	KISS	CLAG	LAWK	**LEP**
KEB	KIST	FLAG	LAWN	LEPS
KEBS	**KIT**	SLAG	LAWS	LEPT
KED	SKIT	LAGS	**LAX**	**LES**
AKED	KITE	**LAH**	FLAX	ALES
EKED	KITH	BLAH	**LAY**	OLES
KEDS	KITS	LAHS	ALAY	ULES
KEF	**KOA**	**LAM**	BLAY	LESS
KEFS	KOAN	BLAM	CLAY	LEST
KEG	KOAP	CLAM	FLAY	**LET**
SKEG	KOAS	FLAM	PLAY	BLET
KEGS	**KOB**	GLAM	SLAY	LETS
KEN	KOBO	SLAM	LAYS	**LEU**
SKEN	KOBS	LAMA	**LEA**	LEUD
KENO	**KOI**	LAMB	FLEA	**LEV**
KENS	KOIS	LAME	ILEA	LEVA
KENT	**KON**	LAMP	OLEA	LEVE
KEP	IKON	LAMS	PLEA	LEVO
SKEP	KOND	**LAP**	LEAD	LEVY
KEPI	KONK	ALAP	LEAF	**LEW**
KEPS	KONS	CLAP	LEAK	ALEW
KEPT	**KOP**	FLAP	LEAL	BLEW
KET	KOPH	KLAP	LEAM	CLEW
SKET	KOPS	PLAP	LEAN	FLEW
KETA	**KOR**	SLAP	LEAP	PLEW
KETE	KORA	LAPS	LEAR	SLEW
KETO	KORE	**LAR**	LEAS	LEWD
KETS	KORO	ALAR	LEAT	**LEX**
KEY	KORS	LARD	**LED**	FLEX
KEYS	KORU	LARE	BLED	ILEX
KHI	**KOS**	LARI	FLED	PLEX
KHIS	KOSS	LARK	GLED	ULEX
KID	**KOW**	LARN	PLED	**LEY**
SKID	KOWS	LARS	SLED	BLEY
KIDS	**KUE**	**LAS**	**LEE**	FLEY
KIF	KUEH	ALAS	ALEE	GLEY
KIFF	KUES	LASE	BLEE	SLEY
KIFS	**KYE**	LASH	FLEE	LEYS
KIN	KYES	LASS	GLEE	**LEZ**
AKIN	**KYU**	LAST	SLEE	LEZZ
SKIN	KYUS	**LAT**	LEED	**LIB**
KINA	**LAB**	BLAT	LEEK	GLIB
KIND	BLAB	CLAT	LEEP	LIBS
KINE	FLAB	FLAT	LEER	**LID**
KING	SLAB	PLAT	LEES	GLID
KINK	LABS	SLAT	LEET	OLID
KINO	**LAC**	LATE	**LEG**	SLID
KINS	LACE	LATH	CLEG	LIDO
KIP	LACK	LATI	FLEG	LIDS
SKIP	LACS	LATS	GLEG	**LIE**
KIPE	LACY	LATU	LEGS	PLIE
KIPP	**LAD**	**LAV**	**LEI**	LIED

LIEF	FLOG	GLOW	MAES	MATY
LIEN	SLOG	PLOW	**MAG**	**MAW**
LIER	VLOG	SLOW	MAGE	MAWK
LIES	LOGE	LOWE	MAGG	MAWN
LIEU	LOGO	LOWN	MAGI	MAWR
LIG	LOGS	LOWP	MAGS	MAWS
LIGS	LOGY	LOWS	**MAK**	**MAX**
LIN	**LOO**	LOWT	MAKE	MAXI
BLIN	ALOO	**LOX**	MAKI	**MAY**
LIND	LOOF	FLOX	MAKO	MAYA
LINE	LOOK	**LOY**	MAKS	MAYO
LING	LOOM	CLOY	**MAL**	MAYS
LINK	LOON	PLOY	MALA	**MED**
LINN	LOOP	LOYS	MALE	MEDS
LINO	LOOR	**LUD**	MALI	**MEE**
LINS	LOOS	LUDE	MALL	SMEE
LINT	LOOT	LUDO	MALM	MEED
LINY	**LOP**	LUDS	MALS	MEEK
LIP	CLOP	**LUG**	MALT	MEER
BLIP	FLOP	GLUG	**MAM**	MEES
CLIP	GLOP	PLUG	IMAM	MEET
FLIP	PLOP	SLUG	MAMA	**MEG**
SLIP	SLOP	LUGE	MAMS	MEGA
LIPA	LOPE	LUGS	**MAN**	MEGS
LIPE	LOPS	**LUM**	MANA	**MEL**
LIPO	**LOR**	ALUM	MAND	MELA
LIPS	FLOR	GLUM	MANE	MELD
LIS	LORD	PLUM	MANG	MELL
LISK	LORE	SLUM	MANI	MELS
LISP	LORN	LUMA	MANO	MELT
LIST	LORY	LUMP	MANS	**MEM**
LIT	**LOS**	LUMS	MANY	MEME
ALIT	LOSE	**LUR**	**MAP**	MEMO
BLIT	LOSH	BLUR	MAPS	MEMS
CLIT	LOSS	SLUR	**MAR**	**MEN**
FLIT	LOST	LURE	MARA	AMEN
GLIT	**LOT**	LURK	MARC	OMEN
SLIT	BLOT	LURS	MARD	MEND
LITE	CLOT	**LUV**	MARE	MENE
LITH	PLOT	LUVS	MARG	MENG
LITS	SLOT	**LUX**	MARK	MENO
LITU	LOTA	FLUX	MARL	MENT
LOB	LOTE	LUXE	MARM	MENU
BLOB	LOTH	**LYE**	MARS	**MES**
FLOB	LOTI	LYES	MART	AMES
GLOB	LOTO	**LYM**	MARY	EMES
SLOB	LOTS	LYME	**MAS**	MESA
LOBE	**LOU**	LYMS	AMAS	MESE
LOBI	CLOU	**MAA**	MASA	MESH
LOBO	LOUD	MAAR	MASE	MESS
LOBS	LOUN	MAAS	MASH	**MET**
LOD	LOUP	**MAC**	MASK	META
ALOD	LOUR	MACE	MASS	METE
CLOD	LOUS	MACH	MAST	METH
PLOD	LOUT	MACK	MASU	METS
LODE	**LOW**	MACS	**MAT**	**MEU**
LODS	ALOW	**MAD**	MATE	EMEU
LOG	BLOW	MADE	MATH	MEUS
BLOG	CLOW	MADS	MATS	**MEW**
CLOG	FLOW	**MAE**	MATT	SMEW

MEWL	MOAS	MORS	MUTE	NEKS
MEWS	MOAT	MORT	MUTI	**NEP**
MHO	**MOB**	**MOS**	MUTS	NEPS
MHOS	MOBE	EMOS	MUTT	**NET**
MIB	MOBS	MOSE	**MYC**	NETE
MIBS	MOBY	MOSH	MYCS	NETS
MIC	**MOC**	MOSK	**NAB**	NETT
EMIC	MOCH	MOSS	SNAB	**NEW**
MICA	MOCK	MOST	NABE	ANEW
MICE	MOCS	**MOT**	NABK	ENEW
MICH	**MOD**	MOTE	NABS	KNEW
MICK	MODE	MOTH	**NAG**	NEWS
MICO	MODI	MOTI	KNAG	NEWT
MICS	MODS	MOTS	SNAG	**NIB**
MID	**MOE**	MOTT	NAGA	SNIB
AMID	MOER	MOTU	NAGS	NIBS
IMID	MOES	**MOU**	**NAM**	**NID**
MIDI	**MOG**	MOUE	NAME	NIDE
MIDS	SMOG	MOUP	NAMS	NIDI
MIG	MOGS	MOUS	NAMU	NIDS
MIGG	**MOI**	**MOW**	**NAN**	**NIE**
MIGS	MOIL	MOWA	ANAN	ONIE
MIL	MOIT	MOWN	NANA	NIED
MILD	**MOL**	MOWS	NANE	NIEF
MILE	MOLA	**MOY**	NANG	NIES
MILF	MOLD	MOYA	NANS	**NIL**
MILK	MOLE	MOYL	**NAP**	ANIL
MILL	MOLL	MOYS	KNAP	NILL
MILO	MOLS	**MOZ**	SNAP	NILS
MILS	MOLT	MOZE	NAPA	**NIM**
MILT	MOLY	MOZO	NAPE	NIMB
MIM	**MOM**	MOZZ	NAPS	NIMS
MIME	MOME	**MUD**	**NAS**	**NIP**
MIR	MOMI	MUDS	ANAS	SNIP
AMIR	MOMS	**MUG**	MNAS	NIPA
EMIR	**MON**	SMUG	**NAT**	NIPS
SMIR	MONA	MUGG	GNAT	**NIS**
MIRE	MONG	MUGS	NATS	ANIS
MIRI	MONK	**MUM**	**NAW**	UNIS
MIRK	MONO	MUMM	GNAW	NISH
MIRO	MONS	MUMP	SNAW	NISI
MIRS	MONY	MUMS	**NAY**	**NIT**
MIRV	**MOO**	MUMU	NAYS	KNIT
MIRY	MOOD	**MUN**	**NEB**	SNIT
MIS	MOOI	MUNG	SNEB	UNIT
AMIS	MOOK	MUNI	NEBS	NITE
MISE	MOOL	MUNS	**NED**	NITS
MISO	MOON	MUNT	SNED	**NIX**
MISS	MOOP	**MUS**	NEDS	NIXE
MIST	MOOR	AMUS	**NEE**	NIXY
MIX	MOOS	EMUS	KNEE	**NOB**
MIXT	MOOT	UMUS	SNEE	KNOB
MIXY	**MOP**	MUSE	NEED	SNOB
MIZ	MOPE	MUSH	NEEM	NOBS
MIZZ	MOPS	MUSK	NEEP	**NOD**
MNA	MOPY	MUSO	**NEF**	SNOD
MNAS	**MOR**	MUSS	NEFS	NODE
MOA	MORA	MUST	**NEG**	NODI
MOAI	MORE	**MUT**	NEGS	NODS
MOAN	MORN	SMUT	**NEK**	**NOG**

SNOG	GNUS	OBOS	**OES**	OKAS
NOGG	ONUS	**OBS**	DOES	OKAY
NOGS	**NUT**	BOBS	FOES	**OKE**
NOM	KNUT	COBS	GOES	BOKE
NOMA	NUTS	DOBS	HOES	COKE
NOME	**NYE**	FOBS	JOES	HOKE
NOMS	SNYE	GOBS	MOES	JOKE
NON	NYED	HOBS	NOES	LOKE
ANON	NYES	JOBS	ROES	MOKE
NONA	**OAF**	KOBS	TOES	POKE
NONE	GOAF	LOBS	VOES	ROKE
NONG	LOAF	MOBS	WOES	SOKE
NONI	OAFS	NOBS	**OFF**	TOKE
NOO	**OAK**	ROBS	BOFF	WOKE
NOOB	BOAK	SOBS	COFF	YOKE
NOOK	SOAK	YOBS	DOFF	OKEH
NOON	OAKS	**OCA**	GOFF	OKES
NOOP	OAKY	COCA	KOFF	**OLD**
NOR	**OAR**	LOCA	TOFF	BOLD
NORI	BOAR	SOCA	OFFS	COLD
NORK	HOAR	OCAS	OFFY	FOLD
NORM	ROAR	**OCH**	**OFT**	GOLD
NOS	SOAR	COCH	COFT	HOLD
ONOS	VOAR	LOCH	LOFT	MOLD
NOSE	OARS	MOCH	SOFT	SOLD
NOSH	OARY	ROCH	TOFT	TOLD
NOSY	**OAT**	OCHE	**OHM**	WOLD
NOT	BOAT	**ODA**	OHMS	YOLD
KNOT	COAT	CODA	**OHO**	OLDE
SNOT	DOAT	SODA	BOHO	OLDS
NOTA	GOAT	ODAH	COHO	OLDY
NOTE	MOAT	ODAL	SOHO	**OLE**
NOTT	OATH	ODAS	TOHO	BOLE
NOW	OATS	**ODD**	**OHS**	COLE
ANOW	OATY	ODDS	BOHS	DOLE
ENOW	**OBA**	**ODE**	DOHS	GOLE
GNOW	BOBA	BODE	HOHS	HOLE
KNOW	SOBA	CODE	OOHS	JOLE
SNOW	OBAS	LODE	SOHS	MOLE
NOWL	**OBE**	MODE	**OIK**	NOLE
NOWN	JOBE	NODE	HOIK	POLE
NOWS	LOBE	RODE	OIKS	ROLE
NOWT	MOBE	YODE	**OIL**	SOLE
NOWY	ROBE	ODEA	BOIL	TOLE
NOY	OBES	ODES	COIL	VOLE
NOYS	OBEY	**ODS**	FOIL	OLEA
NUB	**OBI**	BODS	MOIL	OLEO
KNUB	GOBI	CODS	NOIL	OLES
SNUB	LOBI	DODS	ROIL	**OLM**
NUBS	OBIA	GODS	SOIL	HOLM
NUN	OBIS	HODS	TOIL	OLMS
NUNS	OBIT	LODS	OILS	**OMS**
NUR	**OBO**	MODS	OILY	COMS
KNUR	GOBO	NODS	**OIS**	DOMS
NURD	HOBO	PODS	BOIS	HOMS
NURL	KOBO	RODS	KOIS	MOMS
NURR	LOBO	SODS	POIS	NOMS
NURS	ZOBO	TODS	**OKA**	OOMS
NUS	OBOE	YODS	HOKA	POMS
ANUS	OBOL	ODSO	KOKA	ROMS

SOMS	BOOM	BOOT	TORC	NOSE
TOMS	COOM	COOT	ORCA	OOSE
ONE	DOOM	FOOT	ORCS	POSE
BONE	LOOM	HOOT	**ORD**	ROSE
CONE	ROOM	LOOT	BORD	TOSE
DONE	SOOM	MOOT	CORD	OSES
FONE	TOOM	POOT	FORD	**OUD**
GONE	ZOOM	ROOT	LORD	FOUD
HONE	OOMS	SOOT	SORD	LOUD
LONE	**OON**	TOOT	WORD	OUDS
NONE	BOON	WOOT	ORDO	**OUK**
PONE	COON	ZOOT	ORDS	BOUK
RONE	DOON	OOTS	**ORE**	DOUK
SONE	GOON	**OPE**	BORE	GOUK
TONE	HOON	COPE	CORE	JOUK
ZONE	LOON	DOPE	DORE	POUK
ONER	MOON	HOPE	FORE	SOUK
ONES	NOON	LOPE	GORE	TOUK
ONO	POON	MOPE	HORE	YOUK
MONO	ROON	NOPE	KORE	ZOUK
ONOS	SOON	POPE	LORE	OUKS
ONS	TOON	ROPE	MORE	**OUP**
CONS	WOON	TOPE	PORE	COUP
DONS	ZOON	OPED	RORE	DOUP
EONS	OONS	OPEN	SORE	LOUP
FONS	OONT	OPES	TORE	MOUP
GONS	**OOP**	**OPS**	WORE	NOUP
HONS	COOP	BOPS	YORE	ROUP
IONS	GOOP	COPS	ORES	SOUP
KONS	HOOP	DOPS	**ORF**	OUPA
MONS	LOOP	FOPS	CORF	OUPH
OONS	MOOP	HOPS	ORFE	OUPS
PONS	NOOP	KOPS	ORFS	**OUR**
SONS	POOP	LOPS	**ORS**	COUR
TONS	ROOP	MOPS	BORS	DOUR
WONS	SOOP	OOPS	CORS	FOUR
ONST	YOOP	POPS	DORS	HOUR
ONY	OOPS	SOPS	HORS	JOUR
BONY	**OOR**	TOPS	JORS	LOUR
CONY	BOOR	WOPS	KORS	POUR
MONY	DOOR	**OPT**	MORS	SOUR
PONY	GOOR	OPTS	TORS	TOUR
TONY	HOOR	**ORA**	VORS	YOUR
ONYX	LOOR	BORA	**ORT**	OURN
OOF	MOOR	FORA	BORT	OURS
COOF	POOR	GORA	DORT	**OUS**
GOOF	**OOS**	HORA	FORT	FOUS
HOOF	BOOS	KORA	MORT	LOUS
LOOF	COOS	MORA	PORT	MOUS
POOF	DOOS	SORA	RORT	NOUS
ROOF	GOOS	TORA	SORT	SOUS
WOOF	LOOS	ORAD	TORT	YOUS
YOOF	MOOS	ORAL	WORT	OUST
OOFS	POOS	**ORB**	ORTS	**OUT**
OOFY	ROOS	DORB	**OSE**	BOUT
OOH	WOOS	FORB	COSE	DOUT
BOOH	ZOOS	SORB	DOSE	GOUT
POOH	OOSE	ORBS	HOSE	HOUT
OOHS	OOSY	ORBY	LOSE	LOUT
OOM	**OOT**	**ORC**	MOSE	NOUT

POUT	GOYS	PAST	PELT	**PIN**
ROUT	HOYS	**PAT**	**PEN**	SPIN
SOUT	JOYS	SPAT	OPEN	PINA
TOUT	LOYS	PATE	PEND	PINE
OUTS	MOYS	PATH	PENE	PING
OVA	NOYS	PATS	PENI	PINK
NOVA	SOYS	PATU	PENK	PINS
OVAL	TOYS	PATY	PENS	PINT
OWE	**PAC**	**PAV**	PENT	PINY
HOWE	PACA	PAVE	**PEP**	**PIP**
LOWE	PACE	PAVS	PEPO	PIPA
YOWE	PACK	**PAW**	PEPS	PIPE
OWED	PACO	SPAW	**PER**	PIPI
OWER	PACS	PAWA	APER	PIPS
OWES	PACT	PAWK	PERE	PIPY
OWL	PACY	PAWL	PERI	**PIR**
BOWL	**PAD**	PAWN	PERK	PIRL
COWL	PADI	PAWS	PERM	PIRN
DOWL	PADS	**PAY**	PERN	PIRS
FOWL	**PAH**	APAY	PERP	**PIS**
GOWL	OPAH	SPAY	PERT	PISE
HOWL	PAHS	PAYS	PERV	PISH
JOWL	**PAL**	**PEA**	**PES**	PISO
NOWL	OPAL	PEAG	APES	PISS
SOWL	PALE	PEAK	PESO	**PIT**
YOWL	PALL	PEAL	PEST	SPIT
OWLS	PALM	PEAN	**PET**	PITA
OWLY	PALP	PEAR	PETS	PITH
OWN	PALS	PEAS	**PEW**	PITS
DOWN	PALY	PEAT	SPEW	PITY
GOWN	**PAM**	**PEC**	PEWS	**PIU**
LOWN	SPAM	SPEC	PHI	PIUM
MOWN	PAMS	PECH	PHIS	**PIX**
NOWN	**PAN**	PECK	PHIZ	PIXY
POWN	SPAN	PECS	**PHO**	**PLU**
SOWN	PAND	**PED**	PHOH	PLUE
TOWN	PANE	APED	PHON	PLUG
OWNS	PANG	OPED	PHOS	PLUM
OWT	PANS	SPED	PHOT	PLUS
DOWT	PANT	PEDS	**PIA**	**POA**
LOWT	**PAP**	**PEE**	PIAL	POAS
NOWT	PAPA	EPEE	PIAN	**POD**
ROWT	PAPE	PEED	PIAS	APOD
TOWT	PAPS	PEEK	**PIC**	SPOD
OWTS	**PAR**	PEEL	EPIC	PODS
OXY	SPAR	PEEN	SPIC	**POI**
BOXY	PARA	PEEP	PICA	POIS
COXY	PARD	PEER	PICE	**POL**
DOXY	PARE	PEES	PICK	POLE
FOXY	PARK	**PEG**	PICS	POLK
POXY	PARP	PEGH	**PIE**	POLL
OYE	PARR	PEGS	SPIE	POLO
OYER	PARS	**PEH**	PIED	POLS
OYES	PART	PEHS	PIER	POLT
OYEZ	**PAS**	**PEL**	PIES	POLY
OYS	SPAS	PELA	PIET	**POM**
BOYS	UPAS	PELE	**PIG**	POME
COYS	PASE	PELF	PIGS	POMO
DOYS	PASH	PELL		POMP
FOYS	PASS	PELS		POMS

POO	**PUD**	AQUA	FRAP	REDE
POOD	SPUD	QUAD	TRAP	REDO
POOF	PUDS	QUAG	WRAP	REDS
POOH	PUDU	QUAI	RAPE	**REE**
POOK	**PUG**	QUAT	RAPS	BREE
POOL	SPUG	QUAY	RAPT	CREE
POON	PUGH	**RAD**	**RAS**	DREE
POOP	PUGS	BRAD	BRAS	FREE
POOR	**PUH**	DRAD	ERAS	GREE
POOS	PUHA	GRAD	FRAS	PREE
POOT	**PUL**	ORAD	RASE	TREE
POP	PULA	PRAD	RASH	REED
POPE	PULE	TRAD	RASP	REEF
POPS	PULI	RADE	RAST	REEK
POS	PULK	RADS	**RAT**	REEL
APOS	PULL	**RAG**	BRAT	REEN
EPOS	PULP	BRAG	DRAT	REES
POSE	PULS	CRAG	FRAT	**REF**
POSH	PULU	DRAG	GRAT	TREF
POSS	PULY	FRAG	PRAT	REFS
POST	**PUN**	RAGA	TRAT	REFT
POSY	SPUN	RAGE	RATA	**REG**
POT	PUNA	RAGG	RATE	AREG
SPOT	PUNG	RAGI	RATH	DREG
POTE	PUNK	RAGS	RATO	REGO
POTS	PUNS	RAGU	RATS	REGS
POTT	PUNT	**RAH**	RATU	**REH**
POW	PUNY	RAHS	**RAV**	REHS
POWN	**PUP**	**RAI**	GRAV	**REI**
POWS	PUPA	RAIA	RAVE	BREI
POX	PUPS	RAID	RAVS	REIF
POXY	PUPU	RAIK	**RAW**	REIK
POZ	**PUR**	RAIL	BRAW	REIN
POZZ	SPUR	RAIN	CRAW	REIS
PRE	PURE	RAIS	DRAW	**REM**
PREE	PURI	RAIT	RAWN	CREM
PREM	PURL	**RAJ**	RAWS	PREM
PREP	PURR	RAJA	**RAY**	REMS
PREX	PURS	**RAM**	BRAY	**REN**
PREY	**PUS**	CRAM	CRAY	BREN
PREZ	OPUS	DRAM	DRAY	GREN
PRO	PUSH	GRAM	FRAY	WREN
PROA	PUSS	PRAM	GRAY	REND
PROB	**PUT**	TRAM	PRAY	RENK
PROD	PUTS	RAMI	TRAY	RENS
PROF	PUTT	RAMP	XRAY	RENT
PROG	PUTZ	RAMS	RAYA	RENY
PROM	**PUY**	**RAN**	RAYS	**REO**
PROO	PUYS	BRAN	**REB**	REOS
PROP	**PYA**	CRAN	REBS	**REP**
PROS	PYAS	GRAN	**REC**	PREP
PROW	PYAT	RANA	RECK	REPO
PRY	**PYE**	RAND	RECS	REPP
SPRY	PYES	RANG	**RED**	REPS
PRYS	PYET	RANI	ARED	**RES**
PSI	**QAT**	RANK	BRED	ARES
PSIS	QATS	RANT	CRED	ERES
PUB	**QIN**	**RAP**	ERED	IRES
PUBE	QINS	CRAP	IRED	ORES
PUBS	**QUA**	DRAP	REDD	TRES

URES	BRIM	GROK	TRUE	SALL
RESH	CRIM	ROKE	RUED	SALP
REST	GRIM	ROKS	RUER	SALS
RET	PRIM	ROKY	RUES	SALT
ARET	TRIM	**ROM**	**RUG**	**SAM**
FRET	RIMA	FROM	DRUG	SAMA
TRET	RIME	PROM	FRUG	SAME
RETE	RIMS	ROMA	TRUG	SAMP
RETS	RIMU	ROMP	RUGA	SAMS
REV	RIMY	ROMS	RUGS	**SAN**
EREV	**RIN**	**ROO**	**RUM**	SAND
REVS	BRIN	BROO	ARUM	SANE
REW	GRIN	PROO	DRUM	SANG
AREW	TRIN	ROOD	GRUM	SANK
BREW	RIND	ROOF	RUME	SANS
CREW	RINE	ROOK	RUMP	SANT
DREW	RING	ROOM	RUMS	**SAP**
GREW	RINK	ROON	**RUN**	SAPS
TREW	RINS	ROOP	RUND	**SAR**
REWS	**RIP**	ROOS	RUNE	ASAR
REX	DRIP	ROOT	RUNG	KSAR
GREX	GRIP	**ROT**	RUNS	OSAR
PREX	TRIP	GROT	RUNT	TSAR
REZ	RIPE	TROT	**RUT**	SARD
PREZ	RIPP	VROT	BRUT	SARI
TREZ	RIPS	ROTA	RUTH	SARK
RHO	RIPT	ROTE	RUTS	SARS
RHOS	**RIT**	ROTI	**RYA**	**SAT**
RIA	BRIT	ROTL	RYAL	SATE
ARIA	CRIT	ROTO	RYAS	SATI
CRIA	FRIT	ROTS	**RYE**	**SAU**
RIAD	GRIT	**ROW**	TRYE	SAUL
RIAL	WRIT	AROW	RYES	SAUT
RIAS	RITE	BROW	**SAB**	**SAV**
RIB	RITS	CROW	SABE	SAVE
CRIB	RITT	DROW	SABS	SAVS
DRIB	RITZ	FROW	**SAC**	**SAW**
FRIB	**RIZ**	GROW	SACK	SAWN
RIBA	FRIZ	PROW	SACS	SAWS
RIBS	RIZA	TROW	**SAD**	**SAX**
RID	**ROB**	VROW	SADE	SAXE
ARID	PROB	ROWS	SADI	**SAY**
GRID	ROBE	ROWT	SADO	SAYS
IRID	ROBS	**RUB**	SADS	**SEA**
RIDE	**ROC**	DRUB	**SAG**	ASEA
RIDS	CROC	GRUB	SAGA	SEAL
RIF	ROCH	RUBE	SAGE	SEAM
RIFE	ROCK	RUBS	SAGO	SEAN
RIFF	ROCS	RUBY	SAGS	SEAR
RIFS	**ROD**	**RUC**	SAGY	SEAS
RIFT	BROD	RUCK	**SAI**	SEAT
RIG	PROD	RUCS	SAIC	**SEC**
BRIG	TROD	**RUD**	SAID	SECH
FRIG	RODE	CRUD	SAIL	SECO
GRIG	RODS	RUDD	SAIM	SECS
PRIG	**ROE**	RUDE	SAIN	SECT
TRIG	FROE	RUDS	SAIR	**SED**
RIGG	ROED	**RUE**	SAIS	USED
RIGS	ROES	CRUE	**SAL**	**SEE**
RIM	**ROK**	GRUE	SALE	SEED

SEEK	SHES	**SKY**	SOWM	SUQS
SEEL	SHET	ESKY	SOWN	**SUR**
SEEM	SHEW	SKYF	SOWP	SURA
SEEN	**SHY**	SKYR	SOWS	SURD
SEEP	ASHY	**SNY**	**SOY**	SURE
SEER	**SIB**	SNYE	SOYA	SURF
SEES	SIBB	**SOB**	SOYS	**SUS**
SEG	SIBS	SOBA	**SPA**	SUSS
SEGO	**SIC**	SOBS	SPAE	SUSU
SEGS	SICE	**SOC**	SPAG	**SYE**
SEI	SICH	SOCA	SPAM	SYED
SEIF	SICK	SOCK	SPAN	SYEN
SEIK	SICS	SOCS	SPAR	SYES
SEIL	**SIF**	**SOD**	SPAS	**SYN**
SEIR	SIFT	SODA	SPAT	SYNC
SEIS	**SIK**	SODS	SPAW	SYND
SEL	SIKA	**SOG**	SPAY	SYNE
SELD	SIKE	SOGS	SPAZ	**TAB**
SELE	**SIM**	**SOH**	**SPY**	STAB
SELF	SIMA	SOHO	ESPY	TABI
SELL	SIMI	SOHS	**SRI**	TABS
SELS	SIMP	**SOL**	SRIS	TABU
SEN	SIMS	SOLA	**STY**	**TAD**
SENA	**SIN**	SOLD	STYE	TADS
SEND	SIND	SOLE	**SUB**	**TAE**
SENE	SINE	SOLI	SUBA	TAED
SENS	SING	SOLO	SUBS	TAEL
SENT	SINH	SOLS	**SUD**	TAES
SER	SINK	**SOM**	SUDD	**TAG**
USER	SINS	SOMA	SUDS	STAG
SERA	**SIP**	SOME	**SUE**	TAGS
SERE	SIPE	SOMS	SUED	**TAI**
SERF	SIPS	SOMY	SUER	TAIG
SERK	**SIR**	**SON**	SUES	TAIL
SERR	SIRE	SONE	SUET	TAIN
SERS	SIRI	SONG	**SUG**	TAIS
SET	SIRS	SONS	SUGH	TAIT
SETA	**SIS**	**SOP**	SUGO	**TAK**
SETS	PSIS	SOPH	SUGS	TAKA
SETT	SISS	SOPS	**SUI**	TAKE
SEW	SIST	**SOS**	SUID	TAKI
SEWN	**SIT**	DSOS	SUIT	TAKS
SEWS	ISIT	ISOS	**SUK**	TAKY
SEX	SITE	**SOT**	SUKH	**TAM**
SEXT	SITH	SOTH	SUKS	TAME
SEXY	SITS	SOTS	**SUM**	TAMP
SEY	SITZ	**SOU**	SUMO	TAMS
SEYS	**SKA**	SOUK	SUMP	**TAN**
SHA	SKAG	SOUL	SUMS	TANA
SHAD	SKAS	SOUM	SUMY	TANE
SHAG	SKAT	SOUP	**SUN**	TANG
SHAH	SKAW	SOUR	SUNG	TANH
SHAM	**SKI**	SOUS	SUNI	TANK
SHAN	SKID	SOUT	SUNK	TANS
SHAT	SKIM	**SOV**	SUNN	**TAO**
SHAW	SKIN	SOVS	SUNS	TAOS
SHAY	SKIO	**SOW**	**SUP**	**TAP**
SHE	SKIP	SOWF	SUPE	ATAP
SHEA	SKIS	SOWL	SUPS	STAP
SHED	SKIT		**SUQ**	TAPA

TAPE	TEED	TIDE	TOME	ETUI
TAPS	TEEK	TIDS	TOMO	PTUI
TAPU	TEEL	TIDY	TOMS	TUIS
TAR	TEEM	**TIE**	**TON**	**TUM**
STAR	TEEN	STIE	TONE	STUM
TARA	TEER	TIED	TONG	TUMP
TARE	TEES	TIER	TONK	TUMS
TARN	**TEF**	TIES	TONS	**TUN**
TARO	TEFF	**TIG**	TONY	STUN
TARP	TEFS	TIGE	**TOO**	TUNA
TARS	**TEG**	TIGS	TOOK	TUND
TART	TEGG	**TIK**	TOOL	TUNE
TAS	TEGS	TIKA	TOOM	TUNG
ETAS	TEGU	TIKE	TOON	TUNS
ITAS	**TEL**	TIKI	TOOT	TUNY
UTAS	TELA	TIKS	**TOP**	**TUP**
TASH	TELD	**TIL**	ATOP	TUPS
TASK	TELE	TILE	STOP	**TUT**
TASS	TELL	TILL	TOPE	TUTS
TAT	TELS	TILS	TOPH	TUTU
ETAT	TELT	TILT	TOPI	**TWA**
STAT	**TEN**	**TIN**	TOPO	TWAE
TATE	ETEN	TINA	TOPS	TWAL
TATH	STEN	TIND	**TOR**	TWAS
TATS	TEND	TINE	TORA	TWAT
TATT	TENE	TING	TORC	TWAY
TATU	TENS	TINK	TORE	**TWO**
TAU	TENT	TINS	TORI	TWOS
TAUS	**TES**	TINT	TORN	**TYE**
TAUT	ATES	TINY	TORO	STYE
TAV	UTES	**TIP**	TORR	TYED
TAVA	TEST	TIPI	TORS	TYEE
TAVS	**TET**	TIPS	TORT	TYER
TAW	STET	TIPT	TORY	TYES
STAW	TETE	**TIS**	**TOT**	**TYG**
TAWA	TETH	UTIS	STOT	TYGS
TAWS	TETS	**TIT**	TOTE	**UDO**
TAWT	**TEW**	TITE	TOTS	BUDO
TAX	STEW	TITI	**TOW**	JUDO
TAXA	TEWS	TITS	STOW	KUDO
TAXI	**TEX**	**TOC**	TOWN	LUDO
TAY	TEXT	ATOC	TOWS	UDON
STAY	**THE**	TOCK	TOWT	UDOS
TAYS	ETHE	TOCO	TOWY	**UDS**
TEA	THEE	TOCS	**TOY**	BUDS
TEAD	THEM	**TOD**	TOYO	CUDS
TEAK	THEN	TODS	TOYS	DUDS
TEAL	THEW	TODY	**TRY**	FUDS
TEAM	THEY	**TOE**	TRYE	JUDS
TEAR	**THO**	TOEA	TRYP	LUDS
TEAS	THON	TOED	**TSK**	MUDS
TEAT	THOU	TOES	TSKS	OUDS
TEC	**TIC**	TOEY	**TUB**	PUDS
TECH	ETIC	**TOG**	STUB	RUDS
TECS	OTIC	TOGA	TUBA	SUDS
TED	TICE	TOGE	TUBE	WUDS
STED	TICH	TOGS	TUBS	**UEY**
TEDS	TICK	**TOM**	**TUG**	QUEY
TEDY	TICS	ATOM	TUGS	UEYS
TEE	**TID**	TOMB	**TUI**	**UFO**

BUFO	PUMP	NURD	TUTU	VIDS
UFOS	RUMP	SURD	UTUS	**VIE**
UGH	SUMP	TURD	**UVA**	VIED
EUGH	TUMP	URDE	UVAE	VIER
PUGH	YUMP	URDS	UVAS	VIES
SUGH	UMPH	URDY	**VAC**	VIEW
VUGH	UMPS	**URE**	VACS	**VIG**
UGHS	UMPY	CURE	**VAE**	VIGA
UGS	**UMS**	DURE	UVAE	VIGS
BUGS	BUMS	IURE	VAES	**VIM**
DUGS	CUMS	JURE	**VAG**	VIMS
FUGS	FUMS	LURE	VAGI	**VIN**
HUGS	GUMS	MURE	VAGS	VINA
JUGS	HUMS	PURE	**VAN**	VINE
LUGS	LUMS	SURE	VANE	VINO
MUGS	MUMS	UREA	VANG	VINS
PUGS	RUMS	URES	VANS	VINT
RUGS	SUMS	**URN**	VANT	VINY
SUGS	TUMS	BURN	**VAR**	**VIS**
TUGS	VUMS	CURN	VARA	VISA
VUGS	**UMU**	DURN	VARE	VISE
YUGS	MUMU	GURN	VARS	**VOE**
UKE	UMUS	OURN	VARY	EVOE
BUKE	**UNI**	TURN	**VAS**	VOES
CUKE	MUNI	URNS	AVAS	**VOL**
DUKE	SUNI	**URP**	KVAS	VOLA
JUKE	UNIS	BURP	UVAS	VOLE
LUKE	UNIT	RURP	VASA	VOLK
NUKE	**UNS**	URPS	VASE	VOLS
PUKE	BUNS	**USE**	VAST	VOLT
YUKE	DUNS	FUSE	**VAT**	**VOR**
UKES	FUNS	MUSE	VATS	VORS
ULE	GUNS	RUSE	VATU	**VOW**
DULE	HUNS	USED	**VAU**	AVOW
GULE	MUNS	USER	VAUS	VOWS
HULE	NUNS	USES	VAUT	**VUG**
MULE	PUNS	**UTA**	**VAV**	VUGG
PULE	RUNS	KUTA	VAVS	VUGH
RULE	SUNS	UTAS	**VAW**	VUGS
TULE	TUNS	**UTE**	VAWS	**VUM**
YULE	**UPO**	BUTE	VEE	OVUM
ULES	UPON	CUTE	VEEP	VUMS
ULEX	**UPS**	JUTE	VEER	**WAB**
ULU	CUPS	LUTE	VEES	SWAB
LULU	DUPS	MUTE	**VEG**	WABS
PULU	GUPS	UTES	VEGA	**WAD**
SULU	HUPS	**UTS**	VEGO	SWAD
ZULU	OUPS	BUTS	**VET**	WADD
ULUS	PUPS	CUTS	EVET	WADE
UMM	SUPS	GUTS	VETO	WADI
MUMM	TUPS	HUTS	VETS	WADS
UMMA	YUPS	JUTS	**VEX**	WADT
UMP	UPSY	MUTS	VEXT	WADY
BUMP	**URB**	NUTS	**VIA**	**WAE**
DUMP	BURB	OUTS	VIAE	TWAE
GUMP	CURB	PUTS	VIAL	WAES
HUMP	URBS	RUTS	VIAS	**WAG**
JUMP	**URD**	TUTS	**VID**	SWAG
LUMP	BURD	**UTU**	AVID	WAGE
MUMP	CURD	KUTU	VIDE	WAGS

WAI	OWED	YWIS	**YAD**	WYES	
WAID	WEDS	WISE	DYAD	YESK	
WAIF	**WEE**	WISH	YADS	YEST	
WAIL	AWEE	WISP	**YAG**	**YET**	
WAIN	SWEE	WISS	YAGI	PYET	
WAIR	TWEE	WIST	YAGS	YETI	
WAIS	WEED	**WIT**	**YAH**	YETT	
WAIT	WEEK	TWIT	AYAH	**YEW**	
WAN	WEEL	WITE	YAHS	YEWS	
HWAN	WEEM	WITH	**YAK**	**YGO**	
SWAN	WEEN	WITS	KYAK	YGOE	
WAND	WEEP	**WIZ**	YAKS	**YID**	
WANE	WEER	SWIZ	**YAM**	YIDS	
WANG	WEES	**WOE**	LYAM	**YIN**	
WANK	WEET	WOES	YAMS	AYIN	
WANS	**WEM**	**WOF**	**YAP**	PYIN	
WANT	WEMB	WOFS	YAPP	TYIN	
WANY	WEMS	**WOG**	YAPS	YINS	
WAP	**WEN**	WOGS	**YAR**	**YIP**	
SWAP	WENA	**WOK**	KYAR	YIPE	
WAPS	WEND	WOKE	YARD	YIPS	
WAR	WENS	WOKS	YARE	**YOB**	
WARB	WENT	**WON**	YARK	YOBS	
WARD	**WET**	WONK	YARN	**YOD**	
WARE	WETA	WONS	YARR	YODE	
WARK	WETS	WONT	**YAW**	YODH	
WARM	**WEX**	**WOO**	YAWL	YODS	
WARN	WEXE	WOOD	YAWN	**YOK**	
WARP	**WEY**	WOOF	YAWP	YOKE	
WARS	SWEY	WOOL	YAWS	YOKS	
WART	WEYS	WOON	YAWY	**YOM**	
WARY	**WHA**	WOOS	**YAY**	YOMP	
WAS	WHAE	WOOT	YAYS	**YON**	
TWAS	WHAM	**WOP**	**YEA**	YOND	
WASE	WHAP	SWOP	YEAD	YONI	
WASH	WHAT	WOPS	YEAH	YONT	
WASP	**WHO**	**WOS**	YEAN	**YOU**	
WAST	WHOA	TWOS	YEAR	YOUK	
WAT	WHOM	WOST	YEAS	YOUR	
SWAT	WHOP	**WOT**	**YEN**	YOUS	
TWAT	WHOT	SWOT	EYEN	**YOW**	
WATE	WHOW	WOTS	HYEN	YOWE	
WATS	**WHY**	**WOW**	SYEN	YOWL	
WATT	WHYS	WOWF	YENS	YOWS	
WAW	**WIG**	WOWS	**YEP**	**YUG**	
WAWA	SWIG	**WRY**	YEPS	YUGA	
WAWE	TWIG	AWRY	**YES**	YUGS	
WAWL	WIGS	**WUD**	AYES	**YUK**	
WAWS	**WIN**	WUDS	BYES	YUKE	
WAX	TWIN	WUDU	DYES	YUKO	
WAXY	WIND	**WUS**	EYES	YUKS	
WAY	WINE	WUSS	HYES	YUKY	
AWAY	WING	**WYE**	KYES	**YUM**	
SWAY	WINK	WYES	LYES	YUMP	
TWAY	WINN	**WYN**	NYES	**YUP**	
WAYS	WINO	WYND	OYES	YUPS	
WEB	WINS	WYNN	PYES	**YUS**	
WEBS	WINY	WYNS	RYES	AYUS	
WED	**WIS**	**XIS**	SYES	KYUS	
AWED	IWIS	AXIS	TYES	**ZAG**	

ZAGS	ZEES	**ZIG**	ZITE	ZOOS
ZAP	**ZEK**	ZIGS	ZITI	ZOOT
ZAPS	ZEKS	**ZIN**	ZITS	**ZOS**
ZEA	**ZEL**	ZINC	**ZIZ**	DZOS
ZEAL	ZELS	ZINE	ZIZZ	**ZZZ**
ZEAS	**ZEP**	ZING	**ZOL**	ZZZS
ZED	ZEPS	ZINS	ZOLS	
ZEDS	**ZHO**	**ZIP**	**ZOO**	
ZEE	DZHO	ZIPS	ZOOM	
MZEE	ZHOS	**ZIT**	ZOON	

Four-letter root words

AALS	ABRIS	ACMES	DAFFY	**AGIO**
BAALS	**ABUT**	**ACNE**	TAFFY	AGIOS
DAALS	ABUTS	ACNED	**AFRO**	**AGLU**
PAALS	**ABYE**	ACNES	AFROS	AGLUS
TAALS	ABYES	**ACRE**	**AGAR**	**AGMA**
ABAC	**ABYS**	NACRE	AGARS	MAGMA
ABACA	ABYSM	ACRED	**AGAS**	TAGMA
ABACI	ABYSS	ACRES	JAGAS	AGMAS
ABACK	**ACAI**	**ACTA**	NAGAS	**AGOG**
ABACS	ACAIS	PACTA	RAGAS	AGOGE
ABAS	**ACCA**	**ACTS**	SAGAS	**AGON**
BABAS	BACCA	FACTS	AGAST	WAGON
CABAS	YACCA	PACTS	**AGED**	AGONE
YABAS	ACCAS	TACTS	CAGED	AGONS
ABASE	**ACED**	**ACYL**	GAGED	AGONY
ABASH	FACED	ACYLS	PAGED	**AGUE**
ABASK	LACED	**ADAW**	RAGED	VAGUE
ABBA	MACED	ADAWS	WAGED	AGUED
DABBA	PACED	**ADDS**	**AGEE**	AGUES
GABBA	RACED	WADDS	RAGEE	**AHED**
YABBA	**ACER**	**ADDY**	**AGEN**	AAHED
ABBAS	LACER	BADDY	AGENE	RAHED
ABBE	MACER	CADDY	AGENT	**AIAS**
ABBED	PACER	DADDY	**AGER**	RAIAS
ABBES	RACER	FADDY	CAGER	**AIDA**
ABBEY	ACERB	PADDY	EAGER	AIDAS
ABED	ACERS	WADDY	GAGER	**AIDE**
SABED	**ACES**	**ADIT**	JAGER	WAIDE
ABET	DACES	ADITS	LAGER	AIDED
ABETS	FACES	**ADOS**	PAGER	AIDER
ABID	LACES	DADOS	RAGER	AIDES
RABID	MACES	FADOS	SAGER	**AIDS**
TABID	PACES	SADOS	WAGER	CAIDS
ABIDE	RACES	**ADZE**	YAGER	GAIDS
ABLE	TACES	ADZED	AGERS	KAIDS
CABLE	**ACHE**	ADZES	**AGES**	LAIDS
FABLE	CACHE	**AEON**	CAGES	MAIDS
GABLE	MACHE	PAEON	GAGES	QAIDS
HABLE	NACHE	AEONS	MAGES	RAIDS
SABLE	RACHE	**AERO**	PAGES	SAIDS
TABLE	TACHE	AEROS	RAGES	**AIGA**
ABLED	ACHED	**AERY**	SAGES	SAIGA
ABLER	ACHES	FAERY	WAGES	TAIGA
ABLES	**ACID**	**AFAR**	**AGHA**	AIGAS
ABLET	ACIDS	AFARA	AGHAS	**AILS**
ABRI	ACIDY	AFARS	**AGIN**	BAILS
ABRIM	**ACME**	**AFFY**	FAGIN	FAILS
ABRIN		BAFFY	AGING	HAILS

JAILS	WAITS	PALAY	PALLS	KAMAS
KAILS	**AITU**	ALAYS	TALLS	LAMAS
MAILS	AITUS	**ALBA**	WALLS	MAMAS
NAILS	**AKAS**	ALBAS	**ALLY**	SAMAS
PAILS	HAKAS	**ALBE**	BALLY	AMASS
RAILS	KAKAS	ALBEE	DALLY	**AMBO**
SAILS	TAKAS	**ALCO**	GALLY	GAMBO
TAILS	VAKAS	ALCOS	PALLY	JAMBO
VAILS	WAKAS	**ALEC**	RALLY	MAMBO
WAILS	**AKED**	ALECK	SALLY	SAMBO
AIMS	BAKED	ALECS	TALLY	ZAMBO
KAIMS	CAKED	**ALEF**	WALLY	AMBOS
MAIMS	FAKED	ALEFS	ALLYL	**AMEN**
SAIMS	LAKED	ALEFT	**ALMA**	RAMEN
AINE	NAKED	**ALES**	HALMA	SAMEN
DAINE	OAKED	BALES	TALMA	YAMEN
FAINE	RAKED	DALES	ALMAH	AMEND
RAINE	WAKED	EALES	ALMAS	AMENE
SAINE	**AKEE**	GALES	**ALME**	AMENS
AINEE	RAKEE	HALES	ALMEH	AMENT
AINS	AKEES	KALES	ALMES	**AMES**
CAINS	**AKES**	MALES	**ALMS**	CAMES
FAINS	BAKES	PALES	BALMS	DAMES
GAINS	CAKES	RALES	CALMS	FAMES
HAINS	FAKES	SALES	HALMS	GAMES
KAINS	HAKES	TALES	MALMS	HAMES
MAINS	JAKES	VALES	PALMS	JAMES
PAINS	LAKES	WALES	**ALOD**	KAMES
RAINS	MAKES	YALES	ALODS	LAMES
SAINS	RAKES	**ALEW**	**ALOE**	NAMES
TAINS	SAKES	ALEWS	ALOED	SAMES
WAINS	TAKES	**ALFA**	ALOES	TAMES
AIRN	WAKES	HALFA	**ALOO**	WAMES
BAIRN	**AKIN**	ALFAS	BALOO	**AMIA**
CAIRN	LAKIN	**ALFS**	ALOOF	LAMIA
AIRNS	TAKIN	CALFS	ALOOS	ZAMIA
AIRS	AKING	HALFS	**ALOW**	AMIAS
FAIRS	**ALAN**	**ALGA**	ALOWE	**AMID**
GAIRS	ALAND	ALGAE	**ALPS**	AMIDE
HAIRS	ALANE	ALGAL	CALPS	AMIDO
LAIRS	ALANG	ALGAS	PALPS	AMIDS
MAIRS	ALANS	**ALIF**	SALPS	**AMIE**
PAIRS	ALANT	CALIF	**ALTO**	MAMIE
SAIRS	**ALAP**	KALIF	SALTO	RAMIE
VAIRS	JALAP	ALIFS	ALTOS	AMIES
WAIRS	ALAPA	**ALKO**	**ALTS**	**AMIN**
AIRT	ALAPS	ALKOS	DALTS	GAMIN
AIRTH	**ALAR**	**ALKY**	HALTS	RAMIN
AIRTS	MALAR	BALKY	MALTS	TAMIN
AIRY	TALAR	TALKY	SALTS	AMINE
DAIRY	ALARM	ALKYD	**ALUM**	AMINO
FAIRY	ALARY	ALKYL	ALUMS	AMINS
HAIRY	**ALAS**	**ALLS**	**ALUS**	**AMIR**
LAIRY	BALAS	BALLS	BALUS	AMIRS
VAIRY	GALAS	CALLS	TALUS	**AMIS**
AITS	MALAS	FALLS	**AMAH**	CAMIS
BAITS	NALAS	GALLS	AMAHS	KAMIS
GAITS	PALAS	HALLS	**AMAS**	RAMIS
RAITS	TALAS	LALLS	CAMAS	TAMIS
TAITS	**ALAY**	MALLS	GAMAS	AMISS

AMLA	MANES	**ANTS**	AQUAE	CARES
AMLAS	PANES	BANTS	AQUAS	DARES
AMMO	SANES	CANTS	**ARAK**	FARES
AMMON	VANES	DANTS	ARAKS	HARES
AMMOS	WANES	GANTS	**ARAR**	LARES
AMOK	**ANGA**	HANTS	ARARS	MARES
AMOKS	FANGA	KANTS	**ARBA**	NARES
AMPS	KANGA	LANTS	ARBAS	PARES
CAMPS	MANGA	PANTS	**ARBS**	RARES
DAMPS	PANGA	RANTS	BARBS	TARES
GAMPS	RANGA	SANTS	CARBS	VARES
LAMPS	SANGA	VANTS	DARBS	**ARET**
RAMPS	TANGA	WANTS	GARBS	CARET
SAMPS	ANGAS	**ANTSY**	WARBS	ARETE
TAMPS	**ANIL**	**ANUS**	**ARCH**	ARETS
VAMPS	ANILE	MANUS	LARCH	ARETT
AMUS	ANILS	**APAY**	MARCH	**ARFS**
CAMUS	**ANIS**	APAYD	PARCH	BARFS
NAMUS	MANIS	APAYS	**ARCO**	ZARFS
RAMUS	RANIS	**APED**	NARCO	**ARGH**
WAMUS	ANISE	CAPED	YARCO	AARGH
AMUSE	**ANKH**	GAPED	ARCOS	**ARIA**
AMYL	ANKHS	JAPED	**ARCS**	MARIA
AMYLS	**ANNA**	NAPED	MARCS	VARIA
ANAL	CANNA	RAPED	NARCS	ARIAS
BANAL	MANNA	TAPED	**ARDS**	**ARID**
CANAL	NANNA	**APER**	BARDS	MARID
FANAL	TANNA	CAPER	CARDS	**ARIL**
ANAN	WANNA	GAPER	EARDS	ARILS
ANANA	ANNAL	JAPER	FARDS	**ARIS**
ANAS	ANNAS	PAPER	HARDS	DARIS
KANAS	ANNAT	RAPER	LARDS	GARIS
LANAS	**ANNO**	TAPER	NARDS	LARIS
MANAS	ANNOY	APERS	PARDS	NARIS
NANAS	**ANNS**	APERT	SARDS	PARIS
RANAS	BANNS	APERY	WARDS	SARIS
TANAS	CANNS	**APES**	YARDS	ZARIS
ANCE	JANNS	CAPES	**AREA**	ARISE
DANCE	**ANOA**	GAPES	AREAD	ARISH
HANCE	ANOAS	JAPES	AREAE	**ARKS**
LANCE	**ANON**	NAPES	AREAL	BARKS
NANCE	CANON	PAPES	AREAR	CARKS
PANCE	FANON	RAPES	AREAS	DARKS
RANCE	**ANSA**	TAPES	**ARED**	HARKS
ANDS	HANSA	**APEX**	BARED	JARKS
BANDS	SANSA	CAPEX	CARED	KARKS
FANDS	ANSAE	**APOD**	DARED	LARKS
HANDS	**ANTA**	APODE	EARED	MARKS
LANDS	MANTA	APODS	FARED	NARKS
PANDS	ANTAE	**APOS**	HARED	PARKS
RANDS	ANTAR	CAPOS	OARED	RARKS
SANDS	ANTAS	GAPOS	PARED	SARKS
WANDS	**ANTE**	**APPS**	RARED	WARKS
ANES	ZANTE	YAPPS	SARED	YARKS
BANES	ANTED	**APSE**	TARED	**ARLE**
CANES	ANTES	LAPSE	WARED	CARLE
FANES	**ANTI**	APSES	AREDD	FARLE
JANES	TANTI	**APSO**	AREDE	MARLE
KANES	ANTIC	APSOS	**ARES**	PARLE
LANES	ANTIS	**AQUA**	BARES	PARLE

ARLED	HASHY	CAULD	EAVES	**AWOL**
ARLES	MASHY	FAULD	FAVES	AWOLS
ARMS	WASHY	HAULD	HAVES	**AXED**
BARMS	**ASKS**	TAULD	LAVES	FAXED
FARMS	BASKS	YAULD	NAVES	MAXED
HARMS	CASKS	**AUNE**	OAVES	RAXED
MARMS	HASKS	AUNES	PAVES	TAXED
WARMS	MASKS	**AUNT**	RAVES	WAXED
ARMY	TASKS	DAUNT	SAVES	**AXEL**
BARMY	**ASPS**	GAUNT	WAVES	AXELS
ARNA	GASPS	HAUNT	**AVID**	**AXES**
VARNA	HASPS	JAUNT	PAVID	FAXES
ARNAS	JASPS	NAUNT	**AVOW**	LAXES
ARPA	RASPS	SAUNT	AVOWS	MAXES
ARPAS	WASPS	TAUNT	**AWAY**	PAXES
ARSE	**ATAP**	VAUNT	AWAYS	RAXES
CARSE	WATAP	AUNTS	**AWDL**	SAXES
FARSE	ATAPS	AUNTY	AWDLS	TAXES
MARSE	**ATES**	**AURA**	**AWED**	WAXES
PARSE	BATES	LAURA	CAWED	ZAXES
ARSED	CATES	AURAE	DAWED	**AXIL**
ARSES	DATES	AURAL	HAWED	AXILE
ARSEY	FATES	AURAR	JAWED	AXILS
ARSY	GATES	AURAS	KAWED	**AXIS**
KARSY	HATES	**AUTO**	LAWED	MAXIS
ARTI	MATES	AUTOS	MAWED	TAXIS
AARTI	NATES	**AVAL**	PAWED	**AXLE**
PARTI	PATES	KAVAL	SAWED	AXLED
ARTIC	RATES	NAVAL	TAWED	AXLES
ARTIS	SATES	AVALE	YAWED	**AXON**
ARTS	TATES	**AVAS**	**AWEE**	CAXON
CARTS	YATES	CAVAS	AWEEL	TAXON
DARTS	**ATMA**	FAVAS	**AWES**	AXONE
FARTS	ATMAN	JAVAS	WAWES	AXONS
HARTS	ATMAS	KAVAS	**AWKS**	**AYAH**
KARTS	**ATOC**	LAVAS	CAWKS	RAYAH
MARTS	ATOCS	TAVAS	DAWKS	AYAHS
PARTS	**ATOK**	AVAST	GAWKS	**AYES**
TARTS	ATOKE	**AVEL**	HAWKS	BAYES
WARTS	ATOKS	CAVEL	LAWKS	**AYIN**
ARTSY	**ATOM**	FAVEL	MAWKS	LAYIN
ARTY	ATOMS	GAVEL	PAWKS	ZAYIN
PARTY	ATOMY	JAVEL	**AWLS**	AYINS
TARTY	**ATOP**	NAVEL	BAWLS	**AYRE**
WARTY	ATOPY	RAVEL	PAWLS	FAYRE
ARUM	**ATUA**	AVELS	WAWLS	AYRES
GARUM	ATUAS	**AVER**	YAWLS	**AZAN**
LARUM	**AUAS**	CAVER	**AWNS**	HAZAN
ARUMS	PAUAS	FAVER	BAWNS	AZANS
ARVO	**AUFS**	HAVER	DAWNS	**AZON**
PARVO	HAUFS	LAVER	FAWNS	GAZON
ARVOS	LAUFS	PAVER	LAWNS	AZONS
ARYL	**AUKS**	RAVER	PAWNS	**AZYM**
ARYLS	BAUKS	SAVER	RAWNS	AZYME
ASAR	CAUKS	TAVER	YAWNS	AZYMS
TASAR	JAUKS	WAVER	**AWNY**	**BAAL**
ASCI	WAUKS	AVERS	FAWNY	BAALS
FASCI	**AULA**	AVERT	LAWNY	**BABA**
ASHY	AULAS	**AVES**	TAWNY	BABAS
DASHY	**AULD**	CAVES	YAWNY	**BABE**

BABEL	BALUS	**BASH**	BEANO	BERET
BABES	**BANC**	ABASH	BEANS	**BERG**
BABU	BANCO	BASHO	BEANY	BERGS
BABUL	BANCS	**BASK**	**BEAR**	**BERK**
BABUS	**BAND**	ABASK	ABEAR	BERKO
BACH	ABAND	BASKS	BEARD	BERKS
BACHA	BANDA	**BASS**	BEARE	**BERM**
BACHS	BANDH	BASSE	BEARS	BERME
BACK	BANDS	BASSI	**BEAT**	BERMS
ABACK	BANDY	BASSO	BEATH	**BEST**
BACKS	**BANE**	BASSY	BEATS	BESTI
BACS	BANED	**BAST**	BEATY	BESTS
ABACS	BANES	BASTA	**BEAU**	**BETA**
BAEL	**BANG**	BASTE	BEAUS	BETAS
BAELS	OBANG	BASTI	BEAUT	**BETE**
BAFF	BANGS	BASTO	BEAUX	BETED
BAFFS	**BANI**	BASTS	**BECK**	BETEL
BAFFY	BANIA	**BATE**	BECKE	BETES
BAFT	**BANK**	ABATE	BECKS	**BETH**
ABAFT	BANKS	BATED	**BEDE**	BETHS
BAFTS	**BANT**	BATES	BEDEL	**BETS**
BAGH	BANTS	**BATH**	BEDES	ABETS
BAGHS	BANTU	BATHE	BEDEW	**BEYS**
BAHT	BANTY	BATHS	**BEEF**	OBEYS
BAHTS	**BAPU**	**BATT**	BEEFS	**BHAI**
BAHU	BAPUS	BATTA	BEEFY	BHAIS
BAHUS	**BARB**	BATTS	**BEEP**	**BHEL**
BAHUT	BARBE	BATTU	BEEPS	BHELS
BAIL	BARBS	BATTY	**BEER**	**BHUT**
BAILS	BARBY	**BAUD**	BEERS	BHUTS
BAIT	**BARD**	BAUDS	BEERY	**BIAS**
BAITH	BARDE	**BAUK**	**BEET**	OBIAS
BAITS	BARDO	BAUKS	BEETS	**BIBB**
BAJU	BARDS	**BAUR**	**BEGO**	BIBBS
BAJUS	BARDY	BAURS	BEGOT	**BICE**
BAKE	**BARE**	**BAWD**	**BEIN**	BICEP
BAKED	BARED	BAWDS	BEING	BICES
BAKEN	BARER	BAWDY	**BELL**	**BIDE**
BAKER	BARES	**BAWL**	BELLE	ABIDE
BAKES	**BARF**	BAWLS	BELLS	BIDED
BALD	BARFS	**BAWN**	BELLY	BIDER
BALDS	**BARK**	BAWNS	**BELT**	BIDES
BALDY	BARKS	**BAWR**	BELTS	BIDET
BALE	BARKY	BAWRS	**BEMA**	**BIDI**
BALED	**BARM**	**BAYE**	BEMAD	BIDIS
BALER	BARMS	BAYED	BEMAS	**BIER**
BALES	BARMY	BAYES	**BEND**	BIERS
BALK	**BARN**	**BAYT**	BENDS	**BIFF**
BALKS	BARNS	BAYTS	BENDY	BIFFO
BALKY	BARNY	**BEAD**	BENE	BIFFS
BALL	**BARP**	BEADS	BENES	BIFFY
BALLS	BARPS	BEADY	BENET	**BIGA**
BALLY	**BARS**	**BEAK**	**BENI**	BIGAE
BALM	KBARS	BEAKS	BENIS	**BIGG**
BALMS	**BASE**	BEAKY	**BENT**	BIGGS
BALMY	ABASE	**BEAM**	BENTO	BIGGY
BALS	BASED	ABEAM	BENTS	**BIKE**
BALSA	BASEN	BEAMS	BENTY	BIKED
BALU	BASER	BEAMY	**BERE**	BIKER
BALUN	BASES	**BEAN**	BERES	BIKES

BILE	**BLAD**	BLOWN	OBOLE	BORAS
BILED	BLADE	BLOWS	BOLES	BORAX
BILES	BLADS	BLOWY	**BOLL**	**BORD**
BILK	BLADY	**BLUB**	BOLLS	ABORD
BILKS	**BLAE**	BLUBS	**BOLO**	BORDE
BILL	BLAER	**BLUE**	BOLOS	BORDS
BILLS	BLAES	BLUED	**BOLT**	**BORE**
BILLY	**BLAG**	BLUER	BOLTS	ABORE
BIMA	BLAGS	BLUES	**BOMA**	YBORE
BIMAH	**BLAH**	BLUET	ABOMA	BORED
BIMAS	BLAHS	BLUEY	BOMAS	BOREE
BIND	**BLAM**	**BLUR**	**BOMB**	BOREL
BINDI	BLAME	BLURB	BOMBE	BORER
BINDS	BLAMS	BLURS	BOMBO	BORES
BINE	**BLAT**	BLURT	BOMBS	**BORK**
BINER	BLATE	**BOAB**	**BOND**	BORKS
BINES	BLATS	BOABS	BONDS	**BORM**
BING	BLATT	**BOAK**	**BONE**	BORMS
BINGE	**BLAW**	BOAKS	BONED	**BORN**
BINGO	BLAWN	**BOAR**	BONER	BORNA
BINGS	BLAWS	BOARD	BONES	BORNE
BINGY	**BLAY**	BOARS	BONEY	**BORT**
BINK	BLAYS	BOART	**BONG**	ABORT
BINKS	**BLEB**	**BOAS**	BONGO	BORTS
BINT	BLEBS	BOAST	BONGS	BORTY
BINTS	**BLED**	**BOAT**	**BONK**	BORTZ
BIOG	ABLED	BOATS	BONKS	**BOSK**
BIOGS	**BLEE**	**BOBA**	**BONY**	BOSKS
BIRD	BLEED	BOBAC	EBONY	BOSKY
BIRDS	BLEEP	BOBAK	**BOOB**	**BOSS**
BIRK	BLEES	BOBAS	BOOBS	BOSSY
BIRKS	**BLET**	**BOCK**	BOOBY	**BOTA**
BIRL	ABLET	BOCKS	**BOOH**	BOTAS
BIRLE	BLETS	**BODE**	BOOHS	**BOTE**
BIRLS	**BLEY**	ABODE	**BOOK**	BOTEL
BIRO	BLEYS	BODED	EBOOK	BOTES
BIROS	**BLIN**	BODES	BOOKS	**BOTH**
BIRR	BLIND	**BOEP**	BOOKY	BOTHY
BIRRS	BLING	BOEPS	**BOOL**	**BOTT**
BISE	BLINI	**BOET**	BOOLS	BOTTE
BISES	BLINK	BOETS	**BOOM**	BOTTS
BISK	BLINS	**BOFF**	BOOMS	BOTTY
BISKS	BLINY	BOFFO	BOOMY	**BOUK**
BITE	**BLIP**	BOFFS	**BOON**	BOUKS
BITER	BLIPS	**BOHO**	ABOON	**BOUN**
BITES	**BLIT**	BOHOS	BOONG	BOUND
BITO	BLITE	**BOIL**	BOONS	BOUNS
BITOS	BLITS	ABOIL	**BOOR**	**BOUT**
BITOU	BLITZ	BOILS	BOORD	ABOUT
BITS	**BLOB**	**BOKE**	BOORS	BOUTS
OBITS	BLOBS	BOKED	**BOOS**	**BOWL**
BITSY	**BLOC**	BOKES	BOOSE	BOWLS
BITT	BLOCK	**BOKO**	BOOST	**BOWR**
BITTE	BLOCS	BOKOS	**BOOT**	BOWRS
BITTS	**BLOG**	**BOLA**	BOOTH	**BOWS**
BITTY	BLOGS	BOLAR	BOOTS	BOWSE
BIZE	**BLOT**	BOLAS	BOOTY	**BOYF**
BIZES	BLOTS	**BOLD**	**BORA**	BOYFS
BLAB	**BLOW**	BOLDS	BORAK	**BOYG**
BLABS	ABLOW	**BOLE**	BORAL	BOYGS

BOYO	**BRIG**	BUCKS	BUNTS	**BYES**
BOYOS	BRIGS	BUCKU	BUNTY	ABYES
BOYS	**BRIK**	**BUDA**	**BUOY**	**BYKE**
BOYSY	IBRIK	BUDAS	BUOYS	BYKED
BOZO	BRIKI	**BUDI**	**BURA**	BYKES
BOZOS	BRIKS	BUDIS	BURAN	**BYRE**
BRAD	**BRIM**	**BUDO**	BURAS	BYRES
BRADS	ABRIM	BUDOS	**BURB**	**BYRL**
BRAE	BRIMS	**BUFF**	BURBS	BYRLS
BRAES	**BRIN**	BUFFA	**BURD**	**BYTE**
BRAG	ABRIN	BUFFE	BURDS	BYTES
BRAGS	BRINE	BUFFI	**BURG**	**CABA**
BRAK	BRING	BUFFO	BURGH	CABAL
BRAKE	BRINK	BUFFS	BURGS	CABAS
BRAKS	BRINS	BUFFY	**BURK**	**CABS**
BRAKY	BRINY	**BUFO**	BURKA	SCABS
BRAN	**BRIO**	BUFOS	BURKE	**CACA**
BRAND	BRIOS	**BUHL**	BURKS	CACAO
BRANE	**BRIS**	BUHLS	**BURL**	CACAS
BRANK	ABRIS	**BUHR**	BURLS	**CACK**
BRANS	BRISE	BUHRS	BURLY	CACKS
BRANT	BRISK	**BUIK**	**BURN**	CACKY
BRAS	BRISS	BUIKS	BURNS	**CADE**
BRASH	**BRIT**	**BUKE**	BURNT	CADEE
BRASS	BRITH	BUKES	**BURP**	CADES
BRAST	BRITS	**BULB**	BURPS	CADET
BRAT	BRITT	BULBS	**BURR**	**CADI**
BRATS	**BROD**	**BULK**	BURRO	CADIE
BRAW	BRODS	BULKS	BURRS	CADIS
BRAWL	**BROG**	BULKY	BURRY	**CADS**
BRAWN	BROGH	**BULL**	**BURS**	ECADS
BRAWS	BROGS	BULLA	BURSA	SCADS
BRAY	**BROO**	BULLS	BURSE	**CAFE**
ABRAY	BROOD	BULLY	BURST	CAFES
BRAYS	BROOK	**BUMF**	**BUSH**	**CAFF**
BRED	BROOL	BUMFS	BUSHY	SCAFF
BREDE	BROOM	**BUMP**	**BUSK**	CAFFS
BREDS	BROOS	BUMPH	BUSKS	**CAGE**
BREE	**BROS**	BUMPS	BUSKY	CAGED
BREED	BROSE	BUMPY	**BUSS**	CAGER
BREEM	BROSY	**BUNA**	BUSSU	CAGES
BREER	**BROW**	ABUNA	**BUST**	CAGEY
BREES	BROWN	BUNAS	BUSTI	**CAGS**
BREI	BROWS	**BUND**	BUSTS	SCAGS
BREID	**BRUS**	BUNDE	BUSTY	**CAID**
BREIS	BRUSH	BUNDH	**BUTE**	CAIDS
BREN	BRUSK	BUNDS	BUTEO	**CAIN**
BRENS	BRUST	BUNDT	BUTES	CAINS
BRENT	**BRUT**	BUNDU	**BUTS**	**CAKE**
BRER	BRUTE	BUNDY	ABUTS	CAKED
BRERE	BRUTS	**BUNG**	**BUTT**	CAKES
BRERS	**BUAT**	BUNGS	BUTTE	CAKEY
BREW	BUATS	BUNGY	BUTTS	**CALF**
BREWS	**BUBA**	**BUNK**	BUTTY	CALFS
BREY	BUBAL	BUNKO	**BUZZ**	**CALK**
BREYS	BUBAS	BUNKS	ABUZZ	CALKS
BRIE	**BUBU**	**BUNN**	BUZZY	**CALL**
BRIEF	BUBUS	BUNNS	**BYDE**	SCALL
BRIER	**BUCK**	BUNNY	BYDED	CALLA
BRIES	BUCKO	**BUNT**	BYDES	CALLS

CALM	**CAPO**	**CAUL**	CETES	**CHIC**
CALMS	CAPON	CAULD	**CHAD**	CHICA
CALMY	CAPOS	CAULK	CHADO	CHICH
CALO	CAPOT	CAULS	CHADS	CHICK
CALOS	**CARB**	**CAUM**	**CHAI**	CHICO
CALP	CARBO	CAUMS	CHAIN	CHICS
SCALP	CARBS	**CAUP**	CHAIR	**CHID**
CALPA	CARBY	SCAUP	CHAIS	CHIDE
CALPS	**CARD**	CAUPS	**CHAL**	**CHIK**
CAMA	CARDI	**CAVA**	CHALK	CHIKS
CAMAN	CARDS	CAVAS	CHALS	**CHIN**
CAMAS	CARDY	**CAVE**	**CHAM**	CHINA
CAME	**CARE**	CAVED	CHAMP	CHINE
CAMEL	SCARE	CAVEL	CHAMS	CHINK
CAMEO	CARED	CAVER	**CHAO**	CHINO
CAMES	CARER	CAVES	CHAOS	CHINS
CAMO	CARES	**CAWK**	**CHAP**	**CHIP**
CAMOS	CARET	CAWKS	CHAPE	CHIPS
CAMP	CAREX	**CAWS**	CHAPS	**CHIT**
SCAMP	**CARK**	SCAWS	CHAPT	CHITS
CAMPI	CARKS	**CEAS**	**CHAR**	**CHIV**
CAMPO	**CARL**	CEASE	ACHAR	CHIVE
CAMPS	CARLE	**CECA**	CHARA	CHIVS
CAMPY	CARLS	CECAL	CHARD	CHIVY
CAMS	**CARN**	**CEDE**	CHARE	**CHIZ**
SCAMS	CARNS	CEDED	CHARK	CHIZZ
CANE	CARNY	CEDER	CHARM	**CHOC**
CANED	**CARP**	CEDES	CHARR	CHOCK
CANEH	SCARP	**CEDI**	CHARS	CHOCO
CANER	CARPI	CEDIS	CHART	CHOCS
CANES	CARPS	**CEIL**	CHARY	**CHOG**
CANG	**CARR**	CEILI	**CHAS**	CHOGS
CANGS	CARRS	CEILS	CHASE	**CHOP**
CANN	CARRY	**CELL**	CHASM	CHOPS
CANNA	**CARS**	CELLA	**CHAT**	**CHOU**
CANNS	SCARS	CELLI	CHATS	CHOUT
CANNY	CARSE	CELLO	**CHAV**	CHOUX
CANS	**CART**	CELLS	SCHAV	**CHOW**
SCANS	SCART	**CELT**	CHAVE	CHOWK
CANSO	CARTA	CELTS	CHAVS	CHOWS
CANST	CARTE	**CENS**	**CHAW**	**CHUB**
CANT	CARTS	CENSE	CHAWK	CHUBS
SCANT	**CASA**	**CENT**	CHAWS	**CHUG**
CANTO	CASAS	SCENT	**CHAY**	CHUGS
CANTS	**CASE**	CENTO	CHAYA	**CHUM**
CANTY	CASED	CENTS	CHAYS	CHUMP
CAPA	CASES	CENTU	**CHEF**	CHUMS
SCAPA	**CASK**	**CEPE**	CHEFS	**CHUR**
CAPAS	CASKS	CEPES	**CHER**	CHURL
CAPE	CASKY	**CERE**	OCHER	CHURN
SCAPE	**CAST**	CERED	CHERE	CHURR
CAPED	CASTE	CERES	CHERT	**CHUT**
CAPER	CASTS	**CERO**	**CHEW**	CHUTE
CAPES	**CATE**	CEROS	CHEWS	**CIDE**
CAPEX	CATER	**CERT**	CHEWY	CIDED
CAPH	CATES	CERTS	**CHIA**	CIDER
CAPHS	**CATS**	CERTY	CHIAO	CIDES
CAPI	SCATS	**CESS**	CHIAS	**CIDS**
SCAPI	**CAUK**	CESSE	**CHIB**	ACIDS
CAPIZ	CAUKS	**CETE**	CHIBS	**CIEL**

CIELS	**CLOD**	COEDS	COMPT	CORED
CILL	CLODS	**COFF**	**COND**	CORER
CILLS	**CLOG**	SCOFF	YCOND	CORES
CINE	CLOGS	COFFS	CONDO	COREY
CINES	**CLON**	**COGS**	**CONE**	**CORK**
CION	CLONE	SCOGS	SCONE	CORKS
SCION	CLONK	**COHO**	CONED	CORKY
CIONS	CLONS	COHOE	CONES	**CORM**
CIRE	**CLOP**	COHOG	CONEY	CORMS
CIRES	CLOPS	COHOS	**CONF**	**CORN**
CIRL	**CLOT**	**COIF**	CONFS	ACORN
CIRLS	CLOTE	COIFS	**CONI**	SCORN
CIST	CLOTH	**COIL**	CONIA	CORNI
CISTS	CLOTS	COILS	CONIC	CORNO
CITE	**CLOU**	**COIN**	CONIN	CORNS
CITED	CLOUD	COINS	CONKS	CORNU
CITER	CLOUR	**COIR**	**CONK**	CORNY
CITES	CLOUS	COIRS	CONKS	**CORS**
CIVE	CLOUT	**COIT**	CONKY	CORSE
CIVES	**CLOW**	COITS	**CONN**	CORSO
CIVET	CLOWN	**COKE**	CONNE	**COSE**
CLAD	CLOWS	COKED	CONNS	COSEC
YCLAD	**CLOY**	COKES	**CONS**	COSED
CLADE	CLOYE	**COLA**	ICONS	COSES
CLADS	CLOYS	COLAS	**COOF**	COSET
CLAG	**CLUB**	**COLD**	COOFS	COSEY
CLAGS	CLUBS	ACOLD	**COOK**	**COST**
CLAM	**CLUE**	SCOLD	COOKS	COSTA
CLAME	CLUED	COLDS	COOKY	COSTE
CLAMP	CLUES	**COLE**	**COOL**	COSTS
CLAMS	**COAL**	COLED	COOLS	**COTE**
CLAN	COALA	COLES	COOLY	COTED
CLANG	COALS	COLEY	**COOM**	COTES
CLANK	COALY	**COLL**	COOMB	**COTH**
CLANS	**COAT**	COLLS	COOMS	COTHS
CLAP	COATE	COLLY	COOMY	**COTS**
CLAPS	COATI	**COLT**	**COON**	SCOTS
CLAPT	COATS	COLTS	COONS	**COTT**
CLAT	**COBB**	**COMA**	**COOP**	COTTA
ECLAT	COBBS	COMAE	SCOOP	COTTS
CLATS	COBBY	COMAL	COOPS	**COUP**
CLAW	**COCA**	COMAS	COOPT	SCOUP
CLAWS	COCAS	**COMB**	**COOS**	COUPE
CLAY	**COCK**	COMBE	COOST	COUPS
CLAYS	ACOCK	COMBI	**COOT**	**COUR**
CLEF	COCKS	COMBO	SCOOT	SCOUR
CLEFS	COCKY	COMBS	COOTS	COURB
CLEFT	**COCO**	COMBY	**COPE**	COURD
CLEG	COCOA	**COME**	SCOPE	COURE
CLEGS	COCOS	COMER	COPED	COURS
CLEM	**CODA**	COMES	COPEN	COURT
CLEMS	CODAS	COMET	COPER	**COVE**
CLEW	**CODE**	**COMM**	COPES	COVED
CLEWS	CODEC	COMMA	**COPS**	COVEN
CLIP	CODED	COMMO	SCOPS	COVER
CLIPE	CODEN	COMMS	COPSE	COVES
CLIPS	CODER	COMMY	COPSY	COVET
CLIPT	CODES	**COMP**	**CORD**	COVEY
CLIT	CODEX	COMPO	CORDS	**COWK**
CLITS	**COED**	COMPS	**CORE**	COWKS
			SCORE	

COWL	CREWE	**CUKE**	CUTEY	DANKS
SCOWL	CREWS	CUKES	**CUTS**	**DANT**
COWLS	**CRIA**	**CULL**	SCUTS	IDANT
COWP	CRIAS	SCULL	**CYAN**	DANTS
SCOWP	**CRIB**	CULLS	CYANO	**DARB**
COWPS	CRIBS	CULLY	CYANS	DARBS
COWS	**CRIM**	**CULM**	**CYMA**	**DARE**
SCOWS	SCRIM	CULMS	CYMAE	DARED
COXA	CRIME	**CULT**	CYMAR	DARER
COXAE	CRIMP	CULTI	CYMAS	DARES
COXAL	CRIMS	CULTS	**CYME**	**DARG**
COZE	**CRIS**	CULTY	CYMES	DARGA
COZED	CRISE	**CUMS**	**CYST**	DARGS
COZEN	CRISP	SCUMS	CYSTS	**DARI**
COZES	**CRIT**	**CUNT**	**CYTE**	DARIC
COZEY	CRITH	CUNTS	CYTES	DARIS
CRAB	CRITS	**CUPS**	**CZAR**	**DARK**
SCRAB	**CROC**	SCUPS	CZARS	DARKS
CRABS	CROCI	**CURB**	**DAAL**	DARKY
CRAG	CROCK	CURBS	DAALS	**DARN**
SCRAG	CROCS	**CURD**	**DACE**	DARNS
CRAGS	**CROG**	CURDS	DACES	**DART**
CRAM	SCROG	CURDY	**DACK**	DARTS
SCRAM	CROGS	**CURE**	DACKS	**DASH**
CRAME	**CROP**	CURED	**DADA**	DASHI
CRAMP	CROPS	CURER	DADAH	DASHY
CRAMS	**CROW**	CURES	DADAS	**DATA**
CRAN	SCROW	CURET	**DADO**	DATAL
SCRAN	CROWD	**CURF**	DADOS	**DATE**
CRANE	CROWN	SCURF	**DAFF**	DATED
CRANK	CROWS	CURFS	DAFFS	DATER
CRANS	**CRUD**	**CURL**	DAFFY	DATES
CRAP	CRUDE	CURLI	**DAGO**	**DATO**
SCRAP	CRUDS	CURLS	DAGOS	DATOS
CRAPE	CRUDY	CURLY	**DAHL**	**DAUB**
CRAPS	**CRUE**	**CURN**	DAHLS	DAUBE
CRAPY	CRUEL	CURNS	**DAHS**	DAUBS
CRAW	CRUES	CURNY	ODAHS	DAUBY
SCRAW	CRUET	**CURR**	**DAIS**	**DAUD**
CRAWL	**CRUS**	CURRS	DAISY	DAUDS
CRAWS	ECRUS	CURRY	**DALE**	**DAUR**
CRAY	CRUSE	**CURS**	DALED	DAURS
SCRAY	CRUSH	SCURS	DALES	**DAUT**
CRAYS	CRUST	CURSE	**DALI**	DAUTS
CRED	CRUSY	CURSI	DALIS	**DAWD**
ACRED	**CUBE**	CURST	**DALS**	DAWDS
CREDO	CUBEB	**CUSH**	ODALS	**DAWK**
CREDS	CUBED	CUSHY	UDALS	DAWKS
CREE	CUBER	**CUSK**	**DALT**	**DAWN**
SCREE	CUBES	CUSKS	DALTS	DAWNS
CREED	**CUDS**	**CUSP**	**DAME**	**DAWS**
CREEK	SCUDS	CUSPS	DAMES	ADAWS
CREEL	**CUFF**	CUSPY	**DAMN**	**DAWT**
CREEP	SCUFF	**CUSS**	DAMNS	DAWTS
CREES	CUFFO	CUSSO	**DAMP**	**DAYS**
CREM	CUFFS	**CUTE**	DAMPS	ADAYS
CREME	**CUIF**	ACUTE	DAMPY	**DAZE**
CREMS	CUIFS	SCUTE	**DANG**	DAZED
CREW	**CUIT**	CUTER	DANGS	DAZER
SCREW	CUITS	CUTES	**DANK**	DAZES

DEAD	DEILS	DHOLS	**DIOL**	**DOAB**
DEADS	**DEKE**	**DHOW**	DIOLS	DOABS
DEAL	DEKED	DHOWS	**DIPS**	**DOAT**
IDEAL	DEKES	**DIAL**	DIPSO	DOATS
DEALS	**DELE**	DIALS	**DIRE**	**DOCK**
DEALT	DELED	**DICE**	DIRER	DOCKS
DEAN	DELES	DICED	**DIRK**	**DOCO**
DEANS	**DELF**	DICER	DIRKE	DOCOS
DEAR	DELFS	DICES	DIRKS	**DODO**
DEARE	DELFT	DICEY	**DIRL**	DODOS
DEARN	**DELI**	**DICH**	DIRLS	**DOEK**
DEARS	DELIS	DICHT	**DIRT**	DOEKS
DEARY	**DELL**	**DICK**	DIRTS	**DOER**
DEAW	DELLS	DICKS	DIRTY	DOERS
DEAWS	DELLY	DICKY	**DISA**	**DOES**
DEAWY	**DELO**	**DICT**	DISAS	DOEST
DEBE	DELOS	EDICT	**DISC**	**DOFF**
DEBEL	**DELT**	DICTA	DISCI	DOFFS
DEBES	DELTA	DICTS	DISCO	**DOGE**
DEBT	DELTS	DICTY	DISCS	DOGES
DEBTS	**DEME**	**DIDO**	**DISH**	DOGEY
DECK	DEMES	DIDOS	DISHY	**DOIT**
DECKO	**DEMO**	**DIEB**	**DISK**	DOITS
DECKS	DEMOB	DIEBS	DISKS	**DOJO**
DECO	DEMON	**DIET**	**DITA**	DOJOS
DECOR	DEMOS	DIETS	DITAL	**DOLE**
DECOS	**DENE**	**DIFF**	DITAS	DOLED
DECOY	DENES	DIFFS	**DITE**	DOLES
DEED	DENET	**DIKA**	DITED	**DOLL**
DEEDS	DENI	DIKAS	DITES	DOLLS
DEEDY	DENIM	**DIKE**	**DITS**	DOLLY
DEEM	DENIS	DIKED	ADITS	**DOLS**
ADEEM	**DENS**	DIKER	EDITS	IDOLS
DEEMS	DENSE	DIKES	DITSY	**DOLT**
DEEN	**DENT**	DIKEY	**DITT**	DOLTS
DEENS	IDENT	**DILL**	DITTO	**DOME**
DEEP	DENTS	DILLI	DITTS	DOMED
DEEPS	**DERE**	DILLS	DITTY	DOMES
DEER	DERED	DILLY	**DITZ**	**DONA**
DEERE	DERES	**DIME**	DITZY	DONAH
DEERS	**DERM**	DIMER	**DIVA**	DONAS
DEES	DERMA	DIMES	DIVAN	**DONE**
IDEES	DERMS	**DIMP**	DIVAS	DONEE
DEET	**DERN**	DIMPS	**DIVE**	DONER
DEETS	DERNS	**DINE**	DIVED	**DONG**
DEEV	**DERO**	DINED	DIVER	DONGA
DEEVE	DEROS	DINER	DIVES	DONGS
DEEVS	**DERV**	DINES	**DIVI**	**DONS**
DEFI	DERVS	**DING**	DIVIS	UDONS
DEFIS	**DESK**	DINGE	**DIVO**	DONSY
DEFO	DESKS	DINGO	DIVOS	**DOOB**
DEFOG	**DEVA**	DINGS	DIVOT	DOOBS
DEGU	DEVAS	DINGY	**DIXI**	**DOOK**
DEGUM	**DHAK**	**DINK**	DIXIE	DOOKS
DEGUS	DHAKS	DINKS	DIXIT	**DOOL**
DEID	**DHAL**	DINKY	**DIYA**	DOOLE
DEIDS	DHALS	**DINO**	DIYAS	DOOLS
DEIF	**DHOL**	DINOS	**DJIN**	DOOLY
DEIFY	DHOLE	**DINT**	DJINN	**DOOM**
DEIL	DHOLL	DINTS	DJINS	DOOMS

DOOMY	DOUTS	DREKS	DUMAS	**EACH**
DOON	**DOVE**	**DREY**	**DUMB**	BEACH
DOONA	DOVED	DREYS	DUMBO	LEACH
DOOR	DOVEN	**DRIB**	DUMBS	PEACH
DOORN	DOVER	DRIBS	**DUMP**	REACH
DOORS	DOVES	**DRIP**	DUMPS	TEACH
DOPA	**DOWD**	DRIPS	DUMPY	**EALE**
DOPAS	DOWDS	DRIPT	**DUNE**	VEALE
DOPE	DOWDY	**DROP**	DUNES	EALES
DOPED	**DOWL**	DROPS	**DUNG**	**EANS**
DOPER	DOWLE	DROPT	DUNGS	BEANS
DOPES	DOWLS	**DROW**	DUNGY	DEANS
DOPEY	DOWLY	DROWN	**DUNK**	GEANS
DORB	**DOWN**	DROWS	DUNKS	JEANS
DORBA	ADOWN	**DRUB**	**DUNS**	LEANS
DORBS	DOWNA	DRUBS	DUNSH	MEANS
DORE	DOWNS	**DRUG**	**DUNT**	PEANS
ADORE	DOWNY	DRUGS	DUNTS	REANS
DOREE	**DOWP**	**DRUM**	**DUPE**	SEANS
DORES	DOWPS	DRUMS	DUPED	WEANS
DORK	**DOWS**	**DUAD**	DUPER	YEANS
DORKS	DOWSE	DUADS	DUPES	**EARD**
DORKY	**DOWT**	**DUAL**	**DURA**	BEARD
DORM	DOWTS	DUALS	DURAL	HEARD
DORMS	**DOZE**	**DUAN**	DURAS	YEARD
DORMY	ADOZE	DUANS	**DURE**	EARDS
DORP	DOZED	**DUAR**	DURED	**EARL**
DORPS	DOZEN	DUARS	DURES	PEARL
DORR	DOZER	**DUCE**	**DURN**	EARLS
DORRS	DOZES	DUCES	DURNS	EARLY
DORS	**DRAB**	EDUCE	**DURO**	**EARN**
ODORS	DRABS	**DUCK**	DUROC	DEARN
DORSA	**DRAC**	DUCKS	DUROS	LEARN
DORSE	DRACK	DUCKY	DUROY	YEARN
DORT	DRACO	**DUCT**	**DURR**	EARNS
DORTS	**DRAD**	EDUCT	DURRA	**EARS**
DORTY	ADRAD	DUCTS	DURRS	BEARS
DOSE	YDRAD	**DUDE**	DURRY	DEARS
DOSED	**DRAG**	DUDED	**DUSK**	FEARS
DOSEH	DRAGS	DUDES	DUSKS	GEARS
DOSER	**DRAM**	**DUEL**	DUSKY	HEARS
DOSES	DRAMA	DUELS	**DUST**	LEARS
DOTE	DRAMS	**DUET**	ADUST	NEARS
DOTED	**DRAP**	DUETS	DUSTS	PEARS
DOTER	DRAPE	DUETT	DUSTY	REARS
DOTES	DRAPS	**DUFF**	**DWAM**	SEARS
DOUC	**DRAT**	DUFFS	DWAMS	TEARS
DOUCE	DRATS	**DUIT**	**DYAD**	WEARS
DOUCS	**DRAW**	DUITS	DYADS	YEARS
DOUK	DRAWL	**DUKA**	**DYER**	EARST
DOUKS	DRAWN	DUKAS	DYERS	**EASE**
DOUM	DRAWS	**DUKE**	**DYKE**	CEASE
DOUMA	**DRAY**	DUKED	DYKED	FEASE
DOUMS	DRAYS	DUKES	DYKES	LEASE
DOUP	**DREE**	**DULE**	DYKEY	MEASE
DOUPS	DREED	DULES	**DYNE**	PEASE
DOUR	DREES	**DULL**	DYNEL	SEASE
ODOUR	**DREG**	DULLS	DYNES	TEASE
DOURA	DREGS	DULLY	**DZHO**	EASED
DOUT	**DREK**	**DUMA**	DZHOS	EASEL

EASER	WECHT	**EGAD**	BELLS	DEMPT
EASES	**ECOS**	BEGAD	CELLS	KEMPT
EAST	DECOS	EGADS	DELLS	NEMPT
BEAST	**ECRU**	**EGAL**	FELLS	TEMPT
FEAST	ECRUS	LEGAL	HELLS	EMPTS
HEAST	**EDDY**	REGAL	JELLS	EMPTY
LEAST	NEDDY	**EGER**	KELLS	**EMYD**
REAST	REDDY	LEGER	MELLS	EMYDE
YEAST	TEDDY	EGERS	PELLS	EMYDS
EASTS	**EDGE**	**EGGS**	SELLS	**ENDS**
EATH	HEDGE	TEGGS	TELLS	BENDS
BEATH	KEDGE	YEGGS	VELLS	FENDS
DEATH	LEDGE	**EGGY**	WELLS	HENDS
HEATH	SEDGE	LEGGY	YELLS	LENDS
MEATH	WEDGE	PEGGY	**ELMS**	MENDS
NEATH	EDGED	**EGIS**	HELMS	PENDS
EATHE	EDGER	AEGIS	YELMS	RENDS
EATS	EDGES	**EGMA**	**ELTS**	SENDS
BEATS	**EDGY**	REGMA	BELTS	TENDS
FEATS	HEDGY	EGMAS	CELTS	VENDS
GEATS	KEDGY	**EGOS**	DELTS	WENDS
HEATS	LEDGY	REGOS	FELTS	**ENES**
JEATS	SEDGY	SEGOS	GELTS	BENES
LEATS	WEDGY	VEGOS	KELTS	DENES
MEATS	**EDIT**	**EIDE**	MELTS	GENES
NEATS	EDITS	EIDER	PELTS	LENES
PEATS	**EECH**	**EIKS**	WELTS	MENES
SEATS	BEECH	REIKS	YELTS	NENES
TEATS	KEECH	**EILD**	**EMES**	PENES
EAUS	LEECH	EILDS	DEMES	SENES
BEAUS	REECH	**EINE**	FEMES	TENES
EAUX	**EELS**	SEINE	HEMES	**ENEW**
BEAUX	FEELS	**EISH**	LEMES	RENEW
EAVE	HEELS	LEISH	MEMES	ENEWS
DEAVE	JEELS	**EKED**	SEMES	**ENGS**
HEAVE	KEELS	DEKED	TEMES	LENGS
LEAVE	PEELS	REKED	**EMEU**	MENGS
REAVE	REELS	**EKES**	EMEUS	**ENOL**
WEAVE	SEELS	DEKES	**EMIC**	ENOLS
EAVED	TEELS	PEKES	DEMIC	**ENOW**
EAVES	WEELS	REKES	HEMIC	ENOWS
EBON	**EELY**	**EKKA**	**EMIR**	**ENVY**
EBONS	DEELY	MEKKA	EMIRS	SENVY
EBONY	JEELY	EKKAS	**EMIT**	**EONS**
ECAD	SEELY	**ELAN**	DEMIT	AEONS
DECAD	**EERY**	ELAND	REMIT	NEONS
ECADS	BEERY	ELANS	EMITS	PEONS
ECCE	LEERY	**ELDS**	**EMMA**	**EORL**
RECCE	PEERY	GELDS	GEMMA	CEORL
ECCO	VEERY	MELDS	LEMMA	EORLS
RECCO	**EEVN**	VELDS	EMMAS	**EPEE**
SECCO	EEVNS	WELDS	**EMMY**	TEPEE
ECHE	**EFFS**	**ELFS**	FEMMY	EPEES
ECHED	JEFFS	DELFS	GEMMY	**EPHA**
ECHES	MEFFS	PELFS	JEMMY	EPHAH
ECHO	TEFFS	SELFS	EMMYS	EPHAS
ECHOS	**EFTS**	**ELKS**	**EMOS**	**EPIC**
ECHT	HEFTS	WELKS	DEMOS	SEPIC
FECHT	LEFTS	YELKS	MEMOS	EPICS
HECHT	WEFTS	**ELLS**	**EMPT**	**EPOS**

PEPOS	KERNS	**ETAT**	**EWER**	FACED
REPOS	PERNS	ETATS	FEWER	FACER
ERAS	TERNS	**ETCH**	HEWER	FACES
TERAS	**EROS**	FETCH	NEWER	FACET
ERASE	AEROS	KETCH	SEWER	**FACT**
ERED	CEROS	LETCH	EWERS	FACTS
CERED	DEROS	RETCH	**EWES**	**FADE**
DERED	HEROS	VETCH	EWEST	FADED
LERED	KEROS	**ETEN**	**EWTS**	FADER
MERED	WEROS	ETENS	NEWTS	FADES
SERED	ZEROS	**ETHE**	**EXAM**	**FADO**
ERES	EROSE	LETHE	EXAMS	FADOS
BERES	**ERRS**	ETHER	**EXEC**	**FAFF**
CERES	SERRS	**ETHS**	EXECS	FAFFS
DERES	**ERST**	BETHS	**EXED**	**FAIK**
FERES	PERST	HETHS	HEXED	FAIKS
GERES	VERST	METHS	SEXED	**FAIL**
HERES	**ERUV**	TETHS	VEXED	FAILS
LERES	ERUVS	**ETIC**	WEXED	**FAIN**
MERES	**ESES**	METIC	YEXED	FAINE
PERES	BESES	**ETNA**	**EXES**	FAINS
SERES	LESES	ETNAS	DEXES	FAINT
TERES	MESES	**ETUI**	HEXES	**FAIR**
EREV	RESES	ETUIS	KEXES	FAIRS
EREVS	YESES	**EUGH**	LEXES	FAIRY
ERGO	**ESKY**	HEUGH	REXES	**FAKE**
ERGON	PESKY	LEUGH	SEXES	FAKED
ERGOS	**ESNE**	TEUGH	TEXES	FAKER
ERGOT	MESNE	EUGHS	VEXES	FAKES
ERGS	ESNES	**EUKS**	WEXES	FAKEY
BERGS	**ESSE**	NEUKS	YEXES	**FALL**
ERHU	CESSE	YEUKS	ZEXES	FALLS
ERHUS	DESSE	**EURO**	**EXIT**	**FAME**
ERIC	FESSE	EUROS	EXITS	FAMED
CERIC	GESSE	**EVEN**	**EXON**	FAMES
SERIC	JESSE	EEVEN	EXONS	**FAND**
XERIC	ESSES	SEVEN	**EXPO**	FANDS
ERICA	**ESTS**	YEVEN	EXPOS	**FANE**
ERICK	BESTS	EVENS	**EXUL**	FANES
ERICS	FESTS	EVENT	EXULS	**FANG**
ERKS	GESTS	**EVER**	EXULT	FANGA
BERKS	HESTS	BEVER	**EYAS**	FANGO
JERKS	JESTS	FEVER	EYASS	FANGS
MERKS	KESTS	LEVER	**EYED**	**FANK**
NERKS	LESTS	NEVER	FEYED	FANKS
PERKS	NESTS	SEVER	HEYED	**FANO**
SERKS	PESTS	EVERT	KEYED	FANON
YERKS	RESTS	EVERY	**EYEN**	FANOS
ZERKS	TESTS	**EVES**	SEYEN	**FARD**
ERNE	VESTS	LEVES	**EYER**	FARDS
CERNE	WESTS	MEVES	FEYER	**FARE**
GERNE	YESTS	NEVES	GEYER	FARED
KERNE	ZESTS	YEVES	EYERS	FARER
TERNE	**ETAS**	**EVET**	**EYOT**	FARES
ERNED	BETAS	REVET	EYOTS	**FARL**
ERNES	FETAS	EVETS	**EYRA**	FARLE
ERNS	GETAS	**EVIL**	EYRAS	FARLS
DERNS	KETAS	DEVIL	**EYRE**	**FARM**
FERNS	WETAS	KEVIL	EYRES	FARMS
HERNS	ZETAS	EVILS	**FACE**	**FARO**

FAROS	**FEIS**	FIERE	FISHY	FLICS
FARS	FEIST	FIERS	**FISK**	**FLIM**
AFARS	**FELL**	FIERY	FISKS	FLIMP
FARSE	FELLA	**FIFE**	**FIST**	FLIMS
FART	FELLS	FIFED	FISTS	**FLIP**
FARTS	FELLY	FIFER	FISTY	FLIPS
FAST	**FELT**	FIFES	**FITT**	**FLIR**
FASTI	FELTS	**FIGO**	FITTE	FLIRS
FASTS	FELTY	FIGOS	FITTS	FLIRT
FATE	**FEME**	**FIKE**	**FIVE**	**FLIT**
FATED	FEMES	FIKED	FIVER	FLITE
FATES	**FEND**	FIKES	FIVES	FLITS
FATS	FENDS	**FILA**	**FIZZ**	FLITT
FATSO	FENDY	FILAR	FIZZY	**FLOB**
FAUN	**FENI**	**FILE**	**FLAB**	FLOBS
FAUNA	FENIS	FILED	FLABS	**FLOC**
FAUNS	**FENT**	FILER	**FLAG**	FLOCK
FAUR	FENTS	FILES	OFLAG	FLOCS
FAURD	**FEOD**	FILET	FLAGS	**FLOE**
FAUT	FEODS	**FILL**	**FLAK**	FLOES
FAUTS	**FERE**	FILLE	FLAKE	**FLOG**
FAVA	YFERE	FILLO	FLAKS	FLOGS
FAVAS	FERER	FILLS	FLAKY	**FLOP**
FAVE	FERES	FILLY	**FLAM**	FLOPS
FAVEL	**FERM**	**FILM**	FLAME	**FLOR**
FAVER	FERMI	FILMI	FLAMM	FLORA
FAVES	FERMS	FILMS	FLAMS	FLORS
FAWN	**FERN**	FILMY	FLAMY	FLORY
FAWNS	FERNS	**FILO**	**FLAN**	**FLOW**
FAWNY	FERNY	FILOS	FLANK	FLOWN
FAYS	**FESS**	**FIND**	FLANS	FLOWS
OFAYS	FESSE	FINDS	**FLAP**	**FLUB**
FAZE	**FEST**	**FINE**	FLAPS	FLUBS
FAZED	FESTA	FINED	**FLAT**	**FLUE**
FAZES	FESTS	FINER	FLATS	FLUED
FEAL	FESTY	FINES	**FLAW**	FLUES
FEALS	**FETA**	**FINI**	FLAWN	FLUEY
FEAR	FETAL	FINIS	FLAWS	**FLUS**
AFEAR	FETAS	**FINK**	FLAWY	FLUSH
FEARE	**FETE**	FINKS	**FLAX**	**FOAL**
FEARS	FETED	**FINO**	FLAXY	FOALS
FEART	FETES	FINOS	**FLAY**	**FOAM**
FEAT	**FETT**	**FIQH**	FLAYS	FOAMS
FEATS	FETTA	FIQHS	**FLEA**	FOAMY
FECK	FETTS	**FIRE**	FLEAM	**FOHN**
FECKS	**FEUD**	AFIRE	FLEAS	FOHNS
FEEB	FEUDS	FIRED	**FLEE**	**FOID**
FEEBS	**FIAR**	FIRER	FLEER	FOIDS
FEED	FIARS	FIRES	FLEES	**FOIL**
FEEDS	**FIAT**	**FIRK**	FLEET	FOILS
FEEL	FIATS	FIRKS	**FLEG**	**FOIN**
FEELS	**FICE**	**FIRM**	FLEGS	FOINS
FEEN	FICES	FIRMS	**FLEW**	**FOLD**
FEENS	**FICO**	**FIRN**	FLEWS	FOLDS
FEER	FICOS	FIRNS	**FLEX**	**FOLK**
FEERS	**FIDO**	**FIRS**	FLEXO	FOLKS
FEES	FIDOS	FIRST	**FLEY**	FOLKY
FEESE	**FIEF**	**FISC**	FLEYS	**FOND**
FEHM	FIEFS	FISCS	**FLIC**	FONDA
FEHME	**FIER**	**FISH**	FLICK	FONDS

FONDU	FRATE	**FULL**	**GAGE**	IGAPO
FONT	FRATI	FULLS	GAGED	GAPOS
FONTS	FRATS	FULLY	GAGER	**GARB**
FOOD	**FRAU**	**FUME**	GAGES	GARBE
FOODS	FRAUD	FUMED	**GAID**	GARBO
FOODY	FRAUS	FUMER	GAIDS	GARBS
FOOL	**FRAY**	FUMES	**GAIN**	**GARI**
FOOLS	FRAYS	FUMET	AGAIN	GARIS
FOOT	**FREE**	**FUND**	GAINS	**GARS**
AFOOT	FREED	FUNDI	**GAIR**	AGARS
FOOTS	FREER	FUNDS	GAIRS	**GART**
FOOTY	FREES	FUNDY	**GAIT**	GARTH
FORA	FREET	**FUNG**	GAITA	**GASP**
FORAM	**FRET**	FUNGI	GAITS	GASPS
FORAY	FRETS	FUNGO	GAITT	GASPY
FORB	**FRIB**	FUNGS	**GAJO**	**GAST**
FORBS	FRIBS	**FUNK**	GAJOS	AGAST
FORBY	**FRIG**	FUNKS	**GALA**	GASTS
FORD	FRIGS	FUNKY	GALAH	**GATE**
FORDO	**FRIS**	**FURL**	GALAS	AGATE
FORDS	FRISE	FURLS	GALAX	GATED
FORE	FRISK	**FURR**	**GALE**	GATER
AFORE	FRIST	FURRS	GALEA	GATES
FOREL	**FRIT**	FURRY	GALES	**GATH**
FORES	AFRIT	**FUSE**	**GALL**	GATHS
FOREX	FRITH	FUSED	GALLS	**GAUD**
FORK	FRITS	FUSEE	GALLY	GAUDS
FORKS	FRITT	FUSEL	**GAMA**	GAUDY
FORKY	FRITZ	FUSES	AGAMA	**GAUM**
FORM	**FRIZ**	**FUSS**	GAMAS	GAUMS
FORME	FRIZE	FUSSY	GAMAY	GAUMY
FORMS	FRIZZ	**FUST**	**GAMB**	**GAUN**
FORT	**FROE**	FUSTS	GAMBA	GAUNT
FORTE	FROES	FUSTY	GAMBE	**GAUP**
FORTH	**FROG**	**FUZE**	GAMBO	GAUPS
FORTS	FROGS	FUZED	GAMBS	**GAUR**
FORTY	**FROS**	FUZEE	**GAME**	GAURS
FOSS	AFROS	FUZES	GAMED	**GAUS**
FOSSA	FROSH	**FUZZ**	GAMER	GAUSS
FOSSE	FROST	FUZZY	GAMES	**GAVE**
FOUD	**FROW**	**FYCE**	GAMEY	AGAVE
FOUDS	FROWN	FYCES	**GAMP**	GAVEL
FOUL	FROWS	**FYKE**	GAMPS	**GAWD**
AFOUL	FROWY	FYKED	**GAMS**	GAWDS
FOULE	**FRUG**	FYKES	OGAMS	**GAWK**
FOULS	FRUGS	**FYLE**	**GANE**	GAWKS
FOUR	**FUBS**	FYLES	GANEF	GAWKY
FOURS	FUBSY	**FYRD**	GANEV	**GAWP**
FOWL	**FUCK**	FYRDS	**GANG**	GAWPS
FOWLS	FUCKS	**GADE**	GANGS	**GAWS**
FRAB	**FUEL**	GADES	**GANT**	GAWSY
FRABS	FUELS	**GADI**	GANTS	**GAZE**
FRAG	**FUFF**	GADID	**GAOL**	AGAZE
FRAGS	FUFFS	GADIS	GAOLS	GAZED
FRAP	FUFFY	**GADS**	**GAPE**	GAZER
FRAPE	**FUGU**	EGADS	AGAPE	GAZES
FRAPS	FUGUE	GADSO	GAPED	**GEAL**
FRAS	FUGUS	**GAFF**	GAPER	GEALS
FRASS	**FUJI**	GAFFE	GAPES	**GEAN**
FRAT	FUJIS	GAFFS	**GAPO**	GEANS

GEAR	GIBED	GIVEN	GLUME	**GONK**
GEARE	GIBEL	GIVER	GLUMS	GONKS
GEARS	GIBER	GIVES	**GLUT**	**GONS**
GEAT	GIBES	**GLAD**	GLUTE	AGONS
GEATS	**GIFT**	GLADE	GLUTS	**GOOD**
GECK	GIFTS	GLADS	**GNAR**	AGOOD
GECKO	**GIGA**	GLADY	GNARL	GOODS
GECKS	GIGAS	**GLAM**	GNARR	GOODY
GEED	**GILA**	GLAMS	GNARS	**GOOF**
OGEED	AGILA	**GLED**	**GNAT**	GOOFS
GEEK	GILAS	OGLED	GNATS	GOOFY
GEEKS	**GILD**	GLEDE	**GNAW**	**GOOG**
GEEKY	GILDS	GLEDS	GNAWN	GOOGS
GEEP	**GILL**	**GLEE**	GNAWS	**GOOK**
GEEPS	GILLS	AGLEE	**GNOW**	GOOKS
GEES	GILLY	GLEED	GNOWS	GOOKY
OGEES	**GILT**	GLEEK	**GOAD**	**GOOL**
GEESE	GILTS	GLEES	GOADS	GOOLD
GEEST	**GIMP**	GLEET	**GOAF**	GOOLS
GEIT	GIMPS	**GLEI**	GOAFS	GOOLY
GEITS	GIMPY	GLEIS	**GOAL**	**GOON**
GELD	**GING**	**GLEN**	GOALS	GOONS
GELDS	AGING	GLENS	**GOAT**	GOONY
GELT	GINGE	GLENT	GOATS	**GOOP**
GELTS	GINGS	**GLEY**	GOATY	GOOPS
GENA	**GINK**	AGLEY	**GOBI**	GOOPY
GENAL	GINKS	GLEYS	GOBIS	**GOOR**
GENAS	**GINN**	**GLIA**	**GOBO**	GOORS
GENE	GINNY	GLIAL	GOBOS	GOORY
AGENE	**GIOS**	GLIAS	**GODS**	**GOOS**
GENES	AGIOS	**GLIB**	GODSO	GOOSE
GENET	**GIPS**	GLIBS	**GOEL**	GOOSY
GENT	GIPSY	**GLID**	GOELS	**GORA**
AGENT	**GIRD**	GLIDE	**GOER**	AGORA
GENTS	GIRDS	**GLIM**	GOERS	GORAL
GENTY	**GIRL**	GLIME	**GOES**	GORAS
GENU	GIRLS	GLIMS	GOEST	**GORE**
GENUA	GIRLY	**GLIT**	**GOFF**	GORED
GENUS	**GIRN**	GLITS	GOFFS	GORES
GERE	GIRNS	GLITZ	**GOGO**	**GORI**
GERES	GIRO	**GLOB**	GOGOS	GORIS
GERM	GIRON	GLOBE	**GOJI**	**GORM**
GERMS	GIROS	GLOBI	GOJIS	GORMS
GERMY	**GIRR**	GLOBS	**GOLD**	GORMY
GERS	GIRRS	GLOBY	GOLDS	**GORP**
AGERS	**GIRT**	**GLOM**	GOLDY	GORPS
EGERS	GIRTH	GLOMS	**GOLE**	**GOSH**
GEST	GIRTS	**GLOP**	GOLEM	GOSHT
EGEST	**GISM**	GLOPS	GOLES	**GOSS**
GESTE	AGISM	**GLOW**	**GOLF**	GOSSE
GESTS	GISMO	AGLOW	GOLFS	**GOTH**
GETA	GISMS	GLOWS	**GOLP**	GOTHS
GETAS	**GIST**	**GLUE**	GOLPE	**GOUK**
GEUM	AGIST	GLUED	GOLPS	GOUKS
GEUMS	GISTS	GLUER	**GONE**	**GOUT**
GHAT	**GITE**	GLUES	AGONE	GOUTS
GHATS	GITES	GLUEY	GONEF	GOUTY
GHEE	**GIVE**	**GLUG**	GONER	**GOWD**
GHEES	OGIVE	GLUGS	**GONG**	GOWDS
GIBE	GIVED	**GLUM**	GONGS	**GOWF**

GOWFS	**GRIS**	GULFY	HABUS	SHAKE
GOWK	GRISE	**GULL**	**HACK**	HAKEA
GOWKS	GRIST	GULLS	CHACK	HAKES
GOWL	GRISY	GULLY	SHACK	**HAKU**
GOWLS	**GRIT**	**GULP**	THACK	HAKUS
GOWN	GRITH	GULPH	WHACK	**HALE**
GOWNS	GRITS	GULPS	HACKS	SHALE
GRAB	**GROG**	GULPY	**HADE**	THALE
GRABS	GROGS	**GUMP**	SHADE	WHALE
GRAD	**GROK**	GUMPS	HADED	HALED
GRADE	GROKS	**GUNG**	HADES	HALER
GRADS	**GROT**	GUNGE	**HADJ**	HALES
GRAM	GROTS	GUNGY	HADJI	**HALF**
GRAMA	**GROW**	**GUNK**	**HADS**	HALFA
GRAME	GROWL	GUNKS	CHADS	HALFS
GRAMP	GROWN	GUNKY	SHADS	**HALL**
GRAMS	GROWS	**GURL**	HADST	SHALL
GRAN	**GRRL**	GURLS	**HAEM**	HALLO
GRANA	GRRLS	GURLY	HAEMS	HALLS
GRAND	**GRUB**	**GURN**	**HAET**	**HALM**
GRANS	GRUBS	GURNS	HAETS	SHALM
GRANT	**GRUE**	**GURS**	**HAFF**	HALMA
GRAT	GRUED	GURSH	CHAFF	HALMS
GRATE	GRUEL	**GURU**	HAFFS	**HALO**
GRAV	GRUES	GURUS	**HAFT**	HALON
GRAVE	**GRUM**	**GUSH**	CHAFT	HALOS
GRAVS	GRUME	GUSHY	SHAFT	**HALT**
GRAVY	GRUMP	**GUST**	HAFTS	SHALT
GRAY	**GUAN**	GUSTO	**HAGG**	HALTS
GRAYS	GUANA	GUSTS	HAGGS	**HAME**
GREE	GUANO	GUSTY	**HAGS**	SHAME
AGREE	GUANS	**GUTS**	SHAGS	HAMED
GREED	**GUAR**	GUTSY	**HAHA**	HAMES
GREEK	GUARD	**GUYS**	HAHAS	**HAMS**
GREEN	GUARS	GUYSE	**HAHS**	CHAMS
GREES	**GUCK**	**GYAL**	SHAHS	SHAMS
GREET	GUCKS	GYALS	**HAIK**	WHAMS
GREN	GUCKY	**GYBE**	HAIKA	**HAND**
GRENS	**GUDE**	GYBED	HAIKS	SHAND
GREW	GUDES	GYBES	HAIKU	HANDS
GREWS	**GUES**	**GYMP**	**HAIL**	HANDY
GREY	AGUES	GYMPS	HAILS	**HANG**
GREYS	GUESS	**GYPS**	HAILY	BHANG
GRID	GUEST	GYPSY	**HAIN**	CHANG
GRIDE	**GUFF**	**GYRE**	CHAIN	PHANG
GRIDS	GUFFS	GYRED	HAINS	THANG
GRIG	**GUGA**	GYRES	HAINT	WHANG
GRIGS	GUGAS	**GYRO**	**HAIR**	HANGI
GRIM	**GUID**	GYRON	CHAIR	HANGS
GRIME	GUIDE	GYROS	HAIRS	**HANK**
GRIMY	GUIDS	**GYTE**	HAIRY	CHANK
GRIN	**GULA**	GYTES	**HAJI**	SHANK
AGRIN	GULAG	**GYVE**	BHAJI	THANK
GRIND	GULAR	GYVED	HAJIS	HANKS
GRINS	GULAS	GYVES	**HAJJ**	HANKY
GRIP	**GULE**	**HAAF**	HAJJI	**HANT**
GRIPE	GULES	HAAFS	**HAKA**	CHANT
GRIPS	GULET	**HAAR**	HAKAM	HANTS
GRIPT	**GULF**	HAARS	HAKAS	**HAOS**
GRIPY	GULFS	**HABU**	**HAKE**	CHAOS

HAPS	**HATS**	HEARD	**HEMP**	**HEWS**
CHAPS	CHATS	HEARE	HEMPS	CHEWS
SHAPS	GHATS	HEARS	HEMPY	SHEWS
WHAPS	KHATS	HEART	**HEND**	THEWS
HAPU	WHATS	**HEAT**	SHEND	WHEWS
HAPUS	**HAUD**	CHEAT	HENDS	**HEYS**
HARD	HAUDS	WHEAT	**HENS**	WHEYS
CHARD	**HAUF**	HEATH	THENS	**HICK**
SHARD	HAUFS	HEATS	WHENS	CHICK
HARDS	**HAUL**	**HEBE**	**HENT**	THICK
HARDY	SHAUL	THEBE	AHENT	HICKS
HARE	HAULD	HEBEN	SHENT	**HIDE**
CHARE	HAULM	HEBES	HENTS	CHIDE
PHARE	HAULS	**HECH**	**HERB**	HIDED
SHARE	HAULT	HECHT	HERBS	HIDER
WHARE	**HAUT**	**HECK**	HERBY	HIDES
HARED	GHAUT	CHECK	**HERD**	**HIED**
HAREM	HAUTE	HECKS	SHERD	SHIED
HARES	**HAVE**	**HEED**	HERDS	**HIES**
HARK	CHAVE	THEED	**HERE**	RHIES
CHARK	SHAVE	HEEDS	CHERE	SHIES
SHARK	HAVEN	HEEDY	SHERE	**HIGH**
HARKS	HAVER	**HEEL**	THERE	AHIGH
HARL	HAVES	SHEEL	WHERE	THIGH
HARLS	**HAWK**	WHEEL	HERES	HIGHS
HARM	CHAWK	HEELS	**HERL**	HIGHT
CHARM	HAWKS	**HEFT**	HERLS	**HIKE**
PHARM	**HAWM**	THEFT	**HERM**	HIKED
THARM	SHAWM	WHEFT	THERM	HIKER
HARMS	HAWMS	HEFTE	HERMA	HIKES
HARN	**HAWS**	HEFTS	HERMS	**HILA**
SHARN	CHAWS	HEFTY	**HERN**	HILAR
HARNS	SHAWS	**HEID**	HERNS	**HILD**
HARO	THAWS	HEIDS	**HERO**	CHILD
HAROS	HAWSE	**HEIL**	HERON	**HILI**
HARP	**HAYS**	HEILS	HEROS	CHILI
SHARP	CHAYS	**HEIR**	**HERS**	**HILL**
HARPS	SHAYS	THEIR	HERSE	CHILL
HARPY	**HAZE**	HEIRS	**HERY**	SHILL
HART	HAZED	**HELE**	HERYE	THILL
CHART	HAZEL	HELED	**HESP**	HILLO
HARTS	HAZER	HELES	THESP	HILLS
HASH	HAZES	**HELL**	HESPS	HILLY
SHASH	**HEAD**	SHELL	**HEST**	**HILT**
HASHY	AHEAD	HELLO	CHEST	HILTS
HASK	HEADS	HELLS	GHEST	**HIMS**
HASKS	HEADY	**HELM**	HESTS	SHIMS
HASP	**HEAL**	WHELM	**HETE**	WHIMS
HASPS	SHEAL	HELMS	THETE	**HIND**
HAST	WHEAL	**HELO**	HETES	AHIND
GHAST	HEALD	HELOS	**HETH**	HINDS
HASTA	HEALS	HELOT	CHETH	**HING**
HASTE	**HEAP**	**HELP**	KHETH	AHING
HASTY	AHEAP	CHELP	HETHS	EHING
HATE	CHEAP	WHELP	**HETS**	OHING
HATED	HEAPS	HELPS	KHETS	THING
HATER	HEAPY	**HEME**	SHETS	HINGE
HATES	**HEAR**	RHEME	WHETS	HINGS
HATH	SHEAR	THEME	**HEWN**	**HINS**
HATHA	WHEAR	HEMES	SHEWN	CHINS

SHINS	**HOES**	**HONG**	HORNS	SHOWS
THINS	SHOES	THONG	HORNY	HOWSO
WHINS	**HOGG**	HONGI	**HORS**	**HOYA**
HINT	HOGGS	HONGS	KHORS	HOYAS
AHINT	**HOGH**	**HONK**	HORSE	**HUBS**
HINTS	HOGHS	HONKS	HORST	CHUBS
HIOI	**HOGS**	HONKY	HORSY	**HUCK**
HIOIS	CHOGS	**HONS**	**HOSE**	CHUCK
HIPS	SHOGS	PHONS	CHOSE	SHUCK
CHIPS	**HOIK**	**HOOD**	THOSE	HUCKS
SHIPS	HOIKS	HOODS	WHOSE	**HUER**
WHIPS	**HOKA**	HOODY	HOSED	HUERS
HIPT	HOKAS	**HOOF**	HOSEL	**HUFF**
WHIPT	**HOKE**	CHOOF	HOSEN	CHUFF
HIRE	CHOKE	WHOOF	HOSER	HUFFS
SHIRE	HOKED	HOOFS	HOSES	HUFFY
HIRED	HOKES	**HOOK**	HOSEY	**HUGE**
HIREE	HOKEY	CHOOK	**HOST**	HUGER
HIRER	**HOKI**	SHOOK	GHOST	**HUGS**
HIRES	HOKIS	HOOKA	HOSTA	CHUGS
HISH	**HOLD**	HOOKS	HOSTS	THUGS
SHISH	AHOLD	HOOKY	**HOTE**	**HUHU**
WHISH	HOLDS	**HOON**	SHOTE	HUHUS
HISS	**HOLE**	CHOON	HOTEL	**HUIA**
WHISS	DHOLE	SHOON	HOTEN	HUIAS
HISSY	THOLE	HOONS	**HOTS**	**HULA**
HIST	WHOLE	**HOOP**	PHOTS	HULAS
SHIST	HOLED	WHOOP	SHOTS	**HULE**
WHIST	HOLES	HOOPS	**HOUF**	SHULE
HISTS	HOLEY	**HOOR**	HOUFF	HULES
HITS	**HOLK**	HOORD	HOUFS	**HULK**
CHITS	HOLKS	HOORS	**HOUR**	HULKS
SHITS	**HOLM**	**HOOT**	HOURI	HULKY
WHITS	HOLMS	BHOOT	HOURS	**HULL**
HIVE	**HOLS**	SHOOT	**HOUT**	AHULL
CHIVE	DHOLS	WHOOT	CHOUT	HULLO
SHIVE	**HOLT**	HOOTS	SHOUT	HULLS
HIVED	HOLTS	HOOTY	HOUTS	HULLY
HIVER	**HOMA**	**HOPE**	**HOVE**	**HUMA**
HIVES	HOMAS	SHOPE	SHOVE	HUMAN
HIZZ	**HOME**	HOPED	HOVEA	HUMAS
CHIZZ	HOMED	HOPER	HOVED	**HUMF**
WHIZZ	HOMER	HOPES	HOVEL	HUMFS
HOAR	HOMES	**HOPS**	HOVEN	**HUMP**
HOARD	HOMEY	CHOPS	HOVER	CHUMP
HOARS	**HOMO**	SHOPS	HOVES	THUMP
HOARY	ZHOMO	WHOPS	**HOWE**	WHUMP
HOAS	HOMOS	**HORA**	HOWES	HUMPH
HOAST	**HOND**	HORAH	**HOWF**	HUMPS
HOBO	HONDA	HORAL	HOWFF	HUMPY
HOBOS	HONDS	HORAS	HOWFS	**HUMS**
HOCK	**HONE**	**HORE**	**HOWK**	CHUMS
CHOCK	OHONE	CHORE	CHOWK	**HUNK**
SHOCK	PHONE	SHORE	HOWKS	CHUNK
HOCKS	RHONE	WHORE	**HOWL**	THUNK
HOED	SHONE	**HORI**	THOWL	HUNKS
SHOED	HONED	HORIS	HOWLS	HUNKY
HOER	HONER	**HORN**	**HOWS**	**HUNS**
SHOER	HONES	SHORN	CHOWS	SHUNS
HOERS	HONEY	THORN	DHOWS	**HUNT**

SHUNT	NICER	**IKAT**	IMPIS	LINKY
HUNTS	RICER	IKATS	**IMPS**	PINKY
HUPS	ICERS	**IKON**	DIMPS	SINKY
WHUPS	**ICES**	EIKON	GIMPS	ZINKY
HURL	BICES	IKONS	LIMPS	**INNS**
CHURL	DICES	**ILEA**	NIMPS	JINNS
THURL	FICES	PILEA	PIMPS	LINNS
HURLS	RICES	ILEAC	SIMPS	WINNS
HURLY	SICES	ILEAL	TIMPS	**INTI**
HURT	TICES	**ILEX**	WIMPS	INTIL
HURTS	VICES	SILEX	**INBY**	INTIS
HUSH	**ICKY**	ILIA	INBYE	**INTO**
SHUSH	DICKY	CILIA	**INCH**	PINTO
HUSHY	KICKY	MILIA	CINCH	**IONS**
HUSK	MICKY	ILIAC	FINCH	CIONS
HUSKS	PICKY	ILIAD	LINCH	LIONS
HUSKY	TICKY	ILIAL	PINCH	PIONS
HUSO	WICKY	**ILKS**	WINCH	**IOTA**
HUSOS	**ICON**	BILKS	**INFO**	BIOTA
HUSS	ICONS	MILKS	INFOS	DIOTA
HUSSY	**IDEA**	SILKS	**INGO**	IOTAS
HUTS	IDEAL	**ILLS**	BINGO	**IRED**
BHUTS	IDEAS	BILLS	DINGO	AIRED
PHUTS	**IDEE**	CILLS	JINGO	FIRED
SHUTS	IDEES	DILLS	LINGO	HIRED
HWYL	**IDES**	FILLS	PINGO	MIRED
HWYLS	AIDES	GILLS	INGOT	SIRED
HYEN	BIDES	HILLS	**INGS**	TIRED
HYENA	CIDES	JILLS	BINGS	VIRED
HYENS	FIDES	KILLS	DINGS	WIRED
HYKE	HIDES	LILLS	GINGS	**IRES**
HYKES	NIDES	MILLS	HINGS	CIRES
HYLA	RIDES	NILLS	KINGS	FIRES
PHYLA	SIDES	PILLS	LINGS	HIRES
HYLAS	TIDES	RILLS	MINGS	MIRES
HYLE	WIDES	SILLS	PINGS	SIRES
CHYLE	**IDLE**	TILLS	RINGS	TIRES
PHYLE	SIDLE	VILLS	SINGS	VIRES
HYLEG	IDLED	WILLS	TINGS	WIRES
HYLES	IDLER	YILLS	WINGS	**IRID**
HYMN	IDLES	ZILLS	ZINGS	VIRID
HYMNS	**IDOL**	**ILLY**	**INKS**	IRIDS
HYPE	IDOLA	BILLY	BINKS	**IRIS**
HYPED	IDOLS	DILLY	DINKS	SIRIS
HYPER	**IDYL**	FILLY	FINKS	**IRKS**
HYPES	IDYLL	GILLY	GINKS	BIRKS
HYPO	IDYLS	HILLY	JINKS	DIRKS
HYPOS	**IFFY**	SILLY	KINKS	FIRKS
IAMB	BIFFY	TILLY	LINKS	KIRKS
IAMBI	JIFFY	WILLY	MINKS	LIRKS
IAMBS	MIFFY	**IMAM**	OINKS	MIRKS
IBEX	NIFFY	IMAMS	PINKS	YIRKS
VIBEX	**IGGS**	**IMID**	RINKS	**IRON**
ICED	BIGGS	TIMID	SINKS	GIRON
DICED	MIGGS	IMIDE	TINKS	IRONE
RICED	RIGGS	IMIDO	WINKS	IRONS
TICED	**IGLU**	IMIDS	**INKY**	IRONY
VICED	IGLUS	**IMMY**	DINKY	**ISBA**
ICER	**IKAN**	JIMMY	HINKY	ISBAS
DICER	IKANS	**IMPI**	KINKY	**ISIT**

VISIT	JAKEY	**JESS**	**JOLE**	**JUVE**
ISLE	**JAMB**	JESSE	JOLED	JUVES
AISLE	JAMBE	**JEST**	JOLES	**KACK**
LISLE	JAMBO	JESTS	**JOLL**	KACKS
ISLED	JAMBS	**JETE**	JOLLS	**KADE**
ISLES	JAMBU	JETES	JOLLY	KADES
ISLET	**JANE**	**JIAO**	**JOLT**	**KADI**
ISMS	JANES	JIAOS	JOLTS	KADIS
GISMS	**JANN**	**JIBB**	JOLTY	**KAGO**
JISMS	JANNS	JIBBA	**JOMO**	KAGOS
ISNA	JANNY	JIBBS	JOMON	**KAGU**
ISNAE	**JAPE**	**JIBE**	JOMOS	KAGUS
ISOS	JAPED	JIBED	**JONG**	**KAID**
MISOS	JAPER	JIBER	JONGS	KAIDS
PISOS	JAPES	JIBES	**JOOK**	**KAIE**
ITAS	**JARK**	**JIFF**	JOOKS	KAIES
DITAS	JARKS	JIFFS	**JOTA**	**KAIF**
LITAS	**JARL**	JIFFY	JOTAS	KAIFS
PITAS	JARLS	**JILL**	**JOUK**	**KAIK**
VITAS	**JARP**	JILLS	JOUKS	KAIKA
ITCH	JARPS	**JILT**	**JOUR**	KAIKS
AITCH	**JASP**	JILTS	JOURS	**KAIL**
BITCH	JASPE	**JIMP**	**JOWL**	SKAIL
DITCH	JASPS	JIMPY	JOWLS	KAILS
FITCH	**JATO**	**JINK**	JOWLY	**KAIM**
HITCH	JATOS	JINKS	**JUBA**	KAIMS
MITCH	**JAUK**	**JINN**	JUBAS	**KAIN**
PITCH	JAUKS	DJINN	**JUBE**	KAING
TITCH	**JAUP**	JINNE	JUBES	KAINS
WITCH	JAUPS	JINNI	**JUCO**	**KAKA**
ITCHY	**JAVA**	JINNS	JUCOS	KAKAS
ITEM	JAVAS	**JINS**	**JUDO**	**KAKI**
ITEMS	**JAZZ**	DJINS	JUDOS	KAKIS
IWIS	JAZZY	**JIRD**	**JUGA**	**KALE**
KIWIS	**JEAN**	JIRDS	AJUGA	KALES
IXIA	JEANS	**JISM**	JUGAL	**KALI**
IXIAS	**JEAT**	JISMS	**JUJU**	KALIF
IZAR	JEATS	**JIVE**	JUJUS	KALIS
SIZAR	**JEDI**	JIVED	**JUKE**	**KAMA**
IZARD	JEDIS	JIVER	JUKED	KAMAS
IZARS	**JEEL**	JIVES	JUKES	**KAME**
JAAP	JEELS	JIVEY	**JUKU**	KAMES
JAAPS	JEELY	**JOBE**	JUKUS	**KAMI**
JACK	**JEEP**	JOBED	**JUMP**	KAMIK
JACKS	JEEPS	JOBES	JUMPS	KAMIS
JACKY	**JEER**	**JOCK**	JUMPY	**KANA**
JADE	JEERS	JOCKO	**JUNK**	KANAE
JADED	**JEFE**	JOCKS	JUNKS	KANAS
JADES	JEFES	**JOEY**	JUNKY	**KANE**
JAFA	**JEFF**	JOEYS	**JUPE**	KANEH
JAFAS	JEFFS	**JOHN**	JUPES	KANES
JAGA	**JEHU**	JOHNS	**JURA**	**KANG**
JAGAS	JEHUS	**JOIN**	JURAL	KANGA
JAGG	**JELL**	JOINS	JURAT	KANGS
JAGGS	JELLO	JOINT	**JURE**	**KANS**
JAGGY	JELLS	**JOKE**	JUREL	IKANS
JAIL	JELLY	JOKED	**JUST**	**KANT**
JAILS	**JERK**	JOKER	JUSTS	KANTS
JAKE	JERKS	JOKES	**JUTE**	**KAON**
JAKES	JERKY	JOKEY	JUTES	KAONS

KAPA	SKEGS	**KHOR**	KIPPS	**KOAN**
KAPAS	**KEIR**	KHORS	**KIPS**	KOANS
KAPH	KEIRS	**KHUD**	SKIPS	**KOAP**
KAPHS	**KELL**	KHUDS	**KIRK**	KOAPS
KARA	SKELL	**KIBE**	KIRKS	**KOBO**
KARAS	KELLS	KIBEI	**KIRN**	KOBOS
KARAT	KELLY	KIBES	KIRNS	**KOEL**
KARK	**KELP**	**KICK**	**KISS**	KOELS
KARKS	SKELP	KICKS	KISSY	**KOFF**
KARN	KELPS	KICKY	**KIST**	SKOFF
KARNS	KELPY	**KIDS**	KISTS	KOFFS
KARO	**KELT**	SKIDS	**KITE**	**KOHA**
KAROO	KELTS	**KIEF**	SKITE	KOHAS
KAROS	KELTY	KIEFS	KITED	**KOHL**
KART	**KEMB**	**KIER**	KITER	KOHLS
SKART	KEMBO	SKIER	KITES	**KOJI**
KARTS	KEMBS	KIERS	KITH	KOJIS
KATA	**KEMP**	**KIEV**	KITHE	**KOKA**
KATAL	KEMPS	KIEVE	KITHS	KOKAS
KATAS	KEMPT	KIEVS	**KITS**	**KOLA**
KATI	KEMPY	**KIFF**	SKITS	KOLAS
KATIS	**KENO**	SKIFF	**KIVA**	**KOLO**
KATS	KENOS	**KIKE**	KIVAS	KOLOS
IKATS	**KENS**	KIKES	**KIWI**	**KOND**
SKATS	SKENS	**KILL**	KIWIS	KONDO
KAVA	**KENT**	SKILL	**KLAP**	**KONK**
KAVAL	KENTE	KILLS	KLAPS	KONKS
KAVAS	KENTS	**KILN**	**KLIK**	**KONS**
KAWA	**KEPI**	KILNS	KLIKS	IKONS
KAWAS	KEPIS	**KILO**	**KNAG**	**KOOK**
KAWAU	**KEPS**	KILOS	KNAGS	KOOKS
KAWS	SKEPS	**KILP**	**KNAP**	KOOKY
SKAWS	**KERB**	KILPS	KNAPS	**KOPH**
KAYO	KERBS	**KILT**	**KNAR**	KOPHS
KAYOS	**KERF**	KILTS	KNARL	**KORA**
KAYS	KERFS	KILTY	KNARS	KORAI
OKAYS	**KERN**	**KINA**	**KNEE**	KORAS
KAZI	KERNE	KINAS	KNEED	KORAT
KAZIS	KERNS	**KIND**	KNEEL	**KORE**
KBAR	**KERO**	KINDA	KNEES	KORES
KBARS	KEROS	KINDS	**KNIT**	**KORO**
KECK	**KEST**	KINDY	KNITS	KOROS
KECKS	KESTS	**KINE**	**KNOB**	**KORU**
KEEF	**KETA**	KINES	KNOBS	KORUN
SKEEF	KETAS	**KING**	**KNOP**	KORUS
KEEFS	**KETE**	AKING	KNOPS	**KOTO**
KEEK	KETES	EKING	**KNOT**	KOTOS
KEEKS	**KETO**	KINGS	KNOTS	KOTOW
KEEL	KETOL	**KINK**	**KNOW**	**KRAB**
KEELS	**KETS**	SKINK	KNOWE	KRABS
KEEN	SKETS	KINKS	KNOWN	**KSAR**
SKEEN	**KHAF**	KINKY	KNOWS	KSARS
KEENO	KHAFS	**KINO**	**KNUB**	**KUDO**
KEENS	**KHAN**	KINOS	KNUBS	KUDOS
KEEP	KHANS	**KINS**	**KNUR**	**KUDU**
KEEPS	**KHAT**	SKINS	KNURL	KUDUS
KEET	KHATS	**KIPE**	KNURR	**KUFI**
SKEET	**KHET**	KIPES	KNURS	KUFIS
KEETS	KHETH	**KIPP**	**KNUT**	**KUIA**
KEGS	KHETS	KIPPA	KNUTS	KUIAS

KUKU	CLADE	ULAMA	SLAPS	SLATS
KUKUS	GLADE	LAMAS	LAPSE	**LAUD**
KULA	SLADE	**LAMB**	**LARD**	BLAUD
KULAK	LADED	LAMBS	LARDS	LAUDS
KULAN	LADEN	LAMBY	LARDY	**LAUF**
KULAS	LADER	**LAME**	**LARE**	LAUFS
KURI	LADES	BLAME	BLARE	**LAVA**
KURIS	**LADS**	CLAME	FLARE	FLAVA
KURU	BLADS	FLAME	GLARE	LAVAS
KURUS	CLADS	LAMED	LAREE	**LAVE**
KUTA	GLADS	LAMER	LARES	CLAVE
KUTAS	**LADY**	LAMES	**LARI**	SLAVE
KUTI	BLADY	**LAMP**	LARIS	LAVED
KUTIS	GLADY	CLAMP	**LARK**	LAVER
KUTU	**LAER**	LAMPS	LARKS	LAVES
KUTUS	BLAER	**LAMS**	LARKY	**LAWK**
KUZU	LAERS	BLAMS	**LARN**	LAWKS
KUZUS	**LAGS**	CLAMS	LARNS	**LAWN**
KVAS	BLAGS	FLAMS	**LASE**	BLAWN
KVASS	CLAGS	GLAMS	BLASE	FLAWN
KYAK	FLAGS	SLAMS	LASED	LAWNS
KYAKS	SLAGS	**LANA**	LASER	LAWNY
KYAR	**LAHS**	LANAI	LASES	**LAWS**
KYARS	BLAHS	LANAS	**LASH**	BLAWS
KYAT	**LAIC**	**LAND**	BLASH	CLAWS
KYATS	LAICH	ALAND	CLASH	FLAWS
KYBO	LAICS	BLAND	FLASH	SLAWS
KYBOS	**LAID**	ELAND	PLASH	**LAYS**
KYLE	PLAID	GLAND	SLASH	ALAYS
KYLES	SLAID	LANDE	**LASS**	BLAYS
KYND	LAIDS	LANDS	CLASS	CLAYS
KYNDE	**LAIK**	**LANE**	GLASS	FLAYS
KYNDS	GLAIK	ALANE	LASSI	PLAYS
KYPE	LAIKA	PLANE	LASSO	SLAYS
KYPES	LAIKS	SLANE	LASSU	**LAZE**
KYTE	**LAIN**	LANES	**LAST**	BLAZE
SKYTE	BLAIN	**LANG**	BLAST	GLAZE
KYTES	ELAIN	ALANG	CLAST	LAZED
LABS	PLAIN	CLANG	PLAST	LAZES
BLABS	SLAIN	KLANG	LASTS	**LAZO**
FLABS	**LAIR**	SLANG	**LATE**	LAZOS
SLABS	FLAIR	**LANK**	ALATE	**LAZY**
LACE	GLAIR	BLANK	BLATE	GLAZY
GLACE	LAIRD	CLANK	ELATE	**LEAD**
PLACE	LAIRS	FLANK	PLATE	PLEAD
LACED	LAIRY	PLANK	SLATE	LEADS
LACER	**LAKE**	SLANK	LATED	LEADY
LACES	FLAKE	LANKS	LATEN	**LEAF**
LACET	SLAKE	LANKY	LATER	LEAFS
LACEY	LAKED	**LANT**	LATEX	LEAFY
LACK	LAKER	ALANT	**LATH**	**LEAK**
ALACK	LAKES	PLANT	LATHE	BLEAK
BLACK	**LAKH**	SLANT	LATHI	LEAKS
CLACK	LAKHS	LANTS	LATHS	LEAKY
FLACK	**LAKY**	**LAPS**	LATHY	**LEAL**
PLACK	FLAKY	ALAPS	**LATS**	ILEAL
SLACK	**LALL**	CLAPS	BLATS	**LEAM**
LACKS	LALLS	FLAPS	CLATS	FLEAM
LADE	**LAMA**	KLAPS	FLATS	GLEAM
BLADE	LLAMA	PLAPS	PLATS	LEAMS

LEAN	LEFTY	GLEYS	LIKEN	LINGS
CLEAN	**LEGS**	SLEYS	LIKER	LINGY
GLEAN	CLEGS	**LEZZ**	LIKES	**LINK**
LEANS	FLEGS	LEZZA	**LILL**	BLINK
LEANT	**LEHR**	LEZZY	LILLS	CLINK
LEANY	LEHRS	**LIAR**	**LILT**	PLINK
LEAP	**LEIR**	LIARD	LILTS	SLINK
LEAPS	LEIRS	LIARS	**LILY**	LINKS
LEAPT	**LEIS**	LIART	SLILY	LINKY
LEAR	GLEIS	**LIAS**	**LIMA**	**LINN**
BLEAR	VLEIS	ALIAS	LIMAN	LINNS
CLEAR	LEISH	GLIAS	LIMAS	LINNY
LEARE	**LEME**	**LIBS**	LIMAX	**LINO**
LEARN	FLEME	GLIBS	**LIMB**	LINOS
LEARS	LEMED	**LICE**	CLIMB	**LINS**
LEARY	LEMEL	SLICE	LIMBA	BLINS
LEAS	LEMES	**LICH**	LIMBI	**LINT**
FLEAS	**LEND**	LICHI	LIMBO	CLINT
PLEAS	BLEND	LICHT	LIMBS	ELINT
LEASE	LENDS	**LICK**	LIMBY	FLINT
LEASH	**LENG**	CLICK	**LIME**	GLINT
LEAST	LENGS	FLICK	CLIME	LINTS
LEAT	**LENO**	KLICK	GLIME	LINTY
BLEAT	LENOS	SLICK	SLIME	**LINY**
CLEAT	**LENS**	LICKS	LIMED	BLINY
PLEAT	GLENS	**LIDO**	LIMEN	**LION**
LEATS	LENSE	LIDOS	LIMES	LIONS
LEED	**LENT**	**LIED**	LIMEY	**LIPA**
BLEED	BLENT	CLIED	**LIMN**	LIPAS
GLEED	GLENT	FLIED	LIMNS	**LIPE**
LEEK	OLENT	PLIED	**LIMO**	CLIPE
CLEEK	LENTI	**LIEF**	LIMOS	SLIPE
GLEEK	LENTO	LIEFS	**LIMP**	**LIPO**
SLEEK	**LEPT**	**LIEN**	BLIMP	LIPOS
LEEKS	CLEPT	ALIEN	FLIMP	**LIPS**
LEEP	SLEPT	LIENS	LIMPA	BLIPS
BLEEP	LEPTA	**LIER**	LIMPS	CLIPS
CLEEP	**LERE**	FLIER	**LIMY**	FLIPS
SLEEP	LERED	PLIER	BLIMY	SLIPS
LEEPS	LERES	SLIER	SLIMY	**LIRA**
LEER	**LERP**	LIERS	**LIND**	LIRAS
FLEER	LERPS	**LIES**	BLIND	**LIRK**
SLEER	**LESS**	CLIES	LINDS	LIRKS
LEERS	BLESS	FLIES	LINDY	**LISK**
LEERY	**LEST**	PLIES	**LINE**	FLISK
LEES	BLEST	VLIES	ALINE	GLISK
BLEES	LESTS	**LIEU**	CLINE	LISKS
FLEES	**LETS**	LIEUS	LINED	**LISP**
GLEES	BLETS	**LIFE**	LINEN	LISPS
LEESE	**LEUD**	LIFER	LINER	**LIST**
LEET	LEUDS	LIFES	LINES	ALIST
FLEET	**LEVE**	**LIFT**	LINEY	BLIST
GLEET	CLEVE	CLIFT	**LING**	LISTS
SLEET	LEVEE	GLIFT	BLING	**LITE**
LEETS	LEVEL	LIFTS	CLING	BLITE
LEFT	LEVER	**LIKE**	FLING	ELITE
ALEFT	LEVES	ALIKE	PLING	FLITE
CLEFT	**LEYS**	GLIKE	SLING	LITED
LEFTE	BLEYS	YLIKE	LINGA	LITER
LEFTS	FLEYS	LIKED	LINGO	LITES

LITH	ALODS	LOOFS	**LOSH**	LOVES
LITHE	CLODS	**LOOK**	FLOSH	LOVEY
LITHO	PLODS	BLOOK	SLOSH	**LOWE**
LITHS	**LOFT**	PLOOK	**LOSS**	ALOWE
LITS	ALOFT	LOOKS	FLOSS	LOWED
BLITS	LOFTS	**LOOM**	GLOSS	LOWER
CLITS	LOFTY	BLOOM	LOSSY	LOWES
FLITS	**LOGE**	GLOOM	**LOST**	**LOWN**
GLITS	ELOGE	SLOOM	GLOST	BLOWN
SLITS	LOGES	LOOMS	**LOTA**	CLOWN
LIVE	**LOGO**	**LOON**	FLOTA	FLOWN
ALIVE	LOGOI	LOONS	LOTAH	LOWND
BLIVE	LOGON	LOONY	LOTAS	LOWNE
OLIVE	LOGOS	**LOOP**	**LOTE**	LOWNS
SLIVE	**LOGS**	BLOOP	CLOTE	**LOWP**
LIVED	BLOGS	CLOOP	FLOTE	LOWPS
LIVEN	CLOGS	GLOOP	ZLOTE	**LOWS**
LIVER	FLOGS	SLOOP	LOTES	BLOWS
LIVES	SLOGS	LOOPS	**LOTH**	CLOWS
LOAD	VLOGS	LOOPY	CLOTH	FLOWS
LOADS	**LOGY**	**LOOR**	SLOTH	GLOWS
LOAF	ELOGY	FLOOR	**LOTI**	PLOWS
LOAFS	OLOGY	LOORD	LOTIC	SLOWS
LOAM	**LOID**	**LOOS**	**LOTO**	LOWSE
CLOAM	SLOID	ALOOS	LOTOS	**LOWT**
GLOAM	LOIDS	LOOSE	**LOTS**	LOWTS
LOAMS	**LOIN**	**LOOT**	BLOTS	**LOYS**
LOAMY	ALOIN	CLOOT	CLOTS	CLOYS
LOAN	ELOIN	SLOOT	PLOTS	PLOYS
SLOAN	LOINS	LOOTS	SLOTS	**LUAU**
LOANS	**LOIR**	**LOPE**	**LOUD**	LUAUS
LOBE	LOIRS	ELOPE	ALOUD	**LUBE**
GLOBE	**LOKE**	SLOPE	CLOUD	LUBED
LOBED	BLOKE	LOPED	**LOUN**	LUBES
LOBES	CLOKE	LOPER	LOUND	**LUCE**
LOBI	LOKES	LOPES	LOUNS	LUCES
GLOBI	**LOLL**	**LOPS**	**LOUP**	**LUCK**
LOBO	LOLLS	CLOPS	LOUPE	CLUCK
LOBOS	LOLLY	ELOPS	LOUPS	PLUCK
LOBS	**LOMA**	FLOPS	**LOUR**	LUCKS
BLOBS	LOMAS	GLOPS	CLOUR	LUCKY
FLOBS	**LOME**	PLOPS	FLOUR	**LUDE**
GLOBS	LOMED	SLOPS	LOURE	BLUDE
SLOBS	LOMES	**LORD**	LOURS	ELUDE
LOCA	**LONE**	LORDS	LOURY	LUDES
LOCAL	ALONE	LORDY	**LOUS**	**LUDO**
LOCH	CLONE	**LORE**	CLOUS	LUDOS
LOCHS	LONER	BLORE	LOUSE	**LUES**
LOCK	**LONG**	LOREL	LOUSY	BLUES
BLOCK	ALONG	LORES	**LOUT**	CLUES
CLOCK	FLONG	**LORY**	CLOUT	FLUES
FLOCK	KLONG	FLORY	FLOUT	GLUES
LOCKS	PLONG	GLORY	GLOUT	PLUES
LOCO	LONGA	**LOSE**	LOUTS	SLUES
LOCOS	LONGE	CLOSE	**LOVE**	**LUFF**
LODE	LONGS	LOSED	CLOVE	BLUFF
GLODE	**LOOF**	LOSEL	GLOVE	FLUFF
LODEN	ALOOF	LOSEN	SLOVE	PLUFF
LODES	KLOOF	LOSER	LOVED	SLUFF
LODS	LOOFA	LOSES	LOVER	LUFFA

LUFFS	LUREX	**MACK**	**MAMA**	OMASA
LUGE	**LURK**	SMACK	MAMAS	MASAS
KLUGE	LURKS	MACKS	**MAMS**	**MASE**
LUGED	**LURS**	**MACS**	IMAMS	MASED
LUGER	BLURS	EMACS	**MANA**	MASER
LUGES	SLURS	**MAGE**	MANAS	MASES
LUGS	**LUSH**	IMAGE	MANAT	**MASH**
GLUGS	BLUSH	MAGES	**MAND**	SMASH
PLUGS	FLUSH	**MAGG**	MANDI	MASHY
SLUGS	PLUSH	MAGGS	**MANE**	**MASK**
LUIT	SLUSH	**MAGI**	MANED	MASKS
SLUIT	LUSHY	MAGIC	MANEH	**MASS**
LUKE	**LUSK**	**MAID**	MANES	AMASS
FLUKE	LUSKS	MAIDS	MANET	MASSA
LULL	**LUST**	**MAIK**	**MANG**	MASSE
LULLS	LUSTS	SMAIK	MANGA	MASSY
LULU	LUSTY	MAIKO	MANGE	**MAST**
LULUS	**LUTE**	MAIKS	MANGO	MASTS
LUMA	ELUTE	**MAIL**	MANGS	MASTY
LUMAS	FLUTE	EMAIL	MANGY	**MASU**
LUMP	GLUTE	MAILE	**MANI**	MASUS
CLUMP	LUTEA	MAILL	MANIA	**MATE**
FLUMP	LUTED	MAILS	MANIC	AMATE
PLUMP	LUTER	**MAIM**	MANIS	MATED
SLUMP	LUTES	MAIMS	**MANO**	MATER
LUMPS	**LUTZ**	**MAIN**	MANOR	MATES
LUMPY	KLUTZ	AMAIN	MANOS	MATEY
LUMS	**LUXE**	MAINS	**MANS**	**MATH**
ALUMS	LUXES	MANSE	MANSE	MATHS
GLUMS	**LWEI**	**MAIR**	**MARA**	**MATT**
PLUMS	LWEIS	MAIRE	MARAE	MATTE
SLUMS	**LYAM**	MAIRS	MARAH	MATTS
LUNA	LYAMS	**MAKE**	MARAS	**MAUD**
LUNAR	**LYME**	MAKER	**MARC**	MAUDS
LUNAS	LYMES	MAKES	MARCH	**MAUL**
LUNE	**LYNE**	**MAKI**	MARCS	MAULS
LUNES	LYNES	MAKIS	**MARD**	**MAUN**
LUNET	**LYRE**	**MAKO**	MARDY	MAUND
LUNG	LYRES	MAKOS	**MARE**	**MAUT**
CLUNG	**LYSE**	**MALA**	MARES	AMAUT
FLUNG	LYSED	MALAM	**MARG**	MAUTS
SLUNG	LYSES	MALAR	MARGE	**MAWK**
LUNGE	**LYTE**	MALAS	MARGS	MAWKS
LUNGI	FLYTE	MALAX	**MARK**	MAWKY
LUNGS	LYTED	**MALE**	MARKA	**MAWR**
LUNK	LYTES	MALES	MARKS	MAWRS
BLUNK	**MAAR**	**MALI**	**MARL**	**MAXI**
CLUNK	MAARE	MALIC	MARLE	MAXIM
FLUNK	MAARS	MALIK	MARLS	MAXIS
PLUNK	**MABE**	MALIS	MARLY	**MAYA**
SLUNK	MABES	**MALL**	**MARM**	MAYAN
LUNKS	**MACE**	SMALL	SMARM	MAYAS
LUNT	MACED	MALLS	MARMS	**MAYO**
BLUNT	MACER	**MALM**	**MARS**	MAYOR
LUNTS	MACES	SMALM	MARSE	MAYOS
LURE	**MACH**	MALMS	MARSH	**MAYS**
ALURE	MACHE	MALMY	**MART**	MAYST
LURED	MACHI	**MALT**	SMART	**MAZE**
LURER	MACHO	SMALT	MARTS	AMAZE
LURES	MACHS	MALTS	**MARTS**	SMAZE
		MALTY	**MASA**	

MAZED	AMENE	**MEWL**	MILTS	MISOS
MAZER	MENED	MEWLS	MILTY	**MISS**
MAZES	MENES	**MEWS**	MILTZ	AMISS
MAZEY	**MENG**	SMEWS	**MIME**	MISSA
MEAD	MENGE	**MEZE**	MIMED	MISSY
MEADS	MENGS	MEZES	MIMEO	**MIST**
MEAL	**MENT**	**MEZZ**	MIMER	MISTS
MEALS	AMENT	MEZZE	MIMES	MISTY
MEALY	MENTA	MEZZO	**MINA**	**MITE**
MEAN	MENTO	**MICA**	MINAE	SMITE
MEANE	**MENU**	MICAS	MINAR	MITER
MEANS	MENUS	**MICE**	MINAS	MITES
MEANT	**MEOU**	AMICE	**MIND**	**MITT**
MEANY	MEOUS	**MICH**	MINDS	MITTS
MEAT	**MEOW**	MICHE	**MINE**	**MITY**
MEATH	MEOWS	MICHT	AMINE	AMITY
MEATS	**MERC**	**MICK**	IMINE	**MIXT**
MEATY	MERCH	MICKS	MINED	MIXTE
MECK	MERCS	MICKY	MINER	**MIZZ**
MECKS	MERCY	**MICO**	MINES	MIZZY
MEED	**MERE**	MICOS	**MING**	**MOAN**
MEEDS	MERED	**MIDI**	MINGE	MOANS
MEEK	MEREL	MIDIS	MINGS	**MOAT**
SMEEK	MERER	**MIDS**	MINGY	MOATS
MEER	MERES	AMIDS	**MINI**	**MOBE**
AMEER	**MERI**	IMIDS	MINIM	MOBES
EMEER	MERIL	MIDST	MINIS	MOBEY
MEERS	MERIS	**MIEN**	**MINK**	**MOCH**
MEES	MERIT	MIENS	MINKE	MOCHA
SMEES	**MERK**	**MIFF**	MINKS	MOCHS
MEET	SMERK	MIFFS	**MINO**	MOCHY
MEETS	MERKS	MIFFY	AMINO	**MOCK**
MEFF	**MERL**	**MIGG**	IMINO	SMOCK
MEFFS	MERLE	MIGGS	MINOR	MOCKS
MEGA	MERLS	**MIHA**	MINOS	**MODE**
OMEGA	**MESA**	MIHAS	**MINT**	MODEL
MEIN	MESAL	**MIHI**	MINTS	MODEM
MEINS	MESAS	MIHIS	MINTY	MODER
MEINT	**MESE**	**MIKE**	**MIRE**	MODES
MEINY	MESEL	MIKED	MIRED	**MODI**
MELA	MESES	MIKES	MIRES	MODII
MELAS	**MESH**	**MILD**	MIREX	**MOER**
MELD	MESHY	MILDS	**MIRI**	MOERS
MELDS	**MESS**	**MILE**	MIRIN	**MOFO**
MELL	MESSY	SMILE	**MIRK**	MOFOS
SMELL	**META**	MILER	SMIRK	**MOGS**
MELLS	METAL	MILES	MIRKS	SMOGS
MELT	**METE**	**MILF**	MIRKY	**MOHR**
SMELT	METED	MILFS	**MIRO**	MOHRS
MELTS	METER	**MILK**	MIROS	**MOIL**
MELTY	METES	MILKO	**MIRS**	MOILS
MEME	**METH**	MILKS	AMIRS	**MOIT**
MEMES	METHO	MILKY	EMIRS	MOITS
MEMO	METHS	**MILL**	SMIRS	**MOJO**
MEMOS	**MEUS**	MILLE	**MIRV**	MOJOS
MEND	EMEUS	MILLS	MIRVS	**MOKE**
AMEND	MEUSE	**MILO**	**MISE**	SMOKE
EMEND	**MEVE**	MILOR	MISER	MOKES
MENDS	MEVED	MILOS	MISES	**MOKI**
MENE	MEVES	**MILT**	**MISO**	MOKIS

MOKO	SMOOT	MOTUS	**MUMP**	**MUTE**
SMOKO	MOOTS	**MOUE**	MUMPS	MUTED
MOKOS	**MOPE**	MOUES	**MUMS**	MUTER
MOLA	MOPED	**MOUP**	MUMSY	MUTES
MOLAL	MOPER	MOUPS	**MUMU**	**MUTI**
MOLAR	MOPES	**MOUS**	MUMUS	MUTIS
MOLAS	MOPEY	MOUSE	**MUNG**	**MUTS**
MOLD	**MOPS**	MOUST	MUNGA	SMUTS
MOLDS	MOPSY	MOUSY	MUNGE	**MUTT**
MOLDY	**MORA**	**MOVE**	MUNGO	MUTTS
MOLE	MORAE	AMOVE	MUNGS	**MUZZ**
AMOLE	MORAL	EMOVE	**MUNI**	MUZZY
MOLES	MORAS	MOVED	MUNIS	**MYAL**
MOLL	MORAT	MOVER	**MUNT**	MYALL
MOLLA	MORAY	MOVES	MUNTS	**MYNA**
MOLLS	**MORE**	**MOWA**	MUNTU	MYNAH
MOLLY	SMORE	MOWAS	MUONS	MYNAS
MOLT	MOREL	**MOXA**	**MUON**	**MYTH**
SMOLT	MORES	MOXAS	MUONS	MYTHI
YMOLT	**MORN**	**MOYA**	**MURA**	MYTHS
MOLTO	MORNE	MOYAS	MURAL	MYTHY
MOLTS	MORNS	**MOYL**	MURAS	**MYXO**
MOME	**MORS**	MOYLE	**MURE**	MYXOS
MOMES	MORSE	MOYLS	EMURE	**MZEE**
MONA	**MORT**	**MOZE**	MURED	MZEES
MONAD	AMORT	MOZED	MURES	**NAAM**
MONAL	MORTS	MOZES	MUREX	NAAMS
MONAS	**MOSE**	**MOZO**	**MURK**	**NAAN**
MONG	MOSED	MOZOS	MURKS	NAANS
AMONG	MOSES	**MUCH**	MURKY	**NABE**
EMONG	MOSEY	MUCHO	**MURL**	NABES
MONGO	**MOSK**	**MUCK**	MURLS	**NABK**
MONGS	MOSKS	AMUCK	MURLY	NABKS
MONK	**MOSS**	MUCKS	**MURR**	**NABS**
MONKS	MOSSO	MUCKY	MURRA	SNABS
MONO	MOSSY	**MUFF**	MURRE	**NACH**
MONOS	**MOST**	MUFFS	MURRI	NACHE
MOOD	MOSTE	**MUGG**	MURRS	NACHO
MOODS	MOSTS	MUGGA	MURRY	**NADA**
MOODY	**MOTE**	MUGGS	**MUSE**	NADAS
MOOK	EMOTE	MUGGY	AMUSE	**NAFF**
MOOKS	SMOTE	**MUGS**	MUSED	NAFFS
MOOL	MOTED	SMUGS	MUSER	**NAGA**
MOOLA	MOTEL	**MUID**	MUSES	NAGAS
MOOLI	MOTEN	MUIDS	MUSET	**NAGS**
MOOLS	MOTES	**MUIL**	**MUSH**	KNAGS
MOOLY	MOTET	MUILS	SMUSH	SNAGS
MOON	MOTEY	**MUIR**	MUSHA	**NAIF**
MOONG	**MOTH**	MUIRS	MUSHY	NAIFS
MOONS	MOTHS	**MULE**	**MUSK**	**NAIK**
MOONY	MOTHY	EMULE	MUSKS	NAIKS
MOOP	**MOTI**	MULED	MUSKY	**NAIL**
MOOPS	MOTIF	MULES	**MUSO**	SNAIL
MOOR	MOTIS	MULEY	MUSOS	NAILS
SMOOR	**MOTT**	**MULL**	**MUSS**	**NALA**
MOORS	MOTTE	MULLA	MUSSE	NALAS
MOORY	MOTTO	MULLS	MUSSY	**NAME**
MOOS	MOTTS	**MUMM**	**MUST**	NAMED
MOOSE	MOTTY	MUMMS	MUSTH	NAMER
MOOT	**MOTU**	MUMMY	MUSTS	NAMES
			MUSTY	

NAMU	SNEDS	**NIDE**	**NODS**	NOSES
NAMUS	**NEED**	SNIDE	SNODS	NOSEY
NANA	KNEED	NIDED	**NOEL**	**NOTA**
ANANA	SNEED	NIDES	NOELS	NOTAL
JNANA	NEEDS	**NIEF**	**NOGG**	**NOTE**
NANAS	NEEDY	NIEFS	NOGGS	NOTED
NANE	**NEEM**	**NIES**	**NOGS**	NOTER
INANE	NEEMB	SNIES	SNOGS	NOTES
NAPA	NEEMS	**NIFE**	**NOIL**	**NOUL**
NAPAS	**NEEP**	KNIFE	NOILS	NOULD
NAPE	NEEPS	NIFES	NOILY	NOULE
NAPED	**NEIF**	**NIFF**	**NOIR**	NOULS
NAPES	NEIFS	SNIFF	NOIRS	**NOUN**
NAPS	**NEMA**	NIFFS	**NOLE**	NOUNS
KNAPS	ENEMA	NIFFY	ANOLE	NOUNY
SNAPS	NEMAS	**NIGH**	NOLES	**NOUP**
NARC	**NEMN**	ANIGH	**NOLL**	NOUPS
NARCO	NEMNS	NIGHS	KNOLL	**NOUT**
NARCS	**NENE**	NIGHT	NOLLS	KNOUT
NARD	NENES	**NILL**	**NOLO**	SNOUT
NARDS	**NEON**	NILLS	NOLOS	**NOVA**
NARE	NEONS	**NILS**	**NOMA**	NOVAE
SNARE	**NERD**	ANILS	NOMAD	NOVAS
NARES	NERDS	**NIMB**	NOMAS	**NOWL**
NARK	NERDY	NIMBI	**NOME**	NOWLS
SNARK	**NERK**	NIMBS	GNOME	**NOWN**
NARKS	NERKA	**NINE**	NOMEN	KNOWN
NARKY	NERKS	NINES	NOMES	**NOWS**
NARY	NEST	**NIPA**	**NONA**	ENOWS
SNARY	NESTS	NIPAS	NONAS	GNOWS
UNARY	**NETE**	**NIPS**	**NONE**	KNOWS
NATS	NETES	SNIPS	NONES	SNOWS
GNATS	**NETT**	**NIRL**	NONET	**NOWT**
NAVE	NETTS	NIRLS	**NONG**	NOWTS
KNAVE	NETTY	NIRLY	NONGS	NOWTY
NAVEL	**NEUK**	**NISH**	**NONI**	**NOWY**
NAVES	NEUKS	KNISH	NONIS	SNOWY
NAVEW	**NEUM**	**NITE**	**NOOB**	**NUBS**
NAZE	NEUME	UNITE	NOOBS	KNUBS
NAZES	NEUMS	NITER	**NOOK**	SNUBS
NAZI	**NEVE**	NITES	SNOOK	**NUDE**
NAZIR	NEVEL	**NITS**	NOOKS	NUDER
NAZIS	NEVER	KNITS	NOOKY	NUDES
NEAL	NEVES	SNITS	**NOON**	**NUFF**
NEALS	**NEWS**	UNITS	NOONS	SNUFF
NEAP	ENEWS	**NIXE**	**NOOP**	NUFFS
SNEAP	NEWSY	NIXED	SNOOP	**NUKE**
NEAPS	**NEWT**	NIXER	NOOPS	NUKED
NEAR	NEWTS	NIXES	**NORI**	NUKES
ANEAR	**NEXT**	**NOAH**	NORIA	**NULL**
NEARS	NEXTS	NOAHS	NORIS	NULLA
NEAT	**NGAI**	**NOBS**	**NORK**	NULLS
NEATH	NGAIO	KNOBS	NORKS	**NUMB**
NEATS	**NIBS**	SNOBS	**NORM**	NUMBS
NEBS	SNIBS	**NOCK**	ENORM	**NURD**
SNEBS	**NICE**	KNOCK	NORMA	NURDS
NECK	NICER	NOCKS	NORMS	NURDY
SNECK	**NICK**	**NODE**	**NOSE**	**NURL**
NECKS	SNICK	ANODE	NOSED	KNURL
NEDS	NICKS	NODES	NOSER	NURLS

NURR	COBIA	OFAYS	OKEHS	OLLAV
KNURR	OBIAS	**OFFS**	**OKES**	**OLMS**
NURRS	**OBIS**	BOFFS	BOKES	HOLMS
NURS	GOBIS	COFFS	COKES	**OLPE**
KNURS	**OBIT**	DOFFS	HOKES	GOLPE
NURSE	OOBIT	GOFFS	JOKES	OLPES
NUTS	OBITS	KOFFS	LOKES	**OMBU**
KNUTS	**OBOE**	TOFFS	MOKES	KOMBU
NUTSO	OBOES	**OFFY**	POKES	OMBUS
NUTSY	**OBOL**	TOFFY	ROKES	**OMEN**
NYES	BOBOL	**OGAM**	SOKES	NOMEN
SNYES	OBOLE	OGAMS	TOKES	WOMEN
OAFS	OBOLI	**OGEE**	YOKES	OMENS
GOAFS	OBOLS	YOGEE	**OKRA**	**OMER**
LOAFS	**OBOS**	OGEED	KOKRA	COMER
OAKS	GOBOS	OGEES	OKRAS	GOMER
BOAKS	HOBOS	**OGLE**	**OKTA**	HOMER
SOAKS	KOBOS	BOGLE	OKTAS	VOMER
OARS	LOBOS	FOGLE	**OLDE**	OMERS
BOARS	ZOBOS	OGLED	SOLDE	**OMIT**
HOARS	**OCAS**	OGLER	OLDEN	VOMIT
ROARS	COCAS	OGLES	OLDER	OMITS
SOARS	SOCAS	**OGRE**	**OLDS**	**OMOV**
VOARS	**OCHE**	OGRES	BOLDS	OMOVS
OARY	BOCHE	**OHED**	COLDS	**ONCE**
GOARY	OCHER	HOHED	FOLDS	BONCE
HOARY	OCHES	OOHED	GOLDS	NONCE
ROARY	**OCTA**	**OHIA**	HOLDS	PONCE
OAST	OCTAD	OHIAS	MOLDS	SONCE
BOAST	OCTAL	**OIKS**	SOLDS	ONCER
COAST	OCTAN	HOIKS	WOLDS	ONCES
HOAST	OCTAS	**OILS**	**OLDY**	ONCET
LOAST	**ODAH**	BOILS	GOLDY	**ONER**
ROAST	ODAHS	COILS	MOLDY	BONER
TOAST	**ODAL**	FOILS	**OLEO**	DONER
OASTS	MODAL	MOILS	OLEOS	GONER
OATH	NODAL	NOILS	**OLES**	HONER
LOATH	PODAL	ROILS	BOLES	LONER
OATHS	ODALS	SOILS	COLES	MONER
OATS	**ODAS**	TOILS	DOLES	TONER
BOATS	CODAS	**OILY**	GOLES	ZONER
COATS	SODAS	DOILY	HOLES	ONERS
DOATS	**ODES**	NOILY	JOLES	ONERY
GOATS	BODES	ROILY	MOLES	**ONES**
MOATS	CODES	SOILY	NOLES	BONES
OATY	LODES	**OINK**	POLES	CONES
GOATY	MODES	BOINK	ROLES	HONES
OBAS	NODES	OINKS	SOLES	JONES
BOBAS	RODES	**OINT**	TOLES	NONES
SOBAS	**ODIC**	JOINT	VOLES	PONES
OBES	IODIC	NOINT	**OLID**	RONES
JOBES	SODIC	POINT	SOLID	SONES
LOBES	**ODOR**	OINTS	**OLIO**	TONES
MOBES	ODORS	**OKAS**	FOLIO	ZONES
ROBES	**ODSO**	HOKAS	POLIO	**ONIE**
OBESE	GODSO	KOKAS	OLIOS	BONIE
OBEY	**ODYL**	**OKAY**	**OLLA**	MONIE
MOBEY	ODYLE	TOKAY	HOLLA	**ONLY**
OBEYS	ODYLS	OKAYS	MOLLA	FONLY
OBIA	**OFAY**	**OKEH**	OLLAS	SONLY

ONOS	WOOPS	**OPPO**	**ORRA**	WOULD
MONOS	YOOPS	ZOPPO	MORRA	**OULK**
ONTO	**OOSE**	OPPOS	SORRA	OULKS
CONTO	BOOSE	**OPUS**	**ORTS**	**OUMA**
ONUS	GOOSE	MOPUS	BORTS	DOUMA
BONUS	LOOSE	**ORAD**	DORTS	LOUMA
CONUS	MOOSE	DORAD	FORTS	OUMAS
TONUS	NOOSE	**ORAL**	MORTS	**OUPA**
OOFS	ROOSE	BORAL	PORTS	OUPAS
COOFS	WOOSE	CORAL	RORTS	**OUPH**
GOOFS	OOSES	GORAL	SORTS	OUPHE
HOOFS	**OOSY**	HORAL	TORTS	OUPHS
LOOFS	GOOSY	LORAL	WORTS	**OUPS**
POOFS	**OOTS**	MORAL	**ORZO**	COUPS
ROOFS	BOOTS	PORAL	ORZOS	DOUPS
WOOFS	COOTS	RORAL	**OSES**	LOUPS
YOOFS	FOOTS	SORAL	COSES	MOUPS
OOFY	HOOTS	ORALS	DOSES	NOUPS
BOOFY	LOOTS	**ORBS**	HOSES	ROUPS
GOOFY	MOOTS	DORBS	KOSES	SOUPS
POOFY	POOTS	FORBS	LOSES	**OURN**
ROOFY	ROOTS	SORBS	MOSES	BOURN
WOOFY	SOOTS	**ORBY**	NOSES	MOURN
OOHS	TOOTS	CORBY	OOSES	YOURN
BOOHS	**OOZE**	FORBY	POSES	**OURS**
POOHS	BOOZE	**ORCA**	ROSES	COURS
OOMS	COOZE	ORCAS	TOSES	FOURS
BOOMS	OOZED	**ORCS**	**OSSA**	HOURS
COOMS	OOZES	TORCS	FOSSA	JOURS
DOOMS	**OOZY**	**ORDO**	**OTIC**	LOURS
LOOMS	BOOZY	FORDO	LOTIC	POURS
ROOMS	DOOZY	SORDO	**OTTO**	SOURS
SOOMS	WOOZY	ORDOS	LOTTO	TOURS
TOOMS	**OPAH**	**ORDS**	MOTTO	YOURS
ZOOMS	OPAHS	BORDS	POTTO	**OUST**
OONS	**OPAL**	CORDS	OTTOS	JOUST
BOONS	COPAL	FORDS	**OUCH**	MOUST
COONS	NOPAL	LORDS	COUCH	ROUST
GOONS	OPALS	SORDS	GOUCH	OUSTS
HOONS	**OPED**	WORDS	MOUCH	**OUTS**
LOONS	COPED	**ORES**	POUCH	BOUTS
MOONS	DOPED	BORES	TOUCH	DOUTS
NOONS	HOPED	CORES	VOUCH	GOUTS
POONS	LOPED	DORES	OUCHT	HOUTS
ROONS	MOPED	FORES	**OUDS**	LOUTS
TOONS	OOPED	GORES	FOUDS	POUTS
WOONS	ROPED	KORES	**OUKS**	ROUTS
ZOONS	TOPED	LORES	BOUKS	SOUTS
OONT	**OPEN**	MORES	DOUKS	TOUTS
OONTS	COPEN	PORES	GOUKS	**OUZO**
OOPS	OPENS	RORES	JOUKS	OUZOS
COOPS	**OPES**	SORES	POUKS	**OVAL**
GOOPS	COPES	TORES	SOUKS	OVALS
HOOPS	DOPES	YORES	TOUKS	**OVEL**
LOOPS	HOPES	**ORFE**	YOUKS	HOVEL
MOOPS	LOPES	ORFES	ZOUKS	NOVEL
NOOPS	MOPES	**ORGY**	**OULD**	OVELS
POOPS	POPES	PORGY	COULD	**OVEN**
ROOPS	ROPES	**ORLE**	MOULD	COVEN
SOOPS	TOPES	ORLES	NOULD	DOVEN

HOVEN	**OWNS**	PACED	PALSY	PARSE
ROVEN	DOWNS	PACER	**PAMS**	**PART**
WOVEN	GOWNS	PACES	SPAMS	APART
OVENS	LOWNS	PACEY	**PAND**	SPART
OVER	POWNS	**PACK**	PANDA	PARTI
COVER	TOWNS	PACKS	PANDS	PARTS
DOVER	**OWRE**	**PACO**	PANDY	PARTY
HOVER	HOWRE	PACOS	**PANE**	**PASE**
LOVER	POWRE	**PACT**	SPANE	PASEO
MOVER	OWRES	EPACT	PANED	PASES
ROVER	**OWSE**	PACTA	PANEL	**PASH**
OVERS	BOWSE	PACTS	PANES	PASHA
OVERT	DOWSE	**PACY**	**PANG**	PASHM
OVUM	LOWSE	SPACY	SPANG	**PASS**
NOVUM	SOWSE	**PADI**	PANGA	PASSE
OWED	TOWSE	PADIS	PANGS	**PAST**
BOWED	OWSEN	**PAGE**	**PANS**	PASTA
COWED	**OWTS**	APAGE	SPANS	PASTE
DOWED	DOWTS	PAGED	PANSY	PASTS
JOWED	LOWTS	PAGER	**PANT**	PASTY
LOWED	NOWTS	PAGES	PANTO	**PATE**
MOWED	ROWTS	**PAHS**	PANTS	SPATE
NOWED	TOWTS	OPAHS	PANTY	PATED
ROWED	**OXEN**	**PAID**	**PAPA**	PATEN
SOWED	BOXEN	APAID	PAPAL	PATER
TOWED	WOXEN	**PAIK**	PAPAS	PATES
VOWED	**OXER**	PAIKS	PAPAW	**PATH**
WOWED	BOXER	**PAIL**	**PAPE**	PATHS
YOWED	OXERS	SPAIL	PAPER	**PATS**
OWER	**OXES**	PAILS	PAPES	SPATS
BOWER	BOXES	**PAIN**	**PARA**	PATSY
COWER	COXES	SPAIN	PARAE	**PATU**
DOWER	FOXES	PAINS	PARAS	PATUS
LOWER	GOXES	PAINT	**PARD**	PAUA
MOWER	HOXES	**PAIR**	SPARD	PAUAS
POWER	LOXES	PAIRE	PARDI	**PAUL**
ROWER	NOXES	PAIRS	PARDS	SPAUL
SOWER	POXES	**PAIS**	PARDY	PAULS
TOWER	**OXID**	PAISA	**PARE**	**PAVE**
VOWER	OXIDE	PAISE	SPARE	PAVED
OWES	OXIDS	**PALE**	PARED	PAVEN
BOWES	**OXIM**	SPALE	PAREO	PAVER
HOWES	OXIME	PALEA	PARER	PAVES
LOWES	OXIMS	PALED	PARES	**PAWA**
YOWES	**OYER**	PALER	PAREU	PAWAS
OWLS	COYER	PALES	PAREV	PAWAW
BOWLS	FOYER	PALET	**PARK**	**PAWK**
COWLS	TOYER	**PALL**	SPARK	PAWKS
DOWLS	OYERS	SPALL	PARKA	PAWKY
FOWLS	**OYES**	PALLA	PARKI	**PAWL**
GOWLS	NOYES	PALLS	PARKS	SPAWL
HOWLS	**PAAL**	PALLY	PARKY	PAWLS
JOWLS	PAALS	**PALM**	**PARP**	**PAWN**
NOWLS	**PAAN**	PALMS	PARPS	SPAWN
SOWLS	PAANS	PALMY	**PARR**	PAWNS
YOWLS	**PACA**	**PALP**	PARRA	**PAWS**
OWLY	PACAS	PALPI	PARRS	SPAWS
DOWLY	**PACE**	PALPS	PARRY	**PAYS**
JOWLY	APACE	**PALS**	**PARS**	APAYS
LOWLY	SPACE	OPALS	SPARS	SPAYS

PAYSD	PEINS	PERVS	SPIKE	PIOYE
PEAG	**PEKE**	PERVY	PIKED	PIOYS
PEAGE	PEKES	**PESO**	PIKER	**PIPA**
PEAGS	**PELA**	PESOS	PIKES	PIPAL
PEAK	PELAS	**PEST**	PIKEY	PIPAS
APEAK	**PELE**	PESTO	**PIKI**	**PIPE**
SPEAK	PELES	PESTS	PIKIS	PIPED
PEAKS	**PELF**	PESTY	**PILA**	PIPER
PEAKY	PELFS	**PETS**	PILAF	PIPES
PEAL	**PELL**	SPETS	PILAO	PIPET
SPEAL	SPELL	**PEWS**	PILAR	**PIPI**
PEALS	PELLS	SPEWS	PILAU	PIPIS
PEAN	**PELT**	**PHIS**	PILAW	PIPIT
SPEAN	SPELT	APHIS	**PILE**	**PIRL**
PEANS	PELTA	**PHON**	SPILE	PIRLS
PEAR	PELTS	PHONE	PILEA	**PIRN**
SPEAR	**PEND**	PHONO	PILED	PIRNS
PEARE	SPEND	PHONS	PILEI	**PISE**
PEARL	UPEND	PHONY	PILER	PISES
PEARS	PENDS	**PHOT**	PILES	**PISH**
PEART	PENDU	PHOTO	**PILI**	APISH
PEAS	**PENE**	PHOTS	PILIS	**PISO**
PEASE	PENED	**PHUT**	**PILL**	PISOS
PEAT	PENES	PHUTS	SPILL	**PITA**
SPEAT	**PENI**	**PIAL**	PILLS	PITAS
PEATS	PENIE	SPIAL	**PIMA**	**PITH**
PEATY	PENIS	**PIAN**	PIMAS	PITHS
PEBA	**PENK**	APIAN	**PIMP**	PITHY
PEBAS	PENKS	PIANI	PIMPS	**PITS**
PECH	**PENS**	PIANO	**PINA**	SPITS
PECHS	OPENS	PIANS	SPINA	**PIUM**
PECK	**PENT**	**PICA**	PINAS	OPIUM
SPECK	SPENT	SPICA	**PINE**	PIUMS
PECKE	PENTS	PICAL	OPINE	**PIZE**
PECKS	**PEON**	PICAS	SPINE	PIZED
PECKY	PEONS	**PICE**	PINED	PIZES
PECS	PEONY	SPICE	PINES	**PLAN**
SPECS	**PEPO**	**PICK**	PINEY	PLANE
PEED	PEPOS	SPICK	**PING**	PLANK
SPEED	**PERE**	PICKS	APING	PLANS
PEEK	PEREA	PICKY	OPING	PLANT
APEEK	PERES	**PICS**	PINGO	**PLAP**
PEEKS	**PERI**	EPICS	PINGS	PLAPS
PEEL	PERIL	SPICS	**PINK**	**PLAT**
SPEEL	PERIS	**PIED**	SPINK	SPLAT
PEELS	**PERK**	SPIED	PINKO	PLATE
PEEN	PERKS	**PIER**	PINKS	PLATS
PEENS	PERKY	SPIER	PINKY	PLATY
PEEP	**PERM**	PIERS	**PINS**	**PLAY**
PEEPE	SPERM	PIERT	SPINS	SPLAY
PEEPS	PERMS	**PIES**	**PINT**	UPLAY
PEER	**PERN**	SPIES	PINTA	PLAYA
SPEER	PERNS	**PIET**	PINTO	PLAYS
PEERS	**PERP**	PIETA	PINTS	**PLEA**
PEERY	PERPS	PIETS	**PINY**	PLEAD
PEES	**PERT**	PIETY	SPINY	PLEAS
EPEES	APERT	**PIKA**	**PION**	PLEAT
PEGH	PERTS	PIKAS	PIONS	**PLEB**
PEGHS	**PERV**	PIKAU	PIONY	PLEBE
PEIN	PERVE	**PIKE**	**PIOY**	PLEBS

PLED	**POLK**	SPOOT	POWND	**PROG**
UPLED	POLKA	POOTS	POWNS	SPROG
PLEW	POLKS	**POPE**	POWNY	PROGS
PLEWS	**POLL**	POPES	**POXY**	**PROM**
PLIED	POLLS	**POPS**	EPOXY	PROMO
PLIE	POLLY	POPSY	**POZZ**	PROMS
PLIED	**POLO**	**PORE**	POZZY	**PROO**
PLIER	POLOS	SPORE	**PRAD**	PROOF
PLIES	**POLT**	PORED	SPRAD	**PROP**
PLIM	POLTS	PORER	PRADS	PROPS
PLIMS	**POLY**	PORES	**PRAM**	**PROS**
PLOD	POLYP	**PORK**	PRAMS	PROSE
PLODS	POLYS	SPORK	**PRAO**	PROSO
PLOP	**POME**	PORKS	PRAOS	PROSS
PLOPS	POMES	PORKY	**PRAT**	PROST
PLOT	**POMO**	**PORN**	SPRAT	PROSY
PLOTS	POMOS	PORNO	PRATE	**PROW**
PLOTZ	**POMP**	PORNS	PRATS	PROWL
PLOW	POMPS	PORNY	PRATT	PROWS
PLOWS	**POND**	**PORT**	PRATY	**PRYS**
PLOY	PONDS	APORT	**PRAU**	PRYSE
PLOYS	**PONE**	SPORT	PRAUS	**PSIS**
PLUE	PONES	PORTA	**PRAY**	APSIS
PLUES	PONEY	PORTS	SPRAY	**PUBE**
PLUG	**PONG**	PORTY	PRAYS	PUBES
PLUGS	PONGA	**POSE**	**PREE**	**PUCE**
PLUM	PONGO	POSED	SPREE	PUCER
PLUMB	PONGS	POSER	PREED	PUCES
PLUME	PONGY	POSES	PREEN	**PUCK**
PLUMP	**PONK**	POSEY	PREES	PUCKA
PLUMS	PONKS	**POSH**	**PREM**	PUCKS
PLUMY	**PONT**	SPOSH	PREMS	**PUDS**
PLUS	PONTS	POSHO	PREMY	SPUDS
PLUSH	PONTY	**POSS**	**PREP**	PUDSY
POCK	**POOD**	POSSE	PREPS	**PUDU**
POCKS	POODS	**POST**	**PREX**	PUDUS
POCKY	**POOF**	POSTS	PREXY	**PUER**
PODS	SPOOF	**POTE**	**PREY**	SPUER
APODS	POOFS	POTED	PREYS	PUERS
SPODS	POOFY	POTES	**PRIG**	**PUFF**
POEM	**POOH**	**POTS**	SPRIG	PUFFS
POEMS	POOHS	SPOTS	PRIGS	PUFFY
POEP	**POOK**	POTSY	**PRIM**	**PUGS**
POEPS	SPOOK	**POTT**	PRIMA	SPUGS
POET	POOKA	POTTO	PRIME	**PUHA**
POETS	POOKS	POTTS	PRIMI	PUHAS
POGO	**POOL**	POTTY	PRIMO	**PUJA**
POGOS	SPOOL	**POUF**	PRIMP	PUJAH
POIS	POOLS	POUFF	PRIMS	PUJAS
POISE	**POON**	POUFS	PRIMY	**PUKA**
POKE	SPOON	**POUK**	**PROA**	PUKAS
SPOKE	POONS	POUKE	PROAS	**PUKE**
POKED	**POOP**	POUKS	**PROB**	PUKED
POKER	APOOP	**POUR**	PROBE	PUKER
POKES	POOPS	POURS	PROBS	PUKES
POKEY	**POOR**	**POUT**	**PROD**	PUKEY
POLE	SPOOR	SPOUT	SPROD	**PUKU**
POLED	POORI	POUTS	PRODS	PUKUS
POLER	POORT	POUTY	**PROF**	**PULA**
POLES	**POOT**	**POWN**	PROFS	PULAO
POLEY				

PULAS	**PURS**	QUIMS	**RAFT**	RAJAS
PULE	SPURS	**QUIN**	CRAFT	**RAKE**
SPULE	PURSE	QUINA	DRAFT	BRAKE
PULED	PURSY	QUINE	GRAFT	CRAKE
PULER	**PUSH**	QUINO	KRAFT	DRAKE
PULES	PUSHY	QUINS	RAFTS	RAKED
PULI	**PUSS**	QUINT	**RAGA**	RAKEE
PULIK	PUSSY	**QUIP**	RAGAS	RAKER
PULIS	**PUTT**	EQUIP	**RAGE**	RAKES
PULK	PUTTI	QUIPO	RAGED	**RAKI**
PULKA	PUTTO	QUIPS	RAGEE	RAKIA
PULKS	PUTTS	QUIPU	RAGER	RAKIS
PULL	PUTTY	**QUIT**	RAGES	**RAKU**
PULLI	**PYAT**	SQUIT	**RAGG**	RAKUS
PULLS	PYATS	QUITE	RAGGA	**RALE**
PULP	**PYET**	QUITS	RAGGS	RALES
PULPS	PYETS	**QUIZ**	RAGGY	**RAMI**
PULPY	**PYIN**	SQUIZ	**RAGI**	RAMIE
PULS	PYINS	**QUOD**	TRAGI	RAMIN
PULSE	**PYNE**	QUODS	RAGIS	RAMIS
PULU	PYNED	**QUOP**	**RAGS**	**RAMP**
PULUS	PYNES	QUOPS	BRAGS	CRAMP
PUMA	**PYOT**	**RABI**	CRAGS	GRAMP
PUMAS	PYOTS	RABIC	DRAGS	TRAMP
PUMP	**PYRE**	RABID	FRAGS	RAMPS
PUMPS	SPYRE	RABIS	**RAGU**	**RAMS**
PUMY	PYRES	**RACE**	RAGUS	CRAMS
SPUMY	PYREX	BRACE	**RAIA**	DRAMS
PUNA	**PYRO**	GRACE	RAIAS	GRAMS
PUNAS	PYROS	TRACE	**RAID**	PRAMS
PUNG	**QADI**	RACED	BRAID	TRAMS
PUNGA	QADIS	RACER	RAIDS	**RANA**
PUNGS	**QAID**	RACES	**RAIK**	GRANA
PUNK	QAIDS	**RACH**	TRAIK	PRANA
SPUNK	**QOPH**	BRACH	RAIKS	RANAS
PUNKA	QOPHS	ORACH	**RAIL**	**RAND**
PUNKS	**QUAD**	RACHE	BRAIL	BRAND
PUNKY	SQUAD	**RACK**	DRAIL	GRAND
PUNT	QUADS	BRACK	FRAIL	RANDS
PUNTO	**QUAG**	CRACK	GRAIL	RANDY
PUNTS	QUAGS	DRACK	TRAIL	**RANG**
PUNTY	**QUAI**	FRACK	RAILE	KRANG
PUPA	QUAIL	TRACK	RAILS	ORANG
PUPAE	QUAIR	WRACK	**RAIN**	PRANG
PUPAL	QUAIS	RACKS	BRAIN	WRANG
PUPAS	**QUAT**	**RACY**	DRAIN	RANGA
PUPU	SQUAT	ORACY	GRAIN	RANGE
PUPUS	QUATE	**RADE**	TRAIN	RANGI
PURE	QUATS	GRADE	RAINE	RANGY
PURED	**QUAY**	IRADE	RAINS	**RANI**
PUREE	QUAYD	TRADE	RAINY	RANID
PURER	QUAYS	**RADS**	**RAIS**	RANIS
PURES	**QUEY**	BRADS	RAISE	**RANK**
PURI	QUEYN	GRADS	**RAIT**	BRANK
PURIN	QUEYS	PRADS	KRAIT	CRANK
PURIS	**QUID**	TRADS	TRAIT	DRANK
PURL	EQUID	**RAFF**	RAITA	FRANK
PURLS	SQUID	DRAFF	RAITS	PRANK
PURR	QUIDS	GRAFF	**RAJA**	TRANK
PURRS	**QUIM**	RAFFS	RAJAH	RANKE

RANKS	CRATE	GRAYS	BREDE	REIKS
RANT	FRATE	PRAYS	REDED	**REIN**
BRANT	GRATE	TRAYS	REDES	GREIN
DRANT	IRATE	XRAYS	**REDO**	REINK
GRANT	ORATE	**RAZE**	CREDO	REINS
ORANT	PRATE	BRAZE	UREDO	**REIS**
TRANT	URATE	CRAZE	REDON	BREIS
RANTS	WRATE	GRAZE	REDOS	REIST
RAPE	RATED	RAZED	REDOX	**REKE**
CRAPE	RATEL	RAZEE	**REDS**	REKED
DRAPE	RATER	RAZER	BREDS	REKES
FRAPE	RATES	RAZES	CREDS	REKEY
GRAPE	**RATH**	**READ**	**REED**	**REMS**
TRAPE	WRATH	AREAD	BREED	CREMS
RAPED	RATHA	BREAD	CREED	PREMS
RAPER	RATHE	DREAD	DREED	**REND**
RAPES	RATHS	OREAD	FREED	TREND
RAPS	**RATO**	TREAD	GREED	RENDS
CRAPS	RATOO	READD	PREED	**RENS**
DRAPS	RATOS	READS	TREED	BRENS
FRAPS	**RATS**	READY	REEDE	GRENS
TRAPS	BRATS	**REAK**	REEDS	WRENS
WRAPS	DRATS	BREAK	REEDY	**RENT**
RAPT	FRATS	CREAK	**REEF**	BRENT
TRAPT	PRATS	FREAK	REEFS	DRENT
WRAPT	TRATS	WREAK	REEFY	PRENT
YRAPT	**RATU**	REAKS	**REEK**	URENT
RARE	RATUS	**REAL**	CREEK	YRENT
CRARE	**RAUN**	AREAL	GREEK	RENTE
URARE	RAUNS	UREAL	REEKS	RENTS
RARED	**RAVE**	REALM	REEKY	**REPO**
RAREE	BRAVE	REALO	**REEL**	REPOS
RARER	CRAVE	REALS	CREEL	REPOT
RARES	DRAVE	**REAM**	REELS	**REPP**
RARK	GRAVE	BREAM	**REEN**	REPPS
RARKS	TRAVE	CREAM	GREEN	**REPS**
RASE	RAVED	DREAM	PREEN	CREPS
ERASE	RAVEL	REAME	TREEN	PREPS
PRASE	RAVEN	REAMS	REENS	**RESH**
URASE	RAVER	REAMY	**REES**	FRESH
RASED	RAVES	**REAN**	BREES	**REST**
RASER	**RAVS**	REANS	CREES	CREST
RASES	GRAVS	**REAP**	DREES	DREST
RASH	**RAWN**	REAPS	FREES	PREST
BRASH	BRAWN	**REAR**	GREES	TREST
CRASH	DRAWN	AREAR	PREES	WREST
TRASH	PRAWN	DREAR	TREES	RESTO
RASP	RAWNS	REARM	REEST	RESTS
GRASP	**RAWS**	REARS	**REGO**	RESTY
RASPS	BRAWS	**RECK**	GREGO	**RETE**
RASPY	CRAWS	DRECK	REGOS	ARETE
RAST	DRAWS	TRECK	**REGS**	RETEM
BRAST	**RAYA**	WRECK	DREGS	**RETS**
WRAST	RAYAH	RECKS	**REIF**	ARETS
RASTA	RAYAS	**REDD**	PREIF	FRETS
RATA	**RAYS**	AREDD	TREIF	TRETS
RATAL	BRAYS	REDDS	REIFS	**REVS**
RATAN	CRAYS	REDDY	REIFY	EREVS
RATAS	DRAYS	**REDE**	**REIK**	**REWS**
RATE	FRAYS	AREDE	REIKI	BREWS

CREWS	RIEMS	BRINE	**RITE**	**RODE**
GREWS	**RIFE**	CRINE	TRITE	ERODE
TREWS	RIFER	TRINE	URITE	TRODE
RHEA	**RIFF**	URINE	WRITE	RODED
RHEAS	GRIFF	RINES	RITES	RODEO
RHUS	TRIFF	**RING**	**RITS**	RODES
ERHUS	RIFFS	BRING	BRITS	**RODS**
RIAD	**RIFT**	ERING	CRITS	BRODS
TRIAD	DRIFT	IRING	FRITS	PRODS
RIADS	GRIFT	WRING	GRITS	TRODS
RIAL	RIFTE	RINGS	WRITS	**ROES**
PRIAL	RIFTS	**RINK**	**RITT**	FROES
TRIAL	RIFTY	BRINK	BRITT	**ROIL**
URIAL	**RIGG**	DRINK	FRITT	BROIL
RIALS	RIGGS	PRINK	RITTS	DROIL
RIAS	**RIGS**	RINKS	**RITZ**	ROILS
ARIAS	BRIGS	**RINS**	FRITZ	ROILY
CRIAS	FRIGS	BRINS	RITZY	**ROIN**
RIBA	GRIGS	GRINS	**RIVA**	GROIN
RIBAS	PRIGS	TRINS	RIVAL	PROIN
RIBS	TRIGS	RINSE	RIVAS	ROINS
CRIBS	**RILE**	**RIOT**	**RIVE**	**ROJI**
DRIBS	RILED	ARIOT	DRIVE	ROJIS
FRIBS	RILES	GRIOT	RIVED	**ROKE**
RICE	RILEY	RIOTS	RIVEL	BROKE
DRICE	**RILL**	**RIPE**	RIVEN	PROKE
GRICE	BRILL	CRIPE	RIVER	TROKE
PRICE	DRILL	GRIPE	RIVES	WROKE
TRICE	FRILL	TRIPE	RIVET	ROKED
RICED	GRILL	RIPED	**RIZA**	ROKER
RICER	KRILL	RIPEN	RIZAS	ROKES
RICES	PRILL	RIPER	**ROAD**	**ROKS**
RICEY	TRILL	RIPES	BROAD	GROKS
RICH	RILLE	**RIPP**	TROAD	**ROLE**
RICHT	RILLS	RIPPS	ROADS	DROLE
RICK	**RIMA**	**RIPS**	**ROAM**	PROLE
BRICK	PRIMA	DRIPS	ROAMS	ROLES
CRICK	RIMAE	GRIPS	**ROAN**	**ROLF**
ERICK	**RIME**	TRIPS	GROAN	ROLFS
PRICK	CRIME	**RIPT**	ROANS	**ROLL**
TRICK	GRIME	DRIPT	**ROAR**	DROLL
WRICK	PRIME	GRIPT	ROARS	PROLL
RICKS	RIMED	**RISE**	ROARY	TROLL
RICY	RIMER	ARISE	**ROBE**	ROLLS
PRICY	RIMES	BRISE	PROBE	**ROMA**
RIDE	**RIMS**	CRISE	ROBED	AROMA
BRIDE	BRIMS	FRISE	ROBES	GROMA
GRIDE	CRIMS	GRISE	**ROBS**	ROMAL
PRIDE	PRIMS	PRISE	PROBS	ROMAN
TRIDE	TRIMS	RISEN	**ROCH**	**ROMP**
RIDER	**RIMU**	RISER	BROCH	TROMP
RIDES	RIMUS	RISES	**ROCK**	ROMPS
RIDS	**RIMY**	**RISK**	BROCK	**ROMS**
GRIDS	GRIMY	BRISK	CROCK	PROMS
IRIDS	PRIMY	FRISK	FROCK	**RONE**
RIEL	**RIND**	RISKS	TROCK	CRONE
ARIEL	GRIND	RISKY	ROCKS	DRONE
ORIEL	RINDS	**RISP**	ROCKY	GRONE
RIELS	RINDY	CRISP	**ROCS**	IRONE
RIEM	**RINE**	RISPS	CROCS	KRONE

PRONE	RORES	TROUT	**RUGA**	CRUSE
TRONE	**RORT**	ROUTE	RUGAE	DRUSE
RONEO	RORTS	ROUTH	RUGAL	RUSES
RONES	RORTY	ROUTS	**RUGS**	**RUSH**
RONG	**RORY**	**ROVE**	DRUGS	BRUSH
PRONG	FRORY	DROVE	FRUGS	CRUSH
WRONG	**ROSE**	GROVE	TRUGS	FRUSH
RONT	AROSE	PROVE	**RUIN**	RUSHY
FRONT	BROSE	TROVE	BRUIN	**RUSK**
RONTE	EROSE	ROVED	RUING	BRUSK
RONTS	PROSE	ROVEN	RUINS	RUSKS
ROOD	ROSED	ROVER	**RUKH**	**RUST**
BROOD	ROSES	ROVES	RUKHS	BRUST
ROODS	ROSET	**ROWS**	**RULE**	CRUST
ROOF	**ROST**	BROWS	BRULE	FRUST
GROOF	CROST	CROWS	RULED	TRUST
PROOF	FROST	DROWS	RULER	RUSTS
ROOFS	PROST	FROWS	RULES	RUSTY
ROOFY	ROSTI	GROWS	**RULY**	**RUTH**
ROOK	ROSTS	PROWS	TRULY	TRUTH
BROOK	**ROSY**	TROWS	**RUME**	RUTHS
CROOK	BROSY	VROWS	BRUME	**RUTS**
DROOK	PROSY	**ROWT**	GRUME	BRUTS
ROOKS	**ROTA**	ROWTH	RUMEN	**RYAL**
ROOKY	ROTAL	ROWTS	RUMES	RYALS
ROOM	ROTAN	**RUBE**	**RUMP**	**RYKE**
BROOM	ROTAS	RUBEL	CRUMP	GRYKE
GROOM	**ROTE**	RUBES	FRUMP	TRYKE
VROOM	WROTE	**RUBS**	GRUMP	RYKED
ROOMS	ROTED	DRUBS	TRUMP	RYKES
ROOMY	ROTES	GRUBS	RUMPO	**RYND**
ROON	**ROTI**	**RUCK**	RUMPS	RYNDS
CROON	ROTIS	CRUCK	RUMPY	**RYOT**
KROON	**ROTL**	TRUCK	**RUMS**	RYOTS
ROONS	ROTLS	RUCKS	ARUMS	**RYPE**
ROOP	**ROTO**	**RUDD**	DRUMS	GRYPE
DROOP	PROTO	RUDDS	**RUND**	RYPER
TROOP	ROTON	RUDDY	GRUND	**SAAG**
ROOPS	ROTOR	**RUDE**	RUNDS	SAAGS
ROOPY	ROTOS	CRUDE	**RUNE**	**SABE**
ROOS	**ROTS**	PRUDE	RUNED	SABED
BROOS	GROTS	RUDER	RUNES	SABER
ROOSA	TROTS	RUDES	**RUNG**	SABES
ROOSE	**ROUE**	**RUDS**	BRUNG	**SACK**
ROOST	ROUEN	CRUDS	WRUNG	SACKS
ROOT	ROUES	**RUED**	RUNGS	**SADE**
WROOT	**ROUL**	GRUED	**RUNT**	TSADE
ROOTS	PROUL	TRUED	BRUNT	SADES
ROOTY	ROULE	RUEDA	GRUNT	**SADI**
ROPE	ROULS	**RUER**	PRUNT	TSADI
GROPE	**ROUM**	TRUER	RUNTS	SADIS
TROPE	ROUMS	RUERS	RUNTY	**SADO**
ROPED	**ROUP**	**RUES**	**RURP**	SADOS
ROPER	CROUP	CRUES	RURPS	**SAFE**
ROPES	GROUP	GRUES	**RURU**	SAFED
ROPEY	ROUPS	TRUES	RURUS	SAFER
RORE	ROUPY	**RUFF**	**RUSA**	SAFES
CRORE	**ROUT**	GRUFF	RUSAS	**SAGA**
FRORE	CROUT	RUFFE	**RUSE**	SAGAS
PRORE	GROUT	RUFFS	**RUSE**	**SAGE**

USAGE	SANDS	**SCAM**	**SEAL**	SEMES
SAGER	SANDY	SCAMP	SEALS	**SEMI**
SAGES	**SANE**	SCAMS	**SEAM**	SEMIE
SAGO	SANED	**SCAN**	SEAME	SEMIS
SAGOS	SANER	SCAND	SEAMS	**SENA**
SAIC	SANES	SCANS	SEAMY	SENAS
SAICE	**SANG**	SCANT	**SEAN**	**SEND**
SAICK	SANGA	**SCAR**	SEANS	SENDS
SAICS	SANGH	ESCAR	**SEAR**	**SENE**
SAID	SANGO	OSCAR	SEARE	SENES
SAIDS	SANGS	SCARE	SEARS	**SENS**
SAIL	**SANK**	SCARF	**SEAS**	SENSA
SAILS	SANKO	SCARP	SEASE	SENSE
SAIM	**SANS**	SCARS	**SEAT**	SENSI
SAIMS	SANSA	SCART	SEATS	**SENT**
SAIN	**SANT**	SCARY	**SECH**	SENTE
SAINE	SANTO	**SCAT**	SECHS	SENTI
SAINS	SANTS	SCATH	**SECT**	SENTS
SAINT	**SARD**	SCATS	SECTS	**SEPT**
SAIR	SARDS	SCATT	**SEED**	SEPTA
SAIRS	**SARI**	**SCAW**	SEEDS	SEPTS
SAIS	SARIN	SCAWS	SEEDY	**SERA**
SAIST	SARIS	**SCOG**	**SEEK**	SERAC
SAKE	**SARK**	SCOGS	SEEKS	SERAI
SAKER	SARKS	**SCOP**	**SEEL**	SERAL
SAKES	SARKY	SCOPA	SEELD	**SERE**
SAKI	**SARS**	SCOPE	SEELS	SERED
SAKIA	KSARS	SCOPS	SEELY	SERER
SAKIS	TSARS	**SCOT**	**SEEM**	SERES
SALE	**SASS**	ASCOT	SEEMS	**SERF**
SALEP	SASSE	ESCOT	**SEEP**	SERFS
SALES	SASSY	SCOTS	SEEPS	**SERK**
SALET	**SATE**	**SCOW**	SEEPY	SERKS
SALL	SATED	SCOWL	**SEER**	**SERR**
SALLE	SATEM	SCOWP	SEERS	SERRA
SALLY	SATES	SCOWS	**SEGO**	SERRE
SALP	**SATI**	**SCUD**	SEGOL	SERRS
SALPA	SATIN	SCUDI	SEGOS	SERRY
SALPS	SATIS	SCUDO	**SEIF**	**SERS**
SALS	**SAUL**	SCUDS	SEIFS	USERS
SALSA	SAULS	**SCUG**	**SEIL**	**SESE**
SALSE	SAULT	SCUGS	SEILS	SESEY
SALT	**SAUT**	**SCUL**	**SEIR**	**SESS**
SALTO	SAUTE	SCULK	SEIRS	SESSA
SALTS	SAUTS	SCULL	**SEIS**	**SETA**
SALTY	**SAVE**	SCULP	SEISE	SETAE
SAMA	SAVED	SCULS	SEISM	SETAL
SAMAN	SAVER	**SCUM**	**SEKT**	**SETT**
SAMAS	SAVES	SCUMS	SEKTS	SETTS
SAME	SAVEY	**SCUP**	**SELE**	**SEXT**
YSAME	**SAXE**	SCUPS	SELES	SEXTO
SAMEK	SAXES	**SCUR**	**SELF**	SEXTS
SAMEL	**SAYS**	SCURF	SELFS	**SHAD**
SAMEN	SAYST	SCURS	**SELL**	SHADE
SAMES	**SCAB**	**SCUT**	SELLA	SHADS
SAMEY	SCABS	SCUTA	SELLE	SHADY
SAMP	**SCAD**	SCUTE	SELLS	**SHAG**
SAMPI	SCADS	SCUTS	**SEME**	SHAGS
SAMPS	**SCAG**	**SCYE**	SEMEE	**SHAH**
SAND	SCAGS	SCYES	SEMEN	SHAHS

SHAM	SHOGI	**SIGH**	SIREE	**SKIN**
SHAMA	SHOGS	SIGHS	SIREN	SKINK
SHAME	**SHOO**	SIGHT	SIRES	SKINS
SHAMS	SHOOK	**SIGN**	**SIRI**	SKINT
SHAN	SHOOL	SIGNA	SIRIH	**SKIO**
SHAND	SHOON	SIGNS	SIRIS	SKIOS
SHANK	SHOOS	**SIJO**	**SISS**	**SKIP**
SHANS	SHOOT	SIJOS	SISSY	SKIPS
SHAW	**SHOP**	**SIKA**	**SIST**	**SKIT**
PSHAW	SHOPE	SIKAS	SISTS	SKITE
SHAWL	SHOPS	**SIKE**	**SITE**	SKITS
SHAWM	**SHOT**	SIKER	SITED	**SKOL**
SHAWN	SHOTE	SIKES	SITES	SKOLS
SHAWS	SHOTS	**SILD**	**SITH**	**SKUA**
SHAY	SHOTT	SILDS	SITHE	SKUAS
SHAYA	**SHOW**	**SILE**	**SIZE**	**SKUG**
SHAYS	SHOWD	ESILE	SIZED	SKUGS
SHEA	SHOWN	SILED	SIZEL	**SKYF**
SHEAF	SHOWS	SILEN	SIZER	SKYFS
SHEAL	SHOWY	SILER	SIZES	**SKYR**
SHEAR	**SHRI**	SILES	**SKAG**	SKYRE
SHEAS	SHRIS	SILEX	SKAGS	SKYRS
SHED	**SHUL**	**SILK**	**SKAT**	**SLAB**
ASHED	SHULE	SILKS	SKATE	SLABS
SHEDS	SHULN	SILKY	SKATS	**SLAE**
SHES	SHULS	**SILL**	SKATT	SLAES
ASHES	**SHUN**	SILLS	**SKAW**	**SLAG**
ISHES	SHUNS	SILLY	SKAWS	SLAGS
SHET	SHUNT	**SILO**	**SKEE**	**SLAM**
ASHET	**SHUT**	SILOS	SKEED	SLAMS
SHETS	SHUTE	**SILT**	SKEEF	**SLAP**
SHEW	SHUTS	SILTS	SKEEN	SLAPS
SHEWN	**SHWA**	SILTY	SKEER	**SLAT**
SHEWS	SHWAS	**SIMA**	SKEES	SLATE
SHIM	**SIAL**	SIMAR	SKEET	SLATS
SHIMS	SIALS	SIMAS	**SKEG**	SLATY
SHIN	**SIBB**	**SIMI**	SKEGG	**SLAW**
SHINE	SIBBS	SIMIS	SKEGS	SLAWS
SHINS	**SICE**	**SIMP**	**SKEN**	**SLAY**
SHINY	SICES	SIMPS	SKENE	SLAYS
SHIP	**SICH**	**SIND**	SKENS	**SLEB**
SHIPS	SICHT	SINDS	**SKEO**	SLEBS
SHIR	**SICK**	**SINE**	SKEOS	**SLED**
SHIRE	SICKO	SINED	**SKEP**	ISLED
SHIRK	SICKS	SINES	SKEPS	SLEDS
SHIRR	**SIDA**	SINEW	**SKER**	**SLEE**
SHIRS	SIDAS	**SING**	ASKER	SLEEK
SHIRT	**SIDE**	USING	ESKER	SLEEP
SHIT	ASIDE	SINGE	SKERS	SLEER
SHITE	SIDED	SINGS	**SKET**	SLEET
SHITS	SIDER	**SINH**	SKETS	**SLEW**
SHIV	SIDES	SINHS	**SKEW**	SLEWS
SHIVA	**SIDH**	**SINK**	ASKEW	**SLEY**
SHIVE	SIDHA	SINKS	SKEWS	SLEYS
SHIVS	SIDHE	SINKY	**SKID**	**SLID**
SHOE	**SIEN**	**SIPE**	SKIDS	SLIDE
SHOED	SIENS	SIPED	**SKIM**	**SLIM**
SHOER	SIENT	SIPES	SKIMO	SLIME
SHOES	**SIFT**	**SIRE**	SKIMP	SLIMS
SHOG	SIFTS	SIRED	SKIMS	SLIMY

SLIP	SNABS	**SOCA**	SOOPS	SOWNE
SLIPE	**SNAG**	SOCAS	**SOOT**	**SOWP**
SLIPS	SNAGS	**SOCK**	SOOTE	SOWPS
SLIPT	**SNAP**	SOCKO	SOOTH	**SOWS**
SLIT	SNAPS	SOCKS	SOOTS	SOWSE
SLITS	**SNAR**	**SODA**	SOOTY	**SOYA**
SLOB	SNARE	SODAS	**SOPH**	SOYAS
SLOBS	SNARF	**SOFA**	SOPHS	**SPAE**
SLOE	SNARK	SOFAR	SOPHY	SPAED
SLOES	SNARL	SOFAS	**SORA**	SPAER
SLOG	SNARS	**SOFT**	PSORA	SPAES
SLOGS	SNARY	SOFTA	SORAL	**SPAG**
SLOP	**SNAW**	SOFTS	SORAS	SPAGS
SLOPE	SNAWS	SOFTY	**SORB**	**SPAM**
SLOPS	**SNEB**	**SOIL**	SORBO	SPAMS
SLOPY	SNEBS	SOILS	SORBS	**SPAN**
SLOT	**SNED**	SOILY	**SORD**	SPANE
SLOTH	SNEDS	**SOJA**	SORDA	SPANG
SLOTS	**SNEE**	SOJAS	SORDO	SPANK
SLOW	SNEED	**SOKE**	SORDS	SPANS
SLOWS	SNEER	SOKEN	**SORE**	**SPAR**
SLUB	SNEES	SOKES	SORED	SPARD
SLUBB	**SNIB**	**SOLA**	SOREE	SPARE
SLUBS	SNIBS	SOLAH	SOREL	SPARK
SLUE	**SNIG**	SOLAN	SORER	SPARS
SLUED	SNIGS	SOLAR	SORES	SPART
SLUES	**SNIP**	SOLAS	SOREX	**SPAS**
SLUG	SNIPE	**SOLD**	**SORN**	SPASM
SLUGS	SNIPS	SOLDE	SORNS	**SPAT**
SLUM	SNIPY	SOLDI	**SORT**	SPATE
SLUMP	**SNIT**	SOLDO	SORTA	SPATS
SLUMS	SNITS	SOLDS	SORTS	**SPAW**
SLUR	**SNOB**	**SOLE**	**SOTH**	SPAWL
SLURB	SNOBS	SOLED	SOTHS	SPAWN
SLURP	**SNOD**	SOLEI	**SOUK**	SPAWS
SLURS	SNODS	SOLER	SOUKS	**SPAY**
SLUT	**SNOG**	SOLES	**SOUL**	SPAYD
SLUTS	SNOGS	**SOLI**	SOULS	SPAYS
SMEE	**SNOT**	SOLID	**SOUM**	**SPAZ**
SMEEK	SNOTS	**SOLO**	SOUMS	SPAZA
SMEES	**SNOW**	SOLON	**SOUP**	SPAZZ
SMEW	SNOWK	SOLOS	SOUPS	**SPEC**
SMEWS	SNOWS	**SOMA**	SOUPY	SPECK
SMIR	SNOWY	SOMAN	**SOUR**	SPECS
SMIRK	**SNUB**	SOMAS	SOURS	**SPEK**
SMIRR	SNUBS	**SONE**	**SOUS**	SPEKS
SMIRS	**SNUG**	SONES	SOUSE	**SPET**
SMIT	SNUGS	**SONG**	**SOUT**	SPETS
SMITE	**SNYE**	SONGS	SOUTH	**SPEW**
SMITH	SNYES	**SONS**	SOUTS	SPEWS
SMITS	**SOAK**	SONSE	**SOWF**	SPEWY
SMOG	SOAKS	SONSY	SOWFF	**SPIC**
SMOGS	**SOAP**	**SOOK**	SOWFS	ASPIC
SMUG	SOAPS	SOOKS	**SOWL**	SPICA
SMUGS	SOAPY	**SOOL**	SOWLE	SPICE
SMUR	**SOAR**	SOOLE	SOWLS	SPICK
SMURS	SOARE	SOOLS	**SOWM**	SPICS
SMUT	SOARS	**SOOM**	SOWMS	SPICY
SMUTS	**SOBA**	SOOMS	**SOWN**	**SPIE**
SNAB	SOBAS	**SOOP**	SOWND	SPIED

SPIEL	STATE	**STUD**	**SUNN**	**SWIM**
SPIER	STATS	STUDE	SUNNA	ASWIM
SPIES	**STAW**	STUDS	SUNNS	SWIMS
SPIF	STAWS	STUDY	SUNNY	**SWIZ**
SPIFF	**STAY**	**STUM**	**SUPE**	SWIZZ
SPIFS	STAYS	STUMM	SUPER	**SWOB**
SPIK	**STED**	STUMP	SUPES	SWOBS
SPIKE	STEDD	STUMS	**SURA**	**SWOP**
SPIKS	STEDE	**STUN**	SURAH	SWOPS
SPIKY	STEDS	ASTUN	SURAL	SWOPT
SPIM	**STEM**	STUNG	SURAS	**SWOT**
SPIMS	STEME	STUNK	SURAT	SWOTS
SPIN	STEMS	STUNS	**SURD**	**SYBO**
SPINA	**STEN**	STUNT	SURDS	SYBOE
SPINE	STEND	**STYE**	**SURE**	SYBOW
SPINK	STENO	STYED	USURE	**SYCE**
SPINS	STENS	STYES	SURED	SYCEE
SPINY	STENT	**SUBA**	SURER	SYCES
SPIT	**STEP**	TSUBA	SURES	**SYEN**
SPITE	STEPS	SUBAH	**SURF**	SYENS
SPITS	STEPT	SUBAS	SURFS	**SYKE**
SPITZ	**STET**	**SUCK**	SURFY	SYKER
SPIV	STETS	SUCKS	**SUSU**	SYKES
SPIVS	**STEW**	SUCKY	SUSUS	**SYLI**
SPOD	STEWS	**SUDD**	**SWAB**	SYLIS
SPODE	STEWY	SUDDS	SWABS	**SYNC**
SPODS	**STIE**	**SUDS**	**SWAD**	SYNCH
SPOT	STIED	SUDSY	SWADS	SYNCS
SPOTS	STIES	**SUED**	**SWAG**	**SYND**
SPUD	**STIM**	SUEDE	SWAGE	SYNDS
SPUDS	STIME	**SUER**	SWAGS	**SYNE**
SPUE	STIMS	SUERS	**SWAM**	SYNED
SPUED	STIMY	**SUET**	SWAMI	SYNES
SPUER	**STIR**	SUETS	SWAMP	**SYPE**
SPUES	ASTIR	SUETY	SWAMY	SYPED
SPUG	STIRE	**SUGH**	**SWAN**	SYPES
SPUGS	STIRK	SUGHS	SWANG	**SYPH**
SPUN	STIRP	**SUGO**	SWANK	SYPHS
SPUNK	STIRS	SUGOS	SWANS	**TAAL**
SPUR	**STOA**	**SUID**	**SWAP**	TAALS
SPURN	STOAE	SUIDS	SWAPS	**TABI**
SPURS	STOAI	**SUIT**	SWAPT	TABID
SPURT	STOAS	SUITE	**SWAT**	**TABS**
STAB	STOAT	SUITS	SWATH	STABS
STABS	**STOB**	**SUKH**	SWATS	**TABU**
STAG	STOBS	SUKHS	**SWAY**	TABUN
STAGE	**STOP**	**SULK**	ASWAY	TABUS
STAGS	ESTOP	SULKS	**SWAYL**	**TACE**
STAGY	STOPE	SULKY	SWAYS	TACES
STAP	STOPS	**SULU**	**SWEE**	TACET
STAPH	STOPT	SULUS	SWEED	**TACH**
STAPS	**STOT**	**SUMO**	SWEEL	TACHE
STAR	STOTS	SUMOS	SWEEP	TACHO
STARE	STOTT	**SUMP**	SWEER	TACHS
STARK	**STOW**	SUMPH	SWEES	**TACK**
STARN	STOWN	SUMPS	SWEET	STACK
STARR	STOWP	**SUNI**	**SWEY**	TACKS
STARS	STOWS	SUNIS	SWEYS	TACKY
START	**STUB**	**SUNK**	**SWIG**	**TACO**
STAT	STUBS	SUNKS	SWIGS	TACOS

TACT	STAMP	STASH	**TEDS**	TEMSE
TACTS	TAMPS	**TASK**	STEDS	**TEND**
TAEL	**TANA**	TASKS	**TEED**	STEND
TAELS	TANAS	TASS	STEED	TENDS
TAGS	**TANE**	TASSE	**TEEK**	TENDU
STAGS	STANE	**TATE**	STEEK	**TENE**
TAHA	**TANG**	STATE	**TEEL**	CTENE
TAHAS	STANG	TATER	STEEL	TENES
TAHR	TANGA	TATES	TEELS	TENET
TAHRS	TANGI	**TATH**	**TEEM**	**TENS**
TAIG	TANGO	TATHS	STEEM	ETENS
STAIG	TANGS	**TATS**	TEEMS	STENS
TAIGA	TANGY	ETATS	**TEEN**	TENSE
TAIGS	**TANH**	STATS	STEEN	**TENT**
TAIL	TANHS	**TATT**	TEEND	STENT
TAILS	**TANK**	TATTS	TEENE	TENTH
TAIN	STANK	TATTY	TEENS	TENTS
STAIN	TANKA	**TATU**	TEENY	TENTY
TAINS	TANKS	TATUS	**TEER**	**TEPA**
TAINT	TANKY	**TAUT**	STEER	TEPAL
TAIS	**TANS**	TAUTS	TEERS	TEPAS
TAISH	TANSY	**TAVA**	**TEFF**	**TERF**
TAIT	**TAPA**	TAVAH	TEFFS	TERFE
TAITS	TAPAS	TAVAS	**TEGG**	TERFS
TAKA	**TAPE**	**TAWA**	TEGGS	**TERM**
TAKAS	ETAPE	TAWAI	**TEGU**	TERMS
TAKE	TAPED	TAWAS	TEGUA	**TERN**
STAKE	TAPEN	**TAWS**	TEGUS	STERN
TAKEN	TAPER	STAWS	**TEHR**	TERNE
TAKER	TAPES	TAWSE	TEHRS	TERNS
TAKES	TAPET	**TAWT**	**TEIL**	**TEST**
TAKI	**TAPS**	TAWTS	STEIL	TESTA
TAKIN	ATAPS	**TAXI**	TEILS	TESTE
TAKIS	STAPS	TAXIS	**TEIN**	TESTS
TALA	**TAPU**	**TAYS**	STEIN	TESTY
TALAK	TAPUS	STAYS	TEIND	**TETE**
TALAQ	**TARA**	**TEAD**	TEINS	TETES
TALAR	TARAS	STEAD	**TELA**	**TETH**
TALAS	**TARE**	TEADE	STELA	TETHS
TALC	STARE	TEADS	TELAE	**TETS**
TALCS	TARED	**TEAK**	**TELE**	STETS
TALCY	TARES	STEAK	STELE	**TEWS**
TALE	**TARN**	TEAKS	TELES	STEWS
STALE	STARN	**TEAL**	TELEX	**TEXT**
TALEA	TARNS	STEAL	**TELL**	TEXTS
TALER	**TARO**	TEALS	STELL	**THAN**
TALES	TAROC	**TEAM**	TELLS	THANA
TALK	TAROK	STEAM	TELLY	THANE
STALK	TAROS	TEAMS	**TEME**	THANG
TALKS	TAROT	**TEAR**	STEME	THANK
TALKY	**TARP**	STEAR	TEMED	THANS
TALL	TARPS	TEARS	TEMES	**THAR**
STALL	**TARS**	TEARY	**TEMP**	THARM
TALLS	STARS	**TEAS**	TEMPI	THARS
TALLY	TARSI	TEASE	TEMPO	**THAW**
TAME	**TART**	**TEAT**	TEMPS	THAWS
TAMED	START	TEATS	TEMPT	THAWY
TAMER	TARTS	**TECH**	**TEMS**	**THEE**
TAMES	TARTY	TECHS	ITEMS	THEED
TAMP	**TASH**	TECHY	STEMS	THEEK

THEES	**TIFF**	TIRES	**TOLE**	TOPHS
THEM	STIFF	**TIRL**	STOLE	**TOPI**
THEMA	TIFFS	TIRLS	TOLED	TOPIC
THEME	**TIFT**	**TIRO**	TOLES	TOPIS
THEN	TIFTS	TIROS	**TOLL**	**TOPO**
THENS	**TIGE**	**TIRR**	ATOLL	TOPOI
THEW	TIGER	TIRRS	TOLLS	TOPOS
THEWS	TIGES	**TITE**	TOLLY	**TOPS**
THEWY	**TIKA**	TITER	**TOLT**	STOPS
THIG	TIKAS	**TITI**	TOLTS	**TORA**
THIGH	**TIKE**	TITIS	**TOLU**	TORAH
THIGS	TIKES	**TIVY**	TOLUS	TORAN
THIN	**TIKI**	STIVY	**TOMB**	TORAS
THINE	TIKIS	**TIZZ**	TOMBS	**TORC**
THING	**TILE**	TIZZY	**TOME**	TORCH
THINK	STILE	**TOAD**	TOMES	TORCS
THINS	UTILE	TOADS	**TOMO**	**TORE**
THIO	TILED	TOADY	TOMOS	STORE
THIOL	TILER	**TOCK**	**TOMS**	TORES
THIR	TILES	STOCK	ATOMS	**TORI**
THIRD	**TILL**	TOCKS	**TONE**	TORIC
THIRL	STILL	TOCKY	ATONE	TORII
THON	TILLS	**TOCO**	STONE	**TORO**
THONG	TILLY	TOCOS	TONED	TOROS
THOU	**TILT**	TOCS	TONER	TOROT
THOUS	ATILT	**TOEA**	TONES	**TORR**
THRO	STILT	TOEAS	TONEY	TORRS
THROB	TILTH	**TOFF**	**TONG**	**TORS**
THROE	TILTS	TOFFS	STONG	TORSE
THROW	**TIME**	TOFFY	TONGA	TORSI
THRU	STIME	**TOFT**	TONGS	TORSK
THRUM	TIMED	TOFTS	**TONK**	TORSO
THUD	TIMER	**TOFU**	STONK	**TORT**
THUDS	TIMES	TOFUS	TONKA	TORTA
THUG	**TINA**	**TOGA**	TONKS	TORTE
THUGS	TINAS	TOGAE	**TONY**	TORTS
TIAN	**TIND**	TOGAS	ATONY	**TORY**
TIANS	TINDS	**TOGE**	STONY	STORY
TIAR	**TINE**	TOGED	**TOOK**	**TOSA**
TIARA	TINEA	TOGES	STOOK	TOSAS
TIARS	TINED	**TOIL**	**TOOL**	**TOSE**
TICE	TINES	TOILE	STOOL	TOSED
TICED	**TING**	TOILS	TOOLS	TOSES
TICES	STING	**TOOM**	**TOOM**	**TOSH**
TICH	TINGE	**TOIT**	TOOMS	TOSHY
STICH	TINGS	STOIT	**TOON**	**TOSS**
TICHY	**TINK**	TOITS	TOONS	STOSS
TICK	STINK	**TOKE**	**TOOT**	TOSSY
STICK	TINKS	ATOKE	TOOTH	**TOST**
TICKS	**TINT**	STOKE	TOOTS	YTOST
TICKY	STINT	TOKED	**TOPE**	**TOTE**
TIDE	TINTS	TOKEN	STOPE	TOTED
TIDED	TINTY	TOKER	TOPED	TOTEM
TIDES	**TIPI**	TOKES	TOPEE	TOTER
TIED	TIPIS	**TOKO**	TOPEK	TOTES
STIED	**TIPS**	TOKOS	TOPER	**TOTS**
TIER	TIPSY	**TOLA**	TOPES	STOTS
TIERS	**TIRE**	TOLAN	**TOPH**	**TOUK**
TIES	STIRE	TOLAR	TOPHE	TOUKS
STIES	TIRED	TOLAS	TOPHI	**TOUN**

STOUN	**TRIE**	**TUAN**	TURNS	**TYRE**
TOUNS	TRIED	TUANS	**TUSH**	STYRE
TOUR	TRIER	**TUBA**	TUSHY	TYRED
STOUR	TRIES	TUBAE	**TUSK**	TYRES
TOURS	**TRIG**	TUBAL	TUSKS	**TYRO**
TOUT	STRIG	TUBAR	TUSKY	TYROS
STOUT	TRIGO	TUBAS	**TUTU**	**TYTE**
TOUTS	TRIGS	**TUBE**	TUTUS	STYTE
TOWN	**TRIM**	TUBED	**TWAE**	**TZAR**
STOWN	STRIM	TUBER	TWAES	TZARS
TOWNS	TRIMS	TUBES	**TWAL**	**UDAL**
TOWNY	**TRIN**	**TUBS**	TWALS	UDALS
TOWS	TRINE	STUBS	**TWAT**	**UDON**
STOWS	TRINS	**TUCK**	TWATS	UDONS
TOWSE	**TRIO**	STUCK	**TWAY**	**UDOS**
TOWSY	TRIOL	TUCKS	TWAYS	BUDOS
TOWT	TRIOR	**TUFA**	**TWEE**	JUDOS
TOWTS	TRIOS	TUFAS	ETWEE	KUDOS
TOYO	**TRIP**	**TUFF**	TWEED	LUDOS
TOYON	ATRIP	STUFF	TWEEL	**UEYS**
TOYOS	STRIP	TUFFE	TWEEN	QUEYS
TOZE	TRIPE	TUFFS	TWEER	**UFOS**
TOZED	TRIPS	**TUFT**	TWEET	BUFOS
TOZES	TRIPY	TUFTS	**TWIG**	**UGHS**
TRAD	**TROD**	TUFTY	TWIGS	EUGHS
STRAD	TRODE	**TUIS**	**TWIN**	SUGHS
TRADE	TRODS	ETUIS	TWINE	VUGHS
TRADS	**TROG**	TUISM	TWINK	**UGLY**
TRAM	TROGS	**TULE**	TWINS	FUGLY
TRAMP	**TRON**	TULES	TWINY	**UKES**
TRAMS	TRONA	**TUMP**	**TWIT**	BUKES
TRAP	TRONC	STUMP	TWITE	CUKES
STRAP	TRONE	TUMPS	TWITS	DUKES
TRAPE	TRONK	TUMPY	**TYED**	JUKES
TRAPS	TRONS	**TUMS**	STYED	NUKES
TRAPT	**TROP**	STUMS	**TYEE**	PUKES
TRAT	STROP	**TUNA**	TYEES	YUKES
TRATS	TROPE	TUNAS	**TYER**	**ULAN**
TRATT	**TROT**	**TUND**	TYERS	KULAN
TRAY	TROTH	TUNDS	**TYES**	YULAN
STRAY	TROTS	**TUNE**	STYES	ULANS
TRAYS	**TROW**	TUNED	**TYIN**	**ULES**
TREE	STROW	TUNER	TYING	DULES
TREED	TROWS	TUNES	**TYKE**	GULES
TREEN	**TROY**	**TUNG**	TYKES	HULES
TREES	STROY	STUNG	**TYMP**	MULES
TREF	TROYS	TUNGS	TYMPS	PULES
TREFA	**TRUE**	**TUNS**	**TYND**	RULES
TREK	TRUED	STUNS	TYNDE	TULES
TREKS	TRUER	**TURD**	**TYNE**	YULES
TRES	TRUES	TURDS	TYNED	**ULEX**
TRESS	**TRUG**	**TURF**	TYNES	CULEX
TREST	TRUGO	TURFS	**TYPE**	**ULNA**
TRET	TRUGS	TURFY	TYPED	ULNAD
TRETS	**TRYE**	**TURK**	TYPES	ULNAE
TREW	TRYER	TURKS	TYPEY	ULNAR
STREW	**TRYP**	**TURM**	**TYPO**	ULNAS
TREWS	TRYPS	TURME	TYPOS	**ULUS**
TREY	**TSAR**	TURMS	**TYPP**	LULUS
TREYS	TSARS	**TURN**	TYPPS	PULUS

SULUS	**UNCI**	**URES**	MUTES	VAUTS
ZULUS	**UNCIA**	AURES	**UTIS**	**VEAL**
ULVA	**UNCO**	CURES	CUTIS	UVEAL
VULVA	BUNCO	DURES	KUTIS	VEALE
ULVAS	JUNCO	LURES	MUTIS	VEALS
UMBO	UNCOS	MURES	**UTUS**	VEALY
BUMBO	UNCOY	PURES	KUTUS	**VEEP**
DUMBO	**UNDE**	SURES	TUTUS	VEEPS
GUMBO	BUNDE	**URGE**	**UVEA**	**VEER**
JUMBO	UNDEE	GURGE	UVEAL	VEERS
RUMBO	UNDER	PURGE	UVEAS	VEERY
UMBOS	**UNDY**	SURGE	**VADE**	**VEGA**
UMMA	BUNDY	URGED	EVADE	VEGAN
GUMMA	CUNDY	URGER	VADED	VEGAS
SUMMA	FUNDY	URGES	VADES	**VEGO**
UMMAH	GUNDY	**URIC**	**VAIL**	VEGOS
UMMAS	OUNDY	AURIC	AVAIL	**VEHM**
UMPH	**UNIS**	**URNS**	VAILS	VEHME
BUMPH	MUNIS	BURNS	**VAIR**	**VEIL**
HUMPH	SUNIS	CURNS	VAIRE	VEILS
SUMPH	**UNIT**	DURNS	VAIRS	VEILY
UMPS	UNITE	GURNS	VAIRY	**VEIN**
BUMPS	UNITS	TURNS	**VALE**	VEINS
DUMPS	UNITY	**URPS**	AVALE	VEINY
GUMPS	**UNTO**	BURPS	VALES	**VELA**
HUMPS	JUNTO	CURPS	VALET	VELAR
JUMPS	PUNTO	TURPS	**VALI**	**VELD**
LUMPS	**UPAS**	**URSA**	VALID	VELDS
MUMPS	OUPAS	BURSA	VALIS	VELDT
PUMPS	PUPAS	URSAE	**VAMP**	**VELE**
RUMPS	ZUPAS	**URUS**	VAMPS	VELES
SUMPS	**UPBY**	GURUS	VAMPY	**VELL**
TUMPS	UPBYE	KURUS	**VANE**	KVELL
YUMPS	**UPDO**	RURUS	VANED	VELLS
UMPY	UPDOS	**URVA**	VANES	**VENA**
BUMPY	**UPON**	MURVA	**VANG**	VENAE
DUMPY	JUPON	URVAS	VANGS	VENAL
HUMPY	YUPON	**USED**	**VANT**	**VEND**
JUMPY	**UPTA**	BUSED	AVANT	VENDS
LUMPY	UPTAK	FUSED	VANTS	**VENT**
RUMPY	**URAO**	MUSED	**VARA**	EVENT
TUMPY	URAOS	**USER**	VARAN	VENTS
UMRA	**URBS**	LUSER	VARAS	**VERB**
UMRAH	BURBS	MUSER	**VARE**	VERBS
UMRAS	CURBS	USERS	VAREC	**VERS**
UMUS	**URDE**	**USES**	VARES	AVERS
HUMUS	URDEE	BUSES	**VARY**	OVERS
MUMUS	**URDS**	FUSES	OVARY	VERSE
UNAI	BURDS	MUSES	**VASA**	VERSO
UNAIS	CURDS	PUSES	VASAL	VERST
UNAU	HURDS	RUSES	**VASE**	**VERT**
UNAUS	NURDS	SUSES	VASES	AVERT
UNBE	SURDS	WUSES	**VAST**	EVERT
UNBED	TURDS	**UTAS**	AVAST	OVERT
UNCE	**URDY**	KUTAS	VASTS	VERTS
BUNCE	CURDY	**UTES**	VASTY	VERTU
DUNCE	NURDY	BUTES	**VATU**	**VERY**
OUNCE	**UREA**	CUTES	VATUS	EVERY
PUNCE	UREAL	JUTES	**VAUT**	**VEST**
UNCES	UREAS	LUTES	VAUTE	VESTA

VESTS	VISAS	**VUGH**	WAITS	WARBY
VETS	**VISE**	VUGHS	**WAKA**	**WARD**
EVETS	AVISE	VUGHY	WAKAS	AWARD
VIAL	VISED	**VULN**	**WAKE**	SWARD
VIALS	VISES	VULNS	AWAKE	WARDS
VIBE	**VITA**	**WAAC**	WAKED	**WARE**
VIBES	VITAE	WAACS	WAKEN	AWARE
VIBEX	VITAL	**WABS**	WAKER	SWARE
VIBEY	VITAS	SWABS	WAKES	WARED
VICE	**VITE**	**WACK**	**WAKF**	WARES
VICED	EVITE	SWACK	WAKFS	WAREZ
VICES	VITEX	WACKE	**WALD**	**WARK**
VIDE	**VIVA**	WACKO	WALDO	WARKS
VIDEO	VIVAS	WACKS	WALDS	**WARM**
VIED	VIVAT	WACKY	**WALE**	SWARM
IVIED	**VIVE**	**WADD**	DWALE	WARMS
VIER	VIVER	WADDS	SWALE	**WARN**
VIERS	VIVES	WADDY	WALED	AWARN
VIES	**VLEI**	**WADE**	WALER	WARNS
IVIES	VLEIS	WADED	WALES	**WARP**
VIEW	**VLOG**	WADER	**WALI**	WARPS
VIEWS	VLOGS	WADES	WALIS	**WARS**
VIEWY	**VOAR**	**WADI**	**WALK**	WARST
VIGA	VOARS	WADIS	WALKS	**WART**
VIGAS	**VOID**	**WADS**	**WALL**	SWART
VILD	AVOID	SWADS	WALLA	WARTS
VILDE	OVOID	**WADT**	WALLS	WARTY
VILE	VOIDS	WADTS	WALLY	**WASE**
VILER	**VOIP**	**WAES**	**WALY**	WASES
VILL	VOIPS	TWAES	SWALY	**WASH**
VILLA	**VOLA**	**WAFF**	**WAME**	AWASH
VILLI	VOLAE	WAFFS	WAMED	SWASH
VILLS	VOLAR	**WAFT**	WAMES	WASHY
VINA	**VOLE**	WAFTS	**WAND**	**WASP**
VINAL	VOLED	**WAGE**	WANDS	WASPS
VINAS	VOLES	SWAGE	**WANE**	WASPY
VINE	VOLET	WAGED	WANED	**WAST**
AVINE	**VOLK**	WAGER	WANES	WASTE
OVINE	VOLKS	WAGES	WANEY	WASTS
VINED	**VOLT**	**WAGS**	**WANG**	**WATE**
VINER	VOLTA	SWAGS	DWANG	WATER
VINES	VOLTE	**WAID**	SWANG	**WATS**
VINEW	VOLTI	WAIDE	TWANG	SWATS
VINO	VOLTS	**WAIF**	WANGS	TWATS
VINOS	**VOTE**	WAIFS	**WANK**	WATT
VINT	VOTED	WAIFT	SWANK	WATTS
VINTS	VOTER	**WAIL**	TWANK	**WAUK**
VINY	VOTES	SWAIL	WANKS	WAUKS
VINYL	**VOWS**	WAILS	WANKY	**WAUL**
VIOL	AVOWS	**WAIN**	**WANS**	WAULK
VIOLA	**VRIL**	SWAIN	SWANS	WAULS
VIOLD	VRILS	TWAIN	**WANT**	**WAUR**
VIOLS	**VROU**	WAINS	WANTS	WAURS
VIRE	VROUS	**WAIR**	WANTY	**WAVE**
VIRED	VROUW	WAIRS	**WAPS**	AWAVE
VIREO	**VROW**	**WAIS**	SWAPS	WAVED
VIRES	VROWS	WAIST	**WAQF**	WAVER
VIRL	**VUGG**	**WAIT**	WAQFS	WAVES
VIRLS	VUGGS	AWAIT	**WARB**	WAVEY
VISA	VUGGY	WAITE	WARBS	**WAWA**

WAWAS	**WEIL**	WHETS	WILDS	**WISE**
WAWE	WEILS	**WHEW**	**WILE**	WISED
WAWES	**WEIR**	WHEWS	DWILE	WISER
WAWL	SWEIR	**WHEY**	WILED	WISES
WAWLS	WEIRD	WHEYS	WILES	**WISH**
WAYS	WEIRS	**WHID**	**WILI**	SWISH
AWAYS	**WEKA**	WHIDS	WILIS	WISHA
SWAYS	WEKAS	**WHIG**	**WILL**	WISHT
TWAYS	**WELD**	WHIGS	SWILL	**WISP**
WEAK	WELDS	**WHIM**	TWILL	WISPS
TWEAK	**WELK**	WHIMS	WILLS	WISPY
WEAL	WELKE	**WHIN**	WILLY	**WISS**
SWEAL	WELKS	WHINE	**WILT**	SWISS
WEALD	WELKT	WHINS	TWILT	**WIST**
WEALS	**WELL**	WHINY	WILTS	TWIST
WEAN	DWELL	**WHIO**	**WIMP**	WISTS
WEANS	SWELL	WHIOS	WIMPS	**WITE**
WEAR	WELLS	**WHIP**	WIMPY	TWITE
SWEAR	WELLY	WHIPS	**WIND**	WITED
WEARS	**WELS**	WHIPT	WINDS	WITES
WEARY	WELSH	**WHIR**	WINDY	**WITH**
WEED	**WELT**	WHIRL	**WINE**	SWITH
SWEED	DWELT	WHIRR	DWINE	WITHE
TWEED	SWELT	WHIRS	GWINE	WITHS
WEEDS	WELTS	**WHIT**	SWINE	WITHY
WEEDY	**WEMB**	WHITE	TWINE	**WITS**
WEEK	WEMBS	WHITS	WINED	SWITS
WEEKE	**WEND**	WHITY	WINES	TWITS
WEEKS	WENDS	**WHIZ**	WINEY	**WIVE**
WEEL	WENT	WHIZZ	**WING**	SWIVE
AWEEL	**WEPT**	**WHOM**	AWING	WIVED
SWEEL	SWEPT	WHOMP	OWING	WIVER
TWEEL	**WERO**	**WHOP**	SWING	WIVES
WEELS	WEROS	WHOPS	WINGE	**WOAD**
WEEM	**WEST**	**WHOW**	WINGS	WOADS
WEEMS	EWEST	WHOWS	WINGY	**WOCK**
WEEN	WESTS	EWHOW	WINK	WOCKS
TWEEN	**WETA**	**WHUP**	**WINK**	**WOKE**
WEENS	WETAS	WHUPS	SWINK	AWOKE
WEENY	**WEXE**	**WICE**	TWINK	WOKEN
WEEP	WEXED	TWICE	WINKS	**WOLD**
SWEEP	WEXES	**WICK**	**WINN**	WOLDS
WEEPS	**WEYS**	WICKS	WINNA	**WOLF**
WEEPY	SWEYS	WICKY	WINNS	WOLFS
WEER	**WHAM**	**WIDE**	**WINO**	**WOMB**
SWEER	WHAMO	WIDEN	WINOS	WOMBS
TWEER	WHAMS	WIDER	**WINS**	WOMBY
WEES	**WHAP**	WIDES	TWINS	**WONK**
SWEES	WHAPS	**WIEL**	**WINY**	WONKS
WEEST	**WHAT**	WIELD	TWINY	WONKY
WEET	WHATA	WIELS	**WIPE**	**WONT**
SWEET	WHATS	**WIFE**	SWIPE	WONTS
TWEET	**WHEE**	WIFED	WIPED	**WOOD**
WEETE	WHEEL	WIFES	WIPER	WOODS
WEETS	WHEEN	WIFEY	WIPES	WOODY
WEFT	WHEEP	**WIGS**	**WIRE**	**WOOF**
WEFTE	**WHEN**	SWIGS	SWIRE	WOOFS
WEFTS	WHENS	TWIGS	TWIRE	WOOFY
WEID	**WHET**	**WIKI**	WIRED	**WOOL**
WEIDS		WIKIS	WIRER	WOOLD
		WILD	WIRES	

WOOLS	XYSTI	YEAHS	PYINS	YOURN
WOOLY	XYSTS	**YEAN**	**YIPE**	YOURS
WOON	**YAAR**	YEANS	YIPES	YOURT
SWOON	YAARS	**YEAR**	YIRD	**YOUS**
WOONS	**YABA**	YEARD	YIRDS	YOUSE
WOOS	YABAS	YEARN	**YIRK**	**YOWE**
WOOSE	**YACK**	YEARS	YIRKS	YOWED
WOOSH	KYACK	**YEAS**	**YIRR**	YOWES
WOOT	YACKA	YEAST	YIRRS	**YOWL**
WOOTZ	YACKS	**YECH**	**YITE**	YOWLS
WOPS	**YADS**	YECHS	YITES	**YUAN**
SWOPS	DYADS	YECHY	**YLEM**	YUANS
WORD	**YAFF**	**YEDE**	XYLEM	**YUCA**
SWORD	NYAFF	YEDES	YLEMS	YUCAS
WORDS	YAFFS	**YEED**	**YLKE**	**YUCK**
WORDY	**YAGI**	YEEDS	YLKES	YUCKO
WORE	YAGIS	**YEGG**	**YMPE**	YUCKS
SWORE	**YAHS**	YEGGS	YMPES	YUCKY
WORK	AYAHS	**YELD**	**YOCK**	**YUFT**
AWORK	**YAKS**	GYELD	YOCKS	YUFTS
WORKS	KYAKS	**YELK**	**YODE**	**YUGA**
WORM	**YALE**	YELKS	YODEL	YUGAS
WORMS	YALES	**YELL**	**YODH**	**YUKE**
WORMY	**YAMS**	YELLS	YODHS	YUKED
WORN	LYAMS	**YELM**	**YOGA**	YUKES
SWORN	**YANG**	YELMS	YOGAS	**YUKO**
WORT	KYANG	**YELP**	**YOGH**	YUKOS
WORTH	YANGS	AYELP	YOGHS	**YULE**
WORTS	**YANK**	YELPS	**YOGI**	YULES
WOTS	YANKS	**YELT**	YOGIC	**YUMP**
SWOTS	**YAPP**	YELTS	YOGIN	YUMPS
WOVE	YAPPS	**YENS**	YOGIS	**YURT**
WOVEN	YAPPY	HYENS	**YOKE**	YURTA
WRAP	**YARD**	SYENS	YOKED	YURTS
WRAPS	LYARD	**YERD**	YOKEL	**YUZU**
WRAPT	YARDS	YERDS	YOKER	YUZUS
WREN	**YARE**	**YERK**	YOKES	**ZACK**
WRENS	YARER	YERKS	**YOLK**	ZACKS
WRIT	**YARK**	**YESK**	YOLKS	**ZARF**
WRITE	YARKS	YESKS	YOLKY	ZARFS
WRITS	**YARN**	**YEST**	**YOMP**	**ZARI**
WUDU	YARNS	YESTS	YOMPS	ZARIS
WUDUS	**YARR**	YESTY	**YONI**	**ZATI**
WULL	YARRS	**YETI**	YONIC	ZATIS
WULLS	**YATE**	YETIS	YONIS	**ZEAL**
WUSS	YATES	**YETT**	**YONT**	ZEALS
WUSSY	**YAUD**	YETTS	AYONT	**ZEBU**
WYLE	YAUDS	**YEUK**	**YOOF**	ZEBUB
WYLED	**YAUP**	YEUKS	YOOFS	ZEBUS
WYLES	YAUPS	YEUKY	**YOOP**	**ZEES**
WYND	**YAWL**	**YEVE**	YOOPS	MZEES
WYNDS	YAWLS	YEVEN	**YORE**	**ZEIN**
WYNN	**YAWN**	YEVES	YORES	ZEINS
WYNNS	YAWNS	**YIKE**	**YORK**	**ZERK**
WYTE	YAWNY	YIKED	YORKS	ZERKS
WYTED	**YAWP**	YIKES	**YORP**	**ZERO**
WYTES	YAWPS	**YILL**	YORPS	ZEROS
XRAY	**YEAD**	YILLS	**YOUK**	**ZEST**
XRAYS	YEADS	**YINS**	YOUKS	ZESTS
XYST	**YEAH**	AYINS	**YOUR**	ZESTY

ZETA	ZIMBS	ZOBOS	ZONER	**ZULU**
ZETAS	**ZINC**	**ZOBU**	ZONES	ZULUS
ZEZE	ZINCO	ZOBUS	**ZONK**	**ZUPA**
ZEZES	ZINCS	**ZOEA**	ZONKS	ZUPAN
ZHOS	ZINCY	ZOEAE	**ZOOM**	ZUPAS
DZHOS	**ZINE**	ZOEAL	ZOOMS	**ZURF**
ZIFF	AZINE	ZOEAS	**ZOON**	ZURFS
ZIFFS	ZINEB	**ZOIC**	ZOONS	**ZYGA**
ZILA	ZINES	AZOIC	**ZOOT**	ZYGAL
ZILAS	**ZING**	**ZONA**	ZOOTY	**ZYME**
ZILL	ZINGS	ZONAE	**ZORI**	AZYME
ZILLA	ZINGY	ZONAL	ZORIL	ZYMES
ZILLS	**ZITI**	**ZONE**	ZORIS	
ZIMB	ZITIS	OZONE	**ZOUK**	
ZIMBI	**ZOBO**	ZONED	ZOUKS	

Five-letter root words

ABAKA	**ABLER**	CACHES	ACUTES	ADORER
KABAKA	CABLER	LACHES	**ADDED**	ADORES
ABAKAS	FABLER	MACHES	DADDED	**AECIA**
ABASE	**ABLES**	NACHES	GADDED	AECIAL
ABASED	CABLES	RACHES	MADDED	**AEONS**
ABASER	FABLES	TACHES	PADDED	PAEONS
ABASES	GABLES	**ACING**	RADDED	**AERIE**
ABATE	SABLES	FACING	SADDED	FAERIE
ABATED	TABLES	LACING	WADDED	AERIED
ABATER	ABLEST	MACING	**ADDER**	AERIER
ABATES	**ABLET**	PACING	BADDER	AERIES
ABAYA	CABLET	RACING	GADDER	**AFEAR**
KABAYA	GABLET	**ACINI**	LADDER	AFEARD
ABAYAS	TABLET	ACINIC	MADDER	AFEARS
ABBAS	ABLETS	**ACKEE**	PADDER	**AFTER**
DABBAS	**ABODE**	HACKEE	RADDER	DAFTER
GABBAS	ABODED	ACKEES	SADDER	HAFTER
YABBAS	ABODES	**ACKER**	WADDER	RAFTER
ABBED	**ABOON**	BACKER	ADDERS	SAFTER
CABBED	BABOON	DACKER	**ADDLE**	WAFTER
DABBED	GABOON	HACKER	DADDLE	AFTERS
GABBED	**ABUSE**	JACKER	FADDLE	**AGAMI**
JABBED	ABUSED	LACKER	PADDLE	AGAMIC
NABBED	ABUSER	PACKER	RADDLE	AGAMID
SABBED	ABUSES	RACKER	SADDLE	AGAMIS
TABBED	**ACARI**	SACKER	WADDLE	**AGAZE**
ABELE	ACARID	TACKER	ADDLED	AGAZED
KABELE	**ACCAS**	WACKER	ADDLES	**AGENE**
ABELES	BACCAS	YACKER	**ADIEU**	SAGENE
ABIDE	YACCAS	ACKERS	ADIEUS	AGENES
ABIDED	**ACERS**	**ACRED**	ADIEUX	**AGERS**
ABIDER	FACERS	NACRED	**ADIOS**	CAGERS
ABIDES	LACERS	SACRED	RADIOS	EAGERS
ABIES	MACERS	**ACRES**	**ADMAN**	GAGERS
BABIES	PACERS	NACRES	BADMAN	JAGERS
GABIES	RACERS	**ACTIN**	MADMAN	LAGERS
RABIES	**ACETA**	ACTING	**ADMEN**	PAGERS
ABLED	ACETAL	ACTINS	BADMEN	RAGERS
CABLED	**ACHED**	**ACTOR**	MADMEN	WAGERS
FABLED	BACHED	FACTOR	**ADMIX**	YAGERS
GABLED	CACHED	ACTORS	ADMIXT	**AGGER**
SABLED	**ACHES**	**ACUTE**	**ADORE**	BAGGER
TABLED	BACHES	ACUTER	ADORED	DAGGER

GAGGER	SAIGAS	ALANGS	VALLEY	JAMBER
JAGGER	TAIGAS	**ALANT**	ALLEYS	LAMBER
LAGGER	**AILED**	GALANT	**ALLIS**	TAMBER
NAGGER	BAILED	TALANT	TALLIS	AMBERS
SAGGER	FAILED	ALANTS	**ALLOT**	AMBERY
TAGGER	HAILED	**ALAPA**	BALLOT	**AMBIT**
WAGGER	JAILED	PALAPA	HALLOT	GAMBIT
YAGGER	MAILED	ALAPAS	TALLOT	AMBITS
AGGERS	NAILED	**ALAPS**	ALLOTS	**AMBLE**
AGGIE	RAILED	JALAPS	**ALLOW**	GAMBLE
BAGGIE	SAILED	**ALARY**	BALLOW	HAMBLE
MAGGIE	TAILED	SALARY	CALLOW	RAMBLE
AGGIES	VAILED	**ALATE**	FALLOW	WAMBLE
AGHAS	WAILED	MALATE	GALLOW	AMBLED
AGHAST	**AIMED**	PALATE	HALLOW	AMBLER
AGILE	MAIMED	ALATED	MALLOW	AMBLES
VAGILE	**AIMER**	ALATES	SALLOW	**AMBOS**
AGILER	MAIMER	**ALAYS**	TALLOW	MAMBOS
AGING	AIMERS	PALAYS	WALLOW	SAMBOS
CAGING	**AINGA**	**ALDER**	ALLOWS	ZAMBOS
GAGING	KAINGA	BALDER	**ALMAS**	**AMEBA**
PAGING	AINGAS	ALDERN	HALMAS	AMEBAE
RAGING	**AIRED**	ALDERS	TALMAS	AMEBAN
WAGING	FAIRED	**ALEYE**	**ALMUD**	AMEBAS
AGINGS	HAIRED	ALEYED	TALMUD	**AMEND**
AGISM	LAIRED	ALEYES	ALMUDE	AMENDE
MAGISM	PAIRED	**ALFAS**	ALMUDS	AMENDS
AGISMS	SAIRED	HALFAS	**ALOED**	**AMENE**
AGLET	WAIRED	**ALIFS**	HALOED	AMENED
EAGLET	**AIRER**	CALIFS	**ALOES**	**AMENS**
HAGLET	FAIRER	KALIFS	HALOES	RAMENS
AGLETS	PAIRER	**ALIGN**	**ALONG**	YAMENS
AGMAS	SAIRER	MALIGN	KALONG	**AMENT**
MAGMAS	AIRERS	ALIGNS	**ALOOS**	LAMENT
AGONS	**AIRNS**	**ALINE**	BALOOS	AMENTA
WAGONS	BAIRNS	MALINE	**ALTER**	AMENTS
AGORA	CAIRNS	SALINE	FALTER	**AMIAS**
AGORAE	**AISLE**	VALINE	HALTER	LAMIAS
AGORAS	AISLED	ALINED	PALTER	ZAMIAS
AGREE	AISLES	ALINER	SALTER	**AMIDO**
AGREED	**AIVER**	ALINES	ALTERN	AMIDOL
AGREES	NAIVER	**ALIST**	ALTERS	**AMIDS**
AGUED	TAIVER	MALIST	**ALTOS**	AMIDST
VAGUED	WAIVER	**ALIYA**	SALTOS	**AMIES**
AGUES	AIVERS	ALIYAH	**ALULA**	MAMIES
VAGUES	**AKEES**	ALIYAS	ALULAE	RAMIES
AGUNA	RAKEES	**ALKIE**	ALULAR	**AMINE**
LAGUNA	**AKING**	TALKIE	ALULAS	FAMINE
AGUNAH	BAKING	ALKIES	**AMASS**	GAMINE
AHING	CAKING	**ALLEE**	CAMASS	TAMINE
AAHING	FAKING	CALLEE	**AMATE**	AMINES
RAHING	LAKING	MALLEE	HAMATE	**AMINS**
AIDED	MAKING	SALLEE	RAMATE	GAMINS
LAIDED	RAKING	ALLEES	AMATED	RAMINS
MAIDED	TAKING	**ALLEL**	AMATES	TAMINS
RAIDED	WAKING	HALLEL	**AMAZE**	**AMMON**
AIDER	**AKKAS**	ALLELE	AMAZED	GAMMON
RAIDER	YAKKAS	ALLELS	AMAZES	MAMMON
AIDERS	**ALANG**	**ALLEY**	**AMBER**	AMMONO
AIGAS	LALANG	GALLEY	CAMBER	AMMONS

AMNIO
AMNION
AMNIOS
AMOVE
AMOVED
AMOVES
AMPED
CAMPED
DAMPED
LAMPED
RAMPED
TAMPED
VAMPED
AMPLE
CAMPLE
SAMPLE
AMPLER
AMPLY
CAMPLY
DAMPLY
AMPUL
AMPULE
AMPULS
AMRIT
AMRITA
AMRITS
AMUSE
AMUSED
AMUSER
AMUSES
ANANA
BANANA
MANANA
ZANANA
ANANAS
ANCHO
RANCHO
SANCHO
ANCHOR
ANCHOS
ANCON
ANCONE
ANELE
ANELED
ANELES
ANENT
MANENT
ANGAS
FANGAS
KANGAS
MANGAS
PANGAS
RANGAS
SANGAS
TANGAS
ANGEL
MANGEL
ANGELS
ANGER
BANGER

DANGER
GANGER
HANGER
LANGER
MANGER
RANGER
SANGER
ANGERS
ANGLE
BANGLE
CANGLE
DANGLE
FANGLE
JANGLE
MANGLE
TANGLE
WANGLE
ANGLED
ANGLER
ANGLES
ANGST
ANGSTS
ANGSTY
ANIGH
ANIGHT
ANIMA
ANIMAL
ANIMAS
ANION
WANION
ANIONS
ANKER
BANKER
CANKER
DANKER
HANKER
JANKER
LANKER
RANKER
TANKER
WANKER
YANKER
ANKERS
ANKLE
CANKLE
FANKLE
RANKLE
WANKLE
ANKLED
ANKLES
ANKLET
ANKUS
ANKUSH
ANNAS
CANNAS
MANNAS
NANNAS
TANNAS
ANNEX

ANNEXE
ANNOY
TANNOY
ANNOYS
ANNUL
ANNULI
ANNULS
ANTAR
CANTAR
KANTAR
ANTARA
ANTARS
MANTAS
ANTED
BANTED
CANTED
DANTED
GANTED
HANTED
KANTED
PANTED
RANTED
WANTED
ANTES
MANTES
ZANTES
ANTIC
CANTIC
MANTIC
ANTICK
ANTICS
ANTIS
MANTIS
ANTRA
MANTRA
TANTRA
YANTRA
ANTRAL
ANYON
CANYON
ANYONE
ANYONS
AORTA
AORTAE
AORTAL
AORTAS
APERS
CAPERS
GAPERS
JAPERS
PAPERS
RAPERS
TAPERS
APERY
JAPERY
NAPERY
PAPERY
APHIS
RAPHIS

APING
CAPING
GAPING
JAPING
NAPING
RAPING
TAPING
APISH
PAPISH
APISM
PAPISM
APISMS
APNEA
APNEAL
APNEAS
APPAL
APPALL
APPALS
APPAY
APPAYD
APPAYS
APPEL
LAPPEL
RAPPEL
APPELS
APPLE
DAPPLE
SAPPLE
APPLES
APPLET
APPLEY
APRON
NAPRON
APRONS
APSES
LAPSES
APTLY
RAPTLY
ARBOR
HARBOR
ARBORS
ARCED
FARCED
ARCOS
NARCOS
YARCOS
AREFY
RAREFY
ARETS
CARETS
ARGAL
ARGALA
ARGALI
ARGALS
ARGAN
ARGAND
ARGANS
ARGLE
DARGLE
GARGLE

ARGLED
ARGLES
ARGON
JARGON
ARGONS
ARGUE
ARGUED
ARGUER
ARGUES
ARGUS
SARGUS
ARIAS
VARIAS
ARISE
ARISEN
ARISES
ARISH
BARISH
GARISH
HARISH
MARISH
PARISH
ARKED
BARKED
CARKED
DARKED
HARKED
KARKED
LARKED
MARKED
NARKED
PARKED
RARKED
WARKED
YARKED
ARLED
HARLED
MARLED
PARLED
ARLES
CARLES
FARLES
MARLES
PARLES
ARMED
FARMED
HARMED
WARMED
ARMER
FARMER
HARMER
WARMER
ARMERS
ARMOR
ARMORS
ARMORY
ARNAS
VARNAS
AROID
LAROID

AROIDS	**ARVAL**	**ASSES**	CAUGHT	SAVERS
ARPEN	LARVAL	BASSES	HAUGHT	TAVERS
PARPEN	**ARVOS**	GASSES	NAUGHT	WAVERS
ARPENS	PARVOS	HASSES	RAUGHT	AVERSE
ARPENT	**ASCOT**	JASSES	TAUGHT	**AVERT**
ARRAH	MASCOT	LASSES	WAUGHT	TAVERT
JARRAH	ASCOTS	MASSES	AUGHTS	AVERTS
ARRAS	**ASHED**	PASSES	**AUGUR**	**AVINE**
BARRAS	BASHED	RASSES	AUGURS	RAVINE
NARRAS	CASHED	SASSES	AUGURY	SAVINE
PARRAS	DASHED	TASSES	**AUNTS**	**AVISE**
TARRAS	FASHED	ASSESS	DAUNTS	PAVISE
ARRAY	GASHED	**ASSET**	GAUNTS	AVISED
WARRAY	HASHED	BASSET	HAUNTS	AVISES
ARRAYS	LASHED	TASSET	JAUNTS	**AVIZE**
ARRET	MASHED	ASSETS	NAUNTS	AVIZED
BARRET	PASHED	**ASSOT**	SAUNTS	AVIZES
GARRET	RASHED	ASSOTS	TAUNTS	**AVYZE**
ARRETS	SASHED	ASSOTT	VAUNTS	AVYZED
ARRIS	TASHED	**ASTER**	**AUNTY**	AVYZES
KARRIS	WASHED	BASTER	JAUNTY	**AWAKE**
MARRIS	**ASHEN**	CASTER	VAUNTY	AWAKED
ARRISH	WASHEN	EASTER	**AURAE**	AWAKEN
ARROW	**ASHES**	FASTER	LAURAE	AWAKES
BARROW	BASHES	GASTER	**AURAS**	**AWARD**
FARROW	CASHES	LASTER	LAURAS	VAWARD
HARROW	DASHES	MASTER	**AURIC**	AWARDS
MARROW	FASHES	PASTER	LAURIC	**AWARE**
NARROW	GASHES	RASTER	TAURIC	AWARER
TARROW	HASHES	TASTER	**AURIS**	**AWFUL**
YARROW	LASHES	VASTER	KAURIS	LAWFUL
ARROWS	MASHES	WASTER	MAURIS	**AWING**
ARROWY	PASHES	**ASTERN**	AURIST	CAWING
ARSED	RASHES	ASTERS	**AVAIL**	DAWING
FARSED	SASHES	ASTERT	AVAILE	HAWING
PARSED	TASHES	**ATAPS**	AVAILS	JAWING
ARSES	WASHES	WATAPS	**AVALE**	KAWING
CARSES	**ASKED**	**ATMAN**	AVALED	LAWING
FARSES	BASKED	BATMAN	AVALES	MAWING
MARSES	CASKED	VATMAN	**AVANT**	PAWING
PARSES	MASKED	ATMANS	SAVANT	RAWING
ARSEY	TASKED	**ATOKE**	AVANTI	SAWING
CARSEY	**ASKER**	MATOKE	**AVELS**	TAWING
KARSEY	MASKER	ATOKES	CAVELS	YAWING
ARSON	TASKER	**ATONE**	GAVELS	**AWNED**
PARSON	ASKERS	ATONED	JAVELS	DAWNED
ARSONS	**ASPER**	ATONER	NAVELS	FAWNED
ARTAL	GASPER	ATONES	RAVELS	LAWNED
HARTAL	JASPER	**ATRIA**	**AVENS**	PAWNED
ARTEL	RASPER	LATRIA	DAVENS	YAWNED
CARTEL	ASPERS	ATRIAL	HAVENS	**AWNER**
MARTEL	**ASPIC**	**AUDAD**	MAVENS	DAWNER
ARTELS	ASPICK	CAUDAD	PAVENS	FAWNER
ARTIS	ASPICS	AUDADS	RAVENS	PAWNER
AARTIS	**ASPIS**	**AUGER**	**AVERS**	YAWNER
PARTIS	JASPIS	GAUGER	CAVERS	AWNERS
ARTIST	ASPISH	MAUGER	HAVERS	**AWOKE**
ARUMS	**ASSAI**	SAUGER	LAVERS	AWOKEN
GARUMS	ASSAIL	AUGERS	PAVERS	**AXING**
LARUMS	ASSAIS	**AUGHT**	RAVERS	FAXING

MAXING	ABANDS	BASTED	BELLES	BINGED
RAXING	**BANGS**	BASTER	**BELON**	BINGER
TAXING	OBANGS	BASTES	BELONG	BINGES
WAXING	**BANIA**	**BATED**	BELONS	**BIRLE**
AXITE	BANIAN	ABATED	**BEMIX**	BIRLED
TAXITE	BANIAS	**BATES**	BEMIXT	BIRLER
AXITES	**BANYA**	ABATES	**BENCH**	BIRLES
AXMAN	BANYAN	**BATHE**	BENCHY	**BISES**
TAXMAN	BANYAS	BATHED	**BENNE**	IBISES
AXMEN	**BARBE**	BATHER	BENNES	**BITCH**
TAXMEN	BARBED	BATHES	BENNET	BITCHY
AXONS	BARBEL	**BATTU**	**BENTO**	**BITER**
CAXONS	BARBER	ABATTU	OBENTO	OBITER
TAXONS	BARBES	BATTUE	BENTOS	BITERS
AYAHS	BARBET	**BAULK**	**BERME**	**BITTE**
RAYAHS	**BARDE**	BAULKS	BERMED	BITTED
AYINS	BARDED	BAULKY	BERMES	BITTEN
LAYINS	BARDES	**BEACH**	**BERTH**	BITTER
ZAYINS	**BARES**	BEACHY	BERTHA	**BLADE**
AYRES	BAREST	**BEARD**	BERTHE	BLADED
FAYRES	**BARGE**	BEARDS	BERTHS	BLADER
AZANS	BARGED	BEARDY	**BESEE**	BLADES
HAZANS	BARGEE	**BEARE**	BESEEM	**BLAES**
AZONS	BARGES	BEARED	BESEEN	BLAEST
GAZONS	**BARON**	BEARER	BESEES	**BLAME**
AZOTE	BARONG	BEARES	**BESTI**	BLAMED
AZOTED	BARONS	**BEARS**	BESTIR	BLAMER
AZOTES	BARONY	ABEARS	BESTIS	BLAMES
AZURE	**BARRA**	**BEAUT**	**BETID**	**BLARE**
RAZURE	BARRAS	BEAUTS	BETIDE	BLARED
AZURES	BARRAT	BEAUTY	**BETON**	BLARES
BABOO	**BARRE**	**BECKE**	BETONS	**BLASH**
BABOOL	BARRED	BECKED	BETONY	BLASHY
BABOON	BARREL	BECKES	**BHAJI**	**BLAST**
BABOOS	BARREN	BECKET	BHAJIA	OBLAST
BACCA	BARRES	**BEDEL**	BHAJIS	BLASTS
BACCAE	BARRET	BEDELL	**BICES**	BLASTY
BACCAS	**BARRO**	BEDELS	IBICES	**BLATE**
BADGE	BARROW	**BEDYE**	**BIDED**	ABLATE
BADGED	**BASAL**	BEDYED	ABIDED	OBLATE
BADGER	BASALT	BEDYES	**BIDER**	BLATER
BADGES	**BASAN**	**BEECH**	ABIDER	**BLAZE**
BAIZE	BASANS	BEECHY	BIDERS	ABLAZE
BAIZED	BASANT	**BEEDI**	**BIDES**	BLAZED
BAIZES	**BASED**	BEEDIE	ABIDES	BLAZER
BAKER	ABASED	**BEGUN**	**BIELD**	BLAZES
BAKERS	**BASER**	BEGUNK	BIELDS	**BLEAK**
BAKERY	ABASER	**BEIGE**	BIELDY	BLEAKS
BALLS	**BASES**	BEIGEL	**BIJOU**	BLEAKY
BALLSY	ABASES	BEIGES	BIJOUS	**BLEAR**
BALSA	BASEST	**BELEE**	BIJOUX	BLEARS
BALSAM	**BASIN**	BELEED	**BILBO**	BLEARY
BALSAS	BASING	BELEES	BILBOA	**BLEND**
BALTI	BASINS	**BELIE**	BILBOS	BLENDE
BALTIC	**BASSE**	BELIED	**BILGE**	BLENDS
BALTIS	BASSED	BELIEF	BILGED	**BLENT**
BANDA	BASSER	BELIER	BILGES	YBLENT
BANDAR	BASSES	BELIES	**BILLY**	**BLEST**
BANDAS	BASSET	**BELLE**	BILLYO	ABLEST
BANDS	**BASTE**	BELLED	**BINGE**	**BLETS**

ABLETS	**BOLUS**	BOUGET	**BRAWL**	BRISKS
BLING	OBOLUS	**BOUGH**	BRAWLS	BRISKY
ABLING	**BOMAS**	BOUGHS	BRAWLY	**BROAD**
BLINGS	ABOMAS	BOUGHT	**BRAWN**	ABROAD
BLINGY	**BOMBE**	**BOUND**	BRAWNS	BROADS
BLINS	BOMBED	ABOUND	BRAWNY	**BROCH**
ABLINS	BOMBER	YBOUND	**BRAYS**	BROCHE
BLOCK	BOMBES	**BOUNDS**	ABRAYS	BROCHO
BLOCKS	**BONIE**	**BOURN**	**BRAZE**	BROCHS
BLOCKY	BONIER	BOURNE	BRAZED	**BROKE**
BLOKE	**BONNE**	BOURNS	BRAZEN	BROKED
BLOKES	BONNES	**BOUSE**	BRAZER	BROKEN
BLOKEY	BONNET	BOUSED	BRAZES	BROKER
BLOND	**BONZE**	BOUSES	**BREAD**	BROKES
BLONDE	BONZER	**BOUTS**	BREADS	**BRONC**
BLONDS	BONZES	ABOUTS	BREADY	BRONCO
BLOOD	**BOOKS**	**BOWER**	**BREDE**	BRONCS
BLOODS	EBOOKS	BOWERS	BREDED	**BROOD**
BLOODY	BOOKSY	BOWERY	BREDES	BROODS
BLOOM	**BOONG**	**BOWNE**	**BREES**	BROODY
ABLOOM	BOONGA	BOWNED	BREESE	**BROOM**
BLOOMS	BOONGS	BOWNES	BREEST	BROOMS
BLOOMY	**BOORD**	**BOWSE**	**BREIS**	BROOMY
BLOWS	BOORDE	BOWSED	BREIST	**BROOS**
BLOWSE	BOORDS	BOWSER	**BRENT**	BROOSE
BLOWSY	**BOOSE**	BOWSES	YBRENT	**BROTH**
BLUES	BOOSED	BOWSEY	BRENTS	BROTHS
BLUEST	BOOSES	**BOYAR**	**BREVE**	BROTHY
BLUESY	**BOOZE**	BOYARD	BREVES	**BROWN**
BLUID	BOOZED	BOYARS	BREVET	BROWNS
BLUIDS	BOOZER	**BOYAU**	**BRIAR**	BROWNY
BLUIDY	BOOZES	BOYAUX	BRIARD	**BROWS**
BLUME	BOOZEY	**BRACE**	BRIARS	BROWSE
BLUMED	**BORAL**	BRACED	BRIARY	BROWST
BLUMES	ABORAL	BRACER	**BRIBE**	BROWSY
BLUSH	BORALS	BRACES	BRIBED	**BRUSH**
ABLUSH	**BORDE**	**BRAID**	BRIBEE	BRUSHY
BOARD	BORDEL	ABRAID	BRIBER	**BRUTE**
ABOARD	BORDER	BRAIDE	BRIBES	BRUTED
BOARDS	BORDES	BRAIDS	**BRICK**	BRUTER
BOCCI	**BORDS**	**BRAIN**	BRICKS	BRUTES
BOCCIA	ABORDS	BRAINS	BRICKY	**BUBAL**
BOCCIE	**BOREE**	BRAINY	**BRIDE**	BUBALE
BOCCIS	BOREEN	**BRAKE**	BRIDED	BUBALS
BODED	BOREES	BRAKED	BRIDES	**BUDGE**
ABODED	**BORNE**	BRAKES	**BRIER**	BUDGED
BODES	ABORNE	**BRAND**	BRIERS	BUDGER
ABODES	**BORTS**	BRANDS	BRIERY	BUDGES
BODGE	ABORTS	BRANDY	**BRIKS**	BUDGET
BODGED	**BOSOM**	**BRANK**	IBRIKS	**BUFFE**
BODGER	BOSOMS	BRANKS	**BRILL**	BUFFED
BODGES	BOSOMY	BRANKY	BRILLO	BUFFEL
BOGIE	**BOTCH**	**BRASH**	BRILLS	BUFFER
BOGIED	BOTCHY	BRASHY	**BRINE**	BUFFET
BOGIES	**BOTTE**	**BRASS**	BRINED	**BUGLE**
BOGLE	BOTTED	BRASSY	BRINER	BUGLED
BOGLED	BOTTES	**BRAVE**	BRINES	BUGLER
BOGLES	**BOUGE**	BRAVED	**BRINS**	BUGLES
BOLES	BOUGED	BRAVER	ABRINS	BUGLET
OBOLES	BOUGES	BRAVES	**BRISK**	**BULGE**

BULGED	CACHET	**CAPES**	CATCHT	CESSES
BULGER	**CADGE**	SCAPES	CATCHY	**CETYL**
BULGES	CADGED	**CAPLE**	**CATER**	ACETYL
BULLA	CADGER	CAPLES	ACATER	CETYLS
BULLAE	CADGES	CAPLET	CATERS	**CHACE**
BUNAS	**CAECA**	**CAPOT**	**CATES**	CHACED
ABUNAS	CAECAL	CAPOTE	ACATES	CHACES
BUNCE	**CAFFS**	CAPOTS	**CATTY**	**CHADO**
BUNCED	SCAFFS	**CARAT**	SCATTY	CHADOR
BUNCES	**CAIRN**	CARATE	**CAUDA**	CHADOS
BUNCH	CAIRNS	CARATS	CAUDAD	**CHAFE**
BUNCHY	CAIRNY	**CARBO**	CAUDAE	CHAFED
BUNDE	**CALLA**	CARBON	CAUDAL	CHAFER
BUNDED	CALLAN	CARBOS	**CAUPS**	CHAFES
BUNJE	CALLAS	CARBOY	SCAUPS	**CHAFF**
BUNJEE	**CALLS**	**CARDI**	**CAUSA**	CHAFFS
BUNJES	SCALLS	CARDIA	CAUSAE	CHAFFY
BURKE	**CALPA**	CARDIE	CAUSAL	**CHAIN**
BURKED	CALPAC	CARDIO	**CAUSE**	CHAINE
BURKER	CALPAS	CARDIS	CAUSED	CHAINS
BURKES	**CALPS**	**CARED**	CAUSEN	**CHAIS**
BURRO	SCALPS	SCARED	CAUSER	CHAISE
BURROS	**CALVE**	**CARER**	CAUSES	**CHALK**
BURROW	CALVED	SCARER	CAUSEY	CHALKS
BURSA	CALVER	CARERS	**CAVER**	CHALKY
BURSAE	CALVES	**CARES**	CAVERN	**CHAMP**
BURSAL	**CAMAS**	SCARES	CAVERS	CHAMPS
BURSAR	CAMASH	CARESS	**CAVIE**	CHAMPY
BURSAS	CAMASS	**CARNY**	CAVIER	**CHANG**
BURST	**CAMEL**	CARNYX	CAVIES	CHANGA
ABURST	SCAMEL	**CAROL**	**CEASE**	CHANGE
BURSTS	CAMELS	CAROLI	CEASED	CHANGS
BUSED	**CAMES**	CAROLS	CEASES	**CHANT**
ABUSED	CAMESE	**CARPS**	**CEAZE**	CHANTS
BUSES	**CAMIS**	SCARPS	CEAZED	CHANTY
ABUSES	CAMISA	**CARRY**	CEAZES	**CHAPE**
BUSTI	CAMISE	SCARRY	**CEDAR**	CHAPEL
BUSTIC	**CAMPI**	**CARSE**	CEDARN	CHAPES
BUSTIS	SCAMPI	CARSES	CEDARS	**CHARD**
BUTLE	**CAMPS**	CARSEY	CEDARY	ECHARD
BUTLED	SCAMPS	**CARTE**	**CELLA**	CHARDS
BUTLER	**CANNA**	ECARTE	CELLAE	**CHARE**
BUTLES	CANNAE	CARTED	CELLAR	CHARED
BUTTE	CANNAS	CARTEL	**CELLI**	CHARES
BUTTED	**CANOE**	CARTER	OCELLI	CHARET
BUTTER	CANOED	CARTES	**CENSE**	**CHARK**
BUTTES	CANOER	**CARTS**	CENSED	CHARKA
CABAL	CANOES	SCARTS	CENSER	CHARKS
CABALA	**CANTO**	**CARVE**	CENSES	**CHARR**
CABALS	CANTON	CARVED	**CENTS**	CHARRO
CABBY	CANTOR	CARVEL	SCENTS	CHARRS
SCABBY	CANTOS	CARVEN	**CENTU**	CHARRY
CABLE	**CANTS**	CARVER	CENTUM	**CHARS**
CABLED	SCANTS	CARVES	**CERNE**	ACHARS
CABLER	**CANTY**	**CASTE**	SCERNE	**CHART**
CABLES	SCANTY	CASTED	CERNED	CHARTA
CABLET	**CAPAS**	CASTER	CERNES	CHARTS
CACHE	SCAPAS	CASTES	**CESSE**	**CHASE**
CACHED	**CAPED**	**CATCH**	CESSED	CHASED
CACHES	SCAPED	SCATCH	CESSER	CHASER

CHASES	CHINAS	CIDERS	CLOSER	COLORY
CHASM	**CHINE**	CIDERY	CLOSES	**COMBE**
CHASMS	CHINED	**CIONS**	CLOSET	COMBED
CHASMY	CHINES	SCIONS	**CLOTH**	COMBER
CHAVS	**CHINK**	**CIRCA**	CLOTHE	COMBES
SCHAVS	CHINKS	CIRCAR	CLOTHS	**COMET**
CHEAP	CHINKY	**CLANK**	**CLOUD**	COMETH
CHEAPO	**CHIRP**	CLANKS	CLOUDS	COMETS
CHEAPS	CHIRPS	CLANKY	CLOUDY	**COMIC**
CHEAPY	CHIRPY	**CLART**	**CLOVE**	COMICE
CHECK	**CHIRR**	CLARTS	CLOVEN	COMICS
CHECKS	CHIRRE	CLARTY	CLOVER	**COMMO**
CHECKY	CHIRRS	**CLASP**	CLOVES	COMMON
CHEEK	**CHIVE**	CLASPS	**CLOYE**	COMMOS
CHEEKS	CHIVED	CLASPT	CLOYED	COMMOT
CHEEKY	CHIVES	**CLASS**	CLOYES	**COMPO**
CHEER	**CHOCK**	CLASSY	**CLUCK**	COMPOS
CHEERO	CHOCKO	**CLATS**	CLUCKS	COMPOT
CHEERS	CHOCKS	ECLATS	CLUCKY	**CONCH**
CHEERY	**CHOKE**	**CLAVE**	CLUMP	CONCHA
CHELA	CHOKED	SCLAVE	CLUMPS	CONCHE
CHELAE	CHOKER	CLAVER	CLUMPY	CONCHO
CHELAS	CHOKES	CLAVES	**CLUNK**	CONCHS
CHERT	CHOKEY	**CLAVI**	CLUNKS	CONCHY
CHERTS	**CHOLI**	CLAVIE	CLUNKY	**CONDO**
CHERTY	CHOLIC	CLAVIS	**CLYPE**	CONDOM
CHEST	CHOLIS	**CLECK**	CLYPED	CONDOR
CHESTS	**CHORD**	CLECKS	CLYPEI	CONDOS
CHESTY	CHORDA	CLECKY	CLYPES	**CONES**
CHIAS	CHORDS	**CLEPE**	**CNIDA**	ICONES
CHIASM	**CHORE**	CLEPED	CNIDAE	SCONES
CHICH	CHOREA	CLEPES	**COACH**	**CONGE**
CHICHA	CHORED	**CLEPT**	COACHY	CONGED
CHICHI	CHOREE	YCLEPT	**COATE**	CONGEE
CHICK	CHORES	**CLEVE**	COATED	CONGER
TCHICK	**CHOSE**	CLEVER	COATEE	CONGES
CHICKS	CHOSEN	CLEVES	COATER	**CONGO**
CHICO	CHOSES	**CLIFF**	COATES	CONGOS
CHICON	**CHOUT**	SCLIFF	**COCCI**	CONGOU
CHICOS	SCHOUT	CLIFFS	COCCIC	**CONIC**
CHIDE	CHOUTS	CLIFFY	COCCID	ICONIC
CHIDED	**CHOWS**	**CLIFT**	**COCKS**	CONICS
CHIDER	CHOWSE	CLIFTS	COCKSY	**CONIN**
CHIDES	**CHUCK**	CLIFTY	**COFFS**	CONINE
CHIEL	CHUCKS	**CLING**	SCOFFS	CONING
CHIELD	CHUCKY	CLINGS	**COHOS**	CONINS
CHIELS	**CHUFF**	CLINGY	COHOSH	**CONNE**
CHILD	CHUFFS	**CLIPE**	COHOST	CONNED
CHILDE	CHUFFY	CLIPED	**COIGN**	CONNER
CHILDS	**CHUNK**	CLIPES	COIGNE	CONNES
CHILL	CHUNKS	**CLOKE**	COIGNS	**CONVO**
CHILLI	CHUNKY	CLOKED	**COLDS**	CONVOS
CHILLS	**CHURR**	CLOKES	SCOLDS	CONVOY
CHILLY	CHURRO	**CLONE**	**COLON**	**COOCH**
CHIME	CHURRS	CLONED	COLONE	SCOOCH
CHIMED	**CHUTE**	CLONER	COLONI	**COOEE**
CHIMER	CHUTED	CLONES	COLONS	COOEED
CHIMES	CHUTES	**CLOSE**	COLONY	COOEES
CHINA	**CIDER**	ECLOSE	**COLOR**	**COOMB**
CHINAR	ACIDER	CLOSED	COLORS	COOMBE

COOMBS	COTTAR	**CRAMS**	CREPES	CROWDS
COOPS	COTTAS	SCRAMS	CREPEY	CROWDY
SCOOPS	**COUCH**	**CRANE**	**CRESS**	**CROWS**
COOTS	COUCHE	CRANED	CRESSY	SCROWS
SCOOTS	**COUNT**	CRANES	**CREST**	**CROZE**
COPAL	COUNTS	**CRANK**	CRESTA	CROZER
COPALM	COUNTY	CRANKS	CRESTS	CROZES
COPALS	**COUPE**	CRANKY	**CREWE**	**CRUDE**
COPED	COUPED	**CRANS**	CREWED	CRUDER
SCOPED	COUPEE	SCRANS	CREWEL	CRUDES
COPES	COUPER	**CRAPE**	CREWES	**CRUMB**
SCOPES	COUPES	SCRAPE	**CREWS**	CRUMBS
COPRA	**COUPS**	CRAPED	SCREWS	CRUMBY
COPRAH	SCOUPS	CRAPES	**CRICK**	**CRUMP**
COPRAS	**COURE**	**CRAPS**	CRICKS	SCRUMP
COPSE	COURED	SCRAPS	CRICKY	CRUMPS
COPSED	COURES	**CRATE**	**CRIED**	CRUMPY
COPSES	**COURS**	CRATED	SCRIED	**CRURA**
CORBE	SCOURS	CRATER	**CRIES**	CRURAL
CORBEL	COURSE	CRATES	SCRIES	**CRUSE**
CORBES	**COUTH**	**CRAVE**	**CRIME**	CRUSES
CORED	SCOUTH	CRAVED	CRIMED	CRUSET
SCORED	COUTHS	CRAVEN	CRIMEN	**CRUST**
CORER	COUTHY	CRAVER	CRIMES	CRUSTA
SCORER	**COVEN**	CRAVES	**CRIMP**	CRUSTS
CORERS	COVENS	**CRAWL**	SCRIMP	CRUSTY
CORES	COVENT	ACRAWL	CRIMPS	**CRYPT**
SCORES	**COVER**	SCRAWL	CRIMPY	CRYPTO
CORIA	COVERS	**CRAWLS**	**CRIMS**	CRYPTS
SCORIA	COVERT	CRAWLY	SCRIMS	**CUBIC**
CORNS	**COVIN**	**CRAWS**	**CRINE**	CUBICA
ACORNS	COVING	SCRAWS	SCRINE	CUBICS
SCORNS	COVINS	**CRAYS**	CRINED	**CUBIT**
CORNU	**COWED**	SCRAYS	CRINES	CUBITI
CORNUA	SCOWED	**CRAZE**	**CRISP**	CUBITS
CORNUS	**COWLS**	CRAZED	CRISPS	**CUFFS**
CORPS	SCOWLS	CRAZES	CRISPY	SCUFFS
CORPSE	**COWPS**	**CREAK**	**CROAK**	**CULCH**
CORSE	SCOWPS	SCREAK	CROAKS	SCULCH
SCORSE	**COZIE**	CREAKS	CROAKY	**CULLS**
CORSES	COZIED	CREAKY	**CROGS**	SCULLS
CORSET	COZIER	**CREAM**	SCROGS	**CULPA**
CORSEY	COZIES	SCREAM	**CROME**	CULPAE
COSEC	**CRABS**	CREAMS	SCROME	**CULTI**
COSECH	SCRABS	CREAMY	CROMED	CULTIC
COSECS	**CRACK**	**CREED**	CROMES	**CURAT**
COSIE	CRACKA	SCREED	**CRONE**	CURATE
COSIED	CRACKS	CREEDS	CRONES	CURATS
COSIER	CRACKY	**CREEK**	CRONET	**CURFS**
COSIES	**CRAFT**	CREEKS	**CROSS**	SCURFS
COSTA	CRAFTS	CREEKY	ACROSS	**CURIA**
COSTAE	CRAFTY	**CREEP**	CROSSE	CURIAE
COSTAL	**CRAGS**	CREEPS	**CROUP**	CURIAL
COSTAR	SCRAGS	CREEPY	CROUPE	CURIAS
COSTE	**CRAKE**	**CREES**	CROUPS	**CURIE**
COSTED	CRAKED	SCREES	CROUPY	ECURIE
COSTER	CRAKES	CREESE	**CROUT**	CURIES
COSTES	**CRAMP**	CREESH	CROUTE	CURIET
COTTA	CRAMPS	**CREPE**	CROUTS	**CURRY**
COTTAE	CRAMPY	CREPED	**CROWD**	SCURRY

CURSE	ADAWED	**DENSE**	**DOING**	**DRAFF**
CURSED	**DEALS**	DENSER	DOINGS	DRAFFS
CURSER	IDEALS	**DENTS**	**DOLMA**	DRAFFY
CURSES	**DEARE**	IDENTS	DOLMAN	**DRAFT**
CURVE	DEARED	**DERAT**	DOLMAS	DRAFTS
CURVED	DEARER	DERATE	**DONNA**	DRAFTY
CURVES	DEARES	DERATS	DONNAS	**DRAPE**
CURVET	**DEATH**	**DERMA**	DONNAT	DRAPED
CURVEY	DEATHS	DERMAL	**DONNE**	DRAPER
CURVY	DEATHY	DERMAS	DONNED	DRAPES
SCURVY	**DEAVE**	**DERTH**	DONNEE	DRAPET
CUTCH	DEAVED	DERTHS	DONNES	DRAPEY
SCUTCH	DEAVES	**DEUCE**	**DOOCE**	**DRAWL**
CUTCHA	**DEBAR**	DEUCED	DOOCED	DRAWLS
CUTER	DEBARK	DEUCES	DOOCES	DRAWLY
ACUTER	DEBARS	**DEVOT**	**DOOLE**	**DREAD**
CUTES	**DEBIT**	DEVOTE	DOOLEE	ADREAD
ACUTES	DEBITS	DEVOTS	DOOLES	DREADS
SCUTES	**DEBUG**	**DEWAN**	**DOORS**	**DREAM**
CUTEST	DEBUGS	DEWANI	ADOORS	DREAMS
CUTESY	**DEBUR**	DEWANS	**DORAD**	DREAMT
CUTTO	DEBURR	**DICTS**	DORADO	DREAMY
CUTTOE	DEBURS	EDICTS	DORADS	**DREAR**
CYCLE	**DECAD**	**DIKAS**	**DORES**	DREARE
CYCLED	DECADE	DIKAST	ADORES	DREARS
CYCLER	DECADS	**DILDO**	**DORIS**	DREARY
CYCLES	**DECAF**	DILDOE	DORISE	**DRECK**
DAIKO	DECAFF	DILDOS	**DORSA**	DRECKS
DAIKON	DECAFS	**DIMPS**	DORSAD	DRECKY
DAIKOS	**DEEMS**	DIMPSY	DORSAL	**DRESS**
DAINE	ADEEMS	**DINER**	**DORSE**	DRESSY
SDAINE	**DEEVE**	DINERO	DORSEL	**DRIER**
DAINED	DEEVED	DINERS	DORSER	DRIERS
DAINES	DEEVES	**DINGE**	DORSES	**DRIES**
DAINT	**DEGUS**	DINGED	**DOUCE**	DRIEST
DAINTY	DEGUST	DINGER	DOUCER	**DRIFT**
DALED	**DEICE**	DINGES	DOUCET	ADRIFT
DALEDH	DEICED	DINGEY	**DOUGH**	DRIFTS
DALEDS	DEICER	**DINNA**	DOUGHS	DRIFTY
DAMME	DEICES	DINNAE	DOUGHT	**DRIVE**
DAMMED	**DEIGN**	**DIRKE**	DOUGHY	DRIVEL
DAMMER	SDEIGN	DIRKED	**DOURA**	DRIVEN
DANCE	DEIGNS	DIRKES	DOURAH	DRIVER
DANCED	**DELIS**	**DITED**	DOURAS	DRIVES
DANCER	DELISH	EDITED	**DOUSE**	**DROIT**
DANCES	DELIST	DIVERT	DOUSED	ADROIT
DANCEY	**DELVE**	**DIVES**	DOUSER	DROITS
DANTS	DELVED	DIVEST	DOUSES	**DROLE**
IDANTS	DELVER	**DJINN**	**DOVIE**	DROLER
DARGA	DELVES	DJINNI	DOVIER	DROLES
DARGAH	**DEMAN**	DJINNS	**DOWER**	**DROLL**
DARGAS	DEMAND	DJINNY	DOWERS	DROLLS
DARRE	DEMANS	**DODGE**	DOWERY	DROLLY
DARRED	**DEMUR**	DODGED	**DOWIE**	**DRONE**
DARRES	DEMURE	DODGEM	DOWIER	DRONED
DAUBE	DEMURS	DODGER	**DOWSE**	DRONER
DAUBED	**DENAR**	DODGES	DOWSED	DRONES
DAUBER	DENARI	**DOGMA**	DOWSER	**DROOL**
DAUBES	DENARS	DOGMAN	DOWSES	DROOLS
DAWED	DENARY	DOGMAS	DOWSET	DROOLY

DROOP	MEAGRE	EASELS	PECHED	PEGGED
DROOPS	EAGRES	**EASER**	TECHED	VEGGED
DROOPY	**EALES**	LEASER	**ECHES**	**EGGER**
DROPS	**REALES**	TEASER	EECHES	KEGGER
DROPSY	VEALES	EASERS	LECHES	LEGGER
DROSS	**EANED**	**EASES**	**EDEMA**	EGGERS
DROSSY	BEANED	CEASES	OEDEMA	EGGERY
DROVE	DEANED	FEASES	EDEMAS	**EGRET**
DROVED	JEANED	LEASES	**EDGED**	REGRET
DROVER	LEANED	MEASES	HEDGED	EGRETS
DROVES	MEANED	PEASES	KEDGED	**EIDER**
DROWN	PEANED	SEASES	LEDGED	DEIDER
DROWND	SEANED	TEASES	SEDGED	EIDERS
DROWNS	WEANED	**EASLE**	WEDGED	**EIGHT**
DROWS	YEANED	MEASLE	**EDGER**	HEIGHT
DROWSE	**EARDS**	EASLES	HEDGER	KEIGHT
DROWSY	BEARDS	**EASTS**	KEDGER	WEIGHT
DRUPE	HEARDS	BEASTS	LEDGER	EIGHTH
DRUPEL	YEARDS	FEASTS	EDGERS	EIGHTS
DRUPES	**EARED**	HEASTS	**EDGES**	EIGHTY
DRUSE	BEARED	LEASTS	HEDGES	**EIGNE**
DRUSEN	DEARED	REASTS	KEDGES	BEIGNE
DRUSES	FEARED	YEASTS	LEDGES	**EISEL**
DUCES	GEARED	**EATEN**	SEDGES	EISELL
EDUCES	LEARED	BEATEN	WEDGES	EISELS
DUCTS	NEARED	NEATEN	**EDILE**	**EJECT**
EDUCTS	REARED	**EATER**	AEDILE	DEJECT
DUETT	SEARED	BEATER	SEDILE	REJECT
DUETTI	TEARED	FEATER	EDILES	EJECTA
DUETTO	WEARED	HEATER	**EDUCE**	EJECTS
DUETTS	**EARLS**	NEATER	DEDUCE	**EKING**
DUKKA	PEARLS	SEATER	REDUCE	DEKING
DUKKAH	**EARLY**	EATERS	SEDUCE	REKING
DUKKAS	DEARLY	EATERY	EDUCED	**EKKAS**
DUPER	NEARLY	**EATHE**	EDUCES	MEKKAS
DUPERS	PEARLY	MEATHE	**EDUCT**	**ELAND**
DUPERY	REARLY	**EAVED**	DEDUCT	RELAND
DUPLE	YEARLY	DEAVED	EDUCTS	ELANDS
DUPLET	**EARNS**	HEAVED	**EERIE**	**ELATE**
DUPLEX	DEARNS	LEAVED	FEERIE	BELATE
DURES	LEARNS	REAVED	PEERIE	DELATE
DURESS	YEARNS	WEAVED	EERIER	GELATE
DUSTS	**EARST**	**EAVES**	**EFFED**	RELATE
ADUSTS	PEARST	DEAVES	JEFFED	VELATE
DWEEB	**EARTH**	HEAVES	REFFED	ELATED
DWEEBS	DEARTH	LEAVES	**EGERS**	ELATER
DWEEBY	HEARTH	REAVES	LEGERS	ELATES
DWINE	EARTHS	WEAVES	**EGEST**	**ELCHI**
DWINED	EARTHY	**EBBED**	REGEST	ELCHIS
DWINES	**EASED**	KEBBED	EGESTA	**ELDER**
EAGER	CEASED	NEBBED	EGESTS	GELDER
MEAGER	FEASED	WEBBED	**EGGAR**	MELDER
EAGERS	LEASED	**EBOOK**	BEGGAR	WELDER
EAGLE	MEASED	REBOOK	SEGGAR	ELDERS
BEAGLE	PEASED	EBOOKS	EGGARS	**ELDIN**
TEAGLE	SEASED	**ECADS**	**EGGED**	ELDING
EAGLED	TEASED	DECADS	BEGGED	ELDINS
EAGLES	**EASEL**	**ECHED**	DEGGED	**ELECT**
EAGLET	TEASEL	EECHED	KEGGED	SELECT
EAGRE	WEASEL	LECHED	LEGGED	ELECTS

ELFED
SELFED
ELFIN
ELFING
ELFINS
ELIDE
RELIDE
ELIDED
ELIDES
ELITE
PELITE
ELITES
ELOPE
DELOPE
ELOPED
ELOPER
ELOPES
ELUDE
DELUDE
ELUDED
ELUDER
ELUDES
ELUTE
ELUTED
ELUTES
ELVER
DELVER
ELVERS
ELVES
DELVES
HELVES
PELVES
SELVES
EMAIL
REMAIL
EMAILS
EMBAR
EMBARK
EMBARS
EMBED
KEMBED
EMBEDS
EMBER
MEMBER
EMBERS
EMBUS
EMBUSY
EMCEE
EMCEED
EMCEES
EMEND
REMEND
EMENDS
EMITS
DEMITS
REMITS
EMMAS
LEMMAS
EMMER
HEMMER

YEMMER
EMMERS
EMOTE
DEMOTE
GEMOTE
REMOTE
EMOTED
EMOTER
EMOTES
EMOVE
REMOVE
EMOVED
EMOVES
EMPTS
TEMPTS
EMULE
AEMULE
EMULED
EMULES
EMURE
DEMURE
EMURED
EMURES
ENATE
SENATE
ENATES
ENDED
BENDED
FENDED
HENDED
MENDED
PENDED
RENDED
SENDED
TENDED
VENDED
WENDED
ENDER
BENDER
FENDER
GENDER
LENDER
MENDER
RENDER
SENDER
TENDER
VENDER
ENDERS
ENDUE
VENDUE
ENDUED
ENDUES
ENEWS
RENEWS
ENROL
ENROLL
ENROLS
ENSUE
ENSUED
ENSUES

ENTER
CENTER
RENTER
TENTER
VENTER
ENTERA
ENTERS
ENTIA
KENTIA
ENTRY
CENTRY
GENTRY
SENTRY
ENURE
TENURE
ENURED
ENURES
ENVOI
RENVOI
ENVOIS
ENVOY
LENVOY
RENVOY
ENVOYS
ENZYM
ENZYME
ENZYMS
EORLS
CEORLS
EOSIN
EOSINE
EOSINS
EPEES
TEPEES
EPHOR
EPHORI
EPHORS
EPOCH
EPOCHA
EPOCHS
EPRIS
EPRISE
EQUAL
EQUALI
EQUALS
EQUIP
EQUIPE
EQUIPS
ERASE
ERASED
ERASER
ERASES
ERBIA
TERBIA
ERBIAS
ERING
CERING
DERING
LERING
MERING

SERING
ERINGO
ERNED
CERNED
GERNED
KERNED
TERNED
ERNES
CERNES
GERNES
KERNES
TERNES
ERODE
ERODED
ERODES
EROSE
REROSE
EROSES
ERRED
SERRED
ERROR
TERROR
ERRORS
ERSES
HERSES
MERSES
PERSES
VERSES
ERUGO
AERUGO
ERUGOS
ERVEN
VERVEN
ESCAR
ESCARP
ESCARS
ESILE
RESILE
ESILES
ESKER
ESKERS
ESNES
MESNES
ESSES
CESSES
DESSES
FESSES
GESSES
JESSES
LESSES
MESSES
NESSES
SESSES
YESSES
ESTER
FESTER
JESTER
MESTER
NESTER
PESTER

RESTER
TESTER
WESTER
YESTER
ZESTER
ESTERS
ETAGE
METAGE
ETAGES
ETAPE
RETAPE
ETAPES
ETHAL
LETHAL
ETHALS
ETHER
AETHER
HETHER
NETHER
PETHER
TETHER
WETHER
ETHERS
ETHOS
METHOS
ETHYL
METHYL
ETHYLS
ETTLE
FETTLE
KETTLE
METTLE
NETTLE
PETTLE
SETTLE
ETTLED
ETTLES
ETWEE
ETWEES
EUGHS
HEUGHS
EUKED
YEUKED
EVADE
EVADED
EVADER
EVADES
EVENS
EEVENS
SEVENS
EVERT
REVERT
EVERTS
EVERY
REVERY
SEVERY
EVETS
REVETS
EVILS
DEVILS

KEVILS	FACETE	**FEARE**	FILLER	**FLINT**
EVITE	FACETS	FEARED	FILLES	FLINTS
LEVITE	**FACIA**	FEARER	FILLET	FLINTY
EVITED	FACIAE	FEARES	**FILMI**	**FLIRT**
EVITES	FACIAL	**FEARS**	FILMIC	FLIRTS
EVOKE	FACIAS	AFEARS	FILMIS	FLIRTY
REVOKE	**FADGE**	**FEASE**	**FILOS**	**FLISK**
EVOKED	FADGED	FEASED	FILOSE	FLISKS
EVOKER	FADGES	FEASES	**FILTH**	FLISKY
EVOKES	**FAINE**	**FEAZE**	FILTHS	**FLITE**
EWERS	FAINED	FEAZED	FILTHY	FLITED
HEWERS	FAINER	FEAZES	**FINAL**	FLITES
SEWERS	FAINES	**FEESE**	FINALE	**FLOAT**
EWEST	**FAINT**	FEESED	FINALS	AFLOAT
FEWEST	FAINTS	FEESES	**FINER**	FLOATS
NEWEST	FAINTY	**FEEZE**	FINERS	FLOATY
EXACT	**FAKER**	FEEZED	FINERY	**FLOCK**
HEXACT	FAKERS	FEEZES	**FINES**	FLOCKS
EXACTA	FAKERY	**FEIST**	FINEST	FLOCKY
EXACTS	**FAKIE**	FEISTS	FINIS	**FLORA**
EXEME	FAKIER	FEISTY	FINISH	FLORAE
LEXEME	FAKIES	**FELLA**	**FITCH**	FLORAL
EXEMED	**FALSE**	FELLAH	FITCHE	FLORAS
EXEMES	FALSED	FELLAS	FITCHY	**FLOSS**
EXIES	FALSER	**FELON**	**FITTE**	FLOSSY
DEXIES	FALSES	FELONS	FITTED	**FLOTE**
EXILE	**FARCE**	FELONY	FITTER	FLOTEL
EXILED	FARCED	**FEMAL**	FITTES	FLOTES
EXILER	FARCER	FEMALE	**FIXIT**	**FLOUR**
EXILES	FARCES	FEMALS	FIXITY	FLOURS
EXINE	**FARCI**	**FENCE**	**FLAGS**	FLOURY
REXINE	FARCIE	FENCED	OFLAGS	**FLUFF**
EXINES	FARCIN	FENCER	**FLAKE**	FLUFFS
EXING	**FARSE**	FENCES	FLAKED	FLUFFY
HEXING	FARSED	**FERES**	FLAKER	**FLUKE**
SEXING	FARSES	FEREST	FLAKES	FLUKED
VEXING	**FASCI**	**FERIA**	FLAKEY	FLUKES
WEXING	FASCIA	FERIAE	**FLAME**	FLUKEY
YEXING	FASCIO	FERIAL	AFLAME	**FLUME**
EXIST	FASCIS	FERIAS	FLAMED	FLUMED
SEXIST	**FASTI**	**FESSE**	FLAMEN	FLUMES
EXISTS	FASTIE	FESSED	FLAMER	**FLUNK**
EXPOS	**FATWA**	FESSES	FLAMES	FLUNKS
EXPOSE	FATWAH	**FESTA**	**FLARE**	FLUNKY
EXTOL	FATWAS	FESTAL	FLARED	**FLURR**
EXTOLD	**FAULT**	FESTAS	FLARES	FLURRS
EXTOLL	FAULTS	**FIBRE**	**FLASH**	FLURRY
EXTOLS	FAULTY	FIBRED	FLASHY	**FLUSH**
EXUDE	**FAUNA**	FIBRES	**FLECK**	FLUSHY
EXUDED	FAUNAE	**FIDGE**	FLECKS	**FLUTE**
EXUDES	FAUNAL	FIDGED	FLECKY	FLUTED
EYING	FAUNAS	FIDGES	**FLESH**	FLUTER
FEYING	**FAVEL**	FIDGET	FLESHY	FLUTES
HEYING	FAVELA	**FIELD**	**FLEXO**	FLUTEY
KEYING	FAVELL	AFIELD	FLEXOR	**FLYPE**
FABLE	**FAVES**	FIELDS	FLEXOS	FLYPED
FABLED	FAVEST	**FIEST**	**FLIES**	FLYPES
FABLER	**FAYNE**	FIESTA	FLIEST	**FLYTE**
FABLES	FAYNED	**FILLE**	**FLIMS**	FLYTED
FACET	FAYNES	FILLED	FLIMSY	FLYTES

FOLIA	FRACTI	FROWST	GALEAS	GAZOON
FOLIAR	FRACTS	FROWSY	**GALLY**	GAZOOS
FOLKS	**FRAME**	**FROZE**	EGALLY	**GEARE**
FOLKSY	FRAMED	FROZEN	**GALUT**	GEARED
FONDU	FRAMER	**FRUIT**	GALUTH	GEARES
FONDUE	FRAMES	FRUITS	GALUTS	**GEIST**
FONDUS	**FRANC**	FRUITY	**GAMAS**	AGEIST
FOOTS	FRANCO	**FRUMP**	AGAMAS	GEISTS
FOOTSY	FRANCS	FRUMPS	GAMASH	**GEMMA**
FORBY	**FRATE**	FRUMPY	**GAMBE**	GEMMAE
FORBYE	FRATER	**FRUST**	GAMBES	GEMMAN
FORCE	**FREAK**	FRUSTA	GAMBET	**GEMOT**
FORCED	FREAKS	FRUSTS	**GAMBO**	GEMOTE
FORCER	FREAKY	**FUDGE**	GAMBOL	GEMOTS
FORCES	**FREES**	FUDGED	**GAMES**	**GENES**
FORES	FREEST	FUDGES	GAMEST	AGENES
FOREST	**FREET**	**FUGLE**	GAMESY	**GENOM**
FORGE	AFREET	FUGLED	**GAMIC**	GENOME
FORGED	FREETS	FUGLES	AGAMIC	GENOMS
FORGER	FREETY	**FUGUE**	OGAMIC	**GENTS**
FORGES	**FREIT**	FUGUED	**GAMIN**	AGENTS
FORGET	FREITS	FUGUES	GAMINE	**GERNE**
FORGO	FREITY	**FUNDI**	GAMING	GERNED
FORGOT	**FRESH**	FUNDIC	GAMINS	GERNES
FORME	AFRESH	FUNDIE	**GAMMA**	**GESSE**
FORMED	**FRIAR**	FUNDIS	GAMMAS	GESSED
FORMEE	FRIARS	**FUNGI**	GAMMAT	GESSES
FORMER	FRIARY	FUNGIC	**GAMME**	**GESTS**
FORMES	**FRILL**	**FURAN**	GAMMED	EGESTS
FORTE	FRILLS	FURANE	GAMMER	**GHAST**
FORTED	FRILLY	FURANS	GAMMES	AGHAST
FORTES	**FRISE**	**FURCA**	**GANEF**	GHASTS
FORTH	FRISEE	FURCAE	GANEFS	**GHOST**
FORTHY	FRISES	FURCAL	**GANJA**	GHOSTS
FOSSA	**FRISK**	**FUROL**	GANJAH	GHOSTY
FOSSAE	FRISKA	FUROLE	GANJAS	**GILAS**
FOSSAS	FRISKS	FUROLS	**GAPES**	AGILAS
FOSSE	FRISKY	**FUROR**	AGAPES	**GIMME**
FOSSED	**FRITS**	FURORE	**GAPOS**	GIMMER
FOSSES	AFRITS	FURORS	IGAPOS	GIMMES
FOUET	**FRIZE**	**FUSIL**	**GARBE**	**GINGE**
FOUETS	FRIZED	FUSILE	GARBED	GINGER
FOULE	FRIZER	FUSILS	GARBES	GINGES
FOULED	FRIZES	**GABLE**	**GARDA**	**GINGS**
FOULER	**FRIZZ**	GABLED	GARDAI	AGINGS
FOULES	FRIZZY	GABLES	**GARIS**	**GISMS**
FOVEA	**FRONT**	GABLET	GARISH	AGISMS
FOVEAE	AFRONT	**GADGE**	**GARRE**	**GISTS**
FOVEAL	FRONTS	GADGES	GARRED	AGISTS
FOVEAS	**FRORE**	GADGET	GARRES	**GIUST**
FOXIE	FROREN	**GAFFE**	GARRET	GIUSTO
FOXIER	**FRORN**	GAFFED	**GATES**	GIUSTS
FOXIES	FRORNE	GAFFER	AGATES	**GIVES**
FOYLE	**FROST**	GAFFES	**GAUGE**	OGIVES
FOYLED	FROSTS	**GAINS**	GAUGED	**GLAIR**
FOYLES	FROSTY	GAINST	GAUGER	GLAIRE
FOYNE	**FROTH**	**GALAX**	GAUGES	GLAIRS
FOYNED	FROTHS	GALAXY	**GAZED**	GLAIRY
FOYNES	FROTHY	**GALEA**	AGAZED	**GLARE**
FRACT	**FROWS**	GALEAE	**GAZOO**	AGLARE

GLARED	GNARLY	GRAPED	AGRIZE	GUNGED
GLARES	**GOBAN**	GRAPES	GRIZES	GUNGES
GLASS	GOBANG	GRAPEY	**GRONE**	**GURGE**
GLASSY	GOBANS	**GRASS**	GRONED	GURGED
GLAUR	**GODSO**	GRASSY	GRONES	GURGES
GLAURS	GODSON	**GRATE**	**GROPE**	**GUSLA**
GLAURY	**GOING**	GRATED	GROPED	GUSLAR
GLAZE	AGOING	GRATER	GROPER	GUSLAS
GLAZED	GOINGS	GRATES	GROPES	**GUTTA**
GLAZEN	**GONIF**	**GRAVE**	**GROSZ**	GUTTAE
GLAZER	GONIFF	GRAVED	GROSZE	GUTTAS
GLAZES	GONIFS	GRAVEL	GROSZY	**GUYLE**
GLEAM	**GOOSE**	GRAVEN	**GROUP**	GUYLED
AGLEAM	GOOSED	GRAVER	GROUPS	GUYLER
GLEAMS	GOOSES	GRAVES	GROUPY	GUYLES
GLEAMY	GOOSEY	**GRAZE**	**GROUT**	**GYROS**
GLEBA	**GORAS**	GRAZED	GROUTS	GYROSE
GLEBAE	AGORAS	GRAZER	GROUTY	**HACKS**
GLEET	**GORGE**	GRAZES	**GROVE**	CHACKS
GLEETS	GORGED	**GREED**	GROVED	SHACKS
GLEETY	GORGER	AGREED	GROVEL	THACKS
GLIDE	GORGES	GREEDS	GROVES	WHACKS
GLIDED	GORGET	GREEDY	GROVET	**HADED**
GLIDER	**GOSSE**	**GREEN**	**GROWL**	SHADED
GLIDES	GOSSED	GREENS	GROWLS	**HADES**
GLIME	GOSSES	GREENY	GROWLY	SHADES
GLIMED	**GOUGE**	**GREES**	**GRUFF**	**HAFFS**
GLIMES	GOUGED	AGREES	GRUFFS	CHAFFS
GLINT	GOUGER	GREESE	GRUFFY	**HAFTS**
GLINTS	GOUGES	**GREET**	**GRUMP**	CHAFTS
GLINTY	**GOURD**	GREETE	GRUMPH	SHAFTS
GLITZ	GOURDE	GREETS	GRUMPS	**HAIKA**
GLITZY	GOURDS	**GREGE**	GRUMPY	HAIKAI
GLOBE	GOURDY	AGREGE	**GRYDE**	**HAINS**
GLOBED	**GOUTY**	**GRICE**	GRYDED	CHAINS
GLOBES	AGOUTY	GRICED	GRYDES	CHAIRS
GLOBI	**GOWAN**	GRICER	**GUANA**	HAIRST
GLOBIN	GOWANS	GRICES	IGUANA	**HAJIS**
GLOOM	GOWANY	**GRIDE**	GUANAS	BHAJIS
GLOOMS	**GRACE**	GRIDED	GUANAY	**HAKES**
GLOOMY	GRACED	GRIDES	**GUIDE**	SHAKES
GLOOP	GRACES	**GRIFF**	GUIDED	**HALAL**
GLOOPS	**GRADE**	GRIFFE	GUIDER	HALALA
GLOOPY	GRADED	GRIFFS	GUIDES	HALALS
GLOSS	GRADER	**GRILL**	**GUILE**	**HALED**
GLOSSA	GRADES	GRILLE	GUILED	SHALED
GLOSSY	**GRAIL**	GRILLS	GUILER	WHALED
GLOVE	GRAILE	**GRIME**	GUILES	**HALER**
GLOVED	GRAILS	GRIMED	**GUILT**	THALER
GLOVER	**GRAIN**	GRIMES	GUILTS	WHALER
GLOVES	GRAINE	**GRIPE**	GUILTY	HALERS
GLOZE	GRAINS	GRIPED	**GUIMP**	HALERU
GLOZED	GRAINY	GRIPER	GUIMPE	**HALES**
GLOZES	**GRAMP**	GRIPES	GUIMPS	SHALES
GLUTE	GRAMPA	GRIPEY	**GUISE**	WHALES
GLUTEI	GRAMPS	**GRISE**	AGUISE	HALEST
GLUTEN	**GRAND**	AGRISE	GUISED	**HALID**
GLUTES	GRANDE	GRISED	GUISER	HALIDE
GNARL	GRANDS	GRISES	GUISES	HALIDS
GNARLS	**GRAPE**	**GRIZE**	**GUNGE**	

HALLO	CHARDS	**HAVES**	**HEDER**	HERMAE
HALLOA	SHARDS	SHAVES	CHEDER	HERMAI
HALLOO	**HARED**	**HAWED**	HEDERA	**HERMS**
HALLOS	CHARED	CHAWED	HEDERS	THERMS
HALLOT	SHARED	SHAWED	**HEDGE**	**HERRY**
HALLOW	**HARES**	THAWED	HEDGED	CHERRY
HALMS	CHARES	**HAWKS**	HEDGER	SHERRY
SHALMS	PHARES	CHAWKS	HEDGES	WHERRY
HALSE	**SHARES**	**HAWMS**	**HEELS**	**HERSE**
HALSED	WHARES	SHAWMS	SHEELS	HERSED
HALSER	**HARKS**	**HAWSE**	WHEELS	HERSES
HALSES	CHARKS	HAWSED	**HEEZE**	**HERYE**
HALVA	SHARKS	HAWSER	PHEEZE	HERYED
HALVAH	**HARMS**	HAWSES	WHEEZE	HERYES
HALVAS	CHARMS	**HAZAN**	HEEZED	**HESPS**
HALVE	PHARMS	CHAZAN	HEEZES	THESPS
HALVED	THARMS	HAZANS	**HEFTE**	**HESTS**
HALVER	**HARNS**	**HAZEL**	HEFTED	CHESTS
HALVES	SHARNS	GHAZEL	HEFTER	**HETES**
HAMAL	**HAROS**	HAZELS	**HEFTS**	THETES
SHAMAL	PHAROS	**HEALS**	THEFTS	**HETHS**
HAMALS	**HARPS**	SHEALS	WHEFTS	CHETHS
HAMBA	SHARPS	WHEALS	**HEIGH**	KHETHS
SHAMBA	**HARPY**	**HEAPS**	HEIGHT	**HEUCH**
HAMED	SHARPY	CHEAPS	**HEIRS**	SHEUCH
SHAMED	**HARRY**	**HEAPY**	THEIRS	HEUCHS
HAMES	CHARRY	CHEAPY	**HEIST**	**HEUGH**
SHAMES	GHARRY	**HEARE**	THEIST	SHEUGH
HAMMY	**HARTS**	WHEARE	HEISTS	WHEUGH
CHAMMY	CHARTS	HEARER	**HELLS**	HEUGHS
SHAMMY	**HASTE**	HEARES	SHELLS	**HEWED**
WHAMMY	CHASTE	**HEARS**	**HELMS**	CHEWED
HAMZA	HASTED	SHEARS	WHELMS	SHEWED
HAMZAH	HASTEN	HEARSE	**HELPS**	THEWED
HAMZAS	HASTES	HEARSY	CHELPS	WHEWED
HANCE	**HATCH**	**HEART**	WHELPS	**HEWER**
CHANCE	THATCH	HEARTH	**HELVE**	CHEWER
HANCES	**HAUGH**	HEARTS	SHELVE	SHEWER
HANDS	SHAUGH	HEARTY	HELVED	HEWERS
SHANDS	HAUGHS	**HEAST**	HELVES	**HEXAD**
HANDY	HAUGHT	HEASTE	**HEMES**	HEXADE
SHANDY	**HAULM**	HEASTS	RHEMES	HEXADS
HANGS	HAULMS	**HEATH**	THEMES	**HEXES**
BHANGS	HAULMY	SHEATH	**HEMIC**	RHEXES
CHANGS	**HAULS**	HEATHS	CHEMIC	**HICKS**
PHANGS	SHAULS	HEATHY	**HEMIN**	CHICKS
THANGS	HAULST	**HEATS**	HEMINA	THICKS
WHANGS	**HAUNT**	CHEATS	HEMINS	**HIDED**
HANKS	CHAUNT	WHEATS	**HENCE**	CHIDED
CHANKS	HAUNTS	**HEAVE**	THENCE	**HIDER**
SHANKS	**HAUSE**	SHEAVE	WHENCE	CHIDER
THANKS	HAUSED	THEAVE	**HENDS**	HIDERS
HANSE	HAUSEN	HEAVED	SHENDS	**HIDES**
HANSEL	HAUSES	HEAVEN	**HERDS**	CHIDES
HANSES	**HAVEN**	HEAVER	SHERDS	**HIGHS**
HANTS	SHAVEN	HEAVES	**HERES**	THIGHS
CHANTS	HAVENS	**HEBES**	THERES	**HIGHT**
HAPPY	**HAVER**	THEBES	WHERES	HIGHTH
CHAPPY	SHAVER	**HECKS**	HERESY	HIGHTS
HARDS	HAVERS	CHECKS	**HERMA**	**HIJRA**

HIJRAH	**HOERS**	CHOOKS	SHOUTS	HYDRAE
HIJRAS	SHOERS	SHOOKS	**HOVED**	HYDRAS
HILLO	**HOISE**	**HOOLY**	SHOVED	**HYING**
HILLOA	HOISED	DHOOLY	**HOVEL**	SHYING
HILLOS	HOISES	**HOONS**	SHOVEL	**HYLES**
HILLS	**HOKED**	CHOONS	HOVELS	CHYLES
CHILLS	CHOKED	**HOOPS**	**HOVER**	**HYLIC**
SHILLS	**HOKES**	WHOOPS	SHOVER	PHYLIC
THILLS	CHOKES	**HOOSH**	HOVERS	**HYPHA**
HILLY	**HOKEY**	WHOOSH	**HOVES**	HYPHAE
CHILLY	CHOKEY	**HOOTS**	SHOVES	HYPHAL
WHILLY	**HOLDS**	BHOOTS	**HOWKS**	**IAMBI**
HINGE	AHOLDS	SHOOTS	CHOWKS	IAMBIC
WHINGE	**HOLED**	WHOOTS	**HOWLS**	**ICERS**
HINGED	THOLED	**HOOVE**	THOWLS	DICERS
HINGER	**HOLES**	HOOVED	**HUBBY**	RICERS
HINGES	DHOLES	HOOVEN	CHUBBY	**ICHED**
HINGS	THOLES	HOOVER	**HUCKS**	MICHED
THINGS	WHOLES	HOOVES	CHUCKS	NICHED
HINKY	**HOLLA**	**HOPPY**	SHUCKS	RICHED
CHINKY	CHOLLA	CHOPPY	**HUFFS**	**ICHES**
HINNY	HOLLAS	SHOPPY	CHUFFS	FICHES
SHINNY	**HOLLO**	**HORAL**	**HUFFY**	LICHES
WHINNY	HOLLOA	CHORAL	CHUFFY	MICHES
HINTS	HOLLOO	**HORDE**	**HUGGY**	NICHES
CHINTS	HOLLOS	HORDED	SHUGGY	RICHES
HIPPO	HOLLOW	HORDES	**HULES**	TICHES
SHIPPO	**HOLLY**	**HORNS**	SHULES	WICHES
HIPPOS	WHOLLY	THORNS	**HULLO**	**ICIER**
HIPPY	**HOMIE**	**HORNY**	HULLOA	DICIER
CHIPPY	HOMIER	THORNY	HULLOO	RICIER
WHIPPY	HOMIES	**HORSE**	HULLOS	**ICING**
HIRED	**HOMOS**	AHORSE	**HUMAN**	DICING
SHIRED	ZHOMOS	HORSED	HUMANE	RICING
HIRES	**HONED**	HORSES	HUMANS	TICING
SHIRES	PHONED	HORSEY	**HUMPS**	VICING
HISTS	**HONER**	**HORST**	CHUMPS	ICINGS
SHISTS	PHONER	HORSTE	THUMPS	**ICKER**
WHISTS	HONERS	HORSTS	WHUMPS	BICKER
HITCH	**HONES**	**HOSEN**	**HUMUS**	DICKER
HITCHY	PHONES	CHOSEN	HUMUSY	KICKER
HITHE	RHONES	**HOSES**	**HUNKS**	LICKER
HITHER	HONEST	CHOSES	CHUNKS	NICKER
HITHES	**HONEY**	**HOSTS**	THUNKS	PICKER
HIVED	PHONEY	GHOSTS	**HUNKY**	RICKER
CHIVED	HONEYS	**HOUGH**	CHUNKY	SICKER
HIVER	**HONGS**	CHOUGH	**HUNTS**	TICKER
SHIVER	THONGS	SHOUGH	SHUNTS	WICKER
HIVERS	**HONKY**	THOUGH	**HURLS**	YICKER
HIVES	SHONKY	HOUGHS	CHURLS	ICKERS
CHIVES	**HOOEY**	**HOUSE**	THURLS	**ICKLE**
SHIVES	PHOOEY	CHOUSE	**HURRA**	FICKLE
HOARS	HOOEYS	SHOUSE	DHURRA	MICKLE
HOARSE	**HOOFS**	HOUSED	HURRAH	NICKLE
HOCKS	CHOOFS	HOUSEL	HURRAS	PICKLE
CHOCKS	WHOOFS	HOUSER	HURRAY	RICKLE
SHOCKS	**HOOKA**	HOUSES	**HUZZA**	SICKLE
HODJA	HOOKAH	HOUSEY	HUZZAH	TICKLE
KHODJA	HOOKAS	**HOUTS**	HUZZAS	ICKLER
HODJAS	**HOOKS**	CHOUTS	**HYDRA**	**ICTAL**

RICTAL	IMBARK	LINGOT	TINTER	PISHES
ICTUS	IMBARS	INGOTS	WINTER	WISHES
RICTUS	**IMBED**	**INION**	INTERN	**ISLED**
IDANT	LIMBED	MINION	INTERS	AISLED
AIDANT	NIMBED	PINION	**INTRO**	MISLED
IDANTS	IMBEDS	INIONS	INTRON	**ISLES**
IDENT	**IMBUE**	**INKED**	INTROS	AISLES
BIDENT	IMBUED	DINKED	**INURE**	LISLES
EIDENT	IMBUES	FINKED	INURED	**ISSUE**
RIDENT	**IMPED**	JINKED	INURES	TISSUE
IDENTS	GIMPED	KINKED	**INWIT**	ISSUED
IDLED	LIMPED	LINKED	INWITH	ISSUER
SIDLED	PIMPED	OINKED	INWITS	ISSUES
IDLER	WIMPED	PINKED	**IODID**	**ISTLE**
SIDLER	IMPEDE	RINKED	IODIDE	MISTLE
IDLERS	**IMPIS**	TINKED	IODIDS	ISTLES
IDLES	IMPISH	WINKED	**IODIN**	**ITCHY**
SIDLES	**IMPLY**	ZINKED	IODINE	BITCHY
IDLEST	DIMPLY	**INKER**	IODINS	FITCHY
IDOLA	JIMPLY	DINKER	IONIC	HITCHY
EIDOLA	LIMPLY	JINKER	BIONIC	PITCHY
IGGED	PIMPLY	LINKER	PIONIC	TITCHY
BIGGED	SIMPLY	PINKER	IONICS	WITCHY
DIGGED	**INANE**	SINKER	**IOTAS**	**ITHER**
FIGGED	INANER	TINKER	BIOTAS	CITHER
GIGGED	INANES	WINKER	DIOTAS	DITHER
JIGGED	**INCUS**	INKERS	**IRADE**	EITHER
LIGGED	INCUSE	**INKLE**	TIRADE	HITHER
PIGGED	**INDIE**	KINKLE	IRADES	LITHER
RIGGED	KINDIE	TINKLE	**IRATE**	MITHER
TIGGED	YINDIE	WINKLE	PIRATE	NITHER
WIGGED	INDIES	INKLED	IRATER	TITHER
ZIGGED	**INDOL**	INKLES	**IRING**	WITHER
IKONS	INDOLE	**INNED**	AIRING	ZITHER
EIKONS	INDOLS	BINNED	FIRING	**IVIED**
ILEUM	**INDOW**	DINNED	HIRING	DIVIED
PILEUM	WINDOW	FINNED	MIRING	**IVIES**
ILEUS	INDOWS	GINNED	SIRING	CIVIES
PILEUS	**INDUE**	LINNED	TIRING	**IZARD**
ILIAL	INDUED	PINNED	VIRING	LIZARD
FILIAL	INDUES	SINNED	WIRING	RIZARD
ILIUM	**INFER**	TINNED	**IRKED**	VIZARD
CILIUM	INFERE	WINNED	DIRKED	WIZARD
MILIUM	INFERS	**INNER**	FIRKED	IZARDS
ILLER	**INGAN**	DINNER	KIRKED	**IZARS**
BILLER	FINGAN	FINNER	LIRKED	SIZARS
FILLER	INGANS	GINNER	YIRKED	**JACKS**
GILLER	**INGLE**	PINNER	**IRONE**	JACKSY
HILLER	BINGLE	SINNER	IRONED	**JALOP**
KILLER	DINGLE	TINNER	IRONER	JALOPS
MILLER	GINGLE	WINNER	IRONES	JALOPY
SILLER	JINGLE	INNERS	**IRONS**	**JAMBE**
TILLER	KINGLE	**INTEL**	GIRONS	JAMBED
WILLER	LINGLE	LINTEL	**ISHES**	JAMBEE
IMAGE	MINGLE	INTELS	BISHES	JAMBER
IMAGED	PINGLE	**INTER**	DISHES	JAMBES
IMAGER	SINGLE	HINTER	FISHES	**JAMBO**
IMAGES	TINGLE	LINTER	HISHES	JAMBOK
IMBAR	INGLES	MINTER	KISHES	**JAMBU**
MIMBAR	**INGOT**	SINTER	NISHES	JAMBUL

JAMBUS	**KAING**	SKIERS	**KROON**	**LAIRY**
JAPER	KAINGA	**KILLS**	KROONI	GLAIRY
JAPERS	**KALPA**	SKILLS	KROONS	**LAKED**
JAPERY	KALPAC	**KIMBO**	**KULAK**	FLAKED
JASPE	KALPAK	AKIMBO	KULAKI	SLAKED
JASPER	KALPAS	KIMBOS	KULAKS	**LAKER**
JASPES	**KAPUT**	**KINAS**	**KUTCH**	FLAKER
JAUNT	KAPUTT	KINASE	KUTCHA	SLAKER
JAUNTS	**KARAT**	**KINKS**	**KYBOS**	LAKERS
JAUNTY	KARATE	SKINKS	KYBOSH	**LAKES**
JEBEL	KARATS	**KITED**	**KYNDE**	FLAKES
DJEBEL	**KARTS**	SKITED	KYNDED	SLAKES
JEBELS	SKARTS	**KITES**	KYNDES	**LAKIN**
JEHAD	**KAVAS**	SKITES	**KYTES**	LAKING
JEHADI	KAVASS	**KITHE**	SKYTES	LAKINS
JEHADS	**KECKS**	KITHED	**KYTHE**	**LAMAS**
JEMBE	KECKSY	KITHES	KYTHED	LLAMAS
DJEMBE	**KEDGE**	**KLUGE**	KYTHES	ULAMAS
JEMBES	KEDGED	KLUGED	**LABIA**	**LAMED**
JESSE	KEDGER	KLUGES	LABIAL	BLAMED
JESSED	KEDGES	**KLUTZ**	**LABRA**	FLAMED
JESSES	**KEENS**	KLUTZY	LABRAL	LAMEDH
JIBBA	SKEENS	**KNACK**	**LACED**	LAMEDS
JIBBAH	**KEETS**	KNACKS	PLACED	**LAMER**
JIBBAS	SKEETS	KNACKY	**LACER**	BLAMER
JIHAD	**KELLS**	**KNARL**	PLACER	FLAMER
JIHADI	SKELLS	KNARLS	LACERS	**LAMES**
JIHADS	**KELLY**	KNARLY	**LACES**	BLAMES
JINNE	SKELLY	**KNAWE**	GLACES	CLAMES
JINNEE	**KELPS**	KNAWEL	PLACES	FLAMES
JINNI	SKELPS	KNAWES	**LACET**	LAMEST
DJINNI	**KENTE**	**KNIFE**	PLACET	**LAMIA**
JINNIS	KENTED	KNIFED	LACETS	LAMIAE
JINNS	KENTES	KNIFER	**LACKS**	LAMIAS
DJINNS	**KERNE**	KNIFES	BLACKS	**LAMMY**
JOTUN	KERNED	**KNIVE**	CLACKS	CLAMMY
JOTUNN	KERNEL	KNIVED	FLACKS	GLAMMY
JOTUNS	KERNES	KNIVES	PLACKS	**LAMPS**
JOULE	**KERRY**	**KNOLL**	SLACKS	CLAMPS
JOULED	SKERRY	KNOLLS	**LADED**	**LANCE**
JOULES	**KERVE**	KNOLLY	BLADED	ELANCE
JOWAR	KERVED	**KNOWE**	**LADER**	GLANCE
JOWARI	KERVES	KNOWER	BLADER	LANCED
JOWARS	**KETCH**	KNOWES	LADERS	LANCER
JUDGE	SKETCH	**KNURL**	**LADES**	LANCES
JUDGED	**KHAYA**	KNURLS	BLADES	LANCET
JUDGER	KHAYAL	KNURLY	CLADES	**LANCH**
JUDGES	KHAYAS	**KOBAN**	GLADES	BLANCH
JUICE	**KHEDA**	KOBANG	SLADES	FLANCH
JUICED	KHEDAH	KOBANS	**LADLE**	PLANCH
JUICER	KHEDAS	**KOFFS**	LADLED	**LANDE**
JUICES	**KIBBE**	SKOFFS	LADLER	LANDED
JUMAR	KIBBEH	**KORUN**	LADLES	LANDER
JUMARS	KIBBES	KORUNA	**LAIDS**	LANDES
JUMART	**KIBLA**	KORUNY	PLAIDS	**LANDS**
KAIKA	KIBLAH	**KRANS**	**LAIKS**	ALANDS
KAIKAI	KIBLAS	SKRANS	GLAIKS	BLANDS
KAIKAS	**KIDDY**	**KRONE**	**LAIRS**	ELANDS
KAILS	SKIDDY	KRONEN	FLAIRS	GLANDS
SKAILS	**KIERS**	KRONER	GLAIRS	**LANES**

FLANES	SLATER	**LAZAR**	SLEDGE	**LEUGH**
PLANES	**LATHE**	BLAZAR	LEDGED	CLEUGH
SLANES	LATHED	LAZARS	LEDGER	PLEUGH
LANKS	LATHEE	**LAZED**	LEDGES	**LEVEE**
BLANKS	LATHEN	BLAZED	**LEDGY**	LEVEED
CLANKS	LATHER	GLAZED	FLEDGY	LEVEES
FLANKS	LATHES	**LAZES**	**LEECH**	**LEVER**
PLANKS	**LATTE**	BLAZES	FLEECH	CLEVER
LANKY	LATTEN	GLAZES	SLEECH	LEVERS
CLANKY	LATTER	**LEACH**	**LEEKS**	**LEVES**
LANTS	LATTES	BLEACH	**LEEPS**	CLEVES
ALANTS	**LAUDS**	PLEACH	CLEEKS	**LEVIN**
PLANTS	BLAUDS	LEACHY	GLEEKS	ALEVIN
SLANTS	**LAUGH**	**LEADS**	SLEEKS	LEVINS
LAPSE	LAUGHS	PLEADS	**LEEPS**	**LEVIS**
ELAPSE	LAUGHY	**LEAKS**	BLEEPS	CLEVIS
LAPSED	**LAURA**	BLEAKS	CLEEPS	**LEXES**
LAPSER	LAURAE	**LEAKY**	SLEEPS	FLEXES
LAPSES	LAURAS	BLEAKY	**LEERS**	ILEXES
LARES	**LAVAS**	**LEAMS**	FLEERS	PLEXES
BLARES	FLAVAS	FLEAMS	**LEETS**	ULEXES
FLARES	LAVASH	GLEAMS	FLEETS	**LIBER**
GLARES	**LAVED**	**LEANS**	GLEETS	LIBERO
LARGE	SLAVED	CLEANS	SLEETS	LIBERS
LARGEN	**LAVER**	GLEANS	**LEFTE**	**LIBRA**
LARGER	CLAVER	**LEARE**	LEFTER	LIBRAE
LARGES	SLAVER	LEARED	**LEFTS**	LIBRAS
LARUM	LAVERS	LEARES	CLEFTS	**LICIT**
ALARUM	CLAVES	**LEARN**	**LEGGE**	ELICIT
LARUMS	SLAVES	LEARNS	ALEGGE	**LICKS**
LARVA	**LAWED**	LEARNT	LEGGED	CLICKS
LARVAE	BLAWED	**LEARS**	LEGGER	FLICKS
LARVAL	CLAWED	BLEARS	LEGGES	KLICKS
LARVAS	FLAWED	CLEARS	**LEGIT**	SLICKS
LASER	**LAWER**	**LEARY**	ELEGIT	**LIEGE**
FLASER	CLAWER	BLEARY	LEGITS	LIEGER
LASERS	**LAWIN**	**LEASE**	**LEMES**	LIEGES
LASSI	LAWINE	PLEASE	FLEMES	**LIENS**
LASSIE	LAWING	LEASED	**LEMON**	ALIENS
LASSIS	LAWINS	LEASER	LEMONS	**LIERS**
LASTS	FLAWNS	LEASES	**LEMONY**	FLIERS
BLASTS	**LAWNS**	**LEATS**	LENDS	PLIERS
CLASTS	FLAWNS	BLEATS	BLENDS	**LIEVE**
LATCH	**LAXES**	CLEATS	**LENSE**	SLIEVE
CLATCH	FLAXES	PLEATS	FLENSE	LIEVER
KLATCH	LAXEST	**LEAVE**	LENSED	LIEVES
SLATCH	**LAYED**	CLEAVE	LENSES	**LIFTS**
LATED	ALAYED	GLEAVE	**LENTI**	CLIFTS
ALATED	CLAYED	SLEAVE	LENTIC	GLIFTS
ELATED	FLAYED	LEAVED	LENTIL	**LIGAN**
PLATED	PLAYED	LEAVEN	**LENTO**	LIGAND
SLATED	SLAYED	LEAVER	LENTOR	LIGANS
LATEN	**LAYER**	LEAVES	LENTOS	**LIGGE**
PLATEN	FLAYER	**LEAZE**	**LETCH**	LIGGED
LATENS	PLAYER	SLEAZE	FLETCH	LIGGER
LATENT	SLAYER	LEAZES	**LETHE**	LIGGES
LATER	LAYERS	**LEDGE**	LETHEE	**LIGHT**
BLATER	**LAYIN**	FLEDGE	LETHES	ALIGHT
ELATER	LAYING	GLEDGE	**LEUCH**	BLIGHT
PLATER	LAYINS	PLEDGE	CLEUCH	FLIGHT

PLIGHT	**LININ**	GLOAMS	**LONGA**	SLOPPY
SLIGHT	LINING	**LOANS**	LONGAN	**LORAL**
LIGHTS	LININS	SLOANS	LONGAS	FLORAL
LIKES	**LINKS**	**LOATH**	**LONGE**	**LOREL**
GLIKES	BLINKS	LOATHE	PLONGE	LORELS
LIKEST	CLINKS	LOATHY	LONGED	**LORES**
LIKIN	PLINKS	**LOAVE**	LONGER	BLORES
LIKING	SLINKS	LOAVED	LONGES	**LORIC**
LIKINS	**LINKY**	LOAVES	**LONGS**	LORICA
LIMAX	PLINKY	**LOBBY**	FLONGS	LORICS
CLIMAX	SLINKY	BLOBBY	KLONGS	**LOSED**
LIMBI	**LINTS**	GLOBBY	PLONGS	CLOSED
LIMBIC	CLINTS	SLOBBY	**LOOEY**	**LOSER**
LIMBS	ELINTS	**LOBED**	BLOOEY	CLOSER
CLIMBS	FLINTS	GLOBED	FLOOEY	LOSERS
LIMED	GLINTS	**LOBES**	LOOEYS	**LOSES**
GLIMED	**LINTY**	GLOBES	**LOOFA**	CLOSES
SLIMED	FLINTY	LOBOSE	LOOFAH	ULOSES
LIMES	GLINTY	**LOBOS**	LOOFAS	**LOSSY**
CLIMES	**LIPAS**	LOBUS	**LOOFS**	FLOSSY
GLIMES	LIPASE	GLOBUS	KLOOFS	GLOSSY
SLIMES	**LIPID**	**LOCAL**	**LOOIE**	**LOTAS**
LIMEY	LIPIDE	LOCALE	BLOOIE	FLOTAS
BLIMEY	LIPIDS	LOCALS	FLOOIE	**LOTES**
LIMEYS	**LIPPY**	**LOCKS**	LOOIES	CLOTES
LIMPS	FLIPPY	BLOCKS	**LOOKS**	FLOTES
BLIMPS	SLIPPY	CLOCKS	BLOOKS	**LOTTE**
FLIMPS	**LIROT**	FLOCKS	PLOOKS	LOTTED
LIMPSY	LIROTH	**LOCUS**	**LOOMS**	LOTTER
LINCH	**LISKS**	LOCUST	BLOOMS	LOTTES
CLINCH	FLISKS	**LODGE**	GLOOMS	**LOTTO**
FLINCH	GLISKS	PLODGE	SLOOMS	BLOTTO
LINDS	**LITED**	LODGED	**LOOPS**	LOTTOS
BLINDS	FLITED	LODGER	BLOOPS	**LOUGH**
LINED	**LITES**	LODGES	CLOOPS	CLOUGH
ALINED	BLITES	**LOGAN**	GLOOPS	PLOUGH
LINEN	ELITES	SLOGAN	SLOOPS	SLOUGH
LINENS	FLITES	LOGANS	**LOOPY**	LOUGHS
LINENY	**LITHE**	**LOGES**	GLOOPY	**LOUPE**
LINER	BLITHE	ELOGES	**LOOSE**	LOUPED
ALINER	LITHED	**LOGGY**	LOOSED	LOUPEN
LINERS	LITHER	CLOGGY	LOOSEN	LOUPES
LINES	LITHES	**LOGIA**	LOOSER	**LOURE**
ALINES	**LIVED**	ALOGIA	LOOSES	LOURED
CLINES	SLIVED	**LOGIE**	**LOOTS**	LOURES
LINGA	LIVEDO	LOGIER	CLOOTS	**LOURS**
LINGAM	**LIVEN**	LOGIES	SLOOTS	CLOURS
LINGAS	SLIVEN	**LOIDS**	**LOPED**	FLOURS
LINGO	LIVENS	SLOIDS	ELOPED	**LOURY**
OLINGO	**LIVER**	**LOINS**	SLOPED	FLOURY
LINGOT	OLIVER	ALOINS	**LOPER**	**LOUSE**
LINGS	SLIVER	ELOINS	ELOPER	BLOUSE
BLINGS	LIVERS	**LOIPE**	SLOPER	FLOUSE
CLINGS	LIVERY	LOIPEN	LOPERS	LOUSED
FLINGS	**LIVES**	**LOKES**	**LOPES**	LOUSER
PLINGS	OLIVES	BLOKES	ELOPES	LOUSES
SLINGS	SLIVES	CLOKES	SLOPES	**LOUSY**
LINGY	LIVEST	**LONER**	**LOPPY**	BLOUSY
BLINGY	**LOAMS**	CLONER	FLOPPY	**LOUTS**
CLINGY	CLOAMS	LONERS	GLOPPY	CLOUTS

FLOUTS	SLUMMY	GLUTES	**MANAT**	**MAUVE**
GLOUTS	**LUMPS**	**LUXES**	MANATI	MAUVER
LOVED	CLUMPS	FLUXES	MANATS	MAUVES
GLOVED	FLUMPS	**LYING**	MANATU	**MAXIM**
LOVER	GLUMPS	CLYING	**MANDI**	MAXIMA
CLOVER	PLUMPS	FLYING	MANDIR	MAXIMS
GLOVER	SLUMPS	PLYING	MANDIS	**MAZED**
PLOVER	**LUMPY**	LYINGS	**MANGA**	AMAZED
LOVERS	CLUMPY	**LYSIN**	MANGAL	**MAZES**
LOVES	GLUMPY	LYSINE	MANGAS	AMAZES
CLOVES	PLUMPY	LYSING	**MANGE**	SMAZES
GLOVES	SLUMPY	LYSINS	MANGED	**MEANE**
LOWED	**LUNAR**	**LYTED**	MANGEL	MEANED
BLOWED	LUNARS	FLYTED	MANGER	MEANER
FLOWED	LUNARY	**LYTES**	MANGES	MEANES
GLOWED	**LUNCH**	FLYTES	MANGEY	**MEASE**
PLOWED	CLUNCH	**LYTTA**	**MANIA**	MEASED
SLOWED	GLUNCH	LYTTAE	MANIAC	MEASES
LOWER	**LUNGE**	LYTTAS	MANIAS	**MEATH**
BLOWER	BLUNGE	**MACHE**	**MANNA**	SMEATH
FLOWER	PLUNGE	MACHER	MANNAN	MEATHE
GLOWER	LUNGED	MACHES	MANNAS	MEATHS
PLOWER	LUNGEE	**MACKS**	**MARLE**	**MEDIA**
SLOWER	LUNGER	SMACKS	MARLED	MEDIAD
LOWERS	LUNGES	**MACLE**	MARLES	MEDIAE
LOWERY	**LUNGI**	MACLED	**MARMS**	MEDIAL
LOWES	LUNGIE	MACLES	SMARMS	MEDIAN
LOWEST	LUNGIS	**MACRO**	**MARSH**	MEDIAS
LOWLY	**LUNKS**	MACRON	MARSHY	**MEDIC**
SLOWLY	BLUNKS	MACROS	**MARTS**	MEDICK
LOWNE	CLUNKS	**MADAM**	SMARTS	MEDICO
LOWNED	FLUNKS	MADAME	**MASSE**	MEDICS
LOWNES	PLUNKS	MADAMS	MASSED	**MEDLE**
LOWNS	**LUNTS**	**MAGES**	MASSES	MEDLED
CLOWNS	BLUNTS	IMAGES	**MATCH**	MEDLES
LOWSE	**LUPIN**	**MAIKS**	SMATCH	MEDLEY
BLOWSE	LUPINE	SMAIKS	**MATED**	**MEERS**
LOWSED	LUPINS	**MAILE**	AMATED	AMEERS
LOWSER	**LURES**	MAILED	**MATES**	EMEERS
LOWSES	ALURES	MAILER	AMATES	**MELIC**
LUCKS	**LURRY**	MAILES	**MATIN**	MELICK
CLUCKS	BLURRY	**MAILS**	MATING	MELICS
PLUCKS	FLURRY	EMAILS	MATINS	**MELLS**
LUCKY	PLURRY	**MALIC**	MATLOW	SMELLS
CLUCKY	SLURRY	MALICE	**MATTE**	**MELTS**
PLUCKY	**LUSHY**	**MALIS**	MATTED	SMELTS
LUDES	FLUSHY	MALISM	MATTER	**MENDS**
BLUDES	PLUSHY	MALIST	MATTES	AMENDS
ELUDES	SLUSHY	**MALLS**	**MATZA**	EMENDS
LUFFS	**LUTEA**	SMALLS	MATZAH	**MENED**
BLUFFS	LUTEAL	**MALMS**	MATZAS	AMENED
FLUFFS	**LUTED**	SMALMS	**MATZO**	OMENED
PLUFFS	ELUTED	**MALMY**	MATZOH	**MENGE**
SLUFFS	FLUTED	SMALMY	MATZOS	MENGED
LUGED	**LUTER**	**MALTS**	MATZOT	MENGES
KLUGED	FLUTER	SMALTS	**MAUND**	**MENSA**
LUGES	LUTERS	**MAMMA**	MAUNDS	MENSAE
KLUGES	**LUTES**	MAMMAE	MAUNDY	MENSAL
LUMMY	ELUTES	MAMMAL	**MAUTS**	MENSAS
PLUMMY	FLUTES	MAMMAS	AMAUTS	**MENSE**

MENSED	MIDGES	SMITER	SMOORS	AMOVES
MENSES	MIDGET	MITERS	**MOOTS**	EMOVES
MENTA	**MIDST**	**MITES**	SMOOTS	**MOYLE**
AMENTA	AMIDST	SMITES	MOOVE	SMOYLE
OMENTA	MIDSTS	**MITRE**	AMOOVE	MOYLED
MENTAL	**MIEVE**	MITRED	MOOVED	MOYLES
MENTO	MIEVED	MITRES	MOOVES	**MUCKS**
MENTOR	MIEVES	**MOBLE**	MOPER	AMUCKS
MENTOS	**MIGHT**	MOBLED	MOPERS	**MUDGE**
MEREL	SMIGHT	MOBLES	MOPERY	SMUDGE
MERELL	MIGHTS	**MOCKS**	**MORAL**	MUDGED
MERELS	MIGHTY	SMOCKS	AMORAL	MUDGER
MERELY	**MILER**	**MODER**	MORALE	MUDGES
MERES	SMILER	MODERN	MORALL	**MUGGA**
MEREST	MILERS	MODERS	MORALS	MUGGAR
MERGE	**MILES**	**MODES**	**MORES**	MUGGAS
EMERGE	SMILES	MODEST	SMORES	**MULED**
MERGED	**MILLE**	**MODGE**	**MORNE**	EMULED
MERGEE	MILLED	MODGED	MORNED	**MULES**
MERGER	MILLER	MODGES	MORNES	EMULES
MERGES	MILLES	**MOGGY**	**MORPH**	**MULLA**
MERIS	MILLET	SMOGGY	MORPHO	MULLAH
MERISM	**MILOR**	**MOIRA**	MORPHS	MULLAS
MERKS	MILORD	MOIRAI	**MORRO**	**MUNGE**
SMERKS	MILORS	**MOIST**	MORROS	EMUNGE
MERSE	**MINCE**	MOISTS	MORROW	MUNGED
EMERSE	MINCED	**MOKES**	**MORSE**	MUNGES
MERSES	MINCER	SMOKES	MORSEL	**MURED**
MESES	MINCES	**MOKOS**	MORSES	EMURED
EMESES	**MINES**	SMOKOS	**MOTED**	**MURES**
TMESES	AMINES	**MOLES**	EMOTED	EMURES
MESTO	IMINES	AMOLES	**MOTES**	**MURRA**
MESTOM	**MINGE**	MOLEST	EMOTES	MURRAM
METHO	MINGED	**MOLLA**	**MOTET**	MURRAS
METHOD	MINGER	MOLLAH	MOTETS	MURRAY
METHOS	MINGES	MOLLAS	MOTETT	**MURRE**
METIC	**MINIM**	**MOLTS**	**MOTOR**	MURREE
EMETIC	MINIMA	SMOLTS	MOTORS	MURREN
METICS	MINIMS	**MONER**	MOTORY	MURRES
METRE	**MINIS**	MONERA	**MOUCH**	MURREY
METRED	MINISH	MONGO	SMOUCH	**MURRI**
METRES	**MIRIN**	MONGOE	**MOULD**	MURRIN
MEUSE	MIRING	MONGOL	MOULDS	MURRIS
SMEUSE	MIRINS	MONGOS	MOULDY	**MURRY**
MEUSED	**MIRKS**	MONGS	**MOUNT**	SMURRY
MEUSES	SMIRKS	MONGST	AMOUNT	**MUSCA**
MIASM	**MIRKY**	**MONIE**	MOUNTS	MUSCAE
MIASMA	SMIRKY	MONIED	**MOUSE**	MUSCAT
MIASMS	**MISER**	MONIES	SMOUSE	**MUSED**
MICHE	MISERE	**MONOS**	MOUSED	AMUSED
MICHED	MISERS	MONOSY	MOUSER	**MUSER**
MICHER	MISERY	**MONTE**	MOUSES	AMUSER
MICHES	**MISES**	MONTEM	MOUSEY	MUSERS
MICRO	AMISES	MONTES	**MOUTH**	**MUSES**
MICRON	**MISSA**	**MOOCH**	MOUTHS	AMUSES
MICROS	MISSAE	SMOOCH	MOUTHY	**MUSIC**
MIDDY	MISSAL	**MOOLA**	**MOVED**	AMUSIC
SMIDDY	MISSAW	MOOLAH	AMOVED	MUSICK
MIDGE	MISSAY	MOOLAS	EMOVED	MUSICS
SMIDGE	**MITER**	**MOORS**	**MOVES**	**MUSSE**

MUSSED	**NEATH**	NITERS	NOTCHY	DOATER
MUSSEL	ANEATH	NITERY	**NOULD**	OATERS
MUSSES	SNEATH	**NITES**	NOULDE	**OAVES**
MUTCH	UNEATH	UNITES	NOWED	LOAVES
SMUTCH	**NECKS**	**NITRO**	SNOWED	SOAVES
MUTES	SNECKS	NITROS	UNOWED	**OBANG**
MUTEST	**NEESE**	NITROX	**NUBBY**	GOBANG
MUTIS	NEESED	NITRY	KNUBBY	KOBANG
MUTISM	NEESES	NITRYL	SNUBBY	OBANGS
MYTHI	**NEEZE**	**NKOSI**	**NUCHA**	**OBELI**
MYTHIC	SNEEZE	INKOSI	NUCHAE	OBELIA
NACRE	NEEZED	NKOSIS	NUCHAL	**OBESE**
NACRED	NEEZES	**NOBBY**	**NUDES**	OBESER
NACRES	**NELLY**	KNOBBY	NUDEST	**OBEYS**
NAGGY	SNELLY	SNOBBY	**NUDGE**	MOBEYS
KNAGGY	**NEMAS**	**NOBLE**	SNUDGE	**OBIAS**
SNAGGY	ENEMAS	NOBLER	NUDGED	COBIAS
NAHAL	**NEROL**	NOBLES	NUDGER	**OBITS**
NAHALS	NEROLI	**NOCKS**	NUDGES	OOBITS
NAILS	NEROLS	KNOCKS	**NUFFS**	**OBOES**
SNAILS	**NERTS**	**NODAL**	SNUFFS	GOBOES
NAIVE	INERTS	ANODAL	**NULLA**	HOBOES
NAIVER	**NERVE**	ENODAL	NULLAH	**OBOLE**
NAIVES	ENERVE	**NODES**	NULLAS	SOBOLE
NAKED	NERVED	ANODES	**NURLS**	OBOLES
SNAKED	NERVER	NOINT	KNURLS	**OBOLS**
NALLA	NERVES	ANOINT	**NURRS**	BOBOLS
NALLAH	**NEWED**	NOINTS	KNURRS	**OCCAM**
NALLAS	ENEWED	**NOISE**	**NURSE**	OCCAMS
NAMMA	**NEWEL**	NOISED	NURSED	OCCAMY
GNAMMA	NEWELL	NOISES	NURSER	**OCHER**
NANAS	NEWELS	**NOLES**	NURSES	TOCHER
ANANAS	**NICHE**	ANOLES	**NYALA**	OCHERS
JNANAS	NICHED	**NOLLS**	INYALA	OCHERY
NAPPE	NICHER	KNOLLS	NYALAS	**OCHES**
NAPPED	NICHES	**NOMAD**	**NYMPH**	BOCHES
NAPPER	**NICKS**	NOMADE	NYMPHA	COCHES
NAPPES	KNICKS	NOMADS	NYMPHO	ROCHES
NAPPY	SNICKS	NOMADY	NYMPHS	**OCHRE**
SNAPPY	**NIDED**	**NOMES**	**OAKED**	OCHREA
NARES	SNIDED	GNOMES	BOAKED	OCHRED
SNARES	**NIDES**	**NOMIC**	SOAKED	OCHRES
NARKS	SNIDES	ANOMIC	**OAKEN**	OCHREY
SNARKS	**NIFES**	GNOMIC	SOAKEN	**OCKER**
NARKY	KNIFES	**NOOKS**	**OAKER**	COCKER
SNARKY	**NIFFS**	SNOOKS	SOAKER	DOCKER
NASHI	SNIFFS	**NOOPS**	OAKERS	HOCKER
NASHIS	**NIFFY**	SNOOPS	**OARED**	LOCKER
NATCH	SNIFFY	**NOOSE**	HOARED	MOCKER
SNATCH	**NIFTY**	NOOSED	ROARED	ROCKER
NATES	SNIFTY	NOOSER	SOARED	OCKERS
ENATES	**NIGHT**	NOOSES	**OASTS**	**OCREA**
NATTY	ANIGHT	**NORMA**	BOASTS	OCREAE
GNATTY	KNIGHT	NORMAL	COASTS	**OCTAN**
NAVES	NIGHTS	NORMAN	HOASTS	OCTANE
KNAVES	NIGHTY	NORMAS	ROASTS	OCTANS
NEAPS	**NIPPY**	**NOSES**	TOASTS	OCTANT
SNEAPS	SNIPPY	ENOSES	**OATER**	**OCTET**
NEARS	**NITER**	GNOSES	BOATER	OCTETS
ANEARS	UNITER	**NOTCH**	COATER	OCTETT

OCULI	SOILED	SOLLER	WONNED	BORALS
LOCULI	TOILED	TOLLER	**ONTIC**	CORALS
ODALS	**OILER**	OLLERS	PONTIC	GORALS
MODALS	BOILER	**OLLIE**	**OOHED**	MORALS
ODDER	COILER	COLLIE	BOOHED	**ORANG**
CODDER	MOILER	MOLLIE	POOHED	ORANGE
DODDER	TOILER	TOLLIE	**OOPED**	ORANGS
FODDER	OILERS	OLLIES	COOPED	ORANGY
MODDER	OILERY	**OLOGY**	GOOPED	**ORANT**
NODDER	**OINKS**	OOLOGY	HOOPED	VORANT
ODISM	BOINKS	**OLPES**	LOOPED	ORANTS
IODISM	**OINTS**	GOLPES	MOOPED	**ORATE**
ODISMS	JOINTS	**OMASA**	POOPED	BORATE
ODIST	NOINTS	OMASAL	ROOPED	LORATE
CODIST	POINTS	**OMBER**	SOOPED	ORATED
MODIST	**OKAYS**	BOMBER	**OORIE**	ORATES
ODISTS	TOKAYS	COMBER	COORIE	**ORBED**
ODIUM	**OKRAS**	SOMBER	GOORIE	SORBED
PODIUM	KOKRAS	OMBERS	TOORIE	**ORBIT**
SODIUM	**OLDEN**	**OMBRE**	OORIER	ORBITA
ODIUMS	BOLDEN	HOMBRE	**OOSES**	ORBITS
OFFED	GOLDEN	SOMBRE	BOOSES	ORBITY
BOFFED	HOLDEN	OMBRES	GOOSES	**ORCIN**
COFFED	OLDENS	**OMBUS**	LOOSES	ORCINE
DOFFED	**OLDER**	KOMBUS	NOOSES	ORCINS
GOFFED	BOLDER	**OMERS**	ROOSES	**ORDER**
OFFER	COLDER	COMERS	WOOSES	BORDER
COFFER	FOLDER	GOMERS	**OOZED**	CORDER
DOFFER	GOLDER	HOMERS	BOOZED	ORDERS
GOFFER	HOLDER	VOMERS	**OOZES**	**ORGAN**
OFFERS	MOLDER	**OMITS**	BOOZES	MORGAN
OFFIE	POLDER	VOMITS	COOZES	ORGANA
MOFFIE	SOLDER	**ONCES**	**OPALS**	ORGANS
OFFIES	**OLDIE**	BONCES	COPALS	**ORGIA**
OFTEN	COLDIE	NONCES	NOPALS	GORGIA
SOFTEN	OLDIES	PONCES	**OPENS**	ORGIAC
OFTER	**OLEIN**	SONCES	COPENS	ORGIAS
LOFTER	SOLEIN	**ONELY**	**OPERA**	**ORGUE**
SOFTER	OLEINE	LONELY	POPERA	MORGUE
OGEES	OLEINS	**ONERS**	OPERAS	ORGUES
YOGEES	**OLENT**	BONERS	**OPINE**	**ORMER**
OGGIN	DOLENT	GONERS	OPINED	DORMER
HOGGIN	**OLIOS**	HONERS	OPINES	FORMER
NOGGIN	FOLIOS	LONERS	**OPING**	WORMER
OGGINS	POLIOS	TONERS	COPING	ORMERS
OGLED	**OLIVE**	ZONERS	DOPING	**ORPIN**
BOGLED	SOLIVE	**ONION**	HOPING	ORPINE
OGLES	OLIVER	GONION	LOPING	ORPINS
BOGLES	OLIVES	RONION	MOPING	**ORRIS**
FOGLES	OLIVET	ONIONS	OOPING	MORRIS
OHING	**OLLAS**	ONIONY	ROPING	**OSIER**
HOHING	HOLLAS	**ONIUM**	TOPING	COSIER
OOHING	MOLLAS	CONIUM	**OPPOS**	HOSIER
OILED	**OLLER**	GONIUM	OPPOSE	NOSIER
BOILED	GOLLER	IONIUM	**OPTER**	OOSIER
COILED	HOLLER	ONIUMS	COPTER	POSIER
DOILED	JOLLER	**ONNED**	OPTERS	ROSIER
FOILED	LOLLER	CONNED	**ORACH**	OSIERS
MOILED	POLLER	DONNED	ORACHE	OSIERY
ROILED	ROLLER	FONNED	**ORALS**	**OSMIC**

COSMIC	OUNCES	DOVENS	LOWRIE	SPALLS
OSMICS	**OUNDY**	WOVENS	OWRIER	**PANDA**
OSMOL	WOUNDY	**OVERS**	**OXERS**	PANDAR
OSMOLE	**OUPED**	COVERS	BOXERS	PANDAS
OSMOLS	COUPED	DOVERS	**OXIES**	**PANED**
OSTIA	LOUPED	HOVERS	DOXIES	SPANED
OSTIAL	MOUPED	LOVERS	FOXIES	**PANES**
OTARY	POUPED	MOVERS	MOXIES	SPANES
NOTARY	ROUPED	ROVERS	**OYERS**	**PANGS**
ROTARY	SOUPED	**OVERT**	FOYERS	SPANGS
VOTARY	**OURIE**	COVERT	TOYERS	**PANIC**
OTHER	COURIE	**OVINE**	**OZZIE**	PANICK
BOTHER	LOURIE	BOVINE	MOZZIE	PANICS
FOTHER	POURIE	OVINES	OZZIES	**PANNE**
LOTHER	TOURIE	**OWING**	**PACED**	PANNED
MOTHER	OURIER	BOWING	SPACED	PANNER
NOTHER	**OUSEL**	COWING	**PACER**	PANNES
POTHER	HOUSEL	DOWING	SPACER	**PANTO**
ROTHER	OUSELS	JOWING	PACERS	PANTON
TOTHER	**OUSTS**	LOWING	**PACES**	PANTOS
OTHERS	JOUSTS	MOWING	SPACES	**PAPER**
OTTAR	MOUSTS	ROWING	**PACEY**	PAPERS
COTTAR	ROUSTS	SOWING	SPACEY	PAPERY
OTTARS	**OUTBY**	TOWING	**PACHA**	**PARCH**
OTTER	OUTBYE	VOWING	PACHAK	EPARCH
COTTER	**OUTED**	WOWING	PACHAS	**PARDI**
DOTTER	DOUTED	YOWING	**PACTS**	PARDIE
HOTTER	HOUTED	**OWLED**	EPACTS	**PARED**
JOTTER	LOUTED	BOWLED	**PAEON**	SPARED
LOTTER	POUTED	COWLED	PAEONS	**PARER**
POTTER	ROUTED	FOWLED	PAEONY	SPARER
ROTTER	TOUTED	GOWLED	**PAGOD**	PARERA
TOTTER	**OUTER**	HOWLED	PAGODA	PARERS
OTTERS	COUTER	JOWLED	PAGODS	**PARES**
OTTOS	DOUTER	SOWLED	**PAILS**	SPARES
LOTTOS	FOUTER	YOWLED	SPAILS	**PAREV**
MOTTOS	MOUTER	**OWLER**	**PAINS**	PAREVE
POTTOS	POUTER	BOWLER	SPAINS	**PARGE**
OUBIT	ROUTER	FOWLER	**PAINT**	SPARGE
WOUBIT	SOUTER	HOWLER	PAINTS	PARGED
OUBITS	TOUTER	JOWLER	PAINTY	PARGES
OUENS	OUTERS	YOWLER	**PAIRE**	PARGET
ROUENS	**OUTRE**	OWLERS	PAIRED	**PARIS**
OUGHT	FOUTRE	OWLERY	PAIRER	PARISH
BOUGHT	OUTRED	**OWLET**	PAIRES	**PARKI**
DOUGHT	**OUTRO**	HOWLET	**PAISA**	PARKIE
FOUGHT	OUTROS	OWLETS	PAISAN	PARKIN
MOUGHT	OUTROW	**OWNED**	PAISAS	PARKIS
NOUGHT	**OVARY**	BOWNED	**PALEA**	**PARKS**
ROUGHT	COVARY	DOWNED	PALEAE	SPARKS
SOUGHT	**OVATE**	GOWNED	PALEAL	**PARKY**
OUGHTS	BOVATE	LOWNED	**PALED**	SPARKY
OUMAS	NOVATE	**OWNER**	OPALED	**PARLE**
DOUMAS	OVATED	DOWNER	**PALES**	PARLED
LOUMAS	OVATES	OWNERS	SPALES	PARLES
OUNCE	**OVELS**	**OWRES**	PALEST	PARLEY
BOUNCE	HOVELS	HOWRES	**PALLA**	**PAROL**
JOUNCE	NOVELS	POWRES	PALLAE	PAROLE
POUNCE	**OVENS**	**OWRIE**	PALLAH	PAROLS
ROUNCE	COVENS	COWRIE	**PALLS**	**PARRA**

PARRAL	SPAVIN	PEEVER	PETARS	**PIECE**
PARRAS	PAVING	PEEVES	PETARY	APIECE
PARRY	PAVINS	**PEISE**	**PETIT**	PIECED
SPARRY	**PAVIS**	SPEISE	PETITE	PIECEN
PARSE	PAVISE	PEISED	**PETRE**	PIECER
SPARSE	**PAWLS**	PEISES	PETREL	PIECES
PARSEC	SPAWLS	**PEIZE**	PETRES	**PIERS**
PARSED	**PAWNS**	PEIZED	**PEYSE**	SPIERS
PARSER	SPAWNS	PEIZES	PEYSED	PIERST
PARSES	**PAYED**	**PEKIN**	PEYSES	**PIGHT**
PARTI	SPAYED	PEKINS	**PHANG**	SPIGHT
PARTIM	**PEACE**	**PELLS**	UPHANG	YPIGHT
PARTIS	PEACED	SPELLS	PHANGS	PIGHTS
PARTS	PEACES	**PELTA**	**PHARM**	**PIKED**
SPARTS	**PEACH**	PELTAE	PHARMA	SPIKED
PASES	PEACHY	PELTAS	PHARMS	**PIKER**
UPASES	**PEAKS**	**PELTS**	**PHASE**	SPIKER
PASSE	SPEAKS	SPELTS	PHASED	PIKERS
PASSED	**PEALS**	**PENCE**	PHASES	**PIKES**
PASSEE	SPEALS	SPENCE	**PHEER**	SPIKES
PASSEL	**PEANS**	PENCEL	PHEERE	**PIKEY**
PASSER	SPEANS	PENCES	PHEERS	SPIKEY
PASSES	**PEARL**	**PENDS**	**PHENE**	PIKEYS
PASTE	PEARLS	SPENDS	SPHENE	**PILAF**
PASTED	PEARLY	UPENDS	PHENES	PILAFF
PASTEL	**PEARS**	**PENED**	**PHESE**	PILAFS
PASTER	SPEARS	OPENED	PHESED	**PILED**
PASTES	PEARST	**PENNA**	PHESES	SPILED
PATCH	**PEASE**	PENNAE	**PHOCA**	**PILES**
PATCHY	PEASED	PENNAL	PHOCAE	SPILES
PATEN	PEASEN	**PENNE**	PHOCAS	**PILLS**
PATENS	PEASES	PENNED	**PHONE**	SPILLS
PATENT	**PEATS**	PENNER	PHONED	**PINAS**
PATER	SPEATS	PENNES	PHONER	SPINAS
PATERA	**PEAZE**	**PENNI**	PHONES	**PINED**
PATERS	PEAZED	PENNIA	PHONEY	OPINED
PATES	PEAZES	PENNIS	**PHONO**	SPINED
SPATES	**PECKE**	**PERCE**	PHONON	**PINES**
PATIN	PECKED	PERCED	PHONOS	OPINES
PATINA	PECKER	PERCEN	**PHONY**	SPINES
PATINE	PECKES	PERCES	APHONY	**PINKS**
PATINS	**PECKS**	**PERDU**	**PHOTO**	SPINKS
PATKA	SPECKS	EPERDU	PHOTOG	**PINNA**
PATKAS	**PECKY**	PERDUE	PHOTON	PINNAE
PATTE	SPECKY	PERDUS	PHOTOS	PINNAL
PATTED	**PEDAL**	**PERIS**	**PHYLA**	PINNAS
PATTEE	PEDALO	PERISH	PHYLAE	**PINNY**
PATTEN	PEDALS	**PERMS**	PHYLAR	SPINNY
PATTER	**PEECE**	SPERMS	**PIANI**	**PINTO**
PATTES	PEECES	**PERSE**	PIANIC	SPINTO
PAULS	**PEELS**	SPERSE	**PICAL**	PINTOS
SPAULS	SPEELS	PERSES	APICAL	**PIQUE**
PAUSE	**PEEPE**	**PERST**	EPICAL	PIQUED
PAUSED	PEEPED	SPERST	**PICAS**	PIQUES
PAUSER	PEEPER	**PERVE**	SPICAS	PIQUET
PAUSES	PEEPES	PERVED	**PICKS**	**PIROG**
PAVAN	**PEERS**	PERVES	SPICKS	PIROGI
PAVANE	SPEERS	**PETAR**	**PICOT**	**PITCH**
PAVANE	**PEEVE**	PETARA	PICOTE	PITCHY
PAVANS	PEEVED	PETARD	PICOTS	**PIUMS**
PAVIN				

OPIUMS	PLONKS	PONCES	**POUPE**	PRIEFE
PIZZA	PLONKY	PONCEY	POUPED	PRIEFS
PIZZAS	**PLOOK**	**PONGY**	POUPES	**PRIER**
PIZZAZ	UPLOOK	SPONGY	**POUTS**	SPRIER
PLACE	PLOOKS	**POOFS**	SPOUTS	PRIERS
PLACED	PLOOKY	SPOOFS	**POUTY**	**PRIES**
PLACER	**PLOUK**	**POOFY**	SPOUTY	PRIEST
PLACES	PLOUKS	SPOOFY	**POWRE**	**PRIGS**
PLACET	PLOUKY	**POOJA**	POWRED	SPRIGS
PLAID	**PLUCK**	POOJAH	POWRES	**PRIMA**
UPLAID	PLUCKS	POOJAS	**POYSE**	PRIMAL
PLAIDS	PLUCKY	**POOKS**	POYSED	PRIMAS
PLAIN	**PLUFF**	SPOOKS	**POOLS**	**PRIME**
PLAINS	PLUFFS	**POOLS**	POYSES	PRIMED
PLAINT	PLUFFY	SPOOLS	**PRANG**	PRIMER
PLANE	**PLUME**	**POONS**	SPRANG	PRIMES
PLANED	PLUMED	SPOONS	PRANGS	**PRINT**
PLANER	PLUMES	**POOTS**	**PRANK**	SPRINT
PLANES	**PLUMP**	SPOOTS	PRANKS	PRINTS
PLANET	PLUMPS	**PORAL**	PRANKY	**PRIOR**
PLANT	PLUMPY	SPORAL	**PRATE**	PRIORS
PLANTA	**PLUNK**	**PORED**	UPRATE	PRIORY
PLANTS	PLUNKS	SPORED	PRATED	**PRISE**
PLASH	PLUNKY	**PORES**	PRATER	EPRISE
SPLASH	**PLUSH**	SPORES	PRATES	UPRISE
PLASHY	PLUSHY	**PORGE**	**PRATS**	PRISED
PLASM	**POACH**	PORGED	SPRATS	PRISER
PLASMA	POACHY	PORGES	**PRAYS**	PRISES
PLASMS	**PODAL**	**PORKS**	SPRAYS	**PRISM**
PLAST	APODAL	SPORKS	**PREED**	PRISMS
YPLAST	**PODDY**	**PORTA**	SPREED	PRISMY
PLASTE	SPODDY	PORTAL	**PREES**	**PRISS**
PLATE	**PODIA**	PORTAS	SPREES	PRISSY
PLATED	PODIAL	**PORTS**	**PREIF**	**PRIZE**
PLATEN	**POINT**	SPORTS	PREIFE	PRIZED
PLATER	POINTE	**PORTY**	PREIFS	PRIZER
PLATES	POINTS	SPORTY	**PRENT**	PRIZES
PLATS	POINTY	**POSES**	SPRENT	**PROBE**
SPLATS	**POISE**	EPOSES	PRENTS	PROBED
PLAYS	POISED	**POSSE**	**PRESE**	PROBER
SPLAYS	POISER	POSSED	PRESES	PROBES
UPLAYS	POISES	POSSER	PRESET	**PRODS**
PLEAD	**POKED**	POSSES	**PREST**	SPRODS
UPLEAD	SPOKED	POSSET	UPREST	**PROGS**
PLEADS	**POKES**	**POTCH**	PRESTO	SPROGS
PLEAS	SPOKES	POTCHE	PRESTS	**PROIN**
PLEASE	**POKIE**	**POTIN**	**PREVE**	PROINE
PLICA	POKIER	POTING	PREVED	PROINS
PLICAE	POKIES	POTINS	PREVES	**PROKE**
PLICAL	**POLEY**	**POTTY**	**PRICE**	PROKED
PLINK	POLEYN	SPOTTY	PRICED	PROKER
UPLINK	POLEYS	**POUCH**	PRICER	PROKES
PLINKS	**POLIS**	POUCHY	PRICES	**PROLE**
PLINKY	POLISH	**POUFF**	PRICEY	PROLED
PLONG	**POLYP**	POUFFE	**PRICK**	PROLEG
PLONGD	POLYPE	POUFFS	PRICKS	PROLER
PLONGE	POLYPI	POUFFY	PRICKY	PROLES
PLONGS	POLYPS	**POULP**	**PRIDE**	**PROLL**
PLONK	**PONCE**	POULPE	PRIDED	UPROLL
PLONKO	PONCED	POULPS	PRIDES	PROLLS

PRONE	PUNCES	**QUANT**	EQUIPS	**RAFFS**
PRONER	**PUNCH**	EQUANT	**QUIRE**	DRAFFS
PRONES	PUNCHY	QUANTA	SQUIRE	GRAFFS
PRONG	**PUNKA**	QUANTS	QUIRED	**RAFTS**
SPRONG	PUNKAH	**QUARE**	QUIRES	CRAFTS
PRONGS	PUNKAS	SQUARE	**QUIRK**	DRAFTS
PROSE	**PUNKS**	QUARER	QUIRKS	GRAFTS
UPROSE	SPUNKS	QUARK	QUIRKY	KRAFTS
PROSED	**PUNKY**	SQUARK	**QUIRT**	**RAGEE**
PROSER	SPUNKY	QUARKS	SQUIRT	DRAGEE
PROSES	**PURDA**	**QUART**	QUIRTS	RAGEES
PROTO	PURDAH	QUARTE	**QUITE**	**RAGGY**
PROTON	PURDAS	QUARTO	QUITED	BRAGGY
PROVE	**PUREE**	QUARTS	QUITES	CRAGGY
PROVED	PUREED	QUARTZ	**QUITS**	DRAGGY
PROVEN	PUREES	**QUASH**	SQUITS	**RAGUS**
PROVER	**PURES**	SQUASH	**QUOTE**	TRAGUS
PROVES	PUREST	**QUATE**	QUOTED	**RAIDS**
PROYN	**PURGE**	EQUATE	QUOTER	BRAIDS
PROYNE	SPURGE	**QUATS**	QUOTES	**RAIKS**
PROYNS	PURGED	SQUATS	**QUOTH**	**RAILE**
PRUNE	PURGER	**QUEEN**	QUOTHA	GRAILE
PRUNED	PURGES	QUEENS	**QUYTE**	RAILED
PRUNER	**PURIN**	QUEENY	QUYTED	RAILER
PRUNES	PURINE	**QUEME**	QUYTES	RAILES
PRUTA	PURING	QUEMED	**RABAT**	**RAILS**
PRUTAH	PURINS	QUEMES	RABATO	BRAILS
PRYER	**PURIS**	**QUEUE**	RABATS	DRAILS
SPRYER	PURISM	QUEUED	**RABBI**	FRAILS
PRYERS	PURIST	QUEUER	RABBIN	GRAILS
PRYSE	**PURSE**	QUEUES	RABBIS	TRAILS
PRYSED	PURSED	**QUICH**	RABBIT	**RAINE**
PRYSES	PURSER	QUICHE	**RABIC**	GRAINE
PSEUD	PURSES	**QUICK**	ARABIC	RAINED
PSEUDO	PURSEW	QUICKS	**RABIS**	RAINES
PSEUDS	**PUSES**	QUICKY	ARABIS	**RAINS**
PSYCH	OPUSES	**QUIDS**	**RACED**	BRAINS
PSYCHE	**PUSLE**	EQUIDS	BRACED	DRAINS
PSYCHO	PUSLED	SQUIDS	GRACED	GRAINS
PSYCHS	PUSLES	**QUIFF**	TRACED	TRAINS
PUCES	PUSLEY	SQUIFF	**RACER**	**RAINY**
PUCEST	**PUTTI**	QUIFFS	BRACER	BRAINY
PUDDY	PUTTIE	**QUILL**	TRACER	GRAINY
SPUDDY	**PYRES**	SQUILL	RACERS	**RAIRD**
PUERS	SPYRES	QUILLS	**RACES**	BRAIRD
SPUERS	**QUACK**	**QUINE**	BRACES	RAIRDS
PUGGY	QUACKS	EQUINE	GRACES	**RAISE**
SPUGGY	QUACKY	QUINES	TRACES	ARAISE
PULES	**QUADS**	**QUINO**	**RACHE**	BRAISE
SPULES	SQUADS	QUINOA	ORACHE	FRAISE
PULIS	**QUAIL**	QUINOL	RACHES	PRAISE
EPULIS	SQUAIL	QUINOS	RACHET	RAISED
PULSE	QUAILS	**QUINS**	**RACKS**	RAISER
PULSED	**QUAKE**	QUINSY	BRACKS	RAISES
PULSER	QUAKED	**QUINT**	CRACKS	**RAITS**
PULSES	QUAKER	SQUINT	TRACKS	KRAITS
PULUS	QUAKES	QUINTA	WRACKS	TRAITS
OPULUS	**QUALM**	QUINTE	**RADGE**	**RAKED**
PUNCE	QUALMS	QUINTS	RADGER	BRAKED
PUNCED	QUALMY	**QUIPS**	RADGES	

CRAKED	CRAPED	CRATES	DRAYED	CREAMY
RAKER	DRAPED	GRATES	FRAYED	DREAMY
RAKERS	GRAPED	ORATES	GRAYED	**REARM**
RAKERY	TRAPED	PRATES	PRAYED	PREARM
RAKES	**RAPER**	URATES	**RAYLE**	REARMS
BRAKES	DRAPER	**RATHE**	GRAYLE	**REARS**
CRAKES	RAPERS	RATHER	RAYLED	DREARS
DRAKES	**RAPES**	**RATHS**	RAYLES	**REAST**
RAKIS	CRAPES	WRATHS	RAYLET	BREAST
RAKISH	DRAPES	**RATIO**	**RAYNE**	REASTS
RALLY	GRAPES	RATION	TRAYNE	REASTY
ORALLY	TRAPES	RATIOS	RAYNES	**REATE**
RALLYE	**RAPPE**	**RATOO**	**RAYON**	CREATE
RAMPS	FRAPPE	RATOON	CRAYON	REATES
CRAMPS	RAPPED	RATOOS	RAYONS	**REAVE**
GRAMPS	RAPPEE	**RATTY**	**RAZED**	GREAVE
TRAMPS	RAPPEL	BRATTY	BRAZED	REAVED
RANAS	RAPPEN	**RAVED**	CRAZED	REAVER
PRANAS	RAPPER	BRAVED	GRAZED	REAVES
RANCE	RAPPES	CRAVED	**RAZEE**	**REBEC**
PRANCE	**RARES**	GRAVED	RAZEED	REBECK
TRANCE	CRARES	**RAVEL**	RAZEES	REBECS
RANCED	URARES	GRAVEL	**RAZER**	**REBID**
RANCEL	RAREST	TRAVEL	BRAZER	PREBID
RANCES	**RASED**	RAVELS	GRAZER	REBIDS
RANCH	ERASED	**RAVEN**	RAZERS	**REBIT**
BRANCH	**RASER**	CRAVEN	**RAZES**	REBITE
CRANCH	ERASER	GRAVEN	BRAZES	**REBUY**
RANCHO	RASERS	RAVENS	CRAZES	PREBUY
RANDS	**RASES**	**RAVER**	GRAZES	REBUYS
BRANDS	BRASES	BRAVER	**REACH**	**RECAL**
GRANDS	CRASES	CRAVER	AREACH	RECALL
RANDY	ERASES	GRAVER	BREACH	RECALS
BRANDY	PRASES	RAVERS	CREACH	**RECCE**
RANGE	URASES	**RAVES**	PREACH	RECCED
GRANGE	**RASPS**	BRAVES	**REACT**	RECCES
ORANGE	GRASPS	CRAVES	PREACT	**RECIT**
RANGED	**RASSE**	GRAVES	REACTS	RECITE
RANGER	WRASSE	TRAVES	**READS**	RECITS
RANGES	RASSES	**RAVIN**	AREADS	**RECKS**
RANGY	**RATAN**	RAVINE	BREADS	DRECKS
ORANGY	RATANS	RAVING	DREADS	TRECKS
RANKE	RATANY	RAVINS	OREADS	WRECKS
RANKED	**RATCH**	**RAWER**	TREADS	**RECTA**
RANKER	CRATCH	BRAWER	**READY**	RECTAL
RANKES	FRATCH	DRAWER	BREADY	**RECTO**
RANKS	**RATED**	**RAWIN**	**REAKS**	RECTOR
BRANKS	CRATED	RAWING	BREAKS	RECTOS
CRANKS	GRATED	RAWINS	CREAKS	**RECUR**
FRANKS	ORATED	**RAWLY**	FREAKS	RECURE
PRANKS	PRATED	BRAWLY	WREAKS	RECURS
TRANKS	**RATER**	CRAWLY	**REAME**	**RECUT**
RANTS	CRATER	DRAWLY	REAMED	PRECUT
BRANTS	FRATER	**RAWNS**	REAMER	RECUTS
CRANTS	GRATER	BRAWNS	REAMES	**REDED**
DRANTS	IRATER	PRAWNS	**REAMS**	BREDED
GRANTS	KRATER	**RAXES**	BREAMS	**REDES**
ORANTS	PRATER	PRAXES	CREAMS	AREDES
TRANTS	RATERS	**RAYED**	DREAMS	BREDES
RAPED	**RATES**	BRAYED	**REAMY**	**REDIA**

UREDIA	**REFIX**	RENTES	**RETIE**	GRICER
REDIAE	PREFIX	**RENTS**	RETIED	PRICER
REDIAL	**REGAL**	BRENTS	RETIES	RICERS
REDIAS	REGALE	PRENTS	**RETRO**	**RICES**
REDIP	REGALS	**REPAY**	RETROD	DRICES
REDIPS	**REGAR**	PREPAY	RETROS	GRICES
REDIPT	REGARD	REPAYS	**REUSE**	PRICES
REDON	REGARS	**REPIN**	REUSED	TRICES
REDONE	**REGES**	REPINE	REUSES	**RICEY**
REDONS	REGEST	REPINS	**REVET**	PRICEY
REDOS	**REGMA**	**REPLA**	BREVET	**RICHT**
CREDOS	BREGMA	REPLAN	TREVET	BRICHT
UREDOS	**REGNA**	REPLAY	REVETS	FRICHT
REDRY	REGNAL	**REPOS**	**REVIE**	RICHTS
PREDRY	**REGOS**	REPOSE	REVIED	**RICIN**
REDYE	GREGOS	REPOST	REVIES	RICING
REDYED	**REIFS**	**RESAW**	REVIEW	RICINS
REDYES	PREIFS	RESAWN	**REVUE**	**RICKS**
REECH	**REINS**	RESAWS	PREVUE	BRICKS
BREECH	GREINS	**RESEE**	REVUES	CRICKS
REECHO	**REIST**	RESEED	**REWED**	ERICKS
REECHY	BREIST	RESEEK	BREWED	PRICKS
REEDE	REISTS	RESEEN	CREWED	TRICKS
REEDED	**REIVE**	RESEES	GREWED	WRICKS
REEDEN	REIVED	**RESES**	REWEDS	**RIDER**
REEDER	REIVER	GRESES	**REWIN**	ARIDER
REEDES	REIVES	PRESES	REWIND	RIDERS
REEDS	**RELIC**	URESES	REWINS	**RIDES**
BREEDS	RELICS	**RESET**	**REXES**	BRIDES
CREEDS	RELICT	PRESET	GREXES	GRIDES
GREEDS	**RELIE**	RESETS	PREXES	IRIDES
REEDY	RELIED	**RESEW**	**RHEUM**	PRIDES
GREEDY	RELIEF	RESEWN	RHEUMS	**RIDGE**
REEKS	RELIER	RESEWS	RHEUMY	BRIDGE
BREEKS	RELIES	**RESID**	**RHOMB**	FRIDGE
CREEKS	**REMAN**	RESIDE	RHOMBI	RIDGED
REEKY	PREMAN	RESIDS	RHOMBS	RIDGEL
CREEKY	REMAND	**RESIN**	**RHUMB**	RIDGER
REELS	REMANS	RESINS	RHUMBA	RIDGES
CREELS	**REMEN**	RESINY	RHUMBS	**RIELS**
REENS	PREMEN	**RESIT**	**RHYME**	ARIELS
GREENS	REMEND	RESITE	RHYMED	ORIELS
PREENS	REMENS	RESITS	RHYMER	**RIEVE**
TREENS	**REMIT**	**RESOW**	RHYMES	GRIEVE
REEST	FREMIT	RESOWN	**RIADS**	PRIEVE
BREEST	REMITS	RESOWS	TRIADS	RIEVER
FREEST	**REMIX**	**RESTO**	**RIALS**	RIEVES
REESTS	PREMIX	PRESTO	PRIALS	**RIFFS**
REESTY	REMIXT	RESTOS	TRIALS	GRIFFS
REEVE	**RENDS**	**RESTS**	URIALS	**RIFLE**
PREEVE	TRENDS	CRESTS	**RIANT**	TRIFLE
REEVED	**RENNE**	PRESTS	CRIANT	RIFLED
REEVES	BRENNE	TRESTS	**RIBES**	RIFLER
REFEL	FRENNE	WRESTS	BRIBES	RIFLES
REFELL	RENNED	**RETAX**	TRIBES	**RIFTE**
REFELS	RENNES	PRETAX	**RICED**	RIFTED
REFELT	RENNET	**RETCH**	GRICED	**RIFTS**
REFER	**RENTE**	WRETCH	PRICED	DRIFTS
PREFER	RENTED	**RETIA**	TRICED	GRIFTS
REFERS	RENTER	RETIAL	**RICER**	**RIFTY**

DRIFTY	RINSER	**ROACH**	**ROLLS**	**ROPER**
RIGHT	RINSES	BROACH	DROLLS	GROPER
ARIGHT	**RIOTS**	**ROADS**	PROLLS	PROPER
BRIGHT	GRIOTS	BROADS	TROLLS	ROPERS
FRIGHT	**RIPED**	TROADS	**ROMAL**	ROPERY
WRIGHT	GRIPED	**ROANS**	BROMAL	**ROPES**
RIGHTO	**RIPER**	GROANS	ROMALS	GROPES
RIGHTS	GRIPER	**ROATE**	**ROMAN**	TROPES
RIGHTY	RIPERS	ROATED	ROMANO	**ROQUE**
RIGID	**RIPES**	ROATES	ROMANS	ROQUES
FRIGID	CRIPES	**ROBED**	**ROMPS**	ROQUET
RIGIDS	GRIPES	PROBED	TROMPS	**RORES**
RIGOL	TRIPES	**ROBES**	**RONDE**	CRORES
RIGOLL	RIPEST	PROBES	RONDEL	PRORES
RIGOLS	**RISEN**	**ROBIN**	RONDES	**RORIE**
RILED	ARISEN	ROBING	**RONES**	RORIER
ARILED	**RISER**	ROBINS	CRONES	**ROSED**
RILLE	PRISER	**ROBOT**	DRONES	PROSED
GRILLE	RISERS	ROBOTS	GRONES	**ROSES**
RILLED	**RISES**	**ROCKS**	IRONES	BROSES
RILLES	ARISES	BROCKS	PRONES	EROSES
RILLET	BRISES	CROCKS	TRONES	PROSES
RILLS	CRISES	FROCKS	**RONNE**	UROSES
BRILLS	FRISES	TROCKS	RONNEL	**ROSET**
DRILLS	GRISES	**RODED**	**RONTS**	GROSET
FRILLS	IRISES	ERODED	FRONTS	ROSETS
GRILLS	KRISES	**RODES**	**ROODS**	ROSETY
KRILLS	PRISES	ERODES	BROODS	**ROSIN**
PRILLS	**RISKS**	TRODES	**ROOFS**	ROSING
TRILLS	BRISKS	**ROGER**	GROOFS	ROSINS
RIMED	FRISKS	DROGER	PROOFS	ROSINY
CRIMED	**RISKY**	ROGERS	**ROOKS**	**ROSIT**
GRIMED	BRISKY	**ROGUE**	BROOKS	PROSIT
PRIMED	FRISKY	BROGUE	CROOKS	ROSITS
RIMER	**RISPS**	DROGUE	DROOKS	**ROSTS**
PRIMER	CRISPS	ROGUED	**ROOMS**	FROSTS
TRIMER	**RITES**	ROGUER	BROOMS	**ROTAL**
RIMERS	FRITES	ROGUES	GROOMS	CROTAL
RIMES	TRITES	**ROILS**	VROOMS	**ROTCH**
CRIMES	URITES	BROILS	**ROOMY**	CROTCH
GRIMES	WRITES	DROILS	BROOMY	ROTCHE
PRIMES	**RITTS**	**ROINS**	**ROONS**	**ROTON**
RIMUS	BRITTS	GROINS	CROONS	CROTON
PRIMUS	FRITTS	PROINS	KROONS	PROTON
RINDS	**RIVEL**	**ROKED**	**ROOPS**	ROTONS
GRINDS	DRIVEL	BROKED	DROOPS	**ROTTE**
RINES	RIVELS	GROKED	TROOPS	ROTTED
BRINES	**RIVEN**	PROKED	**ROOPY**	ROTTEN
CRINES	DRIVEN	TROKED	DROOPY	ROTTER
TRINES	**RIVER**	**ROKER**	**ROOSE**	ROTTES
URINES	DRIVER	BROKER	BROOSE	**ROUGE**
RINGS	RIVERS	PROKER	ROOSED	ROUGED
BRINGS	RIVERY	ROKERS	ROOSER	ROUGES
WRINGS	**RIVES**	**ROKES**	ROOSES	**ROUGH**
RINKS	DRIVES	BROKES	**ROOTS**	BROUGH
BRINKS	**RIVET**	PROKES	WROOTS	GROUGH
DRINKS	GRIVET	TROKES	ROOTSY	TROUGH
PRINKS	PRIVET	**ROLES**	**ROPED**	ROUGHS
RINSE	TRIVET	DROLES	GROPED	ROUGHT
RINSED	RIVETS	PROLES	TROPED	ROUGHY

ROULE	**ROWER**	**RUMEN**	**RYMME**	**SAMBA**
TROULE	CROWER	CRUMEN	RYMMED	TSAMBA
ROULES	GROWER	RUMENS	RYMMES	SAMBAL
ROULS	PROWER	**RUMES**	**SABER**	SAMBAR
PROULS	ROWERS	BRUMES	SABERS	SAMBAS
ROUND	**ROWND**	GRUMES	**SABIN**	**SAMEK**
AROUND	DROWND	**RUMLY**	SABINE	SAMEKH
GROUND	ROWNDS	DRUMLY	SABINS	SAMEKS
ROUNDS	**ROWTH**	GRUMLY	**SABLE**	**SAMEL**
ROUPS	GROWTH	**RUMMY**	USABLE	SAMELY
CROUPS	TROWTH	CRUMMY	SABLED	**SANES**
GROUPS	ROWTHS	DRUMMY	SABLES	SANEST
ROUPY	**ROYNE**	**RUMPS**	**SABRE**	**SANGA**
CROUPY	GROYNE	CRUMPS	SABRED	SANGAR
GROUPY	PROYNE	FRUMPS	SABRES	SANGAS
ROUSE	ROYNED	GRUMPS	**SACRA**	**SANGH**
AROUSE	ROYNES	TRUMPS	SACRAL	SANGHA
CROUSE	**RUBBY**	**RUMPY**	**SADES**	SANGHS
GROUSE	GRUBBY	CRUMPY	TSADES	**SANSA**
TROUSE	**RUBIN**	FRUMPY	**SADIS**	SANSAR
ROUSED	RUBINE	GRUMPY	TSADIS	SANSAS
ROUSER	RUBINS	**RUNCH**	SADISM	**SANTO**
ROUSES	**RUBUS**	BRUNCH	SADIST	SANTOL
ROUTE	URUBUS	CRUNCH	**SAFES**	SANTON
CROUTE	**RUCHE**	**RUNED**	SAFEST	SANTOS
ROUTED	RUCHED	PRUNED	**SAGER**	**SARIN**
ROUTER	RUCHES	**RUNES**	USAGER	SARING
ROUTES	**RUCKS**	PRUNES	**SAGES**	SARINS
ROUTH	CRUCKS	**RUNTS**	USAGES	**SAROD**
DROUTH	TRUCKS	BRUNTS	SAGEST	SARODE
ROUTHS	**RUDDY**	GRUNTS	**SAHIB**	SARODS
ROUTS	CRUDDY	PRUNTS	SAHIBA	**SASIN**
CROUTS	**RUDER**	**RUPIA**	SAHIBS	SASINE
GROUTS	CRUDER	RUPIAH	**SAIDS**	SASINS
TROUTS	RUDERY	RUPIAS	SAIDST	**SASSE**
ROVED	**RUDES**	**RURAL**	**SAINE**	SASSED
DROVED	CRUDES	CRURAL	SAINED	SASSES
GROVED	RUDEST	RURALS	**SAITH**	**SATIN**
PROVED	**RUFFE**	**RUSES**	SAITHE	ISATIN
ROVEN	TRUFFE	CRUSES	SAITHS	SATING
PROVEN	RUFFED	DRUSES	**SALAD**	SATINS
ROVER	RUFFES	URUSES	SALADE	SATINY
DROVER	**RUFFS**	**RUSHY**	SALADS	**SATYR**
PROVER	GRUFFS	BRUSHY	**SALLE**	SATYRA
TROVER	RUGAL	**RUSSE**	SALLEE	SATYRS
ROVERS	**RUGAL**	RUSSEL	SALLES	**SAUCE**
ROVES	FRUGAL	RUSSET	SALLET	SAUCED
DROVES	**RUGGY**	**RUSTS**	**SALPA**	SAUCER
GROVES	DRUGGY	BRUSTS	SALPAE	SAUCES
PROVES	**RUING**	CRUSTS	SALPAS	**SAUGH**
TROVES	GRUING	FRUSTS	**SALUE**	SAUGHS
ROWDY	TRUING	TRUSTS	SALUED	SAUGHY
CROWDY	RUINGS	**RUSTY**	SALUES	**SAUTE**
ROWED	**RUINS**	CRUSTY	**SALVE**	SAUTED
BROWED	BRUINS	TRUSTY	SALVED	SAUTES
CROWED	**RULES**	**RUTHS**	SALVER	**SAVIN**
TROWED	BRULES	TRUTHS	SALVES	SAVINE
ROWEL	**RUMAL**	**RYKES**	**SALVO**	SAVING
TROWEL	BRUMAL	GRYKES	SALVOR	SAVINS
ROWELS	RUMALS	TRYKES	SALVOS	**SAVOR**

SAVORS	SCHMOS	SCULPS	SENSES	SHAMAN
SAVORY	**SCHUL**	SCULPT	**SENTE**	SHAMAS
SCALA	SCHULN	**SCURF**	SENTED	**SHAME**
SCALAE	SCHULS	SCURFS	**SEPTA**	ASHAME
SCALAR	**SCOPA**	SCURFY	SEPTAL	SHAMED
SCALE	SCOPAE	**SCUSE**	**SERAI**	SHAMER
SCALED	**SCOPE**	SCUSED	SERAIL	SHAMES
SCALER	SCOPED	SCUSES	SERAIS	**SHAND**
SCALES	SCOPES	**SCUTA**	**SERES**	SHANDS
SCALL	**SCORE**	SCUTAL	SEREST	SHANDY
SCALLS	SCORED	**SCUZZ**	**SERGE**	**SHAPE**
SCALLY	SCORER	SCUZZY	SERGED	SHAPED
SCAMP	SCORES	**SEAME**	SERGER	SHAPEN
SCAMPI	**SCOTS**	SEAMED	SERGES	SHAPER
SCAMPS	ASCOTS	SEAMEN	**SERIN**	SHAPES
SCANT	ESCOTS	SEAMER	SERINE	**SHARE**
SCANTS	**SCOUT**	SEAMES	SERING	SHARED
SCANTY	SCOUTH	**SEARE**	SERINS	SHARER
SCAPE	SCOUTS	SEARED	**SERRA**	SHARES
ESCAPE	**SCRAM**	SEARER	SERRAE	**SHARN**
SCAPED	SCRAMB	**SEASE**	SERRAN	SHARNS
SCAPES	SCRAMS	SEASED	SERRAS	SHARNY
SCARE	**SCRAP**	SEASES	**SERRE**	**SHARP**
SCARED	SCRAPE	**SEAZE**	SERRED	SHARPS
SCARER	SCRAPS	SEAZED	SERRES	SHARPY
SCARES	**SCRAW**	SEAZES	**SERVE**	**SHAVE**
SCAREY	SCRAWL	**SEDGE**	SERVED	SHAVED
SCARP	SCRAWM	SEDGED	SERVER	SHAVEN
ESCARP	SCRAWP	SEDGES	SERVES	SHAVER
SCARPA	SCRAWS	**SEGUE**	**SEVER**	SHAVES
SCARPH	**SCRAY**	SEGUED	SEVERE	**SHAWS**
SCARPS	SCRAYE	SEGUES	SEVERS	PSHAWS
SCARS	SCRAYS	**SEINE**	SEVERY	**SHEAF**
ESCARS	**SCREE**	SEINED	**SEWIN**	SHEAFS
OSCARS	SCREED	SEINER	SEWING	SHEAFY
SCART	SCREEN	SEINES	SEWINS	**SHEEN**
SCARTH	SCREES	**SEISE**	**SEXTO**	SHEENS
SCARTS	SCREET	SEISED	SEXTON	SHEENY
SCATH	**SCREW**	SEISER	SEXTOS	**SHEEP**
SCATHE	SCREWS	SEISES	**SHACK**	SHEEPO
SCATHS	SCREWY	**SEITY**	SHACKO	SHEEPY
SCATT	**SCRIM**	ASEITY	SHACKS	**SHEET**
SCATTS	SCRIMP	**SEIZE**	**SHADE**	SHEETS
SCATTY	SCRIMS	SEIZED	SHADED	SHEETY
SCAUR	**SCRIP**	SEIZER	SHADER	**SHEIK**
SCAURS	SCRIPS	SEIZES	SHADES	SHEIKH
SCAURY	SCRIPT	**SELLA**	**SHAKE**	SHEIKS
SCEAT	**SCROW**	SELLAE	ASHAKE	**SHELF**
SCEATT	ESCROW	SELLAS	SHAKED	SHELFS
SCEND	SCROWL	**SELLE**	SHAKEN	SHELFY
ASCEND	SCROWS	SELLER	SHAKER	**SHELL**
SCENDS	**SCRUM**	SELLES	SHAKES	SHELLS
SCENE	SCRUMP	**SEMEE**	**SHALE**	SHELLY
SCENED	SCRUMS	SEMEED	SHALED	**SHEND**
SCENES	**SCUDO**	**SENOR**	SHALES	YSHEND
SCENT	ESCUDO	SENORA	SHALEY	SHENDS
ASCENT	**SCULL**	SENORS	**SHALL**	**SHENT**
SCENTS	SCULLE	**SENSE**	SHALLI	YSHENT
SCHMO	SCULLS	SENSED	**SHAMA**	**SHETS**
SCHMOE	**SCULP**	SENSEI	SHAMAL	ASHETS

SHIEL	SHOVED	SITHEN	SLANGS	SLOPES
SHIELD	SHOVEL	SITHES	SLANGY	**SLOSH**
SHIELS	SHOVER	**SKANK**	**SLANT**	ASLOSH
SHIER	SHOVES	SKANKS	ASLANT	SLOSHY
ASHIER	**SHREW**	SKANKY	SLANTS	**SLOVE**
SHIERS	SHREWD	**SKART**	SLANTY	SLOVEN
SHIES	SHREWS	SKARTH	**SLATE**	**SLUBB**
SHIEST	**SHROW**	SKARTS	SLATED	SLUBBS
SHIFT	SHROWD	**SKATE**	SLATER	SLUBBY
SHIFTS	SHROWS	SKATED	SLATES	**SLUMP**
SHIFTY	**SHTUM**	SKATER	SLATEY	SLUMPS
SHINE	SHTUMM	SKATES	**SLAVE**	SLUMPY
ASHINE	**SHULE**	**SKEAN**	SLAVED	**SLURP**
SHINED	SHULED	SKEANE	SLAVER	SLURPS
SHINER	SHULES	SKEANS	SLAVES	SLURPY
SHINES	**SHUTE**	**SKEAR**	SLAVEY	**SLUSH**
SHIRE	SHUTED	SKEARS	**SLEEK**	SLUSHY
SHIRED	SHUTES	SKEARY	SLEEKS	**SMALM**
SHIRES	**SIDES**	**SKEER**	SLEEKY	SMALMS
SHIRR	ASIDES	SKEERS	**SLEEP**	SMALMY
SHIRRA	**SIDLE**	SKEERY	ASLEEP	**SMALT**
SHIRRS	SIDLED	**SKELL**	SLEEPS	SMALTI
SHIRT	SIDLER	SKELLS	SLEEPY	SMALTO
SHIRTS	SIDLES	SKELLY	**SLEET**	SMALTS
SHIRTY	**SIEGE**	**SKERS**	SLEETS	**SMARM**
SHISH	SIEGED	ASKERS	SLEETY	SMARMS
SHISHA	SIEGER	ESKERS	**SLICE**	SMARMY
SHITE	SIEGES	**SKIES**	SLICED	**SMART**
SHITED	**SIEVE**	ESKIES	SLICER	SMARTS
SHITES	SIEVED	**SKILL**	SLICES	SMARTY
SHIVA	SIEVES	SKILLS	**SLIDE**	**SMEAR**
SHIVAH	**SIGNA**	SKILLY	SLIDED	ASMEAR
SHIVAS	SIGNAL	**SKIMP**	SLIDER	SMEARS
SHIVE	**SILEN**	SKIMPS	SLIDES	SMEARY
SHIVER	SILENE	SKIMPY	**SLIME**	**SMEKE**
SHIVES	SILENI	**SKITE**	SLIMED	SMEKED
SHLEP	SILENS	SKITED	SLIMES	SMEKES
SHLEPP	SILENT	SKITES	**SLIMS**	**SMELL**
SHLEPS	**SILES**	**SKIVE**	SLIMSY	SMELLS
SHOAL	ESILES	SKIVED	**SLING**	SMELLY
SHOALS	**SILVA**	SKIVER	ISLING	**SMILE**
SHOALY	SILVAE	SKIVES	SLINGS	SMILED
SHOOL	SILVAN	**SKRIK**	**SLINK**	SMILER
SHOOLE	SILVAS	SKRIKE	SLINKS	SMILES
SHOOLS	**SINEW**	SKRIKS	SLINKY	SMILET
SHORE	SINEWS	**SKUNK**	**SLIPE**	SMILEY
ASHORE	SINEWY	SKUNKS	SLIPED	**SMIRK**
SHORED	**SINGE**	SKUNKY	SLIPES	SMIRKS
SHORER	SINGED	**SKYRE**	**SLIVE**	SMIRKY
SHORES	SINGER	SKYRED	SLIVED	**SMIRR**
SHORT	SINGES	SKYRES	SLIVEN	SMIRRS
SHORTS	**SIRRA**	**SKYTE**	SLIVER	SMIRRY
SHORTY	SIRRAH	SKYTED	SLIVES	**SMITE**
SHOTT	SIRRAS	SKYTES	**SLOOM**	SMITER
SHOTTE	**SIRUP**	**SLAKE**	SLOOMS	SMITES
SHOTTS	SIRUPS	ASLAKE	SLOOMY	**SMITH**
SHOUT	SIRUPY	SLAKED	**SLOPE**	SMITHS
SHOUTS	**SITHE**	SLAKER	ASLOPE	SMITHY
SHOUTY	SITHED	SLAKES	SLOPED	**SMOKE**
SHOVE	SITHEE	**SLANG**	SLOPER	SMOKED

SMOKER	SNOOPY	**SORDO**	**SPARS**	SPIKER
SMOKES	**SNOOT**	SORDOR	SPARSE	SPIKES
SMOKEY	SNOOTS	**SOREL**	**SPART**	SPIKEY
SMOOT	SNOOTY	SORELL	SPARTH	**SPILE**
SMOOTH	**SNORE**	SORELS	SPARTS	SPILED
SMOOTS	SNORED	SORELY	**SPAUL**	SPILES
SMORE	SNORER	**SORES**	SPAULD	**SPILT**
SMORED	SNORES	TSORES	SPAULS	SPILTH
SMORES	**SNORT**	SOREST	**SPAWN**	**SPINA**
SNAIL	SNORTS	**SORTA**	SPAWNS	SPINAE
SNAILS	SNORTY	SORTAL	SPAWNY	SPINAL
SNAILY	**SNOUT**	**SOUCE**	**SPEAR**	SPINAR
SNAKE	SNOUTS	SOUCED	SPEARS	SPINAS
SNAKED	SNOUTY	SOUCES	SPEARY	**SPINE**
SNAKES	**SNUFF**	**SOUGH**	**SPECK**	ASPINE
SNAKEY	SNUFFS	SOUGHS	SPECKS	SPINED
SNARE	SNUFFY	SOUGHT	SPECKY	SPINEL
SNARED	**SOARE**	**SOURS**	**SPEED**	SPINES
SNARER	SOARED	SOURSE	SPEEDO	SPINET
SNARES	SOARER	**SOUSE**	SPEEDS	**SPIRE**
SNARK	SOARES	SOUSED	SPEEDY	ASPIRE
SNARKS	**SODOM**	SOUSES	**SPELT**	SPIREA
SNARKY	SODOMS	**SOWCE**	SPELTS	SPIRED
SNARL	SODOMY	SOWCED	SPELTZ	SPIREM
SNARLS	**SOLAN**	SOWCES	**SPEND**	SPIRES
SNARLY	SOLAND	**SOWLE**	SPENDS	**SPITE**
SNATH	SOLANO	SOWLED	SPENDY	SPITED
SNATHE	SOLANS	SOWLES	**SPEUG**	SPITES
SNATHS	**SOLDE**	**SOWSE**	SPEUGS	**SPLAY**
SNEAK	SOLDER	SOWSED	**SPIAL**	SPLAYS
SNEAKS	SOLDES	SOWSES	ESPIAL	**SPOIL**
SNEAKY	**SOLEI**	SOZIN	SPIALS	SPOILS
SNEER	SOLEIN	SOZINE	**SPICA**	SPOILT
SNEERS	**SOLER**	SOZINS	SPICAE	**SPOKE**
SNEERY	SOLERA	**SPACE**	SPICAS	SPOKED
SNEES	SOLERS	SPACED	**SPICE**	SPOKEN
SNEESH	**SOLID**	SPACER	SPICED	SPOKES
SNELL	SOLIDI	SPACES	SPICER	**SPOOF**
SNELLS	SOLIDS	SPACEY	SPICES	SPOOFS
SNELLY	**SOLVE**	**SPADE**	SPICEY	SPOOFY
SNIDE	SOLVED	SPADED	**SPICK**	**SPOOK**
SNIDED	SOLVER	SPADER	ASPICK	SPOOKS
SNIDER	SOLVES	SPADES	SPICKS	SPOOKY
SNIDES	**SONDE**	**SPAIN**	**SPICS**	**SPOON**
SNIDEY	SONDER	SPAING	ASPICS	SPOONS
SNIFF	SONDES	SPAINS	**SPIDE**	SPOONY
SNIFFS	**SONNE**	**SPALL**	SPIDER	**SPORE**
SNIFFY	SONNES	SPALLE	SPIDES	SPORED
SNIFT	SONNET	SPALLS	**SPIED**	SPORES
SNIFTS	**SOOLE**	**SPANE**	ESPIED	**SPORT**
SNIFTY	SOOLED	SPANED	**SPIER**	ASPORT
SNIPE	SOOLES	SPANES	ESPIER	SPORTS
SNIPED	**SOOTE**	**SPARE**	SPIERS	SPORTY
SNIPER	SOOTED	SPARED	**SPIES**	**SPOSH**
SNIPES	SOOTES	SPARER	ESPIES	SPOSHY
SNOKE	**SOOTH**	SPARES	**SPIFF**	**SPOUT**
SNOKED	SOOTHE	**SPARK**	SPIFFS	ASPOUT
SNOKES	SOOTHS	SPARKE	SPIFFY	SPOUTS
SNOOP	**SORAS**	SPARKS	**SPIKE**	SPOUTY
SNOOPS	PSORAS	SPARKY	SPIKED	**SPRED**

SPREDD	**STAVE**	STEREO	STOMAS	**STRAY**
SPREDS	STAVED	STERES	**STOND**	ASTRAY
SPREE	STAVES	**STERN**	STONDS	ESTRAY
SPREED	**STEAD**	ASTERN	**STONE**	STRAYS
SPREES	STEADS	STERNA	ASTONE	**STREW**
SPRIT	STEADY	STERNS	STONED	STREWN
ESPRIT	**STEAL**	**STICK**	STONEN	STREWS
SPRITE	OSTEAL	STICKS	STONER	**STRIA**
SPRITS	STEALE	STICKY	STONES	STRIAE
SPRITZ	STEALS	**STIFF**	STONEY	**STRIG**
SPUME	STEALT	STIFFS	**STONN**	STRIGA
SPUMED	**STEAM**	STIFFY	STONNE	STRIGS
SPUMES	STEAMS	**STILE**	STONNS	**STRIP**
SPUNK	STEAMY	STILED	**STONY**	STRIPE
SPUNKS	**STEAN**	STILES	ASTONY	STRIPS
SPUNKY	STEANE	STILET	**STOOL**	STRIPT
SPURN	STEANS	**STILL**	STOOLS	STRIPY
SPURNE	**STEAR**	STILLS	**STOOP**	**STROW**
SPURNS	STEARD	STILLY	ASTOOP	STROWN
SQUAT	STEARE	**STILT**	STOOPE	STROWS
ASQUAT	STEARS	STILTS	STOOPS	**STRUM**
SQUATS	**STEDD**	STILTY	**STOPE**	ESTRUM
SQUAW	STEDDE	**STIME**	STOPED	STRUMA
SQUAWK	STEDDS	STIMED	STOPER	STRUMS
SQUAWS	STEDDY	STIMES	STOPES	**STRUT**
STAGE	**STEDE**	**STING**	**STOPS**	ASTRUT
STAGED	STEDED	STINGO	ESTOPS	STRUTS
STAGER	STEDES	STINGS	**STORE**	**STUFF**
STAGES	**STEED**	STINGY	STORED	STUFFS
STAGEY	STEEDS	**STINK**	STORER	STUFFY
STAKE	STEEDY	STINKO	STORES	**STUMP**
STAKED	**STEEL**	STINKS	STOREY	STUMPS
STAKES	STEELD	STINKY	**STORM**	STUMPY
STALE	STEELS	**STINT**	STORMS	**STUNS**
STALED	STEELY	STINTS	STORMY	ASTUNS
STALER	**STEEM**	STINTY	**STOTT**	**STUPE**
STALES	ESTEEM	**STIPE**	STOTTS	STUPED
STALK	STEEMS	STIPED	STOTTY	STUPES
STALKO	**STEEP**	STIPEL	**STOUN**	**STYLE**
STALKS	STEEPS	STIPES	STOUND	STYLED
STALKY	STEEPY	**STIRE**	STOUNS	STYLEE
STANE	**STEER**	STIRED	**STOUR**	STYLER
STANED	STEERS	STIRES	STOURE	STYLES
STANES	STEERY	**STIVE**	STOURS	STYLET
STARE	**STELA**	STIVED	STOURY	**STYLI**
ASTARE	STELAE	STIVER	**STOUT**	STYLIE
STARED	STELAI	STIVES	STOUTH	**STYME**
STARER	STELAR	**STOCK**	STOUTS	STYMED
STARES	**STELL**	STOCKS	**STOVE**	STYMES
STARR	STELLA	STOCKY	STOVED	**STYRE**
STARRS	STELLS	**STOKE**	STOVER	STYRED
STARRY	**STEME**	STOKED	STOVES	STYRES
START	STEMED	STOKER	**STOWN**	**STYTE**
ASTART	STEMES	STOKES	STOWND	STYTED
STARTS	**STENO**	**STOLE**	**STRAK**	STYTES
STATE	STENOS	STOLED	STRAKE	**SUAVE**
ESTATE	**STENT**	STOLEN	**STRAW**	SUAVER
STATED	OSTENT	STOLES	STRAWN	**SUBAS**
STATER	STENTS	**STOMA**	STRAWS	TSUBAS
STATES	**STERE**	STOMAL	STRAWY	**SUEDE**

SUEDED	**SWASH**	SWOUNE	TAMALS	**TATER**
SUEDES	SWASHY	SWOUNS	**TAMES**	STATER
SUGAR	**SWATH**	**SYLPH**	TAMEST	TATERS
SUGARS	SWATHE	SYLPHS	**TAMIN**	**TATES**
SUGARY	SWATHS	SYLPHY	ETAMIN	STATES
SUITE	SWATHY	**SYLVA**	TAMINE	**TATUS**
SUITED	**SWEAR**	SYLVAE	TAMING	STATUS
SUITER	SWEARD	SYLVAN	TAMINS	**TAVER**
SUITES	SWEARS	SYLVAS	**TAMIS**	TAVERN
SULPH	SWEARY	**SYRUP**	TAMISE	TAVERS
SULPHA	**SWEAT**	SYRUPS	**TAMPS**	TAVERT
SULPHS	SWEATS	SYRUPY	STAMPS	**TAWED**
SUMAC	SWEATY	**TAATA**	**TANGI**	STAWED
SUMACH	**SWEEP**	ATAATA	TANGIE	**TAWER**
SUMACS	SWEEPS	TAATAS	TANGIS	TAWERS
SUMMA	SWEEPY	**TABER**	**TANGS**	TAWERY
SUMMAE	**SWEER**	TABERS	STANGS	**TAWIE**
SUMMAR	SWEERS	**TABLE**	**TANKS**	TAWIER
SUMMAS	SWEERT	STABLE	STANKS	**TAWSE**
SUMMAT	**SWEET**	TABLED	**TANNA**	TAWSED
SUNNA	SWEETS	TABLES	TANNAH	TAWSES
SUNNAH	SWEETY	TABLET	TANNAS	**TEADS**
SUNNAS	**SWEIR**	**TACKS**	**TAPES**	STEADS
SUPER	SWEIRS	STACKS	ETAPES	**TEAKS**
SUPERB	SWEIRT	**TAGGY**	STAPES	STEAKS
SUPERS	**SWIFT**	STAGGY	**TAPET**	**TEALS**
SURED	SWIFTS	**TAIGS**	TAPETA	STEALS
USURED	SWIFTY	STAIGS	TAPETI	**TEAMS**
SURER	**SWING**	**TAINS**	TAPETS	STEAMS
USURER	ASWING	STAINS	**TAPIS**	**TEARS**
SURES	SWINGE	**TAKES**	TAPIST	STEARS
USURES	SWINGS	STAKES	**TARED**	**TEASE**
SUREST	SWINGY	**TAKIN**	STARED	TEASED
SURGE	**SWIPE**	TAKING	**TARES**	TEASEL
SURGED	SWIPED	TAKINS	STARES	TEASER
SURGER	SWIPER	**TALEA**	**TARGE**	TEASES
SURGES	SWIPES	TALEAE	TARGED	**TEAZE**
SWAGE	SWIPEY	**TALER**	TARGES	TEAZED
SWAGED	**SWIRL**	STALER	TARGET	TEAZEL
SWAGER	ASWIRL	TALERS	**TARNS**	TEAZES
SWAGES	SWIRLS	**TALES**	STARNS	**TECTA**
SWALE	SWIRLY	STALES	**TARRE**	TECTAL
SWALED	**SWISH**	**TALKS**	TARRED	**TEDDY**
SWALES	SWISHY	STALKS	TARRES	STEDDY
SWAMP	**SWITH**	**TALKY**	**TARRY**	**TEELS**
SWAMPS	SWITHE	STALKY	STARRY	STEELS
SWAMPY	**SWIVE**	**TALLS**	**TARSI**	**TEEMS**
SWANK	SWIVED	STALLS	TARSIA	STEEMS
SWANKS	SWIVEL	**TALON**	**TARTS**	**TEENE**
SWANKY	SWIVES	ETALON	STARTS	TEENED
SWARD	SWIVET	TALONS	**TASER**	TEENER
USWARD	**SWOON**	**TALPA**	TASERS	TEENES
SWARDS	ASWOON	TALPAE	**TASSE**	**TEENS**
SWARDY	SWOONS	TALPAS	TASSEL	STEENS
SWARM	SWOONY	**TALUK**	TASSES	TEENSY
ASWARM	**SWOOP**	TALUKA	TASSET	**TEERS**
SWARMS	SWOOPS	TALUKS	**TASTE**	STEERS
SWART	SWOOPY	**TAMAL**	TASTED	**TEETH**
SWARTH	**SWOUN**	TAMALE	TASTER	TEETHE
SWARTY	SWOUND		TASTES	**TEILS**

STEILS	**TESTA**	THROED	**TIRES**	ATOLLS
TEINS	TESTAE	THROES	STIRES	**TOMIA**
STEINS	**TESTE**	**THROW**	**TITCH**	STOMIA
TELAE	TESTED	THROWE	STITCH	TOMIAL
STELAE	TESTEE	THROWN	TITCHY	**TONAL**
TELES	TESTER	THROWS	**TITHE**	ATONAL
STELES	TESTES	**THUMB**	TITHED	**TONED**
TELESM	**TETRA**	THUMBS	TITHER	ATONED
TELIA	TETRAD	THUMBY	TITHES	STONED
TELIAL	TETRAS	**THYME**	**TITIS**	**TONER**
TELIC	**TEWED**	THYMES	OTITIS	ATONER
ATELIC	STEWED	THYMEY	**TITLE**	STONER
STELIC	**THALE**	**THYMI**	TITLED	TONERS
TELLS	THALER	THYMIC	TITLER	**TONES**
STELLS	**THANA**	**TIBIA**	TITLES	ATONES
TEMED	THANAH	TIBIAE	**TITUP**	STONES
ITEMED	THANAS	TIBIAL	TITUPS	**TONEY**
STEMED	**THANE**	TIBIAS	TITUPY	STONEY
TEMES	ETHANE	**TICKS**	**TOAST**	**TONIC**
STEMES	THANES	STICKS	TOASTS	ATONIC
TEMSE	**THECA**	**TICKY**	TOASTY	TONICS
TEMSED	THECAE	STICKY	**TOAZE**	**TONKS**
TEMSES	THECAL	**TIFFS**	TOAZED	STONKS
TENCH	**THEIN**	STIFFS	TOAZES	**TONNE**
STENCH	THEINE	**TIGER**	**TOCKS**	STONNE
TENDS	THEINS	TIGERS	STOCKS	TONNER
STENDS	**THEME**	TIGERY	**TOCKY**	TONNES
TENES	THEMED	**TILED**	STOCKY	**TOOLS**
CTENES	THEMES	STILED	**TODDE**	STOOLS
TENIA	**THERM**	**TILER**	TODDED	**TOOTH**
TENIAE	THERME	TILERS	TODDES	TOOTHS
TENIAS	THERMS	TILERY	**TOGAE**	TOOTHY
TENNE	**THICK**	**TILES**	TOGAED	**TOOTS**
TENNER	THICKO	STILES	**TOILE**	TOOTSY
TENNES	THICKS	**TILLS**	ETOILE	**TOPED**
TENSE	THICKY	STILLS	TOILED	STOPED
TENSED	**THING**	**TILLY**	TOILER	**TOPER**
TENSER	THINGS	STILLY	TOILES	STOPER
TENSES	THINGY	**TILTS**	TOILET	TOPERS
TENTS	**THOLE**	STILTS	**TOISE**	**TOPES**
STENTS	THOLED	**TIMED**	TOISES	STOPES
TERCE	THOLES	STIMED	**TOITS**	**TOPIC**
TERCEL	**THORN**	**TIMES**	STOITS	ATOPIC
TERCES	THORNS	STIMES	**TOKED**	TOPICS
TERCET	THORNY	**TINEA**	STOKED	**TOQUE**
TERES	**THORO**	TINEAL	**TOKER**	TOQUES
STERES	THORON	TINEAS	STOKER	TOQUET
TERGA	**THORP**	**TINGE**	TOKERS	**TORAN**
TERGAL	THORPE	TINGED	**TOKES**	TORANA
TERNE	THORPS	TINGES	ATOKES	TORANS
ETERNE	**THRAW**	**TINGS**	STOKES	**TORCH**
TERNED	THRAWN	STINGS	**TOLAN**	TORCHY
TERNES	THRAWS	**TINKS**	TOLANE	**TORES**
TERNS	**THREE**	STINKS	TOLANS	STORES
STERNS	THREEP	**TINTS**	**TOLED**	**TOROS**
TERRA	THREES	STINTS	STOLED	TOROSE
TERRAE	**THROB**	**TINTY**	TOLEDO	**TOROT**
TERRAS	ATHROB	STINTY	**TOLES**	TOROTH
TERSE	THROBS	**TIRED**	STOLES	**TORSE**
TERSER	**THROE**	STIRED	**TOLLS**	TORSEL

TORSES	STRADS	TRICKY	TROUTY	**TWEED**
TORTE	**TRAGI**	**TRIDE**	**TROVE**	TWEEDS
TORTEN	TRAGIC	STRIDE	STROVE	TWEEDY
TORTES	**TRAIK**	**TRIER**	TROVER	**TWEEL**
TOSES	STRAIK	ETRIER	TROVES	ATWEEL
PTOSES	TRAIKS	TRIERS	**TROWS**	TWEELS
TOTEM	**TRAIN**	**TRIGO**	STROWS	TWEELY
TOTEMS	STRAIN	TRIGON	**TROYS**	**TWEEN**
TOTTY	TRAINS	TRIGOS	STROYS	ATWEEN
STOTTY	**TRAIT**	**TRIGS**	**TRUCE**	TWEENS
TOUCH	STRAIT	STRIGS	TRUCED	TWEENY
TOUCHE	TRAITS	**TRIKE**	TRUCES	**TWERP**
TOUCHY	**TRAMP**	STRIKE	**TRUCK**	TWERPS
TOUGH	STRAMP	TRIKES	STRUCK	TWERPY
TOUGHS	TRAMPS	**TRILL**	TRUCKS	**TWICE**
TOUGHY	TRAMPY	TRILLO	**TRUES**	TWICER
TOUNS	**TRANS**	TRILLS	TRUEST	**TWILL**
STOUNS	TRANSE	**TRIMS**	**TRUST**	TWILLS
TOURS	**TRAPE**	STRIMS	TRUSTS	TWILLY
STOURS	TRAPED	**TRINE**	TRUSTY	**TWINE**
TOUSE	TRAPES	TRINED	**TRUTH**	TWINED
TOUSED	**TRAPS**	TRINES	TRUTHS	TWINER
TOUSER	STRAPS	**TRIOS**	TRUTHY	TWINES
TOUSES	**TRASH**	TRIOSE	**TRYST**	**TWIRE**
TOUTS	TRASHY	**TRIPE**	TRYSTE	TWIRED
STOUTS	**TRASS**	STRIPE	TRYSTS	TWIRES
TOUZE	STRASS	TRIPES	**TUBBY**	**TWIRL**
TOUZED	**TRAVE**	TRIPEY	STUBBY	TWIRLS
TOUZES	TRAVEL	**TRIPS**	**TUCKS**	TWIRLY
TOWED	TRAVES	STRIPS	STUCKS	**TWIRP**
STOWED	**TRAYS**	**TRIPY**	**TUFFE**	TWIRPS
TOWER	STRAYS	STRIPY	TUFFES	TWIRPY
STOWER	**TREAT**	**TRIST**	TUFFET	**TWIST**
TOWERS	TREATS	TRISTE	**TUFFS**	TWISTS
TOWERY	TREATY	**TRITE**	STUFFS	TWISTY
TOWIE	**TREFA**	TRITER	**TUMPS**	**TWIXT**
TOWIER	TREFAH	TRITES	STUMPS	ATWIXT
TOWIES	**TREIF**	**TROAD**	**TUMPY**	**TWYER**
TOWSE	TREIFA	TROADE	STUMPY	TWYERE
TOWSED	**TREND**	TROADS	**TUNIC**	TWYERS
TOWSER	TRENDS	**TRODE**	TUNICA	**TYING**
TOWSES	TRENDY	TRODES	TUNICS	STYING
TOWZE	**TRESS**	**TROKE**	**TURBO**	**TYLER**
TOWZED	STRESS	STROKE	TURBOS	STYLER
TOWZES	TRESSY	TROKED	TURBOT	TYLERS
TOXIN	**TREWS**	TROKES	**TUYER**	**TYPIC**
TOXINE	STREWS	**TROLL**	TUYERE	ATYPIC
TOXINS	**TRIAC**	STROLL	TUYERS	ETYPIC
TRACE	TRIACS	TROLLS	**TWAIN**	**TYRAN**
TRACED	TRIACT	TROLLY	ATWAIN	TYRANS
TRACER	**TRIAL**	**TROMP**	TWAINS	TYRANT
TRACES	ATRIAL	TROMPE	**TWANG**	**TYRED**
TRACK	TRIALS	TROMPS	TWANGS	STYRED
STRACK	**TRICE**	**TROPE**	TWANGY	**TYRES**
TRACKS	TRICED	TROPED	**TWANK**	STYRES
TRADE	TRICEP	TROPES	TWANKS	**TYTHE**
TRADED	TRICES	**TROUT**	TWANKY	TYTHED
TRADER	**TRICK**	STROUT	**TWEAK**	TYTHES
TRADES	STRICK	TROUTS	TWEAKS	**UDDER**
TRADS	TRICKS	TROUTS	TWEAKY	BUDDER

DUDDER	GUMMAS	DUNDER	UNTIES	SURGES
JUDDER	SUMMAS	FUNDER	**UNTIL**	**URIAL**
MUDDER	**UMMED**	SUNDER	UNTILE	BURIAL
PUDDER	BUMMED	UNDERN	**UNTIN**	CURIAL
RUDDER	GUMMED	**UNFIX**	MUNTIN	URIALS
SUDDER	HUMMED	UNFIXT	UNTINS	**URINE**
UDDERS	MUMMED	**UNHAT**	**UNWON**	MURINE
UGGED	SUMMED	SUNHAT	UNWONT	PURINE
BUGGED	VUMMED	UNHATS	**UPPED**	URINED
FUGGED	**UMPED**	**UNIFY**	CUPPED	URINES
HUGGED	BUMPED	MUNIFY	DUPPED	**URITE**
JUGGED	DUMPED	**UNION**	HUPPED	CURITE
LUGGED	GUMPED	BUNION	PUPPED	URITES
MUGGED	HUMPED	UNIONS	SUPPED	**URNED**
PUGGED	JUMPED	**UNITE**	TUPPED	BURNED
RUGGED	LUMPED	DUNITE	**UPPER**	DURNED
SUGGED	MUMPED	GUNITE	CUPPER	GURNED
TUGGED	PUMPED	MUNITE	SUPPER	TURNED
ULANS	RUMPED	UNITED	UPPERS	**URPED**
KULANS	TUMPED	UNITER	**UPTAK**	BURPED
YULANS	YUMPED	UNITES	UPTAKE	**URSAE**
ULNAR	**UMPIE**	**UNKED**	UPTAKS	BURSAE
ULNARE	YUMPIE	BUNKED	**UPTIE**	**URVAS**
ULVAS	UMPIES	DUNKED	UPTIED	MURVAS
VULVAS	**UMPTY**	FUNKED	UPTIES	**USAGE**
UMBER	HUMPTY	JUNKED	**URALI**	USAGER
CUMBER	NUMPTY	**UNKET**	OURALI	USAGES
DUMBER	**UNARY**	JUNKET	URALIS	**USERS**
LUMBER	LUNARY	SUNKET	**URARE**	LUSERS
NUMBER	**UNBAR**	**UNLET**	CURARE	MUSERS
UMBERS	UNBARE	RUNLET	URARES	**USHER**
UMBERY	UNBARK	**UNLIT**	**URARI**	BUSHER
UMBLE	UNBARS	SUNLIT	CURARI	GUSHER
BUMBLE	**UNBED**	**UNMAN**	OURARI	HUSHER
FUMBLE	SUNBED	GUNMAN	URARIS	LUSHER
HUMBLE	UNBEDS	UNMANS	**URATE**	MUSHER
JUMBLE	**UNCAP**	**UNMIX**	AURATE	PUSHER
MUMBLE	UNCAPE	UNMIXT	CURATE	RUSHER
RUMBLE	UNCAPS	**UNPEN**	URATES	USHERS
TUMBLE	**UNCES**	UNPENS	**URBAN**	**USING**
UMBLES	BUNCES	UNPENT	RURBAN	BUSING
UMBOS	DUNCES	**UNRED**	TURBAN	FUSING
BUMBOS	OUNCES	UNREDY	URBANE	MUSING
DUMBOS	PUNCES	**UNRIG**	**UREAS**	**USURE**
GUMBOS	**UNCIA**	RUNRIG	UREASE	USURED
JUMBOS	UNCIAE	UNRIGS	**URENA**	USURER
RUMBOS	UNCIAL	**UNRIP**	MURENA	USURES
UMBRA	**UNCLE**	UNRIPE	URENAS	**UTILE**
UMBRAE	NUNCLE	UNRIPS	**URGED**	FUTILE
UMBRAL	UNCLED	**UNSET**	GURGED	RUTILE
UMBRAS	UNCLES	SUNSET	PURGED	SUTILE
UMBRE	UNCLEW	UNSETS	SURGED	**UTTER**
UMBREL	**UNCOS**	**UNSEW**	**URGER**	BUTTER
UMBRES	BUNCOS	UNSEWN	BURGER	CUTTER
UMIAC	JUNCOS	UNSEWS	PURGER	GUTTER
UMIACK	**UNCUS**	**UNSEX**	SURGER	MUTTER
UMIACS	JUNCUS	UNSEXY	URGERS	NUTTER
UMIAQ	**UNCUT**	**UNTIE**	**URGES**	PUTTER
UMIAQS	UNCUTE	AUNTIE	GURGES	RUTTER
UMMAS	**UNDER**	UNTIED	PURGES	UTTERS

UVULA	**VEALE**	VILLAR	VOLVES	SWALES
UVULAE	VEALED	VILLAS	**VOMIT**	**WALIS**
UVULAR	VEALER	**VINER**	VOMITO	WALISE
UVULAS	VEALES	VINERS	VOMITS	**WALLA**
VADED	**VELLS**	VINERY	**VOUCH**	WALLAH
EVADED	KVELLS	**VINES**	AVOUCH	WALLAS
VADES	**VENGE**	OVINES	**VOWED**	**WANGS**
EVADES	AVENGE	**VIRGE**	AVOWED	DWANGS
VAGUE	VENGED	VIRGER	**VOWER**	TWANGS
VAGUED	VENGER	VIRGES	AVOWER	**WANKS**
VAGUER	VENGES	**VIRTU**	VOWERS	SWANKS
VAGUES	**VENIN**	VIRTUE	**VULVA**	TWANKS
VAILS	VENINE	VIRTUS	VULVAE	**WANKY**
AVAILS	VENINS	**VISED**	VULVAL	SWANKY
VALES	**VENTS**	AVISED	VULVAR	TWANKY
AVALES	EVENTS	**VISES**	VULVAS	**WANZE**
VALET	**VENUE**	AVISES	**WACKE**	WANZED
VALETA	AVENUE	**VISIE**	WACKER	WANZES
VALETE	VENUES	VISIED	WACKES	**WARDS**
VALETS	**VERGE**	VISIER	**WADDY**	AWARDS
VALIS	VERGED	VISIES	SWADDY	SWARDS
VALISE	VERGER	**VISIT**	**WAFER**	**WARMS**
VALSE	VERGES	VISITE	WAFERS	SWARMS
VALSED	**VERSE**	VISITS	WAFERY	**WARNS**
VALSES	AVERSE	**VISTA**	**WAGED**	AWARNS
VALUE	VERSED	VISTAL	SWAGED	**WARRE**
VALUED	VERSER	VISTAS	**WAGER**	WARRED
VALUER	VERSES	**VITAL**	SWAGER	WARREN
VALUES	VERSET	AVITAL	WAGERS	WARREY
VALVE	**VERST**	VITALS	**WAGES**	**WARTY**
VALVED	VERSTE	**VITTA**	SWAGES	SWARTY
VALVES	VERSTS	VITTAE	**WAILS**	**WASHY**
VANDA	**VERTS**	**VODOU**	SWAILS	SWASHY
VANDAL	AVERTS	VODOUN	**WAINS**	**WASTE**
VANDAS	EVERTS	VODOUS	SWAINS	WASTED
VAPOR	**VERTU**	**VOGIE**	TWAINS	WASTEL
VAPORS	VERTUE	VOGIER	**WAIRS**	WASTER
VAPORY	VERTUS	**VOGUE**	WAIRSH	WASTES
VAREC	**VERVE**	VOGUED	**WAITE**	**WATAP**
VARECH	VERVEL	VOGUER	TWAITE	WATAPE
VARECS	VERVEN	VOGUES	WAITED	WATAPS
VARVE	VERVES	VOGUEY	WAITER	**WATCH**
VARVED	VERVET	**VOICE**	WAITES	AWATCH
VARVEL	**VESTA**	VOICED	**WAITS**	SWATCH
VARVES	VESTAL	VOICER	AWAITS	**WATER**
VASES	VESTAS	VOICES	**WAIVE**	WATERS
KVASES	**VETCH**	**VOIDS**	WAIVED	WATERY
VAULT	KVETCH	AVOIDS	WAIVER	**WAUGH**
VAULTS	VETCHY	OVOIDS	WAIVES	WAUGHS
VAULTY	**VICAR**	**VOLAR**	**WAKED**	WAUGHT
VAUNT	VICARS	VOLARY	AWAKED	**WAURS**
AVAUNT	VICARY	**VOLTE**	**WAKEN**	WAURST
VAUNTS	**VIGOR**	VOLTED	AWAKEN	**WAVER**
VAUNTY	VIGORO	VOLTES	WAKENS	WAVERS
VAUTE	VIGORS	**VOLVA**	**WAKES**	WAVERY
VAUTED	**VILER**	VOLVAE	AWAKES	**WAXER**
VAUTES	EVILER	VOLVAS	**WALED**	WAXERS
VAWTE	**VILLA**	**VOLVE**	SWALED	**WAYED**
VAWTED	VILLAE	EVOLVE	**WALES**	SWAYED
VAWTES	VILLAN	VOLVED	DWALES	**WEALS**

SWEALS	WEIZES	WHITER	**WIPER**	WORTHS
WEARS	**WELKE**	WHITES	SWIPER	WORTHY
SWEARS	WELKED	WHITEY	WIPERS	**WOUND**
WEARY	WELKES	**WHIZZ**	**WIPES**	SWOUND
AWEARY	**WELLS**	WHIZZO	SWIPES	WOUNDS
SWEARY	DWELLS	WHIZZY	**WIRED**	WOUNDY
WEAVE	SWELLS	**WHORE**	TWIRED	**WRACK**
WEAVED	**WELTS**	WHORED	**WIRES**	AWRACK
WEAVER	SWELTS	WHORES	SWIRES	WRACKS
WEAVES	**WHACK**	**WICCA**	TWIRES	**WRATH**
WEDEL	WHACKO	WICCAN	**WIRRA**	WRATHS
WEDELN	WHACKS	WICCAS	WIRRAH	WRATHY
WEDELS	WHACKY	**WIDES**	**WISES**	**WRIER**
WEDGE	**WHALE**	WIDEST	WISEST	OWRIER
WEDGED	WHALED	**WIELD**	**WISTS**	**WRIES**
WEDGES	WHALER	WIELDS	TWISTS	WRIEST
WEEDS	WHALES	WIELDY	**WITCH**	**WRIST**
TWEEDS	**WHATS**	**WIFTY**	SWITCH	WRISTS
WEEDY	WHATSO	SWIFTY	TWITCH	WRISTY
TWEEDY	**WHEAR**	**WIGGY**	WITCHY	**WRITE**
WEELS	WHEARE	TWIGGY	**WITES**	WRITER
SWEELS	**WHEAT**	**WIGHT**	TWITES	WRITES
TWEELS	WHEATS	TWIGHT	**WITHE**	**WROKE**
WEENS	WHEATY	WIGHTS	SWITHE	YWROKE
TWEENS	**WHEEL**	**WILES**	WITHED	WROKEN
WEENSY	AWHEEL	DWILES	WITHER	**WRONG**
WEENY	WHEELS	**WILLS**	WITHES	AWRONG
SWEENY	WHEELY	SWILLS	**WIVED**	WRONGS
TWEENY	**WHELK**	TWILLS	SWIVED	**XENIA**
WEEPS	WHELKS	**WILLY**	**WIVER**	XENIAL
SWEEPS	WHELKY	TWILLY	WIVERN	XENIAS
WEEPY	**WHIFF**	**WILTS**	WIVERS	**XENIC**
SWEEPY	WHIFFS	TWILTS	**WIVES**	AXENIC
WEEST	WHIFFY	**WINCE**	SWIVES	**YACKS**
TWEEST	**WHILE**	WINCED	**WOKEN**	KYACKS
WEETE	AWHILE	WINCER	AWOKEN	**YAFFS**
WEETED	WHILED	WINCES	**WOLVE**	NYAFFS
WEETEN	WHILES	WINCEY	WOLVED	**YANGS**
WEETER	**WHIMS**	**WINED**	WOLVER	KYANGS
WEETS	WHIMSY	DWINED	WOLVES	**YCLED**
SWEETS	**WHINE**	TWINED	**WOODS**	CYCLED
TWEETS	WHINED	**WINES**	WOODSY	**YEAST**
WEFTE	WHINER	DWINES	**WOONS**	YEASTS
WEFTED	WHINES	SWINES	SWOONS	YEASTY
WEFTES	WHINEY	TWINES	**WOOPS**	**YESES**
WEIGH	**WHIRL**	**WINGE**	SWOOPS	CYESES
AWEIGH	AWHIRL	SWINGE	**WOOSE**	OYESES
WEIGHS	WHIRLS	TWINGE	WOOSEL	**YLEMS**
WEIGHT	WHIRLY	WINGED	WOOSES	XYLEMS
WEIRD	**WHIRR**	WINGER	**WOOSH**	**YODLE**
WEIRDO	WHIRRS	WINGES	SWOOSH	YODLED
WEIRDS	WHIRRY	**WINGS**	**WORDS**	YODLER
WEIRDY	**WHISH**	SWINGS	SWORDS	YODLES
WEIRS	WHISHT	**WINGY**	**WORSE**	**YOGIN**
SWEIRS	**WHISK**	SWINGY	WORSED	YOGINI
WEISE	WHISKS	**WINKS**	WORSEN	YOGINS
WEISED	WHISKY	SWINKS	WORSER	**YOGIS**
WEISES	**WHITE**	TWINKS	WORSES	YOGISM
WEIZE	WHITED	**WIPED**	WORSET	**YOJAN**
WEIZED	WHITEN	SWIPED	**WORTH**	YOJANA

YOJANS	ZEBECK	**ZINES**	ZOAEAE	OZONES
YOUTH	ZEBECS	AZINES	ZOAEAS	**ZOOEA**
YOUTHS	**ZIBET**	**ZINKE**	**ZOMBI**	ZOOEAE
YOUTHY	ZIBETH	ZINKED	ZOMBIE	ZOOEAL
ZAMAN	ZIBETS	ZINKES	ZOMBIS	ZOOEAS
ZAMANG	**ZILLA**	**ZIZIT**	**ZONAL**	**ZYMES**
ZAMANS	ZILLAH	ZIZITH	AZONAL	AZYMES
ZEBEC	ZILLAS	**ZOAEA**	**ZONES**	

Six-letter root words

AARRGH	ACANTHA	PACTION	SADDING	ADVISES
AARRGHH	ACANTHI	TACTION	WADDING	**ADWARE**
ABAKAS	ACANTHS	ACTIONS	ADDINGS	BADWARE
KABAKAS	**ACATES**	**ACTIVE**	**ADDLED**	ADWARES
ABAYAS	VACATES	FACTIVE	DADDLED	**AEMULE**
KABAYAS	**ACCEDE**	ACTIVES	FADDLED	AEMULED
ABDABS	ACCEDED	**ACTORS**	PADDLED	AEMULES
HABDABS	ACCEDER	FACTORS	RADDLED	**AEONIC**
ABDUCE	ACCEDES	**ACTUAL**	SADDLED	PAEONIC
ABDUCED	**ACCITE**	FACTUAL	WADDLED	**AERATE**
ABDUCES	ACCITED	TACTUAL	**ADDLES**	AERATED
ABELES	ACCITES	ACTUALS	DADDLES	AERATES
KABELES	**ACCRUE**	**ACTURE**	FADDLES	**AERIES**
ABELIA	ACCRUED	FACTURE	PADDLES	FAERIES
ABELIAN	ACCRUES	ACTURES	RADDLES	AERIEST
ABELIAS	**ACCUSE**	**ACUATE**	SADDLES	**AFFAIR**
ABIDER	ACCUSED	VACUATE	WADDLES	AFFAIRE
RABIDER	ACCUSER	**ACUITY**	**ADDUCE**	AFFAIRS
ABIDERS	ACCUSES	VACUITY	ADDUCED	**AFFEAR**
ABJURE	**ACHING**	**ACUMEN**	ADDUCER	AFFEARD
ABJURED	BACHING	CACUMEN	ADDUCES	AFFEARE
ABJURER	CACHING	ACUMENS	**ADHERE**	AFFEARS
ABJURES	ACHINGS	**ACUTES**	ADHERED	**AFFIES**
ABLATE	**ACKEES**	ACUTEST	ADHERER	BAFFIES
ABLATED	HACKEES	**ADDEND**	ADHERES	DAFFIES
ABLATES	**ACKERS**	ADDENDA	**ADJOIN**	TAFFIES
ABLETS	BACKERS	ADDENDS	ADJOINS	WAFFIES
CABLETS	DACKERS	**ADDERS**	ADJOINT	**AFFINE**
GABLETS	HACKERS	GADDERS	**ADJURE**	AFFINED
TABLETS	JACKERS	LADDERS	ADJURED	AFFINES
ABLING	LACKERS	MADDERS	ADJURER	**AFGHAN**
CABLING	PACKERS	PADDERS	ADJURES	AFGHANI
FABLING	RACKERS	WADDERS	**ADLAND**	AFGHANS
GABLING	SACKERS	**ADDIES**	BADLAND	**AFTERS**
SABLING	TACKERS	BADDIES	ADLANDS	HAFTERS
TABLING	WACKERS	CADDIES	**ADMIRE**	RAFTERS
ABLINGS	YACKERS	DADDIES	ADMIRED	WAFTERS
ABOLLA	**ACKNOW**	HADDIES	ADMIRER	**AGENES**
ABOLLAE	ACKNOWN	LADDIES	ADMIRES	SAGENES
ABOLLAS	ACKNOWS	PADDIES	**ADNEXA**	**AGGADA**
ABOMAS	**ACNODE**	SADDIES	ADNEXAL	HAGGADA
ABOMASA	TACNODE	TADDIES	**ADONIS**	AGGADAH
ABOMASI	ACNODES	WADDIES	ADONISE	AGGADAS
ABRADE	**ACQUIS**	**ADDING**	**ADVENE**	**AGGERS**
ABRADED	ACQUIST	DADDING	ADVENED	BAGGERS
ABRADER	**ACQUIT**	GADDING	ADVENES	DAGGERS
ABRADES	ACQUITE	HADDING	**ADVISE**	GAGGERS
ABYING	ACQUITS	MADDING	ADVISED	JAGGERS
BABYING	**ACTION**	PADDING	ADVISEE	LAGGERS
ACANTH	FACTION	RADDING	ADVISER	NAGGERS

SAGGERS	SAILING	ALEGGED	SALLIES	CAMBERS
TAGGERS	TAILING	ALEGGES	TALLIES	JAMBERS
WAGGERS	VAILING	**ALEXIN**	WALLIES	LAMBERS
YAGGERS	WAILING	ALEXINE	**ALLIUM**	TAMBERS
AGGIES	**AIMERS**	ALEXINS	BALLIUM	**AMBITS**
BAGGIES	MAIMERS	**ALGOID**	GALLIUM	GAMBITS
JAGGIES	**AIMING**	VALGOID	PALLIUM	**AMBLED**
MAGGIES	MAIMING	**ALIDAD**	ALLIUMS	GAMBLED
RAGGIES	**AINGAS**	ALIDADE	**ALLONS**	HAMBLED
AGINGS	KAINGAS	ALIDADS	BALLONS	RAMBLED
PAGINGS	**AIREST**	**ALIGNS**	GALLONS	WAMBLED
RAGINGS	FAIREST	MALIGNS	**ALLOTS**	**AMBLER**
AGISMS	PAIREST	**ALINES**	BALLOTS	GAMBLER
MAGISMS	SAIREST	MALINES	TALLOTS	RAMBLER
AGLETS	**AIRIER**	SALINES	**ALLOWS**	AMBLERS
EAGLETS	HAIRIER	VALINES	BALLOWS	**AMBLES**
HAGLETS	LAIRIER	**ALIPED**	FALLOWS	GAMBLES
AGNAME	VAIRIER	TALIPED	GALLOWS	HAMBLES
AGNAMED	**AIRILY**	ALIPEDS	HALLOWS	RAMBLES
AGNAMES	FAIRILY	**ALISON**	MALLOWS	WAMBLES
AGNATE	**AIRING**	MALISON	SALLOWS	**AMELIA**
MAGNATE	FAIRING	ALISONS	TALLOWS	CAMELIA
AGNATES	HAIRING	**ALIYOT**	WALLOWS	AMELIAS
AGNISE	LAIRING	ALIYOTH	**ALLUDE**	**AMENDE**
AGNISED	PAIRING	**ALKALI**	ALLUDED	AMENDED
AGNISES	SAIRING	ALKALIC	ALLUDES	AMENDER
AGNIZE	WAIRING	ALKALIN	**ALLURE**	AMENDES
AGNIZED	AIRINGS	ALKALIS	ALLURED	**AMENTA**
AGNIZES	**AIRNED**	**ALKANE**	ALLURER	RAMENTA
AGOROT	CAIRNED	ALKANES	ALLURES	AMENTAL
AGOROTH	**AIRWAY**	ALKANET	**ALMOND**	**AMENTS**
AGRISE	FAIRWAY	**ALKIES**	ALMONDS	LAMENTS
AGRISED	AIRWAYS	TALKIES	ALMONDY	**AMERCE**
AGRISES	**AIVERS**	WALKIES	**ALMUDS**	AMERCED
AGRIZE	TAIVERS	**ALLEES**	TALMUDS	AMERCER
AGRIZED	WAIVERS	CALLEES	**ALNAGE**	AMERCES
AGRIZES	**ALANGS**	MALLEES	ALNAGER	**AMIDIN**
AGRYZE	LALANGS	SALLEES	ALNAGES	AMIDINE
AGRYZED	**ALANIN**	**ALLEGE**	**ALODIA**	AMIDINS
AGRYZES	ALANINE	ALLEGED	ALODIAL	**AMINES**
AGUISE	ALANINS	ALLEGER	**ALSOON**	FAMINES
AGUISED	**ALANTS**	ALLEGES	ALSOONE	GAMINES
AGUISES	TALANTS	**ALLELS**	**ALTERN**	TAMINES
AGUIZE	**ALAPAS**	HALLELS	SALTERN	**AMISES**
AGUIZED	PALAPAS	**ALLEYS**	ALTERNE	CAMISES
AGUIZES	**ALATED**	GALLEYS	**ALTERS**	KAMISES
AIDERS	PALATED	VALLEYS	FALTERS	TAMISES
RAIDERS	**ALATES**	**ALLIED**	HALTERS	**AMMONS**
AIDING	MALATES	DALLIED	PALTERS	GAMMONS
LAIDING	PALATES	GALLIED	SALTERS	MAMMONS
MAIDING	**ALBERT**	PALLIED	**ALUMIN**	**AMOEBA**
RAIDING	HALBERT	RALLIED	ALUMINA	AMOEBAE
AILING	ALBERTS	SALLIED	ALUMINE	AMOEBAN
BAILING	**ALCADE**	TALLIED	ALUMINS	AMOEBAS
FAILING	FALCADE	**ALLIES**	**ALUMNA**	**AMOOVE**
HAILING	ALCADES	BALLIES	ALUMNAE	AMOOVED
JAILING	**ALCOVE**	DALLIES	**AMATES**	AMOOVES
MAILING	ALCOVED	GALLIES	HAMATES	**AMPING**
NAILING	ALCOVES	PALLIES	**AMBERS**	CAMPING
RAILING	**ALEGGE**	RALLIES		DAMPING

LAMPING	WANGLER	ANTICKS	CARABIN	BARKING
RAMPING	ANGLERS	**ANTING**	ARABINS	CARKING
TAMPING	**ANGLES**	BANTING	**ARABIS**	DARKING
VAMPING	BANGLES	CANTING	MARABIS	HARKING
AMPLER	CANGLES	DANTING	ARABISE	KARKING
SAMPLER	DANGLES	GANTING	**ARABLE**	LARKING
AMTRAC	FANGLES	HANTING	PARABLE	MARKING
AMTRACK	JANGLES	KANTING	ARABLES	NARKING
AMTRACS	MANGLES	PANTING	**ARAISE**	PARKING
AMUSES	TANGLES	RANTING	ARAISED	RARKING
CAMUSES	WANGLES	WANTING	ARAISES	SARKING
WAMUSES	**ANILIN**	ANTINGS	**ARAYSE**	WARKING
ANALLY	ANILINE	**ANTLER**	ARAYSED	YARKING
BANALLY	ANILINS	PANTLER	ARAYSES	**ARLING**
ANALOG	**ANIMIS**	ANTLERS	**ARBORS**	CARLING
ANALOGA	ANIMISM	**ANTLIA**	HARBORS	DARLING
ANALOGS	ANIMIST	ANTLIAE	**ARBOUR**	HARLING
ANALOGY	**ANIONS**	**ANTRUM**	HARBOUR	MARLING
ANANAS	FANIONS	TANTRUM	ARBOURS	PARLING
BANANAS	WANIONS	ANTRUMS	**ARCADE**	WARLING
MANANAS	**ANKERS**	**ANYONS**	ARCADED	**ARMERS**
ZANANAS	BANKERS	CANYONS	ARCADES	FARMERS
ANARCH	CANKERS	**APEXES**	**ARCHED**	HARMERS
ANARCHS	HANKERS	CAPEXES	MARCHED	WARMERS
ANARCHY	JANKERS	**APHTHA**	PARCHED	**ARMFUL**
ANATAS	RANKERS	NAPHTHA	**ARCHER**	HARMFUL
ANATASE	TANKERS	APHTHAE	MARCHER	ARMFULS
ANCHOS	WANKERS	**APISMS**	ARCHERS	**ARMIES**
RANCHOS	YANKERS	PAPISMS	ARCHERY	SARMIES
SANCHOS	**ANKLED**	**APLITE**	**ARCHES**	**ARMING**
ANELED	FANKLED	HAPLITE	LARCHES	FARMING
PANELED	RANKLED	APLITES	MARCHES	HARMING
ANGELS	**ANKLES**	**APNOEA**	PARCHES	WARMING
MANGELS	CANKLES	APNOEAL	ARCHEST	ARMINGS
ANGERS	FANKLES	APNOEAS	**ARCING**	**ARMOUR**
BANGERS	RANKLES	**APOLOG**	FARCING	ARMOURS
DANGERS	**ANLAGE**	APOLOGS	ARCINGS	ARMOURY
GANGERS	ANLAGEN	APOLOGY	**AREOLA**	**ARMURE**
HANGERS	ANLAGES	**APPELS**	AREOLAE	ARMURES
LANGERS	**ANNEXE**	LAPPELS	AREOLAR	**AROUSE**
MANGERS	ANNEXED	RAPPELS	AREOLAS	CAROUSE
RANGERS	ANNEXES	**APPEND**	**ARGENT**	AROUSED
SANGERS	**ANNOYS**	WAPPEND	MARGENT	AROUSER
ANGINA	TANNOYS	APPENDS	ARGENTS	AROUSES
ANGINAL	**ANONYM**	**APPLES**	**ARGLED**	**ARPENS**
ANGINAS	ANONYMA	DAPPLES	GARGLED	PARPENS
ANGLED	ANONYMS	SAPPLES	**ARGLES**	**ARPENT**
BANGLED	**ANSATE**	**APPORT**	DARGLES	PARPENT
CANGLED	ANSATED	RAPPORT	GARGLES	ARPENTS
DANGLED	**ANTARA**	APPORTS	**ARGONS**	**ARRACK**
FANGLED	TANTARA	**APPOSE**	JARGONS	BARRACK
JANGLED	ANTARAS	PAPPOSE	**ARIOSE**	CARRACK
MANGLED	**ANTARS**	APPOSED	CARIOSE	ARRACKS
TANGLED	CANTARS	APPOSER	**ARISES**	**ARRANT**
WANGLED	KANTARS	APPOSES	PARISES	FARRANT
ANGLER	**ANTHER**	**APRONS**	**ARISTA**	WARRANT
DANGLER	PANTHER	NAPRONS	BARISTA	**ARRAYS**
JANGLER	ANTHERS	**ARABIC**	ARISTAE	WARRAYS
MANGLER	**ANTICK**	ARABICA	ARISTAS	**ARRECT**
TANGLER	ANTICKE	**ARABIN**	**ARKING**	CARRECT

ARRETS	**ASHIER**	TASSETS	ATTESTS	**AVAILE**
BARRETS	CASHIER	**ASSIST**	**ATTIRE**	AVAILED
GARRETS	DASHIER	BASSIST	ATTIRED	AVAILES
ARRIDE	HASHIER	ASSISTS	ATTIRES	**AVENGE**
ARRIDED	MASHIER	**ASSIZE**	**ATTONE**	AVENGED
ARRIDES	WASHIER	ASSIZED	ATTONED	AVENGER
ARRIVE	**ASHING**	ASSIZER	ATTONES	AVENGES
ARRIVED	BASHING	ASSIZES	**ATTRAP**	**AVIATE**
ARRIVER	CASHING	**ASSUME**	RATTRAP	AVIATED
ARRIVES	DASHING	ASSUMED	ATTRAPS	AVIATES
ARROWS	FASHING	ASSUMER	**ATTRIT**	**AVISES**
BARROWS	GASHING	ASSUMES	ATTRITE	MAVISES
FARROWS	HASHING	**ASSURE**	ATTRITS	PAVISES
HARROWS	LASHING	ASSURED	**ATTUNE**	**AVULSE**
MARROWS	MASHING	ASSURER	ATTUNED	AVULSED
NARROWS	PASHING	ASSURES	ATTUNES	AVULSES
TARROWS	RASHING	**ASTERN**	**AUDING**	**AWARDS**
YARROWS	SASHING	EASTERN	DAUDING	VAWARDS
ARROWY	TASHING	PASTERN	GAUDING	**AWHAPE**
MARROWY	WASHING	**ASTERS**	HAUDING	AWHAPED
ARSHIN	**ASHMAN**	BASTERS	LAUDING	AWHAPES
ARSHINE	MASHMAN	CASTERS	AUDINGS	**AWLESS**
ARSHINS	**ASHMEN**	EASTERS	**AUGERS**	JAWLESS
ARSIER	MASHMEN	FASTERS	GAUGERS	LAWLESS
TARSIER	**ASHRAM**	GASTERS	SAUGERS	**AWNERS**
ARSING	ASHRAMA	LASTERS	**AUGHTS**	DAWNERS
FARSING	ASHRAMS	MASTERS	NAUGHTS	FAWNERS
PARSING	**ASKERS**	PASTERS	WAUGHTS	PAWNERS
ARSONS	MASKERS	RASTERS	**AUGUST**	YAWNERS
PARSONS	TASKERS	TASTERS	AUGUSTE	**AWNIER**
ARTELS	**ASKING**	WASTERS	AUGUSTS	FAWNIER
CARTELS	BASKING	**ASTONE**	**AULDER**	LAWNIER
MARTELS	CASKING	ASTONED	CAULDER	TAWNIER
ARTFUL	GASKING	ASTONES	**AUNTER**	YAWNIER
CARTFUL	MASKING	**ASTRAL**	DAUNTER	**AWNING**
ARTIER	TASKING	CASTRAL	GAUNTER	DAWNING
PARTIER	ASKINGS	GASTRAL	HAUNTER	FAWNING
TARTIER	**ASLAKE**	ASTRALS	SAUNTER	PAWNING
WARTIER	ASLAKED	**ASTUTE**	TAUNTER	YAWNING
ARTIES	ASLAKES	ASTUTER	VAUNTER	AWNINGS
PARTIES	**ASPERS**	**ATOKES**	AUNTERS	**AXILLA**
ARTIEST	GASPERS	MATOKES	**AUNTIE**	MAXILLA
ARTILY	JASPERS	**ATONED**	JAUNTIE	AXILLAE
TARTILY	RASPERS	BATONED	VAUNTIE	AXILLAR
ARTIST	ASPERSE	**ATRIAL**	AUNTIES	AXILLAS
ARTISTE	**ASPIRE**	PATRIAL	**AUNTLY**	**AXITES**
ARTISTS	ASPIRED	**ATRIUM**	GAUNTLY	TAXITES
ASCENT	ASPIRER	NATRIUM	**AURATE**	**AXLIKE**
NASCENT	ASPIRES	ATRIUMS	AURATED	WAXLIKE
ASCENTS	**ASPISH**	**ATTACH**	AURATES	**AYWORD**
ASCOTS	RASPISH	ATTACHE	**AURORA**	NAYWORD
MASCOTS	WASPISH	**ATTAIN**	AURORAE	AYWORDS
ASEITY	**ASSAIL**	ATTAINS	AURORAL	**AZURES**
GASEITY	VASSAIL	ATTAINT	AURORAS	RAZURES
ASHAME	WASSAIL	**ATTASK**	**AUTEUR**	**BABBLE**
ASHAMED	ASSAILS	ATTASKS	HAUTEUR	BABBLED
ASHAMES	**ASSENT**	ATTASKT	AUTEURS	BABBLER
ASHERY	ASSENTS	**ATTEST**	**AUTUMN**	BABBLES
FASHERY	**ASSETS**	FATTEST	AUTUMNS	**BABIES**
WASHERY	BASSETS	WATTEST	AUTUMNY	BABIEST

BABOOS	BASSEST	**BEJADE**	**BETAKE**	BILLYOS
BABOOSH	**BASSET**	BEJADED	BETAKEN	**BINDER**
BAFFLE	BASSETS	BEJADES	BETAKES	BINDERS
BAFFLED	BASSETT	**BELACE**	**BETEEM**	BINDERY
BAFFLER	**BATEAU**	BELACED	BETEEME	**BINGLE**
BAFFLES	BATEAUX	BELACES	BETEEMS	BINGLED
BAGASS	**BATING**	**BELATE**	**BETIDE**	BINGLES
BAGASSE	ABATING	BELATED	BETIDED	**BIOGEN**
BAGGIE	**BATTER**	BELATES	BETIDES	BIOGENS
BAGGIER	BATTERO	**BELDAM**	**BETIME**	BIOGENY
BAGGIES	BATTERS	BELDAME	BETIMED	**BIOTIC**
BAILLI	BATTERY	BELDAMS	BETIMES	ABIOTIC
BAILLIE	**BATTLE**	**BELEAP**	**BETTED**	BIOTICS
BAILLIS	BATTLED	BELEAPS	ABETTED	**BIRDIE**
BALDIE	BATTLER	BELEAPT	**BETTER**	BIRDIED
BALDIER	BATTLES	**BELONG**	ABETTER	BIRDIES
BALDIES	**BAYING**	BELONGS	**BETTOR**	**BIRKIE**
BALLAD	EBAYING	**BELOVE**	ABETTOR	BIRKIER
BALLADE	**BEAGLE**	BELOVED	BETTORS	BIRKIES
BALLADS	BEAGLED	BELOVES	**BEWARE**	**BIRSLE**
BALLAN	BEAGLER	**BEMEAN**	BEWARED	BIRSLED
BALLANS	BEAGLES	BEMEANS	BEWARES	BIRSLES
BALLANT	**BEAVER**	BEMEANT	**BEWRAP**	**BISTRE**
BALSAM	BEAVERS	**BEMETE**	BEWRAPS	BISTRED
BALSAMS	BEAVERY	BEMETED	BEWRAPT	BISTRES
BALSAMY	**BEDAZE**	BEMETES	**BEYLIC**	**BITTER**
BANDAR	BEDAZED	**BEMIRE**	BEYLICS	BITTERN
BANDARI	BEDAZES	BEMIRED	**BEZZLE**	BITTERS
BANDARS	**BEDLAM**	BEMIRES	BEZZLED	**BITTIE**
BANDED	BEDLAMP	**BEMUSE**	BEZZLES	BITTIER
ABANDED	BEDLAMS	BEMUSED	**BHISTI**	BITTIES
BANDIT	**BEDROP**	BEMUSES	BHISTIE	**BLAGUE**
BANDITO	BEDROPS	**BENAME**	BHISTIS	BLAGUER
BANDITS	BEDROPT	BENAMED	**BIBBER**	BLAGUES
BANGLE	**BEETLE**	BENAMES	BIBBERS	**BLASTS**
BANGLED	BEETLED	**BENTOS**	BIBBERY	OBLASTS
BANGLES	BEETLER	OBENTOS	**BICORN**	**BLENDE**
BARBEL	BEETLES	**BENZIN**	BICORNE	BLENDED
BARBELL	**BEGAZE**	BENZINE	BICORNS	BLENDER
BARBELS	BEGAZED	BENZINS	**BIDDEN**	BLENDES
BARDIE	BEGAZES	**BENZOL**	ABIDDEN	**BLIGHT**
BARDIER	**BEGGAR**	BENZOLE	**BIDENT**	BLIGHTS
BARDIES	BEGGARS	BENZOLS	BIDENTS	BLIGHTY
BARGES	BEGGARY	**BERAKE**	**BIDERS**	**BLINGS**
BARGEST	**BEGRIM**	BERAKED	ABIDERS	ABLINGS
BARMIE	BEGRIME	BERAKES	**BIDING**	**BLINTZ**
BARMIER	BEGRIMS	**BERATE**	ABIDING	BLINTZE
BARRIE	**BEGUIN**	BERATED	BIDINGS	**BLITHE**
BARRIER	BEGUINE	BERATES	**BIFFIN**	BLITHER
BARRIES	BEGUINS	**BERIME**	BIFFING	**BLONDE**
BASHED	**BEHAVE**	BERIMED	BIFFINS	BLONDER
ABASHED	BEHAVED	BERIMES	**BIGGIN**	BLONDES
BASHES	BEHAVER	**BERLIN**	BIGGING	**BLOTCH**
ABASHES	BEHAVES	BERLINE	BIGGINS	BLOTCHY
BASING	**BEHOVE**	BERLINS	**BILLOW**	**BLOUSE**
ABASING	BEHOVED	**BERTHE**	BILLOWS	BLOUSED
BASQUE	BEHOVES	BERTHED	BILLOWY	BLOUSES
BASQUED	**BEIGNE**	BERTHES	**BILLYO**	**BLOWIE**
BASQUES	BEIGNES	**BESPAT**	BILLYOH	BLOWIER
BASSES	BEIGNET	BESPATE	BILLYOS	BLOWIES

BLOWSE	BOOGIED	BRAVERS	BROUGHS	BUREAUS
BLOWSED	BOOGIES	BRAVERY	BROUGHT	BUREAUX
BLOWSES	**BOOKIE**	**BRAVES**	**BROWSE**	**BURGLE**
BLOWZE	BOOKIER	BRAVEST	BROWSED	BURGLED
BLOWZED	BOOKIES	**BRAYED**	BROWSER	BURGLES
BLOWZES	**BORATE**	ABRAYED	BROWSES	**BURREL**
BLUDGE	BORATED	**BREAST**	**BRUCIN**	BURRELL
BLUDGED	BORATES	ABREAST	BRUCINE	BURRELS
BLUDGER	**BORREL**	BREASTS	BRUCINS	**BURSAR**
BLUDGES	BORRELL	**BREATH**	**BRUISE**	BURSARS
BLUDIE	**BORSCH**	BREATHE	BRUISED	BURSARY
BLUDIER	BORSCHT	BREATHS	BRUISER	**BUSHIE**
BLUNGE	**BOSQUE**	BREATHY	BRUISES	BUSHIER
BLUNGED	BOSQUES	**BREEZE**	**BUBBLE**	BUSHIES
BLUNGER	BOSQUET	BREEZED	ABUBBLE	**BUSHWA**
BLUNGES	**BOSSES**	BREEZES	BUBBLED	BUSHWAH
BOBBER	BOSSEST	**BREVET**	BUBBLER	BUSHWAS
BOBBERS	**BOTONE**	BREVETE	BUBBLES	**BUSIES**
BOBBERY	BOTONEE	BREVETS	**BUCKLE**	BUSIEST
BOBBIN	**BOTTLE**	**BREWER**	BUCKLED	**BUSING**
BOBBING	BOTTLED	BREWERS	BUCKLER	ABUSING
BOBBINS	BOTTLER	BREWERY	BUCKLES	BUSINGS
BOBBLE	BOTTLES	**BRIBER**	**BUCKRA**	**BUSKIN**
BOBBLED	**BOUCHE**	BRIBERS	BUCKRAM	BUSKING
BOBBLES	BOUCHEE	BRIBERY	BUCKRAS	BUSKINS
BOCKED	BOUCHES	**BRIDGE**	**BUDDLE**	**BUSTLE**
BOCKEDY	**BOUCLE**	ABRIDGE	BUDDLED	BUSTLED
BODGIE	BOUCLEE	BRIDGED	BUDDLES	BUSTLER
BODGIER	BOUCLES	BRIDGES	**BUDGER**	BUSTLES
BODGIES	**BOUGHT**	**BRIDLE**	BUDGERO	**BUTENE**
BODING	ABOUGHT	BRIDLED	BUDGERS	BUTENES
ABODING	BOUGHTS	BRIDLER	**BUGGAN**	**BUTLER**
BODINGS	**BOUNCE**	BRIDLES	BUGGANE	BUTLERS
BOFFIN	BOUNCED	**BRIGUE**	BUGGANS	BUTLERY
BOFFING	BOUNCER	BRIGUED	**BUGGER**	**BUTTED**
BOFFINS	BOUNCES	BRIGUES	BUGGERS	ABUTTED
BOGGLE	**BOUNDS**	**BROACH**	BUGGERY	**BUTTER**
BOGGLED	ABOUNDS	ABROACH	**BUGGIN**	ABUTTER
BOGGLER	**BOURSE**	**BROADS**	BUGGING	BUTTERS
BOGGLES	BOURSES	ABROADS	BUGGINS	BUTTERY
BOILER	**BOVATE**	**BROCHE**	**BUMBLE**	**BUTTLE**
BOILERS	OBOVATE	BROCHED	BUMBLED	BUTTLED
BOILERY	BOVATES	BROCHES	BUMBLER	BUTTLES
BONIST	**BRACER**	**BROKER**	BUMBLES	**BUTTON**
EBONIST	BRACERO	BROKERS	**BUMMLE**	BUTTONS
BONISTS	BRACERS	BROKERY	BUMMLED	BUTTONY
BONNIE	**BRAHMA**	**BROMAL**	BUMMLES	**BUZUKI**
BONNIER	BRAHMAN	BROMALS	**BUNDLE**	BUZUKIA
BONNIES	BRAHMAS	**BROMID**	BUNDLED	BUZUKIS
BOOBOO	**BRAIDE**	BROMIDE	BUNDLER	**BYLINE**
BOOBOOK	BRAIDED	BROMIDS	BUNDLES	BYLINED
BOOBOOS	BRAIDER	**BROMIN**	**BUNGLE**	BYLINER
BOODIE	**BRAIDS**	BROMINE	BUNGLED	BYLINES
BOODIED	ABRAIDS	BROMINS	BUNGLER	**BYSSAL**
BOODIES	**BRAISE**	**BRONZE**	BUNGLES	ABYSSAL
BOODLE	BRAISED	BRONZED	**BURBLE**	**CABBED**
BOODLED	BRAISES	BRONZEN	BURBLED	SCABBED
BOODLER	**BRANCH**	BRONZER	BURBLER	**CACKLE**
BOODLES	BRANCHY	BRONZES	BURBLES	CACKLED
BOOGIE	**BRAVER**	**BROUGH**	**BUREAU**	CACKLER

CACKLES	CANDLES	CARLINS	**CAUDLE**	CHANGER
CADDIE	**CANGLE**	**CARNIE**	CAUDLED	CHANGES
CADDIED	CANGLED	CARNIED	CAUDLES	**CHAPES**
CADDIES	CANGLES	CARNIER	**CAUTER**	CHAPESS
CADDIS	**CANKER**	CARNIES	CAUTERS	**CHARDS**
CADDISH	CANKERS	**CAROCH**	CAUTERY	ECHARDS
CADEAU	CANKERY	CAROCHE	**CAVIAR**	**CHARGE**
CADEAUX	**CANNED**	**CARPAL**	CAVIARE	CHARGED
CAGOUL	SCANNED	CARPALE	CAVIARS	CHARGER
CAGOULE	**CANNER**	CARPALS	**CELLAR**	CHARGES
CAGOULS	SCANNER	**CARPED**	OCELLAR	**CHASSE**
CAJOLE	CANNERS	SCARPED	CELLARS	CHASSED
CAJOLED	CANNERY	**CARPER**	**CELLOS**	CHASSES
CAJOLER	**CANNIE**	SCARPER	CELLOSE	**CHASTE**
CAJOLES	CANNIER	CARPERS	**CEMENT**	CHASTEN
CALKIN	CANTAL	**CARREL**	CEMENTA	CHASTER
CALKING	CANTALA	CARRELL	CEMENTS	**CHAUFE**
CALKINS	CANTALS	CARRELS	**CENTRA**	CHAUFED
CALLAN	**CANTED**	**CARROT**	CENTRAL	CHAUFER
CALLANS	SCANTED	CARROTS	**CENTRE**	CHAUFES
CALLANT	**CANTER**	CARROTY	CENTRED	**CHEESE**
CALLED	SCANTER	**CARTED**	CENTRES	CHEESED
SCALLED	CANTERS	SCARTED	**CERATE**	CHEESES
CALLOP	**CANTHI**	**CARTES**	ACERATE	**CHEQUE**
SCALLOP	ACANTHI	ECARTES	CERATED	CHEQUER
CALLOPS	**CANTIC**	**CARVER**	CERATES	CHEQUES
CALPAC	CANTICO	CARVERS	**CERNED**	**CHEVRE**
CALPACK	**CANTLE**	CARVERY	SCERNED	CHEVRES
CALPACS	SCANTLE	**CARVES**	**CERNES**	CHEVRET
CALQUE	CANTLED	SCARVES	SCERNES	**CHEWIE**
CALQUED	CANTLES	CASERN	**CEROUS**	CHEWIER
CALQUES	CANTLET	CASERNE	ACEROUS	CHEWIES
CAMBIA	CANULA	CASERNS	**CESTOI**	**CHIASM**
CAMBIAL	CANULAE	**CASQUE**	CESTOID	CHIASMA
CAMELS	CANULAR	CASQUED	**CESURA**	CHIASMI
SCAMELS	CANULAS	CASQUES	CESURAE	CHIASMS
CAMERA	**CAPING**	**CASTLE**	CESURAL	**CHICKS**
CAMERAE	SCAPING	CASTLED	CESURAS	TCHICKS
CAMERAL	**CAPITA**	CASTLES	**CETYLS**	**CHILDE**
CAMERAS	CAPITAL	**CASTOR**	ACETYLS	CHILDED
CAMMED	CAPITAN	CASTORS	**CHAETA**	CHILDER
SCAMMED	**CAPRIC**	CASTORY	CHAETAE	CHILDES
CAMPED	CAPRICE	**CATALO**	CHAETAL	**CHIMER**
SCAMPED	**CARDIA**	CATALOG	**CHAINE**	CHIMERA
CAMPER	CARDIAC	CATALOS	CHAINED	CHIMERE
SCAMPER	CARDIAE	**CATENA**	CHAINES	CHIMERS
CAMPERS	CARDIAS	CATENAE	**CHALLA**	**CHINCH**
CAMPERY	**CARERS**	CATENAS	CHALLAH	CHINCHY
CAMPLE	SCARERS	**CATERS**	CHALLAN	**CHINES**
CAMPLED	**CARINA**	ACATERS	CHALLAS	CHINESE
CAMPLES	OCARINA	**CATLIN**	**CHALOT**	**CHINTZ**
CANDID	CARINAE	CATLING	CHALOTH	CHINTZY
CANDIDA	CARINAL	CATLINS	**CHANCE**	**CHIRAL**
CANDIDS	CARINAS	**CATTED**	CHANCED	ACHIRAL
CANDIE	**CARING**	SCATTED	CHANCEL	**CHIRRE**
CANDIED	SCARING	**CATTIE**	CHANCER	CHIRRED
CANDIES	CARINGS	CATTIER	CHANCES	CHIRREN
CANDLE	**CARLIN**	CATTIES	CHANCEY	CHIRRES
CANDLED	CARLINE	**CAUDAL**	**CHANGE**	**CHOANA**
CANDLER	CARLING	ACAUDAL	CHANGED	CHOANAE

CHOICE	CIRCLED	CLUTCHY	SCOLDER	CONSOLE
CHOICER	CIRCLER	**COARSE**	**COLLAR**	CONSOLS
CHOICES	CIRCLES	COARSEN	COLLARD	**CONSUL**
CHOLER	CIRCLET	COARSER	COLLARS	CONSULS
CHOLERA	**CIRCUS**	**COBBLE**	**COLLIE**	CONSULT
CHOLERS	CIRCUSY	COBBLED	COLLIED	**CONTES**
CHOOSE	**CITHER**	COBBLER	COLLIER	CONTEST
CHOOSER	CITHERN	COBBLES	COLLIES	**CONTRA**
CHOOSES	CITHERS	**COCAIN**	**COLLOP**	CONTRAS
CHOOSEY	**CITRIN**	COCAINE	COLLOPS	CONTRAT
CHOPIN	CITRINE	COCAINS	SCOLLOP	**COOKER**
CHOPINE	CITRINS	**COCKLE**	**COLOBI**	COOKERS
CHOPINS	**CITRUS**	COCKLED	COLOBID	COOKERY
CHORAL	CITRUSY	COCKLER	**COLONE**	**COOPED**
CHORALE	**CLAMBE**	COCKLES	COLONEL	SCOOPED
CHORALS	CLAMBER	**CODDLE**	COLONES	**COOPER**
CHORDA	**CLAQUE**	CODDLED	**COLONI**	SCOOPER
CHORDAE	CLAQUER	CODDLER	COLONIC	COOPERS
CHORDAL	CLAQUES	CODDLES	**COLOUR**	COOPERY
CHOREA	**CLAVES**	**CODEIN**	COLOURS	**COORIE**
CHOREAL	SCLAVES	CODEINA	COLOURY	COORIED
CHOREAS	**CLAVIE**	CODEINE	**COMAKE**	COORIES
CHORIA	CLAVIER	CODEINS	COMAKER	**COOTCH**
CHORIAL	CLAVIES	**CODLIN**	COMAKES	SCOOTCH
CHOUSE	**CLEANS**	CODLING	**COMMER**	**COOTER**
CHOUSED	CLEANSE	CODLINS	COMMERE	SCOOTER
CHOUSER	**CLEAVE**	**COELOM**	COMMERS	COOTERS
CHOUSES	CLEAVED	COELOME	**COMMIX**	**COPING**
CHOUTS	CLEAVER	COELOMS	COMMIXT	SCOPING
SCHOUTS	CLEAVES	**COERCE**	**COMMOT**	COPINGS
CHOWSE	**CLEPED**	COERCED	COMMOTE	**COPPER**
CHOWSED	YCLEPED	COERCER	COMMOTS	COPPERS
CHOWSES	**CLICHE**	COERCES	**COMPAS**	COPPERY
CHRISM	CLICHED	**COFFED**	COMPASS	**COPPIN**
CHRISMA	CLICHES	SCOFFED	COMPAST	COPPING
CHRISMS	**CLIFFS**	**COFFER**	**COMPER**	COPPINS
CHROME	SCLIFFS	SCOFFER	COMPERE	**COPULA**
CHROMED	**CLINIC**	COFFERS	COMPERS	SCOPULA
CHROMEL	ACLINIC	**COFFIN**	**COMPOS**	COPULAE
CHROMES	CLINICS	COFFING	COMPOSE	COPULAR
CHROMY	**CLIQUE**	COFFINS	COMPOST	COPULAS
CHROMYL	CLIQUED	**COFFLE**	**COMPOT**	**CORERS**
CHUKKA	CLIQUES	COFFLED	COMPOTE	SCORERS
CHUKKAR	CLIQUEY	COFFLES	COMPOTS	**CORING**
CHUKKAS	**CLOACA**	**COGGED**	**CONCHA**	SCORING
CHUPPA	CLOACAE	SCOGGED	CONCHAE	**CORNEA**
CHUPPAH	CLOACAL	**COGGLE**	CONCHAL	CORNEAE
CHUPPAS	CLOACAS	COGGLED	CONCHAS	CORNEAL
CHURCH	**CLOSED**	COGGLES	**CONCHE**	CORNEAS
CHURCHY	ECLOSED	**COHERE**	CONCHED	**CORNED**
CICADA	**CLOSES**	COHERED	CONCHES	ACORNED
CICADAE	ECLOSES	COHERER	**CONGEE**	SCORNED
CICADAS	CLOSEST	COHERES	CONGEED	**CORNER**
CINDER	**CLOTHE**	**COIFFE**	CONGEES	SCORNER
CINDERS	CLOTHED	COIFFED	**CONGES**	CORNERS
CINDERY	CLOTHES	COIFFES	CONGEST	**CORNET**
CINEOL	**CLOVER**	**COIGNE**	**CONJEE**	CORNETS
CINEOLE	CLOVERS	COIGNED	CONJEED	CORNETT
CINEOLS	CLOVERY	COIGNES	CONJEES	**CORNUA**
CIRCLE	**CLUTCH**	**COLDER**	**CONSOL**	CORNUAL

CORONA	COURSED	SCREEDS	**CRUSTA**	**CURDLE**
CORONAE	COURSER	**CREESE**	CRUSTAE	CURDLED
CORONAL	COURSES	CREESED	CRUSTAL	CURDLER
CORONAS	**COUTER**	CREESES	**CRYING**	CURDLES
CORPSE	SCOUTER	**CREESH**	SCRYING	**CURIES**
CORPSED	COUTERS	CREESHY	CRYINGS	ECURIES
CORPSES	**COUTHS**	**CRESTA**	**CRYPTO**	**CURIOS**
CORSES	SCOUTHS	CRESTAL	CRYPTON	CURIOSA
SCORSES	**COWING**	**CREWED**	CRYPTOS	**CURRAN**
CORTIN	SCOWING	SCREWED	**CUBICA**	CURRANS
CORTINA	**COWLED**	**CRIMPS**	CUBICAL	CURRANT
CORTINS	SCOWLED	SCRIMPS	CUBICAS	**CURRED**
CORYZA	**COWPED**	**CRIMPY**	**CUDDLE**	SCURRED
CORYZAL	SCOWPED	SCRIMPY	SCUDDLE	**CURRIE**
CORYZAS	**COWRIE**	**CRINES**	CUDDLED	CURRIED
COSHER	SCOWRIE	SCRINES	CUDDLER	CURRIER
COSHERS	COWRIES	**CRINGE**	CUDDLES	CURRIES
COSHERY	**COZIES**	CRINGED	**CUFFED**	**CURSOR**
COSIES	COZIEST	CRINGER	SCUFFED	CURSORS
COSIEST	**CRADLE**	CRINGES	**CUFFIN**	CURSORY
COSMIN	CRADLED	**CRISSA**	CUFFING	**CUSHIE**
COSMINE	CRADLER	CRISSAL	CUFFINS	CUSHIER
COSMINS	CRADLES	**CRISTA**	**CUFFLE**	CUSHIES
COSTAR	**CRAGGY**	CRISTAE	SCUFFLE	**CUTELY**
COSTARD	SCRAGGY	**CROCHE**	CUFFLED	ACUTELY
COSTARS	**CRAMES**	CROCHES	CUFFLES	**CUTEST**
COTEAU	CRAMESY	CROCHET	**CUISSE**	ACUTEST
COTEAUX	**CRANCH**	**CROGGY**	CUISSER	**CUTLER**
COTING	SCRANCH	SCROGGY	CUISSES	CUTLERS
COTINGA	**CRANIA**	**CROMED**	**CULLED**	CUTLERY
COTISE	CRANIAL	SCROMED	SCULLED	**CUTTER**
COTISED	**CRANNY**	**CROMES**	**CULLER**	SCUTTER
COTISES	SCRANNY	SCROMES	SCULLER	CUTTERS
COTTON	**CRAPED**	**CROSSE**	CULLERS	**CUTTLE**
COTTONS	SCRAPED	CROSSED	**CULTCH**	SCUTTLE
COTTONY	**CRAPES**	CROSSER	SCULTCH	CUTTLED
COTYPE	SCRAPES	CROSSES	**CULVER**	CUTTLES
ECOTYPE	**CRAPPY**	**CROTAL**	CULVERS	**CUZZES**
COTYPES	SCRAPPY	SCROTAL	CULVERT	SCUZZES
COUCHE	**CRATCH**	CROTALA	**CUMBER**	**CYANID**
COUCHED	SCRATCH	CROTALS	SCUMBER	CYANIDE
COUCHEE	**CRAWLS**	**CROUPE**	CUMBERS	CYANIDS
COUCHER	SCRAWLS	CROUPED	**CUMMER**	**CYANIN**
COUCHES	**CRAWLY**	CROUPER	SCUMMER	CYANINE
COUPED	SCRAWLY	CROUPES	CUMMERS	CYANINS
SCOUPED	**CREAKS**	**CRUDES**	**CUNNER**	**CYATHI**
COUPLE	SCREAKS	CRUDEST	SCUNNER	CYATHIA
COUPLED	**CREAKY**	**CRUISE**	CUNNERS	**CYCLER**
COUPLER	SCREAKY	CRUISED	**CUPOLA**	CYCLERS
COUPLES	**CREAMS**	CRUISER	CUPOLAR	CYCLERY
COUPLET	SCREAMS	CRUISES	CUPOLAS	**CYCLIC**
COURED	**CREASE**	**CRUMMY**	**CUPPER**	ACYCLIC
SCOURED	CREASED	SCRUMMY	SCUPPER	**CYCLIN**
COURIE	CREASER	**CRUMPS**	CUPPERS	CYCLING
SCOURIE	CREASES	SCRUMPS	**CUPULA**	CYCLINS
COURIED	**CREATE**	**CRUMPY**	CUPULAE	**CYMBAL**
COURIER	OCREATE	SCRUMPY	CUPULAR	CYMBALO
COURIES	CREATED	**CRUNCH**	**CURATE**	CYMBALS
COURSE	CREATES	SCRUNCH	CURATED	**CYMLIN**
SCOURSE	**CREEDS**	CRUNCHY	CURATES	CYMLING

CYMLINS	**DAYGLO**	DEFILES	**DENARI**	DEVISED
CYPRES	DAYGLOW	**DEFINE**	DENARII	DEVISEE
CYPRESS	**DAZZLE**	DEFINED	**DENOTE**	DEVISER
DABBLE	DAZZLED	DEFINER	DENOTED	DEVISES
DABBLED	DAZZLER	DEFINES	DENOTES	**DEVOTE**
DABBLER	DAZZLES	**DEFUSE**	**DENTAL**	DEVOTED
DABBLES	**DEANER**	DEFUSED	EDENTAL	DEVOTEE
DACOIT	DEANERS	DEFUSER	DENTALS	DEVOTES
DACOITS	DEANERY	DEFUSES	**DENTIN**	**DEWLAP**
DACOITY	**DEARES**	**DEFUZE**	DENTINE	DEWLAPS
DACTYL	DEAREST	DEFUZED	DENTING	DEWLAPT
DACTYLI	**DEBASE**	DEFUZES	DENTINS	**DHARMA**
DACTYLS	DEBASED	**DEGREE**	**DENUDE**	ADHARMA
DADDLE	DEBASER	DEGREED	DENUDED	DHARMAS
DADDLED	DEBASES	DEGREES	DENUDER	**DHOOTI**
DADDLES	**DEBATE**	**DEIGNS**	DENUDES	DHOOTIE
DAGGLE	DEBATED	SDEIGNS	**DEODAR**	DHOOTIS
DAGGLED	DEBATER	**DEJECT**	DEODARA	**DIAMIN**
DAGGLES	DEBATES	DEJECTA	DEODARS	DIAMINE
DAIDLE	**DEBONE**	DEJECTS	**DEPONE**	DIAMINS
DAIDLED	DEBONED	**DELATE**	DEPONED	**DIARCH**
DAIDLES	DEBONER	DELATED	DEPONES	DIARCHY
DAINED	DEBONES	DELATES	**DEPOSE**	**DIAZIN**
SDAINED	**DECIDE**	**DELETE**	DEPOSED	DIAZINE
DAINES	DECIDED	DELETED	DEPOSER	DIAZINS
SDAINES	DECIDER	DELETES	DEPOSES	**DIBBLE**
DAKOIT	DECIDES	**DELIME**	**DEPUTE**	DIBBLED
DAKOITI	**DECKLE**	DELIMED	DEPUTED	DIBBLER
DAKOITS	DECKLED	DELIMES	DEPUTES	DIBBLES
DAKOITY	DECKLES	**DELOPE**	**DERATE**	**DICKIE**
DAMAGE	**DECODE**	DELOPED	DERATED	DICKIER
DAMAGED	DECODED	DELOPES	DERATES	DICKIES
DAMAGER	DECODER	**DELUDE**	**DERIDE**	**DIDDLE**
DAMAGES	DECODES	DELUDED	DERIDED	DIDDLED
DANDLE	**DECOKE**	DELUDER	DERIDER	DIDDLER
DANDLED	DECOKED	DELUDES	DERIDES	DIDDLES
DANDLER	DECOKES	**DELUGE**	**DERIVE**	DIDDLEY
DANDLES	**DECREE**	DELUGED	DERIVED	**DILATE**
DANGLE	DECREED	DELUGES	DERIVER	DILATED
DANGLED	DECREER	**DEMAIN**	DERIVES	DILATER
DANGLER	DECREES	DEMAINE	**DESINE**	DILATES
DANGLES	DECREET	DEMAINS	DESINED	**DILUTE**
DAPPLE	**DEDUCE**	**DEMEAN**	DESINES	DILUTED
DAPPLED	DEDUCED	DEMEANE	**DESIRE**	DILUTEE
DAPPLES	DEDUCES	DEMEANS	DESIRED	DILUTER
DARKLE	**DEEMED**	**DEMENT**	DESIRER	DILUTES
DARKLED	ADEEMED	DEMENTI	DESIRES	**DIMPLE**
DARKLES	**DEFACE**	DEMENTS	**DESYNE**	DIMPLED
DARTLE	DEFACED	**DEMISE**	DESYNED	DIMPLES
DARTLED	DEFACER	DEMISED	DESYNES	**DINDLE**
DARTLES	DEFACES	DEMISES	**DETENT**	DINDLED
DAUBER	**DEFAME**	**DEMODE**	DETENTE	DINDLES
DAUBERS	DEFAMED	DEMODED	DETENTS	**DINKIE**
DAUBERY	DEFAMER	**DEMOTE**	**DETENU**	DINKIER
DAWDLE	DEFAMES	DEMOTED	DETENUE	DINKIES
DAWDLED	**DEFAST**	DEMOTES	DETENUS	**DINNLE**
DAWDLER	DEFASTE	**DEMURE**	**DETUNE**	DINNLED
DAWDLES	**DEFILE**	DEMURED	DETUNED	DINNLES
DAWING	DEFILED	DEMURER	DETUNES	**DIOXAN**
ADAWING	DEFILER	DEMURES	**DEVISE**	DIOXANE

DIOXANS	DOMAINE	DROICHY	**EARFUL**	**EATERY**
DIOXID	DOMAINS	**DROLES**	FEARFUL	PEATERY
DIOXIDE	**DOMINE**	DROLEST	TEARFUL	**EATHLY**
DIOXIDS	DOMINEE	**DROMON**	EARFULS	DEATHLY
DIPLON	DOMINES	DROMOND	**EARING**	**EATING**
DIPLONS	**DONATE**	DROMONS	BEARING	BEATING
DIPLONT	ODONATE	**DROUTH**	DEARING	FEATING
DISBAR	DONATED	DROUTHS	FEARING	HEATING
DISBARK	DONATES	DROUTHY	GEARING	SEATING
DISBARS	**DONSIE**	**DROWSE**	HEARING	EATINGS
DISCUS	DONSIER	DROWSED	LEARING	**EBBING**
DISCUSS	**DOODLE**	DROWSES	MEARING	KEBBING
DISMAY	DOODLED	**DRUDGE**	NEARING	NEBBING
DISMAYD	DOODLER	DRUDGED	REARING	WEBBING
DISMAYL	DOODLES	DRUDGER	SEARING	**EBOOKS**
DISMAYS	**DORISE**	DRUDGES	TEARING	REBOOKS
DISPLE	ODORISE	**DUBBIN**	WEARING	**ECBOLE**
DISPLED	DORISED	DUBBING	EARINGS	ECBOLES
DISPLES	DORISES	DUBBINS	**EARNED**	**ECHING**
DISTIL	**DORIZE**	**DUCKIE**	LEARNED	EECHING
DISTILL	ODORIZE	DUCKIER	YEARNED	LECHING
DISTILS	DORIZED	DUCKIES	**EARNER**	PECHING
DISUSE	DORIZES	**DUDDER**	LEARNER	**ECLOSE**
DISUSED	**DOTTLE**	DUDDERS	YEARNER	RECLOSE
DISUSES	DOTTLED	DUDDERY	EARNERS	ECLOSED
DITHER	DOTTLER	**DUDDIE**	**EARTHS**	ECLOSES
DITHERS	DOTTLES	DUDDIER	DEARTHS	**EDDIES**
DITHERY	**DOUBLE**	**DUMPLE**	HEARTHS	NEDDIES
DITING	DOUBLED	DUMPLED	**EASELS**	TEDDIES
EDITING	DOUBLER	DUMPLES	TEASELS	**EDDISH**
DIVERS	DOUBLES	**DURESS**	WEASELS	NEDDISH
DIVERSE	DOUBLET	DURESSE	**EASERS**	REDDISH
DIVIDE	**DOUCHE**	**DUSTED**	LEASERS	**EDEMAS**
DIVIDED	DOUCHED	ADUSTED	TEASERS	OEDEMAS
DIVIDER	DOUCHES	**DYNAST**	**EASIES**	**EDGERS**
DIVIDES	**DOUGHT**	DYNASTS	EASIEST	HEDGERS
DIVINE	DOUGHTY	DYNASTY	**EASING**	KEDGERS
DIVINED	**DOWLNE**	**DYNODE**	CEASING	LEDGERS
DIVINER	DOWLNES	**DYVOURS**	FEASING	**EDGIER**
DIVINES	DOWLNEY	DYVOURY	LEASING	HEDGIER
DOBBIN	**DRACHM**	**EAGLED**	MEASING	KEDGIER
DOBBING	DRACHMA	BEAGLED	PEASING	LEDGIER
DOBBINS	DRACHMS	TEAGLED	SEASING	SEDGIER
DOCILE	**DRAPER**	**EAGLES**	TEASING	WEDGIER
DOCILER	DRAPERS	BEAGLES	EASINGS	**EDGING**
DODDER	DRAPERY	TEAGLES	**EASLES**	HEDGING
DODDERS	**DREADS**	**EAGRES**	MEASLES	KEDGING
DODDERY	ADREADS	MEAGRES	**EASTED**	WEDGING
DODGER	**DREARE**	**EANING**	BEASTED	EDGINGS
DODGERS	DREARER	BEANING	FEASTED	**EDILES**
DODGERY	DREARES	DEANING	REASTED	AEDILES
DOGGER	**DREDGE**	LEANING	YEASTED	**EDUCED**
DOGGERS	DREDGED	MEANING	**EASTER**	DEDUCED
DOGGERY	DREDGER	PEANING	FEASTER	REDUCED
DOGGIE	DREDGES	SEANING	EASTERN	SEDUCED
DOGGIER	**DROGUE**	WEANING	EASTERS	**EDUCES**
DOGGIES	DROGUES	YEANING	**EATERS**	DEDUCES
DOLENT	DROGUET	**EARDED**	BEATERS	REDUCES
DOLENTE	**DROICH**	BEARDED	HEATERS	SEDUCES
DOMAIN	DROICHS	YEARDED	SEATERS	**EDUCTS**

DEDUCTS	KEGGING	MELDING	EMERGED	LEMURES
EECHED	LEGGING	WELDING	EMERGES	**ENABLE**
LEECHED	PEGGING	ELDINGS	**EMERSE**	TENABLE
REECHED	VEGGING	**ELECTS**	DEMERSE	ENABLED
EECHES	**EGISES**	SELECTS	EMERSED	ENABLER
BEECHES	AEGISES	**ELENCH**	NEMESES	ENABLES
KEECHES	**EGOIST**	ELENCHI	**EMESIS**	**ENATES**
LEECHES	EGOISTS	ELENCHS	NEMESIS	PENATES
REECHES	**EGRESS**	**ELFING**	**EMETIC**	SENATES
EELIER	NEGRESS	SELFING	MEMETIC	**ENATIC**
SEELIER	REGRESS	**ELFISH**	EMETICS	VENATIC
EERIER	**EGRETS**	SELFISH	**EMETIN**	**ENCAGE**
BEERIER	REGRETS	**ELITES**	EMETINE	ENCAGED
LEERIER	**EIGHTH**	PELITES	EMETINS	ENCAGES
PEERIER	HEIGHTH	VELITES	**EMMERS**	**ENCASE**
EERILY	**EIGHTHS**	**ELOPED**	HEMMERS	ENCASED
BEERILY	HEIGHTS	DELOPED	YEMMERS	ENCASES
LEERILY	WEIGHTS	**ELOPES**	**EMMOVE**	**ENCAVE**
EFFACE	**EIGHTY**	DELOPES	EMMOVED	ENCAVED
EFFACED	WEIGHTY	**ELUDED**	EMMOVES	ENCAVES
EFFACER	**EITHER**	DELUDED	**EMOTED**	**ENCINA**
EFFACES	NEITHER	**ELUDER**	DEMOTED	ENCINAL
EFFEIR	**EJECTA**	DELUDER	**EMOTER**	ENCINAS
EFFEIRS	DEJECTA	ELUDERS	REMOTER	**ENCODE**
EFFERE	**EJECTS**	**ELUDES**	EMOTERS	ENCODED
EFFERED	DEJECTS	DELUDES	**EMOTES**	ENCODER
EFFERES	REJECTS	**ELUTOR**	GEMOTES	ENCODES
EFFING	**ELANCE**	ELUTORS	REMOTES	**ENCORE**
JEFFING	ELANCED	**ELUVIA**	**EMOVED**	ENCORED
REFFING	ELANCES	ELUVIAL	REMOVED	ENCORES
EFFINGS	**ELANDS**	**ELVERS**	**EMOVES**	**ENDERS**
EFFRAY	RELANDS	DELVERS	REMOVES	BENDERS
EFFRAYS	**ELAPID**	**ELYTRA**	**EMPALE**	FENDERS
EFFUSE	ELAPIDS	ELYTRAL	EMPALED	GENDERS
EFFUSED	**ELAPSE**	**EMAILS**	EMPALER	LENDERS
EFFUSES	DELAPSE	REMAILS	EMPALES	MENDERS
EFTEST	RELAPSE	**EMBALE**	**EMPARE**	RENDERS
DEFTEST	ELAPSED	EMBALED	EMPARED	SENDERS
LEFTEST	ELAPSES	EMBALES	EMPARES	TENDERS
EGALLY	**ELATED**	**EMBASE**	**EMPLOY**	VENDERS
LEGALLY	BELATED	EMBASED	EMPLOYE	**ENDING**
REGALLY	DELATED	EMBASES	EMPLOYS	BENDING
EGENCE	GELATED	**EMBERS**	**EMPTED**	FENDING
REGENCE	RELATED	MEMBERS	TEMPTED	HENDING
EGENCES	VELATED	**EMBLEM**	**EMULED**	LENDING
EGENCY	**ELATER**	EMBLEMA	AEMULED	MENDING
REGENCY	RELATER	EMBLEMS	**EMULES**	PENDING
EGESTS	ELATERS	**EMBOLI**	AEMULES	RENDING
REGESTS	**ELATES**	EMBOLIC	**EMULGE**	SENDING
EGGARS	BELATES	**EMBRUE**	EMULGED	TENDING
BEGGARS	DELATES	EMBRUED	EMULGES	VENDING
SEGGARS	GELATES	EMBRUES	**EMUNGE**	WENDING
EGGERS	RELATES	**EMBRYO**	EMUNGED	ENDINGS
KEGGERS	**ELDERS**	EMBRYON	EMUNGES	**ENDITE**
LEGGERS	GELDERS	EMBRYOS	**EMURED**	ENDITED
EGGIER	MELDERS	**EMENDS**	DEMURED	ENDITES
LEGGIER	WELDERS	REMENDS	**EMURES**	**ENDUES**
EGGING	**ELDING**	**EMERGE**	DEMURES	VENDUES
BEGGING	GELDING	DEMERGE	**EMURES**	**ENDURE**
DEGGING		REMERGE	DEMURES	ENDURED

ENDURER	ENROBES	EONISMS	ERRINGS	LETCHES
ENDURES	**ENSATE**	**EPARCH**	**ERRORS**	RETCHES
ENERVE	SENSATE	EPARCHS	TERRORS	VETCHES
ENERVED	**ENSILE**	EPARCHY	**ERUGOS**	**ETHALS**
ENERVES	PENSILE	**EPAULE**	AERUGOS	LETHALS
ENEWED	SENSILE	EPAULES	**ESCAPE**	**ETHANE**
RENEWED	TENSILE	EPAULET	ESCAPED	METHANE
ENFACE	ENSILED	**EPERDU**	ESCAPEE	**ETHANES**
ENFACED	ENSILES	EPERDUE	ESCAPER	**ETHERS**
ENFACES	**ENSURE**	**EPHEBI**	ESCAPES	AETHERS
ENFIRE	CENSURE	EPHEBIC	**ESCROL**	PETHERS
ENFIRED	ENSURED	**EPIGON**	ESCROLL	TETHERS
ENFIRES	ENSURER	EPIGONE	ESCROLS	WETHERS
ENFOLD	ENSURES	EPIGONI	**ESILES**	**ETHOXY**
PENFOLD	**ENTAIL**	EPIGONS	RESILES	METHOXY
TENFOLD	VENTAIL	**EPIMER**	**ESTATE**	ETHOXYL
ENFOLDS	ENTAILS	EPIMERE	GESTATE	**ETHYLS**
ENFREE	**ENTAME**	EPIMERS	RESTATE	METHYLS
ENFREED	ENTAMED	**EPIZOA**	TESTATE	**ETTLED**
ENFREES	ENTAMES	EPIZOAN	ESTATED	FETTLED
ENGAGE	**ENTERA**	**EPOCHA**	ESTATES	METTLED
ENGAGED	ENTERAL	EPOCHAL	**ESTERS**	NETTLED
ENGAGEE	**ENTERS**	EPOCHAS	FESTERS	PETTLED
ENGAGER	CENTERS	**EPONYM**	JESTERS	SETTLED
ENGAGES	RENTERS	EPONYMS	MESTERS	**ETTLES**
ENGINE	TENTERS	EPONYMY	NESTERS	FETTLES
ENGINED	VENTERS	**EPOSES**	PESTERS	KETTLES
ENGINER	**ENTETE**	DEPOSES	RESTERS	METTLES
ENGINES	ENTETEE	REPOSES	TESTERS	NETTLES
ENGORE	**ENTICE**	**EPRISE**	WESTERS	PETTLES
ENGORED	PENTICE	REPRISE	ZESTERS	SETTLES
ENGORES	ENTICED	**EPUISE**	**ESTRAL**	**EUCAIN**
ENISLE	ENTICER	EPUISEE	OESTRAL	EUCAINE
ENISLED	ENTICES	**EQUATE**	VESTRAL	EUCAINS
ENISLES	**ENURED**	EQUATED	**ESTRIN**	**EUCHRE**
ENLACE	TENURED	EQUATES	OESTRIN	EUCHRED
ENLACED	**ENURES**	**ERBIAS**	ESTRINS	EUCHRES
ENLACES	TENURES	TERBIAS	**ESTRUM**	**EUGHEN**
ENLOCK	**ENVIES**	**ERBIUM**	OESTRUM	LEUGHEN
GENLOCK	SENVIES	TERBIUM	ESTRUMS	**EUKING**
ENLOCKS	**ENVIRO**	ERBIUMS	**ESTRUS**	YEUKING
ENMOVE	ENVIRON	**ERMINE**	OESTRUS	**EUPHON**
ENMOVED	ENVIROS	ERMINED	**ETAGES**	EUPHONS
ENMOVES	**ENVOIS**	ERMINES	METAGES	EUPHONY
ENNUYE	RENVOIS	**ERNING**	**ETAMIN**	**EUREKA**
ENNUYED	**ENVOYS**	CERNING	ETAMINE	HEUREKA
ENNUYEE	LENVOYS	FERNING	ETAMINS	EUREKAS
ENOSES	RENVOYS	GERNING	**ETAPES**	**EVERTS**
KENOSES	**ENZONE**	KERNING	RETAPES	REVERTS
ENOSIS	ENZONED	TERNING	**ETCHED**	**EVILER**
KENOSIS	ENZONES	**EROSES**	FETCHED	REVILER
ENRACE	**EOLIAN**	XEROSES	LETCHED	**EVINCE**
ENRACED	AEOLIAN	**EROTIC**	RETCHED	EVINCED
ENRACES	**EOLITH**	CEROTIC	TETCHED	EVINCES
ENRAGE	NEOLITH	XEROTIC	**ETCHER**	**EVITES**
ENRAGED	EOLITHS	EROTICA	FETCHER	LEVITES
ENRAGES	**EONIAN**	EROTICS	ETCHERS	**EVOKED**
ENROBE	AEONIAN	**ERRING**	**ETCHES**	REVOKED
ENROBED	**EONISM**	HERRING	FETCHES	**EVOKER**
ENROBER	PEONISM	SERRING	KETCHES	REVOKER

EVOKERS	EXPOSES	AFEARED	**FIDGET**	FLEECED
EVOKES	**EXTANT**	**FECKIN**	FIDGETS	FLEECER
REVOKES	SEXTANT	FECKING	FIDGETY	FLEECES
EVOLVE	**EXTERN**	**FECULA**	**FIERCE**	**FLENSE**
DEVOLVE	EXTERNE	FECULAE	FIERCER	FLENSED
REVOLVE	EXTERNS	FECULAS	**FIGURE**	FLENSER
EVOLVED	**EXUVIA**	**FEEBLE**	FIGURED	FLENSES
EVOLVER	EXUVIAE	FEEBLED	FIGURER	**FLIGHT**
EVOLVES	EXUVIAL	FEEBLER	FIGURES	FLIGHTS
EVULSE	**FACETE**	FEEBLES	**FILING**	FLIGHTY
EVULSED	FACETED	**FEERIN**	FILINGS	**FLOUSE**
EVULSES	**FACTOR**	FEERING	**FILLET**	FLOUSED
EXACTS	FACTORS	FEERINS	FILLETS	FLOUSES
HEXACTS	FACTORY	**FEIRIE**	**FILMIS**	**FLOWER**
EXARCH	**FACULA**	FEIRIER	FILMISH	FLOWERS
HEXARCH	FACULAE	**FEMORA**	**FINNAC**	FLOWERY
EXARCHS	FACULAR	FEMORAL	FINNACK	**FOLIOS**
EXARCHY	**FADDLE**	**FERLIE**	FINNACS	FOLIOSE
EXCIDE	FADDLED	FERLIED	**FIRKIN**	**FOLKIE**
EXCIDED	FADDLES	FERLIER	FIRKING	FOLKIER
EXCIDES	**FAGGOT**	FERLIES	FIRKINS	FOLKIES
EXCISE	FAGGOTS	**FERRET**	**FISHER**	**FONDLE**
EXCISED	FAGGOTY	FERRETS	FISHERS	FONDLED
EXCISES	**FAINES**	FERRETY	FISHERY	FONDLER
EXCITE	FAINEST	**FERULA**	**FISSLE**	FONDLES
EXCITED	**FAKIES**	FERULAE	FISSLED	**FONDUE**
EXCITER	FAKIEST	FERULAS	FISSLES	FONDUED
EXCITES	**FALSES**	**FERULE**	**FITCHE**	FONDUES
EXCUSE	FALSEST	FERULED	FITCHEE	**FOOTIE**
EXCUSED	**FANGLE**	FERULES	FITCHES	FOOTIER
EXCUSER	FANGLED	**FETICH**	FITCHET	FOOTIES
EXCUSES	FANGLES	FETICHE	FITCHEW	**FOOTLE**
EXEDRA	**FANKLE**	**FETTLE**	**FITTES**	FOOTLED
EXEDRAE	FANKLED	FETTLED	FITTEST	FOOTLER
EXEMES	FANKLES	FETTLER	**FIXATE**	FOOTLES
LEXEMES	**FANNEL**	FETTLES	FIXATED	**FOOZLE**
EXHALE	FANNELL	**FEUTRE**	FIXATES	FOOZLED
EXHALED	FANNELS	FEUTRED	**FIZZLE**	FOOZLER
EXHALES	**FARCIE**	FEUTRES	FIZZLED	FOOZLES
EXHUME	FARCIED	**FIANCE**	FIZZLES	**FORAGE**
EXHUMED	FARCIES	FIANCEE	**FLAMBE**	FORAGED
EXHUMER	**FARCIN**	FIANCES	FLAMBEE	FORAGER
EXHUMES	FARCING	**FIBBER**	FLAMBES	FORAGES
EXINES	FARCINS	FIBBERS	**FLANGE**	**FORBAD**
REXINES	**FARMER**	FIBBERY	FLANGED	FORBADE
EXISTS	FARMERS	**FIBROS**	FLANGER	**FOREBY**
SEXISTS	FARMERY	FIBROSE	FLANGES	FOREBYE
EXOTIC	**FASCIA**	**FIBULA**	**FLAUNT**	**FORGER**
EXOTICA	FASCIAE	FIBULAE	FLAUNTS	FORGERS
EXOTICS	FASCIAL	FIBULAR	FLAUNTY	FORGERY
EXPERT	FASCIAS	FIBULAS	**FLAVIN**	**FORMAT**
SEXPERT	**FASCIS**	**FICKLE**	FLAVINE	FORMATE
EXPERTS	FASCISM	FICKLED	FLAVINS	FORMATS
EXPIRE	FASCIST	FICKLER	**FLAVOR**	**FORMIC**
EXPIRED	**FAVELL**	FICKLES	FLAVORS	FORMICA
EXPIRER	FAVELLA	**FIDDLE**	FLAVORY	**FOUGHT**
EXPIRES	**FEAGUE**	FIDDLED	**FLEDGE**	FOUGHTY
EXPOSE	FEAGUED	FIDDLER	FLEDGED	**FOULES**
EXPOSED	FEAGUES	FIDDLES	FLEDGES	FOULEST
EXPOSER	**FEARED**	FIDDLEY	**FLEECE**	**FOUTRE**

FOUTRED	FUZZLED	GASKING	GIRDLER	GOODIER
FOUTRES	FUZZLES	GASKINS	GIRDLES	GOODIES
FOXIES	**GABBLE**	**GATEAU**	**GIRLIE**	**GOOGLE**
FOXIEST	GABBLED	GATEAUS	GIRLIER	GOOGLED
FRAISE	GABBLER	GATEAUX	GIRLIES	GOOGLES
FRAISED	GABBLES	**GAUCHE**	**GIRNIE**	**GOONIE**
FRAISES	**GADGET**	GAUCHER	GIRNIER	GOONIER
FRAPPE	GADGETS	**GAUCIE**	**GITTIN**	GOONIES
FRAPPED	GADGETY	GAUCIER	GITTING	**GOPURA**
FRAPPEE	**GAGGER**	**GAWSIE**	**GLAIRE**	GOPURAM
FRAPPES	GAGGERS	GAWSIER	GLAIRED	GOPURAS
FRATCH	GAGGERY	**GEISTS**	GLAIRES	**GOSSIP**
FRATCHY	**GAGGLE**	AGEISTS	**GLAIVE**	GOSSIPS
FRATER	GAGGLED	**GELATE**	GLAIVED	GOSSIPY
FRATERS	GAGGLES	GELATED	GLAIVES	**GOUGER**
FRATERY	**GAINST**	GELATES	**GLANCE**	GOUGERE
FREETS	AGAINST	GELATI	GLANCED	GOUGERS
AFREETS	**GALANT**	GELATIN	GLANCER	**GOWLAN**
FREEZE	GALANTY	GELATIS	GLANCES	GOWLAND
FREEZER	**GALLET**	**GENERA**	**GLEDGE**	GOWLANS
FREEZES	GALLETA	GENERAL	GLEDGED	**GRADIN**
FRIAND	GALLETS	**GENTIL**	GLEDGES	GRADINE
FRIANDE	**GALLIC**	GENTILE	**GLITCH**	GRADING
FRIANDS	GALLICA	**GENTLE**	GLITCHY	GRADINI
FRIDGE	**GALOSH**	GENTLED	**GLOBIN**	GRADINO
FRIDGED	GALOSHE	GENTLER	GLOBING	GRADINS
FRIDGES	**GAMBLE**	GENTLES	GLOBINS	**GRAINE**
FRIEZE	GAMBLED	**GENTRY**	**GLOSSA**	GRAINED
FRIEZED	GAMBLER	AGENTRY	GLOSSAE	GRAINER
FRIEZES	GAMBLES	**GEODES**	GLOSSAL	GRAINES
FRIJOL	**GAMETE**	GEODESY	GLOSSAS	**GRAMAS**
FRIJOLE	AGAMETE	**GERMAN**	**GLYCIN**	GRAMASH
FRINGE	GAMETES	GERMANE	GLYCINE	**GRAMMA**
FRINGED	**GANOIN**	GERMANS	GLYCINS	GRAMMAR
FRINGES	GANOINE	**GERMIN**	**GOATEE**	GRAMMAS
FROWIE	GANOINS	GERMINA	GOATEED	**GRANDE**
FROWIER	**GARAGE**	GERMING	GOATEES	GRANDEE
FROWST	GARAGED	GERMINS	**GOBBLE**	GRANDER
FROWSTS	GARAGES	**GHESSE**	GOBBLED	**GRANGE**
FROWSTY	GARAGEY	GHESSED	GOBBLER	GRANGER
FUDDLE	**GARBLE**	GHESSES	GOBBLES	GRANGES
FUDDLED	GARBLED	**GIGGLE**	**GODDAM**	**GRASTE**
FUDDLER	GARBLER	GIGGLED	GODDAMN	AGRASTE
FUDDLES	GARBLES	GIGGLER	GODDAMS	**GRATIN**
FULFIL	**GARGET**	GIGGLES	**GOGGLE**	GRATINE
FULFILL	GARGETS	**GILLIE**	GOGGLED	GRATING
FULFILS	GARGETY	GILLIED	GOGGLER	GRATINS
FULLER	**GARGLE**	GILLIES	GOGGLES	**GRAVEL**
FULLERS	GARGLED	**GINGAL**	**GOITRE**	GRAVELS
FULLERY	GARGLER	GINGALL	GOITRED	GRAVELY
FUMBLE	GARGLES	GINGALS	GOITRES	**GRAVES**
FUMBLED	**GAROTE**	**GINGER**	**GOLLAN**	GRAVEST
FUMBLER	GAROTED	GINGERS	GOLLAND	**GRAVID**
FUMBLES	GAROTES	GINGERY	GOLLANS	GRAVIDA
FURROW	**GARROT**	**GINNER**	**GOLOSH**	**GREASE**
FURROWS	GARROTE	AGINNER	GOLOSHE	GREASED
FURROWY	GARROTS	GINNERS	GOLOSHE	GREASER
FUTILE	**GASHES**	GINNERY	**GOODBY**	GREASES
FUTILER	GASHEST	**GIRDLE**	GOODBYE	**GREAVE**
FUZZLE	**GASKIN**	GIRDLED	GOODBYS	GREAVED

GREAVES	IGUANAS	HACKERS	SHAMBLE	HARMINE
GREETE	GUANASE	HACKERY	HAMBLED	HARMING
GREETED	**GUANIN**	**HACKLE**	HAMBLES	HARMINS
GREETER	GUANINE	SHACKLE	**HAMING**	**HARPED**
GREETES	GUANINS	HACKLED	SHAMING	SHARPED
GRIECE	**GUDDLE**	HACKLER	**HAMLET**	**HARPER**
GRIECED	GUDDLED	HACKLES	CHAMLET	SHARPER
GRIECES	GUDDLES	HACKLET	HAMLETS	HARPERS
GRIEVE	**GUGGLE**	**HADING**	**HAMMED**	**HARPIN**
GRIEVED	GUGGLED	SHADING	SHAMMED	HARPING
GRIEVER	GUGGLES	**HAFTED**	WHAMMED	HARPINS
GRIEVES	**GUIMPE**	SHAFTED	**HAMMER**	**HASHED**
GRILLE	GUIMPED	**HAFTER**	SHAMMER	SHASHED
GRILLED	GUIMPES	SHAFTER	HAMMERS	**HASHES**
GRILLER	**GUISED**	HAFTERS	**HAMPER**	SHASHES
GRILLES	AGUISED	**HAGGED**	CHAMPER	**HASSES**
GRIPPE	**GUISES**	SHAGGED	HAMPERS	CHASSES
GRIPPED	AGUISES	**HAGGIS**	**HANCES**	**HASSLE**
GRIPPER	**GULLER**	HAGGISH	CHANCES	HASSLED
GRIPPES	GULLERS	**HAGGLE**	**HANDLE**	HASSLES
GRISED	GULLERY	HAGGLED	HANDLED	**HASTED**
AGRISED	**GUNNER**	HAGGLER	HANDLER	GHASTED
GRISES	GUNNERA	HAGGLES	HANDLES	**HASTEN**
AGRISES	GUNNERS	**HAINED**	**HANGED**	CHASTEN
GRIZES	GUNNERY	CHAINED	CHANGED	HASTENS
AGRIZES	**GURGLE**	**HAIRED**	PHANGED	**HATTED**
GROCER	GURGLED	CHAIRED	WHANGED	CHATTED
GROCERS	GURGLES	**HALALA**	**HANGER**	**HATTER**
GROCERY	GURGLET	HALALAH	CHANGER	CHATTER
GROOVE	**GUSSIE**	HALALAS	HANGERS	PHATTER
GROOVED	GUSSIED	**HALERS**	**HANJAR**	SHATTER
GROOVER	GUSSIES	THALERS	KHANJAR	HATTERS
GROOVES	**GUSTIE**	WHALERS	HANJARS	**HAUGHS**
GROSER	GUSTIER	**HALING**	**HANKED**	SHAUGHS
GROSERS	**GUTTER**	SHALING	SHANKED	**HAUGHT**
GROSERT	GUTTERS	WHALING	THANKED	HAUGHTY
GROUCH	GUTTERY	**HALLAH**	**HANKER**	**HAULED**
GROUCHY	**GUTTLE**	CHALLAH	THANKER	SHAULED
GROUND	GUTTLED	HALLAHS	HANKERS	**HAUNTS**
AGROUND	GUTTLER	**HALLAL**	**HANTED**	CHAUNTS
GROUNDS	GUTTLES	HALLALI	CHANTED	**HAVERS**
GROUSE	**GUZZLE**	HALLALS	**HAPPED**	SHAVERS
GROUSED	GUZZLED	**HALLAN**	CHAPPED	**HAVING**
GROUSER	GUZZLER	CHALLAN	WHAPPED	SHAVING
GROUSES	GUZZLES	HALLANS	**HAPTEN**	HAVINGS
GROWTH	**GWEDUC**	**HALLOT**	HAPTENE	**HAWING**
GROWTHS	GWEDUCK	CHALLOT	HAPTENS	CHAWING
GROWTHY	GWEDUCS	SHALLOT	**HARING**	SHAWING
GRUDGE	**GYRATE**	HALLOTH	CHARING	THAWING
GRUDGED	GYRATED	**HALLOW**	SHARING	**HAZANS**
GRUDGER	GYRATES	SHALLOW	**HARKED**	CHAZANS
GRUDGES	**HACHIS**	HALLOWS	CHARKED	**HAZELS**
GRUMPH	RHACHIS	**HALTER**	SHARKED	GHAZELS
GRUMPHS	**HACKED**	HALTERE	**HARMED**	**HAZZAN**
GRUMPHY	CHACKED	HALTERS	CHARMED	CHAZZAN
GRUNGE	SHACKED	**HALUTZ**	PHARMED	HAZZANS
GRUNGER	THACKED	CHALUTZ	**HARMER**	**HEALED**
GRUNGES	WHACKED	**HAMALS**	CHARMER	SHEALED
GRUNGEY	**HACKER**	SHAMALS	HARMERS	**HEALTH**
GUANAS	WHACKER	**HAMBLE**	**HARMIN**	HEALTHS

HEALTHY	SHELLER	WHETHER	SHIPPER	CHOCKED
HEAPED	HELLERI	**HEUCHS**	WHIPPER	SHOCKED
CHEAPED	HELLERS	SHEUCHS	**HIPPIE**	**HOCKER**
HEAPER	HELLERY	**HEUGHS**	CHIPPIE	CHOCKER
CHEAPER	**HELMED**	SHEUGHS	SHIPPIE	SHOCKER
HEAPERS	WHELMED	WHEUGHS	HIPPIER	HOCKERS
HEARER	**HELMET**	**HEWERS**	HIPPIES	**HOCKLE**
SHEARER	HELMETS	CHEWERS	**HIPPIN**	HOCKLED
HEARERS	**HELPED**	SHEWERS	HIPPING	HOCKLES
HEARSE	CHELPED	**HEWING**	*HIPPINS	**HODDEN**
HEARSED	WHELPED	CHEWING	**HIPPOS**	SHODDEN
HEARSES	**HELVED**	SHEWING	SHIPPOS	HODDENS
HEATED	SHELVED	WHEWING	**HIRING**	**HODDIN**
CHEATED	**HELVES**	HEWINGS	SHIRING	HODDING
HEATER	SHELVES	**HICCUP**	HIRINGS	HODDINS
CHEATER	THELVES	HICCUPS	**HIRPLE**	**HODDLE**
THEATER	**HEMPIE**	HICCUPY	HIRPLED	HODDLED
HEATERS	HEMPIER	**HICKIE**	HIRPLES	HODDLES
HEATHS	HEMPIES	THICKIE	**HIRSLE**	**HODJAS**
SHEATHS	**HENNER**	HICKIES	HIRSLED	KHODJAS
HEATHY	HENNERS	**HIDDEN**	HIRSLES	**HOEING**
SHEATHY	HENNERY	CHIDDEN	**HISHED**	SHOEING
HEAVED	**HENNIN**	**HIDDER**	WHISHED	**HOGGED**
SHEAVED	HENNING	SHIDDER	**HISHES**	SHOGGED
HEAVES	HENNINS	WHIDDER	WHISHES	**HOGGER**
SHEAVES	**HERBAR**	HIDDERS	**HISSED**	HOGGERS
THEAVES	HERBARS	**HIDERS**	WHISSED	HOGGERY
HECKLE	HERBARY	CHIDERS	**HISSES**	**HOGGIN**
HECKLED	**HEREAT**	**HIDING**	WHISSES	HOGGING
HECKLER	THEREAT	CHIDING	**HISTED**	HOGGINS
HECKLES	WHEREAT	HIDINGS	WHISTED	**HOGTIE**
HEDDLE	**HEREBY**	**HIGGLE**	**HISTIE**	HOGTIED
HEDDLED	THEREBY	HIGGLED	BHISTIE	HOGTIES
HEDDLES	WHEREBY	HIGGLER	**HITHER**	**HOISIN**
HEDERA	**HEREIN**	HIGGLES	THITHER	HOISING
HEDERAL	THEREIN	**HIGHED**	WHITHER	HOISINS
HEDERAS	WHEREIN	THIGHED	HITHERS	**HOKIER**
HEDERS	**HEREOF**	**HILLED**	**HITTER**	CHOKIER
CHEDERS	THEREOF	CHILLED	CHITTER	**HOKING**
HEELED	WHEREOF	SHILLED	WHITTER	CHOKING
SHEELED	**HEREON**	**HILLER**	HITTERS	**HOLIES**
WHEELED	THEREON	CHILLER	**HIVERS**	HOLIEST
HEELER	WHEREON	THILLER	SHIVERS	**HOLING**
WHEELER	**HERETO**	HILLERS	**HIVING**	THOLING
HEELERS	THERETO	**HINGED**	CHIVING	HOLINGS
HEEZED	WHERETO	WHINGED	**HIZZED**	**HOLISM**
PHEEZED	**HERMAE**	**HINGER**	CHIZZED	WHOLISM
WHEEZED	THERMAE	WHINGER	WHIZZED	HOLISMS
HEEZES	**HERMIT**	HINGERS	**HIZZES**	**HOLIST**
PHEEZES	THERMIT	**HINGES**	CHIZZES	WHOLIST
WHEEZES	HERMITS	WHINGES	PHIZZES	HOLISTS
HEIGHT	**HERNIA**	**HIPPED**	WHIZZES	**HOLLAS**
AHEIGHT	HERNIAE	CHIPPED	**HOARSE**	CHOLLAS
HEIGHTH	HERNIAL	SHIPPED	HOARSEN	**HOMAGE**
HEIGHTS	HERNIAS	WHIPPED	HOARSER	HOMAGED
HEISTS	**HEROIN**	**HIPPEN**	**HOBBLE**	HOMAGER
THEISTS	HEROINE	SHIPPEN	HOBBLED	HOMAGES
HELLED	HEROINS	HIPPENS	HOBBLER	**HOMELY**
SHELLED	**HETHER**	**HIPPER**	HOBBLES	HOMELYN
HELLER	THETHER	CHIPPER	**HOCKED**	**HOMIES**

HOMIEST	**HOSTLY**	WHUMPED	VIBICES	TIGGING
HONDLE	GHOSTLY	**HUMPER**	**ICHING**	WIGGING
HONDLED	**HOTTED**	THUMPER	MICHING	ZIGGING
HONDLES	SHOTTED	HUMPERS	NICHING	**IGNIFY**
HONERS	**HOUGHS**	**HUNGRY**	RICHING	DIGNIFY
PHONERS	CHOUGHS	AHUNGRY	**ICICLE**	LIGNIFY
HONEST	SHOUGHS	**HUNKIE**	ICICLED	SIGNIFY
HONESTY	**HOUSED**	HUNKIER	ICICLES	**IGNITE**
HONEYS	CHOUSED	HUNKIES	**ICIEST**	LIGNITE
PHONEYS	**HOUSER**	**HUNTED**	DICIEST	IGNITED
HONIED	CHOUSER	SHUNTED	RICIEST	IGNITER
PHONIED	HOUSERS	**HUNTER**	**ICINGS**	IGNITES
HONING	**HOUSES**	CHUNTER	DICINGS	**IGNORE**
PHONING	CHOUSES	SHUNTER	**ICKERS**	SIGNORE
HOODIE	SHOUSES	HUNTERS	BICKERS	IGNORED
HOODIER	**HOUTED**	**HUPPAH**	DICKERS	IGNORER
HOODIES	SHOUTED	CHUPPAH	KICKERS	IGNORES
HOOFED	**HOVELS**	HUPPAHS	LICKERS	**ILEXES**
CHOOFED	SHOVELS	**HUPPED**	NICKERS	SILEXES
WHOOFED	**HOVERS**	WHUPPED	PICKERS	**ILICES**
HOOKED	SHOVERS	**HUPPOT**	RICKERS	CILICES
CHOOKED	**HOVING**	CHUPPOT	TICKERS	**ILLEST**
HOOLIE	SHOVING	HUPPOTH	WICKERS	WILLEST
HOOLIER	**HOWDIE**	**HURDLE**	YICKERS	**ILLIPE**
HOOLIES	HOWDIED	HURDLED	**ICKIER**	ILLIPES
HOOPED	HOWDIES	HURDLER	DICKIER	**ILLITE**
WHOOPED	**HUCKED**	HURDLES	KICKIER	TILLITE
HOOPER	CHUCKED	**HURRAS**	PICKIER	ILLITES
WHOOPER	SHUCKED	DHURRAS	**ICKILY**	**ILLUDE**
HOOPERS	**HUCKLE**	**HURTLE**	PICKILY	ILLUDED
HOOPLA	CHUCKLE	HURTLED	**ICKLER**	ILLUDES
WHOOPLA	HUCKLED	HURTLER	FICKLER	**ILLUME**
HOOPLAS	HUCKLES	HURTLES	MICKLER	ILLUMED
HOOTED	**HUDDLE**	**HUSHED**	PICKLER	ILLUMES
WHOOTED	HUDDLED	SHUSHED	TICKLER	**IMAGER**
HOOTER	HUDDLER	**HUSHER**	**IDEATE**	IMAGERS
SHOOTER	HUDDLES	SHUSHER	IDEATED	IMAGERY
HOOTERS	**HUFFED**	**HUSHES**	IDEATES	**IMBARS**
HOPPED	CHUFFED	SHUSHES	**IDENTS**	MIMBARS
CHOPPED	**HUFFER**	**HUSTLE**	BIDENTS	**IMBASE**
SHOPPED	CHUFFER	HUSTLED	**IDLERS**	IMBASED
WHOPPED	HUFFERS	HUSTLER	SIDLERS	IMBASES
HOPPER	**HUGGED**	HUSTLES	**IDLING**	**IMBIBE**
CHOPPER	CHUGGED	**HUTTED**	HIDLING	IMBIBED
SHOPPER	**HUGGER**	PHUTTED	KIDLING	IMBIBER
WHOPPER	CHUGGER	**HUTZPA**	SIDLING	IMBIBES
HOPPERS	HUGGERS	CHUTZPA	**IDOLON**	**IMBRUE**
HOPPLE	**HUMANE**	HUTZPAH	EIDOLON	IMBRUED
HOPPLED	HUMANER	HUTZPAS	**IFFIER**	IMBRUES
HOPPLER	**HUMBLE**	**HYALIN**	MIFFIER	**IMMIES**
HOPPLES	HUMBLED	HYALINE	NIFFIER	GIMMIES
HORDED	HUMBLER	HYALINS	**IGGING**	JIMMIES
CHORDED	HUMBLES	**HYDRAS**	BIGGING	**IMMURE**
HORNED	**HUMMED**	HYDRASE	DIGGING	IMMURED
THORNED	CHUMMED	**HYDRIA**	FIGGING	IMMURES
HOSIER	**HUMMLE**	HYDRIAE	GIGGING	**IMPALE**
HOSIERS	WHUMMLE	**HYDRID**	JIGGING	IMPALED
HOSIERY	**HUMPED**	HYDRIDE	LIGGING	IMPALER
HOSTED	CHUMPED	HYDRIDS	PIGGING	IMPALES
GHOSTED	THUMPED	**IBICES**	RIGGING	**IMPAVE**

IMPAVED	**INCHER**	**INGANS**	PINKIER	INSTALL
IMPAVES	PINCHER	FINGANS	SINKIER	INSTALS
IMPEDE	WINCHER	**INGENU**	ZINKIER	**INSTIL**
IMPEDED	INCHERS	INGENUE	**INKING**	INSTILL
IMPEDER	**INCHES**	INGENUS	DINKING	INSTILS
IMPEDES	CINCHES	**INGEST**	FINKING	**INSULA**
IMPING	FINCHES	INGESTA	JINKING	INSULAE
GIMPING	LINCHES	INGESTS	KINKING	INSULAR
LIMPING	PINCHES	**INGLES**	LINKING	**INSURE**
PIMPING	WINCHES	BINGLES	OINKING	INSURED
WIMPING	**INCISE**	DINGLES	PINKING	INSURER
IMPINGE	INCISED	GINGLES	RINKING	INSURES
IMPINGS	INCISES	JINGLES	SINKING	**INTELS**
IMPISH	**INCITE**	KINGLES	TINKING	LINTELS
WIMPISH	ZINCITE	LINGLES	WINKING	**INTERN**
IMPLED	INCITED	MINGLES	ZINKING	INTERNE
DIMPLED	INCITER	PINGLES	**INKLED**	INTERNS
PIMPLED	INCITES	SINGLES	TINKLED	**INTERS**
RIMPLED	**INCOME**	TINGLES	WINKLED	HINTERS
SIMPLED	INCOMER	**INGOES**	**INKLES**	LINTERS
WIMPLED	INCOMES	BINGOES	KINKLES	MINTERS
IMPLEX	**INCUSE**	DINGOES	TINKLES	SINTERS
SIMPLEX	INCUSED	JINGOES	WINKLES	TINTERS
IMPONE	INCUSES	LINGOES	INKLESS	WINTERS
IMPONED	**INDIES**	PINGOES	**INKPAD**	**INTIMA**
IMPONES	KINDIES	**INGOTS**	INKPADS	INTIMAE
IMPOSE	LINDIES	LINGOTS	**INLACE**	INTIMAL
IMPOSED	YINDIES	**INHALE**	INLACED	INTIMAS
IMPOSER	**INDIGO**	INHALED	INLACES	**INTONE**
IMPOSES	WINDIGO	INHALER	**INNATE**	INTONED
IMPOSEX	INDIGOS	INHALES	PINNATE	INTONER
IMPROV	**INDITE**	**INHERE**	**INNERS**	INTONES
IMPROVE	INDITED	INHERED	DINNERS	**INULAS**
IMPROVS	INDITER	INHERES	FINNERS	INULASE
IMPURE	INDITES	**INHUME**	GINNERS	**INVADE**
IMPURER	**INDOWS**	INHUMED	PINNERS	INVADED
IMPUTE	WINDOWS	INHUMER	SINNERS	INVADER
IMPUTED	**INDUCE**	INHUMES	TINNERS	INVADES
IMPUTER	INDUCED	**INIONS**	WINNERS	**INVITE**
IMPUTES	INDUCER	MINIONS	**INNING**	INVITED
INANES	INDUCES	PINIONS	BINNING	INVITEE
INANEST	**INFALL**	**INISLE**	DINNING	INVITER
INCAGE	PINFALL	INISLED	FINNING	INVITES
INCAGED	INFALLS	INISLES	GINNING	**INVOKE**
INCAGES	**INFAME**	**INJURE**	LINNING	INVOKED
INCASE	INFAMED	INJURED	PINNING	INVOKER
PINCASE	INFAMES	INJURER	RINNING	INVOKES
INCASED	**INFANT**	INJURES	SINNING	**INWORK**
INCASES	INFANTA	**INKERS**	TINNING	PINWORK
INCAVE	INFANTE	JINKERS	WINNING	TINWORK
INCAVED	INFANTS	LINKERS	INNINGS	INWORKS
INCAVES	**INFOLD**	PINKERS	**INSANE**	**INWOVE**
INCEDE	PINFOLD	SINKERS	INSANER	INWOVEN
INCEDED	INFOLDS	TINKERS	**INSHIP**	**IODATE**
INCEDES	**INFULA**	WINKERS	KINSHIP	IODATED
INCHED	INFULAE	**INKIER**	INSHIPS	IODATES
CINCHED	**INFUSE**	DINKIER	**INSIDE**	**IODISE**
FINCHED	INFUSED	HINKIER	INSIDER	IODISED
PINCHED	INFUSER	KINKIER	INSIDES	IODISER
WINCHED	INFUSES	LINKIER	**INSTAL**	IODISES

IODIZE	MISTLES	JAUNSES	**JUBILE**	**KIDDED**
IODIZED	**ITCHED**	**JEBELS**	JUBILEE	SKIDDED
IODIZER	BITCHED	DJEBELS	JUBILES	**KIDDER**
IODIZES	DITCHED	**JEELIE**	**JUDDER**	SKIDDER
IONICS	HITCHED	JEELIED	JUDDERS	KIDDERS
BIONICS	MITCHED	JEELIES	JUDDERY	**KIDDIE**
IONISE	PITCHED	**JEJUNA**	**JUGGLE**	KIDDIED
LIONISE	WITCHED	JEJUNAL	JUGGLED	KIDDIER
IONISED	**ITCHES**	**JEMBES**	JUGGLER	KIDDIES
IONISER	AITCHES	DJEMBES	JUGGLES	**KIDGIE**
IONISES	BITCHES	**JERKIN**	**JUGULA**	KIDGIER
IONIZE	DITCHES	JERKING	JUGULAR	**KILLED**
LIONIZE	FITCHES	JERKINS	**JUMBLE**	SKILLED
IONIZED	HITCHES	**JERQUE**	JUMBLED	**KIMMER**
IONIZER	MITCHES	JERQUED	JUMBLER	SKIMMER
IONIZES	PITCHES	JERQUER	JUMBLES	KIMMERS
IRADES	TITCHES	JERQUES	**JUNGLE**	**KIMONO**
TIRADES	WITCHES	**JIBBAH**	JUNGLED	OKIMONO
IREFUL	**IZARDS**	DJIBBAH	JUNGLES	KIMONOS
DIREFUL	LIZARDS	JIBBAHS	**JUNKIE**	**KINDLE**
IRENIC	RIZARDS	**JIGGLE**	JUNKIER	KINDLED
EIRENIC	VIZARDS	JIGGLED	JUNKIES	KINDLER
SIRENIC	WIZARDS	JIGGLES	**JUSTLE**	KINDLES
IRENICS	**IZZARD**	**JIGSAW**	JUSTLED	**KINGLE**
IRITIS	DIZZARD	JIGSAWN	JUSTLES	KINGLES
MIRITIS	GIZZARD	JIGSAWS	**KAGOUL**	KINGLET
TIRITIS	IZZARDS	**JIMMIE**	KAGOULE	**KINKED**
IRKING	**JABBLE**	JIMMIED	KAGOULS	SKINKED
DIRKING	JABBLED	JIMMIES	**KAIKAI**	**KIPPED**
FIRKING	JABBLES	**JINGAL**	KAIKAIS	SKIPPED
KIRKING	**JAGGER**	JINGALL	**KAINIT**	**KIPPER**
LIRKING	JAGGERS	JINGALS	KAINITE	SKIPPER
YIRKING	JAGGERY	**JINGLE**	KAINITS	KIPPERS
IRONIC	**JAGHIR**	JINGLED	**KAOLIN**	**KIRTLE**
GIRONIC	JAGHIRE	JINGLER	KAOLINE	KIRTLED
TIRONIC	JAGHIRS	JINGLES	KAOLINS	KIRTLES
ISATIN	**JAMBOK**	JINGLET	**KECKLE**	**KITING**
ISATINE	SJAMBOK	**JIRBLE**	KECKLED	SKITING
ISATINS	JAMBOKS	JIRBLED	KECKLES	KITINGS
ISCHIA	**JAMPAN**	JIRBLES	**KEGGER**	**KITSCH**
ISCHIAL	JAMPANI	**JITTER**	SKEGGER	KITSCHY
ISLING	JAMPANS	JITTERS	KEGGERS	**KITTEN**
AISLING	**JANGLE**	JITTERY	**KELPED**	KITTENS
ISOBAR	JANGLED	**JOBBER**	SKELPED	KITTENY
ISOBARE	JANGLER	JOBBERS	**KELTER**	**KITTLE**
ISOBARS	JANGLES	JOBBERY	SKELTER	SKITTLE
ISOGON	**JARGON**	**JOGGLE**	KELTERS	KITTLED
ISOGONE	JARGONS	JOGGLED	**KENNED**	KITTLER
ISOGONS	JARGONY	JOGGLER	SKENNED	KITTLES
ISOGONY	**JASMIN**	JOGGLES	KENNETT	**KLUDGE**
ISOMER	JASMINE	**JOINER**	**KEPPED**	KLUDGED
ISOMERE	JASMINS	JOINERS	SKEPPED	KLUDGES
ISOMERS	**JASPER**	JOINERY	**KERMES**	KLUDGEY
ISSUED	JASPERS	**JOSTLE**	KERMESS	**KOLHOZ**
TISSUED	JASPERY	JOSTLED	**KHALIF**	KOLHOZY
ISSUES	**JAUNCE**	JOSTLER	KHALIFA	**KOLKOZ**
TISSUES	JAUNCED	JOSTLES	KHALIFS	KOLKOZY
ISTHMI	JAUNCES	**JOUNCE**	**KIBBLE**	**KOOKIE**
ISTHMIC	**JAUNSE**	JOUNCED	KIBBLED	KOOKIER
ISTLES	JAUNSED	JOUNCES	KIBBLES	**KOUMIS**

KOUMISS	LAGGINS	ELANCES	PLASHED	**LAURYL**
KREESE	**LAIDED**	GLANCES	SLASHED	LAURYLS
KREESED	PLAIDED	**LANDED**	**LASHER**	**LAVERS**
KREESES	**LAIPSE**	BLANDED	CLASHER	CLAVERS
KVETCH	LAIPSED	**LANDER**	FLASHER	SLAVERS
KVETCHY	LAIPSES	BLANDER	PLASHER	**LAVING**
LACERS	**LAIRED**	SLANDER	SLASHER	SLAVING
PLACERS	GLAIRED	LANDERS	LASHERS	LAVISH
LACETS	**LAKERS**	**LANDES**	**LASHES**	SLAVISH
PLACETS	FLAKERS	GLANDES	BLASHES	**LAVOLT**
LACIER	SLAKERS	**LANGER**	CLASHES	LAVOLTA
GLACIER	**LAKIER**	CLANGER	FLASHES	LAVOLTS
LACING	FLAKIER	FLANGER	PLASHES	**LAWING**
PLACING	**LAKING**	SLANGER	SLASHES	BLAWING
LACINGS	FLAKING	LANGERS	**LASKET**	CLAWING
LACKED	SLAKING	**LANGUE**	FLASKET	FLAWING
BLACKED	LAKINGS	LANGUED	LASKETS	LAWINGS
CLACKED	**LALLAN**	LANGUES	**LASSES**	**LAXISM**
FLACKED	LALLAND	LANGUET	CLASSES	LAXISMS
SLACKED	LALLANS	**LANKED**	GLASSES	**LAYERS**
LACKER	**LAMBER**	BLANKED	**LASSIE**	FLAYERS
BLACKER	CLAMBER	CLANKED	GLASSIE	PLAYERS
CLACKER	LAMBERS	FLANKED	LASSIES	SLAYERS
FLACKER	LAMBERT	PLANKED	**LASSIS**	**LAYING**
SLACKER	**LAMBIE**	**LANKER**	CLASSIS	ALAYING
LACKERS	LAMBIER	BLANKER	**LASTED**	CLAYING
LACUNA	LAMBIES	FLANKER	BLASTED	FLAYING
LACUNAE	**LAMINA**	**LANKLY**	**LASTER**	PLAYING
LACUNAL	LAMINAE	BLANKLY	BLASTER	SLAYING
LACUNAR	LAMINAL	**LANNER**	PLASTER	LAYINGS
LACUNAS	LAMINAR	PLANNER	LASTERS	**LAYOFF**
LADDER	LAMINAS	LANNERS	**LATENS**	PLAYOFF
BLADDER	**LAMING**	**LAPPED**	PLATENS	LAYOFFS
CLADDER	BLAMING	CLAPPED	**LATEST**	**LAZARS**
GLADDER	FLAMING	FLAPPED	BLATEST	BLAZARS
LADDERS	**LAMMED**	KLAPPED	LATESTS	**LAZIER**
LADDERY	CLAMMED	PLAPPED	**LATHER**	GLAZIER
LADDIE	FLAMMED	SLAPPED	BLATHER	**LAZIES**
CLADDIE	GLAMMED	**LAPPER**	SLATHER	LAZIEST
GLADDIE	SLAMMED	CLAPPER	LATHERS	**LAZILY**
LADDIES	**LAMMER**	FLAPPER	LATHERY	GLAZILY
LADERS	CLAMMER	SLAPPER	**LATINA**	**LAZING**
BLADERS	SLAMMER	LAPPERS	PLATINA	BLAZING
LADING	LAMMERS	**LAPSED**	LATINAS	GLAZING
BLADING	**LAMPED**	ELAPSED	**LATTEN**	**LEADED**
LADINGS	CLAMPED	**LAPSES**	FLATTEN	PLEADED
LADRON	**LAMPER**	ELAPSES	LATTENS	**LEADER**
LADRONE	CLAMPER	**LARGES**	**LATTER**	PLEADER
LADRONS	LAMPERN	LARGESS	BLATTER	LEADERS
LAGGED	LAMPERS	LARGEST	CLATTER	**LEAGUE**
BLAGGED	**LANATE**	**LARNEY**	FLATTER	LEAGUED
CLAGGED	PLANATE	BLARNEY	PLATTER	LEAGUER
FLAGGED	LANATED	LARNEYS	SLATTER	LEAGUES
SLAGGED	**LANCED**	**LARUMS**	**LAUDED**	**LEAKER**
LAGGER	ELANCED	ALARUMS	BLAUDED	BLEAKER
BLAGGER	GLANCED	**LASERS**	**LAUNCE**	LEAKERS
FLAGGER	**LANCER**	FLASERS	LAUNCED	**LEAMED**
LAGGERS	GLANCER	**LASHED**	LAUNCES	GLEAMED
LAGGIN	LANCERS	CLASHED	**LAUNCH**	**LEANED**
LAGGING	**LANCES**	FLASHED	FLAUNCH	CLEANED

GLEANED	**LEERED**	LEUCINE	SLIMIER	FLIPPER
LEANER	FLEERED	LEUCINS	**LIMINA**	SLIPPER
CLEANER	**LEFTIE**	**LEVINS**	LIMINAL	LIPPERS
GLEANER	LEFTIES	ALEVINS	**LIMING**	**LIPPIE**
LEANERS	**LEGATE**	**LEXICA**	GLIMING	CLIPPIE
LEANLY	LEGATED	LEXICAL	SLIMING	LIPPIER
CLEANLY	LEGATEE	**LIABLE**	LIMINGS	LIPPIES
LEARED	LEGATES	PLIABLE	**LIMMER**	**LISSES**
BLEARED	**LEGATO**	**LIAISE**	GLIMMER	BLISSES
CLEARED	LEGATOR	LIAISED	SLIMMER	PLISSES
LEASED	LEGATOS	LIAISES	LIMMERS	**LISSOM**
PLEASED	**LEGGED**	**LIASES**	**LIMPED**	LISSOME
LEASER	ALEGGED	ALIASES	FLIMPED	**LISTEL**
PLEASER	FLEGGED	**LIBATE**	**LIMPSY**	LISTELS
LEASERS	**LEGGER**	LIBATED	SLIMPSY	**LISTEN**
LEASES	GLEGGER	LIBATES	**LINERS**	GLISTEN
PLEASES	LEGGERS	**LIBBED**	ALINERS	LISTENS
LEASOW	**LEGGES**	GLIBBED	**LINGER**	**LISTER**
LEASOWE	ALEGGES	**LIBBER**	BLINGER	BLISTER
LEASOWS	**LEGGIE**	GLIBBER	CLINGER	GLISTER
LEAVED	LEGGIER	LIBBERS	FLINGER	KLISTER
CLEAVED	LEGGIES	**LICHES**	SLINGER	LISTERS
SLEAVED	**LEGGIN**	CLICHES	LINGERS	**LITHER**
LEAVER	LEGGING	ELICHES	**LINGUA**	BLITHER
CLEAVER	LEGGINS	**LICKED**	LINGUAE	SLITHER
LEAVERS	**LEGIST**	CLICKED	LINGUAL	**LITHES**
LEAVES	ELEGIST	FLICKED	LINGUAS	LITHEST
CLEAVES	LEGISTS	SLICKED	**LINING**	**LITING**
GLEAVES	**LEGITS**	**LICKER**	ALINING	FLITING
SLEAVES	ELEGITS	CLICKER	LININGS	**LITTER**
LEAZES	**LEMING**	FLICKER	**LINKED**	BLITTER
SLEAZES	FLEMING	SLICKER	BLINKED	CLITTER
LECHER	**LENDER**	LICKERS	CLINKED	FLITTER
LECHERS	BLENDER	**LIEVES**	PLINKED	GLITTER
LECHERY	SLENDER	SLIEVES	SLINKED	SLITTER
LECHES	LENDERS	LIEVEST	**LINKER**	LITTERS
FLECHES	**LENGTH**	**LIFTED**	BLINKER	LITTERY
LECTOR	ALENGTH	CLIFTED	CLINKER	**LITTLE**
ELECTOR	LENGTHS	**LIGATE**	KLINKER	LITTLER
LECTORS	LENGTHY	LIGATED	PLINKER	LITTLES
LEDGED	**LENITE**	LIGATES	SLINKER	**LIVERS**
FLEDGED	LENITED	**LIGHTS**	LINKERS	CLIVERS
GLEDGED	LENITES	ALIGHTS	**LINNED**	OLIVERS
PLEDGED	**LENSED**	BLIGHTS	BLINNED	SLIVERS
SLEDGED	FLENSED	FLIGHTS	**LINTED**	**LIVING**
LEDGER	**LENSES**	PLIGHTS	FLINTED	SLIVING
PLEDGER	FLENSES	SLIGHTS	GLINTED	LIVINGS
SLEDGER	**LESSER**	**LIGULA**	**LINTER**	**LOATHE**
LEDGERS	BLESSER	LIGULAE	SLINTER	LOATHED
LEDGES	**LESSES**	LIGULAR	LINTERS	LOATHER
FLEDGES	BLESSES	LIGULAS	**LINTIE**	LOATHES
GLEDGES	**LESSOR**	**LIMBEC**	LINTIER	**LOBATE**
PLEDGES	PLESSOR	LIMBECK	LINTIES	GLOBATE
SLEDGES	LESSORS	LIMBECS	**LIPPED**	LOBATED
LEEING	**LETTED**	**LIMBED**	BLIPPED	**LOBBED**
FLEEING	BLETTED	CLIMBED	CLIPPED	BLOBBED
GLEEING	**LETTER**	**LIMBER**	FLIPPED	FLOBBED
LEEPED	LETTERN	CLIMBER	SLIPPED	**LOBBER**
BLEEPED	LETTERS	LIMBERS	**LIPPER**	CLOBBER
CLEEPED	**LEUCIN**	**LIMIER**	CLIPPER	SLOBBER

LOBBERS	ALONELY	CLOTTER	LOWINGS	PLUMPED
LOBING	**LONERS**	PLOTTER	**LOWISH**	SLUMPED
GLOBING	CLONERS	SLOTTER	SLOWISH	**LUMPEN**
LOBINGS	**LONGED**	LOTTERS	**LOWNED**	PLUMPEN
LOBOSE	PLONGED	LOTTERY	CLOWNED	LUMPENS
GLOBOSE	**LONGES**	**LOUCHE**	**LOWSED**	**LUMPER**
LOBULE	PLONGES	LOUCHER	BLOWSED	CLUMPER
GLOBULE	LONGEST	**LOUGHS**	**LOWSES**	PLUMPER
LOBULES	**LOOMED**	CLOUGHS	BLOWSES	LUMPERS
LOCATE	BLOOMED	PLOUGHS	LOWSEST	**LUNATE**
LOCATED	GLOOMED	SLOUGHS	**LUBBER**	LUNATED
LOCATER	SLOOMED	**LOUNGE**	BLUBBER	LUNATES
LOCATES	**LOONIE**	LOUNGED	CLUBBER	**LUNGED**
LOCHIA	LOONIER	LOUNGER	FLUBBER	BLUNGED
LOCHIAL	LOONIES	LOUNGES	SLUBBER	PLUNGED
LOCKED	**LOOPED**	LOUNGEY	LUBBERS	**LUNGER**
BLOCKED	BLOOPED	**LOURED**	**LUCERN**	BLUNGER
CLOCKED	GLOOPED	CLOURED	LUCERNE	PLUNGER
FLOCKED	**LOOPER**	FLOURED	LUCERNS	LUNGERS
LOCKER	BLOOPER	**LOURIE**	**LUCHOT**	**LUNGES**
BLOCKER	LOOPERS	LOURIER	LUCHOTH	BLUNGES
CLOCKER	**LOOSES**	LOURIES	**LUCKED**	PLUNGES
LOCKERS	LOOSEST	**LOUSED**	CLUCKED	**LUNIES**
LOCULE	**LOOSIE**	BLOUSED	PLUCKED	LUNIEST
LOCULED	FLOOSIE	FLOUSED	**LUCKIE**	**LUNKER**
LOCULES	LOOSIES	**LOUSES**	LUCKIER	BLUNKER
LOCUST	**LOPERS**	BLOUSES	LUCKIES	CLUNKER
LOCUSTA	ELOPERS	FLOUSES	**LUFFED**	FLUNKER
LOCUSTS	SLOPERS	**LOUTED**	BLUFFED	PLUNKER
LODGED	**LOPING**	CLOUTED	FLUFFED	LUNKERS
PLODGED	ELOPING	FLOUTED	PLUFFED	**LUNTED**
LODGES	SLOPING	GLOUTED	SLUFFED	BLUNTED
PLODGES	**LOPPED**	**LOUVRE**	**LUGGED**	**LUNULA**
LOGANS	CLOPPED	LOUVRED	GLUGGED	LUNULAE
SLOGANS	FLOPPED	LOUVRES	PLUGGED	LUNULAR
LOGGED	GLOPPED	**LOVERS**	SLUGGED	**LURDAN**
BLOGGED	PLOPPED	CLOVERS	**LUGGER**	LURDANE
CLOGGED	SLOPPED	GLOVERS	PLUGGER	LURDANS
FLOGGED	**LOPPER**	PLOVERS	SLUGGER	**LUSHED**
SLOGGED	FLOPPER	**LOVING**	LUGGERS	BLUSHED
LOGGER	LOPPERS	GLOVING	**LUGING**	FLUSHED
BLOGGER	**LORICA**	LOVINGS	KLUGING	SLUSHED
CLOGGER	LORICAE	**LOWBOY**	LUGINGS	**LUSHER**
FLOGGER	**LORIES**	PLOWBOY	**LUMBER**	BLUSHER
SLOGGER	GLORIES	LOWBOYS	CLUMBER	FLUSHER
VLOGGER	**LOSERS**	**LOWERS**	PLUMBER	PLUSHER
LOGGERS	CLOSERS	BLOWERS	SLUMBER	LUSHERS
LOGGIE	**LOSING**	FLOWERS	LUMBERS	**LUSHES**
LOGGIER	CLOSING	GLOWERS	**LUMINA**	BLUSHES
LOGIES	LOSINGS	PLOWERS	ALUMINA	FLUSHES
ELOGIES	**LOSSES**	**LOWERY**	LUMINAL	PLUSHES
OLOGIES	FLOSSES	FLOWERY	**LUMINE**	SLUSHES
LOGIEST	GLOSSES	**LOWEST**	ALUMINE	LUSHEST
LOLLOP	**LOTTED**	SLOWEST	LUMINED	**LUSHLY**
LOLLOPS	BLOTTED	**LOWING**	LUMINES	PLUSHLY
LOLLOPY	CLOTTED	BLOWING	**LUMMOX**	**LUSTER**
LOMENT	PLOTTED	FLOWING	FLUMMOX	BLUSTER
LOMENTA	SLOTTED	GLOWING	**LUMPED**	CLUSTER
LOMENTS	**LOTTER**	PLOWING	CLUMPED	FLUSTER
LONELY	BLOTTER	SLOWING	FLUMPED	LUSTERS

LUSTRA	**MALICE**	MARQUEE	MATTINS	SMELTED
LUSTRAL	MALICED	MARQUES	**MATURE**	**MELTER**
LUSTRE	MALICES	**MARROW**	MATURED	SMELTER
LUSTRED	SMALLED	MARROWS	MATURER	MELTERS
LUSTRES	**MANAGE**	MARROWY	MATURES	**MENACE**
LUTEAL	MANAGED	**MARTED**	**MATZOT**	MENACED
GLUTEAL	MANAGER	SMARTED	MATZOTH	MENACER
PLUTEAL	MANAGES	**MARTEN**	**MAUGRE**	MENACES
LUTERS	**MANCHE**	SMARTEN	MAUGRED	**MENAGE**
FLUTERS	MANCHES	MARTENS	MAUGRES	AMENAGE
LUTING	MANCHET	**MARTIN**	**MAUVES**	MENAGED
ELUTING	**MANDIR**	MARTING	MAUVEST	MENAGES
FLUTING	MANDIRA	MARTINI	**MAUVIN**	**MENDED**
LUTINGS	MANDIRS	MARTINS	MAUVINE	AMENDED
LUTIST	**MANEGE**	**MARTYR**	MAUVINS	EMENDED
FLUTIST	MANEGED	MARTYRS	**MAXIMA**	**MENDER**
LUTISTS	MANEGES	MARTYRY	MAXIMAL	AMENDER
LUTZES	**MANGLE**	**MASCLE**	**MAZING**	EMENDER
KLUTZES	MANGLED	MASCLED	AMAZING	MENDERS
LUXATE	MANGLER	MASCLES	**MEADOW**	**MENING**
LUXATED	MANGLES	**MASHED**	MEADOWS	AMENING
LUXATES	**MANIOC**	SMASHED	MEADOWY	OMENING
LYINGS	MANIOCA	**MASHER**	**MEAGRE**	**MENSCH**
FLYINGS	MANIOCS	SMASHER	MEAGRER	MENSCHY
LYRATE	**MANITO**	MASHERS	MEAGRES	**MENTAL**
LYRATED	MANITOS	**MASHES**	**MEALIE**	AMENTAL
LYTING	MANITOU	SMASHES	MEALIER	OMENTAL
FLYTING	**MANTLE**	**MASHIE**	MEALIES	**MENTUM**
MACKLE	MANTLED	MASHIER	**MEANES**	AMENTUM
MACKLED	MANTLES	MASHIES	MEANEST	OMENTUM
MACKLES	MANTLET	**MASHUP**	**MEASLE**	**MERCER**
MACULA	**MANTRA**	MASHUPS	MEASLED	AMERCER
MACULAE	MANTRAM	MASQUE	MEASLES	MERCERS
MACULAR	MANTRAP	MASQUER	**MEATHS**	MERCERY
MACULAS	MANTRAS	MASQUES	SMEATHS	**MERCES**
MACULE	**MANURE**	**MASSED**	**MEDDLE**	AMERCES
MACULED	MANURED	AMASSED	MEDDLED	**MERGED**
MACULES	MANURER	**MASSES**	MEDDLER	EMERGED
MADAME	MANURES	AMASSES	MEDDLES	**MERGES**
MADAMED	**MAPLES**	**MASTER**	**MEDIAN**	EMERGES
MADAMES	MAPLESS	MASTERS	MEDIANS	**MERLIN**
MADRAS	**MAPPER**	MASTERY	MEDIANT	MERLING
MADRASA	MAPPERS	**MASTIC**	**MEDUSA**	MERLINS
MAGGOT	MAPPERY	MASTICH	MEDUSAE	**MESTOM**
MAGGOTS	**MARBLE**	MASTICS	MEDUSAL	MESTOME
MAGGOTY	MARBLED	**MATIES**	MEDUSAN	MESTOMS
MAGISM	MARBLER	MATIEST	MEDUSAS	**METICS**
IMAGISM	MARBLES	**MATING**	**MEGARA**	EMETICS
MAGISMS	**MARINE**	AMATING	MEGARAD	**METTLE**
MAGNET	MARINER	MATINGS	**MEGASS**	METTLED
MAGNETO	MARINES	**MATRIC**	MEGASSE	METTLES
MAGNETS	**MARKKA**	MATRICE	**MEGILP**	**MEUSES**
MAILED	MARKKAA	MATRICS	MEGILPH	SMEUSES
EMAILED	MARKKAS	**MATTER**	MEGILPS	**MEZUZA**
MAILER	**MARLIN**	SMATTER	**MELLED**	MEZUZAH
EMAILER	MARLINE	MATTERS	SMELLED	MEZUZAS
MAILERS	MARLING	MATTERY	**MELLOW**	**MIASMA**
MALGRE	MARLINS	**MATTIN**	MELLOWS	MIASMAL
MALGRED	**MARQUE**	MATTING	MELLOWY	MIASMAS
MALGRES			**MELTED**	**MICATE**

EMICATE	**MISHAP**	MOLINES	MOTTLED	SMUGGER
MICATED	MISHAPS	MOLINET	MOTTLER	MUGGERS
MICATES	MISHAPT	**MOLTEN**	MOTTLES	**MULING**
MICELL	**MISKEN**	YMOLTEN	**MOUNTS**	EMULING
MICELLA	MISKENS	**MOMENT**	AMOUNTS	**MULMUL**
MICELLE	MISKENT	MOMENTA	**MOUSED**	MULMULL
MICELLS	**MISSEE**	MOMENTO	SMOUSED	MULMULS
MICKLE	MISSEEM	MOMENTS	**MOUSER**	**MUMBLE**
MICKLER	MISSEEN	**MONERA**	SMOUSER	MUMBLED
MICKLES	MISSEES	MONERAN	MOUSERS	MUMBLER
MICRON	**MISSEL**	**MONGER**	MOUSERY	MUMBLES
OMICRON	MISSELL	MONGERS	**MOUSES**	**MUMMER**
MICRONS	MISSELS	MONGERY	SMOUSES	MUMMERS
MIDDLE	**MISSES**	**MONGST**	**MOUSIE**	MUMMERY
MIDDLED	AMISSES	AMONGST	MOUSIER	**MUNGED**
MIDDLER	**MISSIS**	EMONGST	MOUSIES	EMUNGED
MIDDLES	MISSISH	**MONTAN**	**MOUSLE**	**MUNGES**
MIDGES	**MISTER**	MONTANE	MOUSLED	EMUNGES
SMIDGES	MISTERM	MONTANT	MOUSLES	**MUNITE**
MIDGIE	MISTERS	**MOOLVI**	**MOUSME**	MUNITED
MIDGIER	MISTERY	MOOLVIE	MOUSMEE	MUNITES
MIDGIES	**MISTLE**	MOOLVIS	MOUSMES	**MUNTIN**
MIGHTS	MISTLED	**MOORED**	**MOUSSE**	MUNTING
SMIGHTS	MISTLES	SMOORED	MOUSSED	MUNTINS
MIGHTST	**MISUSE**	**MOOTED**	MOUSSES	**MURING**
MIKRON	MISUSED	SMOOTED	**MOVING**	EMURING
OMIKRON	MISUSER	**MOOVED**	AMOVING	**MURLIN**
MIKRONS	MISUSES	AMOOVED	EMOVING	MURLING
MIKVOT	**MITERS**	**MOOVES**	**MOYLED**	MURLINS
MIKVOTH	SMITERS	AMOOVES	SMOYLED	**MURRAM**
MILDEW	**MITTEN**	**MORALL**	**MOYLES**	MURRAMS
MILDEWS	SMITTEN	MORALLS	SMOYLES	**MURREE**
MILDEWY	MITTENS	MORALLY	**MUCHEL**	MURREES
MILERS	**MIZZLE**	**MORASS**	MUCHELL	**MURREY**
SMILERS	MIZZLED	MORASSY	MUCHELS	MURREYS
MILIEU	MIZZLES	**MOROSE**	**MUCOSA**	**MURRIN**
MILIEUS	**MOBBLE**	MOROSER	MUCOSAE	MURRINE
MILIEUX	MOBBLED	**MORTAR**	MUCOSAL	MURRINS
MILLIE	MOBBLES	MORTARS	MUCOSAS	**MUSCLE**
MILLIER	**MOCHIE**	MORTARY	**MUDDLE**	MUSCLED
MILLIES	MOCHIER	**MORULA**	MUDDLED	MUSCLES
MIMOSA	**MOCKED**	MORULAE	MUDDLER	**MUSERS**
MIMOSAE	SMOCKED	MORULAR	MUDDLES	AMUSERS
MIMOSAS	**MOCKER**	MORULAS	**MUDGED**	**MUSHED**
MINGLE	MOCKERS	**MOSSIE**	SMUDGED	SMUSHED
MINGLED	MOCKERY	MOSSIER	**MUDGER**	**MUSHES**
MINGLER	**MODERN**	MOSSIES	SMUDGER	SMUSHES
MINGLES	MODERNE	**MOTHER**	MUDGERS	**MUSING**
MINIMA	MODERNS	SMOTHER	**MUDGES**	AMUSING
MINIMAL	**MODEST**	MOTHERS	SMUDGES	MUSINGS
MINIMAX	MODESTY	MOTHERY	**MUFFIN**	**MUSIVE**
MINUTE	**MODIST**	**MOTION**	MUFFING	AMUSIVE
MINUTED	MODISTE	AMOTION	MUFFINS	**MUSKIE**
MINUTER	MODISTS	EMOTION	**MUFFLE**	MUSKIER
MINUTES	**MOILED**	MOTIONS	MUFFLED	MUSKIES
MIRKER	SMOILED	**MOTIVE**	MUFFLER	**MUTATE**
SMIRKER	**MOLDER**	EMOTIVE	MUFFLES	MUTATED
MISCUE	SMOLDER	MOTIVED	**MUGGED**	MUTATES
MISCUED	MOLDERS	MOTIVES	SMUGGED	**MUTINE**
MISCUES	**MOLINE**	**MOTTLE**	**MUGGER**	MUTINED

MUTINES	ANEARED	KNICKER	NOBLEST	NOUSLES
MUTTON	UNEARED	SNICKER	**NOCKED**	**NOVATE**
MUTTONS	**NEATEN**	NICKERS	KNOCKED	NOVATED
MUTTONY	UNEATEN	**NICKLE**	**NODDED**	NOVATES
MUZZLE	NEATENS	NICKLED	SNODDED	**NOVENA**
MUZZLED	**NEBBED**	NICKLES	**NODDER**	NOVENAE
MUZZLER	SNEBBED	**NIDATE**	SNODDER	NOVENAS
MUZZLES	**NEBULA**	NIDATED	NODDERS	**NUANCE**
MYELIN	NEBULAE	NIDATES	**NODDLE**	NUANCED
MYELINE	NEBULAR	**NIDING**	NODDLED	NUANCES
MYELINS	NEBULAS	SNIDING	NODDLES	**NUBBED**
NAGGED	**NECKED**	NIDINGS	**NODULE**	SNUBBED
SNAGGED	SNECKED	**NIFFED**	NODULED	**NUBBIN**
NAILED	**NECTAR**	SNIFFED	NODULES	NUBBING
SNAILED	NECTARS	**NIFFER**	**NOESES**	NUBBINS
NAILER	NECTARY	SNIFFER	ANOESES	**NUBBLE**
NAILERS	**NEEDLE**	NIFFERS	**NOESIS**	KNUBBLE
NAILERY	NEEDLED	**NIGGER**	ANOESIS	NUBBLED
NAIVES	NEEDLER	SNIGGER	**NOETIC**	NUBBLES
NAIVEST	NEEDLES	NIGGERS	ANOETIC	**NUBBLY**
NANDIN	NEEZED	NIGGERY	**NOGGED**	KNUBBLY
NANDINA	SNEEZED	**NIGGLE**	SNOGGED	**NUCLEI**
NANDINE	**NEEZES**	SNIGGLE	**NOGGIN**	NUCLEIC
NANDINS	SNEEZES	NIGGLED	NOGGING	NUCLEIN
NANISM	**NEGATE**	NIGGLER	NOGGINS	**NUDGED**
ONANISM	NEGATED	NIGGLES	**NOINTS**	SNUDGED
NANISMS	NEGATER	**NIGHTS**	ANOINTS	**NUDGES**
NANNIE	NEGATES	KNIGHTS	**NOMINA**	SNUDGES
NANNIED	**NERVED**	**NIMBLE**	NOMINAL	**NUGGET**
NANNIES	ENERVED	NIMBLER	**NONAGE**	NUGGETS
NAPPED	**NERVES**	**NIPPED**	NONAGED	NUGGETY
KNAPPED	ENERVES	SNIPPED	NONAGES	**NURDLE**
SNAPPED	**NESTLE**	**NIPPER**	**NONUSE**	NURDLED
NAPPER	NESTLED	SNIPPER	NONUSER	NURDLES
KNAPPER	NESTLER	NIPPERS	NONUSES	**NURLED**
SNAPPER	NESTLES	**NIPPLE**	**NOODGE**	KNURLED
NAPPERS	**NETTIE**	NIPPLED	NOODGED	**NURSER**
NAPPIE	NETTIER	NIPPLES	NOODGES	NURSERS
NAPPIER	NETTIES	**NIRLIE**	**NOODLE**	NURSERY
NAPPIES	**NETTLE**	NIRLIER	NOODLED	**NURSLE**
NARCOS	NETTLED	**NISHES**	NOODLES	NURSLED
NARCOSE	NETTLER	KNISHES	**NOOKIE**	NURSLES
NATION	NETTLES	**NITERS**	NOOKIER	**NUTATE**
ENATION	**NEURON**	UNITERS	NOOKIES	NUTATED
NATIONS	NEURONE	**NITRID**	**NOSHER**	NUTATES
NATTER	NEURONS	NITRIDE	NOSHERS	**NUTTER**
NATTERS	**NEWING**	NITRIDS	NOSHERY	NUTTERS
NATTERY	ENEWING	**NITRIL**	**NOSIES**	NUTTERY
NATURA	**NEWSIE**	NITRILE	NOSIEST	**NUZZLE**
NATURAE	NEWSIER	NITRILS	**NOTATE**	SNUZZLE
NATURAL	NEWSIES	**NITROS**	NOTATED	NUZZLED
NATURE	**NIBBED**	NITROSO	NOTATES	NUZZLER
NATURED	SNIBBED	**NKOSIS**	**NOTHER**	NUZZLES
NATURES	**NIBBLE**	INKOSIS	ANOTHER	**NYALAS**
NAUGHT	NIBBLED	**NOBBLE**	**NOTICE**	INYALAS
NAUGHTS	NIBBLER	KNOBBLE	NOTICED	**NYMPHA**
NAUGHTY	NIBBLES	NOBBLED	NOTICER	NYMPHAE
NEAPED	**NICKED**	NOBBLER	NOTICES	NYMPHAL
SNEAPED	SNICKED	NOBBLES	**NOUSLE**	**OAKERS**
NEARED	**NICKER**	**NOBLES**	NOUSLED	SOAKERS

OAKIES	JOCULAR	BOINKED	**ONEYER**	ROOPING
OAKIEST	LOCULAR	**OINTED**	BONEYER	SOOPING
OARIER	VOCULAR	JOINTED	MONEYER	**OORALI**
HOARIER	**OCULARS**	NOINTED	ONEYERS	WOORALI
ROARIER	OCULUS	POINTED	**ONIONS**	OORALIS
OARING	LOCULUS	**OLDENS**	RONIONS	**OORIER**
HOARING	**ODISMS**	BOLDENS	**ONIUMS**	MOORIER
ROARING	IODISMS	GOLDENS	CONIUMS	**OOSIER**
SOARING	**ODISTS**	**OLDEST**	IONIUMS	GOOSIER
OATERS	CODISTS	BOLDEST	**ONLINE**	**OOZIER**
BOATERS	MODISTS	COLDEST	ONLINER	BOOZIER
COATERS	**ODIUMS**	GOLDEST	**ONNING**	WOOZIER
DOATERS	PODIUMS	**OLDIES**	CONNING	**OOZILY**
OATIER	SODIUMS	COLDIES	DONNING	BOOZILY
GOATIER	**OFFERS**	**OLDISH**	FONNING	WOOZILY
OBANGS	COFFERS	COLDISH	KONNING	**OOZING**
GOBANGS	DOFFERS	GOLDISH	RONNING	BOOZING
KOBANGS	GOFFERS	**OLEFIN**	WONNING	**OPAQUE**
OBDURE	**OFFICE**	OLEFINE	**ONUSES**	OPAQUED
OBDURED	OFFICER	OLEFINS	BONUSES	OPAQUER
OBDURES	OFFICES	**OLIVES**	NONUSES	OPAQUES
OBECHE	**OFFIES**	SOLIVES	TONUSES	**OPERAS**
BOBECHE	MOFFIES	**OLLERS**	**OODLES**	POPERAS
OBECHES	TOFFIES	GOLLERS	BOODLES	**OPIATE**
OBELIA	**OFFING**	HOLLERS	DOODLES	OPIATED
LOBELIA	BOFFING	JOLLERS	NOODLES	OPIATES
OBELIAS	COFFING	LOLLERS	POODLES	**OPPOSE**
OBJURE	DOFFING	POLLERS	**OOFIER**	OPPOSED
OBJURED	GOFFING	ROLLERS	BOOFIER	OPPOSER
OBJURES	OFFINGS	SOLLERS	GOOFIER	OPPOSES
OBLAST	**OFFISH**	TOLLERS	POOFIER	**OPTERS**
OBLASTI	TOFFISH	**OLLIES**	ROOFIER	COPTERS
OBLASTS	**OFTEST**	COLLIES	WOOFIER	**OPTIMA**
OBLIGE	SOFTEST	DOLLIES	**OOGAMY**	OPTIMAL
OBLIGED	**OGGINS**	FOLLIES	ZOOGAMY	**OPUSES**
OBLIGEE	HOGGINS	GOLLIES	**OOGENY**	MOPUSES
OBLIGER	NOGGINS	HOLLIES	ZOOGENY	**ORACLE**
OBLIGES	**OGLING**	JOLLIES	**OOHING**	CORACLE
OBOLES	BOGLING	LOLLIES	BOOHING	ORACLED
SOBOLES	OGLINGS	MOLLIES	POOHING	ORACLES
OBTUSE	**OILERS**	POLLIES	**OOIDAL**	**ORALLY**
OBTUSER	BOILERS	TOLLIES	ZOOIDAL	MORALLY
OCCIES	COILERS	WOLLIES	**OOLITE**	**ORANGE**
BOCCIES	MOILERS	**OMBERS**	ZOOLITE	ORANGER
MOCCIES	TOILERS	BOMBERS	OOLITES	ORANGES
OCHERS	**OILERY**	COMBERS	**OOLITH**	ORANGEY
TOCHERS	BOILERY	SOMBERS	ZOOLITH	**ORARIA**
OCHREA	**OILIER**	**OMBRES**	OOLITHS	ORARIAN
OCHREAE	NOILIER	HOMBRES	**OOLOGY**	**ORATED**
OCKERS	ROILIER	SOMBRES	NOOLOGY	BORATED
COCKERS	SOILIER	**OMENTA**	ZOOLOGY	**ORATES**
DOCKERS	**OILING**	LOMENTA	**OOMIAC**	BORATES
HOCKERS	BOILING	MOMENTA	OOMIACK	**ORATOR**
LOCKERS	COILING	TOMENTA	OOMIACS	ORATORS
MOCKERS	FOILING	OMENTAL	**OOPING**	ORATORY
ROCKERS	MOILING	**ONDING**	COOPING	**ORBING**
OCTETT	ROILING	BONDING	HOOPING	SORBING
OCTETTE	SOILING	FONDING	LOOPING	ZORBING
OCTETTS	TOILING	PONDING	MOOPING	**ORBITA**
OCULAR	**OINKED**	ONDINGS	POOPING	ORBITAL

ORBITAS	JOSTLER	LOUPING	OUTRUNS	FOWLING
ORCINE	OSTLERS	MOUPING	**OUTSEE**	GOWLING
PORCINE	**OTHERS**	POUPING	OUTSEEN	HOWLING
ORCINES	BOTHERS	ROUPING	OUTSEES	JOWLING
ORDERS	FOTHERS	SOUPING	**OUTSIN**	SOWLING
BORDERS	MOTHERS	**OURALI**	OUTSING	YOWLING
CORDERS	POTHERS	WOURALI	OUTSINS	**OWNERS**
ORDURE	ROTHERS	OURALIS	**OUTVIE**	DOWNERS
BORDURE	**OTTARS**	**OURIER**	OUTVIED	**OWNING**
ORDURES	COTTARS	COURIER	OUTVIES	BOWNING
ORGANS	**OTTERS**	LOURIER	**OUTWAR**	DOWNING
MORGANS	COTTERS	**OUSELS**	OUTWARD	GOWNING
ORGIAS	DOTTERS	HOUSELS	OUTWARS	LOWNING
GORGIAS	HOTTERS	**OUSTED**	**OUTWIN**	**OXLIKE**
ORGIAST	JOTTERS	JOUSTED	OUTWIND	BOXLIKE
ORGIES	LOTTERS	MOUSTED	OUTWING	FOXLIKE
PORGIES	POTTERS	ROUSTED	OUTWINS	**OXTAIL**
ORGONE	ROTTERS	**OUSTER**	**OUTWIT**	FOXTAIL
FORGONE	TOTTERS	JOUSTER	OUTWITH	OXTAILS
ORGONES	**OUBITS**	ROUSTER	OUTWITS	**OXYGEN**
ORGUES	WOUBITS	OUSTERS	**OUVERT**	LOXYGEN
MORGUES	**OUCHED**	**OUTBAR**	COUVERT	OXYGENS
ORIGAN	COUCHED	OUTBARK	OUVERTE	**OYESES**
ORIGANE	DOUCHED	OUTBARS	**OVATED**	NOYESES
ORIGANS	GOUCHED	**OUTERS**	NOVATED	**OYSTER**
ORMERS	MOUCHED	COUTERS	**OVATES**	ROYSTER
DORMERS	POUCHED	DOUTERS	BOVATES	OYSTERS
FORMERS	TOUCHED	FOUTERS	NOVATES	**OZZIES**
WORMERS	VOUCHED	MOUTERS	**OVENED**	MOZZIES
ORNATE	**OUCHES**	POUTERS	DOVENED	POZZIES
ORNATER	BOUCHES	ROUTERS	**OVERDO**	**PACERS**
OROGEN	COUCHES	SOUTERS	OVERDOG	SPACERS
OROGENS	DOUCHES	TOUTERS	**OVERED**	**PACIER**
OROGENY	GOUCHES	**OUTFLY**	COVERED	SPACIER
ORPHIC	MOUCHES	GOUTFLY	DOVERED	**PACIFY**
MORPHIC	POUCHES	**OUTHER**	HOVERED	OPACIFY
ORPINE	ROUCHES	COUTHER	LOVERED	**PACING**
FORPINE	TOUCHES	MOUTHER	**OVERGO**	SPACING
ORPINES	VOUCHES	POUTHER	OVERGOT	**PADDLE**
ORRICE	**OUGHLY**	SOUTHER	**OVERLY**	PADDLED
MORRICE	ROUGHLY	**OUTING**	LOVERLY	PADDLER
ORRICES	TOUGHLY	DOUTING	**OVINES**	PADDLES
ORTHOS	**OUGHTS**	HOUTING	BOVINES	**PAESAN**
PORTHOS	BOUGHTS	LOUTING	**OVULAR**	PAESANI
OSCULA	NOUGHTS	POUTING	OVULARY	PAESANO
OSCULAR	**OUGLIE**	ROUTING	**OWLERS**	PAESANS
OSIERS	OUGLIED	TOUTING	BOWLERS	**PAINED**
COSIERS	OUGLIES	OUTINGS	FOWLERS	SPAINED
HOSIERS	**OULDER**	**OUTLIE**	HOWLERS	**PAIOCK**
ROSIERS	BOULDER	OUTLIED	JOWLERS	PAIOCKE
OSIERY	FOULDER	OUTLIER	YOWLERS	PAIOCKS
HOSIERY	MOULDER	OUTLIES	**OWLETS**	**PAIRES**
OSMOSE	POULDER	**OUTRAN**	HOWLETS	PAIREST
OSMOSED	**OUNCES**	OUTRANG	**OWLIER**	**PAISAN**
OSMOSES	BOUNCES	OUTRANK	DOWLIER	PAISANA
OSMUND	JOUNCES	**OUTRED**	JOWLIER	PAISANO
OSMUNDA	POUNCES	FOUTRED	LOWLIER	PAISANS
OSMUNDS	ROUNCES	OUTREDS	**OWLING**	**PAJOCK**
OSTLER	**OUPING**	**OUTRUN**	BOWLING	PAJOCKE
HOSTLER	COUPING	OUTRUNG	COWLING	PAJOCKS

PALACE	**PARKED**	SPATTED	**PELTER**	PETITES
PALACED	SPARKED	**PATTEE**	SPELTER	**PETREL**
PALACES	**PARKER**	SPATTEE	PELTERS	PETRELS
PALAMA	SPARKER	**PATTER**	**PENCES**	**PETSAI**
PALAMAE	PARKERS	SPATTER	SPENCES	PETSAIS
PALATE	**PARKIE**	PATTERN	**PENDED**	**PETTLE**
PALATED	SPARKIE	PATTERS	UPENDED	PETTLED
PALATES	PARKIER	**PAUNCH**	**PENING**	PETTLES
PALLED	PARKIES	PAUNCHY	OPENING	**PEYOTE**
SPALLED	**PARKIN**	**PAVINS**	**PENSIL**	PEYOTES
PALLIA	PARKING	SPAVINS	PENSILE	**PEZANT**
PALLIAL	PARKINS	**PAVISE**	PENSILS	PEZANTS
PALMAR	**PARKIS**	PAVISER	**PEOPLE**	**PHALLI**
PALMARY	PARKISH	PAVISES	PEOPLED	PHALLIC
PALMIE	**PARKLY**	**PAWNED**	PEOPLER	PHALLIN
PALMIER	SPARKLY	SPAWNED	PEOPLES	**PHANGS**
PALMIES	**PAROLE**	**PAWNER**	**PEPPER**	UPHANGS
PALMIET	PAROLED	SPAWNER	PEPPERS	**PHASIC**
PAMPER	PAROLEE	PAWNERS	PEPPERY	APHASIC
PAMPERO	PAROLES	**PAYING**	**PEPSIN**	**PHEERE**
PAMPERS	**PARPEN**	APAYING	PEPSINE	PHEERES
PANGED	PARPEND	SPAYING	PEPSINS	**PHEESE**
SPANGED	PARPENS	PAYINGS	**PEPTID**	PHEESED
PANGEN	PARPENT	**PEANED**	PEPTIDE	PHEESES
PANGENE	**PARRED**	SPEANED	PEPTIDS	**PHEEZE**
PANGENS	SPARRED	**PEARCE**	**PERCEN**	PHEEZED
PANICK	**PARROT**	PEARCED	PERCENT	PHEEZES
PANICKS	PARROTS	PEARCES	**PERDUE**	**PHENES**
PANICKY	PARROTY	**PEBBLE**	EPERDUE	SPHENES
PANING	**PARSER**	PEBBLED	PERDUES	**PHENIC**
SPANING	SPARSER	PEBBLES	**PERFIN**	SPHENIC
PANISC	PARSERS	**PECKED**	PERFING	**PHENOM**
PANISCS	**PARTAN**	SPECKED	PERFINS	PHENOMS
PANNED	SPARTAN	**PEDDLE**	**PERKIN**	**PHESES**
SPANNED	PARTANS	PEDDLED	PERKING	APHESES
PANNER	**PARVIS**	PEDDLER	PERKINS	**PHLEGM**
SPANNER	PARVISE	PEDDLES	**PERSES**	PHLEGMS
PANNERS	**PASTER**	**PEDLAR**	SPERSES	PHLEGMY
PAPAYA	PASTERN	PEDLARS	**PERSON**	**PHOBIA**
PAPAYAN	PASTERS	PEDLARY	PERSONA	PHOBIAS
PAPAYAS	**PASTIE**	**PEDLER**	PERSONS	**PHOEBE**
PAPULA	PASTIER	PEDLERS	**PERSUE**	PHOEBES
PAPULAE	PASTIES	PEDLERY	PERSUED	**PHONEY**
PAPULAR	**PASTIL**	**PEELED**	PERSUES	PHONEYS
PARADE	PASTILS	SPEELED	**PERUKE**	**PHONIC**
PARADED	PASTILY	**PEELER**	PERUKED	APHONIC
PARADER	**PATERA**	SPEELER	PERUKES	PHONICS
PARADES	PATERAE	PEELERS	**PERUSE**	**PHOTIC**
PARDAL	**PATHED**	**PEENGE**	PERUSED	APHOTIC
PARDALE	SPATHED	PEENGED	PERUSER	PHOTICS
PARDALS	**PATHIC**	PEENGES	PERUSES	**PHOTON**
PARERS	SPATHIC	**PEERED**	**PESANT**	PHOTONS
SPARERS	PATHICS	SPEERED	PESANTE	**PHRASE**
PARGED	**PATINA**	**PEERIE**	PESANTS	PHRASED
SPARGED	PATINAE	PEERIER	**PESTLE**	PHRASER
PARGES	PATINAS	PEERIES	PESTLED	PHRASES
SPARGES	**PATINE**	**PEISES**	PESTLES	**PHYLLO**
PARING	PATINED	SPEISES	**PETARD**	PHYLLOS
SPARING	PATINES	**PELTAS**	PETARDS	**PIAFFE**
PARINGS	**PATTED**	PELTAST	**PETITE**	PIAFFED

PIAFFER	PILULAS	**PLAGUE**	**PLYING**	POOTLED
PIAFFES	**PIMENT**	PLAGUED	UPLYING	POOTLES
PICENE	PIMENTO	PLAGUER	**PODDIE**	**POPPLE**
EPICENE	PIMENTS	PLAGUES	PODDIER	POPPLED
PICENES	**PIMPLE**	PLAGUEY	PODDIES	POPPLES
PICKAX	PIMPLED	**PLANCH**	**PODDLE**	**PORING**
PICKAXE	PIMPLES	PLANCHE	PODDLED	SPORING
PICKER	**PINGLE**	**PLANTA**	PODDLES	**PORTED**
SPICKER	PINGLED	PLANTAE	**PODIUM**	SPORTED
PICKERS	PINGLER	PLANTAR	SPODIUM	**PORTER**
PICKERY	PINGLES	PLANTAS	PODIUMS	SPORTER
PICKIN	**PINIER**	**PLASHY**	**POINTE**	PORTERS
PICKING	SPINIER	SPLASHY	POINTED	**POSHES**
PICKINS	**PINIES**	**PLASTE**	POINTEL	SPOSHES
PICKLE	PINIEST	PLASTER	POINTER	POSHEST
PICKLED	**PINING**	**PLATAN**	POINTES	**POSIES**
PICKLER	OPINING	PLATANE	**POKIES**	POSIEST
PICKLES	**PINION**	PLATANS	POKIEST	**POSSUM**
PICOTE	OPINION	**PLAYED**	**POKING**	OPOSSUM
PICOTED	PINIONS	SPLAYED	SPOKING	POSSUMS
PICOTEE	**PINKEY**	**PLEADS**	**POLEAX**	**POSTER**
PIDDLE	PINKEYE	UPLEADS	POLEAXE	POSTERN
PIDDLED	PINKEYS	**PLEASE**	**POLICE**	POSTERS
PIDDLER	**PINKIE**	PLEASED	POLICED	**POSTIL**
PIDDLES	PINKIER	PLEASER	POLICER	APOSTIL
PIERCE	PINKIES	PLEASES	POLICES	POSTILS
PIERCED	**PINNER**	**PLEDGE**	**POLITE**	**POSTIN**
PIERCER	SPINNER	PLEDGED	POLITER	POSTING
PIERCES	PINNERS	PLEDGEE	**POLLEN**	POSTINS
PIFFLE	**PINNET**	PLEDGER	POLLENS	**POTAGE**
PIFFLED	SPINNET	PLEDGES	POLLENT	POTAGER
PIFFLER	PINNETS	PLEDGET	**POLYPE**	POTAGES
PIFFLES	**PINTOS**	**PLENTY**	POLYPED	**POTASS**
PIGGIE	SPINTOS	APLENTY	POLYPES	POTASSA
PIGGIER	**PIPPIN**	**PLEURA**	**POMADE**	**POTCHE**
PIGGIES	PIPPING	PLEURAE	POMADED	POTCHED
PIGGIN	PIPPINS	PLEURAL	POMADES	POTCHER
PIGGING	**PIRATE**	PLEURAS	**POMMEL**	POTCHES
PIGGINS	PIRATED	**PLIGHT**	POMMELE	**POTGUN**
PIGHTS	PIRATES	UPLIGHT	POMMELS	POTGUNS
SPIGHTS	**PISTOL**	YPLIGHT	**PONGED**	**POTHER**
PIKERS	PISTOLE	PLIGHTS	SPONGED	POTHERB
SPIKERS	PISTOLS	**PLINKS**	**PONTIL**	POTHERS
PIKING	**PITARA**	UPLINKS	PONTILE	POTHERY
SPIKING	PITARAH	**PLODGE**	PONTILS	**POTJIE**
PIKINGS	PITARAS	SPLODGE	**POOJAH**	POTJIES
PILFER	PITTED	PLODGED	POOJAHS	**POTTED**
PILFERS	SPITTED	PLODGES	**POOLED**	SPOTTED
PILFERY	**PITTEN**	**PLONGE**	SPOOLED	**POTTER**
PILING	SPITTEN	PLONGED	**POOLER**	SPOTTER
SPILING	**PITTER**	PLONGES	SPOOLER	POTTERS
PILINGS	SPITTER	**PLOOKS**	POOLERS	POTTERY
PILLED	PITTERS	UPLOOKS	**POONCE**	**POTZER**
SPILLED	**PIZAZZ**	**PLOVER**	POONCED	POTZERS
PILLOW	PIZAZZY	PLOVERS	POONCES	**POUDRE**
PILLOWS	**PIZZAZ**	PLOVERY	**POORER**	POUDRES
PILLOWY	PIZZAZZ	**PLUNGE**	SPOORER	**POUFFE**
PILULA	**PLACIT**	PLUNGED	**POORIS**	POUFFED
PILULAE	PLACITA	PLUNGER	POORISH	POUFFES
PILULAR	PLACITS	PLUNGES	**POOTLE**	**POUNCE**

POUNCED	**PREPAY**	PROTEIN	PURFLED	**QUAVER**
POUNCER	PREPAYS	**PROTYL**	PURFLER	QUAVERS
POUNCES	**PRESTO**	PROTYLE	PURFLES	QUAVERY
POUNCET	PRESTOS	PROTYLS	**PURGES**	**QUEACH**
POUTED	**PRESTS**	**PROVEN**	SPURGES	QUEACHY
SPOUTED	UPRESTS	PROVEND	**PURLIN**	**QUELCH**
POUTER	**PREVUE**	**PROVER**	PURLINE	SQUELCH
SPOUTER	PREVUED	PROVERB	PURLING	**QUICHE**
POUTERS	PREVUES	PROVERS	PURLINS	QUICHED
POWDER	**PREWAR**	**PROYNE**	**PURPLE**	QUICHES
POWDERS	PREWARM	PROYNED	PURPLED	**QUILLS**
POWDERY	PREWARN	PROYNES	PURPLER	SQUILLS
PRAISE	**PREYER**	**PRUTOT**	PURPLES	**QUINES**
UPRAISE	PREYERS	PRUTOTH	**PURRED**	EQUINES
PRAISED	**PRIAPI**	**PSYCHE**	SPURRED	**QUININ**
PRAISER	PRIAPIC	PSYCHED	**PURSUE**	QUININA
PRAISES	**PRIEFE**	PSYCHES	PURSUED	QUININE
PRANCE	PRIEFES	**PTERIA**	PURSUER	QUININS
PRANCED	**PRIEST**	APTERIA	PURSUES	**QUINTA**
PRANCER	SPRIEST	**PTOTIC**	**PUTTER**	QUINTAL
PRANCES	PRIESTS	APTOTIC	SPUTTER	QUINTAN
PRANCK	**PRIEVE**	PUCKERY	PUTTERS	QUINTAR
PRANCKE	PRIEVED	**PUDDER**	**PUTTIE**	QUINTAS
PRANCKS	PRIEVES	SPUDDER	PUTTIED	**QUINTE**
PRANGS	**PRIMER**	PUDDERS	PUTTIER	QUINTES
SPRANGS	PRIMERO	**PUDDLE**	PUTTIES	QUINTET
PRATED	PRIMERS	SPUDDLE	**PUZZLE**	**QUINTS**
UPRATED	**PRINCE**	PUDDLED	PUZZLED	SQUINTS
PRATES	PRINCED	PUDDLER	PUZZLER	**QUIRED**
UPRATES	PRINCES	PUDDLES	PUZZLES	SQUIRED
PRAYED	**PRINTS**	**PUFFER**	**PYLORI**	**QUIRES**
SPRAYED	SPRINTS	PUFFERS	PYLORIC	SQUIRES
PRAYER	**PRISER**	PUFFERY	**PYRROL**	**QUIRTS**
SPRAYER	UPRISER	**PUFFIN**	PYRROLE	SQUIRTS
PRAYERS	PRISERE	PUFFING	PYRROLS	**QUITCH**
PREACE	PRISERS	PUFFINS	**QABALA**	SQUITCH
PREACED	**PRISES**	**PUGGIE**	QABALAH	**QUITES**
PREACES	UPRISES	PUGGIER	QABALAS	EQUITES
PREACH	**PRIVET**	PUGGIES	**QAWWAL**	**QUIVER**
UPREACH	PRIVETS	**PUGGLE**	QAWWALI	AQUIVER
PREACHY	**PROBER**	PUGGLED	QAWWALS	QUIVERS
PREASE	PROBERS	PUGGLES	**QUAERE**	QUIVERY
PREASED	**PROBIT**	**PUMICE**	QUAERED	**RABBET**
PREASES	PROBITS	PUMICED	QUAERES	DRABBET
PREBUY	PROBITY	PUMICER	**QUAILS**	RABBETS
PREBUYS	**PROINE**	PUMICES	SQUAILS	**RABBIT**
PRECIS	PROINED	**PUMMEL**	**QUANTA**	CRABBIT
PRECISE	PROINES	PUMMELO	QUANTAL	FRABBIT
PREEVE	**PROLLS**	PUMMELS	**QUANTS**	RABBITO
PREEVED	UPROLLS	**PUNGLE**	EQUANTS	RABBITS
PREEVES	**PRONES**	PUNGLED	**QUARER**	RABBITY
PREFER	PRONEST	PUNGLES	SQUARER	**RABBLE**
PREFERS	**PROPYL**	**PUNKIE**	**QUARKS**	BRABBLE
PRELIM	PROPYLA	SPUNKIE	SQUARKS	DRABBLE
PRELIMS	PROPYLS	PUNKIER	**QUARTE**	GRABBLE
PREMIE	**PROTEA**	PUNKIES	QUARTER	PRABBLE
PREMIER	PROTEAN	**PUPATE**	QUARTES	RABBLED
PREMIES	PROTEAS	PUPATED	QUARTET	RABBLER
PREMIX	**PROTEI**	PUPATES	**QUARTZ**	RABBLES
PREMIXT	PROTEID	**PURFLE**	QUARTZY	**RACEME**

RACEMED	**RAFTER**	**RAISIN**	RANKERS	BRASHER
RACEMES	CRAFTER	RAISING	**RANKES**	CRASHER
RACERS	DRAFTER	RAISINS	RANKEST	TRASHER
BRACERS	GRAFTER	RAISINY	**RANKLE**	RASHERS
TRACERS	**RAFTERS**	**RAKING**	CRANKLE	**RASHES**
RACHES	**RAGEES**	BRAKING	PRANKLE	BRASHES
BRACHES	DRAGEES	CRAKING	RANKLED	CRASHES
ORACHES	**RAGGED**	RAKINGS	RANKLES	TRASHES
RACHET	BRAGGED	**RAMBLE**	**RANKLY**	RASHEST
BRACHET	CRAGGED	BRAMBLE	CRANKLY	**RASHLY**
RACHETS	DRAGGED	RAMBLED	FRANKLY	BRASHLY
RACHIS	FRAGGED	RAMBLER	**RANSOM**	**RASING**
ARACHIS	RAGGEDY	RAMBLES	TRANSOM	ERASING
RACING	**RAGGLE**	**RAMMED**	RANSOMS	**RASPED**
BRACING	DRAGGLE	CRAMMED	**RANTED**	GRASPED
GRACING	RAGGLED	DRAMMED	DRANTED	**RASPER**
TRACING	RAGGLES	TRAMMED	GRANTED	GRASPER
RACINGS	**RAGMEN**	**RAMMEL**	TRANTED	RASPERS
RACKED	RAGMENT	TRAMMEL	**RANTER**	**RASSES**
CRACKED	**RAIDED**	RAMMELS	GRANTER	BRASSES
TRACKED	BRAIDED	**RAMMER**	TRANTER	FRASSES
WRACKED	**RAIDER**	CRAMMER	RANTERS	GRASSES
RACKER	BRAIDER	RAMMERS	**RANULA**	TRASSES
CRACKER	RAIDERS	**RAMPED**	RANULAR	WRASSES
TRACKER	**RAIKED**	CRAMPED	RANULAS	**RASSLE**
RACKERS	TRAIKED	TRAMPED	**RAPERS**	WRASSLE
RACKET	**RAILED**	**RAMPER**	DRAPERS	RASSLED
BRACKET	BRAILED	CRAMPER	**RAPIER**	RASSLES
CRACKET	DRAILED	TRAMPER	CRAPIER	**RASURE**
RACKETS	TRAILED	RAMPERS	DRAPIER	ERASURE
RACKETT	**RAILER**	**RANCED**	GRAPIER	RASURES
RACKETY	FRAILER	PRANCED	RAPIERS	**RATERS**
RACKLE	TRAILER	TRANCED	**RAPING**	CRATERS
CRACKLE	RAILERS	**RANCES**	CRAPING	FRATERS
GRACKLE	**RAILES**	PRANCES	DRAPING	GRATERS
RADDED	GRAILES	TRANCES	GRAPING	KRATERS
BRADDED	**RAILLY**	**RANDED**	TRAPING	PRATERS
RADDLE	FRAILLY	BRANDED	**RAPPED**	**RATIFY**
RADDLED	**RAINED**	**RANDIE**	CRAPPED	GRATIFY
RADDLES	BRAINED	RANDIER	DRAPPED	**RATINE**
RADGES	DRAINED	RANDIES	FRAPPED	GRATINE
RADGEST	GRAINED	**RANGED**	TRAPPED	RATINES
RADIAL	TRAINED	PRANGED	WRAPPED	**RATING**
RADIALE	**RAINES**	WRANGED	**RAPPEE**	CRATING
RADIALS	GRAINES	**RANGER**	FRAPPEE	GRATING
RADIAN	**RAIRDS**	FRANGER	RAPPEES	ORATING
RADIANS	BRAIRDS	GRANGER	**RAPPER**	PRATING
RADIANT	**RAISED**	ORANGER	CRAPPER	RATINGS
RADULA	ARAISED	RANGERS	TRAPPER	**RATION**
RADULAE	BRAISED	**RANGES**	WRAPPER	ORATION
RADULAR	FRAISED	GRANGES	RAPPERS	RATIONS
RADULAS	PRAISED	ORANGES	**RAPPES**	**RATLIN**
RAFFLE	**RAISER**	**RANKED**	FRAPPES	RATLINE
RAFFLED	PRAISER	BRANKED	**RASCAL**	RATLING
RAFFLER	RAISERS	CRANKED	ERASERS	RATLINS
RAFFLES	**RAISES**	FRANKED	**RASHED**	**RATTAN**
RAFTED	ARAISES	PRANKED	BRASHED	RATTANS
CRAFTED	BRAISES	**RANKER**	CRASHED	**RATTED**
DRAFTED	FRAISES	CRANKER	TRASHED	DRATTED
GRAFTED	PRAISES	FRANKER	**RASHER**	PRATTED

RATTER	CRAYONS	REBILLS	ERECTOR	REFACED
RATTERS	**RAZERS**	**REBIND**	RECTORS	REFACES
RATTERY	BRAZERS	PREBIND	RECTORY	**REFECT**
RATTLE	GRAZERS	REBINDS	**RECULE**	PREFECT
BRATTLE	**RAZING**	**REBOIL**	RECULED	REFECTS
PRATTLE	BRAZING	PREBOIL	RECULES	**REFERS**
RATTLED	CRAZING	REBOILS	**RECURE**	PREFERS
RATTLER	GRAZING	**REBOOK**	PRECURE	**REFILE**
RATTLES	**RAZZLE**	PREBOOK	RECURED	PREFILE
RAUCLE	FRAZZLE	REBOOKS	RECURES	REFILED
RAUCLER	RAZZLES	**REBORE**	**RECUSE**	REFILES
RAUGHT	**REACTS**	REBORED	RECUSED	**REFINE**
DRAUGHT	PREACTS	REBORES	RECUSES	REFINED
FRAUGHT	**READER**	**REBORN**	**RECUTS**	REFINER
RAUNCH	DREADER	PREBORN	PRECUTS	REFINES
BRAUNCH	TREADER	**REBUKE**	**REDATE**	**REFIRE**
CRAUNCH	READERS	REBUKED	PREDATE	PREFIRE
GRAUNCH	**REAKED**	REBUKER	REDATED	REFIRED
RAUNCHY	CREAKED	REBUKES	REDATES	REFIRES
RAUNGE	FREAKED	**REBUYS**	**REDDLE**	**REFLOW**
RAUNGED	WREAKED	PREBUYS	TREDDLE	REFLOWN
RAUNGES	**REALES**	**RECANE**	REDDLED	REFLOWS
RAVAGE	REALEST	RECANED	REDDLES	**REFORM**
RAVAGED	**REALLY**	RECANES	**REDEAL**	PREFORM
RAVAGER	AREALLY	**RECAST**	REDEALS	REFORMS
RAVAGES	**REAMED**	PRECAST	REDEALT	**REFUGE**
RAVELS	BREAMED	RECASTS	**REDIAL**	REFUGED
GRAVELS	CREAMED	**RECEDE**	PREDIAL	REFUGEE
TRAVELS	DREAMED	PRECEDE	UREDIAL	REFUGES
RAVENS	**REAMER**	RECEDED	REDIALS	**REFUND**
CRAVENS	CREAMER	RECEDES	**REDING**	PREFUND
RAVERS	DREAMER	**RECENT**	AREDING	REFUNDS
BRAVERS	REAMERS	PRECENT	BREDING	**REFUSE**
CRAVERS	**REARER**	**RECEPT**	**REDRAW**	REFUSED
GRAVERS	DREARER	PRECEPT	REDRAWN	REFUSER
RAVINE	REARERS	RECEPTS	REDRAWS	REFUSES
RAVINED	**REARMS**	**RECESS**	**REDUCE**	**REFUTE**
RAVINES	PREARMS	PRECESS	REDUCED	REFUTED
RAVING	**REASON**	**RECIPE**	REDUCER	REFUTER
BRAVING	TREASON	PRECIPE	REDUCES	REFUTES
CRAVING	REASONS	RECIPES	**REEDER**	**REGALE**
GRAVING	**REASTS**	**RECITE**	BREEDER	GREGALE
RAVINGS	BREASTS	RECITED	REEDERS	REGALED
RAWEST	**REATES**	RECITER	**REEDIT**	REGALER
BRAWEST	CREATES	RECITES	PREEDIT	REGALES
RAWING	**REAVED**	**RECKED**	REEDITS	**REGIME**
DRAWING	GREAVED	TRECKED	**REEKED**	REGIMEN
RAWINGS	**REAVER**	WRECKED	GREEKED	REGIMES
RAYING	PREAVER	**RECODE**	**REEKIE**	**REGINA**
BRAYING	REAVERS	PRECODE	REEKIER	REGINAE
DRAYING	**REAVES**	RECODED	**REELED**	REGINAL
FRAYING	GREAVES	RECODES	CREELED	REGINAS
GRAYING	**REBATE**	**RECOOK**	**REESTS**	**REGIVE**
PRAYING	REBATED	PRECOOK	BREESTS	REGIVEN
RAYLES	REBATER	RECOOKS	**REEVED**	REGIVES
GRAYLES	REBATES	**RECOUP**	PREEVED	**REGLUE**
RAYLESS	**REBIDS**	PRECOUP	**REEVES**	REGLUED
RAYNES	PREBIDS	RECOUPE	PREEVES	REGLUES
TRAYNES	**REBILL**	RECOUPS	**REFACE**	**REGROW**
RAYONS	PREBILL	**RECTOR**	PREFACE	REGROWN

REGROWS	REMEETS	**REPAYS**	RESHOES	PRETELL
REGULA	**REMISE**	PREPAYS	**RESHOW**	RETELLS
REGULAE	PREMISE	**REPINE**	PRESHOW	**RETEST**
REGULAR	REMISED	REPINED	RESHOWN	PRETEST
REHEAR	REMISES	REPINER	RESHOWS	RETESTS
REHEARD	**REMISS**	REPINES	**RESIDE**	**RETILE**
REHEARS	PREMISS	**REPLAN**	PRESIDE	RETILED
REHEAT	**REMITS**	PREPLAN	RESIDED	RETILES
PREHEAT	FREMITS	REPLANS	RESIDER	**RETIME**
REHEATS	**REMIXT**	REPLANT	RESIDES	RETIMED
REHIRE	PREMIXT	**REPLUM**	**RESIFT**	RETIMES
REHIRED	**REMOLD**	REPLUMB	RESIFTS	**RETINA**
REHIRES	PREMOLD	**REPONE**	PRESIFT	RETINAE
REHOME	REMOLDS	PREPONE	RESILE	RETINAL
REHOMED	**REMOTE**	REPONED	**RESILE**	RETINAS
REHOMES	REMOTER	REPONES	RESILED	**RETIRE**
REINED	REMOTES	**REPOSE**	RESILES	RETIRED
GREINED	**REMOVE**	PREPOSE	**RESITE**	RETIREE
REISTS	PREMOVE	REPOSED	RESITED	RETIRER
BREISTS	REMOVED	REPOSER	RESITES	RETIRES
RELACE	REMOVER	REPOSES	**RESIZE**	**RETOLD**
RELACED	REMOVES	**REPPED**	RESIZED	PRETOLD
RELACES	**RENAIL**	PREPPED	RESIZES	**RETRIM**
RELATE	TRENAIL	**REPURE**	**RESKUE**	PRETRIM
PRELATE	RENAILS	REPURED	RESKUED	RETRIMS
RELATED	**RENAME**	REPURES	RESKUES	**RETTED**
RELATER	PRENAME	**REPUTE**	**RESOAK**	ARETTED
RELATES	RENAMED	REPUTED	PRESOAK	FRETTED
RELINE	RENAMES	REPUTES	RESOAKS	**RETUNE**
RELINED	**RENDED**	**REQUIT**	**RESOLD**	RETUNED
RELINES	TRENDED	REQUITE	PRESOLD	RETUNES
RELIVE	**RENEGE**	REQUITS	**RESOLE**	**RETURN**
RELIVED	RENEGED	**RERISE**	RESOLED	RETURNS
RELIVER	RENEGER	RERISEN	RESOLES	**RETYPE**
RELIVES	RENEGES	RERISES	**RESORT**	PRETYPE
RELOAD	**RENNED**	**RESALE**	PRESORT	RETYPED
PRELOAD	GRENNED	PRESALE	RESORTS	RETYPES
RELOADS	**RENNES**	RESALES	**RESTED**	**REURGE**
RELUME	BRENNES	**RESCUE**	CRESTED	REURGED
RELUMED	FRENNES	RESCUED	PRESTED	REURGES
RELUMES	**RENNIN**	RESCUER	WRESTED	PREVERB
REMADE	RENNING	RESCUES	**RESTER**	REVERBS
PREMADE	RENNINS	**RESEAU**	PRESTER	**REVERE**
REMADES	**RENTAL**	RESEAUS	WRESTER	REVERED
REMAKE	TRENTAL	RESEAUX	RESTERS	REVERER
REMAKER	RENTALS	**RESELL**	**RESTOS**	REVERES
REMAKES	**RENTED**	PRESELL	PRESTOS	**REVERS**
REMATE	PRENTED	RESELLS	**RESUME**	REVERSE
CREMATE	**RENTER**	**RESENT**	PRESUME	REVERSI
REMATED	BRENTER	PRESENT	RESUMED	REVERSO
REMATES	RENTERS	RESENTS	RESUMER	**REVETS**
REMBLE	**REPACK**	**RESETS**	RESUMES	BREVETS
TREMBLE	PREPACK	PRESETS	**RETAKE**	TREVETS
REMBLED	REPACKS	**RESHES**	RETAKEN	**REVIEW**
REMBLES	**REPAID**	FRESHES	RETAKER	PREVIEW
REMEDE	PREPAID	**RESHIP**	RETAKES	REVIEWS
REMEDED	**REPAVE**	PRESHIP	**RETAPE**	**REVILE**
REMEDES	PREPAVE	RESHIPS	PRETAPE	REVILED
REMEET	REPAVED	**RESHOE**	RETAPED	REVILER
PREMEET	REPAVES	RESHOED	RETAPES	**RETELL**

REVILES	**RIBBON**	FRIDGED	**RIMING**	RIPPLET
REVISE	RIBBONS	**RIDGES**	BRIMING	**RIPSAW**
PREVISE	RIBBONY	BRIDGES	CRIMING	RIPSAWN
REVISED	**RIBLET**	FRIDGES	GRIMING	RIPSAWS
REVISER	DRIBLET	**RIDING**	PRIMING	**RISERS**
REVISES	TRIBLET	BRIDING	**RIMMED**	PRISERS
REVIVE	RIBLETS	GRIDING	BRIMMED	**RISING**
REVIVED	**RICERS**	PRIDING	PRIMMED	ARISING
REVIVER	GRICERS	RIDINGS	TRIMMED	GRISING
REVIVES	PRICERS	**RIEVER**	**RIMMER**	IRISING
REVOKE	**RICHES**	GRIEVER	BRIMMER	KRISING
REVOKED	RICHEST	RIEVERS	CRIMMER	PRISING
REVOKER	**RICHTS**	**RIEVES**	GRIMMER	RISINGS
REVOKES	FRICHTS	GRIEVES	KRIMMER	**RISKED**
REVOTE	**RICIER**	PRIEVES	PRIMMER	BRISKED
REVOTED	PRICIER	**RIFFLE**	TRIMMER	FRISKED
REVOTES	**RICING**	RIFFLED	RIMMERS	**RISKER**
REVUES	GRICING	RIFFLER	**RIMPLE**	BRISKER
PREVUES	PRICING	RIFFLES	CRIMPLE	FRISKER
REWAKE	TRICING	**RIFLED**	RIMPLED	RISKERS
REWAKED	**RICKED**	TRIFLED	RIMPLES	**RISPED**
REWAKEN	BRICKED	**RIFLER**	**RINDED**	CRISPED
REWAKES	CRICKED	TRIFLER	BRINDED	**RITTED**
REWARM	PRICKED	RIFLERS	GRINDED	FRITTED
PREWARM	TRICKED	RIFLERY	**RINGED**	GRITTED
REWARMS	WRICKED	**RIFLES**	CRINGED	**RITTER**
REWASH	**RICKER**	TRIFLES	FRINGED	CRITTER
PREWASH	PRICKER	**RIFTED**	WRINGED	FRITTER
REWIRE	TRICKER	DRIFTED	**RINGER**	GRITTER
PREWIRE	RICKERS	GRIFTED	BRINGER	RITTERS
REWIRED	**RICKET**	**RIGGED**	CRINGER	**RITZES**
REWIRES	CRICKET	FRIGGED	WRINGER	FRITZES
REWOKE	PRICKET	GRIGGED	RINGERS	**RIVELS**
REWOKEN	RICKETS	PRIGGED	**RINKED**	DRIVELS
REWORK	RICKETY	TRIGGED	PRINKED	**RIVERS**
PREWORK	**RICKEY**	**RIGGER**	**RIPERS**	DRIVERS
REWORKS	CRICKEY	FRIGGER	GRIPERS	**RIVETS**
REWORN	RICKEYS	PRIGGER	**RIPING**	GRIVETS
PREWORN	**RICKLE**	TRIGGER	GRIPING	PRIVETS
REWOVE	BRICKLE	RIGGERS	**RIPOST**	TRIVETS
REWOVEN	PRICKLE	**RIGHTS**	RIPOSTE	**RIVING**
REWRAP	TRICKLE	BRIGHTS	RIPOSTS	DRIVING
PREWRAP	RICKLES	FRIGHTS	**RIPPED**	**RIZZAR**
REWRAPS	**RICKLY**	WRIGHTS	DRIPPED	RIZZARS
REWRAPT	PRICKLY	**RIGLIN**	GRIPPED	RIZZART
REZONE	TRICKLY	RIGLING	TRIPPED	**RIZZER**
REZONED	**RIDDED**	RIGLINS	**RIPPER**	FRIZZER
REZONES	GRIDDED	**RILLED**	DRIPPER	RIZZERS
RHOMBI	**RIDDER**	DRILLED	FRIPPER	**ROARIE**
RHOMBIC	GRIDDER	FRILLED	GRIPPER	ROARIER
RHYTHM	RIDDERS	GRILLED	TRIPPER	**ROATED**
RHYTHMI	**RIDDLE**	PRILLED	RIPPERS	TROATED
RHYTHMS	GRIDDLE	TRILLED	**RIPPLE**	**ROBAND**
RIBBED	RIDDLED	**RILLES**	ARIPPLE	PROBAND
CRIBBED	RIDDLER	GRILLES	CRIPPLE	ROBANDS
DRIBBED	RIDDLES	**RIMERS**	GRIPPLE	**ROBBER**
RIBBER	**RIDENT**	PRIMERS	TRIPPLE	ROBBERS
CRIBBER	TRIDENT	TRIMERS	**RIPPLED**	ROBBERY
DRIBBER	**RIDGED**	**RIMIER**	RIPPLER	**ROBBIN**
RIBBERS	BRIDGED	GRIMIER	RIPPLES	ROBBING

ROBBINS	TROLLED	TROPING	BROUGHT	GROWTHS
ROBING	**ROLLER**	ROPINGS	DROUGHT	TROWTHS
PROBING	DROLLER	**ROQUET**	WROUGHT	**ROYNED**
ROBINGS	PROLLER	CROQUET	**ROUGHY**	PROYNED
ROBUST	TROLLER	ROQUETS	FROUGHY	**ROYNES**
ROBUSTA	ROLLERS	**ROSACE**	**ROULES**	GROYNES
ROCHES	**ROMAGE**	ROSACEA	TROULES	PROYNES
BROCHES	FROMAGE	ROSACES	**ROUNCE**	**RUBBED**
CROCHES	ROMAGES	**ROSETS**	FROUNCE	DRUBBED
TROCHES	**ROMALS**	GROSETS	TROUNCE	GRUBBED
ROCHET	BROMALS	**ROSIER**	ROUNCES	**RUBBER**
CROCHET	**ROMPED**	BROSIER	**ROUNDS**	DRUBBER
ROCHETS	TROMPED	CROSIER	GROUNDS	GRUBBER
ROCKED	**RONTES**	PROSIER	**ROUPED**	RUBBERS
BROCKED	FRONTES	ROSIERE	CROUPED	RUBBERY
CROCKED	**RONZER**	ROSIERS	GROUPED	**RUBBIT**
FROCKED	BRONZER	**ROSIES**	TROUPED	RUBBITY
GROCKED	RONZERS	ROSIEST	**ROUSED**	**RUBBLE**
TROCKED	**ROOFED**	**ROSILY**	AROUSED	GRUBBLE
ROCKER	PROOFED	PROSILY	GROUSED	RUBBLED
ROCKERS	**ROOFER**	**ROSING**	**ROUSER**	RUBBLES
ROCKERY	PROOFER	PROSING	AROUSER	**RUBIES**
ROCKET	ROOFERS	**ROSSER**	GROUSER	RUBIEST
BROCKET	**ROOFIE**	CROSSER	TROUSER	**RUBINE**
CROCKET	ROOFIER	GROSSER	ROUSERS	RUBINES
ROCKETS	ROOFIES	ROSSERS	**ROUSES**	**RUCKED**
RODDED	**ROOKED**	**ROSTED**	AROUSES	TRUCKED
BRODDED	BROOKED	FROSTED	GROUSES	**RUCKLE**
PRODDED	CROOKED	**ROSTRA**	TROUSES	BRUCKLE
RODENT	DROOKED	ROSTRAL	**ROUTED**	TRUCKLE
ERODENT	**ROOKIE**	**ROTATE**	GROUTED	RUCKLED
RODENTS	BROOKIE	ROTATED	**ROUTER**	RUCKLES
RODING	ROOKIER	ROTATES	GROUTER	**RUDDED**
ERODING	ROOKIES	**ROTHER**	TROUTER	CRUDDED
RODINGS	**ROOMED**	BROTHER	ROUTERS	**RUDDLE**
ROGERS	BROOMED	FROTHER	**ROUTES**	CRUDDLE
DROGERS	GROOMED	ROTHERS	CROUTES	RUDDLED
ROGUER	VROOMED	**ROTONS**	**ROUTHS**	RUDDLES
ROGUERS	**ROOMER**	CROTONS	DROUTHS	**RUDELY**
ROGUERY	GROOMER	PROTONS	**ROVERS**	CRUDELY
ROGUES	ROOMERS	**ROTTED**	DROVERS	**RUDERY**
BROGUES	**ROOMIE**	TROTTED	PROVERS	PRUDERY
DROGUES	ROOMIER	**ROTTER**	TROVERS	**RUDEST**
ROILED	ROOMIES	TROTTER	**ROVING**	CRUDEST
BROILED	**ROOPED**	ROTTERS	DROVING	**RUDISH**
DROILED	DROOPED	**ROTULA**	PROVING	PRUDISH
ROINED	TROOPED	ROTULAE	ROVINGS	**RUEING**
GROINED	**ROOSES**	ROTULAS	**ROWELS**	GRUEING
PROINED	BROOSES	**ROTUND**	TROWELS	TRUEING
ROKERS	**ROOTED**	OROTUND	**ROWERS**	RUEINGS
BROKERS	WROOTED	ROTUNDA	CROWERS	**RUFFED**
PROKERS	**ROOTLE**	ROTUNDS	GROWERS	GRUFFED
ROKING	ROOTLED	**ROUBLE**	**ROWING**	**RUFFES**
BROKING	ROOTLES	TROUBLE	CROWING	TRUFFES
GROKING	ROOTLET	ROUBLES	GROWING	**RUFFIN**
PROKING	**ROPERS**	**ROUGHS**	TROWING	RUFFING
TROKING	GROPERS	BROUGHS	ROWINGS	RUFFINS
ROLLED	PROPERS	GROUGHS	**ROWNDS**	**RUFFLE**
DROLLED	**ROPING**	TROUGHS	DROWNDS	TRUFFLE
PROLLED	GROPING	**ROUGHT**	**ROWTHS**	RUFFLED

RUFFLER	PRUNTED	SALTIER	**SCERNE**	**SCRIMP**
RUFFLES	**RUSHED**	SALTIES	SCERNED	SCRIMPS
RUFFLY	BRUSHED	**SALUTE**	SCERNES	SCRIMPY
GRUFFLY	CRUSHED	SALUTED	**SCHEME**	**SCRIVE**
RUGGED	FRUSHED	SALUTER	SCHEMED	SCRIVED
DRUGGED	**RUSHER**	SALUTES	SCHEMER	SCRIVES
FRUGGED	BRUSHER	**SAMBAS**	SCHEMES	**SCROLL**
RUGGER	CRUSHER	TSAMBAS	**SCHISM**	ESCROLL
DRUGGER	RUSHERS	**SAMPLE**	SCHISMA	SCROLLS
RUGGERS	**RUSHES**	SAMPLED	SCHISMS	**SCROME**
RUGOLA	BRUSHES	SAMPLER	**SCHIZO**	SCROMED
ARUGOLA	CRUSHES	SAMPLES	SCHIZOS	SCROMES
RUGOLAS	FRUSHES	SANGARS	**SCHLEP**	**SCROTA**
RUMBLE	**RUSSET**	**SANGHA**	SCHLEPP	SCROTAL
CRUMBLE	RUSSETS	SANGHAS	SCHLEPS	**SCROWL**
DRUMBLE	RUSSETY	SANGHAT	**SCHNOZ**	SCROWLE
GRUMBLE	**RUSTED**	**SAPPLE**	SCHNOZZ	SCROWLS
RUMBLED	CRUSTED	SAPPLED	**SCHOOL**	**SCROWS**
RUMBLER	TRUSTED	SAPPLES	SCHOOLE	ESCROWS
RUMBLES	**RUSTLE**	**SATINS**	SCHOOLS	**SCRUFF**
RUMBLY	RUSTLED	ISATINS	**SCLERA**	SCRUFFS
CRUMBLY	RUSTLER	**SATRAP**	SCLERAE	SCRUFFY
GRUMBLY	RUSTLES	SATRAPS	SCLERAL	**SCRUMP**
RUMENS	**RUSTRE**	SATRAPY	SCLERAS	SCRUMPS
CRUMENS	RUSTRED	**SATYRA**	**SCONCE**	SCRUMPY
RUMINA	RUSTRES	SATYRAL	ASCONCE	**SCRUNT**
RUMINAL	**SABBAT**	SATYRAS	SCONCED	SCRUNTS
RUMMER	SABBATH	**SAVAGE**	SCONCES	SCRUNTY
BRUMMER	SABBATS	SAVAGED	**SCORIA**	**SCRUZE**
DRUMMER	**SABKHA**	SAVAGER	SCORIAC	SCRUZED
GRUMMER	SABKHAH	SAVAGES	SCORIAE	SCRUZES
RUMMERS	SABKHAS	**SAVANT**	**SCORSE**	**SCULLE**
RUMPED	SABKHAT	SAVANTE	SCORSED	SCULLED
CRUMPED	**SADDLE**	SAVANTS	SCORSER	SCULLER
FRUMPED	SADDLED	**SAVOUR**	SCORSES	SCULLES
GRUMPED	SADDLER	SAVOURS	**SCOURS**	**SCUNGE**
TRUMPED	SADDLES	SAVOURY	SCOURSE	SCUNGED
RUMPLE	**SAFROL**	**SCALAR**	**SCOUSE**	SCUNGES
CRUMPLE	SAFROLE	SCALARE	SCOUSER	**SCYTHE**
FRUMPLE	SAFROLS	SCALARS	SCOUSES	SCYTHED
RUMPLED	**SAGGAR**	**SCAPED**	**SCRAPE**	SCYTHER
RUMPLES	SAGGARD	ESCAPED	SCRAPED	SCYTHES
RUMPLY	SAGGARS	**SCAPES**	SCRAPER	**SDAINE**
CRUMPLY	**SAHIBA**	ESCAPES	SCRAPES	SDAINED
RUNDLE	SAHIBAH	**SCARCE**	**SCRAWL**	SDAINES
GRUNDLE	SAHIBAS	SCARCER	SCRAWLS	**SDEIGN**
TRUNDLE	**SALIVA**	**SCARED**	SCRAWLY	SDEIGNE
RUNDLED	SALIVAL	ASCARED	SCREAKY	SDEIGNS
RUNDLES	SALIVAS	**SCARPS**	**SCREAM**	**SEALER**
RUNDLET	**SALLOW**	ESCARPS	SCREAMO	SEALERS
RUNKLE	SALLOWS	**SCARRE**	SCREAMS	SEALERY
CRUNKLE	SALLOWY	SCARRED	**SCRIBE**	**SEARCE**
RUNKLED	**SALMON**	SCARRES	ASCRIBE	SEARCED
RUNKLES	SALMONS	**SCATHE**	ESCRIBE	SEARCES
RUNNEL	SALMONY	SCATHED	SCRIBED	**SEAWAN**
TRUNNEL	**SALTER**	SCATHES	SCRIBER	SEAWANS
RUNNELS	PSALTER	**SCENDS**	SCRIBES	SEAWANT
RUNTED	SALTERN	ASCENDS	**SCRIKE**	**SEBATE**
BRUNTED	SALTERS	**SCENTS**	SCRIKED	SEBATES
GRUNTED	**SALTIE**	ASCENTS	SCRIKES	**SECEDE**

SECEDED	**SEPTIC**	SHEATHE	SHOTTES	SILVERY
SECEDER	ASEPTIC	SHEATHS	**SHOWER**	**SIMPLE**
SECEDES	SEPTICS	SHEATHY	SHOWERS	SIMPLED
SECOND	**SEQUEL**	**SHEAVE**	SHOWERY	SIMPLER
SECONDE	SEQUELA	SHEAVED	**SHRIEK**	SIMPLES
SECONDI	SEQUELS	SHEAVES	SHRIEKS	SIMPLEX
SECONDO	**SERENE**	**SHEESH**	SHRIEKY	**SIMURG**
SECONDS	SERENED	SHEESHA	**SHRIKE**	SIMURGH
SECRET	SERENER	**SHEIKH**	SHRIKED	SIMURGS
SECRETA	SERENES	SHEIKHA	SHRIKES	**SINGLE**
SECRETE	**SERINE**	SHEIKHS	**SHRILL**	SINGLED
SECRETS	ESERINE	**SHELVE**	SHRILLS	SINGLES
SECURE	SERINES	SHELVED	SHRILLY	SINGLET
SECURED	**SERING**	SHELVER	**SHRIMP**	**SINTER**
SECURER	SERINGA	SHELVES	SHRIMPS	SINTERS
SECURES	**SEROSA**	**SHENDS**	SHRIMPY	SINTERY
SEDATE	SEROSAE	YSHENDS	**SHRINE**	**SIPPLE**
SEDATED	SEROSAL	**SHERIA**	SHRINED	SIPPLED
SEDATER	SEROSAS	SHERIAS	SHRINES	SIPPLES
SEDATES	**SERRAN**	SHERIAT	**SHRIVE**	**SITULA**
SEDUCE	SERRANO	**SHERIF**	SHRIVED	SITULAE
SEDUCED	SERRANS	SHERIFF	SHRIVEL	**SIXAIN**
SEDUCER	**SERVER**	SHERIFS	SHRIVEN	SIXAINE
SEDUCES	SERVERS	**SHEUCH**	SHRIVER	SIXAINS
SEELIE	SERVERY	SHEUCHS	SHRIVES	**SIZZLE**
SEELIER	**SESTET**	**SHIEST**	**SHROUD**	SIZZLED
SEETHE	SESTETS	ASHIEST	SHROUDS	SIZZLER
SEETHED	SESTETT	**SHIKAR**	SHROUDY	SIZZLES
SEETHER	**SETTLE**	SHIKARI	**SHROVE**	**SKATOL**
SEETHES	SETTLED	SHIKARS	SHROVED	SKATOLE
SEISIN	SETTLER	**SHIKSE**	SHROVES	SKATOLS
SEISING	SETTLES	SHIKSEH	**SHTICK**	**SKETCH**
SEISINS	**SEVERE**	SHIKSES	SHTICKS	SKETCHY
SEIZIN	SEVERED	**SHINNE**	SHTICKY	**SKIING**
SEIZING	SEVERER	SHINNED	**SICKLE**	SKIINGS
SEIZINS	**SEXTAN**	SHINNES	SICKLED	**SKIVIE**
SELECT	SEXTANS	SHINNEY	SICKLES	SKIVIER
SELECTA	SEXTANT	**SHIPPO**	**SIERRA**	**SKLATE**
SELECTS	**SEXTET**	SHIPPON	SIERRAN	SKLATED
SEMBLE	SEXTETS	SHIPPOS	SIERRAS	SKLATES
SEMBLED	SEXTETT	**SHIVER**	**SIFFLE**	**SKLENT**
SEMBLES	**SEXUAL**	ASHIVER	SIFFLED	ASKLENT
SEMINA	ASEXUAL	SHIVERS	SIFFLES	SKLENTS
SEMINAL	**SHADOW**	SHIVERY	**SIGNOR**	**SKRIKE**
SEMINAR	SHADOWS	**SHLOCK**	SIGNORA	SKRIKED
SEMPLE	SHADOWY	SHLOCKS	SIGNORE	SKRIKES
SEMPLER	**SHAMED**	SHLOCKY	SIGNORI	**SLAKED**
SENHOR	ASHAMED	**SHLUMP**	SIGNORS	ASLAKED
SENHORA	**SHAMES**	SHLUMPS	SIGNORY	YSLAKED
SENHORS	ASHAMES	SHLUMPY	**SILAGE**	**SLAKES**
SENSIS	**SHANTI**	**SHOOLE**	SILAGED	ASLAKES
SENSISM	SHANTIH	SHOOLED	SILAGES	**SLAVER**
SENSIST	SHANTIS	SHOOLES	**SILENE**	SLAVERS
SENSOR	**SHARIA**	**SHOPPE**	SILENES	SLAVERY
SENSORS	SHARIAH	SHOPPED	**SILKIE**	**SLEAVE**
SENSORY	SHARIAS	SHOPPER	SILKIER	SLEAVED
SEPSES	SHARIAT	SHOPPES	SILKIES	SLEAVES
ASEPSES	**SHAWED**	**SHOTTE**	**SILVER**	**SLEDGE**
SEPSIS	PSHAWED	SHOTTED	SILVERN	SLEDGED
ASEPSIS	**SHEATH**	SHOTTEN	SILVERS	SLEDGER

SLEDGES	SNEEZED	**SORTIE**	**SPHERE**	ASPREAD
SLEECH	SNEEZER	SORTIED	SPHERED	SPREADS
SLEECHY	SNEEZES	SORTIES	SPHERES	**SPREDD**
SLEEVE	SNIDES	**SOUPLE**	**SPIALS**	SPREDDE
SLEEVED	SNIDEST	SOUPLED	ESPIALS	SPREDDS
SLEEVER	**SNITCH**	SOUPLES	**SPICER**	**SPRING**
SLEEVES	SNITCHY	**SOURCE**	SPICERS	SPRINGE
SLEIGH	**SNOOZE**	SOURCED	SPICERY	SPRINGS
SLEIGHS	SNOOZED	SOURCES	**SPICKS**	SPRINGY
SLEIGHT	SNOOZER	**SOWSSE**	ASPICKS	**SPRITS**
SLOUCH	SNOOZES	SOWSSED	**SPIDER**	ESPRITS
SLOUCHY	**SNUBBE**	SOWSSES	SPIDERS	**SPROUT**
SLOUGH	SNUBBED	**SOZZLE**	SPIDERY	ASPROUT
SLOUGHI	SNUBBER	SOZZLED	**SPIERS**	SPROUTS
SLOUGHS	SNUBBES	SOZZLES	ESPIERS	**SPRUCE**
SLOUGHY	**SNUDGE**	**SPALLE**	**SPIKER**	SPRUCED
SLUDGE	SNUDGED	SPALLED	SPIKERS	SPRUCER
SLUDGED	SNUDGES	SPALLER	SPIKERY	SPRUCES
SLUDGES	**SOAPIE**	SPALLES	**SPINES**	**SPULYE**
SLUICE	SOAPIER	**SPARES**	ASPINES	SPULYED
SLUICED	SOAPIES	SPAREST	**SPIRED**	SPULYES
SLUICES	**SOCAGE**	**SPARGE**	ASPIRED	**SPURNE**
SLUTCH	SOCAGER	SPARGED	**SPIREM**	SPURNED
SLUTCHY	SOCAGES	SPARGER	SPIREME	SPURNER
SMIDGE	**SOCIAL**	SPARGES	SPIREMS	SPURNES
SMIDGEN	ASOCIAL	**SPARKE**	**SPIRES**	**SPYING**
SMIDGES	SOCIALS	SPARKED	ASPIRES	ESPYING
SMOILE	**SODAIN**	SPARKER	**SPIRIT**	SPYINGS
SMOILED	SODAINE	**SPARKES**	SPIRITS	**SQUALL**
SMOILES	**SOIGNE**	**SPARRE**	SPIRITY	SQUALLS
SMOKIE	SOIGNEE	SPARRED	**SPLASH**	SQUALLY
SMOKIER	**SOLACE**	SPARRER	SPLASHY	**SQUAMA**
SMOKIES	SOLACED	SPARRES	**SPLEEN**	SQUAMAE
SMOOCH	SOLACER	**SPARSE**	SPLEENS	**SQUARE**
SMOOCHY	SOLACES	SPARSER	SPLEENY	SQUARED
SMOOGE	**SOLATE**	**SPARTH**	**SPLICE**	SQUARER
SMOOGED	ISOLATE	SPARTHE	SPLICED	SQUARES
SMOOGES	SOLATED	SPARTHS	SPLICER	**SQUASH**
SMOOTH	SOLATES	**SPATHE**	SPLICES	SQUASHY
SMOOTHS	**SOLITO**	SPATHED	**SPLINE**	**SQUAWK**
SMOOTHY	SOLITON	SPATHES	SPLINED	SQUAWKS
SMOUSE	**SOMBRE**	**SPAVIE**	SPLINES	SQUAWKY
SMOUSED	SOMBRED	SPAVIES	**SPONGE**	**SQUEAK**
SMOUSER	SOMBRER	SPAVIET	SPONGED	SQUEAKS
SMOUSES	SOMBRES	**SPENCE**	SPONGER	SQUEAKY
SMOYLE	**SONSIE**	SPENCER	SPONGES	**SQUIFF**
SMOYLED	SONSIER	SPENCES	**SPORTS**	SQUIFFY
SMOYLES	**SOOGEE**	**SPERRE**	ASPORTS	**SQUILL**
SMUDGE	SOOGEED	SPERRED	**SPOUSE**	SQUILLA
SMUDGED	SOOGEES	SPERRES	ESPOUSE	SQUILLS
SMUDGER	**SOOGIE**	**SPERSE**	SPOUSED	**SQUINT**
SMUDGES	SOOGIED	ASPERSE	SPOUSES	ASQUINT
SMUTCH	SOOGIES	SPERSED	**SPRAIN**	SQUINTS
SMUTCHY	**SOOTHE**	SPERSES	SPRAINS	SQUINTY
SNATCH	SOOTHED	**SPHAER**	SPRAINT	**SQUIRE**
SNATCHY	SOOTHER	SPHAERE	**SPRAWL**	ESQUIRE
SNEBBE	SOOTHES	SPHAERS	ASPRAWL	SQUIRED
SNEBBED	**SOPITE**	**SPHEAR**	SPRAWLS	SQUIRES
SNEBBES	SOPITED	SPHEARE	SPRAWLY	**SQUIRM**
SNEEZE	SOPITES	SPHEARS	**SPREAD**	SQUIRMS

SQUIRMY	**STEARE**	STONERN	**STRIGA**	SUCCOSE
SQUISH	STEARED	STONERS	STRIGAE	**SUCCOT**
SQUISHY	STEARES	**STONES**	**STRIKE**	SUCCOTH
STABLE	**STEDDE**	ASTONES	STRIKER	**SUCKLE**
ASTABLE	STEDDED	**STONNE**	STRIKES	SUCKLED
STABLED	STEDDES	STONNED	**STRING**	SUCKLER
STABLER	**STEEMS**	STONNES	STRINGS	SUCKLES
STABLES	ESTEEMS	**STOOGE**	STRINGY	**SUDATE**
STADIA	**STEEVE**	STOOGED	**STRIPE**	SUDATED
STADIAL	STEEVED	STOOGES	STRIPED	SUDATES
STADIAS	STEEVER	**STOOPE**	STRIPER	**SUDDEN**
STAGER	STEEVES	STOOPED	STRIPES	ASUDDEN
STAGERS	**STELIC**	STOOPER	STRIPEY	SUDDENS
STAGERY	ASTELIC	STOOPES	**STRIVE**	**SUKKOT**
STAITH	**STELLA**	**STOOZE**	STRIVED	SUKKOTH
STAITHE	STELLAR	STOOZED	STRIVEN	**SULFID**
STAITHS	STELLAS	STOOZER	STRIVER	SULFIDE
STALES	**STEMME**	STOOZES	STRIVES	SULFIDS
STALEST	STEMMED	**STOUND**	**STROBE**	**SULFUR**
STAPLE	STEMMER	ASTOUND	STROBED	SULFURS
STAPLED	STEMMES	STOUNDS	STROBES	SULFURY
STAPLER	**STENCH**	**STOVER**	**STROKE**	**SULTAN**
STAPLES	STENCHY	ESTOVER	STROKED	SULTANA
STARCH	**STENTS**	STOVERS	STROKEN	SULTANS
STARCHY	OSTENTS	**STRAFE**	STROKER	**SUMMAR**
STARTS	**STEPPE**	STRAFED	STROKES	**SUMMARY**
ASTARTS	STEPPED	STRAFER	**STROMA**	**SUMMAT**
STARTSY	STEPPER	STRAFES	STROMAL	SUMMATE
STARVE	STEPPES	**STRAIN**	**STROOK**	SUMMATS
STARVED	**STERNA**	STRAINS	STROOKE	**SUMMER**
STARVER	STERNAL	STRAINT	**STRUMA**	SUMMERS
STARVES	**STERVE**	**STRAKE**	STRUMAE	SUMMERY
STATED	STERVED	STRAKED	STRUMAS	**SUNDER**
ESTATED	STERVES	STRAKES	**STRUMS**	ASUNDER
STATES	**STIEVE**	**STRAND**	ESTRUMS	SUNDERS
ESTATES	STIEVER	ASTRAND	**STYLAR**	**SUPPLE**
STATIC	**STIFLE**	STRANDS	ASTYLAR	SUPPLED
ASTATIC	STIFLED	**STRANG**	**STYLIE**	SUPPLER
STATICE	STIFLER	STRANGE	STYLIER	SUPPLES
STATICS	STIFLES	**STRATA**	**STYMIE**	**SURFIE**
STATIN	**STIGMA**	STRATAL	STYMIED	SURFIER
STATING	STIGMAL	STRATAS	STYMIES	SURFIES
STATINS	STIGMAS	**STRAYS**	**SUBDUE**	**SURGER**
STATUE	**STIMIE**	ESTRAYS	SUBDUED	SURGERS
STATUED	STIMIED	**STREAK**	SUBDUER	SURGERY
STATUES	STIMIES	STREAKS	SUBDUES	**SURING**
STATUS	**STIRRA**	STREAKY	**SUBMEN**	USURING
STATUSY	STIRRAH	**STREAM**	SUBMENU	**SUTLER**
STAYNE	STIRRAS	STREAMS	**SUBPAR**	SUTLERS
STAYNED	**STIRRE**	STREAMY	SUBPART	SUTLERY
STAYNES	STIRRED	STREETY	**SUBTIL**	**SUTTLE**
STEALE	STIRRER	**STRICH**	SUBTILE	SUTTLED
STEALED	STIRRES	ESTRICH	**SUBTLE**	SUTTLES
STEALER	**STODGE**	OSTRICH	SUBTLER	**SUTURE**
STEALES	STODGED	**STRICT**	**SUCCES**	SUTURED
STEALT	STODGER	ASTRICT	SUCCESS	SUTURES
STEALTH	STODGES	**STRIDE**	**SUCCOR**	**SVELTE**
STEANE	STONED	ASTRIDE	SUCCORS	SVELTER
STEANED	ASTONED	STRIDER	SUCCORY	**SWARDS**
STEANES	**STONER**	STRIDES	**SUCCOS**	USWARDS

SWARTH	ATACTIC	**TANGED**	**TATTER**	TEMPERA
SWARTHS	TACTICS	STANGED	TATTERS	TEMPERS
SWARTHY	**TAENIA**	**TANGIE**	TATTERY	**TEMPLE**
SWARVE	TAENIAE	TANGIER	**TATTIE**	STEMPLE
SWARVED	TAENIAS	TANGIES	TATTIER	TEMPLED
SWARVES	**TAGGED**	**TANGLE**	TATTIES	TEMPLES
SWATHE	STAGGED	TANGLED	**TATTLE**	TEMPLET
SWATHED	**TAGGER**	TANGLER	TATTLED	**TENDED**
SWATHER	STAGGER	TANGLES	TATTLER	STENDED
SWATHES	TAGGERS	**TANKED**	TATTLES	**TENNIS**
SWERVE	**TAIGLE**	STANKED	**TATUED**	TENNIST
SWERVED	TAIGLED	**TANNER**	STATUED	**TENSES**
SWERVER	TAIGLES	TANNERS	**TAVERN**	TENSEST
SWERVES	**TAIVER**	TANNERY	TAVERNA	**TENTED**
SWINGE	TAIVERS	**TANNIC**	TAVERNS	STENTED
SWINGED	TAIVERT	STANNIC	**TAWING**	**TENTIE**
SWINGER	**TAKING**	**TANNIN**	STAWING	TENTIER
SWINGES	STAKING	TANNING	TAWINGS	**TENURE**
SWITCH	TAKINGS	TANNINS	**TAWTIE**	TENURED
SWITCHY	**TALKED**	**TAPETA**	TAWTIER	TENURES
SWITHE	STALKED	TAPETAL	**TAXIES**	**TEREFA**
SWITHER	**TALKER**	**TAPPED**	ATAXIES	TEREFAH
SWOUNE	STALKER	STAPPED	**TEAGLE**	**TERNAL**
SWOUNED	TALKERS	**TAPPET**	TEAGLED	ETERNAL
SWOUNES	**TALKIE**	TAPPETS	TEAGLES	STERNAL
SYLVIA	TALKIER	**TARAND**	**TEAMED**	**TERNED**
SYLVIAS	TALKIES	TARANDS	STEAMED	STERNED
SYLVIN	**TALLIS**	**TARCEL**	**TEAMER**	**TERTIA**
SYLVINE	TALLISH	TARCELS	STEAMER	TERTIAL
SYLVINS	**TALLIT**	**TARIFF**	TEAMERS	TERTIAN
SYMBOL	TALLITH	TARIFFS	**TEARED**	TERTIAS
SYMBOLE	TALLITS	**TARING**	STEARED	**TESTER**
SYMBOLS	**TALLOW**	STARING	**TEAZLE**	TESTERN
SYNURA	TALLOWS	TARINGS	TEAZLED	TESTERS
SYNURAE	TALLOWY	**TARPAN**	TEAZLES	**TEWING**
TAATAS	TALONS	TARPANS	**TECHIE**	STEWING
ATAATAS	ETALONS	**TARRED**	TECHIER	**THALLI**
TABBED	**TAMARA**	STARRED	TECHIES	THALLIC
STABBED	TAMARAO	**TARTAN**	**TEDDED**	**THANES**
TABLED	TAMARAS	TARTANA	STEDDED	ETHANES
STABLED	TAMARAU	TARTANE	**TEEMED**	**THANNA**
TABLES	**TAMARI**	TARTANS	STEEMED	THANNAH
STABLES	TAMARIN	**TARTAR**	**TEENED**	THANNAS
TABULA	TAMARIS	TARTARE	STEENED	**THATCH**
TABULAE	**TAMBUR**	TARTARS	**TEERED**	THATCHT
TABULAR	TAMBURA	**TARTED**	STEERED	THATCHY
TACKED	TAMBURS	STARTED	**TEETHE**	**THEISM**
STACKED	**TAMINE**	**TARTER**	TEETHED	ATHEISM
TACKER	ETAMINE	STARTER	TEETHER	THEISMS
STACKER	TAMINES	**TARTLY**	TEETHES	**THEIST**
TACKERS	**TAMINS**	STARTLY	**TEGULA**	ATHEIST
TACKET	ETAMINS	**TASHED**	TEGULAE	THEISTS
STACKET	**TAMMIE**	STASHED	TEGULAR	**THERME**
TACKETS	TAMMIED	**TASHES**	**TELLAR**	THERMEL
TACKETY	TAMMIES	STASHES	STELLAR	THERMES
TACKLE	**TAMPED**	**TASSEL**	TELLARS	**THIEVE**
TACKLED	STAMPED	TASSELL	**TELLIN**	THIEVED
TACKLER	**TAMPER**	TASSELS	TELLING	THIEVES
TACKLES	STAMPER	**TATERS**	TELLINS	**THIRST**
TACTIC	TAMPERS	STATERS	**TEMPER**	ATHIRST

THIRSTS	TIETACS	TIPPLED	STOMIUM	TORQUES
THIRSTY	**TIFFED**	TIPPLER	**TONERS**	**TORULA**
THOUGH	STIFFED	TIPPLES	ATONERS	TORULAE
THOUGHT	**TIFFIN**	**TIPTOE**	STONERS	TORULAS
THREAD	TIFFING	TIPTOED	**TONGUE**	**TORULI**
THREADS	TIFFINS	TIPTOES	TONGUED	TORULIN
THREADY	**TILING**	**TIRING**	TONGUES	**TOSSES**
THRIFT	STILING	STIRING	**TONICS**	STOSSES
THRIFTS	TILINGS	TIRINGS	ATONICS	**TOTTED**
THRIFTY	**TILLED**	**TIRRED**	**TONIER**	STOTTED
THRILL	STILLED	STIRRED	STONIER	**TOTTER**
ATHRILL	**TILLER**	**TISSUE**	**TONIES**	STOTTER
THRILLS	STILLER	TISSUED	ATONIES	TOTTERS
THRILLY	TILLERS	TISSUES	STONIES	TOTTERY
THRIST	**TILTED**	TISSUEY	TONIEST	**TOTTIE**
THRISTS	STILTED	**TITTLE**	**TONING**	STOTTIE
THRISTY	**TILTER**	TITTLED	ATONING	TOTTIER
THRIVE	STILTER	TITTLES	STONING	TOTTIES
THRIVED	TILTERS	**TITTUP**	TONINGS	**TOUCHE**
THRIVEN	**TIMBAL**	TITTUPS	**TONISH**	TOUCHED
THRIVER	TIMBALE	TITTUPY	STONISH	TOUCHER
THRIVES	TIMBALS	**TITULE**	**TONKED**	TOUCHES
THROAT	**TIMBER**	TITULED	STONKED	**TOUPEE**
THROATS	TIMBERS	TITULES	**TONKER**	TOUPEED
THROATY	TIMBERY	**TOCKED**	STONKER	TOUPEES
THRONE	**TIMBRE**	STOCKED	TONKERS	**TOURIE**
THRONED	TIMBREL	**TODDLE**	**TONNAG**	STOURIE
THRONES	TIMBRES	TODDLED	TONNAGE	TOURIES
THROWE	**TIMING**	TODDLER	TONNAGS	**TOUSLE**
THROWER	STIMING	TODDLES	**TONNES**	TOUSLED
THROWES	TIMINGS	**TODGER**	STONNES	TOUSLES
THWART	**TINDER**	STODGER	**TOOLED**	**TOUTER**
ATHWART	TINDERS	TODGERS	STOOLED	STOUTER
THWARTS	TINDERY	**TOGATE**	**TOOLIE**	TOUTERS
TIBIAL	**TINGED**	TOGATED	STOOLIE	**TOUTIE**
STIBIAL	STINGED	**TOGGER**	TOOLIES	TOUTIER
TICKED	**TINGLE**	TOGGERS	**TOOTLE**	**TOUZLE**
STICKED	ATINGLE	TOGGERY	TOOTLED	TOUZLED
TICKER	TINGLED	**TOGGLE**	TOOTLER	TOUZLES
STICKER	TINGLER	TOGGLED	TOOTLES	**TOWAGE**
TICKERS	TINGLES	TOGGLER	**TOPERS**	STOWAGE
TICKLE	**TINIES**	TOGGLES	STOPERS	TOWAGES
STICKLE	TINIEST	**TOILES**	**TOPFUL**	**TOWERS**
TICKLED	**TINKER**	ETOILES	TOPFULL	STOWERS
TICKLER	STINKER	**TOITED**	**TOPING**	**TOWIES**
TICKLES	TINKERS	STOITED	STOPING	TOWIEST
TIDDLE	**TINKLE**	**TOKERS**	**TOPPED**	**TOWING**
TIDDLED	TINKLED	STOKERS	STOPPED	STOWING
TIDDLER	TINKLER	**TOKING**	**TOPPER**	TOWINGS
TIDDLES	TINKLES	STOKING	STOPPER	**TOWMON**
TIDDLEY	**TINNIE**	TOLUID	TOPPERS	TOWMOND
TIDIES	TINNIER	TOLUIDE	**TOPPLE**	TOWMONS
TIDIEST	TINNIES	TOLUIDS	STOPPLE	TOWMONT
TIERCE	**TINTED**	**TOLUOL**	TOPPLED	**TOWNIE**
TIERCED	STINTED	TOLUOLE	TOPPLES	TOWNIER
TIERCEL	**TINTER**	TOLUOLS	**TORIES**	TOWNIES
TIERCES	STINTER	**TOMBAC**	STORIES	**TRACER**
TIERCET	TINTERS	TOMBACK	**TORQUE**	TRACERS
TIETAC	**TIPPLE**	TOMBACS	TORQUED	TRACERY
TIETACK	STIPPLE	**TOMIUM**	TORQUER	**TRAIKS**

STRAIKS	**TRITON**	**TUNICA**	OUAKARI	PULLING
TRAINS	TRITONE	TUNICAE	UAKARIS	WULLING
STRAINS	TRITONS	**TUNNED**	**UBERTY**	ULLINGS
TRAITS	**TRIVIA**	STUNNED	PUBERTY	**ULOSES**
STRAITS	TRIVIAL	**TURACO**	**UBIETY**	DULOSES
TRAMEL	**TROCHE**	TURACOS	DUBIETY	**ULOSIS**
TRAMELL	TROCHEE	TURACOU	**UCKERS**	DULOSIS
TRAMELS	TROCHES	**TURBAN**	BUCKERS	**UMBERS**
TRAMPS	**TROCHI**	TURBAND	DUCKERS	CUMBERS
STRAMPS	TROCHIL	TURBANS	FUCKERS	LUMBERS
TRANCE	**TROKED**	TURBANT	MUCKERS	NUMBERS
TRANCED	STROKED	**TURBIT**	PUCKERS	**UMBLES**
TRANCES	**TROKES**	TURBITH	SUCKERS	BUMBLES
TRANCEY	STROKES	TURBITS	TUCKERS	FUMBLES
TRAPPY	**TROLLS**	**TURNER**	YUCKERS	HUMBLES
STRAPPY	STROLLS	TURNERS	**UDDERS**	JUMBLES
TRAYNE	**TROMPE**	TURNERY	BUDDERS	MUMBLES
TRAYNED	TROMPED	**TURNIP**	DUDDERS	NUMBLES
TRAYNES	TROMPES	TURNIPS	JUDDERS	RUMBLES
TREBLE	**TROPHI**	TURNIPY	MUDDERS	TUMBLES
TREBLED	TROPHIC	**TURTLE**	PUDDERS	**UMBREL**
TREBLES	**TROPHY**	TURTLED	RUDDERS	TUMBREL
TREPAN	ATROPHY	TURTLER	SUDDERS	UMBRELS
TREPANG	**TROPIN**	TURTLES	**UGGING**	**UMBRIL**
TREPANS	ATROPIN	**TUSHIE**	BUGGING	TUMBRIL
TREVIS	TROPINE	STUSHIE	FUGGING	UMBRILS
TREVISS	TROPING	TUSHIES	HUGGING	**UMMING**
TRIAGE	TROPINS	**TUSSLE**	JUGGING	BUMMING
TRIAGED	**TROULE**	TUSSLED	LUGGING	GUMMING
TRIAGES	TROULED	TUSSLES	MUGGING	HUMMING
TRICKS	TROULES	**TUSSOR**	PUGGING	MUMMING
STRICKS	**TROUPE**	TUSSORE	RUGGING	SUMMING
TRICKSY	TROUPED	TUSSORS	SUGGING	VUMMING
TRIENE	TROUPER	**TWEEZE**	TUGGING	**UMPIES**
TRIENES	TROUPES	TWEEZED	**UGLIED**	DUMPIES
TRIERS	**TROUSE**	TWEEZER	OUGLIED	HUMPIES
ETRIERS	TROUSER	TWEEZES	**UGLIER**	RUMPIES
TRIFLE	TROUSES	**TWIBIL**	FUGLIER	YUMPIES
TRIFLED	**TROUTS**	TWIBILL	**UGLIES**	**UMPING**
TRIFLER	STROUTS	TWIBILS	OUGLIES	BUMPING
TRIFLES	**TROWED**	**TWINGE**	UGLIEST	DUMPING
TRIKES	STROWED	TWINGED	**ULEXES**	GUMPING
STRIKES	**TRUDGE**	TWINGES	CULEXES	HUMPING
TRIPES	TRUDGED	**TWITCH**	**ULICES**	JUMPING
STRIPES	TRUDGEN	TWITCHY	CULICES	LUMPING
TRIPEY	TRUDGER	**TYLERS**	**ULLAGE**	MUMPING
STRIPEY	TRUDGES	STYLERS	FULLAGE	PUMPING
TRIPLE	**TRYSTE**	**TYMPAN**	SULLAGE	RUMPING
TRIPLED	TRYSTED	TYMPANA	ULLAGED	TUMPING
TRIPLES	TRYSTER	TYMPANI	ULLAGES	YUMPING
TRIPLET	TRYSTES	TYMPANO	**ULLING**	**UMPIRE**
TRIPLEX	**TUBBED**	TYMPANS	BULLING	UMPIRED
TRIPOD	STUBBED	TYMPANY	CULLING	UMPIRES
TRIPODS	**TUMBLE**	**TYRING**	DULLING	**UNABLE**
TRIPODY	STUMBLE	STYRING	FULLING	TUNABLE
TRISUL	TUMBLED	**TZADDI**	GULLING	**UNAKIN**
TRISULA	TUMBLER	TZADDIK	HULLING	UNAKING
TRISULS	TUMBLES	TZADDIQ	LULLING	**UNBALE**
TRITES	**TUMPED**	TZADDIS	MULLING	UNBALED
TRITEST	STUMPED	**UAKARI**	NULLING	UNBALES

UNBARE	**UNFREE**	SUNLIKE	**UNSHED**	**UPDIVE**
UNBARED	UNFREED	UNLIKED	DUNSHED	UPDIVED
UNBARES	UNFREES	UNLIKES	**UNSHIP**	UPDIVES
UNBEDS	**UNGIRT**	**UNLIME**	GUNSHIP	**UPDRAW**
SUNBEDS	UNGIRTH	UNLIMED	NUNSHIP	UPDRAWN
UNBELT	**UNGLUE**	UNLIMES	UNSHIPS	UPDRAWS
SUNBELT	UNGLUED	**UNLINE**	**UNSHOE**	**UPGAZE**
UNBELTS	UNGLUES	UNLINED	UNSHOED	UPGAZED
UNBONE	**UNGULA**	UNLINES	UNSHOES	UPGAZES
UNBONED	UNGULAE	**UNLIVE**	**UNSHOT**	**UPGROW**
UNBONES	UNGULAR	UNLIVED	GUNSHOT	UPGROWN
UNBORN	**UNGYVE**	UNLIVES	**UNSUIT**	UPGROWS
UNBORNE	UNGYVED	**UNLOCK**	SUNSUIT	**UPHROE**
UNCAGE	UNGYVES	GUNLOCK	UNSUITS	EUPHROE
UNCAGED	**UNHAND**	UNLOCKS	**UNSURE**	UPHROES
UNCAGES	UNHANDS	**UNLOVE**	UNSURED	**UPLEAN**
UNCAKE	UNHANDY	UNLOVED	UNSURER	UPLEANS
UNCAKED	**UNHASP**	UNLOVES	**UNTAME**	UPLEANT
UNCAKES	SUNHATS	**UNMAKE**	UNTAMED	**UPLEAP**
UNCAPE	**UNHELE**	UNMAKER	UNTAMES	UPLEAPS
UNCAPED	UNHELED	UNMAKES	**UNTENT**	UPLEAPT
UNCAPES	UNHELES	**UNNEST**	UNTENTS	**UPMAKE**
UNCASE	**UNHIVE**	DUNNEST	UNTENTY	UPMAKER
UNCASED	UNHIVED	FUNNEST	**UNTIES**	UPMAKES
UNCASES	UNHIVES	UNNESTS	AUNTIES	**UPPERS**
UNCATE	**UNHOOD**	**UNPILE**	PUNTIES	CUPPERS
JUNCATE	NUNHOOD	UNPILED	**UNTILE**	SUPPERS
UNCLES	UNHOODS	UNPILES	UNTILED	**UPPILE**
NUNCLES	**UNIONS**	**UNPOPE**	UNTILES	UPPILED
UNCLIP	BUNIONS	UNPOPED	**UNTINS**	UPPILES
UNCLIPS	**UNIQUE**	UNPOPES	MUNTINS	**UPPING**
UNCLIPT	UNIQUER	**UNRAKE**	**UNTRUE**	CUPPING
UNCOES	UNIQUES	UNRAKED	UNTRUER	DUPPING
JUNCOES	**UNITED**	UNRAKES	**UNTUNE**	HUPPING
UNCOEST	MUNITED	**UNREAD**	UNTUNED	PUPPING
UNCOPE	**UNITES**	UNREADY	UNTUNES	SUPPING
UNCOPED	DUNITES	**UNRIGS**	**UNVAIL**	TUPPING
UNCOPES	GUNITES	RUNRIGS	UNVAILE	UPPINGS
UNDATE	MUNITES	**UNRIPE**	UNVAILS	**UPRATE**
UNDATED	**UNKING**	UNRIPER	**UNWIRE**	UPRATED
UNDECK	BUNKING	**UNROBE**	UNWIRED	UPRATES
SUNDECK	DUNKING	UNROBED	UNWIRES	**UPRISE**
UNDECKS	FUNKING	UNROBES	**UNWISE**	UPRISEN
UNDIES	JUNKING	**UNROOF**	SUNWISE	UPRISER
BUNDIES	UNKINGS	SUNROOF	UNWISER	UPRISES
CUNDIES	**UNLACE**	UNROOFS	**UNWIVE**	**UPSIZE**
FUNDIES	UNLACED	**UNROPE**	UNWIVED	UPSIZED
GUNDIES	UNLACES	UNROPED	UNWIVES	UPSIZES
UNDINE	**UNLADE**	UNROPES	**UNWOVE**	**UPTAKE**
NUNDINE	UNLADED	**UNROVE**	UNWOVEN	UPTAKEN
UNDINES	UNLADEN	UNROVEN	**UNYOKE**	UPTAKES
UNDRAW	UNLADES	**UNRULE**	UNYOKED	**URALIS**
UNDRAWN	**UNLAST**	UNRULED	UNYOKES	OURALIS
UNDRAWS	UNLASTE	UNRULES	**UPBLOW**	**URANIA**
UNEDGE	**UNLESS**	**UNSAFE**	UPBLOWN	URANIAN
UNEDGED	GUNLESS	UNSAFER	UPBLOWS	URANIAS
UNEDGES	RUNLESS	**UNSEAM**	**UPDATE**	**URANIC**
UNFAIR	SUNLESS	UNSEAMS	UPDATED	PURANIC
FUNFAIR	**UNLIKE**	**UNSETS**	UPDATER	**URARES**
UNFAIRS	NUNLIKE	SUNSETS	UPDATES	CURARES

URARIS	**UTTERS**	**VENTER**	VISAGED	SWADDLE
CURARIS	BUTTERS	EVENTER	VISAGES	TWADDLE
OURARIS	CUTTERS	VENTERS	**VISING**	WADDLED
URATES	GUTTERS	**VENTRE**	AVISING	WADDLER
AURATES	MUTTERS	AVENTRE	**VISITE**	WADDLES
CURATES	NUTTERS	VENTRED	VISITED	**WADDLY**
URBANE	PUTTERS	VENTRES	VISITEE	TWADDLY
URBANER	RUTTERS	**VENUES**	VISITER	**WADMOL**
UREDIA	**VACATE**	AVENUES	VISITES	WADMOLL
UREDIAL	VACATED	**VERBID**	**VITTLE**	WADMOLS
URENAS	VACATES	OVERBID	VITTLED	**WADSET**
MURENAS	**VADING**	VERBIDS	VITTLES	WADSETS
URGENT	EVADING	**VERDIT**	**VIZZIE**	WADSETT
SURGENT	**VAGINA**	VERDITE	VIZZIED	**WAFFLE**
TURGENT	VAGINAE	VERDITS	VIZZIES	WAFFLED
URGERS	VAGINAL	**VERISM**	**VOIDED**	WAFFLER
BURGERS	VAGINAS	VERISMO	AVOIDED	WAFFLES
PURGERS	**VAGUES**	VERISMS	**VOIDER**	**WAGERS**
SURGERS	VAGUEST	**VERMIL**	AVOIDER	SWAGERS
URGING	**VAILED**	VERMILS	VOIDERS	**WAGGED**
GURGING	AVAILED	VERMILY	**VOLANT**	SWAGGED
PURGING	**VALETE**	**VERMIN**	VOLANTE	**WAGGER**
SURGING	VALETED	VERMINS	**VOLUME**	SWAGGER
URGINGS	VALETES	VERMINY	VOLUMED	WAGGERS
URIALS	**VALLAR**	**VERSET**	VOLUMES	WAGGERY
BURIALS	VALLARY	OVERSET	**VOLUTE**	**WAGGLE**
URINES	**VALLUM**	VERSETS	EVOLUTE	WAGGLED
MURINES	VALLUMS	**VERSIN**	VOLUTED	WAGGLER
PURINES	**VAMOSE**	VERSINE	VOLUTES	WAGGLES
URITES	VAMOSED	VERSING	**VOLVED**	**WAGING**
CURITES	VAMOSES	VERSINS	EVOLVED	SWAGING
URNING	**VANISH**	**VERTED**	**VOLVES**	**WAITED**
BURNING	EVANISH	AVERTED	EVOLVES	AWAITED
DURNING	**VAPOUR**	EVERTED	**VOMICA**	**WAITER**
GURNING	VAPOURS	**VESICA**	VOMICAE	AWAITER
TURNING	VAPOURY	VESICAE	VOMICAS	WAITERS
URNINGS	**VARIES**	VESICAL	**VOUDON**	**WAITES**
URPING	OVARIES	**VETCHY**	VOUDONS	TWAITES
BURPING	**VAUNCE**	KVETCHY	**VOUDOU**	**WAKENS**
USEFUL	VAUNCED	**VIATIC**	VOUDOUN	AWAKENS
MUSEFUL	VAUNCES	AVIATIC	VOUDOUS	**WAKING**
USEFULS	**VAUNTS**	VIATICA	**VOWERS**	AWAKING
USHERS	AVAUNTS	**VIATOR**	AVOWERS	WAKINGS
BUSHERS	**VELATE**	AVIATOR	**VOWING**	**WALIER**
GUSHERS	VELATED	VIATORS	AVOWING	SWALIER
HUSHERS	**VELURE**	**VIBRIO**	**VOYAGE**	**WALIES**
LUSHERS	VELURED	VIBRION	VOYAGED	WALIEST
MUSHERS	VELURES	VIBRIOS	VOYAGER	**WALING**
PUSHERS	**VELVET**	**VICTOR**	VOYAGES	SWALING
RUSHERS	VELVETS	EVICTOR	**WABBLE**	**WALLAH**
UTASES	VELVETY	VICTORS	WABBLED	WALLAHS
MUTASES	**VENGED**	VICTORY	WABBLER	**WALLET**
UTISES	AVENGED	**VILEST**	WABBLES	SWALLET
CUTISES	**VENGER**	EVILEST	**WACKES**	WALLETS
UTMOST	AVENGER	**VILLAN**	WACKEST	**WALLIE**
OUTMOST	VENGERS	VILLANS	**WADDIE**	WALLIER
UTMOSTS	**VENGES**	VILLANY	SWADDIE	WALLIES
UTOPIA	AVENGES	**VIMINA**	WADDIED	**WALLOW**
UTOPIAN	**VENTED**	VIMINAL	WADDIES	SWALLOW
UTOPIAS	EVENTED	**VISAGE**	**WADDLE**	WALLOWS

WAMBLE	WASTERS	WEIGHTY	TWIGHTS	WINKLES
WAMBLED	WASTERY	**WEIRED**	**WIGLET**	**WINNED**
WAMBLES	**WATTER**	SWEIRED	TWIGLET	TWINNED
WANGLE	SWATTER	**WELKIN**	WIGLETS	**WINTER**
TWANGLE	**WATTLE**	WELKING	**WILLED**	TWINTER
WANGLED	TWATTLE	WELKINS	SWILLED	WINTERS
WANGLER	WATTLED	**WELLED**	TWILLED	WINTERY
WANGLES	WATTLES	DWELLED	**WILLER**	**WINTLE**
WANKED	**WAVIES**	SWELLED	SWILLER	WINTLED
SWANKED	WAVIEST	**WELTED**	WILLERS	WINTLES
WANKER	**WAYING**	SWELTED	**WILLIE**	**WIPERS**
SWANKER	SWAYING	**WELTER**	WILLIED	SWIPERS
WANKERS	**WEAKER**	SWELTER	WILLIES	**WIPING**
WANNED	TWEAKER	WELTERS	**WILLOW**	SWIPING
SWANNED	**WEALTH**	**WESTER**	WILLOWS	WIPINGS
WAPPED	WEALTHS	WESTERN	WILLOWY	**WIRING**
SWAPPED	WEALTHY	WESTERS	**WILTED**	TWIRING
WAPPER	**WEARER**	**WHALER**	TWILTED	WIRINGS
SWAPPER	SWEARER	WHALERS	**WIMBLE**	**WISHED**
WAPPERS	WEARERS	WHALERY	WIMBLED	SWISHED
WARBLE	**WEASEL**	**WHANAU**	WIMBLES	**WISHER**
WARBLED	WEASELS	WHANAUS	**WIMPLE**	SWISHER
WARBLER	WEASELY	**WHEELS**	WIMPLED	WISHERS
WARBLES	**WEBBIE**	AWHEELS	WIMPLES	**WISHES**
WARDED	WEBBIER	**WHEESH**	**WINDLE**	SWISHES
AWARDED	WEBBIES	WHEESHT	DWINDLE	**WISSES**
SWARDED	**WEDGIE**	**WHEEZE**	SWINDLE	SWISSES
WARDER	WEDGIER	WHEEZED	WINDLED	**WISTED**
AWARDER	WEDGIES	WHEEZER	WINDLES	TWISTED
WARDERS	**WEEDER**	WHEEZES	**WINDOW**	**WITCHY**
WARMED	WEEDERS	**WHERES**	WINDOWS	SWITCHY
SWARMED	WEEDERY	WHERESO	WINDOWY	TWITCHY
WARMER	**WEEING**	**WHINGE**	**WINERY**	**WITHER**
SWARMER	SWEEING	WHINGED	SWINERY	SWITHER
WARMERS	**WEENIE**	WHINGER	**WINGED**	WITHERS
WARNED	TWEENIE	WHINGES	SWINGED	**WITHIN**
AWARNED	WEENIER	**WHITEN**	TWINGED	WITHING
WARRAN	WEENIES	WHITENS	**WINGER**	WITHINS
WARRAND	**WEEPER**	**WHITES**	SWINGER	**WITTED**
WARRANS	SWEEPER	WHITEST	WINGERS	TWITTED
WARRANT	WEEPERS	**WIBBLE**	**WINGES**	**WITTER**
WARSLE	**WEEPIE**	WIBBLED	SWINGES	TWITTER
WARSLED	WEEPIER	WIBBLES	TWINGES	WITTERS
WARSLER	WEEPIES	**WIDDLE**	**WINIER**	**WIVERN**
WARSLES	**WEETED**	TWIDDLE	TWINIER	WIVERNS
WASHED	SWEETED	WIDDLED	**WINING**	**WIVING**
SWASHED	TWEETED	WIDDLES	DWINING	SWIVING
WASHER	**WEETEN**	**WIGGED**	TWINING	**WIZZES**
SWASHER	SWEETEN	SWIGGED	**WINISH**	SWIZZES
WASHERS	**WEETER**	TWIGGED	SWINISH	**WOBBLE**
WASHERY	SWEETER	**WIGGER**	**WINKED**	WOBBLED
WASHES	TWEETER	SWIGGER	SWINKED	WOBBLER
SWASHES	**WEEVIL**	TWIGGER	TWINKED	WOBBLES
WASHIN	WEEVILS	WIGGERS	**WINKER**	**WOODIE**
WASHING	WEEVILY	WIGGERY	SWINKER	WOODIER
WASHINS	**WEEWEE**	**WIGGLE**	WINKERS	WOODIES
WASPIE	WEEWEED	WIGGLED	**WINKLE**	**WOOLIE**
WASPIER	WEEWEES	WIGGLER	TWINKLE	WOOLIER
WASPIES	**WEIGHT**	WIGGLES	WINKLED	WOOLIES
WASTER	WEIGHTS	**WIGHTS**	WINKLER	**WOONED**

SWOONED	**WRAXLE**	**WUZZLE**	DYESTER	**ZONATE**
WOOSEL	WRAXLED	WUZZLED	YESTERN	OZONATE
WOOSELL	WRAXLES	WUZZLES	**YMPING**	ZONATED
WOOSELS	**WREATH**	**YABBIE**	GYMPING	**ZONULA**
WOPPED	WREATHE	YABBIED	**ZADDIK**	ZONULAE
SWOPPED	WREATHS	YABBIES	TZADDIK	ZONULAR
WORDED	WREATHY	**YAFFED**	ZADDIKS	ZONULAS
SWORDED	**WRETHE**	NYAFFED	**ZANIES**	**ZONULE**
WORMER	WRETHED	**YAPPIE**	ZANIEST	ZONULES
WORMERS	WRETHES	YAPPIER	**ZITHER**	ZONULET
WORMERY	**WRIEST**	YAPPIES	ZITHERN	**ZYMITE**
WOTTED	OWRIEST	**YELLOW**	ZITHERS	AZYMITE
SWOTTED	**WRITHE**	YELLOWS	**ZIZZLE**	ZYMITES
WOULDS	WRITHED	YELLOWY	ZIZZLED	
WOULDST	WRITHEN	**YESSES**	ZIZZLES	
WOUNDS	WRITHER	OYESSES	**ZOARIA**	
SWOUNDS	WRITHES	**YESTER**	ZOARIAL	

Seven-letter root words

ABIETIC	**ACCRETE**	ACROMIAL	RADULATE	AGENISES
RABIETIC	ACCRETED	**ACTINIA**	ADULATED	**AGENIZE**
ABILITY	ACCRETES	ACTINIAE	ADULATES	AGENIZED
LABILITY	**ACCURSE**	ACTINIAN	**ADVANCE**	AGENIZES
ABLINGS	ACCURSED	ACTINIAS	ADVANCED	**AGGADAH**
CABLINGS	ACCURSES	**ACTIONS**	ADVANCER	HAGGADAH
FABLINGS	**ACERATE**	FACTIONS	ADVANCES	AGGADAHS
TABLINGS	LACERATE	PACTIONS	**ADVERSE**	**AGGADAS**
ABOMASA	MACERATE	TACTIONS	ADVERSER	HAGGADAS
ABOMASAL	ACERATED	**ACTRESS**	ADVISOR	**AGGADIC**
ABRIDGE	**ACETATE**	ACTRESSY	ADVISORS	HAGGADIC
ABRIDGED	ACETATED	**ACTUATE**	ADVISORY	**AGGADOT**
ABRIDGER	ACETATES	ACTUATED	**ADWARES**	HAGGADOT
ABRIDGES	**ACHENIA**	ACTUATES	BADWARES	AGGADOTH
ABROOKE	ACHENIAL	**ACTURES**	**ADWOMAN**	**AGGRACE**
ABROOKED	**ACHIEVE**	FACTURES	MADWOMAN	AGGRACED
ABROOKES	ACHIEVED	**ACYLATE**	**ADWOMEN**	AGGRACES
ABSCISE	ACHIEVER	ACYLATED	MADWOMEN	**AGGRADE**
ABSCISED	ACHIEVES	ACYLATES	**AECIDIA**	AGGRADED
ABSCISES	**ACICULA**	**ADDINGS**	AECIDIAL	AGGRADES
ABSCISS	ACICULAE	PADDINGS	**AFFEARE**	**AGGRATE**
ABSCISSA	ACICULAR	WADDINGS	AFFEARED	AGGRATED
ABSCISSE	ACICULAS	**ADDLING**	AFFEARES	AGGRATES
ABSINTH	**ACKNOWN**	DADDLING	**AFFORCE**	**AGILITY**
ABSINTHE	ACKNOWNE	FADDLING	AFFORCED	VAGILITY
ABSINTHS	**ACNODES**	PADDLING	AFFORCES	**AGISTER**
ABSOLVE	TACNODES	RADDLING	**AFFRONT**	MAGISTER
ABSOLVED	**ACONITE**	SADDLING	AFFRONTE	AGISTERS
ABSOLVER	TACONITE	WADDLING	AFFRONTS	**AGITATE**
ABSOLVES	ACONITES	**ADJUDGE**	**AGACANT**	AGITATED
ACALEPH	**ACQUEST**	ADJUDGED	AGACANTE	AGITATES
ACALEPHE	ACQUESTS	ADJUDGES	**AGATISE**	**AGITATO**
ACALEPHS	**ACQUIRE**	**ADLANDS**	AGATISED	AGITATOR
ACANTHA	ACQUIRED	BADLANDS	AGATISES	**AGLYCON**
ACANTHAE	ACQUIREE	**ADONISE**	**AGATIZE**	AGLYCONE
ACANTHAS	ACQUIRER	ADONISED	AGATIZED	AGLYCONS
ACANTHI	ACQUIRES	ADONISES	AGATIZES	**AGNATES**
ACANTHIN	**ACRIDIN**	**ADONIZE**	**AGELESS**	MAGNATES
ACCINGE	ACRIDINE	ADONIZED	WAGELESS	**AGONISE**
ACCINGED	ACRIDINS	ADONIZES	**AGENISE**	AGONISED
ACCINGES	**ACROMIA**	**ADULATE**	AGENISED	AGONISES

AGONIZE	ALIPEDS	AMARANTS	**ANETHOL**	**ANTHERS**
AGONIZED	TALIPEDS	**AMASSES**	ANETHOLE	PANTHERS
AGONIZES	**ALISONS**	CAMASSES	ANETHOLS	**ANTHILL**
AIDLESS	MALISONS	**AMBERED**	**ANGELIC**	WANTHILL
MAIDLESS	**ALIZARI**	CAMBERED	ANGELICA	ANTHILLS
AILERON	ALIZARIN	**AMBLERS**	**ANGERED**	**ANTICKE**
TAILERON	ALIZARIS	GAMBLERS	DANGERED	ANTICKED
AILERONS	**ALKALIN**	RAMBLERS	LANGERED	**ANTIGEN**
AILMENT	ALKALINE	**AMBLING**	**ANGLERS**	ANTIGENE
BAILMENT	**ALKALIS**	GAMBLING	DANGLERS	ANTIGENS
AILMENTS	ALKALISE	HAMBLING	JANGLERS	**ANTILOG**
AINSELL	**ALLEDGE**	LAMBLING	MANGLERS	ANTILOGS
NAINSELL	ALLEDGED	RAMBLING	TANGLERS	ANTILOGY
AINSELLS	ALLEDGES	WAMBLING	WANGLERS	**ANTINGS**
AIRIEST	**ALLEGGE**	AMBLINGS	**ANGLING**	BANTINGS
HAIRIEST	ALLEGGED	**AMBONES**	CANGLING	CANTINGS
LAIRIEST	ALLEGGES	HAMBONES	DANGLING	PANTINGS
VAIRIEST	**ALLEYED**	JAMBONES	FANGLING	RANTINGS
AIRINGS	VALLEYED	**AMELIAS**	GANGLING	**ANTIQUE**
FAIRINGS	WALLEYED	CAMELIAS	JANGLING	ANTIQUED
PAIRINGS	**ALLISES**	**AMENAGE**	MANGLING	ANTIQUER
AIRLESS	GALLISES	AMENAGED	TANGLING	ANTIQUES
HAIRLESS	TALLISES	AMENAGES	WANGLING	ANTIQUEY
AIRLIKE	**ALLIUMS**	**AMENTUM**	ANGLINGS	**ANTLERS**
HAIRLIKE	BALLIUMS	RAMENTUM	**ANGRIES**	PANTLERS
AIRLINE	GALLIUMS	**AMMONIA**	ANGRIEST	**ANTONYM**
HAIRLINE	PALLIUMS	AMMONIAC	**ANGUINE**	ANTONYMS
AIRLINER	**ALLNESS**	AMMONIAS	SANGUINE	ANTONYMY
AIRLINES	TALLNESS	**AMNESIA**	**ANGUISH**	**ANTRUMS**
AIRLOCK	**ALLODIA**	AMNESIAC	LANGUISH	TANTRUMS
HAIRLOCK	ALLODIAL	AMNESIAS	**ANIMATE**	**APANAGE**
AIRLOCKS	**ALLOWED**	**AMPHORA**	ANIMATED	APANAGED
AIRWAYS	FALLOWED	AMPHORAE	ANIMATER	APANAGES
FAIRWAYS	GALLOWED	AMPHORAL	ANIMATES	**APELIKE**
AIRWISE	HALLOWED	AMPHORAS	**ANIMATO**	TAPELIKE
PAIRWISE	SALLOWED	**AMPULLA**	ANIMATOR	**APERIES**
ALATION	TALLOWED	AMPULLAE	**ANKLING**	JAPERIES
HALATION	WALLOWED	AMPULLAR	FANKLING	NAPERIES
ALATIONS	**ALLUVIA**	**AMYGDAL**	RANKLING	**APHASIA**
ALBERTS	ALLUVIAL	AMYGDALA	**ANNATES**	APHASIAC
HALBERTS	**ALLYING**	AMYGDALE	TANNATES	APHASIAS
ALCADES	DALLYING	AMYGDALS	**ANNOYED**	**APHELIA**
FALCADES	GALLYING	**ANALITY**	TANNOYED	APHELIAN
ALEURON	PALLYING	BANALITY	**ANNULAR**	**APHIDES**
ALEURONE	RALLYING	**ANALYSE**	CANNULAR	RAPHIDES
ALEURONS	SALLYING	ANALYSED	ANNULARS	**APLITES**
ALEWIFE	TALLYING	ANALYSER	**ANODISE**	HAPLITES
KALEWIFE	**ALMANAC**	ANALYSES	ANODISED	**APLITIC**
ALFAQUI	ALMANACK	**ANALYZE**	ANODISES	HAPLITIC
ALFAQUIN	ALMANACS	ANALYZED	**ANODIZE**	**APOCARP**
ALFAQUIS	**ALTERED**	ANALYZER	ANODIZED	APOCARPS
ALIFORM	FALTERED	ANALYZES	ANODIZES	APOCARPY
PALIFORM	HALTERED	**ANAPHOR**	**ANTARAS**	**APOPLEX**
ALIGNED	PALTERED	ANAPHORA	TANTARAS	APOPLEXY
MALIGNED	**ALTERER**	ANAPHORS	**ANTEFIX**	**APPEASE**
ALIGNER	FALTERER	**ANCILLA**	ANTEFIXA	APPEASED
MALIGNER	PALTERER	ANCILLAE	**ANTENNA**	APPEASER
ALIGNERS	ALTERERS	ANCILLAS	ANTENNAE	APPEASES
ALIMONY	**AMARANT**	**ANELING**	ANTENNAL	**APPERIL**
PALIMONY	AMARANTH	PANELING	ANTENNAS	APPERILL

APPERILS	**AREFIES**	HARROWED	WASSAILS	AUDIBLED
APPORTS	RAREFIES	MARROWED	**ASSIEGE**	AUDIBLES
RAPPORTS	**ARGENTS**	NARROWED	ASSIEGED	**AUDITOR**
APPRISE	MARGENTS	TARROWED	ASSIEGES	AUDITORS
APPRISED	**ARGLING**	**ARTICLE**	**ASSISTS**	AUDITORY
APPRISER	GARGLING	PARTICLE	BASSISTS	**AUGUSTE**
APPRISES	**ARGUSES**	ARTICLED	**ASSUAGE**	AUGUSTER
APPRIZE	SARGUSES	ARTICLES	ASSUAGED	AUGUSTES
APPRIZED	**ARISHES**	**ARTIEST**	ASSUAGER	**AULDEST**
APPRIZER	GARISHES	TARTIEST	ASSUAGES	CAULDEST
APPRIZES	MARISHES	WARTIEST	**ASSWAGE**	**AULNAGE**
APPROVE	PARISHES	**ARTISAN**	ASSWAGED	AULNAGER
APPROVED	**ARISTAS**	BARTISAN	ASSWAGES	AULNAGES
APPROVER	BARISTAS	PARTISAN	**ASTABLE**	**AUNTERS**
APPROVES	**ARMIGER**	ARTISANS	CASTABLE	DAUNTERS
APSIDAL	ARMIGERO	**ARTLESS**	TASTABLE	HAUNTERS
CAPSIDAL	ARMIGERS	WARTLESS	WASTABLE	SAUNTERS
APTNESS	**ARMILLA**	**ARTSIES**	**ASTEISM**	TAUNTERS
RAPTNESS	ARMILLAE	ARTSIEST	CASTEISM	VAUNTERS
AQUARIA	**ARMILLAS**	**ARTWORK**	ASTEISMS	**AUNTIES**
AQUARIAL	**ARMINGS**	PARTWORK	**ATABRIN**	JAUNTIES
AQUARIAN	FARMINGS	ARTWORKS	ATABRINE	**AUREATE**
ARABINS	WARMINGS	**ARUSPEX**	ATABRINS	LAUREATE
CARABINS	**ARMLESS**	HARUSPEX	**ATAGHAN**	**AURELIA**
ARABISE	HARMLESS	**ASCIDIA**	YATAGHAN	AURELIAN
ARABISED	**AROUSAL**	ASCIDIAN	ATAGHANS	AURELIAS
ARABISES	CAROUSAL	**ASCRIBE**	**ATHEISE**	**AUREOLA**
ARABIZE	AROUSALS	ASCRIBED	ATHEISED	AUREOLAE
ARABIZED	**AROUSED**	ASCRIBES	ATHEISES	AUREOLAS
ARABIZES	CAROUSED	**ASHIEST**	**ATHEIZE**	**AUREOLE**
ARABLES	**AROUSER**	DASHIEST	ATHEIZED	AUREOLED
PARABLES	CAROUSER	HASHIEST	ATHEIZES	AUREOLES
ARBORED	AROUSERS	MASHIEST	**ATOMISE**	**AURICLE**
HARBORED	**AROUSES**	WASHIEST	ATOMISED	AURICLED
ARBORET	CAROUSES	**ASHLESS**	ATOMISER	AURICLES
ARBORETA	**ARPENTS**	BASHLESS	ATOMISES	**AUSTERE**
ARBORETS	PARPENTS	CASHLESS	**ATOMIZE**	AUSTERER
ARBOURS	**ARRACKS**	SASHLESS	ATOMIZED	**AUTARCH**
HARBOURS	BARRACKS	**ASKANCE**	ATOMIZER	AUTARCHS
ARCADIA	CARRACKS	ASKANCED	ATOMIZES	AUTARCHY
ARCADIAN	**ARRAIGN**	ASKANCES	**ATONING**	**AUTEURS**
ARCADIAS	DARRAIGN	**ASKINGS**	BATONING	HAUTEURS
ARCHAEA	ARRAIGNS	GASKINGS	**ATRIUMS**	**AUTOCAR**
ARCHAEAL	**ARRANGE**	MASKINGS	NATRIUMS	AUTOCARP
ARCHAEAN	ARRANGED	TASKINGS	**ATROPIN**	AUTOCARS
ARCHERS	ARRANGER	**ASPERGE**	ATROPINE	**AUTOMAT**
MARCHERS	ARRANGES	ASPERGED	ATROPINS	AUTOMATA
ARCHING	**ARRASES**	ASPERGER	**ATTACHE**	AUTOMATE
MARCHING	NARRASES	ASPERGES	ATTACHED	AUTOMATS
PARCHING	TARRASES	**ASPERSE**	ATTACHER	**AUTONYM**
ARCHINGS	**ARRAYED**	ASPERSED	ATTACHES	TAUTONYM
ARCHIVE	WARRAYED	ASPERSER	**ATTRAPS**	AUTONYMS
ARCHIVED	**ARREEDE**	ASPERSES	RATTRAPS	**AVELLAN**
ARCHIVES	ARREEDES	**ASPIRIN**	**ATTRITE**	AVELLANE
ARCINGS	**ARRIAGE**	ASPIRING	ATTRITED	**AVENTRE**
FARCINGS	CARRIAGE	ASPIRINS	ATTRITES	AVENTRED
ARCUATE	MARRIAGE	**ASPISES**	**ATTUITE**	AVENTRES
ARCUATED	ARRIAGES	JASPISES	ATTUITED	**AVERAGE**
AREFIED	**ARROWED**	**ASSAILS**	ATTUITES	AVERAGED
RAREFIED	FARROWED	VASSAILS	**AUDIBLE**	AVERAGES

AWFULLY	BALISTAS	**BATABLE**	BELIEVES	ABETTING
LAWFULLY	**BALLADE**	ABATABLE	**BELOVED**	BETTINGS
AWNIEST	BALLADED	**BATTEAU**	BELOVEDS	**BETTORS**
FAWNIEST	BALLADES	BATTEAUX	**BENEFIC**	ABETTORS
LAWNIEST	**BANDAGE**	**BATTIES**	BENEFICE	**BEWHORE**
TAWNIEST	BANDAGED	BATTIEST	**BEPROSE**	BEWHORED
YAWNIEST	BANDAGER	**BAUCHLE**	BEPROSED	BEWHORES
AWNINGS	BANDAGES	BAUCHLED	BEPROSES	**BICYCLE**
DAWNINGS	**BANDEAU**	BAUCHLES	**BERCEAU**	BICYCLED
FAWNINGS	BANDEAUS	**BAUDRIC**	BERCEAUX	BICYCLER
YAWNINGS	BANDEAUX	BAUDRICK	**BEREAVE**	BICYCLES
AXILLAE	**BANDIES**	BAUDRICS	BEREAVED	**BIDINGS**
MAXILLAE	BANDIEST	**BAWDIES**	BEREAVEN	ABIDINGS
AXILLAR	**BANDING**	BAWDIEST	BEREAVER	**BIENNIA**
MAXILLAR	ABANDING	**BEARDIE**	BEREAVES	BIENNIAL
AXILLARS	BANDINGS	BEARDIER	**BERHYME**	**BIOPHOR**
AXILLARY	**BANDORE**	BEARDIES	BERHYMED	BIOPHORE
AXILLAS	BANDORES	**BEARING**	BERHYMES	BIOPHORS
MAXILLAS	**BAPTISE**	ABEARING	**BESHAME**	**BIRKIES**
AYWORDS	BAPTISED	BEARINGS	BESHAMED	BIRKIEST
NAYWORDS	BAPTISER	**BECRIME**	BESHAMES	**BISCUIT**
AZOTISE	BAPTISES	BECRIMED	**BESIEGE**	BISCUITS
AZOTISED	**BAPTIZE**	BECRIMES	BESIEGED	BISCUITY
AZOTISES	BAPTIZED	**BECURSE**	BESIEGER	**BITTIES**
AZOTIZE	BAPTIZER	BECURSED	BESIEGES	BITTIEST
AZOTIZED	BAPTIZES	BECURSES	**BESLAVE**	**BIVALVE**
AZOTIZES	**BARBATE**	**BEDRAPE**	BESLAVED	BIVALVED
AZURITE	BARBATED	BEDRAPED	BESLAVER	BIVALVES
LAZURITE	**BARCHAN**	BEDRAPES	BESLAVES	**BLADDER**
AZURITES	BARCHANE	**BEDUNCE**	**BESLIME**	BLADDERS
BACCARA	BARCHANS	BEDUNCED	BESLIMED	BLADDERY
BACCARAS	**BARCODE**	BEDUNCES	BESLIMES	**BLANKET**
BACCARAT	BARCODED	**BEELINE**	**BESMILE**	BLANKETS
BACCATE	BARCODES	BEELINED	BESMILED	BLANKETY
BACCATED	**BARDIES**	BEELINES	BESMILES	**BLASTIE**
BACKBIT	BARDIEST	**BEGGING**	**BESMOKE**	BLASTIER
BACKBITE	**BARGEES**	ABEGGING	BESMOKED	BLASTIES
BACKHOE	BARGEESE	BEGGINGS	BESMOKES	**BLATTER**
BACKHOED	**BARRAGE**	**BEGINNE**	**BESPICE**	BLATTERS
BACKHOES	BARRAGED	BEGINNER	BESPICED	**BLISTER**
BAGGIES	BARRAGES	BEGINNES	BESPICES	BLISTERS
BAGGIEST	**BARRIES**	**BEGORRA**	**BESPOKE**	BLISTERY
BAGPIPE	BARRIEST	BEGORRAH	BESPOKEN	**BLOCKIE**
BAGPIPED	**BARYTON**	**BEGRIME**	**BESTREW**	BLOCKIER
BAGPIPER	BARYTONE	BEGRIMED	BESTREWN	BLOCKIES
BAGPIPES	BARYTONS	BEGRIMES	BESTREWS	**BLOOMER**
BALADIN	**BASEMEN**	**BEGUILE**	**BESTRID**	BLOOMERS
BALADINE	BASEMENT	BEGUILED	BESTRIDE	BLOOMERY
BALADINS	**BASHING**	BEGUILER	**BESTROW**	**BLOOSME**
BALANCE	ABASHING	BEGUILES	BESTROWN	BLOOSMED
BALANCED	BASHINGS	**BEHOOVE**	BESTROWS	BLOOSMES
BALANCER	**BASIDIA**	BEHOOVED	**BETEEME**	**BLOSSOM**
BALANCES	BASIDIAL	BEHOOVES	BETEEMED	BLOSSOMS
BALDIES	**BASILAR**	**BEKNAVE**	BETEEMES	BLOSSOMY
BALDIEST	BASILARY	BEKNAVED	**BETITLE**	**BLOWIES**
BALDRIC	**BASILIC**	BEKNAVES	BETITTLED	BLOWIEST
BALDRICK	BASILICA	BELDAMES	BETITLES	**BLUBBER**
BALDRICS	**BASTARD**	**BELIEVE**	**BETTERS**	BLUBBERS
BALISTA	BASTARDS	BELIEVED	ABETTERS	BLUBBERY
BALISTAE	BASTARDY	BELIEVER	**BETTING**	**BLUSTER**

BLUSTERS	BRAILLED	BRITTLED	BUSHIEST	**CAMELIA**
BLUSTERY	BRAILLER	BRITTLER	**BUTCHER**	CAMELIAS
BODGIES	BRAILLES	BRITTLES	BUTCHERS	**CAMMING**
BODGIEST	**BRAMBLE**	**BROADAX**	BUTCHERY	SCAMMING
BOERBUL	BRAMBLED	BROADAXE	**BUTCHES**	**CAMPERS**
BOERBULL	BRAMBLES	**BROCADE**	BUTCHEST	SCAMPERS
BOERBULS	**BRANGLE**	BROCADED	**BUTMENT**	**CAMPING**
BOHEMIA	BRANGLED	BROCADES	ABUTMENT	SCAMPING
BOHEMIAN	BRANGLES	**BRODDLE**	BUTMENTS	CAMPINGS
BOHEMIAS	**BRASHES**	BRODDLED	**BUTTALS**	**CANDENT**
BOLSHIE	BRASHEST	BRODDLES	ABUTTALS	SCANDENT
BOLSHIER	**BRASSIE**	**BROIDER**	**BUTTERS**	**CANDIDA**
BOLSHIES	BRASSIER	BROIDERS	ABUTTERS	CANDIDAL
BOMBARD	BRASSIES	BROIDERY	**BUTTING**	CANDIDAS
BOMBARDE	**BRATTLE**	**BROMATE**	ABUTTING	**CANNERS**
BOMBARDS	BRATTLED	BROMATED	**CABBAGE**	SCANNERS
BONDAGE	BRATTLES	BROMATES	CABBAGED	**CANNING**
BONDAGER	**BRAWLIE**	**BROMISE**	CABBAGES	SCANNING
BONDAGES	BRAWLIER	BROMISED	CABBAGEY	CANNINGS
BONISTS	**BRAYING**	BROMISES	**CABBALA**	**CANNULA**
EBONISTS	ABRAYING	**BROMIZE**	CABBALAH	CANNULAE
BONNIES	**BRAZIER**	BROMIZED	CABBALAS	CANNULAR
BONNIEST	BRAZIERS	BROMIZES	**CABBING**	CANNULAS
BOOKIES	BRAZIERY	**BRONCHI**	SCABBING	**CANTEST**
BOOKIEST	**BREATHE**	BRONCHIA	**CABEZON**	SCANTEST
BOOKSIE	BREATHED	**BROOKED**	CABEZONE	**CANTHUS**
BOOKSIER	BREATHER	ABROOKED	CABEZONS	ACANTHUS
BORSTAL	BREATHES	**BROUGHT**	**CACONYM**	**CANTICO**
BORSTALL	**BRECCIA**	BROUGHTA	CACONYMS	CANTICOS
BORSTALS	BRECCIAL	**BROWNIE**	CACONYMY	CANTICOY
BOSSIES	BRECCIAS	BROWNIER	**CADENCE**	**CANTIER**
BOSSIEST	**BREENGE**	BROWNIES	CADENCED	SCANTIER
BOTANIC	BREENGED	**BRUSQUE**	CADENCES	**CANTILY**
BOTANICA	BREENGES	BRUSQUER	**CAESURA**	SCANTILY
BOTANICS	**BREINGE**	**BUDDIES**	CAESURAE	**CANTING**
BOTCHER	BREINGED	BUDDIEST	CAESURAL	SCANTING
BOTCHERS	BREINGES	**BUDGERO**	CAESURAS	CANTINGS
BOTCHERY	**BREVETE**	BUDGEROS	**CAFFEIN**	**CANTLED**
BOULDER	BREVETED	BUDGEROW	CAFFEINE	SCANTLED
BOULDERS	**BRICKIE**	**BUGGIES**	CAFFEINS	**CANTLES**
BOULDERY	BRICKIER	BUGGIEST	**CAJOLER**	SCANTLES
BOUNDED	BRICKIES	**BULIMIA**	CAJOLERS	**CANZONE**
ABOUNDED	**BRIDGED**	BULIMIAC	CAJOLERY	CANZONES
BOUNDEN	ABRIDGED	BULIMIAS	**CALAMAR**	CANZONET
YBOUNDEN	**BRIDGES**	**BULLIES**	CALAMARI	**CAPABLE**
BRABBLE	ABRIDGES	BULLIEST	CALAMARS	CAPABLER
BRABBLED	**BRIGADE**	**BULLOCK**	CALAMARY	**CAPELIN**
BRABBLER	BRIGADED	BULLOCKS	**CALCINE**	CAPELINE
BRABBLES	BRIGADES	BULLOCKY	CALCINED	CAPELINS
BRACHAH	**BRIMFUL**	**BULRUSH**	CALCINES	**CAPITAN**
BRACHAHS	BRIMFULL	BULRUSHY	**CALIBRE**	CAPITANI
BRACHIA	**BRINDLE**	**BUMBAZE**	CALIBRED	CAPITANO
ABRACHIA	BRINDLED	BUMBAZED	CALIBRES	CAPITANS
BRACHIAL	BRINDLES	BUMBAZES	**CALLOPS**	**CAPSIZE**
BRAHMAN	**BRINIES**	**BURGLAR**	SCALLOPS	CAPSIZED
BRAHMANI	BRINIEST	BURGLARS	**CALYCLE**	CAPSIZES
BRAHMANS	**BRISTLE**	BURGLARY	CALYCLED	**CAPSULE**
BRAIDED	BRISTLED	**BURNOUS**	CALYCLES	CAPSULED
ABRAIDED	BRISTLES	BURNOUSE	**CAMAIEU**	CAPSULES
BRAILLE	**BRITTLE**	**BUSHIES**	CAMAIEUX	**CAPTIVE**

CAPTIVED	SCATTERY	CHAPEAUX	CHINKIES	CISTERNA
CAPTIVES	**CATTIER**	**CHAPPED**	**CHIPPIE**	CISTERNS
CAPTURE	SCATTIER	SCHAPPED	CHIPPIER	**CITATOR**
CAPTURED	**CATTIES**	**CHAPPIE**	CHIPPIES	CITATORS
CAPTURER	CATTIEST	CHAPPIER	**CHIRRUP**	CITATORY
CAPTURES	**CATTILY**	CHAPPIES	CHIRRUPS	**CITRATE**
CAPUCHE	SCATTILY	**CHARISM**	CHIRRUPY	CITRATED
CAPUCHED	**CATTING**	CHARISMA	**CHITLIN**	CITRATES
CAPUCHES	SCATTING	CHARISMS	CHITLING	**CLASSIC**
CARABIN	**CAUDATE**	**CHARLIE**	CHITLINS	CLASSICO
CARABINE	ACAUDATE	CHARLIER	**CHLORID**	CLASSICS
CARABINS	ECAUDATE	CHARLIES	CHLORIDE	**CLASSIS**
CARACOL	CAUDATED	**CHARQUI**	CHLORIDS	CLASSISM
CARACOLE	CAUDATES	CHARQUID	**CHLORIN**	CLASSIST
CARACOLS	**CAULINE**	CHARQUIS	CHLORINE	**CLAVATE**
CARCASE	ACAULINE	**CHATEAU**	CHLORINS	CLAVATED
CARCASED	**CAYENNE**	CHATEAUS	**CHOICES**	**CLEANSE**
CARCASES	CAYENNED	CHATEAUX	CHOICEST	CLEANSED
CARDECU	CAYENNES	**CHATTER**	**CHOKIES**	CLEANSER
CARDECUE	**CENSURE**	CHATTERS	CHOKIEST	CLEANSES
CARDECUS	CENSURED	CHATTERY	**CHONDRI**	**CLEEPED**
CARINAS	CENSURER	**CHAUNCE**	CHONDRIN	YCLEEPED
OCARINAS	CENSURES	CHAUNCED	**CHORAGI**	**CLERUCH**
CARIOSE	**CENTAUR**	CHAUNCES	CHORAGIC	CLERUCHS
SCARIOSE	CENTAURS	**CHAUNGE**	**CHOREGI**	CLERUCHY
CARIOUS	CENTAURY	CHAUNGED	CHOREGIC	**CLIMATE**
SCARIOUS	**CENTRIC**	CHAUNGES	**CHORTLE**	CLIMATED
CARLESS	ACENTRIC	**CHEATER**	CHORTLED	CLIMATES
SCARLESS	**CERATED**	CHEATERS	CHORTLER	**CLOSING**
CARNIES	ACERATED	CHEATERY	CHORTLES	ECLOSING
CARNIEST	**CEREBRA**	**CHEDDAR**	**CHRISMA**	CLOSINGS
CAROUSE	CEREBRAL	CHEDDARS	CHRISMAL	**CLOSURE**
CAROUSED	**CERESIN**	CHEDDARY	**CHROMIC**	CLOSURED
CAROUSEL	CERESINE	**CHELATE**	ACHROMIC	CLOSURES
CAROUSER	CERESINS	CHELATED	**CHUCKLE**	**CLOTURE**
CAROUSES	**CERNING**	CHELATES	CHUCKLED	CLOTURED
CARPERS	SCERNING	**CHEVRON**	CHUCKLER	CLOTURES
SCARPERS	**CHAFFER**	CHEVRONS	CHUCKLES	**CLUSTER**
CARPING	CHAFFERS	CHEVRONY	**CHUPPOT**	CLUSTERS
SCARPING	CHAFFERY	**CHEWIES**	CHUPPOTH	CLUSTERY
CARPINGS	**CHALAZA**	CHEWIEST	**CHUTZPA**	**CLUTTER**
CARRIER	CHALAZAE	**CHIASMA**	CHUTZPAH	CLUTTERS
SCARRIER	CHALAZAL	CHIASMAL	CHUTZPAS	CLUTTERY
CARRIERS	CHALAZAS	CHIASMAS	**CILIATE**	**COALISE**
CARTING	**CHALICE**	CHIASMIC	CILIATED	COALISED
SCARTING	CHALICED	**CHIASMI**	CILIATES	COALISES
CARTOON	CHALICES	CHIASMIC	**CINEAST**	**COALIZE**
CARTOONS	**CHALLOT**	**CHICANE**	CINEASTE	COALIZED
CARTOONY	CHALLOTH	CHICANED	CINEASTS	COALIZES
CASCADE	**CHAMISA**	CHICANER	**CINEREA**	**COBBLER**
CASCADED	CHAMISAL	CHICANES	CINEREAL	COBBLERS
CASCADES	CHAMISAS	**CHIEFER**	CINEREAS	COBBLERY
CASEATE	**CHAMPAC**	CHIEFERY	**CINGULA**	**COCHLEA**
CASEATED	CHAMPACA	**CHIFFON**	CINGULAR	COCHLEAE
CASEATES	CHAMPACS	CHIFFONS	**CIRCUIT**	COCHLEAR
CASEMEN	**CHANCER**	CHIFFONY	CIRCUITS	COCHLEAS
CASEMENT	CHANCERS	**CHILLER**	CIRCUITY	**COCKADE**
CATCHES	CHANCERY	SCHILLER	**CISSIES**	COCKADED
SCATCHES	**CHAPEAU**	CHILLERS	CISSIEST	COCKADES
CATTERY	CHAPEAUS	**CHINKIE**	**CISTERN**	**COCKEYE**
		CHINKIER		

COCKEYED	COMITIAS	CONCERTO	CONNOTED	CORNETTS
COCKEYES	**COMMAND**	CONCERTS	CONNOTES	**CORNICE**
COCKIES	COMMANDO	**CONCISE**	**CONSOLE**	CORNICED
COCKIEST	COMMANDS	CONCISED	CONSOLED	CORNICES
CODRIVE	**COMMOVE**	CONCISER	CONSOLER	**CORNING**
CODRIVEN	COMMOVED	CONCISES	CONSOLES	SCORNING
CODRIVER	COMMOVES	**CONDOLE**	**CONSPUE**	**CORNUTE**
CODRIVES	**COMMUNE**	CONDOLED	CONSPUED	CORNUTED
COFFERS	COMMUNED	CONDOLER	CONSPUES	CORNUTES
SCOFFERS	COMMUNER	CONDOLES	**CONSULT**	**CORPORA**
COFFING	COMMUNES	**CONDONE**	CONSULTA	CORPORAL
SCOFFING	**COMMUTE**	CONDONED	CONSULTS	CORPORAS
COGGING	COMMUTED	CONDONER	**CONSUME**	**CORRADE**
SCOGGING	COMMUTER	CONDONES	CONSUMED	CORRADED
COGGINGS	COMMUTES	**CONDUCE**	CONSUMER	CORRADES
COGNISE	**COMPARE**	CONDUCED	CONSUMES	**CORRODE**
COGNISED	COMPARED	CONDUCER	**CONTRAS**	CORRODED
COGNISER	COMPARER	CONDUCES	CONTRAST	CORRODER
COGNISES	COMPARES	**CONDUCT**	**CONTRAT**	CORRODES
COGNIZE	**COMPERE**	CONDUCTI	CONTRATE	**CORYPHE**
COGNIZED	COMPERED	CONDUCTS	CONTRATS	CORYPHEE
COGNIZER	COMPERES	**CONFIDE**	**CONTROL**	CORYPHES
COGNIZES	**COMPETE**	CONFIDED	CONTROLE	**COSMISM**
COLICIN	COMPETED	CONFIDER	CONTROLS	ACOSMISM
COLICINE	COMPETES	CONFIDES	**CONTUSE**	COSMISMS
COLICINS	**COMPILE**	**CONFINE**	CONTUSED	**COSMIST**
COLLAGE	COMPILED	CONFINED	CONTUSES	ACOSMIST
COLLAGED	COMPILER	CONFINER	**CONVENE**	COSMISTS
COLLAGEN	COMPILES	CONFINES	CONVENED	**COSTATE**
COLLAGES	**COMPLIN**	**CONFUSE**	CONVENER	ECOSTATE
COLLATE	COMPLINE	CONFUSED	CONVENES	COSTATED
COLLATED	COMPLINS	CONFUSES	**CONVIVE**	**COSTUME**
COLLATES	**COMPOSE**	**CONFUTE**	CONVIVED	COSTUMED
COLLEGE	COMPOSED	CONFUTED	CONVIVES	COSTUMER
COLLIDE	COMPOSER	CONFUTER	**CONVOKE**	COSTUMES
COLLIDED	COMPOSES	CONFUTES	CONVOKED	COSTUMEY
COLLIDER	**COMPUTE**	**CONGREE**	CONVOKER	**COTHURN**
COLLIDES	COMPUTED	CONGREED	CONVOKES	COTHURNI
COLLIER	COMPUTER	CONGREES	**COOCHES**	COTHURNS
COLLIERS	COMPUTES	CONGREET	SCOOCHES	**COTTAGE**
COLLIERY	**CONACRE**	**CONGRUE**	**COOPERS**	COTTAGED
COLLOPS	CONACRED	CONGRUED	SCOOPERS	COTTAGER
SCOLLOPS	CONACRES	CONGRUES	**COOPING**	COTTAGES
COLLUDE	**CONARIA**	**CONICAL**	SCOOPING	COTTAGEY
COLLUDED	CONARIAL	ICONICAL	**COOTERS**	**COTTISE**
COLLUDER	**CONCAVE**	**CONIDIA**	SCOOTERS	COTTISED
COLLUDES	CONCAVED	CONIDIAL	**COPPICE**	COTTISES
COLOGNE	CONCAVES	CONIDIAN	COPPICED	**COTYPES**
COLOGNED	**CONCEDE**	**CONJOIN**	COPPICES	ECOTYPES
COLOGNES	CONCEDED	CONJOINS	**COPULAE**	**COUPING**
COMBIES	CONCEDER	CONJOINT	SCOPULAE	SCOUPING
COMBIEST	CONCEDES	**CONJURE**	**COPULAS**	**COURANT**
COMBINE	**CONCEIT**	CONJURED	SCOPULAS	COURANTE
COMBINED	CONCEITS	CONJURER	**CORIOUS**	COURANTO
COMBINER	CONCEITY	CONJURES	SCORIOUS	COURANTS
COMBINES	**CONCEPT**	**CONNIVE**	**CORNERS**	**COURIES**
COMBLES	CONCEPTI	CONNIVED	SCORNERS	SCOURIES
COMBLESS	CONCEPTS	CONNIVER	**CORNETT**	**COURING**
COMITIA	**CONCERT**	CONNIVES	CORNETTI	SCOURING
COMITIAL	CONCERTI	**CONNOTE**	CORNETTO	**COURSED**

SCOURSED	**CREAKED**	CROOKERY	**CULLION**	CUTTIEST
COURSES	SCREAKED	**CROPFUL**	SCULLION	**CUTTLED**
SCOURSES	**CREAMED**	CROPFULL	CULLIONS	SCUTTLED
COUTEAU	SCREAMED	CROPFULS	**CULTURE**	**CUTTLES**
COUTEAUX	**CREAMER**	**CROSSES**	CULTURED	SCUTTLES
COUTERS	SCREAMER	CROSSEST	CULTURES	**CUTWORK**
SCOUTERS	CREAMERS	CRUCIANS	**CUMBERS**	SCUTWORK
COUTHER	CREAMERY	**CRUDDLE**	SCUMBERS	CUTWORKS
SCOUTHER	**CREATIN**	CRUDDLED	**CUMMERS**	**CYANIDE**
COUTHIE	CREATINE	CRUDDLES	SCUMMERS	CYANIDED
COUTHIER	CREATING	**CRUMBLE**	**CUNEATE**	CYANIDES
COUVADE	CREATINS	CRUMBLED	CUNEATED	**CYANISE**
COUVADES	**CREEPIE**	CRUMBLES	**CUNNERS**	CYANISED
COWHIDE	CREEPIER	**CRUMMIE**	SCUNNERS	CYANISES
COWHIDED	CREEPIES	SCRUMMIE	**CUPPERS**	**CYANIZE**
COWHIDES	**CREMATE**	CRUMMIER	SCUPPERS	CYANIZED
COWLING	CREMATED	CRUMMIES	**CURARIS**	CYANIZES
SCOWLING	CREMATES	**CRUMPED**	**CURATOR**	**CYCLASE**
COWLINGS	**CRENATE**	SCRUMPED	CURATORS	CYCLISED
COWPING	CRENATED	**CRUMPLE**	CURATORY	CYCLISES
SCOWPING	**CREVICE**	SCRUMPLE	**CURETTE**	**CYCLIZE**
COWRIES	CREVICED	CRUMPLED	CURETTED	CYCLIZED
SCOWRIES	CREVICES	CRUMPLES	CURETTES	CYCLIZES
COWRITE	**CREWING**	**CRUNCHY**	**CURLIES**	**CYMBALO**
COWRITER	SCREWING	SCRUNCHY	CURLIEST	CYMBALOM
COWRITES	**CRIBBLE**	**CRUNKLE**	**CURRANT**	CYMBALOS
CRABBED	SCRIBBLE	CRUNKLED	CURRANTS	**CYPSELA**
SCRABBED	CRIBBLED	CRUNKLES	CURRANTY	CYPSELAE
CRACKLE	CRIBBLES	**CRUSADE**	**CURRIED**	**CYSTEIN**
CRACKLED	**CRIMINA**	CRUSADED	SCURRIED	CYSTEINE
CRACKLES	CRIMINAL	CRUSADER	**CURRIER**	CYSTEINS
CRAGGED	**CRIMPED**	CRUSADES	SCURRIER	**DACTYLI**
SCRAGGED	SCRIMPED	**CRYINGS**	CURRIERS	DACTYLIC
CRAMMED	**CRIMPER**	SCRYINGS	CURRIERY	**DAINING**
SCRAMMED	SCRIMPER	**CRYOGEN**	**CURRIES**	SDAINING
CRANKLE	CRIMPERS	CRYOGENS	SCURRIES	**DANDIES**
CRANKLED	**CRIMPLE**	CRYOGENY	**CURRING**	DANDIEST
CRANKLES	CRIMPLED	**CUBBIES**	SCURRING	**DARRAIN**
CRANNOG	CRIMPLES	CUBBIEST	**CURVATE**	DARRAINE
CRANNOGE	**CRINATE**	**CUDDLED**	CURVATED	DARRAINS
CRANNOGS	CRINATED	SCUDDLED	**CURVIER**	**DASTARD**
CRAPING	**CRINKLE**	**CUDDLES**	SCURVIER	DASTARDS
SCRAPING	CRINKLED	SCUDDLES	**CUSHIES**	DASTARDY
CRAPPED	CRINKLES	**CUFFING**	CUSHIEST	**DAUPHIN**
SCRAPPED	**CRIPPLE**	SCUFFING	**CUSHION**	DAUPHINE
CRAPPER	CRIPPLED	**CUFFLED**	CUSHIONS	DAUPHINS
SCRAPPER	CRIPPLER	SCUFFLED	CUSHIONY	**DAYTALE**
CRAPPERS	CRIPPLES	**CUFFLES**	**CUSPATE**	DAYTALER
CRAPPIE	**CRISPIN**	SCUFFLES	CUSPATED	DAYTALES
CRAPPIER	CRISPING	CUFFLESS	**CUSTARD**	**DEALATE**
CRAPPIES	CRISPINS	**CUITTLE**	CUSTARDS	DEALATED
CRAUNCH	**CROCEIN**	CUITTLED	CUSTARDY	DEALATES
CRAUNCHY	CROCEINE	CUITTLES	**CUTCHES**	**DEBBIES**
CRAWLED	CROCEINS	**CULCHES**	SCUTCHES	DEBBIEST
SCRAWLED	**CROMING**	SCULCHES	**CUTESIE**	**DEBOUCH**
CRAWLER	SCROMING	**CULLERS**	CUTESIER	DEBOUCHE
SCRAWLER	**CROODLE**	SCULLERS	**CUTTERS**	**DEBRIDE**
CRAWLERS	CROODLED	**CULLING**	SCUTTERS	DEBRIDED
CRAZIES	CROODLES	SCULLING	**CUTTIES**	DEBRIDES
CRAZIEST	**CROOKER**	CULLINGS		DECEASE

DECEASED	DELAPSED	DERANGER	**DIASTEM**	**DISEDGE**
DECEASES	DELAPSES	DERANGES	DIASTEMA	DISEDGED
DECEIVE	**DELEAVE**	**DESCALE**	DIASTEMS	DISEDGES
DECEIVED	DELEAVED	DESCALED	**DICKIES**	**DISHOME**
DECEIVER	DELEAVES	DESCALES	DICKIEST	DISHOMED
DECEIVES	**DELIVER**	**DESERVE**	**DICTATE**	DISHOMES
DECIDUA	DELIVERS	DESERVED	DICTATED	**DISJOIN**
DECIDUAE	DELIVERY	DESERVER	DICTATES	DISJOINS
DECIDUAL	**DELOUSE**	DESERVES	**DIDDIES**	DISJOINT
DECIDUAS	DELOUSED	**DESPISE**	DIDDIEST	**DISLIKE**
DECLARE	DELOUSER	DESPISED	**DIFFUSE**	DISLIKED
DECLARED	DELOUSES	DESPISER	DIFFUSED	DISLIKEN
DECLARER	**DEMAGOG**	DESPISES	DIFFUSER	DISLIKER
DECLARES	DEMAGOGS	**DESPITE**	DIFFUSES	DISLIKES
DECLASS	DEMAGOGY	DESPITED	**DIGGING**	**DISPACE**
DECLASSE	**DEMEANE**	DESPITES	**DIHEDRA**	DISPACED
DECLINE	DEMEANED	**DESTINE**	DIHEDRAL	DISPACES
DECLINED	DEMEANES	DESTINED	**DILATOR**	**DISPONE**
DECLINER	**DEMENTI**	DESTINES	DILATORS	DISPONED
DECLINES	DEMENTIA	**DETERGE**	DILATORY	DISPONEE
DECUPLE	DEMENTIS	DETERGED	**DILLIES**	DISPONER
DECUPLED	**DEMERGE**	DETERGER	DILLIEST	DISPONES
DECUPLES	DEMERGED	DETERGES	**DILUVIA**	**DISPOSE**
DECURVE	DEMERGER	**DETRUDE**	DILUVIAL	DISPOSED
DECURVED	DEMERGES	DETRUDED	DILUVIAN	DISPOSER
DECURVES	**DEMERSE**	DETRUDES	**DINGIES**	DISPOSES
DEEMING	DEMERSED	**DEVALUE**	DINGIEST	**DISPUTE**
ADEEMING	DEMERSES	DEVALUED	**DINKIES**	DISPUTED
DEFENCE	**DEMURES**	DEVALUES	DINKIEST	DISPUTER
DEFENCED	DEMUREST	**DEVELOP**	**DIPLOID**	DISPUTES
DEFENCES	**DENTATE**	DEVELOPE	DIPLOIDS	**DISRATE**
DEFENSE	EDENTATE	DEVELOPS	DIPLOIDY	DISRATED
DEFENSED	DENTATED	**DEVIATE**	**DIPLOMA**	DISRATES
DEFENSES	**DEPLANE**	DEVIATED	DIPLOMAS	**DISROBE**
DEFLATE	DEPLANED	DEVIATES	DIPLOMAT	DISROBED
DEFLATED	DEPLANES	**DEVOICE**	**DIPTERA**	DISROBER
DEFLATER	**DEPLETE**	DEVOICED	DIPTERAL	DISROBES
DEFLATES	DEPLETED	DEVOICES	DIPTERAN	**DISSAVE**
DEFORCE	DEPLETER	**DEVOLVE**	DIPTERAS	DISSAVED
DEFORCED	DEPLETES	DEVOLVED	**DIRTIES**	DISSAVES
DEFORCER	**DEPLORE**	DEVOLVES	DIRTIEST	**DISTUNE**
DEFORCES	DEPLORED	**DEXTRIN**	**DISABLE**	DISTUNED
DEFROZE	DEPLORER	DEXTRINE	DISABLED	DISTUNES
DEFROZEN	DEPLORES	DEXTRINS	DISABLER	**DISYOKE**
DEGLAZE	**DEPLUME**	**DHARMAS**	DISABLES	DISYOKED
DEGLAZED	DEPLUMED	ADHARMAS	**DISCAGE**	DISYOKES
DEGLAZES	DEPLUMES	**DIALYSE**	DISCAGED	**DIVERGE**
DEGRADE	**DEPRAVE**	DIALYSED	DISCAGES	DIVERGED
DEGRADED	DEPRAVED	DIALYSER	**DISCASE**	DIVERGES
DEGRADER	DEPRAVER	DIALYSES	DISCASED	**DIVERSE**
DEGRADES	DEPRAVES	**DIALYZE**	DISCASES	DIVERSED
DEHISCE	**DEPRIVE**	DIALYZED	**DISCIDE**	DIVERSES
DEHISCED	DEPRIVED	DIALYZER	DISCIDED	**DIVINES**
DEHISCES	DEPRIVER	DIALYZES	DISCIDES	DIVINEST
DEIGNED	DEPRIVES	**DIARISE**	**DISCURE**	**DIVORCE**
SDEIGNED	**DEQUEUE**	DIARISED	DISCURED	DIVORCED
DEJEUNE	DEQUEUED	DIARISES	DISCURES	DIVORCEE
DEJEUNER	DEQUEUES	**DIARIZE**	**DISEASE**	DIVORCER
DEJEUNES	**DERANGE**	DIARIZED	DISEASED	DIVORCES
DELAPSE	DERANGED	DIARIZES	DISEASES	**DIVULGE**

DIVULGED	DRAGGLES	DUUMVIRS	**EASINGS**	DECURIES
DIVULGER	**DRAUGHT**	**DUVETYN**	CEASINGS	**EDEMATA**
DIVULGES	DRAUGHTS	DUVETYNE	LEASINGS	OEDEMATA
DIVULSE	DRAUGHTY	DUVETYNS	TEASINGS	**EDGIEST**
DIVULSED	**DREADED**	**DWINDLE**	**EASTERS**	HEDGIEST
DIVULSES	ADREADED	DWINDLED	FEASTERS	KEDGIEST
DIVVIES	**DREAMER**	DWINDLES	**EASTING**	LEDGIEST
DIVVIEST	DREAMERS	**DYNAMIC**	BEASTING	SEDGIEST
DIZZIES	DREAMERY	ADYNAMIC	FEASTING	WEDGIEST
DIZZIEST	**DREARES**	DYNAMICS	REASTING	**EDGINGS**
DOCKISE	DREAREST	**DYSODIL**	YEASTING	HEDGINGS
DOCKISED	**DRIBBLE**	DYSODILE	EASTINGS	WEDGINGS
DOCKISES	DRIBBLED	DYSODILS	**EASTLIN**	**EDITION**
DOCKIZE	DRIBBLER	**DYSPNEA**	EASTLING	SEDITION
DOCKIZED	DRIBBLES	DYSPNEAL	EASTLINS	EDITIONS
DOCKIZES	DRIBBLET	DYSPNEAS	**EATABLE**	**EDUCATE**
DODDIES	**DRIZZLE**	**EAGERLY**	BEATABLE	EDUCATED
DODDIEST	DRIZZLED	MEAGERLY	HEATABLE	EDUCATES
DOGGIES	DRIZZLES	**EAGLING**	EATABLES	**EDUCING**
DOGGIEST	**DROLLER**	BEAGLING	**EATINGS**	DEDUCING
DOGGONE	DROLLERY	TEAGLING	BEATINGS	REDUCING
DOGGONED	**DROUGHT**	**EANLING**	HEATINGS	SEDUCING
DOGGONER	DROUGHTS	WEANLING	SEATINGS	**EDUCTOR**
DOGGONES	DROUGHTY	YEANLING	**EBONISE**	REDUCTOR
DOMICIL	**DRUDGER**	EANLINGS	EBONISED	SEDUCTOR
DOMICILE	DRUDGERS	**EARDING**	EBONISES	EDUCTORS
DOMICILS	DRUDGERY	BEARDING	**EBONITE**	**EECHING**
DOMINEE	DRUGGETS	YEARDING	EBONITES	LEECHING
DOMINEER	**DRUGGIE**	**EARDROP**	**EBONIZE**	REECHING
DOMINEES	DRUGGIER	TEARDROP	EBONIZED	**EELIEST**
DONATES	DRUGGIES	EARDROPS	EBONIZES	SEELIEST
ODONATES	**DRUMBLE**	**EARINGS**	**EBRIATE**	**EERIEST**
DONATOR	DRUMBLED	BEARINGS	EBRIATED	BEERIEST
DONATORS	DRUMBLES	GEARINGS	**ECDYSON**	LEERIEST
DONATORY	**DUALISE**	HEARINGS	ECDYSONE	PEERIEST
DORISED	DUALISED	SEARINGS	ECDYSONS	**EFFORCE**
ODORISED	DUALISES	WEARINGS	**ECHIDNA**	EFFORCED
DORISES	**DUALIZE**	**EARLESS**	ECHIDNAE	EFFORCES
ODORISES	DUALIZED	FEARLESS	ECHIDNAS	**EFFULGE**
DORIZED	DUALIZES	GEARLESS	**ECHOISE**	EFFULGED
ODORIZED	**DUCHESS**	TEARLESS	ECHOISED	EFFULGES
DORIZES	DUCHESSE	**EARLIER**	ECHOISES	**EGALITY**
ODORIZES	**DUCKIES**	NEARLIER	**ECHOIZE**	LEGALITY
DOTTLES	DUCKIEST	PEARLIER	ECHOIZED	REGALITY
DOTTLEST	**DULCIAN**	**EARLIES**	ECHOIZES	**EGENCES**
DOVECOT	DULCIANA	PEARLIES	**ECLIPSE**	REGENCES
DOVECOTE	DULCIANS	YEARLIES	ECLIPSED	**EGGIEST**
DOVECOTS	**DUMMIES**	EARLIEST	ECLIPSER	LEGGIEST
DOWDIES	DUMMIEST	**EARLIKE**	ECLIPSES	**EGOTISE**
DOWDIEST	**DUMPIES**	BEARLIKE	**ECLOSED**	EGOTISED
DRABBLE	DUMPIEST	**EARNERS**	RECLOSED	EGOTISES
DRABBLED	**DUNNIES**	LEARNERS	**ECLOSES**	**EGOTIZE**
DRABBLER	DUNNIEST	YEARNERS	RECLOSES	EGOTIZED
DRABBLES	**DUODENA**	**EARNING**	**ECOLOGY**	EGOTIZES
DRACHMA	DUODENAL	LEARNING	OECOLOGY	**EIGHTHS**
DRACHMAE	**DUSTING**	YEARNING	**ECTASES**	HEIGHTHS
DRACHMAI	ADUSTING	EARNINGS	PECTASES	**EJECTED**
DRACHMAS	DUSTPANS	**EASELED**	**ECTOZOA**	DEJECTED
DRAGGLE	**DUUMVIR**	TEASELED	ECTOZOAN	REJECTED
DRAGGLED	DUUMVIRI	WEASELED	**ECURIES**	**EJECTOR**

REJECTOR	DELUDERS	EMONGEST	ENCHASER	ENGRAVED
EJECTORS	**ELUDING**	**EMOTING**	ENCHASES	ENGRAVEN
ELAPSED	DELUDING	DEMOTING	**ENCLAVE**	ENGRAVER
DELAPSED	**ELUSION**	**EMOTION**	ENCLAVED	ENGRAVES
RELAPSED	DELUSION	DEMOTION	ENCLAVES	**ENHANCE**
ELAPSES	ELUSIONS	REMOTION	**ENCLOSE**	ENHANCED
DELAPSES	**ELUSIVE**	EMOTIONS	ENCLOSED	ENHANCER
RELAPSES	DELUSIVE	**EMOVING**	ENCLOSER	ENHANCES
ELASTIC	**ELUSORY**	REMOVING	ENCLOSES	**ENLARGE**
GELASTIC	DELUSORY	**EMPAIRE**	**ENDARCH**	ENLARGED
ELASTICS	**EMAILED**	EMPAIRED	ENDARCHY	ENLARGEN
ELATERS	REMAILED	EMPAIRES	**ENDINGS**	ENLARGER
RELATERS	**EMANATE**	**EMPAYRE**	BENDINGS	ENLARGES
ELATING	EMANATED	EMPAYRED	LENDINGS	**ENLIGHT**
BELATING	EMANATES	EMPAYRES	MENDINGS	PENLIGHT
DELATING	**EMBATHE**	**EMPERCE**	SENDINGS	ENLIGHTS
GELATING	EMBATHED	EMPERCED	VENDINGS	**ENLOCKS**
RELATING	EMBATHES	EMPERCES	**ENDOGEN**	GENLOCKS
ELATION	**EMBLAZE**	**EMPLACE**	ENDOGENS	**ENNOBLE**
DELATION	EMBLAZED	EMPLACED	ENDOGENY	ENNOBLED
GELATION	EMBLAZER	EMPLACES	**ENDORSE**	ENNOBLER
RELATION	EMBLAZES	**EMPLANE**	ENDORSED	ENNOBLES
ELATIONS	**EMBOGUE**	EMPLANED	ENDORSEE	**ENOLOGY**
ELATIVE	EMBOGUED	EMPLANES	ENDORSER	MENOLOGY
RELATIVE	EMBOGUES	**EMPLOYE**	ENDORSES	OENOLOGY
ELATIVES	**EMBRACE**	EMPLOYED	**ENDWAYS**	PENOLOGY
ELDINGS	EMBRACED	EMPLOYEE	BENDWAYS	VENOLOGY
GELDINGS	EMBRACER	EMPLOYER	**ENDWISE**	**ENOUNCE**
WELDINGS	EMBRACES	EMPLOYES	BENDWISE	DENOUNCE
ELECTED	**EMBRAVE**	**EMPLUME**	**ENEWING**	RENOUNCE
SELECTED	EMBRAVED	EMPLUMED	RENEWING	ENOUNCED
ELECTEE	EMBRAVES	EMPLUMES	**ENFLAME**	ENOUNCES
SELECTEE	**EMBRUTE**	**EMPRESS**	ENFLAMED	**ENPLANE**
ELECTEES	EMBRUTED	EMPRESSE	ENFLAMES	ENPLANED
ELECTOR	EMBRUTES	**EMPTIES**	**ENFOLDS**	ENPLANES
SELECTOR	**EMENDED**	EMPTIEST	PENFOLDS	**ENQUEUE**
ELECTORS	REMENDED	**EMPTING**	TENFOLDS	ENQUEUED
ELECTRO	**EMERGED**	TEMPTING	**ENFORCE**	ENQUEUES
ELECTRON	DEMERGED	EMPTINGS	RENFORCE	**ENQUIRE**
ELECTROS	REMERGED	**EMULATE**	ENFORCED	ENQUIRED
ELEGISE	**EMERGES**	EMULATED	ENFORCER	ENQUIRER
ELEGISED	DEMERGES	EMULATES	ENFORCES	ENQUIRES
ELEGISES	REMERGES	**EMULING**	**ENFRAME**	**ENRANGE**
ELEGIZE	**EMERITA**	AEMULING	ENFRAMED	ENRANGED
ELEGIZED	EMERITAE	**EMURING**	ENFRAMES	ENRANGES
ELEGIZES	EMERITAS	DEMURING	**ENFROZE**	**ENROUND**
ELENCHI	**EMERSED**	**ENACTOR**	ENFROZEN	ENROUNDS
ELENCHIC	DEMERSED	ENACTORS	**ENGINER**	**ENSLAVE**
ELEVATE	**EMETICS**	ENACTORY	ENGINERS	ENSLAVED
ELEVATED	MEMETICS	**ENATION**	ENGINERY	ENSLAVER
ELEVATES	**EMICATE**	VENATION	**ENGLOBE**	ENSLAVES
ELFHOOD	EMICATED	ENATIONS	ENGLOBED	**ENSNARE**
SELFHOOD	EMICATES	**ENCHAFE**	ENGLOBES	ENSNARED
ELFHOODS	**EMITTED**	ENCHAFED	**ENGORGE**	ENSNARER
ELOCUTE	DEMITTED	ENCHAFES	ENGORGED	ENSNARES
ELOCUTED	REMITTED	**ENCHANT**	ENGORGES	**ENSTYLE**
ELOCUTES	**EMITTER**	PENCHANT	**ENGRACE**	ENSTYLED
ELOPING	REMITTER	ENCHANTS	ENGRACED	ENSTYLES
DELOPING	EMITTERS	**ENCHASE**	ENGRACES	**ENSURED**
ELUDERS	**EMONGES**	ENCHASED	**ENGRAVE**	CENSURED

ENSURER	LEPIDOTE	**ESTATES**	ETOURDIE	**EXCERPT**
CENSURER	EPIDOTES	GESTATES	**ETTLING**	EXCERPTA
ENSURERS	**EPIGONI**	RESTATES	FETTLING	EXCERPTS
ENSURES	EPIGONIC	TESTATES	NETTLING	**EXCLUDE**
CENSURES	**EPILATE**	**ESTHETE**	PETTLING	EXCLUDED
ENTAILS	DEPILATE	AESTHETE	SETTLING	EXCLUDEE
VENTAILS	EPILATED	ESTHETES	**EULOGIA**	EXCLUDER
ENTAYLE	EPILATES	**ESTIVAL**	EULOGIAE	EXCLUDES
VENTAYLE	**EPISTLE**	AESTIVAL	EULOGIAS	**EXCRETA**
ENTAYLED	EPISTLED	FESTIVAL	**EUPLOID**	EXCRETAL
ENTAYLES	EPISTLER	**ESTREPE**	EUPLOIDS	**EXCRETE**
ENTERED	EPISTLES	ESTREPED	EUPLOIDY	EXCRETED
CENTERED	**EPITHEM**	ESTREPES	**EUREKAS**	EXCRETER
TENTERED	EPITHEMA	**ESTRINS**	HEUREKAS	EXCRETES
ENTHRAL	EPITHEMS	OESTRINS	**EVANGEL**	**EXCURSE**
ENTHRALL	**EPURATE**	**ESTRIOL**	EVANGELS	EXCURSED
ENTHRALS	DEPURATE	OESTRIOL	EVANGELY	EXCURSES
ENTHUSE	EPURATED	ESTRIOLS	**EVERTED**	**EXECUTE**
ENTHUSED	EPURATES	**ESTRONE**	REVERTED	EXECUTED
ENTHUSES	**EQUITES**	OESTRONE	**EVIRATE**	EXECUTER
ENTICED	REQUITES	ESTRONES	LEVIRATE	EXECUTES
PENTICED	**ERBIUMS**	**ESTROUS**	EVIRATED	**EXEMPLA**
ENTICES	TERBIUMS	OESTROUS	EVIRATES	EXEMPLAR
PENTICES	**ERISTIC**	**ESTRUMS**	**EVITATE**	**EXHEDRA**
ENTITLE	MERISTIC	OESTRUMS	LEVITATE	EXHEDRAE
ENTITLED	VERISTIC	**ETACISM**	EVITATED	**EXORDIA**
ENTITLES	ERISTICS	BETACISM	EVITATES	EXORDIAL
ENTOMIC	**ERMINED**	ETACISMS	**EVOCATE**	**EXPENSE**
PENTOMIC	VERMINED	**ETAMINE**	EVOCATED	EXPENSED
ENTOZOA	**EROTICA**	KETAMINE	EVOCATES	EXPENSES
ENTOZOAL	EROTICAL	ETAMINES	**EVOKERS**	**EXPERTS**
ENTOZOAN	**EROTISE**	**ETATISM**	REVOKERS	SEXPERTS
ENTREAT	EROTISED	ETATISME	**EVOKING**	**EXPIATE**
ENTREATS	EROTISES	ETATISMS	REVOKING	EXPIATED
ENTREATY	**EROTIZE**	**ETATIST**	**EVOLUTE**	EXPIATES
ENTRIES	EROTIZED	ETATISTE	REVOLUTE	**EXPLODE**
CENTRIES	EROTIZES	**ETCHERS**	EVOLUTED	EXPLODED
GENTRIES	**ERRINGS**	FETCHERS	EVOLUTES	EXPLODER
SENTRIES	HERRINGS	**ETCHING**	**EVOLVED**	EXPLODES
ENTRISM	**ESCALOP**	FETCHING	DEVOLVED	**EXPLORE**
CENTRISM	ESCALOPE	KETCHING	REVOLVED	EXPLORED
ENTRISMS	ESCALOPS	LETCHING	**EVOLVER**	EXPLORER
ENTRIST	**ESCRIBE**	RETCHING	REVOLVER	EXPLORES
CENTRIST	DESCRIBE	ETCHINGS	EVOLVERS	**EXPRESS**
ENTRISTS	ESCRIBED	**ETHANAL**	**EVOLVES**	EXPRESSO
ENTWINE	ESCRIBES	METHANAL	DEVOLVES	**EXPULSE**
ENTWINED	**ESLOYNE**	ETHANALS	REVOLVES	EXPULSED
ENTWINES	ESLOYNED	**ETHANES**	**EVULSED**	EXPULSES
ENURING	ESLOYNES	METHANES	REVULSED	**EXPUNGE**
TENURING	**ESPOUSE**	**ETHANOL**	**EXAMINE**	EXPUNGED
ENVELOP	BESPOUSE	METHANOL	HEXAMINE	EXPUNGER
ENVELOPE	ESPOUSED	ETHANOLS	EXAMINED	EXPUNGES
ENVELOPS	ESPOUSER	**ETHERIC**	EXAMINEE	**EXPURGE**
ENVIRON	ESPOUSES	AETHERIC	EXAMINER	EXPURGED
ENVIRONS	**ESQUIRE**	**ETHOXYL**	EXAMINES	EXPURGES
EOLITHS	ESQUIRED	METHOXYL	**EXAMPLE**	**EXTREMA**
NEOLITHS	ESQUIRES	ETHOXYLS	EXAMPLED	EXTREMAL
EONISMS	**ESTATED**	**ETHYLIC**	EXAMPLES	**EXTREME**
PEONISMS	GESTATED	METHYLIC	**EXARCHY**	EXTREMER
EPIDOTE	RESTATED	**ETOURDI**	HEXARCHY	EXTREMES

EXTRUDE	FENNIEST	FLATTERS	**FORESEE**	**FRESHES**
EXTRUDED	**FERLIES**	FLATTERY	FORESEEN	FRESHEST
EXTRUDER	FERLIEST	**FLAVOUR**	FORESEER	**FRIANDE**
EXTRUDES	**FERRULE**	FLAVOURS	FORESEES	FRIANDES
FABLIAU	FERRULED	FLAVOURY	**FORFAIR**	**FRIBBLE**
FABLIAUX	FERRULES	**FLEECIE**	FORFAIRN	FRIBBLED
FALCATE	**FERTILE**	FLEECIER	FORFAIRS	FRIBBLER
FALCATED	FERTILER	FLEECIES	**FORGIVE**	FRIBBLES
FALCULA	**FIBROSE**	**FLICKER**	FORGIVEN	**FRIPPER**
FALCULAE	FIBROSED	FLICKERS	FORGIVER	FRIPPERS
FALCULAS	FIBROSES	FLICKERY	FORGIVES	FRIPPERY
FANCIES	**FICKLES**	**FLITTER**	**FORMATE**	**FRIZZLE**
FANCIEST	FICKLEST	FLITTERN	FORMATED	FRIZZLED
FANFARE	**FILARIA**	FLITTERS	FORMATES	FRIZZLER
FANFARED	FILARIAE	**FLORULA**	**FORMULA**	FRIZZLES
FANFARES	FILARIAL	FLORULAE	FORMULAE	**FROGEYE**
FANGLES	FILARIAN	**FLOSSIE**	FORMULAR	FROGEYED
FANGLESS	**FILIATE**	FLOSSIER	FORMULAS	FROGEYES
FARRIER	FILIATED	FLOSSIES	**FORPINE**	**FROTHER**
FARRIERS	FILIATES	**FLOUNCE**	FORPINED	FROTHERS
FARRIERY	**FIMBRIA**	FLOUNCED	FORPINES	FROTHERY
FASCISM	FIMBRIAE	FLOUNCES	**FORSAKE**	**FROUNCE**
FASCISMI	FIMBRIAL	**FLUORID**	FORSAKEN	FROUNCED
FASCISMO	**FINAGLE**	FLUORIDE	FORSAKER	FROUNCES
FASCISMS	FINAGLED	FLUORIDS	FORSAKES	**FRUITER**
FASCIST	FINAGLER	**FLUORIN**	**FORSLOE**	FRUITERS
FASCISTA	FINAGLES	FLUORINE	FORSLOED	FRUITERY
FASCISTI	**FINALIS**	FLUORINS	FORSLOES	**FRUMPLE**
FASCISTS	FINALISE	**FLUSHES**	**FORTUNE**	FRUMPLED
FASHION	FINALISM	FLUSHEST	FORTUNED	FRUMPLES
FASHIONS	FINALIST	**FLUSTER**	FORTUNES	**FUCHSIA**
FASHIONY	**FINANCE**	FLUSTERS	**FORZATI**	FUCHSIAS
FATIGUE	FINANCED	FLUSTERY	SFORZATI	**FUCHSIN**
FATIGUED	FINANCES	**FLUTTER**	**FORZATO**	FUCHSINE
FATIGUES	**FINESSE**	AFLUTTER	SFORZATO	FUCHSINS
FATTIES	FINESSED	FLUTTERS	FORZATOS	**FULMINE**
FATTIEST	FINESSER	FLUTTERY	**FOSSULA**	FULMINED
FAUNULA	FINESSES	**FLYBLOW**	FOSSULAE	FULMINES
FAUNULAE	**FINIKIN**	FLYBLOWN	**FOVEATE**	**FULSOME**
FEARING	FINIKING	FLYBLOWS	FOVEATED	FULSOMER
AFEARING	**FISSURE**	**FOLIAGE**	**FOVEOLA**	**FUNNIES**
FEATHER	FISSURED	FOLIAGED	FOVEOLAE	FUNNIEST
FEATHERS	FISSURES	FOLIAGES	FOVEOLAR	**FURCATE**
FEATHERY	**FISTULA**	**FOLIATE**	FOVEOLAS	FURCATED
FEATURE	FISTULAE	FOLIATED	**FOVEOLE**	FURCATES
FEATURED	FISTULAR	FOLIATES	FOVEOLES	**FURCULA**
FEATURES	FISTULAS	**FOLKIES**	FOVEOLET	FURCULAE
FEBRILE	**FLACKER**	FOLKIEST	**FRACTUR**	FURCULAR
AFEBRILE	FLACKERS	**FOLKMOT**	FRACTURE	**FURNACE**
FEDAYEE	FLACKERY	FOLKMOTE	FRACTURS	FURNACED
FEDAYEEN	**FLAKIES**	FOLKMOTS	**FRAGILE**	FURNACES
FEEBLES	FLAKIEST	**FOOTIES**	FRAGILER	**FURRIER**
FEEBLEST	**FLAMBEE**	FOOTIEST	**FRAZZLE**	FURRIERS
FELLATE	FLAMBEED	**FOOTLER**	FRAZZLED	FURRIERY
FELLATED	FLAMBEES	FOOTLERS	FRAZZLES	**FURRIES**
FELLATES	**FLAMING**	**FORBODE**	**FRECKLE**	FURRIEST
FENAGLE	FLAMINGO	FORBODED	FRECKLED	**FUSAROL**
FENAGLED	**FLASHES**	FORBODES	FRECKLES	FUSAROLE
FENAGLES	FLASHEST	**FORERAN**	**FRENULA**	FUSAROLS
FENNIES	**FLATTER**	FORERANK	FRENULAR	**GABELLE**

GABELLED	**GEALOUS**	GLAZIERS	GRANDAME	GRUMBLES
GABELLER	GEALOUSY	GLAZIERY	GRANDAMS	**GRUNTLE**
GABELLES	**GELATIN**	**GLIADIN**	**GRANNIE**	GRUNTLED
GALABEA	GELATINE	GLIADINE	GRANNIED	GRUNTLES
GALABEAH	GELATING	GLIADINS	GRANNIES	**GUISING**
GALABEAS	GELATINS	**GLIBBER**	**GRAPHIC**	AGUISING
GALABIA	**GEMMATE**	GLIBBERY	AGRAPHIC	GUISINGS
GALABIAH	GEMMATED	**GLIDDER**	GRAPHICS	**GUMMIES**
GALABIAS	GEMMATES	GLIDDERY	**GRAPLIN**	GUMMIEST
GALANGA	**GENERAL**	**GLIMMER**	GRAPLINE	**GUMSHOE**
GALANGAL	GENERALE	AGLIMMER	GRAPLINS	GUMSHOED
GALANGAS	GENERALS	GLIMMERS	**GRAPPLE**	GUMSHOES
GALEATE	**GENESES**	GLIMMERY	GRAPPLED	**GUTTATE**
GALEATED	AGENESES	**GLIMPSE**	GRAPPLER	GUTTATED
GALLICA	**GENESIS**	GLIMPSED	GRAPPLES	GUTTATES
GALLICAN	AGENESIS	GLIMPSER	**GRATINE**	**GUTTIES**
GALLICAS	**GENETIC**	GLIMPSES	GRATINEE	GUTTIEST
GALLISE	AGENETIC	**GLITTER**	**GRAVIDA**	**GUYLINE**
GALLISED	GENETICS	AGLITTER	GRAVIDAE	GUYLINER
GALLISES	**GENIZOT**	GLITTERS	GRAVIDAS	GUYLINES
GALLIZE	GENIZOTH	GLITTERY	**GRECISE**	**GYRATOR**
GALLIZED	**GENTLES**	**GLOBATE**	GRECISED	GYRATORS
GALLIZES	GENTLEST	GLOBATED	GRECISES	GYRATORY
GALOCHE	**GERMAIN**	**GLOBULE**	**GRECIZE**	**HABITAN**
GALOCHED	GERMAINE	GLOBULES	GRECIZED	HABITANS
GALOCHES	GERMAINS	GLOBULET	GRECIZES	HABITANT
GALOPIN	**GERMINA**	**GLOSSAL**	**GREEING**	**HACHURE**
GALOPING	GERMINAL	AGLOSSAL	AGREEING	HACHURED
GALOPINS	**GESTATE**	**GLUTTON**	**GRIDDLE**	HACHURES
GALOSHE	GESTATED	GLUTTONS	GRIDDLED	**HACKERS**
GALOSHED	GESTATES	GLUTTONY	GRIDDLES	WHACKERS
GALOSHES	**GESTURE**	**GNOSTIC**	**GRILLER**	**HACKING**
GAMETES	GESTURED	AGNOSTIC	GRILLERS	CHACKING
AGAMETES	GESTURER	GNOSTICS	GRILLERY	SHACKING
GANGLIA	GESTURES	**GOLIARD**	**GRIMACE**	THACKING
GANGLIAL	**GHILLIE**	GOLIARDS	GRIMACED	WHACKING
GANGLIAR	GHILLIED	GOLIARDY	GRIMACER	HACKINGS
GARBAGE	GHILLIES	**GOLOSHE**	GRIMACES	**HACKLED**
GARBAGES	**GIDDIES**	GOLOSHED	**GRINDER**	SHACKLED
GARBAGEY	GIDDIEST	GOLOSHES	GRINDERS	**HACKLER**
GARBLES	**GIMMICK**	**GONIDIA**	GRINDERY	SHACKLER
GARBLESS	GIMMICKS	GONIDIAL	**GRISING**	HACKLERS
GAROTTE	GIMMICKY	**GOODIES**	AGRISING	**HACKLES**
GAROTTED	**GINGIVA**	GOODIEST	**GRIZZLE**	SHACKLES
GAROTTER	GINGIVAE	**GOONIES**	GRIZZLED	**HACKSAW**
GAROTTES	GINGIVAL	GOONIEST	GRIZZLER	HACKSAWN
GARROTE	**GINNERS**	**GOOSIES**	GRIZZLES	HACKSAWS
GARROTED	AGINNERS	GOOSIEST	**GROSSES**	**HADARIM**
GARROTER	**GIRASOL**	**GOSPODA**	GROSSEST	CHADARIM
GARROTES	GIRASOLE	GOSPODAR	**GROUSES**	**HADDOCK**
GAUDIES	GIRASOLS	**GRABBLE**	GROUSEST	SHADDOCK
GAUDIEST	**GIRLIES**	GRABBLED	**GROWLER**	HADDOCKS
GAVOTTE	GIRLIEST	GRABBLER	GROWLERS	**HAFTARA**
GAVOTTED	**GLAIRIN**	GRABBLES	GROWLERY	HAFTARAH
GAVOTTES	GLAIRING	**GRADATE**	**GRUBBLE**	HAFTARAS
GAWKIES	GLAIRINS	GRADATED	GRUBBLED	**HAFTERS**
GAWKIEST	**GLASSIE**	GRADATES	GRUBBLES	SHAFTERS
GAZETTE	GLASSIER	**GRAMARY**	**GRUMBLE**	**HAFTING**
GAZETTED	GLASSIES	GRAMARYE	GRUMBLED	SHAFTING
GAZETTES	**GLAZIER**	**GRANDAM**	GRUMBLER	**HAGGADA**

HAGGADAH	HANDLERS	**HARRIES**	**HEATERS**	**HENDING**
HAGGADAS	**HANGERS**	GHARRIES	CHEATERS	SHENDING
HAGGING	CHANGERS	**HARSHES**	THEATERS	**HENNIES**
SHAGGING	**HANGING**	HARSHEST	**HEATHER**	HENNIEST
HAGRIDE	CHANGING	**HASHING**	SHEATHER	**HEPATIC**
HAGRIDER	PHANGING	SHASHING	HEATHERS	HEPATICA
HAGRIDES	WHANGING	HASHINGS	HEATHERY	HEPATICS
HAINING	HANGINGS	**HASSOCK**	**HEATING**	**HERBAGE**
CHAINING	**HANJARS**	HASSOCKS	CHEATING	HERBAGED
HAININGS	KHANJARS	HASSOCKY	HEATINGS	HERBAGES
HAIRING	**HANKERS**	**HASTATE**	**HEAVIES**	**HERMITS**
CHAIRING	THANKERS	HASTATED	HEAVIEST	THERMITS
HALAKHA	**HANKING**	**HASTENS**	**HEAVING**	**HEROISE**
HALAKHAH	SHANKING	CHASTENS	SHEAVING	HEROISED
HALAKHAS	THANKING	**HASTING**	HEAVINGS	HEROISES
HALAVAH	**HANTING**	GHASTING	**HEELERS**	**HEROIZE**
HALAVAHS	CHANTING	HASTINGS	WHEELERS	HEROIZED
HALBERT	**HAPLESS**	**HATCHED**	**HEELING**	HEROIZES
HALBERTS	CHAPLESS	THATCHED	SHEELING	**HERRIED**
HALFLIN	**HAPLOID**	**HATCHER**	WHEELING	CHERRIED
HALFLING	HAPLOIDS	THATCHER	HEELINGS	WHERRIED
HALFLINS	HAPLOIDY	HATCHERS	**HEEZING**	**HERRIES**
HALIDOM	**HAPPIER**	HATCHERY	PHEEZING	CHERRIES
HALIDOME	CHAPPIER	**HATCHES**	WHEEZING	SHERRIES
HALIDOMS	**HAPPIES**	THATCHES	**HEGEMON**	WHERRIES
HALIMOT	CHAPPIES	**HATCHET**	HEGEMONS	**HETAERA**
HALIMOTE	HAPPIEST	HATCHETS	HEGEMONY	HETAERAE
HALIMOTS	**HAPPING**	HATCHETY	**HEGUMEN**	HETAERAS
HALLAHS	CHAPPING	**HATTERS**	HEGUMENE	**HETAIRA**
CHALLAHS	WHAPPING	CHATTERS	HEGUMENS	HETAIRAI
HALLANS	**HARDIES**	SHATTERS	HEGUMENY	HETAIRAS
CHALLANS	HARDIEST	**HATTING**	**HEILING**	**HEWABLE**
HALLOTH	**HARKING**	CHATTING	SHEILING	CHEWABLE
CHALLOTH	CHARKING	HATTINGS	**HELLERS**	**HEXAPLA**
HALLOWS	SHARKING	**HAULING**	SHELLERS	HEXAPLAR
SHALLOWS	**HARMERS**	SHAULING	**HELLIER**	HEXAPLAS
HALTERE	CHARMERS	**HAUNTED**	SHELLIER	**HEXAPOD**
HALTERED	**HARMFUL**	CHAUNTED	HELLIERS	HEXAPODS
HALTERES	CHARMFUL	**HAUNTER**	**HELLING**	HEXAPODY
HAMBLED	**HARMING**	CHAUNTER	SHELLING	**HEXARCH**
SHAMBLED	CHARMING	HAUNTERS	**HELMING**	HEXARCHY
HAMBLES	PHARMING	**HAVINGS**	WHELMING	**HICKIES**
SHAMBLES	**HARMOST**	SHAVINGS	**HELPING**	THICKIES
HAMBONE	HARMOSTS	**HAZANIM**	CHELPING	**HICKISH**
HAMBONED	HARMOSTY	CHAZANIM	WHELPING	THICKISH
HAMBONES	**HAROSET**	**HAZZANS**	HELPINGS	**HICKORY**
HAMLETS	CHAROSET	CHAZZANS	**HELVING**	CHICKORY
CHAMLETS	HAROSETH	**HEADING**	SHELVING	**HIDDERS**
HAMMERS	HAROSETS	SHEADING	**HEMATIC**	SHIDDERS
SHAMMERS	**HARPERS**	HEADINGS	RHEMATIC	WHIDDERS
HAMMING	SHARPERS	**HEALING**	THEMATIC	**HIDINGS**
SHAMMING	**HARPIES**	SHEALING	HEMATICS	CHIDINGS
WHAMMING	CHARPIES	HEALINGS	**HEMATIN**	**HILDING**
HAMPERS	SHARPIES	**HEAPING**	HEMATINE	CHILDING
CHAMPERS	**HARPING**	CHEAPING	HEMATINS	HILDINGS
HANDCAR	SHARPING	**HEARERS**	**HEMIPOD**	**HILLERS**
HANDCARS	HARPINGS	SHEARERS	HEMIPODE	CHILLERS
HANDCART	**HARRIER**	**HEARING**	HEMIPODS	THILLERS
HANDLER	CHARRIER	SHEARING	**HEMPIES**	**HILLIER**
CHANDLER	HARRIERS	HEARINGS	HEMPIEST	CHILLIER

HILLING	WHITHERS	DHOOLIES	CHUCKING	**HUTZPAH**
CHILLING	**HITLESS**	HOOLIEST	SHUCKING	CHUTZPAH
SHILLING	SHITLESS	**HOOPERS**	**HUCKLED**	HUTZPAHS
HILLINGS	**HITTERS**	WHOOPERS	CHUCKLED	**HUTZPAS**
HILLOCK	CHITTERS	**HOOPING**	**HUCKLES**	CHUTZPAS
HILLOCKS	WHITTERS	WHOOPING	CHUCKLES	**HYDRANT**
HILLOCKY	**HITTING**	**HOOPLAS**	**HUFFIER**	HYDRANTH
HINGERS	CHITTING	WHOOPLAS	CHUFFIER	HYDRANTS
WHINGERS	SHITTING	**HOOSHED**	**HUFFING**	**HYDRATE**
HINGING	**HIZZING**	WHOOSHED	CHUFFING	HYDRATED
WHINGING	CHIZZING	**HOOSHES**	HUFFINGS	HYDRATES
HINKIER	WHIZZING	WHOOSHES	**HUGGERS**	**HYDROPS**
CHINKIER	**HOCKERS**	**HOOTERS**	CHUGGERS	HYDROPSY
HINNIED	SHOCKERS	SHOOTERS	**HUGGING**	**HYDROXY**
SHINNIED	**HOCKING**	**HOOTING**	CHUGGING	HYDROXYL
WHINNIED	CHOCKING	SHOOTING	**HUMBLES**	**HYMENIA**
HINNIES	SHOCKING	WHOOTING	HUMBLEST	HYMENIAL
SHINNIES	**HOGGING**	**HOPPERS**	HUMMAUMS	**HYPOGEA**
WHINNIES	SHOGGING	CHOPPERS	**HUMMING**	HYPOGEAL
HIPLESS	HOGGINGS	SHOPPERS	CHUMMING	HYPOGEAN
SHIPLESS	**HOGNOSE**	WHOPPERS	HUMMINGS	**HYPONYM**
WHIPLESS	HOGNOSED	**HOPPIER**	**HUMMOCK**	HYPONYMS
HIPLIKE	HOGNOSES	CHOPPIER	HUMMOCKS	HYPONYMY
WHIPLIKE	**HOGWEED**	SHOPPIER	HUMMOCKY	**ICELESS**
HIPPENS	HOGWEEDS	**HOPPING**	**HUMPERS**	VICELESS
SHIPPENS	**HOKIEST**	CHOPPING	THUMPERS	**ICELIKE**
HIPPIER	CHOKIEST	SHOPPING	**HUMPIES**	VICELIKE
CHIPPIER	**HOLESOM**	WHOPPING	HUMPIEST	**ICKIEST**
WHIPPIER	HOLESOME	HOPPINGS	**HUMPING**	DICKIEST
HIPPIES	**HOLISMS**	**HORDING**	CHUMPING	KICKIEST
CHIPPIES	WHOLISMS	CHORDING	THUMPING	PICKIEST
SHIPPIES	**HOLISTS**	**HORNIER**	WHUMPING	**ICKLEST**
HIPPIEST	WHOLISTS	THORNIER	**HUNKIER**	FICKLEST
HIPPING	**HOLLERS**	**HORNILY**	CHUNKIER	MICKLEST
CHIPPING	CHOLLERS	THORNILY	**HUNKIES**	**ICONISE**
SHIPPING	**HOLYDAM**	**HORNING**	HUNKIEST	ICONISED
WHIPPING	HOLYDAME	THORNING	**HUNTERS**	ICONISES
HIPPINGS	HOLYDAMS	HORNINGS	CHUNTERS	**ICONIZE**
HIPSTER	**HOMININ**	**HORNITO**	SHUNTERS	ICONIZED
WHIPSTER	HOMININE	HORNITOS	**HUNTING**	ICONIZES
HIPSTERS	HOMININS	**HOSANNA**	SHUNTING	**ICTUSES**
HIRLING	**HOMOLOG**	HOSANNAH	HUNTINGS	RICTUSES
CHIRLING	HOMOLOGS	HOSANNAS	**HUPPAHS**	**IDOLISE**
THIRLING	HOMOLOGY	**HOSTING**	CHUPPAHS	IDOLISED
WHIRLING	**HOMONYM**	GHOSTING	**HUPPING**	IDOLISER
HIRLINGS	HOMONYMS	HOSTINGS	WHUPPING	IDOLISES
HISHING	HOMONYMY	**HOTTING**	**HUPPOTH**	**IDOLIZE**
PHISHING	**HONEYED**	SHOTTING	CHUPPOTH	IDOLIZED
WHISHING	PHONEYED	HOTTINGS	**HURRIES**	IDOLIZER
HISSIES	**HOODIES**	**HOUSERS**	DHURRIES	IDOLIZES
HISSIEST	HOODIEST	CHOUSERS	**HUSHERS**	**IFFIEST**
HISSING	**HOOFING**	**HOUSING**	SHUSHERS	MIFFIEST
WHISSING	CHOOFING	CHOUSING	**HUSHING**	NIFFIEST
HISSINGS	WHOOFING	HOUSINGS	SHUSHING	**IGNEOUS**
HISTING	**HOOKIES**	**HOUTING**	**HUSKIES**	LIGNEOUS
WHISTING	CHOOKIES	SHOUTING	HUSKIEST	**IGNITES**
HISTRIO	HOOKIEST	HOUTINGS	**HUTTING**	LIGNITES
HISTRION	**HOOKING**	**HOVELED**	PHUTTING	**IGNOBLE**
HISTRIOS	CHOOKING	SHOVELED	SHUTTING	IGNOBLER
HITHERS	**HOOLIES**	**HUCKING**	HUTTINGS	**IGNORES**

SIGNORES	IMPLORES	INDICANS	INHUMANE	INTITLES
ILLAPSE	**IMPRESS**	INDICANT	**INKIEST**	**INTRADA**
ILLAPSED	IMPRESSE	**INDICIA**	DINKIEST	INTRADAS
ILLAPSES	**IMPROVE**	INDICIAL	HINKIEST	INTRADAY
ILLITES	IMPROVED	INDICIAS	KINKIEST	**INTRUDE**
TILLITES	IMPROVER	**INDIGEN**	LINKIEST	INTRUDED
ILLUVIA	IMPROVES	INDIGENE	PINKIEST	INTRUDER
ILLUVIAL	**IMPULSE**	INDIGENS	SINKIEST	INTRUDES
IMAGINE	IMPULSED	INDIGENT	ZINKIEST	**INTWINE**
IMAGINED	IMPULSES	**INDIGOS**	**INKLING**	INTWINED
IMAGINER	**INBEING**	WINDIGOS	TINKLING	INTWINES
IMAGINES	INBEINGS	**INDORSE**	WINKLING	**INVERSE**
IMBATHE	**INBOARD**	INDORSED	INKLINGS	INVERSED
IMBATHED	PINBOARD	INDORSEE	**INNARDS**	INVERSES
IMBATHES	INBOARDS	INDORSER	WINNARDS	**INVOICE**
IMBLAZE	**INCASES**	INDORSES	**INNERVE**	INVOICED
IMBLAZED	PINCASES	**INDOWED**	INNERVED	INVOICES
IMBLAZES	**INCENSE**	WINDOWED	INNERVES	**INVOLVE**
IMBRUTE	INCENSED	**INDULGE**	**INNINGS**	INVOLVED
IMBRUTED	INCENSER	INDULGED	GINNINGS	INVOLVER
IMBRUTES	INCENSES	INDULGER	PINNINGS	INVOLVES
IMBURSE	**INCHASE**	INDULGES	TINNINGS	**INWEAVE**
IMBURSED	INCHASED	**INDULIN**	WINNINGS	INWEAVED
IMBURSES	INCHASES	INDULINE	**INQUERE**	INWEAVES
IMITATE	**INCHERS**	INDULINS	INQUERED	**INWORKS**
IMITATED	PINCHERS	**INDUSIA**	INQUERES	PINWORKS
IMITATES	WINCHERS	INDUSIAL	**INQUIRE**	TINWORKS
IMMENSE	**INCHING**	**INERTIA**	INQUIRED	**IONISED**
IMMENSER	CINCHING	INERTIAE	INQUIRER	LIONISED
IMMERGE	PINCHING	INERTIAL	INQUIRES	**IONISER**
IMMERGED	WINCHING	INERTIAS	**INSCULP**	LIONISER
IMMERGES	**INCHPIN**	**INFALLS**	INSCULPS	IONISERS
IMMERSE	LINCHPIN	PINFALLS	INSCULPT	**IONISES**
IMMERSED	INCHPINS	**INFAUNA**	**INSHIPS**	LIONISES
IMMERSER	**INCISOR**	INFAUNAE	KINSHIPS	**IONIZED**
IMMERSES	INCISORS	INFAUNAL	**INSNARE**	LIONIZED
IMPASTE	INCISORY	INFAUNAS	INSNARED	**IONIZER**
IMPASTED	**INCITES**	**INFLAME**	INSNARER	LIONIZER
IMPASTES	ZINCITES	INFLAMED	INSNARES	IONIZERS
IMPERIA	**INCLINE**	INFLAMER	**INSPIRE**	**IONIZES**
IMPERIAL	INCLINED	INFLAMES	INSPIRED	LIONIZES
IMPINGE	INCLINER	**INFLATE**	INSPIRER	**IRELESS**
IMPINGED	INCLINES	INFLATED	INSPIRES	FIRELESS
IMPINGER	**INCLOSE**	INFLATER	**INSTATE**	TIRELESS
IMPINGES	INCLOSED	INFLATES	INSTATED	WIRELESS
IMPINGS	INCLOSER	**INFOLDS**	INSTATES	**IRIDIAN**
LIMPINGS	INCLOSES	PINFOLDS	**INTAGLI**	VIRIDIAN
PIMPINGS	**INCLUDE**	**INFORCE**	INTAGLIO	**IRIDISE**
IMPLATE	INCLUDED	INFORCED	**INTENSE**	IRIDISED
IMPLATED	INCLUDES	INFORCES	INTENSER	IRIDISES
IMPLATES	**INCONNU**	**INGLOBE**	**INTERNE**	**IRIDIZE**
IMPLETE	INCONNUE	INGLOBED	INTERNED	IRIDIZED
IMPLETED	INCONNUS	INGLOBES	INTERNEE	IRIDIZES
IMPLETES	**INCURVE**	**INGOING**	INTERNES	**IRISATE**
IMPLODE	INCURVED	DINGOING	INTERNET	IRISATED
IMPLODED	INCURVES	INGOINGS	**INTHRAL**	IRISATES
IMPLODES	**INDAMIN**	**INHERCE**	INTHRALL	**IRONIES**
IMPLORE	INDAMINE	INHERCED	INTHRALS	IRONIEST
IMPLORED	INDAMINS	INHERCES	**INTITLE**	**IRONISE**
IMPLORER	**INDICAN**	**INHUMAN**	INTITLED	SIRONISE

IRONISED	JAMBIYAH	**KABBALA**	OKIMONOS	**LACKERS**
IRONISES	JAMBIYAS	KABBALAH	**KINESES**	CLACKERS
IRONIZE	**JAMBOKS**	KABBALAS	AKINESES	FLACKERS
SIRONIZE	SJAMBOKS	**KALOOKI**	**KINESIS**	SLACKERS
IRONIZED	**JAMMIES**	KALOOKIE	AKINESIS	**LACKING**
IRONIZES	JAMMIEST	KALOOKIS	**KINETIC**	BLACKING
ISOCHOR	**JANIZAR**	**KASHRUT**	AKINETIC	CLACKING
ISOCHORE	JANIZARS	KASHRUTH	KINETICS	FLACKING
ISOCHORS	JANIZARY	KASHRUTS	**KINKING**	SLACKING
ISOGAMY	**JANTIES**	**KEGGERS**	SKINKING	**LACTATE**
MISOGAMY	JANTIEST	SKEGGERS	**KINLESS**	LACTATED
ISOLATE	**JAUNTIE**	**KELLIES**	SKINLESS	LACTATES
ISOLATED	JAUNTIER	SKELLIES	**KIPPERS**	**LACUNAR**
ISOLATES	JAUNTIES	**KELPING**	SKIPPERS	LACUNARS
ISSUING	**JAVELIN**	SKELPING	**KIPPING**	LACUNARY
TISSUING	JAVELINA	**KELTERS**	SKIPPING	**LADDERS**
ITCHIER	JAVELINS	SKELTERS	**KITTLED**	BLADDERS
BITCHIER	**JAWBONE**	**KENNING**	SKITTLED	CLADDERS
HITCHIER	JAWBONED	SKENNING	**KITTLES**	**LADDERY**
PITCHIER	JAWBONER	KENNINGS	SKITTLES	BLADDERY
TITCHIER	JAWBONES	**KEPPING**	KITTLEST	**LADDIES**
WITCHIER	**JEALOUS**	SKEPPING	**KNACKER**	CLADDIES
ITCHILY	JEALOUSE	**KERMESS**	KNACKERS	GLADDIES
BITCHILY	JEALOUSY	KERMESSE	KNACKERY	**LADINGS**
HITCHILY	**JEHADIS**	**KERRIES**	**KNAPPLE**	BLADINGS
PITCHILY	JEHADISM	SKERRIES	KNAPPLED	**LAGGERS**
ITCHING	JEHADIST	**KETCHES**	KNAPPLES	BLAGGERS
BITCHING	**JELLABA**	SKETCHES	**KNOBBLE**	FLAGGERS
DITCHING	DJELLABA	**KETUBOT**	KNOBBLED	**LAGGING**
HITCHING	JELLABAH	KETUBOTH	**KNOBBLES**	BLAGGING
MITCHING	JELLABAS	**KEYNOTE**	**KNUBBLE**	CLAGGING
PITCHING	**JEMMIES**	KEYNOTED	KNUBBLED	FLAGGING
WITCHING	JEMMIEST	KEYNOTER	KNUBBLES	SLAGGING
ITCHINGS	**JEOPARD**	KEYNOTES	**KNUCKLE**	LAGGINGS
ITEMISE	JEOPARDS	**KHALIFA**	KNUCKLED	**LAICISE**
ITEMISED	JEOPARDY	KHALIFAH	KNUCKLER	LAICISED
ITEMISER	**JERKIES**	KHALIFAS	KNUCKLES	LAICISES
ITEMISES	JERKIEST	KHALIFAT	**KOFTGAR**	**LAICIZE**
ITEMIZE	**JETTIES**	**KHEDIVA**	KOFTGARI	LAICIZED
ITEMIZED	JETTIEST	KHEDIVAL	KOFTGARS	LAICIZES
ITEMIZER	**JIBBAHS**	KHEDIVAS	**KOLKHOS**	**LAIDING**
ITEMIZES	DJIBBAHS	**KHIRKAH**	KOLKHOSY	PLAIDING
ITERATE	**JIHADIS**	**KIDDERS**	**KOLKHOZ**	**LAIRIER**
LITERATE	JIHADISM	SKIDDERS	KOLKHOZY	GLAIRIER
ITERATED	JIHADIST	**KIDDIER**	**KYANISE**	**LAIRING**
ITERATES	**JOLLIES**	SKIDDIER	KYANISED	GLAIRING
IZZARDS	JOLLIEST	KIDDIERS	KYANISES	**LAIRISE**
DIZZARDS	**JOYRIDE**	**KIDDING**	**KYANIZE**	LAIRISED
GIZZARDS	JOYRIDER	SKIDDING	KYANIZED	LAIRISES
JACINTH	JOYRIDES	**KILLDEE**	KYANIZES	**LAIRIZE**
JACINTHE	**JUGGLER**	KILLDEER	**LABELLA**	LAIRIZED
JACINTHS	JUGGLERS	KILLDEES	FLABELLA	LAIRIZES
JAGGIES	JUGGLERY	**KILLIES**	GLABELLA	**LAKIEST**
JAGGIEST	**JUNGLIS**	SKILLIES	**LABIATE**	FLAKIEST
JALOUSE	JUNGLIST	**KILLING**	LABIATED	**LAMBAST**
JALOUSED	**JUNKIES**	SKILLING	LABIATES	LAMBASTE
JALOUSES	JUNKIEST	KILLINGS	**LACINGS**	LAMBASTS
JAMBEAU	**JUSTICE**	**KIMMERS**	PLACINGS	**LAMBERS**
JAMBEAUX	JUSTICER	SKIMMERS	**LACINIA**	CLAMBERS
JAMBIYA	JUSTICES	**KIMONOS**	LACINIAE	**LAMBIES**

LAMBIEST	LANOLINS	CLAWLESS	**LEAVERS**	**LETCHES**
LAMELLA	**LAPPERS**	FLAWLESS	CLEAVERS	FLETCHES
LAMELLAE	CLAPPERS	**LAWLIKE**	**LEAVING**	**LETTING**
LAMELLAR	FLAPPERS	CLAWLIKE	CLEAVING	BLETTING
LAMELLAS	SLAPPERS	**LAYBACK**	SLEAVING	LETTINGS
LAMINAR	**LAPPING**	PLAYBACK	LEAVINGS	**LEVATOR**
LAMINARY	CLAPPING	LAYBACKS	**LECTION**	ELEVATOR
LAMITER	FLAPPING	**LAYOFFS**	ELECTION	LEVATORS
LAMITERS	KLAPPING	PLAYOFFS	FLECTION	**LIBBING**
LAMMERS	PLAPPING	**LAYTIME**	LECTIONS	GLIBBING
CLAMMERS	SLAPPING	PLAYTIME	**LECTORS**	**LIBRATE**
SLAMMERS	LAPPINGS	LAYTIMES	ELECTORS	LIBRATED
LAMMING	**LAPSING**	**LAZIEST**	**LECTURE**	LIBRATES
CLAMMING	ELAPSING	GLAZIEST	LECTURED	**LICENCE**
FLAMMING	**LARGESS**	**LEACHED**	LECTURER	LICENCED
GLAMMING	LARGESSE	BLEACHED	LECTURES	LICENCEE
SLAMMING	**LARNEYS**	PLEACHED	**LEDGERS**	LICENCER
LAMMINGS	BLARNEYS	**LEACHER**	PLEDGERS	LICENCES
LAMPERS	**LARVATE**	BLEACHER	SLEDGERS	**LICENSE**
CLAMPERS	LARVATED	LEACHERS	**LEDGIER**	LICENSED
LAMPING	**LASHERS**	**LEACHES**	FLEDGIER	LICENSEE
CLAMPING	CLASHERS	BLEACHES	**LEECHED**	LICENSER
GLAMPING	FLASHERS	PLEACHES	FLEECHED	LICENSES
LAMPINGS	PLASHERS	**LEADERS**	**LEECHES**	**LICHTER**
LANCERS	SLASHERS	PLEADERS	FLEECHES	FLICHTER
GLANCERS	**LASHING**	**LEADING**	SLEECHES	**LICKERS**
LANCHED	CLASHING	PLEADING	**LEEPING**	CLICKERS
BLANCHED	FLASHING	LEADINGS	BLEEPING	FLICKERS
FLANCHED	PLASHING	**LEAMING**	CLEEPING	SLICKERS
PLANCHED	SLASHING	GLEAMING	SLEEPING	**LICKING**
LANCHES	LASHINGS	**LEANERS**	**LEERING**	CLICKING
BLANCHES	**LASKETS**	CLEANERS	FLEERING	FLICKING
FLANCHES	FLASKETS	GLEANERS	LEERINGS	SLICKING
PLANCHES	**LASSIES**	**LEANEST**	**LEGGIER**	LICKINGS
LANCING	GLASSIES	CLEANEST	LEGGIERO	**LIGHTED**
ELANCING	**LASTERS**	**LEANING**	**LEGGIES**	ALIGHTED
GLANCING	BLASTERS	CLEANING	LEGGIEST	BLIGHTED
LANDERS	PLASTERS	GLEANING	**LEGGING**	FLIGHTED
GLANDERS	**LASTING**	LEANINGS	ALEGGING	PLIGHTED
SLANDERS	BLASTING	**LEARIER**	FLEGGING	SLIGHTED
LANDING	LASTINGS	BLEARIER	LEGGINGS	**LIGHTER**
BLANDING	**LATCHED**	**LEARING**	**LEGISTS**	BLIGHTER
LANDINGS	CLATCHED	BLEARING	ELEGISTS	PLIGHTER
LANGERS	**LATCHES**	CLEARING	**LEISURE**	SLIGHTER
CLANGERS	CLATCHES	**LEASERS**	LEISURED	LIGHTERS
FLANGERS	KLATCHES	PLEASERS	LEISURES	**LIGHTLY**
SLANGERS	SLATCHES	**LEASING**	**LEMMING**	SLIGHTLY
LANKEST	**LATHERS**	PLEASING	CLEMMING	**LIGROIN**
BLANKEST	BLATHERS	LEASINGS	LEMMINGS	LIGROINE
LANKIER	SLATHERS	**LEASOWE**	**LENDERS**	LIGROINS
CLANKIER	**LATINAS**	LEASOWED	BLENDERS	**LIMBERS**
LANKING	PLATINAS	LEASOWES	**LENDING**	CLIMBERS
BLANKING	**LATTENS**	**LEASURE**	BLENDING	**LIMBING**
CLANKING	FLATTENS	PLEASURE	LENDINGS	BLIMBING
FLANKING	**LATTICE**	LEASURES	**LENSING**	CLIMBING
PLANKING	LATTICED	**LEATHER**	FLENSING	**LIMIEST**
LANNERS	LATTICES	PLEATHER	**LESSORS**	SLIMIEST
PLANNERS	**LAUDING**	LEATHERN	PLESSORS	**LIMMERS**
LANOLIN	BLAUDING	LEATHERS	**LETCHED**	GLIMMERS
LANOLINE	**LAWLESS**	LEATHERY	FLETCHED	SLIMMERS

LIMPING	FLIPPIER	**LOBULES**	**LOPPERS**	GLOVINGS
FLIMPING	SLIPPIER	GLOBULES	FLOPPERS	**LOWBALL**
LIMPINGS	**LIPPIES**	**LOCKAGE**	**LOPPIER**	BLOWBALL
LINCHES	CLIPPIES	BLOCKAGE	FLOPPIER	LOWBALLS
CLINCHES	LIPPIEST	LOCKAGES	GLOPPIER	**LOWBOYS**
FLINCHES	**LIPPING**	**LOCKERS**	SLOPPIER	PLOWBOYS
LINEATE	BLIPPING	BLOCKERS	**LOPPIES**	**LOWDOWN**
LINEATED	CLIPPING	CLOCKERS	FLOPPIES	BLOWDOWN
LINGERS	FLIPPING	**LOCKING**	LOPPIEST	SLOWDOWN
CLINGERS	SLIPPING	BLOCKING	**LOPPING**	LOWDOWNS
FLINGERS	LIPPINGS	CLOCKING	CLOPPING	**LOWERED**
SLINGERS	**LIQUATE**	FLOCKING	FLOPPING	FLOWERED
LINGIER	LIQUATED	LOCKINGS	GLOPPING	GLOWERED
BLINGIER	LIQUATES	**LOCUSTA**	PLOPPING	**LOWINGS**
CLINGIER	**LISTENS**	LOCUSTAE	SLOPPING	BLOWINGS
LINGULA	GLISTENS	LOCUSTAL	LOPPINGS	SLOWINGS
LINGULAE	**LISTERS**	**LODGING**	**LOSABLE**	**LOWLAND**
LINGULAR	BLISTERS	PLODGING	CLOSABLE	PLOWLAND
LINGULAS	GLISTERS	LODGINGS	**LOSINGS**	LOWLANDS
LINKERS	KLISTERS	**LOGGERS**	CLOSINGS	**LOWLIFE**
BLINKERS	**LITHELY**	BLOGGERS	**LOSSIER**	LOWLIFER
CLINKERS	BLITHELY	CLOGGERS	FLOSSIER	LOWLIFES
KLINKERS	**LITHEST**	FLOGGERS	GLOSSIER	**LOWNESS**
PLINKERS	BLITHEST	SLOGGERS	**LOTTERS**	SLOWNESS
SLINKERS	**LITORAL**	VLOGGERS	BLOTTERS	**LOWNING**
LINKIER	CLITORAL	**LOGGIER**	CLOTTERS	CLOWNING
PLINKIER	**LITTERS**	CLOGGIER	PLOTTERS	**LOZENGE**
SLINKIER	BLITTERS	**LOGGING**	SLOTTERS	LOZENGED
LINKING	CLITTERS	BLOGGING	**LOTTING**	LOZENGES
BLINKING	FLITTERS	CLOGGING	BLOTTING	**LUBBERS**
CLINKING	GLITTERS	FLOGGING	CLOTTING	BLUBBERS
PLINKING	SLITTERS	SLOGGING	PLOTTING	CLUBBERS
SLINKING	**LITTERY**	VLOGGING	SLOTTING	FLUBBERS
LINNING	GLITTERY	LOGGINGS	**LOUCHER**	SLUBBERS
BLINNING	**LITTLES**	**LOGICAL**	SLOUCHER	**LUCKIER**
LINTERS	LITTLEST	ALOGICAL	**LOUNDER**	CLUCKIER
SLINTERS	**LITTLIN**	**LOGROLL**	FLOUNDER	PLUCKIER
LINTIER	LITTLING	BLOGROLL	LOUNDERS	**LUCKIES**
FLINTIER	LITTLINS	LOGROLLS	**LOURIER**	LUCKIEST
GLINTIER	**LIVERED**	**LONGING**	FLOURIER	**LUCKILY**
LINTIES	SLIVERED	PLONGING	**LOURIES**	PLUCKILY
LINTIEST	**LIVEYER**	LONGINGS	LOURIEST	**LUCKING**
LINTING	LIVEYERE	**LOOBIES**	**LOURING**	CLUCKING
FLINTING	LIVEYERS	LOOBIEST	CLOURING	PLUCKING
GLINTING	**LIXIVIA**	**LOOMING**	FLOURING	**LUFFING**
LIONISE	LIXIVIAL	BLOOMING	LOURINGS	BLUFFING
LIONISED	**LOAMING**	GLOOMING	**LOUSIER**	FLUFFING
LIONISER	GLOAMING	SLOOMING	BLOUSIER	PLUFFING
LIONISES	**LOATHES**	**LOONIES**	**LOUSILY**	SLUFFING
LIONIZE	LOATHEST	LOONIEST	BLOUSILY	**LUGGERS**
LIONIZED	**LOBATED**	**LOOPERS**	**LOUSING**	PLUGGERS
LIONIZER	GLOBATED	BLOOPERS	BLOUSING	SLUGGERS
LIONIZES	**LOBBERS**	**LOOPIER**	FLOUSING	**LUGGING**
LIPLESS	CLOBBERS	GLOOPIER	**LOUTING**	GLUGGING
SLIPLESS	SLOBBERS	**LOOPING**	CLOUTING	PLUGGING
LIPPERS	**LOBBING**	BLOOPING	FLOUTING	SLUGGING
CLIPPERS	BLOBBING	GLOOPING	GLOUTING	**LUGHOLE**
FLIPPERS	FLOBBING	LOOPINGS	**LOVERED**	PLUGHOLE
SLIPPERS	**LOBULAR**	**LOOSIES**	CLOVERED	LUGHOLES
LIPPIER	GLOBULAR	FLOOSIES	**LOVINGS**	**LUMBAGO**

PLUMBAGO	FLUSHEST	MANACLED	**MATADOR**	**MELLING**
LUMBAGOS	PLUSHEST	MANACLES	MATADORA	SMELLING
LUMBERS	**LUSHIER**	**MANDATE**	MATADORE	**MELODIC**
CLUMBERS	FLUSHIER	MANDATED	MATADORS	MELODICA
PLUMBERS	PLUSHIER	MANDATES	**MATCHED**	MELODICS
SLUMBERS	SLUSHIER	**MANDIOC**	SMATCHED	**MELTERS**
LUMINES	**LUSHING**	MANDIOCA	**MATCHES**	SMELTERS
ALUMINES	BLUSHING	MANDIOCS	SMATCHES	**MELTING**
LUMMIER	FLUSHING	**MANDRIL**	**MATELOT**	SMELTING
PLUMMIER	SLUSHING	MANDRILL	MATELOTE	MELTINGS
SLUMMIER	**LUSTERS**	MANDRILS	MATELOTS	**MENAGED**
LUMPENS	BLUSTERS	**MANTEAU**	**MATTERS**	AMENAGED
PLUMPENS	CLUSTERS	MANTEAUS	SMATTERS	**MENAGES**
LUMPERS	FLUSTERS	MANTEAUX	**MATURES**	AMENAGES
CLUMPERS	**LUTINGS**	**MARABOU**	MATUREST	**MENDERS**
PLUMPERS	FLUTINGS	MARABOUS	**MAULGRE**	AMENDERS
LUMPIER	**LUTISTS**	MARABOUT	MAULGRED	EMENDERS
CLUMPIER	FLUTISTS	**MARCHES**	MAULGRES	**MENDING**
GLUMPIER	**LYINGLY**	MARCHESA	**MAUVAIS**	AMENDING
PLUMPIER	PLYINGLY	MARCHESE	MAUVAISE	EMENDING
SLUMPIER	**LYOPHIL**	MARCHESI	**MAUVEIN**	MENDINGS
LUMPILY	LYOPHILE	**MARDIES**	MAUVEINE	**MERCERS**
GLUMPILY	**LYSOGEN**	MARDIEST	MAUVEINS	AMERCERS
LUMPING	LYSOGENS	**MARINER**	**MAXILLA**	**MERGING**
CLUMPING	LYSOGENY	MARINERA	MAXILLAE	EMERGING
FLUMPING	**MACHINE**	MARINERS	MAXILLAR	MERGINGS
PLUMPING	MACHINED	**MARKING**	MAXILLAS	**MERONYM**
SLUMPING	MACHINES	**MARMOSE**	**MAZEDLY**	MERONYMS
LUMPISH	**MADRASA**	MARMOSES	AMAZEDLY	MERONYMY
CLUMPISH	MADRASAH	MARMOSET	**MEAGRES**	**MERRIES**
GLUMPISH	MADRASAS	**MARQUIS**	MEAGREST	MERRIEST
PLUMPISH	**MAFFLIN**	MARQUISE	**MEALIES**	**MERSION**
LUNCHED	MAFFLING	**MARSHAL**	MEALIEST	EMERSION
GLUNCHED	MAFFLINS	MARSHALL	**MEARING**	MERSIONS
LUNCHES	**MAGISMS**	MARSHALS	SMEARING	**MESHUGA**
CLUNCHES	IMAGISMS	**MARTENS**	**MEASURE**	MESHUGAH
GLUNCHES	**MAGNETO**	SMARTENS	MEASURED	MESHUGAS
LUNGERS	MAGNETON	**MARTING**	MEASURER	**MESQUIN**
BLUNGERS	MAGNETOS	SMARTING	MEASURES	MESQUINE
PLUNGERS	**MAHJONG**	**MASHERS**	**MEDIATE**	**MESQUIT**
LUNGING	MAHJONGG	SMASHERS	MEDIATED	MESQUITE
BLUNGING	MAHJONGS	**MASHIES**	MEDIATES	MESQUITS
PLUNGING	**MAILERS**	MASHIEST	**MEDULLA**	**MESSAGE**
LUNKERS	EMAILERS	**MASHING**	MEDULLAE	MESSAGED
BLUNKERS	**MAILING**	SMASHING	MEDULLAR	MESSAGES
CLUNKERS	EMAILING	MASHINGS	MEDULLAS	**METAMER**
FLUNKERS	MAILINGS	**MASHUPS**	**MEGAPOD**	METAMERE
PLUNKERS	**MALARIA**	SMASHUPS	MEGAPODE	METAMERS
LUNTING	MALARIAL	**MASSAGE**	MEGAPODS	**METAZOA**
BLUNTING	MALARIAN	MASSAGED	**MEGARON**	METAZOAL
LUPULIN	MALARIAS	MASSAGER	MEGARONS	METAZOAN
LUPULINE	**MALEFIC**	MASSAGES	**MEGATON**	**METHOXY**
LUPULINS	MALEFICE	**MASSING**	MEGATONS	METHOXYL
LURRIES	**MALLING**	AMASSING	**MEGILLA**	**METICAL**
FLURRIES	SMALLING	**MASTABA**	MEGILLAH	EMETICAL
SLURRIES	MALLINGS	MASTABAH	MEGILLAS	METICALS
LUSHERS	**MAMILLA**	MASTABAS	**MEIOSES**	**METONYM**
BLUSHERS	MAMILLAE	**MASTICH**	AMEIOSES	METONYMS
FLUSHERS	MAMILLAR	MASTICHE	**MEIOSIS**	METONYMY
LUSHEST	**MANACLE**	MASTICHS	AMEIOSIS	**MEZQUIT**

MEZQUITE	MINUTEST	**MISPAGE**	SMOILING	**MORPHIN**
MEZQUITS	**MINUTIA**	MISPAGED	**MOLDERS**	MORPHINE
MEZUZOT	MINUTIAE	MISPAGES	SMOLDERS	MORPHING
MEZUZOTH	MINUTIAL	**MISPLAN**	**MOLLUSC**	MORPHINS
MICATED	MINUTIAL	MISPLANS	MOLLUSCA	**MORTICE**
EMICATED	**MIRKIER**	MISPLANT	MOLLUSCS	MORTICED
MICATES	SMIRKIER	MISRATE	**MONARCH**	MORTICER
EMICATES	**MIRKILY**	MISRATED	MONARCHS	MORTICES
MICELLA	SMIRKILY	MISRATES	MONARCHY	**MORTISE**
MICELLAE	**MISCITE**	**MISRULE**	**MONDAIN**	AMORTISE
MICELLAR	MISCITED	MISRULED	MONDAINE	MORTISED
MICELLAS	MISCITES	MISRULES	MONDAINS	MORTISER
MICKLES	**MISCODE**	**MISSIES**	**MONILIA**	MORTISES
MICKLEST	MISCODED	MISSIEST	MONILIAL	**MOSSIES**
MICRONS	MISCODES	**MISSILE**	MONILIAS	MOSSIEST
OMICRONS	**MISDATE**	EMISSILE	**MONITOR**	**MOTHERS**
MICTION	MISDATED	MISSILES	MONITORS	SMOTHERS
EMICTION	MISDATES	**MISSING**	MONITORY	**MOTHERY**
MICTIONS	**MISDEAL**	AMISSING	**MONOCLE**	SMOTHERY
MIDDIES	MISDEALS	**MISSION**	MONOCLED	**MOTIONS**
SMIDDIES	MISDEALT	EMISSION	MONOCLES	AMOTIONS
MIDGIES	**MISDRAW**	OMISSION	**MONOLOG**	EMOTIONS
MIDGIEST	MISDRAWN	MISSIONS	MONOLOGS	**MOTTIES**
MIDLIFE	MISDRAWS	**MISSIVE**	MONOLOGY	MOTTIEST
MIDLIFER	**MISFARE**	EMISSIVE	**MONOPOD**	**MOUCHED**
MIDMOST	MISFARED	OMISSIVE	MONOPODE	SMOUCHED
AMIDMOST	MISFARES	MISSIVES	MONOPODS	**MOUCHES**
MIDMOSTS	**MISFILE**	**MISTAKE**	MONOPODY	SMOUCHES
MIDSHIP	MISFILED	MISTAKEN	**MONSTER**	**MOULDER**
AMIDSHIP	MISFILES	MISTAKER	MONSTERA	SMOULDER
MIDSHIPS	**MISFIRE**	MISTAKES	MONSTERS	MOULDERS
MIDSIZE	MISFIRED	**MISTIME**	**MONTAGE**	**MOUNTED**
MIDSIZED	MISFIRES	MISTIMED	MONTAGED	AMOUNTED
MIDWIFE	**MISGIVE**	MISTIMES	MONTAGES	**MOUSERS**
MIDWIFED	MISGIVEN	**MISTUNE**	**MONTANT**	SMOUSERS
MIDWIFES	MISGIVES	MISTUNED	MONTANTO	**MOUSIES**
MIDWIVE	**MISGROW**	MISTUNES	MONTANTS	MOUSIEST
MIDWIVED	MISGROWN	**MISTYPE**	**MOOCHED**	**MOUSING**
MIDWIVES	MISGROWS	MISTYPED	SMOOCHED	SMOUSING
MIGRANT	**MISHEAR**	MISTYPES	**MOOCHER**	MOUSINGS
EMIGRANT	MISHEARD	**MISWRIT**	SMOOCHER	**MOWBURN**
MIGRANTS	MISHEARS	MISWRITE	MOOCHERS	MOWBURNS
MIGRATE	**MISKNOW**	**MISYOKE**	**MOOCHES**	MOWBURNT
EMIGRATE	MISKNOWN	MISYOKED	SMOOCHES	**MOYLING**
MIGRATED	MISKNOWS	MISYOKES	**MOODIES**	SMOYLING
MIGRATES	**MISLIKE**	**MITHERS**	MOODIEST	**MRIDANG**
MIKRONS	MISLIKED	SMITHERS	**MOONIES**	MRIDANGA
OMIKRONS	MISLIKER	**MITOSES**	MOONIEST	MRIDANGS
MILITAR	MISLIKES	AMITOSES	**MOORING**	**MUDDIES**
MILITARY	**MISLIVE**	**MITOSIS**	SMOORING	MUDDIEST
MILLINE	MISLIVED	AMITOSIS	MOORINGS	**MUDGERS**
MILLINER	MISLIVES	**MITOTIC**	**MOOTING**	SMUDGERS
MILLINES	**MISMATE**	AMITOTIC	SMOOTING	**MUDGING**
MINIATE	MISMATED	**MOCKING**	MOOTINGS	SMUDGING
MINIATED	MISMATES	SMOCKING	**MOOVING**	**MUGGING**
MINIATES	**MISMOVE**	MOCKINGS	AMOOVING	SMUGGING
MINICAM	MISMOVED	**MODERNE**	**MORALLY**	MUGGINGS
MINICAMP	MISMOVES	MODERNER	AMORALLY	**MULLOCK**
MINICAMS	**MISNAME**	MODERNES	**MORCEAU**	MULLOCKS
MINUTES	MISNAMED	**MOILING**	MORCEAUX	MULLOCKY

MULTURE	SNAPPERS	NEGLIGES	SNIPPILY	**NOUVEAU**
MULTURED	**NAPPIER**	**NERVATE**	**NIPPING**	NOUVEAUX
MULTURER	SNAPPIER	ENERVATE	SNIPPING	**NOVELLA**
MULTURES	**NAPPIES**	**NERVING**	**NITPICK**	NOVELLAE
MUNDANE	NAPPIEST	ENERVING	NITPICKS	NOVELLAS
MUNDANER	**NAPPING**	NERVINGS	NITPICKY	**NUBBIER**
MUNGING	KNAPPING	**NETTIES**	**NITRATE**	KNUBBIER
EMUNGING	SNAPPING	NETTIEST	NITRATED	SNUBBIER
MURIATE	**NARCEIN**	**NEURISM**	NITRATES	**NUBBING**
MURIATED	NARCEINE	ANEURISM	**NITRIDE**	SNUBBING
MURIATES	NARCEINS	NEURISMS	NITRIDED	**NUBBLED**
MUSETTE	**NARGILE**	**NEURULA**	NITRIDES	KNUBBLED
AMUSETTE	NARGILEH	NEURULAE	**NOBBIER**	**NUBBLES**
MUSETTES	NARGILES	NEURULAR	KNOBBIER	KNUBBLES
MUSHING	**NARKIER**	NEURULAS	SNOBBIER	**NUDGING**
SMUSHING	SNARKIER	**NEWCOME**	**NOBBILY**	SNUDGING
MUSICAL	**NARRATE**	NEWCOMER	SNOBBILY	**NURAGHI**
MUSICALE	NARRATED	**NEWSIES**	**NOBBLED**	NURAGHIC
MUSICALS	NARRATER	NEWSIEST	KNOBBLED	**NURLING**
MUSKIES	NARRATES	**NIBBING**	**NOBBLES**	KNURLING
MUSKIEST	**NARWHAL**	SNIBBING	KNOBBLES	**NURTURE**
MUSTARD	NARWHALE	**NICKERS**	**NOCKING**	NURTURED
MUSTARDS	NARWHALS	KNICKERS	KNOCKING	NURTURER
MUSTARDY	**NASTIES**	SNICKERS	**NOCTURN**	NURTURES
MUTCHED	NASTIEST	**NICKING**	NOCTURNE	**NUZZLED**
SMUTCHED	**NATCHES**	SNICKING	NOCTURNS	SNUZZLED
MUTCHES	SNATCHES	**NICOTIN**	**NODALLY**	**NUZZLES**
SMUTCHES	**NATIONS**	NICOTINE	ANODALLY	SNUZZLES
MYCELIA	ENATIONS	NICOTINS	**NODDIES**	**NYMPHAE**
MYCELIAL	**NATTIER**	**NICTATE**	NODDIEST	NYMPHAEA
MYCELIAN	GNATTIER	NICTATED	**NODDING**	**OARFISH**
MYLODON	**NAVARCH**	NICTATES	SNODDING	BOARFISH
MYLODONS	NAVARCHS	**NIFFERS**	**NODDINGS**	**OARIEST**
MYLODONT	NAVARCHY	SNIFFERS	**NOGGING**	HOARIEST
MYSPACE	**NEAPING**	**NIFFIER**	SNOGGING	ROARIEST
MYSPACED	SNEAPING	SNIFFIER	NOGGINGS	**OATIEST**
MYSPACES	**NEARING**	**NIFFING**	**NOINTED**	GOATIEST
MYTHISE	ANEARING	SNIFFING	ANOINTED	**OATLIKE**
MYTHISED	**NEBBING**	**NIFTIER**	**NOINTER**	BOATLIKE
MYTHISES	SNEBBING	SNIFTIER	ANOINTER	GOATLIKE
MYTHIZE	**NEBBISH**	**NIFTIES**	NOINTERS	MOATLIKE
MYTHIZED	NEBBISHE	NIFTIEST	**NOMARCH**	**OBECHES**
MYTHIZES	NEBBISHY	**NIGGERS**	NOMARCHS	BOBECHES
NAGGIER	**NECKING**	SNIGGERS	NOMARCHY	**OBELIAS**
KNAGGIER	SNECKING	**NIGGLED**	**NONUPLE**	LOBELIAS
SNAGGIER	**NECKINGS**	SNIGGLED	NONUPLES	**OBELISE**
NAGGING	**NECROSE**	**NIGGLER**	NONUPLET	OBELISED
SNAGGING	NECROSED	SNIGGLER	**NOOKIES**	OBELISES
NAGGINGS	NECROSES	NIGGLERS	NOOKIEST	**OBELIZE**
NAILERY	**NEDDIES**	**NIGGLES**	**NORTHER**	OBELIZED
SNAILERY	NEDDIEST	SNIGGLES	NORTHERN	OBELIZES
NAILING	**NEEDLES**	**NIGHTED**	NORTHERS	**OBLIQUE**
SNAILING	NEEDLESS	KNIGHTED	**NOTITIA**	OBLIQUED
NAILINGS	**NEEZING**	**NIGHTLY**	NOTITIAE	OBLIQUER
NANISMS	SNEEZING	KNIGHTLY	NOTITIAS	OBLIQUES
ONANISMS	**NEGATOR**	**NIPPERS**	**NOUMENA**	**OBSCENE**
NAPLESS	NEGATORS	SNIPPERS	NOUMENAL	OBSCENER
SNAPLESS	NEGATORY	**NIPPIER**	**NOURSLE**	**OBSCURE**
NAPPERS	**NEGLIGE**	SNIPPIER	NOURSLED	OBSCURED
KNAPPERS	NEGLIGEE	**NIPPILY**	NOURSLES	OBSCURER

OBSCURES	GOLDENED	ZOOSPERM	PORTOLAN	OUTDARES
OBSERVE	**OLDNESS**	OOSPERMS	ORTOLANS	**OUTDATE**
OBSERVED	BOLDNESS	**OOSPORE**	**OSMOSES**	OUTDATED
OBSERVER	COLDNESS	ZOOSPORE	COSMOSES	OUTDATES
OBSERVES	**OLOGIES**	OOSPORES	KOSMOSES	**OUTDRAW**
OBTRUDE	OOLOGIES	**OOTHECA**	**OSTLERS**	OUTDRAWN
OBTRUDED	**OLOGIST**	OOTHECAE	HOSTLERS	OUTDRAWS
OBTRUDER	OOLOGIST	OOTHECAL	JOSTLERS	**OUTDURE**
OBTRUDES	OLOGISTS	**OOZIEST**	**OSTMARK**	OUTDURED
OBVIATE	**OLOROSO**	BOOZIEST	POSTMARK	OUTDURES
OBVIATED	DOLOROSO	WOOZIEST	OSTMARKS	**OUTEDGE**
OBVIATES	OLOROSOS	**OPAQUES**	**OTARIES**	OUTEDGES
OCCIPUT	**OMENTUM**	OPAQUEST	NOTARIES	**OUTFACE**
OCCIPUTS	LOMENTUM	**OPERAND**	ROTARIES	OUTFACED
OCCLUDE	MOMENTUM	OPERANDS	VOTARIES	OUTFACES
OCCLUDED	TOMENTUM	**OPERATE**	**OTTERED**	**OUTFIRE**
OCCLUDER	OMENTUMS	OPERATED	COTTERED	OUTFIRED
OCCLUDES	**OMNIFIC**	OPERATES	HOTTERED	OUTFIRES
OCHERED	SOMNIFIC	**OPHIURA**	POTTERED	**OUTFLOW**
TOCHERED	**OMPHALI**	OPHIURAN	TOTTERED	OUTFLOWN
OCREATE	OMPHALIC	OPHIURAS	**OUCHING**	OUTFLOWS
COCREATE	**ONCOGEN**	**ORACLES**	COUCHING	**OUTGAZE**
OCTOPUS	ONCOGENE	CORACLES	DOUCHING	OUTGAZED
OCTOPUSH	ONCOGENS	**ORALISM**	GOUCHING	OUTGAZES
OCTUPLE	**ONDINGS**	MORALISM	MOUCHING	**OUTGIVE**
OCTUPLED	BONDINGS	ORALISMS	POUCHING	OUTGIVEN
OCTUPLES	**ONENESS**	**ORALIST**	TOUCHING	OUTGIVES
OCTUPLET	DONENESS	MORALIST	VOUCHING	**OUTGNAW**
OCTUPLEX	GONENESS	ORALISTS	**OULDEST**	OUTGNAWN
OCULATE	LONENESS	**ORALITY**	COULDEST	OUTGNAWS
LOCULATE	**ONETIME**	MORALITY	WOULDEST	**OUTGROW**
OCULATED	ZONETIME	**ORANGER**	**OURALIS**	OUTGROWN
ODALISK	**ONEYERS**	ORANGERY	WOURALIS	OUTGROWS
ODALISKS	MONEYERS	**ORANGES**	**OURIEST**	**OUTHEAR**
ODORISE	**OOFIEST**	ORANGEST	LOURIEST	OUTHEARD
ODORISED	BOOFIEST	**ORATING**	**OURSELF**	OUTHEARS
ODORISES	GOOFIEST	BORATING	YOURSELF	**OUTHIRE**
ODORIZE	POOFIEST	**ORATORY**	**OUSTERS**	OUTHIRED
ODORIZED	ROOFIEST	MORATORY	JOUSTERS	OUTHIRES
ODORIZES	WOOFIEST	**ORDERED**	ROUSTERS	**OUTHYRE**
OFFERED	**OOGONIA**	BORDERED	**OUSTING**	OUTHYRED
COFFERED	OOGONIAL	**ORDERER**	JOUSTING	OUTHYRES
GOFFERED	**OOLITES**	BORDERER	MOUSTING	**OUTINGS**
OFFSIDE	ZOOLITES	ORDERERS	ROUSTING	HOUTINGS
OFFSIDER	**OOLITHS**	**ORDINAR**	**OUTBAKE**	POUTINGS
OFFSIDES	ZOOLITHS	ORDINARS	OUTBAKED	ROUTINGS
OFTENER	**OOLITIC**	ORDINARY	OUTBAKES	**OUTLEAP**
SOFTENER	ZOOLITIC	**ORDINES**	**OUTBURN**	OUTLEAPS
OILIEST	**OOLOGIC**	SORDINES	OUTBURNS	OUTLEAPT
NOILIEST	ZOOLOGIC	**ORDURES**	OUTBURNT	**OUTLINE**
ROILIEST	**OOPHYTE**	BORDURES	**OUTCAST**	OUTLINED
SOILIEST	ZOOPHYTE	**OROLOGY**	OUTCASTE	OUTLINER
OINKING	OOPHYTES	HOROLOGY	OUTCASTS	OUTLINES
BOINKING	**OORALIS**	**ORPINES**	**OUTCHID**	**OUTLIVE**
OINTING	WOORALIS	FORPINES	OUTCHIDE	OUTLIVED
JOINTING	**OORIEST**	**ORRICES**	**OUTCROW**	OUTLIVER
NOINTING	MOORIEST	MORRICES	OUTCROWD	OUTLIVES
POINTING	**OOSIEST**	**ORRISES**	OUTCROWS	**OUTLOVE**
OLDENED	GOOSIEST	MORRISES	**OUTDARE**	OUTLOVED
BOLDENED	**OOSPERM**	**ORTOLAN**	OUTDARED	OUTLOVES

OUTMODE	OUTWORKS	COVERTLY	**PAINING**	SPARKIES
OUTMODED	**OUTWRIT**	**OVERUSE**	SPAINING	PARKIEST
OUTMODES	OUTWRITE	OVERUSED	**PALLIES**	**PARKING**
OUTMOVE	**OUVRIER**	OVERUSES	PALLIEST	SPARKING
OUTMOVED	OUVRIERE	**OVULATE**	**PALLING**	PARKINGS
OUTMOVES	OUVRIERS	OVULATED	SPALLING	**PARKISH**
OUTNAME	**OVARIES**	OVULATES	**PALMATE**	SPARKISH
OUTNAMED	COVARIES	**OWLIEST**	PALMATED	**PARLING**
OUTNAMES	**OVATING**	DOWLIEST	**PALMIES**	SPARLING
OUTPACE	NOVATING	JOWLIEST	PALMIEST	**PARONYM**
OUTPACED	**OVATION**	LOWLIEST	**PALPATE**	PARONYMS
OUTPACES	NOVATION	**OWLLIKE**	PALPATED	PARONYMY
OUTRACE	OVATIONS	BOWLLIKE	PALPATES	**PARRIER**
OUTRACED	**OVENING**	**OXALATE**	**PALSIES**	SPARRIER
OUTRACES	DOVENING	OXALATED	PALSIEST	PARRIERS
OUTRAGE	**OVERAGE**	OXALATES	**PANACEA**	**PARRING**
OUTRAGED	COVERAGE	**OXIDATE**	PANACEAN	SPARRING
OUTRAGES	OVERAGED	OXIDATED	PANACEAS	**PARTAKE**
OUTRANG	OVERAGES	OXIDATES	**PANCAKE**	PARTAKEN
OUTRANGE	**OVERALL**	**OXIDISE**	PANCAKED	PARTAKER
OUTRATE	COVERALL	OXIDISED	PANCAKES	PARTAKES
OUTRATED	OVERALLS	OXIDISER	**PANGING**	**PARTANS**
OUTRATES	**OVERAWE**	OXIDISES	SPANGING	SPARTANS
OUTRAVE	OVERAWED	**OXIDIZE**	**PANICLE**	**PARVENU**
OUTRAVED	OVERAWES	OXIDIZED	PANICLED	PARVENUE
OUTRAVES	**OVERBID**	OXIDIZER	PANICLES	PARVENUS
OUTRIDE	OVERBIDS	OXIDIZES	**PANNERS**	**PASSAGE**
OUTRIDER	**OVERDYE**	**OXTAILS**	SPANNERS	PASSAGED
OUTRIDES	OVERDYED	FOXTAILS	**PANNING**	PASSAGER
OUTRING	OVERDYER	**OXYGENS**	SPANNING	PASSAGES
FOUTRING	OVERDYES	LOXYGENS	PANNINGS	**PASSMEN**
OUTRINGS	**OVEREYE**	**OXYPHIL**	**PANTILE**	PASSMENT
OUTROPE	OVEREYED	OXYPHILE	PANTILED	**PASTIES**
OUTROPER	OVEREYES	OXYPHILS	PANTILES	PASTIEST
OUTROPES	**OVERFLY**	**OYSTERS**	**PAPILLA**	**PASTINA**
OUTSIDE	HOVERFLY	ROYSTERS	PAPILLAE	PASTINAS
OUTSIDER	**OVERING**	**OZONATE**	PAPILLAR	**PASTURE**
OUTSIDES	COVERING	OZONATED	PAPILLAR	PASTURED
OUTSIZE	DOVERING	OZONATES	**PAPPIES**	PASTURER
OUTSIZED	HOVERING	**OZONISE**	PAPPIEST	PASTURES
OUTSIZES	**OVERLET**	OZONISED	**PARABLE**	**PATAGIA**
OUTTAKE	COVERLET	OZONISER	SPARABLE	PATAGIAL
OUTTAKEN	OVERLETS	OZONISES	PARABLED	**PATCHER**
OUTTAKES	**OVERLIE**	**OZONIZE**	PARABLES	PATCHERS
OUTVOTE	OVERLIER	OZONIZED	**PARADOX**	PATCHERY
OUTVOTED	OVERLIES	OZONIZER	PARADOXY	**PATELLA**
OUTVOTER	**OVERRAN**	OZONIZES	**PARAZOA**	PATELLAE
OUTVOTES	OVERRANK	**PACEMAN**	PARAZOAN	PATELLAR
OUTWEAR	**OVERSEE**	SPACEMAN	**PARBAKE**	PATELLAS
OUTWEARS	OVERSEED	**PACEMEN**	PARBAKED	**PATINAE**
OUTWEARY	OVERSEEN	SPACEMEN	PARBAKES	PATINAED
OUTWEED	OVERSEER	**PACIEST**	**PARCHES**	**PATTERS**
GOUTWEED	OVERSEES	SPACIEST	PARCHESI	SPATTERS
OUTWEEDS	**OVERSEW**	**PACKAGE**	**PARGING**	**PATTING**
OUTWILE	OVERSEWN	PACKAGED	SPARGING	SPATTING
OUTWILED	OVERSEWS	PACKAGER	PARGINGS	**PAWNERS**
OUTWILES	**OVERSOW**	PACKAGES	**PARKERS**	SPAWNERS
OUTWIND	OVERSOWN	**PAENULA**	SPARKERS	**PAWNING**
OUTWINDS	OVERSOWS	PAENULAE	**PARKIER**	SPAWNING
OUTWORK	**OVERTLY**	PAENULAS	SPARKIER	**PEACOCK**

PEACOCKS	PENANCED	PERMUTES	**PICKAXE**	PIPETTES
PEACOCKY	PENANCES	**PEROXID**	PICKAXED	**PIRATED**
PEAKING	**PENDING**	PEROXIDE	PICKAXES	SPIRATED
SPEAKING	SPENDING	PEROXIDS	**PICOLIN**	**PISCINA**
PEANING	UPENDING	**PERSICO**	PICOLINE	PISCINAE
SPEANING	**PENNATE**	PERSICOS	PICOLINS	PISCINAL
PEARLIN	PENNATED	PERSICOT	**PICRATE**	PISCINAS
PEARLING	**PENSION**	**PERSING**	PICRATED	**PISTOLE**
PEARLINS	PENSIONE	SPERSING	PICRATES	PISTOLED
PEASANT	PENSIONS	**PERSONA**	**PICTURE**	PISTOLES
PEASANTS	**PENTICE**	PERSONAE	PICTURED	PISTOLET
PEASANTY	PENTICED	PERSONAL	PICTURES	**PITCHER**
PECKIER	PENTICES	PERSONAS	**PIGGIES**	SPITCHER
SPECKIER	**PENTISE**	**PERTAKE**	PIGGIEST	PITCHERS
PECKING	PENTISED	PERTAKEN	**PIGHTED**	**PITTERS**
SPECKING	PENTISES	PERTAKES	SPIGHTED	SPITTERS
PECKINGS	**PEPTISE**	**PERTUSE**	**PIGNOLI**	**PITTING**
PECTATE	PEPTISED	PERTUSED	PIGNOLIA	SPITTING
SPECTATE	PEPTISER	**PERVADE**	PIGNOLIS	PITTINGS
PECTATES	PEPTISES	PERVADED	**PIKELET**	**PIZZAZZ**
PECTISE	**PEPTIZE**	PERVADER	SPIKELET	PIZZAZZY
PECTISED	PEPTIZED	PERVADES	PIKELETS	**PLACATE**
PECTISES	PEPTIZER	**PESSIMA**	**PILEATE**	PLACATED
PECTIZE	PEPTIZES	PESSIMAL	PILEATED	PLACATER
PECTIZED	**PERCHER**	**PETIOLE**	**PILINGS**	PLACATES
PECTIZES	PERCHERS	PETIOLED	SPILINGS	**PLACCAT**
PECULIA	PERCHERY	PETIOLES	**PILLAGE**	PLACCATE
PECULIAR	**PERDURE**	**PETTIES**	SPILLAGE	PLACCATS
PEDAGOG	PERDURED	PETTIEST	PILLAGED	**PLANCHE**
PEDAGOGS	PERDURES	**PETTING**	PILLAGER	PLANCHED
PEDAGOGY	**PERFECT**	SPETTING	PILLAGES	PLANCHES
PEDDLER	PERFECTA	PETTINGS	**PILLING**	PLANCHET
PEDDLERS	PERFECTI	**PFENNIG**	SPILLING	**PLANULA**
PEDDLERY	PERFECTO	PFENNIGE	PILLINGS	PLANULAE
PEDICEL	PERFECTS	PFENNIGS	**PIMENTO**	PLANULAR
PEDICELS	**PERFUME**	**PHANTOM**	PIMENTON	**PLASHED**
PEDICLE	PERFUMED	PHANTOMS	PIMENTOS	SPLASHED
PEDICLED	PERFUMER	PHANTOMY	**PINIEST**	**PLASHER**
PEDICLES	PERFUMES	**PHILTRE**	SPINIEST	SPLASHER
PEEKABO	**PERFUSE**	PHILTRED	**PINIONS**	PLASHERS
PEEKABOO	PERFUSED	PHILTRES	OPINIONS	**PLASHES**
PEEKABOS	PERFUSES	**PHONATE**	**PINKIES**	SPLASHES
PEELERS	**PERIDIA**	PHONATED	PINKIEST	**PLASTER**
SPEELERS	PERIDIAL	PHONATES	**PINNATE**	PLASTERS
PEELING	**PERIDOT**	**PHONICS**	PINNATED	PLASTERY
SPEELING	PERIDOTE	APHONICS	**PINNERS**	**PLASTIC**
PEELINGS	PERIDOTS	**PHONIES**	SPINNERS	APLASTIC
PEERIES	**PERIGON**	APHONIES	**PINNETS**	PLASTICS
PEERIEST	PERIGONE	PHONIEST	SPINNETS	**PLATEAU**
PEERING	PERIGONS	**PHORATE**	**PINNIES**	PLATEAUS
SPEERING	**PERINEA**	EPHORATE	SPINNIES	PLATEAUX
PEISHWA	PERINEAL	PHORATES	**PINNING**	**PLATIES**
PEISHWAH	**PERIQUE**	**PIANIST**	SPINNING	PLATIEST
PEISHWAS	PERIQUES	PIANISTE	PINNINGS	**PLATTED**
PELORIA	**PERJURE**	PIANISTS	**PINNULA**	SPLATTED
PELORIAN	PERJURED	**PIARIST**	PINNULAE	**PLATTER**
PELORIAS	PERJURER	APIARIST	PINNULAR	SPLATTER
PELTERS	PERJURES	PIARISTS	PINNULAS	PLATTERS
SPELTERS	**PERMUTE**	**PICENES**	**PIPETTE**	**PLAUDIT**
PENANCE	PERMUTED	EPICENES	PIPETTED	PLAUDITE

PLAUDITS	POLEAXES	SPORTIER	PRANKLES	PRELUDES
PLAYING	**POLITIC**	PORTIERE	**PRATING**	**PRELUDI**
SPLAYING	POLITICK	**PORTING**	UPRATING	PRELUDIO
UPLAYING	POLITICO	SPORTING	PRATINGS	PREMIER
PLICATE	POLITICS	**POSSUMS**	**PRATTLE**	PREMIERE
PLICATED	**POLLAXE**	OPOSSUMS	SPRATTLE	PREMIERS
PLICATES	POLLAXED	**POSTILS**	PRATTLED	**PREMISE**
PLIGHTS	POLLAXES	APOSTILS	PRATTLER	PREMISED
UPLIGHTS	**POLLUTE**	**POSTURE**	PRATTLES	PREMISES
PLIMSOL	POLLUTED	POSTURED	**PRAUNCE**	**PREMOVE**
PLIMSOLE	POLLUTER	POSTURER	PRAUNCED	PREMOVED
PLIMSOLL	POLLUTES	POSTURES	PRAUNCES	PREMOVES
PLIMSOLS	**POLYGAM**	**POTHOLE**	**PRAYERS**	**PREPARE**
PLINKED	POLYGAMS	POTHOLED	SPRAYERS	PREPARED
UPLINKED	POLYGAMY	POTHOLER	**PRAYING**	PREPARER
PLODGED	**POLYGON**	POTHOLES	SPRAYING	PREPARES
SPLODGED	POLYGONS	**POTLACH**	PRAYINGS	**PREPAVE**
PLODGES	POLYGONY	POTLACHE	**PREASSE**	PREPAVED
SPLODGES	**POLYMER**	**POTTERS**	PREASSED	PREPAVES
PLOOKIE	POLYMERS	SPOTTERS	PREASSES	**PREPLAN**
PLOOKIER	POLYMERY	**POTTIER**	**PREBAKE**	PREPLANS
PLOTTIE	**POLYPOD**	SPOTTIER	PREBAKED	PREPLANT
PLOTTIER	POLYPODS	**POTTIES**	PREBAKES	**PREPONE**
PLOTTIES	POLYPODY	SPOTTIES	**PRECAVA**	PREPONED
PLOUKIE	**POLYZOA**	POTTIEST	PRECAVAE	PREPONES
PLOUKIER	POLYZOAN	**POTTING**	PRECAVAL	**PREPOSE**
PLUMAGE	**POMMELE**	SPOTTING	**PRECEDE**	PREPOSED
PLUMAGED	POMMELED	**POULARD**	PRECEDED	PREPOSES
PLUMAGES	**PONCEAU**	POULARDE	PRECEDES	**PREPPIE**
PLUMBER	PONCEAUS	POULARDS	**PRECISE**	PREPPIER
PLUMBERS	PONCEAUX	**POURSUE**	PRECISED	PREPPIES
PLUMBERY	**PONGIER**	POURSUED	PRECISER	**PREPUCE**
PLUMPIE	SPONGIER	POURSUES	PRECISES	PREPUCES
PLUMPIER	**PONGING**	**POUTERS**	**PRECODE**	**PREPUPA**
PLUMULA	SPONGING	SPOUTERS	PRECODED	PREPUPAE
PLUMULAE	**PONTOON**	**POUTIER**	PRECODES	PREPUPAL
PLUMULAR	SPONTOON	SPOUTIER	**PRECURE**	PREPUPAS
PLUSHES	PONTOONS	**POUTING**	PRECURED	**PRESAGE**
PLUSHEST	**POOFIER**	SPOUTING	PRECURES	PRESAGED
POCKIES	SPOOFIER	POUTINGS	**PREDATE**	PRESAGER
POCKIEST	**POOKING**	**PRACTIC**	PREDATED	PRESAGES
PODAGRA	SPOOKING	APRACTIC	PREDATES	**PRESHOW**
PODAGRAL	**POOLERS**	PRACTICE	**PREEING**	PRESHOWN
PODAGRAS	SPOOLERS	PRACTICK	SPREEING	PRESHOWS
PODDIER	**POOLING**	PRACTICS	**PREFACE**	**PRESIDE**
SPODDIER	SPOOLING	**PRAIRIE**	PREFACED	PRESIDED
PODDIES	**POPPIES**	PRAIRIED	PREFACER	PRESIDER
PODDIEST	POPPIEST	PRAIRIES	PREFACES	PRESIDES
PODIUMS	**PORKIES**	**PRAISED**	**PREFADE**	**PRESUME**
SPODIUMS	PORKIEST	UPRAISED	PREFADED	PRESUMED
POETISE	**PORPESS**	**PRAISER**	PREFADES	PRESUMER
POETISED	PORPESSE	UPRAISER	**PREFILE**	PRESUMES
POETISER	**PORTAGE**	PRAISERS	PREFILED	**PRETAPE**
POETISES	PORTAGED	**PRAISES**	PREFILES	PRETAPED
POETIZE	PORTAGES	UPRAISES	**PREFIRE**	PRETAPES
POETIZED	**PORTERS**	**PRANCKE**	PREFIRED	**PRETYPE**
POETIZER	SPORTERS	PRANCKED	PREFIRES	PRETYPED
POETIZES	**PORTESS**	PRANCKES	**PRELUDE**	PRETYPES
POLEAXE	PORTESSE	**PRANKLE**	PRELUDED	**PREVENE**
POLEAXED	**PORTIER**	PRANKLED	PRELUDER	PREVENED

PREVENES	PROLONGE	**PSALTER**	APYRETIC	**QUIPPED**
PREVISE	PROLONGS	PSALTERS	**PYREXIA**	EQUIPPED
PREVISED	**PROMISE**	PSALTERY	APYREXIA	**QUIPPER**
PREVISES	PROMISED	**PTERYLA**	PYREXIAL	EQUIPPER
PREWIRE	PROMISEE	PTERYLAE	PYREXIAS	QUIPPERS
PREWIRED	PROMISER	**PTOMAIN**	**QUACKER**	**QUIRING**
PREWIRES	PROMISES	PTOMAINE	QUACKERS	SQUIRING
PRICKLE	**PROMOTE**	PTOMAINS	QUACKERY	**QUIRTED**
PRICKLED	PROMOTED	**PUDDERS**	**QUACKLE**	SQUIRTED
PRICKLES	PROMOTER	SPUDDERS	QUACKLED	**QUIZZER**
PRIGGED	PROMOTES	**PUDDING**	QUACKLES	QUIZZERS
SPRIGGED	**PRONATE**	SPUDDING	**QUADDED**	QUIZZERY
PRIGGER	PRONATED	PUDDINGS	SQUADDED	**QUIZZES**
SPRIGGER	PRONATES	PUDDINGY	**QUADRAT**	SQUIZZES
PRIGGERS	**PRONOTA**	**PUDDLES**	QUADRATE	**QUOITER**
PRIGGERY	PRONOTAL	SPUDDLES	QUADRATS	QUOITERS
PRIMSIE	**PROPAGE**	**PUDENDA**	**QUAILED**	**RABATTE**
PRIMSIER	PROPAGED	PUDENDAL	SQUAILED	RABATTED
PRINTED	PROPAGES	**PUGGIES**	**QUALITY**	RABATTES
SPRINTED	**PROPALE**	SPUGGIES	EQUALITY	**RABBETS**
PRINTER	PROPALED	PUGGIEST	**QUAREST**	DRABBETS
SPRINTER	PROPALES	**PULSATE**	SQUAREST	**RABBITO**
PRINTERS	**PROPINE**	PULSATED	**QUARTER**	RABBITOH
PRINTERY	PROPINED	PULSATES	QUARTERN	RABBITOS
PRISERS	PROPINES	**PUMPKIN**	QUARTERS	**RABBLED**
UPRISERS	**PROPONE**	PUMPKING	**QUARTET**	BRABBLED
PRISING	PROPONED	PUMPKINS	QUARTETS	DRABBLED
UPRISING	PROPONES	**PUNALUA**	QUARTETT	GRABBLED
PRIVATE	**PROPOSE**	PUNALUAN	**QUASHED**	**RABBLER**
PRIVATER	PROPOSED	PUNALUAS	SQUASHED	BRABBLER
PRIVATES	PROPOSER	**PUNKIER**	**QUASHER**	DRABBLER
PRIVIES	PROPOSES	SPUNKIER	SQUASHER	GRABBLER
PRIVIEST	**PRORATE**	**PUNKIES**	QUASHERS	RABBLERS
PROBATE	PRORATED	SPUNKIES	**QUASHES**	**RABBLES**
PROBATED	PRORATES	PUNKIEST	SQUASHES	BRABBLES
PROBATES	**PROSOMA**	**PUPARIA**	**QUEENIE**	DRABBLES
PROCURE	PROSOMAL	PUPARIAL	QUEENIER	GRABBLES
PROCURED	PROSOMAS	**PUPILAR**	QUEENIES	PRABBLES
PROCURER	**PROTEAS**	PUPILARY	**QUIBBLE**	**RACHETS**
PROCURES	PROTEASE	**PURLING**	QUIBBLED	BRACHETS
PRODUCE	**PROTEGE**	SPURLING	QUIBBLER	**RACHIAL**
PRODUCED	PROTEGEE	PURLINGS	QUIBBLES	BRACHIAL
PRODUCER	PROTEGES	**PURPLES**	**QUIDDIT**	**RACINGS**
PRODUCES	**PROTEID**	PURPLEST	QUIDDITS	BRACINGS
PROFANE	PROTEIDE	**PURPOSE**	QUIDDITY	TRACINGS
PROFANED	PROTEIDS	PURPOSED	**QUIDDLE**	**RACKERS**
PROFANER	**PROVIDE**	PURPOSES	QUIDDLED	CRACKERS
PROFANES	PROVIDED	**PURRING**	QUIDDLER	TRACKERS
PROFILE	PROVIDER	SPURRING	QUIDDLES	**RACKETS**
PROFILED	PROVIDES	PURRINGS	**QUIESCE**	BRACKETS
PROFILER	**PROVINE**	**PUSSIES**	QUIESCED	CRACKETS
PROFILES	PROVINED	PUSSIEST	QUIESCES	**RACKFUL**
PROFUSE	PROVINES	**PUSTULE**	**QUILLAI**	WRACKFUL
PROFUSER	**PROVISO**	PUSTULED	QUILLAIA	RACKFULS
PROLATE	PROVISOR	PUSTULES	QUILLAIS	**RACKING**
PROLATED	PROVISOS	**PUTTERS**	**QUINCHE**	CRACKING
PROLATES	**PROVOKE**	SPUTTERS	QUINCHED	FRACKING
PROLLED	PROVOKED	**PYGIDIA**	QUINCHES	TRACKING
UPROLLED	PROVOKER	PYGIDIAL	**QUINIES**	WRACKING
PROLONG	PROVOKES	**PYRETIC**	SQUINIES	RACKINGS

RADDING	**RAINIER**	**RANCING**	TRAPPING	**RATTLIN**
BRADDING	BRAINIER	PRANCING	WRAPPING	RATTLINE
RADIATA	GRAINIER	TRANCING	RAPPINGS	RATTLING
RADIATAS	**RAINILY**	**RANDIES**	**RAPTURE**	RATTLINS
RADIATE	BRAINILY	BRANDIES	RAPTURED	**RAUNCHY**
ERADIATE	**RAINING**	RANDIEST	RAPTURES	CRAUNCHY
RADIATED	BRAINING	**RANDING**	**RASHERS**	**RAVELED**
RADIATES	DRAINING	BRANDING	CRASHERS	GRAVELED
RAFFISH	GRAINING	**RANGERS**	TRASHERS	TRAVELED
DRAFFISH	TRAINING	FRANGERS	**RASHEST**	**RAVELER**
RAFTERS	**RAISERS**	GRANGERS	BRASHEST	TRAVELER
CRAFTERS	PRAISERS	**RANGIER**	**RASHING**	RAVELERS
DRAFTERS	**RAISING**	ORANGIER	BRASHING	**RAVELIN**
GRAFTERS	ARAISING	**RANGING**	CRASHING	RAVELING
RAFTING	BRAISING	PRANGING	TRASHING	RAVELINS
CRAFTING	FRAISING	WRANGING	**RASPERS**	**RAVELLY**
DRAFTING	PRAISING	RANGINGS	GRASPERS	GRAVELLY
GRAFTING	RAISINGS	**RANKERS**	**RASPING**	**RAVENED**
RAFTINGS	**RAKSHAS**	FRANKERS	GRASPING	CRAVENED
RAGGIER	RAKSHASA	**RANKEST**	RASPINGS	**RAVINGS**
BRAGGIER	**RAMBLED**	CRANKEST	**RASSLED**	CRAVINGS
CRAGGIER	BRAMBLED	FRANKEST	WRASSLED	GRAVINGS
DRAGGIER	**RAMBLES**	**RANKING**	**RASSLES**	**RAWBONE**
RAGGIES	BRAMBLES	BRANKING	WRASSLES	RAWBONED
RAGGIEST	**RAMMELS**	CRANKING	**RASURES**	**RAWHIDE**
RAGGING	TRAMMELS	FRANKING	ERASURES	RAWHIDED
BRAGGING	**RAMMERS**	PRANKING	**RATCHES**	RAWHIDES
DRAGGING	CRAMMERS	RANKINGS	CRATCHES	**RAWINGS**
FRAGGING	**RAMMIES**	**RANKISH**	FRATCHES	DRAWINGS
RAGGINGS	TRAMMIES	CRANKISH	**RATCHET**	**RAYLING**
RAGGLED	RAMMIEST	PRANKISH	BRATCHET	GRAYLING
DRAGGLED	**RAMMING**	**RANKLED**	RATCHETS	**RAZZLES**
RAGGLES	CRAMMING	CRANKLED	**RATINGS**	FRAZZLES
DRAGGLES	DRAMMING	PRANKLED	GRATINGS	**REACHED**
RAGMENT	TRAMMING	**RANKLES**	PRATINGS	AREACHED
FRAGMENT	**RAMPAGE**	CRANKLES	**RATIONS**	BREACHED
RAGMENTS	RAMPAGED	PRANKLES	ORATIONS	PREACHED
RAGTIME	RAMPAGER	**RANKLESS**	**RATLING**	**REACHER**
RAGTIMER	RAMPAGES	**RANSOMS**	BRATLING	BREACHER
RAGTIMES	**RAMPERS**	TRANSOMS	RATLINGS	PREACHER
RAIDERS	CRAMPERS	**RANTERS**	**RATPACK**	TREACHER
BRAIDERS	TRAMPERS	GRANTERS	BRATPACK	REACHERS
RAIDING	**RAMPING**	TRANTERS	RATPACKS	**REACHES**
BRAIDING	CRAMPING	**RANTING**	**RATTIER**	AREACHES
RAIDINGS	TRAMPING	DRANTING	BRATTIER	BREACHES
RAIKING	RAMPINGS	GRANTING	**RATTING**	PREACHES
TRAIKING	**RAMPIRE**	TRANTING	DRATTING	**REACTED**
RAILCAR	RAMPIRED	RANTINGS	PRATTING	PREACTED
RAILCARD	RAMPIRES	**RANULAR**	RATTINGS	**READAPT**
RAILCARS	**RANCHED**	GRANULAR	**RATTISH**	PREADAPT
RAILERS	BRANCHED	**RAPIERS**	BRATTISH	READAPTS
TRAILERS	CRANCHED	DRAPIERS	**RATTLED**	**READERS**
RAILING	**RANCHER**	**RAPPERS**	BRATTLED	DREADERS
BRAILING	BRANCHER	CRAPPERS	PRATTLED	TREADERS
DRAILING	RANCHERO	TRAPPERS	**RATTLER**	**READIER**
TRAILING	RANCHERS	WRAPPERS	PRATTLER	BREADIER
RAILINGS	**RANCHES**	**RAPPING**	RATTLERS	**READIES**
RAINBOW	BRANCHES	CRAPPING	**RATTLES**	READIEST
RAINBOWS	CRANCHES	DRAPPING	BRATTLES	**READING**
RAINBOWY	TRANCHES	FRAPPING	PRATTLES	AREADING

BREADING	**REAVERS**	PRECIPES	TREDDLED	PREERECT
DREADING	PREAVERS	**RECITED**	**REDDLES**	REERECTS
TREADING	**REAVING**	PRECITED	TREDDLES	**REEVING**
READINGS	GREAVING	**RECKING**	**REDIALS**	PREEVING
READMIT	**REAWAKE**	TRECKING	PREDIALS	**REEVOKE**
PREADMIT	REAWAKED	WRECKING	**REDLINE**	REEVOKED
READMITS	REAWAKEN	**RECLEAN**	REDLINED	REEVOKES
READOPT	REAWAKES	PRECLEAN	REDLINER	**REFACED**
PREADOPT	**REAWOKE**	RECLEANS	REDLINES	PREFACED
READOPTS	REAWOKEN	**RECLINE**	**REDRAFT**	**REFACES**
REAKING	**REBADGE**	RECLINED	PREDRAFT	PREFACES
BREAKING	REBADGED	RECLINER	REDRAFTS	**REFECTS**
CREAKING	REBADGES	RECLINES	**REDREAM**	PREFECTS
FREAKING	**REBILLS**	**RECLOSE**	REDREAMS	**REFENCE**
WREAKING	PREBILLS	RECLOSED	REDREAMT	REFENCED
REALISE	**REBINDS**	RECLOSES	**REDRIED**	REFENCES
REALISED	PREBINDS	**RECODED**	PREDRIED	**REFEREE**
REALISER	**REBIRTH**	PRECODED	**REDRIES**	REFEREED
REALISES	PREBIRTH	**RECODES**	PREDRIES	REFEREES
REALIST	REBIRTHS	PRECODES	**REDRILL**	**REFIGHT**
REALISTS	**REBOARD**	**RECOOKS**	PREDRILL	PREFIGHT
REALIZE	PREBOARD	PRECOOKS	REDRILLS	REFIGHTS
REALIZED	REBOARDS	**RECOUPE**	**REDRIVE**	**REFILED**
REALIZER	**REBOILS**	RECOUPED	REDRIVEN	PREFILED
REALIZES	PREBOILS	**RECOURE**	REDRIVES	**REFILES**
REALLIE	**REBOOKS**	RECOURED	**REECHED**	PREFILES
REALLIED	PREBOOKS	RECOURES	BREECHED	**REFINER**
REALLIES	**REBOUND**	**RECOVER**	**REECHES**	REFINERS
REALLOT	PREBOUND	RECOVERS	BREECHES	REFINERY
PREALLOT	REBOUNDS	RECOVERY	**REECHIE**	**REFIRED**
REALLOTS	**REBRACE**	**RECOYLE**	REECHIER	PREFIRED
REALTER	REBRACED	RECOYLED	**REEDERS**	**REFIRES**
PREALTER	REBRACES	RECOYLES	BREEDERS	PREFIRES
REALTERS	**REBUILD**	**RECRATE**	**REEDIER**	**REFIXED**
REAMERS	PREBUILD	RECRATED	GREEDIER	PREFIXED
CREAMERS	REBUILDS	RECRATES	**REEDILY**	**REFIXES**
DREAMERS	**REBUILT**	**RECTION**	GREEDILY	PREFIXES
REAMIER	PREBUILT	ERECTION	**REEDING**	**REFLATE**
CREAMIER	**RECASTS**	RECTIONS	BREEDING	REFLATED
DREAMIER	PRECASTS	**RECTORS**	REEDINGS	REFLATES
REAMING	**RECEDED**	ERECTORS	**REEDITS**	**REFOCUS**
BREAMING	PRECEDED	**RECUILE**	PREEDITS	PREFOCUS
CREAMING	**RECEDES**	RECUILED	**REEDMAN**	**REFORGE**
DREAMING	PRECEDES	RECUILES	FREEDMAN	REFORGED
REAPPLY	**RECEIVE**	**RECURED**	**REEDMEN**	REFORGES
PREAPPLY	RECEIVED	PRECURED	FREEDMEN	**REFORMS**
REARGUE	RECEIVER	**RECURES**	**REEKIER**	PREFORMS
REARGUED	RECEIVES	PRECURES	CREEKIER	**REFRAME**
REARGUES	**RECENSE**	**RECURVE**	**REEKING**	REFRAMED
REARING	RECENSED	RECURVED	GREEKING	REFRAMES
DREARING	RECENSES	RECURVES	**REELECT**	**REFROZE**
REARISE	**RECEPTS**	**RECYCLE**	PREELECT	PREFROZE
REARISEN	PRECEPTS	RECYCLED	REELECTS	REFROZEN
REARISES	**RECHECK**	RECYCLER	**REELING**	**REFUNDS**
REARMED	PRECHECK	RECYCLES	CREELING	PREFUNDS
PREARMED	RECHECKS	**REDATED**	REELINGS	**REGALES**
REASONS	**RECHOSE**	PREDATED	**REENACT**	GREGALES
TREASONS	PRECHOSE	**REDATES**	PREENACT	**REGALIA**
REASTED	RECHOSEN	PREDATES	REENACTS	REGALIAN
BREASTED	**RECIPES**	**REDDLED**	**REERECT**	REGALIAS

REGAUGE	RELAPSED	TRENAILS	PREPPING	RESCALED
REGAUGED	RELAPSER	**RENAMES**	REPPINGS	RESCALES
REGAUGES	RELAPSES	PRENAMES	**REPRESS**	**RESCIND**
REGIMEN	**RELATES**	**RENDING**	PREPRESS	PRESCIND
REGIMENS	PRELATES	TRENDING	**REPRICE**	RESCINDS
REGIMENT	**RELAXIN**	**RENEGUE**	PREPRICE	**RESCORE**
REGLAZE	RELAXING	RENEGUED	REPRICED	PRESCORE
REGLAZED	RELAXINS	RENEGUER	REPRICES	RESCORED
REGLAZES	**RELEARN**	RENEGUES	**REPRIME**	RESCORES
REGMATA	RELEARNS	**RENEWER**	REPRIMED	**RESEIZE**
BREGMATA	RELEARNT	RENEWERS	REPRIMES	RESEIZED
REGNANT	**RELEASE**	**RENNING**	**REPRINT**	RESEIZES
PREGNANT	RELEASED	BRENNING	PREPRINT	**RESELLS**
REGORGE	RELEASEE	GRENNING	REPRINTS	PRESELLS
REGORGED	RELEASER	RENNINGS	**REPRISE**	**RESENTS**
REGORGES	RELEASES	**RENTALS**	REPRISED	PRESENTS
REGRADE	**RELIEVE**	TRENTALS	REPRISES	**RESERVE**
REGRADED	RELIEVED	**RENTING**	**REPRIVE**	PRESERVE
REGRADES	RELIEVER	PRENTING	REPRIVED	RESERVED
REGRATE	RELIEVES	RENTINGS	REPRIVES	RESERVER
REGRATED	**RELIVES**	**REORDER**	**REPRIZE**	RESERVES
REGRATER	PRELIVES	PREORDER	REPRIZED	**RESHAPE**
REGRATES	**RELOADS**	REORDERS	REPRIZES	PRESHAPE
REGREDE	PRELOADS	**REPACKS**	**REPROBE**	RESHAPED
REGREDED	**REMAINS**	PREPACKS	REPROBED	RESHAPER
REGREDES	CREMAINS	**REPAVED**	REPROBES	RESHAPES
REGULAR	**REMATED**	PREPAVED	**REPROVE**	**RESHAVE**
REGULARS	CREMATED	**REPAVES**	REPROVED	RESHAVED
REHEARS	**REMATES**	PREPAVES	REPROVER	RESHAVEN
REHEARSE	CREMATES	**REPIQUE**	REPROVES	RESHAVES
REHEATS	**REMBLED**	REPIQUED	**REPRYVE**	**RESHINE**
PREHEATS	TREMBLED	REPIQUES	REPRYVED	RESHINED
REHINGE	**REMBLES**	**REPLACE**	REPRYVES	RESHINES
REHINGED	TREMBLES	PREPLACE	**REPULSE**	**RESHIPS**
REHINGES	**REMERGE**	REPLACED	REPULSED	PRESHIPS
REHOUSE	REMERGED	REPLACER	REPULSER	**RESHOWN**
REHOUSED	REMERGES	REPLACES	REPULSES	PRESHOWN
REHOUSES	**REMISED**	**REPLANS**	**REQUERE**	**RESHOWS**
REIMAGE	PREMISED	PREPLANS	REQUERED	PRESHOWS
REIMAGED	**REMISES**	**REPLANT**	REQUERES	**RESIDED**
REIMAGES	PREMISES	PREPLANT	**REQUIRE**	PRESIDED
REINING	**REMIXED**	REPLANTS	REQUIRED	**RESIDER**
GREINING	PREMIXED	**REPLATE**	REQUIRER	PRESIDER
REISSUE	**REMIXES**	REPLATED	REQUIRES	RESIDERS
REISSUED	PREMIXES	REPLATES	**REQUITE**	**RESIDES**
REISSUER	**REMOLDS**	**REPLETE**	REQUITED	PRESIDES
REISSUES	PREMOLDS	REPLETED	REQUITER	**RESIDUA**
REJOICE	**REMORSE**	REPLETES	REQUITES	RESIDUAL
REJOICED	PREMORSE	**REPONED**	**REQUOTE**	**RESIFTS**
REJOICER	REMORSES	PREPONED	REQUOTED	PRESIFTS
REJOICES	**REMOTES**	**REPONES**	REQUOTES	**RESILIN**
REJOURN	REMOTEST	PREPONES	**RERAISE**	RESILING
REJOURNS	**REMOVED**	**REPOSAL**	RERAISED	RESILINS
REJUDGE	PREMOVED	REPOSALL	RERAISES	**RESLATE**
PREJUDGE	**REMOVES**	REPOSALS	**REROUTE**	RESLATED
REJUDGED	PREMOVES	**REPOSED**	REROUTED	RESLATES
REJUDGES	**RENAGUE**	PREPOSED	REROUTES	**RESOAKS**
RELACHE	RENAGUED	**REPOSES**	**RESALES**	PRESOAKS
RELACHES	RENAGUES	PREPOSES	PRESALES	**RESOLVE**
RELAPSE	**RENAILS**	**REPPING**	**RESCALE**	PRESOLVE

RESOLVED	**RETAPED**	PREVALUE	REWRITER	**RIDGING**
RESOLVER	PRETAPED	REVALUED	REWRITES	BRIDGING
RESOLVES	**RETAPES**	REVALUES	**RHABDOM**	FRIDGING
RESORTS	PRETAPES	**REVENGE**	RHABDOME	RIDGINGS
PRESORTS	**RETASTE**	REVENGED	RHABDOMS	**RIEVERS**
RESPACE	PRETASTE	REVENGER	**RHOMBOI**	GRIEVERS
RESPACED	RETASTED	REVENGES	RHOMBOID	**RIEVING**
RESPACES	RETASTES	**REVENUE**	**RHUBARB**	GRIEVING
RESPADE	**RETCHED**	REVENUED	RHUBARBS	PRIEVING
RESPADED	WRETCHED	REVENUER	RHUBARBY	**RIFFLER**
RESPADES	**RETCHES**	REVENUES	**RHYTHMI**	RIFFLERS
RESPIRE	WRETCHES	**REVERBS**	RHYTHMIC	**RIFLERS**
RESPIRED	**RETELLS**	PREVERBS	**RIBBERS**	TRIFLERS
RESPIRES	PRETELLS	**REVERSE**	CRIBBERS	**RIFLING**
RESPITE	**RETESTS**	REVERSED	DRIBBERS	TRIFLING
RESPITED	PRETESTS	REVERSER	**RIBBING**	RIFLINGS
RESPITES	**RETINUE**	REVERSES	CRIBBING	**RIFTIER**
RESPLIT	RETINUED	**REVIEWS**	DRIBBING	DRIFTIER
PRESPLIT	RETINUES	PREVIEWS	RIBBINGS	**RIFTING**
RESPLITS	**RETITLE**	**REVISAL**	**RIBLETS**	DRIFTING
RESPOKE	RETITLED	REVISALS	DRIBLETS	GRIFTING
RESPOKEN	RETITLES	**REVISED**	TRIBLETS	**RIGGERS**
RESTAGE	**RETRACE**	PREVISED	**RIBSTON**	FRIGGERS
RESTAGED	RETRACED	**REVISES**	RIBSTONE	PRIGGERS
RESTAGES	RETRACER	BREVISES	RIBSTONS	TRIGGERS
RESTAMP	RETRACES	PREVISES	**RIBWORK**	**RIGGING**
PRESTAMP	**RETRAIN**	TREVISES	CRIBWORK	FRIGGING
RESTAMPS	PRETRAIN	**REVISIT**	RIBWORKS	GRIGGING
RESTATE	RETRAINS	PREVISIT	**RICHTED**	PRIGGING
RESTATED	**RETRAIT**	REVISITS	FRICHTED	TRIGGING
RESTATES	RETRAITE	**REVISOR**	**RICHTER**	RIGGINGS
RESTERS	RETRAITS	PREVISOR	BRICHTER	**RIGGISH**
PRESTERS	RETRAITT	REVISORS	**RICIEST**	PRIGGISH
WRESTERS	**RETRATE**	REVISORY	PRICIEST	**RIGHTED**
RESTING	RETRATED	**REVIVER**	**RICKERS**	FRIGHTED
CRESTING	RETRATES	REVIVERS	PRICKERS	**RIGHTEN**
PRESTING	**RETREAT**	**REVOICE**	TRICKERS	BRIGHTEN
WRESTING	PRETREAT	REVOICED	**RICKETS**	FRIGHTEN
RESTINGS	RETREATS	REVOICES	CRICKETS	RIGHTENS
RESTOKE	**RETRIAL**	**REVOLVE**	PRICKETS	**RIGHTER**
RESTOKED	PRETRIAL	REVOLVED	**RICKING**	BRIGHTER
RESTOKES	RETRIALS	REVOLVER	BRICKING	RIGHTERS
RESTORE	**RETRIMS**	REVOLVES	CRICKING	**RIGHTLY**
PRESTORE	PRETRIMS	**REWARMS**	FRICKING	BRIGHTLY
RESTORED	**RETTING**	PREWARMS	PRICKING	**RIGIDER**
RESTORER	ARETTING	**REWEAVE**	TRICKING	FRIGIDER
RESTORES	FRETTING	REWEAVED	WRICKING	**RIGIDLY**
RESTYLE	**RETYPED**	REWEAVES	**RICKLES**	FRIGIDLY
RESTYLED	PRETYPED	**REWEIGH**	BRICKLES	**RILLING**
RESTYLES	**RETYPES**	PREWEIGH	PRICKLES	DRILLING
RESUMED	PRETYPES	REWEIGHS	TRICKLES	FRILLING
PRESUMED	**REUNION**	**REWIRED**	**RICKSHA**	GRILLING
RESUMER	PREUNION	PREWIRED	RICKSHAS	PRILLING
PRESUMER	REUNIONS	**REWIRES**	RICKSHAW	TRILLING
RESUMERS	**REUNITE**	PREWIRES	**RIDDERS**	**RIMIEST**
RESUMES	PREUNITE	**REWORKS**	GRIDDERS	GRIMIEST
PRESUMES	REUNITED	PREWORKS	**RIDDLED**	**RIMLESS**
RESURGE	REUNITER	**REWRAPS**	GRIDDLED	BRIMLESS
RESURGED	REUNITES	PREWRAPS	**RIDDLES**	**RIMMERS**
RESURGES	**REVALUE**	**REWRITE**	GRIDDLES	BRIMMERS

CRIMMERS	FRISKERS	BROGUISH	TROOPING	CROUPIER
KRIMMERS	**RISKFUL**	**ROILING**	**ROOTIES**	**ROUPILY**
PRIMMERS	FRISKFUL	BROILING	ROOTIEST	CROUPILY
TRIMMERS	**RISKIER**	DROILING	**ROOTING**	**ROUPING**
RIMMING	BRISKIER	**ROINING**	WROOTING	CROUPING
BRIMMING	FRISKIER	GROINING	ROOTINGS	GROUPING
PRIMMING	**RISKILY**	PROINING	**ROQUETS**	TROUPING
TRIMMING	FRISKILY	**ROLLERS**	CROQUETS	**ROUSERS**
RIMMINGS	**RISKING**	PROLLERS	**ROSARIA**	AROUSERS
RIMPLED	BRISKING	TROLLERS	ROSARIAN	GROUSERS
CRIMPLED	FRISKING	**ROLLICK**	**ROSEOLA**	TROUSERS
RIMPLES	**RISPING**	ROLLICKS	ROSEOLAR	**ROUSING**
CRIMPLES	CRISPING	ROLLICKY	ROSEOLAS	AROUSING
RINDING	RISPINGS	**ROLLING**	**ROSETTE**	GROUSING
GRINDING	**RITTERS**	DROLLING	ROSETTED	**ROUTERS**
RINGERS	CRITTERS	PROLLING	ROSETTES	GROUTERS
BRINGERS	FRITTERS	TROLLING	**ROSIERS**	TROUTERS
CRINGERS	GRITTERS	ROLLINGS	CROSIERS	**ROUTHIE**
WRINGERS	**RITTING**	**ROMAGES**	**ROSIEST**	ROUTHIER
RINGING	FRITTING	FROMAGES	BROSIEST	**ROUTING**
BRINGING	GRITTING	**ROMANCE**	PROSIEST	GROUTING
CRINGING	**RIZZERS**	ROMANCED	**ROSSERS**	TROUTING
FRINGING	FRIZZERS	ROMANCER	CROSSERS	ROUTINGS
WRINGING	**ROACHED**	ROMANCES	GROSSERS	**ROVINGS**
RINGINGS	BROACHED	**ROMPING**	TROSSERS	DROVINGS
RINKING	**ROACHES**	TROMPING	**ROSTING**	PROVINGS
DRINKING	BROACHES	**RONDEAU**	FROSTING	**ROWABLE**
PRINKING	**ROADWAY**	RONDEAUX	**ROTATOR**	GROWABLE
RINNING	BROADWAY	**RONZERS**	ROTATORS	**ROWDIES**
GRINNING	ROADWAYS	BRONZERS	ROTATORY	CROWDIES
RIPOSTE	**ROARING**	**ROOFERS**	**ROTCHES**	ROWDIEST
RIPOSTED	ROARINGS	PROOFERS	CROTCHES	**ROWELED**
RIPOSTES	**ROATING**	**ROOFIES**	**ROTHERS**	TROWELED
RIPPERS	TROATING	ROOFIEST	BROTHERS	**ROWINGS**
DRIPPERS	**ROBANDS**	**ROOFING**	FROTHERS	GROWINGS
FRIPPERS	PROBANDS	PROOFING	**ROTTERS**	**ROWNDED**
GRIPPERS	**ROCHETS**	ROOFINGS	TROTTERS	DROWNDED
TRIPPERS	CROCHETS	**ROOKERY**	**ROTTING**	**ROYNING**
RIPPIER	**ROCKABY**	CROOKERY	TROTTING	PROYNING
DRIPPIER	ROCKABYE	**ROOKIES**	**ROUBLES**	**ROZELLE**
GRIPPIER	**ROCKERY**	BROOKIES	TROUBLES	ROZELLES
TRIPPIER	CROCKERY	ROOKIEST	**ROUCHES**	**RUBASSE**
RIPPIERS	**ROCKETS**	**ROOKING**	CROUCHES	RUBASSES
RIPPING	BROCKETS	BROOKING	GROUCHES	**RUBBERS**
DRIPPING	CROCKETS	CROOKING	TROUCHES	DRUBBERS
GRIPPING	**ROCKING**	DROOKING	**ROUGHED**	GRUBBERS
TRIPPING	CROCKING	**ROOMERS**	TROUGHED	**RUBBING**
RIPPINGS	FROCKING	GROOMERS	**ROULEAU**	DRUBBING
RIPPLED	GROCKING	**ROOMIER**	ROULEAUS	GRUBBING
CRIPPLED	TROCKING	BROOMIER	ROULEAUX	RUBBINGS
TRIPPLED	ROCKINGS	**ROOMIES**	**ROUNCES**	**RUBBISH**
RIPPLER	**RODDING**	ROOMIEST	FROUNCES	RUBBISHY
CRIPPLER	BRODDING	**ROOMING**	TROUNCES	**RUBBLED**
TRIPPLER	PRODDING	BROOMING	**ROUNDED**	GRUBBLED
RIPPLERS	RODDINGS	GROOMING	GROUNDED	**RUBBLES**
RIPPLES	**RODENTS**	VROOMING	**ROUNDER**	GRUBBLES
CRIPPLES	ERODENTS	**ROOPIER**	GROUNDER	**RUBELLA**
GRIPPLES	**ROGUERY**	DROOPIER	ROUNDERS	RUBELLAN
TRIPPLES	BROGUERY	**ROOPING**	ROUNDLET	RUBELLAS
RISKERS	**ROGUISH**	DROOPING	**ROUPIER**	**RUBEOLA**

RUBEOLAR	DRUMMERS	CRUSTIER	**SAPHENA**	SCANTLED
RUBEOLAS	**RUMMEST**	TRUSTIER	SAPHENAE	SCANTLES
RUCKING	GRUMMEST	**RUSTILY**	SAPHENAS	**SCAPING**
TRUCKING	**RUMMIER**	CRUSTILY	**SAPLING**	ESCAPING
RUCKLED	CRUMMIER	TRUSTILY	SAPLINGS	**SCAPPLE**
TRUCKLED	**RUMMIES**	**RUSTING**	**SAPONIN**	SCAPPLED
RUCKLES	CRUMMIES	BRUSTING	SAPONINE	SCAPPLES
TRUCKLES	DRUMMIES	CRUSTING	SAPONINS	**SCAPULA**
RUCKMAN	RUMMIEST	TRUSTING	**SARCINA**	SCAPULAE
TRUCKMAN	**RUMNESS**	RUSTINGS	SARCINAE	SCAPULAR
RUCKMEN	GRUMNESS	**RUSTLES**	SARCINAS	SCAPULAS
TRUCKMEN	**RUMPING**	RUSTLESS	**SARDINE**	**SCARPED**
RUDDIER	CRUMPING	**RUTHFUL**	SARDINED	ESCARPED
CRUDDIER	FRUMPING	TRUTHFUL	SARDINES	**SCATTER**
RUDDIES	GRUMPING	**SABELLA**	**SARMENT**	SCATTERS
RUDDIEST	KRUMPING	ISABELLA	SARMENTA	SCATTERY
RUDDING	TRUMPING	SABELLAS	SARMENTS	**SCAVAGE**
CRUDDING	**RUMPLED**	**SABURRA**	**SASSIES**	SCAVAGER
RUDDLED	CRUMPLED	SABURRAL	SASSIEST	SCAVAGES
CRUDDLED	FRUMPLED	SABURRAS	**SATIATE**	**SCEDULE**
RUDDLES	**RUMPLES**	**SACRIST**	SATIATED	SCEDULED
CRUDDLES	CRUMPLES	SACRISTS	SATIATES	SCEDULES
RUFFIAN	FRUMPLES	SACRISTY	**SAUTOIR**	**SCENDED**
RUFFIANS	RUMPLESS	**SADDLER**	SAUTOIRE	ASCENDED
RUFFING	**RUNCHES**	SADDLERS	SAUTOIRS	**SCEPTRE**
GRUFFING	BRUNCHES	SADDLERY	**SAVAGER**	SCEPTRED
RUFFLED	CRUNCHES	**SAFARIS**	SAVAGERY	SCEPTRES
TRUFFLED	**RUNDLED**	SAFARIST	**SAVAGES**	**SCHAPPE**
RUFFLES	TRUNDLED	SAFFRONY	SAVAGEST	SCHAPPED
TRUFFLES	**RUNDLES**	**SAGENES**	**SAVANNA**	SCHAPPES
RUGGERS	GRUNDLES	SAGENESS	SAVANNAH	**SCHLEPP**
DRUGGERS	TRUNDLES	**SAGITTA**	SAVANNAS	SCHLEPPS
RUGGIER	**RUNKLED**	SAGITTAL	**SAVVIES**	SCHLEPPY
DRUGGIER	CRUNKLED	SAGITTAS	SAVVIEST	**SCHLOCK**
RUGGING	**RUNKLES**	**SALICET**	**SAWDUST**	SCHLOCKS
DRUGGING	CRUNKLES	SALICETA	SAWDUSTS	SCHLOCKY
FRUGGING	**RUNNELS**	SALICETS	SAWDUSTY	**SCHLUMP**
RUGGINGS	TRUNNELS	**SALICIN**	**SCABBLE**	SCHLUMPS
RUGOLAS	**RUNNION**	SALICINE	SCABBLED	SCHLUMPY
ARUGOLAS	TRUNNION	SALICINS	SCABBLES	**SCHMALZ**
RUINATE	RUNNIONS	**SALTATE**	**SCALADE**	SCHMALZY
RUINATED	**RUPTURE**	SALTATED	ESCALADE	**SCHMELZ**
RUINATES	RUPTURED	SALTATES	SCALADES	SCHMELZE
RUMBLED	RUPTURES	**SALTERS**	**SCALADO**	**SCHMOOS**
CRUMBLED	**RUSHERS**	PSALTERS	ESCALADO	SCHMOOSE
DRUMBLED	BRUSHERS	**SALTIES**	SCALADOS	**SCHMOOZ**
GRUMBLED	CRUSHERS	SALTIEST	**SCALIER**	SCHMOOZE
RUMBLER	**RUSHIER**	**SALVAGE**	ESCALIER	SCHMOOZY
GRUMBLER	BRUSHIER	SALVAGED	**SCALLOP**	**SCHOOLE**
RUMBLERS	**RUSHING**	SALVAGEE	ESCALLOP	SCHOOLED
RUMBLES	BRUSHING	SALVAGER	SCALLOPS	SCHOOLES
CRUMBLES	CRUSHING	SALVAGES	**SCAMBLE**	**SCIATIC**
DRUMBLES	FRUSHING	**SAMPLER**	SCAMBLED	SCIATICA
GRUMBLES	RUSHINGS	SAMPLERS	SCAMBLER	SCIATICS
RUMMAGE	**RUSSELS**	SAMPLERY	SCAMBLES	**SCIENCE**
RUMMAGED	BRUSSELS	**SANDBUR**	**SCAMPIS**	SCIENCED
RUMMAGER	**RUSSULA**	SANDBURR	SCAMPISH	SCIENCES
RUMMAGES	RUSSULAE	SANDBURS	**SCANDIA**	**SCISSIL**
RUMMERS	RUSSULAS	**SAOUARI**	SCANDIAS	SCISSILE
BRUMMERS	**RUSTIER**	SAOUARIS	**SCANTLE**	SCISSILS

SCOPULA	SCUMBLE	SERUEWE	SHINIES	SILICONS
SCOPULAE	SCUMBLED	SERUEWED	SHINIEST	**SILIQUA**
SCOPULAS	SCUMBLES	SERUEWES	**SHIPMEN**	SILIQUAE
SCOTTIE	**SCURRIL**	**SERVEWE**	SHIPMENT	SILIQUAS
SCOTTIES	SCURRILE	SERVEWED	**SHMALTZ**	**SILKIES**
SCOURGE	**SCUTTLE**	SERVEWES	SHMALTZY	SILKIEST
SCOURGED	SCUTTLED	**SERVICE**	**SHMOOSE**	**SILLIES**
SCOURGER	SCUTTLER	SERVICED	SHMOOSED	SILLIEST
SCOURGES	SCUTTLES	SERVICER	SHMOOSER	**SIMPLES**
SCOURSE	**SDEIGNE**	SERVICES	SHMOOSES	SIMPLEST
SCOURSED	SDEIGNED	**SESTETT**	**SHMOOZE**	**SINCERE**
SCOURSES	SDEIGNES	SESTETTE	SHMOOZED	SINCERER
SCRATCH	**SECLUDE**	SESTETTO	SHMOOZER	**SINUATE**
SCRATCHY	SECLUDED	SESTETTS	SHMOOZES	SINUATED
SCREECH	SECLUDES	**SEXTETT**	**SHOEPAC**	SINUATES
SCREECHY	**SECONDE**	SEXTETTE	SHOEPACK	**SIRNAME**
SCREEVE	SECONDED	SEXTETTS	SHOEPACS	SIRNAMED
SCREEVED	SECONDEE	**SHACKLE**	**SHOGGLE**	SIRNAMES
SCREEVER	SECONDER	SHACKLED	SHOGGLED	**SISSIES**
SCREEVES	SECONDES	SHACKLER	SHOGGLES	SISSIEST
SCREIGH	**SECRETE**	SHACKLES	**SHOOGIE**	**SITUATE**
SCREIGHS	SECRETED	**SHAMBLE**	SHOOGIED	SITUATED
SCRIBED	SECRETER	SHAMBLED	SHOOGIES	SITUATES
ASCRIBED	SECRETES	SHAMBLES	**SHOOGLE**	**SKELLIE**
ESCRIBED	**SECURES**	**SHAMING**	SHOOGLED	SKELLIED
SCRIBES	SECUREST	ASHAMING	SHOOGLES	SKELLIER
ASCRIBES	**SEDATES**	**SHAMMAS**	**SHRIEVE**	SKELLIES
ESCRIBES	SEDATEST	SHAMMASH	SHRIEVED	**SKIFFLE**
SCRIEVE	**SEISMIC**	**SHATTER**	SHRIEVES	SKIFFLED
SCRIEVED	ASEISMIC	SHATTERS	**SHUDDER**	SKIFFLES
SCRIEVES	**SEITIES**	SHATTERY	SHUDDERS	**SKITTER**
SCROLLS	ASEITIES	**SHAWING**	SHUDDERY	SKITTERS
ESCROLLS	**SELVAGE**	PSHAWING	**SHUFFLE**	SKITTERY
SCROOGE	SELVAGED	**SHEATHE**	SHUFFLED	**SKITTLE**
SCROOGED	SELVAGEE	SHEATHED	SHUFFLER	SKITTLED
SCROOGES	SELVAGES	SHEATHER	SHUFFLES	SKITTLES
SCROUGE	**SEMIMAT**	SHEATHES	**SHUTTLE**	**SKUTTLE**
SCROUGED	SEMIMATT	**SHEENIE**	SHUTTLED	SKUTTLED
SCROUGER	**SEMINAR**	SHEENIER	SHUTTLER	SKUTTLES
SCROUGES	SEMINARS	SHEENIES	SHUTTLES	**SKYBORN**
SCROWLE	SEMINARY	**SHEHITA**	**SIAMESE**	SKYBORNE
SCROWLED	**SENSATE**	SHEHITAH	SIAMESED	**SKYDIVE**
SCROWLES	SENSATED	SHEHITAS	SIAMESES	SKYDIVED
SCRUNCH	SENSATES	**SHELLAC**	**SIAMEZE**	SKYDIVER
SCRUNCHY	**SEPTATE**	SHELLACK	SIAMEZED	SKYDIVES
SCRUPLE	ASEPTATE	SHELLACS	SIAMEZES	**SLABBER**
SCRUPLED	**SEPTICS**	**SHELTER**	**SIGMATE**	SLABBERS
SCRUPLER	ASEPTICS	SHELTERS	SIGMATED	SLABBERY
SCRUPLES	**SEQUELA**	SHELTERY	SIGMATES	**SLAKING**
SCUDDLE	SEQUELAE	**SHIKSEH**	**SIGNIOR**	ASLAKING
SCUDDLED	**SERENES**	SHIKSEHS	SIGNIORI	**SLANDER**
SCUDDLES	SERENEST	**SHIMMER**	SIGNIORS	ISLANDER
SCUFFLE	**SERIATE**	SHIMMERS	SIGNIORY	SLANDERS
SCUFFLED	SERIATED	SHIMMERY	**SIGNORI**	**SLATTER**
SCUFFLER	SERIATES	**SHINESS**	SIGNORIA	SLATTERN
SCUFFLES	**SERINES**	ASHINESS	**SILENCE**	SLATTERS
SCULLERY	ESERINES	**SHINGLE**	SILENCED	SLATTERY
SCULPIN	**SERRATE**	SHINGLED	SILENCER	**SLEEPER**
SCULPING	SERRATED	SHINGLER	SILENCES	SLEEPERS
SCULPINS	SERRATES	SHINGLES	**SILICON**	SLEEPERY
			SILICONE	

SLIDDER	SNOOZLED	**SPACKLE**	**SPINULA**	SPULZIED
SLIDDERS	SNOOZLES	SPACKLED	SPINULAE	SPULZIES
SLIDDERY	**SNOTTER**	SPACKLES	**SPIRANT**	**SPUNKIE**
SLIPPER	SNOTTERS	**SPAIRGE**	ASPIRANT	SPUNKIER
SLIPPERS	SNOTTERY	SPAIRGED	SPIRANTS	SPUNKIES
SLIPPERY	**SNOTTIE**	SPAIRGES	**SPIRING**	**SPUTTER**
SLITHER	SNOTTIER	**SPAMMIE**	ASPIRING	SPUTTERS
SLITHERS	SNOTTIES	SPAMMIER	**SPIRULA**	SPUTTERY
SLITHERY	**SNUFFLE**	SPAMMIES	SPIRULAE	**SQUARES**
SLOBBER	SNUFFLED	**SPANGLE**	SPIRULAS	SQUAREST
SLOBBERS	SNUFFLER	SPANGLED	**SPITTLE**	**SQUEEZE**
SLOBBERY	SNUFFLES	SPANGLER	SPITTLES	SQUEEZED
SLUMBER	**SNUGGER**	SPANGLES	**SPLENIA**	SQUEEZER
SLUMBERS	SNUGGERY	SPANGLET	SPLENIAL	SQUEEZES
SLUMBERY	**SNUGGLE**	**SPARKIE**	**SPLODGE**	**SQUELCH**
SMARAGD	SNUGGLED	SPARKIER	SPLODGED	SQUELCHY
SMARAGDE	SNUGGLES	SPARKIES	SPLODGES	**SQUIDGE**
SMARAGDS	**SNUZZLE**	**SPARKLE**	**SPLOTCH**	SQUIDGED
SMELLERS	SNUZZLED	ASPARKLE	SPLOTCHY	SQUIDGES
SMELTER	SNUZZLES	SPARKLED	**SPLURGE**	**SQUILLA**
SMELTERS	**SOAPIES**	SPARKLER	SPLURGED	SQUILLAE
SMELTERY	SOAPIEST	SPARKLES	SPLURGER	SQUILLAS
SMOKIES	**SOCIALS**	SPARKLET	SPLURGES	**SQUIRED**
SMOKIEST	ASOCIALS	**SPATULA**	**SPONGIN**	ESQUIRED
SMOODGE	**SODDIES**	SPATULAR	SPONGING	**SQUIRES**
SMOODGED	SODDIEST	SPATULAS	SPONGINS	ESQUIRES
SMOODGES	**SOLANIN**	**SPECIAL**	**SPOOFER**	SQUIRESS
SMOTHER	SOLANINE	ESPECIAL	SPOOFERS	**SQUOOSH**
SMOTHERS	SOLANINS	SPECIALS	SPOOFERY	SQUOOSHY
SMOTHERY	**SOLATED**	**SPECKLE**	**SPORTED**	**STABLES**
SMUGGER	ISOLATED	SPECKLED	ASPORTED	STABLEST
SMUGGERY	**SOLATES**	SPECKLES	**SPOTTIE**	**STAGGER**
SMUGGLE	ISOLATES	**SPECTRA**	SPOTTIER	STAGGERS
SMUGGLED	**SOLDIER**	SPECTRAL	SPOTTIES	STAGGERY
SMUGGLER	SOLDIERS	**SPECULA**	**SPOUSAL**	**STAGGIE**
SMUGGLES	SOLDIERY	SPECULAR	ESPOUSAL	STAGGIER
SNABBLE	**SOLICIT**	**SPELDIN**	SPOUSALS	STAGGIES
SNABBLED	SOLICITS	SPELDING	**SPOUSED**	**STAMINA**
SNABBLES	SOLICITY	SPELDINS	ESPOUSED	STAMINAL
SNAFFLE	**SOLVATE**	**SPERSED**	**SPOUSES**	STAMINAS
SNAFFLED	SOLVATED	ASPERSED	ESPOUSES	**STAMPED**
SNAFFLES	SOLVATES	**SPERSES**	**SPREAZE**	STAMPEDE
SNICKER	**SOMBRER**	ASPERSES	SPREAZED	STAMPEDO
SNICKERS	SOMBRERO	**SPHERIC**	SPREAZES	**STARTED**
SNICKERY	**SOMBRES**	ASPHERIC	**SPREDDE**	ASTARTED
SNIFFLE	SOMBREST	SPHERICS	SPREDDEN	**STARTLE**
SNIFFLED	**SOOTHES**	**SPICATE**	SPREDDES	STARTLED
SNIFFLER	SOOTHEST	SPICATED	**SPREEZE**	STARTLER
SNIFFLES	**SOREDIA**	**SPICULA**	SPREEZED	STARTLES
SNIGGLE	SOREDIAL	SPICULAE	SPREEZES	**STATICE**
SNIGGLED	**SOUFFLE**	SPICULAR	**SPRINGE**	STATICES
SNIGGLER	SOUFFLED	**SPINACH**	SPRINGED	**STATING**
SNIGGLES	SOUFFLES	SPINACHY	SPRINGER	ESTATING
SNIPPET	**SOUPLES**	**SPINDLE**	SPRINGES	**STATURE**
SNIPPETS	SOUPLESS	SPINDLED	**SPRUCES**	STATURED
SNIPPETY	**SOUTHER**	SPINDLER	SPRUCEST	STATURES
SNIRTLE	SOUTHERN	SPINDLES	**SPULYIE**	**STEALTH**
SNIRTLED	SOUTHERS	**SPINNER**	SPULYIED	STEALTHS
SNIRTLES	**SOVKHOZ**	SPINNERS	SPULYIES	STEALTHY
SNOOZLE	SOVKHOZY	SPINNERY	**SPULZIE**	**STEAMIE**

STEAMIER	STONIEST	STYLISES	SUNBAKES	**SWINDGE**
STEAMIES	**STONING**	**STYLIZE**	**SUNBATH**	SWINDGED
STEARIN	ASTONING	STYLIZED	SUNBATHE	SWINDGES
STEARINE	STONINGS	STYLIZER	SUNBATHS	**SWINDLE**
STEARING	**STONISH**	STYLIZES	**SUNBEAM**	SWINDLED
STEARINS	ASTONISH	**SUBDUCE**	SUNBEAMS	SWINDLER
STEELIE	**STOPPED**	SUBDUCED	SUNBEAMY	SWINDLES
STEELIER	ESTOPPED	SUBDUCES	**SUNBURN**	**SWINGLE**
STEELIES	**STOPPLE**	**SUBLATE**	SUNBURNS	SWINGLED
STEEMED	STOPPLED	SUBLATED	SUNBURNT	SWINGLES
ESTEEMED	STOPPLES	SUBLATES	**SUNNIES**	**SWISHES**
STEEPLE	**STOUNDS**	**SUBLIME**	SUNNIEST	SWISHEST
STEEPLED	ASTOUNDS	SUBLIMED	**SUPPLES**	**SWIZZLE**
STEEPLES	**STOURIE**	SUBLIMER	SUPPLEST	SWIZZLED
STEEVES	STOURIER	SUBLIMES	**SUPPOSE**	SWIZZLER
STEEVEST	**STOVERS**	**SUBSIDE**	SUPPOSED	SWIZZLES
STELLIO	ESTOVERS	SUBSIDER	SUPPOSER	SYLLABI
STELLION	**STRANGE**	SUBSIDES	SUPPOSES	SYLLABIC
STEMMER	ESTRANGE	**SUBSUME**	**SUPREME**	**SYLPHID**
STEMMERS	STRANGER	SUBSUMED	SUPREMER	SYLPHIDE
STEMMERY	STRANGES	SUBSUMES	SUPREMES	SYLPHIDS
STERNAL	**STRAYED**	**SUBTILE**	**SURBASE**	**SYMBION**
ASTERNAL	ESTRAYED	SUBTILER	SURBASED	SYMBIONS
STEROID	**STRAYVE**	**SUBVENE**	SURBASES	SYMBIONT
ASTEROID	STRAYVED	SUBVENED	**SURBATE**	**SYMBIOT**
STEROIDS	STRAYVES	SUBVENES	SURBATED	SYMBIOTE
STHENIA	**STRETCH**	**SUCCUBA**	SURBATES	SYMBIOTS
ASTHENIA	STRETCHY	SUCCUBAE	**SURFACE**	**SYMBOLE**
STHENIAS	**STRIATE**	SUCCUBAS	SURFACED	SYMBOLED
STHENIC	STRIATED	**SUFFICE**	SURFACER	SYMBOLES
ASTHENIC	STRIATES	SUFFICED	SURFACES	**SYMITAR**
STIBBLE	**STROBIL**	SUFFICER	**SURFIES**	SYMITARE
STIBBLER	STROBILA	SUFFICES	SURFIEST	SYMITARS
STIBBLES	STROBILE	**SUFFUSE**	**SURMISE**	**SYNAPSE**
STICKLE	STROBILI	SUFFUSED	SURMISED	SYNAPSED
STICKLED	STROBILS	SUFFUSES	SURMISER	SYNAPSES
STICKLER	**STRODLE**	**SUICIDE**	SURMISES	**SYNCARP**
STICKLES	STRODLED	SUICIDED	**SURNAME**	SYNCARPS
STIDDIE	STRODLES	SUICIDES	SURNAMED	SYNCARPY
STIDDIED	**STROOKE**	**SULCATE**	SURNAMER	**SYNERGY**
STIDDIES	STROOKEN	SULCATED	SURNAMES	ASYNERGY
STIPPLE	STROOKES	**SULFATE**	**SURVIVE**	**SYNONYM**
STIPPLED	**STUBBIE**	SULFATED	SURVIVED	SYNONYME
STIPPLER	STUBBIER	SULFATES	SURVIVER	SYNONYMS
STIPPLES	STUBBIES	**SULFURY**	SURVIVES	SYNONYMY
STIPULE	**STUBBLE**	SULFURYL	**SUSPENS**	**SYNOVIA**
STIPULED	STUBBLED	SULKIES	SUSPENSE	SYNOVIAL
STIPULES	STUBBLES	SULKIEST	**SUSPIRE**	SYNOVIAS
STOMACH	**STUDENT**	**SULPHID**	SUSPIRED	**SYNTAGM**
STOMACHS	STUDENTS	SULPHIDE	SUSPIRES	SYNTAGMA
STOMACHY	STUDENTY	SULPHIDS	**SWADDLE**	SYNTAGMS
STOMATA	**STUMBLE**	**SULPHUR**	SWADDLED	**SYRINGE**
STOMATAL	STUMBLED	SULPHURS	SWADDLER	SYRINGED
STOMATE	STUMBLER	SULPHURY	SWADDLES	SYRINGES
OSTOMATE	STUMBLES	**SUMMATE**	**SWANKIE**	**SYSTOLE**
STOMATES	**STUNNED**	SUMMATED	SWANKIER	ASYSTOLE
STONIED	ASTUNNED	SUMMATES	SWANKIES	SYSTOLES
ASTONIED	**STYLISE**	**SUNBAKE**	**SWANNIE**	**TABBING**
STONIES	STYLISED	SUNBAKED	SWANNIER	STABBING
ASTONIES	STYLISER	SUNBAKES	SWANNIES	**TABLEAU**

TABLEAUS	**TAMBOUR**	STEAMING	**THALAMI**	STIFFING
TABLEAUX	TAMBOURA	TEAMINGS	THALAMIC	TIFFINGS
TABLING	TAMBOURS	**TEARING**	**THEISMS**	**TILLAGE**
STABLING	**TAMINES**	STEARING	ATHEISMS	STILLAGE
TABLINGS	ETAMINES	**TECHIES**	**THEISTS**	TILLAGES
TABLOID	**TAMPERS**	TECHIEST	ATHEISTS	**TILLERS**
TABLOIDS	STAMPERS	**TECHNIC**	**THEOLOG**	STILLERS
TABLOIDY	**TAMPING**	ATECHNIC	THEOLOGS	**TILLIER**
TABORIN	STAMPING	TECHNICS	THEOLOGY	STILLIER
TABORINE	TAMPINGS	**TEDDIES**	**THEOREM**	**TILLING**
TABORING	**TANDOOR**	STEDDIES	THEOREMS	STILLING
TABORINS	TANDOORI	**TEDDING**	**THERIAC**	TILLINGS
TACHISM	TANDOORS	STEDDING	THERIACA	**TILTERS**
TACHISME	**TANGIES**	**TEEMING**	THERIACS	STILTERS
TACHISMS	TANGIEST	STEEMING	**THERMIT**	**TILTING**
TACHIST	**TANGING**	**TEENAGE**	THERMITE	STILTING
TACHISTE	STANGING	TEENAGED	THERMITS	TILTINGS
TACHISTS	**TANKING**	TEENAGER	**THIAMIN**	**TINGING**
TACKERS	STANKING	TEENAGES	THIAMINE	STINGING
STACKERS	TANKINGS	**TEENING**	THIAMINS	**TINKERS**
TACKETS	**TANNATE**	STEENING	**THIAZIN**	STINKERS
STACKETS	STANNATE	**TEERING**	THIAZINE	**TINKING**
TACKIES	TANNATES	STEERING	THIAZINS	STINKING
TACKIEST	**TAPPICE**	**TEGMINA**	**THIAZOL**	**TINNIES**
TACKING	TAPPICED	TEGMINAL	THIAZOLE	TINNIEST
STACKING	TAPPICES	**TEGUMEN**	THIAZOLS	**TINTERS**
TACKINGS	**TAPPING**	TEGUMENT	**THICKET**	STINTERS
TAGGERS	STAPPING	**TELETEX**	THICKETS	**TINTIER**
STAGGERS	TAPPINGS	TELETEXT	THICKETY	STINTIER
TAGGIER	**TARDIES**	**TELLING**	**THIMBLE**	**TINTING**
STAGGIER	TARDIEST	STELLING	THIMBLED	STINTING
TAGGING	**TARINGS**	TELLINGS	THIMBLES	TINTINGS
STAGGING	STARINGS	**TEMPLES**	**THIONIN**	**TIPPLED**
TAGGINGS	**TARRIER**	STEMPLES	THIONINE	STIPPLED
TAKEOUT	STARRIER	**TEMPTER**	THIONINS	**TIPPLER**
STAKEOUT	TARRIERS	TEMPTERS	**THROMBI**	STIPPLER
TAKEOUTS	**TARRIES**	**TENCHES**	THROMBIN	TIPPLERS
TALKERS	TARRIEST	STENCHES	**THUNDER**	**TIPPLES**
STALKERS	**TARRING**	**TENDING**	THUNDERS	STIPPLES
TALKIER	STARRING	STENDING	THUNDERY	**TIRRING**
STALKIER	TARRINGS	**TENTING**	**THYLOSE**	STIRRING
TALKIES	**TARTANE**	STENTING	THYLOSES	**TITANIS**
TALKIEST	TARTANED	TENTINGS	**TICKERS**	TITANISM
TALKING	TARTANES	**TEREBRA**	STICKERS	**TITCHES**
STALKING	**TARTING**	TEREBRAE	**TICKIES**	STITCHES
TALKINGS	STARTING	TEREBRAS	STICKIES	**TITRATE**
TALLAGE	**TARTISH**	**TERNING**	**TICKING**	TITRATED
STALLAGE	STARTISH	STERNING	STICKING	TITRATES
TALLAGED	**TASHING**	**TERRACE**	TICKINGS	**TITULAR**
TALLAGES	STASHING	TERRACED	**TICKLED**	TITULARS
TALLITH	**TASSELL**	TERRACES	STICKLED	TITULARY
TALLITHS	TASSELLS	**TESSERA**	**TICKLER**	**TOASTIE**
TAMANDU	TASSELLY	TESSERAE	STICKLER	TOASTIER
TAMANDUA	**TATTIES**	TESSERAL	TICKLERS	TOASTIES
TAMANDUS	TATTIEST	**TESTRIL**	**TICKLES**	**TOCCATA**
TAMARIN	**TAWNIES**	TESTRILL	STICKLES	STOCCATA
TAMARIND	TAWNIEST	TESTRILS	**TIDDIES**	TOCCATAS
TAMARINS	**TEAMERS**	**TEXTURE**	STIDDIES	**TOCKIER**
TAMARIS	STEAMERS	TEXTURED	TIDDIEST	STOCKIER
TAMARISK	**TEAMING**	TEXTURES	**TIFFING**	**TOCKING**

STOCKING	TOPSIDES	**TRAIPSE**	TRIBUTES	STROLLER
TODGERS	**TOPSPIN**	TRAIPSED	**TRICKER**	TROLLERS
STODGERS	TOPSPINS	TRAIPSES	TRICKERS	**TROLLOP**
TOFFIES	**TORCHER**	**TRAMMEL**	TRICKERY	TROLLOPS
TOFFIEST	TORCHERE	STRAMMEL	**TRICKIE**	TROLLOPY
TOITING	TORCHERS	TRAMMELS	TRICKIER	**TROPHIC**
STOITING	**TORDION**	**TRAMPED**	**TRICKLE**	ATROPHIC
TOLIDIN	TORDIONS	STRAMPED	TRICKLED	STROPHIC
TOLIDINE	**TORMENT**	**TRAMPLE**	TRICKLES	**TROPINE**
TOLIDINS	TORMENTA	TRAMPLED	TRICKLET	ATROPINE
TONALLY	TORMENTS	TRAMPLER	**TRICORN**	TROPINES
ATONALLY	**TORMINA**	TRAMPLES	TRICORNE	**TROPINS**
TONIEST	TORMINAL	**TRANCHE**	TRICORNS	ATROPINS
STONIEST	**TORTURE**	TRANCHES	**TRIDENT**	**TROPISM**
TONINGS	TORTURED	TRANCHET	STRIDENT	ATROPISM
STONINGS	TORTURER	**TRANGLE**	TRIDENTS	TROPISMS
TONKERS	TORTURES	STRANGLE	**TRIFFID**	**TROUBLE**
STONKERS	**TOTTERS**	TRANGLES	TRIFFIDS	TROUBLED
TONKING	STOTTERS	**TRAPEZE**	TRIFFIDY	TROUBLER
STONKING	**TOTTIES**	TRAPEZED	**TRIGGED**	TROUBLES
TONNEAU	STOTTIES	TRAPEZES	STRIGGED	**TROUNCE**
TONNEAUS	TOTTIEST	**TRAPPED**	**TRILITH**	TROUNCED
TONNEAUX	**TOTTING**	STRAPPED	TRILITHS	TROUNCER
TONSURE	STOTTING	**TRAPPER**	**TRILOBE**	TROUNCES
TONSURED	TOTTINGS	STRAPPER	TRILOBED	**TROWING**
TONSURES	**TOURIST**	TRAPPERS	TRILOBES	STROWING
TONTINE	TOURISTA	**TRASHER**	TRILOBES	**TRUCKLE**
TONTINER	TOURISTS	TRASHERS	**TRIMMED**	TRUCKLED
TONTINES	TOURISTY	TRASHERY	STRIMMED	TRUCKLER
TOOLIES	**TOUSTIE**	**TRASSES**	**TRINDLE**	TRUCKLES
STOOLIES	TOUSTIER	STRASSES	TRINDLED	**TRUFFLE**
TOOLING	**TOWABLE**	**TRAVOIS**	TRINDLES	TRUFFLED
STOOLING	STOWABLE	TRAVOISE	**TRIOXID**	TRUFFLES
TOOLINGS	**TOWAGES**	**TREACLE**	TRIOXIDE	**TRUMEAU**
TOOSHIE	STOWAGES	TREACLED	TRIOXIDS	TRUMEAUX
STOOSHIE	**TOWAWAY**	TREACLES	**TRIPIER**	**TRUMPET**
TOOSHIER	STOWAWAY	**TREADLE**	STRIPIER	STRUMPET
TOPARCH	TOWAWAYS	TREADLED	**TRIPPED**	TRUMPETS
TOPARCHS	**TOWINGS**	TREADLER	STRIPPED	**TRUNDLE**
TOPARCHY	STOWINGS	TREADLES	**TRIPPER**	TRUNDLED
TOPLESS	**TOWNIES**	**TREDDLE**	STRIPPER	TRUNDLER
STOPLESS	TOWNIEST	TREDDLED	TRIPPERS	TRUNDLES
TOPLINE	**TRACHEA**	TREDDLES	TRIPPERY	**TRUSTEE**
TOPLINED	TRACHEAE	**TREMBLE**	**TRIPPLE**	TRUSTEED
TOPLINER	TRACHEAL	ATREMBLE	TRIPPLED	TRUSTEES
TOPLINES	TRACHEAS	TREMBLED	TRIPPLER	**TSUNAMI**
TOPONYM	**TRACHLE**	TREMBLER	TRIPPLES	TSUNAMIC
TOPONYMS	TRACHLED	TREMBLES	**TRIPTAN**	TSUNAMIS
TOPONYMY	TRACHLES	**TRESSED**	TRIPTANE	**TUBBIER**
TOPPERS	**TRADUCE**	STRESSED	TRIPTANS	STUBBIER
STOPPERS	TRADUCED	**TRESSES**	**TROCHIL**	**TUBBING**
TOPPING	TRADUCER	STRESSES	TROCHILI	STUBBING
STOPPING	TRADUCES	**TRIARCH**	TROCHILS	TUBBINGS
TOPPINGS	**TRAIKED**	TRIARCHS	**TROFFER**	**TUILYIE**
TOPPLED	STRAIKED	TRIARCHY	TROFFERS	TUILYIED
STOPPLED	**TRAINED**	**TRIAZIN**	**TROKING**	TUILYIES
TOPPLES	STRAINED	TRIAZINE	STROKING	**TUILZIE**
STOPPLES	**TRAINER**	TRIAZINS	**TROLLED**	TUILZIED
TOPSIDE	STRAINER	**TRIBUTE**	STROLLED	TUILZIES
TOPSIDER	TRAINERS	TRIBUTER	**TROLLER**	**TUMBLED**

STUMBLED	**TYMPANA**	UNBRACED	UNHINGED	GUNPAPER
TUMBLER	TYMPANAL	UNBRACES	UNHINGES	UNPAPERS
STUMBLER	**TYMPANI**	**UNBRAKE**	**UNHOODS**	**UNPLACE**
TUMBLERS	TYMPANIC	UNBRAKED	NUNHOODS	UNPLACED
TUMBLES	**TYPICAL**	UNBRAKES	**UNHORSE**	UNPLACES
STUMBLES	ATYPICAL	**UNBROKE**	UNHORSED	**UNPLUME**
TUMESCE	ETYPICAL	UNBROKEN	UNHORSES	UNPLUMED
TUMESCED	**TYRANNE**	**UNBURNT**	**UNHOUSE**	UNPLUMES
TUMESCES	TYRANNED	SUNBURNT	FUNHOUSE	**UNPURSE**
TUMPIER	TYRANNES	**UNCHOKE**	GUNHOUSE	UNPURSED
STUMPIER	**TZITZIT**	SUNCHOKE	UNHOUSED	UNPURSES
TUMPING	TZITZITH	UNCHOKED	UNHOUSES	**UNQUOTE**
STUMPING	**UAKARIS**	UNCHOKES	**UNIFIED**	UNQUOTED
TUMULAR	OUAKARIS	**UNCLASP**	MUNIFIED	UNQUOTES
TUMULARY	**UBEROUS**	UNCLASPS	**UNIFIES**	**UNREAVE**
TUNNING	SUBEROUS	**UNCLOSE**	MUNIFIES	UNREAVED
STUNNING	TUBEROUS	UNCLOSED	**UNIFORM**	UNREAVES
TUNNINGS	**UDDERED**	UNCLOSES	CUNIFORM	**UNREEVE**
TURBINE	JUDDERED	**UNCLOUD**	UNIFORMS	UNREEVED
TURBINED	PUDDERED	UNCLOUDS	**UNIQUES**	UNREEVES
TURBINES	**UGLIEST**	UNCLOUDY	UNIQUEST	**UNROOFS**
TUSHIES	FUGLIEST	**UNCRATE**	**UNITING**	SUNROOFS
STUSHIES	**UILLEAN**	UNCRATED	MUNITING	**UNROUND**
TUSSOCK	UILLEANN	UNCRATES	UNITINGS	RUNROUND
TUSSOCKS	**ULLAGES**	**UNCTION**	**UNITION**	UNROUNDS
TUSSOCKY	FULLAGES	FUNCTION	MUNITION	**UNSCALE**
TUTELAR	SULLAGES	JUNCTION	PUNITION	UNSCALED
TUTELARS	**ULLINGS**	UNCTIONS	UNITIONS	UNSCALES
TUTELARY	BULLINGS	**UNCURSE**	**UNITISE**	**UNSENSE**
TWADDLE	CULLINGS	UNCURSED	UNITISED	UNSENSED
TWADDLED	NULLINGS	UNCURSES	UNITISER	UNSENSES
TWADDLER	**ULULATE**	**UNDECKS**	UNITISES	**UNSHALE**
TWADDLES	ULULATED	SUNDECKS	**UNITIVE**	UNSHALED
TWANGLE	ULULATES	**UNDERDO**	PUNITIVE	UNSHALES
TWANGLED	**UMBERED**	UNDERDOG	**UNITIZE**	**UNSHAPE**
TWANGLER	CUMBERED	**UNDERGO**	UNITIZED	UNSHAPED
TWANGLES	LUMBERED	UNDERGOD	UNITIZER	UNSHAPEN
TWATTLE	NUMBERED	**UNDINES**	UNITIZES	UNSHAPES
TWATTLED	**UMBRAGE**	NUNDINES	**UNLEARN**	**UNSHIPS**
TWATTLER	UMBRAGED	**UNDRAPE**	UNLEARNS	GUNSHIPS
TWATTLES	UMBRAGES	UNDRAPED	UNLEARNT	NUNSHIPS
TWEEDLE	**UMBRELS**	UNDRAPES	**UNLOCKS**	**UNSIGHT**
TWEEDLED	TUMBRELS	**UNDRESS**	GUNLOCKS	GUNSIGHT
TWEEDLER	**UMBRILS**	SUNDRESS	**UNLOOSE**	UNSIGHTS
TWEEDLES	TUMBRILS	**UNDYING**	UNLOOSED	**UNSPOKE**
TWIDDLE	**UMBROUS**	BUNDYING	UNLOOSEN	UNSPOKEN
TWIDDLED	CUMBROUS	**UNFAIRS**	UNLOOSES	**UNSTATE**
TWIDDLER	**UNAWAKE**	FUNFAIRS	**UNMAKER**	UNSTATED
TWIDDLES	UNAWAKED	**UNFENCE**	GUNMAKER	UNSTATES
TWINKLE	**UNBAKED**	UNFENCED	UNMAKERS	**UNSTICK**
TWINKLED	SUNBAKED	UNFENCES	**UNMITRE**	GUNSTICK
TWINKLER	**UNBELTS**	**UNFROZE**	UNMITRED	UNSTICKS
TWINKLES	SUNBELTS	UNFROZEN	UNMITRES	**UNSTOCK**
TWITTER	**UNBLIND**	**UNGLOVE**	**UNNERVE**	GUNSTOCK
ATWITTER	SUNBLIND	UNGLOVED	UNNERVED	UNSTOCKS
TWITTERS	UNBLINDS	UNGLOVES	UNNERVES	**UNSUITS**
TWITTERY	**UNBLOCK**	**UNGUENT**	**UNNOBLE**	SUNSUITS
TWIZZLE	SUNBLOCK	UNGUENTA	UNNOBLED	**UNTHINK**
TWIZZLED	UNBLOCKS	UNGUENTS	UNNOBLES	UNTHINKS
TWIZZLES	**UNBRACE**	**UNHINGE**	**UNPAPER**	**UNTRACE**

UNTRACED	**UPSTARE**	MUTTERER	VAUNTIER	**VETCHES**
UNTRACES	UPSTARED	PUTTERER	**VAVASOR**	KVETCHES
UNTRUST	UPSTARES	UTTERERS	VAVASORS	**VETIVER**
UNTRUSTS	**UPSTATE**	**VACCINA**	VAVASORY	VETIVERS
UNTRUSTY	UPSTATER	VACCINAL	**VAWNTIE**	VETIVERT
UNTWINE	UPSTATES	VACCINAS	VAWNTIER	**VETTING**
UNTWINED	**UPSURGE**	**VACCINE**	**VEINULE**	VETTINGS
UNTWINES	UPSURGED	VACCINEE	VEINULES	**VEXILLA**
UNVAILE	UPSURGES	VACCINES	VEINULET	VEXILLAR
UNVAILED	**UPTHROW**	**VACUATE**	**VENGERS**	**VIALFUL**
UNVAILES	UPTHROWN	EVACUATE	AVENGERS	VIALFULS
UNVOICE	UPTHROWS	VACUATED	**VENGING**	**VIATICA**
UNVOICED	**UPVALUE**	VACUATES	AVENGING	VIATICAL
UNVOICES	UPVALUED	**VAILING**	**VENTAIL**	**VIATORS**
UNWARIE	UPVALUES	AVAILING	AVENTAIL	AVIATORS
UNWARIER	**URALITE**	**VALANCE**	VENTAILE	**VIBRATE**
UNWATER	RURALITE	VALANCED	VENTAILS	VIBRATED
UNWATERS	URALITES	VALANCES	**VENTERS**	VIBRATES
UNWATERY	**URETHAN**	**VALUATE**	EVENTERS	**VIBRATO**
UNWORTH	URETHANE	EVALUATE	**VENTING**	VIBRATOR
UNWORTHS	URETHANS	VALUATED	EVENTING	VIBRATOS
UNWORTHY	**URETHRA**	VALUATES	VENTINGS	**VICIATE**
UPBROKE	URETHRAE	**VALVULA**	**VENTRED**	VICIATED
UPBROKEN	URETHRAL	VALVULAE	AVENTRED	VICIATES
UPCLOSE	URETHRAS	VALVULAR	**VENTRES**	**VICTORS**
UPCLOSED	**URGENCY**	**VAMOOSE**	AVENTRES	EVICTORS
UPCLOSES	TURGENCY	VAMOOSED	**VENTURE**	**VIGOROS**
UPCURVE	**URGINGS**	VAMOOSES	AVENTURE	VIGOROSO
UPCURVED	PURGINGS	**VAMPIRE**	VENTURED	**VILAYET**
UPCURVES	SURGINGS	VAMPIRED	VENTURER	VILAYETS
UPGRADE	**URINATE**	VAMPIRES	VENTURES	**VILLAGE**
UPGRADED	URINATED	**VANDYKE**	**VERANDA**	VILLAGER
UPGRADER	URINATES	VANDYKED	VERANDAH	VILLAGES
UPGRADES	**URNINGS**	VANDYKES	VERANDAS	**VILLAIN**
UPHEAVE	BURNINGS	**VANTAGE**	**VERBIDS**	VILLAINS
UPHEAVED	TURNINGS	VANTAGED	OVERBIDS	VILLAINY
UPHEAVER	**UROLOGY**	VANTAGES	**VERBOSE**	**VINEGAR**
UPHEAVES	OUROLOGY	**VARIATE**	VERBOSER	VINEGARS
UPHROES	**USELESS**	VARIATED	**VERDITE**	VINEGARY
EUPHROES	FUSELESS	VARIATES	VERDITER	**VINTAGE**
UPLYING	**USHERED**	**VARICES**	VERDITES	VINTAGED
DUPLYING	HUSHERED	AVARICES	**VERDURE**	VINTAGER
UPPINGS	**UTILISE**	**VARIOLA**	VERDURED	VINTAGES
CUPPINGS	UTILISED	VARIOLAR	VERDURES	**VIOLATE**
UPRAISE	UTILISER	VARIOLAS	**VERRUCA**	VIOLATED
UPRAISED	UTILISES	**VARIOLE**	VERRUCAE	VIOLATER
UPRAISER	**UTILITY**	OVARIOLE	VERRUCAS	VIOLATES
UPRAISES	FUTILITY	VARIOLES	**VERSETS**	**VISCERA**
UPROUSE	**UTILIZE**	**VARIOUS**	OVERSETS	VISCERAL
UPROUSED	UTILIZED	OVARIOUS	**VERSION**	**VITAMIN**
UPROUSES	UTILIZER	**VARNISH**	AVERSION	VITAMINE
UPSCALE	UTILIZES	VARNISHY	EVERSION	VITAMINS
UPSCALED	**UTOPIAS**	**VASCULA**	VERSIONS	**VITELLI**
UPSCALES	UTOPIAST	VASCULAR	**VERTING**	VITELLIN
UPSPOKE	**UTTERED**	**VAUNTED**	AVERTING	**VITIATE**
UPSPOKEN	BUTTERED	AVAUNTED	EVERTING	VITIATED
UPSTAGE	GUTTERED	**VAUNTER**	**VESTURE**	VITIATES
UPSTAGED	MUTTERED	VAUNTERS	VESTURED	**VOCABLE**
UPSTAGER	PUTTERED	VAUNTERY	VESTURER	EVOCABLE
UPSTAGES	**UTTERER**	**VAUNTIE**	VESTURES	VOCABLES

VOIDERS	**WALLOWS**	**WASPIES**	WELCOMED	WHITTLED
AVOIDERS	SWALLOWS	WASPIEST	WELCOMER	WHITTLER
VOIDING	**WAMPISH**	**WATCHES**	WELCOMES	WHITTLES
AVOIDING	SWAMPISH	SWATCHES	**WELLING**	**WHOMBLE**
VOIDINGS	**WANGLED**	**WATTLED**	DWELLING	WHOMBLED
VOLUTED	TWANGLED	TWATTLED	SWELLING	WHOMBLES
EVOLUTED	**WANGLER**	**WATTLES**	WELLINGS	**WHOMMLE**
VOLUTES	TWANGLER	TWATTLES	**WELTERS**	WHOMMLED
EVOLUTES	WANGLERS	WATTLESS	SWELTERS	WHOMMLES
VOLVING	**WANGLES**	**WAYFARE**	**WELTING**	**WHUMMLE**
EVOLVING	TWANGLES	WAYFARED	SWELTING	WHUMMLED
VOUCHED	**WANKERS**	WAYFARER	WELTINGS	WHUMMLES
AVOUCHED	SWANKERS	WAYFARES	**WHAISLE**	**WIDDLED**
VOUCHER	**WANKIER**	**WEARERS**	WHAISLED	TWIDDLED
AVOUCHER	SWANKIER	SWEARERS	WHAISLES	**WIDDLES**
VOUCHERS	**WANKING**	**WEARIED**	**WHAIZLE**	TWIDDLES
VOUCHES	SWANKING	AWEARIED	WHAIZLED	**WIGGERS**
AVOUCHES	**WANNABE**	**WEARIER**	WHAIZLES	SWIGGERS
VULGATE	WANNABEE	SWEARIER	**WHEEDLE**	TWIGGERS
EVULGATE	WANNABES	**WEARIES**	WHEEDLED	**WIGGIER**
VULGATES	**WANNING**	WEARIEST	WHEEDLER	TWIGGIER
WADDIES	SWANNING	**WEARING**	WHEEDLES	**WIGGING**
SWADDIES	**WANTING**	SWEARING	**WHEELIE**	SWIGGING
WADDLED	AWANTING	**WEARINGS**	WHEELIER	TWIGGING
SWADDLED	**WAPPERS**	**WEATHER**	WHEELIES	WIGGINGS
TWADDLED	SWAPPERS	AWEATHER	**WHEENGE**	**WIGHTED**
WADDLER	**WAPPING**	WEATHERS	WHEENGED	TWIGHTED
SWADDLER	SWAPPING	**WEBBIES**	WHEENGES	**WIGLESS**
TWADDLER	**WARDERS**	WEBBIEST	**WHEEPLE**	TWIGLESS
WADDLERS	AWARDERS	**WEBZINE**	WHEEPLED	**WIGLETS**
WADDLES	**WARDING**	WEBZINES	WHEEPLES	TWIGLETS
SWADDLES	AWARDING	**WEDGIES**	**WHEEZLE**	**WIGLIKE**
TWADDLES	SWARDING	WEDGIEST	WHEEZLED	TWIGLIKE
WAGGERS	WARDINGS	**WEEDIER**	WHEEZLES	**WILLERS**
SWAGGERS	**WARFARE**	TWEEDIER	**WHEMMLE**	SWILLERS
WAGGING	WARFARED	**WEEDILY**	WHEMMLED	**WILLIES**
SWAGGING	WARFARER	TWEEDILY	WHEMMLES	TWILLIES
WAINING	WARFARES	**WEENIES**	**WHIFFLE**	**WILLING**
SWAINING	**WARMERS**	SWEENIES	WHIFFLED	SWILLING
WAITERS	SWARMERS	TWEENIES	WHIFFLER	TWILLING
AWAITERS	**WARMING**	WEENIEST	WHIFFLES	**WILTING**
WAITING	SWARMING	**WEEPERS**	**WHIMPLE**	TWILTING
AWAITING	WARMINGS	SWEEPERS	WHIMPLED	**WINDLED**
WAITINGS	**WARNING**	**WEEPIER**	WHIMPLES	DWINDLED
WAKENED	AWARNING	SWEEPIER	**WHIPSAW**	SWINDLED
AWAKENED	WARNINGS	**WEEPIES**	WHIPSAWN	**WINDLES**
WAKENER	**WARRANT**	WEEPIEST	WHIPSAWS	DWINDLES
AWAKENER	WARRANTS	**WEEPING**	**WHISKER**	SWINDLES
WAKENERS	WARRANTY	SWEEPING	WHISKERS	WINDLESS
WAKINGS	**WARSTLE**	WEEPINGS	WHISKERY	**WINGERS**
AWAKINGS	WARSTLED	**WEETEST**	**WHISPER**	SWINGERS
WALIEST	WARSTLER	SWEETEST	WHISPERS	**WINGIER**
SWALIEST	WARSTLES	**WEETING**	WHISPERY	SWINGIER
WALLETS	**WASHERS**	SWEETING	**WHISTLE**	**WINGING**
SWALLETS	SWASHERS	TWEETING	WHISTLED	SWINGING
WALLEYE	**WASHIER**	**WEIGELA**	WHISTLER	TWINGING
WALLEYED	SWASHIER	WEIGELAS	WHISTLES	**WINGMAN**
WALLEYES	**WASHING**	**WEIRING**	**WHITIES**	SWINGMAN
WALLIES	SWASHING	SWEIRING	WHITIEST	**WINGMEN**
WALLIEST	WASHINGS	**WELCOME**	**WHITTLE**	SWINGMEN

WINIEST	TWISTING	SWOOSHED	**WRESTLE**	YCLEEPES
TWINIEST	**WITCHED**	**WOOSHES**	WRESTLED	**YESHIVA**
WINKERS	SWITCHED	SWOOSHES	WRESTLER	YESHIVAH
SWINKERS	TWITCHED	**WOPPING**	WRESTLES	YESHIVAS
WINKING	**WITCHES**	SWOPPING	**WRIGGLE**	**YUMMIES**
SWINKING	SWITCHES	**WORDING**	WRIGGLED	YUMMIEST
TWINKING	TWITCHES	**WORKOUT**	WRIGGLER	**ZADDIKS**
WINKINGS	**WITHERS**	WORKOUTS	WRIGGLES	TZADDIKS
WINKLED	SWITHERS	**WOTTING**	**WRINKLE**	**ZECCHIN**
TWINKLED	**WITHIES**	SWOTTING	WRINKLED	ZECCHINE
WINKLER	WITHIEST	**WOUNDED**	WRINKLES	ZECCHINI
TWINKLER	**WITTERS**	SWOUNDED	**WRITING**	ZECCHINO
WINKLERS	TWITTERS	**WRANGLE**	WRITINGS	ZECCHINS
WINKLES	**WITTING**	WRANGLED	**WUSSIES**	**ZONATED**
TWINKLES	TWITTING	WRANGLER	WUSSIEST	OZONATED
WINNING	WITTINGS	WRANGLES	**XANTHIN**	**ZOOGLEA**
TWINNING	**WOODBIN**	**WRASSLE**	XANTHINE	ZOOGLEAE
WINNINGS	WOODBIND	WRASSLED	XANTHINS	ZOOGLEAL
WINSOME	WOODBINE	WRASSLES	**XYLIDIN**	ZOOGLEAS
WINSOMER	WOODBINS	**WRASTLE**	XYLIDINE	**ZYGOSES**
WINTERS	**WOODIES**	WRASTLED	XYLIDINS	AZYGOSES
TWINTERS	WOODIEST	WRASTLES	**YAFFING**	**ZYMITES**
WISHERS	**WOOLIES**	**WREATHE**	NYAFFING	AZYMITES
SWISHERS	WOOLIEST	WREATHED	**YAPPIES**	**ZYMOGEN**
WISSING	**WOONING**	WREATHEN	YAPPIEST	ZYMOGENE
SWISSING	SWOONING	WREATHER	**YCLEEPE**	ZYMOGENS
WISTING	**WOOSHED**	WREATHES	YCLEEPED	

Eight-letter root words

ABDICATE	ABSOLUTES	TACONITES	ADULATORY	NAINSELLS
ABDICATED	**ABSTERGE**	**ACRODONT**	**ADUNCATE**	**AIRBRUSH**
ABDICATES	ABSTERGED	MACRODONT	ADUNCATED	HAIRBRUSH
ABDOMINA	ABSTERGES	ACRODONTS	**ADVOCATE**	**AIRINESS**
ABDOMINAL	**ABSTRUSE**	**ACTIONED**	ADVOCATED	HAIRINESS
ABERRATE	ABSTRUSER	PACTIONED	ADVOCATES	**AIRLINES**
ABERRATED	**ACANTHIN**	**ACTIVATE**	**AFFIANCE**	HAIRLINES
ABERRATES	ACANTHINE	ACTIVATED	AFFIANCED	**AIRLOCKS**
ABNEGATE	ACANTHINS	ACTIVATES	AFFIANCES	HAIRLOCKS
ABNEGATED	**ACCOLADE**	**ACTIVISE**	**AFFRONTE**	**ALATIONS**
ABNEGATES	ACCOLADED	ACTIVISED	AFFRONTED	HALATIONS
ABOIDEAU	ACCOLADES	ACTIVISES	AFFRONTEE	**ALBITISE**
ABOIDEAUS	**ACCORAGE**	**ACTIVISM**	**AFTEREYE**	ALBITISED
ABOIDEAUX	ACCORAGED	LACTIVISM	AFTEREYED	ALBITISES
ABOITEAU	ACCORAGES	ACTIVISMS	AFTEREYES	**ALBITIZE**
ABOITEAUS	**ACCOUTRE**	**ACTIVIST**	**AGGADAHS**	ALBITIZED
ABOITEAUX	ACCOUTRED	LACTIVIST	HAGGADAHS	ALBITIZES
ABORIGIN	ACCOUTRES	ACTIVISTS	**AGGADOTH**	**ALEWIVES**
ABORIGINE	**ACERATED**	**ACTIVIZE**	HAGGADOTH	KALEWIVES
ABORIGINS	LACERATED	ACTIVIZED	**AGGRIEVE**	**ALIENATE**
ABROGATE	MACERATED	ACTIVIZES	AGGRIEVED	ALIENATED
ABROGATED	**ACERBATE**	**ACTUALLY**	AGGRIEVES	ALIENATES
ABROGATES	ACERBATED	FACTUALLY	**AGISTERS**	**ALIGNERS**
ABSCISIN	ACERBATES	TACTUALLY	MAGISTERS	MALIGNERS
ABSCISING	**ACETAMID**	**ACUITIES**	**AGNOMINA**	**ALIGNING**
ABSCISINS	ACETAMIDE	VACUITIES	AGNOMINAL	MALIGNING
ABSCISSA	ACETAMIDS	**ACULEATE**	**AILERONS**	**ALIZARIN**
ABSCISSAE	**ACIERATE**	ACULEATED	TAILERONS	ALIZARINE
ABSCISSAS	ACIERATED	ACULEATES	**AILMENTS**	ALIZARINS
ABSOLUTE	ACIERATES	**ADULATOR**	BAILMENTS	**ALKALISE**
ABSOLUTER	**ACONITES**	ADULATORS	**AINSELLS**	ALKALISED

ALKALISER	AMMONITES	**ANNULATE**	APHORIZED	**ARILLATE**
ALKALISES	**AMORTISE**	CANNULATE	APHORIZER	ARILLATED
ALKALIZE	AMORTISED	ANNULATED	APHORIZES	**ARMATURE**
ALKALIZED	AMORTISES	ANNULATES	**APHTHOUS**	ARMATURED
ALKALIZER	**AMORTIZE**	**ANOREXIC**	NAPHTHOUS	ARMATURES
ALKALIZES	AMORTIZED	TANOREXIC	**APOLOGIA**	**ARMONICA**
ALKYLATE	AMORTIZES	ANOREXICS	APOLOGIAE	HARMONICA
ALKYLATED	**AMPHIBIA**	**ANTECEDE**	APOLOGIAS	ARMONICAS
ALKYLATES	AMPHIBIAN	ANTECEDED	**APPANAGE**	**AROUSALS**
ALLELUIA	**AMPHORIC**	ANTECEDES	APPANAGED	CAROUSALS
ALLELUIAH	CAMPHORIC	**ANTEDATE**	APPANAGES	**AROUSERS**
ALLELUIAS	**AMPULLAR**	ANTEDATED	**APPETISE**	CAROUSERS
ALLIABLE	AMPULLARY	ANTEDATES	APPETISED	**AROUSING**
TALLIABLE	**AMPUTATE**	**ANTEFIXA**	APPETISER	CAROUSING
ALLIANCE	AMPUTATED	ANTEFIXAE	APPETISES	**ARQUEBUS**
DALLIANCE	AMPUTATES	ANTEFIXAL	**APPETIZE**	HARQUEBUS
ALLIANCES	**AMYGDALA**	**ANTELOPE**	APPETIZED	**ARRAIGNS**
ALLIGATE	AMYGDALAE	GANTELOPE	APPETIZER	DARRAIGNS
ALLIGATED	**ANAGLYPH**	ANTELOPES	APPETIZES	**ARRAYING**
ALLIGATES	ANAGLYPHS	**ANTHILLS**	**APPLIQUE**	WARRAYING
ALLOCATE	ANAGLYPHY	WANTHILLS	APPLIQUED	**ARRIAGES**
ALLOCATED	**ANAPHORA**	**ANTICISE**	APPLIQUES	CARRIAGES
ALLOCATES	ANAPHORAL	ANTICISED	**APPRAISE**	MARRIAGES
ALLOPATH	ANAPHORAS	ANTICISES	APPRAISED	**ARROGATE**
ALLOPATHS	**ANECDOTA**	**ANTICIZE**	APPRAISEE	ARROGATED
ALLOPATHY	ANECDOTAL	ANTICIZED	APPRAISER	ARROGATES
ALLOTTER	**ANGELICA**	ANTICIZES	APPRAISES	**ARROWING**
ALLOTTERS	ANGELICAL	**ANTIDOTE**	**APRICATE**	FARROWING
ALLOTTERY	ANGELICAS	ANTIDOTED	APRICATED	HARROWING
ALLOWING	**ANGERING**	ANTIDOTES	APRICATES	MARROWING
FALLOWING	DANGERING	**ANTILIFE**	**AQUATINT**	NARROWING
GALLOWING	**ANGLINGS**	ANTILIFER	AQUATINTA	TARROWING
HALLOWING	DANGLINGS	**ANTIMONY**	AQUATINTS	**ARSEHOLE**
SALLOWING	JANGLINGS	ANTIMONYL	**ARBORISE**	ARSEHOLED
TALLOWING	TANGLINGS	**ANTINUKE**	ARBORISED	ARSEHOLES
WALLOWING	WANGLINGS	ANTINUKER	ARBORISES	**ARTICLES**
ALTERERS	**ANGUIPED**	ANTINUKES	**ARBORIZE**	PARTICLES
FALTERERS	ANGUIPEDE	**ANTIPHON**	ARBORIZED	**ARTIFICE**
PALTERERS	**ANGULATE**	ANTIPHONS	ARBORIZES	ARTIFICER
ALTERING	MANGULATE	ANTIPHONY	**ARBOROUS**	ARTIFICES
FALTERING	ANGULATED	**ANTIPOLE**	HARBOROUS	**ARTINESS**
HALTERING	ANGULATES	RANTIPOLE	**ARBOURED**	TARTINESS
PALTERING	**ANKYLOSE**	ANTIPOLES	HARBOURED	**ARTISANS**
ALTERNAT	ANKYLOSED	**ANTISTAT**	**ARCHAISE**	BARTISANS
ALTERNATE	ANKYLOSES	ANTISTATS	ARCHAISED	PARTISANS
ALTERNATS	**ANNALISE**	**APERTURE**	ARCHAISER	**ARTWORKS**
AMBLINGS	ANNALISED	APERTURED	ARCHAISES	PARTWORKS
GAMBLINGS	ANNALISES	APERTURES	**ARCHAIZE**	**ASEITIES**
LAMBLINGS	**ANNALIZE**	**APHETISE**	ARCHAIZED	GASEITIES
RAMBLINGS	ANNALIZED	APHETISED	ARCHAIZER	**ASHERIES**
WAMBLINGS	ANNALIZES	APHETISES	ARCHAIZES	FASHERIES
AMBROSIA	**ANNOTATE**	**APHETIZE**	**ARCOLOGY**	WASHERIES
AMBROSIAL	ANNOTATED	APHETIZED	SARCOLOGY	**ASHINESS**
AMBROSIAN	ANNOTATES	APHETIZES	**AREFYING**	WASHINESS
AMBROSIAS	**ANNOUNCE**	**APHORISE**	RAREFYING	**ASPERATE**
AMBULATE	ANNOUNCED	APHORISED	**AREOLATE**	ASPERATED
AMBULATED	ANNOUNCER	APHORISER	AREOLATED	ASPERATES
AMBULATES	ANNOUNCES	APHORISES	**ARGUMENT**	**ASPEROUS**
AMMONITE	**ANNOYING**	**APHORIZE**	ARGUMENTA	JASPEROUS
MAMMONITE	TANNOYING	APHORIZE	ARGUMENTS	**ASPERSOR**

ASPERSORS	AURICULAE	BACKBONED	**BASHLESS**	**BELITTLES**
ASPERSORY	AURICULAR	BACKBONES	ABASHLESS	**BEMINGLE**
ASPHYXIA	AURICULAS	**BACKDATE**	**BASHMENT**	BEMINGLED
ASPHYXIAL	**AURIFORM**	BACKDATED	ABASHMENT	BEMINGLES
ASPHYXIAS	TAURIFORM	BACKDATES	BASHMENTS	**BEMUDDLE**
ASPIRATA	**AUTOLOGY**	**BACKDROP**	**BASILICA**	BEMUDDLED
ASPIRATAE	TAUTOLOGY	BACKDROPS	BASILICAE	BEMUDDLES
ASPIRATE	**AUTOLYSE**	BACKDROPT	BASILICAL	**BEMUFFLE**
ASPIRATED	AUTOLYSED	**BACKFIRE**	BASILICAN	BEMUFFLED
ASPIRATES	AUTOLYSES	BACKFIRED	BASILICAS	BEMUFFLES
ASSAILED	**AUTOLYZE**	BACKFIRES	**BASOPHIL**	**BEMUZZLE**
WASSAILED	AUTOLYZED	**BACKSLID**	BASOPHILE	BEMUZZLED
ASSAILER	AUTOLYZES	BACKSLIDE	BASOPHILS	BEMUZZLES
WASSAILER	**AUTOMATE**	**BACTERIA**	**BATEMENT**	**BENEFICE**
ASSAILERS	AUTOMATED	BACTERIAL	ABATEMENT	BENEFICED
ASSEMBLE	AUTOMATES	BACTERIAN	BATEMENTS	BENEFICES
ASSEMBLED	**AUTONYMS**	BACTERIAS	**BATTLEAX**	**BENZIDIN**
ASSEMBLER	TAUTONYMS	**BACULITE**	BATTLEAXE	BENZIDINE
ASSEMBLES	**AUTOSAVE**	BACULITES	**BAUDRICK**	BENZIDINS
ASSERTOR	AUTOSAVED	**BADINAGE**	BAUDRICKE	**BEPIMPLE**
ASSERTORS	AUTOSAVES	BADINAGED	BAUDRICKS	BEPIMPLED
ASSERTORY	**AUTOTYPE**	BADINAGES	**BEARDIES**	BEPIMPLES
ASSONATE	AUTOTYPED	**BALDPATE**	BEARDIEST	**BEPRAISE**
ASSONATED	AUTOTYPES	BALDPATED	**BECHANCE**	BEPRAISED
ASSONATES	**AUXILIAR**	BALDPATES	BECHANCED	BEPRAISES
ASTEISMS	AUXILIARS	**BALLADIN**	BECHANCES	**BERBERIN**
CASTEISMS	AUXILIARY	BALLADINE	**BECLOTHE**	BERBERINE
ASTRAGAL	**AVENTAIL**	BALLADING	BECLOTHED	BERBERINS
ASTRAGALI	AVENTAILE	BALLADINS	BECLOTHES	**BERGAMAS**
ASTRAGALS	AVENTAILS	**BALLISTA**	**BEDABBLE**	BERGAMASK
ASTRINGE	**AVIANISE**	BALLISTAE	BEDABBLED	**BESMUDGE**
ASTRINGED	AVIANISED	BALLISTAS	BEDABBLES	BESMUDGED
ASTRINGER	AVIANISES	**BANALISE**	**BEDAGGLE**	BESMUDGES
ASTRINGES	**AVIANIZE**	BANALISED	BEDAGGLED	**BESOOTHE**
ATAGHANS	AVIANIZED	BANALISES	BEDAGGLES	BESOOTHED
YATAGHANS	AVIANIZES	**BANALIZE**	**BEDAZZLE**	BESOOTHES
ATCHIEVE	**AVIARIES**	BANALIZED	BEDAZZLED	**BESPOUSE**
ATCHIEVED	CAVIARIES	BANALIZES	BEDAZZLES	BESPOUSED
ATCHIEVES	**AVICULAR**	**BANDEROL**	**BEDIMPLE**	BESPOUSES
ATHETISE	NAVICULAR	BANDEROLE	BEDIMPLED	**BIOGENIC**
ATHETISED	**AVIFAUNA**	BANDEROLS	BEDIMPLES	ABIOGENIC
ATHETISES	AVIFAUNAE	**BARBECUE**	**BEFRINGE**	**BIOGRAPH**
ATHETIZE	AVIFAUNAL	BARBECUED	BEFRINGED	BIOGRAPHS
ATHETIZED	AVIFAUNAS	BARBECUER	BEFRINGES	BIOGRAPHY
ATHETIZES	**AVIGATOR**	BARBECUES	**BEFUDDLE**	**BIRDLIME**
ATMOLYSE	NAVIGATOR	**BARBEQUE**	BEFUDDLED	BIRDLIMED
ATMOLYSED	AVIGATORS	BARBEQUED	BEFUDDLES	BIRDLIMES
ATMOLYSES	**AXILLARY**	BARBEQUES	**BEGIRDLE**	**BLASTEMA**
ATMOLYZE	MAXILLARY	**BAREBONE**	BEGIRDLED	BLASTEMAL
ATMOLYZED	**AZURITES**	BAREBONED	BEGIRDLES	BLASTEMAS
ATMOLYZES	LAZURITES	BAREBONES	**BEGRUDGE**	**BLASTIES**
ATTICISE	**BACCHANT**	**BARNACLE**	BEGRUDGED	BLASTIEST
ATTICISED	BACCHANTE	BARNACLED	BEGRUDGER	**BLASTULA**
ATTICISES	BACCHANTS	BARNACLES	BEGRUDGES	BLASTULAE
ATTICIZE	**BACILLAR**	**BASELINE**	**BEJUMBLE**	BLASTULAR
ATTICIZED	BACILLARY	BASELINER	BEJUMBLED	BLASTULAS
ATTICIZES	**BACKBITE**	BASELINES	BEJUMBLES	**BLEACHER**
AUGUSTES	BACKBITER	**BASEMENT**	**BELITTLE**	BLEACHERS
AUGUSTEST	BACKBITES	ABASEMENT	BELITTLED	BLEACHERY
AURICULA	**BACKBONE**	BASEMENTS	BELITTLER	**BLIZZARD**

BLIZZARDS	**BRAIDING**	**BUTMENTS**	CANONISED	SCARPINGS
BLIZZARDY	ABRAIDING	ABUTMENTS	CANONISER	**CARSHARE**
BLOCKADE	BRAIDINGS	**BUTTHEAD**	CANONISES	CARSHARED
BLOCKADED	**BRANCHER**	BUTTHEADS	**CANONIZE**	CARSHARES
BLOCKADER	BRANCHERS	**BUTYLATE**	CANONIZED	**CARTOUCH**
BLOCKADES	BRANCHERY	BUTYLATED	CANONIZER	CARTOUCHE
BLOCKIES	**BRANCHIA**	BUTYLATES	CANONIZES	**CASEMATE**
BLOCKIEST	BRANCHIAE	**CABALLER**	**CANOODLE**	CASEMATED
BLONDINE	BRANCHIAL	CABALLERO	CANOODLED	CASEMATES
BLONDINED	**BRASSIER**	CABALLERS	CANOODLER	**CASTELLA**
BLONDINES	BRASSIERE	**CABRIOLE**	CANOODLES	CASTELLAN
BLOODIES	**BRASSIES**	CABRIOLES	**CANTHARI**	**CASTRATE**
BLOODIEST	BRASSIEST	CABRIOLET	CANTHARID	CASTRATED
BLOVIATE	**BRATTICE**	**CACOMIXL**	CANTHARIS	CASTRATER
BLOVIATED	BRATTICED	CACOMIXLE	**CANTIEST**	CASTRATES
BLOVIATES	BRATTICES	CACOMIXLS	SCANTIEST	**CASTRATO**
BLUELINE	**BRETTICE**	**CACUMINA**	**CANTLING**	CASTRATOR
BLUELINER	BRETTICED	CACUMINAL	SCANTLING	CASTRATOS
BLUELINES	BRETTICES	**CALAMINE**	**CANULATE**	**CATALYSE**
BLUENOSE	**BRICKIES**	CALAMINED	CANULATED	CATALYSED
BLUENOSED	BRICKIEST	CALAMINES	CANULATES	CATALYSER
BLUENOSES	**BRIDGING**	**CALCANEA**	**CAPITATE**	CATALYSES
BODEMENT	ABRIDGING	CALCANEAL	CAPITATED	**CATALYZE**
ABODEMENT	BRIDGINGS	CALCANEAN	**CAPITULA**	CATALYZED
BODEMENTS	**BRIMFULL**	**CALCEATE**	CAPITULAR	CATALYZER
BOLDFACE	BRIMFULLY	CALCEATED	**CAPONIER**	CATALYZES
BOLDFACED	**BRITTLES**	CALCEATES	CAPONIERE	**CATAPHOR**
BOLDFACES	BRITTLEST	**CALCULAR**	CAPONIERS	CATAPHORA
BOLSHIES	**BROMELIA**	CALCULARY	**CAPONISE**	CATAPHORS
BOLSHIEST	BROMELIAD	**CALORISE**	CAPONISED	**CATENATE**
BOMBARDE	BROMELIAS	CALORISED	CAPONISES	CATENATED
BOMBARDED	**BRONCHIA**	CALORISES	**CAPONIZE**	CATENATES
BOMBARDER	BRONCHIAL	**CALORIZE**	CAPONIZED	**CATHEDRA**
BOMBARDES	**BROOKING**	CALORIZED	CAPONIZES	CATHEDRAE
BORECOLE	ABROOKING	CALORIZES	**CAPRICCI**	CATHEDRAL
BORECOLES	**BROWNIES**	**CALVARIA**	CAPRICCIO	CATHEDRAS
BOTANICA	BROWNIEST	CALVARIAL	**CAPRIOLE**	**CATTIEST**
BOTANICAL	**BRUCELLA**	CALVARIAN	CAPRIOLED	SCATTIEST
BOTANICAS	BRUCELLAE	CALVARIAS	CAPRIOLES	**CAVITATE**
BOTANISE	BRUCELLAS	**CALYPTER**	**CAPSOMER**	CAVITATED
BOTANISED	**BUBBLIES**	CALYPTERA	CAPSOMERE	CAVITATES
BOTANISER	BUBBLIEST	CALYPTERS	CAPSOMERS	**CELLULAR**
BOTANISES	**BUILDING**	**CAMPINGS**	**CAPSULAR**	ACELLULAR
BOTANIZE	ABUILDING	SCAMPINGS	CAPSULARY	CELLULARS
BOTANIZED	BUILDINGS	**CANALISE**	**CARABINE**	**CENTINEL**
BOTANIZER	**BULLDOZE**	CANALISED	CARABINER	CENTINELL
BOTANIZES	BULLDOZED	CANALISES	CARABINES	CENTINELS
BOUNDING	BULLDOZER	**CANALIZE**	**CARACOLE**	**CENTONEL**
ABOUNDING	BULLDOZES	CANALIZED	CARACOLED	CENTONELL
BOUSOUKI	**BULLETIN**	CANALIZES	CARACOLER	CENTONELS
BOUSOUKIA	BULLETING	**CANEPHOR**	CARACOLES	**CENTUPLE**
BOUSOUKIS	BULLETINS	CANEPHORA	**CARAPACE**	CENTUPLED
BOUTIQUE	**BURNOOSE**	CANEPHORE	CARAPACED	CENTUPLES
BOUTIQUES	BURNOOSED	CANEPHORS	CARAPACES	**CEPHALIC**
BOUTIQUEY	BURNOOSES	**CANNELON**	**CARETAKE**	ACEPHALIC
BOUTONNE	**BURNOUSE**	CANNELONI	CARETAKEN	CEPHALICS
BOUTONNEE	BURNOUSED	CANNELONS	**CARINATE**	**CERCARIA**
BOUZOUKI	BURNOUSES	**CANNINGS**	ECARINATE	CERCARIAE
BOUZOUKIA	**BUSINESS**	SCANNINGS	CARINATED	CERCARIAL
BOUZOUKIS	BUSINESSY	**CANONISE**	**CARPINGS**	CERCARIAN

CERCARIAS	CHUMSHIPS	COCREATED	COLONIZES	CONCLUDES
CHANDLER	**CHURINGA**	COCREATES	**COLOPHON**	**CONCOURS**
CHANDLERS	CHURINGAS	**CODERIVE**	COLOPHONS	CONCOURSE
CHANDLERY	**CHYMOSIN**	CODERIVED	COLOPHONY	**CONCRETE**
CHAPERON	CHYMOSINS	CODERIVES	**COLORISE**	CONCRETED
CHAPERONE	**CICERONE**	**COENDURE**	COLORISED	CONCRETES
CHAPERONS	CICERONED	COENDURED	COLORISER	**CONDENSE**
CHAPPIES	CICERONES	COENDURES	COLORISES	CONDENSED
CHAPPIEST	**CINCTURE**	**COEQUATE**	**COLORIZE**	CONDENSER
CHARCOAL	CINCTURED	COEQUATED	COLORIZED	CONDENSES
CHARCOALS	CINCTURES	COEQUATES	COLORIZER	**CONFERVA**
CHARCOALY	**CINNAMON**	**COEVOLVE**	COLORIZES	CONFERVAE
CHAROSET	CINNAMONS	COEVOLVED	**COMANAGE**	CONFERVAL
CHAROSETH	CINNAMONY	COEVOLVES	COMANAGED	CONFERVAS
CHAROSETS	**CIRRIPED**	**COGITATE**	COMANAGER	**CONFLATE**
CHASTISE	CIRRIPEDE	COGITATED	COMANAGES	CONFLATED
CHASTISED	CIRRIPEDS	COGITATES	**COMATULA**	CONFLATES
CHASTISER	**CISTERNA**	**COGNOSCE**	COMATULAE	**CONFRONT**
CHASTISES	CISTERNAE	COGNOSCED	**COMEDDLE**	CONFRONTE
CHATTIES	CISTERNAL	COGNOSCES	COMEDDLED	CONFRONTS
CHATTIEST	**CIVILISE**	**COHOBATE**	COMEDDLES	**CONGLOBE**
CHERRIES	CIVILISED	COHOBATED	**COMINGLE**	CONGLOBED
CHERRIEST	CIVILISER	COHOBATES	COMINGLED	CONGLOBES
CHICANER	CIVILISES	**COIFFURE**	COMINGLES	**CONICITY**
CHICANERS	**CIVILIZE**	COIFFURED	**COMMENCE**	ICONICITY
CHICANERY	CIVILIZED	COIFFURES	COMMENCED	**CONNIVER**
CHILLERS	CIVILIZER	**COINCIDE**	COMMENCER	CONNIVERS
SCHILLERS	CIVILIZES	COINCIDED	COMMENCES	CONNIVERY
CHILLIES	**CLAUSTRA**	COINCIDES	**COMMERCE**	**CONQUEST**
CHILLIEST	CLAUSTRAL	**COINHERE**	ECOMMERCE	CONQUESTS
CHILLING	**CLAUSULA**	COINHERED	COMMERCED	**CONSERVE**
SCHILLING	CLAUSULAE	COINHERES	COMMERCES	CONSERVED
CHILLINGS	CLAUSULAR	**COINSURE**	**COMMERGE**	CONSERVER
CHINKIES	**CLEEPING**	COINSURED	COMMERGED	CONSERVES
CHINKIEST	YCLEEPING	COINSURER	COMMERGES	**CONSPIRE**
CHIPPIES	**CLITELLA**	COINSURES	**COMPESCE**	CONSPIRED
CHIPPIEST	CLITELLAR	**COLLAPSE**	COMPESCED	CONSPIRER
CHITTIES	**CLODPATE**	COLLAPSED	COMPESCES	CONSPIRES
CHITTIEST	CLODPATED	COLLAPSES	**COMPLAIN**	**CONSTATE**
CHIVAREE	CLODPATES	**COLLEGIA**	COMPLAINS	CONSTATED
CHIVAREED	**COACHIES**	COLLEGIAL	COMPLAINT	CONSTATES
CHIVAREES	COACHIEST	COLLEGIAN	**COMPLETE**	**CONSTRUE**
CHLORDAN	**COADMIRE**	**COLLOGUE**	COMPLETED	CONSTRUED
CHLORDANE	COADMIRED	COLLOGUED	COMPLETER	CONSTRUER
CHLORDANS	COADMIRES	COLLOGUES	COMPLETES	CONSTRUES
CHOCCIES	**COALESCE**	**COLLOQUE**	**COMPRIZE**	**CONTINUA**
CHOCCIEST	COALESCED	COLLOQUED	COMPRIZED	CONTINUAL
CHOCKFUL	COALESCES	COLLOQUES	COMPRIZES	**CONTINUE**
CHOCKFULL	**COALHOLE**	**COLLUVIA**	**COMPULSE**	CONTINUED
CHROMISE	COALHOLES	COLLUVIAL	COMPULSED	CONTINUER
CHROMISED	**COALMINE**	**COLOCATE**	COMPULSES	CONTINUES
CHROMISES	COALMINER	COLOCATED	**CONCEIVE**	**CONTRAST**
CHROMIZE	COALMINES	COLOCATES	CONCEIVED	CONTRASTS
CHROMIZED	**COASSUME**	**COLONISE**	CONCEIVER	CONTRASTY
CHROMIZES	COASSUMED	COLONISED	CONCEIVES	**CONTRIVE**
CHROMOUS	COASSUMES	COLONISER	**CONCISES**	CONTRIVED
ACHROMOUS	**COCHLEAR**	COLONISES	CONCISEST	CONTRIVER
CHUMMIES	COCHLEARE	**COLONIZE**	**CONCLUDE**	CONTRIVES
CHUMMIEST	COCHLEARS	COLONIZED	CONCLUDED	**CONVERGE**
CHUMSHIP	**COCREATE**	COLONIZER	CONCLUDER	CONVERGED

CONVERGES	**CRAGGILY**	**CRIBELLA**	**CULLIONS**	**DAHABIYA**
CONVERSE	SCRAGGILY	CRIBELLAR	SCULLIONS	DAHABIYAH
CONVERSED	**CRAMMING**	**CRIMPERS**	**CULTCHES**	DAHABIYAS
CONVERSER	SCRAMMING	SCRIMPERS	SCULTCHES	**DAINTIES**
CONVERSES	**CRANCHED**	**CRIMPIER**	**CULTRATE**	DAINTIEST
CONVINCE	SCRANCHED	SCRIMPIER	CULTRATED	**DAMASKIN**
CONVINCED	**CRANCHES**	**CRIMPING**	**CUMBERED**	DAMASKING
CONVINCER	SCRANCHES	SCRIMPING	SCUMBERED	DAMASKINS
CONVINCES	**CRAPPERS**	**CRISPATE**	**CUMULATE**	**DANCETTE**
CONVOLVE	SCRAPPERS	CRISPATED	CUMULATED	DANCETTEE
CONVOLVED	**CRAPPIER**	**CRISPIES**	CUMULATES	DANCETTES
CONVOLVES	SCRAPPIER	CRISPIEST	**CURARISE**	**DANDRUFF**
CONVULSE	**CRAPPIES**	**CRISTATE**	CURARISED	DANDRUFFS
CONVULSED	CRAPPIEST	CRISTATED	CURARISES	DANDRUFFY
CONVULSES	**CRAPPING**	**CRITERIA**	**CURARIZE**	**DARRAIGN**
COOTCHED	SCRAPPING	CRITERIAL	CURARIZED	DARRAIGNE
SCOOTCHED	**CRATCHES**	**CRITICAL**	CURARIZES	DARRAIGNS
COOTCHES	SCRATCHES	ACRITICAL	**CURCUMIN**	**DARRAINE**
SCOOTCHES	**CRAWLERS**	**CRITIQUE**	CURCUMINE	DARRAINED
COPULATE	SCRAWLERS	CRITIQUED	CURCUMINS	DARRAINES
SCOPULATE	**CRAWLIER**	CRITIQUES	**CURLICUE**	**DATABASE**
COPULATED	SCRAWLIER	**CROSSBIT**	CURLICUED	DATABASED
COPULATES	**CRAWLING**	CROSSBITE	CURLICUES	DATABASES
COQUETTE	SCRAWLING	**CROSSTIE**	**CURRIERS**	**DATELINE**
COQUETTED	CRAWLINGS	CROSSTIED	SCURRIERS	DATELINED
COQUETTES	**CREAKIER**	CROSSTIES	**CURRYING**	DATELINES
CORDELLE	SCREAKIER	**CROTCHET**	SCURRYING	**DAYDREAM**
CORDELLED	**CREAKING**	CROTCHETS	CURRYINGS	DAYDREAMS
CORDELLES	SCREAKING	CROTCHETY	**CURSITOR**	DAYDREAMT
CORELATE	**CREAMERS**	**CRUMMIER**	CURSITORS	DAYDREAMY
CORELATED	SCREAMERS	SCRUMMIER	CURSITORY	**DEADLINE**
CORELATES	**CREAMING**	**CRUMMIES**	**CURTALAX**	DEADLINED
CORELESS	SCREAMING	SCRUMMIES	CURTALAXE	DEADLINES
SCORELESS	**CREASOTE**	CRUMMIEST	**CURVIEST**	**DEAERATE**
CORONATE	CREASOTED	**CRUMPING**	SCURVIEST	DEAERATED
CORONATED	CREASOTES	SCRUMPING	**CUSPIDOR**	DEAERATES
CORONATES	**CREEPIES**	**CRUMPLED**	CUSPIDORE	**DEBONAIR**
COROTATE	CREEPIEST	SCRUMPLED	CUSPIDORS	DEBONAIRE
COROTATED	**CREMATOR**	**CRUMPLES**	**CUTENESS**	**DEBOUCHE**
COROTATES	CREMATORS	SCRUMPLES	ACUTENESS	DEBOUCHED
CORPORAL	CREMATORY	**CRUNCHED**	**CUTICULA**	DEBOUCHES
CORPORALE	**CRENELLE**	SCRUNCHED	CUTICULAE	**DEBRUISE**
CORPORALS	CRENELLED	**CRUNCHES**	CUTICULAR	DEBRUISED
CORVETTE	CRENELLES	SCRUNCHES	**CUTINISE**	DEBRUISES
CORVETTED	**CREOLISE**	**CRUNCHIE**	CUTINISED	**DECEMVIR**
CORVETTES	CREOLISED	SCRUNCHIE	CUTINISES	DECEMVIRI
COSMISMS	CREOLISES	CRUNCHIER	**CUTINIZE**	DECEMVIRS
ACOSMISMS	**CREOLIZE**	CRUNCHIES	CUTINIZED	**DECENNIA**
COSMISTS	CREOLIZED	**CRUSTATE**	CUTINIZES	DECENNIAL
ACOSMISTS	CREOLIZES	CRUSTATED	**CUTTLING**	**DECENTRE**
COSTUMER	**CREOSOTE**	**CRUSTIES**	SCUTTLING	DECENTRED
COSTUMERS	CREOSOTED	CRUSTIEST	**CUTWORKS**	DECENTRES
COSTUMERY	CREOSOTES	**CRYOSTAT**	SCUTWORKS	**DECIMATE**
COURSING	**CREVASSE**	CRYOSTATS	**CYANAMID**	DECIMATED
SCOURSING	CREVASSED	**CUDDLING**	CYANAMIDE	DECIMATES
COURSINGS	CREVASSES	SCUDDLING	CYANAMIDS	**DECLASSE**
CRABBING	**CRIBBLED**	**CUFFLING**	**CZARITSA**	DECLASSED
SCRABBING	SCRIBBLED	SCUFFLING	CZARITSAS	DECLASSEE
CRAGGIER	**CRIBBLES**	**CULLINGS**	**DACTYLIC**	DECLASSES
SCRAGGIER	SCRIBBLES	SCULLINGS	DACTYLICS	**DECORATE**

DECORATED	DENATURES	**DEVELOPE**	**DISBURSE**	DISPENSER
DECORATES	**DENOTATE**	DEVELOPED	DISBURSED	DISPENSES
DECOUPLE	DENOTATED	DEVELOPER	DISBURSER	**DISPERSE**
DECOUPLED	DENOTATES	DEVELOPES	DISBURSES	DISPERSED
DECOUPLER	**DENOUNCE**	**DEVIATOR**	**DISCIPLE**	DISPERSER
DECOUPLES	DENOUNCED	DEVIATORS	DISCIPLED	DISPERSES
DECREASE	DENOUNCER	DEVIATORY	DISCIPLES	**DISPLACE**
DECREASED	DENOUNCES	**DIAGNOSE**	**DISCLOSE**	DISPLACED
DECREASES	**DENUDATE**	DIAGNOSED	DISCLOSED	DISPLACER
DEDICATE	DENUDATED	DIAGNOSES	DISCLOSER	DISPLACES
DEDICATED	DENUDATES	**DIALOGUE**	DISCLOSES	**DISPLODE**
DEDICATEE	**DEPEOPLE**	DIALOGUED	**DISCOURE**	DISPLODED
DEDICATES	DEPEOPLED	DIALOGUER	DISCOURED	DISPLODES
DEFECATE	DEPEOPLES	DIALOGUES	DISCOURES	**DISPLUME**
DEFECATED	**DEPILATE**	**DIAPAUSE**	**DISCOVER**	DISPLUMED
DEFECATES	DEPILATED	DIAPAUSED	DISCOVERS	DISPLUMES
DEFILADE	DEPILATES	DIAPAUSES	DISCOVERT	**DISPONGE**
DEFILADED	**DEPURATE**	**DIARRHEA**	DISCOVERY	DISPONGED
DEFILADES	DEPURATED	DIARRHEAL	**DISCRETE**	DISPONGES
DEGREASE	DEPURATES	DIARRHEAS	DISCRETER	**DISPRIZE**
DEGREASED	**DEPUTISE**	**DICHASIA**	**DISGORGE**	DISPRIZED
DEGREASER	DEPUTISED	DICHASIAL	DISGORGED	DISPRIZES
DEGREASES	DEPUTISES	**DICTATOR**	DISGORGER	**DISPROVE**
DEIGNING	**DEPUTIZE**	DICTATORS	DISGORGES	DISPROVED
SDEIGNING	DEPUTIZED	DICTATORY	**DISGRACE**	DISPROVEN
DEIONISE	DEPUTIZES	**DIDRACHM**	DISGRACED	DISPROVER
DEIONISED	**DEROGATE**	DIDRACHMA	DISGRACER	DISPROVES
DEIONISER	DEROGATED	DIDRACHMS	DISGRACES	**DISPUNGE**
DEIONISES	DEROGATES	**DIGITATE**	**DISGRADE**	DISPUNGED
DEIONIZE	**DESCRIBE**	DIGITATED	DISGRADED	DISPUNGES
DEIONIZED	DESCRIBED	**DIGITISE**	DISGRADES	**DISPURSE**
DEIONIZER	DESCRIBER	DIGITISED	**DISGUISE**	DISPURSED
DEIONIZES	DESCRIBES	DIGITISER	DISGUISED	DISPURSES
DELEGATE	**DESCRIVE**	DIGITISES	DISGUISER	**DISSEISE**
DELEGATED	DESCRIVED	**DIGITIZE**	DISGUISES	DISSEISED
DELEGATEE	DESCRIVES	DIGITIZED	**DISHABLE**	DISSEISEE
DELEGATES	**DESOLATE**	DIGITIZER	DISHABLED	DISSEISES
DELIBATE	DESOLATED	DIGITIZES	DISHABLES	**DISSEIZE**
DELIBATED	DESOLATER	**DIMERISE**	**DISHDASH**	DISSEIZED
DELIBATES	DESOLATES	DIMERISED	DISHDASHA	DISSEIZEE
DEMENTIA	**DESPOTAT**	DIMERISES	**DISHORSE**	DISSEIZES
DEMENTIAL	DESPOTATE	**DIMERIZE**	DISHORSED	**DISSERVE**
DEMENTIAS	DESPOTATS	DIMERIZED	DISHORSES	DISSERVED
DEMERARA	**DESTRUCT**	DIMERIZES	**DISHOUSE**	DISSERVES
DEMERARAN	DESTRUCTO	**DIPLOMAT**	DISHOUSED	**DISSOLVE**
DEMERARAS	DESTRUCTS	DIPLOMATA	DISHOUSES	DISSOLVED
DEMIVOLT	**DETANGLE**	DIPLOMATE	**DISINURE**	DISSOLVER
DEMIVOLTE	DETANGLED	DIPLOMATS	DISINURED	DISSOLVES
DEMIVOLTS	DETANGLER	**DIRECTOR**	DISINURES	**DISSUADE**
DEMOCRAT	DETANGLES	DIRECTORS	**DISLEAVE**	DISSUADED
DEMOCRATS	**DETHRONE**	DIRECTORY	DISLEAVED	DISSUADER
DEMOCRATY	DETHRONED	**DIRIGISM**	DISLEAVES	DISSUADES
DEMONISE	DETHRONER	DIRIGISME	**DISLODGE**	**DISTANCE**
DEMONISED	DETHRONES	DIRIGISMS	DISLODGED	DISTANCED
DEMONISES	**DETONATE**	**DISABUSE**	DISLODGES	DISTANCES
DEMONIZE	DETONATED	DISABUSED	**DISPENCE**	**DISTASTE**
DEMONIZED	DETONATES	DISABUSES	DISPENCED	DISTASTED
DEMONIZES	**DETRAQUE**	**DISAGREE**	DISPENCES	DISTASTES
DENATURE	DETRAQUEE	DISAGREED	**DISPENSE**	**DISTRAIN**
DENATURED	DETRAQUES	DISAGREES	DISPENSED	DISTRAINS

DISTRAINT	DUBITATED	**ECLOSING**	EJECTIONS	EMBATTLES
DISTRAIT	DUBITATES	RECLOSING	**EJECTIVE**	**EMBEZZLE**
DISTRAITE	**DUCHESSE**	**ECOLOGIC**	REJECTIVE	EMBEZZLED
DISULFID	DUCHESSED	OECOLOGIC	EJECTIVES	EMBEZZLER
DISULFIDE	DUCHESSES	**ECSTASIS**	**EJECTORS**	EMBEZZLES
DISULFIDS	**DUNGAREE**	ECSTASISE	REJECTORS	**EMBOLISE**
DISUNITE	DUNGAREED	**ECUMENIC**	**ELAPSING**	EMBOLISED
DISUNITED	DUNGAREES	OECUMENIC	DELAPSING	EMBOLISES
DISUNITER	**DYNAMISE**	ECUMENICS	RELAPSING	**EMBOLIZE**
DISUNITES	DYNAMISED	**EDGEWISE**	**ELATEDLY**	EMBOLIZED
DISVALUE	DYNAMISES	WEDGEWISE	BELATEDLY	EMBOLIZES
DISVALUED	**DYNAMITE**	**EDITIONS**	RELATEDLY	**EMBRACER**
DISVALUES	DYNAMITED	SEDITIONS	**ELATIONS**	EMBRACERS
DIVAGATE	DYNAMITER	**EDUCATOR**	DELATIONS	EMBRACERY
DIVAGATED	DYNAMITES	EDUCATORS	GELATIONS	**EMENDATE**
DIVAGATES	**DYNAMIZE**	EDUCATORY	RELATIONS	EMENDATED
DIVINISE	DYNAMIZED	**EDUCIBLE**	**ELATIVES**	EMENDATES
DIVINISED	DYNAMIZES	DEDUCIBLE	RELATIVES	**EMENDING**
DIVINISES	**DYSPNOEA**	REDUCIBLE	**ELECTEES**	REMENDING
DIVINIZE	DYSPNOEAL	SEDUCIBLE	SELECTEES	**EMERGENT**
DIVINIZED	DYSPNOEAS	**EDUCTION**	**ELECTING**	EMERGENTS
DIVINIZES	**DYSTOCIA**	DEDUCTION	SELECTING	**EMERGING**
DJELLABA	DYSTOCIAL	REDUCTION	**ELECTION**	DEMERGING
DJELLABAH	DYSTOCIAS	SEDUCTION	SELECTION	REMERGING
DJELLABAS	**DYSTOPIA**	EDUCTIONS	ELECTIONS	**EMERSION**
DOGGONES	DYSTOPIAN	**EDUCTIVE**	**ELECTIVE**	DEMERSION
DOGGONEST	DYSTOPIAS	DEDUCTIVE	SELECTIVE	EMERSIONS
DOMICILE	**EANLINGS**	REDUCTIVE	ELECTIVES	**EMIGRATE**
DOMICILED	WEANLINGS	SEDUCTIVE	**ELECTORS**	REMIGRATE
DOMICILES	YEANLINGS	**EDUCTORS**	SELECTORS	EMIGRATED
DOMINATE	**EARDROPS**	REDUCTORS	**ELECTRIC**	EMIGRATES
DOMINATED	TEARDROPS	SEDUCTORS	ELECTRICS	**EMISSION**
DOMINATES	**EARLIEST**	**EERINESS**	**ELEVATED**	DEMISSION
DORISING	NEARLIEST	BEERINESS	ELEVATEDS	REMISSION
ODORISING	PEARLIEST	LEERINESS	**ELEVATOR**	EMISSIONS
DORIZING	**EARNINGS**	**EFFECTOR**	ELEVATORS	**EMISSIVE**
ODORIZING	LEARNINGS	EFFECTORS	ELEVATORY	DEMISSIVE
DOWNCOME	YEARNINGS	**EFFIERCE**	**ELFHOODS**	REMISSIVE
DOWNCOMER	**EASELESS**	EFFIERCED	SELFHOODS	**EMITTERS**
DOWNCOMES	CEASELESS	EFFIERCES	**ELFISHLY**	REMITTERS
DOWNSIZE	**EASTINGS**	**EFFLUVIA**	SELFISHLY	**EMITTING**
DOWNSIZED	BEASTINGS	EFFLUVIAL	**ELONGATE**	DEMITTING
DOWNSIZER	FEASTINGS	**EGENCIES**	ELONGATED	REMITTING
DOWNSIZES	**EATERIES**	REGENCIES	ELONGATES	**EMMARBLE**
DOWNZONE	PEATERIES	**EGGFRUIT**	**ELUSIONS**	EMMARBLED
DOWNZONED	**EBAUCHES**	EGGFRUITS	DELUSIONS	EMMARBLES
DOWNZONES	DEBAUCHES	**EGOMANIA**	**ELUVIATE**	**EMOTIONS**
DRAGGING	**EBIONISE**	EGOMANIAC	ELUVIATED	DEMOTIONS
DRAGGINGS	EBIONISED	EGOMANIAS	ELUVIATES	REMOTIONS
DREADFUL	EBIONISES	**EGRESSED**	**EMACIATE**	**EMPEOPLE**
DREADFULS	**EBIONIZE**	REGRESSED	EMACIATED	EMPEOPLED
DREADING	EBIONIZED	**EGRESSES**	EMACIATES	EMPEOPLES
ADREADING	EBIONIZES	NEGRESSES	**EMAILING**	**EMPERISE**
DREARIES	**ECAUDATE**	REGRESSES	REMAILING	EMPERISED
DREARIEST	DECAUDATE	**EJECTING**	EMAILINGS	EMPERISES
DRICKSIE	**ECCLESIA**	DEJECTING	**EMANATOR**	**EMPERIZE**
DRICKSIER	ECCLESIAE	REJECTING	EMANATORS	EMPERIZED
DRUGGIES	ECCLESIAL	**EJECTION**	EMANATORY	EMPERIZES
DRUGGIEST	**ECHINATE**	DEJECTION	**EMBATTLE**	**EMPHASIS**
DUBITATE	ECHINATED	REJECTION	EMBATTLED	EMPHASISE

EMPIERCE	**ENFIERCE**	**ENSHRINE**	ENWREATHE	ERADIATED
EMPIERCED	ENFIERCED	ENSHRINED	ENWREATHS	ERADIATES
EMPIERCES	ENFIERCES	ENSHRINEE	**EOLIENNE**	**ERGOTISE**
EMPLONGE	**ENFILADE**	ENSHRINES	AEOLIPILE	ERGOTISED
EMPLONGED	ENFILADED	**ENSILAGE**	EOLIPILES	ERGOTISES
EMPLONGES	ENFILADES	ENSILAGED	**EOLITHIC**	**ERGOTIZE**
EMPTINGS	**ENFORCED**	ENSILAGES	NEOLITHIC	ERGOTIZED
TEMPTINGS	RENFORCED	**ENSNARER**	**EPENDYMA**	ERGOTIZES
EMPURPLE	**ENFORCES**	ENSNARERS	EPENDYMAL	**ERRORIST**
EMPURPLED	RENFORCES	**ENSORCEL**	EPENDYMAS	TERRORIST
EMPURPLES	**ENGIRDLE**	ENSORCELL	**EPHEDRIN**	ERRORISTS
EMULSIFY	ENGIRDLED	ENSORCELS	EPHEDRINE	**ERUCTATE**
DEMULSIFY	ENGIRDLES	**ENSPHERE**	EPHEDRINS	ERUCTATED
ENARCHES	**ENGRAMME**	ENSPHERED	**EPHEMERA**	ERUCTATES
MENARCHES	ENGRAMMES	ENSPHERES	EPHEMERAE	**ERYTHEMA**
ENATIONS	**ENGRAVER**	**ENSURERS**	EPHEMERAL	ERYTHEMAL
VENATIONS	ENGRAVERS	CENSURERS	EPHEMERAS	ERYTHEMAS
ENCHANTS	ENGRAVERY	**ENSURING**	**EPICEDIA**	**ESCALADE**
PENCHANTS	**ENGRIEVE**	CENSURING	EPICEDIAL	ESCALADED
ENCHARGE	ENGRIEVED	**ENSWATHE**	EPICEDIAN	ESCALADER
ENCHARGED	ENGRIEVES	ENSWATHED	**EPIDOTES**	ESCALADES
ENCHARGES	**ENGROOVE**	ENSWATHES	LEPIDOTES	**ESCALATE**
ENCIRCLE	ENGROOVED	**ENTAMEBA**	**EPIFAUNA**	ESCALATED
ENCIRCLED	ENGROOVES	ENTAMEBAE	EPIFAUNAE	ESCALATES
ENCIRCLES	**ENHEARSE**	ENTAMEBAS	EPIFAUNAL	**ESCALOPE**
ENCLOTHE	ENHEARSED	**ENTANGLE**	EPIFAUNAS	ESCALOPED
ENCLOTHED	ENHEARSES	PENTANGLE	**EPIGRAPH**	ESCALOPES
ENCLOTHES	**ENKINDLE**	ENTANGLED	EPIGRAPHS	**ESCRIBED**
ENCRADLE	ENKINDLED	ENTANGLER	EPIGRAPHY	DESCRIBED
ENCRADLED	ENKINDLER	ENTANGLES	**EPILATED**	**ESCRIBES**
ENCRADLES	ENKINDLES	**ENTAYLES**	DEPILATED	DESCRIBES
ENCREASE	**ENLIGHTS**	VENTAYLES	**EPILATES**	**ESOPHAGI**
ENCREASED	PENLIGHTS	**ENTERING**	DEPILATES	OESOPHAGI
ENCREASES	**ENLUMINE**	CENTERING	**EPILATOR**	**ESOTERIC**
ENDAMAGE	ENLUMINED	TENTERING	DEPILATOR	ESOTERICA
ENDAMAGED	ENLUMINES	ENTERINGS	EPILATORS	**ESPOUSED**
ENDAMAGES	**ENOPHILE**	**ENTHRONE**	**EPILOGUE**	BESPOUSED
ENDAMEBA	OENOPHILE	ENTHRONED	EPILOGUED	**ESPOUSES**
ENDAMEBAE	XENOPHILE	ENTHRONES	EPILOGUES	BESPOUSES
ENDAMEBAS	ENOPHILES	**ENTICING**	**EPITHECA**	**ESSONITE**
ENDOSMOS	**ENOSISES**	PENTICING	EPITHECAE	HESSONITE
ENDOSMOSE	KENOSISES	ENTICINGS	**EPIZOISM**	ESSONITES
ENDOSTEA	**ENOUNCED**	**ENTRANCE**	EPIZOISMS	**ESTATING**
ENDOSTEAL	DENOUNCED	ENTRANCED	**EPURATED**	GESTATING
ENERGISE	RENOUNCED	ENTRANCES	DEPURATED	RESTATING
ENERGISED	**ENOUNCES**	**ENTRISMS**	**EPURATES**	**ESTHESES**
ENERGISER	DENOUNCES	CENTRISMS	DEPURATES	AESTHESES
ENERGISES	RENOUNCES	**ENTRISTS**	**EQUALISE**	**ESTHESIA**
ENERGIZE	**ENRAUNGE**	CENTRISTS	EQUALISED	AESTHESIA
ENERGIZED	ENRAUNGED	**ENVEIGLE**	EQUALISER	ESTHESIAS
ENERGIZER	ENRAUNGES	ENVEIGLED	EQUALISES	**ESTHESIS**
ENERGIZES	**ENSAMPLE**	ENVEIGLES	**EQUALIZE**	AESTHESIS
ENERVATE	ENSAMPLED	**ENVELOPE**	EQUALIZED	**ESTHETES**
DENERVATE	ENSAMPLES	ENVELOPED	EQUALIZER	AESTHETES
ENERVATED	**ENSCONCE**	ENVELOPER	EQUALIZES	**ESTHETIC**
ENERVATES	ENSCONCED	ENVELOPES	**EQUIPAGE**	AESTHETIC
ENFEEBLE	ENSCONCES	**ENVISAGE**	EQUIPAGED	ESTHETICS
ENFEEBLED	**ENSHEATH**	ENVISAGED	EQUIPAGES	**ESTIMATE**
ENFEEBLER	ENSHEATHE	ENVISAGES	**ERADIATE**	ESTIMATED
ENFEEBLES	ENSHEATHS	**ENWREATH**	RERADIATE	ESTIMATES

ESTIVATE	ETHOXIDES	EVERSIONS	EXIGEANTE	FEDERATED
AESTIVATE	**ETHYLATE**	**EVERTING**	**EXORCISE**	FEDERATES
ESTIVATED	METHYLATE	REVERTING	EXORCISED	**FELLATIO**
ESTIVATES	ETHYLATED	**EVIDENCE**	EXORCISER	FELLATION
ESTRANGE	**ETHYLENE**	EVIDENCED	EXORCISES	FELLATIOS
ESTRANGED	METHYLENE	EVIDENCES	**EXORCIZE**	**FEMINISE**
ESTRANGER	ETHYLENES	**EVIRATES**	EXORCIZED	FEMINISED
ESTRANGES	**ETIOLATE**	LEVIRATES	EXORCIZER	FEMINISES
ESTRIOLS	PETIOLATE	**EVITATED**	EXORCIZES	**FEMINIZE**
OESTRIOLS	ETIOLATED	LEVITATED	**EXPEDITE**	FEMINIZED
ESTROGEN	ETIOLATES	**EVITATES**	EXPEDITED	FEMINIZES
OESTROGEN	**ETIOLOGY**	LEVITATES	EXPEDITER	**FENESTRA**
ESTROGENS	AETIOLOGY	**EVOCABLE**	EXPEDITES	FENESTRAE
ESTRONES	**ETRANGER**	REVOCABLE	**EXPIATOR**	FENESTRAL
OESTRONES	ETRANGERE	**EVOCATOR**	EXPIATORS	FENESTRAS
ESTRUSES	ETRANGERS	EVOCATORS	EXPIATORY	**FIBERISE**
OESTRUSES	**EUCALYPT**	EVOCATORY	**EXTREMES**	FIBERISED
ETACISMS	EUCALYPTI	**EVOLVERS**	EXTREMEST	FIBERISES
BETACISMS	EUCALYPTS	REVOLVERS	**EXTRORSE**	**FIBERIZE**
ETAMINES	**EUCARYOT**	**EVOLVING**	DEXTRORSE	FIBERIZED
KETAMINES	EUCARYOTE	DEVOLVING	**EXTUBATE**	FIBERIZES
ETCHINGS	EUCARYOTS	REVOLVING	EXTUBATED	**FIBRILLA**
LETCHINGS	**EUDAEMON**	**EVULGATE**	EXTUBATES	FIBRILLAE
ETERNISE	EUDAEMONS	EVULGATED	**EXUVIATE**	FIBRILLAR
ETERNISED	EUDAEMONY	EVULGATES	EXUVIATED	**FIGURANT**
ETERNISES	**EUKARYOT**	**EVULSION**	EXUVIATES	FIGURANTE
ETERNIZE	EUKARYOTE	REVULSION	**FABULATE**	FIGURANTS
ETERNIZED	EUKARYOTS	**EVULSIONS**	FABULATED	**FILAGREE**
ETERNIZES	**EULOGISE**	**EXAMINEE**	FABULATES	FILAGREED
ETHANALS	EULOGISED	EXAMINEES	**FABULISE**	FILAGREES
METHANALS	EULOGISER	**EXAMINES**	FABULISED	**FILIGREE**
ETHANOIC	EULOGISES	HEXAMINES	FABULISES	FILIGREED
METHANOIC	**EULOGIUM**	**EXANTHEM**	**FABULIZE**	FILIGREES
ETHANOLS	EULOGIUMS	EXANTHEMA	FABULIZED	**FILTRATE**
METHANOLS	**EULOGIZE**	EXANTHEMS	FABULIZES	FILTRATED
ETHEREAL	EULOGIZED	**EXCAVATE**	**FANFARON**	FILTRATES
AETHEREAL	EULOGIZER	EXCAVATED	FANFARONA	**FINALISE**
ETHERISE	EULOGIZES	EXCAVATES	FANFARONS	FINALISED
ETHERISED	**EUPHUISE**	**EXCHANGE**	**FANTASIE**	FINALISER
ETHERISER	EUPHUISED	EXCHANGED	FANTASIED	FINALISES
ETHERISES	EUPHUISES	EXCHANGER	FANTASIES	**FINALIZE**
ETHERIST	**EUPHUIZE**	EXCHANGES	**FARADISE**	FINALIZED
ETHERISTS	EUPHUIZED	**EXECRATE**	FARADISED	FINALIZER
ETHERIZE	EUPHUIZES	EXECRATED	FARADISER	FINALIZES
ETHERIZED	**EVACUATE**	EXECRATES	FARADISES	**FINICKIN**
ETHERIZER	EVACUATED	**EXECUTOR**	**FARADIZE**	FINICKING
ETHERIZES	EVACUATES	EXECUTORS	FARADIZED	**FISSIPED**
ETHICISE	**EVALUATE**	EXECUTORY	FARADIZER	FISSIPEDE
ETHICISED	DEVALUATE	**EXEMPLAR**	FARADIZES	FISSIPEDS
ETHICISES	REVALUATE	EXEMPLARS	**FASCIATE**	**FLAGELLA**
ETHICIST	EVALUATED	EXEMPLARY	FASCIATED	FLAGELLAR
ETHICISTS	EVALUATES	**EXERCISE**	**FASCICLE**	**FLAMBEAU**
ETHICIZE	**EVANESCE**	SEXERCISE	FASCICLED	FLAMBEAUS
ETHICIZED	EVANESCED	EXERCISED	FASCICLES	FLAMBEAUX
ETHICIZES	EVANESCES	EXERCISER	**FASCISTI**	**FLATLINE**
ETHNARCH	**EVERMORE**	EXERCISES	FASCISTIC	FLATLINED
ETHNARCHS	NEVERMORE	**EXHUMATE**	**FATIGATE**	FLATLINER
ETHNARCHY	**EVERSION**	EXHUMATED	FATIGATED	FLATLINES
ETHOXIDE	REVERSION	EXHUMATES	FATIGATES	**FLEECIES**
METHOXIDE		**EXIGEANT**	**FEDERATE**	FLEECIEST

FLEXTIME	**FORESTAL**	**GAILLARD**	GLISSADED	**HACKINGS**
FLEXTIMER	FORESTALL	GAILLARDE	GLISSADER	WHACKINGS
FLEXTIMES	**FORETIME**	**GALABIYA**	GLISSADES	**HACKLERS**
FLIMSIES	AFORETIME	GALABIYAH	**GLOSSIES**	SHACKLERS
FLIMSIEST	FORETIMES	GALABIYAS	GLOSSIEST	**HACKLING**
FLOPPIES	**FORHAILE**	**GALLABEA**	**GLYCERIN**	SHACKLING
FLOPPIEST	FORHAILED	GALLABEAH	GLYCERINE	**HADDOCKS**
FLOSSIES	FORHAILES	GALLABEAS	GLYCERINS	SHADDOCKS
FLOSSIEST	**FORHOOIE**	**GALLABIA**	**GNOSTICS**	**HAFTOROT**
FLOURISH	FORHOOIED	GALLABIAH	AGNOSTICS	HAFTOROTH
FLOURISHY	FORHOOIES	GALLABIAS	**GOALWARD**	**HAGGADOT**
FLUIDISE	**FORJUDGE**	**GANGRENE**	GOALWARDS	HAGGADOTH
FLUIDISED	FORJUDGED	GANGRENED	**GOSSAMER**	**HALACHOT**
FLUIDISER	FORJUDGES	GANGRENES	GOSSAMERS	HALACHOTH
FLUIDISES	**FORMULAR**	**GARAGIST**	GOSSAMERY	**HALAKHOT**
FLUIDIZE	FORMULARY	GARAGISTE	**GRADUATE**	HALAKHOTH
FLUIDIZED	**FORSPOKE**	GARAGISTS	GRADUATED	**HALLOWED**
FLUIDIZER	FORSPOKEN	**GARGOYLE**	GRADUATES	SHALLOWED
FLUIDIZES	**FORWASTE**	GARGOYLED	**GRAECISE**	**HALLOWER**
FOCALISE	FORWASTED	GARGOYLES	GRAECISED	SHALLOWER
FOCALISED	FORWASTES	**GARROTTE**	GRAECISES	HALLOWERS
FOCALISES	**FORZANDI**	GARROTTED	**GRAECIZE**	**HALUTZIM**
FOCALIZE	SFORZANDI	GARROTTER	GRAECIZED	CHALUTZIM
FOCALIZED	**FORZANDO**	GARROTTES	GRAECIZES	**HAMBLING**
FOCALIZES	SFORZANDO	**GASTNESS**	**GRAFFITI**	SHAMBLING
FOOTNOTE	FORZANDOS	GASTNESSE	SGRAFFITI	**HANDLERS**
FOOTNOTED	**FORZATOS**	**GASTRULA**	GRAFFITIS	CHANDLERS
FOOTNOTES	SFORZATOS	GASTRULAE	**GRAFFITO**	**HANDSOME**
FOOTWEAR	**FRACTURE**	GASTRULAR	SGRAFFITO	HANDSOMER
FOOTWEARS	FRACTURED	GASTRULAS	**GRANDSIR**	HANDSOMES
FOOTWEARY	FRACTURER	**GEFUFFLE**	GRANDSIRE	**HANDWRIT**
FORAMINA	FRACTURES	GEFUFFLED	GRANDSIRS	HANDWRITE
FORAMINAL	**FRANCISE**	GEFUFFLES	**GRANULAR**	**HANUKIAH**
FOREBODE	FRANCISED	**GELASTIC**	GRANULARY	CHANUKIAH
FOREBODED	FRANCISES	AGELASTIC	**GRATINEE**	HANUKIAHS
FOREBODER	**FRANCIZE**	**GEMINATE**	GRATINEED	**HAPHTARA**
FOREBODES	FRANCIZED	GEMINATED	GRATINEES	HAPHTARAH
FOREDATE	FRANCIZES	GEMINATES	**GREASIES**	HAPHTARAS
FOREDATED	**FREEBASE**	**GENERATE**	GREASIEST	**HAPPIEST**
FOREDATES	FREEBASED	GENERATED	**GREENIES**	CHAPPIEST
FOREHAND	FREEBASER	GENERATES	GREENIEST	**HARANGUE**
AFOREHAND	FREEBASES	**GENTRIES**	**GRESSING**	HARANGUED
FOREHANDS	**FREEBOOT**	AGENTRIES	EGRESSING	HARANGUER
FOREKNOW	FREEBOOTS	**GESNERIA**	GRESSINGS	HARANGUES
FOREKNOWN	FREEBOOTY	GESNERIAD	**GREWSOME**	**HARDLINE**
FOREKNOWS	**FRILLIES**	GESNERIAS	GREWSOMER	HARDLINER
FOREMEAN	FRILLIEST	**GLABELLA**	**GRISLIES**	**HARDNOSE**
FOREMEANS	**FRIZZIES**	GLABELLAE	GRISLIEST	HARDNOSED
FOREMEANT	FRIZZIEST	GLABELLAR	**GRIZZLER**	HARDNOSES
FORENAME	**FRONTAGE**	**GLACIATE**	GRIZZLERS	**HARDWIRE**
FORENAMED	FRONTAGER	GLACIATED	**GRUESOME**	HARDWIRED
FORENAMES	FRONTAGES	GLACIATES	GRUESOMER	HARDWIRES
FORESAID	**FROSTBIT**	**GLADIOLA**	**GUANIDIN**	**HARKENER**
AFORESAID	FROSTBITE	GLADIOLAR	GUANIDINE	HARKENERS
FORESHEW	**FUMIGATE**	GLADIOLAS	GUANIDINS	**HARMALIN**
FORESHEWN	FUMIGATED	**GLADSOME**	**GUNKHOLE**	HARMALINE
FORESHEWS	FUMIGATES	GLADSOMER	GUNKHOLED	HARMALINS
FORESHOW	**FURFUROL**	**GLASSIES**	GUNKHOLES	**HARMLESS**
FORESHOWN	FURFUROLE	GLASSIEST	**GYMNASIA**	CHARMLESS
FORESHOWS	FURFUROLS	**GLISSADE**	GYMNASIAL	**HARMONIC**

HARMONICA	HEBETATED	THEREUPON	THITHERTO	**HUCKSTER**
HARMONICS	HEBETATES	WHEREUPON	**HOBBYIST**	HUCKSTERS
HAROSETH	**HEBRAISE**	**HEREWITH**	HOBBYISTS	HUCKSTERY
CHAROSETH	HEBRAISED	THEREWITH	**HOLESOME**	**HUFFIEST**
HAROSETHS	HEBRAISES	WHEREWITH	WHOLESOME	CHUFFIEST
HAROSETS	**HEBRAIZE**	**HERNIATE**	**HOLISTIC**	**HUMANISE**
CHAROSETS	HEBRAIZED	HERNIATED	WHOLISTIC	HUMANISED
HARPINGS	HEBRAIZES	HERNIATES	**HOMINISE**	HUMANISER
SHARPINGS	**HEELINGS**	**HERRYING**	HOMINISED	HUMANISES
HARTBEES	WHEELINGS	CHERRYING	HOMINISES	**HUMANIZE**
HARTBEEST	**HEELLESS**	WHERRYING	**HOMINIZE**	HUMANIZED
HASTENED	WHEELLESS	**HESITATE**	HOMINIZED	HUMANIZER
CHASTENED	**HELLFIRE**	HESITATED	HOMINIZES	HUMANIZES
HASTENER	SHELLFIRE	HESITATER	**HONEYING**	**HUMBLING**
CHASTENER	HELLFIRES	HESITATES	PHONEYING	THUMBLING
HASTENERS	**HELPLESS**	**HIDLINGS**	**HOOKNOSE**	HUMBLINGS
HATCHERS	WHELPLESS	CHIDLINGS	HOOKNOSED	**HUNGERED**
THATCHERS	**HEMATICS**	**HIERARCH**	HOOKNOSES	AHUNGERED
HATCHING	THEMATICS	HIERARCHS	**HOOSHING**	**HUNKIEST**
THATCHING	**HEMOLYSE**	HIERARCHY	WHOOSHING	CHUNKIEST
HATCHINGS	HEMOLYSED	**HIERATIC**	**HOPPIEST**	**HUNTINGS**
HATTERED	HEMOLYSES	HIERATICA	CHOPPIEST	SHUNTINGS
CHATTERED	**HEMOLYZE**	HIERATICS	SHOPPIEST	**HUTZPAHS**
SHATTERED	HEMOLYZED	**HILLIEST**	**HOPPINGS**	CHUTZPAHS
HAUNTERS	HEMOLYZES	CHILLIEST	CHOPPINGS	**HYDROZOA**
CHAUNTERS	**HEMOSTAT**	**HILLINGS**	SHOPPINGS	HYDROZOAN
HAUNTING	CHEMOSTAT	CHILLINGS	WHOPPINGS	**HYPERNYM**
CHAUNTING	HEMOSTATS	SHILLINGS	**HORNBILL**	HYPERNYMS
HAUNTINGS	**HEPATICA**	**HIMATION**	THORNBILL	HYPERNYMY
HAWTHORN	HEPATICAE	HIMATIONS	HORNBILLS	**HYPODERM**
HAWTHORNS	HEPATICAL	**HINKIEST**	**HORNIEST**	HYPODERMA
HAWTHORNY	HEPATICAS	CHINKIEST	THORNIEST	HYPODERMS
HAZZANIM	**HEPATISE**	**HINNYING**	**HORNLESS**	**HYPOGAEA**
CHAZZANIM	HEPATISED	SHINNYING	THORNLESS	HYPOGAEAL
HEADACHE	HEPATISES	WHINNYING	**HORNLIKE**	HYPOGAEAN
HEADACHES	**HEPATIZE**	**HIPPIEST**	THORNLIKE	**HYPOTHEC**
HEADACHEY	HEPATIZED	CHIPPIEST	**HOROLOGE**	HYPOTHECA
HEADINGS	HEPATIZES	WHIPPIEST	HOROLOGER	HYPOTHECS
SHEADINGS	**HEPTARCH**	**HIPPINGS**	HOROLOGES	**IBERISES**
HEADLINE	HEPTARCHS	CHIPPINGS	**HOROLOGY**	FIBERISES
HEADLINED	HEPTARCHY	SHIPPINGS	CHOROLOGY	**ICKINESS**
HEADLINER	**HERBARIA**	WHIPPINGS	**HOSPITAL**	PICKINESS
HEADLINES	HERBARIAL	**HIPSTERS**	HOSPITALE	**IDEALISE**
HEALINGS	HERBARIAN	WHIPSTERS	HOSPITALS	IDEALISED
SHEALINGS	**HEREAWAY**	**HIRLINGS**	**HOSTINGS**	IDEALISER
HEARINGS	THEREAWAY	WHIRLINGS	GHOSTINGS	IDEALISES
SHEARINGS	HEREAWAYS	**HISTAMIN**	**HOTHOUSE**	**IDEALIZE**
HEARTIES	**HEREFROM**	HISTAMINE	HOTHOUSED	IDEALIZED
HEARTIEST	THEREFROM	HISTAMINS	HOTHOUSES	IDEALIZER
HEATABLE	WHEREFROM	**HISTIDIN**	**HOUTINGS**	IDEALIZES
CHEATABLE	**HEREINTO**	HISTIDINE	SHOUTINGS	**IDEOGRAM**
HEATHERS	THEREINTO	HISTIDINS	**HOVELING**	VIDEOGRAM
SHEATHERS	WHEREINTO	**HISTOGEN**	SHOVELING	IDEOGRAMS
HEATHIER	**HERENESS**	HISTOGENS	**HOVELLED**	**IFFINESS**
SHEATHIER	THERENESS	HISTOGENY	SHOVELLED	MIFFINESS
HEATINGS	WHERENESS	**HISTORIC**	**HOVELLER**	**IGNIFIED**
CHEATINGS	**HEREUNTO**	AHISTORIC	SHOVELLER	DIGNIFIED
HEATLESS	THEREUNTO	**HITHERED**	HOVELLERS	LIGNIFIED
WHEATLESS	WHEREUNTO	WHITHERED	**HUCKLING**	SIGNIFIED
HEBETATE	**HEREUPON**	**HITHERTO**	CHUCKLING	**IGNIFIES**

DIGNIFIES	INCONNUES	**INSCRIBE**	INTRIGUER	AISLELESS
LIGNIFIES	**INCORPSE**	INSCRIBED	INTRIGUES	**ISOCHRON**
SIGNIFIES	INCORPSED	INSCRIBER	**INTUBATE**	ISOCHRONE
ILLUMINE	INCORPSES	INSCRIBES	INTUBATED	ISOCHRONS
ILLUMINED	**INCREASE**	**INSETTER**	INTUBATES	**ISOGAMIC**
ILLUMINER	INCREASED	PINSETTER	**INUNDATE**	MISOGAMIC
ILLUMINES	INCREASER	INSETTERS	INUNDATED	**ITCHIEST**
IMITABLE	INCREASES	**INSHEATH**	INUNDATES	BITCHIEST
LIMITABLE	**INCUBATE**	INSHEATHE	**INVEAGLE**	HITCHIEST
IMMANTLE	INCUBATED	INSHEATHS	INVEAGLED	PITCHIEST
IMMANTLED	INCUBATES	**INSHRINE**	INVEAGLES	TITCHIEST
IMMANTLES	**INDAGATE**	INSHRINED	**INVEIGLE**	WITCHIEST
IMMINGLE	INDAGATED	INSHRINES	INVEIGLED	**ITCHINGS**
IMMINGLED	INDAGATES	**INSOLATE**	INVEIGLER	PITCHINGS
IMMINGLES	**INDICATE**	INSOLATED	INVEIGLES	WITCHINGS
IMMODEST	VINDICATE	INSOLATES	**INVENTOR**	**ITCHWEED**
IMMODESTY	INDICATED	**INSOMNIA**	INVENTORS	WITCHWEED
IMMOLATE	INDICATES	INSOMNIAC	INVENTORY	ITCHWEEDS
IMMOLATED	**INDOWING**	INSOMNIAS	**INVERTIN**	**ITERATES**
IMMOLATES	WINDOWING	**INSOURCE**	INVERTING	LITERATES
IMMUNISE	**INDURATE**	INSOURCED	INVERTINS	**JACULATE**
IMMUNISED	INDURATED	INSOURCES	**INVOCATE**	EJACULATE
IMMUNISER	INDURATES	**INSPHERE**	INVOCATED	JACULATED
IMMUNISES	**INFAMISE**	INSPHERED	INVOCATES	JACULATES
IMMUNIZE	INFAMISED	INSPHERES	**INVOLUTE**	**JALOUSIE**
IMMUNIZED	INFAMISES	**INSTANCE**	INVOLUTED	JALOUSIED
IMMUNIZER	**INFAMIZE**	INSTANCED	INVOLUTES	JALOUSIES
IMMUNIZES	INFAMIZED	INSTANCES	**IODINATE**	**JAMBOLAN**
IMPISHLY	INFAMIZES	**INSULATE**	IODINATED	JAMBOLANA
WIMPISHLY	**INFOLDED**	INSULATED	IODINATES	JAMBOLANS
IMPLEDGE	PINFOLDED	INSULATES	**IONISERS**	**JAPANISE**
IMPLEDGED	**INFRINGE**	**INSWATHE**	LIONISERS	JAPANISED
IMPLEDGES	INFRINGED	INSWATHED	**IONISING**	JAPANISES
IMPLEXES	INFRINGER	INSWATHES	LIONISING	**JAPANIZE**
SIMPLEXES	INFRINGES	**INTERESS**	**IONIZERS**	JAPANIZED
IMPLICIT	**INGROOVE**	INTERESSE	LIONIZERS	JAPANIZES
IMPLICITY	INGROOVED	**INTERVAL**	**IONIZING**	**JAROVISE**
IMPLUNGE	INGROOVES	INTERVALE	LIONIZING	JAROVISED
IMPLUNGED	**INHEARSE**	INTERVALS	**IREFULLY**	JAROVISES
IMPLUNGES	INHEARSED	**INTHRONE**	DIREFULLY	**JAROVIZE**
IMPOLITE	INHEARSES	INTHRONED	**IRENICAL**	JAROVIZED
IMPOLITER	**INHUMATE**	INTHRONES	EIRENICAL	JAROVIZES
IMPRESSE	INHUMATED	**INTIFADA**	**IRENICON**	**JAUNDICE**
IMPRESSED	INHUMATES	INTIFADAH	EIRENICON	JAUNDICED
IMPRESSER	**INITIATE**	INTIFADAS	IRENICONS	JAUNDICES
IMPRESSES	INITIATED	**INTIMATE**	**IRONISED**	**JAUNTIES**
IMPURPLE	INITIATES	INTIMATED	SIRONISED	JAUNTIEST
IMPURPLED	**INKINESS**	INTIMATER	**IRONISES**	**JAWBONER**
IMPURPLES	KINKINESS	INTIMATES	SIRONISES	JAWBONERS
INBOARDS	PINKINESS	**INTIMIST**	**IRONIZED**	**JEALOUSE**
PINBOARDS	**INKLINGS**	INTIMISTE	SIRONIZED	JEALOUSED
INCENSOR	TINKLINGS	INTIMISTS	**IRONIZES**	JEALOUSES
INCENSORS	**INNATELY**	**INTITULE**	SIRONIZES	**JELLABAH**
INCENSORY	PINNATELY	INTITULED	**IRRIGATE**	DJELLABAH
INCHOATE	**INNOVATE**	INTITULES	IRRIGATED	JELLABAHS
INCHOATED	INNOVATED	**INTONATE**	IRRIGATES	**JELLABAS**
INCHOATES	INNOVATES	INTONATED	**IRRITATE**	DJELLABAS
INCHPINS	**INSCONCE**	INTONATES	IRRITATED	**JEWELLER**
LINCHPINS	INSCONCED	**INTRIGUE**	IRRITATES	JEWELLERS
INCONNUE	INSCONCES	INTRIGUED	**ISLELESS**	JEWELLERY

JOINTURE	KRUMPINGS	**LAPPERED**	LAVATIONS	FLETCHING
JOINTURED	**LABELLUM**	CLAPPERED	**LAVISHES**	LETCHINGS
JOINTURES	FLABELLUM	**LAPPINGS**	LAVISHEST	**LEVATORS**
JUBILATE	**LACELESS**	CLAPPINGS	**LAVISHLY**	ELEVATORS
JUBILATED	PLACELESS	FLAPPINGS	SLAVISHLY	**LEVERAGE**
JUBILATES	**LACERATE**	SLAPPINGS	**LAYBACKS**	LEVERAGED
JUGULATE	LACERATED	**LASHINGS**	PLAYBACKS	LEVERAGES
JUGULATED	LACERATES	CLASHINGS	**LAYTIMES**	**LEVIGATE**
JUGULATES	**LACKADAY**	FLASHINGS	PLAYTIMES	LEVIGATED
JULIENNE	ALACKADAY	PLASHINGS	**LAZINESS**	LEVIGATES
JULIENNED	**LACKERED**	SLASHINGS	GLAZINESS	**LEVITATE**
JULIENNES	FLACKERED	**LASTINGS**	**LAZURITE**	LEVITATED
JUMBOISE	**LACKLAND**	BLASTINGS	LAZURITES	LEVITATES
JUMBOISED	BLACKLAND	**LATCHING**	**LEACHERS**	LEYLANDI
JUMBOISES	LACKLANDS	CLATCHING	BLEACHERS	LEYLANDII
JUMBOIZE	**LADDERED**	**LATERISE**	**LEACHING**	LEYLANDIS
JUMBOIZED	BLADDERED	LATERISED	BLEACHING	**LIBERATE**
JUMBOIZES	**LAGGINGS**	LATERISES	PLEACHING	LIBERATED
KABELJOU	BLAGGINGS	**LATERITE**	LEACHINGS	LIBERATES
KABELJOUS	FLAGGINGS	ELATERITE	**LEADINGS**	**LICHENIN**
KABELJOUW	SLAGGINGS	LATERITES	PLEADINGS	LICHENING
KEELHALE	**LAIRIEST**	**LATERIZE**	**LEANINGS**	LICHENINS
KEELHALED	GLAIRIEST	LATERIZED	CLEANINGS	**LICKINGS**
KEELHALES	**LAMBASTE**	LATERIZES	GLEANINGS	CLICKINGS
KEFUFFLE	LAMBASTED	**LATHERED**	**LEANNESS**	SLICKINGS
KEFUFFLED	LAMBASTES	BLATHERED	CLEANNESS	**LIENABLE**
KEFUFFLES	**LAMINATE**	SLATHERED	**LEARIEST**	ALIENABLE
KETCHING	LAMINATED	**LATHERER**	BLEARIEST	**LIGATURE**
SKETCHING	LAMINATES	BLATHERER	**LEASABLE**	LIGATURED
KEYSTONE	**LAMMINGS**	LATHERERS	PLEASABLE	LIGATURES
KEYSTONED	SLAMMINGS	**LATINISE**	**LEASINGS**	**LIGHTERS**
KEYSTONES	**LAMPINGS**	PLATINISE	PLEASINGS	BLIGHTERS
KHALIFAT	GLAMPINGS	LATINISED	**LEASURES**	PLIGHTERS
KHALIFATE	**LANCHING**	LATINISES	PLEASURES	SLIGHTERS
KHALIFATS	BLANCHING	**LATINIZE**	**LEATHERS**	**LIGHTEST**
KHANSAMA	FLANCHING	PLATINIZE	PLEATHERS	SLIGHTEST
KHANSAMAH	PLANCHING	LATINIZED	**LEAVINGS**	**LIGHTFUL**
KHANSAMAS	**LANDDROS**	LATINIZES	CLEAVINGS	PLIGHTFUL
KILLINGS	LANDDROST	**LATITUDE**	**LECTIONS**	**LIGHTING**
SKILLINGS	**LANDLESS**	PLATITUDE	ELECTIONS	ALIGHTING
KIPPERED	GLANDLESS	LATITUDES	FLECTIONS	BLIGHTING
SKIPPERED	**LANDMINE**	**LAUDATOR**	**LECTRESS**	FLIGHTING
KITTLING	LANDMINED	LAUDATORS	ELECTRESS	PLIGHTING
SKITTLING	LANDMINES	LAUDATORY	**LEDGIEST**	SLIGHTING
KLONDIKE	**LANDSLID**	**LAUGHTER**	FLEDGIEST	LIGHTINGS
KLONDIKED	LANDSLIDE	FLAUGHTER	**LEECHING**	**LIGHTISH**
KLONDIKER	**LANGUAGE**	SLAUGHTER	FLEECHING	SLIGHTISH
KLONDIKES	SLANGUAGE	LAUGHTERS	**LEERINGS**	**LIGULATE**
KLONDYKE	LANGUAGED	**LAUNCHED**	FLEERINGS	LIGULATED
KLONDYKED	LANGUAGES	FLAUNCHED	**LEGALISE**	**LIKENESS**
KLONDYKER	**LANKIEST**	**LAUNCHES**	LEGALISED	ALIKENESS
KLONDYKES	CLANKIEST	FLAUNCHES	LEGALISER	**LIMINESS**
KREASOTE	**LANKNESS**	**LAUREATE**	LEGALISES	SLIMINESS
KREASOTED	BLANKNESS	LAUREATED	**LEGALIZE**	**LIMPSIER**
KREASOTES	**LAPBOARD**	LAUREATES	LEGALIZED	SLIMPSIER
KREOSOTE	CLAPBOARD	**LAVALIER**	LEGALIZER	**LINDWORM**
KREOSOTED	LAPBOARDS	LAVALIERE	LEGALIZES	BLINDWORM
KREOSOTES	**LAPIDATE**	LAVALIERS	**LENDINGS**	LINDWORMS
KRUMPING	LAPIDATED	**LAVATION**	BLENDINGS	**LINGIEST**
SKRUMPING	LAPIDATES	CLAVATION	**LETCHING**	BLINGIEST

CLINGIEST	**LOCKINGS**	BLOUSIEST	CLUSTERED	MAIASAURA
LINKIEST	BLOCKINGS	**LOVEBITE**	FLUSTERED	MAIASAURS
PLINKIEST	CLOCKINGS	LOVEBITES	**LUSTRATE**	**MAILINGS**
SLINKIEST	FLOCKINGS	**LOVELESS**	FLUSTRATE	EMAILINGS
LINOTYPE	**LOCKLESS**	GLOVELESS	LUSTRATED	**MAINLINE**
LINOTYPED	FLOCKLESS	**LOVELIES**	LUSTRATES	MAINLINED
LINOTYPER	**LOCOMOTE**	LOVELIEST	**LUSTROUS**	MAINLINER
LINOTYPES	LOCOMOTED	**LOWBALLS**	BLUSTROUS	MAINLINES
LINTIEST	LOCOMOTES	BLOWBALLS	**LUXMETER**	**MALAXATE**
FLINTIEST	**LOCULATE**	**LOWDOWNS**	FLUXMETER	MALAXATED
GLINTIEST	LOCULATED	BLOWDOWNS	LUXMETERS	MALAXATES
LIPPERED	**LOCUTION**	SLOWDOWNS	**LYOPHILE**	**MALINGER**
SLIPPERED	ELOCUTION	**LOWERIER**	LYOPHILED	MALINGERS
LIPPIEST	LOCUTIONS	FLOWERIER	**LYRICISE**	MALINGERY
FLIPPIEST	**LOCUTORY**	**LOWERING**	LYRICISED	**MALLEATE**
SLIPPIEST	ELOCUTORY	FLOWERING	LYRICISES	MALLEATED
LIPPINGS	**LODICULA**	GLOWERING	**LYRICIZE**	MALLEATES
CLIPPINGS	LODICULAE	LOWERINGS	LYRICIZED	**MALVASIA**
LIQUESCE	**LOGGIEST**	**LOWLANDS**	LYRICIZES	MALVASIAN
LIQUESCED	CLOGGIEST	PLOWLANDS	**MACARISE**	MALVASIAS
LIQUESCES	**LOGGINGS**	**LUCKIEST**	MACARISED	**MAMILLAR**
LISTENED	BLOGGINGS	CLUCKIEST	MACARISES	MAMILLARY
GLISTENED	CLOGGINGS	PLUCKIEST	**MACARIZE**	**MAMMILLA**
LISTERIA	FLOGGINGS	**LUGGABLE**	MACARIZED	MAMMILLAE
LISTERIAL	VLOGGINGS	GLUGGABLE	MACARIZES	**MANDARIN**
LISTERIAS	**LOGICISE**	LUGGABLES	**MACARONI**	MANDARINE
LITERACY	LOGICISED	**LUGHOLES**	MACARONIC	MANDARINS
ALITERACY	LOGICISES	PLUGHOLES	MACARONIS	**MANDATOR**
LITERATE	**LOGICIZE**	**LUMBAGOS**	**MACERATE**	MANDATORS
ALITERATE	LOGICIZED	PLUMBAGOS	MACERATED	MANDATORY
LITERATES	LOGICIZES	**LUMBERED**	MACERATER	**MANDOLIN**
LITERATI	**LOGOMACH**	SLUMBERED	MACERATES	MANDOLINE
LITERATIM	LOGOMACHS	**LUMBERER**	**MACULATE**	MANDOLINS
LITERATO	LOGOMACHY	SLUMBERER	MACULATED	**MANICURE**
LITERATOR	**LOGROLLS**	LUMBERERS	MACULATES	MANICURED
LITIGATE	BLOGROLLS	**LUMINOUS**	**MADERISE**	MANICURES
LITIGATED	**LONENESS**	ALUMINOUS	MADERISED	**MANIFEST**
LITIGATES	ALONENESS	**LUMMIEST**	**MADERIZE**	MANIFESTO
LITTERED	**LOOPHOLE**	PLUMMIEST	MADERIZED	MANIFESTS
CLITTERED	LOOPHOLED	SLUMMIEST	MADERIZES	**MANUBRIA**
FLITTERED	LOOPHOLES	**LUMMOXES**	**MADRASSA**	MANUBRIAL
GLITTERED	**LOOPIEST**	FLUMMOXES	MADRASSAH	**MARGARIN**
LIVENESS	GLOOPIEST	**LUMPIEST**	MADRASSAS	MARGARINE
ALIVENESS	**LOPPIEST**	CLUMPIEST	**MAGDALEN**	MARGARINS
LIVERING	FLOPPIEST	GLUMPIEST	MAGDALENE	**MARINADE**
SLIVERING	GLOPPIEST	PLUMPIEST	MAGDALENS	MARINADED
LOBULATE	SLOPPIEST	SLUMPIEST	**MAGISTER**	MARINADES
LOBULATED	**LORICATE**	**LUNCHING**	MAGISTERS	**MARINATE**
LOCALISE	LORICATED	GLUNCHING	MAGISTERY	MARINATED
LOCALISED	LORICATES	**LUNULATE**	**MAGNESIA**	MARINATES
LOCALISER	**LOSSIEST**	LUNULATED	MAGNESIAL	**MARSUPIA**
LOCALISES	FLOSSIEST	**LUSHIEST**	MAGNESIAN	MARSUPIAL
LOCALIZE	GLOSSIEST	FLUSHIEST	MAGNESIAS	MARSUPIAN
LOCALIZED	**LOSSLESS**	PLUSHIEST	**MAGNIFIC**	**MASHINGS**
LOCALIZER	GLOSSLESS	SLUSHIEST	MAGNIFICO	SMASHINGS
LOCALIZES	**LOUNDERS**	**LUSHNESS**	**MAHARAJA**	**MASSACRE**
LOCKABLE	FLOUNDERS	FLUSHNESS	MAHARAJAH	MASSACRED
BLOCKABLE	**LOURIEST**	PLUSHNESS	MAHARAJAS	MASSACRER
LOCKAGES	FLOURIEST	**LUSTERED**	**MAIASAUR**	MASSACRES
BLOCKAGES	**LOUSIEST**	BLUSTERED	**MAIASAUR**	**MASTODON**

MASTODONS	SMELTINGS	EMIGRATES	MISJUDGED	**MISSTYLE**
MASTODONT	**MEMBRANE**	**MIGRATOR**	MISJUDGER	MISSTYLED
MATACHIN	MEMBRANED	MIGRATORS	MISJUDGES	MISSTYLES
MATACHINA	MEMBRANES	MIGRATORY	**MISLEARN**	**MISTHROW**
MATACHINI	**MEMORISE**	**MILIARIA**	MISLEARNS	MISTHROWN
MATCHING	MEMORISED	MILIARIAL	MISLEARNT	MISTHROWS
SMATCHING	MEMORISER	MILIARIAS	**MISLEEKE**	**MISTITLE**
MATTERED	MEMORISES	**MILITATE**	MISLEEKED	MISTITLED
SMATTERED	**MEMORIZE**	MILITATED	MISLEEKES	MISTITLES
MATURATE	MEMORIZED	MILITATES	**MISLODGE**	**MISTRACE**
MATURATED	MEMORIZER	**MILLEPED**	MISLODGED	MISTRACED
MATURATES	MEMORIZES	MILLEPEDE	MISLODGES	MISTRACES
MAUSOLEA	**MENAGING**	MILLEPEDS	**MISMETRE**	**MISVALUE**
MAUSOLEAN	AMENAGING	**MILLINER**	MISMETRED	MISVALUED
MAXILLAR	**MENDABLE**	MILLINERS	MISMETRES	MISVALUES
MAXILLARY	AMENDABLE	MILLINERY	**MISPARSE**	**MITIGATE**
MAXIMISE	EMENDABLE	**MILLIPED**	MISPARSED	MITIGATED
MAXIMISED	**MENSTRUA**	MILLIPEDE	MISPARSES	MITIGATES
MAXIMISER	MENSTRUAL	MILLIPEDS	**MISPLACE**	**MOBILISE**
MAXIMISES	**MEPHITIS**	**MINIBIKE**	MISPLACED	MOBILISED
MAXIMIZE	MEPHITISM	MINIBIKER	MISPLACES	MOBILISER
MAXIMIZED	**MERGENCE**	MINIBIKES	**MISPOISE**	MOBILISES
MAXIMIZER	EMERGENCE	**MINIMISE**	MISPOISED	**MOBILIZE**
MAXIMIZES	MERGENCES	MINIMISED	MISPOISES	MOBILIZED
MAZEMENT	**MERSIONS**	MINIMISER	**MISPRICE**	MOBILIZER
AMAZEMENT	EMERSIONS	MINIMISES	MISPRICED	MOBILIZES
MAZEMENTS	**MESCALIN**	**MINIMIZE**	MISPRICES	**MOCKINGS**
MEDIATOR	MESCALINE	MINIMIZED	**MISPRISE**	SMOCKINGS
MEDIATORS	MESCALINS	MINIMIZER	MISPRISED	**MODERATE**
MEDIATORY	**MESHUGGA**	MINIMIZES	MISPRISES	MODERATED
MEDICATE	MESHUGGAH	**MIRKIEST**	**MISPRIZE**	MODERATES
MEDICATED	**MESOGLEA**	SMIRKIEST	MISPRIZED	**MODERATO**
MEDICATES	MESOGLEAL	**MISATONE**	MISPRIZER	MODERATOR
MEDICINE	MESOGLEAS	MISATONED	MISPRIZES	MODERATOS
MEDICINED	**MESOPHYL**	MISATONES	**MISQUOTE**	**MODERNES**
MEDICINER	MESOPHYLL	**MISCEGEN**	MISQUOTED	MODERNEST
MEDICINES	MESOPHYLS	MISCEGENS	MISQUOTER	**MODULATE**
MEDITATE	**METALISE**	**MISCHOSE**	MISQUOTES	MODULATED
MEDITATED	METALISED	MISCHOSEN	**MISRAISE**	MODULATES
MEDITATES	METALISES	**MISDRIVE**	MISRAISED	**MOLDERED**
MEDULLAR	**METALIZE**	MISDRIVEN	MISRAISES	SMOLDERED
MEDULLARY	METALIZED	MISDRIVES	**MISROUTE**	**MOLLUSCA**
MELANISE	METALIZES	**MISENROL**	MISROUTED	MOLLUSCAN
MELANISED	**METHADON**	MISENROLL	MISROUTES	**MONETISE**
MELANISES	METHADONE	MISENROLS	**MISSHAPE**	MONETISED
MELANIZE	METHADONS	**MISFRAME**	MISSHAPED	MONETISES
MELANIZED	**MICATING**	MISFRAMED	MISSHAPEN	**MONETIZE**
MELANIZES	EMICATING	MISFRAMES	MISSHAPER	MONETIZED
MELINITE	**MICROCAR**	**MISGAUGE**	MISSHAPES	MONETIZES
GMELINITE	MICROCARD	MISGAUGED	**MISSIONS**	**MONOTONE**
MELINITES	MICROCARS	MISGAUGES	EMISSIONS	MONOTONED
MELODISE	**MICTIONS**	**MISGRADE**	OMISSIONS	MONOTONES
MELODISED	EMICTIONS	MISGRADED	**MISSPACE**	**MOOCHERS**
MELODISER	**MIDSHIPS**	MISGRADES	MISSPACED	SMOOCHERS
MELODISES	AMIDSHIPS	**MISGUIDE**	MISSPACES	**MOOCHING**
MELODIZE	**MIGRANTS**	MISGUIDED	**MISSPOKE**	SMOOCHING
MELODIZED	EMIGRANTS	MISGUIDER	MISSPOKEN	**MOONFACE**
MELODIZER	**MIGRATED**	MISGUIDES	**MISSTATE**	MOONFACED
MELODIZES	EMIGRATED	**MISJUDGE**	MISSTATED	MOONFACES
MELTINGS	MIGRATES	MISJUDGED	MISSTATES	**MORALISE**

MORALISED	MRIDANGAS	NASALISED	**NIGGERED**	SNUBBIEST
MORALISER	**MUCKRAKE**	NASALISES	SNIGGERED	**NUBBLIER**
MORALISES	MUCKRAKED	**NASALIZE**	**NIGGLERS**	KNUBBLIER
MORALISM	MUCKRAKER	NASALIZED	SNIGGLERS	**NUBBLING**
AMORALISM	MUCKRAKES	NASALIZES	**NIGGLING**	KNUBBLING
MORALISMS	**MUDIRIEH**	**NATTIEST**	SNIGGLING	**NUBECULA**
MORALIST	MUDIRIEHS	GNATTIEST	NIGGLINGS	NUBECULAE
AMORALIST	**MULTIPED**	**NAUSEATE**	**NIGROSIN**	**NUCLEATE**
MORALISTS	MULTIPEDE	NAUSEATED	NIGROSINE	ANUCLEATE
MORALITY	MULTIPEDS	NAUSEATES	NIGROSINS	ENUCLEATE
AMORALITY	**MULTIPLE**	**NAVICULA**	**NIPPIEST**	NUCLEATED
MORALIZE	MULTIPLES	NAVICULAR	SNIPPIEST	NUCLEATES
MORALIZED	MULTIPLET	NAVICULAS	**NOBBIEST**	**NUISANCE**
MORALIZER	MULTIPLEX	**NAVIGATE**	KNOBBIEST	NUISANCER
MORALIZES	**MULTITON**	NAVIGATED	SNOBBIEST	NUISANCES
MORNINGS	MULTITONE	NAVIGATES	**NOBBLING**	**NUMERATE**
AMORNINGS	**MULTIUSE**	**NEBBISHE**	KNOBBLING	ENUMERATE
MOROSITY	MULTIUSER	NEBBISHER	**NODALISE**	NUMERATED
AMOROSITY	**MURICATE**	NEBBISHES	NODALISED	NUMERATES
MORTGAGE	MURICATED	**NEBULISE**	NODALISES	**NUMMULAR**
MORTGAGED	**MUSCADIN**	NEBULISED	**NODALIZE**	NUMMULARY
MORTGAGEE	MUSCADINE	NEBULISER	NODALIZED	**NUZZLING**
MORTGAGER	MUSCADINS	NEBULISES	NODALIZES	SNUZZLING
MORTGAGES	**MUSETTES**	**NEBULIZE**	**NOINTERS**	**OBDURATE**
MORTISED	AMUSETTES	NEBULIZED	ANOINTERS	OBDURATED
AMORTISED	**MUSICALE**	NEBULIZER	**NOINTING**	OBDURATES
MORTISES	MUSICALES	NEBULIZES	ANOINTING	**OBLIGATE**
AMORTISES	**MUSINGLY**	**NECKLACE**	**NOMADISE**	OBLIGATED
MOSASAUR	AMUSINGLY	NECKLACED	NOMADISED	OBLIGATES
MOSASAURI	**MUSTACHE**	NECKLACES	NOMADISES	**OBLIGATO**
MOSASAURS	MUSTACHED	**NEEDFIRE**	**NOMADIZE**	OBLIGATOR
MOSCHATE	MUSTACHES	NEEDFIRES	NOMADIZED	OBLIGATOS
MOSCHATEL	**MUTCHING**	**NEGATIVE**	NOMADIZES	**OBLIQUES**
MOTHERED	SMUTCHING	NEGATIVED	**NOMINATE**	OBLIQUEST
SMOTHERED	**MUTILATE**	NEGATIVES	NOMINATED	**OBSCURES**
MOTIONAL	MUTILATED	**NEUMATIC**	NOMINATES	OBSCUREST
EMOTIONAL	MUTILATES	PNEUMATIC	**NONDANCE**	**OBSOLETE**
MOTIVATE	**MYOGRAPH**	**NEURISMS**	NONDANCER	OBSOLETED
MOTIVATED	MYOGRAPHS	ANEURISMS	NONDANCES	OBSOLETES
MOTIVATES	MYOGRAPHY	**NEUROMAS**	**NONSTICK**	**OBTURATE**
MOTIVITY	**MYOTONIA**	NEUROMAST	NONSTICKY	OBTURATED
EMOTIVITY	AMYOTONIA	**NEVELLED**	**NOSEDIVE**	OBTURATES
MOTORISE	MYOTONIAS	KNEVELLED	NOSEDIVED	**OBVOLUTE**
MOTORISED	**MYSTAGOG**	**NICKERED**	NOSEDIVES	OBVOLUTED
MOTORISES	MYSTAGOGS	KNICKERED	**NOTARISE**	**OCCIPITA**
MOTORIZE	MYSTAGOGY	SNICKERED	NOTARISED	OCCIPITAL
MOTORIZED	**MYXAMEBA**	**NICKNAME**	NOTARISES	**OCCUPATE**
MOTORIZES	MYXAMEBAE	NICKNAMED	**NOTARIZE**	OCCUPATED
MOUCHING	MYXAMEBAS	NICKNAMER	NOTARIZED	OCCUPATES
SMOUCHING	**NAGGIEST**	NICKNAMES	NOTARIZES	**OCELLATE**
MOULDERS	KNAGGIEST	**NICOTIAN**	**NOVELISE**	LOCELLATE
SMOULDERS	SNAGGIEST	NICOTIANA	NOVELISED	OCELLATED
MOUNTAIN	**NAPPIEST**	NICOTIANS	NOVELISER	**OCHERING**
MOUNTAINS	SNAPPIEST	**NICOTINE**	NOVELISES	TOCHERING
MOUNTAINY	**NARKIEST**	NICOTINED	**NOVELIZE**	**OCULARLY**
MOUNTING	SNARKIEST	NICOTINES	NOVELIZED	JOCULARLY
AMOUNTING	**NARRATOR**	**NIFFIEST**	NOVELIZER	**OCULATED**
MOUNTINGS	NARRATORS	SNIFFIEST	NOVELIZES	LOCULATED
MRIDANGA	NARRATORY	**NIFTIEST**	**NUBBIEST**	**ODOGRAPH**
MRIDANGAM	**NASALISE**	SNIFTIEST	KNUBBIEST	HODOGRAPH

ODOGRAPHS	ZOOSPERMS	**ORTHOSES**	**OUTDOORS**	OUTSLEEPS
ODOMETER	**OOSPHERE**	PORTHOSES	OUTDOORSY	**OUTSMILE**
HODOMETER	NOOSPHERE	**ORTOLANS**	**OUTDREAM**	OUTSMILED
ODOMETERS	OOSPHERES	PORTOLANS	OUTDREAMS	OUTSMILES
ODOMETRY	**OOSPORES**	**OSCITATE**	OUTDREAMT	**OUTSMOKE**
HODOMETRY	ZOOSPORES	OSCITATED	**OUTDRIVE**	OUTSMOKED
IODOMETRY	**OOSPORIC**	OSCITATES	OUTDRIVEN	OUTSMOKES
OENOLOGY	ZOOSPORIC	**OSCULATE**	OUTDRIVES	**OUTSNORE**
POENOLOGY	**OOZINESS**	OSCULATED	**OUTFABLE**	OUTSNORED
OENOPHIL	BOOZINESS	OSCULATES	OUTFABLED	OUTSNORES
OENOPHILE	WOOZINESS	**OSIERIES**	OUTFABLES	**OUTSPOKE**
OENOPHILS	**OPALESCE**	HOSIERIES	**OUTFENCE**	OUTSPOKEN
OENOPHILY	OPALESCED	**OSTEOGEN**	OUTFENCED	**OUTSTARE**
OFFERING	OPALESCES	OSTEOGENS	OUTFENCES	OUTSTARED
COFFERING	**OPERCULA**	OSTEOGENY	**OUTFLIES**	OUTSTARES
GOFFERING	OPERCULAR	**OSTMARKS**	GOUTFLIES	**OUTSTATE**
OFFERINGS	**OPPILATE**	POSTMARKS	**OUTGLARE**	OUTSTATED
OFFSHORE	OPPILATED	**OSTRACOD**	OUTGLARED	OUTSTATES
OFFSHORED	OPPILATES	OSTRACODE	OUTGLARES	**OUTTHROW**
OFFSHORES	**OPSIMATH**	OSTRACODS	**OUTGUIDE**	OUTTHROWS
OILERIES	OPSIMATHS	**OTOSCOPE**	OUTGUIDED	OUTTHROWS
BOILERIES	OPSIMATHY	ROTOSCOPE	OUTGUIDES	**OUTTRADE**
OILINESS	**OPSONISE**	OTOSCOPES	**OUTLEARN**	OUTTRADED
SOILINESS	OPSONISED	**OTTERING**	OUTLEARNS	OUTTRADES
OKEYDOKE	OPSONISES	COTTERING	OUTLEARNT	**OUTVALUE**
OKEYDOKEY	**OPSONIZE**	HOTTERING	**OUTPLACE**	OUTVALUED
OLDENING	OPSONIZED	POTTERING	OUTPLACED	OUTVALUES
BOLDENING	OPSONIZES	TOTTERING	OUTPLACER	**OUTVOICE**
GOLDENING	**OPTIMISE**	**OUTARGUE**	OUTPLACES	OUTVOICED
OLIGARCH	OPTIMISED	OUTARGUED	**OUTPRICE**	OUTVOICES
OLIGARCHS	OPTIMISER	OUTARGUES	OUTPRICED	**OUTWASTE**
OLIGARCHY	OPTIMISES	**OUTBLAZE**	OUTPRICES	OUTWASTED
OLOGISTS	**OPTIMIZE**	OUTBLAZED	**OUTPRIZE**	OUTWASTES
OOLOGISTS	OPTIMIZED	OUTBLAZES	OUTPRIZED	**OUTWEEDS**
OMENTUMS	OPTIMIZER	**OUTBRAVE**	OUTPRIZES	GOUTWEEDS
LOMENTUMS	OPTIMIZES	OUTBRAVED	**OUTQUOTE**	**OVATIONS**
MOMENTUMS	**OPUSCULA**	OUTBRAVES	OUTQUOTED	NOVATIONS
OOGAMETE	OPUSCULAR	**OUTBRIBE**	OUTQUOTES	**OVERABLE**
ZOOGAMETE	**ORALISMS**	OUTBRIBED	**OUTRAISE**	COVERABLE
OOGAMETES	MORALISMS	OUTBRIBES	OUTRAISED	**OVERAGES**
OOGAMIES	**ORALISTS**	**OUTBROKE**	OUTRAISES	COVERAGES
ZOOGAMIES	MORALISTS	OUTBROKEN	**OUTRANGE**	**OVERALLS**
OOGAMOUS	**ORDERERS**	**OUTBULGE**	OUTRANGED	COVERALLS
ZOOGAMOUS	BORDERERS	OUTBULGED	OUTRANGES	**OVERBAKE**
OOGENIES	**ORDERING**	OUTBULGES	**OUTSCORE**	OVERBAKED
ZOOGENIES	BORDERING	**OUTCASTE**	OUTSCORED	OVERBAKES
OOLACHAN	ORDERINGS	OUTCASTED	OUTSCORES	**OVERBLOW**
HOOLACHAN	**ORDINATE**	OUTCASTES	**OUTSERVE**	OVERBLOWN
OOLACHANS	ORDINATED	**OUTCHIDE**	OUTSERVED	OVERBLOWS
OOLOGIES	ORDINATES	OUTCHIDED	OUTSERVES	**OVERBORN**
NOOLOGIES	**ORGANISE**	OUTCHIDES	**OUTSHAME**	OVERBORNE
ZOOLOGIES	ORGANISED	**OUTCURSE**	OUTSHAMED	**OVERBURN**
OOLOGIST	ORGANISER	OUTCURSED	OUTSHAMES	OVERBURNS
ZOOLOGIST	ORGANISES	OUTCURSES	**OUTSHINE**	OVERBURNT
OOLOGISTS	**ORGANIZE**	**OUTDANCE**	OUTSHINED	**OVERCOME**
OOPHYTES	ORGANIZED	OUTDANCED	OUTSHINES	OVERCOMER
ZOOPHYTES	ORGANIZER	OUTDANCES	**OUTSKATE**	OVERCOMES
OOPHYTIC	ORGANIZES	**OUTDODGE**	OUTSKATED	**OVERCROW**
ZOOPHYTIC	**ORTHODOX**	OUTDODGED	OUTSKATES	OVERCROWD
OOSPERMS	ORTHODOXY	OUTDODGES	**OUTSLEEP**	OVERCROWS

OVERCURE	**OVERRAKE**	**PACIFIER**	PARALYSED	SPECKIEST
OVERCURED	OVERRAKED	OPACIFIER	PARALYSER	**PECTATES**
OVERCURES	OVERRAKES	PACIFIERS	PARALYSES	SPECTATES
OVERDARE	**OVERRATE**	**PACIFIES**	**PARALYZE**	**PECULATE**
OVERDARED	OVERRATED	OPACIFIES	PARALYZED	SPECULATE
OVERDARES	OVERRATES	**PAGANISE**	PARALYZER	PECULATED
OVERDOSE	**OVERRIDE**	PAGANISED	PARALYZES	PECULATES
OVERDOSED	OVERRIDER	PAGANISER	**PARAMENT**	**PEDERAST**
OVERDOSES	OVERRIDES	PAGANISES	PARAMENTA	PEDERASTS
OVERDRAW	**OVERRIPE**	**PAGANIZE**	PARAMENTS	PEDERASTY
OVERDRAWN	OVERRIPEN	PAGANIZED	**PARANOIA**	**PEDICURE**
OVERDRAWS	**OVERRULE**	PAGANIZER	PARANOIAC	PEDICURED
OVERFLOW	OVERRULED	PAGANIZES	PARANOIAS	PEDICURES
OVERFLOWN	OVERRULER	**PAGINATE**	**PARASHOT**	**PEDIGREE**
OVERFLOWS	OVERRULES	PAGINATED	PARASHOTH	PEDIGREED
OVERGIVE	**OVERSAVE**	PAGINATES	**PARKIEST**	PEDIGREES
OVERGIVEN	OVERSAVED	**PALESTRA**	SPARKIEST	**PEDIPALP**
OVERGIVES	OVERSAVES	PALESTRAE	**PAROCHIN**	PEDIPALPI
OVERGROW	**OVERSIZE**	PALESTRAL	PAROCHINE	PEDIPALPS
OVERGROWN	OVERSIZED	PALESTRAS	PAROCHINS	**PEDUNCLE**
OVERGROWS	OVERSIZES	**PALISADE**	**PAROEMIA**	PEDUNCLED
OVERHALE	**OVERSLIP**	PALISADED	PAROEMIAC	PEDUNCLES
OVERHALED	COVERSLIP	PALISADES	PAROEMIAL	**PEJORATE**
OVERHALES	OVERSLIPS	**PALLIATE**	PAROEMIAS	PEJORATED
OVERHATE	OVERSLIPT	PALLIATED	**PARTICLE**	PEJORATES
OVERHATED	**OVERTAKE**	PALLIATES	SPARTICLE	**PENALISE**
OVERHATES	OVERTAKEN	**PALMIPED**	PARTICLES	PENALISED
OVERHEAR	OVERTAKES	PALMIPEDE	**PARVOLIN**	PENALISES
OVERHEARD	**OVERTHIN**	PALMIPEDS	PARVOLINE	**PENALIZE**
OVERHEARS	OVERTHINK	**PALPATOR**	PARVOLINS	PENALIZED
OVERHOPE	**OVERTIME**	PALPATORS	**PASTICCI**	PENALIZES
OVERHOPED	OVERTIMED	PALPATORY	PASTICCIO	**PENDICLE**
OVERHOPES	OVERTIMER	**PALPEBRA**	**PASTORAL**	PENDICLER
OVERHYPE	OVERTIMES	PALPEBRAE	PASTORALE	PENDICLES
OVERHYPED	**OVERTIRE**	PALPEBRAL	PASTORALI	**PENSIONE**
OVERHYPES	OVERTIRED	PALPEBRAS	PASTORALS	PENSIONED
OVERLADE	OVERTIRES	**PANDEMIA**	**PATHETIC**	PENSIONER
OVERLADED	**OVERTURE**	PANDEMIAN	APATHETIC	PENSIONES
OVERLADEN	COVERTURE	PANDEMIAS	PATHETICS	**PENTARCH**
OVERLADES	OVERTURED	**PANNIKEL**	**PATHOGEN**	PENTARCHS
OVERLEAP	OVERTURES	PANNIKELL	PATHOGENE	PENTARCHY
OVERLEAPS	**OVERTYPE**	PANNIKELS	PATHOGENS	**PENTOSAN**
OVERLEAPT	OVERTYPED	**PANTALON**	PATHOGENY	PENTOSANE
OVERLETS	OVERTYPES	PANTALONE	**PATINATE**	PENTOSANS
COVERLETS	**OVERURGE**	PANTALONS	PATINATED	**PENUMBRA**
OVERLIVE	OVERURGED	**PAPALISE**	PATINATES	PENUMBRAE
OVERLIVED	OVERURGES	PAPALISED	**PATINISE**	PENUMBRAL
OVERLIVES	**OVERVOTE**	PAPALISES	PATINISED	PENUMBRAS
OVERLOVE	OVERVOTED	**PAPALIZE**	PATINISES	**PERCEIVE**
OVERLOVED	OVERVOTES	PAPALIZED	**PATINIZE**	PERCEIVED
OVERLOVES	**OVERWEAR**	PAPALIZES	PATINIZED	PERCEIVER
OVERMINE	OVERWEARS	**PAPILLAR**	PATINIZES	PERCEIVES
OVERMINED	OVERWEARY	PAPILLARY	**PATRIATE**	**PEREGRIN**
OVERMINES	**OYSTERED**	**PARABLES**	PATRIATED	PEREGRINE
OVERNAME	ROYSTERED	SPARABLES	PATRIATES	PEREGRINS
OVERNAMED	**OYSTERER**	**PARAFFIN**	**PATTERED**	**PERFECTO**
OVERNAMES	ROYSTERER	PARAFFINE	SPATTERED	PERFECTOR
OVERPLAN	OYSTERERS	PARAFFINS	**PEARLIES**	PERFECTOS
OVERPLANS	**PACIFIED**	PARAFFINY	PEARLIEST	**PERFUMER**
OVERPLANT	OPACIFIED	**PARALYSE**	**PECKIEST**	PERFUMERS

PERFUMERY	PHILOMELS	**PIPELINE**	POLARISER	PORTOLANI
PERIODIC	**PHORATES**	PIPELINED	POLARISES	PORTOLANO
APERIODIC	EPHORATES	PIPELINES	**POLARIZE**	PORTOLANS
PERIODID	**PHOSPHID**	**PIRLICUE**	POLARIZED	**POSITIVE**
PERIODIDE	PHOSPHIDE	PIRLICUED	POLARIZER	POSITIVER
PERIODIDS	PHOSPHIDS	PIRLICUES	POLARIZES	POSITIVES
PERIPTER	**PHOSPHIN**	**PISCATOR**	**POLEMISE**	**POSSIBLE**
PERIPTERS	PHOSPHINE	PISCATORS	POLEMISED	POSSIBLER
PERIPTERY	PHOSPHINS	PISCATORY	POLEMISES	POSSIBLES
PERMEATE	**PHOSPHOR**	**PISTOLET**	**POLEMIZE**	**POSTCAVA**
PERMEATED	PHOSPHORE	EPISTOLET	POLEMIZED	POSTCAVAE
PERMEATES	PHOSPHORI	**PITTINGS**	POLEMIZES	POSTCAVAL
PERORATE	PHOSPHORS	SPITTINGS	**POLONISE**	POSTCAVAS
PERORATED	**PHOTOGEN**	**PLACENTA**	POLONISED	**POSTCODE**
PERORATES	PHOTOGENE	PLACENTAE	POLONISES	POSTCODED
PEROXIDE	PHOTOGENS	PLACENTAL	**POLONIZE**	POSTCODES
PEROXIDED	PHOTOGENY	PLACENTAS	POLONIZED	**POSTDATE**
PEROXIDES	**PHYLARCH**	**PLANARIA**	POLONIZES	POSTDATED
PERSPIRE	PHYLARCHS	PLANARIAN	**POLYARCH**	POSTDATES
PERSPIRED	PHYLARCHY	PLANARIAS	POLYARCHY	**POSTPONE**
PERSPIRES	**PHYSIQUE**	**PLANETIC**	**POLYGLOT**	POSTPONED
PERSUADE	PHYSIQUED	APLANETIC	POLYGLOTS	POSTPONER
PERSUADED	PHYSIQUES	**PLASHERS**	POLYGLOTT	POSTPONES
PERSUADER	**PIARISTS**	SPLASHERS	**POLYMATH**	**POSTPOSE**
PERSUADES	APIARISTS	**PLASHIER**	POLYMATHS	POSTPOSED
PERSWADE	**PICKADIL**	SPLASHIER	POLYMATHY	POSTPOSES
PERSWADED	PICKADILL	**PLASHING**	**POLYONYM**	**POTTABLE**
PERSWADES	PICKADILS	SPLASHING	POLYONYMS	SPOTTABLE
PERTNESS	**PICOWAVE**	PLASHINGS	POLYONYMY	**POTTIEST**
APERTNESS	PICOWAVED	**PLATTERS**	**POLYPHON**	SPOTTIEST
PERVERSE	PICOWAVES	SPLATTERS	POLYPHONE	**POULTICE**
PERVERSER	**PICRITIC**	**PLATTING**	POLYPHONS	POULTICED
PERVIATE	EPICRITIC	SPLATTING	POLYPHONY	POULTICES
PERVIATED	**PIGHTING**	PLATTINGS	**PONGIEST**	**POURTRAY**
PERVIATES	SPIGHTING	**PLEADING**	SPONGIEST	POURTRAYD
PETALOUS	**PIKELETS**	UPLEADING	**PONTIFIC**	POURTRAYS
APETALOUS	SPIKELETS	PLEADINGS	PONTIFICE	**POUTIEST**
PETECHIA	**PILLAGES**	**PLEASURE**	**PONTOONS**	SPOUTIEST
PETECHIAE	SPILLAGES	PLEASURED	SPONTOONS	**POUTINGS**
PETECHIAL	**PILLINGS**	PLEASURER	**POOFIEST**	SPOUTINGS
PHALANGE	SPILLINGS	PLEASURES	SPOOFIEST	**POZZOLAN**
PHALANGER	**PINAFORE**	**PLEONAST**	POPULATED	POZZOLANA
PHALANGES	PINAFORED	PLEONASTE	POPULATES	POZZOLANS
PHANGING	PINAFORES	PLEONASTS	**PORPOISE**	**PRACTICE**
UPHANGING	**PINDLING**	**PLIGHTED**	PORPOISED	PRACTICED
PHANTASM	SPINDLING	UPLIGHTED	PORPOISES	PRACTICER
PHANTASMA	**PINELIKE**	**PLIGHTER**	**PORTABLE**	PRACTICES
PHANTASMS	SPINELIKE	UPLIGHTER	SPORTABLE	**PRACTISE**
PHENAZIN	**PINIONED**	PLIGHTERS	PORTABLES	PRACTISED
PHENAZINE	OPINIONED	**PLINKING**	**PORTANCE**	PRACTISER
PHENAZINS	**PINNACLE**	UPLINKING	SPORTANCE	PRACTISES
PHENETOL	PINNACLED	PLINKINGS	PORTANCES	**PRAISERS**
PHENETOLE	PINNACLES	**PLODGING**	**PORTIERE**	UPRAISERS
PHENETOLS	**PINNINGS**	SPLODGING	PORTIERED	**PRAISING**
PHERESES	SPINNINGS	**PLOTTIES**	PORTIERES	UPRAISING
APHERESES	**PINNIPED**	PLOTTIEST	**PORTIEST**	PRAISINGS
PHERESIS	PINNIPEDE	**PODDIEST**	SPORTIEST	**PRATTLED**
APHERESIS	PINNIPEDS	SPODDIEST	**PORTLESS**	SPRATTLED
PHILOMEL	**PINTSIZE**	**POLARISE**	SPORTLESS	**PRATTLES**
PHILOMELA	PINTSIZED	POLARISED	**PORTOLAN**	SPRATTLES

PRAYINGS	PRESERVES	**PROCAINE**	PTYALIZES	PYROLIZED
SPRAYINGS	**PRESHAPE**	PROCAINES	**PUDDINGS**	PYROLIZES
PREACHED	PRESHAPED	**PRODITOR**	SPUDDINGS	**PYROLYSE**
UPREACHED	PRESHAPES	PRODITORS	**PUERPERA**	PYROLYSED
PREACHES	PRESIDIA	PRODITORY	PUERPERAE	PYROLYSER
UPREACHES	PRESIDIAL	**PRODNOSE**	PUERPERAL	PYROLYSES
PREAMBLE	**PRESLICE**	PRODNOSED	**PULSATOR**	**PYROLYZE**
PREAMBLED	PRESLICED	PRODNOSES	PULSATORS	PYROLYZED
PREAMBLES	PRESLICES	**PRODROMI**	PULSATORY	PYROLYZER
PRECHOSE	**PRESOLVE**	PRODROMIC	**PULVILLE**	PYROLYZES
PRECHOSEN	PRESOLVED	**PROGNOSE**	PULVILLED	**QUADDING**
PRECISES	PRESOLVES	PROGNOSED	PULVILLES	SQUADDING
PRECISEST	**PRESSURE**	PROGNOSES	PULVILLI	**QUADRATE**
PRECLUDE	PRESSURED	**PROGRADE**	PULVILLIO	QUADRATED
PRECLUDED	PRESSURES	PROGRADED	**PUMICATE**	QUADRATES
PRECLUDES	**PRESTORE**	PROGRADES	PUMICATED	**QUADRIGA**
PREDATOR	PRESTORED	**PROLAMIN**	PUMICATES	QUADRIGAE
PREDATORS	PRESTORES	PROLAMINE	**PUNCTATE**	QUADRIGAS
PREDATORY	**PRETASTE**	PROLAMINS	PUNCTATED	**QUAGMIRE**
PREFROZE	PRETASTED	**PROLAPSE**	**PUNCTURE**	QUAGMIRED
PREFROZEN	PRETASTES	PROLAPSED	PUNCTURED	QUAGMIRES
PREGUIDE	**PRETERIT**	PROLAPSES	PUNCTURER	**QUAILING**
PREGUIDED	PRETERITE	**PROLLING**	PUNCTURES	SQUAILING
PREGUIDES	PRETERITS	UPROLLING	**PUNKIEST**	QUAILINGS
PREJUDGE	**PRETTIES**	**PROLOGUE**	SPUNKIEST	**QUANTISE**
PREJUDGED	PRETTIEST	PROLOGUED	**PUPILLAR**	QUANTISED
PREJUDGER	**PREUNITE**	PROLOGUES	PUPILLARY	QUANTISER
PREJUDGES	PREUNITED	**PROLONGE**	**PURCHASE**	QUANTISES
PREMIERE	PREUNITES	PROLONGED	PURCHASED	**QUANTIZE**
PREMIERED	**PREVALUE**	PROLONGER	PURCHASER	QUANTIZED
PREMIERES	PREVALUED	PROLONGES	PURCHASES	QUANTIZER
PRENTICE	PREVALUES	**PROMULGE**	**PURLICUE**	QUANTIZES
PRENTICED	**PRIEDIEU**	PROMULGED	PURLICUED	**QUARTETT**
PRENTICES	PRIEDIEUS	PROMULGES	PURLICUES	QUARTETTE
PREPASTE	PRIEDIEUX	**PROROGUE**	**PURLINGS**	QUARTETTI
PREPASTED	**PRIGGERS**	PROROGUED	SPURLINGS	QUARTETTO
PREPASTES	SPRIGGERS	PROROGUES	**PURRINGS**	QUARTETTS
PREPENSE	**PRIGGING**	**PROTAMIN**	SPURRINGS	**QUARTILE**
PREPENSED	SPRIGGING	PROTAMINE	**PUTTERED**	QUARTILES
PREPENSES	PRIGGINGS	PROTAMINS	SPUTTERED	**QUASHERS**
PREPLACE	**PRIMROSE**	**PROTOXID**	**PUTTERER**	SQUASHERS
PREPLACED	PRIMROSED	PROTOXIDE	SPUTTERER	**QUASHING**
PREPLACES	PRIMROSES	PROTOXIDS	PUTTERERS	SQUASHING
PREPPIES	**PRINCESS**	**PROTOZOA**	**PYCNIDIA**	**QUEENIES**
PREPPIEST	PRINCESSE	PROTOZOAL	PYCNIDIAL	QUEENIEST
PREPRICE	PRINCIPI	PROTOZOAN	**PYORRHEA**	**QUELCHED**
PREPRICED	PRINCIPIA	**PROTRUDE**	PYORRHEAL	SQUELCHED
PREPRICES	**PRINTERS**	PROTRUDED	PYORRHEAS	**QUELCHES**
PRERINSE	SPRINTERS	PROTRUDES	**PYREXIAS**	SQUELCHES
PRERINSED	**PRINTING**	**PROVEDOR**	APYREXIAS	**QUINCHED**
PRERINSES	SPRINTING	PROVEDORE	**PYRITISE**	SQUINCHED
PRESBYTE	PRINTINGS	PROVEDORS	PYRITISED	**QUINCHES**
PRESBYTER	**PRIORATE**	**PROVISOR**	PYRITISES	SQUINCHES
PRESBYTES	PRIORATES	PROVISORS	**PYRITIZE**	**QUINOLIN**
PRESCORE	**PRIORITY**	PROVISORY	PYRITIZED	QUINOLINE
PRESCORED	APRIORITY	**PTYALISE**	PYRITIZES	QUINOLINS
PRESCORES	**PRISSIES**	PTYALISED	**PYROLISE**	**QUINTETT**
PRESERVE	PRISSIEST	PTYALISES	PYROLISED	QUINTETTE
PRESERVED	**PRIVATES**	**PTYALIZE**	PYROLISES	QUINTETTI
PRESERVER	PRIVATEST	PTYALIZED	**PYROLIZE**	QUINTETTO

QUINTETTS	**RAFTSMEN**	CRANKLING	**RAVELLER**	REASSIGNS
QUIPPERS	CRAFTSMEN	PRANKLING	TRAVELLER	**REASSUME**
EQUIPPERS	DRAFTSMEN	**RANKNESS**	RAVELLERS	REASSUMED
QUIPPING	**RAGGIEST**	CRANKNESS	**RAVENING**	REASSUMES
EQUIPPING	BRAGGIEST	FRANKNESS	CRAVENING	**REASSURE**
QUIRTING	CRAGGIEST	**RANSOMED**	RAVENINGS	PREASSURE
SQUIRTING	DRAGGIEST	TRANSOMED	**RAVISHED**	REASSURED
QUITCHES	**RAGGINGS**	**RAPESEED**	YRAVISHED	REASSURER
SQUITCHES	BRAGGINGS	GRAPESEED	**REABSORB**	REASSURES
QUITTERS	DRAGGINGS	RAPESEEDS	PREABSORB	**REASTING**
SQUITTERS	FRAGGINGS	**RAPPINGS**	REABSORBS	BREASTING
RABBLERS	**RAGGLING**	TRAPPINGS	**REACCEDE**	**REBIDDEN**
BRABBLERS	DRAGGLING	WRAPPINGS	REACCEDED	PREBIDDEN
DRABBLERS	**RAGMENTS**	**RASHNESS**	REACCEDES	**REBILLED**
GRABBLERS	FRAGMENTS	BRASHNESS	**REACCUSE**	PREBILLED
RABBLING	**RAIDINGS**	**RASSLING**	PREACCUSE	**REBIRTHS**
BRABBLING	BRAIDINGS	WRASSLING	REACCUSED	PREBIRTHS
DRABBLING	**RAILCARD**	**RATCHETS**	REACCUSES	**REBOARDS**
GRABBLING	RAILCARDS	BRATCHETS	**REACHERS**	PREBOARDS
RABBLINGS	**RAILHEAD**	**RATCHING**	BREACHERS	**REBOILED**
RACEABLE	TRAILHEAD	FRATCHING	PREACHERS	PREBOILED
TRACEABLE	RAILHEADS	**RATIFIED**	TREACHERS	**REBOOKED**
RACEMISE	**RAILLESS**	GRATIFIED	**REACHING**	PREBOOKED
RACEMISED	TRAILLESS	**RATIFIER**	AREACHING	**REBOTTLE**
RACEMISES	**RAINBAND**	GRATIFIER	BREACHING	REBOTTLED
RACEMIZE	TRAINBAND	RATIFIERS	PREACHING	REBOTTLES
RACEMIZED	RAINBANDS	**RATIFIES**	**REACTING**	**REBOUGHT**
RACEMIZES	**RAINIEST**	GRATIFIES	PREACTING	PREBOUGHT
RACHILLA	BRAINIEST	**RATIONAL**	**READAPTS**	**REBUILDS**
RACHILLAE	GRAINIEST	RATIONALE	PREADAPTS	PREBUILDS
RACHILLAS	**RAINLESS**	RATIONALS	**READIEST**	**REBUTTAL**
RACHISES	BRAINLESS	**RATLINGS**	BREADIEST	PREBUTTAL
ARACHISES	GRAINLESS	BRATLINGS	**READINGS**	REBUTTALS
RACHITIS	TRAINLESS	**RATPACKS**	TREADINGS	**REBUYING**
TRACHITIS	**RAINWASH**	BRATPACKS	**READJUST**	PREBUYING
RACKETED	BRAINWASH	**RATTIEST**	PREADJUST	**RECEDING**
BRACKETED	**RAISINGS**	BRATTIEST	READJUSTS	PRECEDING
RACKINGS	PRAISINGS	**RATTLERS**	**READMITS**	**RECENSOR**
CRACKINGS	**RAKEHELL**	PRATTLERS	PREADMITS	PRECENSOR
FRACKINGS	RAKEHELLS	**RATTLING**	**READOPTS**	RECENSORS
TRACKINGS	RAKEHELLY	BRATTLING	PREADOPTS	**RECENTRE**
RADIATED	**RAMBLING**	PRATTLING	**READVISE**	RECENTRED
ERADIATED	BRAMBLING	RATTLINGS	READVISED	RECENTRES
RADIATES	RAMBLINGS	**RAUNCHED**	READVISES	**RECEPTOR**
ERADIATES	**RAMPAUGE**	BRAUNCHED	**REAEDIFY**	PRECEPTOR
RADIATOR	RAMPAUGED	CRAUNCHED	REAEDIFYE	RECEPTORS
RADIATORS	RAMPAUGES	GRAUNCHED	**REALLOTS**	**RECESSED**
RADIATORY	**RAMPINGS**	**RAUNCHES**	PREALLOTS	PRECESSED
RADICANT	TRAMPINGS	BRAUNCHES	**REALTERS**	**RECESSES**
ERADICANT	**RANCHERS**	CRAUNCHES	PREALTERS	PRECESSES
RADICATE	BRANCHERS	GRAUNCHES	**REAMIEST**	**RECHANGE**
ERADICATE	**RANCHING**	**RAVELERS**	CREAMIEST	RECHANGED
RADICATED	BRANCHING	TRAVELERS	DREAMIEST	RECHANGES
RADICATES	CRANCHING	**RAVELING**	**REARMING**	**RECHARGE**
RAFTINGS	RANCHINGS	GRAVELING	PREARMING	PRECHARGE
DRAFTINGS	**RANGIEST**	TRAVELING	**REAROUSE**	RECHARGED
GRAFTINGS	ORANGIEST	RAVELINGS	REAROUSED	RECHARGER
RAFTSMAN	**RANKINGS**	**RAVELLED**	REAROUSES	RECHARGES
CRAFTSMAN	PRANKINGS	GRAVELLED	**REASSIGN**	**RECHECKS**
DRAFTSMAN	**RANKLING**	TRAVELLED	PREASSIGN	PRECHECKS

RECHOOSE	**REDIGEST**	PREFIGURE	**REHEATED**	REKINDLED
PRECHOOSE	PREDIGEST	REFIGURED	PREHEATED	REKINDLES
RECHOOSES	REDIGESTS	REFIGURES	**REHEATER**	**RELATION**
RECHOSEN	**REDISTIL**	**REFILING**	PREHEATER	PRELATION
PRECHOSEN	REDISTILL	PREFILING	REHEATERS	RELATIONS
RECIRCLE	REDISTILS	**REFILLED**	**REHIRING**	**RELAUNCH**
RECIRCLED	**REDIVIDE**	PREFILLED	PREHIRING	PRELAUNCH
RECIRCLES	REDIVIDED	**REFIRING**	**REIGNITE**	**RELEGATE**
RECISION	REDIVIDES	PREFIRING	REIGNITED	RELEGATED
PRECISION	**REDOUBLE**	**REFIXING**	REIGNITES	RELEGATES
RECISIONS	REDOUBLED	PREFIXING	**REILLUME**	**RELOADED**
RECKLING	REDOUBLER	**REFORMAT**	REILLUMED	PRELOADED
FRECKLING	REDOUBLES	PREFORMAT	REILLUMES	**RELOCATE**
RECKLINGS	**REDRILLS**	REFORMATE	**REIMPOSE**	PRELOCATE
RECLEANS	PREDRILLS	REFORMATS	PREIMPOSE	RELOCATED
PRECLEANS	**REDRYING**	**REFORMED**	REIMPOSED	RELOCATEE
RECLOTHE	PREDRYING	PREFORMED	REIMPOSES	RELOCATES
RECLOTHED	**REDSHIFT**	**REFREEZE**	**REINCITE**	**RELUMINE**
RECLOTHES	REDSHIFTS	PREFREEZE	REINCITED	RELUMINED
RECODING	**REDSTART**	REFREEZES	REINCITES	RELUMINES
PRECODING	REDSTARTS	**REFRINGE**	**REINDUCE**	**REMARKET**
RECOLLET	**REDUVIID**	REFRINGED	REINDUCED	PREMARKET
RECOLLETS	REDUVIIDS	REFRINGES	REINDUCES	REMARKETS
RECONFER	**REECHING**	**REFROZEN**	**REINFORM**	**REMARQUE**
RECONFERS	BREECHING	PREFROZEN	PREINFORM	REMARQUED
RECOOKED	**REEDBUCK**	**REFUNDED**	REINFORMS	REMARQUES
PRECOOKED	REEDBUCKS	PREFUNDED	**REINFUSE**	**REMASTER**
RECOUPLE	**REEDIEST**	**REFUSION**	REINFUSED	CREMASTER
RECOUPLED	GREEDIEST	REFUSIONS	REINFUSES	REMASTERS
RECOUPLES	**REEDINGS**	**REGELATE**	**REINJURE**	**REMATING**
RECOURSE	BREEDINGS	REGELATED	REINJURED	CREMATING
RECOURSED	**REEDITED**	REGELATES	REINJURES	**REMBLING**
RECOURSES	PREEDITED	**REGNANCY**	**REINSERT**	TREMBLING
RECREATE	**REEKIEST**	PREGNANCY	PREINSERT	**REMEDIAT**
RECREATED	CREEKIEST	**REGROOVE**	REINSERTS	REMEDIATE
RECREATES	**REELECTS**	REGROOVED	**REINSTAL**	**REMIGATE**
RECTIONS	PREELECTS	REGROOVES	REINSTALL	REMIGATED
ERECTIONS	**REEMERGE**	**REGROWTH**	REINSTALS	REMIGATES
RECURING	REEMERGED	PREGROWTH	**REINSURE**	**REMISING**
PRECURING	REEMERGES	REGROWTHS	REINSURED	PREMISING
REDAMAGE	**REENACTS**	**REGULATE**	REINSURER	**REMIXING**
REDAMAGED	PREENACTS	REGULATED	REINSURES	PREMIXING
REDAMAGES	**REENGAGE**	REGULATES	**REINVADE**	**REMODIFY**
REDARGUE	GREENGAGE	**REGULISE**	REINVADED	PREMODIFY
REDARGUED	REENGAGED	REGULISED	REINVADES	**REMOLDED**
REDARGUES	REENGAGES	REGULISES	**REINVITE**	PREMOLDED
REDATING	**REERECTS**	**REGULIZE**	PREINVITE	**REMOTION**
PREDATING	PREERECTS	REGULIZED	REINVITED	PREMOTION
REDDLING	**REEXPOSE**	REGULIZES	REINVITES	REMOTIONS
TREDDLING	PREEXPOSE	**REHANDLE**	**REINVOKE**	**REMOVING**
REDECIDE	REEXPOSED	PREHANDLE	REINVOKED	PREMOVING
REDECIDED	REEXPOSES	REHANDLED	REINVOKES	**RENATURE**
REDECIDES	**REFACING**	REHANDLES	**REJUDGED**	CRENATURE
REDEFINE	PREFACING	**REHARDEN**	PREJUDGED	RENATURED
PREDEFINE	**REFERRED**	PREHARDEN	**REJUDGES**	RENATURES
REDEFINED	PREFERRED	REHARDENS	PREJUDGES	**RENEGADE**
REDEFINES	**REFERRER**	**REHEARSE**	**REJUGGLE**	RENEGADED
REDESIGN	PREFERRER	REHEARSED	REJUGGLED	RENEGADES
PREDESIGN	REFERRERS	REHEARSER	REJUGGLES	**RENFORCE**
REDESIGNS	**REFIGURE**	REHEARSES	**REKINDLE**	RENFORCED

RENFORCES	REPLUNGES	PRESEASON	PRESOLVES	**RETICULA**
RENOTIFY	**REPONING**	RESEASONS	**RESONATE**	RETICULAR
PRENOTIFY	PREPONING	**RESECURE**	RESONATED	**RETINOID**
RENOUNCE	**REPOSING**	RESECURED	RESONATES	CRETINOID
RENOUNCED	PREPOSING	RESECURES	**RESORTED**	RETINOIDS
RENOUNCER	**REPREEVE**	**RESELECT**	PRESORTED	**RETINULA**
RENOUNCES	REPREEVED	PRESELECT	**RESOURCE**	RETINULAE
RENOVATE	REPREEVES	RESELECTS	RESOURCED	RETINULAR
RENOVATED	**REPRICED**	**RESEMBLE**	RESOURCES	RETINULAS
RENOVATES	PREPRICED	RESEMBLED	**RESPLICE**	**RETRAINS**
RENUMBER	**REPRICES**	RESEMBLER	RESPLICED	PRETRAINS
PRENUMBER	PREPRICES	RESEMBLES	RESPLICES	**RETREATS**
RENUMBERS	**REPRIEVE**	**RESENTED**	**RESPONSE**	PRETREATS
RENVERSE	REPRIEVED	PRESENTED	RESPONSER	**RETRIALS**
RENVERSED	REPRIEVER	**RESENTER**	RESPONSES	PRETRIALS
RENVERSES	REPRIEVES	PRESENTER	**RESTABLE**	**RETRIEVE**
REOBTAIN	**REPRINTS**	RESENTERS	RESTABLED	RETRIEVED
PREOBTAIN	PREPRINTS	**RESERVED**	RESTABLES	RETRIEVER
REOBTAINS	**REPTILIA**	PRESERVED	**RESTAMPS**	RETRIEVES
REOCCUPY	REPTILIAN	**RESERVER**	PRESTAMPS	**RETYPING**
PREOCCUPY	**REPURSUE**	PRESERVER	**RESTINGS**	PRETYPING
REOPPOSE	REPURSUED	RESERVERS	CRESTINGS	**REUNIONS**
REOPPOSED	REPURSUES	**RESERVES**	**RESTLESS**	PREUNIONS
REOPPOSES	**REQUOYLE**	PRESERVES	CRESTLESS	**REUNITED**
REORDAIN	REQUOYLED	**RESETTLE**	**RESTORED**	PREUNITED
PREORDAIN	REQUOYLES	PRESETTLE	PRESTORED	**REUNITES**
REORDAINS	**RERECORD**	RESETTLED	**RESTORES**	PREUNITES
REORDERS	PRERECORD	RESETTLES	PRESTORES	**REVALUED**
PREORDERS	RERECORDS	**RESHAPED**	**RESTRAIN**	PREVALUED
REPACKED	**REREVIEW**	PRESHAPED	RESTRAINS	**REVALUES**
PREPACKED	PREREVIEW	**RESHAPES**	RESTRAINT	PREVALUES
REPARTEE	REREVIEWS	PRESHAPES	**RESTRESS**	**REVETTED**
REPARTEED	**REREVISE**	**RESHOWED**	PRESTRESS	BREVETTED
REPARTEES	REREVISED	PRESHOWED	**RESTRIKE**	**REVIEWED**
REPASTED	REREVISES	**RESIDENT**	PRESTRIKE	PREVIEWED
PREPASTED	**RESADDLE**	PRESIDENT	RESTRIKES	**REVIEWER**
REPAVING	RESADDLED	**RESIDENTS**	**RESTRING**	PREVIEWER
PREPAVING	RESADDLES	**RESIDERS**	RESTRINGE	REVIEWERS
REPAYING	**RESALUTE**	PRESIDERS	RESTRINGS	**REVISING**
PREPAYING	RESALUTED	**RESIDING**	**RESTRIVE**	PREVISING
REPEOPLE	RESALUTES	PRESIDING	RESTRIVEN	**REVISION**
REPEOPLED	**RESAMPLE**	**RESIFTED**	RESTRIVES	PREVISION
REPEOPLES	RESAMPLED	PRESIFTED	**RESUMERS**	REVISIONS
REPERUSE	RESAMPLES	**RESINATE**	PRESUMERS	**REVISITS**
REPERUSED	**RESCHOOL**	RESINATED	**RESUMING**	PREVISITS
REPERUSES	PRESCHOOL	RESINATES	PRESUMING	**REVISORS**
REPHRASE	RESCHOOLS	**RESINISE**	**RESURVEY**	PREVISORS
REPHRASED	**RESCINDS**	RESINISED	PRESURVEY	**REWARMED**
REPHRASES	PRESCINDS	RESINISES	RESURVEYS	PREWARMED
REPLACED	**RESCORED**	**RESINIZE**	**RETACKLE**	**REWASHED**
PREPLACED	PRESCORED	RESINIZED	RETACKLED	PREWASHED
REPLACES	**RESCORES**	RESINIZES	RETACKLES	**REWASHES**
PREPLACES	PRESCORES	**RESOAKED**	**RETAPING**	PREWASHES
REPLEDGE	**RESCREEN**	PRESOAKED	PRETAPING	**REWEIGHS**
REPLEDGED	PRESCREEN	**RESOLUTE**	**RETASTED**	PREWEIGHS
REPLEDGES	RESCREENS	RESOLUTER	PRETASTED	**REWIRING**
REPLICAS	**RESCRIPT**	RESOLUTES	**RETASTES**	PREWIRING
REPLICASE	PRESCRIPT	**RESOLVED**	PRETASTES	**REWORKED**
REPLUNGE	RESCRIPTS	PRESOLVED	**RETESTED**	PREWORKED
REPLUNGED	**RESEASON**	**RESOLVES**	PRETESTED	**RHEOPHIL**

RHEOPHILE	RIGIDISES	ROBOTIZED	CROUPIEST	**CRUMPLING**
RHIZOBIA	**RIGIDITY**	ROBOTIZES	**ROUSSEAU**	FRUMPLING
RHIZOBIAL	FRIGIDITY	**ROCKETED**	TROUSSEAU	**RUNKLING**
RHODAMIN	**RIGIDIZE**	CROCKETED	ROUSSEAUS	CRUNKLING
RHODAMINE	RIGIDIZED	**ROCKINGS**	**ROUTHIER**	**RUNNIONS**
RHODAMINS	RIGIDIZES	FROCKINGS	DROUTHIER	TRUNNIONS
RHYTHMIC	**RIMELESS**	**ROCKLESS**	**ROUTINGS**	**RURALISE**
ARHYTHMIC	CRIMELESS	FROCKLESS	GROUTINGS	RURALISED
RHYTHMICS	**RIMESTER**	**ROLLINGS**	TROUTINGS	RURALISES
RIBBINGS	TRIMESTER	DROLLINGS	**ROWELING**	**RURALIZE**
CRIBBINGS	RIMESTERS	TROLLINGS	TROWELING	RURALIZED
RIBWORKS	**RIMINESS**	**ROMANISE**	**ROWELLED**	RURALIZES
CRIBWORKS	GRIMINESS	ROMANISED	TROWELLED	**RUSHIEST**
RICERCAR	**RIMMINGS**	ROMANISES	**ROWNDING**	BRUSHIEST
RICERCARE	TRIMMINGS	**ROMANIZE**	DROWNDING	**RUSHINGS**
RICERCARI	**RIMPLING**	ROMANIZED	**ROYALISE**	BRUSHINGS
RICERCARS	CRIMPLING	ROMANIZES	ROYALISED	**RUSHLIKE**
RICHTEST	**RINGINGS**	**ROOFINGS**	ROYALISES	BRUSHLIKE
BRICHTEST	BRINGINGS	PROOFINGS	**ROYALIZE**	**RUSTABLE**
RICHTING	CRINGINGS	**ROOFLESS**	ROYALIZED	TRUSTABLE
FRICHTING	**RINGSIDE**	PROOFLESS	ROYALIZES	**RUSTIEST**
RICKYARD	RINGSIDER	**ROOMIEST**	**RUBBINGS**	CRUSTIEST
BRICKYARD	RINGSIDES	BROOMIEST	DRUBBINGS	TRUSTIEST
RICKYARDS	**RIPPINGS**	**ROOPIEST**	**RUBBLING**	**RUSTLESS**
RIDDLING	DRIPPINGS	DROOPIEST	GRUBBLING	CRUSTLESS
GRIDDLING	TRIPPINGS	**ROQUETED**	**RUCKLING**	TRUSTLESS
RIDDLINGS	**RIPPLERS**	CROQUETED	TRUCKLING	**RUTHLESS**
RIDGINGS	CRIPPLERS	**ROQUETTE**	**RUDDIEST**	TRUTHLESS
BRIDGINGS	TRIPPLERS	CROQUETTE	CRUDDIEST	**SABELLAS**
RIDICULE	**RIPPLING**	ROQUETTES	**RUDDLING**	ISABELLAS
RIDICULED	CRIPPLING	**ROSELIKE**	CRUDDLING	**SABOTAGE**
RIDICULER	TRIPPLING	PROSELIKE	**RUDENESS**	SABOTAGED
RIDICULES	**RIPPLINGS**	**ROSINESS**	CRUDENESS	SABOTAGES
RIFLINGS	**RISKIEST**	PROSINESS	**RUDERIES**	**SACRARIA**
TRIFLINGS	BRISKIEST	**ROSTELLA**	PRUDERIES	SACRARIAL
RIFTIEST	FRISKIEST	ROSTELLAR	**RUFFLING**	**SAFRANIN**
DRIFTIEST	**RITORNEL**	**ROSTRATE**	TRUFFLING	SAFRANINE
RIFTLESS	RITORNELL	EROSTRATE	RUFFLINGS	SAFRANINS
DRIFTLESS	RITORNELS	PROSTRATE	**RUGGIEST**	**SAGINATE**
RIGGINGS	**RIVALISE**	ROSTRATED	DRUGGIEST	SAGINATED
FRIGGINGS	RIVALISED	**ROTAVATE**	**RUMBLERS**	SAGINATES
PRIGGINGS	RIVALISES	ROTAVATED	GRUMBLERS	**SALINISE**
RIGHTENS	**RIVALIZE**	ROTAVATES	**RUMBLIER**	SALINISED
BRIGHTENS	RIVALIZED	**ROTOVATE**	CRUMBLIER	SALINISES
FRIGHTENS	RIVALIZES	ROTOVATED	GRUMBLIER	**SALINIZE**
RIGHTEST	**RIVELLED**	ROTOVATES	**RUMBLING**	SALINIZED
BRIGHTEST	DRIVELLED	**ROUGHHEW**	CRUMBLING	SALINIZES
RIGHTFUL	**RIVETING**	ROUGHHEWN	DRUMBLING	**SALIVATE**
FRIGHTFUL	RIVETINGS	ROUGHHEWS	GRUMBLING	SALIVATED
RIGHTING	**ROACHING**	**ROUGHING**	RUMBLINGS	SALIVATES
FRIGHTING	BROACHING	TROUGHING	**RUMINATE**	**SANDARAC**
RIGHTINGS	**ROADSIDE**	**ROULETTE**	RUMINATED	SANDARACH
RIGHTISH	BROADSIDE	ROULETTED	RUMINATES	SANDARACS
BRIGHTISH	ROADSIDES	ROULETTES	**RUMMIEST**	**SANGUINE**
RIGHTIST	**ROADWAYS**	**ROUNDERS**	CRUMMIEST	SANGUINED
RIGHTISTS	BROADWAYS	GROUNDERS	**RUMPLESS**	SANGUINES
RIGIDEST	**ROBOTISE**	**ROUNDING**	TRUMPLESS	**SANITATE**
FRIGIDEST	ROBOTISED	GROUNDING	**RUMPLIER**	SANITATED
RIGIDISE	ROBOTISES	ROUNDINGS	CRUMPLIER	SANITATES
RIGIDISED	**ROBOTIZE**	**ROUPIEST**	**RUMPLING**	**SANITISE**

SANITISED	SCHMOOSED	**SCURVIES**	SEQUENCER	SIBILATES
SANITISER	SCHMOOSES	SCURVIEST	SEQUENCES	**SICKLIES**
SANITISES	**SCHMOOZE**	**SCUTELLA**	**SERAPHIN**	SICKLIEST
SANITIZE	SCHMOOZED	SCUTELLAR	SERAPHINE	**SIDELINE**
SANITIZED	SCHMOOZER	**SECRETES**	SERAPHINS	SIDELINED
SANITIZER	SCHMOOZES	SECRETEST	**SERENADE**	SIDELINER
SANITIZES	**SCHNECKE**	**SECRETIN**	SERENADED	SIDELINES
SANNYASI	SCHNECKEN	SECRETING	SERENADER	**SIDERATE**
SANNYASIN	**SCIATICA**	SECRETINS	SERENADES	SIDERATED
SANNYASIS	SCIATICAL	**SECRETOR**	SERJEANT	SIDERATES
SAPPHIRE	SCIATICAS	SECRETORS	SERJEANTS	**SIGHTSEE**
SAPPHIRED	**SCLEREID**	SECRETORY	SERJEANTY	SIGHTSEEN
SAPPHIRES	SCLEREIDE	**SEIGNEUR**	**SEROTYPE**	SIGHTSEER
SARABAND	SCLEREIDS	SEIGNEURS	SEROTYPED	SIGHTSEES
SARABANDE	**SCLEROSE**	SEIGNEURY	SEROTYPES	**SIGNORIA**
SARABANDS	SCLEROSED	**SEIGNIOR**	**SEXTUPLE**	SIGNORIAL
SATIRISE	SCLEROSES	SEIGNIORS	SEXTUPLED	SIGNORIAS
SATIRISED	**SCOUTHER**	SEIGNIORY	SEXTUPLES	**SILICATE**
SATIRISER	SCOUTHERS	**SELVEDGE**	SEXTUPLET	SILICATED
SATIRISES	SCOUTHERY	SELVEDGED	**SEXUALLY**	SILICATES
SATIRIZE	**SCRABBLE**	SELVEDGES	ASEXUALLY	**SILICULA**
SATIRIZED	SCRABBLED	**SEMIDOME**	**SHAMIANA**	SILICULAE
SATIRIZER	SCRABBLER	SEMIDOMED	SHAMIANAH	SILICULAS
SATIRIZES	SCRABBLES	SEMIDOMES	SHAMIANAS	**SIMILISE**
SATURATE	**SCRAMBLE**	**SEMIMATT**	**SHAUCHLE**	SIMILISED
SATURATED	SCRAMBLED	SEMIMATTE	SHAUCHLED	SIMILISES
SATURATER	SCRAMBLER	**SEMINATE**	SHAUCHLES	**SIMILIZE**
SATURATES	SCRAMBLES	SEMINATED	**SHECHITA**	SIMILIZED
SAVORIES	**SCRATTLE**	SEMINATES	SHECHITAH	SIMILIZES
SAVORIEST	SCRATTLED	**SEMINOMA**	SHECHITAS	**SIMONISE**
SCALADES	SCRATTLES	SEMINOMAD	**SHEENIES**	SIMONISED
ESCALADES	**SCRIBBLE**	SEMINOMAS	SHEENIEST	SIMONISES
SCALLOPS	SCRIBBLED	**SEMUNCIA**	**SHEEPCOT**	**SIMONIZE**
ESCALLOPS	SCRIBBLER	SEMUNCIAE	SHEEPCOTE	SIMONIZED
SCANTIES	SCRIBBLES	SEMUNCIAL	SHEEPCOTS	SIMONIZES
SCANTIEST	**SCRIBING**	SEMUNCIAS	**SHENDING**	**SIMPLIST**
SCAPULAR	ASCRIBING	**SENSIBLE**	YSHENDING	SIMPLISTE
SCAPULARS	ESCRIBING	SENSIBLER	**SHIGELLA**	SIMPLISTS
SCAPULARY	SCRIBINGS	SENSIBLES	SHIGELLAE	**SIMULATE**
SCARPING	**SCRIGGLE**	**SENSILLA**	SHIGELLAS	SIMULATED
ESCARPING	SCRIGGLED	SENSILLAE	**SHILLALA**	SIMULATES
SCARPINGS	SCRIGGLES	**SENSORIA**	SHILLALAH	**SINGSONG**
SCAVENGE	**SCROBBLE**	SENSORIAL	SHILLALAS	SINGSONGS
SCAVENGED	SCROBBLED	**SENTENCE**	**SHITFACE**	SINGSONGY
SCAVENGER	SCROBBLES	SENTENCED	SHITFACED	**SINGULAR**
SCAVENGES	**SCROGGIE**	SENTENCER	SHITFACES	SINGULARS
SCELERAT	SCROGGIER	SENTENCES	**SHIVAREE**	SINGULARY
SCELERATE	**SCROUNGE**	**SEPALOUS**	SHIVAREED	**SINICISE**
SCELERATS	SCROUNGED	ASEPALOUS	SHIVAREES	SINICISED
SCENDING	SCROUNGER	**SEPARATE**	**SHODDIES**	SINICISES
ASCENDING	SCROUNGES	SEPARATED	SHODDIEST	**SINICIZE**
SCHEDULE	**SCROWDGE**	SEPARATES	**SHOWCASE**	SINICIZED
SCHEDULED	SCROWDGED	**SEPTARIA**	SHOWCASED	SINICIZES
SCHEDULER	SCROWDGES	SEPTARIAN	SHOWCASES	**SIRENISE**
SCHEDULES	**SCRUMMIE**	**SEPTUPLE**	**SHUNPIKE**	SIRENISED
SCHLIERE	SCRUMMIER	SEPTUPLED	SHUNPIKED	SIRENISES
SCHLIEREN	SCRUMMIES	SEPTUPLES	SHUNPIKER	**SIRENIZE**
SCHMALTZ	**SCRUMPLE**	SEPTUPLET	SHUNPIKES	SIRENIZED
SCHMALTZY	SCRUMPLED	**SEQUENCE**	**SIBILATE**	SIRENIZES
SCHMOOSE	SCRUMPLES	SEQUENCED	SIBILATED	**SIRONISE**

SIRONISED	SODOMISED	**SPERSING**	SPRINGALD	STARGAZED
SIRONISES	SODOMISES	ASPERSING	SPRINGALS	STARGAZER
SIRONIZE	**SODOMIZE**	**SPHINGID**	**SPRINGLE**	STARGAZES
SIRONIZED	SODOMIZED	SPHINGIDS	SPRINGLES	STARGAZEY
SIRONIZES	SODOMIZES	**SPIFFIES**	SPRINGLET	**STARTING**
SKELLIES	**SOLARISE**	SPIFFIEST	**SPRINKLE**	ASTARTING
SKELLIEST	SOLARISED	**SPIRANTS**	SPRINKLED	STARTINGS
SKEWNESS	SOLARISES	ASPIRANTS	SPRINKLER	**STEADIES**
ASKEWNESS	**SOLARIZE**	**SPIRATED**	SPRINKLES	STEADIEST
SKILLIES	SOLARIZED	ASPIRATED	**SPUILZIE**	**STEAMIES**
SKILLIEST	SOLARIZES	**SPIRILLA**	SPUILZIED	STEAMIEST
SKINNIES	**SOLATING**	SPIRILLAR	SPUILZIES	**STEELIES**
SKINNIEST	ISOLATING	**SPLENIUM**	**SPUNKIES**	STEELIEST
SKYWRITE	**SOLATION**	ASPLENIUM	SPUNKIEST	**STEEMING**
SKYWRITER	ISOLATION	SPLENIUMS	**SPURRIES**	ESTEEMING
SKYWRITES	SOLATIONS	**SPLINTER**	SPURRIEST	**STEGODON**
SLAISTER	**SOLECISE**	SPLINTERS	**SQUABBLE**	STEGODONS
SLAISTERS	SOLECISED	SPLINTERY	SQUABBLED	STEGODONT
SLAISTERY	SOLECISES	**SPLUTTER**	SQUABBLER	**STELLATE**
SLANDERS	**SOLECIZE**	SPLUTTERS	SQUABBLES	STELLATED
ISLANDERS	SOLECIZED	SPLUTTERY	**SQUADRON**	**STEROIDS**
SLIPCASE	SOLECIZES	**SPOLIATE**	SQUADRONE	ASTEROIDS
SLIPCASED	**SOLFEGGI**	SPOLIATED	SQUADRONS	**STHENIAS**
SLIPCASES	SOLFEGGIO	SPOLIATES	**SQUATTLE**	ASTHENIAS
SLIVOVIC	**SOLIDATE**	**SPOONIES**	SQUATTLED	**STICKIES**
SLIVOVICA	SOLIDATED	SPOONIEST	SQUATTLES	STICKIEST
SLUGHORN	SOLIDATES	**SPORIDIA**	**SQUEAKER**	**STINGIES**
SLUGHORNE	**SOMNIATE**	SPORIDIAL	SQUEAKERS	STINGIEST
SLUGHORNS	SOMNIATED	**SPOROZOA**	SQUEAKERY	**STIPULAR**
SLUSHIES	SOMNIATES	SPOROZOAL	**SQUEEGEE**	STIPULARY
SLUSHIEST	**SONICATE**	SPOROZOAN	SQUEEGEED	**STOCCATA**
SMELLIES	SONICATED	**SPORTIES**	SQUEEGEES	STOCCATAS
SMELLIEST	SONICATES	SPORTIEST	**SQUIGGLE**	**STOCKADE**
SMOOTHES	**SORORISE**	**SPORTING**	SQUIGGLED	STOCKADED
SMOOTHEST	SORORISED	ASPORTING	SQUIGGLER	STOCKADES
SMOULDER	SORORISES	**SPOTTIES**	SQUIGGLES	**STOMATAL**
ASMOULDER	**SORORIZE**	SPOTTIEST	**SQUILGEE**	ASTOMATAL
SMOULDERS	SORORIZED	**SPOUSALS**	SQUILGEED	**STOMATES**
SNAKEBIT	SORORIZES	ESPOUSALS	SQUILGEES	OSTOMATES
SNAKEBITE	**SOUVLAKI**	**SPOUSING**	**SQUIRESS**	**STOMODEA**
SNEESHIN	SOUVLAKIA	ESPOUSING	ESQUIRESS	STOMODEAL
SNEESHING	SOUVLAKIS	**SPRACKLE**	**SQUIRING**	**STONYING**
SNEESHINS	**SPAETZLE**	SPRACKLED	ESQUIRING	ASTONYING
SNOTTIES	SPAETZLES	SPRACKLES	**SQUIRREL**	**STOPPAGE**
SNOTTIEST	**SPAMMIES**	**SPRADDLE**	SQUIRRELS	ESTOPPAGE
SNOWSHOE	SPAMMIEST	SPRADDLED	SQUIRRELY	STOPPAGES
SNOWSHOED	**SPARKIES**	SPRADDLES	**STABLISH**	**STOPPING**
SNOWSHOER	SPARKIEST	**SPRANGLE**	ESTABLISH	ESTOPPING
SNOWSHOES	**SPATLESE**	SPRANGLED	**STAGGIES**	STOPPINGS
SOAPLAND	SPATLESEN	SPRANGLES	STAGGIEST	**STOUNDED**
SOAPLANDS	SPATLESES	**SPRATTLE**	**STAGNATE**	ASTOUNDED
SOAPSUDS	**SPECIATE**	SPRATTLED	STAGNATED	**STRADDLE**
SOAPSUDSY	SPECIATED	SPRATTLES	STAGNATES	ASTRADDLE
SOBERISE	SPECIATES	**SPREATHE**	**STAMPEDE**	STRADDLED
SOBERISED	**SPECTATE**	SPREATHED	STAMPEDED	STRADDLER
SOBERISES	SPECTATED	SPREATHES	STAMPEDER	STRADDLES
SOBERIZE	SPECTATES	**SPREETHE**	STAMPEDES	**STRAGGLE**
SOBERIZED	**SPELDRIN**	SPREETHED	**STANCHES**	STRAGGLED
SOBERIZES	SPELDRING	SPREETHES	STANCHEST	STRAGGLER
SODOMISE	SPELDRINS	**SPRINGAL**	**STARGAZE**	STRAGGLES

STRANGER	**STUNNING**	**SUBVERSE**	ASYMMETRY	TALLIATED
ESTRANGER	ASTUNNING	SUBVERSED	**SYMPODIA**	TALLIATES
STRANGERS	STUNNINGS	SUBVERSES	SYMPODIAL	**TALLITOT**
STRANGES	**STUPRATE**	**SUCURUJU**	**SYMPOSIA**	TALLITOTH
ESTRANGES	STUPRATED	SUCURUJUS	SYMPOSIAC	**TAMPINGS**
STRANGEST	STUPRATES	**SUDAMINA**	SYMPOSIAL	STAMPINGS
STRANGLE	**STURDIES**	SUDAMINAL	**SYNAPSES**	**TANNATES**
STRANGLED	STURDIEST	**SUFFLATE**	ASYNAPSES	STANNATES
STRANGLER	**STYLISER**	SUFFLATED	**SYNAPSIS**	**TAPENADE**
STRANGLES	STYLISERS	SUFFLATES	ASYNAPSIS	TAPENADES
STRAUCHT	**SUBAHDAR**	**SULFINYL**	**SYNCYTIA**	**TARANTAS**
STRAUCHTS	SUBAHDARS	SULFINYLS	SYNCYTIAL	TARANTASS
STRAVAGE	SUBAHDARY	**SULPHATE**	**SYNDETIC**	**TARRIEST**
STRAVAGED	**SUBCOSTA**	SULPHATED	ASYNDETIC	STARRIEST
STRAVAGES	SUBCOSTAE	SULPHATES	**SYNDETON**	**TARRINGS**
STRAYING	SUBCOSTAL	**SULPHURY**	ASYNDETON	STARRINGS
ESTRAYING	**SUBERISE**	SULPHURYL	SYNDETONS	**TARTRATE**
STRAYINGS	SUBERISED	**SUNBATHE**	**SYNEDRIA**	TARTRATED
STREIGNE	SUBERISES	SUNBATHED	SYNEDRIAL	TARTRATES
STREIGNED	**SUBERIZE**	SUNBATHER	**SYNERGIA**	**TAUTONYM**
STREIGNES	SUBERIZED	SUNBATHES	ASYNERGIA	TAUTONYMS
STRELITZ	SUBERIZES	**SUPERATE**	SYNERGIAS	TAUTONYMY
STRELITZI	**SUBITISE**	SUPERATED	**SYNOPSIS**	**TAWDRIES**
STRICHES	SUBITISED	SUPERATES	SYNOPSISE	TAWDRIEST
ESTRICHES	SUBITISES	**SUPERMOM**	**SYPHILIS**	**TEAMINGS**
OSTRICHES	**SUBITIZE**	SUPERMOMS	SYPHILISE	STEAMINGS
STRICKLE	SUBITIZED	**SUPINATE**	**SYSTOLES**	**TEGMENTA**
STRICKLED	SUBITIZES	SUPINATED	ASYSTOLES	TEGMENTAL
STRICKLES	**SUBLEASE**	SUPINATES	**SYSTOLIC**	**TELEPATH**
STRIDDLE	SUBLEASED	**SUPREMES**	ASYSTOLIC	TELEPATHS
STRIDDLED	SUBLEASES	SUPREMEST	**TABLINGS**	TELEPATHY
STRIDDLES	**SUBLIMES**	**SURCEASE**	STABLINGS	**TELESTIC**
STRINGED	SUBLIMEST	SURCEASED	**TABOURIN**	TELESTICH
ASTRINGED	**SUBLIMIT**	SURCEASES	TABOURING	TELESTICS
STRINGER	SUBLIMITS	**SURPLICE**	TABOURINS	**TELETYPE**
ASTRINGER	SUBLIMITY	SURPLICED	**TABULATE**	TELETYPED
STRINGERS	**SUBLUNAR**	SURPLICES	TABULATED	TELETYPES
STRINKLE	SUBLUNARY	**SURPRISE**	TABULATES	**TELEVISE**
STRINKLED	**SUBMENTA**	SURPRISED	**TACKINGS**	TELEVISED
STRINKLES	SUBMENTAL	SURPRISER	STACKINGS	TELEVISER
STROBILA	**SUBMERGE**	SURPRISES	**TACKLESS**	TELEVISES
STROBILAE	SUBMERGED	**SURPRIZE**	STACKLESS	**TEMPORAL**
STROBILAR	SUBMERGES	SURPRIZED	**TAGGIEST**	ATEMPORAL
STRODDLE	**SUBMERSE**	SURPRIZES	STAGGIEST	TEMPORALS
STRODDLED	SUBMERSED	**SUSPENSE**	**TAILGATE**	**TENTACLE**
STRODDLES	SUBMERSES	SUSPENSER	TAILGATED	TENTACLED
STRONGYL	**SUBPHYLA**	SUSPENSES	TAILGATER	TENTACLES
STRONGYLE	SUBPHYLAR	**SWANKIES**	TAILGATES	**TENTORIA**
STRONGYLS	**SUBSERVE**	SWANKIEST	**TAILPIPE**	TENTORIAL
STRONTIA	SUBSERVED	**SWANNIES**	TAILPIPED	**TESSELLA**
STRONTIAN	SUBSERVES	SWANNIEST	TAILPIPES	TESSELLAE
STRONTIAS	**SUBTITLE**	**SYLLABIC**	**TAKEOUTS**	TESSELLAR
STRUGGLE	SUBTITLED	ASYLLABIC	STAKEOUTS	**TETANISE**
STRUGGLED	SUBTITLES	SYLLABICS	**TALKIEST**	TETANISED
STRUGGLER	**SUBTOPIA**	**SYLLABLE**	STALKIEST	TETANISES
STRUGGLES	SUBTOPIAN	SYLLABLED	**TALKINGS**	**TETANIZE**
STUBBIES	SUBTOPIAS	SYLLABLES	STALKINGS	TETANIZED
STUBBIEST	**SUBTRUDE**	**SYMBOLIC**	**TALLAGES**	TETANIZES
STUMPIES	SUBTRUDED	SYMBOLICS	STALLAGES	**TETRAPOD**
STUMPIEST	SUBTRUDES	**SYMMETRY**	**TALLIATE**	TETRAPODS

TETRAPODY	TIDDLIEST	TOPSCORED	STRAPPERS	**TRIPIEST**
TETRARCH	**TIDIVATE**	TOPSCORES	**TRAPPIER**	STRIPIEST
TETRARCHS	TIDIVATED	**TORCHIER**	STRAPPIER	**TRIPLING**
TETRARCHY	TIDIVATES	TORCHIERE	**TRAPPING**	STRIPLING
TETROXID	**TILLAGES**	TORCHIERS	STRAPPING	TRIPLINGS
TETROXIDE	STILLAGES	**TORQUATE**	TRAPPINGS	**TRIPLOID**
TETROXIDS	**TILLIEST**	TORQUATED	**TRAUCHLE**	TRIPLOIDS
THEISTIC	STILLIEST	TORQUATES	TRAUCHLED	TRIPLOIDY
ATHEISTIC	**TILLINGS**	**TOTALISE**	TRAUCHLES	**TRIPPERS**
THEMATIC	STILLINGS	TOTALISED	**TRAVERSE**	STRIPPERS
ATHEMATIC	**TILTINGS**	TOTALISER	TRAVERSED	**TRIPPING**
THEMATICS	STILTINGS	TOTALISES	TRAVERSER	STRIPPING
THEOLOGY	**TINCTURE**	**TOTALIZE**	TRAVERSES	TRIPPINGS
ATHEOLOGY	TINCTURED	TOTALIZED	**TREACHER**	**TRITIATE**
THEORISE	TINCTURES	TOTALIZER	TREACHERS	TRITIATED
THEORISED	**TINPLATE**	TOTALIZES	TREACHERY	TRITIATES
THEORISER	TINPLATED	**TOTTERED**	**TREASURE**	**TRITICAL**
THEORISES	TINPLATES	STOTTERED	TREASURED	TRITICALE
THEORIZE	**TINTIEST**	**TOWAWAYS**	TREASURER	**TRIUMVIR**
THEORIZED	STINTIEST	STOWAWAYS	TREASURES	TRIUMVIRI
THEORIZER	**TINTINGS**	**TOXOCARA**	**TRENDIES**	TRIUMVIRS
THEORIZES	STINTINGS	TOXOCARAL	TRENDIEST	TRIUMVIRY
THEOSOPHY	**TINTLESS**	TOXOCARAS	**TREPHINE**	**TRIVALVE**
THEREFOR	STINTLESS	**TRABEATE**	TREPHINED	TRIVALVED
THEREFORE	**TIPPLERS**	TRABEATED	TREPHINER	TRIVALVES
THERIACA	STIPPLERS	**TRACHEID**	TREPHINES	**TROCHILI**
THERIACAL	**TIPPLING**	TRACHEIDE	**TRESSING**	TROCHILIC
THERIACAS	STIPPLING	TRACHEIDS	STRESSING	**TROCHLEA**
THINGIES	**TIPPYTOE**	**TRAIKING**	**TRESSURE**	TROCHLEAE
THINGIEST	TIPPYTOED	STRAIKING	TRESSURED	TROCHLEAR
THIONINE	TIPPYTOES	**TRAINERS**	TRESSURES	TROCHLEAS
ETHIONINE	**TITIVATE**	STRAINERS	**TRIANGLE**	**TROILISM**
THIONINES	TITIVATED	**TRAINING**	TRIANGLED	TROILISMS
THIOPHEN	TITIVATES	STRAINING	TRIANGLES	**TROLLERS**
THIOPHENE	**TITUBATE**	TRAININGS	**TRICHINA**	STROLLERS
THIOPHENS	TITUBATED	**TRAMLINE**	TRICHINAE	**TROLLING**
THRAPPLE	TITUBATES	TRAMLINED	TRICHINAL	STROLLING
THRAPPLED	**TOASTIES**	TRAMLINES	TRICHINAS	TROLLINGS
THRAPPLES	TOASTIEST	**TRAMMELS**	**TRICKLED**	**TROPHIED**
THROPPLE	**TOCCATAS**	STRAMMELS	STRICKLED	ATROPHIED
THROPPLED	STOCCATAS	**TRAMPING**	**TRICKLES**	**TROPHIES**
THROPPLES	**TOCKIEST**	STRAMPING	STRICKLES	ATROPHIES
THROTTLE	STOCKIEST	TRAMPINGS	TRICKLESS	**TROPINES**
THROTTLED	**TOLERATE**	**TRANGLES**	**TRICYCLE**	ATROPINES
THROTTLER	TOLERATED	STRANGLES	TRICYCLED	**TROPISMS**
THROTTLES	TOLERATES	**TRANSFIX**	TRICYCLER	ATROPISMS
THYROXIN	**TOLUIDIN**	TRANSFIXT	TRICYCLES	**TROSSERS**
THYROXINE	TOLUIDINE	**TRANSUDE**	**TRIENNIA**	STROSSERS
THYROXINS	TOLUIDINS	TRANSUDED	TRIENNIAL	**TROUTING**
TICKINGS	**TONALITY**	TRANSUDES	**TRIFLING**	STROUTING
STICKINGS	ATONALITY	**TRANSUME**	TRIFLINGS	TROUTINGS
TICKLERS	**TONELESS**	TRANSUMED	**TRIFORIA**	**TRUMPETS**
STICKLERS	STONELESS	TRANSUMES	TRIFORIAL	STRUMPETS
TICKLING	**TONICITY**	**TRAPDOOR**	**TRIGGING**	**TRUNCATE**
STICKLING	ATONICITY	TRAPDOORS	STRIGGING	TRUNCATED
TICKLINGS	**TOPPINGS**	**TRAPEZIA**	**TRIHEDRA**	TRUNCATES
TICKSEED	STOPPINGS	TRAPEZIAL	TRIHEDRAL	**TRUSTIES**
STICKSEED	**TOPPLING**	**TRAPLINE**	**TRIMMING**	TRUSTIEST
TICKSEEDS	STOPPLING	STRAPLINE	STRIMMING	**TUBBIEST**
TIDDLIES	**TOPSCORE**	TRAPLINES	TRIMMINGS	STUBBIEST
		TRAPPERS		

TUBERCLE	**UNBRIDLE**	**UNDULATE**	UNPOISONS	UNTHRONED
TUBERCLED	UNBRIDLED	UNDULATED	**UNPRAISE**	UNTHRONES
TUBERCLES	UNBRIDLES	UNDULATES	UNPRAISED	**UNTIDIES**
TUBULATE	**UNBRIGHT**	**UNFOUGHT**	UNPRAISES	UNTIDIEST
TUBULATED	SUNBRIGHT	GUNFOUGHT	**UNPRISON**	**UPBEARER**
TUBULATES	**UNBUCKLE**	**UNGAZING**	UNPRISONS	CUPBEARER
TUMBLERS	UNBUCKLED	SUNGAZING	**UNPUZZLE**	UPBEARERS
STUMBLERS	UNBUCKLES	**UNGENTLY**	UNPUZZLED	**URALITES**
TUMBLING	**UNBUNDLE**	PUNGENTLY	UNPUZZLES	RURALITES
STUMBLING	UNBUNDLED	**UNHEALTH**	**UNREELER**	**URBANISE**
TUMBLINGS	UNBUNDLER	UNHEALTHS	UNREELERS	URBANISED
TUMPIEST	UNBUNDLES	UNHEALTHY	**UNRETIRE**	URBANISES
STUMPIEST	**UNBURNED**	**UNHEARSE**	UNRETIRED	**URBANIZE**
TUNICATE	SUNBURNED	UNHEARSED	UNRETIRES	URBANIZED
TUNICATED	**UNCHARGE**	UNHEARSES	**UNRIDDLE**	URBANIZES
TUNICATES	UNCHARGED	**UNHOUSES**	UNRIDDLED	**UREDINIA**
TUNNINGS	UNCHARGES	FUNHOUSES	UNRIDDLER	UREDINIAL
STUNNINGS	**UNCHASTE**	GUNHOUSES	UNRIDDLES	**URGENTLY**
TURQUOIS	UNCHASTER	**UNICYCLE**	**UNROUNDS**	TURGENTLY
TURQUOISE	**UNCHOKES**	UNICYCLED	RUNROUNDS	**UROBOROS**
TUTORISE	SUNCHOKES	UNICYCLES	**UNRUFFLE**	OUROBOROS
TUTORISED	**UNCINATE**	**UNIFORMS**	UNRUFFLED	**UROPYGIA**
TUTORISES	RUNCINATE	CUNIFORMS	UNRUFFLES	UROPYGIAL
TUTORIZE	UNCINATED	**UNIFYING**	**UNSADDLE**	**UROSCOPY**
TUTORIZED	**UNCLOTHE**	MUNIFYING	UNSADDLED	OUROSCOPY
TUTORIZES	UNCLOTHED	UNIFYINGS	UNSADDLES	**URSIFORM**
TWEENAGE	UNCLOTHES	**UNIONISE**	**UNSETTLE**	BURSIFORM
TWEENAGER	**UNCOUPLE**	UNIONISED	UNSETTLED	**URTICATE**
TYRANNES	UNCOUPLED	UNIONISER	UNSETTLES	URTICATED
TYRANNESS	UNCOUPLER	UNIONISES	**UNSIGHTS**	URTICATES
TYRANNIS	UNCOUPLES	**UNIONIZE**	GUNSIGHTS	**USEFULLY**
TYRANNISE	**UNCREATE**	UNIONIZED	**UNSLUICE**	MUSEFULLY
UBERTIES	UNCREATED	UNIONIZER	UNSLUICED	**USHERING**
PUBERTIES	UNCREATES	UNIONIZES	UNSLUICES	HUSHERING
UBIETIES	**UNCTIONS**	**UNITIONS**	**UNSPHERE**	USHERINGS
DUBIETIES	FUNCTIONS	MUNITIONS	UNSPHERED	**USTULATE**
ULCERATE	JUNCTIONS	PUNITIONS	UNSPHERES	PUSTULATE
ULCERATED	**UNDAZZLE**	**UNIVALVE**	**UNSTABLE**	**UTTERERS**
ULCERATES	UNDAZZLED	UNIVALVED	UNSTABLER	MUTTERERS
ULTIMATE	UNDAZZLES	UNIVALVES	**UNSTICKS**	PUTTERERS
ULTIMATED	**UNDELETE**	**UNMAKERS**	GUNSTICKS	**UTTERING**
ULTIMATES	UNDELETED	GUNMAKERS	**UNSTOCKS**	BUTTERING
UMBERING	UNDELETES	**UNMANTLE**	GUNSTOCKS	GUTTERING
CUMBERING	**UNDERAGE**	UNMANTLED	**UNSTRUCK**	MUTTERING
LUMBERING	UNDERAGED	UNMANTLES	SUNSTRUCK	PUTTERING
NUMBERING	UNDERAGES	**UNMINGLE**	**UNSWATHE**	UTTERINGS
UNBATHED	**UNDERBIT**	UNMINGLED	UNSWATHED	**VACCINIA**
SUNBATHED	UNDERBITE	UNMINGLES	UNSWATHES	VACCINIAL
UNBEATEN	**UNDERLIE**	**UNMUFFLE**	**UNTACKLE**	VACCINIAS
SUNBEATEN	UNDERLIER	UNMUFFLED	UNTACKLED	**VACUATED**
UNBLINDS	UNDERLIES	UNMUFFLES	UNTACKLES	EVACUATED
SUNBLINDS	**UNDERSEA**	**UNMUZZLE**	**UNTANGLE**	**VACUATES**
UNBLOCKS	UNDERSEAL	UNMUZZLED	UNTANGLED	EVACUATES
SUNBLOCKS	UNDERSEAS	UNMUZZLES	UNTANGLES	**VAGINATE**
UNBONNET	**UNDERUSE**	**UNPAPERS**	**UNTANNED**	EVAGINATE
SUNBONNET	UNDERUSED	GUNPAPERS	SUNTANNED	VAGINATED
UNBONNETS	UNDERUSES	**UNPEOPLE**	**UNTHRIFT**	**VAGINULA**
UNBOTTLE	**UNDOUBLE**	UNPEOPLED	UNTHRIFTS	VAGINULAE
UNBOTTLED	UNDOUBLED	UNPEOPLES	UNTHRIFTY	**VALIDATE**
UNBOTTLES	UNDOUBLES	**UNPOISON**	**UNTHRONE**	VALIDATED

VALIDATES	VELARIZES	**VIGNETTE**	**VOLITATE**	WARDROBED
VALLHUND	**VENENATE**	VIGNETTED	VOLITATED	WARDROBER
VALLHUNDS	VENENATED	VIGNETTER	VOLITATES	WARDROBES
VALORISE	VENENATES	VIGNETTES	**VOLPLANE**	**WAREHOUS**
VALORISED	**VENERATE**	**VILLAGER**	VOLPLANED	WAREHOUSE
VALORISES	VENERATED	VILLAGERS	VOLPLANES	**WARFARIN**
VALORIZE	VENERATES	VILLAGERY	**VOLUMISE**	WARFARING
VALORIZED	**VENGEFUL**	**VINCIBLE**	VOLUMISED	WARFARINS
VALORIZES	AVENGEFUL	EVINCIBLE	VOLUMISER	**WARMINGS**
VALUABLE	**VENTAILE**	**VINCIBLY**	VOLUMISES	SWARMINGS
EVALUABLE	AVENTAILE	EVINCIBLY	**VOLUMIZE**	**WASHIEST**
VALUABLES	VENTAILES	**VIRILISE**	VOLUMIZED	SWASHIEST
VALUATED	AVENTAILS	VIRILISED	VOLUMIZER	**WASHINGS**
EVALUATED	**VENTAILS**	VIRILISES	VOLUMIZES	SWASHINGS
VALUATES	**VENTINGS**	**VIRILIZE**	**VOLUTION**	**WATTLING**
EVALUATES	EVENTINGS	VIRILIZED	EVOLUTION	TWATTLING
VALUATOR	**VENTLESS**	VIRILIZES	VOLUTIONS	WATTLINGS
EVALUATOR	EVENTLESS	**VIRTUOSI**	**VOUCHERS**	**WEARIEST**
VALUATORS	**VENTRING**	VIRTUOSIC	AVOUCHERS	SWEARIEST
VAMBRACE	AVENTRING	**VIRULENT**	**VOUCHING**	**WEARINGS**
VAMBRACED	VENTRINGS	AVIRULENT	AVOUCHING	SWEARINGS
VAMBRACES	**VENTURES**	**VISAGIST**	**VOUTSAFE**	**WEEDIEST**
VANISHED	AVENTURES	VISAGISTE	VOUTSAFED	TWEEDIEST
EVANISHED	**VERATRIN**	VISAGISTS	VOUTSAFES	**WEEPIEST**
VANISHES	VERATRINE	**VISCOUNT**	**VOWELISE**	SWEEPIEST
EVANISHES	VERATRINS	VISCOUNTS	VOWELISED	**WEEPINGS**
VAPORISE	**VERJUICE**	VISCOUNTY	VOWELISES	SWEEPINGS
VAPORISED	VERJUICED	**VITALISE**	**VOWELIZE**	**WELLHEAD**
VAPORISER	VERJUICES	VITALISED	VOWELIZED	SWELLHEAD
VAPORISES	**VERMINED**	VITALISER	VOWELIZES	WELLHEADS
VAPORIZE	OVERMINED	VITALISES	**VULGATES**	**WELLINGS**
VAPORIZED	**VERSIONS**	**VITALIZE**	EVULGATES	DWELLINGS
VAPORIZER	AVERSIONS	VITALIZED	**VULSELLA**	SWELLINGS
VAPORIZES	EVERSIONS	VITALIZER	VULSELLAE	**WELTERED**
VAPULATE	**VERTEBRA**	VITALIZES	**WADDLERS**	SWELTERED
VAPULATED	VERTEBRAE	**VITELLIN**	SWADDLERS	**WHEELIES**
VAPULATES	VERTEBRAL	VITELLINE	TWADDLERS	WHEELIEST
VARICOSE	VERTEBRAS	VITELLINS	**WADDLIER**	**WHEREFOR**
VARICOSED	**VESICATE**	**VOCALESE**	TWADDLIER	WHEREFORE
VARICOSES	VESICATED	VOCALESES	**WADDLING**	**WHEYFACE**
VARIOLES	VESICATES	**VOCALISE**	SWADDLING	WHEYFACED
OVARIOLES	**VESICULA**	VOCALISED	TWADDLING	WHEYFACES
VARITYPE	VESICULAE	VOCALISER	**WAKENERS**	**WHIFFLER**
VARITYPED	VESICULAR	VOCALISES	AWAKENERS	WHIFFLERS
VARITYPES	**VESTIGIA**	**VOCALIZE**	**WAKENING**	WHIFFLERY
VASCULAR	VESTIGIAL	VOCALIZED	AWAKENING	**WHIMSIES**
AVASCULAR	**VETCHIER**	VOCALIZER	WAKENINGS	WHIMSIEST
VAUNTING	KVETCHIER	VOCALIZES	**WALLOWED**	**WHINNIES**
AVAUNTING	**VEXILLAR**	**VOCATION**	SWALLOWED	WHINNIEST
VAUNTINGS	VEXILLARY	AVOCATION	**WALLOWER**	**WHIRLIES**
VEGETATE	**VIBRATOR**	EVOCATION	SWALLOWER	WHIRLIEST
VEGETATED	VIBRATORS	VOCATIONS	WALLOWERS	**WIDDLING**
VEGETATES	VIBRATORY	**VOCATIVE**	**WANGLERS**	TWIDDLING
VEGETIVE	**VIBRISSA**	EVOCATIVE	TWANGLERS	**WIGGIEST**
VEGETIVES	VIBRISSAE	VOCATIVES	**WANGLING**	TWIGGIEST
VELARISE	VIBRISSAL	**VOIDABLE**	TWANGLING	**WIGHTING**
VELARISED	**VIDEOTEX**	AVOIDABLE	WANGLINGS	TWIGHTING
VELARISES	VIDEOTEXT	**VOIDANCE**	**WANKIEST**	**WINDBLOW**
VELARIZE	**VIGILANT**	AVOIDANCE	SWANKIEST	WINDBLOWN
VELARIZED	VIGILANTE	VOIDANCES	**WARDROBE**	WINDBLOWS

WINDBURN	**WINNINGS**	**WITTERED**	SWORDLESS	TZADDIKIM
WINDBURNS	TWINNINGS	TWITTERED	**WORDPLAY**	**ZAMINDAR**
WINDBURNT	**WIREDRAW**	**WITTINGS**	SWORDPLAY	ZAMINDARI
WINDLING	WIREDRAWN	TWITTINGS	WORDPLAYS	ZAMINDARS
DWINDLING	WIREDRAWS	**WOBBLIES**	**WORMHOLE**	ZAMINDARY
SWINDLING	**WISELING**	WOBBLIEST	WORMHOLED	**ZEMINDAR**
WINDLINGS	WISELINGS	**WOMANISE**	WORMHOLES	ZEMINDARI
WINERIES	**WISHINGS**	WOMANISED	**WORTHIES**	ZEMINDARS
SWINERIES	SWISHINGS	WOMANISER	WORTHIEST	ZEMINDARY
WINGBEAT	**WITCHIER**	WOMANISES	**WOUNDING**	**ZONATION**
SWINGBEAT	SWITCHIER	**WOMANIST**	SWOUNDING	OZONATION
WINGBEATS	TWITCHIER	WOMANISTS	WOUNDINGS	ZONATIONS
WINGEING	**WITCHING**	**WOMANIZE**	**XYLOIDIN**	**ZOOGLOEA**
SWINGEING	SWITCHING	WOMANIZED	XYLOIDINE	ZOOGLOEAE
TWINGEING	TWITCHING	WOMANIZER	XYLOIDINS	ZOOGLOEAL
WINGIEST	WITCHINGS	WOMANIZES	**YERSINIA**	ZOOGLOEAS
SWINGIEST	**WITHDRAW**	**WOOLLIES**	YERSINIAE	**ZOOMORPH**
WINKLERS	WITHDRAWN	WOOLLIEST	YERSINIAS	ZOOMORPHS
TWINKLERS	WITHDRAWS	**WOOSHING**	**YESHIVOT**	ZOOMORPHY
WINKLING	**WITHERED**	SWOOSHING	YESHIVOTH	**ZOOPHORI**
TWINKLING	SWITHERED	**WORDLESS**	**ZADDIKIM**	ZOOPHORIC

Blockers

Blockers are the opposite of hooks. They are words which cannot have a letter added at the beginning or end. These are extremely useful to know, as they allow you to close down whole sections of the board to your opponents. The following lists show blockers of two to six letters in length. Not included in the five and six-letter lists are words with endings that obviously preclude a single letter being added at the end: -ED, -J, -S, -X, -Y and -Z.

Two-letter words

FY	XU

Three-letter words

AUE	GEY	NTH	SAZ	TWP
BEZ	GOX	NYS	SEZ	VLY
CAZ	HEX	OXO	SHH	VOX
CLY	HMM	PAX	SIX	WOX
CUZ	HOX	PHT	SLY	YAE
DUH	KEX	PLY	SMA	YEH
DUX	LUZ	POH	SOX	YEX
FAE	MEH	PST	SOZ	ZAS
FAP	MUX	PYX	SWY	ZAX
FAX	NAE	QIS	TAJ	ZEX
FEZ	NAH	RAX	THY	ZOA
FLY	NOH	RHY	TIX	ZUZ
FRY	NOX	SAE	TUX	

Four-letter words

AAHS	AHIS	ANEW	AWRY	BANS
ABBS	AHOY	ANOW	AXAL	BAPS
ABLY	AJAR	APTS	AYUS	BATS
ABOS	AJEE	AREG	BAAS	BAYS
ACHY	ALAE	AREW	BABY	BEDS
ADRY	ALBS	AROW	BADE	BEDU
AESC	ALEE	ASEA	BADS	BEEN
AGLY	ALIT	AVOS	BAGS	BEES
AHEM	ALSO	AWFY	BAMS	BEGS

BELS	COAX	DINS	EMYS	FRAE
BENJ	COBS	DIPT	ENUF	FROM
BENS	COCH	DISS	EOAN	FUCI
BEVY	CODS	DIVS	ESPY	FUDS
BHAT	COFT	DIXY	EUGE	FUGS
BIBS	COKY	DOBS	EUOI	FUMS
BIDS	COLS	DOBY	EVOE	FUMY
BIEN	COLY	DOCS	EVOS	FUNS
BIGS	COMS	DODS	EWKS	FURS
BINS	CONY	DOEN	EYES	FURY
BIOS	COPY	DOGS	EYNE	FUSC
BISH	CORF	DOGY	EYRY	FUTZ
BIST	CORY	DOHS	FAAN	GABS
BLEW	COSH	DOMS	FAAS	GABY
BOBS	COSS	DOMY	FABS	GAED
BODS	COSY	DOOS	FADS	GAEN
BODY	COWY	DOPS	FADY	GAES
BOGS	COXY	DOPY	FAGS	GAGA
BOGY	COYS	DORY	FAHS	GAGS
BOHS	COZY	DOSH	FAIX	GAKS
BOIS	CRUX	DOSS	FALX	GALS
BOKS	CUBS	DOST	FANS	GAMY
BONA	CUED	DOTH	FASH	GANS
BOPS	CUES	DOTS	FAUX	GAPS
BORS	CURT	DOTY	FAWS	GAPY
BOSH	CWMS	DOUN	FEDS	GARE
BOTS	DABS	DOUX	FEET	GASH
BOXY	DADS	DOWF	FEGS	GATS
BRRR	DAES	DOXY	FEHS	GAYS
BRUX	DAFT	DOYS	FEMS	GAZY
BUBO	DAGS	DOZY	FENS	GEDS
BUBS	DAKS	DREW	FETS	GEEZ
BUDS	DAMS	DRYS	FEUS	GELS
BUGS	DANS	DSOS	FEWS	GEMS
BUMS	DAPS	DUBS	FEYS	GENS
BUNS	DAVY	DUCI	FIBS	GEOS
BURY	DEAF	DUDS	FIDS	GERT
BUSY	DEBS	DUED	FIGS	GETS
BUYS	DEEK	DUES	FIKY	GHIS
CAAS	DEFT	DUGS	FILS	GIBS
CAGY	DEFY	DULY	FINS	GIDS
CAKY	DEGS	DUOS	FITS	GIED
CALX	DELS	DUPS	FIXT	GIEN
CANY	DEMY	DUSH	FLED	GIES
CAPS	DENY	DUTY	FLIX	GIGS
CASH	DESI	DYED	FLOX	GINS
CAUF	DEUS	DYES	FLUX	GITS
CAVY	DEVS	DZOS	FOBS	GIZZ
CAYS	DEWS	EASY	FOCI	GJUS
CEES	DEWY	EBBS	FOEN	GLEG
CELS	DEXY	ECOD	FOES	GNUS
CEPS	DEYS	ECUS	FOGS	GOAS
CHEZ	DIBS	EDDO	FOGY	GOBS
CHIS	DIDY	EDHS	FONE	GOBY
CHON	DIED	EHED	FONS	GOEY
CIAO	DIEL	EINA	FOPS	GORY
CIGS	DIES	ELHI	FOUS	GOVS
CITO	DIFS	ELMY	FOXY	GOYS
CITS	DIGS	ELSE	FOYS	GREX
CITY	DIMS	EMUS	FOZY	GUBS

GULS	JAWS	KOSS	METS	NOMS
GULY	JAXY	KOWS	MHOS	NOPE
GUMS	JAYS	KRIS	MIBS	NOSH
GUNS	JAZY	KUEH	MICS	NOSY
GUPS	JAZZ	KUES	MIGS	NOTT
GUVS	JEED	KUNA	MILS	NOUS
GYMS	JEES	KUNE	MINX	NOYS
GYNY	JEEZ	KYES	MINY	NUNS
GYRI	JEON	KYNE	MIPS	NYAS
HAED	JETS	KYUS	MIRY	NYED
HAEN	JEUX	LACS	MIXY	OAKY
HAES	JEWS	LACY	MNAS	OCCY
HASS	JIBS	LANX	MOAI	ODDS
HAZY	JIGS	LARS	MOAS	ODEA
HEHS	JINX	LATI	MOBS	OHMS
HELD	JIVY	LATU	MOBY	OLEA
HEMS	JIZZ	LAVS	MOCS	ONST
HEPS	JOBS	LECH	MODS	ONYX
HEPT	JOCO	LEKE	MOES	OPTS
HISN	JOES	LEKS	MOLS	ORFS
HIYA	JOGS	LEKU	MOLY	ORYX
HOAX	JOKY	LEPS	MOMI	OSAR
HOBS	JOLS	LEVA	MOMS	OYEZ
HODS	JORS	LEVO	MONS	PACS
HOHA	JOSH	LEVY	MONY	PADS
HOHS	JOSS	LEWD	MOOI	PALY
HOLP	JOTS	LIDS	MOPY	PAPS
HOLY	JOWS	LIGS	MOSH	PATY
HOMS	JOYS	LIRE	MOTS	PAVS
HOMY	JUDS	LIRI	MOWN	PEDS
HOSS	JUGS	LITU	MOWS	PEGS
HOYS	JURY	LOCI	MOYS	PEHS
HUED	JUTS	LORN	MOZZ	PELS
HUES	JYNX	LUDS	MUDS	PEPS
HUGY	KAAL	LUNY	MUNS	PFFT
HUIC	KAAS	LUVS	MWAH	PFUI
HUIS	KABS	LYCH	MYCS	PHAT
HUNG	KAED	LYES	NADS	PHEW
HUNH	KAES	LYMS	NAIN	PHIZ
HWAN	KAFS	LYNX	NAMS	PHOH
HYED	KAIS	LYRA	NANG	PHOS
HYES	KAKS	MAAS	NANS	PIAS
HYPS	KEAS	MADE	NAOI	PIGS
HYTE	KEBS	MADS	NAOS	PILY
IBIS	KEDS	MAES	NAVY	PIPS
ICHS	KEFS	MAGS	NAYS	PIPY
IDEM	KEKS	MAHA	NEFS	PIRS
IDLY	KEPT	MAKS	NEGS	PISS
IGAD	KESH	MALS	NEKS	PITY
ILKA	KEWL	MANY	NEPS	PIXY
INIA	KEYS	MAPS	NESH	PLEX
INLY	KHIS	MARY	NESS	POAS
INRO	KIFS	MATS	NETS	POCO
IURE	KILD	MATY	NEVI	POGY
JABS	KIRS	MAWN	NIDI	POKY
JAGS	KISH	MAWS	NIDS	POLS
JAKS	KNEW	MAZY	NIED	POMS
JAMS	KOAS	MEDS	NIMS	PONS
JAPS	KOBS	MEGS	NISI	PONY
JARS	KOIS	MELS	NIXY	POOS
JASS	KOPS	MEMS	NODI	PORY
JASY	KORS	MENO	NOES	POSY

POWS	SECO	SUNS	TWAS	WIRY
PREZ	SECS	SUPS	TWOS	WOES
PRUH	SEEN	SUQS	TYDE	WOFS
PSST	SEES	SUSS	TYGS	WOGS
PTUI	SEGS	SWUM	TYPY	WOKS
PUBS	SEIK	SYED	UNDO	WONS
PUGH	SELD	SYES	UPGO	WOST
PUIR	SELS	TADS	UPSY	WOWF
PUKY	SEPS	TAED	UVAE	WOWS
PULY	SESH	TAES	UVAS	WUDS
PUNS	SETS	TAKS	VACS	WYCH
PUNY	SEWN	TAKY	VAES	WYES
PUPS	SEWS	TALI	VAGI	WYNS
PUTS	SEXY	TAMS	VAGS	YAGS
PUTZ	SEYS	TAOS	VAIN	YALD
PUYS	SHAT	TAUS	VANS	YAPS
PYAS	SHMO	TAVS	VARS	YAWS
PYES	SHOD	TAXA	VATS	YAWY
PYIC	SIBS	TECS	VAUS	YAYS
QATS	SICS	TEDY	VAVS	YBET
QINS	SIES	TEES	VAWS	YEBO
QUEP	SIMS	TEFS	VEES	YEPS
RACA	SINS	TEGS	VERA	YEWS
RAHS	SIPS	TELD	VERD	YGOE
RAZZ	SIRS	TELS	VETO	YIDS
REBS	SITS	TELT	VEXT	YIPS
RECS	SITZ	THAE	VIAE	YMPT
REFS	SIZY	THAT	VIAS	YOBS
REFT	SJOE	THEY	VIBS	YODS
REHS	SKAS	THIS	VIDS	YOKS
RELY	SKIS	THUS	VIGS	YOLD
RENK	SKRY	TICS	VIMS	YOND
RENY	SOBS	TIDS	VINS	YOWS
REOS	SOCS	TIDY	VIVO	YUCH
RHOS	SODS	TIGS	VIZY	YUGS
RIFS	SOGS	TIKS	VOES	YUKS
RIVO	SOHO	TILS	VOLS	YUKY
ROED	SOHS	TINS	VORS	YUNX
ROKY	SOLS	TINY	VROT	YUPS
RONZ	SOME	TIPT	VUGS	YUTZ
ROPY	SOMS	TITS	VUMS	YWIS
ROUX	SOMY	TOBY	WADY	ZAGS
RUBY	SOON	TODS	WANY	ZANY
RUCS	SOPS	TODY	WARY	ZAPS
RUNS	SORI	TOED	WAVY	ZEAS
RYAS	SOSS	TOES	WAWS	ZEDS
RYES	SOTS	TOEY	WAXY	ZEKS
RYFE	SOVS	TOGS	WEBS	ZELS
SABS	SOYS	TOHO	WEDS	ZEPS
SACS	SPED	TOLD	WEMS	ZIGS
SADS	SPRY	TONS	WENA	ZINS
SAFT	SRIS	TORN	WENS	ZIPS
SAGS	STEY	TOWY	WERE	ZITE
SAGY	SUBS	TOYS	WERT	ZITS
SAMS	SUCH	TREZ	WETS	ZIZZ
SAPS	SUES	TSKS	WHAE	ZOLS
SASH	SUGS	TUGS	WHOA	ZOOS
SAVS	SUKS	TUNY	WHOT	ZZZS
SAWN	SUMS	TUPS	WHYS	
SAWS	SUMY	TUTS	WICH	
SCRY	SUNG	TUZZ	WILY	

Five-letter words

AARGH	ALOFT	AYONT	CACTI	CYMAE
ABACI	ALONE	AZIDO	CAESE	DAWEN
ABACK	ALOOF	AZOIC	CAJON	DAYCH
ABAFT	ALOUD	AZURN	CAJUN	DAYNT
ABASH	ALOWE	BAITH	CALID	DEALT
ABASK	ALTHO	BAKEN	CANST	DEASH
ABEAM	AMAIN	BANAL	CAPUT	DEDAL
ABLOW	AMICI	BARER	CARPI	DEERE
ABOIL	AMINO	BARIC	CECAL	DEFFO
ABORE	AMNIA	BASEN	CECUM	DEMIC
ABRAM	AMNIC	BASHO	CERIC	DEMPT
ABRIM	AMONG	BASSI	CESTI	DESHI
ABUNE	AMORT	BASTA	CHAPT	DIACT
ACERB	ANILE	BATCH	CHAVE	DIANE
ACHOO	ANSAE	BEDAD	CHERE	DICTA
ACMIC	ANTAE	BEGAD	CHIAO	DIDST
ACOCK	APACE	BEGAN	CHIMO	DINGO
ACOLD	APAGE	BEGAT	CHODE	DIRER
ACRID	APAID	BEGOT	CHOTA	DISCI
ADDIO	APART	BELCH	CHYND	DITCH
ADOWN	APAYD	BERKO	CILIA	DIVNA
ADOZE	APEAK	BESAT	CINCH	DOCHT
ADRAD	APEEK	BESAW	CINCT	DOEST
ADSUM	APERT	BIACH	CIPPI	DOETH
ADUNC	APGAR	BIFID	CIRRI	DOGGO
ADYTA	APIAN	BIGAE	CLAPT	DOILT
AESIR	APOOP	BINAL	CLASH	DOLCI
AFALD	APORT	BIRCH	CLIPT	DOLIA
AFIRE	APTER	BITOU	CLOMB	DOMAL
AFOOT	AQUAE	BIVIA	CLUNG	DOMIC
AFORE	AREAE	BLAER	COMAE	DONER
AFOUL	AREAL	BLASE	COMAL	DORIC
AGAIN	AREAR	BLAWN	COOST	DOTAL
AGAST	AREDD	BLIST	CORAM	DOWNA
AGGRI	AREIC	BLIVE	CORNI	DRACK
AGLEE	ARERE	BLOWN	CORNO	DRACO
AGLOW	ARIOT	BLUER	COUDE	DRANK
AGOOD	AROSE	BODHI	COULD	DRAVE
AGRIN	ASKEW	BOEUF	COURD	DRAWN
AHEAD	ASKOI	BOLAR	COXAE	DRENT
AHEAP	ASTIR	BONZA	COXAL	DREST
AHENT	ASWIM	BOREL	COYER	DRIPT
AHIGH	ASYLA	BORIC	CRASH	DROPT
AHIND	ATILT	BORNA	CREPT	DUCAL
AHINT	ATRIP	BOWIE	CROCI	DUING
AHULL	AULIC	BOXEN	CRONK	DUMKA
AIDOI	AULOI	BRAVI	CROST	DUNCH
AIGHT	AURAL	BREEM	CRUSH	DUNNO
AINEE	AURAR	BREME	CUFFO	DUNSH
AITCH	AUREI	BRUNG	CUING	DUOMI
ALACK	AVAST	BRUSK	CUISH	DURST
ALANE	AWASH	BUFFA	CUNEI	DUTCH
ALBEE	AWAVE	BUFFI	CURCH	DWELT
ALEFT	AWEEL	BUILT	CURLI	EHING
ALGAE	AWORK	BURNT	CURSI	ELMEN
ALGAL	AXIAL	BUTCH	CURST	EMONG
ALGID	AXILE	BUXOM	CWTCH	ENLIT
ALIKE	AYELP	BYSSI	CYANO	ENORM
ALIVE	AYGRE	CABRE	CYBER	ETYMA

EVHOE	GIGHE	ICTIC	LOACH	MUNCH
EVOHE	GINZO	ILEAC	LOAST	MUSHA
EWHOW	GIRSH	ILEAL	LOBAR	MUTER
EYRIR	GLIAL	ILIAC	LOGOI	MYOID
FATAL	GLODE	IMIDO	LOSEN	NAEVI
FAUGH	GNASH	IMINO	LOTIC	NARIC
FAURD	GNAWN	IMSHI	LOYAL	NARRE
FAVER	GOBAR	INAPT	LUACH	NATAL
FAYER	GOBBI	INBYE	LUCID	NAUCH
FEART	GOBBO	INCUT	LUDIC	NAVAL
FECAL	GOEST	INEPT	LUMME	NEGRO
FECIT	GOETH	INERM	LURCH	NEIST
FEHME	GOIER	INFRA	LURID	NEMPT
FELCH	GONIA	INNIT	LYARD	NEVER
FERER	GONNA	INTIL	LYART	NEWER
FETAL	GONZO	INTRA	LYCEA	NGWEE
FETCH	GOTTA	INUST	LYNCH	NICER
FETID	GOUCH	IODIC	LYTIC	NIDAL
FEWER	GOYIM	ISNAE	MAARE	NIMBI
FEYER	GRANA	JAMON	MACHI	NITID
FILAR	GREEK	JEUNE	MADID	NIVAL
FILCH	GRIPT	JINGO	MANET	NOHOW
FILII	GROWN	JIRRE	MARCH	NOMEN
FILUM	GRUND	JOKOL	MARIA	NOMOI
FINCH	GRYPT	JOMON	MAYAN	NOOIT
FLITT	GULAR	JURAL	MAYST	NOTAL
FLOSH	GULCH	KACHA	MEANT	NOTUM
FLOWN	GURSH	KAMME	MEDII	NOVAE
FLUNG	GWINE	KASME	MEINT	NOXAL
FOCAL	GYRAL	KEECH	MELBA	NUDER
FOLIC	HABLE	KEMPT	MENSH	NUDZH
FORDO	HADAL	KENCH	MERCH	NUGAE
FORZA	HADST	KIDGE	MERER	NUMEN
FORZE	HAITH	KINDA	MESAL	NUTSO
FOUER	HANCH	KLIEG	MESIC	NYING
FRACK	HARSH	KNELT	MEYNT	OATEN
FRAPE	HASTA	KNISH	MICRA	OBIIT
FRATI	HATHA	KOHEN	MIKRA	OBOLI
FRENA	HAULT	KORAI	MILCH	OGMIC
FROSH	HAUTE	KOTCH	MILIA	OHMIC
FRUSH	HEAME	KRONA	MINAE	OHONE
FUBAR	HEMAL	KYDST	MISCH	OIDIA
FUGAL	HEWGH	LAEVO	MISDO	OLEIC
FUNGO	HIANT	LAITH	MISGO	OLPAE
FURTH	HILAR	LARCH	MITCH	ONCET
GADJO	HILCH	LAXER	MIXTE	ORGIC
GADSO	HILUM	LAZZI	MODII	OSSIA
GANCH	HOING	LAZZO	MOLAL	OTAKU
GARNI	HOKKU	LEANT	MOLTO	OUTDO
GAYER	HOOCH	LEAPT	MOONG	OUTGO
GEESE	HOTCH	LEASH	MOOSE	OVOLI
GELID	HOTEN	LEEZE	MORAE	OWSEN
GENAL	HOVEN	LEISH	MOSSO	PACTA
GENIC	HOWBE	LEPID	MOSTE	PADRI
GENII	HOWSO	LEPTA	MOTEN	PAISE
GENUA	HUGER	LEUCO	MUCHO	PAKKA
GESSO	HUMIC	LIART	MUCIC	PALER
GEYAN	HUMID	LIBRI	MUCID	PALPI
GEYER	HUNCH	LITAI	MULCH	PAOLI
GHEST	HUTCH	LIVID	MULSH	PAOLO

PAPAL	RAMAL	SHOPE	STUNK	TRUER
PAPPI	RAREE	SHORN	STURE	TRYMA
PARAE	RARER	SHOWN	SUCCI	TUBAE
PARVE	RASTA	SHULN	SUENT	TUBAL
PAVID	RECTI	SHUSH	SULCI	TUBAR
PAYSD	REDID	SIDHE	SULFO	TUMID
PEART	REJON	SIELD	SUPRA	TYNDE
PELON	RELIT	SIKER	SURAL	TYPAL
PENAL	REMET	SINCE	SWACK	ULNAD
PENDU	RENAL	SITKA	SWANG	ULNAE
PEPLA	RERAN	SKEEF	SWAPT	ULPAN
PERCH	RESAT	SKINT	SWARE	UNAPT
PEREA	REWAN	SKOSH	SWEPT	UNBID
PETRI	REWON	SLAID	SWOLN	UNDEE
PETTI	RHYTA	SLAIN	SWOPT	UNDID
PETTO	RIFER	SLANK	SWORE	UNDUE
PHPHT	RIMAE	SLASH	SWORN	UNDUG
PHYLE	RORAL	SLEER	SWUNG	UNETH
PIEZO	RORIC	SLEPT	SYKER	UNGOT
PIING	RORID	SLIER	TABID	UNHIP
PILAR	RUBAI	SLIPT	TACET	UNKID
PILCH	RUGAE	SLISH	TACIT	UNMET
PILEI	RUNIC	SLUNG	TAGMA	UNRID
PILUM	RYPER	SLUNK	TAISH	UNSOD
PINCH	SAFER	SLYER	TAKEN	UNWET
PLENA	SAGUM	SMASH	TANTI	UPBYE
PLESH	SAIST	SMOTE	TANTO	UPLIT
POOCH	SALIC	SMUSH	TAPEN	UPRAN
PORCH	SAMEN	SNASH	TARDO	UPTER
POUPT	SANER	SNOEP	TARGA	URAEI
PRESA	SAPID	SNUCK	TAULD	URDEE
PRIMI	SATEM	SNUSH	TAZZE	UREAL
PROST	SAYNE	SOCKO	TEACH	UREIC
PROUD	SAYST	SODIC	TELOI	URENT
PSOAE	SCAND	SOLDI	TEMPI	URNAL
PSOAI	SCAPI	SOLDO	TEPID	UTERI
PUBIC	SCUDI	SOPRA	TEUCH	UVEAL
PUCER	SEELD	SORAL	TEUGH	VACUA
PUCKA	SEFER	SORBO	THAIM	VAGAL
PUDIC	SEGNI	SORDA	THELF	VAIRE
PUKKA	SENGI	SORER	THEMA	VALID
PULIK	SENSA	SOUCT	THIEF	VAPID
PULLI	SENTI	SPAKE	THILK	VASAL
PULMO	SENZA	SPARD	THINE	VATIC
PUPAE	SEPIC	SPAZA	THOLI	VAUCH
PUPAL	SERAL	SPENT	THOSE	VEHME
PURER	SERER	SPRAD	THRAE	VELUM
PUTID	SERIC	SPUTA	THREW	VENAE
PUTTO	SESSA	STAID	TICCA	VENAL
PYOID	SETAE	STASH	TIDAL	VERRA
PYRAL	SETAL	STEPT	TIMID	VILDE
PYRIC	SHAKT	STOAE	TONDI	VILLI
QUALE	SHALT	STOAI	TONKA	VIMEN
QUASI	SHASH	STOLN	TOPHI	VINIC
QUAYD	SHAWN	STONG	TOPOI	VIOLD
QUOAD	SHERE	STOOD	TORII	VIRAL
QURSH	SHEWN	STOPT	TORSI	VIRID
RABID	SHIUR	STUDE	TRAPT	VITAE
RADII	SHONE	STUMM	TRIFF	VIVID
RAGDE	SHOON	STUNG	TRILD	VOILA

VOLAE	WHILK	WRAPT	YEWEN	YUCKO
VOLTA	WHIPT	WRATE	YFERE	YUMMO
VOLTI	WHOSE	WROTE	YINCE	ZILCH
VOULU	WHOSO	WROTH	YLIKE	ZLOTE
VULGO	WIDER	WRUNG	YMOLT	ZOEAE
WAIDE	WILCO	WRYER	YOGIC	ZOEAL
WANLE	WINCH	XERIC	YOKUL	ZONAE
WANNA	WINNA	XOANA	YOMIM	ZOPPA
WARST	WISER	XYLIC	YONIC	ZOPPO
WAXEN	WISHA	XYSTI	YOURN	ZOWIE
WELCH	WISHT	YARER	YOUSE	ZUZIM
WELKT	WOFUL	YAULD	YRAPT	ZYGAL
WELSH	WOKKA	YBORE	YRENT	ZYGON
WENCH	WOMEN	YCLAD	YRIVD	ZYMIC
WERSH	WOMYN	YCOND	YSAME	
WHAMO	WOWEE	YDRAD	YTOST	
WHICH	WOXEN	YEVEN	YUCCH	

Six-letter words

(The list does not include words ending in -ED, -J, -S, -X, -Y, -Z.).

AAHING	AFFYDE	ALMOST	ANURAL	ASLEEP
ABATTU	AFIELD	ALULAE	ANURIC	ASLOPE
ABEIGH	AFLAME	ALULAR	ANYHOW	ASLOSH
ABLAZE	AFLOAT	ALUMNI	AORTAE	ASMEAR
ABLEST	AFRAID	ALVINE	AORTAL	ASPOUT
ABLOOM	AFRESH	AMARNA	AORTIC	ASQUAT
ABLUSH	AFRONT	AMBACH	APEMAN	ASSOTT
ABOARD	AGAMIC	AMBUSH	APEMEN	ASTARE
ABORAL	AGAPAE	AMEBAE	APIECE	ASTOOP
ABORNE	AGAPAI	AMEBAN	APNEAL	ASTRUT
ABULIC	AGHAST	AMEBIC	APNEIC	ASWARM
ABURST	AGILER	AMIDIC	APODAL	ASWING
ACETIC	AGLARE	AMIDST	APPAID	ASWIRL
ACETUM	AGLEAM	AMINIC	APPAYD	ASWOON
ACHIER	AGOING	AMMINO	APTEST	ATAVIC
ACIDER	AGONAL	AMMONO	APTING	ATELIC
ACIDIC	AGONIC	AMORAL	ARCANE	ATHROB
ACINAR	AGORAE	AMUSIC	ARCHEI	ATOKAL
ACINIC	AGUISH	AMYLIC	ARDENT	ATONAL
ACKNEW	AGUNAH	ANCILE	AREACH	ATOPIC
ACRAWL	AGUNOT	ANCORA	ARGULI	ATWAIN
ACULEI	AHCHOO	ANEATH	ARGUTE	ATWEEL
ACUTER	AHORSE	ANELLI	ARIDER	ATWEEN
ADIPIC	AIDANT	ANEMIC	ARIGHT	ATWIXT
ADMIXT	AIDFUL	ANENST	ARILLI	ATYPIC
ADNATE	AIDMAN	ANETIC	ARIOSI	AUDIAL
ADRIFT	AIDMEN	ANGOLA	ARISEN	AVANTI
ADROIT	AIKONA	ANIGHT	AROUND	AVERSE
ADYTUM	AIMFUL	ANISIC	ARRIBA	AVIDER
ADZING	AIRMAN	ANKUSH	ARRISH	AVITAL
AECIAL	AIRMEN	ANNULI	ARSENO	AVOUCH
AECIUM	AKIMBO	ANODAL	ARSINO	AWARER
AEDINE	ALBEIT	ANODIC	ASHAKE	AWATCH
AEFALD	ALDERN	ANOMIC	ASHINE	AWEIGH
AERIER	ALEXIC	ANOUGH	ASHORE	AWEING
AFAWLD	ALIBLE	ANOXIC	ASHRAF	AWHILE
AFEARD	ALLYOU	ANTRAL	ASLANT	AWHIRL

AWOKEN	BEREFT	BREGMA	CELLAE	COWISH
AWRACK	BESANG	BRICHT	CENDRE	COWMAN
AWRONG	BESEEN	BROKEN	CENTAI	COWMEN
AWSOME	BESTAD	BROMIC	CERCAL	COXIER
AXEMAN	BESUNG	BROOCH	CERING	COXING
AXEMEN	BETCHA	BRUMAL	CERTIE	COYEST
AXENIC	BETING	BRUNCH	CERULE	COYING
AXONAL	BETOOK	BRUTAL	CHADRI	COYISH
AXONIC	BETROD	BUCCAL	CHANGA	COZING
AZONAL	BEWENT	BUFFEL	CHELAE	CREANT
AZONIC	BEWEPT	BULBAR	CHEVAL	CREDAL
AZOTIC	BHAJIA	BULLAE	CHICER	CRIANT
BAALIM	BIATCH	BUMALO	CHOLIC	CRIBLE
BABIER	BIAXAL	BURSAE	CHORIC	CRIMEN
BACCAE	BIFOLD	BURSAL	CHOSEN	CRINAL
BACULA	BIFORM	BUSIER	CHOUSH	CRISIC
BADDER	BIGGER	BUSMAN	CHYLDE	CROTCH
BADMAN	BILING	BUSMEN	CICALE	CROUCH
BADMEN	BIMBLE	BYDING	CIDING	CROUSE
BAGMAN	BINATE	BYKING	CILIUM	CRUDER
BAGMEN	BINMAN	BYLIVE	CISTIC	CRURAL
BAKGAT	BINMEN	BYPAST	CITING	CRUTCH
BALDER	BIRKEN	CAAING	CITRIC	CUBING
BALING	BISSON	CABMAN	CLASPT	CUBITI
BALTIC	BITTEN	CABMEN	CLATCH	CULMEN
BANING	BIVIUM	CADENT	CLECHE	CULPAE
BANISH	BLAEST	CADMIC	CLENCH	CULTIC
BARBAL	BLAISE	CAECAL	CLEVER	CUMULI
BARDIC	BLAIZE	CAECUM	CLINAL	CUNEAL
BAREST	BLANCH	CAGIER	CLINCH	CUPMAN
BARFUL	BLATER	CAGING	CLONAL	CUPMEN
BARING	BLEACH	CAKIER	CLONIC	CUPRIC
BARISH	BLENCH	CALAMI	CLOVEN	CURIAE
BARMAN	BLOOIE	CALASH	CLUING	CURIAL
BARMEN	BLOTTO	CALCIC	CLUNCH	CURING
BASEST	BLUEST	CALLID	CLYING	CURSAL
BASSER	BLUIER	CALMER	CLYPEI	CURTER
BATMAN	BLUISH	CAMASH	CNIDAE	CURULE
BATMEN	BOGMAN	CAMSHO	COAXAL	CUSPAL
BAYMAN	BOGMEN	CANIER	COBRIC	CUTCHA
BAYMEN	BOKING	CANNAE	COCCAL	CYANIC
BEATEN	BOLDER	CANNOT	COCCIC	CYMOID
BECAME	BOLETI	CARDAN	COGENT	CYMOSE
BEDASH	BOLLEN	CARMAN	COHOSH	CYSTIC
BEDIDE	BONIER	CARMEN	COINOP	CYTISI
BEDRID	BONSAI	CAROLI	COITAL	CYTOID
BEDYDE	BONZER	CARRON	COKIER	DADGUM
BEFELD	BOOING	CARTOP	COKING	DAEDAL
BEFELL	BOREAL	CARVEN	COMADE	DAEING
BEFORE	BOSHTA	CASEIC	COMETH	DAFTER
BEGILT	BOSKER	CASINI	COMODO	DAIMEN
BEGIRT	BOSSER	CATCHT	COMOSE	DAMMIT
BEGONE	BOWMAN	CATTLE	CONGII	DANISH
BEHALF	BOWMEN	CAUDAD	CONING	DANKER
BEHELD	BOXIER	CAUDAE	COOCOO	DARKER
BELIKE	BOYING	CAUGHT	COSING	DAWISH
BELIVE	BOYISH	CAUSAE	COSMIC	DAYLIT
BEMATA	BRAWER	CAUSEN	COSTAE	DAZING
BEMIXT	BREACH	CEDARN	COTTAE	DEAFER
BENIGN	BREECH	CEDING	COWIER	DEARER

DEAWIE	DOVIER	ENGILT	FAYING	FOEMEN
DEBILE	DOVING	ENGIRT	FAZING	FOETAL
DEBOSH	DOVISH	ENLEVE	FEATER	FOETID
DECANI	DOWIER	ENMESH	FECUND	FOGASH
DECENT	DOWING	ENODAL	FEEING	FOGMAN
DEEDER	DOZIER	ENOLIC	FEHMIC	FOGMEN
DEEING	DREAMT	ENRAPT	FELSIC	FOLIAR
DEEPER	DREICH	ENRICH	FENMAN	FONDER
DEFFER	DREIGH	EOCENE	FENMEN	FONTAL
DEFTER	DRENCH	EOTHEN	FEODAL	FOOBAR
DEGAGE	DRIEGH	EPHORI	FEREST	FORANE
DEIDER	DRIEST	EPICAL	FERIAE	FORBYE
DEIFER	DRIVEN	EPODIC	FERIAL	FORDID
DEIFIC	DROLER	EQUALI	FERINE	FOREDO
DEKING	DROMIC	EREMIC	FERRIC	FOREGO
DELISH	DROMOI	ERENOW	FERVID	FORGAT
DELTIC	DRUSEN	ERUCIC	FETING	FORGOT
DELUXE	DRYEST	ERUVIM	FETISH	FORMEE
DENSER	DRYISH	ERUVIN	FEUDAL	FORRAD
DERING	DUCTAL	ETERNE	FEUING	FORREN
DERMAL	DUDING	ETYMIC	FEWEST	FORRIT
DERMIC	DUDISH	ETYPIC	FEYEST	FOSSAE
DETACH	DUEFUL	EURIPI	FEYING	FOUEST
DEVOID	DUELLI	EWGHEN	FIFING	FOULER
DEVOUT	DUETTI	EWKING	FIKIER	FOVEAE
DEWIER	DUKING	EXEUNT	FIKING	FOVEAL
DEWING	DULLER	EXILIC	FIKISH	FOXIER
DEXTRO	DUMBER	EXODIC	FILIAL	FOZIER
DIAMYL	DUMELA	EXODOI	FILMIC	FRACTI
DICIER	DUMOSE	EXONIC	FILOSE	FRAENA
DIEING	DUNNER	EXTOLD	FILTRE	FRANCO
DIKIER	DUPING	EYEING	FINEST	FREEST
DIKING	DURING	FAAING	FINISH	FRENCH
DINFUL	DUSKER	FABBER	FINITO	FRIGID
DINING	DYABLE	FACEUP	FINSKO	FROREN
DINKER	DYKIER	FACIAE	FISTIC	FRORNE
DINNAE	DYKING	FACILE	FITFUL	FROZEN
DIREST	EADISH	FADIER	FIXIVE	FRUGAL
DISCAL	EASIER	FAECAL	FLANCH	FRUSTA
DISTAL	EASSEL	FAINER	FLAXEN	FULCRA
DITTIT	EASSIL	FAIRER	FLEECH	FULGID
DJINNI	ECESIC	FAKIER	FLEMIT	FULVID
DOABLE	ECHINI	FAKING	FLENCH	FUMIER
DOGMAN	ECHOIC	FALLEN	FLETCH	FUMING
DOGMEN	EDENIC	FAMING	FLIEST	FUMULI
DOITIT	EFFETE	FAMISH	FLINCH	FUNDIC
DOLING	EGESTA	FAMULI	FLITCH	FUNEST
DOLIUM	EIDENT	FARAND	FLOCCI	FUNGIC
DOMIER	EIDOLA	FARFET	FLOOIE	FUNNER
DOMING	EIKING	FARING	FLORAE	FURCAE
DOMOIC	EKUELE	FASCIO	FLORID	FURCAL
DOPIER	ELDEST	FATING	FLOUSH	FURDER
DORMIE	ELMIER	FATTER	FLUIER	FUSILE
DORSAD	ELVISH	FAUNAE	FLUISH	FUSING
DORSUM	EMBOST	FAUNAL	FLYEST	FUSUMA
DOSING	EMDASH	FAURER	FLYMAN	FUZING
DOTIER	EMMESH	FAVEST	FLYMEN	FYKING
DOTISH	ENARCH	FAVOSE	FLYSCH	GAEING
DOUCER	ENCASH	FAXING	FODGEL	GAGING
DOURER	ENDASH	FAYEST	FOEMAN	GAGMAN

GAGMEN	GRAVEN	HITMAN	INGRAM	KLATCH
GAIJIN	GRAYER	HITMEN	INGRUM	KLOOCH
GALEAE	GREEBO	HOAING	INKJET	KNITCH
GAMASH	GREYER	HODMAN	INLAID	KOUROI
GAMEST	GRINCH	HODMEN	INMESH	KRONEN
GAMGEE	GRIPLE	HOHING	INMOST	KRONER
GAMIER	GROSZE	HOLDEN	INRUSH	KRONOR
GAPIER	GRUING	HOLIER	INTACT	KRONUR
GARDAI	GRUTCH	HOLMIC	INTIME	KROONI
GARISH	GRYSIE	HOLPEN	INTIRE	KULAKI
GASHER	GUNMAN	HOMIER	INTOWN	KUTCHA
GASLIT	GUNMEN	HOOROO	INWITH	KYBOSH
GASMAN	GUNNEN	HOOTCH	INWORN	LABARA
GASMEN	GUTTAE	HOOVEN	IRATER	LABILE
GATVOL	GUYING	HOPING	IRIDAL	LABIUM
GAUNCH	GYBING	HORMIC	IRIDIC	LABRAL
GAYEST	GYLDEN	HORRID	IRITIC	LACTIC
GAZIER	GYMNIC	HOSING	IRREAL	LAESIE
GEASON	GYRANT	HOWZAT	ITERUM	LAICAL
GEDDIT	GYRING	HOWZIT	ITSELF	LAKISH
GEEING	GYROSE	HOXING	JACENT	LAMEST
GEMINI	GYVING	HOYING	JADING	LAMIAE
GEMMAE	HABILE	HUDDEN	JADISH	LAMISH
GEMMAN	HADDEN	HUDDUP	JANTEE	LANOSE
GEMMEN	HAEING	HUGEST	JEEING	LARGER
GENIAL	HAEMAL	HUMERI	JEJUNE	LARINE
GEODIC	HAEMIC	HYDRAE	JEWING	LAROID
GESTIC	HAIKAI	HYDRIC	JIBING	LARVAE
GEYEST	HAINCH	HYEING	JIMPER	LARVAL
GHUBAR	HALERU	HYENIC	JIMSON	LATHEN
GIBING	HALEST	HYETAL	JINGKO	LATISH
GIDDAP	HALFEN	HYMNIC	JINNEE	LAURAE
GIDDUP	HAMOSE	HYPHAE	JIVIER	LAURIC
GIEING	HAMULI	HYPHAL	JIVING	LAVASH
GIGMAN	HANGUL	HYPOID	JOBING	LAWEST
GIGMEN	HANIWA	IATRIC	JOCOSE	LAWFUL
GILDEN	HARDER	IBADAH	JOCUND	LAWMAN
GIUSTO	HARISH	IBADAT	JOKIER	LAWMEN
GLAZEN	HATING	IBIDEM	JOKING	LAXEST
GLEBAE	HAULST	ICEMAN	JOLING	LAYMAN
GLOBAL	HAUNCH	ICEMEN	JOVIAL	LAYMEN
GLUIER	HAWKIT	ICONIC	JOWING	LEALER
GLUING	HAYIER	IDEATA	JOYFUL	LEARNT
GLUISH	HAZIER	IDLEST	JOYING	LEETLE
GLUNCH	HEARIE	IDOLUM	JUBATE	LEFTER
GLUTEI	HEISHI	IMIDIC	JUGATE	LEGMAN
GNAMMA	HELIAC	IMMANE	JUKING	LEGMEN
GNOMAE	HELING	IMMESH	JYMOLD	LEKKER
GNOMIC	HEMOID	INANER	KAEING	LENGER
GOETIC	HEMPEN	INARCH	KAONIC	LENTEN
GOIEST	HEPPER	INBENT	KAPUTT	LENTIC
GOLDER	HERMAI	INBORN	KARMIC	LERING
GONION	HETING	INCAVI	KAWING	LESBIC
GONIUM	HEYING	INCAVO	KEIGHT	LEWDER
GOOIER	HIATAL	INCUBI	KEPPEN	LIBANT
GORIER	HIEING	INCULT	KEPPIT	LIBRAE
GOTTEN	HIEMAL	INDIGN	KEWLER	LIEDER
GOWDER	HIKING	INFELT	KIBOSH	LIEFER
GOYISH	HIPPIC	INFERE	KIPPEN	LIENAL
GRANUM	HISPID	INFIMA	KIRSCH	LIEVER

LIFULL	MAMMAE	MODISH	NIRLIT	OTITIC
LIKEST	MANENT	MODULI	NITRIC	OUTATE
LIKUTA	MANFUL	MODULO	NIXING	OUTBYE
LIMBIC	MANQUE	MOIRAI	NOBBUT	OUTDID
LIMNIC	MANTIC	MONACT	NOBLER	OUTSAT
LIMPID	MARISH	MONISH	NODOSE	OUTSAW
LIMULI	MARMEM	MOOING	NOGAKU	OUTWON
LINEAL	MASING	MOPIER	NONFAT	OWLISH
LINEAR	MATIER	MOPING	NONMAN	OWRIER
LINIER	MAUGER	MOPISH	NONMEN	OXALIC
LINISH	MAUNNA	MORBID	NONPAR	OXIDIC
LIPOIC	MAUVER	MORISH	NORDIC	OZONIC
LIROTH	MAWGER	MORSAL	NOSIER	PACTUM
LITHIC	MAWING	MORYAH	NOSTOI	PAINCH
LITTEN	MAXING	MOSHAV	NOSTRO	PAIRER
LIVEST	MAYEST	MOSING	NOTING	PALEAE
LOBULI	MAYHAP	MOTIER	NOTOUR	PALEAL
LOCULI	MAZIER	MOUGHT	NOULDE	PALEST
LOGIER	MEAGER	MOZING	NOUNAL	PALIER
LOIPEN	MEATAL	MUCOSE	NOWISE	PALISH
LOMATA	MEDIAD	MULISH	NOYING	PALLAE
LOMING	MEDIAE	MUONIC	NUBILE	PALLID
LOOING	MEEKER	MURKER	NUCHAE	PALPAL
LOOSER	MEIKLE	MUSCAE	NUDEST	PANINO
LOOTEN	MENSAE	MUTEST	NUKING	PAPISH
LORATE	MENSAL	MUTING	NUMINA	PAPYRI
LOREAL	MEREST	MUXING	NUTANT	PARDEE
LOTHER	MERMAN	MYSELF	OAFISH	PARDIE
LOUDER	MERMEN	MYTHIC	OAKIER	PAREVE
LOUING	MESIAD	MYTHOI	OBESER	PARISH
LOUPEN	MESIAL	MYXOID	OBIING	PARTIM
LOUPIT	MESIAN	NAFFER	OBITAL	PASSEE
LOWSER	METING	NAIANT	OBITER	PASSIM
LOWSIT	MEVING	NAIFER	OBTECT	PAUSAL
LOXING	MEWING	NAIVER	OCELLI	PAWING
LUBING	MIDCAP	NAPING	OCHONE	PEARST
LUBRIC	MIKING	NARIAL	OCREAE	PEASEN
LUCENT	MILDER	NARINE	OCTOPI	PEASON
LUCKEN	MILIUM	NASIAL	ODDEST	PECTIC
LUITEN	MILKEN	NASTIC	ODDISH	PEDATE
LUNIER	MIMING	NATANT	OGAMIC	PEEING
LUPOID	MIMMER	NAUTCH	OGIVAL	PELTAE
LUPPEN	MINIER	NEANIC	OGRISH	PENIAL
LUTEUM	MINISH	NEARER	OIDIUM	PENILE
LUTTEN	MIRCHI	NEATER	OILMAN	PENILL
LYFULL	MIRIER	NEBISH	OILMEN	PENMAN
LYSING	MIRING	NEFAST	OMASAL	PENMEN
LYTTAE	MISATE	NERVAL	OMASUM	PENNAE
MAAING	MISDID	NESHER	OMIGOD	PENNIA
MACING	MISLIT	NETHER	ONAGRI	PEPFUL
MADMAN	MISMET	NEUMIC	ONIRIC	PERAEA
MADMEN	MISSAE	NEURAL	ONRUSH	PERDIE
MAGYAR	MISSAW	NEVOID	OPTING	PEREIA
MAINER	MISUST	NEWEST	ORBIER	PERFET
MAKUTA	MITIER	NEWISH	ORGANA	PERISH
MALEIC	MITRAL	NICEST	ORGIAC	PERITI
MALIBU	MIXIER	NICISH	OSTEAL	PERNIO
MALIST	MIXING	NIELLI	OSTIAL	PEROGI
MALLEI	MNEMIC	NIGHER	OSTIUM	PEROXO
MALOTI	MODICA	NIOBIC	OTIOSE	PERTER

PHAEIC	POSIER	RAKISH	RETRAL	SAYEST
PHATIC	POTASH	RAMATE	RETROD	SBIRRI
PHOCAE	POTATO	RAMEAL	RETUSE	SBIRRO
PHONAL	POTING	RAMOSE	REWORE	SCALAE
PHWOAH	POTMAN	RAMULI	RHINAL	SCATCH
PHWOAR	POTMEN	RANCID	RHIZIC	SCEATT
PHYLAE	POUKIT	RANINE	RHODIC	SCHTUM
PHYLAR	POWWAW	RAPHAE	RHOTIC	SCHULN
PHYLIC	POXIER	RAPINI	RICHER	SCIENT
PHYLON	POXING	RAPPEN	RICTAL	SCOLIA
PHYLUM	PRELAW	RAREST	RIDDEN	SCOOCH
PIANIC	PREMAN	RARING	RIFEST	SCOOSH
PIAZZE	PREMEN	RATHER	RIGHTO	SCOPAE
PICINE	PREMIA	RAUCID	RILIER	SCORCH
PICRIC	PRIMAL	RAVISH	RILING	SCOTCH
PIEING	PROGUN	RAWISH	RIMOSE	SCRYDE
PIEMAN	PRONER	RAXING	RIPEST	SCULCH
PIEMEN	PRONTO	README	RODMAN	SCUTAL
PIERST	PROSIT	REALER	RODMEN	SCUTCH
PILEUM	PROWAR	REALIA	ROKIER	SCUTUM
PILOSE	PROWER	RECHIE	ROOPIT	SCYPHI
PINETA	PRUTAH	RECKAN	ROPIER	SEAMAN
PINNAE	PSORIC	RECTAL	RORIER	SEAMEN
PINNAL	PUCEST	REDIAE	ROSCID	SEARCH
PINXIT	PUDENT	REDIPT	ROSEAL	SEARER
PINYIN	PUIRER	REDONE	ROTING	SECESH
PIONIC	PUKIER	REDREW	ROUPET	SECUND
PIPIER	PUKING	REECHO	ROUPIT	SEDENT
PIRNIT	PULIER	REEDEN	RUBATI	SEDILE
PIROGI	PULPAL	REFELL	RUBBET	SEIKER
PITHOI	PUNANI	REFELT	RUBIER	SEJANT
PITMEN	PUNCTA	REFLEW	RUEFUL	SELDOM
PIZING	PUNIER	REGAVE	RUGATE	SELLAE
PLACID	PUNISH	REGILT	RUGOSE	SEMEIA
PLAGAL	PUREST	REGNAL	RULIER	SEMPER
PLANAR	PURING	REGNUM	RURBAN	SEMPRE
PLEACH	PUTRID	REGREW	RUSHEN	SENITI
PLENCH	PUTSCH	REGULI	RUSINE	SENRYU
PLEXAL	PUTTEN	REHASH	RYKING	SENSUM
PLIANT	PYCNIC	REHUNG	SACCOI	SEPMAG
PLICAE	PYEING	REKING	SADDER	SEPTAL
PLICAL	PYEMIC	RELAID	SAFEST	SEREST
PLONGD	PYNING	RELATA	SAFING	SERRAE
PLUTEI	PYXING	RELIDE	SAFTER	SETOSE
PODIAL	QUAINT	RELISH	SAGEST	SEXFID
POISHA	QUALIA	REMOUD	SAGIER	SEXIER
POKIER	QUATCH	RENKER	SAIDST	SHAKEN
POLISH	QUEINT	REPAND	SAIRER	SHAPEN
POLYPI	QUENCH	REROSE	SAKKOI	SHARON
POMATO	QUETCH	RESAID	SALEWD	SHAVEN
POMMEE	QUINIC	RESAWN	SALPAE	SHAZAM
PONENT	QUOOKE	RESEEN	SAMIER	SHOULD
PONTAL	QUOTHA	RESEWN	SANCTA	SHRANK
PONTIC	QURUSH	RESHOD	SANEST	SHREWD
POOING	RACIAL	RESHOT	SANING	SHROWD
POOKIT	RACIER	RESOWN	SAPEGO	SHRUNK
POPISH	RADDER	RETIAL	SAPFUL	SHTOOM
POPRIN	RADGER	RETOOK	SARING	SHTUMM
PORIER	RADISH	RETORE	SATING	SHYEST
POSHER	RAHING	RETORN	SATIVE	SHYING

SHYISH	SOLIDI	STROVE	TERGUM	TOZING
SIALIC	SOLING	STROWN	TERRAE	TRAGAL
SICCAN	SOMATA	STRUCK	TERSER	TREFAH
SICCAR	SOMONI	STRUNG	TESTAE	TREIFA
SICKER	SORBIC	STYING	THECAE	TRENCH
SIFREI	SORDID	SUABLE	THECAL	TREPID
SIGLOI	SOREST	SUAVER	THENAL	TRIACT
SIGLUM	SOUGHT	SUBITO	THENCE	TRIFID
SILENI	SOURER	SUBMAN	THETCH	TRILLO
SILING	SPEECH	SUBSEA	THETIC	TRINAL
SILVAE	SPERST	SULCAL	THOLOI	TRISTE
SIMIAL	SPETCH	SUMMAE	THORIC	TRITER
SINFUL	SPICAE	SUNKEN	THRASH	TROPPO
SINING	SPINAE	SUNLIT	THRAWN	TROUCH
SIPING	SPLISH	SUPERB	THRESH	TRUEST
SISTRA	SPLOSH	SURBET	THRICE	TRUING
SITHEE	SPOILT	SUREST	THROVE	TRYPAN
SITING	SPOKEN	SUTILE	THROWN	TSKING
SITTEN	SPORAL	SWATCH	THRUSH	TUBATE
SIWASH	SPRACK	SWEERT	THYINE	TUFOLI
SIZIER	SPRAID	SWEIRT	THYMIC	TUMULI
SKEIGH	SPRENT	SWOOSH	THYRSI	TUNIER
SKITCH	SPRIER	SYEING	TIBIAE	TURBID
SKOLIA	SPRONG	SYLVAE	TICING	TURFEN
SKOOSH	SPRUNG	SYNING	TIEING	TURGID
SKYIER	SPRUSH	SYPING	TIFOSI	TUSSAC
SKYING	SPRYER	TAEING	TIFOSO	TUSSAL
SKYISH	SPUING	TAIHOA	TIGLIC	TUTMAN
SKYLIT	SPUTUM	TAISCH	TINEAL	TUTMEN
SKYMAN	SQUUSH	TAKIER	TINIER	TWEEST
SKYMEN	STALER	TALEAE	TINING	TWILIT
SLATCH	STALKO	TALLER	TINMAN	TYEING
SLEAZO	STANCH	TALPAE	TINMEN	TYKISH
SLEEST	STANCK	TAMEST	TITMAN	TYNING
SLIEST	STATAL	TAPING	TITMEN	TYPIER
SLIVEN	STATIM	TAPPIT	TITULI	UBIQUE
SLOOSH	STEARD	TARNAL	TOEIER	UGSOME
SLOWER	STEELD	TAUGHT	TOEING	ULNARE
SLUING	STELAE	TAURIC	TOFORE	ULTIMO
SLYEST	STELAI	TAUTER	TOLUIC	UMBRAE
SLYISH	STELAR	TAUTIT	TOMATO	UMBRAL
SMALTI	STERIC	TAVERT	TOMBAL	UNBEEN
SMATCH	STEYER	TAWIER	TOMBIC	UNBENT
SMEECH	STINKO	TAXMAN	TOMIAL	UNBORE
SMIRCH	STITCH	TAXMEN	TONANT	UNCAST
SMOOSH	STOBIE	TEAING	TOOMER	UNCHIC
SMOUCH	STOLEN	TECTAL	TOPMAN	UNCIAE
SNEESH	STOLID	TEDIER	TOPMEN	UNCINI
SNIDER	STOMAL	TEEING	TOROSE	UNCLAD
SOAKEN	STOMIA	TEGMEN	TOROTH	UNCOER
SOBEIT	STONEN	TELIAL	TORRID	UNCOOL
SOBFUL	STOUSH	TELIUM	TORTEN	UNCUTE
SOCMAN	STRACK	TEMENE	TOSING	UNDEAD
SOCMEN	STRATI	TENIAE	TOSSEN	UNDEAR
SODAIC	STRAWN	TENSER	TOTHER	UNDONE
SOEVER	STREWN	TENUTI	TOTING	UNDREW
SOFTER	STRIAE	TERAPH	TOWIER	UNEATH
SOLEIN	STRIPT	TERATA	TOYISH	UNEVEN
SOLEMN	STRODE	TERBIC	TOYMAN	UNFELT
SOLGEL	STRONG	TERGAL	TOYMEN	UNFINE

UNFIRM	UNTROD	VANMEN	WANKLE	XENIUM
UNFIXT	UNVEXT	VARSAL	WANNEL	XOANON
UNFOND	UNWELL	VASTER	WANNER	XYLOID
UNGAIN	UNWEPT	VATMAN	WARIER	XYSTOI
UNGILT	UNWISH	VATMEN	WARING	YAKUZA
UNGLAD	UNWIST	VEDUTA	WARMAN	YAREST
UNGORD	UNWONT	VEDUTE	WARMEN	YAWING
UNGUAL	UNWORN	VEGETE	WASHEN	YBLENT
UNHEWN	UPBLEW	VEHMIC	WASSUP	YBOUND
UNHUNG	UPBORE	VEINAL	WAURST	YBRENT
UNHURT	UPDOVE	VELOCE	WAVIER	YCLEPT
UNIFIC	UPDREW	VENIAL	WAXIER	YEDING
UNITAL	UPGIRT	VENOSE	WEXING	YEOMAN
UNJUST	UPGONE	VERIER	WEYARD	YEOMEN
UNKEND	UPGREW	VERLIG	WHATEN	YEVING
UNKENT	UPGUSH	VERMAL	WHATNA	YEXING
UNKEPT	UPHAND	VERNAL	WHATSO	YIKING
UNKIND	UPHELD	VIABLE	WHEARE	YIPPEE
UNLAID	UPHILD	VIBIER	WHILOM	YITTEN
UNLASH	UPHOVE	VICING	WHILST	YOWING
UNLEAL	UPHUNG	VIDUAL	WHITER	YPIGHT
UNLICH	UPLAID	VIENNA	WHIZZO	YPLAST
UNLOST	UPMOST	VILLAE	WHOMSO	YSHENT
UNMADE	UPPISH	VILLAR	WHOOSH	YTTRIC
UNMARD	UPROSE	VINEAL	WIDEST	YUKIER
UNMEEK	UPRUSH	VINIER	WIDISH	YUKING
UNMEET	UPRYST	VINING	WIFING	YWROKE
UNMESH	UPSENT	VIRENT	WILFUL	ZAFTIG
UNMIXT	UPSOLD	VIRILE	WILIER	ZANIER
UNMOWN	UPTOOK	VIRING	WILING	ZAPATA
UNOPEN	UPTORE	VISCID	WIMMIN	ZELOSO
UNPAID	UPTORN	VISIVE	WIRIER	ZEROTH
UNPENT	UPWENT	VISTAL	WISEST	ZINCIC
UNPURE	URACHI	VITTAE	WISING	ZIPTOP
UNREAL	URATIC	VOGIER	WITHAL	ZIZITH
UNRENT	UREMIC	VOLAGE	WITING	ZOAEAE
UNRUDE	URETIC	VOLING	WOEFUL	ZOECIA
UNSAID	URSINE	VOLVAE	WOOHOO	ZOETIC
UNSAWN	USABLE	VORAGO	WORSER	ZOFTIG
UNSENT	UVULAE	VORANT	WOTCHA	ZONOID
UNSEWN	VACANT	VORPAL	WOWFER	ZOOEAE
UNSHOD	VADOSE	VOSTRO	WOWING	ZOOEAL
UNSOFT	VAGILE	VULVAE	WRENCH	ZOOIER
UNSOLD	VAGROM	VULVAL	WRETCH	ZOONAL
UNSOWN	VAGUER	VULVAR	WROKEN	ZOONIC
UNSPUN	VAINER	WABBIT	WRYEST	ZUFOLI
UNSUNG	VALIUM	WAEFUL	WRYING	ZUFOLO
UNSUNK	VALVAL	WAIRSH	WYLING	ZUZZIM
UNTOLD	VALVAR	WANDLE	WYTING	ZYGOID
UNTORN	VANMAN	WANIER	XENIAL	ZYMOID

CHAPTER 9
MISCELLANEOUS LISTS

This section contains a variety of short lists that don't really have a home elsewhere in the book. Not all these lists are of great importance to Scrabble but they may appeal to some players. The section includes lists of words according to their frequency of play over one million simulated computer games, compound words whose two halves can be transposed, lists of place names and personal names that happen to be allowed words, and a fascinating list of words that unexpectedly take an -S hook. Finally there are lists of allowable words whose origins are in overseas English-speaking regions of the world. Most of these lists do not aim to be exhaustive but the contents have been selected in order to maintain some relevance to Scrabble.

Unexpected -S hooks

In a game of Scrabble, it can be a great advantage to be able to surprise the opponent by making a play using an S that unexpectedly hooks an existing word that looks as if it is unextendable. There are three categories of such words selected here: words that have already been pluralized with an S but which can then take a further S hook (eg CITES-S); words that are past tenses in -ED that can be treated as a noun and therefore take an -S hook (e.g. MARRIED-S); those words that end in consonant followed by Y where the plural can be a straight -S, breaking the standard rule of converting Y to I and adding ES (eg TRILBY-S). While all these words will also appear in their appropriate place within the hook word section, it is of value to have them all collected together here in one place, for ease of learning.

Words ending in -S that take another S

ABBES-S	COMBLES-S	HANDLES-S	MIS-S
ABYS-S	COSINES-S	HOS-S	MORAS-S
ADVENTURES-S	CUFFLES-S	HURTLES-S	MOS-S
AMAS-S	DAUPHINES-S	INKLES-S	MUS-S
AMIS-S	DEADLINES-S	JOINTURES-S	NEEDLES-S
ASSES-S	DOS-S	KAROS-S	NERVINES-S
BAS-S	DURES-S	KAVAS-S	OGRES-S
BIBLES-S	ESQUIRES-S	KINDLES-S	PHILOSOPHES-S
BOS-S	FAINNES-S	KINGLES-S	PIS-S
BRAS-S	FANGLES-S	KIS-S	POS-S
BULGINES-S	FES-S	LARGES-S	POSSES-S
BUTTERINES-S	FOGLES-S	LAS-S	PRECES-S
CAMAS-S	FOOTLES-S	LOWNES-S	PRELATES-S
CAPLES-S	FRAS-S	MAPLES-S	PRINCES-S
CARES-S	GAMINES-S	MARQUES-S	PROCURES-S
CARLES-S	GARBLES-S	MAS-S	PROS-S
CAVAS-S	GAUS-S	MES-S	RANKLES-S
CHAPES-S	GOS-S	MILLIONAIRES-S	RAYLES-S
CITES-S	GUES-S	MILLIONNAIRES-S	ROOTLES-S

RUMPLES-S	SOS-S	TACKLES-S	TYRANNES-S
RUSTLES-S	SOUPLES-S	TAILLES-S	USURES-S
SAGENES-S	SPARKLES-S	TARTINES-S	WATTLES-S
SALTINES-S	SPECKLES-S	TAS-S	WINDLES-S
SHINES-S	SPRINGLES-S	TIMELINES-S	ZEBRAS-S
SIGHTLINES-S	SQUIRES-S	TREADLES-S	
SKIFFLES-S	SUCKLES-S	TRICKLES-S	

Words ending in -ED that take an S

ASSURED-S	COMBINED-S	INTENDED-S	MARRIED-S
BELOVED-S	ELEVATED-S	LAMED-S	MOPED-S
BETROTHED-S	FROSTED-S	LIMITED-S	UNLEADED-S
COLOURED-S	INSURED-S	MALTED-S	WICKED-S

Words ending in consonant plus Y that take an S

ABHENRY-S	DARCY-S	MILLIHENRY-S	SWINGBY-S
ABY-S	DROSTDY-S	NY-S	TELLY-S
BENDY-S	DRY-S	PLATY-S	TREVALLY-S
BIALY-S	EMMY-S	POLY-S	TRILBY-S
BLOWBY-S	FLYBY-S	PRY-S	WHY-S
BY-S	GOODBY-S	QWERTY-S	ZLOTY-S
CANTERBURY-S	HENRY-S	SHINDY-S	
COLBY-S	JANSKY-S	STANDBY-S	

Transposals

Some words consist of two elements (compound words) which can be transposed to give a different word. These give you two words for the price of one and it may be that only one of them will fit on a board during a game. This list focuses on transposals where the two halves are equal in length (for example, DOGWATCH and WATCHDOG are omitted) and ignores those that are not compound words (for example, TRYPAN and PANTRY are omitted).

BACKFALL	FALLBACK	FLOODWATER	WATERFLOOD	MATESHIP	SHIPMATE
BACKFIRE	FIREBACK	FORTEPIANO	PIANOFORTE	OFFPUT	PUTOFF
BACKLIFT	LIFTBACK	FRYPAN	PANFRY	OFFSET	SETOFF
BACKSEAT	SEATBACK	FUCKHEAD	HEADFUCK	OUTPUT	PUTOUT
BIRDCAGE	CAGEBIRD	GEARHEAD	HEADGEAR	OUTRIG	RIGOUT
BIRDSONG	SONGBIRD	GUESTHOUSE	HOUSEGUEST	OUTRUN	RUNOUT
BOILOVER	OVERBOIL	GUTROT	ROTGUT	OUTSET	SETOUT
BONEFISH	FISHBONE	HANDOVER	OVERHAND	OVERPASS	PASSOVER
BOOKCASE	CASEBOOK	HANGOVER	OVERHANG	OVERSLIP	SLIPOVER
BOOKWORK	WORKBOOK	HEADLONG	LONGHEAD	OVERTAKE	TAKEOVER
BOOTJACK	JACKBOOT	HEADRAIL	RAILHEAD	OVERTURN	TURNOVER
BUSHFIRE	FIREBUSH	HILLSIDE	SIDEHILL	OVERWING	WINGOVER
BUYOUT	OUTBUY	HOLDOVER	OVERHOLD	OVERWRAP	WRAPOVER
COATTAIL	TAILCOAT	HOMETOWN	TOWNHOME	PARSEC	SECPAR
COMEDOWN	DOWNCOME	HUNGOVER	OVERHUNG	PITSAW	SAWPIT
COMEOVER	OVERCOME	JAYVEE	VEEJAY	RAGTAG	TAGRAG
CUTOFF	OFFCUT	JOYPOP	POPJOY	ROADSIDE	SIDEROAD
DOVERING	RINGDOVE	LAYOUT	OUTLAY	ROOTWORM	WORMROOT
DOWNPLAY	PLAYDOWN	LOCKPICK	PICKLOCK	WOODWORM	WORMWOOD
DOWNTURN	TURNDOWN	LOOKOVER	OVERLOOK		

Placenames

Some placenames can also be valid Scrabble words, either because the word has a meaning related to that place or just through sheer coincidence. Here is selection that may be of interest. The list is by no means exhaustive but represents a selection of words up to eight-letters in length that have some value to the Scrabble player. (The assistance of David Sutton is acknowledged in generating this list.)

ACTON	a stuffed jacket worn under mail	CREWE	a pot
		DERBY	a kind of hat
ALAMO	a kind of poplar	DERRY	a dislike
ALASKA	a heavy fabric	DEVON	a breed of cattle from Devon
AMAZON	a tall, powerful woman	DOVER	to doze
AMMAN	a district magistrate	ETNA	a vessel for heating liquids
ANGOLA	relating to a fabric made from the wool of the Angora goat	FLORENCE	a former gold coin of Europe
		FUJI	a silk fabric
		FULHAM	a loaded die
ARMAGNAC	a kind of brandy	GALILEE	a small chapel or porch at the western end of some medieval English churches
ASCOT	a type of necktie with broad ends		
ASSAM	in Malaysia, tamarind as used in cooking	GAMBIA	the inspissated juice of a plant growing in Malacca
BABEL	a scene of confusion	GENEVA	a spirit distilled from gin
BALBOA	the monetary unit of Panama	GENOA	a large jib which overlaps the mainsail
BALMORAL	a flat Scottish bonnet	GERS	Mongolian tents
BANGKOK	a straw hat	GOA	a kind of Tibetan gazelle with backward-curving horns
BARBICAN	an outer defensive work; esp a tower at a gate or bridge		
		GOBI	Hindi word for cauliflower
BEDLAM	an asylum	GOSPORT	a communication device in an aeroplane
BERLIN	a type of carriage		
BLARNEY	to talk persuasively	GREECE	a flight of steps
BOHEMIA	a community of bohemians	GUERNSEY	a woollen jersey
BOLIVIA	a type of fabric	HACKNEY	a kind of cab
BOLOGNA	a kind of sausage	HAMBURG	a patty of ground beef
BOSTON	a card game	HARROW	a spiked frame for breaking up ground
BOURBON	a kind of whisky		
BOWERY	any area frequented by drunks	HASTINGS	early fruit or vegetables
BRAZIL	a dyewood	HAVERING	present participle of 'to haver'
BRENT	a kind of goose		
BRISTOL	a smooth cardboard	HENLEY	a type of sweater
BRUSSELS	a brussels sprout	HOLLAND	a coarse cotton or linen
CAMELOT	a strong waterproof fabric	HOMBURG	a man's felt hat
CANADA	a narrow canyon	ILLAWARRA	a breed of dairy cattle
CHAD	a punched out piece of paper	INDIA	NATO alphabet code for letter i
CHANTILLY	as in chantilly lace		
CHEDDAR	a type of cheese	JAFFA	a low-bowled ball in Cricket
CHESHIRE	a kind of pig	JAPAN	to coat with glossy, black lacquer
CHILE	chili		
CHINA	fine porcelain ware	JAVA	a kind of coffee
CHUR	New Zealand expression of agreement	JERSEY	a close-fitting, knitted shirt
		JORDAN	a chamber-pot
COLOGNE	a perfumed liquid	KASHMIR	a soft twilled fabric of goat's wool
COLORADO	refers to a medium strength cigar		
		KENT	to punt or pole
CONGO	a kind of black Chinese tea	KIEV	a type of stuffed chicken dish
CORBY	a crow, a raven	LABRADOR	a breed of dog
CORDOBA	the standard monetary unit of Nicaragua	LANGLEY	a unit of illumination used to measure the temperature of a star
CREMONA	an ancient wind instrument		

LEVANT	to abscond
LEWIS	a dovetailed iron tenon made to fit into a stone so that it can be hoisted
LIMA	a kind of bean
LUCERNE	a fodder plant
MACON	smoked salted mutton
MADEIRA	a white wine
MADISON	a type of cycle race, first staged in Madison Square Gardens
MADRAS	a cotton fabric
MALI	one of the gardener class in India
MANILA	a fibre used in making rope
MAYO	mayonnaise
MEDINA	in N. African cities, the ancient native quarter
MINORCA	a type of domestic fowl
MODENA	a dark purple colour
MOLDOVA	a green tektite found in the Czech republic, thought to be the product of an ancient meteorite impact in Germany
MOROCCO	a kind of leather
MUSCAT	muscatel wine; a musky variety of grape or its vine
MUSCOVY	a type of duck
NATAL	relating to birth
NELSON	a wrestling hold
NIGER	a negro
NOME	a province or department esp. in ancient Greece
ORLEANS	a variety of plum
OXFORD	a type of shoe
PAISLEY	a patterned fabric
PANAMA	a kind of straw hat
PARIS	a European herb
PENNINE	a mineral of the chlorite group
PHOENIX	a mythological bird
PINNER	one who impounds cattle
POLISH	to make smooth and lustrous by rubbing
POPLAR	a kind of tree
PORTLAND	a kind of cement, having the color of the Portland stone
QUEBEC	NATO alphabet code for letter q
RABAT	to rotate into coincidence with another plane
RHINE	a drainage channel
RHONE	a roof-gutter
RIALTO	a theatrical district; a marketplace
RIOJA	a Spanish red wine
RIVIERA	any warm coastal district reminiscent of the Riviera
RUBICON	the winning of a game in piquet before one's opponent scores
RUSSIA	a kind of leather
SARK	a shirt, a chemise
SAUTERNE	a white wine
SEINE	to fish with a certain kind of net
SILESIA	a thin twilled cotton or linen
SODOM	any place notorious for vice
SOHO	a hunting cry
SOMERSET	a somersault
SPAIN	to wean
STEPNEY	a spare wheel
STROUD	a kind of coarse blanket made at Stroud
SUMATRA	a short, violent squall in or near the Straits of Malacca
SURREY	a horse-drawn carriage
TELFORD	a road made of stones
TEXAS	the uppermost structure on a steamboat
THEBES	plural of 'thebe', a monetary unit of Botswana
TILBURY	a light open two-wheeled carriage
TOLEDO	a sword made at Toledo
TONGA	a light two-wheeled Indian vehicle
TRIPOLI	an earthy substance originally brought from Tripoli, used in polishing stones and metals
TUPELO	a North American tree
TYNE	to lose
ULSTER	a kind of overcoat
VALENCIA	a kind of woven fabric
VICHY	a kind of mineral water
VICTORIA	a kind of open carriage
VIENNA	a type of steak
VIRGINIA	a type of flue-cured tobacco grown originally in Virginia
VOLTA	a lively dance in 3/4 time
WALES	weals
WALLSEND	a kind of coal
WANTAGE	a deficiency, a shortage
WARSAW	a kind of fish
WATERLOO	a decisive defeat or setback
WELS	an American catfish
WIGAN	a stiff plain-woven cotton
WOOMERA	a stick for launching a spear with greater force
WORTHING	present participle of 'worth', to be, to happen
YORK	to bowl a batsman with a YORKER
ZAIRE	a monetary unit of Zaire

Personal names

Similarly, some personal names can also be valid Scrabble words, either because the familiar personal name has itself been derived from a word (such as girls' names that come from flowers) or because something has been named after someone, or just out of coincidence. Here is selection that may be of interest. The list is by no means exhaustive but represents a selection of words up to eight-letters in length that have some value to the Scrabble player. (The assistance of David Sutton is acknowledged in generating this list.)

ABIGAIL	a lady's maid
ALAN	a large hunting dog
ALBERT	a short kind of watch-chain
ALMA	Egyptian dancing girl
ANNA	a former coin of India
BASIL	an aromatic herb
BEN	a mountain peak
BENEDICT	a newly married man
BENJAMIN	benzoine, a gum resin
BENNY	an amphetamine tablet
BERTHA	a woman's deep collar
BETH	a Hebrew letter
BILL	to present for payment
BILLY	a metal container for cooking outdoors
BOBBY	a policeman
BONNIE	bonny (pretty)
BRAD	a thin nail
BUSTER	something large
CARL	a miser
CAROL	to sing joyously
CELESTE	a keyboard instrument
CHAD	a scrap of paper
CHARLEY	a fool
CHARLIE	a fool
CHUCK	to throw
CICERO	a typeface
CLARENCE	a closed carriage
CLEMENT	merciful
CLIFF	a high steep face of rock
CRISPIN	poetic for a shoemaker
DAISY	a flowering plant
DAPHNE	a flowering shrub
DAVY	a miner's safety lamp
DEXTER	situated on the right
DIANE	a kind of steak
DICK	a detective
DICKENS	a devil
DOLLY	a wheeled platform
DONNA	an Italian lady
DOTTY	crazy
DUSTY	full of dust
ERICA	a shrub of the heath family
FAGIN	one who trains young thieves
FANNY	the buttocks
FAY	to join closely
FELICITY	happiness
FLORENCE	a durable silk fabric
FLOSSIE	a floozy
FRANK	to mark for postage

FRITZ	a state of disrepair
GABBY	talkative
GILBERT	an electromagnetic unit of force
GILLY	to act as a hunting attendant
GLEN	a small valley
GLORIA	a halo
GRAHAM	wholewheat flour
GUY	chap, fellow
HANSEL	to inaugurate with a gift
HECTOR	to bully
HENRY	a unit of inductance
HERBY	abounding in herbs
HOMER	to hit a home run
HYACINTH	a type of flower
JACK	to raise with a type of lever
JACKY	a sailor
JADE	to weary
JAKE	a yokel
JANE	a girl or woman
JEAN	a durable cotton fabric
JEMIMA	an elastic-sided boot
JENNY	a travelling crane
JERRY	a builder of flimsy houses
JESS	to strap the legs of a hawk
JILL	a cart for carrying timber
JIMMY	to pry open with a crowbar
JO	a sweetheart
JOE	a sweetheart
JOEY	a young kangaroo
JOHNNY	a sleeveless hospital gown
JORDAN	a type of chamberpot
JOSEPH	a woman's long cloak
JOSH	to tease
JUDAS	a spyhole in a door
KELLY	a specialist drilling pipe
KELVIN	the SI unit of temperature
KEN	to know
KERRY	one of an Irish breed of cattle
KITTY	a fund of money
LANCE	to pierce with a lance
LAURA	a type of monastery
LOUIE	a lieutenant
LOUIS	a former gold coin of France
LUCIFER	a friction match
MARC	residue after pressing grapes
MARCEL	to give soft waves to hair with heated tongs
MARGE	margarine

MARIA	dark areas of the Moon or Mars	SALLY	to rush out suddenly
MARINA	a berthing area for yachts	SANDY	covered with sand
MARTIN	a small bird	SHAW	a small wood
MARYJANE	marijuana	SHEILA	a young girl or a woman
MATILDA	a hobo's bundle	SHELLY	abounding in seashells
MAXWELL	a unit of magnetic flux	SHERLOCK	a detective
MICHAEL	teasing (as in 'take the michael')	SHYLOCK	a ruthless creditor
		SIBYL	a female prophet
MICKEY	to drug someone's drink	SONNY	a small boy
MOLLY	a tropical fish	SPENCER	a short double-breasted overcoat
MORGAN	a type of saddle horse		
MORRIS	an English folk dance	TAMMY	a fabric of mixed fibers
NANCY	an effeminate young man	TEDDY	a furry, stuffed toy bear.
NAPOLEON	a old French gold coin	TERRY	an absorbent fabric
NELLIE	a weak or foolish person	TIFFANY	a thin, mesh fabric
NELLY	a weak or foolish person	TIMOTHY	a kind of grass
NEWTON	a unit of force	TINA	slang term for crystal meth
NOAH	a shark (Australian slang)	TITAN	anything gigantic
NOEL	any Christmas carol	TOBY	a type of drinking mug
OLIVE	a small fruit	TOMMY	to oppress by paying in goods instead of money
OSCAR	cash		
PAM	a type of card game	TONY	stylish
PATSY	one who is easily fooled	TROY	a system of weights
PATTY	a thin, flat cake of food	VERA	very
PETER	to diminish gradually	VERONICA	a type of herb
RALPH	to vomit	VICTORIA	a gigantic water lily
REG	a regulation	WALDO	a remote control gadget
REX	a king	WALLY	something visually pleasing
ROMEO	a swain, a beau	WARREN	a place where rabbits live
RUTH	compassion	WEBSTER	a weaver

Playability lists

The lists of words given here represent those that have occurred most often in 8 million Scrabble games played by a computer against itself. By definition, all these words are certainly worth knowing because they naturally crop up on a regular basis. To assist, the words have been split into word-length and the most frequent words have been listed for each length. It is perhaps not surprising to see a lot of JQXZ words among these lists. To give a flavour of how the words without JQXZ sit within the most-frequently played words, a list of the top 1,000 irrespective of length is also included. Thanks are due to John O'Laughlin for running the 8 million games and selecting the most frequently played words.

The 250 most frequently played 3-letter words

QIN	ZAG	ONE	WOE	ANE
QAT	ODE	ORE	WOO	JAR
QIS	AHI	IWI	YOU	WEE
EXO	ENE	ZOA	WEX	AMI
OWE	OBE	ERE	ONO	WOF
AXE	EWE	AYU	JOW	ABO
AZO	AIA	AYE	JOR	DZO
AWE	ATE	ETA	JAW	EAU
IDE	ITA	ZOO	URE	AHA
OXO	OPE	ARE	UTE	VEX
JOE	OBI	AWA	WOX	OOF
OYE	ADO	EME	VOX	ABA
JAI	ODA	AGO	EMO	ZAX

QUA	YEA	EMU	ISO	FOB
VOW	WET	BEE	TEE	ANI
ZAP	JEE	ADZ	FEN	APO
OHO	DIF	ERA	NEE	GUV
NYE	ONY	FOX	KOI	TIE
JOT	NOX	GIE	BEZ	DEV
AUA	JAY	HIE	OUR	VET
GOX	OBO	TEF	JAP	GID
GIF	YAE	JEW	AGA	VOR
VAW	FEZ	WEB	BYE	JIG
AME	JIN	FAE	FER	OUT
ZEE	FAX	JOL	BOX	FET
ANA	JOB	ZEA	ZIN	REN
ZOL	AGE	EEN	JEU	WUD
EFT	NEF	WIZ	JIZ	BOW
EYE	EGO	AUE	LOX	PAX
OBA	WAX	ZAS	FOU	GIT
JAG	JOY	AMA	ZIT	FAG
JOG	TAX	REF	FEG	VUG
UPO	WED	OAF	BIO	POI
FEE	UTA	HOX	OKA	REI
JET	FAA	TIX	DIV	EAT
DEX	FEH	ANY	VIN	AMU
FEW	JAB	UEY	RIF	OOR
WAI	APE	HOI	FAB	FAH
REX	ABY	RAX	TWO	WOW
WEN	ORA	YOW	GOE	NAE
OFT	JAM	EEL	VID	LAX
IRE	SUQ	TOE	REH	VAG
GIO	FOE	WEM	HUI	KIF
UNI	TAJ	DEF	GOO	IFS
YEX	DOF	OXY	VOE	FOH
TEX	GOV	WOG	EAR	TEA
ION	FEU	WON	OOH	HER
HEX	ZED	REZ	FED	RET
ALA	XIS	REE	PAV	AKA
FAW	ZEX	HOE	FEM	BIN

The 250 most frequently played 4-letter words

EUOI	ODEA	JOEY	JAPE	OYEZ
QINS	HUIA	OUZO	OBOE	FUJI
QADI	QUOD	YOWE	ADZE	JAGA
QAID	WAQF	JETE	WAIF	JEEZ
QATS	VEXT	JOTA	OFAY	BIZE
JIAO	ANOA	IOTA	OVUM	OWED
AWEE	QUAG	ZOEA	BENJ	FAVA
AVOW	FIVE	LAZO	GREX	JUTE
AJEE	EAUX	AXED	QUEY	AJAR
HIOI	JIVE	JEDI	INIA	QUOP
AQUA	VIAE	DITZ	TOEA	JIBE
IXIA	JOBE	QOPH	OUPA	UVAE
QUAI	FIQH	ETUI	GEEZ	VIBE
EVOE	DJIN	VEGO	AGEE	QUEP
WEXE	JAIL	ZITE	JUVE	ONIE
AGIO	ZITI	VIEW	JOWL	JUDO
EXON	JEFE	TREZ	ZOOT	VROW
OHIA	AZON	IDEE	VIVO	JOLE
OGEE	OBIA	HAJI	QUAD	ZATI

ZAGS	JEEP	ZETA	FEME	JEEL
ZINE	ZEIN	JANE	VROU	WINO
ALOO	ABYE	AVID	VERB	OLIO
VOIP	EOAN	UNAU	JAKE	QUIN
VINT	ROJI	SWIZ	DZHO	ODAH
JEED	JAVA	JILT	JINX	YUGA
VROT	ZORI	TEXT	EAVE	VENT
JIRD	MIRV	YONI	ILEX	FRIZ
MOOI	GOAF	EMEU	YODE	JEHU
WUDU	YAGI	GIFT	PAUA	UNAI
VINO	CIAO	JARL	AUTO	FAIX
WOOF	TWIG	IURE	DZOS	JEAN
QUAY	RONZ	QUAT	JOLT	MAXI
BEAU	AIGA	OWER	AIDA	FEEB
WIFE	WOVE	OLEO	VAGI	WAWE
DIVI	RITZ	NAOI	YOGI	VEEP
ZOON	FADO	KAIE	WAGE	JINN
AXEL	QUIM	UVEA	FIDO	JUGA
EUGE	FAWN	EIDE	JAFA	YETI
AITU	JOIN	VLOG	JATO	AGUE
AWED	AWAY	QUIT	JAWS	AERO
IBEX	IDEA	EINE	GAJO	AIDE
TIVY	FIGO	VEND	OYER	VANT
GOJI	EPEE	HOAX	DIVO	ZEAL
HOWE	RIZA	PERV	AMIE	PFUI
JEON	FAVE	OOZE	VUGH	KIVA
QUIZ	SJOE	KUIA	TAXA	BEEF
AEON	YOUR	MOAI	VIGA	VETO
QUID	DOJO	WEFT	JIVY	ZONE
TAXI	PAVE	JEER	YEVE	JOES
WIVE	JEAT	JADE	FIXT	JEUX

The 250 most frequently played 5-letter words

TRANQ	MIAOU	QUOTA	VROUW	FUGIO
QANAT	YOWIE	FIVER	AVOID	VIDEO
AUDIO	ZAIRE	WIFIE	TOQUE	AUREI
ZOEAE	QUOAD	LOUIE	BOWIE	VELDT
AIOLI	VIGIA	XENIA	QUITE	WOVEN
AINEE	VOGIE	JUVIE	MIAOW	WIVED
FAQIR	EQUID	WAITE	WAQFS	QUEME
NIQAB	LOOIE	EERIE	QUATE	XOANA
OUIJA	ZOWIE	BIVIA	HOURI	FAINE
QORMA	QUOIF	QUENA	YOGEE	JOBED
TALAQ	FAUVE	OURIE	QUIPO	WAIDE
YITIE	FOVEA	AECIA	AIERY	QUAIL
BOOAI	QUAIR	EEJIT	AVIZE	JIGOT
AQUAE	QUEEN	FIQUE	QUEER	VAUTE
OORIE	JIVED	OVOID	VIRTU	BEAUX
QADIS	WAIVE	JIVER	JETON	ZORIL
ADIEU	QUOIT	VIFDA	VIREO	JIRRE
AIDOI	NERTZ	AALII	JEUNE	AWATO
ZOAEA	QUERN	AREAE	VEGIE	JAXIE
OIDIA	AERIE	VITEX	VIBEX	FRITZ
QAIDS	ROQUE	JOINT	ABOVE	VARIX
QIBLA	GUQIN	QUINO	QUIRE	AVION
ZOOEA	FOGIE	HOVEA	ZANTE	QUINA
COOEE	JEWIE	JIAOS	JERID	RIOJA
AULOI	QUOTE	VINEW	OGIVE	DIVOT

WAIFT	OJIME	AVOWS	BEWIG	WIVER
BOVID	AGOOD	VODUN	WEFTE	TOWIE
IVIED	IVORY	BOEUF	DETOX	VOLTI
WAREZ	VOUGE	HUTIA	AWETO	JIRGA
VOEMA	POOVE	ZOOID	VENUE	ZITIS
UMIAQ	JIVEY	KIEVE	JAPED	QOPHS
ATIGI	GAVOT	JIBED	INDEX	QUARE
PIOYE	OBEAH	WEIZE	VIBEY	VENOM
BEVUE	VAGUE	QUEUE	DIAZO	QUIET
QUEYN	ZINEB	WEAVE	JOWED	CIVIE
NOVUM	IGAPO	HERTZ	GLITZ	ALOWE
PIVOT	JAVEL	ZONER	DIOTA	JAWED
VIEWY	VOICE	QUAGS	QUALE	VEENA
ZONAE	ZOEAL	SQUIZ	EVITE	GUIDE
JINNE	FOXIE	QUODS	AWEEL	FAENA
AZINE	BAVIN	VITTA	JINNI	OVATE
QUBIT	QUOIN	HIVED	VIRID	ZERDA
QUEAN	FILII	JIBER	JOULE	DITZY
FIQHS	VAWTE	WIFED	ZONDA	RADIX
WEXED	FOUAT	BITOU	HOOVE	GUIRO
DJINN	ZLOTE	WUXIA	AWAVE	FIRIE
TORII	AJIVA	HINAU	FAVOR	WOOER
EQUIP	VIZOR	AFOOT	FUGIE	FAVER
URAEI	ZONED	QUINE	HOAED	VEINY
VITAE	VOWED	QUAYD	GEOID	OOTID

The 250 most frequently played 6-letter words

EUOUAE	QUOTER	FEIRIE	TOORIE	ENTREZ
ZOAEAE	NIQABS	AVIZED	TOEIER	AERUGO
QINTAR	OPIATE	AUTOED	FAUNAE	OURARI
ZOOEAE	AVIATE	WAIVED	CODEIA	QUINOL
TRANQS	EQUIPE	EQUIDS	QUARTO	FOULIE
QINDAR	QUOTHA	YAUTIA	OUREBI	MOIRAI
FOVEAE	QIVIUT	WOODIE	LOANEE	INWOVE
TAUIWI	JINNEE	HEARIE	NEINEI	QUANGO
QUINOA	VOGIER	ADIEUX	QUEMED	OBELIA
EQUATE	ZOUAVE	EONIAN	QUINIE	FAERIE
OUTVIE	JOWARI	QUITED	BOUGIE	QUAVER
FAQIRS	AEONIC	BOVINE	IDEATA	OURALI
EQUINE	IOLITE	BINIOU	VIGORO	VITTAE
HOAGIE	ATONIA	EURIPI	AGUIZE	IDEATE
AVENUE	QUOTED	ETOILE	IONIZE	OLEATE
FEIJOA	BOATIE	TOQUET	APOGEE	IODIDE
WIENIE	DJINNI	OORIER	AEDINE	COOTIE
IODATE	TENIAE	QUIRED	AWEIGH	TOUTIE
AVOWED	AVOURE	GIAOUR	UNWIVE	FACIAE
VOIDEE	AZIONE	VAUDOO	QUOIFS	HAIQUE
TALAQS	EQUALI	QUAERE	WIVERN	OUTAGE
GOATEE	WAIRUA	QUERNS	DOUANE	VAWTED
AGOUTI	TOITOI	EQUANT	JEELIE	IONONE
QANATS	ZOARIA	GOODIE	AMOOVE	ROADEO
HEINIE	AUGITE	BAGUIO	JARVIE	WOOPIE
VIRTUE	TOONIE	TOETOE	AGORAE	UNWOVE
FOOTIE	WAIVER	QIBLAS	ELUVIA	QUARER
YAQONA	ADAGIO	FOODIE	COATEE	OUIJAS
IODINE	BEANIE	XENIAL	WOOLIE	QUANTA
TIBIAE	ROQUET	ZEATIN	DEAWIE	TOEBIE
QORMAS	QUIVER	OROIDE	ZOOEAL	FEAGUE

QUEENY	QUELEA	AVAILE	OZAENA	EVZONE
EIDOLA	OILIER	FIQUES	DAUTIE	APNOEA
AUDIOS	TAIHOA	JOINER	JOVIAL	VIATOR
WEIZED	VOTEEN	COAITA	AZOTED	OURIER
ZAIRES	ZOECIA	VIRAGO	FOXIER	QUETHE
EXUVIA	OVATED	IODIZE	EXODOI	QUOITS
VAGUED	OREIDE	OCREAE	MEINIE	FAVELA
WURLIE	GOORIE	YITIES	JEWIES	COURIE
FOVEAL	EQUITY	IONIUM	APIECE	EVOLUE
AEROBE	KEAVIE	EGOITY	COORIE	EATAGE
VOMITO	QWERTY	EOCENE	EVOVAE	NOVATE
COOEED	ZOOIER	FLOOIE	OPAQUE	AGOUTA
GAUCIE	GOOIER	VAUTED	HOODIA	JUVIES
QASIDA	JIVIER	AVENGE	LIQUOR	VIRION
QIGONG	GUQINS	QUINTE	OOLITE	BOVATE
AVAUNT	UTOPIA	AGRIZE	APORIA	GOONIE
POURIE	VIGOUR	OLEINE	QUEUER	EJECTA
FERVID	GOALIE	VOGUED	TOURIE	QUINTA
AECIAL	JANTEE	BEEDIE	WEENIE	OUTLIE

The 500 most frequently played 7-letter words

ETAERIO	ALIENER	TORNADE	OUTEARN	ATONERS
ETESIAN	LINEATE	AERATES	TRAINEE	AGENISE
ATONIES	RIOTISE	ELATION	EARLIES	LOANEES
ERASION	NOTAIRE	AUSTERE	EROSION	DIETINE
TAENIAE	RETINAE	ERINITE	AERIALS	EQUINES
EATERIE	EUGARIE	OLEINES	NOILIER	SOAPIER
INERTIA	EUGENIA	ELOINER	EDITION	EERIEST
AEOLIAN	OLEATES	EULOGIA	SOREDIA	SOLERET
OTARINE	DOULEIA	IRISATE	ETIOLIN	DAUTIES
AIERIES	AEROSAT	LAITIES	RATLINS	FOOTIER
OLEARIA	OARIEST	AIRIEST	EXUVIAE	GOATEED
ROSEATE	ORDINEE	ESTRIOL	URALITE	NEGATOR
EROTISE	NEROLIS	GODETIA	OUTLIER	OUTLINE
ISATINE	DENARII	AREOLES	TRITONE	AMNIOTE
ANEROID	TOENAIL	ANTLIAE	ENTASIA	DETRAIN
AEONIAN	EROTICA	URINOSE	ESERINE	SANTERA
SENARII	AQUIVER	ANERGIA	LAIRISE	EUPNOEA
ORIGANE	ATELIER	AUREOLE	GENITOR	NORTENA
EPINAOI	QINDARS	DIORITE	OUTSEEN	AREOLAS
ALIENEE	REGINAE	OREADES	SEQUOIA	SNIRTLE
ANISOLE	INEDITA	LOERIES	TANNERS	TOADIES
ARENOSE	SIENITE	LENTORS	BOATIES	ETOILES
ESTRONE	ANISEED	ENTRAIN	ORATION	STERILE
AIRLINE	TAENIAS	SITULAE	TEARIER	ORNATER
ISOLATE	RETINOL	ATONIAS	AURELIA	ELOINED
OTARIES	ENATION	ALUNITE	OUTVIED	LEANERS
GOATIER	TEENIER	EVASION	LENTIGO	ALSOONE
AREOLAE	NITERIE	TRENISE	SOCIATE	REALTIE
SEALINE	IDEATES	MOINEAU	AUREATE	LINTERS
INOSITE	AENEOUS	DIANOIA	ARENOUS	EGALITE
QINTARS	ARANEID	NEONATE	SOILIER	TERSION
AUDITEE	ROUTINE	ALERION	SINUATE	NAIADES
TINDERS	DARIOLE	NOVATED	SUETIER	AWAITER
AERIEST	EUCAINE	AVIATOR	OPIATED	IRONIST
SERIATE	AUNTIES	TROELIE	DENTILS	RAINOUT
ARENITE	SOUTANE	ROADIES	ANEARED	OREGANO
AEROBIA	EUOUAES	EQUATED	EQUINIA	LINEAGE

AUDIENT	OVARIES	EROTEMA	TOLUENE	GRANITA
ERODENT	BEANIES	ENOLASE	AGEUSIA	OBELIAS
SERRANO	MIAOUED	ANOMIES	STERNED	AILETTE
ENROOTS	OCREATE	INGRATE	ELUSION	SEELIER
ESTOILE	RANDIES	QIVIUTS	ENDORSE	LINNETS
AZIONES	ASTERIA	GENTILE	NERINES	TORANAS
ONERIER	TAUIWIS	REAROSE	DOLENTE	AVENGED
TAURINE	EUTAXIA	SNAILED	TINNIER	ALOETIC
ENTROLD	OSIERED	OBOVATE	AUGITES	RILIEVO
INDARTS	UNWARIE	SNORTER	YAQONAS	WAIVODE
HOAGIES	AILERON	DEASOIL	INUTILE	TONGERS
TARSEAL	ARAISED	TWOONIE	DELIRIA	WIDEOUT
AWAITED	TOONIES	TARAIRE	IODISER	ALDRINS
NAEVOID	EASTERN	ONLINER	GANOINE	UNWIVED
TIARAED	AVIATED	SIERRAN	WAITRON	RONDEAU
ONSTAGE	TALONED	VAUNTIE	ACONITE	OUGLIED
ANESTRA	EQUANTS	DITONES	FOVEATE	NOISIER
HERNIAE	CINEREA	AUDITOR	LIONIZE	NEUTRAL
ACETONE	LAETARE	ONLIEST	TROOLIE	SNARLER
NOSTRIL	SODAINE	AEROGEL	TANGELO	DEJECTA
ALINERS	ONETIME	WOURALI	DINITRO	OPIATES
ARSENAL	OILSEED	REOILED	INTROLD	ANTLERS
GOATEES	STOITER	NEUROID	TERTIAL	GOUTIER
ODONATE	ARISTAE	TESTIER	INTRONS	TOUTIER
ELODEAS	GOONIER	AIRTIME	EIDOLON	CORNEAE
NIOBATE	DOILTER	DEITIES	SILTIER	ARIETTE
NARDINE	OESTRIN	PERINEA	AVENUES	LIERNES
ACINOSE	OVATION	RAOULIA	AGUIZED	ROILIER
DEARIES	OUTLAIN	SENECIO	INWEAVE	GUERITE
RONNIES	AURORAE	ENTICES	RETILED	ORARIAN
ZOARIAL	RATIONS	TOEIEST	AMARONE	GUINEAS
FEIJOAS	ORLEANS	STINGER	OVARIAN	OOGONIA
ODORATE	LADRONE	TRINDLE	COESITE	SCORIAE
ETALONS	DETINUE	BETAINE	INGOTED	LARNIER
NUTRIAS	UNITIVE	STONIER	STONIED	SNIFTER
VAURIEN	AROINTS	RAINIER	OUTGIVE	ACQUITE
SLINTER	UNITAGE	ROADEOS	AURATES	NOVATES
AGONIES	OESTRAL	IGNITES	GENOISE	FLAVINE
IODATES	TENDRIL	LOONIER	BEGONIA	TANGOED
ANOETIC	AMOOVED	UREDIAL	AGISTED	STANNEL
VIOLATE	ANTIAIR	ERUDITE	AERATOR	OVEREAT
TRANNIE	REALISE	TAINTED	RETSINA	TRAILED
EUTEXIA	DOUANES	INLIERS	APTERIA	AROUSED
NAIVETE	BAINITE	ANEURIN	INTERNS	ORIOLES
QUINOAS	OBVIATE	ZOUAVES	TUNICAE	NOTITIA
EVIRATE	SNORTED	AVOIDER	DECIARE	URIDINE
ATEBRIN	VOLANTE	ENDARTS	WOODIER	NASTIER
NOVENAE	COTERIE	SANTERO	IRONIER	ANESTRI
ARIETTA	DIATRON	ISOBARE	ATTIRED	ENRAGES
NITRIDE	INTERNE	ANSATED	ONEIRIC	TAUREAN
EBONITE	AECIDIA	ASTROID	HEINIES	CORONAE
RESIDUA	IOLITES	RADIALE	LIGNITE	AIRSIDE
AUREITY	AUREOLA	ABORTEE	INSTATE	JADEITE
OLESTRA	EMOTIVE	EVICTOR	STARNED	ANILINE
TERRANE	OUTLIES	TREASON	AERATED	QUAERED
PEATIER	TRAINED	SAUTOIR	ENTRIST	INDITER
LEADIER	NITRILE	ERRANTS	SLARTED	DENOTES
FOLIATE	INVITEE	IRONERS	REMANIE	OUTRAVE
HEROINE	ALEURON	ADENINE	OREIDES	LATRINE
ANTIRED	ENACTOR	INWOVEN	SEALANT	LENTOID

NARCIST	EIRENIC	RESILIN	SAOUARI	TONSURE
ROSIERE	EARLOBE	TINNERS	NEURONE	OPALINE
SOLATIA	ADONISE	AGONISE	NEATENS	RETILES

The 500 most frequently played 8-letter words

INERTIAE	TAENIOID	INERRANT	PAEONIES	RETINULA
AERATION	RELATION	ERINITES	RETAILER	AUDITEES
ETAERIOS	AIRLINER	INERTIAS	ACTINIAE	APERIENT
ERIONITE	TERATOID	NONELITE	DENOTIVE	METANOIA
AEROLITE	ENTAILER	RURALITE	RETINOLS	URINATOR
AEROTONE	DERATION	RATTLINE	ANTIWEAR	LINEATED
INERTIAL	NEARLIER	ANOESTRA	LATEENER	NITERIES
REALTONE	ANTIHERO	ORANGIER	EUGARIES	SNIRTLED
ERADIATE	OEDIPEAN	ENDOSTEA	RETIRANT	INITIATE
AREOLATE	ERGATOID	DEVIATOR	AGENETIC	INFLATER
DETAINEE	ELOIGNER	ANTIGENE	EROTICAL	IRISATED
AEGIRINE	ELOINERS	NETTLIER	RENATURE	FAINTIER
ORIENTED	TREENAIL	INTORTED	TAINTURE	OILERIES
ANTERIOR	UREDINIA	ENTOILED	ALGERINE	GREENLIT
EULOGIAE	FOEDARIE	INLANDER	AGENESIA	DIALOGER
ALIENATE	ACIERATE	TROTLINE	AWEARIED	EUGENIAS
EATERIES	DENTALIA	GOITERED	DRAGONET	INTRIGUE
NOTITIAE	RETAINED	REINVADE	VERATRIN	ANOINTER
DOUANIER	ALIENAGE	TOLERATE	NEGATION	REASONED
TENORITE	IODINATE	TOLIDINE	NAUSEATE	ANTIWEED
INAURATE	ABOITEAU	OVERLAIN	REGAINED	STOVAINE
ETIOLATE	LITERATI	CLARINET	EGOITIES	OLEFIANT
RENAILED	INFERIAE	RAINDATE	REARISEN	STEARINE
TENTORIA	LITERATO	CAROTENE	ERECTION	REGAINER
DAINTIER	OUTRAISE	ARANEIDS	ANAEROBE	ODONATES
OLEARIAS	ALIENEES	ENTRESOL	ITERATED	ANEROIDS
RETAINER	TONALITE	DEROGATE	GENITURE	NEOTERIC
AEGIRITE	IDEATION	RETIARII	RATOONER	ORDAINER
DENTARIA	ANTLERED	ORGANDIE	LOITERER	INDAGATE
ETOURDIE	AUREOLAE	LAUREATE	RIGATONI	DEAIRING
UNEASIER	ARTERIAL	ANSERINE	EQUATION	IRENICAL
RITORNEL	INTERVAL	ORATIONS	TIDELINE	DONATIVE
DELATION	EROTISED	AEQUORIN	DEIONISE	TETANOID
RETAILOR	ORIENTER	REGIONAL	RATIONED	ANTIDOTE
INTERNAL	ENARGITE	EGESTION	CINEASTE	INORNATE
ALEURONE	LITREAGE	VIOLATER	RAISONNE	NANOWIRE
SAUTOIRE	OUTEATEN	IDEATING	OESTRONE	NONIDEAL
AURELIAN	TAILORED	ERODENTS	TOENAILS	ENAUNTER
ELONGATE	GAIETIES	NITRATED	EARSTONE	AEROLITH
ORIENTAL	OVARIOLE	THIOUREA	DERACINE	INTERLAY
TRIENNIA	ONERIEST	SERENATE	IRONIEST	VAWNTIER
AERATING	ARENITIC	GRATINEE	AUREOLED	TAGAREEN
AERONAUT	OUTLEARN	ASTONIED	OPTIONEE	RENOVATE
ATROPINE	NEONATES	OUTRANGE	ONIONIER	DOULEIAS
INTERIOR	SEROTINE	DOLERITE	ANTIDORA	REORDAIN
TRIOLEIN	DIGERATI	RELEARNT	RAINIEST	METAIRIE
ADROITER	ORDINATE	TENEBRIO	DELETION	INDENTOR
RETINOID	ALIENERS	LARIATED	RESONATE	DIANOIAS
TAILERON	VAUNTIER	EURONOTE	UINTAITE	ASTEROID
ELATERIN	GAITERED	ELATERID	RENEGADO	RAVIGOTE
DETAINER	SIDENOTE	YEASTIER	SOTERIAL	TRANCIER
TAENIATE	REORIENT	PAINTIER	NOSELITE	GALENOID
OUTLINER	IDOLATER	REANOINT	DENTINAL	ATTAINER

AIRLINES	DATOLITE	ATTORNED	FOLIATED	RINGETTE
AVENTRED	CERATOID	OTTERING	LOITERED	DENTURAL
ABOIDEAU	ERIGERON	GAUNTREE	DEBONAIR	ACRIDINE
GERANIOL	NARCEINE	REDLINER	NEONATAL	ELATIONS
TROILITE	ENTAILED	ELUVIATE	AEROFOIL	AGLITTER
DEAERATE	AURELIAS	RATOONED	TOWNLIER	SENORITA
RETINTED	ISOLATED	OUTEARNS	EUCAINES	PERINEAL
EOLIENNE	AVERSION	ARGENTAL	TAILBONE	FOETIDER
TETRAGON	AUDITION	ANNEALER	INTERTIE	ARSENATE
OLEANDER	AERODYNE	TENDRILS	SOLANINE	LAIRISED
TRINODAL	STONERAW	GERONTIC	IODATION	RETINITE
ANTIMERE	RELOANED	ENTERATE	LIGATURE	GENITORS
INTERAGE	DIRIGENT	ANURETIC	AVENTAIL	RELISTED
OUTLINED	INSOLATE	AUNTLIER	FLOATIER	AVENTURE
ANDESITE	DETRITAL	DEUTERON	DURATION	IRONWARE
FORELAIN	SNARLIER	ANTIRAPE	TENAILLE	INVERTOR
TENURIAL	STRAINED	DRONIEST	SERENATA	ETERNISE
ARANEOUS	TOLEWARE	HAIRLINE	DARTLING	IDEALISE
TRENDIER	ONLINERS	SELENIAN	LAIRIEST	DESOLATE
YERSINIA	DRAISINE	TOILINET	LEGATION	REGENTAL
INTRANET	AGOUTIES	TOLERANT	RETIEING	ELEVATOR
NEUTRINO	DARRAINE	VALERIAN	TARTANED	TRENDOID
ROARIEST	RETINOIC	FLANERIE	CRINATED	RELOADER
LINGERIE	AILLETTES	AVIATORS	LABORITE	STRINGED
DATELINE	IBOGAINE	ERGOTISE	AUROREAN	ELECTRON
GRAINIER	PINOTAGE	FREDAINE	ELECTION	DIAPENTE
TOASTIER	ENDEAVOR	RANDIEST	REINVITE	INVERTED
VENATION	TACONITE	REDISTIL	ANTLIATE	LOUNGIER
TRIAZINE	DICENTRA	RELATIVE	SAUTERNE	SAGENITE
UNTIDIER	INTARSIA	TETRONAL	RETRAITE	DETRAINS
JAUNTIER	ANTHERID	ETHERIAL	ENGAOLED	UNWARIER
GELATION	DISENROL	DIPTERAN	ETRANGER	SIRENIAN
IDEATIVE	GAINLIER	ENTRAINS	NEGATRON	ATTAINED
RITENUTO	AIGRETTE	GRADIENT	OBTAINED	PINDAREE
NOTIFIER	MOINEAUS	ANTEATER	EMERITAE	ELASTANE
TRIGONAL	AROINTED	MEIONITE	INTEGRAL	DIATRIBE
ANORETIC	IRRIGATE	INTERRED	IODYRITE	SELENATE
MEDIATOR	ANOREXIA	TILERIES	ELICITOR	OEILLADE
FETATION	PELORIAN	UNDERLIT	AERODART	AWAITERS
BENITIER	TIMONEER	NAIVETES	ISLANDER	VENETIAN
DIORITES	LEVIRATE	LORINERS	OUTGIVEN	TANDOORI
FARINOSE	ERINGOES	ENDORSEE	ULTERIOR	WAITERED
LANNERET	NARRATED	ANOESTRI	DIATRETA	ROILIEST
ENROOTED	ASTERNAL	SIDERITE	TELETRON	OEDEMATA
NONRATED	UNTAILED	UNDERLIE	URALITES	ANOINTED
GODETIAS	ROTARIES	DELATING	AUREOLES	LENITION
REIGNITE	TORNADES	INTERLAP	REATTAIN	EXORDIAL

The 1000 most frequently played 2-to-8-letter words

QI	TE	EF	ON	AN
RE	NE	FE	XI	AD
IN	ED	DE	GI	OE
ER	OR	EE	AT	BE
WE	IF	TI	DI	UR
IT	ZA	EX	AG	OD
ET	AR	JO	LI	TO
ID	EL	ZO	OW	TA
EN	JA	AW	IO	EA

WO	ST	WOE	YEX	ZAS
QIN	KA	WOO	TEX	AMA
NO	OH	YOU	ION	AWEE
PE	KO	WEX	HEX	REF
AL	AS	ONO	ALA	OAF
AX	UH	JOW	FAW	HOX
NA	MA	JOR	YEA	TIX
OX	OS	JAW	WET	ANY
UT	FY	QAID	JEE	UEY
AE	CH	MM	DIF	HOI
UN	MO	URE	ONY	RAX
YE	SO	UTE	NOX	YOW
DA	UM	WOX	JAY	EEL
FA	US	VOX	OBO	TOE
BI	BY	QATS	YAE	WEM
OF	MU	EMO	FEZ	AVOW
GO	QIS	ANE	JIN	DEF
OI	MY	JAR	FAX	AJEE
AI	HM	WEE	JOB	OXY
LA	SH	AMI	AGE	WOG
LO	EXO	WOF	NEF	WON
DO	OWE	ABO	EGO	REZ
HE	AXE	DZO	WAX	REE
PI	EUOI	EAU	JOY	HOE
EH	AZO	AHA	TAX	ISO
EM	AWE	VEX	WED	TEE
AB	KY	OOF	UTA	FEN
NY	IDE	ABA	FAA	NEE
UG	OXO	ZAX	FEH	KOI
ME	JOE	QUA	JAB	BEZ
HI	OYE	VOW	APE	OUR
OP	JAI	ZAP	ABY	JAP
OU	ZAG	OHO	ORA	AGA
OB	QINS	NYE	JAM	TRANQ
OO	ODE	JOT	SUQ	BYE
NU	AHI	AUA	FOE	FER
MI	ENE	GOX	TAJ	BOX
KI	OBE	GIF	DOF	ZIN
AA	EWE	VAW	GOV	JEU
IS	AIA	AME	FEU	JIZ
ES	ATE	ZEE	ZED	LOX
GU	ITA	ANA	XIS	FOU
YA	OPE	ZOL	ZEX	ZIT
XU	OBI	EFT	EMU	FEG
PA	ADO	EYE	BEE	BIO
AY	ODA	OBA	ADZ	OKA
BA	ONE	JAG	JIAO	DIV
QAT	ORE	JOG	ERA	VIN
UP	IWI	UPO	FOX	RIF
OY	ZOA	FEE	GIE	FAB
YO	ERE	JET	HIE	TWO
AH	AYU	DEX	TEF	HIOI
BO	QADI	FEW	JEW	GOE
YU	AYE	WAI	WEB	VID
HA	ETA	REX	FAE	REH
AM	ZOO	WEN	JOL	HUI
SI	ARE	OFT	ZEA	GOO
OM	AWA	IRE	EEN	VOE
PO	EME	GIO	WIZ	EAR
HO	AGO	UNI	AUE	OOH

FED	OWT	OON	NUR	NEW
PAV	PIU	NOO	FIE	YID
FEM	UMU	BED	KIT	POW
FOB	EVOE	VIG	VEE	AUF
ANI	AIN	YON	NOH	AVO
APO	LIE	YEN	QANAT	KIN
GUV	HEN	WIG	WAE	AUDIO
TIE	JUN	YAW	TAV	FIQH
DEV	HIN	LOR	WAQF	DUH
VET	WEXE	BET	MIZ	KAE
GID	AAH	FOP	HOW	OSE
VOR	ZEL	VEG	LUZ	PIT
JIG	RED	OGEE	FAR	TEW
OUT	AGIO	GOD	JAK	NUT
FET	YET	FAP	PIN	PAW
REN	ALE	ODEA	YEW	YAR
WUD	EAN	EST	DUI	JUD
BOW	HAJ	NAW	NON	GOY
PAX	HID	TOO	VEXT	DJIN
GIT	GIN	WOT	ANOA	OIL
FAG	POX	WAB	GOA	MOZ
VUG	NET	HIT	OOP	TON
POI	MAX	WIN	KOA	LAR
REI	ZOS	TEN	KOW	BAA
EAT	AID	JIB	GUE	YAD
AMU	AIT	DIN	JUG	KOR
OOR	BEN	LID	HAW	PED
FAH	YOD	EDH	KAI	MAW
WOW	REV	HOO	HEW	AAL
NAE	YUG	PEW	TEL	AWL
LAX	WIT	UFO	REO	FIX
VAG	ZIG	FAY	MOI	REM
AQUA	BIT	DIE	BEG	NOY
KIF	LEX	TOR	QUAG	PEH
IFS	EXON	CHI	ZHO	ZOEAE
FOH	NIX	PIE	TAW	LEZ
TEA	NED	TIT	NOD	NUN
HER	DOE	DOO	MOW	LOO
IXIA	UDO	POZ	TOY	RYA
RET	TIN	FAT	ING	CHA
AKA	JUT	VAU	FIVE	FOY
BIN	BID	KID	UVA	JAIL
FIZ	LIN	LIT	EAUX	ZITI
HAE	YEH	GAW	BEL	VAE
CHE	FAN	HUIA	MEE	OVA
UTU	TAI	TET	JIVE	REW
WOP	WEY	GOR	HAO	TAD
BIZ	OWN	TWP	SHE	JEFE
INN	PIX	TOD	RAJ	KON
KEX	NOW	DAW	VIAE	FID
QUAI	DAE	ERR	FIB	RIN
BOI	DIT	LOU	BOP	OOM
AWN	RIZ	IVY	LOW	DEL
TED	VIM	FEY	DID	PIA
OHM	OHIA	QUOD	YAG	PEN
FAD	DOW	HET	DEN	MEW
NOR	PEE	OUP	THE	KEF
TID	VUM	PER	JOBE	AZON
TOW	KYE	PEA	TAE	VAR
DEE	VAN	VAT	DEI	OWL

HUE	TALAQ	RIT	GUP	MEL
ERN	NAT	AQUAE	POD	DOP
DOR	MEN	HON	TAY	ELF
OBIA	BOO	NAY	ADD	FAVA
GON	YAY	JAPE	PIR	JUTE
ZEP	CUZ	FUN	JUVE	AJAR
DUX	WAW	DAB	BAP	ELD
JOEY	OES	HOD	BAG	HEY
EFS	TAR	TOM	NOM	QUOP
EON	AXED	OAR	LAT	CWM
VAV	END	PEL	JOWL	JIBE
GUR	YITIE	OBOE	BOR	UVAE
HOA	WYE	TAG	ORT	WOK
GOB	NOB	ROW	KAF	HIP
AIOLI	OOT	RID	PAD	VIBE
GHI	GIB	ZEK	BAD	WAR
AINEE	GER	ADZE	BEY	ORF
GEE	JEDI	YOM	CEE	QADIS
FAQIR	DITZ	EVO	SHA	LIG
ALU	MIX	OAT	ECH	ADIEU
OUZO	DAN	TUI	DAY	PAN
NAH	TUX	WAIF	ODD	TOT
ELT	OUD	LUV	YGO	AIDOI
YUP	FIT	HAD	NEB	QUEP
NIQAB	YIN	BON	TAO	KOP
NTH	KIR	TEG	POA	DIB
OUIJA	NAB	HAN	ROO	TAN
LOD	VIE	AIR	ZOOT	ERF
FON	KAW	DIG	TAB	ONIE
YOWE	QOPH	GOT	EHS	GUY
DOH	RAI	BAH	OORIE	TAT
YUM	HOY	ZIP	FOG	JUDO
BIG	ETUI	OFAY	VIVO	VROW
DEW	VEGO	GED	SOX	GET
IOS	VLY	OVUM	RAW	MIG
LAW	YAH	DON	QUAD	HOG
JETE	MEH	BENJ	URN	ZOAEA
JOTA	ETH	LAV	DEG	MEU
DAG	MOU	NAG	ICH	NID
PET	ZITE	IFF	ERG	KOB
IOTA	USE	LAD	OYEZ	GIG
PEG	BOH	GREX	HOB	LOP
OUK	FUG	COX	HEM	JOLE
WAG	DAH	EEK	PAR	DIP
YOB	VIEW	PIG	FUJI	NOT
ENG	TREZ	GUN	MAE	AVA
ZOEA	DAL	QUEY	MUX	ART
MOE	GJU	DOD	TOG	SIF
FUB	IDEE	INIA	NEG	ZATI
VIA	OPT	TOEA	JAGA	FOR
QORMA	GIP	OUPA	BAN	OIDIA
GUT	MET	GEEZ	DOM	LOB
LAZO	LOY	ATT	HAT	VOL
POO	OIK	KAT	BAR	ZAGS
DOY	HAJI	AGEE	HEH	ZINE
MID	FIN	ISH	BOA	MYC
KYU	BOD	GEM	JEEZ	TEC
MED	BOOAI	DOB	BIZE	LAH
ROE	TOP	DAD	LOT	EDS
HAG	TIG	WAD	OWED	ALOO

LAG	VINT	RHO	WIFE	WAN
VOIP	BAT	QIBLA	DIVI	FUR
MIR	JEED	ZOOEA	BAY	AULOI
QAIDS	MIB	WUDU	ZOON	ROD
UGH	OIS	RYE	GAB	AITU
COW	VROT	VINO	CAZ	AWED
HAY	JIRD	WOOF	MUN	MIAOU
EFF	PAT	MAA	AXEL	HUN
TIL	FIG	GAE	EUGE	IBEX
REG	MOO	QUAY	NEP	MEG
BOY	MOOI	BEAU	COOEE	ORD

Words from World English

One method of dealing with the awkward tile combinations that inevitably appear on your rack at some point in a game is to memorize a wide selection of words outside the core vocabulary of English. As the most widely spoken language in the world, English is rich in loan-words from other languages, and the versatility of the Roman alphabet and of English pronunciation means that these words tend to be assimilated without much corruption of their original sound. This means that there are many word in English that use 'foreign' letter combinations, which are ideal for Scrabble players. The following lists contain words from Australia, Canada, New Zealand and South Africa, as well as words from the main languages of the Indian Subcontinent - Hindi and Urdu - which have entered British English.

Australian words
Australian English is distinguished not only by the numerous Aboriginal terms for Australia's flora and fauna, but also by a great many shortened forms of commonplace English words. The Australian propensity to slang and short informal words is extremely useful to Scrabble players, especially as many of these words end in O, one of the most common tiles in the game. If you spot an O on the board when you have a difficult set of letters on your rack, there's a good chance that you'll be able to form an informal Aussie word. Native Australian words provide a range of unusual letter combinations, as well as a tendency to include double Os - ideal for rack balancing. Double Rs are also common in Australian English, as are Ks and Ys, so it's well worth acquiring some Antipodean vocabulary.

ADJIGO	yam plant	BRASCO	lavatory
ALF	uncultivated Australian	BROLGA	large grey crane with
ARVO	afternoon		red-and-green head
ASPRO	associate professor	BRUMBY	wild horse
BARRO	embarrassing	BUNYA	tall dome-shaped coniferous
BAUERA	small evergreen shrub		tree
BEAUT	outstanding person or thing	BUNYIP	legendary monster
BELAH	casuarina tree	CADAGI	tropical eucalyptus tree
BERKO	berserk	CARBY	carburettor
BIFFO	fighting or aggressive	CHEWIE	chewing gum
	behaviour	CHIACK	tease or banter
BILBY	burrowing marsupial	CHOCO	conscript or militiaman
BIZZO	empty and irrelevant talk	CHOOK	hen or chicken
BOAB	baobab tree	CHOOM	Englishman
BODGIE	unruly or uncouth man	CONNIE	bus conductor
BOGAN	fool	COMMO	communist
BOOBOOK	small spotted brown owl	COMPO	compensation
BOOFY	strong but stupid	CORREA	evergreen shrub
BOONG	offensive word for a Black	COUCAL	long-legged bird
	person	COUGAN	rowdy person
BOOSHIT	very good	COUTA	type of sailing boat
BORA	native Australian coming-of-	CRONK	unfit or unsound
	age ceremony	CROOL	spoil
BORAK	rubbish or nonsense	CROWEA	pink-flowered shrub

DACK	forcibly remove someone's trousers
DADAH	illegal drugs
DAGGY	untidy or dishevelled
DASYURE	small carnivorous marsupial
DELO	delegate
DERRO	vagrant
DINKUM	genuine or right
DOCO	documentary
DONGA	steep-sided gully
DORBA	stupid, inept, or clumsy person
DRACK	unattractive
DRONGO	slow-witted person
DROOB	pathetic person
DUBBO	stupid
DUGITE	venomous snake
DURRY	cigarette
EARBASH	talk incessantly
EUMUNG	type of acacia
EVO	evening
EXO	excellent
FASTIE	deceitful act
FESTY	dirty or smelly
FIBRO	house built of fibrocement
FIGJAM	very conceited person
FIZGIG	frivolous or flirtatious girl
FOULIE	bad mood
FRIB	short heavy-conditioned piece of wool
FUNDIE	fundamentalist Christian
FURPHY	rumour or fictitious story
GALAH	grey-and-pink cockatoo
GARBO	dustman
GEEBUNG	tree with edible but tasteless fruit
GIDGEE	small acacia tree that sometimes emits an unpleasant smell
GILGAI	natural water hole
GING	child's catapult
GNOW	ground-dwelling bird
GOANNA	monitor lizard
GOOG	egg
GOOLIE	stone or pebble
GUNYAH	bush hut or shelter
GYMPIE	tall tree with stinging hairs on its leaves
HAKEA	type of shrub or tree
HOSTIE	air hostess
HOVEA	plant with purple flowers
HUTCHIE	groundsheet draped over an upright stick as a shelter
JARRAH	type of eucalyptus tree
JEFF	downsize or close down an organization
JUMBUCK	sheep
KARRI	type of eucalyptus tree
KOORI	native Australian
KYBO	temporary lavatory

KYLIE	boomerang that is flat on one side and convex on the other
LOPPY	man employed to do maintenance work on a ranch
LOWAN	ground-dwelling bird
LUBRA	Aboriginal woman
MALLEE	low shrubby eucalyptus tree
MARRI	type of eucalyptus
MELBA	repeated farewell appearances
MIDDY	middle-sized glass of beer
MILKO	milkman
MOLOCH	spiny lizard
MOPOKE	small spotted owl
MOZ	hoodoo or hex
MUGGA	eucalyptus tree with pink flowers and dark bark
MULGA	acacia shrub
MULLOCK	waste material from a mine
MURREE	native Australian
MURRI	native Australian
MYALL	native Australian living independently of society
MYXO	myxomatosis
NANA	head
NARDOO	cloverlike fern
NEDDY	horse
NOAH	shark
NONG	stupid or incompetent person
NORK	female breast
NUMBAT	small marsupial with long snout
OCKER	uncultivated or boorish Australian
PIKER	wild bullock
PINDAN	desert region of Western Australia
PITURI	shrub with narcotic leaves
PLONKO	alcoholic, especially one who drinks wine
PLURRY	euphemism for bloody
PODDY	handfed calf or lamb
POKIE	poker machine
POON	stupid or ineffectual person
POONCE	male homosexual
POSSIE	position
PRELOVED	second-hand
QUOKKA	small wallaby
QUOLL	native cat
RANGA	offensive name for a person with red hair
RAZOO	imaginary coin
REFFO	offensive term for a European refugee after World War Two
REGO	registration of a motor vehicle
RESTO	restored antique, vintage car, etc
ROO	kangaroo

ROUGHIE	something unfair, especially a trick	UPTA	of poor quality
		UPTER	of poor quality
SANGER	sandwich	UTE	utility
SANGO	sandwich	VAG	vagrant
SCOZZA	rowdy person	VEGO	vegetarian
SCUNGY	miserable, sordid or dirty	VIGORO	women's game similar to cricket
SHARPIE	member of a teenage group with short hair and distinctive clothes	WADDY	heavy wooden club used by native Australians
SHERANG	boss	WAGGA	blanket made of sacks stitched together
SHYPOO	liquor of poor quality		
SITELLA	small black-and-white bird	WANDOO	eucalyptus tree with white bark
SKEG	rear fin on the underside of a surfboard	WARATAH	shrub with dark green leaves and crimson flowers
SKITE	boast		
SMOKO	cigarette break	WARB	dirty or insignificant person
SMOODGE	smooch	WHARFIE	wharf labourer
SPAG	offensive term for an Italian	WIDGIE	female bodgie
SPRUIK	speak in public	WILGA	small drought-resistant tree
SWAGGIE	vagrant worker	WIRILDA	acacia tree with edible seeds
SWAGMAN	vagrant worker	WIRRAH	saltwater fish with bright blue spots
SWY	gambling game		
TONK	effeminate man	WOF	fool or idiot
TOOLIE	adult who gatecrashes Schoolies Week	WOOMERA	spear-throwing stick
		WURLEY	Aboriginal hut
TOOSHIE	angry or upset	YABBER	talk or jabber
TRIELLA	three horse races nominated for a bet	YABBY	small freshwater crayfish
		YACCA	grass tree
TROPPO	mentally affected by a tropical climate	YACKA	grass tree
		YARRAN	small hardy tree
TRUCKIE	truck driver	YATE	small eucalyptus tree
TRUGO	game similar to croquet	YIKE	argument, squabble or fight
TUAN	flying phalanger	YUCKO	disgusting
TUART	type of eucalyptus tree	YUMMO	delicious
UMPIE	umpire	ZAMBUCK	St John ambulance attendant
UNCO	awkward or clumsy	ZIFF	beard

Canadian words

Canadian English combines a broad range of British and US terms with words derived from Inuit, as well as from other Native American languages such as Algonquin. Canadian English incorporates many Canadian French words from Quebec, and there are also a number of recently coined Canadian terms. Inuit words can be helpful to Scrabble players because they tend to be quite vowel-heavy. K occurs frequently in Inuit terms, and sometimes appears twice. Such words require a blank tile for the second K if they are to be played during a game.

AGLOO	breathing hole made in ice by a seal	BATEAU	light flat-bottomed boat
AGLU	breathing hole made in ice by a seal	BEIGNET	deep-fried pastry
		BOGAN	sluggish side stream
AMAUT	hood on an Inuit woman's parka for carrying a child	BREWIS	Newfoundland cod stew
		BUMBLEBERRY	mixed berry pie filling
AMOWT	hood on an Inuit woman's parka for carrying a child	BUTTE	isolated steep-sided flat-topped hill
		CANOLA	cooking oil extracted from a variety of rapeseed developed in Canada
ATIGI	Inuit parka		
BABICHE	thongs or lacings of rawhide		
BARACHOIS	shallow lagoon formed by a sand bar	CAYUSE	small Native American pony used by cowboys

CRETONS	shredded pork spread	POGEY	financial relief for the unemployed
COULEE	dry stream valley		
CUSK	gadoid food fish	POGY	financial relief for the unemployed
DEKE	act or instance of feinting in ice hockey		
		POKELOGAN	backwater
ENDORSATION	approval or support	POUTINE	chipped potatoes topped with curd cheese and tomato sauce
HOSER	unsophisticated rural person		
ICEWINE	dessert wine made from frozen grapes		
		PUNG	horse-drawn sleigh
JOUAL	nonstandard Canadian French dialect	REDEYE	drink incorporating beer and tomato juice
KAMIK	Inuit boot made of caribou hide or sealskin	RUBABOO	soup made by boiling pemmican
KLOOCH	North American Indian woman	RUBBY	rubbing alcohol mixed with cheap wine for drinking
KLOOTCH	North American Indian woman		
		SKOOKUM	strong or brave
KUDLIK	Inuit soapstone seal-oil lamp	SNYE	side channel of a river
		SPLAKE	hybrid trout bred by Canadian zoologists
LOGAN	backwater		
LOONIE	Canadian dollar coin with loon bird on one face	STORMSTAYED	isolated due to adverse weather
		SWILER	seal hunter
MUCKAMUCK	food	TILLICUM	friend
MUCKYMUCK	very important person	TOONIE	Canadian two-dollar coin
MUKTUK	beluga skin used as food		
NANOOK	polar bear	TULLIBEE	whitefish found in the Great Lakes
PANZEROTTO	baked turnover with savoury filling		
		TUPEK	Inuit tent of animal skins
PARFLECHE	dried rawhide		
PARKADE	building used as a car park	TUPIK	Inuit tent of animal skins
		TWONIE	Canadian two-dollar coin
PARKETTE	small public park		
PLEW	beaver skin used as standard unit in fur trading	WAWA	speech or language
		WENDIGO	evil spirit or cannibal

Hindi words

After Chinese, Hindi, the dominant language of India, is the most widely spoken language in the world. Many Hindi words entered British English during the Raj, and some have become everyday terms – BUNGALOW and PUNDIT, for example. Others are less common, but are useful to Scrabble players because they provide unusual letter combinations and thus solutions to difficult racks. Combinations such as BH, DH and KH are common in Hindi-derived words, and the preponderance of As, Is and Us can be very helpful in trying to balance a vowel-heavy rack. Above all, Hindi words are useful because they are quite unusual, and so provide a range of options for Scrabble players that aren't immediately obvious - front-hooking onto hang with a B, for example, or end-hooking onto PUNK with an A. Committing some Hindi-derived words to memory will help to keep your opponents on their toes.

AKHARA	gymnasium	BAHADUR	title for distinguished Indians during the Raj
ALAP	vocal music without words		
AMBARY	tropical plant	BAHU	daughter-in-law
ANKUS	elephant goad	BANDH	general strike
ANNA	old copper coin	BANYAN	tree with aerial roots
ARTI	Hindu ritual	BHAI	form of address for a man
AYAH	maidservant or nursemaid	BHAJI	deep-fried vegetable savoury
BABU	Mr	BHANG	psychoactive drug made of hemp
BAEL	spiny tree		

BHANGRA	music combining traditional Punjabi music with Western pop
BHAVAN	large house or building
BHEESTY	water-carrier
BHINDI	okra used in cooking
BHISHTI	water-carrier
BINDI	decorative dot in middle of forehead
BOBBERY	mixed pack of hunting dogs
BUND	embankment
CHAI	tea, especially with added spices
CHAMPAC	tree with fragrant yellow flowers
CHAPATI	flat coarse unleavened bread
CHAPPAL	sandal
CHARAS	hashish
CHARKHA	spinning wheel
CHELA	disciple of a religious teacher
CHICHI	person of mixed British and Indian descent
CHILLUM	pipe for smoking cannabis
CHITAL	the axis deer
CHOLI	short-sleeved bodice
CHOWK	marketplace
CHUDDAR	large shawl or veil
CHUDDIES	underpants
CHUKAR	Indian partridge
COWAGE	tropical climbing plant with stinging pods
COWHAGE	tropical climbing plant with stinging pods
CRORE	ten million
CROREPATI	person who has ten million rupees
DACOIT	member of a gang of armed robbers
DACOITY	robbery by an armed gang
DAK	system of mail delivery
DAL	split grain
DATURA	plant with trumpet-shaped flowers
DEODAR	Himalayan cedar
DEWAN	chief minister of an Indian princedom
DHAK	tropical tree with red flowers
DHAL	curry made from lentils
DHARNA	method of obtaining justice by fasting
DHOBI	washerman
DHOTI	loincloth
DUPATTA	scarf
DURBAR	court of an Indian ruler
DURRIE	cotton carpet
DURZI	Indian tailor
GANJA	potent form of cannabis
GAUR	large wild cow
GARIAL	fish-eating crocodilian with long slender snout
GAVIAL	fish-eating crocodilian with long slender snout
GHARIAL	fish-eating crocodilian with long slender snout
GHARRI	horse-drawn vehicle for hire
GHARRY	horse-drawn vehicle for hire
GHAT	stairs or passage leading down to a river
GHEE	clarified butter
GHERAO	industrial action in which workers imprison their employers
GINGILI	oil obtained from sesame seeds
GORAL	small goat antelope
GUAR	plant that produces gum
GUNNY	coarse fabric used for sacks
HARTAL	act of closing shop or stopping work as a political protest
HOWDAH	seat for riding on an elephant's back
JAGGERY	coarse brown sugar
JAI	victory
KHADDAR	cotton cloth
KHEDA	enclosure for captured elephants
KHEDAH	enclosure for captured elephants
KHEDDAH	enclosure for captured elephants
KIRANA	small, family-owned shop
KOEL	parasitic cuckoo
KOS	Indian unit of distance
KRAIT	brightly coloured venomous snake
KUKRI	Ghurka knife
KULFI	Indian dessert
KURTA	long loose garment like a shirt without a collar
LAC	resinous substance secreted by insects
LAKH	100,000
LANGUR	arboreal monkey
LASSI	yoghurt drink
LATHI	long heavy stick used as a weapon
LUNGI	long piece of cloth worn as loincloth or turban
MACHAN	platform used in tiger hunting
MAHOUT	elephant driver
MAHSEER	large freshwater fish
MANDI	big market
MANDIR	Hindu or Jain temple
MAUND	unit of weight
MEHNDI	practice of painting designs on the hands and feet using henna
MELA	cultural or religious festival
MOHUR	old gold coin

MONAL	Asian pheasant	drawn by horses or bullocks
MORCHA	hostile demonstration against the government	ROTI — type of unleavened bread
MRIDANG	drum used in Indian music	RUPEE — standard monetary unit of India
NAUCH	intricate Indian dance	RYOT — peasant or tenant farmer
NAUTCH	intricate Indian dance	SAMBAR — deer with three-tined antlers
NAWAB	Muslim prince in India	
NEEM	large tree	SAMITI — political association
NILGAI	large Indian antelope	SAMOSA — triangular pastry containing spiced vegetables or meat
NULLAH	stream or drain	
NUMDAH	coarse felt	SARANGI — stringed instrument played with a bow
OONT	camel	
PACHISI	game resembling backgammon	SARDAR — Sikh title
		SARI — traditional dress of Indian women
PAISA	one hundredth of a rupee	
PAKORA	dish of deep-fried chicken or vegetables	SAROD — Indian stringed instrument
		SWAMI — title for a Hindu saint or religious teacher
PANEER	soft white cheese	
PARATHA	flat unleavened bread	TABLA — pair of drums whose pitches can be varied
PEEPUL	tree similar to the banyan	
PUNKA	fan made of palm leaves	THALI — meal consisting of several small dishes
PUNKAH	fan made of palm leaves	
PURDA	custom of keeping women secluded	TIL — sesame
		TOLA — unit of weight
PURDAH	custom of keeping women secluded	TONGA — light two-wheeled vehicle
		TOPEE — pith helmet
PURI	unleavened flaky bread	TOPI — pith helmet
PUTTEE	strip of cloth wound around the leg	URD — bean plant
		VAHANA — vehicle in Indian myth
RAGGEE	cereal grass	VANDA — type of orchid
RAGI	cereal grass	VINA — stringed musical instrument
RAITA	yoghurt-and-vegetable dish served with curry	WALLAH — person in charge of a specific thing
RAJ	government	
RAJAH	ruler or landlord	ZENANA — part of a house reserved for women and girls
RAMTIL	African plant grown in India	
RANEE	queen or princess	ZILA — administrative district in India
RANI	queen or princess	ZILLA — administrative district in India
RATHA	four-wheeled carriage	ZILLAH — administrative district in India

New Zealand words

While New Zealand and Australian English have many words in common, the Kiwi lexicon is greatly enriched by New Zealand's Maori heritage. Maori-derived words are a marvellous resource for the Scrabble player, providing a wealth of unusual vowel combinations, and frequently using consonants that are rarer in European words, such as K, W and H. Maori words are especially good for balancing vowel-heavy racks, as many words use several As, Us or Is – sometimes with three vowels in a row. Relatively high-scoring consonants are also very common, especially K and H. Unfortunately, there is only one K in Scrabble, so many Maori words with two Ks are less useful than they might initially appear. Don't forget blank tiles, however: if you have a blank, a K and a couple of vowels on your rack, there's a good chance that you can find a New Zealand word to play profitably. There are also some unusual words that have entered the vocabulary of New Zealanders from European or Asian languages.

ATUA	spirit or demon	HANGI	open-air cooking pit
BOOHAI	thoroughly lost	HAPU	subtribe
CHUR	expression of agreement	HAPUKA	large fish
COOTIE	body louse	HAPUKU	large fish
GOORIE	mongrel dog	HEITIKI	neck ornament
GRAUNCH	crush or destroy	HIKOI	protest march
HAKA	war dance	HOKONUI	illicit whisky

HONGI	nose-touching greeting	PAUA	edible abalone
HUHU	hairy beetle	PERFING	early retirement from the
HUI	conference or meeting		police force with financial
HUIA	extinct New Zealand bird		compensation
JAFA	offensive term for someone	PIKAU	rucksack
	from Auckland	PIPI	shellfish
JANOLA	household bleach	PIUPIU	leaf skirt
KAHAWAI	large fish	POI	ball of woven flax
KAI	food	PONGA	tall tree fern
KAIK	village	PORAE	edible sea fish
KAINGA	village	PORANGI	crazy
KAKA	long-billed parrot	PORINA	moth larva
KAKAPO	ground-dwelling parrot	POTAE	hat
KARAKIA	prayer	POWHIRI	welcoming ceremony
KARANGA	call or chant of welcome	PUGGY	sticky
KATIPO	small venomous spider	PUHA	sow thistle
KAUPAPA	strategy, policy or cause	PUKEKO	wading bird
KAURI	coniferous tree	PURIRI	forest tree
KAWA	protocol or etiquette	RAHUI	Maori prohibition
KIEKIE	climbing bush plant	RATA	myrtaceous forest tree
KOHA	gift or donation	RAUPATU	seizure of land
KOKAKO	long-tailed crow	RAURIKI	sow thistle
KONEKE	farm vehicle	RONZ	rest of New Zealand
KORU	curved pattern	SHEEPO	person who brings sheep to
KOWHAI	small tree		the catching pen for
KUIA	female elder		shearing
KUNEKUNE	feral pig	TAIAHA	ceremonial fighting staff
KURI	mongrel dog	TAIHOA	hold on!
KUTU	body louse	TAKAHE	rare flightless bird
MANUKA	myrtaceous tree	TANGI	Maori funeral ceremony
MATAI	evergreen tree	TANIWHA	legendary monster
MIHI	ceremonial greeting	TAONGA	treasure
MOA	extinct large flightless bird	TAPU	sacred or forbidden
MOKI	edible sea fish	TARSEAL	bitumen surface of a road
MOKO	Maori tattoo or tattoo	TAUIWI	non-Maori people of New
	pattern		Zealand
MOOLOO	person from Waikato	TIKANGA	Maori customs
MOPOKE	small spotted owl	TOETOE	type of tall grass
MUNGA	army canteen	TOITOI	type of tall grass
NGAI	clan or tribe	TWINK	white correction fluid
NGAIO	small tree	WAKA	Maori canoe
NGATI	tribe or clan	WEKA	flightless bird
NIKAU	palm tree	WERO	warrior's challenge
PAKAHI	acid soil or land	WETA	long-legged wingless insect
PAKAPOO	Chinese lottery	WHANAU	family
PAKOKO	small freshwater fish	WHENAU	native land

South African words

South African English includes words from Nguni languages such as Xhosa and Zulu, as well as Afrikaans, amongst other languages. For Scrabble players, South African English offers a host of useful words for balancing vowel-heavy racks. Many Afrikaans-derived words contain a double A, while Nguni words often contain two or three As. It's a good idea, therefore, to have some South African words up your sleeve for when you find yourself with two or more As on your rack. There are also a lot of K words in South African English. As K can be an awkward letter to use effectively, these can come in very handy, as can the Afrikaans-derived words containing V, which are most helpful in trying to use a difficult tile.

AMADODA	grown men	MUTI	herbal medicine
AMANDLA	politcal slogan calling for power to the Black population	NAARTJIE	tangerine
		NEK	mountain pass
BAAS	boss	NKOSI	master or chief
BABALAS	drunk or hungover	OKE	man
BAKGAT	excellent	OOM	title of respect
BAKKIE	small truck	OUBAAS	person senior in rank or years
BOYKIE	chap or fellow		
BRAAI	grill or roast meat	PADKOS	snacks for a long journey
BRAAIVLEIS	barbecue	PLAAS	farm
BUNDU	wild, remote region	POTJIE	3-legged iron pot
DAGGA	marijuana	ROOIKAT	lynx
DWAAL	state of befuddlement	SCAMTO	argot of urban South African Blacks
FLATSTICK	with great speed		
GEELBEK	yellow-jawed fish	SKOLLY	hooligan
HAMBA	go away	SNOEK	edible marine fish
JA	yes	SPEK	bacon, fat or fatty pork
JAAP	simpleton	STAFFRIDER	person who clings to the side of a train
JEREPIGO	heavy desert wine		
JONG	friend	STEEN	variety of white grape
KAAL	naked	STOKVEL	savings pool or syndicate
KEREL	chap or fellow	TIK	slang for crystal meth
KRAAL	stockaded village	UBUNTU	kindness
KWAITO	type of pop music	VLEI	area of marshy ground
LEGUAAN	large monitor lizard	VOEMA	vigour or energy
MEERKAT	sociable mongoose	VOETSEK	expression of dismissal or rejection
MENEER	Mr or sir		
MEVROU	Mrs or madam	VROU	woman or wife
MOOI	pleasing	YEBO	yes

Urdu words

Urdu, the official language of Pakistan and one of the official languages of India, is closely related to Hindi. Urdu, however, contains many more words derived from Arabic and Persian, and also uses a different system of writing from Hindi, lending a different character to the words that have entered English. Many Urdu culinary terms will be familiar to British Scrabble players from Indian restaurants, while most Anglo-Indian military vocabulary also derives from Urdu rather than Hindi. As with Hindi, the variant spellings of many Urdu words provide opportunities for Scrabble players, as does the frequency of the letter K.

BAGH	garden	INQILAB	revolution
BALTI	spicy Indian dish stewed until most liquid has evaporated	IZZAT	honour or prestige
		JACONET	light cotton fabric
		JEMADAR	officer in the Indian police
BASTI	slum	KAMEEZ	long tunic
BEGUM	woman of high rank	KHARIF	crop harvested at beginning of winter
BIRIANI	Indian dish of highly flavoured rice mixed with meat or fish		
		KHAYAL	kind of Indian classical vocal music
BIRYANI	Indian dish of highly flavoured rice mixed with meat or fish	KINCOB	fine silk fabric embroidered with gold or silver threads
		KOFTA	Indian dish of seasoned minced meat shaped into balls
BUSTEE	slum		
BUSTI	slum		
CHARPAI	bedstead of woven webbing on a wooden frame	KOFTGAR	person skilled in inlaying steel with gold
CHARPOY	bedstead of woven webbing on a wooden frame	KOFTGARI	art of inlaying steel with gold
DAROGHA	manager	KORMA	Indian dish of meat or vegetables braised with yoghurt or cream
DHANSAK	Indian dish of meat or vegetables braised with lentils		

LASCAR	sailor from the East Indies	SHALWAR	loose-fitting trousers
MAIDAN	open space used for meetings and sports	SHIKAR	hunting
		SHIKAREE	hunter
MASALA	mixed spices ground into a paste	SHIKARI	hunter
		SICE	servant who looks after horses
MOOLVI	Muslim doctor of the law		
MOOLVIE	Muslim doctor of the law	SUBADAH	chief native office in a company of sepoys
MURDABAD	down with; death to		
MUSTH	frenzied sexual excitement in male elephants	SUBADAR	chief native office in a company of sepoys
NUMDAH	coarse felt	SUBAH	chief native office in a company of sepoys
QORMA	Indian dish of meat or vegetables braised with yoghurt or cream		
		SYCE	servant who looks after horses
RABI	crop harvested at the end of winter	TAHSIL	administrative division
		TALOOKA	subdivision of a district
SAHIB	title placed after a man's name	TALUK	subdivision of a district
		TALUKA	subdivision of a district
SAICE	servant who looks after horses	TAMASHA	show or entertainment
		TANDOORI	method of cooking on a spit in a clay oven
SARPANCH	head of a village council		
SEPOY	Indian soldier in the service of the British		

CHAPTER 10
ANAGRAMS

A vital skill for the keen Scrabble player is the ability to find words (or anagrams) from given sets of letters. This is the real essence of Scrabble, which, after all, is about rearranging letters on your rack to find the highest scoring combination to place on the board. The most useful words, of course, are those of seven and eight letters, as these are essential for scoring 50-point bonuses. Having the component letters of a bonus word is great – but you still have to be able to get it onto the board to obtain the bonus. And even if there are useful hooks in place on the board, you need these to be in the right place – words already on the board and the limits of board space may well keep your bonus word out of the game. This is where anagrams are so useful. The lists presented in the remainder of this book will enable you to determine if there is a word which can be made from a particular set of letters. For example, is there a valid word that can be made from the letters AEILOPR? How about AEILOPT? (Respectively, yes and no.) If you have the letters for one bonus word, it's invaluable to know if the same letters will work in a different combination which will slot onto the board somewhere. For example, with the letters AEILNST on your rack, you may have spotted SALIENT, but if SALIENT won't fit on the board, have you considered the other eight words which can be made from its letters? A good knowledge of bonus-length anagrams allows you to adapt a good rack to the situation on the board. This enables you to play bonus words more easily - or at the very least, to avoid wasting time hunting for combinations that aren't there. These lists are particularly useful when you are trying to learn from your mistakes after a game or tournament. If you had a rack which you were sure could yield a bonus word, but couldn't find it, you can check the anagram lists to find whether you were on the right lines. The letter sets (so-called 'alphagrams') are listed alphabetically, according to the alphabetical order of their component letters. So, for example, the anagrams of AEINRST all appear together, and these are listed immediately before the anagrams of AEINRSV, and so on.

Seven-letter anagrams

AAAADNP	APADANA	AAAABDJS	BAJADAS		ATABALS
AAAALTY	ATALAYA	AAAABDLM	LAMBADA		BALATAS
AAAARRS	ARAARAS	AAAABDNN	BANDANA	AAAABMOS	ABOMASA
AAAASTT	ATAATAS	AAAABEGL	GALABEA	AAAABMST	MASTABA
AAABBCL	CABBALA	AAAABFLL	FALBALA	AAAABNNR	RABANNA
AAABBKL	KABBALA	AAAABGIL	GALABIA	AAAABNNS	BANANAS
AAABBLS	BABALAS	AAAABHLQ	QABALAH	AAAABORR	ARAROBA
AAABCCR	BACCARA	AAAABILX	ABAXIAL	AAAABRST	BRAATAS
AAABCIR	ARABICA	AAAABIPS	PIASABA	AAAABRSX	ABRASAX
AAABCLO	BACALAO	AAAABISS	ABASIAS		ABRAXAS
AAABCLS	CABALAS	AAAABITV	BATAVIA	AAAABRSZ	BARAZAS
AAABCLV	BACLAVA	AAAABKKS	KABAKAS		BAZAARS
AAABCMR	CARAMBA	AAAABKLS	KABALAS	AAAABSTT	BATATAS
AAABCNR	BARACAN	AAAABKLV	BAKLAVA	AAAACCCH	CACHACA
AAABCNS	CABANAS	AAAABKLW	BAKLAWA	AAAACCIS	ACACIAS
AAABCOR	CARABAO	AAAABKPS	BAASKAP	AAAACCLM	MALACCA
AAABCSS	CASABAS	AAAABKSY	KABAYAS	AAAACCLP	ALPACCA
	CASSABA	AAAABLLW	WALLABA	AAAACCLR	CARACAL
AAABCTW	CATAWBA	AAAABLMT	TAMBALA	AAAACCRS	CASCARA
AAABDFR	ABFARAD	AAAABLPR	PALABRA	AAAACDGS	CADAGAS
AAABDGS	DAGABAS	AAAABLQS	QABALAS	AAAACDIR	ARCADIA
AAABDHS	BAHADAS	AAAABLST	ALBATAS	AAAACDLU	ACAUDAL

AAACDMM	MACADAM		RADIATA	AAAHHLV	HALAVAH
AAACDNS	CANADAS	AAADJMR	JAMADAR	AAAHIKP	APHAKIA
AAACEHR	ARCHAEA	AAADKNW	WAKANDA	AAAHIKW	KAHAWAI
AAACENP	PANACEA	AAADLMN	AMANDLA	AAAHINR	HARIANA
AAACGNT	AGACANT		MANDALA	AAAHIPS	APHASIA
AAACHHL	HALACHA	AAADLMW	WADMAAL	AAAHIST	TAIAHAS
AAACHLZ	CHALAZA	AAADMNT	ADAMANT	AAAHJKW	KAJAWAH
AAACHNT	ACANTHA	AAADMPP	PAPADAM	AAAHKRS	AKHARAS
AAACHRY	ACHARYA	AAADMRS	ARMADAS	AAAHLLS	HALALAS
AAACILM	MALACIA		MADRASA	AAAHLMR	HARMALA
AAACIMR	CARIAMA		RAMADAS	AAAHLNN	ALANNAH
AAACINP	ACAPNIA	AAADNPS	PANADAS	AAAHLSW	HAWALAS
AAACINR	ACARIAN	AAADNRS	SARDANA	AAAHMMT	MAHATMA
AAACIRS	ACRASIA	AAADNRT	TANADAR	AAAHMRS	ASHRAMA
AAACJMR	JACAMAR	AAADWYY	AWAYDAY	AAAHMST	TAMASHA
AAACJNS	JACANAS	AAAEGLT	GALATEA	AAAHNSV	VAHANAS
AAACLLV	CAVALLA	AAAEGNP	APANAGE	AAAHPRT	PARATHA
AAACLMN	ALMANAC	AAAEHLT	ALTHAEA	AAAHRTW	WARATAH
	MANCALA	AAAEIMN	ANAEMIA	AAAIKKR	KARAKIA
AAACLMR	CALAMAR	AAAEKST	AKATEAS	AAAIKLT	LATAKIA
AAACLNT	CANTALA	AAAELMP	PALAMAE	AAAIKRS	AKRASIA
AAACLPS	ALPACAS	AAAELSZ	AZALEAS	AAAILLS	ALALIAS
AAACLPT	CATALPA	AAAEMRT	TARAMEA	AAAILMR	MALARIA
AAACLRZ	ALCAZAR	AAAENST	ANATASE	AAAILNX	ANAXIAL
AAACMNP	CAMPANA	AAAERWY	AREAWAY	AAAILPS	APLASIA
AAACMRS	MARACAS	AAAFFLL	ALFALFA	AAAILRS	ARALIAS
	MARASCA	AAAFHRT	HAFTARA	AAAILRT	TALARIA
	MASCARA	AAAFIRT	RATAFIA	AAAIMNS	MANAIAS
AAACNNR	CARANNA	AAAFNRS	SARAFAN	AAAIMNT	AMANITA
AAACNPT	CATAPAN	AAAFRWY	FARAWAY	AAAINPS	PAISANA
AAACNRS	ARCANAS	AAAGGLN	GALANGA	AAAIPRX	APRAXIA
AAACNRT	NACARAT	AAAGHIP	APHAGIA	AAAIPSV	PIASAVA
AAACNRU	CARAUNA	AAAGHLN	LANGAHA	AAAIQRU	AQUARIA
AAACNRV	CARAVAN	AAAGHNT	ATAGHAN	AAAISST	ASTASIA
AAACNST	CANASTA	AAAGHPR	AGRAPHA	AAAISTW	WAIATAS
AAACNTT	CANTATA	AAAGILN	ANALGIA	AAAISTX	ATAXIAS
AAACPRX	CARAPAX	AAAGINR	ANGARIA	AAAJKST	JATAKAS
AAACPST	PATACAS	AAAGINZ	GAZANIA	AAAJMPS	PAJAMAS
AAACRWY	CARAWAY	AAAGIPT	PATAGIA	AAAJMST	JAMAATS
AAACSST	CASSATA	AAAGISS	ASSAGAI	AAAJMSU	UJAMAAS
AAACSSV	CASAVAS	AAAGJMU	MAJAGUA	AAAKKMR	MARKKAA
	CASSAVA	AAAGKNR	KARANGA	AAAKKNS	KANAKAS
AAACSTT	CATASTA	AAAGLMM	AMALGAM	AAAKKRS	KARAKAS
AAADDMO	AMADODA	AAAGLMN	MALANGA	AAAKLMS	KAMALAS
AAADELM	ALAMEDA		NAGMAAL	AAAKLMY	YAMALKA
AAADFRY	FARADAY	AAAGLNO	ANALOGA	AAAKLSS	ALASKAS
AAADGGH	AGGADAH	AAAGLNS	LASAGNA	AAAKMMU	MAMAKAU
	HAGGADA	AAAGLRS	ARGALAS	AAAKNST	KATANAS
AAADGGS	AGGADAS	AAAGMMT	MAGMATA	AAAKPPU	KAUPAPA
AAADGIL	ADAGIAL	AAAGMNR	ANAGRAM	AAAKPST	PATAKAS
AAADGRS	SAGRADA	AAAGMNS	SAGAMAN	AAALLPT	PALATAL
AAADHHS	SHAHADA	AAAGMTT	TAGMATA	AAALMPT	TAMPALA
AAADHMM	HAMMADA	AAAGNNS	NAGANAS	AAALMRS	MARSALA
AAADHMR	ADHARMA	AAAGNPR	PARGANA	AAALMSS	MASALAS
	HARAMDA	AAAGNRR	NGARARA		SALAAMS
AAADHMS	HAMADAS	AAAGNRT	TANAGRA	AAALNNT	LANTANA
AAADHNS	SADHANA	AAAGNRU	GUARANA	AAALNPT	APLANAT
AAADHWY	HADAWAY	AAAGNTY	YATAGAN	AAALPPS	PALAPAS
AAADILX	ADAXIAL	AAAHHKL	HALAKAH	AAALRRY	ARRAYAL
AAADIMN	DAMIANA		HALAKHA	AAALWYY	LAYAWAY
AAADIRT	DATARIA	AAAHHLL	HALALAH	AAAMMPR	MAMPARA

AAAMNNS	MANANAS	AABCCER	BACCARE	AABDEHS	ABASHED
AAAMNNT	ANATMAN	AABCCET	BACCATE	AABDEIR	BRAAIED
AAAMNPS	PANAMAS	AABCCHH	BACHCHA	AABDEIS	DIABASE
AAAMNRT	AMARANT	AABCCIR	BRACCIA	AABDEKW	DAWBAKE
	MARANTA	AABCDIM	DICAMBA	AABDELL	BALLADE
AAAMNSS	SAMAANS	AABCDIR	CARABID	AABDELT	ABLATED
AAAMNST	ATAMANS	AABCEFR	FACEBAR		DATABLE
AAAMNSW	MANAWAS	AABCEKR	BACKARE	AABDELW	WADABLE
AAAMNTY	MANYATA	AABCELN	BALANCE	AABDEMM	BEMADAM
AAAMORT	TAMARAO	AABCELP	CAPABLE	AABDEMN	BEADMAN
AAAMPPU	PAPAUMA		PACABLE	AABDEMS	SAMBAED
AAAMPRT	PATAMAR	AABCELT	ACTABLE	AABDENU	BANDEAU
AAAMRRZ	ZAMARRA	AABCEMR	MACABER	AABDERR	ABRADER
AAAMRSS	ASRAMAS		MACABRE	AABDERS	ABRADES
	SAMARAS	AABCEMS	AMBSACE	AABDERW	BADWARE
	SAMSARA	AABCEOS	COBAEAS	AABDERY	ABRAYED
AAAMRST	TAMARAS	AABCERR	BARRACE	AABDESU	AUBADES
	TARAMAS	AABCERT	ABREACT	AABDGHN	HANDBAG
AAAMRTU	TAMARAU		BEARCAT	AABDGMO	GAMBADO
AAAMSTT	MATATAS		CABARET	AABDGNS	SANDBAG
AAANNSV	SAVANNA	AABCFKT	FATBACK	AABDGOS	DAGOBAS
AAANNSZ	ZANANAS	AABCHHR	BRACHAH	AABDHMS	BADMASH
AAANNTT	ANNATTA	AABCHIR	BRACHIA	AABDHNT	HATBAND
AAANPPY	PAPAYAN	AABCHMT	AMBATCH	AABDHNY	HAYBAND
AAANRST	ANTARAS	AABCHNR	BARCHAN	AABDHRS	BARDASH
AAANRTT	TANTARA	AABCHOR	ABROACH	AABDHRU	BAHADUR
	TARTANA	AABCHSS	CASBAHS	AABDIIS	BASIDIA
AAANSTT	ANATTAS	AABCILM	CAMBIAL	AABDIKR	BIDARKA
AAAOPRZ	PARAZOA	AABCINR	CARABIN	AABDILN	BALADIN
AAAPPRT	APPARAT	AABCIOP	COPAIBA	AABDIMR	BARMAID
AAAPPSY	PAPAYAS	AABCITX	TAXICAB	AABDINR	BANDARI
AAAPRSS	APSARAS	AABCKLY	LAYBACK	AABDINS	INDABAS
AAAPSST	PASSATA	AABCKNN	CANBANK	AABDINT	TABANID
AAAPTTU	TAUPATA	AABCKPY	PAYBACK	AABDIOT	BIODATA
AAARSST	SATARAS	AABCKRR	BARRACK	AABDIRS	ABRAIDS
AAARSTV	AVATARS	AABCKRS	BACKRAS	AABDLLS	BALLADS
AAARTTT	RATATAT	AABCKSW	BACKSAW	AABDLMS	LAMBDAS
AAARTTU	TUATARA	AABCLMU	CALUMBA	AABDLNS	SALBAND
AAARTXY	ATARAXY	AABCLPY	CAPABLY	AABDLRW	BRADAWL
AABBBOS	BAOBABS	AABCLSY	SCYBALA	AABDMNR	ARMBAND
AABBCEG	CABBAGE	AABCMMU	MACUMBA	AABDNNO	ABANDON
AABBCGY	CABBAGY	AABCMST	TAMBACS	AABDNOR	BANDORA
AABBCMO	CABOMBA	AABCMSU	SAMBUCA	AABDNRS	BANDARS
AABBCOS	BABACOS	AABCNRR	CARBARN		SANDBAR
AABBDGR	GABBARD	AABCORR	CARBORA	AABDNRU	BANDURA
AABBDHS	HABDABS	AABCORT	ABACTOR	AABDNSW	BANDSAW
AABBEGN	BEANBAG		ACROBAT	AABDORS	ABROADS
AABBEIS	BABESIA	AABCOTT	CATBOAT	AABDORV	BRAVADO
AABBELT	BATABLE	AABCRSS	SCARABS	AABDORX	BROADAX
AABBERT	BARBATE	AABCSUU	AUCUBAS	AABDOTY	DAYBOAT
AABBGRT	GABBART	AABCTTU	CATTABU	AABDRRS	DARBARS
AABBHLS	BABLAHS	AABDDEL	ADDABLE	AABDRRW	DRAWBAR
AABBHST	SABBATH	AABDDEN	ABANDED	AABDRST	BASTARD
AABBIJL	JALABIB	AABDDER	ABRADED		TABARDS
AABBLLS	LABLABS	AABDDIK	KABADDI	AABDRSU	SUBADAR
AABBLOR	BARBOLA	AABDDIN	BANDAID	AABDRSY	BAYARDS
AABBLOS	BALBOAS	AABDDLN	BADLAND	AABDSTU	DATABUS
AABBSST	SABBATS	AABDDNS	SANDDAB	AABEELT	EATABLE
AABBSSU	BABASSU	AABDEFL	FADABLE	AABEEMN	AMEBEAN
AABBSTY	BABYSAT	AABDEGM	GAMBADE	AABEEMO	AMOEBAE
AABCCEL	ACCABLE	AABDEGN	BANDAGE	AABEERZ	ZAREEBA

AABEFFL	AFFABLE	AABELST	ABLATES	AABHITT	HABITAT
AABEFFN	BEFFANA		ASTABLE	AABHJNS	BHAJANS
AABEFGL	FLEABAG	AABELSV	SAVABLE	AABHKNR	BARKHAN
AABEFGU	AUFGABE	AABELSY	SAYABLE	AABHKSS	KASBAHS
AABEFNS	BEFANAS	AABELTT	ABETTAL		SABKHAS
	FANBASE	AABELTU	TABLEAU	AABHKST	BHAKTAS
AABEGGG	BAGGAGE		TABULAE		SABKHAT
AABEGGR	GARBAGE	AABELTV	VATABLE	AABHLRS	BHARALS
AABEGLR	ALGEBRA	AABELTX	TAXABLE	AABHLTY	BATHYAL
AABEGMR	BERGAMA	AABELWX	WAXABLE	AABHMNR	BRAHMAN
	MEGABAR	AABEMNO	AMOEBAN	AABHMRS	BRAHMAS
AABEGMS	AMBAGES	AABEMNS	BASEMAN		SAMBHAR
AABEGRR	BAGARRE	AABEMOS	AMOEBAS	AABHMSS	SHAMBAS
	BARRAGE	AABENNW	WANNABE	AABHMTT	BATHMAT
AABEGSS	BAGASSE	AABENPR	PARABEN	AABHNSV	BHAVANS
	SEABAGS	AABENRT	ANTBEAR	AABHNSW	BHAWANS
AABEGST	ATABEGS	AABENTY	ABEYANT	AABHSSW	BASHAWS
	TEABAGS	AABEORT	AEROBAT	AABIILX	BIAXIAL
AABEGSU	ABUSAGE	AABERRW	BARWARE	AABIILZ	ALBIZIA
AABEHLT	HATABLE	AABERSS	ABASERS	AABIJMY	JAMBIYA
AABEHNT	ABTHANE	AABERST	ABATERS	AABIKLM	KALIMBA
AABEHRS	EARBASH		ABREAST	AABIKNS	BANKSIA
AABEHSS	ABASHES		ABREAST	AABILLN	ALBINAL
AABEIKN	IKEBANA	AABERSU	BAUERAS	AABILLR	BARILLA
AABEILM	AMABILE		SUBAREA	AABILLS	LABIALS
	AMIABLE	AABERSZ	ZAREBAS	AABILMN	BIMANAL
AABEILN	ABELIAN	AABERTT	RABATTE	AABILMS	BAALISM
AABEILS	ABELIAS		TABARET	AABILMY	AMIABLY
AABEILT	LABIATE	AABERTU	ABATURE	AABILNS	BASINAL
AABEILX	ABAXILE	AABESTZ	ZABETAS	AABILOU	ABOULIA
AABEIOR	AEROBIA	AABETTU	BATTEAU	AABILRS	BASILAR
AABEIRS	AIRBASE	AABETUX	BATEAUX	AABILST	BALISTA
	ARABISE	AABFFLY	AFFABLY	AABILSU	ABULIAS
AABEIRZ	ARABIZE	AABFILU	FABLIAU	AABIMMR	MARIMBA
AABEJLL	JELLABA	AABFLRU	FABULAR	AABIMNO	AMBOINA
AABEJMU	JAMBEAU	AABGGRS	RAGBAGS		BONAMIA
AABEKLM	MAKABLE	AABGGRY	GARBAGY	AABIMOS	ABOMASI
AABEKLT	TAKABLE	AABGGSS	GASBAGS	AABIMRS	AMBARIS
AABEKNS	SEABANK	AABGHNR	BHANGRA		MARABIS
AABEKPR	PARBAKE	AABGHNS	GABNASH	AABIMST	BASMATI
AABEKRS	ARABESK		NASHGAB	AABINNS	BANIANS
AABEKRY	KERBAYA	AABGHSW	BAGWASH	AABINOU	OUABAIN
AABEKST	ATABEKS	AABGIIL	ABIGAIL	AABINRS	ARABINS
AABELLL	LABELLA	AABGILM	MAILBAG	AABINRT	ATABRIN
AABELLN	BALNEAL	AABGIMS	GAMBIAS	AABINST	ABSTAIN
AABELLO	ABOLLAE	AABGINR	BARGAIN	AABINSW	WABAINS
AABELLR	EARBALL	AABGINS	ABASING	AABINSZ	BANZAIS
AABELLS	SABELLA		BAAINGS	AABIORS	ABROSIA
	SALABLE		BISNAGA	AABIORT	AIRBOAT
AABELMN	NAMABLE	AABGINT	ABATING	AABIPUX	PAXIUBA
AABELMS	MABELAS	AABGINZ	BIZNAGA	AABIRST	BARISTA
AABELMT	TAMABLE	AABGIRS	AIRBAGS		BARTSIA
AABELNO	ABALONE	AABGMNY	MANGABY		
AABELNR	BANALER	AABGOSZ	GAZABOS	AABIRSZ	ZARIBAS
AABELNS	BANSELA	AABGRST	RATBAGS	AABISSW	WASABIS
AABELPP	PAPABLE	AABHHIS	SAHIBAH	AABISTT	ABATTIS
AABELPR	PARABLE	AABHHKS	SABKHAH	AABJMRT	JAMBART
AABELPY	PAYABLE	AABHHRU	BRUHAHA	AABKLSU	KULBASA
AABELRS	ARABLES	AABHHSS	SHABASH	AABKMST	TAMBAKS
AABELRT	RATABLE	AABHINS	HASBIAN	AABKNNS	KANBANS
AABELSS	BALASES	AABHINT	HABITAN	AABKNRS	BARKANS
		AABHISS	SAHIBAS	AABKNRT	TANBARK

AABKOOZ	BAZOOKA	**AABRSTY**	BARYTAS		CARACUL
AABKRST	TASKBAR	**AABSSSY**	SASSABY	**AACCLSU**	ACCUSAL
AABLLNS	BALLANS	**AABSTTW**	ABWATTS	**AACCLTW**	CATCLAW
AABLLNT	BALLANT	**AABSTUX**	SAXTUBA	**AACCMOS**	MACACOS
AABLLNY	BANALLY		SUBTAXA	**AACCNNS**	CANCANS
AABLLOR	ALLOBAR	**AABTTTU**	BATTUTA	**AACCNVY**	VACANCY
AABLLOS	ABOLLAS	**AABZZZZ**	BAZZAZZ	**AACCORU**	CURACAO
AABLLPT	PATBALL	**AACCDEI**	CICADAE		CURACOA
AABLLST	BALLAST	**AACCDEM**	MEDACCA	**AACCOST**	ACCOAST
	BALLATS	**AACCDES**	CASCADE	**AACCOTT**	TOCCATA
AABLLSY	BASALLY		SACCADE	**AACCRRT**	CARRACT
	SALABLY	**AACCDII**	ACCIDIA	**AACCRSS**	CARCASS
AABLLWY	WALLABY	**AACCDIR**	CARDIAC	**AACCRST**	CARACTS
AABLMRS	RAMBLAS	**AACCDIS**	CICADAS	**AACDDEL**	DECADAL
AABLMRU	LABARUM	**AACCDSU**	CADUACS	**AACDDER**	ARCADED
AABLMSS	BALSAMS	**AACCEFT**	CATFACE	**AACDDHR**	CHADDAR
	SAMBALS	**AACCEKR**	CARCAKE	**AACDDIN**	CANDIDA
AABLMST	LAMBAST	**AACCELO**	CLOACAE	**AACDDRW**	CRAWDAD
AABLMSY	ABYSMAL	**AACCENV**	VACANCE	**AACDEEM**	ACADEME
	BALSAMY	**AACCERS**	CARCASE	**AACDEFL**	FALCADE
AABLNTT	BLATANT	**AACCEST**	SACCATE	**AACDEFS**	FACADES
AABLORT	ABLATOR	**AACCESV**	CASEVAC	**AACDEHM**	CHAMADE
AABLOSV	LAVABOS	**AACCHHK**	CHACHKA	**AACDEHR**	CHARADE
AABLPRU	PABULAR		KACHCHA	**AACDEHT**	CATHEAD
AABLPYY	PAYABLY	**AACCHIM**	MACCHIA	**AACDEII**	AECIDIA
AABLRST	ARBLAST	**AACCHIN**	CHICANA	**AACDEIL**	ALCAIDE
AABLRSU	SUBALAR	**AACCHIR**	ARCHAIC	**AACDEIN**	AIDANCE
AABLRSZ	BLAZARS	**AACCHKS**	KACCHAS	**AACDEIR**	CARDIAE
AABLRTU	TABULAR	**AACCHLN**	CLACHAN	**AACDEIS**	ACEDIAS
AABLRTY	RATABLY	**AACCHMP**	CHAMPAC	**AACDELL**	ALCALDE
AABLSST	BASALTS	**AACCHMS**	CHACMAS	**AACDELN**	CANALED
AABLSSY	ABYSSAL	**AACCHNN**	CANNACH		CANDELA
AABLSTU	ABLAUTS	**AACCHNS**	CANCHAS		DECANAL
AABLTTU	ABUTTAL	**AACCHOR**	CAROACH	**AACDELP**	PALACED
AABLTXY	TAXABLY	**AACCHRT**	CHARACT	**AACDELR**	CALDERA
AABMNOT	BOATMAN	**AACCILM**	ACCLAIM		CRAALED
AABMNOY	AMBOYNA	**AACCILS**	ALCAICS	**AACDELS**	ALCADES
AABMNST	BANTAMS		CICALAS		SCALADE
	BATSMAN	**AACCILU**	ACICULA	**AACDELY**	ALCAYDE
AABMORU	MARABOU	**AACCIMS**	CAIMACS	**AACDEMY**	ACADEMY
AABMOSY	BAYAMOS	**AACCIMT**	ACMATIC	**AACDENR**	DRACENA
AABMRSS	SAMBARS	**AACCINS**	ANICCAS	**AACDENV**	ADVANCE
AABMRTU	TAMBURA	**AACCINV**	VACCINA	**AACDENZ**	CADENZA
AABMSST	TSAMBAS	**AACCIOR**	CARIOCA	**AACDEPS**	SCAPAED
AABMSSY	AMBASSY	**AACCIPT**	PICCATA	**AACDERS**	ARCADES
AABNNOZ	BONANZA	**AACCIRT**	ACRATIC		ASCARED
AABNNSY	BANYANS	**AACCITT**	ATACTIC	**AACDERV**	CADAVER
AABNOST	SABATON	**AACCJKR**	CARJACK	**AACDERY**	DAYCARE
AABNOSY	SABAYON	**AACCKLP**	CALPACK	**AACDETU**	CAUDATE
AABNSST	BASANTS	**AACCKRR**	CARRACK	**AACDETV**	VACATED
AABNSYY	BAYYANS	**AACCKRS**	CARACKS	**AACDEUX**	CADEAUX
AABORRS	ARROBAS		CRACKAS	**AACDFIR**	FARADIC
	RASBORA	**AACCLLO**	CLOACAL	**AACDFRS**	CAFARDS
AABORST	ABATORS	**AACCLLT**	CATCALL	**AACDGGI**	AGGADIC
	RABATOS	**AACCLOP**	POLACCA	**AACDGHI**	HAGADIC
AABORSZ	ABRAZOS	**AACCLOR**	CARACOL	**AACDGIS**	CADAGIS
AABOTTY	ATTABOY	**AACCLOS**	CLOACAS	**AACDHMR**	DRACHMA
AABQSUU	SUBAQUA	**AACCLPS**	CALPACS	**AACDHNR**	HANDCAR
AABRRST	BARRATS	**AACCLPT**	PLACCAT	**AACDHRS**	CHADARS
AABRRSU	SABURRA	**AACCLRS**	CALCARS	**AACDHST**	DATCHAS
AABRRUV	BRAVURA	**AACCLRU**	ACCRUAL	**AACDIIS**	ASCIDIA

	DIASCIA	**AACEHNO**	CHOANAE	**AACEMSS**	CAMASES
AACDILR	RADICAL	**AACEHNP**	PANACHE	**AACENPS**	CANAPES
AACDINS	SCANDIA	**AACEHNR**	ACHARNE	**AACENRT**	CATERAN
AACDINT	ANTACID		ARCHEAN	**AACENSS**	CASSENA
AACDINV	VANADIC	**AACEHPP**	APPEACH	**AACENST**	CATENAS
AACDIOR	ACAROID	**AACEHPS**	APACHES	**AACENTT**	CANTATE
AACDIRS	ACARIDS	**AACEHPU**	CHAPEAU	**AACENTY**	CYANATE
	ASCARID	**AACEHRT**	TRACHEA	**AACEOPT**	PEACOAT
	CARDIAS	**AACEHST**	ACHATES	**AACEORS**	ROSACEA
AACDJKW	JACKDAW	**AACEHTT**	ATTACHE	**AACEPRT**	CAPRATE
AACDKPY	DAYPACK	**AACEHTU**	CHATEAU	**AACEPRU**	CAPUERA
AACDKSY	DAYSACK	**AACEILM**	CAMELIA	**AACEPRV**	PRECAVA
AACDLNO	ACNODAL	**AACEIMN**	ANAEMIC	**AACEPSS**	CASPASE
	CALANDO	**AACEIMU**	CAMAIEU	**AACEPWY**	PACEWAY
AACDLNS	SCANDAL	**AACEINR**	ACARINE	**AACERSS**	CAESARS
AACDLOR	CARLOAD		CARINAE	**AACERST**	ACATERS
AACDLOS	SCALADO	**AACEIQU**	ACEQUIA		CARATES
AACDLPR	PLACARD	**AACEIRV**	AVARICE	**AACERSU**	CAESURA
AACDMPS	MADCAPS		CAVIARE	**AACERSZ**	SAZERAC
AACDNRS	CADRANS	**AACEIST**	ECTASIA	**AACERTT**	TEACART
	CANARDS	**AACEJLS**	JACALES	**AACERTU**	ARCUATE
AACDOOV	AVOCADO	**AACEJRS**	JACARES	**AACERWY**	RACEWAY
AACDPRU	CRAPAUD	**AACEKNP**	PANCAKE	**AACESTV**	CAVEATS
AACDRSS	CSARDAS	**AACEKNS**	ASKANCE		VACATES
AACDRSZ	CZARDAS	**AACEKOT**	OATCAKE	**AACESTX**	EXACTAS
AACEEGR	ACREAGE	**AACELLN**	CANELLA	**AACETTU**	ACTUATE
AACEEHR	EARACHE	**AACELLS**	SACELLA	**AACETUV**	VACUATE
AACEEHT	CHAETAE	**AACELLT**	LACTEAL	**AACFFIL**	CAFFILA
AACEEKT	TEACAKE	**AACELMN**	MANACLE	**AACFILS**	CAFILAS
AACEELN	ANELACE	**AACELMR**	CAMERAL		FACIALS
AACEEMR	CAMERAE		CARAMEL		FASCIAL
AACEEMS	AMESACE		CERAMAL	**AACFILU**	FAUCIAL
AACEENT	CATENAE		MACERAL	**AACFINT**	FANATIC
AACEERT	ACERATE			**AACFISS**	FASCIAS
AACEESS	CASEASE	**AACELMU**	MACULAE	**AACFLLT**	CATFALL
AACEEST	CASEATE	**AACELNP**	CAPELAN	**AACFLLU**	FALCULA
AACEETT	ACETATE	**AACELNS**	ANLACES	**AACFLLY**	FALLACY
AACEFIS	FASCIAE	**AACELNT**	LACTEAN	**AACFLPT**	CATFLAP
AACEFLT	FALCATE	**AACELNU**	CANULAE		FLATCAP
AACEFLU	FACULAE		LACUNAE	**AACFLRT**	FLATCAR
AACEFMN	FACEMAN	**AACELNV**	VALANCE		FRACTAL
AACEFRR	CARFARE	**AACELOR**	ACEROLA	**AACFLRU**	FACULAR
AACEFRS	CARAFES	**AACELOV**	COAEVAL	**AACFLSU**	FAUCALS
AACEGGR	AGGRACE	**AACELPR**	CARPALE	**AACFLTU**	FACTUAL
AACEGHN	GANACHE	**AACELPS**	PALACES	**AACFNST**	CAFTANS
AACEGHS	ACHAGES	**AACELPT**	PLACATE	**AACFRRU**	FARRUCA
AACEGIP	AGAPEIC	**AACELRS**	SCALARE	**AACGGMS**	CAGMAGS
AACEGKP	PACKAGE	**AACELRV**	CARAVEL	**AACGHNS**	CHAGANS
AACEGKS	SACKAGE	**AACELSS**	CALESAS	**AACGILL**	GALLICA
AACEGLS	SCALAGE	**AACELST**	ACETALS		GLACIAL
AACEGNR	CAGANER		LACTASE	**AACGILM**	MAGICAL
	CARNAGE	**AACELTT**	LACTATE	**AACGILS**	SCAGLIA
	CRANAGE	**AACELTV**	CLAVATE	**AACGINT**	AGNATIC
AACEGRT	CARTAGE	**AACELTY**	ACYLATE	**AACGIRS**	AGARICS
AACEGSV	SCAVAGE	**AACEMMR**	MACRAME	**AACGIRV**	AGRAVIC
AACEHIN	ACHENIA	**AACEMNP**	PACEMAN	**AACGISU**	GUAIACS
AACEHIR	ARCHAEI	**AACEMNS**	CASEMAN	**AACGJNT**	CATJANG
AACEHKS	ASHCAKE	**AACEMNV**	CAVEMAN	**AACGLOT**	CATALOG
AACEHLP	ACALEPH	**AACEMOS**	CAEOMAS	**AACGLOU**	COAGULA
AACEHLR	ALCHERA	**AACEMPR**	PARACME	**AACGLSY**	GALYACS
AACEHLT	CHAETAL	**AACEMQU**	MACAQUE	**AACGNOU**	GUANACO
		AACEMRS	CAMERAS		

AACHHKR	CHARKHA	**AACHRWY**	ARCHWAY	**AACINST**	SATANIC
AACHHLL	CHALLAH	**AACHSSW**	CASHAWS	**AACIOPT**	TAPIOCA
AACHHLS	CHALAHS	**AACHSTT**	CHATTAS	**AACIOPV**	COPAIVA
AACHIKL	HALAKIC	**AACIILN**	ANCILIA	**AACIOST**	ATOCIAS
AACHIKN	KACHINA		LACINIA		COAITAS
AACHIKR	CHIKARA	**AACIIMS**	CAMISIA	**AACIPPR**	PAPRICA
AACHILO	ACHOLIA	**AACIINP**	APICIAN	**AACIPRS**	PICARAS
AACHILR	ACHIRAL	**AACIINT**	ACTINIA	**AACIPRX**	APRAXIC
	RACHIAL	**AACIITV**	AVIATIC	**AACIQTU**	AQUATIC
AACHILT	CALATHI		VIATICA	**AACIRSS**	ASCARIS
AACHIMR	MACHAIR	**AACIJLP**	JALAPIC	**AACIRST**	CARITAS
AACHIMS	CHAMISA	**AACIJMS**	JICAMAS	**AACIRSV**	CAVIARS
	CHIASMA	**AACIKLL**	ALKALIC	**AACISSS**	CASSIAS
AACHINT	ACANTHI	**AACIKLR**	CLARKIA	**AACISST**	CASITAS
	TACHINA	**AACIKNN**	CANAKIN	**AACISTT**	ASTATIC
AACHIPR	CHARPAI	**AACIKNT**	KATCINA	**AACISTX**	ATAXICS
	HAIRCAP	**AACIKRT**	AKRATIC	**AACJKLS**	JACKALS
AACHIPS	APHASIC	**AACILLN**	ANCILLA	**AACJKMN**	JACKMAN
AACHIPT	CHAPATI	**AACILLS**	CALLAIS		MANJACK
AACHIRS	ARACHIS	**AACILMR**	MAILCAR	**AACJKSS**	JACKASS
AACHIRT	CITHARA	**AACILMS**	CALIMAS	**AACJOSU**	ACAJOUS
AACHITY	CYATHIA		CAMAILS	**AACJPTU**	CAJAPUT
AACHKMN	HACKMAN	**AACILNP**	CALPAIN	**AACKLPS**	KALPACS
AACHKMP	CHAMPAK	**AACILNR**	CARINAL	**AACKLTW**	CATWALK
AACHKNS	ACHKANS		CLARAIN	**AACKMNP**	MANPACK
AACHKPS	CHAPKAS		CRANIAL		PACKMAN
	PACHAKS	**AACILNT**	ACTINAL	**AACKMRT**	AMTRACK
AACHKRS	CHAKRAS		ALICANT	**AACKNRS**	RANSACK
	CHARKAS		ANTICAL	**AACKPRT**	RATPACK
AACHKRT	HATRACK	**AACILOS**	ASOCIAL	**AACKPSZ**	CZAPKAS
AACHKRY	HAYRACK	**AACILOX**	COAXIAL	**AACKPWX**	PACKWAX
AACHKSW	HACKSAW	**AACILPS**	APICALS	**AACKPWY**	PACKWAY
	KWACHAS		SPACIAL	**AACKRRS**	ARRACKS
AACHLLN	CHALLAN	**AACILPT**	CAPITAL	**AACKSTT**	ATTACKS
AACHLLS	CHALLAS		PLACITA	**AACLLNS**	CALLANS
AACHLMS	CHASMAL	**AACILRR**	RAILCAR	**AACLLNT**	CALLANT
AACHLNS	CHALANS	**AACILTT**	CATTAIL	**AACLLNU**	CALLUNA
AACHLNT	CANTHAL	**AACILTV**	VATICAL		LACUNAL
AACHLPP	CHAPPAL	**AACIMMR**	MACRAMI	**AACLLOO**	CALALOO
AACHLPS	PASCHAL	**AACIMNO**	MANIOCA	**AACLLOR**	CORALLA
AACHLPU	CHALUPA	**AACIMNS**	CAIMANS	**AACLLSU**	CALALUS
AACHLST	CALTHAS		MANIACS		CLAUSAL
AACHLSU	ACUSHLA	**AACIMNY**	ANIMACY	**AACLLVY**	CAVALLY
AACHMNP	CHAPMAN	**AACIMOR**	ACROMIA	**AACLMNO**	COALMAN
AACHMNS	MACHANS	**AACIMPR**	PICAMAR	**AACLMNT**	CALMANT
AACHMSY	YASHMAC	**AACIMSS**	CAMISAS		CLAMANT
AACHNOP	PANOCHA	**AACIMTY**	CYMATIA	**AACLMRU**	MACULAR
AACHNOU	HUANACO	**AACINNT**	CANTINA	**AACLMST**	LACTAMS
AACHNPX	PANCHAX	**AACINOR**	CONARIA	**AACLMSU**	CALAMUS
AACHNRS	ANARCHS		OCARINA		MACULAS
AACHNRV	NAVARCH	**AACINPT**	CAPITAN	**AACLNNO**	ANCONAL
AACHNRY	ANARCHY		CAPTAIN	**AACLNNU**	CANNULA
AACHNSS	ASHCANS	**AACINRS**	ACRASIN	**AACLNOS**	CANOLAS
AACHNST	ACANTHS		ARNICAS	**AACLNPY**	CLAYPAN
AACHNSU	ANCHUSA		CARINAS	**AACLNRS**	CARNALS
AACHNSZ	CHAZANS		SARCINA	**AACLNRU**	CANULAR
AACHNZZ	CHAZZAN	**AACINRT**	ANTICAR		LACUNAR
AACHRRT	CATARRH	**AACINRZ**	CZARINA	**AACLNST**	CANTALS
AACHRST	CHARTAS	**AACINSS**	ASCIANS	**AACLNSU**	CANULAS
AACHRSW	CARWASH		CASSINA		LACUNAS
AACHRTU	AUTARCH		SANCAIS	**AACLOPR**	CAPORAL

	CRAPOLA	**AACPSTW**	CATSPAW	**AADEGMS**	DAMAGES
AACLOPT	OCTAPLA	**AACRRST**	CARRATS	**AADEGNS**	AGENDAS
AACLORT	CROTALA	**AACRRSU**	CURARAS	**AADEGRT**	GRADATE
AACLORZ	ALCORZA	**AACRSTV**	CRAVATS	**AADEGRV**	RAVAGED
AACLOST	CATALOS	**AACRTTT**	ATTRACT	**AADEGRY**	DRAYAGE
	COASTAL	**AACRTUV**	VACATUR		YARDAGE
AACLOTT	CATTALO	**AACRTUY**	ACTUARY	**AADEGSV**	SAVAGED
AACLOTV	OCTAVAL	**AACRTWY**	CARTWAY	**AADEHIR**	AIRHEAD
AACLPRS	CARPALS	**AACTUWY**	CUTAWAY	**AADEHJR**	JARHEAD
AACLPRT	CALTRAP	**AADDDEN**	ADDENDA	**AADEHKS**	AKEDAHS
AACLPSS	PASCALS	**AADDEGM**	DAMAGED	**AADEHMN**	HEADMAN
AACLPSU	PASCUAL	**AADDEHH**	HADEDAH	**AADEHMS**	ASHAMED
	PAUCALS	**AADDEIL**	ALIDADE	**AADEHPS**	SAPHEAD
	SCAPULA	**AADDEMM**	MADAMED	**AADEHPW**	AWHAPED
AACLPTY	PLAYACT	**AADDEMN**	DEADMAN	**AADEHRW**	RAWHEAD
AACLRSS	LASCARS	**AADDENP**	DEADPAN		WARHEAD
	RASCALS	**AADDEOR**	DEODARA	**AADEHWY**	HEADWAY
	SACRALS	**AADDEPR**	PARADED	**AADEIKK**	KAIAKED
	SCALARS	**AADDEPT**	ADAPTED	**AADEILR**	RADIALE
AACLRST	CASTRAL	**AADDERS**	ADREADS	**AADEILV**	AVAILED
AACLRTY	LACTARY	**AADDERW**	AWARDED		VEDALIA
AACLRVY	CALVARY	**AADDESX**	ADDAXES	**AADEIMR**	MADEIRA
	CAVALRY	**AADDGNR**	GRADDAN	**AADEIMS**	AMIDASE
AACLSSU	CASUALS		GRANDAD		SEAMAID
	CAUSALS	**AADDHKR**	KHADDAR	**AADEINR**	ARANEID
AACLSTT	SALTCAT	**AADDHRS**	SRADDHA	**AADEINS**	NAIADES
AACLSTU	ACTUALS	**AADDIIK**	DIDAKAI	**AADEINZ**	ZENAIDA
AACLSUV	VASCULA	**AADDIIV**	DAVIDIA	**AADEIPS**	DIAPASE
AACLTTU	TACTUAL	**AADDILS**	ALIDADS	**AADEIRS**	ARAISED
AACMMOT	COMMATA	**AADDIMS**	DADAISM	**AADEIRT**	AIRDATE
AACMNOR	CAMARON	**AADDIST**	DADAIST		RADIATE
	NARCOMA	**AADDLNS**	ADLANDS		TIARAED
AACMNRU	ARCANUM	**AADDMRY**	DRAMADY	**AADEITV**	AVIATED
AACMNSY	CAYMANS	**AADDNVV**	DVANDVA	**AADEITW**	AWAITED
AACMORR	CAMORRA	**AADDOSU**	AOUDADS	**AADEJMR**	JEMADAR
AACMORS	SARCOMA	**AADDRST**	DASTARD	**AADEKKY**	KAYAKED
AACMORT	MARCATO	**AADDRSW**	ADWARDS	**AADEKLR**	KRAALED
AACMOSY	MACOYAS	**AADDSST**	STADDAS	**AADEKLS**	ASLAKED
AACMRRT	TRAMCAR	**AADEEFR**	AFEARED	**AADEKMR**	KAMERAD
AACMRSS	SARCASM	**AADEEGH**	HEADAGE	**AADEKMS**	MEDAKAS
AACMRST	AMTRACS	**AADEELT**	DEALATE		SMAAKED
	RAMCATS	**AADEEMM**	EDAMAME	**AADEKPR**	PARKADE
	TARMACS	**AADEEMT**	EDEMATA	**AADELLP**	PADELLA
AACNNOZ	CANZONA	**AADEENR**	ANEARED	**AADELLY**	ALLAYED
AACNOST	SACATON	**AADEERT**	AERATED	**AADELMN**	LEADMAN
AACNOTZ	ZACATON	**AADEERW**	AWARDEE	**AADELMO**	ALAMODE
AACNPRT	CANTRAP	**AADEFFR**	AFFEARD	**AADELMR**	ALARMED
AACNPST	CAPSTAN	**AADEFGL**	FALDAGE	**AADELMX**	MALAXED
	CAPTANS	**AADEFGR**	FARDAGE	**AADELNR**	ADRENAL
	CATNAPS	**AADEFHT**	FATHEAD	**AADELNT**	LANATED
AACNRST	CANTARS	**AADEFIS**	FADAISE	**AADELNW**	DANELAW
AACNRTU	CURTANA	**AADEFLU**	AEFAULD	**AADELNX**	ADNEXAL
AACNSSV	CANVASS	**AADEFNZ**	FAZENDA	**AADELPR**	PARDALE
AACNSTT	ACTANTS	**AADEGGR**	AGGRADE	**AADELPT**	PALATED
AACNSTU	ASCAUNT		GARAGED	**AADELRT**	LATERAD
AACOPPR	APOCARP	**AADEGHR**	RAGHEAD	**AADELRU**	RADULAE
AACORST	OSTRACA	**AADEGLS**	GELADAS	**AADELRY**	ALREADY
AACORTU	ACATOUR	**AADEGMN**	AGNAMED	**AADELSS**	SALADES
	AUTOCAR		MANAGED		SALSAED
AACOTUV	AUTOVAC	**AADEGMR**	DAMAGER	**AADELTU**	ADULATE
AACPRSS	SCARPAS		MEGARAD	**AADELTY**	DAYTALE

AADEMMN	MANMADE		GRANDMA	AADIMNR	MANDIRA
AADEMMS	MADAMES	AADGMNS	GADSMAN	AADIMNS	MAIDANS
AADEMNO	ADENOMA	AADGMOT	DOGMATA	AADIMNY	DAYANIM
AADEMNS	ANADEMS	AADGMRS	SMARAGD	AADIMOR	DIORAMA
	MAENADS	AADGNPR	GRANDPA	AADIMOT	DOMATIA
AADEMNT	MANDATE	AADGNPS	PADANGS	AADIMRS	ARAMIDS
AADEMRY	DAYMARE		PADNAGS	AADINNN	NANDINA
AADEMSS	AMASSED	AADGNRS	ARGANDS	AADINNP	PANDANI
AADENNT	ANDANTE	AADGNRT	GARDANT	AADINPT	PINTADA
AADENRV	VERANDA	AADGNRY	YARDANG	AADINRR	DARRAIN
AADENRW	AWARNED	AADGOPR	PODAGRA	AADINRS	RADIANS
AADENST	ANSATED	AADGOPS	PAGODAS	AADINRT	INTRADA
AADENSU	SAUNAED	AADGRSU	GARUDAS		RADIANT
AADENSW	WEASAND	AADGRSY	GAYDARS	AADINRV	VIRANDA
AADENWZ	WEAZAND	AADHHPS	PADSHAH	AADINRW	WARDIAN
AADEPRR	PARADER	AADHHRT	HARDHAT	AADINSV	NAVAIDS
AADEPRS	ASPREAD	AADHILS	DAHLIAS	AADINSY	NAYSAID
	PARADES	AADHIMR	HADARIM	AADIOPZ	DOPIAZA
AADEPRT	ADAPTER		HARAMDI	AADIPTX	TAXPAID
	READAPT	AADHIMS	SAMADHI	AADIQSS	QASIDAS
AADEPSS	ESPADAS	AADHINP	DAPHNIA	AADIRRW	AIRWARD
	PASSADE	AADHJNR	HANDJAR	AADIRSU	SUDARIA
AADEPWW	PAWAWED	AADHKNS	DHANSAK	AADISST	STADIAS
AADERRS	ARRASED		KHANDAS	AADKMRY	DAYMARK
AADERRW	AWARDER	AADHKNY	YAKHDAN	AADKMSS	DAMASKS
AADERRY	ARRAYED	AADHLRY	HALYARD	AADKNRT	TANKARD
AADERSW	ADWARES	AADHMMS	DHAMMAS	AADKPSU	PADAUKS
	SEAWARD	AADHMNR	HARDMAN	AADKRWW	AWKWARD
AADERSY	ARAYSED	AADHMRS	DHARMAS	AADLLLN	LALLAND
	DARESAY	AADHNPR	HARDPAN	AADLLMR	MALLARD
AADERTU	AURATED	AADHNRS	DARSHAN	AADLLNW	LAWLAND
AADERWY	DAYWEAR		DHARNAS	AADLLPU	PALUDAL
AADESSY	ASSAYED	AADHNSW	HANDSAW	AADLLSS	SALLADS
AADFLTW	TWAFALD	AADHPRS	PARDAHS	AADLMNN	LANDMAN
AADFMSU	MADAFUS	AADHRSS	HARDASS	AADLMNO	MANDOLA
AADFNRR	FARRAND		SRADHAS		MONADAL
AADFNST	FANTADS	AADHRSZ	HAZARDS	AADLMNU	LADANUM
AADFRST	DAFTARS	AADHRWY	HAYWARD	AADLMOR	ARMLOAD
AADGGHR	HAGGARD	AADHSWY	WASHDAY	AADLMPS	LAMPADS
AADGGLR	LAGGARD	AADIILR	DIARIAL	AADLMSW	WADMALS
AADGGOT	AGGADOT	AADIINO	DIANOIA	AADLNOP	DALAPON
AADGGRS	SAGGARD	AADIINR	DIARIAN	AADLNOV	VANLOAD
AADGHIL	HIDALGA	AADIIPS	ADIPSIA	AADLNOZ	DANAZOL
AADGHOR	DAROGHA		ASPIDIA	AADLNRY	LANYARD
AADGHRS	DARGAHS	AADIJMN	JAMDANI	AADLNSS	SANDALS
AADGIIR	GIARDIA	AADIKLY	ILKADAY	AADLNSU	LANDAUS
AADGIMM	DIGAMMA	AADILLO	ALLODIA	AADLNSV	VANDALS
AADGIMO	AGAMOID		ALODIAL	AADLOPY	PAYLOAD
AADGIMR	DIAGRAM	AADILMR	ADMIRAL	AADLPPU	APPLAUD
AADGIMS	AGAMIDS		AMILDAR	AADLPRS	PARDALS
AADGINW	ADAWING	AADILMT	MATILDA	AADLPYY	PLAYDAY
AADGIOS	ADAGIOS	AADILNP	PALADIN	AADLRRU	RADULAR
AADGIOT	AGATOID	AADILNR	LANIARD	AADLRSU	RADULAS
AADGIRV	GRAVIDA		NADIRAL	AADMMRS	DAMMARS
AADGLLW	GADWALL	AADILPS	APSIDAL	AADMNNO	MADONNA
AADGLMY	AMYGDAL	AADILRS	RADIALS	AADMNNS	SANDMAN
AADGLNO	GONADAL	AADILRT	TAILARD	AADMNOR	MADRONA
AADGLNR	GARLAND	AADILSS	DALASIS		MANDORA
AADGLNS	SLADANG	AADILST	STADIAL		MONARDA
AADGLRU	GRADUAL	AADILTV	DATIVAL		ROADMAN
AADGMNR	GRANDAM	AADILWY	WAYLAID	AADMNOW	ADWOMAN

			AGEMATE	**AAEGINW**	WAINAGE
AADMNRS	MANSARD		AVERAGE	**AAEGIPR**	IGARAPE
AADMNRW	MANWARD	**AAEEGRV**	EATAGES	**AAEGIRR**	ARRIAGE
AADMNRY	DRAYMAN	**AAEEGST**	HETAERA	**AAEGISS**	ASSEGAI
	YARDMAN	**AAEEHRT**	TAENIAE	**AAEGIST**	AGATISE
AADMNSY	DAYSMAN	**AAEEINT**	AKEAKES	**AAEGISU**	AGEUSIA
AADMNTU	MUTANDA	**AAEEKKS**	SEAKALE	**AAEGITT**	AGITATE
	TAMANDU	**AAEEKLS**	REAWAKE	**AAEGITZ**	AGATIZE
AADMOPP	PAPADOM	**AAEEKRW**	MALEATE	**AAEGJTU**	AJUTAGE
AADMOQU	MADOQUA	**AAEELMT**	AREOLAE	**AAEGKNT**	TANKAGE
AADMORT	MATADOR	**AAEELOR**	PALEATE	**AAEGKOS**	SOAKAGE
AADMOSU	AMADOUS	**AAEELPT**	LAETARE	**AAEGLLR**	GLAREAL
AADMPPU	PAPADUM	**AAEELRT**	EMANATE	**AAEGLLT**	GALLATE
AADMRRY	YARDARM	**AAEEMNT**	ENEMATA		GALLETA
AADMRSU	MARAUDS		MANATEE		TALLAGE
AADMRSZ	MAZARDS		AMREETA	**AAEGLMN**	GAMELAN
AADMRZZ	MAZZARD	**AAEEMRT**	MEATAXE	**AAEGLMT**	GAMETAL
AADMSYY	MAYDAYS	**AAEEMTX**	APPEASE	**AAEGLNN**	ANLAGEN
AADNNOT	NOTANDA	**AAEEPPS**	PATERAE	**AAEGLNR**	ALNAGER
AADNNRS	RANDANS	**AAEEPRT**	AERATES	**AAEGLNS**	ALNAGES
AADNOPR	PANDORA	**AAEERST**	SEAWARE		ANLAGES
AADNORT	ONDATRA	**AAEERSW**	AUREATE		GALENAS
AADNORY	ANYROAD	**AAEERTU**	TEAWARE		LAGENAS
AADNPRS	PANDARS	**AAEERTW**	EXARATE		LASAGNE
AADNPRU	PANDURA	**AAEERTX**	AGRAFFE	**AAEGLNU**	AULNAGE
AADNRRW	WARRAND	**AAEFFGR**	AFFAIRE		LEGUAAN
AADNRRY	DARRAYN	**AAEFFIR**	FALAFEL	**AAEGLOP**	APOGEAL
AADNRSS	NASARDS	**AAEFFLL**	FANFARE	**AAEGLRR**	REALGAR
AADNRST	ASTRAND	**AAEFFNR**	AFFEARS	**AAEGLRS**	ALEGARS
	TARANDS	**AAEFFRS**	TAFFETA		LAAGERS
AADNRTY	TANYARD	**AAEFFTT**	FANEGAS	**AAEGLST**	AGELAST
AADNRVW	VANWARD	**AAEFGNS**	AGRAFES		ALGATES
AADNRWY	NAYWARD	**AAEFGRS**	WAFTAGE		LASTAGE
AADOPRR	PARADOR	**AAEFGTW**	AIRFARE	**AAEGLSV**	LAVAGES
AADOPRS	PARADOS	**AAEFIRR**	FAVELLA		SALVAGE
AADOPRT	ADAPTOR	**AAEFLLV**	EARFLAP	**AAEGLSX**	GALAXES
AADOPRX	PARADOX	**AAEFLPR**	PARAFLE	**AAEGMNO**	MANGEAO
AADOPSS	PASSADO		RAFALES	**AAEGMNR**	MANAGER
	POSADAS	**AAEFLRS**	LAWFARE	**AAEGMNS**	AGNAMES
AADOPSU	POUSADA	**AAEFLRW**	FAVELAS		MANAGES
AADOPTT	DOPATTA	**AAEFLSV**	FERMATA		SAGAMEN
AADORWY	ROADWAY	**AAEFMRT**	AQUAFER	**AAEGMNT**	GATEMAN
AADOSTT	TOSTADA	**AAEFQRU**	WARFARE		MAGENTA
AADOWWX	WOADWAX	**AAEFRRW**	WAYFARE		MAGNATE
AADPSSW	PADSAWS	**AAEFRWY**	GALAGES		NAMETAG
AADPSSY	SPAYADS	**AAEGGLS**	ANAGOGE	**AAEGMPR**	RAMPAGE
AADPSYY	PAYDAYS	**AAEGGNO**	APAGOGE	**AAEGMRT**	REGMATA
AADPTTU	DUPATTA	**AAEGGOP**	GARAGES	**AAEGMSS**	MASSAGE
AADQRTU	QUADRAT	**AAEGGRS**	AGGRATE	**AAEGMTT**	METATAG
AADRRSS	SARDARS	**AAEGGRT**	GARAGEY	**AAEGNNP**	PANNAGE
AADRSTU	DATURAS	**AAEGGRY**	GAVAGES	**AAEGNNT**	TANNAGE
AADRSTY	DAYSTAR	**AAEGGSV**	HAULAGE	**AAEGNOP**	APOGEAN
AADRSVW	VAWARDS	**AAEGHLU**	HAYLAGE	**AAEGNPT**	PAGEANT
AADRWWY	WAYWARD	**AAEGHLY**	THANAGE	**AAEGNPW**	PAWNAGE
AAEEFFR	AFFEARE	**AAEGHNT**	LAIRAGE	**AAEGNRR**	ARRANGE
AAEEFGL	LEAFAGE	**AAEGILR**	RAILAGE	**AAEGNRT**	TANAGER
AAEEFRT	RATAFEE		REGALIA	**AAEGNST**	AGNATES
AAEEGKL	LEAKAGE		ALGESIA	**AAEGNSU**	GUANASE
AAEEGLT	ETALAGE	**AAEGILS**	NAGAPIE	**AAEGNTV**	VANTAGE
	GALEATE	**AAEGINP**	ANERGIA	**AAEGNTW**	WANTAGE
AAEEGMN	AMENAGE	**AAEGINR**	VAGINAE	**AAEGORS**	AGAROSE
AAEEGMT	AGAMETE	**AAEGINV**			

	OARAGES	**AAEILNO**	AEOLIAN	**AAEKPRT**	PARTAKE
AAEGPRR	PARERGA	**AAEILNT**	ANTLIAE	**AAEKPTU**	PUKATEA
AAEGPRS	PARAGES	**AAEILOR**	OLEARIA	**AAEKRSS**	KEASARS
AAEGPRW	WARPAGE	**AAEILPX**	EPAXIAL	**AAEKRST**	KARATES
AAEGPSS	PASSAGE	**AAEILRS**	AERIALS	**AAEKSSV**	VAKASES
AAEGPSV	PAVAGES	**AAEILRU**	AURELIA	**AAELLLM**	LAMELLA
AAEGPSY	PAYSAGE	**AAEILRV**	REAVAIL	**AAELLNV**	AVELLAN
AAEGQUY	QUAYAGE		VELARIA	**AAELLNZ**	ZANELLA
AAEGRRV	RAVAGER	**AAEILSS**	ALIASES	**AAELLPR**	PARELLA
AAEGRST	AGRASTE	**AAEILSV**	AVAILES	**AAELLPS**	PAELLAS
	GASTREA	**AAEILSX**	ALEXIAS	**AAELLPT**	PATELLA
	TEARGAS	**AAEIMMT**	IMAMATE	**AAELLRT**	LATERAL
AAEGRSV	RAVAGES	**AAEIMNS**	AMNESIA	**AAELLRY**	ALLAYER
	SAVAGER		ANEMIAS		AREALLY
AAEGRTT	REGATTA	**AAEIMNT**	AMENTIA	**AAELLSW**	SEAWALL
AAEGSSU	ASSUAGE		ANIMATE	**AAELLTV**	VALLATE
	SAUSAGE	**AAEIMPY**	PYAEMIA	**AAELMMR**	ALMEMAR
AAEGSSV	AVGASES	**AAEIMRT**	AMIRATE	**AAELMMT**	LEMMATA
	SAVAGES	**AAEIMRU**	URAEMIA	**AAELMNT**	AMENTAL
AAEGSSW	ASSWAGE	**AAEIMTV**	AMATIVE	**AAELMNU**	ALUMNAE
AAEGSTU	GATEAUS	**AAEINNO**	AEONIAN	**AAELMOT**	OATMEAL
AAEGSTW	WASTAGE	**AAEINPS**	PAESANI	**AAELMPT**	PALMATE
AAEGTTW	WATTAGE	**AAEINPT**	PATINAE	**AAELMRW**	MALWARE
AAEGTUX	GATEAUX	**AAEINST**	ENTASIA	**AAELMST**	MALATES
AAEGTWY	GATEWAY		TAENIAS		MALTASE
	GETAWAY	**AAEIPPS**	APEPSIA		TAMALES
AAEHHPR	RHAPHAE	**AAEIPRR**	PAREIRA	**AAELMSX**	MALAXES
AAEHHPT	APHTHAE	**AAEIPRS**	SPIRAEA	**AAELMSY**	AMYLASE
AAEHILP	APHELIA	**AAEIPRT**	APTERIA	**AAELNNS**	ANNEALS
AAEHIRT	HETAIRA	**AAEIPTT**	APATITE	**AAELNOP**	APNOEAL
AAEHKNT	KHANATE	**AAEIRRT**	TARAIRE	**AAELNOV**	VALONEA
AAEHKPS	PAKEHAS	**AAEIRSS**	ARAISES	**AAELNPR**	PREANAL
AAEHKRY	HAYRAKE	**AAEIRST**	ARISTAE	**AAELNPT**	PLANATE
AAEHKST	TAKAHES		ASTERIA		PLANTAE
AAEHKSW	SEAHAWK		ATRESIA		PLATANE
AAEHLLL	ALLHEAL	**AAEIRSX**	XERASIA	**AAELNPU**	PAENULA
AAEHLMT	HEMATAL	**AAEIRTT**	ARIETTA	**AAELNRS**	ARSENAL
AAEHLNT	ETHANAL	**AAEIRTV**	VARIATE	**AAELNSS**	ANLASES
AAEHLPS	PHASEAL	**AAEIRTW**	AWAITER	**AAELNST**	SEALANT
AAEHLPX	HEXAPLA	**AAEIRVW**	AIRWAVE	**AAELNSY**	ANALYSE
AAEHLRT	TREHALA	**AAEISTT**	SATIATE	**AAELNTT**	TETANAL
AAEHLST	ALTHEAS	**AAEISTV**	AVIATES	**AAELNTY**	ANALYTE
AAEHLTT	ATHLETA	**AAEISTX**	ATAXIES	**AAELNTZ**	ZEALANT
AAEHMSS	ASHAMES	**AAEITUX**	EUTAXIA	**AAELNWY**	LANEWAY
AAEHMST	ATHAMES	**AAEJMST**	MAATJES	**AAELNYZ**	ANALYZE
	HAMATES	**AAEJNRT**	NAARTJE	**AAELORR**	AREOLAR
AAEHMTT	THEMATA	**AAEJOPR**	APAREJO	**AAELORS**	AREOLAS
AAEHNPR	HANAPER	**AAEKKOR**	KARAOKE	**AAELORU**	AUREOLA
AAEHNPS	SAPHENA	**AAEKKRY**	KAYAKER	**AAELOTX**	OXALATE
AAEHNSY	HYAENAS	**AAEKLMS**	KAMELAS	**AAELPPR**	APPAREL
AAEHPRZ	PHEAZAR	**AAEKLNS**	ALKANES	**AAELPPS**	APPEALS
AAEHPSW	AWHAPES	**AAEKLNT**	ALKANET	**AAELPPT**	PALPATE
AAEHPSX	HAPAXES		KANTELA	**AAELPPU**	PAPULAE
AAEHRSY	HEARSAY	**AAEKLSS**	ASLAKES	**AAELPRS**	EARLAPS
AAEHSTT	HASTATE	**AAEKMNW**	WAKEMAN	**AAELPRT**	APTERAL
AAEIKLN	AKENIAL	**AAEKMRR**	EARMARK	**AAELPRV**	PALAVER
AAEILLX	AXILLAE	**AAEKMRS**	SEAMARK	**AAELPSS**	PALASES
AAEILMN	LAMINAE	**AAEKMSW**	WAKAMES		PASELAS
AAEILMS	AMELIAS	**AAEKNNS**	ANANKES		PLAASES
	MALAISE	**AAEKNSW**	AWAKENS	**AAELPST**	PALATES
AAEILNN	ALANINE	**AAEKNUW**	UNAWAKE	**AAELPTT**	TAPETAL

AAELPTU	PLATEAU	AAENRTV	TAVERNA	AAFIKSS	SIFAKAS
AAELPTY	APETALY	AAENRUW	UNAWARE	AAFILNT	FANTAIL
AAELRST	TARSEAL	AAENRUZ	AZUREAN		TAILFAN
AAELRTV	LARVATE	AAENSSU	NAUSEAS	AAFILQU	ALFAQUI
AAELRTZ	LAZARET	AAENSSV	VANESSA	AAFINNT	INFANTA
AAELRVY	ALVEARY	AAENSSW	SEAWANS	AAFINNU	INFAUNA
AAELSST	ATLASES	AAENSTV	SAVANTE	AAFINRS	FARINAS
AAELSTT	SALTATE	AAENSTW	SEAWANT	AAFINTT	ANTIFAT
AAELSTV	VALETAS	AAEOPTZ	ZAPATEO	AAFIPRT	PARFAIT
AAELSTZ	ALTEZAS	AAEORRT	AERATOR	AAFIQTU	AQUAFIT
AAELSUX	ASEXUAL	AAEORRU	AURORAE	AAFIRSS	SAFARIS
AAELSWX	SEALWAX	AAEORST	AEROSAT	AAFIRSU	FUSARIA
AAELTUV	VALUATE	AAEPPRS	APPEARS	AAFIRUY	RUFIYAA
AAELTVV	VALVATE	AAEPPRT	PARAPET	AAFIRWY	FAIRWAY
AAELTZZ	ALTEZZA	AAEPRRS	PARERAS	AAFISST	FATSIAS
AAELWWY	WELAWAY	AAEPRSS	PASEARS	AAFJLLW	JAWFALL
AAEMMMR	MAREMMA		SARAPES	AAFJLOR	ALFORJA
AAEMMMT	MAMMATE	AAEPRST	PETARAS	AAFKNST	KAFTANS
AAEMMNT	MEATMAN	AAEPRSY	APYRASE	AAFLLLS	FALLALS
AAEMMNU	MANUMEA	AAEPRSZ	ZARAPES	AAFLLTY	FATALLY
AAEMMOT	OMMATEA	AAEPRTY	PEATARY	AAFLMPR	FRAMPAL
AAEMNNT	EMANANT	AAEPSTW	WATAPES	AAFLNOR	FORLANA
AAEMNOR	AMARONE	AAEPTTW	WATTAPE	AAFLNRU	FURLANA
AAEMNPP	PAMPEAN	AAERRRS	ARREARS	AAFLNUU	FAUNULA
AAEMNPS	SPAEMAN	AAERRRY	ARRAYER	AAFLSTU	FLAUTAS
AAEMNPT	PEATMAN	AAERRSS	ARRASES	AAFLWYY	FLYAWAY
AAEMNRT	RAMENTA	AAERRST	ERRATAS	AAFMNRT	RAFTMAN
AAEMNRU	MURAENA	AAERRTT	TARTARE	AAFMNST	FANTASM
AAEMNST	NAMASTE	AAERSST	SEARATS	AAFNRRT	FARRANT
AAEMNTU	MANTEAU	AAERSSY	ARAYSES	AAFNSTT	FANTAST
AAEMOTY	ATEMOYA		ASSAYER	AAFNSTY	FANTASY
AAEMOTZ	METAZOA	AAERSTU	AURATES	AAFOSST	AFTOSAS
AAEMPRT	APTAMER	AAERSTW	AWAREST	AAGGHNT	HANGTAG
AAEMQSU	SQUAMAE	AAERTTU	TUATERA	AAGGIJN	JAGAING
AAEMRSS	AMASSER	AAESSTV	SAVATES	AAGGILN	GANGLIA
AAEMRST	AMEARST	AAESSWY	SEAWAYS	AAGGJRY	JAGGARY
	RETAMAS	AAFFILN	AFFINAL	AAGGKSU	GAGAKUS
AAEMRTU	AMATEUR	AAFFILX	AFFIXAL	AAGGLMO	MAGALOG
AAEMSSS	AMASSES	AAFFIMS	MAFFIAS	AAGGLOS	GALAGOS
AAENNNT	ANTENNA	AAFFINS	SAFFIAN	AAGGLRY	GRAYLAG
AAENNST	ANNATES	AAFFINT	AFFIANT	AAGGMNS	MGANGAS
AAENNSZ	ZENANAS	AAFFIRS	AFFAIRS	AAGGNOY	ANAGOGY
AAENNTT	TANNATE		RAFFIAS	AAGGNST	GANGSTA
AAENNTV	VENTANA	AAFFIST	TAFFIAS	AAGGNTT	TAGGANT
AAENOPS	APNOEAS	AAFFLRS	FARFALS	AAGGNWY	GANGWAY
	PAESANO	AAFFPRS	AFFRAPS	AAGGQSU	QUAGGAS
AAENOSZ	OZAENAS	AAFFRSY	AFFRAYS	AAGGRSS	SAGGARS
AAENPPR	PARPANE	AAFFRSZ	ZAFFARS	AAGGRST	RAGTAGS
AAENPSS	PAESANS	AAFGHIN	AFGHANI		TAGRAGS
AAENPST	ANAPEST	AAFGHNS	AFGHANS		
	PEASANT	AAFGLMN	FLAGMAN	AAGHHRR	AARRGHH
AAENPSV	PAVANES	AAFGORR	FARRAGO	AAGHILR	GHARIAL
AAENPSX	PANAXES	AAFHIKL	KHALIFA	AAGHINN	ANHINGA
AAENPTT	EPATANT	AAFHINR	FARINHA	AAGHJNS	GANJAHS
AAENRRT	NARRATE	AAFHLLS	ASHFALL	AAGHKNS	KANGHAS
AAENRSS	NARASES	AAFHLWY	HALFWAY		KHANGAS
AAENRST	ANESTRA	AAFHSTW	FATWAHS	AAGHKNT	THANGKA
	SANTERA	AAFIILR	FILARIA	AAGHLNT	GNATHAL
AAENRTT	TARTANE	AAFIJST	FAJITAS	AAGHLOS	GASAHOL
AAENRTU	NATURAE	AAFIKLS	ALFAKIS	AAGHLSZ	GHAZALS
	TAUREAN		KAFILAS	AAGHMNN	HANGMAN
				AAGHMNU	MAHUANG

AAGHMNW	WHANGAM	**AAGIRRY**	ARGYRIA	**AAGNRSS**	SANGARS
AAGHMRS	GRAHAMS	**AAGIRSW**	WARAGIS	**AAGNRTV**	VAGRANT
	GRAMASH	**AAGISTT**	SAGITTA	**AAGNSST**	SATANGS
AAGHNRS	ARGHANS	**AAGJNRS**	GARJANS	**AAGNSTU**	TAGUANS
	HANGARS	**AAGJRSU**	JAGUARS	**AAGNSUY**	GUANAYS
AAGHNSS	SANGHAS	**AAGKKNO**	ANGAKOK	**AAGOPRU**	GAROUPA
AAGHNST	SANGHAT	**AAGKLSY**	GALYAKS	**AAGOPSS**	SAPSAGO
AAGHQUU	QUAHAUG	**AAGKOOZ**	GAZOOKA	**AAGORSU**	SAGUARO
AAGHRSW	WASHRAG	**AAGKORT**	KATORGA	**AAGOSTU**	AGOUTAS
AAGHSTY	SAGATHY	**AAGLLNS**	LALANGS	**AAGPPRS**	GRAPPAS
AAGIINT	IGNATIA	**AAGLLNT**	GALLANT	**AAGRRSY**	GARRYAS
AAGIKNS	KAINGAS	**AAGLLVY**	VAGALLY	**AAGRSUV**	AVRUGAS
AAGIKNT	TIKANGA	**AAGLMMS**	MALMAGS	**AAGTTUU**	TAUTAUG
AAGIKNW	AWAKING	**AAGLMNS**	MANGALS	**AAHHIRS**	SHARIAH
AAGIKNZ	ZIGANKA	**AAGLNOR**	GRANOLA	**AAHHJJS**	HAJJAHS
AAGILMY	MYALGIA	**AAGLNOS**	ANALOGS	**AAHHLLS**	HALLAHS
AAGILNN	ANGINAL	**AAGLNOY**	ANALOGY	**AAHHLSV**	HALVAHS
AAGILNO	LOGANIA	**AAGLNPS**	LAPSANG	**AAHHMSZ**	HAMZAHS
AAGILNP	PAGINAL	**AAGLNRS**	LANGARS	**AAHHNNT**	THANNAH
AAGILNS	AGNAILS		RAGLANS	**AAHHNPT**	NAPHTHA
AAGILNV	AVALING	**AAGLNRU**	ANGULAR	**AAHHNST**	THANAHS
	VAGINAL	**AAGLNSU**	LAGUNAS	**AAHHOPR**	PHARAOH
AAGILNY	ALAYING	**AAGLNTY**	GALANTY	**AAHIIMT**	HIMATIA
AAGILOS	ALOGIAS	**AAGLORU**	ARUGOLA	**AAHIJNR**	HARIJAN
	LAOGAIS	**AAGLRST**	GASTRAL	**AAHIKMS**	KAMAHIS
	OTALGIA	**AAGLRUU**	ARUGULA	**AAHIKOR**	AKIRAHO
AAGILOT			AUGURAL	**AAHIKPS**	PAKAHIS
AAGILPS	PALAGIS			**AAHIKRS**	HAKARIS
AAGILRS	ARGALIS	**AAGLRVX**	GRAVLAX	**AAHIKRT**	KITHARA
	GARIALS	**AAGLSST**	STALAGS	**AAHILLL**	HALLALI
AAGILSV	GAVIALS	**AAGMMNS**	MAGSMAN	**AAHILLN**	HALLIAN
AAGILTW	WAGTAIL	**AAGMMRR**	GRAMMAR	**AAHILMR**	ALMIRAH
AAGIMNO	ANGIOMA	**AAGMMRS**	GRAMMAS	**AAHILMS**	SHIMAAL
AAGIMNS	MAGIANS	**AAGMMST**	GAMMATS	**AAHILMT**	THALAMI
	SIAMANG	**AAGMMTU**	GUMMATA	**AAHILNT**	THALIAN
AAGIMNT	AMATING	**AAGMMUY**	MAMAGUY	**AAHILPV**	PAHLAVI
AAGIMNZ	AMAZING	**AAGMNNR**	GRANNAM	**AAHILSW**	SAHIWAL
AAGINNS	ANGINAS	**AAGMNOS**	SANGOMA	**AAHILSY**	ALIYAHS
	INANGAS	**AAGMNOT**	AGAMONT	**AAHIMNO**	MAHONIA
AAGINNW	WANIGAN	**AAGMNPR**	PANGRAM	**AAHIMNS**	SHAMINA
AAGINOS	AGNOSIA	**AAGMNPY**	PANGAMY	**AAHIMNZ**	HAZANIM
AAGINPY	APAYING	**AAGMNRS**	RAGMANS	**AAHIMSS**	AHIMSAS
AAGINRR	ARRAIGN	**AAGMNRT**	TANGRAM	**AAHINOP**	APHONIA
AAGINRS	NAGARIS		TRANGAM	**AAHINPP**	PAPHIAN
	SANGRIA	**AAGMNSW**	SWAGMAN	**AAHINPR**	PIRANHA
	SARANGI	**AAGMNSZ**	ZAMANGS	**AAHINST**	SHAITAN
AAGINRT	GRANITA	**AAGMOPY**	APOGAMY		TAHINAS
AAGINRU	GUARANI	**AAGMORS**	MARGOSA	**AAHINTW**	TANIWHA
AAGINRZ	ZINGARA	**AAGMOSU**	AGAMOUS	**AAHIPRS**	PARIAHS
AAGINST	AGAINST	**AAGMPRS**	GRAMPAS		RAPHIAS
	AGITANS	**AAGMRRY**	GRAMARY	**AAHIPRT**	PITARAH
	ANTISAG	**AAGMRSY**	MARGAYS	**AAHIPTZ**	ZAPTIAH
	GITANAS	**AAGNNOS**	GOANNAS	**AAHIRRS**	HARIRAS
AAGINSU	IGUANAS	**AAGNNRU**	RUNANGA	**AAHIRSS**	HARISSA
AAGINSV	VAGINAS	**AAGNNSW**	WANGANS		SHARIAS
AAGINSY	GAINSAY	**AAGNOPR**	PARAGON	**AAHIRST**	SHARIAT
AAGINTY	ANTIGAY	**AAGNORS**	ANGORAS	**AAHIRSV**	VIHARAS
AAGINWW	WAWAING	**AAGNORZ**	ORGANZA	**AAHIRTV**	HAVARTI
AAGIOSS	ASIAGOS	**AAGNOST**	TAONGAS	**AAHISTW**	TAWHAIS
AAGIOTT	AGITATO	**AAGNPRS**	PARANGS	**AAHJKNR**	KHANJAR
AAGIPRS	AIRGAPS	**AAGNRRS**	GARRANS	**AAHJKST**	JHATKAS
AAGIPRU	PIRAGUA	**AAGNRRY**	GRANARY		

AAHJNRS	HANJARS	AAHNRTY	RHATANY	AAILLMN	LAMINAL
	RHANJAS	AAHNSUW	WHANAUS		MANILLA
AAHJRRS	JARRAHS	AAHNSZZ	HAZZANS	AAILLMR	ARMILLA
AAHKKST	KATHAKS	AAHORSU	SAHUARO	AAILLMX	MAXILLA
AAHKLRS	LASHKAR	AAHOSTW	AWHATOS	AAILLNT	LANITAL
AAHKLST	KHALATS	AAHPPRS	PARAPHS	AAILLNV	VANILLA
AAHKLSY	KHAYALS	AAHPRSY	YARPHAS	AAILLPP	PAPILLA
AAHKMSY	YASHMAK	AAHPRTW	WARPATH	AAILLRX	AXILLAR
AAHKNST	KANTHAS	AAHPTWY	PATHWAY	AAILLSV	SALIVAL
AAHKNSU	KAHUNAS	AAHRSSS	HASSARS	AAILLSX	AXILLAS
AAHKPSS	PASHKAS	AAHRSST	SHASTRA	AAILLUV	ALLUVIA
AAHKPSU	HAPUKAS	AAHRSTY	ASHTRAY	AAILLXY	AXIALLY
AAHKRSS	RAKSHAS	AAHRTTW	ATHWART	AAILMMN	MAILMAN
AAHLLLS	HALLALS	AAHSSSY	SASHAYS	AAILMMR	AMMIRAL
AAHLLNS	HALLANS	AAIIKKS	KAIKAIS	AAILMMS	MIASMAL
	NALLAHS	AAIIKSZ	ZAIKAIS	AAILMMX	MAXIMAL
AAHLLOS	HALLOAS	AAIILMR	AIRMAIL	AAILMNR	LAMINAR
AAHLLPS	PALLAHS	AAIILPR	PAIRIAL		RAILMAN
AAHLLSW	WALLAHS	AAIILPT	TILAPIA	AAILMNS	ALMAINS
AAHLLWY	HALLWAY	AAIILRZ	ALIZARI		ANIMALS
AAHLMMS	HAMMALS	AAIINNZ	ANZIANI		LAMINAS
	MAHMALS	AAIINRT	ANTIAIR		MANILAS
	MASHLAM	AAIINTT	TITANIA	AAILMNT	MATINAL
AAHLMRS	MARSHAL	AAIINZZ	ZIZANIA	AAILMNU	ALUMINA
AAHLMRU	HAMULAR	AAIIRVV	VIVARIA	AAILMNV	MAILVAN
AAHLMSS	SHAMALS	AAIJKRS	RAKIJAS	AAILMPS	IMPALAS
AAHLMST	MALTHAS	AAIJLNP	JALAPIN	AAILMQU	MAQUILA
AAHLMSU	HAMAULS	AAIJMNP	JAMPANI	AAILMRT	MARITAL
AAHLNPX	PHALANX	AAIJMNT	ANTIJAM		MARTIAL
AAHLNRW	NARWHAL	AAIJNRS	JARINAS	AAILMSS	ALISMAS
AAHLPRS	PHRASAL	AAIJNRZ	JANIZAR		SALAMIS
AAHLPST	ASPHALT	AAIJNST	TINAJAS	AAILMSU	AUMAILS
	SPATHAL	AAIJPPY	JIPYAPA	AAILNNS	ALANINS
	TAPLASH	AAIJRSW	JAWARIS	AAILNOT	AILANTO
AAHLRSS	ASHLARS	AAIKLLN	ALKALIN		ALATION
AAHLRST	HARTALS	AAIKLLS	ALKALIS	AAILNOV	NOVALIA
AAHLRSW	SHALWAR	AAIKLMS	KALMIAS		VALONIA
AAHMMMS	HAMMAMS		KAMILAS	AAILNPS	SALPIAN
AAHMMNS	MASHMAN	AAIKLNP	PALINKA	AAILNPT	PLATINA
AAHMMSS	SHAMMAS	AAIKLNS	KALIANS	AAILNRU	ULNARIA
AAHMNNU	HANUMAN	AAIKLPR	PALIKAR	AAILNRY	LANIARY
AAHMNRS	HARMANS	AAIKMNN	MANAKIN	AAILNSS	SALINAS
AAHMNSS	SHAMANS	AAIKMNR	RAMAKIN	AAILNST	LATINAS
AAHMNTX	XANTHAM	AAIKMOR	ROMAIKA	AAILNSY	INYALAS
AAHMOPR	AMPHORA	AAIKMOS	AMAKOSI	AAILNTV	VALIANT
AAHMPRS	PHARMAS	AAIKMRS	KARAISM	AAILNTY	ANALITY
AAHMQSU	QUAMASH	AAIKNRS	KINARAS	AAILORS	ROSALIA
AAHMRSS	ASHRAMS		KIRANAS		SOLARIA
AAHMSST	ASTHMAS	AAIKNST	TANKIAS	AAILORU	RAOULIA
	MATSAHS	AAIKORU	OUAKARI	AAILORV	OVARIAL
AAHMSSU	MASHUAS	AAIKOSY	SOKAIYA		VARIOLA
AAHMSTZ	HAZMATS	AAIKPPR	PAPRIKA	AAILORZ	ZOARIAL
	MATZAHS	AAIKPRR	AIRPARK	AAILOST	SOLATIA
AAHNNOS	HOSANNA	AAIKRSS	ASKARIS	AAILPPT	APPALTI
AAHNNST	TANNAHS	AAIKRST	KARAITS	AAILPRS	PARIALS
	THANNAS	AAIKRSU	UAKARIS	AAILPRT	PARTIAL
AAHNNTX	XANTHAN	AAIKSTT	ASTATKI		PATRIAL
AAHNOPR	ANAPHOR	AAIKTVV	AKVAVIT	AAILPRY	AIRPLAY
AAHNORT	ATHANOR	AAILLLP	PALLIAL	AAILPST	SPATIAL
AAHNORV	NAVARHO	AAILLLT	LATILLA	AAILPTT	TALIPAT
AAHNRTX	ANTHRAX	AAILLMM	MAMILLA	AAILPZZ	PALAZZI

AAILQWW	QAWWALI	**AAINRSU**	ANURIAS	**AAKKSUZ**	ZAKUSKA
AAILRRV	ARRIVAL		SAURIAN	**AAKLMPU**	LAMPUKA
AAILRST	LARIATS		URANIAS	**AAKLMRY**	MALARKY
	LATRIAS	**AAINRSV**	SAVARIN	**AAKLMUY**	YAMULKA
AAILRTT	RATTAIL	**AAINRTV**	VARIANT	**AAKLNOO**	OOLAKAN
AAILRTV	TRAVAIL	**AAINRTW**	ANTIWAR	**AAKLNOU**	OULAKAN
AAILRWY	RAILWAY	**AAINRTZ**	TZARINA	**AAKLOOP**	PALOOKA
AAILSSS	ASSAILS	**AAINSST**	ISTANAS	**AAKLOOT**	TALOOKA
AAILSSV	SALIVAS	**AAINSSY**	SANYASI	**AAKLRSU**	KURSAAL
	SALVIAS	**AAINSTT**	ATTAINS		RUSALKA
	VASSAIL	**AAINSTV**	VANITAS	**AAKLSSU**	SAKSAUL
AAILSSW	WASSAIL	**AAINTTT**	ATTAINT	**AAKLSTU**	TALUKAS
AAILTTT	LATITAT	**AAINTTU**	TUTANIA	**AAKLWWY**	WALKWAY
AAIMMMT	MAMMATI	**AAINTTX**	ANTITAX	**AAKMMNR**	MARKMAN
AAIMMNO	AMMONIA	**AAIOPRS**	APORIAS	**AAKMMOS**	MAMAKOS
AAIMMSS	MIASMAS	**AAIOPRT**	ATROPIA	**AAKMMSU**	MAMAKUS
AAIMNNO	OMNIANA	**AAIOPRV**	OVIPARA	**AAKMNSU**	MANUKAS
AAIMNNT	ANTIMAN	**AAIORRS**	ROSARIA	**AAKMORU**	AMOKURA
AAIMNOS	ANOSMIA	**AAIORSU**	SAOUARI	**AAKMOSU**	MOUSAKA
AAIMNOT	AMATION	**AAIORTV**	AVIATOR	**AAKMRSU**	KARAMUS
	ANIMATO	**AAIPPRS**	APPAIRS		KUMARAS
AAIMNPT	TIMPANA	**AAIPPRU**	PUPARIA	**AAKMRUZ**	MAZURKA
AAIMNRS	MARINAS	**AAIPPTT**	PITAPAT	**AAKMRWY**	WAYMARK
AAIMNRT	MARTIAN	**AAIPRST**	PITARAS	**AAKMSSY**	YASMAKS
	TAMARIN	**AAIPRSY**	PIRAYAS	**AAKNNTU**	NUNATAK
AAIMNST	MANATIS	**AAIPRTT**	PARTITA	**AAKNORS**	ANORAKS
	STAMINA	**AAIPSTY**	PITAYAS	**AAKNRST**	KANTARS
AAIMNSV	VIMANAS	**AAIPSZZ**	PIAZZAS	**AAKNSST**	ASKANTS
AAIMNTX	TAXIMAN	**AAIQSSU**	QUASSIA	**AAKNSTW**	WANKSTA
AAIMRRS	MARARIS	**AAIQTUV**	AQUAVIT	**AAKNSWZ**	KWANZAS
AAIMRST	AMRITAS	**AAIRSST**	ARISTAS	**AAKNTWY**	TWANKAY
	TAMARIS		TARSIAS	**AAKOOPP**	PAKAPOO
AAIMRSU	SAMURAI	**AAIRSTT**	STRIATA	**AAKOPRS**	PAKORAS
AAIMRTU	TIMARAU	**AAIRSTY**	RAIYATS	**AAKORST**	OSTRAKA
AAIMSST	STASIMA	**AAIRSUW**	WAIRUAS	**AAKPRWY**	PARKWAY
AAIMSSU	AMUSIAS	**AAIRSWY**	AIRWAYS	**AAKRSTU**	KATSURA
AAIMSTT	TATAMIS	**AAIRSZZ**	RAZZIAS	**AAKRTUY**	AUTARKY
AAIMSTV	ATAVISM	**AAISTTV**	ATAVIST	**AAKSSTT**	ATTASKS
AAIMSUV	MAUVAIS	**AAISTUY**	YAUTIAS	**AAKSTTT**	ATTASKT
AAINNPU	PUNAANI	**AAITWXY**	TAXIWAY	**AAKSTUY**	YUKATAS
AAINNRU	URANIAN	**AAJJMRS**	JAMJARS	**AALLLNS**	LALLANS
AAINNRV	NAVARIN	**AAJKLWY**	JAYWALK	**AALLLSS**	SALLALS
	NIRVANA	**AAJKMNR**	JARKMAN	**AALLMMS**	MALLAMS
AAINOPS	ANOPIAS	**AAJKNSS**	SANJAKS	**AALLMPU**	AMPULLA
	ANOPSIA	**AAJMNPS**	JAMPANS	**AALLNOX**	ALLOXAN
	PAISANO	**AAJMNZZ**	JAZZMAN	**AALLNPU**	PLANULA
AAINORR	ORARIAN	**AAJMORR**	MOJARRA	**AALLNSY**	ALANYLS
AAINORV	OVARIAN	**AAJMORT**	MAJORAT		NASALLY
AAINOST	ATONIAS	**AAJMPSY**	PYJAMAS	**AALLNVY**	NAVALLY
AAINOSX	ANOXIAS	**AAJNNOS**	JOANNAS	**AALLORS**	AROLLAS
AAINPPS	PAPAINS	**AAJNOSW**	AJOWANS	**AALLOSZ**	AZOLLAS
AAINPRS	PARIANS	**AAJNOSY**	YOJANAS	**AALLOTV**	LAVOLTA
	PIRANAS	**AAJNPRS**	PRAJNAS	**AALLPPS**	APPALLS
AAINPSS	PAISANS	**AAJOPSU**	SAPAJOU	**AALLPPY**	PAPALLY
AAINPST	PASTINA	**AAKKLPS**	KALPAKS	**AALLRUY**	AURALLY
	PATINAS	**AAKKLRU**	KARAKUL	**AALLRVY**	VALLARY
	PINATAS	**AAKKMOT**	TOKAMAK	**AALLSTT**	ATLATLS
	TAIPANS	**AAKKMRS**	MARKKAS		TALLATS
AAINRST	ANTIARS	**AAKKNSU**	KANUKAS	**AALLUVV**	VALVULA
	ARTISAN	**AAKKOPS**	KAKAPOS	**AALMMMS**	MAMMALS
	TSARINA	**AAKKPSU**	KAPUKAS	**AALMMNO**	AMMONAL

AALMMNS	ALMSMAN	AALRSTU	AUSTRAL	AANNNOS	ANNONAS
AALMMNT	MALTMAN	AALRSTY	ASTYLAR	AANNOTT	ANNATTO
AALMNOS	SALAMON		SATYRAL	AANNPSS	SANPANS
AALMNOY	ANOMALY	AALSSSV	VASSALS	AANNPSW	SWANPAN
AALMNPS	NAPALMS	AALSSTU	ASSAULT	AANNPUY	PUNAANY
AALMNSU	MANUALS	AALSSUX	SAXAULS	AANNRSU	ANURANS
AALMORT	ALAMORT	AALSTUV	VALUTAS	AANNSYZ	NYANZAS
AALMORY	MAYORAL	AALSWYY	WAYLAYS	AANOQSY	YAQONAS
AALMOST	AMATOLS	AAMMMRY	MAMMARY	AANORST	TORANAS
AALMPRY	PALMARY	AAMMNRT	MANTRAM	AANORTT	ARNATTO
	PALMYRA	AAMMNST	AMTMANS	AANOSST	SONATAS
AALMPSS	PLASMAS	AAMMOOS	MAOMAOS	AANOSTT	ANATTOS
AALMRRU	RAMULAR	AAMMOTY	MYOMATA	AANPPSS	SAPPANS
AALMRSU	ALARUMS	AAMMRRS	MARRAMS	AANPRST	PARTANS
AALMSSU	MASULAS	AAMMRST	RAMSTAM		SPARTAN
AALMTTU	MULATTA		TAMMARS		TARPANS
AALNNRU	ANNULAR	AAMMSUZ	MAZUMAS		TRAPANS
AALNNSU	ANNUALS	AAMNNNS	MANNANS	AANPRSU	PURANAS
AALNPRT	PLANTAR	AAMNNOY	ANONYMA	AANPSST	PASSANT
AALNPRU	LUPANAR	AAMNOOS	MANOAOS	AANQRTU	QUARTAN
AALNPST	PLANTAS	AAMNORR	MARRANO	AANRRSW	WARRANS
	PLATANS		ORRAMAN	AANRRSY	YARRANS
	SALTPAN	AAMNORS	OARSMAN	AANRRTW	WARRANT
AALNPUU	PUNALUA		RAMONAS	AANRSSS	SANSARS
AALNQTU	QUANTAL	AAMNORT	AMORANT	AANRSTT	RATTANS
AALNRRU	RANULAR	AAMNORZ	ROMANZA		TANTRAS
AALNRSU	RANULAS	AAMNOSZ	AMAZONS		TARTANS
AALNRSW	NARWALS	AAMNOTU	AUTOMAN	AANRSTY	YANTRAS
AALNRTT	LATRANT	AAMNOTY	ANATOMY	AANRSTZ	TARZANS
AALNRTU	NATURAL	AAMNPRT	MANTRAP	AANRUWY	RUNAWAY
AALNSST	SANTALS		RAMPANT	AANSSTT	TSANTSA
AALNSTT	SALTANT	AAMNPRY	PARANYM	AANSSTV	SAVANTS
	TALANTS	AAMNPSS	PASSMAN	AANSSTZ	STANZAS
AALNSTU	SULTANA		SAMPANS	AANSSYY	NAYSAYS
AALNSTY	ANALYST	AAMNPST	TAMPANS	AANSTTT	STATANT
AALNTTU	TALAUNT		TAPSMAN	AANSTUV	AVAUNTS
AALOPPT	APPALTO	AAMNPTY	TYMPANA	AANSVWY	ANYWAYS
AALOPRS	PARASOL	AAMNRST	ARTSMAN	AAOORRW	WOORARA
AALOPST	TAPALOS		MANTRAS	AAOPSST	POTASSA
AALOPSY	PAYOLAS	AAMNRUY	MANUARY		SAPOTAS
AALOPVV	PAVLOVA	AAMNSTU	MANATUS	AAOQSSU	OQUASSA
AALOPZZ	PALAZZO		MANTUAS	AAORRSU	AURORAS
AALORRU	AURORAL		TAMANUS	AAORRSV	VARROAS
AALORST	ALASTOR	AAMOORS	AMOROSA	AAORSTT	TOTARAS
AALORSU	AROUSAL	AAMOPRS	PARAMOS	AAORSVV	VAVASOR
AALORTX	LAXATOR	AAMORRZ	ZAMARRO	AAOSTTV	OTTAVAS
AALOSTT	SALTATO	AAMORSV	SAMOVAR	AAOTTUY	TATOUAY
AALOSVW	AVOWALS	AAMORTY	AMATORY	AAOTWWY	TOWAWAY
AALOTTY	TALAYOT	AAMOSSS	SAMOSAS	AAPPSWW	PAWPAWS
AALPPRU	PAPULAR	AAMOSTT	STOMATA	AAPRRSU	PARURAS
AALPPRY	PAPYRAL	AAMOTTU	AUTOMAT	AAPRRTT	RATTRAP
AALPRRS	PARRALS	AAMPRRT	RAMPART	AAPRSST	SATRAPS
AALPRSW	ASPRAWL	AAMPSSY	AMPASSY	AAPRSTT	ATTRAPS
AALPRSY	PARLAYS	AAMRSST	MATRASS	AAPRSTY	SATRAPY
AALPRTY	LAPTRAY	AAMRSSU	ASARUMS	AAPRTUU	RAUPATU
AALPSTU	SPATULA	AAMRSTU	SUMATRA	AAPRTWY	PARTWAY
AALQSWW	QAWWALS		TRAUMAS	AAPZZZZ	PAZZAZZ
AALRSST	ASTRALS	AAMRTTY	TRYMATA	AAQRSSU	QUASARS
	TARSALS	AAMRTWY	TRAMWAY	AARRSSS	SARSARS
AALRSSW	SALWARS	AAMSSTU	SATSUMA	AARRSTT	TARTARS
AALRSTT	STRATAL	AAMSTTU	MATATUS	AARRSUW	RAWARUS

AARRSWY	WARRAYS	**ABBDLRU**	LUBBARD	**ABBGINT**	TABBING
AARSSST	ASSARTS	**ABBDMOR**	BOMBARD	**ABBGINU**	BUBINGA
	SASTRAS	**ABBDMOU**	BABUDOM	**ABBGINY**	BABYING
AARSSTT	ASTARTS	**ABBDNOX**	BANDBOX	**ABBGMSU**	BUMBAGS
	STRATAS	**ABBEESU**	BAUBEES	**ABBGOOU**	BUGABOO
AARSSTY	SATYRAS	**ABBEESW**	BAWBEES	**ABBGORS**	GABBROS
AARSSWW	WARSAWS	**ABBEFIR**	FABBIER	**ABBHIJS**	JIBBAHS
AASSTTU	STATUAS	**ABBEFST**	FABBEST	**ABBHISY**	BABYISH
AASTTUU	TUATUAS	**ABBEGIR**	GABBIER	**ABBHJSU**	JUBBAHS
ABBBDEL	BABBLED	**ABBEGLR**	GABBLER	**ABBHOOS**	BABOOSH
	BLABBED		GRABBLE		HABOOBS
ABBBELR	BABBLER	**ABBEGLS**	GABBLES	**ABBHRRU**	RHUBARB
	BLABBER	**ABBEGNO**	BOGBEAN	**ABBHTTU**	BATHTUB
	BRABBLE	**ABBEGNU**	BUGBANE	**ABBIIMN**	BAMBINI
ABBBELS	BABBLES	**ABBEGRR**	GRABBER	**ABBIJLS**	JILBABS
ABBBELU	ABUBBLE	**ABBEGRS**	GABBERS	**ABBIKNO**	BIOBANK
ABBBITT	BABBITT	**ABBEGRU**	BUGBEAR	**ABBILLS**	LIBLABS
ABBCDER	CRABBED	**ABBEHLS**	SHABBLE	**ABBILOR**	BILOBAR
ABBCDES	SCABBED	**ABBEILT**	BITABLE	**ABBILOS**	BILBOAS
ABBCEHI	BABICHE	**ABBEIRS**	BARBIES	**ABBILOT**	BOBTAIL
ABBCEHU	BABUCHE		RABBIES	**ABBILSU**	BUBALIS
ABBCEIS	CABBIES	**ABBEIST**	BABIEST	**ABBIMNO**	BAMBINO
ABBCELR	CLABBER		TABBIES	**ABBIMSU**	BABUISM
ABBCELS	SCABBLE	**ABBEISW**	SWABBIE	**ABBINOR**	RABBONI
ABBCERR	CRABBER	**ABBEISY**	YABBIES	**ABBINRS**	RABBINS
ABBCGIN	CABBING	**ABBEJLS**	JABBLES	**ABBIORT**	RABBITO
ABBCIIS	BIBASIC	**ABBEJRS**	JABBERS	**ABBIRST**	RABBITS
ABBCIKT	BACKBIT	**ABBELLR**	BARBELL	**ABBIRTY**	RABBITY
ABBCIRS	BICARBS	**ABBELMR**	BRAMBLE	**ABBISTY**	BABYSIT
ABBCIRT	CRABBIT	**ABBELNS**	SNABBLE	**ABBKLOU**	BLAUBOK
ABBCKUY	BUYBACK	**ABBELOR**	BELABOR	**ABBLLOX**	BOXBALL
ABBCOST	BOBCATS	**ABBELPR**	PRABBLE	**ABBLLTU**	BULLBAT
ABBCOTY	ABBOTCY	**ABBELRR**	RABBLER	**ABBLMRY**	BRAMBLY
ABBCRYY	CRYBABY	**ABBELRS**	BARBELS	**ABBLOOS**	BABOOLS
ABBDDEL	DABBLED		RABBLES	**ABBMOOR**	BOMBORA
ABBDDER	DRABBED		SLABBER	**ABBMOOS**	BAMBOOS
ABBDEFR	FRABBED	**ABBELRU**	BARBULE	**ABBMOST**	BOMBAST
ABBDEGL	GABBLED	**ABBELRW**	WABBLER	**ABBMOTU**	BUMBOAT
ABBDEGR	GRABBED	**ABBELSU**	BAUBLES	**ABBNOOS**	BABOONS
ABBDEHT	BEDBATH		BUBALES	**ABBOORU**	RUBABOO
ABBDEIT	TABBIED	**ABBELSW**	BAWBLES	**ABBORSS**	ABSORBS
ABBDEIY	YABBIED		WABBLES	**ABBOSTY**	BATBOYS
ABBDEJL	JABBLED	**ABBELUY**	BUYABLE		BOBSTAY
ABBDELR	DABBLER	**ABBEMUZ**	BUMBAZE	**ABBQSUY**	SQUABBY
	DRABBLE	**ABBENRS**	NABBERS	**ABBRSSU**	BUSBARS
	RABBLED	**ABBEORS**	EARBOBS	**ABBRSTU**	BARBUTS
ABBDELS	DABBLES	**ABBEOTX**	BEATBOX	**ABBSSSU**	SUBBASS
	SLABBED	**ABBERRS**	BARBERS	**ABCCCHI**	BACCHIC
ABBDELW	WABBLED	**ABBERST**	BARBETS	**ABCCEIR**	ACERBIC
ABBDERR	DRABBER		RABBETS		BRECCIA
ABBDERS	DABBERS		STABBER	**ABCCEIS**	BACCIES
ABBDERT	DRABBET	**ABBERSW**	SWABBER		SEBACIC
ABBDEST	STABBED	**ABBERSY**	YABBERS	**ABCCEOS**	BACCOES
	TEBBADS	**ABBESSU**	SUBBASE	**ABCCHII**	BACCHII
ABBDESU	BEDAUBS	**ABBFIRT**	FRABBIT	**ABCCHTY**	BYCATCH
ABBDESW	SWABBED	**ABBGGIN**	GABBING	**ABCCILU**	CUBICAL
ABBDGIN	DABBING	**ABBGHSU**	GUBBAHS	**ABCCIMR**	CAMBRIC
ABBDHIJ	DJIBBAH	**ABBGIJN**	JABBING	**ABCCINU**	BUCCINA
ABBDILR	LIBBARD	**ABBGINN**	NABBING	**ABCCIOR**	BORACIC
ABBDINR	RIBBAND	**ABBGINR**	BARBING		BRACCIO
ABBDITY	DABBITY	**ABBGINS**	SABBING	**ABCCIOS**	BOCCIAS

ABCCISU	CUBICAS	ABCEGOS	BOCAGES	ABCELOP	PLACEBO
ABCCKOW	BAWCOCK		BOSCAGE	ABCELOV	VOCABLE
ABCCKTU	CUTBACK	ABCEGSU	CUBAGES	ABCELPS	BECLASP
ABCCOOR	BAROCCO	ABCEHIS	BIACHES	ABCELPU	BLUECAP
ABCCOOT	TOBACCO	ABCEHKL	BECHALK	ABCELPY	BYPLACE
ABCCSUU	SUCCUBA	ABCEHKO	BACKHOE	ABCELRS	CABLERS
ABCDDEU	ABDUCED	ABCEHLO	CHAEBOL	ABCELRU	CURABLE
ABCDEEH	BEACHED	ABCEHLU	BAUCHLE	ABCELRW	BECRAWL
ABCDEEL	BELACED	ABCEHMR	BECHARM	ABCELST	CABLETS
	DEBACLE		BRECHAM	ABCELSU	BASCULE
ABCDEHT	BATCHED		CHAMBER	ABCEMRS	CAMBERS
ABCDEHU	DEBAUCH		CHAMBRE		CEMBRAS
ABCDEIK	DIEBACK	ABCEHNR	BRECHAN		CRAMBES
ABCDEIN	CABINED	ABCEHOS	BASOCHE	ABCEMSW	WEBCAMS
ABCDEIP	PEDICAB	ABCEHRS	BRACHES	ABCEMSX	EXCAMBS
ABCDEIR	CARBIDE	ABCEHRT	BATCHER	ABCENOR	BACONER
ABCDEKL	BLACKED		BRACHET	ABCENOS	BEACONS
ABCDEKR	REDBACK		BRACHET	ABCENOW	COWBANE
ABCDELO	CODABLE	ABCEHST	BATCHES	ABCENOZ	CABEZON
ABCDEOR	BARCODE	ABCEIIT	ABIETIC	ABCENRU	UNBRACE
	BROCADE	ABCEIKS	BACKIES	ABCENSU	CUBANES
ABCDERS	DECARBS	ABCEIKT	TIEBACK	ABCEOOS	CABOOSE
ABCDERT	BRACTED	ABCEILL	ICEBALL	ABCEORR	BRACERO
ABCDERU	CUDBEAR	ABCEILM	ALEMBIC	ABCEORS	BORACES
ABCDESU	ABDUCES		CEMBALI	ABCEORU	CORBEAU
	SCUBAED	ABCEILR	CALIBER	ABCEORV	CABOVER
ABCDHIO	ICHABOD		CALIBRE	ABCERRS	BRACERS
ABCDHOR	CHOBDAR	ABCEILT	CITABLE	ABCERSU	RUBACES
ABCDHOS	BODACHS	ABCEIMO	AMOEBIC		SUBRACE
ABCDIIS	DIBASIC	ABCEINR	CARBINE	ABCESSS	ABSCESS
ABCDILO	CABILDO	ABCEINT	CABINET	ABCESTW	WEBCAST
ABCDILR	BALDRIC	ABCEIOR	AEROBIC	ABCFIKN	FINBACK
ABCDINS	ABSCIND	ABCEIOT	ICEBOAT	ABCFIKT	BACKFIT
ABCDIRS	SCABRID	ABCEIRS	ASCRIBE	ABCFILO	BIFOCAL
ABCDIRT	CATBIRD		CABRIES	ABCFIOT	BIOFACT
ABCDIRU	BAUDRIC		CARBIES	ABCFIRS	FABRICS
ABCDIRW	BAWDRIC		CARIBES	ABCFKLY	FLYBACK
ABCDISU	SUBACID	ABCEIRZ	ZEBRAIC	ABCFLOO	COBLOAF
ABCDNOS	ABSCOND	ABCEISS	ABSCISE	ABCFNOS	CONFABS
ABCDOOR	CORDOBA		SCABIES	ABCGHIN	BACHING
ABCDORR	BROCARD		SEBASIC	ABCGHKO	HOGBACK
ABCDORU	BUCARDO	ABCEITT	TABETIC	ABCGIKN	BACKING
ABCDSTU	ABDUCTS	ABCEJST	ABJECTS	ABCGILN	CABLING
ABCEEHS	BEACHES	ABCEKLN	BLACKEN	ABCGINR	BRACING
ABCEEHU	EBAUCHE	ABCEKLO	BECLOAK	ABCGKLO	BACKLOG
ABCEELS	BELACES	ABCEKLR	BLACKER	ABCGMSU	SCUMBAG
ABCEEMR	EMBRACE	ABCEKNR	BRACKEN	ABCHHII	HIBACHI
ABCEEMS	EMBACES	ABCEKRS	BACKERS	ABCHILS	CHABLIS
ABCEENR	CARBEEN		REBACKS	ABCHIMT	BATHMIC
	CARBENE	ABCEKRT	BRACKET	ABCHIOT	COHABIT
ABCEENS	ABSENCE	ABCEKST	BACKETS	ABCHKOU	CHABOUK
ABCEERR	ACERBER		BACKSET	ABCHKSU	CHABUKS
	CEREBRA		SETBACK	ABCHKTU	HACKBUT
	REBRACE	ABCEKSY	BACKSEY	ABCHKUW	HAWBUCK
ABCEERU	BERCEAU	ABCEKTW	WETBACK	ABCHNOR	BROCHAN
ABCEESS	BECASSE	ABCELLS	BECALLS	ABCHNRU	BRAUNCH
ABCEESU	BECAUSE	ABCELLU	BULLACE	ABCHNRY	BRANCHY
ABCEFIS	BIFACES	ABCELMO	CEMBALO	ABCHORT	BRACHOT
ABCEGIR	RIBCAGE	ABCELMR	CAMBREL	ABCHOSX	CASHBOX
ABCEGMO	CAMBOGE		CLAMBER	ABCHOTT	CHATBOT
ABCEGOR	BROCAGE	ABCELMS	BECALMS	ABCHPSU	HUBCAPS
			SCAMBLE		

ABCIILL	BACILLI	ABCLOVY	VOCABLY		BEARDIE
ABCIILN	ALBINIC	ABCLRUY	CURABLY	ABDEEJS	BEJADES
ABCIILS	BASILIC	ABCMOPS	MOBCAPS	ABDEEJT	JETBEAD
ABCIILT	ALBITIC	ABCMORS	COMARBS	ABDEEKL	LAKEBED
ABCIIMN	MINICAB		CRAMBOS	ABDEEKR	BERAKED
ABCIIMS	IAMBICS	ABCMOST	COMBATS	ABDEEKS	DEBEAKS
ABCIIOR	CIBORIA		MOBCAST	ABDEELL	LABELED
ABCIIOT	ABIOTIC		TOMBACS	ABDEELM	BELDAME
ABCIJNO	JACOBIN	ABCMRSS	SCRAMBS		BEMEDAL
ABCIKLT	BACKLIT	ABCNORS	CARBONS		EMBALED
ABCIKPS	BIPACKS		CORBANS	ABDEELN	ENABLED
ABCIKSY	SICKBAY	ABCORRW	CROWBAR	ABDEELR	BEDERAL
ABCILNO	COALBIN	ABCORSS	BRASCOS		BLEARED
ABCILOU	ABOULIC	ABCORSX	BOXCARS	ABDEELS	BEADLES
ABCILRS	SCRIBAL	ABCORSY	CARBOYS	ABDEELT	BELATED
ABCILTU	CUBITAL	ABCOSSU	BASUCOS		BLEATED
ABCIMMS	CAMBISM	ABCSSTU	SACBUTS	ABDEELY	BELAYED
ABCIMMU	CAMBIUM		SUBACTS		DYEABLE
ABCIMST	CAMBIST	ABDDDEL	BLADDED	ABDEEMN	BEADMEN
ABCIMSU	CUMBIAS	ABDDDER	BRADDED		BEDEMAN
ABCINOR	CORBINA	ABDDEEH	BEDHEAD		BENAMED
ABCINOS	BONACIS	ABDDEEJ	BEJADED	ABDEEMR	AMBERED
ABCINOT	BOTANIC	ABDDEER	BEARDED		BREAMED
ABCIORR	BARRICO		BREADED		EMBREAD
ABCIORS	CABRIOS		DEBEARD	ABDEEMS	EMBASED
ABCIORU	CARIBOU	ABDDEES	DEBASED	ABDEEMT	BEDMATE
ABCIOUV	BIVOUAC	ABDDEET	DEBATED	ABDEEMY	EMBAYED
ABCIRST	CABRITS	ABDDEEZ	BEDAZED	ABDEEMZ	BEMAZED
ABCIRTY	BARYTIC	ABDDEIL	ADDIBLE	ABDEEPR	BEDRAPE
ABCISSS	ABSCISS	ABDDEIN	ABIDDEN		PREBADE
ABCJOSU	JACOBUS		BANDIED	ABDEERR	BARREED
ABCKLLY	BLACKLY	ABDDEIR	BRAIDED	ABDEERS	BEADERS
ABCKLOT	BACKLOT	ABDDEIS	BADDIES		DEBASER
ABCKMOT	TOMBACK	ABDDELN	BLANDED		SABERED
ABCKMRU	BUCKRAM	ABDDELR	BLADDER	ABDEERT	BERATED
ABCKMUZ	ZAMBUCK	ABDDELU	BLAUDED		BETREAD
ABCKNNO	BANNOCK	ABDDENR	BRANDED		DEBATER
ABCKNRU	RUNBACK	ABDDEOR	ABORDED		REBATED
ABCKNSU	SUNBACK		BOARDED		TABERED
ABCKNTU	CUTBANK		ROADBED	ABDEERW	BEWARED
ABCKORS	BAROCKS	ABDDEOY	DEADBOY	ABDEERY	BEEYARD
ABCKORY	ROCKABY	ABDDERW	BEDWARD		BERAYED
ABCKOSW	SOWBACK	ABDDEST	BADDEST	ABDEESS	DEBASES
ABCKOTU	BACKOUT	ABDDESY	DAYBEDS		SEABEDS
	OUTBACK	ABDDHIS	BADDISH	ABDEEST	BEASTED
ABCKPSU	BACKUPS	ABDDHSU	BUDDHAS		BESTEAD
ABCKRSU	BUCKRAS	ABDDIMN	MIDBAND		DEBATES
ABCKSTU	SACKBUT	ABDDINS	DISBAND	ABDEESZ	BEDAZES
	SUBTACK	ABDDLLO	ODDBALL	ABDEETT	ABETTED
ABCKSUW	BUCKSAW	ABDDMOR	DAMBROD	ABDEETX	BETAXED
	SAWBUCK	ABDEEFG	FEEDBAG	ABDEFFL	BAFFLED
ABCLLOY	CALLBOY	ABDEEFL	FEELBAD	ABDEFLT	FLATBED
ABCLMNU	CLUBMAN	ABDEEGL	BEAGLED	ABDEFLU	LEAFBUD
ABCLMOY	CYMBALO	ABDEEGR	REBADGE	ABDEFOR	FORBADE
ABCLMSY	CYMBALS	ABDEEGZ	BEGAZED	ABDEFOS	SOFABED
ABCLMUU	BACULUM	ABDEEHO	OBEAHED	ABDEFRW	BEDWARF
ABCLNOS	BLANCOS	ABDEEHS	BEHEADS	ABDEFST	BEDFAST
ABCLNOY	BALCONY	ABDEEHT	BEATHED	ABDEGGL	BLAGGED
ABCLNSU	SUBCLAN	ABDEEHV	BEHAVED	ABDEGGR	BRAGGED
ABCLOOX	COALBOX	ABDEEHW	WEBHEAD	ABDEGHI	BIGHEAD
ABCLOST	COBALTS	ABDEEIR	BEADIER	ABDEGHR	BEGHARD

ABDEGIN	BEADING	ABDEIST	BASTIDE	ABDEOOT	TABOOED
ABDEGIR	ABRIDGE	ABDEISU	SUBIDEA	ABDEORR	ARBORED
	BRIGADE	ABDEISW	BAWDIES		BOARDER
ABDEGLM	GAMBLED	ABDEJRU	ABJURED		BROADER
ABDEGLN	BANGLED	ABDEKLN	BLANKED		REBOARD
ABDEGLR	BELGARD	ABDEKLU	BAULKED	ABDEORT	ABORTED
	GARBLED	ABDEKNR	BRANKED		BORATED
ABDEGLS	BEGLADS	ABDEKNU	UNBAKED		TABORED
ABDEGNO	BONDAGE	ABDEKRS	DEBARKS	ABDEORV	BRAVOED
	DOGBANE	ABDELMP	BEDLAMP	ABDEOST	BOASTED
ABDEGOS	BODEGAS	ABDELMR	MARBLED	ABDEOTU	BOUTADE
ABDEGRS	BADGERS		RAMBLED	ABDEQSU	BASQUED
ABDEHIL	HIDABLE	ABDELMS	BEDLAMS	ABDERSS	BRASSED
ABDEHIT	HABITED		BEDLAMS		SERDABS
ABDEHLM	HAMBLED	ABDELMW	WAMBLED	ABDERST	DABSTER
ABDEHLR	HALBERD	ABDELMY	EMBAYLD		TABERDS
ABDEHOW	BOWHEAD	ABDELNR	BLANDER	ABDERSU	DAUBERS
ABDEHRS	BERDASH	ABDELNU	UNBALED		EARBUDS
	BRASHED	ABDELOR	LABORED		SUBEDAR
ABDEHRT	BREADTH	ABDELOS	ALBEDOS	ABDERSV	ADVERBS
ABDEHSU	SUBHEAD	ABDELOT	BLOATED	ABDERSY	REDBAYS
ABDEIIL	ALIBIED		LOBATED	ABDERTY	DRYBEAT
ABDEIKT	BATIKED	ABDELOW	DOWABLE	ABDERUY	DAUBERY
ABDEILP	BIPEDAL	ABDELPU	DUPABLE	ABDETTU	ABUTTED
	PIEBALD	ABDELPY	PYEBALD	ABDFIRT	FATBIRD
ABDEILR	BALDIER	ABDELRR	DRABLER	ABDGGIN	BADGING
	BEDRAIL	ABDELRS	BEDRALS	ABDGGOR	BOGGARD
	BLADIER		BLADERS	ABDGIIN	ABIDING
	BRAILED	ABDELRT	BLARTED	ABDGILN	BALDING
	RAILBED	ABDELRU	DURABLE		BLADING
	RIDABLE	ABDELRW	BRAWLED	ABDGINN	BANDING
ABDEILS	BALDIES		WARBLED	ABDGINO	ABODING
	DIABLES	ABDELRY	DRYABLE	ABDGINR	BARDING
	DISABLE	ABDELST	BALDEST		BRIGAND
ABDEILT	LIBATED		BLASTED	ABDGINT	DINGBAT
ABDEILU	AUDIBLE		STABLED	ABDGINU	DAUBING
ABDEILY	BEADILY	ABDELSU	BELAUDS	ABDGINW	WINDBAG
ABDEIMO	AMEBOID	ABDELTT	BATTLED	ABDGIRT	DIRTBAG
ABDEIMR	EMBRAID		BLATTED	ABDGLNO	BOGLAND
ABDEIMS	IMBASED	ABDELTU	ABLUTED	ABDGLUY	LADYBUG
ABDEINR	BANDIER	ABDEMMO	MAMBOED	ABDGNOS	BANDOGS
	BRAINED	ABDEMNO	ABDOMEN	ABDGORS	BODRAGS
ABDEINS	BANDIES	ABDEMNS	BEDAMNS	ABDHHOS	DOBHASH
	BASINED	ABDEMRU	RUMBAED	ABDHIIT	ADHIBIT
ABDEINW	BEDAWIN	ABDENNR	BRANNED	ABDHILS	BALDISH
ABDEIRR	BARDIER	ABDENOR	BANDORE	ABDHJNO	HANDJOB
	BRAIDER		BROADEN	ABDHMOR	RHABDOM
	BRIARED	ABDENOT	BATONED	ABDHMSU	BUDMASH
	RABIDER	ABDENOY	NAEBODY	ABDHMTU	MUDBATH
ABDEIRS	ABIDERS	ABDENPS	BEDPANS	ABDHNOR	BODHRAN
	BARDIES	ABDENRR	BRANDER	ABDHNSU	HUSBAND
	BRAISED		REBRAND	ABDHOSY	HOBDAYS
	DARBIES	ABDENRS	BANDERS	ABDHRSU	BURDASH
	SEABIRD	ABDENRT	BARTEND		RHABDUS
	SIDEBAR	ABDENRU	UNBARED	ABDIINO	ANOBIID
ABDEIRT	REDBAIT	ABDENRW	BRAWNED	ABDIJRY	JAYBIRD
	TRIBADE	ABDENSS	BADNESS	ABDIKNW	BAWDKIN
ABDEIRU	DAUBIER	ABDENSU	SUBDEAN	ABDIKRS	DISBARK
ABDEIRW	BAWDIER		UNBASED	ABDILMO	BIMODAL
ABDEIRX	AXEBIRD	ABDENSY	BENDAYS	ABDILOO	DIABOLO
ABDEISS	BIASSED	ABDENTU	UNBATED	ABDILOR	LABROID

ABDILOT	TABLOID	**ABDRSTU**	BUSTARD		PREBAKE
ABDILRS	BRIDALS	**ABDRUZZ**	BUZZARD	**ABEEKPS**	BESPAKE
	LABRIDS	**ABEEEGR**	BEERAGE		BESPEAK
	RIBALDS	**ABEEELS**	SEEABLE	**ABEEKRR**	BREAKER
ABDILRW	AWLBIRD	**ABEEELY**	EYEABLE	**ABEEKRS**	BEAKERS
ABDILRY	RABIDLY	**ABEEEMY**	EYEBEAM		BERAKES
ABDILUY	AUDIBLY	**ABEEERV**	BEREAVE	**ABEEKST**	BETAKES
ABDILWY	BAWDILY	**ABEEFFL**	EFFABLE	**ABEELLR**	LABELER
ABDIMNR	BIRDMAN	**ABEEFLM**	FLAMBEE		RELABEL
ABDIMOR	AMBROID	**ABEEFLO**	BEEFALO	**ABEELLY**	EYEBALL
ABDIMRS	BARDISM	**ABEEFLS**	BEFLEAS	**ABEELMM**	EMBLEMA
ABDIMRY	MAYBIRD	**ABEEFTU**	BEAUFET	**ABEELMS**	EMBALES
ABDINOR	INBOARD	**ABEEGGS**	GEEBAGS	**ABEELMT**	BEAMLET
ABDINOT	BANDITO	**ABEEGHR**	HERBAGE	**ABEELMZ**	EMBLAZE
ABDINRS	RIBANDS	**ABEEGHS**	BEEGAHS	**ABEELNP**	PLEBEAN
ABDINRT	ANTBIRD		BHAGEES	**ABEELNR**	ENABLER
ABDINRU	UNBRAID	**ABEEGLL**	GABELLE	**ABEELNS**	BALEENS
ABDINST	BANDITS		GELABLE		ENABLES
ABDIOSU	BADIOUS	**ABEEGLR**	BEAGLER	**ABEELNT**	TENABLE
ABDIPRU	UPBRAID	**ABEEGLS**	BEAGLES	**ABEELNU**	NEBULAE
ABDIRRS	BRAIRDS	**ABEEGLT**	GETABLE	**ABEELOR**	EARLOBE
	BRIARDS	**ABEEGNR**	REBEGAN	**ABEELPR**	BEPEARL
ABDIRRW	WARBIRD	**ABEEGPW**	WEBPAGE	**ABEELPS**	BELEAPS
ABDIRSS	DISBARS	**ABEEGRR**	GERBERA	**ABEELPT**	BELEAPT
ABDIRSU	RIBAUDS	**ABEEGRS**	ABREGES	**ABEELQU**	EQUABLE
	SUBARID		BAREGES	**ABEELRR**	BLEARER
ABDIRTY	TRIBADY		BARGEES		ERRABLE
			BARGEES	**ABEELRT**	BLEATER
ABDKNOO	BANDOOK	**ABEEGRU**	AUBERGE		RETABLE
ABDKOOY	DAYBOOK	**ABEEGRW**	BREWAGE		
ABDLLNY	BLANDLY	**ABEEGSZ**	BEGAZES	**ABEELRY**	BELAYER
ABDLLOR	BOLLARD	**ABEEHJS**	BHAJEES	**ABEELST**	BELATES
ABDLNOR	BANDROL	**ABEEHLR**	HEELBAR	**ABEELSU**	SUEABLE
ABDLORY	BROADLY	**ABEEHLW**	HEWABLE		USEABLE
ABDLOSU	BUSLOAD	**ABEEHMS**	BESHAME	**ABEELSV**	BESLAVE
ABDLOYY	LADYBOY	**ABEEHMT**	EMBATHE	**ABEELSW**	SEWABLE
ABDLRUY	DURABLY	**ABEEHNN**	HENBANE	**ABEEMNS**	BASEMEN
ABDLRYY	BYRLADY	**ABEEHNS**	BANSHEE		BEMEANS
ABDLSUU	SUBDUAL		BEENAHS		BENAMES
ABDMNNO	BONDMAN		SHEBEAN	**ABEEMNT**	BEMEANT
ABDMRUY	MARYBUD	**ABEEHNT**	BENEATH	**ABEEMRS**	AMBEERS
ABDNOOR	BRADOON	**ABEEHRT**	BREATHE		BEAMERS
	ONBOARD	**ABEEHRV**	BEHAVER		BESMEAR
ABDNOPR	PROBAND	**ABEEHSV**	BEHAVES	**ABEEMRV**	EMBRAVE
ABDNORS	ROBANDS	**ABEEHTY**	EYEBATH	**ABEEMSS**	EMBASES
ABDNOSU	ABOUNDS	**ABEEIKR**	BEAKIER	**ABEEMST**	EMBASTE
	BAUSOND	**ABEEILS**	BAILEES	**ABEENNW**	BAWNEEN
ABDNOSX	SANDBOX	**ABEEIMR**	BEAMIER	**ABEENRV**	VERBENA
ABDNOSY	SANDBOY	**ABEEINS**	BEANIES	**ABEENRY**	BEANERY
ABDNOYY	ANYBODY	**ABEEINT**	BETAINE	**ABEEORS**	AEROBES
ABDNRSU	SANDBUR	**ABEEIRT**	BEATIER	**ABEEORT**	ABORTEE
ABDNRTU	TURBAND		EBRIATE	**ABEEPST**	BESPATE
ABDNSTY	STANDBY	**ABEEIST**	BEASTIE	**ABEERRS**	BEARERS
ABDOORW	BARWOOD	**ABEEJMS**	JAMBEES		BREARES
ABDOOWY	BAYWOOD	**ABEEJRS**	BAJREES	**ABEERRT**	REBATER
ABDORRS	BORDARS	**ABEEKLR**	BLEAKER		TABRERE
ABDORSS	ADSORBS	**ABEEKLS**	KABELES		TEREBRA
ABDORSY	BOYARDS	**ABEEKNT**	BETAKEN	**ABEERST**	BEATERS
	BYROADS	**ABEEKNV**	BEKNAVE		BERATES
ABDOSYY	DAYBOYS	**ABEEKNY**	EYEBANK		REBATES
ABDRRSU	DURBARS	**ABEEKOP**	PEEKABO	**ABEERSV**	BEAVERS
ABDRSSU	ABSURDS	**ABEEKPR**	BARKEEP	**ABEERSW**	BEWARES

ABEERSY	EBAYERS	**ABEGINO**	BEGONIA	**ABEHLNT**	BENTHAL
	EYEBARS	**ABEGINR**	BEARING	**ABEHLNU**	UNHABLE
ABEERSZ	ZEREBAS	**ABEGINS**	SABEING	**ABEHLRS**	HERBALS
ABEERTT	ABETTER	**ABEGINT**	BEATING	**ABEHLRT**	BLATHER
	BERETTA	**ABEGINY**	ABYEING		HALBERT
ABEERVY	BEAVERY		EBAYING	**ABEHLSS**	BLASHES
ABEERWY	BEWEARY	**ABEGIPP**	BAGPIPE	**ABEHMNO**	HAMBONE
ABEESST	SEBATES	**ABEGKLU**	BULKAGE	**ABEHNOS**	HEBONAS
ABEESWX	BEESWAX	**ABEGKOR**	BROKAGE	**ABEHNRY**	ABHENRY
ABEETXY	EXABYTE	**ABEGKOS**	BOSKAGE	**ABEHRRS**	BRASHER
ABEFFIS	BAFFIES	**ABEGLLS**	BEGALLS		HERBARS
ABEFFKO	BAKEOFF	**ABEGLMR**	GAMBLER	**ABEHRRY**	HERBARY
ABEFFLR	BAFFLER		GAMBREL	**ABEHRSS**	BASHERS
ABEFFLS	BAFFLES	**ABEGLMS**	GAMBLES		BRASHES
ABEFFOT	OFFBEAT	**ABEGLNR**	BRANGLE	**ABEHRST**	BATHERS
ABEFGIL	FILABEG	**ABEGLNS**	BANGLES		BERTHAS
ABEFGLS	BEFLAGS	**ABEGLOR**	ALBERGO		BREATHS
ABEFGST	GABFEST	**ABEGLOT**	GLOBATE	**ABEHRTY**	BREATHY
ABEFILN	FINABLE	**ABEGLRR**	GARBLER	**ABEIILL**	BAILLIE
ABEFILR	FRIABLE	**ABEGLRS**	GARBLES	**ABEIILS**	ALIBIES
ABEFILS	FAIBLES	**ABEGLRU**	BLAGUER		BAILIES
ABEFILU	FIBULAE	**ABEGLSS**	BAGLESS		BIALIES
ABEFILX	FIXABLE	**ABEGLST**	GABLETS	**ABEIINN**	BIENNIA
ABEFINU	BEAUFIN	**ABEGLSU**	BELUGAS	**ABEIINT**	BAINITE
ABEFIRT	BAREFIT		BLAGUES	**ABEIJMR**	JAMBIER
	FIBRATE	**ABEGMOR**	EMBARGO	**ABEIJNS**	BASENJI
ABEFITY	BEATIFY	**ABEGMOS**	GAMBOES	**ABEIKKS**	BAKKIES
ABEFLLS	BEFALLS	**ABEGMRU**	UMBRAGE	**ABEIKLL**	LIKABLE
ABEFLLU	BALEFUL	**ABEGMST**	GAMBETS	**ABEIKLR**	BALKIER
ABEFLLY	FLYABLE	**ABEGNNT**	BANTENG	**ABEIKLS**	SKIABLE
ABEFLMS	FLAMBES	**ABEGNOR**	BEGROAN	**ABEIKLT**	BATLIKE
ABEFLNU	BANEFUL	**ABEGNOS**	NOSEBAG	**ABEIKNR**	INBREAK
ABEFLNY	FLYBANE	**ABEGNRS**	BANGERS	**ABEIKNT**	BEATNIK
ABEFLRS	FABLERS		GRABENS	**ABEIKRR**	BARKIER
ABEFLRY	FRYABLE	**ABEGNSW**	BEGNAWS		BRAKIER
ABEFMOS	BEFOAMS	**ABEGOPY**	PAGEBOY	**ABEIKWY**	BIKEWAY
ABEFMRS	FERBAMS	**ABEGORR**	BEGORRA	**ABEILLN**	LINABLE
ABEFORR	FORBARE	**ABEGORS**	BORAGES	**ABEILLO**	LOBELIA
	FORBEAR	**ABEGORX**	GEARBOX	**ABEILLP**	PLIABLE
ABEFORX	FAREBOX	**ABEGOSZ**	GAZEBOS	**ABEILLR**	BRAILLE
ABEFORY	FOREBAY	**ABEGOTT**	BOTTEGA		LIBERAL
ABEFPRS	PREFABS	**ABEGOUY**	BUOYAGE	**ABEILLS**	BALLIES
ABEGGIR	BAGGIER	**ABEGRRU**	GARBURE	**ABEILLV**	LIVABLE
ABEGGIS	BAGGIES	**ABEGRST**	BARGEST	**ABEILMN**	MINABLE
ABEGGLR	BLAGGER	**ABEGSTU**	BAGUETS	**ABEILMR**	BALMIER
ABEGGMO	GAMBOGE		TUBAGES		LAMBIER
ABEGGNU	BUGGANE				MIRABLE
ABEGGRR	BRAGGER	**ABEHILR**	HIRABLE		REMBLAI
ABEGGRS	BAGGERS	**ABEHIMO**	BOHEMIA	**ABEILMS**	ABLEISM
	BEGGARS	**ABEHIMS**	BEAMISH		EMBAILS
ABEGGRU	BURGAGE	**ABEHIMT**	IMBATHE		LAMBIES
ABEGGRY	BEGGARY	**ABEHINS**	BANSHIE	**ABEILMT**	BIMETAL
ABEGHNS	SHEBANG	**ABEHIRS**	BEARISH		LIMBATE
ABEGHOR	BEGORAH	**ABEHISU**	BEAUISH		TIMBALE
ABEGHRU	BEARHUG	**ABEHITU**	HABITUE	**ABEILMU**	BUMELIA
ABEGIKL	BAGLIKE	**ABEHITZ**	ZABTIEH	**ABEILMW**	WEBMAIL
ABEGILV	GIVABLE	**ABEHKLS**	KEBLAHS	**ABEILMX**	MIXABLE
ABEGIMN	BEAMING	**ABEHKNT**	BETHANK	**ABEILMY**	BEAMILY
ABEGIMR	GAMBIER	**ABEHKRU**	HAUBERK	**ABEILMZ**	IMBLAZE
ABEGIMT	MEGABIT	**ABEHKTU**	KETUBAH	**ABEILNP**	BIPLANE
ABEGINN	BEANING	**ABEHLMS**	HAMBLES	**ABEILNS**	LESBIAN
			SHAMBLE		

ABEILOS	OBELIAS		BRASSIE	ABELLRU	RUBELLA
ABEILPT	PATIBLE	ABEIRST	BAITERS		RULABLE
ABEILRS	BAILERS		BARITES	ABELLST	BALLETS
ABEILRT	LIBRATE		REBAITS	ABELLTU	BALLUTE
	TABLIER		TERBIAS		BULLATE
	TRIABLE	ABEIRSX	BRAXIES	ABELMMR	MEMBRAL
ABEILRW	BRAWLIE	ABEIRSZ	BRAIZES	ABELMMS	EMBALMS
	WIRABLE		ZERIBAS	ABELMNT	BELTMAN
ABEILRY	BILAYER	ABEIRTT	BATTIER		LAMBENT
ABEILSS	ABSEILS		BIRETTA	ABELMNU	ALBUMEN
	BALISES		RATBITE	ABELMOV	MOVABLE
	ISABELS	ABEIRTV	VIBRATE	ABELMRR	MARBLER
	LABISES	ABEIRUX	EXURBIA		RAMBLER
ABEILST	ABLEIST	ABEISSS	BIASSES	ABELMRS	AMBLERS
	ALBITES	ABEISTT	BATISTE		BLAMERS
	ASTILBE		BATTIES		LAMBERS
	BASTILE		BISTATE		MARBLES
	BESTIAL	ABEISTW	BAWTIES		RAMBLES
	BLASTIE	ABEISUV	ABUSIVE	ABELMRT	LAMBERT
	LIBATES	ABEITUX	BAUXITE	ABELMSU	BEMAULS
	STABILE	ABEJLUY	BLUEJAY	ABELMSW	WAMBLES
ABEILSW	BEWAILS	ABEJMNO	JAMBONE	ABELMTU	MUTABLE
ABEILSY	BAILEYS		JOBNAME	ABELNOS	BONSELA
ABEILSZ	SIZABLE	ABEJMNS	ENJAMBS	ABELNOT	NOTABLE
ABEILVV	BIVALVE	ABEJMRS	JAMBERS	ABELNOW	OWNABLE
ABEIMNP	PEMBINA	ABEJMUX	JAMBEUX	ABELNOY	BALONEY
ABEIMNR	MIRBANE	ABEJNOS	BANJOES	ABELNRS	BRANLES
ABEIMNT	AMBIENT	ABEJNOW	JAWBONE		BRANSLE
ABEIMRR	BARMIER	ABEJNST	BEJANTS	ABELNRT	BRANTLE
ABEIMRS	AMBRIES	ABEJORS	JERBOAS	ABELNRU	NEBULAR
ABEIMSS	IMBASES	ABEJRRU	ABJURER	ABELNRY	BLARNEY
ABEIMSU	MAUBIES	ABEJRSU	ABJURES	ABELNSU	NEBULAS
ABEINOT	NIOBATE	ABEKKKU	BUKKAKE		UNBALES
ABEINPT	BEPAINT	ABEKLLY	BLEAKLY	ABELNSY	BYLANES
ABEINRR	BARNIER	ABEKLMS	KEMBLAS	ABELNSZ	BENZALS
ABEINRT	ATEBRIN	ABEKLNR	BLANKER	ABELNTU	ABLUENT
ABEINRW	WEBINAR	ABEKLNT	BLANKET		TUNABLE
ABEINRZ	ZEBRINA	ABEKLOP	POKABLE	ABELNTY	TENABLY
ABEINSS	SABINES	ABEKLRS	BALKERS	ABELOPR	ROPABLE
ABEINST	BANTIES	ABEKLRU	BAULKER	ABELOPS	POSABLE
	BASINET	ABEKMNS	EMBANKS	ABELOPT	POTABLE
	BESAINT	ABEKMRS	EMBARKS	ABELORR	LABORER
	BESTAIN	ABEKMSU	SAMBUKE	ABELORS	LABROSE
ABEINTT	TABINET	ABEKNRS	BANKERS	ABELORT	BLOATER
ABEIORS	ISOBARE		BARKENS	ABELORU	RUBEOLA
ABEIOSS	ABIOSES	ABEKNRU	UNBRAKE	ABELORW	ROWABLE
	ISOBASE	ABEKNST	BANKETS	ABELOSS	BOLASES
ABEIOST	BOATIES	ABEKNSU	SUNBAKE	ABELOST	BOATELS
ABEIOTV	OBVIATE	ABEKOOR	ABROOKE		OBLATES
ABEIPST	BAPTISE	ABEKOTU	OUTBAKE	ABELOSV	ABSOLVE
ABEIPTZ	BAPTIZE	ABEKPRU	BREAKUP	ABELOSW	SOWABLE
ABEIRRR	BARRIER		UPBREAK	ABELOTT	TOTABLE
ABEIRRS	BARRIES	ABEKRRS	BARKERS	ABELOTV	VOTABLE
	BRASIER	ABEKSST	BASKETS	ABELOTW	TEABOWL
ABEIRRT	ARBITER	ABELLMN	BELLMAN		TOWABLE
	RAREBIT	ABELLMS	EMBALLS	ABELPRU	PUBERAL
ABEIRRW	WARBIER	ABELLNT	NETBALL	ABELPTY	TYPABLE
ABEIRRZ	BIZARRE	ABELLOS	LOSABLE	ABELQUY	EQUABLY
	BRAZIER	ABELLOV	LOVABLE	ABELRRS	BARRELS
ABEIRSS	BASSIER		VOLABLE	ABELRRW	BRAWLER
	BRAISES	ABELLRS	BALLERS		WARBLER

ABELRSS	BARLESS	**ABENPSU**	SUBPENA	BRASSET
	BRALESS	**ABENQTU**	BANQUET	BREASTS
ABELRST	ALBERTS	**ABENRRS**	BARRENS	**ABERSSU**	ABUSERS
	BATLERS	**ABENRRU**	URBANER		BUSERAS
	BLASTER	**ABENRST**	BANTERS		RUBASSE
	LABRETS		BARNETS		SURBASE
	STABLER	**ABENRSU**	UNBARES	**ABERSSZ**	ZEBRASS
ABELRSV	VERBALS		UNBEARS	**ABERSTT**	BATTERS
ABELRSW	BAWLERS	**ABENRSY**	BARNEYS		TABRETS
	WARBLES	**ABENRSZ**	BRAZENS	**ABERSTU**	ARBUTES
ABELRSY	BARLEYS	**ABENRUX**	EXURBAN		BURSATE
ABELRSZ	BLAZERS	**ABENSST**	ABSENTS		SURBATE
ABELRTT	BATTLER		BASNETS	**ABERSTV**	BRAVEST
	BLATTER	**ABENSTT**	BATTENS	**ABERSTW**	BRAWEST
	BRATTLE	**ABENSTU**	BUTANES		WABSTER
ABELRTW	BLEWART		SUNBEAT	**ABERSTX**	BAXTERS
ABELRUZ	ZEBRULA	**ABENSTZ**	BEZANTS	**ABERSTY**	BARYTES
ABELRVY	BRAVELY	**ABENTZZ**	BEZZANT		BETRAYS
ABELSST	BASTLES	**ABEOORT**	AEROBOT	**ABERSUU**	BUREAUS
	STABLES	**ABEOOST**	SEABOOT	**ABERSWY**	BEWRAYS
ABELSSU	SUBSALE	**ABEOOTV**	OBOVATE	**ABERTTU**	ABUTTER
ABELSTT	BATLETS	**ABEOPRS**	SAPROBE	**ABERTTY**	BATTERY
	BATTELS	**ABEOPRT**	PROBATE	**ABERUUX**	BUREAUX
	BATTLES	**ABEOQRU**	BAROQUE	**ABESSST**	BASSEST
	BLATEST	**ABEORRS**	ARBORES		BASSETS
	TABLETS		BRASERO	**ABESSSY**	ABYSSES
ABELSTU	SUBLATE	**ABEORRT**	ABORTER	**ABESSTT**	BASSETT
ABELSTY	BAETYLS		ARBORET	**ABESTTU**	BATTUES
	BEASTLY		TABORER	**ABEZZZZ**	BEZZAZZ
ABELSUY	USEABLY	**ABEORST**	BOASTER	**ABFFGIN**	BAFFING
ABELSWY	BAWLEYS		BOATERS	**ABFFIIL**	BAILIFF
	BYELAWS		BORATES	**ABFFINO**	BANOFFI
ABELTWY	BELTWAY		REBATOS	**ABFFLOO**	BOFFOLA
ABEMMOS	MAMBOES		SORBATE	**ABFFLOU**	BUFFALO
ABEMMRS	BAMMERS	**ABEORSV**	BRAVOES	**ABFGILN**	FABLING
ABEMNOS	AMBONES	**ABEORSX**	BORAXES	**ABFGINR**	BARFING
	BEMOANS	**ABEORSY**	ROSEBAY	**ABFGLSU**	BAGFULS
ABEMNOT	BOATMEN	**ABEORSZ**	BEZOARS		BAGSFUL
ABEMNRY	BYREMAN	**ABEORTT**	ABETTOR	**ABFGOOT**	FOOTBAG
	MYRBANE		BATTERO	**ABFHIST**	BATFISH
ABEMNST	BATSMEN		TABORET		BIFTAHS
ABEMNSU	SUNBEAM	**ABEOSTV**	BOVATES	**ABFHLSU**	BASHFUL
ABEMNSY	BYNAMES	**ABEPRSU**	UPBEARS	**ABFIILR**	BIFILAR
ABEMORT	BROMATE	**ABEPRSW**	BEWRAPS	**ABFIIMR**	FIMBRIA
ABEMOTU	OUTBEAM	**ABEPRTW**	BEWRAPT	**ABFILRU**	FIBULAR
ABEMRST	TAMBERS	**ABEPRTY**	TYPEBAR	**ABFILSU**	FIBULAS
ABEMRSW	BESWARM	**ABEPSTU**	UPBEATS	**ABFIMOR**	FIBROMA
ABEMSSY	EMBASSY	**ABEQRSU**	BARQUES	**ABFLLSU**	FUSBALL
ABENNOR	BARONNE	**ABEQSSU**	BASQUES	**ABFLOTU**	BOATFUL
ABENNOS	NANOBES	**ABERRST**	BARRETS	**ABFLOTW**	BATFOWL
ABENNRR	BRANNER		BARTERS	**ABFLOTY**	FLYBOAT
ABENNRS	BANNERS	**ABERRSU**	BURSERA	**ABFNOSY**	FANBOYS
ABENNST	BANNETS		SABREUR	**ABFNSSU**	FANSUBS
ABENORS	BORANES	**ABERRSV**	BRAVERS	**ABFOORT**	FOOTBAR
ABENORT	BARONET	**ABERRSY**	BRAYERS	**ABFOOTY**	FOYBOAT
	REBOANT	**ABERRSZ**	BRAZERS	**ABFSTTU**	TUBFAST
ABENORW	RAWBONE	**ABERRUV**	BRAVURE	**ABGGGIN**	BAGGING
ABENORZ	ZEBRANO	**ABERRVY**	BRAVERY	**ABGGIIT**	GIGABIT
ABENOST	ONBEATS	**ABERSSS**	BRASSES	**ABGGILN**	GABLING
ABENOSY	SOYBEAN	**ABERSST**	BASTERS	**ABGGILY**	BAGGILY
ABENOTY	BAYONET		BESTARS	**ABGGINN**	BANGING

ABGGINR	BARGING	**ABGINRS**	SABRING	**ABHILTU**	HALIBUT
	GARBING	**ABGINRV**	BRAVING	**ABHIMNR**	BRAHMIN
ABGGIST	BAGGITS	**ABGINRY**	BRAYING	**ABHIMRS**	MIHRABS
ABGGISW	BAGWIGS	**ABGINRZ**	BRAZING	**ABHIMSZ**	MAZHBIS
ABGGNOS	GOBANGS	**ABGINSS**	BASSING	**ABHINST**	ABSINTH
ABGGNSU	BUGGANS	**ABGINST**	BASTING	**ABHIOOS**	BOOHAIS
ABGGORT	BOGGART	**ABGINSU**	ABUSING	**ABHIOPS**	PHOBIAS
ABGHHSU	HAGBUSH	**ABGINTT**	BATTING	**ABHIORS**	BOARISH
ABGHILN	BLAHING	**ABGINTU**	ANTIBUG	**ABHIORT**	BOTHRIA
ABGHINS	BASHING		TABUING	**ABHIOST**	ISOBATH
ABGHINT	BATHING	**ABGINTW**	BATWING	**ABHIOSU**	HAUBOIS
ABGHLOT	HAGBOLT	**ABGINTY**	BAYTING	**ABHISST**	TASBIHS
ABGHLRU	BURGHAL	**ABGIOPT**	PIGBOAT	**ABHISTU**	HABITUS
ABGHMOO	GOOMBAH	**ABGIOSU**	BAGUIOS	**ABHKLSY**	BASHLYK
ABGHMRU	HAMBURG	**ABGKKNO**	BANGKOK	**ABHKORU**	BOURKHA
ABGHNOR	HAGBORN	**ABGKNOS**	KOBANGS	**ABHKRSU**	BURKHAS
	HORNBAG	**ABGKOOS**	BOGOAKS		KURBASH
ABGHOTU	ABOUGHT	**ABGKORW**	WORKBAG	**ABHLMSY**	SHAMBLY
ABGHSSU	BUGSHAS	**ABGLLMU**	GUMBALL	**ABHLOUX**	BOXHAUL
ABGHSTU	HAGBUTS	**ABGLMNU**	LUMBANG	**ABHLRSY**	BRASHLY
ABGIILN	BAILING	**ABGLMOS**	GAMBOLS	**ABHLRTU**	HURLBAT
ABGIINS	BIASING	**ABGLMOU**	LUMBAGO	**ABHMNOS**	BONHAMS
ABGIINT	BAITING	**ABGLMSY**	GYMBALS	**ABHMNSU**	BUSHMAN
ABGIINZ	BAIZING	**ABGLNOO**	BOLOGNA	**ABHMRSU**	RHUMBAS
ABGIJMN	JAMBING	**ABGLOOT**	TOOLBAG		SAMBHUR
ABGIJOO	JIGABOO	**ABGLORS**	BROLGAS	**ABHMSUY**	MAYBUSH
ABGIKLN	BALKING	**ABGLORT**	RAGBOLT	**ABHNOOS**	BHOONAS
ABGIKNN	BANKING	**ABGLOSU**	ALBUGOS	**ABHNOST**	BOTHANS
ABGIKNO	BOAKING		SUBGOAL	**ABHNSTU**	SUNBATH
ABGIKNR	BARKING			**ABHOPRS**	BARHOPS
	BRAKING	**ABGLRRU**	BURGLAR	**ABHORRS**	HARBORS
ABGIKNS	BAKINGS	**ABGMNOY**	BOGYMAN	**ABHORRU**	HARBOUR
	BASKING	**ABGMOOY**	GOOMBAY	**ABHOTUY**	HAUTBOY
ABGIKNU	BAUKING	**ABGMORW**	BAGWORM	**ABHPSTY**	BYPATHS
ABGIKST	KITBAGS	**ABGNOOR**	BARGOON	**ABHQSSU**	BUQSHAS
ABGILLN	BALLING	**ABGNOOS**	BOONGAS	**ABHRSTU**	TARBUSH
ABGILMN	AMBLING		GABOONS	**ABHSSUW**	BUSHWAS
	BALMING	**ABGNOPR**	PROBANG	**ABHSTUW**	WASHTUB
	BLAMING	**ABGNORS**	BARONGS	**ABIIINR**	BIRIANI
	LAMBING		BROGANS	**ABIIKKS**	KABIKIS
ABGILMS	GIMBALS	**ABGNOTU**	GUNBOAT	**ABIIKKT**	KIBITKA
ABGILNR	BLARING	**ABGNOWY**	BOWYANG	**ABIILLS**	BAILLIS
ABGILNS	ABLINGS	**ABGOORT**	BOTARGO	**ABIILMN**	MINILAB
	SABLING	**ABGOPST**	POSTBAG	**ABIILMU**	BULIMIA
ABGILNT	TABLING	**ABGORRU**	GOBURRA	**ABIILNQ**	INQILAB
ABGILNW	BAWLING	**ABGORST**	BOGARTS	**ABIILNS**	AIBLINS
	BLAWING	**ABGORTU**	OUTBRAG		BILIANS
ABGILNZ	BLAZING	**ABGOTTU**	TUGBOAT	**ABIILOV**	BOLIVIA
ABGILOR	GARBOIL	**ABGSSTU**	SAGBUTS	**ABIILRY**	BILIARY
ABGILRT	BATGIRL	**ABHHISS**	SHIBAHS	**ABIILST**	STIBIAL
ABGIMMN	BAMMING	**ABHHJSU**	JUBHAHS	**ABIILTY**	ABILITY
ABGIMRS	GAMBIRS	**ABHHKOT**	KHOTBAH	**ABIIMNR**	MINIBAR
ABGIMST	GAMBIST	**ABHHKTU**	KHUTBAH	**ABIIMSS**	MISBIAS
	GAMBITS	**ABHHSUW**	BUSHWAH	**ABIIMST**	IAMBIST
ABGINNN	BANNING	**ABHHSUY**	HUSHABY	**ABIINNS**	BAININS
ABGINNR	BARNING	**ABHIINT**	INHABIT	**ABIINOR**	ROBINIA
ABGINNT	BANTING	**ABHIKLS**	BASHLIK	**ABIINRY**	BIRYANI
ABGINOS	BAGNIOS		KIBLAHS	**ABIIOSS**	ABIOSIS
	GABIONS	**ABHIKST**	BHAKTIS	**ABIJLNR**	BRINJAL
ABGINOT	BOATING	**ABHIKTW**	HAWKBIT	**ABIJNOT**	ABJOINT
ABGINRR	BARRING	**ABHILNO**	HOBNAIL	**ABIJRSU**	JABIRUS
		ABHILOS	ABOLISH		

ABIKKSU	KABUKIS	**ABIMTTY**	AMBITTY	**ABLLOVY**	LOVABLY
ABIKLLY	BALKILY	**ABINNSU**	BUNNIAS	**ABLLPSU**	BALLUPS
	LIKABLY	**ABINOOR**	BORONIA	**ABLLRUY**	BULLARY
ABIKLMN	LAMBKIN	**ABINOOT**	BONIATO	**ABLMMOU**	BUMMALO
ABIKLOR	KILOBAR	**ABINORT**	TABORIN	**ABLMNOU**	UMBONAL
ABIKLOS	KOLBASI	**ABINORW**	RAINBOW	**ABLMOOT**	TOMBOLA
ABIKMNR	BARMKIN	**ABINOSS**	BASIONS	**ABLMOPS**	APLOMBS
ABIKMRS	IMBARKS	**ABINOST**	BASTION	**ABLMORS**	BROMALS
ABIKNST	BANKITS		BONITAS	**ABLMOSY**	LAMBOYS
ABIKOUZ	BAZOUKI		OBTAINS	**ABLMOVY**	MOVABLY
ABIKRST	BRITSKA	**ABINOSU**	ABUSION	**ABLMPSU**	PABLUMS
ABIKRTZ	BRITZKA	**ABINRST**	BRISANT	**ABLMPUU**	PABULUM
ABIKSTT	BATTIKS	**ABINRTV**	VIBRANT	**ABLMRSU**	LABRUMS
ABIKUUZ	BUZUKIA	**ABIOORR**	ARBORIO		LUMBARS
ABILLMN	BILLMAN	**ABIORRS**	BARRIOS	**ABLMSTY**	TYMBALS
ABILLMU	BALLIUM	**ABIORRZ**	BIZARRO	**ABLMTUY**	MUTABLY
ABILLMY	BALMILY	**ABIORSS**	ISOBARS	**ABLNOOP**	POBLANO
ABILLNP	PINBALL	**ABIORST**	ORBITAS	**ABLNOSZ**	BLAZONS
ABILLPY	PLIABLY	**ABIORTV**	VIBRATO	**ABLNOTU**	BUTANOL
ABILLSW	SAWBILL	**ABIPRTY**	BIPARTY	**ABLNOTY**	NOTABLY
ABILLSY	SYLLABI	**ABIPSTT**	BAPTIST	**ABLNRSU**	SLURBAN
ABILLTT	BATTILL	**ABIRSTU**	ABITURS	**ABLNSTU**	BUNTALS
ABILLWX	WAXBILL	**ABIRTTY**	TRAYBIT		TULBANS
ABILLWY	WAYBILL	**ABISSST**	BASSIST	**ABLNTUY**	TUNABLY
ABILMMS	IMBALMS	**ABISTTU**	TUBAIST	**ABLOORS**	BAROLOS
ABILMNU	ALBUMIN	**ABJJOOS**	JOJOBAS		ROBALOS
ABILMOX	MAILBOX	**ABJKMOS**	JAMBOKS	**ABLOORT**	TOOLBAR
ABILMRT	TIMBRAL		SJAMBOK	**ABLOORY**	OBOLARY
ABILMST	TIMBALS	**ABJLMOO**	JAMBOOL	**ABLOPYY**	PLAYBOY
ABILNOS	ALBINOS	**ABJLMSU**	JAMBULS	**ABLORST**	BORSTAL
ABILNOT	BITONAL		JUMBALS	**ABLORSU**	LABOURS
ABILNOZ	BIZONAL	**ABJOSZZ**	JAZZBOS		SUBORAL
ABILNRY	BAIRNLY	**ABKLLNY**	BLANKLY	**ABLORSW**	BARLOWS
ABILOPR	BIPOLAR	**ABKLOOW**	LAWBOOK	**ABLORTW**	BLAWORT
	PARBOIL	**ABKLORT**	BLOKART	**ABLORUW**	BOURLAW
ABILORS	BAILORS	**ABKLOTX**	TALKBOX	**ABLOSST**	OBLASTS
ABILORT	ORBITAL	**ABKLRUW**	BULWARK	**ABLOSTT**	TALBOTS
ABILORV	BOLIVAR	**ABKLSSY**	SKYLABS	**ABLOSTV**	ABVOLTS
ABILOST	OBLASTI	**ABKLSTY**	BYTALKS	**ABLOSTX**	SALTBOX
ABILOTU	BAILOUT	**ABKMNOO**	BOOKMAN	**ABLOSUV**	SUBOVAL
	OBITUAL	**ABKMOST**	TOMBAKS	**ABLOTUW**	OUTBAWL
	TABOULI	**ABKMSUZ**	ZAMBUKS	**ABLPRSU**	BURLAPS
ABILRRY	LIBRARY	**ABKNNNO**	NONBANK	**ABLPSYY**	BYPLAYS
ABILRSS	BRASILS	**ABKNRSU**	UNBARKS	**ABLRSWY**	BYRLAWS
ABILRST	TRIBALS	**ABKNRUU**	BUNRAKU	**ABLRTUU**	TUBULAR
ABILRSU	BURIALS	**ABKOORS**	BOORKAS	**ABLRTUY**	BUTYRAL
	RAILBUS	**ABKORTU**	OUTBARK	**ABLSTTU**	BUTTALS
ABILRSZ	BRAZILS	**ABKSSTU**	SUBTASK	**ABMMNOS**	MOBSMAN
ABILSTU	TABULIS	**ABLLLOW**	LOWBALL	**ABMNSTU**	NUMBATS
ABILSYZ	SIZABLY	**ABLLLUY**	LULLABY	**ABMNSUY**	YNAMBUS
ABIMMRS	MIMBARS	**ABLLNOO**	BALLOON	**ABMOORR**	BARROOM
ABIMMTU	MITUMBA	**ABLLNOS**	BALLONS	**ABMOOSW**	WABOOMS
ABIMNRS	MINBARS	**ABLLOOS**	LOBOLAS	**ABMOOSZ**	BAZOOMS
ABIMNSU	MIBUNAS	**ABLLOPR**	PROBALL	**ABMOPRT**	BARMPOT
ABIMOSS	BIOMASS	**ABLLORR**	ROLLBAR	**ABMOPST**	BAMPOTS
ABIMPST	BAPTISM	**ABLLORT**	TOLLBAR		SPAMBOT
	BITMAPS	**ABLLORU**	LOBULAR	**ABMORTU**	TAMBOUR
ABIMRSS	BISMARS	**ABLLOST**	BALLOTS	**ABMOSTU**	SUBATOM
ABIMRST	IMBRAST	**ABLLOSU**	BULLOSA	**ABMOSTW**	WOMBATS
ABIMRSU	BARIUMS	**ABLLOSW**	BALLOWS	**ABMRSSU**	SAMBURS
ABIMRTT	TRIMTAB	**ABLLOTY**	TALLBOY	**ABMRSTU**	TAMBURS

ABNNOOT	NANOBOT	**ACCDEOY**	ACCOYED		RACEMIC
ABNOORS	SOROBAN	**ACCDERU**	ACCRUED	**ACCEINO**	COCAINE
ABNOORZ	BORAZON		CARDECU		OCEANIC
ABNOOSS	BASSOON	**ACCDESU**	ACCUSED	**ACCEINV**	VACCINE
ABNOOST	BATOONS		SUCCADE	**ACCEIPR**	CAPRICE
ABNORST	BARTONS	**ACCDFIL**	FLACCID	**ACCEIPS**	ICECAPS
ABNORSY	BARYONS	**ACCDHIL**	CHALCID		IPECACS
ABNORTY	BARYTON	**ACCDILS**	SCALDIC	**ACCEIPV**	PECCAVI
ABNOSSU	BONASUS	**ACCDINS**	SCANDIC	**ACCEIQU**	CACIQUE
ABNOTUY	BUOYANT	**ACCDIOT**	CACTOID	**ACCEIRS**	CARICES
ABNRSTU	TURBANS		OCTADIC	**ACCEIRT**	CREATIC
ABNRSUU	AUBURNS	**ACCDKNO**	CANDOCK	**ACCEIST**	ACCITES
ABNRTTU	TURBANT	**ACCDKOW**	DAWCOCK		ASCETIC
ABNSTUW	BAWSUNT	**ACCDLOY**	ACCOYLD		ECTATIC
ABNSTYZ	BYZANTS		CACODYL	**ACCEKLR**	CACKLER
ABOOPSX	SOAPBOX	**ACCDORS**	ACCORDS		CLACKER
ABOORTW	ROWBOAT	**ACCEEHL**	CALECHE		CRACKLE
ABOOTTW	TOWBOAT	**ACCEEHO**	COACHEE	**ACCEKLS**	CACKLES
ABORRSU	ARBOURS	**ACCEELN**	CENACLE	**ACCEKMO**	MEACOCK
ABORRSW	BARROWS	**ACCEENR**	CREANCE	**ACCEKOP**	PEACOCK
ABORSTU	ABORTUS	**ACCEERT**	ACCRETE	**ACCEKOS**	SEACOCK
	OUTBARS	**ACCEFIT**	FACTICE	**ACCEKPU**	CUPCAKE
	ROBUSTA	**ACCEFLU**	FELUCCA	**ACCEKRR**	CRACKER
	RUBATOS	**ACCEGIN**	ACCINGE	**ACCEKRT**	CRACKET
	TABOURS	**ACCEGOS**	SOCCAGE	**ACCELLY**	CALYCLE
ABORSTW	TOWBARS	**ACCEHHI**	CHECHIA		CECALLY
ABORSTY	TARBOYS	**ACCEHIL**	CALICHE	**ACCELNO**	CONCEAL
ABOSSUU	AUSUBOS		CHALICE	**ACCELNS**	CANCELS
ABOSSWW	BOWSAWS	**ACCEHIM**	MACCHIE	**ACCELOR**	CORACLE
ABOSTUU	AUTOBUS	**ACCEHIN**	CHICANE	**ACCELOT**	CACOLET
ABOTTTU	BATTUTO	**ACCEHLN**	CHANCEL	**ACCELRS**	CARCELS
ABPRSTU	ABRUPTS	**ACCEHLO**	COCHLEA	**ACCELSU**	SACCULE
	SUBPART	**ACCEHNO**	CONCHAE	**ACCELSY**	CALYCES
	UPBRAST	**ACCEHNR**	CHANCER		CYCLASE
ABPRSUY	UPBRAYS		CHANCRE	**ACCEMNU**	CACUMEN
ABRRSSU	BURSARS	**ACCEHNS**	CHANCES	**ACCENOR**	CONACRE
ABRRSUY	BURSARY	**ACCEHNT**	CATCHEN	**ACCENOS**	ASCONCE
ABRRTUY	TURBARY	**ACCEHNU**	CHAUNCE	**ACCENOT**	COENACT
ABRSTUU	ARBUTUS	**ACCEHNY**	CHANCEY	**ACCENOV**	CONCAVE
ABSSUWY	SUBWAYS	**ACCEHOR**	CAROCHE	**ACCENPT**	PECCANT
ACCCILY	ACYCLIC		COACHER	**ACCENRS**	CANCERS
ACCDDEE	ACCEDED	**ACCEHOS**	CHACOES	**ACCENST**	ACCENTS
ACCDDEI	CADDICE		COACHES	**ACCEOPY**	CACOEPY
ACCDEEN	CADENCE	**ACCEHPU**	CAPUCHE	**ACCEORW**	CRACOWE
ACCDEER	ACCEDER	**ACCEHRS**	CREACHS	**ACCEOTT**	TOCCATE
ACCDEES	ACCEDES	**ACCEHRT**	CATCHER	**ACCEPRY**	PECCARY
ACCDEHK	CHACKED		RECATCH	**ACCEPST**	ACCEPTS
ACCDEHN	CHANCED	**ACCEHST**	CACHETS	**ACCERRS**	SCARCER
ACCDEHO	COACHED		CATCHES	**ACCERRT**	CARRECT
ACCDEHT	CATCHED	**ACCEHTT**	CATHECT	**ACCERSS**	ARCSECS
ACCDEII	ACCIDIE	**ACCEHTU**	CATECHU	**ACCERSU**	ACCRUES
ACCDEIO	ACCOIED	**ACCEHXY**	CACHEXY		ACCURSE
ACCDEIT	ACCITED	**ACCEIKP**	ICEPACK		ACCUSER
ACCDEIU	CADUCEI	**ACCEIKR**	CACKIER	**ACCERSW**	ACCREWS
ACCDEKL	CACKLED	**ACCEILL**	CALICLE	**ACCESSU**	ACCUSES
	CLACKED	**ACCEILN**	CALCINE	**ACCESSY**	CYCASES
ACCDEKO	COCKADE	**ACCEILO**	COELIAC	**ACCFIIP**	PACIFIC
ACCDEKR	CRACKED	**ACCEILS**	CALICES	**ACCFILY**	CALCIFY
ACCDENS	ACCENDS		CELIACS	**ACCGHIN**	CACHING
ACCDENY	CADENCY	**ACCEILT**	CALCITE		CHACING
ACCDEOT	COACTED	**ACCEIMR**	CERAMIC	**ACCGNOS**	COGNACS

ACCHHIS	CHICHAS	ACCINSW	WICCANS
ACCHHKU	KUCHCHA	ACCINSY	CYCASIN
ACCHIKS	CHIACKS	ACCIOPR	CAPROIC
ACCHIMS	CHASMIC	ACCIORS	SCORIAC
ACCHINO	CHICANO	ACCIORT	ACROTIC
ACCHIOP	PICACHO	ACCIOST	OCICATS
ACCHIOR	COCHAIR	ACCIPRT	PRACTIC
ACCHIOT	CHAOTIC	ACCIRRS	CIRCARS
ACCHIOU	ACOUCHI		RICRACS
ACCHIRS	SCRAICH	ACCIRST	ARCTICS
ACCHJSU	JACCHUS	ACCISTT	TACTICS
ACCHKOY	HAYCOCK		TICTACS
ACCHKSU	KUCCHAS	ACCISTU	CAUSTIC
ACCHKSY	CHYACKS		CICUTAS
ACCHLNO	CONCHAL	ACCKLOR	CARLOCK
ACCHLTU	CLAUCHT	ACCKLRY	CRACKLY
ACCHNOS	CONCHAS	ACCKMOR	CROMACK
ACCHNRS	SCRANCH	ACCKOPR	CAPROCK
ACCHNRU	CRAUNCH	ACCKOSS	CASSOCK
ACCHOPU	CAPOUCH		COSSACK
	PACHUCO	ACCKOST	CASTOCK
ACCHORR	CARROCH	ACCKPRU	CRACKUP
ACCHOSU	CACHOUS	ACCLOSU	COUCALS
ACCHOTW	CHOCTAW	ACCLOSY	ACCLOYS
ACCHOUY	ACOUCHY	ACCMNOY	CACONYM
ACCHPTU	CATCHUP	ACCMOOT	COCOMAT
	UPCATCH	ACCMOOY	COCOYAM
ACCHRRU	CURRACH	ACCMOPT	ACCOMPT
ACCHRST	SCRATCH		COMPACT
ACCHRSU	SCRAUCH	ACCMRUU	CURCUMA
ACCHSSU	SUCCAHS	ACCNNOO	COONCAN
ACCIILN	ACLINIC	ACCNOOP	COCOPAN
ACCIINT	ACTINIC	ACCNOOR	RACCOON
ACCIIST	ASCITIC	ACCNOOS	CACOONS
	SCIATIC	ACCNOST	CATCONS
ACCIKRR	CARRICK	ACCNOTT	CONTACT
ACCIKRS	CARSICK	ACCNOTU	ACCOUNT
ACCILLU	CALCULI	ACCOORT	COACTOR
ACCILMO	COMICAL	ACCOPTY	COPYCAT
ACCILMU	CALCIUM	ACCOQSU	SQUACCO
ACCILNO	CONICAL	ACCORSS	CORCASS
	LACONIC		CORSACS
ACCILNY	CYNICAL	ACCORTU	ACCOURT
ACCILOR	CALORIC	ACCOSST	ACCOSTS
ACCILOS	ACCOILS	ACCRSTU	ACCURST
	CALICOS	ACDDDEI	CADDIED
ACCILOV	VOCALIC	ACDDDEL	CLADDED
ACCILRU	CRUCIAL	ACDDDEU	ADDUCED
ACCILRY	ACRYLIC	ACDDDKO	DADDOCK
ACCILSS	CLASSIC	ACDDEEF	DEFACED
ACCILST	CLASTIC	ACDDEEL	DECALED
ACCILSU	SACCULI	ACDDEER	CEDARED
ACCIMOT	COMATIC	ACDDEES	DECADES
ACCIMOZ	ZIMOCCA	ACDDEEY	DECAYED
ACCIMRU	CUMARIC	ACDDEHR	CHEDDAR
ACCINNO	CANONIC	ACDDEHY	DAYCHED
ACCINOP	CANOPIC	ACDDEIL	CLADDIE
ACCINOR	ACRONIC	ACDDEIN	CANDIED
ACCINOS	COCAINS	ACDDEIS	CADDIES
ACCINOT	CANTICO	ACDDEIU	DECIDUA
ACCINRU	CRUCIAN	ACDDELN	CANDLED

ACDDELO	CLADODE
ACDDELR	CLADDER
	CRADLED
ACDDELS	SCALDED
ACDDELU	CAUDLED
ACDDEMU	DUCDAME
ACDDEOP	DECAPOD
ACDDERU	ADDUCER
ACDDESU	ADDUCES
	SCAUDED
ACDDHHU	CHUDDAH
ACDDHIS	CADDISH
ACDDHKO	HADDOCK
ACDDHOR	CHADDOR
ACDDHRU	CHUDDAR
ACDDIIS	DIACIDS
ACDDIKZ	ZADDICK
ACDDINS	CANDIDS
ACDDIRS	DISCARD
ACDDIRY	DRYADIC
ACDDIST	ADDICTS
	DIDACTS
ACDDISY	DYADICS
ACDDKMO	MADDOCK
ACDDKOP	PADDOCK
ACDDSSY	CADDYSS
ACDDSTU	ADDUCTS
ACDEEES	DECEASE
ACDEEFF	EFFACED
ACDEEFN	ENFACED
ACDEEFR	DEFACER
	REFACED
ACDEEFS	DEFACES
ACDEEFT	FACETED
ACDEEGL	GLACEED
ACDEEGN	ENCAGED
ACDEEHL	LEACHED
ACDEEHP	CHEAPED
	PEACHED
ACDEEHR	REACHED
ACDEEHT	CHEATED
ACDEEIR	DECIARE
ACDEEJT	DEJECTA
ACDEEKR	CREAKED
ACDEELL	CADELLE
ACDEELN	CLEANED
	ELANCED
	ENLACED
ACDEELR	CLEARED
	CREEDAL
	DECLARE
	RELACED
ACDEELS	DESCALE
ACDEELT	CLEATED
ACDEELV	CLEAVED
ACDEEMN	MENACED
ACDEEMO	CAMEOED
ACDEEMR	AMERCED
	CREAMED
	RACEMED
ACDEEMV	MEDEVAC

ACDEENR	ENRACED	**ACDEHKL**	CHALKED		OCEANID
	RECANED		HACKLED	**ACDEINR**	CAIRNED
ACDEENS	DECANES	**ACDEHKR**	CHARKED		CARNIED
	ENCASED	**ACDEHKS**	SHACKED		DANCIER
ACDEENT	ENACTED	**ACDEHKT**	THACKED	**ACDEINS**	CANDIES
ACDEENV	ENCAVED	**ACDEHKW**	WHACKED		INCASED
	VENDACE	**ACDEHLN**	LANCHED	**ACDEINV**	INCAVED
ACDEEPR	CAPERED	**ACDEHLR**	CHALDER	**ACDEINY**	CYANIDE
	PEARCED	**ACDEHLS**	CLASHED	**ACDEIOS**	CODEIAS
	PREACED	**ACDEHLT**	LATCHED	**ACDEIPR**	EPACRID
ACDEEPS	ESCAPED	**ACDEHMP**	CHAMPED		PERACID
ACDEERS	CREASED	**ACDEHMR**	CHARMED	**ACDEIPS**	DISPACE
	DECARES		MARCHED	**ACDEIRR**	ACRIDER
	SEARCED	**ACDEHMS**	CHASMED		CARRIED
ACDEERT	CATERED	**ACDEHMT**	MATCHED	**ACDEIRS**	CARDIES
	CEDRATE	**ACDEHNR**	ENDARCH		DARCIES
	CERATED		RANCHED		RADICES
	CREATED	**ACDEHNT**	CHANTED		SIDECAR
	REACTED	**ACDEHOP**	POACHED	**ACDEIRU**	DECURIA
ACDEERY	DECAYER	**ACDEHOR**	CHORDAE	**ACDEISS**	DISCASE
ACDEETU	EDUCATE		ROACHED	**ACDEIST**	ACIDEST
ACDEETX	EXACTED	**ACDEHOS**	COHEADS		DACITES
ACDEFFH	CHAFFED	**ACDEHOT**	CATHODE	**ACDEISV**	ADVICES
ACDEFFS	DECAFFS	**ACDEHPP**	CHAPPED	**ACDEITT**	DICTATE
ACDEFGO	DOGFACE	**ACDEHPR**	PARCHED	**ACDEITY**	EDACITY
ACDEFHU	CHAUFED	**ACDEHPT**	PATCHED	**ACDEJLO**	CAJOLED
ACDEFIN	FACIEND	**ACDEHPU**	CUPHEAD	**ACDEJNU**	JAUNCED
	FANCIED	**ACDEHRR**	CHARRED	**ACDEKKN**	KNACKED
ACDEFIR	FARCIED	**ACDEHRS**	CRASHED	**ACDEKLM**	MACKLED
ACDEFKL	FLACKED		ECHARDS	**ACDEKLN**	CLANKED
ACDEFRS	SCARFED	**ACDEHRT**	CHARTED	**ACDEKLO**	CLOAKED
ACDEFRT	CRAFTED		RATCHED	**ACDEKLS**	SLACKED
	FRACTED	**ACDEHSS**	CHASSED	**ACDEKLT**	TACKLED
ACDEGGL	CLAGGED	**ACDEHST**	SCATHED		TALCKED
ACDEGGR	CRAGGED	**ACDEHSY**	DAYCHES	**ACDEKLU**	CAULKED
ACDEGGS	SCAGGED	**ACDEHTT**	CHATTED	**ACDEKMS**	SMACKED
ACDEGHN	CHANGED	**ACDEHTW**	WATCHED	**ACDEKNR**	CRANKED
	GANCHED	**ACDEHTY**	YACHTED	**ACDEKNS**	SNACKED
ACDEGHR	CHARGED	**ACDEHUV**	VAUCHED	**ACDEKNU**	UNCAKED
ACDEGIN	INCAGED	**ACDEIIR**	ACIDIER	**ACDEKOR**	CROAKED
ACDEGIR	CADGIER	**ACDEILL**	CEDILLA	**ACDEKQU**	QUACKED
ACDEGIS	DISCAGE	**ACDEILM**	CAMELID	**ACDEKRS**	DACKERS
ACDEGKO	DOCKAGE		CLAIMED	**ACDEKRT**	TRACKED
ACDEGLN	CANGLED		DECIMAL	**ACDEKRW**	WRACKED
	CLANGED		DECLAIM	**ACDEKRY**	KEYCARD
	GLANCED		MALICED	**ACDEKST**	STACKED
ACDEGLO	DECALOG		MEDICAL	**ACDEKSW**	SWACKED
ACDEGNO	CONGAED	**ACDEILN**	INLACED	**ACDELLS**	SCALLED
	DECAGON	**ACDEILR**	DECRIAL	**ACDELMM**	CLAMMED
ACDEGNU	UNCAGED		RADICEL	**ACDELMP**	CAMPLED
ACDEGOR	CARGOED		RADICLE		CLAMPED
	CORDAGE	**ACDEILS**	SCAILED	**ACDELMS**	MASCLED
ACDEGRS	CADGERS	**ACDEILT**	CITADEL	**ACDELMU**	MACULED
ACDEGST	GEDACTS		DELTAIC	**ACDELNO**	CELADON
ACDEHHN	HANCHED		DIALECT	**ACDELNR**	CANDLER
ACDEHHT	HATCHED		EDICTAL	**ACDELNS**	CALENDS
ACDEHIN	CHAINED	**ACDEILV**	CAVILED		CANDLES
	ECHIDNA	**ACDEIMT**	MICATED	**ACDELNT**	CANTLED
ACDEHIP	EDAPHIC	**ACDEIMV**	MEDIVAC	**ACDELNU**	LAUNCED
ACDEHIR	CHAIRED	**ACDEIMY**	MEDIACY		UNLACED
ACDEHIX	HEXADIC	**ACDEINO**	CODEINA	**ACDELOP**	PEDOCAL

ACDELOR	CAROLED		PEASCOD			SCIARID
	ORACLED	**ACDEOPT**	COAPTED	**ACDIIRT**	ARCTIID
ACDELOS	COLEADS	**ACDEORR**	CERRADO		TRIACID
	SOLACED		CORRADE		TRIADIC
ACDELOT	LOCATED	**ACDEORS**	SARCODE	**ACDIITY**	ACIDITY
ACDELOV	ALCOVED	**ACDEORT**	CORDATE	**ACDIKLS**	SKALDIC
ACDELPP	CLAPPED		REDCOAT	**ACDILLO**	CODILLA
ACDELPS	CLASPED	**ACDEOST**	COASTED	**ACDILMO**	DOMICAL
	SCALPED	**ACDEOTT**	CODETTA	**ACDILMS**	CLADISM
ACDELQU	CALQUED	**ACDEOUV**	COUVADE	**ACDILNO**	NODICAL
ACDELRR	CRADLER	**ACDEPPR**	CRAPPED	**ACDILNU**	DULCIAN
ACDELRS	CRADLES	**ACDEPRS**	REDCAPS		INCUDAL
	RECLADS		SCARPED	**ACDILOP**	PLACOID
	SCALDER		SCRAPED		PODALIC
ACDELRT	CLARTED	**ACDEPSU**	SCAUPED	**ACDILOR**	CORDIAL
ACDELRU	CAULDER	**ACDEQSU**	CASQUED	**ACDILOT**	COTIDAL
ACDELRW	CRAWLED	**ACDERRS**	CARDERS	**ACDILPU**	PALUDIC
ACDELSS	CLASSED		SCARRED	**ACDILRT**	TRICLAD
	DECLASS	**ACDERST**	REDACTS	**ACDILRY**	ACRIDLY
ACDELST	CASTLED		SCARTED	**ACDILST**	CLADIST
ACDELSU	CAUDLES	**ACDERSU**	CRUSADE	**ACDILTW**	WILDCAT
	CEDULAS		SCAURED	**ACDILTY**	DACTYLI
ACDELSW	DECLAWS	**ACDERTT**	DETRACT	**ACDIMMU**	CADMIUM
ACDELTT	CLATTED		TRACTED	**ACDIMNO**	MANDIOC
ACDELTU	CLAUTED	**ACDERTU**	CURATED		MONACID
ACDELWW	DEWCLAW		TRADUCE		MONADIC
ACDEMMR	CRAMMED	**ACDESTT**	SCATTED		NOMADIC
ACDEMMS	SCAMMED	**ACDESTV**	ADVECTS	**ACDIMNY**	DYNAMIC
ACDEMNU	DECUMAN	**ACDFIIT**	FATIDIC	**ACDIMOO**	CAMOODI
ACDEMOR	CAROMED	**ACDFIIY**	ACIDIFY	**ACDIMOT**	COADMIT
	COMRADE	**ACDFIOT**	FACTOID	**ACDINNO**	NONACID
ACDEMPR	CRAMPED	**ACDGGIN**	CADGING	**ACDINRU**	CANDIRU
ACDEMPS	DECAMPS	**ACDGIIM**	DIGICAM		IRACUND
	SCAMPED	**ACDGIKN**	DACKING	**ACDINST**	DISCANT
ACDENNS	SCANNED	**ACDGINN**	DANCING	**ACDINSW**	WINDACS
ACDENNT	CANDENT	**ACDGINO**	GONADIC	**ACDINSY**	CYANIDS
ACDENNU	NUANCED	**ACDGINR**	CARDING	**ACDIOPR**	PARODIC
ACDENOR	ACORNED	**ACDGKLO**	DAGLOCK		PICADOR
	DRACONE	**ACDGNOT**	CANTDOG	**ACDIORR**	CORRIDA
ACDENOS	ACNODES	**ACDGORT**	DOGCART	**ACDIORS**	CARDIOS
	DEACONS	**ACDHIIL**	CHILIAD		SARCOID
ACDENOT	TACNODE	**ACDHIMR**	DHARMIC	**ACDIORT**	ARCTOID
ACDENPR	PRANCED	**ACDHIOP**	PHACOID		CAROTID
ACDENPT	PANDECT	**ACDHIRY**	DIARCHY	**ACDIOST**	DACOITS
ACDENPU	UNCAPED	**ACDHLOR**	CHORDAL	**ACDIOSZ**	ZODIACS
	UNPACED		DORLACH	**ACDIOTY**	DACOITY
ACDENRS	DANCERS	**ACDHMRS**	DRACHMS	**ACDIOXY**	OXYACID
ACDENRT	CANTRED	**ACDHNOW**	COWHAND	**ACDIPRS**	CAPRIDS
	TRANCED	**ACDHOOT**	CATHOOD	**ACDIPSS**	CAPSIDS
ACDENRU	DURANCE	**ACDHOPR**	POCHARD	**ACDIPTY**	DIPTYCA
	UNCARED	**ACDHORR**	ORCHARD	**ACDIQRU**	QUADRIC
	UNRACED	**ACDHORS**	CHADORS	**ACDIRST**	DRASTIC
ACDENRY	ARDENCY	**ACDHRUY**	DUARCHY	**ACDIRTU**	DATURIC
ACDENSS	ASCENDS	**ACDHRYY**	DYARCHY	**ACDISST**	DICASTS
ACDENST	DECANTS	**ACDIIIN**	INDICIA	**ACDITUV**	VIADUCT
	DESCANT	**ACDIIJT**	JADITIC	**ACDJNTU**	ADJUNCT
	SCANTED	**ACDIINN**	INDICAN	**ACDKLOP**	PADLOCK
ACDENSU	UNCASED	**ACDIINO**	CONIDIA	**ACDKLSY**	SKYCLAD
ACDENTU	UNACTED	**ACDIINR**	ACRIDIN	**ACDKMOO**	MOCKADO
ACDENUV	VAUNCED	**ACDIIOS**	ISODICA	**ACDKMPU**	MUDPACK
ACDEOPS	PEACODS	**ACDIIRS**	CIDARIS	**ACDKOPR**	POCKARD

ACDLLOR	COLLARD	ACEEHNP	CHEAPEN	ACEEMNR	MENACER
ACDLLUY	DUCALLY	ACEEHNS	ACHENES	ACEEMNS	CASEMEN
ACDLNOR	CALDRON		ENCHASE		EMACSEN
ACDLNOT	COTLAND	ACEEHOR	OCHREAE		MENACES
ACDLOWY	LADYCOW	ACEEHPP	ECHAPPE	ACEEMNT	CEMENTA
ACDLSTY	DACTYLS	ACEEHPR	CHEAPER	ACEEMNV	CAVEMEN
ACDMMNO	COMMAND		PEACHER	ACEEMRR	AMERCER
ACDMNOP	COMPAND	ACEEHPS	PEACHES		CREAMER
ACDMOOW	CAMWOOD	ACEEHRR	REACHER	ACEEMRS	AMERCES
ACDMORZ	CZARDOM	ACEEHRS	REACHES		CAREMES
ACDMPSU	MUDCAPS	ACEEHRT	CHEATER		RACEMES
ACDMSTU	MUDCATS		HECTARE	ACEEMRT	CREMATE
ACDNOOR	CARDOON		RECHATE		MEERCAT
ACDNORS	CANDORS		RECHEAT	ACEEMSS	CAMESES
	CARDONS		RETEACH	ACEEMSZ	ECZEMAS
	DACRONS		TEACHER	ACEENNP	PENANCE
ACDNORU	CANDOUR	ACEEHST	EATCHES	ACEENNR	NARCEEN
	CAUDRON		ESCHEAT	ACEENNT	CANTEEN
ACDOPST	PODCAST		TEACHES	ACEENNY	CAYENNE
ACDORST	COSTARD	ACEEHTT	THECATE	ACEENOR	CORNEAE
ACDORSU	CRUSADO	ACEEHTX	EXCHEAT	ACEENOT	ACETONE
ACDORSW	COWARDS	ACEEILP	CALIPEE	ACEENRS	CAREENS
ACDORUZ	CRUZADO	ACEEIMT	EMICATE		CASERNE
ACDOSTV	VODCAST	ACEEINR	CINEREA		ENRACES
ACDRSTU	CUSTARD	ACEEINU	EUCAINE		RECANES
ACDRSUU	CARDUUS	ACEEIRR	CARIERE	ACEENRT	CENTARE
ACEEEPS	ESCAPEE	ACEEISV	VESICAE		CRENATE
ACEEEUV	EVACUEE	ACEEJKN	JACKEEN		REENACT
ACEEFFR	EFFACER	ACEEJSY	JAYCEES	ACEENSS	CASSENE
ACEEFFS	EFFACES	ACEEKNP	KNEECAP		ENCASES
ACEEFHN	ENCHAFE	ACEELLN	NACELLE		SEANCES
ACEEFIN	FAIENCE	ACEELLS	CALLEES		SENECAS
	FIANCEE	ACEELMP	EMPLACE	ACEENST	CETANES
ACEEFLU	FECULAE	ACEELMR	RECLAME		TENACES
ACEEFMN	FACEMEN	ACEELNR	CLEANER	ACEENSV	ENCAVES
ACEEFNS	ENFACES		RECLEAN	ACEENTU	CUNEATE
ACEEFNY	FAYENCE	ACEELNS	CLEANSE	ACEEORS	ACEROSE
ACEEFPR	PREFACE		ELANCES	ACEEORT	OCREATE
ACEEFRS	REFACES		ENLACES	ACEEOSS	CASEOSE
ACEEGIL	ELEGIAC		SCALENE	ACEEOST	ACETOSE
ACEEGNR	ENGRACE	ACEELNT	LATENCE		COATEES
ACEEGNS	ENCAGES	ACEELNV	ENCLAVE	ACEEOTV	EVOCATE
ACEEGNT	CENTAGE		VALENCE	ACEEPRR	CAPERER
ACEEGOT	ECOTAGE	ACEELPR	PERCALE		PRERACE
ACEEGPS	CEPAGES		REPLACE	ACEEPRS	ESCAPER
ACEEGSU	ESCUAGE	ACEELPT	CAPELET		PEARCES
ACEEHHT	CHEETAH	ACEELRR	CLEARER		PERCASE
ACEEHIP	CHEAPIE	ACEELRS	ALERCES		PREACES
ACEEHIT	HICATEE		CEREALS		RESPACE
	TEACHIE		RELACES	ACEEPSS	ESCAPES
ACEEHIV	ACHIEVE		RESCALE	ACEEPST	PECTASE
ACEEHKO	HOECAKE		SCLERAE	ACEEPSX	CAPEXES
ACEEHKS	HACKEES	ACEELRT	TREACLE	ACEEPTT	PECTATE
ACEEHLR	LEACHER	ACEELRU	CAERULE	ACEERRS	CAREERS
	RELACHE	ACEELRV	CLEAVER		CREASER
ACEEHLS	LEACHES	ACEELST	CELESTA	ACEERRT	CATERER
ACEEHLT	CHELATE		SELECTA		RECRATE
ACEEHMP	EMPEACH	ACEELSU	EUCLASE		RETRACE
ACEEHMR	MACHREE	ACEELSV	CLEAVES		TERRACE
ACEEHMT	MACHETE	ACEELVX	EXCLAVE	ACEERSS	CREASES
ACEEHNN	ENHANCE	ACEEMNP	PACEMEN		SEARCES

ACEERST	CERATES	**ACEGHNS**	CHANGES	**ACEGOSS**	SOCAGES
	CREATES		GANCHES	**ACEGOSW**	COWAGES
	ECARTES	**ACEGHNU**	CHAUNGE	**ACEGOTT**	COTTAGE
	SECRETA	**ACEGHOU**	GOUACHE	**ACEGRTU**	TRUCAGE
ACEERSU	CESURAE	**ACEGHOW**	COWHAGE	**ACEGSTU**	SCUTAGE
ACEERTX	EXACTER	**ACEGHRR**	CHARGER	**ACEGTTU**	CUTTAGE
	EXCRETA	**ACEGHRS**	CHARGES	**ACEHHLS**	CHALEHS
ACEERVZ	CERVEZA		CREAGHS	**ACEHHLT**	HATCHEL
ACEESSS	ASCESES	**ACEGHRT**	GERTCHA	**ACEHHNS**	HANCHES
ACEESST	ECTASES	**ACEGHRU**	GAUCHER	**ACEHHRT**	HATCHER
ACEESTT	CASETTE	**ACEGILL**	ELLAGIC	**ACEHHRU**	HACHURE
ACEFFHI	AFFICHE	**ACEGILN**	ANGELIC	**ACEHHRX**	HEXARCH
ACEFFHR	CHAFFER		ANGLICE	**ACEHHST**	CHETAHS
ACEFFIN	CAFFEIN		GALENIC		HATCHES
ACEFFIS	SCAFFIE	**ACEGILP**	PELAGIC	**ACEHHTT**	HATCHET
ACEFFOR	AFFORCE	**ACEGILR**	GLACIER	**ACEHIKR**	KACHERI
ACEFFST	AFFECTS		GRACILE	**ACEHIKS**	HACKIES
ACEFGIP	PIGFACE	**ACEGILS**	ALGESIC	**ACEHILL**	CHALLIE
ACEFGLU	CAGEFUL	**ACEGILT**	ALGETIC		HELICAL
ACEFGOT	GEOFACT	**ACEGIMO**	CAMOGIE	**ACEHILM**	LECHAIM
ACEFHMR	CHAMFER	**ACEGIMR**	GRIMACE		MICHAEL
ACEFHOR	ARCHFOE	**ACEGIMT**	GAMETIC	**ACEHILR**	CHARLIE
ACEFHRS	CHAFERS	**ACEGINO**	COINAGE	**ACEHILT**	ALETHIC
ACEFHRU	CHAUFER	**ACEGINP**	PEACING		ETHICAL
ACEFHSU	CHAUFES	**ACEGINR**	ANERGIC	**ACEHIMN**	MACHINE
ACEFIIL	FELICIA		GRECIAN	**ACEHIMP**	IMPEACH
ACEFILL	ICEFALL	**ACEGINS**	CEASING	**ACEHIMR**	CHIMERA
ACEFILM	MALEFIC		INCAGES	**ACEHIMS**	CHAMISE
ACEFILR	FILACER	**ACEGINV**	VEGANIC	**ACEHIMT**	HEMATIC
ACEFILS	FECIALS	**ACEGINY**	GYNECIA	**ACEHINN**	ENCHAIN
ACEFINN	FINANCE	**ACEGINZ**	CEAZING	**ACEHINR**	ARCHINE
ACEFINR	FANCIER	**ACEGIOP**	APOGEIC	**ACEHINS**	CHAINES
ACEFINS	FANCIES	**ACEGIRT**	CIGARET		INCHASE
	FASCINE	**ACEGIRU**	GAUCIER	**ACEHINT**	CHANTIE
	FIANCES	**ACEGIRW**	GAWCIER	**ACEHINY**	HYACINE
ACEFINU	UNIFACE	**ACEGIST**	CAGIEST		HYAENIC
ACEFIRS	FARCIES	**ACEGJKL**	JACKLEG	**ACEHIOT**	ACHIOTE
	FIACRES	**ACEGKLO**	LOCKAGE	**ACEHIPP**	CHAPPIE
ACEFITV	FACTIVE	**ACEGKLR**	GRACKLE	**ACEHIPR**	CHARPIE
ACEFITY	ACETIFY	**ACEGKMO**	MOCKAGE	**ACEHIPT**	APHETIC
ACEFKLR	FLACKER	**ACEGKOR**	CORKAGE		HEPATIC
ACEFKLT	FLACKET	**ACEGLLO**	COLLAGE	**ACEHIRR**	CHARIER
ACEFLRU	CAREFUL	**ACEGLNO**	CONGEAL	**ACEHIRS**	CAHIERS
ACEFLSU	FECULAS	**ACEGLNR**	CLANGER		CASHIER
ACEFNNO	FACONNE		GLANCER		ERIACHS
ACEFNRT	CANTREF	**ACEGLNS**	CANGLES	**ACEHIRT**	THERIAC
ACEFNRU	FURNACE		GLANCES	**ACEHIRV**	ARCHIVE
ACEFOPR	PROFACE	**ACEGLOT**	CATELOG	**ACEHISS**	CHAISES
ACEFORR	FORECAR	**ACEGLOU**	CAGOULE	**ACEHIST**	ACHIEST
ACEFOTU	OUTFACE	**ACEGLPS**	GELCAPS		AITCHES
ACEFRRS	FARCERS	**ACEGMOP**	COMPAGE	**ACEHITY**	YACHTIE
	SCARFER	**ACEGNOR**	ACROGEN	**ACEHITZ**	ZAITECH
ACEFRRT	CRAFTER		CORNAGE	**ACEHKLR**	HACKLER
	REFRACT	**ACEGNOT**	COAGENT	**ACEHKLS**	HACKLES
ACEFRRU	FARCEUR		COGNATE		SHACKLE
ACEFRSU	SURFACE	**ACEGNSU**	CANGUES	**ACEHKLT**	HACKLET
ACEFRTU	FACTURE		UNCAGES	**ACEHKMN**	HACKMEN
	FURCATE	**ACEGORS**	CARGOES	**ACEHKNY**	HACKNEY
ACEFSTU	FAUCETS		CORSAGE	**ACEHKOT**	HOTCAKE
ACEGHLO	GALOCHE		SOCAGER	**ACEHKRS**	HACKERS
ACEGHNR	CHANGER	**ACEGORU**	COURAGE	**ACEHKRW**	WHACKER

ACEHKRY	HACKERY	ACEHNPS	PECHANS	ACEHRTW	WATCHER
ACEHLLP	PELLACH	ACEHNRR	RANCHER	ACEHRTY	YACHTER
ACEHLLS	SHELLAC	ACEHNRS	CHENARS	ACEHRXY	EXARCHY
ACEHLLT	HELLCAT		RANCHES	ACEHSSS	CHASSES
ACEHLMT	CHAMLET	ACEHNRT	CHANTER	ACEHSST	SACHETS
ACEHLMY	ALCHEMY		TRANCHE		SCATHES
ACEHLNN	CHANNEL	ACEHNSS	SCHANSE	ACEHSSW	CASHEWS
ACEHLNO	CHALONE	ACEHNST	CHASTEN	ACEHSTW	WATCHES
ACEHLNP	PLANCHE		NATCHES	ACEHSTX	HEXACTS
ACEHLNR	CHARNEL	ACEHNSU	NAUCHES	ACEHSUV	VAUCHES
	LARCHEN	ACEHNSZ	SCHANZE	ACEHTTU	TEUCHAT
ACEHLNS	LANCHES	ACEHNTT	ETCHANT	ACEHTTW	WATCHET
ACEHLOP	EPOCHAL	ACEHNTU	UNTEACH	ACEIILM	CIMELIA
ACEHLOR	CHOLERA	ACEHNTY	CHANTEY	ACEIILS	LAICISE
	CHORALE	ACEHNZZ	CHAZZEN	ACEIILT	CILIATE
	CHOREAL	ACEHOOT	OOTHECA	ACEIILZ	LAICIZE
ACEHLOS	LOACHES	ACEHOPR	POACHER	ACEIIPS	EPISCIA
	OSCHEAL	ACEHOPS	CHEAPOS	ACEIITV	CAITIVE
ACEHLOT	CATHOLE		EPOCHAS		VICIATE
	CHOLATE		POACHES	ACEIJKS	JACKIES
ACEHLPS	CHAPELS		SHOEPAC		JACKSIE
ACEHLPT	CHAPLET	ACEHORS	CHOREAS	ACEIKLS	SACLIKE
ACEHLPY	CHEAPLY		ORACHES	ACEIKLT	CATLIKE
ACEHLRS	CLASHER		ROACHES	ACEIKMR	KERAMIC
	LARCHES	ACEHOSS	CHAOSES	ACEIKNT	ANTICKE
	RASCHEL	ACEHOTY	CHAYOTE	ACEIKOP	PAIOCKE
ACEHLRT	ARCHLET	ACEHPPS	SCHAPPE	ACEIKPR	EARPICK
	TRACHLE	ACEHPRS	EPARCHS	ACEIKPW	WICKAPE
ACEHLRY	CHARLEY		PARCHES	ACEIKPX	PICKAXE
ACEHLSS	CLASHES	ACEHPRT	CHAPTER	ACEIKRS	CASKIER
	SEALCHS		PATCHER		EIRACKS
ACEHLST	CHALETS		REPATCH	ACEIKRT	TACKIER
	LATCHES	ACEHPRU	UPREACH	ACEIKRW	WACKIER
	SATCHEL	ACEHPRY	EPARCHY	ACEIKSS	SEASICK
ACEHLTT	CHATTEL		PREACHY	ACEIKST	CAKIEST
	LATCHET	ACEHPSS	CHAPESS		TACKIES
ACEHMNP	CHAPMEN	ACEHPST	HEPCATS	ACEIKTT	TIETACK
ACEHMNR	ENCHARM		PATCHES	ACEILLL	ALLELIC
	MARCHEN	ACEHQUY	QUEACHY	ACEILLM	LIMACEL
ACEHMNS	MANCHES	ACEHRRS	ARCHERS		MICELLA
ACEHMNT	MANCHET		CRASHER	ACEILLS	ALLICES
ACEHMPR	CHAMPER	ACEHRRT	CHARTER		CAILLES
ACEHMRR	CHARMER		RECHART	ACEILLX	LEXICAL
	MARCHER	ACEHRRV	CHARVER	ACEILMN	CNEMIAL
ACEHMRS	MACHERS	ACEHRRX	XERARCH		MELANIC
	MARCHES	ACEHRRY	ARCHERY	ACEILMR	CALMIER
	MESARCH	ACEHRSS	CHASERS		CLAIMER
	SCHMEAR		CRASHES		MIRACLE
ACEHMRT	MATCHER		ESCHARS		RECLAIM
	REMATCH	ACEHRST	ARCHEST	ACEILMS	LIMACES
ACEHMRU	CHAUMER		CHARETS		MALICES
ACEHMSS	SACHEMS		CHASTER	ACEILMT	CLIMATE
	SAMECHS		RACHETS		METICAL
	SCHEMAS		RATCHES	ACEILMX	EXCLAIM
ACEHMST	MATCHES	ACEHRSU	ARCHEUS	ACEILMY	MYCELIA
ACEHMTT	MATCHET	ACEHRSV	VARECHS	ACEILNN	ENCINAL
ACEHMTY	ECTHYMA	ACEHRSW	CHAWERS	ACEILNP	CAPELIN
ACEHMTZ	CHAMETZ	ACEHRSX	EXARCHS		PANICLE
ACEHNNR	CHANNER	ACEHRSY	HYRACES		PELICAN
ACEHNNT	ENCHANT	ACEHRTT	CHATTER	ACEILNR	CARLINE
ACEHNOP	PANOCHE		RATCHET	ACEILNS	INLACES

	SANICLE	**ACEIMSU**	CAESIUM	**ACEIPRS**	EPACRIS
	SCALENI	**ACEIMSX**	CASEMIX		SCRAPIE
ACEILNU	CAULINE	**ACEIMTX**	TAXEMIC		SPACIER
ACEILOR	CALORIE	**ACEINNP**	PINNACE	**ACEIPRT**	PARETIC
	CARIOLE	**ACEINNR**	CANNIER		PICRATE
	COALIER		NARCEIN	**ACEIPST**	ASEPTIC
	LORICAE	**ACEINNS**	CANINES		PACIEST
ACEILOS	CELOSIA		ENCINAS		SPICATE
	COALISE		NANCIES	**ACEIPSU**	AUSPICE
ACEILOT	ALOETIC	**ACEINNT**	ANCIENT	**ACEIPSZ**	CAPIZES
ACEILOZ	COALIZE	**ACEINNY**	CYANINE		CAPSIZE
ACEILPR	CALIPER	**ACEINOP**	APNOEIC	**ACEIPTV**	CAPTIVE
	REPLICA		PAEONIC	**ACEIQRU**	ACQUIRE
ACEILPS	PLAICES	**ACEINOS**	ACINOSE	**ACEIQSU**	CAIQUES
	SPECIAL	**ACEINOT**	ACONITE	**ACEIQTU**	ACQUITE
ACEILPT	PLICATE		ANOETIC	**ACEIQUZ**	CAZIQUE
ACEILPU	PECULIA	**ACEINPR**	CAPRINE	**ACEIRRR**	CARRIER
ACEILRR	CERRIAL	**ACEINPS**	INSCAPE	**ACEIRRS**	CARRIES
ACEILRS	CLARIES		PINCASE		SCARIER
	ECLAIRS	**ACEINPT**	PICANTE	**ACEIRRT**	CIRRATE
	SCALIER	**ACEINRR**	CARNIER		ERRATIC
ACEILRT	ARTICLE	**ACEINRS**	ARCSINE	**ACEIRRW**	AIRCREW
	RECITAL		ARSENIC	**ACEIRRZ**	CRAZIER
	TALCIER		CARNIES	**ACEIRST**	ATRESIC
ACEILRU	AURICLE		CERASIN		CRISTAE
ACEILRV	CALIVER	**ACEINRT**	CANTIER		RACIEST
	CAVILER		CERATIN		STEARIC
	CLAVIER		CERTAIN	**ACEIRSU**	SAUCIER
	VALERIC		CREATIN		URICASE
	VELARIC		CRINATE	**ACEIRSV**	CARVIES
ACEILRY	CLAYIER		NACRITE		CAVIERS
ACEILSS	SALICES		TACRINE		VARICES
ACEILST	ASTELIC	**ACEINSS**	CASEINS		VISCERA
	ELASTIC		CASSINE	**ACEIRSZ**	CRAZIES
	LACIEST		INCASES	**ACEIRTT**	ATRETIC
	LATICES	**ACEINST**	ACETINS		CATTIER
	SALICET		CANIEST		CITRATE
ACEILSV	CLAVIES		CINEAST	**ACEISSS**	ASCESIS
	VESICAL	**ACEINSU**	EUCAINS	**ACEISST**	ASCITES
ACEILTT	LATTICE	**ACEINSV**	INCAVES		ECTASIS
	TACTILE	**ACEINSY**	CYANISE	**ACEISTT**	CATTIES
ACEILVW	WAVICLE	**ACEINTT**	NICTATE		STATICE
ACEIMMS	CAMMIES		TETANIC		TIETACS
ACEIMNO	ENCOMIA	**ACEINTU**	TUNICAE	**ACEISTV**	ACTIVES
ACEIMNP	PEMICAN	**ACEINTV**	VENATIC	**ACEISVV**	VIVACES
ACEIMNR	CARMINE	**ACEINTX**	INEXACT	**ACEITTV**	CAVETTI
ACEIMNS	AMNESIC	**ACEINTY**	CYANITE	**ACEITTX**	EXTATIC
	CINEMAS	**ACEINTZ**	ZINCATE	**ACEITUX**	AUXETIC
ACEIMNT	EMICANT	**ACEINYZ**	CYANIZE	**ACEJKMN**	JACKMEN
	NEMATIC	**ACEIOOZ**	ZOOECIA	**ACEJKOP**	PAJOCKE
ACEIMOR	COREMIA	**ACEIOPT**	ECTOPIA	**ACEJKRS**	JACKERS
ACEIMOV	VOMICAE	**ACEIORS**	CARIOSE	**ACEJKST**	JACKETS
ACEIMPR	CAMPIER		ORACIES	**ACEJLOR**	CAJOLER
ACEIMPY	PYAEMIC		SCORIAE	**ACEJLOS**	CAJOLES
ACEIMRT	MATRICE	**ACEIORT**	EROTICA	**ACEJNOS**	CAJONES
ACEIMRU	URAEMIC	**ACEIOST**	SOCIATE	**ACEJNOT**	JACONET
ACEIMSS	CAMISES	**ACEIOTX**	EXOTICA	**ACEJNOY**	JOYANCE
ACEIMST	ACMITES	**ACEIPPR**	CRAPPIE	**ACEJNSU**	JAUNCES
	ETACISM		EPICARP	**ACEJNTU**	JUNCATE
	MICATES	**ACEIPPT**	TAPPICE	**ACEJPTU**	CAJEPUT
	SEMATIC	**ACEIPRR**	CRAPIER	**ACEJRTT**	TRAJECT

ACEKKNR	KNACKER	**ACELLNU**	NUCLEAL	**ACELNSU**	CENSUAL
ACEKLLP	PELLACK	**ACELLNY**	CLEANLY		LACUNES
ACEKLMS	MACKLES	**ACELLOR**	CORELLA		LAUNCES
ACEKLNR	CRANKLE		OCELLAR		UNLACES
ACEKLNS	CANKLES	**ACELLOS**	CALLOSE		UNSCALE
	SLACKEN		LOCALES	**ACELNTT**	CANTLET
ACEKLOR	EARLOCK	**ACELLOT**	COLLATE	**ACELNTY**	LATENCY
ACEKLPS	SPACKLE	**ACELLPS**	SCALPEL	**ACELNVY**	VALENCY
ACEKLPT	PLACKET	**ACELLPY**	CLYPEAL	**ACELOPR**	POLACRE
ACEKLQU	QUACKLE	**ACELLRR**	CARRELL	**ACELOPS**	ESCALOP
ACEKLRS	CALKERS	**ACELLRS**	CALLERS	**ACELOPT**	POLECAT
	LACKERS		CELLARS	**ACELOPU**	COPULAE
	SLACKER		RECALLS	**ACELOQU**	COEQUAL
ACEKLRT	TACKLER		SCLERAL	**ACELORR**	CAROLER
ACEKLRU	CAULKER	**ACELLRY**	CLEARLY	**ACELORS**	CLAROES
ACEKLST	TACKLES	**ACELLST**	CALLETS		COALERS
ACEKLSY	LACKEYS	**ACELMMR**	CLAMMER		ESCOLAR
ACEKMNP	PACKMEN	**ACELMNO**	COALMEN		ORACLES
ACEKMOR	COMAKER	**ACELMNS**	ENCALMS		RECOALS
ACEKMOS	COMAKES	**ACELMOR**	CAROMEL		SOLACER
ACEKMRS	SMACKER	**ACELMOT**	CAMELOT	**ACELORT**	LOCATER
ACEKNOS	NOCAKES	**ACELMOU**	CAULOME	**ACELORY**	CALOYER
ACEKNPR	PRANCKE		LEUCOMA	**ACELOSS**	SOLACES
ACEKNRR	CRANKER	**ACELMPR**	CLAMPER	**ACELOST**	ALECOST
ACEKNRS	CANKERS	**ACELMPS**	CAMPLES		LACTOSE
	SNACKER	**ACELMRS**	MARCELS		LOCATES
ACEKNRY	CANKERY	**ACELMRY**	CAMELRY		SCATOLE
ACEKNST	NACKETS	**ACELMSS**	MASCLES		TALCOSE
ACEKNSU	UNCAKES		MESCALS	**ACELOSV**	ALCOVES
ACEKORR	CROAKER		SCAMELS		COEVALS
ACEKPPR	PREPACK	**ACELMST**	CALMEST	**ACELOTT**	CALOTTE
ACEKPRS	PACKERS		CAMLETS	**ACELOTU**	OCULATE
	REPACKS	**ACELMSU**	ALMUCES	**ACELOTY**	ACOLYTE
ACEKPST	PACKETS		MACULES		COTYLAE
ACEKQRU	QUACKER	**ACELMSZ**	MEZCALS	**ACELOUV**	VACUOLE
ACEKRRS	RACKERS	**ACELMTU**	CALUMET	**ACELPPR**	CLAPPER
	RERACKS	**ACELNNO**	ALENCON	**ACELPPS**	SCAPPLE
ACEKRRT	RETRACK	**ACELNNS**	CANNELS	**ACELPRS**	CARPELS
	TRACKER	**ACELNNU**	UNCLEAN		CLASPER
ACEKRSS	SACKERS	**ACELNNY**	LYNCEAN		CRAPLES
	SCREAKS	**ACELNOP**	NOPLACE		PARCELS
ACEKRST	RACKETS	**ACELNOR**	CORNEAL		PLACERS
	RESTACK	**ACELNOS**	SECONAL		RECLASP
	RETACKS	**ACELNOT**	LACTONE		SCALPER
	STACKER	**ACELNOZ**	CALZONE	**ACELPRT**	PLECTRA
	TACKERS	**ACELNPS**	ENCLASP	**ACELPRY**	PRELACY
ACEKRSU	CAUKERS		SPANCEL	**ACELPSS**	CAPLESS
ACEKRSW	CAWKERS	**ACELNPT**	CLAPNET	**ACELPST**	CAPLETS
	WACKERS	**ACELNPU**	CLEANUP		PLACETS
ACEKRSY	SCREAKY		UNPLACE	**ACELPSU**	CAPSULE
	YACKERS	**ACELNRS**	LANCERS		SCALEUP
ACEKRTT	RACKETT		RANCELS		SPECULA
ACEKRTY	RACKETY	**ACELNRT**	CENTRAL		UPSCALE
ACEKSST	CASKETS	**ACELNRU**	LUCARNE	**ACELPSY**	CYPSELA
ACEKSTT	STACKET		NUCLEAR	**ACELPTY**	ECTYPAL
	TACKETS		UNCLEAR	**ACELPUU**	CUPULAE
ACEKSTW	WACKEST	**ACELNRY**	LARCENY	**ACELQRU**	CLAQUER
ACEKSUW	WAESUCK	**ACELNST**	CANTLES		LACQUER
ACEKTTY	TACKETY		CENTALS	**ACELQSU**	CALQUES
ACELLMO	CALOMEL		LANCETS		CLAQUES
ACELLMY	MYCELLA		SCANTLE	**ACELQUY**	LACQUEY

ACELRRS	CARRELS	**ACEMPST**	CAMPEST	**ACENRTT**	TRANECT
ACELRRU	RAUCLER	**ACEMPSY**	MYSPACE	**ACENRTU**	CENTAUR
ACELRRW	CRAWLER	**ACEMRSS**	SCREAMS		UNCRATE
ACELRSS	CARLESS	**ACEMRST**	MERCATS		UNTRACE
	CLASSER	**ACEMRSY**	CRAMESY	**ACENRTY**	ENCRATY
	SCALERS	**ACEMSSU**	CAMUSES		NECTARY
	SCLERAS	**ACEMSTT**	METCAST		TRANCEY
ACELRST	CARTELS	**ACEMSTU**	MUCATES	**ACENSST**	ASCENTS
	CLARETS	**ACEMSUX**	EXACUMS		SECANTS
	CRESTAL	**ACENNOS**	ANCONES		STANCES
	SCARLET		SONANCE	**ACENSSU**	UNCASES
	TARCELS	**ACENNOT**	CONNATE		USANCES
ACELRSU	CESURAL	**ACENNOX**	COANNEX	**ACENSTT**	CANTEST
	RECUSAL	**ACENNOY**	NOYANCE	**ACENSTU**	NUTCASE
	SECULAR	**ACENNOZ**	CANZONE	**ACENSUU**	USAUNCE
ACELRSV	CALVERS	**ACENNRS**	CANNERS	**ACENSUV**	VAUNCES
	CARVELS		SCANNER	**ACEOOPP**	APOCOPE
	CLAVERS	**ACENNRY**	CANNERY	**ACEOOTZ**	ECTOZOA
ACELRSW	CLAWERS	**ACENNST**	NASCENT	**ACEOPRX**	EXOCARP
ACELRTT	CLATTER	**ACENNSU**	NUANCES	**ACEOPSS**	SCAPOSE
ACELRTY	TREACLY	**ACENNTY**	TENANCY	**ACEOPST**	CAPOTES
ACELSSS	CLASSES	**ACENOOR**	CORONAE		SCOPATE
	SACLESS	**ACENOPT**	PATONCE		TOECAPS
ACELSST	CASTLES	**ACENOPU**	PONCEAU	**ACEOPSW**	COWPEAS
	SCLATES	**ACENORS**	CANOERS	**ACEOPTU**	OUTPACE
ACELSSU	CLAUSES		CARNOSE	**ACEORRS**	COARSER
ACELSSV	SCLAVES		COARSEN		CORREAS
ACELSTU	CAUTELS		CORNEAS	**ACEORRT**	ACROTER
	SULCATE		EARCONS		CREATOR
ACELSTY	ACETYLS		NARCOSE		REACTOR
	SCYTALE	**ACENORT**	ENACTOR	**ACEORSS**	ROSACES
ACELSUU	ACULEUS	**ACENOSS**	CASSONE	**ACEORST**	COASTER
ACELSUX	EXCUSAL	**ACENOST**	COSTEAN		COATERS
ACELSXY	CALYXES		OCTANES		RECOATS
ACELTUY	ACUTELY	**ACENOTT**	ATTONCE	**ACEORSU**	ACEROUS
ACELTXY	EXACTLY	**ACENOTV**	CENTAVO		CAROUSE
ACEMMRR	CRAMMER	**ACENPRR**	PRANCER	**ACEORSW**	CROWEAS
ACEMMRS	SCAMMER	**ACENPRS**	PRANCES	**ACEORSX**	COAXERS
ACEMNOR	CREMONA	**ACENPRU**	PRAUNCE	**ACEORTU**	OUTRACE
	ROMANCE	**ACENPST**	CATNEPS	**ACEORTV**	OVERACT
ACEMNOS	ANCOMES	**ACENPSU**	PAUNCES	**ACEORTX**	EXACTOR
ACEMNPS	ENCAMPS		UNCAPES	**ACEOSSU**	CASEOUS
ACEMNRT	CREMANT	**ACENPSW**	PAWNCES	**ACEOSTT**	COSTATE
ACEMNRW	CREWMAN	**ACENPTT**	PENTACT	**ACEOSTU**	ACETOUS
ACEMNSU	ACUMENS	**ACENPTY**	PATENCY	**ACEOSTV**	AVOCETS
ACEMOPR	COMPARE	**ACENRRY**	ERRANCY		OCTAVES
	COMPEAR	**ACENRSS**	ANCRESS	**ACEOTTV**	CAVETTO
ACEMOPS	ECOMAPS		CASERNS	**ACEOTUU**	AUTOCUE
	POMACES	**ACENRST**	CANTERS		COUTEAU
ACEMORS	AMORCES		CARNETS	**ACEOTUX**	COTEAUX
	SCREAMO		NECTARS	**ACEPPRR**	CRAPPER
ACEMORU	MORCEAU		RECANTS	**ACEPPRS**	CAPPERS
ACEMOSS	COSMEAS		SCANTER	**ACEPRRS**	CARPERS
ACEMOST	CAMOTES		TANRECS		SCARPER
	COMATES		TRANCES		SCRAPER
ACEMOSU	MUCOSAE	**ACENRSU**	SURANCE	**ACEPRSS**	ESCARPS
ACEMPRR	CRAMPER	**ACENRSV**	CAVERNS		PARSECS
ACEMPRS	CAMPERS		CRAVENS		SCRAPES
	SCAMPER	**ACENRSY**	CARNEYS		SECPARS
ACEMPRT	CRAMPET		SCENARY		SPACERS
ACEMPRY	CAMPERY	**ACENRSZ**	ZARNECS	**ACEPRST**	CARPETS

	PREACTS		SCUTATE
	PRECAST	ACESTTY	TESTACY
	SPECTRA	ACESTUY	EUSTACY
ACEPRSU	APERCUS	ACFFHSU	CHAUFFS
	SCAUPER	ACFFIIT	CAITIFF
ACEPRTU	CAPTURE	ACFFIKM	MAFFICK
ACEPSST	ASPECTS	ACFFILT	AFFLICT
ACEPSTU	CUSPATE	ACFFINS	FANFICS
	TEACUPS	ACFFINY	FANCIFY
ACEQRTU	RACQUET	ACFFIRT	TRAFFIC
ACEQSSU	CASQUES	ACFFIRY	FARCIFY
	SACQUES	ACFFLSS	SCLAFFS
ACEQSTU	ACQUEST	ACFFLTU	FACTFUL
ACERRRY	RECARRY	ACFFOST	CASTOFF
ACERRSS	CRASSER		OFFCAST
	SCARERS	ACFGHIN	CHAFING
	SCARRES	ACFGINR	FARCING
ACERRST	CARTERS	ACFGINS	FACINGS
	CRATERS	ACFHIIS	FIASCHI
	TRACERS	ACFHIST	CATFISH
ACERRSU	CURARES	ACFHISU	FUCHSIA
ACERRSV	CARVERS	ACFHLNU	FLAUNCH
	CRAVERS	ACFHNOU	FAUCHON
ACERRSY	CRAYERS	ACFHRTU	FUTHARC
ACERRTT	RETRACT	ACFHRTY	FRATCHY
ACERRTU	TRACEUR	ACFIILN	FINICAL
ACERRTY	TRACERY	ACFIKNN	FINNACK
ACERRUV	VERRUCA	ACFIKNU	FUNCKIA
ACERRVY	CARVERY	ACFIKTY	TACKIFY
ACERSST	ACTRESS	ACFILNO	FOLACIN
	CASTERS	ACFILNY	FANCILY
	RECASTS	ACFILOY	COALIFY
ACERSSU	ARCUSES	ACFILRY	CLARIFY
	CAUSERS	ACFILSS	FISCALS
	CESURAS	ACFIMOR	ACIFORM
	SAUCERS		FORMICA
	SUCRASE	ACFIMRU	FUMARIC
ACERSSV	SCARVES	ACFIMSS	FASCISM
ACERSSY	CARSEYS	ACFINNS	FINNACS
	SCRAYES	ACFINNY	INFANCY
ACERSTT	SCATTER	ACFINOT	FACTION
ACERSTU	ACTURES	ACFINOV	FAVICON
	CAUTERS	ACFINRS	FARCINS
	CRUSTAE	ACFINRT	FRANTIC
	CURATES		INFARCT
ACERSTY	SECTARY		INFRACT
ACERTTT	TETRACT	ACFINRY	CARNIFY
ACERTTU	CURTATE	ACFIOPY	OPACIFY
ACERTTX	EXTRACT	ACFIOSS	FIASCOS
ACERTTY	CATTERY	ACFIPRY	CAPRIFY
ACERTUV	CURVATE	ACFIRSY	SACRIFY
ACERTUX	CURTAXE		SCARIFY
ACERTUY	CAUTERY	ACFISST	FASCIST
ACESSTT	STACTES	ACFKLRU	RACKFUL
ACESSTU	CAESTUS	ACFKLSU	SACKFUL
	CUESTAS	ACFLLOY	FOCALLY
ACESSTY	CYTASES	ACFLNOS	FALCONS
	ECSTASY		FLACONS
ACESSUY	CAUSEYS	ACFLNSU	CANFULS
	CAYUSES		CANSFUL
ACESTTU	ACUTEST	ACFLOPW	COWFLAP

ACFLOST	OLFACTS
ACFLPSU	CAPFULS
ACFLRSU	CARFULS
ACFLRTU	CARTFUL
ACFLRUU	FURCULA
ACFLTTU	TACTFUL
ACFLTUY	FACULTY
ACFMSTU	FACTUMS
ACFNNOT	NONFACT
ACFNNUY	UNFANCY
ACFNRTU	FRUCTAN
ACFNSTU	UNFACTS
ACFORST	FACTORS
	FORCATS
ACFORTY	FACTORY
ACFRRTU	FRACTUR
ACFRSTU	FRACTUS
ACGGHIS	CHIGGAS
ACGGINR	GRACING
ACGGIOS	AGOGICS
ACGGRSY	SCRAGGY
ACGHIKN	HACKING
ACGHIMO	OGHAMIC
ACGHINR	ARCHING
	CHAGRIN
	CHARING
ACGHINS	ACHINGS
	CASHING
	CHASING
ACGHINT	GNATHIC
ACGHINW	CHAWING
	CHINWAG
ACGHIOR	CHORAGI
ACGHIPR	GRAPHIC
ACGHIRS	SCRAIGH
ACGHLTU	CLAUGHT
ACGHNRU	GRAUNCH
ACGHOST	GOTCHAS
ACGHOSU	GAUCHOS
ACGHRRU	CURRAGH
ACGHRSU	CURAGHS
	SCRAUGH
ACGIILN	ALGINIC
ACGIITU	AUGITIC
ACGIJKN	JACKING
ACGIKLN	CALKING
	LACKING
ACGIKNP	PACKING
ACGIKNR	ARCKING
	CARKING
	CRAKING
	RACKING
ACGIKNS	CAKINGS
	CASKING
	SACKING
ACGIKNT	TACKING
ACGIKNV	VACKING
ACGIKNY	YACKING
ACGILLN	CALLING
ACGILLO	LOGICAL
ACGILMN	CALMING

ACGILMY	MYALGIC	ACGKMMO	GAMMOCK	ACHIMRS	CHARISM
ACGILNN	LANCING	ACGKORV	GARVOCK		CHIMARS
ACGILNO	COALING	ACGLLPU	CUPGALL		CHRISMA
ACGILNP	PLACING	ACGLNOR	CLANGOR	ACHIMSS	CHIASMS
ACGILNR	CARLING	ACGLNOY	AGLYCON		SCHISMA
ACGILNS	LACINGS	ACGLNSU	GLUCANS	ACHIMST	MASTICH
	SCALING	ACGLNSY	GLYCANS		TACHISM
ACGILNT	CATLING	ACGLOSU	CAGOULS	ACHINNU	UNCHAIN
	TALCING	ACGLOXY	COXALGY	ACHINOP	APHONIC
ACGILNU	CINGULA	ACGMNOP	CAMPONG	ACHINOY	ONYCHIA
	GLUCINA	ACGNNOR	CRANNOG	ACHINPS	SPINACH
ACGILNV	CALVING	ACGNOOT	OCTAGON	ACHINRS	CHINARS
ACGILNW	CLAWING	ACGNORS	GARCONS	ACHINRU	UNCHAIR
ACGILNY	CLAYING	ACGNOSS	GASCONS	ACHINRZ	ZARNICH
ACGILOS	CALIGOS	ACGNOSU	COUGANS	ACHINTX	XANTHIC
ACGILOT	OTALGIC	ACGORRY	GYROCAR	ACHINUV	CHAUVIN
ACGILRS	GARLICS	ACGORSU	COUGARS	ACHIOPS	ISOPACH
ACGIMMN	CAMMING	ACGORUU	COUGUAR	ACHIOPT	APHOTIC
ACGIMNO	COAMING	ACGOSWY	COGWAYS	ACHIORT	CHARIOT
ACGIMNP	CAMPING	ACGSTTU	CATGUTS		HARICOT
ACGIMNU	CAUMING	ACHHIRS	RHACHIS		ISOTACH
ACGINNN	CANNING	ACHHISV	CHAVISH	ACHIOST	ISOTACH
ACGINNR	CRANING	ACHHLOT	CHALOTH	ACHIPPS	SAPPHIC
	RANCING	ACHHMSU	CHUMASH	ACHIPST	HAPTICS
ACGINNS	CANINGS	ACHHOST	TOSHACH		PATHICS
ACGINNT	CANTING	ACHHPPU	CHUPPAH		SPATHIC
ACGINOR	ORGANIC	ACHHTTT	THATCHT	ACHIPTU	CHUPATI
ACGINOS	AGNOSIC	ACHHTTY	THATCHY	ACHIPTW	WHIPCAT
	ANGICOS	ACHIIKM	KAMICHI	ACHIQRU	CHARQUI
ACGINOT	COATING	ACHIILS	ISCHIAL	ACHIQSU	QUAICHS
	COTINGA	ACHIIMS	CHIASMI	ACHIRRT	TRIARCH
ACGINOX	COAXING	ACHIINT	CHIANTI	ACHIRTU	HAIRCUT
ACGINPP	CAPPING	ACHIIPS	PACHISI	ACHIRTY	CHARITY
ACGINPR	CARPING	ACHIIRV	CHIVARI	ACHISSS	CHASSIS
	CRAPING	ACHIJKS	HIJACKS	ACHISST	SCAITHS
ACGINPS	SCAPING	ACHIJNT	JACINTH	ACHISTT	CATTISH
	SPACING	ACHIKOS	KOCHIAS		CHATTIS
ACGINRS	ARCINGS	ACHIKRS	RICKSHA		TACHIST
	CARINGS	ACHIKRY	HAYRICK	ACHKKRU	CHUKKAR
	RACINGS	ACHIKSS	SHICKSA	ACHKKSU	CHUKKAS
	SACRING	ACHILLO	LOCHIAL	ACHKLST	KLATSCH
	SCARING	ACHILLP	PHALLIC	ACHKMMO	HAMMOCK
ACGINRT	CARTING	ACHILLS	CHALLIS	ACHKOPS	HOPSACK
	CRATING	ACHILLT	THALLIC	ACHKORS	CHOKRAS
	TRACING	ACHILMO	MALICHO	ACHKOSS	HASSOCK
ACGINRV	CARVING		MOCHILA		SHACKOS
	CRAVING	ACHILMS	CHIMLAS	ACHKOSW	WHACKOS
ACGINRZ	CRAZING	ACHILOR	CHORIAL	ACHKOTT	HATTOCK
ACGINSS	CASINGS	ACHILOS	SCHOLIA	ACHKRSU	CHUKARS
ACGINST	ACTINGS	ACHILPS	CALIPHS	ACHKSTW	THWACKS
	CASTING	ACHILRS	ARCHILS	ACHLLOO	ALCOHOL
ACGINSU	CAUSING		CARLISH	ACHLLOR	CHLORAL
	SAUCING	ACHILRY	CHARILY	ACHLLOS	CHOLLAS
ACGINSV	CAVINGS	ACHILST	CHITALS	ACHLLOT	CHALLOT
ACGINSW	CAWINGS	ACHILSY	CLAYISH	ACHLMOP	CAMPHOL
ACGINTT	CATTING	ACHILWY	LICHWAY	ACHLMSY	CHLAMYS
ACGINUV	VICUGNA	ACHIMNO	MANIHOC	ACHLMSZ	SCHMALZ
ACGIORT	ARGOTIC		MOHICAN	ACHLMYY	ALCHYMY
ACGIRST	GASTRIC	ACHIMOS	CHAMISO	ACHLNOS	LOCHANS
	TRAGICS		CHAMOIS	ACHLNOY	HALCYON
ACGKLLO	GALLOCK	ACHIMOX	CHAMOIX	ACHLNSU	NUCHALS
				ACHLNTU	TULCHAN

	UNLATCH	**ACHRSTY**	STARCHY	**ACIKNST**	ANTICKS
ACHLOPR	RAPLOCH	**ACHRSUU**	URACHUS		CATKINS
ACHLOPT	POTLACH	**ACHSSTU**	CUSHATS		CATSKIN
ACHLORS	CHORALS	**ACHSSTY**	STACHYS	**ACIKNTT**	TINTACK
	LORCHAS	**ACHSSUW**	CUSHAWS	**ACIKOPS**	PAIOCKS
	SCHOLAR	**ACHSTUW**	WAUCHTS	**ACIKORS**	ARKOSIC
ACHLORT	TROCHAL	**ACHSTUY**	CYATHUS	**ACIKPRT**	PATRICK
ACHLOSW	SALCHOW	**ACIIKNN**	CANIKIN		TRIPACK
ACHLOTY	ACOLYTH	**ACIIKRS**	AIRSICK	**ACIKPSS**	ASPICKS
ACHLPST	SPLATCH	**ACIILLN**	ALLICIN	**ACIKRST**	KARSTIC
ACHLTUZ	CHALUTZ	**ACIILMM**	MIMICAL	**ACILLLY**	ALLYLIC
ACHMNOR	MONARCH	**ACIILMS**	LAICISM	**ACILLMS**	MISCALL
	NOMARCH	**ACIILNR**	CLARINI	**ACILLRY**	LYRICAL
ACHMNOU	UNMACHO	**ACIILNS**	INCISAL	**ACILLSS**	SCILLAS
ACHMNRU	UNCHARM		SALICIN	**ACILMNO**	LIMACON
ACHMOPR	CAMPHOR		SINICAL		MALONIC
ACHMORS	CHROMAS	**ACIILNV**	VICINAL	**ACILMNU**	CULMINA
	MORCHAS	**ACIILOV**	VILIACO	**ACILMOP**	OILCAMP
ACHMORZ	MACHZOR	**ACIILPT**	APLITIC	**ACILMOT**	COMITAL
ACHMOST	STOMACH	**ACIILPU**	APICULI	**ACILMPS**	PLASMIC
ACHMPTU	MATCHUP	**ACIILRY**	CILIARY		PSALMIC
ACHMSSU	SUMACHS	**ACIILSS**	SILICAS	**ACILMPY**	CAMPILY
ACHMSUW	CUMSHAW	**ACIILST**	ITALICS	**ACILMSU**	MUSICAL
ACHNNOS	CHANSON	**ACIILSU**	ILIACUS	**ACILNNO**	CANNOLI
	NONCASH	**ACIILSV**	CLIVIAS	**ACILNNU**	UNCINAL
ACHNOOY	CHANOYO	**ACIILTY**	LAICITY	**ACILNNY**	CANNILY
ACHNORS	ANCHORS	**ACIIMMN**	MINICAM	**ACILNOR**	CLARINO
	ARCHONS	**ACIIMMS**	MIASMIC		CLARION
	RANCHOS	**ACIIMNR**	CRIMINA	**ACILNOS**	ALNICOS
ACHNORT	CHANTOR		MINICAR		OILCANS
ACHNOSS	SANCHOS	**ACIIMOT**	COMITIA	**ACILNOU**	INOCULA
ACHNOST	CHATONS	**ACIIMST**	ISMATIC	**ACILNOY**	ACYLOIN
ACHNOSY	ONYCHAS		ITACISM	**ACILNOZ**	CALZONI
ACHNOTY	TACHYON		SIMATIC	**ACILNPS**	CAPLINS
ACHNOUY	CHANOYU	**ACIINNO**	ANIONIC		INCLASP
ACHNOVY	ANCHOVY	**ACIINNS**	NIACINS	**ACILNPY**	PLIANCY
ACHNPSS	SCHNAPS	**ACIINOS**	ASINICO	**ACILNRS**	CARLINS
ACHNPUY	PAUNCHY	**ACIINOV**	AVIONIC	**ACILNST**	CATLINS
ACHNRTY	CHANTRY	**ACIINPS**	PISCINA		TINCALS
ACHNRUY	RAUNCHY	**ACIINTT**	TITANIC	**ACILNSU**	UNCIALS
	UNCHARY	**ACIINUX**	AUXINIC	**ACILNTU**	LUNATIC
ACHNSTU	CANTHUS	**ACIIPPR**	PRIAPIC	**ACILNTY**	ANTICLY
	CHAUNTS	**ACIIPRT**	PIRATIC		CANTILY
	STAUNCH	**ACIIRST**	SATIRIC	**ACILNUV**	VINCULA
ACHNSTY	SNATCHY	**ACIIRTT**	TRIATIC	**ACILOPT**	CAPITOL
ACHOOSS	CASHOOS	**ACIITTX**	TAXITIC		COALPIT
ACHOOST	CAHOOTS	**ACIJUZZ**	JACUZZI		OPTICAL
ACHOPRS	CARHOPS	**ACIKLLY**	ALKYLIC		TOPICAL
	COPRAHS	**ACIKLNS**	CALKINS	**ACILORR**	RACLOIR
ACHOPRT	TOPARCH	**ACIKLOR**	AIRLOCK	**ACILORV**	CORIVAL
ACHOPRY	CHARPOY	**ACIKLTY**	TACKILY	**ACILOSS**	SOCIALS
ACHOPSY	POCHAYS	**ACIKLWY**	WACKILY	**ACILOST**	CITOLAS
ACHORRS	CHARROS	**ACIKMOO**	OOMIACK		STOICAL
ACHORRT	TROCHAR	**ACIKMOT**	COMATIK	**ACILOTV**	VOLATIC
ACHORST	ORCHATS	**ACIKMPR**	RAMPICK		VOLTAIC
ACHORSU	AUROCHS	**ACIKMPW**	PICKMAW	**ACILOTX**	TOXICAL
ACHPPSU	CHUPPAS	**ACIKMSU**	UMIACKS	**ACILPRT**	CLIPART
ACHPRSS	SCARPHS	**ACIKNNP**	PANNICK	**ACILPST**	PLACITS
ACHPTUZ	CHUTZPA	**ACIKNPS**	PANICKS		PLASTIC
ACHRRTU	CRATHUR	**ACIKNPY**	PANICKY	**ACILPSU**	SPICULA
ACHRSST	SCARTHS	**ACIKNRS**	NICKARS	**ACILPTY**	TYPICAL

ACILRSS	CRISSAL	ACINNTU	ANNICUT	ACIQSTU	ACQUIST
ACILRST	CITRALS	ACINOPT	CAPTION		ACQUITS
ACILRSU	URACILS		PACTION	ACIRRSS	SIRCARS
ACILRSY	SCARILY	ACINOQU	COQUINA	ACIRRST	TRICARS
ACILRTU	CURTAIL	ACINORR	CARRION	ACIRRSU	CURARIS
	TRUCIAL	ACINORS	AIRCONS	ACIRSST	RACISTS
ACILRTY	CLARITY		RACINOS		SACRIST
ACILRVY	VICARLY		SARONIC	ACIRSSU	CUIRASS
ACILRYZ	CRAZILY	ACINORT	CAROTIN	ACIRSTT	ASTRICT
ACILSSS	CLASSIS		CORTINA	ACIRSTU	URTICAS
ACILSSU	CLUSIAS	ACINORV	CORVINA	ACIRSTW	TWISCAR
ACILSUY	SAUCILY	ACINOSS	CAISSON	ACIRSTY	SATYRIC
ACILTTY	CATTILY		CASINOS	ACIRSTZ	CZARIST
	TACITLY		CASSINO	ACIRTUY	RAUCITY
ACILTUV	VICTUAL	ACINOST	ACTIONS	ACISSTT	STATICS
ACIMMNO	AMMONIC		ATONICS	ACISSTU	CASUIST
ACIMNOP	CAMPION		CATIONS	ACISTTU	CATSUIT
ACIMNOR	MARCONI	ACINOSU	ACINOUS	ACISTUV	VACUIST
	MINORCA	ACINOSY	SYCONIA	ACITUVY	VACUITY
ACIMNOS	ANOSMIC	ACINOTT	TACTION	ACJKKSY	SKYJACK
	CAMIONS	ACINOTU	AUCTION	ACJKLOW	LOCKJAW
	CONIMAS		CAUTION	ACJKNNO	JANNOCK
	MANIOCS	ACINPRT	CANTRIP	ACJKOPS	PAJOCKS
	MASONIC	ACINPRU	PURANIC	ACJKOPT	JACKPOT
ACIMNPU	PANICUM	ACINPRY	CYPRIAN	ACJLORU	JOCULAR
ACIMNRS	ARCMINS	ACINPSS	PANISCS	ACJMNTU	MUNTJAC
	NARCISM	ACINPST	CATNIPS	ACJPTUU	CAJUPUT
ACIMNRT	MANTRIC	ACINQTU	QUANTIC	ACKKLOY	KOLACKY
ACIMNRU	CRANIUM	ACINRST	NARCIST	ACKLLOP	POLLACK
	CUMARIN	ACINRSU	CRUSIAN	ACKLLOY	LAYLOCK
ACIMNTT	CATMINT	ACINRTT	TANTRIC	ACKLLSY	SLACKLY
ACIMOOS	OOMIACS	ACINRTU	CURTAIN	ACKLMNO	LOCKMAN
ACIMOPT	APOMICT		TURACIN	ACKLMOR	ARMLOCK
	POTAMIC	ACINSTU	ANICUTS		LOCKRAM
ACIMOSS	MOSAICS		NAUTICS	ACKLNOU	UNCLOAK
ACIMOST	ATOMICS	ACINSUV	VICUNAS	ACKLNRY	CRANKLY
	MATICOS	ACIOPRS	PICAROS	ACKLOOR	OARLOCK
	OSMATIC		PROSAIC	ACKLORV	LAVROCK
	SOMATIC	ACIOPRT	APRICOT	ACKLORW	WARLOCK
ACIMOSV	VOMICAS		APROTIC	ACKLORY	ROCKLAY
ACIMPRT	CRAMPIT		PAROTIC	ACKLOSS	LASSOCK
	PTARMIC		PATRICO	ACKMMMO	MAMMOCK
ACIMPRY	PRIMACY	ACIOPST	COPITAS	ACKMNOS	SOCKMAN
ACIMPSS	SCAMPIS		PSOATIC	ACKMNRU	RUCKMAN
	SPASMIC	ACIOPTT	APTOTIC	ACKMOST	STOMACK
ACIMPST	IMPACTS	ACIOPTY	OPACITY	ACKMOTT	MATTOCK
ACIMRSS	RACISMS	ACIORRS	CORSAIR	ACKNNOW	ACKNOWN
ACIMRST	MATRICS	ACIORSU	CARIOUS	ACKNOSW	ACKNOWS
ACIMRSY	MYRICAS		CURIOSA	ACKNPRS	PRANCKS
ACIMRSZ	CZARISM	ACIORTT	CITATOR	ACKNPSU	UNPACKS
ACIMSST	MASTICS		RICOTTA	ACKNRTU	UNTRACK
	MISACTS	ACIOSST	SCOTIAS	ACKNSTU	UNSTACK
	MISCAST	ACIOSSV	OVISACS		UNTACKS
ACIMSTT	TACTISM	ACIPRSS	CASSPIR	ACKOPRR	PARROCK
ACINNOT	ACTINON	ACIPRSY	PISCARY	ACKOPSY	YAPOCKS
	CANTION	ACIPRTT	TIPCART	ACKORRT	TARROCK
	CONTAIN	ACIPRVY	PRIVACY	ACKOSTW	TOWSACK
ACINNOZ	CANZONI	ACIPSST	SPASTIC	ACKOWZZ	WAZZOCK
ACINNST	INCANTS	ACIPSTT	TIPCATS	ACKPSSY	SKYCAPS
	STANNIC	ACIPTUY	PAUCITY	ACKPSTU	STACKUP
ACINNSY	CYANINS	ACIQRTU	QUARTIC	ACLLLOY	LOCALLY

ACLLOOR	COROLLA	**ACLOSST**	COSTALS	**ACNORTT**	CONTRAT
ACLLOOS	ALCOOLS	**ACLOSTU**	LOCUSTA	**ACNORTU**	COURANT
ACLLOPS	CALLOPS		TALCOUS	**ACNOSSZ**	SCAZONS
	SCALLOP	**ACLOSTW**	COTWALS	**ACNOSTT**	OCTANTS
ACLLORS	COLLARS	**ACLPRTY**	CRYPTAL	**ACNOSTU**	CONATUS
ACLLORU	LOCULAR	**ACLPRUU**	CUPULAR		NOCTUAS
ACLLOSU	CALLOUS	**ACLRSSW**	SCRAWLS		TOUCANS
ACLLOSW	CALLOWS	**ACLRSSY**	CRASSLY	**ACNOSTW**	SNOWCAT
ACLLOTU	OUTCALL	**ACLRSTU**	CRUSTAL	**ACNPRSY**	SYNCARP
ACLLOVY	VOCALLY		CURTALS	**ACNRRSU**	CURRANS
ACLLRYY	ACRYLYL	**ACLRSTY**	CRYSTAL	**ACNRRTU**	CURRANT
ACLLSUY	CULLAYS	**ACLRSWY**	SCRAWLY	**ACNRSTU**	UNCARTS
ACLMNOO	LOCOMAN	**ACLSSTU**	CUTLASS	**ACNRSUY**	UNSCARY
ACLMNPU	UNCLAMP	**ACMNOPR**	CRAMPON	**ACNRSWY**	SCRAWNY
ACLMNUY	CALUMNY	**ACMNOPY**	COMPANY	**ACNRTUY**	TRUANCY
ACLMOPS	COPALMS	**ACMNORS**	MACRONS	**ACNRUYZ**	UNCRAZY
ACLMORS	CLAMORS	**ACMNORY**	ACRONYM	**ACOOPRR**	CORPORA
ACLMORU	CLAMOUR	**ACMNOSS**	MASCONS	**ACOOPRT**	ROOTCAP
ACLMOSU	MUCOSAL	**ACMNSTU**	SANCTUM	**ACOOPSU**	OPACOUS
ACLMSTU	TALCUMS	**ACMOOST**	SCOTOMA	**ACOOPTT**	TOPCOAT
ACLMSUU	LUCUMAS	**ACMOPRT**	COMPART	**ACOORTU**	TOURACO
ACLMSUY	MASCULY	**ACMOPSS**	COMPASS	**ACOOSTV**	OCTAVOS
ACLNNOO	NONCOLA	**ACMOPST**	COMPAST	**ACOPPRR**	PROCARP
ACLNOOR	CORONAL	**ACMOPTU**	CAMPOUT	**ACOPPRS**	COPPRAS
ACLNOOT	COOLANT	**ACMORRS**	CARROMS	**ACOPPRT**	CARPORT
	OCTANOL	**ACMORST**	COMARTS	**ACOPRST**	CAPTORS
ACLNOOV	VOLCANO	**ACMORTW**	CATWORM	**ACOPSTU**	UPCOAST
ACLNORU	CORNUAL	**ACMOSST**	MASCOTS	**ACOPSTW**	COWPATS
	COURLAN		SCAMTOS	**ACORRST**	CARROTS
ACLNOSS	CLASSON	**ACMOSSU**	MUCOSAS		TROCARS
ACLNOST	COLTANS	**ACMOSTT**	TOMCATS	**ACORRTT**	TRACTOR
ACLNOSX	CLAXONS	**ACMOSTU**	MOTUCAS	**ACORRTU**	CURATOR
ACLNOUV	UNVOCAL	**ACMPSSY**	SPYCAMS	**ACORRTY**	CARROTY
ACLNPSU	UNCLASP	**ACMQTUU**	CUMQUAT	**ACORSST**	CASTORS
ACLNRTU	TRUNCAL	**ACMRSSU**	SACRUMS		COSTARS
ACLNSTY	SCANTLY	**ACMRSSW**	SCRAWMS	**ACORSSU**	SARCOUS
ACLNSUV	VULCANS	**ACMSSTU**	MUSCATS		SOUCARS
ACLOOPP	ALCOPOP	**ACMSTUU**	MUTUCAS	**ACORSSW**	SOWCARS
ACLOOPR	CARPOOL	**ACMSUUV**	VACUUMS	**ACORSTT**	COTTARS
ACLOORT	LOCATOR	**ACNNNOS**	CANNONS	**ACORSTU**	CUATROS
ACLOOSZ	ZOCALOS	**ACNNNUY**	UNCANNY		SURCOAT
ACLOPRT	CALTROP	**ACNNORY**	CANONRY		TURACOS
	PROCTAL	**ACNNOST**	CANTONS	**ACORSTV**	CAVORTS
ACLOPRU	COPULAR	**ACNNOSY**	CANYONS	**ACORSTX**	OXCARTS
	CUPOLAR		SONANCY	**ACORSTY**	CASTORY
ACLOPSU	COPULAS	**ACNNRSY**	SCRANNY	**ACORSUU**	RAUCOUS
	CUPOLAS	**ACNOOPS**	POONACS	**ACORSYZ**	CORYZAS
	SCOPULA	**ACNOORS**	CORONAS	**ACORTUU**	TURACOU
ACLOPSY	CALYPSO		RACOONS	**ACOSSZZ**	SCOZZAS
ACLOPTY	POLYACT	**ACNOORT**	CARTOON	**ACOSTTU**	OUTACTS
ACLORRS	CORRALS		CORANTO		OUTCAST
ACLORST	CARLOTS	**ACNOPSW**	SNOWCAP	**ACOSUUV**	VACUOUS
	CROTALS	**ACNORRS**	RANCORS	**ACPPRSY**	SCRAPPY
	SCROTAL	**ACNORRU**	RANCOUR	**ACPRSSW**	SCRAWPS
ACLORSU	CAROLUS	**ACNORRY**	CARRYON	**ACPSSTU**	CATSUPS
	OCULARS	**ACNORST**	CANTORS		UPCASTS
	OSCULAR		CARTONS	**ACPSTUU**	USUCAPT
	RUCOLAS		CONTRAS	**ACRRSTU**	CRATURS
ACLORTY	ACTORLY		CRATONS	**ACRSTTU**	TRACTUS
ACLORUV	VOCULAR	**ACNORSU**	NACROUS	**ADDDDEL**	DADDLED
ACLORYZ	CORYZAL	**ACNORSY**	CRAYONS	**ADDDDOR**	DODDARD

ADDDEER	DREADED		SEDATED	ADDEIPS	PADDIES
	READDED		STEADED	ADDEIRR	ARRIDED
ADDDEFL	FADDLED	ADDEEVW	ADVEWED	ADDEIRT	TARDIED
ADDDEGL	GLADDED	ADDEEWX	DEWAXED	ADDEISS	SADDIES
ADDDEIL	DAIDLED	ADDEFHN	HANDFED	ADDEIST	TADDIES
ADDDEIS	DADDIES	ADDEFIR	FADDIER	ADDEISV	ADVISED
ADDDEIW	WADDIED	ADDEFLS	FADDLES	ADDEISW	SWADDIE
ADDDELN	DANDLED	ADDEFLY	FADEDLY		WADDIES
ADDDELP	PADDLED	ADDEFNU	UNFADED	ADDEISY	DAYSIDE
ADDDELR	RADDLED	ADDEFRT	DRAFTED	ADDEITU	AUDITED
ADDDELS	DADDLES	ADDEFRU	DEFRAUD	ADDEJLY	JADEDLY
	SADDLED	ADDEFRW	DWARFED	ADDEJNU	UNJADED
ADDDELW	DAWDLED	ADDEGGL	DAGGLED	ADDEJRU	ADJURED
	WADDLED	ADDEGGR	DRAGGED	ADDEKLR	DARKLED
ADDDELY	ADDEDLY	ADDEGHO	GODHEAD	ADDELLU	ALLUDED
ADDDENO	DEODAND	ADDEGIL	GLADDIE		DUALLED
ADDDENS	ADDENDS	ADDEGIN	DEADING	ADDELMW	DWALMED
ADDDENU	UNADDED	ADDEGJU	ADJUDGE	ADDELNR	DANDLER
ADDDEQU	QUADDED	ADDEGLN	DANGLED	ADDELNS	DANDLES
ADDDGIN	DADDING		GLADDEN	ADDELNU	UNLADED
ADDDHOY	HODADDY	ADDEGLR	GLADDER	ADDELPP	DAPPLED
ADDDOOS	DOODADS	ADDEGRS	GADDERS	ADDELPR	PADDLER
ADDEEEM	ADEEMED	ADDEGRU	GUARDED	ADDELPS	PADDLES
ADDEEEY	DEADEYE	ADDEHIR	DIEHARD	ADDELRS	LADDERS
ADDEEFM	DEFAMED		DIHEDRA		RADDLES
ADDEEGR	DEGRADE	ADDEHIS	HADDIES		SADDLER
ADDEEHL	HEALDED	ADDEHKS	KEDDAHS	ADDELRT	DARTLED
ADDEEHN	HEADEND	ADDEHLN	HANDLED	ADDELRW	DAWDLER
ADDEEHR	ADHERED	ADDEHLS	DALEDHS		DRAWLED
	REDHEAD	ADDEHOR	HOARDED		WADDLER
ADDEEHS	DEASHED	ADDEHRS	SHARDED	ADDELRY	DREADLY
ADDEEIR	DEAIRED	ADDEHST	HADDEST		LADDERY
	READIED	ADDEIIK	DIDAKEI	ADDELSS	SADDLES
ADDEEIT	IDEATED	ADDEIIM	DIAMIDE	ADDELST	STADDLE
ADDEEKN	KNEADED	ADDEIIS	DAISIED	ADDELSW	DAWDLES
ADDEEKR	DAKERED	ADDEILL	DALLIED		SWADDLE
ADDEELM	MEDALED		DIALLED		WADDLES
ADDEELN	DELENDA	ADDEILP	PLAIDED	ADDELTW	TWADDLE
	LADENED	ADDEILR	DIEDRAL	ADDELTY	DATEDLY
ADDEELP	PEDALED		DRAILED	ADDELYZ	DAZEDLY
	PLEADED	ADDEILS	DAIDLES	ADDELZZ	DAZZLED
ADDEELS	DELEADS		LADDIES	ADDEMMR	DRAMMED
ADDEELT	DELATED	ADDEILT	DILATED	ADDEMMW	DWAMMED
ADDEELY	DELAYED	ADDEIMR	ADMIRED	ADDEMNS	DEMANDS
ADDEEMN	AMENDED		MARDIED		MADDENS
	DEADMEN	ADDEIMS	DIADEMS	ADDEMNU	MAUNDED
ADDEEMR	DREAMED	ADDEIMX	ADMIXED	ADDEMOP	POMADED
ADDEEMS	ADDEEMS	ADDEINO	ADENOID	ADDEMRS	MADDERS
ADDEENS	DEADENS	ADDEINP	PANDIED	ADDEMRY	DRAMEDY
ADDEENV	ADVENED	ADDEINR	DANDIER	ADDEMST	MADDEST
	DAVENED		DRAINED	ADDEMUW	DWAUMED
ADDEENY	DENAYED	ADDEINS	DANDIES	ADDENOR	ADORNED
ADDEEOT	DEODATE		SDAINED	ADDENOT	DONATED
ADDEERR	DREADER	ADDEINT	NIDATED		NODATED
ADDEERS	DEADERS	ADDEINU	UNAIDED	ADDENOU	DUODENA
ADDEERT	DERATED	ADDEINV	INVADED	ADDENPU	PUDENDA
	REDATED		VIDENDA	ADDENRS	DANDERS
	TREADED	ADDEIOR	RADIOED	ADDENRT	DRANTED
ADDEERY	DERAYED	ADDEIOT	IODATED	ADDENRU	DAUNDER
	YEARDED		TOADIED	ADDENSS	DESANDS
ADDEEST	DEADEST	ADDEIOV	AVOIDED		SADDENS

ADDENSU	ASUDDEN	ADDIKTZ	TZADDIK		ALLEGED
ADDENSY	SDAYNED	ADDILMN	MIDLAND	ADEEGLM	GLEAMED
ADDENTU	DAUNTED	ADDILMS	LADDISM	ADEEGLN	ANGELED
	UNDATED	ADDILNY	DANDILY		GELANDE
ADDEOPT	ADOPTED	ADDILOS	DISLOAD		GLEANED
ADDEORS	DEODARS	ADDIMNO	DIAMOND	ADEEGLR	LAGERED
ADDEOSS	SADDOES	ADDIMOR	DIADROM		REGALED
ADDEPPR	DRAPPED	ADDIMRS	DIRDAMS	ADEEGLT	GELATED
ADDEPRS	PADDERS	ADDIMSS	MISADDS		LEGATED
ADDEPTU	UPDATED	ADDIMSY	DISMAYD		TEAGLED
ADDERSS	ADDRESS		MIDDAYS	ADEEGLU	LEAGUED
ADDERST	ADDREST	ADDINOR	ANDROID	ADEEGLV	GAVELED
	RADDEST	ADDINRY	DIANDRY	ADEEGLZ	DEGLAZE
ADDERSW	SWARDED	ADDIPRS	DISPRAD	ADEEGMN	ENDGAME
	WADDERS	ADDIQST	TSADDIQ		MANEGED
ADDERSY	DRYADES	ADDIQTZ	TZADDIQ		MENAGED
ADDERTT	DRATTED	ADDIRZZ	DIZZARD	ADEEGMS	DEGAMES
ADDESST	SADDEST	ADDISTZ	TZADDIS	ADEEGNR	ANGERED
ADDESTU	ADUSTED	ADDLLRU	DULLARD		DERANGE
	SUDATED	ADDLNRY	DRYLAND		ENRAGED
ADDFHIS	FADDISH	ADDLOOS	SOLDADO		GRANDEE
ADDFIMS	FADDISM	ADDLTWY	TWADDLY		GRENADE
ADDFINY	DANDIFY	ADDMNOS	DODMANS	ADEEGNT	AGENTED
ADDFIST	FADDIST		ODDSMAN		ENDGATE
ADDGGIN	GADDING	ADDMOOS	ADDOOMS		NEGATED
ADDGHIN	HADDING	ADDNNOR	DONNARD	ADEEGNV	AVENGED
ADDGIIR	DIAGRID	ADDOORS	DORADOS		VENDAGE
ADDGILN	ADDLING	ADDOPSY	DASYPOD	ADEEGOT	DOGEATE
ADDGIMN	MADDING	ADDORST	DOTARDS		GOATEED
ADDGINO	DADOING	ADDOSTU	OUTADDS	ADEEGPR	PREAGED
ADDGINP	PADDING	ADDQSUY	SQUADDY	ADEEGRR	REGRADE
ADDGINR	RADDING	ADEEEFY	FEDAYEE	ADEEGRS	DRAGEES
ADDGINS	ADDINGS	ADEEELS	EASELED		GREASED
	SADDING	ADEEELV	DELEAVE	ADEEGRU	GUARDEE
ADDGINU	DAUDING	ADEEEMN	DEMEANE	ADEEGRV	GREAVED
ADDGINW	DAWDING	ADEEERR	ARREEDE	ADEEGRW	RAGWEED
	WADDING	ADEEERX	EXEDRAE		WAGERED
ADDGIOS	GADOIDS	ADEEESW	SEAWEED	ADEEGSS	DEGASES
ADDGIPY	GIDDYAP	ADEEFGU	FEAGUED	ADEEHHS	SHAHEED
ADDGLNO	GLADDON	ADEEFHS	SHEAFED	ADEEHIR	HEADIER
ADDGMNO	GODDAMN	ADEEFIR	AREFIED	ADEEHJS	HADJEES
ADDGMOS	GODDAMS		FEDARIE	ADEEHLR	HEDERAL
ADDGOOS	OGDOADS	ADEEFKR	FREAKED	ADEEHLS	LEASHED
ADDGOOW	DAGWOOD	ADEEFLN	ENDLEAF		SHEALED
ADDGORW	GODWARD	ADEEFLR	FEDERAL	ADEEHLX	EXHALED
ADDHIKS	KADDISH	ADEEFLS	DEFLEAS	ADEEHMN	HEADMEN
ADDHILS	LADDISH	ADEEFLT	DEFLATE	ADEEHNN	HENNAED
ADDHIMS	MADDISH	ADEEFMR	DEFAMER	ADEEHNS	DASHEEN
ADDHINP	DAPHNID	ADEEFMS	DEFAMES	ADEEHNT	NETHEAD
ADDHISS	SADDISH	ADEEFNS	DEAFENS	ADEEHNV	HAVENED
	SIDDHAS	ADEEFPR	PREFADE	ADEEHPR	EPHEDRA
ADDHITY	HYDATID	ADEEFRT	DRAFTEE	ADEEHRR	ADHERER
ADDHLOO	LADHOOD	ADEEFRW	WAFERED		REHEARD
ADDHOOS	DOODAHS	ADEEFST	DEAFEST	ADEEHRS	ADHERES
ADDHOTY	ATHODYD		DEFASTE		HEADERS
ADDHSSU	SADDHUS		DEFEATS		HEARSED
ADDIINS	DISDAIN		FEASTED		HEDERAS
ADDIIPS	DIAPSID	ADEEGGH	EGGHEAD		SHEARED
ADDIKST	TSADDIK	ADEEGGL	ALEGGED	ADEEHRT	EARTHED
ADDIKSZ	ZADDIKS	ADEEGGN	ENGAGED		HEARTED
ADDIKTY	KATYDID	ADEEGLL	ALLEDGE	ADEEHRV	HAVERED

ADEEHRX	EXHEDRA		PEDALER	**ADEEMWY**	MAYWEED
ADEEHSS	DEASHES		PLEADER	**ADEENNS**	ENNEADS
ADEEHST	HEADSET		REPLEAD	**ADEENNX**	ANNEXED
ADEEHSV	SHEAVED	**ADEELPS**	DELAPSE	**ADEENPS**	SNEAPED
ADEEHSX	HEXADES		ELAPSED		SPEANED
ADEEHSY	HAYSEED		PLEASED	**ADEENRS**	DEANERS
ADEEIJT	JADEITE		SEPALED		ENDEARS
ADEEILM	EMAILED	**ADEELPT**	PETALED	**ADEENRU**	UNEARED
	LIMEADE		PLEATED	**ADEENRV**	RAVENED
ADEEILN	ALIENED	**ADEELQU**	EQUALED	**ADEENRY**	DEANERY
	DELAINE	**ADEELRS**	DEALERS		RENAYED
ADEEILR	LEADIER		LEADERS		YEAREND
ADEEILS	AEDILES		REDEALS		YEARNED
	DEISEAL	**ADEELRT**	ALERTED	**ADEENST**	STANDEE
ADEEILY	EYELIAD		ALTERED		STEANED
ADEEIMN	DEMAINE		REDEALT	**ADEENSV**	ADVENES
ADEEIMT	MEDIATE		RELATED	**ADEENSW**	DEEWANS
ADEEINN	ADENINE		TREADLE	**ADEENTT**	DENTATE
ADEEINS	ANISEED	**ADEELRV**	RAVELED	**ADEEOPT**	ADOPTEE
ADEEIRR	READIER	**ADEELRW**	LEEWARD	**ADEEORS**	OREADES
ADEEIRS	DEARIES	**ADEELRX**	RELAXED	**ADEEORW**	OARWEED
	READIES	**ADEELRY**	DELAYER	**ADEEPPR**	PAPERED
ADEEIRW	WEARIED		LAYERED	**ADEEPRS**	PREASED
ADEEISS	DISEASE		RELAYED		RESPADE
	SEASIDE	**ADEELST**	DELATES		SPEARED
ADEEIST	IDEATES		STEALED	**ADEEPRT**	ADEPTER
ADEEISV	ADVISEE	**ADEELSV**	SLEAVED		PREDATE
ADEEITU	AUDITEE	**ADEELSW**	SWEALED		RETAPED
ADEEITV	DEVIATE	**ADEELTT**	LADETTE		TAPERED
ADEEJSY	DEEJAYS	**ADEELTV**	VALETED	**ADEEPRV**	DEPRAVE
ADEEKNP	KNEEPAD		VELATED		PERVADE
ADEEKNR	KNEADER	**ADEELTX**	EXALTED		REPAVED
	NAKEDER	**ADEELTZ**	TEAZLED	**ADEEPSS**	PESADES
ADEEKNS	SNEAKED	**ADEELUV**	DEVALUE	**ADEEPTX**	EXAPTED
ADEEKNW	WAKENED	**ADEELYZ**	LAYDEEZ	**ADEEQRU**	QUAERED
ADEEKRS	DEKARES	**ADEEMNR**	AMENDER	**ADEEQTU**	EQUATED
	SKEARED		ENARMED	**ADEERRR**	DREARER
ADEEKRW	REWAKED		MEANDER	**ADEERRS**	DREARES
	WREAKED		REAMEND		READERS
ADEEKTW	TWEAKED		REEDMAN		REDEARS
ADEEKWY	WEEKDAY		RENAMED		REDSEAR
ADEELLP	LAPELED	**ADEEMNS**	AMENDES		REREADS
ADEELLS	ALLSEED		DEMEANS	**ADEERRT**	RETREAD
ADEELLY	ALLEYED		SEEDMAN		TREADER
ADEELMM	MELAMED	**ADEEMNT**	ENTAMED	**ADEERRV**	AVERRED
ADEELMN	LEADMEN	**ADEEMNY**	DEMAYNE	**ADEERRW**	REDWARE
ADEELMP	EMPALED	**ADEEMOS**	OEDEMAS	**ADEERSS**	RESEDAS
ADEELMR	EMERALD	**ADEEMPR**	EMPARED	**ADEERST**	DEAREST
ADEELMS	MEASLED		PREMADE		DERATES
ADEELMT	MEDALET	**ADEEMRR**	DREAMER		ESTRADE
	METALED		REARMED		REASTED
ADEELMU	AEMULED		REDREAM		REDATES
ADEELMY	YEALMED	**ADEEMRS**	MEDRESA		SEDATER
ADEELNP	DEPLANE		REMADES		STEARED
	PANELED		REMEADS		TASERED
ADEELNR	LEARNED		SMEARED	**ADEERSV**	ADVERSE
ADEELNS	LEADENS	**ADEEMRT**	REMATED		EVADERS
ADEELNT	EDENTAL	**ADEEMST**	STEAMED	**ADEERSW**	DRAWEES
	LATENED	**ADEEMSU**	MEDUSAE		RESAWED
ADEELOS	ELODEAS	**ADEEMSW**	MAWSEED	**ADEERTT**	ARETTED
ADEELPR	PEARLED	**ADEEMTW**	MATWEED		TREATED

ADEERTV	AVERTED	**ADEFIRS**	FARSIDE	**ADEGGPS**	SPAGGED
	TAVERED		FRAISED	**ADEGGRR**	DRAGGER
ADEERTW	DEWATER	**ADEFIST**	DAFTIES	**ADEGGRS**	DAGGERS
	TARWEED		FADIEST	**ADEGGRY**	RAGGEDY
	WATERED	**ADEFITX**	FIXATED	**ADEGGST**	GADGETS
ADEERTX	RETAXED	**ADEFKLN**	FANKLED		STAGGED
ADEERVW	WAVERED		FLANKED	**ADEGGSW**	SWAGGED
ADEERWX	REWAXED	**ADEFKNR**	FRANKED	**ADEGGTY**	GADGETY
ADEESST	SEDATES	**ADEFKNU**	UNFAKED	**ADEGHIN**	HEADING
ADEESSX	AXSEEDS	**ADEFLLN**	ELFLAND	**ADEGHIR**	HAGRIDE
ADEESSY	ESSAYED	**ADEFLLW**	DEWFALL		HEADRIG
ADEESTT	ESTATED	**ADEFLMM**	FLAMMED	**ADEGHIS**	HIDAGES
ADEESTU	SAUTEED	**ADEFLNN**	FENLAND	**ADEGHJU**	JUGHEAD
ADEESTW	SWEATED	**ADEFLOR**	ALFREDO	**ADEGHLU**	LAUGHED
ADEESTY	YEASTED	**ADEFLOT**	FLOATED	**ADEGHMO**	HOMAGED
ADEESVY	SAVEYED	**ADEFLPP**	FLAPPED	**ADEGHNP**	PHANGED
ADEESWX	DEWAXES	**ADEFLRS**	FARDELS	**ADEGHNS**	GNASHED
ADEETUX	EXUDATE	**ADEFLRU**	DAREFUL		HAGDENS
ADEEWWX	WAXWEED	**ADEFLTT**	FLATTED	**ADEGHNW**	WHANGED
ADEFFFL	FLAFFED	**ADEFLTU**	DEFAULT	**ADEGHOR**	HAGRODE
ADEFFGR	GRAFFED		FAULTED	**ADEGHPR**	GRAPHED
ADEFFIN	AFFINED	**ADEFMNU**	UNFAMED	**ADEGHST**	GHASTED
ADEFFIP	PIAFFED	**ADEFMOS**	DEFOAMS	**ADEGHUW**	WAUGHED
ADEFFIR	DAFFIER	**ADEFNRS**	FARDENS	**ADEGILL**	GALLIED
ADEFFIS	DAFFIES		SNARFED	**ADEGILN**	ALIGNED
ADEFFIX	AFFIXED	**ADEFNSU**	SNAFUED		DEALING
ADEFFLM	MAFFLED		UNDEAFS		LEADING
ADEFFLO	LEADOFF	**ADEFNUZ**	UNFAZED	**ADEGILO**	GEOIDAL
ADEFFLR	RAFFLED	**ADEFOOS**	SEAFOOD	**ADEGILR**	GLADIER
ADEFFLW	WAFFLED	**ADEFORS**	FEDORAS		GLAIRED
ADEFFNY	NYAFFED	**ADEFORV**	FAVORED	**ADEGILS**	SILAGED
ADEFFQU	QUAFFED	**ADEFORY**	FEODARY	**ADEGILT**	LIGATED
ADEFFST	STAFFED		FORAYED		TAIGLED
ADEFFUW	WAUFFED	**ADEFOTU**	FADEOUT	**ADEGILV**	GLAIVED
ADEFGGL	FLAGGED	**ADEFPPR**	FRAPPED	**ADEGIMP**	MEDIGAP
ADEFGGR	FRAGGED	**ADEFPRR**	PREFARD	**ADEGIMS**	DEGAMIS
ADEFGLN	FANGLED	**ADEFRRT**	DRAFTER	**ADEGINN**	DEANING
	FLANGED		REDRAFT	**ADEGINR**	AREDING
ADEFGNS	DEFANGS	**ADEFRRW**	DWARFER		DEARING
ADEFGOR	FORAGED	**ADEFRST**	STRAFED		DERAIGN
ADEFGOT	FAGOTED	**ADEFRSU**	FADEURS		EARDING
ADEFGOU	FOUGADE	**ADEFRSW**	SWARFED		GRADINE
ADEFGRS	DEFRAGS	**ADEFRSY**	DEFRAYS		GRAINED
ADEFGRT	GRAFTED	**ADEFRUY**	FEUDARY		READING
ADEFHIS	DEAFISH	**ADEFSTT**	DAFTEST	**ADEGINS**	AGNISED
ADEFHIT	FAITHED	**ADEGGGL**	GAGGLED	**ADEGINV**	DEAVING
ADEFHLS	FLASHED	**ADEGGHL**	HAGGLED		EVADING
	FLEADHS	**ADEGGHS**	SHAGGED	**ADEGINW**	WINDAGE
ADEFHLU	HEADFUL	**ADEGGIR**	DAGGIER	**ADEGINY**	YEADING
ADEFHRW	WHARFED	**ADEGGIS**	GADGIES	**ADEGINZ**	AGNIZED
ADEFHST	SHAFTED	**ADEGGIU**	GAUDGIE	**ADEGIOT**	GODETIA
ADEFIKL	FADLIKE		GUIDAGE	**ADEGIRS**	AGRISED
ADEFILL	FLAILED	**ADEGGLR**	DRAGGLE	**ADEGIRT**	TRIAGED
ADEFILS	DISLEAF		GARGLED	**ADEGIRU**	GAUDIER
ADEFIMN	INFAMED		RAGGLED	**ADEGIRZ**	AGRIZED
ADEFIMS	DISFAME	**ADEGGLS**	DAGGLES	**ADEGIST**	AGISTED
ADEFINN	FANNIED		SLAGGED	**ADEGISU**	AGUISED
ADEFINR	FRIANDE	**ADEGGLW**	WAGGLED		GAUDIES
ADEFINS	FADEINS	**ADEGGMO**	DEMAGOG	**ADEGISV**	VISAGED
ADEFINT	DEFIANT	**ADEGGNS**	SNAGGED	**ADEGIUV**	VIDUAGE
	FAINTED	**ADEGGOP**	PEDAGOG	**ADEGIUZ**	AGUIZED

ADEGJLN	JANGLED		WORDAGE	ADEHKRS	SHARKED
ADEGLLU	ULLAGED	ADEGOSS	DOSAGES	ADEHLLO	HALLOED
ADEGLMM	GLAMMED		SEADOGS		HOLLAED
ADEGLMN	MANGLED	ADEGOST	DOGATES	ADEHLLP	LAPHELD
ADEGLMR	MALGRED		DOTAGES	ADEHLMS	LAMEDHS
ADEGLMU	GLAUMED	ADEGOTT	TOGATED	ADEHLNR	HANDLER
ADEGLNN	ENDLANG	ADEGOVY	VOYAGED	ADEHLNS	HANDLES
ADEGLNR	DANGLER	ADEGPRS	GRASPED		HANDSEL
	GNARLED		SPADGER	ADEHLOS	SHOALED
ADEGLNS	DANGLES		SPARGED	ADEHLOT	LOATHED
	GLANDES	ADEGPRU	UPGRADE	ADEHLPR	RALPHED
	LAGENDS	ADEGPUZ	UPGAZED	ADEHLPS	PLASHED
	SLANGED	ADEGRRS	GRADERS	ADEHLRS	HARELDS
ADEGLNT	TANGLED		REGARDS		HERALDS
ADEGLNU	LANGUED	ADEGRRU	GUARDER	ADEHLSS	HASSLED
ADEGLNW	WANGLED	ADEGRSS	GRASSED		SLASHED
ADEGLOP	GALOPED	ADEGRST	RADGEST	ADEHLST	DALETHS
ADEGLOT	GLOATED	ADEGRSU	DESUGAR	ADEHLSU	SHAULED
ADEGLPU	PLAGUED		SUGARED	ADEHLSW	SHAWLED
ADEGLRS	DARGLES	ADEGRTY	GYRATED	ADEHLTY	DEATHLY
ADEGLRU	RAGULED		TRAGEDY	ADEHMMS	SHAMMED
ADEGLRY	GRADELY	ADEGRUU	AUGURED	ADEHMMW	WHAMMED
ADEGLSS	GLASSED	ADEGRUY	GAUDERY	ADEHMNR	HARDMEN
ADEGLTY	DALGYTE	ADEGRYZ	AGRYZED		HERDMAN
ADEGMNS	GADSMEN	ADEGSSU	DEGAUSS	ADEHMOP	MOPHEAD
ADEGMNU	AGENDUM	ADEHHKS	KHEDAHS	ADEHMOR	HADROME
	GUDEMAN	ADEHHOP	HOPHEAD	ADEHMPR	PHARMED
ADEGMOP	MEGAPOD	ADEHHOT	HOTHEAD	ADEHMRS	DERHAMS
ADEGMRU	MAUGRED	ADEHHRS	HARSHED	ADEHMSS	SMASHED
ADEGNNO	NONAGED	ADEHHSS	SHASHED	ADEHNPS	DAPHNES
ADEGNNU	DUNNAGE	ADEHIJS	JEHADIS	ADEHNRS	HANDERS
ADEGNOP	PONDAGE	ADEHIKS	DASHEKI		HARDENS
ADEGNOR	GROANED	ADEHIKV	KHEDIVA	ADEHNRU	UNHEARD
ADEGNOS	SONDAGE	ADEHILN	HIELAND	ADEHNSS	SNASHED
ADEGNOT	TANGOED		INHALED	ADEHNST	HANDSET
ADEGNOV	DOGVANE	ADEHILP	HELIPAD	ADEHNSU	UNHEADS
ADEGNOW	GOWANED	ADEHILS	HALIDES	ADEHNTU	HAUNTED
	WAGONED	ADEHILY	HEADILY	ADEHOOP	APEHOOD
ADEGNPR	PRANGED	ADEHIMO	HAEMOID	ADEHOPT	POTHEAD
ADEGNPS	SPANGED	ADEHINP	HEADPIN	ADEHOPX	HEXAPOD
ADEGNPU	UNPAGED		PINHEAD	ADEHORR	HOARDER
ADEGNRR	GNARRED	ADEHINR	HANDIER	ADEHOST	HOASTED
	GRANDER	ADEHIPP	HAPPIED	ADEHOSX	OXHEADS
ADEGNRS	DANGERS	ADEHIPR	RAPHIDE	ADEHOTW	TOWHEAD
	GANDERS	ADEHIPS	APHIDES	ADEHPPW	WHAPPED
	GARDENS		DIPHASE	ADEHPRS	PHRASED
ADEGNRT	DRAGNET	ADEHIPT	PITHEAD		SHARPED
	GRANTED	ADEHIRR	HARDIER	ADEHPST	HEPTADS
ADEGNRU	ENGUARD		HARRIED		SPATHED
	RAUNGED	ADEHIRS	AIRSHED	ADEHPSW	PSHAWED
ADEGNRW	WRANGED		DASHIER	ADEHQSU	QUASHED
ADEGNST	STANGED		HARDIES	ADEHRRU	HURRAED
ADEGNSU	AUGENDS		SHADIER	ADEHRSS	DASHERS
ADEGNTU	GAUNTED	ADEHIRT	AIRTHED		SHADERS
	UNGATED	ADEHIRW	RAWHIDE	ADEHRST	DEARTHS
ADEGNTW	TWANGED	ADEHIRY	HAYRIDE		HARDEST
ADEGNUW	UNWAGED		HYDRIAE		HARDSET
ADEGNUZ	UNGAZED	ADEHKNS	SHANKED		HATREDS
ADEGORS	DOGEARS	ADEHKNT	THANKED		THREADS
ADEGORT	GAROTED	ADEHKOR	HARDOKE		TRASHED
ADEGORW	DOWAGER	ADEHKOT	KATHODE	ADEHRSY	HYDRASE

ADEHRTW	THRAWED		UNIDEAL	ADEIMNU	UNAIMED
	WRATHED	ADEILNV	ANDVILE	ADEIMOU	MIAOUED
ADEHRTY	HYDRATE		ANVILED	ADEIMOW	MIAOWED
	THREADY	ADEILNX	INDEXAL	ADEIMPR	DAMPIER
ADEHSST	STASHED	ADEILOP	OEDIPAL	ADEIMPV	IMPAVED
ADEHSSW	SWASHED	ADEILOR	DARIOLE	ADEIMRR	ADMIRER
ADEHSTW	SWATHED	ADEILOS	DEASOIL		MARDIER
ADEHSYY	HEYDAYS		ISOLEAD		MARRIED
ADEHUZZ	HUZZAED	ADEILOU	DOULEIA	ADEIMRS	ADMIRES
ADEIILR	DELIRIA	ADEILOZ	DIAZOLE		MARDIES
	IRIDEAL	ADEILPP	APPLIED		MISREAD
ADEIILS	DAILIES	ADEILPR	LIPREAD		SEDARIM
	LIAISED		PEDRAIL		SIDEARM
	SEDILIA		PREDIAL	ADEIMRT	READMIT
ADEIIMN	AMIDINE	ADEILPS	ALIPEDS	ADEIMRY	MIDYEAR
	DIAMINE		ELAPIDS	ADEIMST	DIASTEM
ADEIINR	DENARII		LAIPSED		MISDATE
ADEIINT	INEDITA		LAPIDES	ADEIMSV	VIDAMES
ADEIINZ	DIAZINE		PAIDLES	ADEIMSX	ADMIXES
ADEIIPR	PERIDIA		PALSIED	ADEIMTU	IDEATUM
ADEIIRS	AIRSIDE		PLEIADS		TAEDIUM
	DAIRIES	ADEILPT	PLAITED	ADEIMTY	DAYTIME
	DIARIES		TALIPED	ADEINNN	NANDINE
	DIARISE	ADEILQU	QUAILED		NANNIED
ADEIIRZ	DIARIZE	ADEILRR	LARDIER	ADEINNR	NARDINE
ADEIISS	DAISIES	ADEILRS	DERAILS	ADEINNS	DANNIES
ADEIJMR	JEMIDAR		DIALERS	ADEINOR	ANEROID
ADEIKLN	KNAIDEL		REDIALS	ADEINOS	ADONISE
ADEIKLS	SKAILED		SIDERAL		ANODISE
ADEIKLY	KAYLIED	ADEILRT	DILATER		SODAINE
ADEIKNS	KANDIES		REDTAIL	ADEINOV	NAEVOID
ADEIKRS	DAIKERS		TRAILED	ADEINOX	DIOXANE
	DARKIES	ADEILRU	UREDIAL	ADEINOZ	ADONIZE
ADEIKRT	TRAIKED	ADEILRV	RIVALED		ANODIZE
ADEILLL	DIALLEL		VALIDER	ADEINPR	PARDINE
ADEILLP	PALLIED	ADEILRY	READILY	ADEINPS	PANDIES
ADEILLR	DALLIER	ADEILSS	AIDLESS		PANSIED
	DIALLER		DEASILS		SPAINED
	RALLIED	ADEILST	DETAILS	ADEINPT	DEPAINT
ADEILLS	DALLIES		DILATES		PAINTED
	DISLEAL	ADEILSU	AUDILES		PATINED
	LALDIES		DEASIUL	ADEINRR	DRAINER
	SALLIED		DUALISE		RANDIER
ADEILLT	TALLIED	ADEILSV	DEVISAL	ADEINRS	RANDIES
ADEILLV	VIALLED	ADEILSY	DIALYSE		SANDIER
ADEILLY	IDEALLY		EYLIADS		SARDINE
ADEILMM	DILEMMA	ADEILUZ	DUALIZE	ADEINRT	ANTIRED
ADEILMO	MELODIA	ADEILYZ	DIALYZE		DETRAIN
ADEILMP	IMPALED	ADEIMMR	MERMAID		TRAINED
	IMPLEAD	ADEIMMS	MISMADE	ADEINRU	UNAIRED
ADEILMS	MAELIDS	ADEIMMT	TAMMIED		URANIDE
	MEDIALS	ADEIMNO	AMIDONE	ADEINRV	INVADER
	MISDEAL		DOMAINE		RAVINED
	MISLEAD	ADEIMNR	ADERMIN	ADEINSS	SDAINES
ADEILMU	MIAULED		INARMED	ADEINST	DESTAIN
ADEILNN	ANNELID	ADEIMNS	DEMAINS		DETAINS
	LINDANE		MAIDENS		INSTEAD
ADEILNP	PLAINED		MEDIANS		NIDATES
ADEILNS	DENIALS		MEDINAS		SAINTED
	SNAILED		SIDEMAN		SATINED
ADEILNU	ALIUNDE	ADEIMNT	MEDIANT		STAINED

ADEINSV	INVADES	ADEISSV	ADVISES	ADELLMU	MEDULLA
ADEINSW	DEWANIS		DISSAVE	ADELLNR	LANDLER
ADEINTT	TAINTED	ADEISSZ	ASSIZED	ADELLNW	ELLWAND
ADEINTU	AUDIENT	ADEISTU	DAUTIES	ADELLOR	ODALLER
ADEINTV	DEVIANT	ADEISTV	AVIDEST	ADELLOW	ALLOWED
ADEINVV	NAVVIED		DATIVES	ADELLOY	ALLOYED
ADEIOPS	ADIPOSE		VISTAED	ADELLPS	SPALLED
ADEIOPT	OPIATED	ADEISTW	DAWTIES	ADELLRS	LADLERS
ADEIORS	ROADIES		WAISTED	ADELLRU	ALLURED
	SOREDIA	ADEISVV	SAVVIED		UDALLER
ADEIORV	AVODIRE	ADEISWY	SIDEWAY	ADELLST	STALLED
	AVOIDER		WAYSIDE	ADELLSU	ALLUDES
ADEIORX	EXORDIA	ADEITUZ	DEUTZIA		ALUDELS
ADEIOST	IODATES	ADEITWY	TIDEWAY	ADELLSV	DEVALLS
	TOADIES	ADEJMOR	MAJORED	ADELMMS	SLAMMED
ADEIOSX	OXIDASE	ADEJMRU	JUMARED		SMALMED
ADEIOSZ	DIAZOES		MUDEJAR	ADELMNN	LANDMEN
ADEIOTX	OXIDATE	ADEJNSU	JAUNSED	ADELMNR	MANDREL
ADEIOVV	VAIVODE	ADEJNTU	JAUNTED	ADELMNT	MANTLED
ADEIOVW	WAIVODE	ADEJOPR	JEOPARD	ADELMOR	EARLDOM
ADEIOWW	WAIWODE	ADEJRRU	ADJURER	ADELMOS	DAMOSEL
ADEIPPR	DRAPPIE	ADEJRSU	ADJURES	ADELMOZ	DAMOZEL
	PREPAID	ADEJSSU	JUDASES	ADELMPS	PSALMED
ADEIPPU	APPUIED	ADEKKNS	SKANKED		SAMPLED
ADEIPRR	DRAPIER	ADEKLNP	PLANKED	ADELMRS	MEDLARS
	PARRIED	ADEKLNR	RANKLED	ADELMRU	MURALED
	RAPIDER	ADEKLNS	KALENDS	ADELMSS	DAMSELS
ADEIPRS	ASPIRED	ADEKLNY	NAKEDLY	ADELMST	MALTEDS
	DESPAIR	ADEKLOP	POLKAED	ADELMSU	ALMUDES
	DIAPERS	ADEKLOS	SKOALED		MEDUSAL
	PRAISED	ADEKLPP	KLAPPED	ADELMSW	WADMELS
ADEIPRT	DIPTERA	ADEKLRS	DARKLES	ADELMYZ	MAZEDLY
	PARTIED	ADEKLST	SKLATED	ADELNNP	PLANNED
	PIRATED		STALKED	ADELNNU	UNLADEN
ADEIPRV	VAPIDER	ADEKLSY	YSLAKED	ADELNOR	LADRONE
ADEIPSS	APSIDES	ADEKLUW	WAULKED	ADELNOS	LOADENS
ADEIQRU	QUERIDA	ADEKMNS	DESKMAN	ADELNOT	TALONED
ADEIRRS	ARRIDES	ADEKMRS	DEMARKS	ADELNOY	YEALDON
	RAIDERS	ADEKNOU	UNOAKED	ADELNPT	PLANTED
ADEIRRT	TARDIER	ADEKNPP	KNAPPED	ADELNPY	ENDPLAY
	TARRIED	ADEKNPR	PRANKED	ADELNRS	DARNELS
ADEIRRV	ARRIVED	ADEKNPS	SPANKED		ENLARDS
ADEIRST	ARIDEST	ADEKNRR	KNARRED		LANDERS
	ASTERID	ADEKNRS	DARKENS		RELANDS
	ASTRIDE	ADEKNRT	DARKNET		SLANDER
	DIASTER	ADEKNRU	UNRAKED		SNARLED
	DISRATE	ADEKNSS	SANDEKS	ADELNRU	LAUNDER
	STAIDER	ADEKNST	DANKEST		LURDANE
	STAIRED		STANKED		RUNDALE
	TARDIES	ADEKNSU	UNASKED	ADELNRY	DEARNLY
	TIRADES	ADEKNSW	SWANKED	ADELNSS	SENDALS
ADEIRSU	RESIDUA	ADEKNUW	UNWAKED	ADELNST	DENTALS
ADEIRSV	ADVISER	ADEKNVY	VANDYKE		SLANTED
	VARDIES	ADEKORT	TROAKED	ADELNSU	UNLADES
ADEIRSX	RADIXES	ADEKPRS	SPARKED		UNLEADS
ADEIRTT	ATTIRED	ADEKPSY	KEYPADS	ADELNSY	ADENYLS
ADEIRTV	TARDIVE	ADEKRST	DARKEST	ADELNTU	LUNATED
ADEIRTY	DIETARY		STARKED		UNDEALT
ADEISSS	DASSIES		STRAKED	ADELNTW	WETLAND
ADEISST	DISSEAT	ADEKRSY	DARKEYS	ADELNUW	UNLAWED
	SAIDEST	ADELLMS	SMALLED	ADELOPR	LEOPARD

	PAROLED	**ADELTUV**	VAULTED		MEDUSAS
	PRELOAD	**ADELTUX**	LUXATED	**ADEMTTU**	MUTATED
ADELOPS	DEPOSAL	**ADELTWZ**	WALTZED	**ADENNOY**	ANNOYED
	PEDALOS	**ADEMMPS**	SPAMMED		ANODYNE
ADELOPT	PLOATED	**ADEMMRS**	DAMMERS	**ADENNPS**	SPANNED
	TADPOLE		SMARMED	**ADENNPT**	PENDANT
ADELORS	LOADERS	**ADEMMRT**	TRAMMED	**ADENNST**	STANDEN
	ORDEALS	**ADEMMNS**	SANDMEN	**ADENNSU**	DUENNAS
	RELOADS	**ADEMMNU**	MUNDANE	**ADENNSW**	SWANNED
ADELORT	DELATOR		UNNAMED	**ADENNWY**	DEWANNY
	LEOTARD	**ADEMNOR**	MADRONE	**ADENOOP**	NAPOOED
ADELORU	ROULADE		ROADMEN	**ADENOOT**	ODONATE
ADELOSS	ALDOSES	**ADEMNOS**	DAEMONS	**ADENOOZ**	ENDOZOA
	LASSOED		MASONED	**ADENOPR**	APRONED
ADELOST	SALTOED		MODENAS		OPERAND
	SOLATED		MONADES		PADRONE
ADELOSV	SALVOED		NOMADES		PANDORE
ADELOSW	WALDOES	**ADEMNOW**	ADWOMEN	**ADENOPS**	DAPSONE
ADELOTT	TOTALED		WOMANED	**ADENOPT**	NOTEPAD
ADELOTU	OUTLEAD	**ADEMNPS**	DAMPENS		TONEPAD
ADELPPP	PLAPPED	**ADEMNRS**	DAMNERS	**ADENORR**	ADORNER
ADELPPS	DAPPLES		MANREDS		READORN
	SAPPLED		RANDEMS	**ADENORT**	TORNADE
	SLAPPED		REMANDS	**ADENORU**	RONDEAU
ADELPRS	PEDLARS	**ADEMNRU**	DURAMEN	**ADENOST**	ASTONED
ADELPRY	PEDLARY		MANURED		DONATES
ADELPST	SPALTED		MAUNDER		ONSTEAD
	STAPLED		UNARMED	**ADENOSU**	DOUANES
ADELPSU	UPLEADS	**ADEMNRY**	DRAYMEN	**ADENOSY**	NOYADES
ADELPSW	DEWLAPS		YARDMEN	**ADENOTT**	ATTONED
	SPAWLED	**ADEMNSS**	DESMANS		NOTATED
ADELPSY	SPLAYED		MADNESS	**ADENOTV**	NOVATED
ADELPTT	PLATTED	**ADEMNST**	TANDEMS	**ADENOTZ**	ZONATED
ADELPTW	DEWLAPT	**ADEMNSU**	MEDUSAN	**ADENPPR**	PARPEND
ADELPTY	ADEPTLY		SUDAMEN	**ADENPPS**	APPENDS
ADELRRS	LARDERS	**ADEMNSY**	DAYSMEN		SNAPPED
ADELRRU	RUDERAL	**ADEMNTU**	UNMATED	**ADENPPW**	WAPPEND
ADELRRW	DRAWLER		UNTAMED	**ADENPRR**	PARDNER
ADELRSS	RASSLED	**ADEMOOV**	AMOOVED	**ADENPRS**	PANDERS
	SARDELS	**ADEMOPS**	APEDOMS	**ADENPRU**	UNDRAPE
ADELRST	DARTLES		POMADES		UNPARED
	SLARTED	**ADEMORR**	ARMORED	**ADENPRW**	PRAWNED
ADELRSU	LAUDERS	**ADEMORS**	RADOMES		PREDAWN
ADELRSW	WARSLED	**ADEMOSV**	VAMOSED	**ADENPST**	PEDANTS
ADELRSZ	DRAZELS	**ADEMOSW**	MEADOWS		PENTADS
ADELRTT	RATTLED	**ADEMOSY**	SAMOYED	**ADENPSW**	SPAWNED
ADELRTW	TRAWLED		SOMEDAY	**ADENPSX**	EXPANDS
ADELRTX	DEXTRAL	**ADEMOWY**	MEADOWY		SPANDEX
ADELRTY	LYRATED	**ADEMPRS**	DAMPERS	**ADENPSY**	DYSPNEA
ADELRWW	WRAWLED	**ADEMPRT**	TRAMPED	**ADENPTU**	UNADEPT
ADELRWX	WRAXLED	**ADEMPSS**	SPASMED	**ADENPUV**	UNPAVED
ADELRZZ	DAZZLER	**ADEMPST**	DAMPEST	**ADENQTU**	QUANTED
ADELSST	DESALTS		STAMPED	**ADENRRS**	DARNERS
ADELSTT	SLATTED	**ADEMPSW**	SWAMPED		ERRANDS
ADELSTU	AULDEST	**ADEMRRU**	EARDRUM		SNARRED
	SALUTED	**ADEMRST**	SMARTED	**ADENRRW**	REDRAWN
ADELSUV	AVULSED	**ADEMRSU**	REMUDAS	**ADENRRY**	REYNARD
ADELSWY	SWAYLED	**ADEMRSW**	SWARMED	**ADENRSS**	SANDERS
ADELSZZ	DAZZLES	**ADEMRTU**	MATURED		SARSDEN
ADELTTT	TATTLED	**ADEMSST**	DEMASTS	**ADENRST**	ENDARTS
ADELTTW	WATTLED	**ADEMSSU**	ASSUMED		STANDER

	STARNED	**ADEORSV**	OVERSAD	SWARVED
ADENRSU	ASUNDER		SAVORED	**ADERWWY**	WEYWARD
	DANSEUR	**ADEORSW**	REDOWAS	**ADESSTU**	SUDATES
	DAUNERS	**ADEORTT**	ROTATED	**ADESSTW**	WADSETS
ADENRSW	DAWNERS		TROATED	**ADESTTU**	STATUED
	WANDERS	**ADEORTU**	OUTDARE	**ADESTTW**	SWATTED
	WARDENS		OUTREAD		WADSETT
ADENRSZ	ZANDERS		READOUT	**ADFFGIN**	DAFFING
ADENRTT	TRANTED	**ADEORWY**	RODEWAY	**ADFFHNO**	HANDOFF
ADENRTU	DAUNTER	**ADEORYZ**	ZEDOARY		OFFHAND
	NATURED	**ADEOSTT**	TOASTED	**ADFFILY**	DAFFILY
	UNRATED	**ADEOTTU**	OUTDATE	**ADFFIST**	DISTAFF
	UNTREAD	**ADEOWWY**	WAYWODE	**ADFFLNO**	FANFOLD
ADENRTV	VERDANT	**ADEPPRS**	DAPPERS	**ADFFLOO**	OFFLOAD
ADENRTX	DEXTRAN	**ADEPPRT**	TRAPPED	**ADFFOOR**	AFFOORD
ADENRTY	DENTARY	**ADEPPRW**	WRAPPED	**ADFFORS**	AFFORDS
	TRAYNED	**ADEPPST**	STAPPED	**ADFGGIN**	FADGING
	TYRANED	**ADEPPSW**	SWAPPED	**ADFGINN**	FANDING
ADENRUY	UNREADY	**ADEPPTU**	PUPATED	**ADFGINR**	FARDING
ADENRUZ	UNRAZED	**ADEPPUY**	APPUYED	**ADFGINS**	FADINGS
ADENSSS	SADNESS	**ADEPRRS**	DRAPERS	**ADFGLLU**	GLADFUL
ADENSSU	SUNDAES		SPARRED	**ADFHLNU**	HANDFUL
ADENSSW	WESANDS	**ADEPRRY**	DRAPERY	**ADFHLNY**	FLYHAND
	WESSAND	**ADEPRSS**	ADPRESS	**ADFHLSY**	SHADFLY
ADENSTT	ATTENDS		SPADERS	**ADFHOOS**	SHADOOF
ADENSTU	SAUNTED		SPREADS	**ADFHSSU**	SHADUFS
	UNSATED	**ADEPRST**	DEPARTS	**ADFILLU**	FLUIDAL
ADENSTV	ADVENTS		DRAPETS	**ADFIMNR**	FINDRAM
ADENSTY	STAYNED		PETARDS	**ADFIMNY**	DAMNIFY
ADENSUV	UNSAVED	**ADEPRSY**	SPRAYED	**ADFINRS**	FRIANDS
ADENSUW	UNSAWED	**ADEPRTT**	PRATTED	**ADFINRT**	INDRAFT
ADENSWY	ENDWAYS	**ADEPRTU**	UPDATER	**ADFIORS**	FORSAID
ADENSWZ	WEZANDS		UPRATED	**ADFLLYY**	LADYFLY
ADENTTU	ATTUNED	**ADEPSTT**	SPATTED	**ADFLMOO**	DAMFOOL
	NUTATED	**ADEPSTU**	UPDATES	**ADFLMPU**	MUDFLAP
	TAUNTED	**ADEPSZZ**	SPAZZED	**ADFLMTU**	MUDFLAT
ADENTUV	VAUNTED	**ADEQRSU**	SQUARED	**ADFLNOP**	PLAFOND
ADENTUX	UNTAXED	**ADERRST**	DARTERS	**ADFLNSY**	SANDFLY
ADENUWX	UNWAXED		DARTRES	**ADFLORU**	FOULARD
ADENUWY	UNWAYED		RETARDS	**ADFMNOS**	FANDOMS
ADEOORS	ROADEOS		STARRED	**ADFMOSU**	FUMADOS
ADEOORT	ODORATE		TRADERS	**ADFNNOT**	FONDANT
ADEOPPS	APPOSED	**ADERRSW**	DRAWERS	**ADFNOST**	FANTODS
	PEAPODS		REDRAWS	**ADFOOPT**	FOOTPAD
ADEOPQU	OPAQUED		REWARDS	**ADFOOTW**	FATWOOD
ADEOPRR	EARDROP		WARDERS	**ADFORRW**	FORWARD
ADEOPRT	ADOPTER	**ADERRSY**	YARDERS		FROWARD
	READOPT	**ADERSSU**	ASSURED	**ADFPRTU**	UPDRAFT
ADEOPRV	VAPORED		RUDASES	**ADGGGIN**	DAGGING
ADEOPSS	SPADOES	**ADERSSW**	SAWDERS	**ADGGHNO**	HANGDOG
ADEOPST	PODESTA		SWEARDS	**ADGGILN**	GADLING
ADEORRS	ADORERS	**ADERSTT**	STARTED	**ADGGILR**	RIGGALD
	DROSERA		TETRADS	**ADGGINN**	DANGING
ADEORRW	ARROWED	**ADERSTV**	ADVERTS	**ADGGINO**	GOADING
ADEORRZ	RAZORED		STARVED	**ADGGINR**	GRADING
ADEORSS	SARODES	**ADERSTW**	STEWARD		NIGGARD
ADEORST	DOATERS		STRAWED	**ADGGINU**	GAUDING
	ROASTED		WRASTED	**ADGHILO**	HIDALGO
	TORSADE	**ADERSTY**	STRAYED	**ADGHINN**	HANDING
	TROADES	**ADERSUY**	DASYURE	**ADGHINS**	DASHING
ADEORSU	AROUSED	**ADERSVW**	DWARVES		SHADING

ADGHINU	HAUDING	ADGINRR	DARRING	ADHIKOP	HAPKIDO
ADGHIPR	DIGRAPH	ADGINRS	DARINGS	ADHIKRS	DARKISH
ADGHIRR	ARDRIGH		GRADINS	ADHIKSU	HAIDUKS
ADGHIRS	DISHRAG	ADGINRT	DARTING	ADHILMO	HALIDOM
ADGHNNU	HANDGUN		TRADING	ADHILNY	HANDILY
ADGHNOS	HAGDONS	ADGINRU	DAURING	ADHILOP	HAPLOID
	SANDHOG	ADGINRW	DRAWING	ADHILOS	HALOIDS
ADGHNOW	HAGDOWN		WARDING	ADHILOY	HOLIDAY
ADGHORW	HOGWARD	ADGINRY	DRAYING		HYALOID
ADGHRSU	DURGAHS		YARDING		HYOIDAL
ADGHRTU	DRAUGHT	ADGINST	DATINGS	ADHILRY	HARDILY
ADGIILN	DIALING	ADGINSU	AUDINGS	ADHILSY	LADYISH
	GLIADIN	ADGINSW	WADINGS		SHADILY
	LAIDING	ADGINTU	DAUTING	ADHIMNS	HANDISM
ADGIILT	DIGITAL	ADGINTW	DAWTING	ADHIMPS	DAMPISH
ADGIIMN	MAIDING	ADGINWY	GWYNIAD		PHASMID
ADGIINN	DAINING	ADGIORT	GORDITA	ADHIMRS	DIRHAMS
ADGIINO	GONIDIA	ADGIPRU	PAGURID		MIDRASH
ADGIINR	GRADINI	ADGIRSU	GUISARD	ADHINOT	ANTHOID
	RAIDING	ADGIRZZ	GIZZARD	ADHINPS	DISHPAN
ADGIINS	SIGANID	ADGLLNO	GOLLAND	ADHINPU	DAUPHIN
ADGIINU	IGUANID	ADGLMNO	MANGOLD	ADHINSS	SANDHIS
ADGIINW	GWINIAD	ADGLNOO	DONGOLA	ADHIOOS	HOODIAS
ADGIIPY	PYGIDIA		GONDOLA	ADHIORS	HAIRDOS
ADGIJOS	ADJIGOS	ADGLNOR	GOLDARN	ADHIOST	TOADISH
ADGIKNR	DARKING	ADGLNOW	GOWLAND	ADHIRSS	SHAIRDS
ADGILLN	LADLING	ADGLNOY	DAYLONG	ADHJKOS	KHODJAS
ADGILMN	MADLING	ADGLNRY	GRANDLY	ADHKKSU	DUKKAHS
ADGILNN	LANDING	ADGLOPS	LAPDOGS		DUKKHAS
ADGILNO	DIGONAL	ADGLOWY	DAYGLOW	ADHKORW	DORHAWK
	LOADING	ADGMNOO	GOODMAN	ADHKOSU	SHAKUDO
ADGILNR	DARLING	ADGMNOR	GORMAND	ADHLLLO	HOLDALL
	LARDING	ADGNOOR	DRAGOON	ADHLLNO	HOLLAND
ADGILNS	LADINGS		GADROON	ADHLMOY	HOLYDAM
	LIGANDS	ADGNOOS	GOONDAS	ADHLMPY	LYMPHAD
ADGILNU	LANGUID	ADGNOPS	DOGNAPS	ADHLORS	HOLARDS
	LAUDING	ADGNORS	DRAGONS	ADHLOYY	HOLYDAY
ADGILOR	GOLIARD	ADGNORU	AGROUND	ADHMNOO	HOODMAN
ADGILOS	DIALOGS	ADGNORY	ORGANDY		MANHOOD
ADGILOV	VALGOID	ADGNRRU	GURNARD	ADHMNSU	NUMDAHS
ADGILRY	DAYGIRL	ADGNRSU	DURGANS	ADHMORY	HYDROMA
ADGILSU	GLADIUS	ADGNRUU	UNGUARD	ADHNNSU	NHANDUS
ADGILUY	GAUDILY	ADGOOPS	GOSPODA		UNHANDS
ADGIMMN	DAMMING	ADGORSW	WARDOGS	ADHNNUY	UNHANDY
ADGIMNN	DAMNING	ADGORTU	OUTDRAG	ADHNOOS	DAHOONS
ADGIMNP	DAMPING	ADGPRSU	UPDRAGS	ADHNORS	HADRONS
ADGIMNR	MRIDANG	ADGRSTU	DUSTRAG	ADHNORU	UNHOARD
ADGINNR	DARNING	ADHHIRS	HARDISH	ADHNOSU	HOUDANS
	NARDING	ADHHISS	SHAHIDS	ADHNOTU	HANDOUT
	RANDING	ADHHIST	HADITHS	ADHNRSU	DHURNAS
ADGINNS	SANDING	ADHHISW	WHIDAHS	ADHNRSY	SHANDRY
ADGINNT	DANTING	ADHHKSU	DUHKHAS	ADHNRTY	HYDRANT
ADGINNW	DAWNING	ADHHMOS	SHAHDOM	ADHNRUY	UNHARDY
ADGINOR	ADORING	ADHHOSU	HOUDAHS	ADHOOPT	HOPTOAD
	GRADINO	ADHHOSW	HOWDAHS	ADHOORR	RHODORA
	ROADING	ADHHSWY	WHYDAHS	ADHOORS	DHOORAS
ADGINOS	GANOIDS	ADHIIJS	JIHADIS	ADHOPRT	HARDTOP
ADGINOT	DOATING	ADHIIJT	IJTIHAD	ADHOPRU	UPHOARD
ADGINPP	DAPPING	ADHIIKS	DASHIKI	ADHOPST	DASHPOT
ADGINPR	DRAPING	ADHIIMS	MAIDISH	ADHORRU	DHOURRA
ADGINPS	SPADING	ADHIKNS	DANKISH	ADHORSU	DOURAHS

ADHOSSW	SHADOWS	**ADIKNRS**	DISRANK	**ADIMNOS**	DAIMONS
ADHOSWY	SHADOWY	**ADIKOST**	DAKOITS		DOMAINS
ADHPRSU	PURDAHS	**ADIKOTY**	DAKOITY		MADISON
ADHPSUU	UPHAUDS	**ADIKPRS**	DISPARK	**ADIMNRS**	MANDIRS
ADHRRSU	DHURRAS	**ADIKQRU**	DIQUARK	**ADIMNSS**	DISMANS
ADIIILR	IRIDIAL	**ADIKSST**	DIKASTS	**ADIMNST**	MANTIDS
ADIIINR	IRIDIAN	**ADIKSSU**	ADSUKIS	**ADIMOOS**	ISODOMA
ADIIKOS	AIKIDOS	**ADIKSTT**	DIKTATS	**ADIMORR**	MIRADOR
ADIIKOT	DAKOITI	**ADIKSUZ**	ADZUKIS	**ADIMOST**	DIATOMS
ADIIKSY	YIDAKIS	**ADIKSWY**	SKIDWAY		MASTOID
ADIILLS	ILLIADS	**ADILLMM**	MILLDAM	**ADIMOSY**	DAIMYOS
ADIILMS	MILADIS	**ADILLRY**	LAIRDLY	**ADIMOTT**	MATTOID
	MISDIAL	**ADILLSY**	DISALLY	**ADIMPRY**	PYRAMID
	MISLAID	**ADILLTY**	TIDALLY	**ADIMQSU**	QUIDAMS
ADIILNO	LIANOID	**ADILLVY**	VALIDLY	**ADIMRSS**	DISARMS
ADIILNV	INVALID	**ADILLYY**	DAYLILY	**ADIMRSU**	RADIUMS
ADIILOS	SIALOID	**ADILMNO**	MONDIAL	**ADIMRSW**	MISDRAW
ADIILRW	WIRILDA	**ADILMNR**	MANDRIL	**ADIMRSY**	MYRIADS
ADIILSS	SIALIDS		RIMLAND	**ADIMSSS**	SADISMS
ADIILST	DIALIST	**ADILMNU**	MAUDLIN	**ADIMSST**	DISMAST
ADIILUV	DILUVIA	**ADILMOP**	DIPLOMA	**ADIMSSY**	DISMAYS
ADIIMMS	MAIDISM	**ADILMOS**	AMIDOLS	**ADIMSTU**	DUMAIST
ADIIMNN	INDAMIN	**ADILMOU**	ALODIUM		STADIUM
ADIIMNS	AMIDINS	**ADILMOY**	AMYLOID	**ADIMSWY**	MIDWAYS
	DIAMINS	**ADILMPS**	PLASMID	**ADINNNS**	NANDINS
ADIIMOS	DAIMIOS	**ADILMSS**	DISMALS	**ADINNOP**	DIPNOAN
ADIIMPV	IMPAVID	**ADILMSU**	DUALISM		NONPAID
ADIIMRS	MIDAIRS	**ADILMSY**	DISMAYL	**ADINNOR**	ANDIRON
ADIIMRU	MUDIRIA		LADYISM	**ADINNPS**	PINDANS
ADIIMSS	MISSAID	**ADILNNS**	INLANDS	**ADINNRS**	INNARDS
ADIINPR	PINDARI	**ADILNOR**	ORDINAL	**ADINNRW**	INDRAWN
	PRIDIAN	**ADILNOS**	DOLINAS		WINNARD
ADIINST	DISTAIN		LADINOS	**ADINNRY**	INNYARD
ADIINSU	INDUSIA	**ADILNRS**	ALDRINS	**ADINNSU**	INDUNAS
	SUIDIAN	**ADILNRU**	DIURNAL	**ADINOOP**	POINADO
ADIINSV	AVIDINS	**ADILNRY**	RANDILY	**ADINOPP**	OPPIDAN
ADIINSZ	DIAZINS	**ADILNSS**	ISLANDS	**ADINOPR**	PADRONI
	DIZAINS	**ADILNST**	TINDALS		PONIARD
ADIIPRS	DIAPIRS	**ADILNSU**	DUALINS	**ADINOPT**	PINTADO
ADIIPXY	PYXIDIA		SUNDIAL	**ADINORR**	ORDINAR
ADIIQRU	DAQUIRI	**ADILOOV**	OVOIDAL	**ADINORS**	INROADS
ADIIRST	DIARIST	**ADILOOZ**	ZOOIDAL		ORDAINS
ADIIRTY	ARIDITY	**ADILOPR**	DIPOLAR		SADIRON
ADIISSY	SAIYIDS	**ADILORT**	DILATOR	**ADINORT**	DIATRON
ADIITVY	AVIDITY	**ADILOSZ**	OZALIDS	**ADINORV**	VIRANDO
ADIJMSS	MASJIDS	**ADILOTU**	OUTLAID	**ADINOSX**	DIAXONS
ADIJNOS	ADJOINS	**ADILPRY**	PYRALID		DIOXANS
ADIJNOT	ADJOINT		RAPIDLY	**ADINOTX**	OXIDANT
ADIJSSS	JASSIDS	**ADILPSS**	SALPIDS	**ADINPST**	PANDITS
ADIKLNY	LADYKIN	**ADILPST**	PLASTID		SANDPIT
ADIKLOR	KILORAD	**ADILPSY**	DISPLAY	**ADINQRS**	QINDARS
ADIKLOS	ODALISK	**ADILPTU**	PLAUDIT	**ADINRRT**	TRIDARN
ADIKLPS	KLIPDAS	**ADILPVY**	VAPIDLY	**ADINRST**	INDARTS
ADIKMNN	MANKIND	**ADILQSU**	SQUALID	**ADINRSU**	DURIANS
ADIKMOS	MIKADOS	**ADILRSZ**	LIZARDS		SUNDARI
ADIKMOU	DAIMOKU	**ADILRTY**	TARDILY	**ADINRSW**	INWARDS
ADIKMSS	DISMASK	**ADILSTU**	DUALIST	**ADINRTU**	TRIDUAN
ADIKNOS	DAIKONS		TULADIS		UNITARD
ADIKNPS	INKPADS	**ADILSTY**	STAIDLY	**ADINSTT**	DISTANT
	KIDNAPS	**ADILTUY**	DUALITY	**ADINSTU**	UNSTAID
	SKIDPAN	**ADIMNNO**	MONDAIN	**ADINTTY**	DITTANY

ADINWWY	WINDWAY	ADLMSTU	TALMUDS	ADNNOOT	NANODOT
ADIOOPR	PARODOI	ADLNNOR	NORLAND	ADNNOOY	NOONDAY
ADIOOSW	WOODSIA	ADLNNSU	SUNLAND	ADNNORS	RANDONS
ADIOPRR	AIRDROP	ADLNOOR	LARDOON	ADNNORT	DONNART
ADIOPRS	SPAROID	ADLNOOS	DOOLANS	ADNNOST	DANTONS
ADIOPRT	PAROTID		ONLOADS		DONNATS
ADIOPRV	PRIVADO	ADLNORS	LADRONS	ADNNOSU	ADNOUNS
ADIOPSU	ADIPOUS		LARDONS	ADNNOTU	DAUNTON
ADIORST	ASTROID	ADLNORT	TROLAND	ADNNRTU	DUNNART
ADIORSU	SAUROID	ADLNORU	NODULAR	ADNNRUW	UNDRAWN
ADIORSV	ADVISOR	ADLNOSS	SOLANDS	ADNOOPR	PANDOOR
ADIORTU	AUDITOR		SOLDANS	ADNOORS	NARDOOS
ADIOSTU	OUTSAID	ADLNOST	DALTONS	ADNOORT	DONATOR
ADIOSVW	DISAVOW		SANDLOT		ODORANT
ADIPRSS	SPARIDS	ADLNOSU	SOULDAN		TANDOOR
ADIPRST	DISPART		UNLOADS		TORNADO
ADIQSTU	DIQUATS	ADLNOSX	OXLANDS	ADNOOSW	WANDOOS
ADIRRSS	SIRDARS	ADLNOSY	SYNODAL	ADNOPRS	PARDONS
ADIRRST	RITARDS	ADLNOTU	OUTLAND	ADNOPRU	PANDOUR
ADIRRSZ	RIZARDS	ADLNPSU	UPLANDS	ADNOPRV	PROVAND
ADIRSSU	SARDIUS	ADLNRSU	LURDANS	ADNOPST	DOPANTS
ADIRSSV	VISARDS	ADLNRUU	UNDULAR	ADNORRW	NORWARD
ADIRSSW	WISARDS	ADLNRUY	LAUNDRY	ADNORSW	ONWARDS
ADIRSTY	SATYRID	ADLNSSU	SULDANS	ADNORTU	ROTUNDA
ADIRSUY	DYSURIA	ADLNTUU	UNADULT	ADNORTY	TARDYON
ADIRSVZ	VIZARDS	ADLOPRU	POULARD	ADNORWY	NAYWORD
ADIRSWZ	WIZARDS	ADLOPSU	UPLOADS	ADNOSSU	SOUDANS
ADIRSZZ	IZZARDS	ADLORRW	WARLORD	ADNOSTT	DOTANTS
ADISSST	SADISTS	ADLORSS	DORSALS	ADNOSTU	ASTOUND
ADISSYY	SAYYIDS	ADLORSU	SUDORAL	ADNPRUW	UPDRAWN
ADISTTY	DITTAYS	ADLOSSS	DOSSALS	ADNPSTU	DUSTPAN
ADJKOSU	JUDOKAS	ADLPSSU	SPAULDS		STANDUP
ADJLMOR	JARLDOM	ADMMNOS	MANDOMS		UPSTAND
ADJLUUW	WUDJULA	ADMMNSU	SUMMAND	ADNRSST	STRANDS
ADJNORS	JORDANS	ADMMOST	MADTOMS	ADNRSSU	SUNDRAS
ADJNORU	ADJOURN	ADMNOOR	DOORMAN	ADNRSTU	DRAUNTS
ADJOPSY	JOYPADS		MADRONO		DURANTS
ADJORRU	ADJUROR	ADMNOOW	WOODMAN		TUNDRAS
ADJSSTU	ADJUSTS	ADMNOOZ	MADZOON	ADNRSUW	SUNWARD
ADKKLOY	KAKODYL	ADMNOQU	QUONDAM		UNDRAWS
ADKLMRU	MUDLARK	ADMNORS	RANDOMS	ADNSSTY	DYNASTS
ADKOPSU	PADOUKS		RODSMAN	ADNSTYY	DYNASTY
ADKORWY	DAYWORK	ADMNORT	DORMANT	ADOOPRS	PARODOS
	WORKDAY		MORDANT	ADOOPSU	APODOUS
ADKRSWY	SKYWARD	ADMNOSS	DAMSONS	ADOOPSW	SAPWOOD
ADLLMOW	WADMOLL	ADMNOSU	OSMUNDA	ADOORSS	DOOSRAS
ADLLMOY	MODALLY	ADMNOSY	DYNAMOS	ADOORTW	WOODRAT
ADLLNOW	LOWLAND	ADMNSTU	DUSTMAN	ADOORWY	DOORWAY
ADLLNOY	NODALLY	ADMOORT	DOORMAT	ADOOSTT	TOSTADO
ADLLOPR	POLLARD	ADMOORY	DAYROOM	ADOOSUV	VAUDOOS
ADLLOPS	DALLOPS	ADMOPPU	POPADUM	ADOOWWX	WOODWAX
ADLLORS	DOLLARS	ADMORRS	RAMRODS	ADOPRRW	WARDROP
ADLLRWY	DRYWALL	ADMORST	STARDOM	ADORRSU	ARDOURS
ADLLTUY	ADULTLY		TSARDOM	ADORSTW	TOWARDS
ADLMNOS	ALMONDS	ADMORSU	MADUROS	ADORSUU	ARDUOUS
	DOLMANS	ADMORTW	MADWORT	ADORSWY	AYWORDS
ADLMNOY	ALMONDY	ADMORTZ	TZARDOM	ADORTUW	OUTDRAW
ADLMOOR	LORDOMA	ADMRSTU	DURMAST		OUTWARD
	MALODOR		MUSTARD	ADOUUVX	VAUDOUX
ADLMORU	MODULAR			ADPRSTU	UPDARTS
ADLMOSW	WADMOLS	ADNNOOS	NANDOOS	ADPRSUW	UPDRAWS

	UPWARDS	AEEFSTT	FEATEST	AEEGLRZ	REGLAZE
ADRSSUW	USWARDS	AEEGGLL	ALLEGGE	AEEGLSS	AGELESS
ADSSTUW	SAWDUST	AEEGGLR	GREGALE		ALGESES
AEEEFLR	EELFARE	AEEGGLS	ALEGGES	AEEGLST	EAGLETS
AEEEGGN	ENGAGEE	AEEGGLT	GATELEG		GELATES
AEEEGKL	KEELAGE	AEEGGNR	ENGAGER		LEGATES
AEEEGLT	LEGATEE	AEEGGNS	ENGAGES		SEGETAL
AEEEGNT	TEENAGE	AEEGGOP	EPAGOGE		TEAGLES
AEEEGPR	PEERAGE	AEEGGRS	AGREGES		TELEGAS
AEEEGPS	SEEPAGE		RAGGEES	AEEGLSU	LEAGUES
AEEEGRR	EAGERER		REGGAES	AEEGLSV	GLEAVES
AEEEGRT	ETAGERE	AEEGGRU	REGAUGE		SELVAGE
AEEEHLS	HEALEES	AEEGGST	TAGGEES	AEEGLTT	GALETTE
AEEEILN	ALIENEE	AEEGGSW	GEEGAWS	AEEGLTU	TEGULAE
AEEEIRT	EATERIE	AEEGHIR	HIREAGE	AEEGLTV	VEGETAL
AEEELRS	RELEASE	AEEGHNT	THENAGE	AEEGMMT	GEMMATE
AEEELTV	ELEVATE	AEEGHNW	WHANGEE		TAGMEME
AEEERVW	REWEAVE	AEEGHSZ	GEEZAHS	AEEGMNR	GERMANE
AEEERWY	EYEWEAR	AEEGILL	GALILEE	AEEGMNS	MANEGES
AEEFFLL	FELAFEL	AEEGILM	MILEAGE		MENAGES
AEEFFNS	NEAFFES	AEEGILN	LINEAGE	AEEGMNT	GATEMEN
AEEFFRS	AFFEERS	AEEGILP	EPIGEAL	AEEGMPR	PREGAME
AEEFGLN	FENAGLE	AEEGILT	EGALITE	AEEGMRR	MEAGRER
AEEFGNR	FREEGAN	AEEGILW	WEIGELA	AEEGMRS	MEAGRES
AEEFGNT	FANTEEG	AEEGIMR	REIMAGE	AEEGMRU	REMUAGE
AEEFGRS	SERFAGE	AEEGINP	EPIGEAN	AEEGMSS	MEGASSE
AEEFGSU	FEAGUES	AEEGINR	REGINAE		MESSAGE
AEEFGTW	WEFTAGE	AEEGINS	AGENISE	AEEGMST	GAMETES
AEEFHRT	FEATHER	AEEGINU	EUGENIA		METAGES
	TEREFAH	AEEGINZ	AGENIZE	AEEGNNP	PANGENE
AEEFILR	FILAREE	AEEGIPP	PIPEAGE	AEEGNNR	ENRANGE
	LEAFIER	AEEGIPR	PIERAGE	AEEGNNS	ENNAGES
AEEFILW	ALEWIFE	AEEGIRU	EUGARIE	AEEGNOP	PEONAGE
AEEFIRS	AREFIES	AEEGISS	AEGISES	AEEGNPP	GENAPPE
	FAERIES		ASSIEGE	AEEGNRS	ENRAGES
	FREESIA	AEEGJRS	JAEGERS	AEEGNRT	GRANTEE
AEEFISW	SEAWIFE	AEEGJSY	JAYGEES		GREATEN
AEEFKRS	FAKEERS	AEEGKLL	KLEAGLE		NEGATER
AEEFLLT	FELLATE	AEEGLLR	ALLEGER		REAGENT
	LEAFLET	AEEGLLS	ALLEGES	AEEGNRU	RENAGUE
AEEFLMN	ENFLAME	AEEGLLZ	GAZELLE		UNEAGER
AEEFLMS	FEMALES	AEEGLMN	GLEEMAN	AEEGNRV	AVENGER
AEEFLRT	REFLATE		MELANGE		ENGRAVE
AEEFLRU	FERULAE	AEEGLMR	GLEAMER	AEEGNSS	SAGENES
AEEFLRW	WELFARE	AEEGLMT	MELTAGE		SENEGAS
AEEFLRY	LEAFERY	AEEGLNR	ENLARGE	AEEGNST	NEGATES
AEEFLRZ	ALFEREZ		GENERAL		SANGEET
AEEFLSU	EASEFUL		GLEANER	AEEGNSV	AVENGES
AEEFLTX	TELEFAX	AEEGLNT	ELEGANT		GENEVAS
AEEFMNR	ENFRAME	AEEGLNU	EUGLENA	AEEGNTT	TENTAGE
	FREEMAN	AEEGLNV	EVANGEL	AEEGNTV	VENTAGE
AEEFMRR	REFRAME	AEEGLOR	AEROGEL	AEEGOPS	APOGEES
AEEFMRT	FERMATE	AEEGLPR	PEREGAL	AEEGORV	OVERAGE
AEEFOTV	FOVEATE	AEEGLPS	PELAGES	AEEGOST	GOATEES
AEEFPPR	FRAPPEE	AEEGLRR	REGALER	AEEGPRS	ASPERGE
AEEFRRS	FEARERS	AEEGLRS	GALERES		PRESAGE
AEEFRRT	FERRATE		REGALES	AEEGPRU	PUGAREE
AEEFRST	AFREETS	AEEGLRU	LEAGUER	AEEGPST	SEPTAGE
	FEASTER		REGULAE	AEEGRRS	GREASER
AEEFRTU	FEATURE	AEEGLRW	LEGWEAR		REGEARS
AEEFRWY	FREEWAY	AEEGLRY	EAGERLY	AEEGRRT	GREATER

	REGRATE		RESHAPE	**AEEIMNR**	REMANIE
AEEGRRU	REARGUE		SPHAERE	**AEEIMNS**	MEANIES
AEEGRRW	WAGERER		SPHEARE		NEMESIA
AEEGRSS	GREASES	**AEEHPRT**	PREHEAT	**AEEIMNT**	ETAMINE
AEEGRST	ERGATES	**AEEHPSS**	APHESES		MATINEE
	RESTAGE		SPAHEES	**AEEIMNX**	EXAMINE
AEEGRSV	GREAVES	**AEEHPUV**	UPHEAVE	**AEEIMPR**	EMPAIRE
AEEGRTU	TREAGUE	**AEEHQSU**	QUASHEE	**AEEIMRR**	REAMIER
AEEGRUZ	GUEREZA	**AEEHRRS**	HEARERS		REREMAI
AEEGSSW	SEWAGES		REHEARS	**AEEIMRS**	SEAMIER
AEEGSTT	GESTATE		SHEARER		SERIEMA
	TAGETES	**AEEHRSS**	HEARSES	**AEEIMRT**	EMERITA
AEEGTTZ	GAZETTE	**AEEHRST**	AETHERS		EMIRATE
AEEHHNT	HEATHEN		HEATERS		MEATIER
AEEHHRT	HEATHER		REHEATS	**AEEIMSS**	MISEASE
AEEHHSS	SHEESHA	**AEEHRSV**	HEAVERS		SIAMESE
AEEHHST	SHEATHE		RESHAVE	**AEEIMST**	STEAMIE
AEEHHSW	HEEHAWS	**AEEHRSW**	WHEREAS	**AEEIMSZ**	SIAMEZE
AEEHINR	HERNIAE	**AEEHRTT**	THEATER	**AEEIMTT**	TEATIME
AEEHIPR	HEAPIER		THEATRE	**AEEINPR**	PERINEA
AEEHIRV	HEAVIER		THEREAT	**AEEINRT**	ARENITE
AEEHIST	ATHEISE	**AEEHRTV**	THREAVE		RETINAE
AEEHISV	HEAVIES	**AEEHRTW**	WEATHER		TRAINEE
AEEHITZ	ATHEIZE		WHEREAT	**AEEINST**	ETESIAN
AEEHKMS	HAKEEMS		WREATHE	**AEEINTV**	NAIVETE
AEEHKNR	HEARKEN	**AEEHSST**	HEASTES	**AEEINVW**	INWEAVE
AEEHKNT	THANKEE	**AEEHSSV**	SHEAVES	**AEEIORT**	ETAERIO
AEEHKRT	HEKTARE	**AEEHSTV**	THEAVES	**AEEIPRR**	PEREIRA
AEEHKRU	HEUREKA	**AEEHSWY**	EYEWASH	**AEEIPRS**	APERIES
AEEHLMS	SHEMALE	**AEEIIRS**	AIERIES		EPEIRAS
AEEHLNT	LETHEAN	**AEEIKLP**	APELIKE	**AEEIPRT**	PEATIER
AEEHLPT	HEELTAP		PEALIKE	**AEEIPSV**	PEAVIES
AEEHLRS	HEALERS	**AEEIKLR**	EARLIKE	**AEEIPTX**	EXPIATE
AEEHLRT	HALTERE		LEAKIER	**AEEIRRR**	ARRIERE
	LEATHER	**AEEIKLT**	TEALIKE	**AEEIRRS**	REARISE
AEEHLRV	HAVEREL	**AEEIKPR**	PEAKIER		RERAISE
AEEHLSS	LEASHES	**AEEIKSV**	KEAVIES	**AEEIRRT**	TEARIER
AEEHLST	LATHEES	**AEEILLR**	REALLIE	**AEEIRRW**	WEARIER
AEEHLSW	AWHEELS	**AEEILMR**	EMAILER	**AEEIRST**	AERIEST
AEEHLSX	EXHALES		MEALIER		SERIATE
AEEHLSY	EYELASH	**AEEILMS**	MEALIES	**AEEIRSW**	WEARIES
AEEHLTT	ATHLETE	**AEEILNP**	ALEPINE	**AEEIRTT**	ARIETTE
AEEHMNT	METHANE		ELAPINE		ITERATE
AEEHMRS	HAREEMS	**AEEILNR**	ALIENER	**AEEIRTV**	EVIRATE
	MAHSEER	**AEEILNS**	SEALINE	**AEEISST**	EASIEST
AEEHMRT	ERATHEM	**AEEILNT**	LINEATE	**AEEISVV**	EVASIVE
	THERMAE	**AEEILNX**	ALEXINE	**AEEITTV**	AVIETTE
AEEHMST	MEATHES	**AEEILPT**	EPILATE		EVITATE
AEEHMSU	HEAUMES		PILEATE	**AEEITUX**	EUTEXIA
AEEHNPS	PEAHENS	**AEEILRR**	EARLIER	**AEEIUVX**	EXUVIAE
AEEHNPT	HAPTENE		LEARIER	**AEEJKSS**	JAKESES
	HEPTANE	**AEEILRS**	EARLIES	**AEEJMSS**	JAMESES
	PHENATE		REALISE	**AEEJNST**	SEJEANT
AEEHNRS	ARSHEEN	**AEEILRT**	ATELIER	**AEEJNTU**	JAUNTEE
AEEHNRT	EARTHEN		REALTIE	**AEEJRSV**	EVEJARS
	HEARTEN	**AEEILRV**	LEAVIER	**AEEJSVY**	JAYVEES
AEEHNST	ETHANES		VEALIER		VEEJAYS
AEEHNSV	HEAVENS	**AEEILRZ**	REALIZE	**AEEKKNO**	KOKANEE
AEEHNSX	HEXANES	**AEEILTT**	AILETTE	**AEEKKOO**	KOEKOEA
AEEHNTW	WHEATEN	**AEEILTV**	ELATIVE	**AEEKLLT**	LAKELET
AEEHPRS	HEAPERS	**AEEIMNN**	ENAMINE	**AEEKLMN**	KEELMAN

AEEKLNS	ALKENES	AEELNNP	ENPLANE		REALEST
AEEKLNT	KANTELE	AEELNOS	ENOLASE		RELATES
AEEKLPS	PALKEES		LOANEES		RESLATE
AEEKLRS	LEAKERS	AEELNPR	REPANEL		STEALER
AEEKLSV	VAKEELS	AEELNPS	ALPEENS	AEELRSU	LEASURE
AEEKMNS	KAMSEEN		SPELEAN	AEELRSV	LAVEERS
AEEKMNW	WAKEMEN	AEELNRR	LEARNER		LEAVERS
AEEKMRR	REMAKER		RELEARN		REVEALS
AEEKMRS	REMAKES	AEELNRS	LEANERS		SEVERAL
AEEKMRT	MEERKAT	AEELNRT	ALTERNE		VEALERS
AEEKNNN	NANKEEN		ENTERAL	AEELRSX	RELAXES
AEEKNNP	KNEEPAN		ETERNAL	AEELRSY	SEALERY
AEEKNRS	SNEAKER		TELERAN	AEELRTX	EXALTER
AEEKNRT	RETAKEN	AEELNRW	RENEWAL	AEELRUV	REVALUE
AEEKNRW	REWAKEN	AEELNSS	ENSEALS	AEELSST	ALTESSE
	WAKENER	AEELNST	ELANETS		STEALES
AEEKNSS	SKEANES		LATEENS		TEASELS
AEEKNSW	WEAKENS		LEANEST	AEELSSV	SLEAVES
AEEKNSY	YANKEES	AEELNSV	ENSLAVE	AEELSSW	AWELESS
AEEKORW	REAWOKE		LEAVENS		WEASELS
AEEKPRS	PARKEES	AEELNSW	WEANELS	AEELSSY	ASYLEES
	RESPEAK	AEELNTY	ENTAYLE	AEELSSZ	SLEAZES
	SPEAKER	AEELOPR	PAROLEE	AEELSTU	ELUATES
AEEKPRT	PERTAKE	AEELOPX	POLEAXE		SETUALE
AEEKRRT	RETAKER	AEELORS	AREOLES	AEELSTV	SALVETE
AEEKRRW	WREAKER	AEELORU	AUREOLE		VALETES
AEEKRST	RETAKES	AEELOST	OLEATES		VELETAS
	SAKERET	AEELOSW	LEASOWE	AEELSTX	LATEXES
AEEKRSU	EUREKAS	AEELPRR	PEARLER	AEELSTY	EYALETS
AEEKRSW	REWAKES	AEELPRS	LEAPERS	AEELSTZ	TEAZELS
AEEKRTW	TWEAKER		PLEASER		TEAZLES
AEEKSSS	ASKESES		PRESALE	AEELSWY	LEEWAYS
AEEKSTW	WEAKEST		RELAPSE		WEASELY
AEELLLS	ALLELES		REPEALS	AEELTTY	LAYETTE
AEELLMS	MALLEES	AEELPRT	PETRALE	AEELTVW	WAVELET
AEELLOV	ALVEOLE		PLEATER	AEEMMMR	MAREMME
AEELLPR	PARELLE		PRELATE	AEEMMMS	MAMMEES
AEELLSS	SALLEES		REPLATE	AEEMMNT	MEATMEN
AEELLST	LEALEST	AEELPRU	PLEURAE	AEEMMPY	EMPYEMA
AEELLWY	WALLEYE	AEELPSS	ELAPSES	AEEMMRT	AMMETER
AEELMNP	EMPANEL		PLEASES		METAMER
	EMPLANE		SAPELES	AEEMMSY	MAMEYES
AEELMNR	REELMAN	AEELPSU	EPAULES	AEEMNNO	ANEMONE
AEELMNS	ENAMELS	AEELPTT	PALETTE	AEEMNNP	PENNAME
	MELENAS		PELTATE	AEEMNOX	AXONEME
AEELMNT	MANTEEL	AEELPTU	EPAULET	AEEMNPR	PRENAME
	TELEMAN	AEELQRU	LEQUEAR	AEEMNPS	SPAEMEN
AEELMNV	VELAMEN	AEELQSU	QUELEAS	AEEMNPT	PEATMEN
AEELMNY	AMYLENE		SEQUELA	AEEMNRS	MEANERS
AEELMPR	EMPALER	AEELRRT	ALERTER		RENAMES
	PREMEAL		ALTERER	AEEMNRT	REMANET
AEELMPS	EMPALES		REALTER	AEEMNSS	ENSEAMS
AEELMPX	EXAMPLE		RELATER	AEEMNST	ENTAMES
	EXEMPLA	AEELRRV	RAVELER		MEANEST
AEELMRS	MEALERS	AEELRRX	RELAXER	AEEMNSX	EXAMENS
AEELMRT	LAMETER	AEELRSS	EARLESS	AEEMOPT	METOPAE
AEELMSS	MEASLES		LEASERS	AEEMORT	EROTEMA
AEELMST	MALTESE		RESALES	AEEMOSW	AWESOME
AEELMSU	AEMULES		RESEALS		WAESOME
AEELMSZ	MEAZELS		SEALERS	AEEMPRS	AMPERES
AEELMTU	EMULATE	AEELRST	ELATERS		EMPARES

AEEMPRT	TEMPERA	AEENSST	ENTASES	AEERRSU	ERASURE
AEEMPRY	EMPAYRE		SATEENS	AEERRSV	REAVERS
AEEMPST	METEPAS		SENATES	AEERRSW	REWEARS
AEEMPSW	WAMPEES		SENSATE		SWEARER
AEEMPTU	AMPUTEE		STEANES		WEARERS
AEEMQRU	MARQUEE	AEENSSU	UNEASES	AEERRTT	RETRATE
AEEMRRS	REAMERS	AEENSSV	AVENSES		RETREAT
	SMEARER	AEENSSW	WAENESS		TREATER
AEEMRSS	SEAMERS	AEENSTT	NEATEST	AEERRTV	AVERTER
AEEMRST	REMATES	AEENSUV	AVENUES	AEERRTW	REWATER
	RETEAMS	AEENSWZ	WEAZENS		WATERER
	STEAMER	AEENTTV	NAVETTE	AEERRVW	WAVERER
	TEAMERS	AEENUVW	UNWEAVE	AEERSST	EASTERS
AEEMRSU	MEASURE	AEEOPRT	OPERATE		RESEATS
AEEMRTX	EXTREMA	AEEOPTZ	EPAZOTE		SAETERS
AEEMRTY	METAYER	AEEORRS	REAROSE		SEAREST
AEEMSSS	SESAMES	AEEORSS	SEROSAE		SEATERS
AEEMSST	MESETAS	AEEORST	ROSEATE		STEARES
	SEAMSET	AEEORSV	OVERSEA		TEASERS
AEEMSTT	METATES	AEEORTV	OVERATE		TESSERA
AEEMSTX	TAXEMES		OVEREAT	AEERSSU	RESEAUS
AEENNOT	NEONATE	AEEORVW	OVERAWE		SEASURE
AEENNOV	NOVENAE	AEEOSUU	EUOUAES		UREASES
AEENNPT	PENNATE	AEEOSVV	EVOVAES	AEERSSV	ASSEVER
	PENTANE	AEEPPRR	PAPERER	AEERSSY	ESSAYER
AEENNRS	ENSNARE		PREPARE	AEERSTT	ESTREAT
	RENNASE		REPAPER		RESTATE
AEENNRX	REANNEX	AEEPPRS	RAPPEES		RETASTE
AEENNST	NEATENS	AEEPPRT	PRETAPE	AEERSTU	AUSTERE
AEENNSX	ANNEXES	AEEPPRV	PREPAVE	AEERSTW	SWEATER
AEENNTU	UNEATEN	AEEPRRS	REAPERS	AEERSTX	RETAXES
AEENOPR	PERAEON		SPEARER	AEERSUV	VAREUSE
AEENOPU	EUPNOEA	AEEPRRT	PEARTER	AEERSUX	RESEAUX
AEENORS	ARENOSE		TAPERER	AEERSVW	WEAVERS
AEENOSS	ANOESES	AEEPRRV	PREAVER	AEERSWX	REWAXES
AEENOSU	AENEOUS	AEEPRSS	ASPERSE	AEERTTX	EXTREAT
AEENPRS	PANEERS		PARESES	AEERTWW	WETWARE
AEENPST	NEPETAS		PRAESES	AEERTWX	TREEWAX
	PENATES		PREASES	AEESSSW	SEESAWS
	PESANTE		PREASSE	AEESSSY	EYASSES
AEENPSU	EUPNEAS		SERAPES	AEESSTT	ESTATES
AEENPSW	PAWNEES	AEEPRST	REPEATS	AEESSTX	TEXASES
AEENPSX	EXPANSE		RETAPES	AEESSUX	AUXESES
AEENRRS	EARNERS	AEEPRSV	REPAVES	AEESTTT	TESTATE
	REEARNS	AEEPRSZ	SPREAZE	AEESWXY	WAXEYES
AEENRRT	TERRANE	AEEPRTU	EPURATE	AEFFFLR	FLAFFER
AEENRRV	RAVENER	AEEPRTY	PEATERY	AEFFGIR	GIRAFFE
AEENRRY	YEARNER	AEEPRTZ	TRAPEZE		RIFFAGE
AEENRSS	ENSEARS	AEEPSSS	ASEPSES	AEFFGNR	ENGRAFF
AEENRST	EARNEST	AEEPSST	PESETAS	AEFFGRS	GAFFERS
	EASTERN	AEEPSSW	PESEWAS	AEFFGRU	GAUFFER
	NEAREST	AEEPSTT	SEPTATE	AEFFHST	HAFFETS
	RATEENS		SPATTEE	AEFFINS	AFFINES
AEENRSW	WEANERS	AEEPSVY	PEAVEYS	AEFFIPR	PIAFFER
AEENRTT	ENTREAT	AEEQRSU	QUAERES	AEFFIPS	PIAFFES
	RATTEEN	AEEQSTU	EQUATES	AEFFIRX	AFFIXER
	TERNATE	AEERRRS	REARERS		REAFFIX
AEENRTV	AVENTRE	AEERRSS	ERASERS	AEFFIST	TAFFIES
	NERVATE	AEERRST	RETEARS	AEFFISW	WAFFIES
	VETERAN		SERRATE	AEFFISX	AFFIXES
AEENRUV	UNREAVE		TEARERS	AEFFKOP	OFFPEAK

AEFFKOR	RAKEOFF	AEFGORT	FAGOTER	AEFINNS	FAINNES
AEFFKOT	OFFTAKE	AEFGORV	FORGAVE		FANNIES
	TAKEOFF	AEFGRRT	GRAFTER	AEFINNT	INFANTE
AEFFLLY	FLYLEAF		REGRAFT	AEFINNZ	FANZINE
AEFFLMW	FLAMFEW	AEFGRSU	GAUFERS	AEFINPR	FIREPAN
AEFFLNS	SNAFFLE		GAUFRES	AEFINRR	REFRAIN
AEFFLRR	RAFFLER	AEFHIRT	FAITHER	AEFINRS	INFARES
AEFFLRS	FARFELS	AEFHIRW	WHARFIE		SERAFIN
	RAFFLES	AEFHISZ	HAFIZES	AEFINRT	FAINTER
AEFFLRU	FEARFUL	AEFHLLS	FELLAHS		FENITAR
AEFFLRW	WAFFLER	AEFHLOR	FAHLORE	AEFINRW	FAWNIER
AEFFLSW	WAFFLES	AEFHLRS	FLASHER	AEFINRX	XERAFIN
AEFFLSY	YAFFLES	AEFHLRT	FARTHEL	AEFINST	FAINEST
AEFFLTU	FATEFUL	AEFHLRZ	FAHLERZ		FANSITE
AEFFMRU	EARMUFF	AEFHLSS	FLASHES		NAIFEST
AEFFNST	NAFFEST	AEFHLTU	HATEFUL	AEFINSW	FANWISE
AEFFOVW	WAVEOFF	AEFHRRT	FARTHER	AEFINTX	ANTEFIX
AEFFQRU	QUAFFER	AEFHRST	FATHERS	AEFIQRU	AQUIFER
AEFFRST	AFFRETS		HAFTERS	AEFIRRR	FARRIER
	RESTAFF		SHAFTER	AEFIRSS	FRAISES
	STAFFER	AEFHRSY	FASHERY	AEFIRST	FAIREST
AEFFRSY	EFFRAYS	AEFIILT	FILIATE	AEFIRTT	FATTIER
AEFFRSZ	ZAFFERS	AEFIIRS	FAIRIES	AEFISST	FASTIES
	ZAFFRES	AEFIJLO	JEOFAIL		FIESTAS
AEFFTTY	TAFFETY	AEFIJOS	FEIJOAS		FISSATE
AEFGGGO	FOGGAGE	AEFIKLN	FANLIKE	AEFISTT	FATTIES
AEFGGIR	FAGGIER	AEFIKLR	FLAKIER	AEFISTX	FIXATES
AEFGGLR	FLAGGER	AEFIKLS	FLAKIES	AEFJNST	FANJETS
AEFGGMO	MEGAFOG	AEFIKLT	FATLIKE	AEFKLNN	FLANKEN
AEFGGRY	FAGGERY	AEFIKST	FAKIEST	AEFKLNR	FLANKER
AEFGILN	FEALING	AEFILLM	FAMILLE	AEFKLNS	FANKLES
	FINAGLE	AEFILLS	FAILLES	AEFKLOS	SEAFOLK
	LEAFING	AEFILMN	FEMINAL	AEFKLRS	FLAKERS
AEFGILO	FOLIAGE		INFLAME	AEFKLRT	FARTLEK
AEFGILR	FRAGILE	AEFILMR	FLAMIER	AEFKLST	FLASKET
AEFGINR	FEARING	AEFILNN	FLANNIE	AEFKLUW	WAKEFUL
AEFGINS	FEASING	AEFILNS	FINALES	AEFKNRR	FRANKER
AEFGINT	FEATING	AEFILNT	INFLATE	AEFKORS	FORSAKE
AEFGINZ	FEAZING	AEFILNU	INFULAE	AEFLLNN	FANNELL
AEFGIRT	FRIGATE	AEFILNV	FLAVINE		FLANNEL
AEFGIRU	REFUGIA	AEFILOT	FOLIATE	AEFLLOT	FLOATEL
AEFGITU	FATIGUE	AEFILPT	FLEAPIT	AEFLLRS	FALLERS
AEFGLLU	FULLAGE	AEFILRR	FLARIER		REFALLS
AEFGLMN	FLAGMEN		FRAILER	AEFLLSY	FALSELY
AEFGLNR	FLANGER	AEFILRU	FAILURE	AEFLLTT	FLATLET
AEFGLNS	FANGLES	AEFILRV	FAVRILE	AEFLLTU	TALEFUL
	FLANGES	AEFILRW	FLAWIER	AEFLLUZ	ZEALFUL
AEFGLOT	FLOTAGE	AEFILRX	FLAXIER	AEFLMNS	FLAMENS
AEFGLOW	FLOWAGE	AEFILRZ	FILAZER	AEFLMOR	FEMORAL
AEFGLPU	PAGEFUL	AEFILSS	FALSIES	AEFLMRS	FLAMERS
AEFGLRS	REFLAGS		FILASSE	AEFLMUW	WAMEFUL
AEFGLRU	RAGEFUL	AEFILST	FETIALS	AEFLMUZ	MAZEFUL
AEFGLUZ	GAZEFUL		SEALIFT	AEFLNNN	FLANNEN
AEFGMOR	FROMAGE	AEFILTT	FLATTIE	AEFLNNS	FANNELS
AEFGMSU	FUMAGES	AEFILWY	LIFEWAY	AEFLNOV	FLAVONE
AEFGNRR	FRANGER	AEFIMNR	FIREMAN	AEFLNRS	SALFERN
	GRANFER	AEFIMNS	FAMINES	AEFLNRU	FLANEUR
AEFGNRT	ENGRAFT		INFAMES		FRENULA
AEFGOOT	FOOTAGE	AEFIMOR	FOAMIER		FUNERAL
AEFGORR	FORAGER	AEFIMRR	FIREARM	AEFLNSU	FLAUNES
AEFGORS	FORAGES	AEFIMRS	MISFARE	AEFLNTT	FLATTEN

AEFLNUU	FAUNULE	AEFORTV	OVERFAT	AEGGMNY	YEGGMAN
AEFLOOV	FOVEOLA	AEFOSST	FATSOES	AEGGMSS	EGGMASS
AEFLOPW	PEAFOWL		FOSSATE	AEGGNNU	GUNNAGE
AEFLORS	LOAFERS	AEFOSTU	FEATOUS	AEGGNRR	GRANGER
	SAFROLE	AEFPPRS	FRAPPES	AEGGNRS	GANGERS
AEFLORT	FLOATER	AEFRRST	FRATERS		GRANGES
	FLOREAT		RAFTERS		NAGGERS
	REFLOAT		STRAFER	AEGGNSU	GANGUES
AEFLORY	FORELAY	AEFRRTY	FRATERY	AEGGRRY	RAGGERY
AEFLOST	FOLATES	AEFRRSS	FRASSES	AEGGRSS	AGGRESS
AEFLOSW	SEAFOWL	AEFRSST	FASTERS		SAGGERS
AEFLPPR	FLAPPER		STRAFES		SEGGARS
AEFLPRS	FELSPAR	AEFRSTU	FAUREST	AEGGRST	GAGSTER
AEFLPRU	FLAREUP	AEFRSTW	FRETSAW		GARGETS
AEFLPRY	PALFREY		WAFTERS		STAGGER
AEFLRSS	FALSERS	AEFRTTU	TARTUFE		TAGGERS
	FLASERS	AEFRTUW	WAFTURE	AEGGRSU	GAUGERS
AEFLRST	FALTERS	AEFRWYZ	FRAWZEY	AEGGRSW	SWAGGER
AEFLRSU	EARFULS	AEFSSTT	FASTEST		WAGGERS
	FERULAS		SAFTEST	AEGGRSY	YAGGERS
	REFUSAL	AEFSSUV	FAVUSES	AEGGRTY	GARGETY
AEFLRSY	FLAYERS	AEFSTTT	FATTEST	AEGGRWY	WAGGERY
AEFLRTT	FLATTER	AEGGGLS	GAGGLES	AEGGSWW	GEWGAWS
AEFLRTU	REFUTAL	AEGGGLU	LUGGAGE	AEGHHIT	AHEIGHT
	TEARFUL	AEGGGRS	GAGGERS	AEGHIJR	JAGHIRE
AEFLRZZ	FRAZZLE	AEGGGRY	GAGGERY	AEGHIKL	HAGLIKE
AEFLSST	FALSEST	AEGGHLR	HAGGLER	AEGHILN	HEALING
	FATLESS	AEGGHLS	HAGGLES	AEGHILR	LAIGHER
	FESTALS	AEGGHMO	HEMAGOG	AEGHIMT	MEGAHIT
AEFLSTU	FLUATES	AEGGHRS	SHAGGER	AEGHINP	HEAPING
	SULFATE	AEGGHSW	EGGWASH	AEGHINR	HEARING
AEFMNOR	FORAMEN	AEGGIJR	JAGGIER	AEGHINT	GAHNITE
	FOREMAN	AEGGIJS	JAGGIES		HEATING
AEFMNRT	RAFTMEN	AEGGILN	EAGLING	AEGHINV	HEAVING
AEFMNRU	FRAENUM		GEALING	AEGHINZ	GENIZAH
AEFMORR	FOREARM		LIGNAGE	AEGHIOS	HOAGIES
AEFMORS	FOAMERS	AEGGIMS	MAGGIES	AEGHIRS	HEGARIS
AEFMORT	FORMATE	AEGGINR	GEARING		HEGIRAS
AEFMOUW	WAMEFOU		NAGGIER		HIRAGES
AEFMRRS	FARMERS	AEGGINS	AGEINGS	AEGHISS	GEISHAS
	FRAMERS		SIGNAGE	AEGHISZ	GHAZIES
AEFMRRY	FARMERY	AEGGIOS	ISAGOGE	AEGHLNO	HALOGEN
AEFNNRS	FANNERS	AEGGIRR	RAGGIER	AEGHLNT	ALENGTH
AEFNNST	ENFANTS	AEGGIRS	RAGGIES	AEGHLOS	GALOSHE
AEFNOPR	PROFANE		SAGGIER	AEGHLRU	LAUGHER
AEFNOPY	PAYFONE	AEGGIRT	TAGGIER	AEGHLSS	SEALGHS
AEFNORR	FORERAN	AEGGIRU	GARIGUE	AEGHLST	HAGLETS
AEFNRRS	FARRENS	AEGGIST	STAGGIE	AEGHLSZ	GHAZELS
AEFNRSS	FARNESS	AEGGISW	SWAGGIE	AEGHLTW	THALWEG
AEFNRSU	FURANES	AEGGJRS	JAGGERS	AEGHMNN	HANGMEN
	UNSAFER	AEGGJRY	JAGGERY	AEGHMNO	HOGMANE
AEFNRSW	FAWNERS	AEGGLNO	AGELONG	AEGHMOR	HOMAGER
AEFNSST	FASTENS	AEGGLNR	GANGREL	AEGHMOS	HOMAGES
	FATNESS	AEGGLNS	LAGGENS		OHMAGES
AEFNSTT	FATTENS	AEGGLRR	GARGLER	AEGHMSU	MESHUGA
AEFOPRW	FOREPAW	AEGGLRS	GARGLES	AEGHNOX	HEXAGON
AEFORRV	FAVORER		LAGGERS	AEGHNRS	GNASHER
	OVERFAR		RAGGLES		HANGERS
AEFORRY	FORAYER	AEGGLRW	WAGGLER		REHANGS
AEFORSW	FORESAW	AEGGLRY	GREYLAG		SHERANG
AEFORSY	FORESAY	AEGGLSW	WAGGLES	AEGHNRU	NURAGHE

AEGHNSS	GNASHES		GENITAL		SIGMATE
AEGHNST	STENGAH		TAGLINE	AEGIMSV	MISGAVE
AEGHOPY	HYPOGEA	AEGILNU	LINGUAE	AEGINNO	GANOINE
AEGHORS	GHERAOS		UNAGILE	AEGINNP	NEAPING
AEGHOSS	SEAHOGS	AEGILNV	LEAVING		PEANING
AEGHOST	HOSTAGE		VEALING	AEGINNR	AGINNER
AEGHPRS	SPREAGH	AEGILNY	ALEYING		EARNING
AEGHPST	HATPEGS		YEALING		ENGRAIN
AEGHRST	GATHERS	AEGILOS	GOALIES		GRANNIE
AEGHSST	GASHEST		SOILAGE		NEARING
AEGIIMN	IMAGINE	AEGILOU	EULOGIA	AEGINNS	INNAGES
AEGIKLN	LEAKING	AEGILPS	PAIGLES		SEANING
	LINKAGE	AEGILRR	GLARIER	AEGINNT	ANTEING
AEGIKLT	GLAIKET	AEGILRS	GLAIRES		ANTIGEN
	TAGLIKE		GRAILES		GENTIAN
AEGIKNP	PEAKING	AEGILRZ	GLAZIER	AEGINNU	ANGUINE
AEGIKNR	REAKING	AEGILSS	ALGESIS		GUANINE
AEGIKNS	SINKAGE		GLASSIE	AEGINNW	WEANING
AEGIKPP	KIPPAGE		LIGASES	AEGINNY	YEANING
AEGIKPR	GARPIKE		SILAGES	AEGINOR	ORIGANE
AEGIKRW	GAWKIER	AEGILST	AGILEST	AEGINOS	AGONIES
AEGIKSW	GAWKIES		AIGLETS		AGONISE
AEGILLL	ILLEGAL		GELATIS	AEGINOZ	AGONIZE
AEGILLM	MEGILLA		LIGATES	AEGINPP	GENIPAP
	MILLAGE		TAIGLES	AEGINPR	REAPING
AEGILLN	GALLEIN	AEGILSV	GLAIVES	AEGINPS	PEASING
	NIGELLA	AEGILTU	GLUTAEI		SPAEING
AEGILLP	PILLAGE	AEGILTY	EGALITY		SPINAGE
AEGILLS	GALLIES	AEGIMMR	GAMMIER	AEGINPZ	PEAZING
	GALLISE	AEGIMNN	AMENING	AEGINRR	ANGRIER
AEGILLT	TILLAGE		MEANING		EARRING
AEGILLU	LIGULAE	AEGIMNP	PIGMEAN		GRAINER
AEGILLV	VILLAGE	AEGIMNR	GERMAIN		RANGIER
AEGILLY	AGILELY		GERMINA		REARING
AEGILLZ	GALLIZE		MANGIER	AEGINRS	ANGRIES
AEGILMN	GEMINAL		MEARING		EARINGS
	LEAMING		REAMING		ERASING
	MEALING	AEGIMNS	ENIGMAS		GAINERS
AEGILMR	GREMIAL		GAMINES		GRAINES
	LAMIGER		MEASING		REAGINS
AEGILMS	MILAGES		SEAMING		REGAINS
AEGILNN	ANELING	AEGIMNT	MINTAGE		REGINAS
	EANLING		TEAMING		SEARING
	LEANING		TEGMINA		SERINGA
	NEALING	AEGIMOS	IMAGOES	AEGINRT	GRANITE
AEGILNP	LEAPING	AEGIMPR	EPIGRAM		GRATINE
	PEALING		PRIMAGE		INGRATE
	PLEAING	AEGIMPS	MAGPIES		TANGIER
AEGILNR	ALIGNER		MISPAGE		TEARING
	ENGRAIL	AEGIMPT	PIGMEAT	AEGINRV	REAVING
	LAERING	AEGIMRR	ARMIGER		VINEGAR
	LEARING	AEGIMRS	GISARME	AEGINRW	WEARING
	NARGILE		IMAGERS	AEGINRZ	ZINGARE
	REALIGN		MAIGRES	AEGINSS	AGNISES
	REGINAL		MIRAGES		EASINGS
AEGILNS	LEASING	AEGIMRT	MIGRATE		SEASING
	LINAGES		RAGTIME	AEGINST	EASTING
	SEALING	AEGIMRU	GAUMIER		EATINGS
AEGILNT	ATINGLE	AEGIMRY	IMAGERY		GAINEST
	ELATING	AEGIMSS	AGEISMS		GENISTA
	GELATIN	AEGIMST	GAMIEST		INGATES

	INGESTA	**AEGKMSS**	MASKEGS	**AEGLNTU**	LANGUET
	SEATING	**AEGKNOR**	KARENGO	**AEGLNTW**	TWANGLE
	TAGINES	**AEGKNRS**	SKANGER	**AEGLNUU**	UNGULAE
	TANGIES	**AEGKRSW**	GAWKERS	**AEGLNUW**	GUNWALE
	TEASING	**AEGKSST**	GASKETS	**AEGLOOZ**	ZOOGLEA
	TSIGANE	**AEGLLLY**	LEGALLY	**AEGLOPR**	PERGOLA
AEGINSU	GUINEAS	**AEGLLNO**	ALLONGE	**AEGLORS**	GALORES
AEGINSY	EASYING		GALLEON		GAOLERS
AEGINSZ	AGNIZES	**AEGLLNR**	LANGREL	**AEGLORT**	GLOATER
	SEAZING	**AEGLLNS**	LEGLANS		LEGATOR
AEGINTU	UNITAGE	**AEGLLNT**	GELLANT	**AEGLORV**	VORLAGE
AEGINTV	VINTAGE	**AEGLLNY**	LANGLEY	**AEGLOSS**	GLOSSAE
AEGINTZ	TEAZING	**AEGLLOR**	ALLEGRO	**AEGLOST**	GELATOS
	TZIGANE	**AEGLLOT**	TOLLAGE		LEGATOS
AEGINVW	WEAVING	**AEGLLRY**	ALLERGY	**AEGLOSU**	GEALOUS
AEGIORT	GOATIER		GALLERY	**AEGLOSV**	LOVAGES
AEGIPPR	GAPPIER		LARGELY	**AEGLOTV**	VOLTAGE
AEGIPPS	PIPAGES		REGALLY	**AEGLPPR**	GRAPPLE
AEGIPRR	GRAPIER	**AEGLLST**	GALLETS	**AEGLPRS**	GRAPLES
AEGIPRS	GASPIER	**AEGLLSU**	SEAGULL	**AEGLPRU**	EARPLUG
	PRISAGE		SULLAGE		GRAUPEL
	SPAIRGE		ULLAGES		PLAGUER
AEGIPST	GAPIEST	**AEGLLSY**	GALLEYS	**AEGLPSS**	GAPLESS
AEGIRRZ	GRAZIER	**AEGLLTU**	GLUTEAL	**AEGLPSU**	PLAGUES
AEGIRSS	AGRISES	**AEGLMNR**	MANGLER		PLUSAGE
	GASSIER	**AEGLMNS**	MANGELS	**AEGLPUY**	PLAGUEY
AEGIRST	AGISTER		MANGLES	**AEGLRRU**	REGULAR
	AIGRETS	**AEGLMOR**	GLOMERA	**AEGLRSS**	LARGESS
	GAITERS		GOMERAL	**AEGLRST**	LARGEST
	SEAGIRT	**AEGLMOU**	MOULAGE	**AEGLRSV**	GRAVELS
	STAGIER	**AEGLMPU**	PLUMAGE		VERGLAS
	STRIGAE	**AEGLMRS**	MALGRES	**AEGLRSY**	ARGYLES
	TIRAGES	**AEGLMRU**	MAULGRE		GRAYLES
	TRIAGES	**AEGLMSV**	MAGLEVS	**AEGLRSZ**	GLAZERS
AEGIRSV	GARVIES	**AEGLMSY**	MYGALES	**AEGLRTU**	GAULTER
	GRAVIES	**AEGLNOS**	ENGAOLS		TEGULAR
	RIVAGES	**AEGLNOT**	TANGELO		TRAGULE
AEGIRSW	EARWIGS	**AEGLNPR**	GRAPNEL	**AEGLRTY**	GREATLY
	GAWSIER	**AEGLNPS**	SPANGLE	**AEGLRVY**	GRAVELY
AEGIRSZ	AGRIZES	**AEGLNRS**	ANGLERS	**AEGLSSS**	GASLESS
AEGIRTV	VIRGATE		ERLANGS		GLASSES
	VITRAGE		LANGERS	**AEGLSST**	TAGLESS
AEGIRUY	YUGARIE		LARGENS	**AEGLSSU**	SAULGES
AEGIRUZ	GAUZIER		SLANGER	**AEGLSTT**	GESTALT
AEGISST	AGEISTS	**AEGLNRT**	TANGLER	**AEGLSTW**	TALWEGS
	SAGIEST		TRANGLE	**AEGLTUV**	VULGATE
AEGISSU	AGUISES	**AEGLNRU**	GRANULE	**AEGLUUY**	GUAYULE
AEGISSV	VISAGES	**AEGLNRW**	WANGLER	**AEGLUVY**	VAGUELY
AEGISTU	AUGITES		WRANGLE	**AEGMMNS**	MAGSMEN
AEGISTY	GASEITY	**AEGLNRY**	ANGERLY	**AEGMMRS**	GAMMERS
AEGISTZ	GAZIEST	**AEGLNSS**	GLASSEN		GRAMMES
AEGISUZ	AGUIZES	**AEGLNST**	GELANTS	**AEGMMRU**	RUMMAGE
AEGISYZ	AZYGIES		LANGEST	**AEGMMSS**	SMEGMAS
AEGJLNR	JANGLER		TANGLES	**AEGMNNO**	AGNOMEN
AEGJLNS	JANGLES	**AEGLNSU**	ANGELUS		NONGAME
AEGJLSS	JAGLESS		LAGUNES	**AEGMNOR**	MARENGO
AEGJLST	JETLAGS		LANGUES		MEGARON
AEGKKNO	ANGEKOK		LEGUANS	**AEGMNOS**	GAMONES
AEGKLOU	KAGOULE	**AEGLNSW**	WANGLES		MANGOES
AEGKLRS	GRAKLES	**AEGLNSY**	LYNAGES	**AEGMNOT**	GEOMANT
AEGKMRY	KERYGMA	**AEGLNTT**	GANTLET		MAGNETO

	MEGATON	AEGNRTY	AGENTRY	AEGRSSU	ARGUSES
	MONTAGE	AEGNSSY	GANSEYS		SAUGERS
AEGMNPY	PYGMEAN		GAYNESS		USAGERS
AEGMNRS	ENGRAMS	AEGNSTT	GESTANT	AEGRSSW	SWAGERS
	GERMANS	AEGNTTU	TUTENAG	AEGRSSY	GYRASES
	MANGERS	AEGOORT	ROOTAGE	AEGRSTT	TARGETS
AEGMNRT	GARMENT	AEGOPPR	PROPAGE	AEGRSTV	GRAVEST
	MARGENT	AEGOPRT	PORTAGE	AEGRSTY	GRAYEST
	RAGMENT		POTAGER		GYRATES
AEGMNST	MAGNETS	AEGOPST	GESTAPO		STAGERY
AEGMNSW	SWAGMEN		POSTAGE	AEGRSUV	SEVRUGA
AEGMNTU	AUGMENT		POTAGES	AEGRSVY	GARVEYS
	MUTAGEN	AEGOPTT	POTTAGE	AEGRSYZ	AGRYZES
AEGMOOR	MOORAGE	AEGORRT	GARROTE	AEGSSSU	GAUSSES
AEGMORS	ROMAGES	AEGORSS	SORAGES	AEGSTUU	AUGUSTE
AEGMOSW	WAGSOME	AEGORST	GAROTES	AEGSTUV	VAGUEST
AEGMOSY	GAYSOME		ORGEATS	AEGTTTU	GUTTATE
AEGMOXY	EXOGAMY		STORAGE	AEHHIKS	SHEIKHA
AEGMRSU	MAUGRES		TOERAGS	AEHHIRS	HASHIER
	MURAGES	AEGORSU	AERUGOS	AEHHIST	SHEHITA
AEGMSUY	MAGUEYS	AEGORTT	GAROTTE	AEHHLST	HEALTHS
AEGMSUZ	ZEUGMAS	AEGORTU	OUTRAGE	AEHHLTY	HEALTHY
AEGNNOS	NONAGES	AEGORUV	OUVRAGE	AEHHNRS	HARSHEN
AEGNNOT	NEGATON	AEGORVY	VOYAGER	AEHHPRS	RHAPHES
	TONNAGE	AEGOSSU	GASEOUS	AEHHRRS	HARSHER
AEGNNOW	NONWAGE	AEGOSTU	OUTAGES	AEHHRSS	HARSHES
AEGNNPS	PANGENS	AEGOSTW	STOWAGE	AEHHRST	HEARTHS
	PENANGS		TOWAGES	AEHHSSS	SHASHES
AEGNNRT	REGNANT	AEGOSTX	OXGATES	AEHHSST	SHEATHS
AEGNNRU	GUNNERA	AEGOSVY	VOYAGES	AEHHSTY	SHEATHY
AEGNNST	GANNETS	AEGOTTU	OUTGATE	AEHIILR	HAILIER
AEGNNTT	TANGENT	AEGOTTV	GAVOTTE	AEHIIRR	HAIRIER
AEGNNTU	TUNNAGE	AEGOTUV	OUTGAVE	AEHIJRS	HEJIRAS
AEGNOOR	OREGANO	AEGOTUZ	OUTGAZE	AEHIKLT	HATLIKE
AEGNOPT	PONTAGE	AEGPPRS	GAPPERS	AEHIKNS	HANKIES
AEGNORR	GROANER	AEGPRRS	GRASPER	AEHIKPS	PEAKISH
	ORANGER		SPARGER	AEHIKRS	SHAKIER
AEGNORS	ONAGERS	AEGPRRY	GRAPERY	AEHIKSS	SAKIEHS
	ORANGES	AEGPRSS	GASPERS	AEHIKST	SHITAKE
AEGNORT	NEGATOR		SPARGES	AEHIKSW	HAWKIES
AEGNORW	WAGONER	AEGPRST	PARGETS		WEAKISH
AEGNORY	ORANGEY	AEGPRSU	GAUPERS	AEHIKSY	SAKIYEH
AEGNOST	ONSTAGE	AEGPRSW	GAWPERS	AEHILMN	HELIMAN
AEGNOSY	NOSEGAY	AEGPSSU	PEGASUS	AEHILMO	HEMIOLA
AEGNOWY	WAYGONE	AEGPSTU	UPSTAGE	AEHILMS	LEHAIMS
AEGNPRS	ENGRASP	AEGPSUZ	UPGAZES	AEHILMY	LEHAYIM
AEGNPRT	TREPANG	AEGRRSS	GRASSER	AEHILNR	HERNIAL
AEGNRRS	GARNERS	AEGRRST	GARRETS		INHALER
	RANGERS		GARTERS	AEHILNS	INHALES
AEGNRRT	GRANTER		GRATERS	AEHILNY	HYALINE
	REGRANT	AEGRRSU	ARGUERS	AEHILOR	AIRHOLE
AEGNRSS	SANGERS		SUGARER	AEHILPR	HARELIP
	SERANGS	AEGRRSV	GRAVERS	AEHILPT	HAPLITE
AEGNRST	ARGENTS	AEGRRSZ	GRAZERS	AEHILRS	HAILERS
	GARNETS	AEGRRUU	AUGURER		SHALIER
	STRANGE	AEGRRUV	GRAVURE	AEHILRT	LATHIER
AEGNRSU	RAUNGES		VERRUGA	AEHILRU	HAULIER
	UNGEARS	AEGRSSS	GASSERS	AEHILSS	SHEILAS
AEGNRSW	GNAWERS		GRASSES	AEHILST	HALITES
AEGNRTU	GAUNTER	AEGRSST	GASTERS		HELIAST
AEGNRTW	TWANGER		STAGERS	AEHILSW	SHAWLIE

	WHAISLE	**AEHISSV**	SHAVIES	**AEHLRSS**	ASHLERS
AEHILTT	LITHATE	**AEHISTT**	ATHEIST		HALSERS
AEHILTY	HYALITE		STAITHE		LASHERS
					SLASHER
AEHILUV	VIHUELA	**AEHISTY**	HAYIEST		
AEHILVY	HEAVILY	**AEHISTZ**	HAZIEST	**AEHLRST**	HALTERS
AEHILWZ	WHAIZLE	**AEHISVY**	YESHIVA		HARSLET
AEHIMMR	HAMMIER	**AEHITTW**	THWAITE		LATHERS
AEHIMMS	MAIHEMS	**AEHJLOW**	JAWHOLE		SLATHER
AEHIMNR	HARMINE	**AEHKMSS**	SAMEKHS		THALERS
AEHIMNS	HAEMINS	**AEHKNRS**	HANKERS	**AEHLRSU**	HAULERS
	HEMINAS		HARKENS	**AEHLRSV**	HALVERS
AEHIMNT	HEMATIN	**AEHKNRT**	THANKER	**AEHLRSW**	WHALERS
AEHIMNY	HYMENIA	**AEHKNSZ**	KHAZENS	**AEHLRTY**	EARTHLY
AEHIMPS	PHAEISM	**AEHKOOR**	HOROEKA		HARTELY
AEHIMRS	MASHIER	**AEHKOSS**	SHAKOES		HEARTLY
	MISHEAR	**AEHKPRS**	PHREAKS		LATHERY
AEHIMSS	MASHIES	**AEHKPSU**	SHAKEUP	**AEHLRWY**	WHALERY
	MESSIAH	**AEHKRRS**	SHARKER	**AEHLSSS**	ASHLESS
AEHIMST	ATHEISM	**AEHKRSS**	KASHERS		HASSELS
AEHINPR	HEPARIN		SHAKERS		HASSLES
AEHINPS	INPHASE	**AEHKRSW**	HAWKERS		SLASHES
AEHINPT	PENTHIA	**AEHKSSY**	ASHKEYS	**AEHLSST**	HASLETS
AEHINRS	ARSHINE	**AEHKSWY**	HAWKEYS		HATLESS
	HERNIAS	**AEHLLLS**	HALLELS		SHELTAS
AEHINRT	HAIRNET	**AEHLLOS**	HALLOES	**AEHLSSY**	HAYSELS
	INEARTH	**AEHLLOV**	HELLOVA	**AEHLSTT**	STEALTH
	THERIAN	**AEHLLRS**	HERSALL	**AEHLSTW**	WEALTHS
AEHINSS	HESSIAN	**AEHLLST**	LETHALS	**AEHLSWY**	SHAWLEY
AEHINST	SHEITAN	**AEHLLUV**	HELLUVA	**AEHLTWY**	WEALTHY
	STHENIA	**AEHLLYZ**	HAZELLY	**AEHMMNS**	MASHMEN
AEHINSV	EVANISH	**AEHLMNO**	MANHOLE	**AEHMMRS**	HAMMERS
	VAHINES	**AEHLMNY**	HYMENAL		SHAMMER
AEHINSW	WAHINES	**AEHLMOR**	ARMHOLE	**AEHMMSS**	SHAMMES
AEHIORR	HOARIER	**AEHLMPS**	PELHAMS	**AEHMMSY**	MAYHEMS
AEHIPPR	HAPPIER	**AEHLMPW**	WHAMPLE	**AEHMNOR**	MENORAH
AEHIPPS	HAPPIES	**AEHLMRS**	HARMELS	**AEHMNOS**	HOSEMAN
AEHIPPT	EPITAPH	**AEHLMRT**	THERMAL	**AEHMNOT**	NATHEMO
AEHIPRS	HARPIES	**AEHLMRU**	HUMERAL	**AEHMNOY**	HAEMONY
	SHARPIE	**AEHLMST**	HAMLETS	**AEHMNPY**	NYMPHAE
AEHIPSS	APHESIS	**AEHLNOS**	ENHALOS	**AEHMNRU**	HUMANER
AEHIPST	APESHIT	**AEHLNOT**	ANETHOL	**AEHMNST**	ANTHEMS
AEHIPSW	PEISHWA		ETHANOL		HETMANS
AEHIPTZ	ZAPTIEH	**AEHLNRT**	ENTHRAL	**AEHMOPT**	APOTHEM
AEHIQSU	HAIQUES	**AEHLNSS**	HANSELS	**AEHMORT**	TERAOHM
	QUASHIE	**AEHLNST**	HANTLES	**AEHMPRS**	HAMPERS
AEHIRRR	HARRIER	**AEHLNSU**	UNHEALS	**AEHMPTY**	EMPATHY
AEHIRRS	HARRIES		UNLEASH	**AEHMRRS**	HARMERS
AEHIRSS	ARISHES		UNSHALE	**AEHMRSS**	MARSHES
	RASHIES	**AEHLOPR**	EPHORAL		MASHERS
	SHERIAS	**AEHLOPT**	TAPHOLE		SHAMERS
AEHIRST	HASTIER	**AEHLORS**	SHOALER		SHMEARS
	SHERIAT	**AEHLORT**	LOATHER		SMASHER
AEHIRSV	ASHIVER		RATHOLE	**AEHMRST**	HAMSTER
AEHIRSW	WASHIER	**AEHLOSS**	ASSHOLE	**AEHMRTU**	MAUTHER
	WEARISH	**AEHLOST**	LOATHES	**AEHMRTW**	MAWTHER
AEHIRTW	THAWIER	**AEHLPRS**	PLASHER	**AEHMSSS**	SMASHES
AEHIRWY	HAYWIRE		SPHERAL	**AEHMSST**	SMEATHS
AEHISST	ASHIEST	**AEHLPSS**	HAPLESS	**AEHMSTT**	SHMATTE
	SAITHES		PLASHES	**AEHMSTU**	HUMATES
	STASHIE	**AEHLPST**	PLASHET	**AEHMSUW**	MAHEWUS
	TAISHES	**AEHLPSY**	SHAPELY	**AEHMUZZ**	MEZUZAH

AEHNNTU	UNNEATH		SPHAERS			MINIATE
AEHNNWY	ANYWHEN		SPHEARS	AEIIMPR	IMPERIA
AEHNOPT	PHAETON	AEHPRST	SPARTHE	AEIIMRT	AIRTIME
	PHONATE		TEPHRAS	AEIIMRV	VIREMIA
AEHNOPW	WANHOPE		THREAPS	AEIIMST	AMITIES
AEHNOPY	HYPONEA	AEHPRSW	PREWASH		ATIMIES
AEHNORS	HOARSEN	AEHPRTT	PHATTER	AEIIMTT	IMITATE
	SENHORA	AEHPRTY	THERAPY	AEIINNS	ASININE
AEHNORT	ANOTHER	AEHPSST	SPATHES		INSANIE
AEHNOSX	HEXOSAN	AEHPSSW	PESHWAS	AEIINOP	EPINAOI
AEHNPPS	HAPPENS	AEHPSTY	HYPATES	AEIINQU	EQUINIA
AEHNPRS	SHARPEN	AEHQRSU	QUASHER	AEIINRR	RAINIER
AEHNPRT	PANTHER	AEHQSSU	QUASHES	AEIINRS	SENARII
AEHNPST	HAPTENS	AEHRRSS	RASHERS	AEIINRT	INERTIA
AEHNPSU	UNSHAPE		SHARERS	AEIINST	ISATINE
AEHNPTY	PHYTANE	AEHRRST	TRASHER	AEIINSX	SIXAINE
AEHNRSS	HARNESS	AEHRRTU	URETHRA	AEIINTX	AXINITE
AEHNRST	ANTHERS	AEHRSST	RASHEST	AEIIPRR	PRAIRIE
	HARTENS		SHASTER	AEIIRRV	RIVIERA
	THENARS		TRASHES		VAIRIER
AEHNRTU	HAUNTER	AEHRSSV	SHAVERS	AEIIRST	AIRIEST
	UNEARTH	AEHRSSW	HAWSERS		IRISATE
	UNHEART		SWASHER	AEIIRSW	AIRWISE
	URETHAN		WASHERS	AEIITTV	VITIATE
AEHNRTX	NARTHEX	AEHRSTT	HATTERS	AEIJKLM	JAMLIKE
AEHNSSS	SNASHES		RATHEST	AEIJKLW	JAWLIKE
AEHNSST	HASTENS		SHATTER	AEIJLNV	JAVELIN
	SNATHES		THREATS	AEIJLNW	JAWLINE
	SNEATHS	AEHRSTV	HARVEST	AEIJLRS	JAILERS
AEHNSSU	HAUSENS		THRAVES	AEIJLSZ	JEZAILS
AEHNSSZ	SAZHENS	AEHRSTW	SWATHER	AEIJMMR	JAMMIER
AEHNSTY	ASTHENY		THAWERS	AEIJMMS	JAMMIES
	SHANTEY		WREATHS		JEMIMAS
AEHNSUW	WHENUAS	AEHRSVW	WHARVES	AEIJMNS	JASMINE
AEHNSUY	HAUYNES	AEHRSWY	WASHERY	AEIJNNS	JANNIES
AEHNTTW	WHATTEN	AEHRSXY	HYRAXES	AEIJNRS	INJERAS
AEHOORT	TOHEROA	AEHRTUU	HAUTEUR	AEIJNRT	JANTIER
AEHOPRT	PHORATE	AEHRTWY	WREATHY		NARTJIE
AEHOPST	TEASHOP	AEHSSST	STASHES	AEIJNST	JANTIES
AEHORRS	HOARSER	AEHSSSW	SWASHES		TAJINES
AEHORST	ASTHORE	AEHSSTW	SWATHES	AEIJNTU	JAUNTIE
	EARSHOT	AEHSTUX	EXHAUST	AEIJRSV	JARVIES
	HAROSET	AEIIKLR	AIRLIKE	AEIJRZZ	JAZZIER
AEHORSX	HOAXERS	AEIIKNT	KAINITE	AEIJSSV	JIVEASS
AEHORTU	OUTHEAR	AEIIKSS	SAIKEIS	AEIKKLO	OAKLIKE
AEHORTX	OXHEART	AEIILLT	TAILLIE	AEIKKPS	PIKAKES
AEHORUV	HAVEOUR	AEIILMP	LIPEMIA	AEIKKST	TAKKIES
AEHORUW	WAREHOU	AEIILMR	RAMILIE	AEIKLLW	LAWLIKE
AEHOSTU	ATHEOUS	AEIILNN	ANILINE	AEIKLLY	LEAKILY
AEHOSTW	AWHETOS	AEIILNR	AIRLINE	AEIKLMN	MANLIKE
AEHPPRS	PERHAPS	AEIILNX	EXILIAN	AEIKLMP	MAPLIKE
AEHPPRW	WHAPPER	AEIILRR	LAIRIER	AEIKLMR	ARMLIKE
AEHPPSU	SHAPEUP	AEIILRS	LAIRISE	AEIKLNO	KAOLINE
	UPHEAPS	AEIILRV	VIRELAI	AEIKLNR	LANKIER
AEHPRRS	HARPERS	AEIILRZ	LAIRIZE	AEIKLNS	ALKINES
	PHRASER	AEIILSS	LIAISES	AEIKLNT	ANTLIKE
	SHARPER		SILESIA	AEIKLNU	UNALIKE
AEHPRSS	PHRASES	AEIILST	LAITIES	AEIKLOR	OARLIKE
	SERAPHS	AEIILSW	LEWISIA	AEIKLOT	KEITLOA
	SHAPERS	AEIILTZ	TAILZIE		OATLIKE
	SHERPAS	AEIIMNT	INTIMAE	AEIKLRR	LARKIER

AEIKLRS	LAIKERS	**AEILLNU**	UILLEAN				MALTIER
	SERKALI	**AEILLNY**	ALIENLY				MARLITE
AEIKLRT	RATLIKE	**AEILLOV**	ALVEOLI	**AEILMSS**	AIMLESS		
	TALKIER	**AEILLPR**	PALLIER		MESAILS		
AEIKLRV	KLAVIER		PERILLA		SAMIELS		
AEIKLRW	WARLIKE	**AEILLPS**	ILLAPSE		SEISMAL		
AEIKLRY	RAYLIKE		PALLIES	**AEILMSZ**	MEZAILS		
AEIKLSS	ALSIKES	**AEILLPU**	PILULAE	**AEILMTY**	LAYTIME		
	ASSLIKE	**AEILLPY**	EPYLLIA		MEATILY		
AEIKLST	LAKIEST	**AEILLQU**	LALIQUE	**AEILNNY**	INANELY		
	TALKIES	**AEILLRR**	RALLIER	**AEILNOP**	OPALINE		
AEIKLSW	SAWLIKE	**AEILLRS**	RALLIES	**AEILNOR**	AILERON		
	WALKIES		SALLIER		ALERION		
AEIKLWX	WAXLIKE	**AEILLRT**	LITERAL		ALIENOR		
AEIKMMS	MISMAKE		TALLIER	**AEILNOS**	ANISOLE		
AEIKMNP	PIKEMAN		TRIELLA	**AEILNOT**	ELATION		
AEIKMNR	MANKIER	**AEILLRU**	RUELLIA		TOENAIL		
	RAMEKIN	**AEILLRW**	WALLIER	**AEILNPR**	PEARLIN		
AEIKMNS	KINEMAS	**AEILLSS**	ALLISES		PLAINER		
AEIKMPR	RAMPIKE		SALLIES		PRALINE		
AEIKMRW	MAWKIER	**AEILLST**	SITELLA	**AEILNPS**	ALPINES		
AEIKMSS	KAMISES		TAILLES		PINEALS		
AEIKMST	KETMIAS		TALLIES		SPANIEL		
	MISTAKE	**AEILLSW**	WALLIES		SPLENIA		
AEIKNNT	NEATNIK	**AEILLUV**	ELUVIAL	**AEILNPT**	PANTILE		
AEIKNPR	RANPIKE	**AEILLVX**	VEXILLA	**AEILNPW**	PINWALE		
AEIKNRR	NARKIER	**AEILMMN**	MAILMEN	**AEILNPX**	EXPLAIN		
AEIKNRS	SNAKIER	**AEILMMR**	MALMIER	**AEILNQU**	EQUINAL		
AEIKNRT	KERATIN	**AEILMMS**	LAMMIES		QUINELA		
AEIKNRW	WANKIER		MELISMA	**AEILNRR**	LARNIER		
AEIKNSS	KINASES	**AEILMNN**	LINEMAN	**AEILNRS**	ALINERS		
AEIKNST	INTAKES		MELANIN		NAILERS		
	KENTIAS	**AEILMNO**	MINEOLA		RENAILS		
	TANKIES	**AEILMNP**	IMPANEL	**AEILNRT**	ENTRAIL		
AEIKNSW	SWANKIE		MANIPLE		LATRINE		
AEIKNSY	KYANISE	**AEILMNR**	MANLIER		RATLINE		
	YANKIES		MARLINE		RELIANT		
AEIKNSZ	KAIZENS		MINERAL		RETINAL		
AEIKNTU	UNAKITE		RAILMEN		TRENAIL		
AEIKNTY	KYANITE	**AEILMNS**	ISLEMAN	**AEILNRV**	RAVELIN		
AEIKNYZ	KYANIZE		MALINES	**AEILNRW**	LAWNIER		
AEIKOST	OAKIEST		MENIALS	**AEILNRX**	RELAXIN		
AEIKPRR	PARKIER		SEMINAL	**AEILNRY**	INLAYER		
AEIKPRS	PARKIES	**AEILMNT**	AILMENT		NAILERY		
	SPARKIE		ALIMENT	**AEILNSS**	SALINES		
AEIKPRW	PAWKIER	**AEILMNU**	ALUMINE		SILANES		
AEIKQRU	QUAKIER	**AEILMOR**	LOAMIER	**AEILNST**	EASTLIN		
AEIKRRS	KERRIAS	**AEILMPR**	IMPALER		ELASTIN		
	SARKIER		IMPEARL		ENTAILS		
AEIKRSS	KAISERS		LEMPIRA		NAILSET		
	KARSIES		PALMIER		SALIENT		
AEIKRST	ARKITES	**AEILMPS**	IMPALES		SALTINE		
	KARITES		PALMIES		SLAINTE		
AEIKRSU	KAURIES	**AEILMPT**	IMPLATE		STANIEL		
AEIKRSW	SKIWEAR		PALMIET		TENAILS		
AEIKRSZ	KARZIES	**AEILMRR**	LARMIER	**AEILNSU**	INSULAE		
AEIKSSS	ASKESIS		MARLIER		INULASE		
AEIKSTT	TAKIEST	**AEILMRS**	MAILERS	**AEILNSV**	ALEVINS		
AEILLMN	MANILLE		REALISM		VALINES		
AEILLNR	RALLINE		REMAILS	**AEILNSW**	LAWINES		
AEILLNS	AINSELL	**AEILMRT**	LAMITER	**AEILNSX**	ALEXINS		

AEILNSY	ELYSIAN	AEILRWY	WEARILY	MAUVINE
AEILNTU	ALUNITE	AEILSSS	LAISSES	AEIMOOP	IPOMOEA
AEILNTV	VENTAIL		LASSIES	AEIMOPR	EMPORIA
AEILNUV	UNALIVE	AEILSST	SALTIES		MEROPIA
	UNVAILE	AEILSSU	SAULIES	AEIMORR	ARMOIRE
AEILNUW	LAUWINE	AEILSSV	VALISES	AEIMOST	AMOSITE
AEILNVY	NAIVELY		VESSAIL		ATOMIES
AEILOPR	PELORIA	AEILSSW	WALISES		ATOMISE
AEILOPS	LEIPOAS	AEILSTU	SITULAE		OSMIATE
AEILORV	VARIOLE	AEILSTV	ESTIVAL	AEIMOTX	TOXEMIA
AEILOST	ISOLATE	AEILSTW	WALIEST	AEIMOTZ	ATOMIZE
AEILOTV	VIOLATE	AEILSTY	TAILYES	AEIMPRR	RAMPIRE
AEILPPR	APPERIL	AEILSTZ	LAZIEST	AEIMPRS	IMPRESA
	APPLIER	AEILSVV	LAVVIES		SAMPIRE
	ARIPPLE	AEILTVY	VILAYET	AEIMPRT	PRIMATE
AEILPPS	APPLIES	AEILUVX	EXUVIAL	AEIMPRV	VAMPIER
	LAPPIES	AEIMMMS	MAMMIES		VAMPIRE
AEILPRS	PALSIER	AEIMMNS	AMMINES	AEIMPSS	IMPASSE
	PARLIES		MISNAME		PESSIMA
AEILPRT	PLAITER	AEIMMOS	MIMOSAE	AEIMPST	IMPASTE
	PLATIER	AEIMMPS	SPAMMIE		PASTIME
AEILPRV	PREVAIL	AEIMMRR	RAMMIER	AEIMPSV	IMPAVES
AEILPSS	ESPIALS	AEIMMRS	MAIMERS	AEIMPSW	MAPWISE
	LAIPSES		RAMMIES	AEIMPSY	PYEMIAS
	LAPISES	AEIMMRT	MARMITE		YAMPIES
	LIPASES		TRAMMIE	AEIMRRR	MARRIER
	PALSIES	AEIMMSS	SAMMIES	AEIMRRS	MARRIES
AEILPST	APLITES	AEIMMST	MISMATE		SIMARRE
	PALIEST		SEMIMAT	AEIMRRV	MARVIER
	PLATIES		TAMMIES	AEIMRSS	MASSIER
	TALIPES	AEIMMZZ	MIZMAZE		SARMIES
AEILPSY	PAISLEY	AEIMNNT	MANNITE	AEIMRST	IMARETS
AEILQTU	LIQUATE	AEIMNOR	MORAINE		MAESTRI
	TEQUILA		ROMAINE		MAISTER
AEILRRS	RAILERS	AEIMNOS	ANOMIES		MASTIER
	RERAILS	AEIMNOT	AMNIOTE		MISRATE
AEILRRT	RETIRAL	AEIMNOU	MOINEAU		SEMITAR
	RETRIAL	AEIMNPR	PERMIAN		SMARTIE
	TRAILER	AEIMNRR	MARINER	AEIMRSU	UREMIAS
AEILRSS	AIRLESS	AEIMNRS	MARINES	AEIMRSV	MISAVER
	RESAILS		REMAINS	AEIMRSW	AWMRIES
	SAILERS		SEMINAR		SEMIRAW
	SERAILS		SIRNAME	AEIMRSY	RIMAYES
	SERIALS	AEIMNRT	MERANTI	AEIMRTU	MURIATE
AEILRST	REALIST		MINARET	AEIMRTV	VITAMER
	RETAILS		RAIMENT	AEIMRTW	WARTIME
	SALTIER	AEIMNRV	VERMIAN	AEIMSSS	AMISSES
	SALTIRE	AEIMNRW	WIREMAN		MESSIAS
	SLATIER	AEIMNSS	INSEAMS	AEIMSST	ASTEISM
	TAILERS		SAMISEN		MISEATS
AEILRSV	REVISAL	AEIMNST	ETAMINS		MISSEAT
AEILRSW	SWALIER		INMATES		SAMIEST
	WAILERS		MAINEST		SAMITES
AEILRTT	TERTIAL		MANTIES		TAMISES
AEILRTU	URALITE		TAMEINS	AEIMSSV	MASSIVE
AEILRTW	WALTIER		TAMINES		MAVISES
AEILRTY	IRATELY	AEIMNSW	MANWISE	AEIMSSW	SWAMIES
	REALITY	AEIMNTX	TAXIMEN	AEIMSSY	MYIASES
	TEARILY	AEIMNTY	AMENITY	AEIMSTT	ETATISM
AEILRVV	REVIVAL		ANYTIME		MATIEST
AEILRVY	VIRELAY	AEIMNUV	MAUVEIN		MATTIES

AEIMSTZ	MAZIEST		TERRAIN	AEINTUV	VAUNTIE
	MESTIZA		TRAINER	AEINTVW	VAWNTIE
AEIMSUV	AMUSIVE	AEINRSS	ARSINES	AEINTVY	NAIVETY
AEIMSXX	MAXIXES		SARNIES	AEINTXY	ANXIETY
AEIMTYZ	AZYMITE	AEINRST	ANESTRI	AEIOPRS	SOAPIER
AEINNNS	NANNIES		ANTSIER	AEIOPSS	SOAPIES
AEINNOT	ENATION		NASTIER	AEIOPST	ATOPIES
AEINNPR	PANNIER		RATINES		OPIATES
AEINNPT	PANTINE		RESIANT	AEIOQSU	SEQUOIA
	PINNATE		RETAINS	AEIORRR	ARRIERO
AEINNRS	INSANER		RETINAS		ROARIER
	INSNARE		RETSINA	AEIORST	OARIEST
AEINNRT	ENTRAIN		STAINER		OTARIES
	TRANNIE		STARNIE	AEIORSV	OVARIES
AEINNRU	ANEURIN		STEARIN	AEIOSST	SOSATIE
AEINNSS	SANNIES	AEINRSV	AVENIRS	AEIOSTT	OATIEST
	SIENNAS		RAVINES		OSTIATE
AEINNST	INANEST	AEINRTT	INTREAT		TOASTIE
	NANITES		ITERANT	AEIOSTZ	AZOTISE
	STANINE		NATTIER	AEIOTZZ	AZOTIZE
	TANNIES		NITRATE	AEIPPPR	PAPPIER
AEINNSW	SWANNIE		TARTINE	AEIPPPS	PAPPIES
AEINNSZ	ENZIANS		TERTIAN	AEIPPRS	APPRISE
AEINNTT	ANTIENT	AEINRTU	RUINATE		SAPPIER
AEINOPS	EPINAOS		TAURINE	AEIPPRT	PERIAPT
	SENOPIA		URANITE	AEIPPRY	YAPPIER
AEINOPZ	APIEZON		URINATE	AEIPPRZ	APPRIZE
	EPIZOAN	AEINRTW	TAWNIER		ZAPPIER
AEINORS	ERASION		TINWARE	AEIPPSS	PASPIES
AEINORT	NOTAIRE	AEINRUV	VAURIEN	AEIPPSY	YAPPIES
	OTARINE	AEINRUW	UNWARIE	AEIPRRR	PARRIER
AEINOSS	ANOESIS	AEINRUZ	AZURINE	AEIPRRS	ASPIRER
AEINOST	ATONIES	AEINRVV	VERVAIN		PARRIES
AEINOSV	EVASION	AEINRWY	YAWNIER		PRAISER
AEINOSZ	AZIONES	AEINSSS	SANSEIS		RAPIERS
AEINOXZ	OXAZINE		SASINES		RASPIER
AEINPPP	PANPIPE	AEINSST	ENTASIS		REPAIRS
AEINPPR	NAPPIER		NASTIES	AEIPRRT	PARTIER
AEINPPS	NAPPIES		SEITANS	AEIPRSS	ASPIRES
	PINESAP		SESTINA		PARESIS
AEINPRS	PANIERS		TANSIES		PARISES
	RAPINES		TISANES		PRAISES
AEINPRT	PAINTER	AEINSSV	SAVINES		SPIREAS
	PERTAIN		VINASSE	AEIPRST	PAIREST
	REPAINT	AEINSTT	INSTATE		PARTIES
AEINPSS	ASPINES		SATINET		PASTIER
	PANSIES	AEINSTU	AUNTIES		PIASTER
	SAPIENS		SINUATE		PIASTRE
AEINPST	PANTIES	AEINSTV	NAIVEST		PIRATES
	PATINES		NATIVES		PRATIES
	SAPIENT		VAINEST		TRAIPSE
	SPINATE	AEINSTW	AWNIEST	AEIPRSU	SPURIAE
AEINPSW	WINESAP		TAWNIES		UPRAISE
AEINPTT	PATIENT		WANIEST	AEIPRSV	PARVISE
AEINPTU	PETUNIA		WANTIES		PAVISER
AEINPTY	PANEITY	AEINSTX	ANTISEX	AEIPRSW	WASPIER
AEINQTU	ANTIQUE		SEXTAIN	AEIPRTT	PARTITE
	QUINATE	AEINSTZ	ZANIEST	AEIPRTV	PRIVATE
AEINRRS	SIERRAN		ZEATINS	AEIPRTW	WIRETAP
	SNARIER	AEINSVV	NAVVIES	AEIPRXY	PYREXIA
AEINRRT	RETRAIN	AEINSWY	ANYWISE	AEIPSSS	ASEPSIS

	ASPISES		TATTIER	**AEKLNRS**	RANKLES
AEIPSST	PASTIES		TITRATE	**AEKLNRV**	KLAVERN
	PATSIES	**AEIRTTV**	TAIVERT	**AEKLNST**	ANKLETS
	PETSAIS	**AEIRTTW**	TAWTIER		ASKLENT
	TAPISES	**AEIRTTX**	EXTRAIT		LANKEST
AEIPSSV	PASSIVE	**AEIRTUY**	AUREITY	**AEKLNSW**	KNAWELS
	PAVISES	**AEIRTUZ**	AZURITE	**AEKLNSY**	ALKYNES
	PAVISSE	**AEIRTVY**	VARIETY	**AEKLORY**	ROKELAY
	SPAVIES	**AEIRWWY**	WIREWAY	**AEKLOST**	SKATOLE
AEIPSSW	WASPIES	**AEISSSS**	SASSIES	**AEKLOVZ**	ZELKOVA
AEIPSTT	PATTIES	**AEISSST**	SIESTAS	**AEKLPPT**	PEPTALK
	TAPETIS		TASSIES	**AEKLPRS**	SPARKLE
AEIPSTU	TAUPIES	**AEISSSW**	WISEASS	**AEKLPSS**	SPLAKES
AEIPSTV	SPAVIET	**AEISSSZ**	ASSIZES	**AEKLPSY**	KEYPALS
AEIPSTW	TAWPIES	**AEISSUV**	SUASIVE	**AEKLRRS**	LARKERS
AEIPTXY	EPITAXY	**AEISSUX**	AUXESIS	**AEKLRSS**	SLAKERS
AEIQRUV	AQUIVER	**AEISSVV**	SAVVIES	**AEKLRST**	STALKER
AEIQSSU	SAIQUES	**AEISTTT**	ETATIST		TALKERS
AEIRRRT	TARRIER		TATTIES	**AEKLRSV**	LEKVARS
AEIRRRV	ARRIVER	**AEISTTU**	SITUATE	**AEKLRSW**	WALKERS
AEIRRSS	ARRISES	**AEISTTV**	STATIVE	**AEKLRUW**	WAULKER
	RAISERS	**AEISTTW**	TAWIEST	**AEKLSST**	LASKETS
	SIERRAS		TWAITES		SKLATES
AEIRRST	ARTSIER	**AEISTTX**	TAXITES	**AEKLSTU**	AUKLETS
	SERRATI	**AEISTTY**	SATIETY	**AEKMMNR**	MARKMEN
	TARRIES	**AEISTVW**	WAVIEST	**AEKMNOS**	SOKEMAN
	TARSIER	**AEISTWX**	TAXWISE	**AEKMNRU**	UNMAKER
AEIRRSV	ARRIVES		WAXIEST	**AEKMNSU**	UNMAKES
	VARIERS	**AEITTTU**	ATTUITE	**AEKMOOT**	MATOOKE
AEIRRTT	RATTIER	**AEITTTV**	VITTATE	**AEKMOST**	MATOKES
	RETRAIT	**AEJJLNU**	JEJUNAL	**AEKMPRU**	UPMAKER
	TARTIER	**AEJKMNR**	JARKMEN	**AEKMPSU**	MAKEUPS
AEIRRTW	WARTIER	**AEJKNRS**	JANKERS		UPMAKES
AEIRRTY	RETIARY	**AEJKPTU**	KAJEPUT	**AEKMRRS**	MARKERS
AEIRRVV	VIVERRA	**AEJLNUV**	JUVENAL		REMARKS
AEIRSSS	SASSIER	**AEJLOSU**	JALOUSE	**AEKMRSS**	MASKERS
AEIRSST	ARSIEST		JEALOUS	**AEKMRST**	MARKETS
	ARTSIES	**AEJLOUZ**	AZULEJO	**AEKMRSU**	KUMERAS
	SAIREST	**AEJLSSW**	JAWLESS	**AEKNNOP**	NONPEAK
	SATIRES	**AEJMMRS**	JAMMERS	**AEKNNRS**	ENRANKS
	TIRASSE	**AEJMNZZ**	JAZZMEN	**AEKNNST**	KANTENS
AEIRSSU	SAURIES	**AEJMRST**	RAMJETS	**AEKNNTU**	UNTAKEN
AEIRSSZ	ASSIZER	**AEJMSST**	JETSAMS	**AEKNOSW**	WEAKONS
AEIRSTT	ARTIEST	**AEJMSSY**	JESSAMY	**AEKNPPR**	KNAPPER
	ARTISTE	**AEJMSTY**	MAJESTY	**AEKNPRS**	SPANKER
	ATTIRES	**AEJNNOS**	JOANNES	**AEKNPSU**	UNSPEAK
	IRATEST	**AEJNORZ**	ZANJERO	**AEKNPTU**	UPTAKEN
	RATITES	**AEJNSST**	JESSANT	**AEKNRRS**	RANKERS
	STRIATE	**AEJNSSU**	JAUNSES	**AEKNRSS**	KRANSES
	TASTIER	**AEJPRSS**	JASPERS	**AEKNRST**	RANKEST
	TERTIAS	**AEJPRSY**	JASPERY		STARKEN
AEIRSTV	TAIVERS	**AEJRSVY**	JARVEYS		TANKERS
	VASTIER	**AEJRSZZ**	JAZZERS	**AEKNRSU**	UNRAKES
	VERITAS	**AEJSTWY**	JETWAYS	**AEKNRSW**	SWANKER
AEIRSTW	WAISTER	**AEKKNRS**	KRAKENS		WANKERS
	WAITERS		SKANKER	**AEKNRSY**	YANKERS
	WARIEST	**AEKKRSY**	YAKKERS	**AEKNRSZ**	KRANZES
	WASTRIE	**AEKLLTU**	KELLAUT	**AEKNRVY**	KNAVERY
AEIRSVV	SAVVIER	**AEKLMOU**	LEUKOMA	**AEKNSSU**	ANKUSES
AEIRSVW	WAIVERS	**AEKLNPP**	KNAPPLE	**AEKNSWY**	SWANKEY
AEIRTTT	ATTRITE	**AEKLNPR**	PRANKLE	**AEKOPRS**	PRESOAK

AEKORRS	ROSAKER	**AELLPPS**	LAPPELS		RAMPOLE
AEKORSS	ARKOSES	**AELLPRS**	SPALLER	**AELMOPU**	AMPOULE
	RESOAKS	**AELLPRU**	PLEURAL	**AELMOPY**	MAYPOLE
	SOAKERS	**AELLPSS**	SPALLES	**AELMORS**	MORALES
AEKORST	KOTARES	**AELLPST**	PALLETS	**AELMORU**	MORULAE
AEKOSTV	VOETSAK	**AELLPTU**	PLUTEAL	**AELMORV**	REMOVAL
AEKOTTU	OUTTAKE	**AELLPTY**	PLAYLET	**AELMOSS**	MOLASSE
	TAKEOUT	**AELLQUY**	EQUALLY	**AELMOST**	MALTOSE
AEKPPSU	UPSPAKE	**AELLRRU**	ALLURER	**AELMOSY**	AMYLOSE
	UPSPEAK	**AELLRST**	STELLAR	**AELMOTT**	MATELOT
AEKPRRS	PARKERS		TELLARS	**AELMPRS**	EMPARLS
	REPARKS	**AELLRSU**	ALLURES		LAMPERS
	SPARKER		LAURELS		PALMERS
AEKPRSS	SPARKES	**AELLRSW**	WALLERS		SAMPLER
AEKPSSY	PASSKEY	**AELLRSY**	RALLYES	**AELMPRT**	TEMPLAR
AEKPSTU	TAKEUPS	**AELLRTY**	ALERTLY		TRAMPLE
	UPTAKES		ELYTRAL	**AELMPRY**	LAMPREY
AEKQRSU	QUAKERS		RETALLY	**AELMPSS**	MAPLESS
AEKQSSU	SQUEAKS	**AELLRVY**	RAVELLY		SAMPLES
AEKQSUY	SQUEAKY	**AELLSST**	SALLETS	**AELMPST**	AMPLEST
AEKRRST	KARTERS		STELLAS	**AELMPSU**	AMPULES
	KRATERS		TASSELL	**AELMPTU**	PLUMATE
	STARKER	**AELLSSW**	LAWLESS	**AELMRRS**	MARRELS
AEKRSST	SKATERS	**AELLSTT**	TALLEST	**AELMRSS**	ARMLESS
	STRAKES		TALLETS	**AELMRST**	ARMLETS
	STREAKS	**AELLSTW**	SETWALL		LAMSTER
	TASKERS		SWALLET		MARTELS
AEKRSSY	KARSEYS		WALLETS		TRAMELS
AEKRSTY	STREAKY	**AELLSTY**	STALELY	**AELMRSU**	MAULERS
AEKRSUW	WAUKERS	**AELLSVY**	VALLEYS		SERUMAL
AEKSSSV	KVASSES	**AELLTUU**	ULULATE	**AELMRSV**	MARVELS
AEKSSTT	TSATSKE	**AELLUVV**	VALVULE	**AELMRTT**	MARTLET
AEKSWYY	KEYWAYS	**AELMMNO**	MAMELON	**AELMRTU**	RELATUM
AELLMNU	LUMENAL	**AELMMNS**	ALMSMEN	**AELMSST**	MATLESS
AELLMRS	SMALLER	**AELMMNT**	MALTMEN		SAMLETS
AELLMRT	TRAMELL	**AELMMOY**	MYELOMA	**AELMSTU**	AMULETS
AELLMST	MALLETS	**AELMMRS**	LAMMERS		MULETAS
AELLMSU	MALLEUS		RAMMELS	**AELNNPR**	PLANNER
AELLMSY	MELLAYS		RAMMLES	**AELNNPS**	PENNALS
	MESALLY		SLAMMER	**AELNNPU**	UNPANEL
AELLMTY	METALLY	**AELMMRT**	TRAMMEL	**AELNNRS**	ENSNARL
AELLMWX	MAXWELL	**AELMMST**	STAMMEL		LANNERS
AELLNOP	PALLONE	**AELMMSY**	MALMSEY	**AELNNRT**	LANTERN
	PLEONAL	**AELMNNS**	LENSMAN	**AELNNRU**	UNLEARN
AELLNOR	LLANERO	**AELMNOR**	ALMONER	**AELNNST**	STANNEL
AELLNOV	NOVELLA		NEMORAL	**AELNNTU**	ANNULET
AELLNOY	ALONELY	**AELMNOS**	MELANOS	**AELNOOS**	ALSOONE
AELLNPY	PENALLY	**AELMNOT**	LOMENTA	**AELNOPS**	ESPANOL
AELLNRT	ENTRALL		OMENTAL		NOPALES
AELLNSS	ALLNESS		TELAMON	**AELNOPT**	POLENTA
AELLNSW	ENWALLS	**AELMNPR**	LAMPERN	**AELNOPU**	APOLUNE
AELLNTT	TALLENT	**AELMNRS**	ALMNERS	**AELNORS**	LOANERS
AELLNUU	LUNULAE	**AELMNRU**	NUMERAL		ORLEANS
AELLNVY	VENALLY	**AELMNSS**	MANLESS		RELOANS
AELLOPX	POLLAXE	**AELMNST**	LAMENTS	**AELNORU**	ALEURON
AELLORS	ROSELLA		MANTELS	**AELNORV**	VERONAL
AELLORT	REALLOT		MANTLES	**AELNOST**	ETALONS
AELLORV	ALLOVER	**AELMNSU**	MENSUAL		TOLANES
	OVERALL	**AELMNTT**	MANTLET	**AELNOTV**	VOLANTE
AELLORY	LOYALER	**AELMNTU**	NUTMEAL	**AELNOTY**	ANOLYTE
AELLOSS	LOESSAL	**AELMOPR**	PLEROMA	**AELNOUZ**	ZONULAE

AELNPPR	PREPLAN	AELOPSX	EXPOSAL		REPLAYS
AELNPPY	PLAYPEN	AELOPTT	PALETOT		SPARELY
AELNPRS	PLANERS	AELOPTU	OUTLEAP	AELPRTT	PARTLET
	REPLANS	AELORRT	REALTOR		PLATTER
AELNPRT	PANTLER		RELATOR		PRATTLE
	PLANTER	AELORSS	LASSOER	AELPRTY	PEARTLY
	REPLANT		OARLESS		PEYTRAL
AELNPRY	PLENARY		SEROSAL		PRELATY
AELNPSS	NAPLESS		SOLERAS		PTERYLA
AELNPST	PLANETS	AELORST	OESTRAL	AELPRUY	EPULARY
	PLATENS		OLESTRA	AELPSSS	PASSELS
AELNPSU	UPLEANS	AELORTT	RETOTAL		SAPLESS
AELNPTU	UPLEANT	AELORTU	ROTULAE	AELPSST	PASTELS
AELNPTX	EXPLANT		TORULAE		STAPLES
AELNPTY	APLENTY	AELORTV	LEVATOR	AELPSTT	PATTLES
	PENALTY	AELORTY	ROYALET		PELTAST
AELNQUU	UNEQUAL	AELORTZ	ZELATOR	AELPSTU	PULSATE
AELNRRS	SNARLER	AELORUU	ROULEAU		PUTEALS
AELNRSS	RANSELS	AELORVX	OVERLAX		SPATULE
AELNRST	ANTLERS	AELORVY	LAYOVER	AELPSTZ	SPATZLE
	RENTALS		OVERLAY	AELPUUV	UPVALUE
	SALTERN	AELORWY	OWRELAY	AELQRRU	QUARREL
	SLANTER	AELOSSS	LASSOES	AELQSSU	LASQUES
	STERNAL	AELOSST	SOLATES		SQUEALS
AELNRSV	VERLANS	AELOSSV	SALVOES	AELQSUZ	QUEZALS
AELNRSY	LARNEYS	AELOSSW	LEASOWS	AELQTUZ	QUETZAL
AELNRSZ	RANZELS	AELOSTV	SOLVATE	AELRRSU	SURREAL
AELNRTT	TRENTAL	AELOSTZ	ZEALOTS	AELRRSW	WARSLER
AELNRTU	NEUTRAL	AELOSUZ	ZEALOUS	AELRRTT	RATTLER
AELNRTV	VENTRAL	AELOSVY	SAVELOY	AELRRTW	TRAWLER
AELNRUU	NEURULA	AELOTTU	TOLUATE	AELRSSS	RASSLES
AELNRUV	UNRAVEL	AELOTUV	OVULATE	AELRSST	ARTLESS
	VENULAR	AELOTVV	VOLVATE		LASTERS
AELNSSU	SENSUAL	AELOTVY	OVATELY		SALTERS
	UNSEALS	AELPPRS	LAPPERS		SLATERS
AELNSSW	AWNLESS		RAPPELS		TARSELS
AELNSSX	LAXNESS		SLAPPER	AELRSSU	SAURELS
AELNSTT	LATENTS	AELPPRY	REAPPLY	AELRSSV	SALVERS
	LATTENS	AELPPSS	SAPPLES		SERVALS
	TALENTS	AELPPST	APPLETS		SLAVERS
AELNSTU	ELUANTS		LAPPETS		VERSALS
	LUNATES		STAPPLE	AELRSSW	WARLESS
	UNLASTE	AELPPSU	APPULSE		WARSLES
AELNSTV	LEVANTS		PAPULES		WRASSLE
AELNSTY	STANYEL		UPLEAPS	AELRSSY	RAYLESS
AELNSTZ	ZELANTS	AELPPTU	UPLEAPT		SLAYERS
AELNSUW	UNWEALS	AELPQSU	PLAQUES	AELRSTT	RATTLES
AELNTUV	ENVAULT	AELPRRS	PARRELS		SLATTER
AELOORS	AEROSOL	AELPRSS	LAPSERS		STARLET
	ROSEOLA	AELPRST	PALTERS		STARTLE
AELOPPR	PROPALE		PERSALT		TATLERS
AELOPPX	APOPLEX		PLASTER	AELRSTU	ESTRUAL
AELOPRR	PERORAL		PLATERS		SALUTER
	PREORAL		PSALTER	AELRSTV	TRAVELS
AELOPRS	PAROLES		STAPLER		VARLETS
	REPOSAL	AELPRSU	PERUSAL		VESTRAL
AELOPRT	PROLATE		PLEURAS	AELRSTW	WARSTLE
AELOPRV	OVERLAP	AELPRSW	PRAWLES		WASTREL
AELOPST	APOSTLE	AELPRSY	PARLEYS		WRASTLE
	PELOTAS		PARSLEY	AELRSTY	RAYLETS
	POTALES		PLAYERS	AELRSUV	VALUERS

AELRSVV	VARVELS	**AEMNNRT**	MANRENT	**AEMORRW**	EARWORM
AELRSVY	SLAVERY		REMNANT	**AEMORST**	AMORETS
AELRSWX	WRAXLES	**AEMNNSW**	NEWSMAN		MAESTRO
AELRSWY	LAWYERS	**AEMNNTU**	UNMEANT		OMERTAS
AELRSZZ	RAZZLES	**AEMNOPP**	PAMPOEN	**AEMORSU**	RAMEOUS
AELRTTT	TARTLET	**AEMNOPR**	MANROPE	**AEMORSW**	SEAWORM
	TATTLER		REPOMAN		WOMERAS
AELRTTU	TUTELAR	**AEMNOPS**	MOPANES	**AEMORSX**	XEROMAS
AELRTUV	VAULTER	**AEMNOPZ**	ZAMPONE	**AEMOSST**	OSMATES
AELRTWY	TRAWLEY	**AEMNORR**	ORRAMEN	**AEMOSSV**	VAMOSES
AELRTWZ	WALTZER	**AEMNORS**	ENAMORS	**AEMOSTT**	STOMATE
AELSSST	TASSELS		MOANERS	**AEMOSTW**	TWASOME
AELSSTT	LATESTS		OARSMEN	**AEMOSUZ**	ZAMOUSE
	SALTEST	**AEMNORT**	TONEARM	**AEMOSWY**	SOMEWAY
	STALEST	**AEMNORU**	ENAMOUR	**AEMOTTZ**	MOZETTA
	TASLETS		NEUROMA	**AEMPPRS**	MAPPERS
AELSSTU	SALUTES	**AEMNORV**	OVERMAN		PAMPERS
	TALUSES	**AEMNORY**	ANYMORE		PREAMPS
AELSSTV	VESTALS		ROMNEYA	**AEMPPRY**	MAPPERY
AELSSTW	WASTELS	**AEMNOSS**	MONASES	**AEMPRRS**	PREARMS
AELSSTX	TAXLESS	**AEMNOST**	MANTOES		RAMPERS
AELSSTY	LYSATES	**AEMNOTT**	TOMENTA	**AEMPRRT**	TRAMPER
AELSSUV	AVULSES	**AEMNOTU**	AUTOMEN	**AEMPRRW**	PREWARM
AELSSVY	SLAVEYS		NOTAEUM	**AEMPRST**	EMPARTS
AELSSWY	WAYLESS		OUTNAME		RESTAMP
AELSTTT	TATTLES	**AEMNPSS**	PASSMEN		STAMPER
AELSTTW	WATTLES	**AEMNPST**	ENSTAMP		TAMPERS
AELSTTY	STATELY		TAPSMEN	**AEMPRSU**	SUPREMA
	STYLATE	**AEMNPSU**	PNEUMAS	**AEMPRSV**	REVAMPS
AELSTUX	LUXATES	**AEMNPTU**	PUTAMEN		VAMPERS
AELSTWZ	WALTZES	**AEMNPTY**	PAYMENT	**AEMPRSW**	SWAMPER
AELSUVY	SUAVELY	**AEMNRRU**	MANURER	**AEMPRTT**	TRAMPET
AELSWZZ	SWAZZLE	**AEMNRST**	ARTSMEN	**AEMPRTU**	TEMPURA
AELTTTW	TWATTLE		MARTENS	**AEMPSSU**	EMPUSAS
AELTTUX	TEXTUAL		SARMENT	**AEMPTTT**	ATTEMPT
AELTUVV	VULVATE		SMARTEN	**AEMPTTU**	TAPETUM
AEMMMRS	MAMMERS	**AEMNRSU**	MANURES	**AEMQRSU**	MARQUES
AEMMMST	MAMMETS		MURENAS		MASQUER
AEMMMSY	MAMMEYS		SURNAME	**AEMQSSU**	MASQUES
AEMMNOT	MOMENTA	**AEMNRTU**	TRUEMAN		SQUAMES
AEMMNSS	MESSMAN	**AEMNRTV**	VARMENT	**AEMRRRS**	MARRERS
AEMMNTU	AMENTUM	**AEMNSSS**	MESSANS	**AEMRRRY**	REMARRY
AEMMOPR	MAMPOER	**AEMNSST**	STAMENS	**AEMRRST**	ARMREST
AEMMORS	MARMOSE	**AEMNSSU**	UNSEAMS		SMARTER
AEMMORW	WOMMERA	**AEMNSTU**	UNTAMES	**AEMRRSU**	ARMURES
AEMMPRS	SPAMMER		UNTEAMS	**AEMRRSV**	MARVERS
AEMMRRS	RAMMERS	**AEMNSTY**	AMNESTY	**AEMRRSW**	REWARMS
AEMMRST	STAMMER	**AEMNTTU**	NUTMEAT		SWARMER
AEMMRSY	YAMMERS	**AEMNTWY**	WAYMENT		WARMERS
AEMMRSZ	MAMZERS	**AEMOORT**	TEAROOM	**AEMRRTU**	ERRATUM
AEMMSST	STEMMAS	**AEMOORW**	WOOMERA		MATURER
AEMMSTU	MAUMETS	**AEMOOST**	OSTEOMA	**AEMRSST**	MASTERS
	SUMMATE	**AEMOOSV**	AMOOVES		STREAMS
AEMMSTW	MAWMETS		VAMOOSE	**AEMRSSU**	AMUSERS
AEMNNOR	MONERAN	**AEMOPPR**	PAMPERO		ASSUMER
AEMNNOS	MANNOSE	**AEMOPSZ**	APOZEMS		MASSEUR
AEMNNOT	MONTANE	**AEMORRR**	ARMORER	**AEMRSTT**	MATTERS
	NONMEAT	**AEMORRS**	MAREROS		SMATTER
AEMNNOU	NOUMENA		REMORAS	**AEMRSTU**	MATURES
AEMNNOZ	MENAZON		ROAMERS		STRUMAE
AEMNNRS	MANNERS	**AEMORRV**	OVERARM	**AEMRSTW**	WARMEST

AEMRSTY	MASTERY	AENORXY	ANOREXY	AENRSTT	NATTERS
	MAYSTER	AENOSSS	SEASONS		RATTENS
	STREAMY	AENOSST	ASTONES	AENRSTU	AUNTERS
AEMRTTX	MARTEXT	AENOSSW	WEASONS		NATURES
AEMRTTY	MATTERY	AENOSTT	ATTONES		SAUNTER
AEMRTUU	TRUMEAU		NOTATES	AENRSTV	SERVANT
AEMSSSU	ASSUMES	AENOSTU	SOUTANE		TAVERNS
AEMSSTU	MUTASES	AENOSTV	NOVATES		VERSANT
AEMSSUW	WAMUSES	AENOSVW	WAVESON	AENRSTW	STRAWEN
AEMSSYZ	ZYMASES	AENOUUV	NOUVEAU		WANTERS
AEMSTTU	MUTATES	AENPPRS	NAPPERS	AENRSTY	TRAYNES
AEMSTUV	MAUVEST		PARPENS	AENRSUW	UNSWEAR
AEMSTVZ	ZEMSTVA		PARSNEP		UNWARES
AEMSUZZ	MEZUZAS		SNAPPER	AENRSUY	SYNURAE
AENNNOS	NONANES	AENPPRT	PARPENT	AENRSWY	YAWNERS
AENNNPT	PENNANT	AENPPRU	UNPAPER	AENRTTU	TAUNTER
AENNOPS	PANNOSE	AENPPST	PETNAPS	AENRTTY	NATTERY
AENNORT	NORTENA	AENPRRT	PARTNER	AENRTUV	VAUNTER
AENNORY	ANNOYER	AENPRRW	PRAWNER	AENRTUW	UNWATER
AENNOSS	NOSEANS		PREWARN	AENRUWY	UNWEARY
AENNOSV	NOVENAS	AENPRST	ARPENTS	AENSSST	ASSENTS
AENNOSY	ANYONES		ENTRAPS		SNASTES
AENNOTU	TONNEAU		PANTERS	AENSSTU	NASUTES
AENNPRS	PANNERS		PARENTS		UNSEATS
	SPANNER		PASTERN	AENSSTX	SEXTANS
AENNQTU	QUANNET		PERSANT	AENSSTY	STAYNES
AENNRST	TANNERS		TREPANS	AENSSTZ	STANZES
AENNRSV	VANNERS	AENPRSW	ENWRAPS	AENSSWY	SAWNEYS
AENNRTT	ENTRANT		PAWNERS	AENSSXY	SYNAXES
AENNRTV	VERNANT		SPAWNER	AENSTTT	ATTENTS
AENNRTY	TANNERY	AENPRSZ	PANZERS	AENSTTU	ATTUNES
	TYRANNE	AENPRTT	PATTERN		NUTATES
AENNSSW	WANNESS		REPTANT		TAUTENS
AENNSTT	TANNEST	AENPRUV	PARVENU		TETANUS
	TENANTS	AENPSST	APTNESS		UNSTATE
AENNSTW	WANNEST		PATNESS	AENSTTX	SEXTANT
AENOOTZ	ENTOZOA		PESANTS	AENSTUX	UNTAXES
	OZONATE	AENPSSY	SYNAPSE	AENSTWY	TAWNEYS
AENOPPR	PROPANE	AENPSTT	PATENTS	AENTTTU	ATTUENT
AENOPRS	PERSONA		PATTENS	AEOOPPS	PAPOOSE
AENOPRT	OPERANT	AENPSTU	PEANUTS	AEOOPRS	OROPESA
	PRONATE		PESAUNT	AEOPPPS	PAPPOSE
	PROTEAN	AENPSTW	STEWPAN	AEOPPRS	APPOSER
AENOPST	TEOPANS	AENPSTY	SYNAPTE		POPERAS
AENOPSU	POSAUNE	AENPSTZ	PEZANTS	AEOPPRV	APPROVE
AENOPSV	PAVONES	AENQSTU	EQUANTS	AEOPPSS	APPOSES
AENOPSW	WEAPONS	AENRRSS	SERRANS	AEOPQRU	OPAQUER
AENOPTU	AUTOPEN		SNARERS	AEOPQSU	OPAQUES
AENORRS	SERRANO	AENRRST	ERRANTS	AEOPRRS	PARORES
AENORRT	ORNATER		RANTERS	AEOPRRT	PRAETOR
AENORRV	OVERRAN	AENRRSW	WARNERS		PRORATE
AENORSS	REASONS		WARRENS	AEOPRRV	VAPORER
	SENORAS	AENRRSY	YARNERS	AEOPRSS	SOAPERS
AENORST	ATONERS	AENRRTT	TRANTER	AEOPRST	ESPARTO
	SANTERO	AENRRTY	TERNARY		PROTEAS
	SENATOR	AENRSSS	SARSENS		SEAPORT
	TREASON	AENRSST	SARSNET	AEOPRTT	PORTATE
AENORSU	ARENOUS		TRANSES	AEOPRTV	OVERAPT
AENORTU	OUTEARN	AENRSSW	ANSWERS	AEOPRVY	OVERPAY
AENORTV	VENATOR		RAWNESS	AEOPRWY	ROPEWAY
AENORWZ	WARZONE	AENRSSY	SARNEYS	AEOPSSS	PSOASES

AEOPSST	PETASOS		PRATERS	AERSSST	ASSERTS
	SAPOTES	AEPRRSU	PARURES		TRASSES
AEOPSTT	APTOTES		UPREARS	AERSSSU	ASSURES
	TEAPOTS	AEPRRSW	REWRAPS		SARUSES
AEOPSTY	TEAPOYS		WARPERS	AERSSSW	WRASSES
AEOPSTZ	TOPAZES	AEPRRSY	PRAYERS	AERSSTT	ASTERTS
AEOQRTU	EQUATOR		RESPRAY		STARETS
	QUORATE		SPRAYER		STATERS
AEOQRUV	VAQUERO	AEPRRTU	PARTURE		TASTERS
AEOQSUU	AQUEOUS		RAPTURE	AERSSTV	STARVES
AEORRRS	ROARERS	AEPRRTW	REWRAPT	AERSSTW	WASTERS
AEORRSS	SOARERS	AEPRRTY	PARTYER	AERSSTY	ESTRAYS
AEORRST	ROASTER		PETRARY		STAYERS
AEORRSU	AROUSER	AEPRSSS	PASSERS		STAYRES
AEORRSV	SAVORER	AEPRSST	PASTERS	AERSSUV	VARUSES
	SEROVAR		REPASTS	AERSSVW	SWARVES
AEORSSS	SAROSES		SPAREST	AERSSWY	SAWYERS
	SEROSAS	AEPRSSU	PAUSERS		SWAYERS
AEORSST	OSETRAS	AEPRSSY	PESSARY	AERSTTT	STRETTA
	OSSETRA	AEPRSTT	PATTERS		TARTEST
AEORSSU	AROUSES		SPATTER		TATTERS
AEORSTT	ROTATES		TAPSTER	AERSTTU	ASTUTER
	TOASTER	AEPRSTU	PASTURE		STATURE
AEORSUV	AVOURES		UPRATES	AERSTTV	VATTERS
AEORSVW	AVOWERS		UPSTARE	AERSTTW	SWATTER
	OVERSAW		UPTEARS		TEWARTS
	REAVOWS	AEPRSTY	YAPSTER	AERSTTY	YATTERS
AEORSVY	AVOYERS	AEPRSTZ	PATZERS	AERSTTZ	STARETZ
AEORTTU	OUTRATE	AEPRSUX	ARUSPEX	AERSTUU	AUTEURS
AEORTUV	OUTRAVE	AEPRSUY	YAUPERS	AERSTUY	ESTUARY
AEORTUW	OUTWEAR	AEPRSWY	SPYWARE	AERSTVY	STRAYVE
AEORTVX	OVERTAX		YAWPERS	AERSTWY	WASTERY
AEOSSTV	AVOSETS	AEPRSYY	SPRAYEY	AERTTTY	TATTERY
AEOSTTU	OUTEATS	AEPRTXY	APTERYX	AERTTUV	VETTURA
AEOSUVZ	ZOUAVES	AEPSSTU	PETASUS	AESSSTT	TASSETS
AEPPPRU	PREPUPA	AEPSSZZ	SPAZZES	AESSTTT	ATTESTS
AEPPRRS	RAPPERS	AEPSSTU	UPSTATE	AESSTTU	STATUES
AEPPRRT	TRAPPER	AEPSZZZ	PZAZZES	AESSTTV	VASTEST
AEPPRRW	PREWRAP	AEQRRSU	SQUARER	AESSTUV	SUAVEST
	WRAPPER	AEQRRTU	QUARTER	AESSTUY	EUSTASY
AEPPRSS	APPRESS	AEQRSSU	SQUARES	AESSVVY	SAVVEYS
	SAPPERS	AEQRSTU	QUAREST	AESTTTU	STATUTE
AEPPRST	TAPPERS		QUARTES		TAUTEST
AEPPRSU	PAUPERS		QUATRES	AESTTTW	WATTEST
	UPSPEAR	AEQRSUV	QUAVERS	AFFFGIN	FAFFING
AEPPRSW	SWAPPER	AEQRTTU	QUARTET	AFFFLLO	FALLOFF
	WAPPERS	AEQRUVY	QUAVERY	AFFGGIN	GAFFING
AEPPRSY	PREPAYS	AEQSSSU	QUASSES	AFFGINN	NAFFING
	YAPPERS	AERRSST	ARRESTS	AFFGINW	WAFFING
AEPPRSZ	ZAPPERS		RASTERS	AFFGINY	AFFYING
AEPPSTT	TAPPETS		STARERS		YAFFING
AEPPSTU	PASTEUP	AERRSSU	ASSURER	AFFGSUW	GUFFAWS
	PUPATES		RASURES	AFFHILN	HAFFLIN
AEPQRTU	PARQUET	AERRSTT	RATTERS	AFFHIRS	RAFFISH
AEPRRRS	SPARRER		RESTART	AFFHIST	HAFFITS
AEPRRSS	PARSERS		STARTER	AFFIITX	FIXATIF
	RASPERS	AERRSTV	STARVER	AFFIKRS	KAFFIRS
	SPARERS	AERRSTY	STRAYER	AFFILMN	MAFFLIN
	SPARRES	AERRSUZ	RAZURES	AFFILOR	RIFFOLA
	SPARSER	AERRSWY	WARREYS	AFFILPS	PILAFFS
AEPRRST	PARTERS	AERRTTY	RATTERY	AFFILSY	FALSIFY

AFFIMRS	AFFIRMS		RAFTING	**AFIKLOT**	FLOKATI
AFFIMST	MASTIFF	**AFGINRY**	FRAYING	**AFIKMNR**	FINMARK
AFFINRU	FUNFAIR	**AFGINST**	FASTING	**AFIKNRT**	RATFINK
	RUFFIAN	**AFGINTT**	FATTING	**AFIKNSU**	FUNKIAS
AFFINTY	TIFFANY	**AFGINTU**	FAUTING	**AFIKRSS**	FRISKAS
AFFIORR	FORFAIR	**AFGINTW**	WAFTING	**AFILLMS**	MISFALL
AFFIRRU	FURFAIR	**AFGIOTT**	FAGOTTI	**AFILLNP**	PINFALL
AFFIRST	TARIFFS	**AFGIRTY**	GRATIFY	**AFILLNS**	INFALLS
AFFIRSU	SUFFARI	**AFGKNOP**	PAKFONG	**AFILLNY**	FINALLY
AFFIRSZ	ZAFFIRS	**AFGKORT**	KOFTGAR	**AFILLPT**	PITFALL
AFFLOPY	PLAYOFF	**AFGLLLY**	GALLFLY	**AFILLPU**	PAILFUL
AFFLOSY	LAYOFFS	**AFGLLUY**	FUGALLY	**AFILLRY**	FRAILLY
AFFMOPR	OFFRAMP	**AFGLNOS**	FLAGONS	**AFILLTY**	TAILFLY
AFFNORS	SAFFRON	**AFGLNSU**	FUNGALS	**AFILLUV**	FLUVIAL
AFFNORT	AFFRONT	**AFGLRYY**	GRAYFLY		VIALFUL
AFFOPSY	PAYOFFS	**AFGMNOR**	FROGMAN	**AFILLUW**	WAILFUL
AFFRSST	STRAFFS	**AFGMORS**	FOGRAMS	**AFILMNT**	LIFTMAN
AFGGGIN	FAGGING	**AFGOOTT**	FAGOTTO	**AFILMOR**	ALIFORM
AFGGINN	FANGING	**AFGORRS**	FRAGORS	**AFILMOY**	FOAMILY
AFGGOST	FAGGOTS	**AFGOSTU**	FUGATOS	**AFILMPY**	AMPLIFY
AFGGOTY	FAGGOTY	**AFHIIRS**	FAIRISH	**AFILMSS**	FALSISM
AFGHHIS	HAGFISH		HAIRIFS	**AFILNPU**	PAINFUL
AFGHINS	FASHING	**AFHIISW**	WAIFISH	**AFILNSV**	FLAVINS
AFGHINT	HAFTING	**AFHIKLS**	KHALIFS	**AFILNTU**	ANTIFLU
AFGHIRS	GARFISH	**AFHIKRS**	KHARIFS		FLUTINA
AFGHLSU	GASHFUL	**AFHIKUY**	KUFIYAH	**AFILNTY**	FAINTLY
AFGHLTU	FLAUGHT	**AFHILLN**	HALFLIN	**AFILORW**	AIRFLOW
AFGHRTU	FRAUGHT	**AFHILSS**	FALSISH	**AFILOTX**	FOXTAIL
AFGIIKN	FAIKING	**AFHILTW**	HALFWIT	**AFILQUY**	QUALIFY
AFGIILN	FAILING	**AFHIMNU**	HAFNIUM	**AFILRRY**	FRIARLY
AFGIINN	FAINING	**AFHINOS**	FASHION	**AFILRSZ**	FRAZILS
AFGIINR	FAIRING	**AFHINPS**	PANFISH	**AFILRTY**	FRAILTY
AFGIINT	FIATING	**AFHINTU**	UNFAITH	**AFILSSY**	SALSIFY
AFGIINW	WAIFING	**AFHIORS**	OARFISH	**AFILSTU**	FISTULA
AFGIJMS	FIGJAMS	**AFHIRSS**	SHARIFS	**AFILSTY**	FALSITY
AFGIKLN	FLAKING	**AFHIRST**	RATFISH	**AFILTTY**	FATTILY
AFGILLN	FALLING	**AFHISST**	FASTISH	**AFIMNRS**	FIRMANS
AFGILMN	FLAMING	**AFHISSW**	SAWFISH	**AFIMOOS**	MAFIOSO
AFGILNO	FOALING	**AFHISTT**	FATTISH	**AFIMORV**	AVIFORM
	LOAFING	**AFHISWY**	FISHWAY	**AFIMRST**	MAFTIRS
AFGILNR	FLARING	**AFHKORY**	HAYFORK	**AFIMSSS**	MASSIFS
AFGILNS	FALSING	**AFHKRTU**	FUTHARK	**AFIMSSV**	FAVISMS
AFGILNT	FATLING	**AFHLMRU**	HARMFUL	**AFIMSTT**	FATTISM
AFGILNU	GAINFUL	**AFHLMSU**	FULHAMS	**AFIMSUV**	FAUVISM
AFGILNW	FLAWING	**AFHLOOS**	LOOFAHS	**AFIMSUZ**	UMFAZIS
AFGILNY	ANGLIFY	**AFHLOTY**	HAYLOFT	**AFIMTTY**	MATTIFY
	FLAYING	**AFHLSTU**	HATFULS	**AFINNNS**	FINNANS
AFGILRU	FIGURAL		HATSFUL	**AFINNOR**	FRANION
AFGIMNO	FOAMING	**AFHMOST**	FATHOMS	**AFINNOS**	FANIONS
AFGIMNR	FARMING	**AFHOOPT**	POOFTAH	**AFINNOT**	FONTINA
	FRAMING	**AFHOPTU**	POUFTAH	**AFINNST**	INFANTS
AFGIMNY	MAGNIFY	**AFHORSS**	SHOFARS	**AFINORS**	INSOFAR
AFGINNN	FANNING	**AFIILNS**	FINALIS	**AFINRSU**	UNFAIRS
AFGINNS	FINGANS		FINIALS	**AFINRTU**	ANTIFUR
AFGINNW	FAWNING	**AFIILNT**	TAILFIN	**AFINSSU**	FUSAINS
AFGINNY	FAYNING	**AFIILOR**	AIRFOIL	**AFINSTU**	FAUNIST
AFGINOT	ANTIFOG	**AFIILRT**	AIRLIFT		FIAUNTS
AFGINRR	FARRING	**AFIILRY**	FAIRILY		FUSTIAN
AFGINRS	FARSING	**AFIIMOS**	MAFIOSI		INFAUST
AFGINRT	FARTING	**AFIJNNS**	FINJANS	**AFIORST**	FAITORS
	INGRAFT	**AFIKLLY**	FLAKILY	**AFIORTU**	FAITOUR

AFIORTZ	FORZATI	**AFMNORT**	FORMANT	**AGGIKNW**	GAWKING
AFIQRSU	FAQUIRS	**AFMNOST**	FANTOMS	**AGGILLN**	GALLING
AFISSTT	SITFAST	**AFMNRSU**	SURFMAN		GINGALL
AFISSTY	SATISFY	**AFMNRTU**	TURFMAN	**AGGILLN**	ANGLING
AFISTTT	FATTIST	**AFMOOSS**	SAMFOOS	**AGGILNO**	GAOLING
AFISTUV	FAUVIST	**AFMORST**	FARMOST		GOALING
AFITTUY	FATUITY		FORMATS	**AGGILNR**	ARGLING
AFJLRSU	JARFULS	**AFMORSU**	AUSFORM		GLARING
	JARSFUL	**AFMORTU**	FOUMART	**AGGILNS**	GINGALS
AFKLNRY	FRANKLY	**AFMOSTT**	AFTMOST		LAGGINS
AFKLNTU	TANKFUL	**AFMOSTU**	SFUMATO	**AGGILNT**	GATLING
AFKLOWY	FOLKWAY	**AFNNNOS**	NONFANS	**AGGILNZ**	GLAZING
AFKRRTU	FRAKTUR	**AFNORRW**	FORWARN	**AGGILOS**	LOGGIAS
AFLLMPU	PALMFUL	**AFNORTW**	FANWORT	**AGGIMMN**	GAMMING
AFLLMSU	FULLAMS	**AFNOTUW**	OUTFAWN	**AGGIMMN**	MANGING
AFLLNOS	ONFALLS	**AFNPRSY**	FRYPANS	**AGGIMNS**	GAMINGS
AFLLNSU	FULLANS	**AFNSSTU**	SUNFAST	**AGGIMNU**	GAUMING
AFLLOOY	ALOOFLY	**AFOOPPR**	APPROOF	**AGGINNN**	GANNING
AFLLORS	FLORALS	**AFOORST**	FOOTRAS	**AGGINNP**	PANGING
AFLLORU	FLORULA	**AFOORTZ**	FORZATO	**AGGINNR**	RANGING
AFLLOSW	FALLOWS	**AFOOTWY**	FOOTWAY	**AGGINNT**	GANTING
AFLLOTU	FALLOUT	**AFORRSW**	FARROWS		TANGING
	OUTFALL	**AFORRSY**	FORRAYS	**AGGINNU**	UNAGING
AFLLPSU	LAPFULS		ORFRAYS	**AGGINNW**	GNAWING
AFLLPUY	PLAYFUL	**AFORSSY**	FORSAYS	**AGGINOT**	GIGATON
AFLLUWY	AWFULLY	**AFORSTU**	FAUTORS	**AGGINPP**	GAPPING
AFLMNOU	MOANFUL		FOUTRAS	**AGGINPR**	GRAPING
AFLMORS	FORMALS	**AFORSUV**	FAVOURS		PARGING
AFLMORU	FORMULA	**AFORTTU**	TARTUFO	**AGGINPS**	GAPINGS
AFLMORW	WOLFRAM	**AFOSSSU**	FOUSSAS		GASPING
AFLMOST	FLOTSAM	**AFOSTTU**	OUTFAST		PAGINGS
AFLMRSU	ARMFULS	**AFOSTUU**	FATUOUS	**AGGINPU**	GAUPING
	ARMSFUL	**AFPSTUW**	UPWAFTS	**AGGINPW**	GAWPING
	FULMARS	**AGGGGIN**	GAGGING	**AGGINRR**	GARRING
AFLMSTU	MASTFUL	**AGGGHIN**	HAGGING	**AGGINRS**	GRINGAS
AFLMSUU	FAMULUS	**AGGGIJN**	JAGGING		RAGINGS
AFLNORT	FRONTAL	**AGGGILN**	LAGGING		SIRGANG
AFLNOTT	FLOTANT	**AGGGIMN**	MAGGING	**AGGINRT**	GRATING
AFLNPSU	PANFULS	**AGGGINN**	GANGING		TARGING
AFLNRTU	RUNFLAT		NAGGING	**AGGINRU**	ARGUING
AFLNSTU	FLAUNTS	**AGGGINR**	RAGGING	**AGGINRV**	GRAVING
AFLNTUY	FLAUNTY	**AGGGINS**	SAGGING	**AGGINRY**	GRAYING
AFLOOTW	WOOLFAT	**AGGGINT**	TAGGING	**AGGINRZ**	GRAZING
AFLOPTT	FLATTOP	**AGGGINU**	GAUGING	**AGGINSS**	GASSING
AFLORSS	SAFROLS	**AGGGINV**	VAGGING	**AGGINST**	GASTING
AFLORSU	FUSAROL	**AGGGINW**	WAGGING		GATINGS
AFLORSV	FLAVORS	**AGGGINZ**	ZAGGING		STAGING
AFLORUV	FLAVOUR	**AGGHHIS**	HAGGISH	**AGGINSW**	SWAGING
AFLORVY	FLAVORY	**AGGHIIL**	GHILGAI	**AGGINSZ**	GAZINGS
AFLORWW	WARWOLF	**AGGHIMN**	GINGHAM	**AGGINUV**	VAGUING
AFLOSSU	FOSSULA	**AGGHINN**	HANGING	**AGGIORS**	GORGIAS
AFLPRTY	FLYTRAP	**AGGHINS**	GASHING	**AGGISWW**	WIGWAGS
AFLPSTY	FLYPAST	**AGGHISW**	WAGGISH	**AGGISZZ**	ZIGZAGS
AFLRTUU	FUTURAL	**AGGIIJJ**	JIGAJIG	**AGGLOST**	LOGGATS
AFLRTUY	TRAYFUL	**AGGIILS**	GILGAIS	**AGGMNOS**	MOGGANS
AFLSSTU	FUTSALS	**AGGIIMN**	IMAGING	**AGGMORR**	GROGRAM
AFLSTUV	VATFULS	**AGGIINN**	GAINING	**AGGMOST**	MAGGOTS
AFLSUWY	SWAYFUL	**AGGIINT**	GAITING	**AGGMOTY**	MAGGOTY
AFLSWYY	FLYWAYS	**AGGIINV**	GINGIVA	**AGGMRSU**	MUGGARS
AFMNNOR	NONFARM	**AGGIJJO**	JIGAJOG	**AGGNOSU**	GUANGOS
AFMNOOT	FOOTMAN	**AGGIKNS**	GASKING	**AGGNOSW**	WAGGONS

AGGNOSX	OXGANGS	AGHINSS	SASHING		NAILING
AGGNOSY	SYNAGOG	AGHINST	HASTING	AGIILNR	GLAIRIN
AGGNPSU	UPGANGS		TASHING		LAIRING
AGGNRSU	NUGGARS	AGHINSU	ANGUISH		RAILING
AGGPRSY	PYGARGS		HAUSING	AGIILNS	AISLING
AGHHIMN	HIGHMAN	AGHINSV	HAVINGS		NILGAIS
AGHHINS	HASHING		SHAVING		SAILING
AGHHIWY	HIGHWAY	AGHINSW	HAWSING	AGIILNT	INTAGLI
AGHHOSW	HOGWASH		SHAWING		TAILING
AGHHSSU	SHAUGHS		WASHING	AGIILNV	VAILING
AGHHTUY	HAUGHTY	AGHINSY	HAYINGS		VIALING
AGHIILN	HAILING	AGHINSZ	HAZINGS	AGIILNW	WAILING
	NILGHAI	AGHINTT	HATTING	AGIILOV	VILIAGO
AGHIINN	HAINING		TATHING	AGIILPT	PIGTAIL
AGHIINR	HAIRING	AGHINTW	THAWING	AGIILTY	AGILITY
AGHIJRS	JAGHIRS	AGHIOST	GOATISH	AGIIMMN	MAIMING
AGHIKNN	HANKING	AGHIPSW	PIGWASH	AGIIMMS	IMAGISM
AGHIKNR	HARKING	AGHIQSU	QUAIGHS	AGIIMNN	MAINING
AGHIKNS	SHAKING	AGHIRRS	GHARRIS	AGIIMOR	ORIGAMI
AGHIKNW	HAWKING	AGHIRST	GRAITHS	AGIIMST	IMAGIST
AGHIKSU	KIAUGHS	AGHIRSU	GUARISH	AGIINNP	PAINING
AGHIKSW	GAWKISH	AGHIRSY	GRAYISH	AGIINNR	AIRNING
AGHILLN	HALLING	AGHJMNO	MAHJONG		INGRAIN
AGHILNO	HALOING	AGHKOSW	GOSHAWK		RAINING
AGHILNR	HARLING	AGHLMPU	GALUMPH	AGIINNS	SAINING
AGHILNS	HALSING	AGHLMSU	MUGHALS	AGIINNW	WAINING
	LASHING	AGHLNUY	NYLGHAU	AGIINNZ	ZINGANI
	SHALING	AGHLOOS	GASOHOL	AGIINPR	PAIRING
AGHILNT	HALTING	AGHLOSU	GOULASH	AGIINRS	AIRINGS
	LATHING	AGHLSTU	GALUTHS		ARISING
AGHILNU	HAULING	AGHLSTY	GHASTLY		RAGINIS
	NILGHAU	AGHMORY	HYGROMA		RAISING
AGHILNV	HALVING	AGHMRRU	MURRAGH		SAIRING
AGHILNW	WHALING	AGHNNOU	HOUNGAN	AGIINRT	AIRTING
AGHILNY	NYLGHAI	AGHNNSU	HUNGANS		RAITING
AGHILOT	GOLIATH		UNHANGS	AGIINRW	WAIRING
AGHILRS	LARGISH	AGHNOTU	HANGOUT	AGIINRZ	ZINGARI
AGHILRT	ALRIGHT		TOHUNGA	AGIINSV	AVISING
AGHILST	ALIGHTS	AGHNPSU	HANGUPS		VISAING
AGHIMMN	HAMMING		UPHANGS	AGIINTW	WAITING
AGHIMNR	HARMING	AGHNRST	THRANGS	AGIINTX	TAXIING
AGHIMNS	MASHING	AGHNRSU	NURHAGS	AGIINVV	VIVAING
	SHAMING	AGHNRUY	AHUNGRY	AGIINVW	WAIVING
AGHIMNW	HAWMING	AGHNSTU	NAUGHTS	AGIINVZ	AVIZING
AGHIMPS	GAMPISH	AGHNSUY	GUNYAHS	AGIJKNU	JAUKING
AGHINNO	NIHONGA	AGHNTUY	NAUGHTY	AGIJLLN	JINGALL
AGHINNT	HANTING	AGHOORT	AGOROTH	AGIJLNS	JINGALS
	TANGHIN	AGHOQSU	QUAHOGS	AGIJMMN	JAMMING
AGHINOR	HOARING	AGHORTW	WARTHOG	AGIJNPP	JAPPING
AGHINOX	HOAXING	AGHPTUY	PAUGHTY	AGIJNPR	JARPING
AGHINPP	HAPPING	AGHRRSU	GURRAHS	AGIJNPS	JAPINGS
AGHINPR	HARPING	AGHRSTU	TUGHRAS	AGIJNPU	JAUPING
AGHINPS	HASPING	AGHRSTY	GYTRASH	AGIJNRR	JARRING
	PASHING	AGHSTUW	WAUGHTS	AGIJNSW	JAWINGS
	PHASING	AGIIJLN	JAILING		JIGSAWN
	SHAPING	AGIIKLN	LAIKING	AGIJNZZ	JAZZING
AGHINPT	PATHING	AGIIKLT	GLAIKIT	AGIJSSW	JIGSAWS
AGHINRS	GARNISH	AGIIKNP	PAIKING	AGIKKNR	KARKING
	RASHING	AGIIKNR	RAIKING	AGIKKNY	YAKKING
	SHARING	AGIILMN	MAILING	AGIKLNN	ANKLING
AGHINRU	NURAGHI	AGIILNN	ALINING		LANKING

AGIKLNO	OAKLING	**AGILMNY**	MANGILY		LATIGOS
AGIKLNR	LARKING	**AGILMOS**	GLIOMAS		SALIGOT
AGIKLNS	LAKINGS	**AGILMPS**	MAGILPS	**AGILRSS**	SLAIRGS
	SLAKING	**AGILMPU**	PLAGIUM	**AGILSSY**	GASSILY
AGIKLNT	TALKING	**AGILMST**	STIGMAL	**AGILSTY**	STAGILY
AGIKLNW	WALKING	**AGILNNO**	LOANING	**AGILUYZ**	GAUZILY
AGIKLWY	GAWKILY	**AGILNNP**	PLANING	**AGIMMNR**	RAMMING
AGIKMNR	MARKING	**AGILNNR**	LARNING	**AGIMMNS**	SAMMING
AGIKMNS	MAKINGS	**AGILNNS**	LIGNANS	**AGIMMSS**	MAGISMS
	MASKING		LINSANG	**AGIMNNN**	MANNING
AGIKNNR	NARKING	**AGILNNT**	TANLING	**AGIMNNO**	MOANING
	RANKING	**AGILNOP**	GALOPIN	**AGIMNNR**	RINGMAN
AGIKNNS	SNAKING	**AGILNOR**	RANGOLI	**AGIMNNS**	NAMINGS
AGIKNNT	KANTING	**AGILNOT**	ANTILOG	**AGIMNNW**	WINGMAN
	TANKING	**AGILNOV**	LOAVING	**AGIMNOR**	ROAMING
AGIKNNU	UNAKING	**AGILNOZ**	LAZOING	**AGIMNOT**	MOATING
AGIKNNW	WANKING	**AGILNPP**	LAPPING	**AGIMNOV**	AMOVING
AGIKNNY	YANKING		PALPING	**AGIMNPP**	MAPPING
AGIKNOS	SOAKING	**AGILNPR**	GRAPLIN	**AGIMNPR**	GRIPMAN
AGIKNOY	KAYOING		PARLING		RAMPING
	OKAYING	**AGILNPS**	LAPSING	**AGIMNPT**	TAMPING
AGIKNPR	PARKING		PALINGS	**AGIMNPV**	VAMPING
AGIKNQU	QUAKING		SAPLING	**AGIMNRR**	MARRING
AGIKNRR	RARKING	**AGILNPT**	PLATING	**AGIMNRS**	ARMINGS
AGIKNRS	RAKINGS	**AGILNPW**	LAPWING		MARGINS
	SARKING	**AGILNPY**	PLAYING	**AGIMNRT**	MARTING
AGIKNRT	KARTING	**AGILNRT**	RATLING		MIGRANT
AGIKNRW	WARKING	**AGILNRW**	WARLING	**AGIMNRW**	WARMING
AGIKNRY	YARKING	**AGILNRY**	ANGRILY	**AGIMNRY**	MYRINGA
AGIKNSS	ASKINGS		NARGILY	**AGIMNSS**	MASSING
	GASKINS		RANGILY	**AGIMNST**	MASTING
AGIKNST	SKATING		RAYLING		MATINGS
	STAKING	**AGILNSS**	LASINGS		TAMINGS
	TAKINGS		SIGNALS	**AGIMNSU**	AMUSING
	TASKING	**AGILNST**	ANGLIST	**AGIMNSY**	MAYINGS
AGIKNSW	WAKINGS		LASTING	**AGIMNTT**	MATTING
AGIKNUW	WAUKING		SALTING	**AGIMORS**	ISOGRAM
AGILLLN	LALLING		SLATING	**AGIMORU**	GOURAMI
AGILLMN	MALLING		STALING	**AGIMOSY**	ISOGAMY
AGILLMU	GALLIUM	**AGILNSU**	LINGUAS	**AGIMRRT**	TRIGRAM
AGILLNP	PALLING		NILGAUS	**AGIMRSU**	GURAMIS
AGILLNU	LINGUAL		SALUING	**AGIMRTY**	TRIGAMY
	LINGULA	**AGILNSV**	SALVING	**AGIMSST**	STIGMAS
AGILLNW	WALLING		SLAVING	**AGIMSWW**	WIGWAMS
AGILLNY	ALLYING		VALSING	**AGINNNP**	PANNING
AGILLOR	GORILLA	**AGILNSW**	LAWINGS	**AGINNNT**	TANNING
AGILLOT	GALLIOT		SWALING	**AGINNNV**	VANNING
AGILLRU	LIGULAR	**AGILNSY**	LAYINGS	**AGINNNW**	WANNING
AGILLSU	LIGULAS		SLAYING	**AGINNOS**	GANOINS
	LUGSAIL	**AGILNTY**	GIANTLY	**AGINNOT**	ATONING
AGILLYZ	GLAZILY	**AGILNUV**	VALUING	**AGINNOZ**	ZINGANO
AGILMMN	LAMMING	**AGILNUW**	WAULING	**AGINNPP**	NAPPING
AGILMMS	GIMMALS	**AGILNVV**	VALVING	**AGINNPS**	PINANGS
AGILMNO	LOAMING	**AGILNWW**	WAWLING		SPANING
AGILMNP	LAMPING	**AGILNWY**	YAWLING	**AGINNPT**	PANTING
	PALMING	**AGILNYZ**	LAZYING	**AGINNPW**	PAWNING
AGILMNR	MARLING	**AGILOPT**	GALIPOT	**AGINNRS**	SNARING
AGILMNS	LINGAMS	**AGILORS**	GIRASOL	**AGINNRT**	RANTING
	MALIGNS		GLORIAS	**AGINNRW**	WARNING
AGILMNT	MALTING	**AGILORW**	AIRGLOW	**AGINNRY**	YARNING
AGILMNU	MAULING	**AGILOST**	GALIOTS	**AGINNST**	ANTINGS

	STANING	**AGINRRT**	TARRING	**AGIRTVY**	GRAVITY
AGINNSU	GUANINS	**AGINRRW**	WARRING	**AGISTTW**	WITGATS
AGINNSW	AWNINGS	**AGINRST**	GASTRIN	**AGISTUV**	VAGITUS
	SNAWING		GRATINS	**AGJLMOS**	LOGJAMS
	WANINGS		RATINGS	**AGJLRUU**	JUGULAR
AGINNTU	ANTIGUN		STARING	**AGJNOOR**	JARGOON
AGINNTW	WANTING		TARINGS	**AGJNORS**	JARGONS
AGINNWY	YAWNING	**AGINRSU**	AIRGUNS	**AGJNORY**	JARGONY
AGINNWZ	WANZING	**AGINRSV**	RAVINGS	**AGJSTTY**	GYTTJAS
AGINNYZ	ZANYING	**AGINRSW**	RAWINGS	**AGKLNNO**	ANKLONG
AGINOOO	OOGONIA	**AGINRSY**	SIGNARY	**AGKLNNU**	ANKLUNG
AGINOOP	POGONIA		SYRINGA	**AGKLNOS**	KALONGS
AGINOPR	PIGNORA	**AGINRTT**	RATTING	**AGKLOOS**	KAGOOLS
	PORANGI		TARTING	**AGKLOST**	KGOTLAS
AGINOPS	SOAPING	**AGINRTW**	RINGTAW	**AGKLOSU**	KAGOULS
AGINORR	ROARING	**AGINRTY**	GIANTRY	**AGKMNOP**	KAMPONG
AGINORS	IGNAROS	**AGINRUW**	WAURING	**AGKMPRU**	PUGMARK
	ORIGANS	**AGINRVY**	VARYING	**AGKNOPT**	PAKTONG
	SIGNORA	**AGINRWY**	RINGWAY	**AGKNRSU**	KURGANS
	SOARING	**AGINRZZ**	RAZZING	**AGKORRW**	RAGWORK
AGINORT	ORATING	**AGINSSS**	ASSIGNS	**AGLLNOO**	GALLOON
	ROATING		SASSING	**AGLLNOS**	GALLONS
AGINORZ	ZINGARO	**AGINSSU**	SAGUINS		GOLLANS
AGINOSS	SAGOINS	**AGINSSV**	SAVINGS	**AGLLNTU**	GALLNUT
AGINOST	AGONIST	**AGINSSW**	SAWINGS		NUTGALL
	GITANOS	**AGINSSY**	SAYINGS	**AGLLOOR**	ROGALLO
AGINOSU	SAGOUIN	**AGINSTT**	STATING	**AGLLOOT**	GALLOOT
AGINOTU	AUTOING		TASTING	**AGLLOPS**	GALLOPS
	OUTGAIN	**AGINSTU**	SAUTING	**AGLLOPU**	PLUGOLA
AGINOTV	OVATING	**AGINSTV**	STAVING	**AGLLORS**	GOLLARS
AGINOTZ	TOAZING	**AGINSTW**	STAWING	**AGLLOSS**	GLOSSAL
AGINOVW	AVOWING		TAWINGS	**AGLLOSU**	GALLOUS
AGINPPP	PAPPING		TAWSING	**AGLLOSW**	GALLOWS
AGINPPR	PARPING		WASTING	**AGLLOTT**	GLOTTAL
	RAPPING	**AGINSTX**	TAXINGS	**AGLLPTY**	GLYPTAL
AGINPPS	SAPPING	**AGINSTY**	STAYING	**AGLLRSY**	ARGYLLS
AGINPPT	TAPPING		STYGIAN	**AGLLRYY**	GYRALLY
AGINPPW	WAPPING	**AGINSUX**	GUANXIS	**AGLMMSY**	GYMMALS
AGINPPY	YAPPING	**AGINSVW**	WAVINGS	**AGLMOPY**	POLYGAM
AGINPPZ	ZAPPING	**AGINSWX**	WAXINGS	**AGLMORS**	GLAMORS
AGINPRR	PARRING	**AGINSWY**	SWAYING	**AGLMORU**	GLAMOUR
AGINPRS	PARINGS	**AGINTTT**	TATTING	**AGLNNOS**	LONGANS
	PARSING	**AGINTTU**	TATUING	**AGLNNSU**	LUNGANS
	RASPING		TAUTING	**AGLNOOO**	OLOGOAN
	SPARING	**AGINTTV**	VATTING	**AGLNOOS**	LAGOONS
AGINPRT	PARTING	**AGINTTW**	TAWTING	**AGLNORU**	LANGUOR
	PRATING	**AGINTUV**	VAUTING	**AGLNOSS**	SLOGANS
	TRAPING	**AGINTVW**	VAWTING	**AGLNOST**	ALONGST
AGINPRW	WARPING	**AGINTXY**	TAXYING	**AGLNOSU**	LANUGOS
AGINPRY	PRAYING	**AGINTYZ**	TZIGANY	**AGLNOSW**	GOWLANS
AGINPSS	PASSING	**AGINVYZ**	AVYZING	**AGLNPSY**	SPANGLY
	SPAINGS	**AGINWWX**	WAXWING	**AGLNPUY**	GUNPLAY
AGINPST	PASTING	**AGIOPPT**	AGITPOP	**AGLNRSU**	LANGURS
AGINPSU	PAUSING	**AGIOPSS**	GAPOSIS	**AGLNRUU**	UNGULAR
AGINPSV	PAVINGS	**AGIORST**	AGISTOR	**AGLNTUY**	GAUNTLY
AGINPSY	PAYINGS		ORGIAST	**AGLOOPS**	APOLOGS
	SPAYING	**AGIORSU**	GIAOURS	**AGLOOPY**	APOLOGY
AGINPTT	PATTING	**AGIORSV**	VIRAGOS	**AGLOORS**	GOORALS
AGINPTU	TAPUING	**AGIOSTU**	AGOUTIS	**AGLOOST**	GALOOTS
AGINPUY	YAUPING	**AGIOUUY**	OUGUIYA	**AGLORSU**	RUGOLAS
AGINPWY	YAWPING	**AGIRSTU**	GUITARS	**AGLOSSS**	GLOSSAS

AGLOSSW	SAWLOGS	AGORRST	GARROTS	AHIKORS	KAROSHI
AGLOSUV	VALGOUS	AGORRTW	RAGWORT	AHIKOSW	KOWHAIS
AGLOSWY	LOGWAYS	AGORRTY	GYRATOR	AHIKPRS	PARKISH
AGLRSSU	GUSLARS	AGORSSU	RUGOSAS	AHIKRSS	SHIKARS
AGLRSUU	ARGULUS	AGORSTU	RAGOUTS	AHIKRSW	RIKSHAW
AGLRSUV	VULGARS	AGORTUY	GRAYOUT	AHIKSSS	SHIKSAS
AGLSYYZ	SYZYGAL	AGOSTTU	TAUTOGS	AHIKSST	SKAITHS
AGMMNOS	GAMMONS	AGOSUYZ	AZYGOUS	AHILLNO	HALLION
AGMMNSU	MAGNUMS	AGSSTUU	AUGUSTS	AHILLNP	PHALLIN
AGMMORY	MYOGRAM	AHHHISS	HASHISH	AHILLNT	ANTHILL
AGMNNOR	GRANNOM	AHHIIMS	HAIMISH	AHILLOS	HILLOAS
AGMNNOS	MAGNONS	AHHIJRS	HIJRAHS	AHILLRT	ATHRILL
	SONGMAN	AHHIKKR	KHIRKAH	AHILLSS	SHALLIS
AGMNNOT	TONGMAN	AHHIKSS	SHAIKHS	AHILLST	TALLISH
AGMNNOW	GOWNMAN	AHHIKSW	HAWKISH	AHILLSZ	ZILLAHS
AGMNORS	MORGANS	AHHIMNU	HAHNIUM	AHILLTT	TALLITH
AGMNORU	ORGANUM	AHHINST	SHANTIH	AHILLTY	LAITHLY
AGMNOST	AMONGST	AHHIPRS	RHAPHIS	AHILMMO	MOHALIM
AGMNSSU	MUSANGS	AHHISSS	SHISHAS	AHILMMS	MASHLIM
AGMNSTU	MUSTANG	AHHISSV	SHIVAHS	AHILMMY	HAMMILY
AGMNSTY	GYMNAST	AHHISTT	SHITTAH	AHILMNS	MASHLIN
	SYNTAGM	AHHKOOS	HOOKAHS	AHILMOP	OMPHALI
AGMNSYY	SYNGAMY	AHHLLOT	HALLOTH	AHILMOS	HOLMIAS
AGMOOYZ	ZOOGAMY	AHHLRSY	HARSHLY	AHILMOT	HALIMOT
AGMOPRR	PROGRAM	AHHMPRU	HARUMPH	AHILMOU	HALOUMI
AGMOPRU	GOPURAM	AHHOORS	HOORAHS	AHILMSU	ALUMISH
AGMORRW	RAGWORM	AHHOPRS	SHOPHAR	AHILNPS	PLANISH
AGMORSS	ORGASMS	AHHPPSU	HUPPAHS	AHILNRS	SHRINAL
AGMORSY	MORGAYS	AHHPTUZ	HUTZPAH	AHILNRT	INTHRAL
AGMOSYZ	ZYGOMAS	AHHRRSU	HURRAHS	AHILNSS	LASHINS
AGMPRSU	GRAMPUS	AHHSUZZ	HUZZAHS	AHILNSU	INHAULS
AGMPSUZ	GAZUMPS	AHIIKPS	PAKIHIS	AHILNSY	HYALINS
AGMRSSU	GRASSUM	AHIIKRS	RIKISHA		LINHAYS
AGNNNOO	NONAGON		SHIKARI	AHILORY	HOARILY
AGNNOOR	ARGONON	AHIILPS	SILPHIA	AHILOTY	ALIYOTH
	ORGANON	AHIILST	LITHIAS	AHILOTZ	THIAZOL
AGNNOST	TONNAGS	AHIIMNT	THIAMIN	AHILPPS	PALSHIP
AGNNOSY	NONGAYS	AHIIMSS	SASHIMI		SHIPLAP
AGNNSSU	UNSNAGS	AHIIMST	SAMITHI	AHILPPY	HAPPILY
AGNNSTU	TANGUNS	AHIINPR	HAIRPIN	AHILPRT	PHILTRA
AGNNSUW	WANGUNS	AHIINST	TAHINIS	AHILPSY	APISHLY
AGNOOSZ	GAZOONS	AHIINTU	HUITAIN	AHILSST	SALTISH
AGNOQSU	QUANGOS	AHIINTZ	THIAZIN		TAHSILS
AGNORRS	GARRONS	AHIIPRS	AIRSHIP	AHILSSV	SLAVISH
AGNORRT	GRANTOR	AHIIRTW	TAWHIRI	AHILSTU	HALITUS
AGNORSS	SARONGS	AHIKKSS	KISHKAS		THULIAS
AGNORST	SNOTRAG	AHIKLPS	KALIPHS	AHILSTY	HASTILY
AGNORSU	OURANGS	AHIKLRS	LARKISH	AHILSWY	WASHILY
AGNORTU	OUTRANG	AHIKLSS	SHASLIK	AHILSYZ	LAZYISH
AGNOSSS	GOSSANS	AHIKLST	KHILATS	AHIMMRS	RAMMISH
AGNOSST	SONTAGS	AHIKLSY	SHAKILY	AHIMNNS	MANNISH
AGNOSTU	NOUGATS	AHIKMNO	KOHANIM	AHIMNNU	INHUMAN
	OUTSANG	AHIKMNS	KHAMSIN	AHIMNOT	MANIHOT
AGNOSZZ	GOZZANS	AHIKMRS	KASHMIR	AHIMNPS	SHIPMAN
AGNOTUW	OUTGNAW		KHIMARS	AHIMNRS	HARMINS
AGNPRSS	SPRANGS	AHIKMSV	MIKVAHS	AHIMOPR	MORPHIA
AGNRSSU	SUNGARS	AHIKMSW	MAWKISH	AHIMORS	MOHAIRS
AGNRTUY	GAUNTRY	AHIKNRS	RANKISH	AHIMORZ	RHIZOMA
AGOPPST	STOPGAP	AHIKNSS	SNAKISH	AHIMOSS	SHAMOIS
AGOPRST	RAGTOPS	AHIKNSV	KNAVISH	AHIMPSS	MISHAPS
AGOPRSU	GOPURAS	AHIKNTT	THANKIT		PASHIMS

Key	Word(s)
AHIMPST	MISHAPT
AHIMPSV	VAMPISH
AHIMPSW	WAMPISH
AHIMRSS	MAHSIRS
AHIMRST	THAIRMS
	THIRAMS
	THRIMSA
AHIMRSW	WARMISH
AHIMSSU	HASSIUM
AHIMSTV	MITSVAH
AHIMTUZ	AZIMUTH
AHIMTVZ	MITZVAH
AHINNST	TANNISH
AHINNSW	WANNISH
AHINNTX	XANTHIN
AHINORT	ORTHIAN
AHINOTZ	HOATZIN
AHINPRS	HARPINS
AHINPST	HATPINS
AHINRSS	ARSHINS
	SHAIRNS
AHINRST	TARNISH
AHINRSU	UNHAIRS
AHINRSV	VARNISH
AHINRTY	RHYTINA
AHINRVY	HRYVNIA
AHINSST	SHANTIS
AHINSSW	WASHINS
AHINSTU	INHAUST
AHINSYZ	ZANYISH
AHINTUU	TAUHINU
AHIOOST	ATISHOO
AHIOPRU	OPHIURA
AHIOPXY	HYPOXIA
AHIORSS	ORISHAS
AHIORST	AIRSHOT
	SHORTIA
	THORIAS
AHIORSV	HAVIORS
AHIORSW	AIRSHOW
AHIORUV	HAVIOUR
AHIPRSS	RASPISH
AHIPRST	HARPIST
AHIPRSU	RUPIAHS
AHIPRSW	WARSHIP
AHIPRWY	WHIPRAY
AHIPSSW	WASPISH
AHIPSWW	WHIPSAW
AHIPSWY	SHIPWAY
AHIRRSS	SHIRRAS
	SIRRAHS
AHIRRST	STIRRAH
AHIRRSW	WIRRAHS
AHIRSST	HAIRSTS
AHIRSTT	ATHIRST
	RATTISH
	TARTISH
AHIRSTW	TRISHAW
	WRAITHS
AHISSTT	STAITHS
AHISSTU	SHIATSU
	THIASUS
AHISSTW	WHATSIS
AHISTTW	WHATSIT
AHISTUZ	SHIATZU
AHITTWW	WHITTAW
AHJOOPS	POOJAHS
AHKKSSU	SUKKAHS
AHKLOOS	KOOLAHS
AHKLPSU	PULKHAS
AHKMNSU	KHANUMS
AHKMORR	MARKHOR
AHKMOSS	MOKSHAS
AHKMOSW	MOHAWKS
AHKMRTU	MUKHTAR
AHKNPSU	PUNKAHS
AHKPSUU	HAPUKUS
AHKRSST	SKARTHS
AHKRSSU	KASHRUS
AHKRSTU	KASHRUT
	KHURTAS
	TUSHKAR
AHLLMOS	MOLLAHS
	OLLAMHS
AHLLMSU	MULLAHS
AHLLNOS	SHALLON
AHLLNOY	HALLYON
AHLLNSU	NULLAHS
AHLLOOS	HALLOOS
	HOLLOAS
AHLLOPS	SHALLOP
AHLLOST	SHALLOT
AHLLOSU	HULLOAS
AHLLOSW	HALLOWS
	SHALLOW
AHLLOTY	LOATHLY
	TALLYHO
AHLLPSU	PHALLUS
AHLLPSY	ALPHYLS
AHLLPYY	APHYLLY
AHLLRST	THRALLS
AHLLSTU	THALLUS
AHLMMSU	MASHLUM
AHLMNPY	NYMPHAL
AHLMNSY	HYMNALS
AHLMNUY	HUMANLY
AHLMOOS	MOOLAHS
AHLMORU	HUMORAL
AHLMOSS	SHALOMS
AHLMSTZ	SHMALTZ
AHLMSUU	HAMULUS
AHLNOPR	ALPHORN
AHLNOPT	HAPLONT
	NAPHTOL
AHLNORT	ALTHORN
AHLOOPS	HOOPLAS
AHLOOPW	WHOOPLA
AHLOOTW	WOOLHAT
AHLORST	HARLOTS
AHLOSST	SHALOTS
AHLOSTU	OUTLASH
AHLOTUU	OUTHAUL
AHLPRSY	SHARPLY
AHLPRUY	HYPURAL
AHLPSSU	SULPHAS
AHLPSSY	SPLASHY
AHMMMOT	MAMMOTH
AHMMMUU	HUMMAUM
AHMMOSS	SHAMMOS
AHMMOSW	WHAMMOS
AHMNNSU	NUMNAHS
AHMNNTU	MANHUNT
AHMNNUU	UNHUMAN
AHMNOPS	SHOPMAN
AHMNOPT	PHANTOM
AHMNORY	HARMONY
AHMNOSS	HANSOMS
AHMNOSW	SHOWMAN
AHMNRSU	RHAMNUS
AHMNRYY	HYMNARY
AHMOOPS	OOMPAHS
	SHAMPOO
AHMOOSS	SAMSHOO
AHMORRU	MORRHUA
AHMORST	HARMOST
AHMORSZ	MAHZORS
AHMOSSY	SHAMOYS
AHMOSTU	MAHOUTS
AHMOSTZ	MATZOHS
AHMOSWY	HAYMOWS
AHMOTTZ	MATZOTH
AHMPSSU	MASHUPS
	SMASHUP
AHMRRSU	MURRHAS
AHMRSTW	WARMTHS
AHMRSTY	THRYMSA
AHMSSSU	SAMSHUS
AHNNSSU	SUNNAHS
AHNOOPR	HARPOON
AHNOPRS	ORPHANS
AHNORSS	SHORANS
AHNORSX	SAXHORN
AHNOTTW	WHATNOT
AHNPPSS	SHNAPPS
AHNPPUU	PUPUNHA
AHNPPUY	UNHAPPY
AHNPRSU	UNSHARP
AHNPRXY	PHARYNX
AHNPSSU	UNHASPS
AHNRSVY	HRYVNAS
AHNRVYY	HRYVNYA
AHNSSTU	SUNHATS
AHNSTUW	UNTHAWS
AHNSTUY	UNHASTY
AHOORSS	SHOORAS
AHOORSY	HOORAYS
AHOPRSS	PHASORS
AHOPRTY	ATROPHY
AHOPSTW	WASHPOT
AHOPTTW	TOWPATH
AHORRSW	HARROWS
AHORSTT	THROATS
AHORSTU	AUTHORS

AHORSTW	WROATHS	AIILRTV	TRIVIAL	AIKKLOO	KALOOKI
AHORTTY	THROATY		VITRAIL	AIKKLSU	KALUKIS
AHOSTUU	TAUHOUS	AIIMMNS	ANIMISM	AIKKMNR	KIRKMAN
AHOSTUW	OUTWASH	AIIMMNX	MAXIMIN	AIKKMOT	KOMATIK
	WASHOUT		MINIMAX	AIKKNOS	KONAKIS
AHPRRTY	PHRATRY	AIIMMSS	MISAIMS	AIKKOOW	KOKOWAI
AHPRSST	SPARTHS	AIIMNNV	MINIVAN	AIKKOPY	KOPIYKA
AHPSSUW	WASHUPS	AIIMNOR	AMORINI	AIKKSUZ	ZAKUSKI
AHPSTUZ	HUTZPAS	AIIMNPS	PAINIMS	AIKLLNY	LANKILY
AHPSXYY	ASPHYXY		PIANISM	AIKLMMN	MILKMAN
AHQSSUY	SQUASHY	AIIMNPT	IMPAINT	AIKLMNN	LINKMAN
AHRRSUY	HURRAYS		TIMPANI	AIKLMNS	MALKINS
AHRSSSU	HUSSARS	AIIMNRT	MARTINI	AIKLMPU	LAMPUKI
AHRSSTT	STRATHS	AIIMNSS	SAIMINS	AIKLMSS	MISKALS
AHRSSTW	SWARTHS		SIMIANS	AIKLMSU	KALIUMS
AHRSTTW	THWARTS	AIIMNST	ANIMIST	AIKLNOS	KAOLINS
AHRSTWY	SWARTHY		INTIMAS	AIKLNSY	SNAKILY
AHRTUWY	THRUWAY		SANTIMI	AIKLPWY	PAWKILY
AHSSSTU	TUSSAHS	AIIMNTT	IMITANT	AIKLQUY	QUAKILY
AIIILMT	MILITIA	AIIMNTU	MINUTIA	AIKLRSY	SARKILY
AIIILNT	INITIAL	AIIMNTV	VITAMIN	AIKLRTT	TITLARK
AIIILVX	LIXIVIA	AIIMNTY	AMINITY	AIKLSSU	SALUKIS
AIIIMRS	SAIMIRI	AIIMPRS	IMPAIRS	AIKLSSY	SKYSAIL
AIIKKSW	WAKIKIS	AIIMPSS	SIMPAIS	AIKMMRS	MISMARK
AIIKMMS	SKIMMIA	AIIMRST	SIMITAR	AIKMMSS	IMMASKS
AIIKMNN	MANIKIN	AIIMSST	SAMITIS	AIKMNNS	KINSMAN
	MANKINI	AIIMSSY	MYIASIS	AIKMNRS	RANKISM
AIIKNNT	TANKINI	AIINNOP	PIANINO	AIKMNSS	KAMSINS
AIIKNST	KAINITS	AIINNPS	PANINIS	AIKMNSW	MAWKINS
AIIKPST	PATIKIS	AIINNQU	QUININA	AIKMOOS	OOMIAKS
AIIKRRU	RAURIKI	AIINNSZ	ZINNIAS	AIKMPRS	IMPARKS
AIIKRTT	TRAIKIT	AIINNTY	INANITY	AIKMRSU	KUMARIS
AIILLLP	LAPILLI	AIINOPS	SINOPIA		RUMAKIS
AIILLMN	LIMINAL	AIINOTT	NOTITIA	AIKMSST	KISMATS
AIILLMS	LIMAILS	AIINPPR	RAPPINI	AIKNNNS	NANKINS
AIILLMW	WILLIAM	AIINPRS	ASPIRIN	AIKNNPS	NAPKINS
AIILLNV	VILLAIN	AIINPST	PIANIST	AIKNOST	KATIONS
AIILLQU	QUILLAI	AIINRSS	RAISINS	AIKNPRS	KIRPANS
AIILLUV	ILLUVIA	AIINRSY	RAISINY		PARKINS
AIILMMN	MINIMAL	AIINRTV	VITRAIN	AIKNPSS	PANISKS
AIILMNN	LAMININ	AIINRTZ	TRIAZIN	AIKNRST	KIRTANS
AIILMNO	MONILIA	AIINSST	ISATINS	AIKNSTU	TANUKIS
AIILMNS	MISLAIN	AIINSSX	SIXAINS	AIKOORT	ROOIKAT
AIILMNT	INTIMAL	AIINSTT	TITANIS	AIKOORW	KOROWAI
AIILMNV	VIMINAL		TITIANS	AIKOPST	KATIPOS
AIILMRS	SIMILAR	AIINSTV	NAIVIST	AIKORRS	KORARIS
AIILMRT	MILITAR	AIIPRST	PIARIST	AIKORST	TROIKAS
AIILMRY	MILIARY	AIIPSTW	WAPITIS	AIKOSTW	KWAITOS
AIILNNS	ANILINS	AIIPTTU	PITUITA	AIKRRSS	SIRKARS
AIILNOS	LIAISON	AIISTUW	TAUIWIS	AIKRSST	STRAIKS
AIILNPT	PINTAIL	AIJJMMS	JIMJAMS	AIKRTUZ	ZIKURAT
AIILNPU	NAUPLII	AIJLORS	JAILORS	AILLLNO	LINALOL
AIILNRY	RAINILY	AIJLORT	TOLARJI	AILLMNU	LUMINAL
AIILNTU	NAUTILI	AIJLSTW	WILTJAS	AILLMNY	MANLILY
AIILNTV	INVITAL	AIJLYZZ	JAZZILY	AILLMOT	MAILLOT
AIILNTY	ANILITY	AIJMNSS	JASMINS	AILLMPT	LAMPLIT
AIILOPP	PAPILIO	AIJMORS	ROMAJIS	AILLMPU	PALLIUM
AIILORV	RAVIOLI	AIJNORT	JANITOR	AILLMSU	ALLIUMS
AIILPRU	LIPURIA	AIJORSW	JOWARIS	AILLMSW	SAWMILL
AIILQSU	SILIQUA	AIJPRSU	PUJARIS	AILLMSY	MISALLY
AIILRST	LIATRIS	AIJPSTU	JUPATIS	AILLNNO	LANOLIN

AILLNOP	PAILLON	**AILNNOS**	SOLANIN	**AILOSTU**	OUTSAIL
AILLNPY	PLAINLY	**AILNNOT**	ANTLION	**AILOSTX**	OXTAILS
AILLNST	INSTALL	**AILNNPU**	PINNULA	**AILOSWY**	OILWAYS
AILLNSV	VILLANS	**AILNNSU**	UNNAILS	**AILOTVY**	OVALITY
AILLNSW	INWALLS		UNSLAIN	**AILPPRU**	PUPILAR
AILLNVY	VILLANY	**AILNOPY**	POLYNIA	**AILPPSU**	SUIPLAP
AILLORT	LITORAL	**AILNOQU**	AQUILON	**AILPPSY**	PAYSLIP
AILLORZ	ZORILLA	**AILNOSS**	ALISONS		SAPPILY
AILLPRS	PILLARS		SIALONS	**AILPPTY**	PLATYPI
AILLPRU	PILULAR	**AILNOST**	LATINOS	**AILPQSU**	PASQUIL
AILLPSU	PILLAUS		TALIONS	**AILPRSS**	SPIRALS
	PILULAS	**AILNOTU**	OUTLAIN	**AILPRSU**	PARULIS
AILLPUV	PLUVIAL	**AILNPRW**	PRAWLIN		SPIRULA
AILLQSU	SQUILLA	**AILNPSS**	SPINALS		UPRISAL
AILLRSU	ARILLUS	**AILNPST**	PLAINTS	**AILPRSY**	PYRALIS
AILLRVY	VIRALLY	**AILNPSU**	PAULINS	**AILPSST**	PASTILS
AILLSTT	TALLITS		SPINULA		SPITALS
AILLSTY	SALTILY	**AILNPSX**	SALPINX	**AILPSTU**	TIPULAS
AILLSUZ	LAZULIS	**AILNPTU**	NUPTIAL	**AILPSTY**	PASTILY
AILLTVY	VITALLY		PATULIN		PAYLIST
AILLTWW	WITWALL		UNPLAIT	**AILPSWY**	SLIPWAY
AILMMOR	IMMORAL	**AILNPTY**	INAPTLY		WASPILY
AILMMSS	MALISMS		PTYALIN	**AILQSSU**	SQUAILS
AILMMSY	MYALISM	**AILNPUV**	PLUVIAN	**AILQTTU**	QUITTAL
AILMMUU	ALUMIUM	**AILNQTU**	QUINTAL	**AILQTUY**	QUALITY
AILMMUW	MWALIMU	**AILNRST**	RATLINS	**AILRRVY**	RIVALRY
AILMNNO	NOMINAL	**AILNRSU**	INSULAR	**AILRSTT**	STARLIT
AILMNOP	LAMPION		URINALS	**AILRSTU**	RITUALS
AILMNOS	MALISON	**AILNRTT**	RATTLIN		TRISULA
	MONIALS	**AILNRTY**	RIANTLY	**AILRSTY**	TRYSAIL
	SOMNIAL	**AILNSST**	INSTALS	**AILRTTU**	TITULAR
AILMNOY	ALIMONY	**AILNSSV**	SILVANS	**AILRTTY**	RATTILY
AILMNPS	MISPLAN	**AILNSTT**	LATTINS		TARTILY
	PLASMIN	**AILNSTU**	UNALIST	**AILRTUV**	VIRTUAL
AILMNPT	IMPLANT	**AILNSTY**	NASTILY		VITULAR
AILMNPU	ULPANIM		SAINTLY	**AILSSSY**	SASSILY
AILMNRS	MARLINS	**AILNSUV**	UNVAILS	**AILSSTU**	TISSUAL
AILMNRU	MURLAIN	**AILNTTY**	NATTILY	**AILSSTX**	LAXISTS
	RUMINAL	**AILNTUV**	UNVITAL	**AILSSUV**	VISUALS
AILMNSS	MASLINS	**AILNTWY**	TAWNILY	**AILSSVY**	SYLVIAS
AILMNSU	ALUMINS	**AILOORS**	OORALIS	**AILSSVZ**	VIZSLAS
AILMOOV	MOVIOLA		OORIALS	**AILSTTY**	TASTILY
AILMOPS	LIPOMAS	**AILOORW**	WOORALI	**AILSTUW**	LAWSUIT
AILMOPT	OPTIMAL	**AILOPST**	APOSTIL	**AILSVVY**	SAVVILY
AILMORS	ORALISM		TOPSAIL	**AILTTTY**	TATTILY
AILMOST	SOMITAL	**AILOPSY**	SOAPILY	**AIMMMSU**	MUMMIAS
AILMOSY	ISOAMYL	**AILOPTT**	TALIPOT	**AIMMMUX**	MAXIMUM
AILMPRS	IMPARLS	**AILOPTV**	PIVOTAL	**AIMMNTU**	MANUMIT
AILMPRU	PRIMULA	**AILOQTU**	ALIQUOT	**AIMMORS**	AMORISM
AILMPST	PALMIST	**AILORSS**	SAILORS	**AIMMOSS**	MIMOSAS
AILMPSY	MISPLAY	**AILORST**	ORALIST	**AIMMOST**	ATOMISM
AILMRST	MISTRAL		RIALTOS	**AIMMSUX**	MAXIMUS
	RAMTILS		SLIOTAR	**AIMNNOR**	IRONMAN
AILMRSU	SIMULAR		TAILORS	**AIMNNOS**	AMNIONS
AILMSSS	MISSALS	**AILORSU**	OURALIS		MANSION
AILMSST	MISTALS	**AILORTY**	ORALITY		ONANISM
AILMSSX	LAXISMS	**AILORUW**	WOURALI	**AIMNNSS**	NANISMS
AILMSSY	MISLAYS	**AILORUX**	UXORIAL	**AIMNNSY**	MINYANS
AILMSTU	ULTIMAS	**AILORVY**	OLIVARY	**AIMNOOR**	AMORINO
AILMSTY	MYALIST	**AILOSSS**	ASSOILS	**AIMNOOT**	AMOTION
AILMSUV	MAULVIS	**AILOSTT**	ALTOIST	**AIMNOPR**	RAMPION

AIMNOPS	MOPANIS	**AINNOPT**	PINTANO	**AINQSSU**	QUASSIN
AIMNOPT	MAINTOP	**AINNOSS**	NASIONS	**AINQSTU**	ASQUINT
	PTOMAIN	**AINNOST**	ANOINTS		QUINTAS
	TAMPION		NATIONS	**AINQSUY**	YANQUIS
	TIMPANO		ONANIST	**AINRRTY**	TRINARY
AIMNOPZ	ZAMPONI	**AINNOSW**	WANIONS	**AINRRUY**	URINARY
AIMNORS	MAINORS	**AINNPSS**	INSPANS	**AINRSST**	INSTARS
AIMNORT	TORMINA	**AINNPST**	SNAPTIN		SANTIRS
AIMNORU	MAINOUR	**AINNPTU**	UNPAINT		STRAINS
AIMNOST	MANITOS	**AINNQTU**	QUINNAT	**AINRSTT**	STRAINT
	STAMNOI		QUINTAN		TRANSIT
AIMNOTU	MANITOU	**AINNRSU**	URANINS	**AINRSTU**	NUTRIAS
	TINAMOU	**AINNRTT**	INTRANT	**AINRTTT**	TITRANT
AIMNPST	PITMANS	**AINNRTU**	URINANT	**AINRTUY**	UNITARY
AIMNPSW	IMPAWNS	**AINNSTT**	INSTANT	**AINSSTT**	STATINS
AIMNPSY	PAYNIMS	**AINNSTU**	UNSAINT		TANISTS
AIMNPTY	TYMPANI	**AINNTUY**	ANNUITY	**AINSSTU**	ISSUANT
AIMNRRU	MURRAIN	**AINOOPR**	PRONAOI		SUSTAIN
AIMNRST	MARTINS	**AINOORR**	ORARION	**AINSSXY**	SYNAXIS
AIMNRSU	SURAMIN	**AINOORT**	ORATION	**AINTTVY**	TANTIVY
	URANISM	**AINOOTV**	OVATION	**AIOORRW**	WOORARI
AIMNRTU	NATRIUM	**AINOPPT**	APPOINT	**AIOORSS**	ARIOSOS
AIMNRTV	VARMINT	**AINOPRS**	PARISON	**AIOPPRR**	PROPRIA
AIMNRUU	URANIUM		PORINAS	**AIOPRRT**	AIRPORT
AIMNSST	SANTIMS		SOPRANI		PARITOR
AIMNSTT	MATTINS	**AINOPRT**	ATROPIN	**AIOPRRX**	AIRPROX
AIMNSTU	MANITUS	**AINOPSS**	PASSION	**AIOPRST**	AIRPOST
	SANTIMU	**AINOPTT**	ANTIPOT		AIRSTOP
	TSUNAMI	**AINOPTU**	OPUNTIA		PAROTIS
AIMNSUV	MAUVINS		UTOPIAN	**AIOPRSV**	PAVIORS
AIMNSUZ	MIZUNAS	**AINOQSU**	QUINOAS	**AIOPRTT**	PATRIOT
AIMNSVY	MAYVINS	**AINORST**	AROINTS	**AIOPRTY**	TOPIARY
AIMNSYZ	ZANYISM		RATIONS	**AIOPRUV**	PAVIOUR
AIMOPST	IMPASTO	**AINORSW**	WARISON	**AIOPSTU**	UTOPIAS
	MATIPOS	**AINORTU**	RAINOUT	**AIORRRW**	WARRIOR
AIMOPSY	MYOPIAS	**AINORTW**	WAITRON	**AIORRSU**	OURARIS
AIMORRU	ORARIUM	**AINORTX**	TRIAXON	**AIORRTT**	TRAITOR
AIMORST	AMORIST	**AINOSSU**	SANIOUS	**AIORRTX**	ORATRIX
AIMORTT	TRITOMA		SUASION	**AIORSST**	AORISTS
AIMORUZ	ZOARIUM	**AINOSTT**	STATION		ARISTOS
AIMOSTT	ATOMIST	**AINOSUX**	ANXIOUS		SATORIS
AIMPPSS	PAPISMS	**AINOSVY**	SYNOVIA	**AIORSSU**	SOUARIS
AIMPPST	MAPPIST	**AINPPRS**	PARSNIP	**AIORSSV**	SAVIORS
AIMPRRY	PRIMARY	**AINPQTU**	PIQUANT	**AIORSTU**	SAUTOIR
AIMPRST	ARMPITS	**AINPRSS**	SPINARS	**AIORSTV**	TRAVOIS
	IMPARTS		SPRAINS		VIATORS
	MISPART	**AINPRST**	SPIRANT	**AIORSTY**	OSTIARY
AIMPRSY	PYRAMIS		SPRAINT	**AIORSUV**	SAVIOUR
AIMQRSU	MARQUIS	**AINPRSU**	PRUINAS		VARIOUS
AIMRSST	TSARISM	**AINPRSW**	INWRAPS	**AIOSSTT**	TATSOIS
AIMRSTU	ATRIUMS		RIPSAWN	**AIOSSYZ**	ZOYSIAS
	MATSURI	**AINPRTT**	TRIPTAN	**AIOTTUW**	OUTWAIT
AIMRSTY	MAISTRY	**AINPRTU**	PURITAN	**AIPPRRS**	RIPRAPS
	SYMITAR		UPTRAIN	**AIPPRSU**	PRIAPUS
AIMRSTZ	TZARISM	**AINPSST**	PISSANT	**AIPPSST**	PAPISTS
AIMSSSY	MISSAYS		PTISANS	**AIPRRTT**	TRIPART
AIMSSTT	STATISM	**AINPSSV**	SPAVINS	**AIPRSST**	RAPISTS
AIMSSTU	AUTISMS	**AINPSTU**	TIPUNAS	**AIPRSSW**	RIPSAWS
AINNNOW	WANNION	**AINQRST**	QINTARS	**AIPRSTU**	UPSTAIR
AINNNST	TANNINS	**AINQRTU**	QUINTAR	**AIPRSUY**	PYURIAS
AINNOPS	SAPONIN	**AINQRUY**	QUINARY	**AIPRTVY**	PRAVITY

AIPSSTT	TAPISTS	**AKLRSVY**	VALKYRS	**ALLORWY**	ROLLWAY
AIPSSTW	PITSAWS	**AKMNORW**	WORKMAN	**ALLORYY**	ROYALLY
	SAWPITS	**AKMNRTU**	TRANKUM	**ALLOSSW**	SALLOWS
AIPYZZZ	PIZAZZY	**AKMNSSU**	UNMASKS	**ALLOSTT**	TALLOTS
AIPZZZZ	PIZZAZZ	**AKMOORT**	MOOKTAR	**ALLOSTU**	SOLUTAL
AIRRSST	RISTRAS	**AKMOOSS**	OAKMOSS	**ALLOSTV**	LAVOLTS
	STIRRAS	**AKMORST**	OSTMARK	**ALLOSTW**	TALLOWS
AIRRSZZ	RIZZARS	**AKMPRSU**	MARKUPS	**ALLOSWW**	SWALLOW
AIRRTZZ	RIZZART	**AKMQTUU**	KUMQUAT		WALLOWS
AIRSSSU	RUSSIAS	**AKMRSTU**	MUSKRAT	**ALLOSWY**	SALLOWY
AIRSSTT	ARTISTS	**AKMSTUU**	MAKUTUS	**ALLOTTY**	TOTALLY
	SITTARS	**AKNNOOS**	NANOOKS	**ALLOTWY**	TALLOWY
	STRAITS	**AKNORSU**	KORUNAS		TOLLWAY
	TSARIST	**AKNORSY**	KARYONS	**ALLOTYY**	LOYALTY
AIRSSTU	AURISTS		RYOKANS	**ALLPRSU**	PLURALS
AIRSTTT	ATTRIST	**AKNORTU**	OUTRANK	**ALLPSSY**	PSYLLAS
	ATTRITS	**AKOOPRT**	PARTOOK	**ALLQSSU**	SQUALLS
AIRSTTU	TURISTA	**AKOORRS**	KAROROS	**ALLQSUY**	SQUALLY
AIRSTTY	YTTRIAS		KARROOS	**ALLRRUY**	RURALLY
AIRSTTZ	TZARIST		KORORAS	**ALLRSTU**	LUSTRAL
AIRSTVY	VARSITY	**AKOOSTU**	ATOKOUS	**ALLRSUY**	LAURYLS
AIRTUVX	VITRAUX	**AKOPRRU**	PARKOUR	**ALLSUUY**	USUALLY
AISSSST	ASSISTS	**AKORRTW**	ARTWORK	**ALMMSUW**	WAMMULS
AISSTTT	STATIST	**AKORRWW**	WARWORK	**ALMMSUY**	AMYLUMS
AISSTTU	AUTISTS	**AKORWWX**	WAXWORK	**ALMNNUY**	UNMANLY
AISTTVY	VASTITY	**AKOSSTU**	OUTASKS	**ALMNOOP**	LAMPOON
AISTUVY	SUAVITY	**AKOSTTU**	OUTTASK	**ALMNOOT**	TOOLMAN
AJKMNNU	JUNKMAN	**AKOSTWY**	TOWKAYS	**ALMNOOW**	WOOLMAN
AJKMNTU	MUNTJAK	**AKQRSSU**	SQUARKS	**ALMNOPS**	PLASMON
AJKNSSY	JANSKYS	**AKQOSSUW**	SQUAWKS	**ALMNOPW**	PLOWMAN
AJLLRUY	JURALLY	**AKQSUWY**	SQUAWKY	**ALMNORS**	NORMALS
AJLMORY	MAJORLY	**AKRSSTU**	TUSKARS	**ALMNORU**	UNMORAL
AJLNORU	JOURNAL	**AKSSWYY**	SKYWAYS	**ALMNORY**	ALMONRY
AJLOORS	JAROOLS	**ALLLOST**	TALLOLS	**ALMNOSS**	SALMONS
AJLOPPY	JALOPPY	**ALLLOYY**	LOYALLY	**ALMNOSU**	MONAULS
AJMNRUY	JURYMAN	**ALLMNOP**	POLLMAN		SOLANUM
AJMOPST	JAMPOTS	**ALLMNOT**	TOLLMAN	**ALMNOSY**	SALMONY
AJMRSTU	JUMARTS	**ALLMNOY**	ALLONYM	**ALMNOWY**	WOMANLY
AJNRSTU	JURANTS	**ALLMNPU**	PULLMAN	**ALMNPSU**	SUNLAMP
AKKKOOS	KOKAKOS	**ALLMOOS**	OSMOLAL	**ALMNRSU**	MURLANS
AKKKORU	ROKKAKU	**ALLMORS**	MORALLS	**ALMNSUU**	ALUMNUS
AKKLRSY	SKYLARK	**ALLMORY**	MORALLY	**ALMOOPY**	POLYOMA
AKKLSWY	SKYWALK	**ALLMOSS**	SLALOMS	**ALMOORS**	OSMOLAR
AKKMOOT	TOKOMAK	**ALLMOST**	MALTOLS	**ALMOPPT**	PALMTOP
AKKNRSU	KUNKARS	**ALLMOSW**	MALLOWS	**ALMOPRT**	MARPLOT
AKKOOPS	PAKOKOS	**ALLMPUU**	PLUMULA	**ALMORRU**	MORULAR
AKKOQSU	QUOKKAS	**ALLMSUV**	VALLUMS	**ALMORSS**	SAMLORS
AKKORSU	KAKUROS	**ALLNOPS**	POLLANS	**ALMORST**	MORTALS
AKLMMSU	MAMLUKS	**ALLNOTY**	TONALLY		STROMAL
AKLNOSU	KOULANS	**ALLNOYZ**	ZONALLY	**ALMORSU**	MORULAS
AKLNOSX	KLAXONS	**ALLNRUU**	LUNULAR	**ALMORTU**	TUMORAL
AKLOPRW	LAPWORK	**ALLNSTY**	SLANTLY	**ALMOSST**	SMALTOS
AKLOSST	SKATOLS	**ALLNTUU**	ULULANT	**ALMOSTW**	MATLOWS
AKLOSTW	KOTWALS	**ALLOOPS**	APOLLOS	**ALMOSXY**	XYLOMAS
AKLOTTU	OUTTALK		PALOLOS	**ALMOTTU**	MULATTO
AKLOTUW	OUTWALK	**ALLOOST**	LATOSOL	**ALMRSTY**	SMARTLY
	WALKOUT	**ALLOOTX**	AXOLOTL	**ALMRSUU**	RAMULUS
AKLPRSY	SPARKLY	**ALLOPRS**	PALLORS	**ALMRTUU**	MUTULAR
AKLPSTU	UPTALKS	**ALLOPRY**	PAYROLL		TUMULAR
AKLPSUW	WALKUPS	**ALLOPSW**	WALLOPS	**ALMSSUY**	ALYSSUM
AKLRSTY	STARKLY	**ALLORSS**	SOLLARS		ASYLUMS

ALMSTUU	MUTUALS	ALORSUV	LOUVARS	AMNORRS	MARRONS
	UMLAUTS		VALOURS	AMNORSS	RAMSONS
ALNNOOR	NONORAL	ALORTWW	AWLWORT		RANSOMS
ALNNOPY	NONPLAY	ALORTYY	ROYALTY	AMNORST	MATRONS
ALNNRSU	UNSNARL	ALORUVY	OVULARY		TRANSOM
ALNNSUU	ANNULUS	ALOSTTU	OUTLAST	AMNORSY	MASONRY
ALNOOPR	POLARON	ALOSTUW	OUTLAWS		MORNAYS
ALNOOPT	PLATOON	ALOSTUY	LAYOUTS	AMNORTU	ROMAUNT
ALNOOPV	VANPOOL		OUTLAYS	AMNOSST	STAMNOS
ALNOORT	ORTOLAN	ALOSTXY	OXYSALT	AMNOSTU	AMOUNTS
ALNOOSS	SALOONS	ALPRRSU	LARRUPS		MOUTANS
	SOLANOS	ALPRSSU	PULSARS		OUTMANS
ALNOPPY	PANOPLY	ALPRSSW	SPRAWLS	AMNOSYZ	ZYMOSAN
ALNOPRS	PROLANS	ALPRSTY	PSALTRY	AMNOTUY	AUTONYM
ALNOPSS	SPONSAL	ALPRSUU	PURSUAL	AMNPSTY	TYMPANS
ALNOPTU	OUTPLAN	ALPRSUW	PULWARS	AMNPTYY	TYMPANY
ALNOPYY	POLYNYA	ALPRSWY	SPRAWLY	AMNQTUU	QUANTUM
ALNORST	LATRONS	ALQSTUY	SQUATLY	AMNRRUY	UNMARRY
ALNORSU	SOLUNAR	ALRSSUU	RUSSULA	AMNRSTU	ANTRUMS
ALNORUY	UNROYAL	ALRSTTY	STARTLY		UNSMART
ALNORUZ	ZONULAR	ALRSTUU	SUTURAL	AMNRTTU	TANTRUM
ALNOSST	SANTOLS	ALRSTUW	TULWARS	AMNSTTU	MUTANTS
	STANOLS	ALRSUUV	UVULARS	AMNSTUU	AUTUMNS
ALNOSUZ	ZONULAS	AMMMNOS	MAMMONS	AMNTUUY	AUTUMNY
ALNPRUY	PLANURY	AMMMOSU	AMOMUMS	AMOOORS	AMOROSO
ALNPSTU	PULSANT	AMMNOOR	MOORMAN	AMOOPRS	PROSOMA
	PULTANS	AMMNOOT	MOOTMAN	AMOOPRT	TAPROOM
ALNPTUY	UNAPTLY	AMMNOPS	PSAMMON	AMOORSU	AMOROUS
ALNPTXY	PLANXTY	AMMNRUY	NUMMARY	AMOORSV	MOORVAS
ALNRSUY	URANYLS	AMMOORR	MAORMOR		VAROOMS
ALNSSTU	SULTANS		MORMAOR	AMOORXY	OXYMORA
ALNSSVY	SYLVANS	AMMOPTU	POMATUM	AMOPPSY	MAYPOPS
ALNSTUW	WALNUTS	AMMORST	MARMOTS	AMOPSTT	TOPMAST
ALNSUUU	UNUSUAL	AMMOSXY	MYXOMAS	AMORRST	MORTARS
ALOOPSS	SALOOPS	AMMPSUW	WAMPUMS	AMORRSU	ARMOURS
ALOOPYZ	POLYZOA	AMMRRSU	MARRUMS	AMORRSW	MARROWS
ALOORRS	SORORAL		MURRAMS	AMORRTY	MORTARY
ALOPPRS	POPLARS	AMMRSUY	SUMMARY	AMORRUY	ARMOURY
ALOPPRU	POPULAR	AMMSSTU	SUMMATS	AMORRWY	MARROWY
ALOPPRY	PROPYLA	AMNNOOX	MONAXON	AMORSST	MATROSS
ALOPPST	LAPTOPS	AMNNORS	NORMANS		STROAMS
ALOPRRS	PARLORS	AMNNOSW	SNOWMAN	AMORSSY	MORASSY
ALOPRRU	PARLOUR	AMNNOSY	ANONYMS	AMORWWX	WAXWORM
ALOPRST	PATROLS	AMNNOTT	MONTANT	AMOSTUW	OUTSWAM
	PORTALS	AMNNOTY	ANTONYM	AMOSTUZ	MAZOUTS
ALOPRSU	PARLOUS	AMNNOUW	UNWOMAN	AMOSUYZ	AZYMOUS
ALOPRSY	PYROLAS	AMNNSTU	STANNUM	AMPRSST	STRAMPS
ALOPSST	POSTALS	AMNOOOS	MONOAOS	AMPRSUW	WARMUPS
ALOPSSU	SPOUSAL	AMNOOPP	POMPANO	AMRRSTU	RASTRUM
ALOPSUV	VOLUSPA	AMNOORS	MAROONS	AMRRSTY	MARTYRS
ALOPTUY	OUTPLAY		ROMANOS	AMRRSUY	MURRAYS
ALOQRRU	RORQUAL	AMNOOTT	OTTOMAN	AMRRTYY	MARTYRY
ALOQRSU	SQUALOR	AMNOOTZ	MATZOON	AMRSSTU	STRUMAS
ALOQSTU	LOQUATS	AMNOPPR	PROPMAN	AMRSTTU	STRATUM
ALORRST	ROSTRAL	AMNOPRT	PORTMAN	ANNNOSY	SYNANON
ALORRSW	WORRALS	AMNOPRY	PARONYM	ANNOPRS	NAPRONS
ALORSST	SORTALS	AMNOPST	POSTMAN	ANNOPSS	SANNOPS
ALORSSU	ROSULAS		TAMPONS	ANNOPST	NONPAST
ALORSSV	SALVORS		TOPSMAN		PANTONS
ALORSTU	ROTULAS	AMNOPTU	PANTOUM	ANNOPTY	POYNANT
	TORULAS	AMNOPTY	TYMPANO	ANNORST	NATRONS

	NONARTS	**AOOPPRS**	APROPOS	**APPRSTY**	STRAPPY
ANNORSW	NONWARS	**AOOPRTT**	TAPROOT	**APPRSUW**	UPWRAPS
ANNOSST	SANTONS	**AOORRST**	ORATORS	**APPRSUY**	PAPYRUS
	SONANTS	**AOORRSY**	ARROYOS	**APRSSSU**	SURPASS
ANNOSTW	WANTONS	**AOORRTT**	ROTATOR	**APRSSWY**	PSYWARS
ANNOSTY	TANNOYS	**AOORRTU**	OUTROAR	**APRSTTU**	STARTUP
ANNOTTY	TANTONY	**AOORRTY**	ORATORY		UPSTART
ANNPSSU	SANNUPS	**AOORSTT**	TOOARTS	**APRSTTY**	TAPSTRY
	UNSNAPS	**AOORSTU**	OUTSOAR	**APRSUWY**	SPURWAY
ANNPSTU	PANTUNS	**AOORSTV**	OVATORS	**APSSTUY**	UPSTAYS
ANNRTYY	TYRANNY	**AOOSTTT**	TATTOOS	**APSSUWY**	UPSWAYS
ANNSSTU	SUNTANS	**AOOSTUZ**	AZOTOUS	**AQRTUYZ**	QUARTZY
ANNSSTY	SYNTANS	**AOOTXYZ**	ZOOTAXY	**AQSTTUY**	SQUATTY
ANOOPRS	PRONAOS	**AOPPPSU**	PAPPOUS	**ARSSSTU**	TUSSARS
	SOPRANO	**AOPPRRT**	RAPPORT	**ARSSTTU**	STRATUS
ANOOPRT	PATROON	**AOPPRST**	APPORTS	**ARSSTTY**	STARTSY
	PRONOTA	**AOPPRST**	PARROTS	**ASSTTUY**	STATUSY
ANOORST	RATOONS		RAPTORS	**AVYYZZZ**	ZYZZYVA
	SANTOOR	**AOPRRSU**	UPROARS	**BBBDELO**	BLOBBED
ANOORTT	ARNOTTO	**AOPRRSW**	SPARROW		BOBBLED
	RATTOON	**AOPRRTY**	PARROTY	**BBBDELU**	BLUBBED
ANOPRRS	SPORRAN		PORTRAY		BUBBLED
ANOPRSS	PARSONS	**AOPRSST**	ASPORTS	**BBBEILS**	BIBBLES
	SANPROS		PASTORS	**BBBEIOS**	BOBBIES
ANOPRST	PARTONS	**AOPRSSU**	SAPOURS	**BBBEIRS**	BIBBERS
	PATRONS		UPSOARS	**BBBEIRY**	BIBBERY
	TARPONS	**AOPRSTU**	ASPROUT	**BBBEISU**	BUBBIES
ANOPRSW	PAWNORS	**AOPRSTW**	POSTWAR	**BBBELOS**	BOBBLES
ANOPRTV	PROVANT	**AOPRSUV**	VAPOURS	**BBBELRU**	BLUBBER
ANOPSTT	OPTANTS	**AOPRTTU**	OUTPART		BUBBLER
ANOPSTU	OUTSPAN	**AOPRTUY**	OUTPRAY	**BBBELSU**	BUBBLES
ANOPSUY	YAUPONS	**AOPRUVY**	VAPOURY	**BBBEORS**	BOBBERS
ANORRSW	NARROWS	**AOPSSTU**	OUTPASS	**BBBEORY**	BOBBERY
ANORRWW	WARWORN		PASSOUT	**BBBGIIN**	BIBBING
ANORSSV	SOVRANS	**AOPSTTX**	POSTTAX	**BBBGINO**	BOBBING
ANORSTT	ATTORNS	**AOPSTUY**	AUTOPSY	**BBBHIOS**	BOBBISH
	RATTONS		PAYOUTS	**BBBHSUU**	HUBBUBS
	ROTTANS	**AOPSTWY**	WAYPOST	**BBBINOS**	BOBBINS
ANORSTU	ROUSANT	**AOPTTUU**	AUTOPUT	**BBBIOTT**	BOBBITT
	SANTOUR	**AOQRSTU**	QUARTOS	**BBCCIKO**	BIBCOCK
ANORSTY	AROYNTS	**AORRSST**	SARTORS	**BBCDEHI**	CHIBBED
ANORSUU	ANUROUS	**AORRSSU**	ASSUROR	**BBCDEIR**	CRIBBED
	URANOUS	**AORRSTW**	TARROWS	**BBCDELO**	COBBLED
ANORWWY	WAYWORN	**AORRSWY**	SOWARRY	**BBCDELU**	CLUBBED
ANOSSTZ	STANZOS		YARROWS	**BBCEEHO**	BOBECHE
ANOSTTU	TOTANUS	**AORSSST**	ASSORTS	**BBCEEIR**	BERBICE
ANPPSUW	SUPPAWN	**AORSSTT**	STATORS	**BBCEHIN**	NEBBICH
ANPRSSU	UNSPARS	**AORSSTU**	SOUTARS	**BBCEILR**	CRIBBLE
ANPRSTU	SUNTRAP	**AORSSUV**	SAVOURS	**BBCEIOR**	COBBIER
	UNSTRAP	**AORSSUY**	OSSUARY	**BBCEIRR**	CRIBBER
			SUASORY	**BBCEIRU**	CUBBIER
ANPRSUW	UNWRAPS	**AORSTUW**	OUTWARS	**BBCEISU**	CUBBIES
ANPRSUY	UNPRAYS	**AORSTUY**	YAOURTS	**BBCEKKO**	KEBBOCK
ANPSSUW	SUPAWNS	**AORSUVY**	SAVOURY	**BBCEKKU**	KEBBUCK
ANPSTUU	TUPUNAS	**AORTUVY**	AVOUTRY	**BBCELOR**	CLOBBER
ANRSSTU	SANTURS	**AORUVVY**	VOUVRAY		COBBLER
	SUNSTAR	**AOSSTTT**	STATTOS	**BBCELOS**	COBBLES
ANRSSUY	SUNRAYS	**AOSSTUY**	OUTSAYS	**BBCELRU**	CLUBBER
ANRSTTU	TRUANTS	**AOSTTTW**	TATTOWS	**BBCEORS**	COBBERS
ANRSTTY	TYRANTS	**AOSTTUY**	OUTSTAY	**BBCEOSW**	COBWEBS
ANRSUWY	RUNWAYS	**APPRRUU**	PURPURA	**BBCGINO**	COBBING
ANSSTTU	TUTSANS				

BBCGINU	CUBBING	BBDIOOR	BOOBIRD	BBEILRT	TRIBBLE
BBCHISU	CUBBISH	BBDIRUY	RUBBIDY	BBEILSS	BIBLESS
BBCINOU	BUBONIC	BBDKSUY	DYBBUKS	BBEILST	STIBBLE
BBCRSUY	SCRUBBY	BBEEEES	BEEBEES	BBEILSW	WIBBLES
BBDDEIL	DIBBLED	BBEEERR	BERBERE	BBEILSY	YIBBLES
BBDDEIR	DRIBBED	BBEEERU	BEBEERU	BBEIMOS	BIMBOES
BBDDERU	DRUBBED	BBEEIKS	KEBBIES		MOBBIES
BBDEEIR	DEBBIER	BBEEIRS	BRIBEES	BBEINOR	NOBBIER
BBDEEIS	DEBBIES	BBEEIRW	WEBBIER	BBEINRU	NUBBIER
BBDEELP	PEBBLED	BBEEISW	WEBBIES	BBEIOOS	BOOBIES
BBDEENS	SNEBBED	BBEEKLS	LEBBEKS	BBEIOOT	BOBOTIE
BBDEEOR	BEROBED	BBEELPS	PEBBLES	BBEIRRS	BRIBERS
BBDEFLO	FLOBBED	BBEELSS	EBBLESS		RIBBERS
BBDEFLU	FLUBBED	BBEENSS	SNEBBES	BBEIRRY	BRIBERY
BBDEGIL	GLIBBED	BBEFILR	FRIBBLE	BBEIRSU	RUBBIES
BBDEGLO	GOBBLED	BBEFIRS	FIBBERS	BBEIRTU	TUBBIER
BBDEGRU	GRUBBED	BBEFIRU	FUBBIER	BBEISSU	BUSBIES
BBDEGSU	BEDBUGS	BBEFIRY	FIBBERY		SUBBIES
BBDEHLO	HOBBLED	BBEFLRU	FLUBBER	BBEISTU	STUBBIE
BBDEIIM	IMBIBED	BBEFRUY	FUBBERY	BBEJORS	JOBBERS
BBDEIKL	KIBBLED	BBEGIKN	KEBBING	BBEJORY	JOBBERY
BBDEILN	NIBBLED	BBEGILR	GLIBBER	BBEKLNO	KNOBBLE
BBDEILO	BILOBED		GRIBBLE	BBEKLNU	KNUBBLE
	LOBBIED	BBEGINN	NEBBING	BBEKLOS	BLESBOK
BBDEILR	DIBBLER	BBEGINW	WEBBING	BBEKLUU	BUBUKLE
	DRIBBLE	BBEGIOR	GOBBIER	BBEKNOR	KNOBBER
BBDEILS	DIBBLES	BBEGIOS	GIBBOSE	BBEKNSU	NEBBUKS
BBDEILW	WIBBLED	BBEGIRS	GIBBERS	BBELLOY	BELLBOY
BBDEINS	SNIBBED	BBEGIST	GIBBETS	BBELLSU	BULBELS
BBDEIOS	DOBBIES	BBEGLOR	GOBBLER	BBELLTU	BULBLET
BBDEIRR	DRIBBER	BBEGLOS	GOBBLES	BBELMOS	MOBBLES
BBDEIRS	DIBBERS	BBEGLRU	GRUBBLE	BBELMOT	BOMBLET
BBDEKNO	KNOBBED	BBEGNSU	BEBUNGS	BBELMRU	BUMBLER
BBDELMO	MOBBLED	BBEGOST	GOBBETS	BBELMSU	BUMBLES
BBDELMU	BUMBLED	BBEGRRU	GRUBBER	BBELNOR	NOBBLER
BBDELNO	NOBBLED	BBEHIKS	KIBBEHS	BBELNOS	NOBBLES
BBDELNU	NUBBLED	BBEHINS	NEBBISH	BBELNSU	NUBBLES
BBDELOO	BEBLOOD	BBEHIOS	HOBBIES	BBELNSY	NYBBLES
BBDELOS	BOBSLED	BBEHISU	HUBBIES	BBELORS	LOBBERS
BBDELOW	WOBBLED	BBEHLOR	HOBBLER		SLOBBER
BBDELRU	BLURBED	BBEHLOS	HOBBLES	BBELORU	BOERBUL
	BURBLED	BBEHMTU	BETHUMB	BBELORW	WOBBLER
	RUBBLED	BBEHORS	HOBBERS	BBELORY	LOBBYER
BBDELSU	SLUBBED	BBEIIKL	BIBLIKE	BBELOST	BOBLETS
BBDEMSU	BEDUMBS	BBEIILR	RIBIBLE	BBELOSW	WOBBLES
BBDENSU	SNUBBED	BBEIILS	BILBIES	BBELRRU	BURBLER
BBDEORS	DOBBERS	BBEIIMR	IMBIBER	BBELRSU	BURBLES
BBDEOST	STOBBED	BBEIIMS	IMBIBES		LUBBERS
BBDEOSW	SWOBBED	BBEIIRR	RIBBIER		RUBBLES
BBDERRU	DRUBBER	BBEIIRS	RIBIBES		SLUBBER
BBDERSU	DUBBERS	BBEIJOS	JOBBIES	BBELSTU	STUBBLE
BBDESSU	SUBDEBS	BBEIJRS	JIBBERS	BBEMNSU	BENUMBS
BBDESTU	STUBBED	BBEIKLS	KIBBLES	BBEMORS	BOMBERS
BBDFLUU	FLUBDUB	BBEILNR	NIBBLER		MOBBERS
BBDGIIN	DIBBING	BBEILNS	NIBBLES	BBENOTW	BOWBENT
BBDGINO	DOBBING	BBEILOS	BILBOES	BBENRSU	SNUBBER
BBDGINU	DUBBING		LOBBIES	BBENSSU	SNUBBES
BBDIKSU	DIBBUKS	BBEILOT	BIBELOT	BBEOOSY	YOBBOES
BBDILRY	DRIBBLY	BBEILPR	PRIBBLE	BBEORRS	ROBBERS
BBDINOS	DOBBINS	BBEILQU	QUIBBLE	BBEORRY	ROBBERY
BBDINSU	DUBBINS	BBEILRS	LIBBERS	BBEORSS	SOBBERS

BBEORSW	SWOBBER	**BBIMOSY**	YOBBISM	**BCDEKLU**	BUCKLED
BBEORYY	YOBBERY	**BBINNSU**	NUBBINS	**BCDEKOR**	BEDROCK
BBEPRUW	BREWPUB	**BBINORS**	RIBBONS		BROCKED
BBERRSU	RUBBERS		ROBBINS	**BCDEKOY**	BOCKEDY
BBERRUY	RUBBERY	**BBINORY**	RIBBONY	**BCDEKSU**	BEDUCKS
BBERSTU	TUBBERS	**BBIRTUY**	RUBBITY	**BCDELOU**	BECLOUD
BBFGIIN	FIBBING	**BBJLOOW**	BLOWJOB	**BCDEMOR**	CROMBED
BBFGINO	FOBBING	**BBKLNOY**	KNOBBLY	**BCDEMRU**	CRUMBED
BBFGINU	FUBBING	**BBKLNUY**	KNUBBLY	**BCDENOU**	BOUNCED
BBFILSU	BIBFULS	**BBKLOOU**	BLOUBOK		BUNCOED
BBGGIIN	GIBBING	**BBKOOOO**	BOOBOOK	**BCDEORU**	COURBED
BBGGINO	GOBBING	**BBKOOSS**	BOSBOKS	**BCDEORW**	BECROWD
BBGGINU	GUBBING	**BBLLSUU**	BULBULS	**BCDEOSU**	SUBCODE
BBGHINO	HOBBING	**BBLOSUU**	BULBOUS	**BCDESUU**	SUBDUCE
BBGIIJN	JIBBING	**BBLOSWY**	BLOWBYS	**BCDHIOR**	BICHORD
BBGIILN	LIBBING	**BBLSTUY**	STUBBLY	**BCDHIRU**	BRUCHID
BBGIINN	NIBBING	**BBMOOOX**	BOOMBOX	**BCDHOOU**	CUBHOOD
BBGIINR	BRIBING	**BBNNOOS**	BONBONS	**BCDIIRU**	RUBIDIC
	RIBBING	**BBNOOOS**	BONOBOS	**BCDILOO**	COLOBID
BBGIJNO	JOBBING	**BBNOORU**	BOURBON	**BCDINOW**	COWBIND
BBGILLU	BILLBUG	**BBOOOOS**	BOOBOOS	**BCDIORW**	COWBIRD
BBGILNO	LOBBING	**BBOOSSY**	BOSSBOY	**BCDIOSU**	CUBOIDS
BBGILNU	BULBING	**BBOOSUU**	BOUBOUS	**BCDIRSY**	CYBRIDS
BBGIMNO	BOMBING	**BBORSTU**	BURBOTS	**BCDKORU**	BURDOCK
	MOBBING	**BBOSSUY**	BUSBOYS	**BCDNOSU**	BONDUCS
BBGINNU	NUBBING	**BBRSSUU**	SUBURBS	**BCDSTUU**	SUBDUCT
BBGINOO	BOOBING	**BCCEEHS**	CHEBECS	**BCEEEHN**	BEECHEN
BBGINOR	ROBBING	**BCCEIIS**	BICCIES	**BCEEEHS**	BEECHES
BBGINOS	GIBBONS	**BCCEILO**	ECBOLIC		BESEECH
	SOBBING	**BCCEILU**	CUBICLE	**BCEEFIN**	BENEFIC
BBGINPU	PUBBING	**BCCEILY**	BICYCLE	**BCEEFKL**	BEFLECK
BBGINRU	RUBBING	**BCCEIOS**	BOCCIES	**BCEEGIR**	ICEBERG
BBGINSU	GUBBINS	**BCCEMOR**	CROMBEC	**BCEEHIP**	EPHEBIC
	SUBBING	**BCCILOU**	BUCOLIC	**BCEEHIT**	HEBETIC
BBGINTU	TUBBING	**BCCILUY**	CUBICLY	**BCEEHLR**	BELCHER
BBGIOSU	GIBBOUS	**BCCINOO**	OBCONIC	**BCEEHLS**	BELCHES
BBGIOSW	BOBWIGS	**BCCISUU**	SUCCUBI	**BCEEHNR**	BENCHER
BBHHIOS	HOBBISH	**BCCMOOX**	COXCOMB	**BCEEHNS**	BENCHES
BBHIMOS	MOBBISH	**BCCMSUU**	SUCCUMB	**BCEEHOS**	OBECHES
BBHIOOS	BOOBISH	**BCCNOOR**	CORNCOB	**BCEEHOU**	BOUCHEE
BBHIOST	HOBBITS	**BCDEEHL**	BELCHED	**BCEEIMR**	BECRIME
BBHIOSY	YOBBISH	**BCDEEHN**	BENCHED	**BCEEIPS**	BESPICE
BBHIRSU	RUBBISH	**BCDEEIL**	DECIBEL	**BCEEIRS**	ESCRIBE
BBHISTU	TUBBISH	**BCDEEKS**	BEDECKS	**BCEEIRT**	TEREBIC
BBHJOOS	HOBJOBS	**BCDEENU**	BEDUNCE	**BCEEKNS**	NEBECKS
BBHKOOS	BOSHBOK	**BCDEHIR**	BIRCHED	**BCEEKNU**	BUCKEEN
BBHNOOS	HOBNOBS	**BCDEHIT**	BITCHED	**BCEEKRS**	REBECKS
BBHOOUW	WHOOBUB	**BCDEHNU**	BUNCHED	**BCEEKST**	BECKETS
BBIIILM	BILIMBI	**BCDEHOR**	BROCHED	**BCEEKSZ**	ZEBECKS
BBIIKTZ	KIBBITZ	**BCDEHOT**	BOTCHED	**BCEEKUY**	BUCKEYE
BBIILST	BIBLIST	**BCDEHOU**	DEBOUCH	**BCEELOS**	ECBOLES
BBIISUU	BUIBUIS	**BCDEIIO**	BIOCIDE	**BCEELOU**	BOUCLEE
BBIJMOO	JIBBOOM	**BCDEIKR**	BRICKED	**BCEEMOS**	BECOMES
BBIJNOS	JIBBONS	**BCDEIKS**	SICKBED	**BCEENOS**	OBSCENE
BBIKOSS	SKIBOBS	**BCDEIKT**	BEDTICK	**BCEENRU**	CRUBEEN
BBIKTUZ	KIBBUTZ	**BCDEILM**	CLIMBED	**BCEEQSU**	QUEBECS
BBILLSU	BULBILS	**BCDEILO**	DOCIBLE	**BCEERSU**	BECURSE
BBILLUU	LULIBUB	**BCDEIOS**	BODICES	**BCEFIIS**	SEBIFIC
BBILNOY	NOBBILY		CEBOIDS	**BCEGIKN**	BECKING
BBIMMOS	MOBBISM	**BCDEIRS**	SCRIBED	**BCEGLOS**	BECLOGS
		BCDEKLO	BLOCKED	**BCEHINR**	BIRCHEN

BCEHINT	BENTHIC	BCEKMOS	BEMOCKS	BCHLSSU	SCHLUBS
	BITCHEN	BCEKNOS	BECKONS	BCHNOOR	BRONCHO
BCEHIOR	BRIOCHE	BCEKORT	BROCKET	BCHOORS	BROCHOS
BCEHIOT	BIOTECH	BCEKORU	ROEBUCK	BCHORST	BORSCHT
BCEHIRS	BIRCHES	BCEKOSU	BUCKOES		BORTSCH
BCEHIST	BITCHES	BCEKOTY	BYCOKET	BCIIKLN	NIBLICK
BCEHITW	BEWITCH	BCEKRSU	BUCKERS	BCIILMU	BULIMIC
BCEHLRU	BLUCHER	BCEKSTU	BESTUCK	BCIILOR	COLIBRI
BCEHNSU	BUNCHES		BUCKETS	BCIILSY	SIBYLIC
BCEHORS	BROCHES	BCELLOW	COWBELL	BCIINOS	BIONICS
BCEHORT	BOTCHER	BCELLSU	SUBCELL	BCIINOT	BIONTIC
BCEHORW	COWHERB	BCELMNU	CLUBMEN	BCIIOPS	BIOPICS
BCEHOSS	BOSCHES	BCELMOS	COMBLES		BIOPSIC
BCEHOST	BOTCHES	BCELMRU	CLUMBER	BCIIOPT	BIOPTIC
BCEHOSU	BOUCHES		CRUMBLE	BCIIOST	BIOTICS
	SUBECHO	BCELMSU	SCUMBLE	BCIISTU	BISCUIT
BCEHRSU	CHERUBS	BCELNOW	BECLOWN	BCIKKOX	KICKBOX
BCEHRTU	BUTCHER	BCELORS	CORBELS	BCIKNOS	KINCOBS
BCEHSTU	BUTCHES	BCELOSU	BOUCLES	BCIKORT	BROCKIT
BCEIIKR	BRICKIE	BCELRSU	BECURLS	BCIKOTT	BITTOCK
BCEIIKS	BICKIES	BCELSSU	CUBLESS	BCILMPU	PLUMBIC
BCEIISV	VIBICES	BCEMNTU	CUMBENT		UPCLIMB
BCEIKLM	LIMBECK	BCEMOOS	COOMBES	BCILOOR	BICOLOR
BCEIKLO	BLOCKIE	BCEMORS	COMBERS		BROCOLI
BCEIKLR	BRICKLE		RECOMBS	BCILPSU	PUBLICS
BCEIKNR	BRICKEN	BCEMRRU	CRUMBER	BCIMNOU	UMBONIC
BCEIKRS	BICKERS	BCEMRSU	CUMBERS	BCIMSSU	CUBISMS
BCEIKST	BESTICK		SCUMBER	BCINOOR	BORONIC
BCEIKSU	BUCKIES	BCENORU	BOUNCER	BCINOOS	BOSONIC
BCEILMO	EMBOLIC	BCENOSU	BOUNCES	BCINORS	BICORNS
BCEILMR	CLIMBER	BCEORSS	SCROBES		BICRONS
	RECLIMB	BCEORSU	BESCOUR	BCINORU	RUBICON
BCEILMS	EMBLICS		OBSCURE	BCINRSU	BRUCINS
	LIMBECS	BCERRSU	CURBERS	BCINSUU	INCUBUS
BCEILNO	BINOCLE	BCERSTU	BECRUST	BCIOORT	ROBOTIC
BCEILOR	BRICOLE		BECURST	BCIORSS	BORSICS
	CORBEIL	BCESSTU	SUBSECT	BCIORST	STROBIC
BCEILOS	COLBIES	BCFKMUU	BUMFUCK	BCIOSTY	SYBOTIC
BCEILOU	CIBOULE	BCFSSUU	SUBFUSC	BCIRRSU	RUBRICS
BCEILSY	BEYLICS	BCGIKNO	BOCKING	BCIRTUY	BUTYRIC
BCEIMNO	COMBINE	BCGIKNU	BUCKING	BCISSTU	BUSTICS
BCEIMOR	COMBIER	BCGIMNO	COMBING		CUBISTS
	MICROBE	BCGINNU	BUNCING	BCISTUU	CUBITUS
BCEIMOS	COMBIES	BCGINRU	CURBING	BCJKMUU	JUMBUCK
BCEINOR	BICORNE	BCGORSU	COBURGS	BCKLLOO	BOLLOCK
BCEINOS	EBONICS	BCGORSY	CYBORGS	BCKLLOU	BULLOCK
BCEINOZ	BENZOIC	BCHHORS	BORSHCH	BCKLNOU	UNBLOCK
BCEINRU	BRUCINE	BCHIIOP	BIOCHIP	BCKLOOX	LOCKBOX
BCEIORS	CORBIES	BCHIIOT	COHIBIT	BCKMMOU	BUMMOCK
BCEIRRS	SCRIBER	BCHIIRR	BIRCHIR	BCKMOSU	BUCKSOM
BCEIRSS	SCRIBES	BCHIIRS	BICHIRS	BCKNNOO	BONNOCK
BCEIRSU	SUBERIC	BCHIKOU	CHIBOUK	BCKNSUU	NUBUCKS
BCEIRTU	BRUCITE	BCHIKOY	BOYCHIK	BCKOTTU	BUTTOCK
BCEISST	BISECTS	BCHIKSU	BUCKISH	BCLMOOU	COULOMB
BCEJOST	OBJECTS	BCHILMY	CHIMBLY	BCLMRUY	CRUMBLY
BCEJSTU	SUBJECT	BCHILOS	CHIBOLS	BCLOOSU	COLOBUS
BCEKLLO	BELLOCK	BCHIMOR	RHOMBIC		SUBCOOL
BCEKLOR	BLOCKER	BCHINOR	BRONCHI	BCLORTU	CLOTBUR
BCEKLRU	BRUCKLE	BCHIOPR	PIBROCH	BCLSTUU	SUBCULT
	BUCKLER	BCHIOPS	PHOBICS	BCMMRUU	CRUMBUM
BCEKLSU	BUCKLES	BCHLOTY	BLOTCHY	BCMOOST	TOMBOCS

BCMORSY	CORYMBS	BDEEEIS	BEEDIES		ELBOWED
BCMOSTU	COMBUST	BDEEELL	DELEBLE	BDEELRT	TREBLED
BCNOORS	BRONCOS	BDEEELP	BLEEPED	BDEELSS	BEDLESS
BCNOSTU	COBNUTS	BDEEELR	BLEEDER		BLESSED
BCNRSUU	UNCURBS	BDEEELT	BEETLED	BDEELTT	BLETTED
BCOOOOS	BOOCOOS	BDEEELV	BEVELED	BDEELZZ	BEZZLED
BCOOPYY	COPYBOY	BDEEEMN	BEDEMEN	BDEEMOS	BESOMED
BCOOSWY	COWBOYS	BDEEEMT	BEMETED	BDEEMOW	EMBOWED
BCOOTTU	BOOTCUT	BDEEENS	BENDEES	BDEEMOX	EMBOXED
BCOOTTY	BOYCOTT	BDEEEPS	BESPEED	BDEEMRU	EMBRUED
BCTUUZZ	BUZZCUT	BDEEERR	BREEDER		UMBERED
BDDDEIU	BUDDIED		BREERED	BDEEMSU	BEMUSED
BDDDELU	BUDDLED		REBREED		EMBUSED
BDDDEOR	BRODDED	BDEEERZ	BREEZED	BDEENOR	DEBONER
BDDEEER	REEDBED	BDEEEST	DEBTEES		ENROBED
BDDEEES	SEEDBED	BDEEFIR	BRIEFED		REDBONE
BDDEEEW	BEDEWED		DEBRIEF	BDEENOS	DEBONES
BDDEEIL	BIELDED		FIBERED	BDEENPR	PREBEND
BDDEEIR	DEBRIDE	BDEEFOX	FEEDBOX	BDEENRR	BREDREN
BDDEEIS	BEDSIDE	BDEEGOR	BEGORED	BDEENRS	BENDERS
BDDEEIT	BETIDED	BDEEGOY	BOGEYED	BDEEORR	REBORED
	DEBITED	BDEEGSU	BUGSEED	BDEEORS	BEDSORE
BDDEELN	BLENDED	BDEEHOV	BEHOVED		SOBERED
BDDEENO	DEBONED	BDEEHRT	BERTHED	BDEEORV	OVERBED
BDDEERS	BEDDERS	BDEEIKL	BEDLIKE	BDEEORW	BOWERED
BDDEESU	DEBUSED	BDEEIKN	BEINKED	BDEEOSX	SEEDBOX
BDDEETU	DEBUTED	BDEEILL	BELLIED	BDEERSU	BURSEED
BDDEGIN	BEDDING		DELIBLE	BDEERUW	BURWEED
BDDEGIR	BRIDGED		LIBELED	BDEESSU	DEBUSES
BDDEGLU	BLUDGED	BDEEILS	EDIBLES	BDEFFLU	BLUFFED
BDDEIIR	BIRDIED	BDEEILV	BEDEVIL	BDEFILR	FILBERD
BDDEIIS	BIDDIES	BDEEIMR	BEMIRED	BDEFLMU	FUMBLED
BDDEILN	BLINDED		BERIMED	BDEFLOU	BODEFUL
BDDEILR	BRIDLED	BDEEIMT	BEDTIME	BDEFOOR	FORBODE
BDDEILU	BUILDED		BETIMED	BDEGGLO	BLOGGED
BDDEINR	BRINDED	BDEEIMX	BEMIXED		BOGGLED
BDDEINU	BUNDIED	BDEEINR	BENDIER	BDEGGOR	BROGGED
BDDEIOO	BOODIED		INBREED	BDEGHIT	BEDIGHT
BDDEIRR	REDBIRD	BDEEINZ	BEDIZEN		BIGHTED
BDDEIRS	BIDDERS	BDEEIRR	BERRIED	BDEGHOU	BOUGHED
BDDEIRU	BUDDIER		BRIERED	BDEGILN	BINGLED
BDDEISU	BUDDIES	BDEEIRS	BREDIES	BDEGILO	OBLIGED
BDDELNU	BUNDLED		DERBIES	BDEGILS	BEGILDS
BDDELOO	BLOODED	BDEEIRT	BEDRITE	BDEGINN	BENDING
	BOODLED	BDEEISS	BESIDES	BDEGINO	BOINGED
BDDELOR	BRODDLE	BDEEIST	BETIDES	BDEGINR	BREDING
BDDELOS	BODDLES	BDEEIVV	BEVVIED	BDEGIOO	BOOGIED
BDDELOU	DOUBLED	BDEEJLS	DJEBELS	BDEGIOR	BODGIER
BDDELSU	BUDDLES	BDEEJMS	DJEMBES	BDEGIOS	BODGIES
BDDENOU	BOUNDED	BDEEKMO	KEMBOED	BDEGIOT	BIGOTED
BDDEOOR	BROODED	BDEEKRU	REBUKED	BDEGIRS	BEGIRDS
BDDEORU	OBDURED	BDEELLS	BEDELLS		BRIDGES
BDDEOTU	DOUBTED	BDEELMR	REMBLED	BDEGIRU	BRIGUED
BDDERSU	BUDDERS	BDEELMS	SEMBLED	BDEGISU	BUDGIES
	REDBUDS	BDEELMU	UMBELED	BDEGLNU	BLUNGED
BDDESUU	SUBDUED	BDEELNR	BLENDER		BUNGLED
BDDGIIN	BIDDING		REBLEND	BDEGLRU	BLUDGER
BDDGINU	BUDDING	BDEELNS	BLENDES		BURGLED
BDDGIOR	BIRDDOG	BDEELNT	BENDLET	BDEGLSU	BLUDGES
BDDISSU	DISBUDS	BDEELOV	BELOVED	BDEGNOW	BEDGOWN
BDEEEFL	FEEBLED	BDEELOW	BOWELED	BDEGNSU	BEDUNGS

BDEGOOY	GOODBYE	BDEINRY	BINDERY	BDELOST	BOLDEST
BDEGORS	BODGERS	BDEINST	BIDENTS	BDELOSU	BLOUSED
BDEGORU	BUDGERO	BDEINSU	BEDUINS		DOUBLES
BDEGRSU	BEDRUGS		BUNDIES	BDELOSW	BLOWSED
	BUDGERS	BDEIOOR	DOOBRIE	BDELOTT	BLOTTED
	REDBUGS	BDEIOOS	BOODIES		BOTTLED
BDEGSTU	BUDGETS		DOOBIES	BDELOTU	BOULTED
BDEHINS	BEHINDS	BDEIORR	BROIDER		DOUBLET
BDEHIRT	BIRTHED	BDEIORS	BORIDES	BDELOWZ	BLOWZED
BDEHLMU	HUMBLED		DISROBE	BDELRRU	BLURRED
BDEHLOS	BEHOLDS	BDEIORT	DEBITOR	BDELRTU	BLURTED
BDEHLSU	BLUSHED		DEORBIT	BDELSSU	BUDLESS
BDEHMTU	THUMBED		ORBITED	BDELSTU	BUSTLED
BDEHORY	HERDBOY	BDEIORV	OVERBID	BDELSWY	LEWDSBY
BDEHOST	HOTBEDS	BDEIORZ	ZEBROID	BDELTTU	BUTTLED
BDEHRSU	BRUSHED	BDEIOSY	DISOBEY	BDEMNNO	BONDMEN
BDEIIRS	BIRDIES	BDEIPRS	PREBIDS	BDEMNOU	EMBOUND
	BRIDIES	BDEIRRS	BIRDERS	BDEMOOR	BEDROOM
BDEIIVV	BIVVIED	BDEIRST	BESTRID		BOREDOM
BDEIJLR	JIRBLED		BISTRED		BROOMED
BDEIKLN	BLINKED	BDEIRSU	BRUISED	BDEMOOS	BOSOMED
BDEIKLU	BUDLIKE		BURDIES	BDEMORS	SOMBRED
BDEIKMO	KIMBOED	BDEIRSV	VERBIDS	BDEMSTU	DUMBEST
BDEIKNO	BOINKED	BDEIRTU	BRUITED	BDENNOU	BOUNDEN
BDEIKRS	BRISKED	BDEIRTY	BEDIRTY		UNBONED
BDEILLU	BULLIED	BDEISST	BEDSITS	BDENNSU	UNBENDS
BDEILMS	DIMBLES	BDEISSU	SUBSIDE	BDENORS	BONDERS
BDEILMW	WIMBLED	BDEISTU	BUISTED	BDENORU	BOUNDER
BDEILNN	BLINNED		SUBEDIT		REBOUND
BDEILNR	BLINDER	BDEITUY	DUBIETY		UNROBED
	BRINDLE	BDEJLMU	JUMBLED	BDENORW	BROWNED
BDEILNS	BINDLES	BDEJORU	OBJURED	BDENORZ	BRONZED
BDEILNY	BYLINED	BDEKLNU	BLUNKED	BDENOST	OBTENDS
BDEILOP	LOBIPED	BDEKNOO	BOOKEND	BDENOSY	BEYONDS
BDEILOR	BROILED	BDEKNOU	BUNKOED	BDENOUW	UNBOWED
BDEILOS	BOLIDES	BDEKNSU	DEBUNKS	BDENOUX	UNBOXED
BDEILOX	BOLIXED	BDEKOOR	BROOKED	BDENRSU	BURDENS
BDEILPP	BLIPPED	BDELLOR	BEDROLL	BDENRTU	BRUNTED
BDEILRR	BRIDLER	BDELMMU	BUMMLED	BDENSSU	SUNBEDS
BDEILRS	BIRSLED		MUMBLED	BDENSTU	SUBTEND
	BRIDLES	BDELMOO	BLOOMED	BDENSUY	SEBUNDY
BDEILRT	DRIBLET	BDELMPU	PLUMBED	BDEOORR	BROODER
BDEILRU	BLUDIER	BDELMRU	DRUMBLE	BDEOORS	BOORDES
	BUILDER		RUMBLED	BDEOORY	DOOBREY
	REBUILD	BDELMTU	TUMBLED	BDEOOST	BOOSTED
BDEILSS	BLISSED	BDELNOR	BLONDER	BDEOPRS	BEDROPS
BDEILST	BILSTED	BDELNOS	BLONDES	BDEOPRT	BEDROPT
BDEILTT	BLITTED		BOLDENS	BDEOPST	BEDPOST
BDEILTZ	BLITZED	BDELNOU	UNLOBED	BDEORRS	BORDERS
BDEIMMR	BRIMMED	BDELNRU	BLUNDER	BDEORRU	BORDURE
BDEIMNR	BIRDMEN		BUNDLER		BOURDER
BDEIMOR	BROMIDE	BDELNSU	BUNDLES	BDEORSS	DESORBS
BDEIMRU	IMBRUED	BDELNTU	BLUNTED	BDEORST	DEBTORS
BDEIMTU	BITUMED	BDELOOP	BLOOPED		STROBED
BDEINOR	INORBED	BDELOOR	BOODLER	BDEORSU	OBDURES
BDEINOU	BEDOUIN	BDELOOS	BOODLES		ROSEBUD
BDEINPR	PREBIND	BDELORS	BORDELS	BDEORSW	BROWSED
BDEINRR	BREDRIN	BDELORU	BOULDER	BDEORTU	DOUBTER
BDEINRS	BINDERS		DOUBLER		OBTRUDE
	INBREDS	BDELORW	BOWLDER		OUTBRED
	REBINDS		LOWBRED		REDOUBT

BDEORUV	OVERDUB	**BDIMNPU**	DUMPBIN	**BEEEJLW**	BEJEWEL
BDEPSTU	DUBSTEP	**BDIMNUU**	DUBNIUM	**BEEEJLZ**	JEZEBEL
BDERRSU	DEBURRS	**BDIMORS**	BROMIDS	**BEEEKLL**	BELLEEK
BDERSSU	SURBEDS	**BDINNOU**	INBOUND	**BEEEKLS**	KEBELES
BDERSTU	BURSTED	**BDINNSU**	UNBINDS	**BEEELPR**	BLEEPER
BDERSUU	SUBDUER	**BDINOOR**	BRIDOON	**BEEELRT**	BEETLER
BDERSUY	RUDESBY	**BDINOOW**	WOODBIN	**BEEELRV**	BEVELER
BDESSTU	BEDUSTS	**BDINOSU**	BOUDINS	**BEEELST**	BEETLES
	BESTUDS	**BDINOUY**	UNIBODY	**BEEEMOS**	BEESOME
BDESSUU	SUBDUES	**BDINPSU**	UPBINDS	**BEEEMRS**	BERSEEM
BDESSUW	SUBDEWS	**BDINRSU**	SUNBIRD	**BEEEMSS**	BESEEMS
BDFIILY	BIFIDLY	**BDINSTU**	BUNDIST	**BEEEMST**	BEMETES
BDFIIOR	FIBROID		DUSTBIN		BETEEMS
BDFIISU	FIDIBUS	**BDIOOOV**	OBOVOID	**BEEENNZ**	BENZENE
BDFIORS	FORBIDS	**BDIOORU**	BOUDOIR	**BEEENTW**	BETWEEN
BDGGINO	BODGING	**BDIOOST**	BIODOTS	**BEEEPRS**	BEEPERS
BDGGINU	BUDGING	**BDIORSW**	WOSBIRD	**BEEEPSW**	BEWEEPS
BDGGLOU	GOLDBUG	**BDIOSSY**	BYSSOID	**BEEERSS**	BREESES
BDGIINN	BINDING	**BDIOSTU**	OUTBIDS	**BEEERSZ**	BEEZERS
BDGIINR	BIRDING	**BDIOSUU**	DUBIOUS		BREEZES
	BRIDING	**BDIRSTU**	DISTURB	**BEEERTV**	BREVETE
BDGIINS	BIDINGS	**BDISSUY**	SUBSIDY	**BEEFGIN**	BEEFING
BDGIIOO	GOBIOID	**BDKLOOS**	KOBOLDS	**BEEFGIT**	BIGFEET
BDGIIOS	GOBIIDS	**BDKNOOU**	BUNDOOK	**BEEFILR**	FEBRILE
BDGILOO	GLOBOID	**BDLOOOX**	OXBLOOD	**BEEFILS**	BELIEFS
BDGIMNU	DUMBING	**BDMOOSS**	BOSSDOM	**BEEFILY**	BEEFILY
BDGINNO	BONDING	**BDMORUW**	BUDWORM	**BEEFINT**	BENEFIT
BDGINNU	BUNDING	**BDNNOOY**	NONBODY	**BEEFIRR**	BRIEFER
BDGINOS	BODINGS	**BDNNOUU**	UNBOUND	**BEEFIRS**	FRISBEE
BDGINOY	BODYING	**BDNOORU**	BOURDON	**BEEFLTY**	BEETFLY
BDGLLOU	BULLDOG	**BDNOOSS**	DOBSONS	**BEEFNRU**	FUNEBRE
BDGLOOT	DOGBOLT	**BDNOOWW**	DOWNBOW	**BEEFORY**	FOREBYE
BDGMSUU	MUDBUGS	**BDNOPUU**	UPBOUND	**BEEFRST**	BEFRETS
BDGOOOW	BOGWOOD	**BDNORTU**	TURBOND	**BEEGGNU**	GEEBUNG
BDGOOSY	GOODBYS	**BDNORUW**	RUBDOWN	**BEEGIIR**	BEIGIER
BDGORSU	DORBUGS	**BDNOSTU**	OBTUNDS	**BEEGILL**	LEGIBLE
BDHIINS	BHINDIS	**BDNOOWX**	BOXWOOD	**BEEGILO**	OBLIGEE
	BINDHIS		WOODBOX	**BEEGILR**	GLEBIER
BDHINOP	HOPBIND			**BEEGILS**	BEIGELS
BDHIOSU	BUSHIDO	**BDORSWY**	BYWORDS	**BEEGILU**	BEGUILE
BDHIRSY	HYBRIDS	**BEEEEFR**	FREEBEE	**BEEGIMR**	BEGRIME
BDHMOOO	HOBODOM	**BEEEEKS**	BESEEKE	**BEEGINN**	BEGINNE
BDHNSUU	BUHUNDS	**BEEEEMT**	BETEEME	**BEEGINP**	BEEPING
BDHOOOY	BOYHOOD	**BEEEENP**	PEEBEEN	**BEEGINR**	BIGENER
BDIIKNO	BODIKIN	**BEEEFIR**	BEEFIER		BREINGE
BDIILMS	DISLIMB		FREEBIE		REBEGIN
BDIILOR	OILBIRD	**BEEEFLR**	FEEBLER	**BEEGINS**	BEIGNES
BDIILOS	LIBIDOS	**BEEEFLS**	FEEBLES	**BEEGINT**	BEETING
BDIIMNS	MISBIND	**BEEEFTW**	WEBFEET		BEIGNET
BDIIMRS	MIDRIBS	**BEEEGIS**	BESIEGE	**BEEGINU**	BEGUINE
BDIISTT	TIDBITS	**BEEEGKL**	GEELBEK	**BEEGISY**	BIGEYES
BDIKNOR	BRODKIN	**BEEEGNR**	BREENGE	**BEEGLNO**	ENGLOBE
BDIKNOS	BODKINS	**BEEEGRR**	BERGERE	**BEEGMNO**	GOMBEEN
BDILLNY	BLINDLY	**BEEEHIV**	BEEHIVE	**BEEGMOU**	EMBOGUE
BDILNNU	UNBLIND	**BEEEHNS**	SHEBEEN	**BEEGNOO**	GOBONEE
BDILNUU	UNBUILD	**BEEEHPS**	EPHEBES	**BEEGNOS**	ENGOBES
BDILOOS	DIOBOLS	**BEEEIKL**	BEELIKE	**BEEGNRS**	BERGENS
BDILPUU	BUILDUP	**BEEEILL**	LIBELEE	**BEEGNRU**	REBEGUN
	UPBUILD	**BEEEILN**	BEELINE	**BEEGNSU**	BUNGEES
BDILRUY	BUIRDLY	**BEEEILV**	BELIEVE	**BEEGNTU**	UNBEGET
BDILTUY	DIBUTYL	**BEEEIRR**	BEERIER	**BEEGRSU**	BURGEES

BEEGSUY	BUGEYES	**BEEIRRS**	BERRIES	**BEENORY**	BONEYER
BEEHINS	BESHINE	**BEEIRRV**	BREVIER	**BEENOST**	BEENTOS
BEEHIOP	EPHEBOI	**BEEIRST**	REBITES		BONESET
BEEHIRR	HERBIER	**BEEIRSY**	RIBEYES	**BEENRRT**	BRENTER
BEEHIST	BHISTEE	**BEEIRTY**	EBRIETY	**BEENSTU**	BUTENES
BEEHKSU	BUKSHEE	**BEEISST**	BETISES		SUBTEEN
BEEHLRT	BLETHER	**BEEISTT**	BETTIES		
	HERBLET	**BEEISTW**	WEBSITE	**BEENSUV**	SUBVENE
BEEHLST	BETHELS	**BEEISVV**	BEVVIES	**BEEOOST**	BOOTEES
BEEHMRY	BERHYME	**BEEJNSU**	BUNJEES	**BEEOPPS**	BOPEEPS
BEEHNNO	HEBENON	**BEEJSSU**	BEJESUS	**BEEOPRR**	REPROBE
BEEHNOS	BESHONE	**BEEKMOS**	BESMOKE	**BEEOPRS**	BEPROSE
BEEHOOV	BEHOOVE	**BEEKNOT**	BETOKEN	**BEEORRS**	REBORES
BEEHOPS	EPHEBOS	**BEEKOPS**	BESPOKE		SOBERER
	PHOEBES	**BEEKORS**	REEBOKS	**BEEORRU**	BOURREE
BEEHORS	HERBOSE	**BEEKRRS**	BERSERK	**BEEORSV**	OBSERVE
BEEHORW	BEWHORE	**BEEKRRU**	REBUKER		OBVERSE
BEEHOST	BEHOTES	**BEEKRSU**	REBUKES		VERBOSE
BEEHOSV	BEHOVES	**BEELLMN**	BELLMEN	**BEEORSY**	OBEYERS
BEEHPSU	EPHEBUS	**BEELLOT**	LOBELET	**BEEORTV**	OVERBET
BEEHRST	BERTHES	**BEELMMS**	EMBLEMS	**BEEORWY**	EYEBROW
	SHERBET	**BEELMNT**	BELTMEN	**BEEOSST**	OBESEST
BEEHRSW	BESHREW	**BEELMOW**	EMBOWEL	**BEEPRRV**	PREVERB
BEEHRTY	THEREBY	**BEELMRS**	REMBLES	**BEEPRSU**	BURPEES
BEEHRWY	WHEREBY	**BEELMRT**	TREMBLE	**BEEQSTU**	BEQUEST
BEEHSST	BEHESTS	**BEELMSS**	SEMBLES	**BEERRST**	BERRETS
BEEHSTY	BHEESTY	**BEELNNO**	ENNOBLE	**BEERRSU**	BEURRES
BEEIJLU	JUBILEE	**BEELNOZ**	BENZOLE	**BEERRSV**	REVERBS
BEEIKLW	WEBLIKE	**BEELNRT**	REBLENT	**BEERRSW**	BREWERS
BEEILLR	LIBELER	**BEELNSU**	NEBULES	**BEERRWY**	BREWERY
BEEILLS	BELLIES	**BEELOST**	BOLETES	**BEERSST**	BREESTS
BEEILLV	BILEVEL	**BEELOSV**	BELOVES	**BEERSSU**	REBUSES
BEEILMP	EPIBLEM	**BEELOSY**	OBESELY		SUBSERE
BEEILMS	BESLIME	**BEELOTY**	EYEBOLT	**BEERSTT**	BETTERS
	BESMILE	**BEELPST**	BEPELTS	**BEERSTV**	BREVETS
BEEILNR	BERLINE	**BEELRSS**	BLESSER	**BEERSTW**	BESTREW
BEEILOS	OBELISE	**BEELRST**	BELTERS		WEBSTER
BEEILOZ	OBELIZE		TREBLES	**BEERTTU**	BURETTE
BEEILRS	BELIERS	**BEELRSY**	BERLEYS	**BEESSTU**	BUSTEES
BEEILRV	VERBILE	**BEELRUZ**	ZEBRULE	**BEETTUV**	BUVETTE
BEEILRY	BEERILY	**BEELSSS**	BLESSES	**BEFFIIS**	BIFFIES
BEEILTT	BETITLE	**BEELSSW**	WEBLESS	**BEFFIRS**	BIFFERS
BEEIMRS	BEMIRES	**BEELSZZ**	BEZZLES	**BEFFIRU**	BUFFIER
	BERIMES	**BEELTTU**	BLUETTE	**BEFFLRU**	BLUFFER
	BIREMES	**BEEMMRS**	MEMBERS	**BEFFOSU**	BOUFFES
BEEIMST	BETIMES	**BEEMNPT**	BENEMPT	**BEFFPSU**	BEPUFFS
BEEIMSX	BEMIXES	**BEEMNRY**	BYREMEN	**BEFFRSU**	BUFFERS
BEEINNS	BENNIES	**BEEMORW**	EMBOWER		REBUFFS
BEEINNZ	BENZINE	**BEEMOSS**	MEBOSES	**BEFFSTU**	BUFFEST
BEEINOS	EBONIES	**BEEMOSX**	EMBOXES		BUFFETS
	EBONISE	**BEEMRRU**	UMBRERE		
BEEINOT	EBONITE	**BEEMRSU**	EMBRUES	**BEFGIIL**	FILIBEG
BEEINOZ	EBONIZE	**BEEMRTU**	EMBRUTE	**BEFGIRU**	FIREBUG
BEEINPR	PEBRINE	**BEEMSSU**	BEMUSES	**BEFGIST**	BEGIFTS
BEEINRT	BENTIER		EMBUSES	**BEFGLSU**	BEGULFS
BEEINRZ	ZEBRINE	**BEENNRS**	BRENNES	**BEFHOOS**	BEHOOFS
BEEINSW	NEWBIES	**BEENNST**	BENNETS	**BEFILMS**	FIMBLES
BEEINWZ	WEBZINE	**BEENOOT**	BOTONEE	**BEFILNO**	LOBEFIN
BEEIORS	EBRIOSE	**BEENORR**	ENROBER	**BEFILNU**	BLUEFIN
BEEIOST	TOEBIES	**BEENORS**	BOREENS	**BEFILOS**	FOIBLES
BEEIQUZ	BEZIQUE		ENROBES	**BEFILOU**	BIOFUEL
				BEFILPY	PLEBIFY
				BEFILRT	FILBERT

BEFILRY	BRIEFLY	BEGILOS	OBLIGES	BEGNOTU	UNBEGOT
BEFILSU	FUSIBLE	BEGILRS	GERBILS	BEGNRSU	BUNGERS
	SUBFILE	BEGILRT	GILBERT	BEGNSUY	BUNGEYS
BEFINOR	BONFIRE	BEGILRU	BULGIER	BEGOORS	BOOGERS
BEFIOOR	BOOFIER	BEGILST	GIBLETS		GOOBERS
BEFIORS	FIBROSE	BEGIMNR	BERMING	BEGOOSY	BOOGEYS
BEFIORX	FIREBOX	BEGIMRS	BEGRIMS	BEGORSU	BROGUES
BEFIRST	BIFTERS	BEGINNU	UNBEING	BEGOSTU	BOUGETS
	FIBSTER	BEGINOS	BINGOES		OUTBEGS
BEFIRSU	FUBSIER		BIOGENS	BEGOSTW	BOWGETS
BEFIRVY	VERBIFY	BEGINOY	BIOGENY	BEGRRSU	BURGERS
BEFISTU	BUFTIES		OBEYING	BEGRSSU	BURGESS
BEFITUX	TUBIFEX	BEGINRR	BRINGER	BEHHKOT	KHOTBEH
BEFLLTY	FLYBELT	BEGINRS	BINGERS	BEHIIST	BHISTIE
BEFLLWY	FLYBLEW	BEGINRV	VERBING	BEHIITX	EXHIBIT
BEFLMRU	FUMBLER	BEGINRW	BREWING	BEHIKLO	HOBLIKE
BEFLMSU	BEFLUMS		WEBRING	BEHIKNT	BETHINK
	FUMBLES	BEGINRY	BREYING	BEHIKRS	KIRBEHS
BEFLOOS	BEFOOLS	BEGINSS	BESINGS	BEHILMS	BLEMISH
BEFLOSU	BEFOULS		BIGNESS	BEHILMT	THIMBLE
BEFLTUU	TUBEFUL	BEGINST	BESTING	BEHILOS	BOLSHIE
BEFOORR	FORBORE	BEGINSU	BEGUINS	BEHILRT	BLITHER
BEFOOTW	WEBFOOT		BUNGIES	BEHILST	THIBLES
BEFSSUU	SUBFEUS	BEGINTT	BETTING	BEHILSU	BLUEISH
BEGGGIN	BEGGING	BEGIOOS	BOOGIES		HELIBUS
BEGGIIS	BIGGIES		GOOBIES	BEHILSW	WEBLISH
BEGGINO	BEGOING	BEGIORV	OVERBIG	BEHIMOR	BIOHERM
BEGGIOR	BOGGIER	BEGIOSS	BIGOSES	BEHIMOY	YOHIMBE
BEGGIRU	BUGGIER	BEGIOSU	BOUGIES	BEHINOP	HIPBONE
BEGGIST	BIGGEST	BEGIRSU	BRIGUES		HOPBINE
BEGGISU	BUGGIES		RUGBIES	BEHINST	HENBITS
BEGGITY	BIGGETY	BEGISSU	GIBUSES	BEHIOST	BOTHIES
BEGGLOR	BLOGGER	BEGKMOS	GEMSBOK	BEHIOTW	HOWBEIT
	BOGGLER	BEGKNSU	BEGUNKS	BEHIRRT	REBIRTH
BEGGLOS	BOGGLES	BEGLLOU	GLOBULE	BEHIRST	HERBIST
BEGGORS	BOGGERS	BEGLMOO	BEGLOOM	BEHIRSU	BUSHIER
BEGGRSU	BUGGERS	BEGLMRU	GRUMBLE	BEHISSU	BUSHIES
BEGGRUY	BUGGERY	BEGLMUU	BLUEGUM	BEHISTT	THIBETS
BEGHHIT	BEHIGHT	BEGLNOS	BELONGS	BEHISTZ	ZIBETHS
BEGHINT	BENIGHT	BEGLNRU	BLUNGER	BEHKKOO	KOKOBEH
BEGHISS	BESIGHS		BUNGLER	BEHKORS	RHEBOKS
BEGHITT	BETIGHT	BEGLNSU	BLUNGES	BEHLLOP	BELLHOP
BEGHRRU	BURGHER		BUNGLES	BEHLLOX	HELLBOX
BEGIILR	BILGIER	BEGLOOS	GLOBOSE	BEHLMOW	WHOMBLE
BEGIIMT	BIGTIME	BEGLOOT	BOOTLEG	BEHLMRU	HUMBLER
BEGIINN	INBEING	BEGLOST	GOBLETS	BEHLMSU	HUMBLES
BEGIINR	BREIING	BEGLOSU	GLEBOUS	BEHLOOT	BOTHOLE
BEGIINS	BINGIES	BEGLOSW	BOWLEGS	BEHLORT	BROTHEL
BEGIKMN	KEMBING		WEBLOGS	BEHLOSW	BEHOWLS
BEGIKNR	KERBING	BEGLOUV	LOVEBUG	BEHLRRU	BURRHEL
BEGILLN	BELLING	BEGLRSU	BUGLERS	BEHLRSU	BLUSHER
BEGILLY	LEGIBLY		BULGERS		BURHELS
BEGILNO	IGNOBLE		BURGLES	BEHLSSU	BLUSHES
	INGLOBE	BEGLRTY	BERGYLT		BUSHELS
BEGILNR	BLINGER	BEGLSTU	BUGLETS	BEHLSTU	BLUSHET
BEGILNS	BINGLES	BEGMNOY	BOGYMEN	BEHMNSU	BUSHMEN
BEGILNT	BELTING	BEGNNUU	UNBEGUN	BEHMOOY	HOMEBOY
BEGILNU	BLUEING	BEGNOOS	BONGOES	BEHMORS	HOMBRES
	BULGINE	BEGNORU	BURGEON	BEHMOTU	BEMOUTH
BEGILNY	BELYING	BEGNOSY	BYGONES	BEHMPTU	BETHUMP
BEGILOR	OBLIGER	BEGNOTT	BETTONG	BEHNNOT	BENTHON

BEHNORS	BREHONS		BOOKSIE			BRITTLE
BEHNORT	BETHORN	BEIKORS	BOSKIER			TRIBLET
BEHNOST	BENTHOS	BEIKORT	REITBOK	BEILRTU	REBUILT
BEHNRTU	BURTHEN	BEIKOSY	BOYKIES	BEILRTY	LIBERTY
BEHOORT	THEORBO	BEIKRRS	BRISKER	BEILRTZ	BLITZER
BEHOOSX	SHOEBOX	BEIKRST	BRISKET	BEILRUY	BRULYIE
BEHOPRT	POTHERB	BEIKRSW	BREWSKI	BEILRUZ	BRULZIE
BEHOPSU	PHOEBUS	BEIKRTU	BURKITE	BEILSSS	BLISSES
BEHORRT	BROTHER	BEILLMN	BILLMEN	BEILSST	BITLESS
BEHORST	BOSHTER	BEILLPR	PREBILL	BEILSTU	BLUIEST
	BOTHERS	BEILLRR	BRILLER		SUBTILE
BEHORSU	HERBOUS	BEILLRS	BILLERS	BEILSTW	BLEWITS
BEHORTT	BETROTH		REBILLS	BEILSTZ	BLITZES
BEHOSTU	BESHOUT	BEILLRU	BULLIER	BEILTTU	BLUETIT
BEHRRSU	BRUSHER	BEILLST	BESTILL	BEIMMOS	BOMMIES
BEHRSSU	BRUSHES		BILLETS	BEIMMRR	BRIMMER
	BUSHERS	BEILLSU	BULLIES	BEIMNOR	BROMINE
BEHRTTU	TURBETH	BEILMNR	NIMBLER	BEIMNTU	BITUMEN
BEIIKKS	BIKKIES	BEILMNS	MILNEBS	BEIMOOR	BOOMIER
BEIIKLN	NIBLIKE	BEILMOR	EMBROIL	BEIMORS	BROMISE
BEIIKLR	RIBLIKE	BEILMOS	BEMOILS	BEIMORW	IMBOWER
BEIIKRR	BIRKIER		EMBOILS		WOMBIER
BEIIKRS	BIRKIES		MOBILES	BEIMORZ	BROMIZE
BEIILLS	BILLIES		OBELISM	BEIMOSS	OBEISMS
BEIILMR	LIMBIER	BEILMRS	LIMBERS	BEIMOSZ	ZOMBIES
BEIILMX	MIXIBLE	BEILMRT	TIMBREL	BEIMOTV	BEVOMIT
BEIILRS	RISIBLE	BEILMRW	WIMBREL	BEIMPRU	BUMPIER
BEIILSV	VISIBLE	BEILMSU	SUBLIME	BEIMRST	BETRIMS
BEIINOT	NIOBITE	BEILMSW	WIMBLES		TIMBERS
BEIINRR	BRINIER	BEILNOO	OBELION		TIMBRES
BEIINRS	BRINIES	BEILNOS	BOLINES	BEIMRSU	ERBIUMS
BEIINST	STIBINE	BEILNOW	BOWLINE		IMBRUES
BEIIOTT	BIOTITE	BEILNRS	BERLINS		IMBURSE
BEIIRRS	BIRSIER	BEILNRY	BYLINER	BEIMRTU	IMBRUTE
	RIBIERS	BEILNSU	SUBLINE		TERBIUM
BEIIRST	BITSIER	BEILNSY	BYLINES	BEIMRTY	TIMBERY
BEIIRTT	BITTIER	BEILNSZ	BENZILS	BEIMSST	BEMISTS
BEIISTT	BITTIES	BEILNTZ	BLINTZE	BEIMSTU	SUBITEM
BEIISTV	VIBIEST	BEILOOR	LOOBIER	BEINNOP	PINBONE
BEIISVV	BIVVIES	BEILOOS	LOOBIES	BEINNOR	BONNIER
BEIISZZ	BIZZIES	BEILOPR	PREBOIL	BEINNOS	BENISON
BEIJLRS	JERBILS	BEILOPY	EPIBOLY		BONNIES
	JIRBLES	BEILOQU	OBLIQUE	BEINNOZ	BENZOIN
BEIJLSU	JUBILES	BEILORR	BROILER	BEINNSU	BUNNIES
BEIJMSU	JUMBIES	BEILORS	BOILERS	BEINNSZ	BENZINS
BEIJNSU	BUNJIES		LIBEROS	BEINOOS	BOONIES
BEIKLMS	BLIKSEM		REBOILS	BEINOOT	EOBIONT
BEIKLNR	BLINKER	BEILORT	TRILOBE	BEINORT	BORNITE
BEIKLNS	LIBKENS	BEILORW	BLOWIER	BEINORW	BROWNIE
BEIKLOR	BLOKIER	BEILORY	BOILERY	BEINOSS	BESOINS
BEIKLOS	OBELISK	BEILOST	BETOILS	BEINOST	BONIEST
BEIKLOW	BOWLIKE	BEILOSW	BLOWIES		EBONIST
BEIKLOX	BOXLIKE	BEILOSX	BOLIXES	BEINOSV	BOVINES
BEIKLRS	BILKERS	BEILRRS	BIRLERS	BEINOSX	BONXIES
BEIKLRU	BULKIER	BEILRRU	BURLIER		INBOXES
BEIKLSY	BEYLIKS	BEILRSS	BIRSLES	BEINOSZ	BIZONES
BEIKLTU	TUBLIKE		RIBLESS	BEINOTT	BOTTINE
BEIKNRS	BRISKEN	BEILRST	BLISTER	BEINRRS	BRINERS
BEIKOOR	BOOKIER		BRISTLE	BEINRSU	BURNIES
	BROOKIE		RIBLETS		RUBINES
BEIKOOS	BOOKIES	BEILRTT	BLITTER		SUBERIN

BEINRSY	BYRNIES	**BEJORSU**	OBJURES	**BELMRTU**	TUMBLER
BEINRTT	BITTERN	**BEKLNRU**	BLUNKER		TUMBREL
BEINRTU	BUNTIER	**BEKLOOT**	BOOKLET	**BELMRTY**	TREMBLY
	TRIBUNE	**BEKLRSU**	BULKERS	**BELMSTU**	STUMBLE
	TURBINE		BURLESK		TUMBLES
BEINSSY	BYSSINE	**BEKMNNO**	BOOKMEN	**BELNNOU**	UNNOBLE
BEIOOPT	BIOTOPE	**BEKMOSS**	EMBOSKS	**BELNNTU**	UNBLENT
BEIOORZ	BOOZIER	**BEKMOST**	STEMBOK	**BELNOOR**	BORNEOL
BEIOOST	BOOTIES	**BEKNNOW**	BEKNOWN	**BELNOOY**	BOLONEY
BEIOPTY	BIOTYPE	**BEKNORS**	BONKERS	**BELNOST**	NOBLEST
BEIORRS	BROSIER	**BEKNORU**	UNBROKE	**BELNOSZ**	BENZOLS
BEIORRT	BORTIER	**BEKNOST**	BEKNOTS	**BELNOYZ**	BENZOYL
	ORBITER	**BEKNRSU**	BUNKERS	**BELNRTU**	BLUNTER
BEIORSS	BOSSIER	**BEKOOPR**	PREBOOK	**BELNSSU**	UNBLESS
	RIBOSES	**BEKOORS**	BOOKERS	**BELNSTU**	SUNBELT
BEIORST	ORBIEST		REBOOKS		UNBELTS
	SORBITE	**BEKOPRU**	UPBROKE		UNBLEST
BEIORSU	BOUSIER	**BEKORRS**	BROKERS	**BELNSYZ**	BENZYLS
	OUREBIS	**BEKORRY**	BROKERY	**BELOOPR**	BLOOPER
BEIORSY	BOYSIER	**BEKORWW**	WEBWORK	**BELOORS**	BOLEROS
BEIORUV	BOUVIER	**BEKOSST**	BOSKETS	**BELOOSS**	SOBOLES
BEIOSSS	BOSSIES	**BEKOTTU**	KETUBOT	**BELOPSU**	PUEBLOS
BEIOSSU	SOUBISE	**BEKRRSU**	BRUSKER	**BELORSS**	ORBLESS
BEIOSSW	BOWSIES		BURKERS	**BELORST**	BOLSTER
BEIOSTT	BOTTIES	**BEKRSSU**	BUSKERS		BOLTERS
BEIOSTX	BOXIEST	**BEKSSTU**	BUSKETS		LOBSTER
	BOXTIES	**BELLLMU**	BLELLUM	**BELORSU**	ROUBLES
BEIOSTY	OBESITY	**BELLNPU**	BULLPEN	**BELORSW**	BLOWERS
BEIPPSU	BUPPIES	**BELLORR**	BORRELL		BOWLERS
BEIPSST	BESPITS	**BELLOSU**	BOULLES	**BELORSY**	SOBERLY
BEIPSSU	PUBISES		LOBULES	**BELORTT**	BLOTTER
BEIQRTU	BRIQUET		SOLUBLE		BOTTLER
BEIQSSU	BISQUES	**BELLOSW**	BELLOWS	**BELORTU**	BOULTER
BEIRRRU	BURRIER	**BELLOUV**	VOLUBLE		TROUBLE
BEIRRSU	BRISURE	**BELLRRU**	BURRELL	**BELOSSU**	BLOUSES
	BRUISER	**BELLRSU**	BULLERS		BOLUSES
	BURIERS	**BELLSTU**	BULLETS	**BELOSSW**	BLOWSES
BEIRRTU	BRUITER	**BELMMOO**	EMBLOOM		BOWLESS
BEIRSSS	BRISSES	**BELMMRU**	MUMBLER	**BELOSTT**	BOTTLES
BEIRSST	BESTIRS	**BELMMSU**	BUMMELS	**BELOSTU**	BOLETUS
	BISTERS		BUMMLES	**BELOSWZ**	BLOWZES
	BISTRES		MUMBLES	**BELRRSU**	BURLERS
	BITSERS	**BELMNOS**	NOMBLES		BURRELS
	BREISTS	**BELMNOU**	NELUMBO	**BELRRTU**	BLURTER
BEIRSSU	BRUISES	**BELMNOY**	BENOMYL	**BELRSTU**	BLUSTER
BEIRSTT	BITTERS	**BELMNSU**	NUMBLES		BUSTLER
BEIRSTU	BUSTIER	**BELMOOR**	BLOOMER		BUTLERS
	RUBIEST		REBLOOM		SUBTLER
BEIRTTU	TRIBUTE	**BELMOOS**	BLOOSME	**BELRSUU**	SUBRULE
BEIRTTY	TREYBIT	**BELMOOT**	BOOMLET	**BELRSUY**	BURLEYS
BEIRTVY	BREVITY	**BELMOPR**	PROBLEM	**BELRTUY**	BRUTELY
BEIRUZZ	BUZZIER	**BELMORT**	TEMBLOR		BUTLERY
BEISSTU	BUSIEST	**BELMOSU**	EMBOLUS	**BELSSTU**	BUSTLES
	SUBSITE	**BELMOSY**	SYMBOLE		SUBLETS
BEISTTU	BUTTIES	**BELMPRU**	PLUMBER	**BELSTTU**	BUTTLES
BEITTWX	BETWIXT		REPLUMB	**BELSTUU**	TUBULES
BEJJSUU	JUJUBES	**BELMRRU**	RUMBLER	**BEMMNOS**	MOBSMEN
BEJKOUX	JUKEBOX	**BELMRSU**	LUMBERS	**BEMMOOS**	EMBOSOM
BEJLMRU	JUMBLER		RUMBLES	**BEMMORR**	BROMMER
BEJLMSU	JUMBLES		SLUMBER	**BEMMRRU**	BRUMMER
BEJLOSS	JOBLESS		UMBRELS	**BEMMRSU**	BUMMERS

BEMMSTU	BUMMEST		BURSTEN	**BESTTUX**	SUBTEXT
BEMNORW	EMBROWN		SUBRENT	**BFFGIIN**	BIFFING
BEMNORY	EMBRYON	**BENSSTU**	SUBNETS	**BFFGINO**	BOFFING
BEMNOST	ENTOMBS	**BEOORSS**	BROOSES	**BFFGINU**	BUFFING
BEMNOSU	UMBONES		SORBOSE	**BFFIINS**	BIFFINS
BEMNOSW	ENWOMBS	**BEOORST**	BOOSTER	**BFFILOO**	BOILOFF
BEMNPTY	BYNEMPT		REBOOTS	**BFFINOS**	BOFFINS
BEMNRSU	NUMBERS	**BEOORSZ**	BOOZERS	**BFFLLUY**	BLUFFLY
BEMNSTU	NUMBEST		REBOZOS	**BFFLOOW**	BLOWOFF
BEMNSUU	SUBMENU	**BEOORTY**	BOOTERY	**BFFNOOU**	BUFFOON
BEMNTTU	BUTMENT	**BEOPPRS**	BOPPERS	**BFFORSU**	RUBOFFS
BEMOOPR	PREBOOM	**BEOPRRS**	PROBERS	**BFFOSUY**	BUYOFFS
BEMOORS	BOOMERS	**BEOPRRV**	PROVERB	**BFGIOOT**	BIGFOOT
BEMORRS	SOMBRER	**BEOPRST**	BESPORT	**BFGIORT**	FROGBIT
BEMORSS	SOMBERS	**BEOPSST**	BESPOTS	**BFGOOSW**	FOGBOWS
	SOMBRES	**BEOPSTU**	BESPOUT	**BFHILSU**	LUBFISH
BEMORST	BESTORM	**BEOQSSU**	BOSQUES	**BFHIOSX**	BOXFISH
	MOBSTER	**BEOQSTU**	BOSQUET	**BFHIRSU**	FURBISH
BEMORSU	UMBROSE	**BEOQSUY**	OBSEQUY	**BFHISTU**	TUBFISH
BEMORSW	BEWORMS	**BEOQTUU**	BOUQUET	**BFHLSUY**	BUSHFLY
BEMORSY	EMBRYOS	**BEORRSS**	RESORBS	**BFIILMO**	BIOFILM
BEMORUX	BUXOMER	**BEORRSW**	BROWSER	**BFIILRS**	FIBRILS
BEMORWW	WEBWORM	**BEORRWY**	BEWORRY	**BFIINOR**	FIBROIN
BEMOTUY	MYOTUBE	**BEORSST**	BESORTS	**BFIINRS**	FIBRINS
BEMPRSU	BUMPERS		SORBETS	**BFILMRU**	BRIMFUL
BEMRSTU	BUMSTER		STROBES	**BFILOTY**	LIFTBOY
BEMSSTU	BESMUTS	**BEORSSU**	BOURSES	**BFILSUY**	FUSIBLY
BEMSSUU	SUBSUME	**BEORSSW**	BOWSERS	**BFIMOYZ**	ZOMBIFY
BEMSTUW	STEWBUM		BROWSES	**BFINNSU**	SNUBFIN
BENNORU	UNBORNE	**BEORSTT**	BETTORS	**BFINOSW**	BOWFINS
BENNORW	NEWBORN	**BEORSTU**	OBTUSER	**BFIORSS**	ROSBIFS
BENNORZ	BRONZEN	**BEORSTV**	OBVERTS	**BFIORSU**	FIBROUS
BENNOST	BONNETS	**BEORSTW**	BESTROW	**BFIRTUY**	BRUTIFY
BENNOSU	UNBONES	**BEORSTZ**	BORTZES	**BFKLOOU**	BOOKFUL
BENNSSU	BUNSENS	**BEORSUU**	UBEROUS	**BFKLOOY**	FLYBOOK
BENNSTU	BUNNETS	**BEORSUZ**	BROUZES	**BFKSSUU**	SUBFUSK
BENOORS	BOONERS		SUBZERO	**BFLLOUW**	BOWLFUL
BENOOST	OBENTOS	**BEORSVV**	BOVVERS	**BFLLOWY**	BLOWFLY
BENOPRR	PREBORN	**BEORSWY**	BOWYERS		FLYBLOW
BENOPRU	UPBORNE	**BEORUVY**	OVERBUY	**BFLOSUX**	BOXFULS
BENORRW	BROWNER	**BEOSSST**	BOSSEST	**BFLOSYY**	FLYBOYS
BENORRZ	BRONZER		BOSSETS	**BFLSTUU**	TUBFULS
BENORST	BRETONS	**BEOSSTT**	OBTESTS	**BFOOOTY**	FOOTBOY
	SORBENT	**BEOSSTW**	BESTOWS	**BFOUXZZ**	FUZZBOX
BENORSU	BOURNES	**BEOSSWY**	BOWSEYS	**BGGGIIN**	BIGGING
	UNROBES	**BEPRRTU**	PERTURB	**BGGGINO**	BOGGING
	UNSOBER	**BEPRSUY**	PREBUYS	**BGGGINU**	BUGGING
BENORSZ	BRONZES	**BEPRTUY**	PUBERTY	**BGGHIIS**	BIGGISH
BENORWY	BYWONER	**BEPSTUY**	SUBTYPE	**BGGHIOS**	BOGGISH
BENOSSU	BONUSES	**BEQRSUU**	BRUSQUE	**BGGIILN**	BILGING
BENOSSW	BESNOWS	**BEQSTUY**	QUBYTES	**BGGIINN**	BINGING
BENOSTT	BOTNETS	**BERRRSU**	BURRERS	**BGGIINS**	BIGGINS
BENOSTU	SUBTONE	**BERRSTU**	BRUTERS	**BGGIISW**	BIGWIGS
BENOSUX	UNBOXES		BURSTER	**BGGIITY**	BIGGITY
BENOSUZ	SUBZONE	**BERSSTU**	BUSTERS	**BGGILNO**	BOGLING
BENOSWY	NEWSBOY	**BERSTTU**	BUTTERS		GLOBING
BENRRSU	BURNERS	**BERSTUV**	SUBVERT	**BGGILNU**	BUGLING
BENRSSU	BRUSSEN	**BERSUZZ**	BUZZERS		BULGING
BENRSTU	BRUNETS	**BERTTUY**	BUTTERY	**BGGINNO**	BONGING
	BUNTERS	**BESSSTU**	SUBSETS	**BGGINNU**	BUNGING
	BURNETS	**BESSTTU**	SUBTEST	**BGGINOS**	BIGGONS

BGGINOU	BOUGING	**BGILNOY**	IGNOBLY	**BGKLOOO**	LOGBOOK
BGGINSU	BUGGINS	**BGILNRU**	BURLING	**BGKORSY**	GRYSBOK
BGGNOOS	BOGONGS	**BGILNRY**	BYRLING	**BGLMOOS**	MOBLOGS
BGGNOSU	BUGONGS	**BGILNSU**	BLUINGS	**BGLMRUY**	GRUMBLY
BGHHIOY	HIGHBOY	**BGILNTU**	BUTLING	**BGLNOOS**	OBLONGS
BGHIILS	GHIBLIS	**BGILOOR**	OBLIGOR	**BGLNOOW**	LONGBOW
BGHIINS	BINGHIS	**BGILOOY**	BIOLOGY	**BGLNOUW**	BLOWGUN
BGHILST	BLIGHTS	**BGILRSU**	BUSGIRL	**BGLOOSU**	GLOBOUS
BGHILTY	BLIGHTY	**BGIMMNU**	BUMMING	**BGLOSSU**	BUGLOSS
BGHINOO	BOOHING	**BGIMNNU**	NUMBING	**BGLOSUY**	BOGUSLY
	HOBOING	**BGIMNOO**	BOOMING	**BGLRSUU**	BULGURS
BGHINOR	BIGHORN	**BGIMNOR**	BORMING	**BGMOORS**	GOMBROS
BGHINSU	BUSHING	**BGIMNOT**	TOMBING	**BGMOOTU**	GUMBOOT
BGHIPSU	BUSHPIG	**BGIMNOW**	WOMBING	**BGMSSUU**	SUBGUMS
BGHIRST	BRIGHTS	**BGIMNPU**	BUMPING	**BGNOOWY**	GOWNBOY
BGHLRUU	BULGHUR	**BGIMOSY**	BOGYISM	**BGNOSSU**	SUBSONG
	BURGHUL	**BGINNOS**	BONINGS	**BGOORSU**	BURGOOS
BGHMORU	HOMBURG	**BGINNOU**	BOUNING	**BGORTUU**	BURGOUT
BGHMSUU	HUMBUGS	**BGINNOW**	BOWNING	**BGORTUW**	BUGWORT
BGHNORU	HORNBUG	**BGINNRU**	BURNING	**BGOSTUU**	BUGOUTS
BGHOORU	BOROUGH	**BGINNTU**	BUNTING	**BHHIIST**	BHISHTI
BGHORSU	BROUGHS	**BGINOOS**	BOOSING	**BHHIKSU**	BHIKHUS
BGHORTU	BROUGHT	**BGINOOT**	BOOTING	**BHIIINN**	INHIBIN
BGHOSTU	BOUGHTS	**BGINOOZ**	BOOZING	**BHIIINT**	INHIBIT
BGIIKLN	BILKING	**BGINOPP**	BOPPING	**BHIINRS**	BRINISH
BGIIKNS	BIKINGS	**BGINOPR**	PROBING	**BHIIPSS**	SIBSHIP
BGIILLN	BILLING	**BGINOOS**	BORINGS	**BHIISST**	BHISTIS
BGIILMN	LIMBING		ROBINGS	**BHIKLOS**	BLOKISH
BGIILNO	BOILING		SORBING	**BHIKOOS**	BOOKISH
BGIILNR	BIRLING	**BGINORZ**	ZORBING	**BHIKSSU**	BUKSHIS
BGIILNS	SIBLING	**BGINOSS**	BOSSING	**BHILLOY**	BILLYOH
BGIIMNR	BRIMING		GIBSONS	**BHILLSU**	BULLISH
BGIIMNU	IMBUING		OBSIGNS	**BHILOTU**	HOLIBUT
BGIINNN	BINNING	**BGINOSU**	BOUSING	**BHILPSU**	PUBLISH
BGIINNR	BRINING	**BGINOSW**	BOWINGS	**BHILSUY**	BUSHILY
	INBRING		BOWSING	**BHIMOOR**	RHOMBOI
BGIINRR	BIRRING	**BGINOSX**	BOXINGS	**BHIMOOS**	HOBOISM
BGIINRT	RINGBIT	**BGINOTT**	BOTTING	**BHIMOPR**	BIMORPH
BGIINST	BITINGS	**BGINOUY**	BUOYING	**BHIMOPS**	PHOBISM
BGIINTT	BITTING	**BGINOWW**	WINGBOW	**BHIMORT**	THROMBI
BGIKLNU	BULKING	**BGINPRU**	BURPING	**BHIMORU**	BOHRIUM
BGIKNNO	BONKING		UPBRING	**BHIMSTU**	BISMUTH
BGIKNNU	BUNKING	**BGINRRU**	BURRING	**BHINRSU**	BURNISH
BGIKNOO	BOOKING	**BGINRSU**	SUBRING	**BHIOOPR**	BIOPHOR
BGIKNOR	BORKING	**BGINRTU**	BRUTING	**BHIOORS**	BOORISH
	BROKING	**BGINRUX**	BRUXING	**BHIOOST**	BOOSHIT
BGIKNRU	BURKING	**BGINRUY**	BURYING	**BHIOPSS**	BISHOPS
BGIKNSU	BUSKING		RUBYING	**BHIOPST**	PHOBIST
BGILLNO	BOLLING	**BGINSSU**	BUSINGS	**BHIOSWZ**	SHOWBIZ
BGILLNU	BULLING		BUSSING	**BHIRSTU**	BRUTISH
BGILMNO	MOBLING	**BGINSTU**	BUSTING	**BHIRTTU**	TURBITH
BGILMNU	BLUMING		TUBINGS	**BHISTTU**	BUSHTIT
BGILMOU	GUMBOIL	**BGINSUY**	BUSYING	**BHKNOSU**	BOHUNKS
BGILNOO	BOOLING		BUYINGS	**BHLRSUU**	BULRUSH
BGILNOS	GLOBINS	**BGINSWY**	SWINGBY	**BHMOORS**	RHOMBOS
	GOBLINS	**BGINTTU**	BUTTING	**BHMORSU**	RHOMBUS
	LOBINGS	**BGINUZZ**	BUZZING	**BHMUUZZ**	HUMBUZZ
BGILNOT	BILTONG	**BGIORSU**	RUBIGOS	**BHOOOOS**	BOOHOOS
	BOLTING	**BGIORTY**	BIGOTRY	**BHOOPST**	SHOPBOT
BGILNOW	BLOWING	**BGIOSSS**	GOSSIBS	**BHOOPSY**	SHOPBOY
	BOWLING	**BGIUWZZ**	BUZZWIG	**BHOOSTW**	BOWSHOT

BHOOSWX	SHOWBOX	BILNOTU	BOTULIN	BIRSTTU	BITTURS
BHORSST	BORSHTS	BILNTUU	TUBULIN		TURBITS
BHPRSUU	BRUSHUP		UNBUILT	BISSSTU	SUBSIST
BIIIKNS	BIKINIS	BILOOPT	POTBOIL	BISSTTU	TUBISTS
BIIKLOT	KILOBIT	BILOOYZ	BOOZILY	BISTUUU	BUSUUTI
BIILLMS	MISBILL	BILOPSU	UPBOILS	BJMOOSU	BOOJUMS
BIILLNO	BILLION	BILORST	BRISTOL	BJNOORU	BONJOUR
BIILLOU	BOUILLI		STROBIL	BJNOSTU	NUTJOBS
BIILLTW	TWIBILL	BILOSSU	SUBSOIL	BKLNUUY	UNBULKY
BIILNNR	BIRLINN	BILOSSY	BOSSILY	BKLOTUU	OUTBULK
BIILNQU	QUIBLIN	BILPTUU	UPBUILT	BKMNSUU	BUNKUMS
BIILNTU	INBUILT	BILRSTY	BRISTLY	BKNNOOO	NONBOOK
BIILNVY	BIVINYL		TRILBYS	BKNOOTW	BOWKNOT
BIILOSU	BILIOUS	BILRTTY	BRITTLY	BKNORSY	SKYBORN
BIILRSY	RISIBLY	BILRTUY	TILBURY	BKOOOOS	BOOKOOS
BIILSTW	TWIBILS	BIMMOOS	IMBOSOM	BKOORWX	WORKBOX
BIILSVY	VISIBLY		MIOMBOS	BKORSWY	BYWORKS
BIIMNOU	NIOBIUM	BIMMORS	BROMISM	BKRSTUU	KRUBUTS
BIIMNSU	MINIBUS	BIMNOOY	BIONOMY	BLLNTUY	BLUNTLY
BIIMOSS	OBIISMS	BIMNORS	BROMINS	BLLOOOS	LOBOLOS
BIIMOSZ	IMBIZOS		MISBORN	BLLOSUU	BULLOUS
BIIMPRS	BIPRISM	BIMNORW	IMBROWN		LOBULUS
BIIMSTU	STIBIUM	BIMNOSS	BONISMS	BLLOSUY	SOLUBLY
BIINORV	VIBRION	BIMNOST	INTOMBS	BLLOUVY	VOLUBLY
BIINOST	BIOTINS	BIMNOSU	OMNIBUS	BLMMPUU	PLUMBUM
BIINOSU	BINIOUS	BIMNOSY	SYMBION	BLMNPUU	UNPLUMB
BIIORSV	VIBRIOS	BIMOSSS	BOSSISM	BLMOOOT	TOMBOLO
BIIOSUV	BIVIOUS	BIMOSTW	MISTBOW	BLMOORW	LOBWORM
BIIRSTU	BURITIS	BIMOSTY	SYMBIOT	BLMOOSS	BLOSSOM
BIISSTV	VIBISTS	BIMRSTU	BRUTISM	BLMOSSY	SYMBOLS
BIISTTT	TITBITS	BIMRSUX	BRUXISM	BLMOUXY	BUXOMLY
BIJNOSU	SUBJOIN	BIMSSSU	SUBMISS	BLMRSUY	SLUMBRY
BIKLLUY	BULKILY	BIMSSTU	SUBMITS	BLMSTUY	STUMBLY
BIKLNOT	INKBLOT	BINNOSU	BUNIONS	BLNNOUW	UNBLOWN
BIKLNOY	LINKBOY	BINOORS	BONSOIR	BLNOORW	LOWBORN
BIKLRSY	BRISKLY	BINOORT	BIOTRON	BLNOOSS	BOLSONS
BIKMNOO	BOOMKIN	BINOOST	BONITOS	BLNOOSU	BLOUSON
BIKMNPU	BUMPKIN	BINOOSU	NIOBOUS	BLNOPUW	UPBLOWN
BIKMNSU	BUMKINS	BINORST	RIBSTON	BLNORSY	BORNYLS
BIKMOSS	IMBOSKS	BINORSU	BOURSIN	BLNOSTU	UNBOLTS
BIKNSSU	BUSKINS	BINORUW	UNIBROW	BLOOOTX	TOOLBOX
BIKORRW	RIBWORK	BINOSST	BONISTS	BLOOPTX	BOXPLOT
BIKSUUZ	BUZUKIS	BINPSUY	BUNYIPS	BLOOPWY	PLOWBOY
BILLNOS	BILLONS	BINRSTU	INBURST	BLOOQUY	OBLOQUY
BILLNOU	BULLION	BINRTUY	BUTYRIN	BLOORWW	LOWBROW
BILLOOY	LOOBILY	BINSTTU	UNBITTS	BLOOSWY	LOWBOYS
BILLOPX	PILLBOX	BINSTUU	SUBUNIT	BLOOTUW	BLOWOUT
BILLORS	BRILLOS	BIOOORS	ROOIBOS	BLOPSTU	SUBPLOT
BILLOSW	BILLOWS	BIOORSZ	BORZOIS	BLOPSUW	BLOWUPS
BILLOSY	BILLYOS	BIOOSST	OBOISTS		UPBLOWS
BILLOUV	VOLUBIL	BIOOSUV	OBVIOUS	BLORSTU	BRULOTS
BILLOWY	BILLOWY	BIOPRST	PROBITS	BLOSSTU	SUBLOTS
BILLRUY	BURLILY	BIOPRTY	PROBITY	BLRTUYY	BUTYRYL
BILLRWY	WRYBILL	BIORRTU	BURRITO	BMNOOOW	MOONBOW
BILMNOR	NOMBRIL	BIORRTW	RIBWORT	BMNOOSU	UNBOSOM
BILMOSU	LIMBOUS	BIORSST	BISTROS	BMNORUW	MOWBURN
BILMPUY	BUMPILY	BIORSTT	BISTORT	BMNOSTU	UNTOMBS
BILMRSU	UMBRILS		BITTORS	BMOOORX	BOXROOM
BILMRTU	TUMBRIL	BIORSUU	RUBIOUS	BMOORSY	BYROOMS
BILMSUU	BULIMUS	BIORTTU	BITTOUR	BMOOSTT	BOTTOMS
BILNNOY	BONNILY	BIOSTUW	WOUBITS	BMOOSTY	TOMBOYS

BMORSST	STROMBS	CCDEIKL	CLICKED	CCEHINT	TECHNIC
BMORSUU	BRUMOUS	CCDEIKR	CRICKED	CCEHINZ	ZECCHIN
	UMBROUS	CCDEILR	CIRCLED	CCEHIOR	CHOICER
BNNRSUU	SUNBURN	CCDEIMO	COMEDIC		CHOREIC
BNNRTUU	UNBURNT	CCDEIOS	CODICES	CCEHIOS	CHOICES
BNOOSST	BOSTONS	CCDEIOT	DOCETIC	CCEHIRS	SCREICH
BNOOSTU	BOUTONS	CCDEKLO	CLOCKED		SCRIECH
	UNBOOTS		COCKLED	CCEHIST	CHICEST
BNOOTTY	BOTTONY	CCDEKLU	CLUCKED		HECTICS
BNORSSU	SUBORNS	CCDEKOR	CROCKED	CCEHKLU	CHUCKLE
BNORSTU	BURTONS	CCDELOU	OCCLUDE	CCEHKMS	SCHMECK
BNORSUU	BURNOUS	CCDENOO	CONCEDO	CCEHKNU	UNCHECK
BNORTUU	BURNOUT	CCDENOS	SCONCED	CCEHKOR	CHOCKER
	OUTBURN	CCDENOU	CONDUCE	CCEHKPU	CHECKUP
BNOSSUW	SUNBOWS	CCDEOST	DECOCTS	CCEHKRU	CHUCKER
BNOSTTU	BUTTONS	CCDHIIL	CICHLID	CCEHLOS	CLOCHES
BNOTTUY	BUTTONY	CCDIILO	CODICIL	CCEHLRU	CLERUCH
BNSTUUU	UBUNTUS	CCDIILU	CULICID	CCEHLSU	CLEUCHS
BOOPSTW	BOWPOTS	CCDIIOR	CRICOID		CULCHES
BOOPSTX	POSTBOX	CCDILOY	CYCLOID	CCEHNOS	CONCHES
BOOPSTY	POSTBOY	CCDILYY	DICYCLY	CCEHOOS	COOCHES
	POTBOYS	CCDKLOU	CUCKOLD	CCEHORS	CROCHES
BOORRSW	BORROWS	CCDNOOR	CONCORD	CCEHORT	CROCHET
BOORRTY	ROBOTRY	CCDNOTU	CONDUCT	CCEHORU	COUCHER
BOOSTUW	WOOBUTS	CCEEGNO	COGENCE	CCEHOSS	COSECHS
BOOSWWW	BOWWWS	CCEEHIK	CHICKEE	CCEHOSU	COUCHES
BOPSSTU	POSTBUS	CCEEHIV	CEVICHE	CCEHRSU	CURCHES
BORRSUW	BURROWS	CCEEHKR	CHECKER	CCEHSTU	CUTCHES
BORSSTW	BROWSTS		RECHECK	CCEHSTW	CWTCHES
BORSTTU	TURBOTS	CCEEHOR	ECORCHE	CCEIILS	CILICES
BORSTUU	RUBOUTS	CCEEHOU	COUCHEE		ICICLES
BOSTRXY	BOSTRYX	CCEEHRS	CRECHES	CCEIIMS	CIMICES
BOSTUUY	BUYOUTS		SCREECH	CCEIIPS	PICCIES
	OUTBUYS	CCEEILN	LICENCE	CCEIIRT	ICTERIC
BPRSTUU	UPBURST	CCEEILS	LECCIES	CCEIIST	CECITIS
CCCDIOO	COCCOID	CCEEINR	ECCRINE	CCEIKLR	CLICKER
CCCDIOS	COCCIDS	CCEEINS	SCIENCE	CCEIKLT	CLICKET
CCCNOOT	CONCOCT	CCEEIOR	CICOREE	CCEIKOR	COCKIER
CCCOOSU	COCCOUS	CCEEIRS	RECCIES	CCEIKOS	COCKIES
CCDEEER	RECCEED	CCEEIRV	CREVICE	CCEIKRT	CRICKET
CCDEEHK	CHECKED	CCEEKOY	COCKEYE	CCEIKRY	CRICKEY
CCDEEIM	ECDEMIC	CCEELNU	LUCENCE	CCEILMO	CELOMIC
CCDEEIO	ECOCIDE	CCEELRY	RECYCLE	CCEILNU	NUCLEIC
CCDEEIR	RECCIED	CCEENRY	RECENCY	CCEILOT	COCTILE
CCDEEIS	DECCIES	CCEEORR	COERCER	CCEILRR	CIRCLER
CCDEEKL	CLECKED	CCEEORS	COERCES	CCEILRS	CIRCLES
CCDEENO	CONCEDE	CCEEORT	COERECT		CLERICS
CCDEENY	DECENCY	CCEERSY	SECRECY	CCEILRT	CIRCLET
CCDEEOR	COERCED	CCEFHRU	CURCHEF	CCEILSU	CULICES
CCDEEPS	SPECCED	CCEFNOT	CONFECT	CCEILSY	CYCLISE
CCDEESU	SUCCEED	CCEGINY	GYNECIC		CYLICES
CCDEFLO	FLOCCED	CCEGNOY	COGENCY	CCEILTU	CUTICLE
CCDEHIL	CLICHED	CCEHHIS	CHICHES	CCEILYZ	CYCLIZE
CCDEHIN	CINCHED	CCEHIKN	CHICKEN	CCEIMNO	MECONIC
CCDEHKO	CHOCKED	CCEHIKU	CHUCKIE	CCEIMOS	COMICES
CCDEHKU	CHUCKED	CCEHILS	CHICLES		MOCCIES
CCDEHNO	CONCHED		CLICHES	CCEIMOT	COMETIC
CCDEHOU	COUCHED	CCEHILU	CULCHIE	CCEIMST	SMECTIC
CCDEHTW	CWTCHED	CCEHIMS	CHEMICS	CCEINOR	CORNICE
CCDEIIL	ICICLED	CCEHINO	CONCHIE		CROCEIN
CCDEIIT	DEICTIC	CCEHINS	CINCHES		CROCINE

CCEINOS	CONCISE	CCHHOOS	CHOCHOS	CCIORSS	SCIROCS
CCEINOT	CONCEIT	CCHHRUY	CHURCHY	CCIOSTT	TICTOCS
CCEINRT	CENTRIC	CCHIIST	STICHIC	CCIPRTY	CRYPTIC
CCEINSS	SCENICS	CCHIKMS	SCHMICK	CCIRSUY	CIRCUSY
CCEIOPP	COPPICE	CCHIKOS	COCKISH	CCKMOOS	MOCOCKS
CCEIOPT	ECTOPIC	CCHIKST	SCHTICK	CCKMOSU	MOCUCKS
CCEIORS	CICEROS		TCHICKS	CCKNOSU	UNCOCKS
CCEIORT	CEROTIC	CCHILOR	CHLORIC	CCKOOSU	CUCKOOS
	ORECTIC	CCHIMOR	CHROMIC	CCKOPSU	COCKUPS
CCEIOSS	CISCOES	CCHIMSY	CHYMICS	CCKOSTU	CUSTOCK
CCEIPST	SCEPTIC	CCHINOR	CHRONIC	CCLMSUU	MUCLUCS
CCEIRST	CRETICS	CCHINOS	CHICONS	CCLOOOZ	ZOCCOLO
CCEISSU	SUCCISE		COCHINS	CCLOPSY	CYCLOPS
CCEJNOT	CONJECT	CCHINSU	SCUCHIN	CCLOSTU	OCCULTS
CCEKLOR	CLOCKER	CCHIORY	CHICORY	CCMOOOR	MOROCCO
	COCKLER	CCHIOTW	COWITCH	CCNOOOS	COCOONS
CCEKLOS	COCKLES	CCHIPSU	HICCUPS	CCNOOPU	PUCCOON
CCEKNOT	CONTECK	CCHIPSY	PSYCHIC	CCNOOTU	COCONUT
CCEKNOY	COCKNEY	CCHIPUY	HICCUPY	CCNOPUY	CONCUPY
CCEKOPS	COPECKS	CCHIRST	SCRITCH	CCNORSU	CONCURS
CCEKOPT	PETCOCK	CCHKLOS	SCHLOCK	CCNOSSU	CONCUSS
CCEKORS	COCKERS	CCHKMOS	SCHMOCK	CCOOORS	ROCOCOS
	RECOCKS	CCHKMSU	SCHMUCK	CCORSSU	SUCCORS
CCEKORT	CROCKET	CCHKOOS	CHOCKOS	CCORSUU	SUCCOUR
CCEKOST	COCKETS	CCHKOSY	COCKSHY	CCORSUY	SUCCORY
CCELLOT	COLLECT	CCHKPUU	UPCHUCK	CCOSSTU	STUCCOS
CCELNOY	CYCLONE	CCHKSTU	SCHTUCK	CCOSSUU	SUCCOUS
CCELNUY	LUCENCY	CCHLSTU	SCULTCH	CCSSSUU	SUCCUSS
CCELRSY	CYCLERS	CCHLTUY	CLUTCHY	CDDDEEI	DECIDED
CCELRYY	CYCLERY	CCHNOOS	CONCHOS	CDDDEEO	DECODED
CCENNOR	CONCERN	CCHNRSU	SCRUNCH	CDDDEEU	DEDUCED
CCENNOT	CONCENT	CCHNRUY	CRUNCHY	CDDDELO	CLODDED
	CONNECT	CCHOORS	SCROOCH		CODDLED
CCENOPT	CONCEPT	CCHOOST	SCOOTCH	CDDDELU	CUDDLED
CCENORT	CONCERT	CCHOSTU	SUCCOTH	CDDDERU	CRUDDED
CCENORW	CONCREW	CCIIILS	SILICIC	CDDDESU	SCUDDED
CCENOSS	SCONCES	CCIILNO	COLICIN	CDDEEER	DECREED
CCENOTV	CONVECT	CCIILNS	CLINICS		RECEDED
CCEOOTT	COCOTTE	CCIILOT	COLITIC	CDDEEES	SECEDED
CCEOPRT	PERCOCT	CCIILPR	CIRCLIP	CDDEEII	DEICIDE
CCEORRT	CORRECT	CCIILST	CLITICS	CDDEEIN	INCEDED
CCEORRU	REOCCUR	CCIINPS	PICNICS	CDDEEIR	DECIDER
CCEORSS	ESCROCS	CCIIRST	CRITICS		DECRIED
	SOCCERS	CCIIRTU	CIRCUIT	CDDEEIS	DECIDES
CCEORTW	TWOCCER	CCIISTY	SICCITY	CDDEEIX	EXCIDED
CCEOSSU	SUCCOSE	CCIKLOW	COWLICK	CDDEEKL	DECKLED
CCERTUW	CREWCUT	CCIKLOY	COCKILY	CDDEEKO	DECKOED
CCESSSU	SUCCESS		COLICKY		DECOKED
CCFIRUY	CRUCIFY	CCIKOPT	COCKPIT	CDDEENO	ENCODED
CCFLOSU	FLOCCUS	CCILNOO	COLONIC	CDDEENS	DESCEND
CCGHINO	GNOCCHI	CCILNOU	COUNCIL		SCENDED
CCGIINS	SICCING	CCILNSY	CYCLINS	CDDEENU	UNCEDED
CCGIINT	TICCING	CCILOOP	PICCOLO	CDDEEOR	DECODER
CCGIKNO	COCKING	CCILSTY	CYCLIST		RECODED
CCGIKNU	CUCKING	CCIMNOU	UNCOMIC	CDDEEOS	DECODES
CCGILNY	CYCLING	CCIMOTY	MYCOTIC	CDDEEOY	DECOYED
CCGKOOR	GORCOCK	CCINOOT	COCTION	CDDEERU	REDUCED
CCHHIIS	CHICHIS	CCINORY	CRYONIC	CDDEESU	DEDUCES
CCHHIIT	ICHTHIC	CCINOTV	CONVICT		SEDUCED
CCHHILS	SCHLICH	CCIOORS	SIROCCO	CDDEEUW	CUDWEED
CCHHINY	CHINCHY	CCIOPTU	OCCIPUT	CDDEHIL	CHILDED

CDDEHIN	CHIDDEN		SECEDER		EXCISED
CDDEHIT	DICHTED	CDEEERT	DECREET	CDEEITV	EVICTED
	DITCHED		ERECTED	CDEEITX	EXCITED
CDDEHNU	DUNCHED	CDEEESS	SECEDES	CDEEJNO	CONJEED
CDDEHOR	CHORDED	CDEEESX	EXCEEDS	CDEEJST	DEJECTS
CDDEHOU	DOUCHED	CDEEFFH	CHEFFED	CDEEKKL	KECKLED
CDDEHRU	CHUDDER	CDEEFHL	FELCHED	CDEEKLR	CLERKED
CDDEIIS	DISCIDE	CDEEFHT	FETCHED	CDEEKLS	DECKELS
CDDEINU	INDUCED	CDEEFII	EDIFICE		DECKLES
CDDEIOS	DISCOED	CDEEFKL	FLECKED	CDEEKNR	REDNECK
CDDEISU	CUDDIES	CDEEFLT	CLEFTED	CDEEKNS	SNECKED
CDDELOR	CODDLER		DEFLECT	CDEEKOS	DECOKES
CDDELOS	CODDLES	CDEEFOR	DEFORCE	CDEEKPS	SPECKED
	SCOLDED	CDEEFST	DEFECTS	CDEEKRS	DECKERS
CDDELOU	CLOUDED	CDEEGIR	GRIECED	CDEEKRT	TRECKED
CDDELRU	CRUDDLE	CDEEGKT	GEDECKT	CDEEKRW	WRECKED
	CUDDLER	CDEEGNO	CONGEED	CDEELMM	CLEMMED
	CURDLED	CDEEHIP	CEPHEID	CDEELOS	ECLOSED
CDDELSU	CUDDLES	CDEEHIS	DEHISCE	CDEELPU	CUPELED
	SCUDDLE	CDEEHIT	CHEDITE		DECUPLE
CDDENOU	UNCODED	CDEEHIV	CHEVIED	CDEELPY	YCLEPED
CDDENSU	CUDDENS	CDEEHKL	HECKLED	CDEELRU	RECULED
CDDEORS	CODDERS	CDEEHLP	CHELPED		ULCERED
CDDEORW	CROWDED	CDEEHLT	LETCHED	CDEELSU	SCEDULE
CDDERSU	SCUDDER	CDEEHLW	WELCHED		SECLUDE
CDDESTU	DEDUCTS	CDEEHMS	SCHEMED	CDEELUX	EXCLUDE
CDDGINO	CODDING	CDEEHNW	WENCHED	CDEENOR	ENCODER
CDDHIOR	DICHORD	CDEEHOR	CHORDEE		ENCORED
CDDIIIO	DIDICOI		COHERED	CDEENOS	ENCODES
CDDIIKN	NIDDICK		OCHERED		SECONDE
CDDIIOP	DIPODIC	CDEEHPR	PERCHED	CDEENOZ	COZENED
CDDIIOS	DISCOID	CDEEHRS	CHEDERS	CDEENRS	DECERNS
CDDIIOY	DIDICOY	CDEEHRT	RETCHED		SCERNED
CDDIIRU	DRUIDIC	CDEEHRU	EUCHRED	CDEENRT	CENTRED
CDDIKOP	PIDDOCK	CDEEHST	CHESTED		CREDENT
CDDINSU	CUDDINS	CDEEHTT	TETCHED	CDEENST	DESCENT
CDDIORS	DISCORD	CDEEIIT	EIDETIC		SCENTED
CDDKOPU	PUDDOCK	CDEEILN	DECLINE	CDEEOOY	COOEYED
CDDKORU	RUDDOCK	CDEEILP	PEDICEL	CDEEOPR	COPERED
CDEEEFL	FLEECED		PEDICLE		PRECODE
CDEEEFN	DEFENCE		DECILES		PROCEED
CDEEEHK	CHEEKED	CDEEILS	DELICES	CDEEORS	RECODES
CDEEEHL	LEECHED		DELICES	CDEEORV	COVERED
CDEEEHP	CHEEPED	CDEEIMN	ENDEMIC	CDEEORW	COWERED
	DEPECHE	CDEEIMS	DECIMES	CDEEORY	DECOYER
CDEEEHR	CHEERED	CDEEINO	CODEINE	CDEEOST	CESTODE
	REECHED	CDEEINR	CEDRINE		ESCOTED
CDEEEHS	CHEESED	CDEEINS	INCEDES	CDEEOTV	COVETED
CDEEEIP	EPICEDE	CDEEINT	ENTICED	CDEERRU	RECURED
CDEEEIV	DECEIVE	CDEEINV	EVINCED		REDUCER
CDEEEJT	EJECTED	CDEEIOS	DIOCESE	CDEERSS	SCREEDS
CDEEEKL	CLEEKED	CDEEIOV	DEVOICE	CDEERST	CRESTED
CDEEELP	CLEEPED	CDEEIPR	PIERCED	CDEERSU	RECUSED
CDEEELR	CREELED	CDEEIPT	PEDETIC		REDUCES
CDEEELT	ELECTED	CDEEIRR	DECRIER		RESCUED
CDEEEPR	CREEPED	CDEEIRS	DECRIES		SECURED
	PRECEDE		DEICERS		SEDUCER
CDEEERR	DECREER	CDEEIRT	RECITED	CDEERSW	DECREWS
CDEEERS	CREESED		TIERCED		SCREWED
	DECREES	CDEEIST	DECEITS	CDEERTU	ERUCTED
	RECEDES	CDEEISV	DEVICES	CDEERUV	DECURVE
		CDEEISX	EXCIDES		

CDEESSU	SEDUCES	CDEHHOT	HOTCHED	CDEHMOU	MOUCHED
CDEESSY	ECDYSES	CDEHHTU	HUTCHED	CDEHMPU	CHUMPED
CDEESTT	DECTETS	CDEHIIL	CEILIDH	CDEHMTU	MUTCHED
	DETECTS	CDEHIIV	CHIVIED	CDEHNOR	CHONDRE
CDEESUX	EXCUSED	CDEHIKN	CHINKED	CDEHNOT	NOTCHED
CDEFFHU	CHUFFED	CDEHIKO	HOICKED	CDEHNPU	PUNCHED
CDEFFIL	CLIFFED	CDEHIKR	CHIRKED	CDEHNRU	CHUNDER
CDEFFIO	COIFFED	CDEHIKT	THICKED		CHURNED
CDEFFLO	COFFLED	CDEHILL	CHILLED	CDEHNSU	DUNCHES
CDEFFLU	CUFFLED	CDEHILO	CHELOID	CDEHNSY	SYNCHED
CDEFFOS	SCOFFED		HELCOID	CDEHOOP	POOCHED
CDEFFSU	SCUFFED	CDEHILP	DELPHIC	CDEHOPP	CHOPPED
CDEFHIL	FILCHED	CDEHILR	CHILDER	CDEHOPT	POTCHED
CDEFHIN	FINCHED		CHIRLED	CDEHOPU	POUCHED
CDEFHMO	CHEFDOM		ELDRICH	CDEHORT	TORCHED
CDEFHOO	CHOOFED	CDEHILS	CHIELDS	CDEHORW	CHOWDER
CDEFIIT	DEFICIT		CHILDES		COWHERD
CDEFIKL	FICKLED	CDEHILT	LICHTED	CDEHOSU	CHOUSED
	FLICKED	CDEHIMR	CHIRMED		DOUCHES
CDEFILT	CLIFTED	CDEHIMT	MITCHED		HOCUSED
CDEFINO	CONFIDE	CDEHINN	CHINNED	CDEHOSW	CHOWSED
CDEFKLO	FLOCKED	CDEHINO	HEDONIC		COWSHED
CDEFKOR	DEFROCK	CDEHINP	PINCHED	CDEHOTU	TOUCHED
	FROCKED	CDEHINW	WINCHED	CDEHOUV	VOUCHED
CDEFNOR	CORNFED	CDEHIOR	CHOIRED	CDEHPSY	PSYCHED
CDEFNTU	DEFUNCT	CDEHIOW	COWHIDE	CDEHRRU	CHURRED
CDEFORT	CROFTED	CDEHIPP	CHIPPED	CDEHRSU	CRUSHED
CDEFOSU	DEFOCUS	CDEHIPR	CHIRPED	CDEHSSU	DUCHESS
	FOCUSED	CDEHIPT	PITCHED	CDEHSTU	DUTCHES
CDEFRTU	FRUCTED	CDEHIQU	QUICHED	CDEHSTY	SCYTHED
CDEFSUU	FUCUSED	CDEHIRR	CHIRRED	CDEIIKR	DICKIER
CDEGGHU	CHUGGED	CDEHIRS	CHIDERS	CDEIIKS	DICKIES
CDEGGLO	CLOGGED		HERDICS	CDEIILO	EIDOLIC
	COGGLED	CDEHIRT	CHIRTED	CDEIIMR	DIMERIC
CDEGGOR	CROGGED		DITCHER	CDEIINR	DINERIC
CDEGGOS	SCOGGED		RICHTED	CDEIINS	INCISED
CDEGGSU	SCUGGED	CDEHIST	DITCHES		INDICES
CDEGHLU	GULCHED		SICHTED	CDEIINT	IDENTIC
CDEGHOU	COUGHED	CDEHITT	CHITTED		INCITED
	GOUCHED	CDEHITW	WITCHED	CDEIIOR	ERICOID
CDEGIIN	DEICING	CDEHIVV	CHIVVED	CDEIIOV	OVICIDE
CDEGIKN	DECKING	CDEHIZZ	CHIZZED	CDEIIRT	DICTIER
CDEGILN	CLINGED	CDEHKLO	HOCKLED		ICTERID
CDEGILU	CLUDGIE	CDEHKLU	HUCKLED	CDEIIRV	VERIDIC
CDEGINO	COIGNED	CDEHKNU	CHUNKED	CDEIIST	DEISTIC
CDEGINR	CRINGED	CDEHKOO	CHOOKED		DICIEST
CDEGINU	DEUCING	CDEHKOS	SHOCKED	CDEIISU	SUICIDE
	EDUCING	CDEHKOT	KOTCHED	CDEIJST	DISJECT
CDEGIOR	ERGODIC	CDEHKSU	SHUCKED	CDEIKLN	CLINKED
CDEGKOR	GROCKED	CDEHKUY	HEYDUCK		NICKLED
CDEGKOU	GEODUCK	CDEHLMU	MULCHED	CDEIKLP	PICKLED
CDEGKUW	GWEDUCK	CDEHLNU	LUNCHED	CDEIKLS	SICKLED
CDEGLSU	CUDGELS	CDEHLNY	LYNCHED		SLICKED
CDEGNSU	SCUNGED	CDEHLOT	CLOTHED	CDEIKLT	TICKLED
CDEGOOS	SCOOGED	CDEHLRU	LURCHED	CDEIKMS	MEDICKS
CDEGORS	CODGERS	CDEHMMU	CHUMMED	CDEIKNS	DICKENS
CDEGOSU	SCOUGED	CDEHMNU	MUNCHED		SNICKED
CDEGSUW	GWEDUCS	CDEHMOO	MOOCHED	CDEIKNZ	ZINCKED
CDEHHIL	HILCHED	CDEHMOP	CHOMPED	CDEIKOS	DOCKISE
CDEHHIT	HITCHED	CDEHMOR	CHROMED	CDEIKOY	YOICKED
CDEHHNU	HUNCHED			CDEIKOZ	DOCKIZE

CDEIKPR	PRICKED	CDEINSZ	DEZINCS	CDELMOP	CLOMPED
CDEIKRR	DERRICK	CDEINTT	TINCTED	CDELMPU	CLUMPED
CDEIKRS	DICKERS	CDEINTU	UNCITED	CDELMSU	MUSCLED
	SCRIKED	CDEIOOR	COORIED	CDELMTU	MULCTED
CDEIKRT	TRICKED	CDEIOPR	PERCOID	CDELNOO	CONDOLE
CDEIKRU	DUCKIER	CDEIOPT	PICOTED	CDELNOU	ENCLOUD
CDEIKRW	WRICKED	CDEIORS	DISCOER	CDELNOW	CLOWNED
CDEIKST	DETICKS		SCODIER	CDELNOY	CONDYLE
	STICKED	CDEIORT	CORDITE	CDELOOR	COLORED
CDEIKSU	DUCKIES	CDEIORU	COURIED		CROODLE
CDEIKSW	WICKEDS	CDEIORV	CODRIVE		CROOLED
CDEIKSY	DICKEYS		DIVORCE		DECOLOR
CDEILLO	CODILLE	CDEIORW	CROWDIE	CDELOPP	CLOPPED
	COLLIDE	CDEIOST	CESTOID	CDELOPU	COUPLED
	COLLIED		COEDITS	CDELORS	SCOLDER
CDEILLU	CULLIED		COTISED	CDELORU	CLOURED
CDEILMO	MELODIC	CDEIPRS	CRISPED	CDELORW	CLOWDER
CDEILNU	INCLUDE		DISCERP	CDELOST	COLDEST
	NUCLIDE	CDEIPRT	PREDICT	CDELOSU	DULCOSE
CDEILOO	OCELOID	CDEIPST	DEPICTS	CDELOSW	SCOWLED
CDEILOP	POLICED		DISCEPT	CDELOTT	CLOTTED
CDEILOR	DOCILER	CDEIRRU	CURDIER	CDELOTU	CLOUTED
CDEILOS	COLDIES		CURRIED	CDELOUY	DOUCELY
CDEILPP	CLIPPED	CDEIRST	CREDITS	CDELOWY	COWEDLY
CDEILPS	SPLICED		DIRECTS	CDELPSU	SCULPED
CDEILPU	CLUPEID	CDEIRSU	CRUISED	CDELRRU	CURDLER
CDEILQU	CLIQUED		DISCURE	CDELRSU	CURDLES
CDEILRS	CLERIDS	CDEIRSV	CERVIDS		SCUDLER
CDEILRU	LUCIDER		SCRIVED	CDELRUY	CRUDELY
CDEILST	DELICTS	CDEIRTV	VERDICT	CDELSTU	DULCETS
CDEILSU	SLUICED	CDEISST	DISSECT	CDELTTU	CUTTLED
CDEILTU	DUCTILE	CDEISSY	ECDYSIS	CDELTUU	DUCTULE
	DULCITE	CDEITUX	EXCUDIT	CDEMMNO	COMMEND
CDEIMNO	DEMONIC	CDEJNOU	JOUNCED	CDEMMOO	COMMODE
CDEIMOR	DORMICE	CDEKKNO	KNOCKED	CDEMMSU	SCUMMED
CDEIMOS	MEDICOS	CDEKLNO	CLONKED	CDEMNNO	CONDEMN
	MISCODE	CDEKLNU	CLUNKED	CDEMNOP	COMPEND
CDEIMOT	DEMOTIC	CDEKLOW	WEDLOCK	CDEMOOS	COMEDOS
CDEIMPR	CRIMPED	CDEKLPU	PLUCKED	CDEMOPT	COMPTED
CDEIMPU	PUMICED	CDEKLRU	RUCKLED	CDEMORS	SCROMED
CDEIMSU	MISCUED	CDEKLSU	SCULKED	CDEMORU	DECORUM
CDEINOS	CODEINS		SUCKLED	CDEMPRU	CRUMPED
	CONDIES	CDEKMOS	SMOCKED	CDENNOO	CONDONE
	SECONDI	CDEKNOR	DORNECK	CDENNOT	CONTEND
CDEINOT	CTENOID	CDEKNOS	DOCKENS	CDENOOP	POONCED
	DEONTIC	CDEKNRU	CRUNKED	CDENOOR	CROONED
	NOTICED		DRUCKEN	CDENOOS	CONDOES
CDEINOU	DOUCINE	CDEKNSU	SUNDECK		SECONDO
CDEINOZ	ZINCODE		UNDECKS	CDENOPU	POUNCED
CDEINPR	PRINCED	CDEKOOR	CROOKED		UNCOPED
CDEINRS	CINDERS	CDEKORS	DOCKERS	CDENORS	CONDERS
	DISCERN		REDOCKS		CORSNED
	NERDICS	CDEKORT	TROCKED		SCORNED
	RESCIND	CDEKOST	DESTOCK	CDENORU	CRUNODE
CDEINRU	INDUCER		DOCKETS	CDENORW	CROWNED
CDEINRY	CINDERY		STOCKED		DECROWN
CDEINSU	CUNDIES	CDEKRSU	DUCKERS	CDENOSS	SECONDS
	INCUDES	CDEKRTU	TRUCKED	CDENOST	DOCENTS
	INCUSED	CDELLOU	COLLUDE	CDENOSY	ECDYSON
	INDUCES		LOCULED	CDENOTU	COUNTED
CDEINSX	EXSCIND	CDELLSU	SCULLED	CDENPUY	PUDENCY

CDENRUU	UNCURED		LINGCOD	CDIMNOO	MONODIC
CDENRUY	DUNCERY	CDGINNO	CONDIGN	CDIMNSU	MUNDICS
CDEOOPP	COPEPOD	CDGINOO	DOOCING	CDIMOOR	CORMOID
CDEOOPS	OPCODES	CDGINOR	CORDING	CDIMOOS	COSMOID
	SCOOPED	CDGINOS	CODINGS	CDIMOSS	COSMIDS
CDEOOPT	COOPTED	CDGINRU	CURDING	CDIMOSU	MUCOIDS
CDEOORR	CORRODE	CDGINTU	DUCTING		MUSCOID
CDEOORV	CODROVE	CDGNOOO	COONDOG	CDIMSSU	MUSCIDS
	VOCODER	CDGOOSY	COYDOGS	CDIMSTU	DICTUMS
CDEOOST	SCOOTED	CDHIMO	DOCHMII	CDINOOS	CONOIDS
CDEOOTV	DOVECOT	CDHIINT	CHINDIT	CDINOOT	ODONTIC
CDEOPPR	CROPPED	CDHIIST	DISTICH	CDINOSY	SYNODIC
CDEOPRS	CORPSED	CDHILLY	CHILDLY	CDINOTU	CONDUIT
CDEOPRU	CROUPED	CDHILNU	UNCHILD		NOCTUID
	PRODUCE	CDHILOR	CHLORID	CDINSSY	SYNDICS
CDEOPSU	SCOUPED	CDHILOS	COLDISH	CDINSTU	INDUCTS
CDEOPSW	SCOWPED	CDHINOR	CHONDRI	CDIOOTT	COTTOID
CDEOQTU	DOCQUET	CDHINSU	DUNCISH	CDIOPRR	RIPCORD
CDEORRS	CORDERS	CDHIOOR	CHOROID	CDIOPSS	PSOCIDS
	RECORDS		OCHROID	CDIORSV	CORVIDS
CDEORRW	CROWDER	CDHIORS	DROICHS	CDIOSST	CODISTS
CDEORSS	CROSSED		ORCHIDS	CDIOSTT	COTTIDS
	SCORSED	CDHIORY	DROICHY	CDIOSTY	CYSTOID
CDEORSU	COURSED	CDHIOTU	OUTCHID	CDIOTUV	OVIDUCT
	SCOURED	CDHIPTY	DIPTYCH	CDIPRSY	CYPRIDS
	SOURCED	CDHIRTY	CHYTRID	CDIPSSU	CUSPIDS
CDEORSW	SCOWDER	CDHKOOR	HORDOCK	CDIRSUY	DYSURIC
CDEORTU	COURTED	CDHORSS	SCHRODS	CDIRTUY	CRUDITY
	EDUCTOR	CDIIILP	LIPIDIC	CDISSSU	DISCUSS
CDEORUU	DOUCEUR	CDIIIOT	IDIOTIC	CDISSTY	CYSTIDS
CDEOSSU	ESCUDOS	CDIIJRU	JURIDIC	CDKMORU	MUDROCK
CDEOSTU	CUSTODE	CDIILLY	IDYLLIC	CDKNNOU	DUNNOCK
	DOUCEST	CDIILMO	DOMICIL	CDKNOOR	DORNOCK
	DOUCETS	CDIILNY	DICLINY	CDKNOSU	UNDOCKS
	SCOUTED	CDIILOP	DIPLOIC	CDLNOUU	UNCLOUD
CDEOSTY	CYTODES	CDIIMOS	DISOMIC	CDLOOPY	LYCOPOD
CDEOSYZ	ZYDECOS	CDIINOR	CRINOID	CDLOSTU	COULDST
CDEPRSU	SPRUCED	CDIINOT	DICTION	CDMMOOO	COMMODO
CDEPRTY	DECRYPT	CDIINOV	VIDICON	CDMNOOS	CONDOMS
CDERRSU	SCURRED	CDIINOZ	ZINCOID	CDMNSUU	CUNDUMS
CDERSTU	CRUDEST	CDIINST	INDICTS	CDMOOST	DOTCOMS
	CRUSTED	CDIINTU	DUNITIC		TOMCODS
CDERSUZ	SCRUZED	CDIIOPT	PODITIC	CDMOSUW	MUDSCOW
CDFHIOS	CODFISH	CDIIORS	CIRSOID	CDNNOTU	CONTUND
CDFIILU	FLUIDIC	CDIIORX	CORIXID	CDNOORS	CONDORS
CDFIISU	FUSIDIC	CDIIOSS	CISSOID		CORDONS
CDFIJOR	FJORDIC	CDIIOSV	VISCOID	CDNORSU	UNCORDS
CDFILUY	DULCIFY	CDIIOTY	IDIOTCY	CDNOTUW	CUTDOWN
CDFIOOT	OCTOFID	CDIIPRY	PYRIDIC	CDOOOPT	OCTOPOD
CDFIOSU	FUCOIDS	CDIIRSU	SCIURID	CDOOOST	DOOCOTS
CDFNOOU	COFOUND	CDIKNNU	NUDNICK	CDOOPST	POSTDOC
CDGHIIN	CHIDING	CDIKNOR	DORNICK	CDOORRY	CORRODY
CDGHILO	GLOCHID	CDIKNOW	WINDOCK	CDOORST	DOCTORS
CDGIIKN	DICKING	CDIKNPU	DUCKPIN	CDOOTUW	WOODCUT
CDGIINO	GONIDIC	CDILLOO	COLLOID	CDOPRTU	PRODUCT
CDGIINS	DICINGS	CDILLUY	LUCIDLY	CDOSTUY	CUSTODY
	DISCING	CDILMTU	MIDCULT	CEEEEGH	GEECHEE
CDGIINT	DICTING	CDILNOS	CODLINS	CEEEEHL	LEECHEE
CDGIKNO	DOCKING	CDILOTU	DULOTIC	CEEEELT	ELECTEE
CDGIKNU	DUCKING	CDILOTY	DICOTYL	CEEEFIL	FLEECIE
CDGILNO	CODLING	CDIMMOU	MODICUM	CEEEFLR	FLEECER

CEEEFLS	FLEECES	CEEFSSU	FESCUES	CEEHLRS	LECHERS
CEEEFNR	REFENCE	CEEGHIN	EECHING	CEEHLRW	WELCHER
CEEEGNR	REGENCE	CEEGHOS	CHEGOES	CEEHLRY	CHEERLY
CEEEGNS	EGENCES	CEEGIIP	EPIGEIC		LECHERY
CEEEGRS	GREECES	CEEGINR	CREEING	CEEHLSS	CHESSEL
CEEEHIR	REECHIE		ENERGIC	CEEHLST	LETCHES
CEEEHKS	KEECHES		GENERIC	CEEHLSW	LECHWES
CEEEHLL	ECHELLE	CEEGINT	GENETIC		WELCHES
CEEEHLS	ELCHEES	CEEGINU	EUGENIC	CEEHLSY	LYCHEES
	LEECHES	CEEGIRS	CIERGES		SLEECHY
CEEEHNR	ENCHEER		GRECISE	CEEHMRS	MERCHES
CEEEHPR	CHEEPER		GRIECES		SCHEMER
CEEEHRR	CHEERER	CEEGIRZ	GRECIZE		SCHMEER
CEEEHRS	REECHES	CEEGKOS	GECKOES	CEEHMRT	MERCHET
CEEEHSS	CHEESES	CEEGLLO	COLLEGE	CEEHMSS	SCHEMES
CEEEINP	EPICENE	CEEGLNT	NEGLECT	CEEHNOP	PENOCHE
CEEEIPR	CREEPIE	CEEGLOU	ECLOGUE	CEEHNPU	PENUCHE
CEEEIRV	RECEIVE	CEEGNOR	COGENER	CEEHNRW	WENCHER
CEEEITV	EVICTEE		CONGREE	CEEHNST	CHENETS
CEEEJRT	REEJECT	CEEGNOS	CONGEES		TENCHES
CEEELLU	ECUELLE	CEEGNRU	URGENCE	CEEHNSV	CHEVENS
CEEELPY	YCLEEPE	CEEGNRY	REGENCY	CEEHNSW	WENCHES
CEEELRT	REELECT	CEEGORT	CORTEGE		WHENCES
CEEELST	CELESTE	CEEGQRU	GRECQUE	CEEHNTU	CHUTNEE
CEEELSV	CLEEVES	CEEHHSW	WHEECHS	CEEHORR	COHERER
CEEEMPR	EMPERCE	CEEHIKM	KIMCHEE	CEEHORS	CHEEROS
CEEENRS	RECENSE	CEEHILN	ELENCHI		CHOREES
CEEENSS	ESSENCE	CEEHILS	ELICHES		COHERES
CEEEPRR	CREEPER		HELICES		ECHOERS
CEEERRT	ERECTER		LICHEES		RECHOSE
	REERECT	CEEHILV	VEHICLE	CEEHORT	TROCHEE
CEEERSS	CREESES	CEEHIMR	CHIMERE	CEEHOUV	VOUCHEE
CEEERST	SECRETE	CEEHIMS	CHEMISE	CEEHPRR	PERCHER
CEEERSV	SCREEVE		SCHEMIE	CEEHPRS	PERCHES
CEEERTX	EXCRETE	CEEHINR	INHERCE	CEEHPRU	UPCHEER
CEEETUX	EXECUTE	CEEHINS	CHINESE	CEEHQRU	CHEQUER
CEEFFNO	OFFENCE	CEEHIOR	CHEERIO	CEEHQSU	CHEQUES
CEEFFOR	EFFORCE		ECHOIER	CEEHQUY	QUEECHY
CEEFFOS	COFFEES	CEEHIOS	ECHOISE	CEEHRST	ETCHERS
CEEFFST	EFFECTS	CEEHIOZ	ECHOIZE		RETCHES
CEEFHIR	CHIEFER	CEEHIRT	ERETHIC	CEEHRSU	EUCHRES
CEEFHIT	FETICHE		ETHERIC	CEEHRSV	CHEVRES
	FITCHEE		HERETIC	CEEHRSW	CHEWERS
CEEFHLS	FELCHES		TECHIER		RECHEWS
	FLECHES	CEEHIRW	CHEWIER	CEEHRSY	CREESHY
CEEFHRT	FECHTER	CEEHIRY	YECHIER	CEEHRTU	TEUCHER
	FETCHER	CEEHISS	SEICHES	CEEHRTV	CHEVRET
CEEFHST	FETCHES	CEEHIST	TECHIES	CEEHSSS	CHESSES
CEEFINV	VENEFIC	CEEHISV	CHEVIES	CEEHSSW	ESCHEWS
CEEFIRR	FIERCER		SEVICHE	CEEHSTV	CHEVETS
CEEFKLR	FLECKER	CEEHISW	CHEWIES		VETCHES
	FRECKLE	CEEHKLR	HECKLER	CEEHSTW	CHEWETS
CEEFLNU	FLUENCE	CEEHKLS	HECKLES	CEEIIKL	ICELIKE
CEEFLRT	REFLECT	CEEHKNP	HENPECK	CEEIINR	EIRENIC
CEEFNNS	FENNECS	CEEHKNS	KENCHES	CEEIINW	ICEWINE
CEEFNNU	UNFENCE	CEEHKST	KETCHES	CEEIIPR	EPEIRIC
CEEFNOR	ENFORCE	CEEHLNO	CHELONE		EPICIER
CEEFNRS	FENCERS		ECHELON	CEEIJOR	REJOICE
CEEFPRT	PERFECT	CEEHLNS	ELENCHS	CEEIKLT	CLEEKIT
	PREFECT	CEEHLNU	LEUCHEN	CEEIKNT	NECKTIE
CEEFRST	REFECTS	CEEHLOW	COWHEEL	CEEIKPR	PECKIER

	PICKEER	**CEEIPST**	PECTISE			PRELECT
CEEIKSS	SICKEES	**CEEIPTZ**	PECTIZE	**CEELPRU**	CUPELER
CEEILLM	MICELLE	**CEEIQSU**	QUIESCE	**CEELRRU**	CRUELER
CEEILMX	LEXEMIC	**CEEIRRT**	RECITER	**CEELRSS**	SCLERES
CEEILNO	CINEOLE	**CEEIRSS**	CERISES	**CEELRST**	TERCELS
CEEILNR	RECLINE	**CEEIRST**	CERITES	**CEELRSU**	RECLUSE
CEEILNS	LICENSE		RECITES		RECULES
	SELENIC		TIERCES	**CEELRSW**	CREWELS
	SILENCE	**CEEIRSU**	ECURIES	**CEELRTU**	LECTURE
CEEILNT	CENTILE	**CEEIRSV**	SCRIEVE	**CEELRTY**	ERECTLY
	LICENTE		SERVICE	**CEELSST**	SELECTS
CEEILNU	LEUCINE	**CEEIRTT**	TIERCET	**CEELSUX**	CULEXES
CEEILPS	ECLIPSE	**CEEIRTU**	EUCRITE	**CEELTTU**	LETTUCE
CEEILPT	TELEPIC	**CEEIRTX**	EXCITER	**CEEMMOR**	COMMERE
CEEILPX	EXCIPLE	**CEEISSX**	EXCISES	**CEEMNOW**	NEWCOME
CEEILRS	CEILERS	**CEEISTU**	CUTESIE	**CEEMNRU**	CERUMEN
CEEILRT	RETICLE	**CEEISTX**	EXCITES	**CEEMNRW**	CREWMEN
	TIERCEL	**CEEITTT**	TECTITE	**CEEMNST**	CEMENTS
CEEILRU	RECUILE	**CEEITTZ**	ZETETIC	**CEEMNSY**	CYMENES
CEEILSS	ICELESS	**CEEJNOS**	CONJEES	**CEEMOPR**	COMPEER
	SIECLES	**CEEJORT**	EJECTOR		COMPERE
CEEILST	SECTILE	**CEEJRST**	REJECTS	**CEEMOPT**	COMPETE
CEEILSV	VESICLE	**CEEKKLS**	KECKLES	**CEEMRRS**	MERCERS
CEEILTU	LEUCITE	**CEEKKSS**	KECKSES	**CEEMRRY**	MERCERY
CEEIMMS	SEMEMIC	**CEEKLNT**	NECKLET		REMERCY
CEEIMMT	MEMETIC	**CEEKLPS**	SPECKLE	**CEEMRST**	CERMETS
CEEIMNO	MIOCENE	**CEEKLSS**	SECKELS	**CEEMSTU**	TUMESCE
CEEIMNT	CENTIME		SECKLES	**CEEMSTY**	MYCETES
CEEIMRS	MERCIES	**CEEKLST**	TECKELS	**CEENNOU**	ENOUNCE
CEEIMRX	EXCIMER	**CEEKNRS**	NECKERS	**CEENNOV**	CONVENE
CEEIMST	EMETICS	**CEEKOSS**	COKESES	**CEENNRT**	CENTNER
CEEINNS	INCENSE	**CEEKOSY**	SOCKEYE	**CEENOOT**	ECOTONE
CEEINOS	SENECIO	**CEEKPRS**	PECKERS	**CEENOPT**	POTENCE
CEEINPR	PERCINE	**CEEKPRY**	RYEPECK	**CEENORS**	ENCORES
CEEINPS	PICENES	**CEEKRRW**	WRECKER		NECROSE
	PIECENS	**CEELLLU**	CELLULE	**CEENORU**	COENURE
CEEINPT	PENTICE	**CEELLNO**	COLLEEN	**CEENORZ**	COZENER
CEEINPU	EUPNEIC	**CEELLOS**	CELLOSE	**CEENOST**	CENOTES
CEEINRS	CERESIN	**CEELLPU**	PUCELLE	**CEENPRS**	SPENCER
	SCRIENE	**CEELMNT**	CLEMENT	**CEENPRT**	PERCENT
	SINCERE	**CEELMOO**	COELOME		PRECENT
CEEINRT	ENTERIC	**CEELMOS**	CLEOMES	**CEENPSS**	SPENCES
	ENTICER	**CEELMOT**	TELECOM	**CEENPST**	PECTENS
CEEINRV	CERVINE	**CEELMOW**	WELCOME	**CEENRSS**	CENSERS
CEEINST	ENTICES	**CEELMSY**	MYCELES		SCERNES
CEEINSV	EVINCES	**CEELNOS**	ENCLOSE		SCREENS
CEEIOPT	PICOTEE	**CEELNPS**	PENCELS		SECERNS
CEEIORT	COTERIE	**CEELNRS**	CRENELS	**CEENRST**	CENTERS
CEEIORV	REVOICE	**CEELNRT**	LECTERN		CENTRES
CEEIOST	COESITE	**CEELNRU**	LUCERNE		TENRECS
CEEIPPR	PRECIPE	**CEELORS**	CREOLES	**CEENRSU**	CENSURE
CEEIPRR	CREPIER		RECLOSE	**CEENRSY**	SCENERY
	PIERCER	**CEELORT**	ELECTOR	**CEENTTU**	CUNETTE
	REPRICE		ELECTRO	**CEEOPRU**	RECOUPE
CEEIPRS	PIECERS	**CEELORY**	RECOYLE	**CEEOPST**	PECTOSE
	PIERCES	**CEELOSS**	ECLOSES	**CEEOPSU**	COUPEES
	PRECISE	**CEELOSU**	COULEES	**CEEOPTY**	ECOTYPE
	RECIPES	**CEELOTU**	ELOCUTE	**CEEORRS**	RESCORE
CEEIPRT	RECEIPT	**CEELOTV**	COVELET	**CEEORRT**	ERECTOR
CEEIPRU	EPICURE	**CEELOTX**	CELOTEX	**CEEORRU**	RECOURE
CEEIPSS	SPECIES	**CEELPRT**	PLECTRE	**CEEORRV**	COVERER

	RECOVER	**CEFGIKN**	FECKING	**CEGGIOR**	GEORGIC
CEEORRW	RECOWER	**CEFGINN**	FENCING	**CEGGIOS**	COGGIES
CEEORSU	CEREOUS	**CEFHILR**	FILCHER	**CEGGLOR**	CLOGGER
CEEORSV	CORVEES	**CEFHILS**	FILCHES	**CEGGLOS**	COGGLES
CEEORTV	COVETER	**CEFHILY**	CHIEFLY	**CEGGORS**	COGGERS
CEEORTW	COWTREE	**CEFHINS**	FINCHES	**CEGGPSU**	EGGCUPS
CEEORTX	COEXERT	**CEFHIRY**	CHIEFRY	**CEGHILN**	LECHING
CEEOTTT	OCTETTE	**CEFHIST**	FITCHES	**CEGHINO**	ECHOING
CEEPPRT	PERCEPT	**CEFHITT**	FITCHET	**CEGHINP**	PECHING
	PRECEPT	**CEFHITW**	FITCHEW	**CEGHINT**	ETCHING
CEEPPRU	PREPUCE	**CEFHLTU**	FUTCHEL	**CEGHINW**	CHEWING
CEEPRRU	PRECURE	**CEFIILT**	FICTILE	**CEGHIOR**	CHOREGI
CEEPRSS	PRECESS	**CEFIIOR**	ORIFICE	**CEGHIOS**	CHIGOES
CEEPRST	RECEPTS	**CEFIITV**	FICTIVE	**CEGHIRS**	CHIGRES
	RESPECT	**CEFIKLR**	FICKLER		SCREIGH
	SCEPTER		FLICKER	**CEGHITU**	GUICHET
	SCEPTRE	**CEFIKLS**	FICKLES	**CEGHLSU**	CLEUGHS
	SPECTER	**CEFILNT**	INFLECT		GULCHES
	SPECTRE	**CEFILNU**	FUNICLE	**CEGHORU**	COUGHER
CEEPRTX	EXCERPT	**CEFILRU**	FLUERIC	**CEGHOSU**	GOUCHES
CEEPSTX	EXCEPTS		LUCIFER	**CEGHRTU**	GUTCHER
	EXPECTS	**CEFIMOR**	COMFIER	**CEGIILN**	CEILING
CEEPSTY	ECTYPES	**CEFIMRY**	MERCIFY		CIELING
CEEPSUY	EYECUPS	**CEFINNO**	CONFINE	**CEGIINP**	PIECING
CEERRSU	RECURES	**CEFINOR**	COINFER	**CEGIKKN**	KECKING
	RESCUER		CONIFER	**CEGIKNN**	NECKING
	SECURER		INFORCE	**CEGIKNP**	PECKING
CEERRSW	SCREWER	**CEFINST**	INFECTS	**CEGIKNR**	RECKING
CEERRUV	RECURVE	**CEFIPSY**	SPECIFY	**CEGIKRU**	GUCKIER
CEERSSS	CESSERS	**CEFIRSS**	SFERICS	**CEGILLN**	CELLING
	CRESSES	**CEFIRTY**	CERTIFY	**CEGILMP**	GEMCLIP
CEERSST	CRESSET		RECTIFY	**CEGILNP**	CLEPING
	RESECTS	**CEFISSU**	FICUSES	**CEGILNR**	CLINGER
	SCREETS	**CEFKLLO**	ELFLOCK		CRINGLE
	SECRETS	**CEFKLOT**	FETLOCK	**CEGILNU**	CLUEING
CEERSSU	CERUSES	**CEFKLRY**	FRECKLY		LUCIGEN
	CESURES	**CEFKRSU**	FUCKERS	**CEGILNW**	CLEWING
	RECUSES	**CEFLNOU**	FLOUNCE	**CEGILNY**	GLYCINE
	RESCUES	**CEFLNTU**	UNCLEFT	**CEGIMNO**	GENOMIC
	SECURES	**CEFLNUY**	FLUENCY	**CEGIMNU**	MUCIGEN
CEERSTT	TERCETS	**CEFMORY**	COMFREY	**CEGINNR**	CERNING
CEERSUX	EXCURSE	**CEFNORS**	CONFERS	**CEGINNS**	CENSING
	EXCUSER	**CEFNORU**	FROUNCE		SCENING
CEERTTU	CURETTE	**CEFNOSS**	CONFESS	**CEGINOR**	COREIGN
CEESSTX	EXSECTS	**CEFNOST**	CONFEST	**CEGINOS**	COGNISE
CEESSUX	EXCUSES	**CEFNOSU**	CONFUSE		COIGNES
CEETTUV	CUVETTE	**CEFNOTU**	CONFUTE	**CEGINOZ**	COGNIZE
CEFFHRU	CHUFFER	**CEFOPRS**	FORCEPS	**CEGINPR**	CREPING
CEFFIOR	OFFICER	**CEFORRS**	FORCERS		PERCING
CEFFIOS	COIFFES	**CEFORRT**	CROFTER	**CEGINRR**	CRINGER
	OFFICES	**CEFORSS**	FRESCOS	**CEGINRS**	CRINGES
CEFFISU	SUFFICE	**CEFORSU**	FOCUSER	**CEGINRW**	CREWING
CEFFLOS	COFFLES		REFOCUS	**CEGINSS**	CESSING
CEFFLSU	CUFFLES	**CEFOSSU**	FOCUSES	**CEGINSU**	CUEINGS
	SCUFFLE		FUCOSES	**CEGIORT**	ERGOTIC
CEFFORS	COFFERS	**CEFRSUW**	CURFEWS	**CEGIRRS**	GRICERS
	SCOFFER	**CEFSSUU**	FUCUSES	**CEGKLNO**	GENLOCK
CEFFORT	COFFRET	**CEGGHIR**	CHIGGER	**CEGKLOR**	GROCKLE
CEFFRSU	SCUFFER	**CEGGHRU**	CHUGGER	**CEGLNOO**	COLOGNE
CEFFSTU	SUFFECT	**CEGGIIS**	CIGGIES	**CEGLOOY**	ECOLOGY
CEFGHIN	CHEFING	**CEGGIKN**	GECKING	**CEGLOSU**	GLUCOSE

CEGLOSY	GLYCOSE	CEHILNS	LICHENS	CEHIORS	COHEIRS
CEGNNOO	ONCOGEN		LINCHES		HEROICS
CEGNOOS	CONGOES	CEHILNT	LINCHET	CEHIORT	ROTCHIE
CEGNORS	CONGERS		TINCHEL		THEORIC
CEGNORU	CONGRUE	CEHILPR	PILCHER	CEHIOST	ECHOIST
CEGNORY	CRYOGEN	CEHILPS	PILCHES		TOISECH
CEGNOST	CONGEST	CEHILRT	LICHTER	CEHIOTU	COUTHIE
CEGNRUY	URGENCY	CEHILRV	CHERVIL	CEHIOTV	CHEVIOT
CEGNSSU	SCUNGES	CEHILSS	CHESILS	CEHIPPR	CHIPPER
CEGNSTY	CYGNETS		CHISELS	CEHIPRR	CHIRPER
CEGOORS	SCROOGE	CEHILST	ELTCHIS	CEHIPRS	CERIPHS
CEGORRS	GROCERS	CEHILSZ	ZILCHES		CIPHERS
CEGORRY	GROCERY	CEHILTY	ETHYLIC		RECHIPS
CEGORSU	SCOURGE		LECYTHI		SPHERIC
	SCROUGE		TECHILY	CEHIPRT	PITCHER
CEHHILS	HILCHES	CEHILXY	HEXYLIC	CEHIPST	CHIPSET
CEHHIOO	HOOCHIE	CEHIMMO	CHOMMIE		PITCHES
CEHHIRS	CHERISH	CEHIMMS	CHEMISM	CEHIQSU	QUICHES
	SHRIECH	CEHIMNY	CHIMNEY	CEHIRRS	CHIRRES
CEHHIRT	HITCHER	CEHIMOR	HOMERIC	CEHIRRT	RICHTER
CEHHIST	HITCHES		MOCHIER	CEHIRST	CITHERS
CEHHITU	HUTCHIE		MORICHE		ESTRICH
CEHHNSU	HUNCHES	CEHIMOS	ECHOISM		RICHEST
CEHHOOS	HOOCHES	CEHIMRS	CHIMERS	CEHIRSU	CUSHIER
CEHHOST	HOTCHES		MICHERS	CEHIRSZ	SCHERZI
	SHOCHET	CEHIMRT	THERMIC	CEHIRTT	CHITTER
CEHHSSU	SHEUCHS	CEHIMRU	RHEUMIC	CEHISSU	CUISHES
CEHHSTU	HUTCHES	CEHIMST	CHEMIST		CUSHIES
CEHIIKN	CHINKIE		MITCHES	CEHISTT	TITCHES
CEHIIKS	HICKIES	CEHIMSU	ECHIUMS	CEHISTW	WITCHES
CEHIIKT	THICKIE	CEHINNO	CHINONE	CEHISZZ	CHIZZES
CEHIILS	CHILIES	CEHINOP	CHOPINE	CEHKKRU	CHUKKER
CEHIINR	HIRCINE		PHOCINE	CEHKLMO	HEMLOCK
CEHIINS	NICEISH	CEHINOR	CHORINE	CEHKLOS	HOCKLES
CEHIINT	ICHNITE	CEHINOT	HENOTIC	CEHKLSU	HUCKLES
	NITCHIE	CEHINOX	CHOENIX	CEHKNOU	UNCHOKE
CEHIIPP	CHIPPIE	CEHINPR	NEPHRIC	CEHKNSU	KUCHENS
CEHIIRT	ITCHIER		PHRENIC	CEHKOOR	KERCHOO
	TICHIER		PINCHER	CEHKORS	CHOKERS
CEHIISV	CHIVIES	CEHINPS	PINCHES		HOCKERS
	VICHIES		SPHENIC		SHOCKER
CEHIKNT	CHETNIK	CEHINPU	PENUCHI	CEHKOST	KOTCHES
	KITCHEN	CEHINQU	QUINCHE	CEHKOSY	CHOKEYS
	THICKEN	CEHINRR	CHIRREN		HOCKEYS
CEHIKNW	CHEWINK	CEHINRS	INCHERS	CEHKPTU	KETCHUP
CEHIKOO	CHOOKIE		NICHERS	CEHKRSU	SHUCKER
CEHIKOR	CHOKIER		RICHENS	CEHKRUY	HUCKERY
CEHIKOS	CHOKIES	CEHINRT	CITHERN	CEHKSTU	KUTCHES
CEHIKPS	PECKISH		CITHREN	CEHKSTY	SKETCHY
CEHIKRR	CHIRKER	CEHINRW	WINCHER	CEHKTVY	KVETCHY
CEHIKRS	SHICKER	CEHINST	ETHNICS	CEHLLMO	MOCHELL
	SKRIECH		STHENIC	CEHLLMU	MUCHELL
CEHIKRT	THICKER	CEHINSU	ECHINUS	CEHLLNS	SCHNELL
CEHIKRW	WHICKER	CEHINSV	CHEVINS	CEHLLOY	YELLOCH
CEHIKST	CHEKIST	CEHINSW	WINCHES	CEHLLPU	CHELLUP
CEHIKSY	HICKEYS	CEHINSZ	ZECHINS	CEHLLSY	SCHELLY
CEHIKTT	THICKET	CEHINTW	WITCHEN	CEHLMOR	CHROMEL
CEHILLR	CHILLER	CEHIOPS	HOSPICE	CEHLMSS	SCHELMS
CEHILMY	CHIMLEY	CEHIOPT	POTICHE	CEHLMSU	MUCHELS
CEHILNO	CHOLINE	CEHIOPU	COPIHUE		MULCHES
	HELICON	CEHIORR	CHORRIE	CEHLMSZ	SCHMELZ

CEHLMUY	CHUMLEY	CEHOOSS	CHOOSES	CEIILPP	CLIPPIE
CEHLNNU	CHUNNEL	CEHOOSY	CHOOSEY	CEIILPT	PELITIC
CEHLNOS	NOCHELS	CEHOOTU	OUTECHO	CEIILST	ELICITS
CEHLNOT	CHOLENT	CEHOPPR	CHOPPER	CEIILTV	LEVITIC
	NOTCHEL	CEHOPRS	PORCHES	CEIIMMT	MIMETIC
CEHLNRU	LUNCHER	CEHOPRT	POTCHER	CEIIMNR	CREMINI
CEHLNRY	LYNCHER	CEHOPRY	CORYPHE		CRIMINE
CEHLNSU	LUNCHES	CEHOPST	POTCHES		MINCIER
CEHLNSY	LYNCHES	CEHOPSU	POUCHES	CEIIMNS	MENISCI
CEHLNTY	LYNCHET	CEHORRT	TORCHER	CEIIMOT	MEIOTIC
CEHLOOS	SCHOOLE	CEHORSS	COSHERS	CEIIMPR	EMPIRIC
CEHLORS	CHOLERS	CEHORST	HECTORS	CEIIMPS	EPICISM
	ORCHELS		ROCHETS	CEIIMRS	CIMIERS
CEHLORT	CHORTLE		ROTCHES	CEIIMRV	VIREMIC
CEHLORU	LOUCHER		TOCHERS	CEIIMSS	SEISMIC
CEHLOST	CLOTHES		TORCHES	CEIIMST	MISCITE
CEHLPPS	SCHLEPP		TROCHES	CEIIMTT	TITMICE
CEHLPSS	SCHLEPS	CEHORSU	CHOREUS	CEIINNO	CONIINE
CEHLPSU	PLEUCHS		CHOUSER		INCONIE
CEHLQSU	SQUELCH		ROUCHES	CEIINNR	CINERIN
CEHLRRU	LURCHER	CEHORSY	COSHERY	CEIINOR	ONEIRIC
CEHLRSU	LURCHES	CEHORSZ	SCHERZO	CEIINOS	EOSINIC
CEHMNRU	MUNCHER	CEHORTU	COUTHER		ICONISE
CEHMNSU	MUNCHES		RETOUCH		NICOISE
CEHMNSY	MENSCHY		TOUCHER	CEIINOV	INVOICE
CEHMOOR	MOOCHER	CEHORTW	WOTCHER	CEIINOZ	ICONIZE
CEHMOOS	MOOCHES	CEHORUV	VOUCHER	CEIINPS	PISCINE
CEHMOPR	CHOMPER	CEHOSSU	CHOUSES	CEIINRS	IRENICS
CEHMORS	CHROMES		HOCUSES		SERICIN
CEHMORU	MOUCHER	CEHOSSW	CHOWSES		SIRENIC
CEHMOSS	SCHMOES	CEHOSTU	TOUCHES	CEIINRT	CITRINE
CEHMOSU	MOUCHES	CEHOSUV	VOUCHES		CRINITE
CEHMOTZ	CHOMETZ	CEHPRSU	CHERUPS		INCITER
CEHMRTU	CHETRUM	CEHPRSY	CHYPRES		NERITIC
CEHMSTU	HUMECTS		CYPHERS	CEIINRZ	ZINCIER
	MUTCHES	CEHPRTU	PUTCHER	CEIINSS	ICINESS
CEHNNRU	CHUNNER	CEHPSSY	PSYCHES		INCISES
CEHNOOP	HENCOOP	CEHQSTU	QUETSCH	CEIINST	INCITES
CEHNOOR	COEHORN	CEHRRSU	CRUSHER	CEIINSU	CUISINE
CEHNOOT	THEOCON	CEHRSSU	CRUSHES	CEIINTZ	CITIZEN
CEHNORT	CHORTEN	CEHRSTT	STRETCH		ZINCITE
	NOTCHER	CEHRSTY	SCYTHER	CEIIOPZ	EPIZOIC
CEHNORV	CHEVRON	CEHSSTU	TUSCHES	CEIIPPR	PIPERIC
CEHNOST	NOTCHES	CEHSSTY	SCYTHES	CEIIPRR	PRICIER
	TECHNOS	CEIIJRU	JUICIER	CEIIPRS	SPICIER
CEHNOSU	COHUNES	CEIIKKR	KICKIER	CEIIPRT	PICRITE
CEHNPRU	PUNCHER	CEIIKLS	SICLIKE	CEIIPST	EPICIST
	UNPERCH	CEIIKMS	MICKIES	CEIIRSS	CISSIER
CEHNPST	PSCHENT	CEIIKNS	KINESIC	CEIIRST	ERISTIC
CEHNPSU	PUNCHES	CEIIKNT	KINETIC		RICIEST
CEHNRRU	CHURNER	CEIIKPR	PICKIER	CEIIRSU	CRUISIE
CEHNRSU	RUNCHES	CEIIKQU	QUICKIE	CEIIRUZ	CRUIZIE
CEHNRTU	CHUNTER	CEIIKRT	TRICKIE	CEIISSS	CISSIES
CEHNSTU	CHESNUT	CEIIKSS	SICKIES	CEIISVV	CIVVIES
CEHNSTY	STENCHY	CEIIKST	EKISTIC	CEIITUV	UVEITIC
CEHNSUU	EUNUCHS		ICKIEST	CEIJNST	INJECTS
CEHNTUY	CHUTNEY		TICKIES	CEIJRSU	JUICERS
CEHOOPS	POOCHES	CEIIKSW	WICKIES	CEIJSTU	JUSTICE
CEHOORS	CHOOSER	CEIILLS	SILICLE	CEIKKNR	KNICKER
	SOROCHE	CEIILNN	INCLINE	CEIKKRS	KICKERS
CEHOORT	CHEROOT	CEIILNP	PENICIL	CEIKLMR	MICKLER

CEIKLMS	MELICKS	**CEIKRSU**	SUCKIER	**CEILQSU**	CLIQUES
	MICKLES	**CEIKRSW**	WICKERS	**CEILQUY**	CLIQUEY
CEIKLNR	CLINKER	**CEIKRSY**	RICKEYS	**CEILRRU**	CURLIER
	CRINKLE		YICKERS	**CEILRSS**	SLICERS
CEIKLNS	NICKELS	**CEIKRTU**	TRUCKIE	**CEILRST**	RELICTS
	NICKLES	**CEIKRTY**	RICKETY	**CEILRSU**	CURLIES
	SLICKEN	**CEIKRUY**	YUCKIER	**CEILRSV**	CLIVERS
CEIKLPR	PICKLER	**CEIKSST**	SICKEST	**CEILRSY**	CLERISY
	PRICKLE	**CEIKSTT**	TICKETS	**CEILRTT**	CLITTER
CEIKLPS	PICKLES	**CEIKSTW**	WICKETS	**CEILRTU**	CULTIER
CEIKLPU	CUPLIKE	**CEIKSTY**	TICKEYS		UTRICLE
CEIKLRS	LICKERS	**CEILLMS**	MICELLS	**CEILSSS**	SCISSEL
	RICKLES	**CEILLNO**	LIONCEL	**CEILSSU**	SLUICES
	SLICKER	**CEILLNU**	NUCELLI	**CEILSTU**	LUCITES
CEIKLRT	TICKLER	**CEILLOR**	COLLIER		LUETICS
	TRICKLE	**CEILLOS**	COLLIES	**CEILTTU**	CUITTLE
CEIKLRU	LUCKIER	**CEILLST**	CELLIST	**CEIMMOS**	COMMIES
CEIKLSS	SICKLES	**CEILLSU**	CULLIES	**CEIMMRR**	CRIMMER
CEIKLST	ICKLEST	**CEILMOP**	COMPILE	**CEIMMRU**	CRUMMIE
	STICKLE		POLEMIC	**CEIMNNO**	MECONIN
	TICKLES	**CEILMOT**	TELOMIC	**CEIMNOR**	INCOMER
CEIKLSU	LUCKIES	**CEILMPR**	CRIMPLE	**CEIMNOS**	COSMINE
CEIKLSY	KYLICES	**CEILNNU**	NUCLEIN		INCOMES
CEIKMRS	SMICKER	**CEILNOP**	PINOCLE		MESONIC
CEIKMRU	MUCKIER		PLEONIC	**CEIMNOT**	CENTIMO
CEIKMRY	MICKERY	**CEILNOS**	CINEOLS		ENTOMIC
CEIKMST	SMICKET		CONSEIL		TONEMIC
CEIKMSY	MICKEYS		INCLOSE	**CEIMNRS**	CREMSIN
CEIKNOR	CONKIER	**CEILNOT**	LECTION		MINCERS
CEIKNOT	KENOTIC	**CEILNOX**	LEXICON	**CEIMNRU**	MINCEUR
	KETONIC	**CEILNPS**	PENCILS		NUMERIC
CEIKNQU	QUICKEN		SPLENIC	**CEIMNYZ**	ENZYMIC
CEIKNRS	NICKERS	**CEILNST**	CLIENTS	**CEIMOOR**	COOMIER
	SNICKER		LECTINS	**CEIMOPR**	MEROPIC
CEIKNSS	SICKENS		LENTISC	**CEIMOPT**	METOPIC
CEIKNST	SNICKET		STENCIL	**CEIMOQU**	COMIQUE
	TICKENS	**CEILNSU**	LEUCINS	**CEIMORR**	MORRICE
CEIKNSW	WICKENS	**CEILNTU**	CUTLINE	**CEIMORT**	MORTICE
CEIKOOS	COOKIES		LINECUT	**CEIMOSX**	EXOSMIC
CEIKOPR	POCKIER		TUNICLE	**CEIMOTT**	TOTEMIC
CEIKOPS	POCKIES	**CEILOOS**	COOLIES	**CEIMOTV**	VICOMTE
CEIKORR	CORKIER	**CEILOOT**	CLOOTIE	**CEIMOTX**	TOXEMIC
	ROCKIER	**CEILOPR**	PELORIC	**CEIMOUZ**	ZOECIUM
CEIKORT	TOCKIER		POLICER	**CEIMPRR**	CRIMPER
CEIKOST	COKIEST	**CEILOPS**	POLICES	**CEIMPRS**	SPERMIC
CEIKOTT	KETOTIC	**CEILOPT**	TOECLIP	**CEIMPRU**	PUMICER
CEIKPRR	PRICKER	**CEILORS**	COILERS	**CEIMPSU**	PUMICES
CEIKPRS	PICKERS		RECOILS	**CEIMRST**	CRETISM
	RIPECKS	**CEILORT**	CORTILE		METRICS
	SPICKER	**CEILORU**	URCEOLI	**CEIMRSU**	CERIUMS
CEIKPRT	PRICKET	**CEILOSS**	LOESSIC		MURICES
CEIKPRY	PICKERY		OSSICLE	**CEIMSSU**	CESIUMS
CEIKPST	PICKETS	**CEILOST**	CITOLES		MISCUES
	SKEPTIC	**CEILOTT**	COLETIT	**CEINNOS**	CONINES
CEIKQRU	QUICKER	**CEILPPR**	CLIPPER		CONNIES
CEIKRRS	RICKERS		CRIPPLE	**CEINNOV**	CONNIVE
CEIKRRT	TRICKER	**CEILPRS**	SPLICER	**CEINNST**	INCENTS
CEIKRSS	SCRIKES	**CEILPSS**	SPLICES	**CEINOOT**	COONTIE
CEIKRST	RICKETS	**CEILPSU**	SPICULE	**CEINOPR**	PERICON
	STICKER	**CEILPSV**	PELVICS		PONCIER
	TICKERS	**CEILPTU**	PICULET		PORCINE

CEINOPT	ENTOPIC	CEIOPPS	COPPIES	CEIPSST	CESSPIT
	NEPOTIC	CEIOPRS	COPIERS		SEPTICS
CEINORR	CORNIER		COPSIER	CEIQRSU	CIRQUES
CEINORS	COINERS		PERSICO	CEIRRRU	CURRIER
	CRINOSE	CEIOPRT	PTEROIC	CEIRRSU	CRUISER
	CRONIES	CEIOPST	POETICS		CURRIES
	ORCEINS	CEIOPSU	PICEOUS		SUCRIER
	ORCINES	CEIOPSW	COWPIES	CEIRRTT	CRITTER
	RECOINS	CEIORRS	CIRROSE	CEIRRTU	RECRUIT
	SERICON		CORRIES	CEIRRTX	RECTRIX
CEINORT	COINTER		CROSIER	CEIRRUV	CURVIER
	NOTICER		ORRICES	CEIRSSU	CRUISES
	RECTION	CEIORRU	COURIER		CRUSIES
CEINORU	COENURI	CEIORRZ	CROZIER		CUISSER
	NOURICE	CEIORSS	COSIERS	CEIRSSV	SCRIVES
CEINORV	CORVINE		CRIOSES	CEIRSTT	TRISECT
CEINORY	ORIENCY	CEIORST	EROTICS	CEIRSTU	CUITERS
CEINOSS	CESSION		TERCIOS		CURIETS
	COSINES	CEIORSU	COURIES		CURITES
	OSCINES		SCOURIE		ICTERUS
CEINOST	NOTICES	CEIORSV	CORSIVE	CEIRSTW	TWICERS
	SECTION		VOICERS	CEIRSUV	CRUIVES
CEINOSV	NOVICES	CEIORSW	COWRIES		CURSIVE
CEINOTT	ENTOTIC		SCOWRIE	CEIRSUZ	CRUZIES
	TONETIC	CEIORSZ	COZIERS	CEIRTTU	CUTTIER
CEINOTX	EXCITON	CEIORTT	COTTIER	CEIRTTX	TECTRIX
CEINOUV	UNVOICE	CEIORTV	EVICTOR	CEISSSU	CUISSES
CEINOVV	CONVIVE	CEIORTW	COWRITE	CEISSTU	CESTUIS
CEINPRS	CRISPEN	CEIORTX	EXCITOR		CUEISTS
	PINCERS		XEROTIC		CUTISES
	PRINCES	CEIORVY	VICEROY		ICTUSES
CEINPRY	CYPRINE	CEIOSSS	COSSIES	CEISTTU	CUTTIES
CEINPST	INCEPTS	CEIOSST	COSIEST	CEISUZZ	CUZZIES
	INSPECT		COTISES	CEJKOSY	JOCKEYS
	PECTINS		OECISTS	CEJNOOS	COJONES
	PEINCTS	CEIOSSU	CESIOUS	CEJNORU	CONJURE
CEINPTY	PYCNITE	CEIOSSV	VISCOSE	CEJNOSU	JOUNCES
CEINQSU	CINQUES	CEIOSTT	COTTISE		JUNCOES
	QUINCES		SCOTTIE	CEJOPRT	PROJECT
CEINRRU	CURNIER	CEIOSTV	COSTIVE	CEKKLNU	KNUCKLE
	REINCUR	CEIOSTW	COWIEST	CEKKNOR	KNOCKER
CEINRSS	SCRINES	CEIOSTX	COEXIST	CEKKOPS	KOPECKS
CEINRST	CISTERN		COXIEST	CEKLLOP	PELLOCK
	CRETINS		EXOTICS	CEKLLRY	CLERKLY
CEINRSV	CRIVENS	CEIOSTY	SOCIETY	CEKLMNO	LOCKMEN
CEINRSW	WINCERS	CEIOSTZ	COZIEST	CEKLMSU	MUCKLES
CEINRTT	CITTERN	CEIOTTY	TOYETIC	CEKLNOS	ENLOCKS
CEINRUV	INCURVE	CEIPPRU	CUPPIER		SLOCKEN
CEINSST	INCESTS	CEIPPST	PEPTICS	CEKLNRU	CLUNKER
	INSECTS	CEIPQTU	PICQUET		CRUNKLE
CEINSSU	INCUSES	CEIPRRS	CRISPER	CEKLORS	LOCKERS
CEINSTU	NEUSTIC		PRICERS		RELOCKS
CEINSTY	CYSTEIN	CEIPRSS	SPICERS	CEKLOST	LOCKETS
	CYSTINE	CEIPRST	TRICEPS		LOCKSET
CEINSWY	WINCEYS	CEIPRSU	CUSPIER	CEKLOTY	TOCKLEY
CEINTTX	EXTINCT	CEIPRSY	SPICERY	CEKLPRU	PLUCKER
CEINVVY	VIVENCY	CEIPRTU	CUPRITE	CEKLPSU	PUCKLES
CEIOOPR	OPORICE		PICTURE	CEKLRSU	RUCKLES
CEIOORS	COORIES	CEIPRTY	PYRETIC		SCULKER
CEIOOST	COOTIES	CEIPRXY	PYREXIC		SUCKLER
CEIOPPR	CROPPIE	CEIPSSS	SCEPSIS	CEKLRTU	TRUCKLE

CEKLSSU	SUCKLES	**CELMOOS**	COELOMS	**CELORVY**	CLOVERY
CEKMNOS	SOCKMEN	**CELMOPS**	COMPELS	**CELOSST**	CLOSEST
CEKMNOY	MOCKNEY	**CELMOPX**	COMPLEX		CLOSETS
CEKMNRU	RUCKMEN	**CELMORS**	CORMELS	**CELOSSU**	OSCULES
CEKMORS	MOCKERS	**CELMPRU**	CLUMPER	**CELOSSX**	COXLESS
CEKMORY	MOCKERY		CRUMPLE	**CELOSTY**	COTYLES
CEKMRSU	MUCKERS	**CELMSSU**	MUSCLES	**CELOSUV**	VOCULES
CEKNNSU	UNSNECK	**CELMSUU**	SECULUM	**CELOTTU**	CULOTTE
CEKNOOV	CONVOKE	**CELMSUY**	LYCEUMS	**CELPRSU**	CURPELS
CEKNORR	CRONKER	**CELMTUU**	CUMULET		SCRUPLE
CEKNORS	CONKERS	**CELNNOU**	NUCLEON	**CELPSUU**	CUPULES
	RECKONS	**CELNNSU**	NUNCLES	**CELPSUY**	CLYPEUS
CEKNORT	TROCKEN	**CELNOOR**	CORONEL	**CELRRSU**	CURLERS
CEKNOST	NOCKETS	**CELNOOS**	COLONES	**CELRSSY**	CRESYLS
CEKNRWY	WRYNECK		CONSOLE	**CELRSTU**	CLUSTER
CEKNSSU	SUCKENS	**CELNORS**	CLONERS		CULTERS
CEKOOPR	PRECOOK		CORNELS		CUSTREL
CEKOOPW	COWPOKE	**CELNOSU**	COUNSEL		CUTLERS
CEKOORR	CROOKER		UNCLOSE		RELUCTS
CEKOORS	COOKERS	**CELNOTU**	NOCTULE	**CELRSTY**	CLYSTER
	RECOOKS	**CELNRSU**	LUCERNS	**CELRSUV**	CULVERS
CEKOORY	COOKERY	**CELNRTU**	LECTURN	**CELRSUW**	CURLEWS
CEKOOSY	COOKEYS	**CELNSUU**	NUCLEUS	**CELRTTU**	CLUTTER
CEKOPRR	PREROCK		NUCULES	**CELRTUU**	CULTURE
CEKOPST	POCKETS	**CELNSUW**	UNCLEWS	**CELRTUV**	CULVERT
CEKORRS	CORKERS	**CELOOPR**	PRECOOL	**CELRTUY**	CRUELTY
	RECORKS	**CELOORR**	COLORER		CUTLERY
	ROCKERS		RECOLOR	**CELSTTU**	CUTLETS
CEKORRY	ROCKERY	**CELOORS**	COOLERS		CUTTLES
CEKORST	RESTOCK		CREOSOL		SCUTTLE
	ROCKETS	**CELOOST**	COOLEST	**CEMMNOT**	COMMENT
	STOCKER		OCELOTS	**CEMMNOU**	COMMUNE
CEKORTW	TWOCKER	**CELOPPS**	COPPLES	**CEMMOOT**	COMMOTE
CEKOSST	SOCKETS	**CELOPRU**	COUPLER	**CEMMOOV**	COMMOVE
CEKPRSU	PUCKERS	**CELOPSU**	CLOSEUP	**CEMMORS**	COMMERS
CEKPRSY	RYPECKS		COUPLES	**CEMMOTU**	COMMUTE
CEKPRUY	PUCKERY		OPUSCLE	**CEMMRSU**	CUMMERS
CEKRRTU	TRUCKER		UPCLOSE		SCUMMER
CEKRSSU	SUCKERS	**CELOPTU**	COUPLET	**CEMNNOT**	CONTEMN
CEKRSTU	TUCKERS		OCTUPLE	**CEMNOOP**	COMPONE
CEKRSUY	YUCKERS	**CELOQSU**	CLOQUES	**CEMNOOS**	ONCOMES
CEKSSTU	SUCKETS	**CELORRU**	CORULER	**CEMNOOY**	ECONOMY
CEKSTTU	TUCKETS	**CELORSS**	CLOSERS		MONOECY
CELLMOU	COLUMEL		CRESOLS	**CEMNOSU**	CONSUME
CELLNOO	COLONEL		ESCROLS		MUSCONE
CELLORS	ESCROLL	**CELORST**	COLTERS	**CEMNRSU**	CRUMENS
CELLOST	COLLETS		CORSLET	**CEMNRTU**	CENTRUM
CELLOSU	LOCULES		COSTREL	**CEMNSTU**	CENTUMS
	OCELLUS		LECTORS	**CEMOOPS**	COMPOSE
CELLOSY	CLOSELY	**CELORSU**	CLOSURE	**CEMOOPT**	COMPOTE
CELLRRU	CRULLER		COLURES	**CEMOOTU**	OUTCOME
CELLRSU	CRUELLS	**CELORSV**	CLOVERS	**CEMOPRS**	COMPERS
	CULLERS		VELCROS	**CEMOPRT**	COMPTER
	SCULLER	**CELORSW**	SCOWLER	**CEMOPST**	COEMPTS
CELLRUY	CRUELLY		SCROWLE	**CEMOPSU**	UPCOMES
CELLSSU	SCULLES	**CELORSY**	SCROYLE	**CEMOPTU**	COMPUTE
CELLSTU	CULLETS	**CELORTT**	CLOTTER	**CEMORRS**	CREMORS
CELMMSU	MESCLUM		CROTTLE	**CEMORSS**	SCROMES
CELMNOO	LOCOMEN	**CELORTU**	CLOTURE	**CEMOSSU**	COMUSES
	MONOCLE		CLOUTER		MUSCOSE
CELMNSU	MESCLUN		COULTER	**CEMOSSY**	MYCOSES

CEMOSTU	COSTUME	**CENOTTX**	CONTEXT	**CEORSST**	CORSETS
CEMPRRU	CRUMPER	**CENPRTY**	ENCRYPT		COSTERS
CEMPRTU	CRUMPET	**CENPTUX**	EXPUNCT		ESCORTS
CEMRRUY	MERCURY	**CENRRTU**	CURRENT		SCOTERS
CEMRSTU	RECTUMS	**CENRSSY**	SCRYNES		SCROTES
CEMSSUU	MUCUSES	**CENRSTU**	ENCRUST		SECTORS
CEMSTTU	TECTUMS	**CENRSUU**	UNCURSE	**CEORSSU**	COURSES
CENNOOR	NONCORE	**CENRSUW**	UNSCREW		SCOURSE
CENNOOS	NEOCONS	**CENRTUY**	CENTURY		SCOUSER
CENNOOT	CONNOTE	**CENSSTY**	ENCYSTS		SOURCES
CENNORS	CONNERS	**CEOOPRS**	COOPERS		SUCROSE
CENNOST	CONSENT		SCOOPER	**CEORSSW**	ESCROWS
	NOCENTS	**CEOOPRY**	COOPERY	**CEORSSY**	CORSEYS
CENNOTT	CONTENT	**CEOORSS**	COOSERS	**CEORSTT**	COTTERS
CENNOTV	CONVENT		ROSCOES	**CEORSTU**	COUTERS
CENNRSU	CUNNERS	**CEOORST**	COOTERS		CROUTES
	SCUNNER		SCOOTER		SCOUTER
CENOOPS	POCOSEN	**CEOORSV**	CROOVES	**CEORSTV**	CORVETS
	POONCES	**CEOORTU**	ECOTOUR		COVERTS
CENOORR	CORONER	**CEOORTW**	COWROTE		VECTORS
	CROONER	**CEOORVY**	OVERCOY	**CEORTUU**	COUTURE
CENOORS	CEROONS	**CEOOSTY**	COYOTES	**CEORTUV**	COUVERT
CENOORT	CORONET		OOCYTES		CUTOVER
CENOOSS	COOSENS	**CEOPPRR**	CROPPER		OVERCUT
CENOPRS	CREPONS	**CEOPPRS**	COPPERS	**CEOSSST**	COSSETS
CENOPRU	POUNCER	**CEOPPRU**	PRECOUP	**CEOSSSU**	SCOUSES
CENOPSU	CONSPUE	**CEOPPRY**	COPPERY	**CEOSSSY**	SYCOSES
	POUNCES	**CEOPRRS**	SCORPER	**CEOSTTT**	OCTETTS
	UNCOPES	**CEOPRRT**	PORRECT	**CEOSTTU**	CUTTOES
CENOPSY	SYNCOPE	**CEOPRRU**	CROUPER	**CEPPRRU**	CRUPPER
CENOPTU	POUNCET		PROCURE	**CEPPRSU**	CUPPERS
CENOPTY	POTENCY	**CEOPRSS**	CORPSES		SCUPPER
CENOQRU	CONQUER		PROCESS		SPRUCER
CENORRS	CORNERS	**CEOPRST**	COPTERS	**CEPRSSU**	PERCUSS
	SCORNER		PROSECT		SPRUCES
CENORRW	CROWNER	**CEOPRSU**	COUPERS	**CEPRSSY**	CYPRESS
	RECROWN		CROUPES	**CEPRSTU**	PRECUTS
CENORSS	CENSORS		RECOUPS	**CEPRSTY**	SCEPTRY
CENORST	CONSTER	**CEOPRTT**	PROTECT	**CEPRSUW**	SCREWUP
	CORNETS	**CEOPRUU**	COUPURE	**CEPRUUV**	UPCURVE
	CRESTON	**CEOPRUV**	COVERUP	**CEPSSTU**	SUSPECT
	CRETONS	**CEOPSTY**	COTYPES	**CERRSSU**	CURSERS
	CRONETS	**CEOQRTU**	CROQUET	**CERRSSY**	SCRYERS
CENORSU	CONURES		ROCQUET	**CERRSSU**	CUSSERS
	ROUNCES	**CEOQSTU**	COQUETS	**CERSSTU**	CRUSETS
CENORTT	CORNETT	**CEORRSS**	CROSSER	**CERSSUZ**	SCRUZES
CENORTU	CORNUTE		RECROSS	**CERSTTU**	CURTEST
	COUNTER		SCORERS		CUTTERS
	RECOUNT		SCORSER		SCUTTER
	TROUNCE	**CEORRST**	RECTORS	**CERSTUV**	CURVETS
CENORTV	CONVERT	**CEORRSU**	COURSER	**CERSTUY**	CURTESY
CENORTW	CROWNET		CRUORES		CURTSEY
CENORUV	UNCOVER		SCOURER	**CESSUZZ**	SCUZZES
CENOSSY	COYNESS	**CEORRSW**	CROWERS	**CFFFKOU**	FUCKOFF
CENOSTT	CONTEST		SCOWRER	**CFFGINO**	COFFING
CENOSTU	CONTUSE	**CEORRSY**	SORCERY	**CFFGINU**	CUFFING
	ECONUTS	**CEORRSZ**	CROZERS	**CFFHINO**	CHIFFON
	UNCOEST	**CEORRTU**	COURTER	**CFFIIRT**	TRIFFIC
CENOSTV	COVENTS	**CEORRTY**	RECTORY	**CFFIKKO**	KICKOFF
CENOSVY	CONVEYS	**CEORRSS**	CROSSES	**CFFIKOP**	PICKOFF
	COVYNES		SCORSES	**CFFILSS**	SCLIFFS

CFFINOS	COFFINS	**CGGIINR**	GRICING	**CGIKMNO**	MOCKING
CFFINSU	CUFFINS	**CGGORSY**	SCROGGY	**CGIKMNU**	MUCKING
CFFKOOO	COOKOFF	**CGHHOSU**	CHOUGHS	**CGIKNNO**	CONKING
CFFMOSU	OFFSCUM	**CGHIILM**	MILCHIG		NOCKING
CFFNSUU	UNCUFFS	**CGHIIMN**	CHIMING	**CGIKNOO**	COOKING
CFFOSTU	CUTOFFS		MICHING	**CGIKNOP**	POCKING
	OFFCUTS	**CGHIINN**	CHINING	**CGIKNOR**	CORKING
CFFRSSU	SCRUFFS		INCHING		ROCKING
CFFRSUY	SCRUFFY		NICHING	**CGIKNOS**	SOCKING
CFGIINO	COIFING	**CGHIINR**	RICHING	**CGIKNOT**	TOCKING
CFGIKNU	FUCKING	**CGHIINT**	ITCHING	**CGIKNOW**	COWKING
CFGINOR	FORCING	**CGHIINV**	CHIVING	**CGIKNOY**	YOCKING
CFHILYY	CHYLIFY	**CGHIKNO**	CHOKING	**CGIKNPU**	KINGCUP
CFHIMYY	CHYMIFY		HOCKING		PUCKING
CFHINSU	FUCHSIN	**CGHIKNU**	HUCKING	**CGIKNRU**	RUCKING
CFHIOSW	COWFISH	**CGHILPY**	GLYPHIC	**CGIKNSU**	SUCKING
CFHIRST	FRICHTS	**CGHILTY**	GLITCHY	**CGIKNTU**	TUCKING
CFHORTU	FUTHORC	**CGHINNO**	CHIGNON	**CGIKNUY**	YUCKING
CFIIIMR	MIRIFIC	**CGHINOR**	CHORING	**CGILLNO**	COLLING
CFIIIVV	VIVIFIC		OCHRING	**CGILLNU**	CULLING
CFIIKNY	FINICKY	**CGHINOS**	COSHING	**CGILMNU**	CULMING
CFIILNT	INFLICT	**CGHINOU**	OUCHING	**CGILMNY**	CYMLING
CFIIMNO	OMNIFIC	**CGHINOW**	CHOWING	**CGILNNO**	CLONING
CFIIMOT	MOTIFIC	**CGHINRU**	RUCHING	**CGILNNU**	UNCLING
CFIIMRY	MICRIFY	**CGHINSU**	CHUSING	**CGILNOO**	COOLING
CFIINOT	FICTION	**CGHINTU**	CHUTING		LOCOING
CFIINOY	ICONIFY	**CGHIOST**	GOTHICS	**CGILNOS**	CLOSING
CFIINYZ	ZINCIFY	**CGHIOSY**	GOYISCH	**CGILNOT**	COLTING
CFIIOSS	OSSIFIC	**CGHLNOS**	SCHLONG	**CGILNOW**	COWLING
CFIKNNO	FINNOCK	**CGHLOSU**	CLOUGHS	**CGILNOY**	CLOYING
CFIKOSS	FOSSICK	**CGHOORT**	TORGOCH	**CGILNPY**	CLYPING
CFIKTUW	FUCKWIT	**CGHORUY**	GROUCHY	**CGILNRU**	CURLING
CFILORS	FROLICS	**CGIIJNU**	JUICING	**CGILNSY**	GLYCINS
CFILORU	FLUORIC	**CGIIKKN**	KICKING	**CGILOOO**	OOLOGIC
CFIMNOR	CONFIRM	**CGIIKLN**	LICKING	**CGILORW**	COWGIRL
CFIMOST	COMFITS	**CGIIKMM**	GIMMICK	**CGILOTT**	GLOTTIC
CFINORY	CORNIFY	**CGIIKNN**	NICKING	**CGILPSU**	GILCUPS
CFINOST	CONFITS	**CGIIKNP**	PICKING	**CGILPTU**	GILTCUP
CFIORST	FICTORS	**CGIIKNR**	RICKING	**CGILPTY**	GLYPTIC
CFIORSY	SCORIFY	**CGIIKNS**	SICKING	**CGIMNOO**	COOMING
CFIRSTU	FRUICTS	**CGIIKNT**	TICKING	**CGIMNOP**	COMPING
CFISSTU	FUSTICS	**CGIIKNW**	WICKING	**CGIMNOR**	CROMING
CFKLLOU	LOCKFUL	**CGIILLO**	ILLOGIC	**CGIMNOS**	COMINGS
CFKNORU	UNFROCK	**CGIILNO**	COILING	**CGINNNO**	CONNING
CFKOTTU	FUTTOCK	**CGIILNP**	CLIPING	**CGINNNU**	CUNNING
CFKPSUU	FUCKUPS	**CGIILNS**	SLICING	**CGINNOP**	PONCING
CFLMRUU	FULCRUM	**CGIIMNN**	MINCING	**CGINNOR**	CORNING
CFLNORY	CORNFLY	**CGIIMNR**	CRIMING	**CGINNOS**	CONSIGN
CFLNOUX	CONFLUX	**CGIINNO**	COINING	**CGINNPU**	PUNCING
CFLNOUY	FLOUNCY	**CGIINNR**	CRINING	**CGINNSY**	SYNCING
CFLOOPW	COWFLOP	**CGIINNW**	WINCING	**CGINOOP**	COOPING
CFLOPRU	CROPFUL	**CGIINNZ**	ZINCING	**CGINOOS**	COOINGS
CFLPSUU	CUPFULS	**CGIINOR**	GIRONIC	**CGINOPP**	COPPING
	CUPSFUL	**CGIINOV**	VOICING	**CGINOPS**	COPINGS
CFMNOOR	CONFORM	**CGIINPR**	PRICING		COPSING
CFMNOUY	UNCOMFY	**CGIINPS**	SPICING		PICONGS
CFMOORT	COMFORT	**CGIINRT**	TRICING		SCOPING
CFNORTU	FUNCTOR	**CGIINSS**	CISSING	**CGINOPU**	COUPING
CFOSSTU	FUSTOCS	**CGIKLNO**	CLOKING	**CGINOPW**	COWPING
CFOSSUU	FUSCOUS		LOCKING	**CGINOPY**	COPYING
CGGGINO	COGGING	**CGIKLNU**	LUCKING	**CGINORS**	SCORING

CGINORU	COURING	CHIJKOS	JOCKISH	CHIPRRY	PYRRHIC
CGINORW	CROWING	CHIKLLO	HILLOCK	CHIPSSY	PHYSICS
CGINORY	GYRONIC	CHIKLTY	THICKLY	CHIQSTU	SQUITCH
CGINOSS	COSIGNS	CHIKNOO	CHINOOK	CHIRRSU	CURRISH
CGINOST	COSTING	CHIKORS	CHIKORS	CHIRSTY	CHRISTY
	GNOSTIC		CHOKRIS	CHISSST	SCHISTS
CGINOSU	CONGIUS	CHIKORY	HICKORY	CHISSTU	SCHUITS
	SOUCING	CHIKOST	THICKOS	CHISTTU	CHUTIST
CGINOSV	COVINGS	CHIKPSU	PUCKISH	CHISTWY	SWITCHY
CGINOSW	SCOWING	CHIKRSS	SCHRIKS	CHISYZZ	SCHIZZY
	SOWCING	CHIKSST	SCHTIKS	CHITTWY	TWITCHY
CGINOSY	COSYING		SHTICKS	CHKLOOO	HOOLOCK
CGINOTT	COTTING	CHIKSTY	KITSCHY	CHKLOOT	KLOOTCH
CGINOYZ	COZYING		SHTICKY	CHKLOSS	SHLOCKS
CGINPPU	CUPPING	CHILLMU	CHILLUM	CHKLOSY	SHLOCKY
CGINRRU	CURRING	CHILLTY	LICHTLY		SHYLOCK
CGINRSU	CURSING	CHILNOO	HOLONIC	CHKMMOO	HOMMOCK
CGINRSY	CRYINGS	CHILNOR	CHLORIN	CHKMMOU	HUMMOCK
	SCRYING	CHILNSY	LYCHNIS	CHKMOSS	SHMOCKS
CGINRTU	TRUCING	CHILOOS	COOLISH	CHKMSSU	SHMUCKS
CGINRUV	CURVING	CHILORS	ORCHILS	CHKNOOS	SCHNOOK
CGINSSU	CUSSING	CHILORT	TROCHIL	CHKOOST	SCHTOOK
	SCUSING	CHILOST	COLTISH	CHKORSU	CHUKORS
CGINTTU	CUTTING	CHILPSY	SYLPHIC	CHKPTUU	PUTCHUK
CGIOOOS	GIOCOSO	CHILSTU	CULTISH	CHKSSTU	SHTUCKS
CGIOOST	COGITOS	CHILSUY	CUSHILY	CHLMOOS	MOLOCHS
CGIOTYZ	ZYGOTIC	CHIMMOR	MICROHM	CHLMORY	CHROMYL
CGKLNOU	GUNLOCK	CHIMNPY	NYMPHIC	CHLMPSU	SCHLUMP
CGLLOSY	GLYCOLS	CHIMOPR	MORPHIC	CHLOOSS	SCHOOLS
CGLLSYY	GLYCYLS	CHIMORS	CHORISM	CHLOOST	COOLTHS
CGLNOSU	UNCLOGS		CHRISOM	CHLOPST	SPLOTCH
CGLOOSU	COLUGOS	CHIMRRY	MYRRHIC	CHLORSS	SCHORLS
CGNOOSU	CONGOUS	CHIMRSS	CHRISMS	CHLORTY	CHOLTRY
CGOORRW	GORCROW	CHIMSSS	SCHISMS	CHLOSSS	SCHLOSS
CHHIIKS	HICKISH	CHIMSTY	CHYMIST	CHLOSUY	CHYLOUS
CHHIKOR	CHIKHOR		TYCHISM		SLOUCHY
CHHINOR	RHONCHI	CHINOOR	CHORION	CHLOTYZ	ZLOTYCH
CHHINTU	UNHITCH	CHINOPS	CHOPINS	CHLSTUY	SLUTCHY
CHHIRST	SHRITCH		PHONICS	CHMOORS	CHROMOS
CHHISST	SHTCHIS	CHINOPY	CIPHONY	CHMOOSS	SCHMOOS
CHHISTY	ICHTHYS	CHINORS	CRONISH	CHMOOST	SCHTOOM
CHHLOTU	LUCHOTH	CHINOST	CHITONS	CHMOOSY	SMOOCHY
CHHNOOS	HONCHOS	CHINOSU	CUSHION	CHMOOSZ	SCHMOOZ
CHHRTTU	THRUTCH	CHINPSY	HYPNICS	CHMOSUY	CHYMOUS
CHIIKLM	MILCHIK	CHINQSU	SQUINCH	CHMSTUY	SMUTCHY
CHIIKMS	KIMCHIS	CHINRSU	URCHINS	CHNNOOR	CHRONON
CHIIKNN	KINCHIN	CHINSTY	SNITCHY	CHNNOSU	NONSUCH
CHIIKSS	SICKISH	CHINTUW	UNWITCH	CHNOOPS	PONCHOS
CHIILLS	CHILLIS	CHINTYZ	CHINTYZ	CHNOORS	COHORNS
CHIILNT	CHITLIN	CHIOOPR	POCHOIR	CHNOORT	TORCHON
CHIILOT	THIOLIC	CHIOORS	ISOCHOR	CHNORRS	SCHNORR
CHIILST	LITCHIS	CHIOORZ	CHORIZO	CHNORSY	SYNCHRO
CHIILTY	ITCHILY	CHIOPRT	TROPHIC	CHNORTU	COTHURN
CHIIMST	ISTHMIC	CHIOPST	PHOTICS	CHNOSZZ	SCHNOZZ
CHIIMSU	ISCHIUM	CHIOPXY	HYPOXIC	CHNOTUU	UNCOUTH
CHIINNP	INCHPIN	CHIORST	CHORIST	CHNSTUU	TUCHUNS
CHIINOT	THIONIC		OSTRICH	CHOOPPS	COPSHOP
CHIINST	CHITINS	CHIORSW	CHOWRIS	CHOORST	COHORTS
CHIIOPT	OPHITIC	CHIOSST	STICHOS	CHOORSU	OCHROUS
CHIIOST	STICHOI	CHIOSSZ	SCHIZOS	CHOOSST	COHOSTS
CHIIRRS	SCIRRHI	CHIPRRU	CHIRRUP	CHOPPTU	CHUPPOT

CHOPSSY	PSYCHOS	**CIINNTU**	TUNICIN	**CIKNSTU**	UNSTICK
CHOPTUU	TOUCHUP	**CIINOOT**	COITION	**CIKOPPT**	POCKPIT
CHORRSU	CHURROS	**CIINOPR**	PORCINI	**CIKORRS**	CORKIRS
CHORSTU	TROCHUS	**CIINOPS**	PSIONIC	**CIKOSTU**	SICKOUT
CHOSSTU	SCHOUTS	**CIINORS**	INCISOR	**CIKOTUW**	OUTWICK
	SCOUTHS	**CIINORT**	NORITIC	**CIKPPSU**	PICKUPS
CHOSSTW	SCOWTHS		TIRONIC	**CIKPSTU**	STICKUP
CHPSSUY	SCYPHUS	**CIINPRS**	CRISPIN		UPTICKS
CHRRSUU	CHURRUS	**CIINQTU**	QUINTIC	**CIKPUWY**	WICKYUP
CHSSTUY	SCHUYTS	**CIINRST**	CITRINS	**CIKRSST**	STRICKS
CIIILLT	ILLICIT	**CIINRSU**	RICINUS	**CIKRSTY**	TRICKSY
	ILLITIC	**CIINSSV**	VISCINS	**CILLNOS**	COLLINS
CIIILNV	INCIVIL	**CIINTUY**	UNICITY	**CILLNOU**	CULLION
CIIIMNR	CRIMINI	**CIIORST**	SORITIC	**CILLOOR**	CRIOLLO
CIIINPT	INCIPIT	**CIIOSTX**	COXITIS	**CILLOPY**	POLLICY
CIIJLUY	JUICILY	**CIIOSUV**	VICIOUS	**CILLRUY**	CURLILY
CIIKKLL	KILLICK	**CIIPRSS**	SPIRICS	**CILMNOP**	COMPLIN
CIIKKMS	MISKICK	**CIIPRTY**	PYRITIC	**CILMNOS**	CLONISM
CIIKLPY	PICKILY	**CIIRSTV**	VITRICS	**CILMNSY**	CYMLINS
CIIKMMM	MIMMICK	**CIIRTVX**	VICTRIX	**CILMOOS**	LOCOISM
CIIKMNN	MINNICK	**CIJKORS**	CROJIKS	**CILMSTU**	CULTISM
CIIKNPS	PICKINS	**CIJNNOO**	CONJOIN	**CILNOOR**	ORCINOL
CIIKNPT	NITPICK	**CIJNNTU**	INJUNCT	**CILNOOS**	CLOISON
CIIKNSW	INWICKS	**CIJNOOS**	COJOINS		SCOLION
CIIKNTU	CUTIKIN	**CIKKLLO**	KILLOCK	**CILNOPR**	PILCORN
CIIKPUW	WICKIUP	**CIKKOPT**	TOPKICK	**CILNORY**	CORNILY
CIIKSST	TISICKS	**CIKKOTU**	KICKOUT		LYRICON
CIIKSTT	STICKIT		OUTKICK	**CILNOSU**	ULICONS
CIILLTY	LICITLY	**CIKKPSU**	KICKUPS		UNCOILS
CIILLVY	CIVILLY	**CIKLLOP**	PILLOCK	**CILNOTU**	LINOCUT
CIILNOP	CIPOLIN	**CIKLLOR**	ROLLICK	**CILNOXY**	XYLONIC
	PICOLIN	**CIKLLOS**	SILLOCK	**CILNPSU**	INSCULP
CIILNOS	SILICON	**CIKLLOW**	KILLCOW		SCULPIN
CIILNPS	INCLIPS	**CIKLLSY**	SLICKLY		UNCLIPS
CIILNUV	UNCIVIL	**CIKLLUY**	LUCKILY	**CILNPTU**	UNCLIPT
CIILNVY	VINYLIC	**CIKLMSU**	MISLUCK	**CILNSTU**	LINCTUS
CIILOOT	OOLITIC	**CIKLMSY**	SMICKLY	**CILOOPT**	COPILOT
CIILOPT	POLITIC	**CIKLMUY**	MUCKILY	**CILOORU**	COULOIR
CIILORT	CORTILI	**CIKLNOS**	INLOCKS	**CILOOSS**	COLOSSI
CIILOST	COLITIS	**CIKLNRY**	CRINKLY	**CILOOST**	SCIOLTO
	SOLICIT	**CIKLNSU**	UNSLICK	**CILOPRW**	PILCROW
CIILOTT	LITOTIC	**CIKLOOO**	OLICOOK	**CILOPRY**	PYLORIC
CIILPRY	PRICILY	**CIKLOPY**	POCKILY	**CILOPSU**	OILCUPS
CIILPSY	SPICILY	**CIKLOPZ**	ZIPLOCK		UPCOILS
CIILSSS	SCISSIL	**CIKLORY**	ROCKILY	**CILOPSW**	COWSLIP
CIILSSV	SILVICS	**CIKLPRY**	PRICKLY	**CILORST**	LICTORS
CIIMMNO	MINICOM	**CIKLQUY**	QUICKLY	**CILOSTU**	COUTILS
CIIMMRY	MIMICRY	**CIKLRTY**	TRICKLY		OCULIST
CIIMNNO	NIMONIC	**CIKLSTU**	LUSTICK	**CILPRSY**	CRISPLY
CIIMNOS	MISCOIN	**CIKMNNO**	MINNOCK	**CILPRTU**	CULPRIT
CIIMNOT	MICTION	**CIKMNSU**	NICKUMS	**CILRRSU**	SCURRIL
CIIMNRY	CRIMINY	**CIKMOOS**	MISCOOK	**CILRSUU**	SURCULI
CIIMOST	MIOTICS	**CIKMORR**	RIMROCK	**CILRSUY**	CRUSILY
	MISTICO	**CIKMSSU**	MUSICKS	**CILSTTU**	CULTIST
	SOMITIC	**CIKMSTU**	STICKUM	**CIMMNSU**	CUMMINS
CIIMOTT	MITOTIC	**CIKNNOP**	PINNOCK	**CIMMOSS**	COSMISM
CIIMOTV	MOTIVIC	**CIKNNOW**	WINNOCK	**CIMMOST**	COMMITS
CIIMRST	TRISMIC	**CIKNOSW**	COWSKIN	**CIMMOTX**	COMMIXT
CIIMSSV	CIVISMS	**CIKNPSU**	UNPICKS	**CIMNNOS**	NINCOMS
CIIMSTV	VICTIMS	**CIKNPSY**	PYKNICS	**CIMNNSU**	NINCUMS
CIINNOT	NICOTIN	**CIKNPTU**	NUTPICK	**CIMNOOR**	MORONIC

	OMICRON	CIOPRST	TROPICS		SCOLLOP
CIMNORS	CRIMSON	CIOPSTY	COPYIST	CLLORSS	SCROLLS
	MICRONS	CIOQRSU	CROQUIS	CLLOSUU	LOCULUS
CIMNOSS	COSMINS	CIORRSU	CIRROUS	CLMNOSU	COLUMNS
CIMNOSU	CONIUMS	CIORSSS	SCISSOR	CLMOOPT	COMPLOT
CIMNRSU	CRINUMS	CIORSTT	TRICOTS	CLMOPTU	PLUMCOT
CIMOORS	MORISCO	CIORSTU	CITROUS	CLMOSUU	LUCUMOS
CIMOORT	MOTORIC	CIORSTV	VICTORS		OSCULUM
CIMOOST	OSMOTIC	CIORSUU	CURIOUS	CLMPRUY	CRUMPLY
CIMOPSY	COPYISM	CIORTVY	VICTORY	CLMSUUU	CUMULUS
	MISCOPY	CIOSSSY	SYCOSIS	CLNOORT	CONTROL
	MYOPICS	CIOSSUV	VISCOUS	CLNOOSS	CONSOLS
CIMORSU	CORIUMS	CIOTTUY	OUTCITY	CLNOOSU	COLONUS
CIMOSST	COSMIST	CIPRSST	SCRIPTS	CLNOSSU	CONSULS
	SITCOMS	CIPRSSU	PRUSSIC	CLNOSTU	CONSULT
CIMOSSY	MYCOSIS	CIPRTTY	TRYPTIC		UNCOLTS
CIMOSTY	MYOTICS	CIPRUVY	PYRUVIC	CLNOSUW	UNCOWLS
CIMOTYZ	ZYMOTIC	CIPSTTY	STYPTIC	CLNRSUU	UNCURLS
CIMPRSS	SCRIMPS	CIRRTTU	CRITTUR	CLOOPPW	COWPLOP
CIMPRSY	SCRIMPY	CIRSSTU	RUSTICS	CLOOPST	COPLOTS
CIMRSSU	CRISSUM	CIRSTUY	CITRUSY	CLOOPTY	POLYCOT
CIMRSUU	CURIUMS	CIRTUVY	CURVITY	CLOORSU	COLOURS
CIMSSTU	MISCUTS	CISSTUY	CYTISUS	CLOORUY	COLOURY
CIMSSTY	MYSTICS	CJKNNOO	JONNOCK	CLOOSTY	CYTOSOL
CIMSSUV	VISCUMS	CJNORUY	CONJURY	CLOPTUY	OCTUPLY
CINNNOU	INCONNU	CKKLNUY	KNUCKLY	CLORSSW	SCROWLS
CINNORU	UNICORN	CKLLMOU	MULLOCK	CLORSSY	CROSSLY
CINNOSU	NUNCIOS	CKLLOOP	POLLOCK	CLORSUY	CORYLUS
CINNOTU	UNCTION	CKLLOOR	ROLLOCK	CLORTUY	COURTLY
CINNSUU	UNCINUS	CKLLORU	RULLOCK	CLOSSTU	LOCUSTS
CINOOPR	PORCINO	CKLNOSU	UNLOCKS	CLPRSUU	UPCURLS
CINOOPS	OPSONIC	CKLNOTU	LOCKNUT	CLPSSTU	SCULPTS
	POCOSIN	CKLNUUY	UNLUCKY	CMMNOOS	COMMONS
CINOORS	CORONIS	CKLOOOY	OLYCOOK	CMMOORS	ROMCOMS
CINOOSS	COOSINS	CKLOOPR	PORLOCK	CMMOOST	COMMOTS
CINOOSV	OVONICS	CKLOORW	ROWLOCK	CMMOPSY	COMSYMP
CINOPPS	COPPINS	CKLOOTU	LOCKOUT	CMMRSUY	SCRUMMY
CINOPRX	PRINCOX	CKLOPSU	LOCKUPS	CMNNOOS	NONCOMS
CINORRT	TRICORN		UPLOCKS	CMNOOOT	MONOCOT
CINORSS	INCROSS	CKLOPTU	POTLUCK	CMNOOPY	COMPONY
CINORST	CISTRON		PUTLOCK	CMNOSSY	SYNCOMS
	CITRONS	CKMMMOU	MUMMOCK	CMNPTUU	PUNCTUM
	CORNIST	CKMOPSU	MOCKUPS	CMOOPRT	COMPORT
	CORTINS	CKNOOOR	ROCKOON	CMOOPST	COMPOST
CINORSZ	ZIRCONS	CKNORSU	UNCORKS		COMPOTS
CINORTU	RUCTION	CKNOSTU	UNSTOCK	CMOORSU	CORMOUS
CINORTY	TYRONIC	CKNSTUU	UNSTUCK	CMOOSTY	SCOTOMY
CINOSST	CONSIST		UNTUCKS	CMORSTU	SCROTUM
	TOCSINS	CKOOOPT	COOKTOP	CMORTUW	CUTWORM
CINOSSU	COUSINS	CKOOOTU	COOKOUT	CMOSSTU	CUSTOMS
CINOSTU	SUCTION		OUTCOOK	CMOSUVY	MUSCOVY
CINOSUZ	COUZINS	CKOOPPS	POPSOCK	CMPRSSU	SCRUMPS
	ZINCOUS	CKOORSU	SOUROCK	CMPRSUU	CUPRUMS
CINOTXY	OXYNTIC	CKOORTU	OUTROCK	CMPRSUY	SCRUMPY
CINRSTU	INCRUST	CKOPTTU	PUTTOCK	CNNOPSY	PYCNONS
CIOOPRT	PORTICO	CKOPTUU	PUCKOUT	CNNORTU	NOCTURN
	PROOTIC	CKORTUW	CUTWORK	CNNORUW	UNCROWN
CIOOPSU	COPIOUS	CKOSSTU	TUSSOCK	CNNOSUY	UNSONCY
CIOOQTU	COQUITO	CKSSTUU	TUSSUCK	CNOOOPS	POCOSON
CIOORST	OCTROIS	CLLMOSU	MOLLUSC	CNOOPPR	POPCORN
CIOORSU	CORIOUS	CLLOOPS	COLLOPS	CNOOPRU	CROUPON

CNOOPSU	COUPONS	**DDDEFLU**	FUDDLED	**DDEEEST**	DEEDEST
	SOUPCON	**DDDEGII**	GIDDIED		STEEDED
CNOORRW	CORNROW	**DDDEGIR**	GRIDDED	**DDEEESX**	DESEXED
CNOORST	CONSORT	**DDDEGLU**	GUDDLED	**DDEEEWY**	DYEWEED
	CROTONS	**DDDEGRU**	DRUDGED	**DDEEFGL**	FLEDGED
CNOORTT	CONTORT	**DDDEHIW**	WHIDDED	**DDEEFII**	DEIFIED
CNOORTU	CONTOUR	**DDDEHLO**	HODDLED		EDIFIED
	CORNUTO	**DDDEHLU**	HUDDLED	**DDEEFIL**	DEFILED
	CROUTON	**DDDEHTU**	THUDDED		FIELDED
CNOOSST	NOSTOCS	**DDDEIIK**	KIDDIED	**DDEEFIN**	DEFINED
	ONCOSTS	**DDDEIIR**	DIDDIER	**DDEEFLU**	DEEDFUL
CNOOSTT	COTTONS	**DDDEIIS**	DIDDIES	**DDEEFNS**	DEFENDS
CNOOSTY	TYCOONS	**DDDEIIV**	DIVIDED	**DDEEFSU**	DEFUSED
CNOOSUU	NOCUOUS	**DDDEIKS**	SKIDDED	**DDEEFUZ**	DEFUZED
CNOOSVY	CONVOYS	**DDDEILM**	MIDDLED	**DDEEGGL**	GLEDGED
CNOOTTW	COTTOWN	**DDDEILN**	DINDLED	**DDEEGIN**	DEEDING
CNOOTTY	COTTONY	**DDDEILP**	PIDDLED		DEIGNED
CNOPRTY	CRYPTON	**DDDEILR**	DIDDLER	**DDEEGIS**	DISEDGE
CNOPSTU	PUNCTOS		RIDDLED	**DDEEGLP**	PLEDGED
CNORSSU	UNCROSS	**DDDEILS**	DIDDLES	**DDEEGLS**	SLEDGED
CNORSSY	SYNROCS	**DDDEILT**	TIDDLED	**DDEEGLU**	DELUGED
CNORTUY	COUNTRY	**DDDEILW**	WIDDLED	**DDEEGNU**	UNEDGED
CNRSSTU	SCRUNTS	**DDDEILY**	DIDDLEY	**DDEEGRR**	DREDGER
CNRSTUY	SCRUNTY	**DDDEIMU**	MUDDIED	**DDEEGRS**	DREDGES
COOORSZ	COROZOS	**DDDEIOR**	DODDIER	**DDEEHLS**	HEDDLES
COOPRRT	PROCTOR	**DDDEIOS**	DODDIES	**DDEEHNU**	DUDHEEN
COOPRSS	SCROOPS	**DDDEIRS**	DIDDERS	**DDEEHRS**	SHEDDER
COOPRTU	OUTCROP	**DDDEIRU**	DUDDIER	**DDEEILM**	DELIMED
COOPSTU	COPOUTS		RUDDIED	**DDEEILR**	DREIDEL
	OCTOPUS	**DDDELMU**	MUDDLED	**DDEEILS**	SLEIDED
COOPSUY	COYPOUS	**DDDELNO**	NODDLED	**DDEEILV**	DEVILED
COORSTU	OCTUORS	**DDDELOO**	DOODLED	**DDEEILW**	WIELDED
COORSUU	ROUCOUS	**DDDELOP**	PLODDED	**DDEEILY**	DEEDILY
COORTUW	OUTCROW		PODDLED		YIELDED
COOSSTY	OOCYSTS	**DDDELOS**	DODDLES	**DDEEIMN**	DENIMED
COOSTTY	OTOCYST	**DDDELOT**	TODDLED	**DDEEIMP**	IMPEDED
COPRRSS	SCRORPS	**DDDELPU**	PUDDLED	**DDEEIMS**	DEMISED
COPRRTU	CORRUPT	**DDDELRU**	RUDDLED		MISDEED
COPRSTY	CRYPTOS	**DDDENOS**	SNODDED	**DDEEINR**	NEDDIER
COPRSUU	CUPROUS	**DDDEOPR**	PRODDED	**DDEEINS**	DESINED
COPRTUU	UPCOURT	**DDDEOQU**	QUODDED		NEDDIES
CORRSSU	CURSORS	**DDDEORS**	DODDERS		SDEINED
CORRSUY	CURSORY	**DDDEORY**	DODDERY	**DDEEINT**	ENDITED
CORSSTU	SCRUTOS	**DDDEPSU**	SPUDDED		TEINDED
COSTTUU	CUTOUTS	**DDDERSU**	DUDDERS	**DDEEINW**	INDEWED
DDDDEIL	DIDDLED	**DDDERUY**	DUDDERY		WIDENED
DDDEEGR	DREDGED	**DDDESTU**	STUDDED	**DDEEINX**	DEINDEX
DDDEEHL	HEDDLED	**DDDGINO**	DODDING		INDEXED
DDDEEHS	SHEDDED	**DDEEEFX**	FEDEXED	**DDEEINZ**	DIZENED
DDDEEIR	DERIDED	**DDEEEGR**	DEGREED	**DDEEIOV**	VIDEOED
DDDEELM	MEDDLED	**DDEEEIR**	DEEDIER	**DDEEIPR**	PREDIED
DDDEELP	PEDDLED	**DDEEELN**	NEEDLED	**DDEEIPS**	DEPSIDE
DDDEELR	REDDLED	**DDEEELT**	DELETED	**DDEEIRR**	DERIDER
DDDEELS	SLEDDED	**DDEEELV**	DEVELED		REDDIER
DDDEELU	DELUDED	**DDEEELW**	WEDELED		REDRIED
DDDEEMO	DEMODED	**DDEEEMN**	EMENDED		RIDERED
DDDEENS	SNEDDED	**DDEEEMR**	REMEDED	**DDEEIRS**	DERIDES
DDDEENU	DENUDED	**DDEEENT**	TEENDED		DESIRED
DDDEERU	UDDERED	**DDEEENW**	ENDEWED		DIEDRES
DDDEEST	STEDDED	**DDEEEPS**	SPEEDED		RESIDED
DDDEFIL	FIDDLED	**DDEEESS**	DESEEDS	**DDEEIRV**	DERIVED

DDEEIRW	WEIRDED	DDEESST	STEDDES		SHIDDER
DDEEIST	DEIDEST	DDEETTU	DUETTED	DDEHIRT	THIRDED
	TEDDIES	DDEFGIR	FRIDGED	DDEHIRW	WHIDDER
DDEEISV	DEVISED	DDEFILR	FIDDLER	DDEHIRY	HYDRIDE
DDEEKKO	DEKKOED	DDEFILS	FIDDLES	DDEHLNO	HONDLED
DDEELLU	DUELLED	DDEFILY	FIDDLEY	DDEHLOS	HODDLES
DDEELLW	DWELLED	DDEFIOR	FOREDID	DDEHLRU	HUDDLER
DDEELMO	MODELED	DDEFIRT	DRIFTED		HURDLED
DDEELMR	MEDDLER	DDEFISU	FUDDIES	DDEHLSU	HUDDLES
DDEELMS	MEDDLES	DDEFLNO	FONDLED	DDEHNOS	HODDENS
DDEELNO	OLDENED	DDEFLOO	FLOODED		SHODDEN
DDEELNS	LEDDENS	DDEFLRU	FUDDLER	DDEHNOU	HOUNDED
DDEELOP	DELOPED	DDEFLSU	FUDDLES	DDEHNRU	HUNDRED
DDEELOW	DOWELED	DDEFNOR	FRONDED	DDEHNSU	DUNSHED
DDEELOY	YODELED	DDEFNOU	FONDUED	DDEHNUZ	NUDZHED
DDEELPR	PEDDLER		FOUNDED	DDEHOSW	SHOWDED
DDEELPS	PEDDLES	DDEFNSU	DEFUNDS	DDEHRSU	SHUDDER
	SPELDED	DDEFORS	FODDERS	DDEHRSY	SHREDDY
DDEELRS	REDDLES	DDEGGRU	DRUGGED	DDEIIKR	KIDDIER
	SLEDDER		GRUDGED	DDEIIKS	KIDDIES
DDEELRT	TREDDLE	DDEGHIT	DIGHTED	DDEIIMS	MIDDIES
DDEELRU	DELUDER	DDEGIIN	DINGIED	DDEIINT	INDITED
DDEELSU	DELUDES	DDEGIIR	GIDDIER	DDEIINV	DIVINED
DDEEMMO	MODEMED	DDEGIIS	GIDDIES	DDEIIOS	IODIDES
DDEEMOT	DEMOTED	DDEGILR	GIRDLED		IODISED
DDEEMRU	DEMURED		GLIDDER	DDEIIOX	DIOXIDE
DDEENNU	UNENDED		GRIDDLE	DDEIIOZ	IODIZED
DDEENOP	DEPONED	DDEGIMO	DEMIGOD	DDEIIRT	DIRTIED
DDEENOT	DENOTED	DDEGINO	DINGOED		TIDDIER
DDEENOV	DOVENED	DDEGINR	GRINDED	DDEIIRV	DIVIDER
DDEENOW	ENDOWED		REDDING	DDEIIST	STIDDIE
DDEENOZ	DOZENED	DDEGINT	TEDDING		TIDDIES
DDEENPS	DEPENDS	DDEGINW	WEDDING	DDEIISV	DIVIDES
DDEENPU	UPENDED	DDEGINY	EDDYING	DDEIISW	WIDDIES
DDEENRS	REDDENS	DDEGIOR	DODGIER	DDEIITT	DITTIED
DDEENRT	TRENDED	DDEGIRR	GRIDDER	DDEIIVV	DIVVIED
DDEENRU	DENUDER	DDEGKLU	KLUDGED	DDEIIZZ	DIZZIED
	ENDURED	DDEGLOP	PLODGED	DDEIKLN	KINDLED
DDEENST	STENDED	DDEGLOS	DOGSLED	DDEIKLS	KIDDLES
DDEENSU	DENUDES	DDEGLSU	GUDDLES	DDEIKNR	KINDRED
	DUDEENS		SLUDGED	DDEIKOS	KIDDOES
	DUENDES	DDEGMOO	DOGEDOM	DDEIKRS	KIDDERS
DDEENSY	DESYNED	DDEGMOS	DODGEMS		SKIDDER
DDEENTU	DETUNED	DDEGMSU	SMUDGED	DDEILLO	DOLLIED
DDEEOOR	RODEOED	DDEGNOO	NOODGED	DDEILLR	DRILLED
DDEEOPS	DEPOSED	DDEGNOS	GODDENS	DDEILLU	ILLUDED
	SEEDPOD		GODSEND	DDEILMP	DIMPLED
DDEEORR	ORDERED	DDEGNOU	DUDGEON	DDEILMR	MIDDLER
DDEEORV	DOVERED	DDEGNSU	SNUDGED	DDEILMS	MIDDLES
DDEEORW	DOWERED	DDEGORS	DODGERS	DDEILNN	DINNLED
DDEEOTV	DEVOTED		GORSEDD	DDEILNS	DINDLES
DDEEOTX	DETOXED	DDEGORY	DODGERY		SLIDDEN
DDEEPRS	PEDDERS	DDEGOSS	GODDESS	DDEILNW	DWINDLE
	SPREDDE	DDEGOST	STODGED		WINDLED
DDEEPTU	DEPUTED	DDEGRRU	DRUDGER	DDEILOR	DROILED
DDEERRS	REDDERS	DDEGRSU	DRUDGES	DDEILOS	DILDOES
DDEERSS	DRESSED	DDEGRTU	TRUDGED	DDEILOT	DELTOID
DDEERST	REDDEST	DDEHINS	NEDDISH	DDEILPR	PIDDLER
	TEDDERS	DDEHIOW	HOWDIED	DDEILPS	DISPLED
DDEERSW	WEDDERS	DDEHIRS	HIDDERS		PIDDLES
DDEERTU	DETRUDE		REDDISH	DDEILPU	DUPLIED

DDEILQU	QUIDDLE	**DDEKMOU**	DUKEDOM	**DDENPSU**	PUDDENS
DDEILRR	RIDDLER	**DDEKOOR**	DROOKED	**DDENRSU**	DUNDERS
DDEILRS	DREIDLS	**DDEKORU**	DROUKED	**DDENSSU**	SUDDENS
	RIDDLES	**DDELLOR**	DROLLED	**DDENSTU**	STUDDEN
	SLIDDER	**DDELMOU**	MOULDED	**DDEOOPR**	DROOPED
DDEILRT	TIDDLER	**DDELMPU**	DUMPLED	**DDEOORU**	ODOURED
DDEILST	TIDDLES	**DDELMRU**	MUDDLER	**DDEOORW**	REDWOOD
DDEILSW	WIDDLES	**DDELMSU**	MUDDLES	**DDEOOWY**	DYEWOOD
DDEILTU	DILUTED	**DDELNOO**	NOODLED	**DDEOPPR**	DROPPED
DDEILTW	TWIDDLE	**DDELNOS**	NODDLES	**DDEOPPR**	PRODDER
DDEILTY	LYDDITE	**DDELNOU**	LOUNDED	**DDEOPRW**	DEWDROP
	TIDDLEY		NODULED	**DDEORSW**	DROWSED
DDEIMMU	DUMMIED	**DDELNOW**	LOWNDED		SWORDED
DDEIMNS	MIDDENS	**DDELNRU**	NURDLED	**DDEPRSS**	SPREDDS
DDEIMNU	MUEDDIN		RUNDLED	**DDEPRSU**	PUDDERS
DDEIMOO	MOODIED	**DDELOOR**	DOODLER		SPUDDER
DDEIMOR	DERMOID		DROOLED	**DDERRSU**	RUDDERS
DDEIMOS	DESMOID	**DDELOOS**	DOODLES	**DDERSSU**	SUDDERS
DDEIMRU	MUDDIER	**DDELOOW**	WOOLDED	**DDGGINO**	DODGING
DDEIMSS	DESMIDS	**DDELOPR**	PLODDER		GODDING
DDEIMST	MIDDEST	**DDELOPS**	PODDLES	**DDGHINO**	HODDING
DDEIMSU	DEDIMUS	**DDELORT**	TODDLER	**DDGHOOO**	GODHOOD
	MUDDIES	**DDELORW**	WORLDED	**DDGIIKN**	KIDDING
DDEINOP	POINDED	**DDELOST**	TODDLES	**DDGIILN**	LIDDING
DDEINOR	NODDIER	**DDELOTT**	DOTTLED	**DDGIILY**	GIDDILY
DDEINOS	NODDIES	**DDELPRU**	PUDDLER	**DDGIINR**	RIDDING
DDEINOT	DENTOID	**DDELPSU**	PUDDLES	**DDGIMNO**	MODDING
DDEINOW	INDOWED		SPUDDLE	**DDGIMNU**	MUDDING
DDEINPS	DISPEND	**DDELRSU**	RUDDLES	**DDGINNO**	NODDING
DDEINRU	UNDRIED	**DDELSTU**	STUDDLE	**DDGINOP**	PODDING
DDEINST	DISTEND	**DDEMMRU**	DRUMMED	**DDGINOR**	RODDING
DDEINSU	NUDDIES	**DDEMMSU**	SMEDDUM	**DDGINOS**	SODDING
DDEINSW	SWIDDEN	**DDEMNOS**	ODDSMEN	**DDGINOT**	TODDING
DDEIOOS	DOODIES	**DDEMNOT**	ODDMENT	**DDGINPU**	PUDDING
DDEIOPR	PODDIER	**DDEMNOU**	MOUNDED	**DDGINRU**	RUDDING
DDEIOPS	PODDIES	**DDEMORS**	MODDERS	**DDGINUW**	WUDDING
DDEIORS	DORISED	**DDEMRSU**	MUDDERS	**DDGIPUY**	GIDDYUP
	SODDIER	**DDENNOR**	DENDRON	**DDGMOOS**	DOGDOMS
DDEIORV	OVERDID		DONNERD	**DDGOOOW**	DOGWOOD
DDEIORW	DOWDIER	**DDENOOP**	ENDOPOD	**DDHIIKS**	KIDDISH
DDEIORZ	DORIZED	**DDENOOS**	DESNOOD	**DDHIISS**	SIDDHIS
DDEIOSS	SODDIES		SNOODED	**DDHIKSU**	KIDDUSH
DDEIOST	TODDIES	**DDENOPS**	DESPOND	**DDHINOS**	HODDINS
DDEIOSV	VODDIES	**DDENOPU**	POUNDED	**DDHIORY**	HYDROID
DDEIOSW	DOWDIES	**DDENOPW**	POWNDED	**DDHIRSY**	HYDRIDS
DDEIOTT	DITTOED	**DDENORS**	DONDERS	**DDIIIOO**	OIDIOID
DDEIOWW	WIDOWED		NODDERS	**DDIIKKS**	DIKDIKS
DDEIPPR	DRIPPED		SNODDER	**DDIIKLS**	SKIDLID
DDEIPRS	DISPRED	**DDENORT**	TRODDEN	**DDIIKSV**	KIDVIDS
DDEIPRU	UPDRIED	**DDENORU**	REDOUND	**DDIILOP**	DIPLOID
DDEIPSU	PUDDIES		ROUNDED	**DDIIOSX**	DIOXIDS
DDEIPUV	UPDIVED		UNDERDO		IXODIDS
DDEIRRS	RIDDERS	**DDENORW**	DROWNED	**DDIIQTU**	QUIDDIT
DDEIRRU	RUDDIER		ROWNDED	**DDIKNOS**	DODKINS
DDEIRSU	RUDDIES		WONDRED	**DDIKOOS**	SKIDDOO
DDEIRSW	WIDDERS	**DDENOSS**	ODDNESS	**DDILMUY**	MUDDILY
DDEISSU	DISUSED		SODDENS	**DDILNRS**	DIRNDLS
DDEISTU	STUDDIE	**DDENOSU**	SOUNDED	**DDILOSY**	DYSODIL
	STUDIED	**DDENOSW**	SOWNDED	**DDILOWY**	DOWDILY
DDEJRSU	JUDDERS	**DDENOSY**	DYNODES	**DDILRUY**	RUDDILY
DDEJRUY	JUDDERY	**DDENOUW**	WOUNDED	**DDILTWY**	TWIDDLY

DDIMOOS DODOISM	**DEEEISV** DEVISEE	**DEEENTV** EVENTED
DDIMRSU DIRDUMS	**DEEEJLW** JEWELED	**DEEEORW** OREWEED
DDIMSSU DUDISMS	**DEEEJNU** DEJEUNE	**DEEEOTV** DEVOTEE
DDINOST SNODDIT	**DEEEJRR** JERREED	**DEEEPRS** SPEEDER
DDIORTU TURDOID	**DEEEJRS** JEREEDS	SPEERED
DDIRRUY DRUIDRY	**DEEEKLN** KNEELED	**DEEEPRT** PETERED
DDIRSSU SIDDURS	**DEEEKLS** SLEEKED	**DEEEPRU** EPERDUE
DDLLMOO DOLLDOM	**DEEEKMS** SMEEKED	**DEEEPRV** PREEVED
DDMMSUU DUMDUMS	**DEEEKNW** WEEKEND	**DEEEPSS** PEDESES
DDMNOOR DROMOND	**DEEEKRS** KREESED	**DEEEPST** DEEPEST
DDMRSUU DURDUMS	SKEERED	STEEPED
DDNORSW DROWNDS	**DEEEKRY** REKEYED	**DEEEQRU** QUEERED
DDOOOOS DOODOOS	**DEEEKST** STEEKED	**DEEEQUU** DEQUEUE
DDORSTY DROSTDY	**DEEELLV** LEVELED	**DEEERRS** REEDERS
DEEEEMX EXEEMED	**DEEELMS** MESELED	**DEEERRV** REVERED
DEEEEWW WEEWEED	**DEEELNR** NEEDLER	**DEEERSS** RESEEDS
DEEEFFR EFFERED	**DEEELNS** NEEDLES	SEEDERS
DEEEFLR FLEERED	**DEEELPS** SPEELED	**DEEERST** REESTED
DEEEFLT FLEETED	**DEEELPT** DEPLETE	STEERED
DEEEFNR ENFREED	**DEEELRT** DEERLET	**DEEERSV** DESERVE
DEEEFNS DEFENSE	**DEEELRV** LEVERED	SEVERED
DEEEFRS FEEDERS	REVELED	**DEEERSW** RESEWED
REFEEDS	**DEEELST** DELETES	SEWERED
DEEEFRV FEVERED	SLEETED	SWEERED
DEEEFSX FEDEXES	STEELED	WEEDERS
DEEEGKL GLEEKED	**DEEELSV** SLEEVED	**DEEERSY** REDEYES
DEEEGKR GREEKED	**DEEELSW** SWEELED	**DEEERTV** EVERTED
DEEEGLP PLEDGEE	**DEEELTW** TWEEDLE	**DEEERTW** TWEERED
DEEEGLT GLEETED	TWEELED	**DEEERTX** EXERTED
DEEEGMR DEMERGE	**DEEELTX** TELEXED	**DEEERWY** WEEDERY
EMERGED	**DEEEMMW** EMMEWED	**DEEESSX** DESEXES
DEEEGNP PEENGED	**DEEEMNR** EMENDER	**DEEESTV** STEEVED
DEEEGNR GREENED	REEDMEN	**DEEESTW** SWEETED
RENEGED	**DEEEMNS** DEMESNE	**DEEETTV** VEDETTE
DEEEGRR REGREDE	SEEDMEN	**DEEETTW** TWEETED
DEEEGRS DEGREES	**DEEEMNW** ENMEWED	**DEEETWZ** TWEEZED
DEEEGRT DETERGE	**DEEEMRS** DEMERSE	**DEEFFFO** FEOFFED
GREETED	EMERSED	**DEEFFIN** EFFENDI
DEEEGST EGESTED	MEDRESE	**DEEFFOR** OFFERED
DEEEHKT THEEKED	REDEEMS	**DEEFFST** DEFFEST
DEEEHLS SHEELED	REMEDES	**DEEFFSU** EFFUSED
DEEEHLW WHEEDLE	**DEEEMRT** METERED	**DEEFGGL** FLEGGED
WHEELED	**DEEEMST** STEEMED	**DEEFGIN** FEEDING
DEEEHNS SHEENED	**DEEENPR** PREENED	FEIGNED
DEEEHPS PHEESED	PRENEED	**DEEFGIP** PIGFEED
DEEEHPW WHEEPED	**DEEENPS** DEEPENS	**DEEFGLS** FLEDGES
DEEEHPZ PHEEZED	**DEEENQU** QUEENED	**DEEFGRU** REFUGED
DEEEHRS HEEDERS	**DEEENRS** NEEDERS	**DEEFHLS** FLESHED
HEREDES	SERENED	SHELFED
SHEERED	SNEERED	**DEEFHLU** HEEDFUL
DEEEHST SEETHED	**DEEENRT** ENTERED	**DEEFHRS** FRESHED
SHEETED	**DEEENRV** ENERVED	**DEEFIIR** DEIFIER
DEEEHTT TEETHED	**DEEENRW** RENEWED	EDIFIER
DEEEHWZ WHEEZED	**DEEENRY** RENEYED	REIFIED
DEEEIJL JEELIED	**DEEENST** STEENED	**DEEFIIS** DEIFIES
DEEEIMR EMERIED	**DEEENSV** VENDEES	EDIFIES
DEEEINR NEEDIER	**DEEENSW** ENSEWED	**DEEFILN** ENFILED
DEEEIPS DEEPIES	**DEEENSZ** SNEEZED	**DEEFILR** DEFILER
DEEEIRR REEDIER	**DEEENTT** DETENTE	FERLIED
DEEEIRS SEEDIER	NEDETTE	FIELDER
DEEEIRW WEEDIER	**DEEENTU** DETENUE	REFILED

DEEFILS	DEFILES	**DEEGIMN**	DEEMING	**DEEHIKV**	KHEDIVE
DEEFILT	FILETED	**DEEGIMV**	DEMIVEG	**DEEHILS**	SHIELED
DEEFIMS	MISFEED	**DEEGINN**	ENGINED	**DEEHILT**	LETHIED
DEEFINR	DEFINER		NEEDING	**DEEHINR**	INHERED
	ENFIRED	**DEEGINR**	DREEING	**DEEHIRR**	HERRIED
	FENDIER		ENERGID		REHIRED
	REFINED		GREINED	**DEEHIRT**	DIETHER
DEEFINS	DEFINES		REEDING	**DEEHIST**	HEISTED
DEEFINT	FEINTED		REIGNED	**DEEHITV**	THIEVED
DEEFINX	ENFIXED	**DEEGINS**	SDEIGNE	**DEEHKLW**	WHELKED
DEEFIRR	FERRIED		SEEDING	**DEEHLLO**	HELLOED
	REFIRED	**DEEGINV**	DEEVING	**DEEHLLS**	SHELLED
	REFRIED	**DEEGINW**	WEEDING	**DEEHLMW**	WHELMED
DEEFIRS	DEFIERS	**DEEGINY**	YEEDING	**DEEHLNU**	UNHELED
	SERIFED	**DEEGIPW**	PIGWEED	**DEEHLOV**	HOVELED
DEEFIRT	FETIDER	**DEEGIRS**	SEDGIER	**DEEHLPW**	WHELPED
DEEFIRX	REFIXED	**DEEGIRV**	DIVERGE	**DEEHLSV**	SHELVED
DEEFIRY	REEDIFY		GRIEVED	**DEEHLSW**	WELSHED
DEEFIRZ	FRIEZED	**DEEGIRW**	WEDGIER	**DEEHMNR**	HERDMEN
DEEFIST	DEIFEST	**DEEGIST**	EDGIEST	**DEEHMNS**	MENSHED
DEEFLLU	FUELLED	**DEEGISW**	WEDGIES	**DEEHMOR**	HOMERED
DEEFLNS	FLENSED	**DEEGJRU**	REJUDGE		REHOMED
DEEFLNU	NEEDFUL	**DEEGKMO**	GEEKDOM	**DEEHMRU**	RHEUMED
DEEFLOT	FEEDLOT	**DEEGKRS**	KEDGERS	**DEEHMUX**	EXHUMED
DEEFLOY	EYEFOLD	**DEEGLMU**	EMULGED	**DEEHNOY**	HONEYED
DEEFLRU	FERULED	**DEEGLNS**	LEGENDS	**DEEHNPR**	PREHEND
DEEFLRY	DEERFLY	**DEEGLNT**	GENTLED	**DEEHNRS**	HERDENS
DEEFLSU	DEFUELS		GLENTED	**DEEHNUY**	UNHEEDY
DEEFLTT	FETTLED	**DEEGLOY**	GOLDEYE	**DEEHORS**	RESHOED
DEEFMOR	FREEDOM	**DEEGLPR**	PLEDGER	**DEEHORV**	HOVERED
DEEFNRS	FENDERS	**DEEGLPS**	PLEDGES	**DEEHOSY**	HOSEYED
DEEFNRU	UNFREED	**DEEGLPT**	PLEDGET	**DEEHPRS**	SPHERED
DEEFNUU	UNFEUED	**DEEGLRS**	GELDERS	**DEEHRRS**	HERDERS
DEEFORV	OVERFED		LEDGERS	**DEEHRSS**	HERDESS
DEEFORZ	DEFROZE		REDLEGS	**DEEHRSU**	USHERED
DEEFRSU	DEFUSER		SLEDGER	**DEEHRSW**	SHREWED
	REFUSED	**DEEGLRU**	GRUELED	**DEEHRTW**	WRETHED
DEEFRSW	SWERFED		GUELDER	**DEEHSYY**	HEYDEYS
DEEFRTT	FRETTED		REGLUED	**DEEHTTW**	WHETTED
DEEFRTU	FEUTRED	**DEEGLRW**	WERGELD	**DEEIINT**	DIETINE
	REFUTED	**DEEGLSS**	SLEDGES	**DEEIIPR**	EPEIRID
DEEFSSU	DEFUSES	**DEEGLSU**	DELUGES	**DEEIIRW**	WEIRDIE
DEEFSTT	DEFTEST	**DEEGMNU**	EMUNGED	**DEEIIST**	DEITIES
DEEFSUZ	DEFUZES		GUDEMEN	**DEEIJLL**	JELLIED
DEEGGIS	GIDGEES	**DEEGMRS**	DEGERMS	**DEEIJMM**	JEMMIED
DEEGGLS	GLEDGES	**DEEGMUW**	GUMWEED	**DEEIJTT**	JETTIED
DEEGHIN	HEEDING	**DEEGNNO**	ENDOGEN	**DEEIKLL**	KILLDEE
	NEIGHED	**DEEGNNR**	GRENNED	**DEEIKLN**	KNEIDEL
DEEGHIR	HEDGIER	**DEEGNOR**	ENGORED		LIKENED
DEEGHIW	WEIGHED	**DEEGNRS**	GENDERS	**DEEIKMS**	SMEIKED
DEEGHOW	HOGWEED	**DEEGNSU**	DENGUES	**DEEIKMW**	MIDWEEK
DEEGHRS	HEDGERS		UNEDGES	**DEEIKNR**	REINKED
DEEGHSS	GHESSED	**DEEGOOS**	SOOGEED	**DEEIKNS**	ENSKIED
DEEGIJS	GIDJEES	**DEEGORR**	ROGERED		SKEINED
DEEGIKN	DEKEING	**DEEGOSS**	GESSOED	**DEEIKOV**	DOVEKIE
DEEGIKR	KEDGIER	**DEEGOSY**	GEODESY	**DEEILLS**	DELLIES
DEEGILN	DELEING	**DEEGOTU**	OUTEDGE	**DEEILMS**	DELIMES
DEEGILR	GELIDER	**DEEGRRU**	REURGED	**DEEILNO**	ELOINED
	LEDGIER	**DEEGRSW**	SWEDGER	**DEEILNR**	REDLINE
	LEIDGER	**DEEGSSU**	GUESSED		RELINED
DEEGILS	LEGSIDE	**DEEGSTU**	GUESTED	**DEEILNS**	ENISLED

	ENSILED	**DEEINOR**	ORDINEE	**DEEIRRV**	DERIVER
	LINSEED	**DEEINPR**	REPINED		REDRIVE
DEEILNT	LENITED		RIPENED		RIVERED
DEEILNV	LIVENED	**DEEINPW**	PINWEED	**DEEIRRW**	REWIRED
DEEILNY	DYELINE	**DEEINRR**	DERNIER		WEIRDER
	NEEDILY		NERDIER	**DEEIRSS**	DESIRES
DEEILOR	REOILED	**DEEINRS**	DENIERS		RESIDES
DEEILOS	OILSEED		NEREIDS	**DEEIRST**	DIESTER
DEEILPR	PERILED		RESINED		DIETERS
	REPLIED	**DEEINRU**	UREDINE		REEDITS
DEEILPS	SEEDLIP	**DEEINRW**	REWIDEN		REISTED
	SPEILED		WIDENER		RESITED
	SPIELED	**DEEINRX**	INDEXER	**DEEIRSU**	RESIDUE
DEEILRS	RESILED		REINDEX		UREIDES
DEEILRT	RETILED	**DEEINSS**	DESINES	**DEEIRSV**	DERIVES
DEEILRV	DELIVER	**DEEINST**	DESTINE		DEVISER
	LIVERED		ENDITES		DIVERSE
	RELIVED		STEINED		REVISED
	REVILED	**DEEINSV**	DEVEINS	**DEEIRSW**	SWEIRED
DEEILRW	WIELDER	**DEEINSW**	ENDIVES	**DEEIRSZ**	RESIZED
DEEILRY	REEDILY		ENDWISE	**DEEIRTU**	ERUDITE
	YIELDER		SINEWED	**DEEIRTV**	RIVETED
DEEILSS	DIESELS	**DEEINSX**	INDEXES		VERDITE
	IDLESSE	**DEEINTT**	DINETTE	**DEEIRVV**	REVIVED
	SEIDELS	**DEEINTU**	DETINUE	**DEEISSU**	DISEUSE
DEEILST	ISLETED	**DEEINTV**	EVIDENT	**DEEISSV**	DEVISES
DEEILSY	EYELIDS	**DEEINVW**	VINEWED	**DEEISTT**	TEDIEST
	SEEDILY	**DEEINVX**	INVEXED	**DEEISTW**	DEWIEST
DEEILTU	DILUTEE	**DEEINWZ**	WIZENED	**DEEISTX**	EXISTED
DEEILTV	DEVILET	**DEEIOPS**	EPISODE	**DEEITTV**	VIDETTE
DEEILWY	WEEDILY		POESIED	**DEEJNOS**	JONESED
DEEIMMO	MIMEOED	**DEEIOPT**	EPIDOTE	**DEEJNOY**	ENJOYED
DEEIMMS	MISDEEM	**DEEIOPX**	EPOXIDE	**DEEJQRU**	JERQUED
DEEIMMW	IMMEWED		EPOXIED	**DEEKKRT**	TREKKED
DEEIMNO	DOMINEE	**DEEIORS**	OREIDES	**DEEKLLN**	KNELLED
DEEIMNR	ERMINED		OSIERED	**DEEKLLV**	KVELLED
DEEIMNS	DESMINE	**DEEIOSV**	VOIDEES	**DEEKLPS**	SKELPED
	SIDEMEN	**DEEIPPT**	PEPTIDE	**DEEKLRS**	SKELDER
DEEIMNT	DEMENTI	**DEEIPRS**	PREDIES	**DEEKMNS**	DESKMEN
DEEIMOR	EMEROID		PRESIDE	**DEEKMRS**	SMERKED
DEEIMPR	DEMIREP		SPEIRED	**DEEKNNS**	SKENNED
	EPIDERM		SPIERED	**DEEKNOT**	TOKENED
	IMPEDER	**DEEIPRT**	PREEDIT	**DEEKNSY**	ENSKYED
DEEIMPS	IMPEDES		TEPIDER	**DEEKORV**	REVOKED
	SEMIPED	**DEEIPRV**	DEPRIVE	**DEEKORY**	YOKERED
DEEIMPT	EMPTIED		PREDIVE	**DEEKOVY**	DOVEKEY
DEEIMRS	REMEIDS		PRIEVED	**DEEKPPS**	SKEPPED
	REMISED	**DEEIPRX**	EXPIRED	**DEEKPRU**	PERUKED
DEEIMRT	DEMERIT	**DEEIPSS**	DESPISE	**DEEKRRS**	SKERRED
	DIMETER		PEDESIS	**DEEKRSU**	RESKUED
	MERITED	**DEEIPST**	DESPITE	**DEEKSTT**	SKETTED
	MITERED	**DEEIQRU**	QUERIED	**DEELLMS**	SMELLED
	RETIMED	**DEEIQTU**	QUIETED	**DEELLNS**	SNELLED
DEEIMRX	REMIXED	**DEEIRRS**	DERRIES	**DEELLPS**	SPELLED
DEEIMSS	DEMISES		DESIRER	**DEELLQU**	QUELLED
DEEIMTT	EMITTED		REDRIES	**DEELLRU**	DUELLER
DEEINNP	PENNIED		RESIDER	**DEELLRW**	DWELLER
DEEINNS	INDENES		SERRIED	**DEELLRY**	ELDERLY
DEEINNT	DENTINE	**DEEIRRT**	RETIRED	**DEELLST**	STELLED
DEEINNU	ENNUIED		RETRIED	**DEELLSW**	SWELLED
DEEINNZ	DENIZEN		TIREDER	**DEELMNO**	LEMONED

DEELMOR	MODELER	**DEEMMOV**	EMMOVED	**DEENRST**	STERNED
	REMODEL	**DEEMMST**	STEMMED		TENDERS
DEELMPT	TEMPLED	**DEEMNOR**	MODERNE		TENDRES
DEELMPU	DEPLUME	**DEEMNOT**	DEMETON	**DEENRSU**	ENDURES
DEELMRS	MELDERS	**DEEMNOU**	EUDEMON		ENSURED
DEELMRU	RELUMED	**DEEMNOV**	ENMOVED	**DEENRSV**	VENDERS
DEELMST	SMELTED		VENOMED	**DEENRSZ**	DZERENS
DEELMSU	MULESED	**DEEMNOY**	MONEYED	**DEENRTU**	DENTURE
DEELMSY	MEDLEYS	**DEEMNRS**	MENDERS		RETUNED
DEELMTT	METTLED		REMENDS		TENURED
DEELNOT	DOLENTE	**DEEMNST**	DEMENTS	**DEENRTV**	VENTRED
DEELNPU	PENDULE	**DEEMNTU**	UNMETED	**DEENSST**	DENSEST
DEELNRS	LENDERS	**DEEMNUW**	UNMEWED	**DEENSSU**	DUENESS
	RELENDS	**DEEMORS**	EMERODS	**DEENSSY**	DESYNES
	SLENDER	**DEEMORV**	REMOVED		ENDYSES
DEELNSS	ENDLESS	**DEEMORX**	EXODERM	**DEENSTT**	DETENTS
DEELNST	DENTELS	**DEEMOSS**	DEMOSES		STENTED
	NESTLED	**DEEMOST**	DEMOTES	**DEENSTU**	DETENUS
DEELNSW	WEDELNS	**DEEMOSY**	MOSEYED		DETUNES
DEELNSY	DENSELY	**DEEMPRS**	DEPERMS	**DEENSTX**	EXTENDS
DEELNTT	NETTLED		PREMEDS	**DEENSUV**	VENDUES
DEELOOS	DOOLEES	**DEEMPSU**	DUMPEES	**DEENSUW**	UNSEWED
DEELOPP	PEOPLED	**DEEMPTT**	TEMPTED	**DEENSUX**	UNSEXED
DEELOPR	DEPLORE	**DEEMRRU**	DEMURER	**DEENUVX**	UNVEXED
DEELOPS	DELOPES	**DEEMRSU**	DEMURES	**DEEOPPY**	POPEYED
DEELOPV	DEVELOP		RESUMED	**DEEOPRR**	PEDRERO
DEELOPX	EXPLODE	**DEEMSUY**	MUDEYES	**DEEOPRS**	DEPOSER
DEELORS	RESOLED	**DEENNOR**	ENDERON		REPOSED
DEELORU	URODELE	**DEENNOS**	DONNEES	**DEEOPRW**	POWERED
DEELORV	LOVERED	**DEENNOT**	ENDNOTE	**DEEOPSS**	DEPOSES
DEELORW	LOWERED		TENONED		SPEEDOS
	ROWELED	**DEENNOY**	DOYENNE	**DEEOPSX**	EXPOSED
DEELORY	YODELER	**DEENNOZ**	ENDZONE		PODEXES
DEELOSU	DELOUSE		ENZONED	**DEEOPTU**	TOUPEED
DEELOTV	DOVELET		ENZONED	**DEEOPXY**	EPOXYED
DEELOTW	TOWELED	**DEENNPT**	PENDENT	**DEEORRR**	ORDERER
DEELOVV	DEVOLVE	**DEENNRU**	ENURNED		REORDER
	EVOLVED	**DEENNST**	DENNETS	**DEEORRS**	REREDOS
DEELPRS	PEDLERS		STENNED	**DEEORRV**	OVERRED
	SPELDER	**DEENNTZ**	TENDENZ		REDROVE
DEELPRU	PRELUDE	**DEENNUY**	ENNUYED	**DEEORST**	OERSTED
DEELPRY	PEDLERY	**DEENOOR**	RONEOED		ROSETED
DEELPST	PESTLED	**DEENOPR**	REPONED		TEREDOS
DEELPTT	PETTLED	**DEENOPS**	DEPONES	**DEEORSV**	DEVORES
DEELRRU	RULERED		SPONDEE	**DEEORSW**	RESOWED
DEELRSS	ELDRESS	**DEENOPT**	PENTODE	**DEEORSX**	REDOXES
DEELRSU	DUELERS	**DEENORS**	ENDORSE	**DEEORTT**	OTTERED
	ELUDERS	**DEENORT**	ERODENT		TETRODE
DEELRSV	DELVERS	**DEENORW**	ENDOWER	**DEEORTV**	REVOTED
DEELRSW	REWELDS		REENDOW	**DEEORTW**	TOWERED
	WELDERS	**DEENORZ**	REZONED	**DEEORTX**	OXTERED
DEELRUV	VELURED	**DEENOST**	DENOTES	**DEEORTZ**	ROZETED
DEELSSW	DEWLESS	**DEENPPR**	PERPEND	**DEEORUV**	OVERDUE
DEELSTT	SETTLED	**DEENPRS**	SPENDER	**DEEORVY**	OVERDYE
DEELSTU	TELEDUS	**DEENPRT**	PRENTED	**DEEORXX**	XEROXED
DEELSTW	LEWDEST		PRETEND	**DEEOSTV**	DEVOTES
	SWELTED	**DEENPSX**	EXPENDS	**DEEOSTX**	DETOXES
DEELSUV	EVULSED	**DEENRRS**	RENDERS	**DEEOTUW**	OUTWEED
DEELSVV	DEVVELS	**DEENRRU**	ENDURER	**DEEPPPR**	PREPPED
DEELTUX	EXULTED	**DEENRSS**	REDNESS	**DEEPPST**	STEPPED
DEELVXY	VEXEDLY		RESENDS	**DEEPPSU**	SPEEDUP
			SENDERS		

DEEPRRS	SPERRED	**DEFFNOR**	FORFEND	**DEFILTY**	FETIDLY
DEEPRRU	PERDURE	**DEFFNOS**	OFFENDS	**DEFILXY**	FIXEDLY
	REPURED		SENDOFF	**DEFILZZ**	FIZZLED
DEEPRSS	DEPRESS	**DEFFNSU**	SNUFFED	**DEFIMOR**	DEIFORM
	PRESSED	**DEFFOPU**	POUFFED	**DEFIMOW**	WIFEDOM
	SPERSED	**DEFFORS**	DOFFERS	**DEFINRS**	FINDERS
DEEPRST	PRESTED	**DEFFOSW**	SOWFFED		FRIENDS
DEEPRSU	PERDUES	**DEFFRSU**	DUFFERS		REDFINS
	PERSUED	**DEFFSTU**	DUFFEST		REFINDS
	PERUSED		STUFFED	**DEFINRU**	UNFIRED
	SUPERED	**DEFGGIR**	FRIGGED	**DEFINST**	SNIFTED
DEEPRTU	ERUPTED	**DEFGGLO**	FLOGGED	**DEFINSU**	FUNDIES
	REPUTED	**DEFGGOR**	FROGGED		INFUSED
DEEPRTY	RETYPED	**DEFGGRU**	FRUGGED	**DEFINSY**	DENSIFY
DEEPRUV	PREVUED	**DEFGINN**	FENDING	**DEFINUX**	UNFIXED
DEEPSTU	DEPUTES	**DEFGINR**	FRINGED	**DEFINUY**	UNDEIFY
DEEQSTU	QUESTED	**DEFGINU**	FEUDING	**DEFIOOS**	FOODIES
DEERRSS	DRESSER	**DEFGINY**	DEFYING	**DEFIOQU**	QUOIFED
	REDRESS	**DEFGIOR**	FIREDOG	**DEFIORU**	FOUDRIE
DEERRUV	VERDURE	**DEFGIRS**	FRIDGES	**DEFIOST**	FOISTED
DEERSSS	DRESSES	**DEFGIRT**	GRIFTED	**DEFIPRY**	PERFIDY
DEERSST	DESERTS	**DEFGIRU**	FIGURED	**DEFIRRT**	DRIFTER
	DESSERT	**DEFGIST**	FIDGETS	**DEFIRST**	FRISTED
	TRESSED	**DEFGITY**	FIDGETY	**DEFIRTT**	FRITTED
DEERSSU	DURESSE	**DEFGRTU**	GRUFTED	**DEFIRTU**	FRUITED
DEERSTV	STERVED	**DEFHIRS**	REDFISH	**DEFIRZZ**	FRIZZED
	VERDETS	**DEFHIST**	SHIFTED	**DEFISTU**	FEUDIST
DEERSTW	STREWED	**DEFHLOO**	ELFHOOD	**DEFISTW**	SWIFTED
	WRESTED	**DEFHLSU**	FLUSHED	**DEFKLNU**	FLUNKED
DEERSTX	DEXTERS		SHEDFUL	**DEFLLOU**	DOLEFUL
DEERSTY	DYESTER	**DEFHOOW**	WHOOFED	**DEFLLUW**	DEWFULL
DEERSVW	SWERVED	**DEFHORT**	FROTHED	**DEFLMOS**	SELFDOM
DEERTTU	UTTERED	**DEFHRSU**	FRUSHED	**DEFLMPU**	FLUMPED
DEERTUX	EXTRUDE	**DEFIILM**	MIDLIFE	**DEFLNOO**	ONEFOLD
DEESSTT	DETESTS	**DEFIILN**	INFIDEL	**DEFLNOP**	PENFOLD
DEESSTV	DEVESTS		INFIELD	**DEFLNOR**	FONDLER
DEESTTT	STETTED	**DEFIIMS**	FIDEISM		FORLEND
DEFFFLU	FLUFFED	**DEFIIMW**	MIDWIFE	**DEFLNOS**	ENFOLDS
DEFFGRU	GRUFFED	**DEFIINU**	UNIFIED		FONDLES
DEFFHIW	WHIFFED	**DEFIINX**	INFIXED	**DEFLNOT**	TENFOLD
DEFFHOU	HOUFFED	**DEFIIST**	FIDEIST	**DEFLNRU**	DERNFUL
DEFFHOW	HOWFFED	**DEFIKLS**	FLISKED	**DEFLOOR**	FLOODER
DEFFIKS	SKIFFED	**DEFIKRS**	FRISKED		FLOORED
DEFFILP	PIFFLED	**DEFILLO**	FOLLIED		REFLOOD
DEFFILR	RIFFLED	**DEFILLR**	FRILLED	**DEFLOOT**	FOOTLED
DEFFILS	SIFFLED	**DEFILMP**	FLIMPED	**DEFLOOZ**	FOOZLED
DEFFIMO	FIEFDOM	**DEFILNR**	FLINDER	**DEFLOPP**	FLOPPED
DEFFINS	SNIFFED	**DEFILNT**	FLINTED	**DEFLORS**	FOLDERS
DEFFIOS	DIEOFFS	**DEFILNU**	UNFILDE		REFOLDS
	OFFSIDE		UNFILED	**DEFLORT**	TELFORD
DEFFIPS	SPIFFED	**DEFILOO**	FOLIOED	**DEFLORU**	FLOURED
DEFFIRS	DIFFERS	**DEFILOW**	OLDWIFE		FOULDER
DEFFIST	STIFFED	**DEFILPP**	FLIPPED	**DEFLOSS**	FLOSSED
DEFFISU	DIFFUSE	**DEFILPU**	UPFIELD	**DEFLOSU**	DEFOULS
DEFFKOS	SKOFFED	**DEFILRT**	FLIRTED		FLOUSED
DEFFLMU	MUFFLED		TRIFLED	**DEFLOTU**	FLOUTED
DEFFLPU	PLUFFED	**DEFILRU**	DIREFUL	**DEFLPRU**	PURFLED
DEFFLRU	RUFFLED	**DEFILSS**	FISSLED	**DEFLRRU**	FLURRED
DEFFLSU	DUFFELS	**DEFILST**	STIFLED	**DEFLRUU**	DUREFUL
	DUFFLES	**DEFILSU**	SULFIDE	**DEFLUZZ**	FUZZLED
	SLUFFED	**DEFILTT**	FLITTED	**DEFMNUU**	UNFUMED

DEFMORS	DEFORMS	**DEGGLSU**	SLUGGED	**DEGILLO**	GOLLIED
	SERFDOM	**DEGGMSU**	SMUGGED	**DEGILLR**	GRILLED
DEFMPRU	FRUMPED	**DEGGNOO**	DOGGONE	**DEGILLU**	GULLIED
DEFNOOR	FORDONE	**DEGGNOS**	SNOGGED	**DEGILLY**	GELIDLY
DEFNORT	FRONTED	**DEGGNOU**	GUDGEON	**DEGILMN**	MEDLING
DEFNORU	FOUNDER	**DEGGNSU**	SNUGGED		MELDING
	REFOUND	**DEGGOPR**	PROGGED		MINGLED
DEFNORW	FROWNED	**DEGGORS**	DOGGERS	**DEGILMS**	MIDLEGS
DEFNOST	FONDEST	**DEGGORT**	TROGGED	**DEGILNN**	LENDING
DEFNOSU	FONDUES	**DEGGORY**	DOGGERY	**DEGILNO**	GLENOID
DEFNPRU	PREFUND	**DEGGOSS**	DOGGESS	**DEGILNP**	PINGLED
DEFNRSU	FUNDERS	**DEGGRRU**	DRUGGER	**DEGILNS**	DINGLES
	REFUNDS		GRUDGER		ELDINGS
DEFNSUU	UNFUSED	**DEGGRSU**	GRUDGES		ENGILDS
DEFOOPR	PROOFED	**DEGGRTU**	DRUGGET		SINGLED
DEFOOPS	SPOOFED	**DEGHHIT**	HIGHTED	**DEGILNT**	GLINTED
DEFOORS	DOOFERS		THIGHED		TINGLED
	FORDOES	**DEGHHOU**	HOUGHED	**DEGILNU**	DUELING
DEFOORT	REDFOOT	**DEGHILN**	HINDLEG		ELUDING
DEFORST	DEFROST	**DEGHILT**	DELIGHT		INDULGE
	FROSTED		LIGHTED	**DEGILNV**	DELVING
DEFORTU	FOUTRED	**DEGHINN**	HENDING		DEVLING
DEFSSUU	DUFUSES	**DEGHINO**	HONGIED	**DEGILNW**	WELDING
DEGGGIL	GIGGLED	**DEGHINR**	HERDING	**DEGILOR**	GLORIED
DEGGGIN	DEGGING	**DEGHINT**	NIGHTED		GODLIER
DEGGGIR	GRIGGED	**DEGHINW**	WHINGED		GOLDIER
DEGGGLO	GOGGLED	**DEGHIOT**	HOGTIED	**DEGILOU**	OUGLIED
DEGGGLU	GLUGGED	**DEGHIPT**	PIGHTED	**DEGILRR**	GIRDLER
	GUGGLED	**DEGHIRT**	GIRTHED	**DEGILRS**	GILDERS
DEGGGOR	GROGGED		RIGHTED		GIRDLES
DEGGHIL	HIGGLED	**DEGHIST**	SIGHTED		GLIDERS
DEGGHIN	HEDGING	**DEGHITW**	WIGHTED		GRISLED
DEGGHIW	WHIGGED	**DEGHLOO**	DOGHOLE		LIDGERS
DEGGHOS	SHOGGED	**DEGHNOT**	THONGED		REGILDS
DEGGIJL	JIGGLED	**DEGHORR**	DROGHER		RIDGELS
DEGGIKN	KEDGING	**DEGHORU**	ROUGHED		RIDGELS
DEGGILN	GELDING	**DEGHOST**	GHOSTED	**DEGILRU**	GUILDER
	NIGGLED	**DEGHOSU**	SOUGHED	**DEGILRW**	WERGILD
DEGGILW	WIGGLED	**DEGHOTU**	OUGHTED	**DEGILTZ**	GLITZED
DEGGINS	EDGINGS		TOUGHED	**DEGILUV**	DIVULGE
	SNIGGED	**DEGIIKR**	KIDGIER	**DEGIMNN**	MENDING
DEGGINW	WEDGING	**DEGIILL**	GILLIED	**DEGIMNO**	DEMOING
DEGGIOR	DOGGIER	**DEGIILN**	EILDING		MENDIGO
DEGGIOS	DOGGIES		ELIDING	**DEGIMNS**	SMIDGEN
DEGGIPR	PRIGGED	**DEGIIMR**	MIDGIER	**DEGIMPU**	GUIMPED
DEGGIRS	DIGGERS	**DEGIIMS**	MIDGIES	**DEGIMSS**	SMIDGES
DEGGIRT	TRIGGED	**DEGIINN**	INDIGEN	**DEGIMST**	MIDGETS
DEGGIRU	DRUGGIE	**DEGIINR**	DINGIER	**DEGINNN**	DENNING
DEGGISW	SWIGGED	**DEGIINS**	DINGIES	**DEGINNP**	PENDING
DEGGITW	TWIGGED	**DEGIINT**	DIETING	**DEGINNR**	GRINNED
DEGGJLO	JOGGLED		EDITING		RENDING
DEGGJLU	JUGGLED		IGNITED	**DEGINNS**	ENDINGS
DEGGKSU	SKUGGED	**DEGIIPS**	GIPSIED		SENDING
DEGGLOO	GOOGLED	**DEGIIRR**	RIDGIER	**DEGINNT**	DENTING
DEGGLOR	DOGGREL		RIGIDER		TENDING
DEGGLOS	DOGLEGS	**DEGIIRS**	DIRIGES	**DEGINNU**	ENDUING
	SLOGGED	**DEGIISW**	WIDGIES	**DEGINNV**	VENDING
DEGGLOT	TOGGLED	**DEGIJLN**	JINGLED	**DEGINNW**	WENDING
DEGGLPU	PLUGGED	**DEGIKLO**	DOGLIKE	**DEGINNY**	DENYING
	PUGGLED		GODLIKE	**DEGINOP**	PIDGEON
DEGGLRU	GURGLED	**DEGIKNS**	DESKING	**DEGINOR**	ERODING
					GROINED

	IGNORED
	NEGROID
	REDOING
DEGINOS	DINGOES
DEGINOT	INGOTED
DEGINOW	WENDIGO
	WIDGEON
	WONGIED
DEGINRR	GRINDER
	REGRIND
DEGINRS	DINGERS
	ENGIRDS
DEGINRU	DUNGIER
DEGINRW	REDWING
	WRINGED
DEGINRY	YERDING
DEGINSS	DESIGNS
	SDEIGNS
DEGINST	NIDGETS
	STEDING
	STINGED
DEGINSU	GUNDIES
	SUEDING
DEGINSW	SWINDGE
	SWINGED
DEGINSY	DINGEYS
	DYEINGS
DEGINTU	DUETING
DEGINTW	TWINGED
DEGINUX	EXUDING
DEGIOOR	GOODIER
DEGIOOS	GOODIES
	SOOGIED
DEGIOPR	PODGIER
DEGIORR	GRODIER
DEGIORT	GOITRED
DEGIPPR	GRIPPED
DEGIPRU	PUDGIER
DEGIPSY	GYPSIED
DEGIQSU	SQUIDGE
DEGIRRS	GIRDERS
	RIDGERS
DEGIRRU	DURGIER
DEGIRSS	DIGRESS
DEGIRSU	GUIDERS
DEGIRTT	GRITTED
DEGISST	DIGESTS
	DISGEST
DEGISSU	GUSSIED
DEGISTU	DUGITES
	GIUSTED
DEGISTW	WIDGETS
DEGJLNU	JUNGLED
DEGJRSU	JUDGERS
DEGKKOR	GROKKED
DEGKLSU	KLUDGES
DEGKLUY	KLUDGEY
DEGLMMO	GLOMMED
DEGLMOO	GLOOMED
DEGLMOU	MOGULED
DEGLNNO	ENDLONG

DEGLNOP	PLONGED
DEGLNOS	DONGLES
	GOLDENS
DEGLNOU	LOUNGED
DEGLNPU	PLUNGED
	PUNGLED
DEGLNRU	GRUNDLE
DEGLNSU	GULDENS
DEGLNUU	UNGLUED
	UNGLUED
DEGLOOP	GLOOPED
DEGLOPP	GLOPPED
DEGLOPR	PLEDGOR
DEGLOPS	PLODGES
	SPLODGE
DEGLORS	LODGERS
DEGLORW	GROWLED
DEGLOSS	GLOSSED
	GODLESS
DEGLOST	GOLDEST
DEGLOTU	GLOUTED
DEGLSSU	SLUDGES
DEGLTTU	GLUTTED
	GUTTLED
DEGLUZZ	GUZZLED
DEGMNOO	GOODMEN
DEGMOOR	GROOMED
DEGMOOS	SMOODGE
	SMOOGED
DEGMPRU	GRUMPED
DEGMRSU	MUDGERS
	SMUDGER
DEGMSSU	SMUDGES
DEGNNOU	DUNGEON
DEGNOOS	NOODGES
DEGNOPR	PRONGED
DEGNOPS	SPONGED
DEGNORU	GUERDON
	UNDERGO
	UNGORED
DEGNORW	WRONGED
DEGNOTU	TONGUED
DEGNRSU	DUNGERS
	GERUNDS
	NUDGERS
DEGNRTU	GRUNTED
	TRUDGEN
DEGNRUU	UNURGED
DEGNSSU	SNUDGES
DEGNUVY	UNGYVED
DEGOORV	GROOVED
	OVERDOG
DEGOOST	STOOGED
DEGOPRU	GROUPED
DEGORRS	DROGERS
DEGORSS	GROSSED
	SODGERS
DEGORST	STODGER
	TODGERS
DEGORSU	DROGUES
	GOURDES

	GROUSED
DEGORTU	DROGUET
	GROUTED
DEGOSST	STODGES
DEGOSTU	DEGOUTS
DEGOSTW	GOWDEST
DEGRRTU	TRUDGER
DEGRSTU	TRUDGES
DEGSSTU	DEGUSTS
DEHHISW	WHISHED
DEHHMPU	HUMPHED
DEHHOOS	HOOSHED
DEHHSSU	SHUSHED
DEHIIKO	HIKOIED
DEHIINN	HINNIED
DEHIIPS	PIEDISH
DEHIIRS	DISHIER
DEHIKRS	SHIRKED
	SHRIKED
DEHIKSW	WHISKED
DEHILLO	HILLOED
DEHILLS	SHILLED
DEHILMS	DISHELM
DEHILNP	DELPHIN
DEHILOT	LITHOED
DEHILPR	HIRPLED
DEHILRS	HIRSLED
DEHILRT	THIRLED
DEHILRW	WHIRLED
DEHILSS	SHIELDS
DEHILTY	DIETHYL
DEHIMMS	SHIMMED
DEHIMMW	WHIMMED
DEHIMNS	MEHNDIS
DEHIMNU	INHUMED
DEHIMOP	HEMIPOD
DEHIMOR	HEIRDOM
DEHIMOS	DISHOME
DEHIMOT	ETHMOID
DEHIMRS	DIRHEMS
DEHIMRU	HUMIDER
DEHIMST	SMITHED
DEHIMUX	HUMIDEX
DEHINNS	SHINNED
DEHINNT	THINNED
DEHINOP	DIPHONE
	PHONIED
DEHINOR	HORDEIN
DEHINOS	HOIDENS
DEHINOY	HYENOID
DEHINPS	ENDSHIP
DEHINRS	HINDERS
	NERDISH
	SHRINED
DEHINRU	UNHIRED
DEHINUV	UNHIVED
DEHIOOR	HOODIER
DEHIOOS	HOODIES
DEHIOOT	DHOOTIE
DEHIORS	RHODIES
DEHIORT	THEROID

DEHIOST	HOISTED		THONDER	DEIIMNO	DOMINIE
DEHIOSU	HIDEOUS		THORNED	DEIIMRT	TIMIDER
DEHIOSV	DOVEISH		THRONED	DEIIMST	MISDIET
DEHIOSW	HOWDIES	DEHNORU	HOUNDER		MISEDIT
DEHIOSX	OXHIDES	DEHNOSU	UNSHOED		STIMIED
DEHIOTU	HIDEOUT	DEHNOSY	HOYDENS	DEIIMSZ	MIDSIZE
DEHIPPS	SHIPPED	DEHNOTZ	DOZENTH	DEIIMVW	MIDWIVE
DEHIPPW	WHIPPED	DEHNRSU	HURDENS	DEIINOS	IODINES
DEHIRRS	SHIRRED	DEHNRTU	THUNDER		IONISED
DEHIRRU	DHURRIE	DEHNSSU	DUNSHES	DEIINOT	EDITION
	HURRIED		SNUSHED		TENIOID
DEHIRRW	WHIRRED	DEHNSSY	YSHENDS	DEIINOZ	IONIZED
DEHIRST	DITHERS	DEHNSTU	SHUNTED	DEIINRR	RINDIER
	SHIRTED	DEHNSUZ	NUDZHES	DEIINRS	INSIDER
DEHIRSU	HURDIES	DEHNSYY	HYDYNES		SNIDIER
DEHIRSV	DERVISH	DEHOOPT	PHOTOED	DEIINRT	INDITER
	SHRIVED	DEHOOPW	WHOOPED		NITRIDE
DEHIRTV	THRIVED	DEHOOST	SOOTHED	DEIINRU	URIDINE
DEHIRTW	WRITHED	DEHOOSW	WOOSHED	DEIINRV	DIVINER
DEHIRTY	DITHERY	DEHOOTT	TOOTHED	DEIINRW	WINDIER
DEHISSW	SWISHED	DEHOOTW	WHOOTED	DEIINSS	INSIDES
	WHISSED	DEHOPPS	SHOPPED	DEIINST	INDITES
DEHISTT	SHITTED	DEHOPPW	WHOPPED		TINEIDS
DEHISTW	WHISTED	DEHORSS	SHODERS	DEIINSV	DIVINES
DEHISVV	SHIVVED	DEHORST	DEHORTS	DEIINSY	YINDIES
DEHIWZZ	WHIZZED		SHORTED	DEIINTV	INVITED
DEHKNTU	THUNKED	DEHORSV	SHROVED	DEIIORS	IODISER
DEHLLOO	HOLLOED	DEHORSW	SHROWED	DEIIORT	DIORITE
DEHLLOU	HULLOED	DEHORTT	TROTHED	DEIIORV	IVORIED
DEHLMOU	MUDHOLE	DEHORTW	WORTHED	DEIIORZ	IODIZER
DEHLMSU	MULSHED	DEHOSTT	SHOTTED	DEIIOSS	IODISES
DEHLNOS	HONDLES	DEHOSTU	SHOUTED	DEIIOSZ	IODIZES
DEHLOOS	SHOOLED		SOUTHED	DEIIOSX	OXIDISE
DEHLOOT	TOEHOLD	DEHOSTW	SOWTHED	DEIIOXZ	OXIDIZE
DEHLOPP	HOPPLED	DEHPPUW	WHUPPED	DEIIPPR	DIPPIER
DEHLORS	HOLDERS	DEHPSSY	PHYSEDS	DEIIPRS	PIERIDS
DEHLORW	WHORLED	DEHPTTU	PHUTTED	DEIIPRT	RIPTIDE
DEHLOSS	SLOSHED	DEIIIRS	IRIDISE		TIDERIP
DEHLOST	SLOTHED	DEIIIRZ	IRIDIZE	DEIIRRT	DIRTIER
DEHLRRU	HURDLER	DEIIJMM	JIMMIED	DEIIRST	DIRTIES
DEHLRSU	HURDLES	DEIIKKL	KIDLIKE		DITSIER
DEHLRTU	HURTLED	DEIIKLS	DISLIKE		TIDIERS
DEHLSSU	SLUSHED	DEIIKNR	DINKIER	DEIIRTT	TRITIDE
DEHLSTU	HUSTLED	DEIIKNS	DINKIES	DEIIRTX	EDITRIX
DEHMNOO	HOODMEN		KINDIES	DEIIRTZ	DITZIER
DEHMNSU	MUDHENS	DEIIKST	DIKIEST	DEIIRVV	DIVVIER
DEHMOPR	MORPHED	DEIILLR	DILLIER		VIVIDER
DEHMOPW	WHOMPED	DEIILLS	DILLIES	DEIIRZZ	DIZZIER
DEHMORU	HUMORED	DEIILLW	WILLIED	DEIISTT	DIETIST
DEHMOST	METHODS	DEIILMN	MIDLINE		DITTIES
DEHMOTU	MOUTHED	DEIILMP	IMPLIED		TIDIEST
DEHMPTU	THUMPED	DEIILMT	DELIMIT	DEIISTV	VISITED
DEHMPUW	WHUMPED		LIMITED	DEIISVV	DIVVIES
DEHMSSU	SMUSHED	DEIILNS	INISLED	DEIISZZ	DIZZIES
DEHNNSU	SHUNNED		LINDIES	DEIIVZZ	VIZZIED
DEHNOOR	HONORED	DEIILOS	DOILIES	DEIJLLO	JOLLIED
DEHNOOW	HOEDOWN		IDOLISE	DEIJNOR	JOINDER
	WOODHEN	DEIILOZ	IDOLIZE	DEIJNOT	JOINTED
DEHNOPU	UNHOPED	DEIILPS	LIPIDES	DEIJNRU	INJURED
DEHNORS	DEHORNS	DEIILRV	LIVIDER	DEIJNSU	DISJUNE
DEHNORT	NORTHED	DEIIMMX	IMMIXED	DEIJORY	JOYRIDE

DEIJOST	JOISTED	DEILLRT	TRILLED		DIPOLES
DEIJRRS	JERRIDS	DEILLRU	DULLIER		PELOIDS
DEIJTTU	JUTTIED	DEILLRV	DREVILL		SOLIPED
DEIKKNS	SKINKED	DEILLSS	LIDLESS		SPOILED
DEIKKRS	SKRIKED	DEILLST	STILLED	DEILOPT	PILOTED
DEIKLLS	DESKILL	DEILLSU	ILLUDES	DEILOPU	EUPLOID
	SKILLED		SULLIED	DEILORS	SOLDIER
DEIKLNP	PLINKED	DEILLSW	SWILLED		SOLIDER
DEIKLNR	KINDLER	DEILLTW	TWILLED	DEILORT	DOILTER
DEIKLNS	KINDLES	DEILMMP	PLIMMED	DEILORW	DOWLIER
	SLINKED	DEILMMS	SLIMMED	DEILOSV	LIVEDOS
DEIKLNT	TINKLED	DEILMNS	MILDENS	DEILOSY	DOYLIES
DEIKLNU	UNLIKED	DEILMNU	LUMINED	DEILOTU	OUTLIED
DEIKLNW	WINKLED		UNLIMED		TOLUIDE
DEIKLOP	PODLIKE	DEILMOP	IMPLODE	DEILPPR	RIPPLED
DEIKLOR	RODLIKE	DEILMOR	MOLDIER	DEILPPS	SIPPLED
DEIKLOS	KELOIDS	DEILMOS	MELOIDS		SLIPPED
DEIKLRS	SKIRLED		MIDSOLE	DEILPPT	TIPPLED
DEIKLRT	KIRTLED		SMOILED	DEILPPU	UPPILED
DEIKLST	KIDLETS	DEILMOY	MYELOID	DEILPRT	TRIPLED
DEIKLTT	KITTLED	DEILMPP	PIMPLED	DEILPRU	PRELUDI
DEIKMMS	SKIMMED	DEILMPR	RIMPLED	DEILPSS	DISPELS
DEIKMPS	SKIMPED	DEILMPS	DIMPLES		DISPLES
DEIKMRS	SMIRKED		MISPLED	DEILPSU	DUPLIES
DEIKNNS	SKINNED		SIMPLED	DEILPTY	TEPIDLY
DEIKNOS	DOESKIN	DEILMPW	WIMPLED	DEILQTU	QUILTED
DEIKNOV	INVOKED	DEILMST	MILDEST	DEILRRU	LURIDER
DEIKNPR	PRINKED		MISTLED	DEILRSS	SIDLERS
DEIKNRR	DRINKER	DEILMSW	MILDEWS		SLIDERS
DEIKNRS	KINDERS	DEILMWY	MILDEWY	DEILRSV	DRIVELS
	KINREDS	DEILMXY	MIXEDLY	DEILRSW	SWIRLED
	REDSKIN	DEILMZZ	MIZZLED		WILDERS
DEIKNST	DINKEST	DEILNNS	DINNLES	DEILRSY	RIDLEYS
	KINDEST		LINDENS	DEILRTU	DILUTER
DEIKNSW	SWINKED	DEILNNU	UNLINED	DEILRTW	TWIRLED
DEIKNSY	DINKEYS	DEILNOO	EIDOLON	DEILRTY	TIREDLY
	KIDNEYS	DEILNOS	DOLINES	DEILRVY	DEVILRY
DEIKNSZ	ZENDIKS		INDOLES	DEILRWY	WEIRDLY
DEIKNTT	KNITTED		SONDELI	DEILRWZ	WRIZLED
DEIKNTW	TWINKED	DEILNOT	LENTOID	DEILRZZ	DRIZZLE
DEIKORR	DORKIER	DEILNOU	UNOILED	DEILSST	DELISTS
DEIKOSY	DISYOKE	DEILNPP	NIPPLED	DEILSTT	SLITTED
DEIKPPS	SKIPPED	DEILNPS	SPELDIN		STILTED
DEIKQRU	QUIRKED		SPINDLE	DEILSTU	DILUTES
DEIKRRS	SKIRRED		SPLINED		DUELIST
DEIKRST	SKIRTED	DEILNPU	UNPILED	DEILSTW	WILDEST
DEIKRSU	DUIKERS	DEILNRT	TENDRIL	DEILSTY	DISTYLE
	DUSKIER		TRINDLE	DEILSUV	DIVULSE
DEIKSTY	DYKIEST	DEILNST	DENTILS	DEILSZZ	SIZZLED
DEIKSVY	SKYDIVE	DEILNSW	SWINDLE	DEILTTT	TITTLED
DEILLMO	MODELLI		WINDLES	DEILTTU	TITULED
DEILLMU	ILLUMED	DEILNSY	SNIDELY	DEILTTV	VITTLED
DEILLNW	INDWELL	DEILNTU	DILUENT	DEILTTW	TWILTED
DEILLOR	DOLLIER		UNTILED	DEILZZZ	ZIZZLED
DEILLOS	DOLLIES	DEILNTW	INDWELT	DEIMMMU	MUMMIED
DEILLOV	LIVELOD		WINTLED	DEIMMOT	TOMMIED
DEILLPR	PRILLED	DEILNUV	UNLIVED	DEIMMPR	PRIMMED
DEILLPS	SPILLED	DEILOOS	DOOLIES	DEIMMRS	DIMMERS
DEILLQU	QUILLED	DEILOPR	LEPORID	DEIMMRT	MIDTERM
DEILLRR	DRILLER	DEILOPS	DESPOIL		TRIMMED
	REDRILL		DIPLOES	DEIMMRU	DUMMIER

	IMMURED	**DEINNOO**	ONIONED			UNTRIED
DEIMMST	DIMMEST	**DEINNOP**	PINNOED	**DEINRTX**	DEXTRIN
DEIMMSU	DUMMIES	**DEINNOR**	ENDIRON	**DEINRTY**	TINDERY
	MEDIUMS	**DEINNOS**	DONNIES	**DEINRUW**	UNWIRED
DEIMNNU	MINUEND		ONDINES	**DEINSST**	DISNEST
	UNMINED	**DEINNOT**	INTONED		DISSENT
DEIMNOP	IMPONED		NOINTED		SNIDEST
DEIMNOR	MINORED	**DEINNRS**	DINNERS	**DEINSSU**	NIDUSES
DEIMNOS	DOMINES		ENDRINS	**DEINSSV**	VENDISS
	EMODINS	**DEINNRU**	DUNNIER	**DEINSSW**	WINDSES
	MISDONE		INURNED	**DEINSSY**	ENDYSIS
DEIMNPS	IMPENDS	**DEINNST**	DENTINS	**DEINSTT**	DENTIST
DEIMNRS	MINDERS		INDENTS		DISTENT
	REMINDS		INTENDS		STINTED
DEIMNRU	UNRIMED	**DEINNSU**	DUNNIES	**DEINSTU**	DISTUNE
DEIMNSS	DIMNESS		UNDINES		DUNITES
	MISSEND	**DEINNSW**	ENWINDS	**DEINSTY**	DENSITY
DEIMNST	MINDSET	**DEINNSY**	DYNEINS		DESTINY
	MISTEND	**DEINNTU**	DUNNITE	**DEINSUZ**	UNSIZED
DEIMNSW	MISWEND	**DEINNTW**	TWINNED	**DEINUVW**	UNWIVED
DEIMNTU	MINUTED	**DEINOOZ**	OZONIDE	**DEIOORS**	ODORISE
	MUNITED	**DEINOPR**	POINDER		OROIDES
	MUTINED		PROINED	**DEIOORW**	WOODIER
	UNTIMED	**DEINOPS**	DISPONE	**DEIOORZ**	ODORIZE
DEIMNUX	UNMIXED		SPINODE	**DEIOOSS**	ISODOSE
DEIMOOR	DOOMIER	**DEINOPT**	POINTED	**DEIOOST**	OSTEOID
	MOIDORE		POINTED	**DEIOOSW**	WOODIES
	MOODIER	**DEINOQU**	QUOINED	**DEIOOSZ**	DOOZIES
DEIMOOS	MOODIES	**DEINORR**	DRONIER	**DEIOOVV**	VOIVODE
DEIMOPR	IMPEDOR	**DEINORS**	DINEROS	**DEIOOWW**	WOIWODE
DEIMOPS	IMPOSED		DONSIER	**DEIOPPP**	POPPIED
DEIMORR	REMORID		INDORSE	**DEIOPPS**	DOPPIES
DEIMORS	MISDOER		ORDINES	**DEIOPRS**	PERIODS
	MOIDERS		ROSINED	**DEIOPRT**	DIOPTER
DEIMORU	ERODIUM		SORDINE		DIOPTRE
DEIMOSS	MISDOES	**DEINORU**	DOURINE		PERIDOT
DEIMOST	DISTOME		NEUROID		PROTEID
	DOMIEST	**DEINORW**	DOWNIER	**DEIOPRV**	PROVIDE
	MODISTE		WINDORE	**DEIOPRX**	PEROXID
	MOISTED	**DEINOSS**	ONSIDES	**DEIOPSS**	DISPOSE
DEIMOSW	MOWDIES	**DEINOST**	DITONES	**DEIOPST**	DEPOSIT
DEIMOTT	OMITTED		STONIED		DOPIEST
DEIMOTV	MOTIVED	**DEINPPS**	SNIPPED		PODITES
	VOMITED	**DEINPRS**	PINDERS		POSITED
DEIMPPR	PRIMPED	**DEINPRT**	PRINTED		SOPITED
DEIMPRT	DIREMPT	**DEINPST**	DIPNETS		TOPSIDE
DEIMPRU	DUMPIER		STIPEND	**DEIOPSV**	VESPOID
	UMPIRED	**DEINPSU**	UNIPEDS	**DEIOPTT**	TIPTOED
DEIMPSU	DUMPIES		UNSPIDE	**DEIOPTV**	PIVOTED
DEIMPTU	IMPUTED		UNSPIED	**DEIOQTU**	QUOITED
DEIMRRS	SMIRRED	**DEINPUW**	UNWIPED	**DEIORRT**	DORTIER
DEIMRSW	MISDREW	**DEINRRU**	NURDIER	**DEIORRW**	ROWDIER
DEIMRSY	SEMIDRY	**DEINRST**	TINDERS		WORDIER
DEIMRUU	UREDIUM	**DEINRSU**	INSURED		WORRIED
DEIMSST	DEMISTS	**DEINRSV**	VERDINS	**DEIORSS**	DORISES
DEIMSSU	MISUSED	**DEINRSW**	REWINDS		DOSSIER
DEIMSTT	SMITTED		WINDERS	**DEIORST**	EDITORS
DEIMSTU	MUISTED	**DEINRTT**	TRIDENT		ROISTED
	TEDIUMS	**DEINRTU**	INTRUDE		ROSITED
DEIMSTY	STYMIED		TURDINE		SORTIED
DEINNNU	NUNDINE		UNTIRED		STEROID
			UNTRIDE		

	STORIED	**DEIRRUX**	DRUXIER	**DEKPRSU**	PREDUSK
	TRIODES	**DEIRSST**	DISSERT	**DEKRSUY**	DUYKERS
DEIORSV	DEVISOR		STRIDES	**DEKSSTU**	DUSKEST
	DEVOIRS	**DEIRSSU**	DISEURS	**DELLMOO**	MODELLO
	VISORED		SUDSIER	**DELLOOW**	WOOLLED
	VOIDERS	**DEIRSTU**	DUSTIER	**DELLOPR**	PROLLED
DEIORSW	DOWRIES		REDUITS		REDPOLL
	ROWDIES		STUDIER	**DELLORR**	DROLLER
	WEIRDOS	**DEIRSTV**	DIVERTS	**DELLORT**	TROLLED
DEIORSZ	DORIZES		VERDITS	**DELLOSU**	DUELLOS
DEIORTT	DOTTIER	**DEISSST**	DESISTS	**DELLOVW**	LOWVELD
DEIORTU	ETOURDI	**DEISSSU**	DISUSES	**DELLRWY**	DRYWELL
	IODURET	**DEISSTU**	STUDIES	**DELLSTU**	DULLEST
	OUTRIDE		TISSUED	**DELMMSU**	SLUMMED
DEIORTZ	ROZITED	**DEISSTV**	DIVESTS	**DELMNOS**	DOLMENS
DEIORVZ	VIZORED	**DEISTTW**	DEWITTS	**DELMOOS**	SLOOMED
DEIORWW	WIDOWER		TWISTED	**DELMOOW**	ELMWOOD
DEIOSTT	DOTIEST	**DEISWZZ**	SWIZZED	**DELMOPR**	PREMOLD
	STOITED	**DEITTTW**	TWITTED	**DELMORS**	MOLDERS
DEIOSTU	OUTSIDE	**DEJLOST**	JOSTLED		REMOLDS
	TEDIOUS	**DEJLSTU**	JUSTLED		SLORMED
DEIOSTV	DOVIEST	**DEJOORY**	JOYRODE	**DELMORU**	MOULDER
DEIOSTW	DOWIEST	**DEJOSTU**	JOUSTED		REMOULD
DEIOSTX	EXODIST	**DEKKLSU**	SKULKED	**DELMOSU**	MODULES
DEIOSTZ	DOZIEST	**DEKKNRU**	KRUNKED		MOUSLED
DEIOSUV	DEVIOUS	**DEKKNSU**	SKUNKED	**DELMOSY**	SMOYLED
DEIOTUV	OUTVIED	**DEKLLNO**	KNOLLED	**DELMOTT**	MOTTLED
DEIOTUW	WIDEOUT	**DEKLLOS**	SKOLLED	**DELMOTU**	MOULTED
DEIPPPU	PUPPIED	**DEKLLSU**	SKULLED	**DELMOUV**	VOLUMED
DEIPPQU	QUIPPED	**DEKLNOP**	PLONKED	**DELMPPU**	PLUMPED
DEIPPRR	DRIPPER	**DEKLNPU**	PLUNKED	**DELMPRU**	RUMPLED
DEIPPRS	DIPPERS	**DEKLNRU**	KNURLED	**DELMPSU**	DUMPLES
DEIPPRT	TRIPPED		RUNKLED		SLUMPED
DEIPPST	PEPTIDS	**DEKLRSU**	SKUDLER	**DELMTUY**	MUTEDLY
DEIPPSU	DUPPIES	**DEKNNOS**	NONSKED	**DELMUZZ**	MUZZLED
DEIPRSS	PRISSED	**DEKNNRU**	DRUNKEN	**DELNOOS**	NOODLES
	SPIDERS	**DEKNOOS**	SNOOKED		SNOOLED
DEIPRST	SPIRTED	**DEKNOPP**	KNOPPED	**DELNORS**	RONDELS
	STRIPED	**DEKNOPR**	PRONKED	**DELNORT**	ENTROLD
DEIPRSU	PUDSIER	**DEKNOQU**	QUONKED	**DELNORU**	LOUNDER
	SIRUPED	**DEKNOST**	STONKED		ROUNDEL
	UPDRIES	**DEKNOSW**	SNOWKED		ROUNDLE
DEIPRSY	SPIDERY	**DEKNOSY**	DONKEYS	**DELNOSS**	OLDNESS
DEIPSSU	UPSIDES	**DEKNOTT**	KNOTTED	**DELNOSU**	LOUDENS
DEIPSSV	VESPIDS	**DEKNOTU**	KNOUTED		NODULES
DEIPSTT	SPITTED	**DEKNOUY**	UNYOKED		NOUSLED
DEIPSTU	DISPUTE	**DEKNPSU**	SPUNKED	**DELNOSW**	DOWLNES
DEIPSUV	UPDIVES	**DEKNRRU**	DRUNKER	**DELNOSZ**	DONZELS
DEIPSUZ	UPSIZED	**DEKNRSU**	DUNKERS	**DELNOTW**	LETDOWN
DEIPSXY	PYXIDES	**DEKNRTU**	TRUNKED	**DELNOTY**	NOTEDLY
DEIPTTU	PUTTIED	**DEKNSSU**	DUSKENS	**DELNOUV**	UNLOVED
	TITUPED	**DEKOOPS**	SPOOKED	**DELNOWY**	DOWLNEY
DEIQRSU	SQUIRED	**DEKOOST**	DOOKETS	**DELNPRU**	PLUNDER
DEIQRTU	QUIRTED		STOOKED	**DELNRSU**	LURDENS
DEIQTTU	QUITTED	**DEKOOTW**	KOTOWED		NURDLES
DEIQUZZ	QUIZZED	**DEKOPST**	DESKTOP		NURSLED
DEIRRST	STIRRED	**DEKORST**	STROKED		RUNDLES
	STRIDER	**DEKORWY**	KEYWORD	**DELNRTU**	RUNDLET
DEIRRSU	DRUSIER	**DEKOSSU**	KUDOSES		TRUNDLE
	DURRIES	**DEKOSVY**	SKYDOVE	**DELNRUU**	UNRULED
DEIRRSV	DRIVERS				

DELNSSU	DULNESS	**DELPRSU**	DRUPELS		TENDRON
DELNUWY	UNWELDY		SLURPED	**DENNORU**	ENROUND
DELNUZZ	NUZZLED	**DELPSSU**	PLUSSED	**DENNOST**	STONNED
DELOOPP	PLEOPOD	**DELPSTU**	DUPLETS		TENDONS
DELOOPS	POODLES	**DELPSUY**	SPULYED	**DENNOTU**	UNNOTED
	SPOOLED	**DELPUZZ**	PUZZLED		UNTONED
DELOOPT	POOTLED	**DELRRSU**	SLURRED	**DENNOUW**	ENWOUND
DELOORT	ROOTLED	**DELRSTU**	LUSTRED		UNOWNED
DELOORW	WOOLDER		RUSTLED	**DENNOUZ**	UNZONED
DELOOSS	DOLOSSE		STRUDEL	**DENNRSU**	UNDERNS
DELOOST	STOOLED	**DELRTTU**	TURTLED	**DENNSSU**	DUNNESS
	TOLEDOS	**DELSSTU**	TUSSLED	**DENNSTU**	DUNNEST
DELOOSW	DEWOOLS	**DELSTTU**	SUTTLED		STUNNED
DELOOTT	TOOTLED	**DELUWZZ**	WUZZLED	**DENNTUU**	UNTUNED
DELOPPP	PLOPPED	**DEMMRRU**	DRUMMER	**DENOOPS**	SNOOPED
	POPPLED	**DEMMSTU**	STUMMED		SPOONED
DELOPPR	DROPPLE	**DEMNOOR**	DOORMEN	**DENOOSS**	NOSODES
DELOPPS	SLOPPED		MORENDO	**DENOOST**	SNOOTED
DELOPPT	TOPPLED	**DEMNOOW**	WOODMEN		STOODEN
DELOPPY	POLYPED	**DEMNORS**	MODERNS	**DENOOSW**	SWOONED
DELOPRS	POLDERS		RODSMEN		WOODENS
	PRESOLD	**DEMNORT**	MORDENT	**DENOOSZ**	SNOOZED
DELOPRT	DROPLET	**DEMNORU**	MOURNED	**DENOOTU**	DUOTONE
	PRETOLD	**DEMNORY**	DEMONRY		OUTDONE
DELOPRU	POULDER	**DEMNOST**	ENDMOST	**DENOOUW**	UNWOOED
	POULDRE	**DEMNOSU**	MENUDOS	**DENOPPR**	PROPEND
	PROULED	**DEMNOTU**	DEMOUNT	**DENOPPU**	UNPOPED
DELOPRW	PROWLED		MOUNTED	**DENOPRS**	PERNODS
DELOPSU	SOUPLED	**DEMNOUV**	UNMOVED		PONDERS
DELOPSY	DEPLOYS	**DEMNSTU**	DUSTMEN		RESPOND
	PODLEYS	**DEMOOPP**	POPEDOM	**DENOPRT**	PORTEND
DELOPTT	PLOTTED	**DEMOOPR**	PREDOOM		PROTEND
DELOPTZ	PLOTZED		PROMOED	**DENOPRU**	POUNDER
DELORRY	ORDERLY	**DEMOOPS**	SPOOMED		UNROPED
DELORSS	DORSELS	**DEMOORS**	DROOMES	**DENOPRV**	PROVEND
	RODLESS		SMOORED	**DENOPRY**	PROYNED
	SOLDERS	**DEMOORT**	MOTORED	**DENOPSU**	UNPOSED
DELORST	DROLEST	**DEMOORV**	VROOMED	**DENOPTY**	POYNTED
	OLDSTER	**DEMOOSS**	OSMOSED	**DENOPUX**	EXPOUND
	STRODLE	**DEMOOST**	SMOOTED	**DENORRS**	DRONERS
DELORSW	WELDORS	**DEMOOTT**	MOTTOED	**DENORRU**	RONDURE
DELORSY	YODLERS	**DEMOOTU**	OUTMODE		ROUNDER
DELORTT	DOTTLER	**DEMOPRT**	TROMPED		UNORDER
	DOTTREL	**DEMOPST**	STOMPED	**DENORRW**	DROWNER
DELORTU	TROULED	**DEMORRS**	DORMERS	**DENORSS**	SONDERS
DELORUV	LOUVRED	**DEMORRU**	RUMORED	**DENORST**	RODENTS
DELOSSS	DOSSELS	**DEMORST**	STORMED		SNORTED
DELOSSU	DULOSES	**DEMORSW**	DEWORMS	**DENORSU**	ENDUROS
DELOSTT	DOTTELS	**DEMOSSU**	MOUSSED		RESOUND
	DOTTLES		SMOUSED		SOUNDER
	SLOTTED	**DEMOSTT**	DOMETTS		UNDOERS
DELOSTU	LOUDEST	**DEMOSTU**	MOUSTED	**DENORSV**	VENDORS
	OULDEST		SMOUTED	**DENORSW**	DOWNERS
	TOUSLED	**DEMOSTY**	MODESTY		WONDERS
DELOSYY	DOYLEYS	**DEMPRSU**	DUMPERS	**DENORSY**	YONDERS
DELOSZZ	SOZZLED	**DEMPRTU**	TRUMPED	**DENORUW**	REWOUND
DELOTUU	OUTDUEL	**DEMPSTU**	STUMPED		WOUNDER
DELOTUV	VOLUTED	**DEMRRSU**	MURDERS	**DENOSTT**	SNOTTED
DELOTUZ	TOUZLED		SMURRED	**DENOSTU**	DEUTONS
DELPPRU	PURPLED	**DEMSTTU**	SMUTTED		SNOUTED
DELPPSU	SUPPLED	**DENNORT**	DONNERT	**DENOSUW**	SWOUNED

	UNSOWED
DENPRSU	SPURNED
DENPRTU	PRUDENT
	PRUNTED
	UPTREND
DENPSSU	SENDUPS
	SUSPEND
	UPSENDS
DENRSSU	SUNDERS
	UNDRESS
DENRSSY	DRYNESS
DENRSTU	RETUNDS
	UNDREST
DENRSUU	UNSURED
DENSSTY	SYNDETS
DENSSUW	SUNDEWS
DENSTTU	STUDENT
	STUNTED
DENTUVY	DUVETYN
DEOOPPS	OPPOSED
DEOOPRS	SPOORED
DEOOPRT	TORPEDO
	TROOPED
DEOOPST	STOOPED
DEOOPSW	SWOOPED
	WOOPSED
DEOOPSX	EXOPODS
DEOORRT	REDROOT
DEOORST	ROOSTED
DEOORSZ	DOOZERS
DEOORTU	OUTDOER
	OUTRODE
DEOORTW	WROOTED
DEOOSTT	TOOTSED
DEOOSTU	OUTDOES
DEOOSTZ	STOOZED
DEOPPPR	PROPPED
DEOPPQU	QUOPPED
DEOPPRR	DROPPER
DEOPPRS	DOPPERS
DEOPPST	STOPPED
DEOPPSW	SWOPPED
DEOPRRS	DORPERS
DEOPRRU	PROUDER
DEOPRST	DEPORTS
	REDTOPS
	SPORTED
DEOPRSU	POUDERS
	POUDRES
DEOPRSW	POWDERS
DEOPRTU	TROUPED
DEOPRWY	POWDERY
DEOPSST	DESPOTS
DEOPSSU	PSEUDOS
	SPOUSED
DEOPSTT	SPOTTED
DEOPSTU	OUTSPED
	SPOUTED
DEOPTTY	TYPTOED
DEOQRTU	TORQUED
DEORRSS	DORSERS
DEORRST	DORTERS
	RODSTER
DEORRSU	ORDURES
DEORRSV	DROVERS
DEORRSW	REWORDS
	SWORDER
DEORRVY	OVERDRY
DEORSSS	DOSSERS
	DROSSES
DEORSSU	DOUSERS
DEORSSW	DOWSERS
	DROWSES
	SOWDERS
DEORSTT	DETORTS
	DOTTERS
DEORSTU	DETOURS
	DOUREST
	DOUTERS
	OUTREDS
	REDOUTS
	ROUSTED
DEORSTW	STROWED
	WORSTED
DEORSTY	DESTROY
	ROYSTED
	STROYED
DEORSUV	DEVOURS
DEORTTT	TROTTED
DEORTTU	TUTORED
DEORTUU	OUTDURE
DEORTUW	OUTDREW
DEOSSSW	SOWSSED
DEOSSTW	DOWSETS
DEOSSYY	ODYSSEY
DEOSTTT	STOTTED
DEOSTTU	DUETTOS
	TESTUDO
DEOSTTW	SWOTTED
DEOSTUU	DUTEOUS
DEOSTUX	TUXEDOS
DEOTTUY	TUTOYED
DEPRRSU	SPURRED
DEPRRUY	PRUDERY
DEPRSTU	SPURTED
DEPRSUU	PURSUED
	USURPED
DEPRSUY	SYRUPED
DERRSTU	RUSTRED
DERSSSU	SUDSERS
DERSSTU	DUSTERS
	TRUSSED
DERSTTU	STURTED
	TRUSTED
DERSTTY	TRYSTED
DERSTUU	SUTURED
DERSTUY	RESTUDY
DFFGINO	DOFFING
DFFGINU	DUFFING
DFFIIMR	MIDRIFF
DFFIIRT	TRIFFID
DFFIMOR	DIFFORM
DFFLOOU	FOODFUL
DFFOSTU	DUSTOFF
DFGGIIN	FIDGING
DFGGINU	FUDGING
DFGGOOS	FOGDOGS
DFGHIOS	DOGFISH
DFGIINN	FINDING
DFGIINY	DIGNIFY
DFGILNO	FOLDING
DFGINNO	FONDING
DFGINNU	FUNDING
DFGINOR	FORDING
DFGINOU	FUNGOID
DFGMOOY	FOGYDOM
DFHILSU	DISHFUL
DFHIMSU	MUDFISH
DFIKRSU	FURKIDS
DFILLUY	FLUIDLY
DFILMMO	FILMDOM
DFILMNU	MINDFUL
DFILNOP	PINFOLD
DFILNOS	INFOLDS
DFILORT	TRIFOLD
DFILORU	FLUORID
DFILOSX	SIXFOLD
DFILOTW	TWIFOLD
DFILSSU	SULFIDS
DFILTUU	DUTIFUL
DFIMNUY	MUNDIFY
DFIMOOS	FOODISM
DFIMORS	DISFORM
DFINOTU	OUTFIND
DFIOORW	FIRWOOD
DFLMOOU	DOOMFUL
DFLMOUW	MUDFLOW
DFLNOSU	UNFOLDS
DFLOORU	ODORFUL
DFLOOTU	FOLDOUT
DFLOOTW	TWOFOLD
DFLOPRY	DROPFLY
DFLOPSU	FOLDUPS
	UPFOLDS
DFLOTWY	TWYFOLD
DFNNOOO	NONFOOD
DFNNOUU	UNFOUND
DFNORUY	FOUNDRY
DFOORSX	OXFORDS
DGGGIIN	DIGGING
DGGGINO	DOGGING
DGGHIOS	DOGGISH
DGGIILN	GILDING
	GLIDING
DGGIINN	DINGING
DGGIINR	GIRDING
	GRIDING
	RIDGING
DGGIINU	GUIDING
DGGIJNU	JUDGING
DGGILNO	GODLING
	LODGING
DGGIMNO	MODGING

DGGIMNU	MUDGING	**DGIINOW**	WINDIGO				PONGIDS
DGGINNO	DONGING	**DGIINOX**	DIGOXIN	**DGINORR**	DORRING
DGGINNU	DUNGING	**DGIINPP**	DIPPING	**DGINORS**	RODINGS
	NUDGING	**DGIINPR**	PRIDING	**DGINORT**	DORTING
DGGINRY	GRYDING	**DGIINPS**	PIDGINS	**DGINORV**	DROVING
DGGNOSU	DUGONGS	**DGIINPU**	PINGUID	**DGINORW**	WORDING
	GUNDOGS	**DGIINRS**	RIDINGS	**DGINOSS**	DOSSING
DGHHOOO	HOGHOOD	**DGIINRT**	DIRTING	**DGINOST**	DOTINGS
DGHIILN	HIDLING	**DGIINRV**	DRIVING	**DGINOSU**	DOUSING
	HILDING	**DGIINRY**	YIRDING		GUIDONS
DGHIINS	DISHING	**DGIINSS**	DISSING	**DGINOSW**	DISGOWN
	HIDINGS		SIDINGS		DOWSING
	SHINDIG	**DGIINST**	TIDINGS	**DGINOSZ**	DOZINGS
DGHILNO	HOLDING	**DGIINSV**	DIVINGS	**DGINOTT**	DOTTING
DGHILNY	HYLDING	**DGIINTT**	DITTING	**DGINOTU**	DOUTING
DGHILOS	GOLDISH	**DGIINTY**	DIGNITY	**DGINPPU**	DUPPING
DGHILPY	DIGLYPH		TIDYING	**DGINRSU**	UNGIRDS
DGHINOO	HOODING	**DGIINVY**	DIVYING	**DGINRSY**	DRYINGS
DGHINOR	HORDING	**DGIIORT**	TIGROID	**DGINSSU**	SUDSING
DGHINSU	DUSHING	**DGIJOSU**	JUDOGIS	**DGINSTU**	DUSTING
DGHINTU	HINDGUT	**DGIKMNO**	KINGDOM	**DGIOPRY**	PRODIGY
	UNDIGHT	**DGIKNNU**	DUNKING	**DGIOSTW**	GODWITS
DGHIOOS	GOODISH	**DGIKNNY**	KYNDING	**DGIPRSU**	UPGIRDS
DGHIOPS	DOGSHIP	**DGIKNOO**	DOOKING	**DGIQSUY**	SQUIDGY
	GODSHIP	**DGIKNOS**	DOGSKIN	**DGISSTU**	DISGUST
DGHOOPS	HOPDOGS	**DGIKNOU**	DOUKING	**DGLNORU**	GOLDURN
DGHOOST	HOTDOGS	**DGIKNSU**	DUSKING	**DGLNOUY**	UNGODLY
DGHORTU	DROUGHT	**DGILLNO**	DOLLING	**DGLOOOW**	LOGWOOD
DGHOTUY	DOUGHTY	**DGILLNU**	DULLING	**DGLOOST**	GODSLOT
DGIIKLN	KIDLING	**DGILLOY**	GODLILY	**DGLOOSU**	DUOLOGS
DGIIKNN	DINKING	**DGILMNO**	MOLDING	**DGLOPSY**	SPLODGY
	KINDING	**DGILNOR**	GIRLOND	**DGLOSYY**	DYSLOGY
DGIIKNR	DIRKING		LORDING	**DGMOOUW**	GUMWOOD
DGIIKNS	DISKING	**DGILNOY**	YODLING	**DGMOPRU**	GUMDROP
DGIILLN	DILLING	**DGILNSU**	UNGILDS	**DGMORUU**	GURUDOM
DGIILMN	MILDING	**DGILNYY**	DYINGLY	**DGNNORU**	NONDRUG
DGIILNO	LOIDING	**DGILOPY**	PODGILY	**DGNOOOP**	GONOPOD
DGIILNR	DIRLING	**DGILOST**	DIGLOTS	**DGNOOOR**	GODROON
DGIILNS	SIDLING	**DGILPUY**	PUDGILY	**DGNOORS**	DRONGOS
	SLIDING	**DGILRUY**	GUILDRY	**DGNOOSS**	GODSONS
DGIILNW	WILDING	**DGIMNOO**	DOOMING	**DGNOOSW**	GODOWNS
DGIILNY	DINGILY	**DGIMNPU**	DUMPING	**DGNOOTW**	DOGTOWN
DGIILRS	RIDGILS	**DGIMOPY**	PYGMOID	**DGNORSU**	GROUNDS
DGIILRY	RIGIDLY	**DGIMSTU**	MIDGUTS	**DGNOSSU**	SUNDOGS
DGIIMMN	DIMMING	**DGINNNO**	DONNING	**DGOORTT**	DOGTROT
DGIIMNN	MINDING	**DGINNNU**	DUNNING	**DGOPRRU**	PRODRUG
DGIIMNS	SMIDGIN	**DGINNOP**	PONDING	**DGOSTUU**	DUGOUTS
DGIIMOP	PIGMOID	**DGINNOR**	DRONING	**DHIILNS**	HIDLINS
DGIIMOS	SIGMOID	**DGINNOS**	DONINGS	**DHIILOT**	DITHIOL
DGIINNN	DINNING		ONDINGS		LITHOID
DGIINNR	RINDING	**DGINNOU**	UNDOING	**DHIILSW**	WILDISH
DGIINNS	NIDINGS	**DGINNOW**	DOWNING	**DHIIMMS**	DHIMMIS
	SINDING	**DGINNRU**	DURNING		DIMMISH
	SNIDING	**DGINNSY**	SYNDING	**DHIIMNO**	HOMINID
DGIINNT	DINTING	**DGINNTU**	DUNTING	**DHIIMPS**	MIDSHIP
	TINDING		TUNDING	**DHIINRU**	HIRUDIN
DGIINNU	INDUING	**DGINNUW**	WINDGUN	**DHIIOPX**	XIPHOID
DGIINNW	DWINING	**DGINNUY**	UNDYING	**DHIIORZ**	RHIZOID
	WINDING	**DGINOOW**	WOODING	**DHIIOST**	HISTOID
DGIINOS	INDIGOS	**DGINOPP**	DOPPING	**DHIIPST**	DIPSHIT
DGIINOV	VOIDING	**DGINOPS**	DOPINGS	**DHIKORS**	DORKISH

DHIKSSU	DUSKISH	**DIIJNOS**	DISJOIN	**DILLOSY**	SOLIDLY
DHILLOS	DOLLISH	**DIIKKNS**	KIDSKIN	**DILLPSY**	PSYLLID
DHILLPY	PHYLLID	**DIIKLNS**	DISLINK	**DILLRUY**	LURIDLY
DHILLSU	DULLISH	**DIIKNOT**	DOITKIN	**DILMNRU**	DRUMLIN
DHILMUY	HUMIDLY	**DIILLST**	DISTILL	**DILMOOY**	DOOMILY
DHILNOP	DOLPHIN	**DIILLVY**	LIVIDLY		MOODILY
DHILOST	DOLTISH	**DIILMNS**	DISLIMN	**DILMORS**	MILORDS
DHILOSU	LOUDISH	**DIILMOO**	MODIOLI	**DILMOSS**	MISSOLD
DHILPSU	LUDSHIP	**DIILMOS**	IDOLISM	**DILMOST**	MISTOLD
	SULPHID	**DIILMST**	MIDLIST	**DILMOSU**	SOLIDUM
DHILPSY	SYLPHID	**DIILMTY**	TIMIDLY	**DILMOSY**	ODYLISM
DHILRTY	THIRDLY	**DIILNNU**	INDULIN	**DILMPUY**	DUMPILY
DHIMOPR	DIMORPH	**DIILNOT**	TOLIDIN	**DILMTUY**	TUMIDLY
DHIMORU	HUMIDOR	**DIILNWY**	WINDILY	**DILNNSU**	DUNLINS
	RHODIUM	**DIILNXY**	XYLIDIN	**DILNOOS**	OODLINS
DHIMOSS	MISSHOD	**DIILOPS**	LIPOIDS	**DILNOPS**	DIPLONS
DHIMPSU	DUMPISH	**DIILOST**	IDOLIST	**DILNOPT**	DIPLONT
DHINNOS	DONNISH	**DIILQSU**	LIQUIDS	**DILNOQU**	QUODLIN
DHINNSU	DUNNISH	**DIILRSU**	SILURID	**DILNORT**	INTROLD
DHINOPS	DONSHIP	**DIILRTY**	DIRTILY	**DILNOSU**	UNSOLID
DHINOPY	HYPNOID	**DIILSST**	DISTILS	**DILNOXY**	INDOXYL
DHINORS	DISHORN	**DIILSTY**	IDYLIST	**DILNPSU**	LISPUND
	DRONISH	**DIILVVY**	VIVIDLY	**DILNPSY**	SPINDLY
DHINRSU	NURDISH	**DIILYZZ**	DIZZILY	**DILNSTU**	INDULTS
DHINSSY	SHINDYS	**DIIMNOR**	MIDIRON	**DILORTU**	DILUTOR
DHINSTU	TUNDISH	**DIIMNSU**	INDIUMS	**DILORWY**	ROWDILY
DHIOOST	DHOOTIS	**DIIMORS**	DIORISM		WORDILY
DHIOPTY	PHYTOID	**DIIMOSS**	IODISMS	**DILOSSS**	DOSSILS
	TYPHOID	**DIIMSSS**	DISMISS	**DILOSSU**	DULOSIS
DHIORSW	WORDISH	**DIIMSTW**	DIMWITS		SOLIDUS
DHIORTY	THYROID	**DIIMSUV**	VIDIMUS	**DILOSTU**	TOLUIDS
DHIPRSU	PRUDISH	**DIINNOT**	TONDINI	**DILOSTY**	STYLOID
DHIPRSY	SYRPHID	**DIINNSW**	INWINDS	**DILOTTY**	DOTTILY
DHJOPRU	JODHPUR	**DIINOQU**	QUINOID	**DILRYZZ**	DRIZZLY
DHKMOOU	MUDHOOK	**DIINORS**	SORDINI	**DILSTUY**	DUSTILY
DHKORSY	DROSHKY	**DIINORT**	DINITRO	**DIMMOST**	MIDMOST
DHLMOOU	HOODLUM	**DIINOSX**	DIOXINS	**DIMNNOO**	MIDNOON
DHLMOOU	HOODLUM	**DIINRST**	NITRIDS	**DIMNNOS**	DONNISM
DHLOOTU	HOLDOUT	**DIIOOPS**	OPIOIDS	**DIMNNOT**	DINMONT
DHLOPSU	HOLDUPS	**DIIOPRS**	SPIROID	**DIMNOOS**	DOMINOS
	UPHOLDS	**DIIORSV**	DIVISOR	**DIMNOPU**	IMPOUND
DHMMRUU	HUMDRUM		VIROIDS	**DIMNORS**	DORMINS
DHMNOYY	HYMNODY	**DIIORTX**	TRIOXID		NIMRODS
DHNNOOU	NUNHOOD	**DIIRSTX**	DISTRIX	**DIMNOTW**	MIDTOWN
DHNOOOS	SONHOOD	**DIITUVY**	VIDUITY	**DIMNOWX**	MIXDOWN
DHNOOSU	UNHOODS	**DIJMSSU**	MUSJIDS	**DIMNSSU**	NUDISMS
DHOOOOS	HOODOOS	**DIJOSTU**	JUDOIST	**DIMOPSU**	PODIUMS
DHOOPRU	UPHOORD	**DIKKLSU**	KUDLIKS		SPODIUM
DHOORST	HOTRODS	**DIKKOPS**	DIKKOPS	**DIMORSW**	MISWORD
DHOORSU	RHODOUS	**DIKLNOR**	LORDKIN	**DIMOSST**	MODISTS
DHOPRSU	PUSHROD	**DIKLSTU**	KIDULTS	**DIMOSSU**	SODIUMS
DHOPRSY	HYDROPS	**DIKLSUY**	DUSKILY	**DIMOSSW**	WISDOMS
DHORSSU	SHROUDS	**DIKMNSU**	DINKUMS	**DIMOSTU**	DIMOUTS
DHORSTU	DROUTHS	**DIKNNOS**	NONSKID	**DIMRTUU**	TRIDUUM
DHORSUY	HYDROUS	**DIKNNSU**	NUDNIKS	**DIMRUUV**	DUUMVIR
	SHROUDY	**DIKNOOW**	INKWOOD	**DINNOOR**	RONDINO
DHORTUY	DROUTHY	**DIKNORV**	DVORNIK	**DINNOOT**	TONDINO
DHORXYY	HYDROXY	**DIKOORT**	DROOKIT	**DINNOPR**	NONDRIP
DIIIMOS	SIMIOID	**DIKOOSS**	SKIDOOS	**DINNOPW**	PINDOWN
DIIIMRU	IRIDIUM	**DIKORTU**	DROUKIT	**DINNOSS**	SINDONS
DIIIMSV	DIVISIM	**DILLMSU**	MUDSILL	**DINNOUW**	INWOUND
DIIINPS	INSIPID				

DINNSUW	UNWINDS	DLOOPTU	OUTPLOD	EEEEPSW	PEEWEES
DINOORS	INDOORS	DLOOPTY	TYLOPOD	EEEESWW	WEEWEES
	SORDINO	DLOOPUY	DUOPOLY	EEEFFFO	FEOFFEE
DINOORT	TORDION	DLOOPWY	PLYWOOD	EEEFFOR	OFFEREE
DINOOST	ISODONT	DLOORSU	DOLOURS	EEEFFRS	EFFERES
DINOPSU	DUPIONS	DLOOSTU	OUTSOLD	EEEFGRU	REFUGEE
	UNIPODS	DLOOTTU	OUTTOLD	EEEFHRS	SHEREEF
DINORSU	DIURONS	DLOPRUY	PROUDLY	EEEFIRR	REEFIER
	DURIONS	DLORSTY	DRYLOTS	EEEFIRS	FEERIES
DINORTU	TURDION	DLOSTUW	WOULDST	EEEFLRR	FLEERER
DINORWW	WINDROW	DMMOORU	MUDROOM	EEEFLRS	FEELERS
DINOSSW	DISOWNS	DMNOOOP	MONOPOD		REFEELS
DINOSWW	WINDOWS	DMNOORS	DROMONS	EEEFLRT	FLEETER
DINOTUW	OUTWIND	DMNOOTW	TOWMOND	EEEFLSS	FEELESS
DINOWWY	WINDOWY	DMNOSSU	OSMUNDS	EEEFMNR	FREEMEN
DINPSTU	PUNDITS	DMOOOQU	QUOMODO	EEEFNRS	ENFREES
DINPSUW	UPWINDS	DMORTUW	MUDWORT	EEEFNRV	ENFEVER
	WINDUPS	DNNOORW	NONWORD	EEEFORS	FORESEE
DINRSSU	SUNDRIS	DNNOOST	DONNOTS	EEEFRRS	REEFERS
DINSSTU	NUDISTS	DNNORUU	UNROUND	EEEFRRZ	FREEZER
DIOOPPS	DOPPIOS	DNNORUW	RUNDOWN	EEEFRSZ	FREEZES
DIOOPRS	SPOROID	DNNOSUU	UNSOUND	EEEGHNW	WHEENGE
DIOOPSS	ISOPODS	DNNOSUW	SUNDOWN	EEEGIKR	GEEKIER
DIOORST	DISROOT	DNNOUUW	UNWOUND	EEEGILN	GLEENIE
	TOROIDS	DNNRTUU	TURNDUN	EEEGILS	ELEGIES
DIOORTT	RIDOTTO	DNNSTUU	TUNDUNS		ELEGISE
DIOOSTX	TOXOIDS	DNOORTU	OROTUND	EEEGILZ	ELEGIZE
DIOPRST	DISPORT	DNOOSUV	VODOUNS	EEEGINP	EPIGENE
	TORPIDS		VOUDONS	EEEGINR	GREENIE
	TRIPODS	DNOOTUW	NUTWOOD	EEEGIPR	PERIGEE
DIOPRTY	TRIPODY	DNOOUUV	VOUDOUN	EEEGKLR	KEGELER
DIOPSST	DISPOST	DNOPRUU	ROUNDUP	EEEGLMN	GLEEMEN
DIORRST	STRIDOR	DNOPTUW	PUTDOWN	EEEGLNT	GENTEEL
DIORSTT	DISTORT	DNOPUUW	UPWOUND	EEEGMRR	REMERGE
DIOSSTU	STUDIOS	DNORSST	STRONDS	EEEGMRS	EMERGES
DIOSUUV	VIDUOUS	DNORSTU	ROTUNDS		MERGEES
DIPRSTU	DISRUPT	DNOSSTU	STOUNDS	EEEGNNO	NEOGENE
DIPSSTU	STUPIDS	DNOSSTW	STOWNDS	EEEGNPR	EPERGNE
DIRSTUY	DRYSUIT	DNOSSUW	SWOUNDS	EEEGNPS	PEENGES
	SURDITY	DNOSSWW	SWOWNDS	EEEGNRR	GREENER
DJNNOOS	DONJONS	DOOOOSV	VOODOOS		REGREEN
DKNNRUU	UNDRUNK	DOOOPSW	DOOWOPS		RENEGER
DKNOOPS	PONDOKS	DOOORSU	ODOROUS	EEEGNRS	RENEGES
DKOOOOS	KOODOOS	DOOORTU	OUTDOOR	EEEGNRU	RENEGUE
DKOOOSZ	ODZOOKS	DOOPRSU	UROPODS	EEEGNRV	REVENGE
DLLOOPS	DOLLOPS	DOOPRSY	PROSODY	EEEGNSS	GENESES
DLLORWY	WORLDLY	DOOPRTU	DROPOUT	EEEGNTT	GENETTE
DLMNOOY	MYLODON		OUTDROP	EEEGRRT	GREETER
DLMNOSU	UNMOLDS	DOOPSTU	UPSTOOD		REGREET
DLMNOUU	UNMOULD	DOORRSS	SORDORS	EEEGRSS	GREESES
DLMOSUU	MODULUS	DOORRTU	DORTOUR	EEEGRST	GREETES
DLNOOWW	LOWDOWN	DOOSUUV	VOUDOUS	EEEGRSZ	GEEZERS
DLNOPRU	PULDRON	DORSSTU	STROUDS	EEEGRUX	EXERGUE
DLNOPSY	SPONDYL	DORSUVY	DYVOURS	EEEHILW	WHEELIE
DLNORSU	UNLORDS	DORUVYY	DYVOURY	EEEHINS	SHEENIE
DLNORUY	ROUNDLY	DPSSTUU	DUSTUPS	EEEHIRX	HEXEREI
DLNOSUY	SOUNDLY	EEEEFRR	REFEREE	EEEHISZ	HEEZIES
DLOOOTW	WOODLOT	EEEEGTX	EXEGETE	EEEHLNW	ENWHEEL
DLOOPPY	POLYPOD	EEEENTT	ENTETEE	EEEHLOY	EYEHOLE
DLOOPSS	PODSOLS	EEEEPST	TEEPEES	EEEHLPS	SHEEPLE
DLOOPSZ	PODZOLS	EEEEPSV	VEEPEES	EEEHLPW	WHEEPLE

EEEHLRS	HEELERS	**EEEJSST**	JESTEES			REMEETS
	REHEELS	**EEEKKRS**	KEEKERS			TEEMERS
EEEHLRW	WHEELER	**EEEKLLU**	UKELELE	**EEEMRTX**	EXTREME
EEEHLST	LETHEES	**EEEKLMN**	KEELMEN	**EEEMSST**	ESTEEMS
EEEHLWZ	WHEEZLE	**EEEKLNR**	KNEELER			MESTEES
EEEHNST	ETHENES	**EEEKLNS**	SLEEKEN	**EEEMSTT**	MEETEST
EEEHNSX	HEXENES	**EEEKLNX**	KLEENEX	**EEEMSTU**	EMEUTES
EEEHNSY	SHEENEY	**EEEKLPW**	EKPWELE	**EEENNPT**	PENTENE
EEEHPRS	PHEERES	**EEEKLRS**	KEELERS	**EEENNRT**	ETRENNE
EEEHPSS	PHEESES			SLEEKER	**EEENNSV**	VENENES
EEEHPSZ	PHEEZES	**EEEKMNS**	MEEKENS	**EEENNTT**	ENTENTE
EEEHRRS	SHEERER	**EEEKMST**	MEEKEST	**EEENNUY**	ENNUYEE
EEEHRST	SEETHER	**EEEKNPT**	KEEPNET	**EEENPRR**	PREENER
	SHEETER	**EEEKNRS**	KEENERS	**EEENPRT**	PRETEEN
EEEHRTT	TEETHER	**EEEKNST**	KEENEST			TERPENE
EEEHRWZ	WHEEZER			KETENES	**EEENPRV**	PREVENE
EEEHSST	SEETHES	**EEEKORV**	REEVOKE	**EEENPSS**	PENSEES
EEEHSSV	SHEEVES	**EEEKPRS**	KEEPERS	**EEENPST**	ENSTEEP
EEEHSTT	ESTHETE	**EEEKRRS**	REEKERS			STEEPEN
	TEETHES	**EEEKRSS**	KREESES	**EEENPSW**	ENSWEEP
EEEHSWZ	WHEEZES			RESEEKS	**EEENPSX**	EXPENSE
EEEIJLS	JEELIES			SEEKERS	**EEENQUU**	ENQUEUE
EEEIKLL	EELLIKE	**EEEKRST**	KEESTER	**EEENRRS**	SERENER
EEEIKLS	KEELIES			SKEETER			SNEERER
EEEIKLY	EYELIKE	**EEELLRV**	LEVELER	**EEENRRT**	ENTERER
EEEIKRR	REEKIER	**EEELMNR**	REELMEN			REENTER
EEEILRR	LEERIER	**EEELMNT**	ELEMENT			TERREEN
EEEILRS	SEELIER			TELEMEN			TERRENE
EEEILRV	RELIEVE	**EEELMPX**	EXEMPLE	**EEENRRV**	VENERER
EEEILST	EELIEST	**EEELMSX**	LEXEMES	**EEENRRW**	RENEWER
	STEELIE	**EEELNST**	STELENE	**EEENRSS**	SERENES
EEEIMMS	MEEMIES	**EEELNSV**	ELEVENS	**EEENRST**	ENTREES
EEEIMNS	ENEMIES	**EEELPRS**	PEELERS			RETENES
EEEIMNT	EMETINE			SLEEPER			TEENERS
EEEIMPR	EPIMERE			SPEELER	**EEENRSV**	ENERVES
	PREEMIE	**EEELPRT**	REPLETE			EVENERS
EEEIMRS	EMERIES	**EEELPRX**	REEXPEL			VENEERS
EEEIMRT	EREMITE	**EEELPST**	STEEPLE	**EEENRSZ**	SNEEZER
EEEINQU	QUEENIE	**EEELRRS**	REELERS	**EEENRTV**	EVENTER
EEEINRS	ESERINE	**EEELRRV**	REVELER			EVERNET
EEEINRT	TEENIER	**EEELRSV**	RELEVES	**EEENRTW**	TWEENER
EEEINRW	WEENIER			SLEEVER	**EEENRTX**	EXTERNE
EEEINSW	WEENIES	**EEELRTV**	LEVERET	**EEENRUV**	REVENUE
EEEINTW	TWEENIE	**EEELSSS**	LESSEES			UNREEVE
EEEIPRR	PEERIER	**EEELSST**	TELESES	**EEENSSZ**	SNEEZES
EEEIPRS	PEERIES	**EEELSSV**	SLEEVES	**EEENSTV**	EVENEST
	SEEPIER	**EEELSSY**	EYELESS	**EEENSTW**	SWEETEN
EEEIPRW	WEEPIER	**EEELSTU**	EUSTELE	**EEENSTX**	EXTENSE
EEEIPST	EPEEIST	**EEELSTX**	TELEXES	**EEENSVW**	VENEWES
EEEIPSU	EPUISEE	**EEELSTY**	EYELETS	**EEENSWY**	SWEENEY
EEEIPSW	WEEPIES	**EEELTTX**	TELETEX	**EEEOPPS**	EPOPEES
EEEIRRT	RETIREE	**EEEMMSS**	MESEEMS	**EEEORSV**	OVERSEE
EEEIRRV	REVERIE			SEMEMES	**EEEORSY**	EYESORE
EEEIRST	EERIEST	**EEEMNRS**	MENEERS	**EEEORVY**	OVEREYE
EEEIRSV	VEERIES	**EEEMNSS**	NEMESES	**EEEPPRS**	PEEPERS
EEEIRSZ	RESEIZE	**EEEMNST**	MENTEES	**EEEPRSS**	PEERESS
EEEISTW	SWEETIE	**EEEMORT**	EROTEME	**EEEPRST**	ESTREPE
EEEJLRW	JEWELER	**EEEMOSY**	EYESOME			STEEPER
EEEJNPY	JEEPNEY	**EEEMPRT**	PREMEET	**EEEPRSV**	PEEVERS
EEEJPRS	JEEPERS	**EEEMRSS**	SEEMERS			PREEVES
EEEJRRS	JEERERS	**EEEMRST**	MEETERS	**EEEPRSW**	SWEEPER

	WEEPERS	**EEFHISY**	FISHEYE	**EEFIRST**	FESTIER
EEEPRSZ	SPREEZE	**EEFHLMN**	FLEHMEN	**EEFIRSX**	REFIXES
EEEQRRU	QUEERER	**EEFHLNS**	ENFLESH	**EEFIRSZ**	FRIEZES
	REQUERE	**EEFHLRS**	FLESHER	**EEFISTV**	FESTIVE
EEEQSUZ	SQUEEZE		HERSELF	**EEFLLOS**	FELLOES
EEERRRV	REVERER	**EEFHLSS**	FLESHES	**EEFLLRS**	FELLERS
EEERRST	RETREES	**EEFHNRS**	FRESHEN	**EEFLLRU**	FUELLER
	STEERER	**EEFHORT**	THEREOF	**EEFLLST**	FELLEST
EEERRSV	RESERVE	**EEFHORW**	WHEREOF	**EEFLLTY**	FLEETLY
	REVERES	**EEFHRRS**	FRESHER	**EEFLMTU**	TEEMFUL
	REVERSE		REFRESH	**EEFLNNO**	ENFELON
	SEVERER	**EEFHRRU**	FUEHRER	**EEFLNNS**	FENNELS
EEERSSS	SEERESS	**EEFHRSS**	FRESHES	**EEFLNOS**	ONESELF
EEERSTT	TEETERS	**EEFHRST**	FRESHET	**EEFLNRS**	FLENSER
	TERETES		HEFTERS		FRESNEL
EEERSTV	STEEVER	**EEFIIMN**	FEMINIE	**EEFLNSS**	FLENSES
EEERSTW	SWEETER	**EEFIIRR**	FEIRIER	**EEFLNTU**	TEENFUL
EEERSUV	REVEUSE		FIERIER	**EEFLOOV**	FOVEOLE
EEERSUW	SERUEWE		REIFIER	**EEFLOTU**	OUTFEEL
EEERSVW	SERVEWE	**EEFIIRS**	REIFIES	**EEFLRRS**	FERRELS
	WEEVERS	**EEFIKLL**	ELFLIKE	**EEFLRRU**	FERRULE
EEERTTW	TWEETER	**EEFILLS**	FELLIES	**EEFLRST**	FELTERS
EEERTWZ	TWEEZER	**EEFILLX**	FLEXILE		REFLETS
EEESSTT	SETTEES	**EEFILNO**	OLEFINE		TELFERS
	TESTEES	**EEFILNS**	FELINES	**EEFLRSU**	FERULES
EEESSTV	STEEVES	**EEFILOR**	FORELIE		FUELERS
	VESTEES	**EEFILPR**	PREFILE		REFUELS
EEESTTW	WEETEST		PRELIFE	**EEFLRTT**	FETTLER
EEESTWZ	TWEEZES	**EEFILRR**	FERLIER	**EEFLRTU**	FLEURET
EEFFFNO	ENFEOFF	**EEFILRS**	FERLIES	**EEFLRUX**	FLEXURE
EEFFFOR	FEOFFER		REFILES	**EEFLSTT**	FETTLES
EEFFGLU	EFFULGE		REFLIES		LEFTEST
EEFFINT	FIFTEEN		RELIEFS	**EEFLSUY**	EYEFULS
EEFFIRS	EFFEIRS	**EEFILRT**	FELTIER	**EEFMNOR**	FOREMEN
EEFFKLS	KEFFELS		FERTILE	**EEFMNRT**	FERMENT
EEFFNOS	OFFENSE	**EEFILST**	FELSITE	**EEFMOTT**	MOFETTE
EEFFORR	OFFERER		LEFTIES	**EEFMPRU**	PERFUME
	REOFFER		LIEFEST	**EEFMSTW**	FEWMETS
EEFFOST	TOFFEES	**EEFILTY**	EYELIFT	**EEFMTTU**	FUMETTE
EEFFSSU	EFFUSES	**EEFIMMR**	FEMMIER	**EEFNNRS**	FRENNES
EEFFSTU	SUFFETE	**EEFIMNR**	FIREMEN	**EEFNORT**	OFTENER
EEFGILN	FEELING	**EEFIMRT**	FEMITER	**EEFNORZ**	ENFROZE
	FLEEING	**EEFINNR**	FENNIER	**EEFNRRY**	FERNERY
EEFGILT	GEFILTE	**EEFINNS**	FENNIES	**EEFNRSS**	ENSERFS
EEFGINR	FEERING	**EEFINRR**	FERNIER	**EEFNRSU**	UNFREES
	FEIGNER		REFINER	**EEFNRTV**	FERVENT
	FREEING	**EEFINRS**	ENFIRES	**EEFNSSW**	FEWNESS
	REEFING		FEERINS	**EEFNSSY**	FEYNESS
EEFGINS	FEESING		FINEERS	**EEFORRV**	FOREVER
EEFGINZ	FEEZING		REFINES	**EEFORRZ**	REFROZE
EEFGIRR	GRIEFER	**EEFINRT**	FEINTER	**EEFORSX**	FOREXES
EEFGIST	GIFTEES	**EEFINSS**	FINESSE	**EEFOTTU**	FOUETTE
EEFGLLU	GLEEFUL	**EEFINSX**	ENFIXES	**EEFPRRS**	PREFERS
EEFGLOR	FORELEG	**EEFIPRR**	PREFIRE	**EEFPRSU**	PERFUSE
EEFGLOS	SOLFEGE		PREIFES	**EEFRRST**	FERRETS
EEFGORR	REFORGE	**EEFIPRS**	PREIFES	**EEFRRSU**	REFUSER
EEFGORY	FROGEYE		PRIEFES	**EEFRRTT**	FRETTER
EEFGRSU	REFUGES	**EEFIRRS**	FERRIES	**EEFRRTU**	REFUTER
EEFHIRS	FRESHIE		REFIRES	**EEFRRTY**	FERRETY
	HEIFERS		REFRIES	**EEFRSST**	FESTERS
EEFHIRT	HEFTIER	**EEFIRRT**	FERRITE	**EEFRSSU**	REFUSES
		EEFIRSS	FRISEES		

EEFRSTT	FETTERS	**EEGIKNS**	SEEKING		REGIVEN
EEFRSTU	FEUTRES		SKEEING		VEERING
	REFUTES	**EEGIKNT**	KITENGE	**EEGINSS**	GENESIS
EEFRSTW	FEWTERS	**EEGILLS**	GELLIES		SEEINGS
EEFSSTU	FETUSES	**EEGILNP**	LEEPING		SIGNEES
EEGGGIS	GEGGIES		PEELING	**EEGINSW**	SEEWING
EEGGGLR	GLEGGER	**EEGILNR**	LEERING		SWEEING
EEGGHTU	THUGGEE		REELING	**EEGINTV**	VENTIGE
EEGGILN	GLEEING	**EEGILNS**	LEESING	**EEGINTW**	WEETING
	NEGLIGE		SEELING	**EEGINTX**	EXIGENT
EEGGILR	LEGGIER	**EEGILNT**	GENTILE	**EEGIOST**	EGOTISE
EEGGILS	LEGGIES	**EEGILOS**	ELOGIES		GOETIES
EEGGINR	GREEING	**EEGILPS**	SPIEGEL	**EEGIOTZ**	EGOTIZE
EEGGIPS	PEGGIES	**EEGILRS**	LEIGERS	**EEGIRRV**	GRIEVER
EEGGIRS	GREIGES		LIEGERS	**EEGIRSS**	SIEGERS
EEGGIST	EGGIEST	**EEGILRV**	VELIGER	**EEGIRSV**	GRIEVES
EEGGISV	VEGGIES	**EEGILST**	ELEGIST		REGIVES
EEGGKRS	KEGGERS		ELEGITS	**EEGIRTT**	TERGITE
	SKEGGER	**EEGIMMR**	GEMMIER	**EEGIRTU**	GUERITE
EEGGLRS	EGGLERS		GREMMIE	**EEGISTV**	VESTIGE
	LEGGERS		IMMERGE	**EEGKLRS**	KEGLERS
EEGGLSS	EGGLESS	**EEGIMNR**	MEERING	**EEGKNOR**	KEROGEN
EEGGMNY	YEGGMEN		REGIMEN	**EEGKNRU**	GERENUK
EEGGMSU	MUGGEES	**EEGIMNS**	SEEMING	**EEGLLNS**	LEGLENS
EEGGNNS	GENSENG	**EEGIMNT**	MEETING	**EEGLLSS**	LEGLESS
EEGGNOR	ENGORGE		TEEMING	**EEGLLST**	LEGLETS
EEGGNOY	GEOGENY	**EEGIMNX**	EXEMING	**EEGLMMU**	GEMMULE
EEGGORR	REGORGE	**EEGIMRR**	GERMIER	**EEGLMOR**	GOMEREL
EEGGORU	GOUGERE	**EEGIMRS**	EMIGRES	**EEGLMSU**	EMULGES
EEGGORV	OVEREGG		REGIMES		LEGUMES
EEGGPRU	PUGGREE		REMIGES	**EEGLNNS**	GENNELS
EEGHILN	HEELING	**EEGINNP**	PEENING	**EEGLNOR**	ERELONG
EEGHINR	REHINGE	**EEGINNR**	ENGINER	**EEGLNOU**	EUGENOL
EEGHINT	THEEING		INGENER	**EEGLNOZ**	LOZENGE
EEGHINY	HYGIENE	**EEGINNS**	ENGINES	**EEGLNRT**	GENTLER
EEGHINZ	HEEZING		GENNIES	**EEGLNRY**	GREENLY
EEGHIRW	REWEIGH		NEESING	**EEGLNST**	GENTLES
	WEIGHER		SNEEING		LENGEST
EEGHKRS	SKREEGH	**EEGINNT**	TEENING	**EEGLNSU**	LUNGEES
EEGHLNU	LEUGHEN	**EEGINNU**	GENUINE	**EEGLOSS**	EGOLESS
EEGHMNO	HEGEMON		INGENUE	**EEGLPSS**	PEGLESS
EEGHMNU	HEGUMEN	**EEGINNV**	EEVNING	**EEGLRRU**	GRUELER
EEGHNRT	GREENTH		EVENING	**EEGLRST**	REGLETS
EEGHNRY	GREYHEN	**EEGINNW**	ENEWING	**EEGLRSU**	REGLUES
EEGHRTU	TEUGHER		WEENING	**EEGLRTW**	WERGELT
EEGHSSS	GHESSES	**EEGINNZ**	NEEZING	**EEGLRTY**	TELERGY
EEGHSTZ	SHEGETZ	**EEGINOP**	EPIGONE	**EEGMMRY**	GEMMERY
EEGIIRS	GRIESIE	**EEGINOS**	GENOISE	**EEGMNOS**	EMONGES
EEGIJLN	JEELING		SOIGNEE		GENOMES
EEGIJNP	JEEPING	**EEGINPP**	PEEPING	**EEGMNRS**	GERMENS
EEGIJNR	JEERING	**EEGINPR**	PEERING	**EEGMNST**	SEGMENT
EEGIKKN	KEEKING		PREEING	**EEGMNSU**	EMUNGES
EEGIKLL	LEGLIKE	**EEGINPS**	SEEPING	**EEGMNTU**	TEGUMEN
EEGIKLM	GEMLIKE	**EEGINPV**	PEEVING	**EEGMOST**	GEMOTES
EEGIKLN	KEELING	**EEGINPW**	WEEPING	**EEGMRRS**	MERGERS
EEGIKLP	PEGLIKE	**EEGINRS**	GREISEN	**EEGMRTU**	GUMTREE
EEGIKNN	KEENING	**EEGINRT**	GENTIER	**EEGNNRU**	UNGREEN
	KNEEING		INTEGER	**EEGNNST**	GENNETS
EEGIKNP	KEEPING		TEERING	**EEGNOPS**	PONGEES
	PEEKING		TREEING	**EEGNORS**	ENGORES
EEGIKNR	REEKING	**EEGINRV**	REEVING		NEGROES

EEGNOSX	EXOGENS	EEHINRS	HENRIES	EEHMNRY	MYNHEER
EEGNPUX	EXPUNGE		INHERES	EEHMNSS	MENSHES
EEGNRSS	NEGRESS		RESHINE	EEHMORS	REHOMES
EEGNRST	GERENTS	EEHINRT	NEITHER	EEHMORT	THEOREM
	REGENTS		THEREIN	EEHMPST	TEMPEHS
EEGNRSV	VENGERS	EEHINRW	WHEREIN	EEHMRST	THERMES
EEGNRSY	GYRENES	EEHINST	THEINES	EEHMRUX	EXHUMER
EEGNSSU	GENUSES	EEHIORS	HEROISE	EEHMSST	SMEETHS
	NEGUSES	EEHIORZ	HEROIZE	EEHMSUV	HUMVEES
EEGNSTU	GUESTEN	EEHIPRT	PRITHEE	EEHMSUX	EXHUMES
EEGOOSS	SOOGEES	EEHIPSV	PEEVISH	EEHNNOS	SHONEEN
EEGOPRT	PROTEGE	EEHIPTT	EPITHET	EEHNNRS	HENNERS
EEGORTV	OVERGET	EEHIRRS	HERRIES	EEHNNRY	HENNERY
EEGOSSS	GESSOSS		REHIRES	EEHNOOR	HONOREE
EEGPPRR	PREPREG	EEHIRSS	HEIRESS	EEHNOPT	POTHEEN
EEGPRSU	PUGREES		HERISSE	EEHNORS	RESHONE
EEGPRUX	EXPURGE	EEHIRST	HEISTER	EEHNORT	THEREON
EEGRRSS	REGRESS	EEHIRSV	SHRIEVE	EEHNORW	NOWHERE
	SERGERS	EEHIRTW	THEWIER		WHEREON
EEGRRST	REGRETS	EEHIRWY	WHEYIER	EEHNOSX	HEXONES
EEGRRSU	RESURGE	EEHISST	HESSITE	EEHNPSS	SEPHENS
	REURGES	EEHISTT	HETTIES		SPHENES
EEGRRSV	VERGERS	EEHISTV	THIEVES	EEHNPSW	NEPHEWS
EEGRRUY	GRUYERE	EEHKLOY	KEYHOLE	EEHNRST	THRENES
EEGRSST	REGESTS	EEHKLSS	SHEKELS	EEHNSST	NESHEST
EEGRSSU	GUESSER	EEHKOOY	EYEHOOK	EEHNSTU	ENTHUSE
EEGRSSY	GEYSERS	EEHKRSS	SHREEKS	EEHNSTV	SEVENTH
EEGRSTT	GETTERS	EEHLLMP	PHELLEM	EEHNSTY	ETHYNES
EEGRSTU	GESTURE	EEHLLNS	ENSHELL	EEHNSWW	WHENWES
EEGRSTY	GREYEST	EEHLLOS	HELLOES	EEHOOPW	WHOOPEE
EEGSSSU	GUESSES	EEHLLOT	THEELOL	EEHOOST	TOESHOE
EEHHORU	HOUHERE	EEHLLRS	HELLERS	EEHOPRU	EUPHROE
EEHHRTT	THETHER		SHELLER	EEHOPSS	SHEEPOS
EEHHRTW	WHETHER	EEHLLRY	HELLERY	EEHOPST	HEPTOSE
EEHHSTW	WHEESHT	EEHLMMW	WHEMMLE	EEHORRV	HOVERER
EEHIINS	HEINIES	EEHLMRS	HELMERS	EEHORSS	RESHOES
EEHIKLN	HENLIKE	EEHLMRT	THERMEL	EEHORST	HETEROS
EEHIKLO	HOELIKE	EEHLMST	HELMETS	EEHORSU	REHOUSE
EEHILLR	HELLERI	EEHLNSU	UNHELES	EEHORSW	WHERESO
	HELLIER	EEHLNSY	HENLEYS	EEHORTT	THERETO
EEHILMN	HELIMEN	EEHLORY	HOLEYER	EEHORTW	WHERETO
	HEMLINE	EEHLPRS	HELPERS	EEHORVW	HOWEVER
EEHILNT	THEELIN	EEHLPRT	TELPHER		WHOEVER
EEHILOP	PIEHOLE	EEHLPSS	PLESHES	EEHOSST	ETHOSES
EEHILPS	EPHELIS	EEHLQSS	SHEQELS	EEHOSSX	HEXOSES
EEHILRS	LEISHER	EEHLRST	SHELTER	EEHOSTW	TOWHEES
EEHILRW	WHILERE	EEHLRSV	SHELVER	EEHOSTY	EYESHOT
EEHILST	SHELTIE	EEHLRSW	WELSHER	EEHPPST	HEPPEST
EEHILSX	HELIXES	EEHLRSY	SHEERLY	EEHPRSS	SPHERES
EEHIMMS	MISHMEE	EEHLSSU	HUELESS	EEHPRST	HEPSTER
EEHIMNO	HEMIONE	EEHLSSV	SHELVES		PETHERS
EEHIMPR	HEMPIER	EEHLSSW	SHEWELS		SPERTHE
EEHIMPS	HEMPIES		WELSHES		THREEPS
	IMPHEES	EEHLSTT	SHTETEL	EEHPRTY	PRYTHEE
EEHIMPT	EPITHEM	EEHLSTV	THELVES	EEHQSTU	QUETHES
EEHIMRS	MESHIER	EEHMMRS	HEMMERS	EEHRRSW	WERSHER
EEHINNR	HENNIER	EEHMNNO	NONHEME	EEHRRTW	WHERRET
EEHINNS	HENNIES	EEHMNNS	MENSHEN	EEHRSSU	RUSHEES
EEHINNY	HYENINE	EEHMNOP	PHONEME	EEHRSSW	SHEWERS
EEHINOR	HEROINE	EEHMNOS	HOSEMEN	EEHRSTT	TETHERS
EEHINRR	ERRHINE	EEHMNRU	ENRHEUM	EEHRSTW	WETHERS

	WRETHES	**EEIKPRR**	PERKIER		ETOILES
EEHRSTZ	HERTZES	**EEIKPRS**	PESKIER	**EEILOTZ**	ZEOLITE
EEHRSVW	WHERVES	**EEIKPSW**	KEWPIES	**EEILPRR**	REPLIER
EEHRTTW	WHETTER	**EEIKRRS**	KERRIES	**EEILPRS**	REPLIES
EEHRVWY	WHYEVER	**EEIKRST**	KEISTER		SPIELER
EEHSTUY	SHUTEYE		KIESTER	**EEILPRT**	PERLITE
EEIIKKS	KIEKIES	**EEIKRSY**	SKIEYER		REPTILE
EEIIKRS	KIERIES	**EEIKRUY**	YEUKIER	**EEILPRU**	PUERILE
EEIILMS	MIELIES	**EEIKSST**	SEIKEST	**EEILPSS**	PELISSE
EEIILRV	VEILIER	**EEIKSTT**	STEEKIT	**EEILPST**	EPISTLE
EEIIMNS	MEINIES	**EEIKTTT**	TEKTITE		PELITES
EEIIMPR	RIEMPIE	**EEILLMT**	MELLITE	**EEILPWY**	WEEPILY
EEIIMRT	EMERITI	**EEILLNS**	NELLIES	**EEILQRU**	RELIQUE
EEIIMST	ITEMISE	**EEILLPS**	ELLIPSE	**EEILRRS**	RELIERS
EEIIMTZ	ITEMIZE	**EEILLRS**	LEISLER	**EEILRRV**	RELIVER
EEIINNS	NEINEIS		RELLIES		REVILER
EEIINRT	ERINITE	**EEILLRT**	TREILLE	**EEILRSS**	IRELESS
	NITERIE	**EEILLRV**	EVILLER		RESILES
EEIINRV	VEINIER	**EEILLRY**	LEERILY	**EEILRST**	LEISTER
EEIINST	SIENITE	**EEILLSS**	EISELLS		RETILES
EEIINSW	EISWEIN	**EEILLST**	TELLIES		STERILE
	WIENIES	**EEILLSV**	VIELLES	**EEILRSU**	LEISURE
EEIINTV	INVITEE	**EEILLSW**	WELLIES	**EEILRSV**	LEVIERS
EEIIPST	PIETIES	**EEILMMT**	MELTEMI		RELIVES
EEIIRRV	RIVIERE	**EEILMNN**	LINEMEN		REVILES
EEIIRVW	VIEWIER	**EEILMNR**	ERMELIN		SERVILE
EEIISST	SEITIES	**EEILMNS**	ISLEMEN		VEILERS
EEIISTV	VISITEE	**EEILMNY**	MYELINE	**EEILRSX**	EXILERS
EEIJKLT	JETLIKE	**EEILMPT**	IMPLETE	**EEILRTT**	RETITLE
EEIJKRR	JERKIER	**EEILMRT**	MELTIER	**EEILRVY**	LIVEYER
EEIJKRS	JERKIES	**EEILMRV**	VERMEIL	**EEILSSS**	SESELIS
EEIJLLS	JELLIES	**EEILMST**	ELMIEST		SESSILE
EEIJMMR	JEMMIER	**EEILNNO**	LEONINE	**EEILSST**	LISTEES
EEIJMMS	JEMMIES	**EEILNNT**	LENIENT		TELESIS
EEIJNNS	JENNIES	**EEILNNV**	ENLIVEN		TIELESS
EEIJRRS	JERRIES	**EEILNOR**	ELOINER	**EEILSSU**	ILEUSES
EEIJRTT	JETTIER	**EEILNOS**	OLEINES	**EEILSSV**	SLIEVES
EEIJSSS	JESSIES	**EEILNPS**	PENSILE	**EEILSSW**	LEWISES
EEIJSTT	JETTIES	**EEILNPT**	PENLITE	**EEILSSX**	LEXISES
EEIKKRR	KERKIER	**EEILNRS**	LIERNES		SILEXES
EEIKKST	TEKKIES		RELINES	**EEILSTV**	EVILEST
EEIKLLS	KELLIES	**EEILNRV**	LIVENER		LEVITES
	SKELLIE	**EEILNSS**	ENISLES		LIEVEST
EEIKLNT	NETLIKE		ENSILES		VELITES
EEIKLNY	KEYLINE		SENILES	**EEILSTX**	SEXTILE
EEIKLOT	TOELIKE		SENSILE	**EEILSUV**	ELUSIVE
EEIKLPS	KELPIES		SILENES	**EEILSVW**	WEEVILS
EEIKLPT	PIKELET	**EEILNST**	LENITES	**EEILSZZ**	LEZZIES
EEIKLSS	SELKIES		LISENTE	**EEILTTX**	TEXTILE
EEIKLST	KELTIES		SETLINE	**EEILTUX**	ULEXITE
	SLEEKIT		TENSILE	**EEILVWY**	WEEVILY
EEIKMNP	PIKEMEN	**EEILNSY**	YEELINS	**EEIMMNS**	IMMENSE
EEIKMPR	KEMPIER	**EEILNTT**	ENTITLE	**EEIMMRS**	IMMERSE
EEIKMPS	MISKEEP	**EEILNTV**	VEINLET	**EEIMMSS**	MIMESES
EEIKNOS	EIKONES	**EEILNUV**	VEINULE		MISSEEM
EEIKNPY	PINKEYE	**EEILOPT**	PETIOLE	**EEIMMST**	MISMEET
EEIKNRS	KEIRENS	**EEILORS**	LOERIES	**EEIMNNO**	NOMINEE
EEIKNRT	KERNITE	**EEILORT**	TROELIE	**EEIMNNT**	EMINENT
EEIKNSS	ENSKIES	**EEILORV**	OVERLIE	**EEIMNOS**	SEMEION
	KINESES		RELIEVO	**EEIMNOT**	ONETIME
EEIKNWY	EYEWINK	**EEILOST**	ESTOILE	**EEIMNRS**	ERMINES

EEIMNRV	MINEVER		NERVINE	**EEINSST**	SEITENS
EEIMNRW	WIREMEN	**EEINNRW**	WENNIER		SESTINE
EEIMNSS	INSEEMS	**EEINNST**	INTENSE	**EEINSSV**	SENVIES
	MISSEEN		TENNIES	**EEINSSW**	NEWSIES
	NEMESIS	**EEINNSV**	VENINES	**EEINSTT**	NETTIES
	SIEMENS	**EEINNTW**	ENTWINE	**EEINSTV**	TENSIVE
EEIMNST	EMETINS	**EEINNTZ**	NETIZEN		VENITES
EEIMNSW	MISWEEN	**EEINOPR**	PEREION	**EEINSTX**	EXTINES
EEIMNSY	MEINEYS		PIONEER		SIXTEEN
	MENYIES	**EEINOPS**	PEONIES	**EEINSTY**	SYENITE
EEIMNTT	MINETTE	**EEINORR**	ONERIER	**EEIOPPT**	EPITOPE
EEIMOPS	EPISOME	**EEINOSS**	EOSINES	**EEIOPSS**	POESIES
EEIMOPT	EPITOME	**EEINPPS**	PEPSINE	**EEIOPST**	POETISE
EEIMORS	ISOMERE	**EEINPRR**	REPINER	**EEIOPSX**	EPOXIES
EEIMOSS	MEIOSES		RIPENER	**EEIOPTZ**	POETIZE
EEIMOTV	EMOTIVE	**EEINPRS**	EREPSIN	**EEIORRS**	ROSIERE
EEIMPRR	PREMIER		REPINES	**EEIORSS**	SOIREES
	REPRIME	**EEINPRT**	INEPTER	**EEIORST**	EROTISE
EEIMPRS	EMPIRES	**EEINPRZ**	PRENZIE	**EEIORSV**	EROSIVE
	EMPRISE	**EEINPSS**	PENISES	**EEIORTZ**	EROTIZE
	EPIMERS	**EEINPST**	PENTISE	**EEIOSST**	ISOETES
	IMPRESE	**EEINPSV**	PENSIVE	**EEIOSTT**	TOEIEST
	PERMIES		VESPINE	**EEIPPPR**	PEPPIER
	PREMIES	**EEINQRU**	ENQUIRE		PREPPIE
	PREMISE		INQUERE	**EEIPPST**	PEPTISE
	SPIREME	**EEINQSU**	EQUINES		TIPPEES
EEIMPRT	EMPTIER	**EEINQTU**	QUIETEN	**EEIPPTT**	PIPETTE
EEIMPRZ	EMPRIZE	**EEINQUY**	QUEYNIE	**EEIPPTZ**	PEPTIZE
EEIMPST	EMPTIES	**EEINRRS**	RERISEN	**EEIPQRU**	PERIQUE
	SEPTIME		RESINER		REEQUIP
EEIMQRU	REQUIEM	**EEINRRT**	INERTER		REPIQUE
EEIMRRR	MERRIER		REINTER	**EEIPQSU**	EQUIPES
EEIMRRS	MERRIES		RENTIER	**EEIPRRR**	PERRIER
EEIMRRT	MITERER		TERRINE	**EEIPRRS**	PERRIES
	TRIREME	**EEINRRV**	NERVIER		PRISERE
EEIMRRU	EREMURI		VERNIER		REPRISE
EEIMRSS	MERISES	**EEINRSS**	SEINERS		RESPIRE
	MESSIER		SEREINS	**EEIPRRV**	PERVIER
	MISERES		SERINES		REPRIVE
	REMISES	**EEINRST**	ENTIRES	**EEIPRRW**	PREWIRE
EEIMRST	MEISTER		ENTRIES	**EEIPRRX**	EXPIRER
	METIERS		NERITES	**EEIPRRZ**	REPRIZE
	REEMITS		RETINES	**EEIPRSS**	ESPIERS
	RETIMES		TRENISE		PRESSIE
	TREMIES		TRIENES	**EEIPRST**	PESTIER
	TRISEME	**EEINRSV**	ENVIERS		RESPITE
EEIMRSX	MIREXES		INVERSE	**EEIPRSV**	PREVISE
	REMIXES		VEINERS		PRIEVES
EEIMRTT	EMITTER		VENIRES	**EEIPRSW**	SPEWIER
	TERMITE		VERSINE	**EEIPRSX**	EXPIRES
EEIMSSS	MISSEES	**EEINRSW**	NEWSIER		PREXIES
	SEMISES		WEINERS	**EEIPRTT**	PETTIER
EEIMSST	METISSE		WIENERS	**EEIPRTY**	YPERITE
EEINNNP	PENNINE	**EEINRSX**	REXINES	**EEIPRVW**	PREVIEW
EEINNPS	PENNIES	**EEINRTT**	NETTIER	**EEIPRZZ**	PREZZIE
	PINENES		TENTIER	**EEIPSSS**	SPEISES
EEINNRS	NERINES	**EEINRTU**	NEURITE	**EEIPSTT**	PETITES
EEINNRT	INTERNE		RETINUE		PETTIES
EEINNRU	NEURINE		REUNITE	**EEIPSTW**	PEEWITS
EEINNRV	ENRIVEN		UTERINE	**EEIQRRU**	QUERIER
	INNERVE	**EEINSSS**	SENSEIS		REQUIRE

EEIQRSU	ESQUIRE	EEJNORS	REJONES	EEKRSSW	RESKEWS
	QUERIES	EEJNORY	ENJOYER		SKEWERS
EEIQRTU	QUIETER		REENJOY	EEKRSSY	KERSEYS
	REQUITE	EEJNOSS	JONESES	EEKRSTY	KEYSTER
EEIQSTU	EQUITES	EEJORST	RESOJET	EEKSSTW	SKEWEST
EEIRRRT	RETIRER	EEJPRRU	PERJURE	EEKSSTY	KEYSETS
	TERRIER	EEJQRRU	JERQUER	EELLLVY	LEVELLY
EEIRRSS	RERISES	EEJQRSU	JERQUES	EELLMOR	MORELLE
	SERRIES	EEJRSST	JESTERS	EELLMOS	MOSELLE
	SIRREES	EEJRSSY	JERSEYS	EELLMRS	MERELLS
EEIRRST	ETRIERS	EEKKNOS	KEKENOS		SMELLER
	REITERS		KONEKES	EELLMRV	VERMELL
	RESTIER	EEKKOTV	VETKOEK	EELLNOR	RELLENO
	RETIRES	EEKKRRT	TREKKER	EELLNOV	NOVELLE
	RETRIES	EEKKSSY	KEKSYES	EELLNRS	SNELLER
	TERRIES	EEKLLNV	KNEVELL	EELLNST	TELLENS
EEIRRSV	REIVERS	EEKLLSY	SLEEKLY	EELLNSW	NEWELLS
	REVERSI	EEKLLUU	UKULELE	EELLNUV	UNLEVEL
	REVISER	EEKLMPS	KEMPLES	EELLOPS	POLLEES
	RIEVERS	EEKLMRZ	KLEZMER	EELLORS	ROSELLE
EEIRRSW	REWIRES	EEKLNNS	KENNELS	EELLORZ	ROZELLE
	SWEIRER	EEKLNOS	KEELSON	EELLPRS	PRESELL
EEIRRTV	RIVERET	EEKLNRS	KERNELS		RESPELL
	RIVETER	EEKLPRS	KELPERS		SPELLER
EEIRRTW	REWRITE	EEKLRST	KELTERS	EELLPRT	PRETELL
EEIRRVV	REVIVER		KESTREL	EELLPST	PELLETS
EEIRSSS	SEISERS		SKELTER	EELLQRU	QUELLER
EEIRSST	RESITES	EEKLSSY	KEYLESS	EELLRSS	RESELLS
EEIRSSU	REISSUE	EEKLSTT	KETTLES		SELLERS
	SEISURE	EEKLSTW	KEWLEST	EELLRST	RETELLS
EEIRSSV	IVRESSE	EEKMNOS	SOKEMEN		TELLERS
	REVISES	EEKMPRS	KEMPERS	EELLRSU	RUELLES
EEIRSSZ	RESIZES	EEKMRSS	KERMESS	EELLRSW	SWELLER
	SEIZERS	EEKNNRS	KENNERS	EELLRSY	YELLERS
EEIRSTT	TESTIER	EEKNNST	KENNETS	EELLSTV	VELLETS
EEIRSTU	SUETIER	EEKNNTT	KENNETT	EELMMOP	POMMELE
EEIRSTV	RESTIVE	EEKNORW	REWOKEN	EELMMPU	EMPLUME
	SIEVERT	EEKNOSS	KENOSES	EELMNNS	LENSMEN
	STIEVER	EEKNOST	KETONES	EELMNOO	OENOMEL
	VERIEST	EEKNOTY	KEYNOTE	EELMOPR	PLEROME
	VERITES	EEKNRSS	SKREENS	EELMOPT	LEPTOME
EEIRSTW	STEWIER	EEKNRST	RENKEST	EELMOPY	EMPLOYE
EEIRSTZ	ZESTIER	EEKNSST	KNESSET	EELMORW	EELWORM
EEIRSUZ	SEIZURE	EEKNSTU	NETSUKE	EELMOST	OMELETS
EEIRSVV	REVIVES	EEKOOPP	PEKEPOO		TELOMES
EEIRSVW	REVIEWS	EEKOPRS	RESPOKE	EELMPRS	SEMPLER
	VIEWERS	EEKOPTU	OUTKEEP	EELMPST	PELMETS
EEIRTVV	VETIVER	EEKORRV	REVOKER		STEMPEL
EEISSSV	ESSIVES	EEKORST	RESTOKE		STEMPLE
EEISSTV	VITESSE	EEKORSV	EVOKERS		TEMPLES
EEISSTW	WESTIES		REVOKES	EELMPTT	TEMPLET
EEISSTX	SEXIEST	EEKOSSS	SEKOSES	EELMRST	MELTERS
EEISTTW	WETTIES	EEKOSST	KETOSES		REMELTS
EEISTTY	YETTIES	EEKOSTV	VOETSEK		RESMELT
EEISTVX	VITEXES	EEKPPSU	UPKEEPS		SMELTER
EEITUXZ	ZEUXITE	EEKPRRS	REPERKS	EELMRSU	LEMURES
EEJKRRS	JERKERS	EEKPRSU	PERUKES		RELUMES
EEJLLMU	JUMELLE	EEKRRSU	KERERUS	EELMRSW	MEWLERS
EEJLRWY	JEWELRY	EEKRRUZ	KREUZER	EELMSST	TELESMS
EEJNNST	JENNETS	EEKRSST	STREEKS	EELMSSU	MULESES
EEJNOOR	REJONEO	EEKRSSU	RESKUES	EELMSTT	METTLES

	STEMLET		RESPELT	EEMNOOS	SOMEONE
EELNNSV	VENNELS		SPELTER	EEMNOOY	MOONEYE
EELNOPV	ENVELOP	EELPRSU	REPULSE	EEMNOPR	REPOMEN
EELNOPY	POLYENE	EELPRSY	SLEEPRY	EEMNORS	MOREENS
EELNOSV	ELEVONS		YELPERS	EEMNORV	OVERMEN
EELNOSY	ESLOYNE	EELPRTY	PEYTREL		VENOMER
EELNOTT	NOTELET	EELPRTZ	PRETZEL	EEMNORY	MONEYER
EELNOTU	TOLUENE	EELPRUX	PLEXURE	EEMNOST	TEMENOS
EELNPSS	PENSELS	EELPRVY	REPLEVY		TONEMES
	SPLEENS	EELPSST	PESTLES	EEMNOSV	ENMOVES
EELNPSY	SPLEENY	EELPSTT	PETTLES	EEMNPRU	PREMUNE
EELNQUY	QUEENLY	EELPSTY	STEEPLY	EEMNPTU	UMPTEEN
EELNRST	NESTLER	EELPSUX	EXPULSE	EEMNRTU	TRUEMEN
	RELENTS	EELQRUY	QUEERLY	EEMNSYZ	ENZYMES
	SLENTER	EELQSSU	SEQUELS	EEMOOSW	WOESOME
EELNRSU	UNREELS	EELRRSV	VERRELS	EEMOPRR	EMPEROR
EELNRTT	LETTERN	EELRRVY	REVELRY	EEMOPRT	TEMPORE
	NETTLER	EELRSST	STREELS	EEMOPRV	PREMOVE
EELNRUV	NERVULE		TRESSEL	EEMOPRW	EMPOWER
EELNSSS	LESSENS	EELRSSU	RULESSE	EEMOPST	METOPES
EELNSST	NESTLES	EELRSTT	LETTERS	EEMORRS	REMORSE
	NETLESS		LETTRES		ROEMERS
EELNSSU	UNSEELS		SETTLER	EEMORRT	REMOTER
EELNSTT	NETTLES		STERLET	EEMORRU	UROMERE
	TELNETS		TRESTLE	EEMORRV	REMOVER
EELNSTU	ELUENTS	EELRSTV	SERVLET	EEMORST	EMOTERS
	UNSTEEL		SVELTER		METEORS
EELNSTY	ENSTYLE	EELRSTW	SWELTER		REMOTES
	TENSELY		WELTERS	EEMORSV	REMOVES
EELNSUV	VENULES		WRESTLE	EEMOSST	MESTESO
EELNSXY	XYLENES	EELRSTY	RESTYLE	EEMOTTZ	MOZETTE
EELNTTU	LUNETTE		TERSELY	EEMPPRT	PREEMPT
EELOPPR	PEOPLER	EELRSTZ	SELTZER	EEMPRRT	PRETERM
EELOPPS	PEOPLES	EELRSUV	VELURES	EEMPRSS	EMPRESS
EELOPPZ	ZEPPOLE	EELRSUX	LUREXES	EEMPRST	TEMPERS
EELOPRS	ELOPERS	EELRSVV	VERVELS	EEMPRSU	PRESUME
	LEPROSE	EELSSSU	USELESS		SUPREME
EELOPRX	EXPLORE	EELSSSV	VESSELS	EEMPRTT	TEMPTER
EELOPSS	ELOPSES	EELSSSX	SEXLESS	EEMPRTU	PERMUTE
EELOPTU	EELPOUT	EELSSTT	SETTLES	EEMPSSU	EMPUSES
EELORSS	RESOLES	EELSSTU	SETULES	EEMPSST	TEMPEST
EELORST	SOLERET	EELSSTY	STYLEES	EEMPSTX	EXEMPTS
EELORSV	RESOLVE	EELSSUV	EVULSES	EEMRRST	TERMERS
EELORSY	EROSELY	EELSTUY	EUSTYLE	EEMRRSU	MURREES
EELORTT	LORETTE	EELSTVV	VELVETS		RESUMER
EELORTV	OVERLET	EELSTVW	TWELVES	EEMRRUU	REMUEUR
EELORVV	EVOLVER	EELSTWY	SWEETLY	EEMRSST	MESTERS
	REVOLVE	EELTVVY	VELVETY		RESTEMS
EELOSSS	LOESSES	EEMMNOS	MONEMES	EEMRSSU	RESUMES
EELOSST	OSSELET	EEMMNOT	MEMENTO	EEMRSUX	MUREXES
	TOELESS	EEMMNSS	MESSMEN	EEMSSSU	SMEUSES
EELOSTT	TELEOST	EEMMORS	MEROMES	EEMSSTU	MUSTEES
EELOSUV	EVOLUES	EEMMOST	MESTOME	EEMSTTU	MUSETTE
EELOSVV	EVOLVES	EEMMOSU	MOUSMEE	EENNORT	ENTERON
EELOTUV	EVOLUTE	EEMMOSV	EMMOVES		TENONER
	VELOUTE	EEMMRST	STEMMER	EENNORU	NEURONE
EELPPRX	PERPLEX	EEMMRSY	YEMMERS	EENNOSS	ONENESS
EELPPSU	PEEPULS	EEMMSSS	SEMSEMS	EENNOSZ	ENZONES
EELPQRU	PREQUEL	EEMMSST	STEMMES	EENNOTT	NONETTE
EELPRST	PELTERS	EEMNNOV	ENVENOM	EENNOTY	NEOTENY
	PETRELS	EEMNNSW	NEWSMEN	EENNPRS	PENNERS

EENNQUU	UNQUEEN		RENESTS	**EEORSST**	OSSETER
EENNRST	RENNETS		RESENTS		STEREOS
	TENNERS		STRENES	**EEORSSX**	SOREXES
EENNRUV	UNNERVE	**EENRSSU**	ENSURES		XEROSES
EENNSST	SENNETS	**EENRSTT**	NETTERS	**EEORSTT**	ROSETTE
EENNSSU	UNSEENS		TENTERS	**EEORSTV**	ESTOVER
	UNSENSE		TESTERN		OVERSET
EENNSSW	NEWNESS	**EENRSTU**	NEUTERS		REVOTES
EENOPPR	PREPONE		RETUNES		VETOERS
	PROPONE		TENURES	**EEORSTX**	XEROTES
EENOPPT	PEPTONE		TUREENS	**EEORSTY**	ESOTERY
EENOPRS	OPENERS	**EENRSTV**	VENTERS	**EEORSUV**	OEUVRES
	PEREONS		VENTRES		OVERUSE
	PERONES	**EENRSTW**	WESTERN	**EEORSVW**	OVERSEW
	REOPENS	**EENRSTX**	EXTERNS	**EEORSXX**	XEROXES
	REPONES	**EENRSTY**	STYRENE	**EEORTUV**	OUVERTE
EENOPST	OPENEST		YESTERN	**EEORTVW**	OVERWET
	PENTOSE	**EENRSVV**	VERVENS	**EEOSSSY**	OYESSES
	POSTEEN	**EENRTUV**	VENTURE	**EEOSSTU**	OUTSEES
	POTEENS	**EENSSST**	SETNESS	**EEPPPRS**	PEPPERS
EENOPTT	POTTEEN	**EENSSSY**	SYNESES	**EEPPPRY**	PEPPERY
EENOPTY	NEOTYPE	**EENSSTT**	TENSEST	**EEPPRST**	STEPPER
EENORRV	OVERREN	**EENSSTV**	STEVENS	**EEPPRSX**	PERSPEX
EENORSS	SENORES	**EENSSTW**	WETNESS	**EEPPRTY**	PRETYPE
EENORST	ESTRONE	**EENSSUV**	VENUSES	**EEPPSST**	STEPPES
EENORSY	ONEYERS	**EENSSUX**	NEXUSES	**EEPPSTU**	STEEPUP
	ONEYRES		UNSEXES	**EEPPSUW**	UPSWEEP
EENORSZ	REZONES	**EENSSVW**	SWEVENS	**EEPPSUY**	EUPEPSY
EENORTV	OVERNET	**EENSTTX**	EXTENTS	**EEPRRSS**	PRESSER
EENORVW	OVERNEW	**EENSTTY**	TEENTSY		REPRESS
	REWOVEN	**EENSTUW**	UNSWEET		SPERRES
EENOSSW	WOENESS	**EENSTVY**	SEVENTY	**EEPRRST**	PRESTER
EENOSSY	ESSOYNE	**EEOOPRS**	OPEROSE	**EEPRRSU**	PERUSER
	NOYESES	**EEOOSTT**	TOETOES		REPURES
EENOSTU	OUTSEEN	**EEOPPRS**	PREPOSE	**EEPRRSY**	PREYERS
EENOSTV	VENTOSE	**EEOPPTT**	POPETTE	**EEPRRTV**	PERVERT
	VOTEENS	**EEOPPTU**	OUTPEEP	**EEPRRVY**	REPRYVE
EENOSTW	TOWNEES	**EEOPRRS**	REPOSER	**EEPRSSS**	PRESSES
EENOSVZ	EVZONES	**EEOPRRV**	REPROVE		SPERSES
EENOTTT	TONETTE	**EEOPRRW**	REPOWER	**EEPRSST**	PESTERS
EENPPRT	PERPENT	**EEOPRSS**	REPOSES		PRESETS
EENPRST	PENSTER	**EEOPRSX**	EXPOSER	**EEPRSSU**	PERSUES
	PRESENT	**EEOPRTT**	PROETTE		PERUSES
	REPENTS		TREETOP	**EEPRSSV**	VESPERS
	SERPENT	**EEOPRTU**	OUTPEER	**EEPRSSW**	SPEWERS
EENPRSY	PYRENES	**EEOPSSS**	SPEOSES	**EEPRSSX**	EXPRESS
EENPRTV	PREVENT	**EEOPSST**	POETESS	**EEPRSTT**	PERTEST
EENPRTY	PERENTY	**EEOPSSU**	ESPOUSE		PETTERS
EENPSSS	SPENSES		POSEUSE		PRETEST
EENPSTU	PUNTEES	**EEOPSSX**	EXPOSES	**EEPRSTU**	PERTUSE
EENPSTW	ENSWEPT	**EEOPSTU**	TOUPEES		REPUTES
EENPSTY	STEPNEY	**EEOPSTY**	EYESPOT	**EEPRSTW**	PEWTERS
EENQSTU	SEQUENT		PEYOTES	**EEPRSTX**	EXPERTS
EENRRST	RENTERS	**EEOPTUW**	OUTWEEP		SEXPERT
	RERENTS	**EEOQRTU**	REQUOTE	**EEPRSTY**	RETYPES
	STERNER	**EEORRST**	RESTORE	**EEPRSUV**	PREVUES
EENRRSU	ENSURER	**EEORRSV**	REVERSO	**EEPRSXY**	PYREXES
EENRRSV	NERVERS	**EEORRSZ**	REZEROS	**EEPRTTX**	PRETEXT
EENRRTY	REENTRY	**EEORRTU**	REROUTE	**EEPSSTT**	SEPTETS
EENRRUV	NERVURE	**EEORRTV**	EVERTOR	**EEPSTTU**	PUTTEES
EENRSST	NESTERS	**EEORRTW**	REWROTE	**EEPSTTY**	TYPESET

EEQRRUY	EQUERRY	EESTTTX	SEXTETT	EFFNRUU	UNRUFFE
EEQRSTU	QUESTER	EESTTZZ	TZETZES	EFFNSTU	FUNFEST
	REQUEST	EFFFINO	INFEOFF	EFFOORR	OFFEROR
EEQRSUU	QUEUERS	EFFFIRU	FUFFIER	EFFOPRR	PROFFER
EEQSSTU	QUEESTS	EFFFLRU	FLUFFER	EFFOPSU	POUFFES
EEQSUYZ	SQUEEZY	EFFFOOR	FEOFFOR	EFFORRT	TROFFER
EERRSST	RESTERS	EFFGIJN	JEFFING	EFFORST	EFFORTS
EERRSSV	SERVERS	EFFGINR	REFFING	EFFORSW	SWOFFER
	VERSERS	EFFGINS	EFFINGS	EFFOSST	OFFSETS
EERRSTT	TERRETS	EFFGIRS	GRIFFES		SETOFFS
EERRSTU	URETERS	EFFGISU	GUFFIES	EFFPRSU	PUFFERS
EERRSTV	REVERTS	EFFGORS	GOFFERS	EFFPRUY	PUFFERY
EERRSTW	STREWER	EFFGRRU	GRUFFER	EFFRSSU	SUFFERS
	WRESTER	EFFHILW	WHIFFLE	EFFRSTU	RESTUFF
EERRSUV	REVEURS	EFFHIRS	SHERIFF		STUFFER
EERRSVW	SWERVER	EFFHIRU	HUFFIER		TRUFFES
EERRSVY	SERVERY	EFFHIRW	WHIFFER	EFFSSUU	SUFFUSE
EERRTTU	REUTTER	EFFHITW	WHIFFET	EFFSTTU	TUFFETS
	UTTERER	EFFHLSU	SHUFFLE	EFGGIOR	FOGGIER
EERRTTY	RETTERY	EFFHRSU	HUFFERS	EFGGIRR	FRIGGER
EERSSST	TRESSES	EFFIIJS	JIFFIES	EFGGIRU	FUGGIER
EERSSTT	RETESTS	EFFIIMR	MIFFIER	EFGGIRY	FIGGERY
	SETTERS	EFFIINR	NIFFIER	EFGGLOR	FLOGGER
	STREETS	EFFIIST	FIFTIES	EFGGORS	FOGGERS
	TERSEST		IFFIEST	EFGHIMS	GEMFISH
	TESTERS		STIFFIE	EFGHINT	HEFTING
EERSSTV	REVESTS	EFFIKLS	SKIFFLE	EFGHIRT	FIGHTER
	STERVES	EFFILLU	LIFEFUL		FREIGHT
	VERSETS	EFFILNO	OFFLINE		REFIGHT
	VERSTES	EFFILNS	SNIFFLE	EFGIKNR	KERFING
EERSSTW	STEWERS	EFFILPR	PIFFLER	EFGILLN	FELLING
	WESTERS	EFFILPS	PIFFLES	EFGILMN	FLEMING
EERSSTX	EXSERTS	EFFILRR	RIFFLER	EFGILNR	FLINGER
EERSSTZ	ZESTERS	EFFILRS	RIFFLES	EFGILNS	SELFING
EERSSUX	XERUSES	EFFILRY	FIREFLY	EFGILNT	FELTING
EERSSUY	SEYSURE	EFFILSS	SIFFLES	EFGILNU	FUELING
EERSSVW	SWERVES	EFFIMOS	MOFFIES	EFGILNX	FLEXING
EERSTTT	STRETTE	EFFINRS	NIFFERS	EFGILNY	FLEYING
	TETTERS		SNIFFER	EFGILRU	FUGLIER
EERSTTU	TRUSTEE	EFFINST	INFEFTS		GULFIER
EERSTTV	TREVETS		STIFFEN	EFGIMNT	FIGMENT
	VETTERS	EFFIOPR	PIFFERO	EFGINNP	PFENNIG
EERSTTW	WETTERS	EFFIORT	FORFEIT	EFGINNR	FERNING
EERSTTX	TEXTERS		TOFFIER	EFGINOR	FOREIGN
EERSTTY	STREETY	EFFIORX	FOXFIRE	EFGINPR	PERFING
	SYRETTE	EFFIOST	TOFFIES	EFGINRS	FINGERS
EERSTUV	VERSUTE	EFFIPRU	PUFFIER		FRINGES
	VERTUES	EFFIRRT	TRIFFER	EFGINRU	GUNFIRE
	VESTURE	EFFIRST	RESTIFF	EFGINSS	FESSING
EERSTUY	TUYERES		STIFFER	EFGINTT	FETTING
EERSTVV	VERVETS	EFFLLOS	SELLOFF	EFGINTW	WEFTING
EERSTWY	TWYERES	EFFLMRU	MUFFLER	EFGIOOR	GOOFIER
EERTTUX	TEXTURE	EFFLMSU	MUFFLES	EFGIORV	FORGIVE
EESSSTT	SESTETS	EFFLNSU	SNUFFLE	EFGIRRT	GRIFTER
	TSETSES	EFFLOPS	POFFLES	EFGIRRU	FIGURER
EESSTTT	SESTETT	EFFLOSU	SOUFFLE	EFGIRST	REGIFTS
EESSTTU	SUTTEES	EFFLRRU	RUFFLER	EFGIRSU	FIGURES
EESSTTX	SEXTETS	EFFLRSU	RUFFLES	EFGKOOP	OPGEFOK
EESSTTY	STEYEST	EFFLRTU	FRETFUL	EFGLLSU	FLUGELS
EESSTTZ	TZETSES		TRUFFLE	EFGLNSU	ENGULFS
EESTTTW	WETTEST	EFFNRSU	SNUFFER	EFGLNTU	FULGENT

EFGLORS	GOLFERS	EFIIMST	SEMIFIT	EFILPPR	FLIPPER
EFGLORT	FROGLET	EFIINNR	FINNIER	EFILPPS	FIPPLES
EFGLOSS	FOGLESS	EFIINPV	FIVEPIN	EFILPPU	PIPEFUL
EFGMNOR	FROGMEN	EFIINRT	NIFTIER	EFILPRS	PILFERS
EFGNOOR	FORGONE	EFIINRU	UNIFIER	EFILPRY	PILFERY
EFGNOSU	FUNGOES	EFIINSS	FINISES	EFILQUY	LIQUEFY
EFGOORR	FORGOER	EFIINST	FINITES	EFILRRS	RIFLERS
EFGOORS	FORGOES		NIFTIES	EFILRRT	FLIRTER
EFGORRS	FORGERS	EFIINSU	UNIFIES		TRIFLER
EFGORRU	FERRUGO	EFIINSX	INFIXES	EFILRRY	RIFLERY
EFGORRY	FORGERY	EFIIRRR	FIRRIER	EFILRST	FILTERS
EFGORST	FORGETS	EFIIRRT	RIFTIER		LIFTERS
EFGORSW	GOWFERS	EFIIRST	FISTIER		STIFLER
EFGORTU	FOREGUT	EFIIRTW	WIFTIER		TRIFLES
EFHIINS	FINEISH	EFIIRZZ	FIZZIER	EFILRTT	FLITTER
EFHIIRS	FISHIER	EFIISSV	FISSIVE	EFILRTU	FLUTIER
EFHIJSW	JEWFISH	EFIISTW	SWIFTIE		FUTILER
EFHILMS	FLEMISH	EFIJLLY	JELLIFY	EFILRTY	FLYTIER
	HIMSELF	EFIJLOR	FRIJOLE	EFILRVV	FLIVVER
EFHILSS	HISSELF	EFIJLOT	JETFOIL	EFILRZZ	FRIZZLE
	SELFISH	EFIKLNU	FLUNKIE	EFILSSS	FISSLES
EFHILST	LEFTISH	EFIKLOR	FOLKIER	EFILSST	SELFIST
EFHILTY	HEFTILY	EFIKLOS	FOLKIES		STIFLES
EFHINNS	FENNISH	EFIKLOX	FOXLIKE	EFILSTT	LEFTIST
EFHINST	FISHNET	EFIKLRU	FLUKIER	EFILSTU	FLUIEST
EFHIRSS	FISHERS	EFIKNRS	KNIFERS		SULFITE
	SERFISH	EFIKNRU	FUNKIER	EFILSZZ	FIZZLES
	SHERIFS	EFIKORR	FORKIER	EFILUVX	FLUXIVE
EFHIRST	SHIFTER	EFIKRRS	FRISKER	EFIMMRU	FERMIUM
EFHIRSY	FISHERY	EFIKRST	FRISKET	EFIMNOR	FERMION
EFHISUW	HUSWIFE	EFILLMS	MISFELL	EFIMNTT	FITMENT
EFHLLPU	HELPFUL	EFILLOO	FOLIOLE	EFIMOST	FOMITES
EFHLLSY	FLESHLY	EFILLOS	FOLLIES	EFIMRRS	FIRMERS
EFHLNSU	UNFLESH	EFILLOW	LOWLIFE	EFIMRST	FIRMEST
EFHLOOX	FOXHOLE	EFILLRR	FRILLER		FREMITS
EFHLOPU	HOPEFUL	EFILLRS	FILLERS	EFIMRTY	METRIFY
EFHLOSS	FLOSHES		REFILLS	EFIMSTU	FUMIEST
EFHLRSU	FLUSHER	EFILLST	FILLETS	EFIMTTU	FUMETTI
EFHLRSY	FRESHLY	EFILLUW	WILEFUL	EFINNOR	INFERNO
EFHLSSU	FLUSHES	EFILMNT	LIFTMEN	EFINNRS	FINNERS
EFHLSTY	THYSELF	EFILMNU	FULMINE	EFINNRU	FUNNIER
EFHLTTW	TWELFTH	EFILMOT	FILEMOT	EFINNSU	FUNNIES
EFHNORT	FORHENT	EFILMRS	FILMERS	EFINOPR	FORPINE
EFHOORS	HOOFERS		REFILMS	EFINPRS	PERFINS
EFHORRT	FROTHER	EFILMSS	SELFISM	EFINRST	SNIFTER
EFHORSS	FROSHES	EFILMST	FILMSET	EFINRSU	INFUSER
EFHORST	FOTHERS		LEFTISM	EFINRUY	REUNIFY
EFHRRSU	FUHRERS	EFILNNO	NONLIFE	EFINSST	FITNESS
EFHRRTU	FURTHER	EFILNOS	OLEFINS		INFESTS
EFHRSSU	FRUSHES	EFILNOX	FLEXION	EFINSSU	INFUSES
EFIIKLN	FINLIKE	EFILNSS	FINLESS	EFINSUX	UNFIXES
EFIIKST	FIKIEST	EFILOOS	FLOOSIE	EFINSZZ	FIZZENS
EFIILLS	FILLIES		FOLIOSE	EFIOOPR	POOFIER
EFIILMR	FILMIER	EFILOOZ	FLOOZIE	EFIOORR	ROOFIER
EFIILMS	MISFILE	EFILOPR	PROFILE	EFIOORS	ROOFIES
EFIILRT	FIRELIT	EFILORR	FLORIER	EFIOORT	FOOTIER
	FITLIER	EFILORT	LOFTIER	EFIOORW	WOOFIER
EFIILRY	FIERILY		TREFOIL	EFIOOST	FOOTIES
EFIILSS	FISSILE	EFILOSS	FLOSSIE		FOOTSIE
EFIIMRR	RIMFIRE	EFILOSU	FOULIES		OOFIEST
EFIIMRS	MISFIRE	EFILOSX	SEXFOIL	EFIOPRR	PORIFER

EFIOPRT	FIREPOT	**EFLLORU**	FLORULE	**EFLOTUW**	OUTFLEW
	PIEFORT	**EFLLOST**	FLOTELS	**EFLPRRU**	PURFLER
EFIORRT	ROTIFER	**EFLLOSW**	FELLOWS	**EFLPRSU**	PURFLES
EFIORRW	FROWIER	**EFLLRSU**	FULLERS	**EFLPRUY**	PREYFUL
EFIORSS	FROISES	**EFLLRUY**	FULLERY	**EFLPSTU**	PESTFUL
EFIORST	FOISTER	**EFLLSSY**	FLYLESS	**EFLRRSU**	FURLERS
	FORTIES	**EFLLSTU**	FULLEST	**EFLRSSU**	FURLESS
EFIORTU	OUTFIRE	**EFLMOSU**	FULSOME	**EFLRSTU**	FLUSTER
EFIORTV	OVERFIT	**EFLMPRU**	FRUMPLE		FLUTERS
EFIOSST	SOFTIES	**EFLMSUU**	MUSEFUL		RESTFUL
EFIOSTX	FOXIEST	**EFLNNOS**	NONSELF	**EFLRTTU**	FLUTTER
EFIOSTZ	FOZIEST	**EFLNNOU**	NONFUEL	**EFLSSUU**	USEFULS
EFIPPRR	FRIPPER	**EFLNNSU**	FUNNELS	**EFLSTUZ**	ZESTFUL
EFIPPRT	FRIPPET	**EFLNORT**	FORLENT	**EFLSUZZ**	FUZZLES
EFIPRST	PRESIFT	**EFLNORU**	FLEURON	**EFMNOOT**	FOOTMEN
EFIPRTY	PETRIFY	**EFLNORW**	REFLOWN	**EFMNORS**	ENFORMS
EFIRRRU	FURRIER	**EFLNORY**	FELONRY	**EFMNOST**	FOMENTS
EFIRRSU	FRISEUR	**EFLNOST**	TEFLONS	**EFMNRSU**	FRENUMS
	FRISURE	**EFLNOSU**	SULFONE		SURFMEN
	FURRIES	**EFLNOTT**	FLETTON	**EFMNRTU**	TURFMEN
	SURFIER		FONTLET	**EFMOORZ**	ZOEFORM
EFIRRSZ	FRIZERS	**EFLNPSU**	PENFULS	**EFMOPRR**	PERFORM
EFIRRTT	FRITTER	**EFLNPUX**	FUNPLEX		PREFORM
EFIRRTU	FRITURE	**EFLNSSU**	FULNESS	**EFMOPRT**	POMFRET
	FRUITER		UNSELFS	**EFMORRS**	FORMERS
	TURFIER	**EFLNSTU**	FLUENTS		REFORMS
EFIRRTY	TERRIFY		NESTFUL	**EFMOTTU**	FUMETTO
EFIRRUZ	FURZIER		NETFULS	**EFMPRUY**	PERFUMY
EFIRRZZ	FRIZZER	**EFLNSUY**	SYNFUEL	**EFMRRSU**	FERRUMS
EFIRSST	RESIFTS	**EFLNTTU**	TENTFUL	**EFMRTUY**	FURMETY
	SIFTERS	**EFLNTUU**	TUNEFUL	**EFNNORT**	FORNENT
	STRIFES	**EFLOORR**	FLOORER	**EFNNORU**	FENURON
EFIRSSU	FISSURE	**EFLOORS**	FORSLOE	**EFNNOTU**	UNOFTEN
	FUSSIER	**EFLOORT**	FOOTLER	**EFNNSTU**	FUNNEST
	SURFIES	**EFLOORY**	FOOLERY	**EFNOOST**	EFTSOON
EFIRSTT	FITTERS	**EFLOORZ**	FOOZLER		FESTOON
	TITFERS	**EFLOOST**	FOOTLES	**EFNORRT**	FRONTER
EFIRSTU	FUSTIER	**EFLOOSZ**	FOOZLES		REFRONT
	SURFEIT	**EFLOPPR**	FLOPPER	**EFNORRU**	FORERUN
EFIRSTW	SWIFTER	**EFLORRS**	ROLFERS	**EFNORRW**	FROWNER
EFIRSTZ	FRITZES	**EFLORSS**	FLOSSER	**EFNORST**	FRONTES
EFIRSUX	FIXURES	**EFLORST**	FLORETS	**EFNORTU**	FORTUNE
EFIRSVY	VERSIFY		LOFTERS	**EFNORTW**	FORWENT
EFIRSZZ	FIZZERS	**EFLORSU**	FUROLES	**EFNORUZ**	UNFROZE
	FRIZZES		OURSELF	**EFNOSST**	SOFTENS
EFIRTTU	TUFTIER	**EFLORSW**	FLOWERS	**EFNRSTU**	FUNSTER
	TURFITE		FOWLERS	**EFOOPRR**	PROOFER
EFIRTUV	FURTIVE		REFLOWS		REPROOF
EFIRTUX	FIXTURE		WOLFERS	**EFOOPRS**	SPOOFER
EFIRUZZ	FUZZIER	**EFLORSX**	FLEXORS	**EFOOPRT**	FORETOP
EFISTTT	FITTEST	**EFLORTT**	FORTLET		POOFTER
EFISTTY	TESTIFY	**EFLORTU**	FLOUTER	**EFOORRS**	REROOFS
EFJLSTU	JESTFUL	**EFLORTW**	FELWORT		ROOFERS
EFKLMNO	MENFOLK	**EFLORVY**	FLYOVER	**EFOORST**	FOETORS
EFKLMOR	MERFOLK		OVERFLY		FOOTERS
EFKLNRU	FLUNKER	**EFLORWW**	WERWOLF		REFOOTS
EFKLNUY	FLUNKEY	**EFLORWY**	FLOWERY	**EFOORSW**	WOOFERS
EFKLOPU	POKEFUL	**EFLOSSS**	FLOSSES	**EFOORTW**	WOOFTER
EFKLPSU	SKEPFUL	**EFLOSSU**	FLOUSES	**EFOPPRY**	FOPPERY
EFKNRSU	FUNKERS	**EFLOSTU**	FOULEST	**EFOPRSS**	PROFESS
EFKORRS	FORKERS	**EFLOTTU**	OUTFELT	**EFOPRST**	FORPETS

EFOPRSU	PROFUSE		LEGGINS	**EGGLORS**	LOGGERS
EFOPRTU	POUFTER		NIGGLES		SLOGGER
EFOPRTY	TORPEFY		SNIGGLE	**EGGLORT**	TOGGLER
EFORRSU	FERROUS	**EGGILNU**	GLUEING	**EGGLORV**	VLOGGER
	FURORES		LUGEING	**EGGLOST**	GOGLETS
EFORRSV	FERVORS	**EGGILNY**	GINGELY		LOGGETS
EFORRTY	TORREFY		GLEYING		TOGGLES
EFORRUV	FERVOUR	**EGGILOR**	LOGGIER	**EGGLOSW**	WOGGLES
EFORSST	FORESTS	**EGGILRS**	LIGGERS	**EGGLPRU**	PLUGGER
	FOSTERS	**EGGILRW**	WIGGLER	**EGGLPSU**	PUGGLES
EFORSSU	FOURSES		WRIGGLE	**EGGLRSU**	GLURGES
EFORSTU	FOUTERS	**EGGILST**	GIGLETS		GURGLES
	FOUTRES	**EGGILSU**	LUGGIES		LUGGERS
EFORSTW	TWOFERS	**EGGILSW**	WIGGLES		SLUGGER
EFOSSTT	SOFTEST	**EGGIMMN**	GEMMING	**EGGLRTU**	GURGLET
EFOSTWW	WOWFEST	**EGGIMNN**	MENGING	**EGGLSTU**	GUGLETS
EFPRTUY	PUTREFY	**EGGIMNR**	GERMING	**EGGMRSU**	MUGGERS
EFPSTUY	STUPEFY		MERGING		SMUGGER
EFRRSSU	SURFERS	**EGGIMOS**	MOGGIES	**EGGNOOY**	GEOGONY
EFRRSTU	RETURFS	**EGGIMRU**	MUGGIER	**EGGNRRU**	GRUNGER
EFRRSUU	FUREURS	**EGGINNN**	GENNING	**EGGNRSU**	GRUNGES
EFRSSSU	FUSSERS	**EGGINNR**	GERNING		SNUGGER
EFRSTTU	TUFTERS	**EGGINNS**	GINSENG	**EGGNRUY**	GRUNGEY
EFRSTUU	FUTURES	**EGGINNV**	VENGING	**EGGNSTU**	NUGGETS
EFSSTTU	FUSTETS	**EGGINRS**	GINGERS	**EGGNTUY**	NUGGETY
EGGGIKN	KEGGING		NIGGERS	**EGGOPRR**	PROGGER
EGGGILN	LEGGING		SERGING	**EGGORRS**	GORGERS
EGGGILR	GIGGLER		SNIGGER	**EGGORST**	GORGETS
EGGGILS	GIGGLES	**EGGINRU**	GRUEING		TOGGERS
EGGGINP	PEGGING		GUNGIER	**EGGORSU**	GOUGERS
EGGGINV	VEGGING	**EGGINRV**	VERGING	**EGGORTY**	TOGGERY
EGGGLOR	GOGGLER	**EGGINRW**	GREWING	**EGGPRUY**	PUGGERY
EGGGLOS	GOGGLES	**EGGINRY**	GINGERY	**EGGRRSU**	RUGGERS
EGGGLSU	GUGGLES		GREYING	**EGGRSTU**	TUGGERS
EGGGNOS	EGGNOGS		NIGGERY	**EGGSSTU**	SUGGEST
EGGHILR	HIGGLER	**EGGINSS**	GESSING	**EGHHHIT**	HEIGHTH
EGGHILS	HIGGLES	**EGGINTT**	GETTING	**EGHHIMN**	HIGHMEN
EGGHINP	PEGHING	**EGGINTW**	TWIGGEN	**EGHHIRS**	HIGHERS
EGGHIRT	THIGGER	**EGGIORS**	SOGGIER	**EGHHIST**	EIGHTHS
EGGHIRU	HUGGIER	**EGGIPRR**	PRIGGER		HEIGHTS
EGGHLOS	SHOGGLE	**EGGIPRU**	PUGGIER		HIGHEST
EGGHORS	HOGGERS	**EGGIPRY**	PIGGERY	**EGHHOSW**	SHOWGHE
EGGHORY	HOGGERY	**EGGIPSU**	PUGGIES	**EGHHSSU**	SHEUGHS
EGGHOST	HOGGETS	**EGGIRRS**	RIGGERS	**EGHHSUW**	WHEUGHS
EGGHRSU	HUGGERS	**EGGIRRT**	TRIGGER	**EGHIILL**	GHILLIE
EGGIIJR	JIGGIER	**EGGIRRU**	RUGGIER	**EGHIILN**	HEILING
EGGIILN	GINGELI	**EGGIRSW**	SWIGGER	**EGHIINR**	HEIRING
EGGIILS	GILGIES		WIGGERS	**EGHIINT**	NIGHTIE
EGGIINS	SIEGING	**EGGIRTW**	TWIGGER	**EGHIINV**	INVEIGH
EGGIIPR	PIGGIER	**EGGIRUV**	VUGGIER	**EGHIKLO**	HOGLIKE
EGGIIPS	PIGGIES	**EGGIRWY**	WIGGERY	**EGHIKNR**	GHERKIN
EGGIIRW	WIGGIER	**EGGJLOR**	JOGGLER	**EGHIKRS**	SKREIGH
EGGIJLS	JIGGLES	**EGGJLOS**	JOGGLES		SKRIEGH
EGGIJRS	JIGGERS	**EGGJLRU**	JUGGLER	**EGHILLN**	HELLING
EGGIKLN	KEGLING	**EGGJLSU**	JUGGLES	**EGHILMN**	HELMING
EGGILLN	GELLING	**EGGJORS**	JOGGERS	**EGHILMP**	MEGILPH
EGGILMS	LEGGISM	**EGGLMSU**	SMUGGLE	**EGHILNP**	HELPING
	MIGGLES	**EGGLNOS**	LEGONGS	**EGHILNR**	GHRELIN
EGGILNN	LENGING	**EGGLNSU**	SNUGGLE		HERLING
EGGILNR	NIGGLER	**EGGLOOS**	GOOGLES	**EGHILNS**	ENGLISH
EGGILNS	GINGLES	**EGGLOOY**	GEOLOGY		SHINGLE

EGHILNT	ENLIGHT		THEGNLY	EGIINRR	GIRNIER
	LIGHTEN	EGHLOOS	GOLOSHE	EGIINRT	IGNITER
EGHILNV	HELVING		SHOOGLE		TIERING
EGHILOU	GHOULIE	EGHLOOT	THEOLOG		TIGRINE
EGHILPT	PIGHTLE	EGHLOSS	SEGHOLS	EGIINRV	REIVING
EGHILRT	LIGHTER	EGHLPSU	PLEUGHS		RIEVING
	RELIGHT	EGHLTUY	TEUGHLY	EGIINRW	WEIRING
EGHILSS	SLEIGHS	EGHMMOS	MEGOHMS		WINGIER
EGHILST	SLEIGHT	EGHMNOU	HUMOGEN	EGIINRZ	ZINGIER
EGHIMMN	HEMMING	EGHMOSU	GUMSHOE	EGIINSS	SEISING
EGHIMNS	MESHING	EGHNOOS	HOGNOSE	EGIINST	IGNITES
EGHIMNT	THEMING	EGHNORS	GORHENS	EGIINSV	SIEVING
EGHIMPT	EMPIGHT	EGHNORU	ENROUGH		VISEING
EGHINNN	HENNING		ROUGHEN	EGIINSW	WEISING
EGHINNT	HENTING	EGHNOSU	ENOUGHS	EGIINSZ	SEIZING
EGHINNU	UNHINGE	EGHNOTU	TOUGHEN	EGIINTV	EVITING
EGHINOS	HONGIES	EGHNRSU	HUNGERS	EGIINTX	EXITING
	SHOEING	EGHOPRS	GOPHERS	EGIINVW	VIEWING
EGHINPS	HESPING	EGHORRU	ROUGHER	EGIINWZ	WEIZING
	PHESING	EGHORTU	TOUGHER	EGIIOPR	PIEROGI
EGHINRR	HERRING	EGHOSTT	GHETTOS	EGIIPPS	GIPPIES
EGHINRS	HINGERS	EGHOSUU	HUGEOUS	EGIIPRR	GRIPIER
EGHINRT	RIGHTEN	EGHRSSU	GURSHES	EGIIPRW	PERIWIG
EGHINRW	WHINGER		GUSHERS	EGIIPSS	GIPSIES
EGHINRY	HERYING	EGHRTUY	THEURGY	EGIJKNR	JERKING
EGHINST	NIGHEST	EGIIJKL	JIGLIKE	EGIJLLN	JELLING
EGHINSW	HEWINGS	EGIIJLS	JILGIES	EGIJLNR	JINGLER
	SHEWING	EGIIKLP	PIGLIKE	EGIJLNS	JINGLES
	WHINGES	EGIIKLW	WIGLIKE	EGIJLNT	JINGLET
EGHINSX	HEXINGS	EGIILLS	GILLIES	EGIJNOS	JINGOES
EGHINTT	TIGHTEN	EGIILMT	LEGITIM	EGIJNSS	JESSING
EGHINWW	WHEWING	EGIILNR	LEIRING	EGIJNST	JESTING
EGHIOOS	SHOOGIE		LINGIER	EGIJNTT	JETTING
EGHIOPS	PISHEOG	EGIILNS	SEILING	EGIKKLN	LEKKING
	PISHOGE	EGIILNT	LIGNITE	EGIKLMU	GUMLIKE
EGHIORS	OGREISH	EGIILNV	VEILING	EGIKLNP	KELPING
EGHIORU	ROUGHIE	EGIILNX	EXILING	EGIKLNR	ERLKING
EGHIOST	HOGTIES	EGIILPS	GILPIES	EGIKLNS	KINGLES
EGHIOTT	GOTHITE	EGIILRR	GIRLIER	EGIKLNT	KINGLET
EGHIOTU	TOUGHIE	EGIILRS	GIRLIES	EGIKLNW	WELKING
EGHIOTV	EIGHTVO	EGIIMMS	GIMMIES	EGIKLRS	KILERGS
EGHIRRT	RIGHTER	EGIIMMN	MEINING	EGIKLRU	RUGLIKE
EGHIRSS	GIRSHES	EGIIMNP	IMPINGE	EGIKLTU	GUTLIKE
	SIGHERS	EGIIMNR	MINGIER	EGIKMNP	KEMPING
EGHIRST	RESIGHT	EGIIMNT	ITEMING	EGIKMNS	SMEKING
	SIGHTER	EGIIMNV	MIEVING	EGIKNNN	KENNING
EGHIRSU	GRUSHIE	EGIIMPR	GIMPIER	EGIKNNR	KERNING
	GUSHIER	EGIIMPS	PIGMIES	EGIKNNT	KENTING
EGHIRSY	GREYISH	EGIIMRR	GRIMIER	EGIKNOV	EVOKING
EGHIRTT	TIGHTER	EGIIMSV	MISGIVE	EGIKNPP	KEPPING
EGHIRUV	VUGHIER	EGIINNP	PEINING	EGIKNPR	PERKING
EGHISTW	WEIGHTS	EGIINNR	GINNIER	EGIKNRU	GUNKIER
EGHISTY	HYGEIST		REINING	EGIKNRV	KERVING
EGHITWY	WEIGHTY	EGIINNS	INGINES	EGIKNRY	KEYRING
EGHLLOU	LUGHOLE		INSIGNE		YERKING
EGHLMPS	PHLEGMS		SEINING	EGIKNST	KESTING
EGHLMPY	PHLEGMY	EGIINNV	VEINING	EGIKNSW	SKEWING
EGHLNOR	LEGHORN	EGIINOP	EPIGONI	EGIKNSY	KEYINGS
EGHLNPU	ENGULPH	EGIINPS	PEISING		YESKING
EGHLNST	LENGTHS		PIGSNIE	EGIKNUY	YEUKING
EGHLNTY	LENGTHY	EGIINPZ	PEIZING	EGILLMN	MELLING

EGILLNO	LOGLINE		SINGLET	EGIMNOS	MISGONE
EGILLNS	LEGLINS		SNIGLET	EGIMNOT	EMOTING
	LINGELS		TINGLES		MITOGEN
	LINGLES	EGILNSU	LUNGIES	EGIMNOU	MEOUING
	SELLING		SLUEING	EGIMNOV	EMOVING
EGILLNT	GILLNET	EGILNSW	SLEWING	EGIMNOW	MEOWING
	TELLING		SWINGLE	EGIMNPR	GRIPMEN
EGILLNW	WELLING	EGILNSZ	ZINGELS		IMPREGN
EGILLNY	YELLING	EGILNTT	ETTLING		PERMING
EGILLOR	GIROLLE		LETTING	EGIMNPT	EMPTING
EGILLOS	GOLLIES	EGILNTU	ELUTING		PIGMENT
EGILLRR	GRILLER	EGILNTW	WELTING		TEMPING
EGILLRS	GILLERS		WINGLET	EGIMNQU	QUEMING
	GRILLES	EGILNUY	GUYLINE	EGIMNRS	GERMINS
EGILLST	GILLETS	EGILNVY	LEVYING		MERINGS
EGILLSU	GULLIES	EGILOOS	GOOLIES		MINGERS
	LIGULES		OLOGIES	EGIMNRT	METRING
EGILMMN	LEMMING	EGILOPS	EPILOGS		TERMING
EGILMMR	GLIMMER	EGILORS	GLOIRES	EGIMNRU	EMURING
EGILMMY	GEMMILY		GLORIES	EGIMNSS	MESSING
EGILMNR	GREMLIN	EGILOSS	GLIOSES	EGIMNST	STEMING
	MERLING	EGILOST	ELOGIST		TEMSING
	MINGLER		LOGIEST	EGIMNSU	MEUSING
EGILMNS	MINGLES	EGILOSU	OUGLIES	EGIMNSW	MEWSING
EGILMNT	MELTING	EGILPPR	GRIPPLE	EGIMORR	GORMIER
EGILMNU	EMULING	EGILPRU	GULPIER	EGIMORS	OGREISM
	GUMLINE	EGILPST	PIGLETS	EGIMOSS	EGOISMS
	LEGUMIN	EGILPSY	GILPEYS		MISGOES
EGILMNW	MEWLING	EGILRRU	GURLIER	EGIMOST	EGOTISM
EGILMNY	YELMING	EGILRSS	GRILSES	EGIMPSU	GUIMPES
EGILMOR	GOMERIL	EGILRST	GLISTER	EGIMPSY	GYMPIES
EGILMOS	SEMILOG		GRISTLE		PYGMIES
EGILMOU	ELOGIUM	EGILRSU	GUILERS	EGIMRSW	MISGREW
EGILMPS	GLIMPSE		LIGURES	EGIMSST	STIGMES
	MEGILPS		LURGIES	EGINNNP	PENNING
EGILMST	GIMLETS	EGILRSY	GREISLY	EGINNNR	RENNING
EGILNNS	GINNELS		GRIESLY	EGINNNY	YENNING
	LENSING		GRISELY	EGINNOO	IONOGEN
EGILNOP	ELOPING	EGILRTT	GLITTER	EGINNOP	OPENING
EGILNOS	ELOIGNS	EGILRTY	TIGERLY	EGINNOR	NEGRONI
	LEGIONS	EGILRUV	VIRGULE	EGINNOV	OVENING
	LIGNOSE	EGILRZZ	GRIZZLE	EGINNPU	PENGUIN
	LINGOES	EGILSST	LEGISTS	EGINNRR	GRINNER
	LONGIES	EGILSSW	WIGLESS	EGINNRS	ENRINGS
EGILNOT	LENTIGO	EGILSTU	GLUIEST		GINNERS
EGILNPP	LEPPING		UGLIEST	EGINNRT	RENTING
EGILNPR	PINGLER	EGILSTW	WIGLETS		RINGENT
EGILNPS	PINGLES	EGILSTZ	GLITZES		TERNING
	SPIGNEL	EGILTTW	TWIGLET	EGINNRU	ENURING
EGILNPT	PELTING	EGIMMRR	GRIMMER	EGINNRV	NERVING
EGILNPY	YELPING	EGIMMRS	GIMMERS	EGINNRY	GINNERY
EGILNRS	GIRNELS		MEGRIMS		RENYING
	LINGERS	EGIMMRU	GUMMIER	EGINNSS	ENSIGNS
	SLINGER	EGIMMSU	GUMMIES		SENSING
EGILNRT	RINGLET	EGIMMTU	GUMMITE	EGINNST	NESTING
	TINGLER	EGIMNNN	NEMNING		SENTING
	TRINGLE	EGIMNNO	OMENING		TENSING
EGILNRY	RELYING	EGIMNNR	RINGMEN	EGINNSU	ENSUING
EGILNSS	SINGLES	EGIMNNS	MENSING		GUNNIES
EGILNST	GLISTEN	EGIMNNW	WINGMEN		INGENUS
	LESTING	EGIMNOR	MOERING	EGINNSW	NEWSING

EGINNSY	GYNNIES		RUEINGS			GRIPPES
EGINNTT	NETTING		SIGNEUR	EGIPPSU	GUPPIES
	TENTING	EGINRSV	SERVING	EGIPPSY	GYPPIES
EGINNTV	VENTING		VERSING	EGIPRRS	GRIPERS
EGINNVY	ENVYING	EGINRSW	SWINGER	EGIPRUU	GUIPURE
EGINOOR	GOONIER		WINGERS	EGIPSSY	GYPSIES
EGINOOS	GOONIES	EGINRSY	SYRINGE	EGIRRRU	GURRIER
	ISOGONE	EGINRSZ	ZINGERS	EGIRRST	GRISTER
	NOOGIES	EGINRTT	GITTERN	EGIRRSU	GURRIES
EGINOPR	PERIGON		RETTING		SURGIER
	PIROGEN	EGINRTU	TRUEING	EGIRRSV	VIRGERS
	PONGIER	EGINRTV	VERTING	EGIRRTT	GRITTER
EGINOPS	EPIGONS	EGINRTY	RETYING	EGIRSST	TIGRESS
	PIGEONS	EGINRVV	REVVING	EGIRSSU	GUISERS
	PINGOES	EGINRVY	REVYING	EGIRSTU	GUSTIER
EGINORR	IGNORER	EGINSST	INGESTS		GUTSIER
EGINORS	ERINGOS		SIGNETS	EGIRSTV	GRIVETS
	IGNORES	EGINSSW	SEWINGS	EGIRSUZ	GUIZERS
	REGIONS		SWINGES	EGIRTTU	GUTTIER
	SIGNORE	EGINSSX	SEXINGS		TURGITE
EGINORT	GENITOR	EGINSSY	YESSING	EGISSSU	GUSSIES
EGINORV	OVERING	EGINSTT	SETTING	EGISTTU	GUTTIES
EGINORZ	ZEROING		TESTING	EGISUWY	WISEGUY
EGINOSU	IGNEOUS	EGINSTU	GUNITES	EGJLNSU	JUNGLES
EGINOSW	WIGEONS	EGINSTV	VESTING	EGJLSTU	JUGLETS
EGINOSY	ISOGENY	EGINSTW	STEWING	EGJOSTT	GJETOST
EGINOSZ	GINZOES		TWINGES	EGKLORW	LEGWORK
EGINOTT	TENTIGO		WESTING	EGKMSSU	MUSKEGS
EGINOTV	VETOING	EGINSTZ	ZESTING	EGKNOSY	KYOGENS
EGINOTZ	GENIZOT	EGINSVX	VEXINGS	EGLLORS	GOLLERS
EGINPPP	PEPPING	EGINSWY	SWEYING	EGLLOSY	SYLLOGE
EGINPPR	REPPING	EGINSZZ	GIZZENS	EGLLRSU	GULLERS
EGINPPS	PIGPENS	EGINTTV	VETTING	EGLLRUY	GULLERY
EGINPRS	PERSING	EGINTTW	WETTING	EGLLSTU	GULLETS
	PINGERS	EGINTTX	TEXTING	EGLLSUY	GULLEYS
	SPRINGE	EGIOOPR	GOOPIER	EGLMMRU	GLUMMER
EGINPRU	PUERING	EGIOORS	GOORIES	EGLMNOO	ENGLOOM
EGINPRV	PERVING		GOOSIER	EGLMNOR	MONGREL
	PREVING	EGIOOSS	GOOSIES	EGLMOOR	LEGROOM
EGINPRY	PREYING		SOOGIES	EGLMSSU	GUMLESS
EGINPSS	GIPSENS	EGIOOST	GOOIEST	EGLNNSU	GUNNELS
EGINPSU	SPUEING	EGIOPPS	GIPPOES	EGLNOOV	VONGOLE
EGINPSW	SPEWING	EGIOPRS	PORGIES	EGLNOOY	ENOLOGY
EGINPSY	ESPYING		SERPIGO		NEOLOGY
	PEYSING	EGIOPRU	GROUPIE	EGLNOPS	PLONGES
	PIGSNEY		PIROGUE	EGLNORS	LONGERS
EGINPTT	PETTING	EGIORRS	GORSIER	EGLNORU	LOUNGER
EGINPYY	EPIGYNY	EGIORST	GOITERS	EGLNOST	LONGEST
EGINQUU	QUEUING		GOITRES	EGLNOSU	LOUNGES
EGINRRS	ERRINGS		GORIEST	EGLNOSY	LYSOGEN
	GIRNERS	EGIORTU	GOUTIER	EGLNOUV	UNGLOVE
	RINGERS	EGIORTV	VERTIGO	EGLNOUY	LOUNGEY
	SERRING	EGIORTZ	ZORGITE	EGLNOXY	LOXYGEN
EGINRRW	WRINGER	EGIORUV	VOGUIER		XYLOGEN
EGINRSS	INGRESS	EGIOSST	EGOISTS	EGLNOYZ	LOZENGY
	RESIGNS		STOGIES	EGLNPRU	PLUNGER
	SIGNERS	EGIOSTT	EGOTIST	EGLNPSU	PLUNGES
	SINGERS	EGIOSTV	VOGIEST		PUNGLES
EGINRST	RESTING	EGIOTUV	OUTGIVE	EGLNRSU	LUNGERS
	STINGER	EGIPPRR	GRIPPER	EGLNRTU	GRUNTLE
EGINRSU	REUSING	EGIPPRS	GIPPERS	EGLNSSU	GUNLESS

	GUNSELS	**EGNNOOS**	NONEGOS	**EGORRST**	GROSERT
EGLNSTU	ENGLUTS	**EGNNORT**	RONTGEN	**EGORRSU**	GROUSER
	GLUTENS	**EGNNOSU**	GUENONS		ROGUERS
EGLNSUU	UNGLUES	**EGNNPTU**	PUNGENT	**EGORRSW**	GROWERS
EGLOORS	REGOSOL	**EGNNRSU**	GUNNERS		REGROWS
EGLOOSY	GOOLEYS	**EGNNRUY**	GUNNERY	**EGORRTU**	GROUTER
EGLOPRS	PROLEGS	**EGNNSYY**	GYNNEYS	**EGORRUY**	ROGUERY
EGLOPSS	GOSPELS	**EGNNTUU**	UNGUENT	**EGORSSS**	GROSSES
EGLOPTU	GLUEPOT	**EGNOOPS**	PONGOES	**EGORSST**	GOSTERS
EGLORRW	GROWLER	**EGNOORS**	ORGONES		GROSETS
EGLORSS	GLOSSER		OROGENS		STORGES
	REGLOSS	**EGNOORY**	OROGENY	**EGORSSU**	GROUSES
EGLORSU	REGULOS	**EGNOOST**	GENTOOS	**EGORSTV**	GROVETS
EGLORSV	GLOVERS	**EGNOOSY**	GOONEYS	**EGORSUV**	VOGUERS
	GROVELS	**EGNOOTU**	OUTGONE	**EGORTUW**	OUTGREW
EGLORSW	GLOWERS	**EGNOOYZ**	ZOOGENY	**EGOSSTU**	GUSTOES
	REGLOWS	**EGNOPRS**	PRESONG	**EGOSSTY**	STOGEYS
EGLOSSS	GLOSSES		SPONGER	**EGOSSYZ**	ZYGOSES
EGLOSST	GOSLETS	**EGNOPRY**	PROGENY	**EGOSTTU**	GOUTTES
EGLOSUV	VOULGES		PYROGEN	**EGOSTYZ**	ZYGOTES
EGLPRSU	GULPERS	**EGNOPSS**	SPONGES	**EGPPRSY**	GYPPERS
	SPLURGE	**EGNOPSW**	GOWPENS	**EGPRRSU**	PURGERS
EGLPRUY	GYPLURE	**EGNORRW**	REGROWN	**EGPRSSU**	SPURGES
EGLRSTU	GURLETS		WRONGER	**EGPRSTY**	GYPSTER
EGLRSUU	REGULUS	**EGNORSS**	ENGROSS	**EGPRSUU**	UPSURGE
EGLRSUY	GUYLERS	**EGNORST**	TONGERS	**EGRRSSU**	SURGERS
EGLRSYY	GRYSELY	**EGNORSU**	SURGEON	**EGRRSUY**	SURGERY
EGLRTTU	GUTTLER	**EGNORSV**	GOVERNS	**EGRSSTU**	GUTSERS
EGLRUZZ	GUZZLER	**EGNORSY**	ERYNGOS	**EGRSSUY**	GYRUSES
EGLSSTU	GUTLESS		GROYNES	**EGRSTTU**	GUTTERS
	TUGLESS	**EGNORUY**	YOUNGER	**EGRSTUZ**	GUTZERS
EGLSTTU	GUTTLES	**EGNOSSY**	GONYSES	**EGRTTUY**	GUTTERY
EGLSTUU	GLUTEUS	**EGNOSTU**	TONGUES	**EGSSSTU**	GUSSETS
EGLSUZZ	GUZZLES	**EGNOSXY**	OXYGENS	**EHHIIMS**	HEIMISH
EGMMORT	GROMMET	**EGNPRSU**	REPUGNS	**EHHIKSS**	SHEIKHS
EGMMOSU	GUMMOSE	**EGNPSSU**	SPUNGES		SHIKSEH
EGMMRRU	GRUMMER	**EGNPSUX**	EXPUGNS	**EHHILLS**	HELLISH
EGMMRSU	GUMMERS	**EGNRRTU**	GRUNTER	**EHHINNS**	HENNISH
EGMMRTU	GRUMMET	**EGNRSTU**	GUNTERS	**EHHIPRS**	HERSHIP
EGMNNOS	SONGMEN		GURNETS	**EHHIPSY**	HYPHIES
EGMNNOT	TONGMEN		SURGENT	**EHHIRST**	HITHERS
EGMNNOW	GOWNMEN	**EGNRSUY**	GURNEYS	**EHHIRSU**	HUSHIER
EGMNOOS	MONGOES	**EGNRSYY**	SYNERGY	**EHHIRTT**	THITHER
EGMNORS	MONGERS	**EGNRTTU**	GRUTTEN	**EHHIRTW**	WHITHER
	MORGENS		TURGENT	**EHHISSW**	WHISHES
EGMNORU	MURGEON	**EGNSUVY**	UNGYVES	**EHHISWY**	WHEYISH
EGMNORY	MONGERY	**EGOOPRS**	POGOERS	**EHHNPSY**	HYPHENS
EGMNOST	EMONGST	**EGOOPSY**	POOGYES	**EHHOOSS**	HOOSHES
EGMNOSU	EUMONGS	**EGOORRV**	GROOVER	**EHHORTT**	THOTHER
	MUNGOES	**EGOORSV**	GROOVES	**EHHRSSU**	HUSHERS
EGMNOSY	MYOGENS	**EGOORSY**	GOOSERY		SHUSHER
EGMNOYZ	ZYMOGEN	**EGOORTU**	OUTGOER	**EHHSSSU**	SHUSHES
EGMNSTU	NUTMEGS	**EGOORTV**	OVERGOT	**EHIIIKT**	HEITIKI
EGMNSUU	EUMUNGS	**EGOOSST**	STOOGES	**EHIIKLP**	HIPLIKE
EGMOORR	GROOMER	**EGOOSSY**	GOOSEYS	**EHIIKNR**	HINKIER
	REGROOM	**EGOOSTU**	OUTGOES	**EHIILLR**	HILLIER
EGMOOSS	SMOOGES	**EGOPRRS**	GROPERS	**EHIILNP**	HIPLINE
EGMORST	GROMETS	**EGOPRRU**	GROUPER	**EHIILTT**	LITHITE
EGMORSU	GRUMOSE		REGROUP	**EHIIMSS**	MEISHIS
	MORGUES	**EGORRSS**	GROSERS	**EHIINNS**	HINNIES
EGMORTU	GOURMET		GROSSER	**EHIINRS**	SHINIER

EHIINRT	INHERIT	EHILMSU	HELIUMS	EHIMRST	HERMITS
EHIINRW	WHINIER		HUMLIES		MITHERS
EHIINRZ	RHIZINE		MUHLIES	EHIMRSU	HEURISM
EHIINSS	SHINIES	EHILMTT	MELTITH		MUSHIER
EHIIPPR	HIPPIER	EHILMUW	UMWHILE	EHIMRTT	THERMIT
EHIIPPS	HIPPIES	EHILNOP	PINHOLE	EHIMRTY	MYTHIER
	SHIPPIE	EHILNOT	HOTLINE		THYMIER
EHIIPRT	PITHIER		NEOLITH	EHIMSST	THEISMS
EHIIPTT	PITIETH	EHILNPS	PLENISH	EHIMSTU	HUMITES
EHIIRSS	HISSIER	EHILNSS	ELSHINS		TUMSHIE
EHIIRST	HIRSTIE	EHILNTY	ETHINYL	EHIMSTY	MYTHISE
EHIIRTW	WHITIER	EHILOOR	HOOLIER	EHIMSWY	WHIMSEY
	WITHIER	EHILOOS	HOOLIES	EHIMTYZ	MYTHIZE
EHIISSS	HISSIES	EHILOPT	HOPLITE	EHINNNS	HENNINS
EHIISST	STISHIE	EHILOSS	ISOHELS	EHINNRT	THINNER
EHIISTW	WHITIES	EHILOST	EOLITHS	EHINNSS	SHINNES
	WITHIES		HOLIEST	EHINNSW	WENNISH
EHIJNNO	JOHNNIE		HOSTILE	EHINNSY	SHINNEY
EHIKKRS	SHIKKER	EHILPRS	HIRPLES	EHINOPR	PHONIER
EHIKKSS	KISHKES	EHILPRT	PHILTER	EHINOPS	PHONIES
EHIKLRU	HULKIER		PHILTRE	EHINOPX	PHOENIX
EHIKLTU	HUTLIKE	EHILPSS	HIPLESS	EHINORR	HORNIER
EHIKLTY	LEKYTHI	EHILRRW	WHIRLER	EHINORS	HEROINS
EHIKMNT	METHINK	EHILRSS	HIRSELS		INSHORE
EHIKMSV	MIKVEHS		HIRSLES	EHINOST	ETHIONS
EHIKNOS	HONKIES	EHILRST	SLITHER		HISTONE
EHIKNRS	KERNISH	EHILRSU	HURLIES	EHINOSU	HEINOUS
EHIKNRT	RETHINK		LUSHIER	EHINPPS	HIPPENS
	THINKER	EHILRSV	SHRIVEL		SHIPPEN
EHIKNRU	HUNKIER	EHILRTU	LUTHIER	EHINPSS	HIPNESS
EHIKNSS	KNISHES	EHILRTW	WHIRTLE	EHINRSS	SHINERS
EHIKNSU	HUNKIES	EHILSSS	SLISHES		SHRINES
EHIKOOR	HOOKIER	EHILSST	HITLESS	EHINRST	HINTERS
EHIKOOS	HOOKIES		TEHSILS		NITHERS
EHIKOST	HOKIEST	EHILSTT	LISTETH	EHINRSV	SHRIVEN
EHIKPRS	KEPHIRS		LITHEST	EHINRSW	WHINERS
	PERKISH		THISTLE	EHINRTV	THRIVEN
EHIKRRS	SHIRKER	EHILSTV	THIVELS	EHINRTW	WRITHEN
EHIKRSS	SHREIKS	EHILSTW	WHISTLE	EHINRTZ	ZITHERN
	SHRIEKS	EHILTTU	THULITE	EHINSSS	SHINESS
	SHRIKES	EHILTTW	WHITTLE	EHINSST	SITHENS
EHIKRSU	HUSKIER	EHILTWY	WHITELY	EHINSTW	WHITENS
EHIKRSW	WHISKER	EHIMMRS	SHIMMER	EHINSTZ	ZENITHS
EHIKRSY	SHRIEKY	EHIMMSY	SHIMMEY	EHINSUV	UNHIVES
EHIKSSS	SHIKSES	EHIMNOS	HOMINES	EHINTUW	UNWHITE
EHIKSSU	HUSKIES	EHIMNPS	SHIPMEN	EHIOOPW	WHOOPIE
EHIKSTW	WHISKET	EHIMNRS	MENHIRS	EHIOORT	HOOTIER
EHIKSWY	WHISKEY	EHIMNRU	INHUMER	EHIOOST	TOOSHIE
EHILLMN	HILLMEN		RHENIUM	EHIOPPR	HOPPIER
EHILLNO	HELLION	EHIMNSU	INHUMES	EHIOPRS	ROSEHIP
EHILLNS	INSHELL	EHIMNTY	THYMINE	EHIOPSS	SOPHIES
EHILLOO	OILHOLE	EHIMORS	HEROISM	EHIOPST	ETHIOPS
EHILLOS	HILLOES		MOREISH		OPHITES
	HOLLIES	EHIMORT	MOITHER	EHIORRS	HORSIER
EHILLRS	HILLERS		MOTHIER	EHIORRT	HERITOR
	RELLISH	EHIMORZ	RHIZOME	EHIORSS	HOSIERS
EHILLRT	THILLER	EHIMOST	HOMIEST	EHIORST	HERIOTS
EHILLRU	HULLIER	EHIMPPX	PEMPHIX		HOISTER
EHILLTY	LITHELY	EHIMPRU	HUMPIER		SHORTIE
EHILMMO	MOHELIM	EHIMPRW	WHIMPER		TOSHIER
EHILMPW	WHIMPLE	EHIMPSU	HUMPIES	EHIORSU	HOUSIER

EHIORSW	SHOWIER	EHJORSS	JOSHERS	EHLOSTY	THYLOSE
EHIORSY	HOSIERY	EHKLNOR	ELKHORN	EHLOTXY	ETHOXYL
EHIORTT	THORITE	EHKLNOS	LOKSHEN	EHLPPSS	SHLEPPS
EHIORTU	OUTHIRE	EHKLOOT	HOOKLET	EHLPRSU	PLUSHER
	ROUTHIE	EHKLPST	KLEPHTS	EHLPSSU	PLUSHES
EHIORTV	OVERHIT	EHKMOOS	SMOKEHO	EHLRRSU	HURLERS
EHIOSST	HOSTIES	EHKMOSY	SKYHOME	EHLRSSU	LUSHERS
EHIOSTT	HOTTIES	EHKNORS	HONKERS	EHLRSTU	HURTLES
EHIOSTY	ISOHYET	EHKNOSY	HONKEYS		HUSTLER
EHIPPRS	PRESHIP	EHKNRSU	HUNKERS	EHLRSUY	HURLEYS
	SHIPPER	EHKNSSU	HUNKSES	EHLSSSU	SLUSHES
EHIPPRW	WHIPPER	EHKNSUY	HUNKEYS	EHLSSTT	SHTETLS
EHIPPST	HIPPEST	EHKOORS	HOOKERS	EHLSSTU	HUSTLES
EHIPPTW	WHIPPET	EHKOOSY	HOOKEYS		LUSHEST
EHIPRSS	PISHERS	EHKORSS	KOSHERS		SLEUTHS
	RESHIPS	EHKORSW	HOWKERS	EHLSTTU	SHUTTLE
	SERIPHS	EHKORSY	HORKEYS	EHMMRSU	HUMMERS
EHIPRST	HIPSTER	EHKOSSS	SKOSHES	EHMNNOO	NONHOME
EHIPRSU	PUSHIER	EHKRSSU	HUSKERS	EHMNOOR	HORMONE
EHIPRSW	WHISPER	EHKRSTU	TUSHKER		MOORHEN
EHIPSTT	PETTISH	EHLLNSU	UNSHELL	EHMNOPS	PHENOMS
EHIPSZZ	PHIZZES	EHLLOOS	HOLLOES		SHOPMEN
EHIRRRU	HURRIER	EHLLORS	HOLLERS	EHMNOST	MONETHS
EHIRRSS	SHERRIS	EHLLOSU	HULLOES	EHMNOSW	SHOWMEN
EHIRRSU	HURRIES	EHLLRSU	HULLERS	EHMNPSU	HUMPENS
	RUSHIER	EHLMMOW	WHOMMLE	EHMNPTY	NYMPHET
EHIRRSV	SHRIVER	EHLMMSU	HUMMELS	EHMNTTU	HUTMENT
EHIRRTV	THRIVER	EHLMMUW	WHUMMLE	EHMOOSS	SHMOOSE
EHIRRTW	WHERRIT	EHLMNOT	MENTHOL	EHMOOSW	SOMEHOW
	WHIRRET	EHLMNOY	HOMELYN	EHMOOSX	HOMOSEX
	WRITHER	EHLMNSU	UNHELMS	EHMOOSZ	SHMOOZE
EHIRSSS	HISSERS	EHLMOOS	HOLESOM	EHMOPRW	MORPHEW
EHIRSSV	SHIVERS	EHLMOPS	PHLOEMS	EHMORSS	MOSHERS
	SHRIVES	EHLMSSU	MULSHES	EHMORST	MOTHERS
EHIRSSW	SWISHER	EHLMSTY	METHYLS		SMOTHER
	WISHERS	EHLNOPS	PHENOLS		THERMOS
EHIRSTT	HITTERS	EHLNORT	HORNLET	EHMORTU	MOUTHER
	TITHERS	EHLNPSY	PHENYLS	EHMORTY	MOTHERY
EHIRSTU	HIRSUTE	EHLNRTU	LUTHERN	EHMOSWY	SOMEWHY
EHIRSTV	THRIVES	EHLNTTY	TENTHLY	EHMOTXY	METHOXY
EHIRSTW	SWITHER	EHLNTYY	ETHYNYL	EHMPRSU	HUMPERS
	WITHERS	EHLOOPT	POTHOLE	EHMPRTU	THUMPER
	WRITHES	EHLOOSS	SHOOLES	EHMRRSY	RHYMERS
EHIRSTZ	ZITHERS	EHLOOSY	HOOLEYS	EHMRRTU	MURTHER
EHIRSVY	SHIVERY	EHLOPPR	HOPPLER	EHMRSSU	MUSHERS
EHIRTTW	WHITRET	EHLOPPS	HOPPLES	EHMRSUU	HUMERUS
	WHITTER	EHLOPSX	PHLOXES	EHMRTUV	VERMUTH
EHIRWZZ	WHIZZER	EHLOPSY	SPYHOLE	EHMSSSU	SMUSHES
EHISSSU	HUSSIES	EHLORST	HOLSTER	EHMSSUU	HUMUSES
EHISSSW	SWISHES		HOSTLER	EHNNOOR	NONHERO
	WHISSES	EHLORSW	HOWLERS	EHNNOPR	NEPHRON
EHISSTT	THEISTS	EHLORTW	WHORTLE	EHNNOPY	HYPNONE
EHISSTU	STUSHIE	EHLORTY	HELOTRY	EHNNRSU	SHUNNER
	TUSHIES	EHLOSSS	SLOSHES	EHNNSTU	UNSHENT
EHISTTW	TEWHITS	EHLOSST	HOSTELS	EHNNSUW	UNSHEWN
	WETTISH	EHLOSSU	HOUSELS	EHNOORR	HONORER
	WHITEST	EHLOSSV	SHOVELS	EHNOORS	HEROONS
EHISTWY	WHITEYS	EHLOSTT	LOTHEST		ONSHORE
EHISUZZ	HUZZIES		SHOTTLE		SOREHON
EHISWZZ	WHIZZES	EHLOSTW	HOWLETS	EHNOPRS	PHONERS
EHJOPSS	JOSEPHS		THOWELS	EHNOPRY	HYPERON

EHNOPSU	EUPHONS	**EHORRSS**	SHORERS	**EIIKNPR**	PINKIER
EHNOPSY	PHONEYS	**EHORRST**	RHETORS	**EIIKNPS**	PINKIES
EHNOPUY	EUPHONY		ROTHERS	**EIIKNRS**	KEIRINS
EHNOPXY	PHENOXY		SHORTER		SINKIER
EHNORRS	HORNERS	**EHORRTW**	THROWER	**EIIKNRZ**	ZINKIER
EHNORRT	HORRENT	**EHORSST**	HORSTES	**EIIKNSS**	KINESIS
	NORTHER		TOSHERS	**EIIKNST**	INKIEST
EHNORRY	HERONRY	**EHORSSU**	HOUSERS	**EIIKNTW**	TWINKIE
EHNORSS	NOSHERS	**EHORSSV**	SHOVERS	**EIIKPRS**	SPIKIER
	SENHORS		SHROVES	**EIIKPSS**	PISKIES
EHNORST	HORNETS	**EHORSSW**	RESHOWS	**EIIKRRS**	RISKIER
	SHORTEN		SHOWERS	**EIIKRSS**	KISSIER
	THRENOS	**EHORSTT**	HOTTERS	**EIIKRSV**	SKIVIER
	THRONES	**EHORSTU**	SHOUTER	**EIIKSTT**	KITTIES
EHNORSU	UNHORSE		SOUTHER	**EIILLMM**	MILLIME
EHNORSW	RESHOWN	**EHORSTW**	THROWES	**EIILLMN**	MILLINE
EHNORSY	NOSHERY	**EHORSTX**	EXHORTS	**EIILLMR**	MILLIER
EHNOSST	HOTNESS	**EHORSWY**	SHOWERY	**EIILLMS**	MILLIES
EHNOSSU	UNSHOES	**EHORTUY**	OUTHYRE	**EIILLMT**	LIMELIT
EHNOSTT	SHOTTEN	**EHOSSST**	HOSTESS	**EIILLNV**	VILLEIN
EHNOSTY	HONESTY	**EHOSSSU**	SHOUSES	**EIILLPS**	ILLIPES
EHNOSUU	UNHOUSE	**EHOSSTT**	SHOTTES		PILLIES
EHNOTUY	YOUTHEN	**EHOSTTT**	HOTTEST	**EIILLRS**	SILLIER
EHNPRSY	PHRENSY	**EHOTTTW**	WOTTETH	**EIILLRT**	TILLIER
EHNRSTU	HUNTERS	**EHPRSSU**	PUSHERS	**EIILLSS**	SILLIES
	SHUNTER	**EHPRSSY**	SYPHERS	**EIILLST**	ILLITES
	UNHERST	**EHPRSYZ**	ZEPHYRS	**EIILLSW**	WILLIES
EHNRTWY	WRYTHEN	**EHPRTTU**	TURPETH	**EIILLTT**	LITTLIE
EHNSSSU	SNUSHES	**EHPRTUW**	UPTHREW		TILLITE
EHNSSSY	SHYNESS	**EHQRSSU**	QURSHES	**EIILLTV**	VITELLI
EHOOOPS	HOOPOES	**EHRRSSU**	RUSHERS	**EIILMNV**	MILVINE
EHOOPRS	HOOPERS	**EHRRSTU**	HURTERS	**EIILMPR**	IMPERIL
EHOOPRW	WHOOPER	**EHRSSTY**	SHYSTER	**EIILMPS**	IMPLIES
EHOOPTY	OOPHYTE		THYRSES	**EIILMPT**	LIMEPIT
EHOORST	HOOTERS	**EHRSTTU**	SHUTTER	**EIILMRR**	MIRLIER
	RESHOOT	**EHRSTTW**	STREWTH	**EIILMRS**	MILREIS
	SHEROOT	**EHRSTUW**	WUTHERS		SLIMIER
	SHOOTER	**EHRSTUY**	TUSHERY		SMILIER
	SOOTHER	**EHRTTTY**	THRETTY	**EIILMRT**	LIMITER
EHOORSV	HOOVERS	**EHSSSTU**	TUSSEHS		MILTIER
EHOORTV	OVERHOT	**EIIILRV**	RILIEVI	**EIILMSS**	MISLIES
EHOOSST	SOOTHES	**EIIILST**	ILEITIS		MISSILE
EHOOSSW	WOOSHES	**EIIINPR**	RIPIENI		SIMILES
EHOPPRS	HOPPERS	**EIIJMMS**	JIMMIES	**EIILMST**	ELITISM
	SHOPPER	**EIIJMPR**	JIMPIER		LIMIEST
EHOPPRT	PROPHET	**EIIJSTV**	JIVIEST		LIMITES
EHOPPRW	WHOPPER	**EIIKKLN**	INKLIKE	**EIILMSU**	MILIEUS
EHOPPSS	SHOPPES	**EIIKKNR**	KINKIER	**EIILMSV**	MISLIVE
EHOPRRY	ORPHREY	**EIIKKLP**	LIPLIKE	**EIILMUX**	MILIEUX
EHOPRST	POTHERS	**EIIKLLS**	KILLIES	**EIILNNS**	LINNIES
	STROPHE	**EIIKLMR**	MILKIER	**EIILNOR**	NOILIER
	THORPES	**EIIKLMS**	MISLIKE	**EIILNOS**	ELISION
EHOPRSU	UPHROES	**EIIKLNR**	LINKIER		ISOLINE
EHOPRSW	PRESHOW	**EIIKLNT**	TINLIKE		LIONISE
EHOPRSY	PHORESY	**EIIKLPS**	PLISKIE	**EIILNOT**	ETIOLIN
EHOPRTU	POUTHER	**EIIKLRS**	SILKIER	**EIILNOV**	OLIVINE
EHOPRTY	POTHERY	**EIIKLSS**	SILKIES	**EIILNOZ**	LIONIZE
EHOPRUY	EUPHORY	**EIIKLST**	KILTIES	**EIILNPS**	SPLENII
EHOPSSS	SPOSHES	**EIIKLVY**	IVYLIKE	**EIILNRR**	NIRLIER
EHOPSST	POSHEST	**EIIKMRR**	MIRKIER	**EIILNRS**	INLIERS
EHOPSTY	TYPHOSE	**EIIKNNT**	KINETIN		RESILIN

EIILNRT	LINTIER	EIINNNP	NINEPIN	EIIPPRZ	ZIPPIER
	NITRILE	EIINNNS	NINNIES	EIIPPST	PIPIEST
EIILNSS	INISLES	EIINNOS	INOSINE	EIIPPSY	YIPPIES
EIILNST	LINIEST	EIINNPS	PINNIES	EIIPRRS	SPIRIER
	LINTIES	EIINNQU	QUININE	EIIPRRT	TRIPIER
EIILNTT	INTITLE	EIINNRT	TINNIER	EIIPRRV	PRIVIER
EIILNTU	INUTILE	EIINNST	INTINES	EIIPRST	PITIERS
EIILOPR	LIRIOPE		TINNIES		TIPSIER
EIILORR	ROILIER	EIINNSW	INSINEW	EIIPRSV	PRIVIES
EIILORS	SOILIER	EIINNTV	INVENIT	EIIPRSW	SWIPIER
EIILORV	RILIEVO	EIINNTW	INTWINE		WISPIER
EIILOST	IOLITES	EIINOPR	RIPIENO	EIIPSTT	PIETIST
	OILIEST	EIINOPS	PIONIES	EIIPTTT	PITTITE
EIILPPR	LIPPIER		SINOPIE	EIIPTTU	PITUITE
EIILPPS	LIPPIES	EIINORR	IRONIER	EIIRRTZ	RITZIER
EIILPST	SPILITE	EIINORS	IONISER	EIIRSSS	SISSIER
EIILQSU	SILIQUE		IRONIES	EIIRSSV	VISIERS
EIILRST	RILIEST		IRONISE	EIIRSTV	REVISIT
	SILTIER		NOISIER		STIVIER
EIILRSV	LIVIERS	EIINORZ	IONIZER		VISITER
EIILRSX	ELIXIRS		IRONIZE	EIIRSTW	WIRIEST
EIILSSV	VISILES	EIINOSS	IONISES	EIIRSVZ	VIZIERS
EIILSTT	ELITIST	EIINOST	INOSITE	EIIRSWZ	WIZIERS
EIILSTU	UTILISE	EIINOSZ	IONIZES	EIIRTTW	WITTIER
EIILSTW	WILIEST	EIINPPR	NIPPIER	EIISSSS	SISSIES
EIILSZZ	LIZZIES	EIINPRS	INSPIRE	EIISSTV	VISITES
EIILTUY	TUILYIE		PIRNIES	EIISSTX	SIXTIES
EIILTUZ	TUILZIE		SNIPIER	EIISSTZ	SIZEIST
	UTILIZE		SPINIER		SIZIEST
EIILTXY	EXILITY	EIINPST	PINIEST	EIISTTT	TITTIES
EIIMMRS	MIMSIER		PINITES	EIISTUV	UVEITIS
EIIMMSS	MIMESIS		TIEPINS	EIISTZZ	TIZZIES
EIIMMST	MISTIME	EIINPTT	PENTITI	EIISVZZ	VIZZIES
EIIMMSX	IMMIXES	EIINQRU	INQUIRE	EIJKKSU	JUKSKEI
EIIMNNS	MINNIES	EIINQSU	QUINIES	EIJKLRY	JERKILY
EIIMNPR	PRIMINE	EIINQTU	INQUIET	EIJKNPR	PERJINK
EIIMNRT	INTERIM	EIINRTT	NITRITE		PREJINK
	MINTIER		NITTIER	EIJKNRS	JERKINS
	TERMINI		TINTIER		JINKERS
EIIMNRV	MINIVER	EIINRTV	INVITER	EIJKNRU	JUNKIER
EIIMNST	MINIEST		VITRINE	EIJKNSU	JUNKIES
EIIMNTV	MINIVET	EIINRTW	TWINIER	EIJKOST	JOKIEST
EIIMNTY	NIMIETY	EIINSSS	SEISINS	EIJLLNY	INJELLY
EIIMOSS	MEIOSIS	EIINSSZ	SEIZINS	EIJLLOR	JOLLIER
EIIMPRS	PISMIRE	EIINSTT	SITTINE	EIJLLOS	JOLLIES
	PRIMSIE		TINIEST	EIJLLST	JILLETS
EIIMPRW	WIMPIER	EIINSTU	UNITIES	EIJLORT	JOLTIER
EIIMPST	PIETISM		UNITISE	EIJLORW	JOWLIER
EIIMPTY	IMPIETY	EIINSTV	INVITES	EIJLRST	JILTERS
EIIMRSS	MERISIS		VINIEST	EIJLSTU	JULIETS
	MISSIER	EIINSTW	WINIEST	EIJMPRU	JUMPIER
EIIMRST	MIRIEST	EIINSUZ	UNISIZE	EIJMPST	JIMPEST
	MISTIER	EIINTUV	UNITIVE	EIJNNOS	ENJOINS
	RIMIEST	EIINTUZ	UNITIZE	EIJNORS	JOINERS
EIIMSSS	MISSIES	EIIORST	RIOTISE		REJOINS
EIIMSST	MITISES	EIIORSV	IVORIES	EIJNORT	JOINTER
	STIMIES	EIIORTZ	RIOTIZE	EIJNORY	JOINERY
EIIMSSV	MISSIVE	EIIOSTZ	ZOISITE	EIJNOST	JONTIES
EIIMSSZ	SIZEISM	EIIPPPR	PIPPIER	EIJNPRU	JUNIPER
EIIMSTT	MITIEST	EIIPPRR	RIPPIER	EIJNRRU	INJURER
EIIMSTX	MIXIEST	EIIPPRT	TIPPIER	EIJNRSU	INJURES

EIJNSTY	JITNEYS	**EIKLPST**	SKELPIT		STINKER
EIJNTTW	TWINJET	**EIKLPSU**	PUSLIKE		TINKERS
EIJOPST	POTJIES	**EIKLPSY**	PESKILY	**EIKNRSW**	SWINKER
EIJORTT	JOTTIER	**EIKLRST**	KILTERS		WINKERS
EIJRSTT	JITTERS		KIRTLES	**EIKNRTT**	KNITTER
	TRIJETS		KLISTER		TRINKET
EIJRTTY	JITTERY	**EIKLRSU**	SULKIER	**EIKNSSU**	SUNKIES
EIJSSTU	JESUITS	**EIKLRTT**	KITTLER	**EIKNSTT**	KITTENS
EIJSSUV	JUSSIVE	**EIKLSSS**	KISSELS	**EIKNTTY**	KITTENY
EIJSTTU	JUTTIES	**EIKLSSU**	SULKIES	**EIKNTUZ**	KUNZITE
EIKKLNR	KLINKER	**EIKLSTT**	KITTELS	**EIKOORR**	ROOKIER
EIKKLNS	KINKLES		KITTLES	**EIKOORS**	KOORIES
EIKKLSY	KYLIKES		SKITTLE		ROOKIES
	SKYLIKE	**EIKMMRR**	KRIMMER	**EIKOOST**	STOOKIE
EIKKMNR	KIRKMEN	**EIKMMRS**	KIMMERS	**EIKOPPR**	PORKPIE
EIKKNRS	SKINKER		SKIMMER	**EIKOPPS**	KOPPIES
EIKKOOR	KOOKIER	**EIKMNNS**	KINSMEN	**EIKOPRR**	PORKIER
EIKKRSS	SKRIKES	**EIKMNOR**	MONIKER	**EIKOPRS**	PORKIES
EIKKRSY	YIKKERS	**EIKMNRS**	MERKINS	**EIKOPST**	POKIEST
EIKKRUY	YUKKIER	**EIKMNSS**	MISKENS	**EIKORST**	ROKIEST
EIKLLNW	INKWELL	**EIKMNST**	MISKENT	**EIKORSY**	YORKIES
EIKLLOS	SKOLLIE	**EIKMNSW**	MISKNEW	**EIKOSST**	KETOSIS
EIKLLOW	OWLLIKE	**EIKMORS**	IRKSOME	**EIKPPRS**	KIPPERS
EIKLLRS	KILLERS		SMOKIER		SKIPPER
	RESKILL	**EIKMOSS**	SMOKIES	**EIKPPST**	SKIPPET
	SKILKILL	**EIKMOSY**	MISYOKE	**EIKPRSS**	SPIKERS
EIKLLST	SKILLET	**EIKMPST**	MISKEPT	**EIKPRSY**	SPIKERY
EIKLMMN	MILKMEN	**EIKMPSU**	MUSPIKE	**EIKPSSS**	SKEPSIS
EIKLMNN	LINKMEN	**EIKMRRS**	SMIRKER	**EIKPSTU**	PUKIEST
EIKLMNR	KREMLIN	**EIKMRRU**	MURKIER	**EIKRRSS**	RISKERS
EIKLMRS	MILKERS	**EIKMRSS**	KIRMESS	**EIKRRST**	SKIRRET
EIKLNNS	ENLINKS	**EIKMRST**	MIRKEST		SKIRTER
EIKLNNU	NUNLIKE	**EIKMRSU**	MUSKIER		STRIKER
EIKLNOS	SONLIKE	**EIKMSST**	KISMETS	**EIKRSSS**	KISSERS
EIKLNPR	PLINKER	**EIKMSSU**	MUSKIES	**EIKRSST**	STRIKES
EIKLNRS	LINKERS	**EIKMSSY**	MISKEYS	**EIKRSSV**	SKIVERS
	RELINKS	**EIKMSTU**	KUMITES	**EIKRSTT**	SKITTER
	SLINKER		MISTEUK	**EIKRSTU**	TURKIES
EIKLNRT	TINKLER	**EIKNNOR**	EINKORN		TUSKIER
EIKLNRU	URNLIKE	**EIKNNOS**	KINONES	**EIKSSTT**	KITSETS
EIKLNRW	WINKLER	**EIKNNPS**	PINKENS	**EIKSSTW**	WESKITS
	WRINKLE	**EIKNNRS**	SKINNER		WISKETS
EIKLNSS	INKLESS	**EIKNOOR**	NOOKIER	**EIKSSTY**	SKYIEST
	KINLESS		ROOINEK	**EIKSTUY**	YUKIEST
	SILKENS	**EIKNOOS**	NOOKIES	**EILLLOS**	LOLLIES
EIKLNST	LENTISK	**EIKNOPS**	PINKOES	**EILLMNU**	MULLEIN
	TINKLES	**EIKNORV**	INVOKER	**EILLMOS**	MOLLIES
EIKLNSU	SUNLIKE	**EIKNORW**	WONKIER	**EILLMOT**	MELILOT
	UNLIKES	**EIKNOSS**	KENOSIS	**EILLMOU**	MOUILLE
EIKLNSV	KELVINS	**EIKNOSV**	INVOKES	**EILLMRS**	MILLERS
EIKLNSW	WELKINS	**EIKNPRR**	PRINKER	**EILLMSS**	MISSELL
	WINKLES	**EIKNPRS**	PERKINS	**EILLMST**	MILLETS
EIKLNSY	SKYLINE		PINKERS		MISTELL
EIKLNTT	KNITTLE	**EIKNPRU**	PUNKIER	**EILLMSU**	ILLUMES
EIKLNTU	NUTLIKE	**EIKNPST**	PINKEST	**EILLMTU**	MULLITE
EIKLNTW	TWINKLE	**EIKNPSU**	PUNKIES	**EILLNNP**	PENNILL
EIKLOOP	PLOOKIE		SPUNKIE	**EILLNOS**	LIONELS
EIKLOPT	POTLIKE	**EIKNPSY**	PINKEYS		NIELLOS
EIKLOPU	PLOUKIE	**EIKNRSS**	SINKERS	**EILLNSS**	ILLNESS
EIKLORY	YOLKIER	**EIKNRST**	REKNITS	**EILLNST**	LENTILS
EIKLOTY	TOYLIKE		SKINTER		LINTELS
EIKLPRY	PERKILY				

	TELLINS	
EILLNUV	LEVULIN	
EILLOPS	POLLIES	
EILLORU	ROUILLE	
EILLORW	LOWLIER	
EILLORZ	ZORILLE	
EILLOST	OILLETS	
	STELLIO	
	TOLLIES	
EILLOSV	VILLOSE	
EILLOSW	WOLLIES	
EILLPPR	PREPILL	
EILLPRS	SPILLER	
EILLPSS	LIPLESS	
EILLPSU	PILULES	
EILLQTU	QUILLET	
EILLRRT	TRILLER	
EILLRSS	SILLERS	
EILLRST	RILLETS	
	STILLER	
	TILLERS	
	TRELLIS	
EILLRSW	SWILLER	
	WILLERS	
EILLRTT	LITTLER	
EILLSST	LISTELS	
EILLSSU	SULLIES	
EILLSTT	LITTLES	
EILLSTU	TUILLES	
EILLSTW	WILLEST	
	WILLETS	
EILLSWY	WILLEYS	
EILMMNO	MOLIMEN	
EILMMRS	LIMMERS	
	SLIMMER	
EILMMRU	LUMMIER	
EILMNOO	OINOMEL	
EILMNOS	LOMEINS	
	MOLINES	
EILMNOT	MOLINET	
EILMNPS	PLENISM	
EILMNRS	LIMNERS	
	MERLINS	
EILMNSS	SIMNELS	
EILMNSU	EMULSIN	
	LUMINES	
	UNLIMES	
EILMNSY	MYELINS	
EILMOOS	MOOLIES	
EILMOOV	MOOLVIE	
EILMOPR	IMPLORE	
EILMORR	LORIMER	
EILMORS	MOILERS	
EILMORT	MOTLIER	
EILMOSS	LIMOSES	
	LISSOME	
	SMOILES	
EILMOST	MOTILES	
EILMPPS	PIMPLES	
EILMPPU	PLUMPIE	
EILMPRS	LIMPERS	

	PRELIMS	
	RIMPLES	
	SIMPLER	
EILMPRU	LUMPIER	
	PLUMIER	
EILMPRY	PRIMELY	
EILMPSS	SIMPLES	
EILMPST	LIMPEST	
	LIMPETS	
EILMPSU	IMPULSE	
EILMPSW	WIMPLES	
EILMPSX	SIMPLEX	
EILMPSY	LIMPSEY	
EILMPTY	EMPTILY	
EILMRRU	MURLIER	
EILMRRY	MERRILY	
EILMRSS	RIMLESS	
	SMILERS	
EILMRST	MILTERS	
EILMRSU	MISRULE	
EILMRSV	VERMILS	
EILMRSY	MISERLY	
	MISRELY	
EILMRTY	LYMITER	
EILMRVY	VERMILY	
EILMSSS	MISSELS	
EILMSST	MISTLES	
	SMILETS	
EILMSSU	MUESLIS	
EILMSSY	MESSILY	
	MILSEYS	
	SMILEYS	
EILMSTT	SMITTLE	
EILMSTZ	MILTZES	
EILMSZZ	MIZZLES	
EILMUUV	ELUVIUM	
EILNNOR	ONLINER	
EILNNPU	PINNULE	
EILNNRY	INNERLY	
EILNNSS	INNLESS	
EILNNST	LINNETS	
EILNNSU	UNLINES	
EILNNSW	WINNLES	
EILNNSY	LINNEYS	
EILNOOP	POLONIE	
EILNOOR	LOONIER	
EILNOOS	LOONIES	
EILNOOV	VIOLONE	
EILNOPP	PLENIPO	
EILNOPR	PLERION	
	PROLINE	
EILNOPS	EPSILON	
	PINOLES	
EILNOPT	POINTEL	
	PONTILE	
	POTLINE	
	TOPLINE	
EILNORR	LORINER	
EILNORS	NEROLIS	
EILNORT	RETINOL	
EILNOSS	ESLOINS	

	INSOLES	
	LESIONS	
	LIONESS	
EILNOST	ENTOILS	
	LIONETS	
	ONLIEST	
EILNOSU	ELUSION	
EILNOTU	ELUTION	
	OUTLINE	
EILNOTV	VIOLENT	
EILNOTW	TOWLINE	
EILNOVV	INVOLVE	
EILNPPS	LIPPENS	
	NIPPLES	
EILNPRS	PILSNER	
EILNPRU	PURLINE	
EILNPSS	PENSILS	
	SPINELS	
	SPLINES	
EILNPST	LEPTINS	
	PINTLES	
	PLENIST	
EILNPSU	LINEUPS	
	LUPINES	
	SPINULE	
	UNPILES	
EILNPTY	INEPTLY	
EILNPUV	VULPINE	
EILNRST	LINTERS	
	SLINTER	
	SNIRTLE	
EILNRSV	SILVERN	
EILNRTY	INERTLY	
EILNRVY	NERVILY	
EILNSSS	SINLESS	
EILNSST	ENLISTS	
	LISTENS	
	SILENTS	
	TINSELS	
EILNSSU	INSULSE	
	SILENUS	
EILNSSV	SNIVELS	
EILNSSW	WINLESS	
EILNSSY	LINSEYS	
	LYSINES	
EILNSTU	LUNIEST	
	LUTEINS	
	UNTILES	
	UTENSIL	
EILNSTV	VENTILS	
EILNSTW	WESTLIN	
	WINTLES	
EILNSUV	UNLIVES	
	UNVEILS	
EILNSUX	LINUXES	
EILNSUY	LUNYIES	
EILNSVY	SYLVINE	
EILNVXY	VIXENLY	
EILOOPR	LOOPIER	
EILOORS	ORIOLES	
EILOORT	TROOLIE	

EILOORW	WOOLIER	EILPPST	STIPPLE		TITULES
EILOOSS	LOOSIES		TIPPLES	EILSTTV	VITTLES
EILOOST	OOLITES	EILPPSU	PILEUPS	EILSTTY	STYLITE
	OSTIOLE		UPPILES		TESTILY
	STOOLIE	EILPPSW	SWIPPLE	EILSTVY	SYLVITE
	TOOLIES	EILPRSS	LISPERS	EILSTYZ	STYLIZE
EILOOSW	WOOLIES	EILPRST	RESPLIT		ZESTILY
EILOOTZ	ZOOLITE		SPIRTLE	EILSUVV	LUVVIES
EILOPPR	LOPPIER		TRIPLES	EILSWZZ	SWIZZLE
EILOPPS	LOPPIES	EILPRTT	TRIPLET	EILSZZZ	ZIZZLES
EILOPPZ	ZEPPOLI	EILPRTX	TRIPLEX	EILTWZZ	TWIZZLE
EILOPRS	SLOPIER	EILPRUU	PURLIEU	EIMMMOS	MOMMIES
	SPOILER	EILPSSS	PLISSES	EIMMMST	MIMMEST
EILOPRT	POITREL	EILPSST	STIPELS	EIMMMSU	MUMMIES
	POLITER		TIPLESS	EIMMNRS	NIMMERS
EILOPSS	POLISES	EILPSSW	SWIPLES	EIMMNSU	IMMUNES
EILOPST	PIOLETS	EILPSSZ	ZIPLESS	EIMMOPS	POMMIES
	PISTOLE	EILPSTT	SPITTLE	EIMMORS	MEMOIRS
EILOPSU	PILEOUS	EILPSTU	PULIEST	EIMMOST	TOMMIES
EILOPSV	PLOSIVE		PUTELIS	EIMMOSV	MISMOVE
EILOPTT	PLOTTIE		STIPULE	EIMMPRR	PRIMMER
EILOPTX	EXPLOIT	EILPSUY	SPULYIE	EIMMPRU	PREMIUM
EILORRS	LORRIES	EILPSUZ	SPULZIE	EIMMRRS	RIMMERS
EILORRU	LOURIER	EILPSZZ	PIZZLES	EIMMRRT	TRIMMER
EILORSS	LORISES	EILPTTY	PETTILY	EIMMRRU	RUMMIER
	LOSSIER	EILQRTU	QUILTER	EIMMRSS	MERISMS
	RISSOLE	EILQRUU	LIQUEUR		SIMMERS
EILORST	ESTRIOL	EILQTUY	QUIETLY	EIMMRST	MISTERM
	LOITERS	EILRRSU	LURRIES	EIMMRSU	IMMURES
	TOILERS		SURLIER		MUMSIER
EILORSU	LOURIES	EILRRTW	TWIRLER		RUMMIES
	LOUSIER	EILRSST	LISTERS	EIMMRSW	SWIMMER
	SOILURE		RELISTS	EIMMRUY	YUMMIER
EILORSV	OLIVERS	EILRSSV	SILVERS	EIMMSST	SEMMITS
	VIOLERS		SLIVERS		TSIMMES
EILORSW	LOWRIES	EILRSSW	SWILERS	EIMMSTU	TUMMIES
EILORTT	TORTILE	EILRSTT	LITTERS	EIMMSTZ	TZIMMES
	TRIOLET		SLITTER	EIMMSUY	YUMMIES
EILORTU	OUTLIER		TESTRIL	EIMNNOR	IRONMEN
EILORTV	OVERLIT		TILTERS	EIMNNOT	MENTION
EILOSSV	SOLIVES		TITLERS	EIMNOOR	IONOMER
EILOSTT	LITOTES	EILRSTU	LUSTIER		MOONIER
	TOILETS		RULIEST	EIMNOOS	ISONOME
EILOSTU	OUTLIES		RUTILES		MOONIES
EILOSTV	OLIVETS	EILRSTY	STYLIER		NOISOME
	VIOLETS	EILRSUV	SURVEIL	EIMNOOT	EMOTION
EILOSTW	OWLIEST	EILRSUW	WURLIES	EIMNOOX	EXOMION
EILOSTZ	ZLOTIES	EILRSVY	LIVYERS	EIMNOPR	PROMINE
EILOTUV	OUTLIVE		SILVERY	EIMNOPS	IMPONES
EILOTUW	OUTWILE	EILRSZZ	SIZZLER		PEONISM
EILPPPY	PEPPILY	EILRTTY	LITTERY	EIMNOPT	EMPTION
EILPPRR	RIPPLER		TRITELY		PIMENTO
EILPPRS	LIPPERS	EILRTUV	RIVULET	EIMNORS	MERINOS
	RIPPLES	EILSSTT	STILETS		MERSION
	SLIPPER	EILSSTW	WITLESS	EIMNOSS	EONISMS
EILPPRT	RIPPLET	EILSSTY	STYLISE	EIMNOST	MESTINO
	TIPPLER	EILSSVW	SWIVELS		MOISTEN
	TRIPPLE	EILSSZZ	SIZZLES		MONTIES
EILPPRU	PULPIER	EILSTTT	TITTLES		SENTIMO
EILPPSS	PIPLESS	EILSTTU	LUTITES	EIMNOSW	WINSOME
	SIPPLES			EIMNOTY	OMNEITY

	OMNIETY	**EIMORSV**	VERISMO	**EIMSSST**	MISSETS
EIMNPSS	MISPENS	**EIMORTT**	MOTTIER	**EIMSSSU**	MISUSES
EIMNPST	EMPTINS		OMITTER	**EIMSSSX**	SEXISMS
	PIMENTS	**EIMORTV**	VOMITER	**EIMSSTY**	STYMIES
EIMNPTU	PINETUM	**EIMORVX**	OVERMIX	**EIMSTYZ**	ZYMITES
EIMNQSU	MESQUIN	**EIMOSSS**	MOSSIES	**EIMUUVX**	EXUVIUM
EIMNRRU	MURRINE	**EIMOSST**	MITOSES	**EINNNOS**	NONNIES
EIMNRST	ENTRISM		SOMITES	**EINNNRS**	RENNINS
	MINSTER	**EIMOSSU**	MOUSIES	**EINNOOS**	IONONES
	MINTERS	**EIMOSTT**	MOTIEST	**EINNOPS**	PENSION
	REMINTS		MOTTIES		PINONES
EIMNRSU	MUREINS		TITMOSE		SPINONE
	MURINES	**EIMOSTU**	TIMEOUS	**EINNOPT**	PONTINE
	NEURISM	**EIMOSTV**	MOTIVES	**EINNOQU**	QUINONE
EIMNRSV	VERMINS	**EIMOSTX**	EXOTISM	**EINNORS**	RONNIES
EIMNRTU	MINUTER	**EIMOSTZ**	MESTIZO	**EINNORT**	INTONER
	MUNTRIE	**EIMOSYZ**	ISOZYME		NOINTER
	UNMITER	**EIMOSZZ**	MOZZIES		TERNION
	UNMITRE	**EIMOTTU**	TIMEOUT	**EINNORU**	NOUNIER
EIMNRVY	VERMINY	**EIMPRRS**	PRIMERS		REUNION
EIMNSSS	SENSISM	**EIMPRRT**	PRETRIM	**EINNORV**	ENVIRON
EIMNSST	MISSENT	**EIMPRRU**	IMPURER	**EINNOSS**	SONNIES
EIMNSSU	MINUSES		PRIMEUR	**EINNOST**	INTONES
EIMNSTT	MITTENS	**EIMPRSS**	IMPRESS		TENSION
	SMITTEN		PREMISS	**EINNOSV**	VENISON
EIMNSTU	MINUETS		SIMPERS	**EINNOSY**	YONNIES
	MINUTES		SPIREMS	**EINNOTT**	NONETTI
	MISTUNE	**EIMPRST**	IMPREST		TONTINE
	MUNITES		PERMITS	**EINNOVW**	INWOVEN
	MUTINES	**EIMPRSU**	RUMPIES	**EINNPRS**	PINNERS
EIMNSTW	MISWENT		SPUMIER		SPINNER
EIMNSUX	UNMIXES		UMPIRES	**EINNPRT**	ENPRINT
EIMNSZZ	MIZZENS	**EIMPRTU**	IMPUTER	**EINNPRU**	PUNNIER
EIMNUZZ	MUEZZIN		TUMPIER	**EINNPST**	PINNETS
EIMOORR	MOORIER	**EIMPRTX**	PREMIXT		SPINNET
	ROOMIER	**EIMPSST**	MISSTEP		TENPINS
EIMOORS	ROOMIES	**EIMPSSU**	SEPIUMS	**EINNPSY**	SPINNEY
EIMOPPR	MOPPIER	**EIMPSTU**	IMPETUS	**EINNRRU**	RUNNIER
	POMPIER		IMPUTES	**EINNRSS**	SINNERS
EIMOPRR	PRIMERO		UPTIMES	**EINNRST**	INTERNS
EIMOPRS	IMPOSER	**EIMPSTY**	MISTYPE		TINNERS
	PROMISE	**EIMPSUY**	YUMPIES	**EINNRSU**	SUNNIER
	SEMIPRO	**EIMQSTU**	MESQUIT		UNREINS
EIMOPRV	IMPROVE	**EIMQTUZ**	MEZQUIT		UNRISEN
EIMOPRW	IMPOWER	**EIMRRST**	RETRIMS	**EINNRSW**	WINNERS
EIMOPSS	IMPOSES		TRIMERS	**EINNRTV**	VINTNER
	MOPSIES	**EIMRRSU**	MURRIES	**EINNRUV**	UNRIVEN
EIMOPST	MOPIEST	**EIMRSST**	MISTERS	**EINNSST**	SENNITS
	OPTIMES		SMITERS		SINNETS
	STOMPIE	**EIMRSSU**	MISUSER	**EINNSSU**	SUNNIES
EIMOPSX	IMPOSEX		MUSSIER	**EINNSSY**	SINSYNE
EIMOPSY	MYOPIES		SURMISE	**EINNSTT**	INTENTS
EIMORRW	WORMIER	**EIMRSSV**	VERISMS		TENNIST
EIMORSS	ISOMERS	**EIMRSTT**	METRIST	**EINNSTU**	TUNNIES
	MOISERS	**EIMRSTU**	MUSTIER	**EINNSTV**	INVENTS
	MOSSIER	**EIMRSTY**	MISTERY	**EINNSUW**	UNSINEW
EIMORST	EROTISM		SMYTRIE	**EINNSWY**	SWINNEY
	MOISTER	**EIMRTTU**	TERTIUM	**EINNTUW**	UNTWINE
	MORTISE	**EIMRTUV**	VITREUM	**EINOOPZ**	EPIZOON
	TRISOME	**EIMRTUX**	MIXTURE	**EINOORS**	EROSION
EIMORSU	MOUSIER	**EIMRUZZ**	MUZZIER	**EINOOST**	ISOTONE

	TOONIES		TONITES	**EINRSTW**	TWINERS
EINOOSZ	OZONISE	**EINOSTW**	TOWNIES		WINTERS
EINOOTW	TWOONIE		TWONIES	**EINRSTY**	SINTERY
EINOOTZ	ZOONITE	**EINOSTX**	TOXINES	**EINRSUW**	UNWIRES
EINOOZZ	OZONIZE	**EINOSUV**	ENVIOUS		UNWISER
EINOPPR	POPERIN		NIVEOUS	**EINRSVW**	WIVERNS
	PROPINE		VEINOUS	**EINRSWY**	SWINERY
EINOPPS	PEPINOS	**EINOTTT**	TOTIENT	**EINRTTU**	NUTTIER
EINOPRR	PORNIER	**EINPPRS**	NIPPERS	**EINRTTW**	TWINTER
EINOPRS	ORPINES		SNIPPER		WRITTEN
	PIONERS	**EINPPSS**	PEPSINS	**EINRTUV**	UNRIVET
	PROINES	**EINPPST**	SNIPPET		VENTURI
EINOPRT	POINTER	**EINPPSW**	WIPPENS	**EINRTUW**	UNWRITE
	PROTEIN	**EINPRRT**	PRINTER	**EINRTWY**	WINTERY
	PTERION		REPRINT	**EINSSST**	SENSIST
	REPOINT	**EINPRRU**	UNRIPER	**EINSSSU**	SINUSES
	TROPINE	**EINPRSS**	SNIPERS	**EINSSSY**	SYNESIS
EINOPRV	PROVINE	**EINPRST**	NIPTERS	**EINSSTU**	INTUSES
EINOPSS	SPINOSE		PTERINS	**EINSSTV**	INVESTS
EINOPST	PINTOES	**EINPRSU**	PRUINES	**EINSSTW**	WISENTS
	POINTES		PURINES		WITNESS
	PONTIES		UPRISEN	**EINSSTY**	TINSEYS
EINOPSW	POWNIES	**EINPRTU**	REPUNIT	**EINSSUW**	SUNWISE
	WINESOP	**EINPSST**	INSTEPS	**EINSSWY**	WINSEYS
EINOPSY	PIONEYS		SPINETS	**EINSTTU**	TUNIEST
EINOPTT	PENTITO	**EINPSSU**	PUISNES	**EINSTTW**	ENTWIST
EINOPTU	POUTINE		SUPINES		TWINSET
EINOQUX	EQUINOX	**EINPSTT**	SPITTEN	**EINSTTY**	TENSITY
EINORRS	IRONERS	**EINPSTU**	PUNIEST	**EINSTWY**	WITNEYS
	ROSINER		PUNTIES	**EINSUVW**	UNWIVES
EINORSS	ORNISES	**EINPSTW**	INSWEPT	**EINSWZZ**	WIZZENS
	SENIORS	**EINPTTY**	TINTYPE	**EINTTTW**	TWITTEN
	SONERIS	**EINQRSU**	REQUINS	**EINTTUY**	TENUITY
	SONSIER	**EINQRUU**	UNIQUER	**EIOOPRR**	ROOPIER
EINORST	NORITES	**EINQRUY**	ENQUIRY	**EIOOPRV**	POOVIER
	OESTRIN	**EINQSSU**	SEQUINS	**EIOOPST**	ISOTOPE
	ORIENTS	**EINQSTU**	INQUEST	**EIOOPSW**	WOOPIES
	STONIER		QUINTES	**EIOORRT**	ROOTIER
	TERSION	**EINQSUU**	UNIQUES	**EIOORST**	OORIEST
	TRIONES	**EINQSUZ**	QUINZES		ROOTIES
EINORSU	URINOSE	**EINQTTU**	QUINTET		SOOTIER
EINORSV	ENVIROS	**EINQTUU**	UNQUIET		TOORIES
	RENVOIS	**EINRRSS**	RINSERS	**EIOORTZ**	ZOOTIER
	VERSION	**EINRRSU**	INSURER	**EIOORWZ**	WOOZIER
EINORSW	SNOWIER		RUINERS	**EIOOSST**	OOSIEST
EINORSX	OREXINS	**EINRRTU**	RUNTIER	**EIOOSTT**	TOOTSIE
EINORTT	TRITONE	**EINRSST**	ESTRINS	**EIOOSTZ**	OOZIEST
EINORTU	ROUTINE		INSERTS		ZOOIEST
EINORTW	NOWTIER		SINTERS	**EIOPPPR**	POPPIER
	TOWNIER	**EINRSSU**	INSURES	**EIOPPPS**	POPPIES
EINORTZ	TRIZONE		SUNRISE	**EIOPPRS**	SOPPIER
EINOSSS	ESSOINS	**EINRSSV**	VERSINS	**EIOPPRT**	TOPPIER
	OSSEINS	**EINRSTT**	ENTRIST	**EIOPPSS**	POPSIES
	SESSION		RETINTS	**EIOPPST**	POTPIES
EINOSST	NOSIEST		STINTER	**EIOPQRU**	PIROQUE
	SONTIES		TINTERS	**EIOPRRS**	PROSIER
	STONIES	**EINRSTU**	NUTSIER	**EIOPRRT**	PIERROT
EINOSSU	SINUOSE		TRIUNES		PORTIER
EINOSSZ	SOZINES		UNITERS		PRERIOT
EINOSTT	SNOTTIE	**EINRSTV**	INVERTS	**EIOPRRU**	ROUPIER
	TONIEST		STRIVEN	**EIOPRSS**	POISERS

	PROSSIE		TOURIES
EIOPRST	PERIOST		TOUSIER
	PORIEST	**EIORSTV**	TORSIVE
	PROSTIE	**EIORSTW**	OWRIEST
	REPOSIT		TOWSIER
	RIPOSTE	**EIORTTT**	TOTTIER
	ROPIEST	**EIORTTU**	TOUTIER
EIOPRSU	POURIES	**EIORTTV**	TORTIVE
	SOUPIER		VIRETOT
EIOPRSX	PROXIES	**EIORTUV**	VOITURE
EIOPRTT	POTTIER	**EIORTUZ**	TOUZIER
EIOPRTU	POUTIER	**EIORTWZ**	TOWZIER
EIOPRTV	OVERTIP	**EIOSSTU**	SOUTIES
	PIVOTER	**EIOSSTV**	SOVIETS
EIOPSSS	POSSIES		STOVIES
EIOPSST	POSIEST	**EIOSTTT**	STOTTIE
	POSTIES		TOTTIES
	POTSIES	**EIOSTTU**	TOUSTIE
	SEPIOST	**EIOSTTW**	TOWIEST
	SOPITES	**EIOSTUV**	OUTVIES
EIOPSSU	POUSSIE	**EIOSTUZ**	OUTSIZE
EIOPSTT	POTTIES	**EIOSTVV**	VOTIVES
	SPOTTIE	**EIPPPSU**	PUPPIES
	TIPTOES	**EIPPQRU**	QUIPPER
EIOPSTU	PITEOUS	**EIPPRRS**	RIPPERS
EIOPSTX	EXPOSIT	**EIPPRRT**	TRIPPER
	POXIEST	**EIPPRSS**	SIPPERS
EIOPSTY	ISOTYPE	**EIPPRST**	TIPPERS
EIOPSZZ	POZZIES	**EIPPRSU**	PURPIES
EIOPTUW	WIPEOUT	**EIPPRSY**	YIPPERS
EIOQRTU	QUOITER	**EIPPRSZ**	ZIPPERS
EIOQTUX	QUIXOTE	**EIPPRTT**	TRIPPET
EIORRRS	SORRIER	**EIPPSST**	SIPPETS
EIORRRT	RORTIER	**EIPPSTT**	TIPPETS
	TERROIR	**EIPPSUY**	YUPPIES
EIORRRW	WORRIER	**EIPQSTU**	PIQUETS
EIORRSS	ORRISES	**EIPRRSS**	PRISERS
	ROSIERS	**EIPRRST**	STRIPER
EIORRST	RIOTERS	**EIPRRSU**	PURSIER
	ROISTER		UPRISER
	RORIEST	**EIPRRSZ**	PRIZERS
EIORRSV	REVISOR	**EIPRRTU**	PURTIER
EIORRSW	WORRIES	**EIPRRTY**	TRIPERY
EIORRUV	OUVRIER	**EIPRRUV**	UPRIVER
EIORRVV	REVIVOR	**EIPRSSS**	PISSERS
EIORSSS	SEISORS	**EIPRSST**	ESPRITS
EIORSST	ROESTIS		PERSIST
	ROSIEST		PRIESTS
	SIROSET		SITREPS
	SORITES		SPRIEST
	SORTIES		SPRITES
	STORIES		STIRPES
	TOSSIER		STRIPES
	TRIOSES		TRIPSES
EIORSSU	SERIOUS	**EIPRSSU**	PUSSIER
EIORSSV	VIROSES		SUSPIRE
EIORSSX	XEROSIS		UPRISES
EIORSSZ	SEIZORS	**EIPRSSW**	SWIPERS
EIORSTT	STOITER	**EIPRSTT**	PITTERS
EIORSTU	OURIEST		SPITTER
	STOURIE		

	TIPSTER		
EIPRSTU	PERITUS		
	PUIREST		
EIPRSTV	PRIVETS		
EIPRSTX	EXTIRPS		
EIPRSTY	PYRITES		
	STRIPEY		
EIPRSUU	EURIPUS		
EIPRTTU	PUTTIER		
EIPRUVW	PURVIEW		
EIPSSSU	PUSSIES		
EIPSSTZ	SPITZES		
EIPSSUZ	UPSIZES		
EIPSTTU	PUTTIES		
EIPSTTY	TYPIEST		
EIQRSSU	RISQUES		
	SQUIERS		
	SQUIRES		
EIQRSTU	QUERIST		
	REQUITS		
EIQRSUV	QUIVERS		
EIQRTTU	QUITTER		
EIQRUVY	QUIVERY		
EIQRUZZ	QUIZZER		
EIQSTUU	QUIETUS		
EIQSUZZ	QUIZZES		
EIRRRST	STIRRER		
EIRRSST	STIRRES		
EIRRSTT	RITTERS		
	TERRITS		
EIRRSTU	RUSTIER		
EIRRSTV	STRIVER		
EIRRSTW	WRITERS		
EIRRSZZ	RIZZERS		
EIRRTTU	RUTTIER		
EIRSSST	RESISTS		
	SISTERS		
EIRSSSU	ISSUERS		
	RISUSES		
EIRSSTT	SITTERS		
EIRSSTU	SUITERS		
EIRSSTV	STIVERS		
	STRIVES		
	TREVISS		
	VERISTS		
EIRSSUU	USURIES		
EIRSSUV	VIRUSES		
EIRSSUW	WUSSIER		
EIRSTTT	STRETTI		
	TITTERS		
	TRITEST		
EIRSTTU	TERTIUS		
EIRSTTV	TRIVETS		
EIRSTTW	RETWIST		
	TWISTER		
	WITTERS		
EIRSTUV	REVUIST		
	STUIVER		
	VIRTUES		
EIRSUVV	SURVIVE		
EIRSUVW	SURVIEW		

EIRTTTW	TWITTER	**EKLNOSS**	KELSONS	**EKORRST**	STROKER
EIRTTUV	VUTTIER		SLOKENS	**EKORRSW**	REWORKS
EISSSSW	SWISSES	**EKLNOSU**	LEUKONS		WORKERS
EISSSTU	SITUSES	**EKLNPRU**	PLUNKER	**EKORRSY**	YORKERS
	TISSUES	**EKLNPSU**	SPELUNK	**EKORRST**	STOKERS
EISSSTW	SWITSES	**EKLNRSU**	LUNKERS		STROKES
EISSSTX	SEXISTS		RUNKLES	**EKORUYY**	EURYOKY
EISSSUW	WUSSIES	**EKLNSST**	SKLENTS	**EKPPSUU**	SEPPUKU
EISSTTY	TYSTIES	**EKLOORS**	LOOKERS	**EKPRSSY**	KRYPSES
EISSTUV	TUSSIVE		RELOOKS	**EKRRSSY**	SKRYERS
EISSTUY	TISSUEY	**EKLOPST**	KLEPTOS	**EKRSSTU**	TUSKERS
EISSTVW	SWIVETS	**EKLOSTV**	STOKVEL	**EKRSTUY**	TURKEYS
EISSWZZ	SWIZZES	**EKLRRSU**	LURKERS	**EKRSUVY**	KURVEYS
EISTTTU	TUTTIES	**EKLRSSU**	SULKERS	**ELLLORR**	LORRELL
EISTTUW	WETSUIT	**EKLSSSY**	SKYLESS	**ELLLORS**	LOLLERS
EJJMNUU	JEJUNUM	**EKLSTTU**	SKUTTLE	**ELLLOSZ**	LOZELLS
EJKMNNU	JUNKMEN	**EKLSTUZ**	KLUTZES	**ELLLRSU**	LULLERS
EJKNRSU	JUNKERS	**EKMMRSU**	SKUMMER	**ELLMNOO**	MOELLON
EJKNSTU	JUNKETS	**EKMNORW**	WORKMEN	**ELLMNOP**	POLLMEN
EJKOORY	JOOKERY	**EKMNORY**	MONKERY	**ELLMNOT**	TOLLMEN
EJKORUY	JOUKERY	**EKMNOSU**	MUSKONE	**ELLMNSU**	MULLENS
EJLLORS	JOLLERS	**EKMNOSY**	MONKEYS	**ELLMOOR**	MORELLO
EJLLORY	JOLLYER	**EKMNPTU**	UNKEMPT	**ELLMORR**	MORRELL
EJLLOSY	JOLLEYS	**EKMOOPS**	MOPOKES	**ELLMOSW**	MELLOWS
EJLORST	JOLTERS	**EKMORSS**	SMOKERS	**ELLMOWY**	MELLOWY
	JOSTLER	**EKMPRRU**	KRUMPER	**ELLMPSU**	PELLUMS
EJLORSW	JOWLERS	**EKMRSTU**	MURKEST	**ELLMPUU**	PLUMULE
EJLOSST	JOSTLES	**EKMSSTU**	MUSKETS	**ELLMRSU**	MULLERS
EJLOSSY	JOYLESS	**EKMSSUY**	KUMYSES	**ELLMSTU**	MULLETS
EJLSSTU	JUSTLES	**EKNNOST**	NEKTONS	**ELLMSUV**	VELLUMS
EJMNRUY	JURYMEN	**EKNOORS**	SNOOKER	**ELLMSUY**	MULLEYS
EJMOSST	JETSOMS	**EKNOPSU**	UNSPOKE	**ELLNNOT**	TONNELL
EJMPRSU	JUMPERS	**EKNORST**	REKNOTS	**ELLNOOW**	WOOLLEN
EJNORRU	REJOURN		STONKER	**ELLNOPS**	POLLENS
EJNORUY	JOURNEY		STROKEN	**ELLNOPT**	POLLENT
EJNOSST	JETSONS		TONKERS	**ELLNORS**	ENROLLS
EJNOSTT	JETTONS	**EKNORSW**	KNOWERS	**ELLNOST**	STOLLEN
EJOORVY	OVERJOY	**EKNORSY**	YONKERS	**ELLNOSU**	NOUSELL
EJOOSSY	SOOJEYS	**EKNORTT**	KNOTTER	**ELLNOSV**	VELLONS
EJOPPRT	PROPJET	**EKNORTW**	NETWORK	**ELLNOSW**	SWOLLEN
EJOPRST	PROJETS	**EKNORUY**	YOUNKER	**ELLNOVY**	NOVELLY
EJOPRTT	JETPORT	**EKNOSTY**	STENOKY	**ELLNOXY**	XYLENOL
EJORSSS	JOSSERS	**EKNOSUY**	UNYOKES	**ELLNPSU**	UNSPELL
EJORSTT	JOTTERS	**EKNPRSU**	PUNKERS	**ELLNSSU**	SULLENS
EJORSTU	JOUSTER	**EKNPSTU**	PUNKEST		UNSELLS
EJOSTTU	OUTJEST	**EKNPSUY**	PUNKEYS	**ELLNSUU**	LUNULES
	OUTJETS	**EKNRTUY**	TURNKEY	**ELLOOSW**	WOOSELL
EJPRRUY	PERJURY	**EKNSSTU**	SUNKETS	**ELLOOSY**	LOOSELY
EJRSSTU	JUSTERS	**EKOOPRT**	PERTOOK	**ELLOOTU**	TOLUOLE
EJSSTTU	JUSTEST	**EKOOPRV**	PROVOKE	**ELLOPRR**	PROLLER
EKKLOOY	OLYKOEK	**EKOORRS**	KOREROS	**ELLOPRS**	POLLERS
EKKLRSU	SKULKER	**EKOORRY**	ROOKERY		REPOLLS
EKKOPSU	PUKEKOS	**EKOORST**	STOOKER	**ELLOPTU**	POLLUTE
EKLLMSU	SKELLUM		STROOKE	**ELLORRS**	REROLLS
EKLLNOR	KNOLLER	**EKOORTW**	KOTOWER		ROLLERS
EKLLRRU	KRULLER	**EKOPPSU**	UPSPOKE	**ELLORRT**	TROLLER
EKLMMSU	KUMMELS	**EKOPRRS**	PORKERS	**ELLORSS**	SOLLERS
EKLMSSU	MUSKLES		PROKERS		SORELLS
	SKELUMS	**EKOPRRW**	PREWORK	**ELLORST**	TOLLERS
EKLNOPR	PLONKER	**EKOPRUY**	KOUPREY	**ELLORTY**	TROLLEY
EKLNORS	SNORKEL	**EKOPTTU**	OUTKEPT	**ELLORVY**	LOVERLY

ELLOSST	TOLSELS
ELLOSTU	OUTSELL
	SELLOUT
ELLOSTX	EXTOLLS
ELLOSTY	TOLLEYS
ELLOSVY	VOLLEYS
ELLOSWY	YELLOWS
ELLOTTU	OUTTELL
ELLOTUW	OUTWELL
ELLOTUY	OUTYELL
ELLOVWY	VOWELLY
ELLOWYY	YELLOWY
ELLPRSU	PULLERS
ELLPSSU	UPSELLS
ELLPSTU	PULLETS
ELLPSUW	UPSWELL
	UPWELLS
ELLPSUY	PULLEYS
ELMMOPS	POMMELS
ELMMOPU	PUMMELO
ELMMORT	TROMMEL
ELMMPRU	PLUMMER
ELMMPSU	PUMMELS
ELMMPTU	PLUMMET
ELMMRSU	SLUMMER
ELMMRTU	TUMMLER
ELMMSTU	STUMMEL
ELMNOOT	MOONLET
	TOOLMEN
ELMNOOW	WOOLMEN
ELMNOPW	PLOWMEN
ELMNORS	MERLONS
ELMNOST	LOMENTS
	MELTONS
ELMNOSY	MYELONS
ELMNOTU	MOULTEN
ELMNOTY	YMOLTEN
ELMNPPU	PLUMPEN
ELMNPSU	LUMPENS
	PLENUMS
ELMNPUU	UNPLUME
ELMOOPP	POMPELO
ELMOOPS	POMELOS
ELMOORT	TREMOLO
ELMOOSS	OSMOLES
ELMOOSY	MOOLEYS
ELMOPRT	PREMOLT
ELMOPRY	POLYMER
ELMOPSU	PLUMOSE
	PUMELOS
ELMOPSY	EMPLOYS
ELMORSS	MORSELS
ELMORST	MERLOTS
	MOLTERS
ELMORSU	EMULSOR
ELMORTT	MOTTLER
ELMORTU	MOULTER
ELMOSST	MOLESTS
ELMOSSU	MOUSLES
ELMOSSY	SMOYLES
ELMOSTT	MOTTLES

ELMOSTY	MOTLEYS
ELMOSUU	EMULOUS
ELMOSUV	VOLUMES
ELMOSXY	OXYMELS
ELMOSZZ	MOZZLES
ELMPPRU	PLUMPER
ELMPPSU	PEPLUMS
ELMPRSU	LUMPERS
	RUMPLES
ELMPRUY	PLUMERY
ELMRSTY	MYRTLES
ELMRTUU	MULTURE
ELMRTUY	ELYTRUM
ELMRUZZ	MUZZLER
ELMSSSU	MUSSELS
	SUMLESS
ELMSTUU	MUTUELS
	MUTULES
ELMSTUW	UMWELTS
ELMSUZZ	MUZZLES
ELNNOPU	NONUPLE
ELNNORS	RONNELS
ELNNOSS	NELSONS
ELNNRSU	RUNNELS
ELNNRTU	TRUNNEL
ELNNSTU	TUNNELS
ELNOOPT	PELOTON
ELNOOSS	LOOSENS
ELNOOSU	NEOSOUL
	UNLOOSE
ELNOOSW	WOOLENS
ELNOOSY	LOONEYS
ELNOOSZ	SNOOZLE
ELNOPRU	PLEURON
ELNOPRY	PRONELY
ELNOPST	LEPTONS
ELNOPSY	POLEYNS
ELNOPTU	OPULENT
ELNORSS	NORSELS
ELNORST	LENTORS
ELNORSU	NOURSLE
ELNORTY	ELYTRON
ELNOSSS	LESSONS
	SONLESS
ELNOSST	TELSONS
ELNOSSU	ENSOULS
	NOUSLES
ELNOSSV	SLOVENS
ELNOSSW	LOWNESS
ELNOSTT	TONLETS
ELNOSTU	LENTOUS
ELNOSTV	SOLVENT
ELNOSUV	UNLOVES
ELNOSUZ	ZONULES
ELNOSVY	LENVOYS
ELNOSZZ	NOZZLES
ELNOTTW	TOWNLET
ELNOTUZ	ZONULET
ELNOTVY	NOVELTY
ELNPSST	SPLENTS
ELNPSTU	PENULTS

ELNPSTY	PENTYLS
ELNRSSU	NURSLES
	RUNLESS
ELNRSTU	RUNLETS
ELNRSTY	STERNLY
ELNRSUU	UNRULES
ELNRSUZ	LUZERNS
ELNRUZZ	NUZZLER
ELNSSSU	SUNLESS
ELNSSSY	SELSYNS
	SLYNESS
ELNSTTU	NUTLETS
ELNSUZZ	NUZZLES
	SNUZZLE
ELOOPPS	POEPOLS
ELOOPRS	LOOPERS
	POOLERS
	RESPOOL
	SPOOLER
ELOOPSS	POSOLES
ELOOPST	POOTLES
ELOOPSZ	POZOLES
ELOORST	LOOTERS
	RETOOLS
	ROOTLES
	TOOLERS
ELOORSW	WOOLERS
ELOORTT	ROOTLET
	TOOTLER
ELOOSST	LOOSEST
	LOTOSES
ELOOSSW	WOOSELS
ELOOSTT	TOOLSET
	TOOTLES
ELOOSTU	OUTSOLE
ELOOSWY	WOOLSEY
ELOOTUV	OUTLOVE
ELOPPPS	POPPLES
ELOPPRS	LOPPERS
	PROPELS
ELOPPST	STOPPLE
	TOPPLES
ELOPPSU	POULPES
	UPSLOPE
ELOPPSY	POLYPES
ELOPRRS	PROLERS
ELOPRRU	PROULER
ELOPRRW	PROWLER
ELOPRRY	PYRROLE
ELOPRSS	PLESSOR
	SLOPERS
	SPLORES
ELOPRST	PETROLS
	REPLOTS
ELOPRSU	LEPROUS
	PELORUS
	PERLOUS
	SPORULE
ELOPRSV	PLOVERS
ELOPRSW	PLOWERS
	REPLOWS

ELOPRSX	PLEXORS	**ELOSWZZ**	SWOZZLE	**EMMNOTY**	METONYM
ELOPRSY	LEPROSY	**ELPPRRU**	PURPLER	**EMMOOTY**	MYOTOME
ELOPRTT	PLOTTER	**ELPPRSU**	PULPERS	**EMMOPRR**	PROMMER
ELOPRTU	PLOUTER		PURPLES	**EMMORSS**	MOMSERS
	POULTER		REPULPS	**EMMORSZ**	MOMZERS
ELOPRTW	PLOWTER		SUPPLER	**EMMOSST**	MESTOMS
ELOPRTY	PROTYLE	**ELPPSSU**	SUPPLES	**EMMOSSU**	MOMUSES
ELOPRVY	OVERPLY	**ELPQSUU**	PULQUES		MOUSMES
	PLOVERY	**ELPRRSU**	PURLERS	**EMMOSYZ**	ZYMOMES
ELOPSST	TOPLESS		SLURPER	**EMMPRSU**	MUMPERS
ELOPSSU	SOUPLES	**ELPRSSU**	PULSERS	**EMMPSTU**	METUMPS
ELOPSTT	POTTLES	**ELPRSTU**	SPURTLE	**EMMRRSU**	RUMMERS
ELOPSTU	TUPELOS	**ELPRSUV**	PULVERS	**EMMRSSU**	SUMMERS
ELOPSTY	PEYOTLS	**ELPRTUU**	PULTURE	**EMMRSTU**	RUMMEST
ELOPSTZ	PLOTZES	**ELPRUZZ**	PUZZLER	**EMMRSUY**	SUMMERY
ELOPTUY	OUTYELP	**ELPSSSU**	PLUSSES	**EMMSSUU**	MUSEUMS
ELORRSS	SORRELS		PUSSELS	**EMNNOOR**	MONERON
ELORRSW	WORRELS	**ELPSSUU**	LUPUSES	**EMNNOSW**	SNOWMEN
ELORSSS	LESSORS	**ELPSSUY**	PUSLEYS	**EMNNOWW**	NEWMOWN
ELORSST	OSTLERS		PUSSLEY	**EMNOOPT**	METOPON
	STEROLS		SPULYES	**EMNOORS**	MOONERS
	TORSELS	**ELPSTUU**	PLUTEUS	**EMNOORT**	MONTERO
ELORSSU	LOUSERS		PUSTULE	**EMNOOSS**	MONOSES
ELORSSV	SOLVERS	**ELPSUZZ**	PUZZELS	**EMNOOST**	MOONSET
ELORSTT	LOTTERS		PUZZLES	**EMNOOSY**	NOYSOME
	SETTLOR	**ELRRSTU**	RUSTLER	**EMNOOTY**	ENOMOTY
	SLOTTER	**ELRRTTU**	TURTLER	**EMNOPPR**	PROPMEN
	TOLTERS	**ELRSSSU**	RUSSELS	**EMNOPRT**	PORTMEN
ELORSTU	ELUTORS	**ELRSSTU**	LUSTERS	**EMNOPST**	POSTMEN
	OUTLERS		LUSTRES		TOPSMEN
	TROULES		RESULTS	**EMNOPSU**	SPUMONE
ELORSTV	REVOLTS		RUSTLES	**EMNOPSY**	EPONYMS
ELORSTW	TROWELS		SUTLERS	**EMNOPYY**	EPONYMY
	WORTLES		ULSTERS	**EMNORRU**	MOURNER
ELORSUV	LOUVERS	**ELRSSTY**	STYLERS	**EMNORSS**	SERMONS
	LOUVRES	**ELRSTTU**	TURTLES	**EMNORST**	MENTORS
	VELOURS	**ELRSTTY**	TETRYLS		MONSTER
ELORSUY	ELUSORY	**ELRSTUY**	SUTLERY		MONTRES
ELORSVW	WOLVERS	**ELRSTWY**	SWELTRY	**EMNORTT**	TORMENT
ELORSWY	YOWLERS	**ELRSUWY**	WURLEYS	**EMNORTU**	MONTURE
ELORTTY	LOTTERY	**ELRSUWZ**	WURZELS		MOUNTER
ELORTVY	OVERTLY	**ELRTTUY**	UTTERLY		REMOUNT
ELOSSTU	LOTUSES	**ELRTUUV**	VULTURE	**EMNOSST**	STEMSON
	SOLUTES	**ELSSSTU**	TUSSLES	**EMNOSTU**	UNSMOTE
	TOUSLES	**ELSSSUU**	LUSUSES	**EMNOSTY**	ETYMONS
ELOSSTW	LOWSEST	**ELSSTTU**	SUTTLES	**EMNOSXY**	EXONYMS
	SLOWEST	**ELSSTTY**	STYLETS	**EMNPSSU**	PENSUMS
ELOSSTY	SYSTOLE	**ELSSTYY**	SYSTYLE	**EMNRRSU**	MURRENS
	TOLSEYS	**ELSUWZZ**	WUZZLES	**EMNRRUY**	UNMERRY
	TOYLESS	**EMMMOST**	MOMMETS	**EMNRSSU**	RUMNESS
	TYLOSES	**EMMMRSU**	MUMMERS	**EMNRSTU**	MUNSTER
ELOSSVW	VOWLESS	**EMMMRUY**	MUMMERY		MUNTERS
ELOSSXY	XYLOSES	**EMMNNOS**	MNEMONS		STERNUM
ELOSSZZ	SOZZLES	**EMMNOOR**	MONOMER	**EMOOPRS**	OOSPERM
ELOSTTU	OUTLETS		MOORMEN	**EMOOPRT**	PROMOTE
ELOSTTY	TYLOTES	**EMMNOOT**	MOMENTO	**EMOOPRY**	POMEROY
ELOSTUU	LUTEOUS		MOOTMEN	**EMOORRS**	MOROSER
ELOSTUV	VOLUTES	**EMMNORY**	MERONYM		ROOMERS
ELOSTUZ	TOUZLES	**EMMNOST**	MOMENTS	**EMOORST**	MOOTERS
ELOSTYZ	TOLZEYS		MONTEMS	**EMOORSU**	UROSOME
ELOSWYY	YOWLEYS	**EMMNOTU**	OMENTUM	**EMOOSSS**	OSMOSES

Code	Word(s)
EMOOSTT	MOOTEST
	MOTTOES
	TOOMEST
EMOOSTW	TWOSOME
EMOOSTY	MYOSOTE
	TOYSOME
EMOOSXY	OXYSOME
EMOOTUV	OUTMOVE
EMOPPRS	MOPPERS
EMOPPST	MOPPETS
EMOPPSY	POMPEYS
EMOPPTU	UPTEMPO
EMOPRRS	ROMPERS
EMOPRST	STOMPER
	TROMPES
EMOPRSU	SUPREMO
EMOPSSU	MOPUSES
EMOPSSY	MYOPSES
EMOQSSU	MOSQUES
EMORRST	STORMER
	TERMORS
	TREMORS
EMORRSU	MORSURE
EMORRSW	WORMERS
EMORRWY	WORMERY
EMORSSS	MOSSERS
EMORSST	MOTSERS
EMORSSU	MOUSERS
	SMOUSER
EMORSTU	MOUTERS
	OESTRUM
EMORSUV	MEVROUS
EMORSUY	MOUSERY
EMOSSSU	MOUSSES
	SMOUSES
EMOSSTT	MOSTEST
EMOSSYZ	ZYMOSES
EMOSTTT	MOTETTS
EMOSTVZ	ZEMSTVO
EMOTTTU	TETOTUM
EMOTUZZ	MEZUZOT
EMPPRSU	PUMPERS
	REPUMPS
EMPPSTU	MUPPETS
EMPRSTU	RESTUMP
	STUMPER
	SUMPTER
EMPRTTU	TRUMPET
EMPSSTU	SEPTUMS
EMRRSTU	STURMER
EMRRSUY	MURREYS
EMRSSTU	ESTRUMS
	MUSTERS
	STUMERS
EMRSTTU	MUTTERS
EMRSTYY	MYSTERY
EMSSSTY	SYSTEMS
ENNNOPS	PENNONS
ENNNOSW	NONNEWS
ENNNRUY	NUNNERY
ENNOOPR	PRENOON
ENNOORS	NOONERS
ENNOORT	NORTENO
ENNOORZ	NONZERO
ENNOOTT	NONETTO
ENNORST	STONERN
	TONNERS
ENNORSU	NEURONS
	NONUSER
ENNORSW	RENOWNS
	WONNERS
ENNORTU	NEUTRON
ENNORUV	UNROVEN
ENNOSST	SONNETS
	STONNES
	TENSONS
ENNOSSU	NONUSES
ENNOSSW	NOWNESS
ENNOSTU	NEUSTON
ENNOSTW	NEWTONS
ENNOSTZ	TENZONS
ENNOUVW	UNWOVEN
ENNPRSU	PUNNERS
ENNPSTU	PUNNETS
	UNSPENT
ENNRRSU	RUNNERS
ENNRSTU	RUNNETS
	STUNNER
ENNRSUW	WUNNERS
ENNSSTU	UNNESTS
ENNSTTU	UNTENTS
ENNSTUU	UNTUNES
ENNSTYY	SYNTENY
ENNTTUY	UNTENTY
ENOOPPR	PROPONE
ENOOPRS	OPERONS
	SNOOPER
ENOOPSY	SPOONEY
ENOORSS	NOOSERS
	SEROONS
	SOONERS
ENOORST	ENROOTS
ENOORSU	ONEROUS
ENOORSW	SWOONER
ENOORSZ	SNOOZER
ENOORTT	NETROOT
ENOOSST	SOONEST
ENOOSSZ	SNOOZES
ENOOSTT	TESTOON
ENOOSTU	UNSOOTE
ENOOTXY	OXYTONE
ENOPPSU	UNPOPES
ENOPRRS	PERRONS
ENOPRRU	PRONEUR
ENOPRRW	PREWORN
ENOPRSS	PERSONS
ENOPRST	POSTERN
	PRONEST
ENOPRSU	UNROPES
ENOPRSY	PROYNES
	PYONERS
	PYRONES
ENOPRTT	PORTENT
ENOPRTY	ENTROPY
ENOPSST	POSNETS
	STEPSON
ENOPSTT	POTENTS
ENOPSUX	XENOPUS
ENOPSWY	POWNEYS
ENOQTUU	UNQUOTE
ENORRSS	SNORERS
	SORNERS
ENORRST	SNORTER
ENORRSZ	RONZERS
ENORRTT	TORRENT
ENORRUV	OVERRUN
	RUNOVER
ENORSSS	SENSORS
ENORSST	NESTORS
	STONERS
	TENSORS
ENORSSW	WORSENS
ENORSSY	SENSORY
ENORSTT	ROTTENS
	SNOTTER
	STENTOR
ENORSTU	TENOURS
	TONSURE
ENORSTY	TYRONES
ENORSUV	NERVOUS
ENORSUW	UNSWORE
ENORSUZ	ZONURES
ENORSVY	RENVOYS
ENORSZZ	NOZZERS
ENORTUW	UNWROTE
ENORTUY	TOURNEY
ENOSSST	SESTONS
ENOSSTT	OSTENTS
	STETSON
	TESTONS
ENOSSTU	OUTNESS
	TONUSES
ENOSSTW	TWONESS
ENOSSTX	SEXTONS
ENOSSUW	SWOUNES
ENOSSWW	SWOWNES
ENOSTTU	STOUTEN
	TENUTOS
ENOSTUU	TENUOUS
ENOTTUW	OUTWENT
ENPPRSU	PRENUPS
ENPRRSU	PRUNERS
	SPURNER
ENPRSSU	SPURNES
ENPRSTU	PUNSTER
	PUNTERS
ENPRSUU	UNPURSE
ENPRSWY	PREWYNS
ENPSSSU	SUSPENS
ENPSSTU	UNSTEPS
ENPSTTU	STUPENT
ENPSTUU	TUNEUPS
ENPSTUW	UNSWEPT

ENRRSSU	NURSERS	**EOPPRST**	POPSTER	**EOPTTUW**	OUTWEPT
ENRRSTU	RETURNS		STOPPER	**EOQRRTU**	TORQUER
	TURNERS		TOPPERS	**EOQRSTU**	QUESTOR
ENRRSUU	UNSURER	**EOPPRSU**	PURPOSE		QUOTERS
ENRRSUY	NURSERY	**EOPPRSW**	SWOPPER		ROQUETS
ENRRTUU	NURTURE	**EOPPRSY**	PYROPES		TORQUES
	UNTRUER	**EOPPSSU**	SUPPOSE	**EOQSTTU**	TOQUETS
ENRRTUY	TURNERY	**EOPRRSS**	PRESSOR	**EORRRST**	RORTERS
ENRSSTU	UNRESTS		PROSERS		TERRORS
ENRSSWY	WRYNESS	**EOPRRST**	PORTERS	**EORRSSS**	ROSSERS
ENRSTTU	ENTRUST		PRESORT	**EORRSST**	RESORTS
	NUTTERS		PRETORS		ROSTERS
ENRSUZZ	NUZZERS		REPORTS		SORTERS
ENRSVWY	WYVERNS		SPORTER		STORERS
ENRTTUY	NUTTERY	**EOPRRSU**	POURERS	**EORRSSU**	ROUSERS
ENSSSTU	SUNSETS		REPOURS	**EORRSTT**	RETORTS
EOOOPRS	OOSPORE	**EOPRRSV**	PROVERS		ROTTERS
EOOPPRS	OPPOSER	**EOPRRTU**	TROUPER		STERTOR
	POOPERS	**EOPRSSS**	POSSERS		TORRETS
	PROPOSE		PROSSES	**EORRSTU**	RETOURS
EOOPPRU	EUROPOP	**EOPRSST**	PORTESS		ROUSTER
EOOPPRV	POPOVER		POSTERS		ROUTERS
EOOPPSS	OPPOSES		PRESTOS		TOURERS
EOOPRRS	SPOORER		REPOSTS		TROUSER
EOOPRRT	PROTORE		RESPOTS	**EORRSTV**	TROVERS
	TROOPER		STOPERS	**EORRSTW**	STROWER
EOOPRSS	POROSES	**EOPRSSU**	POSEURS	**EORRSTY**	ROYSTER
EOOPRST	POOREST		SEROPUS		STROYER
	POOTERS		SOUPERS	**EORRSZZ**	ROZZERS
	STOOPER	**EOPRSSW**	PROWESS	**EORRTTT**	TROTTER
EOOPRSW	SWOOPER	**EOPRSSY**	OSPREYS	**EORRTTU**	TORTURE
EOOPRTU	OUTROPE		PYROSES		TROUTER
EOOPRTV	OVERTOP	**EOPRSTT**	POTTERS	**EORSSST**	TOSSERS
EOOPRTW	TOWROPE		PROTEST	**EORSSSU**	SOURSES
EOOPRVY	POOVERY		SPOTTER	**EORSSTU**	ESTROUS
EOOPRYZ	ZOOPERY	**EOPRSTU**	PETROUS		OESTRUS
EOOPSST	STOOPES		POSTURE		OUSTERS
EOOPSSW	WOOPSES		POUTERS		SOUREST
EOOPTYZ	ZOOTYPE		PROTEUS		SOUTERS
EOORRSS	ROOSERS		SEPTUOR		STOURES
EOORRST	ROOSTER		SPOUTER		TOUSERS
	ROOTERS		TROUPES		TROUSES
	TOREROS	**EOPRSTW**	POWTERS		TUSSORE
EOORRVW	ROWOVER		PROWEST	**EORSSTV**	STOVERS
EOORSSS	SOROSES	**EOPRSTX**	EXPORTS		VOTRESS
EOORSTT	TOOTERS	**EOPRSTZ**	POTZERS	**EORSSTW**	SOWTERS
EOORSTZ	STOOZER	**EOPRSUU**	POURSUE		STOWERS
EOORSVW	OVERSOW		UPROUSE		STOWRES
EOORTUW	OUTWORE	**EOPRSUV**	OVERSUP		TOWSERS
EOOSSST	OSTOSES	**EOPRSUW**	POURSEW		WORSETS
EOOSSSU	OSSEOUS	**EOPRTTY**	POTTERY	**EORSSTY**	OYSTERS
EOOSSTT	TOOTSES	**EOPRTUY**	EUTROPY		STOREYS
EOOSSTZ	STOOZES	**EOPRTVY**	POVERTY	**EORSSTZ**	ZOSTERS
EOOSTWZ	WOOTZES	**EOPSSSS**	POSSESS	**EORSSWW**	WOWSERS
EOOTTUV	OUTVOTE	**EOPSSST**	POSSETS	**EORSTTT**	STOTTER
EOPPPRS	POPPERS	**EOPSSSU**	POUSSES		STRETTO
EOPPPST	POPPETS		SPOUSES		TOTTERS
EOPPRRS	PROPERS	**EOPSSTX**	SEXPOTS	**EORSTTU**	OUTSERT
	PROSPER	**EOPSTTU**	OUTSTEP		STOUTER
EOPPRSS	OPPRESS		TOUPETS		TOUTERS
	PORPESS	**EOPSTTW**	STEWPOT	**EORSTTW**	SWOTTER

EORSTTX	EXTORTS	FFGIIMN	MIFFING	FFNORSU	RUNOFFS
EORSTTY	ROSETTY	FFGIINN	NIFFING	FFNORTU	TURNOFF
EORSTUX	SEXTUOR	FFGIINR	GRIFFIN	FFOOPST	STOPOFF
EORSUVY	VOYEURS		RIFFING	FFOPSTU	OFFPUTS
EORTTTY	TOTTERY	FFGIINT	TIFFING		PUTOFFS
EORTTUY	TUTOYER	FFGILNU	LUFFING	FFRRSUU	FURFURS
EOSSSST	STOSSES	FFGIMNU	MUFFING	FGGGIIN	FIGGING
EOSSSSW	SOWSSES	FFGINOR	GRIFFON	FGGGINO	FOGGING
EOSSTTU	OUTSETS	FFGINOS	GONIFFS	FGGGINU	FUGGING
	SETOUTS		OFFINGS	FGGHIIS	FISHGIG
EOSSUYZ	SOYUZES	FFGINPU	PUFFING	FGGIINT	GIFTING
EOSTTTW	WOTTEST	FFGINRU	RUFFING	FGGIISS	FISGIGS
EPPPSTU	PUPPETS	FFGLOOS	LOGOFFS	FGGIISZ	FIZGIGS
EPPRRTU	PRERUPT	FFGLRUY	GRUFFLY	FGGIIZZ	FIZZGIG
EPPRRUU	PURPURE	FFHHISU	HUFFISH	FGGILNO	GOLFING
EPPRSSU	SUPPERS	FFHIINS	FINFISH	FGGILNU	FUGLING
EPPSSTU	UPSTEPS	FFHIISY	FISHIFY		GULFING
EPPSTUW	UPSWEPT	FFHIKNU	HUFFKIN	FGGILOY	FOGGILY
EPRRRSU	SPURRER	FFHILSU	FISHFUL	FGGILUY	FUGGILY
EPRRSSU	PURSERS	FFHILTY	FIFTHLY	FGGINOO	GOOFING
EPRRSTU	SPURTER	FFHILUY	HUFFILY	FGGINOR	FORGING
EPRRSUU	PURSUER	FFHIMSU	MUFFISH	FGGINOW	GOWFING
	USURPER	FFHIOST	TOFFISH	FGGINUU	FUGUING
EPRRSUY	SPURREY	FFHIOSX	FOXFISH	FGHHIOS	HOGFISH
EPRRTUU	RUPTURE	FFHOOSW	SHOWOFF	FGHIINS	FISHING
EPRSSSU	PUSSERS	FFHORSS	SHROFFS	FGHIINT	INFIGHT
EPRSSTU	UPRESTS	FFHOSTU	SHUTOFF	FGHIIPS	PIGFISH
EPRSSTY	SPRYEST	FFIILMY	MIFFILY	FGHILST	FLIGHTS
EPRSSUU	PURSUES	FFIINST	TIFFINS	FGHILSU	SIGHFUL
EPRSSUW	PURSEWS	FFIISUZ	ZIFFIUS	FGHILTY	FLIGHTY
EPRSTTU	PUTTERS	FFIKLSS	SKLIFFS	FGHIMNU	HUMFING
	SPUTTER	FFILLLU	FULFILL	FGHINOO	HOOFING
EPRSTUU	PUTURES	FFILLSU	FULFILS	FGHINOU	HOUFING
EPRSTUY	YUPSTER	FFILNSY	SNIFFLY	FGHINOW	HOWFING
EPRSUVY	PURVEYS	FFILOST	FILFOTS	FGHIOSY	FOGYISH
EQRSTWY	QWERTYS	FFILOUZ	ZUFFOLI	FGHIRST	FRIGHTS
ERRSSTU	RUSTRES	FFILPSS	SPLIFFS	FGHNOOR	FOGHORN
	TRUSSER	FFILPUY	PUFFILY	FGHORUY	FROUGHY
ERRSSUU	USURERS	FFILRTY	FRITFLY	FGHOTUY	FOUGHTY
ERRSSUY	SURREYS	FFILSTU	FISTFUL	FGIIKNN	FINKING
ERRSTTU	RUTTERS	FFILSTY	STIFFLY		KNIFING
	TRUSTER	FFIMNSU	MUFFINS	FGIIKNR	FIRKING
	TURRETS	FFINNSU	NUFFINS	FGIIKNS	FISKING
ERRSTTY	TRYSTER	FFINOOT	FINFOOT	FGIILLN	FILLING
ERSSSTU	RUSSETS	FFINOPS	SPINOFF	FGIILMN	FILMING
	TRUSSES	FFINOPT	PONTIFF	FGIILNO	FOILING
	TUSSERS	FFINPSU	PUFFINS	FGIILNR	RIFLING
ERSSSUU	USURESS	FFINRSU	RUFFINS	FGIILNS	FILINGS
ERSSTTU	TUTRESS	FFIOPRS	RIPOFFS	FGIILNT	FLITING
ERSSTTY	TRYSTES	FFIOPST	TIPOFFS		LIFTING
ERSSTUU	SUTURES	FFIORTY	FORTIFY	FGIILNX	FLIXING
ERSSTUY	RUSSETY	FFIOSST	SOFFITS	FGIILNY	LIGNIFY
ERSSTXY	XYSTERS	FFIQSUY	SQUIFFY	FGIIMNR	FIRMING
ERSSUVY	SURVEYS	FFIRTUY	FRUTIFY	FGIINNN	FINNING
ERSTTTU	STUTTER	FFJMOPU	JUMPOFF	FGIINNO	FOINING
ERSTTUX	URTEXTS	FFKLORU	FORKFUL	FGIINNS	FININGS
FFFGINU	FUFFING	FFLLOOU	LOOFFUL	FGIINRR	FIRRING
FFFILOT	LIFTOFF	FFLMORU	FORMFUL	FGIINRS	FIRINGS
FFFLOSY	FLYOFFS	FFLNSUY	SNUFFLY	FGIINRT	RIFTING
FFGGINO	GOFFING	FFLOOUZ	ZUFFOLO	FGIINRY	NIGRIFY
FFGHINU	HUFFING	FFLOSTY	FYLFOTS	FGIINRZ	FRIZING

FGIINST	FISTING	**FGLLNUU**	LUNGFUL	**FIIKNRS**	FIRKINS
	SIFTING	**FGLLOWY**	GLOWFLY	**FIIKNYZ**	ZINKIFY
FGIINSX	FIXINGS	**FGLMSUU**	MUGFULS	**FIILLMO**	MILFOIL
FGIINSY	SIGNIFY	**FGLNORU**	FURLONG	**FIILLMY**	FILMILY
FGIINTT	FITTING	**FGLNOSU**	SONGFUL	**FIILLNS**	INFILLS
	TIFTING	**FGLNPUU**	UPFLUNG	**FIILLPS**	FILLIPS
FGIINZZ	FIZZING	**FGLOOUY**	UFOLOGY	**FIILLSU**	FUSILLI
FGIKLNU	FLUKING	**FGLORSU**	FULGORS	**FIILNOT**	TINFOIL
FGIKNNU	FUNKING	**FGLORUU**	FULGOUR	**FIILNTY**	NIFTILY
FGIKNOR	FORKING	**FGLOTUY**	GOUTFLY	**FIILPRS**	RIFLIPS
FGIKNSY	SKYFING	**FGLSTUU**	GUSTFUL	**FIILPTU**	PITIFUL
FGILLNU	FULLING		GUTFULS	**FIILQUY**	LIQUIFY
FGILMNU	FLUMING		GUTSFUL	**FIIMMNU**	INFIMUM
FGILNOO	FOOLING	**FGNOORU**	FOURGON	**FIIMNRS**	INFIRMS
FGILNOP	FOPLING	**FGNORSY**	GRYFONS	**FIIMSST**	MISFITS
FGILNOR	ROLFING	**FGNOSUU**	FUNGOUS	**FIINORS**	FIORINS
FGILNOT	LOFTING	**FHHLSUU**	HUSHFUL	**FIINOSS**	FISSION
FGILNOU	FOULING	**FHIILMS**	FILMISH	**FIINRTY**	NITRIFY
FGILNOW	FLOWING	**FHIILSY**	FISHILY	**FIIOPST**	POSITIF
	FOWLING	**FHIILTY**	LITHIFY	**FIIPSTY**	TIPSIFY
	WOLFING	**FHIINPS**	PINFISH	**FIIRTVY**	VITRIFY
FGILNOY	FOYLING	**FHIKLOS**	FOLKISH	**FIJLLOY**	JOLLIFY
FGILNPU	UPFLING	**FHILLSU**	FULLISH	**FIJSTUY**	JUSTIFY
FGILNPY	FLYPING	**FHILOOS**	FOOLISH	**FIKKLNO**	KINFOLK
FGILNRU	FURLING	**FHILOSW**	WOLFISH	**FIKLLSU**	SKILFUL
FGILNSU	INGULFS	**FHILPSU**	SHIPFUL	**FIKLLUY**	FLUKILY
FGILNSY	FLYINGS	**FHILPTU**	PITHFUL	**FIKLNOW**	WOLFKIN
FGILNTU	FLUTING	**FHILSUW**	WISHFUL	**FIKLNSU**	SKINFUL
FGILNTY	FLYTING	**FHINOSU**	FUSHION	**FIKLNUY**	FUNKILY
FGILNUX	FLUXING	**FHINRSU**	FURNISH	**FIKLRSU**	RISKFUL
FGILOOY	GOOFILY	**FHINSSU**	SUNFISH	**FIKLSTU**	KISTFUL
FGILORY	GLORIFY	**FHINSTU**	UNSHIFT		LUTFISK
FGIMNOR	FORMING	**FHIOOST**	OOFTISH	**FIKNNOS**	FINNSKO
FGIMOSY	FOGYISM	**FHIOPPS**	FOPPISH	**FIKNOSX**	FOXSKIN
FGINNNO	FONNING	**FHIOPSX**	FOXSHIP	**FIKRSTU**	TURFSKI
FGINNNU	FUNNING	**FHIORRY**	HORRIFY	**FILLLUW**	WILLFUL
FGINNOY	FOYNING	**FHIOSST**	SOFTISH	**FILLMOY**	MOLLIFY
FGINOOR	ROOFING	**FHIOSTU**	OUTFISH	**FILLNUY**	NULLIFY
FGINOOT	FOOTING	**FHIPPSU**	PUPFISH	**FILLOTU**	TOILFUL
FGINOOW	WOOFING	**FHIPSTU**	UPSHIFT	**FILLOTY**	LOFTILY
FGINOPP	FOPPING	**FHIRRST**	SHRIFTS	**FILLPSU**	UPFILLS
FGINOPU	POUFING	**FHIRSTT**	THRIFTS	**FILLSTU**	LISTFUL
FGINORS	FROINGS	**FHIRTTY**	THRIFTY	**FILMNOO**	MONOFIL
FGINORT	FORTING	**FHIRTUY**	THURIFY	**FILMOSU**	FOLIUMS
FGINOST	SOFTING	**FHISSSU**	HUSSIFS	**FILMSTU**	MISTFUL
FGINOSW	SOWFING	**FHISSTU**	SHUFTIS	**FILNNUY**	FUNNILY
FGINOSX	FOXINGS	**FHKORTU**	FUTHORK	**FILNORS**	FLORINS
FGINRRU	FURRING	**FHLNORU**	HORNFUL	**FILNORU**	FLUORIN
FGINRSU	SURFING	**FHLNSUU**	UNFLUSH	**FILNOSW**	INFLOWS
FGINRSY	FRYINGS	**FHLOOSY**	SHOOFLY	**FILNOUX**	FLUXION
FGINRTU	TURFING	**FHLOPSU**	SHOPFUL	**FILNSTU**	TINFULS
FGINSSU	FUSSING	**FHLPSUU**	PUSHFUL	**FILNTUY**	UNFITLY
FGINSTU	FUSTING	**FHLRTUU**	HURTFUL	**FILOOSU**	FOLIOUS
FGINTTU	TUFTING		RUTHFUL	**FILOOTW**	WITLOOF
FGINTUZ	FUTZING	**FHNOTUX**	FOXHUNT	**FILORST**	FIRLOTS
FGINUZZ	FUZZING	**FHOOORS**	FORHOOS		FLORIST
FGIORST	FRIGOTS	**FHOOORT**	HOOFROT	**FILORSV**	FRIVOLS
FGIORTW	FIGWORT	**FHOOOTT**	HOTFOOT	**FILORTU**	FLORUIT
FGISTUU	FUGUIST	**FHOORSW**	FORHOWS	**FILORTY**	TRIFOLY
FGJLSUU	JUGFULS	**FHORSTU**	FOURTHS	**FILOSSS**	FOSSILS
	JUGSFUL	**FIIIKNN**	FINIKIN	**FILPPUY**	PULPIFY

FILPSTU	UPLIFTS	**FLMORWY**	WORMFLY	**GGGINOU**	GOUGING
FILRRUY	FURRILY	**FLMSUUU**	FUMULUS	**GGGINPU**	PUGGING
FILRSTY	FIRSTLY	**FLNOORR**	FORLORN	**GGGINRU**	GURGING
FILRYZZ	FRIZZLY	**FLNOOSU**	UNFOOLS		RUGGING
FILSSUY	FUSSILY	**FLNOOSW**	ONFLOWS	**GGGINSU**	SUGGING
FILSTTU	FLUTIST	**FLNRSUU**	UNFURLS	**GGGINTU**	TUGGING
FILSTUW	WISTFUL		URNFULS	**GGHHIIN**	HIGHING
FILSTUY	FUSTILY	**FLOOOTU**	OUTFOOL	**GGHHIOS**	HOGGISH
FILSTWY	SWIFTLY	**FLOOPWX**	FOWLPOX	**GGHIIJS**	JIGGISH
FILTTUY	TUFTILY	**FLOORSW**	FORSLOW	**GGHIINN**	HINGING
FILUYZZ	FUZZILY	**FLOOTUW**	OUTFLOW		NIGHING
FIMMMUY	MUMMIFY	**FLOPSTU**	POTFULS	**GGHIINS**	SIGHING
FIMMORS	MISFORM	**FLOPSUW**	UPFLOWS	**GGHIIPS**	PIGGISH
FIMNORS	INFORMS	**FLOPTUU**	POUTFUL	**GGHIIRS**	RIGGISH
FIMNORU	UNIFORM	**FLOSUUV**	FULVOUS	**GGHIITT**	THIGGIT
FIMOORS	ISOFORM	**FLPRSUU**	UPFURLS	**GGHILOS**	LOGGISH
FIMOORV	OVIFORM	**FLRSSUU**	SULFURS	**GGHIMSU**	MUGGISH
FIMORRT	TRIFORM	**FLRSUUY**	SULFURY	**GGHINNO**	HONGING
FIMORTY	MORTIFY	**FMNORSU**	UNFORMS	**GGHINOS**	HOGGINS
FIMRTUY	FURMITY	**FMRSTUU**	FRUSTUM	**GGHINSU**	GUSHING
FIMSTYY	MYSTIFY	**FNNNUUY**	UNFUNNY		SUGHING
FINOOSS	FOISONS	**FNNOORT**	FRONTON	**GGHIOSW**	WOGGISH
FINOPRS	FRIPONS	**FNOORRW**	FORWORN	**GGHIPSU**	PUGGISH
FINOPSU	SOUPFIN	**FNOORSU**	SUNROOF	**GGHLOSY**	SHOGGLY
FINOPTY	PONTIFY		UNROOFS	**GGHORSU**	GROUGHS
FINORSS	FRISSON	**FNOPRTU**	UPFRONT	**GGHOSTU**	THUGGOS
FINORST	FORINTS	**FNRSTUU**	UNTURFS	**GGIIILN**	GINGILI
FINORTY	INTROFY	**FNSSUUY**	UNFUSSY	**GGIIJJS**	JIGJIGS
FINOSSU	FUSIONS	**FNSTTUU**	UNSTUFT	**GGIIKNN**	KINGING
FIOORSU	FURIOSO	**FOOOPRT**	ROOFTOP	**GGIILLN**	GILLING
FIOPRST	FORPITS	**FOOOTTU**	OUTFOOT	**GGIILMN**	GLIMING
	PROFITS	**FOORSSS**	FOSSORS	**GGIILNP**	PIGLING
	SPORTIF	**FOORTTX**	FOXTROT	**GGIILNR**	RIGLING
FIOPRSY	PROSIFY	**FOPSSTU**	FUSSPOT	**GGIILNU**	GUILING
FIOPSTX	POSTFIX	**FORRSUW**	FURROWS	**GGIIMNN**	MINGING
FIORRTY	TORRIFY	**FORRUWY**	FURROWY	**GGIIMNP**	GIMPING
FIORSUU	FURIOUS	**FORSSTW**	FROWSTS	**GGIIMNR**	GRIMING
FIOSTTU	OUTFITS	**FORSTWY**	FROWSTY	**GGIINNN**	GINNING
FIOTTTU	TOFUTTI	**GGGGIIN**	GIGGING	**GGIINNO**	INGOING
FIPPUYY	YUPPIFY	**GGGHINO**	HOGGING	**GGIINNP**	PINGING
FIRSSTT	STRIFTS	**GGGHINU**	HUGGING	**GGIINNR**	GIRNING
FIRSSUY	RUSSIFY	**GGGIIJN**	JIGGING		RINGING
FKLMOOT	FOLKMOT	**GGGIILN**	LIGGING	**GGIINNS**	SIGNING
FKLORUW	WORKFUL	**GGGIINP**	PIGGING		SINGING
FKNOSTY	KONFYTS	**GGGIINR**	RIGGING	**GGIINNT**	TINGING
FKOOORS	FORSOOK	**GGGIINT**	TIGGING	**GGIINNW**	WINGING
FKRSSUY	SKYSURF	**GGGIINW**	WIGGING	**GGIINNZ**	ZINGING
FLLOOSW	FOLLOWS	**GGGIINZ**	ZIGGING	**GGIINPP**	GIPPING
FLLOPTU	PLOTFUL	**GGGIIST**	GIGGITS	**GGIINPR**	GRIPING
	TOPFULL	**GGGIJNO**	JOGGING	**GGIINPS**	PIGGINS
FLLOSSY	LOSLYFS	**GGGIJNU**	JUGGING	**GGIINRS**	GRISING
FLLOSUU	SOULFUL	**GGGILNO**	LOGGING	**GGIINRT**	GIRTING
FLLOUWY	WOFULLY	**GGGILNU**	LUGGING		RINGGIT
FLLSTUU	LUSTFUL	**GGGIMNO**	MOGGING	**GGIINSU**	GUISING
FLMMOUX	FLUMMOX	**GGGIMNU**	MUGGING	**GGIINSV**	GIVINGS
FLMNOOU	MOUFLON	**GGGINNO**	GONGING	**GGIINTT**	GITTING
FLMNOSU	MUFLONS		NOGGING	**GGIIRRS**	GRIGRIS
FLMOOOT	TOMFOOL			**GGIJNSU**	JUGGINS
FLMOORS	FORMOLS	**GGGINNU**	GUNGING	**GGIKLNU**	KLUGING
FLMOORU	ROOMFUL	**GGGINOR**	GORGING	**GGIKNOR**	GROKING
FLMORSY	FORMYLS	**GGGINOS**	SOGGING	**GGIKNOS**	GINGKOS
		GGGINOT	TOGGING		

	GINKGOS	**GGNOORS**	GORGONS	**GHILNOW**	HOWLING
GGILLNU	GULLING	**GGNOOSY**	GONGYOS	**GHILNPU**	INGULPH
GGILMUY	MUGGILY	**GGRRSUU**	GRUGRUS	**GHILNRU**	HURLING
GGILNNO	LONGING	**GHHIIIS**	HIGHISH	**GHILNSU**	LUSHING
GGILNNU	LUNGING	**GHHIIST**	HIGHTHS		SHULING
GGILNOS	GOSLING	**GHHIINS**	HISHING	**GHILNSY**	SHINGLY
	OGLINGS	**GHHINSU**	HUSHING	**GHILNTY**	NIGHTLY
GGILNOV	GLOVING	**GHHIOPT**	HIGHTOP	**GHILOSU**	SLOUGHI
GGILNOW	GLOWING	**GHHIRST**	SHRIGHT	**GHILPST**	PLIGHTS
	GOWLING	**GHHORTU**	THROUGH	**GHILPTU**	UPLIGHT
GGILNOZ	GLOZING	**GHHOSSU**	SHOUGHS	**GHILPTY**	YPLIGHT
GGILNPU	GULPING	**GHHOTTU**	THOUGHT	**GHILRTY**	RIGHTLY
GGILNRU	GURLING	**GHIIIMN**	MIHIING	**GHILSST**	SLIGHTS
GGILNSU	LUGINGS	**GHIIKNO**	HOIKING	**GHILSTY**	SIGHTLY
GGILNUY	GUYLING	**GHIIKNT**	KITHING	**GHILSUY**	GUSHILY
	UGLYING	**GHIILLN**	HILLING	**GHILTTY**	TIGHTLY
GGILOOS	GIGOLOS	**GHIILNR**	HIRLING	**GHILTWY**	WIGHTLY
GGILOST	GIGLOTS	**GHIILNT**	HILTING	**GHIMMNU**	HUMMING
GGILOSY	SOGGILY		LITHING	**GHIMNNY**	HYMNING
GGILRWY	WRIGGLY	**GHIILNW**	WHILING	**GHIMNOS**	GNOMISH
GGIMMNU	GUMMING	**GHIILRS**	GIRLISH		HOMINGS
GGIMNNU	MUNGING	**GHIINNS**	SHINING		MOSHING
GGIMNOR	GORMING	**GHIINNT**	HINTING	**GHIMNPU**	HUMPING
GGIMNPU	GUMPING		NITHING	**GHIMNRY**	RHYMING
GGIMNPY	GYMPING	**GHIINNW**	WHINING	**GHIMNSU**	MUSHING
GGIMNSU	MUGGINS	**GHIINOS**	HOISING	**GHIMRSU**	SIMURGH
GGINNNU	GUNNING	**GHIINPP**	HIPPING	**GHIMSST**	SMIGHTS
GGINNOO	ONGOING	**GHIINPS**	PISHING	**GHIMSTT**	MIGHTST
GGINNOP	PONGING	**GHIINPT**	PITHING	**GHINNOO**	HOONING
GGINNOR	GRONING	**GHIINRS**	HIRINGS	**GHINNOP**	PHONING
GGINNOS	NOGGINS		SHIRING	**GHINNOR**	HORNING
GGINNOT	TONGING	**GHIINSS**	HISSING	**GHINNOS**	NOSHING
GGINNOW	GOWNING	**GHIINST**	HISTING	**GHINNOT**	NOTHING
GGINNRU	GURNING		INSIGHT	**GHINNTU**	HUNTING
GGINOOP	POGOING		SHITING	**GHINOOP**	HOOPING
GGINOOS	GOOSING		SITHING		POOHING
GGINOPR	GORPING	**GHIINSV**	VISHING	**GHINOOS**	SHOOING
	GROPING	**GHIINSW**	WISHING	**GHINOOT**	HOOTING
	PORGING	**GHIINTT**	HITTING	**GHINOOV**	HOOVING
GGINOPU	UPGOING		TITHING	**GHINOPP**	HOPPING
GGINOQS	QIGONGS	**GHIINTW**	WHITING	**GHINOPS**	GINSHOP
GGINORS	GORINGS		WITHING		POSHING
	GRINGOS	**GHIINZZ**	HIZZING	**GHINOPY**	HYPOING
GGINORU	ROGUING	**GHIIOPR**	PIROGHI	**GHINORS**	HORSING
	ROUGING	**GHIIRST**	TIGRISH		SHORING
GGINORW	GROWING	**GHIJNOS**	JOSHING	**GHINORW**	WHORING
GGINORZ	GROZING	**GHIKLNO**	HOLKING	**GHINOST**	HOSTING
GGINOSS	GOSSING	**GHIKLNU**	HULKING		TOSHING
GGINOUV	VOGUING	**GHIKNNO**	HONKING	**GHINOSU**	HOUSING
GGINPPY	GYPPING	**GHIKNOO**	HOOKING	**GHINOSV**	SHOVING
GGINPRU	PURGING	**GHIKNOW**	HOWKING	**GHINOSW**	SHOWING
GGINRSU	SURGING	**GHIKNST**	KNIGHTS	**GHINOTT**	HOTTING
	URGINGS	**GHIKNSU**	HUSKING		TONIGHT
GGINSTU	GUSTING	**GHIKNTY**	KYTHING	**GHINOTU**	HOUTING
	GUTSING	**GHIKRTU**	TUGHRIK		THOUING
GGINTTU	GUTTING	**GHILLNU**	HULLING	**GHINPPU**	HUPPING
GGIOORS	GORGIOS	**GHILLSU**	GULLISH	**GHINPPY**	HYPPING
GGIPRSY	SPRIGGY	**GHILLTY**	LIGHTLY	**GHINPSU**	GUNSHIP
GGLLOOS	LOGLOGS	**GHILNOS**	HOLINGS		PUSHING
GGLOOOS	GOOGOLS		LONGISH	**GHINPSY**	HYPINGS
GGMRSUU	MUGGURS	**GHILNOT**	THOLING	**GHINRSU**	RUSHING

GHINRTU	HURTING	GIIKLMN	MILKING	GIILNOR	LIGROIN
	UNGIRTH	GIIKLNN	INKLING		ROILING
	UNRIGHT		KILNING	GIILNOS	SILOING
GHINSTU	SHUTING		LINKING		SOILING
	TUSHING	GIIKLNR	LIRKING	GIILNOT	TOILING
	UNSIGHT	GIIKLNS	LIKINGS	GIILNPP	LIPPING
GHINTTU	HUTTING		SILKING	GIILNPS	LISPING
GHINTTY	TYTHING	GIIKLNT	KILTING		PILINGS
GHIOPSZ	PHIZOGS		KITLING		SLIPING
GHIORSU	ROGUISH	GIIKNNO	OINKING		SPILING
GHIOSUV	VOGUISH	GIIKNNP	KINGPIN	GIILNRS	RIGLINS
GHIPRST	SPRIGHT		PINKING	GIILNRT	TIRLING
GHIPRTU	UPRIGHT	GIIKNNR	KIRNING	GIILNST	LISTING
GHIPSST	SPIGHTS		RINKING		SILTING
GHIPTTU	UPTIGHT	GIIKNNS	SINKING		STILING
GHIQSTU	QUIGHTS	GIIKNNT	TINKING		TILINGS
GHIRSTW	WRIGHTS	GIIKNNV	KNIVING	GIILNSV	LIVINGS
GHISTTW	TWIGHTS	GIIKNNW	WINKING		SLIVING
GHLMOOO	HOMOLOG	GIIKNNZ	ZINKING	GIILNTT	TILTING
GHLMOSU	MOGHULS	GIIKNPP	KIPPING		TITLING
GHLOOSY	SHOOGLY	GIIKNPS	PIGSKIN	GIILNTW	WILTING
GHLOPSU	PLOUGHS		PIKINGS		WITLING
GHLORUY	ROUGHLY		SPIKING	GIILOSS	GLIOSIS
GHLOSSU	SLOUGHS	GIIKNRS	GIRKINS	GIILOST	OLIGIST
GHLOSTY	GHOSTLY		GRISKIN	GIILRST	STRIGIL
GHLOSUY	SLOUGHY		KRISING	GIIMMNN	NIMMING
GHLOTUY	TOUGHLY		RISKING	GIIMMNR	RIMMING
GHMORSU	SORGHUM	GIIKNRY	YIRKING	GIIMNNS	MININGS
GHMOSTU	MUGSHOT	GIIKNSS	KISSING	GIIMNNT	MINTING
GHMPRSU	GRUMPHS		SKIINGS	GIIMNPP	PIMPING
GHMPRUY	GRUMPHY	GIIKNST	KISTING	GIIMNPR	PRIMING
GHNOOPS	GONOPHS		KITINGS	GIIMNPS	IMPINGS
GHNOPRY	GRYPHON		SKITING	GIIMNPW	WIMPING
GHNORST	THRONGS	GIIKNSV	SKIVING	GIIMNRT	MITRING
GHNORUU	UNROUGH		VIKINGS	GIIMNRV	MIRVING
GHNOSSU	SHOGUNS	GIIKNTT	KITTING	GIIMNSS	MISSING
GHNOSTU	GUNSHOT	GIILLLN	LILLING	GIIMNST	MISTING
	HOGNUTS	GIILLMN	MILLING		SMITING
	NOUGHTS	GIILLNN	NILLING		STIMING
	SHOTGUN	GIILLNO	GILLION		TIMINGS
GHNOTUY	YOUNGTH	GIILLNP	PILLING	GIINNNP	PINNING
GHOOOSW	HOOSGOW	GIILLNR	RILLING	GIINNNR	RINNING
GHOOPST	PHOTOGS	GIILLNT	LILTING	GIINNNS	INNINGS
GHOOQSU	QUOHOGS		TILLING		SINNING
GHOORSS	SORGHOS	GIILLNW	WILLING	GIINNNT	TINNING
GHORSTU	TROUGHS	GIILMNN	LIMNING	GIINNNW	WINNING
GHORSTW	GROWTHS	GIILMNO	MOILING	GIINNOP	OPINING
GHORTUW	WROUGHT	GIILMNP	LIMPING		PIONING
GHORTUY	YOGHURT	GIILMNS	LIMINGS	GIINNOR	IRONING
GHORTWY	GROWTHY		SLIMING		ROINING
GHOSTUU	OUTGUSH		SMILING	GIINNOS	NOISING
GIIIKNT	TIKIING	GIILMNT	MILTING	GIINNOT	OINTING
GIIINRS	IRISING	GIILMPR	PILGRIM	GIINNPP	NIPPING
	NIGIRIS	GIILMRY	GRIMILY	GIINNPS	SNIPING
GIIJKNN	JINKING	GIILNNN	LINNING	GIINNPU	PINGUIN
GIIJLNT	JILTING	GIILNNR	NIRLING	GIINNRS	RINSING
GIIJNNO	JOINING	GIILNNS	LIGNINS	GIINNRT	TRINING
GIIJNNX	JINXING		LININGS	GIINNRU	INURING
GIIKKNN	KINKING	GIILNNT	LINTING		RUINING
GIIKKNR	KIRKING	GIILNNY	INLYING		URINING
GIIKLLN	KILLING	GIILNOP	PIGNOLI	GIINNSW	INSWING

GIINNTT	TINTING	**GIJKNOO**	JOOKING	**GILLNYY**	LYINGLY
GIINNTU	UNITING	**GIJKNOU**	JOUKING	**GILLOOS**	LOLIGOS
GIINNTV	VINTING	**GIJLLNO**	JOLLING	**GILLORS**	RIGOLLS
GIINNTW	TWINING	**GIJLNOT**	JOLTING	**GILMMUY**	GUMMILY
GIINOPS	POISING	**GIJLNOU**	JOULING	**GILMNOO**	LOOMING
GIINORS	ORIGINS	**GIJLNOW**	JOWLING		MOOLING
	SIGNIOR	**GIJLNSU**	JUNGLIS	**GILMNOR**	MORLING
	SIGNORI	**GIJMNPU**	JUMPING	**GILMNOT**	MOLTING
GIINORT	IGNITOR	**GIJNOTT**	JOTTING	**GILMNOY**	MOYLING
	RIOTING	**GIJNRUY**	JURYING	**GILMNPU**	LUMPING
GIINOSY	YOGINIS	**GIJNSTU**	JUSTING		PLUMING
GIINOTT	TOITING	**GIJNTTU**	JUTTING	**GILMNRU**	MURLING
GIINPPP	PIPPING	**GIKKNNO**	KONKING	**GILMNSU**	LIGNUMS
GIINPPR	RIPPING	**GIKKNOO**	KOOKING	**GILMPSY**	GYMSLIP
GIINPPS	PIPINGS	**GIKKNOY**	YOKKING	**GILNNOO**	GLONOIN
	SIPPING	**GIKKNUY**	YUKKING		LOONING
GIINPPT	TIPPING	**GIKLNOO**	LOOKING	**GILNNOU**	LOUNING
GIINPPY	YIPPING	**GIKLNOP**	POLKING	**GILNNOW**	LOWNING
GIINPPZ	ZIPPING	**GIKLNRU**	LURKING	**GILNNRU**	NURLING
GIINPQU	PIQUING	**GIKLNSU**	LUSKING	**GILNNSU**	UNSLING
GIINPRS	PRISING		SULKING	**GILNNTU**	LUNTING
	RISPING	**GIKMNOS**	SMOKING	**GILNNUV**	VULNING
	SPIRING	**GIKMNSU**	MUSKING	**GILNOOP**	LOOPING
GIINPRZ	PRIZING	**GIKNNNO**	KONNING		POOLING
GIINPSS	PISSING	**GIKNNOO**	KONGONI	**GILNOOS**	LOGIONS
GIINPST	SPITING	**GIKNNOP**	PONKING		LOOSING
GIINPSW	SWIPING	**GIKNNOS**	SNOKING		OLINGOS
	WIPINGS	**GIKNNOT**	TONKING		SOLOING
	WISPING	**GIKNNOW**	KNOWING		SOOLING
GIINPTT	PITTING	**GIKNNOZ**	ZONKING	**GILNOOT**	LOOTING
GIINPTW	WINGTIP	**GIKNNSU**	UNKINGS		TOOLING
GIINPTY	PITYING	**GIKNOOP**	POOKING	**GILNOPP**	LOPPING
GIINQRU	QUIRING	**GIKNOOR**	ROOKING	**GILNOPR**	PROLING
GIINQTU	QUITING	**GIKNOOS**	SOOKING	**GILNOPS**	POLINGS
GIINRRS	SIRRING	**GIKNOPR**	PORKING		SLOPING
GIINRRT	TIRRING		PROKING	**GILNOPT**	POLTING
GIINRRY	YIRRING	**GIKNOPS**	SPOKING	**GILNOPU**	LOUPING
GIINRSS	RISINGS	**GIKNOPU**	POUKING	**GILNOPW**	LOWPING
	SIRINGS	**GIKNORT**	TROKING		PLOWING
GIINRST	STIRING	**GIKNORW**	WORKING	**GILNOPY**	PLOYING
	TIRINGS	**GIKNORY**	YORKING	**GILNORS**	LORINGS
GIINRSV	VIRGINS	**GIKNOST**	STOKING	**GILNORU**	LOURING
GIINRSW	WIRINGS	**GIKNOSU**	SOUKING	**GILNORY**	YORLING
GIINRTT	RITTING	**GIKNOSY**	YOKINGS	**GILNOSS**	LOSINGS
GIINRTW	TWIRING	**GIKNOTU**	TOUKING	**GILNOST**	LINGOTS
	WRITING	**GIKNOUY**	YOUKING		TIGLONS
GIINSST	SISTING	**GIKNRSY**	SKRYING		TOLINGS
GIINSSU	ISSUING		SKRYING	**GILNOSU**	LOUSING
GIINSSW	WISSING	**GIKNSTU**	TUSKING	**GILNOSV**	LOVINGS
GIINSSZ	SIZINGS	**GIKNSTY**	SKYTING		SOLVING
GIINSTT	SITTING	**GIKRSTU**	TUGRIKS	**GILNOSW**	LOWINGS
GIINSTU	SUITING	**GILLLNO**	LOLLING		LOWSING
GIINSTV	STIVING	**GILLLNU**	LULLING		SLOWING
GIINSTW	WISTING	**GILLMNU**	MULLING		SOWLING
GIINSVW	SWIVING	**GILLNNU**	NULLING	**GILNOTT**	LOTTING
GIINTTT	TITTING	**GILLNOP**	POLLING	**GILNOTU**	LOUTING
GIINTTW	WITTING	**GILLNOR**	ROLLING	**GILNOTV**	VOLTING
GIINVYZ	VIZYING	**GILLNOT**	TOLLING	**GILNOTW**	LOWTING
GIINZZZ	ZIZZING	**GILLNPU**	PULLING	**GILNOVV**	VOLVING
GIIORSV	ISOGRIV	**GILLNSU**	ULLINGS	**GILNOVW**	WOLVING
GIJKNNU	JUNKING	**GILLNUW**	WULLING	**GILNOWY**	YOWLING

GILNPPU	PULPING	GIMNPPU	PUMPING	GINOOSY	ISOGONY
GILNPRU	PURLING	GIMNPRU	RUMPING	GINOOTT	TOOTING
GILNPSU	PLUSING	GIMNPSU	IMPUGNS	GINOPPP	POPPING
	PULINGS		SPUMING	GINOPPS	SOPPING
	PULSING	GIMNPTU	TUMPING	GINOPPT	TOPPING
	PUSLING	GIMNPUY	YUMPING	GINOPPU	POUPING
GILNPUY	UPLYING	GIMNSSU	MUSINGS	GINOPPW	WOPPING
GILNRSU	LURINGS		MUSSING	GINOPRS	PROIGNS
	RULINGS	GIMNSTU	MUSTING		PROSING
GILNSSU	NISGULS	GIMNSTY	STYMING		ROPINGS
GILNSTU	LUSTING	GIMNUZZ	MUZZING		SPORING
	LUTINGS	GIMORSS	OGRISMS	GINOPRT	PORTING
	SINGULT		SIMORGS		TROPING
GILNSTY	STYLING	GIMORSW	MISGROW	GINOPRU	INGROUP
GILNSUY	LUNGYIS	GIMOSSY	YOGISMS		POURING
GILNVYY	VYINGLY	GIMOSTU	GOMUTIS		ROUPING
GILOORS	GIROSOL	GIMRSSU	SIMURGS	GINOPRV	PROVING
GILOOSS	ISOLOGS	GIMRSUU	GURUISM	GINOPRW	POWRING
GILOOST	OLOGIST	GINNNOO	NOONING	GINOPRY	YORPING
GILOOTW	TWIGLOO	GINNNOR	RONNING	GINOPSS	POSINGS
GILORTT	TRIGLOT	GINNNOW	WONNING		POSSING
GILORTY	TRILOGY	GINNNPU	PUNNING	GINOPST	POSTING
GILOSTT	GLOTTIS	GINNNRU	RUNNING		STOPING
GILOTUY	GOUTILY	GINNNSU	SUNNING	GINOPSU	SOUPING
GILRSTY	GRISTLY	GINNNTU	TUNNING	GINOPSY	POYSING
GILRTUY	LITURGY	GINNOOS	NOOSING	GINOPTT	POTTING
GILRYZZ	GRIZZLY	GINNOOW	WOONING	GINOPTU	POUTING
GILSTUY	GUSTILY	GINNOOZ	ZOONING	GINOQTU	QUOTING
	GUTSILY	GINNOPS	SPONGIN	GINORRT	RORTING
GIMMMNU	MUMMING	GINNOPY	PONYING	GINORRV	VORRING
GIMMNOT	TOMMING	GINNORS	SNORING	GINORSS	GRISONS
GIMMNPU	MUMPING		SORNING		INGROSS
GIMMNRY	RYMMING	GINNORU	GRUNION		SIGNORS
GIMMNSU	SUMMING	GINNORW	INGROWN		SORINGS
GIMMNUV	VUMMING	GINNORY	GIRONNY	GINORST	ROSTING
GIMMORS	GIMMORS		ROYNING		SORTING
GIMNNOO	MOONING	GINNOSS	NOSINGS		STORING
GIMNNOR	MORNING	GINNOST	STONING		TRIGONS
GIMNNOS	MIGNONS		TONINGS	GINORSU	ROUSING
GIMNNTU	MUNTING	GINNOSW	SNOWING		SOURING
GIMNOOP	MOOPING		WONINGS	GINORSV	ROVINGS
GIMNOOR	MOORING	GINNOSZ	ZONINGS	GINORSW	ROWINGS
	ROOMING	GINNOTW	WONTING		WORSING
GIMNOOS	SOOMING	GINNPRU	PRUNING	GINORSY	ROSYING
GIMNOOT	MOOTING	GINNPTU	PUNTING		SIGNORY
	TOOMING	GINNRSU	NURSING	GINORTT	ROTTING
GIMNOOV	MOOVING		URNINGS	GINORTU	OUTGRIN
GIMNOOZ	ZOOMING	GINNRTU	TURNING		OUTRING
GIMNOPP	MOPPING	GINNSTU	TUNINGS		ROUTING
GIMNOPR	ROMPING	GINNTTU	NUTTING		TOURING
GIMNOPU	MOUPING	GINNTUY	UNTYING	GINORTW	ROWTING
GIMNOPY	YOMPING	GINOOPP	POGONIP		TROWING
GIMNORS	SMORING		POOPING	GINOSSS	SOSSING
GIMNORU	ROUMING	GINOOPR	ROOPING	GINOSST	STINGOS
GIMNORW	WORMING	GINOOPS	SOOPING		TOSSING
GIMNOSS	MOSSING	GINOOPT	POOTING	GINOSSU	SOUSING
GIMNOST	GNOMIST	GINOORS	ROOSING	GINOSSW	SOWINGS
GIMNOSU	MOUSING	GINOORT	ROOTING		SOWSING
	SOUMING	GINOOSS	ISOGONS	GINOSTT	SOTTING
GIMNOSW	MOWINGS	GINOOST	SOOTING	GINOSTU	OUSTING
	SOWMING	GINOOSW	WOOINGS		OUTINGS

	OUTSING	**GJOORTT**	JOGTROT	**GNOPRUW**	GROWNUP
	TOUSING	**GKKNOOS**	SONGKOK		UPGROWN
GINOSTV	STOVING	**GKMOOSU**	GOMOKUS	**GNOPSTU**	POTGUNS
	VOTINGS	**GLLLOOR**	LOGROLL	**GNORTUU**	OUTRUNG
GINOSTW	STOWING	**GLLOOPS**	GOLLOPS	**GNOSTUU**	OUTGUNS
	TOWINGS	**GLMMSUU**	SLUMGUM		OUTSUNG
	TOWSING	**GLMNOOO**	MONOLOG	**GNPSUUW**	UPSWUNG
GINOSTY	TOYINGS	**GLMNOOS**	MONGOLS	**GOOOORS**	GOOROOS
GINOTTT	TOTTING	**GLMNUUU**	UMLUNGU	**GOOPRST**	GOSPORT
GINOTTU	TOUTING	**GLMOOOR**	MOORLOG	**GOORSTT**	GROTTOS
GINOTTW	TOWTING	**GLMOOYY**	MYOLOGY	**GOORTUW**	OUTGROW
	WOTTING	**GLMORUW**	LUGWORM	**GOPRSUW**	UPGROWS
GINOTUW	OUTWING	**GLNNOOR**	LORGNON	**GORRSTU**	TURGORS
GINOTUZ	TOUZING	**GLNNSUU**	UNSLUNG	**GORSTTU**	GUTROTS
GINOTWZ	TOWZING	**GLNOOOS**	OOLONGS		ROTGUTS
GINPPPU	PUPPING	**GLNOOOY**	NOOLOGY	**GORSTUY**	YOGURTS
GINPPSU	SUPPING	**GLNOOPR**	PROLONG	**HHIIPPS**	HIPPISH
	UPPINGS	**GLNOOPY**	POLYGON	**HHIISTW**	WHITISH
GINPPTU	TUPPING	**GLNOOSU**	OULONGS	**HHIMRTY**	RHYTHMI
GINPRRU	PURRING	**GLNORWY**	WRONGLY	**HHINNSU**	HUNNISH
GINPRSS	SPRINGS	**GLNOSUW**	SUNGLOW	**HHINORS**	HORNISH
GINPRSU	PURSING	**GLNOTTU**	GLUTTON	**HHIOPST**	HIPSHOT
GINPRSY	PRYINGS	**GLNOUYY**	YOUNGLY	**HHIORSW**	WHORISH
	PRYSING	**GLNPSUU**	UNPLUGS	**HHIOSTT**	HOTTISH
	SPRINGY	**GLOOORY**	OROLOGY	**HHISSTW**	WHISHTS
GINPSSY	SPYINGS	**GLOOOTY**	OTOLOGY	**HHMMSUU**	HUMHUMS
GINPSTU	PIGNUTS	**GLOOOYZ**	ZOOLOGY	**HHMRSTY**	RHYTHMS
	STUPING	**GLOOPRS**	PROLOGS	**HHOOSTT**	HOTSHOT
GINPSTY	TYPINGS	**GLOORUY**	UROLOGY	**HHOPPTU**	HUPPOTH
GINPSUW	UPSWING	**GLOOSTU**	LOGOUTS	**HIIIKRS**	RIKISHI
GINPTTU	PUTTING	**GLOOTUW**	OUTGLOW	**HIIISTV**	SHIVITI
GINPTUY	UPTYING	**GLOPSTU**	PUTLOGS	**HIIJKNS**	HIJINKS
GINPTUZ	PUTZING	**GLORSSY**	GROSSLY	**HIIKLMS**	KHILIMS
GINQTUY	QUYTING	**GLPRSUY**	SPLURGY	**HIIKMOS**	MOKIHIS
GINRRSU	RUNRIGS	**GMMOSUU**	GUMMOUS	**HIIKNNS**	SHINKIN
GINRSST	STRINGS	**GMMPUUW**	MUGWUMP	**HIIKNOS**	INKHOSI
GINRSTU	RUSTING	**GMNNOOS**	GNOMONS	**HIIKNPS**	KINSHIP
GINRSTY	STRINGY	**GMNOORU**	GUNROOM		PINKISH
	STYRING	**GMNOORW**	MORWONG	**HIILMTU**	LITHIUM
	TRYINGS	**GMNSTUU**	GUMNUTS	**HIILNSY**	SHINILY
GINRSUU	USURING	**GMNSUUZ**	MZUNGUS	**HIILPST**	SHILPIT
GINRTTU	RUTTING	**GMOOPRS**	POGROMS	**HIILPSU**	HUIPILS
GINSSSU	SUSSING	**GMOOSTU**	GOMUTOS	**HIILPTY**	PITHILY
GINSTTU	TUTSING	**GMORSUU**	GRUMOUS	**HIILRTT**	TRILITH
GINSTTY	STYTING	**GMORTUW**	MUGWORT	**HIIMMSS**	MISHMIS
GINTTTU	TUTTING	**GMPSSUY**	GYPSUMS	**HIIMNNO**	HOMININ
GIOOPRR	PORRIGO	**GMRUYYZ**	ZYMURGY	**HIIMNSX**	MINXISH
GIOORSV	VIGOROS	**GNNOORS**	ROGNONS	**HIIMPSW**	WIMPISH
GIOPRRU	PRURIGO	**GNNORUW**	UNGROWN	**HIIMRSU**	SHIURIM
GIOPSSS	GOSSIPS	**GNNORYY**	GYRONNY	**HIIMSSS**	MISSISH
GIOPSST	SPIGOTS	**GNNOSUW**	UNGOWNS	**HIIMSST**	MISHITS
GIOPSSY	GOSSIPY	**GNNOUUY**	UNYOUNG	**HIIMSTT**	SHITTIM
GIOPSTU	PIGOUTS	**GNNRUUW**	UNWRUNG	**HIINNOT**	THIONIN
GIORRSU	RIGOURS	**GNNSTUU**	UNSTUNG	**HIINORS**	NOIRISH
GIORSTU	OUTRIGS	**GNOOORS**	GORSOON		ROINISH
	RIGOUTS	**GNOOOSS**	GOSSOON	**HIINOSS**	HOISINS
GIORSUV	VIGOURS	**GNOOOYZ**	ZOOGONY	**HIINPPS**	HIPPINS
GIOSSYZ	ZYGOSIS	**GNOORST**	TROGONS	**HIINPSS**	INSHIPS
GJLMUUU	JUGULUM	**GNOPPSU**	OPPUGNS	**HIINSSW**	SWINISH
GJNOOSU	GOUJONS		POPGUNS	**HIINSTW**	WITHINS
GJNRSUU	GURJUNS	**GNOPRTU**	GUNPORT	**HIIOPRS**	POHIRIS

HIIOPRW	POWHIRI		STYLISH	HIORSSU	SOURISH
HIIOPRZ	RHIZOPI	HILSTTY	THISTLY	HIORSTY	HISTORY
HIIORST	HISTRIO	HILSTWY	SWITHLY	HIOSSTT	SOTTISH
HIIPSSW	WISPISH	HILSTXY	SIXTHLY	HIOSTTU	OUTHITS
HIIPSXY	PIXYISH	HIMMPSU	MUMPISH	HIOSTUW	OUTWISH
HIISTTT	TITTISH	HIMMRSU	RUMMISH	HIOTTUW	OUTWITH
HIJNSSU	SHINJUS	HIMMSTY	MYTHISM		WITHOUT
HIKLNOT	HOTLINK	HIMNOOS	MOONISH	HIPPSTU	PUSHPIT
HIKLSSU	LUSKISH	HIMNOPR	MORPHIN	HIQSSUY	SQUISHY
HIKLSUY	HUSKILY	HIMNRSU	MUNSHIS	HIRSSTT	THIRSTS
HIKMNOS	MONKISH	HIMNSTU	HUMINTS		THRISTS
HIKMOTV	MIKVOTH	HIMNSTY	HYMNIST	HIRSTTU	RUTTISH
HIKMRSU	MURKISH	HIMOORS	MOORISH	HIRSTTY	THIRSTY
HIKMSUZ	MUZHIKS	HIMOPRS	ORPHISM		THRISTY
HIKNNOR	INKHORN		ROMPISH	HISSTUZ	SHITZUS
HIKNNTU	UNTHINK	HIMOPSS	SOPHISM	HJNNOOS	JOHNSON
HIKNOOU	HOKONUI	HIMOPST	PHOTISM	HKKLOOS	KOLKHOS
HIKNPSU	PUNKISH	HIMORST	RIMSHOT	HKKLOOZ	KOLKHOZ
HIKNRSS	SHRINKS	HIMORSW	WORMISH	HKKOOSY	SKYHOOK
HIKOORS	ROOKISH	HIMORTU	THORIUM	HKKOSTU	SUKKOTH
HIKOPSY	SKYPHOI	HIMOTTY	TIMOTHY	HKLOOYZ	KOLHOZY
HILLOPT	HILLTOP	HIMPRSS	SHRIMPS	HKNOOSS	SHNOOKS
HILLOPY	LYOPHIL	HIMPRSY	SHRIMPY	HKNOOSU	UNHOOKS
HILLPSU	UPHILLS	HIMPRTU	TRIUMPH	HKNOOWW	KNOWHOW
HILLRSS	SHRILLS	HIMPTUY	PYTHIUM	HKNSSUU	UNHUSKS
HILLRST	THRILLS	HIMRSTY	RHYMIST	HKOOOPT	POTHOOK
HILLRSY	SHRILLY	HIMSSTU	ISTHMUS	HKOOPSU	HOOKUPS
HILLRTY	THRILLY	HIMSTTY	MYTHIST	HKOOSST	SHTOOKS
HILMMOU	HOLMIUM	HINNNSU	NUNNISH	HKOOSVZ	SOVKHOZ
HILMOPS	LOMPISH	HINNORT	TINHORN	HKOPSSY	SKYPHOS
	PHLOMIS	HINNOST	TONNISH	HKORSWY	WORKSHY
HILMOSS	HOLISMS	HINNPSU	NUNSHIP	HLLOOOS	HOLLOOS
HILMOSW	WHOLISM	HINOOPS	INHOOPS	HLLOOSU	HULLOOS
HILMPSU	LUMPISH	HINOORT	HORNITO	HLLOOSW	HOLLOWS
HILMSSY	HYLISMS	HINOORZ	HORIZON	HLLOPSY	PHYLLOS
HILMSUY	MUSHILY	HINOOST	INSOOTH	HLLPSUY	PLUSHLY
HILMTUU	THULIUM	HINOPPS	SHIPPON	HLMNOTY	MONTHLY
HILNNTY	NINTHLY	HINOPSS	SIPHONS	HLMNPYY	NYMPHLY
HILNOPY	PHONILY		SONSHIP	HLMOOSS	SHOLOMS
HILNORY	HORNILY	HINORST	HORNIST	HLMORRY	MYRRHOL
HILNOTY	THIONYL	HINORSU	NOURISH	HLMOSTY	THYMOLS
HILNPST	PLINTHS	HINORSY	ROYNISH	HLMPSSU	SHLUMPS
HILOOST	OOLITHS	HINOSST	STONISH	HLMPSUY	SHLUMPY
HILOOTT	OTOLITH	HINOSSW	SNOWISH	HLOOPSS	SPLOOSH
HILOOTZ	ZOOLITH	HINOSTW	TOWNISH	HLOOSTY	SOOTHLY
HILOPST	LITHOPS	HINPPSU	PUSHPIN	HLOOTUW	OUTHOWL
HILOPXY	OXYPHIL	HINPSSU	UNSHIPS	HLOPRTY	PROTHYL
HILORSY	HORSILY	HINPSTY	PHYTINS	HLOPSTY	PHYTOLS
HILORTU	UROLITH	HINPTUW	UNWHIPT	HLORSTY	SHORTLY
HILOSST	HOLISTS	HINRSTU	RUNTISH	HLOTUYY	YOUTHLY
HILOSSW	SLOWISH	HIOOPRS	POORISH	HLPRSUU	SULPHUR
HILOSTU	LOUTISH	HIOORSU	ORIHOUS		UPHURLS
HILOSTW	WHOLIST	HIOOSSV	SHIVOOS	HMMMSUU	HUMMUMS
HILOSTY	HYLOIST	HIOOSSW	WHOOSIS	HMMNOOY	HOMONYM
HILOSVW	WOLVISH	HIOPPPS	POPPISH	HMMOOSU	HOUMMOS
HILOSWY	SHOWILY	HIOPPSS	SHIPPOS	HMMRTUY	THRUMMY
HILOTWW	WHITLOW	HIOPRSU	HUPIROS	HMNOPSY	NYMPHOS
HILPRUW	UPWHIRL	HIOPRSW	WORSHIP	HMNOPYY	HYPONYM
HILPSST	SPILTHS	HIOPSST	SOPHIST	HMNPSUY	HYPNUMS
HILPSUY	PUSHILY	HIOPSSY	PHYSIOS	HMOOPRS	MORPHOS
HILSSTY	HYLISTS	HIOPSTU	UPHOIST	HMOORSS	SHROOMS

HMOOSST	SMOOTHS	IIIORRS	RISORII	IILPRVY	PRIVILY
HMOOSTY	SMOOTHY	IIIRSTT	TIRITIS	IILPSST	PISTILS
HMOOSUU	HOUMOUS	IIISTTW	WISTITI	IILPSTY	TIPSILY
HMORSUU	HUMOURS	IIJKNPU	KIPUNJI	IILPSWY	WISPILY
HMSTUYZ	ZYTHUMS	IIJKOPR	PIROJKI	IILRTYZ	RITZILY
HNNOOPS	PHONONS	IIJLLNO	JILLION	IILSTTT	TITLIST
HNNORSU	UNSHORN	IIJMMNY	JIMMINY	IILTTUY	UTILITY
HNNOSTY	SYNTHON	IIJMNOS	MISJOIN	IILTTWY	WITTILY
HNNOSUW	UNSHOWN	IIJNNOT	INJOINT	IIMMMNU	MINIMUM
HNOOPST	PHOTONS	IIKKLNY	KINKILY	IIMMNSU	MINIMUS
HNOOPSU	UNHOOPS	IIKKNPS	KIPSKIN		MINIUMS
HNOOPTY	TYPHOON	IIKKORS	KOKIRIS	IIMNNOS	MINIONS
HNOORSS	HORSONS	IIKLLMY	MILKILY	IIMNOSS	MISSION
HNOORST	THORONS	IIKLLSY	SILKILY	IIMNOSU	IONIUMS
HNOORSU	HONOURS	IIKLMNP	LIMPKIN		NIMIOUS
HNOOSTU	UNSHOOT	IIKLMRY	MIRKILY	IIMNOTX	MIXTION
HNOPSSY	SYPHONS	IIKLNOS	OILSKIN	IIMNPRT	IMPRINT
HNOPSTY	PHYTONS	IIKLPSY	SPIKILY	IIMOPSU	IMPIOUS
	PYTHONS	IIKLRSY	RISKILY	IIMOSST	MITOSIS
	TYPHONS	IIKMNOR	KIRIMON	IIMOSSU	SIMIOUS
HNORSTY	RHYTONS	IIKMNPS	SIMPKIN	IIMRSST	SMRITIS
HNORTUW	UNWORTH	IIKMNSS	SIMKINS	IIMRSSU	SURIMIS
HNOSTUU	UNSHOUT	IIKNNOS	KONINIS	IIMRSTW	MISWRIT
HNOSUWY	UNSHOWY	IIKNOSS	INKOSIS	IIMRTTU	TRITIUM
HNOTTUU	OUTHUNT	IIKNPPS	PIPKINS	IIMRTUV	TRIVIUM
HNRTTUU	UNTRUTH	IIKNSSS	SISKINS	IIMSSSZ	SIZISMS
HNSSTUU	UNSHUTS	IIKOSST	OIKISTS	IIMSSTT	TIMISTS
HOOOOPS	HOOPOOS	IIKOSTT	TITOKIS	IIMSSTU	MISSUIT
HOOPPST	POTSHOP	IIKPSUW	WIKIUPS	IINNOOP	OPINION
HOOPRST	PORTHOS	IILLLSY	SILLILY	IINNOPS	PINIONS
HOOPSSY	SHYPOOS	IILLMNO	MILLION		SPINONI
HOOPSTT	HOTPOTS	IILLMSY	SLIMILY	IINNOTU	UNITION
	HOTSPOT	IILLNOP	PILLION	IINNQSU	QUININS
	POTSHOT	IILLNOZ	ZILLION	IINNQTU	QUINTIN
HOOPSTU	UPSHOOT	IILLNST	INSTILL	IINOPSS	ISOSPIN
HOOPSTY	TOYSHOP	IILLNTT	LITTLIN		SINOPIS
HOOQSSU	SQUOOSH	IILLPSU	ILLUPIS	IINOPST	POITINS
HOORRRS	HORRORS	IILMNOS	LIONISM	IINORST	IRONIST
HOORRST	ORTHROS	IILMNSS	SIMLINS	IINORSV	VIRINOS
HOORSUZ	HUZOORS	IILMORS	SIMILOR		VIRIONS
HOOSTTU	OUTSHOT	IILMOSS	LIMOSIS	IINORTT	INTROIT
HOPRSTU	HOTSPUR	IILMSTU	STIMULI	IINOSSV	VISIONS
HOPRTTU	PRUTOTH	IILMSTY	MISTILY	IINOSUV	INVIOUS
HOPRTUW	UPTHROW	IILNNOT	NITINOL	IINOTTU	TUITION
HOPSSSY	HYSSOPS	IILNNSU	INSULIN	IINPPPS	PIPPINS
HOPSSTU	UPSHOTS		INULINS	IINQRUY	INQUIRY
HOPSTUU	OUTPUSH	IILNNTY	TINNILY	IINRSTU	SIRTUIN
HOPSTUY	TYPHOUS	IILNOPT	PINITOL	IINRTTY	TRINITY
HORSTTW	TROWTHS	IILNORS	SIRLOIN	IINSSST	INSISTS
HORSTUU	OUTRUSH	IILNOSV	VIOLINS	IINSTTU	INTUITS
HOSSTTU	STOUTHS	IILNOSY	NOISILY	IINSTTW	INTWIST
HOSTTUU	SHUTOUT	IILNPPY	NIPPILY		NITWITS
HPPSSUU	PUSHUPS	IILNPTU	PILINUT	IIOOPPS	PIOPIOS
HPRTTUU	THRUPUT	IILNPUV	PULVINI	IIOOSTT	TOITOIS
HRSSTTU	THRUSTS	IILNRST	NITRILS	IIOPRSS	PISSOIR
HRSSTUY	THYRSUS	IILNRSV	RIVLINS	IIOPSTY	PIOSITY
IIIJJLN	JINJILI	IILNSST	INSTILS	IIORSSV	VIROSIS
IIIKMNN	MINIKIN	IILOPRT	TRIPOLI	IIORSTV	IVORIST
IIIKMNS	MINISKI	IILOPST	PILOTIS		VISITOR
IIIMRST	MIRITIS	IILORTV	VITRIOL	IIOSTTU	OUSTITI
		IILOSTV	VIOLIST	IIOSTUV	VITIOUS

IIPPSUU	PIUPIUS
IIPRRSU	PURIRIS
IIPRSST	SPIRITS
	TRIPSIS
IIPRSTU	PITURIS
IIPRSTY	SPIRITY
IIPRTVY	PRIVITY
IIQSTUV	QIVIUTS
IIRRSTT	TIRRITS
IISSSTZ	SIZISTS
IISTTZZ	TZITZIS
IITTTZZ	TZITZIT
IJJMSUU	JUJUISM
IJJSTUU	JUJUIST
	JUJUIST
IJKLLOY	KILLJOY
IJKMOSU	MOUJIKS
IJKMSUZ	MUZJIKS
IJKNOSS	JOSKINS
IJLLLOY	JOLLILY
IJLLOTY	JOLLITY
	JOLTILY
IJLMPUY	JUMPILY
IJLNOQU	JONQUIL
IJLNOTY	JOINTLY
IJMNOPS	JIMPSON
IJMOOST	MOJITOS
IJMOSSS	JISSOMS
IJNNOTU	UNJOINT
IJNORSU	JUNIORS
IJNOTUX	OUTJINX
IJRSSTU	JURISTS
IKKLOOY	KOOKILY
IKKMNOU	KIKUMON
IKKNNSU	UNKINKS
IKKNORT	KIRKTON
IKKOOPY	KOPIYOK
IKKORRS	KORKIRS
IKKSUUY	KIKUYUS
IKLLOTU	OUTKILL
IKLLPSU	UPSKILL
IKLLSTU	KILLUTS
IKLLSUY	SULKILY
IKLMNPU	LUMPKIN
IKLMOOS	LOOKISM
IKLMOPS	MILKSOP
IKLMOSY	SMOKILY
	SOYMILK
IKLMRUY	MURKILY
IKLMSUY	MUSKILY
IKLNNSU	UNLINKS
IKLNOOS	SKOLION
IKLNOOT	KILOTON
IKLNORT	LINKROT
IKLNOSU	ULIKONS
IKLNPSU	LINKUPS
	SKULPIN
	UPLINKS
IKLNRWY	WRINKLY
IKLNTWY	TWINKLY
IKLOOST	LOOKIST
IKLOOTT	TOOLKIT
IKLOSSU	SOUSLIK
IKLSSSU	SUSLIKS
IKLSTTU	KITTULS
IKMNOOO	OKIMONO
IKMNOOR	OMIKRON
IKMNOOS	KIMONOS
	MONOSKI
IKMNORS	MIKRONS
	MORKINS
IKMNOSW	MISKNOW
IKMNPPU	PUMPKIN
IKMNRSU	RUMKINS
IKMNRTU	TRINKUM
IKMOOST	MISTOOK
IKMOSSU	KOUMISS
IKMPRSS	SKRIMPS
IKMSSTU	MUSKITS
IKNNPSU	PUNKINS
IKNNPTU	UNPINKT
IKNNSTU	UNKNITS
IKNOOST	ISOKONT
IKNOPRW	PINWORK
IKNOPST	INKPOTS
	INKSPOT
IKNORSW	INWORKS
IKNORTW	TINWORK
IKNPSTU	SPUTNIK
	UPKNITS
IKOORTT	ROOTKIT
IKORSTU	TURKOIS
IKOSSTU	OUTKISS
IKPRSSU	PRUSIKS
	SPRUIKS
IKPRSSY	KRYPSIS
ILLLOWY	LOWLILY
ILLMNOU	MULLION
ILLMNRU	MILLRUN
ILLMOOR	MOORILL
ILLMOOT	TIMOLOL
ILLMOPS	PLIMSOL
ILLMOSU	LOLIUMS
ILLMPUY	LUMPILY
ILLMSUU	LIMULUS
ILLNOOY	LOONILY
ILLNOQU	QUILLON
ILLNORU	RULLION
ILLNOST	LINTOLS
ILLNPUU	LUPULIN
ILLNSUW	UNWILLS
ILLNTUY	NULLITY
ILLOOPY	LOOPILY
ILLOORZ	ZORILLO
ILLOPRY	PILLORY
ILLOPST	POLLIST
ILLOPSW	PILLOWS
ILLOPWY	PILLOWY
ILLOSUV	VILLOUS
ILLOSUY	LOUSILY
ILLOSWW	WILLOWS
ILLOTUW	OUTWILL
ILLOTXY	XYLITOL
ILLOUVV	VOLVULI
ILLOWWY	WILLOWY
ILLPPUY	PULPILY
ILLPSUV	PULVILS
ILLQSSU	SQUILLS
ILLRSUY	SURLILY
ILLSTUY	LUSTILY
ILMMRUY	RUMMILY
ILMMSSU	SLUMISM
ILMMSUU	MIMULUS
ILMNOOT	MOONLIT
ILMNOOY	MOONILY
ILMNOSU	MOULINS
ILMNRSU	MURLINS
ILMNSSU	MUSLINS
ILMOORY	ROOMILY
ILMOOSS	MOLOSSI
ILMOOSV	MOOLVIS
ILMORSW	WORMILS
ILMORTU	TURMOIL
ILMOSTY	MOISTLY
ILMOSUY	MOUSILY
ILMPSSY	SLIMPSY
ILMPSTU	PLUMIST
ILMRSSY	LYRISMS
ILMSSUY	MUSSILY
ILMSTUY	MUSTILY
ILMUYZZ	MUZZILY
ILNNOOY	NONOILY
ILNNOPS	NONSLIP
ILNNORU	LINURON
ILNNSUY	SUNNILY
ILNOOPS	PLOSION
ILNOOPV	VOLPINO
ILNOORS	ROSINOL
ILNOOSS	SOLIONS
ILNOOST	LOTIONS
	SOLITON
ILNOPPS	POPLINS
ILNOPRU	PURLOIN
ILNOPST	PONTILS
ILNOPSU	PULSION
	UPSILON
ILNOPSY	YPSILON
ILNOPYY	POLYNYI
ILNOQSU	QUINOLS
ILNORST	NOSTRIL
ILNORSU	SURLOIN
ILNORTU	TORULIN
ILNOSST	TONSILS
ILNOSSU	INSOULS
ILNOSTU	OILNUTS
	ULTIONS
ILNOSTY	STONILY
	TYLOSIN
ILNOSWY	SNOWILY
ILNOTUV	VOLUTIN
ILNPRSU	PURLINS
ILNPSST	SPLINTS
ILNPSTU	UNSPILT

	UNSPLIT	**IMNOORR**	MORRION	**INNQSUY**	SQUINNY
ILNRSTY	NITRYLS	**IMNOORS**	MORIONS	**INNRSTU**	INTURNS
ILNSSTU	INSULTS	**IMNOORT**	MONITOR	**INOOPRT**	PORTION
ILNSSVY	SYLVINS		TROMINO	**INOOPSS**	POISONS
ILNTTUY	NUTTILY	**IMNOOSS**	MONOSIS		POISSON
ILOOORS	ROSOLIO		SIMOONS	**INOOPST**	OPTIONS
ILOOPST	POLOIST	**IMNOOST**	MOTIONS		POSITON
	TOPSOIL	**IMNOOSU**	OMINOUS		POTIONS
ILOORST	LORIOTS	**IMNOOSY**	ISONOMY	**INOORSS**	ORISONS
ILOORTY	OLITORY	**IMNOOUX**	OXONIUM	**INOORST**	ISOTRON
ILOOSST	SOLOIST	**IMNOPPU**	PUMPION		NITROSO
ILOOSTY	SOOTILY	**IMNOPRW**	PINWORM		TORSION
ILOOWYZ	WOOZILY	**IMNOPSU**	SPUMONI	**INOORSZ**	ZORINOS
ILOPPSY	SOPPILY	**IMNORRU**	MURRION	**INOORTT**	TORTONI
ILOPRRY	PRIORLY	**IMNORTY**	TRIONYM	**INOOSST**	TOISONS
ILOPRSY	PROSILY	**IMNOSST**	MONISTS	**INOOSUX**	NOXIOUS
ILOPRUY	ROUPILY	**IMNOSSY**	MYOSINS	**INOPPST**	TOPSPIN
ILOPSST	PISTOLS	**IMNOSVY**	VISNOMY	**INOPRSS**	PRISONS
	POSTILS	**IMNRRSU**	MURRINS		SPINORS
ILOPSSX	OXSLIPS	**IMNRSTU**	UNTRIMS	**INOPRST**	TROPINS
ILOPSTT	SPOTLIT	**IMOOPRX**	PROXIMO	**INOPRSU**	INPOURS
ILOPSTU	SLIPOUT	**IMOOSSS**	OSMOSIS	**INOPSST**	PISTONS
ILOPSUY	PIOUSLY	**IMOOSSU**	OSMIOUS		POSTINS
ILOQRSU	LIQUORS	**IMOOSTV**	VOMITOS		SPINTOS
ILORRSY	SORRILY	**IMOPRSS**	PORISMS	**INOPSSU**	POUSSIN
ILORSTU	TROILUS	**IMOPRST**	IMPORTS		SPINOUS
ILOSSTY	TOSSILY		TROPISM	**INOPSTT**	TINPOTS
	TYLOSIS	**IMOPRSV**	IMPROVS	**INOPSTU**	SPINOUT
ILOSTTW	WITTOLS	**IMOPRTU**	PROTIUM	**INORSTT**	INTORTS
ILPPSSU	SLIPUPS	**IMOPSST**	IMPOSTS		TRITONS
ILPPSTU	PULPITS		MISSTOP	**INORSTU**	NITROUS
ILPRSUY	PURSILY	**IMOPSTU**	UTOPISM		TURIONS
ILPSTTU	UPTILTS	**IMORRRS**	MIRRORS	**INORSUU**	RUINOUS
ILPSUUV	PLUVIUS	**IMORSST**	MISSORT		URINOUS
ILRSSTU	TRISULS	**IMORSTU**	TOURISM	**INORSUV**	UNVISOR
ILRSSTY	LYRISTS	**IMORSTY**	TRISOMY	**INOSSTT**	STOTINS
ILRSTUY	RUSTILY	**IMOSSTU**	MISSOUT	**INOSSTU**	OUTSINS
ILRTTUY	RUTTILY		SUMOIST		USTIONS
ILSSTTU	LUTISTS	**IMOSSYZ**	ZYMOSIS	**INOSSUU**	SINUOUS
ILSSTTY	STYLIST	**IMOSTTT**	TOMTITS	**INOSTUW**	OUTWINS
ILSTTUU	TITULUS	**IMOSTUV**	VOMITUS	**INPRSST**	SPRINTS
IMMMOSS	MOMISMS	**IMOSTUW**	OUTSWIM	**INPRSTU**	TURNIPS
IMMNOSS	MONISMS	**IMPRSSU**	PURISMS		UNSTRIP
	NOMISMS	**IMPSSTU**	SUMPITS	**INPRSTY**	TRYPSIN
IMMNOSU	MUSIMON	**IMQRSSU**	SQUIRMS	**INPRTUY**	TURNIPY
	OMNIUMS	**IMQRSUY**	SQUIRMY	**INQSSTU**	SQUINTS
IMMNOUU	MUONIUM	**IMRSSTU**	SISTRUM	**INQSTUY**	SQUINTY
IMMOOSS	SIMOOSS		TRISMUS	**INRSTTU**	INTRUST
IMMOPTU	OPTIMUM		TRUISMS	**INSSTUU**	SUNSUIT
IMMOSSU	OSMIUMS	**IMRTTUY**	YTTRIUM		UNSUITS
IMMOSTU	STOMIUM	**INNNOOR**	NONIRON	**INSTTUW**	UNTWIST
IMMOSTW	WOMMITS	**INNNORU**	RUNNION	**INTTUWY**	UNWITTY
IMMSSTU	MUTISMS	**INNOOPS**	OPSONIN	**IOOPRSS**	POROSIS
	SUMMIST	**INNOORS**	RONIONS	**IOOPRSV**	PROVISO
	SUMMITS	**INNOOST**	NOTIONS	**IOOPSTY**	ISOTOPY
IMNNNOU	MUNNION	**INNOPSY**	PINYONS	**IOORSSS**	SOROSIS
IMNNOOR	NORIMON	**INNORST**	INTRONS	**IOORSST**	TSOORIS
IMNNOSW	MINNOWS	**INNOSSU**	UNISONS	**IOORSTT**	RISOTTO
IMNNSTU	MUNTINS	**INNOSTU**	NONSUIT	**IOORSTU**	RIOTOUS
IMNOOPP	POMPION	**INNOSUY**	UNNOISY	**IOOSSSS**	SISSOOS
IMNOOPT	TOMPION	**INNOSWW**	WINNOWS	**IOOSSST**	OSTOSIS

Code	Word(s)
IOPPPRT	PITPROP
IOPPPST	POPPITS
IOPPRST	RIPSTOP
IOPPSTT	TIPTOPS
IOPRSST	RIPOSTS
IOPRSSY	PYROSIS
IOPRSTT	PROTIST, TROPIST
IOPSSTU	PISTOUS
IOPSTTU	UTOPIST
IOPTTUY	OUTPITY
IOQRTTU	QUITTOR
IOQSSTU	QUOISTS
IORRSTW	WORRITS
IORRSZZ	RIZZORS
IORRTTX	TORTRIX
IORSSTU	SUITORS, TSOURIS
IORSTTU	TOURIST
IORSTTW	TWISTOR
IORTTUW	OUTWRIT
IOSSSTT	TSOTSIS
IOSSTTU	OUTSITS
IOSTTUW	OUTWITS
IPPQSUU	QUIPPUS
IPRRSTU	IRRUPTS, STIRRUP
IPRSSTU	PURISTS, SPRUITS, UPRISTS, UPSTIRS
IPRSTUU	PURSUIT
IPSSSTY	STYPSIS
IPSSTTY	TYPISTS
IPSTTTU	TITTUPS
IPTTTUY	TITTUPY
IQRRSSU	SQUIRRS
IQRSSTU	SQUIRTS
JJSTUUU	JUJUTSU
JKNOOSU	KUNJOOS
JLLOOPS	JOLLOPS
JMOPTUU	OUTJUMP
JNNORUY	NONJURY
JNNOSTU	JOTUNNS
JNOORSU	JOURNOS, SOJOURN
JOOPPSY	JOYPOPS, POPJOYS
JOSTTUU	OUTJUTS
KKLMSUU	MUKLUKS
KKLOOYZ	KOLKOZY
KKMOOSU	SKOOKUM
KKMSTUU	MUKTUKS
KKNORSS	SKRONKS
KKNRSUU	KUNKURS
KKOOPSU	KOKOPUS
KKOSTUU	KOTUKUS
KKSSSTT	TSKTSKS
KLLMOSU	MOLLUSK
KLNOOPS	PLONKOS
KLOOOTU	LOOKOUT, OUTLOOK
KLOOPSU	LOOKUPS, UPLOOKS
KLOSTUU	OUTSULK
KLRSTUU	KULTURS
KMOOORS	MOKOROS
KMOSSUY	KOUMYSS
KMPRSSU	SKRUMPS
KNNNOUW	UNKNOWN
KNNOORW	NONWORK
KNNOSTU	UNKNOTS
KNOOPTT	TOPKNOT
KNOPRTY	KRYPTON
KNORRTY	KRYTRON
KNORSUW	UNWORKS
KOOOTTU	OUTTOOK
KOOPRTW	TOPWORK, WORKTOP
KOORTUW	OUTWORK, WORKOUT
KOOSSSU	KOUSSOS
KOOSSUU	SOUKOUS
KOOSTTU	TUKTOOS
KOOSTWW	KOWTOWS
KOPRSUW	WORKUPS
KORTTUW	TUTWORK
LLLMMUU	MULMULL
LLLOOPS	LOLLOPS
LLLOOPY	LOLLOPY
LLMMSUU	MULMULS
LLMOOPR	ROLLMOP
LLMPPUY	PLUMPLY
LLNORSU	UNROLLS
LLOOPRT	ROLLTOP, TROLLOP
LLOOPSY	POLYOLS
LLOOPTU	OUTPOLL
LLOORTU	OUTROLL, ROLLOUT
LLOOSTU	TOLUOLS
LLOPRSU	UPROLLS
LLOPTUU	OUTPULL, PULLOUT
LLORSST	STROLLS
LLOSTUY	TOLUYLS
LLPPSUU	PULLUPS
LMMSTUU	MULTUMS
LMOOOOS	MOOLOOS
LMOORSU	ORMOLUS
LMOOSTY	TOYLSOM
LMOPSUU	PLUMOUS
LMORSSU	MUSROLS
LMRSTUU	LUSTRUM
LMSTTUU	TUMULTS
LMSTUUU	TUMULUS
LNNOOOW	NONWOOL
LNNOPSU	NONPLUS
LNOOPSU	UNSPOOL
LNOOPTU	PULTOON
LNOOSST	STOLONS
LNOPSTU	PLUTONS, PULTONS
LNOSSUU	UNSOULS
LNPSTUU	PULTUNS
LNRTUUV	VULTURN
LNRTUUY	UNTRULY
LOOOORS	OLOROSO
LOOORST	ROTOLOS
LOOPTTU	OUTPLOT
LOOSSTV	VOLOSTS
LOPPRSY	PROPYLS
LOPPSUU	PULPOUS
LOPPSUY	POLYPUS
LOPRRSY	PYRROLS
LOPRSTY	PROTYLS
LOPRSUY	PYLORUS
LOPRTUY	POULTRY
LOPSSTY	STYLOPS
LORSTTY	TROTYLS
LORSTUU	TORULUS
LOSTTUY	STOUTLY
LPRSSUU	SURPLUS
MMNNOOY	MONONYM
MMNOSSU	MUSMONS, SUMMONS
MMOOPPS	POMPOMS
MMOOSTT	MOTMOTS
MMOPSTY	SYMPTOM
MMRRSUU	MURMURS
MMSTUUU	MUTUUMS
MMSUUUU	MUUMUUS
MNNOOOS	MONSOON
MNNOORU	MONURON
MNNOSYY	SYNONYM
MNNOTUU	UNMOUNT
MNOOOPP	POMPOON
MNOOOYZ	ZOONOMY
MNOOPPS	POMPONS
MNOOPST	TOMPONS
MNOOPTY	TOPONYM
MNOORSU	SUNROOM, UNMOORS
MNOOSTU	MOUTONS
MNOOSTW	TOWMONS
MNOOSUY	ONYMOUS
MNOOTTW	TOWMONT
MNORSTU	NOSTRUM
MNOSTTU	MUTTONS
MNOTTUY	MUTTONY
MOOOTYZ	ZOOTOMY
MOOPPSU	POMPOUS
MOOPRSY	POMROYS
MOOPSSU	OPOSSUM
MOOPSTT	TOPMOST
MOORRSW	MORROWS
MOOSTTU	OUTMOST
MOPPRST	PROMPTS
MOPSSSU	POSSUMS
MOPSSUU	SPUMOUS
MOQRSUU	QUORUMS
MOQSTUU	QUOTUMS
MORRSTU	ROSTRUM

MORRSUU	RUMOURS		UNROOTS	**OOPRTUU**	OUTPOUR
MORSTUU	TUMOURS	**NOORTUW**	OUTWORN	**OOPSSTT**	TOSSPOT
MOSSSTY	MYSOSTS	**NOOTTWY**	TOYTOWN	**OOPSTTU**	OUTPOST
MOSSTTU	UTMOSTS	**NOPPRSU**	UNPROPS		OUTTOPS
MOSSTUU	OUTSUMS	**NOPSSTU**	SUNSPOT	**OOPSWWW**	POWWOWS
MOSTUUW	OUTSWUM		UNSTOPS	**OORRSSW**	SORROWS
NNNSUUY	UNSUNNY	**NOPSTUW**	UPTOWNS	**OORSTUU**	ROUTOUS
NNOOOPR	NONPOOR	**NORSTUU**	OUTRUNS	**OORSTUW**	OUTROWS
NNOOOPT	PONTOON		RUNOUTS	**OORTTTU**	OUTTROT
NNOOPRS	NONPROS	**NORTTUU**	OUTTURN	**OPPPRSU**	UPPROPS
NNOOPRU	PRONOUN		TURNOUT	**OPPRRTU**	PURPORT
NNOOPSS	SPONSON	**NOSSTUW**	UNSTOWS	**OPPRSTU**	SUPPORT
NNOOPST	NONSTOP	**NPRSTUU**	TURNUPS	**OPPRSTY**	STROPPY
	PONTONS		UPTURNS	**OPPRSUY**	PYROPUS
NNOORSY	RONYONS	**NRSSTTU**	STRUNTS	**OPRSSTU**	SPROUTS
NNOOSTW	WONTONS	**NRSSTUU**	STURNUS		STROUPS
NNORSTU	TURNONS		UNTRUSS		STUPORS
NNORSUW	UNSWORN	**NRSTTUU**	UNTRUST	**OPSSSTU**	TOSSUPS
NNOSSUY	UNSONSY	**OOOOPRT**	POTOROO	**OPSTTUU**	OUTPUTS
NNOSTYY	SYNTONY	**OOOOSZZ**	ZOOZOOS		PUTOUTS
NNRSTUU	UNTURNS	**OOOPRTU**	OUTROOP	**ORRSTTU**	TRUSTOR
NOOOSUZ	OZONOUS	**OOORTTU**	OUTROOT	**ORSSSTU**	TUSSORS
NOOOSVX	SONOVOX	**OOPPSST**	POSTOPS	**ORSSTTU**	STROUTS
NOOPRSS	SPONSOR	**OOPRRST**	TORPORS	**ORSSUUU**	USUROUS
NOOPRST	PROTONS	**OOPRSSU**	SOURSOP	**ORSTTUU**	SURTOUT
NOOPSSY	POYSONS	**OOPRSTU**	PORTOUS	**ORSTTUY**	TRYOUTS
NOOPSUY	YOUPONS		UPROOTS	**RSSSTUU**	TUSSURS
NOORSST	TONSORS	**OOPRSTV**	PROVOST		
NOORSTU	UNROOST	**OOPRTTU**	OUTPORT		

Eight-letter anagrams

AAAABCLZ	CALABAZA	**AAABBILT**	ABBATIAL	**AAABDLMS**	LAMBADAS
AAAABENN	ANABAENA	**AAABBKLS**	KABBALAS	**AAABDNNN**	BANDANNA
AAAABKPS	BAASKAAP	**AAABCCMW**	MACCABAW	**AAABDNNS**	BANDANAS
AAAACCRR	CARACARA	**AAABCCRS**	BACCARAS	**AAABDNRS**	SARABAND
AAAACGNR	CARAGANA	**AAABCCRT**	BACCARAT	**AAABDNRT**	ABRADANT
AAAACJRR	JARARACA	**AAABCHIR**	ABRACHIA	**AAABEGHL**	GALABEAH
AAAACLMT	CALAMATA	**AAABCHLS**	CALABASH	**AAABEGLL**	GALLABEA
AAAACNRS	ANASARCA	**AAABCHMU**	MACAHUBA	**AAABEGLS**	GALABEAS
AAAADMTV	AMADAVAT	**AAABCILP**	ABAPICAL	**AAABEHNR**	HABANERA
AAAADNPS	APADANAS	**AAABCINT**	ANABATIC	**AAABEHRT**	BARATHEA
AAAADTVV	AVADAVAT	**AAABCIRS**	ARABICAS	**AAABEMPR**	PARABEMA
AAAAHJMR	MAHARAJA	**AAABCITT**	CIABATTA	**AAABENSS**	ANABASES
AAAAIKMN	KAMAAINA	**AAABCLOS**	BACALAOS	**AAABFLLS**	FALBALAS
AAAAIMPR	ARAPAIMA	**AAABCLSV**	BACLAVAS	**AAABGHIL**	GALABIAH
AAAAIRTX	ATARAXIA	**AAABCNRR**	BARRACAN	**AAABGILL**	GALLABIA
AAAAJKRR	JARARAKA		BARRANCA	**AAABGILS**	GALABIAS
AAAAKKMT	TAKAMAKA	**AAABCNRS**	BARACANS	**AAABGILY**	GALABIYA
AAAAKKNT	KATAKANA	**AAABCNRU**	CARNAUBA	**AAABGLNY**	BANGALAY
AAAAKKVV	KAVAKAVA	**AAABCORS**	CARABAOS	**AAABGLOR**	ALGAROBA
AAAAKKWW	KAWAKAWA	**AAABCPRY**	CAPYBARA	**AAABGMNQ**	MBAQANGA
AAAAKLMT	KALAMATA	**AAABCSSS**	CASSABAS	**AAABGRTU**	RUTABAGA
AAAALLVV	LAVALAVA	**AAABCSTW**	CATAWBAS	**AAABHLQS**	QABALAHS
AAAALSTY	ATALAYAS	**AAABDEHH**	DAHABEAH	**AAABHMST**	MASTABAH
AAAAMMTT	MATAMATA	**AAABDEST**	DATABASE	**AAABILTT**	BATTALIA
AAAAPPRR	PARAPARA	**AAABDFRS**	ABFARADS	**AAABINSS**	ANABASIS
AAAARRSS	SASARARA	**AAABDHHI**	DAHABIAH	**AAABIPSS**	PIASABAS
AAABBCHL	CABBALAH	**AAABDHHL**	HABDALAH		PIASSABA
AAABBCLS	CABBALAS	**AAABDHIY**	DAHABIYA	**AAABISTV**	BATAVIAS
AAABBELT	ABATABLE	**AAABDIKR**	BAIDARKA	**AAABKLSV**	BAKLAVAS
AAABBHKL	KABBALAH	**AAABDKNT**	DATABANK	**AAABKLSW**	BAKLAWAS

AAABKPSS	BAASKAPS	AAACHLSZ	CHALAZAS	AAADGGHH	HAGGADAH
	BAASSKAP	AAACHNST	ACANTHAS	AAADGGHS	AGGADAHS
AAABLLSW	WALLABAS	AAACHRSY	ACHARYAS		HAGGADAS
AAABLMOS	ABOMASAL	AAACILMN	MANIACAL	AAADGIMM	GAMMADIA
AAABLMST	TAMBALAS	AAACILMR	CALAMARI	AAADGLMY	AMYGDALA
AAABLOPR	PARABOLA	AAACILMS	MALACIAS	AAADGLNS	SALADANG
AAABLPRS	PALABRAS	AAACILOS	ALOCASIA	AAADGMRT	DATAGRAM
AAABMSST	MASTABAS	AAACILPR	CARPALIA	AAADHHLV	HAVDALAH
AAABNNRS	RABANNAS	AAACILRV	CALVARIA	AAADHHSS	SHAHADAS
AAABORRS	ARAROBAS	AAACILSY	CALISAYA	AAADHMMS	HAMMADAS
AAACCCHS	CACHACAS	AAACIMRS	CARIAMAS	AAADHMRS	ADHARMAS
AAACCELN	CALCANEA	AAACINPS	ACAPNIAS		HARAMDAS
AAACCEPR	CARAPACE	AAACINTV	CAVATINA		MADRASAH
AAACCHMP	CHAMPACA	AAACIPSU	SAPUCAIA	AAADHNRT	THANADAR
AAACCILR	CALCARIA	AAACIRRS	SACRARIA	AAADHNSS	SADHANAS
AAACCIMM	CAIMACAM	AAACIRSS	ACRASIAS	AAADIILR	RADIALIA
AAACCLMS	MALACCAS	AAACIRTX	ATARAXIC	AAADILLP	PALLADIA
AAACCLPS	ALPACCAS	AAACJMRS	JACAMARS	AAADILRU	ADULARIA
AAACCLRS	CARACALS	AAACKLMN	ALMANACK	AAADIMNS	DAMIANAS
AAACCRSS	CASCARAS	AAACKMRT	TAMARACK	AAADIMNY	ADYNAMIA
AAACCRTT	CATARACT	AAACLLSV	CAVALLAS	AAADIRST	DATARIAS
AAACDDRT	DATACARD	AAACLMNS	ALMANACS		RADIATAS
AAACDEIM	ACADEMIA		MANCALAS	AAADJMRS	JAMADARS
AAACDELM	ACELDAMA	AAACLMRS	CALAMARS	AAADKLMN	KALAMDAN
AAACDEMN	ADAMANCE	AAACLMRY	CALAMARY	AAADKNSW	WAKANDAS
AAACDENR	DRACAENA	AAACLNST	CANTALAS	AAADKRRV	AARDVARK
AAACDEQU	AQUACADE	AAACLPST	CATALPAS	AAADLMNQ	QALAMDAN
AAACDETU	ACAUDATE	AAACLRST	ALCATRAS	AAADLMNS	AMANDLAS
AAACDFIR	FARADAIC	AAACLRSZ	ALCAZARS		MANDALAS
AAACDILR	CALDARIA	AAACMNPS	CAMPANAS	AAADLMSW	WADMAALS
AAACDINR	ACARIDAN	AAACMOST	ATAMASCO	AAADMNST	ADAMANTS
	ARCADIAN	AAACMRSS	MACASSAR	AAADMNTU	TAMANDUA
AAACDIRS	ARCADIAS		MARASCAS	AAADMORT	MATADORA
AAACDKLY	LACKADAY		MASCARAS	AAADMPPP	PAPPADAM
AAACDMMS	MACADAMS	AAACMRSU	AMARACUS	AAADMPPS	PAPADAMS
AAACDMNY	ADAMANCY	AAACNNRS	CARANNAS	AAADMRSS	MADRASAS
AAACDNNO	ANACONDA	AAACNOPT	CAPONATA		MADRASSA
AAACDNRS	SANDARAC	AAACNPST	CATAPANS	AAADNRSS	SARDANAS
AAACDOTV	ADVOCAAT	AAACNRST	NACARATS	AAADNRST	TANADARS
AAACEGNT	AGACANTE	AAACNRSU	CARAUNAS	AAADSWYY	AWAYDAYS
AAACEGTU	AGUACATE	AAACNRSV	CARAVANS	AAAEEKRR	KAREAREA
AAACEHIN	ACHAENIA	AAACNSST	CANASTAS	AAAEGISS	ASSEGAAI
AAACEHLR	ARCHAEAL	AAACNSTT	CANTATAS	AAAEGLMX	MALAXAGE
AAACEHLT	CALATHEA	AAACRRWY	CARRAWAY	AAAEGLRT	ALTARAGE
AAACEHLZ	CHALAZAE	AAACRSWY	CARAWAYS	AAAEGLST	GALATEAS
AAACEHNR	ARCHAEAN	AAACSSST	CASSATAS	AAAEGNPP	APPANAGE
AAACEHNT	ACANTHAE	AAACSSSV	CASSAVAS	AAAEGNPS	APANAGES
AAACELNT	ANALECTA	AAACSSTT	CATASTAS	AAAEGRST	GASTRAEA
AAACELST	CATALASE	AAACSTWY	CASTAWAY	AAAEHLMT	HAEMATAL
AAACENNP	PANACEAN	AAADEFGN	FANEGADA	AAAEHLST	ALTHAEAS
AAACENPS	PANACEAS	AAADEFWY	FADEAWAY	AAAEHMNT	ANATHEMA
AAACGHNR	CHARANGA	AAADEGNP	APANAGED	AAAEHNPS	ANAPHASE
AAACGINT	CAATINGA	AAADEIMZ	MAZAEDIA	AAAEHPTU	PAHAUTEA
AAACGLSW	SCALAWAG	AAADEJMP	PAJAMAED	AAAEIMNS	ANAEMIAS
AAACGMNP	CAMPAGNA	AAADELMS	ALAMEDAS	AAAEKKRT	KARATEKA
AAACGMNR	ARMAGNAC		SALAAMED	AAAEKTWY	TAKEAWAY
AAACHHLS	HALACHAS	AAADEMNP	EMPANADA	AAAELMMN	ANALEMMA
AAACHILZ	CHALAZIA	AAADEMTT	METADATA	AAAELMPT	PALAMATE
AAACHIPS	APHASIAC	AAADENTV	VANADATE	AAAELMTX	MALAXATE
AAACHLLZ	CHALAZAL	AAADEPRT	TAPADERA	AAAELNPT	PANATELA
AAACHLNR	ANARCHAL	AAADFRSY	FARADAYS	AAAELRTV	LAVATERA

AAAEMRST	TARAMEAS	**AAAHHKLS**	HALAKAHS	**AAAIPRST**	ASPIRATA
AAAENNSS	ANANASES		HALAKAHS	**AAAIPRSX**	APRAXIAS
AAAENOPR	PARANOEA	**AAAHHLLS**	HALALAHS	**AAAIPSSV**	PIASAVAS
AAAENPRV	PARAVANE	**AAAHHLSV**	HALAVAHS		PIASSAVA
AAAENPST	ANAPAEST	**AAAHHPRS**	PARASHAH	**AAAISSST**	ASTASIAS
AAAENSST	ANATASES	**AAAHHPRT**	HAPHTARA	**AAAKKTZZ**	KAZATZKA
AAAEPRST	SEPARATA	**AAAHHSTT**	TATAHASH	**AAAKLMSY**	YAMALKAS
AAAERSWY	AREAWAYS	**AAAHIKPS**	APHAKIAS	**AAAKLWWY**	WALKAWAY
AAAERTWY	TEARAWAY	**AAAHIKSW**	KAHAWAIS	**AAAKMMSU**	MAMAKAUS
AAAFFLLS	ALFALFAS	**AAAHIMNR**	MAHARANI	**AAAKMNRS**	NAMASKAR
AAAFHHRT	HAFTARAH	**AAAHIMNS**	SHAMIANA	**AAAKMTUU**	KAUMATUA
AAAFHRST	HAFTARAS	**AAAHIMRT**	HAMARTIA	**AAAKOSWY**	SOAKAWAY
AAAFINST	FANTASIA	**AAAHINPR**	RAPHANIA	**AAAKPPSU**	KAUPAPAS
AAAFINUV	AVIFAUNA	**AAAHINRS**	HARIANAS	**AAALLPRX**	PARALLAX
AAAFIRST	RATAFIAS	**AAAHIPSS**	APHASIAS	**AAALLPST**	PALATALS
AAAFLLWY	FALLAWAY	**AAAHIPTY**	PITAHAYA	**AAALMMOR**	MALAROMA
AAAFMQRU	AQUAFARM	**AAAHJKSW**	KAJAWAHS	**AAALMPST**	TAMPALAS
AAAFNRSS	SARAFANS	**AAAHKMNS**	KHANSAMA	**AAALMRSS**	MARSALAS
AAAFRSWY	FARAWAYS	**AAAHKRSS**	RAKSHASA	**AAALNNPT**	PLATANNA
AAAGGLLN	GALANGAL	**AAAHLMRS**	HARMALAS	**AAALNNST**	LANTANAS
AAAGGLNS	GALANGAS	**AAAHLNNS**	ALANNAHS	**AAALNPRT**	RATAPLAN
AAAGGLOP	GALAPAGO	**AAAHMMST**	MAHATMAS	**AAALNPST**	APLANATS
AAAGHINR	HIRAGANA	**AAAHMNRT**	AMARANTH	**AAALNRTT**	TARLATAN
AAAGHIPR	AGRAPHIA	**AAAHMRSS**	ASHRAMAS	**AAALPRST**	SATRAPAL
AAAGHIPS	APHAGIAS	**AAAHMSST**	TAMASHAS	**AAALRRSY**	ARRAYALS
AAAGHLNS	LANGAHAS	**AAAHNNSV**	SAVANNAH	**AAALSWYY**	LAYAWAYS
AAAGHNNT	AGNATHAN	**AAAHNOPR**	ANAPHORA	**AAAMMPRS**	MAMPARAS
AAAGHNSS	SAGANASH	**AAAHNSTY**	ATHANASY	**AAAMNNST**	ANATMANS
AAAGHNST	ASHTANGA	**AAAHPRST**	PARATHAS	**AAAMNOPR**	PANORAMA
	ATAGHANS	**AAAHRSTW**	WARATAHS	**AAAMNRRY**	YARRAMAN
AAAGHNTY	YATAGHAN	**AAAHSWWY**	WASHAWAY	**AAAMNRST**	AMARANTS
AAAGILMM	MAMALIGA	**AAAHTTWY**	THATAWAY		MARANTAS
AAAGILNS	ANALGIAS	**AAAIIMNP**	APIMANIA	**AAAMNSTY**	MANYATAS
AAAGILPT	PATAGIAL	**AAAIINPR**	APIARIAN	**AAAMNTTY**	MANYATTA
AAAGILRT	ALIGARTA	**AAAIKKMM**	KAIMAKAM	**AAAMORST**	TAMARAOS
AAAGIMMT	GAMMATIA	**AAAIKKRS**	KARAKIAS	**AAAMOTTU**	AUTOMATA
AAAGINRR	AGRARIAN	**AAAIKLST**	LATAKIAS	**AAAMPPSU**	PAPAUMAS
AAAGINRS	ANGARIAS	**AAAIKRSS**	AKRASIAS	**AAAMPRST**	PATAMARS
AAAGINSZ	GAZANIAS	**AAAILLMR**	MALARIAL	**AAAMPRTT**	PATTAMAR
AAAGISSS	ASSAGAIS	**AAAILLPT**	PALATIAL	**AAAMRRSZ**	ZAMARRAS
AAAGJMSU	MAJAGUAS	**AAAILMNR**	MALARIAN	**AAAMRSSS**	SAMSARAS
AAAGKNRS	KARANGAS	**AAAILMRS**	MALARIAS	**AAAMRSTU**	TAMARAUS
AAAGLMMS	AMALGAMS		RASMALAI	**AAAMRTTU**	TRAUMATA
AAAGLMNS	MALANGAS	**AAAILMSV**	MALVASIA	**AAAMRTTZ**	RAZMATAZ
	NAGMAALS	**AAAILNPR**	PLANARIA	**AAANNSSV**	SAVANNAS
AAAGLMST	STALAGMA	**AAAILNRU**	AULARIAN	**AAANNSTT**	ANNATTAS
AAAGLNSS	LASAGNAS	**AAAILPRS**	PARASAIL	**AAANOPRZ**	PARAZOAN
AAAGLNTV	GALAVANT	**AAAILPRV**	PARAVAIL	**AAANORSY**	SAYONARA
AAAGLRRW	WARRAGAL	**AAAILPRX**	PARAXIAL	**AAANPRTV**	PARAVANT
AAAGLRST	ASTRAGAL	**AAAILPSS**	APLASIAS	**AAANQTUU**	AQUANAUT
AAAGMNRS	ANAGRAMS	**AAAILQRU**	AQUARIAL	**AAANRSTT**	TANTARAS
AAAGMPRR	PARAGRAM	**AAAILRST**	SALARIAT		TARANTAS
AAAGNOPR	ARAPONGA	**AAAIMMQQ**	QAIMAQAM		TARTANAS
AAAGNPRS	PARASANG	**AAAIMMST**	MIASMATA	**AAANTWWY**	WANTAWAY
	PARGANAS	**AAAIMNRR**	MARINARA	**AAAORSWY**	SOARAWAY
AAAGNPRU	ARAPUNGA	**AAAIMNST**	AMANITAS	**AAAPPRST**	APPARATS
AAAGNRRS	NGARARAS	**AAAIMRSU**	MAIASAUR	**AAAPQRTU**	PARAQUAT
AAAGNRST	TANAGRAS	**AAAINNRR**	RANARIAN	**AAAPSSST**	PASSATAS
AAAGNRSU	GUARANAS	**AAAINOPR**	PARANOIA	**AAAPSTTU**	TAUPATAS
AAAGNSTY	YATAGANS	**AAAINPSS**	PAISANAS	**AAARSTTT**	RATATATS
AAAHHHKL	HALAKHAH	**AAAINQRU**	AQUARIAN	**AAARSTTU**	TUATARAS

AAASTWYY	STAYAWAY	**AABCCINN**	CANNABIC	**AABCELNS**	BALANCES
AABBBDEK	KABABBED	**AABCCKKP**	BACKPACK	**AABCELOR**	ALBACORE
AABBBELS	BABBELAS	**AABCCKLL**	CALLBACK	**AABCELPR**	CAPABLER
AABBCDEG	CABBAGED	**AABCCKLP**	BLACKCAP	**AABCELPS**	SPACELAB
AABBCDKN	BACKBAND	**AABCCKLW**	CLAWBACK	**AABCELRS**	BERASCAL
AABBCDRS	SCABBARD	**AABCCKST**	BACKCAST	**AABCELRT**	BRACTEAL
AABBCEGS	CABBAGES		SCATBACK		CARTABLE
AABBCEGY	CABBAGEY	**AABCCMOT**	CATACOMB	**AABCELST**	CASTABLE
AABBCEIS	ABBACIES	**AABCCMOY**	MACCABOY	**AABCELSU**	CAUSABLE
AABBCEKR	BAREBACK	**AABCDEIN**	ABIDANCE	**AABCELWY**	CABLEWAY
AABBCEKT	BACKBEAT	**AABCDEIT**	ABDICATE	**AABCEMRT**	CRABMEAT
AABBCINR	BARBICAN	**AABCDEKT**	BACKDATE	**AABCEMRV**	VAMBRACE
AABBCIRR	BARBARIC	**AABCDELL**	CABALLED	**AABCEMSS**	AMBSACES
AABBCIST	SABBATIC	**AABCDELN**	BALANCED	**AABCENYY**	ABEYANCY
AABBCKST	BACKSTAB	**AABCDHKN**	BACKHAND	**AABCEORS**	ACARBOSE
AABBCMOS	CABOMBAS	**AABCDHKR**	HARDBACK	**AABCERRS**	BARRACES
AABBCORS	BARBASCO	**AABCDIIS**	DIABASIC	**AABCERST**	ABREACTS
AABBDENS	BASEBAND	**AABCDILL**	BALLADIC		BEARCATS
AABBDERT	BARBATED	**AABCDILR**	ALDICARB		CABARETS
AABBDGRS	GABBARDS	**AABCDILU**	BICAUDAL		CABRESTA
AABBEELR	BEARABLE	**AABCDIMS**	DICAMBAS		CABRETTA
AABBEELT	BEATABLE	**AABCDINT**	ABDICANT	**AABCERTT**	CABRETTA
AABBEGNS	BEANBAGS	**AABCDIRS**	CARABIDS	**AABCESSU**	ABACUSES
AABBEILL	BAILABLE	**AABCDKLN**	BACKLAND	**AABCFHKL**	HALFBACK
AABBEISS	BABESIAS	**AABCDKLO**	BACKLOAD	**AABCFIIL**	BIFACIAL
AABBEKLN	BANKABLE	**AABCDKNR**	BANKCARD	**AABCFKLL**	BACKFALL
AABBELLM	BLAMABLE	**AABCDKRW**	BACKWARD		FALLBACK
AABBELLN	BEANBALL		DRAWBACK	**AABCFKLT**	FLATBACK
AABBELLS	BASEBALL	**AABCDKRY**	BACKYARD	**AABCFKST**	FASTBACK
AABBELNN	BANNABLE	**AABCDLNS**	SCABLAND		FATBACKS
AABBELOS	BAALEBOS	**AABCDNRR**	BRANCARD	**AABCGIMO**	CAMBOGIA
AABBELOT	BOATABLE	**AABCDNST**	CABSTAND	**AABCGKRY**	GRAYBACK
AABBELRR	BARRABLE	**AABCEEFL**	FACEABLE	**AABCHHRS**	BRACHAHS
AABBELRY	BEARABLY	**AABCEEHS**	SEABEACH	**AABCHILR**	BRACHIAL
AABBELSU	ABUSABLE	**AABCEELR**	RACEABLE	**AABCHINR**	BRANCHIA
AABBEORT	BAREBOAT	**AABCEENY**	ABEYANCE	**AABCHKLS**	BACKLASH
AABBGRST	GABBARTS	**AABCEERS**	SCARABEE	**AABCHKLU**	BACKHAUL
AABBHKSU	BABUSHKA	**AABCEERT**	ACERBATE	**AABCHKRS**	SHABRACK
AABBHSST	SABBATHS	**AABCEFRS**	FACEBARS	**AABCHKSW**	BACKWASH
AABBIILL	BILABIAL	**AABCEGOT**	CABOTAGE	**AABCHLOO**	COOLABAH
AABBIKLT	BARBITAL	**AABCEHKL**	HACKABLE	**AABCHMRY**	CHAMBRAY
AABBIRSU	BABIRUSA	**AABCEHLS**	CASHABLE	**AABCHNRS**	BARCHANS
AABBLLMY	BLAMABLY	**AABCEHMS**	AMBACHES	**AABCIILR**	BIRACIAL
AABBLORS	BARBOLAS	**AABCEHNR**	BARCHANE	**AABCIILS**	BASILICA
AABBLSSU	SUBBASAL	**AABCEILM**	AMICABLE	**AABCIINR**	BRAINIAC
AABBMMOZ	ZAMBOMBA	**AABCEIMN**	AMBIANCE	**AABCIKLT**	TAILBACK
AABBSSSU	BABASSUS	**AABCEINR**	CARABINE	**AABCILLR**	BACILLAR
AABCCCHI	BACCHIAC	**AABCEIRT**	BACTERIA		CABRILLA
AABCCDET	BACCATED	**AABCEITT**	CIABATTE	**AABCILMS**	BALSAMIC
AABCCEHK	BACKACHE	**AABCEKLM**	CLAMBAKE		CABALISM
AABCCELS	CASCABEL	**AABCEKLP**	PACKABLE	**AABCILMY**	AMICABLY
	CASCABLE	**AABCEKLR**	LACEBARK	**AABCILNN**	CANNIBAL
AABCCERT	BRACCATE	**AABCEKLS**	SACKABLE	**AABCILNO**	ANABOLIC
AABCCHHS	BACHCHAS	**AABCEKST**	BACKSEAT	**AABCILOR**	BRACIOLA
AABCCHIN	BACCHIAN		SEATBACK	**AABCILST**	BASALTIC
AABCCHIS	BISCACHA	**AABCELLL**	CALLABLE		CABALIST
AABCCHIZ	BIZCACHA	**AABCELLP**	PLACABLE	**AABCINNN**	CANNABIN
AABCCHKS	CASHBACK	**AABCELLR**	CABALLER	**AABCINNR**	CINNABAR
AABCCHKT	BACKCHAT	**AABCELLS**	SCALABLE	**AABCINNS**	CANNABIS
AABCCHNT	BACCHANT	**AABCELNR**	BALANCER	**AABCINOT**	BOTANICA
AABCCIMR	CARBAMIC		BARNACLE	**AABCINRS**	CARABINS
				AABCINSU	BANAUSIC

AABCIOPS	COPAIBAS	**AABDEELW**	WADEABLE	**AABDERTT**	RABATTED
AABCIOSS	SCABIOSA	**AABDEEMN**	ENDAMEBA	**AABDERTV**	VARTABED
AABCIRSS	BRASSICA	**AABDEERT**	TEABREAD	**AABDERWY**	WAYBREAD
AABCISSS	ABSCISSA	**AABDEERY**	BAYADEER	**AABDESSS**	BADASSES
AABCISTX	TAXICABS		BAYADERE	**AABDFHLN**	FAHLBAND
AABCKKLT	TALKBACK	**AABDEGHN**	HEADBANG	**AABDGHNS**	HANDBAGS
AABCKLNO	LOANBACK	**AABDEGIN**	BADINAGE	**AABDGINN**	ABANDING
AABCKLNY	CLAYBANK	**AABDEGIR**	BIGARADE	**AABDGINR**	ABRADING
AABCKLPS	BACKSLAP	**AABDEGLR**	GRADABLE	**AABDGLNR**	LANDGRAB
AABCKLPY	PLAYBACK	**AABDEGMS**	GAMBADES	**AABDGMOS**	GAMBADOS
AABCKLSY	LAYBACKS	**AABDEGNR**	BANDAGER	**AABDGNOV**	VAGABOND
AABCKNNS	CANBANKS	**AABDEGNS**	BANDAGES	**AABDGNSS**	SANDBAGS
AABCKNPS	SNAPBACK	**AABDEGRR**	BARRAGED	**AABDGORR**	GARBOARD
AABCKPRT	BRATPACK	**AABDEHHI**	DAHABIEH	**AABDGORT**	TAGBOARD
AABCKPRW	BACKWRAP	**AABDEHKR**	HARDBAKE	**AABDGOTU**	GADABOUT
AABCKPSY	PAYBACKS	**AABDEHMR**	HARDBEAM	**AABDHINR**	HAIRBAND
AABCKRRS	BARRACKS	**AABDEHNR**	BAREHAND	**AABDHLLN**	HANDBALL
AABCKSSW	BACKSAWS	**AABDEILN**	BALADINE	**AABDHLLR**	HARDBALL
AABCKSTY	BACKSTAY	**AABDEILR**	RADIABLE	**AABDHNST**	HATBANDS
AABCKSWY	SWAYBACK	**AABDEILT**	LABIATED	**AABDHNSY**	HAYBANDS
AABCLLLO	COALBALL	**AABDEINR**	BANDEIRA	**AABDHRSU**	BAHADURS
AABCLLLY	BALLCLAY	**AABDEIOU**	ABOIDEAU		SUBAHDAR
AABCLLPY	PLACABLY	**AABDEIRS**	ARABISED	**AABDIILR**	BIRADIAL
AABCLLSY	SCALABLY	**AABDEIRZ**	ARABIZED	**AABDIILS**	BASIDIAL
AABCLMRY	CARBAMYL	**AABDEISS**	DIABASES	**AABDIKRS**	BIDARKAS
AABCLMSU	CALUMBAS	**AABDEJLL**	DJELLABA	**AABDILLN**	BALLADIN
AABCLNTY	BLATANCY	**AABDEJNX**	BANJAXED	**AABDILNS**	BALADINS
AABCLNUU	CUNABULA	**AABDEKPR**	PARBAKED	**AABDIMNO**	ABDOMINA
AABCLRRY	CARBARYL	**AABDEKRY**	DAYBREAK	**AABDIMNR**	MADBRAIN
AABCLRSU	LABRUSCA	**AABDEKSW**	DAWBAKES	**AABDIMRS**	BARMAIDS
AABCMMSU	MACUMBAS	**AABDELLS**	BALLADES	**AABDINNR**	RAINBAND
AABCMSSU	SAMBUCAS	**AABDELLT**	BALLATED	**AABDINRS**	BANDARIS
AABCNORR	BARRANCO	**AABDELLU**	LAUDABLE	**AABDINST**	TABANIDS
AABCNRRS	CARBARNS	**AABDELMN**	DAMNABLE	**AABDIORR**	AIRBOARD
AABCORRS	CARBORAS	**AABDELMS**	BALSAMED	**AABDKNNS**	SANDBANK
AABCORST	ABACTORS	**AABDELNR**	BARELAND	**AABDLLRY**	BALLADRY
	ACROBATS	**AABDELNS**	SANDABLE		BALLYARD
AABCOSTT	CATBOATS	**AABDELOR**	ADORABLE	**AABDLLUY**	LAUDABLY
AABCRSTT	ABSTRACT	**AABDELPR**	DRAPABLE	**AABDLMNU**	LABDANUM
AABCSTTU	CATTABUS		PARABLED	**AABDLMNY**	DAMNABLY
AABDDEET	DEADBEAT	**AABDELPT**	BALDPATE	**AABDLMRU**	ADUMBRAL
AABDDEGN	BANDAGED	**AABDELRS**	BASELARD	**AABDLNPT**	PLATBAND
AABDDEHL	BALDHEAD	**AABDELRT**	TRADABLE	**AABDLNSS**	SALBANDS
AABDDEHN	HEADBAND	**AABDELRW**	DRAWABLE	**AABDLOOT**	BOATLOAD
AABDDEIR	ABRAIDED	**AABDELRY**	READABLY	**AABDLOPR**	LAPBOARD
AABDDELL	BALLADED	**AABDELSW**	SAWBLADE	**AABDLORR**	LABRADOR
AABDDENR	BRANDADE	**AABDELSY**	ABASEDLY		LARBOARD
AABDDERT	TABARDED	**AABDEMMS**	BEMADAMS	**AABDLORY**	ADORABLY
AABDDESS	BADASSED	**AABDEMNS**	BEADSMAN	**AABDLRSW**	BRADAWLS
AABDDIKS	KABADDIS	**AABDEMNT**	BANDMATE	**AABDMNNS**	BANDSMAN
AABDDINZ	ZINDABAD	**AABDENSU**	BANDEAUS	**AABDMNNY**	BANDYMAN
AABDDLNS	BADLANDS	**AABDENTU**	UNABATED	**AABDMNOR**	BOARDMAN
AABDDMOR	DAMBOARD	**AABDENUX**	BANDEAUX	**AABDMNRS**	ARMBANDS
AABDDMRU	MURDABAD	**AABDENVW**	WAVEBAND	**AABDNNOS**	ABANDONS
AABDDNSS	SANDDABS	**AABDEORS**	SEABOARD	**AABDNNTU**	ABUNDANT
AABDEEHL	BEHEADAL	**AABDEORT**	TEABOARD	**AABDNORS**	BANDORAS
AABDEEHR	BAREHEAD	**AABDEORX**	BROADAXE	**AABDNPSS**	PASSBAND
AABDEELR	READABLE	**AABDERRS**	ABRADERS	**AABDNRRY**	BARNYARD
AABDEELT	DATEABLE	**AABDERRT**	TABERDAR	**AABDNRSS**	SANDBARS
	DEALBATE	**AABDERRW**	BEARWARD	**AABDNRSU**	BANDURAS
AABDEELV	EVADABLE	**AABDERSW**	BADWARES	**AABDNSSW**	BANDSAWS

AABDORSV	BRAVADOS	**AABEGGLY**	GAGEABLY	**AABEIMRS**	AMBARIES
AABDORTY	BOATYARD	**AABEGGRS**	GARBAGES	**AABEINOZ**	ZABAIONE
AABDORWY	BROADWAY	**AABEGGRY**	GARBAGEY	**AABEINRT**	ATABRINE
	WAYBOARD	**AABEGHIL**	GALABIEH		RABATINE
AABDOSTY	DAYBOATS	**AABEGHLN**	HANGABLE	**AABEINST**	BASANITE
AABDRRSS	BRASSARD	**AABEGHNR**	BERGHAAN	**AABEIOTU**	ABOITEAU
AABDRRSW	DRAWBARS	**AABEGILN**	GAINABLE	**AABEIRSS**	AIRBASES
AABDRSST	BASTARDS	**AABEGILT**	AGITABLE		ARABISES
AABDRSSU	SUBADARS	**AABEGINR**	ABEARING	**AABEIRSV**	ABRASIVE
AABDRSTY	BASTARDY	**AABEGLLL**	GLABELLA	**AABEIRSZ**	ARABIZES
AABEEFLN	FLEABANE	**AABEGLLM**	BALLGAME	**AABEIRTU**	AUBRETIA
AABEEGGL	GAGEABLE	**AABEGLNW**	GNAWABLE		AUBRIETA
AABEEGKR	BRAKEAGE	**AABEGLRS**	ALGEBRAS	**AABEISST**	ABATISES
	BREAKAGE	**AABEGLRT**	GLABRATE	**AABEJLLS**	JELLABAS
AABEEGLT	ABLEGATE	**AABEGLRU**	ARGUABLE	**AABEJLMM**	JAMMABLE
AABEEGNT	ABNEGATE	**AABEGLRZ**	GRAZABLE	**AABEJMUX**	JAMBEAUX
AABEEHLL	HEALABLE	**AABEGMNR**	BARGEMAN	**AABEJNOZ**	ZABAJONE
AABEEHLR	HEARABLE	**AABEGMNY**	MANGABEY	**AABEJNSX**	BANJAXES
AABEEHLT	HATEABLE	**AABEGMRS**	BERGAMAS	**AABEKLLS**	SLAKABLE
	HEATABLE		MEGABARS	**AABEKLLT**	TALKABLE
AABEEHMR	HARAMBEE	**AABEGMRT**	BREGMATA	**AABEKLLW**	WALKABLE
AABEEKLM	MAKEABLE	**AABEGMTT**	GAMBETTA	**AABEKLMS**	MASKABLE
AABEEKLT	TAKEABLE	**AABEGNOR**	BARONAGE	**AABEKMNR**	BRAKEMAN
AABEEKMT	BAKEMEAT	**AABEGORT**	ABROGATE	**AABEKNSS**	SEABANKS
	MAKEBATE	**AABEGOST**	SABOTAGE	**AABEKPRR**	PARBREAK
AABEEKRW	BAKEWARE	**AABEGOSZ**	GAZABOES	**AABEKPRS**	PARBAKES
AABEELLS	LEASABLE	**AABEGRRS**	BAGARRES	**AABEKRRS**	BARESARK
	SALEABLE		BARRAGES	**AABEKRSS**	ARABESKS
	SEALABLE	**AABEGRSS**	BRASSAGE	**AABEKRSY**	KERBAYAS
AABEELMN	AMENABLE	**AABEGSSS**	BAGASSES	**AABELLMT**	MEATBALL
	NAMEABLE	**AABEGSSU**	ABUSAGES	**AABELLNO**	LOANABLE
AABEELMT	TAMEABLE	**AABEHIRR**	HERBARIA	**AABELLPP**	PALPABLE
AABEELPR	REAPABLE	**AABEHJLL**	JELLABAH	**AABELLPS**	LAPSABLE
AABEELPT	TAPEABLE	**AABEHKLS**	SHAKABLE	**AABELLPY**	PLAYABLE
AABEELRS	ERASABLE	**AABEHLMS**	SHAMABLE	**AABELLRS**	EARBALLS
AABEELRT	RATEABLE	**AABEHLOT**	OATHABLE	**AABELLSS**	SABELLAS
	TEARABLE	**AABEHLPS**	SHAPABLE	**AABELLSV**	SALVABLE
AABEELRW	WEARABLE	**AABEHLPT**	ALPHABET	**AABELLSY**	SALEABLY
AABEELST	EATABLES	**AABEHLRS**	SHARABLE		SLAYABLE
	TEASABLE	**AABEHLRW**	WARHABLE	**AABELLUV**	VALUABLE
AABEELSV	SAVEABLE	**AABEHLSV**	SHAVABLE	**AABELMNY**	AMENABLY
AABEEMNO	AMOEBEAN	**AABEHLSW**	WASHABLE	**AABELMPP**	MAPPABLE
AABEEMNT	ENTAMEBA	**AABEHNOR**	HABANERO	**AABELMST**	BLASTEMA
AABEEMPR	ABAMPERE	**AABEHNST**	ABTHANES		LAMBASTE
AABEENNW	WANNABEE	**AABEIJLL**	JAILABLE	**AABELMSU**	AMUSABLE
AABEENOR	ANAEROBE	**AABEIKLS**	KIELBASA	**AABELMTU**	AMBULATE
AABEERRT	ABERRATE	**AABEIKNS**	IKEBANAS	**AABELNNT**	TANNABLE
AABEERSZ	ZAREEBAS	**AABEILLL**	ALLIABLE	**AABELNOS**	ABALONES
AABEERTT	TRABEATE	**AABEILLM**	MAILABLE	**AABELNOT**	ATONABLE
AABEFFNS	BEFFANAS	**AABEILLS**	ISABELLA	**AABELNPS**	ANABLEPS
AABEFGLS	FLEABAGS		SAILABLE	**AABELNPT**	PANTABLE
AABEFGSU	AUFGABES	**AABEILNR**	INARABLE	**AABELNPW**	PAWNABLE
AABEFHKL	HALFBEAK	**AABEILNS**	BANALISE	**AABELNRY**	BALNEARY
AABEFLLL	FLABELLA	**AABEILNZ**	BANALIZE	**AABELNSS**	BANSELAS
AABEFLMO	FOAMABLE	**AABEILRS**	RAISABLE	**AABELNST**	BANALEST
AABEFLMR	FARMABLE	**AABEILRV**	VARIABLE	**AABELOPR**	PARABOLE
	FRAMABLE	**AABEILST**	BALISTAE	**AABELORR**	ARBOREAL
AABEFLMU	FLAMBEAU		LABIATES	**AABELORS**	BRESAOLA
AABEFLTU	FABULATE		SATIABLE	**AABELOSV**	LAVABOES
AABEFNSS	FANBASES	**AABEILTV**	ABLATIVE	**AABELOVW**	AVOWABLE
AABEGGGS	BAGGAGES	**AABEIMNR**	AMBERINA	**AABELPPR**	PALPEBRA

AABELPPT	TAPPABLE	**AABGINRY**	ABRAYING	**AABILOSU**	ABOULIAS
AABELPRS	PARABLES	**AABGINSS**	BISNAGAS	**AABILOTT**	BOATTAIL
	PARSABLE	**AABGINSZ**	BIZNAGAS	**AABILQST**	QABALIST
	PREBASAL	**AABGLLLO**	GOALBALL	**AABILRRT**	ARBITRAL
	SPARABLE	**AABGLLRY**	BALLYRAG	**AABILRST**	ARBALIST
AABELPSS	PASSABLE	**AABGLMNU**	GALBANUM	**AABILRSU**	BALISAUR
AABELPSY	PAYABLES	**AABGLNOW**	BANGALOW	**AABILRSY**	BASILARY
AABELRST	ARBALEST	**AABGLRUY**	ARGUABLY	**AABILRVY**	VARIABLY
	RATABLES	**AABGMORR**	BAROGRAM	**AABILSST**	BALISTAS
AABELRTY	BETRAYAL	**AABGNORZ**	GARBANZO	**AABILSTY**	SATIABLY
	RATEABLY	**AABGORTT**	BOTTARGA	**AABILSUX**	SUBAXIAL
AABELSST	BASALTES	**AABHHISS**	SAHIBAHS	**AABIMMRS**	MARIMBAS
AABELSTT	ABETTALS	**AABHHKSS**	SABKHAHS	**AABIMNNO**	BONAMANI
	STATABLE	**AABHHORU**	BROUHAHA	**AABIMNOS**	AMBOINAS
	TASTABLE	**AABHHRSU**	BRUHAHAS		BONAMIAS
AABELSTU	TABLEAUS	**AABHIIMP**	AMPHIBIA	**AABIMNRU**	MANUBRIA
AABELSTW	WASTABLE	**AABHIINU**	BAUHINIA	**AABIMORS**	AMBROSIA
AABELSTX	TAXABLES	**AABHIJMY**	JAMBIYAH	**AABIMRSU**	SIMARUBA
AABELSWY	SWAYABLE	**AABHILLR**	HAIRBALL	**AABIMSST**	BASMATIS
AABELTTU	TABULATE	**AABHILTU**	HABITUAL	**AABINNPR**	BRAINPAN
AABELTTX	BATTLEAX	**AABHIMNR**	BRAHMANI	**AABINORS**	ABRASION
AABELTUX	TABLEAUX	**AABHINSS**	HASBIANS	**AABINOSU**	OUABAINS
AABEMMXY	MYXAMEBA	**AABHINST**	HABITANS	**AABINRST**	ATABRINS
AABENNSW	WANNABES	**AABHINTT**	HABITANT		BARTISAN
AABENPRS	PARABENS	**AABHIRST**	TABASHIR	**AABINRTZ**	BARTIZAN
AABENRRT	ABERRANT	**AABHISTT**	HABITATS	**AABINSST**	ABSTAINS
AABENRST	ANTBEARS	**AABHKLLW**	BALLHAWK	**AABIORRS**	SORBARIA
	RATSBANE	**AABHKNRS**	BARKHANS	**AABIORSS**	ABROSIAS
AABENRTU	ARBUTEAN	**AABHKSST**	SABKHATS	**AABIORST**	AIRBOATS
AABEORRT	ARBORETA	**AABHLLSW**	WASHBALL	**AABIORSV**	BAVAROIS
AABEORST	AEROBATS	**AABHLMSY**	SHAMABLY	**AABIORTT**	ABATTOIR
	RABATOES	**AABHMNRS**	BRAHMANS	**AABIOSSY**	BIOASSAY
AABEOSSU	OUBAASES	**AABHMRSS**	SAMBHARS	**AABIPSUX**	PAXIUBAS
AABEQSUU	USQUABAE	**AABHMSTT**	BATHMATS	**AABIRSST**	BARISTAS
AABERRRT	BARRATER	**AABHNOTU**	AUTOBAHN		BARTSIAS
AABERRSW	BARWARES	**AABHQSSU**	SQUABASH		
AABERSSU	SUBAREAS	**AABHRRSU**	SURBAHAR	**AABIRTUY**	RUBAIYAT
AABERSTT	RABATTES	**AABIIJLT**	JAILBAIT	**AABISTUZ**	ZAIBATSU
	TABARETS	**AABIILSZ**	ALBIZIAS	**AABJLMNO**	JAMBOLAN
AABERSTU	ABATURES	**AABIILZZ**	ALBIZZIA	**AABJMRST**	JAMBARTS
AABESZZZ	BAZAZZES	**AABIINST**	ANTIBIAS	**AABKLLPR**	BALLPARK
AABETTUX	BATTEAUX	**AABIIPST**	BAPTISIA	**AABKLSSU**	KULBASAS
AABFILUX	FABLIAUX	**AABIJMSY**	JAMBIYAS	**AABKMNNS**	BANKSMAN
AABFLLST	FASTBALL	**AABIKLMS**	KABALISM	**AABKNRST**	TANBARKS
AABFLOTT	FALTBOAT		KALIMBAS	**AABKOOSZ**	BAZOOKAS
	FLATBOAT	**AABIKLST**	KABALIST	**AABKOPRS**	SOAPBARK
AABGGGNN	GANGBANG	**AABIKNSS**	BANKSIAS	**AABKRSST**	TASKBARS
AABGGNOT	TABOGGAN	**AABILLLY**	LABIALLY	**AABLLMOR**	BALMORAL
AABGGRRT	BRAGGART	**AABILLRS**	BARILLAS	**AABLLNST**	BALLANTS
AABGHINS	ABASHING	**AABILLST**	BALLISTA	**AABLLORS**	ALLOBARS
AABGHKRS	SHAGBARK	**AABILMNS**	BAILSMAN	**AABLLORY**	ABORALLY
AABGHNRS	BHANGRAS	**AABILMNU**	BIMANUAL	**AABLLPPY**	PALPABLY
AABGHNSS	NASHGABS	**AABILMQS**	QABALISM	**AABLLPRT**	TRAPBALL
AABGIILS	ABIGAILS	**AABILMSS**	BAALISMS	**AABLLPST**	PATBALLS
AABGIINR	BRAAIING	**AABILNNU**	BIANNUAL	**AABLLSST**	BALLASTS
AABGILMS	MAILBAGS	**AABILNOR**	BARONIAL	**AABLLSTU**	BLASTULA
AABGILNT	ABLATING	**AABILNOT**	ABLATION	**AABLLSVY**	SALVABLY
	BANGTAIL	**AABILNRT**	BRANTAIL	**AABLLUVY**	VALUABLY
AABGIMNS	SAMBAING	**AABILNRU**	BINAURAL	**AABLMNOR**	ABNORMAL
AABGIMSU	GAMBUSIA	**AABILNTY**	BANALITY	**AABLMNTU**	AMBULANT
AABGINRS	BARGAINS	**AABILOST**	SAILBOAT	**AABLMOST**	BLASTOMA
				AABLMRSU	LABARUMS

AABLMSST	LAMBASTS	**AACCEGOR**	ACCORAGE	**AACCIRTY**	CARYATIC
AABLNSSU	SUBNASAL	**AACCEGRU**	CARUCAGE	**AACCISTT**	STACCATI
AABLNTTT	BLATTANT	**AACCEHIX**	CACHEXIA	**AACCJKRS**	CARJACKS
AABLORST	ABLATORS	**AACCEILN**	CALCANEI	**AACCJKRW**	CRACKJAW
AABLOTUY	LAYABOUT	**AACCEILU**	ACICULAE	**AACCJORU**	CARCAJOU
AABLOVWY	AVOWABLY	**AACCEIRR**	CERCARIA		CARJACOU
AABLPSSY	PASSABLY	**AACCEKRS**	CARCAKES		
AABLRRSU	SABURRAL	**AACCELLY**	CAECALLY	**AACCKKPS**	PACKSACK
AABLRSST	ARBLASTS		CALYCEAL	**AACCKLOS**	COALSACK
AABLRSTU	SUBTALAR	**AACCELOR**	CARACOLE	**AACCKLPS**	CALPACKS
AABLRSUU	SUBAURAL	**AACCELPT**	PLACCATE	**AACCKORT**	COATRACK
AABLSTTU	ABUTTALS	**AACCELRR**	CARCERAL	**AACCKRRS**	CARRACKS
AABMMOSU	ABOMASUM	**AACCELTY**	CALYCATE	**AACCLLRU**	CALCULAR
AABMNNOO	BONAMANO	**AACCEMNU**	CUMACEAN	**AACCLLST**	CATCALLS
AABMNOST	BOATSMAN	**AACCENRT**	CARCANET	**AACCLMNY**	CLAMANCY
AABMNOSY	AMBOYNAS	**AACCENSV**	VACANCES	**AACCLOPS**	POLACCAS
AABMNOTW	BATWOMAN	**AACCENTU**	ACUTANCE	**AACCLORS**	CARACOLS
AABMNRTU	RAMBUTAN	**AACCERSS**	CARCASES	**AACCLPRS**	CALCSPAR
AABMORSU	MARABOUS	**AACCERTU**	ACCURATE	**AACCLPST**	PLACCATS
AABMORTU	MARABOUT		CARUCATE	**AACCLRSU**	ACCRUALS
	TAMBOURA	**AACCESSV**	CASEVACS		CARACULS
AABMOSSU	ABOMASUS	**AACCFGOO**	CACAFOGO		SACCULAR
AABMRSTU	TAMBURAS	**AACCFILR**	FARCICAL	**AACCLSSU**	ACCUSALS
AABNNOST	ABSONANT	**AACCFLTU**	CALCTUFA	**AACCLSTW**	CATCLAWS
AABNNOSZ	BONANZAS	**AACCGILT**	GALACTIC	**AACCNSTU**	ACCUSANT
AABNOSST	SABATONS	**AACCHHIL**	HALACHIC	**AACCOPRS**	ASCOCARP
AABNOSSY	SABAYONS	**AACCHHKS**	CHACHKAS	**AACCORSU**	CURACAOS
AABORRRT	BARRATOR	**AACCHHKT**	CHATCHKA		CURACAOS
AABORRSS	RASBORAS	**AACCHHMU**	MUCHACHA	**AACCOSST**	ACCOASTS
AABORRSU	BAROSAUR	**AACCHILL**	CAILLACH	**AACCOSTT**	STACCATO
AABORSTT	BAROSTAT	**AACCHILP**	PACHALIC		STOCCATA
AABRRRTY	BARRATRY	**AACCHINR**	ANARCHIC		TOCCATAS
AABRRSST	BRASSART		CHARACIN	**AACCRRST**	CARRACTS
AABRRSSU	SABURRAS	**AACCHINS**	CHICANAS	**AACDDEHI**	ACIDHEAD
AABRRSUV	BRAVURAS	**AACCHIOR**	AIRCOACH	**AACDDEIL**	DAEDALIC
AABSSTUX	SAXTUBAS	**AACCHISV**	VISCACHA	**AACDDENV**	ADVANCED
AABSTTTU	BATTUTAS	**AACCHIVZ**	VIZCACHA	**AACDDETU**	CAUDATED
AACCCDIS	SACCADIC	**AACCHKOZ**	KAZACHOC	**AACDDGHL**	CLADDAGH
AACCCFIO	FOCACCIA	**AACCHLLT**	CATCHALL	**AACDDHRS**	CHADDARS
AACCCHHR	CRACHACH	**AACCHLNS**	CLACHANS	**AACDDILN**	CANDIDAL
AACCCHHU	CACHUCHA	**AACCHLOR**	CHARCOAL	**AACDDINR**	RADICAND
AACCCRUY	ACCURACY	**AACCHLOT**	CACHALOT	**AACDDINS**	CANDIDAS
AACCDDES	CASCADED	**AACCHLRS**	CLARSACH	**AACDDRSW**	CRAWDADS
AACCDEIM	ACADEMIC	**AACCHMNO**	COACHMAN	**AACDEEHH**	HEADACHE
AACCDELO	ACCOLADE	**AACCHMPS**	CHAMPACS	**AACDEEHR**	AREACHED
AACCDEMS	MEDACCAS	**AACCHNNS**	CANNACHS		HEADRACE
AACCDENU	CADUCEAN	**AACCHNOR**	CORANACH	**AACDEEHS**	HEADCASE
AACCDERR	RACECARD	**AACCHRST**	CHARACTS	**AACDEELS**	ESCALADE
AACCDERS	CARCASED	**AACCIINV**	VACCINIA	**AACDEEMS**	ACADEMES
	CARDCASE	**AACCIIST**	SCIATICA	**AACDEEPS**	ESCAPADE
AACCDESS	CASCADES	**AACCILMS**	ACCLAIMS	**AACDEERT**	ACERATED
	SACCADES	**AACCILNV**	VACCINAL	**AACDEEST**	CASEATED
AACCDHIR	CHARACID	**AACCILRU**	ACICULAR		ESTACADE
AACCDIIS	ACCIDIAS	**AACCILSU**	ACICULAS	**AACDEETT**	ACETATED
AACCDILN	DANCICAL	**AACCILTT**	TACTICAL	**AACDEETU**	ECAUDATE
AACCDIRS	CARDIACS	**AACCIMNU**	CACUMINA	**AACDEETV**	CAVEATED
AACCDOVY	ADVOCACY	**AACCINSV**	VACCINAS	**AACDEFHR**	HARDFACE
AACCEELT	CALCEATE	**AACCIORS**	CARIOCAS	**AACDEFLS**	FALCADES
AACCEENT	CETACEAN	**AACCIORU**	CARIACOU	**AACDEFLT**	FALCATED
AACCEFLO	COALFACE	**AACCIPRT**	APRACTIC	**AACDEFNT**	CAFTANED
AACCEFST	CATFACES	**AACCIPTY**	CAPACITY	**AACDEGGR**	AGGRACED
				AACDEGKP	PACKAGED

AACDEGMR	DECAGRAM	AACDESTU	CAUDATES	AACDJQRU	JACQUARD
AACDEHHY	HEADACHY	AACDETTU	ACTUATED	AACDKLLN	LACKLAND
AACDEHIN	HACIENDA	AACDETUV	VACUATED	AACDKPRT	TRACKPAD
AACDEHLP	CEPHALAD	AACDFLNR	FLANCARD	AACDKPSY	DAYPACKS
AACDEHMR	DRACHMAE	AACDGGHI	HAGGADIC	AACDKSSY	DAYSACKS
AACDEHMS	CHAMADES	AACDGINR	ARCADING	AACDLLUY	CAUDALLY
AACDEHRS	CHARADES		CARANGID	AACDLNSS	SCANDALS
	HARDCASE		CARDIGAN	AACDLORS	CARLOADS
AACDEHRT	CATHEDRA	AACDHHKR	HARDHACK	AACDLORT	CARTLOAD
AACDEHST	CATHEADS	AACDHHNS	SHADCHAN	AACDLORY	COALYARD
AACDEHTT	ATTACHED	AACDHHRS	SHADRACH	AACDLOSS	SCALADOS
AACDEIIL	AECIDIAL	AACDHIIS	DICHASIA	AACDLOSV	CALVADOS
AACDEIIM	ACIDEMIA	AACDHILL	CHILLADA	AACDLPRS	PLACARDS
AACDEILM	CAMAILED	AACDHILR	DIARCHAL	AACDLRTY	DACTYLAR
AACDEILS	ALCAIDES	AACDHIMR	CHADARIM	AACDMMOR	CARDAMOM
	SIDALCEA		DRACHMAI	AACDMMRU	CARDAMUM
AACDEIMN	MAENADIC	AACDHINP	HANDICAP	AACDMNNO	MANCANDO
AACDEIMS	CAMISADE	AACDHINR	ARACHNID	AACDMNNY	CANDYMAN
AACDEIMT	ACETAMID	AACDHKPR	HARDPACK	AACDMNOR	CARDAMON
AACDEINR	CANARIED	AACDHKRT	HARDTACK	AACDOOSV	AVOCADOS
	RADIANCE	AACDHLNP	HANDCLAP	AACDORRT	CARTROAD
AACDEINS	AIDANCES	AACDHLOT	CATHODAL	AACDPRSU	CRAPAUDS
AACDEIRT	RADICATE	AACDHLRY	CHARLADY	AACEEFIT	FACETIAE
AACDEJNT	ADJACENT		DYARCHAL	AACEEFLP	PALEFACE
AACDEKNP	PANCAKED	AACDHMMR	DRAMMACH	AACEEFNS	FEASANCE
AACDEKNS	ASKANCED	AACDHMOP	PACHADOM	AACEEGIR	ACIERAGE
AACDEKTT	ATTACKED	AACDHMRS	DRACHMAS		AGACERIE
AACDELLN	CALENDAL	AACDHNOW	WAHCONDA	AACEEGLR	CLEARAGE
	CANALLED	AACDHNRS	HANDCARS	AACEEGLV	CLEAVAGE
AACDELLS	ALCALDES	AACDHNRT	HANDCART	AACEEGNR	CARAGEEN
AACDELMN	MANACLED	AACDHPRS	CRASHPAD	AACEEGNY	GYNAECEA
AACDELNR	CALENDAR	AACDIINS	ASCIDIAN	AACEEGRS	ACREAGES
	LANDRACE	AACDIIRU	ACIDURIA		GEARCASE
AACDELNS	CANDELAS	AACDIISS	DIASCIAS	AACEEHLP	ACALEPHE
AACDELNV	VALANCED	AACDILLP	PALLADIC	AACEEHLT	LEACHATE
AACDELOS	CASELOAD	AACDILMN	MANDALIC	AACEEHRS	AREACHES
	ESCALADO	AACDILMT	DALMATIC		EARACHES
AACDELPT	PLACATED	AACDILMU	CALADIUM	AACEEHRT	TRACHEA
AACDELRS	CALDERAS	AACDILNO	DIACONAL	AACEEIMT	EMACIATE
AACDELSS	SCALADES	AACDILNR	CARDINAL	AACEEINN	ENCAENIA
AACDELSY	ALCAYDES	AACDILNU	DULCIANA	AACEEIRT	ACIERATE
AACDELTT	LACTATED	AACDILNV	VANDALIC	AACEEKRT	CARETAKE
AACDELTV	CLAVATED	AACDILOZ	ZODIACAL	AACEEKST	TEACAKES
AACDELTY	ACYLATED	AACDILPS	CAPSIDAL	AACEELNS	ANELACES
AACDENOT	ANECDOTA	AACDILRT	RAILCARD	AACEELRT	LACERATE
AACDENRS	DRACENAS	AACDILRS	RADICALS	AACEELST	ESCALATE
AACDENRV	ADVANCER	AACDIMNO	MANDIOCA	AACEELTU	ACULEATE
AACDENSV	ADVANCES	AACDIMNY	ADYNAMIC	AACEEMRT	MACERATE
	CANVASED		CYANAMID		RACEMATE
AACDENSZ	CADENZAS	AACDIMOS	CAMISADO	AACEEMSS	AMESACES
AACDENTU	ADUNCATE	AACDIMRT	DRAMATIC	AACEEMST	CASEMATE
AACDEOPS	ESCAPADO	AACDINRT	RADICANT	AACEENNT	CATENANE
AACDEOTU	AUTOCADE		TRIDACNA	AACEENRS	CESAREAN
AACDEOTV	ADVOCATE	AACDINRY	RADIANCY	AACEENRW	CANEWARE
AACDEPRS	SCARPAED	AACDINSS	SCANDIAS	AACEENTT	CATENATE
AACDEQUY	ADEQUACY	AACDINST	ANTACIDS	AACEEPRV	PRECAVAE
AACDERST	CADASTER	AACDIOTU	AUTACOID	AACEEPSS	SEASCAPE
	CADASTRE	AACDIRSS	ASCARIDS	AACEERRW	CAREWARE
AACDERSV	CADAVERS	AACDIRTY	CARYATID	AACEERSU	CAESURAE
AACDERSY	DAYCARES	AACDITUY	AUDACITY	AACEERTV	ACERVATE
AACDERTU	ARCUATED	AACDJKSW	JACKDAWS	AACEESSS	CASEASES

AACEESST	CASEATES	**AACEHLST**	ALCAHEST	**AACEIPPS**	PAPACIES
AACEESTT	ACETATES	**AACEHMNP**	CAMPHANE	**AACEIPRS**	AIRSCAPE
AACEETUV	EVACUATE	**AACEHMRS**	MARCHESA		AIRSPACE
AACEETVX	EXCAVATE	**AACEHMSS**	CAMASHES	**AACEIPRT**	APRICATE
AACEFFIN	AFFIANCE	**AACEHMST**	SCHEMATA	**AACEIPSS**	CAPIASES
AACEFHLP	HALFPACE	**AACEHNOR**	ARCHAEON	**AACEIPTT**	APATETIC
AACEFILM	FACEMAIL	**AACEHNPS**	PANACHES		CAPITATE
AACEFILT	CALIFATE	**AACEHPRT**	RACEPATH	**AACEIQSU**	ACEQUIAS
AACEFIST	FASCIATE	**AACEHPSU**	CHAPEAUS	**AACEIRSV**	AVARICES
AACEFKMS	FACEMASK	**AACEHPUX**	CHAPEAUX		CAVIARES
AACEFLLU	FALCULAE	**AACEHQTU**	CHAQUETA	**AACEIRTV**	VICARATE
AACEFRRS	CARFARES	**AACEHRRS**	CARSHARE	**AACEISST**	ECTASIAS
AACEFRRU	FURCRAEA	**AACEHRSS**	CHARASES	**AACEITTV**	ACTIVATE
AACEFRSS	FRACASES	**AACEHRST**	TRACHEAS		CAVITATE
AACEFRST	SEACRAFT	**AACEHRSU**	ARCHAEUS	**AACEJLTU**	JACULATE
AACEFRSX	CARFAXES	**AACEHRTT**	ATTACHER	**AACEKKLW**	CAKEWALK
AACEFRTT	ARTEFACT		REATTACH	**AACEKLRW**	RACEWALK
AACEGGRS	AGGRACES	**AACEHSTT**	ATTACHES	**AACEKMPR**	CAPMAKER
AACEGHNS	GANACHES	**AACEHSTU**	CHATEAUS	**AACEKMRR**	CARMAKER
AACEGHNT	CHANTAGE	**AACEHTUX**	CHATEAUX	**AACEKNPS**	PANCAKES
AACEGILN	ANGELICA	**AACEIILN**	LACINIAE	**AACEKNSS**	ASKANCES
AACEGILT	GLACIATE	**AACEIINT**	ACTINIAE	**AACEKOST**	OATCAKES
AACEGINR	CANAIGRE	**AACEIIRV**	CAVIARIE	**AACEKRTT**	ATTACKER
AACEGINY	GYNAECIA	**AACEIKMT**	KAMACITE		REATTACK
AACEGIOP	APOGAEIC	**AACEILLM**	CAMELLIA	**AACELLMR**	MARCELLA
AACEGIRR	CARRIAGE	**AACEILLN**	ALLIANCE	**AACELLNR**	CANALLER
AACEGIRV	VICARAGE		ANCILLAE	**AACELLNS**	CANELLAS
AACEGKPR	PACKAGER		CANAILLE	**AACELLOT**	ALLOCATE
AACEGKPS	PACKAGES	**AACEILMN**	ANALCIME	**AACELLST**	CASTELLA
AACEGKRT	TRACKAGE		CALAMINE		LACTEALS
AACEGKSS	SACKAGES	**AACEILMS**	CAMELIAS	**AACELLTY**	ALLEYCAT
AACEGLNY	LANCEGAY	**AACEILMT**	CALAMITE	**AACELMNP**	PLACEMAN
AACEGLSS	SCALAGES	**AACEILNS**	CANALISE	**AACELMNS**	MANACLES
AACEGMNO	COMANAGE	**AACEILNT**	ANALCITE	**AACELMOT**	CELOMATA
AACEGMNP	CAMPAGNE		LAITANCE	**AACELMRS**	CARAMELS
AACEGNRS	CAGANERS	**AACEILNU**	ACAULINE		CERAMALS
	CARNAGES	**AACEILNV**	VALENCIA		MACERALS
	CRANAGES		VALIANCE	**AACELMTU**	MACULATE
AACEGRST	CARTAGES	**AACEILNZ**	CANALIZE	**AACELNNO**	ANCONEAL
AACEGRSV	SCAVAGER	**AACEILOP**	ALOPECIA	**AACELNNU**	CANNULAE
AACEGSSV	SCAVAGES	**AACEILRT**	TAILRACE	**AACELNOR**	LECANORA
AACEHHRU	HUARACHE	**AACEILRV**	CAVALIER	**AACELNPR**	PARLANCE
AACEHIKN	ICEKHANA		VARICEAL	**AACELNPS**	CAPELANS
AACEHILL	ACHILLEA	**AACEILST**	SALICETA		SCALEPAN
	HELIACAL	**AACEIMNS**	AMNESIAC	**AACELNPT**	PLACENTA
AACEHILN	ACHENIAL	**AACEIMRS**	MACARISE	**AACELNPY**	ANYPLACE
AACEHILP	PHACELIA		MESARAIC	**AACELNRT**	LACERANT
AACEHIMR	CHIMAERA	**AACEIMRZ**	MACARIZE	**AACELNRY**	ARCANELY
AACEHIMT	HAEMATIC	**AACEIMTT**	CATAMITE	**AACELNST**	ANALECTS
AACEHIPT	HEPATICA	**AACEIMUX**	CAMAIEUX	**AACELNSV**	VALANCES
AACEHIRS	ARCHAISE	**AACEINNT**	ANTIACNE	**AACELNTU**	CANULATE
AACEHIRT	THERIACA	**AACEINRS**	ACARINES		LACUNATE
AACEHIRZ	ARCHAIZE		CANARIES		TENACULA
AACEHKSS	ASHCAKES		CESARIAN	**AACELORS**	ACEROLAS
AACEHLNT	CALANTHE		SARCINAE	**AACELORV**	CAVALERO
AACEHLNU	EULACHAN	**AACEINRT**	CARINATE	**AACELOST**	CATALOES
AACEHLPS	ACALEPHS		CRANIATE	**AACELOSU**	ACAULOSE
AACEHLRS	ALCHERAS	**AACEINRV**	VARIANCE	**AACELOSV**	COAEVALS
AACEHLRT	TRACHEAL	**AACEINST**	ESTANCIA	**AACELPRS**	CARPALES
AACEHLRX	EXARCHAL	**AACEINTV**	CAVATINE	**AACELPRT**	PLACATER
AACEHLSS	CALASHES	**AACEIOPR**	CAPOEIRA	**AACELPRV**	PRECAVAL

AACELPST	PLACATES	AACESTTU	ACTUATES	AACGJNST	CATJANGS
AACELPSU	SCAPULAE	AACESTUV	VACUATES	AACGLMOU	GLAUCOMA
AACELRSS	SCALARES	AACESUWY	CAUSEWAY	AACGLOST	CATALOGS
AACELRSU	CAESURAL	AACFFILS	CAFFILAS	AACGMNRS	CRAGSMAN
AACELRSV	CARAVELS	AACFGRST	CRAGFAST	AACGNOSU	GUANACOS
AACELRTY	ACRYLATE	AACFHMST	CAMSHAFT	AACGNRVY	VAGRANCY
AACELRWY	CLAYWARE	AACFILLY	FACIALLY	AACHHIKL	HALAKHIC
	CLEARWAY	AACFILOS	FASCIOLA	AACHHIKR	KACHAHRI
AACELSST	LACTASES	AACFINST	FANATICS	AACHHILR	RHACHIAL
AACELSTT	LACTATES	AACFIRRT	AIRCRAFT	AACHHIMS	MASHIACH
AACELSTY	ACYLATES	AACFIRST	FRASCATI	AACHHKRS	CHARKHAS
	CATALYSE	AACFIRTT	ARTIFACT	AACHHLLS	CHALLAHS
AACELTTY	CATTLEYA	AACFISST	FASCISTA	AACHHLOT	HALACHOT
AACELTYZ	CATALYZE	AACFJKLP	FLAPJACK	AACHHORU	HUARACHO
AACEMMRS	MACRAMES	AACFKLPT	FLATPACK	AACHHTWY	HATCHWAY
AACEMNOR	AMORANCE	AACFLLST	CATFALLS	AACHIIMR	MARIACHI
AACEMNPS	SPACEMAN	AACFLLSU	FALCULAS	AACHIKKZ	KAZACHKI
AACEMNST	CAMSTANE	AACFLOPR	PARFOCAL	AACHIKNR	CHINKARA
AACEMPRS	PARACMES	AACFLPST	CATFLAPS	AACHIKNS	KACHINAS
AACEMQSU	MACAQUES		FLATCAPS	AACHIKNT	KATCHINA
AACEMRSS	MASSACRE	AACFLRST	FLATCARS	AACHIKRS	CHIKARAS
AACEMSSS	CAMASSES		FRACTALS	AACHILLP	CALIPHAL
AACENOTU	OCEANAUT	AACFRRSU	FARRUCAS	AACHILLR	RACHILLA
AACENPRS	PANCREAS	AACFRRTW	WARCRAFT	AACHILMS	CHAMISAL
AACENPRT	CATNAPER	AACGGINO	ANAGOGIC		CHIASMAL
AACENPST	PASTANCE	AACGGIOP	APAGOGIC	AACHILMT	THALAMIC
AACENPSU	SAUCEPAN	AACGHILT	TAIGLACH	AACHILNP	CHAPLAIN
AACENPTT	PANCETTA	AACGHIPR	AGRAPHIC	AACHILOS	ACHOLIAS
AACENRST	CANASTER	AACGHIRR	CHIRAGRA	AACHILPS	CALIPASH
	CATERANS	AACGHLLO	AGALLOCH		PASHALIC
AACENRSV	CANVASER	AACGHLRU	RUGALACH	AACHILPT	HAPTICAL
AACENRTT	REACTANT	AACGHNOR	CHARANGO	AACHILRV	ARCHIVAL
AACENRTY	CATENARY	AACGHOPZ	GAZPACHO	AACHIMNN	CHAINMAN
AACENRVZ	CZAREVNA	AACGHORU	GUACHARO		CHINAMAN
AACENSSS	CASSENAS	AACGIIMN	MAGICIAN	AACHIMNP	CHINAMPA
AACENSSV	CANVASES	AACGIINR	GARCINIA	AACHIMNR	CHAIRMAN
AACENSTT	CANTATES	AACGILLN	GALLICAN	AACHIMNS	SHAMANIC
	CASTANET	AACGILLO	ALOGICAL	AACHIMNT	MATACHIN
AACENSTY	CYANATES	AACGILLS	GALLICAS	AACHIMNZ	CHAZANIM
AACENTUV	EVACUANT		GLACIALS	AACHIMRR	ARMCHAIR
AACEOPPR	COAPPEAR	AACGILLU	ALGUACIL	AACHIMRS	ARCHAISM
AACEOPRT	CAPROATE	AACGILNN	CANALING		CHARISMA
AACEOPST	PEACOATS	AACGILNO	ANALOGIC		MACHAIRS
AACEORSS	ROSACEAS	AACGILNR	CRAALING	AACHIMSS	CHAMISAS
AACEORSU	ARACEOUS	AACGILNT	ANTALGIC		CHIASMAS
AACEORTV	CAVEATOR	AACGILNV	GALVANIC	AACHIMST	CATHISMA
AACEOSST	SEACOAST	AACGILOU	GUAIACOL	AACHINNT	ACANTHIN
AACEPRST	CAPRATES	AACGILOX	COXALGIA	AACHINRT	CANTHARI
AACEPRSU	CAPUERAS	AACGILRT	TRAGICAL	AACHINSW	CHAINSAW
AACEPSSS	CASPASES	AACGILSS	SCAGLIAS	AACHIPPT	CHAPPATI
AACEPSWY	PACEWAYS	AACGIMMT	MAGMATIC	AACHIPRS	CHARPAIS
AACERRTU	ARCATURE	AACGIMNN	MANGANIC		HAIRCAPS
AACERSSS	RASCASSE	AACGIMNP	CAMPAIGN	AACHIPSS	APHASICS
AACERSSU	CAESURAS		PANGAMIC	AACHIPST	CHAPATIS
AACERSSZ	SAZERACS	AACGIMOP	APOGAMIC	AACHIPTT	CHAPATTI
AACERSTT	CASTRATE	AACGIMRR	MARGARIC	AACHIRST	ARCHAIST
	TEACARTS	AACGIMUU	GUAIACUM		CITHARAS
AACERSWY	RACEWAYS	AACGINOT	CONTAGIA	AACHIRTX	TAXIARCH
AACERTTT	TRACTATE	AACGINPS	SCAPAING	AACHKKOZ	KAZACHOK
AACESSSV	CAVASSES	AACGINTV	VACATING	AACHKMPS	CHAMPAKS
AACESSTT	SCEATTAS	AACGISTY	SAGACITY	AACHKNSW	HACKSAWN

AACHKPSS	SCHAPSKA	AACIKLRS	CLARKIAS		PACATION
AACHKRST	HATRACKS	AACIKMNW	MACKINAW	AACINORS	OCARINAS
AACHKRSY	HAYRACKS	AACIKNNS	CANAKINS	AACINORT	RAINCOAT
AACHKSSW	HACKSAWS	AACIKNST	KATCINAS	AACINOTV	VACATION
AACHKSTY	HAYSTACK	AACIKRTU	AUTARKIC	AACINPRT	CANTRAIP
AACHLLLU	HALLUCAL	AACILLLY	LAICALLY	AACINPST	CAPITANS
AACHLLNS	CHALLANS	AACILLMR	LACRIMAL		CAPTAINS
AACHLLOR	ALACHLOR	AACILLMT	CLIMATAL	AACINPTY	CAPITAYN
AACHLMNO	MONACHAL	AACILLNS	ANCILLAS	AACINQTU	ACQUAINT
AACHLMOS	CHLOASMA	AACILLPY	APICALLY	AACINRSS	ACRASINS
AACHLNOO	OOLACHAN	AACILLRY	RACIALLY		SARCINAS
AACHLORT	THORACAL	AACILMNT	CALAMINT	AACINRST	ARCANIST
AACHLOST	CALATHOS		CLAIMANT	AACINRSZ	CZARINAS
AACHLPPS	CHAPPALS	AACILMOR	ACROMIAL	AACINSSS	CASSINAS
AACHLPSS	PASCHALS	AACILMOT	ATOMICAL	AACINSTZ	STANZAIC
AACHLPSU	CHALUPAS	AACILMRS	MAILCARS	AACIOPST	TAPIOCAS
AACHLSSU	ACUSHLAS	AACILMTY	CALAMITY	AACIOPSV	COPAIVAS
AACHLSTU	CALATHUS	AACILNOR	CONARIAL	AACIPPRS	PAPRICAS
AACHMMNR	MARCHMAN	AACILNPS	CALPAINS	AACIPRST	ASPARTIC
AACHMNNR	RANCHMAN	AACILNRS	CLARAINS	AACIPRTY	RAPACITY
AACHMNTW	WATCHMAN	AACILNRV	CARNIVAL	AACIQSTU	AQUATICS
AACHMNTY	YACHTMAN	AACILNST	ALICANTS	AACIRRTT	TARTARIC
AACHMNUY	NAUMACHY		SANTALIC	AACIRSTT	CASTRATI
AACHMORT	ACHROMAT	AACILNTT	TANTALIC	AACIRSTZ	CZARITSA
	TRACHOMA	AACILNTU	NAUTICAL	AACIRTVY	CAVITARY
AACHMPRT	CHAMPART	AACILNTY	ANALYTIC	AACIRTZZ	CZARITZA
AACHMPRY	PHARMACY	AACILNUV	NAVICULA	AACISSTW	SWASTICA
AACHMSSY	YASHMACS	AACILNVY	VALIANCY	AACJKLPS	SLAPJACK
AACHNOPS	PANOCHAS	AACILOSS	ASOCIALS	AACJKMNS	MANJACKS
AACHNOSU	HUANACOS	AACILOTT	COATTAIL	AACJKOOR	JACKAROO
AACHNPRS	SARPANCH		TAILCOAT	AACJKSTY	JACKSTAY
AACHNRST	TRASHCAN	AACILPRU	PIACULAR	AACJPSTU	CAJAPUTS
AACHNRSV	NAVARCHS	AACILPST	APLASTIC	AACKKNPS	KNAPSACK
AACHNRVY	NAVARCHY		CAPITALS	AACKLOWY	LOCKAWAY
AACHNSSU	ANCHUSAS	AACILPSZ	CAPSIZAL	AACKLSTW	CATWALKS
AACHNSTU	ACANTHUS	AACILPTU	CAPITULA	AACKMNPS	MANPACKS
AACHNSZZ	CHAZZANS	AACILPTY	ATYPICAL	AACKMNRT	TRACKMAN
AACHOPPR	APPROACH	AACILQRU	ACQUIRAL	AACKMNST	TACKSMAN
AACHOPRR	PARACHOR	AACILRRS	RAILCARS	AACKMRST	AMTRACKS
AACHOPRT	CATAPHOR	AACILRTY	ALACRITY	AACKNRSS	RANSACKS
AACHORTU	RACAHOUT	AACILRUU	AURICULA	AACKORWY	ROCKAWAY
AACHOTTU	TACAHOUT	AACILRUV	AVICULAR	AACKPRST	RATPACKS
AACHRRST	CATARRHS	AACILSTT	CATTAILS	AACKPSWY	PACKWAYS
AACHRSTU	AUTARCHS		STATICAL	AACKRTWY	TRACKWAY
AACHRSWY	ARCHWAYS	AACILSTY	SALACITY	AACLLLOO	CALLALOO
AACHRTUY	AUTARCHY	AACIMMNO	AMMONIAC	AACLLMMU	MACALLUM
AACIILMN	ANIMALIC	AACIMMRS	MACARISM	AACLLMRY	LACRYMAL
AACIILMO	MAIOLICA		MACRAMIS	AACLLNRY	CARNALLY
AACIILRT	IATRICAL		MARASMIC	AACLLNST	CALLANTS
AACIILRV	VICARIAL	AACIMNOR	ARMONICA	AACLLNSU	CALLUNAS
AACIILTV	VIATICAL		MACARONI	AACLLOOS	CALALOOS
AACIIMNT	ANIMATIC		MAROCAIN	AACLLRRY	CARRYALL
AACIIMSS	CAMISIAS	AACIMNOS	MANIOCAS	AACLLRSY	RASCALLY
AACIINNT	ACTINIAN	AACIMNOT	ANATOMIC	AACLLSUU	CLAUSULA
AACIINPR	PICARIAN	AACIMORT	AROMATIC	AACLLSUY	CASUALLY
AACIINPT	CAPITANI	AACIMOTX	MAXICOAT		CAUSALLY
AACIINST	ACTINIAS	AACIMPRS	PICAMARS	AACLLTUY	ACTUALLY
AACIIRSV	VISCARIA	AACIMRSS	SAMSARIC	AACLMNNS	CLANSMAN
AACIJLMO	MAJOLICA	AACINNST	CANTINAS	AACLMNSS	CLASSMAN
AACIJNOP	JAPONICA	AACINOPR	PARANOIC	AACLMNST	CALMANTS
AACIKLMS	MAILSACK	AACINOPT	CAPITANO	AACLMOTU	COMATULA

AACLMRRU	MACRURAL	**AACOPSTV**	POSTCAVA	**AADDNSVV**	DVANDVAS
AACLNNOT	CANTONAL	**AACOPSTY**	APOSTACY	**AADDRSST**	DASTARDS
AACLNNRU	CANNULAR	**AACORRTV**	VARACTOR	**AADDRSTY**	DASTARDY
AACLNNSU	CANNULAS	**AACORSSW**	CARASSOW	**AADEEERT**	DEAERATE
AACLNOPR	COPLANAR	**AACORSTT**	CASTRATO	**AADEEFFR**	AFFEARED
AACLNOTT	OCTANTAL	**AACORSTU**	ACATOURS	**AADEEGHR**	GEARHEAD
AACLNPSY	CLAYPANS		AUTOCARS		HEADGEAR
AACLNRSU	LACUNARS	**AACORTTU**	ACTUATOR	**AADEEGHS**	HEADAGES
AACLNRUY	LACUNARY		AUTOCRAT	**AADEEGHT**	HEADGATE
AACLNTVY	VACANTLY	**AACOSTUV**	AUTOVACS	**AADEEGLM**	MEGADEAL
AACLOOPT	TAPACOLO	**AACPSSTW**	CATSPAWS	**AADEEGLR**	LAAGERED
AACLOPRS	CAPORALS	**AACRSTTT**	ATTRACTS	**AADEEGLT**	GALEATED
	CRAPOLAS	**AACRSTUV**	VACATURS	**AADEEGMN**	AMENAGED
AACLOPST	OCTAPLAS	**AACRSTWY**	CARTWAYS		ENDAMAGE
AACLOPTU	TAPACULO	**AACSTUWY**	CUTAWAYS	**AADEEGMR**	REDAMAGE
AACLORRU	ORACULAR	**AADDDEEH**	DEADHEAD	**AADEEGNR**	GADARENE
AACLORSU	CAROUSAL	**AADDDEER**	ADREADED	**AADEEGRV**	AVERAGED
AACLORSZ	ALCORZAS	**AADDDERW**	ADWARDED	**AADEEHMT**	MEATHEAD
AACLORUV	VACUOLAR	**AADDDGNR**	GRANDDAD	**AADEEIRT**	ERADIATE
AACLOSTT	CATTALOS	**AADDEELT**	DEALATED	**AADEEIRW**	AWEARIED
AACLOSUU	ACAULOUS	**AADDEFLL**	DEADFALL	**AADEEKNW**	AWAKENED
AACLPPRT	CLAPTRAP	**AADDEGGR**	AGGRADED	**AADEEKRW**	REAWAKED
AACLPRST	CALTRAPS	**AADDEGRT**	GRADATED	**AADEELNN**	ANNEALED
AACLPRSU	CAPSULAR	**AADDEHHR**	HARDHEAD	**AADEELPP**	APPEALED
	SCAPULAR	**AADDEHHS**	HADEDAHS	**AADEELST**	DEALATES
AACLPRTY	CALYPTRA	**AADDEHLN**	HEADLAND	**AADEELTV**	ALVEATED
AACLPSSU	SCAPULAS	**AADDEHMN**	HANDMADE	**AADEEMMS**	EDAMAMES
AACLPSTY	PLAYACTS	**AADDEHRW**	HEADWARD	**AADEEMNS**	MAENADES
AACLPTTU	CATAPULT	**AADDEHRZ**	HAZARDED	**AADEEMNT**	EMANATED
AACLRSTU	CLAUSTRA	**AADDEILN**	DEDALIAN	**AADEEMOT**	OEDEMATA
AACLRSUV	VASCULAR	**AADDEILS**	ALIDADES	**AADEEMRR**	DEMERARA
AACLRTUX	CURTALAX	**AADDEIRT**	RADIATED	**AADEENPT**	TAPENADE
AACLRWWY	CRAWLWAY	**AADDEKMS**	DAMASKED	**AADEENTT**	ANTEDATE
AACLSSTT	SALTCATS	**AADDELNS**	SANDALED	**AADEEPPR**	APPEARED
AACLSTTY	CATALYST	**AADDELTU**	ADULATED	**AADEEPPS**	APPEASED
AACLSTUY	CASUALTY	**AADDEMNT**	MANDATED	**AADEEPRS**	PASEARED
AACMNOOR	MACAROON	**AADDEMRU**	MARAUDED	**AADEEQTU**	ADEQUATE
AACMNORS	CAMARONS	**AADDEMRY**	DAYDREAM	**AADEERSW**	AWARDESS
	MASCARON	**AADDENPR**	PANDARED	**AADEFFLT**	AFFLATED
	NARCOMAS	**AADDENPS**	DEADPANS	**AADEFFNR**	FANFARED
AACMNPRY	RAMPANCY	**AADDEORS**	DEODARAS	**AADEFFRY**	AFFRAYED
AACMNRRU	MACRURAN	**AADDGMNR**	GRANDDAM	**AADEFGLS**	FALDAGES
AACMNRSU	ARCANUMS	**AADDGNRS**	GRADDANS	**AADEFGRS**	FARDAGES
AACMORRS	CAMORRAS		GRANDADS	**AADEFHLT**	FLATHEAD
AACMORSS	SARCOMAS	**AADDGNRU**	GRADUAND	**AADEFHST**	FATHEADS
AACMORST	MARCATOS	**AADDHHRS**	SHRADDHA		HEADFAST
AACMRRST	TRAMCARS	**AADDHIMN**	HANDMAID	**AADEFHTW**	FATWAHED
AACMRSSS	SARCASMS	**AADDHKRS**	KHADDARS	**AADEFIJO**	FEIJOADA
AACNNOSZ	CANZONAS	**AADDHRSS**	SRADDHAS	**AADEFILR**	FAIRLEAD
AACNOSST	SACATONS	**AADDIIKS**	DIDAKAIS	**AADEFIRS**	FARADISE
AACNOSTZ	ZACATONS	**AADDIISV**	DAVIDIAS		SAFARIED
AACNOTTY	CATATONY	**AADDILNO**	DIANODAL	**AADEFIRZ**	FARADIZE
AACNPRST	CANTRAPS	**AADDIMSS**	DADAISMS	**AADEFISS**	FADAISES
AACNPSST	CAPSTANS	**AADDISST**	DADAISTS	**AADEFLLR**	FALDERAL
AACNRSTT	TRANSACT	**AADDKMMO**	MOKADDAM	**AADEFLRY**	DEFRAYAL
AACNRSTU	CURTANAS	**AADDLLNY**	LANDLADY	**AADEFLTT**	FALDETTA
AACOORTX	TOXOCARA	**AADDLNRW**	LANDWARD	**AADEFNSZ**	FAZENDAS
AACOPPRS	APOCARPS	**AADDLNRY**	YARDLAND	**AADEFRRW**	WARFARED
AACOPPRY	APOCARPY	**AADDMMQU**	MUQADDAM	**AADEFRWY**	WAYFARED
AACOPRSU	ACARPOUS	**AADDNRST**	STANDARD	**AADEGGRS**	AGGRADES
AACOPRTU	AUTOCARP	**AADDNRWY**	YARDWAND		SAGGARED

AADEGGRT	AGGRATED	AADEHMNS	HEADSMAN	AADEJMPY	PYJAMAED
AADEGGRU	GUARDAGE	AADEHMST	MASTHEAD	AADEJMRS	JEMADARS
AADEGHLN	DANELAGH	AADEHNPS	SANDHEAP	AADEJNNP	JAPANNED
AADEGHNR	HANGARED	AADEHNRV	VERANDAH	AADEKLLN	LAKELAND
AADEGHRS	RAGHEADS	AADEHNSX	HANDAXES	AADEKLNR	KALENDAR
	RHAGADES	AADEHPPR	PARAPHED	AADEKLRY	KALEYARD
AADEGILL	DIALLAGE	AADEHPSS	SAPHEADS	AADEKMNR	MANDRAKE
AADEGILT	GLADIATE	AADEHRRW	HARDWARE	AADEKMRS	KAMERADS
AADEGINR	AREADING	AADEHRRZ	HAZARDER	AADEKNST	ASKANTED
	DRAINAGE	AADEHRSS	HARASSED	AADEKNUW	UNAWAKED
	GARDENIA	AADEHRSW	RAWHEADS	AADEKPRS	PARKADES
AADEGINT	INDAGATE		WARHEADS	AADEKSTT	ATTASKED
AADEGIRR	GERARDIA	AADEHSSY	SASHAYED	AADELLOS	ALDOLASE
AADEGIRV	GRAVIDAE	AADEHSTT	HASTATED	AADELLPP	APPALLED
AADEGIST	AGATISED	AADEHSTY	HEADSTAY	AADELLPS	PADELLAS
AADEGITT	AGITATED	AADEHSWY	HEADWAYS	AADELLRT	DATALLER
AADEGITV	DIVAGATE	AADEILMS	MALADIES	AADELLWY	WELLADAY
AADEGITZ	AGATIZED	AADEILMU	AUMAILED	AADELMNP	NAPALMED
AADEGJTU	ADJUTAGE	AADEILNT	DENTALIA	AADELMNR	ALDERMAN
AADEGKMR	DEKAGRAM	AADEILPR	PRAEDIAL		MALANDER
AADEGLLT	TALLAGED	AADEILPS	PALISADE	AADELMNS	DALESMAN
AADEGLMN	MAGDALEN	AADEILPT	LAPIDATE		LEADSMAN
AADEGLMY	AMYGDALE	AADEILRS	SALARIED	AADELMOS	ALAMODES
AADEGLNS	SELADANG	AADEILRT	LARIATED	AADELMPT	PALMATED
AADEGLOP	GALOPADE	AADEILSS	ASSAILED	AADELMRU	ALARUMED
AADEGLSV	SALVAGED	AADEILSV	VEDALIAS	AADELMYZ	AMAZEDLY
AADEGMNR	GRANDAME	AADEILTT	DILATATE	AADELNPT	PEATLAND
AADEGMPR	RAMPAGED	AADEILTV	VALIDATE	AADELNRS	ADRENALS
AADEGMRS	DAMAGERS	AADEIMNN	AMANDINE	AADELNST	EASTLAND
	MEGARADS	AADEIMNP	PANDEMIA	AADELNSW	DANELAWS
	SMARAGDE	AADEIMNR	MARINADE	AADELNSY	ANALYSED
AADEGMSS	MASSAGED	AADEIMNT	ANIMATED	AADELNYZ	ANALYZED
AADEGNRR	ARRANGED		DIAMANTE	AADELOTX	OXALATED
AADEGNTV	VANTAGED	AADEIMPZ	DIAZEPAM	AADELPPT	PALPATED
AADEGPRY	PAYGRADE	AADEIMRS	MADEIRAS	AADELPRS	PARDALES
AADEGPSS	PASSAGED	AADEIMRV	MARAVEDI	AADELPRY	PARLAYED
AADEGRST	GRADATES	AADEIMSS	AMIDASES	AADELPTY	PLAYDATE
AADEGRSV	SAVEGARD		SEAMAIDS	AADELQUU	QUAALUDE
AADEGRSY	DRAYAGES	AADEIMST	ADAMSITE	AADELRSY	SALEYARD
	YARDAGES		DIASTEMA	AADELRTU	RADULATE
AADEGRTU	GRADUATE	AADEINPT	PATINAED	AADELRTV	LARVATED
AADEGSSU	ASSUAGED	AADEINRR	DARRAINE	AADELRTY	DAYTALER
AADEGSSW	ASSWAGED	AADEINRS	ARANEIDS	AADELSTT	SALTATED
AADEHHHS	HASHHEAD	AADEINRT	DENTARIA	AADELSTU	ADULATES
AADEHHOR	HOARHEAD		RAINDATE	AADELSTY	DAYTALES
AADEHILN	NAILHEAD	AADEINSZ	ZENAIDAS	AADELTUV	VALUATED
AADEHILR	HEADRAIL	AADEINTT	ATTAINED	AADEMNOS	ADENOMAS
	RAILHEAD	AADEIPPR	APPAIRED	AADEMNPS	SPADEMAN
AADEHILS	HEADSAIL	AADEIPRS	PARADISE	AADEMNST	MANDATES
AADEHIRR	DIARRHEA	AADEIPSS	DIAPASES	AADEMNUZ	UNAMAZED
AADEHIRS	AIRHEADS	AADEIPSU	DIAPAUSE	AADEMORT	MATADORE
AADEHIWY	HIDEAWAY	AADEIPTV	ADAPTIVE	AADEMRRU	MARAUDER
AADEHJRS	JARHEADS	AADEIRST	AIRDATES	AADEMRSS	MADRASES
AADEHKMR	HEADMARK		DATARIES	AADEMRSY	DAYMARES
AADEHLLL	HALALLED		RADIATES	AADEMSSS	ADMASSES
AADEHLLO	HALLOAED	AADEIRTT	DIATRETA	AADEMWZZ	ZAMZAWED
AADEHLLW	HEADWALL	AADEIRTV	VARIATED	AADENNST	ANDANTES
AADEHLMP	HEADLAMP	AADEISST	DIASTASE	AADENRRT	NARRATED
AADEHLNR	ANHEDRAL	AADEISTT	ASTATIDE	AADENRRW	WARRANED
AADEHLPS	SLAPHEAD		SATIATED	AADENRSV	VERANDAS
AADEHLRS	ASHLARED	AADEITVW	VIEWDATA	AADENRTT	TARTANED

AADENSSW	WEASANDS	**AADGIMMN**	MADAMING	**AADHLMOY**	DALMAHOY
AADENSTY	ASYNDETA	**AADGIMMS**	DIGAMMAS	**AADHLNPY**	HANDPLAY
AADENSTZ	STANZAED	**AADGIMNR**	MRIDANGA	**AADHLNSW**	WASHLAND
AADENSWZ	WEAZANDS	**AADGIMOS**	AGAMOIDS	**AADHLPSS**	SLAPDASH
AADENTUV	AVAUNTED	**AADGIMPR**	PARADIGM	**AADHLRSY**	HALYARDS
AADEOPRT	TAPADERO	**AADGIMRS**	DIAGRAMS	**AADHLRUY**	HAULYARD
AADEOPST	ADESPOTA	**AADGIMRT**	GRADATIM	**AADHMNNY**	HANDYMAN
AADEORRT	AERODART	**AADGINPR**	PARADING	**AADHMNOU**	OMADHAUN
AADEPPRT	PREADAPT	**AADGINPT**	ADAPTING	**AADHMOPS**	PASHADOM
AADEPRRS	PARADERS	**AADGINRR**	DARRAIGN	**AADHNPRS**	HARDPANS
AADEPRST	ADAPTERS	**AADGINRU**	GUARDIAN	**AADHNPSS**	HANDPASS
	READAPTS	**AADGINRW**	AWARDING	**AADHNRSS**	DARSHANS
AADEPSSS	PASSADES	**AADGIQRU**	QUADRIGA	**AADHNSSW**	HANDSAWS
AADEQRTU	QUADRATE	**AADGIRSV**	GRAVIDAS	**AADHNSTT**	HATSTAND
AADERRRW	REARWARD	**AADGLLSW**	GADWALLS	**AADHRRTW**	THRAWARD
AADERRSW	AWARDERS	**AADGLMOR**	MALGRADO	**AADHRRYZ**	HAZARDRY
AADERRWY	WARRAYED	**AADGLMSY**	AMYGDALS	**AADHRSWY**	HAYWARDS
AADERSST	ASSARTED	**AADGLNOR**	LARGANDO	**AADHSSWY**	WASHDAYS
AADERSSW	SEAWARDS	**AADGLNRS**	GARLANDS	**AADIIINR**	ANIRIDIA
AADERSTT	ASTARTED	**AADGLNSS**	SLADANGS	**AADIILNS**	SIALIDAN
AADERSTW	EASTWARD	**AADGLOOW**	AGALWOOD	**AADIINOS**	DIANOIAS
	RADWASTE	**AADGLOPR**	PODAGRAL	**AADIIPSS**	ADIPSIAS
AADERSWY	DAYWEARS	**AADGLORW**	GOALWARD	**AADIJMNS**	JAMDANIS
AADERUVY	AYURVEDA	**AADGLPRW**	GLADWRAP	**AADIKLLO**	ALKALOID
AADFGNNO	FANDANGO	**AADGLRSU**	GRADUALS	**AADIKLLR**	KILLADAR
AADFGRSU	SAUFGARD	**AADGMNOP**	PAGANDOM	**AADIKLRY**	KAILYARD
AADFHMNR	FARMHAND	**AADGMNOR**	DRAGOMAN	**AADIKLSY**	ILKADAYS
AADFHNST	HANDFAST	**AADGMNOS**	GOADSMAN	**AADIKMNS**	DAMASKIN
AADFIINT	INTIFADA	**AADGMNRS**	DRAGSMAN	**AADIKNQR**	QINDARKA
AADFIMRS	FARADISM		GRANDAMS	**AADILLLO**	ALLODIAL
AADFINRU	UNAFRAID		GRANDMAS	**AADILLNR**	LANDRAIL
AADFLLLN	LANDFALL	**AADGMRSS**	SMARAGDS	**AADILLPR**	PAILLARD
AADFLLNT	FLATLAND	**AADGNNQU**	QUANDANG		PALLIARD
AADFLMNR	FARMLAND	**AADGNPRS**	GRANDPAS	**AADILLRS**	SILLADAR
AADFLORW	AARDWOLF	**AADGNRST**	GARDANTS	**AADILLRY**	RADIALLY
AADFLOTW	DATAFLOW	**AADGNRSY**	YARDANGS	**AADILLSY**	DYSLALIA
AADFLOTX	TOADFLAX	**AADGNRTU**	GUARDANT	**AADILMNN**	MAINLAND
AADFLOWY	FOLDAWAY	**AADGNRUV**	VANGUARD	**AADILMNO**	DOMAINAL
AADFMRRY	FARMYARD	**AADGNRWY**	DRANGWAY		DOMANIAL
AADGGHOT	AGGADOTH	**AADGOPRS**	PODAGRAS	**AADILMNP**	PLAIDMAN
	HAGGADOT	**AADGRRUW**	GURDWARA	**AADILMRS**	ADMIRALS
AADGGHRS	HAGGARDS	**AADHHIPS**	PADISHAH		AMILDARS
AADGGIMN	DAMAGING	**AADHHKNS**	SHADKHAN	**AADILMST**	MATILDAS
AADGGLNN	GANGLAND	**AADHHNSW**	WASHHAND	**AADILNNV**	LAVANDIN
AADGGLRS	LAGGARDS	**AADHHPSS**	PADSHAHS	**AADILNOR**	ORDALIAN
AADGGRSS	SAGGARDS	**AADHHRST**	HARDHATS	**AADILNPR**	PRANDIAL
AADGGRST	STAGGARD	**AADHIINP**	APHIDIAN	**AADILNPS**	PALADINS
AADGHILS	HIDALGAS	**AADHILLR**	HALLIARD	**AADILNRS**	LANIARDS
AADGHIPR	DIAGRAPH	**AADHILNR**	HANDRAIL	**AADILNTT**	DILATANT
AADGHIST	HAGADIST	**AADHILRT**	HARDTAIL	**AADILOPS**	PALISADO
AADGHORS	DAROGHAS	**AADHILRV**	HAVILDAR	**AADILORR**	RAILROAD
AADGHRTU	HATGUARD	**AADHIMRS**	HARAMDIS	**AADILPRS**	PARDALIS
AADGIINS	GAINSAID	**AADHIMSS**	SAMADHIS	**AADILPRY**	LAPIDARY
AADGIIRS	GIARDIAS	**AADHINOT**	ANTHODIA	**AADILRRS**	RISALDAR
AADGILLO	GLADIOLA	**AADHINPS**	DAPHNIAS	**AADILRST**	DIASTRAL
AADGILLR	GAILLARD	**AADHINRR**	HARRIDAN		TAILARDS
	GALLIARD	**AADHIPRS**	PARISHAD	**AADILSST**	STADIALS
AADGILMR	MADRIGAL	**AADHJNRS**	HANDJARS	**AADIMNNR**	MANDARIN
AADGILNO	DIAGONAL	**AADHKLOT**	KATHODAL	**AADIMNOR**	RADIOMAN
	GONADIAL	**AADHKNSS**	DHANSAKS	**AADIMNOT**	MANATOID
AADGILNS	SALADING	**AADHKNSY**	YAKHDANS	**AADIMNRS**	MANDIRAS

AADIMNRT	TAMARIND	AADLNRSY	LANYARDS	AAEEFFRS	AFFEARES
AADIMNRY	DAIRYMAN	AADLOPSY	PAYLOADS	AAEEFGLS	LEAFAGES
	MAINYARD	AADLORST	LOADSTAR	AAEEFRRS	SEAFARER
AADIMNRZ	ZAMINDAR	AADLORTU	ADULATOR	AAEEFRST	RATAFEES
AADIMNSS	DAMASSIN		LAUDATOR	AAEEGILN	ALIENAGE
AADIMNSU	SUDAMINA	AADLPPRW	WALDRAPP	AAEEGILP	EPIGAEAL
AADIMNUV	VANADIUM	AADLPPSU	APPLAUDS	AAEEGINP	EPIGAEAN
AADIMORS	DIORAMAS	AADLPQUY	QUADPLAY	AAEEGINS	AGENESIA
AADIMPST	MISADAPT	AADLPSYY	PLAYDAYS	AAEEGKLS	LEAKAGES
AADIMRSW	MISAWARD	AADMMNOW	MADWOMAN	AAEEGLLN	ENALLAGE
AADIMSTZ	SAMIZDAT	AADMMNSU	MANDAMUS	AAEEGLRY	LAYERAGE
AADINNNS	NANDINAS	AADMNNOS	MADONNAS	AAEEGLST	ETALAGES
AADINNOT	ADNATION	AADMNORS	MADRONAS		STEALAGE
AADINOPR	PARANOID		MANDORAS	AAEEGLSV	SALVAGEE
AADINOPS	DIAPASON		MONARDAS	AAEEGMNS	AMENAGES
AADINOPT	ADAPTION		ROADSMAN	AAEEGMPR	AMPERAGE
AADINORT	ANTIDORA	AADMNORT	MANDATOR	AAEEGMST	AGAMETES
AADINOTV	AVOIDANT	AADMNRSS	MANSARDS		AGEMATES
AADINPST	PINTADAS	AADMNRSW	MANWARDS	AAEEGMTY	METAYAGE
AADINRRS	DARRAINS	AADMNSTU	TAMANDUS	AAEEGNRS	SANGAREE
AADINRRW	AIRDRAWN	AADMOPPP	PAPPADOM	AAEEGNRT	TAGAREEN
AADINRST	INTRADAS	AADMOPPS	PAPADOMS	AAEEGRST	STEARAGE
	RADIANTS	AADMOPRX	DOXAPRAM	AAEEGRSV	AVERAGES
AADINRSV	VIRANDAS	AADMOQSU	MADOQUAS	AAEEGRTW	WATERAGE
AADINRTY	INTRADAY	AADMORRT	TRAMROAD	AAEEHIMR	HAEREMAI
AADIOPRS	DIASPORA	AADMORST	MATADORS	AAEEHKKR	HARAKEKE
AADIOPSZ	DOPIAZAS	AADMPPSU	PAPADUMS	AAEEHKRT	HEKETARA
AADIORRT	RADIATOR	AADMRRSY	YARDARMS	AAEEHLMR	AHEMERAL
AADIPSUY	UPADAISY	AADMRSZZ	MAZZARDS	AAEEHMNR	HERMAEAN
AADIRRSW	AIRWARDS	AADNNPSU	PANDANUS	AAEEHNPS	SAPHENAE
AADIRRSY	DISARRAY	AADNOPRS	PANDORAS	AAEEHPRT	EARTHPEA
AADISTXY	DYSTAXIA	AADNOPSS	SANDSOAP		HEARTPEA
AADJNTTU	ADJUTANT	AADNORST	ONDATRAS	AAEEHRST	HETAERAS
AADJNTUV	ADJUVANT	AADNORTY	DONATARY	AAEEHRTW	AWEATHER
AADKLMNR	LANDMARK	AADNOSUV	VANADOUS		WHEATEAR
AADKLNPR	PARKLAND	AADNOSWY	NOWADAYS	AAEEHRWY	HEREAWAY
AADKLRTU	TALUKDAR	AADNPRSU	PANDURAS	AAEEHTVW	HEATWAVE
AADKMNRS	DARKMANS	AADNPSTT	STANDPAT	AAEEILNT	ALIENATE
AADKMRSY	DAYMARKS	AADNQRSU	QUADRANS	AAEEINTT	TAENIATE
AADKNRST	TANKARDS	AADNQRTU	QUADRANT	AAEEJMNP	JAMPANEE
AADKORWY	WORKADAY	AADNQRUY	QUANDARY	AAEEKLSS	SEAKALES
AADKPRRW	PARKWARD	AADNRRSW	WARRANDS	AAEEKLTW	LATEWAKE
AADLLLNS	LALLANDS	AADNRRSY	DARRAYNS	AAEEKMNS	NAMESAKE
AADLLMPY	LADYPALM	AADNRSTY	TANYARDS	AAEEKMRT	TEAMAKER
AADLLMRS	MALLARDS	AADNRSWY	NAYWARDS	AAEEKNRW	AWAKENER
AADLLNOY	ANODALLY	AADOPPRR	PARADROP		REAWAKEN
AADLLNPY	PLAYLAND	AADOPRRS	PARADORS	AAEEKPRT	PARAKEET
AADLLNSW	LAWLANDS	AADOPRST	ADAPTORS	AAEEKPSS	SEASPEAK
AADLMNNS	LANDSMAN	AADOPRXY	PARADOXY	AAEEKQSU	SEAQUAKE
AADLMNOR	MANDORLA	AADOPSSS	PASSADOS	AAEEKRSW	REAWAKES
AADLMNOS	MANDOLAS	AADOPSSU	POUSADAS	AAEELLLM	LAMELLAE
AADLMNSS	LANDMASS	AADOPSTT	DOPATTAS	AAEELLMR	AMARELLE
AADLMNSU	LADANUMS	AADOPSUY	PADUASOY	AAEELLMT	MALLEATE
AADLMNUU	LAUDANUM	AADORSVY	SAVOYARD	AAEELLNV	AVELLANE
AADLMORS	ARMLOADS	AADORSWY	ROADWAYS	AAEELLPT	PATELLAE
AADLNOPR	PARLANDO	AADOSSTT	TOSTADAS	AAEELMMT	METAMALE
AADLNOPS	DALAPONS	AADPSTTU	DUPATTAS	AAEELMST	MALEATES
	SOAPLAND	AADQRSTU	QUADRATS	AAEELNNR	ANNEALER
AADLNOST	SALTANDO	AADRSSTY	DAYSTARS	AAEELNPS	SEAPLANE
AADLNOSV	VANLOADS	AAEEEHRT	HETAERAE		SPELAEAN
AADLNOSZ	DANAZOLS	AAEEEMRT	AMEERATE	AAEELNPT	PANETELA

AAEELNPU	PAENULAE	AAEFIKLT	KALIFATE	AAEGILTT	TAILGATE
AAEELNST	ELASTANE	AAEFILTY	FAYALITE	AAEGIMNO	EGOMANIA
AAEELORT	AREOLATE	AAEFIMRR	AIRFRAME	AAEGIMNP	PIGMAEAN
AAEELORU	AUREOLAE	AAEFINNT	FAINEANT	AAEGIMNS	MAGNESIA
AAEELPPR	APPEALER	AAEFINNU	INFAUNAE	AAEGIMNT	AGMINATE
AAEELRST	LAETARES	AAEFINPU	EPIFAUNA		ENIGMATA
AAEELRTU	LAUREATE	AAEFINST	FANTASIE	AAEGIMNZ	MAGAZINE
AAEELRTV	VALERATE	AAEFINTX	ANTEFIXA	AAEGIMRR	MARRIAGE
AAEELSST	ELASTASE	AAEFIRRS	AIRFARES	AAEGIMRT	GEMATRIA
AAEELTUV	EVALUATE	AAEFKMST	MAKEFAST		MARITAGE
AAEELVWY	WAYLEAVE	AAEFLLSV	FAVELLAS	AAEGINNR	ANEARING
AAEEMMTT	TEAMMATE	AAEFLMOT	MEATLOAF	AAEGINPS	NAGAPIES
AAEEMNPT	NAMETAPE	AAEFLMTT	FLATMATE		PAGANISE
AAEEMNST	EMANATES	AAEFLNUU	FAUNULAE	AAEGINPT	PAGINATE
	MANATEES	AAEFLPRS	EARFLAPS	AAEGINPZ	PAGANIZE
AAEEMPRS	PARAMESE		PARAFLES	AAEGINRS	ANERGIAS
AAEEMRST	AMREETAS	AAEFLRSW	LAWFARES		ANGARIES
AAEEMSTT	SEATMATE	AAEFLRTW	FLATWARE		ARGINASE
AAEEMSTX	MEATAXES	AAEFMRST	FERMATAS	AAEGINRT	AERATING
AAEENNNT	ANTENNAE	AAEFMRSU	FUMARASE	AAEGINST	SAGINATE
AAEENPRT	PARANETE	AAEFMRTU	FUMARATE	AAEGINSW	WAINAGES
AAEENRRS	ARRASENE	AAEFQRSU	AQUAFERS	AAEGINTV	NAVIGATE
AAEENRST	ARSENATE	AAEFRRRW	WARFARER		VAGINATE
	SERENATA	AAEFRRSW	WARFARES	AAEGIPRS	IGARAPES
AAEENRTT	ANTEATER	AAEFRRWY	WAYFARER	AAEGIPRU	PERIAGUA
AAEENSTU	NAUSEATE	AAEFRSWY	WAYFARES	AAEGIRRS	ARRIAGES
AAEENSTX	ANATEXES	AAEFRTTX	AFTERTAX	AAEGIRSV	VAGARIES
AAEEPPRR	APPEARER	AAEGGINR	GRAINAGE	AAEGISSS	ASSEGAIS
	RAPPAREE	AAEGGIOT	AGIOTAGE	AAEGISST	AGATISES
	REAPPEAR	AAEGGLNR	LANGRAGE	AAEGISSU	AGEUSIAS
AAEEPPRS	APPEASER	AAEGGLNU	LANGUAGE	AAEGISTT	AGITATES
AAEEPPSS	APPEASES	AAEGGMMR	GRAMMAGE	AAEGISTZ	AGATIZES
AAEEPRST	ASPERATE	AAEGGNOS	ANAGOGES	AAEGIVWY	GIVEAWAY
	SEPARATE	AAEGGNOW	WAGONAGE	AAEGJSTU	AJUTAGES
AAEEPSTT	ASEPTATE	AAEGGNRY	GARGANEY	AAEGKNST	TANKAGES
AAEERRWW	REWAREWA	AAEGGOPR	PARAGOGE	AAEGKOSS	SOAKAGES
AAEERSSW	SEAWARES	AAEGGOPS	APAGOGES	AAEGLLMS	SMALLAGE
AAEERSTT	STEARATE	AAEGGRST	AGGRATES	AAEGLLPR	PELLAGRA
AAEERSTW	SEAWATER	AAEGHLNP	PHALANGE	AAEGLLSS	GALLEASS
	TEAWARES	AAEGHLSU	HAULAGES	AAEGLLST	GALLATES
AAEERSWX	EARWAXES	AAEGHLSY	HAYLAGES		GALLETAS
AAEERSYY	YEASAYER	AAEGHMRX	HEXAGRAM		STALLAGE
AAEFFGRS	AGRAFFES	AAEGHMSS	GAMASHES		TALLAGES
AAEFFGST	STAFFAGE	AAEGHNRU	HARANGUE	AAEGLLTU	GLUTAEAL
AAEFFIRS	AFFAIRES	AAEGHNST	THANAGES	AAEGLMNS	GAMELANS
AAEFFLLR	FARFALLE	AAEGHOPY	HYPOGAEA	AAEGLMNV	GAVELMAN
AAEFFLLS	FALAFELS	AAEGILLP	PELAGIAL	AAEGLMPY	GAMEPLAY
AAEFFLPR	PARAFFLE	AAEGILLR	GALLERIA	AAEGLMST	ALMAGEST
AAEFFLRT	TAFFAREL	AAEGILLT	ALLIGATE	AAEGLNOU	ANALOGUE
AAEFFNRS	FANFARES	AAEGILMS	SEMIGALA	AAEGLNPP	LAGNAPPE
AAEFFRRY	AFFRAYER	AAEGILNP	PELAGIAN	AAEGLNPT	PLANTAGE
AAEFFSTT	TAFFETAS	AAEGILNR	GERANIAL	AAEGLNRS	ALNAGERS
AAEFGGRT	GRAFTAGE		REGALIAN	AAEGLNRT	ARGENTAL
AAEFGHRW	WHARFAGE	AAEGILNT	AGENTIAL	AAEGLNRU	AULNAGER
AAEFGINR	AFEARING		ALGINATE	AAEGLNSS	LASAGNES
AAEFGITT	FATIGATE	AAEGILRS	GASALIER	AAEGLNSU	AULNAGES
AAEFGLLL	FLAGELLA		LAIRAGES		LEGUAANS
AAEFGLOT	FLOATAGE		RAILAGES	AAEGLNTU	ANGULATE
AAEFGRTU	FRAUTAGE		REGALIAS	AAEGLOSV	AASVOGEL
AAEFGSTW	WAFTAGES	AAEGILSS	ALGESIAS	AAEGLRRS	REALGARS
AAEFIILR	FILARIAE	AAEGILSX	GALAXIES		RESALGAR

AAEGLRRW	WARRAGLE	AAEGRSTZ	STARGAZE	AAEHNPST	PHEASANT
AAEGLRST	AGRESTAL	AAEGRSVY	SAVAGERY	AAEHNPSY	SYNAPHEA
AAEGLRSV	SALVAGER	AAEGSSSU	ASSUAGES	AAEHNTTX	XANTHATE
AAEGLRTY	LEGATARY		SAUSAGES	AAEHPRSZ	PHEAZARS
AAEGLSST	AGELASTS	AAEGSSSV	AVGASSES	AAEHRRSS	HARASSER
	LASTAGES	AAEGSSSW	ASSWAGES	AAEHRSSS	HARASSES
AAEGLSSV	SALVAGES	AAEGSSTV	SAVAGEST	AAEHRSSY	HEARSAYS
AAEGLSVY	SAVAGELY	AAEGSSTW	WASTAGES	AAEHRSTU	ARETHUSA
AAEGLTUV	VAULTAGE	AAEGSTTW	WATTAGES	AAEHRTWX	EARTHWAX
AAEGMMNR	ENGRAMMA	AAEGSTWY	GATEWAYS	AAEIIKNS	AKINESIA
AAEGMMNS	GAMESMAN		GETAWAYS	AAEIILMP	LIPAEMIA
AAEGMNOS	MANGEAOS	AAEHIIRT	HETAIRAI	AAEIIMRV	VIRAEMIA
AAEGMNPY	PYGMAEAN		HETAIRIA	AAEIINSV	AVIANISE
AAEGMNRS	MANAGERS	AAEHILMN	HIELAMAN	AAEIINVZ	AVIANIZE
AAEGMNRT	MAGNETAR	AAEHILNP	APHELIAN	AAEIIPRS	APIARIES
AAEGMNRV	GRAVAMEN	AAEHILNT	ANTHELIA	AAEIIRSV	AVIARIES
AAEGMNST	MAGENTAS	AAEHILPR	PARHELIA	AAEIJLNV	JAVELINA
	MAGNATES	AAEHIMNT	ANTHEMIA	AAEIJNPS	JAPANISE
	NAMETAGS		HAEMATIN	AAEIJNPZ	JAPANIZE
AAEGMORR	AEROGRAM	AAEHIMRU	MAIREHAU	AAEIJNRT	NAARTJIE
AAEGMORS	SAGAMORE	AAEHINPT	APHANITE	AAEIKKMZ	KAMIKAZE
AAEGMPRR	RAMPAGER	AAEHINST	ASTHENIA	AAEIKLLN	ALKALINE
AAEGMPRS	RAMPAGES	AAEHIPST	APATHIES	AAEIKLLS	ALKALIES
AAEGMPRU	RAMPAUGE	AAEHIRST	HETAIRAS		ALKALISE
AAEGMRRV	MARGRAVE	AAEHIRTT	HATTERIA	AAEIKLLV	LAVALIKE
AAEGMRRY	GRAMARYE	AAEHKLST	ALKAHEST	AAEIKLLZ	ALKALIZE
AAEGMRSS	MASSAGER	AAEHKMRT	HATMAKER	AAEIKLNT	ANTILEAK
AAEGMRST	MEGASTAR	AAEHKMRY	HAYMAKER	AAEIKMRR	KRAMERIA
AAEGMRTU	AGERATUM	AAEHKNST	KHANATES	AAEIKPRT	PARAKITE
AAEGMSSS	MASSAGES	AAEHKRSY	HAYRAKES	AAEILLLU	ALLELUIA
AAEGMSTT	METATAGS	AAEHKSSW	SEAHAWKS	AAEILLMM	MAMILLAE
AAEGMTTW	MEGAWATT	AAEHLLLS	ALLHEALS	AAEILLMR	ARMILLAE
AAEGNNOP	NEOPAGAN	AAEHLMNT	METHANAL	AAEILLMX	MAXILLAE
AAEGNNPS	PANNAGES	AAEHLMNW	WHALEMAN	AAEILLNT	ALLANITE
AAEGNNST	TANNAGES	AAEHLMSY	SEALYHAM	AAEILLPP	PAPILLAE
AAEGNPST	PAGEANTS	AAEHLMTU	HAMULATE	AAEILLPT	PALLIATE
AAEGNPSW	PAWNAGES	AAEHLNOZ	HALAZONE	AAEILLRT	ARILLATE
AAEGNRRR	ARRANGER	AAEHLNRT	ANTHERAL	AAEILLRV	LAVALIER
AAEGNRRS	ARRANGES	AAEHLNRW	NARWHALE	AAEILLRY	AERIALLY
AAEGNRST	STARAGEN	AAEHLNST	ETHANALS	AAEILLTT	TALLIATE
	TANAGERS	AAEHLNTX	EXHALANT	AAEILLTV	ALLATIVE
AAEGNRTU	RUNAGATE	AAEHLOPT	APHOLATE	AAEILMMX	AXILEMMA
AAEGNSSU	GUANASES	AAEHLPRS	PEARLASH	AAEILMNN	MELANIAN
AAEGNSTT	STAGNATE	AAEHLPRX	HEXAPLAR	AAEILMNT	ALAIMENT
AAEGNSTV	VANTAGES	AAEHLPSX	HEXAPLAS		ANTIMALE
AAEGNSTW	WANTAGES	AAEHLPUV	UPHEAVAL		LAMINATE
AAEGNTUV	VAUNTAGE	AAEHLRST	TREHALAS	AAEILMNV	VELAMINA
AAEGORRT	ARROGATE	AAEHLRTT	THEATRAL	AAEILMRT	MATERIAL
AAEGORSS	AGAROSES	AAEHLSSV	LAVASHES	AAEILMSS	MALAISES
AAEGORTT	AEGROTAT	AAEHLSTT	ATHLETAS	AAEILNNS	ALANINES
AAEGPPRW	WRAPPAGE	AAEHMMOT	HEMATOMA		ANNALISE
AAEGPRSS	PASSAGER	AAEHMNPT	PATHNAME	AAEILNNZ	ANNALIZE
AAEGPRSW	WARPAGES	AAEHMNPY	NYMPHAEA	AAEILNPR	AIRPLANE
AAEGPSSS	PASSAGES	AAEHMNRS	SHAREMAN	AAEILNPT	PALATINE
AAEGPSSY	PAYSAGES		SHEARMAN	AAEILNRU	AURELIAN
AAEGQSUY	QUAYAGES	AAEHMNRT	EARTHMAN	AAEILNRV	VALERIAN
AAEGRRSV	RAVAGERS	AAEHMOPR	AMPHORAE	AAEILNSS	NASALISE
AAEGRSST	GASTREAS	AAEHMOPT	HEPATOMA	AAEILNSZ	NASALIZE
AAEGRSSU	ASSUAGER	AAEHMORT	ATHEROMA	AAEILNTT	ANTLIATE
AAEGRSTT	REGATTAS	AAEHNPRS	HANAPERS	AAEILNTV	AVENTAIL
AAEGRSTV	STRAVAGE	AAEHNPSS	SAPHENAS	AAEILORS	OLEARIAS

AAEILPPS	PAPALISE	AAEINSTT	ASTATINE	AAELLLMS	LAMELLAS
AAEILPPZ	PAPALIZE		SANITATE	AAELLLPR	PARALLEL
AAEILPRT	PARIETAL	AAEINSTV	SANATIVE	AAELLMPU	AMPULLAE
AAEILPRX	PREAXIAL	AAEINSTX	ANATEXIS	AAELLNPU	PLANULAE
AAEILPST	STAPELIA	AAEINTTT	TITANATE	AAELLNSS	NASSELLA
AAEILRRT	ARTERIAL	AAEIPPRS	APPRAISE	AAELLNSZ	ZANELLAS
AAEILRSS	ASSAILER	AAEIPPSS	APEPSIAS	AAELLORV	ALVEOLAR
	REASSAIL	AAEIPRRS	PAREIRAS	AAELLPRS	PARELLAS
	SALARIES	AAEIPRSS	SPIRAEAS	AAELLPRT	PATELLAR
AAEILRSU	AURELIAS	AAEIPRST	ASPIRATE	AAELLPST	PATELLAS
AAEILRSV	REAVAILS		PARASITE	AAELLRST	LATERALS
AAEILRTV	VARIETAL		SEPTARIA	AAELLRSY	ALLAYERS
AAEILSTV	AESTIVAL	AAEIPRTT	PATRIATE	AAELLSSW	SEAWALLS
	SALIVATE	AAEIPRTZ	TRAPEZIA	AAELLUVV	VALVULAE
AAEILSTX	SAXATILE	AAEIPRXY	APYREXIA	AAELLWWY	WELLAWAY
AAEILSWY	AISLEWAY	AAEIPSTT	APATITES	AAELLWYY	ALLEYWAY
AAEILTVX	LAXATIVE	AAEIQRTU	TAQUERIA	AAELMMNO	MELANOMA
AAEIMMST	IMAMATES	AAEIRRRT	TERRARIA	AAELMMOX	AXOLEMMA
AAEIMNOT	METANOIA	AAEIRRST	TARAIRES	AAELMMRS	ALMEMARS
AAEIMNOX	ANOXEMIA	AAEIRRTV	VERATRIA	AAELMMTU	MALAMUTE
AAEIMNPR	PEARMAIN	AAEIRSST	ASTERIAS	AAELMNOT	MALONATE
AAEIMNPS	PAEANISM		ATRESIAS	AAELMNOX	AXONEMAL
AAEIMNPT	IMPANATE	AAEIRSSX	XERASIAS	AAELMNPT	PLATEMAN
AAEIMNRR	MARINERA	AAEIRSTT	ARIETTAS	AAELMNRT	MATERNAL
AAEIMNRT	ANIMATER		ARISTATE	AAELMNSS	SALESMAN
	MARINATE	AAEIRSTV	VARIATES	AAELMNST	TALESMAN
AAEIMNRZ	MAZARINE	AAEIRSTW	AWAITERS	AAELMNSW	WEALSMAN
AAEIMNSS	AMNESIAS	AAEIRSVW	AIRWAVES	AAELMNSY	SEAMANLY
AAEIMNST	AMENTIAS	AAEIRTTZ	ZARATITE	AAELMOST	OATMEALS
	ANIMATES	AAEISSTT	SATIATES	AAELMOSU	MAUSOLEA
AAEIMNTZ	NIZAMATE	AAEISTUX	EUTAXIAS	AAELMOTZ	METAZOAL
AAEIMOPR	PAROEMIA	AAEITTVX	TAXATIVE	AAELMPPY	MAYAPPLE
AAEIMOTX	TOXAEMIA	AAEJLNOP	JALAPENO	AAELMPRT	MALAPERT
AAEIMOTZ	AZOTEMIA	AAEJMNRY	MARYJANE	AAELMPRX	EXAMPLAR
AAEIMPRS	ASPERMIA	AAEJNNPR	JAPANNER	AAELMPSS	LAMPASES
	SAPREMIA	AAEJNRST	NAARTJES		LAMPASSE
AAEIMPSY	PYAEMIAS	AAEJNRTZ	JAZERANT	AAELMPST	PLATEASM
AAEIMRST	AMIRATES	AAEJOPRS	APAREJOS	AAELMPTV	VAMPLATE
AAEIMRSU	URAEMIAS	AAEJRSSV	SVARAJES	AAELMPTY	PLAYMATE
AAEIMRTT	AMARETTI	AAEJRSSW	SWARAJES	AAELMRSW	MALWARES
AAEIMSUV	MAUVAISE	AAEKKORS	KARAOKES	AAELMRSY	LAMASERY
AAEINNTT	ANTENATI	AAEKKRSY	KAYAKERS	AAELMRTT	MALTREAT
AAEINORT	AERATION	AAEKLLTY	ALKYLATE	AAELMSST	MALTASES
AAEINORX	ANOREXIA	AAEKLMRW	LAWMAKER	AAELMSSY	AMYLASES
AAEINPPR	PRIAPEAN	AAEKLMRY	MALARKEY	AAELNNNT	ANTENNAL
AAEINPRS	PANARIES	AAEKLNRS	LARNAKES	AAELNNOT	NEONATAL
AAEINPRT	ANTIRAPE	AAEKLNST	ALKANETS	AAELNNTU	ANNULATE
AAEINPTT	PATINATE		KANTELAS	AAELNOSS	SEASONAL
AAEINRRW	RAINWEAR	AAEKLPRS	ASPARKLE	AAELNOSV	VALONEAS
AAEINRST	ANTISERA	AAEKMMPR	MAPMAKER	AAELNPRS	PRENASAL
	ARTESIAN	AAEKMORT	KERATOMA	AAELNPRT	PARENTAL
	RATANIES	AAEKMRRS	EARMARKS		PARLANTE
	RESINATA	AAEKMRRW	WARMAKER		PATERNAL
	SANTERIA	AAEKMRSS	SEAMARKS		PRENATAL
	SEATRAIN	AAEKNPRT	PARTAKEN	AAELNPRW	WARPLANE
AAEINRTT	ATTAINER	AAEKORTY	AKARYOTE	AAELNPST	PLATANES
	REATTAIN	AAEKPRRT	PARTAKER		PLEASANT
AAEINRTU	INAURATE	AAEKPRST	PARTAKES	AAELNPSU	PAENULAS
AAEINRTW	ANTIWEAR	AAEKPSTU	PUKATEAS	AAELNPTT	PANTALET
AAEINRTZ	ATRAZINE	AAEKSSSV	KAVASSES	AAELNRSS	ARSENALS
AAEINSST	ENTASIAS	AAELLLMR	LAMELLAR	AAELNRST	ASTERNAL

AAELNRSY	ANALYSER	AAEMNSST	NAMASTES	AAEOSTUV	AUTOSAVE
AAELNRTT	ALTERANT	AAEMNSTU	MANTEAUS	AAEPPRRT	TARPAPER
	ALTERNAT	AAEMNTUX	MANTEAUX	AAEPPRST	PARAPETS
	TARLETAN	AAEMOPXZ	OXAZEPAM	AAEPPSTT	APPESTAT
AAELNRTX	RELAXANT	AAEMORTT	AMARETTO	AAEPQRTU	PARAQUET
AAELNRYZ	ANALYZER		TERATOMA	AAEPRSSY	APYRASES
AAELNSST	SEALANTS	AAEMORTX	XEROMATA	AAEPRTXY	TAXPAYER
AAELNSSV	ENVASSAL	AAEMOSTT	STEATOMA	AAEPSTTW	WATTAPES
AAELNSSY	ANALYSES	AAEMOSTY	ATEMOYAS	AAEPSWXX	PAXWAXES
AAELNSTT	ATLANTES	AAEMOTTU	AUTOMATE	AAEPSZZZ	PAZAZZES
AAELNSTY	ANALYTES	AAEMPPSS	PAMPASES	AAERRRSY	ARRAYERS
AAELNSTZ	ZEALANTS	AAEMPRST	APTAMERS	AAERRSST	TARRASES
AAELNSWY	LANEWAYS	AAEMPTTU	AMPUTATE	AAERRSTT	TARTARES
AAELNSYZ	ANALYZES	AAEMQSTU	SQUAMATE	AAERRTTT	TARTRATE
AAELOPRS	PSORALEA	AAEMRRTU	ARMATURE	AAERSSSY	ASSAYERS
AAELORSU	AUREOLAS	AAEMRSSS	AMASSERS	AAERSTTU	SATURATE
AAELORTY	ALEATORY	AAEMRSTU	AMATEURS		TUATERAS
AAELOSTX	OXALATES	AAEMRTTU	MATURATE	AAERTTTW	TERAWATT
AAELPPRS	APPARELS	AAENNNST	ANTENNAS	AAERTWWY	WATERWAY
AAELPPST	PALPATES	AAENNOTT	ANNOTATE	AAESTWWY	WASTEWAY
AAELPPSU	APPLAUSE	AAENNSTT	STANNATE	AAFFGILS	GAFFSAIL
AAELPRST	PALESTRA		TANNATES	AAFFHIKY	KAFFIYAH
AAELPRSV	PALAVERS	AAENNSTU	NAUSEANT	AAFFIILX	AFFIXIAL
AAELPRSY	PARALYSE	AAENNSTV	VENTANAS	AAFFILRT	TAFFRAIL
AAELPRTT	TETRAPLA	AAENOPSS	PAESANOS	AAFFINPR	PARAFFIN
AAELPRWY	PLAYWEAR	AAENOQTU	AQUATONE	AAFFINSS	SAFFIANS
AAELPRYZ	PARALYZE	AAENORRU	AUROREAN	AAFFINST	AFFIANTS
AAELPSTU	PLATEAUS	AAENORST	ANOESTRA	AAFFLPST	PALSTAFF
AAELPSTV	PALSTAVE	AAENORSU	ARANEOUS	AAFFLSTU	AFFLATUS
AAELPSWY	PALEWAYS	AAENORTU	AERONAUT	AAFFMNST	STAFFMAN
AAELPTUV	VAPULATE	AAENOSST	ASSONATE	AAFFNNOR	FANFARON
AAELPTUX	PLATEAUX	AAENPPRS	PARPANES	AAFFOORW	FOOFARAW
AAELRSST	TARSEALS	AAENPPRT	APPARENT	AAFGHINS	AFGHANIS
AAELRSTZ	LAZARETS		TRAPPEAN	AAFGHNRU	FRAUGHAN
AAELRTUV	VELATURA	AAENPRTY	PRYTANEA	AAFGILNO	GOLFIANA
AAELRUZZ	ZARZUELA	AAENPSST	ANAPESTS	AAFGINTW	FATWAING
AAELRWYY	WAYLAYER		PEASANTS	AAFGLLNU	LANGLAUF
AAELSSTT	SALTATES	AAENPSTT	ANTEPAST	AAFGLNRT	FLAGRANT
AAELSTUV	VALUATES	AAENPSTY	PEASANTY	AAFGNRRT	FRAGRANT
AAELSTZZ	ALTEZZAS	AAENRRRT	NARRATER	AAFGORRS	FARRAGOS
AAEMMMRS	MAREMMAS	AAENRRSS	NARRASES	AAFHHIKL	KHALIFAH
AAEMMNOT	AMMONATE	AAENRRST	NARRATES	AAFHHORT	HAFTORAH
AAEMMNRT	ARMAMENT	AAENRRSST	SANTERAS	AAFHIKLS	KHALIFAS
AAEMMNSU	MANUMEAS	AAENRSTT	TARTANES	AAFHIKLT	KHALIFAT
AAEMMOST	METASOMA	AAENRSTV	TAVERNAS		KHILAFAT
AAEMMSTT	STEMMATA		TSAREVNA	AAFHINRS	FARINHAS
AAEMNORS	AMARONES	AAENRSUW	UNAWARES	AAFHIRST	AIRSHAFT
AAEMNORT	EMANATOR	AAENRSYY	NAYSAYER	AAFHLLSS	ASHFALLS
AAEMNOSW	SEAWOMAN	AAENRTVZ	TZAREVNA	AAFHLSTW	FLATWASH
AAEMNOTZ	METAZOAN	AAENSSSV	VANESSAS	AAFHLSTY	LAYSHAFT
AAEMNPPS	PAMPEANS	AAENSSTV	SAVANTES	AAFHORTT	HAFTAROT
AAEMNPRS	PARMESAN	AAENSSTW	SEAWANTS	AAFHRSUU	HAUSFRAU
	SPEARMAN	AAENSSWY	AWAYNESS	AAFIILLM	FAMILIAL
AAEMNPRT	PARAMENT	AAENTTTT	ATTENTAT	AAFIILLR	FILARIAL
	PERMATAN	AAEOPPSS	APOAPSES	AAFIILMR	FAMILIAR
AAEMNRRY	YARRAMEN	AAEOPSTT	APOSTATE	AAFIILNR	FILARIAN
AAEMNRST	SARMENTA	AAEOPSTZ	ZAPATEOS	AAFIINST	FISTIANA
	SEMANTRA	AAEORRST	AERATORS	AAFIKLLY	ALKALIFY
AAEMNRSU	MURAENAS	AAEORSST	AEROSATS	AAFILLNR	RAINFALL
AAEMNRTT	ATRAMENT	AAEORSTT	AEROSTAT	AAFILLUV	AVAILFUL
AAEMNRTW	WATERMAN	AAEORTTV	ROTAVATE	AAFILMST	FATALISM

AAFILNNU	INFAUNAL	AAGGNSTT	TAGGANTS		MARGINAL
AAFILNQU	ALFAQUIN	AAGGNSWY	GANGWAYS	AAGILMNX	MALAXING
AAFILNST	FANTAILS	AAGGRSTT	STAGGART	AAGILMOT	GLIOMATA
	TAILFANS	AAGHHIMS	MASHGIAH	AAGILMRY	GRAYMAIL
AAFILOPR	PARAFOIL	AAGHHINS	SHANGHAI	AAGILMSY	MYALGIAS
AAFILQSU	ALFAQUIS	AAGHHNOS	OANSHAGH	AAGILNOS	LOGANIAS
AAFILSTT	FATALIST	AAGHILNN	HANGNAIL	AAGILNOT	GALTONIA
AAFILTTY	FATALITY	AAGHILPY	HYPALGIA	AAGILNPT	PALATING
AAFIMNOR	FORAMINA	AAGHILRS	GHARIALS	AAGILNRR	LARRIGAN
AAFIMNOT	ANTIFOAM		HARIGALS	AAGILNSS	SALSAING
AAFINNOV	FAVONIAN	AAGHIMNS	ASHAMING	AAGILNTV	GALIVANT
AAFINNRS	SAFRANIN	AAGHIMRT	TAGHAIRM	AAGILNUV	VAGINULA
AAFINNST	INFANTAS	AAGHINNS	ANHINGAS	AAGILOOP	APOLOGIA
AAFINNSU	INFAUNAS	AAGHINPS	PAGANISH	AAGILOPT	TOPALGIA
AAFINRRW	WARFARIN	AAGHINPW	AWHAPING	AAGILOSS	AGLOSSIA
AAFINSTU	FAUSTIAN	AAGHIPRR	AIRGRAPH	AAGILOST	OTALGIAS
AAFIPRST	PARFAITS	AAGHIRSV	VAGARISH	AAGILPRY	PLAGIARY
AAFIQSTU	AQUAFITS	AAGHKMNY	GYMKHANA	AAGILRRW	WARRIGAL
AAFIRSST	SAFARIST	AAGHKNST	THANGKAS	AAGILRTT	ATTAGIRL
AAFIRSUY	RUFIYAAS	AAGHLNNS	LANGSHAN	AAGILSTT	SAGITTAL
AAFIRSWY	FAIRWAYS	AAGHLNPY	ANAGLYPH	AAGILSTW	WAGTAILS
AAFIRTTT	FRITTATA	AAGHLOSS	GASAHOLS	AAGIMMRR	MARIGRAM
AAFJLLSW	JAWFALLS	AAGHMNOY	HOGMANAY	AAGIMNNN	MANGANIN
AAFJLORS	ALFORJAS		MAHOGANY	AAGIMNNO	AGNOMINA
AAFLLNOV	FLAVANOL	AAGHMNSU	MAHUANGS	AAGIMNOS	ANGIOMAS
AAFLLNUY	FAUNALLY	AAGHMNSW	WHANGAMS	AAGIMNPS	PAGANISM
AAFLLPRT	PRATFALL	AAGHNOPR	AGRAPHON	AAGIMNRR	MARGARIN
	TRAPFALL	AAGHNPRY	PHRYGANA	AAGIMNSS	AMASSING
AAFLLPST	SPATFALL	AAGHNSST	SANGHATS		SIAMANGS
AAFLMORV	LAVAFORM	AAGHOPPR	APOGRAPH	AAGIMNSY	GYMNASIA
AAFLNNOT	NONFATAL	AAGHQSUU	QUAHAUGS	AAGIMPTU	PATAGIUM
AAFLNORS	FORLANAS	AAGHRRTU	ARRAUGHT	AAGIMSSV	SAVAGISM
	SAFRONAL	AAGHRSSW	WASHRAGS	AAGIMSTT	STIGMATA
AAFLNOTT	FLOATANT	AAGIIKKN	KAIAKING	AAGINNNW	WANNIGAN
AAFLNRSU	FURLANAS	AAGIILMN	IMAGINAL	AAGINNNY	NANNYGAI
AAFLSTWY	FLATWAYS	AAGIILNS	ALIASING	AAGINNOT	AGNATION
AAFLSWYY	FLYAWAYS	AAGIILNV	AVAILING	AAGINNRW	AWARNING
AAFMNRST	RAFTSMAN	AAGIIMNN	MAGAININ	AAGINNSU	SAUNAING
AAFMNSST	FANTASMS	AAGIIMST	ASTIGMIA	AAGINNSW	WANIGANS
AAFMOPRR	PARAFORM	AAGIINNU	IGUANIAN	AAGINNSY	SYNANGIA
AAFNPPRT	FRAPPANT	AAGIINRS	ARAISING	AAGINNTV	VAGINANT
AAFNSSTT	FANTASTS	AAGIINST	IGNATIAS	AAGINNTW	AWANTING
AAGGGHNS	GANGSHAG	AAGIINTV	AVIATING	AAGINORR	RANGIORA
AAGGGINR	GARAGING	AAGIINTW	AWAITING	AAGINOSS	AGNOSIAS
AAGGHNST	HANGTAGS	AAGIKKNY	KAYAKING	AAGINPPY	APPAYING
AAGGILLN	GANGLIAL	AAGIKLNO	KAOLIANG	AAGINPRU	PAGURIAN
AAGGILNR	GANGLIAR	AAGIKLNR	KRAALING	AAGINPRW	PARAWING
AAGGIMNN	MANAGING	AAGIKLNS	ASLAKING	AAGINPRY	AGRYPNIA
AAGGIMNR	MARAGING	AAGIKMNS	SMAAKING	AAGINPST	PAGANIST
AAGGINNT	ANTIGANG	AAGIKMRS	SKIAGRAM	AAGINPWW	PAWAWING
AAGGINRV	RAVAGING	AAGIKNST	TIKANGAS	AAGINRRS	ARRAIGNS
AAGGINSV	SAVAGING	AAGIKNSW	AWAKINGS	AAGINRRY	ARRAYING
AAGGIRST	GARAGIST	AAGIKNSZ	ZIGANKAS	AAGINRSS	SANGRIAS
AAGGITTW	GIGAWATT	AAGILLNU	UNIALGAL		SARANGIS
AAGGLLLY	LALLYGAG	AAGILLNY	ALLAYING	AAGINRST	GRANITAS
AAGGLMOS	MAGALOGS	AAGILLSS	GALLIASS	AAGINRSU	GUARANIS
AAGGLNOT	TAGALONG	AAGILLTV	GALLIVAT	AAGINRSY	ARAYSING
AAGGLRSY	GRAYLAGS	AAGILLUZ	ALGUAZIL	AAGINSST	ASSIGNAT
AAGGMNNS	GANGSMAN	AAGILMMR	MAILGRAM	AAGINSSU	GAUSSIAN
AAGGNNOO	ONGAONGA	AAGILMNO	MAGNOLIA	AAGINSSY	ASSAYING
AAGGNSST	GANGSTAS	AAGILMNR	ALARMING		GAINSAYS

AAGIORTT	AGITATOR	AAGOPSSS	SAPSAGOS	AAHIRSST	SHARIATS
AAGIORTV	AVIGATOR	AAGORSSS	SARGASSO	AAHIRSTV	HAVARTIS
AAGIPRSU	PIRAGUAS	AAGORSSU	SAGUAROS	AAHISTWY	THISAWAY
AAGIRRSY	ARGYRIAS	AAGRRSSY	RAYGRASS	AAHJKNRS	KHANJARS
AAGIRSTV	GRAVITAS	AAGRSSSW	SAWGRASS	AAHJOPRT	JATROPHA
	STRAVAIG	AAGRSSTU	SASTRUGA	AAHKKOOR	HOROKAKA
AAGISSTT	SAGITTAS	AAGRSTUZ	ZASTRUGA	AAHKLLMR	HALLMARK
AAGKKNOS	ANGAKOKS	AAGSTTUU	TAUTAUGS	AAHKLRSS	LASHKARS
AAGKLRSV	GRAVLAKS	AAHHIIMM	MAHIMAHI	AAHKMOTW	TOMAHAWK
AAGKNOOR	KANGAROO	AAHHIINN	HINAHINA	AAHKMSSY	YASHMAKS
AAGKOOSZ	GAZOOKAS	AAHHIKNU	HANUKIAH	AAHKRSSW	SAWSHARK
AAGKORST	KATORGAS	AAHHIRSS	SHARIAHS	AAHLLLOO	HALLALOO
AAGLLMOY	ALLOGAMY	AAHHKLOT	HALAKHOT	AAHLLMRS	MARSHALL
AAGLLNOO	LAGOONAL		HALAKOTH	AAHLLOPT	ALLOPATH
AAGLLNRY	LARYNGAL	AAHHKMRS	HASHMARK	AAHLLSWY	HALLWAYS
AAGLLNST	GALLANTS	AAHHKSWW	HAWKSHAW	AAHLMMSS	MASHLAMS
AAGLLOOP	APOLOGAL	AAHHMMSS	SHAMMASH	AAHLMOOS	MASOOLAH
AAGLLOPY	POLYGALA	AAHHNNOS	HOSANNAH	AAHLMOPR	AMPHORAL
AAGLLOSS	AGLOSSAL	AAHHNNST	THANNAHS	AAHLMRSS	MARSHALS
AAGLMNSS	GLASSMAN	AAHHNPST	NAPHTHAS	AAHLMSTU	THALAMUS
AAGLNNOO	ANALOGON	AAHHOPRS	PHARAOHS	AAHLNPST	ASHPLANT
AAGLNORS	GRANOLAS	AAHIIKRT	TARAKIHI	AAHLNRSW	NARWHALS
AAGLNPSS	LAPSANGS	AAHIILRT	HAIRTAIL	AAHLPRRT	PHRATRAL
AAGLNQUU	AQUALUNG	AAHIJNRS	HARIJANS	AAHLPSST	ASPHALTS
AAGLNRRU	GRANULAR	AAHIJPRS	RAJASHIP	AAHLRSSW	SHALWARS
AAGLOPRY	PARALOGY	AAHIKLPS	PASHALIK	AAHMNNPU	PANHUMAN
AAGLORSU	ARUGOLAS	AAHIKLST	HALAKIST	AAHMNNSU	HANUMANS
AAGLRRUW	WARRAGUL	AAHIKORS	AKIRAHOS	AAHMNORT	MARATHON
AAGLRSTU	GASTRULA	AAHIKORW	WHAKAIRO	AAHMNOST	HOASTMAN
AAGLRSUU	ARUGULAS	AAHIKRST	KITHARAS	AAHMNOTX	XANTHOMA
AAGMMRRS	GRAMMARS	AAHILLLS	HALLALIS	AAHMNPST	PHANTASM
AAGMMSUY	MAMAGUYS		SHILLALA	AAHMNRST	TRASHMAN
AAGMNNOR	NANOGRAM	AAHILLNS	HALLIANS	AAHMNSTX	XANTHAMS
AAGMNNRS	GRANNAMS	AAHILMNR	HARMALIN	AAHMOPRS	AMPHORAS
AAGMNOPZ	ZAMPOGNA	AAHILMRS	ALMIRAHS	AAHMRSST	STRAMASH
AAGMNORT	MARTAGON	AAHILMSS	SHIMAALS	AAHNNOSS	HOSANNAS
AAGMNOSS	SANGOMAS	AAHILNNT	INHALANT	AAHNNPSW	SHWANPAN
AAGMNOST	AGAMONTS	AAHILNOT	HALATION	AAHNNSTX	XANTHANS
AAGMNPRS	PANGRAMS	AAHILOPP	HAPLOPIA	AAHNOPRS	ANAPHORS
AAGMNRST	TANGRAMS	AAHILPSV	PAHLAVIS	AAHNORST	ATHANORS
	TRANGAMS	AAHILPSY	PHYSALIA	AAHNORSV	NAVARHOS
AAGMNRTU	ARMGAUNT	AAHILRRZ	ARRHIZAL	AAHNOSTT	THANATOS
AAGMNSSW	SWAGSMAN	AAHILSSW	SAHIWALS	AAHNPSTT	PHANTAST
AAGMNSTY	SYNTAGMA	AAHIMNOS	MAHONIAS	AAHNPSTY	PHANTASY
AAGMORSS	MARGOSAS	AAHIMNPS	PASHMINA	AAHNTUWY	HUNTAWAY
AAGMOTUY	AUTOGAMY	AAHIMNSS	SHAMINAS	AAHOPRST	PARASHOT
AAGMOTYZ	ZYGOMATA	AAHIMNZZ	HAZZANIM	AAHOPRTU	AUTOHARP
AAGMRSST	MATGRASS	AAHIMRSW	RAWMAISH	AAHOQSUW	AQUASHOW
AAGNNNOP	NONPAGAN	AAHIMRTY	ARYTHMIA	AAHORSSU	SAHUAROS
AAGNNRSU	RUNANGAS	AAHINOPS	APHONIAS	AAHPRSTW	WARPATHS
AAGNNSTT	STAGNANT	AAHINPPS	PAPHIANS	AAHPSTWY	PATHWAYS
AAGNOPRS	PARAGONS	AAHINPRS	PIRANHAS	AAHRRTTW	THRAWART
AAGNOPRT	TRAGOPAN	AAHINRSW	RAINWASH	AAHRSSST	SHASTRAS
AAGNORRT	ARROGANT	AAHINRTU	HAURIANT	AAHRSSTY	ASHTRAYS
	TARRAGON	AAHINSST	SHAITANS	AAHRSTTW	STRAWHAT
AAGNORSZ	ORGANZAS	AAHINSTW	TANIWHAS	AAIIILMR	MILIARIA
AAGNORTU	ARGONAUT	AAHIOPRT	ATROPHIA	AAIIIMNR	NIRAMIAI
AAGNRSTV	VAGRANTS	AAHIPRST	PITARAHS	AAIIJJPP	JIPIJAPA
AAGNRTUY	GUARANTY	AAHIPSTZ	ZAPTIAHS	AAIIKKKR	KAKARIKI
AAGNRTYZ	ZYGANTRA	AAHIPSXY	ASPHYXIA	AAIIKKNN	KINAKINA
AAGOPRSU	GAROUPAS	AAHIRSSS	HARISSAS	AAIILLQU	QUILLAIA

AAIILMNS	MAINSAIL	**AAILLMNS**	LAMINALS	**AAILNQTU**	ALIQUANT
AAIILMRS	AIRMAILS		MANILLAS	**AAILNSSY**	ANALYSIS
AAIILNRZ	ALIZARIN	**AAILLMNT**	MANTILLA	**AAILNSTV**	VALIANTS
AAIILNUX	UNIAXIAL	**AAILLMNY**	ANIMALLY	**AAILNSTY**	NASALITY
AAIILPRR	RIPARIAL	**AAILLMPT**	TAILLAMP	**AAILNTTT**	LATITANT
AAIILPRS	PAIRIALS	**AAILLMRS**	ARMILLAS	**AAILNTTY**	NATALITY
AAIILPST	TILAPIAS	**AAILLMRT**	RAMTILLA	**AAILORRS**	RASORIAL
AAIILRSZ	ALIZARIS	**AAILLMRX**	MAXILLAR	**AAILORRV**	VARIOLAR
AAIILRTX	TRIAXIAL	**AAILLMSX**	MAXILLAS	**AAILORSS**	ROSALIAS
AAIILRUX	AUXILIAR	**AAILLNOV**	VALLONIA	**AAILORSU**	RAOULIAS
AAIILTXY	AXIALITY	**AAILLNPU**	NAUPLIAL	**AAILORSV**	VARIOLAS
AAIIMNNT	AMANITIN	**AAILLNST**	LANITALS	**AAILPPRU**	PUPARIAL
	MAINTAIN	**AAILLNSV**	VANILLAS	**AAILPPST**	PAPALIST
AAIIMNPX	PANMIXIA	**AAILLPPR**	PAPILLAR	**AAILPRST**	PARTIALS
AAIINNRT	ANTIARIN	**AAILLRRY**	ARILLARY		PATRIALS
AAIINOTV	AVIATION	**AAILLRSX**	AXILLARS		TRIAPSAL
AAIINPRR	RIPARIAN	**AAILLRXY**	AXILLARY	**AAILPRSY**	AIRPLAYS
AAIINPZZ	PIAZZIAN	**AAILMMRS**	ALARMISM	**AAILPSTT**	TALIPATS
AAIINRST	INTARSIA		AMMIRALS	**AAILQRSU**	SQUARIAL
AAIINSTT	TITANIAS	**AAILMMSX**	MAXIMALS	**AAILQSWW**	QAWWALIS
AAIINSZZ	ZIZANIAS	**AAILMNNT**	LAMANTIN	**AAILRRSV**	ARRIVALS
AAIIOPST	APOSITIA	**AAILMNOP**	PALAMINO	**AAILRSTT**	RATTAILS
AAIIORTZ	ZOIATRIA	**AAILMNOR**	MANORIAL	**AAILRSTV**	TRAVAILS
AAIIPRST	APIARIST		MORAINAL	**AAILRSVY**	SALIVARY
AAIIPRVV	VIVIPARA	**AAILMNOX**	MONAXIAL	**AAILRSWY**	RAILWAYS
AAIIRSTV	AVIARIST	**AAILMNRU**	MANURIAL	**AAILRTUY**	AURALITY
AAIIRSTW	WISTARIA	**AAILMNRY**	LAMINARY	**AAILSSSV**	VASSAILS
AAIIRTVX	AVIATRIX	**AAILMNSS**	NASALISM	**AAILSSSW**	WASSAILS
AAIJLLQU	QUILLAJA	**AAILMNST**	STAMINAL	**AAILSSTY**	STAYSAIL
AAIJLNPS	JALAPINS		TALISMAN	**AAILSTTT**	LATITATS
AAIJMNPS	JAMPANIS	**AAILMNSU**	ALUMINAS	**AAIMMNOS**	AMMONIAS
AAIJNRSY	JANISARY	**AAILMNSV**	MAILVANS	**AAIMMNST**	MAINMAST
AAIJNRSZ	JANIZARS		NAVALISM	**AAIMMRSU**	SAMARIUM
AAIJNRYZ	JANIZARY	**AAILMOPT**	LIPOMATA	**AAIMNNRT**	TRAINMAN
AAIJPPSY	JIPYAPAS	**AAILMORR**	ARMORIAL	**AAIMNOOZ**	ZOOMANIA
AAIKKNOS	SKOKIAAN	**AAILMPPS**	PAPALISM	**AAIMNORT**	ANIMATOR
AAIKKSTZ	KAZATSKI	**AAILMPRT**	PRIMATAL		MONTARIA
AAIKLNNN	ALKANNIN	**AAILMQSU**	MAQUILAS		TAMANOIR
AAIKLNPS	PALINKAS	**AAILMRST**	ALARMIST	**AAIMNORW**	AIRWOMAN
AAIKLNST	NASTALIK		ALASTRIM	**AAIMNOSS**	ANOSMIAS
AAIKLPRS	PALIKARS		MARTIALS	**AAIMNOST**	AMATIONS
AAIKMNNS	MANAKINS	**AAILMTTU**	ULTIMATA	**AAIMNOTT**	ANTIATOM
AAIKMNRS	RAMAKINS	**AAILNNOT**	NATIONAL	**AAIMNPRZ**	MARZIPAN
AAIKMNST	ANTIMASK	**AAILNNPT**	PLAINANT	**AAIMNPST**	ANTISPAM
AAIKMORS	ROMAIKAS		PLANTAIN	**AAIMNPTU**	PUTAMINA
AAIKMRSS	KARAISMS	**AAILNNRU**	LUNARIAN	**AAIMNRRT**	TRIMARAN
AAIKMRST	TAMARISK	**AAILNNST**	ANNALIST	**AAIMNRRU**	RANARIUM
AAIKNNTT	ANTITANK		SANTALIN	**AAIMNRST**	MARTIANS
AAIKNQRT	QINTARKA	**AAILNOPS**	SALOPIAN		TAMARINS
AAIKORSU	OUAKARIS	**AAILNOPT**	TALAPOIN	**AAIMNSST**	MANTISSA
AAIKPPRS	PAPRIKAS	**AAILNORS**	ORINASAL		SATANISM
AAIKPRRS	AIRPARKS	**AAILNORT**	NOTARIAL		STAMINAS
AAIKSSTT	ASTATKIS		RATIONAL	**AAIMNSTU**	AMIANTUS
AAIKSSTV	SVASTIKA	**AAILNOST**	AILANTOS	**AAIMNSTY**	MAINSTAY
AAIKSSTW	SWASTIKA		ALATIONS	**AAIMOPRS**	MARIPOSA
AAIKSTVV	AKVAVITS	**AAILNOSV**	VALONIAS		PAROSMIA
AAILLLSS	SALSILLA	**AAILNOTV**	LAVATION	**AAIMPRST**	PASTRAMI
AAILLLST	LATILLAS	**AAILNOTX**	LAXATION	**AAIMPRSU**	MARSUPIA
AAILLLUV	ALLUVIAL	**AAILNPRU**	PLANURIA	**AAIMQRUU**	AQUARIUM
AAILLMMM	MAMMILLA	**AAILNPSS**	SALPIANS	**AAIMRRSY**	MISARRAY
AAILLMMR	MAMILLAR	**AAILNPST**	PLATINAS	**AAIMRRTY**	MARTYRIA

AAIMRSSU	SAMURAIS	AAIRSSTT	TSARITSA	AALLRSTY	ASTRALLY
AAIMRSTU	TIMARAUS	AAIRSTTZ	TSARITZA	AALLRUVV	VALVULAR
AAIMSSSY	MISASSAY	AAIRSTWY	STAIRWAY	AALMMNOS	AMMONALS
AAIMSSTV	ATAVISMS	AAIRTTZZ	TZARITZA	AALMNORT	MATRONAL
AAINNOPV	PAVONIAN	AAISSTTV	ATAVISTS	AALMNORU	MONAURAL
AAINNOST	SONATINA	AAISTWXY	TAXIWAYS	AALMNOSS	SALAMONS
AAINNOTT	NATATION	AAJKLSWY	JAYWALKS	AALMNOWY	LAYWOMAN
AAINNOTX	ANATOXIN	AAJMMORR	MARJORAM	AALMNPTY	TYMPANAL
AAINNRSV	NAVARINS	AAJMORRS	MOJARRAS	AALMNTTU	TANTALUM
	NIRVANAS	AAJMORST	MAJORATS	AALMNTUU	AUTUMNAL
AAINNRTU	NUTARIAN	AAJOPSSU	SAPAJOUS	AALMOOSS	MASSOOLA
AAINNSST	NAISSANT	AAKKLRSU	KARAKULS	AALMOPPR	MALAPROP
AAINNSSY	SANNYASI	AAKKMMOO	KAMOKAMO	AALMOPSX	AXOPLASM
AAINOOPS	ANOOPSIA	AAKKMOST	TOKAMAKS	AALMOSTT	STOMATAL
AAINOPSS	ANOPSIAS	AAKKOSUZ	ZAKOUSKA	AALMOTXY	XYLOMATA
	PAISANOS	AAKKSTYZ	KAZATSKY	AALMPPSU	PASPALUM
AAINORRS	ORARIANS	AAKLMPSU	LAMPUKAS	AALMPRSY	PALMYRAS
	ROSARIAN	AAKLMRUY	YARMULKA	AALMPSTY	PLATYSMA
AAINOTTX	TAXATION	AAKLMSUY	YAMULKAS	AALMQSUU	SQUAMULA
AAINPPRY	PAPYRIAN	AAKLNOOS	OOLAKANS	AALMSTTU	MULATTAS
AAINPRST	ASPIRANT	AAKLNOSU	OULAKANS	AALNNNOS	NONNASAL
	PARTISAN	AAKLOOPS	PALOOKAS	AALNNNOV	NONNAVAL
	SPARTINA	AAKLOOST	TALOOKAS	AALNNOPP	NONPAPAL
AAINPRTZ	PARTIZAN	AAKLPRTY	KALYPTRA	AALNNOPT	PANTALON
AAINPSST	PASTINAS	AAKLRSSU	KURSAALS	AALNNOST	SONANTAL
AAINPTTT	ANTPITTA		RUSALKAS	AALNNPUU	PUNALUAN
AAINQRRU	QUARRIAN	AAKLSSSU	SAKSAULS	AALNNRSU	ANNULARS
AAINQRTU	QUATRAIN	AAKLSWWY	WALKWAYS	AALNNTTY	NATANTLY
AAINQTTU	AQUATINT	AAKMMNRS	MARKSMAN	AALNNTUU	LUNANAUT
AAINRRSS	SARRASIN	AAKMORSU	AMOKURAS	AALNOORS	ORONASAL
AAINRRSZ	SARRAZIN	AAKMORUZ	MAZOURKA	AALNOPRT	PATRONAL
AAINRSST	ARTISANS	AAKMOSSU	MOUSAKAS	AALNOPST	POSTANAL
	TSARINAS		MOUSSAKA	AALNORUV	ANOVULAR
AAINRSSU	SAURIANS	AAKMRSUZ	MAZURKAS	AALNPRSU	LUPANARS
AAINRSSV	SAVARINS	AAKMRSWY	WAYMARKS	AALNPSST	SALTPANS
AAINRSTV	VARIANTS	AAKNNSTU	NUNATAKS	AALNPSUU	PUNALUAS
AAINRSTY	SANITARY	AAKNRSYY	SYNKARYA	AALNPTWX	WAXPLANT
AAINRSTZ	TZARINAS	AAKNSSTW	WANKSTAS	AALNRRTY	ARRANTLY
AAINRTWY	TRAINWAY	AAKNSTWY	TWANKAYS	AALNRSTU	NATURALS
AAINSSSS	ASSASSIN	AAKOOPPS	PAKAPOOS	AALNSSTT	SALTANTS
AAINSSSY	SANYASIS	AAKOPPRT	PORTAPAK	AALNSSTU	SULTANAS
AAINSSTT	SATANIST	AAKPRSWY	PARKWAYS	AALNSSTY	ANALYSTS
AAINSTTT	ANTISTAT	AAKRSSTU	KATSURAS	AALNSTTU	TALAUNTS
	ATTAINTS	AALLLSTY	LAYSTALL		TANTALUS
AAINSTTU	TUTANIAS	AALLMNST	STALLMAN	AALOPPRT	PALPATOR
AAINSTTV	AVANTIST	AALLMNTY	TALLYMAN	AALOPPRV	APPROVAL
AAINSTTY	SATANITY	AALLMNUY	MANUALLY	AALOPPST	APOPLAST
AAIOPPSS	APOAPSIS	AALLMORY	AMORALLY	AALOPRSS	PARASOLS
AAIOPRRT	TROPARIA	AALLMPRU	AMPULLAR	AALOPRST	PASTORAL
AAIOPRST	ATROPIAS	AALLMSST	SMALLSAT	AALOPSVV	PAVLOVAS
AAIOPRSU	PAROUSIA	AALLNNUY	ANNUALLY	AALOPSZZ	PALAZZOS
AAIOPSTU	AUTOPSIA	AALLNOST	SANTALOL	AALORSST	ALASTORS
AAIORSSU	SAOUARIS	AALLNOSX	ALLOXANS	AALORSSU	AROUSALS
AAIORSTV	AVIATORS	AALLNOTY	ATONALLY	AALORSTX	LAXATORS
AAIORTUZ	AZOTURIA	AALLNPRU	PLANULAR	AALORTUV	VALUATOR
AAIPPSTT	PITAPATS	AALLNRTY	TARNALLY	AALORTVY	LAVATORY
AAIPRSSX	SPARAXIS	AALLOORW	WALLAROO	AALOSTTY	TALAYOTS
AAIPRSTT	PARTITAS	AALLORSU	ALLOSAUR	AALPRSTU	PASTURAL
AAIQRSTU	AQUARIST	AALLORWY	ROLLAWAY		SPATULAR
AAIQSSSU	QUASSIAS	AALLOSTV	LAVOLTAS	AALPRSTY	LAPTRAYS
AAIQSTUV	AQUAVITS	AALLPRST	PLASTRAL	AALPSSTU	SPATULAS

AALRRTTY	TARTARLY	**AAORSVVY**	VAVASORY	**ABBCKLOY**	BLACKBOY
AALRSSTU	AUSTRALS	**AAOSTTUY**	TATOUAYS	**ABBCKNRU**	BACKBURN
AALRSSTY	SATYRALS	**AAOSTWWY**	STOWAWAY	**ABBCKSUY**	BUYBACKS
AALRSSVY	VASSALRY		TOWAWAYS	**ABBCLRSY**	SCRABBLY
AALRSTTW	STALWART	**AAPRRSTT**	RATTRAPS	**ABBDDEEL**	BEDDABLE
AALRSTUY	SALUTARY	**AAPRSTUU**	RAUPATUS	**ABBDDEEU**	BEDAUBED
AALSSSTU	ASSAULTS	**AARSTTUY**	STATUARY	**ABBDDEIL**	BIDDABLE
AAMMMSTU	MAMMATUS	**ABBBCDEO**	CABOBBED	**ABBDDELR**	DRABBLED
AAMMNPRS	RAMPSMAN	**ABBBDEEK**	KEBABBED	**ABBDDEOR**	BEDBOARD
AAMMNRST	MANTRAMS	**ABBBDEEL**	BEDABBLE	**ABBDDILY**	BIDDABLY
AAMMOTXY	MYXOMATA	**ABBBDEKO**	KABOBBED	**ABBDEEER**	BEEBREAD
AAMMRSSU	MARASMUS	**ABBBDELR**	BRABBLED	**ABBDEEHR**	REHABBED
AAMNNORS	SONARMAN	**ABBBEILR**	BABBLIER	**ABBDEEJR**	JABBERED
AAMNNOSY	ANONYMAS		BRIBABLE	**ABBDEELN**	BENDABLE
AAMNORRS	MARRANOS	**ABBBELMO**	BOMBABLE	**ABBDEERR**	BARBERED
AAMNORSZ	ROMANZAS	**ABBBELRR**	BRABBLER	**ABBDEERT**	RABBETED
AAMNPRST	MANTRAPS	**ABBBELRS**	BABBLERS	**ABBDEERY**	YABBERED
AAMNPRSY	PARANYMS		BLABBERS	**ABBDEGLR**	GRABBLED
AAMNQSUW	SQUAWMAN		BRABBLES	**ABBDEHOO**	BOOBHEAD
AAMOORSS	AMOROSAS	**ABBBELTU**	TUBBABLE	**ABBDEHST**	BEDBATHS
AAMOPRRU	PARAMOUR	**ABBBGILN**	BABBLING	**ABBDEILN**	BINDABLE
AAMORRSZ	ZAMARROS		BLABBING	**ABBDEIRR**	DRABBIER
AAMORSSU	MOSASAUR	**ABBBHSUY**	BUSHBABY	**ABBDEIRT**	RABBITED
AAMORSSV	SAMOVARS	**ABBBIRTY**	BABBITRY	**ABBDELMO**	BABELDOM
AAMORSTT	STROMATA	**ABBBISTT**	BABBITTS	**ABBDELMR**	BRAMBLED
AAMOSTTU	AUTOMATS	**ABBBOORU**	RUBBABOO	**ABBDELNO**	BONDABLE
AAMPRRST	RAMPARTS	**ABBBOSTU**	SUBABBOT	**ABBDELNS**	SNABBLED
AAMRSSST	SMARTASS	**ABBCCKMO**	BACKCOMB	**ABBDELRR**	DRABBLER
AAMRSSTT	MATTRASS	**ABBCDEKN**	BACKBEND	**ABBDELRS**	DABBLERS
AAMRSSTU	SUMATRAS	**ABBCDELS**	SCABBLED		DRABBLES
AAMRSTWY	TRAMWAYS	**ABBCDERS**	SCRABBED	**ABBDEMOR**	BOMBARDE
AAMSSSTU	SATSUMAS	**ABBCDKNO**	BACKBOND	**ABBDEMUZ**	BUMBAZED
AANNOSST	ASSONANT	**ABBCEERU**	BARBECUE	**ABBDENRU**	UNBARBED
AANNOSTT	ANNATTOS	**ABBCEGIR**	CRIBBAGE	**ABBDEORS**	ABSORBED
AANNOTTW	NANOWATT	**ABBCEHIS**	BABICHES	**ABBDEORX**	BREADBOX
AANNPSSW	SWANPANS	**ABBCEHOU**	BABOUCHE	**ABBDEQSU**	SQUABBED
AANNRSTY	STANNARY	**ABBCEHOY**	BEACHBOY	**ABBDERRS**	DRABBERS
AANOOPPX	OPOPANAX	**ABBCEHSU**	BABUCHES	**ABBDERST**	DRABBEST
AANOOPRZ	PARAZOON	**ABBCEHTU**	BATHCUBE		DRABBETS
AANOPRTY	ANATROPY	**ABBCEIKT**	BACKBITE	**ABBDFOOY**	BABYFOOD
AANORRRT	NARRATOR	**ABBCEILR**	BARBICEL	**ABBDGILN**	DABBLING
AANORSTT	ARNATTOS	**ABBCEIRR**	CRABBIER	**ABBDGINR**	DRABBING
AANORSTY	SANATORY	**ABBCEIRS**	SCABBIER	**ABBDGIOR**	GABBROID
AANORTTY	NATATORY	**ABBCEKLU**	BLUEBACK	**ABBDHIJS**	DJIBBAHS
AANPPTTY	PATTYPAN	**ABBCEKNO**	BACKBONE	**ABBDHIRS**	DRABBISH
AANPRSST	SPARTANS	**ABBCEKNU**	BUCKBEAN	**ABBDHIRT**	BIRDBATH
AANQRSTU	QUARTANS	**ABBCELLU**	CLUBABLE	**ABBDHOOY**	BABYHOOD
AANRRSTW	WARRANTS	**ABBCELRS**	CLABBERS	**ABBDILNO**	BAILBOND
AANRRTTY	TARTANRY		SCRABBLE	**ABBDILRS**	LIBBARDS
AANRRTWY	WARRANTY	**ABBCELRU**	CURBABLE	**ABBDINRS**	RIBBANDS
AANRSTTU	SATURANT	**ABBCELSS**	SCABBLES	**ABBDLLOY**	BABYDOLL
AANRSUWY	RUNAWAYS	**ABBCERRS**	CRABBERS	**ABBDLMOO**	BOMBLOAD
AANSSSTT	TSANTSAS	**ABBCGINR**	CRABBING	**ABBDLRSU**	LUBBARDS
AAOORRSW	WOORARAS	**ABBCGINS**	SCABBING	**ABBDMORS**	BOMBARDS
AAOPSSST	POTASSAS	**ABBCGIOR**	GABBROIC	**ABBDMOSU**	BABUDOMS
AAOPSSTY	APOSTASY	**ABBCIILL**	BIBLICAL	**ABBDNORW**	BROWBAND
AAOQSSSU	OQUASSAS	**ABBCIINR**	RABBINIC	**ABBDOORX**	BOXBOARD
AAORSSTT	STAROSTA	**ABBCIKRT**	BRICKBAT	**ABBDORRU**	RUBBOARD
AAORSSVV	VAVASORS	**ABBCILRY**	CRABBILY	**ABBEEHRR**	REHABBER
	VAVASSOR	**ABBCILSY**	SCABBILY	**ABBEEILT**	BITEABLE
AAORSUVV	VAVASOUR	**ABBCKLOW**	BLOWBACK	**ABBEEINR**	BEARBINE

ABBEEJRR	JABBERER	ABBEMSUZ	BUMBAZES	ABBLLSUY	SYLLABUB
ABBEEJRS	BEJABERS	ABBENORS	BASEBORN	ABBLLOPRY	PROBABLY
ABBEELOY	OBEYABLE	ABBENORY	NABOBERY	ABBMOORS	BOMBORAS
ABBEELTU	BLUEBEAT	ABBENOSS	NABOBESS	ABBMOSST	BOMBASTS
ABBEENOR	BAREBONE	ABBEORRS	ABSORBER	ABBMOSTU	BUMBOATS
ABBEEQRU	BARBEQUE		REABSORB	ABBNRSUU	SUBURBAN
ABBEERTT	BARBETTE	ABBEORTW	BROWBEAT	ABBOORSU	RUBABOOS
ABBEESSS	ABBESSES	ABBEQRSU	SQUABBER	ABBOSSTY	BOBSTAYS
ABBEFFLU	BUFFABLE	ABBERRRY	BARBERRY	ABCCCIOO	BOCACCIO
ABBEFILR	FLABBIER	ABBERRYY	BAYBERRY	ABCCDEHO	CABOCHED
ABBEFIST	FABBIEST	ABBERSST	STABBERS	ABCCDHIK	DABCHICK
ABBEGIRR	GRABBIER	ABBERSSW	SWABBERS	ABCCEEHN	BECHANCE
ABBEGIST	GABBIEST	ABBESSSU	SUBBASES	ABCCEELP	PECCABLE
ABBEGLRR	GRABBLER	ABBFGINR	FRABBING	ABCCEEOR	CABOCEER
ABBEGLRS	GABBLERS	ABBFILLY	FLABBILY	ABCCEFLU	CLUBFACE
	GRABBLES	ABBFLOOT	BOBFLOAT	ABCCEILR	BRECCIAL
ABBEGNOS	BOGBEANS	ABBGGILN	GABBLING	ABCCEILY	CELIBACY
ABBEGNSU	BUGBANES	ABBGGINR	GRABBING	ABCCEIRS	BRECCIAS
ABBEGRRS	GRABBERS	ABBGIJLN	JABBLING	ABCCEIRT	BACTERIC
ABBEGRSU	BUGBEARS	ABBGILNR	RABBLING	ABCCEKMO	COMEBACK
ABBEHILS	BABELISH	ABBGILNS	SLABBING	ABCCESUU	SUCCUBAE
ABBEHIRS	SHABBIER	ABBGILNU	BAUBLING	ABCCHISU	BACCHIUS
ABBEHLSS	SHABBLES	ABBGILNW	WABBLING	ABCCHNOO	CABOCHON
ABBEHORT	BATHROBE	ABBGINSS	SABBINGS	ABCCHOSU	CHUBASCO
ABBEILLL	BILLABLE	ABBGINST	STABBING	ABCCIISS	ABSCISIC
ABBEILLO	BOILABLE	ABBGINSU	BUBINGAS	ABCCIKKK	KICKBACK
ABBEILMS	BABELISM	ABBGINSW	SWABBING	ABCCIKKP	PICKBACK
ABBEILNU	BUBALINE	ABBGINTY	TABBYING	ABCCIKOR	ABRICOCK
ABBEILOT	BILOBATE	ABBGINYY	YABBYING	ABCCILOR	CARBOLIC
ABBEILOV	OBVIABLE	ABBGOOSU	BUGABOOS	ABCCILOT	COBALTIC
ABBEILRS	SLABBIER	ABBHIIMS	BIMBASHI	ABCCILUU	CUBICULA
ABBEILRW	WABBLIER	ABBHILSY	SHABBILY	ABCCIMRS	CAMBRICS
ABBEILST	BISTABLE	ABBHINOS	NABOBISH	ABCCINOR	CARBONIC
ABBEIMRU	BERIMBAU	ABBHIORT	RABBITOH	ABCCINSU	BUCCINAS
ABBEINTT	TABBINET	ABBHRRSU	RHUBARBS	ABCCIORS	ASCORBIC
ABBEIRRT	RABBITER	ABBHRRUY	RHUBARBY	ABCCKLLO	BALLCOCK
ABBEIRRW	BARBWIRE	ABBHSTTU	BATHTUBS	ABCCKLOX	CLACKBOX
ABBEISST	TABBISES	ABBIINOT	BIBATION	ABCCKOOT	COCKBOAT
ABBEISSW	SWABBIES	ABBIKNOS	BIOBANKS	ABCCKOSW	BAWCOCKS
ABBEKLOO	BOOKABLE	ABBILLOT	BOATBILL	ABCCKSTU	CUTBACKS
ABBELLLU	BLUEBALL	ABBILLSU	SILLABUB	ABCCLLUY	BUCCALLY
ABBELLRS	BARBELLS	ABBILOST	BIOBLAST	ABCCLOOO	COCOBOLA
ABBELMRS	BRAMBLES		BOBTAILS	ABCCMOOY	MACCOBOY
ABBELNRU	BURNABLE	ABBILOTU	TABBOULI	ABCCOORS	BAROCCOS
ABBELNSS	SNABBLES	ABBIMNOS	BAMBINOS	ABCCOOST	TOBACCOS
ABBELOOT	BOOTABLE		NABOBISM	ABCCSSUU	SUCCUBAS
ABBELOPR	PROBABLE	ABBIMSSU	BABUISMS	ABCDDEER	DECARBED
ABBELORS	BELABORS	ABBINORS	RABBONIS	ABCDDEOR	BARCODED
	SORBABLE	ABBINORX	BRAINBOX		BROCADED
ABBELORU	BELABOUR	ABBINSSU	SUBBASIN	ABCDDETU	ABDUCTED
ABBELPRS	PRABBLES	ABBIORST	RABBITOS	ABCDEEFK	FEEDBACK
ABBELQSU	SQUABBLE	ABBIRRTY	RABBITRY	ABCDEEHL	BLEACHED
ABBELRRS	RABBLERS	ABBIRSUU	SUBURBIA	ABCDEEHR	BERDACHE
ABBELRSS	BARBLESS	ABBISSTY	BABYSITS		BREACHED
	SLABBERS	ABBITUZZ	BUZZBAIT	ABCDEEJT	ABJECTED
ABBELRSU	BARBULES	ABBKKNOO	BANKBOOK	ABCDEEKR	REBACKED
ABBELRSW	WABBLERS	ABBKLOSU	BLAUBOKS	ABCDEELL	BECALLED
ABBELRSY	SLABBERY	ABBLLLOW	BLOWBALL	ABCDEELM	BECALMED
ABBELSUY	BUYABLES	ABBLLOSX	BOXBALLS	ABCDEELS	DEBACLES
ABBEMOOR	AEROBOMB	ABBLLRSU	BULLBARS	ABCDEELU	EDUCABLE
ABBEMOSX	BOMBAXES	ABBLLSTU	BULLBATS	ABCDEEMR	CAMBERED

	EMBRACED	**ABCDILRS**	BALDRICS	**ABCEGIMN**	EMBACING
ABCDEEMX	EXCAMBED	**ABCDINOR**	BRACONID	**ABCEGIRS**	RIBCAGES
ABCDEENO	BEACONED	**ABCDINSS**	ABSCINDS	**ABCEGKLL**	BLACKLEG
ABCDEEPP	BECAPPED	**ABCDIRST**	CATBIRDS	**ABCEGKLO**	BLOCKAGE
ABCDEERR	REBRACED	**ABCDIRSU**	BAUDRICS	**ABCEGKMU**	MEGABUCK
ABCDEETU	ABDUCTEE		SUBACRID	**ABCEGKOR**	BROCKAGE
ABCDEFLO	BOLDFACE	**ABCDIRSW**	BAWDRICS	**ABCEGKRY**	GREYBACK
ABCDEGIR	BIRDCAGE	**ABCDKNOW**	BACKDOWN	**ABCEGMOS**	CAMBOGES
ABCDEHIR	BEDCHAIR	**ABCDKOOR**	BACKDOOR	**ABCEGNOR**	BONGRACE
ABCDEHKO	BACKHOED	**ABCDKOOW**	BACKWOOD	**ABCEGNRU**	CANEGRUB
ABCDEHLN	BLANCHED	**ABCDKOPR**	BACKDROP	**ABCEGORS**	BROCAGES
ABCDEHLU	BAUCHLED	**ABCDKORW**	BACKWORD	**ABCEGOSS**	BOSCAGES
	CLUBHEAD	**ABCDLLNU**	CLUBLAND	**ABCEHIST**	BIATCHES
ABCDEHNR	BRANCHED	**ABCDNOSS**	ABSCONDS	**ABCEHITT**	BATHETIC
ABCDEHOR	BROACHED	**ABCDOORS**	CORDOBAS	**ABCEHKLS**	BECHALKS
ABCDEHOS	CABOSHED	**ABCDOORW**	CRABWOOD	**ABCEHKOS**	BACKHOES
ABCDEIIT	DIABETIC	**ABCDOPRU**	CUPBOARD	**ABCEHKTW**	BETHWACK
ABCDEIKS	BACKSIDE	**ABCDORRS**	BROCARDS	**ABCEHLNR**	BLANCHER
	DIEBACKS	**ABCDORSU**	BUCARDOS	**ABCEHLNS**	BLANCHES
ABCDEILR	CALIBRED	**ABCDORTU**	ABDUCTOR	**ABCEHLOR**	BACHELOR
ABCDEIPS	PEDICABS	**ABCDORUY**	OBDURACY	**ABCEHLOS**	CHAEBOLS
ABCDEIRS	ASCRIBED	**ABCEEEFK**	BEEFCAKE	**ABCEHLSU**	BAUCHLES
	CARBIDES	**ABCEEFNT**	BENEFACT		CHASUBLE
ABCDEISS	ABSCISED	**ABCEEHIR**	BEACHIER	**ABCEHMOT**	HECATOMB
ABCDEKLO	BLOCKADE	**ABCEEHLM**	BECHAMEL	**ABCEHMRS**	BECHARMS
ABCDEKLV	BACKVELD	**ABCEEHLN**	ALEBENCH		BRECHAMS
ABCDEKNN	NECKBAND	**ABCEEHLR**	BLEACHER		CHAMBERS
ABCDEKNU	UNBACKED	**ABCEEHLS**	BLEACHES	**ABCEHNRR**	BRANCHER
ABCDEKRS	REDBACKS	**ABCEEHLW**	CHEWABLE		REBRANCH
ABCDEKRT	TRACKBED	**ABCEEHRR**	BREACHER	**ABCEHNRS**	BRANCHES
ABCDELMS	SCAMBLED	**ABCEEHRS**	BREACHES		BRECHANS
ABCDELNO	BLANCOED	**ABCEEHSU**	EBAUCHES	**ABCEHOOT**	COHOBATE
ABCDELOO	CABOODLE	**ABCEEILT**	CELIBATE	**ABCEHOPU**	PABOUCHE
ABCDELRU	BARLEDUC		CITEABLE	**ABCEHORR**	BROACHER
ABCDEMNU	DUMBCANE	**ABCEEIMN**	AMBIENCE	**ABCEHORS**	BROACHES
ABCDEMOT	COMBATED	**ABCEEKLY**	EYEBLACK	**ABCEHORU**	BAROUCHE
ABCDEMRS	SCRAMBED	**ABCEELOV**	EVOCABLE	**ABCEHOSS**	BASOCHES
ABCDENRU	UNBRACED	**ABCEELRR**	CEREBRAL	**ABCEHRST**	BATCHERS
ABCDENSU	ABDUCENS	**ABCEELRT**	BRACELET		BRACHETS
ABCDENTU	ABDUCENT	**ABCEEMRR**	EMBRACER	**ABCEHRTT**	BRATCHET
ABCDEORS	BARCODES	**ABCEEMRS**	EMBRACES	**ABCEIIRT**	RABIETIC
	BROCADES	**ABCEENOZ**	CABEZONE	**ABCEIKKL**	KICKABLE
ABCDEORW	BECOWARD	**ABCEENRS**	CARBEENS	**ABCEIKLP**	PICKABLE
ABCDEORY	CARBOYED		CARBENES	**ABCEIKLR**	CRABLIKE
ABCDERSU	CUDBEARS	**ABCEENRT**	CABERNET	**ABCEIKLS**	SCABLIKE
ABCDESTU	SUBACTED	**ABCEENSS**	ABSENCES	**ABCEIKST**	TIEBACKS
ABCDFKLO	FOLDBACK	**ABCEEPRT**	BECARPET	**ABCEIKWZ**	ZWIEBACK
ABCDGINU	ABDUCING	**ABCEERRS**	REBRACES	**ABCEILLR**	CRIBELLA
ABCDHKLO	HOLDBACK	**ABCEERST**	ACERBEST	**ABCEILLS**	ICEBALLS
ABCDHLNU	CLUBHAND	**ABCEERUX**	BERCEAUX	**ABCEILLT**	BALLETIC
ABCDHORS	CHOBDARS	**ABCEESSS**	BECASSES	**ABCEILMS**	ALEMBICS
ABCDIILO	BIOCIDAL	**ABCEFIIT**	BEATIFIC	**ABCEILNN**	BINNACLE
	DIABOLIC	**ABCEFIKL**	BACKFILE	**ABCEILNO**	BIOCLEAN
ABCDIIMY	CYMBIDIA	**ABCEFIKR**	BACKFIRE		COINABLE
ABCDIIRT	TRIBADIC		FIREBACK	**ABCEILNU**	BACULINE
ABCDIKLR	BALDRICK	**ABCEFINO**	BONIFACE	**ABCEILOR**	ALBICORE
ABCDIKLS	BACKSLID	**ABCEFKOO**	FACEBOOK		BRACIOLE
ABCDIKRU	BAUDRICK	**ABCEFLNO**	BACLOFEN		CABRIOLE
ABCDILLR	BIRDCALL	**ABCEGHIN**	BEACHING	**ABCEILOS**	SOCIABLE
ABCDILOS	CABILDOS	**ABCEGIKV**	GIVEBACK	**ABCEILRS**	CALIBERS
ABCDILOU	CUBOIDAL	**ABCEGILN**	BELACING		CALIBRES

ABCEILST	BASILECT		SCAMBLER	ABCFKLSY	FLYBACKS
ABCEILTT	BITTACLE		SCRAMBLE	ABCFKOST	SOFTBACK
ABCEILTU	BACULITE	ABCELMRY	CYMBALER	ABCGGIMO	GAMBOGIC
ABCEILTY	BIACETYL	ABCELMSS	SCAMBLES	ABCGHINT	BATCHING
ABCEIMRW	MICAWBER	ABCELNOT	BALCONET	ABCGHKOS	HOGBACKS
ABCEIMST	BETACISM	ABCELNUU	NUBECULA	ABCGHNPU	PUNCHBAG
ABCEINOO	COENOBIA	ABCELOOT	BOOTLACE	ABCGIINN	CABINING
ABCEINRS	BRISANCE	ABCELOPS	PLACEBOS	ABCGIKLN	BLACKING
	CARBINES	ABCELOPY	COPYABLE	ABCGIKNS	BACKINGS
ABCEINRT	BACTERIN	ABCELORT	BROCATEL	ABCGIKNW	WINGBACK
ABCEINRV	VIBRANCE	ABCELOST	OBSTACLE	ABCGILNS	CABLINGS
ABCEINST	BASCINET	ABCELOSV	VOCABLES	ABCGINRS	BRACINGS
	CABINETS	ABCELOTU	BLUECOAT	ABCGINSU	SCUBAING
ABCEINTU	INCUBATE	ABCELPSS	BECLASPS	ABCGKLMU	BLACKGUM
ABCEIORS	AEROBICS	ABCELPSU	BLUECAPS	ABCGKLOS	BACKLOGS
ABCEIORT	BORACITE	ABCELPSY	BYPLACES	ABCGLNOX	CLANGBOX
ABCEIOST	ICEBOATS	ABCELRSU	ARBUSCLE	ABCGMSSU	SCUMBAGS
ABCEIRRT	CATBRIER	ABCELRSW	BECRAWLS	ABCGSUZZ	SCUZZBAG
	CRIBRATE		BESCRAWL	ABCHHIIS	HIBACHIS
ABCEIRSS	ASCRIBES	ABCELRTT	BRACTLET	ABCHIIPS	BIPHASIC
ABCEIRSW	CRABWISE	ABCELSSU	BASCULES	ABCHIKLS	BLACKISH
ABCEIRTT	BRATTICE		SUBSCALE	ABCHIKRS	BRACKISH
ABCEIRTY	ACERBITY	ABCELTTU	CUTTABLE	ABCHILMO	CHOLIAMB
ABCEISSS	ABSCISES	ABCEMOOS	CAMBOOSE	ABCHILOO	COOLIBAH
	ABSCISSE	ABCEMORS	CRAMBOES	ABCHIMOR	CHORIAMB
ABCEISST	ASBESTIC	ABCEMORT	COMBATER	ABCHIMRU	BRACHIUM
ABCEISTT	TABETICS	ABCENORS	BACONERS	ABCHINOR	BRONCHIA
ABCEJKLU	BLUEJACK	ABCENOSU	SUBOCEAN	ABCHIOOR	BORACHIO
ABCEJLTY	ABJECTLY	ABCENOSW	COWBANES	ABCHIOST	COHABITS
ABCEKKRU	BUCKRAKE	ABCENOSZ	CABEZONS	ABCHIRRT	TRIBRACH
ABCEKKSW	SKEWBACK	ABCENOUY	BUOYANCE	ABCHKLOT	HACKBOLT
ABCEKLLO	LOCKABLE	ABCENRSU	UNBRACES	ABCHKLOW	HOWLBACK
ABCEKLMO	MOCKABLE	ABCENTUX	EXCUBANT	ABCHKMPU	HUMPBACK
ABCEKLNS	BLACKENS	ABCEOOSS	CABOOSES	ABCHKOOP	CHAPBOOK
ABCEKLOO	COOKABLE	ABCEOPUU	BEAUCOUP	ABCHKOOS	CASHBOOK
ABCEKLOR	ROCKABLE	ABCEORRS	BRACEROS	ABCHKOSU	CHABOUKS
ABCEKLOS	BECLOAKS	ABCEORST	CABESTRO	ABCHKRSU	BACKRUSH
ABCEKLPU	PALEBUCK		CABRESTO	ABCHKSTU	HACKBUTS
ABCEKLSS	BACKLESS	ABCEORSU	CORBEAUS	ABCHKSUW	HAWBUCKS
ABCEKLST	BLACKEST	ABCEOSUX	SAUCEBOX	ABCHLLUU	CLUBHAUL
ABCEKNOT	BOATNECK	ABCEPSSU	SUBSPACE	ABCHMOTX	MATCHBOX
ABCEKNRS	BRACKENS	ABCERRTU	CARBURET	ABCHNORS	BROCHANS
ABCEKOOS	BOOKCASE	ABCERRWY	CYBERWAR	ABCHOORR	ROORBACH
	CASEBOOK	ABCERSSU	SUBRACES	ABCHOSTT	CHATBOTS
ABCEKORY	ROCKABYE	ABCERTUU	CUBATURE	ABCHOTWX	WATCHBOX
ABCEKRST	BACKREST	ABCESSTU	SUBCASTE	ABCIIKRR	AIRBRICK
	BRACKETS	ABCESSTW	WEBCASTS	ABCIILMU	BULIMIAC
ABCEKSST	BACKSETS	ABCESSUU	SUBCAUSE	ABCIILOT	BIOTICAL
	SETBACKS	ABCESTUU	SUBACUTE	ABCIIMNS	MINICABS
ABCEKSSY	BACKSEYS	ABCFIKLL	BACKFILL	ABCIINOT	CIBATION
ABCEKSTW	WETBACKS	ABCFIKLN	BLACKFIN	ABCIINSS	ABSCISIN
ABCELLOS	CLOSABLE	ABCFIKLP	BACKFLIP	ABCIINTU	BUCATINI
ABCELLPU	CULPABLE	ABCFIKLT	BACKLIFT	ABCIIORS	ISOBARIC
ABCELLRU	BRUCELLA		LIFTBACK	ABCIIRST	TRIBASIC
ABCELLSU	BUCELLAS	ABCFIKNS	FINBACKS	ABCIISTY	BASICITY
	BULLACES	ABCFIKST	BACKFITS	ABCIITUX	BAUXITIC
ABCELMNY	LAMBENCY	ABCFILOS	BIFOCALS	ABCIJNOS	JACOBINS
ABCELMOR	BECLAMOR	ABCFIOST	BIOFACTS	ABCIKKLL	KICKBALL
ABCELMOS	CEMBALOS	ABCFKLLU	FULLBACK	ABCIKLST	BACKLIST
ABCELMRS	CAMBRELS	ABCFKLLY	BLACKFLY	ABCIKLTU	BUCKTAIL
	CLAMBERS	ABCFKLOW	BACKFLOW	ABCIKNPS	BACKSPIN

ABCIKSSY	SICKBAYS	ABCKORUY	BUCKAYRO	ABDDEILU	AUDIBLED
ABCILLNY	BILLYCAN	ABCKOSSW	SOWBACKS		BUDDLEIA
ABCILLRU	LUBRICAL	ABCKOSTU	BACKOUTS	ABDDEINR	BRANDIED
ABCILLSU	BACILLUS		OUTBACKS	ABDDEINS	SIDEBAND
ABCILLSY	SYLLABIC	ABCKSSTU	SACKBUTS	ABDDEINW	WIDEBAND
ABCILMMO	CIMBALOM		SUBTACKS	ABDDEIRR	BRAIRDED
ABCILMSU	SUBCLAIM	ABCKSSUW	BUCKSAWS	ABDDELOT	DEADBOLT
ABCILNOR	CARBINOL		SAWBUCKS	ABDDELRS	BLADDERS
ABCILNOS	COALBINS	ABCLLNOR	CORNBALL	ABDDELRY	BLADDERY
ABCILNPU	PUBLICAN	ABCLLOSY	CALLBOYS	ABDDENNU	UNBANDED
ABCILOOR	COOLIBAR	ABCLLPUY	CULPABLY	ABDDENOU	ABOUNDED
ABCILOSY	SOCIABLY	ABCLMMOY	CYMBALOM	ABDDENST	BEDSTAND
ABCILRRU	RUBRICAL	ABCLMOOO	COLOBOMA	ABDDEORS	ADSORBED
ABCIMMSS	CAMBISMS	ABCLMOSY	CYMBALOS		ROADBEDS
ABCIMMSU	CAMBIUMS	ABCLMSUU	BACULUMS	ABDDEOSY	DEADBOYS
ABCIMORR	MICROBAR	ABCLMSUY	SCYBALUM	ABDDERSW	BEDWARDS
ABCIMRTU	UMBRATIC	ABCLNORY	CARBONYL	ABDDGILN	BLADDING
ABCIMSST	CAMBISTS	ABCLNSSU	SUBCLANS	ABDDGINR	BRADDING
ABCINNOS	NONBASIC	ABCLORXY	CARBOXYL	ABDDHIOR	RHABDOID
ABCINORS	CORBINAS	ABCLOSUV	SUBVOCAL	ABDDILMO	LAMBDOID
ABCINORU	CONURBIA	ABCLSSSU	SUBCLASS	ABDDILRY	LADYBIRD
ABCINORY	BARYONIC	ABCLSUUU	SUBUCULA	ABDDIMNO	BONDMAID
ABCINOST	BOTANICS	ABCMOORT	MOBOCRAT	ABDDINSS	DISBANDS
ABCINOTU	BUTANOIC	ABCMOSST	MOBCASTS	ABDDIRRY	YARDBIRD
ABCINRVY	VIBRANCY	ABCNNORU	CONURBAN	ABDDLLOS	ODDBALLS
ABCIOPRS	SAPROBIC	ABCNORTY	CORYBANT	ABDDLUWY	BULWADDY
ABCIORRS	BARRICOS	ABCNOUYY	BUOYANCY	ABDDMORS	DAMBRODS
ABCIORSU	CARIBOUS	ABCORRSS	CROSSBAR		
ABCIOSSU	SCABIOUS	ABCORRSW	CROWBARS	ABDEEEFL	BEFLEAED
ABCIOSUV	BIVOUACS	ABCORRTU	TURBOCAR		FEEDABLE
ABCIRSTT	ABSTRICT	ABCORSSU	SCABROUS	ABDEEEFN	BEDEAFEN
ABCIRSUV	SUBVICAR	ABCOSSTU	SUBCOSTA	ABDEEEHR	BEHEADER
ABCJKOOT	BOOTJACK	ABCOSTTU	COTTABUS	ABDEEELP	BELEAPED
	JACKBOOT	ABCRSTTU	SUBTRACT	ABDEEEMN	BEMEANED
ABCKKOOR	BOOKRACK	ABDDDEEM	BEMADDED	ABDEEERV	BEAVERED
ABCKKORW	BACKWORK	ABDDDEET	ADDEBTED		BEREAVED
ABCKLLOR	ROLLBACK	ABDDEEEH	BEHEADED	ABDEEFGS	FEEDBAGS
ABCKLLOS	BALLOCKS	ABDDEEEK	DEBEAKED	ABDEEFIT	TABEFIED
ABCKLLPU	PULLBACK	ABDDEEGG	DEBAGGED	ABDEEFLM	FLAMBEED
ABCKLNNO	NONBLACK	ABDDEEGR	BADGERED	ABDEEFMO	BEFOAMED
ABCKLOPT	BLACKTOP		REBADGED	ABDEEFMR	BEDFRAME
ABCKLOPW	PLOWBACK	ABDDEEHS	BEDASHED	ABDEEGGL	BEDAGGLE
ABCKLOST	BACKLOTS		BEDHEADS	ABDEEGGR	BEGGARED
	SLOTBACK	ABDDEEHT	DEATHBED	ABDEEGHR	HERBAGED
ABCKLOSW	SLOWBACK	ABDDEEIL	BELADIED	ABDEEGLL	BEGALLED
ABCKLOTU	BLACKOUT	ABDDEEKR	DEBARKED		GABELLED
ABCKMOOR	BACKROOM	ABDDEELU	BELAUDED	ABDEEGNW	BEGNAWED
ABCKMORR	BROCKRAM	ABDDEEMN	BEDAMNED	ABDEEGRS	REBADGES
ABCKMOSS	MOSSBACK		BEMADDEN	ABDEEGRU	BEDEGUAR
ABCKMOST	BACKMOST	ABDDEENY	BENDAYED	ABDEEHIR	BRAEHEID
	TOMBACKS	ABDDEEPR	BEDRAPED	ABDEEHLS	SHEDABLE
ABCKMRSU	BUCKRAMS	ABDDEERR	DEBARRED	ABDEEHLU	BLUEHEAD
ABCKMSUZ	ZAMBUCKS	ABDDEERS	DEBEARDS	ABDEEHMS	BESHAMED
ABCKNNOS	BANNOCKS	ABDDEEST	BEDSTEAD	ABDEEHMT	EMBATHED
ABCKNORY	CRYOBANK		BESTADDE	ABDEEHNO	BONEHEAD
ABCKNRSU	RUNBACKS	ABDDEGIR	ABRIDGED	ABDEEHRT	BREATHED
ABCKNRTU	TURNBACK		BRIGADED	ABDEEHSS	BEDASHES
ABCKNSTU	CUTBANKS	ABDDEHMO	HEBDOMAD	ABDEEHST	BETHESDA
ABCKOORR	ROORBACK	ABDDEHMU	DUMBHEAD	ABDEEHSW	WEBHEADS
ABCKOORU	BUCKAROO	ABDDEHOY	HOBDAYED	ABDEEHTT	BEHATTED
ABCKOPST	BACKSTOP	ABDDEILS	DISABLED	ABDEEIKL	BEADLIKE
				ABDEEIKR	BIDARKEE

ABDEEILM	EMBAILED	ABDEEMST	BEDMATES	ABDEGLRS	BELGARDS
ABDEEILN	DENIABLE	ABDEENNR	BANNERED	ABDEGLRY	BADGERLY
ABDEEILR	RIDEABLE	ABDEENRT	BANTERED	ABDEGLSU	SLUGABED
ABDEEILS	ABSEILED	ABDEENRU	UNBEARED	ABDEGMRU	UMBRAGED
	BELADIES	ABDEENRY	BARNEYED	ABDEGNOR	BONDAGER
ABDEEILT	DELIBATE	ABDEENRZ	BRAZENED	ABDEGNOS	BONDAGES
	EDITABLE	ABDEENST	ABSENTED		DOGBANES
ABDEEILV	EVADIBLE	ABDEENTT	BATTENED	ABDEGNRU	UNGARBED
ABDEEILW	BEWAILED	ABDEEPRS	BEDRAPES	ABDEGOPR	PEGBOARD
ABDEEIPR	BEDIAPER		BESPREAD	ABDEGORT	BOGARTED
ABDEEIRR	BEARDIER	ABDEEPTT	BEPATTED	ABDEGRSU	SUBGRADE
	BREADIER	ABDEERRT	BARTERED	ABDEHILL	BILLHEAD
ABDEEIRS	BEARDIES	ABDEERRY	RYEBREAD	ABDEHILS	DISHABLE
ABDEEIRT	EBRIATED	ABDEERSS	DEBASERS	ABDEHIMT	IMBATHED
	REBAITED	ABDEERST	BETREADS	ABDEHINS	BANISHED
ABDEEIST	BEADIEST		BREASTED	ABDEHITU	HABITUDE
	DIABETES		DEBATERS	ABDEHKLU	BULKHEAD
ABDEEITU	BEAUTIED	ABDEERSY	BEEYARDS	ABDEHKNO	KNOBHEAD
ABDEEJMN	ENJAMBED	ABDEERTT	BATTERED	ABDEHLLN	HANDBELL
ABDEEJST	JETBEADS		DRABETTE	ABDEHLLO	HOLDABLE
ABDEEKLS	LAKEBEDS	ABDEERTW	WATERBED	ABDEHLLU	BULLHEAD
ABDEEKMN	EMBANKED	ABDEERTY	BETRAYED	ABDEHLMS	SHAMBLED
ABDEEKMR	BEDMAKER	ABDEERWY	BEWRAYED	ABDEHLOT	BOLTHEAD
	EMBARKED	ABDEESST	BASSETED	ABDEHLRS	HALBERDS
ABDEEKNR	BARKENED		BESTEADS	ABDEHMNO	HAMBONED
	BEDARKEN	ABDEFHOO	BOOFHEAD	ABDEHMOR	RHABDOME
ABDEEKNV	BEKNAVED	ABDEFIIS	BASIFIED	ABDEHMRU	RHUMBAED
ABDEEKPR	PREBAKED	ABDEFILN	FINDABLE	ABDEHMSU	AMBUSHED
ABDEEKRR	DEBARKER	ABDEFLLO	FOLDABLE	ABDEHNTU	UNBATHED
ABDEELLL	LABELLED	ABDEFLNU	FUNDABLE	ABDEHORR	ABHORRED
ABDEELLM	EMBALLED		UNFABLED		HARBORED
ABDEELLN	LENDABLE	ABDEFLOR	FORDABLE	ABDEHOSW	BESHADOW
ABDEELLT	BALLETED	ABDEFLST	FLATBEDS		BOWHEADS
ABDEELLW	WELDABLE	ABDEFLSU	LEAFBUDS	ABDEHRST	BREADTHS
ABDEELMM	EMBALMED	ABDEFNRU	FABURDEN	ABDEHSSU	SUBHEADS
ABDEELMN	MENDABLE	ABDEFOSS	SOFABEDS	ABDEHTTU	BUTTHEAD
ABDEELMS	BELDAMES	ABDEFRRY	FRYBREAD	ABDEIIRT	DIATRIBE
	BEMEDALS	ABDEFRSW	BEDWARFS	ABDEIKMR	IMBARKED
ABDEELMU	BEMAULED	ABDEGGIL	DIGGABLE	ABDEIKNS	BANKSIDE
ABDEELMZ	EMBLAZED	ABDEGGNU	UNBAGGED	ABDEIKNU	BAUDEKIN
ABDEELNS	SENDABLE	ABDEGHIS	BIGHEADS	ABDEILLR	BRAILLED
ABDEELNT	BANDELET	ABDEGHRS	BEGHARDS	ABDEILLS	SLIDABLE
ABDEELNV	VENDABLE	ABDEGIJN	BEJADING	ABDEILMM	DIMMABLE
ABDEELOR	ERODABLE	ABDEGILM	GIMBALED		IMBALMED
	LEEBOARD	ABDEGILN	BLINDAGE	ABDEILMN	MANDIBLE
ABDEELOS	ALBEDOES	ABDEGILU	GUIDABLE	ABDEILMS	SEMIBALD
ABDEELPT	BEDPLATE	ABDEGIMT	GAMBITED	ABDEILMZ	IMBLAZED
ABDEELRR	BARRELED	ABDEGINO	GABIONED	ABDEILNR	BILANDER
ABDEELRS	BEDERALS	ABDEGINR	BEARDING	ABDEILNT	BIDENTAL
ABDEELRV	DEVERBAL		BREADING	ABDEILNW	WINDABLE
ABDEELRZ	BLAZERED	ABDEGINS	BEADINGS	ABDEILNY	DENIABLY
ABDEELSV	BESLAVED		DEBASING	ABDEILOV	VOIDABLE
ABDEELTT	BATTELED	ABDEGINT	DEBATING	ABDEILOX	OXIDABLE
	TABLETED	ABDEGINZ	BEDAZING	ABDEILPP	DIPPABLE
ABDEELZZ	BEDAZZLE	ABDEGIPP	BAGPIPED	ABDEILPS	PIEBALDS
ABDEEMNO	BEMOANED	ABDEGIRR	ABRIDGER	ABDEILRS	BEDRAILS
ABDEEMNS	BEADSMEN	ABDEGIRS	ABRIDGES		DISABLER
	BEDESMAN		BRIGADES		RAILBEDS
ABDEEMRR	EMBARRED	ABDEGLMO	GAMBOLED	ABDEILRT	LIBRATED
ABDEEMRS	EMBREADS	ABDEGLNR	BRANGLED	ABDEILRV	DRIVABLE
ABDEEMRV	EMBRAVED	ABDEGLOT	GLOBATED	ABDEILRY	DIABLERY

ABDEILSS	DISABLES	**ABDELNOR**	BANDEROL	**ABDEPSSY**	BYPASSED
ABDEILST	BALDIEST	**ABDELNOU**	UNDOABLE	**ABDERRSU**	ABSURDER
	BLADIEST	**ABDELNOZ**	BLAZONED	**ABDERSST**	DABSTERS
ABDEILSU	AUDIBLES	**ABDELNRY**	BENADRYL	**ABDERSSU**	SUBEDARS
ABDEILSY	BIASEDLY		BYLANDER		SURBASED
ABDEILTU	DUTIABLE	**ABDELNSS**	BALDNESS	**ABDERSTU**	SURBATED
ABDEILTU	BIVALVED	**ABDELNST**	BLANDEST	**ABDERSTW**	BEDSTRAW
ABDEIMNR	BRIDEMAN	**ABDELORU**	LABOURED	**ABDERSTY**	DRYBEATS
ABDEIMOO	AMOEBOID	**ABDELOSV**	ABSOLVED	**ABDERTUW**	DRAWTUBE
ABDEIMOR	AMBEROID	**ABDELOSW**	DOWSABEL	**ABDESUWY**	SUBWAYED
ABDEIMRR	IMBARRED	**ABDELPSY**	PYEBALDS	**ABDFHINS**	BANDFISH
ABDEIMRS	EMBRAIDS	**ABDELRRS**	DRABLERS	**ABDFILOR**	FORBIDAL
ABDEINNR	ENDBRAIN	**ABDELRSU**	DURABLES	**ABDFIMRR**	BIRDFARM
ABDEINOR	DEBONAIR	**ABDELRTT**	BRATTLED	**ABDFIRST**	FATBIRDS
ABDEINOS	BEDSONIA	**ABDELSTU**	SUBLATED	**ABDFLOOT**	FOLDBOAT
ABDEINOT	OBTAINED	**ABDEMNNS**	BANDSMEN	**ABDFNORU**	FUNBOARD
ABDEINRS	BRANDIES	**ABDEMNNY**	BANDYMEN	**ABDFRSUW**	SUBDWARF
	BRANDISE	**ABDEMNOR**	BOARDMEN	**ABDGGORS**	BOGGARDS
ABDEINST	BANDIEST	**ABDEMNOS**	ABDOMENS	**ABDGHINR**	HANGBIRD
ABDEINSU	UNBIASED	**ABDEMORT**	BROMATED	**ABDGIINR**	BRAIDING
ABDEINSW	BEDAWINS	**ABDEMRSU**	BERMUDAS	**ABDGIINS**	ABIDINGS
ABDEINTU	UNBAITED	**ABDEMRTU**	DRUMBEAT	**ABDGILNN**	BLANDING
ABDEIOTV	OBVIATED		UMBRATED	**ABDGILNR**	BARDLING
ABDEIPRT	BIPARTED	**ABDENNNU**	UNBANNED	**ABDGILNS**	BLADINGS
ABDEIPST	BAPTISED	**ABDENNOS**	NOSEBAND	**ABDGILNU**	BLAUDING
ABDEIPTZ	BAPTIZED	**ABDENOOT**	BATOONED	**ABDGILOR**	GAOLBIRD
ABDEIRRS	BRAIDERS	**ABDENORS**	BANDORES	**ABDGIMRU**	GUIMBARD
ABDEIRSS	SEABIRDS		BROADENS	**ABDGINNR**	BRANDING
	SIDEBARS	**ABDENORW**	RAWBONED	**ABDGINNS**	BANDINGS
ABDEIRST	BARDIEST	**ABDENORY**	BONEYARD	**ABDGINNY**	BANDYING
	BRAIDEST	**ABDENOTW**	DOWNBEAT	**ABDGINOR**	ABORDING
	RABIDEST	**ABDENRRS**	BRANDERS		BOARDING
	REDBAITS		REBRANDS	**ABDGINRS**	BRIGANDS
	TRIBADES	**ABDENRRU**	UNBARRED	**ABDGINST**	DINGBATS
ABDEIRSU	DAUBRIES	**ABDENRSS**	DRABNESS	**ABDGINSU**	DAUBINGS
ABDEIRSW	BAWDRIES	**ABDENRST**	BANDSTER	**ABDGINSW**	WINDBAGS
	DAWBRIES		BARTENDS	**ABDGIRST**	DIRTBAGS
ABDEIRSX	AXEBIRDS	**ABDENRTU**	BREADNUT	**ABDGLNOS**	BOGLANDS
ABDEIRTV	VIBRATED		TURBANED	**ABDGLOOR**	LOGBOARD
ABDEISST	BASTIDES	**ABDENSSU**	SUBDEANS	**ABDGLSUY**	LADYBUGS
ABDEISSU	DISABUSE	**ABDENSTU**	UNBASTED	**ABDHHSSU**	SHADBUSH
	SUBIDEAS	**ABDENSUU**	UNABUSED	**ABDHIIST**	ADHIBITS
ABDEISTU	DAUBIEST	**ABDENSWY**	BENDWAYS		DISHABIT
ABDEISTW	BAWDIEST	**ABDENTTU**	DEBUTANT	**ABDHILLN**	HANDBILL
ABDEITTU	DUBITATE	**ABDEOORW**	BEARWOOD	**ABDHILNS**	BLANDISH
ABDEJNOW	JAWBONED	**ABDEOPRR**	PREBOARD	**ABDHINRS**	BRANDISH
ABDEKLSW	SKEWBALD	**ABDEOPRT**	PROBATED	**ABDHIORS**	BROADISH
ABDEKNNU	UNBANKED	**ABDEORRS**	ADSORBER	**ABDHIPRS**	BARDSHIP
ABDEKNRU	UNBARKED		BOARDERS	**ABDHIRTY**	BIRTHDAY
	UNBRAKED		REBOARDS	**ABDHJNOS**	HANDJOBS
ABDEKNSU	SUNBAKED	**ABDEORRU**	ARBOURED	**ABDHKNOO**	HANDBOOK
ABDEKOOR	ABROOKED	**ABDEORRW**	DRAWBORE	**ABDHLNSU**	BUSHLAND
ABDEKOOT	DATEBOOK		WARDROBE	**ABDHLORW**	BLOWHARD
ABDEKORW	BEADWORK	**ABDEORST**	BROADEST	**ABDHLOSW**	SHADBLOW
ABDEKORY	KEYBOARD	**ABDEORSW**	SOWBREAD	**ABDHMORS**	RHABDOMS
ABDEKOTU	OUTBAKED	**ABDEORTU**	OBDURATE	**ABDHMOTU**	BADMOUTH
ABDELLMO	MOLDABLE		TABOURED	**ABDHMSTU**	MUDBATHS
ABDELLOR	BEADROLL	**ABDEORUX**	BORDEAUX	**ABDHNORS**	BODHRANS
ABDELLOT	BALLOTED	**ABDEOSTU**	BOUTADES	**ABDHNSSU**	HUSBANDS
ABDELMNU	UNBLAMED	**ABDEPRSU**	SUPERBAD	**ABDHOORT**	HARDBOOT
ABDELMPS	BEDLAMPS	**ABDEPRUY**	UPBRAYED	**ABDIIJLR**	JAILBIRD

ABDIILLR	BILLIARD	ABDMRSUY	MARYBUDS	ABEEGMNR	BARGEMEN
ABDIILRR	RAILBIRD	ABDNNNOR	NONBRAND	ABEEGMRT	BREGMATE
ABDIIMNR	MIDBRAIN	ABDNOORS	BRADOONS	ABEEGMTY	MEGABYTE
ABDIIMSU	BASIDIUM	ABDNOPRS	PROBANDS	ABEEGNTT	BAGNETTE
ABDIINOS	ANOBIIDS	ABDNORSU	BAUDRONS	ABEEGOSZ	GAZEBOES
	OBSIDIAN	ABDNORUY	BOUNDARY	ABEEGPSW	WEBPAGES
ABDIINRR	RAINBIRD	ABDNOSSY	SANDBOYS	ABEEGRRS	GERBERAS
ABDIINTT	BANDITTI	ABDNRRSU	SANDBURR	ABEEGRST	ABSTERGE
ABDIIORT	ORIBATID	ABDNRSSU	SANDBURS	ABEEGRSU	AUBERGES
ABDIIRTY	RABIDITY	ABDNRSTU	TURBANDS	ABEEGRSW	BREWAGES
ABDIJRSY	JAYBIRDS	ABDNSSTY	STANDBYS	ABEEGTTU	BAGUETTE
ABDIKLNR	BLINKARD	ABDNSTUU	BUTSUDAN	ABEEHILR	HIREABLE
ABDIKLOU	KILOBAUD	ABDOORSW	BARWOODS	ABEEHINT	THEBAINE
ABDIKNSW	BAWDKINS	ABDOORTU	OUTBOARD	ABEEHIRS	HEBRAISE
ABDIKRSS	DISBARKS	ABDOOSSW	BASSWOOD	ABEEHIRZ	HEBRAIZE
ABDILLRY	BRIDALLY	ABDOOSWY	BAYWOODS	ABEEHLLL	HEELBALL
	RIBALDLY	ABDRSSTU	BUSTARDS	ABEEHLLP	HELPABLE
ABDILOOS	DIABOLOS	ABDRSUZZ	BUZZARDS	ABEEHLLR	BEERHALL
ABDILORS	LABROIDS	ABEEEFLR	REEFABLE		HAREBELL
ABDILOST	BLASTOID	ABEEEFRS	FREEBASE	ABEEHLRS	HEELBARS
	TABLOIDS	ABEEEGRS	BARGEESE	ABEEHLSV	BEHALVES
ABDILOTY	TABLOIDY		BEERAGES	ABEEHMSS	BESHAMES
ABDILRRY	RIBALDRY	ABEEEGRV	BEVERAGE	ABEEHMST	EMBATHES
ABDILRSW	AWLBIRDS	ABEEEHTT	HEBETATE	ABEEHNNS	HENBANES
ABDILRZZ	BLIZZARD	ABEEEKLP	KEEPABLE	ABEEHNPP	BEHAPPEN
ABDILSTU	SUBTIDAL	ABEEELLP	PEELABLE	ABEEHNSS	BANSHEES
ABDIMNRS	MISBRAND	ABEEELLR	REELABLE		SHEBEANS
ABDIMORS	AMBROIDS	ABEEEMSY	EYEBEAMS	ABEEHNTT	HEBETANT
ABDIMRSS	BARDISMS	ABEEENRT	TENEBRAE	ABEEHORS	RHEOBASE
ABDIMRSY	MAYBIRDS	ABEEENRV	BEREAVEN	ABEEHQTU	BEQUEATH
ABDINOPR	PINBOARD	ABEEENST	ABSENTEE	ABEEHRRT	BREATHER
ABDINORS	INBOARDS	ABEEERRT	TEREBRAE	ABEEHRST	BREATHES
ABDINORU	AIRBOUND	ABEEERRV	BEREAVER		HARTBEES
ABDINOST	BANDITOS	ABEEERSV	BEREAVES	ABEEHRSV	BEHAVERS
ABDINOTY	ANTIBODY	ABEEFFNO	BANOFFEE	ABEEHSTY	EYEBATHS
ABDINRST	ANTBIRDS	ABEEFFTU	BEAUFFET	ABEEIKKL	BEAKLIKE
ABDINRSU	UNBRAIDS	ABEEFILL	FILEABLE	ABEEIKLL	LIKEABLE
ABDINRTY	BANDITRY	ABEEFILN	FINEABLE	ABEEIKLM	BEAMLIKE
ABDIOSUU	SUBAUDIO	ABEEFILR	AFEBRILE	ABEEIKLN	BEANLIKE
ABDIPRSU	UPBRAIDS		BALEFIRE	ABEEIKLR	BEARLIKE
ABDIRRSW	WARBIRDS		FIREABLE	ABEEIKLT	BAKELITE
ABDIRRUY	RIBAUDRY	ABEEFILS	FEASIBLE	ABEEIKRS	BAKERIES
ABDJMOOR	DOORJAMB	ABEEFILT	FLEABITE	ABEEIKRT	TIEBREAK
ABDKLNOO	BOOKLAND	ABEEFIRS	FIREBASE	ABEEIKST	BEAKIEST
ABDKNOOS	BANDOOKS	ABEEFIST	TABEFIES	ABEEILLN	LIENABLE
ABDKOOSY	DAYBOOKS	ABEEFLLL	FELLABLE		LINEABLE
ABDKORSY	SKYBOARD	ABEEFLLN	BEFALLEN	ABEEILLR	RELIABLE
ABDLLNOS	SLOBLAND	ABEEFLMS	FLAMBEES	ABEEILLV	LEVIABLE
ABDLLNUW	BUNDWALL	ABEEFLOS	BEEFALOS		LIVEABLE
ABDLLORS	BOLLARDS	ABEEFORR	FOREBEAR	ABEEILLX	EXILABLE
ABDLNORS	BANDROLS	ABEEFSTU	BEAUFETS	ABEEILMN	MINEABLE
ABDLNOSU	SUBNODAL	ABEEGHRS	HERBAGES	ABEEILMS	BELAMIES
ABDLOSSU	BUSLOADS	ABEEGHRT	BERTHAGE	ABEEILNN	BIENNALE
ABDLOSYY	LADYBOYS	ABEEGILV	GIVEABLE	ABEEILNP	PLEBEIAN
ABDLRSUU	SUBDURAL	ABEEGINR	BAREGINE	ABEEILNS	BASELINE
ABDLRSUY	ABSURDLY		BERGENIA	ABEEILNU	BANLIEUE
ABDLSSUU	SUBDUALS	ABEEGIRV	VERBIAGE	ABEEILNV	ENVIABLE
ABDLSTUU	SUBADULT	ABEEGLLR	GABELLER	ABEEILPW	WIPEABLE
ABDMNNOS	BONDSMAN	ABEEGLLS	GABELLES	ABEEILPX	EXPIABLE
ABDMNOUW	MAWBOUND	ABEEGLRS	BEAGLERS	ABEEILRR	BLEARIER
ABDMOOPR	MOPBOARD	ABEEGLTT	GETTABLE	ABEEILRT	LIBERATE

ABEEILRW	BEWAILER	ABEELNOP	BEANPOLE	ABEENSTW	NEWSBEAT
ABEEILSS	SEISABLE		OPENABLE	ABEEORRV	OVERBEAR
ABEEILST	SEABLITE	ABEELNOV	OVENABLE	ABEEORSS	BOREASES
ABEEILSV	EVASIBLE	ABEELNRS	ENABLERS	ABEEORST	ABORTEES
ABEEILSZ	SEIZABLE	ABEELNRT	RENTABLE		REBATOES
	SIZEABLE	ABEELNST	NESTABLE	ABEEORTV	OVERBEAT
ABEEILTV	EVITABLE	ABEELNTT	NETTABLE	ABEEOSTX	TEABOXES
ABEEILVW	VIEWABLE	ABEELNTU	TUNEABLE	ABEEPRRU	UPBEARER
ABEEIMRS	AMBERIES	ABEELOPR	OPERABLE	ABEEPRRY	PEABERRY
ABEEIMRT	AMBERITE		ROPEABLE	ABEEPTTY	PETABYTE
ABEEIMST	BEAMIEST	ABEELOPS	POSEABLE	ABEEQSUU	USQUEBAE
ABEEINST	BETAINES	ABEELORS	EARLOBES	ABEERRRT	BARTERER
ABEEINTY	AYENBITE	ABEELORV	OVERABLE	ABEERRST	REBATERS
ABEEIPRS	BEPRAISE	ABEELORX	EXORABLE		TABRERES
ABEEIRTT	BATTERIE	ABEELOTT	TOTEABLE		TEREBRAS
ABEEIRTV	BREVIATE	ABEELOTV	VOTEABLE	ABEERRTT	BARRETTE
ABEEISST	BEASTIES	ABEELPRS	BEPEARLS		BATTERER
ABEEISSV	ABESSIVE	ABEELPTT	PETTABLE		BERRETTA
ABEEISTT	BEATIEST	ABEELPTY	TYPEABLE	ABEERRTV	VERTEBRA
ABEEISTU	BEAUTIES	ABEELRST	ARBELEST	ABEERRTY	BETRAYER
ABEEITUX	BEAUXITE		BLEAREST		TEABERRY
ABEEJMOR	JAMBOREE		BLEATERS	ABEERRWY	BEWRAYER
ABEEKLOT	KEELBOAT		RESTABLE	ABEERSTT	ABETTERS
ABEEKLSS	BEAKLESS		RETABLES		BERETTAS
ABEEKLST	BLEAKEST	ABEELRSU	REUSABLE	ABEERSTU	SUBERATE
ABEEKMNR	BRAKEMEN	ABEELRSV	BESLAVER	ABEERTTT	BETATTER
	EMBANKER		SERVABLE	ABEERTTY	TERABYTE
ABEEKMRR	REEMBARK	ABEELRSY	BELAYERS	ABEESTXY	EXABYTES
ABEEKNSV	BEKNAVES	ABEELRTT	BATTELER	ABEESZZZ	BEZAZZES
ABEEKNSY	EYEBANKS	ABEELRTU	BATELEUR	ABEETTUX	EXTUBATE
ABEEKOOP	PEEKABOO		BLEUATRE	ABEFFKOR	BREAKOFF
ABEEKOPS	PEEKABOS	ABEELSSS	BASELESS	ABEFFKOS	BAKEOFFS
ABEEKORV	OVERBAKE	ABEELSST	BATELESS	ABEFFLRS	BAFFLERS
ABEEKPRS	BARKEEPS		BEATLESS	ABEFFOST	OFFBEATS
	PREBAKES	ABEELSSU	SUBLEASE	ABEFGILS	FILABEGS
ABEEKPSS	BESPEAKS	ABEELSSV	BESLAVES	ABEFGILT	GIFTABLE
ABEEKRRS	BREAKERS	ABEELSTT	SEATBELT	ABEFGLLR	BERGFALL
ABEEKRST	BESTREAK		TESTABLE	ABEFGSST	GABFESTS
ABEELLLR	LABELLER	ABEELSTW	STEWABLE	ABEFHILS	FISHABLE
ABEELLLS	SELLABLE	ABEELTTW	WETTABLE	ABEFHOOT	HOOFBEAT
ABEELLLT	TELLABLE	ABEEMMNR	MEMBRANE	ABEFIIMR	FIMBRIAE
ABEELLMT	MELTABLE	ABEEMMRU	BUMMAREE	ABEFIIRS	BASIFIER
ABEELLNP	BALLPEEN	ABEEMNOR	BEMOANER	ABEFIISS	BASIFIES
ABEELLOT	BALLOTEE	ABEEMNST	BASEMENT	ABEFILLL	FALLIBLE
ABEELLOV	LOVEABLE	ABEEMNTT	ABETMENT		FILLABLE
ABEELLRS	LABELERS		BATEMENT	ABEFILLM	FILMABLE
	RELABELS	ABEEMRSS	BESMEARS	ABEFILLO	FOILABLE
ABEELLSY	EYEBALLS	ABEEMRSV	EMBRAVES	ABEFILLR	FIREBALL
ABEELLTT	LETTABLE	ABEENNRT	BANNERET	ABEFILLT	LIFTABLE
ABEELMMR	EMBALMER	ABEENNRU	EBURNEAN	ABEFILOT	LIFEBOAT
	EMMARBLE	ABEENNSW	BAWNEENS	ABEFILRS	BARFLIES
ABEELMNO	BONEMEAL	ABEENNTU	UNBEATEN	ABEFILSU	FABULISE
ABEELMOV	MOVEABLE	ABEENORS	SEABORNE	ABEFILSY	FEASIBLY
ABEELMPR	PREAMBLE	ABEENOTZ	BENZOATE	ABEFILTT	FITTABLE
ABEELMRT	ATREMBLE	ABEENRRR	BARRENER	ABEFILUZ	FABULIZE
ABEELMRZ	EMBLAZER	ABEENRRT	BANTERER	ABEFINNR	FIBRANNE
ABEELMSS	ASSEMBLE	ABEENRSS	BARENESS	ABEFINSU	BEAUFINS
	BEAMLESS	ABEENRST	ABSENTER	ABEFIORT	BIFORATE
ABEELMST	BEAMLETS	ABEENRSV	VERBENAS		FIREBOAT
ABEELMSZ	EMBLAZES	ABEENRTT	BATTENER	ABEFIRRT	FIREBRAT
ABEELMTT	EMBATTLE	ABEENSSS	BASENESS	ABEFIRST	FIBRATES

ABEFITUY	BEAUTIFY	ABEGIMNY	EMBAYING	ABEHIKLS	BLEAKISH
ABEFLLMU	BLAMEFUL	ABEGIMRS	GAMBIERS	ABEHILLR	HAIRBELL
ABEFLLRU	FURLABLE	ABEGIMST	MEGABITS	ABEHILNR	HIBERNAL
ABEFLLTU	TABLEFUL	ABEGIMUX	GIAMBEUX	ABEHILRS	BLASHIER
ABEFLMOR	FORMABLE	ABEGINOR	ABORIGEN	ABEHILTT	HITTABLE
ABEFLNRU	FUNEBRAL	ABEGINOS	BEGONIAS		TITHABLE
ABEFLNSY	FLYBANES	ABEGINRR	BARREING	ABEHIMMS	MEMSAHIB
ABEFLOTU	OUTFABLE		BERRIGAN	ABEHIMNO	BOHEMIAN
ABEFLRSU	SURFABLE	ABEGINRS	BEARINGS	ABEHIMOS	BOHEMIAS
ABEFMRSU	SUBFRAME		SABERING		OBEAHISM
ABEFOORT	BAREFOOT	ABEGINRT	BERATING	ABEHIMST	IMBATHES
ABEFORRS	FORBEARS		REBATING	ABEHINRS	BANISHER
ABEFORSY	FOREBAYS		TABERING	ABEHINSS	BANISHES
ABEGGGIN	ABEGGING	ABEGINRW	BEWARING		BANSHIES
ABEGGHLU	HUGGABLE	ABEGINRY	BERAYING	ABEHINST	ABSINTHE
ABEGGILN	BEAGLING	ABEGINST	BEASTING	ABEHIOPU	EUPHOBIA
ABEGGINZ	BEGAZING		BEATINGS	ABEHIORV	BEHAVIOR
ABEGGIRR	BRAGGIER	ABEGINSY	EBAYINGS	ABEHIRRS	BRASHIER
ABEGGIST	BAGGIEST	ABEGINTT	ABETTING	ABEHISTU	HABITUES
ABEGGITY	GIGABYTE	ABEGINTW	WINGBEAT	ABEHISTZ	ZABTIEHS
ABEGGLLU	LUGGABLE	ABEGIOSS	BIOGASES	ABEHJORS	JOBSHARE
ABEGGLRS	BLAGGERS	ABEGIPPR	BAGPIPER	ABEHKLLW	HAWKBELL
ABEGGLRY	BEGGARLY	ABEGIPPS	BAGPIPES	ABEHKNOR	HORNBEAK
ABEGGMOS	GAMBOGES	ABEGKLSU	BULKAGES	ABEHKNST	BETHANKS
ABEGGNSU	BUGGANES	ABEGKORS	BROKAGES	ABEHKOPS	BAKESHOP
ABEGGRRS	BRAGGERS		GROSBEAK	ABEHKRSU	HAUBERKS
ABEGGRST	BRAGGEST	ABEGKOSS	BOSKAGES	ABEHKSTU	KETUBAHS
ABEGGRSU	BURGAGES	ABEGLLLU	GLUEBALL	ABEHLLRT	BETHRALL
ABEGHILP	PHILABEG		GULLABLE	ABEHLMMU	HUMMABLE
ABEGHILR	ALBERGHI	ABEGLLOR	BARGELLO	ABEHLMSS	SHAMBLES
ABEGHINO	OBEAHING	ABEGLMOR	BEGLAMOR	ABEHLNOT	BENTHOAL
ABEGHINT	BEATHING	ABEGLMRS	GAMBLERS	ABEHLNTU	HUNTABLE
ABEGHINV	BEHAVING		GAMBRELS	ABEHLOSW	SHOWABLE
ABEGHNSS	SHEBANGS	ABEGLMUY	MEALYBUG	ABEHLOTU	TABOULEH
ABEGHORR	BEGORRAH	ABEGLNRS	BRANGLES	ABEHLOTY	HYLOBATE
ABEGHOSU	BAGHOUSE	ABEGLORW	GROWABLE	ABEHLRST	BLATHERS
ABEGHRRY	HAGBERRY	ABEGLRRS	GARBLERS		HALBERTS
ABEGHRST	BARGHEST	ABEGLRSS	GARBLESS	ABEHLSSS	BASHLESS
ABEGHRSU	BEARHUGS	ABEGLRSU	BLAGUERS	ABEHLSST	BATHLESS
ABEGIIMS	BIGAMIES	ABEGLRUU	BLAGUEUR	ABEHMNOR	HORNBEAM
ABEGIINO	IBOGAINE	ABEGLSTU	GUSTABLE	ABEHMNOS	HAMBONES
ABEGIJTU	BIJUGATE	ABEGMNOS	GAMBESON	ABEHMNST	BASHMENT
ABEGIKNR	BERAKING	ABEGMNOY	BOGEYMAN	ABEHMOOR	REHOBOAM
	BREAKING		MONEYBAG	ABEHMRSU	AMBUSHER
ABEGIKNT	BETAKING	ABEGMORT	BERGAMOT	ABEHMSSU	AMBUSHES
ABEGILLN	LABELING	ABEGMRSU	UMBRAGES	ABEHMSTU	BUSHMEAT
ABEGILMN	EMBALING	ABEGNNST	BANTENGS	ABEHNRSY	ABHENRYS
ABEGILNN	ENABLING	ABEGNORS	BEGROANS	ABEHNSTU	SUNBATHE
ABEGILNR	BLEARING	ABEGNOSS	NOSEBAGS	ABEHORRR	ABHORRER
ABEGILNS	SIGNABLE	ABEGNRST	BANGSTER		HARBORER
	SINGABLE	ABEGNRTU	BURGANET	ABEHORST	BATHORSE
ABEGILNT	BELATING	ABEGNSTU	SUBAGENT	ABEHOSST	BATHOSES
	BLEATING	ABEGOORS	BARGOOSE	ABEHOSTX	HATBOXES
	TANGIBLE	ABEGOPSY	PAGEBOYS	ABEHOSXY	HAYBOXES
ABEGILNY	BELAYING	ABEGOSTT	BOTTEGAS	ABEHPSSU	SUBPHASE
ABEGILOT	OBLIGATE	ABEGOSUY	BUOYAGES	ABEHRSST	BRASHEST
ABEGIMNN	BENAMING	ABEGRRSU	GARBURES	ABEHRTUY	EURYBATH
ABEGIMNR	BREAMING	ABEGRRUV	BURGRAVE	ABEIIKLS	KIELBASI
ABEGIMNS	BEAMINGS	ABEGRSST	BARGESTS	ABEIILLS	BAILLIES
	EMBASING	ABEGRSTU	BARGUEST	ABEIILMT	IMITABLE
	MISBEGAN	ABEGSSTU	SUBSTAGE	ABEIILNN	BIENNIAL

ABEIILNR	BILINEAR		LISTABLE		SUASIBLE
ABEIILNV	INVIABLE	ABEILLTT	TILTABLE	ABEILSTU	SUITABLE
ABEIILPT	PITIABLE	ABEILMMR	IMBALMER	ABEILSTY	BEASTILY
ABEIILRR	LIBRAIRE	ABEILMNS	BAILSMEN	ABEILSUX	BISEXUAL
ABEIILRS	BISERIAL		BIMENSAL	ABEILSVV	BIVALVES
ABEIILST	ALBITISE	ABEILMNT	BAILMENT	ABEILSYZ	SIZEABLY
	SIBILATE	ABEILMOR	BROMELIA	ABEIMNPS	PEMBINAS
ABEIILTV	VITIABLE	ABEILMRR	MARBLIER	ABEIMNRS	MIRBANES
ABEIILTZ	ALBITIZE	ABEILMRS	REMBLAIS	ABEIMNST	AMBIENTS
ABEIINRR	BRAINIER	ABEILMRW	WAMBLIER	ABEIMORS	BIRAMOSE
ABEIINRS	BINARIES	ABEILMSS	ABLEISMS	ABEIMORU	AEROBIUM
ABEIINST	BAINITES		MISSABLE	ABEIMRST	BARMIEST
ABEIJLNO	JOINABLE	ABEILMST	BALMIEST	ABEIMRSU	AUMBRIES
ABEIJLTU	JUBILATE		BIMETALS	ABEIMRTV	AMBIVERT
ABEIJMNN	BENJAMIN		LAMBIEST		VERBATIM
ABEIJMRS	JAMBIERS		TIMBALES	ABEIMSSU	IAMBUSES
ABEIJNSS	BASENJIS	ABEILMSU	BUMELIAS	ABEINNOS	BESONIAN
ABEIKLLL	KILLABLE	ABEILMSW	WEBMAILS	ABEINNOZ	BEZONIAN
ABEIKLLM	BALMLIKE	ABEILMSZ	IMBLAZES	ABEINNRR	BRANNIER
	LAMBLIKE	ABEILNNW	WINNABLE	ABEINNRU	INURBANE
ABEIKLLN	BALKLINE	ABEILNOP	OPINABLE	ABEINORR	AIRBORNE
	LINKABLE	ABEILNOT	TAILBONE	ABEINORS	BARONIES
ABEIKLLS	SLABLIKE	ABEILNPS	BIPLANES		SEAROBIN
ABEIKLLY	LIKEABLY	ABEILNPT	PINTABLE	ABEINORT	BARITONE
ABEIKLNR	BARNLIKE	ABEILNRS	RINSABLE		OBTAINER
ABEIKLNS	SINKABLE	ABEILNRU	RUINABLE		REOBTAIN
ABEIKLOS	KILOBASE	ABEILNSS	ALBINESS		TABORINE
ABEIKLOT	BOATLIKE		BASSLINE	ABEINOST	BOTANIES
ABEIKLRU	BAULKIER		LESBIANS		BOTANISE
ABEIKLSS	KISSABLE	ABEILNST	INSTABLE		NIOBATES
ABEIKLST	BALKIEST	ABEILNSU	SABULINE		OBEISANT
ABEIKLSY	KIELBASY	ABEILNTV	BIVALENT	ABEINOTZ	BOTANIZE
ABEIKNNR	NINEBARK	ABEILNTY	BINATELY	ABEINPST	BEPAINTS
ABEIKNRR	BRANKIER	ABEILNUV	UNVIABLE	ABEINQSU	BASQUINE
ABEIKNRS	BEARSKIN	ABEILNVY	ENVIABLY	ABEINRRW	BRAWNIER
	INBREAKS	ABEILORR	BORRELIA	ABEINRST	ATEBRINS
ABEIKNST	BEATNIKS	ABEILORS	BOREALIS		BANISTER
	SNAKEBIT	ABEILORT	LABORITE		BARNIEST
ABEIKRST	BARKIEST	ABEILOTV	BLOVIATE	ABEINRSU	ANBURIES
	BRAKIEST	ABEILPPR	RIPPABLE		URBANISE
	BREASKIT	ABEILPPT	TIPPABLE	ABEINRSW	WEBINARS
ABEIKSWY	BIKEWAYS	ABEILPRT	PARTIBLE	ABEINRSZ	ZEBRINAS
ABEILLLM	MILLABLE	ABEILPRZ	PRIZABLE	ABEINRTU	BRAUNITE
ABEILLLT	TILLABLE	ABEILPSS	PASSIBLE		URBANITE
ABEILLLW	WILLABLE	ABEILPST	EPIBLAST	ABEINRUZ	URBANIZE
ABEILLMM	LIMBMEAL	ABEILRRU	REBURIAL	ABEINSSS	BIASNESS
ABEILLMS	MISLABEL	ABEILRRW	BRAWLIER	ABEINSST	BASINETS
ABEILLNT	LIBELANT	ABEILRST	BLASTIER		BASSINET
ABEILLOS	ISOLABLE		LIBRATES		BESAINTS
	LOBELIAS		TABLIERS		BESTAINS
ABEILLOV	VIOLABLE	ABEILRSY	BILAYERS	ABEINSSU	UNBIASES
ABEILLPS	LAPSIBLE	ABEILRTT	TITRABLE	ABEINSTT	TABINETS
ABEILLQU	LIQUABLE	ABEILRTW	WRITABLE	ABEINTTU	INTUBATE
ABEILLRR	BRAILLER	ABEILRYY	BIYEARLY	ABEIORRS	ARBORISE
ABEILLRS	BALLSIER	ABEILSST	ABLEISTS	ABEIORRZ	ARBORIZE
	BRAILLES		ASTILBES	ABEIORSS	ISOBARES
	LIBERALS		BASTILES	ABEIORST	SABOTIER
ABEILLRY	BERYLLIA		BESTIALS	ABEIORTV	ABORTIVE
	BLEARILY		BLASTIES	ABEIOSSS	ISOBASES
	RELIABLY		STABILES	ABEIOSTV	OBVIATES
ABEILLST	BASTILLE	ABEILSSU	ISSUABLE	ABEIPRRS	SPARERIB

ABEIPRST	BAPTISER	**ABEKOORY**	YEARBOOK	**ABELNRUY**	URBANELY
ABEIPRTZ	BAPTIZER	**ABEKORTU**	BREAKOUT	**ABELNRYZ**	BRAZENLY
ABEIPSST	BAPTISES		OUTBREAK	**ABELNSTU**	ABLUENTS
ABEIPSTZ	BAPTIZES	**ABEKOSTU**	OUTBAKES		UNSTABLE
ABEIRRRS	BARRIERS	**ABEKPRSU**	BREAKUPS	**ABELNSTY**	ABSENTLY
ABEIRRSS	BRASIERS		UPBREAKS	**ABELNSUU**	UNUSABLE
	BRASSIER	**ABEKRSTY**	BASKETRY	**ABELNTUY**	TUNEABLY
ABEIRRST	ARBITERS	**ABELLLMU**	LABELLUM	**ABELOOTY**	TABOOLEY
	BARRIEST	**ABELLLOR**	ROLLABLE	**ABELOPRT**	PORTABLE
	RAREBITS	**ABELLLOT**	TOLLABLE	**ABELOPRU**	POURABLE
ABEIRRSZ	BIZARRES	**ABELLLSY**	SYLLABLE	**ABELOPRV**	PROVABLE
	BRAZIERS	**ABELLMOR**	OMBRELLA	**ABELOPRY**	OPERABLY
ABEIRRTT	BIRRETTA	**ABELLMRU**	UMBELLAR	**ABELOPST**	POTABLES
	BRATTIER		UMBRELLA	**ABELOPTT**	POTTABLE
ABEIRRVY	BREVIARY	**ABELLNNO**	BALLONNE	**ABELOQTU**	QUOTABLE
ABEIRRYZ	BRAZIERY	**ABELLNOS**	BONSELLA	**ABELORRS**	LABORERS
ABEIRSSS	BRASSIES	**ABELLNOT**	BALLONET	**ABELORRU**	LABOURER
ABEIRSSU	AIRBUSES	**ABELLNRU**	RUBELLAN		RUBEOLAR
ABEIRSTT	BIRETTAS	**ABELLNST**	NETBALLS	**ABELORST**	BLOATERS
ABEIRSTV	VIBRATES	**ABELLOPW**	PLOWABLE		SORTABLE
ABEIRSTW	WARBIEST	**ABELLORT**	BALLOTER		STORABLE
ABEIRSTY	BESTIARY	**ABELLOSV**	SOLVABLE	**ABELORSU**	RUBEOLAS
	SYBARITE	**ABELLOTU**	LOBULATE	**ABELORSV**	ABSOLVER
ABEIRSUX	EXURBIAS	**ABELLOTY**	LOBATELY	**ABELOSSU**	SABULOSE
ABEIRTTY	YTTERBIA		OBLATELY	**ABELOSSV**	ABSOLVES
ABEISSST	BASSIEST	**ABELLOVY**	LOVEABLY	**ABELOSTU**	ABSOLUTE
ABEISSTT	BATISTES	**ABELLRSU**	RUBELLAS	**ABELOSTW**	BESTOWAL
ABEISTTT	BATTIEST	**ABELLRVY**	VERBALLY		STOWABLE
ABEISTUX	BAUXITES	**ABELLSTU**	BALLUTES		TEABOWLS
ABEISZZZ	BIZAZZES	**ABELMMSU**	SUMMABLE	**ABELOTTU**	OUTBLEAT
ABEITTTU	TITUBATE	**ABELMNNO**	NOBLEMAN	**ABELOTUZ**	OUTBLAZE
ABEJKLOU	KABELJOU	**ABELMNOZ**	EMBLAZON	**ABELPRTU**	PUBERTAL
ABEJLMPU	JUMPABLE	**ABELMNST**	SEMBLANT	**ABELQSUU**	SUBEQUAL
ABEJLSUY	BLUEJAYS	**ABELMNSU**	ALBUMENS	**ABELRRSW**	BRAWLERS
ABEJMNOS	JAMBONES		BLUESMAN		WARBLERS
	JOBNAMES	**ABELMOOT**	MOOTABLE	**ABELRRTU**	BARRULET
ABEJMOOR	JEROBOAM	**ABELMOSU**	ALBUMOSE	**ABELRSST**	BLASTERS
ABEJNORW	JAWBONER	**ABELMOSV**	MOVABLES		STABLERS
ABEJNOSW	JAWBONES	**ABELMOTY**	METABOLY	**ABELRSSY**	LABRYSES
ABEJOSWX	JAWBOXES	**ABELMOVY**	MOVEABLY	**ABELRSTT**	BATTLERS
ABEJRRSU	ABJURERS	**ABELMPTU**	PLUMBATE		BLATTERS
ABEKKKSU	BUKKAKES	**ABELMRRS**	MARBLERS		BRATTLES
ABEKLMOS	ABELMOSK		RAMBLERS	**ABELRSTU**	BALUSTER
	SMOKABLE	**ABELMRST**	LAMBERTS		RUSTABLE
ABEKLNOW	KNOWABLE	**ABELMSSY**	ASSEMBLY	**ABELRSTW**	BLEWARTS
ABEKLNRY	BANKERLY	**ABELNNOR**	BANNEROL	**ABELRSUZ**	ZEBRULAS
ABEKLNST	BLANKEST	**ABELNNRU**	RUNNABLE	**ABELRTTU**	BURLETTA
	BLANKETS	**ABELNORZ**	BLAZONER		REBUTTAL
ABEKLNTY	BLANKETY	**ABELNOSS**	BONSELAS	**ABELSSSU**	SUBSALES
ABEKLORW	WORKABLE	**ABELNOST**	NEOBLAST	**ABELSSTT**	STABLEST
ABEKLRSS	BARKLESS		NOTABLES	**ABELSSTU**	SUBLATES
ABEKLRSU	BAULKERS		STONABLE	**ABELSTUU**	SUBULATE
ABEKMNNS	BANKSMEN	**ABELNOSY**	BALONEYS	**ABELSTWY**	BELTWAYS
ABEKMNTU	BUNKMATE	**ABELNPRU**	PRUNABLE	**ABELTTUU**	TUBULATE
ABEKMSSU	SAMBUKES	**ABELNPSU**	SUBPANEL	**ABELTTUY**	BUTYLATE
ABEKNNOT	BANKNOTE	**ABELNQTU**	BLANQUET	**ABEMMNOO**	MOONBEAM
ABEKNORV	OVERBANK	**ABELNRRY**	BARRENLY	**ABEMNOST**	BOATSMEN
ABEKNRSU	UNBRAKES	**ABELNRSS**	BRANSLES	**ABEMNOTU**	UMBONATE
ABEKNSSU	SUNBAKES	**ABELNRST**	BRANTLES	**ABEMNOTW**	BATWOMEN
ABEKNSSY	SNEAKSBY	**ABELNRSY**	BLARNEYS	**ABEMNPRU**	PENUMBRA
ABEKOORS	ABROOKES	**ABELNRTU**	TURNABLE	**ABEMNRSY**	MYRBANES

ABEMNSSU	SUNBEAMS	**ABEQRSUU**	ARQUEBUS	**ABFOOSTY**	FOYBOATS
ABEMNSTU	SUBMENTA	**ABERRRTY**	BARRETRY	**ABFORSTU**	SURFBOAT
ABEMNSUY	SUNBEAMY	**ABERRSSU**	SABREURS	**ABFSSTTU**	TUBFASTS
ABEMNTTU	ABUTMENT	**ABERRSSU**	RUBASSES	**ABGGGILN**	BLAGGING
ABEMORRS	EMBRASOR	**ABERRTYY**	TAYBERRY	**ABGGGINR**	BRAGGING
ABEMORST	BROMATES	**ABERRWXY**	WAXBERRY	**ABGGGINS**	BAGGINGS
ABEMORSU	AMBEROUS	**ABERSSST**	BRASSETS	**ABGGIIST**	GIGABITS
ABEMORTZ	BAROMETZ	**ABERSSSU**	RUBASSES	**ABGGIJNN**	JINGBANG
ABEMOSTU	OUTBEAMS		SURBASES	**ABGGILMN**	GAMBLING
ABEMRSSW	BESWARMS	**ABERSSTU**	ABSTRUSE	**ABGGILNR**	GARBLING
ABENNORS	BARONNES		SURBATES	**ABGGNNUY**	GUNNYBAG
ABENNOTU	BUTANONE	**ABERSSTW**	WABSTERS	**ABGGNOOT**	TOBOGGAN
	NANOTUBE	**ABERSTTU**	ABUTTERS	**ABGGORST**	BOGGARTS
ABENNRRS	BRANNERS	**ABERSTUW**	WATERBUS	**ABGHHILL**	HIGHBALL
ABENOPSU	SUBPOENA	**ABERTTUY**	BUTYRATE	**ABGHIINT**	HABITING
ABENORSS	BARONESS	**ABESSSTT**	BASSETTS	**ABGHILMN**	HAMBLING
ABENORST	BARONETS	**ABESSSTU**	ASBESTUS	**ABGHINRS**	BRASHING
ABENORSZ	ZEBRANOS	**ABESSTTU**	SUBSTATE	**ABGHINSS**	BASHINGS
ABENORTT	BETATRON	**ABFFGILN**	BAFFLING	**ABGHINWZ**	WHIZBANG
ABENORTV	BEVATRON	**ABFFIILS**	BAILIFFS	**ABGHIOPR**	BIOGRAPH
ABENORTY	BARYTONE	**ABFFINOS**	BANOFFIS	**ABGHLOST**	HAGBOLTS
ABENOSSW	SAWBONES	**ABFFLLPU**	PUFFBALL	**ABGHMOOS**	GOOMBAHS
ABENOSSY	SOYBEANS	**ABFFLOOS**	BOFFOLAS	**ABGHMORU**	BROUGHAM
ABENOSTY	BAYONETS	**ABFFLOST**	BLASTOFF	**ABGHMRSU**	HAMBURGS
ABENPSSU	SUBPENAS	**ABFFLOSU**	BUFFALOS	**ABGHNORS**	HORNBAGS
ABENQSTU	BANQUETS	**ABFFNOTU**	BOUFFANT	**ABGHORTU**	BROUGHTA
ABENRRYZ	BRAZENRY	**ABFGILNS**	FABLINGS	**ABGHOSTU**	BUSHGOAT
ABENRSTU	UNBRASTE	**ABFGLLOO**	GOOFBALL	**ABGHPRSU**	SUBGRAPH
	URBANEST	**ABFGOOST**	FOOTBAGS	**ABGIIILN**	ALIBIING
ABENSSSS	BASSNESS	**ABFGORUU**	FAUBOURG	**ABGIIKNT**	BATIKING
ABENSTZZ	BEZZANTS	**ABFHIIST**	BAITFISH	**ABGIILNR**	BRAILING
ABEOORST	AEROBOTS	**ABFHILLS**	FISHBALL	**ABGIILNS**	SAIBLING
ABEOOSST	SEABOOTS	**ABFHINNO**	INFOBAHN	**ABGIILNT**	LIBATING
ABEOPPRY	PAPERBOY	**ABFHIORS**	BOARFISH	**ABGIILOT**	OBLIGATI
ABEOPRSS	SAPROBES	**ABFHOOTT**	FOOTBATH	**ABGIIMNS**	IMBASING
ABEOPRST	PROBATES	**ABFHSSTU**	SUBSHAFT	**ABGIIMST**	BIGAMIST
ABEOPSST	POSTBASE	**ABFIILLR**	FIBRILLA	**ABGIINNO**	BIGNONIA
ABEOQRSU	BAROQUES	**ABFIILMR**	FIMBRIAL	**ABGIINNR**	BRAINING
ABEORRRT	BARRETOR	**ABFIILRR**	FIBRILAR	**ABGIINOR**	ABORIGIN
ABEORRSS	BRASEROS	**ABFILLLY**	FALLIBLY	**ABGIINRS**	BRAISING
ABEORRST	ABORTERS	**ABFILNSU**	BASINFUL	**ABGIINSS**	BIASINGS
	ARBORETS	**ABFILOTT**	BOATLIFT		BIASSING
	TABORERS	**ABFILSTU**	FABULIST	**ABGIINST**	BAITINGS
ABEORRTU	TABOURER	**ABFIMORS**	FIBROMAS	**ABGIJNRU**	ABJURING
ABEORSST	BOASTERS	**ABFJORSU**	FRABJOUS	**ABGIJOOS**	JIGABOOS
	SORBATES	**ABFKLLOR**	FORKBALL	**ABGIKLNN**	BLANKING
ABEORSSY	ROSEBAYS		KORFBALL	**ABGIKLNS**	BALKINGS
ABEORSTT	ABETTORS	**ABFLLOOS**	FOOSBALL	**ABGIKLNU**	BAULKING
	BATTEROS	**ABFLLOOT**	FOOTBALL	**ABGIKNNR**	BRANKING
	TABORETS	**ABFLLORU**	FOURBALL	**ABGIKNNS**	BANKINGS
ABEORSTU	SABOTEUR	**ABFLLOST**	SOFTBALL	**ABGIKNRR**	RINGBARK
ABEORTTU	OBTURATE	**ABFLLSSU**	FUSBALLS	**ABGILLMN**	LAMBLING
	TABOURET		FUSSBALL	**ABGILLNS**	BALLINGS
ABEORTUV	OUTBRAVE	**ABFLMORY**	FORMABLY	**ABGILMNR**	MARBLING
ABEOSSST	ASBESTOS	**ABFLNSUU**	BUSULFAN		RAMBLING
ABEOSTUV	SUBOVATE	**ABFLOSTU**	BOASTFUL	**ABGILMNS**	AMBLINGS
ABEOSTWX	SWEATBOX		BOATFULS		LAMBINGS
ABEPRRTU	ABRUPTER	**ABFLOSTW**	BATFOWLS	**ABGILMNW**	WAMBLING
ABEPRSSY	PASSERBY	**ABFLOSTY**	FLYBOATS	**ABGILNNT**	BANTLING
ABEPRSTY	TYPEBARS	**ABFLOSUU**	FABULOUS	**ABGILNNU**	UNBALING
ABEPSSSY	BYPASSES	**ABFNORTU**	TURBOFAN	**ABGILNOR**	LABORING
		ABFOORST	FOOTBARS		

ABGILNOT	BLOATING	**ABGLOOST**	TOOLBAGS	**ABHLLSTU**	BULLSHAT
	OBLIGANT	**ABGLOOTY**	BATOLOGY	**ABHLORTW**	WHORLBAT
ABGILNRT	BLARTING	**ABGLORST**	RAGBOLTS	**ABHLOSUX**	BOXHAULS
	BRATLING	**ABGLORSU**	GLABROUS	**ABHLOSWW**	WASHBOWL
ABGILNRW	BRAWLING	**ABGLOSSU**	SUBGOALS	**ABHLPSUY**	SUBPHYLA
	WARBLING	**ABGLRRSU**	BURGLARS	**ABHLRSTU**	HURLBATS
ABGILNST	BLASTING	**ABGLRRUY**	BURGLARY	**ABHLSSTU**	SALTBUSH
	STABLING	**ABGMNOOR**	GAMBROON	**ABHMNOTY**	BOTHYMAN
	TABLINGS	**ABGMNOOY**	BOOGYMAN	**ABHMNSUU**	SUBHUMAN
ABGILNSW	BAWLINGS	**ABGMOOSY**	GOOMBAYS	**ABHMOORT**	BATHROOM
ABGILNTT	BATTLING	**ABGMORSW**	BAGWORMS	**ABHMRSSU**	SAMBHURS
	BLATTING	**ABGNOORS**	BARGOONS	**ABHNSSTU**	SUNBATHS
ABGILNTY	TANGIBLY	**ABGNOORY**	BOONGARY	**ABHOORST**	TARBOOSH
ABGILOOT	OBLIGATO	**ABGNOPRS**	PROBANGS	**ABHOOSTW**	SHOWBOAT
ABGILORS	GARBOILS	**ABGNORSU**	OSNABURG	**ABHORRSU**	HARBOURS
ABGILORW	BRIGALOW	**ABGNOSTU**	GUNBOATS	**ABHORSTU**	TARBOUSH
ABGILRST	BATGIRLS	**ABGNOSWY**	BOWYANGS	**ABHOSTUY**	HAUTBOYS
ABGIMMNO	MAMBOING	**ABGOORST**	BOTARGOS	**ABHSSTUW**	WASHTUBS
ABGIMNRU	RUMBAING	**ABGOPSST**	POSTBAGS	**ABIIINRS**	BIRIANIS
ABGIMOSU	BIGAMOUS	**ABGORRSU**	GOBURRAS	**ABIIINRY**	BIRIYANI
	SUBIMAGO	**ABGORSTU**	OUTBRAGS	**ABIIKKST**	KIBITKAS
ABGIMSST	GAMBISTS	**ABGOSTTU**	TUGBOATS	**ABIIKLSS**	BASILISK
ABGINNNR	BRANNING	**ABHHIKSS**	BAKSHISH	**ABIILLMR**	MILLIBAR
ABGINNOR	ABORNING	**ABHHKOST**	KHOTBAHS	**ABIILLTY**	LABILITY
ABGINNOT	BATONING	**ABHHKSTU**	KHUTBAHS	**ABIILMNO**	BINOMIAL
ABGINNRU	UNBARING	**ABHHRRSTU**	HATBRUSH	**ABIILMNS**	ALBINISM
ABGINNRX	BANXRING	**ABHHSSUW**	BUSHWAHS		MINILABS
ABGINNST	BANTINGS	**ABHIINRS**	BAIRNISH	**ABIILMSU**	BULIMIAS
ABGINOOR	BIGAROON		BRAINISH	**ABIILNOT**	LIBATION
ABGINOOT	TABOOING	**ABHIINST**	INHABITS	**ABIILNQS**	INQILABS
ABGINORT	ABORTING	**ABHIIORZ**	RHIZOBIA	**ABIILNRS**	BRASILIN
	BORATING	**ABHIKLLW**	HAWKBILL	**ABIILNRY**	BRAINILY
	TABORING	**ABHIKLOR**	KOHLRABI	**ABIILNRZ**	BRAZILIN
ABGINORV	BRAVOING	**ABHIKLSS**	BASHLIKS	**ABIILNST**	SIBILANT
ABGINOST	BOASTING	**ABHIKSTW**	HAWKBITS	**ABIILNVY**	INVIABLY
	BOATINGS	**ABHIKSUZ**	BUZKASHI	**ABIILOSV**	BOLIVIAS
	BOSTANGI	**ABHILLPT**	PITHBALL	**ABIILPTY**	PITIABLY
ABGINRRS	BARRINGS	**ABHILNOS**	HOBNAILS	**ABIIMNOT**	AMBITION
ABGINRSS	BRASSING	**ABHILNOT**	BIATHLON	**ABIIMNRS**	BINARISM
ABGINRST	BRASTING	**ABHILOPS**	BASOPHIL		MINIBARS
ABGINSST	BASTINGS	**ABHILRTW**	WHIRLBAT	**ABIIMSST**	IAMBISTS
ABGINSTT	BATTINGS	**ABHILSST**	STABLISH	**ABIINORS**	ROBINIAS
ABGINSTW	BATSWING	**ABHILSTU**	HALIBUTS	**ABIINRSY**	BIRYANIS
ABGINTTU	ABUTTING	**ABHIMMST**	BATHMISM	**ABIIRSSV**	VIBRISSA
ABGIOPST	PIGBOATS	**ABHIMNRS**	BRAHMINS	**ABIJLNRS**	BRINJALS
ABGIRRSS	RIBGRASS	**ABHINSST**	ABSINTHS	**ABIJLNTU**	JUBILANT
ABGKKNOS	BANGKOKS	**ABHIOSST**	ISOBATHS	**ABIJNOOT**	JOBATION
ABGKORSW	WORKBAGS	**ABHIOSTU**	HAUTBOIS	**ABIJNOST**	ABJOINTS
ABGLLLOY	GLOBALLY	**ABHIRRSU**	AIRBRUSH		BANJOIST
ABGLLLUY	GULLABLY	**ABHIRSSS**	BRASSISH	**ABIKLLLM**	LAMBKILL
ABGLLMSU	GUMBALLS	**ABHIRSTT**	BRATTISH	**ABIKLLUY**	BAULKILY
ABGLLNUW	BUNGWALL	**ABHJNOOT**	JOHNBOAT	**ABIKLMNS**	LAMBKINS
ABGLLORU	GLOBULAR	**ABHKLSSY**	BASHLYKS		LAMBSKIN
ABGLLRUY	BULLYRAG	**ABHKLSUW**	BUSHWALK	**ABIKLMOU**	KUMBALOI
ABGLMNSU	LUMBANGS	**ABHKOOOT**	BOATHOOK	**ABIKLNRY**	BYRLAKIN
ABGLMOPU	PLUMBAGO	**ABHKORSU**	BOURKHAS	**ABIKLORS**	KILOBARS
ABGLMOSU	LUMBAGOS		KOURBASH	**ABIKLOSS**	KOLBASIS
ABGLNOOS	BOLOGNAS				KOLBASSI
ABGLNOOT	LONGBOAT	**ABHKORSV**	BOSHVARK	**ABIKLSSY**	KISSABLY
ABGLNOUW	BUNGALOW	**ABHLLMOT**	MOTHBALL	**ABIKMNNR**	BRINKMAN
ABGLOOOO	BOOGALOO	**ABHLLOOY**	BALLYHOO	**ABIKMNRS**	BARMKINS
		ABHLLPSU	PUSHBALL		

ABIKNORR	IRONBARK	**ABINOPTX**	PAINTBOX	**ABLMNRUU**	ALBURNUM
ABIKOSUZ	BAZOUKIS	**ABINORST**	TABORINS		LABURNUM
ABIKRSST	BRITSKAS	**ABINORSW**	RAINBOWS	**ABLMOOST**	TOMBOLAS
ABIKRSTZ	BRITZKAS	**ABINORTU**	TABOURIN	**ABLMOSTY**	MYOBLAST
	BRITZSKA	**ABINORWY**	RAINBOWY	**ABLMPSUU**	PABULUMS
ABILLLPY	PLAYBILL	**ABINOSST**	ANTIBOSS	**ABLNNOOR**	NONLABOR
ABILLMSU	BALLIUMS		BASTIONS	**ABLNOOPS**	POBLANOS
ABILLNPS	PINBALLS	**ABINOSSU**	ABUSIONS	**ABLNORST**	LASTBORN
ABILLORT	TRILOBAL	**ABINOSTT**	BOTANIST	**ABLNORYZ**	BLAZONRY
ABILLOVY	VIOLABLY	**ABINRSTU**	URBANIST	**ABLNOSTU**	BUTANOLS
ABILLPST	SPITBALL	**ABINRSTV**	VIBRANTS	**ABLNOSUZ**	SUBZONAL
ABILLRTY	TRIBALLY	**ABINRTUY**	URBANITY	**ABLNRSUU**	SUBLUNAR
ABILLSSW	SAWBILLS	**ABINTTTU**	TITUBANT	**ABLNSTUY**	UNSTABLY
ABILLSTT	BATTILLS	**ABIOORRS**	ARBORIOS	**ABLNSUUY**	UNUSABLY
ABILLSWX	WAXBILLS	**ABIOORTV**	OBVIATOR	**ABLOOPRR**	PROLABOR
ABILLSWY	WAYBILLS	**ABIOPRSU**	BIPAROUS	**ABLOORST**	BARSTOOL
ABILMNOU	OLIBANUM	**ABIOPSTU**	SUBTOPIA		TOOLBARS
ABILMNSU	ALBUMINS	**ABIORRST**	ARBORIST	**ABLOORTY**	OBLATORY
ABILMOPS	BIOPLASM	**ABIORRSZ**	BIZARROS	**ABLOOSTT**	BOOTLAST
ABILMORS	LABORISM	**ABIORRTV**	VIBRATOR	**ABLOOSTZ**	ZOOBLAST
	MISLABOR	**ABIORSTV**	VIBRATOS	**ABLOPRSU**	SUBPOLAR
ABILMOTU	BUMALOTI	**ABIORTUY**	OBITUARY	**ABLOPRTY**	PORTABLY
ABILNOOT	BOLTONIA	**ABIPSSTT**	BAPTISTS	**ABLOPRVY**	PROVABLY
	LOBATION	**ABIRRSTU**	AIRBURST	**ABLOPSUU**	PABULOUS
	OBLATION	**ABIRSSUZ**	SUBSIZAR	**ABLOPSYY**	PLAYBOYS
ABILNOPR	PANBROIL	**ABIRSTTY**	TRAYBITS	**ABLOQTUY**	QUOTABLY
ABILNORU	UNILOBAR	**ABISSSST**	BASSISTS	**ABLORSST**	BORSTALS
ABILNOTU	ABLUTION	**ABISSTTU**	TUBAISTS	**ABLORSSU**	SUBSOLAR
	ABUTILON	**ABJKMOSS**	SJAMBOKS	**ABLORSTW**	BLAWORTS
ABILNRTU	TRIBUNAL	**ABJLMOOS**	JAMBOOLS	**ABLORSTY**	SORTABLY
	TURBINAL	**ABKKMOOR**	BOOKMARK	**ABLORSUW**	BOURLAWS
ABILNRWY	BRAWNILY	**ABKLLNOR**	BANKROLL	**ABLORTUW**	OUTBRAWL
ABILOPRS	PARBOILS	**ABKLOOPY**	PLAYBOOK	**ABLOSSUU**	SABULOUS
ABILOPST	BIOPLAST	**ABKLOOSW**	LAWBOOKS	**ABLOSTTU**	SUBTOTAL
ABILORST	LABORIST	**ABKLORST**	BLOKARTS	**ABLOSTUW**	OUTBAWLS
	ORBITALS	**ABKLORWY**	WORKABLY	**ABLPRTUY**	ABRUPTLY
	STROBILA	**ABKLRSUW**	BULWARKS	**ABLRSTUY**	BUTYRALS
ABILORSV	BOLIVARS	**ABKNNNOS**	NONBANKS	**ABMNTTUY**	BUTTYMAN
ABILORTY	LIBATORY	**ABKNNOSW**	SNOWBANK	**ABMOORRS**	BARROOMS
ABILORUV	BIOVULAR	**ABKNOPST**	STOPBANK	**ABMOPRST**	BARMPOTS
ABILOSTU	BAILOUTS	**ABKNPRTU**	BANKRUPT	**ABMOPSST**	SPAMBOTS
	TABOULIS	**ABKNRSUU**	BUNRAKUS	**ABMORSTU**	TAMBOURS
ABILPSSY	PASSIBLY	**ABKOOPSS**	PASSBOOK	**ABMOSSTU**	SUBATOMS
ABILRSSY	BRASSILY	**ABKOORTW**	WORKBOAT	**ABMRRSUY**	BURRAMYS
ABILRSUV	SUBVIRAL	**ABKOOSTT**	KOTTABOS	**ABNNNORU**	NONURBAN
ABILSSUY	ISSUABLY	**ABKORSTU**	OUTBARKS	**ABNNOOST**	NANOBOTS
ABILSTUY	SUITABLY	**ABKSSSTU**	SUBTASKS	**ABNOORRT**	ROBORANT
ABIMMNOO	MAINBOOM	**ABLLLOSW**	LOWBALLS	**ABNOORSS**	SOROBANS
ABIMMSTU	MITUMBAS	**ABLLMOOR**	BALLROOM	**ABNOORSZ**	BORAZONS
ABIMNOSU	BIMANOUS	**ABLLMOPW**	BLOWLAMP	**ABNOORYZ**	BRYOZOAN
ABIMNRSU	URBANISM	**ABLLMOSY**	SMALLBOY	**ABNOOSSS**	BASSOONS
ABIMNRTU	TAMBURIN	**ABLLNOOS**	BALLOONS	**ABNORSTY**	BARYTONS
ABIMORSU	BIRAMOUS	**ABLLNOSW**	SNOWBALL	**ABNORTUU**	RUNABOUT
ABIMORSY	BOYARISM	**ABLLORRS**	ROLLBARS	**ABNOSSSU**	BONASSUS
ABIMPSST	BAPTISMS	**ABLLORST**	BORSTALL	**ABNOSTUX**	SUBTAXON
ABIMRSST	STRABISM		TOLLBARS	**ABNRSTTU**	TURBANTS
ABIMRSTT	TRIMTABS	**ABLLORSU**	SOURBALL	**ABOORRSU**	ARBOROUS
ABINNOST	ANTISNOB	**ABLLOSTY**	TALLBOYS	**ABOORRSW**	ROWBOATS
ABINOORS	BORONIAS	**ABLLRTUY**	BRUTALLY	**ABOOSTTU**	OUTBOAST
ABINOORT	ABORTION	**ABLLSSUY**	SYLLABUS	**ABOOSTTW**	TOWBOATS
ABINOOST	BONIATOS	**ABLMMOSU**	BUMMALOS	**ABORSSTU**	ROBUSTAS

ABOSTTTU	BATTUTOS	ACCDESSU	SUCCADES	ACCEFILS	FASCICLE
ABPRSSTU	SUBPARTS	ACCDESUU	CADUCEUS	ACCEFIST	FACTICES
ACCCDIIO	COCCIDIA		CAUCUSED	ACCEFLSU	FELUCCAS
ACCCEHIX	CACHEXIC	ACCDGHOO	COACHDOG	ACCEGINS	ACCINGES
ACCCELRY	CYCLECAR	ACCDHIIR	DIARCHIC	ACCEGKMO	GAMECOCK
ACCCENPY	PECCANCY	ACCDHILS	CHALCIDS	ACCEGNOY	COAGENCY
ACCCFIIL	CALCIFIC	ACCDHIMO	DOCHMIAC	ACCEGOSS	SOCCAGES
ACCCHILO	COLCHICA	ACCDHIOR	CHAORDIC	ACCEHHIS	CHECHIAS
ACCCHRTY	CATCHCRY	ACCDHIOT	CATHODIC	ACCEHHKO	CHECHAKO
ACCCIILT	CALCITIC	ACCDHIRY	DYARCHIC	ACCEHHKT	CHATCHKE
ACCCIIPR	CAPRICCI	ACCDHLOR	CLOCHARD		HATCHECK
ACCCILLY	CYCLICAL	ACCDIINU	UNACIDIC	ACCEHIKP	CHICKPEA
ACCCIOPU	CAPUCCIO	ACCDIIOT	ACIDOTIC	ACCEHIKR	AIRCHECK
ACCDDEEN	ACCENDED	ACCDIIRT	CARDITIC	ACCEHILM	ALCHEMIC
	CADENCED	ACCDIIST	DICASTIC		CHEMICAL
ACCDDEIS	CADDICES	ACCDIITY	DICACITY	ACCEHILP	CEPHALIC
ACCDDEKO	COCKADED	ACCDILNU	DUNCICAL	ACCEHILS	CALICHES
ACCDDEOR	ACCORDED	ACCDILOY	CALYCOID		CHALICES
ACCDDIII	DIACIDIC	ACCDILTY	DACTYLIC	ACCEHILT	HECTICAL
ACCDDIIT	DIDACTIC	ACCDINOR	CANCROID	ACCEHIMN	MECHANIC
ACCDEEER	REACCEDE		DRACONIC	ACCEHIMS	SACHEMIC
ACCDEEHT	CACHETED	ACCDIOOR	CORACOID	ACCEHINO	ANECHOIC
ACCDEELN	CANCELED	ACCDIORS	SARCODIC	ACCEHINR	CHANCIER
ACCDEENR	CANCERED	ACCDIOST	STICCADO		CHICANER
ACCDEENS	CADENCES	ACCDITUY	CADUCITY	ACCEHINS	CHICANES
ACCDEENT	ACCENTED	ACCDKNOS	CANDOCKS	ACCEHINT	ATECHNIC
ACCDEEPT	ACCEPTED	ACCDKOSW	DAWCOCKS		CATECHIN
ACCDEERS	ACCEDERS	ACCDLOSY	CACODYLS	ACCEHIOR	COACHIER
ACCDEERT	ACCRETED	ACCDOOST	STOCCADO	ACCEHIOS	COACHIES
ACCDEERU	CARDECUE	ACCDOOXY	CACODOXY	ACCEHIRT	CATCHIER
ACCDEERW	ACCREWED	ACCDOSUU	CADUCOUS	ACCEHKPY	PAYCHECK
ACCDEESS	ACCESSED	ACCEEEPT	ACCEPTEE	ACCEHLNS	CHANCELS
ACCDEGIN	ACCEDING	ACCEEHIT	HICCATEE	ACCEHLOR	COCHLEAR
	ACCINGED	ACCEEHLO	COCHLEAE	ACCEHLOS	COCHLEAS
ACCDEHIK	CHIACKED	ACCEEHLS	CALECHES	ACCEHLOT	CATECHOL
ACCDEHIL	CHALICED	ACCEEHOS	COACHEES	ACCEHLST	CLATCHES
ACCDEHIN	CHICANED	ACCEEHRT	CETERACH	ACCEHMNO	COACHMEN
ACCDEHKY	CHYACKED	ACCEEHST	SEECATCH	ACCEHNNO	CHACONNE
ACCDEHLT	CLATCHED	ACCEEILR	CELERIAC	ACCEHNNY	CYNANCHE
ACCDEHNR	CRANCHED	ACCEEILS	ECCLESIA	ACCEHNOR	CHARNECO
ACCDEHNU	CHAUNCED	ACCEEINV	VACCINEE		ENCROACH
ACCDEHPU	CAPUCHED	ACCEEKLN	NECKLACE	ACCEHNOT	CONCHATE
ACCDEIIS	ACCIDIES	ACCEELNO	COENACLE	ACCEHNRS	CHANCERS
ACCDEILN	CALCINED	ACCEELNR	CANCELER		CHANCRES
ACCDEILO	ECOCIDAL		CLARENCE		CRANCHES
ACCDEILU	CAUDICLE	ACCEELNS	CENACLES	ACCEHNRY	CHANCERY
ACCDEILY	DELICACY	ACCEELOS	COALESCE	ACCEHNSU	CHAUNCES
ACCDEINO	DECANOIC	ACCEELRT	CALCRETE	ACCEHOPT	CACHEPOT
ACCDEINT	ACCIDENT	ACCEENNS	NASCENCE	ACCEHORS	CAROCHES
ACCDEIRT	ACCREDIT	ACCEENPR	CREPANCE		COACHERS
ACCDEISU	CAUDICES	ACCEENRS	CREANCES	ACCEHPSU	CAPUCHES
ACCDEKLR	CRACKLED	ACCEENRT	REACCENT	ACCEHRST	CATCHERS
ACCDEKOS	COCKADES	ACCEENST	ACESCENT		CRATCHES
ACCDELLY	CALYCLED	ACCEEORT	COCREATE	ACCEHSST	SCATCHES
ACCDELOY	ACCLOYED		CROCEATE	ACCEHSTT	CATHECTS
ACCDENOR	CONACRED	ACCEEPRT	ACCEPTER	ACCEHSTU	CATECHUS
ACCDENOV	CONCAVED		REACCEPT	ACCEIIST	CAECITIS
ACCDEORR	ACCORDER	ACCEERST	ACCRETES	ACCEIKLT	TICKLACE
ACCDEOST	ACCOSTED	ACCEERSU	REACCUSE	ACCEIKPS	ICEPACKS
ACCDERSU	ACCURSED	ACCEESSS	ACCESSES	ACCEIKST	CACKIEST
	CARDECUS	ACCEFFIY	EFFICACY	ACCEILLN	CANCELLI

ACCEILLR	CLERICAL	**ACCELSSY**	CYCLASES	**ACCHIORT**	THORACIC
ACCEILLS	CALICLES	**ACCELWYY**	CYCLEWAY		TROCHAIC
ACCEILLU	CAULICLE	**ACCENNSY**	NASCENCY	**ACCHIOSU**	ACOUCHIS
ACCEILLV	CLAVICLE	**ACCENORR**	CORNACRE	**ACCHIRRT**	CARRITCH
ACCEILNS	CALCINES	**ACCENORS**	CONACRES	**ACCHIRSS**	SCRAICHS
	SCENICAL	**ACCENORT**	ACCENTOR	**ACCHKLOR**	CHARLOCK
ACCEILNT	CANTICLE	**ACCENOST**	COENACTS	**ACCHKOSY**	HAYCOCKS
ACCEILNV	CLAVECIN		COSECANT	**ACCHLOOT**	CACHOLOT
ACCEILNY	CALYCINE	**ACCENOSU**	CONCAUSE	**ACCHLSTU**	CLAUCHTS
ACCEILOP	ALOPECIC	**ACCENOSV**	CONCAVES	**ACCHMORS**	CASCHROM
ACCEILOS	CALICOES	**ACCEOPRT**	ACCEPTOR	**ACCHNNUY**	UNCHANCY
	COELIACS	**ACCEOPTU**	OCCUPATE	**ACCHNOOR**	COANCHOR
ACCEILRV	CERVICAL	**ACCEORST**	ECTOSARC		CORONACH
ACCEILST	CALCITES	**ACCEORSW**	CRACOWES	**ACCHNOTU**	COUCHANT
ACCEILTY	ACETYLIC	**ACCEORTU**	ACCOUTER	**ACCHNRUY**	CRAUNCHY
ACCEIMOS	OCCAMIES		ACCOUTRE	**ACCHNTUY**	UNCATCHY
ACCEIMRS	CERAMICS	**ACCEOSSS**	SACCOSES	**ACCHOOTU**	OUTCOACH
ACCEINNR	CANCRINE	**ACCERRST**	CARRECTS	**ACCHOPSU**	PACHUCOS
ACCEINOR	COCINERA	**ACCERSST**	SCARCEST	**ACCHORTU**	CARTOUCH
ACCEINOS	COCAINES	**ACCERSSU**	ACCURSES	**ACCHORTY**	OCTARCHY
ACCEINOT	ACETONIC		ACCUSERS	**ACCHOSTW**	CHOCTAWS
ACCEINRT	ACENTRIC	**ACCESSTU**	CACTUSES	**ACCHOTTU**	OUTCATCH
ACCEINSV	VACCINES	**ACCESSUU**	CAUCUSES	**ACCHPSTU**	CATCHUPS
ACCEINTU	CUNEATIC	**ACCFFLTU**	CALCTUFF	**ACCHRRSU**	CURRACHS
ACCEIOPR	CECROPIA	**ACCFHLTY**	CATCHFLY	**ACCHRSSU**	SCRAUCHS
ACCEIOTV	COACTIVE	**ACCFIILT**	LACTIFIC	**ACCHRSTY**	SCRATCHY
ACCEIPRS	CAPRICES	**ACCFIKLL**	CALFLICK	**ACCHRTWY**	WATCHCRY
ACCEIPRT	PRACTICE	**ACCFLNOO**	CONFOCAL	**ACCIIIOT**	OITICICA
ACCEIPSV	PECCAVIS	**ACCFOORT**	COFACTOR	**ACCIILLN**	CLINICAL
ACCEIQSU	CACIQUES	**ACCGHIKN**	CHACKING	**ACCIILMT**	CLIMATIC
ACCEIRRR	RICERCAR	**ACCGHINN**	CHANCING	**ACCIILNO**	ICONICAL
ACCEIRSU	CAESURIC	**ACCGHINO**	COACHING	**ACCIILRT**	CRITICAL
	CURACIES	**ACCGHINT**	CATCHING	**ACCIIMNN**	CINNAMIC
ACCEIRTU	CRUCIATE	**ACCGHIOR**	CHORAGIC	**ACCIINNO**	ANICONIC
ACCEISST	ASCETICS	**ACCGIINT**	ACCITING	**ACCIINNP**	PICCANIN
ACCEISTT	ECSTATIC	**ACCGIKLN**	CACKLING	**ACCIINOT**	ACONITIC
ACCEKLNR	CRACKNEL		CLACKING		CATIONIC
ACCEKLRS	CACKLERS	**ACCGIKMR**	GIMCRACK		ITACONIC
	CLACKERS	**ACCGIKNR**	CRACKING	**ACCIINPS**	CAPSICIN
	CRACKLES	**ACCGILOX**	COXALGIC	**ACCIINTY**	CYANITIC
ACCEKMOS	MEACOCKS	**ACCGINOT**	COACTING	**ACCIIOPT**	OCCIPITA
ACCEKNOR	CORNCAKE	**ACCGINOY**	ACCOYING	**ACCIIPST**	PASTICCI
ACCEKOPS	PEACOCKS	**ACCGINRU**	ACCRUING	**ACCIIRTX**	CICATRIX
ACCEKOPY	PEACOCKY	**ACCGINSU**	ACCUSING	**ACCIISST**	SCIATICS
ACCEKOSS	SEACOCKS	**ACCGLOOY**	CACOLOGY	**ACCIJKMR**	JIMCRACK
ACCEKPSU	CUPCAKES	**ACCHHITT**	CHITCHAT	**ACCIKKNN**	NICKNACK
ACCEKRRS	CRACKERS	**ACCHHMOS**	CAMSHOCH	**ACCIKKRR**	RICKRACK
ACCEKRST	CRACKETS	**ACCHHMOU**	MUCHACHO	**ACCIKKTT**	TICKTACK
ACCELLSY	CALYCLES	**ACCHIIMS**	CHIASMIC	**ACCIKLOT**	COCKTAIL
ACCELLUY	CALYCULE	**ACCHIIRT**	RACHITIC	**ACCIKNST**	CANSTICK
ACCELMNY	CYCLAMEN	**ACCHIIST**	CHIASTIC	**ACCIKOPR**	APRICOCK
ACCELNOS	CONCEALS	**ACCHILNO**	CHALONIC	**ACCIKPRT**	PRACTICK
ACCELNOV	CONCLAVE	**ACCHILNY**	CHANCILY	**ACCILLUY**	CALYCULI
ACCELNRU	CARUNCLE	**ACCHILOR**	ORICHALC	**ACCILMOS**	COSMICAL
ACCELOOT	COLOCATE	**ACCHILOT**	CATHOLIC	**ACCILMOX**	CACOMIXL
ACCELORS	CORACLES	**ACCHIMOR**	ACHROMIC	**ACCILMSU**	CALCIUMS
ACCELORT	ACROLECT	**ACCHINNO**	CINCHONA	**ACCILMUU**	ACICULUM
ACCELOST	CACOLETS	**ACCHINOS**	CHICANOS	**ACCILNOT**	CICLATON
ACCELRSY	SCARCELY	**ACCHINPU**	CAPUCHIN		LACTONIC
ACCELRTU	CLEARCUT	**ACCHIOPS**	PICACHOS	**ACCILNOV**	VOLCANIC
ACCELSSU	SACCULES	**ACCHIORS**	COCHAIRS	**ACCILNUV**	VULCANIC

ACCILORS	CALORICS
ACCILORT	CORTICAL
ACCILOSS	CLASSICO
ACCILOSV	VOCALICS
ACCILPRY	CAPRYLIC
ACCILRRU	CIRCULAR
ACCILRSY	ACRYLICS
ACCILSSS	CLASSICS
ACCILSST	CLASTICS
ACCILTUU	CUTICULA
ACCIMNOS	MOCCASIN
ACCIMNTU	CANTICUM
ACCIMOPR	MICROCAP
ACCIMORR	MICROCAR
ACCIMORU	COUMARIC
ACCIMOSZ	ZIMOCCAS
ACCIMPSU	CAPSICUM
ACCIMSTY	CYMATICS
ACCINOOS	OCCASION
ACCINOOT	COACTION
ACCINORT	CRATONIC
	NARCOTIC
ACCINORV	CAVICORN
ACCINOST	CANTICOS
ACCINOTY	CANTICOY
	CYANOTIC
ACCINRSU	CRUCIANS
ACCINSSY	CYCASINS
ACCIOOPP	APOCOPIC
ACCIOPST	SPICCATO
ACCIORST	ACROSTIC
ACCIORSY	ISOCRACY
ACCIOSTT	STICCATO
ACCIOSTU	ACOUSTIC
ACCIPRST	PRACTICS
ACCIRRTT	TRICTRAC
ACCIRSTY	SCARCITY
ACCISSTU	CAUSTICS
ACCKKRSU	RUCKSACK
ACCKLLOO	ALCOLOCK
ACCKLORS	CARLOCKS
ACCKMMRU	CRUMMACK
ACCKMORS	CROMACKS
ACCKOOOP	COCKAPOO
ACCKOOOT	COCKATOO
ACCKOPRS	CAPROCKS
ACCKOPRT	CRACKPOT
ACCKORST	STOCKCAR
ACCKOSSS	CASSOCKS
	COSSACKS
ACCKOSST	CASTOCKS
ACCKPRSU	CRACKUPS
ACCLLNOY	CYCLONAL
ACCLLOSU	OCCLUSAL
ACCLLSUU	CALCULUS
ACCLSSUU	SACCULUS
ACCMNOSY	CACONYMS
ACCMNOYY	CACONYMY
ACCMOOST	COCOMATS
ACCMOOSY	COCOYAMS
ACCMOPST	ACCOMPTS
	COMPACTS
ACCMOSTU	ACCUSTOM
ACCMRSUU	CURCUMAS
ACCNNOOS	COONCANS
ACCNOOPS	COCOPANS
ACCNOORS	RACCOONS
ACCNOOTU	COCOANUT
ACCNOPTU	OCCUPANT
ACCNORTT	CONTRACT
ACCNOSTT	CONTACTS
ACCNOSTU	ACCOUNTS
ACCOORST	COACTORS
ACCOPSTY	COPYCATS
ACCOQSSU	SQUACCOS
ACCORRTY	CARRYCOT
ACCORSTU	ACCOURTS
ACDDDEIS	CADDISED
ACDDDEIT	ADDICTED
ACDDDETU	ADDUCTED
ACDDDKOS	DADDOCKS
ACDDEEES	DECEASED
ACDDEEHO	COHEADED
ACDDEEHT	DETACHED
ACDDEEIT	DEDICATE
ACDDEEIU	DECIDUAE
ACDDEEKR	DACKERED
ACDDEELL	DECALLED
ACDDEELR	DECLARED
ACDDEELS	DESCALED
ACDDEELW	DECLAWED
ACDDEEMP	DECAMPED
ACDDEENO	DEACONED
ACDDEENR	CREDENDA
ACDDEENS	ASCENDED
ACDDEENT	DECADENT
	DECANTED
ACDDEERT	REDACTED
ACDDEETU	EDUCATED
ACDDEETV	ADVECTED
ACDDEGIS	DISCAGED
ACDDEHIK	DICKHEAD
ACDDEHKN	DECKHAND
ACDDEHRS	CHEDDARS
ACDDEHRY	CHEDDARY
ACDDEIIL	DEICIDAL
ACDDEIIM	MEDICAID
ACDDEILS	CLADDIES
ACDDEILU	DECIDUAL
ACDDEINR	CANDIDER
	RIDDANCE
ACDDEINT	DEDICANT
ACDDEINY	CYANIDED
ACDDEIPS	DISPACED
ACDDEIRT	READDICT
ACDDEISS	CADDISES
	DISCASED
ACDDEISU	DECIDUAS
ACDDEITT	DICTATED
ACDDEKLO	DEADLOCK
ACDDEKOR	RADDOCKE
ACDDELOS	CLADODES
ACDDELRS	CLADDERS
ACDDENRU	UNCARDED
ACDDENTU	ADDUCENT
ACDDEOPS	DECAPODS
ACDDEORR	CORRADED
ACDDEORW	COWARDED
ACDDERSU	ADDUCERS
	CRUSADED
ACDDERTU	TRADUCED
ACDDGILN	CLADDING
ACDDGINU	ADDUCING
ACDDGINY	CADDYING
ACDDHHSU	CHUDDAHS
ACDDHIIO	DIADOCHI
ACDDHIMR	DIDRACHM
ACDDHIOY	DIADOCHY
ACDDHIRY	HYDRACID
ACDDHKNO	DOCKHAND
ACDDHKOS	HADDOCKS
	SHADDOCK
ACDDHORS	CHADDORS
ACDDHRSU	CHUDDARS
ACDDIIOR	CARDIOID
ACDDILNY	CANDIDLY
ACDDILRW	WILDCARD
ACDDILTY	DIDACTYL
ACDDINNU	UNCANDID
ACDDINSY	DISCANDY
ACDDIRSS	DISCARDS
ACDDKLNO	DOCKLAND
ACDDKMOS	MADDOCKS
ACDDKOPS	PADDOCKS
ACDDKORY	DOCKYARD
ACDDORTU	ADDUCTOR
ACDEEEFT	DEFECATE
ACDEEEKS	SEEDCAKE
ACDEEENR	CAREENED
ACDEEENT	ANTECEDE
ACDEEERR	CAREERED
ACDEEERS	DECREASE
ACDEEESS	DECEASES
	SEEDCASE
ACDEEFFT	AFFECTED
ACDEEFHN	ENCHAFED
ACDEEFIL	CALEFIED
ACDEEFIN	DEFIANCE
ACDEEFIS	CASEFIED
ACDEEFPR	PREFACED
ACDEEFRS	DEFACERS
	FRESCADE
ACDEEFRY	FEDERACY
ACDEEFTT	FACETTED
ACDEEGLY	DELEGACY
ACDEEGNR	ENGRACED
ACDEEHIN	ECHIDNAE
ACDEEHIR	CHARIDEE
ACDEEHIV	ACHIEVED
ACDEEHKO	COKEHEAD
ACDEEHLP	PLEACHED
ACDEEHLT	CHELATED
ACDEEHMR	DEMARCHE

ACDEEHNN	ENHANCED	**ACDEEMNO**	CODENAME	**ACDEFNOW**	FACEDOWN
ACDEEHNR	ENARCHED	**ACDEEMNP**	ENCAMPED	**ACDEFNRU**	FURNACED
ACDEEHNS	ENCASHED	**ACDEEMRS**	SCREAMED	**ACDEFORT**	FACTORED
	ENCHASED	**ACDEEMRT**	CREMATED	**ACDEFOTU**	OUTFACED
ACDEEHPR	PREACHED	**ACDEEMSV**	MEDEVACS	**ACDEFRSU**	SURFACED
ACDEEHRS	SEARCHED	**ACDEENNP**	PENANCED	**ACDEFRTU**	FURCATED
ACDEEHRT	DETACHER	**ACDEENNT**	TENDANCE	**ACDEGGRS**	SCRAGGED
	RACHETED	**ACDEENNY**	CAYENNED	**ACDEGHLO**	GALOCHED
ACDEEHSS	CHASSEED	**ACDEENOT**	ANECDOTE	**ACDEGHNU**	CHAUNGED
ACDEEHST	DETACHES	**ACDEENRS**	ASCENDER		GAUNCHED
	SACHETED		REASCEND	**ACDEGIIL**	ALGICIDE
ACDEEIIP	EPICEDIA	**ACDEENRT**	CANTERED	**ACDEGIKM**	MAGICKED
ACDEEILT	DELICATE		CRENATED	**ACDEGILN**	DECALING
ACDEEILU	AEDICULE		DECANTER	**ACDEGIMR**	DECIGRAM
ACDEEIMR	CERAMIDE		NECTARED		GRIMACED
	MEDICARE		RECANTED	**ACDEGINU**	GUIDANCE
ACDEEIMT	DECIMATE	**ACDEENRV**	CAVERNED	**ACDEGINY**	DECAYING
	EMICATED		CRAVENED	**ACDEGIRS**	DISGRACE
	MEDICATE	**ACDEENRY**	CARNEYED	**ACDEGISS**	DISCAGES
ACDEEINN	DECENNIA		DECENARY	**ACDEGIST**	CADGIEST
	ENNEADIC	**ACDEENRZ**	CREDENZA	**ACDEGKOS**	DOCKAGES
ACDEEINR	DERACINE	**ACDEENSV**	VENDACES	**ACDEGLLO**	COLLAGED
ACDEEINU	AUDIENCE	**ACDEENTT**	DANCETTE	**ACDEGLOS**	DECALOGS
ACDEEINV	DEVIANCE	**ACDEENTU**	CUNEATED	**ACDEGLOU**	CLOUDAGE
ACDEEIPS	DISPEACE	**ACDEEOPS**	PEASECOD	**ACDEGNOS**	DECAGONS
ACDEEIRS	DECIARES	**ACDEEORT**	DECORATE	**ACDEGNRU**	UNGRACED
ACDEEJKT	JACKETED		RECOATED	**ACDEGORS**	CORDAGES
ACDEEKLR	LACKERED	**ACDEEOTV**	EVOCATED	**ACDEGOTT**	COTTAGED
ACDEEKLY	LACKEYED	**ACDEEPPR**	RECAPPED	**ACDEHHIN**	HAINCHED
ACDEEKNR	CANKERED	**ACDEEPRS**	ESCARPED	**ACDEHHNU**	HAUNCHED
ACDEEKPR	REPACKED		RESPACED	**ACDEHHRU**	HACHURED
ACDEEKPT	PACKETED	**ACDEEPRT**	CARPETED	**ACDEHHTT**	DETHATCH
ACDEEKRR	RERACKED		PREACTED		THATCHED
ACDEEKRS	SCREAKED	**ACDEEPST**	ASPECTED	**ACDEHIIP**	APHICIDE
ACDEEKRT	RACKETED	**ACDEERRS**	SCAREDER	**ACDEHIJK**	HIJACKED
	RETACKED	**ACDEERRT**	CRATERED	**ACDEHILR**	HERALDIC
ACDEEKST	CASKETED		RECRATED	**ACDEHILT**	DITHECAL
ACDEELLR	CELLARED		RETRACED	**ACDEHIMM**	CHAMMIED
	RECALLED		TERRACED	**ACDEHIMN**	MACHINED
ACDEELLS	CADELLES	**ACDEERSS**	CARESSED	**ACDEHIMS**	SCHIEDAM
ACDEELMN	ENCALMED	**ACDEERST**	CEDRATES	**ACDEHINR**	INARCHED
ACDEELMP	EMPLACED	**ACDEERSY**	DECAYERS	**ACDEHINS**	ECHIDNAS
ACDEELNR	CALENDER	**ACDEESTU**	EDUCATES		INCHASED
	ENCRADLE	**ACDEESUX**	CAUDEXES	**ACDEHIRS**	RACHIDES
ACDEELNS	CLEANSED	**ACDEESUY**	CAUSEYED	**ACDEHIRT**	THRIDACE
ACDEELNT	LANCETED	**ACDEFFHU**	CHAUFFED		TRACHEID
ACDEELNV	ENCLAVED	**ACDEFFLS**	SCLAFFED	**ACDEHIRV**	ARCHIVED
ACDEELOR	COLEADER	**ACDEFFOR**	AFFORCED	**ACDEHIST**	SCAITHED
	RECOALED	**ACDEFGIN**	DEFACING	**ACDEHISU**	CHIAUSED
ACDEELPR	PARCELED	**ACDEFGOS**	DOGFACES	**ACDEHKLO**	HEADLOCK
	REPLACED	**ACDEFHKU**	FUCKHEAD	**ACDEHKLS**	SHACKLED
ACDEELRR	DECLARER		HEADFUCK	**ACDEHKNU**	UNHACKED
ACDEELRS	DECLARES	**ACDEFHLN**	FLANCHED	**ACDEHKOV**	HAVOCKED
	RESCALED	**ACDEFIIL**	DEIFICAL	**ACDEHKRU**	ARCHDUKE
ACDEELRT	CLARETED	**ACDEFIIP**	PACIFIED	**ACDEHKTW**	THWACKED
	DECRETAL	**ACDEFILN**	CANFIELD	**ACDEHLNP**	PLANCHED
	TREACLED	**ACDEFILR**	FILECARD	**ACDEHLNR**	CHANDLER
ACDEELRV	CALVERED		FRICADEL	**ACDEHLNU**	LAUNCHED
	CLAVERED	**ACDEFINN**	FINANCED	**ACDEHLOS**	COALSHED
ACDEELSS	DECLASSE	**ACDEFINS**	FACIENDS	**ACDEHLRS**	CHALDERS
	DESCALES	**ACDEFLOT**	OLFACTED	**ACDEHLRT**	TRACHLED

ACDEHLSS	CHADLESS	ACDEILNP	PANICLED	ACDEIOSS	ACIDOSES
ACDEHMST	SMATCHED	ACDEILNU	DULCINEA	ACDEIOSU	EDACIOUS
ACDEHNOR	ANCHORED	ACDEILNY	ADENYLIC	ACDEIPPT	TAPPICED
	RONDACHE		LYCAENID	ACDEIPRS	EPACRIDS
ACDEHNPU	PAUNCHED	ACDEILOS	COALISED		PERACIDS
ACDEHNRU	RAUNCHED	ACDEILOZ	COALIZED	ACDEIPRT	PICRATED
	UNARCHED	ACDEILPR	PLACIDER	ACDEIPSS	DISPACES
ACDEHNRY	ENDARCHY	ACDEILPS	DISPLACE		SPADICES
ACDEHNST	SNATCHED	ACDEILPT	PLICATED	ACDEIPST	SPICATED
	STANCHED	ACDEILRS	DECRIALS	ACDEIPSZ	CAPSIZED
ACDEHNSU	UNCASHED		RADICELS	ACDEIPTV	CAPTIVED
ACDEHNTU	CHAUNTED		RADICLES	ACDEIQRU	ACQUIRED
ACDEHORR	HARDCORE	ACDEILRT	ARTICLED	ACDEIRSS	SIDECARS
ACDEHORT	CHORDATE		LACERTID	ACDEIRST	ACRIDEST
ACDEHORW	COWHEARD	ACDEILRU	AURICLED	ACDEIRSU	DECURIAS
ACDEHOST	CATHODES		RADICULE	ACDEIRTT	CITRATED
ACDEHOUV	AVOUCHED	ACDEILST	CITADELS		TETRACID
ACDEHPPS	SCHAPPED		DIALECTS		TETRADIC
ACDEHPRS	SCARPHED	ACDEILSY	ECDYSIAL	ACDEISSS	DISCASES
ACDEHPST	DESPATCH	ACDEILTT	LATTICED	ACDEISTT	DICTATES
ACDEHPSU	CUPHEADS	ACDEILTY	DIACETYL	ACDEKLNR	CRANKLED
ACDEHPTU	DEATHCUP	ACDEIMNO	COMEDIAN	ACDEKLPS	SPACKLED
ACDEHQTU	QUATCHED		DAEMONIC	ACDEKLQU	QUACKLED
ACDEHRRS	CHRESARD		DEMONIAC	ACDEKNPR	PRANCKED
ACDEHRST	STARCHED	ACDEIMNP	PANDEMIC	ACDEKNPU	UNPACKED
ACDEHTUW	WAUCHTED	ACDEIMNT	MEDICANT	ACDEKNRU	UNRACKED
ACDEIILN	ALCIDINE	ACDEIMOR	COADMIRE	ACDEKNSU	UNCASKED
ACDEIILS	LAICISED		RACEMOID	ACDEKNTU	UNTACKED
ACDEIILT	CILIATED	ACDEIMPS	MIDSPACE	ACDEKOST	STOCKADE
ACDEIILZ	LAICIZED	ACDEIMPT	IMPACTED	ACDEKRSY	KEYCARDS
ACDEIIMU	AECIDIUM	ACDEIMRT	DERMATIC	ACDELLNU	UNCALLED
ACDEIINR	ACRIDINE		TIMECARD	ACDELLOR	CAROLLED
ACDEIINS	SCIAENID	ACDEIMST	MISACTED		COLLARED
ACDEIINT	ACTINIDE	ACDEIMSV	MEDIVACS	ACDELLOT	COLLATED
	CTENIDIA	ACDEINNR	CRANNIED	ACDELLSU	CALLUSED
	DIACTINE	ACDEINNT	INCANTED	ACDELMOR	CLAMORED
	INDICATE	ACDEINOP	CANOPIED	ACDELMSU	MUSCADEL
ACDEIINU	INDUCIAE	ACDEINOS	CODEINAS	ACDELNOO	CANOODLE
ACDEIIRT	RATICIDE		DIOCESAN	ACDELNOR	COLANDER
ACDEIIST	ACIDIEST		OCEANIDS		CONELRAD
ACDEIITV	CAVITIED	ACDEINOT	ACTIONED	ACDELNOS	CELADONS
	VATICIDE		CATENOID	ACDELNPU	UNPLACED
	VICIATED	ACDEINOV	VOIDANCE	ACDELNRS	CANDLERS
ACDEIJNU	JAUNDICE	ACDEINPT	PEDANTIC	ACDELNRY	CALENDRY
ACDEIKNP	PANICKED		PENTADIC	ACDELNST	SCANTLED
ACDEIKNT	ANTICKED	ACDEINRR	RANCIDER	ACDELNSU	UNSCALED
ACDEIKPX	PICKAXED	ACDEINRT	CRINATED	ACDELNUW	UNCLAWED
ACDEILLM	MEDALLIC		DICENTRA	ACDELOOW	LACEWOOD
ACDEILLN	DECLINAL	ACDEINSS	ACIDNESS	ACDELOPS	PEDOCALS
ACDEILLS	CEDILLAS	ACDEINST	DANCIEST	ACDELOPT	CLODPATE
ACDEILLV	CAVILLED		DISTANCE	ACDELOPU	CUPOLAED
ACDEILMN	MEDCINAL	ACDEINSY	CYANIDES	ACDELORV	OVERCLAD
ACDEILMO	CAMELOID		CYANISED	ACDELOTU	OCULATED
	MELODICA	ACDEINTT	NICTATED	ACDELPPS	SCAPPLED
ACDEILMS	CAMELIDS	ACDEINTU	INCUDATE	ACDELPSU	CAPSULED
	DECIMALS	ACDEINVY	DEVIANCY		UPSCALED
	DECLAIMS	ACDEINYZ	CYANIZED	ACDELRRS	CRADLERS
	MEDICALS	ACDEIOPS	DIASCOPE	ACDELRSS	SCALDERS
ACDEILMT	CLIMATED	ACDEIORS	IDOCRASE	ACDELRSW	SCRAWLED
	MALEDICT	ACDEIORT	CERATOID	ACDELRSY	SACREDLY
ACDEILMX	CLIMAXED	ACDEIORV	COVARIED	ACDELSTU	CAULDEST

	SULCATED	**ACDEORST**	REDCOATS		RHODANIC
ACDELSWW	DEWCLAWS	**ACDEORSU**	CAROUSED	**ACDHINRY**	DINARCHY
ACDEMMRS	SCRAMMED	**ACDEORTU**	AERODUCT	**ACDHINST**	HINDCAST
ACDEMNNY	CANDYMEN		EDUCATOR	**ACDHINSW**	SANDWICH
ACDEMNOR	ROMANCED		OUTRACED	**ACDHIOPS**	SCAPHOID
ACDEMNSU	DECUMANS	**ACDEORTV**	CAVORTED	**ACDHIOPY**	HYPOACID
ACDEMOPR	COMPADRE	**ACDEOSTT**	CODETTAS	**ACDHIORY**	HYRACOID
	COMPARED		COSTATED	**ACDHIPST**	DISPATCH
ACDEMORR	CARROMED	**ACDEOSUV**	COUVADES	**ACDHIQRU**	CHARQUID
ACDEMORS	COMRADES	**ACDEOTTU**	OUTACTED	**ACDHIRRU**	CHURIDAR
ACDEMORT	DEMOCRAT	**ACDEPPRS**	SCRAPPED	**ACDHKORR**	HARDROCK
ACDEMPSU	CAMPUSED	**ACDEPRSW**	SCRAWPED	**ACDHLNOR**	CHALDRON
ACDEMPSY	MYSPACED	**ACDEPRTU**	CAPTURED		CHLORDAN
ACDEMRSW	SCRAWMED	**ACDEPSTU**	CUSPATED		CHONDRAL
ACDEMSTU	MUSCADET	**ACDEQTUU**	AQUEDUCT	**ACDHLORS**	DORLACHS
ACDEMUUV	VACUUMED	**ACDERRSU**	CRUSADER	**ACDHMNTU**	DUTCHMAN
ACDENNNO	CANNONED	**ACDERRTU**	TRADUCER	**ACDHMORU**	MOUCHARD
	NONDANCE	**ACDERSSU**	CRUSADES	**ACDHNORW**	CHAWDRON
ACDENNNU	UNCANNED	**ACDERSTT**	DETRACTS	**ACDHNOSW**	COWHANDS
ACDENNOR	ORDNANCE		SCRATTED	**ACDHOOST**	CATHOODS
ACDENNOT	CANTONED	**ACDERSTU**	TRADUCES	**ACDHOOTW**	WOODCHAT
ACDENNST	SCANDENT	**ACDERTUV**	CURVATED	**ACDHOPRS**	POCHARDS
ACDENOPR	ENDOCARP	**ACDFFHNU**	HANDCUFF	**ACDHOPTU**	TOUCHPAD
ACDENORR	RANCORED	**ACDFFIRT**	DIFFRACT	**ACDHORRS**	ORCHARDS
ACDENORS	DRACONES	**ACDFFLOS**	SCAFFOLD	**ACDHORSY**	DYSCHROA
	ENDOSARC	**ACDFIILU**	FIDUCIAL	**ACDIIILN**	INDICIAL
ACDENORT	CARTONED	**ACDFILMR**	FILMCARD	**ACDIIINR**	ANIRIDIC
	NOTECARD	**ACDFILOU**	FUCOIDAL	**ACDIIINS**	INDICIAS
ACDENORY	CRAYONED	**ACDFINOR**	FRICANDO	**ACDIIIPR**	DIAPIRIC
	DEACONRY	**ACDFIOST**	FACTOIDS	**ACDIIJLU**	JUDICIAL
ACDENOST	ENDOCAST	**ACDGHINY**	DAYCHING	**ACDIIKLP**	PICKADIL
	TACNODES	**ACDGHOTW**	DOGWATCH	**ACDIILMS**	DISCLAIM
ACDENOSY	CYANOSED		WATCHDOG	**ACDIILNO**	CONIDIAL
ACDENOTT	COATTEND	**ACDGIIKP**	DIGIPACK	**ACDIILNS**	SCALDINI
ACDENOTU	OUTDANCE	**ACDGIILO**	DIALOGIC	**ACDIILOV**	OVICIDAL
	UNCOATED	**ACDGIIMS**	DIGICAMS	**ACDIILSU**	SUICIDAL
ACDENPPU	UNCAPPED	**ACDGILNN**	CANDLING	**ACDIILTY**	CALIDITY
ACDENPRU	PRAUNCED	**ACDGILNR**	CRADLING		DIALYTIC
ACDENPST	PANDECTS	**ACDGILNS**	SCALDING	**ACDIIMNO**	DAIMONIC
ACDENRST	CANTREDS	**ACDGILNU**	CAUDLING	**ACDIIMOR**	CORMIDIA
ACDENRSU	DURANCES	**ACDGIMOT**	DOGMATIC		DIORAMIC
ACDENRTU	UNCARTED	**ACDGINNS**	DANCINGS	**ACDIIMOT**	DIATOMIC
	UNCRATED	**ACDGINNY**	CANDYING	**ACDIIMSU**	ASCIDIUM
	UNDERACT	**ACDGINRS**	CARDINGS	**ACDIINNO**	CONIDIAN
	UNTRACED	**ACDGINSU**	SCAUDING	**ACDIINNS**	INDICANS
ACDENRUV	UNCARVED	**ACDGIOPR**	PODAGRIC	**ACDIINNT**	INDICANT
ACDENRVY	VERDANCY	**ACDGKLOS**	DAGLOCKS	**ACDIINOP**	PINACOID
ACDENSST	DESCANTS	**ACDGLNOO**	GOLCONDA	**ACDIINOT**	ACTINOID
ACDENSUU	UNCAUSED	**ACDGNOST**	CANTDOGS		DIATONIC
ACDENTTY	DANCETTY	**ACDGORST**	DOGCARTS	**ACDIINPY**	PYCNIDIA
ACDEOORS	DOORCASE	**ACDHIILS**	CHILIADS	**ACDIINRS**	ACRIDINS
ACDEOPRS	SCOREPAD	**ACDHIINT**	TACHINID	**ACDIIORV**	VARICOID
ACDEOPRU	CROUPADE	**ACDHIIPS**	DIPHASIC	**ACDIIOSS**	ACIDOSIS
ACDEOPRY	COPYREAD	**ACDHIKNP**	HANDPICK	**ACDIIOSX**	OXIDASIC
ACDEOPSS	PEASCODS	**ACDHIKOR**	CHOKIDAR	**ACDIIRSS**	SCIARIDS
ACDEOPTT	CAPOTTED	**ACDHIKOT**	KATHODIC	**ACDIIRST**	ARCTIIDS
ACDEOPTU	OUTPACED	**ACDHILNT**	THINCLAD		CARDITIS
ACDEORRS	CERRADOS	**ACDHILPR**	PILCHARD		TRIACIDS
	CORRADES	**ACDHILPS**	CLAPDISH		TRIADICS
ACDEORRT	REDACTOR	**ACDHIMTW**	MIDWATCH	**ACDIIRTY**	ACRIDITY
ACDEORSS	SARCODES	**ACDHINOR**	HADRONIC	**ACDIISST**	SADISTIC

ACDIKLTU	DUCKTAIL	ACDIOSXY	OXYACIDS	ACDRSTTU	DUSTCART
ACDIKMOO	COOKMAID	ACDIPRST	ADSCRIPT	ACDRSTUY	CUSTARDY
ACDIKRRY	RICKYARD	ACDIPSTY	DIPTYCAS	ACEEEFRR	CAREFREE
ACDILLOS	CODILLAS	ACDIQRSU	QUADRICS	ACEEEGLN	ELEGANCE
ACDILLOU	CAUDILLO	ACDIRSST	DRASTICS	ACEEEGPR	CREEPAGE
	LODICULA	ACDIRSTT	DISTRACT	ACEEEGRS	CARGEESE
ACDILLPY	PLACIDLY	ACDIRTWY	CITYWARD	ACEEEIPR	EARPIECE
ACDILMOR	DROMICAL	ACDISTUV	VIADUCTS	ACEEEIPS	SEAPIECE
ACDILMOU	MUCOIDAL	ACDJNSTU	ADJUNCTS	ACEEEKNT	NECKATEE
ACDILMSS	CLADISMS	ACDKKLUW	DUCKWALK	ACEEELMR	CAMELEER
ACDILMTU	TALMUDIC	ACDKLOPS	PADLOCKS	ACEEENRR	CAREENER
ACDILNOO	CONOIDAL	ACDKMMOR	DRAMMOCK	ACEEENRS	ENCREASE
ACDILNOR	IRONCLAD	ACDKMPSU	MUDPACKS	ACEEENSV	EVANESCE
ACDILNOS	SCALDINO	ACDKOPRS	POCKARDS	ACEEEPSS	ESCAPEES
ACDILNOT	ANTICOLD	ACDLLORS	COLLARDS	ACEEERRR	CAREERER
	DALTONIC	ACDLNNOR	CORNLAND	ACEEERRT	RECREATE
ACDILNRY	RANCIDLY	ACDLNOPR	CROPLAND	ACEEERTT	ETCETERA
ACDILNSU	DULCIANS	ACDLNORS	CALDRONS	ACEEERTX	EXECRATE
ACDILNSY	SYNDICAL	ACDLNORU	CAULDRON	ACEEESUV	EVACUEES
ACDILNUU	NUDICAUL		CRUNODAL	ACEEFFIN	CAFFEINE
ACDILOPS	PLACOIDS	ACDLNORY	CONDYLAR	ACEEFFOR	FOREFACE
ACDILOPY	POLYACID	ACDLNOST	COTLANDS	ACEEFFRS	EFFACERS
	POLYADIC	ACDLNSSU	SUNSCALD	ACEEFFRT	AFFECTER
ACDILORS	CORDIALS	ACDLNORY	CONDYLAR	ACEEFHNS	ENCHAFES
ACDILORT	DICROTAL	ACDLOOOR	COLORADO	ACEEFHWY	WHEYFACE
ACDILOUV	OVIDUCAL	ACDLOORT	DOCTORAL	ACEEFILM	MALEFICE
ACDILPSU	CUSPIDAL	ACDLORWY	COWARDLY	ACEEFILR	LIFECARE
ACDILRST	TRICLADS	ACDLOSWY	LADYCOWS	ACEEFILS	CALEFIES
ACDILSST	CLADISTS	ACDLSTUY	DACTYLUS	ACEEFINS	FAIENCES
ACDILSTW	WILDCATS	ACDMMNOO	COMMANDO		FIANCEES
ACDIMMSU	CADMIUMS	ACDMMNOS	COMMANDS	ACEEFISS	CASEFIES
ACDIMNOO	CODOMAIN	ACDMNOPS	COMPANDS	ACEEFKOR	ECOFREAK
	MONOACID	ACDMNORY	DORMANCY	ACEEFLPU	PEACEFUL
ACDIMNOS	MANDIOCS		MORDANCY	ACEEFLSS	FACELESS
	MONACIDS	ACDMOOPR	MACROPOD	ACEEFLTY	FACETELY
ACDIMNSU	MUSCADIN	ACDMOOSW	CAMWOODS	ACEEFNSY	FAYENCES
	SCANDIUM	ACDMORSZ	CZARDOMS	ACEEFPRR	PREFACER
ACDIMNSY	DYNAMICS	ACDMPRTU	DUMPCART	ACEEFPRS	PREFACES
ACDIMOOS	CAMOODIS	ACDNOORR	RONCADOR	ACEEFPRT	PERFECTA
ACDIMOST	COADMITS	ACDNOORS	CARDOONS		PRAEFECT
ACDIMOSY	DOCIMASY	ACDNOORT	ACRODONT	ACEEFPTY	TYPEFACE
ACDINNOO	ANCONOID	ACDNOORV	CORDOVAN	ACEEFRSU	FARCEUSE
ACDINNOS	NONACIDS	ACDNOOTU	DUCATOON	ACEEGHNR	ENCHARGE
ACDINNOY	ANODYNIC	ACDNORRW	WARDCORN		GRENACHE
ACDINOPS	SPONDAIC	ACDNORSU	CANDOURS		RECHANGE
ACDINORS	SARDONIC		CAUDRONS	ACEEGHNX	EXCHANGE
ACDINORT	TORNADIC	ACDNOSTW	DOWNCAST	ACEEGHRR	RECHARGE
ACDINORW	CORDWAIN	ACDNOSUU	ADUNCOUS	ACEEGIKL	CAGELIKE
ACDINRSU	CANDIRUS	ACDOOPPR	PODOCARP	ACEEGILS	ELEGIACS
ACDINSST	DISCANTS	ACDOOPSU	DOCUSOAP		LEGACIES
ACDINSTY	DYNASTIC	ACDOOPTY	OCTAPODY	ACEEGINS	AGENCIES
ACDINTUY	ADUNCITY	ACDOORST	OSTRACOD	ACEEGINT	AGENETIC
ACDIOOTU	AUTOCOID		SCORDATO	ACEEGIRS	GRAECISE
ACDIOPRS	PICADORS	ACDOPRST	POSTCARD	ACEEGIRZ	GRAECIZE
	SPORADIC	ACDOPSST	PODCASTS	ACEEGKNR	NECKGEAR
ACDIORRS	CORRIDAS	ACDORRWY	COWARDRY	ACEEGKRW	WRECKAGE
ACDIORSS	SARCOIDS	ACDORSST	COSTARDS	ACEEGLNY	ELEGANCY
ACDIORST	CAROTIDS	ACDORSSU	CRUSADOS	ACEEGLPU	PUCELAGE
ACDIORTT	DICTATOR	ACDORSUZ	CRUZADOS	ACEEGNNT	TANGENCE
ACDIOSTX	DOXASTIC	ACDOSSTV	VODCASTS	ACEEGNOZ	COZENAGE
ACDIOSTY	DYSTOCIA	ACDOSTTU	DUSTCOAT	ACEEGNRS	ENGRACES
		ACDRSSTU	CUSTARDS		

ACEEGNRY	REAGENCY		SEARCHER		CREASIER
ACEEGNST	CENTAGES	ACEEHRRT	TREACHER	ACEEIRSU	CAUSERIE
ACEEGNSV	SCAVENGE	ACEEHRSS	SEARCHES	ACEEIRSW	WISEACRE
ACEEGORR	RACEGOER	ACEEHRST	CHEATERS	ACEEIRTV	CREATIVE
ACEEGORV	COVERAGE		HECTARES		REACTIVE
ACEEGOST	ECOTAGES		RECHATES	ACEEISTV	VESICATE
ACEEGSSU	ESCUAGES		RECHEATS	ACEEJKNS	JACKEENS
ACEEHHRU	HEUCHERA		TEACHERS	ACEEJKRT	REJACKET
ACEEHHST	CHEETAHS	ACEEHRTT	CATHETER	ACEEKLMR	MACKEREL
ACEEHILR	LEACHIER	ACEEHRTY	CHEATERY	ACEEKLRT	RETACKLE
ACEEHILS	HELICASE	ACEEHSST	ESCHEATS	ACEEKLRW	EELWRACK
ACEEHINT	ECHINATE	ACEEHSTX	CATHEXES	ACEEKMPT	EMPACKET
ACEEHIPR	PEACHIER		EXCHEATS	ACEEKNPS	KNEECAPS
ACEEHIPS	CHEAPIES	ACEEHTTV	CHAVETTE	ACEEKNRW	NECKWEAR
ACEEHIPT	EPITHECA	ACEEHTWY	WATCHEYE	ACEEKRRT	RACKETER
	PETECHIA	ACEEIKLL	LACELIKE	ACEELLMT	CELLMATE
ACEEHIRT	AETHERIC	ACEEIKLV	CAVELIKE	ACEELLNS	NACELLES
	HETAERIC	ACEEIKMR	ICEMAKER	ACEELLNT	LANCELET
ACEEHIRV	ACHIEVER	ACEEIKNP	PEACENIK	ACEELLOT	OCELLATE
	CHIVAREE	ACEEIKRR	CREAKIER	ACEELLPT	CAPELLET
ACEEHIST	HICATEES	ACEEILLM	MICELLAE	ACEELLRR	CELLARER
ACEEHISV	ACHIEVES	ACEEILLP	CALLIPEE		RECALLER
ACEEHITV	ATCHIEVE	ACEEILMN	CAMELINE	ACEELLRT	CELLARET
ACEEHKNS	SKEECHAN	ACEEILMT	EMETICAL	ACEELLRV	CREVALLE
ACEEHKOS	HOECAKES	ACEEILMU	LEUCEMIA	ACEELLSS	LACELESS
ACEEHKTT	HACKETTE	ACEEILNP	CAPELINE	ACEELMNO	CAMELEON
ACEEHLMP	EMPLEACH	ACEEILNR	CARELINE	ACEELMNP	PLACEMEN
ACEEHLOS	SHOELACE		CINEREAL	ACEELMPS	EMPLACES
ACEEHLPS	PLEACHES		RELIANCE	ACEELMRS	RECLAMES
ACEEHLRS	LEACHERS	ACEEILNS	SALIENCE		SCLEREMA
	RELACHES	ACEEILPS	CALIPEES	ACEELNPR	PRECLEAN
ACEEHLSS	LACHESES		ESPECIAL	ACEELNPT	PENTACLE
ACEEHLST	CHELATES	ACEEILRS	ESCALIER	ACEELNRR	LARCENER
ACEEHLSW	ESCHEWAL	ACEEILRV	RECEIVAL	ACEELNRS	CLEANERS
ACEEHLTV	CHEVALET	ACEEIMOT	ACOEMETI		CLEANSER
ACEEHMNP	CAMPHENE	ACEEIMRR	CREAMIER		RECLEANS
ACEEHMNR	MENARCHE		REARMICE	ACEELNRU	CERULEAN
ACEEHMRS	CASHMERE		RECAMIER	ACEELNRV	VERNACLE
	MACHREES	ACEEIMRS	CASIMERE	ACEELNSS	CLEANSES
	MARCHESE		RACEMISE	ACEELNST	CLEANEST
ACEEHMST	MACHETES	ACEEIMRT	CEMITARE		LATENCES
ACEEHNNR	ENHANCER	ACEEIMRZ	RACEMIZE	ACEELNSU	NUCLEASE
ACEEHNNS	ENHANCES	ACEEIMST	EMICATES	ACEELNSV	ENCLAVES
ACEEHNPS	CHEAPENS	ACEEINNR	NARCEINE		VALENCES
ACEEHNRS	ENARCHES	ACEEINPS	SAPIENCE	ACEELNTT	TENTACLE
	ENCHASER	ACEEINPT	PATIENCE	ACEELNTU	NUCLEATE
ACEEHNRV	REVANCHE	ACEEINRS	CINEREAS	ACEELOPS	ESCALOPE
ACEEHNSS	ENCASHES		INCREASE		OPALESCE
	ENCHASES		RESIANCE	ACEELORS	ESCAROLE
ACEEHOOT	OOTHECAE	ACEEINRT	CENTIARE	ACEELORT	CORELATE
ACEEHOPT	APOTHECE		CREATINE		RELOCATE
ACEEHORT	OCHREATE		INCREATE	ACEELOSS	SECALOSE
ACEEHPPS	ECHAPPES		ITERANCE	ACEELOSV	VOCALESE
ACEEHPRR	PREACHER	ACEEINST	CINEASTE	ACEELPPR	PREPLACE
ACEEHPRS	PEACHERS	ACEEINSU	EUCAINES	ACEELPRR	PRECLEAR
	PREACHES	ACEEINTV	ENACTIVE		REPLACER
ACEEHPRT	ETHERCAP	ACEEINTX	EXITANCE	ACEELPRS	PERCALES
ACEEHPST	CHEAPEST	ACEEIPRP	PRAECIPE		REPLACES
ACEEHQSU	QUEACHES	ACEEIPST	SPECIATE	ACEELPRT	PRAELECT
ACEEHRRS	REACHERS	ACEEIQRU	ACQUIREE	ACEELPST	CAPELETS
	RESEARCH	ACEEIRRS	CARIERES	ACEELPSY	CYPSELAE

ACEELPTU	PECULATE	**ACEEORST**	CREASOTE	**ACEFHIST**	SHITFACE
ACEELPTY	CLYPEATE	**ACEEOSSS**	CASEOSES	**ACEFHISV**	CAVEFISH
ACEELRRS	CLEARERS	**ACEEOSTT**	ECOSTATE	**ACEFHLNS**	FLANCHES
ACEELRSS	CARELESS	**ACEEOSTV**	EVOCATES	**ACEFHMRS**	CHAMFERS
	RESCALES	**ACEEPRRS**	CAPERERS	**ACEFHORS**	ARCHFOES
ACEELRST	CLEAREST	**ACEEPRRT**	RECARPET	**ACEFHORU**	FAROUCHE
	SCELERAT	**ACEEPRSS**	ESCAPERS	**ACEFHRST**	FRATCHES
	TREACLES		RESPACES	**ACEFHRSU**	CHAUFERS
ACEELRSV	CERVELAS	**ACEEPRTT**	ETTERCAP	**ACEFIILS**	FELICIAS
	CLEAVERS	**ACEEPRTU**	PERACUTE	**ACEFIIPR**	PACIFIER
ACEELRTT	RACLETTE	**ACEEPRTX**	EXCERPTA	**ACEFIIPS**	PACIFIES
ACEELRTU	ULCERATE	**ACEEPSST**	PECTASES	**ACEFIIRT**	ARTIFICE
ACEELRTV	CERVELAT	**ACEEPSSU**	AUCEPSES	**ACEFIKLL**	CALFLIKE
ACEELRTX	EXCRETAL	**ACEEPSTT**	PECTATES	**ACEFILLS**	ICEFALLS
ACEELSST	CELESTAS		SPECTATE	**ACEFILLY**	FACILELY
	SELECTAS	**ACEEPSTY**	TYPECASE	**ACEFILOP**	EPIFOCAL
ACEELSSU	EUCLASES	**ACEERRRT**	RETRACER	**ACEFILOS**	FASCIOLE
ACEELSTT	TELECAST	**ACEERRSS**	CARESSER		FOCALISE
ACEELSVX	EXCLAVES		CREASERS	**ACEFILOZ**	FOCALIZE
ACEEMMOT	AMMOCETE	**ACEERRST**	CATERERS	**ACEFILRS**	FILACERS
ACEEMNNS	SCENEMAN		RECRATES	**ACEFILRY**	FIRECLAY
ACEEMNOT	MECONATE		RETRACES	**ACEFIMNY**	FEMINACY
ACEEMNPS	SPACEMEN		TERRACES	**ACEFIMPR**	CAMPFIRE
ACEEMNRS	MENACERS	**ACEERRSU**	ECRASEUR	**ACEFINNS**	FINANCES
ACEEMNST	CASEMENT	**ACEERRTU**	CREATURE	**ACEFINRS**	FANCIERS
ACEEMOPR	CAMPOREE	**ACEERRUV**	VERRUCAE		FRANCISE
ACEEMOPT	COPEMATE	**ACEERSSS**	CARESSES	**ACEFINRX**	CARNIFEX
ACEEMORS	RACEMOSE	**ACEERSST**	CATERESS	**ACEFINRZ**	FRANCIZE
ACEEMORV	OVERCAME		CERASTES	**ACEFINSS**	FASCINES
ACEEMRRS	AMERCERS	**ACEERSSU**	SURCEASE	**ACEFINST**	FANCIEST
	CREAMERS	**ACEERSSV**	CREVASSE	**ACEFINSU**	UNIFACES
	SCREAMER	**ACEERSTU**	SECATEUR	**ACEFIOSS**	FIASCOES
ACEEMRRY	CREAMERY	**ACEERSTX**	EXACTERS	**ACEFIPRY**	REPACIFY
ACEEMRST	CREMATES	**ACEERSVZ**	CERVEZAS	**ACEFIRRT**	CRAFTIER
	MEERCATS	**ACEERTTU**	ERUCTATE	**ACEFIRTT**	TRIFECTA
ACEEMRTW	CREWMATE	**ACEESSST**	ECSTASES	**ACEFIRTY**	FERACITY
ACEENNPS	PENANCES	**ACEESSTT**	CASETTES	**ACEFISST**	FACTISES
ACEENNRS	NARCEENS		CASSETTE	**ACEFKLRS**	FLACKERS
ACEENNRT	ENTRANCE	**ACEESTTX**	EXACTEST	**ACEFKLRY**	FLACKERY
ACEENNST	CANTEENS	**ACEFFGIN**	EFFACING	**ACEFKLST**	FLACKETS
ACEENNSY	CAYENNES	**ACEFFHIR**	CHAFFIER	**ACEFLLSS**	CALFLESS
ACEENOPT	CONEPATE	**ACEFFHIS**	AFFICHES	**ACEFLMNO**	FLAMENCO
ACEENORT	CAROTENE	**ACEFFHRS**	CHAFFERS	**ACEFLNOR**	FALCONER
ACEENOST	ACETONES	**ACEFFHRU**	CHAUFFER	**ACEFLNOT**	CONFLATE
	NOTECASE	**ACEFFHRY**	CHAFFERY		FALCONET
ACEENPRR	PARCENER	**ACEFFILT**	FACELIFT	**ACEFLNRY**	CRANEFLY
ACEENPRT	PERCEANT	**ACEFFIMS**	CAFFEISM	**ACEFLORS**	ALFRESCO
	PREENACT	**ACEFFINS**	CAFFEINS	**ACEFLRTU**	CRATEFUL
ACEENRRT	RECANTER	**ACEFFISS**	SCAFFIES		FULCRATE
	RECREANT	**ACEFFLLU**	FULLFACE	**ACEFLRUU**	FURCULAE
ACEENRSS	CASERNES	**ACEFFLRS**	SCLAFFER	**ACEFMNOO**	MOONFACE
ACEENRST	CENTARES	**ACEFFORS**	AFFORCES	**ACEFNNOS**	FACONNES
	ENCASTRE	**ACEFGINN**	ENFACING	**ACEFNORV**	CONFERVA
	REASCENT	**ACEFGINR**	REFACING	**ACEFNPRT**	PENCRAFT
	REENACTS	**ACEFGINT**	FACETING	**ACEFNRST**	CANTREFS
	SARCENET	**ACEFGIPS**	PIGFACES	**ACEFNRSU**	FURNACES
ACEENRTU	ENACTURE	**ACEFGLRU**	GRACEFUL	**ACEFOOPT**	FOOTPACE
	UNCREATE	**ACEFGLSU**	CAGEFULS	**ACEFOORT**	FOOTRACE
ACEENSSS	CASSENES	**ACEFGOST**	GEOFACTS	**ACEFOPST**	POSTFACE
ACEENSTX	EXSECANT	**ACEFHIKL**	LIFEHACK	**ACEFORRS**	FORECARS
ACEEOQTU	COEQUATE	**ACEFHIKS**	FISHCAKE	**ACEFORST**	FORECAST

ACEFORSX	CARFOXES	**ACEGILPS**	PELAGICS	**ACEGLLOS**	COLLAGES
ACEFOSTU	OUTFACES	**ACEGILRS**	GLACIERS	**ACEGLNOS**	CONGEALS
ACEFRRSS	SCARFERS		GRACILES		LONGCASE
ACEFRRST	CRAFTERS	**ACEGILRV**	CLAVIGER	**ACEGLNOT**	OCTANGLE
	REFRACTS	**ACEGILRY**	GLYCERIA	**ACEGLNOY**	AGLYCONE
ACEFRRSU	FARCEURS	**ACEGILSS**	GLACISES	**ACEGLNRS**	CLANGERS
	SURFACER	**ACEGILST**	GELASTIC		GLANCERS
ACEFRRTU	FRACTURE		GESTICAL	**ACEGLOST**	CATELOGS
ACEFRSSU	SURFACES	**ACEGIMMT**	TAGMEMIC	**ACEGLOSU**	CAGOULES
ACEFRSTU	FACTURES	**ACEGIMNN**	MENACING	**ACEGMNOY**	GEOMANCY
	FURCATES	**ACEGIMNO**	CAMEOING	**ACEGMNRS**	CRAGSMEN
ACEGGILN	CAGELING	**ACEGIMNR**	AMERCING	**ACEGMOPS**	COMPAGES
	GLACEING		CREAMING	**ACEGMORS**	SCARMOGE
ACEGGILR	CLAGGIER		GERMANIC	**ACEGMRRY**	GRAMERCY
ACEGGINN	ENCAGING	**ACEGIMNS**	MAGNESIC	**ACEGNNOR**	CRANNOGE
ACEGGIOP	EPAGOGIC	**ACEGIMNT**	MAGNETIC	**ACEGNNOY**	CYANOGEN
ACEGGIRR	CRAGGIER	**ACEGIMOS**	CAMOGIES	**ACEGNNRY**	REGNANCY
ACEGHIIT	CHIGETAI	**ACEGIMOX**	EXOGAMIC	**ACEGNNTY**	TANGENCY
ACEGHILN	LEACHING	**ACEGIMRR**	GRIMACER	**ACEGNORS**	ACROGENS
ACEGHILT	LICHGATE	**ACEGIMRS**	GRIMACES		CORNAGES
	TEIGLACH	**ACEGIMTY**	MEGACITY	**ACEGNOST**	COAGENTS
ACEGHINP	CHEAPING	**ACEGINNO**	CANOEING		COGNATES
	PEACHING	**ACEGINNR**	ENRACING	**ACEGNSSY**	CAGYNESS
ACEGHINR	REACHING		RECANING	**ACEGOORS**	CARGOOSE
ACEGHINT	CHEATING	**ACEGINNS**	ENCASING	**ACEGOPRY**	GEOCARPY
	TEACHING	**ACEGINNT**	ENACTING	**ACEGORSS**	CORSAGES
ACEGHLOS	GALOCHES	**ACEGINNV**	ENCAVING		SOCAGERS
ACEGHLRS	SCHLAGER	**ACEGINOS**	COINAGES	**ACEGORST**	ESCARGOT
ACEGHLRU	RUGELACH	**ACEGINOY**	GYNOECIA	**ACEGORSU**	COURAGES
ACEGHLTY	LYCHGATE	**ACEGINPR**	CAPERING	**ACEGORTT**	COTTAGER
ACEGHLUY	GAUCHELY		PEARCING	**ACEGORTY**	CATEGORY
ACEGHMMU	CHUMMAGE		PREACING	**ACEGOSTT**	COTTAGES
ACEGHMOR	ECHOGRAM	**ACEGINPS**	ESCAPING	**ACEGOTTY**	COTTAGEY
	GRAMOCHE	**ACEGINRS**	CREASING	**ACEGPRSTU**	TRUCAGES
ACEGHNPU	CHANGEUP		GRECIANS	**ACEGSSTU**	SCUTAGES
ACEGHNRS	CHANGERS		SEARCING	**ACEGSTTU**	CUTTAGES
ACEGHNRU	UNCHARGE	**ACEGINRT**	ARGENTIC	**ACEHHINS**	HAINCHES
ACEGHNSU	CHAUNGES		CATERING	**ACEHHIPS**	CHEAPISH
	GAUNCHES		CITRANGE	**ACEHHIRR**	HIERARCH
ACEGHOSU	GOUACHES		CREATING	**ACEHHIST**	SHECHITA
ACEGHOSW	COWHAGES		REACTING	**ACEHHISU**	HUISACHE
ACEGHRRS	CHARGERS	**ACEGINSS**	CAGINESS	**ACEHHLST**	HATCHELS
ACEGHRTU	RECAUGHT		CEASINGS	**ACEHHLSU**	SHAUCHLE
ACEGHSTU	GAUCHEST	**ACEGINTX**	EXACTING	**ACEHHMNN**	HENCHMAN
ACEGIIMP	EPIGAMIC	**ACEGIOTT**	COGITATE	**ACEHHNRT**	ETHNARCH
ACEGIINR	REAGINIC	**ACEGIPRS**	SPAGERIC	**ACEHHNSU**	HAUNCHES
ACEGIINV	VICINAGE	**ACEGIRST**	AGRESTIC	**ACEHHPRT**	HEPTARCH
ACEGIKNR	CREAKING		CIGARETS	**ACEHHRST**	HATCHERS
ACEGILLO	COLLEGIA		ERGASTIC	**ACEHHRSU**	HACHURES
ACEGILLR	ALLERGIC	**ACEGISTU**	GAUCIEST	**ACEHHRTT**	THATCHER
ACEGILMU	MUCILAGE	**ACEGISTW**	GAWCIEST	**ACEHHRTY**	HATCHERY
ACEGILMY	GLYCEMIA	**ACEGJKLS**	JACKLEGS		THEARCHY
ACEGILNN	CLEANING	**ACEGKLOS**	LOCKAGES	**ACEHHRXY**	HEXARCHY
	ELANCING	**ACEGKLOV**	GAVELOCK	**ACEHHSTT**	HATCHETS
	ENLACING	**ACEGKLRS**	GRACKLES		THATCHES
ACEGILNR	CLEARING	**ACEGKMOS**	MOCKAGES	**ACEHHTTY**	HATCHETY
	RELACING	**ACEGKORS**	CORKAGES	**ACEHIIMN**	CHIMINEA
ACEGILNT	CLEATING	**ACEGKORW**	CAGEWORK	**ACEHIIMS**	ISCHEMIA
ACEGILNV	CLEAVING	**ACEGKOST**	STOCKAGE	**ACEHIINT**	ETHICIAN
ACEGILNW	LACEWING	**ACEGKRTU**	TRUCKAGE	**ACEHIIRT**	HETAIRIC
ACEGILOS	CALIGOES	**ACEGLLNO**	COLLAGEN		HIERATIC

ACEHIJKR	HIJACKER	**ACEHINRU**	ECHIURAN	**ACEHKOSW**	WHACKOES
ACEHIJNT	JACINTHE	**ACEHINRV**	VACHERIN	**ACEHKOTU**	TUCKAHOE
ACEHIKLP	KEPHALIC	**ACEHINSS**	ACHINESS	**ACEHKRSW**	WHACKERS
ACEHIKLR	CHALKIER		INCHASES	**ACEHKRTW**	THWACKER
	HACKLIER	**ACEHINST**	ASTHENIC	**ACEHLLMO**	MALLECHO
ACEHIKLW	LICHWAKE		CHANTIES	**ACEHLLOO**	COALHOLE
ACEHIKRS	KACHERIS	**ACEHINSY**	HYACINES	**ACEHLLOR**	ORCHELLA
ACEHIKRW	WHACKIER		SYNECHIA	**ACEHLLPS**	PELLACHS
ACEHILLS	CHALLIES	**ACEHIOPR**	POACHIER	**ACEHLLSS**	SHELLACS
ACEHILLT	HELLICAT	**ACEHIOST**	ACHIOTES	**ACEHLLST**	HELLCATS
ACEHILMN	INCHMEAL		TOISEACH	**ACEHLLSU**	HALLUCES
ACEHILMO	CHOLEMIA	**ACEHIPPR**	CHAPPIER	**ACEHLMOT**	CHAMELOT
ACEHILMP	IMPLEACH	**ACEHIPPS**	CHAPPIES	**ACEHLMST**	CHAMLETS
ACEHILMS	CAMELISH	**ACEHIPRS**	ASPHERIC	**ACEHLNNS**	CHANNELS
	LECHAIMS		CHARPIES	**ACEHLNOS**	CHALONES
	MICHAELS		PARCHESI	**ACEHLNOU**	EULACHON
ACEHILMY	LECHAYIM		SERAPHIC	**ACEHLNPS**	PLANCHES
ACEHILNP	CEPHALIN	**ACEHIPRT**	CHAPITER	**ACEHLNPT**	PLANCHET
ACEHILNT	CHAINLET		PATCHIER	**ACEHLNRS**	CHARNELS
	CHATLINE		PHREATIC	**ACEHLNRU**	LAUNCHER
	ETHNICAL	**ACEHIPST**	HEPATICS		RELAUNCH
ACEHILOR	HALICORE		PASTICHE	**ACEHLNST**	STANCHEL
	HEROICAL		PISTACHE	**ACEHLNSU**	LAUNCHES
ACEHILPR	PARHELIC	**ACEHIPTT**	PATHETIC	**ACEHLOOT**	OOTHECAL
ACEHILPY	PEACHILY	**ACEHIPTW**	WHITECAP	**ACEHLOPT**	POTLACHE
ACEHILRR	CHARLIER	**ACEHIQSU**	QUAICHES	**ACEHLORS**	CHOLERAS
ACEHILRS	CHARLIES	**ACEHIRRR**	CHARRIER		CHORALES
ACEHILST	ETHICALS	**ACEHIRSS**	CASHIERS	**ACEHLORT**	CHELATOR
ACEHILTT	ATHLETIC		RACHISES		CHLORATE
	THETICAL	**ACEHIRST**	CHARIEST		TROCHLEA
ACEHIMMS	CHAMMIES		STICHERA	**ACEHLORU**	LEACHOUR
ACEHIMNN	CHAINMEN		THERIACS	**ACEHLOST**	CATHOLES
	CHINAMEN	**ACEHIRSU**	EUCHARIS		CHOLATES
ACEHIMNP	CAMPHINE	**ACEHIRSV**	ARCHIVES		ESCHALOT
ACEHIMNR	CHAIRMEN	**ACEHIRSW**	ARCHWISE	**ACEHLPRT**	CHAPTREL
ACEHIMNS	MACHINES	**ACEHIRTT**	CHATTIER	**ACEHLPRY**	CHAPELRY
ACEHIMNT	ANTHEMIC		THEATRIC	**ACEHLPSS**	CHAPLESS
ACEHIMNU	ACHENIUM	**ACEHIRVV**	CHAVVIER	**ACEHLPST**	CHAPLETS
ACEHIMPR	CAMPHIRE	**ACEHISST**	CHASTISE	**ACEHLRSS**	CLASHERS
	CHAMPIER		TAISCHES		RASCHELS
ACEHIMPT	EMPATHIC	**ACEHISSU**	CHIAUSES	**ACEHLRST**	ARCHLETS
	EMPHATIC	**ACEHISTT**	CHATTIES		TRACHLES
ACEHIMRS	CHASMIER		TACHISTE	**ACEHLRSY**	CHARLEYS
	CHIMERAS	**ACEHISTX**	CATHEXIS	**ACEHLRTU**	ARCHLUTE
	MARCHESI	**ACEHISTY**	YACHTIES		TRAUCHLE
ACEHIMRT	RHEMATIC	**ACEHISTZ**	ZAITECHS	**ACEHLSSS**	CASHLESS
ACEHIMSS	CHAMISES	**ACEHKLLS**	SHELLACK	**ACEHLSST**	SATCHELS
ACEHIMST	HEMATICS	**ACEHKLOV**	HAVELOCK		SLATCHES
	MASTICHE	**ACEHKLPR**	KREPLACH	**ACEHLSTT**	CHATTELS
	MISTEACH	**ACEHKLRS**	HACKLERS		LATCHETS
	TACHISME		SHACKLER	**ACEHLSTY**	CHASTELY
ACEHIMTT	THEMATIC	**ACEHKLSS**	SHACKLES	**ACEHMMNR**	MARCHMEN
ACEHIMTZ	MECHITZA	**ACEHKLST**	HACKLETS	**ACEHMNNR**	RANCHMEN
ACEHINNS	ENCHAINS		KLATCHES	**ACEHMNOP**	CAMPHONE
ACEHINOT	ETHANOIC	**ACEHKLTY**	LATCHKEY		PHONECAM
	INCHOATE	**ACEHKMPU**	MUCKHEAP	**ACEHMNOR**	CHOREMAN
ACEHINOX	HEXANOIC	**ACEHKNSY**	HACKNEYS	**ACEHMNRS**	ENCHARMS
ACEHINPS	PAINCHES	**ACEHKOPS**	SHOEPACK	**ACEHMNRT**	MERCHANT
ACEHINPT	HAPTENIC	**ACEHKORV**	HAVOCKER	**ACEHMNSS**	CHESSMAN
ACEHINRS	ARCHINES	**ACEHKOSS**	SHACKOES	**ACEHMNST**	MANCHETS
	INARCHES	**ACEHKOST**	HOTCAKES	**ACEHMNTW**	WATCHMEN

ACEHMNTY	YACHTMEN	**ACEHOSSW**	SHOWCASE	**ACEIIPTX**	EPITAXIC
ACEHMORT	CHROMATE	**ACEHOSTU**	CATHOUSE	**ACEIIRRT**	CRITERIA
ACEHMOST	MOSCHATE		SOUTACHE	**ACEIIRSV**	VICARIES
ACEHMPRS	CHAMPERS	**ACEHOSTY**	CHAYOTES	**ACEIISTT**	ATTICISE
ACEHMRRS	CHARMERS	**ACEHOSUV**	AVOUCHES	**ACEIISTU**	ACUITIES
	MARCHERS	**ACEHOTTU**	OUTCHEAT	**ACEIISTV**	ACTIVISE
ACEHMRSS	SCHMEARS	**ACEHPPSS**	CHAPPESS		CAITIVES
ACEHMRST	MATCHERS		SCHAPPES		CAVITIES
ACEHMRSU	CHAUMERS	**ACEHPRRS**	PRECRASH		VICIATES
ACEHMSST	SMATCHES	**ACEHPRST**	CHAPTERS	**ACEIITTV**	VITICETA
ACEHMSTT	MATCHETS		PATCHERS	**ACEIITTZ**	ATTICIZE
	SCHMATTE	**ACEHPRSU**	PURCHASE	**ACEIITVZ**	ACTIVIZE
ACEHMSTU	MUSTACHE	**ACEHPRTY**	PATCHERY	**ACEIJKSS**	JACKSIES
ACEHMSTY	ECTHYMAS		PETCHARY	**ACEIJMST**	MAJESTIC
ACEHNNOP	PANCHEON	**ACEHPSTY**	SCYPHATE	**ACEIJNRR**	JERRICAN
ACEHNNOT	NANOTECH	**ACEHQSTU**	QUATCHES	**ACEIKKLS**	SACKLIKE
ACEHNNPT	PENCHANT	**ACEHRRSS**	CRASHERS	**ACEIKKNR**	KNACKIER
ACEHNNRS	CHANNERS	**ACEHRRST**	CHARTERS	**ACEIKLLM**	CLAMLIKE
ACEHNNST	ENCHANTS		RECHARTS		MILLCAKE
ACEHNOPR	CANEPHOR		STARCHER	**ACEIKLLW**	CLAWLIKE
	CARPHONE	**ACEHRRSV**	CHARVERS	**ACEIKLLY**	CLAYLIKE
	CHAPERON	**ACEHRRTT**	TETRARCH	**ACEIKLNR**	CLANKIER
ACEHNOPS	PANOCHES	**ACEHRRSST**	STARCHES	**ACEIKLRT**	TALCKIER
ACEHNOPT	CENOTAPH	**ACEHRSSU**	CHASSEUR	**ACEIKLRY**	CREAKILY
ACEHNORR	RANCHERO	**ACEHRSTT**	CHATTERS	**ACEIKMNN**	NICKNAME
ACEHNORT	ANCHORET		RATCHETS	**ACEIKMRS**	KERAMICS
ACEHNPRT	PENTARCH	**ACEHRSTW**	WATCHERS	**ACEIKMRV**	MAVERICK
ACEHNPRU	UNPREACH	**ACEHRSTY**	YACHTERS	**ACEIKNPS**	CAPESKIN
ACEHNPSU	PAUNCHES	**ACEHRTTY**	CHATTERY	**ACEIKNRR**	CRANKIER
ACEHNRRS	RANCHERS		TRACHYTE	**ACEIKNRS**	SKINCARE
ACEHNRSS	ARCHNESS	**ACEHSSSU**	CHAUSSES	**ACEIKNSS**	CAKINESS
ACEHNRST	CHANTERS	**ACEHSSTT**	CHASTEST	**ACEIKOPS**	PAIOCKES
	SNATCHER	**ACEHSSTW**	SWATCHES	**ACEIKORR**	CROAKIER
	STANCHER	**ACEHSTTU**	CATHETUS	**ACEIKPRS**	EARPICKS
	TRANCHES		TEUCHATS	**ACEIKPSW**	WICKAPES
ACEHNRSU	RAUNCHES	**ACEHSTTW**	WATCHETS	**ACEIKPSX**	PICKAXES
ACEHNRSW	CRENSHAW	**ACEHTTUZ**	ZUCHETTA	**ACEIKQRU**	QUACKIER
ACEHNRTT	TRANCHET	**ACEIIKNT**	AKINETIC	**ACEIKRRV**	VRAICKER
ACEHNRTU	CHAUNTER	**ACEIILMN**	LIMACINE	**ACEIKSST**	CASKIEST
ACEHNSSS	SCHANSES	**ACEIILNR**	IRENICAL	**ACEIKSTT**	TACKIEST
ACEHNSST	CHASTENS	**ACEIILNS**	SALICINE		TIETACKS
	SNATCHES	**ACEIILNX**	ALEXINIC	**ACEIKSTW**	WACKIEST
	STANCHES	**ACEIILSS**	LAICISES	**ACEILLLT**	CLITELLA
ACEHNSSZ	SCHANZES	**ACEIILST**	CILIATES	**ACEILLMR**	MICELLAR
ACEHNSTT	ETCHANTS		SILICATE		MILLRACE
ACEHNSTU	NAUTCHES	**ACEIILSZ**	LAICIZES	**ACEILLMS**	LIMACELS
	UNCHASTE	**ACEIIMRS**	CASIMIRE		MICELLAS
ACEHNSTY	CHANTEYS	**ACEIIMRV**	VIRAEMIC	**ACEILLMT**	CALLTIME
ACEHNSTZ	SCHANTZE	**ACEIIMSS**	ASEISMIC		METALLIC
ACEHNSZZ	CHAZZENS	**ACEIIMST**	METICAIS	**ACEILLMY**	MYCELIAL
ACEHOPPR	COPPERAH	**ACEIIMTU**	MAIEUTIC	**ACEILLNT**	CLIENTAL
ACEHOPRR	REPROACH	**ACEIINPS**	PISCINAE	**ACEILLOP**	CALLIOPE
ACEHOPRS	POACHERS	**ACEIINRR**	CAIRNIER	**ACEILLOR**	ROCAILLE
ACEHOPSS	SHOEPACS	**ACEIINRS**	RIANCIES	**ACEILLOS**	LOCALISE
ACEHORRS	HORSECAR	**ACEIINRT**	ARENITIC	**ACEILLOT**	LOCALITE
ACEHORRV	OVERARCH	**ACEIINST**	ANTICISE		TEOCALLI
ACEHORST	CHAROSET		CANITIES	**ACEILLOZ**	LOCALIZE
	THORACES	**ACEIINTV**	INACTIVE	**ACEILLPR**	CALLIPER
ACEHORTT	THEOCRAT	**ACEIINTZ**	ANTICIZE	**ACEILLPS**	ALLSPICE
ACEHORTU	OUTREACH	**ACEIIPRS**	PIRACIES	**ACEILLPY**	EPICALLY
ACEHORUV	AVOUCHER	**ACEIIPSS**	EPISCIAS	**ACEILLRV**	CAVILLER

ACEILLSS	SCALLIES		SOCIETAL	**ACEIMNST**	AMNESTIC
ACEILMMO	CAMOMILE	**ACEILOSU**	EUSOCIAL		SEMANTIC
ACEILMMR	CLAMMIER	**ACEILOSV**	VOCALISE	**ACEIMNSU**	SEMUNCIA
ACEILMNN	CLINAMEN	**ACEILOSX**	SAXICOLE	**ACEIMNSY**	SYCAMINE
ACEILMNO	COALMINE	**ACEILOSZ**	COALIZES	**ACEIMNTU**	NEUMATIC
ACEILMNP	MANCIPLE	**ACEILOTV**	LOCATIVE	**ACEIMOPR**	COPREMIA
ACEILMNS	MELANICS	**ACEILOVZ**	VOCALIZE	**ACEIMOPT**	POEMATIC
	MENISCAL	**ACEILPPY**	PIPECLAY	**ACEIMOTX**	TOXAEMIC
	MESCALIN	**ACEILPRS**	CALIPERS	**ACEIMOTZ**	AZOTEMIC
ACEILMNY	MYCELIAN		REPLICAS		METAZOIC
ACEILMOS	CAMISOLE		SPIRACLE	**ACEIMPRR**	CRAMPIER
ACEILMPS	MISPLACE	**ACEILPRT**	PARTICLE		MERICARP
ACEILMPT	PELMATIC		PRELATIC	**ACEIMPRS**	PARECISM
ACEILMRS	CLAIMERS	**ACEILPRU**	PECULIAR		SAPREMIC
	MIRACLES	**ACEILPSS**	SLIPCASE	**ACEIMPRT**	IMPACTER
	RECLAIMS		SPECIALS	**ACEIMPSS**	ESCAPISM
ACEILMRT	METRICAL	**ACEILPST**	PLICATES		MISSPACE
ACEILMRY	CREAMILY		SEPTICAL		SCAMPIES
ACEILMST	CALMIEST		TIECLASP	**ACEIMPST**	CAMPIEST
	CLEMATIS	**ACEILPSU**	SPICULAE		CAMPSITE
	CLIMATES	**ACEILPTY**	ETYPICAL	**ACEIMPTU**	PUMICATE
	METICALS	**ACEILPXY**	EPICALYX	**ACEIMRST**	CERAMIST
ACEILMSU	MUSICALE	**ACEILRRT**	CLARTIER		MATRICES
ACEILMSX	CLIMAXES	**ACEILRRW**	CRAWLIER		MISTRACE
	EXCLAIMS	**ACEILRSS**	CLASSIER		SCIMETAR
ACEILMTU	AMULETIC	**ACEILRST**	ALTRICES	**ACEIMRTT**	TREMATIC
ACEILNNP	PANNICLE		ARTICLES	**ACEIMRTU**	MURICATE
	PINNACLE		RECITALS	**ACEIMSST**	CASTEISM
ACEILNNR	ENCRINAL		SELICTAR		ETACISMS
ACEILNOR	ACROLEIN		STERICAL	**ACEIMSSU**	CAESIUMS
	COLINEAR	**ACEILRSU**	AURICLES	**ACEIMSTU**	AUTECISM
	CREOLIAN	**ACEILRSV**	CALIVERS	**ACEIMTTU**	MUTICATE
	LONICERA		CAVILERS	**ACEINNOS**	CANONISE
ACEILNPS	CAPELINS		CLAVIERS	**ACEINNOT**	ENACTION
	PANICLES		VISCERAL	**ACEINNOZ**	CANONIZE
	PELICANS	**ACEILRTT**	TRACTILE	**ACEINNPS**	PINNACES
ACEILNPT	PECTINAL	**ACEILRTU**	RETICULA	**ACEINNRS**	CRANNIES
	PLANETIC	**ACEILRTV**	VERTICAL		NARCEINS
ACEILNRS	CARLINES	**ACEILRTY**	LITERACY	**ACEINNST**	ANCIENTS
	LANCIERS	**ACEILRUV**	ACERVULI		CANNIEST
ACEILNRT	CLARINET	**ACEILSST**	ELASTICS		INSECTAN
ACEILNSS	LACINESS		SALICETS		INSTANCE
	SANICLES		SCALIEST	**ACEINNSU**	NUISANCE
ACEILNST	CANISTEL	**ACEILSTT**	LATTICES	**ACEINNSY**	CYANINES
ACEILNSU	AESCULIN		TALCIEST	**ACEINNTU**	UNCINATE
	LUNACIES	**ACEILSTY**	CLAYIEST	**ACEINOPR**	APOCRINE
ACEILNSY	SALIENCY	**ACEILSUV**	VESICULA		CAPONIER
ACEILOPR	CAPRIOLE	**ACEILSVW**	WAVICLES		PROCAINE
ACEILOPT	POETICAL	**ACEILTVY**	ACTIVELY	**ACEINOPS**	CANOPIES
ACEILORR	CARRIOLE	**ACEIMMNP**	PEMMICAN		CAPONISE
ACEILORS	CALORIES	**ACEIMMOS**	SEMICOMA		PAEONICS
	CALORISE	**ACEIMMRS**	RACEMISM	**ACEINOPZ**	CAPONIZE
	CARIOLES	**ACEIMMTT**	METAMICT	**ACEINORS**	SCENARIO
ACEILORT	EROTICAL	**ACEIMNNO**	MONECIAN	**ACEINORT**	ACTIONER
	LORICATE	**ACEIMNOT**	COINMATE		ANORETIC
ACEILORV	ARVICOLE	**ACEIMNOX**	ANOXEMIC		CREATION
ACEILORZ	CALORIZE	**ACEIMNPS**	PEMICANS		REACTION
ACEILOSS	CELOSIAS	**ACEIMNRS**	CARMINES	**ACEINORV**	VERONICA
	COALISES		CREMAINS	**ACEINORX**	ANOREXIC
ACEILOST	ALOETICS	**ACEIMNRU**	MANICURE	**ACEINOST**	ACONITES
	COALIEST	**ACEIMNSS**	AMNESICS		CANOEIST

	SONICATE		PERICARP	**ACEJMRST**	SCRAMJET
ACEINOTT	TACONITE	**ACEIPPRS**	CRAPPIES	**ACEJNNOO**	JONCANOE
ACEINOTV	CONATIVE		EPICARPS	**ACEJNOST**	JACONETS
	INVOCATE	**ACEIPPST**	TAPPICES	**ACEJNOSY**	JOYANCES
ACEINOTX	EXACTION	**ACEIPRRS**	PERISARC	**ACEJNRRY**	JERRYCAN
ACEINPQU	PIQUANCE	**ACEIPRSS**	SCRAPIES	**ACEJNSTU**	JUNCATES
ACEINPSS	INSCAPES	**ACEIPRST**	CRAPIEST	**ACEJPSTU**	CAJEPUTS
	PINCASES		CRISPATE	**ACEJRSTT**	TRAJECTS
ACEINPSY	SAPIENCY		PARETICS	**ACEKKMRU**	MUCKRAKE
ACEINPTT	PITTANCE		PICRATES	**ACEKKNRS**	KNACKERS
ACEINPUY	PICAYUNE		PRACTISE	**ACEKKNRY**	KNACKERY
ACEINRRT	TRANCIER	**ACEIPRTV**	PRACTIVE	**ACEKLLPS**	PELLACKS
ACEINRRU	CURARINE	**ACEIPRTY**	APYRETIC	**ACEKLMPU**	PACKMULE
ACEINRRY	CINERARY	**ACEIPSST**	ASEPTICS	**ACEKLNRS**	CRANKLES
ACEINRSS	ARCSINES		ESCAPIST	**ACEKLNSS**	SLACKENS
	ARSENICS		SPACIEST	**ACEKLNTU**	UNTACKLE
	CERASINS	**ACEIPSSU**	AUSPICES	**ACEKLORS**	EARLOCKS
	RACINESS	**ACEIPSSZ**	CAPSIZES	**ACEKLORV**	LAVEROCK
ACEINRST	CANISTER	**ACEIPSTV**	CAPTIVES	**ACEKLORW**	LACEWORK
	CARNIEST	**ACEIQRRU**	ACQUIRER	**ACEKLPRS**	SPRACKLE
	CERATINS	**ACEIQRSU**	ACQUIRES	**ACEKLPSS**	SPACKLES
	CISTERNA	**ACEIQSTU**	ACQUITES	**ACEKLPST**	PLACKETS
	CREATINS	**ACEIQSUZ**	CAZIQUES	**ACEKLQSU**	QUACKLES
	NACRITES	**ACEIRRRS**	CARRIERS	**ACEKLRSS**	SLACKERS
	SCANTIER		SCARRIER	**ACEKLRST**	TACKLERS
	TACRINES	**ACEIRRST**	ERRATICS	**ACEKLRSU**	CAULKERS
ACEINRTT	INTERACT	**ACEIRRSU**	CURARISE	**ACEKLSSS**	SACKLESS
ACEINRTU	ANURETIC	**ACEIRRSW**	AIRCREWS	**ACEKLSST**	SLACKEST
ACEINRTV	NAVICERT		AIRSCREW		TACKLESS
ACEINRTX	XERANTIC	**ACEIRRTT**	RETRAICT	**ACEKMNOO**	MOONCAKE
ACEINRVY	VICENARY	**ACEIRRTX**	CREATRIX	**ACEKMNRT**	TRACKMEN
ACEINSSS	CASSINES	**ACEIRRTY**	RETIRACY	**ACEKMNST**	TACKSMEN
ACEINSST	CINEASTS	**ACEIRRUZ**	CURARIZE	**ACEKMORS**	COMAKERS
	SCANTIES	**ACEIRSST**	SCARIEST	**ACEKMRSS**	SMACKERS
ACEINSSU	ISSUANCE	**ACEIRSSU**	SAUCIERS	**ACEKNNOW**	ACKNOWNE
ACEINSSY	CYANISES		SCAURIES	**ACEKNPRS**	PRANCKES
ACEINSTT	CANTIEST		URICASES	**ACEKNPRU**	UNPACKER
	ENTASTIC	**ACEIRSSV**	VICARESS	**ACEKNPSS**	PACKNESS
	NICTATES	**ACEIRSTT**	CITRATES	**ACEKNRSS**	SNACKERS
	TETANICS		CRISTATE	**ACEKNRST**	CRANKEST
ACEINSTV	CISTVAEN		SCATTIER	**ACEKOORT**	CARETOOK
	VESICANT	**ACEIRSTU**	SURICATE	**ACEKOORW**	COOKWARE
ACEINSTY	CYANITES	**ACEIRSTZ**	CRAZIEST	**ACEKOPRV**	OVERPACK
ACEINSTZ	ZINCATES	**ACEIRTTU**	URTICATE	**ACEKOPRW**	CAPEWORK
ACEINSYZ	CYANIZES	**ACEIRTTV**	TRACTIVE	**ACEKORRS**	CROAKERS
ACEINTTU	TUNICATE	**ACEIRTUV**	CURATIVE	**ACEKORRV**	OVERRACK
ACEINTTX	EXCITANT	**ACEIRTVY**	VERACITY	**ACEKORSW**	CASEWORK
ACEINTTY	TENACITY	**ACEISSSS**	CASSISES	**ACEKPPRS**	PREPACKS
ACEINTUV	UNACTIVE	**ACEISSST**	ECSTASIS	**ACEKPSSY**	SKYSCAPE
ACEIOPRT	APORETIC	**ACEISSSU**	SAUCISSE	**ACEKQRSU**	QUACKERS
	OPERATIC	**ACEISSTT**	STATICES	**ACEKQRUY**	QUACKERY
ACEIOPST	ECTOPIAS	**ACEISSTU**	SAUCIEST	**ACEKRRST**	RETRACKS
ACEIOPVW	PICOWAVE		SUITCASE		TRACKERS
ACEIORSS	SCARIOSE	**ACEISTTT**	CATTIEST	**ACEKRRTY**	RACKETRY
ACEIORSV	COVARIES	**ACEISTTU**	EUSTATIC	**ACEKRSST**	RESTACKS
	VARICOSE	**ACEISTTW**	SCAWTITE		STACKERS
ACEIOSST	SOCIATES	**ACEISTUX**	AUXETICS	**ACEKRSTT**	RACKETTS
ACEIOSSU	CAESIOUS	**ACEJKOOR**	JACKEROO	**ACEKRSTU**	RUCKSEAT
ACEIOSTT	OSCITATE	**ACEJKOPS**	PAJOCKES	**ACEKSSTT**	STACKETS
ACEIOTVV	VOCATIVE	**ACEJLORS**	CAJOLERS	**ACEKSSUW**	WAESUCKS
ACEIPPRR	CRAPPIER	**ACEJLORY**	CAJOLERY	**ACELLLRU**	CELLULAR

ACELLMOR	MALLCORE	ACELNOSZ	CALZONES	ACELPSSU	CAPSULES
ACELLMOS	CALOMELS	ACELNOTV	COVALENT		SCALEUPS
ACELLMSU	SACELLUM	ACELNOVY	CONVEYAL		UPSCALES
ACELLMSY	MYCELLAS	ACELNPSS	ENCLASPS	ACELPTUU	CUPULATE
ACELLNRU	NUCELLAR		SPANCELS	ACELPTUY	EUCALYPT
ACELLOPS	COLLAPSE	ACELNPST	CLAPNETS	ACELQRSU	CLAQUERS
	ESCALLOP	ACELNPSU	CLEANUPS		LACQUERS
ACELLORR	CAROLLER		UNPLACES	ACELQRUU	CLAQUEUR
ACELLORS	CORELLAS	ACELNRST	CENTRALS	ACELQSUY	LACQUEYS
ACELLORT	COLLARET	ACELNRSU	LUCARNES	ACELRRSW	CRAWLERS
ACELLORV	COVERALL	ACELNRVY	CRAVENLY		SCRAWLER
	OVERCALL	ACELNSST	SCANTLES	ACELRSSS	CLASSERS
ACELLORW	CALLOWER	ACELNSSU	SCALENUS		SCARLESS
ACELLOSS	CALLOSES		UNSCALES	ACELRSST	SCARLETS
	COALLESS	ACELNSTT	CANTLETS	ACELRSSU	RECUSALS
ACELLOST	COLLATES	ACELNSTY	SECANTLY		SECULARS
ACELLOSW	COLESLAW	ACELOOSU	ACOELOUS	ACELRSTT	CLATTERS
ACELLOTU	LOCULATE	ACELOPPU	POPULACE		SCRATTLE
ACELLOVY	COEVALLY	ACELOPRS	PARCLOSE	ACELRSTU	RAUCLEST
ACELLPSS	SCALPELS		POLACRES	ACELRTTU	CULTRATE
ACELLRRS	CARRELLS	ACELOPRT	PECTORAL	ACELRTTY	CLATTERY
ACELLRTY	RECTALLY	ACELOPRU	OPERCULA	ACELSSTT	TACTLESS
ACELLSSU	CALLUSES	ACELOPSS	ESCALOPS	ACELSSTU	CUTLASES
ACELLSSW	CLAWLESS	ACELOPST	POLECATS	ACELSSTY	SCYTALES
ACELLSTU	SCUTELLA	ACELOPSU	SCOPULAE	ACELSSUX	EXCUSALS
ACELLTWY	CETYWALL	ACELOPTU	COPULATE	ACEMMOTY	MYCETOMA
ACELMMOU	MAMELUCO		OUTPLACE	ACEMMRRS	CRAMMERS
ACELMMRS	CLAMMERS	ACELOPTY	CALOTYPE	ACEMMRSS	SCAMMERS
ACELMNNS	CLANSMEN	ACELOQSU	COEQUALS	ACEMNOOR	COENAMOR
ACELMNOR	AMELCORN	ACELORRS	CAROLERS	ACEMNORR	ROMANCER
	CORNMEAL	ACELORRT	RECTORAL	ACEMNORS	CREMONAS
ACELMNOU	COLUMNEA	ACELORSS	ESCOLARS		ROMANCES
ACELMNRU	CRUMENAL		LACROSSE	ACEMNORU	CUMARONE
ACELMNSS	CALMNESS		SOLACERS	ACEMNOST	CAMSTONE
	CLASSMEN	ACELORST	LOCATERS	ACEMNPSS	CAMPNESS
ACELMOPT	COMPLEAT		SECTORAL	ACEMNRUY	NUMERACY
ACELMORR	CLAMORER	ACELORSU	CAROUSEL	ACEMNSSU	MANCUSES
ACELMORS	CAROMELS	ACELORSY	CALOYERS	ACEMOORS	ACROSOME
	SCLEROMA		COARSELY	ACEMOOST	COMATOSE
ACELMORY	CLAYMORE	ACELOSST	ALECOSTS	ACEMOPRR	COMPARER
ACELMOST	CAMELOTS		COATLESS	ACEMOPRS	CAPSOMER
	MOLECAST		LACTOSES		COMPARES
ACELMOSU	CAULOMES		SCATOLES		COMPEARS
	LEUCOMAS	ACELOSTT	CALOTTES		MESOCARP
	MACULOSE	ACELOSTU	LACTEOUS	ACEMOPRT	MERCAPTO
ACELMPRS	CLAMPERS		LOCUSTAE	ACEMORRT	CREMATOR
ACELMPSY	ECLAMPSY		OSCULATE	ACEMORRV	OVERCRAM
ACELMSSU	LACMUSES	ACELOSTY	ACOLYTES	ACEMORSS	SCREAMOS
ACELMSTU	CALUMETS	ACELOSUV	VACUOLES	ACEMORSU	RACEMOUS
	MUSCATEL	ACELOTTY	CATOLYTE	ACEMORSW	CASEWORM
ACELMSUU	SAECULUM	ACELOTXY	ACETOXYL	ACEMORSY	SYCAMORE
ACELMTUU	CUMULATE	ACELPPRS	CLAPPERS	ACEMORTY	COMETARY
ACELNNNO	CANNELON		SCRAPPLE	ACEMORUX	MORCEAUX
ACELNNOS	ALENCONS	ACELPPSS	SCAPPLES	ACEMOSSU	COASSUME
ACELNNRS	SCRANNEL	ACELPRSS	CLASPERS	ACEMPRRS	CRAMPERS
ACELNOOT	ECOTONAL		RECLASPS	ACEMPRSS	SCAMPERS
ACELNOPT	CONEPATL		SCALPERS	ACEMPRST	CRAMPETS
ACELNORV	NOVERCAL	ACELPRST	SCEPTRAL	ACEMPSSU	CAMPUSES
ACELNOSS	SECONALS		SPECTRAL	ACEMPSSY	MYSPACES
ACELNOST	LACTONES	ACELPRSU	SPECULAR	ACEMRSST	SCAMSTER
ACELNOSU	LACUNOSE	ACELPRTY	CALYPTER	ACEMSSTT	METCASTS

ACENNNOU	ANNOUNCE	ACENSSTT	SCANTEST	ACERSTTT	TETRACTS
ACENNOSS	CANONESS	ACENSSTU	NUTCASES	ACERSTTU	CRUSTATE
	SONANCES	ACENSSTW	NEWSCAST	ACERSTTX	EXTRACTS
ACENNOSY	NOYANCES	ACENSSUU	USAUNCES	ACERSTTY	CYTASTER
ACENNOSZ	CANZONES	ACEOOPPS	APOCOPES		SCATTERY
ACENNOTT	COTENANT	ACEOOPSU	POACEOUS	ACERSTUX	CURTAXES
ACENNOTV	COVENANT	ACEOORTT	COROTATE	ACERTTUW	CUTWATER
ACENNOTZ	CANZONET	ACEOORTV	EVOCATOR	ACFFGHIN	CHAFFING
ACENNPRY	PERNANCY		OVERCOAT	ACFFHNOR	CHAFFRON
ACENNRSS	SCANNERS	ACEOPPRS	COPPERAS	ACFFIILO	OFFICIAL
ACENNSUY	SEACUNNY	ACEOPRRT	RECAPTOR	ACFFIIST	CAITIFFS
ACENOORT	CORONATE	ACEOPRST	POSTRACE	ACFFIKMS	MAFFICKS
ACENOOTZ	ECTOZOAN	ACEOPRSX	EXOCARPS	ACFFILNU	FANCIFUL
ACENOPRT	COPARENT	ACEOPRTT	ATTERCOP	ACFFILST	AFFLICTS
	PORTANCE	ACEOPRTU	OUTCAPER	ACFFIRST	TRAFFICS
ACENOPST	CAPSTONE	ACEOPSTU	OUTPACES	ACFFKORT	OFFTRACK
	OPENCAST		SAUCEPOT	ACFFLOSW	SCOFFLAW
ACENOPSU	PONCEAUS	ACEORRST	ACROTERS	ACFFOSST	CASTOFFS
ACENOPUX	PONCEAUX		CREATORS		OFFCASTS
ACENOQTU	COTQUEAN		REACTORS	ACFGHINU	CHAUFING
ACENORRW	CAREWORN	ACEORRSU	CAROUSER	ACFGHITT	CATFIGHT
ACENORRY	CRAYONER	ACEORRTT	RETROACT	ACFGIIMN	MAGNIFIC
ACENORSS	COARSENS	ACEORRTU	EUROCRAT	ACFGIIPR	CAPRIFIG
	NARCOSES	ACEORRTV	CAVORTER	ACFGIKLN	FLACKING
ACENORST	ANCESTOR	ACEORRVW	OVERCRAW	ACFGIKNR	FRACKING
	ENACTORS	ACEORSST	COARSEST	ACFGINNY	FANCYING
	SARCONET		COASTERS	ACFGINRS	FARCINGS
	SORTANCE	ACEORSSU	CAROUSES		SCARFING
ACENORSU	CARNEOUS	ACEORSTT	SECTATOR	ACFGINRT	CRAFTING
	NACREOUS	ACEORSTU	OUTRACES		FRACTING
ACENORTT	CONTRATE	ACEORSTV	OVERACTS	ACFGITUY	FUGACITY
ACENORTU	COURANTE		OVERCAST	ACFGKNOP	PACKFONG
	OUTRANCE	ACEORSTX	EXACTORS	ACFGLNOR	CORNFLAG
ACENORTY	ENACTORY	ACEORTUY	EUCARYOT	ACFHHINW	HAWFINCH
ACENORUY	EUCARYON	ACEOSSTU	SEASCOUT	ACFHIJKS	JACKFISH
ACENOSSS	CASSONES	ACEOSTTT	COATTEST	ACFHILNO	FALCHION
ACENOSST	CONTESSA	ACEOSTTU	OUTCASTE	ACFHILOS	COALFISH
	COSTEANS	ACEOSTTV	CAVETTOS	ACFHINOU	FAUCHION
ACENOSSV	CAVESSON	ACEOSTUU	AUTOCUES	ACFHIRSS	SCARFISH
ACENOSSY	CYANOSES	ACEOTUUX	COUTEAUX	ACFHIRSW	CRAWFISH
ACENOSTT	CONSTATE	ACEOTUXY	AUXOCYTE	ACFHIRSY	CRAYFISH
ACENOSTV	CENTAVOS	ACEPPRRS	CRAPPERS	ACFHISSU	FUCHSIAS
ACENOTTU	TOUCANET		SCRAPPER	ACFHLMRU	CHARMFUL
ACENPRRS	PRANCERS	ACEPRRSS	SCARPERS	ACFHLTUW	WATCHFUL
ACENPRSU	ENCARPUS		SCRAPERS	ACFHMNOR	CHAMFRON
	PRAUNCES	ACEPRRSU	SUPERCAR	ACFHNNOR	CHANFRON
ACENPSTT	PENTACTS	ACEPRRTU	CAPTURER	ACFHNOSU	FAUCHONS
ACENPTTU	PUNCTATE	ACEPRSST	PRECASTS	ACFHRSTU	FUTHARCS
ACENRSST	CRANTSES	ACEPRSSU	SCAUPERS	ACFIILST	FISTICAL
ACENRSSU	SURANCES	ACEPRSTU	CAPTURES	ACFIILSV	SALVIFIC
ACENRSTT	TRANECTS		PRESCUTA	ACFIILTY	FACILITY
	TRANSECT	ACEPSTTY	TYPECAST	ACFIIMPS	PACIFISM
ACENRSTU	CENTAURS	ACEQRSTU	RACQUETS	ACFIIMSS	FASCISMI
	RECUSANT	ACEQSSTU	ACQUESTS	ACFIIPST	PACIFIST
	UNCRATES	ACERRSTT	RETRACTS	ACFIISST	FASCISTI
	UNTRACES	ACERRSTU	TRACEURS		FASCITIS
ACENRSTY	ANCESTRY	ACERRSUV	VERRUCAS	ACFIKLNS	CALFSKIN
ACENRSXY	CARNYXES	ACERSSST	CRASSEST	ACFIKNNS	FINNACKS
ACENRTTU	TRUNCATE	ACERSSSU	SUCRASES	ACFIKNSU	FUNCKIAS
ACENRTUY	CENTAURY	ACERSSTT	SCATTERS	ACFILLSY	FISCALLY
	CYANURET	ACERSSTY	ACTRESSY	ACFILNOR	FORNICAL

ACFILNOS	FOLACINS	ACGGLNOU	GLUCAGON	ACGHRSSU	SCRAUGHS
ACFILNOT	CALIFONT	ACGGLRSY	SCRAGGLY	ACGIILMN	CLAIMING
ACFILORT	TRIFOCAL	ACGHHIJK	HIGHJACK		MALICING
ACFILOTU	CLAFOUTI	ACGHHINN	HANCHING	ACGIILNN	INLACING
ACFILRTY	CRAFTILY	ACGHHINT	HATCHING	ACGIILNO	LOGICIAN
ACFILSSY	CLASSIFY	ACGHIIMN	MICHIGAN	ACGIILNS	SCAILING
ACFILSTU	SULFATIC	ACGHIINN	CHAINING	ACGIILNU	LINGUICA
ACFIMNRU	FRANCIUM	ACGHIINR	CHAIRING	ACGIILNV	CAVILING
ACFIMORR	ARCIFORM	ACGHIKLN	CHALKING	ACGIILRS	GRACILIS
ACFIMORS	FORMICAS		HACKLING	ACGIIMNT	MICATING
ACFIMOSS	FASCISMO	ACGHIKNR	CHARKING	ACGIIMOS	ISOGAMIC
ACFIMSSS	FASCISMS	ACGHIKNS	HACKINGS	ACGIIMST	SIGMATIC
ACFINORT	FRACTION		SHACKING	ACGIINNS	INCASING
ACFINOST	FACTIONS	ACGHIKNT	THACKING	ACGIINNV	INCAVING
ACFINOSV	FAVICONS	ACGHIKNW	WHACKING	ACGIINRT	GRANITIC
ACFINPRS	SCARFPIN	ACGHILNN	LANCHING	ACGIIPRS	SPAGIRIC
ACFINRST	INFARCTS	ACGHILNS	CLASHING	ACGIJJKO	JICKAJOG
	INFRACTS	ACGHILNT	LATCHING	ACGIJKNS	JACKINGS
ACFINSTY	SANCTIFY	ACGHILNU	LAUCHING	ACGIJLNO	CAJOLING
ACFIOSTU	FACTIOUS	ACGHILNY	ACHINGLY	ACGIJNNU	JAUNCING
ACFIRTUY	FURACITY	ACGHILOR	OLIGARCH	ACGIKKNN	KNACKING
ACFISSST	FASCISTS	ACGHIMNP	CHAMPING	ACGIKLMN	MACKLING
ACFKLLOR	ROCKFALL	ACGHIMNR	CHARMING	ACGIKLNN	CLANKING
ACFKLORS	FORSLACK		MARCHING	ACGIKLNO	CLOAKING
ACFKLOST	LOCKFAST	ACGHIMNT	MATCHING	ACGIKLNS	CALKINGS
ACFKLRSU	RACKFULS	ACGHINNR	RANCHING		SLACKING
ACFKLRUW	WRACKFUL	ACGHINNT	CHANTING	ACGIKLNT	TACKLING
ACFKLSSU	SACKFULS	ACGHINNU	UNACHING		TALCKING
	SACKSFUL	ACGHINOP	POACHING	ACGIKLNU	CAULKING
ACFKOSTT	FATSTOCK	ACGHINOR	ROACHING	ACGIKLRY	GARLICKY
ACFLLMRU	CRAMFULL	ACGHINPP	CHAPPING	ACGIKMNO	COMAKING
ACFLMNOO	MOONCALF	ACGHINPR	PARCHING	ACGIKMNS	SMACKING
ACFLNNOO	NONFOCAL	ACGHINPT	NIGHTCAP	ACGIKNNR	CRANKING
ACFLNORY	FALCONRY		PATCHING	ACGIKNNS	SNACKING
ACFLOOPS	FOOLSCAP	ACGHINRR	CHARRING	ACGIKNNU	UNCAKING
ACFLOPSW	COWFLAPS	ACGHINRS	ARCHINGS	ACGIKNOR	CROAKING
ACFLORSU	SCROFULA		CHAGRINS	ACGIKNPS	PACKINGS
ACFLOTTU	FLOATCUT		CRASHING	ACGIKNQU	QUACKING
ACFLRRUU	FURCULAR	ACGHINRT	CHARTING	ACGIKNRS	ARCKINGS
ACFLRSTU	CARTFULS		RATCHING		RACKINGS
ACFMOTTU	FACTOTUM	ACGHINRU	CHURINGA	ACGIKNRT	TRACKING
ACFNNOST	NONFACTS		NURAGHIC	ACGIKNRW	WRACKING
ACFNRSTU	FRUCTANS	ACGHINSS	CHASINGS	ACGIKNSS	SACKINGS
ACFRRSTU	FRACTURS	ACGHINST	SCATHING	ACGIKNST	STACKING
ACGGGILN	CLAGGING	ACGHINSW	CHINWAGS		TACKINGS
ACGGGINS	SCAGGING	ACGHINTT	CHATTING	ACGIKPRS	GRIPSACK
ACGGHINN	CHANGING	ACGHINTW	WATCHING	ACGILLNS	CALLINGS
	GANCHING	ACGHINTY	YACHTING	ACGILMMN	CLAMMING
ACGGHINR	CHARGING	ACGHINUV	VAUCHING	ACGILMNO	GNOMICAL
ACGGHLUU	CHUGALUG	ACGHIPRS	GRAPHICS	ACGILMNP	CAMPLING
ACGGIINN	INCAGING	ACGHIQTU	ACQUIGHT		CLAMPING
ACGGIINT	GIGANTIC	ACGHIRSS	SCRAIGHS	ACGILMNS	CALMINGS
ACGGIIOS	ISAGOGIC	ACGHLLOR	GRALLOCH	ACGILMNU	MACULING
ACGGILNN	CANGLING	ACGHLMOO	LOGOMACH	ACGILMTU	GLUTAMIC
	CLANGING	ACGHLOOY	CHAOLOGY	ACGILNNT	CANTLING
	GLANCING	ACGHLSTU	CLAUGHTS	ACGILNNU	LAUNCING
ACGGILRY	CRAGGILY	ACGHNRYY	GYNARCHY		UNLACING
ACGGINNO	CONGAING	ACGHNTUU	UNCAUGHT	ACGILNOR	CAROLING
ACGGINNU	UNCAGING	ACGHORSU	CHORAGUS		ORACLING
ACGGINOR	CARGOING	ACGHPTUU	UPCAUGHT	ACGILNOS	SOLACING
ACGGIOOR	CORAGGIO	ACGHRRSU	CURRAGHS	ACGILNOT	LOCATING

ACGILNPP	CLAPPING			
ACGILNPS	CLASPING	ACGINRSU	SCAURING	ACHIKKNS	KNACKISH
	PLACINGS	ACGINRSV	CARVINGS	ACHIKKSW	KICKSHAW
	SCALPING		CRAVINGS	ACHIKLLW	HICKWALL
ACGILNQU	CALQUING	ACGINRTT	TRACTING	ACHIKLMY	HICKYMAL
ACGILNRS	CARLINGS	ACGINRTU	CURATING	ACHIKLOR	HAIRLOCK
ACGILNRT	CLARTING	ACGINSST	CASTINGS	ACHIKLPT	CHALKPIT
ACGILNRU	CINGULAR	ACGINSTT	SCATTING	ACHIKNOP	PACHINKO
ACGILNRW	CRAWLING	ACGINSUV	VICUGNAS	ACHIKNRS	CRANKISH
ACGILNRY	CARINGLY	ACGIOORS	GRACIOSO	ACHIKQSU	QUACKISH
ACGILNSS	CLASSING	ACGIORST	ORGASTIC	ACHIKRSS	RICKSHAS
	SCALINGS	ACGIORSU	GRACIOUS	ACHIKRSW	RICKSHAW
ACGILNST	CASTLING	ACGIPRSY	SPAGYRIC	ACHIKRSY	HAYRICKS
	CATLINGS	ACGJLNOU	CONJUGAL	ACHIKRTW	WHITRACK
ACGILNSU	GLUCINAS	ACGKMMOS	GAMMOCKS	ACHIKSSS	SHICKSAS
ACGILNTT	CLATTING	ACGKORSV	GARVOCKS	ACHILLOR	ORCHILLA
ACGILNTU	CLAUTING	ACGLLPSU	CUPGALLS	ACHILLRT	CLITHRAL
ACGILNUY	GUANYLIC	ACGLMOUU	COAGULUM	ACHILMOP	OMPHALIC
ACGILRSU	SURGICAL	ACGLNORS	CLANGORS	ACHILMOS	MALICHOS
ACGIMMNR	CRAMMING	ACGLNORU	CLANGOUR		MOCHILAS
ACGIMMNS	SCAMMING	ACGLNOSY	AGLYCONS	ACHILMRS	CHRISMAL
ACGIMNOR	CAROMING	ACGLOORY	ARCOLOGY	ACHILMTY	MYTHICAL
ACGIMNOS	COAMINGS	ACGLOSUU	GLAUCOUS	ACHILNNS	CLANNISH
ACGIMNPR	CRAMPING	ACGLSSTU	CUTGLASS	ACHILNOO	HOOLICAN
ACGIMNPS	CAMPINGS	ACGMNOPS	CAMPONGS	ACHILNOS	LICHANOS
	SCAMPING	ACGNNOOT	CONTANGO	ACHILNPS	CLANSHIP
ACGIMNSY	GYMNASIC	ACGNNORS	CRANNOGS	ACHILOPR	ORPHICAL
	SYNGAMIC	ACGNOOST	OCTAGONS		RHOPALIC
ACGIMOPR	PICOGRAM	ACGNORST	CONGRATS	ACHILOPU	PACHOULI
ACGIMORS	ORGASMIC	ACGORRSY	GYROCARS	ACHILORT	ACROLITH
ACGIMOUU	GUAIOCUM	ACGORSSW	COWGRASS	ACHILPSY	PHYSICAL
ACGINNNS	CANNINGS	ACGORSUU	COUGUARS	ACHILPTY	PATCHILY
	SCANNING	ACGPPSUU	SCUPPAUG	ACHILRUY	CHYLURIA
ACGINNNU	NUANCING	ACGRSSTU	CUTGRASS	ACHILRVY	CHIVALRY
ACGINNPR	PRANCING	ACHHILPT	PHTHALIC	ACHILSWY	LICHWAYS
ACGINNPU	UNCAPING	ACHHINTW	WHINCHAT	ACHILTTY	CHATTILY
ACGINNRT	TRANCING	ACHHINTY	HYACINTH		
ACGINNRU	UNCARING	ACHHIPPR	HIPPARCH	ACHIMMOS	MACHISMO
ACGINNRY	CARNYING	ACHHLLOT	CHALLOTH		MACHOISM
ACGINNST	CANTINGS	ACHHLMOS	MASHLOCH	ACHIMMST	MISMATCH
	SCANTING	ACHHLNOR	RHONCHAL	ACHIMNNW	WINCHMAN
ACGINNSU	UNCASING	ACHHLORY	HOLARCHY	ACHIMNOP	CHAMPION
ACGINNUV	VAUNCING	ACHHLPRY	PHYLARCH	ACHIMNOR	CHOIRMAN
ACGINOPT	COAPTING	ACHHLSUY	SHAUCHLY		HARMONIC
ACGINORS	ORGANICS	ACHHNTTU	NUTHATCH		OMNIARCH
ACGINORY	CONGIARY		UNTHATCH	ACHIMNOS	MANIHOCS
ACGINOST	AGNOSTIC	ACHHOSST	TOSHACHS		MOHICANS
	COASTING	ACHHPPSU	CHUPPAHS	ACHIMNPT	PITCHMAN
	COATINGS	ACHHPTUZ	CHUTZPAH	ACHIMNSU	INASMUCH
	COTINGAS	ACHIIKMS	KAMICHIS	ACHIMOPR	AMPHORIC
ACGINPPR	CRAPPING	ACHIILMS	CHILIASM	ACHIMOSS	CHAMISOS
ACGINPPS	CAPPINGS	ACHIILPT	HAPLITIC		ISOCHASM
ACGINPRS	CARPINGS	ACHIILST	CHILIAST	ACHIMPSS	SCAMPISH
	SCARPING	ACHIINRT	TRICHINA	ACHIMPST	MISPATCH
	SCRAPING	ACHIINST	CHIANTIS	ACHIMRSS	CHARISMS
ACGINPSS	SPACINGS	ACHIIPRS	PARCHISI	ACHIMRST	CHARTISM
ACGINPSU	SCAUPING	ACHIIPSS	PACHISIS	ACHIMRTY	ARYTHMIC
ACGINRRS	SCARRING	ACHIIRST	RACHITIS	ACHIMSSS	SCHISMAS
ACGINRRY	CARRYING	ACHIIRSU	ISCHURIA	ACHIMSST	MASTICHS
ACGINRSS	SACRINGS	ACHIJKPW	WHIPJACK		TACHISMS
ACGINRST	SCARTING	ACHIJNST	JACINTHS	ACHIMSSU	CHIASMUS
				ACHIMTUY	CYATHIUM
				ACHINNOP	PANCHION

ACHINNSU	ANCHUSIN	**ACHLOSTY**	ACOLYTHS	**ACIILMPT**	PALMITIC
	UNCHAINS	**ACHLOTWX**	WAXCLOTH	**ACIILMRT**	MARLITIC
ACHINOPR	PAROCHIN	**ACHMNORS**	MONARCHS	**ACIILMSS**	LAICISMS
	PROCHAIN		NOMARCHS	**ACIILNOR**	IRONICAL
ACHINOPS	APHONICS	**ACHMNORY**	MONARCHY	**ACIILNOT**	TALIONIC
ACHINORT	ANORTHIC		NOMARCHY	**ACIILNPS**	PISCINAL
ACHINOST	CHITOSAN	**ACHMNRSU**	UNCHARMS	**ACIILNPT**	PLATINIC
ACHINOSY	ONYCHIAS	**ACHMNRTU**	TRUCHMAN	**ACIILNSS**	SALICINS
ACHINOTZ	HOACTZIN	**ACHMOORT**	CHATROOM	**ACIILOSV**	VILIACOS
ACHINPSY	SPINACHY	**ACHMOPRS**	CAMPHORS	**ACIILRTT**	TRITICAL
ACHINRSU	UNCHAIRS	**ACHMORSZ**	MACHZORS	**ACIILRTU**	URALITIC
ACHINRSZ	ZARNICHS	**ACHMORTU**	OUTCHARM	**ACIILSST**	SILASTIC
ACHINSUV	CHAUVINS		OUTMARCH	**ACIILSTV**	SILVATIC
ACHIOPRT	ATROPHIC	**ACHMOSST**	STOMACHS	**ACIIMMNP**	MINICAMP
ACHIOPSS	ISOPACHS	**ACHMOSTY**	STOMACHY	**ACIIMMNS**	MINICAMS
ACHIORSS	COARSISH	**ACHMOTTU**	OUTMATCH	**ACIIMNNO**	AMNIONIC
ACHIORST	ACTORISH	**ACHMPSTU**	MATCHUPS	**ACIIMNNT**	MANNITIC
	CHARIOTS	**ACHMSSUW**	CUMSHAWS	**ACIIMNOR**	MORAINIC
	HARICOTS	**ACHNNORU**	UNANCHOR	**ACIIMNOS**	SIMONIAC
ACHIORTV	TOVARICH	**ACHNNOSS**	CHANSONS	**ACIIMNOT**	AMNIOTIC
ACHIOSST	ISOTACHS	**ACHNOOSY**	CHANOYOS	**ACIIMNRS**	MINICARS
ACHIPPSS	SAPPHICS	**ACHNORST**	CHANTORS	**ACIIMNST**	ACTINISM
ACHIPRRT	PARRITCH	**ACHNORXY**	CHRONAXY	**ACIIMNSU**	MUSICIAN
	PHRATRIC	**ACHNOSTY**	TACHYONS	**ACIIMNTU**	ACTINIUM
ACHIPSTU	CHUPATIS	**ACHNOSUY**	CHANOYUS	**ACIIMNTY**	IMITANCY
ACHIPSTW	WHIPCATS	**ACHNPPSS**	SCHNAPPS		INTIMACY
ACHIPTTU	CHUPATTI	**ACHNRSTU**	UNSTARCH		MINACITY
ACHIQRSU	CHARQUIS	**ACHNRSYY**	SYNARCHY	**ACIIMOST**	COMITIAS
ACHIRRST	TRIARCHS	**ACHNRTUY**	CHAUNTRY		IOTACISM
ACHIRRTY	TRIARCHY	**ACHOORTU**	COAUTHOR	**ACIIMOTT**	AMITOTIC
ACHIRSTT	CHARTIST	**ACHOORTY**	CHAYROOT	**ACIIMPRT**	PRIMATIC
	STRAICHT	**ACHOPRST**	TOPARCHS	**ACIIMPRV**	VAMPIRIC
ACHIRSTU	HAIRCUTS	**ACHOPRSY**	CHARPOYS	**ACIIMRST**	SCIMITAR
ACHISSTT	TACHISTS	**ACHOPRTY**	TOPARCHY	**ACIIMRTU**	MURIATIC
ACHISTTY	CHASTITY	**ACHORRST**	TROCHARS	**ACIIMSST**	ITACISMS
ACHKKORW	HACKWORK	**ACHOTTUW**	OUTWATCH	**ACIIMSTT**	ATTICISM
ACHKKRSU	CHUKKARS		WATCHOUT		MASTITIC
ACHKMMOS	HAMMOCKS	**ACHPRSTU**	PUSHCART	**ACIIMSTV**	ACTIVISM
ACHKMORS	SHAMROCK	**ACHPSTUZ**	CHUTZPAS	**ACIIMTUV**	VIATICUM
ACHKNNUU	NUNCHAKU	**ACHPTTUY**	CHUPATTY	**ACIINNOT**	INACTION
ACHKNOOT	CANTHOOK	**ACHRRSTU**	CRATHURS		NICOTIAN
ACHKOPSS	HOPSACKS	**ACHRRTUY**	CRAYTHUR	**ACIINNQU**	CINQUAIN
ACHKOSSS	HASSOCKS	**ACHRSTTU**	STRAUCHT	**ACIINNRV**	NIRVANIC
ACHKOSSY	HASSOCKY	**ACIIILMN**	INIMICAL	**ACIINNTT**	INCITANT
ACHKOSTT	HATTOCKS	**ACIIILNV**	CIVILIAN	**ACIINNTY**	CANINITY
ACHLLOOS	ALCOHOLS	**ACIIINST**	ISATINIC	**ACIINOOP**	IOPANOIC
ACHLLORS	CHLORALS	**ACIIKLNO**	KAOLINIC	**ACIINOPT**	OPTICIAN
ACHLLORY	CHORALLY	**ACIIKNNN**	CANNIKIN	**ACIINORZ**	ZIRCONIA
ACHLMOPS	CAMPHOLS	**ACIIKNNS**	CANIKINS	**ACIINOSS**	ASINICOS
ACHLMSTZ	SCHMALTZ	**ACIIKNTY**	KYANITIC	**ACIINOSV**	AVIONICS
ACHLMSYZ	SCHMALZY	**ACIIKPRT**	PAITRICK	**ACIINOTT**	CITATION
ACHLNOOU	OULACHON	**ACIILLNS**	ALLICINS	**ACIINPSS**	PISCINAS
ACHLNOSY	HALCYONS	**ACIILLNV**	VANILLIC	**ACIINPTY**	ANTIPYIC
ACHLNSTU	TULCHANS	**ACIILLOV**	VILLIACO	**ACIINRSS**	NARCISSI
ACHLNSTY	STANCHLY	**ACIILLSU**	SILICULA	**ACIINRSU**	URANISCI
ACHLOPRS	RAPLOCHS	**ACIILLSV**	SILVICAL	**ACIINRTU**	URANITIC
ACHLOPRT	CALTHROP	**ACIILLTV**	VILLATIC	**ACIINTTY**	ANTICITY
ACHLOPRY	POLYARCH	**ACIILMMS**	MISCLAIM	**ACIIOPST**	APOSITIC
ACHLOPTT	POTLATCH	**ACIILMNR**	CRIMINAL	**ACIIORST**	AORISTIC
ACHLORSS	SCHOLARS	**ACIILMNU**	ALUMINIC	**ACIIORTV**	VICTORIA
ACHLOSSW	SALCHOWS	**ACIILMOT**	COMITIAL	**ACIIPPST**	PAPISTIC

ACIIRSST	TRIASSIC	ACILMOSV	VOCALISM	ACIMNOOR	ACROMION
ACIIRSTT	ARTISTIC	ACILMPTU	PLACITUM	ACIMNOPS	CAMPIONS
	TRIATICS	ACILMRTU	MULTICAR	ACIMNORS	MARCONIS
ACIISTTT	ATTICIST	ACILMSSS	CLASSISM		MINORCAS
ACIISTTU	AUTISTIC		MISCLASS	ACIMNORT	ROMANTIC
ACIISTTV	ACTIVIST	ACILMSSU	MUSICALS	ACIMNORU	CONARIUM
ACIITTVY	ACTIVITY	ACILMSTY	MYSTICAL		COUMARIN
ACIITVVY	VIVACITY	ACILMTUY	ULTIMACY	ACIMNORY	ACRIMONY
ACIJKKPS	SKIPJACK	ACILNNOS	CANNOLIS	ACIMNOSS	MOCASSIN
ACIJKSTW	STICKJAW	ACILNOOT	LOCATION	ACIMNOST	MONASTIC
ACIJRSSU	JURASSIC	ACILNOOV	VOCALION	ACIMNOTU	ACONITUM
ACIJSUZZ	JACUZZIS	ACILNOPS	SALPICON	ACIMNPSU	PANICUMS
ACIKLMOT	MOCKTAIL	ACILNOPT	PLATONIC	ACIMNPTY	TYMPANIC
ACIKLMST	MALSTICK	ACILNORS	CLARINOS	ACIMNRSS	NARCISMS
ACIKLNOT	ANTILOCK		CLARIONS	ACIMNRSU	CRANIUMS
ACIKLNRY	CRANKILY	ACILNORT	CILANTRO		CUMARINS
ACIKLORS	AIRLOCKS		CONTRAIL	ACIMNSTT	CATMINTS
ACIKLORY	CROAKILY	ACILNOSU	UNSOCIAL	ACIMNSTU	TSUNAMIC
ACIKMNST	STICKMAN	ACILNOSY	ACYLOINS	ACIMOOST	SCOTOMIA
ACIKMOOS	OOMIACKS	ACILNOUV	UNIVOCAL	ACIMOPRT	IMPACTOR
ACIKMOST	COMATIKS	ACILNPSS	INCLASPS	ACIMOPST	APOMICTS
ACIKMPRS	RAMPICKS		SCALPINS	ACIMORST	ACROTISM
ACIKMPST	MAPSTICK	ACILNRSU	CISLUNAR	ACIMORSY	CRAMOISY
ACIKMPSW	PICKMAWS	ACILNRUY	CULINARY	ACIMOSST	ACOSMIST
ACIKMQSU	QUACKISM		URANYLIC		MASSICOT
ACIKNNPR	CRANKPIN	ACILNSTU	LUNATICS	ACIMOSTT	MASTICOT
ACIKNNPS	PANNICKS		SULTANIC		STOMATIC
ACIKNORT	ANTIROCK	ACILNSTY	SCANTILY	ACIMPRST	CRAMPITS
ACIKNPST	PANSTICK	ACILNTTU	ANTICULT		PTARMICS
ACIKNSST	CATSKINS	ACILNTTY	INTACTLY	ACIMRRSY	MISCARRY
ACIKNSTT	TINTACKS	ACILOPRT	TROPICAL	ACIMRSSZ	CZARISMS
ACIKPRST	PATRICKS	ACILOPRV	VALPROIC	ACIMSSST	MISCASTS
	TRIPACKS	ACILOPST	CAPITOLS	ACIMSSTT	TACTISMS
ACIKSTTY	STATICKY		COALPITS	ACINNNOO	NONANOIC
ACILLLNY	CLINALLY		POSTICAL	ACINNOOT	CONATION
ACILLLOP	POLLICAL	ACILORRS	RACLOIRS		INTONACO
ACILLMMY	CLAMMILY	ACILORRV	CORRIVAL	ACINNOQU	CONQUIAN
ACILLMOS	LOCALISM	ACILORST	CALORIST	ACINNORR	NARICORN
ACILLMSS	MISCALLS	ACILORSV	CORIVALS	ACINNOSS	SCANSION
ACILLNOO	COLONIAL	ACILORTV	VORTICAL	ACINNOST	ACTINONS
ACILLNOR	CARILLON	ACILORYZ	ZIRCALOY		CANONIST
ACILLNOS	SCALLION	ACILOSTV	VOCALIST		CANTIONS
ACILLNUY	UNCIALLY	ACILOTUV	OUTCAVIL		CONTAINS
ACILLOQU	COQUILLA	ACILOTVY	VOCALITY		SANCTION
ACILLORT	CLITORAL	ACILPRST	CLIPARTS		SONANTIC
ACILLORY	COLLYRIA	ACILPRSU	SPICULAR	ACINNOTU	CONTINUA
ACILLOST	LOCALIST	ACILPRTU	PICTURAL		COUNTIAN
ACILLOSY	SOCIALLY	ACILPSST	PLASTICS	ACINNRTY	TYRANNIC
ACILLOTY	COITALLY	ACILPSUU	APICULUS	ACINNSTU	ANNICUTS
	LOCALITY	ACILRRTU	TURRICAL	ACINNSTY	INSTANCY
ACILLOUV	COLLUVIA	ACILRSTU	CURTAILS	ACINOOPR	PICAROON
ACILLSSY	CLASSILY		RUSTICAL	ACINOOTV	VOCATION
ACILMNNY	CINNAMYL	ACILRTUV	CULTIVAR	ACINOPPT	PANOPTIC
ACILMNOP	COMPLAIN		CURVITAL	ACINOPRS	PARSONIC
ACILMNOS	LACONISM	ACILSSST	CLASSIST	ACINOPST	CAPTIONS
	LIMACONS	ACILSTTY	SCATTILY		PACTIONS
ACILMOOS	SCOLIOMA	ACILSTUV	VICTUALS	ACINOPTU	ACUPOINT
ACILMOPR	PICLORAM	ACILSTVY	SYLVATIC	ACINOQSU	COQUINAS
	PROCLAIM	ACIMMOSS	ACOSMISM	ACINORRS	CARRIONS
ACILMOPS	OILCAMPS	ACIMMTUY	CYMATIUM	ACINORRT	CARROTIN
ACILMOPT	COMPITAL	ACIMNNNO	CINNAMON		CONTRAIR

ACINORSS	NARCOSIS	**ACIQSSTU**	ACQUISTS	**ACLLOSTU**	LOCUSTAL
ACINORST	CANTORIS	**ACIRRTTX**	TRACTRIX		OUTCALLS
	CAROTINS	**ACIRRTUX**	CURATRIX	**ACLLOSTY**	COSTALLY
	CORTINAS	**ACIRSSST**	SACRISTS	**ACLLRSYY**	ACRYLYLS
ACINORSV	CORVINAS	**ACIRSSTT**	ASTRICTS	**ACLLRTUU**	CULTURAL
ACINORTT	TRACTION	**ACIRSSTW**	TWISCARS	**ACLMMNOU**	COMMUNAL
ACINORTU	NOCTURIA	**ACIRSSTY**	SACRISTY	**ACLMMORW**	CLAMWORM
ACINORTY	CARYOTIN	**ACIRSSTZ**	CZARISTS	**ACLMNOOO**	COOLAMON
ACINOSSS	CAISSONS	**ACISSSTU**	CASUISTS	**ACLMNOOR**	COLORMAN
	CASSINOS	**ACISSTTU**	CATSUITS	**ACLMNORU**	COLUMNAR
ACINOSSY	CYANOSIS	**ACISSTUV**	VACUISTS	**ACLMNORY**	NORMALCY
ACINOSTT	OSCITANT	**ACISTTUY**	ASTUCITY	**ACLMNPSU**	UNCLAMPS
	TACTIONS	**ACJKKSSY**	SKYJACKS	**ACLMORSU**	CLAMOURS
ACINOSTU	ANTICOUS	**ACJKLLOR**	JACKROLL	**ACLMORTU**	CROTALUM
	AUCTIONS	**ACJKLOSW**	LOCKJAWS	**ACLMPRSU**	SCALPRUM
	CAUTIONS	**ACJKNNOS**	JANNOCKS	**ACLMRSUU**	MUSCULAR
ACINOSTW	WAINSCOT	**ACJKOPST**	JACKPOTS	**ACLMSSTU**	MASSCULT
ACINOSWX	COXSWAIN	**ACJMNSTU**	MUNTJACS	**ACLMSTUU**	CUSTUMAL
ACINOTTX	TOXICANT	**ACJPSTUU**	CAJUPUTS	**ACLMSUUV**	VASCULUM
ACINPQUY	PIQUANCY	**ACKKMOPR**	POCKMARK	**ACLNNOOS**	NONCOLAS
ACINPRST	CANTRIPS	**ACKKORRW**	RACKWORK	**ACLNNOOV**	NONVOCAL
ACINPRSY	CYPRIANS	**ACKLLOPS**	POLLACKS	**ACLNNOSS**	NONCLASS
ACINPSTY	SYNAPTIC	**ACKLLOSY**	LAYLOCKS	**ACLNOORS**	CORONALS
ACINQSTU	QUANTICS	**ACKLLPSU**	SKULLCAP	**ACLNOORT**	COLORANT
ACINRSST	NARCISTS	**ACKLMNOS**	LOCKSMAN	**ACLNOOST**	COOLANTS
ACINRSSU	CRUSIANS	**ACKLMORS**	ARMLOCKS		OCTANOLS
ACINRSTU	CURTAINS		LOCKRAMS	**ACLNOOSV**	VOLCANOS
	SATURNIC	**ACKLNOSU**	UNCLOAKS	**ACLNOPSY**	SYNCOPAL
	TURACINS	**ACKLOOPW**	WOOLPACK	**ACLNORSU**	CONSULAR
ACINRTTU	TACITURN	**ACKLOORS**	OARLOCKS		COURLANS
	URTICANT	**ACKLOOSW**	WOOLSACK	**ACLNORTU**	CALUTRON
ACINSTTY	SANCTITY	**ACKLORSV**	LAVROCKS	**ACLNOSSS**	CLASSONS
	SCANTITY	**ACKLORSW**	WARLOCKS	**ACLNOSTU**	CONSULTA
ACINSTYY	SYNCYTIA	**ACKLORSY**	ROCKLAYS		OSCULANT
ACIOOPST	SCOTOPIA	**ACKLOSSS**	LASSOCKS	**ACLNPSSU**	UNCLASPS
ACIOOTYZ	ZOOCYTIA	**ACKMMMOS**	MAMMOCKS	**ACLNPTUU**	PUNCTUAL
ACIOPRST	APRICOTS	**ACKMNOST**	STOCKMAN	**ACLNSSUY**	UNCLASSY
	PISCATOR	**ACKMNRTU**	TRUCKMAN	**ACLOOPPS**	ALCOPOPS
ACIOPRTT	PROTATIC	**ACKMOSST**	STOMACKS	**ACLOOPRR**	CORPORAL
ACIOPRTY	POTICARY	**ACKMOSTT**	MATTOCKS	**ACLOOPRS**	CARPOOLS
ACIOPSST	POTASSIC	**ACKNOPSW**	SNOWPACK	**ACLOORST**	LOCATORS
ACIOPRSU	SPACIOUS	**ACKNORSU**	CRANKOUS	**ACLOORWY**	COLORWAY
ACIOPSTU	AUTOPSIC	**ACKNRSTU**	UNTRACKS	**ACLOPRRU**	PROCURAL
	CAPTIOUS	**ACKNSSTU**	UNSTACKS	**ACLOPRST**	CALTROPS
ACIOPTTU	AUTOPTIC	**ACKOPRRS**	PARROCKS	**ACLOPRXY**	XYLOCARP
ACIORRSS	CORSAIRS	**ACKOPRRT**	TRAPROCK	**ACLOPSSU**	SCOPULAS
ACIORSSU	SCARIOUS	**ACKORRST**	TARROCKS	**ACLOPSSY**	CALYPSOS
ACIORSTT	CITATORS	**ACKORSTW**	CATWORKS	**ACLOPSUU**	OPUSCULA
	RICOTTAS	**ACKOSSTW**	TOWSACKS	**ACLORRTU**	TORCULAR
ACIORTTY	ATROCITY	**ACKOSWZZ**	WAZZOCKS	**ACLORTUW**	LAWCOURT
	CITATORY	**ACKPSSTU**	STACKUPS		OUTCRAWL
ACIORTVY	VORACITY	**ACLLLNOY**	CLONALLY	**ACLOSSTU**	OUTCLASS
ACIOSSST	COASSIST	**ACLLMNOU**	COLUMNAL	**ACLRSSTY**	CRYSTALS
ACIOSSTY	ISOSTACY	**ACLLMORU**	CORALLUM	**ACMMNOSY**	SCAMMONY
ACIOSTUU	CAUTIOUS	**ACLLMOSU**	MOLLUSCA	**ACMMNOYY**	MYOMANCY
ACIPRRUU	PIRARUCU	**ACLLNNOO**	NONLOCAL	**ACMNOOPR**	CRAMPOON
ACIPRSSS	CASSPIRS	**ACLLOORS**	COROLLAS		MONOCARP
ACIPRSTT	TIPCARTS	**ACLLOORT**	COLLATOR	**ACMNOORR**	CROMORNA
ACIPRTTY	TRIPTYCA	**ACLLOOSS**	COLOSSAL	**ACMNOORT**	MONOCRAT
ACIPSSST	SPASTICS	**ACLLOPSS**	SCALLOPS	**ACMNOOYZ**	ZOOMANCY
ACIQRSTU	QUARTICS	**ACLLORUY**	OCULARLY	**ACMNOPRS**	CORPSMAN

	CRAMPONS	**ACPSSTUU**	USUCAPTS	**ADDEEGOR**	DOGEARED
ACMNORSY	ACRONYMS	**ACPSSTUY**	PUSSYCAT	**ADDEEGRR**	DEGRADER
ACMNSSTU	SANCTUMS	**ADDDEEEL**	DELEADED		REGARDED
ACMOOORT	COATROOM	**ADDDEEEM**	ADDEEMED		REGRADED
ACMOOPRS	COPROSMA	**ADDDEEEN**	DEADENED	**ADDEEGRS**	DEGRADES
ACMOORRT	MOTORCAR	**ADDDEEGR**	DEGRADED	**ADDEEGSS**	DEGASSED
ACMOORUU	COUMAROU	**ADDDEEIM**	DIADEMED	**ADDEEHLR**	HERALDED
ACMOOSST	SCOTOMAS	**ADDDEELR**	LADDERED	**ADDEEHLY**	ALDEHYDE
ACMOPRST	COMPARTS	**ADDDEEMN**	DEMANDED	**ADDEEHNR**	ADHEREND
ACMOPSTU	CAMPOUTS		MADDENED		HARDENED
ACMORRSS	CROSSARM	**ADDDEENR**	DANDERED	**ADDEEHNS**	HEADENDS
ACMORSTW	CATWORMS		REDDENDA	**ADDEEHNU**	UNHEADED
	WORMCAST	**ADDDEENS**	DESANDED	**ADDEEHOP**	DOPEHEAD
ACMORSTY	COSTMARY		SADDENED	**ADDEEHRS**	REDHEADS
ACMQSTUU	CUMQUATS	**ADDDEEPS**	SEPADDED	**ADDEEHRT**	THREADED
ACNNNORY	CANNONRY	**ADDDEGJU**	ADJUDGED	**ADDEEIKR**	DAIKERED
ACNNOORT	NONACTOR	**ADDDEIMS**	MISADDED	**ADDEEILN**	DEADLINE
ACNNOSTT	CONSTANT	**ADDDELSW**	SWADDLED	**ADDEEILR**	DEADLIER
ACNOOORT	OCTAROON	**ADDDELTW**	TWADDLED		DERAILED
ACNOOPRT	COPATRON	**ADDDEMNU**	ADDENDUM		REDIALED
ACNOORRY	CORONARY	**ADDDEMOO**	ADDOOMED	**ADDEEILT**	DETAILED
ACNOORST	CARTOONS	**ADDDENOS**	DEODANDS	**ADDEEIMT**	MEDIATED
	CORANTOS	**ADDDENPU**	UNPADDED	**ADDEEINT**	DETAINED
	OSTRACON	**ADDDENRU**	DEUDDARN	**ADDEEINU**	UNIDEAED
ACNOORSU	CANOROUS	**ADDDEOOW**	DEADWOOD	**ADDEEIPR**	DIAPERED
ACNOORTU	COURANTO	**ADDDEORS**	ADDORSED	**ADDEEISS**	DISEASED
ACNOORTY	CARTOONY	**ADDDEOTU**	OUTADDED	**ADDEEIST**	STEADIED
	OCTONARY	**ADDDEQSU**	SQUADDED	**ADDEEITV**	DEVIATED
ACNOPSSW	SNOWCAPS	**ADDDGILN**	DADDLING	**ADDEEKMR**	DEMARKED
ACNORRSU	RANCOURS	**ADDEEEFL**	DEFLEAED	**ADDEEKNR**	DARKENED
ACNORRSY	CARRYONS	**ADDEEEFN**	DEAFENED	**ADDEELLM**	MEDALLED
ACNORRTY	CONTRARY	**ADDEEEFT**	DEFEATED	**ADDEELLP**	PEDALLED
ACNORSTT	CONTRAST	**ADDEEEJY**	DEEJAYED	**ADDEELLV**	DEVALLED
	CONTRATS	**ADDEEELN**	LEADENED	**ADDEELNO**	LOADENED
ACNORSTU	COURANTS	**ADDEEELV**	DELEAVED	**ADDEELNP**	DEPLANED
ACNORTTU	TURNCOAT	**ADDEEEMN**	DEMEANED	**ADDEELNR**	ENLARDED
ACNORTUY	NOCTUARY	**ADDEEEMR**	REMEADED		RELANDED
ACNOSSTW	SNOWCATS	**ADDEEENR**	DEADENER	**ADDEELNU**	UNLEADED
ACNPRSSY	SYNCARPS		ENDEARED	**ADDEELOR**	RELOADED
ACNPRSUY	SPRAUNCY	**ADDEEENW**	DANEWEED	**ADDEELPS**	DELAPSED
ACNPRSYY	SYNCARPY	**ADDEEESY**	DEADEYES	**ADDEELRS**	RESADDLE
ACNRRSTU	CURRANTS	**ADDEEFGN**	DEFANGED	**ADDEELRT**	TREADLED
ACNRRTUY	CURRANTY	**ADDEEFHN**	HANDFEED	**ADDEELST**	DESALTED
ACOOPRRS	CORPORAS	**ADDEEFIL**	DEFILADE	**ADDEELUV**	DEVALUED
ACOOPRST	COPASTOR	**ADDEEFIM**	MADEFIED	**ADDEEMNN**	DEMANNED
	ROOTCAPS	**ADDEEFLT**	DEFLATED	**ADDEEMNP**	DAMPENED
ACOOPSTT	TOPCOATS	**ADDEEFMO**	DEFOAMED	**ADDEEMNR**	DAMNEDER
ACOORSTU	TOURACOS	**ADDEEFNU**	UNDEAFED		DEMANDER
ACOPPRRS	PROCARPS	**ADDEEFPR**	PREFADED		REDEMAND
ACOPRRST	CARPORTS	**ADDEEFRY**	DEFRAYED		REMANDED
ACOPRRTT	PROTRACT		FEEDYARD	**ADDEEMST**	DEMASTED
ACORRSTT	TRACTORS	**ADDEEFTT**	DEFATTED	**ADDEENPP**	APPENDED
ACORRSTU	CURATORS	**ADDEEGGR**	DAGGERED	**ADDEENPR**	PANDERED
ACORRTUY	CARRYOUT	**ADDEEGHR**	HARDEDGE	**ADDEENPX**	EXPANDED
	CURATORY	**ADDEEGLL**	ALLEDGED	**ADDEENRR**	DARNEDER
ACORSSTU	SURCOATS	**ADDEEGLN**	DANEGELD	**ADDEENRT**	ENDARTED
ACORSSUW	CURASSOW	**ADDEEGLZ**	DEGLAZED	**ADDEENRU**	DAUNERED
ACORSSWY	CROSSWAY	**ADDEEGNR**	DANGERED	**ADDEENRW**	DAWNERED
ACORSTTY	CRYOSTAT		DERANGED		WANDERED
ACORSTUU	TURACOUS		GANDERED		WARDENED
ACOSSTTU	OUTCASTS		GARDENED	**ADDEENSS**	DEADNESS

ADDEENTT	ATTENDED	ADDEIJNO	ADJOINED		WADDLERS
	DENTATED	ADDEIKNP	KIDNAPED	ADDELRSY	SADDLERY
ADDEENTU	DENUDATE	ADDEILNS	ISLANDED	ADDELRTW	TWADDLER
ADDEENUV	UNEVADED		LANDSIDE	ADDELSST	STADDLES
ADDEEOST	DEODATES	ADDEILNT	TIDELAND	ADDELSSW	SWADDLES
ADDEEPRS	RESPADED	ADDEILRS	DIEDRALS	ADDELSTW	TWADDLES
ADDEEPRT	DEPARTED	ADDEILRW	WADDLIER	ADDEMMNU	UNDAMMED
	PREDATED	ADDEILSU	DUALISED	ADDEMNNU	UNDAMNED
ADDEEPRV	DEPRAVED	ADDEILSY	DIALYSED	ADDEMNPU	UNDAMPED
	PERVADED	ADDEILUZ	DUALIZED	ADDEMNST	DAMNDEST
ADDEERRS	DREADERS	ADDEILYZ	DIALYZED	ADDEMOSY	DOMESDAY
ADDEERRT	RETARDED	ADDEIMOS	SODAMIDE	ADDENNOT	DANTONED
ADDEERRW	REWARDED	ADDEIMRS	DISARMED	ADDENOPR	PARDONED
	WARDERED		MISDREAD	ADDENORU	UNADORED
ADDEERRY	DEERYARD	ADDEIMST	MISDATED	ADDENPRU	UNDRAPED
ADDEERSW	SAWDERED	ADDEIMSY	DISMAYED	ADDENRST	DARNDEST
ADDEERTT	DERATTED	ADDEIMTT	ADMITTED		STRANDED
ADDEERTV	ADVERTED	ADDEINOR	ORDAINED	ADDENRSU	DAUNDERS
ADDEFFOR	AFFORDED	ADDEINOS	ADENOIDS	ADDENRTU	DRAUNTED
ADDEFIIL	LADIFIED		ADONISED		UNTRADED
ADDEFILT	DEADLIFT		ANODISED	ADDENRUW	UNWARDED
ADDEFILY	LADYFIED	ADDEINOZ	ADONIZED	ADDEORTU	OUTDARED
ADDEFIST	FADDIEST		ANODIZED	ADDEOTTU	OUTDATED
ADDEFLRU	DREADFUL	ADDEINPR	DREPANID	ADDEPRSU	SUPERADD
ADDEFRSU	DEFRAUDS	ADDEINRS	SARDINED	ADDEPRTU	UPDATERD
ADDEGGLR	DRAGGLED	ADDEINRT	INDARTED	ADDFFILO	DAFFODIL
ADDEGHOS	GODHEADS	ADDEINST	DANDIEST	ADDFFINR	DANDRIFF
ADDEGILO	DIALOGED	ADDEIOPR	PARODIED	ADDFFNRU	DANDRUFF
ADDEGILS	GLADDIES	ADDEIORS	ROADSIDE	ADDFGILN	FADDLING
ADDEGINR	DREADING		SIDEROAD	ADDFIMSS	FADDISMS
	READDING	ADDEIOTX	OXIDATED	ADDFISST	FADDISTS
ADDEGIRS	DISGRADE	ADDEIPPR	DIDAPPER	ADDGGILN	GLADDING
ADDEGJSU	ADJUDGES	ADDEIPRS	DISPREAD	ADDGGORU	GUARDDOG
ADDEGLNS	GLADDENS	ADDEIPSS	DIPSADES	ADDGIILN	DAIDLING
ADDEGLST	GLADDEST	ADDEIQSU	SQUADDIE	ADDGIIRS	DIAGRIDS
ADDEGNOP	DOGNAPED	ADDEIRST	DISRATED	ADDGIKNR	GRANDKID
ADDEGNRU	UNGRADED	ADDEIRSW	SIDEWARD	ADDGILNN	DANDLING
ADDEGPRU	UPGRADED	ADDEIRVZ	VIZARDED	ADDGILNP	PADDLING
ADDEHHIN	HINDHEAD	ADDEISSU	DISSUADE	ADDGILNR	RADDLING
ADDEHHLN	HANDHELD	ADDEISSV	DISSAVED	ADDGILNS	SADDLING
ADDEHHNS	SHEDHAND	ADDEISSW	SWADDIES	ADDGILNW	DAWDLING
ADDEHILR	DIHEDRAL	ADDEISSY	DAYSIDES		WADDLING
ADDEHINW	HEADWIND	ADDEJSTU	ADJUSTED	ADDGINPS	PADDINGS
ADDEHIRS	DIEHARDS	ADDEKNVY	VANDYKED	ADDGINQU	QUADDING
ADDEHIRW	RAWHIDED	ADDELLOR	DOLLARED	ADDGINSW	WADDINGS
ADDEHLOS	SHEDLOAD	ADDELMOS	DOLMADES	ADDGINWY	WADDYING
ADDEHMRU	DRUMHEAD	ADDELNNU	DUNELAND	ADDGLNOS	GLADDONS
ADDEHNNU	UNHANDED	ADDELNOO	ONLOADED	ADDGMNOS	GODDAMNS
ADDEHNSU	UNDASHED	ADDELNOU	DUODENAL	ADDGMRUU	MUDGUARD
	UNSHADED		UNLOADED	ADDGOOSW	DAGWOODS
ADDEHOPR	DROPHEAD	ADDELNPU	PUDENDAL	ADDGOQSU	GODSQUAD
ADDEHORW	HEADWORD	ADDELNRS	DANDLERS	ADDGORSW	GODWARDS
ADDEHOSW	SHADOWED	ADDELNSU	UNSADDLE	ADDHHISS	DISHDASH
ADDEHPRU	PURDAHED	ADDELOOR	ELDORADO	ADDHHLNO	HANDHOLD
ADDEHRTY	HYDRATED	ADDELOPU	UPLOADED	ADDHIMOO	MAIDHOOD
ADDEIIKS	DIDAKEIS	ADDELPRS	PADDLERS	ADDHINPS	DAPHNIDS
ADDEIIMS	DIAMIDES		SPRADDLE	ADDHINRW	HINDWARD
ADDEIINZ	DAIDZEIN	ADDELRSS	SADDLERS	ADDHINSY	DANDYISH
ADDEIIRS	DIARISED	ADDELRST	STRADDLE	ADDHIOTY	HYDATOID
ADDEIIRZ	DIARIZED	ADDELRSW	DAWDLERS	ADDHISTY	HYDATIDS
ADDEIITV	ADDITIVE		SWADDLER	ADDHLOOS	LADHOODS

ADDHLOOY	LADYHOOD	ADEEEHHW	HEEHAWED	ADEEFLRR	DEFERRAL
ADDHOORW	HARDWOOD	ADEEEHJN	JEHADEEN	ADEEFLRS	FEDERALS
ADDHOSTY	ATHODYDS	ADEEEHRS	HAEREDES	ADEEFLRT	DEFLATER
ADDIIKMZ	ZADDIKIM	ADEEEHRT	REHEATED		FALTERED
ADDIILUV	DIVIDUAL	ADEEEHRX	EXHEDRAE		REFLATED
ADDIINOT	ADDITION	ADEEEHSY	EYESHADE	ADEEFLSS	FADELESS
ADDIINSS	DISDAINS	ADEEEINT	DETAINEE	ADEEFLST	DEFLATES
ADDIINTV	DIVIDANT	ADEEEKNW	WEAKENED	ADEEFLSX	FLAXSEED
ADDIIPSS	DIAPSIDS	ADEEELMN	ENAMELED	ADEEFMNR	ENFRAMED
ADDIKSST	TSADDIKS	ADEEELNS	ENSEALED		FREEDMAN
ADDIKSTY	KATYDIDS	ADEEELNV	LEAVENED	ADEEFMOR	DEFOAMER
ADDIKSTZ	TZADDIKS	ADEEELPR	REPEALED	ADEEFMRR	REFRAMED
ADDILLNS	LANDSLID	ADEEELRS	RELEASED	ADEEFMRS	DEFAMERS
ADDILLNW	WILDLAND		RESEALED	ADEEFNRU	UNFEARED
ADDILMNS	MIDLANDS	ADEEELRV	LAVEERED	ADEEFNSS	DEAFNESS
ADDILMSS	LADDISMS		REVEALED	ADEEFNST	FASTENED
ADDILNNW	LANDWIND	ADEEELST	TEASELED	ADEEFNTT	FATTENED
ADDILOSS	DISLOADS	ADEEELSV	DELEAVES	ADEEFORR	FOREREAD
ADDIMNOS	DIAMONDS	ADEEELSW	WEASELED	ADEEFORT	FOREDATE
ADDIMNSY	DANDYISM	ADEEELTV	ELEVATED	ADEEFOTV	FOVEATED
ADDIMNYY	DIDYNAMY	ADEEELTZ	TEAZELED	ADEEFPRS	PREFADES
ADDIMROS	DIADROMS	ADEEEMNS	DEMEANES	ADEEFRRT	RAFTERED
ADDINNOR	ORDINAND		ENSEAMED	ADEEFRRY	DEFRAYER
ADDINORS	ANDROIDS	ADEEEMNT	EMENDATE		FEDERARY
	DISADORN	ADEEEMRT	RETEAMED	ADEEFRST	DRAFTEES
ADDINQUY	QUIDDANY	ADEEEMRU	EMERAUDE	ADEEFRTU	FEATURED
ADDINRWW	WINDWARD	ADEEENNT	NEATENED	ADEEGGHS	EGGHEADS
ADDIORTY	ADDITORY	ADEEENRR	REEARNED	ADEEGGJR	JAGGEDER
ADDIQSST	TSADDIQS	ADEEENRS	ENSEARED	ADEEGGLL	ALLEGGED
ADDIQSTZ	TZADDIQS		SERENADE	ADEEGGRR	RAGGEDER
ADDIRSZZ	DIZZARDS	ADEEENTT	ATTENDEE	ADEEGGRS	SAGGERED
ADDKNRRU	DRUNKARD		EDENTATE	ADEEGGRT	RETAGGED
ADDLLNOR	LANDLORD	ADEEENWZ	WEAZENED	ADEEGGRU	REGAUGED
ADDLLRSU	DULLARDS	ADEEEPRS	RAPESEED	ADEEGGWW	GEWGAWED
ADDLNNOW	DOWNLAND	ADEEEPRT	DEPARTEE	ADEEGHNR	REHANGED
ADDLNOOW	DOWNLOAD		REPEATED	ADEEGHOR	GHERAOED
	WOODLAND	ADEEERRS	ARREEDES	ADEEGHRT	GATHERED
ADDLNORR	RANDLORD	ADEEERST	RESEATED	ADEEGIMN	ADEEMING
ADDLNORS	LANDDROS	ADEEERVW	REWEAVED	ADEEGIMR	REIMAGED
ADDLOOSS	SOLDADOS	ADEEESSW	SEAWEEDS	ADEEGINR	REGAINED
ADDLORTY	DOTARDLY		SEESAWED	ADEEGINS	AGENISED
ADDMOOSY	DOOMSDAY	ADEEFFIR	EFFRAIDE	ADEEGINZ	AGENIZED
ADDNOPWY	PANDOWDY	ADEEFGLN	FENAGLED	ADEEGIRS	DISAGREE
ADDNORWW	DOWNWARD	ADEEFHNR	FREEHAND	ADEEGIRT	GAITERED
	DRAWDOWN	ADEEFHOR	FOREHEAD	ADEEGISS	ASSIEGED
ADDOORRY	DOORYARD	ADEEFHRT	FATHERED	ADEEGLLS	ALLEDGES
ADDOORWW	WOODWARD	ADEEFIIR	AERIFIED	ADEEGLLT	GALLETED
ADDOORWY	WOODYARD	ADEEFILN	ENFILADE	ADEEGLLV	GAVELLED
ADDOPSSY	DASYPODS	ADEEFIMS	MADEFIES	ADEEGLNO	ENGAOLED
ADEEEFFR	AFFEERED		SEMIDEAF	ADEEGLNR	ENLARGED
ADEEEFNY	FEDAYEEN	ADEEFINR	FREDAINE		LANGERED
ADEEEFRT	DEFEATER	ADEEFIOR	FOEDARIE		LARGENED
	FEDERATE	ADEEFIRR	RAREFIED	ADEEGLNT	DANEGELT
	REDEFEAT	ADEEFIRS	FEDARIES		DETANGLE
ADEEEGLT	DELEGATE	ADEEFIRY	REAEDIFY	ADEEGLRV	GRAVELED
ADEEEGNR	RENEGADE	ADEEFIST	SAFETIED	ADEEGLRZ	REGLAZED
ADEEEGNT	TEENAGED	ADEEFLLT	FELLATED	ADEEGLSV	SELVAGED
ADEEEGPS	GAPESEED	ADEEFLMN	ENFLAMED	ADEEGLSZ	DEGLAZES
ADEEEGRR	REGEARED	ADEEFLNS	ENDLEAFS	ADEEGMMO	GAMODEME
ADEEEGRS	DEGREASE	ADEEFLOR	FREELOAD	ADEEGMMT	GEMMATED
ADEEEGUW	AGUEWEED	ADEEFLPR	PEDALFER	ADEEGMNR	GENDARME

ADEEGMNS	ENDGAMES	**ADEEHISV**	ADHESIVE	**ADEEHSSY**	HAYSEEDS
ADEEGMNY	GANYMEDE	**ADEEHITZ**	ATHEIZED	**ADEEIILS**	IDEALISE
	MEGADYNE	**ADEEHKNR**	DAKERHEN	**ADEEIILZ**	IDEALIZE
ADEEGMOP	MEGAPODE		HANKERED	**ADEEIITV**	IDEATIVE
ADEEGMOS	MEGADOSE		HARKENED	**ADEEIJKL**	JADELIKE
ADEEGMSS	MESSAGED	**ADEEHKPR**	PHREAKED	**ADEEIJMR**	JEREMIAD
ADEEGNNR	ENDANGER	**ADEEHKRS**	KASHERED	**ADEEIJRS**	JADERIES
	ENRANGED	**ADEEHKWW**	HAWKWEED	**ADEEIJST**	JADEITES
ADEEGNNV	VENDANGE	**ADEEHKWY**	HAWKEYED	**ADEEIKLS**	LAKESIDE
ADEEGNOR	RENEGADO	**ADEEHLLW**	WELLHEAD	**ADEEIKMR**	DIEMAKER
ADEEGNRR	DERANGER	**ADEEHLNO**	ENHALOED	**ADEEIKNP**	KIDNAPEE
	GARDENER	**ADEEHLNR**	REHANDLE	**ADEEIKSW**	WEAKSIDE
	GARNERED	**ADEEHLNS**	HANSELED	**ADEEILLO**	OEILLADE
ADEEGNRS	DERANGES	**ADEEHLNU**	UNHEALED	**ADEEILLR**	REALLIED
	GRANDEES	**ADEEHLRS**	ASHLERED	**ADEEILMN**	ENDEMIAL
	GRENADES	**ADEEHLRT**	HALTERED	**ADEEILMR**	REMAILED
ADEEGNRU	DUNGAREE		LATHERED		REMEDIAL
	RENAGUED	**ADEEHLSS**	HEADLESS	**ADEEILMS**	LIMEADES
	UNAGREED	**ADEEHLTY**	HEATEDLY	**ADEEILMV**	MEDIEVAL
	UNDERAGE	**ADEEHMMO**	HOMEMADE	**ADEEILNR**	RENAILED
	UNGEARED	**ADEEHMMR**	HAMMERED	**ADEEILNS**	DELAINES
ADEEGNRV	ENGRAVED	**ADEEHMNN**	MENHADEN	**ADEEILNT**	DATELINE
ADEEGNSS	AGEDNESS	**ADEEHMNS**	HEADSMEN		ENTAILED
ADEEGNST	ENDGATES	**ADEEHMNT**	ANTHEMED		LINEATED
ADEEGNSV	VENDAGES	**ADEEHMPR**	HAMPERED	**ADEEILPR**	PEDALIER
ADEEGORT	DEROGATE	**ADEEHMSS**	EMDASHES	**ADEEILPS**	PLEIADES
ADEEGORV	OVERAGED	**ADEEHMST**	STEMHEAD	**ADEEILPT**	DEPILATE
ADEEGOST	DOGEATES	**ADEEHNOT**	HEADNOTE		EPILATED
ADEEGOTW	GOATWEED	**ADEEHNPP**	HAPPENED		PILEATED
ADEEGPRS	ASPERGED	**ADEEHNRR**	HARDENER	**ADEEILRR**	DERAILER
	PRESAGED		REHARDEN		RERAILED
ADEEGPRT	PARGETED	**ADEEHNRT**	ADHERENT	**ADEEILRS**	REALISED
ADEEGRRR	REGARDER		HARTENED		RESAILED
ADEEGRRS	REGRADES		NEATHERD		SIDEREAL
ADEEGRRT	GARRETED		THREADEN	**ADEEILRT**	DETAILER
	GARTERED	**ADEEHNSS**	DASHEENS		ELATERID
	REGRATED		ENDASHES		RETAILED
ADEEGRRU	REARGUED	**ADEEHNST**	HASTENED	**ADEEILRZ**	REALIZED
	REDARGUE		NETHEADS	**ADEEILSS**	DEISEALS
ADEEGRSS	DEGASSER	**ADEEHNTU**	UNHEATED		IDEALESS
	DRESSAGE	**ADEEHOPR**	HEADROPE	**ADEEILST**	LEADIEST
ADEEGRST	RESTAGED	**ADEEHORS**	SOREHEAD	**ADEEILSV**	DISLEAVE
ADEEGRSU	GUARDEES	**ADEEHORV**	OVERHEAD	**ADEEILSY**	EYELIADS
ADEEGRSW	RAGWEEDS	**ADEEHPPU**	UPHEAPED	**ADEEIMNR**	REMAINED
ADEEGRTT	TARGETED	**ADEEHPRS**	EPHEDRAS	**ADEEIMNS**	DEMAINES
ADEEGSSS	DEGASSES		RESHAPED		INSEAMED
ADEEGSTT	GESTATED	**ADEEHPRT**	PREDEATH	**ADEEIMNT**	DEMENTIA
ADEEGSWY	EDGEWAYS		THREAPED	**ADEEIMNX**	EXAMINED
ADEEGTTZ	GAZETTED	**ADEEHPUV**	UPHEAVED	**ADEEIMPR**	EMPAIRED
ADEEHHRS	REHASHED	**ADEEHRRS**	ADHERERS	**ADEEIMRR**	DREAMIER
ADEEHHSS	SHAHEEDS		REDSHARE	**ADEEIMRS**	MADERISE
ADEEHHST	SHEATHED	**ADEEHRRT**	RETHREAD	**ADEEIMRT**	DIAMETER
ADEEHIJN	JIHADEEN		THREADER		REMEDIAT
ADEEHIKL	HEADLIKE	**ADEEHRST**	HEADREST	**ADEEIMRZ**	MADERIZE
ADEEHILN	HEADLINE	**ADEEHRSV**	RESHAVED	**ADEEIMSS**	SIAMESED
ADEEHILS	DEISHEAL	**ADEEHRSW**	REWASHED	**ADEEIMST**	MEDIATES
ADEEHIPR	PIERHEAD		WASHERED	**ADEEIMSZ**	SIAMEZED
ADEEHIRT	DEATHIER	**ADEEHRTT**	HATTERED	**ADEEIMTT**	ADMITTEE
ADEEHISS	EADISHES		THREATED		MEDITATE
ADEEHIST	ATHEISED	**ADEEHRTW**	WREATHED	**ADEEINNS**	ADENINES
	HEADIEST	**ADEEHSST**	HEADSETS		ANDESINE

ADEEINOP	OEDIPEAN	ADEELLPR	PEDALLER		PLEADERS
ADEEINPR	PINDAREE		PREDELLA		RELAPSED
ADEEINPT	DIAPENTE	ADEELLPS	SEPALLED		REPLEADS
ADEEINRS	ARSENIDE	ADEELLPT	PALLETED	ADEELPRT	PALTERED
	DENARIES		PETALLED		REPLATED
	DRAISENE	ADEELLQU	EQUALLED	ADEELPRY	PARLEYED
	NEARSIDE	ADEELLRS	SARDELLE		REPLAYED
ADEEINRT	DETAINER	ADEELLRT	TELLARED	ADEELPSS	DELAPSES
	RETAINED	ADEELLRU	LAURELED	ADEELPST	PEDESTAL
ADEEINRV	REINVADE	ADEELLRV	RAVELLED	ADEELPTY	PEDATELY
ADEEINSS	ANISEEDS	ADEELLSS	ALLSEEDS	ADEELQSU	SQUEALED
ADEEINST	ANDESITE		LEADLESS	ADEELRRR	LARDERER
ADEEINTW	ANTIWEED	ADEELLTY	ELATEDLY	ADEELRRT	TREADLER
ADEEINVW	INWEAVED	ADEELLVY	VALLEYED	ADEELRRY	READERLY
ADEEIPRR	RAPIERED	ADEELLWY	WALLEYED	ADEELRST	DESALTER
	REPAIRED	ADEELMNO	LEMONADE		RESLATED
ADEEIPRS	AIRSPEED	ADEELMNP	EMPLANED		TREADLES
ADEEIPTX	EXPIATED	ADEELMNR	ALDERMEN	ADEELRSV	SLAVERED
ADEEIRRR	DREARIER	ADEELMNS	DALESMEN	ADEELRSW	LEEWARDS
ADEEIRRS	DREARIES		EMENDALS	ADEELRSY	DELAYERS
	RERAISED		LEADSMEN	ADEELRTV	TRAVELED
ADEEIRST	READIEST	ADEELMNT	LAMENTED	ADEELRUV	REVALUED
	SERIATED	ADEELMOR	REMOLADE	ADEELRWY	LAWYERED
	SIDERATE	ADEELMOS	SOMEDEAL	ADEELSST	DATELESS
	STEADIER	ADEELMPR	EMPARLED		DETASSEL
ADEEIRSV	READVISE	ADEELMPX	EXAMPLED		TASSELED
ADEEIRTT	ITERATED	ADEELMRS	DEMERSAL	ADEELSTT	LADETTES
ADEEIRTV	DERIVATE		EMERALDS	ADEELSTY	SEDATELY
	EVIRATED	ADEELMRT	TRAMELED	ADEELSUV	DEVALUES
	TAIVERED	ADEELMRV	MARVELED	ADEEMMMR	MAMMERED
ADEEIRTW	WAITERED	ADEELMST	MEDALETS	ADEEMMRY	YAMMERED
ADEEISSS	DISEASES	ADEELMTU	EMULATED	ADEEMMSS	MESDAMES
	SEASIDES	ADEELNNP	ENPLANED	ADEEMMXY	MYXEDEMA
ADEEISST	STEADIES	ADEELNNU	UNANELED	ADEEMNNR	MANNERED
ADEEISSV	ADESSIVE	ADEELNOR	OLEANDER		REMANNED
	ADVISEES		RELOANED	ADEEMNOR	DEMEANOR
ADEEISTU	AUDITEES	ADEELNPS	DEPLANES		ENAMORED
ADEEISTV	DEVIATES		SPALDEEN	ADEEMNOS	DAEMONES
	SEDATIVE	ADEELNPT	ENDPLATE	ADEEMNOT	NEMATODE
ADEEITTV	EVITATED	ADEELNPU	UPLEANED	ADEEMNOU	EUDAEMON
ADEEITVW	TIDEWAVE	ADEELNRT	ANTLERED	ADEEMNPR	DAMPENER
ADEEKMRR	REMARKED	ADEELNRV	LAVENDER	ADEEMNPS	SPADEMEN
ADEEKMRT	DEMARKET	ADEELNSU	UNLEASED	ADEEMNPY	EPENDYMA
	MARKETED		UNSEALED	ADEEMNRS	AMENDERS
ADEEKNNR	ENRANKED	ADEELNSV	ENSLAVED		MEANDERS
ADEEKNPS	KNEEPADS	ADEELNTT	TALENTED		REAMENDS
ADEEKNPW	KNAPWEED	ADEELNTU	UNELATED	ADEEMNSS	SEEDSMAN
ADEEKNRR	DARKENER	ADEELNTV	LEVANTED	ADEEMNST	STAMENED
ADEEKNRS	KNEADERS	ADEELNTY	ENTAYLED	ADEEMNSU	UNSEAMED
ADEEKNST	NAKEDEST	ADEELOPS	PEDALOES	ADEEMNSY	DEMAYNES
ADEEKORS	RESOAKED	ADEELOPX	POLEAXED	ADEEMNTU	UNTEAMED
ADEEKPRR	REPARKED	ADEELORR	RELOADER	ADEEMNTW	METEWAND
ADEEKQSU	SQUEAKED	ADEELORU	AUREOLED	ADEEMORS	SEADROME
ADEEKRST	STREAKED	ADEELORV	OVERLADE	ADEEMORT	MODERATE
ADEEKSWY	WEEKDAYS	ADEELOST	DESOLATE	ADEEMPPR	PAMPERED
ADEELLLP	LAPELLED	ADEELOSW	LEASOWED		REMAPPED
ADEELLMT	METALLED	ADEELPPR	LAPPERED	ADEEMPRR	PREARMED
ADEELLMU	MEDULLAE		RAPPELLED	ADEEMPRT	EMPARTED
ADEELLNP	PANELLED	ADEELPPT	LAPPETED		TAMPERED
ADEELLNW	ENWALLED	ADEELPPU	UPLEAPED	ADEEMPRV	REVAMPED
ADEELLNY	LEADENLY	ADEELPRS	PEDALERS	ADEEMPRY	EMPAYRED

ADEEMPST	STAMPEDE	ADEENSTY	ANDESYTE	ADEERSST	ASSERTED
	STEPDAME	ADEENTTU	TAUTENED		DEARESTS
ADEEMRRS	DREAMERS	ADEENTTV	VENDETTA		ESTRADES
	REDREAMS	ADEEOPRR	PADERERO	ADEERSTT	ASTERTED
ADEEMRRT	REDREAMT	ADEEOPRT	OPERATED		RESTATED
ADEEMRRV	MARVERED	ADEEOPST	ADOPTEES		RETASTED
ADEEMRRW	REWARMED	ADEEOORV	OVERDARE	ADEERSTW	DEWATERS
ADEEMRRY	DREAMERY		OVERDEAR		TARWEEDS
ADEEMRSS	MEDRESAS		OVERREAD		WASTERED
ADEEMRST	MASTERED	ADEEORSW	OARWEEDS	ADEERSTY	ESTRAYED
	STREAMED	ADEEORVW	OVERAWED	ADEERTTT	TATTERED
ADEEMRSU	MEASURED		REAVOWED	ADEERTTY	YATTERED
ADEEMRTT	MATTERED	ADEEPPRR	DAPPERER	ADEERTWW	WARTWEED
ADEEMRTY	METEYARD		PREPARED	ADEERVYY	EVERYDAY
ADEEMSSW	MAWSEEDS	ADEEPPRT	PRETAPED	ADEESSSS	ASSESSED
ADEEMSTW	MATWEEDS	ADEEPPRU	PAUPERED	ADEESSTT	SEDATEST
ADEEMSWY	MAYWEEDS	ADEEPPRV	PREPAVED	ADEESTTT	ATTESTED
ADEENNPT	PENNATED	ADEEPPRW	WAPPERED	ADEESTUX	EXUDATES
ADEENNRS	ENSNARED	ADEEPRRS	RESPREAD	ADEESVVY	SAVVEYED
ADEENNRU	UNEARNED		SPREADER	ADEESWWX	WAXWEEDS
ADEENNTT	TENANTED	ADEEPRRT	DEPARTER	ADEFFGUW	GUFFAWED
ADEENNUW	UNWEANED	ADEEPRRU	UPREARED	ADEFFIMR	AFFIRMED
ADEENNUY	UNYEANED	ADEEPRRV	DEPRAVER	ADEFFIRR	DRAFFIER
ADEENOPW	WEAPONED		PERVADER	ADEFFIRT	TARIFFED
ADEENORS	REASONED	ADEEPRSS	ASPERSED	ADEFFIST	DAFFIEST
ADEENORV	ENDEAVOR		PREASSED	ADEFFLNS	SNAFFLED
ADEENORY	AERODYNE		REPASSED	ADEFFLOS	LEADOFFS
ADEENOSS	ADENOSES		RESPADES	ADEFFORT	TRADEOFF
	SEASONED	ADEEPRST	PEDERAST	ADEFFRST	STRAFFED
ADEENOST	ENDOSTEA		PREDATES	ADEFGGOT	FAGGOTED
ADEENOTT	DENOTATE		REPASTED	ADEFGIIS	GASIFIED
	DETONATE		TRAPESED	ADEFGILN	FINAGLED
ADEENOPR	ENDPAPER	ADEEPRSU	PERSUADE	ADEFGILO	FOLIAGED
ADEENPPS	SANDPEEP	ADEEPRSV	DEPRAVES	ADEFGILS	GADFLIES
ADEENPRR	PANDERER		PERVADES		GASFIELD
ADEENPRT	PARENTED	ADEEPRSW	PERSWADE	ADEFGIMN	DEFAMING
ADEENPRU	UNREAPED	ADEEPRSZ	SPREAZED	ADEFGIRT	DRIFTAGE
ADEENPRX	EXPANDER	ADEEPRTT	PATTERED	ADEFGIRU	ARGUFIED
ADEENPSW	SNAPWEED	ADEEPRTU	DEPURATE	ADEFGITU	FATIGUED
ADEENPTT	PATENTED		EPURATED	ADEFGLOT	GATEFOLD
	PATTENED	ADEEPRTZ	TRAPEZED	ADEFGLRU	FELDGRAU
ADEENRRW	WANDERER	ADEEPSST	STAPEDES	ADEFGNOR	FRONDAGE
ADEENRSS	DEARNESS	ADEEPSTT	ADEPTEST	ADEFGOSU	FOUGADES
ADEENRSU	UNDERSEA	ADEEPSWY	SPEEDWAY	ADEFHHIS	HEADFISH
	UNERASED	ADEEQRTU	DETRAQUE	ADEFHILS	DEALFISH
	UNSEARED	ADEEQRUV	QUAVERED	ADEFHILY	HAYFIELD
ADEENRSW	ANSWERED	ADEERRRT	RETARDER	ADEFHIMS	FAMISHED
ADEENRSY	YEARENDS	ADEERRRW	REDRAWER	ADEFHKOR	FORKHEAD
ADEENRTT	ATTENDER		REREWARD	ADEFHLSU	HEADFULS
	NATTERED		REWARDER	ADEFHLTU	DEATHFUL
	RATTENED	ADEERRST	ARRESTED	ADEFHMOT	FATHOMED
ADEENRTU	DENATURE		DREAREST	ADEFHNOR	FOREHAND
	UNDERATE		RASTERED	ADEFHOST	SOFTHEAD
	UNDEREAT		RETREADS	ADEFIILN	FINIALED
ADEENRTV	AVENTRED		SERRATED	ADEFIILR	AIRFIELD
ADEENRUV	UNREAVED		TREADERS	ADEFIILS	LADIFIES
ADEENSST	ASSENTED	ADEERRSV	ADVERSER		SALIFIED
	SENSATED	ADEERRSW	REDWARES	ADEFIILT	FILIATED
	STANDEES	ADEERRTT	RETRATED	ADEFIIMR	RAMIFIED
ADEENSSU	DANSEUSE	ADEERRTW	REDWATER	ADEFIINS	SANIFIED
ADEENSTU	UNSEATED	ADEERRWY	WARREYED	ADEFIINZ	NAZIFIED

ADEFIIRR	RARIFIED	ADEFORUV	FAVOURED	ADEGIKLO	GOADLIKE
ADEFIIRT	RATIFIED	ADEFOSTU	FADEOUTS	ADEGIKNN	KNEADING
ADEFIIRU	AURIFIED	ADEFPRRT	PREDRAFT	ADEGIKNR	DAKERING
ADEFILMN	INFLAMED	ADEFPTUW	UPWAFTED	ADEGILLO	GLADIOLE
ADEFILNR	FILANDER	ADEFRRST	DRAFTERS	ADEGILLP	PILLAGED
ADEFILNT	INFLATED		REDRAFTS	ADEGILLR	GLADLIER
ADEFILOR	FORELAID	ADEFRSTW	DWARFEST		GRILLADE
ADEFILOT	FOLIATED	ADEFSSTT	STEDFAST	ADEGILLS	GALLISED
ADEFILSS	DISLEAFS	ADEGGGNU	UNGAGGED	ADEGILLZ	GALLIZED
ADEFILSY	DAYFLIES	ADEGGIRR	DRAGGIER	ADEGILMN	MALIGNED
	LADYFIES	ADEGGIST	DAGGIEST		MEDALING
ADEFIMPR	FIREDAMP	ADEGGISU	GAUDGIES	ADEGILNN	LADENING
ADEFIMRS	MISFARED		GUIDAGES	ADEGILNO	GALENOID
ADEFIMSS	DISFAMES	ADEGGJLY	JAGGEDLY	ADEGILNP	PEDALING
ADEFINPR	PANFRIED	ADEGGLNU	ANGLEDUG		PLEADING
ADEFINRR	INFRARED	ADEGGLRS	DRAGGLES	ADEGILNR	DANGLIER
ADEFINRS	FRIANDES	ADEGGLRY	RAGGEDLY		DEARLING
ADEFINRU	UNFAIRED	ADEGGMOS	DEMAGOGS		DRAGLINE
ADEFINYZ	DENAZIFY	ADEGGMOY	DEMAGOGY	ADEGILNS	DEALINGS
ADEFIORS	FORESAID	ADEGGNOW	WAGGONED		LEADINGS
ADEFIRRT	DRAFTIER	ADEGGNTU	UNTAGGED		SIGNALED
ADEFIRSS	FARSIDES	ADEGGNUU	UNGAUGED	ADEGILNT	DELATING
ADEFKSST	DESKFAST	ADEGGOPS	PEDAGOGS	ADEGILNY	DELAYING
ADEFLLLU	LADLEFUL	ADEGGOPY	PEDAGOGY	ADEGILOR	DIALOGER
ADEFLLNS	ELFLANDS	ADEGGPRS	SPRAGGED	ADEGILOS	GOLIASED
ADEFLLOR	FALDEROL	ADEGGRRS	DRAGGERS	ADEGILOU	DIALOGUE
ADEFLLOW	FALLOWED	ADEGGRTY	GADGETRY	ADEGILOY	IDEALOGY
ADEFLLRY	ALDERFLY	ADEGHHOS	HOGSHEAD	ADEGILRS	SLAIRGED
ADEFLLSW	DEWFALLS	ADEGHILN	HEALDING	ADEGILSS	GLISSADE
ADEFLLUY	FEUDALLY	ADEGHILT	ALIGHTED	ADEGILST	GLADIEST
ADEFLMRU	DREAMFUL		GILTHEAD	ADEGILSV	DISGAVEL
ADEFLNNS	FENLANDS	ADEGHINR	ADHERING	ADEGIMNN	AMENDING
ADEFLNOR	FORELAND		HEADRING	ADEGIMNO	AMIDOGEN
ADEFLNRU	DEARNFUL	ADEGHINS	DEASHING	ADEGIMNR	DREAMING
ADEFLNTU	FLAUNTED		HEADINGS		MARGINED
ADEFLNUU	UNFEUDAL		SHEADING		MIDRANGE
ADEFLNUW	UNFLAWED	ADEGHIRR	HAGRIDER	ADEGIMOR	IDEOGRAM
ADEFLORT	DEFLATOR	ADEGHIRS	GARISHED	ADEGIMPS	MEDIGAPS
ADEFLORV	FLAVORED		HAGRIDES		MISPAGED
ADEFLORY	FORELADY		HEADRIGS	ADEGIMRS	MISGRADE
ADEFLPRS	FELDSPAR	ADEGHIRT	GRAITHED	ADEGIMRT	MIGRATED
ADEFLPSU	SPADEFUL	ADEGHJSU	JUGHEADS	ADEGIMST	SIGMATED
ADEFLRSW	SELFWARD	ADEGHLNO	HEADLONG	ADEGINNR	GRANNIED
ADEFLRTU	TRADEFUL		LONGHEAD	ADEGINNV	ADVENING
ADEFLRTW	LEFTWARD	ADEGHLOS	GALOSHED		DAVENING
ADEFLRZZ	FRAZZLED	ADEGHNNU	UNHANGED	ADEGINNW	AWNINGED
ADEFLSTU	DEFAULTS	ADEGHNPU	DUNGHEAP	ADEGINNY	DENAYING
	SULFATED	ADEGHNRT	THRANGED	ADEGINOR	ORGANDIE
ADEFMNRU	UNFRAMED	ADEGHOOP	PAGEHOOD	ADEGINOS	AGONISED
ADEFMORT	FORMATED	ADEGHORT	GOATHERD		DIAGNOSE
ADEFMOSU	FAMOUSED	ADEGHRTU	DAUGHTER	ADEGINOZ	AGONIZED
	FUMADOES	ADEGHTUW	WAUGHTED	ADEGINPU	ANGUIPED
ADEFNNNU	UNFANNED	ADEGIILN	GLIADINE	ADEGINRR	DREARING
ADEFNOPR	PROFANED	ADEGIILP	DIPLEGIA	ADEGINRS	DERAIGNS
ADEFNSST	DAFTNESS	ADEGIIMN	IMAGINED		GRADINES
ADEFOOSS	SEAFOODS	ADEGIIMS	DIGAMIES		READINGS
ADEFORRR	FORRADER	ADEGIINR	DEAIRING	ADEGINRT	DERATING
ADEFORRW	FARROWED	ADEGIINT	IDEATING		GRADIENT
	FOREWARD	ADEGIIRT	DIGERATI		REDATING
ADEFORRY	FOREYARD	ADEGIITT	DIGITATE		TREADING
	FORRAYED	ADEGIJSW	JIGSAWED	ADEGINRY	DERAYING

	READYING	ADEGNOPR	DOGNAPER		PILLHEAD
	YEARDING	ADEGNOPS	PONDAGES	ADEHILMO	HALIDOME
ADEGINSS	ASSIGNED	ADEGNOPU	POUNDAGE	ADEHILNO	LIONHEAD
ADEGINST	SEDATING	ADEGNORT	DRAGONET	ADEHILNR	HARDLINE
	STEADING	ADEGNOSS	SONDAGES	ADEHILNU	UNHAILED
ADEGINSW	WINDAGES	ADEGNOSV	DOGVANES	ADEHILPS	HELIPADS
ADEGINTV	VINTAGED	ADEGNPUY	PYENGADU	ADEHILSV	LAVISHED
ADEGINVW	ADVEWING	ADEGNRRU	GRANDEUR	ADEHILSW	WHAISLED
ADEGINWX	DEWAXING	ADEGNRST	DRAGNETS	ADEHILWZ	WHAIZLED
ADEGINYZ	ZYGAENID		GRANDEST	ADEHIMMS	SHAMMIED
ADEGIORT	ERGATOID	ADEGNRSU	ENGUARDS	ADEHIMOT	HEMATOID
ADEGIOST	GODETIAS	ADEGNRUU	UNARGUED	ADEHIMRS	MISHEARD
ADEGIPRR	PARRIDGE	ADEGNRUZ	GAZUNDER		SEMIHARD
ADEGIPRS	SPAIRGED		UNGRAZED	ADEHIMRY	HYDREMIA
ADEGIRWY	RIDGEWAY	ADEGOORV	OVERGOAD	ADEHINOP	DIAPHONE
ADEGISSU	DISUSAGE	ADEGOORY	GOODYEAR	ADEHINOS	ADHESION
ADEGISTU	GAUDIEST	ADEGOPPR	PROPAGED	ADEHINOY	HYOIDEAN
ADEGISUV	VIDUAGES	ADEGOPRR	DRAGROPE	ADEHINPS	DEANSHIP
ADEGIUWY	GUIDEWAY		PROGRADE		HEADPINS
ADEGJNOR	JARGONED	ADEGOPRT	PORTAGED		PINHEADS
ADEGKLOY	DEKALOGY	ADEGORRT	GARROTED	ADEHINPU	DAUPHINE
ADEGLLNU	GLANDULE	ADEGORST	GOADSTER	ADEHINRT	ANTHERID
	UNGALLED	ADEGORSW	DOWAGERS	ADEHINRU	UNHAIRED
ADEGLLOP	GALLOPED		WORDAGES	ADEHINSS	DANISHES
ADEGLLOR	GOLLARED	ADEGORTT	GAROTTED		SHANDIES
ADEGLLOW	GALLOWED	ADEGORTU	OUTRAGED	ADEHINST	HANDIEST
ADEGLLSU	GALLUSED		RAGOUTED	ADEHINSV	VANISHED
ADEGLMOR	GLAMORED	ADEGORTW	WATERDOG	ADEHIOTT	ATHETOID
ADEGLMOS	GLADSOME	ADEGOTTV	GAVOTTED	ADEHIPRS	RAPHIDES
ADEGLMPU	PLUMAGED	ADEGOTUZ	OUTGAZED	ADEHIPSS	PISSHEAD
ADEGLMRU	MAULGRED	ADEGPRRU	UPGRADER	ADEHIPST	PITHEADS
ADEGLMUY	AMYGDULE	ADEGPRSS	SPADGERS		SIDEPATH
ADEGLNOP	ANGLEPOD	ADEGPRSU	UPGRADES	ADEHIRRT	TRIHEDRA
ADEGLNOY	GONDELAY	ADEGPSTU	UPSTAGED	ADEHIRRW	HARDWIRE
ADEGLNPS	SPANGLED	ADEGRRST	DRAGSTER	ADEHIRSS	AIRSHEDS
ADEGLNRS	DANGLERS	ADEGRRSU	GUARDERS		RADISHES
	GLANDERS	ADEGRSSU	DESUGARS	ADEHIRST	HAIRSTED
ADEGLNRW	WRANGLED		GRADUSES		HARDIEST
ADEGLNSS	GLADNESS	ADEGTTTU	GUTTATED	ADEHIRSV	RAVISHED
ADEGLNTW	TWANGLED	ADEHHIPR	RHAPHIDE	ADEHIRSW	DISHWARE
ADEGLNUZ	UNGLAZED	ADEHHIPS	HEADSHIP		RAWHIDES
ADEGLOPP	GALOPPED	ADEHHIST	SHITHEAD	ADEHIRSY	HAYRIDES
ADEGLORV	OVERGLAD	ADEHHNTU	HEADHUNT	ADEHIRVW	HIVEWARD
ADEGLPPR	GRAPPLED	ADEHHOOR	HOORAHED	ADEHISST	DASHIEST
ADEGLSTY	DALGYTES	ADEHHOPS	HOPHEADS		SHADIEST
ADEGMMNO	GAMMONED	ADEHHOST	HEADSHOT	ADEHISSW	SIWASHED
ADEGMMRU	RUMMAGED		HOTHEADS	ADEHJLOT	JOLTHEAD
ADEGMNOR	DRAGOMEN	ADEHHRRU	HURRAHED	ADEHKLNU	LUNKHEAD
ADEGMNOS	GOADSMEN	ADEHHRST	THRASHED	ADEHKNRS	REDSHANK
ADEGMNOT	MONTAGED	ADEHHUZZ	HUZZAHED	ADEHKNSU	UNSHAKED
ADEGMNOY	ENDOGAMY	ADEHIITZ	THIAZIDE	ADEHKORS	HARDOKES
ADEGMNRS	DRAGSMEN	ADEHIJMS	JEHADISM	ADEHKORW	HEADWORK
ADEGMNSU	AGENDUMS	ADEHIJST	JEHADIST	ADEHKOST	KATHODES
ADEGMOPS	MEGAPODS	ADEHIKLN	HANDLIKE	ADEHLLMU	MULLAHED
ADEGMORS	ORGASMED	ADEHIKLV	KHEDIVAL	ADEHLLOO	HALLOOED
ADEGMORW	WORDGAME	ADEHIKNS	SKINHEAD		HOLLOAED
ADEGMPUZ	GAZUMPED	ADEHIKSS	DASHEKIS	ADEHLLOU	HULLOAED
ADEGNNOR	ANDROGEN	ADEHIKST	SKAITHED	ADEHLLOW	HALLOWED
	DRAGONNE	ADEHIKSV	KHEDIVAS	ADEHLLRT	THRALLED
ADEGNNPU	UNPANGED	ADEHILLO	HILLOAED	ADEHLLRW	HELLWARD
ADEGNNSU	DUNNAGES	ADEHILLP	PHIALLED	ADEHLLSY	DAYSHELL

ADEHLMNO	HOMELAND	**ADEHOPXY**	HEXAPODY	**ADEIKLNW**	DAWNLIKE
ADEHLMOY	HOLYDAME	**ADEHORRS**	HOARDERS		WANDLIKE
ADEHLNRS	HANDLERS	**ADEHORRV**	OVERHARD	**ADEIKLOT**	TOADLIKE
ADEHLNSS	HANDLESS	**ADEHORRW**	HARROWED	**ADEIKLOX**	ALKOXIDE
	HANDSELS	**ADEHORSW**	SHADOWER	**ADEIKLRR**	DARKLIER
ADEHLNST	SHETLAND	**ADEHORTT**	THROATED	**ADEIKLSW**	SIDEWALK
ADEHLNSU	UNHALSED	**ADEHORTU**	AUTHORED	**ADEIKMMS**	IMMASKED
	UNLASHED		OUTHEARD	**ADEIKMPR**	IMPARKED
	UNSHALED	**ADEHOSTW**	TOWHEADS	**ADEIKMRT**	TIDEMARK
ADEHLNUV	UNHALVED	**ADEHPSTU**	DUSTHEAP	**ADEIKNPR**	KIDNAPER
ADEHLOOR	HORDEOLA	**ADEHQSSU**	SQUASHED	**ADEIKNSY**	KYANISED
ADEHLOOT	TOOLHEAD	**ADEHRRUY**	HURRAYED	**ADEIKNYZ**	KYANIZED
ADEHLOPS	ASPHODEL	**ADEHRSSY**	HYDRASES	**ADEIKORT**	KERATOID
	PHOLADES	**ADEHRSTY**	HYDRATES	**ADEIKRST**	STRAIKED
ADEHLOPW	PLOWHEAD	**ADEHRTTW**	THWARTED	**ADEILLMY**	MEDIALLY
ADEHLPSS	SPLASHED	**ADEIILMN**	LIMNAEID	**ADEILLNN**	LANDLINE
ADEHLRRY	HERALDRY	**ADEIILMS**	IDEALISM	**ADEILLNU**	UNALLIED
ADEHMNNY	HANDYMEN		MILADIES	**ADEILLNV**	ANVILLED
ADEHMNOS	HANDSOME	**ADEIILPR**	PERIDIAL	**ADEILLNW**	INWALLED
ADEHMNOT	METHADON	**ADEIILRS**	LAIRISED	**ADEILLNY**	LEYLANDI
	THANEDOM	**ADEIILRZ**	LAIRIZED	**ADEILLOR**	ARILLODE
ADEHMNRS	HERDSMAN	**ADEIILST**	IDEALIST	**ADEILLPR**	PALLIDER
ADEHMNRU	UNHARMED	**ADEIILTV**	DILATIVE		PILLARED
ADEHMNSU	UNSHAMED	**ADEIILTY**	IDEALITY	**ADEILLPS**	ILLAPSED
ADEHMOOP	OOMPAHED	**ADEIIMMS**	MISAIMED		SPADILLE
ADEHMOOR	HEADROOM	**ADEIIMNN**	INDAMINE	**ADEILLRS**	DALLIERS
ADEHMOPS	MOPHEADS	**ADEIIMNR**	MERIDIAN		DIALLERS
ADEHMORS	HADROMES	**ADEIIMNS**	AMIDINES	**ADEILLRT**	TRIALLED
ADEHMORW	HOMEWARD		DIAMINES	**ADEILLRV**	RIVALLED
ADEHMOST	HEADMOST	**ADEIIMNT**	MINIATED	**ADEILLSW**	SIDEWALL
ADEHMOSU	MADHOUSE	**ADEIIMPR**	IMPAIRED	**ADEILMMM**	MELAMDIM
ADEHMOSY	SHAMOYED	**ADEIIMRS**	SEMIARID	**ADEILMMS**	DILEMMAS
ADEHNNSW	HANDSEWN	**ADEIIMTT**	IMITATED	**ADEILMNN**	LANDMINE
ADEHNOPR	ORPHANED	**ADEIINNS**	SANIDINE	**ADEILMNO**	MELANOID
ADEHNOPT	PHONATED	**ADEIINOT**	IDEATION	**ADEILMNP**	PLAIDMEN
ADEHNORS	HARDNOSE		IODINATE	**ADEILMNU**	UNMAILED
ADEHNORV	HANDOVER		TAENIOID	**ADEILMNY**	MAIDENLY
	OVERHAND	**ADEIINRS**	DRAISINE		MEDIANLY
ADEHNOSS	SANDSHOE	**ADEIINRT**	DAINTIER	**ADEILMOS**	DAMOISEL
ADEHNOSU	SEAHOUND	**ADEIINRU**	UREDINIA		MELODIAS
ADEHNPSU	UNHASPED	**ADEIINST**	ADENITIS	**ADEILMOX**	ALDOXIME
	UNSHAPED		DAINTIES	**ADEILMPP**	PALMIPED
ADEHNRSS	HARDNESS	**ADEIINSZ**	DIAZINES	**ADEILMPR**	IMPARLED
ADEHNRSU	UNSHARED	**ADEIINTV**	VANITIED	**ADEILMPS**	IMPLEADS
ADEHNRSW	SWANHERD	**ADEIINUV**	INDUVIAE		MISPLEAD
ADEHNRTU	UNTHREAD	**ADEIIPRR**	PERRADII	**ADEILMPT**	IMPLATED
ADEHNSST	HANDSETS		PRAIRIED	**ADEILMRS**	DISMALER
ADEHNSSU	SUNSHADE	**ADEIIPRS**	PRESIDIA	**ADEILMRY**	DREAMILY
	UNSASHED	**ADEIIPST**	STAPEDII	**ADEILMSS**	MAIDLESS
ADEHNSUV	UNSHAVED	**ADEIIRSS**	AIRSIDES		MISDEALS
			DIARISES		MISLEADS
ADEHNSUW	UNWASHED	**ADEIIRST**	IRISATED	**ADEILMST**	MEDALIST
ADEHNTTU	UNHATTED	**ADEIIRSZ**	DIARIZES		MISDEALT
ADEHNTUW	UNTHAWED	**ADEIITTV**	TIDIVATE	**ADEILMSY**	DYSMELIA
ADEHOOPS	APEHOODS		VITIATED	**ADEILNNO**	NONIDEAL
ADEHOORW	HAREWOOD	**ADEIITUV**	AUDITIVE	**ADEILNNP**	PINELAND
ADEHOORY	HOORAYED	**ADEIJMRS**	JEMIDARS	**ADEILNNR**	INLANDER
ADEHOPRS	RHAPSODE	**ADEIKLLO**	KELOIDAL	**ADEILNNS**	ANNELIDS
ADEHOPST	POTASHED	**ADEIKLLR**	LARDLIKE		LINDANES
	POTHEADS	**ADEIKLLY**	LADYLIKE	**ADEILNNT**	DENTINAL
ADEHOPSX	HEXAPODS	**ADEIKLNS**	SANDLIKE	**ADEILNNU**	UNNAILED

ADEILNOP	PALINODE
ADEILNOS	NODALISE
ADEILNOT	DELATION
ADEILNOZ	NODALIZE
ADEILNPS	SANDPILE
ADEILNPT	PANTILED
ADEILNPU	PALUDINE
ADEILNRS	ISLANDER
ADEILNSU	UNSAILED
ADEILNSV	ANDVILES
ADEILNTU	UNTAILED
ADEILNTV	DIVALENT
ADEILNUV	UNVAILED
ADEILOPS	EPISODAL
	OPALISED
	SEPALOID
ADEILOPT	PETALOID
ADEILOPZ	OPALIZED
ADEILOQU	ODALIQUE
ADEILORS	DARIOLES
	SOLIDARE
	SOREDIAL
ADEILORT	IDOLATER
	TAILORED
ADEILORV	OVERLAID
ADEILORX	EXORDIAL
ADEILOSS	ASSOILED
	DEASOILS
	ISOLEADS
ADEILOST	DIASTOLE
	ISOLATED
	SODALITE
	SOLIDATE
ADEILOSU	DOULEIAS
ADEILOSZ	DIAZOLES
	SLEAZOID
ADEILOTT	DATOLITE
ADEILOTV	DOVETAIL
	VIOLATED
ADEILPPP	PEDIPALP
ADEILPRS	LIPREADS
	PARSLIED
	PEDRAILS
	PREDIALS
	SPIRALED
ADEILPRT	DIPTERAL
	TRIPEDAL
ADEILPRU	EPIDURAL
ADEILPRV	DEPRIVAL
ADEILPSS	DESPISAL
ADEILPST	TALIPEDS
ADEILPTU	PLAUDITE
ADEILQSU	SQUAILED
ADEILQTU	LIQUATED
ADEILRRW	DRAWLIER
ADEILRRY	DREARILY
ADEILRST	DILATERS
	LARDIEST
	REDTAILS
ADEILRSU	RESIDUAL
ADEILRSY	DIALYSER
ADEILRTT	DETRITAL
ADEILRTY	DIELYTRA
ADEILRVY	VARIEDLY
ADEILRYZ	DIALYZER
ADEILSSU	DEASIULS
	DUALISES
ADEILSSV	DEVISALS
ADEILSSY	DIALYSES
ADEILSTV	VALIDEST
ADEILSTY	DIASTYLE
	STEADILY
ADEILSUV	DISVALUE
ADEILSUZ	DUALIZES
ADEILSWY	SLIDEWAY
ADEILSXY	DYSLEXIA
ADEILSYZ	DIALYZES
ADEILTTU	ALTITUDE
	LATITUDE
ADEILTVY	DATIVELY
ADEIMMNS	MISNAMED
ADEIMMNU	UNMAIMED
ADEIMMRS	MERMAIDS
ADEIMMST	MISMATED
ADEIMNNO	DEMONIAN
	MONDAINE
ADEIMNOP	DOPAMINE
ADEIMNOR	RADIOMEN
ADEIMNOS	AMIDONES
	DAIMONES
	DOMAINES
	NOMADIES
	NOMADISE
ADEIMNOT	DOMINATE
	NEMATOID
ADEIMNOU	EUDAIMON
ADEIMNOZ	NOMADIZE
ADEIMNPW	IMPAWNED
ADEIMNRR	MANRIDER
ADEIMNRS	ADERMINS
	SIRNAMED
ADEIMNRU	MURAENID
ADEIMNRY	DAIRYMEN
ADEIMNRZ	ZEMINDAR
ADEIMNSS	SIDESMAN
ADEIMNST	MEDIANTS
	TIDESMAN
ADEIMNSU	MAUNDIES
ADEIMNSY	DYNAMISE
ADEIMNTY	DYNAMITE
ADEIMNYZ	DYNAMIZE
ADEIMORR	AIRDROME
ADEIMORT	MEDIATOR
ADEIMOSS	SESAMOID
ADEIMOST	ATOMISED
ADEIMOTZ	ATOMIZED
ADEIMPRR	RAMPIRED
ADEIMPRT	IMPARTED
	PREADMIT
ADEIMPRV	VAMPIRED
ADEIMPST	DAMPIEST
	IMPASTED
ADEIMRRS	ADMIRERS
	DISARMER
	MARRIEDS
ADEIMRSS	MISREADS
	SIDEARMS
ADEIMRST	MARDIEST
	MISRATED
	READMITS
ADEIMRSY	MIDYEARS
ADEIMRTT	ADMITTER
ADEIMRTU	MURIATED
ADEIMSST	DIASTEMS
	MISDATES
ADEIMSTU	TAEDIUMS
ADEIMSTY	DAYTIMES
ADEINNNS	NANDINES
ADEINNOT	ANOINTED
	ANTINODE
ADEINNOV	DEVONIAN
ADEINNPT	PINNATED
ADEINNPU	UNPAINED
ADEINNRS	INSNARED
ADEINNRZ	RENDZINA
ADEINNSU	UNSAINED
ADEINNSX	DISANNEX
ADEINNTU	ANTIDUNE
	INUNDATE
ADEINOPP	PEPONIDA
ADEINOPT	ANTIPODE
ADEINORR	ORDAINER
	REORDAIN
ADEINORS	ANEROIDS
	DONARIES
ADEINORT	AROINTED
	DERATION
	ORDINATE
	RATIONED
ADEINORU	DOUANIER
ADEINOSS	ADENOSIS
	ADONISES
	ANODISES
ADEINOST	ASTONIED
	SEDATION
ADEINOSX	DIOXANES
ADEINOSZ	ADONIZES
	ANODIZES
ADEINOTT	ANTIDOTE
	TETANOID
ADEINOTV	DONATIVE
ADEINPPX	APPENDIX
ADEINPRS	SPRAINED
ADEINPRT	DIPTERAN
ADEINPRU	UNPAIRED
	UNREPAID
ADEINPST	DEPAINTS
ADEINPSV	SPAVINED
ADEINQTU	ANTIQUED
ADEINRRS	DRAINERS
	SERRANID
ADEINRSS	ARIDNESS
	SARDINES

ADEINRST	DETRAINS	ADEIPSSX	SPADIXES	ADEKNOSU	UNSOAKED
	RANDIEST	ADEIPSTV	VAPIDEST	ADEKNOTW	TAKEDOWN
	STRAINED	ADEIPTTU	APTITUDE	ADEKNRSS	DARKNESS
ADEINRSU	DENARIUS	ADEIQRRU	QUARRIED	ADEKNRST	DARKNETS
	UNRAISED	ADEIQRSU	QUERIDAS	ADEKNSVY	VANDYKES
	URANIDES	ADEIQSUY	QUAYSIDE	ADEKOOTW	TEAKWOOD
ADEINRSV	INVADERS	ADEIRRSW	SWARDIER	ADEKOSTU	OUTASKED
	SANDIVER	ADEIRRTW	TAWDRIER	ADEKQSUW	SQUAWKED
ADEINRSY	SYNEDRIA	ADEIRRWW	WIREDRAW	ADELLMOR	MORALLED
ADEINRTT	NITRATED	ADEIRRZZ	RIZZARED	ADELLMOS	SLALOMED
ADEINRTU	DATURINE	ADEIRSST	ASTERIDS	ADELLMRU	MEDULLAR
	INDURATE		DIASTERS		MURALLED
	RUINATED		DISASTER	ADELLMSU	MEDULLAS
	URINATED		DISRATES	ADELLNNU	ANNULLED
ADEINRUV	UNVARIED	ADEIRSSU	RADIUSES	ADELLNPS	SPENDALL
ADEINRVY	VINEYARD		SUDARIES	ADELLNRS	LANDLERS
ADEINSST	DESTAINS	ADEIRSSV	ADVISERS	ADELLNSS	LANDLESS
	SANDIEST	ADEIRSTT	STRAITED	ADELLNSW	ELLWANDS
ADEINSSV	AVIDNESS		STRIATED		WALLSEND
	VANESSID		TARDIEST	ADELLNTY	DENTALLY
ADEINSSW	WINDASES	ADEIRSTW	TAWDRIES	ADELLNUW	UNWALLED
ADEINSTT	INSTATED	ADEIRTTT	ATTRITED	ADELLOPW	WALLOPED
ADEINSTU	AUDIENTS		TITRATED	ADELLOPX	POLLAXED
	SINUATED	ADEIRTUV	DURATIVE	ADELLORS	ODALLERS
ADEINSTV	DEVIANTS	ADEIRVWY	DRIVEWAY	ADELLOSW	SALLOWED
ADEINSTY	DESYATIN	ADEISSST	ASSISTED	ADELLOTT	ALLOTTED
ADEIOPRR	PRERADIO		DISSEATS		TOTALLED
ADEIOPRS	DIASPORE	ADEISSSV	DISSAVES	ADELLOTV	LAVOLTED
	PARODIES	ADEISSTT	DISTASTE	ADELLOTW	TALLOWED
ADEIOPRV	OVERPAID		STAIDEST	ADELLOVY	LADYLOVE
ADEIOPSS	ADIPOSES	ADEISSTV	DISTAVES	ADELLOWW	WALLOWED
ADEIOPST	DIOPTASE	ADEISSWY	SIDEWAYS	ADELLQSU	SQUALLED
ADEIOPTV	ADOPTIVE		WAYSIDES	ADELLRSU	UDALLERS
ADEIORRT	ADROITER	ADEISTTU	SITUATED	ADELLTUU	ULULATED
ADEIORST	ASTEROID	ADEISTUZ	DEUTZIAS	ADELMNNS	LANDSMEN
ADEIORSV	AVODIRES	ADEISTWY	TIDEWAYS	ADELMNOS	LODESMAN
	AVOIDERS	ADEITTTU	ATTITUDE	ADELMNRS	MANDRELS
ADEIORTT	TERATOID		ATTUITED	ADELMOOW	WOODMEAL
ADEIORTV	DEVIATOR	ADEJLOSU	JALOUSED	ADELMOPS	MALPOSED
ADEIOSSX	OXIDASES	ADEJMMNU	UNJAMMED	ADELMORS	EARLDOMS
ADEIOSTX	OXIDATES	ADEJMRRU	JUMARRED	ADELMOSS	DAMOSELS
ADEIOSTZ	AZOTISED	ADEJNRUW	UNDERJAW	ADELMOSZ	DAMOZELS
ADEIOSVV	VAIVODES	ADEJOPRS	JEOPARDS	ADELMOTU	MODULATE
ADEIOSVW	WAIVODES	ADEJOPRY	JEOPARDY	ADELMPRT	TRAMPLED
ADEIOSWW	WAIWODES	ADEJRRSU	ADJURERS	ADELMRRU	DEMURRAL
ADEIOTZZ	AZOTIZED	ADEJRSTU	ADJUSTER	ADELMSSY	MASSEDLY
ADEIPPRS	APPRISED		READJUST	ADELMSUY	AMUSEDLY
	DRAPPIES	ADEKLMRY	MARKEDLY	ADELMTTY	MATTEDLY
ADEIPPRZ	APPRIZED	ADEKLNOX	KLAXONED	ADELMTUU	UMLAUTED
ADEIPRRS	DRAPIERS	ADEKLNPP	KNAPPLED	ADELNNNU	UNNANELD
ADEIPRSS	DESPAIRS	ADEKLNPR	PRANKLED	ADELNNOT	LENTANDO
ADEIPRST	DIPTERAS	ADEKLNSU	UNSLAKED	ADELNOPR	PONDERAL
	DRAPIEST	ADEKLORW	LEADWORK	ADELNORS	LADRONES
	RAPIDEST	ADEKLPRS	SPARKLED		SOLANDER
	SPIRATED	ADEKLPTU	UPTALKED	ADELNORU	UNLOADER
	TARSIPED	ADEKMNRU	UNMARKED		URODELAN
	TRAIPSED	ADEKMNSU	UNMASKED	ADELNORV	OVERLAND
ADEIPRSU	UPRAISED	ADEKMORS	DARKSOME		RONDAVEL
ADEIPRSW	RIPSAWED	ADEKMTUU	MAKUTUED	ADELNOSY	YEALDONS
ADEIPRTU	EUPATRID	ADEKNNRU	UNRANKED	ADELNPRS	SPANDREL
	PREAUDIT	ADEKNNSS	DANKNESS	ADELNPRU	PENDULAR

	UNDERLAP	**ADELRRSW**	DRAWLERS	**ADENNOTY**	TANNOYED
	UPLANDER	**ADELRRTU**	ULTRARED	**ADENNPST**	PENDANTS
ADELNPRY	PANDERLY	**ADELRSSW**	WARDLESS	**ADENNRRU**	UNDERRAN
	REPANDLY		WRASSLED	**ADENNRTY**	TYRANNED
ADELNPSY	DYSPNEAL	**ADELRSTT**	STARTLED	**ADENNRUW**	UNWARNED
	ENDPLAYS	**ADELRSTW**	WARSTLED	**ADENNSTU**	ASTUNNED
ADELNPUY	UNPLAYED		WRASTLED	**ADENNTUW**	UNWANTED
ADELNRSS	SLANDERS	**ADELRSZZ**	DAZZLERS	**ADENOOPS**	EPANODOS
ADELNRSU	LAUNDERS	**ADELRTUY**	ADULTERY	**ADENOORT**	RATOONED
	LURDANES	**ADELSTTY**	STATEDLY	**ADENOORW**	WANDEROO
	RUNDALES	**ADELTTTW**	TWATTLED	**ADENOOST**	ODONATES
ADELNRTU	DENTURAL	**ADEMMNOW**	MADWOMEN	**ADENOOTZ**	OZONATED
ADELNRTY	ARDENTLY	**ADEMMSTU**	SUMMATED	**ADENOPRR**	PARDONER
ADELNRUY	UNDERLAY	**ADEMNNNU**	UNMANNED	**ADENOPRS**	OPERANDS
ADELNSSS	SANDLESS	**ADEMNNOR**	NORMANDE		PADRONES
ADELNSTU	UNSALTED	**ADEMNNOU**	UNMOANED		PANDORES
ADELNSTW	WETLANDS	**ADEMNNRU**	MUNDANER	**ADENOPRT**	PRONATED
ADELNTUU	UNDULATE		UNDERMAN	**ADENOPRX**	EXPANDOR
ADELNUUV	UNVALUED	**ADEMNOOR**	MAROONED	**ADENOPSS**	DAPSONES
ADELNUZZ	UNDAZZLE	**ADEMNOPR**	POMANDER		SPADONES
ADELOOPV	LEVODOPA	**ADEMNOPT**	TAMPONED	**ADENOPST**	NOTEPADS
ADELOORV	OVERLOAD	**ADEMNORS**	MADRONES		TONEPADS
ADELOOTW	LATEWOOD		RANSOMED	**ADENOPSU**	UNSOAPED
ADELOOWW	WOODWALE		ROADSMEN	**ADENOPSY**	DYSPNOEA
ADELOPPR	PROPALED	**ADEMNOTU**	AMOUNTED	**ADENORRS**	ADORNERS
ADELOPRS	LEOPARDS		OUTNAMED		READORNS
	PRELOADS	**ADEMNPPU**	UNMAPPED	**ADENORRW**	NARROWED
ADELOPRT	PORTALED	**ADEMNPSS**	DAMPNESS	**ADENORST**	TORNADES
	PROLATED	**ADEMNRRU**	UNDERARM	**ADENORTT**	ATTORNED
ADELOPRU	POULARDE		UNMARRED	**ADENORTW**	DANEWORT
ADELOPRW	POLEWARD	**ADEMNRSU**	DURAMENS		TEARDOWN
ADELOPSS	DEPOSALS		MAUNDERS	**ADENORTY**	AROYNTED
ADELOPST	TADPOLES		SURNAMED	**ADENORUX**	RONDEAUX
ADELOPSU	PALUDOSE	**ADEMNRTU**	UNDREAMT	**ADENOSST**	ONSTEADS
ADELOPSY	SEPALODY	**ADEMNRUW**	UNWARMED	**ADENOTUY**	AUTODYNE
ADELOPTY	PETALODY	**ADEMNSSU**	MEDUSANS	**ADENOUVW**	UNAVOWED
ADELORRV	OVERLARD	**ADEMNSUU**	UNAMUSED	**ADENPPRS**	PARPENDS
ADELORSS	ROADLESS	**ADEMNTTU**	UNMATTED	**ADENPPSU**	UNSAPPED
ADELORST	DELATORS	**ADEMOORT**	MODERATO	**ADENPPTU**	UNTAPPED
	LEOTARDS	**ADEMOORV**	VAROOMED	**ADENPRRS**	PARDNERS
	LODESTAR	**ADEMOOST**	STOMODEA	**ADENPRSU**	UNDRAPES
ADELORSU	ROULADES	**ADEMOOSV**	VAMOOSED		UNSPARED
ADELORTW	LEADWORT	**ADEMOPRY**	PYODERMA	**ADENPRSW**	PREDAWNS
ADELOSSS	SODALESS	**ADEMOPST**	STAMPEDO	**ADENPRTU**	DEPURANT
ADELOSST	TOADLESS	**ADEMOPSU**	MOUSEPAD		UNPARTED
ADELOSSW	DOWLASES	**ADEMORRT**	MORTARED	**ADENPRTY**	PEDANTRY
ADELOSTU	OUTLEADS	**ADEMORRU**	ARMOURED	**ADENPRUW**	UNWARPED
ADELOSTV	SOLVATED	**ADEMORRW**	MARROWED	**ADENPRUY**	UNDERPAY
ADELOTUV	OVULATED	**ADEMORST**	STROAMED		UNPRAYED
ADELOTUW	OUTLAWED	**ADEMORTU**	OUTDREAM	**ADENPSSY**	DYSPNEAS
ADELOVWY	AVOWEDLY	**ADEMORTW**	DAMEWORT		SYNAPSED
ADELPPRY	DAPPERLY		WARDMOTE	**ADENQRSU**	SQUANDER
ADELPQUX	QUADPLEX	**ADEMOSSY**	SAMOYEDS	**ADENRRST**	STRANDER
ADELPRRU	LARRUPED	**ADEMPRST**	STRAMPED	**ADENRRSY**	REYNARDS
ADELPRSW	SPRAWLED	**ADEMRRSU**	EARDRUMS	**ADENRRTU**	UNTARRED
ADELPRTT	PRATTLED	**ADEMRRTY**	MARTYRED	**ADENRRWY**	WARDENRY
ADELPRTU	PREADULT	**ADENNNTU**	UNTANNED	**ADENRSSS**	SARSDENS
ADELPSTT	SPLATTED	**ADENNORT**	NONRATED	**ADENRSST**	STANDERS
ADELPSTU	PULSATED	**ADENNOSY**	ANODYNES	**ADENRSSU**	DANSEURS
ADELPUUV	UPVALUED	**ADENNOTU**	UNATONED	**ADENRSTU**	DAUNTERS
ADELRRSU	RUDERALS	**ADENNOTW**	WANTONED		TRANSUDE

	UNTREADS	**ADEPSTUY**	UPSTAYED	**ADFLORSU**	FOULARDS
ADENRSTX	DEXTRANS	**ADEPSUWY**	UPSWAYED	**ADFMRSTU**	STUDFARM
ADENRSUY	UNDERSAY	**ADEQSTTU**	SQUATTED	**ADFNNOST**	FONDANTS
ADENRTTU	TRUANTED	**ADERRSSW**	WARDRESS	**ADFNOORZ**	FORZANDO
ADENRTTY	TYRANTED	**ADERRSTT**	REDSTART	**ADFOOPST**	FOOTPADS
ADENRTUX	UNDERTAX	**ADERSSSU**	ASSUREDS	**ADFOOSTW**	FATWOODS
ADENRUWY	UNDERWAY	**ADERSSTW**	STEWARDS	**ADFOOSWY**	FOODWAYS
ADENSSSW	WESSANDS	**ADERSSUY**	DASYURES	**ADFORRSW**	FORWARDS
ADENSTTU	UNSTATED	**ADERSTTU**	STATURED		FROWARDS
	UNTASTED	**ADERSTUX**	SURTAXED	**ADFPRSTU**	UPDRAFTS
ADENSTUW	UNWASTED	**ADERSTVY**	STRAYVED	**ADGGGILN**	DAGGLING
ADENSTUY	UNSTAYED	**ADERSTWW**	WESTWARD	**ADGGGINR**	DRAGGING
	UNSTEADY	**ADESSTTW**	WADSETTS	**ADGGGINS**	DAGGINGS
ADENSUWY	UNSWAYED	**ADFFGIIR**	GIRAFFID	**ADGGHNOS**	HANGDOGS
ADEOOPRW	PEARWOOD	**ADFFGINS**	DAFFINGS	**ADGGHORY**	HYDRAGOG
ADEOOPSS	APODOSES	**ADFFHIRS**	DRAFFISH	**ADGGILNN**	DANGLING
ADEOORRT	TOREADOR	**ADFFHNOS**	HANDOFFS	**ADGGILNS**	GADLINGS
ADEOOTTT	TATTOOED	**ADFFISST**	DISTAFFS	**ADGGILRS**	RIGGALDS
ADEOPPRT	PREADOPT	**ADFFLNOS**	FANFOLDS	**ADGGINRS**	GRADINGS
ADEOPPRV	APPROVED	**ADFFLOOS**	OFFLOADS		NIGGARDS
ADEOPRRS	EARDROPS	**ADFFLRUU**	FRAUDFUL	**ADGGINRU**	GUARDING
ADEOPRRT	PARROTED	**ADFFNOST**	STANDOFF	**ADGGLRSU**	SLUGGARD
	PREDATOR	**ADFFOORS**	AFFOORDS	**ADGHHILN**	HIGHLAND
	PRORATED	**ADFGINNU**	UNFADING	**ADGHHIOR**	HIGHROAD
	PROTRADE	**ADFGINRS**	FARDINGS	**ADGHILLL**	GILDHALL
	TEARDROP	**ADFGINRT**	DRAFTING	**ADGHILNN**	HANDLING
ADEOPRRU	UPROARED	**ADFGINRW**	DWARFING	**ADGHILOS**	HIDALGOS
ADEOPRST	ADOPTERS	**ADFHILSY**	LADYFISH	**ADGHILPY**	DIAGLYPH
	ASPORTED	**ADFHINSS**	SANDFISH	**ADGHILTY**	DAYLIGHT
	PASTORED	**ADFHIOST**	TOADFISH	**ADGHINOR**	HOARDING
	READOPTS	**ADFHIRSW**	DWARFISH	**ADGHINPR**	HANDGRIP
ADEOPRSU	UPSOARED	**ADFHLNSU**	HANDFULS	**ADGHINSS**	SHADINGS
ADEOPRTT	TETRAPOD		HANDSFUL	**ADGHIPRS**	DIGRAPHS
ADEOPRUV	VAPOURED	**ADFHLNSY**	FLYHANDS	**ADGHIRRS**	ARDRIGHS
ADEOPSST	PODESTAS	**ADFHLOST**	HOLDFAST	**ADGHIRSS**	DISHRAGS
ADEOPSTT	DESPOTAT	**ADFHOOSS**	SHADOOFS	**ADGHITTW**	TIGHTWAD
	POSTDATE	**ADFIIILR**	FILARIID	**ADGHLNNO**	LONGHAND
ADEORRSS	DROSERAS	**ADFIILPY**	LAPIDIFY	**ADGHNNSU**	HANDGUNS
ADEORRST	ROADSTER	**ADFILLLN**	LANDFILL	**ADGHNOSS**	SANDHOGS
ADEORRTW	TARROWED	**ADFILLMN**	FILMLAND	**ADGHNOSW**	HAGDOWNS
ADEORRVW	OVERDRAW	**ADFILLNO**	NAILFOLD	**ADGHOOPR**	ODOGRAPH
ADEORSST	ASSORTED	**ADFILLNW**	WINDFALL	**ADGHORSW**	HOGWARDS
	TORSADES	**ADFILMNO**	MANIFOLD	**ADGHPSYY**	DYSPHAGY
ADEORSTU	OUTDARES	**ADFILMRU**	FLUIDRAM	**ADGHRSTU**	DRAUGHTS
	OUTREADS	**ADFILNWW**	WINDFLAW	**ADGHRTUY**	DRAUGHTY
	READOUTS	**ADFILRTY**	DRAFTILY	**ADGIIIRT**	TIGRIDIA
ADEORSTX	EXTRADOS	**ADFIMNRS**	FINDRAMS	**ADGIILLN**	DIALLING
ADEORSUV	SAVOURED	**ADFIMORY**	FAIRYDOM	**ADGIILLO**	GLADIOLI
ADEORSWY	RODEWAYS	**ADFIMRSW**	DWARFISM	**ADGIILNO**	GONIDIAL
ADEORTTU	OUTRATED	**ADFINORZ**	FORZANDI	**ADGIILNP**	PLAIDING
	OUTTRADE	**ADFINRST**	INDRAFTS	**ADGIILNR**	DRAILING
ADEORTUV	OUTRAVED	**ADFIORSV**	DISFAVOR	**ADGIILNS**	DIALINGS
ADEOSSTT	ASSOTTED	**ADFKLLNO**	FOLKLAND		GLIADINS
ADEOSTTU	OUTDATES	**ADFLLNOW**	DOWNFALL	**ADGIILNT**	DILATING
ADEOSWWY	WAYWODES	**ADFLMNOR**	LANDFORM	**ADGIILPY**	PYGIDIAL
ADEOTTTW	TATTOWED	**ADFLMNOY**	MANYFOLD	**ADGIILST**	DIGITALS
ADEPPRST	STRAPPED	**ADFLMOPR**	FRAMPOLD	**ADGIILTY**	ALGIDITY
ADEPRRTU	RAPTURED	**ADFLMPSU**	MUDFLAPS	**ADGIIMNR**	ADMIRING
ADEPRSTU	PASTURED	**ADFLMSTU**	MUDFLATS	**ADGIIMNX**	ADMIXING
	UPDATERS	**ADFLNOPS**	PLAFONDS	**ADGIIMOR**	IDIOGRAM
	UPSTARED	**ADFLOOWY**	FLOODWAY	**ADGIIMST**	DIGAMIST

ADGIINNR	DRAINING	ADGINNST	STANDING	ADHIIJST	IJTIHADS
ADGIINNS	SDAINING	ADGINNSW	DAWNINGS		JIHADIST
ADGIINNT	NIDATING	ADGINNSY	SDAYNING	ADHIIKSS	DASHIKIS
ADGIINNU	GUANIDIN	ADGINNTU	DAUNTING	ADHIIMPS	AMIDSHIP
ADGIINNV	INVADING	ADGINOOP	POIGNADO	ADHIINOP	OPHIDIAN
ADGIINNY	DIGYNIAN	ADGINOOR	RIGADOON	ADHIINRW	WHINIARD
ADGIINOR	RADIOING	ADGINOPT	ADOPTING	ADHIJLSY	JADISHLY
ADGIINOT	IODATING	ADGINORS	ROADINGS	ADHIKNNT	HANDKNIT
ADGIINOV	AVOIDING	ADGINORU	RIGAUDON	ADHIKOPS	HAPKIDOS
ADGIINRR	ARRIDING	ADGINOST	DOATINGS	ADHILLMN	MILLHAND
ADGIINRS	RAIDINGS	ADGINOTY	TOADYING	ADHILLMO	HOLLIDAM
ADGIINRY	DAIRYING	ADGINPPR	DRAPPING	ADHILLNS	SANDHILL
ADGIINSS	SIGANIDS	ADGINPTU	UPDATING	ADHILLOP	PHALLOID
ADGIINSU	IGUANIDS	ADGINRRS	GRANDSIR	ADHILLOT	THALLOID
ADGIINSV	ADVISING	ADGINRST	TRADINGS	ADHILLRY	HYDRILLA
ADGIINSW	GWINIADS	ADGINRSW	DRAWINGS	ADHILMOO	HOMALOID
ADGIINTU	AUDITING		SWARDING	ADHILMOS	HALIDOMS
ADGIJNRU	ADJURING		WARDINGS	ADHILNOR	RHODINAL
ADGIKLNR	DARKLING	ADGINRSY	YARDINGS	ADHILNST	HANDLIST
ADGILLNU	ALLUDING	ADGINRTT	DRATTING	ADHILOPS	HAPLOIDS
	DUALLING	ADGINRTU	ANTIDRUG		SHIPLOAD
ADGILLNW	WINDGALL	ADGINRTY	TARDYING	ADHILOPY	HAPLOIDY
ADGILLNY	DALLYING	ADGINSTU	ADUSTING	ADHILOST	SHITLOAD
ADGILLOT	GOLDTAIL		SUDATING	ADHILOSY	HOLIDAYS
ADGILMNS	GILDSMAN	ADGINSWY	GWYNIADS		HYALOIDS
	MADLINGS	ADGIORST	GORDITAS	ADHILPSY	LADYSHIP
ADGILMNW	DWALMING	ADGIPRSU	PAGURIDS	ADHIMNOR	RHODAMIN
ADGILMOR	MARIGOLD	ADGIRSSU	GUISARDS	ADHIMNOS	ADMONISH
ADGILNNS	LANDINGS	ADGIRSZZ	GIZZARDS	ADHIMNOU	HUMANOID
	SANDLING	ADGKOOSZ	GADZOOKS	ADHIMNSS	HANDISMS
ADGILNNU	UNLADING	ADGLLNOS	GOLLANDS	ADHIMOPP	AMPHIPOD
ADGILNOS	LOADINGS	ADGLMNOS	MANGOLDS	ADHIMPSS	PHASMIDS
ADGILNPP	DAPPLING	ADGLMNSU	GUMLANDS	ADHIMRTY	MYRIADTH
ADGILNRS	DARLINGS	ADGLNOOS	DONGOLAS	ADHINOPY	DIAPHONY
ADGILNRT	DARTLING		GONDOLAS	ADHINPSS	DISHPANS
ADGILNRW	DRAWLING	ADGLNORS	GOLDARNS	ADHINPSU	DAUPHINS
ADGILNRY	DARINGLY	ADGLNOSW	GOWLANDS	ADHINRTW	HANDWRIT
ADGILNZZ	DAZZLING	ADGLOORY	GARDYLOO	ADHINRWY	WHINYARD
ADGILOOS	SOLIDAGO	ADGLOSWY	DAYGLOWS	ADHINSST	STANDISH
ADGILOPR	PRODIGAL	ADGMNOOR	ONDOGRAM	ADHINSSY	SANDYISH
ADGILORS	GOLIARDS	ADGMNORS	GORMANDS	ADHINSTU	DIANTHUS
ADGILORY	GOLIARDY	ADGMNORU	GOURMAND	ADHIOSTY	TOADYISH
	GYROIDAL	ADGNNOQU	QUANDONG	ADHIPRSW	WARDSHIP
ADGILRSY	DAYGIRLS	ADGNNORS	GRANDSON	ADHIPRSY	SHIPYARD
ADGILRVY	GRAVIDLY	ADGNNRYY	GYNANDRY	ADHIPSTY	DISPATHY
ADGIMMNR	DRAMMING	ADGNOORS	DRAGOONS	ADHIRTWW	WITHDRAW
ADGIMMNW	DWAMMING		GADROONS	ADHITWWY	WIDTHWAY
ADGIMNNU	MAUNDING	ADGNRRSU	GURNARDS	ADHKNORW	HANDWORK
ADGIMNOP	POMADING	ADGNRSUU	UNGUARDS	ADHKORSW	DORHAWKS
ADGIMNPS	DAMPINGS	ADGOOPRS	GOSPODAR	ADHKOSSU	SHAKUDOS
ADGIMNRS	MRIDANGS	ADGOPRST	POSTGRAD	ADHLLLOS	HOLDALLS
ADGIMNRY	MARDYING	ADGOPRSU	PODARGUS	ADHLLNOR	HANDROLL
ADGIMNUW	DWAUMING	ADGORSTU	OUTDRAGS	ADHLLNOS	HOLLANDS
ADGIMOSU	DIGAMOUS	ADGORTUU	OUTGUARD	ADHLLNUV	VALLHUND
ADGINNOR	ADORNING	ADGRSSTU	DUSTRAGS	ADHLMNOO	HANDLOOM
ADGINNOT	DONATING	ADHHIPRS	HARDSHIP	ADHLMORT	THRALDOM
ADGINNPY	PANDYING	ADHHLOOV	HAVDOLOH	ADHLMOSY	HOLYDAMS
ADGINNRS	DARNINGS	ADHHMOSS	SHAHDOMS	ADHLMPSY	LYMPHADS
ADGINNRT	DRANTING	ADHHNRTY	HYDRANTH	ADHLNORW	WALDHORN
ADGINNRU	UNDARING	ADHIIIKS	DAISHIKI	ADHLNOTU	DUATHLON
ADGINNSS	SANDINGS	ADHIIJMS	JIHADISM	ADHLNOUW	DOWNHAUL

ADHLOSYY	HOLYDAYS	ADIIMRST	TRIADISM	ADILMOOR	MODIOLAR
ADHMNOOS	MANHOODS	ADIIMRSU	MUDIRIAS	ADILMOPS	DIPLOMAS
ADHMOPRS	DRAMSHOP	ADIINNOT	NIDATION		PLASMOID
ADHMORSY	HYDROMAS	ADIINNOZ	DIAZINON	ADILMOPT	DIPLOMAT
ADHNNOOR	HONORAND	ADIINOOT	IODATION	ADILMOPY	OLYMPIAD
ADHNNORY	NONHARDY	ADIINOTU	AUDITION	ADILMORU	ORDALIUM
ADHNOOTU	AUNTHOOD	ADIINPRS	PINDARIS	ADILMOST	MODALIST
ADHNORSU	UNHOARDS	ADIINRST	DISTRAIN	ADILMOSU	ALODIUMS
ADHNOSTU	HANDOUTS	ADIINSST	DISTAINS	ADILMOSY	AMYLOIDS
	THOUSAND	ADIINSSU	SUIDIANS	ADILMOTY	MODALITY
ADHNOSUW	UNSHADOW	ADIIOPRS	SPORIDIA	ADILMPRY	LAMPYRID
ADHNOSWW	DOWNWASH	ADIIOPRT	TAPIROID	ADILMPSS	PLASMIDS
ADHNRSTY	HYDRANTS	ADIIOPSS	ADIPOSIS	ADILMPSU	PALUDISM
ADHOOPRS	HOSPODAR	ADIIORST	TARSIOID	ADILMSSU	DUALISMS
ADHOOPST	HOPTOADS	ADIIPRTU	TRIPUDIA	ADILMSSY	DISMAYLS
ADHOORRS	RHODORAS	ADIIPRTY	RAPIDITY		LADYISMS
ADHOORSW	ROADSHOW	ADIIPSTY	SAPIDITY	ADILMTUY	MULTIDAY
ADHOORYZ	HYDROZOA	ADIIPTVY	VAPIDITY	ADILNNNU	NUNDINAL
ADHOPRST	HARDTOPS	ADIIQRSU	DAQUIRIS	ADILNNOT	NONTIDAL
	POTSHARD	ADIIRSST	DIARISTS	ADILNNOV	NONVALID
ADHOPRSU	UPHOARDS	ADIIRSTT	DARTITIS	ADILNNSU	DISANNUL
ADHOPRSY	RHAPSODY		DISTRAIT	ADILNOOR	DOORNAIL
ADHOPSST	DASHPOTS		TRIADIST	ADILNOOV	VINDALOO
ADHORRSU	DHOURRAS	ADIJNOST	ADJOINTS	ADILNOPY	PALINODY
ADHORRTY	HYDRATOR	ADIKKRRW	KIRKWARD	ADILNORS	ORDINALS
ADHORSTU	TOADRUSH	ADIKKRRY	KIRKYARD	ADILNORT	TRINODAL
ADHORSWY	SHOWYARD	ADIKLLOR	ROADKILL	ADILNOTY	NODALITY
ADHPSTYY	DYSPATHY	ADIKLNSP	LANDSKIP	ADILNPRS	SPANDRIL
ADIIINRV	VIRIDIAN	ADIKLNSY	LADYKINS	ADILNPST	DISPLANT
ADIIIQRU	DAIQUIRI	ADIKLORS	KILORADS	ADILNRSU	DIURNALS
ADIIKLLN	KALLIDIN	ADIKLOSS	ODALISKS	ADILNRWY	INWARDLY
ADIIKLMM	MILKMAID	ADIKMNNS	MANKINDS	ADILNSSU	SUNDIALS
ADIIKLST	TAILSKID	ADIKMOSU	DAIMOKUS	ADILNSSW	WINDLASS
ADIIKNOP	PINAKOID	ADIKMSSS	DISMASKS	ADILOOPZ	DIPLOZOA
ADIIKNST	ANTISKID	ADIKNNNU	DUNNAKIN	ADILOORT	IDOLATOR
ADIIKOST	DAKOITIS	ADIKNNST	INKSTAND		TOROIDAL
ADIILLMR	MILLIARD	ADIKNOPY	PYINKADO	ADILOOSV	OVOIDALS
ADIILLNY	IDYLLIAN	ADIKNPSS	SKIDPANS	ADILOPRT	DIOPTRAL
ADIILLOP	LIPOIDAL	ADIKNRSS	DISRANKS		TRIPODAL
ADIILLOR	ARILLOID	ADIKNRST	STINKARD	ADILOPSS	DISPOSAL
ADIILLST	DIALLIST	ADIKPRSS	DISPARKS	ADILOQSU	SQUALOID
ADIILLUV	DILUVIAL	ADIKQRSU	DIQUARKS	ADILORST	DILATORS
ADIILMSS	MISDIALS	ADIKSSWY	SKIDWAYS	ADILORSY	SOLIDARY
ADIILNOT	DILATION	ADILLLPY	PALLIDLY	ADILORTY	ADROITLY
ADIILNSU	INDUSIAL	ADILLMMS	MILLDAMS		DILATORY
ADIILNSV	INVALIDS	ADILLMNR	MANDRILL		IDOLATRY
ADIILNSW	WINDSAIL	ADILLMOU	ALLODIUM	ADILOSST	SODALIST
ADIILNTW	TAILWIND	ADILLMOV	VILLADOM	ADILOSTY	SODALITY
ADIILNTY	DAINTILY	ADILLMSY	DISMALLY	ADILPPSY	DISAPPLY
ADIILNUV	DILUVIAN	ADILLNPS	LANDSLIP	ADILPRSY	PYRALIDS
	INDUVIAL	ADILLOOP	POLOIDAL	ADILPSST	PLASTIDS
ADIILOPP	DIPLOPIA	ADILLOPS	SPADILLO	ADILPSSY	DISPLAYS
ADIILPST	LAPIDIST	ADILLOSW	DISALLOW	ADILPSTU	PLAUDITS
ADIILRST	DISTRAIL	ADILLOSY	DISLOYAL	ADILRTTY	TILTYARD
ADIILRSW	WIRILDAS	ADILLRWY	WILLYARD	ADILRTWY	TAWDRILY
ADIILSST	DIALISTS	ADILLSTY	DISTALLY	ADILRWYZ	WIZARDLY
ADIILSSY	DIALYSIS	ADILMMOS	MODALISM	ADILSSTU	DUALISTS
ADIILTVY	VALIDITY	ADILMNNO	MANDOLIN	ADIMMNOO	AMMONOID
ADIIMMSS	MAIDISMS	ADILMNOS	SALMONID	ADIMMNOS	MONADISM
ADIIMNNS	INDAMINS	ADILMNRS	MANDRILS		NOMADISM
ADIIMPSU	ASPIDIUM		RIMLANDS	ADIMMNSY	DYNAMISM

ADIMMOST	AMIDMOST	ADINRUVZ	UNVIZARD	ADLMOPRW	MOLDWARP
ADIMMOTU	DOMATIUM	ADINSWWY	WINDWAYS	ADLMOPSY	PSALMODY
ADIMNNOS	MONDAINS	ADIOOPRT	PAROTOID	ADLMORSU	MODULARS
ADIMNNOT	DOMINANT	ADIOOPSS	APODOSIS	ADLNNORS	NORLANDS
ADIMNOOR	MAINDOOR	ADIOOSSW	WOODSIAS	ADLNNOSW	SNOWLAND
ADIMNOSS	MADISONS	ADIOPPST	POSTPAID	ADLNNOTU	NONADULT
ADIMNOST	DONATISM	ADIOPRRS	AIRDROPS	ADLNNOTW	TOWNLAND
	SAINTDOM	ADIOPRSS	SPAROIDS	ADLNNSSU	SUNLANDS
ADIMNOWW	WIDOWMAN	ADIOPRST	PARODIST	ADLNNTUU	UNDULANT
ADIMNRSW	MISDRAWN		PAROTIDS	ADLNOORS	LARDOONS
ADIMNRSY	MISANDRY	ADIOPRSV	PRIVADOS	ADLNOORW	LOANWORD
ADIMNSSY	SYSADMIN	ADIOPRTY	PODIATRY	ADLNOPRT	PORTLAND
ADIMNSTY	DYNAMIST	ADIOPSTY	DYSTOPIA	ADLNOPRU	PAULDRON
ADIMOPRY	MYRIAPOD	ADIORRTT	TRADITOR	ADLNOPSU	POUNDALS
ADIMOPSY	SYMPODIA	ADIORSST	ASTROIDS	ADLNOPWY	DOWNPLAY
ADIMORRS	MIRADORS		SARODIST		PLAYDOWN
ADIMOSST	MASTOIDS	ADIORSSV	ADVISORS	ADLNORST	TROLANDS
ADIMOSTT	MATTOIDS	ADIORSTT	STRADIOT	ADLNORWY	ONWARDLY
ADIMOSTY	TOADYISM	ADIORSTU	AUDITORS	ADLNOSST	SANDLOTS
ADIMPRSY	PYRAMIDS	ADIORSVY	ADVISORY	ADLNOSSU	SOULDANS
ADIMRSSW	MISDRAWS	ADIORTUY	AUDITORY	ADLNOSSY	SYNODALS
ADIMRSUU	SUDARIUM	ADIOSSVW	DISAVOWS	ADLNOSTU	OUTLANDS
ADIMSSST	DISMASTS	ADIPRRTU	PURTRAID	ADLOOPRU	UROPODAL
ADIMSSTU	DUMAISTS	ADIPRSST	DISPARTS	ADLOORWW	WOOLWARD
	STADIUMS	ADIRRWYZ	WIZARDRY	ADLOPRSU	POULARDS
ADINNNTU	INUNDANT	ADIRSSTY	SATYRIDS	ADLOPRWY	WORDPLAY
ADINNOOT	DONATION	ADIRSSUY	DYSURIAS	ADLOPSUU	PALUDOUS
	NODATION	ADJKNRUY	JUNKYARD	ADLOQSUW	OLDSQUAW
ADINNOPS	DIPNOANS	ADJLMORS	JARLDOMS	ADLORRSW	WARLORDS
ADINNORS	ANDIRONS	ADJLSUUW	WUDJULAS	ADLORTWY	TOWARDLY
ADINNORT	ORDINANT	ADJNORSU	ADJOURNS	ADLPRUWY	UPWARDLY
ADINNORY	NONDAIRY	ADJORRSU	ADJURORS	ADLRRTUY	ULTRADRY
ADINNOTU	NUDATION	ADJORSTU	ADJUSTOR	ADMMNOOS	DOOMSMAN
ADINNRSW	WINNARDS	ADKKLOSY	KAKODYLS	ADMMNSSU	SUMMANDS
ADINNRSY	INNYARDS	ADKLMRSU	MUDLARKS	ADMMNTUU	MUTANDUM
ADINOOPS	ISOPODAN	ADKLNOPR	DRONKLAP	ADMMNORY	MONANDRY
ADINOOPT	ADOPTION	ADKLOORW	WOODLARK	ADMMNOSU	SOUNDMAN
ADINOORT	TANDOORI		WORKLOAD	ADMMNOTU	NOTANDUM
ADINOOTT	DOTATION	ADKMNORW	MARKDOWN	ADMNOOOT	ODONTOMA
ADINOPPS	OPPIDANS	ADKMOORR	DARKROOM	ADMNOORS	DOORSMAN
ADINOPRR	RAINDROP	ADKNORTU	OUTDRANK		MADRONOS
ADINOPRS	PONIARDS	ADKNRSTU	STUNKARD	ADMNOORW	MOONWARD
ADINOPRY	PYRANOID	ADKOORRW	ROADWORK	ADMNOOST	MASTODON
ADINOPST	PINTADOS	ADKORRWY	YARDWORK	ADMNOOSW	WOODSMAN
	SATINPOD	ADKORSWY	DAYWORKS	ADMNOOSZ	MADZOONS
ADINORRS	ORDINARS		WORKDAYS	ADMNORST	DORMANTS
ADINORRY	ORDINARY	ADKRSSWY	SKYWARDS		MORDANTS
ADINORSS	SADIRONS	ADLLLOOY	DOOLALLY	ADMNORSW	SANDWORM
ADINORST	DIATRONS	ADLLMOSW	WADMOLLS		SWORDMAN
	INTRADOS	ADLLNOPW	PLOWLAND	ADMNOSSU	OSMUNDAS
ADINORSU	DINOSAUR	ADLLNOSW	LOWLANDS	ADMNPPSU	SANDPUMP
ADINORSV	VIRANDOS	ADLLOPRS	POLLARDS	ADMOOPPP	POPPADOM
ADINORTU	DURATION	ADLLORSY	DORSALLY	ADMOORRW	WARDROOM
ADINOSTU	SUDATION	ADLLRSWY	DRYWALLS	ADMOORST	DOORMATS
ADINOSTX	OXIDANTS	ADLMNNOO	NONMODAL	ADMOORSY	DAYROOMS
ADINOSTY	DYSTONIA	ADLMNOOR	MOORLAND	ADMOPPPU	POPPADUM
ADINPSST	SANDPITS	ADLMNORY	RANDOMLY	ADMOPPSU	POPADUMS
ADINPSSY	SYNAPSID	ADLMNOSS	MOSSLAND	ADMORSST	STARDOMS
ADINRRST	TRIDARNS	ADLMOORS	LORDOMAS		TSARDOMS
ADINRSSU	SUNDARIS		MALODORS	ADMORSTW	MADWORTS
ADINRSTU	UNITARDS	ADLMOORU	MALODOUR	ADMORSTZ	TZARDOMS

ADMRSSTU	DURMASTS	**AEEEFRRW**	FREEWARE	**AEEEMPRS**	PERMEASE
	MUSTARDS	**AEEEFRTY**	AFTEREYE	**AEEEMPRT**	PERMEATE
ADMRSTUY	MUSTARDY	**AEEEGGNR**	REENGAGE	**AEEENNRV**	VENEREAN
ADNNOOST	NANODOTS	**AEEEGKLS**	KEELAGES	**AEEENNTV**	VENENATE
ADNNOOSY	NOONDAYS	**AEEEGLLS**	LEGALESE	**AEEENPTT**	PATENTEE
ADNNORTY	DYNATRON	**AEEEGLNR**	GENERALE	**AEEENRST**	SERENATE
ADNNOSTU	DAUNTONS	**AEEEGLRT**	EGLATERE	**AEEENRTT**	ENTERATE
ADNNRSTU	DUNNARTS		REGELATE	**AEEENRTV**	ENERVATE
ADNOOPRS	PANDOORS		RELEGATE		VENERATE
	SPADROON	**AEEEGLRV**	LEVERAGE	**AEEEPRRT**	REPARTEE
ADNOOQRU	QUADROON	**AEEEGLST**	LEGATEES		REPEATER
ADNOORST	DONATORS	**AEEEGLSV**	SELVAGEE		REREPEAT
	ODORANTS	**AEEEGLTV**	VEGELATE	**AEEERRST**	ARRESTEE
	TANDOORS	**AEEEGMRT**	METERAGE	**AEEERRTW**	TREEWARE
	TORNADOS	**AEEEGNRT**	GENERATE	**AEEERSST**	ESTERASE
ADNOORTY	DONATORY		RENEGATE		TESSERAE
ADNOOSVW	ADVOWSON		TEENAGER	**AEEERSVW**	REWEAVES
ADNOPRSU	PANDOURS	**AEEEGNSS**	AGENESES	**AEEERSWY**	EYEWEARS
ADNOPRSV	PROVANDS	**AEEEGNST**	TEENAGES	**AEEERTWY**	EYEWATER
ADNOQRSU	SQUADRON	**AEEEGNTW**	TWEENAGE	**AEEFFLLS**	FELAFELS
ADNORRSW	NORWARDS	**AEEEGPRS**	PEERAGES	**AEEFFLRT**	TAFFEREL
ADNORSTU	ROTUNDAS	**AEEEGPSS**	SEEPAGES	**AEEFFLTT**	FLATFEET
ADNORSTW	SANDWORT	**AEEEGRST**	EAGEREST	**AEEFFNRT**	AFFERENT
ADNORSTY	TARDYONS		ETAGERES	**AEEFGILR**	FILAGREE
ADNORSWY	NAYWORDS		STEERAGE	**AEEFGIRR**	FERRIAGE
ADNORSXY	SARDONYX	**AEEEGRSW**	SEWERAGE	**AEEFGIRS**	FEGARIES
ADNORTUW	OUTDRAWN	**AEEEGTTV**	VEGETATE	**AEEFGIRT**	FIGEATER
	UNTOWARD	**AEEEHKLL**	KEELHALE	**AEEFGLNS**	FENAGLES
ADNORWWY	WANWORDY	**AEEEHLRT**	ETHEREAL	**AEEFGLSU**	FUSELAGE
ADNOSSTU	ASTOUNDS	**AEEEHMPR**	EPHEMERA	**AEEFGNRS**	FREEGANS
ADNOSTTU	OUTSTAND	**AEEEHNRS**	ENHEARSE	**AEEFGNST**	FANTEEGS
	STANDOUT	**AEEEHRRS**	REHEARSE	**AEEFGRSS**	SERFAGES
ADNPRSSU	SANDSPUR	**AEEEHRRT**	REHEATER	**AEEFGSTW**	WEFTAGES
ADNPSSTU	DUSTPANS	**AEEEHSTT**	AESTHETE	**AEEFHIRS**	SHEAFIER
	STANDUPS	**AEEEILNS**	ALIENEES	**AEEFHLLS**	SELFHEAL
	UPSTANDS	**AEEEIMNX**	EXAMINEE	**AEEFHRST**	FEATHERS
ADNRSSUW	SUNWARDS	**AEEEIMRT**	EMERITAE	**AEEFHRTY**	FEATHERY
ADOOPPRU	PAUROPOD	**AEEEIRST**	EATERIES	**AEEFIINR**	INFERIAE
ADOOPRRT	TRAPDOOR	**AEEEJNTT**	JEANETTE	**AEEFIIRS**	AERIFIES
ADOOPRSU	SAUROPOD	**AEEEKKPS**	KEEPSAKE	**AEEFIKLL**	LEAFLIKE
ADOOPSSW	SAPWOODS	**AEEEKMSS**	KAMEESES	**AEEFIKLW**	KALEWIFE
ADOORSTW	WOODRATS	**AEEEKMSZ**	KAMEEZES	**AEEFIKRR**	FREAKIER
ADOORSWY	DOORWAYS	**AEEEKNRW**	WEAKENER	**AEEFIKRS**	FAKERIES
ADOOSSSW	SASSWOOD	**AEEELLPP**	APPELLEE	**AEEFIKRW**	WAKERIFE
ADOOSSTT	TOSTADOS	**AEEELLST**	TELESALE	**AEEFILMN**	FILENAME
ADOPRRSW	WARDROPS	**AEEELMNR**	ENAMELER	**AEEFILMT**	METAFILE
ADOPRSSW	PASSWORD	**AEEELNRT**	LATEENER	**AEEFILNR**	FLANERIE
ADOPSSSU	SOAPSUDS	**AEEELNRV**	VENEREAL	**AEEFILRS**	FILAREES
ADORRSTU	DARTROUS	**AEEELNST**	SELENATE		SERAFILE
ADORSTUW	OUTDRAWS	**AEEELPRR**	REPEALER	**AEEFILRT**	FEATLIER
	OUTWARDS	**AEEELQSU**	SEQUELAE		FRAILTEE
ADORSTUY	SUDATORY	**AEEELRRS**	RELEASER	**AEEFILST**	FEALTIES
ADORTUVY	ADVOUTRY	**AEEELRRV**	REVEALER		FETIALES
ADPRRTUY	PURTRAYD	**AEEELRSS**	RELEASES		LEAFIEST
ADRSSTTU	STARDUST	**AEEELRST**	TEASELER	**AEEFIPSW**	SPAEWIFE
ADSSSTUW	SAWDUSTS	**AEEELRSW**	WEASELER	**AEEFIRRR**	RAREFIER
ADSSTUWY	SAWDUSTY	**AEEELRTX**	AXLETREE	**AEEFIRRS**	RAREFIES
AEEEELRS	RELEASEE	**AEEELSSS**	EASELESS	**AEEFIRSS**	FREESIAS
AEEEEMRT	EMEERATE	**AEEELSTV**	ELEVATES	**AEEFIRTT**	FETERITA
AEEEFLRS	EELFARES	**AEEEMMRT**	METAMERE	**AEEFISST**	SAFETIES
AEEEFMRS	SEAMFREE	**AEEEMNST**	EASEMENT	**AEEFKMNT**	FAKEMENT

AEEFKOPR	FOREPEAK	AEEGHMPR	GRAPHEME	AEEGINTX	EXIGEANT
AEEFKRRY	FREAKERY	AEEGHNPR	GRAPHENE	AEEGIPPS	PIPEAGES
AEEFLLMR	FEMERALL	AEEGHNRS	SHAGREEN	AEEGIPQU	EQUIPAGE
AEEFLLMT	FLAMELET	AEEGHNST	THENAGES	AEEGIPRS	PIERAGES
AEEFLLNR	REFALLEN	AEEGHNSW	WHANGEES	AEEGIPVW	PAGEVIEW
AEEFLLNV	EVENFALL	AEEGHORS	GHERAOES	AEEGIRRS	GREASIER
AEEFLLRW	FAREWELL	AEEGHRRT	GATHERER	AEEGIRSS	GREASIES
AEEFLLSS	LEAFLESS		REGATHER	AEEGIRSU	EUGARIES
AEEFLLST	FELLATES	AEEGIILW	WEIGELIA	AEEGIRTT	AIGRETTE
	LEAFLETS	AEEGIINR	AEGIRINE	AEEGIRTV	ERGATIVE
AEEFLMNS	ENFLAMES	AEEGIIRT	AEGIRITE	AEEGISSS	ASSIEGES
AEEFLMOS	FLEASOME	AEEGIIST	GAIETIES	AEEGISTY	GAYETIES
AEEFLMPR	PREFLAME	AEEGIKLM	GAMELIKE	AEEGKLLS	KLEAGLES
AEEFLMSS	FAMELESS	AEEGIKLT	GATELIKE	AEEGKMRR	REGMAKER
	SELFSAME	AEEGIKLU	AGUELIKE	AEEGKNNR	GENNAKER
AEEFLNRU	FUNEREAL	AEEGILLS	GALILEES	AEEGLLNR	ALLERGEN
AEEFLOOV	FOVEOLAE		LEGALISE	AEEGLLPR	PRELEGAL
AEEFLORV	OVERLEAF	AEEGILLZ	LEGALIZE	AEEGLLRS	ALLEGERS
AEEFLRRR	REFERRAL	AEEGILMN	LIEGEMAN	AEEGLLSZ	GAZELLES
AEEFLRRT	FALTERER	AEEGILMR	GLEAMIER	AEEGLMNS	MELANGES
AEEFLRSS	FEARLESS	AEEGILMS	GELSEMIA	AEEGLMNV	GAVELMEN
AEEFLRST	REFLATES		MILEAGES	AEEGLMOS	MESOGLEA
AEEFLRSW	WELFARES	AEEGILNR	ALGERINE	AEEGLMPX	MEGAPLEX
AEEFLTTT	FLATETTE	AEEGILNS	ENSILAGE	AEEGLMRS	GLEAMERS
AEEFMNOR	FOREMEAN		LINEAGES	AEEGLMRT	TELEGRAM
	FORENAME	AEEGILNT	GALENITE	AEEGLMRY	MEAGERLY
AEEFMNRS	ENFRAMES		GELATINE		MEAGRELY
AEEFMORS	FEARSOME		LEGATINE	AEEGLMST	MELTAGES
AEEFMRRS	REFRAMES	AEEGILNV	INVEAGLE	AEEGLNNR	ENLARGEN
AEEFMRTY	FEMETARY	AEEGILOU	EULOGIAE	AEEGLNNT	ENTANGLE
AEEFNRST	FASTENER	AEEGILPR	PERIGEAL	AEEGLNOS	GASOLENE
	FENESTRA	AEEGILRS	GASELIER	AEEGLNOT	ELONGATE
	REFASTEN	AEEGILRT	LITREAGE	AEEGLNRR	ENLARGER
AEEFNRTT	FATTENER	AEEGILST	EGALITES	AEEGLNRS	ENLARGES
AEEFNSSS	SAFENESS		ELEGIAST		GENERALS
AEEFORRV	OVERFEAR	AEEGILSW	WEIGELAS		GLEANERS
AEEFOSTU	FEATEOUS	AEEGILTV	LEVIGATE	AEEGLNRT	REGENTAL
AEEFRRST	FERRATES	AEEGIMNR	GERMAINE	AEEGLNSU	EUGLENAS
AEEFRSST	FEASTERS	AEEGIMNT	GEMINATE	AEEGLNSV	EVANGELS
AEEFRSTU	FEATURES	AEEGIMRS	GAMESIER	AEEGLNVY	EVANGELY
AEEFRSWY	FREEWAYS		REIMAGES	AEEGLOOZ	ZOOGLEAE
AEEFTTUV	FAUVETTE	AEEGIMRT	EMIGRATE	AEEGLORS	AEROGELS
AEEGGHIW	WEIGHAGE		REMIGATE	AEEGLOST	SEGOLATE
AEEGGINR	AGREEING	AEEGINNT	ANTIGENE	AEEGLPRS	PEREGALS
AEEGGIRV	AGGRIEVE	AEEGINPR	PERIGEAN	AEEGLRRS	REGALERS
AEEGGLLS	ALLEGGES	AEEGINRR	REGAINER	AEEGLRSS	EELGRASS
AEEGGLOU	AEGLOGUE	AEEGINRS	ANERGIES		GEARLESS
AEEGGLRS	GREGALES		GESNERIA		LARGESSE
AEEGGNNR	GANGRENE	AEEGINRT	ENARGITE	AEEGLRSU	LEAGUERS
AEEGGNOS	GASOGENE		GRATINEE	AEEGLRSW	LEGWEARS
AEEGGNOZ	GAZOGENE		INTERAGE	AEEGLRSZ	REGLAZES
AEEGGNRS	ENGAGERS	AEEGINRZ	RAZEEING	AEEGLRTU	REGULATE
AEEGGOPS	EPAGOGES	AEEGINSS	AGENESIS	AEEGLRUX	EXERGUAL
AEEGGPRU	PUGGAREE		AGENISES	AEEGLSST	GATELESS
AEEGGRSU	REGAUGES		ASSIGNEE	AEEGLSSV	SELVAGES
AEEGHIRS	HIREAGES	AEEGINST	SAGENITE	AEEGLSSW	WAGELESS
AEEGHIRT	HERITAGE	AEEGINSU	EUGENIAS	AEEGLSSY	EYEGLASS
AEEGHLOT	HELOTAGE	AEEGINSV	ENVISAGE	AEEGLSTT	GALETTES
AEEGHLRS	SHEARLEG	AEEGINSZ	AGENIZES	AEEGLSTV	VEGETALS
AEEGHLRW	RAGWHEEL	AEEGINTV	AGENTIVE	AEEGLTTU	TUTELAGE
AEEGHMOP	HOMEPAGE		NEGATIVE	AEEGLTUV	EVULGATE

AEEGMMNR	ENGRAMME	**AEEGPSST**	SEPTAGES	**AEEHITTZ**	ATHETIZE
AEEGMMNS	GAMESMEN	**AEEGRRRT**	REGRATER	**AEEHKLLR**	RAKEHELL
AEEGMMOS	GAMESOME	**AEEGRRSS**	GREASERS	**AEEHKLLU**	KEELHAUL
AEEGMMST	GEMMATES	**AEEGRRSS**	REGRATES	**AEEHKMNS**	KHAMSEEN
	TAGMEMES	**AEEGRRSU**	REARGUES	**AEEHKNRR**	HANKERER
AEEGMNOR	ARGEMONE	**AEEGRRSW**	WAGERERS		HARKENER
AEEGMNRS	AGREMENS	**AEEGRRTT**	RETARGET	**AEEHKNRS**	HEARKENS
AEEGMNRT	AGREMENT	**AEEGRSST**	RESTAGES	**AEEHKPRR**	PHREAKER
AEEGMNSS	GAMENESS	**AEEGRSTT**	GREATEST	**AEEHKRST**	HEKTARES
	MAGNESES	**AEEGRSTU**	TREAGUES	**AEEHKRSU**	HEUREKAS
AEEGMNTT	TEGMENTA	**AEEGRSTW**	STREWAGE	**AEEHLLSS**	SEASHELL
AEEGMNTZ	GAZEMENT	**AEEGRSUZ**	GUEREZAS	**AEEHLMNW**	WHALEMEN
AEEGMOOT	OOGAMETE	**AEEGSSTT**	GESTATES		WHEELMAN
AEEGMOST	SOMEGATE	**AEEGSTTT**	STAGETTE	**AEEHLMNY**	HYMENEAL
AEEGMPRS	PREGAMES	**AEEGSTTZ**	GAZETTES	**AEEHLMOS**	HEALSOME
AEEGMRST	GAMESTER	**AEEHHHSS**	HASHEESH	**AEEHLMPT**	HELPMATE
	MEAGREST	**AEEHHIRT**	HEATHIER	**AEEHLMSS**	SHEMALES
AEEGMRSU	REMUAGES	**AEEHHLNZ**	HAZELHEN	**AEEHLNOS**	ENHALOES
AEEGMSSS	MEGASSES	**AEEHHNST**	ENSHEATH	**AEEHLNOT**	ANETHOLE
	MESSAGES		HEATHENS	**AEEHLNPT**	ELEPHANT
AEEGMSSU	MESSUAGE	**AEEHHOOP**	PAHOEHOE	**AEEHLNRT**	LEATHERN
AEEGNNNO	ENNEAGON	**AEEHHRSS**	REHASHES	**AEEHLNSS**	HALENESS
AEEGNNPS	PANGENES	**AEEHHRST**	HEATHERS	**AEEHLNTX**	EXHALENT
AEEGNNRS	ENRANGES		SHEATHER	**AEEHLNVY**	HEAVENLY
AEEGNNRT	GENERANT	**AEEHHRTY**	HEATHERY	**AEEHLORS**	ARSEHOLE
AEEGNNRU	ENRAUNGE	**AEEHHSSS**	SHEESHAS		HALOSERE
AEEGNNRV	ENGRAVEN	**AEEHHSST**	SHEATHES	**AEEHLORV**	OVERHALE
AEEGNOPS	PEONAGES	**AEEHIKLR**	HARELIKE	**AEEHLOSU**	ALEHOUSE
AEEGNPPS	GENAPPES	**AEEHIKRS**	SHIKAREE	**AEEHLPRT**	PLEATHER
AEEGNRRT	ETRANGER	**AEEHILNP**	ELAPHINE	**AEEHLPST**	HEELTAPS
AEEGNRRV	ENGRAVER	**AEEHILRS**	SHIRALEE		PLEASETH
AEEGNRST	ESTRANGE	**AEEHILRT**	ETHERIAL	**AEEHLPTT**	TELEPATH
	GRANTEES	**AEEHIMNT**	HEMATEIN	**AEEHLRRT**	LATHERER
	GREATENS		HEMATINE	**AEEHLRST**	HALTERES
	NEGATERS	**AEEHIMNX**	HEXAMINE		LEATHERS
	REAGENTS	**AEEHIMPT**	EPITHEMA	**AEEHLRSV**	HAVERELS
	SEGREANT	**AEEHIMTT**	HEMATITE	**AEEHLRTT**	HEARTLET
	SERGEANT	**AEEHINRS**	INHEARSE	**AEEHLRTY**	LEATHERY
	STERNAGE	**AEEHINRT**	ATHERINE	**AEEHLSST**	HATELESS
AEEGNRSU	RENAGUES		HERNIATE		HEATLESS
AEEGNRSV	AVENGERS	**AEEHIPRS**	PHARISEE	**AEEHLSTT**	ATHLETES
	ENGRAVES		SPHAIREE	**AEEHLTTY**	ETHYLATE
AEEGNRTU	GAUNTREE	**AEEHIPST**	APHETISE	**AEEHMMRR**	HAMMERER
AEEGNRWY	GREENWAY		HEAPIEST		REHAMMER
AEEGNSSS	SAGENESS		HEPATISE	**AEEHMNNY**	HYMENEAN
AEEGNSST	SANGEETS	**AEEHIPTT**	HEPATITE	**AEEHMNPS**	SHEEPMAN
AEEGNSTT	TENTAGES	**AEEHIPTZ**	APHETIZE	**AEEHMNRS**	SHAREMEN
AEEGNSTV	VENTAGES		HEPATIZE		SHEARMEN
AEEGNTTV	VEGETANT	**AEEHIRRS**	HEARSIER	**AEEHMNRT**	EARTHMEN
AEEGOPRV	OVERPAGE	**AEEHIRRT**	EARTHIER	**AEEHMNST**	METHANES
AEEGOPSS	SAPEGOES		HEARTIER	**AEEHMNTU**	ATHENEUM
AEEGORRV	OVERGEAR	**AEEHIRSS**	ASHERIES	**AEEHMNTX**	EXANTHEM
AEEGORSV	OVERAGES	**AEEHIRST**	HEARTIES	**AEEHMORW**	HOMEWARE
AEEGORVV	OVERGAVE	**AEEHIRSV**	SHIVAREE	**AEEHMPRR**	HAMPERER
AEEGOSTX	GEOTAXES	**AEEHIRTW**	WHEATIER	**AEEHMPSS**	EMPHASES
AEEGPRRS	ASPERGER	**AEEHISST**	ATHEISES	**AEEHMRSS**	MAHSEERS
	PRESAGER		ESTHESIA	**AEEHMRST**	ERATHEMS
AEEGPRRT	PARGETER	**AEEHISTT**	ATHETISE	**AEEHMRTY**	ERYTHEMA
AEEGPRSS	ASPERGES		HESITATE	**AEEHMSST**	MATHESES
	PRESAGES	**AEEHISTV**	HEAVIEST	**AEEHMTUX**	EXHUMATE
AEEGPRSU	PUGAREES	**AEEHISTZ**	ATHEIZES	**AEEHNNSS**	SNEESHAN

AEEHNNTX	XANTHENE	AEEIKKLL	LAKELIKE	AEEILPRR	PEARLIER
AEEHNOPR	EARPHONE	AEEIKKLP	PEAKLIKE	AEEILPRS	ESPALIER
AEEHNPST	HAPTENES	AEEIKKLW	LIKEWAKE		PEARLIES
	HEPTANES	AEEIKLLS	SEALLIKE	AEEILPRT	PEARLITE
	PHENATES	AEEIKLMS	SEAMLIKE	AEEILPST	EPILATES
	STEPHANE	AEEIKLMU	LEUKEMIA	AEEILPSW	PALEWISE
AEEHNRSS	ARSHEENS	AEEIKLMZ	MAZELIKE	AEEILQSU	EQUALISE
AEEHNRST	HASTENER	AEEIKLPT	TAPELIKE	AEEILQUX	EXEQUIAL
	HEARTENS	AEEIKLRW	WEAKLIER	AEEILQUZ	EQUALIZE
AEEHNRSU	UNHEARSE	AEEIKLST	LEAKIEST	AEEILRRS	REALISER
AEEHNRSV	RESHAVEN	AEEIKLSV	VASELIKE	AEEILRRT	RETAILER
AEEHNRTT	HATERENT	AEEIKLVW	WAVELIKE	AEEILRRZ	REALIZER
	THREATEN	AEEIKMMR	MERIMAKE	AEEILRSS	REALISES
AEEHNRTU	URETHANE	AEEIKMNT	KETAMINE	AEEILRST	ATELIERS
AEEHNRTW	ENWREATH	AEEIKNRS	SNEAKIER		EARLIEST
	WATERHEN	AEEIKNRT	ANKERITE		LATERISE
	WREATHEN		KREATINE		LEARIEST
AEEHNRWY	ANYWHERE	AEEIKNSS	AKINESES		REALTIES
AEEHNSST	ANTHESES	AEEIKPST	PEAKIEST	AEEILRSV	VELARISE
AEEHNSTU	UNEATHES	AEEIKRRS	RAKERIES	AEEILRSY	YEARLIES
AEEHNSTW	ENSWATHE		SKEARIER	AEEILRSZ	REALIZES
	WHEATENS	AEEIKRTW	TWEAKIER		SLEAZIER
AEEHOPRT	EPHORATE	AEEILLNT	TENAILLE	AEEILRTT	LATERITE
AEEHOPRV	OVERHEAP	AEEILLRS	REALLIES		LITERATE
AEEHORRV	OVERHEAR	AEEILLRT	LAETRILE	AEEILRTV	LEVIRATE
AEEHORSS	SEAHORSE	AEEILLST	LEALTIES		RELATIVE
	SEASHORE	AEEILMMN	MELAMINE	AEEILRTZ	LATERIZE
AEEHORTV	OVERHATE	AEEILMMT	MEALTIME	AEEILRVW	LIVEWARE
	OVERHEAT	AEEILMNS	MELANISE		REVIEWAL
AEEHOSTU	TEAHOUSE	AEEILMNT	MELANITE	AEEILRVZ	VELARIZE
AEEHPPRS	PRESHAPE	AEEILMNZ	MELANIZE	AEEILSST	ASTELIES
AEEHPRRS	REPHRASE	AEEILMRS	ALMERIES	AEEILSTT	AILETTES
	RESHAPER		EMAILERS	AEEILSTV	ELATIVES
AEEHPRRT	THREAPER		MEASLIER		LEAVIEST
AEEHPRSS	RESHAPES	AEEILMRT	EREMITAL		VEALIEST
	SPHAERES		MATERIEL	AEEILSVW	ALEWIVES
	SPHEARES		REALTIME	AEEILTTV	LEVITATE
AEEHPRST	PREHEATS	AEEILMST	MEALIEST	AEEILTUV	ELUVIATE
	SPREATHE		METALISE	AEEIMMNT	MEANTIME
AEEHPRUV	UPHEAVER	AEEILMSV	MALVESIE	AEEIMNNS	ENAMINES
AEEHPSUV	UPHEAVES	AEEILMTZ	METALIZE	AEEIMNRS	REMANIES
AEEHQSSU	QUASHEES	AEEILNNS	SELENIAN	AEEIMNRT	ANTIMERE
AEEHRRSS	SHEARERS	AEEILNPR	PERINEAL	AEEIMNRX	EXAMINER
AEEHRRTU	URETHRAE	AEEILNPS	ALEPINES	AEEIMNSS	NEMESIAS
AEEHRRTW	WREATHER		PENALISE	AEEIMNST	ETAMINES
AEEHRSSV	RESHAVES		SEPALINE		MATINEES
AEEHRSSW	REWASHES	AEEILNPT	PETALINE		MISEATEN
AEEHRSTT	EARTHSET		TAPELINE		SEMINATE
	THEATERS	AEEILNPZ	PENALIZE	AEEIMNSX	EXAMINES
	THEATRES	AEEILNRR	NEARLIER	AEEIMNUV	MAUVEINE
AEEHRSTV	THREAVES	AEEILNRS	ALIENERS	AEEIMOSS	AMEIOSES
AEEHRSTW	WEATHERS	AEEILNRT	ELATERIN	AEEIMPRS	EMPAIRES
	WREATHES		ENTAILER	AEEIMRRS	REREMAIS
AEEHRTVW	WHATEVER		TREENAIL		SMEARIER
AEEHRTXZ	EXAHERTZ	AEEILNSS	SEALINES	AEEIMRSS	SERIEMAS
AEEHSTTW	SAWTEETH	AEEILNSV	VASELINE	AEEIMRST	EMERITAS
AEEHSTVY	HEAVYSET	AEEILNSX	ALEXINES		EMIRATES
AEEIIMRT	METAIRIE	AEEILNTV	ELVANITE		REAMIEST
AEEIINRT	INERTIAE		VENTAILE		STEAMIER
AEEIISST	ASEITIES	AEEILORT	AEROLITE	AEEIMRTV	VIAMETER
AEEIJPRS	JAPERIES	AEEILOTT	ETIOLATE	AEEIMSSS	MISEASES

	SIAMESES		REASTIER	**AEEKNPSU**	SNEAKEUP
AEEIMSST	SEAMIEST	**AEEIRRSW**	SWEARIER	**AEEKNPSW**	NEWSPEAK
	STEAMIES	**AEEIRRTT**	RETRAITE	**AEEKNRSS**	SNEAKERS
AEEIMSSZ	SIAMEZES	**AEEIRRTW**	WATERIER	**AEEKNRSW**	REWAKENS
AEEIMSTT	ESTIMATE	**AEEIRRVW**	WAVERIER		WAKENERS
	ETATISME	**AEEIRSST**	SERIATES	**AEEKNSSW**	WEAKNESS
	MEATIEST	**AEEIRSST**	SERIATES	**AEEKOOPP**	PEEKAPOO
	TEATIMES		ITERATES	**AEEKORRV**	OVERRAKE
AEEIMSTW	TEAMWISE		TEARIEST	**AEEKORST**	KERATOSE
AEEINNRS	ANSERINE		TREATIES		KREASOTE
AEEINNTV	VENETIAN		TREATISE	**AEEKORTV**	OVERTAKE
AEEINOPS	PAEONIES	**AEEIRSTV**	EVIRATES		TAKEOVER
AEEINPRS	NAPERIES	**AEEIRSTW**	SWEATIER	**AEEKORVW**	OVERWEAK
AEEINPRT	APERIENT		TAWERIES	**AEEKPRSS**	RESPEAKS
AEEINPTT	PIANETTE		WASTERIE		SPEAKERS
AEEINRRS	REARISEN		WEARIEST	**AEEKPRST**	PERTAKES
AEEINRRT	RETAINER	**AEEIRSTY**	YEASTIER	**AEEKPRTT**	PARKETTE
AEEINRSS	SENARIES	**AEEIRSVV**	AVERSIVE	**AEEKPRTU**	REUPTAKE
AEEINRST	ARENITES	**AEEISSTX**	EXTASIES	**AEEKQRSU**	SQUEAKER
	ARSENITE	**AEEISSVW**	SEAWIVES	**AEEKRRST**	RETAKERS
	RESINATE	**AEEISTTT**	ETATISTE		STREAKER
	STEARINE		STEATITE	**AEEKRRSW**	WREAKERS
	TRAINEES	**AEEISTTV**	AVIETTES	**AEEKRSST**	SAKERETS
AEEINRSU	UNEASIER		ESTIVATE	**AEEKRSTW**	TWEAKERS
AEEINSSS	EASINESS		EVITATES	**AEELLLPT**	PELLETAL
AEEINSST	ETESIANS	**AEEISTUX**	EUTAXIES	**AEELLLTT**	TELLTALE
	TENIASES		EUTEXIAS	**AEELLMMS**	MAMSELLE
AEEINSSV	VAINESSE	**AEEISTUX**	EUTAXITE	**AEELLMSS**	MEALLESS
AEEINSTT	ANISETTE	**AEEITTUX**	EXUVIATE	**AEELLNOV**	NOVELLAE
	TETANIES	**AEEITUVX**	EXUVIATE	**AEELLOSV**	ALVEOLES
	TETANISE	**AEEJLOSU**	JEALOUSE	**AEELLOTT**	ALLOTTEE
AEEINSTV	NAIVETES	**AEEJNRST**	SERJEANT	**AEELLPRS**	PARELLES
AEEINSVW	INWEAVES	**AEEJOPRT**	PEJORATE	**AEELLPTT**	PALLETTE
AEEINTTZ	TETANIZE	**AEEJRTTW**	WATERJET		PLATELET
AEEIOOPP	EPOPOEIA	**AEEKKLWY**	LYKEWAKE	**AEELLPTY**	TELEPLAY
AEEIORST	ETAERIOS	**AEEKKNOS**	KOKANEES	**AEELLRRT**	TERRELLA
AEEIPPRR	PAPERIER	**AEEKKOOS**	KOEKOEAS	**AEELLRRV**	RAVELLER
AEEIPPSS	APEPSIES	**AEEKKPSY**	KEEPSAKY	**AEELLSST**	SATELLES
AEEIPPST	APPETISE	**AEEKLLSS**	LEAKLESS		TESSELLA
AEEIPPSU	EUPEPSIA	**AEEKLLST**	LAKELETS	**AEELLSSZ**	ZEALLESS
AEEIPPTT	APPETITE		SKELETAL	**AEELLSTT**	STELLATE
AEEIPPTZ	APPETIZE	**AEEKLMMU**	MAMELUKE	**AEELLSWY**	WALLEYES
AEEIPRRR	RARERIPE	**AEEKLMRT**	TELEMARK		WEASELLY
	REPAIRER	**AEEKLMRY**	YARMELKE	**AEELLTVV**	VALVELET
AEEIPRRS	PEREIRAS	**AEEKLMSS**	MAKELESS	**AEELMMTU**	MALEMUTE
	SPEARIER	**AEEKLNST**	KANTELES	**AEELMNPS**	EMPANELS
AEEIPRST	PARIETES	**AEEKLPSS**	PEAKLESS		EMPLANES
	PETARIES	**AEEKLSSW**	WAKELESS		ENSAMPLE
AEEIPRTV	PERVIATE	**AEEKLSTY**	EYESTALK	**AEELMNPT**	PLATEMEN
AEEIPSST	EPITASES	**AEEKMNSS**	KAMSEENS	**AEELMNRT**	LAMENTER
AEEIPSTT	PEATIEST	**AEEKMORV**	MAKEOVER	**AEELMNSS**	LAMENESS
AEEIPSTX	EPITAXES	**AEEKMOTY**	YOKEMATE		MALENESS
	EXPIATES	**AEEKMRRR**	REMARKER		MANELESS
AEEIPTVX	EXAPTIVE	**AEEKMRRS**	REMAKERS		NAMELESS
AEEIQRSU	QUEASIER	**AEEKMRRT**	MARKETER		SALESMEN
AEEIQRUZ	QUEAZIER		REMARKET	**AEELMNST**	MANTEELS
AEEIQSTU	EQUISETA	**AEEKMRST**	MEERKATS		STEELMAN
AEEIQTUV	EQUATIVE	**AEEKNNSU**	NANKEENS		TALESMEN
AEEIRRSS	REARISES	**AEEKNNPS**	KNEEPANS	**AEELMNSW**	WEALSMEN
	RERAISES	**AEEKNORW**	REAWOKEN	**AEELMNSY**	AMYLENES
AEEIRRST	ARTERIES	**AEEKNPRT**	PERTAKEN	**AEELMNTT**	MANTELET
		AEEKNPST	NETSPEAK		

AEELMNTV	LAVEMENT		OVERLATE	AEELSTVW	WAVELETS
AEELMOTT	MATELOTE	AEELORTW	TOLEWARE	AEEMMNRS	MERESMAN
AEELMPRS	EMPALERS	AEELORVZ	OVERZEAL	AEEMMNTZ	MAZEMENT
	RESAMPLE	AEELOSSW	LEASOWES	AEEMMPSY	EMPYEMAS
AEELMPRX	EXEMPLAR	AEELOSTV	LOVESEAT	AEEMMRRY	YAMMERER
AEELMPRY	EMPYREAL	AEELOTTT	TEETOTAL	AEEMMRST	AMMETERS
AEELMPSX	EXAMPLES	AEELPRRS	PEARLERS		METAMERS
AEELMPTT	PALMETTE		RELAPSER	AEEMMSST	MESSMATE
	TEMPLATE	AEELPRRT	PALTERER	AEEMNNOS	ANEMONES
AEELMRST	LAMETERS		PREALTER	AEEMNNPS	PENNAMES
AEELMRTX	EXTREMAL	AEELPRRY	PARLEYER	AEEMNNRT	REMANENT
AEELMSSS	SEAMLESS	AEELPRSS	PLEASERS	AEEMNNSS	MEANNESS
AEELMSST	MATELESS		PRESALES	AEEMNORV	OVERNAME
	MEATLESS		RELAPSES	AEEMNORZ	ARMOZEEN
	TAMELESS	AEELPRST	PETRALES	AEEMNOSS	ANEMOSES
AEELMSTU	EMULATES		PLEATERS	AEEMNOSW	SEAWOMEN
AEELNNPS	ENPLANES		PRELATES	AEEMNOSX	AXONEMES
AEELNNRT	LANNERET		REPLATES	AEEMNPRS	PRENAMES
AEELNNSS	LEANNESS	AEELPRSU	PLEASURE		SPEARMEN
AEELNOPR	PERONEAL	AEELPRSV	VESPERAL	AEEMNPRT	PERMEANT
AEELNOPT	ANTELOPE	AEELPRTY	PTERYLAE		PETERMAN
AEELNORT	REALTONE	AEELPRUV	PREVALUE	AEEMNPRY	EMPYREAN
AEELNORU	ALEURONE	AEELPSST	SPATLESE	AEEMNPTV	PAVEMENT
AEELNOSS	ENOLASES		TAPELESS	AEEMNRST	REMANETS
AEELNPPS	SPALPEEN	AEELPSTT	PALETTES	AEEMNRSU	USERNAME
AEELNPRR	PRERENAL	AEELPSTU	EPAULETS	AEEMNRSV	VERSEMAN
AEELNPRS	REPANELS	AEELPSTV	SEPTLEVA	AEEMNRSW	MENSWEAR
AEELNPSS	PALENESS	AEELPSTZ	SPAETZLE	AEEMNRTU	NUMERATE
	PANELESS	AEELQRSU	LEQUEARS	AEEMNRTV	AVERMENT
AEELNQSU	SQUALENE		SQUEALER	AEEMNRTW	WATERMEN
AEELNRRS	LEARNERS	AEELQSUZ	QUEZALES	AEEMNRUV	MANEUVER
	RELEARNS	AEELRRST	ALTERERS	AEEMNRVY	EVERYMAN
AEELNRRT	RELEARNT		REALTERS	AEEMNSSS	SAMENESS
AEELNRSS	REALNESS		RELATERS	AEEMNSST	TAMENESS
AEELNRST	ALTERNES	AEELRRSV	RAVELERS	AEEMNSTU	MANSUETE
	ETERNALS		REVERSAL	AEEMNSTW	SWEETMAN
	TELERANS		SLAVERER	AEEMORST	EROTEMAS
AEELNRSV	ENSLAVER	AEELRRSX	RELAXERS	AEEMORTV	OVERTAME
AEELNRSW	RENEWALS	AEELRRTU	URETERAL	AEEMPPRR	PAMPERER
AEELNRTV	LEVANTER	AEELRRTV	TRAVELER	AEEMPRRT	TAMPERER
	RELEVANT	AEELRSST	RESLATES	AEEMPRRV	REVAMPER
AEELNRTW	TREELAWN		STEALERS	AEEMPRST	TEMPERAS
AEELNRTX	EXTERNAL		TEARLESS	AEEMPRSY	EMPAYRES
AEELNRUU	NEURULAE		TESSERAL	AEEMPRTT	ATTEMPER
AEELNRUV	REVENUAL	AEELRSSU	LEASURES	AEEMPSTU	AMPUTEES
AEELNSST	LATENESS	AEELRSSV	SEVERALS	AEEMQRRU	REMARQUE
AEELNSSV	ENSLAVES	AEELRSSW	WARELESS	AEEMQRSU	MARQUEES
	VANELESS	AEELRSTT	ALERTEST	AEEMQTTU	MAQUETTE
AEELNSTY	ENTAYLES	AEELRSTU	RESALUTE	AEEMRRSS	SMEARERS
AEELNTUV	EVENTUAL	AEELRSTX	EXALTERS	AEEMRRST	REMASTER
AEELNTVY	VENTAYLE	AEELRSTY	EASTERLY		STREAMER
AEELOPRS	PAROLEES	AEELRSUV	REVALUES	AEEMRRSU	MEASURER
AEELOPRV	OVERLEAP	AEELRSVY	AVERSELY	AEEMRRTT	TETRAMER
AEELOPSX	POLEAXES	AEELSSST	ALTESSES	AEEMRSST	MASSETER
AEELOPTT	TOEPLATE		SATELESS		SEAMSTER
AEELORRS	RELEASOR		SEATLESS		STEAMERS
AEELORST	OLEASTER	AEELSSTU	SETUALES	AEEMRSSU	MEASURES
AEELORSU	AUREOLES	AEELSSTV	SALVETES		REASSUME
AEELORSV	OVERSALE	AEELSSVW	WAVELESS	AEEMRSTT	TEAMSTER
AEELORTT	TOLERATE	AEELSTTT	STATELET	AEEMRSTW	STEMWARE
AEELORTV	ELEVATOR	AEELSTTY	LAYETTES	AEEMRSTY	METAYERS

AEEMRTWY	YAWMETER	AEENRTTV	ANTEVERT		REASSURE
AEEMSSST	SEAMSETS	AEENRTTX	EXTERNAT	AEERRSSW	SWEARERS
AEEMSSSU	MASSEUSE		EXTRANET	AEERRSTT	RETRATES
AEEMSSTU	MEATUSES	AEENRTTY	ENTREATY		RETREATS
AEEMSTTU	AMUSETTE	AEENRTUV	AVENTURE		TREATERS
AEENNOST	NEONATES	AEENRVWW	NEWWAVER	AEERRSTU	AUSTERER
AEENNPST	PENTANES	AEENSSST	SENSATES		TREASURE
AEENNRRS	ENSNARER	AEENSTTV	NAVETTES	AEERRSTV	AVERTERS
AEENNRSS	ENSNARES	AEENSUVW	UNWEAVES		TRAVERSE
	NEARNESS	AEEOPRRT	PATERERO	AEERRSTW	REWATERS
	RENNASES		PERORATE		WATERERS
AEENNRTU	ENAUNTER	AEEOPRST	OPERATES	AEERRSVW	WAVERERS
AEENNRTV	REVENANT		PROTEASE	AEERSSSS	REASSESS
AEENNRUX	ANNEXURE	AEEOPRTT	OPERETTA	AEERSSSU	SEASURES
AEENNSSS	SANENESS	AEEOPSTZ	EPAZOTES	AEERSSSV	ASSEVERS
AEENNSST	NEATNESS	AEEORRSU	REAROUSE	AEERSSSY	ESSAYERS
AEENNSTT	SETENANT	AEEORRSW	SOWARREE	AEERSSTT	ESTREATS
AEENOORT	AEROTONE	AEEORRTV	OVERRATE		RESTATES
AEENOPRS	PERAEONS	AEEORRVW	OVERWEAR		RETASTES
	PERSONAE	AEEORRVY	OVERYEAR	AEERSSTW	SWEATERS
AEENOPSU	EUPNOEAS	AEEORSSV	OVERSEAS	AEERSSTZ	ERSATZES
AEENORRS	REASONER	AEEORSTV	OVEREATS	AEERSSUU	URAEUSES
AEENORRV	OVERNEAR	AEEORSVV	OVERSAVE	AEERSSUV	VAREUSES
AEENORSS	RESEASON	AEEORSVW	OVERAWES	AEERSTTT	ATTESTER
	SEASONER	AEEORSVY	OVEREASY	AEERSTTX	EXTREATS
AEENORST	EARSTONE	AEEPPPRU	PREPUPAE	AEERSTWW	WETWARES
	RESONATE	AEEPPRRR	PREPARER	AEERTTTZ	TERZETTA
AEENORTV	OVERNEAT		PREPARES	AEERVWYY	EVERYWAY
	RENOVATE		REPAPERS	AEESSSSS	ASSESSES
AEENORVW	OVENWARE	AEEPPRRU	PUERPERA	AEESSTTT	TESTATES
AEENOTTU	OUTEATEN	AEEPPRST	PREPASTE	AEFFFLRS	FLAFFERS
AEENPPRT	PETNAPER		PRETAPES	AEFFGIIL	EFFIGIAL
AEENPPTT	APPETENT	AEEPPRSV	PREPAVES	AEFFGINR	FIREFANG
AEENPQTU	PETANQUE	AEEPRRRT	PARTERRE	AEFFGIRS	GIRAFFES
AEENPRUV	PARVENUE	AEEPRRRS	ASPERSER		RIFFAGES
AEENPSSU	APNEUSES		SPEARERS	AEFFGNRS	ENGRAFFS
AEENPSSX	EXPANSES	AEEPRRST	TAPERERS	AEFFGOST	OFFSTAGE
AEENPTTY	ANTETYPE	AEEPRRSV	PREAVERS	AEFFGRSU	GAUFFERS
AEENRRRW	WARRENER	AEEPRRTT	PATTERER		SUFFRAGE
AEENRRSS	RARENESS		PRETREAT	AEFFHIKY	KAFFIYEH
AEENRRST	TERRANES	AEEPRRTU	APERTURE		KEFFIYAH
AEENRRSV	RAVENERS	AEEPRSSS	ASPERSES	AEFFHILL	HALFLIFE
AEENRRSW	ANSWERER		PREASSES	AEFFILNY	AFFINELY
	REANSWER		REPASSES	AEFFILRW	WAFFLIER
AEENRRSY	YEARNERS	AEEPRSST	TRAPESES	AEFFILUV	EFFLUVIA
AEENRRTT	NATTERER	AEEPRSSZ	SPREAZES	AEFFIMRR	AFFIRMER
	RATTENER	AEEPRSTT	PEARTEST		REAFFIRM
AEENRRTU	RENATURE		PRETASTE	AEFFIMRW	FARMWIFE
AEENRRTV	TAVERNER	AEEPRSTU	EPURATES	AEFFIPRS	PIAFFERS
AEENRSSS	SEARNESS		SUPERATE	AEFFIRSX	AFFIXERS
AEENRSST	ASSENTER	AEEPRSTZ	TRAPEZES	AEFFKLRU	FREAKFUL
	EARNESTS	AEEPSSTT	SPATTEES	AEFFKORS	RAKEOFFS
	SARSENET	AEEQRRUV	QUAVERER	AEFFKOST	OFFTAKES
AEENRSSU	ANURESES	AEERRRST	ARRESTER		TAKEOFFS
AEENRSSX	XERANSES		REARREST	AEFFLMSW	FLAMFEWS
AEENRSTT	ENTREATS	AEERRSST	ASSERTER	AEFFLNSS	SNAFFLES
	RATTEENS		REASSERT	AEFFLNTU	AFFLUENT
AEENRSTU	SAUTERNE		SERRATES	AEFFLRRS	RAFFLERS
AEENRSTV	AVENTRES		TERRASES	AEFFLRSW	WAFFLERS
	VETERANS	AEERRSSU	ERASURES	AEFFLSTU	FEASTFUL
AEENRSUV	UNREAVES				SUFFLATE

AEFFLSUX	AFFLUXES	AEFGMNOR	FORGEMAN	AEFIINRT	FAINTIER
AEFFMNST	STAFFMEN	AEFGMNRT	FRAGMENT	AEFIINRV	VINIFERA
AEFFMRSU	EARMUFFS	AEFGMORS	FROMAGES	AEFIINSS	SANIFIES
AEFFNNSS	NAFFNESS	AEFGNNOT	FONTANGE	AEFIINST	FAINITES
AEFFNORT	AFFRONTE	AEFGNORT	FRONTAGE	AEFIINSZ	NAZIFIES
AEFFORST	AFFOREST	AEFGNRRS	FRANGERS	AEFIIPRT	APERITIF
AEFFOSVW	WAVEOFFS		GRANFERS	AEFIIRRS	FRIARIES
AEFFQRSU	QUAFFERS	AEFGNRST	ENGRAFTS		RARIFIES
AEFFRSST	RESTAFFS	AEFGOOPT	FOOTPAGE	AEFIIRRT	RATIFIER
	STAFFERS	AEFGOORT	FOOTGEAR	AEFIIRST	RATIFIES
AEFFRTTU	TARTUFFE	AEFGOOST	FOOTAGES	AEFIIRSU	AURIFIES
AEFGGGOS	FOGGAGES	AEFGORRS	FORAGERS	AEFIITVX	FIXATIVE
AEFGGILR	FLAGGIER	AEFGORST	FAGOTERS	AEFIJLOS	JEOFAILS
AEFGGINU	FEAGUING	AEFGORTT	FROTTAGE	AEFIJLRZ	JALFREZI
AEFGGIST	FAGGIEST	AEFGOSSU	FOUGASSE	AEFIKLMO	FOAMLIKE
AEFGGLRS	FLAGGERS	AEFGRRST	GRAFTERS	AEFIKLNU	FAUNLIKE
AEFGGMOS	MEGAFOGS		REGRAFTS	AEFIKLNW	FAWNLIKE
AEFGHINR	HANGFIRE	AEFHIKRS	FREAKISH	AEFIKLRY	FREAKILY
AEFGHINS	SHEAFING	AEFHIKSW	WEAKFISH	AEFIKLST	FLAKIEST
AEFGHOSS	FOGASHES	AEFHILLN	FELLAHIN	AEFIKMNN	KNIFEMAN
AEFGHTTU	FUGHETTA	AEFHILLR	FIREHALL	AEFIKMRR	FIREMARK
AEFGIRS	GASIFIER	AEFHILLT	TEFILLAH	AEFIKRUW	WAUKRIFE
AEFGIISS	GASIFIES	AEFHILMS	FISHMEAL	AEFILLMS	FAMILLES
AEFGIKLN	FANGLIKE	AEFHILMT	HALFTIME	AEFILLNT	FLATLINE
AEFGIKNR	FREAKING	AEFHILNS	SHINLEAF	AEFILLOT	FELLATIO
AEFGILNR	FINAGLER	AEFHILOR	FORHAILE	AEFILLRW	FIREWALL
AEFGILNS	FINAGLES	AEFHILOX	HEXAFOIL	AEFILMNR	INFLAMER
AEFGILOS	FOLIAGES	AEFHILPP	HALFPIPE		RIFLEMAN
AEFGILRR	FRAGILER	AEFHILRS	FLASHIER	AEFILMNS	FLAMINES
AEFGILTT	LIFTGATE	AEFHIMSS	FAMISHES		INFLAMES
AEFGIMTU	FUMIGATE	AEFHIRST	FAITHERS		MISFALNE
AEFGINRW	WAFERING	AEFHIRSW	WHARFIES	AEFILMNT	FILAMENT
AEFGINRY	AREFYING	AEFHLMSU	SHAMEFUL	AEFILMST	FLAMIEST
AEFGINST	FEASTING	AEFHLNOT	HALFTONE	AEFILMSY	MAYFLIES
AEFGINTU	FANTIGUE	AEFHLNSS	HALFNESS	AEFILMTY	FEMALITY
AEFGIORR	FAIRGOER	AEFHLORS	FAHLORES	AEFILNNR	INFERNAL
AEFGIRRU	ARGUFIER	AEFHLPRS	PARFLESH	AEFILNNS	FLANNIES
AEFGIRSS	FRIGATES	AEFHLRSS	FLASHERS	AEFILNOR	FORELAIN
AEFGIRSU	ARGUFIES	AEFHLRST	FARTHELS	AEFILNOT	OLEFIANT
AEFGIRTU	FIGURATE	AEFHLRTY	FATHERLY	AEFILNPS	LIFESPAN
	FRUITAGE	AEFHLSST	FLASHEST	AEFILNRT	INFLATER
AEFGIRTW	GIFTWARE	AEFHLSTU	HASTEFUL	AEFILNRU	FRAULEIN
AEFGISTU	FATIGUES	AEFHMNRS	FRESHMAN	AEFILNST	INFLATES
AEFGLLNO	LONGLEAF	AEFHMORT	FATHOMER	AEFILNSV	FLAVINES
AEFGLLOP	FLAGPOLE	AEFHNRSW	FERNSHAW	AEFILNTT	ANTILEFT
AEFGLLSS	FLAGLESS	AEFHRSST	SHAFTERS	AEFILOOR	AEROFOIL
AEFGLLSU	FULLAGES	AEFHRSTT	FARTHEST	AEFILORS	FORESAIL
AEFGLMNU	FUGLEMAN	AEFIIKLW	WAIFLIKE	AEFILORT	FLOATIER
AEFGLMOP	MEGAFLOP	AEFIILLN	NAILFILE	AEFILOST	FOLIATES
AEFGLNOX	FLEXAGON	AEFIILMS	FAMILIES	AEFILPPR	FLAPPIER
AEFGLNRS	FLANGERS	AEFIILNS	FINALISE	AEFILPRX	PREFIXAL
AEFGLNSS	FANGLESS	AEFIILNT	ANTILIFE	AEFILPST	FLEAPITS
AEFGLOOR	FLOORAGE	AEFIILNZ	FINALIZE	AEFILRST	FLARIEST
AEFGLOPR	LEAPFROG	AEFIILSS	SALIFIES		FRAILEST
AEFGLORW	GAREFOWL	AEFIILST	FETIALIS	AEFILRSU	FAILURES
AEFGLOST	FLOTAGES		FILIATES	AEFILRSV	FAVRILES
AEFGLOSW	FLOWAGES	AEFIIMNS	INFAMIES	AEFILRSZ	FILAZERS
AEFGLPSU	PAGEFULS		INFAMISE	AEFILRTT	FILTRATE
AEFGLRTU	GRATEFUL	AEFIIMNZ	FEMINAZI	AEFILRTU	FAULTIER
AEFGLSTU	STAGEFUL		INFAMIZE		FILATURE
AEFGLTUX	FLUXGATE	AEFIIMRS	RAMIFIES	AEFILRUW	WEARIFUL

AEFILSSS	FILASSES	AEFKNRRS	FRANKERS	AEFLORRV	FLAVORER
AEFILSST	SEALIFTS	AEFKNRST	FRANKEST	AEFLORSS	SAFROLES
AEFILSSW	SAWFLIES	AEFKOPRS	FORSPEAK	AEFLORST	FLOATERS
AEFILSTT	FLATTIES	AEFKORRS	FORSAKER		FORESTAL
AEFILSTU	FISTULAE	AEFKORRW	WORKFARE		REFLOATS
AEFILSTV	FESTIVAL	AEFKORSS	FORSAKES	AEFLORSU	FUSAROLE
AEFILSTW	FLATWISE	AEFKORSW	WORKSAFE	AEFLORSY	FORELAYS
	FLAWIEST	AEFKORTU	FREAKOUT	AEFLORTW	FLEAWORT
AEFILSTX	FLAXIEST	AEFLLMMU	FLAMMULE	AEFLOSSU	FOSSULAE
AEFILSWY	LIFEWAYS	AEFLLNNS	FANNELLS	AEFLOSSW	SEAFOWLS
AEFILTUU	FAUTEUIL		FLANNELS	AEFLOSTT	FALSETTO
AEFIMMMR	MAMMIFER	AEFLLNNU	UNFALLEN	AEFLPPRS	FLAPPERS
AEFIMMRS	MISFRAME	AEFLLNRY	FERNALLY	AEFLPPRY	FLYPAPER
AEFIMNST	MANIFEST	AEFLLORT	FELLATOR	AEFLPRSS	FELSPARS
AEFIMORR	AERIFORM	AEFLLORU	FLORULAE	AEFLPRSU	FLAREUPS
AEFIMORT	FORMIATE	AEFLLORV	OVERFALL	AEFLPRSY	PALFREYS
AEFIMOST	FOAMIEST	AEFLLORW	FALLOWER	AEFLPSUU	PAUSEFUL
AEFIMRRS	FIREARMS	AEFLLOST	FLOATELS	AEFLRSSU	REFUSALS
AEFIMRRW	FIRMWARE	AEFLLPRT	PRATFELL	AEFLRSTT	FATTRELS
AEFIMRSS	MISFARES	AEFLLPSS	FLAPLESS		FLATTERS
AEFINNSS	FAINNESS	AEFLLPTU	PLATEFUL	AEFLRSTU	REFUTALS
	NAIFNESS	AEFLLRUW	AWFULLER	AEFLRSZZ	FRAZZLES
AEFINNST	INFANTES	AEFLLRUX	FLEXURAL	AEFLRTTU	AFLUTTER
AEFINNSZ	FANZINES	AEFLLSSW	FLAWLESS	AEFLRTTY	FLATTERY
AEFINOPR	PINAFORE	AEFLLSTT	FLATLETS	AEFLSSTU	FLATUSES
AEFINORS	FARINOSE	AEFLLSTY	FESTALLY		SULFATES
AEFINOTT	FETATION	AEFLMNOT	MATFELON	AEFLSTTT	FLATTEST
AEFINPRS	FIREPANS	AEFLMORU	FORMULAE	AEFLSTTU	TASTEFUL
	PANFRIES		FUMAROLE	AEFLSTUW	WASTEFUL
AEFINRRS	REFRAINS	AEFLMORW	LEAFWORM	AEFMNORS	FORAMENS
AEFINRRU	UNFAIRER	AEFLMOSS	FOAMLESS	AEFMNRRY	FERRYMAN
AEFINRRZ	FRANZIER	AEFLMOSY	FLAYSOME	AEFMNRST	RAFTSMEN
AEFINRSS	FAIRNESS	AEFLMOTU	FLAMEOUT	AEFMNRSU	FRAENUMS
	SANSERIF	AEFLMPRR	FRAMPLER	AEFMORRS	FOREARMS
	SERAFINS	AEFLMSUW	WAMEFULS	AEFMORRT	REFORMAT
AEFINRST	FAINTERS	AEFLNNNS	FLANNENS	AEFMORST	FOREMAST
	FENITARS	AEFLNNOT	FONTANEL		FORMATES
AEFINRSX	XERAFINS	AEFLNNOY	NONLEAFY		MORTSAFE
AEFINSST	FANSITES	AEFLNNTY	FENTANYL	AEFMORVW	WAVEFORM
AEFINSTT	FAINTEST	AEFLNOPR	FLAPERON	AEFMOSSU	FAMOUSES
AEFINSTW	FAWNIEST		FOREPLAN	AEFMOSUW	WAMEFOUS
AEFIORTV	FAVORITE	AEFLNOPT	PANTOFLE	AEFNNSTU	UNFASTEN
AEFIPRRT	FIRETRAP	AEFLNORS	FARNESOL	AEFNOPRR	PROFANER
AEFIQRSU	AQUIFERS	AEFLNORT	FLOREANT	AEFNOPRS	PROFANES
AEFIRRRS	FARRIERS	AEFLNOSV	FLAVONES	AEFNOPSY	PAYFONES
AEFIRRRY	FARRIERY	AEFLNRRU	FRENULAR	AEFNORRW	FOREWARN
AEFIRRST	FRATRIES	AEFLNRSS	SALFERNS	AEFNORST	SEAFRONT
AEFIRSTW	WASTRIFE	AEFLNRSU	FLANEURS	AEFNORSU	FURANOSE
AEFIRTUX	FIXATURE		FUNERALS	AEFNPRSU	SUPERFAN
AEFISTTT	FATTIEST	AEFLNRTU	FLAUNTER	AEFNRRST	TRANSFER
AEFKLLOT	FOLKTALE	AEFLNSST	FLATNESS	AEFNRRUY	FUNERARY
AEFKLMRY	FLYMAKER	AEFLNSTT	FLATTENS	AEFNRSTU	AFTERSUN
AEFKLNRS	FLANKERS	AEFLNSUU	FAUNULES	AEFNSSST	FASTNESS
AEFKLOSS	SEAFOLKS	AEFLNSUY	UNSAFELY	AEFNSSTU	UNSAFEST
AEFKLRST	FARTLEKS	AEFLOORS	SEAFLOOR	AEFNSTUY	UNSAFETY
AEFKLRUW	WREAKFUL	AEFLOORV	FOVEOLAR	AEFOORTW	FOOTWEAR
AEFKLSST	FLASKETS	AEFLOOSV	FOVEOLAS	AEFOPRRT	FOREPART
AEFKLSTT	TALKFEST	AEFLOPPT	PETAFLOP	AEFOPRST	FOREPAST
AEFKNORR	FORERANK	AEFLOPRT	TERAFLOP	AEFOPRSW	FOREPAWS
AEFKNORS	FORSAKEN	AEFLOPRY	FOREPLAY	AEFORRSV	FAVORERS
AEFKNPRR	PREFRANK	AEFLOPSW	PEAFOWLS	AEFORRSW	FORSWEAR

AEFORRSY	FORAYERS		GREASING	**AEGHIMST**	MEGAHITS
AEFORRUV	FAVOURER		SNAGGIER	**AEGHINNN**	HENNAING
AEFORRWY	FORWEARY	**AEGGINRV**	GREAVING	**AEGHINNT**	NAETHING
AEFORSSY	FORESAYS	**AEGGINRW**	WAGERING	**AEGHINNV**	HAVENING
AEFORSTV	OVERFAST	**AEGGINSS**	SIGNAGES	**AEGHINRS**	HEARINGS
AEFORSTW	FORWASTE	**AEGGINST**	NAGGIEST		HEARSING
	SOFTWARE	**AEGGIOPR**	ARPEGGIO		SHEARING
AEFORSTY	FORESTAY		GEROPIGA	**AEGHINRT**	EARTHING
AEFOSTTU	OUTFEAST	**AEGGIOSS**	ISAGOGES		HEARTING
AEFOSTUU	FEATUOUS	**AEGGIQRU**	QUAGGIER		INGATHER
AEFOSTUV	VOUTSAFE	**AEGGIRRU**	GARRIGUE	**AEGHINRV**	HAVERING
AEFPRSST	PRESSFAT	**AEGGIRST**	RAGGIEST	**AEGHINST**	GAHNITES
AEFRRSST	STRAFERS		STAGGIER		HEATINGS
AEFRSSTW	FRETSAWS	**AEGGIRSU**	GARIGUES	**AEGHINSV**	HEAVINGS
AEFRSTTU	TARTUFES	**AEGGIRWY**	EARWIGGY		SHEAVING
AEFRSTUW	WAFTURES	**AEGGISST**	SAGGIEST	**AEGHINSZ**	GENIZAHS
AEFRSWYZ	FRAWZEYS		STAGGIES	**AEGHINTT**	GNATHITE
AEGGGILN	ALEGGING	**AEGGISSW**	SWAGGIES	**AEGHIOPS**	ESOPHAGI
AEGGGINN	ENGAGING	**AEGGISTT**	TAGGIEST	**AEGHIPPR**	EPIGRAPH
AEGGGLSU	LUGGAGES	**AEGGLNPT**	EGGPLANT	**AEGHIPRT**	GRAPHITE
AEGGHIRS	SHAGGIER	**AEGGLNRS**	GANGRELS	**AEGHIRRS**	GHARRIES
AEGGHISS	HAGGISES	**AEGGLORY**	GARGOYLE	**AEGHIRSS**	GARISHES
AEGGHJRY	JAGGHERY	**AEGGLOWY**	WAYLEGGO	**AEGHLNOS**	HALOGENS
AEGGHLRS	HAGGLERS	**AEGGLRRS**	GARGLERS	**AEGHLNOY**	HYALOGEN
AEGGHMOS	HEMAGOGS	**AEGGLRST**	STRAGGLE	**AEGHLOPY**	HYPOGEAL
AEGGHMSU	MESHUGGA	**AEGGLRSW**	WAGGLERS	**AEGHLOSS**	GALOSHES
AEGGHOPY	GEOPHAGY	**AEGGLRSY**	GREYLAGS	**AEGHLRSU**	LAUGHERS
AEGGHORU	ROUGHAGE	**AEGGMNNS**	GANGSMEN	**AEGHLRTU**	LAUGHTER
AEGGHRSS	SHAGGERS	**AEGGMNOR**	GENOGRAM	**AEGHLRTY**	LETHARGY
AEGGIINV	GINGIVAE	**AEGGMORR**	ERGOGRAM	**AEGHLSTW**	THALWEGS
AEGGIJST	JAGGIEST	**AEGGMORT**	MORTGAGE	**AEGHMNOP**	PHENOGAM
AEGGIKNR	KNAGGIER	**AEGGNNSU**	GUNNAGES	**AEGHMNOS**	HOGMANES
AEGGILLN	ALLEGING	**AEGGNORV**	OVERGANG	**AEGHMNOY**	HOGMENAY
AEGGILLR	GRILLAGE	**AEGGNORW**	WAGGONER	**AEGHMOPT**	APOTHEGM
AEGGILMN	GLEAMING	**AEGGNRRS**	GRANGERS	**AEGHMORS**	HOMAGERS
AEGGILNN	ANGELING	**AEGGNRST**	GANGSTER	**AEGHMORT**	ETHOGRAM
	GLEANING	**AEGGOPRU**	GROUPAGE	**AEGHMSSU**	MESHUGAS
AEGGILNR	GANGLIER	**AEGGRSST**	GAGSTERS	**AEGHNNST**	HANGNEST
	LAGERING		STAGGERS	**AEGHNOPT**	HEPTAGON
	REGALING	**AEGGRSSW**	SWAGGERS		PATHOGEN
AEGGILNS	LIGNAGES	**AEGGRSTY**	STAGGERY	**AEGHNOPY**	HYPOGEAN
AEGGILNT	GELATING	**AEGHHMSU**	MESHUGAH	**AEGHNORV**	HANGOVER
	LEGATING	**AEGHIJRS**	JAGHIRES		OVERHANG
	TEAGLING	**AEGHILLM**	MEGILLAH	**AEGHNOSX**	HEXAGONS
AEGGILNU	LEAGUING	**AEGHILLS**	SHIGELLA	**AEGHNPSW**	SPANGHEW
AEGGILNV	GAVELING	**AEGHILMT**	MEGALITH	**AEGHNRSS**	GNASHERS
AEGGILOT	TALEGGIO	**AEGHILNR**	NARGHILE		SHERANGS
AEGGILRS	SLAGGIER		NARGILEH	**AEGHNSST**	STENGAHS
AEGGILRW	WAGGLIER	**AEGHILNS**	HEALINGS	**AEGHOPPR**	PROPHAGE
AEGGIMNN	MANEGING		LEASHING	**AEGHOPPY**	APOPHYGE
	MENAGING		SHEALING	**AEGHOPXY**	EXOPHAGY
AEGGIMRT	GREGATIM	**AEGHILNT**	ATHELING	**AEGHORST**	SHORTAGE
AEGGIMSU	MISGAUGE	**AEGHILNX**	EXHALING	**AEGHOSST**	HOSTAGES
AEGGINNR	ANGERING	**AEGHILPS**	SHAGPILE	**AEGHOSSU**	GASHOUSE
	ENRAGING	**AEGHILRT**	LITHARGE	**AEGHPRSS**	SPREAGHS
AEGGINNT	AGENTING		THIRLAGE	**AEGHPRTU**	UPGATHER
	NEGATING	**AEGHILRU**	LAUGHIER	**AEGHRTTU**	RETAUGHT
AEGGINNU	UNAGEING	**AEGHILST**	LAIGHEST	**AEGIILLU**	AIGUILLE
AEGGINNV	AVENGING	**AEGHILTT**	TEALIGHT	**AEGIILMN**	EMAILING
AEGGINOS	SEAGOING	**AEGHIMNW**	WEIGHMAN	**AEGIILMO**	OLIGEMIA
AEGGINRS	GEARINGS	**AEGHIMPS**	MAGESHIP	**AEGIILMR**	REMIGIAL

AEGIILNN	ALIENING		MALIGNER		STEALING
AEGIILNR	GAINLIER		MALINGER		TAGLINES
AEGIILRR	GLAIRIER	AEGILMNS	MEASLING	AEGILNSV	LEAVINGS
AEGIILTT	LITIGATE	AEGILMNT	LIGAMENT		SLEAVING
AEGIILTV	LIGATIVE		METALING	AEGILNSW	SWEALING
AEGIIMNR	IMAGINER		TEGMINAL	AEGILNSY	YEALINGS
	MIGRAINE	AEGILMNU	AEMULING	AEGILNTV	VALETING
AEGIIMNS	IMAGINES	AEGILMNY	YEALMING	AEGILNTX	EXALTING
AEGIIMTT	MITIGATE	AEGILMRS	GREMIALS	AEGILNTZ	TEAZLING
AEGIINNN	NENNIGAI		LAMIGERS	AEGILNUV	VAGINULE
AEGIINNR	ARGININE		REGALISM	AEGILOPS	SPOILAGE
AEGIINRR	GRAINIER	AEGILMRX	LEXIGRAM	AEGILOPT	PILOTAGE
AEGIIRRT	IRRIGATE	AEGILMTU	MULTIAGE	AEGILORS	GASOLIER
AEGIISTV	VESTIGIA	AEGILNNP	PANELING		GIRASOLE
AEGIJLNR	JANGLIER	AEGILNNR	LEARNING		SERAGLIO
AEGIKLNS	LINKAGES	AEGILNNS	EANLINGS	AEGILOSS	GOLIASES
	SNAGLIKE		LEANINGS		OILGASES
AEGIKLNT	GNATLIKE	AEGILNNT	GANTLINE		SOILAGES
AEGIKLNW	WEAKLING		LATENING	AEGILOST	LATIGOES
AEGIKLOT	GOATLIKE	AEGILNNU	UNGENIAL		OTALGIES
AEGIKMNR	REMAKING	AEGILNNW	WEANLING	AEGILOSU	EULOGIAS
AEGIKMRW	WIGMAKER	AEGILNNY	YEANLING	AEGILPPS	SLIPPAGE
AEGIKNNS	SNEAKING	AEGILNOR	GERANIOL	AEGILPPU	PUPILAGE
AEGIKNNW	WAKENING		REGIONAL	AEGILPRU	PLAGUIER
AEGIKNPS	SPEAKING	AEGILNOS	GASOLINE	AEGILRRU	GLAURIER
AEGIKNRS	SKEARING	AEGILNOT	GELATION	AEGILRSS	GLASSIER
AEGIKNRT	RETAKING		LEGATION	AEGILRST	GLARIEST
AEGIKNRW	REWAKING	AEGILNPR	GRAPLINE		REGALIST
	WREAKING		PEARLING	AEGILRSY	GREASILY
AEGIKNSS	SINKAGES	AEGILNPS	ELAPSING	AEGILRSZ	GLAZIERS
AEGIKNTW	TWEAKING		PLEASING	AEGILRTT	AGLITTER
AEGIKPPS	KIPPAGES	AEGILNPT	PLEATING	AEGILRTU	LIGATURE
AEGIKPRS	GARPIKES	AEGILNQU	EQUALING	AEGILRTY	REGALITY
AEGIKSTW	GAWKIEST	AEGILNRR	GNARLIER	AEGILRVW	LAWGIVER
AEGILLLS	ILLEGALS	AEGILNRS	ALIGNERS	AEGILRYZ	GLAZIERY
AEGILLMS	LEGALISM		ENGRAILS	AEGILSSS	GLASSIES
	MEGILLAS		NARGILES	AEGILSTZ	GLAZIEST
	MILLAGES		REALIGNS	AEGIMMST	GAMMIEST
AEGILLNR	ALLERGIN		SALERING	AEGIMNNO	NONIMAGE
AEGILLNS	GALLEINS		SANGLIER	AEGIMNNR	ENARMING
	NIGELLAS		SIGNALER		RENAMING
AEGILLNU	LINGULAE		SLANGIER	AEGIMNNS	MEANINGS
AEGILLNY	GENIALLY	AEGILNRT	ALERTING	AEGIMNNT	ENTAMING
AEGILLPR	PILLAGER		ALTERING	AEGIMNPR	EMPARING
AEGILLPS	PILLAGES		INTEGRAL	AEGIMNRR	REARMING
	SPILLAGE		RELATING	AEGIMNRS	GERMAINS
AEGILLRU	GUERILLA		TANGLIER		SMEARING
AEGILLRV	VILLAGER		TERAGLIN	AEGIMNRT	EMIGRANT
AEGILLSS	GALLISES		TRIANGLE		REMATING
AEGILLST	LEGALIST	AEGILNRV	RAVELING	AEGIMNRU	GERANIUM
	STILLAGE	AEGILNRX	RELAXING		MAUNGIER
	TILLAGES	AEGILNRY	LAYERING	AEGIMNSS	GAMINESS
AEGILLSV	VILLAGES		RELAYING		SEAMINGS
AEGILLSZ	GALLIZES		YEARLING	AEGIMNST	MANGIEST
AEGILLTU	LIGULATE	AEGILNSS	GAINLESS		MINTAGES
AEGILLTY	LEGALITY		GLASSINE		MISAGENT
AEGILMMR	AGLIMMER		LEASINGS		STEAMING
	GLAMMIER		SEALINGS		TEAMINGS
	LAMMIGER	AEGILNST	EASTLING	AEGIMNSV	VEGANISM
AEGILMNP	EMPALING		GELATINS	AEGIMNTU	TEGUMINA
AEGILMNR	GERMINAL		GENITALS		UMANGITE

AEGIMOOS	OOGAMIES	**AEGINRRS**	EARRINGS	**AEGIOSTX**	GEOTAXIS
AEGIMORR	ARMIGERO		GRAINERS	**AEGIPPRT**	GRIPTAPE
AEGIMORS	GORAMIES	**AEGINRRV**	AVERRING	**AEGIPPST**	GAPPIEST
AEGIMORW	WAGMOIRE	**AEGINRSS**	ASSIGNER	**AEGIPRSS**	PRISAGES
AEGIMPRS	EPIGRAMS		REASSIGN		SPAIRGES
	PRIMAGES		SEARINGS	**AEGIPRST**	GRAPIEST
AEGIMPRU	UMPIRAGE		SERINGAS	**AEGIPRTY**	PTERYGIA
AEGIMPSS	MISPAGES	**AEGINRST**	ANGRIEST	**AEGIPSST**	GASPIEST
AEGIMPST	PIGMEATS		ANGSTIER	**AEGIQRSU**	SQUIRAGE
AEGIMQRU	QUAGMIRE		ASTRINGE	**AEGIRRSS**	GRASSIER
AEGIMRRS	ARMIGERS		GANISTER	**AEGIRRSU**	SUGARIER
AEGIMRRT	RAGTIMER		GANTRIES	**AEGIRRSZ**	GRAZIERS
AEGIMRSS	GISARMES		GRANITES	**AEGIRRTY**	ARGYRITE
AEGIMRST	MAGISTER		INGRATES	**AEGIRSST**	AGISTERS
	MIGRATES		RANGIEST	**AEGIRSTT**	STRIGATE
	RAGTIMES		REASTING	**AEGIRSTV**	VIRGATES
	STERIGMA		STEARING		VITRAGES
AEGIMSST	MASSTIGE		TASERING	**AEGIRSUU**	AUGURIES
	SIGMATES	**AEGINRSV**	VINEGARS	**AEGIRSUY**	YUGARIES
AEGIMSSU	MISUSAGE	**AEGINRSW**	RESAWING	**AEGISSST**	GASSIEST
AEGIMSTU	GAUMIEST		SWEARING	**AEGISSTT**	STAGIEST
AEGINNNX	ANNEXING		WEARINGS	**AEGISSTW**	GAWSIEST
AEGINNOS	ANGINOSE	**AEGINRSY**	RESAYING	**AEGISTUZ**	GAUZIEST
	GANOINES		SYNERGIA	**AEGJLNOR**	JARGONEL
AEGINNOT	NEGATION	**AEGINRTT**	ARETTING	**AEGJLNRS**	JANGLERS
AEGINNPS	SNEAPING		GNATTIER	**AEGJLTUU**	JUGULATE
	SPEANING		TREATING	**AEGKKKNO**	ANGEKKOK
AEGINNRS	AGINNERS	**AEGINRTV**	AVERTING	**AEGKKNOS**	ANGEKOKS
	EARNINGS		GRIEVANT	**AEGKLLOT**	LEKGOTLA
	ENGRAINS		TAVERING	**AEGKLOSU**	KAGOULES
	GRANNIES		VINTAGER	**AEGKMNRU**	GUNMAKER
AEGINNRV	RAVENING	**AEGINRTW**	TWANGIER	**AEGKMRSY**	KERYGMAS
AEGINNRY	RENAYING		WATERING	**AEGKNORS**	KARENGOS
	YEARNING	**AEGINRTX**	RETAXING	**AEGKNRSS**	SKANGERS
AEGINNST	ANTIGENS	**AEGINRVW**	WAVERING	**AEGLLLMU**	GLUMELLA
	GENTIANS	**AEGINRVY**	VINEGARY	**AEGLLNNO**	NONLEGAL
	STEANING	**AEGINRWX**	REWAXING	**AEGLLNOS**	ALLONGES
AEGINNSU	GUANINES	**AEGINRWY**	WEARYING		GALLEONS
	SANGUINE	**AEGINSST**	EASTINGS	**AEGLLNOV**	LONGEVAL
AEGINNSW	WEANINGS		GENISTAS	**AEGLLNPS**	LANGSPEL
AEGINOPT	PINOTAGE		GIANTESS	**AEGLLNRS**	LANGRELS
AEGINORR	ORANGIER		SEATINGS	**AEGLLNST**	GELLANTS
AEGINORS	IGNAROES		TEASINGS	**AEGLLNSY**	LANGLEYS
	ORGANISE		TSIGANES	**AEGLLOOZ**	ZOOGLEAL
	ORIGANES	**AEGINSSY**	ESSAYING	**AEGLLOPR**	GALLOPER
AEGINORZ	ORGANIZE	**AEGINSTT**	ESTATING	**AEGLLORS**	ALLEGROS
AEGINOSS	AGONISES		TANGIEST	**AEGLLORV**	OVERGALL
AEGINOSZ	AGONIZES	**AEGINSTU**	SAUTEING	**AEGLLORY**	ALLEGORY
AEGINPPR	PAPERING		UNITAGES	**AEGLLOSS**	GAOLLESS
AEGINPPS	GENIPAPS	**AEGINSTV**	VINTAGES		GOALLESS
AEGINPRS	PREASING	**AEGINSTW**	SWEATING	**AEGLLOST**	TOLLAGES
	SPEARING	**AEGINSTY**	YEASTING	**AEGLLOTT**	TOLLGATE
AEGINPRT	RETAPING	**AEGINSTZ**	TZIGANES	**AEGLLRVY**	GRAVELLY
	TAPERING	**AEGINSVW**	WEAVINGS	**AEGLLSSU**	GALLUSES
AEGINPRV	REPAVING	**AEGINSVY**	SAVEYING		SEAGULLS
AEGINPRY	REPAYING	**AEGIOPRR**	PROGERIA		SULLAGES
AEGINPSS	SPAEINGS	**AEGIORSS**	ARGOSIES	**AEGLMNNO**	MANGONEL
	SPINAGES	**AEGIORSV**	VIRAGOES	**AEGLMNOY**	AMYLOGEN
AEGINPSY	GYPSEIAN	**AEGIORTV**	RAVIGOTE	**AEGLMNRS**	MANGLERS
AEGINPTY	EGYPTIAN	**AEGIOSTT**	GOATIEST	**AEGLMNSS**	GLASSMEN
AEGINQTU	EQUATING	**AEGIOSTU**	AGOUTIES	**AEGLMNTU**	GUNMETAL

AEGLMOPS	MEGALOPS		GRAUPELS	**AEGNORRY**	ORANGERY
AEGLMORS	GOMERALS		PLAGUERS	**AEGNORST**	ESTRAGON
AEGLMOSU	MOULAGES	**AEGLPSSU**	PLUSAGES		NEGATORS
AEGLMOTU	OUTGLEAM		PLUSSAGE		ORANGEST
AEGLMOTV	MEGAVOLT	**AEGLRRSU**	REGULARS		RAGSTONE
AEGLMPSU	PLUMAGES	**AEGLRRUV**	VULGARER		STONERAG
AEGLMRSU	MAULGRES	**AEGLRSTU**	GAULTERS	**AEGNORSW**	WAGONERS
AEGLMSSU	GAUMLESS		GESTURAL	**AEGNORTT**	TETRAGON
AEGLNNOR	NONGLARE		TRAGULES	**AEGNORTU**	OUTRANGE
AEGLNNPT	PLANGENT	**AEGLRTUY**	ARGUTELY	**AEGNORTY**	NEGATORY
AEGLNNSY	LANGSYNE	**AEGLSSTT**	GESTALTS	**AEGNORUV**	VARGUENO
AEGLNNTU	UNTANGLE	**AEGLSSUV**	VALGUSES	**AEGNOSSY**	NOSEGAYS
AEGLNOPT	GANTLOPE	**AEGLSTUU**	GLUTAEUS	**AEGNOTUY**	AUTOGENY
AEGLNORY	YEARLONG	**AEGLSTUV**	VULGATES	**AEGNPPRU**	GUNPAPER
AEGLNOST	TANGELOS	**AEGLSUUY**	GUAYULES	**AEGNPRRS**	RESPRANG
AEGLNOSU	ANGULOSE	**AEGMMNOR**	GAMMONER	**AEGNPRSS**	ENGRASPS
AEGLNPRS	GRAPNELS	**AEGMMRRU**	RUMMAGER	**AEGNPRST**	TREPANGS
	SPANGLER	**AEGMMRSU**	RUMMAGES	**AEGNPRSU**	SPEARGUN
	SPRANGLE	**AEGMNNOS**	AGNOMENS	**AEGNPRYY**	PANEGYRY
AEGLNPSS	PANGLESS	**AEGMNNOT**	MAGNETON	**AEGNRRST**	GRANTERS
	SPANGLES	**AEGMNORR**	RENOGRAM		REGRANTS
AEGLNPST	SPANGLET	**AEGMNORS**	MEGARONS		STRANGER
AEGLNRRW	WRANGLER	**AEGMNORV**	MANGROVE	**AEGNRSST**	STRANGES
AEGLNRSS	SLANGERS		VENOGRAM	**AEGNRSSY**	GRAYNESS
AEGLNRST	STRANGLE	**AEGMNOST**	GEOMANTS	**AEGNRSTU**	STRAUNGE
	TANGLERS		MAGNETOS	**AEGNRSTW**	TWANGERS
	TRANGLES		MEGATONS	**AEGNRSUZ**	SUNGAZER
AEGLNRSU	GRANULES		MONTAGES	**AEGNRSYY**	ASYNERGY
AEGLNRSW	WANGLERS	**AEGMNOSX**	MAGNOXES	**AEGNSSST**	GASTNESS
	WRANGLES	**AEGMNOXY**	XENOGAMY	**AEGNSSSY**	SYNGASES
AEGLNRSY	LARYNGES	**AEGMNRST**	GARMENTS	**AEGNSTTU**	GAUNTEST
AEGLNRTW	TWANGLER		MARGENTS		TUTENAGS
AEGLNRUY	GUNLAYER		RAGMENTS	**AEGOORST**	ROOTAGES
AEGLNSTT	GANTLETS	**AEGMNRTU**	ARGUMENT	**AEGOORSV**	VORAGOES
AEGLNSTU	LANGUETS		ARGUMENT	**AEGOOSWY**	WAYGOOSE
AEGLNSTW	TWANGLES	**AEGMNSSW**	SWAGSMEN	**AEGOPPRS**	PROPAGES
AEGLNSUW	GUNWALES	**AEGMNSSY**	GAMYNESS	**AEGOPPST**	STOPPAGE
AEGLNTTU	GAUNTLET	**AEGMNSTU**	AUGMENTS	**AEGOPPSU**	SUPPEAGO
AEGLNTUU	UNGULATE		MUTAGENS	**AEGOPRST**	PORTAGES
AEGLOOOZ	ZOOGLOEA	**AEGMOORS**	MOORAGES		POTAGERS
AEGLOOPU	APOLOGUE	**AEGMOPRW**	GAPEWORM	**AEGOPRTU**	PORTAGUE
AEGLOORY	AEROLOGY	**AEGMOPST**	POSTGAME	**AEGOPSST**	GESTAPOS
	AREOLOGY	**AEGMORRW**	WORMGEAR		POSTAGES
AEGLOOSZ	ZOOGLEAS	**AEGMORSS**	GOSSAMER	**AEGOPSSU**	SPOUSAGE
AEGLOPRS	PERGOLAS	**AEGMPRUZ**	GAZUMPER	**AEGOPSTT**	GATEPOST
AEGLOPRY	PLAYGOER	**AEGMPSTU**	STUMPAGE		POTTAGES
AEGLOPTT	PLOTTAGE	**AEGNNOPT**	PENTAGON	**AEGORRRT**	GARROTER
AEGLORST	GLOATERS	**AEGNNORT**	NEGATRON		REGRATOR
	LEGATORS	**AEGNNOST**	NEGATONS	**AEGORRST**	GARROTES
AEGLORSU	GLAREOUS		TONNAGES	**AEGORRTT**	GAROTTER
AEGLORSV	VORLAGES	**AEGNNPRT**	PREGNANT		GARROTTE
AEGLORTU	OUTGLARE	**AEGNNRSU**	GUNNERAS	**AEGORSSS**	SARGOSES
AEGLORTV	TRAVELOG	**AEGNNRTW**	GNATWREN	**AEGORSST**	STORAGES
AEGLORTW	WATERLOG	**AEGNNRTY**	GANNETRY	**AEGORSTT**	GAROTTES
AEGLORTY	GEOLATRY	**AEGNNSTT**	TANGENTS	**AEGORSTU**	OUTRAGES
AEGLOSSW	GALOWSES	**AEGNNSTU**	TUNNAGES	**AEGORSUV**	OUVRAGES
AEGLOSTV	VOLTAGES	**AEGNNTUU**	UNGUENTA	**AEGORSVY**	VOYAGERS
AEGLOSUY	GEALOUSY	**AEGNOORS**	OREGANOS	**AEGORTTU**	TUTORAGE
AEGLPPRR	GRAPPLER	**AEGNOPRR**	PARERGON	**AEGORTUU**	OUTARGUE
AEGLPPRS	GRAPPLES	**AEGNOPST**	PONTAGES	**AEGORUVY**	VOYAGEUR
AEGLPRSU	EARPLUGS	**AEGNORRS**	GROANERS	**AEGOSSTU**	OUTGASES

AEGOSSTW	STOWAGES	AEHIKSST	SHAKIEST
AEGOSSYZ	AZYGOSES		SHITAKES
AEGOSTTU	OUTGATES	AEHIKSSY	SAKIYEHS
AEGOSTTV	GAVOTTES	AEHILLNT	THALLINE
AEGOSTUZ	OUTGAZES	AEHILMNY	HYMENIAL
AEGPRRSS	GRASPERS	AEHILMOS	HEMIOLAS
	SPARGERS	AEHILMOT	HALIMOTE
AEGPRSTU	UPSTAGER	AEHILMQS	SHEQALIM
AEGPSSTU	UPSTAGES	AEHILMRU	HAULMIER
AEGPSSUU	GAUPUSES	AEHILMSW	LIMEWASH
AEGPSSUW	GAWPUSES	AEHILMSY	LEHAYIMS
AEGQRTUU	TRUQUAGE	AEHILNOP	APHELION
AEGRRSSS	GRASSERS		PHELONIA
AEGRRSSU	SUGARERS	AEHILNRS	INHALERS
AEGRRSSY	RYEGRASS	AEHILNRU	INHAULER
AEGRRSUU	AUGURERS	AEHILNSY	HYALINES
AEGRRSUV	GRAVURES	AEHILNTX	ANTHELIX
	VERRUGAS	AEHILNTZ	ZENITHAL
AEGRSSSU	SARGUSES	AEHILORS	AIRHOLES
AEGRSSUV	SEVRUGAS		SHOALIER
AEGRSTTY	STRATEGY	AEHILORT	AEROLITH
AEGRSTUU	AUGUSTER	AEHILOTZ	THIAZOLE
AEGSSTUU	AUGUSTES	AEHILPRS	EARLSHIP
AEGSTTTU	GUTTATES		HARELIPS
AEHHHIST	SHEHITAH		PLASHIER
AEHHIKSS	SHEIKHAS	AEHILPST	HAPLITES
AEHHIMPY	HYPHEMIA	AEHILRSS	HAIRLESS
AEHHIMTW	HAMEWITH	AEHILRSU	HAULIERS
AEHHINST	INSHEATH	AEHILRSV	LAVISHER
AEHHIPSW	PEISHWAH		SHRIEVAL
AEHHISST	HASHIEST	AEHILRTY	EARTHILY
	SHEHITAS		HEARTILY
AEHHISVY	YESHIVAH	AEHILSST	HELIASTS
AEHHLNTU	UNHEALTH		SHALIEST
AEHHNRSS	HARSHENS	AEHILSSV	LAVISHES
AEHHNRSW	HERNSHAW	AEHILSSW	SHAWLIES
AEHHORST	HAROSETH		WHAISLES
AEHHRRST	THRASHER	AEHILSTT	LATHIEST
AEHHRSST	HARSHEST		LITHATES
	THRASHES	AEHILSTY	HYALITES
AEHIIKLR	HAIRLIKE	AEHILSUV	VIHUELAS
AEHIIKRT	TERAKIHI	AEHILSWZ	WHAIZLES
AEHIIKST	SHIITAKE	AEHIMMSS	SHAMMIES
AEHIILMO	HEMIOLIA	AEHIMMST	HAMMIEST
AEHIILMT	LITHEMIA	AEHIMMSW	WHAMMIES
AEHIILNR	HAIRLINE	AEHIMNNU	INHUMANE
AEHIILST	HAILIEST	AEHIMNRS	HARMINES
AEHIIMNT	THIAMINE		SHIREMAN
AEHIIMOP	HEMIOPIA	AEHIMNSS	SHAMISEN
AEHIINNT	IANTHINE	AEHIMNST	HEMATINS
AEHIINTZ	THIAZINE	AEHIMNSU	HUMANISE
AEHIIRRW	WIREHAIR	AEHIMNTU	INHUMATE
AEHIIRST	HAIRIEST	AEHIMNUZ	HUMANIZE
AEHIKKLW	HAWKLIKE	AEHIMPRS	SAMPHIRE
AEHIKLLO	HALOLIKE		SERAPHIM
AEHIKLLT	LATHLIKE	AEHIMPRT	TERAPHIM
AEHIKLMS	SHEKALIM	AEHIMPSS	EMPHASIS
AEHIKLNP	KEPHALIN		MISSHAPE
AEHIKLRS	RASHLIKE		PHAEISMS
AEHIKMNZ	KHAZENIM	AEHIMPST	MATESHIP
AEHIKNSS	SNEAKISH		SHIPMATE

AEHIMRRS	MARSHIER
AEHIMRSS	MARISHES
	MISHEARS
AEHIMSSS	MESSIAHS
AEHIMSST	ATHEISMS
	MASHIEST
	MATHESIS
AEHIMTUY	EUTHYMIA
AEHINNPZ	PHENAZIN
AEHINNSS	SHANNIES
AEHINNTX	XANTHEIN
	XANTHINE
AEHINOPS	APHONIES
AEHINOPU	EUPHONIA
AEHINORT	ANTIHERO
AEHINOTT	THIONATE
AEHINPPY	EPIPHANY
AEHINPRS	HEPARINS
	PARISHEN
	SERAPHIN
AEHINPRT	PERIANTH
AEHINPRX	XERAPHIN
AEHINPST	PENTHIAS
	THESPIAN
AEHINRRS	SHARNIER
AEHINRRU	UNHAIRER
AEHINRSS	ARSHINES
AEHINRST	HAIRNETS
	INEARTHS
	THERIANS
AEHINRSV	ENRAVISH
	VANISHER
AEHINRSW	SHERWANI
AEHINRTU	HAURIENT
AEHINRTW	TARWHINE
AEHINRUW	WHARENUI
AEHINSSS	ASHINESS
	HESSIANS
AEHINSST	ANTHESIS
	SHANTIES
	SHEITANS
	STHENIAS
AEHINSSV	VANISHES
AEHINSSZ	HAZINESS
AEHINSTT	HESITANT
AEHINSTW	INSWATHE
AEHINTTT	ANTITHET
AEHIOPRS	APHORISE
AEHIOPRU	EUPHORIA
AEHIOPRZ	APHORIZE
AEHIOPTT	THIOTEPA
AEHIORRV	OVERHAIR
AEHIORST	HOARIEST
AEHIORTU	THIOUREA
AEHIPPRS	PAPISHER
	SAPPHIRE
AEHIPPSS	PAPISHES
AEHIPPST	EPITAPHS
	HAPPIEST
	PEATSHIP
AEHIPRRS	PHRASIER

AEHIPRRT	RATHRIPE	**AEHLMORS**	ARMHOLES	**AEHMOSTU**	OUTSHAME
AEHIPRSS	PARISHES	**AEHLMOSU**	HAMULOSE	**AEHMOSTW**	SOMEWHAT
	SHARPIES	**AEHLMPPT**	PAMPHLET	**AEHMOSTY**	HOMESTAY
AEHIPRST	TRIPHASE	**AEHLMPSW**	WHAMPLES	**AEHMPPRY**	PAMPHREY
AEHIPRTT	THREAPIT	**AEHLMRSS**	HARMLESS	**AEHMPRST**	HAMPSTER
AEHIPSSW	PEISHWAS	**AEHLMRST**	THERMALS	**AEHMRSSS**	SMASHERS
AEHIPSTZ	ZAPTIEHS	**AEHLMRSU**	HUMERALS	**AEHMRSST**	HAMSTERS
AEHIPSWW	WASHWIPE	**AEHLNOST**	ANETHOLS	**AEHMRSTU**	MAUTHERS
AEHIQSSU	QUASHIES		ETHANOLS	**AEHMRSTW**	MAWTHERS
AEHIRRRS	HARRIERS	**AEHLNOTY**	ETHANOYL	**AEHMSSSU**	SHAMUSES
AEHIRRSS	ARRISHES	**AEHLNPRS**	SHRAPNEL	**AEHMSSTT**	SHMATTES
AEHIRRST	TRASHIER	**AEHLNPTY**	ENTHALPY	**AEHMSTTY**	AMETHYST
AEHIRRSV	RAVISHER	**AEHLNRST**	ENTHRALS	**AEHMSUZZ**	MEZUZAHS
AEHIRRSW	WAIRSHER	**AEHLNSST**	NATHLESS	**AEHNNOPT**	PANTHEON
AEHIRRTW	WRATHIER	**AEHLNSSU**	UNLASHES	**AEHNNOTX**	XANTHONE
AEHIRSST	SHERIATS		UNSHALES	**AEHNNPRU**	NENUPHAR
AEHIRSSV	RAVISHES	**AEHLNSTY**	NAYTHLES	**AEHNNPSU**	UNSHAPEN
AEHIRSSW	SWASHIER	**AEHLNTUZ**	HAZELNUT	**AEHNNSUV**	UNSHAVEN
AEHIRSTU	THESAURI	**AEHLOPRT**	PLETHORA	**AEHNNSUW**	UNWASHEN
AEHIRSTW	SWATHIER	**AEHLOPSS**	HAPLOSES	**AEHNOOPT**	HANEPOOT
	WATERISH	**AEHLOPST**	TAPHOLES	**AEHNOPPY**	HYPOPNEA
AEHIRSTY	HYSTERIA	**AEHLOPTT**	HOTPLATE		PAYPHONE
AEHIRSWY	HAYWIRES	**AEHLORST**	LOATHERS	**AEHNOPRT**	HAPTERON
AEHIRTYZ	YAHRZEIT		RATHOLES	**AEHNOPST**	PHAETONS
AEHISSST	STASHIES	**AEHLORSY**	HOARSELY		PHONATES
AEHISSSW	SIWASHES	**AEHLORUV**	OVERHAUL		STANHOPE
AEHISSSY	ESSAYISH	**AEHLOSSS**	ASSHOLES	**AEHNOPSW**	WANHOPES
AEHISSTT	ATHEISTS	**AEHLOSST**	SHOALEST	**AEHNOPSY**	HYPONEAS
	HASTIEST	**AEHLOSTT**	LOATHEST	**AEHNOPXY**	XENOPHYA
	STAITHES	**AEHLPPRT**	THRAPPLE	**AEHNOQTU**	HAQUETON
AEHISSTU	HIATUSES	**AEHLPRSS**	PLASHERS	**AEHNORSS**	HOARSENS
AEHISSTW	WASHIEST		SPLASHER		SENHORAS
AEHISSVY	YESHIVAS	**AEHLPSSS**	SPLASHES	**AEHNOSSX**	HEXOSANS
AEHISTTW	THAWIEST	**AEHLPSST**	PATHLESS	**AEHNPRSS**	SHARPENS
	THWAITES		PLASHETS	**AEHNPRST**	PANTHERS
AEHJLOSW	JAWHOLES	**AEHLPSTU**	SULPHATE	**AEHNPSSU**	UNSHAPES
AEHJNNOS	JOHANNES	**AEHLRRTU**	URETHRAL	**AEHNPSTY**	PHYTANES
AEHKMOPW	MOPEHAWK	**AEHLRSSS**	SLASHERS	**AEHNRSSS**	RASHNESS
AEHKNNSU	UNSHAKEN	**AEHLRSST**	HARSLETS	**AEHNRSTU**	HAUNTERS
AEHKNOSW	HAWKNOSE		SLATHERS		UNEARTHS
AEHKNRST	THANKERS	**AEHLSSSS**	SASHLESS		UNHEARTS
AEHKNSSU	ANKUSHES	**AEHLSSTT**	STEALTHS		URETHANS
AEHKNSWW	NEWSHAWK	**AEHLSSTW**	THAWLESS	**AEHNRTTU**	EARTHNUT
AEHKOOPR	REAPHOOK	**AEHLSSWY**	SHAWLEYS	**AEHNSSTT**	THATNESS
AEHKOORS	HOROEKAS	**AEHLSTTY**	STEALTHY	**AEHNSSTW**	WHATNESS
AEHKOSTU	SHAKEOUT	**AEHMMRSS**	SHAMMERS	**AEHNSSTY**	SHANTEYS
AEHKPSSU	SHAKEUPS	**AEHMNNPY**	NYMPHEAN		SYNTHASE
AEHKRRSS	SHARKERS	**AEHMNOPR**	MORPHEAN	**AEHNSTUW**	UNSWATHE
AEHLLLTY	LETHALLY	**AEHMNORS**	HORSEMAN	**AEHOORST**	TOHEROAS
AEHLLMOP	LAMPHOLE		MENORAHS	**AEHOPPRS**	PROPHASE
AEHLLMTY	METHYLAL		RHAMNOSE	**AEHOPRRY**	PYORRHEA
AEHLLNRT	ENTHRALL		SHOREMAN	**AEHOPRSS**	PHAROSES
AEHLLNTU	UNLETHAL	**AEHMNOST**	HOASTMEN	**AEHOPRST**	PHORATES
AEHLLORW	HALLOWER	**AEHMNOSU**	HOUSEMAN		POTSHARE
AEHLLRSS	HERSALLS	**AEHMNPRU**	PREHUMAN	**AEHOPSST**	PATHOSES
AEHLLSST	HALTLESS	**AEHMNRST**	TRASHMEN		POTASHES
AEHLMMNS	HELMSMAN	**AEHMNSTU**	HUMANEST		SPATHOSE
AEHLMNOS	MANHOLES	**AEHMOPRT**	METAPHOR		TEASHOPS
AEHLMNOT	HOTELMAN	**AEHMOPST**	APOTHEMS	**AEHOPSTT**	HEATSPOT
	METHANOL	**AEHMORST**	TERAOHMS		POSTHEAT
AEHLMNUY	HUMANELY	**AEHMOSTT**	HEMOSTAT	**AEHOPSTU**	PHASEOUT

	TAPHOUSE		MILESIAN	**AEIINPST**	PATINISE
AEHOQRUU	HUAQUERO	**AEIILMPR**	IMPERIAL		PIANISTE
AEHORRRW	HARROWER	**AEIILMPS**	LIPEMIAS	**AEIINPTZ**	PATINIZE
AEHORRSV	OVERRASH	**AEIILMRS**	RAMILIES	**AEIINQSU**	EQUINIAS
AEHORRSW	WARHORSE	**AEIILMTT**	MILITATE	**AEIINRRV**	RIVERAIN
AEHORSST	ASTHORES	**AEIILNNS**	ANILINES	**AEIINRSS**	AIRINESS
	EARSHOTS	**AEIILNQU**	AQUILINE	**AEIINRST**	INERTIAS
	HAROSETS		QUINIELA		RAINIEST
	HOARSEST	**AEIILNRR**	AIRLINER	**AEIINRSY**	YERSINIA
AEHORSSW	SAWHORSE	**AEIILNRS**	AIRLINES	**AEIINRTZ**	TRIAZINE
AEHORSTT	RHEOSTAT		SNAILIER	**AEIINSST**	ISATINES
AEHORSTU	ARTHOUSE	**AEIILNRT**	INERTIAL		SANITIES
	OUTHEARS	**AEIILNSS**	SALINISE		SANITISE
	RATHOUSE	**AEIILNST**	ALIENIST		TENIASIS
AEHORSTX	OXHEARTS		LATINISE	**AEIINSSX**	SIXAINES
	THORAXES		LITANIES	**AEIINSTV**	VANITIES
AEHORSUV	HAVEOURS	**AEIILNSZ**	SALINIZE	**AEIINSTX**	AXINITES
AEHORSUW	WAREHOUS	**AEIILNTZ**	LATINIZE	**AEIINSTZ**	SANITIZE
AEHORSVW	OVERWASH	**AEIILPPT**	TAILPIPE	**AEIINSVV**	INVASIVE
AEHORSWY	HORSEWAY	**AEIILPRT**	LIPARITE	**AEIINTTT**	TITANITE
AEHOSSTU	HOUSESAT		REPTILIA	**AEIINTTU**	UINTAITE
AEHPPRSW	WHAPPERS	**AEIILQSU**	SILIQUAE	**AEIIPRRS**	PRAIRIES
AEHPPSSU	SHAPEUPS	**AEIILRSS**	LAIRISES	**AEIIPRST**	PARITIES
AEHPRRSS	PHRASERS	**AEIILRST**	LAIRIEST	**AEIIPRSW**	PAIRWISE
	SHARPERS		LISTERIA	**AEIIPRTZ**	TRAPEZII
AEHPRSST	SHARPEST	**AEIILRSV**	RIVALISE	**AEIIPRZZ**	PIZZERIA
	SPARTHES		VIRELAIS	**AEIIPSST**	EPITASIS
AEHPRSUX	HARUSPEX	**AEIILRSZ**	LAIRIZES	**AEIIPSTX**	EPITAXIS
AEHPRSUY	EUPHRASY	**AEIILRTT**	LITERATI	**AEIIRRST**	RARITIES
AEHPSTTT	PHATTEST	**AEIILRTZ**	RIVALIZE	**AEIIRRSV**	RIVIERAS
AEHQRSSU	QUASHERS	**AEIILSSS**	SILESIAS	**AEIIRRTT**	IRRITATE
	SQUASHER	**AEIILSSW**	LEWISIAS	**AEIIRSSS**	SIRIASES
AEHQSSSU	SQUASHES	**AEIILSTV**	VITALISE	**AEIIRSST**	IRISATES
AEHRRSST	TRASHERS	**AEIILSTX**	LAXITIES		SATIRISE
AEHRRSTU	URETHRAS	**AEIILSTZ**	TAILZIES	**AEIIRSTV**	VAIRIEST
AEHRRSTY	TRASHERY	**AEIILTVZ**	VITALIZE	**AEIIRSTW**	WISTERIA
AEHRRTTW	THWARTER	**AEIIMMRT**	MARITIME	**AEIIRSTX**	SEXTARII
AEHRSSST	SHASTERS	**AEIIMMSX**	MAXIMISE	**AEIIRSTZ**	SATIRIZE
AEHRSSSW	SWASHERS	**AEIIMMTX**	MAXIMITE	**AEIIRSVV**	VIVARIES
AEHRSSTT	SHATTERS	**AEIIMMXZ**	MAXIMIZE	**AEIIRTTT**	TRITIATE
AEHRSSTV	HARVESTS	**AEIIMNNT**	ANTIMINE	**AEIIRTVZ**	VIZIRATE
AEHRSSTW	SWATHERS	**AEIIMNRU**	URINEMIA	**AEIISTTV**	VITIATES
AEHRSTTY	SHATTERY	**AEIIMNST**	MINIATES	**AEIISTVZ**	IZVESTIA
AEHRSTUU	HAUTEURS	**AEIIMNSZ**	SIMAZINE	**AEIITTTV**	TITIVATE
AEHRSTVZ	SHVARTZE	**AEIIMNTT**	INTIMATE	**AEIITTVV**	VITATIVE
AEHSSTUX	EXHAUSTS	**AEIIMNTU**	MINUTIAE	**AEIJKLZZ**	JAZZLIKE
AEIIINTT	INITIATE	**AEIIMNTV**	VITAMINE	**AEIJLLSS**	JAILLESS
AEIIIRRT	RETIARII	**AEIIMOSS**	AMEIOSIS	**AEIJLMSS**	MAJLISES
AEIIKLLT	TAILLIKE	**AEIIMPRR**	IMPAIRER	**AEIJLNSV**	JAVELINS
AEIIKLNT	KALINITE	**AEIIMPSY**	EPIMYSIA	**AEIJLNSW**	JAWLINES
AEIIKNRS	KAISERIN	**AEIIMRSS**	MISRAISE	**AEIJLOPS**	JALOPIES
AEIIKNSS	AKINESIS	**AEIIMRST**	AIRTIMES	**AEIJLOSU**	JALOUSIE
AEIIKNST	KAINITES		SERIATIM	**AEIJMMST**	JAMMIEST
AEIIKRTY	TERIYAKI	**AEIIMRSV**	VIREMIAS	**AEIJMNSS**	JASMINES
AEIILLMR	MILLIARE	**AEIIMSTT**	IMITATES	**AEIJNRST**	NARTJIES
	RAMILLIE	**AEIINNRS**	SIRENIAN	**AEIJNRTU**	JAUNTIER
AEIILLRS	RAILLIES	**AEIINNRT**	TRIENNIA	**AEIJNSTT**	JANTIEST
AEIILLST	TAILLIES	**AEIINNSS**	INSANIES	**AEIJNSTU**	JAUNTIES
AEIILLTV	ILLATIVE	**AEIINNTV**	INNATIVE	**AEIJORST**	JAROSITE
AEIILMNN	MAINLINE	**AEIINOTT**	NOTITIAE	**AEIJORSV**	JAROVISE
AEIILMNS	ALIENISM	**AEIINPRT**	PAINTIER	**AEIJORVZ**	JAROVIZE

AEIJPSSS	JASPISES	**AEIKNRST**	KERATINS	**AEILLRSU**	RUELLIAS
AEIJSTZZ	JAZZIEST		NARKIEST	**AEILLRSY**	SERIALLY
AEIKKLLW	LIKEWALK	**AEIKNRSW**	SWANKIER	**AEILLRTU**	TAILLEUR
AEIKKLMS	MASKLIKE	**AEIKNRTW**	KNITWEAR	**AEILLRVX**	VEXILLAR
AEIKKLNT	TANKLIKE	**AEIKNSST**	SNAKIEST	**AEILLSSS**	SAILLESS
AEIKKLOO	KALOOKIE	**AEIKNSSW**	SWANKIES	**AEILLSST**	SITELLAS
AEIKKLPR	PARKLIKE	**AEIKNSSY**	KYANISES		TAILLESS
AEIKKMNO	KAKIEMON	**AEIKNSTU**	UNAKITES		TALLISES
AEIKKNRS	SKANKIER	**AEIKNSTV**	KISTVAEN	**AEILLSTT**	SITTELLA
AEIKLLMP	PALMLIKE	**AEIKNSTW**	TWANKIES		TALLITES
AEIKLLMS	SELAMLIK		WANKIEST	**AEILLSTW**	WALLIEST
AEIKLLPY	PLAYLIKE	**AEIKNSTY**	KYANITES	**AEILLSUV**	ALLUSIVE
AEIKLLSS	KILLASES	**AEIKNSYZ**	KYANIZES	**AEILLSYZ**	SLEAZILY
AEIKLLST	SALTLIKE	**AEIKOSST**	STOKESIA	**AEILLTUZ**	LAZULITE
AEIKLMOT	MOATLIKE	**AEIKPRRS**	SPARKIER	**AEILMMNS**	MELANISM
AEIKLMST	MASTLIKE	**AEIKPRSS**	SPARKIES	**AEILMMNT**	IMMANTLE
AEIKLMTT	TALKTIME	**AEIKPRST**	PARKIEST	**AEILMMNY**	IMMANELY
AEIKLNNP	PANNIKEL	**AEIKPSTW**	PAWKIEST	**AEILMMOR**	MEMORIAL
AEIKLNOS	KAOLINES	**AEIKQSTU**	QUAKIEST	**AEILMMOT**	IMMOLATE
AEIKLNOV	NOVALIKE	**AEIKRSST**	ASTERISK	**AEILMMRT**	TRILEMMA
AEIKLNPS	SKIPLANE		SARKIEST	**AEILMMSS**	MELISMAS
AEIKLNRR	KNARLIER	**AEIKRSTW**	WATERSKI	**AEILMMST**	MALMIEST
AEIKLNSS	SEALSKIN			**AEILMMTU**	MALEMIUT
AEIKLNST	LANKIEST	**AEILLLMO**	MALLEOLI	**AEILMNNO**	MINNEOLA
AEIKLNSW	SWANLIKE	**AEILLLMS**	ALLELISM	**AEILMNNP**	IMPANNEL
AEIKLNSY	SNEAKILY	**AEILLLNY**	LINEALLY	**AEILMNNS**	LINESMAN
AEIKLNTU	AUNTLIKE	**AEILLMNS**	MANILLES		MELANINS
AEIKLOPS	SOAPLIKE	**AEILLMNY**	MENIALLY	**AEILMNOS**	LAMINOSE
AEIKLOST	KEITLOAS	**AEILLMSS**	MAILLESS		MINEOLAS
AEIKLPRS	SPARLIKE	**AEILLMSY**	MESIALLY		SEMOLINA
AEIKLPRT	TRAPLIKE	**AEILLNNO**	LANOLINE	**AEILMNPS**	IMPANELS
AEIKLPSS	KALPISES	**AEILLNNS**	NAINSELL		MANIPLES
AEIKLPSW	WASPLIKE	**AEILLNNU**	UILLEANN	**AEILMNRS**	MARLINES
AEIKLQUY	QUAYLIKE		UNLINEAL		MINERALS
AEIKLRSS	SERKALIS	**AEILLNOR**	ALLERION		MISLEARN
AEIKLRST	LARKIEST	**AEILLNPS**	SPLENIAL	**AEILMNRT**	TERMINAL
	STALKIER	**AEILLNPY**	ALPINELY		TRAMLINE
	STARLIKE	**AEILLNQU**	QUINELLA	**AEILMNRU**	LEMURIAN
AEIKLRSV	KLAVIERS	**AEILLNRY**	LINEARLY	**AEILMNSS**	ISLESMAN
AEIKLRTW	WARTLIKE	**AEILLNSS**	AINSELLS	**AEILMNST**	AILMENTS
AEIKLRVY	VALKYRIE		NAILLESS		ALIMENTS
AEIKLRWY	WALKYRIE		SENSILLA		MANLIEST
AEIKLSSS	SAIKLESS	**AEILLNUV**	LAEVULIN		MELANIST
AEIKLSTT	TALKIEST	**AEILLNVY**	VENIALLY		SMALTINE
AEIKMMSS	MISMAKES	**AEILLOSS**	LOESSIAL	**AEILMNSU**	ALUMINES
AEIKMNRS	RAMEKINS	**AEILLOTV**	VOLATILE	**AEILMOOV**	MOVIEOLA
AEIKMNST	MANKIEST	**AEILLPPR**	APPERILL	**AEILMOPR**	PROEMIAL
	MISTAKEN	**AEILLPRS**	PERILLAS	**AEILMOPS**	EPISOMAL
AEIKMPRS	RAMPIKES	**AEILLPSS**	ILLAPSES	**AEILMORS**	MORALISE
AEIKMPSS	MISSPEAK	**AEILLPST**	PALLIEST	**AEILMORT**	AMITROLE
AEIKMRST	MISTAKER		PASTILLE		ROLAMITE
	SITKAMER	**AEILLPSV**	LIPSALVE	**AEILMORZ**	MORALIZE
AEIKMSST	MISTAKES	**AEILLQSU**	LALIQUES	**AEILMOST**	LOAMIEST
AEIKMSTW	MAWKIEST		SQUILLAE	**AEILMOSV**	SEMIOVAL
AEIKNNST	NEATNIKS	**AEILLQTU**	TEQUILLA	**AEILMOSW**	WAILSOME
AEIKNNTU	ANTINUKE	**AEILLRRS**	RALLIERS	**AEILMPRS**	IMPALERS
AEIKNPRR	PRANKIER	**AEILLRRY**	RAILLERY		IMPEARLS
AEIKNPRS	RANPIKES	**AEILLRSS**	RAILLESS		LEMPIRAS
AEIKNPST	SNAKEPIT		SALLIERS	**AEILMPRU**	PLUMERIA
AEIKNRRR	KNARRIER	**AEILLRST**	LITERALS	**AEILMPRV**	PRIMEVAL
AEIKNRRS	SNARKIER		TALLIERS	**AEILMPSS**	PESSIMAL
			TRIELLAS		

AEILMPST	IMPLATES		PLAINEST			VARIOLES
	PALMIEST	**AEILNPSU**	SPINULAE			VOLARIES
	PALMIETS	**AEILNPSW**	PINWALES	**AEILORSY**	ROYALISE
	PETALISM	**AEILNPSX**	EXPLAINS	**AEILORSZ**	SOLARIZE
	SEPTIMAL	**AEILNPTT**	TINPLATE	**AEILORTT**	LITERATO
AEILMPTY	PLAYTIME	**AEILNPTY**	PENALITY	**AEILORTV**	VIOLATER
AEILMQRU	QUALMIER	**AEILNQSU**	QUINELAS	**AEILORTZ**	TRIAZOLE
AEILMRRS	LARMIERS	**AEILNQTU**	QUANTILE	**AEILORVZ**	VALORIZE
AEILMRSS	REALISMS	**AEILNRRS**	SNARLIER	**AEILORYZ**	ROYALIZE
AEILMRST	LAMISTER	**AEILNRSS**	RAINLESS	**AEILOSST**	ISOLATES
	LAMITERS	**AEILNRST**	ENTRAILS	**AEILOSSX**	OXALISES
	MARLIEST		LARNIEST	**AEILOSTT**	TOTALISE
	MARLITES		LATRINES	**AEILOSTV**	VIOLATES
	MISALTER		RATLINES	**AEILOTTV**	VOLITATE
AEILMRSY	MISLAYER		REINSTAL	**AEILOTTZ**	TOTALIZE
	SMEARILY		RETINALS	**AEILPPQU**	APPLIQUE
AEILMRTT	REMITTAL		SLANTIER	**AEILPPRS**	APPERILS
AEILMRUV	VELARIUM		TRENAILS		APPLIERS
AEILMSSX	SMILAXES	**AEILNRSU**	LUNARIES	**AEILPRRS**	REPRISAL
AEILMSTT	MALTIEST	**AEILNRSV**	RAVELINS	**AEILPRRT**	PALTRIER
	METALIST	**AEILNRSX**	RELAXINS		PRETRIAL
	SMALTITE	**AEILNRSY**	INLAYERS	**AEILPRST**	PILASTER
AEILMSTU	SIMULATE		SNAILERY		PLAISTER
AEILMSTY	LAYTIMES	**AEILNRTT**	RATTLINE		PLAITERS
	STEAMILY	**AEILNRTU**	AUNTLIER	**AEILPRSU**	SPIRULAE
	TALEYSIM		RETINULA	**AEILPRSV**	PREVAILS
AEILMSUV	MISVALUE		TENURIAL	**AEILPRSW**	SLIPWARE
AEILMTTU	MUTILATE	**AEILNRTV**	INTERVAL	**AEILPRTV**	LIVETRAP
	ULTIMATE	**AEILNRTY**	INTERLAY	**AEILPRXY**	PYREXIAL
AEILNNOS	SOLANINE	**AEILNSST**	EASTLINS	**AEILPSST**	PALSIEST
AEILNNPU	PINNULAE		ELASTINS	**AEILPSSY**	PAISLEYS
AEILNNRT	INTERNAL		NAILSETS	**AEILPSTT**	PLATIEST
AEILNNSY	INSANELY		SALIENTS	**AEILPSTY**	PTYALISE
AEILNNTY	INNATELY		SALTINES	**AEILPSUV**	PLAUSIVE
AEILNOPR	PELORIAN		STANIELS	**AEILPTYZ**	PTYALIZE
AEILNOPS	OPALINES	**AEILNSSU**	INULASES	**AEILQRSU**	SQUAILER
AEILNOPT	ANTIPOLE	**AEILNSSZ**	LAZINESS	**AEILQRTU**	QUARTILE
AEILNOPU	POULAINE	**AEILNSTU**	ALUNITES		REQUITAL
AEILNORS	AILERONS		INSULATE	**AEILQSTU**	LIQUATES
	ALERIONS	**AEILNSTV**	VENTAILS		TEQUILAS
	ALIENORS	**AEILNSTW**	LAWNIEST	**AEILQSUY**	QUEASILY
AEILNORT	ORIENTAL	**AEILNSUV**	UNVAILES	**AEILQTUY**	EQUALITY
	RELATION	**AEILNSUW**	LAUWINES	**AEILRRST**	RETIRALS
	TAILERON	**AEILNSUY**	UNEASILY		RETRIALS
AEILNORV	OVERLAIN	**AEILNTVY**	NATIVELY		TRAILERS
AEILNOSS	ANISOLES		VENALITY	**AEILRRSU**	RURALISE
AEILNOST	ELATIONS	**AEILNUVV**	UNIVALVE	**AEILRRTT**	RATTLIER
	INSOLATE	**AEILOORV**	OVARIOLE	**AEILRRTU**	RURALITE
	TOENAILS	**AEILOPPR**	OILPAPER	**AEILRRTY**	LITERARY
AEILNOSX	SILOXANE	**AEILOPPT**	OPPILATE	**AEILRRUZ**	RURALIZE
AEILNOTT	TONALITE	**AEILOPRS**	PELORIAS	**AEILRSST**	REALISTS
AEILNPPT	PIEPLANT		POLARISE		SALTIERS
AEILNPRS	PEARLINS	**AEILOPRT**	EPILATOR		SALTIRES
	PRALINES		PETIOLAR		SLAISTER
AEILNPRT	INTERLAP	**AEILOPRZ**	POLARIZE	**AEILRSSV**	REVISALS
	TRAPLINE	**AEILOPST**	SPOLIATE		RIVALESS
	TRIPLANE	**AEILORRT**	RETAILOR	**AEILRSTT**	TERTIALS
AEILNPSS	PAINLESS	**AEILORSS**	SOLARISE	**AEILRSTU**	URALITES
	SPANIELS	**AEILORST**	SOTERIAL	**AEILRSVV**	REVIVALS
AEILNPST	PANELIST	**AEILORSV**	OVERSAIL	**AEILRSVY**	VIRELAYS
	PANTILES		VALORISE	**AEILRTTY**	ALTERITY

AEILRTUV	VAULTIER	AEIMNRSU	ANEURISM		TERATISM
AEILRTUZ	LAZURITE	AEIMNRSY	SEMINARY	AEIMRSTU	MURIATES
AEILRTVV	TRIVALVE	AEIMNRTT	INTERMAT		SEMITAUR
AEILRTWY	WATERILY		MARTINET	AEIMRSTV	MARVIEST
AEILRTXZ	ZELATRIX	AEIMNRTU	RUMINATE		VITAMERS
AEILSSSV	VESSAILS	AEIMNRTW	WARIMENT	AEIMRSTW	WARTIMES
AEILSSTT	SALTIEST	AEIMNRTY	TYRAMINE	AEIMRSTX	MATRIXES
	SLATIEST	AEIMNSSS	SAMISENS	AEIMRSTY	SYMITARE
AEILSSTW	SWALIEST	AEIMNSST	MANTISES	AEIMRSWW	SWIMWEAR
AEILSTTW	WALTIEST		MATINESS	AEIMSSST	ASTEISMS
AEILSTVY	VILAYETS	AEIMNSSU	ANIMUSES		MASSIEST
AEILSTWY	SWEATILY	AEIMNSSZ	MAZINESS		MISSEATS
AEILSTYY	YEASTILY	AEIMNSUV	MAUVEINS	AEIMSSSV	MASSIVES
AEIMMMRZ	MAMZERIM		MAUVINES	AEIMSSTT	ETATISMS
AEIMMNNT	IMMANENT	AEIMNTTU	MATUTINE		MASTIEST
AEIMMNOS	SEMINOMA	AEIMNTVZ	VIZAMENT		MISSTATE
AEIMMNOT	AMMONITE	AEIMOOPS	IPOMOEAS	AEIMSSTX	MASTIXES
AEIMMNSS	MISNAMES	AEIMOPRS	MEROPIAS	AEIMSSTZ	MESTIZAS
AEIMMPRS	SPAMMIER	AEIMOPSX	APOMIXES	AEIMSTYZ	AZYMITES
AEIMMPSS	SPAMMIES	AEIMOPTT	OPTIMATE	AEIMTTUV	MUTATIVE
AEIMMPST	PSAMMITE	AEIMORRS	ARMOIRES	AEINNNOX	ANNEXION
AEIMMRRS	SMARMIER		ARMORIES	AEINNOPS	SAPONINE
AEIMMRST	MARMITES	AEIMORST	AMORTISE	AEINNOPV	PAVONINE
	RAMMIEST		ATOMISER	AEINNORS	RAISONNE
	TRAMMIES	AEIMORTT	AMORETTI	AEINNORT	ANOINTER
AEIMMRTU	IMMATURE	AEIMORTZ	AMORTIZE		INORNATE
AEIMMSST	MISMATES		ATOMIZER		REANOINT
AEIMMSTT	SEMIMATT	AEIMOSST	AMITOSES	AEINNORW	NANOWIRE
AEIMMSZZ	MIZMAZES		AMOSITES	AEINNOST	ENATIONS
AEIMNNOT	ANTINOME		ATOMISES		SONATINE
	NOMINATE		OSMIATES	AEINNOTT	INTONATE
AEIMNNRS	REINSMAN	AEIMOSTX	TOXEMIAS	AEINNOTV	INNOVATE
AEIMNNRT	TRAINMEN	AEIMOSTZ	ATOMIZES		VENATION
AEIMNNST	MANNITES	AEIMOTTV	MOTIVATE	AEINNPRS	PANNIERS
AEIMNOPT	PTOMAINE	AEIMPRRS	RAMPIRES	AEINNPST	PANTINES
AEIMNORS	MORAINES	AEIMPRRT	IMPARTER	AEINNRRS	INSNARER
	ROMAINES		TRAMPIER	AEINNRRT	INERRANT
	ROMANISE	AEIMPRSS	IMPRESAS	AEINNRRS	INSNARES
AEIMNORW	AIRWOMEN		MISPARSE	AEINNRST	ENTRAINS
AEIMNORZ	ARMOZINE		SAMPIRES		TRANNIES
	ROMANIZE	AEIMPRST	APTERISM	AEINNRSU	ANEURINS
AEIMNOSS	ANEMOSIS		PRIMATES		UNARISEN
AEIMNOST	AMNIOTES	AEIMPRSV	VAMPIRES	AEINNRSW	SWANNIER
	MASONITE	AEIMPRSW	SWAMPIER	AEINNRTT	INTRANET
	MISATONE	AEIMPRTU	APTERIUM	AEINNSST	INSANEST
	SOMNIATE	AEIMPSSS	IMPASSES		STANINES
AEIMNOSU	MOINEAUS	AEIMPSST	IMPASTES	AEINNSSV	VAINNESS
AEIMNOSW	WOMANISE		PASTIMES	AEINNSSW	SWANNIES
AEIMNOTZ	MONAZITE		TIMEPASS	AEINNSSZ	ZANINESS
AEIMNOUX	EXONUMIA	AEIMPSTV	VAMPIEST	AEINNSTT	ANTIENTS
AEIMNOWZ	WOMANIZE	AEIMQRSU	MARQUISE		STANNITE
AEIMNPRZ	PRIZEMAN	AEIMRRRS	MARRIERS	AEINNTUV	UNNATIVE
AEIMNPSX	PANMIXES	AEIMRRSS	SIMARRES	AEINOPPR	ROANPIPE
AEIMNQRU	RAMEQUIN	AEIMRSST	ASTERISM	AEINOPPT	ANTIPOPE
AEIMNRRS	MARINERS		MAISTERS	AEINOPRT	ATROPINE
AEIMNRRV	RIVERMAN		MISRATES	AEINOPSS	SENOPIAS
AEIMNRSS	SEMINARS		SEMITARS	AEINOPST	SAPONITE
	SIRNAMES		SMARTIES	AEINOPSZ	EPIZOANS
AEIMNRST	MERANTIS	AEIMRSSV	MISAVERS	AEINOPTZ	TOPAZINE
	MINARETS	AEIMRSSY	EMISSARY	AEINOQRU	AEQUORIN
	RAIMENTS	AEIMRSTT	MISTREAT	AEINOQTU	EQUATION

AEINORRT	ANTERIOR			TRAINERS		**AEIOPSST**	SOAPIEST
AEINORRW	IRONWARE			TRANSIRE		**AEIOPTTV**	OPTATIVE
AEINORSS	ERASIONS		**AEINRRTT**	RETIRANT		**AEIOQSSU**	SEQUOIAS
	SENSORIA		**AEINRRTV**	VERATRIN		**AEIORRRS**	ARRIEROS
AEINORST	ANOESTRI		**AEINRRTW**	INTERWAR		**AEIORRSS**	ROSARIES
	ARSONITE		**AEINRRUW**	UNWARIER		**AEIORRST**	ROARIEST
	NOTAIRES		**AEINRSST**	ARTINESS			ROTARIES
	NOTARIES			RESIANTS		**AEIORRSV**	SAVORIER
	NOTARISE			RETSINAS		**AEIORSSV**	SAVORIES
	ROSINATE			SNARIEST		**AEIORSTT**	TOASTIER
	SENORITA			STAINERS		**AEIORSTU**	OUTRAISE
AEINORSV	AVERSION			STARNIES			SAUTOIRE
AEINORTT	TENTORIA			STEARINS		**AEIORSTV**	TRAVOISE
AEINORTZ	NOTARIZE		**AEINRSSU**	ANURESIS			VIATORES
AEINOSST	ASSIENTO			SENARIUS			VOTARIES
	ASTONIES		**AEINRSSW**	WARINESS		**AEIORSVW**	AVOWRIES
AEINOSSV	EVASIONS		**AEINRSSX**	XERANSIS		**AEIORTTV**	ROTATIVE
AEINOSSX	SAXONIES		**AEINRSTT**	INTREATS		**AEIOSSST**	SOSATIES
AEINOSTV	STOVAINE			NITRATES		**AEIOSSTT**	TOASTIES
AEINOSTX	SAXONITE			STRAITEN		**AEIOSSTZ**	AZOTISES
AEINOSXZ	OXAZINES			TARTINES		**AEIOSTZZ**	AZOTIZES
AEINOTVX	VEXATION			TERTIANS		**AEIPPPST**	PAPPIEST
AEINPPPS	PANPIPES		**AEINRSTU**	RUINATES		**AEIPPRRS**	APPRISER
AEINPPRS	SNAPPIER			TAURINES		**AEIPPRRT**	TRAPPIER
AEINPPRY	PAPYRINE			URANITES		**AEIPPRRZ**	APPRIZER
AEINPPSS	PINESAPS			URINATES		**AEIPPRSS**	APPRISES
AEINPPST	NAPPIEST		**AEINRSTW**	TINWARES		**AEIPPRST**	PERIAPTS
AEINPRRT	PRETRAIN		**AEINRSUV**	VAURIENS		**AEIPPRSZ**	APPRIZES
	TERRAPIN		**AEINRSUZ**	AZURINES		**AEIPPSST**	SAPPIEST
AEINPRRU	UNREPAIR			SUZERAIN		**AEIPPSTY**	YAPPIEST
AEINPRST	PAINTERS		**AEINRSVV**	VERVAINS		**AEIPPSTZ**	ZAPPIEST
	PANTRIES		**AEINRSZZ**	SNAZZIER		**AEIPQRTU**	PRATIQUE
	PERTAINS		**AEINRTTU**	TAINTURE		**AEIPRRRS**	PARRIERS
	PINASTER		**AEINRTUV**	VAUNTIER			SPARRIER
	PRISTANE		**AEINRTVW**	VAWNTIER		**AEIPRRSS**	ASPIRERS
	REPAINTS		**AEINSSST**	SAINTESS			PRAISERS
AEINPRSU	UNPRAISE			SESTINAS		**AEIPRRST**	PARTIERS
AEINPRSW	SPAWNIER		**AEINSSSV**	VINASSES		**AEIPRRSU**	UPRAISER
AEINPRTT	TRIPTANE		**AEINSSTT**	ANTSIEST		**AEIPRRSY**	SPRAYIER
AEINPRTU	PAINTURE			INSTATES		**AEIPRRTV**	PRIVATER
AEINPRTX	EXPIRANT			NASTIEST		**AEIPRSST**	PASTRIES
AEINPSST	SAPIENTS			SATINETS			PIASTERS
	STEAPSIN			TITANESS			PIASTRES
AEINPSSU	APNEUSIS		**AEINSSTU**	SINUATES			RASPIEST
AEINPSSW	WINESAPS		**AEINSSTX**	SEXTANS			TRAIPSES
AEINPSTT	PATIENTS		**AEINSSVW**	WAVINESS		**AEIPRSSU**	UPRAISES
AEINPSTU	PETUNIAS		**AEINSSWX**	WAXINESS		**AEIPRSSV**	PARVISES
	SUPINATE		**AEINSTTT**	NATTIEST			PAVISERS
AEINPSTY	EPINASTY		**AEINSTTV**	TASTEVIN		**AEIPRSSX**	PRAXISES
AEINPTTY	ANTITYPE		**AEINSTTW**	TAWNIEST		**AEIPRSTV**	PRIVATES
AEINQRTU	ANTIQUER		**AEINSTUV**	SUIVANTE		**AEIPRSTW**	WIRETAPS
	QUAINTER		**AEINSTWY**	YAWNIEST		**AEIPRSTY**	ASPERITY
AEINQSTU	ANTIQUES		**AEINSUVV**	VESUVIAN		**AEIPRSVY**	VESPIARY
	QUANTISE		**AEINTTUU**	AUTUNITE		**AEIPRSWW**	WARPWISE
AEINQTTU	EQUITANT		**AEIOOPTT**	PATOOTIE		**AEIPRSXY**	PYREXIAS
AEINQTUY	ANTIQUEY		**AEIOPPST**	APPOSITE		**AEIPRTVY**	VARITYPE
AEINQTUZ	QUANTIZE		**AEIOPRRT**	PRIORATE		**AEIPSSST**	PASTISES
AEINRRST	RESTRAIN		**AEIOPRRW**	AIRPOWER		**AEIPSSSV**	PASSIVES
	RETRAINS		**AEIOPRSV**	VAPORISE			PAVISSES
	STRAINER		**AEIOPRTX**	EXPIATOR		**AEIPSSTT**	PASTIEST
	TERRAINS		**AEIOPRVZ**	VAPORIZE		**AEIPSSTW**	WASPIEST

AEIPSSTY	EPISTASY	AEJLOSUY	JEALOUSY	AEKOPRRT	PARROKET
AEIPSZZZ	PIZAZZES	AEJLOSUZ	AZULEJOS	AEKOPRSS	PRESOAKS
	PIZZAZES	AEJNORSZ	ZANJEROS	AEKOPSTU	OUTSPEAK
AEIPTTUV	PUTATIVE	AEKKKMRU	KRUMKAKE		SPEAKOUT
AEIQRRRU	QUARRIER	AEKKLLWY	LYKEWALK	AEKORRSS	ROSAKERS
AEIQRRSU	QUARRIES	AEKKMNOO	KAKEMONO	AEKORRWW	WORKWEAR
AEIQRRTU	QUARTIER	AEKKNRSS	SKANKERS	AEKORSSS	KAROSSES
AEIQRUZZ	QUAZZIER	AEKKOSSS	SAKKOSES	AEKORSTV	OVERTASK
AEIRRRST	STARRIER	AEKLLSTU	KELLAUTS		VOERTSAK
	TARRIERS	AEKLMORS	LARKSOME	AEKORSTW	SEATWORK
AEIRRRSV	ARRIVERS	AEKLMOSU	LEUKOMAS	AEKORTUY	EUKARYOT
AEIRRSST	TARSIERS	AEKLMRUW	LUKEWARM	AEKOSTTU	OUTSKATE
AEIRRSSY	SISERARY	AEKLMRUY	YARMULKE		OUTTAKES
AEIRRSTT	RETRAITS	AEKLNNSS	LANKNESS		STAKEOUT
	STRAITER	AEKLNOSY	ANKYLOSE		TAKEOUTS
	TARRIEST	AEKLNPPS	KNAPPLES	AEKPPSSU	UPSPEAKS
AEIRRSTW	STRAWIER	AEKLNPRS	PRANKLES	AEKPRRSS	SPARKERS
AEIRRSVV	VIVERRAS	AEKLNPRT	PLANKTER	AEKPRSSY	PASSKEYS
AEIRRTTT	RETRAITT	AEKLNRSS	RANKLESS	AEKQRSUW	SQUAWKER
AEIRRTTY	TERTIARY	AEKLNRSV	KLAVERNS	AEKRRSST	STARKERS
AEIRRVWY	RIVERWAY	AEKLNSST	TANKLESS	AEKRSSTT	STARKEST
AEIRSSST	ASSISTER	AEKLOPRT	LAKEPORT	AEKSSSTT	TSATSKES
	TIRASSES	AEKLOPRW	ROPEWALK	AELLLORY	LOYALLER
AEIRSSSZ	ASSIZERS	AEKLOPTY	KALOTYPE	AELLLRTU	TELLURAL
AEIRSSTT	ARTISTES	AEKLORSY	ROKELAYS	AELLLSUV	VULSELLA
	ARTSIEST	AEKLORTV	OVERTALK	AELLMNOO	ALLOMONE
	STRIATES	AEKLORVW	WALKOVER	AELLMNOZ	MANZELLO
AEIRSSTV	TRAVISES	AEKLOSST	SKATOLES	AELLMNST	STALLMEN
AEIRSSTW	WAISTERS		STALKOES	AELLMNTY	MENTALLY
	WAITRESS	AEKLOSVZ	ZELKOVAS		TALLYMEN
	WASTRIES	AEKLPPST	PEPTALKS	AELLMORR	MORALLER
AEIRSTTT	ATTRITES	AEKLPRRS	SPARKLER	AELLMORS	SLALOMER
	RATTIEST	AEKLPRRS	SPARKLES	AELLMORT	MARTELLO
	TARTIEST	AEKLPRST	SPARKLET	AELLMOSS	LOAMLESS
	TITRATES	AEKLRSST	STALKERS	AELLMOTY	TOMALLEY
	TRISTATE	AEKLRSUW	WAULKERS	AELLMOYZ	ALLOZYME
AEIRSTTW	SWATTIER	AEKLSSST	TASKLESS	AELLMPUU	PLUMULAE
	WARTIEST	AEKMMNRS	MARKSMEN	AELLMRST	TRAMELLS
AEIRSTTX	EXTRAITS	AEKMNRSU	UNMAKERS	AELLMRSY	MERSALYL
AEIRSTTZ	TRISTEZA		UNMASKER	AELLMSST	SMALLEST
AEIRSTUZ	AZURITES	AEKMOOST	MATOOKES	AELLMSWX	MAXWELLS
AEIRSTVY	VESTIARY	AEKMOPRT	TOPMAKER	AELLNOOT	ATENOLOL
AEIRSWWY	WAYWISER	AEKMORTW	TEAMWORK	AELLNOPS	PALLONES
	WIREWAYS		WORKMATE	AELLNOPV	VOLPLANE
AEIRTTTW	ATWITTER	AEKMPRRV	VERKRAMP	AELLNORS	LLANEROS
AEISSSST	SASSIEST	AEKMPRSU	UPMAKERS	AELLNOSV	NOVELLAS
AEISSSTW	TISWASES	AEKMPRTU	UPMARKET	AELLNOWW	ENWALLOW
AEISSSTY	ESSAYIST	AEKNNRSS	RANKNESS	AELLNPRU	PRUNELLA
AEISSTTT	TASTIEST	AEKNORRV	OVERRANK	AELLNPSS	PLANLESS
AEISSTTU	SITUATES	AEKNORUY	EUKARYON	AELLNPTT	PLANTLET
AEISSTTV	STATIVES	AEKNOTTU	OUTTAKEN	AELLNPTU	PLANTULE
	VASTIEST	AEKNPPRS	KNAPPERS	AELLNRUY	NEURALLY
AEISSTVV	SAVVIEST	AEKNPPSS	SPANSPEK		UNREALLY
AEISSTWZ	TIZWASES	AEKNPRSS	SPANKERS	AELLNRVY	VERNALLY
AEISTTTT	TATTIEST	AEKNPSSU	UNSPEAKS	AELLNSST	TALLNESS
AEISTTTU	ATTUITES	AEKNRSST	STARKENS	AELLNSTT	TALLENTS
AEISTTTW	TAWTIEST	AEKNRSSW	SWANKERS	AELLNTTY	LATENTLY
AEJKPSTU	KAJEPUTS	AEKNRSTZ	KRANTZES	AELLNTUU	LUNULATE
AEJLNSUV	JUVENALS	AEKNSSTW	SWANKEST	AELLNTUY	LUNATELY
AEJLORTV	TOLARJEV	AEKNSSWY	SWANKEYS	AELLOOPS	PALEOSOL
AEJLOSSU	JALOUSES	AEKOORSV	OVERSOAK	AELLOPPR	APPELLOR

AELLOPRS	REPOSALL	AELMOOPT	OMOPLATE	AELNOPPY	POLYPNEA
AELLOPRT	PREALLOT	AELMOORS	SALEROOM	AELNOPRS	PERSONAL
AELLOPRW	WALLOPER	AELMOPRR	PREMOLAR		PSORALEN
AELLOPSX	POLLAXES		PREMORAL	AELNOPRV	OVERPLAN
AELLOPTY	ALLOTYPE	AELMOPRS	PLEROMAS	AELNOPST	LAPSTONE
AELLORRY	ROYALLER		RAMPOLES		PLEONAST
AELLORSS	ROSELLAS	AELMOPRT	PROMETAL		POLENTAS
AELLORST	REALLOTS		TEMPORAL	AELNOPSU	APOLUNES
	ROSTELLA	AELMOPSU	AMPOULES	AELNOPTW	TOWPLANE
AELLORSV	ALLOVERS	AELMOPSX	EXOPLASM	AELNORSU	ALEURONS
	OVERALLS	AELMOPSY	MAYPOLES		NEUROSAL
AELLORSW	SALLOWER		PLAYSOME	AELNORSV	VERONALS
AELLORTT	ALLOTTER	AELMOPTT	METAPLOT	AELNORTT	TETRONAL
AELLORWW	WALLOWER		PALMETTO		TOLERANT
AELLOSTY	LOYALEST	AELMORSU	RAMULOSE	AELNORTU	OUTLEARN
AELLOSUV	ALVEOLUS	AELMORSV	REMOVALS	AELNORTY	ORNATELY
AELLPRSS	SPALLERS	AELMORSY	RAMOSELY	AELNOSSV	OVALNESS
AELLPSSY	PLAYLESS	AELMORTU	EMULATOR	AELNOSTV	VOLANTES
AELLPSTY	PLAYLETS	AELMORTZ	METRAZOL	AELNOSTY	ANOLYTES
AELLQRSU	SQUALLER	AELMOSSS	MOLASSES	AELNPPRS	PREPLANS
AELLRRSU	ALLURERS	AELMOSST	MALTOSES	AELNPPRT	PREPLANT
AELLRRTY	RETRALLY	AELMOSSY	AMYLOSES	AELNPPSY	PLAYPENS
AELLRTTY	LATTERLY	AELMOSTT	MATELOTS		SPYPLANE
AELLRTVY	TREVALLY	AELMOSTU	SOULMATE	AELNPRST	PANTLERS
AELLRTYY	LYRATELY	AELMOSTY	ATMOLYSE		PLANTERS
AELLRWYY	LAWYERLY	AELMOTVZ	MAZELTOV		REPLANTS
AELLSSST	SALTLESS	AELMOTYZ	ATMOLYZE	AELNPRSU	PURSLANE
	TASSELLS	AELMPRRT	TRAMPLER		SUPERNAL
AELLSSTW	SETWALLS	AELMPRSS	SAMPLERS	AELNPRTY	PLENARTY
	SWALLETS	AELMPRST	TEMPLARS	AELNPSSS	SNAPLESS
AELLSSTY	TASSELLY		TRAMPLES		SPANLESS
AELLSTUU	ULULATES	AELMPRSY	LAMPREYS	AELNPSSU	SPANSULE
AELLSTVY	VESTALLY		SAMPLERY	AELNPSTX	EXPLANTS
AELLSUVV	VALVULES	AELMPSUX	AMPLEXUS	AELNPTTU	PATULENT
AELLSUXY	SEXUALLY	AELMQSUU	SQUAMULE		PETULANT
AELMMNOS	MAMELONS	AELMRSST	LAMSTERS	AELNPTTY	PATENTLY
AELMMORW	MEALWORM		TRAMLESS	AELNQSUU	UNEQUALS
AELMMOSY	MYELOMAS	AELMRSTT	MALTSTER	AELNRRSS	SNARLERS
AELMMRSS	SLAMMERS		MARTLETS	AELNRRTY	ERRANTLY
AELMMRST	STRAMMEL	AELMRSTU	STAUMREL	AELNRRUU	NEURULAR
	TRAMMELS	AELMRSTY	MASTERLY	AELNRRUV	NERVULAR
AELMMSST	STAMMELS	AELMRTUY	MATURELY	AELNRSST	SALTERNS
AELMMSSY	MALMSEYS	AELMSSSS	MASSLESS		SLANTERS
AELMNNOT	NONMETAL	AELMSSST	MASTLESS	AELNRSTT	SLATTERN
AELMNNOU	NOUMENAL	AELNNNPU	UNPANNEL		TRENTALS
AELMNNRY	MANNERLY	AELNNOOP	NAPOLEON	AELNRSTU	NEUTRALS
AELMNNTU	UNMANTLE	AELNNOOX	NALOXONE	AELNRSTV	VENTRALS
AELMNOPS	NEOPLASM	AELNNOPT	PENTANOL	AELNRSUU	NEURULAS
	PLEONASM	AELNNOQU	NONEQUAL	AELNRSUV	UNRAVELS
AELMNORS	ALMONERS	AELNNORU	NEURONAL	AELNRSVY	SYLVANER
AELMNOST	SALMONET	AELNNOSU	ANNULOSE	AELNRSXY	LARYNXES
	TELAMONS	AELNNPRS	PLANNERS	AELNRTTW	TRAWLNET
AELMNOSU	MELANOUS	AELNNPSU	UNPANELS	AELNRUWY	UNWARELY
AELMNOWY	LAYWOMEN	AELNNRSS	ENSNARLS	AELNSSST	SALTNESS
AELMNOYY	YEOMANLY	AELNNRST	LANTERNS	AELNSSTY	STANYELS
AELMNPRS	LAMPERNS	AELNNRSU	UNLEARNS	AELNSTUV	ENVAULTS
AELMNRSU	MENSURAL	AELNNRTU	UNLEARNT	AELNSSUX	UNSEXUAL
	NUMERALS	AELNNSST	STANNELS	AELNTTUX	EXULTANT
AELMNSTT	MANTLETS	AELNNSTU	ANNULETS	AELOOPRZ	ZOOPERAL
AELMNSTU	NUTMEALS	AELNOOTZ	ENTOZOAL	AELOORRS	ROSEOLAR
AELMNSTY	MESNALTY	AELNOPPR	PROPENAL	AELOORSS	AEROSOLS

	ROSEOLAS	**AELPRRSW**	SPRAWLER	**AELRTTUX**	TEXTURAL
AELOORTW	WATERLOO	**AELPRRTT**	PRATTLER	**AELRTTUY**	TUTELARY
AELOORTZ	ZOOLATER	**AELPRSST**	PERSALTS	**AELSSSTU**	SALTUSES
AELOPPRS	PROLAPSE		PLASTERS	**AELSSSTY**	STAYLESS
	PROPALES		PSALTERS	**AELSSTTW**	WATTLESS
	SAPROPEL		STAPLERS	**AELSSWZZ**	SWAZZLES
AELOPPSU	PAPULOSE	**AELPRSSU**	PERUSALS	**AELSTTTW**	TWATTLES
AELOPPTU	POPULATE	**AELPRSSY**	PARSLEYS	**AELSTTUU**	USTULATE
AELOPPXY	APOPLEXY		SPARSELY	**AELSTTUY**	ASTUTELY
AELOPQUY	OPAQUELY	**AELPRSTT**	PARTLETS	**AELUUVVZ**	VUVUZELA
AELOPRRV	REPROVAL		PLATTERS	**AEMMMOTU**	OMMATEUM
AELOPRSS	REPOSALS		PRATTLES	**AEMMMRTY**	MAMMETRY
AELOPRST	PETROSAL		SPLATTER	**AEMMNNOY**	MONEYMAN
	POLESTAR		SPRATTLE	**AEMMNPRS**	RAMPSMEN
	PROLATES	**AELPRSTU**	APLUSTRE	**AEMMNRRY**	MERRYMAN
AELOPRSU	LEAPROUS	**AELPRSTY**	PEYTRALS	**AEMMNRTU**	RAMENTUM
AELOPRSV	OVERLAPS		PLASTERY	**AEMMOORT**	ROOMMATE
AELOPRVY	OVERPLAY		PSALTERY	**AEMMOPRS**	MAMPOERS
AELOPRYZ	PYRAZOLE	**AELPRSUY**	SUPERLAY	**AEMMORSS**	MARMOSES
AELOPSSS	SOAPLESS	**AELPSSSS**	PASSLESS	**AEMMORST**	MARMOSET
AELOPSST	APOSTLES	**AELPSSST**	PASTLESS	**AEMMORSW**	WOMMERAS
AELOPSSU	ESPOUSAL	**AELPSSTT**	PELTASTS	**AEMMOSTU**	MOUSEMAT
	SEPALOUS	**AELPSSTU**	PULSATES	**AEMMPRSS**	SPAMMERS
AELOPSSX	EXPOSALS		SPATULES	**AEMMRSST**	STAMMERS
AELOPSTT	PALETOTS	**AELPSSTZ**	SPATZLES	**AEMMRTUY**	MAUMETRY
AELOPSTU	OUTLEAPS	**AELPSUUV**	UPVALUES	**AEMMRTWY**	MAWMETRY
	PETALOUS	**AELQRRSU**	QUARRELS	**AEMMSSTU**	SUMMATES
AELOPTTU	OUTLEAPT	**AELQRSUV**	SERVQUAL	**AEMMSSUW**	WAMMUSES
AELORRST	REALTORS	**AELQRSUY**	SQUARELY	**AEMNNOPW**	PENWOMAN
	RELATORS	**AELQSTTU**	SQUATTLE	**AEMNNORS**	MONERANS
	RESTORAL	**AELQSTUZ**	QUETZALS		SONARMEN
AELORSSS	LASSOERS	**AELRRSSU**	SURREALS	**AEMNNORT**	ORNAMENT
AELORSST	OLESTRAS	**AELRRSSW**	WARSLERS	**AEMNNOSS**	MANNOSES
AELORSTT	RETOTALS	**AELRRSTT**	RATTLERS	**AEMNNOST**	MONTANES
AELORSTU	ROSULATE		STARTLER	**AEMNNOSZ**	MENAZONS
AELORSTV	LEVATORS	**AELRRSTW**	TRAWLERS	**AEMNNRST**	MANRENTS
	OVERSALT		WARSTLER		REMNANTS
AELORSTY	ROYALETS	**AELRRTVY**	VARLETRY	**AEMNOORR**	MAROONER
AELORSTZ	ZELATORS	**AELRSSST**	STARLESS	**AEMNOORT**	ANTEROOM
AELORSUU	ROULEAUS	**AELRSSSW**	WRASSLES	**AEMNOORY**	AERONOMY
AELORSVY	LAYOVERS	**AELRSSTT**	SLATTERS	**AEMNOOSZ**	MESOZOAN
	OVERLAYS		STARLETS	**AEMNOOTZ**	METAZOON
AELORSWY	OWRELAYS		STARTLES	**AEMNOPPS**	PAMPOENS
AELORTTV	VARLETTO	**AELRSSTU**	SALUTERS	**AEMNOPRS**	MANROPES
AELORTYZ	ZEALOTRY	**AELRSSTW**	WARSTLES		PROSEMAN
AELORUUX	ROULEAUX		WARTLESS	**AEMNOPRT**	EMPATRON
AELOSSTV	SOLVATES		WASTRELS	**AEMNOPRW**	MANPOWER
AELOSSTY	ASYSTOLE		WRASTLES	**AEMNORRS**	RANSOMER
AELOSSVY	SAVELOYS	**AELRSSUU**	RUSSULAE	**AEMNORST**	MONSTERA
AELOSTTU	TOLUATES	**AELRSSUW**	WALRUSES		ONSTREAM
AELOSTTW	WASTELOT	**AELRSTTT**	TARTLETS		STOREMAN
AELOSTUV	OVULATES		TATTLERS		TONEARMS
AELOSTUY	AUTOLYSE	**AELRSTTU**	LUSTRATE	**AEMNORSU**	ENAMOURS
AELOTUUV	OUTVALUE		TUTELARS		NEUROMAS
AELOTUYZ	AUTOLYZE	**AELRSTTY**	SLATTERY	**AEMNORSV**	OVERMANS
AELPPPRU	PREPUPAL	**AELRSTUV**	VAULTERS		OVERSMAN
AELPPPRY	PREAPPLY		VESTURAL	**AEMNORSY**	ROMNEYAS
AELPPRSS	SLAPPERS	**AELRSTWY**	TRAWLEYS	**AEMNORTT**	TORMENTA
AELPPSST	STAPPLES	**AELRSTWZ**	WALTZERS	**AEMNORTU**	ROUTEMAN
AELPPSSU	APPULSES	**AELRSUVY**	SURVEYAL	**AEMNORTY**	MONETARY
AELPRRRU	LARRUPER	**AELRTTTW**	TWATTLER	**AEMNORVY**	OVERMANY

AEMNORYY	YEOMANRY	AEMOSSUZ	ZAMOUSES	AENNRTTY	TENANTRY
AEMNOSTU	NOTAEUMS	AEMOSSWY	SOMEWAYS	AENOOPST	TEASPOON
	OUTNAMES	AEMOSTTZ	MOZETTAS	AENOORRT	RATOONER
	SEAMOUNT	AEMOTTZZ	MOZETTA	AENOOSTZ	OZONATES
AEMNOSWY	YAWNSOME	AEMPPRST	PRESTAMP	AENOPPRS	PROPANES
AEMNPRSS	PRESSMAN	AEMPRRST	TRAMPERS	AENOPRSS	PERSONAS
AEMNPRSU	SUPERMAN	AEMPRRSW	PREWARMS		RESPONSA
AEMNPSST	ENSTAMPS	AEMPRRSY	SPERMARY	AENOPRST	OPERANTS
	PASSMENT	AEMPRSST	RESTAMPS		PRONATES
AEMNPSTU	SPUMANTE		STAMPERS		PROTEANS
AEMNPSTY	PAYMENTS	AEMPRSSW	SWAMPERS	AENOPRSY	PYRANOSE
AEMNQSUW	SQUAWMEN	AEMPRSTT	TRAMPETS	AENOPRTT	PATENTOR
AEMNRRSU	MANURERS	AEMPRSTU	TEMPURAS	AENOPRWY	WEAPONRY
	SURNAMER		UPSTREAM	AENOPSSU	POSAUNES
AEMNRRUY	NUMERARY	AEMPRSUX	SUPERMAX	AENOPSTU	AUTOPENS
AEMNRSST	SARMENTS	AEMPSSUW	MAWPUSES	AENORRRW	NARROWER
	SMARTENS		WAMPUSES	AENORRSS	SERRANOS
AEMNRSSU	SURNAMES	AEMPSTTT	ATTEMPTS	AENORRST	ANTRORSE
AEMNRSSW	WARMNESS	AEMQRSSU	MARQUESS	AENORSST	ASSENTOR
AEMNRSTU	ANESTRUM		MASQUERS		SANTEROS
	MENSTRUA	AEMRRSST	ARMRESTS		SENATORS
	TRANSUME	AEMRRSSW	SWARMERS		STARNOSE
AEMNRSTV	VARMENTS	AEMRRSTU	MATURERS		TREASONS
AEMNRSTW	TRANSMEW	AEMRRTUV	VERATRUM	AENORSSU	ANSEROUS
	TREWSMAN	AEMRSSSU	ASSUMERS		ARSENOUS
AEMNRSUY	ANEURYSM		MASSEURS	AENORSTT	ORNATEST
AEMNSTTU	NUTMEATS	AEMRSSTT	MATTRESS	AENORSTU	OUTEARNS
AEMNSTWY	WAYMENTS		SMARTEST	AENORSTV	VENATORS
AEMOOPST	POMATOES		SMATTERS	AENORSTW	STONERAW
AEMOORRW	WAREROOM	AEMRSSTY	MAYSTERS	AENORSUV	RAVENOUS
AEMOORST	TEAROOMS	AEMRSTTU	MATUREST	AENORSWZ	WARZONES
AEMOORSW	WOOMERAS		TESTAMUR	AENORTTV	TEVATRON
AEMOORTT	AMORETTO	AEMRSTTX	MARTEXTS	AENORTTX	TETRAXON
AEMOOSST	MAESTOSO	AEMRTUUX	TRUMEAUX	AENORTTY	ATTORNEY
	OSTEOMAS	AEMSTTTU	TESTATUM	AENORTWW	TOWNWEAR
AEMOOSSV	VAMOOSES	AENNNPST	PENNANTS	AENOSSTU	SOUTANES
AEMOOSTT	OSTOMATE	AENNNTTU	UNTENANT	AENOSSTZ	STANZOES
	TOMATOES	AENNOOPR	NANOPORE	AENOSSUU	NAUSEOUS
AEMOOSTU	AUTOSOME	AENNOOTZ	ENTOZOAN	AENOSSVW	WAVESONS
AEMOOTTY	TOMATOEY	AENNOPRT	PATRONNE	AENOTTUU	AUTOTUNE
AEMOPPRS	PAMPEROS	AENNOPRX	NAPROXEN	AENOUUVX	NOUVEAUX
AEMOPRTW	POMWATER	AENNOPST	PENTOSAN	AENPPRSS	PARSNEPS
	TAPEWORM	AENNOPUW	UNWEAPON		SNAPPERS
AEMOQSSU	SQUAMOSE	AENNORST	NORTENAS	AENPPRST	PARPENTS
AEMORRRS	ARMORERS		RESONANT	AENPPRSU	UNPAPERS
AEMORRRU	ARMOURER	AENNORSU	UNREASON	AENPRRST	PARTNERS
AEMORRST	REARMOST	AENNORSY	ANNOYERS	AENPRRSW	PRAWNERS
AEMORRSV	OVERARMS	AENNORTU	UNORNATE		PREWARNS
AEMORRSW	EARWORMS	AENNORTW	WANTONER	AENPRSST	PASTERNS
AEMORRSY	ROSEMARY	AENNORUX	NEURAXON		RAPTNESS
AEMORRVW	OVERWARM	AENNORVY	NOVENARY	AENPRSSW	SPAWNERS
AEMORSSS	MORASSES	AENNOSSU	UNSEASON	AENPRSTT	PATTERNS
AEMORSST	MAESTROS	AENNOSTU	TONNEAUS		TRANSEPT
AEMORSSW	SEAWORMS	AENNOSTX	NONTAXES		TRAPNEST
AEMORSSY	MAYORESS	AENNOTUX	TONNEAUX	AENPRSTU	PERSAUNT
AEMORSTV	OVERMAST	AENNPRSS	SPANNERS	AENPRSUV	PARVENUS
AEMORSVW	OVERSWAM	AENNPSSU	PANNUSES	AENPSSST	PASTNESS
AEMORTTU	TAUTOMER	AENNQSTU	QUANNETS	AENPSSSY	SYNAPSES
AEMOSSTT	EASTMOST	AENNRSTT	ENTRANTS	AENPSSTU	PESAUNTS
	STOMATES	AENNRSTY	TYRANNES	AENPSSTW	STEWPANS
AEMOSSTW	TWASOMES	AENNRSWY	SWANNERY		WASPNEST

AENPSSTY	SYNAPTES	AEOPRSVY	OVERPAYS	AEPRRRSS	SPARRERS
AENPSSTZ	SPETSNAZ	AEOPRSWY	ROPEWAYS	AEPRRSSY	RESPRAYS
AENPSTZZ	SPETZNAZ	AEOPRTWX	WATERPOX		SPRAYERS
AENQRRTU	QUARTERN	AEOPSSST	POTASSES	AEPRRSTU	PARTURES
AENQSTTU	QUESTANT	AEOPTTUY	AUTOTYPE		PASTURER
AENRRRTY	ERRANTRY	AEOQRSTU	EQUATORS		RAPTURES
AENRRSTT	TRANTERS		QUAESTOR	AEPRRSTY	PARTYERS
AENRSSST	SARSNETS	AEOQRSUV	VAQUEROS	AEPRSSST	SPARSEST
AENRSSTT	TARTNESS	AEOQRTTU	TORQUATE		TRESPASS
AENRSSTU	ANESTRUS	AEOQRTUZ	QUATORZE	AEPRSSTT	PATTRESS
	SAUNTERS	AEORRRST	ARRESTOR		SPATTERS
AENRSSTV	SERVANTS	AEORRSST	ASSERTOR		TAPSTERS
	VERSANTS		ASSORTER	AEPRSSTU	PASTURES
AENRSSUW	UNSWEARS		ORATRESS		UPSTARES
AENRSTTU	TAUNTERS		REASSORT	AEPRSSTY	YAPSTERS
AENRSTUV	VAUNTERS		ROASTERS	AEPRSSWY	SPYWARES
AENRSTUW	UNWATERS	AEORRSSU	AROUSERS	AEPRSTTU	STUPRATE
AENRSTWY	STERNWAY	AEORRSSV	SAVORERS		UPSTATER
AENRTUVY	VAUNTERY		SEROVARS	AEPRSTTY	TAPESTRY
AENRTUWY	UNWATERY	AEORRSTT	ROSTRATE	AEPRSTUX	SUPERTAX
AENRTWYY	ENTRYWAY	AEORRSUV	SAVOURER	AEPRTUVY	PYRUVATE
AENSSSTV	VASTNESS	AEORRTTV	OVERTART	AEPSSSSU	PASSUSES
AENSSSTW	WASTNESS	AEORRTUV	AVOUTRER	AEPSSTTU	UPSTATES
AENSSTTU	TAUTNESS	AEORRTZZ	TERRAZZO	AEQRRSSU	SQUARERS
	UNSTATES	AEORRVWY	OVERWARY	AEQRRSTU	QUARTERS
AENSSTTX	SEXTANTS	AEORSSSS	ASSESSOR	AEQRSSTU	SQUAREST
AENSSTXY	SYNTAXES	AEORSSST	OSSETRAS	AEQRSTTU	QUARTETS
AEOOPPPS	PAPPOOSE	AEORSSTT	STRATOSE		SQUATTER
AEOOPPSS	PAPOOSES		TOASTERS	AEQRSTUZ	QUARTZES
AEOOPRRT	OPERATOR	AEORSSTU	OSSATURE	AEQRTTTU	QUARTETT
AEOOPRSS	OROPESAS	AEORSSTV	VOTARESS	AERRSSSU	ASSURERS
AEOOPSTT	POTATOES	AEORSSTX	STORAXES	AERRSSTT	RESTARTS
AEOORRST	SORORATE	AEORSSUU	ROUSSEAU		STARTERS
AEOORTTT	TATTOOER	AEORSTTT	ATTESTOR	AERRSSTU	SERRATUS
AEOORTTV	ROTOVATE		TESTATOR	AERRSSTV	STARVERS
AEOPPRRV	APPROVER	AEORSTTU	OUTRATES	AERRSSTY	STRAYERS
AEOPPRSS	APPOSERS		OUTSTARE	AERRSTUY	TREASURY
AEOPPRST	TRAPPOSE		SEATROUT	AERSSSST	STRASSES
AEOPPRSV	APPROVES	AEORSTUV	OUTRAVES	AERSSSTY	SATYRESS
AEOPQRTU	PAROQUET	AEORSTUW	OUTSWARE	AERSSTTT	STRETTAS
AEOPQSTU	OPAQUEST		OUTSWEAR	AERSSTTU	STATURES
AEOPRRRT	PARROTER		OUTWEARS	AERSSTTW	SWATTERS
AEOPRRSS	ASPERSOR	AEORSTVY	OVERSTAY	AERSSTUX	SURTAXES
AEOPRRST	PRAETORS	AEORSUVW	WAVEROUS	AERSSTVY	STRAYVES
	PRORATES	AEORSVWY	OVERSWAY	AERSSTXY	STYRAXES
AEOPRRSV	VAPORERS	AEORTUWY	OUTWEARY	AERSTTUV	VETTURAS
AEOPRRTV	OVERPART		ROUTEWAY	AERSTTVY	TRAVESTY
AEOPRRUV	VAPOURER	AEORTVXY	VEXATORY	AERTTUXY	TEXTUARY
AEOPRRVW	OVERWRAP	AEOSTTTU	AUTOTEST	AESSSTTU	STATUSES
	WRAPOVER		OUTSTATE	AESSTTTU	ASTUTEST
AEOPRRWW	WARPOWER	AEOSTTUW	OUTWASTE		STATUTES
AEOPRSST	ESPARTOS	AEPPPRSU	PREPUPAS	AFFFFINN	NIFFNAFF
	PORTASES	AEPPPSSU	PAPPUSES	AFFFFIRR	RIFFRAFF
	PROTASES	AEPPRRST	STRAPPER	AFFFGILN	FLAFFING
	SEAPORTS		TRAPPERS	AFFFLLOS	FALLOFFS
AEOPRSSU	ASPEROUS	AEPPRRSW	PREWRAPS	AFFGGINR	GRAFFING
AEOPRSSV	OVERPASS		WRAPPERS	AFFGGINS	GAFFINGS
	PASSOVER	AEPPRSSU	UPSPEARS	AFFGHIRT	AFFRIGHT
AEOPRSTT	PROSTATE	AEPPRSSW	SWAPPERS	AFFGIINP	PIAFFING
AEOPRSTU	APTEROUS	AEPPSSTU	PASTEUPS	AFFGIINX	AFFIXING
AEOPRSTV	OVERPAST	AEPQRSTU	PARQUETS	AFFGIIRT	GRAFFITI

AFFGILMN	MAFFLING	AFGHLNSU	FLASHGUN	AFGLNORU	GROANFUL
AFFGILNR	RAFFLING	AFGHLSTU	FLAUGHTS	AFGLNOUW	WAGONFUL
AFFGILNW	WAFFLING		GHASTFUL	AFGNNNOO	GONFANON
AFFGIMRS	MISGRAFF	AFGHRSTU	FRAUGHTS	AFGOORTZ	ZOOGRAFT
AFFGINNY	NYAFFING	AFGIILLN	FLAILING	AFHIILRS	FRAILISH
AFFGINQU	QUAFFING	AFGIILNS	FAILINGS	AFHIILSS	SAILFISH
AFFGINST	STAFFING	AFGIIMMN	INFAMING	AFHIILST	FISHTAIL
AFFGINUW	WAUFFING	AFGIINNT	FAINTING	AFHIIMST	MISFAITH
AFFGIORT	GRAFFITO	AFGIINRS	FAIRINGS	AFHIINST	FAINTISH
AFFHILLS	FALLFISH		FRAISING	AFHIKSUY	KUFIYAHS
AFFHILNS	HAFFLINS	AFGIINTX	FIXATING	AFHILLNS	HALFLINS
AFFHILST	FLATFISH	AFGIKLNN	FANKLING	AFHILLSW	WALLFISH
AFFHILTU	FAITHFUL		FLANKING	AFHILLSY	FLASHILY
AFFIINTY	AFFINITY	AFGIKNNR	FRANKING	AFHILOSY	OAFISHLY
AFFIISTX	FIXATIFS	AFGIKORT	KOFTGARI	AFHILSST	SALTFISH
AFFILLMM	FLIMFLAM	AFGILLNS	FALLINGS	AFHILSTT	FLATTISH
AFFILMNS	MAFFLINS	AFGILLNT	FLATLING	AFHILSTW	HALFWITS
AFFILORS	RIFFOLAS	AFGILMMN	FLAMMING	AFHIMNST	MANSHIFT
AFFILSUX	SUFFIXAL	AFGILMNO	FLAMINGO	AFHIMNSU	HAFNIUMS
AFFIMSST	MASTIFFS	AFGILNOS	LOAFINGS	AFHINOSS	FASHIONS
AFFINORR	FORFAIRN	AFGILNOT	FLOATING	AFHINOSY	FASHIONY
AFFINOSU	AFFUSION	AFGILNPP	FLAPPING	AFHINSTU	UNFAITHS
AFFINRSU	FUNFAIRS	AFGILNRU	INFRUGAL	AFHIOSSU	FASHIOUS
	RUFFIANS	AFGILNST	FATLINGS	AFHIRSST	STARFISH
AFFIORRS	FORFAIRS	AFGILNTT	FLATTING	AFHISSWY	FISHWAYS
AFFIPSTT	TIPSTAFF	AFGILNTU	FAULTING	AFHKLNTU	THANKFUL
AFFIRRSU	FURFAIRS	AFGILORW	GAIRFOWL	AFHKORSX	FOXSHARK
AFFIRSSU	SUFFARIS	AFGILSSY	GLASSIFY	AFHKORSY	HAYFORKS
AFFLLOOT	FOOTFALL	AFGIMNOS	FOAMINGS	AFHKRSTU	FUTHARKS
AFFLLTUU	FAULTFUL	AFGIMNRS	FARMINGS	AFHLLOTU	LOATHFUL
AFFLOOOT	FOALFOOT		FRAMINGS	AFHLNSUY	UNFLASHY
AFFLOOTT	FLATFOOT	AFGIMNTU	FUMIGANT	AFHLOSTU	OUTFLASH
AFFLOPSY	PLAYOFFS	AFGIMORS	GASIFORM	AFHLOSTY	HAYLOFTS
AFFLORTU	FORFAULT	AFGIMRST	MISGRAFT	AFHLRTUW	WRATHFUL
AFFLRRUU	FURFURAL	AFGINNNS	FANNINGS	AFHNOOST	FANTOOSH
AFFMOPRS	OFFRAMPS	AFGINNNY	FANNYING	AFHOOPST	POOFTAHS
AFFNORSS	SAFFRONS	AFGINNRS	SNARFING	AFHOOPTT	FOOTPATH
AFFNORST	AFFRONTS	AFGINNSU	SNAFUING	AFHOORST	HAFTOROS
AFFNORSY	SAFFRONY	AFGINNSW	FAWNINGS	AFHOORTT	HAFTOROT
AFFNRRUU	FURFURAN	AFGINORV	FAVORING	AFHOPSTU	POUFTAHS
AFGGGILN	FLAGGING	AFGINORY	FORAYING	AFIIKMRS	FAKIRISM
AFGGGINR	FRAGGING	AFGINPPR	FRAPPING	AFIILLLY	FILIALLY
AFGGGINS	FAGGINGS	AFGINRST	INGRAFTS	AFIILLNU	UNFILIAL
AFGGILNN	FANGLING		RAFTINGS	AFIILMMS	FAMILISM
	FLANGING		STRAFING	AFIILMNS	FINALISM
AFGGILOP	GIGAFLOP	AFGINRSW	SWARFING	AFIILNRU	UNIFILAR
AFGGINOR	FORAGING	AFGINRSY	FRAYINGS	AFIILNST	FINALIST
AFGGINOT	FAGOTING	AFGINRTU	FIGURANT		TAILFINS
AFGGINRT	GRAFTING	AFGINSST	FASTINGS	AFIILNTY	FINALITY
AFGGORTY	FAGGOTRY	AFGINSTW	WAFTINGS	AFIILORS	AIRFOILS
AFGHIINT	FAITHING	AFGINSUY	SANGUIFY	AFIILRST	AIRLIFTS
AFGHILLN	HALFLING	AFGIORST	ISOGRAFT	AFIIMNPR	RIFAMPIN
AFGHILNS	FLASHING	AFGIPRTW	GIFTWRAP	AFIIMRSY	FAIRYISM
AFGHILNT	FANLIGHT	AFGKNOPS	PAKFONGS	AFIINNOS	SAINFOIN
AFGHILPS	FLAGSHIP	AFGKORST	KOFTGARS		SINFONIA
AFGHINRT	FARTHING	AFGLLNOT	FLATLONG	AFIINOTX	FIXATION
AFGHINRW	WHARFING	AFGLLRUU	FULGURAL	AFIIORRT	TRIFORIA
AFGHINST	SHAFTING	AFGLLRUY	FRUGALLY	AFIJKRTU	JAKFRUIT
AFGHIOST	GOATFISH	AFGLLSSU	GLASSFUL	AFIJMNOR	JANIFORM
AFGHIRSY	GRAYFISH	AFGLLSTU	GASTFULL	AFIKLNNR	FRANKLIN
AFGHLLUU	LAUGHFUL	AFGLNNOO	GONFALON	AFIKLORT	FORKTAIL

AFIKLOST	FLOKATIS	**AFIORSTU**	FAITOURS	**AFMNOSUU**	UNFAMOUS
AFIKMNNR	FINNMARK	**AFIORSTZ**	SFORZATI	**AFMOOPRR**	PROFORMA
AFIKMNRS	FINMARKS	**AFIRSTTY**	STRATIFY	**AFMORSSU**	AUSFORMS
AFIKNRST	RATFINKS	**AFISSSTT**	SITFASTS	**AFMORSTU**	FOUMARTS
AFIKRSTY	KARSTIFY	**AFISSTTT**	FATTISTS	**AFMORTUY**	FUMATORY
AFILLLOT	FLOTILLA	**AFISSTUV**	FAUVISTS	**AFMOSSTU**	SFUMATOS
AFILLMSS	MISFALLS	**AFKLNOTU**	OUTFLANK	**AFNNOTTY**	NONFATTY
AFILLMUY	AIMFULLY	**AFKLNPRU**	PRANKFUL	**AFNORRSW**	FORWARNS
AFILLNPS	PINFALLS	**AFKLNSTU**	TANKFULS	**AFNORSTW**	FANWORTS
AFILLNPU	PLAINFUL	**AFKLORTW**	FLATWORK	**AFNOSTUW**	OUTFAWNS
AFILLPST	PITFALLS	**AFKLOSWY**	FOLKWAYS	**AFOOPPRS**	APPROOFS
AFILLPSU	PAILFULS	**AFKMOORT**	FOOTMARK	**AFOOPRRT**	RATPROOF
	PAILSFUL	**AFKMORRW**	FARMWORK	**AFOORSTZ**	FORZATOS
AFILLSUV	VIALFULS	**AFKRRSTU**	FRAKTURS		SFORZATO
AFILLTUY	FAULTILY	**AFLLLORY**	FLORALLY	**AFOOSTWY**	FOOTWAYS
AFILMNOR	FORMALIN	**AFLLLUWY**	LAWFULLY	**AFORSTTU**	TARTUFOS
	INFORMAL	**AFLLMNUY**	MANFULLY	**AFORSTTW**	FORSWATT
AFILMNOS	FOILSMAN	**AFLLMORY**	FORMALLY	**AFOSSTTU**	OUTFASTS
AFILMOPR	PALIFORM	**AFLLMPSU**	PALMFULS	**AFOSSTUU**	FASTUOUS
AFILMSSS	FALSISMS	**AFLLNOOV**	FLAVONOL	**AGGGGILN**	GAGGLING
AFILNNNO	NONFINAL	**AFLLNOSW**	SNOWFALL	**AGGGHILN**	HAGGLING
AFILNORT	FLATIRON	**AFLLNUUW**	UNLAWFUL	**AGGGHINS**	SHAGGING
	INFLATOR	**AFLLOOTW**	FOOTWALL	**AGGGILNN**	GANGLING
AFILNOSU	FUSIONAL	**AFLLOSTU**	FALLOUTS	**AGGGILNR**	GARGLING
AFILNPPT	FLIPPANT		OUTFALLS		RAGGLING
AFILNRTU	TRAINFUL	**AFLLRTUY**	ARTFULLY	**AGGGILNS**	LAGGINGS
AFILNRUY	UNFAIRLY	**AFLLSTUW**	WASTFULL		SLAGGING
AFILNSTU	FLUTINAS	**AFLMNNUU**	UNMANFUL	**AGGGILNW**	WAGGLING
	INFLATUS	**AFLMNOPR**	PLANFORM	**AGGGINNS**	GANGINGS
AFILOORT	FAROLITO	**AFLMNORU**	UNFORMAL		NAGGINGS
AFILORSW	AIRFLOWS	**AFLMNOST**	LOFTSMAN		SNAGGING
AFILORTY	FILATORY	**AFLMOPRT**	PLATFORM	**AGGGINPS**	SPAGGING
AFILOSTX	FOXTAILS	**AFLMORRU**	FORMULAR	**AGGGINRS**	RAGGINGS
AFILRSSU	FISSURAL	**AFLMORSU**	FORMULAS	**AGGGINSS**	SAGGINGS
AFILRSTU	FISTULAR	**AFLMORSW**	WOLFRAMS	**AGGGINST**	STAGGING
AFILSSTU	FISTULAS	**AFLMORTU**	FOULMART		TAGGINGS
AFILSTTU	FLAUTIST	**AFLMORTW**	FLATWORM	**AGGGINSU**	GAUGINGS
AFIMMNOR	MANIFORM	**AFLMOSST**	FLOTSAMS	**AGGGINSW**	SWAGGING
AFIMMNOY	AMMONIFY	**AFLMOSUY**	FAMOUSLY	**AGGGIYZZ**	ZIGZAGGY
AFIMMORR	RAMIFORM	**AFLNOPRU**	APRONFUL	**AGGHIILS**	GHILGAIS
AFIMNOPR	NAPIFORM	**AFLNORST**	FRONTALS	**AGGHILNU**	LAUGHING
AFIMNORR	RANIFORM	**AFLNRSTU**	RUNFLATS	**AGGHILST**	GASLIGHT
AFIMNORT	NATIFORM	**AFLNRTUU**	UNARTFUL	**AGGHILSY**	SHAGGILY
AFIMNOSU	INFAMOUS	**AFLNTUUV**	VAUNTFUL	**AGGHIMNO**	HOMAGING
AFIMOOSS	MAFIOSOS	**AFLNTUUY**	UNFAULTY	**AGGHIMNS**	GINGHAMS
AFIMORRU	AURIFORM	**AFLOOSTW**	WOOLFATS	**AGGHINNP**	PHANGING
AFIMORRV	VARIFORM	**AFLOOTTU**	OUTFLOAT	**AGGHINNS**	GNASHING
AFIMORSV	VASIFORM	**AFLOPRUY**	FOURPLAY		HANGINGS
AFIMRSUU	FUSARIUM	**AFLOPSTT**	FLATTOPS	**AGGHINNW**	WHANGING
AFIMSSTT	FATTISMS	**AFLORSSU**	FUSAROLS	**AGGHINPR**	GRAPHING
AFIMSSUV	FAUVISMS	**AFLORSUV**	FLAVOURS	**AGGHINST**	GHASTING
AFINNORS	FRANIONS	**AFLORUVY**	FLAVOURY	**AGGHINUW**	WAUGHING
AFINNOST	FONTINAS	**AFLOSTUU**	FLATUOUS	**AGGHISTT**	GASTIGHT
AFINNOTU	FOUNTAIN	**AFLPRSTY**	FLYTRAPS	**AGGHJMNO**	MAHJONGG
AFINNRTY	INFANTRY	**AFLPRSYY**	FLYSPRAY	**AGGHLOOT**	GOLGOTHA
AFINOPSY	SAPONIFY	**AFLPSSTY**	FLYPASTS	**AGGIIJJS**	JIGAJIGS
AFINQTUY	QUANTIFY	**AFLRSTTU**	STARTFUL	**AGGIILNN**	ALIGNING
AFINRSTX	TRANSFIX	**AFLRSTUY**	TRAYFULS	**AGGIILNR**	GLAIRING
AFINSSTU	FAUNISTS	**AFMNNNUY**	FUNNYMAN	**AGGIILNS**	SILAGING
	FUSTIANS	**AFMNNORT**	FRONTMAN	**AGGIILNT**	LIGATING
AFIOOPRR	AIRPROOF	**AFMNORST**	FORMANTS		TAIGLING

AGGIILNV	GINGIVAL	AGGINPRS	GRASPING	AGHILNSS	HASSLING
AGGIIMNS	IMAGINGS		PARGINGS		LASHINGS
AGGIINNR	GRAINING		SPARGING		SLANGISH
AGGIINNS	AGNISING	AGGINPSS	GASPINGS		SLASHING
	GAININGS	AGGINPUZ	UPGAZING	AGHILNST	HALTINGS
AGGIINNZ	AGNIZING	AGGINRSS	GRASSING		LATHINGS
AGGIINRS	AGRISING		SIRGANGS	AGHILNSU	LANGUISH
AGGIINRT	TRIAGING	AGGINRST	GRATINGS		NILGHAUS
AGGIINRZ	AGRIZING	AGGINRSU	SUGARING		SHAULING
AGGIINST	AGISTING	AGGINRSV	GRAVINGS	AGHILNSW	SHAWLING
AGGIINSU	AGUISING	AGGINRSZ	GRAZINGS		WHALINGS
AGGIINUZ	AGUIZING	AGGINRTY	GYRATING	AGHILNSY	NYLGHAIS
AGGIJJOS	JIGAJOGS	AGGINRUU	AUGURING	AGHILOST	GOLIATHS
AGGIJLNN	JANGLING	AGGINRYZ	AGRYZING	AGHILRSY	GARISHLY
AGGIKNSS	GASKINGS	AGGINSSS	GASSINGS	AGHILRTY	GRAITHLY
AGGILLNS	GINGALLS	AGGINSST	STAGINGS	AGHILSUY	AGUISHLY
AGGILLNU	ULLAGING	AGGINSWY	GAYWINGS	AGHIMMNS	SHAMMING
AGGILLNY	GALLYING	AGGIRTUZ	ZIGGURAT	AGHIMMNW	WHAMMING
AGGILMMN	GLAMMING	AGGKLNNU	ANGKLUNG	AGHIMNPR	PHARMING
AGGILMNN	MANGLING	AGGLLLOY	LOLLYGAG	AGHIMNSS	MASHINGS
AGGILMNO	GLOAMING	AGGLLOOY	ALGOLOGY		SMASHING
AGGILMNP	GLAMPING	AGGLMOOR	LOGOGRAM	AGHIMNTY	THINGAMY
AGGILMNR	MALGRING	AGGLNOPW	GANGPLOW	AGHIMOST	OGHAMIST
AGGILMNU	GLAUMING	AGGLOORY	AGROLOGY	AGHIMPRU	GRAPHIUM
AGGILNNO	GANGLION	AGGLRSTY	STRAGGLY	AGHINNOS	NIHONGAS
AGGILNNR	GNARLING	AGGMORRS	GROGRAMS	AGHINNOT	GNATHION
AGGILNNS	ANGLINGS	AGGMOSTY	MYSTAGOG	AGHINNSS	SNASHING
	SLANGING	AGGNOSSY	SYNAGOGS	AGHINNST	TANGHINS
AGGILNNT	GNATLING	AGGNUWZZ	ZUGZWANG	AGHINNTU	HAUNTING
	TANGLING	AGHHIILT	HIGHTAIL	AGHINNTY	ANYTHING
AGGILNNW	WANGLING	AGHHINRS	HARSHING	AGHINORS	ORANGISH
AGGILNOP	GALOPING	AGHHINSS	HASHINGS	AGHINOST	HOASTING
AGGILNOT	GLOATING		SHASHING	AGHINPPW	WHAPPING
	GOATLING	AGHHISWY	HIGHWAYS	AGHINPPY	HAPPYING
AGGILNPU	PLAGUING	AGHHLOTU	ALTHOUGH	AGHINPRS	HARPINGS
AGGILNPY	GAPINGLY	AGHIILNN	INHALING		PHRASING
AGGILNRY	GRAYLING	AGHIILNS	NILGHAIS		SHARPING
	RAGINGLY	AGHIINNS	HAININGS	AGHINPSS	PHASINGS
AGGILNSS	GLASSING	AGHIINRT	AIRTHING		SHAPINGS
AGGILNSZ	GLAZINGS	AGHIIPRR	HAIRGRIP	AGHINPSW	PSHAWING
AGGIMNRU	MAUGRING	AGHIIRTT	AIRTIGHT	AGHINQSU	QUASHING
AGGINNOR	GROANING	AGHIJNRT	NIGHTJAR	AGHINRRU	HURRAING
AGGINNOT	TANGOING	AGHIKNNS	SHANKING	AGHINRRY	HARRYING
AGGINNOW	WAGONING	AGHIKNNT	THANKING	AGHINRSS	SHARINGS
AGGINNPR	PRANGING	AGHIKNRS	SHARKING	AGHINRST	TRASHING
AGGINNPS	SPANGING	AGHIKNSS	SHAKINGS	AGHINRTW	THRAWING
AGGINNRR	GNARRING	AGHIKNSW	HAWKINGS		WRATHING
AGGINNRS	RANGINGS	AGHILLNO	HALLOING	AGHINSST	HASTINGS
AGGINNRT	GRANTING		HOLLAING		STASHING
AGGINNRU	RAUNGING	AGHILLNS	HALLINGS	AGHINSSV	SHAVINGS
AGGINNRW	WRANGING	AGHILLNT	ALLNIGHT	AGHINSSW	SWASHING
AGGINNST	STANGING	AGHILMTY	ALMIGHTY		WASHINGS
AGGINNSW	GNAWINGS	AGHILNOO	HOOLIGAN	AGHINSTT	HATTINGS
AGGINNTU	GAUNTING	AGHILNOR	LONGHAIR	AGHINSTW	SWATHING
AGGINNTW	TWANGING	AGHILNOS	SHOALING		THAWINGS
AGGINNUZ	UNGAZING	AGHILNOT	LOATHING	AGHINUZZ	HUZZAING
AGGINORT	GAROTING	AGHILNPR	RALPHING	AGHIOPRS	ISOGRAPH
AGGINOST	GIGATONS	AGHILNPS	PLASHING	AGHIPRRT	TRIGRAPH
AGGINOVY	VOYAGING	AGHILNRS	HARLINGS	AGHIRSTT	STRAIGHT
AGGINOWY	WAYGOING		RINGHALS	AGHISSTT	TIGHTASS
AGGINPPS	GAPPINGS	AGHILNRY	NARGHILY	AGHISSTW	SIGHTSAW

AGHJMNOS	MAHJONGS	AGIILNRT	RINGTAIL	AGIJNRRS	JARRINGS
AGHKNOPT	PAKTHONG		TRAILING	AGIKKNNS	SKANKING
AGHKOSSW	GOSHAWKS	AGIILNRV	RIVALING	AGIKLMOR	KILOGRAM
AGHLLMPU	GALLUMPH		VIRGINAL	AGIKLNNP	PLANKING
AGHLMOOR	HOLOGRAM	AGIILNSS	AISLINGS	AGIKLNNR	RANKLING
AGHLMOOY	HOLOGAMY		SAILINGS	AGIKLNOP	POLKAING
AGHLMPSU	GALUMPHS	AGIILNST	TAILINGS	AGIKLNOS	OAKLINGS
AGHLNOSU	SHOGUNAL	AGIILNSU	LINGUISA		SKOALING
AGHLNSUY	NYLGHAUS	AGIILNSW	WAILINGS	AGIKLNPP	KLAPPING
AGHLOOSS	GASOHOLS	AGIILNTT	LITIGANT	AGIKLNST	SKLATING
AGHLOTUU	OUTLAUGH	AGIILNTV	VIGILANT		STALKING
AGHMMOOY	HOMOGAMY	AGIILORU	OLIGURIA		TALKINGS
AGHMNPSU	SPHAGNUM	AGIILOSV	VILIAGOS	AGIKLNSW	WALKINGS
AGHMOOPY	OMOPHAGY	AGIILPST	PIGTAILS	AGIKLNTY	TAKINGLY
AGHMOPRY	MYOGRAPH	AGIILTVY	VAGILITY	AGIKLNUW	WAULKING
AGHMORSY	HYGROMAS	AGIIMMNS	MAIMINGS	AGIKLORY	KILOGRAY
AGHMRRSU	MURRAGHS	AGIIMMSS	IMAGISMS	AGIKMNNU	UNMAKING
AGHNNOSU	HOUNGANS	AGIIMNNR	INARMING	AGIKMNPU	UPMAKING
AGHNNSTU	SHANTUNG	AGIIMNOR	IGNORAMI	AGIKMNRS	MARKINGS
AGHNOORS	SHAGROON	AGIIMNOU	MIAOUING	AGIKMNSS	MASKINGS
AGHNORST	STAGHORN	AGIIMNOW	MIAOWING	AGIKNNPP	KNAPPING
AGHNOSTU	HANGOUTS	AGIIMNPV	IMPAVING	AGIKNNPR	PRANKING
	TOHUNGAS	AGIIMNSS	AMISSING	AGIKNNPS	SPANKING
AGHNPRSY	SYNGRAPH	AGIIMNST	GIANTISM	AGIKNNRR	KNARRING
AGHNTTUU	UNTAUGHT	AGIIMNTT	MITIGANT	AGIKNNRS	RANKINGS
AGHOOPYZ	ZOOPHAGY	AGIIMORS	ORIGAMIS	AGIKNNRU	UNRAKING
AGHOPSSW	SWAGSHOP	AGIIMSST	IMAGISTS	AGIKNNST	STANKING
AGHORSTW	WARTHOGS	AGIINNPS	SPAINING		TANKINGS
AGHRSTTU	STRAUGHT	AGIINNPT	PAINTING	AGIKNNSW	SWANKING
AGIIIKMR	KIRIGAMI		PATINING	AGIKNORT	TROAKING
AGIIILNS	LIAISING	AGIINNRS	INGRAINS	AGIKNOSS	SOAKINGS
AGIIINNS	INSIGNIA	AGIINNRT	TRAINING	AGIKNOST	GOATSKIN
AGIIINRV	VIRGINIA	AGIINNRV	RAVINING	AGIKNOSY	KAYOINGS
AGIIKLNS	SKAILING	AGIINNST	SAINTING	AGIKNPRS	PARKINGS
AGIIKNNT	ANTIKING		SATINING		SPARKING
AGIIKNRT	TRAIKING		STAINING	AGIKNPTU	UPTAKING
AGIILLLM	MILLIGAL	AGIINNSW	SWAINING	AGIKNQSU	QUAKINGS
AGIILLNV	VIALLING	AGIINNTT	TAINTING	AGIKNRSS	SARKINGS
AGIILLOV	VILLAGIO	AGIINOPT	OPIATING	AGIKNRST	KARTINGS
	VILLIAGO	AGIINORS	SIGNORIA		STARKING
AGIILMNP	IMPALING	AGIINORT	RIGATONI	AGIKNSST	SKATINGS
AGIILMNS	MAILINGS	AGIINPRS	ASPIRING		TASKINGS
	MISALIGN		PAIRINGS	AGILLLNS	LALLINGS
AGIILMNU	MIAULING		PRAISING	AGILLMNS	MALLINGS
AGIILNNP	PLAINING	AGIINPRT	PIRATING		SMALLING
AGIILNNS	NAILINGS	AGIINRRV	ARRIVING	AGILLMNU	MULLIGAN
	SNAILING	AGIINRSS	RAISINGS	AGILLMNY	MALIGNLY
AGIILNNU	INGUINAL	AGIINRTT	ATTIRING	AGILLMSU	GALLIUMS
AGIILNNV	ANVILING	AGIINSSZ	ASSIZING	AGILLNOW	ALLOWING
AGIILNNY	INLAYING	AGIINSTV	VISTAING	AGILLNOY	ALLOYING
AGIILNOP	PIGNOLIA	AGIINSTW	WAISTING	AGILLNPS	SPALLING
AGIILNOR	ORIGINAL		WAITINGS	AGILLNPY	PALLYING
AGIILNOT	INTAGLIO	AGIISSTV	VISAGIST	AGILLNRU	ALLURING
	LIGATION	AGIJLLNS	JINGALLS		LINGULAR
	TAGLIONI	AGIJLNPY	JAPINGLY	AGILLNRY	RALLYING
AGIILNOX	GLOXINIA	AGIJMMNS	JAMMINGS	AGILLNST	STALLING
AGIILNPS	LAIPSING	AGIJMNOR	MAJORING	AGILLNSU	LINGUALS
AGIILNPT	PLAITING	AGIJMNRU	JUMARING		LINGULAS
AGIILNQU	QUAILING	AGIJNNSU	JAUNSING	AGILLNSW	WALLINGS
AGIILNRS	GLAIRINS	AGIJNNTT	TJANTING	AGILLNSY	SALLYING
	RAILINGS	AGIJNNTU	JAUNTING		SIGNALLY

	SLANGILY	AGILNPSW	LAPWINGS	AGIMNORS	ORGANISM
AGILLLNTY	TALLYING		SPAWLING		ROAMINGS
AGILLOOR	GILLAROO	AGILNPSY	PALSYING	AGIMNORU	ORIGANUM
AGILLOPT	GALLIPOT		SPLAYING	AGIMNORY	AGRIMONY
AGILLORS	GORILLAS	AGILNPTT	PLATTING	AGIMNOST	ANTISMOG
AGILLOST	GALLIOTS	AGILNPUY	UPLAYING	AGIMNOSV	VAMOSING
AGILLPRY	PLAYGIRL	AGILNRSS	RASSLING	AGIMNPPS	MAPPINGS
AGILLPUY	PLAGUILY	AGILNRST	RATLINGS	AGIMNPRS	RAMPINGS
AGILLSSU	LUGSAILS		SLARTING	AGIMNPRT	TRAMPING
AGILLSSY	GLASSILY		STARLING	AGIMNPSS	SPASMING
AGILMMNS	LAMMINGS	AGILNRSU	SINGULAR	AGIMNPST	STAMPING
	SLAMMING	AGILNRSW	WARLINGS		TAMPINGS
	SMALMING		WARSLING	AGIMNPSV	VAMPINGS
AGILMNNT	MANTLING	AGILNRTT	RATTLING	AGIMNPSW	SWAMPING
AGILMNPS	LAMPINGS	AGILNRTW	TRAWLING	AGIMNRRY	MARRYING
	PSALMING	AGILNRVY	RAVINGLY	AGIMNRST	MIGRANTS
	SAMPLING	AGILNRWW	WRAWLING		SMARTING
AGILMNQU	QUALMING	AGILNRWX	WRAXLING	AGIMNRSW	SWARMING
AGILMNRS	MARLINGS	AGILNSST	ANGLISTS		SWINGARM
AGILMNST	MALTINGS		LASTINGS		WARMINGS
AGILMOPR	LIPOGRAM		SALTINGS	AGIMNRSY	MYRINGAS
AGILMORS	ALGORISM		SLATINGS	AGIMNRTU	MATURING
AGILMPSU	PLAGIUMS	AGILNSSV	SALVINGS	AGIMNSSU	ASSUMING
AGILNNNP	PLANNING	AGILNSSW	SWALINGS	AGIMNSTT	MATTINGS
AGILNNOP	PANGOLIN	AGILNSTT	SLATTING	AGIMNTTU	MUTATING
AGILNNOS	LOANINGS	AGILNSTU	SALUTING	AGIMORRT	MIGRATOR
AGILNNPT	PLANTING	AGILNSUV	AVULSING	AGIMORSS	ISOGRAMS
AGILNNRS	SNARLING	AGILNSUW	WAULINGS	AGIMORSU	GOURAMIS
AGILNNSS	LINSANGS	AGILNSVY	SAVINGLY	AGIMQRUY	QUAGMIRY
AGILNNST	SLANTING	AGILNSWW	WAWLINGS	AGIMRRST	TRIGRAMS
	TANLINGS	AGILNSWY	SWAYLING	AGINNNNY	NANNYING
AGILNNUW	UNLAWING	AGILNTTT	TATTLING	AGINNNOY	ANNOYING
AGILNNUY	UNGAINLY	AGILNTTW	WATTLING	AGINNNPS	PANNINGS
	UNLAYING	AGILNTUV	VAULTING		SPANNING
AGILNOOO	OOGONIAL	AGILNTUX	LUXATING	AGINNNST	TANNINGS
AGILNOOS	ISOGONAL	AGILNTWZ	WALTZING	AGINNNSV	VANNINGS
AGILNOPR	PAROLING	AGILNTXY	TAXINGLY	AGINNNSW	SWANNING
AGILNOPS	GALOPINS	AGILOOPY	APIOLOGY	AGINNNUW	UNWANING
AGILNOPT	PLOATING	AGILOORS	GLORIOSA	AGINNOOP	NAPOOING
AGILNORS	RANGOLIS	AGILOOXY	AXIOLOGY	AGINNOPR	APRONING
AGILNORT	TRIGONAL	AGILOPST	GALIPOTS	AGINNOPT	POIGNANT
AGILNOSS	GLOSSINA	AGILORSS	GIRASOLS	AGINNORT	IGNORANT
	LASSOING	AGILORSW	AIRGLOWS	AGINNOST	ASTONING
AGILNOST	ANTILOGS	AGILOSST	SALIGOTS	AGINNOSU	ANGINOUS
	SALTOING	AGILRSSY	GRASSILY	AGINNOTT	ATTONING
	SOLATING	AGILSYYZ	SYZYGIAL		NOTATING
AGILNOSV	SALVOING	AGIMMNPS	SPAMMING	AGINNOTV	NOVATING
AGILNOTT	TOTALING	AGIMMNRS	SMARMING	AGINNPPS	SNAPPING
AGILNOTY	ANTILOGY	AGIMMNRT	TRAMMING	AGINNPRW	PRAWNING
AGILNPPP	PLAPPING	AGIMMNTY	TAMMYING	AGINNPST	PANTINGS
AGILNPPS	LAPPINGS	AGIMMOSY	MISOGAMY	AGINNPSW	SPAWNING
	SAPPLING	AGIMNNOS	MASONING		WINGSPAN
	SLAPPING		MOANINGS	AGINNPUY	UNPAYING
AGILNPPY	APPLYING	AGIMNNOW	WOMANING	AGINNQTU	QUANTING
AGILNPRS	GRAPLINS	AGIMNNRU	MANURING	AGINNRRS	SNARRING
	SPARLING		UNARMING	AGINNRSS	SNARINGS
	SPRINGAL	AGIMNNSW	SWINGMAN	AGINNRST	RANTINGS
AGILNPSS	SAPLINGS	AGIMNNTU	UNTAMING		STARNING
AGILNPST	PLATINGS	AGIMNOOV	AMOOVING	AGINNRSW	WARNINGS
	SPALTING	AGIMNORR	ARMORING	AGINNRTT	TRANTING
	STAPLING		ROARMING	AGINNRTU	NATURING

AGINNRTY	TRAYNING	AGINPSSS	PASSINGS		NUTGALLS
	TYRANING	AGINPSST	PASTINGS	AGLLOORS	ROGALLOS
AGINNSTU	SAUNTING	AGINPSSU	PAUSINGS	AGLLOOST	GALLOOTS
	STAUNING	AGINPSTT	SPATTING	AGLLOPSU	PLUGOLAS
	UNSATING	AGINPSWY	YAWPINGS	AGLLPRSU	SPURGALL
AGINNSTY	STAYNING	AGINPSZZ	SPAZZING	AGLLPSTY	GLYPTALS
AGINNSUY	UNSAYING	AGINQRSU	SQUARING	AGLLRUVY	VULGARLY
AGINNSWY	YAWNINGS	AGINRRST	STARRING	AGLMOOTY	ATMOLOGY
AGINNTTU	ATTUNING		TARRINGS	AGLMOPSY	POLYGAMS
	NUTATING	AGINRRTY	TARRYING	AGLMOPYY	POLYGAMY
	TAUNTING	AGINRSST	GASTRINS	AGLMORSU	GLAMOURS
AGINNTUV	VAUNTING		STARINGS	AGLNOOOS	OLOGOANS
AGINNTUX	UNTAXING	AGINRSSU	ASSURING	AGLNORSU	LANGUORS
AGINNVVY	NAVVYING	AGINRSSY	SYRINGAS	AGLNOSST	GLASNOST
AGINOOPS	POGONIAS	AGINRSTT	RATTINGS	AGLNOSUU	ANGULOUS
AGINOORT	ROGATION		STARTING	AGLNOSWY	LONGWAYS
AGINOPPS	APPOSING	AGINRSTV	STARVING	AGLNPSUY	GUNPLAYS
AGINOPQU	OPAQUING	AGINRSTW	RINGTAWS	AGLNRUUV	UNVULGAR
AGINOPRV	VAPORING		STRAWING	AGLNSSSU	SUNGLASS
AGINORRS	GARRISON		WRASTING	AGLNSTUY	YGLAUNST
	ROARINGS	AGINRSTY	STINGRAY	AGLOOPST	GOALPOST
AGINORRW	ARROWING		STRAYING	AGLOOTUY	AUTOLOGY
AGINORRZ	RAZORING	AGINRSVW	SWARVING	AGLOPRSS	LOPGRASS
AGINORSS	ASSIGNOR	AGINRSVY	VARYINGS	AGLORSSY	GLOSSARY
	SIGNORAS	AGINRSWY	RINGWAYS	AGLPSSSY	SPYGLASS
	SOARINGS	AGINRTYY	GYNIATRY	AGLRTTUU	GUTTURAL
AGINORST	ORGANIST	AGINSSTT	TASTINGS	AGLSTUUY	AUGUSTLY
	ROASTING	AGINSSTW	WASTINGS	AGMMNOOR	MONOGRAM
AGINORSU	AROUSING	AGINSSWY	SWAYINGS		NOMOGRAM
AGINORSV	SAVORING	AGINSTTT	TATTINGS	AGMMNOOY	MONOGAMY
AGINORTT	ROTATING	AGINSTTW	SWATTING	AGMMOORT	TOMOGRAM
	TROATING	AGINSVVY	SAVVYING	AGMMORSY	MYOGRAMS
AGINORTV	GRAVITON	AGINSWWX	WAXWINGS	AGMMORYZ	ZYMOGRAM
AGINORTY	GYRATION	AGIOORSU	ORAGIOUS	AGMNNORS	GRANNOMS
	ORGANITY	AGIOORSZ	GRAZIOSO	AGMNNOSW	GOWNSMAN
AGINOSST	AGONISTS	AGIOORTU	AUTOGIRO	AGMNOORS	SONOGRAM
AGINOSSU	SAGOUINS	AGIOPPRT	AGITPROP	AGMNOORY	AGRONOMY
AGINOSTT	TANGOIST	AGIOPPST	AGITPOPS	AGMNORST	ANGSTROM
	TOASTING	AGIOPRUY	UROPYGIA	AGMNORSU	ORGANUMS
AGINOSTU	OUTGAINS	AGIORRTT	GRATTOIR	AGMNSSTU	MUSTANGS
AGINPPRS	RAPPINGS	AGIORSST	AGISTORS	AGMNSSTY	GYMNASTS
AGINPPRT	TRAPPING		ORGIASTS		SYNTAGMS
AGINPPRW	WRAPPING	AGIOSUUY	OUGUIYAS	AGMOOOSU	OOGAMOUS
AGINPPST	STAPPING	AGIRSSTU	SASTRUGI	AGMOOPRY	POROGAMY
	TAPPINGS	AGIRSTUZ	ZASTRUGI	AGMOOTVY	VAGOTOMY
AGINPPSW	SWAPPING	AGIRTTUY	GRATUITY	AGMOPRRS	PROGRAMS
AGINPPTU	PUPATING	AGJLRSUU	JUGULARS	AGMOPRSU	GOPURAMS
AGINPPUY	APPUYING	AGJNOORS	JARGOONS	AGMORRSW	RAGWORMS
AGINPRRS	SPARRING	AGJNOPST	JOGPANTS	AGMRSSSU	GRASSUMS
AGINPRRY	PARRYING	AGKLNNOS	ANKLONGS	AGNNNOOS	NONAGONS
AGINPRSS	PARSINGS	AGKLNNSU	ANKLUNGS	AGNNOOPT	POONTANG
	PINGRASS	AGKMMORY	KYMOGRAM	AGNNOORS	ARGONONS
	RASPINGS	AGKMNOPS	KAMPONGS		ORGANONS
AGINPRST	PARTINGS	AGKMPRSU	PUGMARKS	AGNNOQTU	QUANTONG
	PRATINGS	AGKNOPST	PAKTONGS	AGNNORSU	NONSUGAR
AGINPRSW	WARPINGS	AGKORRSW	RAGWORKS	AGNNOSSW	SWANSONG
AGINPRSY	PRAYINGS	AGKORSSW	GASWORKS	AGNNOTUW	OUTGNAWN
	SPRAYING	AGLLLNOW	LONGWALL	AGNORRST	GRANTORS
AGINPRTT	PRATTING	AGLLMOPW	GLOWLAMP	AGNORSST	SNOTRAGS
AGINPRTU	UPRATING	AGLLNOOS	GALLOONS	AGNORTUY	NUGATORY
AGINPRTY	PARTYING	AGLLNSTU	GALLNUTS	AGNOSTUW	OUTGNAWS

AGNPPRSU	UPSPRANG	**AHIIRSTW**	TAWHIRIS		MORPHIAS
AGNRSSTU	NUTGRASS	**AHIKLNRS**	RINKHALS	**AHIMOPST**	OPSIMATH
AGOORRTY	ROGATORY	**AHIKLRSY**	RAKISHLY	**AHIMORRW**	HAIRWORM
AGOORTUY	AUTOGYRO	**AHIKLSSS**	SHASLIKS	**AHIMPPSS**	SAPPHISM
AGOPPSST	STOPGAPS	**AHIKMNSS**	KHAMSINS	**AHIMPRST**	TRAMPISH
AGORRSST	GROSSART	**AHIKMRSS**	KASHMIRS	**AHIMPSSW**	SWAMPISH
	ROTGRASS	**AHIKNPRS**	PRANKISH	**AHIMRSST**	SMARTISH
AGORRSTW	RAGWORTS	**AHIKNPST**	TANKSHIP		THRIMSAS
AGORRSTY	GYRATORS	**AHIKORRW**	HAIRWORK	**AHIMSSSU**	HASSIUMS
AGORRTYY	GYRATORY	**AHIKORSS**	KAROSHIS	**AHIMSSTV**	MITSVAHS
AGORSTTY	GYROSTAT	**AHIKPRSS**	SPARKISH	**AHIMSTUZ**	AZIMUTHS
AGORSTUY	GRAYOUTS	**AHIKRSSW**	RIKSHAWS	**AHIMSTVZ**	MITZVAHS
AHHIKKRS	KHIRKAHS	**AHILLMOU**	HALLOUMI	**AHINNNSY**	NANNYISH
AHHIKLSS	SHASHLIK	**AHILLMPS**	PHALLISM	**AHINNOPT**	ANTIPHON
AHHILNPT	PHTHALIN	**AHILLMSS**	SMALLISH	**AHINNSTX**	XANTHINS
AHHILOST	HAILSHOT	**AHILLMTU**	THALLIUM	**AHINOOPY**	HYPONOIA
AHHILPSW	WHIPLASH	**AHILLNOS**	HALLIONS	**AHINOPRU**	OPHIURAN
AHHIMMSS	MISHMASH	**AHILLNPS**	PHALLINS	**AHINORST**	TRAHISON
AHHIMNSU	HAHNIUMS	**AHILLNRT**	INTHRALL	**AHINOSST**	ASTONISH
AHHINSST	SHANTIHS	**AHILLNST**	ANTHILLS	**AHINOSTZ**	HOATZINS
AHHIPRSS	SHARPISH	**AHILLNTW**	WANTHILL	**AHINPPSS**	SNAPPISH
AHHISSTT	SHITTAHS	**AHILLPST**	PHALLIST	**AHINPRST**	TRANSHIP
AHHKMOTW	HAWKMOTH	**AHILLSTT**	TALLITHS	**AHINPRSY**	SYRPHIAN
AHHKRSTU	KASHRUTH	**AHILLSVY**	LAVISHLY	**AHINPSWW**	WHIPSAWN
AHHLMRTY	RHYTHMAL	**AHILMMSS**	MASHLIMS	**AHINQSUV**	VANQUISH
AHHLNOPT	NAPHTHOL	**AHILMNSS**	MASHLINS	**AHINRSTY**	RHYTINAS
AHHLNPTY	NAPHTHYL	**AHILMOPT**	PHILAMOT	**AHINRSVY**	HRYVNIAS
AHHMPRRU	HARRUMPH	**AHILMOST**	HALIMOTS		VARNISHY
AHHMPRSU	HARUMPHS		MAILSHOT	**AHINSSTU**	INHAUSTS
AHHNORTW	HAWTHORN	**AHILMOSU**	HALOUMIS	**AHINSTUU**	TAUHINUS
AHHOOSST	SHATOOSH	**AHILMQSU**	QUALMISH	**AHIOOPPT**	PHOTOPIA
AHHOPRSS	SHOPHARS	**AHILMTUZ**	HALUTZIM	**AHIOOSST**	ATISHOOS
AHHOPSTU	APHTHOUS	**AHILNOPS**	SIPHONAL	**AHIOPRST**	APHORIST
AHHPSTUZ	HUTZPAHS	**AHILNOPT**	OLIPHANT	**AHIOPRSU**	OPHIURAS
AHIIILMN	MALIHINI	**AHILNORT**	HORNTAIL	**AHIOPRSV**	VAPORISH
AHIIKRSS	RIKISHAS	**AHILNRST**	INTHRALS	**AHIOPSXY**	HYPOXIAS
	SHIKARIS	**AHILOORT**	LOTHARIO	**AHIORSST**	AIRSHOTS
AHIILNPS	PLAINISH	**AHILOPSS**	ALPHOSIS		SHORTIAS
AHIILOST	HALIOTIS		HAPLOSIS	**AHIORSSW**	AIRSHOWS
AHIILPTW	WHIPTAIL	**AHILOPST**	HOSPITAL	**AHIORSTV**	TOVARISH
AHIILRTY	HILARITY	**AHILOSTU**	HALITOUS	**AHIORSUV**	HAVIOURS
AHIIMNNO	HOMINIAN	**AHILOSTZ**	THIAZOLS	**AHIOSTWY**	HOISTWAY
AHIIMNOT	HIMATION	**AHILPPSS**	PALSHIPS	**AHIPPSST**	SAPPHIST
AHIIMNRU	MANUHIRI		SHIPLAPS	**AHIPRSST**	HARPISTS
AHIIMNST	HISTAMIN	**AHILPRTU**	ULTRAHIP		STARSHIP
	ISTHMIAN	**AHILPSSY**	PHYSALIS	**AHIPRSSW**	WARSHIPS
	THIAMINS	**AHILPSXY**	PHYLAXIS	**AHIPRSWY**	WHIPRAYS
AHIIMOPX	AMPHIOXI	**AHILRSTY**	TRASHILY	**AHIPSSWW**	WHIPSAWS
AHIIMRST	ISARITHM	**AHILRTWY**	WRATHILY	**AHIPSSWY**	SHIPWAYS
AHIIMSSS	SASHIMIS	**AHIMMNSU**	HUMANISM	**AHIQRSSU**	SQUARISH
AHIIMSST	SAMITHIS	**AHIMMORZ**	MAHZORIM	**AHIRRSST**	STIRRAHS
AHIINOPT	PHOTINIA	**AHIMMOSS**	SHAMOSIM	**AHIRSSTT**	STARTISH
AHIINOTT	TITHONIA	**AHIMMOSV**	MOSHAVIM	**AHIRSSTW**	TRISHAWS
AHIINPRS	HAIRPINS	**AHIMNOST**	HOISTMAN	**AHISSSTU**	SHIATSUS
AHIINPST	ANTISHIP		MANIHOTS	**AHISSTTW**	WHATSITS
AHIINSST	SAINTISH	**AHIMNOSW**	WOMANISH	**AHISSTUZ**	SHIATZUS
AHIINSSW	SWAINISH	**AHIMNSTU**	HUMANIST	**AHISTTWW**	WHITTAWS
AHIINSTU	HUITAINS	**AHIMNSTX**	XANTHISM	**AHKLOPST**	SHOPTALK
AHIINSTZ	THIAZINS	**AHIMNTUY**	HUMANITY	**AHKLORTW**	LATHWORK
AHIIOPST	HOSPITIA	**AHIMOOSY**	YAHOOISM	**AHKMOORR**	MARKHOOR
AHIIPRSS	AIRSHIPS	**AHIMOPRS**	APHORISM	**AHKMORRS**	MARKHORS

AHKMRSTU	MUKHTARS	**AHMQSSUU**	MUSQUASH		SPIRILLA
AHKNOTTU	OUTTHANK	**AHMRSSTY**	THRYMSAS	**AIILLQSU**	QUILLAIS
AHKNOTUY	THANKYOU	**AHNNSTYY**	SYNANTHY	**AIILLUWW**	WILLIWAU
AHKRSSTU	KASHRUTS	**AHNOOPPY**	APOPHONY	**AIILLWWW**	WILLIWAW
	TUSHKARS	**AHNOOPRS**	HARPOONS	**AIILMMNS**	MINIMALS
AHLLLOOP	POOLHALL	**AHNOOPSU**	APHONOUS	**AIILMNNS**	LAMININS
AHLLNOOS	SHALLOON	**AHNOORRY**	HONORARY	**AIILMNOS**	MONILIAS
AHLLNOSS	SHALLONS	**AHNOPPSW**	PAWNSHOP	**AIILMNOT**	LIMATION
AHLLNOSY	HALLYONS	**AHNOPPSY**	PANSOPHY		MILTONIA
AHLLNOTW	TOWNHALL	**AHNOPSST**	SNAPSHOT	**AIILMNPS**	ALPINISM
AHLLNOUW	UNHALLOW	**AHNORSSX**	SAXHORNS	**AIILMNPT**	PALMITIN
AHLLNRTU	TURNHALL	**AHNORTWW**	WANWORTH	**AIILMNTT**	MILITANT
AHLLOPSS	SHALLOPS	**AHNOSTTW**	WHATNOTS	**AIILMNTU**	MINUTIAL
AHLLOSST	SHALLOTS	**AHNOSTUX**	XANTHOUS	**AIILMPUV**	IMPLUVIA
AHLLOSSW	SHALLOWS	**AHNPPSUU**	PUPUNHAS	**AIILMRST**	MISTRIAL
AHLLOSTU	THALLOUS	**AHNRSVYY**	HRYVNYAS		TRIALISM
AHLLOSTY	TALLYHOS	**AHOOPTYZ**	ZOOPATHY	**AIILMRTY**	LIMITARY
AHLLPRYY	PHYLLARY	**AHOOSSTY**	SOOTHSAY		MILITARY
AHLMMOPY	LYMPHOMA	**AHOOSTTW**	SAWTOOTH	**AIILMSTV**	VITALISM
AHLMMSSU	MASHLUMS	**AHOPSSTW**	WASHPOTS	**AIILNOPV**	PAVILION
AHLMNOOR	HORMONAL	**AHOPSTTW**	TOWPATHS	**AIILNOSS**	LIAISONS
AHLMOOPS	OMPHALOS	**AHOPSTUW**	SOUTHPAW	**AIILNOSV**	VISIONAL
AHLMOPTY	POLYMATH	**AHORTTUW**	WATTHOUR	**AIILNPST**	ALPINIST
AHLMOSUU	HAMULOUS	**AHOSSTUW**	WASHOUTS		ANTISLIP
AHLMSTYZ	SHMALTZY	**AHOSSTUY**	SOUTHSAY		PINTAILS
AHLNNORT	LANTHORN	**AHRSTUWY**	THRUWAYS		TAILSPIN
AHLNOPRS	ALPHORNS	**AIIILLVX**	LIXIVIAL	**AIILNRSU**	SILURIAN
AHLNOPST	HAPLONTS	**AIIILMST**	MILITIAS	**AIILNSTY**	SALINITY
	NAPHTOLS	**AIIILNST**	INITIALS	**AIILNTTY**	LATINITY
AHLNORST	ALTHORNS	**AIIILRVZ**	VIZIRIAL	**AIILOPPS**	PAPILIOS
AHLNRTWY	THRAWNLY	**AIIIMRSS**	SAIMIRIS	**AIILORSV**	RAVIOLIS
AHLOOPSW	WHOOPLAS	**AIIIRSSS**	SIRIASIS	**AIILPRSU**	LIPURIAS
AHLOOSTW	WOOLHATS	**AIIJKMOT**	KOMITAJI	**AIILQSSU**	SILIQUAS
AHLOPSST	SLAPSHOT	**AIIJNRTX**	JANITRIX	**AIILRSTT**	TRIALIST
AHLORRTY	HARLOTRY	**AIIKKSUY**	SUKIYAKI	**AIILRTTY**	TRIALITY
AHLORTTU	ULTRAHOT	**AIIKLLST**	SILKTAIL	**AIILRTVY**	RIVALITY
AHLOSTUU	OUTHAULS	**AIIKLNRR**	LARRIKIN	**AIILSTTV**	VITALIST
AHLRSTUY	LATHYRUS	**AIIKMMSS**	SKIMMIAS	**AIILSTTW**	WAITLIST
AHLRTTWY	THWARTLY	**AIIKMNNN**	MANNIKIN	**AIILTTVY**	VITALITY
AHMMMOST	MAMMOTHS	**AIIKMNNS**	MANIKINS	**AIIMMMST**	MAMMITIS
AHMMMSUU	HUMMAUMS		MANKINIS	**AIIMMNNY**	MINYANIM
AHMNNNOU	NONHUMAN	**AIIKMNPR**	MINIPARK	**AIIMMNRT**	MINIMART
AHMNNSTU	HUNTSMAN	**AIIKNNNP**	PANNIKIN	**AIIMMNSS**	ANIMISMS
	MANHUNTS	**AIIKNNST**	TANKINIS	**AIIMMNSX**	MAXIMINS
AHMNOPST	PHANTOMS	**AIIKORTY**	YAKITORI	**AIIMMNTY**	IMMANITY
AHMNOPTY	PHANTOMY	**AIIKRRSU**	RAURIKIS	**AIIMMSTX**	MAXIMIST
AHMNORRS	RAMSHORN	**AIIKTTZZ**	TZATZIKI	**AIIMNNOS**	INSOMNIA
AHMOOPPT	PHOTOMAP	**AIILLLMT**	MILLTAIL	**AIIMNNSV**	MINIVANS
AHMOOPSS	SHAMPOOS	**AIILLLUV**	ILLUVIAL	**AIIMNPSS**	PIANISMS
AHMOORSW	WASHROOM	**AIILLMNO**	MONILIAL		SINAPISM
AHMOOSSS	SAMSHOOS	**AIILLMRY**	MILLIARY	**AIIMNPST**	IMPAINTS
AHMOPTYY	MYOPATHY	**AIILLMST**	TALLISIM		MISPAINT
AHMORRST	SHORTARM	**AIILLMSW**	WILLIAMS	**AIIMNPSX**	PANMIXIS
AHMORRSU	MORRHUAS	**AIILLMTT**	TALLITIM	**AIIMNRST**	MARTINIS
AHMORSST	HARMOSTS	**AIILLNNV**	VANILLIN		MISTRAIN
AHMORSTY	HARMOSTY	**AIILLNOP**	POLLINIA	**AIIMNSST**	ANIMISTS
AHMORTTW	TAMWORTH	**AIILLNOT**	ILLATION		SAINTISM
AHMORTUW	WARMOUTH	**AIILLNPT**	ANTIPILL		SAMNITIS
AHMOSTTW	MOSTWHAT	**AIILLNSV**	VILLAINS	**AIIMNSTT**	IMITANTS
AHMPSSSU	SMASHUPS	**AIILLNVY**	VILLAINY		TITANISM
AHMPSTYY	SYMPATHY	**AIILLPRS**	SLIPRAIL	**AIIMNSTV**	NATIVISM

	VITAMINS	**AIKLLMUW**	WAUKMILL	**AILLOSTY**	LOYALIST
AIIMNTTU	TITANIUM	**AIKLLSTY**	STALKILY	**AILLOTTT**	TALLITOT
AIIMOPSX	APOMIXIS	**AIKLMNNS**	LINKSMAN	**AILLPPRU**	PUPILLAR
AIIMORTT	IMITATOR	**AIKLMPSU**	LAMPUKIS	**AILLPPSU**	SUPPLIAL
	TIMARIOT	**AIKLMPTU**	KALUMPIT	**AILLPPSY**	PLAYSLIP
AIIMOSST	AMITOSIS	**AIKLNNPS**	LINKSPAN	**AILLPPTU**	PULPITAL
AIIMPPRS	PRIAPISM		SNAPLINK	**AILLPRSY**	SPIRALLY
AIIMPRTY	IMPARITY	**AIKLNPST**	LANTSKIP	**AILLPRTY**	PALTRILY
AIIMRSST	SIMITARS	**AIKLNRSY**	SNARKILY	**AILLPSTY**	PLAYLIST
AIIMRSTU	TIRAMISU	**AIKLNSWY**	SWANKILY	**AILLPSUV**	PLUVIALS
AIIMRUVV	VIVARIUM	**AIKLOSUV**	SOUVLAKI	**AILLPSWY**	SPILLWAY
AIIMSSTT	MASTITIS	**AIKLOTTW**	KILOWATT	**AILLQSSU**	SQUILLAS
AIINNOPS	PIANINOS	**AIKLPRSY**	SPARKILY	**AILLRSTY**	RALLYIST
AIINNOSV	INVASION	**AIKLRSTT**	TITLARKS	**AILLRTUY**	RITUALLY
AIINNOTV	NIVATION	**AIKLSSSY**	SKYSAILS	**AILLRTWY**	WILLYART
AIINNQSU	QUININAS	**AIKMMNOO**	MAKIMONO	**AILLSTWW**	WITWALLS
AIINNQTU	QUINTAIN	**AIKMMRSS**	MISMARKS	**AILLSUVY**	VISUALLY
AIINNSTY	INSANITY	**AIKMNOOY**	YAKIMONO	**AILLWWWY**	WILLYWAW
AIINOOSV	AVOISION	**AIKMNRSS**	RANKISMS	**AILMMNOO**	MONOMIAL
AIINOPSS	SINOPIAS	**AIKMORSS**	KOMISSAR	**AILMMNUU**	ALUMINUM
AIINORTT	ANTIRIOT	**AIKMRSTZ**	SITZMARK	**AILMMOOR**	MAILROOM
	TRITONIA	**AIKNNOOS**	NAINSOOK	**AILMMORS**	MORALISM
AIINOSTT	NOTITIAS	**AIKNNSSW**	SWANSKIN	**AILMMORT**	IMMORTAL
	OSTINATI	**AIKNORST**	SKIATRON	**AILMMRSY**	SMARMILY
AIINPRSS	ASPIRINS	**AIKNORTY**	KARYOTIN	**AILMMSSY**	MYALISMS
AIINPSST	PIANISTS	**AIKNOSTT**	STOTINKA	**AILMMSTU**	SUMMITAL
AIINRRTT	IRRITANT	**AIKOORST**	ROOIKATS	**AILMMSUU**	ALUMIUMS
AIINRSTV	VITRAINS	**AIKOORSW**	KOROWAIS	**AILMMSUW**	MWALIMUS
AIINRSTZ	TRIAZINS	**AIKPTTUU**	PATUTUKI	**AILMNNOS**	NOMINALS
AIINSTTV	NATIVIST	**AIKRSSTY**	SATYRISK	**AILMNNOT**	MANNITOL
	VISITANT	**AIKRSTUZ**	ZIKURATS	**AILMNNTU**	LUMINANT
AIINTTVY	NATIVITY	**AILLLNOO**	LINALOOL	**AILMNOOP**	PALOMINO
AIIORRST	SARTORII	**AILLLNOS**	LINALOLS	**AILMNOOR**	MONORAIL
AIIORSTT	AORTITIS	**AILLLPSU**	LAPILLUS	**AILMNOOS**	MOONSAIL
AIIORSTV	OVARITIS	**AILLMMSY**	SMALMILY	**AILMNOOT**	MOTIONAL
AIIORTTV	VITIATOR	**AILLMNQU**	QUILLMAN	**AILMNOPR**	PROLAMIN
AIIPPRST	AIRSTRIP	**AILLMNST**	STILLMAN	**AILMNOPS**	LAMPIONS
AIIPRSST	PIARISTS	**AILLMOST**	MAILLOTS	**AILMNOPT**	PILOTMAN
AIIPRVVY	VIVIPARY		MISALLOT	**AILMNOPY**	PALIMONY
AIIPSTTU	PITUITAS	**AILLMOSY**	LOYALISM	**AILMNORT**	TORMINAL
AIIRSSTT	SATIRIST	**AILLMOTY**	MOLALITY	**AILMNOSS**	MALISONS
	SITARIST	**AILLMPRY**	PRIMALLY	**AILMNOSU**	LAMINOUS
AIISSSTY	SYSSITIA	**AILLMPSU**	PALLIUMS	**AILMNPSS**	MISPLANS
AIJKKNOU	KINKAJOU	**AILLMSSW**	SAWMILLS		PLASMINS
AIJLLOOR	JILLAROO	**AILLMUUV**	ALLUVIUM	**AILMNPST**	IMPLANTS
AIJLLOVY	JOVIALLY	**AILLNNOS**	LANOLINS		MISPLANT
AIJLNTUY	JAUNTILY	**AILLNOPP**	PAPILLON	**AILMNPTU**	PLATINUM
AIJLOTVY	JOVIALTY	**AILLNOPS**	PAILLONS	**AILMNRSU**	MURLAINS
AIJMORTY	MAJORITY	**AILLNOPV**	PAVILLON	**AILMNRUY**	LUMINARY
AIJNOPPY	POPINJAY	**AILLNORT**	ANTIROLL	**AILMNSTU**	SIMULANT
AIJNORST	JANITORS	**AILLNOST**	STALLION	**AILMOORS**	SAILROOM
AIKKLOOS	KALOOKIS	**AILLNOSU**	ALLUSION	**AILMOORT**	MOTORAIL
AIKKMOOR	KORIMAKO	**AILLNOUV**	ALLUVION		MOTORIAL
AIKKMOST	KOMATIKS	**AILLNPSY**	SPINALLY	**AILMOOSV**	MOVIOLAS
AIKKNOTY	KANTIKOY	**AILLNPTY**	PLIANTLY	**AILMOPRX**	PROXIMAL
AIKKOOSW	KOKOWAIS	**AILLNSST**	INSTALLS	**AILMORSS**	ORALISMS
AIKKOPSY	KOPIYKAS	**AILLOQTU**	TOQUILLA		SOLARISM
AIKKOSUZ	ZAKOUSKI	**AILLORSY**	SAILORLY	**AILMORST**	MORALIST
AIKKRTUZ	ZIKKURAT	**AILLORSZ**	ZORILLAS	**AILMORSU**	SOLARIUM
AIKLLLMW	WALKMILL	**AILLORTT**	LITTORAL	**AILMORSY**	ROYALISM
AIKLLMRR	RILLMARK		TORTILLA	**AILMORTY**	MOLARITY

	MORALITY	**AILNQSTU**	QUINTALS		ULTRAIST
AILMOSSY	ISOAMYLS	**AILNQTUY**	QUAINTLY	**AILRSTTY**	STRAITLY
AILMOSTT	TOTALISM	**AILNRSSU**	INSULARS	**AILRSUVV**	SURVIVAL
AILMOSTU	SOLATIUM	**AILNRSTT**	RATTLINS	**AILRTTUY**	TITULARY
AILMOSTV	VOLTAISM	**AILNRSTU**	LUNARIST	**AILSSTUW**	LAWSUITS
AILMPPSY	MISAPPLY	**AILNRTTU**	RUTILANT	**AIMMMNOU**	AMMONIUM
AILMPRSU	PRIMULAS	**AILNRUWY**	UNWARILY	**AIMMMSUX**	MAXIMUMS
AILMPSST	PALMISTS	**AILNSSTU**	STUNSAIL	**AIMMNORT**	MORTMAIN
	PSALMIST		UNALISTS	**AIMMNOSW**	WOMANISM
AILMPSSY	MISPLAYS	**AILNSTTU**	LUTANIST	**AIMMNPTU**	TIMPANUM
AILMPSTY	PTYALISM	**AILNSTUU**	NAUTILUS	**AIMMNSTU**	MANUMITS
AILMRRSU	RURALISM	**AILNSYZZ**	SNAZZILY	**AIMMORSS**	AMORISMS
AILMRSST	MISTRALS	**AILOOPRT**	TROOPIAL	**AIMMOSST**	ATOMISMS
AILMRSSU	SIMULARS	**AILOORRS**	SORORIAL		SOMATISM
	SURMISAL	**AILOORST**	ISOLATOR	**AIMMOSSU**	MIASMOUS
AILMRSTU	ALTRUISM		OSTIOLAR	**AIMMPSST**	MISSTAMP
	MURALIST	**AILOORSW**	WOORALIS	**AIMMRRSY**	MISMARRY
	ULTRAISM	**AILOORTV**	VIOLATOR	**AIMMRSUU**	MASURIUM
AILMSSTY	MYALISTS	**AILOPRRV**	PROVIRAL	**AIMNNOPT**	POINTMAN
AILNNOOT	NOTIONAL	**AILOPRSU**	PLIOSAUR	**AIMNNOSS**	MANSIONS
AILNNORV	NONRIVAL	**AILOPRTU**	TROUPIAL		ONANISMS
	NONVIRAL	**AILOPRTY**	POLARITY	**AIMNNOTU**	ANTIMUON
AILNNOSS	SOLANINS	**AILOPRUY**	POLYURIA		MOUNTAIN
AILNNOST	ANTLIONS	**AILOPSST**	APOSTILS	**AIMNNOTY**	ANTIMONY
AILNNOSU	UNISONAL		TOPSAILS		ANTINOMY
AILNNOTU	LUNATION	**AILOPSTT**	TALIPOTS	**AIMNNRTU**	RUMINANT
AILNNOTV	NONVITAL	**AILOQSTU**	ALIQUOTS	**AIMNOOOZ**	ZOONOMIA
AILNNPRU	PINNULAR	**AILORSST**	ORALISTS	**AIMNOORV**	OMNIVORA
AILNNPSU	PINNULAS		SLIOTARS	**AIMNOOST**	AMOTIONS
AILNNPTU	UNPLIANT		SOLARIST	**AIMNOOTY**	MYOTONIA
AILNNSTU	INSULANT	**AILORSTT**	ORLISTAT	**AIMNOPRS**	RAMPIONS
AILNOOPT	NOPALITO	**AILORSTU**	SUTORIAL	**AIMNOPRT**	PROTAMIN
	OPTIONAL	**AILORSTY**	ROYALIST	**AIMNOPST**	MAINTOPS
AILNOOST	SOLATION		SOLITARY		PTOMAINS
AILNOPPT	OPPILANT	**AILORSUW**	WOURALIS		TAMPIONS
AILNOPRU	UNIPOLAR	**AILORSVY**	SAVORILY	**AIMNOPTV**	PIVOTMAN
AILNOPRV	PARVOLIN	**AILORTTU**	TUTORIAL	**AIMNOQRU**	MAROQUIN
AILNOPSY	POLYNIAS	**AILORTUV**	OUTRIVAL	**AIMNORSU**	MAINOURS
AILNOPTV	ANVILTOP	**AILOSSTT**	ALTOISTS	**AIMNORTU**	MINOTAUR
AILNOPTY	PONYTAIL	**AILOSSTU**	OUTSAILS	**AIMNORTY**	MINATORY
AILNOQSU	AQUILONS	**AILOSTTT**	TOTALIST	**AIMNOSST**	STASIMON
AILNORST	TONSILAR	**AILOTTTY**	TOTALITY	**AIMNOSTU**	MANITOUS
AILNORTZ	TRIZONAL	**AILPPRUY**	PUPILARY		TINAMOUS
AILNOSSS	SASSOLIN	**AILPPSSU**	SUIPLAPS	**AIMNOSTW**	WOMANIST
AILNOSSY	LANOSITY	**AILPPSSY**	PAYSLIPS	**AIMNOTTU**	MUTATION
AILNOSUV	AVULSION	**AILPQSSU**	PASQUILS	**AIMNPRYY**	PAYNIMRY
AILNOSVY	SYNOVIAL	**AILPRSSU**	SPIRULAS	**AIMNPSTU**	SUMPITAN
AILNOTTV	VOLITANT		UPRISALS	**AIMNRRSU**	MURRAINS
AILNOTTY	TONALITY	**AILPRSTU**	STIPULAR	**AIMNRSSU**	SURAMINS
AILNOTUX	LUXATION	**AILPSSTY**	PAYLISTS		URANISMS
AILNPPSY	SNAPPILY	**AILPSSWY**	SLIPWAYS	**AIMNRSTT**	TANTRISM
AILNPRSU	PURSLAIN	**AILPSTUY**	PLAYSUIT		TRANSMIT
AILNPRSW	PRAWLINS	**AILQSTTU**	QUITTALS	**AIMNRSTU**	NATRIUMS
AILNPRUV	PULVINAR	**AILRRSTU**	RURALIST		NATURISM
AILNPSTU	NUPTIALS	**AILRRSTY**	STARRILY	**AIMNRSTV**	VARMINTS
	PATULINS	**AILRRTUY**	RURALITY	**AIMNRSUU**	URANIUMS
	UNPLAITS	**AILRSSTU**	TISSURAL	**AIMNSSTU**	TSUNAMIS
AILNPSTY	PTYALINS		TRISULAS	**AIMNSSYZ**	ZANYISMS
AILNPSUU	NAUPLIUS	**AILRSSTY**	TRYSAILS	**AIMNSTTU**	ANTISMUT
AILNPTTU	TULIPANT	**AILRSTTU**	ALTRUIST	**AIMOPRSS**	PROSAISM
AILNQRTU	TRANQUIL		TITULARS	**AIMOPRST**	ATROPISM

	PASTROMI		UTOPIANS	**AIORRTWY**	RYOTWARI
AIMOPSST	IMPASTOS	**AINOPSTW**	SWAPTION	**AIORSSST**	ASSISTOR
AIMOPSSY	SYMPOSIA	**AINOPTTU**	OUTPAINT	**AIORSSTU**	SAUTOIRS
AIMORRST	ARMORIST	**AINOPTWY**	WAYPOINT	**AIORSSUV**	SAVIOURS
AIMORRSU	ORARIUMS	**AINOQRRU**	QUARRION	**AIORSTTU**	TOURISTA
	ROSARIUM	**AINOQRSU**	NARQUOIS	**AIORSTTV**	VOTARIST
AIMORRUV	VARIORUM	**AINORRSW**	WARRISON	**AIORSTUV**	VIRTUOSA
AIMORSST	AMORISTS	**AINORRTT**	NITRATOR	**AIOSSSTY**	ISOSTASY
AIMORSSU	OSSARIUM	**AINORRTU**	URINATOR	**AIOSTTUW**	OUTWAITS
AIMORSTT	TRITOMAS	**AINORSST**	ARSONIST	**AIPPRSTY**	PAPISTRY
AIMORSTY	RAMOSITY	**AINORSSW**	WARISONS	**AIPRSSTU**	UPSTAIRS
AIMOSSTT	ATOMISTS	**AINORSTT**	STRONTIA	**AIPRSSTY**	SPARSITY
	SOMATIST	**AINORSTU**	RAINOUTS	**AIPYZZZZ**	PIZZAZZY
AIMPPRUU	PUPARIUM		SUTORIAN	**AIRRSTTY**	ARTISTRY
AIMPPSST	MAPPISTS	**AINORSTW**	WAITRONS	**AIRRSTZZ**	RIZZARTS
AIMPRSST	MISPARTS	**AINORSTX**	TRIAXONS	**AIRSSSTT**	TSARISTS
AIMPRSTY	PARTYISM	**AINORTVY**	VANITORY	**AIRSSTTT**	ATTRISTS
AIMRSSST	TSARISMS	**AINOSSSU**	SUASIONS	**AIRSSTTU**	TURISTAS
AIMRSSTT	MISSTART	**AINOSSTT**	STATIONS	**AIRSSTTZ**	TZARISTS
AIMRSSTU	MATSURIS	**AINOSSVY**	SYNOVIAS	**AISSSTTT**	STATISTS
AIMRSSTY	SYMITARS	**AINOSTTU**	TITANOUS	**AJKMNSTU**	MUNTJAKS
AIMRSSTZ	TZARISMS	**AINPPRSS**	PARSNIPS	**AJKNNOOU**	JUNKANOO
AIMRSTTU	STRIATUM	**AINPPRTT**	TRIPPANT	**AJLNORSU**	JOURNALS
AIMRTTUY	MATURITY	**AINPRSST**	SPIRANTS	**AJMNNOOR**	NONMAJOR
AIMSSSTT	STATISMS		SPRAINTS	**AJMRSTUY**	JURYMAST
AINNNOST	SANTONIN	**AINPRSSU**	PRUSSIAN	**AJORRTUY**	JURATORY
AINNNOSW	WANNIONS	**AINPRSTT**	TRIPTANS	**AKKLRSSY**	SKYLARKS
AINNOOTT	NOTATION	**AINPRSTU**	PURITANS	**AKKLSSWY**	SKYWALKS
AINNOOTV	NOVATION		UPTRAINS	**AKKMOOST**	TOKOMAKS
AINNOOTZ	ZONATION	**AINPSSST**	PISSANTS	**AKKORSTW**	TASKWORK
AINNOPRT	ANTIPORN	**AINPSSSY**	SYNAPSIS	**AKKOSUVZ**	KUVASZOK
AINNOPSS	SAPONINS	**AINPSSTU**	PUISSANT	**AKLLMRUY**	MULLARKY
AINNOPST	PINTANOS	**AINPSTTU**	PANTSUIT	**AKLMNOOW**	MOONWALK
AINNOSST	ONANISTS	**AINQRSTU**	QUINTARS	**AKLNNOPT**	PLANKTON
AINNOTTU	NUTATION	**AINQSSSU**	QUASSINS	**AKLOPRSW**	LAPWORKS
AINNPSST	SNAPTINS	**AINQTTUY**	QUANTITY	**AKLORSTW**	SALTWORK
AINNPSTU	UNPAINTS	**AINRSSTT**	STRAINTS	**AKLOSTTU**	OUTTALKS
AINNQSTU	QUINNATS		TRANSITS	**AKLOSTUW**	OUTWALKS
	QUINTANS	**AINRSTTT**	TITRANTS		WALKOUTS
AINNRSTT	INTRANTS	**AINRSTTU**	ANTIRUST	**AKLPRRSU**	LARKSPUR
AINNRSTU	INSURANT		NATURIST	**AKMMNOOR**	MONOMARK
AINNRSTY	TYRANNIS	**AINRSTTY**	TANISTRY	**AKMNOOOT**	TOKONOMA
AINNSSTT	INSTANTS	**AINSSSTU**	SUSTAINS	**AKMNOOPU**	MOKOPUNA
AINNSSTU	UNSAINTS	**AIOOORRT**	ORATORIO	**AKMNOOST**	MONOTASK
AINNSTTY	NYSTATIN	**AIOORRSW**	WOORARIS	**AKMNRSTU**	TRANKUMS
AINOOPTT	POTATION	**AIOORSUV**	OVARIOUS	**AKMOORST**	MOOKTARS
AINOORRS	ORARIONS	**AIOPRRST**	AIRPORTS	**AKMOPRST**	POSTMARK
AINOORST	ORATIONS		PARITORS	**AKMORSST**	OSTMARKS
AINOORTT	ROTATION	**AIOPRRTT**	PORTRAIT	**AKMQSTUU**	KUMQUATS
AINOOSTT	OSTINATO	**AIOPRSST**	AIRPOSTS	**AKMRSSTU**	MUSKRATS
AINOOSTV	OVATIONS		AIRSTOPS	**AKNOORST**	OSTRAKON
AINOOTTV	OTTAVINO		PROSAIST	**AKNOOUYZ**	YOKOZUNA
AINOPPRT	PARPOINT		PROTASIS	**AKNOPSTW**	SWANKPOT
AINOPPST	APPOINTS	**AIOPRSTT**	PATRIOTS	**AKNORSTU**	OUTRANKS
AINOPPTU	PUPATION	**AIOPRSUV**	PAVIOURS	**AKOPRRSU**	PARKOURS
AINOPRSS	PARISONS	**AIOPSSTT**	PASTITSO	**AKOPRRTW**	PARTWORK
AINOPRST	ATROPINS	**AIOPSTTU**	UTOPIAST	**AKORRSTW**	ARTWORKS
AINOPRTV	PROVIANT	**AIORRRSW**	WARRIORS	**AKORRSWW**	WARWORKS
AINOPSSS	PASSIONS	**AIORRSTT**	TRAITORS	**AKORSWWX**	WAXWORKS
AINOPSTT	POSTNATI	**AIORRSTV**	VARISTOR	**AKOSSTTU**	OUTTASKS
AINOPSTU	OPUNTIAS	**AIORRTTT**	TITRATOR	**ALLLOSWY**	SALLOWLY

ALLLPPUY	PULPALLY	**ALNOOPST**	PLATOONS
ALLLPRUY	PLURALLY	**ALNOOPSV**	VANPOOLS
ALLMNORY	NORMALLY	**ALNOOPXY**	POLYAXON
ALLMNOSY	ALLONYMS	**ALNOOPYZ**	POLYZOAN
ALLMNPSU	PULLMANS	**ALNOOPZZ**	POZZOLAN
ALLMOPSX	SMALLPOX	**ALNOORST**	ORTOLANS
ALLMORTY	MORTALLY	**ALNOPRST**	PLASTRON
ALLMOUWY	MULLOWAY	**ALNOPRTU**	PORTULAN
ALLMPRUU	PLUMULAR	**ALNOPRTY**	PATRONLY
ALLMTUUY	MUTUALLY	**ALNOPSTU**	OUTPLANS
ALLNNOOY	NONLOYAL	**ALNOPSYY**	POLYNYAS
ALLNNOUY	NOUNALLY	**ALNORRWY**	NARROWLY
ALLNOOPS	PLANOSOL	**ALNORSVY**	SOVRANLY
ALLNORSS	LASSLORN	**ALNPPSTU**	SUPPLANT
ALLOOSST	LATOSOLS	**ALNRRTUU**	NURTURAL
ALLOOSTX	AXOLOTLS	**ALNRTTUY**	TRUANTLY
ALLOPRSY	PAYROLLS	**ALOOPPRS**	PROPOSAL
ALLOPSTY	POSTALLY	**ALOOPRST**	POSTORAL
ALLOPTYY	ALLOTYPY	**ALOOPRTU**	UPROOTAL
ALLORSST	ALLSORTS	**ALOORSUV**	VALOROUS
ALLORSWY	ROLLWAYS	**ALOORTYZ**	ZOOLATRY
ALLORTUW	ULTRALOW	**ALOPPRSU**	POPULARS
ALLORTWW	WALLWORT	**ALOPPRYY**	POLYPARY
ALLOSSWW	SWALLOWS	**ALOPPSSU**	SUPPOSAL
ALLOSTWY	TOLLWAYS	**ALOPPSUU**	PAPULOUS
ALLRUUVY	UVULARLY	**ALOPRRSU**	PARLOURS
ALMMNRUU	NUMMULAR		SPORULAR
ALMMORTW	MALTWORM	**ALOPRSTT**	PORTLAST
ALMNNOOR	NONMORAL	**ALOPRSTU**	POSTURAL
ALMNOOPS	LAMPOONS		PULSATOR
ALMNOPSS	PLASMONS	**ALOPRSTY**	PASTORLY
ALMNORTY	MATRONLY	**ALOPSSSU**	SPOUSALS
ALMNOSSU	SOLANUMS	**ALOPSSUV**	VOLUSPAS
ALMNPSSU	SUNLAMPS	**ALOPSTUU**	PATULOUS
ALMOOPRS	PROSOMAL	**ALOPSTUY**	OUTPLAYS
ALMOOPRY	PLAYROOM	**ALOQRRSU**	RORQUALS
ALMOOPSY	POLYOMAS	**ALOQRSSU**	SQUALORS
ALMOORTU	ALUMROOT	**ALORRSUY**	SURROYAL
ALMOPPST	LAMPPOST	**ALORSTTW**	SALTWORT
	PALMTOPS	**ALORSTWW**	AWLWORTS
ALMOPRST	MARPLOTS	**ALORSUVY**	SAVOURLY
ALMORSUU	RAMULOUS	**ALORTUWY**	OUTLAWRY
ALMORSUY	RAMOUSLY	**ALOSSTTU**	OUTLASTS
ALMOSTTU	MULATTOS	**ALOSSTXY**	OXYSALTS
ALMPRSTU	PLASTRUM	**ALPPSTUY**	PLATYPUS
ALMPSSTY	SYMPLAST	**ALPRSSUU**	PURSUALS
ALMRRTYY	MARTYRLY	**ALPRSTUU**	PUSTULAR
ALMRTUUY	TUMULARY	**ALRSSSUU**	RUSSULAS
ALMSSSUY	ALYSSUMS	**AMMNOORT**	MOTORMAN
ALNNNOOT	NONTONAL	**AMMNOPSS**	PSAMMONS
ALNNOOPR	NONPOLAR	**AMMNPTUY**	TYMPANUM
ALNNOORS	NONSOLAR	**AMMOORRS**	MAORMORS
ALNNOORY	NONROYAL		MORMAORS
ALNNOPSY	NONPLAYS	**AMMOPSTU**	POMATUMS
ALNNORRU	NONRURAL	**AMMORRWY**	ARMYWORM
ALNNOTWY	WANTONLY	**AMNNOOSX**	MONAXONS
ALNNRSSU	UNSNARLS	**AMNNOOTT**	MONTANTO
ALNOOPPR	PROPANOL	**AMNNORSW**	MANSWORN
ALNOOPRS	POLARONS	**AMNNORSY**	MANSONRY
ALNOOPRT	PORTOLAN	**AMNNOSTT**	MONTANTS
	PRONOTAL	**AMNNOSTW**	TOWNSMAN

AMNNOSTY	ANTONYMS
AMNNOSUW	UNWOMANS
AMNNOTTU	MOUNTANT
AMNNOTYY	ANTONYMY
AMNNPSTU	PUNTSMAN
AMNNSSTU	STANNUMS
AMNNSTTU	STUNTMAN
AMNOOPPS	POMPANOS
AMNOOSTT	OTTOMANS
AMNOOSTZ	MATZOONS
AMNOOTUY	AUTONOMY
AMNOOTWY	TOYWOMAN
AMNOOTXY	TAXONOMY
AMNOPRSW	SPANWORM
AMNOPRSY	PARONYMS
AMNOPRYY	PARONYMY
AMNOPSTU	PANTOUMS
AMNORSST	TRANSOMS
AMNORSTU	ROMAUNTS
AMNORSTY	STRAMONY
AMNOSSYZ	ZYMOSANS
AMNOSTUY	AUTONYMS
AMNOTTUY	TAUTONYM
AMNQSTUU	QUANTUMS
AMNRSTTU	TANTRUMS
AMOOORSS	AMOROSOS
AMOOPRSS	PROSOMAS
AMOOPRST	TAPROOMS
AMOORRTY	MORATORY
AMOORSTZ	SMORZATO
AMOORTWY	MOTORWAY
AMOOSSTU	ASTOMOUS
AMOOSTVY	VASOTOMY
AMOOTTUY	AUTOTOMY
AMOPRRST	MARSPORT
AMOPRSXY	PAROXYSM
AMOPSSTT	TOPMASTS
AMOQSSUU	SQUAMOUS
AMORRTUY	MORTUARY
AMORSTTU	OUTSMART
AMORSWWX	WAXWORMS
AMORTTUY	MUTATORY
AMPRSTYY	SYMPATRY
AMRRSSTU	RASTRUMS
AMRSSTTU	STRATUMS
ANNNOSSY	SYNANONS
ANNOOQTU	NONQUOTA
ANNOORST	SONORANT
ANNOPRTY	NONPARTY
ANNOPSST	NONPASTS
ANNOSSTU	STANNOUS
ANNPRSUY	SPUNYARN
ANOOPRRT	PRONATOR
ANOOPRSS	SOPRANOS
ANOOPRST	PATROONS
ANOORSST	SANTOORS
ANOORSSU	ARSONOUS
ANOORSTT	ARNOTTOS
	RATTOONS
ANOORSUU	ANOUROUS
ANOPPPRT	PROPPANT

ANOPRRSS	SPORRANS	BBBCEOWY	COBWEBBY	BBDDEEMO	DEMOBBED
ANOPRSTU	STROUPAN	BBBDEEKO	KEBOBBED	BBDDEEMU	BEDUMBED
ANOPRTTU	TRAPUNTO	BBBDEEOR	BEROBBED	BBDDEERU	REDUBBED
ANOPSSTU	OUTSPANS	BBBDENOU	UNBOBBED	BBDDEILR	DRIBBLED
ANOQRSSU	SQUARSON	BBBEEILR	BLEBBIER	BBDDENUU	UNDUBBED
ANORSSTU	SANTOURS	BBBEGILN	BLEBBING	BBDEEGIR	GIBBERED
ANORSTVY	SOVRANTY	BBBEILOR	BLOBBIER	BBDEEGIT	GIBBETED
ANORSUVY	UNSAVORY		BOBBLIER	BBDEEIJR	JIBBERED
ANOTTUUV	OUTVAUNT	BBBEILRU	BUBBLIER	BBDEEIST	DEBBIEST
ANPPSSUW	SUPPAWNS	BBBEILSU	BUBBLIES	BBDEEMNU	BENUMBED
ANPRSSTU	SUNTRAPS	BBBEINOT	BOBBINET	BBDEENUW	UNWEBBED
	UNSTRAPS	BBBELRSU	BLUBBERS	BBDEEOPP	BEBOPPED
ANPRSTUU	PURSUANT		BUBBLERS	BBDEERRU	RUBBERED
ANRRSTUY	UNSTARRY	BBBELRUY	BLUBBERY	BBDEERSU	SUBBREED
ANRRTTUY	TRUANTRY	BBBGILNO	BLOBBING	BBDEFILR	FRIBBLED
ANRSSSTU	SUNSTARS		BOBBLING	BBDEGLRU	GRUBBLED
ANRSSTYY	SYNASTRY	BBBGILNU	BLUBBING	BBDEHORT	THROBBED
AOOOPRST	SOAPROOT		BUBBLING	BBDEHRSU	SHRUBBED
AOOOPRSZ	SPOROZOA	BBBHNOOY	HOBNOBBY	BBDEILLN	BELLBIND
AOOOPRTZ	PROTOZOA	BBBHOOUU	HUBBUBOO	BBDEILLR	BELLBIRD
AOOPPRSY	APOSPORY	BBBIOSTT	BOBBITTS	BBDEILQU	QUIBBLED
AOOPRSSU	SAPOROUS	BBBOOSXY	BOBBYSOX	BBDEILRR	DRIBBLER
AOOPRSTT	TAPROOTS	BBCCIKOS	BIBCOCKS	BBDEILRS	DIBBLERS
AOOPRSTU	ATROPOUS	BBCDEILR	CRIBBLED		DRIBBLES
AOOPRSTW	SOAPWORT	BBCDERSU	SCRUBBED	BBDEILRT	DRIBBLET
AOOPRSUV	VAPOROUS	BBCDIMOY	BOMBYCID	BBDEILRU	BLUEBIRD
AOOPRTTY	POTATORY	BBCEEHOS	BOBECHES	BBDEIMOV	DIVEBOMB
AOORRSTT	ROTATORS	BBCEHINS	NEBBICHS	BBDEINOR	RIBBONED
AOORRSTU	OUTROARS	BBCEHIRU	CHUBBIER	BBDEINRU	UNRIBBED
AOORRTTY	ROTATORY	BBCEILRS	CRIBBLES	BBDEIQSU	SQUIBBED
AOORSSTU	OUTSOARS		SCRIBBLE	BBDEIRRS	DRIBBERS
AOORSSUV	SAVOROUS	BBCEILRU	CLUBBIER	BBDEKLNO	KNOBBLED
AOORSTUV	OUTSAVOR	BBCEIOST	COBBIEST	BBDEKLNU	KNUBBLED
AOPPRRST	RAPPORTS	BBCEIRRS	CRIBBERS	BBDELLMU	DUMBBELL
AOPPRSST	PASSPORT	BBCEISTU	CUBBIEST	BBDELLOO	BOBOLLED
AOPPRSTU	TRAPPOUS	BBCEKKOS	KEBBOCKS	BBDELOOS	BEBLOODS
AOPRRRTY	PARROTRY	BBCEKKSU	KEBBUCKS	BBDELOSS	BOBSLEDS
AOPRRSSW	SPARROWS	BBCEKLSU	BLESBUCK	BBDELSTU	STUBBLED
AOPRRSSY	PORTRAYS	BBCEKLUU	BLUEBUCK	BBDENRUU	UNRUBBED
AOPRRTUY	POURTRAY	BBCELORS	CLOBBERS	BBDERRSU	DRUBBERS
AOPRSSTT	STARSPOT		COBBLERS	BBDERSUU	SUBURBED
AOPRSTTU	OUTPARTS		SCROBBLE	BBDFLSUU	FLUBDUBS
AOPRSTTY	PYROSTAT	BBCELORY	COBBLERY	BBDGIILN	DIBBLING
AOPRSTUY	OUTPRAYS	BBCELRSU	CLUBBERS	BBDGIINR	DRIBBING
AOPSSSTU	PASSOUTS	BBCEMNOU	BUNCOMBE	BBDGINRU	DRUBBING
AOPSSTWY	WAYPOSTS	BBCERRSU	SCRUBBER	BBDGINSU	DUBBINGS
AOPSTTUU	AUTOPUTS	BBCGHIIN	CHIBBING	BBDIIKMU	DIBBUKIM
AOPTTUYY	AUTOTYPY	BBCGIINR	CRIBBING	BBDIKMUY	DYBBUKIM
AORRSSSU	ASSURORS	BBCGILNO	COBBLING	BBDIOORS	BOOBIRDS
AORRSTTW	STARWORT	BBCGILNU	CLUBBING	BBDOSUYY	BUSYBODY
AORRTTWW	WARTWORT	BBCGINSU	CUBBINGS	BBEEEMSX	BEMBEXES
AORSSTTU	STRATOUS	BBCHILSU	CLUBBISH	BBEEERRS	BERBERES
AORSSTTY	STAROSTY	BBCHILUY	CHUBBILY	BBEEERSU	BEBEERUS
AORSTTTU	OUTSTART	BBCHKOOS	BOSCHBOK	BBEEHINS	NEBBISHE
AORSUVVY	VOUVRAYS	BBCHKSUU	BUSHBUCK	BBEEHLOW	BOBWHEEL
AOSSTTUY	OUTSTAYS	BBCILLUY	CLUBBILY	BBEEIIRR	BERIBERI
APPRRSUU	PURPURAS	BBCILMSU	CLUBBISM	BBEEILPR	PEBBLIER
APRSSTTU	STARTUPS	BBCILRSY	SCRIBBLY		PLEBBIER
	UPSTARTS	BBCILSTU	CLUBBIST	BBEEIMSX	BEMBIXES
APRSSUWY	SPURWAYS	BBCIPSUU	SUBPUBIC	BBEEIMTT	BIMBETTE
ASVYYZZZ	ZYZZYVAS	BBCKLOSU	SUBBLOCK	BBEEINRR	BERBERIN

BBEEIRRS	BERBERIS	BBEIOOST	BOBOTIES			RUBBLING
BBEEISTW	WEBBIEST	BBEIORTU	OUTBRIBE	BBGILNSU	SLUBBING
BBEEJLMU	BEJUMBLE	BBEIRSTU	STUBBIER	BBGILRUY	GRUBBILY
BBEELLLU	BLUEBELL		SUBTRIBE	BBGIMNOS	BOMBINGS
BBEEOPPR	BEBOPPER	BBEISSTU	STUBBIES		MOBBINGS
BBEFILRR	FRIBBLER	BBEISTTU	TUBBIEST	BBGINNSU	SNUBBING
BBEFILRS	FRIBBLES	BBEKLNOS	KNOBBLES	BBGINOSS	SOBBINGS
BBEFILRT	FLIBBERT	BBEKLNSU	KNUBBLES	BBGINOST	STOBBING
BBEFIMOR	FIREBOMB	BBEKLOOU	BLUEBOOK	BBGINOSW	SWOBBING
BBEFISTU	FUBBIEST	BBEKLOSS	BLESBOKS	BBGINPSU	PUBBINGS
BBEFLRSU	FLUBBERS	BBEKLSUU	BUBUKLES	BBGINRSU	RUBBINGS
BBEGIIST	GIBBSITE	BBEKNOOT	BONTEBOK	BBGINSSU	SUBBINGS
BBEGILNP	PEBBLING	BBEKNORS	KNOBBERS	BBGINSTU	STUBBING
BBEGILOR	GLOBBIER	BBELLORU	BOERBULL		TUBBINGS
BBEGILRS	GRIBBLES	BBELLOSY	BELLBOYS	BBGLOOWY	LOBBYGOW
BBEGILRY	GLIBBERY	BBELLRUY	LUBBERLY	BBHILOSS	SLOBBISH
BBEGILST	GLIBBEST	BBELLSTU	BULBLETS	BBHIMOSY	HOBBYISM
BBEGINNS	SNEBBING	BBELMOST	BOMBLETS	BBHINOSS	SNOBBISH
BBEGINSW	WEBBINGS	BBELMRSU	BUMBLERS	BBHINSSU	SNUBBISH
BBEGIOST	GOBBIEST	BBELNORS	NOBBLERS	BBHIOOSY	BOOBYISH
BBEGIRRU	GRUBBIER	BBELOORW	BOBOWLER	BBHIORTY	HOBBITRY
BBEGLORS	GOBBLERS	BBELORSS	SLOBBERS	BBHIOSTY	HOBBYIST
BBEGLRSU	GRUBBLES	BBELORSU	BOERBULS	BBHIRSUY	RUBBISHY
BBEGRRSU	GRUBBERS	BBELORSW	WOBBLERS	BBHKOOSS	BOSHBOKS
BBEHINSY	NEBBISHY	BBELORSY	LOBBYERS	BBHOOSUW	WHOOBUBS
BBEHIOTW	BOBWHITE		SLOBBERY	BBHRSSUU	SUBSHRUB
BBEHLORS	HOBBLERS	BBELOTUW	BLOWTUBE	BBIIILMS	BILIMBIS
BBEHLSUU	BLUEBUSH	BBELRRSU	BURBLERS	BBIILLSU	SILLIBUB
BBEHMSTU	BETHUMBS	BBELRSSU	SLUBBERS	BBIILSST	BIBLISTS
BBEHORRT	THROBBER	BBELSSTU	STUBBLES	BBIJMOOS	JIBBOOMS
BBEIILRS	RIBIBLES	BBEMOSXY	BOMBYXES	BBIKLLOO	BILLBOOK
BBEIIMRS	IMBIBERS	BBENORSY	SNOBBERY	BBIKLNOO	BOBOLINK
BBEIIRST	RIBBIEST	BBENRSSU	SNUBBERS	BBILLOYY	BILLYBOY
BBEIKNOR	KNOBBIER	BBEORRXY	BOXBERRY	BBILLSUU	LULIBUBS
BBEIKNRU	KNUBBIER	BBEORSSW	SWOBBERS	BBILMOSY	LOBBYISM
BBEILLLU	BLUEBILL	BBEPRSUW	BREWPUBS	BBILNOSY	SNOBBILY
BBEILLNO	BONIBELL	BBFGILNO	FLOBBING	BBILOSTY	LOBBYIST
BBEILNRS	NIBBLERS	BBFGILNU	FLUBBING	BBILOSUU	BIBULOUS
BBEILNRU	NUBBLIER	BBGGIILN	GLIBBING	BBILRSTU	BLURBIST
BBEILORS	SLOBBIER	BBGGILNO	GOBBLING	BBILSTUY	STUBBILY
BBEILORW	WOBBLIER	BBGGINRU	GRUBBING	BBIMMOSS	MOBBISMS
BBEILOST	BIBELOTS	BBGHILNO	HOBBLING	BBIMNOSS	SNOBBISM
BBEILOSW	WOBBLIES	BBGIIIMN	IMBIBING	BBIMOOSY	BOOBYISM
BBEILPRS	PRIBBLES	BBGIIJNS	JIBBINGS	BBIMOSSY	YOBBISMS
BBEILQRU	QUIBBLER	BBGIIKLN	KIBBLING	BBINORRY	RIBBONRY
BBEILQSU	QUIBBLES	BBGIILMN	BLIMBING	BBJLOOSW	BLOWJOBS
BBEILRRU	BURBLIER	BBGIILNN	NIBBLING	BBKLOOSU	BLOUBOKS
	RUBBLIER	BBGIILNW	WIBBLING	BBKOOOOS	BOOBOOKS
BBEILRRY	BILBERRY	BBGIINNS	SNIBBING	BBLLNNUU	BULNBULN
BBEILRST	STIBBLER	BBGIINRS	RIBBINGS	BBLLOUYY	BULLYBOY
	TRIBBLES	BBGIJNOS	JOBBINGS	BBNOORSU	BOURBONS
BBEILRSU	SLUBBIER	BBGIKNNO	KNOBBING	BBNORSTU	STUBBORN
BBEILSST	STIBBLES	BBGILLSU	BILLBUGS	BBOOSSSY	BOSSBOYS
BBEIMMOT	TIMEBOMB	BBGILMNO	MOBBLING	BCCCIILY	BICYCLIC
BBEIMNOS	BOMBESIN	BBGILMNU	BUMBLING	BCCDEILY	BICYCLED
BBEIMOST	BOMBSITE	BBGILNNO	NOBBLING	BCCDHIKO	DOBCHICK
BBEIMRSU	BRUMBIES	BBGILNNU	NUBBLING	BCCDIKOR	COCKBIRD
BBEINORS	SNOBBIER	BBGILNOW	WOBBLING	BCCEEIRR	CEREBRIC
BBEINOST	NOBBIEST	BBGILNOY	LOBBYING	BCCEHIRU	CHERUBIC
BBEINRSU	SNUBBIER	BBGILNRU	BLURBING	BCCEHORS	BESCORCH
BBEINSTU	NUBBIEST		BURBLING	BCCEIIIS	CICISBEI

BCCEIILO	LIBECCIO	BCDEHLOT	BLOTCHED	BCEEHNRS	BENCHERS
BCCEIIOS	CICISBEO	BCDEHNRU	BRUNCHED	BCEEHNRU	UNBREECH
BCCEILOS	ECBOLICS	BCDEHOOR	BROOCHED	BCEEHNTU	BEECHNUT
BCCEILOY	BIOCYCLE	BCDEIIOS	BIOCIDES	BCEEHOSU	BOUCHEES
BCCEILRU	CRUCIBLE	BCDEIIRR	RICEBIRD	BCEEIILM	IMBECILE
BCCEILRY	BICYCLER	BCDEIITU	DECUBITI	BCEEIKRR	BICKERER
BCCEILSU	CUBICLES	BCDEIKRR	REDBRICK	BCEEILNR	BERNICLE
BCCEILSY	BICYCLES	BCDEIKSS	SICKBEDS	BCEEIMRS	BECRIMES
BCCEMORS	CROMBECS	BCDEIKST	BEDTICKS	BCEEINOT	CENOBITE
BCCEMRUU	CUCUMBER	BCDEILRY	CREDIBLY	BCEEIOSX	ICEBOXES
BCCHIKOY	BOYCHICK	BCDEIMNO	COMBINED	BCEEIPSS	BESPICES
BCCIIMOR	MICROBIC	BCDEINOU	ICEBOUND		BICEPSES
BCCIISTU	CUBISTIC	BCDEIRSU	CURBSIDE	BCEEIRSS	ESCRIBES
BCCIITUY	CUBICITY	BCDEKOOO	CODEBOOK	BCEEIRTT	BRETTICE
BCCIKLLO	COCKBILL	BCDEKORS	BEDROCKS	BCEEJORT	REOBJECT
BCCILMOU	COLUMBIC	BCDEKOSS	BEDSOCKS	BCEEKNOR	BECKONER
BCCILOOR	BROCCOLI	BCDELMRU	CRUMBLED	BCEEKNSU	BUCKEENS
BCCILOSU	BUCOLICS	BCDELMSU	SCUMBLED	BCEEKSUY	BUCKEYES
BCCINORR	CORNCRIB	BCDELOSU	BECLOUDS	BCEELLOT	BELLCOTE
BCCIRTUU	CUCURBIT	BCDEMNOU	UNCOMBED	BCEELOOR	BORECOLE
BCCLOOOO	COCOBOLO	BCDEMOOY	COEMBODY	BCEELOSU	BOUCLEES
BCCMOOSX	COXCOMBS	BCDEMORY	CORYMBED	BCEELRTU	TUBERCLE
BCCMSSUU	SUCCUMBS	BCDENRUU	UNCURBED	BCEEMMOR	COMEMBER
BCCNOORS	CORNCOBS	BCDEOORT	CODEBTOR	BCEEMNRU	ENCUMBER
BCCSSUUU	SUCCUBUS	BCDEOOWY	COWBOYED	BCEEMRRU	CEREBRUM
BCDDEEEK	BEDECKED	BCDEORSU	OBSCURED		CUMBERER
BCDDEEKU	BEDUCKED	BCDEORSW	BECROWDS	BCEENORS	OBSCENER
BCDDEENU	BEDUNCED	BCDEOSSU	SUBCODES	BCEENRSU	CRUBEENS
BCDDEHIL	CHILDBED	BCDESSUU	SUBDUCES	BCEEPRTY	CYBERPET
BCDDESUU	SUBDUCED	BCDHIRSU	BRUCHIDS	BCEERSSU	BECURSES
BCDEEEHR	BREECHED	BCDHOOSU	CUBHOODS	BCEERSTU	SUBERECT
BCDEEGLU	BECUDGEL	BCDHORSU	SUBCHORD	BCEERSXY	CYBERSEX
BCDEEHLN	BLENCHED	BCDIIMOR	BROMIDIC	BCEERTVY	BREVETCY
BCDEEHNR	BEDRENCH	BCDIIPSU	BICUSPID	BCEFFIIR	FEBRIFIC
BCDEEHOU	DEBOUCHE	BCDIKLLU	DUCKBILL	BCEFHISU	SUBCHIEF
BCDEEIKN	BENEDICK	BCDILMOY	MOLYBDIC	BCEFILOR	FORCIBLE
BCDEEIKR	BICKERED	BCDILORU	COLUBRID	BCEGHILN	BELCHING
BCDEEILR	CREDIBLE	BCDIMOOR	COMORBID	BCEGHINN	BENCHING
BCDEEILS	DECIBELS	BCDIMORS	SCOMBRID	BCEGIINO	BIOGENIC
BCDEEILU	EDUCIBLE	BCDINOSW	COWBINDS	BCEGIMNO	BECOMING
BCDEEIMR	BECRIMED	BCDINRUU	RUBICUND	BCEGKMSU	GEMSBUCK
BCDEEINT	BENEDICT	BCDIORSW	COWBIRDS	BCEGLNOO	CONGLOBE
BCDEEIPS	BESPICED	BCDKNOOO	BOONDOCK	BCEHIIOT	BIOETHIC
BCDEEIRS	DESCRIBE	BCDKORSU	BURDOCKS	BCEHIIRT	BITCHIER
	ESCRIBED	BCDSSTUU	SUBDUCTS	BCEHILMY	CHIMBLEY
BCDEEIST	BISECTED	BCEEEFIN	BENEFICE	BCEHIMOR	BICHROME
BCDEEJOT	OBJECTED	BCEEEFKN	NECKBEEF	BCEHIMRS	BESMIRCH
BCDEEKMO	BEMOCKED	BCEEEHIR	BEECHIER	BCEHIMRU	CHERUBIM
BCDEEKNO	BECKONED	BCEEEHRS	BREECHES	BCEHINNO	CHINBONE
BCDEEKRU	REEDBUCK	BCEEENRS	BESCREEN	BCEHINRU	BUNCHIER
BCDEEKTU	BUCKETED	BCEEERSU	BERCEUSE		CHERUBIN
BCDEELNU	BEUNCLED	BCEEFILN	FENCIBLE	BCEHINSU	SUBNICHE
BCDEELOR	CORBELED	BCEEFKLS	BEFLECKS	BCEHIORS	BRIOCHES
BCDEELRU	BECURLED	BCEEFLTU	CLUBFEET	BCEHIORT	BOTCHIER
BCDEEMOR	RECOMBED	BCEEGIRS	ICEBERGS	BCEHIOST	BIOTECHS
BCDEEMRU	CUMBERED	BCEEHINR	BENCHIER	BCEHIRRT	BRICHTER
BCDEENSU	BEDUNCES	BCEEHKSU	BUCKSHEE	BCEHIRST	BRITCHES
BCDEEORV	BEDCOVER	BCEEHLNR	BLENCHER	BCEHIRTY	BITCHERY
BCDEEOTT	OBTECTED	BCEEHLNS	BLENCHES	BCEHLOST	BLOTCHES
BCDEERSU	BECURSED	BCEEHLOT	BECLOTHE	BCEHLRSU	BLUCHERS
BCDEHINS	DISBENCH	BCEEHLRS	BELCHERS	BCEHMSTU	BESMUTCH

BCEHNOPT	BENCHTOP	**BCEKLNOT**	BLONCKET	**BCGINORU**	COURBING
BCEHNRRU	BRUNCHER	**BCEKLNNU**	UNBUCKLE	**BCGINRSU**	CURBINGS
BCEHNRSU	BRUNCHES	**BCEKLORS**	BLOCKERS	**BCHIILTY**	BITCHILY
BCEHOORS	BROOCHES	**BCEKLRSU**	BUCKLERS	**BCHIIOPS**	BIOCHIPS
BCEHOPSU	SUBEPOCH		SUBCLERK	**BCHIIOST**	COHIBITS
BCEHORRU	BROCHURE	**BCEKMSTU**	STEMBUCK	**BCHIIRRS**	BIRCHIRS
BCEHORSS	BORSCHES	**BCEKOORU**	BUCKEROO	**BCHIISSU**	HIBISCUS
BCEHORST	BOTCHERS	**BCEKORST**	BROCKETS	**BCHIKLOS**	BLOCKISH
BCEHORSW	COWHERBS	**BCEKORSU**	ROEBUCKS	**BCHIKOSU**	CHIBOUKS
BCEHORTY	BOTCHERY	**BCEKOSTY**	BYCOKETS	**BCHIKOSY**	BOYCHIKS
BCEHRSTU	BUTCHERS	**BCELLOSW**	COWBELLS	**BCHILNUY**	BUNCHILY
BCEHRTUY	BUTCHERY	**BCELLRUW**	WELLCURB	**BCHILOTY**	BOTCHILY
BCEHSTTU	BUTCHEST	**BCELLSSU**	SUBCELLS	**BCHIOORY**	CHOIRBOY
BCEIIKLN	ICEBLINK	**BCELMOSS**	COMBLESS	**BCHIOPRS**	PIBROCHS
BCEIIKRR	BRICKIER	**BCELMRSU**	CLUMBERS	**BCHIORRT**	BIRROTCH
BCEIIKRS	BRICKIES		CRUMBLES	**BCHIOTTU**	OUTBITCH
BCEIILMS	MISCIBLE	**BCELMSSU**	SCUMBLES	**BCHKNORU**	BUCKHORN
BCEIILNV	VINCIBLE	**BCELNOSW**	BECLOWNS	**BCHKOSTU**	BUCKSHOT
BCEIILOP	EPIBOLIC	**BCELORUV**	OVERCLUB	**BCHLNOUX**	LUNCHBOX
BCEIIMRS	IMBRICES	**BCELRSSU**	CURBLESS	**BCHLRSUU**	CLUBRUSH
BCEIINRS	INSCRIBE	**BCEMOORV**	COMBOVER	**BCHNOORS**	BRONCHOS
BCEIKLMO	COMBLIKE	**BCEMRRSU**	CRUMBERS	**BCHNORSU**	BRONCHUS
BCEIKLMS	LIMBECKS	**BCEMRSSU**	SCUMBERS	**BCHORSST**	BORSCHTS
BCEIKLOO	BOOKLICE	**BCENOOOX**	ECONOBOX	**BCIIILMU**	UMBILICI
BCEIKLOR	BLOCKIER	**BCENORSU**	BOUNCERS	**BCIIIOTT**	BIOTITIC
BCEIKLOS	BLOCKIES	**BCEORRSU**	OBSCURER	**BCIIKLNS**	NIBLICKS
BCEIKLRS	BRICKLES	**BCEORRWY**	COWBERRY	**BCIILLSY**	SIBYLLIC
BCEIKLTU	BLUETICK	**BCEORSSU**	BESCOURS	**BCIILMRU**	LUMBRICI
BCEIKSST	BESTICKS		OBSCURES	**BCIILMSU**	BULIMICS
BCEILMRS	CLIMBERS	**BCERSSTU**	BECRUSTS	**BCIILNVY**	VINCIBLY
	RECLIMBS	**BCESSSTU**	SUBSECTS	**BCIILORS**	COLIBRIS
BCEILNOS	BINOCLES	**BCESSTUU**	SUBCUTES	**BCIILOTY**	BIOLYTIC
BCEILNRU	RUNCIBLE	**BCFIIMOR**	MORBIFIC	**BCIIMNOO**	BIONOMIC
BCEILNYZ	BENZYLIC	**BCFIIORT**	FIBROTIC	**BCIIMORU**	CIBORIUM
BCEILORS	BRICOLES	**BCFILORY**	FORCIBLY	**BCIIMRSS**	SCRIBISM
	CORBEILS	**BCFIMORU**	CUBIFORM	**BCIINORT**	BORNITIC
BCEILOSU	CIBOULES	**BCFKMSUU**	BUMFUCKS	**BCIINORV**	VIBRONIC
BCEILOTU	TUBICOLE	**BCFLOOTU**	CLUBFOOT	**BCIIOPTY**	BIOTYPIC
BCEILPRU	REPUBLIC	**BCFSSSUU**	SUBFUSCS	**BCIIORST**	BISTROIC
BCEIMNOR	COMBINER	**BCGHIINR**	BIRCHING		SORBITIC
BCEIMNOS	COMBINES	**BCGHIINT**	BITCHING	**BCIIOSTT**	BISCOTTI
BCEIMNRU	INCUMBER	**BCGHINNU**	BUNCHING	**BCIISSTU**	BISCUITS
BCEIMORS	MICROBES	**BCGHINOR**	BROCHING	**BCIISTUY**	BISCUITY
BCEIMOST	COMBIEST	**BCGHINOT**	BOTCHING	**BCIKKNSU**	BUCKSKIN
BCEIMOSW	COMBWISE	**BCGHINPU**	PINCHBUG	**BCIKLOOT**	BOOTLICK
BCEIMRRU	CRUMBIER	**BCGHINTU**	BUTCHING	**BCIKLOST**	LOBSTICK
BCEINORS	BICORNES	**BCGIIKNR**	BRICKING	**BCIKORRW**	CRIBWORK
BCEINORU	BOUNCIER	**BCGIIKST**	BIGSTICK	**BCIKOSTT**	BITSTOCK
BCEINOVX	BICONVEX	**BCGIILMN**	CLIMBING		BITTOCKS
BCEINRSU	BRUCINES	**BCGIILOO**	BIOLOGIC	**BCILLPUY**	PUBLICLY
BCEIOOPS	BIOSCOPE	**BCGIINRS**	SCRIBING	**BCILMOSY**	SYMBOLIC
BCEIOOSS	SCOOBIES	**BCGIKLNO**	BLOCKING	**BCILMOTU**	OUTCLIMB
BCEIORRS	CRIBROSE	**BCGIKLNU**	BUCKLING	**BCILMPSU**	UPCLIMBS
BCEIORST	BISECTOR	**BCGIKNSU**	BUCKINGS	**BCILNOUY**	BOUNCILY
BCEIRRSS	SCRIBERS	**BCGILMNY**	CYMBLING	**BCILOORS**	BICOLORS
BCEIRSTU	BRUCITES	**BCGIMNOR**	CROMBING		BROCOLIS
BCEIRTTY	YTTERBIC	**BCGIMNOS**	COMBINGS	**BCILOORU**	BICOLOUR
BCEJOORT	OBJECTOR	**BCGIMNRU**	CRUMBING	**BCIMORSU**	MICROBUS
BCEJSSTU	SUBJECTS	**BCGIMNUU**	CUMBUNGI	**BCINORSU**	BURSICON
BCEKLLNU	BULLNECK	**BCGINNOU**	BOUNCING		RUBICONS
BCEKLLOS	BELLOCKS		BUNCOING	**BCINOSSU**	SUBSONIC

BCINOSTU	SUBTONIC	BDDEEIMO	EMBODIED	BDEEEGRU	BUDGEREE
BCINOSUU	INCUBOUS	BDDEEINR	REBIDDEN	BDEEEHST	BEDSHEET
BCINSTUU	SUBTUNIC	BDDEEINT	INDEBTED	BDEEEHTU	HEBETUDE
BCIOOPSY	BIOSCOPY	BDDEEINW	BINDWEED	BDEEEILN	BEELINED
BCIOORST	ROBOTICS	BDDEEIOR	REBODIED	BDEEEILV	BELIEVED
BCIOOSTT	BISCOTTO	BDDEEIRR	REEDBIRD	BDEEEINS	BENISEED
BCIOPSTU	SUBOPTIC	BDDEEIRS	BIRDSEED	BDEEEIRW	DWEEBIER
	SUBTOPIC		DEBRIDES	BDEEEIRW	
BCIORRSU	CRIBROUS	BDDEEISS	BEDSIDES	BDEEELLR	REBELLED
BCIORSST	CROSSBIT	BDDEEKNU	DEBUNKED	BDEEELLV	BEVELLED
BCISSTUU	SUBCUTIS	BDDEELMU	BEMUDDLE	BDEEELMM	EMBLEMED
BCJKMSUU	JUMBUCKS	BDDEELNO	BOLDENED	BDEEELPT	BEPELTED
BCKKOOOO	COOKBOOK	BDDEENNU	UNBENDED	BDEEELRS	BLEEDERS
BCKLLOOS	BOLLOCKS	BDDEENOT	OBTENDED	BDEEELRY	BERLEYED
BCKLLOSU	BULLOCKS	BDDEENRU	BURDENED	BDEEELUW	BLUEWEED
BCKLLOUY	BULLOCKY	BDDEEORR	BORDERED	BDEEEMMR	MEMBERED
BCKLNOSU	SUNBLOCK	BDDEEORS	DESORBED	BDEEEMNS	BEDESMEN
	UNBLOCKS	BDDEEOSS	DEBOSSED	BDEEENTT	BENETTED
BCKMMOSU	BUMMOCKS	BDDEEOTT	BEDOTTED	BDEEEPSS	BESPEEDS
BCKNNOOS	BONNOCKS	BDDEERRU	DEBURRED	BDEEERRS	BREEDERS
BCKOOOPY	COPYBOOK	BDDEESSU	DEBUSSED		REBREEDS
BCKOSTTU	BUTTOCKS	BDDEESTU	BEDUSTED	BDEEERRV	REVERBED
BCLMOORU	CLUBROOM	BDDEESUW	SUBDEWED	BDEEERTT	BETTERED
BCLMOOSU	COULOMBS	BDDEFOOR	FORBODED	BDEEERTV	BREVETED
BCLMOOTU	OUTCLOMB	BDDEGINS	BEDDINGS	BDEEETTW	BEWETTED
BCLOORTU	CLUBROOT	BDDEIIMO	IMBODIED	BDEEFFPU	BEPUFFED
BCLOOSSU	SUBCOOLS	BDDEILNR	BRINDLED	BDEEFFRU	BUFFERED
BCLORSTU	CLOTBURS	BDDEILOO	BLOODIED		REBUFFED
BCLSSTUU	SUBCULTS	BDDEINNU	UNBIDDEN	BDEEFFTU	BUFFETED
BCMMRSUU	CRUMBUMS	BDDEINOU	UNBODIED	BDEEFGGO	BEFOGGED
BCMORSUU	CUMBROUS	BDDEINRU	UNDERBID	BDEEFGIT	BEGIFTED
BCMOSSTU	COMBUSTS	BDDEIORS	DISORBED	BDEEFGLU	BEGULFED
BCNNOUUY	UNBOUNCY		DISROBED	BDEEFIIW	WEBIFIED
BCOOOORTW	CROWBOOT	BDDEIOWY	WIDEBODY	BDEEFILR	BELFRIED
BCOOOSSU	OSSOBUCO	BDDEIRRS	REDBIRDS	BDEEFINN	BEFINNED
BCOOPSYY	COPYBOYS	BDDEISSU	SUBSIDED	BDEEFINR	BEFRIEND
BCOORSSW	CROSSBOW	BDDEISTU	BUDDIEST	BDEEFIRS	DEBRIEFS
BCOOSTTY	BOYCOTTS	BDDELMRU	DRUMBLED	BDEEFIRU	RUBEFIED
BCORSTTU	OBSTRUCT	BDDELOOR	BLOODRED	BDEEFITT	BEFITTED
BCRSSTUU	SUBCRUST	BDDELORS	BRODDLES	BDEEFLOO	BEFOOLED
BCSTUUZZ	BUZZCUTS	BDDENNOU	UNBONDED	BDEEFLOU	BEFOULED
BDDDDEEU	DEBUDDED	BDDENOTU	OBTUNDED	BDEEFOOR	FOREBODE
BDDDEEEM	EMBEDDED	BDDENRUU	UNDERBUD	BDEEFOOW	BEEFWOOD
BDDDEEIM	IMBEDDED	BDDEORTU	OBTRUDED	BDEEFSUU	SUBFEUED
BDDDEEIR	DEBRIDED	BDDGIINS	BIDDINGS	BDEEGGIW	BEWIGGED
BDDDEEMU	BEMUDDED	BDDGILNU	BUDDLING	BDEEGGMO	EMBOGGED
BDDDEENU	UNBEDDED	BDDGINOR	BRODDING	BDEEGGNU	UNBEGGED
BDDEEELL	DEBELLED	BDDGINSU	BUDDINGS	BDEEGGRU	BEGRUDGE
BDDEEERS	REEDBEDS	BDDGINUY	BUDDYING		BUGGERED
BDDEEESS	SEEDBEDS	BDDGIORS	BIRDDOGS		DEBUGGER
BDDEEFIR	BIRDFEED	BDDGOOSY	DOGSBODY	BDEEGHIS	BESIGHED
BDDEEFLU	BEFUDDLE	BDDHIIRY	DIHYBRID	BDEEGILN	BLEEDING
BDDEEGGU	DEBUGGED	BDDINOOW	WOODBIND	BDEEGILR	BEGIRDLE
BDDEEGIL	BEGILDED	BDDINOSU	DISBOUND	BDEEGILU	BEGUILED
BDDEEGIR	BEGIRDED	BDDINPUU	PUDIBUND	BDEEGIMR	BEGRIMED
BDDEEGNU	BEDUNGED	BDEEEEMS	BESEEMED	BDEEGINR	BERINGED
BDDEEGTU	BUDGETED	BDEEEEMT	BETEEMED		BREEDING
BDDEEHOS	DEBOSHED	BDEEEGIS	BESIEGED		BREINGED
BDDEEIMM	BEDIMMED	BDEEEGMM	BEGEMMED	BDEEGINW	BEDEWING
		BDEEEGNO	EDGEBONE		BEWINGED
		BDEEEGNR	BREENGED	BDEEGINY	BEDYEING
				BDEEGKNU	BEGUNKED

BDEEGLNO	BELONGED				
	ENGLOBED	BDEEINST	BENDIEST	BDEENPRS	PREBENDS
BDEEGMOU	EMBOGUED	BDEEINSW	BENDWISE	BDEENRRS	BREDRENS
BDEEGMSU	BESMUDGE	BDEEINSZ	BEDIZENS	BDEENRRU	BURDENER
BDEEGOOY	BOOGEYED	BDEEIORS	REBODIES	BDEEOORT	REBOOTED
BDEEGORU	BEROUGED	BDEEIORU	BOUDERIE	BDEEOPRR	REPROBED
BDEEGRSV	SVEDBERG	BDEEIOSW	WEBISODE	BDEEOPRS	BEPROSED
BDEEGRTU	BUDGETER	BDEEIRRU	REBURIED	BDEEOPRW	BEPOWDER
BDEEGSSU	BUGSEEDS	BDEEIRRV	RIVERBED	BDEEORRR	BORDERER
BDEEHISW	DWEEBISH	BDEEIRST	BEDRITES	BDEEORRS	RESORBED
BDEEHLNO	BEHOLDEN		BESTRIDE	BDEEORRV	OVERBRED
BDEEHLOR	BEHOLDER		BISTERED	BDEEORSS	BEDSORES
BDEEHLOW	BEHOWLED	BDEEIRSU	DEBRUISE	BDEEORST	BESORTED
BDEEHLSU	BUSHELED	BDEEIRSY	BIRDSEYE		BESTRODE
BDEEHMOR	HOMEBRED	BDEEIRTT	BITTERED	BDEEORSV	OBSERVED
BDEEHMRY	BERHYMED	BDEEISTU	BESUITED	BDEEORTU	OUTBREED
BDEEHOOV	BEHOOVED	BDEEKMOS	BESMOKED	BDEEORTV	OBVERTED
BDEEHORT	BOTHERED		EMBOSKED	BDEEOSSS	DEBOSSES
BDEEHORW	BEWHORED	BDEEKNRU	BUNKERED		OBSESSED
BDEEHOSS	DEBOSHES		DEBUNKER	BDEEOSST	BETOSSED
BDEEIILL	ELIDIBLE	BDEEKOOR	REBOOKED	BDEEOSTT	BESOTTED
BDEEIILN	INEDIBLE	BDEEKORR	BROKERED		OBTESTED
BDEEIILR	BIELDIER	BDEELLMU	UMBELLED	BDEEOSTW	BESTOWED
BDEEIIPT	BEPITIED	BDEELLOW	BELLOWED	BDEEPRRU	PUREBRED
BDEEIKRS	KERBSIDE		BOWELLED	BDEERRTU	TRUEBRED
BDEEIKSS	BEKISSED	BDEELLRU	BULLERED	BDEERRWY	DEWBERRY
BDEEILLL	LIBELLED	BDEELLRY	REDBELLY	BDEERSSU	BURSEEDS
BDEEILLR	REBILLED	BDEELLTU	BULLETED	BDEERSUW	BURWEEDS
BDEEILLT	BILLETED	BDEELLUW	BULLWEED	BDEERTTU	BUTTERED
BDEEILLU	ELUDIBLE	BDEELMNO	EMBOLDEN		REBUTTED
BDEEILMO	BEMOILED	BDEELMOR	REBELDOM	BDEESSSU	DEBUSSES
	EMBOILED	BDEELMPU	BEPLUMED	BDEFIILR	BIRDLIFE
BDEEILMP	BEDIMPLE	BDEELMRT	TREMBLED	BDEFIIRR	FIREBIRD
BDEEILMR	LIMBERED	BDEELMRU	LUMBERED	BDEFIIRU	RUBIFIED
BDEEILMS	BESLIMED	BDEELNNO	ENNOBLED	BDEFIKOR	BIFORKED
	BESMILED	BDEELNRS	BLENDERS	BDEFILRS	FILBERDS
BDEEILNR	LINEBRED		REBLENDS	BDEFILSU	SUBFIELD
	RENDIBLE	BDEELNST	BENDLETS	BDEFIMOR	BIFORMED
BDEEILNU	UNEDIBLE	BDEELNTU	UNBELTED	BDEFINRR	FERNBIRD
BDEEILNV	VENDIBLE	BDEELORU	REDOUBLE	BDEFIORS	FIBROSED
BDEEILOR	ERODIBLE	BDEELOSU	BESOULED	BDEFOORS	FORBODES
	REBOILED	BDEELOSV	BELOVEDS	BDEFOORY	FOREBODY
BDEEILOS	OBELISED	BDEELRTU	BUTLERED	BDEGHHIR	HIGHBRED
BDEEILOT	BETOILED	BDEELRUY	BURLEYED	BDEGHILT	BLIGHTED
BDEEILOZ	OBELIZED	BDEELSST	DEBTLESS	BDEGHIRT	BEDRIGHT
BDEEILRV	BEDRIVEL	BDEEMNOT	BODEMENT	BDEGHIST	BEDIGHTS
BDEEILRW	BEWILDER		ENTOMBED	BDEGIILN	BIELDING
BDEEILSV	BEDEVILS	BDEEMNOW	ENWOMBED	BDEGIINT	BETIDING
BDEEILTT	BETITLED	BDEEMNRU	NUMBERED		DEBITING
BDEEIMNR	BRIDEMEN	BDEEMORR	EMBORDER	BDEGILNN	BLENDING
BDEEIMOR	EMBODIER	BDEEMORS	SOMBERED	BDEGILNO	INGLOBED
BDEEIMOS	EMBODIES	BDEEMORW	BEWORMED	BDEGINNO	DEBONING
BDEEIMRT	TIMBERED	BDEEMORY	REEMBODY	BDEGINNS	BENDINGS
BDEEIMST	BEDTIMES	BDEEMOSS	EMBOSSED	BDEGINOS	OBSIGNED
	BEMISTED	BDEEMPRU	BUMPERED	BDEGINSU	DEBUSING
BDEEIMSU	EMBUSIED	BDEEMRTU	EMBRUTED	BDEGINTU	DEBUTING
BDEEINOS	EBONISED	BDEEMSSU	EMBUSSED	BDEGIOST	BODGIEST
BDEEINOT	OBEDIENT	BDEENNOT	BONNETED	BDEGLMRU	GRUMBLED
BDEEINOZ	EBONIZED	BDEENORS	DEBONERS	BDEGLNOU	BLUDGEON
BDEEINRS	INBREEDS		REDBONES	BDEGLRSU	BLUDGERS
BDEEINRT	INTERBED	BDEENOSW	BESNOWED	BDEGNOSW	BEDGOWNS
		BDEENOUY	UNOBEYED		

BDEGOOSY	GOODBYES	BDEILSST	BILSTEDS	BDELNOSS	BOLDNESS
BDEGORRY	DOGBERRY	BDEILSTU	BLUDIEST		BONDLESS
BDEGORSU	BUDGEROS	BDEIMNOT	INTOMBED	BDELNOST	BLONDEST
BDEGORUW	BUDGEROW	BDEIMNSU	NIMBUSED	BDELNOTU	UNBOLTED
BDEHIKOS	KIBOSHED	BDEIMNUU	UNIMBUED	BDELNOUU	UNDOUBLE
BDEHILMT	THIMBLED	BDEIMORR	IMBORDER	BDELNOUW	UNBLOWED
BDEHIOPS	BISHOPED		MORBIDER	BDELNRSU	BLUNDERS
BDEHKOSY	KYBOSHED	BDEIMORS	BROMIDES		BUNDLERS
BDEHLMOW	WHOMBLED		BROMISED	BDELOORS	BOODLERS
BDEHLSUV	BUSHVELD	BDEIMORY	EMBRYOID	BDELOORV	OVERBOLD
BDEHMOOY	HOMEBODY	BDEIMORZ	BROMIZED	BDELOOUW	BLUEWOOD
BDEHOOOO	BOOHOOED	BDEIMOSS	IMBOSSED	BDELORSU	BOULDERS
BDEHORSU	BESHROUD	BDEIMRSU	IMBURSED		DOUBLERS
BDEHORSY	HERDBOYS	BDEIMRTU	IMBRUTED	BDELORSW	BOWLDERS
BDEIIIKN	BIKINIED	BDEINOOS	NOBODIES	BDELORTU	TROUBLED
BDEIIKLR	BIRDLIKE	BDEINOOW	WOODBINE	BDELORUU	DOUBLURE
BDEIIKTZ	KIBITZED	BDEINORV	OVENBIRD	BDELORUY	BOULDERY
BDEIILMR	BIRDLIME	BDEINOSU	BEDOUINS	BDELOSTU	DOUBLETS
BDEIILNY	INEDIBLY	BDEINOTU	BOUNTIED	BDELPSUU	SUBDUPLE
BDEIILRU	BLUIDIER	BDEINPRS	PREBINDS	BDEMNNOS	BONDSMEN
BDEIILTY	DEBILITY	BDEINRRS	BREDRINS	BDEMNOSU	EMBOUNDS
BDEIIMOS	IMBODIES	BDEINRSU	BURNSIDE	BDEMNOTU	UNTOMBED
BDEIINNZ	BENZIDIN	BDEINRTU	TURBINED	BDEMNSSU	DUMBNESS
BDEIIOPS	BIOPSIED		UNDERBIT	BDEMOORS	BEDROOMS
BDEIKMOS	IMBOSKED	BDEINRUU	UNBURIED		BOREDOMS
BDEIKNOR	BRODEKIN	BDEINSUX	SUBINDEX	BDEMOOSY	SOMEBODY
BDEIKNSU	BUSKINED	BDEINTTU	UNBITTED	BDEMOOTT	BOTTOMED
BDEILLMU	BDELLIUM	BDEIOORR	BROODIER	BDEMSSUU	SUBSUMED
BDEILLNU	UNBILLED	BDEIOORS	DOOBRIES	BDENNOTU	DUBONNET
BDEILLNW	WINDBELL	BDEIORRS	BROIDERS	BDENNOUY	YBOUNDEN
BDEILLOW	BILLOWED		DISROBER	BDENNRUU	UNBURDEN
BDEILLOX	BOLLIXED	BDEIORRU	BOURRIDE		UNBURNED
BDEILMNO	IMBOLDEN	BDEIORRY	BROIDERY	BDENOORU	EUROBOND
BDEILMOS	SEMIBOLD	BDEIORSS	DISROBES	BDENOOTU	UNBOOTED
BDEILMSU	SUBLIMED	BDEIORST	DEBITORS	BDENOOTW	BENTWOOD
BDEILNNO	BLONDINE		DEORBITS	BDENOPRU	PREBOUND
BDEILNOU	UNBOILED	BDEIORSV	OVERBIDS		UNPROBED
	UNILOBED	BDEIORTU	TUBEROID	BDENORSU	BOUNDERS
BDEILNOY	BODYLINE	BDEIOSSY	DISOBEYS		REBOUNDS
BDEILNRS	BLINDERS	BDEIOSUX	SUBOXIDE		SUBORNED
	BRINDLES	BDEIRSSU	DISBURSE	BDENOTTU	BUTTONED
BDEILNRU	UNBRIDLE		SUBSIDER	BDENRSTU	SUBTREND
BDEILNST	BLINDEST	BDEISSSU	SUBSIDES	BDENRSUU	UNBRUSED
BDEILNVY	VENDIBLY	BDEISSTU	SUBEDITS	BDENRUUY	UNDERBUY
BDEILOOR	BLOODIER	BDEKLLUY	BULLDYKE	BDENSSTU	SUBTENDS
BDEILOOS	BLOODIES	BDEKLMOO	BLOKEDOM	BDENSTUU	UNBUSTED
BDEILOPU	UPBOILED	BDEKNOOS	BOOKENDS	BDEOORRS	BROODERS
BDEILOQU	OBLIQUED	BDEKNOOU	UNBOOKED	BDEOORRW	BORROWED
BDEILORT	TRILOBED	BDELLOOR	BORDELLO	BDEOORSY	DOOBREYS
BDEILORV	LOVEBIRD		DOORBELL	BDEOOTUX	OUTBOXED
BDEILOSS	BODILESS	BDELLOOX	BOLLOXED	BDEOOWWW	BOWWOWED
BDEILOSW	DISBOWEL	BDELLORS	BEDROLLS	BDEOPSST	BEDPOSTS
BDEILPRU	PREBUILD	BDELLOUZ	BULLDOZE	BDEOPSTU	SUBDEPOT
BDEILQTU	BEDQUILT	BDELMOOS	BLOOSMED	BDEORRSU	BORDURES
BDEILRRS	BRIDLERS	BDELMOSY	SYMBOLED		BOURDERS
BDEILRRY	LYREBIRD	BDELMRSU	DRUMBLES		SUBORDER
BDEILRST	BRISTLED	BDELMRUU	DELUBRUM	BDEORRTU	OBTRUDER
	DRIBLETS	BDELMSTU	STUMBLED	BDEORRUW	BURROWED
BDEILRSU	BUILDERS	BDELNNOU	UNNOBLED	BDEORSSU	ROSEBUDS
	REBUILDS	BDELNNUU	UNBUNDLE	BDEORSTU	DOUBTERS
BDEILRTT	BRITTLED	BDELNOOS	DOBLONES		OBTRUDES

	REDOUBTS	BDHLOOOT	HOTBLOOD	BDLOOOSX	OXBLOODS
BDEORSUV	OVERDUBS	BDHMOOOS	HOBODOMS	BDLORSUW	SUBWORLD
BDEPSSTU	DUBSTEPS	BDHMOSUW	DUMBSHOW	BDMOORRS	SMORBROD
BDERSSUU	SUBDUERS	BDHNRSUU	UNSHRUBD	BDMOOSSS	BOSSDOMS
BDERSTUU	SUBTRUDE	BDHOOOSY	BOYHOODS	BDMORSUW	BUDWORMS
BDFFIPRU	PUFFBIRD	BDIIINRS	BRINDISI	BDNNOOTU	BUNODONT
BDFGNOOU	FOGBOUND	BDIIIORV	VIBRIOID	BDNOOPTU	POTBOUND
BDFIIITY	BIFIDITY	BDIIKNOS	BODIKINS	BDNOORSU	BOURDONS
BDFIIORS	FIBROIDS	BDIILLNW	WINDBILL	BDNOOSUX	SOUNDBOX
BDFILLLO	BILLFOLD	BDIILMSS	DISLIMBS	BDNOOSWW	DOWNBOWS
BDFILNOO	BLOODFIN	BDIILMSU	MISBUILD	BDNOOTUU	OUTBOUND
BDFILSUU	SUBFLUID	BDIILOOS	BIOSOLID	BDNORSTU	TURBONDS
BDFINORU	UNFORBID	BDIILOQU	OBLIQUID	BDNORSUW	RUBDOWNS
BDFINRUU	FURIBUND	BDIILORS	OILBIRDS	BDOOOSWX	BOXWOODS
BDFIRRSU	SURFBIRD	BDIIMNSS	MISBINDS	BDORUWZZ	BUZZWORD
BDFLOTUU	DOUBTFUL	BDIIMRUU	RUBIDIUM	BEEEEFLN	ENFEEBLE
BDFORSUY	BODYSURF	BDIKNORS	BRODKINS	BEEEEFRS	FREEBEES
BDGGIINR	BRIDGING	BDILLOOY	BLOODILY	BEEEEKSS	BESEEKES
BDGGILNU	BLUDGING	BDILMORY	MORBIDLY	BEEEEMST	BETEEMES
BDGGLOSU	GOLDBUGS	BDILNNSU	SUNBLIND	BEEEENPS	PEEBEENS
BDGHOOUY	DOUGHBOY		UNBLINDS	BEEEENRT	TEREBENE
BDGIIKNR	KINGBIRD	BDILNOOO	DIOBOLON	BEEEENRZ	EBENEZER
BDGIILNN	BLINDING	BDILNOWW	WINDBLOW	BEEEFIRS	FREEBIES
BDGIILNR	BRIDLING	BDILNPRU	PURBLIND	BEEEFIST	BEEFIEST
BDGIILNU	BUILDING	BDILNSUU	UNBUILDS	BEEEFLSS	BEEFLESS
BDGIINNS	BINDINGS	BDILOORY	BROODILY		FEBLESSE
BDGIINRS	BIRDINGS	BDILOPRY	POLYBRID	BEEEFLST	FEEBLEST
BDGIINRW	BIRDWING	BDILOTUU	OUTBUILD	BEEEGILN	BELEEING
BDGIIOOS	GOBIOIDS	BDILPSUU	BUILDUPS	BEEEGINS	BESEEING
BDGILNNO	BLONDING		UPBUILDS	BEEEGIRS	BESIEGER
BDGILNNU	BUNDLING	BDILRTUY	TURBIDLY	BEEEGISS	BESIEGES
BDGILNOO	BLOODING	BDIMNORU	MORIBUND	BEEEGKLS	GEELBEKS
	BOODLING	BDIMNOSU	MISBOUND	BEEEGNRS	BREENGES
BDGILNOU	DOUBLING	BDIMNPSU	DUMPBINS	BEEEGORS	GREEBOES
BDGILNOY	BODINGLY	BDIMNSUU	DUBNIUMS	BEEEGRRS	BERGERES
BDGILNTU	BLINDGUT	BDIMOOSS	DISBOSOM	BEEEGRTT	BEGETTER
BDGILOOS	GLOBOIDS	BDIMOSTU	MISDOUBT	BEEEHIST	BHEESTIE
BDGINNOS	BONDINGS	BDINNOSU	INBOUNDS	BEEEHISV	BEEHIVES
BDGINNOU	BOUNDING	BDINNRUW	WINDBURN	BEEEHLRT	HERBELET
	UNBODING	BDINOORS	BRIDOONS	BEEEHLWW	WEBWHEEL
BDGINNUY	BUNDYING	BDINOOSW	WOODBINS	BEEEHNOY	HONEYBEE
BDGINOOR	BROODING	BDINORSW	SNOWBIRD	BEEEHNSS	SHEBEENS
BDGINOOY	BOODYING	BDINRSSU	SUNBIRDS	BEEEILLL	LIBELLEE
BDGINORS	BIRDSONG	BDINRTUU	UNTURBID	BEEEILLS	LIBELEES
	SONGBIRD	BDINSSTU	BUNDISTS	BEEEILLT	BILLETEE
BDGINORU	OBDURING		DUSTBINS	BEEEILNS	BEELINES
BDGINOTU	DOUBTING	BDIOORSU	BOUDOIRS	BEEEILRV	BELIEVER
BDGINSUU	SUBDUING	BDIOORTY	BOTRYOID	BEEEILSV	BELIEVES
BDGLLOSU	BULLDOGS	BDIORSSW	WOSBIRDS	BEEEINST	EBENISTE
BDGLOOST	DOGBOLTS	BDIORUZZ	BURDIZZO	BEEEIRRZ	BREEZIER
BDGNRUUY	BURGUNDY	BDIOSTUY	BODYSUIT	BEEEIRST	BEERIEST
BDGOOOSW	BOGWOODS	BDIRSSTU	DISTURBS	BEEEJLSW	BEJEWELS
BDHIIPRW	WHIPBIRD	BDKNOOOR	DOORKNOB	BEEEJLSZ	JEZEBELS
BDHILNOS	BLONDISH	BDKNOOSU	BUNDOOKS	BEEEJSUZ	BEJEEZUS
BDHIMOOR	RHOMBOID	BDKOOORW	WORDBOOK	BEEEKLLS	BELLEEKS
BDHIMORT	BIRTHDOM	BDKOORWY	BODYWORK	BEEELLRR	REBELLER
BDHIMSTU	DUMBSHIT	BDKOOSTU	STUDBOOK	BEEELLRT	BELLETER
BDHIMSUU	SUBHUMID	BDLLSTUU	BULLDUST	BEEELLRV	BEVELLER
BDHINOPS	HOPBINDS	BDLNOOOU	DOUBLOON	BEEELMNS	ENSEMBLE
BDHIORST	BIRDSHOT	BDLNOOUY	UNBLOODY	BEEELMRS	RESEMBLE
BDHIOSSU	BUSHIDOS	BDLNOOWW	BLOWDOWN	BEEELMSY	BESEEMLY

Alphagram	Word(s)
BEEEELMZZ	EMBEZZLE
BEEEELPRS	BLEEPERS
BEEEELRST	BEETLERS
BEEEELRSV	BEVELERS
BEEEMMRR	REMEMBER
BEEEMNSU	UNBESEEM
BEEEMRSS	BERSEEMS
BEEENNSZ	BENZENES
BEEENSST	SEBESTEN
BEEENSTW	BETWEENS
BEEEPPPR	BEPEPPER
BEEEPRST	BEPESTER
BEEERSST	BRETESSE
BEEERSTT	BESETTER
BEEESSST	TSESSEBE
BEEFFLMU	BEMUFFLE
BEEFFRTU	BUFFETER
BEEFGILN	FEEBLING
BEEFGINR	BEFINGER
	BEFRINGE
BEEFHILS	FEEBLISH
BEEFIIRS	FIBERISE
BEEFIIRZ	FIBERIZE
BEEFIISW	WEBIFIES
BEEFILLT	LIFEBELT
BEEFILLX	FLEXIBLE
BEEFILNU	UNBELIEF
BEEFILRS	BELFRIES
BEEFINST	BENEFITS
BEEFIRRS	BRIEFERS
BEEFIRSS	FRISBEES
BEEFIRST	BRIEFEST
BEEFIRSU	RUBEFIES
BEEFLORU	BEFOULER
BEEFLORW	BEFLOWER
BEEFNORR	FREEBORN
BEEFNRTU	UNBEREFT
BEEFOORT	FREEBOOT
BEEGGNRU	GREENBUG
BEEGGNSU	GEEBUNGS
BEEGHLMR	BERGMEHL
BEEGIILL	ELIGIBLE
BEEGIILX	EXIGIBLE
BEEGIIST	BEIGIEST
BEEGILLR	GERBILLE
BEEGILMN	BEMINGLE
BEEGILNP	BLEEPING
BEEGILNT	BEETLING
BEEGILNV	BEVELING
BEEGILOS	OBLIGEES
BEEGILRU	BEGUILER
BEEGILST	GLEBIEST
BEEGILSU	BEGUILES
BEEGIMNT	BEMETING
BEEGIMRS	BEGRIMES
BEEGINNR	BEGINNER
	BENIGNER
BEEGINNS	BEGINNES
BEEGINRR	BREERING
BEEGINRS	BIGENERS
	BREINGES
	REBEGINS
BEEGINRZ	BREEZING
BEEGINST	BEESTING
	BEIGNETS
BEEGINSU	BEGUINES
BEEGINSW	BEESWING
BEEGKLUY	KEYBUGLE
BEEGLNOR	BELONGER
BEEGLNOS	ENGLOBES
BEEGMNOS	GOMBEENS
BEEGMNOY	BOGEYMEN
BEEGMOSU	EMBOGUES
BEEGMRSU	SUBMERGE
BEEGNOOW	WOBEGONE
BEEGNOTT	BEGOTTEN
BEEGNRSU	SUBGENRE
	SUNGREBE
BEEGNSTU	BEESTUNG
	UNBEGETS
BEEGOOPR	GEOPROBE
BEEGOPSX	PEGBOXES
BEEHHMOT	BEHEMOTH
BEEHIKLR	HERBLIKE
BEEHIMOT	BOEHMITE
BEEHINSS	BESHINES
	NEBISHES
BEEHIRST	HERBIEST
BEEHIRSV	BESHIVER
BEEHISST	BHISTEES
BEEHKSSU	BUKSHEES
BEEHLLNT	HELLBENT
BEEHLOOR	BOREHOLE
BEEHLOVY	BEHOVELY
BEEHLRSS	HERBLESS
BEEHLRST	BLETHERS
	HERBLETS
BEEHLRSU	BUSHELER
BEEHMORW	HOMEBREW
BEEHMRSY	BERHYMES
BEEHMSTU	SUBTHEME
BEEHNNOS	HEBENONS
BEEHNOOP	NEOPHOBE
BEEHNRRT	BRETHREN
BEEHOOST	BESOOTHE
BEEHOOSV	BEHOOVES
BEEHORSW	BEWHORES
BEEHRRST	SHERBERT
BEEHRSST	SHERBETS
BEEHRSSW	BESHREWS
BEEIILNZ	ZIBELINE
BEEIINOS	EBIONISE
BEEIINOZ	EBIONIZE
BEEIINRT	BENITIER
BEEIIORS	BOISERIE
BEEIIPST	BEPITIES
BEEIIRRR	BRIERIER
BEEIIRSS	IBERISES
BEEIISTU	UBIETIES
BEEIISTZ	BITESIZE
BEEIJLSU	JUBILEES
BEEIJORT	BOERTJIE
BEEIJSTU	BEJESUIT
BEEIKKRS	BREKKIES
BEEIKLNY	EYEBLINK
BEEIKLTU	TUBELIKE
BEEIKLWY	BIWEEKLY
BEEIKORS	BROEKIES
BEEIKSSS	BEKISSES
BEEILLLR	LIBELLER
BEEILLNO	LOBELINE
BEEILLNT	BELTLINE
BEEILLNU	BLUELINE
BEEILLRS	LIBELERS
BEEILLRT	BILLETER
BEEILLSV	BILEVELS
BEEILLTT	BELITTLE
BEEILLTU	TULLIBEE
BEEILMOS	EMBOLIES
	EMBOLISE
BEEILMOZ	EMBOLIZE
BEEILMPP	BEPIMPLE
BEEILMPR	PERIBLEM
BEEILMPS	EPIBLEMS
BEEILMRR	LIMBERER
BEEILMSS	BESLIMES
	BESMILES
BEEILNNS	BLENNIES
BEEILNRS	BERLINES
BEEILNRY	BERYLINE
BEEILNSS	SENSIBLE
BEEILNST	STILBENE
	TENSIBLE
BEEILNSU	NEBULISE
BEEILNUZ	NEBULIZE
BEEILORS	EROSIBLE
BEEILOSS	OBELISES
BEEILOSZ	OBELIZES
BEEILOTV	LOVEBITE
BEEILRRT	TERRIBLE
BEEILRSU	BLUESIER
BEEILRSV	VERBILES
BEEILRYZ	BREEZILY
BEEILSTT	BETITLES
BEEIMORT	BIOMETER
BEEIMRRU	UMBRIERE
BEEIMRST	BIMESTER
BEEIMRTT	EMBITTER
BEEIMSSU	EMBUSIES
BEEINNSS	BEINNESS
BEEINNSZ	BENZINES
BEEINORT	TENEBRIO
BEEINOSS	EBONISES
BEEINOST	BETONIES
	EBONITES
BEEINOSZ	EBONIZES
BEEINPRS	PEBRINES
BEEINRSS	NEBRISES
BEEINRSZ	ZEBRINES
BEEINRTT	REBITTEN
BEEINRTW	INTERWEB
BEEINSTT	BENTIEST
BEEINSWZ	WEBZINES

BEEIOQSU	OBSEQUIE	BEELSTTU	BLUETTES	BEERSSSU	SUBSERES
BEEIORSS	SOBERISE	BEEMNORV	NOVEMBER	BEERSSTW	BESTREWS
BEEIORSW	BOWERIES	BEEMNRRU	NUMBERER		WEBSTERS
BEEIORSZ	SOBERIZE		RENUMBER	BEERSSUV	SUBSERVE
BEEIORTV	OVERBITE	BEEMOORS	BORESOME		SUBVERSE
BEEIQSUZ	BEZIQUES	BEEMOPRT	OBTEMPER	BEERSTTU	BURETTES
BEEIRRSU	REBURIES	BEEMORRS	SOMBERER	BEERSTTY	BYSTREET
BEEIRRSV	BREVIERS	BEEMORSS	EMBOSSER	BEESTTUV	BUVETTES
BEEIRRTT	BITTERER	BEEMORSW	EMBOWERS	BEFFISTU	BUFFIEST
BEEIRSSU	SUBERISE	BEEMOSSS	EMBOSSES	BEFFLRSU	BLUFFERS
BEEIRSSV	BREVISES	BEEMQSUU	EMBUSQUE	BEFFLSTU	BLUFFEST
BEEIRSSW	BREWISES	BEEMRRSU	UMBRERES	BEFGIILL	FILLIBEG
BEEIRSTU	UBERTIES	BEEMRSSU	SUBMERSE	BEFGIILS	FILIBEGS
BEEIRSUZ	SUBERIZE	BEEMRSTU	EMBRUTES	BEFGIINR	BRIEFING
BEEISSTW	WEBSITES	BEEMRTTU	UMBRETTE	BEFGILNU	FUNGIBLE
BEEKMOPR	PEMBROKE	BEEMRTUZ	ZERUMBET	BEFGIRSU	FIREBUGS
BEEKMOSS	BESMOKES	BEEMRSSU	EMBUSSES	BEFHILSU	BLUEFISH
BEEKNOPS	BESPOKEN	BEENNOOS	NONOBESE	BEFHINOS	BONEFISH
BEEKNOST	BETOKENS	BEENNOOT	BOTONNEE		FISHBONE
	STEENBOK	BEENOPTY	TEENYBOP	BEFHIRSU	BUSHFIRE
BEEKRRSS	BERSERKS	BEENORRS	ENROBERS		FIREBUSH
BEEKRRSU	REBUKERS	BEENORTU	BOUNTREE	BEFIIRSU	RUBIFIES
BEELLMTU	UMBELLET	BEENORTV	VERBOTEN	BEFILLXY	FLEXIBLY
BEELLORW	BELLOWER	BEENOSST	BONESETS	BEFILMOR	FORELIMB
	REBELLOW	BEENOSTU	TUBENOSE	BEFILNOS	LOBEFINS
BEELLOSS	LOBELESS	BEENOSTY	BONEYEST	BEFILNSU	BLUEFINS
BEELLOST	LOBELETS	BEENPRST	BESPRENT	BEFILOST	BOTFLIES
BEELLSST	BELTLESS	BEENRSTT	BRENTEST	BEFILOSU	BIOFUELS
BEELLSUV	SUBLEVEL	BEENRSTW	BESTREWN	BEFILOUY	LIFEBUOY
BEELMMOP	BEPOMMEL	BEENRTTU	BRUNETTE	BEFILRST	FILBERTS
BEELMNNO	NOBLEMEN	BEENSSSU	SUBSENSE	BEFILSSU	SUBFILES
BEELMNSU	BLUESMEN	BEENSSTU	SUBTEENS	BEFINORS	BONFIRES
BEELMOSW	EMBOWELS		SUBTENSE	BEFIOOST	BOOFIEST
BEELMRRT	TREMBLER	BEENSSUV	SUBVENES	BEFIORSS	FIBROSES
BEELMRRU	LUMBERER	BEEOORRT	BOORTREE	BEFIORTT	FOREBITT
BEELMRST	TREMBLES	BEEOORRV	OVERBORE	BEFIRSST	FIBSTERS
BEELMSTU	BLUESTEM	BEEOORTT	BEETROOT	BEFISSTU	FUBSIEST
BEELMUZZ	BEMUZZLE	BEEOPRRS	REPROBES	BEFISSUX	SUBFIXES
BEELNNOR	ENNOBLER	BEEOPRSS	BEPROSES	BEFLLLUY	BELLYFUL
BEELNNOS	ENNOBLES	BEEOPSSU	BESPOUSE	BEFLLSTY	FLYBELTS
BEELNOSS	BONELESS	BEEORRSU	BOURREES	BEFLMRSU	FUMBLERS
	NOBLESSE	BEEORRSV	OBSERVER	BEFLORUW	FURBELOW
BEELNOSU	BLUENOSE		VERBOSER	BEFLSTUU	TUBEFULS
	NEBULOSE	BEEORRTU	BOURTREE	BEFMOOOR	FOREBOOM
BEELNOSZ	BENZOLES	BEEORSST	SOBEREST	BEFNOORR	FORBORNE
BEELNSSU	BLUENESS	BEEORSSU	SUBEROSE	BEFNOSSY	FYNBOSES
BEELNTTU	BETELNUT	BEEORSSV	OBSERVES	BEFORRXY	FOXBERRY
BEELNTUY	BUTYLENE		OBVERSES	BEGGGINS	BEGGINGS
BEELOOST	OBSOLETE	BEEORSTU	TUBEROSE	BEGGIINN	BINGEING
BEELOQRU	BRELOQUE	BEEORSTV	OVERBETS	BEGGIINO	BOGIEING
BEELORTT	REBOTTLE	BEEORSTW	BESTOWER	BEGGILRU	BLUGGIER
BEELORVW	OVERBLEW	BEEORSWY	EYEBROWS	BEGGINOY	BOGEYING
BEELOSTW	STEELBOW	BEEOSSSS	OBSESSES	BEGGIOST	BOGGIEST
BEELOSTY	EYEBOLTS	BEEOSSST	BETOSSES	BEGGISTU	BUGGIEST
BEELPRSS	PREBLESS	BEEPPRSU	PREPUBES	BEGGLORS	BLOGGERS
BEELPRUV	BUPLEVER	BEEPRRSU	SUPERBER		BOGGLERS
BEELRSSS	BLESSERS	BEEPRRSV	PREVERBS	BEGGOOOS	GOOSEGOB
BEELRSSV	VERBLESS	BEEPRSTY	PRESBYTE	BEGHHIST	BEHIGHTS
BEELRSUZ	ZEBRULES	BEEQSSTU	BEQUESTS	BEGHIILP	PHILIBEG
BEELRTUU	TRUEBLUE	BEERRSTW	BREWSTER	BEGHIKNT	BEKNIGHT
BEELSSTU	TUBELESS	BEERRTTU	REBUTTER	BEGHILRT	BLIGHTER

	THERBLIG	**BEGIMNOW**	EMBOWING	**BEHILMST**	THIMBLES
BEGHINOR	NEIGHBOR	**BEGIMNOX**	EMBOXING	**BEHILMTY**	BIMETHYL
BEGHINOT	BEHOTING	**BEGIMNRU**	EMBRUING	**BEHILNPY**	BIPHENYL
BEGHINOV	BEHOVING		UMBERING	**BEHILORR**	HORRIBLE
BEGHINRT	BERTHING	**BEGIMNSU**	BEMUSING	**BEHILORS**	BOLSHIER
	BRIGHTEN		EMBUSING	**BEHILOSS**	BOLSHIES
BEGHINST	BENIGHTS		MISBEGUN	**BEHILPRU**	BHELPURI
BEGHIOST	GOBSHITE	**BEGIMOST**	MISBEGOT	**BEHILRST**	BLITHERS
BEGHIRRT	BRIGHTER	**BEGIMOSY**	BOGEYISM	**BEHILRTU**	THURIBLE
BEGHLNOU	BUNGHOLE	**BEGINNNO**	NONBEING	**BEHILSTT**	BLITHEST
BEGHNOTU	BOUGHTEN	**BEGINNNR**	BRENNING	**BEHIMNOO**	BONHOMIE
BEGHORTU	REBOUGHT	**BEGINNNU**	UNBENIGN	**BEHIMOOS**	SEMIHOBO
BEGHOSTU	BESOUGHT	**BEGINNOR**	ENROBING	**BEHIMORS**	BIOHERMS
BEGHOSUU	BUGHOUSE		RINGBONE	**BEHIMOSY**	YOHIMBES
BEGHRRSU	BURGHERS	**BEGINNSU**	UNBEINGS	**BEHIMRTU**	THUMBIER
BEGIIISS	SIGISBEI	**BEGINOOS**	BESOGNIO	**BEHINNOS**	SHINBONE
BEGIILLN	LIBELING	**BEGINORR**	REBORING	**BEHINOPS**	HIPBONES
BEGIILLY	ELIGIBLY	**BEGINORS**	SOBERING		HOPBINES
BEGIILNR	BLINGIER	**BEGINORW**	BOWERING	**BEHINOSW**	WISHBONE
BEGIILST	BILGIEST	**BEGINRRS**	BRINGERS	**BEHIOOPR**	BIOPHORE
BEGIIMNR	BEMIRING	**BEGINRRY**	BERRYING	**BEHIORRT**	BROTHIER
	BERIMING	**BEGINRSV**	VERBINGS	**BEHIPRRT**	PREBIRTH
BEGIIMNS	MISBEGIN	**BEGINRSW**	BREWINGS	**BEHIRRST**	REBIRTHS
BEGIIMNT	BETIMING		WEBRINGS	**BEHIRRSU**	BRUSHIER
BEGIIMNX	BEMIXING	**BEGINRUY**	REBUYING	**BEHIRSST**	HERBISTS
BEGIIMNY	BIGEMINY	**BEGINSTT**	BETTINGS	**BEHIRSSU**	HUBRISES
BEGIINNS	INBEINGS	**BEGINVVY**	BEVVYING	**BEHIRSSY**	HYBRISES
BEGIINRT	REBITING	**BEGKMOSS**	GEMSBOKS	**BEHISSTU**	BUSHIEST
BEGIINRZ	ZINGIBER	**BEGLLORY**	GORBELLY	**BEHKOSSY**	KYBOSHES
BEGIINTW	BITEWING	**BEGLLOSU**	GLOBULES	**BEHKOTTU**	KETUBOTH
BEGIIOSS	SIGISBEO	**BEGLLOTU**	GLOBULET	**BEHLLOOT**	BOLTHOLE
BEGIKMNO	KEMBOING	**BEGLMOOS**	BEGLOOMS	**BEHLLOOW**	BLOWHOLE
BEGIKNRS	KERBINGS	**BEGLMORU**	GRUMBLER	**BEHLLOPS**	BELLHOPS
BEGIKNRU	REBUKING	**BEGLMRSU**	GRUMBLES	**BEHLLSSU**	SUBSHELL
BEGILLLU	BLUEGILL	**BEGLMSUU**	BLUEGUMS	**BEHLMOSW**	WHOMBLES
	GULLIBLE	**BEGLNOUW**	BLUEGOWN	**BEHLMRSU**	HUMBLERS
BEGILLNS	BELLINGS	**BEGLNRSU**	BLUNGERS	**BEHLMSTU**	HUMBLEST
BEGILLNU	BULLGINE		BUNGLERS	**BEHLOOPY**	HYPOBOLE
BEGILLNY	BELLYING	**BEGLOOST**	BOOTLEGS		LYOPHOBE
BEGILMNR	REMBLING	**BEGLOSUV**	LOVEBUGS	**BEHLOOST**	BOTHOLES
BEGILMNS	SEMBLING	**BEGLOTUU**	OUTBULGE	**BEHLORST**	BROTHELS
BEGILNNY	BENIGNLY	**BEGLRSTY**	BERGYLTS	**BEHLOSSU**	SLOEBUSH
BEGILNOR	IGNOBLER	**BEGMNOOY**	BOOGYMEN	**BEHLRRSU**	BURRHELS
BEGILNOS	INGLOBES	**BEGNOORU**	BOURGEON	**BEHLRSSU**	BLUSHERS
BEGILNOV	BELOVING	**BEGNORSU**	BURGEONS	**BEHLSSSU**	BUSHLESS
BEGILNOW	BOWELING	**BEGNORTU**	BURGONET	**BEHLSSTU**	BLUSHETS
	ELBOWING	**BEGNOSTT**	BETTONGS	**BEHMNOTY**	BOTHYMEN
BEGILNRT	TREBLING	**BEGNSSUU**	SUBGENUS	**BEHMOOOX**	HOMEOBOX
BEGILNSS	BLESSING	**BEGORRUY**	BROGUERY	**BEHMOOST**	BESMOOTH
	GLIBNESS	**BEGPRSUU**	SUPERBUG	**BEHMOOSY**	HOMEBOYS
BEGILNST	BELTINGS	**BEHHKOST**	KHOTBEHS	**BEHMOSTU**	BEMOUTHS
	BLINGEST	**BEHIISST**	BHISTIES	**BEHMPSTU**	BETHUMPS
BEGILNSU	BLUEINGS	**BEHIISTX**	EXHIBITS	**BEHNNOST**	BENTHONS
	BULGINES	**BEHIKLOS**	BLOKEISH	**BEHNNOUY**	HONEYBUN
BEGILNTT	BLETTING	**BEHIKLSU**	BUSHLIKE	**BEHNORST**	BETHORNS
BEGILNUW	BLUEWING	**BEHIKNST**	BETHINKS	**BEHNRSTU**	BURTHENS
BEGILNZZ	BEZZLING	**BEHIKOSS**	KIBOSHES	**BEHOOOPZ**	ZOOPHOBE
BEGILORS	OBLIGERS	**BEHIKPSU**	PUSHBIKE	**BEHOOOST**	BOOTHOSE
BEGILRST	GILBERTS	**BEHILLOS**	SHOEBILL	**BEHOORST**	THEORBOS
BEGILSTU	BULGIEST	**BEHILLTY**	BLITHELY	**BEHOORSX**	HORSEBOX
BEGIMNOS	BESOMING	**BEHILMRW**	WHIMBREL	**BEHOOSTX**	HOTBOXES

BEHOOSUY	HOUSEBOY	**BEIKMNNR**	BRINKMEN	**BEILOQRU**	BELIQUOR
BEHOPRST	POTHERBS	**BEIKNOST**	STEINBOK		OBLIQUER
BEHORRST	BROTHERS	**BEIKNRRY**	INKBERRY	**BEILOQSU**	OBLIQUES
BEHORSSU	ROSEBUSH	**BEIKNRSS**	BRISKENS	**BEILORRS**	BROILERS
BEHORSTT	BETROTHS	**BEIKOORS**	BOOKSIER	**BEILORST**	STROBILE
BEHOSSTU	BESHOUTS		BROOKIES		TRILOBES
BEHRRSSU	BRUSHERS	**BEIKOORT**	BROOKITE	**BEILORSU**	BLOUSIER
BEHRSTTU	TURBETHS	**BEIKOOST**	BOOKIEST	**BEILORSW**	BLOWSIER
BEIIIKMN	MINIBIKE	**BEIKORST**	REITBOKS	**BEILORTT**	BLOTTIER
BEIIKRRS	BRISKIER	**BEIKOSST**	BOSKIEST		LIBRETTO
BEIIKRST	BIRKIEST	**BEIKRSST**	BRISKEST		
BEIIKRTZ	KIBITZER		BRISKETS	**BEILORWZ**	BLOWZIER
BEIIKSTZ	KIBITZES	**BEIKRSSW**	BREWSKIS	**BEILOSSY**	BIOLYSES
BEIILLST	LIBELIST	**BEIKRSTU**	BURKITES	**BEILOSTW**	BLOWIEST
BEIILMMO	IMMOBILE	**BEILLMRY**	LIMBERLY	**BEILPRTU**	PREBUILT
BEIILMOS	MOBILISE	**BEILLMSS**	LIMBLESS	**BEILPRTV**	BLIPVERT
BEIILMOZ	MOBILIZE	**BEILLMSU**	SEMIBULL	**BEILRRRU**	BLURRIER
BEIILMST	LIMBIEST	**BEILLNTU**	BULLETIN	**BEILRRTT**	BRITTLER
BEIILMSU	BULIMIES	**BEILLORS**	BROLLIES	**BEILRRTY**	TERRIBLY
BEIILNRS	RINSIBLE	**BEILLORV**	OVERBILL	**BEILRSST**	BLISTERS
BEIILOPR	PERIBOLI	**BEILLOSU**	LIBELOUS		BRISTLES
BEIILRSS	RISIBLES	**BEILLOSX**	BOLLIXES	**BEILRSTT**	BLITTERS
BEIILRST	TRILBIES	**BEILLPRS**	PREBILLS		BRITTLES
BEIILRTT	LIBRETTI	**BEILLRST**	BRILLEST		TRIBLETS
BEIILRUZ	BRUILZIE	**BEILLSST**	BESTILLS	**BEILRSTU**	BURLIEST
BEIILSSV	VISIBLES	**BEILLSTU**	BULLIEST		SUBTILER
BEIILSTT	STILBITE	**BEILMMOS**	EMBOLISM	**BEILRSTY**	BLISTERY
BEIIMNNR	RENMINBI	**BEILMMRU**	MUMBLIER	**BEILRSTZ**	BLITZERS
BEIIMNNU	BIENNIUM	**BEILMNOR**	BROMELIN	**BEILRSUY**	BRULYIES
BEIIMNOS	EBIONISM	**BEILMNOU**	NOBELIUM	**BEILRSUZ**	BRULZIES
BEIIMRTT	IMBITTER	**BEILMNRU**	UNLIMBER	**BEILRTTY**	BITTERLY
BEIINNRS	BRINNIES	**BEILMNST**	NIMBLEST	**BEILSTTU**	BLUETITS
BEIINORS	BRIONIES	**BEILMNUU**	NEBULIUM		SUBTITLE
BEIINOST	NIOBITES	**BEILMOOR**	BLOOMIER	**BEIMMRRS**	BRIMMERS
BEIINQUU	BIUNIQUE	**BEILMORS**	EMBROILS	**BEIMNORS**	BROMINES
BEIINRST	BRINIEST	**BEILMOSS**	OBELISMS	**BEIMNRUZ**	BRUNIZEM
BEIINSST	STIBINES	**BEILMPTU**	PLUMBITE	**BEIMNSSU**	NIMBUSES
BEIINSTT	STIBNITE	**BEILMRRU**	RUMBLIER	**BEIMNSTU**	BITUMENS
BEIIOPSS	BIOPSIES	**BEILMRSS**	BRIMLESS	**BEIMOORR**	BROOMIER
BEIIORST	ORBITIES	**BEILMRST**	TIMBRELS	**BEIMOORS**	BOSOMIER
BEIIOSTT	BIOTITES	**BEILMRSU**	SUBLIMER		RIBOSOME
BEIIRSST	BIRSIEST	**BEILMRSW**	WIMBRELS	**BEIMOOST**	BOOMIEST
BEIISSTT	BITSIEST	**BEILMSSU**	LIMBUSES	**BEIMORRV**	OVERBRIM
BEIISSTU	SUBITISE		SUBLIMES	**BEIMORSS**	BROMISES
BEIISTTT	BITTIEST	**BEILNNTU**	BUNTLINE	**BEIMORSW**	IMBOWERS
BEIISTUZ	SUBITIZE	**BEILNOPS**	BONSPIEL	**BEIMORSZ**	BROMIZES
BEIJLMRU	JUMBLIER	**BEILNOSU**	NUBILOSE	**BEIMORTY**	BIOMETRY
BEIJMOSU	JUMBOISE	**BEILNOSW**	BOWLINES	**BEIMORYZ**	RIBOZYME
BEIJMOUZ	JUMBOIZE	**BEILNOVY**	BOVINELY	**BEIMOSSS**	IMBOSSES
BEIJNORW	BIJWONER	**BEILNRSY**	BYLINERS	**BEIMOSTV**	BEVOMITS
BEIKKLNO	KNOBLIKE	**BEILNSSU**	SUBLINES	**BEIMOSTW**	WOMBIEST
BEIKLLOT	BOLTLIKE	**BEILNSSY**	SENSIBLY	**BEIMOSTY**	SYMBIOTE
BEIKLLOW	BOWLLIKE	**BEILNSTU**	BUSTLINE	**BEIMPRSU**	SUBPRIME
BEIKLMOT	TOMBLIKE	**BEILNSTY**	TENSIBLY	**BEIMPSTU**	BUMPIEST
BEIKLMOW	WOMBLIKE	**BEILNSTZ**	BLINTZES	**BEIMRSSU**	IMBURSES
BEIKLNRS	BLINKERS	**BEILOORV**	BOILOVER	**BEIMRSTU**	IMBRUTES
BEIKLOSS	OBELISKS		OVERBOIL		RESUBMIT
BEIKLOST	BLOKIEST	**BEILOOST**	LOOBIEST		TERBIUMS
BEIKLOTY	KILOBYTE	**BEILOPPW**	BLOWPIPE	**BEIMSSTU**	SUBITEMS
BEIKLRUY	RUBYLIKE	**BEILOPRS**	PREBOILS	**BEINNOPS**	PINBONES
BEIKLSTU	BULKIEST	**BEILOPSS**	POSSIBLE	**BEINNOSS**	BENISONS
					BONINESS

BEINNOST	BONNIEST	BEJLMRSU	JUMBLERS	BELMOSSY	SYMBOLES
BEINNOSZ	BENZOINS	BEJORTTU	TURBOJET	BELMPRSU	PLUMBERS
BEINNRYZ	ZEBRINNY	BEKLNORY	BROKENLY		REPLUMBS
BEINNTTU	UNBITTEN	BEKLNRSU	BLUNKERS	BELMPRUY	PLUMBERY
BEINOOST	BONITOES	BEKLOOOR	BOOKLORE	BELMRRSU	RUMBLERS
	EOBIONTS	BEKLOORT	BROOKLET	BELMRRUY	MULBERRY
BEINORRW	BROWNIER	BEKLOOSS	BOOKLESS	BELMRSSU	SLUMBERS
BEINORRZ	BRONZIER	BEKLOOST	BOOKLETS	BELMRSTU	STUMBLER
BEINORST	BORNITES	BEKLORUV	OVERBULK		TUMBLERS
	RIBSTONE	BEKLRSSU	BURLESKS		TUMBRELS
BEINORSW	BROWNIES	BEKMOOPS	SPEKBOOM	BELMRSUY	SLUMBERY
BEINORSY	BRYONIES	BEKMOOSX	SMOKEBOX	BELMSSTU	STUMBLES
BEINORTZ	BRONZITE	BEKMOSST	STEMBOKS	BELNNNOO	NONNOBLE
BEINOSST	EBONISTS	BEKNNORU	UNBROKEN	BELNNOSU	UNNOBLES
BEINOSSX	BOXINESS	BEKNOOOT	NOTEBOOK	BELNOORS	BORNEOLS
BEINOSTT	BOTTINES	BEKNOPRU	UPBROKEN	BELNOOSS	BOONLESS
BEINOSTU	BOUNTIES	BEKNORSY	SKYBORNE	BELNOOSY	BOLONEYS
BEINRRSY	NISBERRY	BEKOOORV	OVERBOOK	BELNOSTW	SNOWBELT
BEINRSSU	SUBERINS	BEKOOPRS	PREBOOKS	BELNOSUU	NEBULOUS
BEINRSTT	BITTERNS	BEKOORST	BOOKREST	BELNOSYZ	BENZOYLS
BEINRSTU	TRIBUNES	BEKOORTU	OUTBROKE	BELNOTTU	UNBOTTLE
	TURBINES	BEKOOTTX	TEXTBOOK	BELNSSTU	SUNBELTS
BEINRSUU	UNBURIES	BEKORSWW	WEBWORKS	BELNSTTU	BLUNTEST
BEINRTTU	UNBITTER	BEKORTUW	TUBEWORK	BELNSTUU	UNSUBTLE
BEINSSSU	BUSINESS	BEKOSSXY	SKYBOXES	BELOOOSX	LOOSEBOX
BEINSTTU	BUNTIEST	BEKRSSTU	BRUSKEST	BELOOPRS	BLOOPERS
BEIOOPST	BIOTOPES	BELLLLPU	BELLPULL	BELOOPRT	BOLTROPE
BEIOORST	ROBOTISE	BELLLMSU	BLELLUMS	BELOORSW	ROSEBOWL
BEIOORTZ	ROBOTIZE	BELLMORT	MORTBELL	BELOORVW	OVERBLOW
BEIOOSSV	OVIBOSES	BELLMORU	UMBRELLO	BELOOSST	BOOTLESS
BEIOOSTZ	BOOZIEST	BELLMRUY	LUMBERLY	BELOOTUV	OBVOLUTE
BEIOPSTY	BIOTYPES	BELLNOPS	BONSPELL	BELORRTU	TROUBLER
BEIOQTUU	BOUTIQUE	BELLNORW	WELLBORN	BELORSST	BOLSTERS
BEIORRST	ORBITERS	BELLNOSU	BULLNOSE		LOBSTERS
BEIORRSU	BOURSIER	BELLNOSW	SNOWBELL	BELORSSW	BROWLESS
BEIORRSW	BROWSIER	BELLNPSU	BULLPENS	BELORSTT	BLOTTERS
BEIORRTU	ROBURITE	BELLNTUY	TUNBELLY		BOTTLERS
BEIORSST	BROSIEST	BELLOOSU	LOBULOSE	BELORSTU	BOULTERS
	SORBITES	BELLOOSX	BOLLOXES		TROUBLES
BEIORSTT	BORTIEST	BELLOPTY	POTBELLY	BELOSSTU	OUTBLESS
BEIORSTY	SOBRIETY	BELLORTW	BELLWORT	BELOSTUU	TUBULOSE
BEIORSUV	BOUVIERS	BELLOSST	BLOTLESS	BELOSTUY	OBTUSELY
BEIOSSST	BOSSIEST		BOLTLESS	BELPRSUY	SUPERBLY
BEIOSSSU	SOUBISES	BELLOSSU	SOLUBLES	BELRRSTU	BLURTERS
BEIOSSTU	BOUSIEST	BELLOSWY	SOWBELLY	BELRSSSU	BRUSSELS
BEIOSSTY	BOYSIEST	BELLRRSU	BURRELLS	BELRSSTU	BLUSTERS
BEIOTTZZ	BOZZETTI	BELMMOOS	EMBLOOMS		BUSTLERS
BEIPPRSU	PREPUBIS	BELMMRSU	MUMBLERS	BELRSSUU	SUBRULES
BEIQRSTU	BRIQUETS	BELMNOSU	NELUMBOS	BELRSTUY	BLUSTERY
BEIRRSSU	BRISURES	BELMNOSY	BENOMYLS	BELRTUUU	TUBULURE
	BRUISERS	BELMOORS	BLOOMERS	BELSSTTU	SUBTLEST
BEIRRSTU	BRUITERS		REBLOOMS	BELSSTUY	SUBSTYLE
	BURRIEST	BELMOORY	BLOOMERY	BELSTTUY	SUBTLETY
BEIRRTTU	TRIBUTER	BELMOOSS	BLOOSMES	BEMMOOSS	EMBOSOMS
BEIRSSTU	BUSTIERS	BELMOOST	BOOMLETS	BEMMORRS	BROMMERS
BEIRSTTU	TRIBUTES	BELMOPRS	PROBLEMS	BEMMRRSU	BRUMMERS
BEIRSTTY	TREYBITS	BELMORST	TEMBLORS	BEMMRRUU	BEMURMUR
BEISSSTU	SUBSITES	BELMORSY	SOMBERLY	BEMNNSSU	NUMBNESS
BEISSTTU	BUSTIEST		SOMBRELY	BEMNOORT	TROMBONE
BEISTUZZ	BUZZIEST	BELMORUW	RUMBELOW	BEMNORSW	EMBROWNS
BEJKOOST	JESTBOOK	BELMOSST	TOMBLESS	BEMNORSY	EMBRYONS

BEMNSSUU	SUBMENUS	BEORSSSU	SORBUSES	BGGGINOR	BROGGING
BEMNSTTU	BUTMENTS	BEORSSTW	BESTROWS	BGGGINSU	BUGGINGS
BEMNTTUY	BUTTYMEN	BEORSSUU	SUBEROUS	BGGHIINT	BIGHTING
BEMOORRS	SOMBRERO	BEORSTUU	TUBEROUS	BGGIILNN	BINGLING
BEMOORTT	BOTTOMER	BEORSUVY	OVERBUSY		BLINGING
BEMORSST	BESTORMS		OVERBUYS	BGGIILNO	OBLIGING
	MOBSTERS	BEOSSTTU	OBTUSEST	BGGIILNY	GIBINGLY
	SOMBREST	BEPRRSTU	PERTURBS	BGGIINNO	BOINGING
BEMORSSU	MORBUSES	BEPSSTUY	SUBTYPES	BGGIINNR	BRINGING
BEMORSWW	WEBWORMS	BEQRRSSU	BRUSQUER	BGGIINRU	BRIGUING
BEMORTUW	TUBEWORM	BERRSSTU	BURSTERS	BGGILNNU	BLUNGING
BEMOSTUX	BUXOMEST	BERRSTUU	SURREBUT		BUNGLING
BEMOSTUY	MYOTUBES	BERSSTTU	BUTTRESS	BGGILNOR	BLOGRING
BEMRSSTU	BUMSTERS	BERSSTUV	SUBVERST	BGGILNRU	BURGLING
BEMSSSUU	SUBSUMES		SUBVERTS	BGGINOOT	TOBOGGIN
BEMSSTUW	STEWBUMS	BESSSSUY	BYSSUSES	BGGINOOY	BOOGYING
BENNNOTU	UNBONNET	BESSSTTU	SUBTESTS	BGHHHISU	HIGHBUSH
BENNOOTU	BOUTONNE	BESSTTUX	SUBTEXTS	BGHHINOR	HIGHBORN
BENNOPYY	PENNYBOY	BFFFLMUU	BUMFLUFF	BGHHIORW	HIGHBROW
BENNORSW	NEWBORNS	BFFGILNU	BLUFFING	BGHHIOSY	HIGHBOYS
BENNSSSU	SNUBNESS	BFFGINSU	BUFFINGS	BGHIINRT	BIRTHING
BENOORRV	OVERBORN	BFFHORSU	BRUSHOFF	BGHILMNU	HUMBLING
BENOORSU	BURNOOSE	BFFILOOS	BOILOFFS	BGHILNSU	BLUSHING
BENORRSU	SUBORNER	BFFLOOSW	BLOWOFFS	BGHILRTY	BRIGHTLY
BENORRSZ	BRONZERS	BFFLOTUU	OUTBLUFF	BGHIMNTU	THUMBING
BENORRTU	TRUEBORN	BFFNOOSU	BUFFOONS	BGHIMOTU	BIGMOUTH
BENORRUV	OVERBURN	BFFNOSUX	SNUFFBOX	BGHINORS	BIGHORNS
BENORSST	SORBENTS	BFGHINTU	BUNFIGHT	BGHINRSU	BRUSHING
BENORSTU	BURSTONE	BFGILMNU	FUMBLING	BGHINRTU	UNBRIGHT
	RUBSTONE	BFGIOOST	BIGFOOTS	BGHINSSU	BUSHINGS
BENORSTW	BESTROWN	BFGIORST	FROGBITS	BGHIORSU	BROGUISH
	BROWNEST	BFGLLORU	BULLFROG	BGHIPSSU	BUSHPIGS
BENORSUU	BURNOUSE	BFHIILLS	BILLFISH	BGHLRSUU	BULGHURS
BENORSWY	BYWONERS	BFHILOST	FISHBOLT		BURGHULS
BENORTTU	BUTTONER	BFHILOSW	BLOWFISH	BGHMORSU	HOMBURGS
	REBUTTON		FISHBOWL	BGHNORSU	HORNBUGS
BENOSSTU	SUBTONES	BFHIMNSU	NUMBFISH	BGHNOTUU	UNBOUGHT
BENOSSUZ	SUBZONES	BFHLLSUU	BLUSHFUL	BGHOOPTU	BOUGHPOT
BENOSSWY	NEWSBOYS	BFIILMOS	BIOFILMS	BGHOORSU	BOROUGHS
BENRRSUY	SUNBERRY	BFIINORS	FIBROINS	BGIIJLNR	JIRBLING
BENRRSTU	SUBRENTS	BFIIORSS	FIBROSIS	BGIIJLNY	JIBINGLY
BENRSTUY	SUBENTRY	BFIKLOOP	FLIPBOOK	BGIIKLNN	BLINKING
BENSSSUY	BUSYNESS	BFILLMRU	BRIMFULL	BGIIKMNO	KIMBOING
BEOOORTV	OVERBOOT	BFILLSSU	BLISSFUL	BGIIKNNO	BOINKING
BEOORRRW	BORROWER	BFILOSTY	LIFTBOYS	BGIIKNRS	BRISKING
	REBORROW	BFIMNORU	NUBIFORM	BGIILLNS	BILLINGS
BEOORRVW	OVERBROW	BFIMORTU	TUBIFORM	BGIILMNW	WIMBLING
BEOORSSS	OBSESSOR	BFINORYZ	BRONZIFY	BGIILNNN	BLINNING
	SORBOSES	BFIORSTT	FROSTBIT	BGIILNNY	BYLINING
BEOORSST	BOOSTERS	BFKLOOSU	BOOKFULS	BGIILNOR	BROILING
BEOORSTY	BOTRYOSE	BFKLOOSY	FLYBOOKS	BGIILNOS	BOILINGS
BEOOSTUX	OUTBOXES	BFKSSSUU	SUBFUSKS	BGIILNOX	BOLIXING
BEOOTTZZ	BOZZETTO	BFLLNOWY	FLYBLOWN	BGIILNPP	BLIPPING
BEOPRRSV	PROVERBS	BFLLOSUW	BOWLFULS	BGIILNRS	BIRLINGS
BEOPRSST	BESPORTS	BFLLOSWY	FLYBLOWS		BIRSLING
BEOPSSTU	BESPOUTS	BFLOORSU	SUBFLOOR		BRISLING
BEOQSSTU	BOSQUETS	BFNOORTW	BOWFRONT	BGIILNSS	BLISSING
BEOQSTUU	BOUQUETS	BFOOOSTY	FOOTBOYS		SIBLINGS
BEORRRUW	BURROWER	BGGGIINS	BIGGINGS	BGIILNTT	BLITTING
BEORRSSW	BROWSERS	BGGGILNO	BLOGGING	BGIILNTY	BITINGLY
BEORRSTU	ROBUSTER		BOGGLING	BGIILNTZ	BLITZING

BGIIMMNR	BRIMMING	**BGIMNOOS**	BOOMINGS	**BHILLPUW**	BULLWHIP
BGIIMNRS	BRIMINGS		BOSOMING	**BHILLSTU**	BULLSHIT
BGIIMNRU	IMBRUING	**BGIMNORS**	SOMBRING	**BHILNSTU**	BLUNTISH
BGIINNOR	INORBING	**BGIMNORW**	RINGWOMB	**BHILORRY**	HORRIBLY
BGIINNRS	INBRINGS	**BGIMNPSU**	BUMPINGS	**BHILORUY**	BIHOURLY
BGIINNSW	SWINGBIN	**BGIMOSSY**	BOGYISMS	**BHILOSTU**	HOLIBUTS
BGIINORT	ORBITING	**BGINNNOU**	UNBONING	**BHILOSYY**	BOYISHLY
BGIINRST	RINGBITS	**BGINNORU**	UNROBING	**BHIMNORT**	THROMBIN
BGIINRSU	BRUISING	**BGINNORW**	BROWNING	**BHIMOOPR**	BIOMORPH
BGIINRTU	BRUITING	**BGINNORZ**	BRONZING	**BHIMOOSS**	HOBOISMS
BGIINSTT	BITTINGS	**BGINNOUW**	UNBOWING	**BHIMOPRS**	BIMORPHS
BGIINSTU	BUISTING	**BGINNOUX**	UNBOXING	**BHIMOPSS**	PHOBISMS
BGIINVVY	BIVVYING	**BGINNRSU**	BURNINGS	**BHIMORSU**	BOHRIUMS
BGIJLMNU	JUMBLING	**BGINNRTU**	BRUNTING	**BHIMORTU**	BOTHRIUM
BGIJNORU	OBJURING	**BGINNSTU**	BUNTINGS	**BHIMSSTU**	BISMUTHS
BGIJOSUU	BIJUGOUS	**BGINOOST**	BONGOIST	**BHINOPSU**	UNBISHOP
BGIKLNNU	BLUNKING		BOOSTING	**BHINORSW**	BROWNISH
BGIKLNOT	KINGBOLT	**BGINOOSZ**	BOOZINGS	**BHIOOPRS**	BIOPHORS
BGIKLNSU	BULKINGS	**BGINORST**	STROBING	**BHIOOPRT**	BIOTROPH
BGIKNNOS	BONKINGS	**BGINORSW**	BROWSING	**BHIOPSST**	PHOBISTS
BGIKNNOU	BUNKOING	**BGINORSZ**	ZORBINGS	**BHIRSTTU**	TURBITHS
BGIKNOOR	BROOKING	**BGINOSSS**	BOSSINGS	**BHISSTTU**	BUSHTITS
BGIKNOOS	BOOKINGS	**BGINOSWW**	WINGBOWS	**BHKLORUW**	BUHLWORK
BGIKNORS	BROKINGS	**BGINPRSU**	UPBRINGS	**BHKMNOOY**	HYMNBOOK
BGIKNSSU	BUSKINGS	**BGINRSSU**	SUBRINGS	**BHKNOOOR**	HORNBOOK
BGIKNSTU	STINKBUG	**BGINRSTU**	BRUSTING	**BHKOOOPS**	BOOKSHOP
BGILLLUY	GULLIBLY		BRUTINGS	**BHLLNORU**	BULLHORN
BGILLNOU	GLOBULIN		BURSTING	**BHLLOSTU**	BULLSHOT
BGILLNRU	BULLRING	**BGINSSSU**	BUSSINGS	**BHLLRSUU**	BULLRUSH
BGILLNSU	BULLINGS	**BGINSSTU**	BUSTINGS	**BHLOOOTT**	TOLBOOTH
BGILLNUY	BULLYING	**BGINSSWY**	SWINGBYS	**BHLOSTUU**	OUTBLUSH
BGILMMNU	BUMMLING	**BGINSUZZ**	BUZZINGS	**BHLRSUUY**	BULRUSHY
	MUMBLING	**BGISUWZZ**	BUZZWIGS	**BHMNTTUU**	THUMBNUT
BGILMNOO	BLOOMING	**BGKLOOOS**	LOGBOOKS	**BHMOPTTU**	THUMBPOT
BGILMNPU	PLUMBING	**BGKNOOOS**	SONGBOOK	**BHMORSTU**	THROMBUS
BGILMNRU	RUMBLING	**BGKORSSY**	GRYSBOKS	**BHNOOOST**	BOSTHOON
BGILMNTU	TUMBLING	**BGLLLOOR**	BLOGROLL	**BHNOORTX**	BOXTHORN
BGILMORY	GORBLIMY	**BGLLNOOY**	OBLONGLY	**BHNOSSUW**	SNOWBUSH
BGILMOSU	GUMBOILS	**BGLNOOSW**	LONGBOWS	**BHOOPSST**	SHOPBOTS
BGILMOTU	GUMBOTIL	**BGLNOSUW**	BLOWGUNS	**BHOOPSSY**	SHOPBOYS
BGILNNOS	SNOBLING	**BGLOORYY**	BRYOLOGY	**BHOORTTU**	OUTTHROB
BGILNNTU	BLUNTING	**BGMNOOOR**	GOMBROON	**BHOOSSTW**	BOWSHOTS
BGILNOOP	BLOOPING	**BGMOOSTU**	GUMBOOTS	**BHPRSSUU**	BRUSHUPS
BGILNORT	RINGBOLT	**BGMORRUW**	GRUBWORM	**BIIKLOST**	KILOBITS
BGILNORY	BORINGLY	**BGNOOSWY**	GOWNBOYS	**BIIKNOOT**	BOOTIKIN
BGILNOST	BILTONGS	**BGNOSSSU**	SUBSONGS	**BIILLMOR**	MORBILLI
	BOLTINGS	**BGOPRSUU**	SUBGROUP	**BIILLMSS**	MISBILLS
BGILNOSU	BLOUSING	**BGORSTUU**	BURGOUTS	**BIILLNOS**	BILLIONS
BGILNOSW	BLOWINGS	**BGORSTUW**	BUGWORTS	**BIILLOSU**	BOUILLIS
	BOWLINGS	**BHHIISST**	BHISHTIS	**BIILLSTW**	TWIBILLS
BGILNOTT	BLOTTING	**BHIIINNS**	INHIBINS	**BIILMOTY**	MOBILITY
	BOTTLING	**BHIIINST**	INHIBITS	**BIILMSTU**	MISBUILT
BGILNOTU	BOULTING	**BHIIKRSS**	BRISKISH		SUBLIMIT
BGILNOWY	BOWINGLY	**BHIILMPS**	BLIMPISH		
BGILNRRU	BLURRING	**BHIIMRST**	MISBIRTH	**BIILNNRS**	BIRLINNS
BGILNRTU	BLURTING	**BHIIOPRT**	PROHIBIT	**BIILNOOV**	OBLIVION
BGILNSTU	BUSTLING	**BHIIPSSS**	SIBSHIPS	**BIILNORU**	UROBILIN
BGILNTTU	BUTTLING	**BHIKLLOO**	BILLHOOK	**BIILNOTY**	NOBILITY
BGILOORS	OBLIGORS	**BHIKMNTU**	THUMBKIN	**BIILNQSU**	QUIBLINS
BGILRSSU	BUSGIRLS	**BHILLNOR**	HORNBILL	**BIILNSTU**	SUBTILIN
BGIMNOOR	BROOMING	**BHILLOSY**	BILLYOHS	**BIILNSVY**	BIVINYLS
				BIILNTUY	NUBILITY

BIILORST	STROBILI	**BIMOSSTY**	SYBOTISM	**BMNOORRU**	MOORBURN
BIILOSSU	SIBILOUS		SYMBIOTS	**BMNOOSSU**	UNBOSOMS
BIILOSSY	BIOLYSIS	**BIMRSSTU**	BRUTISMS	**BMNORSUW**	MOWBURNS
BIILSTTW	WITBLITS	**BIMRSSUX**	BRUXISMS	**BMNORTUW**	MOWBURNT
BIIMMNSY	NIMBYISM	**BINNORTW**	TWINBORN	**BMOOORSX**	BOXROOMS
BIIMMOSZ	ZOMBIISM	**BINOORST**	BIOTRONS	**BMOORSSU**	SOMBROUS
BIIMNOSU	NIOBIUMS		ISOBRONT	**BMOORSTU**	MOTORBUS
BIIMPRSS	BIPRISMS	**BINORSST**	RIBSTONS	**BMOORTTY**	BOTTOMRY
BIIMSSTU	STIBIUMS	**BINORSSU**	BOURSINS	**BMORSSTU**	STROMBUS
BIINOOTX	BIOTOXIN	**BINORSUW**	UNIBROWS	**BNNORTUW**	NUTBROWN
BIINORSV	VIBRIONS	**BINRSSTU**	INBURSTS	**BNNOTTUU**	UNBUTTON
BIINOTVY	BOVINITY	**BINRSTUY**	BUTYRINS	**BNNRSSUU**	SUNBURNS
BIINRSTU	BURINIST	**BINSSTUU**	SUBUNITS	**BNNRSTUU**	SUNBURNT
BIIQTUUY	UBIQUITY	**BIOPRRSU**	SUBPRIOR	**BNOOOSTW**	SNOWBOOT
BIIRSSTU	BURSITIS	**BIOPRSTW**	BOWSPRIT	**BNOOOSUY**	SONOBUOY
BIJNOSSU	SUBJOINS	**BIORRSTU**	BURRITOS	**BNOORTUW**	BROWNOUT
BIKLLSSU	SUBSKILL	**BIORRSTW**	RIBWORTS	**BNOPRSTU**	POSTBURN
BIKLLUZZ	BUZZKILL	**BIORSSTT**	BISTORTS	**BNORRUUW**	UNBURROW
BIKLNOST	INKBLOTS	**BIORSTTU**	BITTOURS	**BNORSTUU**	BURNOUTS
BIKLNOSY	LINKBOYS	**BIORSTTY**	BOTRYTIS		OUTBURNS
BIKMNOOS	BOOMKINS	**BIORSTUY**	BISTOURY	**BNORTTUU**	OUTBURNT
BIKMNPSU	BUMPKINS	**BIOSTTUY**	OBTUSITY	**BNRSSTUU**	SUNBURST
BIKOOSUU	BOUSOUKI	**BIRSSTTU**	SUBTRIST	**BOOOORRSU**	UROBOROS
BIKOOUUZ	BOUZOUKI	**BIRSSUUV**	SUBVIRUS	**BOOPSSTY**	POSTBOYS
BIKORRSW	RIBWORKS	**BISSSSTU**	SUBSISTS	**BORSTTUU**	OUTBURST
BILLMSUY	BULLYISM	**BISSTUUU**	BUSUUTIS	**BORSTUUY**	BUTYROUS
BILLNOOU	BOUILLON	**BKKOOORW**	BOOKWORK	**BPRSSTUU**	UPBURSTS
BILLNOSU	BULLIONS		WORKBOOK	**CCCDIILY**	DICYCLIC
BILLOSUY	BLOUSILY	**BKLOSTUU**	OUTBULKS	**CCCDIOOS**	COCCOIDS
BILLOSWY	BLOWSILY	**BKMOOORW**	BOOKWORM	**CCCDKLOO**	COLDCOCK
BILLOWYZ	BLOWZILY	**BKMOORUZ**	ZOMBORUK	**CCCEEILT**	ECLECTIC
BILLRRUY	BLURRILY	**BKNNOOOS**	NONBOOKS	**CCCEGOSY**	COCCYGES
BILLRSWY	WRYBILLS	**BKNOOSTW**	BOWKNOTS	**CCCEHIOR**	CHOCCIER
BILMMPSU	PLUMBISM	**BKORSUWY**	BUSYWORK	**CCCEHIOS**	CHOCCIES
BILMNORS	NOMBRILS	**BLLLLOOY**	LOBLOLLY	**CCCEIIRT**	ECCRITIC
BILMOSTU	BOTULISM	**BLLMOORW**	BOLLWORM	**CCCEILNY**	ENCYCLIC
BILMRSTU	TUMBRILS	**BLLOPTUU**	BULLPOUT	**CCCEILUY**	EUCYCLIC
BILNOSTU	BOTULINS	**BLLOTUUY**	OUTBULLY	**CCCEOSXY**	COCCYXES
BILNOSUU	NUBILOUS	**BLMMPSUU**	PLUMBUMS	**CCCHIORY**	CHICCORY
BILNSTUU	TUBULINS	**BLMNPSUU**	UNPLUMBS	**CCCIINSU**	SUCCINIC
BILOOPST	POTBOILS	**BLMOOOST**	TOMBOLOS	**CCCILLYY**	CYCLICLY
BILOORST	SORBITOL	**BLMOOOTU**	OUTBLOOM	**CCCILNOY**	CYCLONIC
BILOORTT	BORLOTTI	**BLMOOOTY**	LOBOTOMY	**CCCILOPY**	CYCLOPIC
BILOPSSY	POSSIBLY	**BLMOORSW**	LOBWORMS	**CCCINSTU**	SUCCINCT
BILORSST	BRISTOLS	**BLMOOSSS**	BLOSSOMS	**CCCIOORS**	SCIROCCO
	STROBILS	**BLMOOSSY**	BLOSSOMY	**CCCKOORW**	COCKCROW
BILOSSSU	SUBSOILS	**BLMOPSUU**	PLUMBOUS	**CCCNOOST**	CONCOCTS
BILOSTUY	ISOBUTYL	**BLNOOSSU**	BLOUSONS	**CCDDEENO**	CONCEDED
BILOTTUU	OUTBUILT	**BLNSTUUY**	UNSUBTLY	**CCDDEEOT**	DECOCTED
BILSTTUY	SUBTILTY	**BLOOPSTX**	BOXPLOTS	**CCDDELOU**	OCCLUDED
BIMMOOSS	IMBOSOMS	**BLOOPSWY**	PLOWBOYS	**CCDDENOU**	CONDUCED
BIMMORSS	BROMISMS	**BLOORSWW**	LOWBROWS	**CCDEEENR**	CREDENCE
BIMNNUUU	UNUNBIUM	**BLOOSSTY**	SLYBOOTS	**CCDEEHIL**	CLICHEED
BIMNORSW	IMBROWNS	**BLOOSTUW**	BLOWOUTS	**CCDEEHLN**	CLENCHED
BIMNOSSY	SYMBIONS	**BLOPSSTU**	SUBPLOTS	**CCDEEILN**	LICENCED
BIMNOSTY	SYMBIONT	**BLORSTUY**	ROBUSTLY	**CCDEEINS**	SCIENCED
BIMNRRUU	MUIRBURN	**BLOSTUUU**	TUBULOUS	**CCDEEIOP**	CODPIECE
BIMNRUUV	VIBURNUM	**BLRSTUYY**	BUTYRYLS	**CCDEEIOS**	ECOCIDES
BIMOORST	ROBOTISM	**BMNOOORW**	MONOBROW	**CCDEEIRV**	CREVICED
BIMOSSSS	BOSSISMS	**BMNOOOSW**	MOONBOWS	**CCDEEKOR**	COCKERED
BIMOSSTW	MISTBOWS	**BMNOOOTW**	BOOMTOWN		RECOCKED

CCDEEKOY	COCKEYED	**CCDILOSY**	CYCLOIDS	**CCEENORT**	CONCRETE
CCDEELRY	RECYCLED	**CCDINOTU**	CONDUCTI	**CCEENRST**	CRESCENT
CCDEENOR	CONCEDER	**CCDKLOSU**	CUCKOLDS	**CCEEORRS**	COERCERS
CCDEENOS	CONCEDES	**CCDKOOOW**	WOODCOCK	**CCEEORST**	COERECTS
CCDEESSU	SUCCEEDS	**CCDNOORS**	CONCORDS	**CCEFFHKO**	CHECKOFF
CCDEHHRU	CHURCHED	**CCDNOSTU**	CONDUCTS	**CCEFHRSU**	CURCHEFS
CCDEHIKT	TCHICKED	**CCEEEILN**	LICENCEE	**CCEFIIPS**	SPECIFIC
CCDEHILN	CLINCHED	**CCEEFFOT**	COEFFECT	**CCEFINOT**	COINFECT
CCDEHIPU	HICCUPED	**CCEEGINR**	RECCEING	**CCEFIRRU**	CRUCIFER
CCDEHKLU	CHUCKLED	**CCEEGNOS**	COGENCES	**CCEFLLOU**	FLOCCULE
CCDEHLTU	CLUTCHED	**CCEEHIKR**	CHECKIER	**CCEFLOOS**	FLOCCOSE
	DECLUTCH	**CCEEHIKS**	CHICKEES	**CCEFNOST**	CONFECTS
CCDEHNRU	CRUNCHED	**CCEEHILN**	ELENCHIC	**CCEGHIKN**	CHECKING
CCDEHOOS	SCOOCHED	**CCEEHINZ**	ZECCHINE	**CCEGHIOR**	CHOREGIC
CCDEHOOT	COOTCHED	**CCEEHISV**	CEVICHES	**CCEGIKLN**	CLECKING
CCDEHORS	SCORCHED	**CCEEHKNS**	SCHNECKE	**CCEGILMY**	GLYCEMIC
CCDEHORT	CROTCHED	**CCEEHKPR**	PRECHECK	**CCEGILOO**	ECOLOGIC
CCDEHORU	CROUCHED	**CCEEHKRS**	CHECKERS	**CCEGILRY**	GLYCERIC
CCDEHOST	SCOTCHED		RECHECKS	**CCEGINNO**	CONGENIC
CCDEHRTU	CRUTCHED	**CCEEHLNR**	CLENCHER	**CCEGINOR**	COERCING
CCDEHSTU	SCUTCHED	**CCEEHLNS**	CLENCHES	**CCEGINPS**	SPECCING
CCDEIILO	CLEIDOIC	**CCEEHORS**	ECORCHES	**CCEGINRY**	RECCYING
CCDEIINO	COINCIDE	**CCEEHOSU**	COUCHEES	**CCEGNOOS**	COGNOSCE
CCDEIIRT	CRICETID	**CCEEHRSY**	SCREECHY	**CCEHHIIR**	CHICHIER
CCDEIIST	DEICTICS	**CCEEIILS**	CICELIES	**CCEHHINS**	CHINCHES
CCDEILOS	SCOLECID	**CCEEIIST**	CECITIES	**CCEHHRSU**	CHURCHES
CCDEILSY	CYCLISED	**CCEEIKLR**	CLECKIER	**CCEHIIMR**	CHIMERIC
CCDEILYZ	CYCLIZED	**CCEEILMU**	LEUCEMIC	**CCEHIIMS**	ISCHEMIC
CCDEINOR	CORNICED	**CCEEILNR**	ENCIRCLE	**CCEHIINZ**	ZECCHINI
CCDEINOS	CONCISED		LICENCER	**CCEHIKNP**	PINCHECK
CCDEINOT	OCCIDENT	**CCEEILNS**	LICENCES	**CCEHIKNS**	CHICKENS
CCDEIOPP	COPPICED	**CCEEILNT**	ELENCTIC	**CCEHIKSU**	CHUCKIES
CCDEIOPR	CERCOPID	**CCEEILPY**	EPICYCLE	**CCEHILNR**	CLINCHER
CCDEIOPU	OCCUPIED	**CCEEILRR**	RECIRCLE	**CCEHILNS**	CLINCHES
CCDEIORT	CODIRECT	**CCEEILRT**	ELECTRIC	**CCEHILOR**	CHOLERIC
CCDEKNOU	UNCOCKED	**CCEEIMNU**	ECUMENIC	**CCEHILOY**	CHOICELY
CCDEKOOU	CUCKOOED	**CCEEINOR**	CICERONE	**CCEHILSU**	CULCHIES
CCDELNOU	CONCLUDE		CROCEINE	**CCEHILTY**	HECTICLY
CCDELORU	OCCLUDER	**CCEEINOV**	CONCEIVE	**CCEHINOR**	CORNICHE
CCDELOSU	OCCLUDES	**CCEEINSS**	SCIENCES		ENCHORIC
CCDELOTU	OCCULTED	**CCEEIORS**	CICOREES	**CCEHINOS**	CONCHIES
CCDENOOO	COCOONED	**CCEEIORV**	COERCIVE	**CCEHINOZ**	ZECCHINO
CCDENORU	CONDUCER	**CCEEIPSS**	SPECCIES	**CCEHINRU**	CRUNCHIE
CCDENOSU	CONDUCES	**CCEEIRSS**	CERCISES	**CCEHINSS**	CHICNESS
CCDEORRU	OCCURRED		ECCRISES	**CCEHINST**	TECHNICS
CCDEORSU	SUCCORED	**CCEEIRSV**	CERVICES	**CCEHINSZ**	ZECCHINS
CCDEOSTU	STUCCOED		CRESCIVE	**CCEHIORT**	RICOCHET
CCDHIIKP	DIPCHICK		CREVICES	**CCEHIOST**	CHOICEST
CCDHIILO	CICHLOID	**CCEEITTU**	EUTECTIC	**CCEHIRSS**	SCREICHS
CCDHIILS	CICHLIDS	**CCEEKLOR**	COCKEREL		SCRIECHS
CCDHIIOR	DICHROIC	**CCEEKNRW**	CREWNECK	**CCEHKLRU**	CHUCKLER
CCDHIIOT	DICHOTIC	**CCEEKOSY**	COCKEYES	**CCEHKLSU**	CHUCKLES
CCDHINOO	CONCHOID	**CCEELMNY**	CLEMENCY	**CCEHKMSS**	SCHMECKS
CCDIILNU	NUCLIDIC	**CCEELNSU**	LUCENCES	**CCEHKMSU**	CHECKSUM
CCDIILOS	CODICILS	**CCEELOSS**	SCOLECES	**CCEHKNSU**	UNCHECKS
CCDIILSU	CULICIDS	**CCEELRRY**	RECYCLER	**CCEHKORW**	CHECKROW
CCDIINOO	CONOIDIC	**CCEELRSY**	RECYCLES	**CCEHKOTU**	CHECKOUT
CCDIINOS	SCINCOID	**CCEEMMNO**	COMMENCE	**CCEHKPSU**	CHECKUPS
CCDIINST	DISCINCT	**CCEEMMOR**	COMMERCE	**CCEHKRSU**	CHUCKERS
CCDIIORS	CRICOIDS	**CCEEMOPS**	COMPESCE	**CCEHLMOR**	CROMLECH
CCDIIORT	DICROTIC	**CCEENNOS**	ENSCONCE	**CCEHLNNU**	UNCLENCH

CCEHLNSU	CLUNCHES	CCEIMOPR	COPREMIC	CCENORTY	CORNETCY
CCEHLRSU	CLERUCHS	CCEIMOST	COSMETIC	CCENOSTV	CONVECTS
CCEHLRUY	CLERUCHY	CCEIMRRU	MERCURIC	CCENRRUY	CURRENCY
CCEHLSSU	SCULCHES	CCEIMRUV	CERVICUM	CCEOOORR	COROCORE
CCEHLSTU	CLUTCHES	CCEINNOS	INSCONCE	CCEOOPRS	PROSECCO
	CULTCHES	CCEINNOV	CONVINCE	CCEOORSU	CROCEOUS
CCEHNRRU	CRUNCHER	CCEINOOR	COERCION	CCEOOSTT	COCOTTES
CCEHNRSU	CRUNCHES	CCEINOOZ	CENOZOIC	CCEOPRUY	REOCCUPY
CCEHOOSS	SCOOCHES	CCEINOPR	CECROPIN	CCEORRST	CORRECTS
CCEHOOST	COOTCHES		COPRINCE	CCEORRSU	REOCCURS
CCEHORRS	SCORCHER	CCEINOPT	CONCEPTI		SUCCORER
CCEHORSS	SCORCHES	CCEINORS	CONCISER	CCEORSSU	CROCUSES
CCEHORST	CROCHETS		CORNICES	CCEORSTU	STUCCOER
	CROTCHES		CROCEINS	CCEORSTW	TWOCCERS
CCEHORSU	COUCHERS	CCEINORT	CONCERTI	CCEOSSTU	STUCCOES
	CROUCHES		NECROTIC	CCERSTUW	CREWCUTS
CCEHORTT	CROTCHET	CCEINOSS	CONCISES	CCESSSUU	CUSCUSES
CCEHOSST	SCOTCHES	CCEINOST	CONCEITS	CCFGILNO	FLOCCING
CCEHRSTU	CRUTCHES	CCEINOTT	CONCETTI	CCFHKLOU	CHOCKFUL
	SCUTCHER		TECTONIC	CCFIINOR	CORNIFIC
CCEHRTUY	CUTCHERY	CCEINOTY	CONCEITY	CCFIIRUX	CRUCIFIX
CCEHSSTU	SCUTCHES	CCEINPRT	PRECINCT	CCFIKNOY	COCKNIFY
CCEIIKLN	NICKELIC	CCEINRTU	CINCTURE	CCFILLOU	FLOCCULI
CCEIILNO	COLICINE	CCEINSTY	SYNECTIC	CCFILNOT	CONFLICT
CCEIILNT	ENCLITIC	CCEIOORT	CROCOITE	CCFKLOOT	COCKLOFT
CCEIILNU	CULICINE	CCEIOOTX	ECOTOXIC	CCFLOOOO	LOCOFOCO
CCEIILOR	LICORICE	CCEIOOTZ	ECTOZOIC	CCGHHIOU	HICCOUGH
CCEIILPT	ECLIPTIC	CCEIOPPS	COPPICES	CCGHIINN	CINCHING
CCEIILST	SCILICET	CCEIOPRT	ECTROPIC	CCGHIKNO	CHOCKING
CCEIILTU	LEUCITIC	CCEIOPRU	OCCUPIER	CCGHIKNU	CHUCKING
CCEIINNO	CONICINE	CCEIOPSU	OCCUPIES	CCGHINNO	CONCHING
CCEIINNR	ENCRINIC	CCEIOPTY	ECOTYPIC	CCGHINOU	COUCHING
CCEIINOR	CICERONI	CCEIORST	CORTICES	CCGHINTW	CWTCHING
CCEIINTU	CICUTINE	CCEIOTXY	EXOCYTIC	CCGIIKLN	CLICKING
CCEIIRRT	CIRCITER	CCEIPSST	SCEPTICS	CCGIIKNR	CRICKING
CCEIIRSS	ECCRISIS	CCEIRSSU	CIRCUSES	CCGIILNR	CIRCLING
CCEIIRST	ICTERICS	CCEJNOST	CONJECTS	CCGIILNU	GLUCINIC
CCEIIRTT	RECTITIC	CCEKLORS	CLOCKERS	CCGIKLNO	CLOCKING
CCEIIRTU	EUCRITIC		COCKLERS		COCKLING
CCEIKKLO	COCKLIKE	CCEKNOST	CONTECKS	CCGIKLNU	CLUCKING
CCEIKLRS	CLICKERS	CCEKNOSY	COCKNEYS	CCGIKNOR	CROCKING
CCEIKLRU	CLUCKIER	CCEKOPST	PETCOCKS	CCGILLOY	GLYCOLIC
CCEIKLST	CLICKETS	CCEKORRY	CROCKERY	CCGILNOY	GLYCONIC
CCEIKORS	COCKSIER	CCEKORST	CROCKETS	CCGILNSY	CYCLINGS
CCEIKOST	COCKIEST	CCEKORSU	COCKSURE	CCGILOSU	GLUCOSIC
CCEIKRST	CRICKETS	CCELLOST	COLLECTS	CCGINNOS	SCONCING
CCEILMOO	COELOMIC	CCELMOPT	COMPLECT	CCGINOTW	TWOCCING
CCEILMOP	COMPLICE	CCELNOSY	CYCLONES	CCGKOORS	GORCOCKS
CCEILNOR	CORNICLE	CCELOPSY	CYCLOPES	CCHHIITY	ICHTHYIC
CCEILNUY	UNICYCLE	CCELORTU	OCCULTER	CCHHILSS	SCHLICHS
CCEILOSS	SCOLICES	CCELOSSY	CYCLOSES	CCHHINOT	CHTHONIC
CCEILRRS	CIRCLERS	CCELRUUY	CURLYCUE	CCHHLRUY	CHURCHLY
CCEILRRU	CURRICLE	CCELSSUY	CYCLUSES	CCHHNRUU	UNCHURCH
CCEILRST	CIRCLETS	CCENNORS	CONCERNS	CCHHOOWW	CHOWCHOW
CCEILRSY	CRESYLIC	CCENNOST	CONCENTS	CCHIINUZ	ZUCCHINI
CCEILRTY	TRICYCLE		CONNECTS	CCHIIORT	ORCHITIC
CCEILRUU	CURLICUE	CCENOORT	CONCERTO	CCHIKMPU	CHIPMUCK
CCEILSSY	CYCLISES	CCENOOTT	CONCETTO	CCHIKORY	CHICKORY
CCEILSTU	CUTICLES	CCENOPST	CONCEPTS	CCHIKSST	SCHTICKS
CCEILSYZ	CYCLIZES	CCENORST	CONCERTS	CCHILNNU	UNCLINCH
CCEIMNOO	ECONOMIC	CCENORSW	CONCREWS	CCHILNUY	UNCHICLY

CCHINORS	CHRONICS	**CCKMOOOR**	MOORCOCK	**CDDEEKOR**	REDOCKED
CCHINSSU	SCUCHINS	**CCKNORTU**	TURNCOCK	**CDDEEKOT**	DOCKETED
CCHIPSSY	PSYCHICS	**CCKOOPRT**	CROCKPOT	**CDDEEKUW**	DUCKWEED
CCHKLOSS	SCHLOCKS	**CCKOOPST**	STOPCOCK	**CDDEELMO**	COMEDDLE
CCHKLOSY	SCHLOCKY	**CCKOPRSU**	COCKSPUR	**CDDEELPU**	DECUPLED
CCHKMNUU	NUMCHUCK	**CCKOSSTU**	CUSTOCKS	**CDDEELSU**	SCEDULED
CCHKMOSS	SCHMOCKS	**CCLLOTUY**	OCCULTLY		SECLUDED
CCHKMSSU	SCHMUCKS	**CCLMOOPU**	COCOPLUM	**CDDEELUX**	EXCLUDED
CCHKOOST	COCKSHOT	**CCLNOOOR**	CONCOLOR	**CDDEELUY**	DEUCEDLY
CCHKOPTU	PUTCHOCK	**CCLOOOSZ**	ZOCCOLOS	**CDDEENOS**	SECONDED
CCHKOSTU	COCKSHUT	**CCLOORSU**	OCCLUSOR	**CDDEENSS**	DESCENDS
CCHKPSUU	UPCHUCKS	**CCMOOORS**	MOROCCOS	**CDDEEOPR**	PRECODED
CCHKSSTU	SCHTUCKS	**CCNOOPSU**	PUCCOONS	**CDDEEORR**	RECORDED
CCHLNTUU	UNCLUTCH	**CCNOORSU**	CONCOURS	**CDDEEORS**	DECODERS
CCHNRSUY	SCRUNCHY	**CCNOOSTU**	COCONUTS	**CDDEERUV**	DECURVED
CCHOORST	SCROOTCH	**CCOOOORR**	COROCORO	**CDDEESUW**	CUDWEEDS
CCIIIMSV	CIVICISM	**CCOOSSUU**	COUSCOUS	**CDDEFIIO**	CODIFIED
CCIIIPRT	PICRITIC	**CCOOTTUU**	TUCOTUCO	**CDDEFINO**	CONFIDED
CCIIKKPW	PICKWICK	**CCORSSTU**	CROSSCUT	**CDDEGIIN**	DECIDING
CCIIKNPY	PICNICKY	**CCORSSUU**	SUCCOURS	**CDDEGINO**	DECODING
CCIILNOS	COLICINS	**CCOTTUUU**	TUCOTUCO	**CDDEGINU**	DEDUCING
CCIILORT	CLITORIC	**CCRSUUUU**	SURUCUCU	**CDDEHIOW**	COWHIDED
CCIILPRS	CIRCLIPS	**CCTTUUUU**	TUCUTUCU	**CDDEHISU**	CHUDDIES
CCIIMNSY	CYNICISM	**CDDDEETU**	DEDUCTED	**CDDEHRSU**	CHUDDERS
CCIINNSU	CICINNUS	**CDDDEIIS**	DISCIDED	**CDDEIINT**	INDICTED
CCIINORZ	ZIRCONIC	**CDDDELRU**	CRUDDLED	**CDDEIISS**	DISCIDES
CCIINOTY	CONICITY	**CDDDELSU**	SCUDDLED	**CDDEIISU**	SUICIDED
CCIIRSTU	CIRCUITS	**CDDDIIOY**	DIDDICOY	**CDDEIKOS**	DOCKISED
CCIIRTUY	CIRCUITY	**CDDEEEEX**	EXCEEDED		DOCKSIDE
CCIKKLOP	LOCKPICK	**CDDEEEFN**	DEFENCED	**CDDEIKOZ**	DOCKIZED
	PICKLOCK	**CDDEEEFT**	DEFECTED	**CDDEILLO**	COLLIDED
CCIKKOTT	TICKTOCK	**CDDEEEIR**	REDECIDE	**CDDEILNU**	INCLUDED
CCIKLOSW	COWLICKS	**CDDEEEIV**	DECEIVED	**CDDEILOR**	CLODDIER
CCIKNOPR	PRINCOCK	**CDDEEEJT**	DEJECTED	**CDDEILRU**	CUDDLIER
CCIKOPRS	CROPSICK	**CDDEEENR**	DECERNED	**CDDEIMOS**	MISCODED
CCIKOPST	COCKPITS	**CDDEEENT**	DECEDENT	**CDDEINTU**	INDUCTED
CCILLOTY	CYCLITOL	**CDDEEEPR**	PRECEDED	**CDDEIORV**	DIVORCED
CCILNOOS	COLONICS	**CDDEEERS**	SCREEDED	**CDDEIRRU**	CRUDDIER
CCILNOSU	COUNCILS	**CDDEEERW**	DECREWED	**CDDEIRSU**	DISCURED
CCILNSUY	SUCCINYL	**CDDEEETT**	DETECTED	**CDDEKNOU**	UNDOCKED
CCILOOPS	PICCOLOS	**CDDEFOOR**	DEFORCED	**CDDELLOU**	COLLUDED
CCILORUU	CURCULIO	**CDDEEGLU**	CUDGELED	**CDDELNOO**	CONDOLED
CCILOSSY	CYCLOSIS	**CDDEEHIS**	DEHISCED	**CDDELOOR**	CROODLED
CCILSSTY	CYCLISTS	**CDDEEHIT**	CHEDDITE	**CDDELORS**	CODDLERS
CCIMNRUU	CURCUMIN	**CDDEEHNR**	DRENCHED	**CDDELRSU**	CRUDDLES
CCINOORT	CROTONIC	**CDDEEIIM**	MEDICIDE		CUDDLERS
CCINOOST	COCTIONS	**CDDEEIIS**	DEICIDES	**CDDELSSU**	SCUDDLES
CCINOPRT	PROCINCT	**CDDEEIKR**	DICKERED	**CDDEMNOU**	DUNCEDOM
CCINOPSY	SYNCOPIC	**CDDEEIKT**	DETICKED	**CDDENNOO**	CONDONED
CCINOPTY	PYCNOTIC	**CDDEEILN**	DECLINED	**CDDENOOR**	CORDONED
CCINORSY	CRYONICS	**CDDEEILP**	PEDICLED	**CDDENORU**	UNCORDED
CCINOSTV	CONVICTS	**CDDEEINR**	CINDERED	**CDDEOORR**	CORRODED
CCIOOPST	SCOTOPIC	**CDDEEINZ**	DEZINCED	**CDDEOORT**	DOCTORED
CCIOORSS	SIROCCOS	**CDDEEIOT**	COEDITED	**CDDEOORW**	CODEWORD
CCIOOTXY	OXYTOCIC	**CDDEEIOV**	DEVOICED	**CDDEOPRU**	PRODUCED
CCIOPRST	COSCRIPT	**CDDEEIPT**	DEPICTED	**CDDERSSU**	SCUDDERS
CCIOPSTU	OCCIPUTS	**CDDEEIRS**	DECIDERS	**CDDGHILO**	GODCHILD
CCIRSSUY	CIRCUSSY		DESCRIED	**CDDGILNO**	CLODDING
CCJNNOTU	CONJUNCT	**CDDEEIRT**	CREDITED		CODDLING
CCKKLMUU	MUCKLUCK		DIRECTED	**CDDGILNU**	CUDDLING
CCKMMORU	CRUMMOCK	**CDDEEKNU**	UNDECKED	**CDDGINRU**	CRUDDING

CDDGINSU	SCUDDING		EXPECTED		DECIPHER
CDDHHISU	SHIDDUCH	CDEEERRS	DECREERS	CDEEHIPS	CEPHEIDS
CDDHIIRY	DIHYDRIC		SCREEDER	CDEEHIRR	CHERRIED
CDDHILOS	CLODDISH	CDEEERSS	RECESSED		DREICHER
CDDHIORS	DICHORDS		SECEDERS	CDEEHIRW	RICHWEED
CDDIIIOS	DIDICOIS	CDEEERST	DECREETS	CDEEHISS	DEHISCES
CDDIIKNS	NIDDICKS		RESECTED	CDEEHIST	CHEDITES
CDDIIOSS	DISCOIDS		SCREETED	CDEEHITW	ITCHWEED
CDDIIOSY	DIDICOYS		SECRETED	CDEEHKST	SKETCHED
CDDIISTY	DYTISCID	CDEEERSV	SCREEVED	CDEEHKTV	KVETCHED
CDDIKOPS	PIDDOCKS	CDEEERTT	DETECTER	CDEEHLMO	LEECHDOM
CDDIORSS	DISCORDS	CDEEERTX	EXCRETED	CDEEHLNO	NOCHELED
CDDKOPSU	PUDDOCKS	CDEEESSX	EXCESSED	CDEEHLPU	PLEUCHED
CDDKORSU	RUDDOCKS	CDEEESTX	EXSECTED	CDEEHLQU	QUELCHED
CDDMMOUU	MOCUDDUM	CDEEETUX	EXECUTED	CDEEHLSU	SCHEDULE
CDDOOORW	CORDWOOD	CDEEFFOR	COFFERED	CDEEHMTU	HUMECTED
CDEEEERX	EXCEEDER		EFFORCED	CDEEHNQU	QUENCHED
CDEEEFFT	EFFECTED	CDEEFHLN	FLENCHED	CDEEHNRR	DRENCHER
CDEEEFHL	FLEECHED	CDEEFHLT	FLETCHED	CDEEHNRS	DRENCHES
CDEEEFNR	REFENCED	CDEEFHNR	FRENCHED	CDEEHNRT	TRENCHED
CDEEEFNS	DEFENCES	CDEEFIIL	ICEFIELD	CDEEHNRW	WRENCHED
CDEEEFRT	REDEFECT	CDEEFIIM	FEMICIDE	CDEEHNST	STENCHED
	REFECTED	CDEEFIIS	EDIFICES	CDEEHNUW	UNCHEWED
CDEEEHHW	WHEECHED	CDEEFIIT	FETICIDE	CDEEHORS	CHORDEES
CDEEEHLR	CHEERLED	CDEEFINT	INFECTED		COSHERED
	LECHERED	CDEEFKLR	FRECKLED	CDEEHORT	HECTORED
CDEEEHMS	SMEECHED	CDEEFKOR	FOREDECK		TOCHERED
CDEEEHOR	REECHOED	CDEEFLST	DEFLECTS	CDEEHPRU	CHERUPED
CDEEEHPS	DEPECHES	CDEEFNNU	UNFENCED	CDEEHPRY	CYPHERED
	SPEECHED	CDEEFNOR	ENFORCED	CDEEHQTU	QUETCHED
CDEEEHRS	CREESHED	CDEEFORR	DEFORCER	CDEEHRTW	WRETCHED
CDEEEHRW	RECHEWED	CDEEFORS	DEFORCES	CDEEHSSU	DUCHESSE
CDEEEHSW	ESCHEWED		FRESCOED	CDEEIILT	ELICITED
CDEEEINP	PIECENED	CDEEFORT	DEFECTOR	CDEEIIMN	MEDICINE
CDEEEINV	EVIDENCE	CDEEGIIR	REGICIDE	CDEEIIMP	EPIDEMIC
CDEEEIPS	EPICEDES	CDEEGIIT	DIEGETIC	CDEEIINT	INDICTEE
CDEEEIRV	DECEIVER	CDEEGINO	GENOCIDE	CDEEIIOS	DIOECIES
	RECEIVED	CDEEGINR	RECEDING	CDEEIIRT	DIERETIC
CDEEEISV	DECEIVES	CDEEGINS	SECEDING	CDEEIIST	EIDETICS
CDEEEJRT	REJECTED	CDEEGIOS	GEODESIC	CDEEIISV	DECISIVE
CDEEEKNW	NECKWEED	CDEEGIOT	GEODETIC	CDEEIITT	DIETETIC
CDEEELLX	EXCELLED	CDEEGIRS	GRECISED	CDEEIJNT	INJECTED
CDEEELNR	CRENELED	CDEEGIRU	CUDGERIE	CDEEIJOR	REJOICED
CDEEELOS	COLESEED	CDEEGIRZ	GRECIZED	CDEEIKLN	NICKELED
CDEEELPY	YCLEEPED	CDEEGKST	GEDECKTS	CDEEIKMY	MICKEYED
CDEEELST	DESELECT	CDEEGLOO	ECOLODGE	CDEEIKNR	NICKERED
	SELECTED	CDEEGLRU	CUDGELER	CDEEIKNS	SICKENED
CDEEELUX	EXCLUDEE	CDEEGNOR	CONGREED	CDEEIKNV	INVECKED
CDEEEMNT	CEMENTED	CDEEHHSU	SHEUCHED	CDEEIKPT	PICKETED
CDEEEMOR	COREDEEM	CDEEHHTT	THETCHED	CDEEIKRR	DRECKIER
CDEEEMPR	EMPERCED	CDEEHIKL	HELIDECK	CDEEIKRT	DETICKER
CDEEENNT	TENDENCE	CDEEHILN	LICHENED	CDEEIKRW	WICKEDER
CDEEENOS	SECONDEE	CDEEHILP	CHELIPED		WICKERED
CDEEENRS	RECENSED	CDEEHILS	CHISELED	CDEEIKRY	YICKERED
	SCREENED	CDEEHINR	ENRICHED	CDEEIKST	TICKSEED
	SECERNED		INHERCED	CDEEIKTT	TICKETED
CDEEENRT	CENTERED		NICHERED	CDEEILNP	PENCILED
	DECENTER		RICHENED		PENDICLE
	DECENTRE	CDEEHIOS	ECHOISED	CDEEILNR	DECLINER
CDEEEPRS	PRECEDES	CDEEHIOZ	ECHOIZED		RECLINED
CDEEEPTX	EXCEPTED	CDEEHIPR	CIPHERED	CDEEILNS	DECLINES

	LICENSED
	SILENCED
CDEEILNT	DENTICLE
CDEEILNU	NUCLEIDE
CDEEILOR	RECOILED
CDEEILPS	ECLIPSED
	PEDICELS
	PEDICLES
CDEEILRS	SCLEREID
CDEEILRT	DERELICT
CDEEILRU	RECUILED
CDEEIMNR	ENDERMIC
CDEEIMNS	CNEMIDES
	ENDEMICS
CDEEIMOR	MEDIOCRE
CDEEIMOS	COMEDIES
CDEEIMPR	PREMEDIC
CDEEIMRS	MISCREED
CDEEIMRV	DECEMVIR
CDEEINNS	INCENSED
CDEEINNT	INCENTED
	INDECENT
CDEEINOR	RECOINED
CDEEINOS	CODEINES
CDEEINPR	PINCERED
CDEEINPS	DISPENCE
CDEEINPT	DEPEINCT
	INCEPTED
	PEINCTED
	PENTICED
CDEEINRU	REINDUCE
CDEEINTU	INDUCTEE
CDEEINTV	INVECTED
CDEEIOPR	RECOPIED
CDEEIORV	CODERIVE
	DIVORCEE
	REVOICED
CDEEIOSS	DIOCESES
CDEEIOSV	DEVOICES
CDEEIPRR	REPRICED
CDEEIPRS	PRECISED
CDEEIPRT	DECREPIT
	DEPICTER
	PRECITED
CDEEIPRU	PEDICURE
CDEEIPST	PECTISED
CDEEIPTZ	PECTIZED
CDEEIQSU	QUIESCED
CDEEIRRS	DECRIERS
	DESCRIER
CDEEIRRT	DIRECTER
	REDIRECT
CDEEIRSS	DESCRIES
CDEEIRST	DESERTIC
	DISCREET
	DISCRETE
CDEEIRSU	DECURIES
CDEEIRSV	DESCRIVE
	SCRIEVED
	SERVICED
CDEEIRTU	CUITERED
	DEUTERIC
CDEEISUV	SEDUCIVE
CDEEITUV	EDUCTIVE
CDEEJKOY	JOCKEYED
CDEEKLNO	ENLOCKED
CDEEKLOR	RELOCKED
CDEEKLPS	SPECKLED
CDEEKMOR	MOCKERED
CDEEKMRU	MUCKERED
CDEEKNOR	RECKONED
CDEEKNRS	REDNECKS
CDEEKNRU	UNRECKED
CDEEKOOR	RECOOKED
CDEEKOPT	POCKETED
CDEEKORR	RECORKED
CDEEKORT	ROCKETED
CDEEKORV	OVERDECK
CDEEKORW	ROCKWEED
CDEEKOST	SOCKETED
CDEEKPRU	PUCKERED
CDEEKRSU	SUCKERED
CDEEKRTU	TUCKERED
CDEELLOR	CORDELLE
CDEELLOT	COLLETED
CDEELLPU	CUPELLED
CDEELMOW	WELCOMED
CDEELNOS	ENCLOSED
CDEELNPU	PEDUNCLE
CDEELNTY	DECENTLY
CDEELNUW	UNCLEWED
CDEELOOW	LOCOWEED
CDEELOPU	DECOUPLE
CDEELORS	RECLOSED
CDEELORV	CLOVERED
CDEELORY	RECOYLED
CDEELOSS	CODELESS
CDEELOST	CLOSETED
CDEELOTU	ELOCUTED
CDEELPRU	PRECLUDE
CDEELPSU	DECUPLES
CDEELRTU	LECTURED
	RELUCTED
CDEELRUX	EXCLUDER
CDEELSSU	SCEDULES
	SECLUDES
CDEELSUX	EXCLUDES
CDEEMOPR	COMPERED
CDEEMOPT	COEMPTED
	COMPETED
CDEEMORT	ECTODERM
CDEEMSTU	TUMESCED
CDEENNOR	RECONNED
CDEENNOS	CONDENSE
CDEENNOU	DENOUNCE
	ENOUNCED
CDEENNOV	CONVENED
CDEENNPY	PENDENCY
CDEENNTU	UNDECENT
CDEENNTY	TENDENCY
CDEENOOS	COOSENED
CDEENORR	CORNERED
CDEENORS	CENSORED
	ENCODERS
	NECROSED
	SECONDER
CDEENORT	CENTRODE
CDEENORU	COENDURE
CDEENOSS	SECONDES
CDEENOSY	ECDYSONE
CDEENOTU	DUECENTO
CDEENOTX	COEXTEND
CDEENOVX	CONVEXED
CDEENOVY	CONVEYED
CDEENPRU	PRUDENCE
CDEENRSU	CENSURED
CDEENRUV	VERECUND
CDEENRUW	UNCREWED
CDEENSST	DESCENTS
CDEENSSU	CENSUSED
CDEENSTY	ENCYSTED
CDEEOOPR	COOPERED
CDEEOOTV	DOVECOTE
CDEEOPPR	COPPERED
CDEEOPRS	PRECODES
	PROCEEDS
CDEEOPRU	RECOUPED
CDEEORRR	RECORDER
	RERECORD
CDEEORRS	RESCORED
CDEEORRU	RECOURED
CDEEORST	CORSETED
	ESCORTED
	SECTORED
CDEEORSV	COVERSED
CDEEORSW	ESCROWED
CDEEORSY	DECOYERS
CDEEORTT	COTTERED
	DETECTOR
CDEEORTV	CORVETED
	VECTORED
CDEEOSST	CESTODES
	COSSETED
CDEEOSTT	ESCOTTED
CDEEPRRU	PRECURED
CDEEPRST	SCEPTRED
CDEERRRU	RECURRED
CDEERRSU	CURSEDER
	REDUCERS
CDEERRUV	RECURVED
CDEERSSU	SEDUCERS
CDEERSUV	DECURVES
CDEERSUX	EXCURSED
CDEERTTU	CURETTED
CDEERTUV	CURVETED
CDEFFINO	COFFINED
CDEFFISU	SUFFICED
CDEFFLSU	SCUFFLED
CDEFFNUU	UNCUFFED
CDEFHILN	FLINCHED
CDEFHILT	FLITCHED
CDEFHIMO	CHIEFDOM
CDEFHIRT	FRICHTED

CDEFHMOS	CHEFDOMS	CDEHIKOS	HOICKSED	CDEIIKRS	DRICKSIE
CDEFIIIL	FILICIDE	CDEHIKRW	HERDWICK	CDEIIKRT	DICKTIER
CDEFIIIT	CITIFIED	CDEHIKST	SKITCHED	CDEIIKST	DICKIEST
CDEFIIOR	CODIFIER	CDEHILMR	MERCHILD		STICKIED
CDEFIIOS	CODIFIES	CDEHILNR	CHILDREN	CDEIILMM	DILEMMIC
CDEFIIST	DEFICITS	CDEHILOR	CHLORIDE	CDEIILMO	DOMICILE
CDEFIITY	CITYFIED	CDEHILOS	CHELOIDS	CDEIILNN	INCLINED
CDEFINNO	CONFINED	CDEHILRT	ELDRITCH	CDEIILNO	INDOCILE
CDEFINNU	INFECUND	CDEHIMOR	CHROMIDE	CDEIILOT	IDIOLECT
CDEFINOR	CONFIDER	CDEHIMOT	METHODIC	CDEIILPS	DISCIPLE
	INFORCED	CDEHIMRS	SMIRCHED	CDEIILPU	PEDICULI
CDEFINOS	CONFIDES	CDEHINNR	INDRENCH		PULICIDE
CDEFINOX	CONFIXED	CDEHINOS	HEDONICS	CDEIILRU	RIDICULE
CDEFIORY	RECODIFY	CDEHINQU	QUINCHED	CDEIIMOS	DIOECISM
CDEFKORS	DEFROCKS	CDEHINST	SNITCHED	CDEIIMRT	DIMETRIC
CDEFLNOU	FLOUNCED	CDEHIOOR	CHOREOID	CDEIIMST	MISCITED
CDEFLORY	FORCEDLY		OCHIDORE	CDEIINNT	INCIDENT
CDEFNORU	FROUNCED	CDEHIOSW	COWHIDES	CDEIINOS	DECISION
	UNFORCED	CDEHIOTU	OUTCHIDE		ICONISED
CDEFNOSU	CONFUSED	CDEHIOTY	THEODICY	CDEIINOV	INVOICED
CDEFNOTU	CONFUTED	CDEHIQTU	QUITCHED	CDEIINOZ	ICONIZED
CDEFNSTU	DEFUNCTS	CDEHIRST	DITCHERS	CDEIINRT	INDICTER
CDEFOSSU	FOCUSSED	CDEHISTT	STITCHED		INDIRECT
CDEGHLNU	GLUNCHED	CDEHISTW	SWITCHED		REINDICT
CDEGHORU	GROUCHED	CDEHITTW	TWITCHED	CDEIINTY	CYTIDINE
CDEGHRTU	GRUTCHED	CDEHKLSU	SHELDUCK	CDEIIOPR	PERIODIC
CDEGIILP	DIPLEGIC	CDEHKNOU	UNCHOKED	CDEIIOPS	EPISODIC
CDEGIINN	INCEDING	CDEHKSUY	HEYDUCKS	CDEIIOPT	EPIDOTIC
CDEGIINX	EXCIDING	CDEHLOOR	COHOLDER	CDEIIOSU	DIECIOUS
CDEGIKNO	DECKOING	CDEHLOOS	DESCHOOL	CDEIIOSV	OVICIDES
	DECOKING		SCHOOLED	CDEIIPPT	PEPTIDIC
CDEGIKNS	DECKINGS	CDEHLORT	CHORTLED	CDEIIPRR	CIRRIPED
CDEGILSU	CLUDGIES	CDEHLOSU	SLOUCHED	CDEIIRST	ICTERIDS
CDEGINNO	ENCODING	CDEHMNTU	DUTCHMEN	CDEIIRTU	DIURETIC
CDEGINNS	SCENDING	CDEHMOOS	SMOOCHED	CDEIIRUV	VIRUCIDE
CDEGINOR	RECODING	CDEHMOSU	SMOUCHED	CDEIISSU	SUICIDES
CDEGINOS	CODESIGN	CDEHMSTU	SMUTCHED	CDEIISTT	DICTIEST
	COGNISED	CDEHNOOP	CHENOPOD	CDEIITWY	CITYWIDE
	COSIGNED		PONCHOED	CDEIJNOO	COJOINED
CDEGINOY	DECOYING	CDEHNRS	CHONDRES	CDEIJSST	DISJECTS
	GYNECOID	CDEHNRSU	CHUNDERS	CDEIKLNO	INLOCKED
CDEGINOZ	COGNIZED	CDEHOORR	RHEOCORD	CDEIKLNR	CRINKLED
CDEGINRU	REDUCING	CDEHOOSS	SCOOSHED	CDEIKLNU	UNLICKED
CDEGINRY	DECRYING	CDEHOOST	COHOSTED	CDEIKLOR	CORDLIKE
CDEGINSU	SEDUCING	CDEHORSU	CHORUSED	CDEIKLOS	SIDELOCK
CDEGINSY	DYSGENIC	CDEHORSW	CHOWDERS	CDEIKLPR	PRICKLED
CDEGKOSU	GEODUCKS		COWHERDS	CDEIKLRT	TRICKLED
CDEGKSUW	GWEDUCKS	CDEHOSSU	HOCUSSED	CDEIKLRU	LUDERICK
CDEGLNOO	COLOGNED	CDEHOSSW	COWSHEDS	CDEIKLST	STICKLED
CDEGNORU	CONGRUED	CDEHSSSU	SCHUSSED	CDEIKLWY	WICKEDLY
CDEGOORS	SCROOGED	CDEIIILS	SILICIDE	CDEIKMSU	MUSICKED
CDEGORSU	SCOURGED	CDEIIIMT	MITICIDE	CDEIKNPU	UNPICKED
	SCROUGED	CDEIIIOS	IDIOCIES	CDEIKNTU	TUNICKED
CDEGORSW	SCROWDGE	CDEIIIRV	VIRICIDE	CDEIKOSS	DOCKISES
CDEHHNOO	HONCHOED	CDEIIITV	VITICIDE	CDEIKOST	DIESTOCK
CDEHIILO	HELICOID	CDEIIKKS	SIDEKICK	CDEIKOSY	YOICKSED
CDEHIILS	CEILIDHS	CDEIIKLS	DISCLIKE	CDEIKOSZ	DOCKIZES
CDEHIIMO	HOMICIDE		SICKLIED	CDEIKRRS	DERRICKS
CDEHIIMR	CHIMERID	CDEIIKMM	MIMICKED	CDEIKSTU	DUCKIEST
CDEHIINO	ECHINOID	CDEIIKNR	CIDERKIN	CDEILLOR	COLLIDER
CDEHIIVV	CHIVVIED	CDEIIKNW	INWICKED	CDEILLOS	CODILLES

Code	Anagram(s)
	COLLIDES
CDEILLOU	LODICULE
CDEILLOY	DOCILELY
CDEILLPU	PELLUCID
CDEILMMS	SCLIMMED
CDEILMNO	DOLMENIC
CDEILMOP	COMPILED
	COMPLIED
CDEILMOS	MELODICS
CDEILMOY	MYCELOID
CDEILMPR	CRIMPLED
CDEILMRU	DULCIMER
CDEILMSY	DYSMELIC
CDEILNOS	INCLOSED
CDEILNOU	NUCLEOID
	UNCOILED
	UNDOCILE
CDEILNRY	CYLINDER
CDEILNSU	INCLUDES
	NUCLIDES
	UNSLICED
CDEILOOW	WOODLICE
CDEILOPS	SCOPELID
CDEILOPU	CLUPEOID
	UPCOILED
CDEILORS	SCLEROID
CDEILORU	CLOUDIER
CDEILORV	COVERLID
CDEILOSS	DISCLOSE
CDEILOST	DOCILEST
CDEILPPR	CRIPPLED
CDEILPSU	CLUPEIDS
CDEILRTY	DIRECTLY
CDEILSTU	DULCITES
	LUCIDEST
CDEILSXY	DYSLEXIC
CDEILTTU	CUITTLED
CDEIMMOT	DECOMMIT
CDEIMMOX	COMMIXED
CDEIMOOW	WOODMICE
CDEIMORT	MORTICED
CDEIMOSS	MISCODES
CDEIMOST	DEMOTICS
	DOMESTIC
CDEIMPRS	SCRIMPED
CDEINNOU	UNCOINED
CDEINNOV	CONNIVED
CDEINOOS	COOSINED
CDEINOOZ	ENDOZOIC
CDEINORR	CORDINER
CDEINORS	CONSIDER
CDEINORT	CENTROID
	DOCTRINE
CDEINORU	DECURION
CDEINORV	CODRIVEN
CDEINOST	DEONTICS
CDEINOSU	DOUCINES
CDEINOSZ	ZINCODES
CDEINOTU	EDUCTION
CDEINOUV	UNVOICED
CDEINOVV	CONVIVED
CDEINPRS	PRESCIND
CDEINPRU	UNPRICED
CDEINPSY	DYSPNEIC
CDEINRRU	INCURRED
CDEINRSS	DISCERNS
	RESCINDS
CDEINRSU	INDUCERS
CDEINRTU	REINDUCT
CDEINRUV	INCURVED
CDEINSSX	EXSCINDS
CDEINSTY	SYNDETIC
CDEIOORS	CORODIES
CDEIOORT	COEDITOR
CDEIOPRS	PERCOIDS
CDEIOPRT	DEPICTOR
CDEIOPST	DESPOTIC
CDEIOPTY	COPYEDIT
CDEIORRT	CREDITOR
	DIRECTOR
CDEIORRV	CODRIVER
	DIVORCER
CDEIORSS	DISCOERS
CDEIORST	CORDITES
CDEIORSU	DISCOURE
CDEIORSV	CODRIVES
	DISCOVER
	DIVORCES
CDEIORSW	CROWDIES
CDEIORSY	DECISORY
CDEIORTU	OUTCRIED
CDEIOSST	CESTOIDS
	SCODIEST
CDEIOSTT	COTTISED
CDEIPRSS	DISCERPS
CDEIPRST	PREDICTS
	SCRIPTED
CDEIPRSY	CYPRIDES
CDEIPRTU	PICTURED
CDEIPSST	DISCEPTS
CDEIPSSU	CUSPIDES
CDEIRRSU	SCURRIED
CDEIRSSU	DISCURES
CDEIRSTU	CRUDITES
	CURDIEST
	CURTSIED
CDEIRSTV	VERDICTS
CDEISSST	DISSECTS
CDEISSSU	DISCUSES
CDEJNORU	CONJURED
CDEKKLNU	KNUCKLED
CDEKLMOR	CLERKDOM
CDEKLMOU	DUCKMOLE
CDEKLNOU	UNLOCKED
CDEKLNRU	CRUNKLED
CDEKLOPU	UPLOCKED
CDEKLORY	YELDROCK
CDEKLOSW	WEDLOCKS
CDEKLRTU	TRUCKLED
CDEKNOOU	UNCOOKED
CDEKNOOV	CONVOKED
CDEKNORS	DORNECKS
CDEKNORU	UNCORKED
CDEKNSSU	SUNDECKS
CDEKNSUU	UNSUCKED
CDEKNTUU	UNTUCKED
CDEKOPSY	COPYDESK
CDEKOSST	DESTOCKS
CDELLNUU	UNCULLED
CDELLOOP	CLODPOLE
CDELLORS	SCROLLED
CDELLORU	COLLUDER
CDELLOSU	COLLUDES
CDELLOTU	CLOUDLET
CDELLTUY	DULCETLY
CDELMNOO	MONOCLED
CDELMNOU	COLUMNED
CDELMPRU	CRUMPLED
CDELNOOR	CONDOLER
CDELNOOS	CONDOLES
	CONSOLED
CDELNOOU	UNCOOLED
CDELNOSS	COLDNESS
CDELNOSU	ENCLOUDS
	UNCLOSED
CDELNOSY	CONDYLES
	SECONDLY
CDELNOTU	UNCOLTED
CDELNOUW	UNCOWLED
CDELNOUY	UNCLOYED
CDELNRUU	UNCURLED
CDELNSUY	SECUNDLY
CDELOORS	COLOREDS
	CROODLES
	DECOLORS
CDELOORU	COLOURED
	DECOLOUR
CDELOORV	OVERCOLD
CDELOOTT	DOLCETTO
CDELOPSU	UPCLOSED
CDELOPTU	OCTUPLED
CDELORSS	CORDLESS
	SCOLDERS
CDELORSU	CLOSURED
CDELORSW	CLOWDERS
	SCROWLED
CDELORTU	CLOTURED
CDELORZZ	CROZZLED
CDELOSSU	DULCOSES
CDELOSTU	COULDEST
	LOCUSTED
CDELPRSU	SCRUPLED
CDELPRUU	UPCURLED
CDELPSTU	SCULPTED
CDELRRSU	CURDLERS
CDELRSSU	SCUDLERS
CDELRSUY	CURSEDLY
CDELRTUU	CULTURED
CDELRUVY	CURVEDLY
CDELSSTU	DUCTLESS
CDELSSUY	CUSSEDLY
CDELSTTU	SCUTTLED
CDELSTUU	DUCTULES

CDEMMNOO	COMMONED	CDEOSSTU	CUSTODES	CDHIRSTY	CHYTRIDS
CDEMMNOS	COMMENDS	CDEPRSTY	DECRYPTS	CDHKOORS	HORDOCKS
CDEMMNOU	COMMUNED	CDEPRUUV	UPCURVED	CDHLOOPY	COPYHOLD
CDEMMOOS	COMMODES	CDERSTTU	DESTRUCT	CDHNORSU	CHONDRUS
CDEMMOOV	COMMOVED	CDFIILSU	FLUIDICS	CDHOOOPW	WOODCHOP
CDEMMOTU	COMMUTED	CDFIKMNU	MINDFUCK	CDHOORRU	UROCHORD
CDEMMRSU	SCRUMMED	CDFIKORS	DISFROCK	CDIIIMNS	MINIDISC
CDEMNNOS	CONDEMNS	CDFKOOTU	DUCKFOOT	CDIIIMNU	INDICIUM
CDEMNOOW	COMEDOWN	CDFNNOOU	CONFOUND	CDIIINSV	INVISCID
	DOWNCOME	CDFNOOSU	COFOUNDS	CDIIIORT	DIORITIC
CDEMNOPS	COMPENDS	CDGHIILN	CHILDING	CDIIKMNO	DOMINICK
CDEMNOSU	CONSUMED	CDGHIILO	CHILIDOG	CDIIKPST	DIPSTICK
CDEMNOTU	DOCUMENT	CDGHIINS	CHIDINGS	CDIILMOS	DOMICILS
CDEMNSUU	SECUNDUM	CDGHIINT	DICHTING	CDIILOPP	DIPLOPIC
CDEMOOPS	COMPOSED		DITCHING	CDIILOTY	DOCILITY
CDEMOPTU	COMPUTED	CDGHILOS	GLOCHIDS	CDIILRUY	URIDYLIC
CDEMORSU	DECORUMS	CDGHINNU	DUNCHING	CDIILSVY	VISCIDLY
CDEMOSTU	COSTUMED	CDGHINOR	CHORDING	CDIILTUY	LUCIDITY
	CUSTOMED	CDGHINOU	DOUCHING	CDIIMNOU	CONIDIUM
CDEMPRSU	SCRUMPED	CDGIIKNS	DICKINGS		MUCINOID
CDENNOOR	CONDONER	CDGIINNU	INDUCING		ONCIDIUM
CDENNOOS	CONDONES	CDGIINOS	DISCOING	CDIIMTUY	MUCIDITY
CDENNOOT	CONNOTED	CDGIKLNU	DUCKLING	CDIINOOS	ISODICON
CDENNOST	CONTENDS	CDGIKLOR	GRIDLOCK		ONISCOID
CDENNOUY	UNCOYNED	CDGIKNOS	DOCKINGS	CDIINORS	CRINOIDS
CDENOORS	CONDORES	CDGIKNSU	DUCKINGS	CDIINORT	INDICTOR
CDENOORT	CREODONT	CDGILNOS	CODLINGS	CDIINOST	DICTIONS
CDENOOST	SECODONT		LINGCODS	CDIINOSV	VIDICONS
CDENOOTT	COTTONED		SCOLDING	CDIINPRY	CYPRINID
CDENOOVY	CONVOYED	CDGILNOU	CLOUDING	CDIINPTU	PUNDITIC
CDENOPSU	CONSPUED	CDGILNRU	CURDLING	CDIINSTT	DISTINCT
CDENORSS	CORSNEDS	CDGINORS	CORDINGS	CDIIOORS	SORICOID
CDENORSU	CRUNODES	CDGINORW	CROWDING	CDIIOOSU	DIOICOUS
CDENORSW	DECROWNS	CDGINSTU	DUCTINGS	CDIIOPRT	DIOPTRIC
CDENORTU	CORNUTED	CDGLOOOY	CODOLOGY		DIPROTIC
	TROUNCED	CDGNOOOS	COONDOGS		TRIPODIC
CDENOSSY	ECDYSONS	CDGNOOTU	GONODUCT	CDIIORSU	SCIUROID
CDENOSTU	CONTUSED	CDHHIILS	CHILDISH	CDIIORSX	CORIXIDS
CDENRSUU	UNCURSED	CDHIILTW	TWICHILD	CDIIOSSS	CISSOIDS
CDENRTUU	UNDERCUT	CDHIINST	CHINDITS	CDIIOSTY	SODICITY
CDENRUUV	UNCURVED	CDHIIOOR	CHORIOID	CDIIPTUY	CUPIDITY
CDEOOPPS	COPEPODS	CDHIIORT	HIDROTIC		PUDICITY
CDEOOPRS	SCROOPED		TRICHOID	CDIIRSSU	SCIURIDS
CDEOOPST	POSTCODE	CDHIIOSZ	SCHIZOID	CDIIRSTT	DISTRICT
CDEOORRR	CORRODER	CDHIISST	DISTICHS	CDIJNSTU	DISJUNCT
CDEOORRS	CORRODES	CDHILNSU	UNCHILDS	CDIKKNOW	KICKDOWN
CDEOORSU	DECOROUS	CDHILOOP	CHILOPOD	CDIKKOPR	DROPKICK
CDEOORSV	VOCODERS	CDHILOOS	DOLICHOS	CDIKNNSU	NUDNICKS
CDEOOSTV	DOVECOTS	CDHILORS	CHLORIDS	CDIKNORS	DORNICKS
CDEOPRRU	PROCURED	CDHIMOSU	DOCHMIUS	CDIKNOSW	WINDOCKS
	PRODUCER	CDHINNOR	CHONDRIN		WINDSOCK
CDEOPRSU	PRODUCES	CDHINORY	HYDRONIC	CDIKNOTW	DOWNTICK
CDEOQSTU	DOCQUETS	CDHIOOPW	WOODCHIP	CDIKNPSU	DUCKPINS
CDEORRSW	CROWDERS	CDHIOORS	CHOROIDS	CDILLOOS	COLLOIDS
CDEORRTU	REDUCTOR	CDHIOORT	TROCHOID	CDILLOTU	DULCITOL
CDEORSST	DOCTRESS	CDHIOPRW	WHIPCORD	CDILLOUY	CLOUDILY
CDEORSSU	SCOURSED	CDHIOPRY	HYDROPIC	CDILMSTU	MIDCULTS
CDEORSSW	SCOWDERS	CDHIOPSY	PSYCHOID	CDILOOPS	PODSOLIC
CDEORSTU	EDUCTORS	CDHIORRT	TRICHORD	CDILOOPZ	PODZOLIC
	SEDUCTOR	CDHIOSUV	DISVOUCH	CDILOORS	DISCOLOR
CDEORSUU	DOUCEURS	CDHIPSTY	DIPTYCHS	CDILOORT	LORDOTIC

CDILOOTY	COTYLOID	**CEEEEPRS**	PRECEESE	**CEEEIRSX**	EXERCISE
CDILOSST	DISCLOST	**CEEEFFIR**	EFFIERCE	**CEEEIRTV**	ERECTIVE
CDILOSTY	DICOTYLS	**CEEEFFRT**	EFFECTER	**CEEEISSS**	ECESISES
	SCOLYTID	**CEEEFHLS**	FLEECHES	**CEEEISTV**	EVICTEES
CDIMMOSU	MODICUMS	**CEEEFILR**	FLEECIER	**CEEEJRRT**	REJECTER
CDIMOORT	MICRODOT	**CEEEFILS**	FLEECIES	**CEEEJRST**	REEJECTS
CDINNQUU	QUIDNUNC	**CEEEFINR**	ENFIERCE	**CEEEKNNP**	PENNEECK
CDINOOOR	CORONOID	**CEEEFLRS**	FLEECERS	**CEEELLNR**	CRENELLE
CDINOOTU	NOCTUOID	**CEEEFNOR**	CONFEREE	**CEEELLSU**	ECUELLES
CDINOPSY	DYSPNOIC	**CEEEFNRS**	REFENCES	**CEEELOPR**	OPERCELE
CDINORSW	DISCROWN	**CEEEGIMN**	EMCEEING	**CEEELOSS**	COLESSEE
CDINORTU	INDUCTOR	**CEEEGINS**	EGENCIES	**CEEELPRT**	PREELECT
CDINOSTU	CONDUITS	**CEEEGINX**	EXIGENCE	**CEEELPSY**	YCLEEPES
	DISCOUNT	**CEEEGITX**	EXEGETIC	**CEEELRRV**	CLEVERER
	NOCTUIDS	**CEEEGMNR**	MERGENCE	**CEEELRST**	REELECTS
CDINOSTY	DYSTONIC	**CEEEGNRS**	REGENCES		RESELECT
CDIOOOPT	OCTOPOID	**CEEEGNRV**	VERGENCE	**CEEELRTT**	ELECTRET
CDIOOPRS	PROSODIC	**CEEEHIKR**	CHEEKIER		TERCELET
CDIOORRR	CORRIDOR	**CEEEHIRR**	CHEERIER	**CEEELSST**	CELESTES
CDIOPRRS	RIPCORDS		REECHIER	**CEEEMNNS**	SCENEMEN
CDIOPRSU	CUSPIDOR	**CEEEHIRS**	CHEESIER	**CEEEMNRT**	CEMENTER
CDIOSSTY	CYSTOIDS	**CEEEHLLS**	ECHELLES		CEREMENT
CDIOSTUV	OVIDUCTS	**CEEEHLRV**	CHEVEREL		RECEMENT
CDJLNOUY	JOCUNDLY	**CEEEHLSS**	SLEECHES	**CEEEMORT**	ECTOMERE
CDKLNOOW	LOCKDOWN	**CEEEHMSS**	SMEECHES	**CEEEMPRS**	EMPERCES
CDKLOOOS	OCKODOLS	**CEEEHNNP**	PENNEECH	**CEEEMRTY**	CEMETERY
CDKLOOPR	DROPLOCK	**CEEEHNRS**	ENCHEERS	**CEEENNPT**	TENPENCE
CDKMMORU	DRUMMOCK	**CEEEHORS**	REECHOES	**CEEENNST**	SENTENCE
CDKMORSU	MUDROCKS	**CEEEHPRS**	CHEEPERS	**CEEENPRS**	PRESENCE
CDKNNOSU	DUNNOCKS	**CEEEHPSS**	SPEECHES	**CEEENPRT**	PRETENCE
CDKNOORS	DORNOCKS	**CEEEHRRS**	CHEERERS	**CEEENQSU**	SEQUENCE
CDKOOORW	CORKWOOD	**CEEEHRSS**	CREESHES	**CEEENRRS**	RESCREEN
CDKORTUW	DUCTWORK		SECESHER		SCREENER
CDLLLOOP	CLODPOLL	**CEEEHRSW**	ESCHEWER	**CEEENRRT**	RECENTER
CDLNOOOW	COOLDOWN	**CEEEHRVY**	CHEVERYE		RECENTRE
CDLNOSUU	UNCLOUDS	**CEEEHSSS**	SECESHES	**CEEENRSS**	RECENSES
CDLNOUUY	UNCLOUDY	**CEEEIJTV**	EJECTIVE	**CEEENSSS**	ESSENCES
CDLOOOTW	COLTWOOD	**CEEEIKRR**	CREEKIER	**CEEENSST**	CENTESES
CDLOOPSY	LYCOPODS	**CEEEILNN**	LENIENCE	**CEEEPRRS**	CREEPERS
CDLOORTY	DOCTORLY	**CEEEILNS**	LICENSEE	**CEEEPRRT**	PREERECT
CDLOOSTU	OUTSCOLD	**CEEEILNT**	TELECINE	**CEEEPRTX**	EXPECTER
CDMNOOPU	COMPOUND	**CEEEILRS**	CELERIES	**CEEERRST**	ERECTERS
CDMNORUU	CORUNDUM	**CEEEILRT**	ERECTILE		REERECTS
CDMOSSUW	MUDSCOWS	**CEEEILTV**	CLEVEITE		SECRETER
CDNNOOOT	CONODONT		ELECTIVE	**CEEERRSU**	RESECURE
CDNNOOTY	CYNODONT	**CEEEIMNN**	EMINENCE	**CEEERRSV**	SCREEVER
CDNNOSTU	CONTUNDS	**CEEEIMPR**	EMPIERCE	**CEEERRTX**	EXCRETER
CDNOSTUW	CUTDOWNS	**CEEEIMRR**	REREMICE	**CEEERSSS**	RECESSES
CDOOOPST	OCTOPODS	**CEEEINNT**	ENCEINTE	**CEEERSST**	SECRETES
CDOOPSST	POSTDOCS	**CEEEINPR**	PIECENER		SESTERCE
CDOORRUY	CORDUROY	**CEEEINPS**	EPICENES	**CEEERSSU**	CEREUSES
CDOORTUW	OUTCROWD	**CEEEINRS**	CERESINE	**CEEERSSV**	SCREEVES
CDOOSTUW	WOODCUTS		SCREENIE	**CEEERSTX**	EXCRETES
CDOPRSTU	PRODUCTS	**CEEEINSS**	ESNECIES	**CEEERTTV**	CREVETTE
CDORSSUW	CUSSWORD	**CEEEIOPT**	TOEPIECE	**CEEERTUX**	EXECUTER
CEEEEGHS	GEECHEES	**CEEEIPRR**	CREEPIER	**CEEESSSX**	EXCESSES
CEEEEHLS	LEECHEES		CREEPERIE	**CEEESTUX**	EXECUTES
CEEEEIPY	EYEPIECE	**CEEEIPRS**	CREEPIES	**CEEFFNOS**	OFFENCES
CEEEEJRT	REJECTEE	**CEEEIPRV**	PERCEIVE	**CEEFFORS**	EFFORCES
CEEEELST	ELECTEES	**CEEEIRRV**	RECEIVER	**CEEFFORT**	EFFECTOR
	SELECTEE	**CEEEIRSV**	RECEIVES	**CEEFGILN**	FLEECING

CEEFHIKR	KERCHIEF	CEEGILNT	ELECTING	CEEHINOR	COINHERE
CEEFHIRY	CHIEFERY	CEEGILOT	ECLOGITE	CEEHINPR	ENCIPHER
CEEFHISS	CHIEFESS	CEEGILRS	CLERGIES	CEEHINPT	PHENETIC
CEEFHIST	CHIEFEST	CEEGILRT	TELERGIC	CEEHINPU	EUPHENIC
	FETICHES	CEEGIMNS	MISCEGEN	CEEHINRR	ENRICHER
CEEFHKLU	CHEEKFUL	CEEGINOO	COOEEING	CEEHINRS	ENRICHES
CEEFHLNR	FLENCHER	CEEGINOR	EROGENIC		INHERCES
CEEFHLNS	FLENCHES	CEEGINPR	CREEPING	CEEHINST	SITHENCE
CEEFHLRT	FLETCHER	CEEGINRS	CREESING	CEEHINSX	CHENIXES
CEEFHLRU	CHEERFUL		GENERICS	CEEHINTT	ENTHETIC
CEEFHLST	FLETCHES	CEEGINRT	ERECTING	CEEHIORS	CHEERIOS
CEEFHNRS	FRENCHES		GENTRICE	CEEHIOSS	ECHOISES
CEEFHORU	FOURCHEE	CEEGINST	GENETICS	CEEHIOST	ECHOIEST
CEEFHRST	FECHTERS	CEEGINSU	EUGENICS	CEEHIOSU	ICEHOUSE
	FETCHERS	CEEGINXY	EXIGENCY	CEEHIOSV	COHESIVE
CEEFIINT	INFICETE	CEEGIORX	EXOERGIC	CEEHIOSZ	ECHOIZES
CEEFIKLR	FLECKIER	CEEGIRSS	GRECISES	CEEHIPRR	CIPHERER
CEEFILLY	FLEECILY	CEEGIRSZ	GRECIZES	CEEHIPRT	HERPETIC
CEEFILRT	TELFERIC	CEEGLLOR	COLLEGER	CEEHIQRU	CHEQUIER
CEEFILRY	FIERCELY	CEEGLLOS	COLLEGES	CEEHIRRR	CHERRIER
CEEFINPP	FIPPENCE	CEEGLNST	NEGLECTS	CEEHIRRS	CHERRIES
CEEFINRT	FRENETIC	CEEGLOSU	ECLOGUES	CEEHIRRT	CHERTIER
	INFECTER	CEEGMMOR	COMMERGE	CEEHIRSS	RICHESSE
	REINFECT	CEEGMNOY	CYMOGENE	CEEHIRST	CHESTIER
CEEFIPRT	PERFECTI	CEEGNNOO	ONCOGENE		HERETICS
CEEFIRST	FIERCEST	CEEGNNOR	CONGENER	CEEHIRTT	TETCHIER
CEEFKLRS	FLECKERS	CEEGNNPU	PUNGENCE	CEEHIRTU	HEURETIC
	FRECKLES	CEEGNORS	COGENERS	CEEHIRTV	VETCHIER
CEEFKLSS	FECKLESS		CONGREES	CEEHISSV	SEVICHES
CEEFLNOR	FLORENCE	CEEGNORT	CONGREET	CEEHISTT	ESTHETIC
CEEFLNSU	FLUENCES		COREGENT		TECHIEST
CEEFLNTU	FECULENT	CEEGNORV	CONVERGE	CEEHISTW	CHEWIEST
CEEFLRST	REFLECTS	CEEGNOTY	ECTOGENY	CEEHISTY	YECHIEST
CEEFNNSU	UNFENCES	CEEGNRSU	URGENCES	CEEHKLPR	KREPLECH
CEEFNORR	CONFRERE	CEEGNRVY	VERGENCY	CEEHKLRS	HECKLERS
	ENFORCER	CEEGORST	CORTEGES	CEEHKNPS	HENPECKS
	RECONFER	CEEGQRSU	GRECQUES	CEEHKRST	RESKETCH
	RENFORCE	CEEHHIRS	CHESHIRE		SKETCHER
CEEFNORS	ENFORCES	CEEHHMNN	HENCHMEN	CEEHKRTV	KVETCHER
CEEFNORW	FENCEROW	CEEHHSTT	THETCHES	CEEHKSST	SKETCHES
CEEFNOTU	OUTFENCE	CEEHIIST	ETHICISE	CEEHKSTV	KVETCHES
CEEFNRVY	FERVENCY	CEEHIITZ	ETHICIZE	CEEHLMOO	HEMOCOEL
CEEFOPRR	PERFORCE	CEEHIKLY	CHEEKILY	CEEHLMSZ	SCHMELZE
CEEFOPRT	PERFECTO	CEEHIKMS	KIMCHEES	CEEHLNOO	HOLOCENE
CEEFORRS	FRESCOER	CEEHIKNW	CHEEWINK	CEEHLNOS	CHELONES
CEEFORSS	FRESCOES	CEEHILLN	CHENILLE		ECHELONS
CEEFORTW	CROWFEET	CEEHILLV	CHEVILLE	CEEHLNOT	ENCLOTHE
CEEFPRST	PERFECTS	CEEHILRS	CHISELER	CEEHLNPS	PLENCHES
	PREFECTS		SCHLIERE	CEEHLNPU	PENUCHLE
CEEGHIKN	CHEEKING	CEEHILRT	TELECHIR	CEEHLNSU	ELENCHUS
CEEGHILN	LEECHING	CEEHILRV	CHEVERIL	CEEHLORT	RECLOTHE
CEEGHINP	CHEEPING	CEEHILRW	CLERIHEW	CEEHLOSS	ECHOLESS
CEEGHINR	CHEERING	CEEHILRY	CHEERILY	CEEHLOSW	COWHEELS
	REECHING	CEEHILSV	VEHICLES	CEEHLQSU	QUELCHES
CEEGHINS	CHEESING	CEEHILSW	SWELCHIE	CEEHLRSU	HERCULES
CEEGHLOW	COGWHEEL	CEEHILSY	CHEESILY	CEEHLRSW	WELCHERS
CEEGIINP	EPIGENIC	CEEHIMMS	CHEMMIES	CEEHLSSS	CHESSELS
CEEGIJNT	EJECTING	CEEHIMRS	CHIMERES	CEEHMNNS	MENSCHEN
CEEGIKLN	CLEEKING	CEEHIMRT	HERMETIC	CEEHMNOR	CHOREMEN
CEEGILNP	CLEEPING	CEEHIMSS	CHEMISES		CHROMENE
CEEGILNR	CREELING		SCHEMIES	CEEHMNSS	CHESSMEN

	MENSCHES	**CEEIJRUV**	VERJUICE	**CEEILRTU**	RETICULE
CEEHMORT	COMETHER	**CEEIKKLN**	NECKLIKE	**CEEILRTY**	CELERITY
CEEHMOTY	HEMOCYTE	**CEEIKKLO**	COKELIKE	**CEEILSSV**	CLEVISES
CEEHMRSS	SCHEMERS	**CEEIKKSS**	KECKSIES		VESICLES
	SCHMEERS	**CEEIKLMU**	LEUKEMIC		VICELESS
CEEHMRST	MERCHETS	**CEEIKLNN**	NECKLINE	**CEEILSTT**	TELESTIC
CEEHNNOW	NOWHENCE	**CEEIKLPR**	PICKEREL		TESTICLE
CEEHNNRT	ENTRENCH	**CEEIKNRS**	SICKENER	**CEEILSTU**	LEUCITES
CEEHNOPS	PENOCHES	**CEEIKNST**	NECKTIES	**CEEIMMPY**	EMPYEMIC
CEEHNORS	RECHOSEN	**CEEIKPRS**	PICKEERS	**CEEIMMRS**	MESMERIC
CEEHNORT	COHERENT		SPECKIER	**CEEIMMST**	MEMETICS
CEEHNORV	CHEVERON	**CEEIKPRT**	PICKETER	**CEEIMNNY**	EMINENCY
CEEHNPSU	PENUCHES	**CEEIKPST**	PECKIEST	**CEEIMNPS**	SPECIMEN
CEEHNQRU	QUENCHER	**CEEILLLP**	PELLICLE	**CEEIMNST**	CENTIMES
CEEHNQSU	QUENCHES	**CEEILLMS**	MICELLES		TENESMIC
CEEHNRRT	RETRENCH	**CEEILLNT**	LENTICEL	**CEEIMORT**	METEORIC
	TRENCHER		LENTICLE	**CEEIMOTY**	MEIOCYTE
CEEHNRRW	WRENCHER	**CEEILMOR**	COMELIER	**CEEIMRSX**	EXCIMERS
CEEHNRST	TRENCHES	**CEEILMPS**	SEMPLICE	**CEEIMSTT**	SMECTITE
CEEHNRSW	WENCHERS	**CEEILNNT**	CENTINEL	**CEEINNOP**	PINECONE
	WRENCHES	**CEEILNNY**	LENIENCY	**CEEINNOT**	NEOTENIC
CEEHNSST	STENCHES	**CEEILNOP**	PLIOCENE	**CEEINNRS**	INCENSER
CEEHNSTU	CHUTNEES	**CEEILNOS**	CINEOLES	**CEEINNRT**	INCENTER
CEEHOOPR	POECHORE	**CEEILNOT**	COTELINE		INCENTRE
CEEHOORS	RECHOOSE		ELECTION	**CEEINNSS**	INCENSES
CEEHOPRS	PRECHOSE		VIOLENCE		NICENESS
CEEHOPRY	CORYPHEE	**CEEILNOV**	PENCILER	**CEEINNST**	NESCIENT
CEEHOPST	SHEEPCOT	**CEEILNPR**	PENCILER	**CEEINOPU**	EUPNOEIC
CEEHOPTT	POCHETTE	**CEEILNPU**	PULICENE	**CEEINORR**	ENCIERRO
CEEHORRS	COHERERS	**CEEILNPX**	CINEPLEX	**CEEINORT**	ERECTION
	COSHERER	**CEEILNRR**	RECLINER		NEOTERIC
CEEHORRT	HECTORER	**CEEILNRS**	LICENSER	**CEEINORV**	OVERNICE
	TORCHERE		RECLINES	**CEEINORX**	EXOCRINE
CEEHORSS	ORCHESES		SILENCER	**CEEINOSS**	SENECIOS
CEEHORST	TROCHEES	**CEEILNRU**	CERULEIN	**CEEINOST**	ICESTONE
CEEHOSUV	VOUCHEES	**CEEILNRV**	VERNICLE		SEICENTO
CEEHPRRS	PERCHERS	**CEEILNSS**	ENCLISES	**CEEINOTV**	EVECTION
CEEHPRRY	PERCHERY		LICENSES	**CEEINPRT**	PRENTICE
CEEHPRSU	UPCHEERS		SILENCES		TERPENIC
CEEHPSST	SPETCHES	**CEEILNST**	CENTILES	**CEEINPST**	PECTINES
CEEHQRSU	CHEQUERS	**CEEILNSU**	LEUCINES		PENTICES
CEEHQSTU	QUETCHES	**CEEILORR**	RECOILER	**CEEINPSX**	SIXPENCE
CEEHRSTV	CHEVRETS	**CEEILORS**	CREOLISE	**CEEINQRU**	QUERCINE
CEEHRSTW	WRETCHES	**CEEILORZ**	CREOLIZE	**CEEINRRS**	SINCERER
CEEHRTTU	TEUCHTER	**CEEILOSS**	SOLECISE	**CEEINRSS**	CERESINS
CEEHSTTU	TEUCHEST	**CEEILOSZ**	SOLECIZE		SCRIENES
CEEIIKLP	EPICLIKE	**CEEILPRS**	ECLIPSER	**CEEINRST**	CENTRIES
CEEIIKLV	VICELIKE		PRESLICE		ENTERICS
CEEIIMPR	EPIMERIC		RESPLICE		ENTICERS
CEEIIMRT	EREMITIC	**CEEILPRY**	CREEPILY		SCIENTER
CEEIINRT	ICTERINE	**CEEILPSS**	ECLIPSES		SECRETIN
	REINCITE	**CEEILPST**	TELEPICS	**CEEINRSU**	INSECURE
CEEIINST	NICETIES	**CEEILPSX**	EXCIPLES		SINECURE
CEEIINSW	ICEWINES	**CEEILQSU**	LIQUESCE	**CEEINRTT**	RETICENT
CEEIINVV	EVINCIVE	**CEEILRST**	RETICLES	**CEEINRTU**	CEINTURE
CEEIIPRS	EPICIERS		SCLERITE		ENURETIC
CEEIIRST	SERICITE		TIERCELS	**CEEINSST**	CENTESIS
CEEIJNOT	EJECTION		TRISCELE	**CEEINSTY**	CYSTEINE
CEEIJNRT	REINJECT	**CEEILRSU**	CISELEUR	**CEEIOPPR**	PERICOPE
CEEIJORR	REJOICER		CISELURE	**CEEIOPPS**	EPISCOPE
CEEIJORS	REJOICES		RECUILES	**CEEIOPRS**	RECOPIES
		CEEILRSV	VERSICLE		

CEEIOPST	ECTOPIES	CEEKORRT	CORKTREE	CEELRSSU	CURELESS
	PICOTEES		ROCKETER		RECLUSES
CEEIORST	COTERIES	CEEKOSSY	SOCKEYES	CEELRSSW	CREWLESS
	ESOTERIC	CEEKOSTT	SOCKETTE	CEELRSTU	CRUELEST
CEEIORSV	REVOICES	CEEKPRRU	PUCKERER		LECTURES
CEEIORSX	EXORCISE	CEEKPRSY	RYEPECKS	CEELRSTY	SECRETLY
CEEIORTT	EROTETIC	CEEKRRSW	WRECKERS	CEELRSUY	SECURELY
CEEIORTV	ORECTIVE	CEELLLSU	CELLULES	CEELSTTU	LETTUCES
CEEIORTX	EXOTERIC	CEELLMOU	MOLECULE	CEEMMNTU	CEMENTUM
CEEIORXZ	EXORCIZE	CEELLNOS	COLLEENS	CEEMMORS	COMMERES
CEEIOSST	COESITES	CEELLNOU	NUCLEOLE	CEEMNORR	CREMORNE
CEEIOSTV	COVETISE	CEELLORT	RECOLLET	CEEMNORW	NEWCOMER
CEEIPPRR	PREPRICE	CEELLOSS	CELLOSES	CEEMNORY	CEREMONY
CEEIPPRS	PRECIPES	CEELLPRU	CUPELLER	CEEMNOYZ	COENZYME
CEEIPPRT	PRECEPIT	CEELLPSU	PUCELLES	CEEMNRSU	CERUMENS
CEEIPPTU	EUPEPTIC	CEELLRRU	CRUELLER	CEEMOORV	COMEOVER
CEEIPRRS	PIERCERS	CEELLRVY	CLEVERLY		OVERCOME
	PRECISER	CEELLSSU	CLUELESS	CEEMOORW	OWRECOME
	REPRICES	CEELLSTY	SELECTLY	CEEMOOTY	OOMYCETE
CEEIPRSS	PRECISES	CEELMOOS	COELOMES	CEEMOPRS	COMPEERS
CEEIPRST	CREPIEST	CEELMOPT	COMPLETE		COMPERES
	RECEIPTS	CEELMORW	WELCOMER	CEEMOPST	COMPETES
CEEIPRSU	EPICURES	CEELMOST	TELECOMS	CEEMOSSS	COSMESES
CEEIPRUX	PRECIEUX	CEELMOSW	WELCOMES	CEEMSSTU	TUMESCES
CEEIPSST	PECTISES	CEELMRTU	ELECTRUM	CEENNOOS	CONENOSE
CEEIPSTZ	PECTIZES	CEELNNOP	PENONCEL	CEENNORS	ONSCREEN
CEEIQSSU	QUIESCES	CEELNNOT	CENTONEL	CEENNORT	CRETONNE
CEEIRRSS	CERRISES		NONELECT	CEENNORU	RENOUNCE
	CRESSIER	CEELNOPU	OPULENCE	CEENNORV	CONVENER
CEEIRRST	RECITERS	CEELNOPY	LYCOPENE	CEENNOST	CENTONES
CEEIRRSV	SERVICER	CEELNORS	ENCLOSER	CEENNOSU	ENOUNCES
CEEIRRSW	SCREWIER		ENSORCEL	CEENNOSV	CONVENES
CEEIRRTU	URETERIC	CEELNORT	ELECTRON	CEENNRST	CENTNERS
CEEIRSSV	SCRIEVES	CEELNORU	ENCOLURE	CEENOOST	ECOTONES
	SERVICES	CEELNOSS	ENCLOSES	CEENOPST	POTENCES
CEEIRSTT	TIERCETS	CEELNPTU	CENTUPLE	CEENOPTW	TWOPENCE
CEEIRSTU	CERUSITE	CEELNRST	LECTERNS	CEENORRS	RECENSOR
	CUTESIER	CEELNRSU	LUCERNES	CEENORRS	NECROSES
	EUCRITES	CEELNRTU	RELUCENT	CEENORSU	COENURES
CEEIRSTV	VERTICES	CEELNRTY	RECENTLY	CEENORSV	CONSERVE
CEEIRSTX	EXCITERS	CEELNSTU	ESCULENT		CONVERSE
CEEIRSVX	CERVIXES	CEELOOVV	COEVOLVE	CEENORSZ	COZENERS
CEEISSST	CITESSES	CEELOPRU	OPERCULE	CEENORTT	TRECENTO
CEEISTTT	TECTITES		RECOUPLE	CEENORVY	CONVEYER
CEEISTTZ	ZETETICS	CEELORSS	CORELESS		RECONVEY
CEEISUVX	EXCUSIVE		RECLOSES	CEENOSVX	CONVEXES
CEEJKOTT	JOCKETTE		SCLEROSE	CEENPPTU	TUPPENCE
CEEJORRT	REJECTOR	CEELORST	CORSELET	CEENPRSS	SPENCERS
CEEJORST	EJECTORS		ELECTORS	CEENPRST	PERCENTS
CEEKKNOS	KNEESOCK		ELECTROS		PRECENTS
CEEKKNPS	KENSPECK		SELECTOR	CEENPSSU	SUSPENCE
CEEKLNPU	PENUCKLE	CEELORSY	RECOYLES	CEENQSUY	SEQUENCY
CEEKLNSS	NECKLESS	CEELORTV	COVERLET	CEENRRSU	CENSURER
CEEKLNST	NECKLETS	CEELOSSU	COLEUSES	CEENRRSU	CENSURES
CEEKLPSS	SPECKLES	CEELOSTU	ELOCUTES	CEENRSTU	UNSECRET
CEEKLRSS	CLERKESS	CEELOSTV	COVELETS	CEENSSSU	CENSUSES
	RECKLESS	CEELPRST	PLECTRES	CEENSSTU	CUTENESS
CEEKNORR	RECKONER		PRELECTS	CEENSTTU	CUNETTES
CEEKNRSU	SUCKENER	CEELPRSU	CUPELERS	CEEOORST	CREOSOTE
CEEKOPRT	POCKETER	CEELRRTU	LECTURER	CEEOPRRS	PRESCORE
CEEKOPRX	OXPECKER	CEELRSST	LECTRESS	CEEOPRRT	RECEPTOR

CEEOPRTX	EXCEPTOR	CEFFLORU	FORCEFUL	FORINSEC
CEEOPRTY	CEROTYPE	CEFFLRSU	SCUFFLER	FORNICES
CEEOPSST	PECTOSES	CEFFLSSU	CUFFLESS	INFORCES
CEEOPSTY	ECOTYPES		SCUFFLES	CEFINORT	INFECTOR
CEEOQTTU	COQUETTE	CEFFORSS	SCOFFERS	CEFINOSX	CONFIXES
CEEORRRS	SORCERER	CEFFORST	COFFRETS	CEFINOTT	CONFETTI
CEEORRSS	RESCORES	CEFFRSSU	SCUFFERS	CEFIOPRS	FORCIPES
CEEORRST	ERECTORS	CEFGHILN	FELCHING	CEFIORTY	FEROCITY
	SECRETOR	CEFGHINT	FECHTING	CEFIRRSU	SCURFIER
CEEORRSU	RECOURES		FETCHING	CEFIRSTU	FRUTICES
	RECOURSE	CEFGIKLN	FLECKING	CEFIRTUV	FRUCTIVE
	RESOURCE	CEFGILNT	CLEFTING	CEFKLLOS	ELFLOCKS
CEEORRSV	COVERERS	CEFGINNS	FENCINGS	CEFKLOOR	FORELOCK
	RECOVERS	CEFGLNUY	FULGENCY	CEFKLOST	FETLOCKS
CEEORRSW	RECOWERS	CEFHIIMS	MISCHIEF	CEFKLPSY	FLYSPECK
CEEORRUV	OVERCURE	CEFHILNR	FLINCHER	CEFKLRUW	WRECKFUL
CEEORRVY	RECOVERY	CEFHILNS	FLINCHES	CEFLLOSU	FLOSCULE
CEEORSTV	COVETERS	CEFHILRS	FILCHERS	CEFLNOSU	FLOUNCES
CEEORSTW	COWTREES	CEFHILRT	FLICHTER	CEFLNRUU	FURUNCLE
CEEORSTX	COEXERTS	CEFHILST	FLITCHES	CEFLNSTU	SCENTFUL
	CORTEXES	CEFHINOT	INFOTECH	CEFLOPTY	COPYLEFT
CEEORTTV	CORVETTE	CEFHINSU	FUCHSINE	CEFMORSY	COMFREYS
CEEORTUX	EXECUTOR	CEFHISTT	FITCHETS	CEFNOOTT	CONFETTO
CEEOSSST	CESTOSES	CEFHISTU	FUCHSITE	CEFNORSU	FROUNCES
CEEOSTTT	OCTETTES	CEFHISTW	FITCHEWS	CEFNORTU	CONFUTER
CEEPPRST	PERCEPTS	CEFHKOOR	FOREHOCK	CEFNOSSU	CONFUSES
	PRECEPTS	CEFHLSSY	FLYSCHES	CEFNOSTU	CONFUTES
CEEPPRSU	PREPUCES	CEFHLSTU	CHESTFUL	CEFOORST	SOFTCORE
CEEPRRSU	PRECURES		FUTCHELS	CEFOPRSU	PREFOCUS
	PRECURSE	CEFIIIST	CITIFIES	CEFORRST	CROFTERS
CEEPRSST	RESPECTS	CEFIILLM	MELLIFIC	CEFORSSU	FOCUSERS
	SCEPTERS	CEFIILNO	OLEFINIC	CEFORSTU	FRUCTOSE
	SCEPTRES	CEFIILRT	CLIFTIER	CEFOSSSU	FOCUSSES
	SPECTERS	CEFIILST	FELSITIC	CEGGHIRS	CHIGGERS
	SPECTRES	CEFIILTY	FELICITY	CEGGHRSU	CHUGGERS
CEEPRSSY	CYPRESES	CEFIIOPR	OPIFICER	CEGGILOO	GEOLOGIC
CEEPRSTX	EXCERPTS	CEFIIORS	ORIFICES	CEGGILOR	CLOGGIER
CEERRSST	RECTRESS	CEFIIPRT	PETRIFIC		COGGLIER
CEERRSSU	RESCUERS	CEFIIRRT	FERRITIC	CEGGILRS	SCRIGGLE
	SECURERS		TERRIFIC	CEGGINNO	CONGEING
CEERRSSW	SCREWERS	CEFIISTY	CITYFIES	CEGGINOO	GEOGONIC
CEERRSUV	RECURVES	CEFIKLOR	FIRELOCK	CEGGIORS	CROGGIES
CEERRTUZ	CREUTZER		FLOCKIER		GEORGICS
CEERSSST	CRESSETS	CEFIKLRS	FLICKERS		SCROGGIE
CEERSSTU	SECUREST	CEFIKLRY	FLICKERY	CEGGLNOY	GLYCOGEN
CEERSSTW	SETSCREW	CEFIKLST	FICKLEST	CEGGLORS	CLOGGERS
CEERSSUX	EXCURSES	CEFILLLO	FOLLICLE	CEGHHINT	HECHTING
	EXCUSERS	CEFILMRU	CRIMEFUL	CEGHIINY	HYGIENIC
CEERSTTU	CURETTES		MERCIFUL	CEGHIKLN	HECKLING
CEERTUXY	EXECUTRY	CEFILNOT	FLECTION	CEGHIKNT	KETCHING
CEESSSTU	CESTUSES	CEFILNST	INFLECTS	CEGHILNP	CHELPING
CEESTTUV	CUVETTES	CEFILNSU	FUNICLES	CEGHILNT	LETCHING
CEFFGHIN	CHEFFING	CEFILOUV	VOICEFUL	CEGHILNW	WELCHING
CEFFHIRU	CHUFFIER	CEFILRSU	FLUERICS	CEGHILST	GLITCHES
CEFFHSTU	CHUFFEST		LUCIFERS	CEGHIMNS	SCHEMING
CEFFIILR	CLIFFIER	CEFIMOST	COMFIEST	CEGHIMNS	WENCHING
CEFFIORS	OFFICERS	CEFINNOR	CONFINER	CEGHINOR	COHERING
CEFFIORU	COIFFEUR	CEFINNOS	CONFINES		OCHERING
	COIFFURE	CEFINORS	COINFERS	CEGHINPR	PERCHING
CEFFIRSU	SUFFICER		CONIFERS	CEGHINQU	CHEQUING
CEFFISSU	SUFFICES		FORENSIC	CEGHINRS	GRINCHES

CEGHINRT	RETCHING	CEGILNTU	CULTIGEN		SCROUNGE
CEGHINRU	EUCHRING	CEGILRSY	LYSERGIC	CEGNORSY	CRYOGENS
CEGHINST	CHESTING	CEGIMNOS	GENOMICS	CEGNORYY	CRYOGENY
	ETCHINGS	CEGIMNOY	MYOGENIC	CEGNOSST	CONGESTS
CEGHINVY	CHEVYING	CEGIMNSU	MUCIGENS	CEGNOTYY	CYTOGENY
CEGHIRSS	SCREIGHS	CEGIMNUY	GYNECIUM	CEGNRTUY	TURGENCY
CEGHIRTU	THEURGIC	CEGINNOR	ENCORING	CEGOORSS	SCROOGES
CEGHISTU	GUICHETS	CEGINNOZ	COZENING	CEGORRSU	SCOURGER
CEGHLNSU	GLUNCHES	CEGINNRS	SCERNING		SCROUGER
CEGHMRUY	CHEMURGY	CEGINNRT	CENTRING	CEGORSSU	SCOURGES
CEGHNORS	GROSCHEN	CEGINNST	SCENTING		SCROUGES
CEGHORSU	CHOREGUS	CEGINNSY	ENSIGNCY	CEHHIIRT	HITCHIER
	COUGHERS		SYNGENIC	CEHHINPY	HYPHENIC
	GROUCHES	CEGINOOP	GEOPONIC	CEHHIOOS	HOOCHIES
CEGHRSTU	GRUTCHES	CEGINOOR	OROGENIC	CEHHIRST	HITCHERS
	GUTCHERS	CEGINOOY	COOEYING	CEHHISTU	HUTCHIES
CEGIILMO	OLIGEMIC	CEGINOOZ	ZOOGENIC	CEHHNORU	HURCHEON
CEGIILNR	CLINGIER	CEGINOPR	COPERING	CEHHOOSS	COHOSHES
CEGIILNS	CEILINGS	CEGINOPY	PYOGENIC	CEHHOOST	HOOTCHES
	CIELINGS	CEGINORS	COGNISER	CEHHOPTY	HYPOTHEC
CEGIILNT	GENTILIC		COREIGNS	CEHHOSST	SHOCHETS
CEGIILOP	EPILOGIC		COSIGNER	CEHHOSSU	CHOUSHES
CEGIILOS	LOGICISE	CEGINORT	GERONTIC	CEHIIKNR	CHINKIER
CEGIILOZ	LOGICIZE	CEGINORV	COVERING	CEHIIKNS	CHINKIES
CEGIINNT	ENTICING	CEGINORW	COWERING	CEHIIKST	THICKIES
CEGIINNV	EVINCING	CEGINORZ	COGNIZER	CEHIILLR	CHILLIER
CEGIINOP	EPIGONIC	CEGINOSS	COGNISES	CEHIILLS	CHILLIES
CEGIINOS	ISOGENIC	CEGINOST	ESCOTING	CEHIILMO	HEMIOLIC
CEGIINPR	PIERCING	CEGINOSZ	COGNIZES	CEHIILMT	LITHEMIC
CEGIINPS	PIECINGS	CEGINOTV	COVETING	CEHIILNN	LICHENIN
CEGIINRT	RECITING	CEGINOXY	OXYGENIC	CEHIILNT	LECITHIN
CEGIINSS	GNEISSIC	CEGINRRS	CRINGERS	CEHIILOT	EOLITHIC
CEGIINSX	EXCISING	CEGINRRU	RECURING	CEHIILTY	HELICITY
CEGIINTV	EVICTING	CEGINRST	CRESTING	CEHIIMOP	HEMIOPIC
CEGIINTX	EXCITING	CEGINRSU	RECUSING	CEHIIMOS	ISOCHEIM
CEGIIOST	EGOISTIC		RESCUING		ISOCHIME
CEGIJLOU	LOGJUICE		SCUNGIER	CEHIIMPT	MEPHITIC
CEGIKKLN	KECKLING		SECURING	CEHIIMRT	HERMITIC
CEGIKLNR	CLERKING	CEGINRSW	SCREWING	CEHIIMST	ETHICISM
	RECKLING	CEGINRSY	SYNERGIC	CEHIINST	ICHNITES
CEGIKNNR	RINGNECK	CEGINRTU	ERUCTING		NITCHIES
CEGIKNNS	NECKINGS	CEGINSUX	EXCUSING	CEHIIPPR	CHIPPIER
	SNECKING	CEGIRSTU	SCUTIGER	CEHIIPPS	CHIPPIES
CEGIKNPS	PECKINGS	CEGKLNNO	LONGNECK	CEHIIPRR	CHIRPIER
	SPECKING	CEGKLNOS	GENLOCKS	CEHIIPRT	PITCHIER
CEGIKNRT	TRECKING	CEGKLORS	GROCKLES	CEHIIRST	CHRISTIE
CEGIKNRW	WRECKING	CEGLLOOU	COLLOGUE	CEHIIRSZ	SCHIZIER
CEGIKSTU	GUCKIEST	CEGLLORY	GLYCEROL	CEHIIRTT	CHITTIER
CEGILMMN	CLEMMING	CEGLLRYY	GLYCERYL		TITCHIER
CEGILMNO	COMINGLE	CEGLNOOS	COLOGNES		TRICHITE
CEGILMPS	GEMCLIPS	CEGLNOTY	COGENTLY	CEHIIRTW	WITCHIER
CEGILNOO	NEOLOGIC	CEGLOOOY	OECOLOGY	CEHIISTT	CHITTIES
CEGILNOS	ECLOSING	CEGLOOTY	CETOLOGY		ETHICIST
CEGILNPU	CUPELING	CEGLOSSU	GLUCOSES		ITCHIEST
CEGILNRS	CLINGERS	CEGLOSSY	GLYCOSES		THEISTIC
	CRINGLES	CEGMNNOO	COGNOMEN		TICHIEST
CEGILNRU	RECULING	CEGNNOOS	ONCOGENS	CEHIISVV	CHIVVIES
	ULCERING	CEGNNPUY	PUNGENCY	CEHIKLPT	KLEPHTIC
CEGILNRY	GLYCERIN	CEGNOOTY	GONOCYTE	CEHIKLRS	CLERKISH
CEGILNSU	LUCIGENS	CEGNORSS	CONGRESS	CEHIKLSU	SUCHLIKE
CEGILNSY	GLYCINES	CEGNORSU	CONGRUES	CEHIKMOS	HOMESICK

CEHIKNRU	CHUNKIER	**CEHIMNPT**	PITCHMEN		TORCHIER
CEHIKNST	CHETNIKS	**CEHIMNSU**	MUNCHIES	**CEHIORRV**	OVERRICH
	KITCHENS	**CEHIMNSY**	CHIMNEYS	**CEHIORSS**	CHORISES
	KNITCHES	**CEHIMOOT**	HOMEOTIC		ORCHESIS
	THICKENS	**CEHIMORR**	CHROMIER		ORCHISES
CEHIKNSW	CHEWINKS	**CEHIMORS**	CHROMISE	**CEHIORST**	ROTCHIES
CEHIKOOS	CHOOKIES		MORICHES		THEORICS
CEHIKOSS	HOICKSES	**CEHIMORT**	CHROMITE	**CEHIORSW**	CHOWRIES
CEHIKOST	CHOKIEST		HORMETIC	**CEHIORTT**	TROCHITE
	THICKOES		TRICHOME	**CEHIORTU**	COUTHIER
CEHIKRSS	KIRSCHES	**CEHIMORZ**	CHROMIZE		TOUCHIER
	SHICKERS	**CEHIMOSS**	ECHOISMS	**CEHIOSST**	ECHOISTS
	SKRIECHS		MISCHOSE		TOISECHS
CEHIKRST	CHIRKEST	**CEHIMOST**	MOCHIEST	**CEHIOSTV**	CHEVIOTS
CEHIKRSW	WHICKERS	**CEHIMOTW**	CHOWTIME	**CEHIPPRS**	CHIPPERS
CEHIKSST	CHEKISTS	**CEHIMRRS**	SMIRCHER	**CEHIPRRS**	CHIRPERS
	KITSCHES	**CEHIMRSS**	SMIRCHES	**CEHIPRSS**	SPHERICS
	SKITCHES	**CEHIMSST**	CHEMISTS	**CEHIPRST**	PITCHERS
CEHIKSTT	THICKEST	**CEHINNOS**	CHINONES		SPITCHER
	THICKETS	**CEHINNRT**	INTRENCH	**CEHIPSST**	CHIPSETS
	THICKSET	**CEHINOOS**	COHESION	**CEHIQSTU**	QUITCHES
CEHIKTTY	THICKETY	**CEHINOPR**	PROCHEIN	**CEHIRSST**	STRICHES
CEHILLPR	PRECHILL	**CEHINOPS**	CHOPINES	**CEHIRSTT**	CHITTERS
CEHILLRS	CHILLERS	**CEHINOPT**	PHONETIC		RESTITCH
	SCHILLER	**CEHINOPU**	EUPHONIC		RICHTEST
CEHILLST	CHILLEST	**CEHINORS**	CHORINES		STITCHER
CEHILMMS	SCHIMMEL	**CEHINORT**	NOTCHIER	**CEHIRSTW**	SWITCHER
CEHILMOU	HUMICOLE	**CEHINORU**	UNHEROIC	**CEHIRSTY**	HYSTERIC
CEHILMSY	CHIMLEYS	**CEHINOSY**	HYOSCINE	**CEHIRTTW**	TWITCHER
CEHILMTY	METHYLIC	**CEHINOTY**	ONYCHITE	**CEHIRTWY**	WITCHERY
CEHILNOP	PHENOLIC	**CEHINPRS**	PHRENICS	**CEHISSTT**	STITCHES
	PINOCHLE		PINCHERS	**CEHISSTU**	CUSHIEST
CEHILNOR	CHLORINE		PINSCHER	**CEHISSTW**	SWITCHES
CEHILNOS	CHOLINES	**CEHINPRU**	PUNCHIER	**CEHISSUW**	SUCHWISE
	HELICONS		UNCIPHER	**CEHISTTW**	TWITCHES
CEHILNPY	PHENYLIC	**CEHINPSU**	PENUCHIS	**CEHKKRSU**	CHUKKERS
CEHILNSS	CHINLESS	**CEHINQSU**	QUINCHES	**CEHKLLOS**	SKELLOCH
CEHILNST	LINCHETS	**CEHINRSS**	RICHNESS	**CEHKLMOS**	HEMLOCKS
	TINCHELS	**CEHINRST**	CHRISTEN	**CEHKLOOS**	KLOOCHES
CEHILOOS	SCHOOLIE		CITHERNS	**CEHKLORS**	SHERLOCK
CEHILOPT	CHIPOTLE		CITHRENS	**CEHKLOSU**	SUCKHOLE
	HELICOPT		SNITCHER	**CEHKNOSU**	SUNCHOKE
CEHILORS	CEORLISH	**CEHINRSW**	WINCHERS		UNCHOKES
CEHILORT	CHLORITE	**CEHINRTU**	RUTHENIC	**CEHKNPUY**	KEYPUNCH
	CLOTHIER	**CEHINSST**	CHINTSES	**CEHKORSS**	SHOCKERS
CEHILORY	HEROICLY		SNITCHES	**CEHKPSTU**	KETCHUPS
CEHILPRS	PILCHERS	**CEHINSTW**	WITCHENS	**CEHKRSSU**	SHUCKERS
CEHILPTY	PHYLETIC	**CEHINSTZ**	CHINTZES	**CEHKRSTU**	HUCKSTER
CEHILRSV	CHERVILS	**CEHIOORS**	CHOOSIER	**CEHLLMOS**	MOCHELLS
CEHILSTT	LICHTEST		ISOCHORE	**CEHLLMSU**	MUCHELLS
CEHILSTW	SWITCHEL	**CEHIOPPR**	CHOPPIER		SCHELLUM
CEHILSTY	CHESTILY	**CEHIOPRS**	SOPHERIC	**CEHLLORS**	CHOLLERS
	LECYTHIS	**CEHIOPRU**	EUPHORIC	**CEHLLOSY**	YELLOCHS
CEHILTTY	TETCHILY		POUCHIER	**CEHLLOUY**	LOUCHELY
CEHIMMOS	CHOMMIES	**CEHIOPSS**	HOSPICES	**CEHLLPSU**	CHELLUPS
CEHIMMRU	CHUMMIER	**CEHIOPST**	POSTICHE	**CEHLMNOU**	HOMUNCLE
CEHIMMSS	CHEMISMS		POTICHES	**CEHLMORS**	CHROMELS
CEHIMMSU	CHUMMIES	**CEHIOPSU**	COPIHUES	**CEHLMSUY**	CHUMLEYS
CEHIMNNW	WINCHMEN	**CEHIOPTU**	EUPHOTIC	**CEHLNNOU**	LUNCHEON
CEHIMNOP	PHONEMIC	**CEHIORRS**	CHORRIES	**CEHLNNSU**	CHUNNELS
CEHIMNOR	CHOIRMEN	**CEHIORRT**	RHETORIC	**CEHLNOST**	CHOLENTS

	NOTCHELS	**CEHOORSS**	CHOOSERS	**CEIILLSS**	SILICLES
CEHLNOTU	UNCLOTHE		SOROCHES	**CEIILLSU**	SILICULE
CEHLNPRU	PRELUNCH	**CEHOORST**	CHEROOTS	**CEIILMNS**	LEMNISCI
CEHLNRSU	LUNCHERS	**CEHOORSU**	OCHEROUS	**CEIILMNT**	LIMNETIC
CEHLNRSY	LYNCHERS		OCHREOUS	**CEIILMNY**	MYELINIC
CEHLNSTY	LYNCHETS	**CEHOOSSS**	SCOOSHES	**CEIILMOT**	CIMOLITE
CEHLOORS	RESCHOOL	**CEHOOSUW**	COWHOUSE	**CEIILNNR**	INCLINER
CEHLOOSS	SCHOOLES	**CEHOPPRS**	CHOPPERS	**CEIILNNS**	INCLINES
CEHLORRT	CHORTLER	**CEHOPPRY**	PROPHECY	**CEIILNOP**	PICOLINE
CEHLORST	CHORTLES	**CEHOPRST**	POTCHERS	**CEIILNOS**	ISOCLINE
CEHLORSU	SLOUCHER	**CEHOPRSY**	CORYPHES		SILICONE
CEHLORTY	HECTORLY	**CEHORRST**	TORCHERS	**CEIILNPS**	PENICILS
CEHLOSSU	SLOUCHES	**CEHORSSU**	CHORUSES	**CEIILNQU**	CLINIQUE
CEHLOSTU	LOUCHEST		CHOUSERS	**CEIILNSS**	ENCLISIS
	SELCOUTH	**CEHORSSZ**	SCHERZOS	**CEIILOPP**	EPIPLOIC
CEHLPPSS	SCHLEPPS	**CEHORSTU**	SCOUTHER		EPIPOLIC
CEHLPPSY	SCHLEPPY		TOUCHERS	**CEIILOPS**	POLICIES
CEHLQSUY	SQUELCHY		TROUCHES	**CEIILORT**	ELICITOR
CEHLRRSU	LURCHERS	**CEHORSTW**	SCOWTHER	**CEIILOTZ**	ZEOLITIC
CEHLSSTU	SLUTCHES	**CEHORSUV**	VOUCHERS	**CEIILPPS**	CLIPPIES
CEHLSTUY	LECYTHUS	**CEHOSSSU**	HOCUSSES	**CEIILPRT**	PERLITIC
CEHMNRSU	MUNCHERS	**CEHOSTTU**	COUTHEST	**CEIILPRU**	PIRLICUE
CEHMNRTU	TRUCHMEN	**CEHOTTUZ**	ZUCHETTO	**CEIILPSS**	ECLIPSIS
CEHMNSSU	MUCHNESS	**CEHPRSTU**	PUTCHERS	**CEIILPTX**	EXPLICIT
CEHMOORS	MOOCHERS	**CEHPSSTU**	PUTSCHES	**CEIILPTY**	PYELITIC
	SMOOCHER	**CEHRRSSU**	CRUSHERS	**CEIILQRU**	CLIQUIER
CEHMOOSS	SCHMOOSE	**CEHRSSSU**	SCHUSSER	**CEIILRSU**	SLUICIER
	SMOOCHES	**CEHRSSTY**	SCYTHERS	**CEIILRSY**	LYRICISE
CEHMOOSZ	SCHMOOZE	**CEHRSTTY**	STRETCHY	**CEIILRTV**	VERTICIL
CEHMOPRS	CHOMPERS	**CEHSSSSU**	SCHUSSES	**CEIILRYZ**	LYRICIZE
CEHMORSU	MOUCHERS	**CEIIILSV**	CIVILISE	**CEIILSSS**	SCISSILE
CEHMORUV	OVERMUCH	**CEIIILVZ**	CIVILIZE	**CEIIMNOT**	EMICTION
CEHMOSSU	SMOUCHES	**CEIIIMNT**	CIMINITE	**CEIIMNRS**	CREMINIS
CEHMRSTU	CHETRUMS	**CEIIINSS**	SINICISE	**CEIIMNRU**	URINEMIC
CEHMSSTU	SMUTCHES	**CEIIINSV**	INCISIVE	**CEIIMNST**	MINCIEST
CEHNNNOU	NUNCHEON	**CEIIINSZ**	SINICIZE	**CEIIMOPT**	EPITOMIC
CEHNNOPU	PUNCHEON	**CEIIJSTU**	JESUITIC	**CEIIMORS**	ISOMERIC
CEHNNOSU	NONESUCH		JUICIEST	**CEIIMOST**	COMITIES
	UNCHOSEN	**CEIIKKST**	KICKIEST		SEMIOTIC
CEHNNRSU	CHUNNERS	**CEIIKLMR**	LIMERICK	**CEIIMPRR**	CRIMPIER
CEHNOOPS	HENCOOPS	**CEIIKLRS**	SICKLIER	**CEIIMPRS**	EMPIRICS
CEHNOORS	COEHORNS	**CEIIKLRT**	TICKLIER		MISPRICE
	SCHOONER	**CEIIKLSS**	SICKLIES	**CEIIMPSS**	EPICISMS
CEHNOOST	THEOCONS	**CEIIKMMR**	MIMICKER	**CEIIMPTU**	PUMICITE
CEHNOPTU	PUTCHEON	**CEIIKMST**	KISMETIC	**CEIIMRRT**	TRIMERIC
CEHNORST	CHORTENS	**CEIIKNRZ**	ZINCKIER	**CEIIMRST**	MERISTIC
	NOTCHERS	**CEIIKNSS**	ICKINESS		SCIMITER
CEHNORSV	CHEVRONS		KINESICS		TRISEMIC
CEHNORTU	CHOUNTER	**CEIIKNST**	KINETICS	**CEIIMRTT**	TERMITIC
CEHNORVY	CHEVRONY	**CEIIKPRR**	PRICKIER	**CEIIMSST**	MISCITES
CEHNOSSZ	SCHNOZES	**CEIIKPST**	PICKIEST	**CEIINNOP**	NEPIONIC
CEHNPPRU	PREPUNCH	**CEIIKQSU**	QUICKIES	**CEIINNOR**	IRENICON
CEHNPRSU	PUNCHERS	**CEIIKRRT**	TRICKIER	**CEIINNOS**	CONIINES
CEHNPSST	PSCHENTS	**CEIIKRST**	STICKIER		OSCININE
CEHNRRSU	CHURNERS	**CEIIKSST**	EKISTICS	**CEIINNOT**	COTININE
CEHNRSTU	CHUNTERS		STICKIES		NICOTINE
CEHNSSSU	SUCHNESS	**CEIIKTTT**	TEKTITIC	**CEIINNRS**	CINERINS
CEHNSSTU	CHESNUTS	**CEIILLMT**	MELLITIC	**CEIINNRT**	INTRINCE
CEHNSTTU	CHESTNUT	**CEIILLNO**	LINOLEIC	**CEIINNST**	INSCIENT
CEHNSTUY	CHUTNEYS	**CEIILLOP**	POLLICIE	**CEIINOPR**	PECORINI
CEHOOORZ	ZOOCHORE	**CEIILLPT**	ELLIPTIC	**CEIINOPS**	EPINOSIC

CEIINOPT	EPITONIC	CEIKLNRS	CLINKERS	CEILLMOY	COMELILY
CEIINORS	RECISION		CRINKLES	CEILLNOS	LIONCELS
	SORICINE	CEIKLNRU	CLUNKIER	CEILLNOU	NUCLEOLI
CEIINORT	RETINOIC	CEIKLNSS	SLICKENS	CEILLOPS	POLLICES
CEIINOSS	ICONISES	CEIKLOSV	LOVESICK	CEILLOQU	COQUILLE
CEIINOSV	INVOICES	CEIKLOTU	LEUKOTIC	CEILLORS	COLLIERS
CEIINOSX	EXCISION	CEIKLPRS	PICKLERS		ORSELLIC
CEIINOSZ	ICONIZES		PRICKLES	CEILLORY	COLLIERY
CEIINOTV	EVICTION	CEIKLPRU	PLUCKIER	CEILLOTU	COUTILLE
CEIINPPR	PRINCIPE	CEIKLRSS	SLICKERS	CEILLRTU	TELLURIC
CEIINPSS	PISCINES	CEIKLRST	STICKLER	CEILLSST	CELLISTS
CEIINRSS	SERICINS		STRICKLE	CEILLSSU	CULLISES
CEIINRST	CITRINES		TICKLERS	CEILMMUY	MYCELIUM
	CRINITES		TRICKLES	CEILMNOP	COMPLINE
	INCITERS	CEIKLRSY	SICKERLY	CEILMNOT	MONTICLE
CEIINRSU	INCISURE	CEIKLRTT	TRICKLET	CEILMOOP	PICOMOLE
	SCIURINE	CEIKLSST	SLICKEST	CEILMOPR	COMPILER
CEIINRTU	NEURITIC		STICKLES		COMPLIER
CEIINSSU	CUISINES	CEIKLSSW	WICKLESS	CEILMOPS	COMPILES
CEIINSTU	CUTINISE	CEIKLSTU	LUCKIEST		COMPLIES
CEIINSTY	CYTISINE	CEIKMNOR	MONICKER		POLEMICS
	SYENITIC	CEIKMNST	STICKMEN	CEILMOSS	SOLECISM
CEIINSTZ	CITIZENS	CEIKMOPT	IMPOCKET	CEILMOSU	COLISEUM
	ZINCIEST	CEIKMORS	OCKERISM	CEILMPRS	CRIMPLES
	ZINCITES	CEIKMRSS	SMICKERS	CEILMPRU	CLUMPIER
CEIINTUZ	CUTINIZE	CEIKMRSU	MUSICKER	CEILMPUU	PECULIUM
CEIIOPRS	IRISCOPE	CEIKMSST	SMICKETS	CEILMRSU	CLUMSIER
CEIIOPRT	PERIOTIC	CEIKMSTU	MUCKIEST		MUSCLIER
CEIIOPSW	WICOPIES	CEIKNNOT	NEKTONIC	CEILMTUU	LUTECIUM
CEIIOPTT	PICOTITE	CEIKNNSU	INSUCKEN	CEILNNOT	CONTLINE
CEIIOSTT	OSTEITIC	CEIKNOST	CONKIEST	CEILNNSU	NUCLEINS
CEIIOSTV	SOVIETIC		KENOTICS	CEILNNSY	SYNCLINE
CEIIPRRS	CRISPIER	CEIKNOTY	CYTOKINE	CEILNOOS	COLONIES
CEIIPRSS	CRISPIES	CEIKNQSU	QUICKENS		COLONISE
CEIIPRST	PICRITES	CEIKNRSS	SNICKERS		ECLOSION
	PRICIEST	CEIKNRST	STRICKEN	CEILNOOZ	COLONIZE
CEIIPSST	EPICISTS	CEIKNRSU	UNSICKER	CEILNOPR	PERCOLIN
	SPICIEST	CEIKNRSY	SNICKERY		REPLICON
CEIIQRTU	CRITIQUE	CEIKNSSS	SICKNESS	CEILNOPS	PINOCLES
CEIIRSST	ERISTICS	CEIKNSST	SNICKETS	CEILNOPT	LEPTONIC
CEIIRSSU	CRUISIES	CEIKOPST	POCKIEST	CEILNOPY	POLYENIC
CEIIRSTT	RECTITIS	CEIKORRS	ROCKIERS	CEILNORS	INCLOSER
CEIIRSTV	VERISTIC	CEIKORST	CORKIEST		LICENSOR
CEIIRSUZ	CRUIZIES		ROCKIEST	CEILNOSS	CONSEILS
CEIISSST	CISSIEST		STOCKIER		INCLOSES
CEIISTVV	VIVISECT	CEIKORSV	OVERSICK	CEILNOST	LECTIONS
CEIJMORT	MICROJET	CEIKOSSY	YOICKSES		TELSONIC
CEIJNORT	INJECTOR	CEIKOSTT	TOCKIEST	CEILNOSU	LEUCOSIN
CEIJNORU	JOUNCIER	CEIKPRRS	PRICKERS	CEILNOSX	LEXICONS
CEIJNOUV	CUNJEVOI	CEIKPRST	PRICKETS	CEILNPRY	PRINCELY
CEIJRSTU	JUSTICER	CEIKPSST	SKEPTICS	CEILNRTU	LINCTURE
CEIJSSTU	JUSTICES		SPICKEST	CEILNRUV	CULVERIN
CEIKKLOR	CORKLIKE	CEIKQSTU	QUICKEST	CEILNSST	LENTISCS
	ROCKLIKE		QUICKSET		STENCILS
CEIKKNRS	KNICKERS	CEIKRRST	TRICKERS	CEILNSTU	CUTLINES
CEIKKRRS	SKERRICK	CEIKRRTY	TRICKERY		LINECUTS
CEIKLLTU	CULTLIKE	CEIKRSST	STICKERS		TUNICLES
CEIKLMOR	CORMLIKE	CEIKRSTU	TRUCKIES	CEILNSUU	UNSLUICE
CEIKLMST	MICKLEST	CEIKRTTY	RICKETTY	CEILOORS	COLORISE
CEIKLMSU	SCUMLIKE	CEIKSSTU	SUCKIEST	CEILOORZ	COLORIZE
CEIKLNPS	SPICKNEL	CEIKSTUY	YUCKIEST	CEILOPPS	POPSICLE

CEILOPRS	POLICERS
CEILOPRT	LEPROTIC
	PETROLIC
CEILOPRV	PROCLIVE
CEILOPST	TOECLIPS
CEILOPTU	EPULOTIC
	POULTICE
CEILOPTY	EPICOTYL
	LIPOCYTE
CEILORST	CLOISTER
	COISTREL
	COSTLIER
	CREOLIST
CEILORTT	CLOTTIER
CEILORTY	CRYOLITE
CEILOSSS	OSSICLES
CEILOSST	SOLECIST
	SOLSTICE
CEILOSSU	COULISSE
CEILOSTT	COLETITS
CEILOTVY	VELOCITY
CEILPPRR	CRIPPLER
CEILPPRS	CLIPPERS
	CRIPPLES
CEILPRSS	SPLICERS
CEILPRSU	SURPLICE
CEILPRUU	PURLICUE
CEILPSSU	SPICULES
CEILPSTU	PICULETS
CEILRRSU	SCURRILE
CEILRSTT	CLITTERS
CEILRSTU	CURLIEST
	UTRICLES
CEILSSSS	SCISSELS
CEILSTTU	CUITTLES
	CULTIEST
CEIMMNNO	MNEMONIC
CEIMMNOU	ENCOMIUM
	MECONIUM
CEIMMORT	RECOMMIT
CEIMMORU	COREMIUM
CEIMMOSX	COMMIXES
CEIMMRRS	CRIMMERS
CEIMMRRU	CRUMMIER
CEIMMRSU	CRUMMIES
	SCRUMMIE
	SCUMMIER
CEIMMRSY	MERYCISM
CEIMNNOO	ENCOMION
CEIMNNOR	NONCRIME
CEIMNNOS	MECONINS
CEIMNNOY	NEOMYCIN
CEIMNOOT	EMOTICON
CEIMNOPT	PENTOMIC
CEIMNOPY	EPONYMIC
CEIMNORS	CREMOSIN
	INCOMERS
	SERMONIC
CEIMNORT	INTERCOM
CEIMNOSS	COSMINES
CEIMNOST	CENTIMOS
CEIMNRST	CENTRISM
CEIMNRSU	NUMERICS
CEIMNSSU	MENISCUS
CEIMOOST	COOMIEST
CEIMOOSZ	MESOZOIC
CEIMOOUZ	ZOOECIUM
CEIMOPRS	COMPRISE
CEIMOPRX	PROXEMIC
CEIMOPRZ	COMPRIZE
CEIMOQSU	COMIQUES
CEIMORRS	MORRICES
CEIMORRT	MORTICER
CEIMORST	MORTICES
CEIMORSX	EXORCISM
CEIMORSY	ISOCRYME
CEIMORTY	EMICTORY
CEIMOSSS	COSMESIS
CEIMOSTV	VICOMTES
CEIMPRRS	CRIMPERS
	SCRIMPER
CEIMPRRU	CRUMPIER
CEIMPRSU	PUMICERS
CEIMRRSU	SCRIMURE
CEIMRRTU	TURMERIC
CEIMRSST	CRETISMS
CEIMSSTY	SYSTEMIC
CEINNNOT	INNOCENT
CEINNNOU	INCONNUE
CEINNORS	INCENSOR
CEINNORU	NEURONIC
CEINNORV	CONNIVER
CEINNORW	COWINNER
CEINNOSV	CONNIVES
CEINNOTU	CONTINUE
CEINNOTV	COINVENT
CEINNSTY	SYNTENIC
CEINOOPR	PECORINO
CEINOOSS	CONIOSES
CEINOOST	COONTIES
CEINOOTZ	ENTOZOIC
	ENZOOTIC
CEINOPPR	CORNPIPE
CEINOPPT	PEPTONIC
CEINOPRS	CONSPIRE
	INCORPSE
CEINOPRT	ENTROPIC
	INCEPTOR
	PRETONIC
CEINOPRV	PROVINCE
CEINOPST	PONCIEST
CEINOPTT	ENTOPTIC
CEINOPTU	UNPOETIC
CEINORRS	RESORCIN
CEINORRT	TRICORNE
CEINORSS	NECROSIS
	SERICONS
CEINORST	COINTERS
	CORNIEST
	NOTICERS
	RECTIONS
CEINORSU	COINSURE
	INSOURCE
	NOURICES
	ROUNCIES
CEINORTT	CONTRITE
	CORNETTI
CEINORTU	NEUROTIC
	UNEROTIC
CEINORTV	CONTRIVE
CEINOSSS	CESSIONS
	COSINESS
CEINOSST	SECTIONS
CEINOSSX	COXINESS
CEINOSSZ	COZINESS
CEINOSTT	CENTOIST
	STENOTIC
	TONETICS
CEINOSTU	COUNTIES
CEINOSTX	EXCITONS
CEINOSTY	CYTOSINE
CEINOSUV	UNVOICES
CEINOSVV	CONVIVES
CEINOTUX	UNEXOTIC
CEINPRSS	CRISPENS
	PRINCESS
CEINPRST	SPECTRIN
CEINPSST	INSPECTS
CEINPSTY	PYCNITES
CEINRRSU	REINCURS
CEINRSST	CISTERNS
CEINRSTT	CENTRIST
	CITTERNS
CEINRSTU	CURNIEST
CEINRSUV	INCURVES
CEINRSVV	CRIVVENS
CEINRTTU	INTERCUT
	TINCTURE
CEINSSTY	CYSTEINS
	CYSTINES
CEINSTTX	EXTINCTS
CEIOOPRS	OPORICES
CEIOOTUV	OUTVOICE
CEIOOTXX	EXOTOXIC
CEIOPPRS	CROPPIES
CEIOPPSY	EPISCOPY
CEIOPRRU	CROUPIER
CEIOPRSS	PERSICOS
CEIOPRST	PERSICOT
CEIOPRSU	PRECIOUS
CEIOPRTU	EUTROPIC
	OUTPRICE
CEIOPSST	COPSIEST
CEIOPSSU	SPECIOUS
CEIORRSS	CROSIERS
CEIORRSU	COURIERS
CEIORRSZ	CROZIERS
CEIORRTU	COURTIER
CEIORRTW	COWRITER
CEIORRUZ	CRUZEIRO
CEIORSST	CROSSTIE
CEIORSSU	SCOURIES
CEIORSSV	CORSIVES

CEIORSSW	SCOWRIES	**CEJNORSU**	CONJURES	**CELLNSUU**	NUCELLUS
CEIORSSX	SIXSCORE	**CEJNRTUU**	JUNCTURE	**CELLNTUU**	LUCULENT
CEIORSTT	COTTIERS	**CEJNSSUU**	JUNCUSES	**CELLNTUY**	LUCENTLY
CEIORSTU	CITREOUS	**CEJOPRST**	PROJECTS	**CELLOOQU**	COLLOQUE
	OUTCRIES	**CEKKLNRU**	KNUCKLER	**CELLORRS**	SCROLLER
CEIORSTV	EVICTORS	**CEKKLNSU**	KNUCKLES	**CELLORSS**	ESCROLLS
	VORTICES	**CEKKNORS**	KNOCKERS	**CELLOSSY**	CLOYLESS
CEIORSTW	COWRITES	**CEKKLNOR**	ROLLNECK	**CELLRRSU**	CRULLERS
CEIORSTX	EXCITORS	**CEKLLOOV**	LOVELOCK	**CELLRSSU**	SCULLERS
	EXORCIST	**CEKLLOPS**	PELLOCKS	**CELLRSUY**	SCULLERY
CEIORSVY	VICEROYS	**CEKLLOSS**	LOCKLESS	**CELMMSSU**	MESCLUMS
CEIORTTU	TOREUTIC	**CEKLLSSU**	LUCKLESS	**CELMNOOR**	COLORMEN
CEIOSSSV	VISCOSES	**CEKLMNOS**	LOCKSMEN	**CELMNOOS**	MONOCLES
CEIOSSTT	COTTISES	**CEKLNOSS**	SLOCKENS	**CELMNOTY**	CLOYMENT
	SCOTTIES	**CEKLNOST**	STENLOCK	**CELMNOUY**	UNCOMELY
CEIOSSTU	COITUSES	**CEKLNRSU**	CLUNKERS	**CELMNSSU**	MESCLUNS
CEIOSSTX	COEXISTS		CRUNKLES	**CELMNTUU**	MUCULENT
CEIPPSTU	CUPPIEST	**CEKLOORV**	OVERLOCK	**CELMOOOT**	LOCOMOTE
CEIPQSTU	PICQUETS	**CEKLOOSS**	COOKLESS	**CELMOOPY**	COEMPLOY
CEIPRRSS	CRISPERS	**CEKLOPST**	LOCKSTEP	**CELMOOSY**	CLOYSOME
CEIPRRST	RESCRIPT	**CEKLORSS**	ROCKLESS	**CELMOPSU**	COMPULSE
	SCRIPTER	**CEKLOSSS**	SOCKLESS	**CELMOPSY**	SYMPLOCE
CEIPRRSU	SPRUCIER	**CEKLOSST**	LOCKSETS	**CELMOSUU**	CUMULOSE
CEIPRSST	CRISPEST	**CEKLOSTY**	TOCKLEYS	**CELMOSYY**	CYMOSELY
CEIPRSTU	CREPITUS	**CEKLPRSU**	PLUCKERS	**CELMPRSU**	CLUMPERS
	CUPRITES	**CEKLRRTU**	TRUCKLER		CRUMPLES
	PICTURES	**CEKLRSSU**	SCULKERS		SCRUMPLE
	PIECRUST		SUCKLERS	**CELMPRTU**	PLECTRUM
CEIPSSST	CESSPITS	**CEKLRSTU**	TRUCKLES	**CELMPSUU**	SPECULUM
CEIPSSTU	CUSPIEST	**CEKLSSSU**	SUCKLESS	**CELMSSSU**	SCUMLESS
CEIRRRSU	CURRIERS	**CEKMNOST**	STOCKMEN	**CELMSSUU**	SECULUMS
	SCURRIER	**CEKMNOSY**	MOCKNEYS	**CELMSTUU**	CUMULETS
CEIRRRUY	CURRIERY	**CEKMNRTU**	TRUCKMEN	**CELNNOSU**	NUCLEONS
CEIRRSSU	CRUISERS	**CEKNNSSU**	UNSNECKS	**CELNNOTY**	NOCENTLY
	SCURRIES	**CEKNOORV**	CONVOKER	**CELNNOUV**	UNCLOVEN
	SUCRIERS	**CEKNOOSV**	CONVOKES	**CELNOORS**	CONSOLER
CEIRRSTT	CRITTERS	**CEKNOPST**	PENSTOCK		CORONELS
	RESTRICT	**CEKNORST**	CRONKEST	**CELNOORT**	CONTROLE
	STRICTER	**CEKNORTU**	COKERNUT	**CELNOORU**	ENCOLOUR
CEIRRSTU	CRUSTIER	**CEKNOSTU**	UNSOCKET	**CELNOOSS**	CONSOLES
	RECRUITS	**CEKNPRUU**	UNPUCKER		COOLNESS
CEIRRSUV	SCURVIER	**CEKNRSTU**	STRUCKEN	**CELNOOVV**	CONVOLVE
CEIRSSSU	CUISSERS	**CEKNRSWY**	WRYNECKS	**CELNOPRT**	PLECTRON
	SCISSURE	**CEKOOORV**	OVERCOOK	**CELNOPUU**	UNCOUPLE
CEIRSSTT	TRISECTS	**CEKOOPRS**	PRECOOKS	**CELNOPUY**	OPULENCY
CEIRSSTU	CITRUSES	**CEKOOPSW**	COWPOKES	**CELNORTW**	CROWNLET
	CRUSTIES	**CEKOORRS**	ROCKROSE	**CELNORWY**	CLOWNERY
	CURTSIES	**CEKOORRW**	COWORKER	**CELNOSSU**	CLONUSES
	RICTUSES	**CEKOORRY**	CROOKERY		COUNSELS
CEIRSSTV	VICTRESS	**CEKOORST**	CROOKEST		UNCLOSES
CEIRSSUV	CURSIVES	**CEKOPRST**	SPROCKET	**CELNOSTU**	NOCTULES
	SCURVIES	**CEKORRTY**	ROCKETRY	**CELNOSUV**	CONVULSE
CEIRSTTU	TUTRICES	**CEKORSST**	RESTOCKS	**CELNOSVY**	SOLVENCY
CEIRSTUV	CURVIEST		STOCKERS	**CELNOVXY**	CONVEXLY
CEIRSTUY	SECURITY	**CEKORSTW**	TWOCKERS	**CELNPTUU**	PUNCTULE
CEIRSUZZ	SCUZZIER	**CEKRRSTU**	RESTRUCK	**CELNRSTU**	LECTURNS
CEISSSSU	CISSUSES		TRUCKERS	**CELOOORV**	OVERCOOL
CEISSSTU	CISTUSES	**CEKRSSUU**	RUCKUSES	**CELOOPRS**	PRECOOLS
CEISTTTU	CUTTIEST	**CELLMOSU**	COLUMELS	**CELOOPSS**	CESSPOOL
CEJLOOSY	JOCOSELY	**CELLNOOS**	COLONELS	**CELOORRS**	COLORERS
CEJNORRU	CONJURER	**CELLNORS**	ENSCROLL		RECOLORS

CELOORRU	COLOURER	CEMMORTU	COMMUTER	CENORRSW	CROWNERS
CELOORSS	COLESSOR	CEMMOSTU	COMMUTES		RECROWNS
	CREOSOLS	CEMMRSSU	SCUMMERS	CENORRTU	TROUNCER
CELOORTW	COLEWORT	CEMNNOST	CONTEMNS	CENORSST	CONSTERS
CELOORVY	OVERCLOY	CEMNNOPT	CONTEMPO		CRESTONS
CELOOSTU	CLOSEOUT	CEMNOORR	CROMORNE	CENORSSU	CORNUSES
CELOPRSS	CROPLESS	CEMNOOTY	MONOCYTE	CENORSTT	CORNETTS
CELOPRSU	COUPLERS	CEMNOPRS	CORPSMEN	CENORSTU	CONSTRUE
CELOPSSU	CLOSEUPS	CEMNOPTT	CONTEMPT		CORNUTES
	OPUSCLES	CEMNORSU	CONSUMER		COUNTERS
	UPCLOSES		MUCRONES		RECOUNTS
CELOPSTU	COUPLETS	CEMNOSSU	CONSUMES		TROUNCES
	OCTUPLES		MUSCONES	CENORSTV	CONVERTS
CELOPSUU	OPUSCULE	CEMNRSTU	CENTRUMS	CENORSTW	CROWNETS
CELOPTTU	OCTUPLET	CEMOOPRS	COMPOSER	CENORSUU	CERNUOUS
CELOPTUX	OCTUPLEX	CEMOOPSS	COMPOSES		COENURUS
CELORRSU	CORULERS	CEMOOPST	COMPOTES	CENORSUV	UNCOVERS
CELORSST	CORSLETS	CEMOOPSY	MYOSCOPE	CENORSUY	CYNOSURE
	COSTRELS	CEMOORSY	SYCOMORE	CENOSSTT	CONTESTS
	CROSSLET	CEMOOSSS	COSMOSES	CENOSSTU	CONTUSES
CELORSSU	CLOSURES	CEMOOSTU	OUTCOMES		COUNTESS
	SCLEROUS	CEMOOSTY	CYTOSOME	CENOSTTX	CONTEXTS
CELORSSW	SCOWLERS	CEMOPRSS	COMPRESS	CENPRSTY	ENCRYPTS
	SCROWLES	CEMOPRST	COMPTERS	CENPRTUU	PUNCTURE
CELORSSY	SCROYLES	CEMOPRTU	COMPUTER	CENPSTUX	EXPUNCTS
CELORSTT	CLOTTERS	CEMOPSTU	COMPUTES	CENRRSTU	CURRENTS
	CROTTLES	CEMORSSU	CORMUSES	CENRSSTU	CURTNESS
CELORSTU	CLOTURES	CEMORSTU	COSTUMER		ENCRUSTS
	CLOUTERS		CUSTOMER	CENRSSUU	UNCURSES
	COULTERS	CEMOSSTU	COSTUMES	CENRSSUW	UNSCREWS
CELORSTY	COYSTREL	CEMOSTUY	COSTUMEY	CEOOOPST	OTOSCOPE
CELORSUU	ULCEROUS	CEMOTXYY	MYXOCYTE	CEOOPRRV	OVERCROP
	URCEOLUS	CEMPRSTU	CRUMPEST	CEOOPRSS	SCOOPERS
CELORSUY	CROUSELY		CRUMPETS	CEOOPRST	TOPSCORE
CELORTTU	COURTLET		SPECTRUM	CEOOPSWX	COWPOXES
CELORTVY	COVERTLY			CEOORRVW	OVERCROW
CELOSSST	COSTLESS	CENNOOPR	CORNPONE	CEOORSST	SCOOTERS
CELOSTTU	CULOTTES	CENNOORV	CONVENOR	CEOORSTU	ECOTOURS
CELPRRSU	SCRUPLER	CENNOOST	CONNOTES		OUTSCORE
CELPRSSU	SCRUPLES	CENNORTU	NOCTURNE	CEOOSTUV	COVETOUS
CELPRSTU	RESCULPT	CENNOSST	CONSENTS	CEOPPRRS	CROPPERS
CELPRSUY	SPRUCELY	CENNOSTT	CONTENTS	CEOPPRST	PROSPECT
CELRSSTU	CLUSTERS	CENNOSTV	CONVENTS	CEOPPRSU	SUPERCOP
	CUSTRELS	CENNRSSU	SCUNNERS	CEOPRRRU	PROCURER
CELRSSTY	CLYSTERS	CENOOOTZ	ECTOZOON	CEOPRRSS	SCORPERS
CELRSTTU	CLUTTERS	CENOOPSS	POCOSENS	CEOPRRST	PORRECTS
	SCUTTLER	CENOORRS	CORONERS	CEOPRRSU	CROUPERS
CELRSTUU	CULTURES		CROONERS		PROCURES
CELRSTUV	CULVERTS	CENOORST	CORONETS	CEOPRRST	PROSECTS
CELRSTUY	CLUSTERY	CENOORSU	CORNEOUS	CEOPRSSU	CORPUSES
CELRTTUY	CLUTTERY	CENOORSV	CONVERSO	CEOPRSTT	PROTECTS
CELSSTTU	SCUTTLES	CENOORTT	CORNETTO	CEOPRSTW	CROWSTEP
CELSSTUU	CULTUSES	CENOORVY	CONVEYOR		SCREWTOP
CEMMNOOR	COMMONER	CENOPRSU	POUNCERS	CEOPRSUU	COUPURES
CEMMNOOS	CONSOMME	CENOPRSY	NECROPSY		CUPREOUS
CEMMNOOY	COMMONEY	CENOPSSU	CONSPUES	CEOPRSUV	COVERUPS
CEMMNORU	COMMUNER	CENOPSSY	PYCNOSES	CEOPRSUW	SUPERCOW
CEMMNOST	COMMENTS		SYNCOPES	CEOQRSTU	CROQUETS
CEMMNOSU	COMMUNES	CENOPSTU	POUNCETS		ROCQUETS
CEMMOOST	COMMOTES	CENOQRSU	CONQUERS	CEOQRTUY	COQUETRY
CEMMOOSV	COMMOVES	CENOQSTU	CONQUEST	CEORRSSS	CROSSERS
		CENORRSS	SCORNERS		

	SCORSERS	**CFGIKNSU**	FUCKINGS	**CFNNOORT**	CONFRONT
CEORRSSU	COURSERS	**CFGINORT**	CROFTING	**CFNORSTU**	FUNCTORS
	CURSORES	**CFGINOSU**	FOCUSING	**CFOOORTW**	CROWFOOT
	SCOURERS	**CFHIINOO**	FINOCHIO	**CFRSTUUU**	USUFRUCT
CEORRSSW	SCOWRERS	**CFHIIORR**	HORRIFIC	**CGGGHINU**	CHUGGING
CEORRSTU	COURTERS	**CFHIKORS**	ROCKFISH	**CGGGILNO**	CLOGGING
CEORRSTY	CORSETRY	**CFHIKSSU**	SUCKFISH		COGGLING
CEORSSST	CROSSEST	**CFHILPTY**	FLYPITCH	**CGGGINOR**	CROGGING
CEORSSSU	SCOURSES	**CFHIMOSS**	SCOMFISH	**CGGGINOS**	COGGINGS
	SCOUSERS	**CFHIMSSU**	SCUMFISH		SCOGGING
	SUCROSES	**CFHINSSU**	FUCHSINS	**CGGGINSU**	SCUGGING
CEORSSTU	CRUSTOSE	**CFHLOPUU**	POUCHFUL	**CGGHILNU**	GULCHING
	SCOUTERS	**CFHORSTU**	FUTHORCS	**CGGHINOU**	COUGHING
CEORSSUV	CORVUSES	**CFIIIKNN**	FINICKIN		GOUCHING
CEORSTUU	COUTURES	**CFIIILSY**	SILICIFY	**CGGIILNN**	CLINGING
	OUTCURSE	**CFIIKKLP**	KICKFLIP	**CGGIINNO**	COIGNING
CEORSTUV	COUVERTS	**CFIIKNNY**	FINNICKY	**CGGIINNR**	CRINGING
	CUTOVERS	**CFIIKNYZ**	ZINCKIFY	**CGGIINRS**	GRICINGS
	OVERCUTS	**CFIILMNU**	FULMINIC	**CGGIKNOR**	GROCKING
CEORSTUY	COURTESY	**CFIILNST**	INFLICTS	**CGGILLOY**	CLOGGILY
CEORTUUV	OUTCURVE	**CFIILNUU**	FUNICULI	**CGGILRSY**	SCRIGGLY
CEOSSSTU	COSTUSES	**CFIILOPR**	PROLIFIC	**CGGINNSU**	SCUNGING
CEOSSTTU	COTTUSES	**CFIILPSU**	PULSIFIC	**CGGINOOS**	SCOOGING
CEPPRRSU	CRUPPERS	**CFIILSTU**	SULFITIC	**CGGINORS**	SCROGGIN
CEPPRSSU	SCUPPERS	**CFIIMNOS**	SOMNIFIC	**CGGINOSU**	SCOUGING
CEPPRTUU	UPPERCUT	**CFIIMOPR**	PICIFORM	**CGHHIILN**	HILCHING
CEPRSSTU	SPRUCEST	**CFIIMORT**	MORTIFIC	**CGHHIINT**	HITCHING
CEPRSSUW	SCREWUPS	**CFIINOPT**	PONTIFIC	**CGHHINNU**	HUNCHING
CEPRSSUY	CYPRUSES	**CFIINORT**	FRICTION	**CGHHINOT**	HOTCHING
CEPRSTUU	CUTPURSE	**CFIINOST**	FICTIONS	**CGHHINTU**	HUTCHING
CEPRSUUV	UPCURVES	**CFIKLORY**	FROLICKY	**CGHIIKNN**	CHINKING
CEPSSSTU	SUSPECTS	**CFIKLSTU**	STICKFUL	**CGHIIKNO**	HOICKING
CERSSSUU	RUSCUSES	**CFIKNNOS**	FINNOCKS	**CGHIIKNR**	CHIRKING
CERSSTTU	SCUTTERS	**CFIKOSSS**	FOSSICKS	**CGHIIKNT**	THICKING
CERSSTUY	CURTSEYS	**CFIKPSTU**	PUCKFIST	**CGHIILLN**	CHILLING
CERSSUUX	EXCURSUS	**CFIKSTUW**	FUCKWITS	**CGHIILNR**	CHIRLING
CFFFKOSU	FUCKOFFS	**CFILMOOR**	COLIFORM	**CGHIILNT**	CHITLING
CFFGHINU	CHUFFING	**CFILNOSU**	SULFONIC		LICHTING
CFFGIINO	COIFFING	**CFILOSUU**	SULFURIC	**CGHIIMNR**	CHIRMING
CFFGILNO	COFFLING	**CFIMNOOR**	CONIFORM	**CGHIIMNS**	MICHINGS
CFFGILNU	CUFFLING	**CFIMNORS**	CONFIRMS	**CGHIIMNT**	MITCHING
CFFGINOS	SCOFFING	**CFIMNORU**	CUNIFORM	**CGHIINNN**	CHINNING
CFFGINSU	SCUFFING		UNCIFORM	**CGHIINNP**	PINCHING
CFFHINOS	CHIFFONS	**CFIMOSSU**	MISFOCUS	**CGHIINNW**	WINCHING
CFFHINOY	CHIFFONY	**CFINNOTU**	FUNCTION	**CGHIINOR**	CHOIRING
CFFIKKOS	KICKOFFS	**CFIOPRUY**	COPURIFY	**CGHIINPP**	CHIPPING
CFFIKLNU	CUFFLINK	**CFKLLOSU**	LOCKFULS	**CGHIINPR**	CHIRPING
CFFIKOPS	PICKOFFS	**CFKLRTUU**	TRUCKFUL	**CGHIINPT**	PITCHING
CFFINNOU	UNCOFFIN	**CFKNORSU**	UNFROCKS	**CGHIINQU**	QUICHING
CFFIRTUY	FRUCTIFY	**CFKOSTTU**	FUTTOCKS	**CGHIINRR**	CHIRRING
CFFKKNOO	KNOCKOFF	**CFLLOORU**	COLORFUL	**CGHIINRT**	CHIRTING
CFFKOOOS	COOKOFFS	**CFLLOPRU**	CROPFULL		RICHTING
CFFMOSSU	OFFSCUMS	**CFLMRSUU**	FULCRUMS	**CGHIINST**	ITCHINGS
CFGHIILN	FILCHING	**CFLMRUUU**	FURCULUM		SICHTING
CFGHINOO	CHOOFING	**CFLNOORT**	CORNLOFT	**CGHIINTT**	CHITTING
CFGIIKLN	FICKLING	**CFLNORSU**	SCORNFUL	**CGHIINTW**	WITCHING
	FLICKING	**CFLOOPSU**	SCOOPFUL	**CGHIINVV**	CHIVVING
CFGIIKNR	FRICKING	**CFLOPRSU**	CROPFULS	**CGHIINVY**	CHIVYING
CFGIINOR	COFIRING	**CFLOPRSU**	COWFLOPS	**CGHIINZZ**	CHIZZING
CFGIKLNO	FLOCKING	**CFMNOORS**	CONFORMS	**CGHIKLNO**	HOCKLING
CFGIKNOR	FROCKING	**CFMOORST**	COMFORTS	**CGHIKLNU**	HUCKLING

CGHIKNNU	CHUNKING	CGIIKNPS	PICKINGS	CGIKNSSU	SUCKINGS
CGHIKNOO	CHOOKING	CGIIKNRS	SCRIKING	CGIKNSTU	GUNSTICK
CGHIKNOS	SHOCKING	CGIIKNRT	TRICKING	CGIKPSTU	PIGSTUCK
CGHIKNOT	KOTCHING	CGIIKNRW	WRICKING	CGILLNOS	COLLINGS
CGHIKNSU	SHUCKING	CGIIKNST	STICKING	CGILLNOY	COLLYING
CGHILMNU	MULCHING		TICKINGS	CGILLNSU	CULLINGS
CGHILNNU	LUNCHING	CGIIKNSW	WICKINGS		SCULLING
CGHILNNY	LYNCHING	CGIIKPST	PIGSTICK	CGILLNUY	CULLYING
CGHILNOT	CLOTHING	CGIILLOS	ILLOGICS	CGILMNOP	CLOMPING
CGHILNRU	LURCHING	CGIILMOS	LOGICISM	CGILMNPU	CLUMPING
CGHIMMNU	CHUMMING	CGIILNOP	POLICING	CGILMNSU	MUSCLING
CGHIMNNU	MUNCHING	CGIILNPP	CLIPPING	CGILMNSY	CYMLINGS
CGHIMNOO	MOOCHING	CGIILNPS	SPLICING	CGILMNTU	MULCTING
CGHIMNOP	CHOMPING	CGIILNQU	CLIQUING	CGILMNUU	CINGULUM
CGHIMNOR	CHROMING	CGIILNSS	SLICINGS		GLUCINUM
CGHIMNOU	MOUCHING	CGIILNSU	SLUICING	CGILMOOY	MYOLOGIC
CGHIMNPU	CHUMPING	CGIILORU	OLIGURIC	CGILNNNO	NONCLING
CGHIMNTU	MUTCHING	CGIILOST	LOGICIST	CGILNNOS	CLONINGS
CGHIMPSY	SPHYGMIC		LOGISTIC	CGILNNOW	CLOWNING
CGHINNOS	CHIGNONS	CGIILRTU	LITURGIC	CGILNOOR	COLORING
CGHINNOT	NOTCHING	CGIIMNNO	INCOMING		CROOLING
CGHINNPU	PUNCHING	CGIIMNPR	CRIMPING	CGILNOOS	COOLINGS
CGHINNRU	CHURNING	CGIIMNPU	PUMICING	CGILNOOY	COOINGLY
CGHINNSY	SYNCHING	CGIIMNSU	MISCUING	CGILNOPP	CLOPPING
CGHINOOP	POOCHING	CGIINNOS	COININGS	CGILNOPU	COUPLING
CGHINOOS	CHOOSING	CGIINNOT	NOTICING	CGILNORU	CLOURING
CGHINOPP	CHOPPING	CGIINNPR	PRINCING	CGILNOSS	CLOSINGS
CGHINOPT	POTCHING	CGIINNSU	INCUSING	CGILNOSW	COWLINGS
CGHINOPU	POUCHING	CGIINNSW	WINCINGS		SCOWLING
CGHINORT	TORCHING	CGIINNTT	TINCTING	CGILNOTT	CLOTTING
CGHINOSU	CHOUSING	CGIINOOS	ISOGONIC	CGILNOTU	CLOUTING
	HOCUSING	CGIINOPT	PICOTING	CGILNPSU	SCULPING
CGHINOSW	CHOWSING	CGIINORT	TRIGONIC	CGILNRSU	CURLINGS
CGHINOTU	TOUCHING	CGIINOST	COTISING	CGILNRYY	CRYINGLY
CGHINOUV	VOUCHING	CGIINOSV	VOICINGS	CGILNTTU	CUTTLING
CGHINPSY	PSYCHING	CGIINPRS	CRISPING	CGILOOOZ	ZOOLOGIC
CGHINPTU	PINCHGUT		PRICINGS	CGILOORU	UROLOGIC
CGHINRRU	CHURRING	CGIINRSU	CRUISING	CGILOPRY	COPYGIRL
CGHINRSU	CRUSHING	CGIINRSV	SCRIVING	CGILORSW	COWGIRLS
	RUCHINGS	CGIINSSS	CISSINGS	CGILPSTU	GILTCUPS
CGHINSTY	SCYTHING	CGIJNNOU	JOUNCING	CGILPSTY	GLYPTICS
CGHLNOSS	SCHLONGS	CGIKKNNO	KNOCKING	CGIMMNSU	SCUMMING
CGHNOOOS	SOOCHONG	CGIKLNNO	CLONKING	CGIMNNOO	GNOMONIC
CGHNOOSU	SOUCHONG	CGIKLNNU	CLUNKING		ONCOMING
CGHOORST	TORGOCHS	CGIKLNOR	ROCKLING	CGIMNOPT	COMPTING
CGIIILNT	LIGNITIC	CGIKLNOS	LOCKINGS	CGIMNOPU	UPCOMING
CGIIINNS	INCISING	CGIKLNPU	PLUCKING	CGIMNORS	SCROMING
CGIIINNT	INCITING	CGIKLNRU	RUCKLING	CGIMNPRU	CRUMPING
CGIIKLNN	CLINKING	CGIKLNSU	SCULKING	CGIMRRUY	MICRURGY
	NICKLING		SUCKLING	CGINNNOS	CONNINGS
CGIIKLNP	PICKLING	CGIKMNOS	MOCKINGS	CGINNNSU	CUNNINGS
CGIIKLNS	LICKINGS		SMOCKING	CGINNOOP	POONCING
	SICKLING	CGIKNOOR	CROOKING	CGINNOOR	CROONING
	SLICKING	CGIKNOOS	COOKINGS	CGINNOPU	POUNCING
CGIIKLNT	TICKLING	CGIKNORS	ROCKINGS		UNCOPING
CGIIKMMS	GIMMICKS	CGIKNORT	TROCKING	CGINNORS	SCORNING
CGIIKMMY	GIMMICKY	CGIKNORW	CORKWING	CGINNORW	CROWNING
CGIIKNNS	SNICKING	CGIKNOST	STOCKING	CGINNOSS	CONSIGNS
CGIIKNNZ	ZINCKING	CGIKNOTW	TWOCKING	CGINNOTU	COUNTING
CGIIKNOY	YOICKING	CGIKNPSU	KINGCUPS	CGINOOPS	SCOOPING
CGIIKNPR	PRICKING	CGIKNRTU	TRUCKING	CGINOOPT	COOPTING

CGINOOST	SCOOTING	**CHIILPRY**	CHIRPILY	**CHIMOSTU**	MISTOUCH
CGINOOTV	COGNOVIT	**CHIILPTY**	PITCHILY	**CHIMPSSY**	PSYCHISM
CGINOPPR	CROPPING	**CHIILQSU**	CLIQUISH	**CHIMSSTY**	CHYMISTS
CGINOPRS	CORPSING	**CHIILSTY**	HYLICIST		TYCHISMS
CGINOPRU	CROUPING	**CHIIMOPT**	PHIMOTIC	**CHINOOPT**	PHOTONIC
CGINOPSU	SCOUPING	**CHIIMORZ**	RHIZOMIC	**CHINOORS**	CHORIONS
CGINOPSW	SCOWPING	**CHIIMPRU**	PICHURIM		ISOCHRON
CGINORSS	CROSSING	**CHIINNPS**	INCHPINS	**CHINOORT**	ORTHICON
	SCORINGS	**CHIINOPS**	SIPHONIC	**CHINOPTY**	HYPNOTIC
	SCORSING	**CHIINORT**	ORNITHIC		PHYTONIC
CGINORSU	COURSING	**CHIIORSS**	CHORISIS		PYTHONIC
	SCOURING	**CHIIORST**	HISTORIC		TYPHONIC
	SOURCING		ORCHITIS	**CHINORTU**	COTHURNI
CGINORTU	COURTING	**CHIIPPRU**	HIPPURIC	**CHINOSSU**	CUSHIONS
CGINOSST	COSTINGS	**CHIIRSTT**	TRISTICH	**CHINOSTZ**	SCHIZONT
	GNOSTICS	**CHIKLLOS**	HILLOCKS	**CHINOSUY**	CUSHIONY
CGINOSTU	SCOUTING	**CHIKLLOY**	HILLOCKY	**CHINSTTU**	UNSTITCH
CGINPPSU	CUPPINGS	**CHIKLNUY**	CHUNKILY	**CHIOOPPT**	PHOTOPIC
CGINPRSU	SPRUCING	**CHIKLORS**	HORLICKS	**CHIOOPRS**	POCHOIRS
CGINRRSU	SCURRING	**CHIKMNNU**	MUNCHKIN	**CHIOOPTY**	OOPHYTIC
CGINRRUY	CURRYING	**CHIKMNPU**	CHIPMUNK	**CHIOORSS**	ISOCHORS
CGINRSSU	CURSINGS	**CHIKMNTU**	MUTCHKIN	**CHIOORSU**	ICHOROUS
CGINRSSY	SCRYINGS	**CHIKNNOP**	PHINNOCK	**CHIOORSZ**	CHORIZOS
CGINRSTU	CRUSTING	**CHIKNOOS**	CHINOOKS	**CHIOORTT**	ORTHOTIC
CGINRSUZ	SCRUZING	**CHIKOPTY**	KYPHOTIC	**CHIOPRST**	STROPHIC
CGINSTTU	CUTTINGS	**CHIKORST**	TROCHISK	**CHIOPSTY**	HYPOCIST
	TUNGSTIC	**CHIKOSST**	STOCKISH	**CHIOPTTU**	OUTPITCH
CGKLNOSU	GUNLOCKS	**CHIKPSYY**	PHYSICKY		PITCHOUT
CGKNOSTU	GUNSTOCK	**CHILLMSU**	CHILLUMS	**CHIORSSS**	CROSSISH
CGLLOSYY	GLYCOSYL	**CHILLOOT**	OILCLOTH	**CHIORSST**	CHORISTS
CGLMOOYY	MYCOLOGY	**CHILMMUY**	CHUMMILY	**CHIPRRSU**	CHIRRUPS
CGLNOOOY	ONCOLOGY	**CHILMOPS**	COMPLISH	**CHIPRRSY**	PYRRHICS
CGLOOOTY	TOCOLOGY	**CHILMOSU**	SCHOLIUM	**CHIPRRUY**	CHIRRUPY
CGLOOTYY	CYTOLOGY	**CHILMPSU**	CLUMPISH	**CHIPRTTY**	TRIPTYCH
CGMNNOOR	MONGCORN	**CHILNNPY**	LYNCHPIN	**CHIPSSTY**	PSYCHIST
CGMNNORU	MUNGCORN	**CHILNOOS**	SCHOLION	**CHIRRSSU**	SCIRRHUS
CGNORSUY	SCROUNGY	**CHILNORS**	CHLORINS	**CHISSTTU**	CHUTISTS
CGOORRSW	GORCROWS	**CHILNOSW**	CLOWNISH	**CHKLOOOS**	HOOLOCKS
CHHIIKST	THICKISH	**CHILNPUY**	PUNCHILY	**CHKLOSSY**	SHYLOCKS
CHHIILTY	HITCHILY	**CHILOOOZ**	HOLOZOIC	**CHKMMOOS**	HOMMOCKS
CHHIIPST	PHTHISIC	**CHILOOPT**	HOLOPTIC	**CHKMMOSU**	HUMMOCKS
CHHIKORS	CHIKHORS	**CHILOOYZ**	HYLOZOIC	**CHKMMOUY**	HUMMOCKY
CHHILRSU	CHURLISH	**CHILOPPY**	CHOPPILY	**CHKNOOSS**	SCHNOOKS
CHHIMPSU	CHUMSHIP	**CHILORST**	TROCHILS	**CHKNORSU**	CORNHUSK
CHHIMRTY	RHYTHMIC	**CHILOSTT**	CLOTTISH	**CHKOOOPS**	COOKSHOP
CHHKOOPS	HOCKSHOP	**CHILOSYY**	COYISHLY	**CHKOOSST**	SCHTOOKS
CHHNORSU	RHONCHUS	**CHILOTUY**	TOUCHILY	**CHKOPSTU**	TUCKSHOP
CHHOOPTT	HOTCHPOT	**CHIMMOOR**	MICROMHO	**CHKPSTUU**	PUTCHUKS
CHHOPPTU	CHUPPOTH	**CHIMMORS**	MICROHMS	**CHLMORSY**	CHROMYLS
CHIIINRT	RHINITIC	**CHIMMORU**	CHROMIUM	**CHLMPSSU**	SCHLUMPS
CHIIKLST	TICKLISH	**CHIMNNOO**	NONOHMIC	**CHLMPSUY**	SCHLUMPY
CHIIKNNS	KINCHINS	**CHIMNOOR**	HORMONIC	**CHLNOOOP**	COLOPHON
CHIIKRST	TRICKISH	**CHIMNORS**	CHRISMON	**CHLOORSU**	CHLOROUS
CHIIKRTW	WHITRICK	**CHIMNORW**	INCHWORM	**CHLOPSTY**	SPLOTCHY
CHIILLLY	CHILLILY	**CHIMNOSU**	INSOMUCH	**CHLORTUY**	CHOULTRY
CHIILMSY	HYLICISM	**CHIMNOSY**	CHYMOSIN	**CHMNOORT**	CORNMOTH
CHIILNNP	LINCHPIN	**CHIMNOUY**	ONYCHIUM	**CHMNORRU**	CRUMHORN
CHIILNST	CHITLINS	**CHIMOORU**	MOUCHOIR	**CHMOORSU**	CHROMOUS
CHIILOPT	HOPLITIC	**CHIMORSS**	CHORISMS	**CHMOOSYZ**	SCHMOOZY
CHIILORT	TROCHILI		CHRISOMS	**CHNNOORS**	CHRONONS
CHIILOST	HOLISTIC	**CHIMORST**	CHRISTOM	**CHNOOPTT**	TOPNOTCH

CHNOORST	TORCHONS
CHNOPRSU	SUNPORCH
CHNOPTUU	OUTPUNCH
CHNORRSS	SCHNORRS
CHNORSSY	SYNCHROS
CHNORSTU	COTHURNS
CHOOORYZ	ZOOCHORY
CHOOPSSS	COPSHOPS
CHOOPSTU	OCTOPUSH
CHOPSTUU	TOUCHUPS
CHORSTTU	SHORTCUT
CIIIKNTU	CUITIKIN
CIIILMPT	IMPLICIT
CIIILMSU	SILICIUM
CIIILNOV	OLIVINIC
CIIILPST	SPILITIC
CIIILSTV	CIVILIST
CIIILTVY	CIVILITY
CIIIMNRS	CRIMINIS
CIIIMNSV	INCIVISM
CIIINNOS	INCISION
CIIINNRT	CITRININ
CIIINOTY	IONICITY
CIIINPPR	PRINCIPI
CIIINPST	INCIPITS
CIIINTVY	VICINITY
CIIJRSTU	JURISTIC
CIIKKLLS	KILLICKS
CIIKKMSS	MISKICKS
CIIKLLSY	SICKLILY
CIIKLOPT	POLITICK
CIIKLPST	LICKSPIT
	LIPSTICK
CIIKLRTY	TRICKILY
CIIKLSTY	STICKILY
CIIKMMMS	MIMMICKS
CIIKMNNS	MINNICKS
CIIKNOOT	COOTIKIN
CIIKNPPR	PINPRICK
CIIKNPST	NITPICKS
	STICKPIN
CIIKNPTY	NITPICKY
CIIKNSTU	CUTIKINS
CIIKPSUW	WICKIUPS
CIILLMTU	TILLICUM
CIILLNOP	POLLINIC
CIILMOPY	IMPOLICY
CIILMOSS	SCIOLISM
CIILMQSU	CLIQUISM
CIILMRSY	LYRICISM
CIILNOOT	NOCTILIO
CIILNOPS	CIPOLINS
	PICOLINS
	PSILOCIN
CIILNORT	NITROLIC
CIILNOSS	SILICONS
CIILNOST	COLISTIN
CIILOOPT	POLITICO
CIILOOTZ	ZOOLITIC
CIILOPPT	POPLITIC
CIILOPST	COLPITIS
	POLITICS
	PSILOTIC
CIILORST	CLITORIS
	COISTRIL
CIILOSST	SCIOLIST
	SOLICITS
CIILOSTY	SOLICITY
CIILOSVV	SLIVOVIC
CIILPRSY	CRISPILY
CIILRSTY	LYRICIST
CIILRTUU	UTRICULI
CIILSSSS	SCISSILS
CIILSTTY	STYLITIC
CIIMMNOS	MINICOMS
CIIMNOOS	ISONOMIC
CIIMNOSS	MISCOINS
CIIMNOST	MICTIONS
	MONISTIC
	NOMISTIC
CIIMNOVY	VIOMYCIN
CIIMORST	TRISOMIC
CIIMOSST	MISTICOS
	STOICISM
CIIMOSYZ	ISOZYMIC
CIIMPRST	SCRIMPIT
CIIMRSTY	MYRISTIC
CIIMRTTU	TRITICUM
CIINNNOO	NONIONIC
CIINNORU	UNIRONIC
CIINNOST	NICOTINS
CIINNSTT	INSTINCT
CIINNSTU	TUNICINS
CIINOOPP	CIOPPINO
CIINOOSS	CONIOSIS
CIINOOST	COITIONS
	ISOTONIC
CIINOOTZ	ZOONITIC
CIINOPRS	PORCINIS
CIINOPSS	PSIONICS
CIINOPSU	OPINICUS
CIINORSS	INCISORS
CIINORST	CROSTINI
CIINORSY	INCISORY
CIINOSSS	SCISSION
CIINOSTT	STICTION
CIINOTTY	TONICITY
CIINPRSS	CRISPINS
CIINPSTU	SINCIPUT
CIINQSTU	QUINTICS
CIIOOPST	ISOTOPIC
CIIOPRST	PORISTIC
CIIOPSTT	OPTICIST
CIIOPSTY	ISOTYPIC
CIIOQTUX	QUIXOTIC
CIIORRWW	WIRRICOW
CIIOTTXY	TOXICITY
CIIPRRTU	PRURITIC
CIIPRSTU	PURISTIC
CIIRSTTU	TRUISTIC
CIISSTTY	CYSTITIS
CIJKOSTY	JOYSTICK
CIJNNOOS	CONJOINS
CIJNNOOT	CONJOINT
CIJNNOTU	JUNCTION
CIJNNSTU	INJUNCTS
CIJOOSTY	JOCOSITY
CIKKLLOS	KILLOCKS
CIKKOPST	TOPKICKS
CIKKOSTU	KICKOUTS
	OUTKICKS
CIKLLOPR	KILLCROP
CIKLLOPS	PILLOCKS
CIKLLORS	ROLLICKS
CIKLLORY	ROLLICKY
CIKLLOSS	SILLOCKS
CIKLLOSW	KILLCOWS
CIKLLPUY	PLUCKILY
CIKLMSSU	MISLUCKS
CIKLNOST	LINSTOCK
CIKLOOOS	OLICOOKS
CIKLOPST	LOPSTICK
CIKLOPSU	LIPOSUCK
CIKLOPSZ	ZIPLOCKS
CIKLOSTU	OUTSLICK
CIKLOSTY	STOCKILY
CIKMNNOS	MINNOCKS
CIKMOORS	SICKROOM
CIKMOOSS	MISCOOKS
CIKMOPST	MOPSTICK
CIKMORRS	RIMROCKS
CIKMSSTU	STICKUMS
CIKNNOOS	COONSKIN
CIKNNOPS	PINNOCKS
CIKNNOST	NONSTICK
CIKNNOSW	WINNOCKS
CIKNOPTY	PYKNOTIC
CIKNOSSW	COWSKINS
CIKNPSTU	NUTPICKS
CIKNSSTU	UNSTICKS
CIKOPPST	POCKPITS
CIKOPSTT	TIPSTOCK
CIKORTTU	OUTTRICK
CIKOSSTT	STOCKIST
CIKOSSTU	SICKOUTS
CIKOSTTU	STICKOUT
CIKOSTUW	OUTWICKS
CIKPSSTU	STICKUPS
CIKPSUWY	WICKYUPS
CILLMNOR	CORNMILL
CILLMSUY	CLUMSILY
	CULLYISM
CILLNOOT	COTILLON
CILLNORS	INSCROLL
CILLNOSU	CULLIONS
	SCULLION
CILLOOOT	OCOTILLO
CILLOORS	CRIOLLOS
CILMMSUY	SCUMMILY
CILMNOPS	COMPLINS
CILMNOPU	PULMONIC
CILMNOSS	CLONISMS
CILMNOUU	INOCULUM

CILMNUUV	VINCULUM	CIMOOOTZ	ZOOTOMIC	CJNOORRU	CONJUROR
CILMOORS	COLORISM	CIMOORSS	MORISCOS	CJRSUUUU	SUCURUJU
	MISCOLOR	CIMOPSSY	COPYISMS	CKKNOOTU	KNOCKOUT
CILMOOSS	LOCOISMS	CIMOSSST	COSMISTS	CKKOORRW	ROCKWORK
CILMOPSY	OLYMPICS	CIMOSTUU	MUTICOUS	CKLLMOSU	MULLOCKS
CILMORUX	MICROLUX	CIMOSTUY	MUCOSITY	CKLLMOUY	MULLOCKY
CILMPRSY	SCRIMPLY	CIMOSTYZ	ZYMOTICS	CKLLOOPS	POLLOCKS
CILMPSUU	SPICULUM	CINNNOOT	NONTONIC	CKLLOORS	ROLLOCKS
CILMSSTU	CULTISMS	CINNNOSU	INCONNUS	CKLLORSU	RULLOCKS
CILMSTYY	MYSTICLY	CINNOOSS	SCOINSON	CKLMMOOS	SLOMMOCK
CILNNORY	NONLYRIC	CINNOOST	SCONTION	CKLMMOSU	SLUMMOCK
CILNOORS	ORCINOLS	CINNOOTU	CONTINUO	CKLNOSTU	LOCKNUTS
CILNOORU	UNICOLOR	CINNOOTX	NONTOXIC	CKLOOOSY	OLYCOOKS
CILNOOSS	CLOISONS	CINNORSU	UNICORNS	CKLOOPRS	PORLOCKS
CILNOOST	COLONIST	CINNOSTU	UNCTIONS	CKLOORSW	ROWLOCKS
	STOLONIC	CINNOSTY	SYNTONIC	CKLOOSTU	LOCKOUTS
CILNOOTU	LOCUTION	CINNQUUX	QUINCUNX	CKLOPSTU	POTLUCKS
CILNOPRS	PILCORNS	CINOOOPT	COOPTION		PUTLOCKS
CILNOPTU	PLUTONIC	CINOOOTZ	ZOONOTIC	CKMMMOSU	MUMMOCKS
CILNORSY	LYRICONS	CINOOPRS	SCORPION	CKMMORUW	MUCKWORM
CILNOSTU	LINOCUTS	CINOOPRT	PROTONIC	CKMNOOOR	MOONROCK
CILNOSUY	COUSINLY	CINOOPSS	POCOSINS	CKMOOOOR	COOKROOM
CILNPSSU	INSCULPS	CINOORST	CROSTINO	CKNOOORS	ROCKOONS
	SCULPINS	CINOOSUV	COVINOUS	CKNOSSTU	UNSTOCKS
CILNPSTU	INSCULPT	CINOOTXY	OXYTOCIN	CKNRSTUU	UNSTRUCK
CILOOPST	COPILOTS		OXYTONIC	CKOOOPST	COOKTOPS
CILOOPYZ	POLYZOIC	CINOPSSY	PYCNOSIS	CKOOOSTU	COOKOUTS
CILOORRT	TRICOLOR	CINOPSTY	SYNOPTIC		OUTCOOKS
CILOORST	COLORIST	CINORRST	TRICORNS	CKOOPPSS	POPSOCKS
	CORTISOL	CINORSST	CISTRONS	CKOOPSTT	STOCKPOT
CILOORSU	COULOIRS		CORNISTS	CKOORSSU	SOUROCKS
CILOOSSU	SCIOLOUS	CINORSTT	CONTRIST	CKOORSTU	OUTROCKS
CILOPPRY	PROPYLIC		STRONTIC	CKOPSTTU	PUTTOCKS
CILOPRRY	PYRROLIC	CINORSTU	RUCTIONS	CKOPSTUU	PUCKOUTS
CILOPRSW	PILCROWS	CINORSUY	COUSINRY	CKORSTUW	CUTWORKS
CILOPRUY	CROUPILY	CINORTUX	COTURNIX		SCUTWORK
	POLYURIC	CINOSSST	CONSISTS	CKOSSSTU	TUSSOCKS
CILOPSSW	COWSLIPS	CINOSSTU	SUCTIONS	CKOSSTUY	TUSSOCKY
CILORSTY	COYSTRIL	CINOSTUV	VISCOUNT	CKSSSTUU	TUSSUCKS
CILOSSTU	OCULISTS	CINRSSTU	INCRUSTS	CLLLOOPT	CLOTPOLL
CILOSSTY	SYSTOLIC	CINRSTTU	INSTRUCT	CLLMOSSU	MOLLUSCS
CILOSSUU	LUSCIOUS	CINRSTUY	SCRUTINY	CLLOOPSS	SCOLLOPS
CILPRSTU	CULPRITS	CIOOOPRS	OOSPORIC	CLLOOQUY	COLLOQUY
CILPSSTU	SCULPSIT	CIOOOTTX	OTOTOXIC	CLMMNOOY	COMMONLY
CILRSTTY	STRICTLY	CIOOOTXZ	ZOOTOXIC	CLMOOOTY	COLOTOMY
CILRSTUY	CRUSTILY	CIOOPRST	PORTICOS	CLMOOPST	COMPLOTS
	RUSTICLY		PROOTICS	CLMOSUUU	CUMULOUS
CILRSUVY	SCURVILY	CIOOPTYZ	ZOOTYPIC	CLNNOOOR	NONCOLOR
CILSSTTU	CULTISTS	CIOOQSTU	COQUITOS	CLNOORST	CONTROLS
CIMMOSSS	COSMISMS	CIOORRWW	WORRICOW	CLNOORTU	CONTROUL
CIMNNOSU	NONMUSIC	CIOORSSU	SCORIOUS		COUNTROL
CIMNOOOZ	ZOONOMIC	CIOOSSTU	STOCIOUS	CLNOSSTU	CONSULTS
CIMNOORS	OMICRONS	CIOPSSTY	COPYISTS	CLNOSTUY	UNCOSTLY
CIMNOORU	CORONIUM	CIORRSTU	CURSITOR	CLOOOPRT	PROTOCOL
CIMNOOTY	MYOTONIC	CIORSSSS	SCISSORS	CLOOPPSW	COWPLOPS
CIMNOPRT	COMPRINT	CIORSTUU	RUCTIOUS	CLOOPSTY	POLYCOTS
CIMNORSS	CRIMSONS	CIPPRRUU	PURPURIC	CLOORTUY	LOCUTORY
CIMNORSY	CRONYISM	CIPSSTTY	STYPTICS	CLOOSSSU	COLOSSUS
CIMNOSTU	MISCOUNT	CIRRSTTU	CRITTURS	CLOOSSTY	CYTOSOLS
CIMNOSUU	MUCINOUS	CIRSSTUY	CITRUSSY	CLOPRSTU	SCULPTOR
CIMNOSUY	SYCONIUM	CJNNOOTU	CONJUNTO		

CLRSSUUU	SURCULUS	DDDEEIST	STEDDIED		STEEDIED
CMMNNOOU	UNCOMMON	DDDEEJRU	JUDDERED	DDEEELLV	DEVELLED
CMMOPSSY	COMSYMPS	DDDEELRT	TREDDLED	DDEEEELNW	WEDELNED
CMNOOOST	MONOCOTS	DDDEENOR	DONDERED	DDEEELPT	DEPLETED
CMNOOOTY	ONCOTOMY		REDDENDO	DDEEELRW	REWELDED
CMNOORRW	CORNWORM	DDDEENOS	SODDENED	DDEEELSS	DEEDLESS
CMNOPSTU	CONSUMPT	DDDEENUW	UNWEDDED	DDEEELTW	TWEEDLED
CMOOPRST	COMPORTS	DDDEEORR	DODDERER	DDEEEMNR	REMENDED
CMOOPSST	COMPOSTS	DDDEEORS	RESODDED	DDEEEMNT	DEMENTED
CMOPRSUX	SCRUMPOX	DDDEEPRU	PUDDERED	DDEEEMPR	DEPERMED
CMORSSTU	SCROTUMS	DDDEERTU	DETRUDED	DDEEEMRS	DEMERSED
CMORSTUW	CUTWORMS	DDDEGILR	GRIDDLED	DDEEENNU	UNNEEDED
CNNOOORT	CONTORNO	DDDEGNOU	UNGODDED	DDEEENPX	EXPENDED
CNNORSTU	NOCTURNS	DDDEHIRT	THRIDDED	DDEEENRR	RENDERED
CNNORSUW	UNCROWNS	DDDEIILS	DIDDLIES	DDEEENRT	TENDERED
CNOOOORT	OCTOROON	DDDEIIMS	SMIDDIED	DDEEENSU	UNSEEDED
CNOOOPSS	POCOSONS	DDDEIINV	DIVIDEND	DDEEENTT	DENETTED
CNOOPPRS	POPCORNS	DDDEIIST	DIDDIEST	DDEEENTX	EXTENDED
CNOOPRSU	CROUPONS		STIDDIED	DDEEENUW	UNWEEDED
CNOOPSSU	SOUPCONS	DDDEILNU	UNLIDDED	DDEEEQUU	DEQUEUED
CNOORRSW	CORNROWS	DDDEILNW	DWINDLED	DDEEERRT	DETERRED
CNOORRTY	CRYOTRON	DDDEILQU	QUIDDLED	DDEEERST	DESERTED
CNOORSST	CONSORTS	DDDEILRS	DIDDLERS	DDEEERSV	DESERVED
CNOORSTT	CONTORTS	DDDEILSY	DIDDLEYS	DDEEESTT	DETESTED
CNOORSTU	CONTOURS	DDDEILTW	TWIDDLED	DDEEESTV	DEVESTED
	CORNUTOS	DDDEIMOS	DISMODED	DDEEESWY	DYEWEEDS
	CROUTONS	DDDEINOR	DENDROID	DDEEFFIR	DIFFERED
	OUTSCORN	DDDEINRU	UNDERDID	DDEEFFNO	OFFENDED
CNOOSTTW	COTTOWNS	DDDEIOST	DODDIEST	DDEEFGGO	DEFOGGED
CNOOTTUU	OUTCOUNT	DDDEIQSU	SQUIDDED	DDEEFGIT	FIDGETED
CNOPRSTY	CRYPTONS	DDDEISTU	DUDDIEST	DDEEFINR	FRIENDED
CNOPSSTY	POSTSYNC	DDDENORW	DROWNDED	DDEEFINU	UNDEFIDE
CNOSTUUU	UNCTUOUS	DDDGIILN	DIDDLING		UNDEFIED
COOOPSTU	OUTSCOOP	DDDIIOOR	DORIDOID	DDEEFLNO	ENFOLDED
COOOPSTY	OTOSCOPY	DDEEEEMR	REDEEMED	DDEEFLOR	REFOLDED
COOOPSYZ	ZOOSCOPY	DDEEEENP	DEEPENED	DDEEFLOU	DEFOULED
COOPPSTU	POSTCOUP	DDEEEERS	RESEEDED	DDEEFMOR	DEFORMED
COOPRRST	PROCTORS	DDEEEERW	DEERWEED	DDEEFNRU	REFUNDED
COOPRSST	TOPCROSS	DDEEEFIR	REDEFIED		UNDERFED
COOPRSTU	OUTCROPS	DDEEEFLU	DEFUELED	DDEEFORR	FODDERER
COOPRSUU	CROUPOUS	DDEEEFLX	DEFLEXED	DDEEGGIR	DERIGGED
COOPRSUY	UROSCOPY	DDEEEFNR	DEFENDER	DDEEGGOR	DOGGEDER
COORRWWY	WORRYCOW		FENDERED	DDEEGHNU	UNHEDGED
COORSSTU	OUTCROSS	DDEEEFNS	DEFENSED	DDEEGILN	ENGILDED
COORSTUW	OUTCROWS	DDEEEFRR	DEFERRED	DDEEGILR	REGILDED
COOSSTTY	OTOCYSTS	DDEEEGLR	LEDGERED	DDEEGINR	ENGIRDED
COPRRSTU	CORRUPTS	DDEEEGMR	DEGERMED		ENRIDGED
DDDDEEIR	DIDDERED		DEMERGED	DDEEGINS	DESIGNED
DDDDEEOR	DODDERED	DDEEEGNR	DEGENDER		SDEIGNED
DDDEEEES	DESEEDED		GENDERED	DDEEGIRV	DIVERGED
DDDEEEFN	DEFENDED	DDEEEGRR	REGREDED	DDEEGISS	DISEDGES
DDDEEENP	DEPENDED	DDEEEGRT	DETERGED	DDEEGIST	DIGESTED
DDDEEENR	REDDENED	DDEEEHLW	WHEEDLED	DDEEGJRU	REJUDGED
DDDEEENU	UNDEEDED	DDEEEHNU	UNHEEDED	DDEEGLNO	GOLDENED
DDDEEERT	TEDDERED	DDEEEILS	DIESELED	DDEEGLNU	UNGELDED
DDDEEERW	REWEDDED	DDEEEIMR	REMEDIED	DDEEGMMU	DEGUMMED
	WEDDERED		REMEDIED	DDEEGOPS	GODSPEED
DDDEEFNU	DEFUNDED	DDEEEINR	REDENIED	DDEEGORS	SODGERED
DDDEEFOR	FODDERED	DDEEEINV	DEVEINED	DDEEGRRS	DREDGERS
DDDEEGIS	DISEDGED	DDEEEIRT	REEDITED	DDEEGRSU	DEGUSTED
DDDEEHRS	SHREDDED	DDEEEIST	DEEDIEST	DDEEHILS	SHIELDED

DDEEHINO	HOIDENED	DDEELNOU	LOUDENED	DDEFILRS	FIDDLERS
DDEEHINR	HINDERED	DDEELNUW	UNWELDED	DDEFILSY	FIDDLEYS
DDEEHIRT	DITHERED	DDEELOOW	DEWOOLED	DDEFLNOU	UNFOLDED
DDEEHISS	EDDISHES	DDEELOPR	DEPLORED	DDEFLOPU	UPFOLDED
DDEEHNOR	DEHORNED		POLDERED	DDEFLRSU	FUDDLERS
DDEEHNOY	HOYDENED	DDEELOPX	EXPLODED	DDEFLRUU	UDDERFUL
DDEEHNSU	DUDHEENS	DDEELOPY	DEPLOYED	DDEFNNUU	UNFUNDED
DDEEHORT	DEHORTED	DDEELORS	SOLDERED	DDEGGINR	DREDGING
DDEEHRRS	SHREDDER	DDEELOSU	DELOUSED	DDEGGLOY	DOGGEDLY
DDEEHRSS	SHEDDERS	DDEELOVV	DEVOLVED	DDEGGNOO	DOGGONED
DDEEIINT	INEDITED	DDEELPRS	PEDDLERS	DDEGHILN	HEDDLING
DDEEIIRV	REDIVIDE	DDEELPRU	PRELUDED	DDEGHINS	SHEDDING
DDEEILLV	DEVILLED	DDEELPRY	PEDDLERY	DDEGIINR	DERIDING
DDEEILMN	MILDENED	DDEELPUX	DUPLEXED	DDEGIIST	GIDDIEST
DDEEILMW	MILDEWED	DDEELRSS	SLEDDERS	DDEGILMN	MEDDLING
DDEEILNR	REDLINED	DDEELRST	TREDDLES	DDEGILNP	PEDDLING
DDEEILNT	DENTILED	DDEELRSU	DELUDERS	DDEGILNR	REDDLING
DDEEILRS	DREIDELS	DDEEMNNU	UNMENDED	DDEGILNS	SLEDDING
DDEEILRV	DRIVELED	DDEEMNOR	ENDODERM	DDEGILNU	DELUDING
DDEEILRW	WILDERED	DDEEMORR	DORMERED		INDULGED
DDEEILST	DELISTED	DDEEMORW	DEWORMED		UNGILDED
DDEEIMNP	IMPENDED	DDEEMRRU	DEMURRED	DDEGILOS	DISLODGE
DDEEIMNR	REMINDED		MURDERED	DDEGILRS	GRIDDLES
DDEEIMOR	MOIDERED	DDEENNOR	DONNERED	DDEGILRY	GLIDDERY
DDEEIMSS	MISDEEDS		REDONNED	DDEGILST	GLIDDEST
DDEEIMST	DEMISTED	DDEENNOY	ENDODYNE	DDEGILUV	DIVULGED
DDEEIMTT	DEMITTED	DDEENNTU	UNDENTED	DDEGIMOS	DEMIGODS
DDEEINNR	DINNERED		UNTENDED	DDEGINNS	SNEDDING
DDEEINNT	INDENTED	DDEENOOW	WOODENED	DDEGINNU	DENUDING
	INTENDED	DDEENOPR	PERDENDO	DDEGINRS	REDDINGS
DDEEINNU	UNDENIED		PONDERED	DDEGINRU	UNGIRDED
DDEEINRT	DENDRITE	DDEENOPW	PONDWEED	DDEGINST	STEDDING
DDEEINRW	REWINDED	DDEENORS	ENDORSED	DDEGINSW	SWINDGED
DDEEINST	DESTINED	DDEENORW	WONDERED		WEDDINGS
	NEDDIEST	DDEENOSS	ENDOSSED	DDEGINUU	UNGUIDED
DDEEINTU	UNEDITED	DDEENPRS	SPREDDEN	DDEGIOST	DODGIEST
DDEEIOPR	PERIODED	DDEENRRU	DURNEDER	DDEGIPRU	UPGIRDED
DDEEIPPR	REDIPPED	DDEENRSU	DENUDERS	DDEGIQSU	SQUIDGED
DDEEIPRR	PREDRIED		SUNDERED	DDEGIRRS	GRIDDERS
DDEEIPRS	PRESIDED	DDEENRTU	RETUNDED	DDEGJNUU	UNJUDGED
DDEEIPRV	DEPRIVED	DDEEOPRT	DEPORTED	DDEGLOPS	SPLODGED
DDEEIPSS	DEPSIDES	DDEEOPRW	POWDERED	DDEGLOSS	DOGSLEDS
	DESPISED	DDEEOPSS	SEEDPODS	DDEGMOOS	DOGEDOMS
DDEEIPST	DESPITED	DDEEORRW	REWORDED		SMOODGED
DDEEIRRS	DERIDERS	DDEEORTT	DETORTED	DDEGNORU	GROUNDED
DDEEIRST	REDDIEST	DDEEORTU	DETOURED		UNDERDOG
DDEEIRSV	DIVERSED	DDEEORUV	DEVOURED		UNDERGOD
DDEEIRTV	DIVERTED	DDEEORVY	OVERDYED	DDEGNOSS	GODSENDS
DDEEISST	DESISTED	DDEEOTUX	TUXEDOED	DDEGNOSU	DUDGEONS
	STEDDIES	DDEEPRRU	PERDURED	DDEGOOTU	OUTDODGE
DDEEISTV	DIVESTED	DDEEPRSS	SPREDDES	DDEGORSS	GORSEDDS
DDEEITTW	DEWITTED	DDEERRUV	VERDURED	DDEGRRSU	DRUDGERS
DDEEJLLO	JODELLED	DDEERSTU	DETRUDES	DDEGRRUY	DRUDGERY
DDEEKNSU	DUSKENED	DDEERTUX	EXTRUDED	DDEHILNY	HIDDENLY
DDEELLMO	MODELLED	DDEFFISU	DIFFUSED	DDEHILOO	IDLEHOOD
DDEELLOW	DOWELLED	DDEFIIIN	NIDIFIED	DDEHIMOS	DISHOMED
DDEELLOY	YODELLED	DDEFIILM	MIDFIELD	DDEHINNU	UNHIDDEN
DDEELMOR	MOLDERED	DDEFIILR	FIDDLIER	DDEHINOR	DIHEDRON
	REMOLDED	DDEFIIMO	MODIFIED	DDEHIORS	SHODDIER
DDEELMPU	DEPLUMED	DDEFIIMW	MIDWIFED	DDEHIOSS	SHODDIES
DDEELMRS	MEDDLERS	DDEFILNO	INFOLDED	DDEHIRSS	SHIDDERS

DDEHIRSW	WHIDDERS	DDEILQSU	QUIDDLES	DDELNOSY	SODDENLY
DDEHIRSY	HYDRIDES	DDEILRRS	RIDDLERS	DDELNRTU	TRUNDLED
DDEHLRSU	HUDDLERS	DDEILRSS	SLIDDERS	DDELNSUY	SUDDENLY
DDEHNOOU	UNHOODED	DDEILRST	STRIDDLE	DDELOORS	DOODLERS
DDEHNPUU	UPHUDDEN		TIDDLERS	DDELOPRS	PLODDERS
DDEHNRSU	HUNDREDS	DDEILRSY	SLIDDERY	DDELORST	STRODDLE
DDEHOOOO	HOODOOED	DDEILRTW	TWIDDLER		STRODLED
DDEHOOSW	WOODSHED	DDEILRZZ	DRIZZLED		TODDLERS
DDEHORSU	SHROUDED	DDEILSTW	TWIDDLES	DDELOSYY	DYSODYLE
DDEHRSSU	SHUDDERS	DDEILSTY	LYDDITES	DDELPRSU	PUDDLERS
DDEHRSUY	SHUDDERY		TIDDLEYS	DDELPSSU	SPUDDLES
DDEIIIRS	IRIDISED	DDEILSUV	DIVULSED	DDELSSTU	STUDDLES
DDEIIIRZ	IRIDIZED	DDEIMMNU	UNDIMMED	DDEMMSSU	SMEDDUMS
DDEIIKLS	DISLIKED	DDEIMNNU	UNMINDED	DDEMNOOU	UNDOOMED
DDEIIKRS	KIDDIERS	DDEIMNSU	MUEDDINS	DDEMNOST	ODDMENTS
	SKIDDIER	DDEIMNUV	VIDENDUM	DDEMNOUU	DUODENUM
DDEIILNR	DIELDRIN	DDEIMORS	DERMOIDS	DDEMNPUU	PUDENDUM
DDEIILOS	IDOLISED	DDEIMOSS	DESMOIDS	DDEMOOTU	OUTMODED
DDEIILOZ	IDOLIZED	DDEIMOSU	MEDUSOID	DDENNORS	DENDRONS
DDEIILPR	PIDDLIER	DDEIMSTU	MUDDIEST	DDENNOSU	UNSODDEN
DDEIILRT	TIDDLIER	DDEINNRU	UNRIDDEN	DDENOOPS	ENDOPODS
DDEIILST	TIDDLIES	DDEINNTU	UNDINTED	DDENOOSS	DESNOODS
DDEIIMSS	SMIDDIES	DDEINOPS	DISPONED	DDENOOUW	UNWOODED
DDEIIMSZ	MIDSIZED	DDEINORS	INDORSED	DDENOPSS	DESPONDS
DDEIIMVW	MIDWIVED	DDEINORT	TRENDOID	DDENORSU	REDOUNDS
DDEIINRT	NITRIDED	DDEINOST	NODDIEST	DDENORTU	ROTUNDED
DDEIINTU	UNTIDIED	DDEINOSW	DISENDOW	DDENORUW	UNWORDED
DDEIIOPR	PERIODID		DISOWNED	DDENOSST	SNODDEST
DDEIIOPS	DIOPSIDE		DOWNSIDE	DDENOSTU	STOUNDED
	DIPODIES	DDEINOWW	WINDOWED	DDENOSTW	STOWNDED
DDEIIOST	ODDITIES	DDEINPPU	UNDIPPED	DDENOSUW	SWOUNDED
DDEIIOSX	DIOXIDES	DDEINPSS	DISPENDS	DDENOTTU	DONUTTED
	OXIDISED	DDEINRST	STRIDDEN		UNDOTTED
DDEIIOXZ	OXIDIZED	DDEINRTU	INTRUDED	DDENRSTU	DURNDEST
DDEIIRSV	DIVIDERS	DDEINSST	DISTENDS	DDENSTUY	SUDDENTY
DDEIIRUV	REDUVIID	DDEINSSW	SWIDDENS	DDEOOOOV	VOODOOED
DDEIISST	STIDDIES	DDEINSTU	DISTUNED	DDEOORSW	REDWOODS
DDEIISTT	TIDDIEST	DDEIOORS	ODORISED	DDEOORWW	ROWDEDOW
DDEIKNRS	KINDREDS	DDEIOORZ	ODORIZED	DDEOOSWY	DYEWOODS
DDEIKOOS	SKIDOOED	DDEIOPRS	DROPSIED	DDEOOUUV	VOUDOUED
DDEIKOSY	DISYOKED		SPODDIER	DDEOPRRS	PRODDERS
DDEIKRSS	SKIDDERS	DDEIOPRV	PROVIDED	DDEOPRSW	DEWDROPS
DDEIKSVY	SKYDIVED	DDEIOPSS	DISPOSED	DDEORTUU	OUTDURED
DDEILMOP	IMPLODED	DDEIOPST	PODDIEST	DDEPRSSU	SPUDDERS
DDEILMOV	DEVILDOM	DDEIORRS	DISORDER	DDFGIILN	FIDDLING
DDEILMRS	MIDDLERS		SORDIDER	DDFGILNU	FUDDLING
DDEILMRU	MUDDLIER	DDEIOSST	SODDIEST	DDFIILSU	DISULFID
DDEILMSU	MUDSLIDE	DDEIOSTW	DOWDIEST	DDFIIOSU	FIDDIOUS
DDEILNPS	SPINDLED	DDEIPRSS	DISPREDS	DDFMNOUU	DUMFOUND
	SPLENDID	DDEIPRSU	SPUDDIER	DDGIIINY	GIDDYING
DDEILNRT	TRINDLED	DDEIPSTU	DISPUTED	DDGGILNU	GUDDLING
DDEILNRU	UNRIDDLE	DDEIRSSU	DRUIDESS	DDGGINNO	DINGDONG
DDEILNSW	DWINDLES	DDEIRSTU	RUDDIEST	DDGGINOS	DODGINGS
	SWINDLED		STURDIED	DDGGINRU	DRUDGING
DDEILOPS	DISPLODE	DDEISSTU	STUDDIES	DDGHIINW	WHIDDING
	LOPSIDED	DDEKMOSU	DUKEDOMS	DDGHILNO	HODDLING
DDEILOST	DELTOIDS	DDELLNUU	UNDULLED	DDGHILNU	HUDDLING
DDEILOSY	DYSODILE	DDELLOOP	DOLLOPED	DDGHINTU	THUDDING
DDEILPRS	PIDDLERS	DDELMNOU	UNMOLDED	DDGHOOOS	GODHOODS
DDEILPRU	PUDDLIER	DDELMRSU	MUDDLERS	DDGIIINO	INDIGOID
DDEILQRU	QUIDDLER	DDELNORU	UNLORDED	DDGIIINV	DIVIDING

DDGIIKNS	SKIDDING	DDLMORSU	DOLDRUMS	DEEEGMRR	DEMERGER
DDGIIKNY	KIDDYING	DDMNOORS	DROMONDS		REMERGED
DDGIILMN	MIDDLING	DDNOORTW	DOWNTROD	DEEEGMRS	DEMERGES
DDGIILNN	DINDLING	DDOORWWY	ROWDYDOW	DEEEGNNR	ENGENDER
DDGIILNP	PIDDLING	DDORSSTY	DROSTDYS	DEEEGNRU	RENEGUED
DDGIILNR	RIDDLING	DEEEEFRR	REFEREED	DEEEGNRV	REVENGED
DDGIILNT	TIDDLING	DEEEEFRZ	DEFREEZE	DEEEGRRS	REGREDES
DDGIILNW	WIDDLING	DEEEEGKR	KEDGEREE	DEEEGRRT	DETERGER
DDGILMNU	MUDDLING	DEEEEHLR	REHEELED	DEEEGRSS	EGRESSED
DDGILNNO	NODDLING	DEEEEKMN	MEEKENED	DEEEGRST	DETERGES
DDGILNOO	DOODLING	DEEEELTY	EYELETED	DEEEGRTT	GETTERED
DDGILNOP	PLODDING	DEEEEMMS	MESEEMED	DEEEHHSW	WHEESHED
	PODDLING	DEEEEMRR	REDEEMER	DEEEHKRS	SHREEKED
DDGILNOT	TODDLING	DEEEEMST	ESTEEMED	DEEEHLMT	HELMETED
DDGILNPU	PUDDLING	DEEEENPR	DEEPENER	DEEEHLPW	WHEEPLED
DDGILNRU	RUDDLING	DEEEENRV	VENEERED	DEEEHLRW	WHEEDLER
DDGIMNOS	MODDINGS	DEEEERTT	TEETERED	DEEEHLSS	HEEDLESS
DDGIMNUY	MUDDYING	DEEEFFIR	EFFEIRED	DEEEHLSW	WHEEDLES
DDGIMRSU	DRUDGISM	DEEEFHLO	FEEDHOLE	DEEEHLWZ	WHEEZLED
DDGINNOS	NODDINGS	DEEEFHST	SHEETFED	DEEEHMMR	REHEMMED
	SNODDING	DEEEFINR	FINEERED	DEEEHMMS	EMMESHED
DDGINOPR	PRODDING		NEEDFIRE	DEEEHMNS	ENMESHED
DDGINOQU	QUODDING		REDEFINE	DEEEHMPS	HEMPSEED
DDGINORS	RODDINGS	DEEEFIPT	TEPEFIED	DEEEHMPW	HEMPWEED
DDGINPSU	PUDDINGS	DEEEFIRR	FREERIDE	DEEEHPRT	THREEPED
	SPUDDING	DEEEFIRS	REDEFIES	DEEEHRTT	TETHERED
DDGINPUY	PUDDINGY	DEEEFIRW	FIREWEED	DEEEIKLR	DEERLIKE
DDGINRUY	RUDDYING	DEEEFKST	KEFTEDES		REEDLIKE
DDGINSTU	STUDDING	DEEEFLLR	REFELLED	DEEEIKLS	SEEDLIKE
DDGLORRU	DRUGLORD	DEEEFLPT	DEEPFELT	DEEEIKLW	WEEDLIKE
DDGOOOSW	DOGWOODS	DEEEFLRR	FERRELED	DEEEILNR	NEEDLIER
DDHILOSY	SHODDILY	DEEEFLRT	FELTERED	DEEEILNS	SELENIDE
DDHILSUY	DUDISHLY		TELFERED	DEEEILRV	RELIEVED
DDHIORSY	HYDROIDS	DEEEFLRU	REFUELED	DEEEILTV	DELETIVE
DDHIOSWY	DOWDYISH	DEEEFLRX	REFLEXED	DEEEILVW	WEEVILED
DDHLLOOO	DOLLHOOD	DEEEFLSX	DEFLEXES	DEEEIMNS	INSEEMED
DDHLMOOO	HOODMOLD	DEEEFMNR	FREEDMEN	DEEEIMRS	REMEDIES
DDHLNOOW	HOLDDOWN	DEEEFNRS	ENSERFED	DEEEIMST	SEEDTIME
DDIIIIVV	DIVIDIVI	DEEEFNRT	DEFERENT	DEEEINNX	ENDEXINE
DDIIKLSS	SKIDLIDS	DEEEFNSS	DEFENSES	DEEEINRR	REINDEER
DDIILOPS	DIPLOIDS	DEEEFNST	ENFESTED	DEEEINRS	NEREIDES
DDIILOPY	DIPLOIDY	DEEEFORV	OVERFEED		REDENIES
DDIIMMUY	DIDYMIUM	DEEEFRRR	DEFERRER	DEEEINST	NEEDIEST
DDIIMOSU	DISODIUM		REFERRED	DEEEINSX	ENDEIXES
DDIIMRSU	DRUIDISM	DEEEFRRT	FERRETED	DEEEINTV	EVENTIDE
	SIDDURIM	DEEEFRST	FESTERED	DEEEIPRS	SPEEDIER
DDIINOPU	DUPONDII	DEEEFRTT	FETTERED	DEEEIPTX	EXPEDITE
DDIIQSTU	QUIDDITS	DEEEFRTW	FEWTERED	DEEEIRRR	DERRIERE
DDIIQTUY	QUIDDITY	DEEEGGPR	REPEGGED	DEEEIRSS	DIERESES
DDIKOOSS	SKIDDOOS	DEEEGHNW	WHEENGED	DEEEIRST	REEDIEST
DDILOOPP	DIPLOPOD	DEEEGILS	ELEGISED	DEEEIRSZ	RESEIZED
DDILOOWW	WILDWOOD	DEEEGILZ	ELEGIZED	DEEEIRTW	TWEEDIER
DDILORSY	SORDIDLY	DEEEGINS	DESIGNEE	DEEEIRVW	REVIEWED
DDILOSSY	DYSODILS	DEEEGIPR	PEDIGREE	DEEEISST	SEEDIEST
DDIMOOSS	DODOISMS	DEEEGIRR	GREEDIER		STEEDIES
DDIMOSUY	DIDYMOUS	DEEEGISS	DIEGESES	DEEEISSV	DEVISEES
DDIMOSWY	DOWDYISM	DEEEGISW	EDGEWISE	DEEEISTW	WEEDIEST
DDINNOWW	DOWNWIND	DEEEGLPR	REPLEDGE	DEEEJLLW	JEWELLED
DDINOOOT	ODONTOID	DEEEGLPS	PLEDGEES	DEEEJNRU	DEJEUNER
DDINOOWW	WOODWIND	DEEEGLSS	EDGELESS	DEEEJNSU	DEJEUNES
DDLLMOOS	DOLLDOMS	DEEEGLSV	SELVEDGE	DEEEJRRS	JERREEDS

DEEEJRSY	JERSEYED	DEEENNRT	ENTENDER	DEEERSTW	WESTERED
DEEEKLNN	KENNELED	DEEENNUW	UNWEENED	DEEERSTX	EXSERTED
DEEEKLNR	KERNELED	DEEENOPR	REOPENED	DEEERSUW	SERUEWED
DEEEKLNU	UNKEELED	DEEENORS	ENDORSEE	DEEERSVW	SERVEWED
DEEEKNSW	WEEKENDS	DEEENPRT	REPENTED	DEEERTTT	TETTERED
DEEEKOPW	POKEWEED		REPETEND	DEEERTTV	REVETTED
DEEEKORV	REEVOKED	DEEENPRU	UNPEERED	DEEERTTW	REWETTED
DEEEKPRR	REPERKED	DEEENPRV	PREVENED	DEEESTTU	SUEDETTE
DEEEKRST	STREEKED	DEEENPRX	EXPENDER	DEEESTTV	VEDETTES
DEEEKRSW	RESKEWED	DEEENPSS	DEEPNESS	DEEFFGLU	EFFULGED
	SKEWERED	DEEENPSX	EXPENSED	DEEFFGOR	GOFFERED
DEEELLLV	LEVELLED	DEEENQUU	ENQUEUED	DEEFFINR	NIFFERED
DEEELLNT	DENTELLE	DEEENRRR	RENDERER	DEEFFINS	EFFENDIS
DEEELLNV	NEVELLED	DEEENRRT	RERENTED	DEEFFINT	INFEFTED
DEEELLNW	NEWELLED		TENDERER	DEEFFIRS	SERIFFED
DEEELLPR	PREDELLE	DEEENRRV	REVEREND	DEEFFNOR	FOREFEND
	REPELLED	DEEENRST	RENESTED		OFFENDER
DEEELLPT	PELLETED		RESENTED		REOFFEND
DEEELLPX	EXPELLED	DEEENRTT	TENTERED	DEEFFRSU	SUFFERED
DEEELLRT	TELLERED	DEEENRTU	NEUTERED	DEEFGGOR	DEFOGGER
DEEELLRV	REVELLED	DEEENRTX	EXTENDER	DEEFGILR	FLEDGIER
DEEELMOS	SOMEDELE	DEEENRUV	REVENUED	DEEFGINR	FINGERED
DEEELMRT	REMELTED		UNREEVED	DEEFGINS	FEEDINGS
DEEELNPU	UNPEELED	DEEENSSS	SEEDNESS	DEEFGINX	FEDEXING
DEEELNRS	NEEDLERS	DEEENSSY	EYEDNESS	DEEFGIPS	PIGFEEDS
DEEELNRT	RELENTED	DEEENSTT	DETENTES	DEEFGIRT	FIDGETER
DEEELNRU	UNREELED		NEDETTES		REGIFTED
DEEELNSS	LESSENED	DEEENSTU	DETENUES	DEEFGIUW	GUDEWIFE
	NEEDLESS	DEEENSTX	DENTEXES	DEEFGLNU	ENGULFED
	SELDSEEN	DEEENSUV	VENDEUSE	DEEFGLOO	FEELGOOD
DEEELNSU	UNSEELED	DEEEOPRR	PEDERERO	DEEFGLUW	GULFWEED
DEEELNTT	TELNETED	DEEEOPRT	DEPORTEE	DEEFGORR	REFORGED
DEEELNTU	UNDELETE	DEEEORRZ	REZEROED	DEEFGORY	FROGEYED
DEEELOPP	DEPEOPLE	DEEEORST	STEREOED	DEEFHIMU	HUMEFIED
DEEELOPV	DEVELOPE	DEEEORSV	OVERSEED	DEEFHINT	HINDFEET
DEEELPRT	DEPLETER	DEEEORSW	OREWEEDS	DEEFHLOR	FREEHOLD
	PELTERED	DEEEORVY	OVEREYED	DEEFHLRS	FELDSHER
	REPLETED	DEEEOSTV	DEVOTEES	DEEFHORT	FOTHERED
DEEELPST	DEPLETES	DEEEPPPR	PEPPERED	DEEFIILN	FEDELINI
	STEEPLED	DEEEPRSS	SPEEDERS		LENIFIED
DEEELRSS	REDELESS	DEEEPRST	ESTREPED	DEEFIINT	DEFINITE
DEEELRST	DEERLETS		PESTERED	DEEFIIRS	DEIFIERS
	STREELED	DEEEPRSZ	SPREEZED		EDIFIERS
DEEELRTT	LETTERED	DEEEPRTX	EXPERTED		FIRESIDE
DEEELRTW	TWEEDLER	DEEEQRRU	REQUERED	DEEFIIRV	VERIFIED
	WELTERED	DEEEQSUU	DEQUEUES	DEEFILLR	REFILLED
DEEELSSS	SEEDLESS	DEEEQSUZ	SQUEEZED	DEEFILLT	FILLETED
DEEELSSV	VESSELED	DEEERRRT	DETERRER	DEEFILMR	REFILMED
DEEELSSW	WEEDLESS	DEEERRRV	VERDERER	DEEFILMS	MEDFLIES
DEEELSTW	TWEEDLES	DEEERRST	DESERTER	DEEFILNX	INFLEXED
DEEELTVV	VELVETED	DEEERRRV	VERDERER	DEEFILPR	PILFERED
DEEEMNNT	NEEDMENT	DEEERRSV	DESERVER		PREFILED
DEEEMNRS	EMENDERS		RESERVED	DEEFILRS	DEFILERS
DEEEMNSS	DEMESNES		REVERSED		FIELDERS
	SEEDSMEN	DEEERRTV	REVERTED	DEEFILRT	FILTERED
DEEEMPRT	TEMPERED	DEEERSSV	DESERVES	DEEFIMSS	MISFEEDS
DEEEMPTX	EXEMPTED	DEEERSTT	DETESTER	DEEFIMTU	TUMEFIED
DEEEMRRU	MURDEREE		RESETTED	DEEFINRR	INFERRED
DEEEMRSS	DEMERSES		RETESTED	DEEFINRS	DEFINERS
	MEDRESES		SETTERED	DEEFINRZ	FRENZIED
DEEEMRST	DEEMSTER		STREETED	DEEFINSS	FINESSED
		DEEERSTV	REVESTED		

DEEFINST	FENDIEST		RERIGGED	DEEGINRS	DESIGNER
	INFESTED	DEEGGLOR	DOGGEREL		ENERGIDS
DEEFIORS	FORESIDE	DEEGGNOR	ENGORGED		REDESIGN
DEEFIORT	FOETIDER	DEEGGNPU	UNPEGGED		REEDINGS
DEEFIPRR	PREFIRED	DEEGGNTU	NUGGETED		RESIGNED
DEEFIPRX	PREFIXED	DEEGGORR	REGORGED	DEEGINRY	REDYEING
DEEFIRRV	FERVIDER	DEEGGORT	GORGETED	DEEGINSS	DINGESES
DEEFIRST	RESIFTED		TOGGERED		EDGINESS
DEEFIRTT	REFITTED	DEEGGQSU	SQUEGGED		SDEIGNES
DEEFISTT	FETIDEST	DEEGGRRU	RUGGEDER		SEEDINGS
DEEFLLNU	UNFELLED	DEEGHHIR	HIGHERED	DEEGINST	INGESTED
DEEFLLOW	FELLOWED	DEEGHHOP	HEDGEHOP		SIGNETED
DEEFLLRU	FULLERED	DEEGHHSU	SHEUGHED		STEEDING
DEEFLNNU	FUNNELED	DEEGHHUW	WHEUGHED	DEEGINSW	WEEDINGS
DEEFLNOR	ENFOLDER	DEEGHILS	SLEIGHED	DEEGINSX	DESEXING
	FORELEND	DEEGHINR	REHINGED	DEEGINZZ	GIZZENED
DEEFLNSU	NEEDFULS	DEEGHIRR	DREIGHER	DEEGIORT	GOITERED
	UNSELFED	DEEGHIST	HEDGIEST	DEEGIOST	EGOTISED
DEEFLNTU	DEFLUENT	DEEGHITW	WEIGHTED	DEEGIOTZ	EGOTIZED
	UNFELTED	DEEGHLPU	PLEUGHED	DEEGIPRU	PREGUIDE
DEEFLNUX	UNFLEXED	DEEGHNRU	HUNGERED	DEEGIPSW	PIGWEEDS
DEEFLORW	DEFLOWER	DEEGHOPR	GOPHERED	DEEGIRST	DIGESTER
	FLOWERED	DEEGHOPS	SHEEPDOG		ESTRIDGE
	REFLOWED	DEEGHORW	HEDGEROW		REDIGEST
DEEFLOST	FEEDLOTS	DEEGHOSW	HOGWEEDS	DEEGIRSU	GUDESIRE
DEEFLOSY	EYEFOLDS	DEEGHOTT	DOGTEETH	DEEGIRSV	DIVERGES
DEEFLPSU	SPEEDFUL		GHETTOED	DEEGISST	SEDGIEST
DEEFLRRU	FERRULED	DEEGIINN	INDIGENE	DEEGISTW	WEDGIEST
DEEFLRUX	REFLUXED	DEEGIISS	DIEGESIS	DEEGJPRU	PREJUDGE
DEEFMNOR	ENFORMED	DEEGIKST	KEDGIEST	DEEGJRSU	REJUDGES
DEEFMNOT	FOMENTED	DEEGILMO	LIEGEDOM	DEEGKMOS	GEEKDOMS
DEEFMORR	DEFORMER	DEEGILMP	IMPLEDGE	DEEGLLOR	GOLLERED
	REFORMED	DEEGILMT	GIMLETED	DEEGLLRU	GRUELLED
DEEFMORS	FREEDOMS	DEEGILNN	NEEDLING	DEEGLLUY	GULLEYED
DEEFMPRU	PERFUMED	DEEGILNO	ELOIGNED	DEEGLNOR	GOLDENER
DEEFNOOR	FOREDONE		LEGIONED	DEEGLNOU	ENGOULED
DEEFNORZ	DEFROZEN	DEEGILNR	ENGIRDLE	DEEGLNOZ	LOZENGED
DEEFNOST	SOFTENED		LINGERED	DEEGLNRY	LEGENDRY
DEEFNRRU	REFUNDER		REEDLING	DEEGLOPR	PLEDGEOR
DEEFNSST	DEFTNESS	DEEGILNS	SEEDLING	DEEGLOPS	DOGSLEEP
DEEFOORR	REROOFED	DEEGILNT	DELETING	DEEGLORV	GROVELED
DEEFOORS	FOREDOES	DEEGILNU	EUGLENID	DEEGLORW	GLOWERED
DEEFOORT	FOOTERED	DEEGILNV	DEVELING		REGLOWED
	REFOOTED	DEEGILNW	WEDELING	DEEGLOSY	GOLDEYES
DEEFOORW	WOODFREE	DEEGILRS	LEIDGERS	DEEGLPRS	PLEDGERS
DEEFORST	DEFOREST	DEEGILRW	WEREGILD	DEEGLPST	PLEDGETS
	FORESTED	DEEGILRY	GREEDILY	DEEGLRSS	SLEDGERS
	FOSTERED	DEEGILSS	LEGSIDES	DEEGLRSW	WERGELDS
DEEFORTU	FOUTERED	DEEGILST	GELIDEST	DEEGMNOR	MONGERED
DEEFORUY	FOUREYED		LEDGIEST	DEEGMNRU	DUNGMERE
DEEFPRSU	PERFUSED			DEEGMSUW	GUMWEEDS
DEEFRRTU	RETURFED	DEEGIMMR	IMMERGED	DEEGNNOS	ENDOGENS
DEEFRSSU	DEFUSERS	DEEGIMNN	EMENDING	DEEGNNOY	ENDOGENY
DEEGGHHO	HEDGEHOG	DEEGIMNR	REMEDING	DEEGNOPU	GEEPOUND
DEEGGHIP	HEDGEPIG	DEEGIMRU	DEMIURGE	DEEGNORV	GOVERNED
DEEGGIJR	JIGGERED	DEEGINNR	ENRINGED	DEEGNPRU	REPUGNED
	REJIGGED	DEEGINNS	ENSIGNED	DEEGNPUX	EXPUGNED
DEEGGINR	GINGERED	DEEGINNT	TEENDING		EXPUNGED
	NIGGERED	DEEGINNW	ENDEWING	DEEGNRUY	UNGREEDY
	RENIGGED	DEEGINOP	PIGEONED	DEEGNSTU	NUTSEDGE
DEEGGIRR	DREGGIER	DEEGINPS	SPEEDING	DEEGORST	GOSTERED
		DEEGINRR	DERINGER		

DEEGOSTU	OUTEDGES	**DEEHLOSU**	HOUSELED	**DEEIKLNR**	REKINDLE
DEEGOTUW	GOUTWEED	**DEEHLOSV**	SHOVELED		RELINKED
DEEGPRUX	EXPURGED	**DEEHLPPS**	SHLEPPED	**DEEIKLNS**	KNEIDELS
DEEGRRSU	RESURGED	**DEEHLSTU**	SLEUTHED		SILKENED
DEEGRSSW	SWEDGERS	**DEEHMNRS**	HERDSMEN	**DEEIKLNU**	DUNELIKE
DEEGRSTU	GESTURED	**DEEHMNSU**	UNMESHED	**DEEIKLOV**	DOVELIKE
DEEGRTTU	GUTTERED	**DEEHMORT**	MOTHERED	**DEEIKLSW**	SILKWEED
DEEGSSTU	GUSSETED	**DEEHNOPY**	PHONEYED	**DEEIKMSW**	MIDWEEKS
DEEHHIRT	HITHERED	**DEEHNORR**	DEHORNER	**DEEIKMSY**	MISKEYED
DEEHHNPY	HYPHENED	**DEEHNORT**	DETHRONE	**DEEIKNNP**	PINKENED
DEEHHPRS	SHEPHERD		THRENODE	**DEEIKNOT**	DIKETONE
DEEHHRST	THRESHED	**DEEHNOWY**	HONEYDEW	**DEEIKNRS**	DEERSKIN
DEEHHRSU	HUSHERED	**DEEHNPRS**	PREHENDS	**DEEIKNRT**	TINKERED
DEEHIKLR	HERDLIKE	**DEEHNSTU**	ENTHUSED	**DEEIKNTT**	KITTENED
DEEHIKLS	SHEDLIKE	**DEEHOORV**	HOOVERED	**DEEIKOSV**	DOVEKIES
DEEHIKRS	SHREIKED	**DEEHOPRT**	POTHERED	**DEEIKPPR**	KIPPERED
	SHRIEKED	**DEEHORRS**	REDHORSE	**DEEIKRSU**	DUKERIES
DEEHIKSV	KHEDIVES	**DEEHORRT**	DEHORTER	**DEEIKRSV**	SKIVERED
DEEHILNS	ENSHIELD	**DEEHORSU**	REHOUSED	**DEEIKSTT**	DISKETTE
DEEHILRS	HIRSELED	**DEEHORSW**	RESHOWED	**DEEILLMP**	IMPELLED
	RELISHED		SHOWERED		MILLEPED
	SHIELDER	**DEEHORTT**	HOTTERED	**DEEILLNO**	NIELLOED
DEEHILSS	HIDELESS	**DEEHORTX**	EXHORTED	**DEEILLOR**	ORIELLED
DEEHILSV	DISHEVEL	**DEEHPRSY**	SYPHERED	**DEEILLPR**	PERILLED
DEEHIMMS	IMMESHED	**DEEHRRSW**	SHREWDER	**DEEILLRT**	TILLERED
DEEHIMNS	INMESHED	**DEEHRTUW**	WUTHERED		TREDILLE
DEEHIMOP	HEMIPODE	**DEEIIKLT**	TIDELIKE	**DEEILLRV**	RIVELLED
DEEHIMRT	MITHERED	**DEEIILNS**	SIDELINE	**DEEILLVY**	VEILEDLY
DEEHINPR	EPHEDRIN	**DEEIILNT**	TIDELINE	**DEEILLWY**	WILLEYED
DEEHINRR	HINDERER	**DEEIILRV**	LIVERIED	**DEEILMNU**	DEMILUNE
DEEHINRS	DRISHEEN	**DEEIILRW**	WIELDIER	**DEEILMOS**	MELODIES
	RESHINED	**DEEIIMRS**	DIMERISE		MELODISE
DEEHINRT	NITHERED	**DEEIIMRZ**	DIMERIZE	**DEEILMOZ**	MELODIZE
DEEHINST	DISTHENE	**DEEIIMST**	ITEMISED	**DEEILMPT**	IMPLETED
DEEHINTW	WHITENED	**DEEIIMTZ**	ITEMIZED	**DEEILNOS**	ESLOINED
DEEHIORS	HEROISED	**DEEIINOS**	DEIONISE		LESIONED
DEEHIORZ	HEROIZED	**DEEIINOZ**	DEIONIZE	**DEEILNOT**	DELETION
DEEHIOTX	ETHOXIDE	**DEEIINST**	DIETINES		ENTOILED
DEEHIPRS	HESPERID	**DEEIINSX**	ENDEIXIS	**DEEILNPP**	LIPPENED
	PERISHED	**DEEIIPRS**	EPEIRIDS	**DEEILNRR**	REDLINER
DEEHIRRS	REDSHIRE	**DEEIIPRU**	PRIEDIEU	**DEEILNRS**	REDLINES
DEEHIRRT	DITHERER	**DEEIIRSS**	DIERESIS	**DEEILNRU**	UNDERLIE
DEEHIRRW	WHERRIED	**DEEIIRST**	SIDERITE	**DEEILNSS**	IDLENESS
DEEHIRST	DIETHERS	**DEEIIRSV**	DERISIVE		LINSEEDS
DEEHIRSV	SHIVERED	**DEEIIRSW**	WEIRDIES	**DEEILNST**	ENLISTED
	SHRIEVED	**DEEIISSS**	DISSEISE		LINTSEED
DEEHIRSW	SHREWDIE	**DEEIISSW**	SIDEWISE		LISTENED
DEEHIRTW	WITHERED	**DEEIISSX**	DEIXISES		TINSELED
DEEHIRTY	HEREDITY	**DEEIISSZ**	DISSEIZE	**DEEILNSV**	SNIVELED
DEEHKLPS	HELPDESK	**DEEIJKNR**	JINKERED	**DEEILNSY**	DYELINES
DEEHKNOS	KEESHOND	**DEEIJNNO**	ENJOINED	**DEEILNTT**	ENTITLED
DEEHKNRU	HUNKERED	**DEEIJNOR**	REJOINED	**DEEILNUV**	UNLEVIED
DEEHKORS	KOSHERED	**DEEIJRTT**	JITTERED		UNVEILED
DEEHLLOR	HOLLERED	**DEEIKKRY**	YIKKERED	**DEEILOPT**	LEPIDOTE
DEEHLLOV	HOVELLED	**DEEIKLLR**	KILLDEER		PETIOLED
DEEHLMMW	WHEMMLED	**DEEIKLLS**	KILLDEES	**DEEILORT**	DOLERITE
DEEHLMNU	UNHELMED		SKELLIED		LOITERED
DEEHLNPU	UNHELPED	**DEEIKLMO**	DOMELIKE	**DEEILORV**	EVILDOER
DEEHLORV	OVERHELD	**DEEIKLMW**	MILKWEED		OVERIDLE
	VERDELHO	**DEEIKLNN**	ENKINDLE	**DEEILOSS**	OILSEEDS
DEEHLOST	HOSTELED		ENLINKED	**DEEILOTT**	TOILETED

DEEILPPR	LIPPERED	
DEEILPRX	DIPLEXER	
DEEILPSS	SEEDLIPS	
DEEILPST	EPISTLED	
DEEILPSU	EPULIDES	
DEEILPSY	SPEEDILY	
DEEILRRV	DRIVELER	
DEEILRST	RELISTED	
DEEILRSU	LEISURED	
DEEILRSV	DELIVERS	
	DESILVER	
	SILVERED	
	SLIVERED	
DEEILRSW	WIELDERS	
DEEILRSY	YIELDERS	
DEEILRTT	LITTERED	
	RETITLED	
DEEILRVY	DELIVERY	
DEEILSSS	IDLESSES	
DEEILSST	TIDELESS	
DEEILSSV	DEVILESS	
DEEILSTU	DILUTEES	
DEEILSTV	DEVILETS	
DEEILSUV	DELUSIVE	
DEEILSVW	SWIVELED	
DEEILTUY	YULETIDE	
DEEILTWY	TWEEDILY	
DEEIMMNS	ENDEMISM	
DEEIMMOS	SEMIDOME	
DEEIMMRS	IMMERSED	
	SIMMERED	
DEEIMMSS	MISDEEMS	
DEEIMNOR	DOMINEER	
DEEIMNOS	DEMONISE	
	DOMINEES	
DEEIMNOZ	DEMONIZE	
DEEIMNPT	PEDIMENT	
DEEIMNRR	REMINDER	
	REREMIND	
DEEIMNRT	REMINTED	
DEEIMNRV	VERMINED	
DEEIMNSS	DESMINES	
	SIDESMEN	
DEEIMNST	DEMENTIS	
	SEDIMENT	
	TIDESMEN	
DEEIMNSU	SEMINUDE	
DEEIMNTT	MITTENED	
DEEIMORS	EMEROIDS	
DEEIMOST	TEDISOME	
DEEIMPRR	PERIDERM	
	REPRIMED	
DEEIMPRS	DEMIREPS	
	EPIDERMS	
	IMPEDERS	
	PREMISED	
	SIMPERED	
DEEIMPRX	PREMIXED	
DEEIMPSS	SEMIPEDS	
DEEIMRSS	DERMISES	
DEEIMRST	DEMERITS	
	DEMISTER	
	DIMETERS	
	MISTERED	
DEEIMRTT	REMITTED	
DEEIMSSU	MEDIUSES	
DEEINNPR	REPINNED	
DEEINNRS	SINNERED	
DEEINNRT	INDENTER	
	INTENDER	
	INTERNED	
DEEINNRU	UNREINED	
DEEINNRV	INNERVED	
DEEINNST	DENTINES	
	DESINENT	
DEEINNSZ	DENIZENS	
DEEINNTV	INVENTED	
DEEINNTW	ENTWINED	
DEEINNUV	UNENVIED	
	UNVEINED	
DEEINOPS	DISPONEE	
	OPENSIDE	
DEEINORS	INDORSEE	
	ORDINEES	
DEEINORT	ORIENTED	
DEEINORW	IRONWEED	
DEEINOST	SIDENOTE	
DEEINOSV	NOSEDIVE	
DEEINOTV	DENOTIVE	
DEEINPPR	NIPPERED	
DEEINPRS	SPENDIER	
DEEINPSS	DISPENSE	
	PIEDNESS	
DEEINPST	PENTISED	
DEEINPSU	UNESPIED	
DEEINPSW	PINWEEDS	
DEEINQRU	ENQUIRED	
	INQUERED	
DEEINQSU	SEQUINED	
DEEINRRT	INTERRED	
	TRENDIER	
DEEINRRV	REDRIVEN	
DEEINRRW	REWINDER	
DEEINRSS	DIRENESS	
DEEINRST	INSERTED	
	NERDIEST	
	RESIDENT	
	SINTERED	
	TRENDIES	
DEEINRSU	UREDINES	
DEEINRSV	INVERSED	
DEEINRSW	REWIDENS	
	WIDENERS	
DEEINRSX	INDEXERS	
DEEINRTT	RETINTED	
DEEINRTU	RETINUED	
	REUNITED	
DEEINRTV	INVERTED	
DEEINRTW	WINTERED	
DEEINRTX	DEXTRINE	
DEEINSST	DESTINES	
DEEINSSV	VENDISES	
DEEINSSW	DEWINESS	
	WIDENESS	
DEEINSTT	DINETTES	
	INSETTED	
DEEINSTU	DETINUES	
DEEINSTV	EVIDENTS	
	INVESTED	
DEEINSUZ	UNSEIZED	
DEEINTUV	DUVETINE	
DEEINUVW	UNVIEWED	
DEEIOPRT	PERIDOTE	
	PROTEIDE	
DEEIOPRX	PEROXIDE	
DEEIOPSS	EPISODES	
DEEIOPST	EPIDOTES	
	POETISED	
DEEIOPSX	EPOXIDES	
DEEIOPTZ	POETIZED	
DEEIORRV	OVERRIDE	
DEEIORST	EROTISED	
DEEIORSV	OVERSIDE	
DEEIORSW	DOWERIES	
	WEIRDOES	
DEEIORTU	ETOURDIE	
DEEIORTV	OVEREDIT	
DEEIORTZ	EROTIZED	
DEEIORVW	OVERWIDE	
DEEIOTVX	VIDEOTEX	
DEEIPPQU	EQUIPPED	
DEEIPPRZ	ZIPPERED	
DEEIPPST	PEPTIDES	
	PEPTISED	
DEEIPPTT	PIPETTED	
DEEIPPTZ	PEPTIZED	
DEEIPQRU	REPIQUED	
DEEIPQTU	PIQUETED	
DEEIPRRS	PREDRIES	
	PRESIDER	
	REPRISED	
	RESPIRED	
DEEIPRRV	DEPRIVER	
	REPRIVED	
DEEIPRRW	PREWIRED	
DEEIPRRZ	REPRIZED	
DEEIPRSS	DESPISER	
	DISPERSE	
	PRESIDES	
DEEIPRST	PREEDITS	
	PRIESTED	
	RESPITED	
DEEIPRSU	DUPERIES	
DEEIPRSV	DEPRIVES	
	PREVISED	
DEEIPRTT	PITTERED	
	PRETTIED	
DEEIPRTX	EXTIRPED	
DEEIPSSS	DESPISES	
DEEIPSST	DESPITES	
	SIDESTEP	
DEEIPSTT	TEPIDEST	
DEEIPSTU	DEPUTIES	

	DEPUTISE	**DEELLMRU**	MULLERED		EXPLORED
DEEIPTUZ	DEPUTIZE	**DEELLNOP**	POLLENED	**DEELOPRY**	DEPLOYER
DEEIQRRU	REQUIRED	**DEELLNOR**	ENROLLED		REDEPLOY
DEEIQRSU	ESQUIRED		RONDELLE	**DEELOPSV**	DEVELOPS
DEEIQRTU	REQUITED	**DEELLOPR**	REPOLLED	**DEELOPSX**	EXPLODES
DEEIQRUV	QUIVERED	**DEELLORR**	REROLLED	**DEELORRS**	RESOLDER
DEEIQTUU	QUIETUDE	**DEELLORW**	ROWELLED		SOLDERER
DEEIRRSS	DERRISES		WELLDOER	**DEELORSU**	DELOUSER
	DESIRERS	**DEELLORY**	YODELLER		URODELES
	DRESSIER	**DEELLOTW**	TOWELLED	**DEELORSV**	RESOLVED
	RESIDERS	**DEELLOTX**	EXTOLLED	**DEELORSY**	YODELERS
DEEIRRST	DESTRIER	**DEELLOVW**	VOWELLED	**DEELORTT**	DOTTEREL
DEEIRRSU	RUDERIES	**DEELLOVY**	VOLLEYED		TOLTERED
DEEIRRSV	DERIVERS	**DEELLOWY**	YELLOWED	**DEELORTV**	REVOLTED
	REDRIVES	**DEELLPUW**	UPWELLED	**DEELORTW**	TROWELED
DEEIRRTV	DIVERTER	**DEELLRSU**	DUELLERS	**DEELORTY**	DELETORY
	VERDITER	**DEELLRSW**	DWELLERS	**DEELORUV**	LOUVERED
DEEIRRWW	WIREDREW	**DEELLSSW**	WELDLESS	**DEELORVV**	REVOLVED
DEEIRRZZ	RIZZERED	**DEELLSUX**	DUXELLES	**DEELORVW**	OVERLEWD
DEEIRSST	DIESTERS	**DEELMMOP**	POMMELED	**DEELOSSU**	DELOUSES
	EDITRESS	**DEELMMPU**	EMPLUMED	**DEELOSTV**	DOVELETS
	RESISTED		PUMMELED	**DEELOSVV**	DEVOLVES
	SISTERED	**DEELMNOO**	MELODEON	**DEELOTUV**	EVOLUTED
DEEIRSSU	DIURESES	**DEELMNOS**	LODESMEN	**DEELPPRU**	REPULPED
	REISSUED	**DEELMNTU**	UNMELTED	**DEELPRRU**	PRELUDER
	RESIDUES	**DEELMNTW**	WELDMENT	**DEELPRSS**	SPELDERS
DEEIRSSV	DEVISERS	**DEELMOOS**	DOLESOME	**DEELPRSU**	PRELUDES
	DISSERVE	**DEELMOPR**	EMPOLDER		REPULSED
	DISSEVER	**DEELMOPY**	EMPLOYED	**DEELPRTU**	DRUPELET
	DIVERSES	**DEELMORS**	MODELERS	**DEELPRUV**	PULVERED
DEEIRSTT	TIREDEST		MORSELED	**DEELPRUX**	DUPLEXER
DEEIRSTU	ERUDITES		REMODELS	**DEELPSUX**	DUPLEXES
	SURETIED	**DEELMOST**	MOLESTED		EXPULSED
DEEIRSTV	VERDITES	**DEELMOSU**	DUELSOME	**DEELPTTY**	PETTEDLY
DEEIRSTW	WEIRDEST	**DEELMPPU**	PEPLUMED	**DEELRSTU**	DELUSTER
DEEIRTTT	TITTERED	**DEELMPSU**	DEPLUMES		LUSTERED
DEEIRTTV	RIVETTED	**DEELMRUY**	DEMURELY		RESULTED
DEEIRTTW	WITTERED	**DEELNNTU**	TUNNELED		ULSTERED
DEEISSSU	DISEUSES	**DEELNOOS**	LOOSENED	**DEELRSTW**	LEWDSTER
DEEISTTV	VIDETTES	**DEELNORT**	REDOLENT		WRESTLED
DEEJKNTU	JUNKETED		RONDELET	**DEELRSTY**	RESTYLED
DEEJPRRU	PERJURED	**DEELNORV**	OVERLEND	**DEELRSUV**	REVULSED
DEEJPTTU	UPJETTED	**DEELNOSS**	LESSONED	**DEEMMORS**	MESODERM
DEEKKOOY	OKEYDOKE	**DEELNOSU**	ENSOULED	**DEEMMRRU**	DUMMERER
DEEKLNOS	SLOKENED	**DEELNOSY**	ESLOYNED	**DEEMMRSU**	SUMMERED
DEEKLNST	SKLENTED	**DEELNPRS**	RESPLEND	**DEEMNNRU**	UNDERMEN
DEEKLOOR	RELOOKED	**DEELNPRY**	DEPRENYL	**DEEMNNTU**	TENENDUM
DEEKLRSS	SKELDERS	**DEELNPSU**	PENDULES	**DEEMNOOS**	ENDOSOME
DEEKMNOY	MONKEYED	**DEELNRTU**	UNDERLET		MOONSEED
DEEKNNNU	UNKENNED	**DEELNRTY**	TENDERLY	**DEEMNOQU**	QUEENDOM
DEEKNOST	DESKNOTE	**DEELNSSW**	LEWDNESS	**DEEMNORR**	MODERNER
DEEKNOTW	KNOTWEED	**DEELNSTY**	ENSTYLED	**DEEMNORS**	MODERNES
DEEKNOTY	KEYNOTED	**DEELNTTU**	UNLETTED		SERMONED
DEEKNSSW	NEWSDESK	**DEELNWWY**	NEWLYWED	**DEEMNORT**	ENTODERM
DEEKOORR	KOREROED	**DEELOORT**	RETOOLED		MENTORED
DEEKORRW	REWORKED	**DEELOPPR**	LOPPERED	**DEEMNOSS**	DEMONESS
DEEKORST	RESTOKED	**DEELOPRR**	DEPLORER		ENMOSSED
DEEKOSVY	DOVEKEYS	**DEELOPRS**	DEPLORES	**DEEMNOST**	DEMETONS
DEEKRUVY	KURVEYED	**DEELOPRV**	PRELOVED	**DEEMNOSU**	EUDEMONS
DEELLMOR	MODELLER	**DEELOPRW**	REPLOWED	**DEEMOOPR**	PODOMERE
DEELLMOW	MELLOWED	**DEELOPRX**	EXPLODER	**DEEMOORT**	ODOMETER

DEEMOPPY	POMPEYED	**DEENOSST**	STENOSED	**DEEORRTU**	REROUTED
DEEMOPRV	PREMOVED	**DEENPPRS**	PERPENDS		RETOURED
DEEMOPST	DEEPMOST	**DEENPRSS**	SPENDERS	**DEEORRUV**	DEVOURER
DEEMOQRU	QUEERDOM	**DEENPRST**	PRETENDS		OVERRUDE
DEEMORRT	TREMORED	**DEENRRSU**	ENDURERS	**DEEORRVW**	OVERDREW
DEEMORRW	DEWORMER		SUNDERER	**DEEORRVY**	OVERDYER
DEEMORST	MODESTER	**DEENRRTU**	RETURNED	**DEEORSST**	DOSSERET
DEEMORSW	WORMSEED	**DEENRSSU**	RUDENESS		OERSTEDS
DEEMORSX	EXODERMS	**DEENRSTU**	DENTURES	**DEEORSTT**	ROSETTED
DEEMORTU	MOUTERED		SEDERUNT		TETRODES
	UDOMETER		UNDERSET	**DEEORSTX**	DEXTROSE
DEEMPPRU	REPUMPED		UNDESERT	**DEEORSTY**	OYSTERED
DEEMPRST	DEMPSTER		UNRESTED		STOREYED
DEEMPRSU	PRESUMED	**DEENRSUU**	UNDERUSE	**DEEORSUV**	OVERUSED
DEEMPRTU	PERMUTED	**DEENRSUV**	UNSERVED	**DEEORSVY**	OVERDYES
DEEMPSUW	SUMPWEED		UNVERSED	**DEEORTTT**	TOTTERED
DEEMRRRU	DEMURRER	**DEENRTUV**	VENTURED	**DEEORTTX**	EXTORTED
	MURDERER	**DEENSSSY**	SYNDESES	**DEEORTUV**	DEVOUTER
DEEMRSTU	DEMUREST	**DEENSTTU**	UNTESTED	**DEEOSSUX**	EXODUSES
	MUSTERED	**DEENSTUV**	UNVESTED	**DEEOSTUW**	OUTWEEDS
DEEMRTTU	MUTTERED	**DEENTTUV**	UNVETTED	**DEEOSTUX**	TUXEDOES
DEEMSSTY	SYSTEMED	**DEENTTUW**	UNWETTED	**DEEPPRSU**	SUPPERED
DEENNNOP	PENNONED	**DEENTUVW**	DUVETYNE	**DEEPPRTY**	PRETYPED
DEENNNPU	UNPENNED	**DEEOOPPR**	PEREOPOD	**DEEPPSSU**	SPEEDUPS
DEENNOPT	DEPONENT	**DEEOORRV**	OVERDOER	**DEEPRRSU**	PERDURES
DEENNOPU	UNOPENED		OVERRODE	**DEEPRRVY**	REPRYVED
DEENNORS	ENDERONS	**DEEOORSV**	OVERDOES	**DEEPRSTU**	PERTUSED
DEENNORW	RENOWNED		OVERDOSE	**DEEPRSUW**	PURSEWED
DEENNOSS	DONENESS	**DEEOPPRS**	PREPOSED	**DEEPRSUY**	PSEUDERY
DEENNOST	ENDNOTES	**DEEOPPST**	ESTOPPED	**DEEPRTTU**	PUTTERED
	SONNETED	**DEEOPRRR**	PREORDER	**DEEPRUVY**	PURVEYED
DEENNOSY	DOYENNES	**DEEOPRRS**	PEDREROS	**DEERRSSS**	DRESSERS
DEENNOSZ	ENDZONES	**DEEOPRRT**	DEPORTER	**DEERRSUV**	VERDURES
DEENNPST	PENDENTS		PORTERED	**DEERRTTU**	TURRETED
DEENNRTU	UNRENTED		REPORTED	**DEERRTUX**	EXTRUDER
	UNTENDER	**DEEOPRRU**	REPOURED	**DEERSSST**	DESSERTS
DEENNRUV	UNNERVED	**DEEOPRRV**	REPROVED		STRESSED
DEENNSSU	NUDENESS	**DEEOPRRW**	POWDERER	**DEERSSSU**	DURESSES
	UNSENSED	**DEEOPRSS**	DEPOSERS	**DEERSSTU**	RUSSETED
DEENNSTU	UNNESTED	**DEEOPRST**	DOPESTER	**DEERSSTY**	DYESTERS
DEENNTTU	UNNETTED		POSTERED	**DEERSTTU**	TRUSTEED
	UNTENTED		REPOSTED	**DEERSTUV**	VESTURED
DEENNTUV	UNVENTED	**DEEOPRSY**	EYEDROPS	**DEERSTUX**	EXTRUDES
DEENOORT	ENROOTED	**DEEOPRTT**	POTTERED	**DEERSUVY**	SURVEYED
DEENOORV	OVERDONE		REPOTTED	**DEERTTUX**	TEXTURED
DEENOORW	WOODENER	**DEEOPRTW**	POWTERED	**DEFFHILW**	WHIFFLED
DEENOOSV	NOSEDOVE	**DEEOPRTX**	EXPORTED	**DEFFHLSU**	SHUFFLED
DEENOPPR	PREPONED	**DEEOPRUZ**	DOUZEPER	**DEFFHORS**	SHROFFED
DEENOPRR	PONDERER	**DEEOPSST**	POSSETED	**DEFFIINT**	TIFFINED
DEENOPRW	PREOWNED	**DEEOPSSU**	ESPOUSED	**DEFFIIPS**	SPIFFIED
DEENOPSS	SPONDEES	**DEEOPSTU**	OUTSPEED	**DEFFIKLS**	SKIFFLED
DEENOPST	PENTODES	**DEEOQRTU**	REQUOTED	**DEFFILNS**	SNIFFLED
DEENORRS	ENDORSER		ROQUETED	**DEFFILOV**	FIVEFOLD
DEENORRW	WONDERER	**DEEORRRS**	ORDERERS	**DEFFIMOS**	FIEFDOMS
DEENORSS	ENDORSES		REORDERS	**DEFFIORS**	OFFSIDER
DEENORST	ERODENTS	**DEEORRRV**	VERDEROR	**DEFFIOSS**	OFFSIDES
DEENORSW	ENDOWERS	**DEEORRST**	RESORTED	**DEFFIQSU**	SQUIFFED
	REENDOWS		RESTORED	**DEFFIRSU**	DIFFUSER
	WORSENED		ROSTERED	**DEFFISSU**	DIFFUSES
DEENORTU	DEUTERON	**DEEORRSV**	OVERREDS	**DEFFISUX**	SUFFIXED
DEENOSSS	ENDOSSES	**DEEORRTT**	RETORTED	**DEFFLNSU**	SNUFFLED

DEFFLOSU	SOUFFLED	DEFIILOR	OILFIRED	DEFIOPRT	PIEDFORT
DEFFLRTU	TRUFFLED	DEFIILPS	FLIPSIDE		PROFITED
DEFFNORS	FORFENDS	DEFIILRW	WILDFIRE	DEFIORRU	FROIDEUR
DEFFNOSS	SENDOFFS	DEFIILSU	FLUIDISE	DEFIORSU	FOUDRIES
DEFFSSUU	SUFFUSED	DEFIILTY	FIDELITY	DEFIORTU	OUTFIRED
DEFFSTUY	DYESTUFF	DEFIILUZ	FLUIDIZE	DEFIOTXY	DETOXIFY
DEFGGILN	FLEDGING	DEFIIMNO	OMNIFIED	DEFIRRST	DRIFTERS
DEFGHILT	FLIGHTED	DEFIIMNR	INFIRMED	DEFIRSSU	FISSURED
DEFGHIRT	FRIGHTED	DEFIIMNU	MUNIFIED		SURFSIDE
DEFGIIIN	IGNIFIED	DEFIIMOR	MODIFIER	DEFISSTU	FEUDISTS
DEFGIILN	DEFILING	DEFIIMOS	MODIFIES	DEFKLORY	FORKEDLY
	FIELDING	DEFIIMRS	MISFIRED	DEFKNORU	UNFORKED
DEFGIILU	UGLIFIED	DEFIIMSS	FIDEISMS	DEFLLOOR	FOLDEROL
DEFGIINN	DEFINING	DEFIIMSW	MIDWIFES	DEFLLOOW	FOLLOWED
DEFGIINY	DEIFYING	DEFIINOT	NOTIFIED	DEFLMOSS	SELFDOMS
	EDIFYING	DEFIINTU	FINITUDE	DEFLMPRU	FRUMPLED
DEFGIIRR	FRIGIDER	DEFIINTY	IDENTIFY	DEFLNOOU	UNFOOLED
DEFGIIST	DIGESTIF	DEFIIOSS	OSSIFIED	DEFLNOPS	PENFOLDS
DEFGILNU	INGULFED	DEFIIOTV	VIDEOFIT	DEFLNORS	FONDLERS
DEFGILRU	DIRGEFUL	DEFIIPRU	PURIFIED		FORLENDS
DEFGILTY	GIFTEDLY	DEFIIPSS	FISSIPED	DEFLNORU	FLOUNDER
DEFGINSU	DEFUSING	DEFIIPTY	TYPIFIED		UNFOLDER
	FEUDINGS	DEFIIRRT	DRIFTIER	DEFLNOST	TENFOLDS
DEFGINTU	UNGIFTED	DEFIISST	FIDEISTS	DEFLNRUU	UNFURLED
DEFGINUZ	DEFUZING	DEFIITTY	FETIDITY	DEFLNSSU	FUNDLESS
DEFGIOOW	GOODWIFE	DEFILLNU	UNFILLED	DEFLNTUU	UNFLUTED
DEFGIORS	FIREDOGS	DEFILLPU	UPFILLED	DEFLOORS	FLOODERS
DEFGJORU	FORJUDGE	DEFILMNU	FULMINED		FORSLOED
DEFGMOOY	FOGEYDOM		UNFILMED		REFLOODS
DEFGNORU	UNFORGED	DEFILNNO	NINEFOLD	DEFLOORT	FORETOLD
DEFGOOSX	DOGFOXES	DEFILNOR	INFOLDER	DEFLOORV	OVERFOLD
DEFHIIMU	HUMIFIED	DEFILNOU	UNFOILED	DEFLOOSS	FOODLESS
DEFHIINS	FIENDISH	DEFILNRS	FLINDERS	DEFLOOUW	FUELWOOD
	FINISHED	DEFILNRU	UNRIFLED	DEFLOPUW	UPFLOWED
DEFHILLO	LIFEHOLD		URNFIELD	DEFLORSS	FORDLESS
DEFHILSS	DISFLESH	DEFILNRY	FRIENDLY	DEFLORST	TELFORDS
DEFHINSU	UNFISHED	DEFILOPR	PROFILED	DEFLORSU	FOULDERS
DEFHIOOW	WIFEHOOD	DEFILORR	FLORIDER	DEFLPRUU	UPFURLED
DEFHIRST	REDSHIFT	DEFILORU	FLUORIDE	DEFLRSUU	DESULFUR
DEFHLOOS	ELFHOODS	DEFILORV	FRIVOLED		SULFURED
	SELFHOOD	DEFILOTU	OUTFIELD	DEFMNORU	UNFORMED
DEFHLOSU	FLOUSHED	DEFILOTY	FOETIDLY	DEFMOOOR	FOREDOOM
DEFHLSSU	SHEDFULS	DEFILPRU	PRIDEFUL	DEFMORSS	SERFDOMS
DEFHOOOR	FORHOOED	DEFILPTU	UPLIFTED	DEFNNOOR	FORDONNE
DEFHOORS	SERFHOOD	DEFILRRU	FLURRIED	DEFNNORT	FRONDENT
DEFHOORW	FORHOWED	DEFILRVY	FERVIDLY	DEFNNOSS	FONDNESS
DEFIIILV	VILIFIED	DEFILRZZ	FRIZZLED	DEFNNOUW	NEWFOUND
DEFIIIMN	MINIFIED	DEFILSSU	SULFIDES	DEFNOOPS	SPOONFED
DEFIIINS	NIDIFIES	DEFIMNOR	INFORMED	DEFNOORS	FRONDOSE
DEFIIINV	VINIFIED	DEFIMOPR	PEDIFORM	DEFNOORU	UNROOFED
DEFIIIVV	VIVIFIED	DEFIMORY	REMODIFY	DEFNOORV	OVERFOND
DEFIILLN	INFILLED	DEFIMOSW	WIFEDOMS	DEFNOOTU	UNFOOTED
DEFIILLO	OILFIELD	DEFIMRRU	DRUMFIRE	DEFNOPRS	FORSPEND
DEFIILLP	FILLIPED	DEFINNRU	REINFUND	DEFNORRU	FRONDEUR
DEFIILLW	WILDLIFE		UNFRIEND	DEFNORSU	FOUNDERS
DEFIILMR	MIDLIFER	DEFINOPR	FORPINED		REFOUNDS
DEFIILMS	MISFIELD	DEFINORW	FOREWIND	DEFNORTU	FORTUNED
	MISFILED	DEFINRTY	TRENDIFY	DEFNORUV	OVERFUND
DEFIILNO	DIOLEFIN	DEFINSTU	UNSIFTED	DEFNOSSW	DOWFNESS
DEFIILNS	INFIDELS	DEFINTTU	UNFITTED	DEFNPRSU	PREFUNDS
	INFIELDS	DEFIOORW	FIREWOOD	DEFNRRUU	UNDERFUR

Key	Anagram(s)
	UNFURRED
DEFNRTUU	UNTURFED
DEFNTTUU	UNTUFTED
DEFOORRW	FOREWORD
DEFOORST	REDFOOTS
DEFOOSSU	DOOFUSES
DEFOOTUX	OUTFOXED
DEFORRUW	FURROWED
DEFORSST	DEFROSTS
	FROSTEDS
DEFORSTW	FROWSTED
DEGGGIIT	GIGGITED
DEGGGILN	GLEDGING
DEGGHINS	HEDGINGS
DEGGHIRS	DREGGISH
DEGGHLOS	SHOGGLED
DEGGHRSU	SHRUGGED
DEGGIINN	DEIGNING
DEGGILNP	PLEDGING
DEGGILNS	GELDINGS
	SLEDGING
	SNIGGLED
DEGGILNU	DELUGING
DEGGILRW	WRIGGLED
DEGGINNU	UNEDGING
DEGGINRU	UNRIGGED
DEGGINSW	WEDGINGS
DEGGINUW	UNWIGGED
DEGGIORS	DISGORGE
DEGGIOST	DOGGIEST
DEGGIPRS	SPRIGGED
DEGGIRRU	DRUGGIER
DEGGIRST	STRIGGED
DEGGIRSU	DRUGGIES
DEGGLMSU	SMUGGLED
DEGGLNSU	SNUGGLED
DEGGLORS	DOGGRELS
DEGGLORY	GORGEDLY
DEGGLRUY	RUGGEDLY
DEGGNOOR	DOGGONER
DEGGNOOS	DOGGONES
DEGGNORU	UNGORGED
DEGGNOSU	GUDGEONS
DEGGRRSU	DRUGGERS
	GRUDGERS
DEGGRSTU	DRUGGETS
DEGHHILV	HIGHVELD
DEGHIILL	GHILLIED
DEGHIINS	DINGHIES
DEGHIKNT	KNIGHTED
DEGHILNS	HINDLEGS
	SHINGLED
DEGHILOU	OUGHLIED
DEGHILPT	PLIGHTED
DEGHILST	DELIGHTS
	SLIGHTED
DEGHINNS	SHENDING
DEGHINNU	UNHINGED
DEGHIOOS	SHOOGIED
DEGHIOPS	DOGESHIP
DEGHIORU	DOUGHIER
DEGHIPST	DESPIGHT
	SPIGHTED
DEGHIQTU	QUIGHTED
DEGHITTW	TWIGHTED
DEGHLNOR	HORNGELD
DEGHLOOS	DOGHOLES
	GOLOSHED
	SHOOGLED
DEGHLOPU	PLOUGHED
DEGHLORY	HYDROGEL
DEGHLOSU	SLOUGHED
DEGHMOSU	GUMSHOED
DEGHMPRU	GRUMPHED
DEGHNOOS	HOGNOSED
DEGHNORT	THRONGED
DEGHNORY	HYDROGEN
DEGHOOSU	DOGHOUSE
DEGHORRS	DROGHERS
DEGHORTU	TROUGHED
DEGHPSUU	UPGUSHED
DEGIIIRS	RIGIDISE
DEGIIIRZ	RIGIDIZE
DEGIIIST	DIGITISE
DEGIIITZ	DIGITIZE
DEGIIKNS	KINGSIDE
DEGIIKST	KIDGIEST
DEGIILMN	DELIMING
DEGIILNR	GRIDELIN
DEGIILNS	EILDINGS
	SIDELING
DEGIILNT	DILIGENT
DEGIILNV	DEVILING
DEGIILNW	WIELDING
DEGIILNY	YIELDING
DEGIILTU	DIGITULE
DEGIILTY	GELIDITY
DEGIIMNP	IMPEDING
	IMPINGED
DEGIIMNS	DEMISING
DEGIIMST	MIDGIEST
DEGIIMSU	MISGUIDE
DEGIINNR	NIDERING
DEGIINNS	DESINING
	INDIGENS
	SDEINING
DEGIINNT	ENDITING
	INDIGENT
	TEINDING
DEGIINNW	INDEWING
	WIDENING
DEGIINNX	INDEXING
DEGIINNZ	DIZENING
DEGIINOS	INDIGOES
DEGIINOV	VIDEOING
DEGIINRS	DESIRING
	RESIDING
	RINGSIDE
DEGIINRT	DIRIGENT
DEGIINRV	DERIVING
	VIRGINED
DEGIINRW	WEIRDING
DEGIINST	DIETINGS
	DINGIEST
	EDITINGS
	INDIGEST
DEGIINSV	DEVISING
DEGIIRST	RIDGIEST
	RIGIDEST
DEGIISSU	DISGUISE
DEGIJMSU	MISJUDGE
DEGIKKNO	DEKKOING
DEGIKLNU	DUKELING
DEGIKLOV	KIDGLOVE
DEGIKLRU	KLUDGIER
DEGIKNNU	UNKINGED
DEGIKNSS	DESKINGS
DEGILLNU	DUELLING
DEGILLNW	DWELLING
DEGILMNO	MODELING
DEGILMNS	GILDSMEN
DEGILMOS	MISLODGE
DEGILMPS	GLIMPSED
DEGILNNO	OLDENING
DEGILNNS	LENDINGS
DEGILNOP	DELOPING
	DIPLOGEN
DEGILNOS	GLENOIDS
	SIDELONG
DEGILNOW	DOWELING
DEGILNOY	YODELING
DEGILNPS	SPELDING
DEGILNRU	INDULGER
DEGILNRY	YELDRING
DEGILNSU	INDULGES
DEGILNSV	DEVLINGS
DEGILNSW	SWINGLED
	WELDINGS
DEGILNWY	WINGEDLY
DEGILOOR	GOODLIER
DEGILOOY	IDEOLOGY
DEGILORV	OVERGILD
DEGILOST	GODLIEST
	GOLDIEST
DEGILOSZ	GOLDSIZE
DEGILPSU	PULSIDGE
DEGILRRS	GIRDLERS
DEGILRSU	GUILDERS
	SLUDGIER
DEGILRSW	WERGILDS
DEGILRUV	DIVULGER
DEGILRZZ	GRIZZLED
DEGILSUV	DIVULGES
DEGIMMNO	MODEMING
DEGIMNNS	MENDINGS
DEGIMNOS	MENDIGOS
	SMIDGEON
DEGIMNOT	DEMOTING
DEGIMNPU	IMPUGNED
DEGIMNRU	DEMURING
DEGIMNSS	SMIDGENS
DEGIMOOT	GOODTIME
DEGIMOOY	GEOMYOID

DEGIMRSU	SMUDGIER	DEGIORST	DIGESTOR	DEHIIMMS	SHIMMIED
DEGIMNNU	UNENDING		GRODIEST	DEHIIMNS	MINISHED
DEGINNOP	DEPONING		STODGIER	DEHIIMRU	MUDIRIEH
DEGINNOT	DENOTING	DEGIOTUU	OUTGUIDE	DEHIIMST	DITHEISM
DEGINNOV	DOVENING	DEGIPSTU	PUDGIEST		SMITHIED
DEGINNOW	ENDOWING	DEGIQSSU	SQUIDGES	DEHIIMSW	WHIMSIED
DEGINNOZ	DOZENING	DEGIRRTU	TURGIDER	DEHIINNS	SHINNIED
DEGINNPS	SPENDING	DEGIRSTU	DURGIEST	DEHIINNW	WHINNIED
DEGINNPU	UPENDING	DEGISSST	DISGESTS	DEHIINSS	SHINDIES
DEGINNRT	TRENDING	DEGJMNTU	JUDGMENT	DEHIINST	SHINTIED
DEGINNRU	ENDURING	DEGLLNOY	GOLDENLY	DEHIIPSS	SHIPSIDE
	UNRINGED	DEGLLOOP	GOLLOPED	DEHIIRRW	WHIRRIED
DEGINNSS	SENDINGS	DEGLLOSS	GOLDLESS	DEHIIRST	DISHERIT
DEGINNST	STENDING	DEGLMNOT	LODGMENT	DEHIISST	DISHIEST
DEGINNSU	UNSIGNED	DEGLMOOY	DEMOLOGY	DEHIISTT	DITHEIST
DEGINNSV	VENDINGS	DEGLNOOT	GOLDTONE		STITHIED
DEGINNSY	DESYNING	DEGLNOUV	UNGLOVED	DEHIJMNO	DEMIJOHN
DEGINNTU	DETUNING	DEGLNRSU	GRUNDLES	DEHIKLMS	MILKSHED
	UNTINGED	DEGLNRTU	GRUNTLED	DEHIKLOO	HOODLIKE
DEGINNUW	UNWINGED	DEGLOOPR	PROLOGED	DEHIKMOS	SHEIKDOM
DEGINOOR	RODEOING	DEGLOOPY	PEDOLOGY	DEHIKPSU	DUKESHIP
DEGINOPR	PROIGNED	DEGLOOUU	DUOLOGUE	DEHILLOP	PHELLOID
DEGINOPS	DEPOSING	DEGLOPRS	PLEDGORS	DEHILLRS	SHRILLED
	DISPONGE	DEGLOPSS	SPLODGES	DEHILLRT	THRILLED
	PIDGEONS	DEGLPRSU	SPLURGED	DEHILMOS	DEMOLISH
DEGINORR	ORDERING	DEGMMNUU	UNGUMMED	DEHILMPW	WHIMPLED
DEGINORS	NEGROIDS	DEGMOOPR	POGROMED	DEHILMSS	DISHELMS
DEGINORU	GUERIDON	DEGMOOSS	SMOODGES	DEHILMTY	DIMETHYL
DEGINORV	DOVERING	DEGMRSSU	SMUDGERS	DEHILNOR	INHOLDER
	RINGDOVE	DEGNNORU	GROUNDEN	DEHILNOY	HONIEDLY
DEGINORW	DOWERING	DEGNNOSU	DUNGEONS	DEHILNPY	DIPHENYL
DEGINOSW	WENDIGOS	DEGNNOUW	UNGOWNED	DEHILOOR	HELIODOR
	WIDGEONS	DEGNOORS	DRONGOES	DEHILOOS	DHOOLIES
DEGINOTV	DEVOTING	DEGNOOSS	GOODNESS	DEHILOPS	DEPOLISH
DEGINOTX	DETOXING	DEGNOOST	STEGODON		POLISHED
DEGINPRS	SPRINGED	DEGNOPPU	OPPUGNED	DEHILOTY	HOLYTIDE
DEGINPRY	PREDYING	DEGNORRU	GROUNDER	DEHILPRT	PHILTRED
DEGINPSU	DISPUNGE		REGROUND	DEHILPSS	SPLISHED
DEGINPTU	DEPUTING	DEGNORSU	GUERDONS	DEHILPSU	SULPHIDE
DEGINRRS	GRINDERS	DEGNORTU	TRUDGEON	DEHILPSY	SYLPHIDE
	REGRINDS	DEGNORUU	UNROUGED	DEHILRTW	WRITHLED
DEGINRRY	GRINDERY	DEGNORYY	GYRODYNE	DEHILSTW	WHISTLED
	REDRYING	DEGNPRUU	UNPURGED	DEHILSTY	DIETHYLS
DEGINRSS	DRESSING	DEGNRSTU	TRUDGENS	DEHILTTW	WHITTLED
DEGINRST	STRINGED	DEGOORSV	OVERDOGS	DEHIMNOS	HEDONISM
DEGINRSU	GRUNDIES	DEGOORTT	GROTTOED		MONISHED
DEGINRSW	REDWINGS	DEGORSST	STODGERS	DEHIMOPS	HEMIPODS
DEGINRSY	SYNERGID	DEGORSTU	DROGUETS	DEHIMORS	HEIRDOMS
	SYRINGED	DEGPRSUU	UPSURGED	DEHIMOSS	DISHOMES
DEGINSSU	DINGUSES	DEGRRSTU	TRUDGERS	DEHIMOST	ETHMOIDS
DEGINSSW	SWINDGES	DEHHILTW	WITHHELD	DEHIMPRS	SHRIMPED
DEGINSTU	DUNGIEST	DEHHISTW	WHISHTED	DEHIMPSY	DEMYSHIP
DEGINTTU	DUETTING	DEHHLSUY	HUSHEDLY	DEHIMSTU	HUMIDEST
DEGIOORS	GOODSIRE	DEHHMRTY	RHYTHMED	DEHIMSTY	MYTHISED
DEGIOOST	GOODIEST	DEHHOOSW	WHOOSHED	DEHIMTYZ	MYTHIZED
DEGIOPRR	PORRIDGE	DEHIIKLS	DISHLIKE	DEHINOOP	INHOOPED
DEGIOPRT	RIDGETOP	DEHIILLS	HILLSIDE	DEHINOPR	NEPHROID
DEGIOPSS	GOSSIPED		SIDEHILL	DEHINOPS	DIPHONES
DEGIOPST	PODGIEST	DEHIILLW	WHILLIED		SIPHONED
DEGIORRU	GOURDIER	DEHIILNS	LINISHED		SPHENOID
DEGIORRV	OVERGIRD	DEHIILSV	DEVILISH	DEHINORS	HORDEINS

DEHINOST	HEDONIST	DEHMOORS	SHROOMED	DEIILMST	DELIMITS
DEHINPSS	ENDSHIPS	DEHMOORW	WHOREDOM		LIMITEDS
DEHINPSU	PUNISHED	DEHMOOSS	SHMOOSED	DEIILMSU	SEDILIUM
DEHINSUW	UNWISHED		SMOOSHED	DEIILMSV	DEVILISM
DEHIOOST	DHOOTIES	DEHMOOST	SMOOTHED		MIDLIVES
	HOODIEST	DEHMOOSZ	SHMOOZED		MISLIVED
DEHIOOVW	WIVEHOOD	DEHMOPRY	HYPODERM	DEIILMSW	SEMIWILD
DEHIOPRS	SPHEROID	DEHMORUU	HUMOURED	DEIILNNU	INDULINE
DEHIOPRT	TROPHIED	DEHNNTUU	UNHUNTED	DEIILNOS	LIONISED
DEHIORRR	HORRIDER	DEHNOOPU	UNHOOPED	DEIILNOT	TOLIDINE
DEHIORSS	DISHORSE	DEHNOORU	HONOURED	DEIILNOZ	LIONIZED
	HIDROSES	DEHNOOSW	HOEDOWNS	DEIILNPV	VILIPEND
DEHIORTU	OUTHIRED		WOODHENS	DEIILNTT	INTITLED
DEHIORTW	WITHEROD	DEHNOPSY	SYPHONED	DEIILNVY	DIVINELY
	WORTHIED	DEHNORSU	ENSHROUD	DEIILNXY	XYLIDINE
DEHIORTY	THYREOID		HOUNDERS	DEIILOPS	PLOIDIES
DEHIOSSU	DISHOUSE		UNHORSED	DEIILORS	IDOLISER
DEHIOSSW	SIDESHOW	DEHNORSY	ENHYDROS	DEIILORZ	IDOLIZER
DEHIOSTU	HIDEOUTS	DEHNORTY	THRENODY	DEIILOSS	IDOLISES
DEHIPSSU	PSEUDISH	DEHNOSSW	SNOWSHED	DEIILOSZ	IDOLIZES
DEHIQSSU	SQUISHED	DEHNOSTZ	DOZENTHS	DEIILPRT	TRIPLIED
DEHIRRST	REDSHIRT	DEHNOSUU	UNHOUSED	DEIILPSS	SIDESLIP
DEHIRRSU	DHURRIES	DEHNRSTU	THUNDERS	DEIILRST	REDISTIL
DEHIRSTT	THIRSTED	DEHNRSUU	UNRUSHED	DEIILSTU	UTILISED
	THRISTED	DEHNRTUY	THUNDERY	DEIILSTV	LIVIDEST
DEHIRTWW	WITHDREW	DEHOOOPP	POPEHOOD	DEIILTUV	DILUTIVE
DEHKLNOU	ELKHOUND	DEHOOPRT	THEROPOD	DEIILTUY	TUILYIED
DEHKNOOU	UNHOOKED	DEHOOSSW	SWOOSHED	DEIILTUZ	TUILZIED
DEHKNSUU	UNHUSKED	DEHOPRST	POTSHERD		UTILIZED
DEHKOOSS	SKOOSHED	DEHORRST	REDSHORT	DEIIMMRS	DIMERISM
DEHLLOOO	HOLLOOED	DEHORTUY	OUTHYRED	DEIIMMST	MISTIMED
DEHLLOOU	HULLOOED	DEHOSSTU	STOUSHED	DEIIMMTT	IMMITTED
DEHLLOOW	HOLLOWED	DEHPPSTU	SHTUPPED	DEIIMNOS	DOMINIES
DEHLLOPY	PHYLLODE	DEHPRSSU	SPRUSHED	DEIIMNRT	DIRIMENT
DEHLMMOW	WHOMMLED	DEHPRSUU	UPRUSHED	DEIIMNTU	MUTINIED
DEHLMMUW	WHUMMLED	DEHQSSUU	SQUUSHED	DEIIMNUV	VENIDIUM
DEHLMOOT	HOTELDOM	DEHRRSTU	DRUTHERS	DEIIMOSS	DISOMIES
DEHLMORY	HYDROMEL	DEHRSTTU	THRUSTED	DEIIMPRU	PERIDIUM
DEHLMOSU	MUDHOLES	DEIIIMST	DIMITIES	DEIIMPSS	DIMPSIES
DEHLMPSU	SHLUMPED	DEIIINSV	DIVINISE	DEIIMRSV	MISDRIVE
DEHLNOOW	DOWNHOLE	DEIIINVZ	DIVINIZE	DEIIMSST	MISDIETS
DEHLNTUY	HUNTEDLY	DEIIIRRS	IRIDISES		MISEDITS
DEHLOOOW	WOODHOLE	DEIIIRSZ	IRIDIZES	DEIIMSTT	TIMIDEST
DEHLOOPT	POTHOLED	DEIIIRTV	VIRIDITE	DEIIMSVW	MIDWIVES
DEHLOORV	HOLDOVER	DEIIISVV	DIVISIVE	DEIINNOP	PINIONED
	OVERHOLD	DEIIKKLS	DISKLIKE	DEIINNPP	PINNIPED
DEHLOOSS	HOODLESS	DEIIKLMS	MISLIKED	DEIINNTW	INTWINED
	SLOOSHED	DEIIKLNR	KINDLIER	DEIINNUV	UNDIVINE
DEHLOOST	TOEHOLDS	DEIIKLNS	DISLIKEN	DEIINORS	DERISION
	TOOLSHED	DEIIKLNV	DEVILKIN		IRONISED
DEHLOOSW	WOOLSHED	DEIIKLRS	DISLIKER		IRONSIDE
DEHLOPRU	UPHOLDER	DEIIKLSS	DISLIKES		RESINOID
DEHLOPSS	SPLOSHED	DEIIKNST	DINKIEST	DEIINORT	RETINOID
DEHLORSU	SHOULDER	DEIIKSVV	SKIVVIED	DEIINORZ	IRONIZED
DEHLPRUU	UPHURLED	DEIILLMP	MILLIPED	DEIINOST	EDITIONS
DEHLRRSU	HURDLERS	DEIILLMT	TIDEMILL		SEDITION
DEHLRSWY	SHREWDLY	DEIILLST	DILLIEST	DEIINOSV	VISIONED
DEHLSTTU	SHUTTLED	DEIILMMS	SEMIMILD	DEIINOTY	IDONEITY
DEHMMRTU	THRUMMED	DEIILMNS	MIDLINES	DEIINPPW	WINDPIPE
DEHMNOOY	HOMODYNE	DEIILMPR	DIMPLIER	DEIINPRS	INSPIRED
DEHMNRUY	UNRHYMED	DEIILMRU	DELIRIUM	DEIINPRT	INTREPID

DEIINPRY	PYRIDINE	DEIJNORS	JOINDERS	DEILMNOO	MELODION
DEIINPSS	SIDESPIN	DEIJNSSU	DISJUNES	DEILMNSS	MILDNESS
DEIINPTU	UNPITIED	DEIJORRY	JOYRIDER		MINDLESS
DEIINQRU	INQUIRED	DEIJORSY	JOYRIDES	DEILMNSU	MUSLINED
DEIINQSU	QUINSIED	DEIKKLNO	KLONDIKE	DEILMOOT	DOLOMITE
	SQUINIED	DEIKKNNU	UNKINKED	DEILMOPR	IMPLORED
DEIINRSS	INDRISES	DEIKLLOR	LORDLIKE		IMPOLDER
	INSIDERS	DEIKLLSS	DESKILLS	DEILMOPS	IMPLODES
DEIINRST	DISINTER	DEIKLMMS	SKLIMMED	DEILMOPZ	ZOLPIDEM
	INDITERS	DEIKLMNU	UNMILKED	DEILMORU	LEMUROID
	NITRIDES	DEIKLMRU	DRUMLIKE		MOULDIER
	RINDIEST	DEIKLNNU	UNLINKED	DEILMORV	OVERMILD
DEIINRSU	DISINURE	DEIKLNOW	DOWNLIKE	DEILMOSS	MIDSOLES
	URIDINES	DEIKLNPU	UPLINKED	DEILMOST	MELODIST
DEIINRSV	DIVINERS	DEIKLNRS	KINDLERS		MODELIST
DEIINRTU	UNTIDIER	DEIKLNRW	WRINKLED		MOLDIEST
DEIINSST	INSISTED	DEIKLNSS	KINDLESS	DEILMOSU	EMULSOID
	SNIDIEST	DEIKLNTW	TWINKLED	DEILMOTV	DEMIVOLT
	TIDINESS	DEIKLSSS	DISKLESS	DEILMPPU	PLUMIPED
DEIINSTU	DISUNITE	DEIKLSTT	SKITTLED	DEILMPSU	DISPLUME
	NUDITIES	DEIKLSTU	DUSTLIKE		IMPULSED
	UNITISED	DEIKMNOO	KIMONOED	DEILMPTU	MULTIPED
	UNTIDIES	DEIKMOSY	MISYOKED	DEILMRRU	DRUMLIER
DEIINSTV	DIVINEST	DEIKMPRS	SKRIMPED	DEILMRSU	MISRULED
DEIINSTW	WINDIEST	DEIKNNOR	DONNIKER	DEILMSSY	DEMISSLY
DEIINTTU	INTUITED	DEIKNNPU	UNPINKED	DEILMSTU	MUSTELID
DEIINTTY	IDENTITY	DEIKNNRU	UNKINDER	DEILNNOT	INDOLENT
DEIINTUZ	UNITIZED	DEIKNNSS	KINDNESS	DEILNOOS	EIDOLONS
DEIIOPRS	PRESIDIO	DEIKNORV	OVERKIND		SOLENOID
DEIIOPRT	DIPTEROI	DEIKNORW	INWORKED	DEILNOPT	TOPLINED
DEIIOPTY	IDIOTYPE	DEIKNOSS	DOESKINS	DEILNORS	DISENROL
DEIIOPZZ	PEZIZOID	DEIKNRRS	DRINKERS	DEILNOSS	SONDELIS
DEIIORSS	IODISERS	DEIKNRSS	REDSKINS	DEILNOST	LENTOIDS
DEIIORST	DIORITES	DEIKNSSU	UNKISSED	DEILNOSU	DELUSION
DEIIORSX	OXIDISER	DEIKORSS	DROSKIES		INSOULED
DEIIORSZ	IODIZERS	DEIKORST	DORKIEST		UNSOILED
DEIIORTX	TRIOXIDE	DEIKOSSY	DISYOKES	DEILNOTU	OUTLINED
DEIIORTY	IODYRITE	DEIKPRSU	PRUSIKED	DEILNOVV	INVOLVED
DEIIORXZ	OXIDIZER		SPRUIKED	DEILNPRS	SPELDRIN
DEIIOSSX	OXIDISES	DEIKRRSU	SKURRIED		SPINDLER
DEIIOSTT	OTITIDES	DEIKRSVY	SKYDIVER	DEILNPRU	UNDERLIP
DEIIOSXZ	OXIDIZES	DEIKSSTU	DUSKIEST	DEILNPSS	SPELDINS
DEIIPPRR	DRIPPIER	DEIKSSVY	SKYDIVES		SPINDLES
DEIIPPST	DIPPIEST	DEILLMNU	UNMILLED	DEILNPST	SPLINTED
DEIIPRST	RIPTIDES	DEILLNSW	INDWELLS	DEILNRSS	RINDLESS
	SPIRITED	DEILLNTU	UNTILLED	DEILNRST	SNIRTLED
	TIDERIPS	DEILLNUW	UNWILLED		TENDRILS
DEIIPRSZ	DISPRIZE	DEILLOOV	LIVELOOD		TRINDLES
DEIIPTTY	TEPIDITY	DEILLOPW	PILLOWED	DEILNRSW	SWINDLER
DEIIQSTU	DISQUIET	DEILLORR	LORDLIER	DEILNRTU	UNDERLIT
DEIIRRVV	VIVERRID	DEILLORS	DOLLIERS	DEILNRTY	TRENDILY
DEIIRSSU	DIURESIS	DEILLORT	TROLLIED	DEILNSST	DINTLESS
DEIIRSTT	DIRTIEST	DEILLORU	LOUDLIER	DEILNSSV	VILDNESS
	TRITIDES	DEILLOSV	LIVELODS	DEILNSSW	SWINDLES
DEIISSTT	DIETISTS	DEILLOWW	WILLOWED		WILDNESS
	DITSIEST	DEILLPRR	PREDRILL		WINDLESS
DEIISTTZ	DITZIEST	DEILLRRS	DRILLERS	DEILNSTU	DILUENTS
DEIISTVV	DIVVIEST		REDRILLS		INSULTED
	VIVIDEST	DEILLRSV	DREVILLS		UNLISTED
DEIISTZZ	DIZZIEST	DEILLSTU	DUELLIST	DEILNTTU	UNTILTED
DEIJNNOU	UNJOINED		DULLIEST		UNTITLED

DEILNTUY	UNITEDLY	DEIMMOOV	MOVIEDOM	DEIMPSTY	MISTYPED
DEILNUWY	UNWIELDY	DEIMMOST	IMMODEST	DEIMQRSU	SQUIRMED
DEILOOPS	POOLSIDE	DEIMMOSV	MISMOVED	DEIMRSSU	SURMISED
DEILOOPW	WOODPILE	DEIMMPST	MISDEMPT	DEIMRSTU	DIESTRUM
DEILOORR	DROOLIER	DEIMMRST	MIDTERMS	DEIMRSUU	RESIDUUM
DEILOPPY	POLYPIDE		STRIMMED	DEINNNOU	INNUENDO
DEILOPRS	LEPORIDS	DEIMMRSU	DRUMMIES	DEINNNPU	UNPINNED
DEILOPRU	PRELUDIO	DEIMMSTU	DUMMIEST	DEINNNSU	NUNDINES
DEILOPSS	DESPOILS		SUMMITED	DEINNNTU	UNTINNED
	DIPLOSES	DEIMNNOS	MISDONNE	DEINNOOT	NOONTIDE
	SOLIPEDS	DEIMNNOU	UNMONIED	DEINNOPT	ENDPOINT
DEILOPST	PISTOLED	DEIMNNSU	MINUENDS	DEINNORS	ENDIRONS
	POSTILED	DEIMNOOS	DOMINOES	DEINNORT	INDENTOR
DEILOPSU	EUPLOIDS		MONODIES	DEINNORU	UNIRONED
DEILOPUY	EUPLOIDY	DEIMNOOT	DEMOTION	DEINNOWW	WINNOWED
DEILOQRU	LIQUORED		MOTIONED	DEINNPRU	UNDERPIN
DEILORRW	LOWRIDER	DEIMNOOX	MONOXIDE	DEINNRSU	UNRINSED
DEILORSS	SOLDIERS	DEIMNOPT	PIEDMONT	DEINNRTU	INTURNED
DEILORST	STOLIDER	DEIMNORT	DORMIENT	DEINNRUU	UNINURED
DEILORSU	SOULDIER	DEIMNOST	DEMONIST	DEINNRUV	UNDRIVEN
DEILORSY	SOLDIERY	DEIMNOTW	DOWNTIME	DEINNRUW	UNWINDER
DEILORTY	ELYTROID	DEIMNOWW	WIDOWMEN	DEINNSTU	DUNNIEST
DEILOSST	SOLIDEST	DEIMNPRU	UNPRIMED		DUNNITES
DEILOSSV	DISSOLVE	DEIMNPSS	MISSPEND	DEINNTUU	UNUNITED
DEILOSTT	DOILTEST	DEIMNPTU	IMPUDENT	DEINNTUW	UNTWINED
DEILOSTU	SOLITUDE	DEIMNRTU	RUDIMENT	DEINOOPS	POISONED
	TOLUIDES		UNMITRED	DEINOOPT	OPTIONED
DEILOSTW	DOWLIEST	DEIMNSSS	MISSENDS	DEINOOPW	PINEWOOD
DEILOSVW	OLDWIVES	DEIMNSST	MINDSETS	DEINOOSU	IDONEOUS
DEILOTUV	OUTLIVED		MISTENDS	DEINOOSZ	OZONIDES
DEILOTUW	OUTWILED	DEIMNSSU	UNMISSED		OZONISED
DEILOTUY	OUTYIELD	DEIMNSSW	MISWENDS	DEINOOTV	DEVOTION
DEILPPRT	TRIPPLED	DEIMNSTU	MISTUNED	DEINOOZZ	OZONIZED
DEILPPST	STIPPLED	DEIMOORS	MOIDORES	DEINOPPR	PROPINED
DEILPPSU	SUPPLIED	DEIMOOSS	SODOMIES	DEINOPPW	DOWNPIPE
DEILPPTU	PULPITED		SODOMISE	DEINOPRS	DISPONER
DEILPRSS	DRIPLESS	DEIMOOST	DOOMIEST		POINDERS
DEILPRSU	SERPULID		MOODIEST		PRISONED
DEILPSTT	SPLITTED		SODOMITE	DEINOPRT	DIPTERON
DEILPSTU	STIPULED	DEIMOOSZ	SODOMIZE	DEINOPRU	INPOURED
DEILPSUY	SPULYIED	DEIMOPRS	IMPEDORS	DEINOPRV	PROVINED
DEILPSUZ	SPULZIED		PROMISED	DEINOPRY	PYRENOID
DEILPTTU	UPTILTED	DEIMOPRT	IMPORTED	DEINOPSS	DISPONES
DEILRRSU	SLURRIED	DEIMOPRV	IMPROVED		DOPINESS
DEILRSSY	DRESSILY	DEIMOPST	IMPOSTED		SPINODES
DEILRSTU	DILUTERS	DEIMORRR	MIRRORED	DEINOPSU	UNPOISED
	LURIDEST	DEIMORRS	MISORDER	DEINOPTW	DEWPOINT
	STUDLIER		MORRISED	DEINORRS	INDORSER
DEILRSVY	DIVERSLY	DEIMORSS	MISDOERS	DEINORSS	INDORSES
DEILRSZZ	DRIZZLES	DEIMORST	MORTISED		SORDINES
DEILRTVY	DEVILTRY	DEIMORSU	DIMEROUS	DEINORST	DRONIEST
DEILSSTU	DUELISTS		ERODIUMS	DEINORSU	DOURINES
DEILSSTY	DISTYLES		SOREDIUM		SOURDINE
	STYLISED	DEIMORSV	MISDROVE	DEINORSW	DISOWNER
DEILSSUV	DIVULSES	DEIMORUX	EXORDIUM		WINDORES
DEILSTUY	SEDULITY	DEIMOSST	DISTOMES	DEINORTT	INTORTED
DEILSTYZ	STYLIZED		MODISTES	DEINORVW	OVERWIND
DEILSWZZ	SWIZZLED	DEIMOSTT	DEMOTIST	DEINOSST	DONSIEST
DEILTWZZ	TWIZZLED	DEIMPRST	DIREMPTS	DEINOSSV	VOIDNESS
DEIMMNOO	OMNIMODE	DEIMPSTU	DUMPIEST	DEINOSSZ	DOZINESS
DEIMMNOS	DEMONISM		DUMPSITE	DEINOSTW	DOWNIEST

DEINOSWZ	DOWNSIZE	**DEIORRSY**	DERISORY	**DEKLSTTU**	SKUTTLED
DEINOTTU	DUETTINO	**DEIORRTU**	OUTRIDER	**DEKMNOSU**	UNSMOKED
DEINOTUV	INDEVOUT	**DEIORRTW**	WORRITED	**DEKMPRSU**	SKRUMPED
DEINPPRU	UNRIPPED	**DEIORRZZ**	RIZZORED	**DEKNNOSS**	NONSKEDS
DEINPPTU	UNTIPPED	**DEIORSSS**	DOSSIERS	**DEKNORUW**	UNWORKED
DEINPPUZ	UNZIPPED	**DEIORSST**	STEROIDS	**DEKNRSTU**	DRUNKEST
DEINPRST	SPRINTED	**DEIORSSU**	DESIROUS	**DEKNRSUY**	UNDERSKY
DEINPRTU	TURNIPED	**DEIORSSV**	DEVISORS	**DEKNSSSU**	DUSKNESS
DEINPRUZ	UNPRIZED	**DEIORSTT**	DORTIEST	**DEKOOPRV**	PROVOKED
DEINPSST	STIPENDS	**DEIORSTU**	IODURETS	**DEKOOTWW**	KOWTOWED
DEINPTTU	INPUTTED		OUTRIDES	**DEKOPSST**	DESKTOPS
	UNPITTED		OUTSIDER	**DEKORSWY**	KEYWORDS
DEINQSTU	SQUINTED		SUITORED	**DEKPRSSU**	PREDUSKS
DEINRRTU	INTRUDER	**DEIORSTW**	ROWDIEST	**DELLLOOP**	LOLLOOP
DEINRSSU	INSUREDS		WORDIEST	**DELLMOOS**	MODELLOS
	SUNDRIES	**DEIORSWW**	WIDOWERS	**DELLMOSW**	SWELLDOM
DEINRSTT	STRIDENT	**DEIORTTX**	TETROXID	**DELLMOSY**	SELDOMLY
	TRIDENTS	**DEIORTUV**	OUTDRIVE	**DELLNOPU**	UNPOLLED
DEINRSTU	INTRUDES	**DEIOSSTU**	OUTSIDES	**DELLNORU**	UNROLLED
	NURDIEST	**DEIOSSTX**	EXODISTS	**DELLNORW**	ROWNDELL
DEINRSTX	DEXTRINS	**DEIOSTTT**	DOTTIEST	**DELLNPUU**	UNPULLED
DEINRTUW	UNDERWIT	**DEIOSTUW**	WIDEOUTS	**DELLOPRS**	REDPOLLS
DEINSSST	DISNESTS	**DEIOSTUZ**	OUTSIZED	**DELLOPRU**	UPROLLED
	DISSENTS	**DEIPPRRS**	DRIPPERS	**DELLOPTU**	POLLUTED
DEINSSSY	SYNDESIS	**DEIPPRST**	STRIPPED	**DELLORRY**	DROLLERY
DEINSSTT	DENTISTS	**DEIPPTTU**	TITUPPED	**DELLORSS**	LORDLESS
DEINSSTU	DISTUNES	**DEIPRRTU**	IRRUPTED	**DELLORST**	DROLLEST
DEINSSUU	UNISSUED		PUTRIDER		STROLLED
DEINSTUU	UNSUITED	**DEIPRSSU**	DISPURSE	**DELLOSTY**	OLDSTYLE
DEINTTUW	UNWITTED		SUSPIRED	**DELLOSVW**	LOWVELDS
DEIOOPRR	DROOPIER	**DEIPRSTU**	DISPUTER	**DELLOTUW**	OUTDWELL
DEIOORSS	ODORISES		STUPIDER	**DELLRSWY**	DRYWELLS
DEIOORSW	WOODSIER	**DEIPRSTZ**	SPRITZED	**DELMNOOV**	NOVELDOM
DEIOORSZ	ODORIZES	**DEIPSSTU**	DISPUTES	**DELMNORY**	MODERNLY
DEIOOSSS	ISODOSES		PUDSIEST	**DELMNOSU**	UNSELDOM
DEIOOSST	OSTEOIDS	**DEIPTTTU**	TITTUPED	**DELMNOTW**	MELTDOWN
DEIOOSTW	WOODIEST	**DEIQRRSU**	SQUIRRED	**DELMNPUU**	PENDULUM
DEIOOSVV	VOIVODES	**DEIQRSTU**	SQUIRTED		UNPLUMED
DEIOOSWW	WOIWODES	**DEIRRSST**	STRIDERS	**DELMOOSW**	ELMWOODS
DEIOPRRV	PROVIDER	**DEIRRSTU**	STURDIER	**DELMOPRS**	PREMOLDS
DEIOPRSS	DISPOSER	**DEIRSSST**	DISSERTS	**DELMORSS**	SMOLDERS
	DROPSIES		DISTRESS	**DELMORSU**	MOULDERS
DEIOPRST	DIOPTERS	**DEIRSSTU**	DIESTRUS		REMOULDS
	DIOPTRES		DRUSIEST		SMOULDER
	DIPTEROS		STUDIERS	**DELMOSTY**	MODESTLY
	PERIDOTS		STURDIES	**DELMRTUU**	MULTURED
	PORTSIDE	**DEIRSSUY**	DYSURIES	**DELMTTUU**	TUMULTED
	PROTEIDS	**DEIRSTTU**	DETRITUS	**DELNOOSU**	NODULOSE
	RIPOSTED	**DEIRSTUX**	DRUXIEST		UNLOOSED
	TOPSIDER	**DEIRSUVV**	SURVIVED	**DELNOOSZ**	SNOOZLED
DEIOPRSV	DISPROVE	**DEISSSTU**	SUDSIEST	**DELNOOWY**	WOODENLY
	PROVIDES	**DEISSTTU**	DUSTIEST	**DELNOPPU**	UNLOPPED
DEIOPRSW	DROPWISE	**DEISTTTU**	DUETTIST	**DELNOPRS**	SPLENDOR
DEIOPRSX	PEROXIDS	**DEJLOOOR**	JORDELOO	**DELNOPUW**	UNPLOWED
DEIOPSSS	DISPOSES	**DEJOOPPY**	POPJOYED	**DELNORSU**	LOUNDERS
DEIOPSST	DEPOSITS	**DEKKLNOY**	KLONDYKE		NOURSLED
	TOPSIDES	**DEKKNSTU**	STUKKEND		ROUNDELS
DEIOPSTV	POSTDIVE	**DEKKSSTT**	TSKTSKED		ROUNDLES
DEIORRRT	TORRIDER	**DEKLNOOU**	UNLOOKED		UNSOLDER
DEIORRSS	DROSSIER	**DEKLOOPU**	UPLOOKED	**DELNORTU**	ROUNDLET
DEIORRSW	DROWSIER	**DEKLRSSU**	SKUDLERS		

DELNORYY	YONDERLY	DEMNOORU	UNMOORED	DENORRSU	RONDURES
DELNOSSU	LOUDNESS	DEMNOOSS	ENDOSMOS		ROUNDERS
DELNOSSW	DOWNLESS	DEMNOOSW	SNOWDOME		UNORDERS
DELNOSTW	LETDOWNS		WOODSMEN	DENORRSW	DROWNERS
DELNOSUU	UNDULOSE	DEMNORST	MORDENTS	DENORRTU	ROTUNDER
	UNSOULED	DEMNORSW	SWORDMEN	DENORRUU	ROUNDURE
DELNOSUV	UNSOLVED	DEMNORSY	SYNDROME	DENORSSU	DOURNESS
DELNOTWY	WONTEDLY	DEMNORUW	UNWORMED		RESOUNDS
DELNPRSU	PLUNDERS	DEMNOSTU	DEMOUNTS		SOUNDERS
DELNRRTU	TRUNDLER		MUDSTONE	DENORSTU	ROUNDEST
DELNRSTU	RUNDLETS	DEMOOPPS	POPEDOMS		TONSURED
	TRUNDLES	DEMOOPRR	PRODROME		UNSORTED
DELNSUZZ	SNUZZLED	DEMOOPRS	PREDOOMS	DENORSTY	DRYSTONE
DELOOORW	WOODLORE	DEMOOPRT	PROMOTED	DENORSUU	UNROUSED
DELOOPPS	PLEOPODS	DEMOORST	DOOMSTER		UNSOURED
DELOORRV	OVERLORD	DEMOORSU	DORMOUSE	DENORSUW	WOUNDERS
DELOORRW	WORDLORE	DEMOORTY	ODOMETRY	DENORTTU	UNROTTED
DELOORSS	DOORLESS	DEMOOSTU	OUTMODES	DENORTUW	UNDERTOW
	LORDOSES	DEMOOTUV	OUTMOVED	DENOSSTU	SOUNDEST
	ODORLESS	DEMOPPRT	PROMPTED	DENOSTUW	UNSTOWED
DELOORSV	OVERSOLD	DEMOPSSU	POSSUMED	DENOTUUV	UNDEVOUT
DELOORSW	WOOLDERS	DEMORRUU	RUMOURED	DENPRSTU	UPTRENDS
DELOORTY	ROOTEDLY	DEMORTUY	UDOMETRY	DENPRSUU	UNPURSED
DELOORUV	OVERLOUD	DEMPRSTU	DUMPSTER	DENPRTUU	UPTURNED
DELOOSSW	WOODLESS	DENNNSUU	UNSUNNED	DENPSSSU	SUSPENDS
DELOOTUV	OUTLOVED	DENNOOOZ	ENDOZOON	DENRRTUU	NURTURED
DELOPPRS	DROPPLES	DENNOOWZ	DOWNZONE	DENRSSSU	SUNDRESS
DELOPPST	STOPPLED	DENNORST	TENDRONS	DENRSTTU	STRUNTED
DELOPPSY	POLYPEDS	DENNORSU	ENROUNDS	DENRSTUU	UNRUSTED
DELOPRST	DROPLETS	DENNOSTU	UNSTONED	DENSSTTU	STUDENTS
DELOPRSU	POULDERS	DENNOSTY	SYNDETON	DENSTTUY	STUDENTY
	POULDRES	DENNOTUW	UNWONTED	DENSTUVY	DUVETYNS
DELOPSTU	POSTLUDE	DENNPRUU	UNPRUNED	DEOOORSW	ROSEWOOD
DELORSST	OLDSTERS	DENNRRUU	UNDERRUN	DEOOOSWW	WOODWOSE
	STRODLES	DENNRTUU	UNTURNED	DEOOPPRS	PROPOSED
DELORSSW	WORDLESS	DENNRTUY	UNTRENDY	DEOOPPRT	PTEROPOD
DELORSTT	DOTTRELS	DENOOORT	OREODONT	DEOOPRRV	PROVEDOR
DELORSUV	SOURVELD	DENOOOTW	WOODNOTE	DEOOPRST	DOORSTEP
DELORSUY	DELUSORY		WOODTONE		TORPEDOS
DELOSSUU	SEDULOUS	DENOOOVW	OVENWOOD	DEOOPRTU	UPROOTED
DELOSTTT	DOTTLEST	DENOOPPR	PROPONED	DEOOPWWW	POWWOWED
DELOSTTY	SOTTEDLY	DENOOPRS	PRODNOSE	DEOORRST	REDROOTS
DELOSTUU	OUTDUELS	DENOOPSY	POYSONED	DEOORRSW	SORROWED
DELOSTUW	WOULDEST	DENOORRS	ENDORSOR	DEOORRVW	OVERWORD
DELOTTUW	OUTDWELT	DENOORTU	UNROOTED	DEOORRWW	OWREWORD
DELOTUVY	DEVOUTLY	DENOORTX	NEXTDOOR	DEOORSTU	OUTDOERS
DELPSTUU	PUSTULED	DENOOSSW	WOODNESS	DEOORTUV	OUTDROVE
DELRSSTU	STRUDELS	DENOOSTU	DUOTONES	DEOORTUW	OUTROWED
DELSSSSU	SUDSLESS	DENOPPRS	PROPENDS	DEOOTTUV	OUTVOTED
DELSSSTU	DUSTLESS	DENOPRSS	RESPONDS	DEOPPRRS	DROPPERS
DEMMNOOO	MONOMODE	DENOPRST	PORTENDS	DEOPPRST	STROPPED
DEMMNOOS	DOOMSMEN		PROTENDS	DEOPPRSU	PURPOSED
DEMMNOSU	SUMMONED	DENOPRSU	POUNDERS	DEOPPSSU	SUPPOSED
DEMMNSUU	UNSUMMED	DENOPRSV	PROVENDS	DEOPRRTU	PROTRUDE
DEMMRRSU	DRUMMERS	DENOPRUV	UNPROVED	DEOPRSTU	POSTURED
DEMMRRUU	MURMURED	DENOPSTU	OUTSPEND		PROUDEST
DEMMRSTU	STRUMMED		UNPOSTED		SPROUTED
DEMNNOSU	SOUNDMEN	DENOPSTW	STEWPOND	DEOPRSUU	POURSUED
DEMNOOOP	MONOPODE	DENOPSUX	EXPOUNDS		UPROUSED
DEMNOOPT	TOMPONED	DENOPTTU	UNPOTTED	DEOPSSTU	UPTOSSED
DEMNOORS	DOORSMEN	DENOQTUU	UNQUOTED	DEORRSST	RODSTERS

DEORRSSW	SWORDERS	**DFILNOPS**	PINFOLDS	**DGHILNNO**	HONDLING
DEORRSTU	DETRUSOR	**DFILORSU**	FLUORIDS	**DGHILNOS**	HOLDINGS
DEORRTTU	TORTURED	**DFIMOOOR**	IODOFORM	**DGHILNRU**	HURDLING
DEORSSTU	OUTDRESS	**DFIMOOSS**	FOODISMS	**DGHILNSY**	HYLDINGS
DEORSSTW	WORSTEDS	**DFIMORSS**	DISFORMS	**DGHILOOR**	GIRLHOOD
DEORSSTY	DESTROYS	**DFINOSTU**	OUTFINDS	**DGHILPSY**	DIGLYPHS
DEORSSUV	OVERSUDS	**DFINRSUW**	WINDSURF	**DGHINNOU**	HOUNDING
DEORSTTU	STROUTED	**DFIOOPRS**	DISPROOF	**DGHINNSU**	DUNSHING
DEORSTUU	OUTDURES	**DFIOORSW**	FIRWOODS	**DGHINNUZ**	NUDZHING
DEORSTUV	OVERDUST	**DFKMMOPU**	DUMMKOPF	**DGHINOSW**	SHOWDING
DEORSTUX	DEXTROUS	**DFLMOSUW**	MUDFLOWS	**DGHINOWY**	HOWDYING
DEOSSSYY	ODYSSEYS	**DFLNOOWW**	DOWNFLOW	**DGHINSTU**	HINDGUTS
DEOSSTTU	TESTUDOS	**DFLOORUU**	ODOURFUL		UNDIGHTS
DEPPSSSY	DYSPEPSY	**DFLOOSTU**	FOLDOUTS	**DGHIOORS**	DROOGISH
DEPRRTUU	RUPTURED	**DFLOOSTW**	TWOFOLDS	**DGHIOPSS**	DOGSHIPS
DEQRSUUY	SURQUEDY	**DFLOPRUU**	PROUDFUL		GODSHIPS
DERSTTTU	STRUTTED	**DFNOOPRU**	PROFOUND	**DGHNOTUU**	DOUGHNUT
DFFGINSU	DUFFINGS	**DFNOORSU**	FRONDOUS	**DGHOOOTT**	DOGTOOTH
DFFIILUY	FLUIDIFY	**DFNOOTUU**	OUTFOUND	**DGHORRUY**	ROUGHDRY
DFFIIMRS	MIDRIFFS	**DFOOOORW**	WOODROOF	**DGHORSTU**	DROUGHTS
DFFIIRST	TRIFFIDS	**DFOOOSTW**	SOFTWOOD	**DGHORTUY**	DROUGHTY
DFFIIRTY	TRIFFIDY	**DGGGIINS**	DIGGINGS	**DGIIIMRS**	DIRIGISM
DFFIORSU	DIFFUSOR	**DGGGINOS**	DOGGINGS	**DGIIINNT**	INDITING
DFFLOORU	FOURFOLD	**DGGGINRU**	DRUGGING	**DGIIINNV**	DIVINING
DFFOORUW	WOODRUFF		GRUDGING	**DGIIINOS**	IODISING
DFFOSSTU	DUSTOFFS	**DGGHIINT**	DIGHTING	**DGIIINOZ**	IODIZING
DFGGHIOT	DOGFIGHT	**DGGIILNR**	GIRDLING	**DGIIIRTY**	RIGIDITY
DFGGIINR	FRIDGING		RIDGLING	**DGIIKLNN**	KINDLING
DFGHILOS	GOLDFISH	**DGGIILNS**	GILDINGS	**DGIIKLNS**	KIDLINGS
DFGIIIRY	RIGIDIFY		GLIDINGS	**DGIIKNNR**	DRINKING
DFGIILRY	FRIGIDLY	**DGGIINNO**	DINGOING	**DGIILLNR**	DRILLING
DFGIINNS	FINDINGS	**DGGIINNR**	GRINDING	**DGIILLNS**	DILLINGS
DFGIINRT	DRIFTING	**DGGIINNW**	WINGDING	**DGIILLNU**	ILLUDING
DFGILNNO	FONDLING	**DGGIINNY**	DINGYING	**DGIILLNW**	WILDLING
DFGILNOO	FLOODING	**DGGIINRS**	GIRDINGS	**DGIILLOU**	LIGULOID
DFGILNOS	FOLDINGS		RIDGINGS	**DGIILMNP**	DIMPLING
DFGINNOU	FONDUING	**DGGIINSU**	GUIDINGS	**DGIILNNN**	DINNLING
	FOUNDING	**DGGIKLNU**	KLUDGING	**DGIILNNP**	PINDLING
DFGINNSU	FUNDINGS	**DGGILNOP**	PLODGING	**DGIILNNW**	WINDLING
DFGINOOR	FORDOING	**DGGILNOS**	GODLINGS	**DGIILNNY**	INDIGNLY
DFGINOSU	FUNGOIDS		LODGINGS	**DGIILNOR**	DROILING
DFGMOOSY	FOGYDOMS	**DGGILNSU**	SLUDGING	**DGIILNOS**	DISLOIGN
DFHIIMUY	HUMIDIFY	**DGGIMNSU**	SMUDGING	**DGIILNPS**	DISPLING
DFHILSSU	DISHFULS	**DGGINNOO**	NOODGING	**DGIILNSS**	SLIDINGS
DFHIMRSU	DRUMFISH	**DGGINNSU**	SNUDGING	**DGIILNSW**	WILDINGS
DFHINOOT	HINDFOOT	**DGGINOST**	STODGING	**DGIILNTU**	DILUTING
DFHINOPS	FISHPOND	**DGGINRTU**	TRUDGING	**DGIIMMNS**	DIMMINGS
DFHISSTU	STUDFISH	**DGGIRSTU**	DRUGGIST	**DGIIMNNS**	MINDINGS
DFHLOOOT	FOOTHOLD	**DGHHOOOS**	HOGHOODS	**DGIIMNOS**	MISDOING
DFHNOOUX	FOXHOUND	**DGHIILNS**	HIDLINGS	**DGIIMNOU**	GONIDIUM
DFIIINVY	DIVINIFY		HILDINGS	**DGIIMNSS**	SMIDGINS
DFIILMTU	MULTIFID	**DGHIIMNT**	MIDNIGHT	**DGIIMOSS**	SIGMOIDS
DFIILOSY	SOLIDIFY	**DGHIIMST**	MISDIGHT	**DGIIMPUY**	PYGIDIUM
DFIILTUY	FLUIDITY	**DGHIINNW**	HINDWING	**DGIINNOP**	POINDING
DFIINPRT	DRIFTPIN	**DGHIINPS**	SPHINGID	**DGIINNOR**	NONRIGID
DFIKNOOS	SKINFOOD	**DGHIINRT**	THIRDING	**DGIINNOW**	INDOWING
DFILLOOT	FLOODLIT	**DGHIINSS**	DISHINGS	**DGIINNRW**	WINDRING
DFILLORY	FLORIDLY		SHINDIGS	**DGIINNSS**	SINDINGS
DFILLOWW	WILDFOWL	**DGHIISST**	DISSIGHT	**DGIINNSW**	WINDINGS
DFILMMOS	FILMDOMS	**DGHIKNOO**	KINGHOOD	**DGIINORR**	GRIDIRON
DFILNNOU	NONFLUID	**DGHILLNU**	DUNGHILL	**DGIINORS**	DORISING

DGIINORT	DIGITRON		UNDOINGS	DHIIOPSX	XIPHOIDS
DGIINORZ	DORIZING	DGINNOSW	SOWNDING	DHIIORSS	HIDROSIS
DGIINOSV	VOIDINGS	DGINNOUW	WOUNDING	DHIIORSZ	RHIZOIDS
DGIINOSW	WINDIGOS	DGINNSSY	SYNDINGS	DHIIPSST	DIPSHITS
DGIINOSX	DIGOXINS	DGINNSUW	WINDGUNS	DHIKNOOW	HOODWINK
DGIINOTT	DITTOING	DGINOOPR	DROOPING	DHIKORSY	HYDROSKI
DGIINOWW	WIDOWING	DGINOOPS	GOSPODIN	DHILLNOW	DOWNHILL
DGIINPPR	DRIPPING		SPONGOID	DHILLOPY	PHYLLOID
DGIINPPS	DIPPINGS	DGINOOTU	OUTDOING	DHILLORS	DROLLISH
DGIINPUV	UPDIVING	DGINOPPR	DROPPING	DHILLOST	TOLLDISH
DGIINRST	STRIDING	DGINOPPS	DOPPINGS	DHILLPSY	PHYLLIDS
DGIINRSV	DRIVINGS	DGINORSV	DROVINGS	DHILMOPY	LYMPHOID
DGIINRTY	DIRTYING	DGINORSW	DROWSING	DHILMOSY	MODISHLY
DGIINSSU	DISUSING		SWORDING	DHILNOPS	DOLPHINS
DGIINTTY	DITTYING		WORDINGS	DHILOPRS	LORDSHIP
DGIINVVY	DIVVYING	DGINOSSW	DISGOWNS	DHILOPSS	SLIPSHOD
DGIINYZZ	DIZZYING	DGINOSUY	DIGYNOUS	DHILORRY	HORRIDLY
DGIKLOOY	KIDOLOGY	DGINPRUY	UPDRYING	DHILPSSU	LUDSHIPS
DGIKMNOS	KINGDOMS	DGINSSTU	DUSTINGS		SULPHIDS
DGIKNOOR	DROOKING	DGINSTUY	STUDYING	DHILPSSY	SYLPHIDS
DGIKNOOW	KINGWOOD	DGIOOPRU	GROUPOID	DHIMMNOT	MIDMONTH
DGIKNORU	DROUKING	DGIOPRRY	PORRIDGY	DHIMNOST	HINDMOST
DGIKNOSS	DOGSKINS	DGIOSUYZ	DIZYGOUS	DHIMNOSU	UNMODISH
DGILLNOR	DROLLING	DGISSSTU	DISGUSTS	DHIMOOOY	OMOHYOID
	LORDLING	DGKLOORW	GOLDWORK	DHIMOOSS	MISSHOOD
DGILLNOY	DOLLYING	DGLNORSU	GOLDURNS	DHIMOPPY	HIPPYDOM
DGILLOOW	GOODWILL	DGLOOOPY	PODOLOGY	DHIMOPRS	DIMORPHS
DGILMNOS	MOLDINGS	DGLOOOSW	LOGWOODS	DHIMORSU	HUMIDORS
DGILMNOU	MOULDING	DGLOOOSY	DOSOLOGY		RHODIUMS
DGILMNPU	DUMPLING	DGLOOOXY	DOXOLOGY	DHINNOTW	THINDOWN
DGILMSUY	SMUDGILY	DGLOOSST	GODSLOTS	DHINOOPR	PHORONID
DGILNNOO	NOODLING	DGMNNOUU	MUNDUNGO	DHINOORS	DISHONOR
DGILNNOU	LOUNDING	DGMOOSUW	GUMWOODS	DHINOPSS	DONSHIPS
DGILNNOW	LOWNDING	DGMOPRSU	GUMDROPS	DHINORSS	DISHORNS
DGILNNRU	NURDLING	DGMOPSYY	GYPSYDOM	DHINORSU	ROUNDISH
DGILNOOR	DROOLING	DGMORSUU	GURUDOMS	DHINOTUW	WHODUNIT
DGILNOOW	WOOLDING	DGNNORUU	UNGROUND	DHINTUWY	WHYDUNIT
DGILNORS	GIRLONDS	DGNOOOPS	GONOPODS	DHIOOOPR	IODOPHOR
	LORDINGS	DGNOOORS	GODROONS	DHIOOPRZ	RHIZOPOD
DGILNORY	YOLDRING	DGNOOSTW	DOGTOWNS	DHIOPRSU	PROUDISH
DGILNOTY	DOTINGLY	DGNOOTYZ	ZYGODONT	DHIOPSTY	TYPHOIDS
DGILNPUY	DUPLYING	DGOORSTT	DOGTROTS	DHIORSTY	THYROIDS
DGILOOTW	GILTWOOD	DGOPRRSU	PRODRUGS		THYRSOID
DGILOPSU	SOLPUGID	DGOPRSTU	POSTDRUG	DHIORSWY	ROWDYISH
DGILOSTY	STODGILY	DHHILOTW	WITHHOLD	DHIPRSSY	SYRPHIDS
DGILRTUY	TURGIDLY	DHHIOPPS	PHOSPHID	DHJOPRSU	JODHPURS
DGIMMNRU	DRUMMING	DHIIIMNS	DIMINISH	DHKMNOOO	MONKHOOD
DGIMMNUY	DUMMYING		MINIDISH	DHKMOOSU	MUDHOOKS
DGIMNNOU	MOUNDING	DHIIINST	HISTIDIN	DHLLOPYY	PHYLLODY
DGIMNOOY	MOODYING	DHIIIOST	HISTIOID	DHLMOOSU	HOODLUMS
DGIMNPSU	DUMPINGS		IDIOTISH	DHLOOORT	ROOTHOLD
DGIMOPSY	GIPSYDOM	DHIILOSS	SOLIDISH	DHLOORSY	HYDROSOL
DGINNNSU	DUNNINGS	DHIIMNOO	HOMINOID	DHLOOSTU	HOLDOUTS
DGINNOOS	SNOODING	DHIIMNOS	HOMINIDS	DHLORXYY	HYDROXYL
DGINNOPU	POUNDING	DHIIMOST	ISTHMOID	DHLOSSTU	SHOULDST
DGINNOPW	POWNDING	DHIIMPSS	MIDSHIPS	DHMMRSUU	HUMDRUMS
DGINNORU	INGROUND	DHIIMTUY	HUMIDITY	DHMNOOOT	HOMODONT
	ROUNDING	DHIINPSW	WINDSHIP	DHMOOPPU	PUMPHOOD
DGINNORW	DROWNING	DHIINRSU	HIRUDINS	DHMORTUY	DRYMOUTH
	ROWNDING	DHIINTWW	WITHWIND	DHNNOOSU	NUNHOODS
DGINNOSU	SOUNDING	DHIIOPRU	OPHIURID	DHNOOOSS	SONHOODS

DHNOOSWW	SHOWDOWN	**DIILQSUU**	LIQUIDUS	**DILOOSUY**	ODIOUSLY
DHNOPSUW	PUSHDOWN	**DIILRSSU**	SILURIDS	**DILOOTUV**	VOLUTOID
DHNORSUU	UNSHROUD	**DIILSSTY**	IDYLISTS	**DILOPRTY**	TORPIDLY
DHNORSUW	DOWNRUSH	**DIIMMNOU**	DOMINIUM	**DILORRTY**	TORRIDLY
DHNOSTUW	SHUTDOWN	**DIIMNNOO**	DOMINION	**DILORSTU**	DILUTORS
DHOOOPRT	ORTHOPOD	**DIIMNNSU**	UNDINISM	**DILORSWY**	DROWSILY
DHOOORTX	ORTHODOX	**DIIMNOPT**	MIDPOINT	**DILOSSTY**	STYLOIDS
DHOOPRST	DROPSHOT	**DIIMNORS**	MIDIRONS	**DILPRTUY**	PUTRIDLY
DHOOPRSU	UPHOORDS	**DIIMNSUU**	INDUSIUM	**DILPSTUY**	STUPIDLY
DHOORSUW	WOODRUSH	**DIIMOPRS**	PRISMOID	**DILRSTUY**	STURDILY
DHOPRSSU	PUSHRODS	**DIIMORSS**	DIORISMS	**DIMMNORY**	MYRMIDON
DHOPRSYY	HYDROPSY	**DIIMPUXY**	PYXIDIUM	**DIMMOOSU**	ISODOMUM
DIIIKMNS	MINIDISK	**DIIMRUUV**	DUUMVIRI	**DIMMOSST**	MIDMOSTS
DIIILLQU	ILLIQUID	**DIIMTTUY**	TUMIDITY	**DIMNNOOS**	MIDNOONS
DIIILTVY	LIVIDITY	**DIINNOSU**	DISUNION	**DIMNNOST**	DINMONTS
DIIIMOST	IDIOTISM	**DIINOOPS**	IODOPSIN	**DIMNOOOS**	ISODOMON
DIIIMRSU	IRIDIUMS	**DIINOOPU**	DOUPIONI	**DIMNOOST**	MONODIST
DIIIMTTY	TIMIDITY	**DIINOQSU**	QUINOIDS	**DIMNOPSU**	IMPOUNDS
DIIINOSV	DIVISION	**DIINOSSU**	SINUSOID	**DIMNOSSU**	MISSOUND
DIIINTVY	DIVINITY	**DIINSTUY**	DISUNITY	**DIMNOSTU**	DISMOUNT
DIIIPRST	DISPIRIT	**DIIOPRTY**	PITYROID	**DIMNOSTW**	MIDTOWNS
DIIIRTVY	VIRIDITY	**DIIORSST**	SISTROID	**DIMNOSUW**	UNWISDOM
DIIITVVY	VIVIDITY	**DIIORSSV**	DIVISORS	**DIMNOSWX**	MIXDOWNS
DIIJNOSS	DISJOINS	**DIIORSTX**	TRIOXIDS	**DIMOOPRR**	PRODROMI
DIIJNOST	DISJOINT	**DIIORSUV**	VIRUSOID	**DIMOOPRY**	MYRIOPOD
DIIKKNSS	KIDSKINS	**DIIPSTTY**	TIDYTIPS	**DIMOORTW**	MODIWORT
DIIKLLNY	KINDLILY	**DIJOSSTU**	JUDOISTS	**DIMOOSST**	SODOMIST
DIIKLNSS	DISLINKS	**DIKLMOOW**	MILKWOOD	**DIMOPRSU**	MISPROUD
DIIKNOST	DOITKINS	**DIKLNNOW**	DOWNLINK	**DIMOPSSU**	SPODIUMS
DIILLMNR	MILLRIND	**DIKLNNUY**	UNKINDLY	**DIMORSSW**	MISWORDS
DIILLMNW	WINDMILL	**DIKLNOOP**	KILOPOND	**DIMORSTY**	MIDSTORY
DIILLMOU	LIMULOID	**DIKLNORS**	LORDKINS	**DIMORSWY**	ROWDYISM
DIILLMPY	LIMPIDLY	**DIKLRUUU**	DURUKULI	**DIMOSTUY**	DUMOSITY
DIILLQUY	LIQUIDLY	**DIKNOOSW**	INKWOODS	**DIMRSTUU**	TRIDUUMS
DIILLSST	DISTILLS		WOODSKIN	**DIMRSUUV**	DUUMVIRS
DIILLSTY	IDYLLIST	**DIKNORSV**	DVORNIKS	**DINNOORS**	RONDINOS
DIILMNSS	DISLIMNS	**DIKNORTU**	OUTDRINK	**DINNOOST**	TONDINOS
DIILMOPP	POMPILID	**DIKOOSTU**	DITOKOUS	**DINNOPSW**	DOWNSPIN
DIILMOSS	IDOLISMS	**DILLMNOP**	MILLPOND		PINDOWNS
	SOLIDISM	**DILLMSSU**	MUDSILLS	**DINOOORW**	IRONWOOD
DIILMOTY	MYTILOID	**DILLOORS**	DOORSILL	**DINOOPSU**	DIPNOOUS
DIILMSST	MIDLISTS	**DILLOSTY**	STOLIDLY	**DINOORRS**	INDORSOR
DIILMUUV	DILUVIUM	**DILLPSSY**	PSYLLIDS	**DINOORST**	TORDIONS
DIILNNSU	INDULINS	**DILMNOOS**	SMILODON	**DINOORSU**	NIDOROUS
DIILNOST	TOLIDINS	**DILMNORW**	LINDWORM	**DINOOSST**	ISODONTS
DIILNOTU	DILUTION	**DILMNOSW**	SLIMDOWN	**DINOOSTT**	ODONTIST
	TOLUIDIN	**DILMNRSU**	DRUMLINS	**DINOOSTY**	NODOSITY
DIILNOUV	DILUVION	**DILMOOSU**	MODIOLUS	**DINOPRTY**	DRYPOINT
DIILNOXY	XYLOIDIN	**DILMOSSU**	SOLIDUMS	**DINORSTU**	STURNOID
DIILNSXY	XYLIDINS	**DILMOSSY**	ODYLISMS		TURDIONS
DIILNTUY	UNTIDILY	**DILNNOOS**	NONSOLID	**DINORSWW**	WINDROWS
DIILOPRT	TRIPLOID	**DILNOPST**	DIPLONTS	**DINOSTUW**	OUTWINDS
DIILOPSS	DIPLOSIS	**DILNOOPS**	LISPOUND	**DINPRTUY**	PUNDITRY
DIILOPSY	YPSILOID	**DILNOQSU**	QUODLINS	**DINRSTUY**	INDUSTRY
DIILOQSU	SOLIQUID	**DILNOSXY**	INDOXYLS	**DIOOPRRT**	PRODITOR
DIILORSU	SILUROID	**DILNOUWY**	WOUNDILY	**DIOOPRRV**	PROVIDOR
DIILORTU	UTILIDOR	**DILNPRSU**	LISPUNDS	**DIOOPRTX**	PROTOXID
DIILOSST	IDOLISTS	**DILNRSUY**	SUNDRILY	**DIOORSST**	DISROOTS
	SOLIDIST	**DILOOPPY**	POLYPOID	**DIOORSTT**	RIDOTTOS
DIILOSTY	SOLIDITY	**DILOOPRY**	DROOPILY	**DIOPRSST**	DISPORTS
DIILPPRY	DRIPPILY	**DILOORSS**	LORDOSIS		

DIOPSSST	DISPOSTS	DNNORTUW	DOWNTURN	EEEFGRSU	REFUGEES
DIORRSST	STRIDORS		TURNDOWN	EEEFHRSS	SHEREEFS
DIORSSTT	DISTORTS	DNNOSSUW	SUNDOWNS	EEEFIPRR	REPRIEFE
DIOSSTUU	STUDIOUS	DNNRSTUU	TURNDUNS	EEEFIPST	TEPEFIES
DIPRSSTU	DISRUPTS	DNOOPPRU	PROPOUND	EEEFIRRT	FREETIER
DIRSSTTU	DISTRUST	DNOOPRSW	SNOWDROP	EEEFIRST	REEFIEST
DIRSSTUY	DRYSUITS	DNOOPRUW	DOWNPOUR	EEEFLRRS	FLEERERS
DKLNOOOW	LOOKDOWN	DNOOPSUY	DUOPSONY	EEEFLRSX	REFLEXES
DKMNOOOR	KOMONDOR	DNOORSUW	WONDROUS	EEEFLSST	FEETLESS
DKNORTUU	OUTDRUNK	DNOOSTUW	NUTWOODS	EEEFLSTT	FLEETEST
DKOOOPRW	PORKWOOD	DNOOSTWW	STOWDOWN	EEEFNNPY	PENNYFEE
DKOOORWW	WOODWORK	DNOOSUUV	VOUDOUNS	EEEFNORS	FORESEEN
DKORSTUW	STUDWORK	DNOOTUUW	OUTWOUND	EEEFNRRT	REFERENT
DLLMORRSU	DRUMROLL	DNOPRSSU	SUNDROPS	EEEFNRSS	FREENESS
DLLMORSU	SLUMLORD	DNOPRSUU	ROUNDUPS	EEEFNRSV	ENFEVERS
DLLNORUY	UNLORDLY	DNOPSTUW	PUTDOWNS	EEEFNRTT	ENFETTER
DLMNOOSW	SNOWMOLD	DNORRSUU	SURROUND	EEEFNRUZ	UNFREEZE
DLMNOOSY	MYLODONS	DNORSSUY	UNDROSSY	EEEFORRS	FORESEER
DLMNOOTY	MYLODONT	DOOOPPRT	PROTOPOD	EEEFORRV	OVERFREE
DLMNOSUU	UNMOULDS	DOOOPRST	DOORPOST	EEEFORSS	FORESEES
DLMORSUY	SMOULDRY		DOORSTOP	EEEFRRRR	REFERRER
DLNOOPRU	POULDRON	DOOORSTU	OUTDOORS	EEEFRRRT	FERRETER
DLNOOSUU	NODULOUS	DOOORSUW	SOURWOOD	EEEFRRSZ	FREEZERS
DLNOOSWW	LOWDOWNS	DOOOSTTU	OUTSTOOD	EEEFRRTT	FETTERER
	SLOWDOWN	DOOPRRTW	DROPWORT	EEEGGILN	NEGLIGEE
DLNOPRSU	PULDRONS	DOOPRSTU	DROPOUTS	EEEGGIRS	EGGERIES
DLNOPSSY	SPONDYLS		OUTDROPS	EEEGHINT	EIGHTEEN
DLNORTUY	ROTUNDLY	DOOPRSTW	STOPWORD	EEEGHLRS	SHEERLEG
DLNOSUUU	UNDULOUS	DOOPSWWY	POWSOWDY	EEEGHMNU	HEGUMENE
DLOOOORS	DOLOROSO	DOORRSTU	DORTOURS	EEEGHNSW	WHEENGES
DLOOOPSS	SPODOSOL	DOORRSUU	ORDUROUS	EEEGIKST	GEEKIEST
DLOOORSU	DOLOROUS	DOORSSUU	SUDOROUS	EEEGILMN	LIEGEMEN
DLOOOSTW	WOODLOTS	DOSTTUUY	OUTSTUDY	EEEGILNS	GLEENIES
DLOOPPSY	POLYPODS	EEEEFNRZ	ENFREEZE	EEEGILNV	ENVEIGLE
DLOOPPUW	PULPWOOD	EEEEFRRS	REFEREES		LEVEEING
DLOOPPYY	POLYPODY	EEEEFRRZ	REFREEZE	EEEGILPS	ESPIEGLE
DLOOPSTU	OUTPLODS	EEEEGGRR	GREEGREE	EEEGILRT	GLEETIER
DLOOPSTY	TYLOPODS	EEEEGMRR	REEMERGE	EEEGILSS	ELEGISES
DLOOPSWY	PLYWOODS	EEEEGNRY	GREENEYE	EEEGILSZ	ELEGIZES
DMMOOORT	MOTORDOM	EEEEGQSU	SQUEEGEE	EEEGIMNX	EXEEMING
DMMOORSU	MUDROOMS	EEEEGSSX	EXEGESES	EEEGIMTV	VEGEMITE
DMNNOOOT	MONODONT	EEEEGSTX	EXEGETES	EEEGINNR	ENGINEER
DMNOOOPS	MONOPODS	EEEEHTTY	EYETEETH	EEEGINRR	GREENIER
DMNOOOPY	MONOPODY	EEEELLPX	EXPELLEE	EEEGINRS	ENERGIES
DMNOOSTU	MOONDUST	EEEELLVY	EYELEVEL		ENERGISE
DMNOOSTW	DOWNMOST	EEEELMST	TELESEME		GREENIES
	TOWMONDS	EEEELNSV	SLEEVEEN		RESEEING
DMOOOQSU	QUOMODOS	EEEENRRV	VENEERER	EEEGINRV	ENGRIEVE
DMOOORWW	WOODWORM	EEEEPPRR	REPEREPE	EEEGINRZ	ENERGIZE
	WORMWOOD	EEEEPPSW	PEESWEEP	EEEGIPRS	PERIGEES
DMOPPPUU	PUPPODUM	EEEEPRRV	REPREEVE	EEEGIRSX	EXERGIES
DMOPPPUY	PUPPYDOM	EEEEPTTW	PEETWEET	EEEGIRTY	TIGEREYE
DMORSTUW	MUDWORTS	EEEFFFOS	FEOFFEES	EEEGISSX	EXEGESIS
DMPPPUUY	MUDPUPPY	EEEFFLOR	FOREFEEL	EEEGISTV	EGESTIVE
DNNOOOWY	NONWOODY	EEEFFLTY	EFFETELY	EEEGITVV	VEGETIVE
DNNOOPRU	PUNDONOR	EEEFFNRT	EFFERENT	EEEGKLRS	KEGELERS
DNNOORSW	NONWORDS	EEEFFORS	OFFEREES	EEEGLMOS	GLEESOME
DNNOOTWW	DOWNTOWN	EEEFFORT	FOREFEET	EEEGLNRT	GREENLET
DNNORRUU	RUNROUND	EEEFFOTU	ETOUFFEE	EEEGMNOS	MONGEESE
DNNORSUU	UNROUNDS	EEEFFRVW	FEVERFEW	EEEGMNRT	EMERGENT
DNNORSUW	RUNDOWNS	EEEFGMRR	GERMFREE	EEEGMNRU	MERENGUE

EEEGMORT	GEOMETER	EEEHPRRT	THREEPER	EEEINRSS	EERINESS
EEEGMRRS	REMERGES	EEEHPRSS	HERPESES		ESERINES
EEEGNNRS	SENGREEN		PHERESES	EEEINRST	ETERNISE
EEEGNPRS	EPERGNES	EEEHPRST	SPREETHE		TEENSIER
EEEGNRRS	GREENERS	EEEHRRVW	WHEREVER	EEEINRSV	VENERIES
	REGREENS	EEEHRSST	SEETHERS	EEEINRSW	WEENSIER
	RENEGERS		SHEEREST	EEEINRSZ	SNEEZIER
EEEGNRRU	RENEGUER		SHEETERS	EEEINRTT	REINETTE
EEEGNRRV	REVENGER	EEEHRSTT	TEETHERS		TEENTIER
EEEGNRRY	GREENERY	EEEHRSWZ	WHEEZERS	EEEINRTZ	ETERNIZE
EEEGNRST	GREENEST	EEEHSSST	ESTHESES	EEEINSSW	SWEENIES
EEEGNRSU	RENEGUES	EEEHSSTT	ESTHETES	EEEINSTT	TEENIEST
EEEGNRSV	REVENGES	EEEIKLMS	MISLEEKE	EEEINSTW	TWEENIES
EEEGNSTT	GENETTES	EEEIKLRS	SKEELIER		WEENIEST
EEEGOPRT	PROTEGEE		SLEEKIER	EEEINTUX	EUXENITE
EEEGRRST	GREETERS	EEEIKLRT	TREELIKE	EEEIPRRV	REPRIEVE
	REGREETS	EEEIKLSW	WEEKLIES	EEEIPRST	PEERIEST
EEEGRSSS	EGRESSES	EEEIKNSS	KNEESIES		STEEPIER
EEEGRSUX	EXERGUES	EEEIKNTX	EKTEXINE	EEEIPRSW	SWEEPIER
EEEHHSSW	WHEESHES	EEEIKRRS	SKEERIER	EEEIPSST	EPEEISTS
EEEHILRW	EREWHILE	EEEIKRST	REEKIEST		SEEPIEST
	WHEELIER	EEEILLRV	REVEILLE	EEEIPSTW	WEEPIEST
EEEHILSW	WHEELIES	EEEILMRS	SEEMLIER	EEEIQSUX	EXEQUIES
EEEHINRS	SHEENIER	EEEILNNO	EOLIENNE	EEEIRRST	REESTIER
EEEHINSS	SHEENIES	EEEILNPR	PELERINE		RETIREES
EEEHINSY	EYESHINE	EEEILNRY	EYELINER	EEEIRRSV	REREVISE
EEEHIPRS	SHEEPIER	EEEILNST	ENLISTEE		REVERIES
EEEHIRSS	HERESIES		SELENITE	EEEIRRTV	RETRIEVE
EEEHIRST	ETHERISE	EEEILNSU	UNSEELIE	EEEIRRVW	REREVIEW
	SHEETIER	EEEILPRS	SLEEPIER		REVIEWER
EEEHIRSX	HEXEREIS	EEEILRRV	RELIEVER	EEEIRSST	STEERIES
EEEHIRTZ	ETHERIZE	EEEILRST	LEERIEST	EEEIRSSV	SEVERIES
EEEHIRWZ	WHEEZIER		SLEETIER	EEEIRSSZ	RESEIZES
EEEHKLNO	KNEEHOLE		STEELIER	EEEIRTVX	EXERTIVE
EEEHLLSS	HEELLESS	EEEILRSV	RELIEVES	EEEISSTW	SWEETIES
EEEHLMNW	WHEELMEN	EEEILRSZ	SLEEZIER	EEEJKKNR	KNEEJERK
EEEHLMPT	HELPMEET	EEEILRVY	LIVEYERE	EEEJLLRW	JEWELLER
EEEHLNSW	ENWHEELS	EEEILSST	SEELIEST	EEEJLRSW	JEWELERS
EEEHLNTV	ELEVENTH		STEELIES	EEEJNPSY	JEEPNEYS
EEEHLNTY	ETHYLENE	EEEILSSW	ELSEWISE	EEEKLLSS	KEELLESS
EEEHLNXY	HEXYLENE	EEEILSTV	TELEVISE	EEEKLLSU	UKELELES
EEEHLOPP	PEEPHOLE	EEEILTVW	TELEVIEW	EEEKLNNR	ENKERNEL
EEEHLOPW	WEEPHOLE	EEEIMNRU	MEUNIERE	EEEKLNRS	KNEELERS
EEEHLOSY	EYEHOLES	EEEIMNST	EMETINES	EEEKLNSS	SLEEKENS
EEEHLPSW	WHEEPLES	EEEIMPRR	PREMIERE	EEEKLPSW	EKPWELES
EEEHLRSW	WHEELERS	EEEIMPRS	EMPERIES	EEEKLRSS	SLEEKERS
EEEHLSWZ	WHEEZLES		EMPERISE	EEEKLSST	SLEEKEST
EEEHMMSS	EMMESHES		PREEMIES	EEEKMNSS	MEEKNESS
EEEHMNNT	MENTHENE	EEEIMPRZ	EMPERIZE	EEEKMORV	OVERMEEK
EEEHMNPS	SHEEPMEN	EEEIMRRS	MISERERE	EEEKMRRS	KERMESSE
EEEHMNSS	ENMESHES	EEEIMRST	EREMITES	EEEKNNSS	KEENNESS
EEEHMNTV	VEHEMENT	EEEIMRTT	REMITTEE	EEEKNORS	KEROSENE
EEEHNNPT	NEPENTHE	EEEINNNT	NINETEEN	EEEKNORV	OVERKEEN
EEEHNNQU	HENEQUEN	EEEINNRT	INTERNEE		OVERKNEE
EEEHNPRS	ENSPHERE		RETINENE	EEEKNPST	KEEPNETS
EEEHNRSS	HERENESS	EEEINPRT	PERENTIE	EEEKOPRV	OVERKEEP
EEEHNRTV	REVEHENT	EEEINQRU	QUEENIER	EEEKORSV	REEVOKES
EEEHNRVW	WHENEVER	EEEINQSU	QUEENIES	EEEKRRST	STREEKER
EEEHNSSS	SNEESHES	EEEINQTU	QUEENITE	EEEKRSST	KEESTERS
EEEHNSSY	SHEENEYS	EEEINRRS	SNEERIER		SKEETERS
EEEHORST	SHOETREE			EEELLLRV	LEVELLER

Code	Word	Code	Word	Code	Word
EEELLLSW	SEWELLEL	EEEMNSST	MEETNESS	EEENSSWY	SWEENEYS
EEELLNOR	ENROLLEE	EEEMNSTW	SWEETMEN	EEEOPPSY	POPESEYE
EEELLNQU	QUENELLE	EEEMORRV	EVERMORE	EEEOPRRV	OVERPEER
EEELLPRR	REPELLER	EEEMORST	EROTEMES	EEEOPRSX	REEXPOSE
EEELLPRX	EXPELLER		STEREOME	EEEORRSV	OVERSEER
EEELLRRS	RESELLER	EEEMORTV	OVERTEEM	EEEORRSX	XEROSERE
EEELLRRT	RETELLER	EEEMPRRT	RETEMPER	EEEORRSZ	REZEROES
EEELLRRV	REVELLER		TEMPERER	EEEORSST	EROTESES
EEELLRSV	LEVELERS	EEEMPRSS	EMPRESSE	EEEORSSV	OVERSEES
EEELMNST	ELEMENTS	EEEMPSSY	EMPYESES	EEEORSSY	EYESORES
	STEELMEN	EEEMRRTX	EXTREMER	EEEORSVY	OVEREYES
EEELMOPP	EMPEOPLE	EEEMRSST	SEMESTER	EEEPPPRR	PEPPERER
EEELMOPY	EMPLOYEE	EEEMRSTX	EXTREMES	EEEPPSTU	STEEPEUP
EEELMORT	TELOMERE	EEENNOPR	NEOPRENE	EEEPRRST	PESTERER
EEELMOTT	OMELETTE	EEENNOSV	VENENOSE	EEEPRRSU	REPERUSE
EEELMPSX	EXEMPLES	EEENNPST	PENTENES	EEEPRRSV	PERVERSE
EEELMRTU	MULETEER	EEENNRST	ETRENNES		PRESERVE
EEELMSSS	SEEMLESS	EEENNRUV	UNEVENER	EEEPRRTW	PEWTERER
EEELMSST	TEEMLESS	EEENNSSV	EVENNESS	EEEPRSST	ESTREPES
EEELNOPV	ENVELOPE	EEENNSTT	ENTENTES		STEEPERS
EEELNOSV	NOVELESE	EEENOPRR	REOPENER	EEEPRSSW	SWEEPERS
EEELNQTU	QUEENLET	EEENORSV	OVERSEEN	EEEPRSSZ	SPREEZES
EEELNRRU	UNREELER	EEENORVW	OVERWEEN	EEEPSSTT	STEEPEST
EEELNRSW	NEWSREEL	EEENORVY	EVERYONE	EEEPSTTT	SEPTETTE
EEELNRSY	SERENELY	EEENOSTY	EYESTONE	EEEQRRSU	REQUERES
EEELNRTV	NERVELET	EEENPPRS	PREPENSE	EEEQRRUV	VERQUERE
EEELNRTY	TERYLENE	EEENPRRS	PREENERS	EEEQRSTU	QUEEREST
EEELOPPR	REPEOPLE	EEENPRRT	REPENTER	EEEQRSUZ	SQUEEZER
EEELORST	SLOETREE	EEENPRST	PRETEENS	EEEQSSUZ	SQUEEZES
EEELPPRS	PRESLEEP		PRETENSE	EEERRRSV	RESERVER
EEELPRSS	PEERLESS		TERPENES		REVERERS
	SLEEPERS		PREVENES		REVERSER
	SPEELERS	EEENPSST	ENSTEEPS		REVERTER
EEELPRST	REPLETES		STEEPENS	EEERRSST	STEERERS
EEELPRSX	REEXPELS	EEENPSSW	ENSWEEPS	EEERRSSV	RESERVES
EEELPRSY	SLEEPERY	EEENPSSX	EXPENSES		REVERSES
EEELPSST	STEEPLES	EEENQSUU	ENQUEUES	EEERRSTT	RESETTER
EEELPTTY	TELETYPE	EEENRRSS	SNEERERS	EEERSSTV	SEVEREST
EEELRRSV	REVELERS	EEENRRST	ENTERERS	EEERSSUV	REVEUSES
EEELRRTT	LETTERER		REENTERS	EEERSSUW	SERUEWES
	RELETTER		RESENTER	EEERSSVW	SERVEWES
EEELRSST	TREELESS		TERREENS	EEERSTTW	TWEETERS
EEELRSSV	SLEEVERS		TERRENES	EEERSTVX	VERTEXES
EEELRSTT	RESETTLE	EEENRRSV	RENVERSE	EEERSTWZ	TWEEZERS
EEELRSTV	LEVERETS		VENERERS	EEESSTTT	SESTETTE
	VERSELET	EEENRRSW	RENEWERS	EEESSTTV	STEEVEST
EEELRSVY	SEVERELY	EEENRRTU	RETURNEE	EEESSTTW	SWEETEST
EEELRTVV	VELVERET	EEENRRTV	REVERENT	EEESTTTX	SEXTETTE
EEELSSTU	EUSTELES	EEENRRUV	REVENUER	EEFFFGLU	GEFUFFLE
EEELSSTW	WEETLESS	EEENRSST	SERENEST	EEFFFKLU	KEFUFFLE
EEELSTVY	STEEVELY	EEENRSSU	ENURESES	EEFFFNOS	ENFEOFFS
EEELTTTX	TELETEXT	EEENRSSZ	SNEEZERS	EEFFFORS	FEOFFERS
EEEMMNRS	MERESMEN	EEENRSTV	EVENTERS	EEFFGIIS	EFFIGIES
EEEMMORS	MESOMERE		EVERNETS	EEFFGINR	EFFERING
EEEMMRUZ	MEZEREUM	EEENRSTW	TWEENERS	EEFFGIRR	GREFFIER
EEEMNNTT	TENEMENT	EEENRSTX	EXTERNES	EEFFGLSU	EFFULGES
EEEMNORZ	MEZEREON	EEENRSTY	YESTREEN	EEFFHIKY	KEFFIYEH
EEEMNPRT	PETERMEN	EEENRSUV	REVENUES	EEFFINST	FIFTEENS
EEEMNRST	ENTREMES		UNREEVES	EEFFISUV	EFFUSIVE
EEEMNRSV	VERSEMEN	EEENSSTW	SWEETENS	EEFFLNTU	EFFLUENT
EEEMNRVY	EVERYMEN		TWEENESS	EEFFLORT	FOREFELT

EEFFLSUX	EFFLUXES	EEFHRSST	FRESHEST	EEFINRRR	INFERRER
EEFFMORR	FREEFORM		FRESHETS	EEFINRRS	REFINERS
EEFFMOTT	MOFFETTE	EEFIIKLL	LIFELIKE	EEFINRRY	REFINERY
EEFFNOSS	OFFENSES	EEFIIKLW	WIFELIKE	EEFINRSS	FINESSER
EEFFORRS	OFFERERS	EEFIIKRS	FIKERIES		RIFENESS
	REOFFERS	EEFIILLN	LIFELINE	EEFINRST	FERNIEST
EEFFORSX	FORFEXES	EEFIILMT	LIFETIME		INFESTER
EEFFRRSU	SUFFERER	EEFIILNS	LENIFIES	EEFINRSU	REINFUSE
EEFFSSTU	SUFFETES	EEFIILRW	WIFELIER	EEFINRSZ	FRENZIES
EEFGIILR	FILIGREE	EEFIIMNN	FEMININE	EEFINSSS	FINESSES
EEFGILNR	FLEERING	EEFIIMNS	FEMINISE	EEFINSTT	FEINTEST
EEFGILNS	FEELINGS	EEFIIMNZ	FEMINIZE	EEFIORRV	OVERRIFE
EEFGILNT	FLEETING	EEFIINRS	FINERIES	EEFIORSX	ORIFEXES
EEFGINNP	PFENNIGE	EEFIIRRS	REIFIERS	EEFIPRRS	PREFIRES
EEFGINRR	FINGERER	EEFIIRRT	FREITIER	EEFIPRSX	PREFIXES
	REFRINGE	EEFIIRRV	VERIFIER	EEFIRRST	FERRITES
EEFGINRS	FEERINGS	EEFIIRST	FEIRIEST	EEFIRRSU	SUREFIRE
	FEIGNERS		FEISTIER	EEFIRRTT	FRETTIER
	REEFINGS		FERITIES	EEFIRRVY	REVERIFY
EEFGINRV	FEVERING		FIERIEST	EEFIRSTT	FRISETTE
EEFGINRZ	FREEZING	EEFIIRSV	VERIFIES	EEFIRSTY	ESTERIFY
EEFGIRRS	GRIEFERS	EEFIKLLT	FELTLIKE	EEFIRTTZ	FRIZETTE
EEFGIRRU	REFIGURE	EEFIKLMU	FUMELIKE	EEFISSSW	FESSWISE
EEFGLLTU	GEFULLTE	EEFIKLNR	FERNLIKE	EEFISSTT	FESTIEST
EEFGLMNU	FUGLEMEN	EEFIKLRS	SERFLIKE	EEFISTWW	WEFTWISE
EEFGLNRY	GREENFLY	EEFIKLSU	FUSELIKE	EEFKNORW	FOREKNEW
EEFGLNUV	VENGEFUL	EEFIKMNN	KNIFEMEN	EEFLLLNU	FLUELLEN
EEFGLORS	FORELEGS	EEFIKNNP	PENKNIFE	EEFLLNSS	FELLNESS
EEFGLOSS	SOLFEGES	EEFILLMT	TELEFILM	EEFLLORT	FORETELL
EEFGMNOR	FORGEMEN	EEFILLNY	FELINELY	EEFLLORV	OVERFELL
EEFGNOOR	FOREGONE	EEFILLRW	FREEWILL	EEFLLRSU	FUELLERS
EEFGOORR	FOREGOER	EEFILLSS	LIFELESS	EEFLLRXY	REFLEXLY
EEFGOORS	FOREGOES	EEFILMNR	RIFLEMEN	EEFLLSSS	SELFLESS
EEFGORRS	REFORGES	EEFILMOS	LIFESOME	EEFLMNSU	MENSEFUL
EEFGORSY	FROGEYES	EEFILMST	FISTMELE	EEFLMORU	FUMEROLE
EEFHILLR	HELLFIRE	EEFILMTX	FLEXTIME	EEFLMSSU	FUMELESS
EEFHILRS	FLESHIER	EEFILNOS	FELONIES	EEFLNNOS	ENFELONS
	SHELFIER		OLEFINES	EEFLNORT	FORELENT
EEFHIMSU	HUMEFIES	EEFILNSS	FINELESS	EEFLNORU	FLUORENE
EEFHIRSS	FRESHIES	EEFILNUV	NIEVEFUL	EEFLNORW	ENFLOWER
EEFHIRSV	FEVERISH	EEFILORS	FORELIES	EEFLNOST	FELSTONE
EEFHIRTY	ETHERIFY	EEFILPRR	PILFERER	EEFLNRSS	FERNLESS
EEFHISST	FETISHES	EEFILPRS	PREFILES		FLENSERS
EEFHISSY	FISHEYES	EEFILRRT	FERTILER		FRESNELS
EEFHISTT	HEFTIEST		FILTERER	EEFLNRSU	SNEERFUL
EEFHLLWY	FLYWHEEL		REFILTER	EEFLNRTU	REFLUENT
EEFHLMNS	FLEHMENS	EEFILRSS	FIRELESS	EEFLNSSS	SELFNESS
EEFHLMOT	HOMEFELT	EEFILRST	FERLIEST	EEFLNSSU	SENSEFUL
EEFHLMST	THEMSELF	EEFILRSU	FUSILEER	EEFLNTUV	EVENTFUL
EEFHLNSU	SHEENFUL	EEFILSST	FELSITES	EEFLOOSV	FOVEOLES
EEFHLRSS	FLESHERS	EEFILSSW	WIFELESS	EEFLOOTV	FOVEOLET
EEFHLSTY	FLYSHEET	EEFILSTT	FELTIEST	EEFLOPTT	POLTFEET
EEFHMNRS	FRESHMEN	EEFILSTY	EYELIFTS	EEFLORRW	FLOWERER
EEFHMORR	HEREFROM	EEFIMMST	FEMMIEST		REFLOWER
EEFHNORT	FOREHENT	EEFIMORT	FORETIME	EEFLORTV	LEFTOVER
EEFHNRSS	FRESHENS	EEFIMRRS	MISREFER	EEFLORTW	FLOWERET
EEFHORRT	THEREFOR	EEFIMRST	FEMITERS	EEFLORVW	OVERFLEW
EEFHORRW	WHEREFOR	EEFIMSTU	TUMEFIES	EEFLORWW	WEREWOLF
EEFHORSW	FORESHEW	EEFINNSS	FINENESS	EEFLOSTU	OUTFEELS
EEFHRRSS	FRESHERS	EEFINNST	FENNIEST	EEFLOSTV	LOVEFEST
EEFHRRSU	FUEHRERS	EEFINORV	OVERFINE	EEFLOSUX	FLEXUOSE

EEFLRRSU	FERRULES	EEGGINRS	GREESING	EEGHORTT	TOGETHER
EEFLRSST	FRETLESS	EEGGINRT	GREETING	EEGHOSTT	GHETTOES
EEFLRSTT	FETTLERS	EEGGINST	EGESTING	EEGHSTTU	TEUGHEST
EEFLRSTU	FLEURETS	EEGGINSU	SEGUEING	EEGIILNR	LINGERIE
EEFLRSUX	FLEXURES	EEGGIPRR	PREGGIER	EEGIILNV	INVEIGLE
	REFLUXES	EEGGJLRU	REJUGGLE	EEGIIMNS	GEMINIES
EEFLSSSU	FUSELESS	EEGGKRSS	SKEGGERS	EEGIINRT	REIGNITE
EEFMNORT	FOMENTER	EEGGLNSS	GLEGNESS		RETIEING
EEFMNRRY	FERRYMEN	EEGGLOOR	GEOLOGER	EEGIINTV	GENITIVE
EEFMNRST	FERMENTS	EEGGNNSS	GENSENGS	EEGIIOST	EGOITIES
EEFMORRR	REFORMER	EEGGNORS	ENGORGES	EEGIJLNW	JEWELING
EEFMORST	FRETSOME	EEGGORRS	REGORGES	EEGIJLNY	JEELYING
EEFMOSTT	MOFETTES	EEGGORSU	GOUGERES	EEGIJNRS	JEERINGS
EEFMPRRU	PERFUMER	EEGGORSV	OVEREGGS	EEGIJOPR	JEREPIGO
EEFMPRSU	PERFUMES	EEGGPRRS	PREGGERS	EEGIKLLN	GLENLIKE
EEFMSTTU	FUMETTES	EEGGPRSU	PUGGREES	EEGIKLLU	GLUELIKE
EEFNNORS	ENFROSEN	EEGGQRSU	SQUEGGER	EEGIKLMR	GERMLIKE
EEFNNORZ	ENFROZEN	EEGHHINT	HEIGHTEN	EEGIKLNN	KNEELING
EEFNORRZ	REFROZEN	EEGHIIST	EIGHTIES	EEGIKLNS	KEELINGS
EEFNORST	ENFOREST	EEGHIKNT	THEEKING		SLEEKING
	RESOFTEN	EEGHIKRS	SKEIGHER	EEGIKLOT	EKLOGITE
	SOFTENER	EEGHILNS	HEELINGS	EEGIKMNS	SMEEKING
EEFNORTU	FOURTEEN		SHEELING	EEGIKNNS	KEENINGS
EEFNORTW	FOREWENT	EEGHILNW	WHEELING	EEGIKNPS	KEEPINGS
EEFNOSTT	OFTENEST	EEGHILRS	SLEIGHER	EEGIKNRS	KREESING
EEFNQRTU	FREQUENT	EEGHIMNW	WEIGHMEN		SKEERING
EEFNRTTU	UNFETTER	EEGHINNS	SHEENING	EEGIKNRY	REKEYING
EEFOORRT	ROOFTREE	EEGHINPS	PHEESING	EEGIKNST	KITENGES
EEFOPRRZ	PREFROZE	EEGHINPT	PHENGITE		STEEKING
EEFORRST	FORESTER	EEGHINPW	WHEEPING	EEGILLNV	LEVELING
	FOSTERER	EEGHINPZ	PHEEZING	EEGILMOS	EGLOMISE
	REFOREST	EEGHINRS	GREENISH	EEGILNOR	ELOIGNER
EEFORRSU	FERREOUS		REHINGES	EEGILNPS	PEELINGS
EEFORRSV	FOREVERS		SHEERING		SLEEPING
EEFORRTY	FERETORY	EEGHINST	SEETHING		SPEELING
EEFORSUV	FEVEROUS		SHEETING	EEGILNRR	LINGERER
EEFOSSTT	FOSSETTE	EEGHINSY	HYGIENES	EEGILNRS	LEERINGS
EEFOSSTU	FOETUSES	EEGHINTT	TEETHING		REELINGS
EEFOSTTU	FOUETTES	EEGHINWZ	WHEEZING	EEGILNRT	GREENLIT
EEFPRSSU	PERFUSES	EEGHIOTT	GOETHITE	EEGILNRU	REGULINE
EEFRRSSU	REFUSERS	EEGHIPRW	PREWEIGH	EEGILNRV	LEVERING
EEFRRSTT	FRETTERS	EEGHIRSW	REWEIGHS		REVELING
EEFRRSTU	REFUTERS		WEIGHERS	EEGILNSS	SEELINGS
EEGGGLST	GLEGGEST	EEGHIRTW	WEIGHTER	EEGILNST	GENTILES
EEGGHLLS	EGGSHELL	EEGHISST	SIGHTSEE		SLEETING
EEGGHLOR	HOGGEREL	EEGHISTY	EYESIGHT		STEELING
EEGGHMSU	MESHUGGE	EEGHKRSS	SKREEGHS	EEGILNSV	SLEEVING
EEGGHSTU	THUGGEES	EEGHLNNT	LENGTHEN	EEGILNSW	SWEELING
EEGGIJRR	REJIGGER	EEGHMNOS	HEGEMONS	EEGILNTW	TWEELING
EEGGIKLN	GLEEKING	EEGHMNOY	HEGEMONY	EEGILNTX	TELEXING
EEGGIKNR	GREEKING	EEGHMNSU	HEGUMENS	EEGILOPU	EPILOGUE
EEGGILNR	LEGERING	EEGHMNUY	HEGUMENY	EEGILOSS	GELOSIES
EEGGILNS	NEGLIGES	EEGHMORT	GEOTHERM	EEGILOSU	EULOGIES
EEGGILNT	GLEETING	EEGHNNRU	ENHUNGER		EULOGISE
EEGGILNY	GINGELEY	EEGHNOOP	GEOPHONE	EEGILOUZ	EULOGIZE
EEGGILOR	LEGGIERO	EEGHNOPS	PHOSGENE	EEGILPSS	SPIEGELS
EEGGILST	LEGGIEST	EEGHNOPY	HYPOGENE	EEGILQSU	SQUILGEE
EEGGIMNR	EMERGING	EEGHNRST	GREENTHS	EEGILRSU	REGULISE
EEGGINNP	PEENGING	EEGHNRSY	GREYHENS	EEGILRSV	VELIGERS
EEGGINNR	GREENING	EEGHNSSU	HUGENESS	EEGILRTV	VERLIGTE
	RENEGING	EEGHOPTY	GEOPHYTE	EEGILRTY	LEGERITY

EEGILRUZ	REGULIZE		REESTING	EEGLORVY	LEVOGYRE
EEGILSST	ELEGISTS		STEERING	EEGLRRSU	GRUELERS
EEGIMMNW	EMMEWING		STREIGNE	EEGLRSTW	WERGELTS
EEGIMMRS	GREMMIES	EEGINRSU	SEIGNEUR	EEGMMOSU	GEMMEOUS
	IMMERGES	EEGINRSV	SEVERING	EEGMNOST	EMONGEST
EEGIMMST	GEMMIEST		VEERINGS		GEMSTONE
EEGIMNNS	MENINGES	EEGINRSW	RESEWING	EEGMNOYZ	ZYMOGENE
EEGIMNNW	ENMEWING		SEWERING	EEGMNSST	SEGMENTS
EEGIMNRS	REGIMENS		SWEERING	EEGMNTTU	TEGUMENT
EEGIMNRT	METERING	EEGINRTT	RINGETTE	EEGMORSU	GRUESOME
	REGIMENT	EEGINRTU	GENITURE	EEGMORSW	GREWSOME
EEGIMNRU	MERINGUE	EEGINRTV	EVERTING	EEGMORTY	GEOMETRY
EEGIMNRY	EMERYING	EEGINRTW	TWEERING	EEGMRSTU	GUMTREES
EEGIMNSS	SEEMINGS	EEGINRTX	EXERTING	EEGNNNOR	NONGREEN
EEGIMNST	MEETINGS		GENETRIX	EEGNNORT	ROENTGEN
	STEEMING	EEGINSSS	GNEISSES	EEGNNOSS	GONENESS
EEGIMNSU	EUGENISM	EEGINSSU	GENIUSES	EEGNNOSV	EVENSONG
EEGIMRST	GERMIEST	EEGINSTT	GENTIEST	EEGNNOXY	XENOGENY
EEGINNPR	PREENING	EEGINSTU	EUGENIST	EEGNOORV	ENGROOVE
EEGINNQU	QUEENING	EEGINSTV	STEEVING		OVERGONE
EEGINNRS	ENGINERS		VENTIGES	EEGNOOST	OSTEOGEN
	INGENERS	EEGINSTW	SWEETING	EEGNOPTY	GENOTYPE
	SERENING	EEGINSTX	EXIGENTS	EEGNORST	ESTROGEN
	SNEERING	EEGINTTV	VIGNETTE	EEGNORSU	GENEROUS
EEGINNRT	ENTERING	EEGINTTW	TWEETING	EEGNORSY	ERYNGOES
EEGINNRV	ENERVING	EEGINTUX	TEGUEXIN	EEGNOTYZ	ZYGOTENE
EEGINNRW	RENEWING	EEGINTWZ	TWEEZING	EEGNPRUX	EXPUNGER
EEGINNRY	ENGINERY	EEGIOPRS	PEROGIES	EEGNPSUX	EXPUNGES
	RENEYING	EEGIOPSU	EPIGEOUS	EEGNRSSY	GREYNESS
EEGINNST	STEENING	EEGIORST	ERGOTISE	EEGNRSUY	GUERNSEY
EEGINNSU	INGENUES	EEGIORTZ	ERGOTIZE	EEGNSSTU	GUESTENS
	UNSEEING	EEGIORVV	OVERGIVE	EEGOORRV	REGROOVE
EEGINNSV	EEVNINGS	EEGIOSST	EGOTISES	EEGOORSV	OVERGOES
	EVENINGS	EEGIOSTZ	EGOTIZES	EEGOPRST	PROTEGES
EEGINNSW	ENSEWING	EEGIPRST	PRESTIGE	EEGOPRSU	SUPEREGO
EEGINNSZ	SNEEZING	EEGIRRST	REGISTER	EEGORRST	OSTREGER
EEGINNTV	EVENTING	EEGIRRSV	GRIEVERS	EEGORRUV	OVERURGE
EEGINOOS	OOGENIES	EEGIRSTT	GRISETTE	EEGORRVW	OVERGREW
EEGINOPR	PERIGONE		TERGITES	EEGORSSS	OGRESSES
EEGINOPS	EPIGONES	EEGIRSTU	GUERITES	EEGORSTU	UROSTEGE
EEGINORR	ERIGERON	EEGISSTV	VESTIGES	EEGORSTV	OVERGETS
EEGINORS	ERINGOES	EEGISTTV	VEGETIST	EEGPPRRS	PREPREGS
EEGINORV	VIROGENE	EEGJORSU	GOUJEERS	EEGPRSUX	EXPURGES
EEGINOSS	GENOISES	EEGKLNOW	WEEKLONG	EEGRRSSU	RESURGES
EEGINOST	EGESTION	EEGKNORS	KEROGENS	EEGRRSTU	GESTURER
EEGINPRR	PEREGRIN	EEGKNRSU	GERENUKS	EEGRRSUY	GRUYERES
EEGINPRS	SPEERING	EEGLLRRU	GRUELLER	EEGRSSSU	GUESSERS
	SPREEING	EEGLMMSU	GEMMULES	EEGRSSTU	GESTURES
EEGINPRT	PETERING	EEGLMNOP	EMPLONGE	EEHHIPSS	SHEEPISH
EEGINPRU	PUREEING	EEGLMNTU	EMULGENT	EEHHIRST	ETHERISH
EEGINPRV	PREEVING	EEGLMORS	GOMERELS	EEHHIRTW	HEREWITH
EEGINPST	STEEPING	EEGLMOSS	GLOSSEME	EEHHKKOO	KOHEKOHE
EEGINPSW	SWEEPING	EEGLNNTU	UNGENTLE	EEHHLLLO	HELLHOLE
	WEEPINGS	EEGLNOPY	POLYGENE	EEHHLRST	THRESHEL
EEGINQRU	QUEERING	EEGLNOSU	EUGENOLS	EEHHNOPT	ETHEPHON
EEGINQUU	QUEUEING	EEGLNOSZ	LOZENGES	EEHHNOSU	HENHOUSE
EEGINRRS	RESIGNER	EEGLNOTY	TELEGONY	EEHHORSU	HOUHERES
EEGINRRV	REVERING	EEGLNPRU	REPLUNGE	EEHHRRST	THRESHER
EEGINRSS	GREISENS	EEGLNSTT	GENTLEST	EEHHRSST	THRESHES
EEGINRST	GENTRIES	EEGLOPRS	GOSPELER	EEHHSSTW	WHEESHTS
	INTEGERS	EEGLORRV	GROVELER	EEHHSSWW	SHWESHWE

EEHIIKLV	HIVELIKE	EEHINPRT	NEPHRITE	EEHLMOOS	HOLESOME
EEHIJMNR	MIJNHEER		PREHNITE	EEHLMOSS	HOMELESS
EEHIKLLT	HELLKITE		TREPHINE	EEHLMOSY	HEMOLYSE
EEHIKLMO	HOMELIKE	EEHINPSX	PHENIXES	EEHLMOYZ	HEMOLYZE
EEHIKLMP	HEMPLIKE	EEHINRRS	ERRHINES	EEHLMRST	THERMELS
EEHIKLMS	SHEKELIM	EEHINRSS	RESHINES	EEHLNOPT	PHENETOL
EEHIKLOS	HOSELIKE	EEHINRTT	THIRTEEN	EEHLNOTT	TELETHON
EEHIKLRW	WHELKIER	EEHINRTW	WHITENER	EEHLOPSS	HOPELESS
EEHIKLWY	WHEYLIKE	EEHIOPPS	HOSEPIPE	EEHLOPST	HEELPOST
EEHIKRRS	SHRIEKER	EEHIORSS	HEROISES		PESTHOLE
EEHILLMS	SHLEMIEL	EEHIORST	ISOTHERE		TELESHOP
EEHILLNP	HELPLINE		THEORIES	EEHLORST	HOSTELER
EEHILLRS	HELLERIS		THEORISE	EEHLORSV	SHOVELER
	HELLIERS	EEHIORSZ	HEROIZES	EEHLOSSS	SHOELESS
	SHELLIER	EEHIORTZ	THEORIZE	EEHLOSTY	HOLEYEST
EEHILMNS	HEMLINES	EEHIOSTX	ETHOXIES	EEHLPPRS	SHLEPPER
EEHILMNU	HELENIUM	EEHIPPST	PSEPHITE	EEHLPRST	TELPHERS
EEHILMOR	HOMELIER	EEHIPPTY	EPIPHYTE	EEHLPRSU	SPHERULE
EEHILNOP	ENOPHILE	EEHIPRRS	PERISHER	EEHLPSSY	PHYLESES
	NEOPHILE		SPHERIER	EEHLRSST	SHELTERS
EEHILNPW	PINWHEEL	EEHIPRSS	PERISHES	EEHLRSSV	SHELVERS
EEHILNST	THEELINS		PHERESIS	EEHLRSSW	WELSHERS
EEHILOPS	PIEHOLES	EEHIPRST	TREESHIP	EEHLRSTY	SHELTERY
EEHILORT	HOTELIER	EEHIPRTT	PERTHITE	EEHLSSTT	SHTETELS
EEHILOSS	HELIOSES		TEPHRITE	EEHLSSTW	THEWLESS
EEHILPRT	HERPTILE		THREEPIT	EEHMMOPR	MORPHEME
EEHILRSS	HEIRLESS	EEHIPSST	STEEPISH	EEHMMORT	OHMMETER
	RELISHES	EEHIPSTT	EPITHETS	EEHMNOOS	MOONSHEE
EEHILRSV	SHELVIER		TIPSHEET	EEHMNOPS	PHONEMES
EEHILSST	LEISHEST	EEHIPSUU	EUPHUISE	EEHMNORS	HORSEMEN
	SHELTIES	EEHIPUUZ	EUPHUIZE		SHOREMEN
EEHILSSV	HIVELESS	EEHIQRSU	QUEERISH	EEHMNOSU	HOUSEMEN
EEHILWYZ	WHEEZILY	EEHIRRSS	SHERRIES	EEHMNOSW	SOMEWHEN
EEHIMMSS	IMMESHES	EEHIRRSV	SHIVERER	EEHMNRSU	ENRHEUMS
	MISHMEES	EEHIRRSW	WHERRIES	EEHMNRSY	MYNHEERS
EEHIMNOS	HEMIONES	EEHIRRTW	WITHERER	EEHMNSSU	UNMESHES
EEHIMNRS	SHIREMEN	EEHIRRTX	HERETRIX	EEHMNTTU	UMTEENTH
EEHIMNRT	THEREMIN	EEHIRSST	HEISTERS	EEHMOORT	RHEOTOME
EEHIMNSS	INMESHES	EEHIRSSV	SHRIEVES	EEHMOOSS	HOMEOSES
EEHIMOST	HOMESITE	EEHIRSSX	RHEXISES	EEHMORSS	HORMESES
EEHIMPRS	EMPERISH	EEHIRSTT	ETHERIST	EEHMORST	THEOREMS
EEHIMPRT	HEMIPTER	EEHIRTVY	THIEVERY	EEHMORVW	WHOMEVER
EEHIMPST	EPITHEMS	EEHISSST	ESTHESIS	EEHMRSUX	EXHUMERS
	HEMPIEST		HESSITES	EEHMSSTY	METHYSES
EEHIMQUV	VEHMIQUE	EEHISSTW	SWEETISH	EEHNNOOT	ETHONONE
EEHIMRRU	RHEUMIER	EEHISTTW	THEWIEST	EEHNNORT	ENTHRONE
EEHIMRST	ERETHISM	EEHISTWY	WHEYIEST	EEHNNOSS	SHONEENS
	ETHERISM	EEHKLOSY	KEYHOLES	EEHNNPPU	UNHEPPEN
EEHIMRTT	THERMITE	EEHKOOSY	EYEHOOKS	EEHNNSSS	NESHNESS
EEHIMSST	MESHIEST	EEHLLLOW	WELLHOLE	EEHNNSTU	UNNETHES
EEHINNQU	HENEQUIN	EEHLLMPS	PHELLEMS	EEHNOORS	HONOREES
	HENIQUEN	EEHLLMSS	HELMLESS	EEHNOORU	HONOUREE
EEHINNRS	ENSHRINE	EEHLLNSS	ENSHELLS	EEHNOPRU	HEREUPON
EEHINNRT	INHERENT	EEHLLORV	HOVELLER	EEHNOPST	POSHTEEN
EEHINNSS	SNEESHIN	EEHLLOSS	HOLELESS		POTHEENS
EEHINNST	HENNIEST	EEHLLOST	THEELOLS	EEHNOPTY	HYPNOTEE
EEHINORS	HEROINES	EEHLLPSS	HELPLESS		NEOPHYTE
	NOSHERIE	EEHLLRSS	SHELLERS	EEHNORSS	SENHORES
EEHINORT	ETHERION	EEHLMMNS	HELMSMEN	EEHNORST	HONESTER
	HEREINTO	EEHLMMSW	WHEMMLES	EEHNORSW	HERONSEW
EEHINPRS	INSPHERE	EEHLMNOT	HOTELMEN		NOWHERES

EEHNORTU	HEREUNTO	EEIILNST	LENITIES	EEIJLNRT	JETLINER
EEHNORTV	OVERHENT	EEIILNTV	LENITIVE	EEIJLNUV	JUVENILE
EEHNOSST	ETHNOSES	EEIILORS	OILERIES	EEIJMMST	JEMMIEST
EEHNPRSU	UNSPHERE	EEIILRST	TILERIES	EEIJNNOR	ENJOINER
EEHNRTTU	UNTETHER	EEIILRSV	LIVERIES	EEIJNRRU	REINJURE
EEHNSSTU	ENTHUSES	EEIILRSW	WISELIER	EEIJSTTT	JETTIEST
EEHNSSTV	SEVENTHS	EEIILSTV	LEVITIES	EEIKKRST	KERKIEST
EEHOOPRS	OOSPHERE		VEILIEST	EEIKLLRS	SKELLIER
EEHOOPRV	OVERHOPE	EEIILSTW	LEWISITE	EEIKLLRY	KYRIELLE
EEHOOPSW	WHOOPEES	EEIIMMTT	MIMETITE	EEIKLLSS	SKELLIES
EEHOORSV	OVERSHOE	EEIIMNOT	MEIONITE	EEIKLMST	STEMLIKE
EEHOOSST	TOESHOES	EEIIMNST	ENMITIES	EEIKLNOS	NOSELIKE
EEHOOTTY	EYETOOTH	EEIIMOST	MOIETIES	EEIKLNOV	OVENLIKE
EEHOPPRY	HYPEROPE	EEIIMPRS	RIEMPIES	EEIKLNRU	RUNELIKE
EEHOPPSW	PEEPSHOW	EEIIMRSS	MISERIES	EEIKLNSS	LIKENESS
EEHOPRSU	EUPHROES	EEIIMRST	ITEMISER	EEIKLNST	NESTLIKE
EEHOPRVY	OVERHYPE	EEIIMRTZ	ITEMIZER	EEIKLNSY	KEYLINES
EEHOPSST	HEPTOSES	EEIIMSST	ITEMISES	EEIKLNTT	TENTLIKE
EEHORRSV	HOVERERS	EEIIMSSV	EMISSIVE	EEIKLOPP	POPELIKE
EEHORRSW	RESHOWER	EEIIMSTZ	ITEMIZES	EEIKLOPR	ROPELIKE
	SHOWERER	EEIINNST	EINSTEIN	EEIKLOPT	POETLIKE
EEHORRTX	EXHORTER		NINETIES	EEIKLORS	ROSELIKE
EEHORSSU	REHOUSES	EEIINORT	ERIONITE	EEIKLORT	LORIKEET
EEHORSVW	WHOSEVER	EEIINPPR	PIPERINE	EEIKLPST	PIKELETS
EEHORTTU	THEREOUT	EEIINPRS	PINERIES		SPIKELET
EEHORTUW	WHEREOUT	EEIINPRV	VIPERINE		STEPLIKE
EEHOSSTY	EYESHOTS	EEIINRRV	RIVERINE	EEIKLRST	TRISKELE
EEHPRSST	HEPSTERS	EEIINRSS	RESINISE	EEIKLSTV	VESTLIKE
	SPERTHES		SIRENISE	EEIKMOOV	MOVIEOKE
EEHPRSTU	SUPERHET	EEIINRST	ERINITES	EEIKMOTX	KETOXIME
EEHPRSTY	HYPESTER		NITERIES	EEIKMPSS	MISKEEPS
	PHYSETER	EEIINRSV	VINERIES	EEIKMPST	KEMPIEST
EEHRRSTW	WHERRETS	EEIINRSW	SINEWIER	EEIKMRSS	KERMISES
EEHRSSSU	RHESUSES		WINERIES	EEIKNORS	KEROSINE
	USHERESS	EEIINRSZ	RESINIZE	EEIKNORV	REINVOKE
EEHRSSTW	WERSHEST		SIRENIZE	EEIKNPSY	PINKEYES
EEHRSTTW	WHETTERS	EEIINRTT	INTERTIE	EEIKNRRT	TINKERER
EEHSSTUY	SHUTEYES		RETINITE	EEIKNRST	KERNITES
EEIIKKLT	KITELIKE	EEIINRTV	REINVITE	EEIKNSWY	EYEWINKS
EEIIKLLN	LINELIKE	EEIINSST	SIENITES	EEIKOQUV	EQUIVOKE
EEIIKLLR	LIKELIER	EEIINSSV	INESSIVE	EEIKORSU	EUROKIES
EEIIKLLT	TILELIKE	EEIINSSW	EISWEINS	EEIKPPRR	KIPPERER
EEIIKLLV	VEILLIKE	EEIINSTT	ENTITIES	EEIKPRST	PERKIEST
EEIIKLNP	PINELIKE	EEIINSTV	INVITEES	EEIKPSST	PESKIEST
EEIIKLNV	VEINLIKE		VEINIEST	EEIKRRSS	SKERRIES
	VINELIKE	EEIIOPTZ	EPIZOITE	EEIKRRST	RESTRIKE
EEIIKLPP	PIPELIKE	EEIIORSS	OSIERIES	EEIKRSST	KEISTERS
EEIIKLRW	WIRELIKE	EEIIPRSS	PIERISES		KIESTERS
EEIIKLSV	VISELIKE	EEIIPRSX	EXPIRIES	EEIKRSTU	KEIRETSU
EEIIKLSW	LIKEWISE	EEIIPRTT	EPITRITE	EEIKSSTY	SKIEYEST
EEIILLMM	MILLIEME	EEIIQSTU	EQUITIES	EEIKSTTT	TEKTITES
EEIILLMT	MELILITE	EEIIQTUV	QUIETIVE	EEIKSTUY	YEUKIEST
EEIILLOP	EOLIPILE	EEIIRRSV	RIVIERES	EEILLMPR	IMPELLER
EEIILLRV	LIVELIER	EEIIRRTV	TIRRIVEE	EEILLMRS	SMELLIER
EEIILMNT	ILMENITE	EEIIRSTV	VERITIES	EEILLMRU	REILLUME
	MELINITE	EEIISSTV	VISITEES	EEILLMSS	LIMELESS
	MENILITE	EEIISTVW	VIEWIEST		SMELLIES
	TIMELINE	EEIJKLTU	JUTELIKE	EEILLMST	MELLITES
EEIILMRT	TIMELIER	EEIJKRST	JERKIEST	EEILLNOR	LONELIER
EEIILMSS	EMISSILE	EEIJLMSS	MEJLISES	EEILLNPS	SPINELLE
EEIILNPP	PIPELINE	EEIJLNNU	JULIENNE	EEILLNSS	LINELESS

EEILLNSY	SENILELY		PLENTIES	EEILPSTY	EPISTYLE
EEILLNVV	VENVILLE	EEILNQUY	EQUINELY	EEILQRSU	RELIQUES
EEILLOOP	EOLOPILE	EEILNRSS	REINLESS	EEILRRSV	RELIVERS
EEILLORS	ORSEILLE	EEILNRST	ENLISTER		RESILVER
EEILLORV	LOVELIER		LISTENER		REVILERS
EEILLOSV	LOVELIES		REENLIST		SILVERER
EEILLPSS	ELLIPSES		SILENTER		SLIVERER
	PILELESS	EEILNRSV	LIVENERS	EEILRRTT	LITTERER
EEILLPSY	SLEEPILY		SNIVELER	EEILRSST	LEISTERS
EEILLPZZ	PIZZELLE	EEILNRTT	NETTLIER		RITELESS
EEILLRSS	LEISLERS	EEILNRTY	ENTIRELY		TIRELESS
EEILLRST	TREILLES		LIENTERY	EEILRSSU	LEISURES
EEILLSSS	ISLELESS	EEILNRUV	UNVEILER	EEILRSSV	SERVILES
EEILLSSV	VEILLESS	EEILNSST	LITENESS	EEILRSSW	WIRELESS
EEILLSTT	STELLITE		SETLINES	EEILRSTT	RETITLES
EEILLSTV	EVILLEST	EEILNSSV	EVILNESS	EEILRSVY	LIVEYERS
EEILLSTW	WELLSITE		LIVENESS	EEILSSTW	WITELESS
EEILLTVY	VELLEITY		VEINLESS	EEILSSTX	EXITLESS
EEILLVWY	WEEVILLY		VILENESS		SEXTILES
EEILMMST	MELTEMIS		VINELESS	EEILSSVW	VIEWLESS
EEILMNNO	LIMONENE	EEILNSSW	WINELESS	EEILSSVX	SILVEXES
EEILMNNS	LINESMEN	EEILNSTT	ENTITLES	EEILSTTX	TEXTILES
EEILMNNU	ENLUMINE	EEILNSTV	VEINLETS	EEILSTUX	ULEXITES
EEILMNOP	PEMOLINE	EEILNSUV	VEINULES	EEILSTVY	STIEVELY
EEILMNOR	LEMONIER	EEILNTUV	VEINULET	EEIMMNRS	IMMENSER
EEILMNRS	ERMELINS	EEILOPRS	PELORIES	EEIMMORS	MEMORIES
EEILMNRU	LEMURINE	EEILOPST	PETIOLES		MEMORISE
	RELUMINE	EEILORRT	LOITERER	EEIMMORZ	MEMORIZE
EEILMNSS	ISLESMEN	EEILORRV	OVERLIER	EEIMMOST	SOMETIME
EEILMNSU	SELENIUM	EEILORRW	LOWERIER	EEIMMRRS	IMMERSER
	SEMILUNE	EEILORST	LITEROSE	EEIMMRSS	IMMERSES
EEILMNSY	MYELINES		TROELIES	EEIMMRST	MERISTEM
EEILMOPS	POLEMISE	EEILORSV	OVERLIES		MIMESTER
EEILMOPZ	POLEMIZE		RELIEVOS		MISMETRE
EEILMORT	MOTELIER		VOLERIES		STEMMIER
EEILMOST	MESOLITE	EEILORSW	OWLERIES	EEIMMRSU	EUMERISM
	MISLETOE	EEILORVV	OVERLIVE	EEIMMRTT	TERMTIME
EEILMPST	IMPLETES		OVERVEIL	EEIMMSSS	MISSEEMS
EEILMPSX	IMPLEXES	EEILOSST	ESTOILES	EEIMMSST	MISMEETS
EEILMQTU	MIQUELET	EEILOSSX	ISOLEXES	EEIMMSTU	SEMIMUTE
EEILMRSS	RIMELESS	EEILOSTW	OWELTIES	EEIMNNOS	NOMINEES
EEILMRST	TERMLIES	EEILOSTZ	ZEOLITES	EEIMNNRS	REINSMEN
EEILMRSV	VERMEILS	EEILOSVW	VOWELISE	EEIMNOPS	EPISEMON
EEILMSST	TIMELESS	EEILOTTT	TOILETTE		SEMIOPEN
EEILMSTT	MELTIEST	EEILOVWZ	VOWELIZE	EEIMNORS	EMERSION
EEILMSUV	EMULSIVE	EEILPPSS	PIPELESS	EEIMNORT	TIMONEER
EEILNNOT	NONELITE	EEILPPSY	EPILEPSY	EEIMNORV	OVERMINE
EEILNNST	LENIENTS	EEILPPRRS	REPLIERS		VOMERINE
	SENTINEL	EEILPRSS	SPIELERS	EEIMNOST	MONETISE
EEILNNSV	ENLIVENS	EEILPRST	EPISTLER		SEMITONE
EEILNOPR	LEPORINE		PELTRIES	EEIMNOTX	XENOTIME
EEILNORS	ELOINERS		PERLITES	EEIMNOTZ	MONETIZE
EEILNOST	NOSELITE		REPTILES		ZONETIME
EEILNOSV	NOVELISE		SPIRELET	EEIMNPRS	SPERMINE
EEILNOVV	LOVEVINE	EEILPRSU	SUPERLIE	EEIMNPRU	PERINEUM
EEILNOVZ	NOVELIZE	EEILPRSV	PRELIVES	EEIMNPRZ	PRIZEMEN
EEILNPPZ	ZEPPELIN	EEILPSSS	PELISSES	EEIMNPST	SEPIMENT
EEILNPRS	PILSENER	EEILPSST	EPISTLES	EEIMNQSU	MESQUINE
EEILNPRU	PERILUNE	EEILPSSU	EPULISES	EEIMNRRT	TERMINER
EEILNPRV	REPLEVIN	EEILPSSV	PELVISES	EEIMNRRV	RIVERMEN
EEILNPST	PENLITES	EEILPSTW	SWEETLIP	EEIMNRST	MISENTER

EEIMNRSV	MINEVERS	EEINNPTT	PENITENT			RENTIERS
EEIMNRTU	MUTINEER	EEINNRST	INTENSER			TERRINES
EEIMNRTV	VIREMENT		INTERNES	EEINRRSU	REINSURE	
EEIMNSSS	MISSENSE	EEINNRSU	NEURINES	EEINRRSV	VERNIERS	
EEIMNSSW	MISWEENS	EEINNRSV	INNERVES	EEINRRTU	REUNITER	
EEIMNSTT	MINETTES		NERVINES		UNRETIRE	
EEIMNSTV	MISEVENT	EEINNRTT	INTERNET	EEINRRTV	INVERTER	
EEIMOPRS	MOPERIES		RENITENT	EEINRRTW	WINTERER	
	PROMISEE	EEINNRTV	INVENTER	EEINRRTX	INTERREX	
	REIMPOSE		REINVENT	EEINRSST	INTERESS	
EEIMOPSS	EPISOMES	EEINNRUX	XENURINE		SENTRIES	
EEIMOPST	EPISTOME	EEINNSST	TENNISES		TRENISES	
	EPITOMES	EEINNSTT	SENTIENT	EEINRSSU	ENURESIS	
	EPSOMITE	EEINNSTW	ENTWINES		ERINUSES	
EEIMORSS	ISOMERES		WENNIEST	EEINRSSV	INVERSES	
EEIMORST	TIRESOME	EEINNSTZ	NETIZENS		VERSINES	
EEIMORSZ	SIEROZEM	EEINOOPT	OPTIONEE	EEINRSTT	INERTEST	
EEIMORTV	OVERTIME	EEINOPPR	PEPERINO		INSETTER	
EEIMORTX	OXIMETER		PEPERONI		INTEREST	
EEIMOSSS	SEMIOSES		RONEPIPE		STERNITE	
EEIMOSSW	SOMEWISE	EEINOPRS	ISOPRENE		TRIENTES	
EEIMOSSX	EXOMISES		PEREIONS	EEINRSTU	ESURIENT	
EEIMOTTT	TOTEMITE		PIONEERS		NEURITES	
EEIMPPRS	EPISPERM	EEINOPTY	EYEPOINT		RETINUES	
EEIMPPST	PIPESTEM	EEINORRR	ORNERIER		REUNITES	
EEIMPRRS	PREMIERS	EEINORRT	ORIENTER	EEINRSTV	NERVIEST	
	REPRIMES		REORIENT		REINVEST	
	SIMPERER	EEINORSS	ESSOINER		SERVIENT	
EEIMPRSS	EMPRISES	EEINORST	ONERIEST		SIRVENTE	
	IMPRESES		SEROTINE	EEINRSTX	INTERSEX	
	IMPRESSE	EEINORSV	EVERSION	EEINRSTY	SERENITY	
	MESPRISE	EEINORTT	TENORITE	EEINRSUV	UNIVERSE	
	PREMISES	EEINORTX	EXERTION	EEINRSVX	VERNIXES	
	SPIREMES	EEINOSSS	ENOSISES	EEINRSWW	NEWSWIRE	
EEIMPRST	EMPTIERS		NOESISES	EEINRTTY	ENTIRETY	
EEIMPRSX	PREMIXES	EEINOSST	ESSONITE		ETERNITY	
EEIMPRSZ	EMPRIZES	EEINOSTT	NOISETTE	EEINSSST	SESTINES	
	MESPRIZE		TEOSINTE	EEINSSSW	WISENESS	
EEIMPSST	SEPTIMES	EEINPPSS	PEPSINES	EEINSSSX	SEXINESS	
EEIMPSSY	EMPYESIS	EEINPRRS	PRERINSE	EEINSSTW	NEWSIEST	
EEIMPSTT	EMPTIEST		REPINERS	EEINSSTX	SIXTEENS	
EEIMQRSU	REQUIEMS		RIPENERS	EEINSSTY	SYENITES	
EEIMQSTU	MESQUITE	EEINPRSS	EREPSINS	EEINSSUX	UNISEXES	
EEIMQTUZ	MEZQUITE		RIPENESS	EEINSTTT	NETTIEST	
EEIMRRST	MERRIEST	EEINPRSU	PENURIES		TENTIEST	
	MITERERS		RESUPINE	EEINSTTW	TENTWISE	
	RIMESTER	EEINPRTU	PREUNITE		TWENTIES	
	TRIREMES	EEINPRTX	INEXPERT	EEINSTTX	EXISTENT	
EEIMRRTT	REMITTER	EEINPSST	PENTISES	EEIOPPRS	EPISPORE	
	TRIMETER	EEINPSTT	INEPTEST		POPERIES	
EEIMRSST	MEISTERS		SPINETTE	EEIOPPST	EPITOPES	
	MISSTEER	EEINQRRU	ENQUIRER	EEIOPRRS	ROPERIES	
	TRISEMES	EEINQRSU	ENQUIRES	EEIOPRRT	PORTIERE	
EEIMRSTT	EMITTERS		INQUERES	EEIOPRRV	OVERRIPE	
	TERMITES		SQUIREEN	EEIOPRST	POETISER	
EEIMRSTU	EMERITUS	EEINQSTU	QUIETENS		POETRIES	
EEIMRTTY	TEMERITY	EEINQSUY	QUEYNIES	EEIOPRTZ	POETIZER	
EEIMSSST	MESSIEST	EEINRRSS	RESINERS	EEIOPSST	POETISES	
	METISSES	EEINRRST	INSERTER	EEIOPSTZ	POETIZES	
EEINNNPS	PENNINES		REINSERT	EEIORRRS	ORRERIES	
EEINNOPS	PENSIONE		REINTERS	EEIORRSS	ROSERIES	

	ROSIERES		VERQUIRE	**EEJQRRSU**	JERQUERS
EEIORRTV	OVERTIRE	**EEIQRSSU**	ESQUIRES	**EEKKNNUU**	KUNEKUNE
EEIORRTW	TOWERIER	**EEIQRSTU**	QUIETERS	**EEKKORWW**	WORKWEEK
EEIORRTX	EXTERIOR		REQUITES	**EEKKOSTV**	VETKOEKS
EEIORRUV	OUVRIERE	**EEIQRSTW**	QWERTIES	**EEKKRRST**	TREKKERS
EEIORSST	EROTESIS	**EEIQRTUY**	QUEERITY	**EEKLLNRY**	KERNELLY
	EROTISES	**EEIQSSSU**	ESQUISSE	**EEKLLNSS**	KNEVELLS
EEIORSSX	OREXISES	**EEIQSTTU**	QUIETEST	**EEKLLSUU**	UKULELES
EEIORSTZ	EROTIZES	**EEIRRRST**	RETIRERS	**EEKLMRSZ**	KLEZMERS
EEIORSVW	OVERWISE		TERRIERS	**EEKLNNNU**	UNKENNEL
EEIORSVZ	OVERSIZE	**EEIRRRTW**	REWRITER	**EEKLNOSS**	KEELSONS
EEIORVVW	OVERVIEW	**EEIRRSST**	RESISTER	**EEKLNOST**	SKELETON
EEIORVWW	WIREWOVE		TRESSIER	**EEKLNOSV**	VELSKOEN
EEIPPPRR	PREPPIER	**EEIRRSSU**	REISSUER	**EEKLORTW**	TELEWORK
EEIPPPRS	PREPPIES	**EEIRRSSV**	REVERSIS	**EEKLOSSU**	LEUKOSES
EEIPPPST	PEPPIEST		REVISERS	**EEKLOSSY**	YOKELESS
EEIPPQRU	EQUIPPER	**EEIRRSSW**	WERRISES	**EEKLRSST**	KESTRELS
EEIPPRRS	PERSPIRE	**EEIRRSTV**	RESTRIVE		SKELTERS
EEIPPRRT	PERIPTER		REVERIST	**EEKNNSTT**	KENNETTS
EEIPPRST	PEPTISER		RIVERETS	**EEKNOPRS**	RESPOKEN
EEIPPRTY	PERIPETY		RIVETERS	**EEKNORTY**	KEYNOTER
EEIPPRTZ	PEPTIZER	**EEIRRSTW**	REWRITES	**EEKNOSTY**	KEYNOTES
EEIPPSST	PEPTISES	**EEIRRSVV**	REVIVERS		KEYSTONE
EEIPPSTT	PIPETTES	**EEIRRTTT**	TITTERER	**EEKNSSST**	KNESSETS
EEIPPSTZ	PEPTIZES	**EEIRSSSU**	REISSUES	**EEKNSSSW**	SKEWNESS
EEIPQRSU	PERIQUES		SEISURES	**EEKNSSTU**	NETSUKES
	REEQUIPS	**EEIRSSSV**	IVRESSES	**EEKOOPPS**	PEKEPOOS
	REPIQUES	**EEIRSSTT**	RESTIEST	**EEKOORST**	KREOSOTE
EEIPQSTU	PEQUISTE	**EEIRSSTU**	SURETIES	**EEKOPRTV**	OVERKEPT
EEIPRRRS	PERRIERS	**EEIRSSTV**	SIEVERTS	**EEKOPSTU**	OUTKEEPS
EEIPRRSS	PRISERES		TREVISES	**EEKORRSV**	REVOKERS
	REPRISES		VESTRIES	**EEKORSST**	RESTOKES
	RESPIRES	**EEIRSSTW**	SWEIREST	**EEKORSTV**	OVERKEST
EEIPRRSV	REPRIVES	**EEIRSSUZ**	SEIZURES		VOERTSEK
EEIPRRSW	PREWIRES	**EEIRSTTU**	SUETTIER	**EEKRRSUZ**	KREUZERS
EEIPRRSX	EXPIRERS	**EEIRSTVV**	VETIVERS	**EEKRRTUZ**	KREUTZER
EEIPRRSZ	REPRIZES	**EEIRSTVY**	SEVERITY	**EEKRSSTY**	KEYSTERS
EEIPRRTT	PRETERIT	**EEIRTTTZ**	TERZETTI	**EELLLLMP**	PELLMELL
	PRETTIER	**EEIRTTVV**	VETIVERT	**EELLMORS**	MORELLES
EEIPRRTW	TWERPIER	**EEISSSTV**	VITESSES	**EELLMORW**	MELLOWER
EEIPRSSS	PRESSIES	**EEISSTTT**	TESTIEST	**EELLMOSS**	MOSELLES
EEIPRSST	RESPITES	**EEISSTTU**	SUETIEST	**EELLMPTU**	PLUMELET
EEIPRSSV	PREVISES	**EEISSTTV**	STIEVEST	**EELLMRSS**	SMELLERS
EEIPRSTT	PRETTIES	**EEISSTTW**	STEWIEST	**EELLMRSV**	VERMELLS
EEIPRSTV	PERVIEST	**EEISSTTZ**	ZESTIEST	**EELLNNOV**	NONLEVEL
EEIPRSTX	PREEXIST	**EEISTTTX**	TETTIXES	**EELLNORR**	ENROLLER
EEIPRSTY	PERSEITY	**EEISTUXZ**	ZEUXITES		REENROLL
	YPERITES	**EEJJLNUY**	JEJUNELY	**EELLNORS**	RELLENOS
EEIPRSVW	PREVIEWS	**EEJKMOOS**	JOKESOME	**EELLNOUV**	NOUVELLE
EEIPRSZZ	PREZZIES	**EEJKNRTU**	JUNKETER	**EELLNPRU**	PRUNELLE
EEIPRTUV	ERUPTIVE	**EEJKORST**	JOKESTER	**EELLNRSU**	SULLENER
EEIPSSSS	SPEISSES	**EEJLLMSU**	JUMELLES	**EELLNSSS**	LENSLESS
EEIPSSTT	PESTIEST	**EEJLLORY**	JOLLEYER	**EELLNSST**	SNELLEST
EEIPSSTW	SPEWIEST	**EEJLPSTU**	PULSEJET	**EELLNSSW**	WELLNESS
	STEPWISE	**EEJNOORS**	REJONEOS	**EELLNSTU**	ENTELLUS
EEIPSTTT	PETTIEST	**EEJNORSY**	ENJOYERS	**EELLNSUV**	UNLEVELS
EEIQRRRU	REQUIRER		REENJOYS	**EELLOPSS**	ELLOPSES
EEIQRRSU	QUERIERS	**EEJORSST**	RESOJETS		POLELESS
	REQUIRES	**EEJPRRRU**	PERJURER	**EELLORRR**	REROLLER
EEIQRRTU	REQUITER	**EEJPRRSU**	PERJURES	**EELLORSS**	ROSELLES
EEIQRRUV	QUIVERER	**EEJPRSTU**	SUPERJET	**EELLORST**	SOLLERET

EELLORSV	OVERSELL	**EELNOPSY**	POLYENES			TRUELOVE
EELLORSZ	ROZELLES	**EELNOPTY**	POLYTENE	**EELOSSST**	OSSELETS
EELLORTX	EXTOLLER	**EELNOQTU**	ELOQUENT	**EELOSSSU**	SOLEUSES
EELLORVY	VOLLEYER	**EELNORST**	ENTRESOL	**EELOSSTT**	TELEOSTS
EELLORWY	YELLOWER	**EELNORTT**	TELETRON	**EELOSSTU**	SETULOSE
EELLOSSS	SOLELESS	**EELNORTV**	OVERLENT	**EELOSSTV**	VETOLESS
EELLOSSV	LOVELESS	**EELNOSSS**	NOSELESS			VOTELESS
EELLOSUV	LEVULOSE			SOLENESS	**EELOSTTX**	SEXTOLET
EELLPRSS	PRESELLS	**EELNOSST**	NOTELESS	**EELOSTUV**	EVOLUTES
	RESPELLS		TONELESS			VELOUTES
	SPELLERS	**EELNOSSU**	SELENOUS	**EELPPSSU**	PEPLUSES
EELLPRST	PRETELLS	**EELNOSSY**	ESLOYNES	**EELPPSTU**	SEPTUPLE
EELLPSST	PELTLESS	**EELNOSSZ**	ZONELESS	**EELPQRSU**	PREQUELS
EELLQRSU	QUELLERS	**EELNOSTT**	NOTELETS	**EELPRRSU**	REPULSER
EELLRSSU	RULELESS	**EELNOSTU**	TOLUENES	**EELPRSST**	SPELTERS
EELLRSSW	SWELLERS	**EELNOSUV**	VENULOSE	**EELPRSSU**	REPULSES
EELLSSTU	TELLUSES	**EELNOTVV**	EVOLVENT	**EELPRSTY**	PEYTRELS
EELLSSTW	SWELLEST	**EELNRSST**	NESTLERS	**EELPRSTZ**	PRETZELS
EELLSTVY	SVELTELY		SLENTERS	**EELPRSUX**	PLEXURES
EELMMPSU	EMPLUMES	**EELNRSTT**	LETTERNS	**EELPRTXY**	EXPERTLY
EELMMPUX	EXEMPLUM		NETTLERS	**EELPSSTZ**	SPELTZES
EELMNOOS	LONESOME	**EELNRSUV**	NERVULES	**EELPSSUX**	EXPULSES
	OENOMELS	**EELNSSSW**	NEWSLESS			PLEXUSES
EELMNORS	SOLEMNER	**EELNSSTT**	TENTLESS			SUPLEXES
EELMNSUY	UNSEEMLY	**EELNSSTU**	TUNELESS	**EELPSTUX**	SEXTUPLE
EELMNTTU	TEMULENT		UNSTEELS	**EELRRSTW**	WRESTLER
EELMNTUY	UNMEETLY	**EELNSSTV**	VENTLESS	**EELRSSST**	RESTLESS
EELMOOSV	LOVESOME	**EELNSSTY**	ENSTYLES			TRESSELS
EELMOPRS	PLEROMES	**EELNSSUV**	UNSELVES	**EELRSSTT**	SETTLERS
EELMOPRY	EMPLOYER	**EELNSTTU**	LUNETTES			STERLETS
	REEMPLOY		UNSETTLE			TRESTLES
EELMOPST	LEPTOMES	**EELOORVV**	OVERLOVE	**EELRSSTU**	STREUSEL
EELMOPSY	EMPLOYES	**EELOPPRS**	PEOPLERS	**EELRSSTV**	SERVLETS
	POLYSEME	**EELOPPSS**	PEPLOSES	**EELRSSTW**	SWELTERS
EELMORST	MOLESTER		POPELESS			WRESTLES
EELMORSW	EELWORMS	**EELOPPST**	ESTOPPEL	**EELRSSTY**	RESTYLES
EELMORTV	OVERMELT	**EELOPPSZ**	ZEPPOLES			TYRELESS
EELMORTY	MOTLEYER	**EELOPRRX**	EXPLORER	**EELRSSTZ**	SELTZERS
	REMOTELY	**EELOPRSV**	PRESOLVE	**EELRSTWY**	WESTERLY
EELMOSSV	MOVELESS	**EELOPRSX**	EXPLORES	**EELSSSTV**	VESTLESS
EELMOTVW	TWELVEMO	**EELOPRTT**	TELEPORT	**EELSSSTZ**	ZESTLESS
EELMPPRU	EMPURPLE	**EELOPSST**	POETLESS	**EELSSTTV**	SVELTEST
EELMPSST	SEMPLEST	**EELOPSTU**	EELPOUTS	**EELSSTTX**	TEXTLESS
	STEMPELS		OUTSLEEP	**EELSSTUY**	EUSTYLES
	STEMPLES		SLEEPOUT	**EEMMNNOY**	MONEYMEN
EELMPSTT	TEMPLETS	**EELOQRUY**	REQUOYLE	**EEMMNOOP**	MENOPOME
EELMRRTU	MURRELET	**EELORRSV**	RESOLVER	**EEMMNOST**	MEMENTOS
EELMRSST	RESMELTS	**EELORRTV**	REVOLTER	**EEMMNOTV**	MOVEMENT
	SMELTERS	**EELORRTW**	TROWELER	**EEMMNRRY**	MERRYMEN
	TERMLESS	**EELORRUV**	OVERRULE	**EEMMOORS**	MEROSOME
EELMRSTY	SMELTERY	**EELORRVV**	REVOLVER	**EEMMOOSS**	MESOSOME
EELMRTUX	LUXMETER	**EELORSSS**	ROSELESS	**EEMMOSST**	MESTOMES
EELMSSST	STEMLESS	**EELORSST**	SOLERETS	**EEMMOSSU**	MOUSMEES
EELMSSTT	STEMLETS	**EELORSSV**	RESOLVES	**EEMMRSST**	STEMMERS
EELNNOSS	LONENESS	**EELORSTT**	LORETTES	**EEMMRSTY**	STEMMERY
EELNNRTU	TUNNELER	**EELORSTU**	RESOLUTE	**EEMMRTUX**	EXTREMUM
EELNNUVY	UNEVENLY	**EELORSTV**	OVERLETS	**EEMNNOPR**	PRENOMEN
EELNOORS	LOOSENER	**EELORSVV**	EVOLVERS	**EEMNNOPW**	PENWOMEN
EELNOPPU	UNPEOPLE		REVOLVES	**EEMNNOSV**	ENVENOMS
EELNOPRT	PETRONEL	**EELORTTU**	ROULETTE	**EEMNOOSS**	SOMEONES
EELNOPSV	ENVELOPS	**EELORTUV**	REVOLUTE	**EEMNOOSY**	MOONEYES

EEMNOPRS	PROSEMEN	**EENNOORT**	ROTENONE	**EENRRSTV**	RENVERST
EEMNORRS	SERMONER	**EENNOPSS**	OPENNESS	**EENRRSUV**	NERVURES
EEMNORSS	MORENESS	**EENNOPTX**	EXPONENT	**EENRRTUV**	VENTURER
EEMNORST	SERMONET	**EENNORRW**	RENOWNER	**EENRSSSU**	SURENESS
	STOREMEN	**EENNORST**	ENTERONS	**EENRSSTT**	STERNEST
EEMNORSU	MOUNSEER		TENONERS		TESTERNS
EEMNORSV	OVERSMEN	**EENNORSU**	NEURONES	**EENRSSTU**	TRUENESS
	VENOMERS	**EENNOSTT**	NONETTES	**EENRSSTW**	WESTERNS
EEMNORSY	MONEYERS	**EENNQSUU**	UNQUEENS	**EENRSSTY**	STYRENES
EEMNORTU	ROUTEMEN	**EENNRSUV**	UNNERVES	**EENRSTUV**	VENTURES
EEMNPRSS	PRESSMEN	**EENNSSSU**	UNSENSES	**EEOOPPRS**	REOPPOSE
EEMNPRSU	SUPERMEN	**EENNSSTX**	NEXTNESS	**EEOOPRST**	PROTEOSE
EEMNPRTU	ERUMPENT	**EENOORST**	OESTRONE	**EEOOPRSX**	EXOSPORE
	UNTEMPER		ROESTONE	**EEOOPRTZ**	ZOETROPE
EEMNRSTU	MUENSTER	**EENOORTU**	EURONOTE	**EEOORRVW**	OVERWORE
EEMNRSTW	TREWSMEN	**EENOORTV**	OVERTONE	**EEOORTVV**	OVERVOTE
EEMNSSTU	MUTENESS	**EENOPPRS**	PREPONES	**EEOOSSST**	OSTEOSES
	TENESMUS		PROPENES	**EEOPPRRR**	PROPERER
EEMNSTTV	VESTMENT		PROPENSE	**EEOPPRSS**	PORPESSE
EEMOOPRT	PROTEOME	**EENOPPST**	PEPTONES		PREPOSES
EEMOORRT	OROMETER	**EENOPRSS**	RESPONSE	**EEOPPSTT**	POPETTES
EEMOORRV	MOREOVER	**EENOPRST**	PROTENSE	**EEOPPSTU**	OUTPEEPS
EEMOORTT	ROOMETTE	**EENOPRSU**	PERONEUS	**EEOPRRRT**	REPORTER
EEMOOSSX	EXOSMOSE	**EENOPRTT**	ENTREPOT	**EEOPRRRV**	REPROVER
EEMOPRRS	EMPERORS	**EENOPRTU**	OUTPREEN	**EEOPRRSS**	REPOSERS
	PREMORSE	**EENOPRXY**	PYROXENE	**EEOPRRST**	PRESTORE
EEMOPRSV	PREMOVES	**EENOPSST**	PENTOSES	**EEOPRRSU**	REPOSURE
EEMOPRSW	EMPOWERS		POSTEENS	**EEOPRRSV**	REPROVES
EEMOQRSU	MORESQUE		POSTTEEN	**EEOPRRSW**	REPOWERS
EEMOQTTU	MOQUETTE	**EENOPSTT**	POSTTEEN	**EEOPRRTT**	POTTERER
EEMORRSS	REMORSES		POTTEENS	**EEOPRRTV**	OVERPERT
EEMORRSU	UROMERES	**EENOPSTY**	NEOTYPES	**EEOPRRTX**	EXPORTER
EEMORRSV	REMOVERS	**EENORRSV**	OVERRENS		REEXPORT
EEMORRTU	MOUTERER	**EENORRTT**	ROTTENER	**EEOPRSSS**	ESPRESSO
	OUTREMER	**EENORSSS**	SORENESS	**EEOPRSST**	PORTESSE
EEMORSST	SOMERSET	**EENORSST**	ESTRONES	**EEOPRSSU**	ESPOUSER
EEMORSTT	REMOTEST	**EENORSSU**	NEUROSES		REPOUSSE
EEMORSTU	TEMEROUS	**EENORSTT**	ONSETTER	**EEOPRSSX**	EXPOSERS
EEMOSSST	MESTESOS	**EENORSTV**	OVERNETS		EXPRESSO
EEMOTTTU	TEETOTUM	**EENORSTX**	EXTENSOR	**EEOPRSTT**	PROETTES
EEMOTTZZ	MOZZETTE	**EENORSVW**	OVERSEWN		TREETOPS
EEMPPRST	PREEMPTS	**EENORTVW**	OVERWENT	**EEOPRSTU**	OUTPEERS
EEMPRRST	PRETERMS	**EENOSSST**	STENOSES	**EEOPRSTV**	OVERSTEP
EEMPRRSU	PRESUMER	**EENOSSSY**	ESSOYNES		STEPOVER
	SUPREMER	**EENOSTTT**	TONETTES	**EEOPRSTY**	SEROTYPE
EEMPRSST	SEMPSTER	**EENOSTUV**	VENTOUSE	**EEOPRSUX**	EXPOSURE
EEMPRSSU	PRESUMES	**EENPPRST**	PERPENTS	**EEOPRTVY**	OVERTYPE
	SUPREMES	**EENPRSST**	PENSTERS	**EEOPSSSU**	ESPOUSES
EEMPRSTT	TEMPTERS		PERTNESS		POSEUSES
EEMPRSTU	PERMUTES		PRESENTS	**EEOPSSTW**	SWEETSOP
EEMPSSTT	TEMPESTS		SERPENTS	**EEOPSSTY**	EYESPOTS
EEMPSSTY	EMPTYSES	**EENPRSSU**	PURENESS	**EEOPSTUW**	OUTSWEEP
EEMRRSSU	RESUMERS	**EENPRSTT**	STREPENT		OUTWEEPS
EEMRRSTU	MUSTERER	**EENPRSTV**	PREVENTS	**EEOQRSTU**	REQUOTES
EEMRRSUU	EREMURUS	**EENPRTUX**	UNEXPERT	**EEOQRTTU**	ROQUETTE
	REMUEURS	**EENPSSSU**	SUSPENSE	**EEORRRST**	RESORTER
EEMRRTTU	MUTTERER	**EENPSSTY**	STEPNEYS		RESTORER
EEMSSTTU	MUSETTES	**EENPSTTU**	PETUNTSE		RETRORSE
EENNNOSS	NONSENSE	**EENPTTUZ**	PETUNTZE	**EEORRRTT**	RETORTER
EENNNOTV	NONEVENT	**EENQSSTU**	SEQUENTS	**EEORRSST**	RESTORES
EENNNPTY	TENPENNY	**EENRRRTU**	RETURNER	**EEORRSSV**	REVERSOS
		EENRRSSU	ENSURERS		

EEORRSTU	REROUTES	EERSTTTU	UTTEREST	EFFISSTT	STIFFEST
EEORRSTV	EVERTORS	EERSTTUX	TEXTURES	EFFISSUX	SUFFIXES
	RESTROVE	EESSSTTT	SESTETTS	EFFLLOSS	SELLOFFS
EEORRSTX	EXTRORSE	EESSTTTX	SEXTETTS	EFFLMNUU	UNMUFFLE
EEORRSTY	OYSTERER	EFFFGINO	FEOFFING	EFFLMRSU	MUFFLERS
EEORRSUV	OVERSURE	EFFFILRU	FLUFFIER	EFFLNRSU	SNUFFLER
EEORRTTT	TOTTERER	EFFFINOS	INFEOFFS	EFFLNRUU	UNRUFFLE
EEORRTTX	EXTORTER	EFFFISTU	FUFFIEST	EFFLNSSU	SNUFFLES
EEORRTUV	OVERTURE	EFFFLRSU	FLUFFERS	EFFLOSSU	SOUFFLES
	TROUVERE	EFFFOORS	FEOFFORS	EFFLRRSU	RUFFLERS
EEORRSSST	OSSETERS	EFFGILRU	GRIEFFUL	EFFLRSTU	TRUFFLES
EEORRSTT	ROSETTES	EFFGINOR	OFFERING	EFFNRSSU	SNUFFERS
EEORRSTV	ESTOVERS	EFFGINSU	EFFUSING	EFFNSSTU	FUNFESTS
	OVERSETS	EFFGIRRU	GRUFFIER	EFFOOORT	FOREFOOT
EEORRSUV	OVERUSES	EFFGRSTU	GRUFFEST	EFFOORRS	OFFERORS
EEORRSSVW	OVERSEWS	EFFHIILS	FILEFISH	EFFOPRRS	PROFFERS
EEORRSTTU	OUTSTEER	EFFHIIRW	WHIFFIER	EFFORRST	TROFFERS
EEORRSTUV	OUTSERVE	EFFHIISW	FISHWIFE	EFFORRUV	OVERRUFF
EEORRSTVW	OVERWETS	EFFHIITT	FIFTIETH	EFFORSSW	SWOFFERS
EEORRSTVX	VORTEXES	EFFHILRW	WHIFFLER	EFFRRSUU	FURFURES
EEORRTTTZ	TERZETTO	EFFHILLS	WHIFFLES	EFFRSSTU	RESTUFFS
EEOSSSSVW	VOWESSES	EFFHIRSS	SHERIFFS		STUFFERS
EEOSSTTT	SESTETTO	EFFHIRSW	WHIFFERS	EFFSSSUU	SUFFUSES
EEPPRRSS	PREPRESS	EFFHISTU	HUFFIEST	EFGGGILN	FLEGGING
EEPPRSST	STEPPERS	EFFHISTW	WHIFFETS	EFGGIINN	FEIGNING
EEPPRSTY	PRETYPES	EFFHLLSU	SHELFFUL	EFGGILOS	SOLFEGGI
EEPPSSUW	UPSWEEPS	EFFHLRSU	SHUFFLER	EFGGINRU	REFUGING
EEPQRRUU	PERRUQUE	EFFHLSSU	SHUFFLES	EFGGIORR	FROGGIER
EEPRRSSS	PRESSERS	EFFHOOOR	FOREHOOF	EFGGIOST	FOGGIEST
EEPRRSST	PRESTERS	EFFHOORS	OFFSHORE	EFGGIRRS	FRIGGERS
EEPRRSSU	PERUSERS	EFFIIMST	MIFFIEST	EFGGIRTU	EGGFRUIT
	PRESSURE	EFFIINRS	SNIFFIER	EFGGISTU	FUGGIEST
EEPRRSTV	PERVERTS	EFFIINSS	IFFINESS	EFGGLORS	FLOGGERS
EEPRRSUU	REPURSUE	EFFIINST	NIFFIEST	EFGGORRY	FROGGERY
EEPRRSVY	REPRYVES	EFFIIPRS	SPIFFIER	EFGHHIIL	HIGHLIFE
EEPRRTTU	PUTTERER	EFFIIPSS	SPIFFIES	EFGHIILS	FLEISHIG
EEPRSSTT	PRETESTS	EFFIISST	STIFFIES	EFGHILNS	FLESHING
EEPRSSTX	SEXPERTS	EFFIKLLO	FOLKLIFE		SHELFING
EEPRSSUX	SUPERSEX	EFFIKLRU	RUFFLIKE	EFGHINRS	FRESHING
EEPRSTTU	UPSETTER	EFFIKLSS	SKIFFLES	EFGHINRT	FRIGHTEN
EEPRSTTX	PRETEXTS	EFFILNRS	SNIFFLER	EFGHIOSY	FOGEYISH
EEPSSTTY	TYPESETS	EFFILNSS	SNIFFLES	EFGHIPRT	PREFIGHT
EEQRRSSTU	QUESTERS	EFFILORT	FORELIFT	EFGHIRST	FIGHTERS
	REQUESTS	EFFILPRS	PIFFLERS		FREIGHTS
EERRSSST	RESTRESS	EFFILPRU	PLUFFIER		REFIGHTS
EERRSSTU	TRESSURE	EFFILRRS	RIFFLERS	EFGHNOTU	FOUGHTEN
EERRSSTW	STREWERS	EFFILRRU	RUFFLIER	EFGHORTU	REFOUGHT
	WRESTERS	EFFILRSU	SIFFLEUR	EFGIIINS	IGNIFIES
EERRSSVW	SWERVERS	EFFINOSU	EFFUSION	EFGIILNR	REFILING
EERRSTTU	REUTTERS	EFFINRSS	SNIFFERS	EFGIILNT	FILETING
	UTTERERS	EFFINRSU	SNUFFIER	EFGIILNU	FIGULINE
EERRSTUV	VESTURER	EFFINSST	STIFFENS	EFGIILRU	UGLIFIER
EERRSTVY	REVESTRY	EFFIOPRS	PIFFEROS	EFGIILSU	UGLIFIES
EERRSUVY	RESURVEY	EFFIOPRU	POUFFIER	EFGIIMNS	MISFEIGN
EERSSSST	STRESSES	EFFIORST	FORFEITS	EFGIINNR	ENFIRING
EERSSSTU	ESTRUSES	EFFIORSX	FOXFIRES		INFRINGE
EERSSSUY	SEYSURES	EFFIOSTT	TOFFIEST		REFINING
EERSSTTU	TRUSTEES	EFFIPSTU	PUFFIEST	EFGIINNT	FEINTING
EERSSTTY	SYRETTES	EFFIQRSU	SQUIFFER	EFGIINNX	ENFIXING
EERSSTUU	UTERUSES	EFFIRSTT	TRIFFEST	EFGIINRR	FRINGIER
EERSSTUV	VESTURES	EFFIRSTU	STUFFIER		REFIRING

EFGIINRU	FIGURINE	EFGORSTU	FOREGUTS	EFIIILSV	VILIFIES
EFGIINRX	REFIXING	EFHHIRSS	FRESHISH	EFIIIMNS	MINIFIES
EFGIINRY	REIFYING	EFHIIKLS	FISHLIKE	EFIIINNT	INFINITE
EFGIINRZ	FRIEZING		FLEISHIK	EFIIINSV	VINIFIES
EFGIITUV	FUGITIVE	EFHIILLT	HELILIFT	EFIIIRVV	VIVIFIER
EFGIKLLU	GULFLIKE	EFHIILNS	FISHLINE	EFIIISTX	FIXITIES
EFGIKLOR	FROGLIKE	EFHIILRT	FILTHIER	EFIIISVV	VIVIFIES
EFGIKNOR	FOREKING	EFHIILST	TILEFISH	EFIIKLLM	FILMLIKE
EFGILLNO	LIFELONG	EFHIIMSU	HUMIFIES	EFIIKLNT	FLINKITE
EFGILLNS	FELLINGS	EFHIINRS	FINISHER	EFIIKLRS	FLISKIER
EFGILLNU	FUELLING		REFINISH	EFIIKNPR	FIREPINK
EFGILLUU	GUILEFUL	EFHIINSS	FINISHES	EFIIKRRS	FRISKIER
EFGILMOR	FILMGOER	EFHIIPPS	PIPEFISH	EFIILLNT	TEFILLIN
EFGILNNS	FLENSING	EFHIIPRS	FIRESHIP	EFIILLRR	FRILLIER
EFGILNOR	FLORIGEN	EFHIIRST	SHIFTIER	EFIILLRS	FRILLIES
EFGILNRS	FLINGERS	EFHIISST	FISHIEST	EFIILMRS	FLIMSIER
EFGILNRU	FERULING	EFHIKLOO	HOOFLIKE	EFIILMSS	FLIMSIES
EFGILNRY	FERLYING	EFHILLSY	ELFISHLY		MISFILES
	REFLYING		FLESHILY	EFIILMST	FILMIEST
EFGILNSS	SELFINGS	EFHILOPS	FISHPOLE	EFIILNRT	FLINTIER
EFGILNST	FELTINGS	EFHILRSU	FLUSHIER	EFIILNTY	FELINITY
EFGILNTT	FETTLING	EFHILSSS	FISHLESS		FINITELY
EFGILNTW	LEFTWING	EFHILTWY	WHITEFLY	EFIILOQU	FILIOQUE
EFGILPRU	FIREPLUG	EFHINNOT	FENTHION	EFIILPPR	FLIPPIER
EFGILSST	GIFTLESS	EFHINSST	FISHNETS	EFIILRRT	FLIRTIER
EFGILSTU	FUGLIEST	EFHIOOOR	FORHOOIE	EFIILRST	FILISTER
	GULFIEST	EFHIOPRS	FORESHIP	EFIILRSU	FUSILIER
EFGIMNST	FIGMENTS	EFHIORRT	FROTHIER	EFIILSTT	FITLIEST
EFGIMOSY	FOGEYISM	EFHIORSS	ROSEFISH	EFIILSTY	FEISTILY
EFGIMRUU	REFUGIUM	EFHIORSV	OVERFISH	EFIIMMNS	FEMINISM
EFGINNNP	PFENNING	EFHIORTT	FORTIETH	EFIIMNOS	FISNOMIE
EFGINNPS	PFENNIGS	EFHIPRSS	SERFSHIP		OMNIFIES
EFGINNRS	FERNINGS	EFHIPRSU	FURPHIES	EFIIMNRR	INFIRMER
EFGINORV	FORGIVEN	EFHIRRTU	THURIFER	EFIIMNRS	MISINFER
EFGINORW	FOREWING	EFHIRSST	SHIFTERS	EFIIMNST	FEMINIST
EFGINPRS	PERFINGS	EFHISSTU	SHUFTIES	EFIIMNSU	MUNIFIES
EFGINPUY	PINGUEFY	EFHISSUW	HUSWIFES	EFIIMNTY	FEMINITY
EFGINRRY	FERRYING	EFHKLNOU	FUNKHOLE	EFIIMRRS	RIMFIRES
	REFRYING	EFHLLLSU	SHELLFUL	EFIIMRSS	MISFIRES
EFGINRSU	GUNFIRES	EFHLNORS	HORNFELS	EFIINNOS	SINFONIE
	REFUSING	EFHLNOUY	HONEYFUL	EFIINNST	FINNIEST
EFGINRSW	SWERFING	EFHLOOSS	HOOFLESS	EFIINORR	INFERIOR
EFGINRTT	FRETTING	EFHLOOSX	FOXHOLES	EFIINORT	NOTIFIER
EFGINRTU	FEUTRING	EFHLOPST	FLESHPOT	EFIINOST	NOTIFIES
	REFUTING	EFHLOPSU	HOPEFULS	EFIINPSV	FIVEPINS
EFGINRTY	GENTRIFY	EFHLORSY	HORSEFLY	EFIINPSX	SPINIFEX
EFGIOOST	GOOFIEST	EFHLORVY	HOVERFLY	EFIINRRT	FERRITIN
EFGIOPTT	PETTIFOG	EFHLOSSU	FLOUSHES	EFIINRST	SNIFTIER
EFGIORRV	FORGIVER	EFHLOSUU	HOUSEFUL	EFIINRSU	UNIFIERS
EFGIORSV	FORGIVES	EFHLOSUY	HOUSEFLY	EFIINRSY	RESINIFY
EFGIRRST	GRIFTERS	EFHLRSSU	FLUSHERS	EFIINSTT	NIFTIEST
EFGIRRSU	FIGURERS	EFHLSSTU	FLUSHEST	EFIINSUV	INFUSIVE
EFGLOOTY	FETOLOGY	EFHLSTTW	TWELFTHS	EFIIORSS	OSSIFIER
EFGLOOVX	FOXGLOVE	EFHNORST	FORHENTS	EFIIOSSS	OSSIFIES
EFGLORST	FROGLETS	EFHNOSUU	FUNHOUSE	EFIIPRRU	PURIFIER
EFGLRSUU	SURGEFUL	EFHOORSW	FORESHOW	EFIIPRST	SPITFIRE
EFGLSSTU	SLUGFEST	EFHORRST	FROTHERS	EFIIPRSU	PURIFIES
EFGNOSST	SONGFEST	EFHORRTY	FROTHERY	EFIIPRTY	TYPIFIER
EFGNSSUU	FUNGUSES	EFHRRSTU	FURTHERS	EFIIPSTY	TYPIFIES
EFGOORRS	FORGOERS	EFHRSTTU	FURTHEST	EFIIRRST	FIRRIEST
EFGORRSU	FERRUGOS	EFIIILRV	VILIFIER	EFIIRRTU	FRUITIER

EFIIRRZZ	FRIZZIER	EFILNUWY	UNWIFELY	EFINOPTX	PONTIFEX
EFIIRSTT	RIFTIEST	EFILOOSS	FLOOSIES	EFINORRT	FRONTIER
EFIIRSZZ	FRIZZIES	EFILOOSZ	FLOOZIES	EFINORSU	REFUSION
EFIIRTUV	FRUITIVE	EFILOPPR	FLOPPIER	EFINORTY	RENOTIFY
EFIIRVVY	REVIVIFY	EFILOPPS	FLOPPIES	EFINOSSX	FOXINESS
EFIISSTT	FISTIEST	EFILOPRR	PROFILER	EFINOSSZ	FOZINESS
EFIISSTW	SWIFTIES	EFILOPRS	PROFILES	EFINOSTT	FISTNOTE
EFIISTTW	WIFTIEST	EFILORRU	FLOURIER	EFINRRRU	FURRINER
EFIISTZZ	FIZZIEST	EFILORRV	FRIVOLER	EFINRSST	SNIFTERS
EFIJLORS	FRIJOLES	EFILORSS	FLOSSIER	EFINRSSU	INFUSERS
EFIJLOST	JETFOILS	EFILORST	FLORIEST	EFINRTTU	UNFITTER
EFIKKLLO	FOLKLIKE		TREFOILS	EFIOOPRS	SPOOFIER
EFIKKLOR	FORKLIKE	EFILORTU	FLUORITE	EFIOOPST	POOFIEST
EFIKLLOT	LOFTLIKE	EFILOSSS	FLOSSIES	EFIOORST	ROOFIEST
EFIKLLOW	WOLFLIKE	EFILOSSX	SEXFOILS	EFIOOSST	FOOTSIES
EFIKLMOR	FOREMILK	EFILOSTT	LOFTIEST	EFIOOSTT	FOOTIEST
EFIKLNSU	FLUNKIES	EFILOSTU	OUTFLIES	EFIOOSTW	WOOFIEST
EFIKLOOR	ROOFLIKE	EFILPPRS	FLIPPERS	EFIOPRRS	PORIFERS
EFIKLOOT	FOOTLIKE	EFILPPST	FLIPPEST	EFIOPRRT	PORTFIRE
EFIKLORS	FOLKSIER	EFILPPSU	PIPEFULS		PROFITER
EFIKLORW	LIFEWORK	EFILPRTU	UPLIFTER	EFIOPRST	FIREPOTS
EFIKLOST	FOLKIEST	EFILPSTU	SPITEFUL		PIEFORTS
EFIKLRSU	SURFLIKE	EFILRRST	FLIRTERS		POSTFIRE
EFIKLRTU	TURFLIKE		TRIFLERS	EFIORRST	FROSTIER
EFIKLSTU	FLUKIEST	EFILRRSU	FLURRIES		ROTIFERS
	LUTEFISK	EFILRRZZ	FRIZZLER	EFIORRSW	FROWSIER
EFIKNNOS	FINNESKO	EFILRSST	RIFTLESS	EFIORRTT	RETROFIT
EFIKNORS	FORESKIN		STIFLERS	EFIORRUZ	FROUZIER
EFIKNRSU	REFUSNIK	EFILRSTT	FLITTERS	EFIORRWZ	FROWZIER
EFIKNSTU	FUNKIEST	EFILRSTW	FEWTRILS	EFIORSST	FOISTERS
EFIKORRW	FIREWORK	EFILRSTY	FLYTIERS	EFIORSTU	FOUSTIER
EFIKORST	FORKIEST	EFILRSVV	FLIVVERS		OUTFIRES
EFIKRRSS	FRISKERS	EFILRSZZ	FRIZZLES	EFIORSTW	FROWIEST
EFIKRSST	FRISKETS	EFILRTTU	FRUITLET	EFIORTTU	REOUTFIT
EFILLLNU	FLUELLIN	EFILSSST	SELFISTS	EFIPPRRS	FRIPPERS
EFILLMSS	FILMLESS	EFILSSTT	LEFTISTS	EFIPPRRY	FRIPPERY
EFILLMSU	SMILEFUL	EFILSSTU	SULFITES	EFIPPRST	FRIPPETS
EFILLOOS	FOLIOLES	EFILSTTU	FLUTIEST	EFIPRRUY	REPURIFY
EFILLORV	OVERFILL		FUTILEST	EFIPRSST	PRESIFTS
EFILLORW	LOWLIFER	EFILSTTW	SWIFTLET	EFIPRSTU	SUPERFIT
EFILLOSW	LOWLIFES	EFIMMRSU	FERMIUMS	EFIPRSUX	SUPERFIX
EFILLRRS	FRILLERS	EFIMNORR	INFORMER	EFIPRTTY	PRETTIFY
EFILLRUY	IREFULLY		REINFORM	EFIRRRSU	FURRIERS
EFILLSTY	STELLIFY		RENIFORM	EFIRRRUY	FURRIERY
EFILLTUY	FUTILELY	EFIMNORS	ENSIFORM	EFIRRSSU	FRISEURS
EFILMNOS	FOILSMEN		FERMIONS		FRISURES
EFILMNSU	FULMINES	EFIMNRSS	FIRMNESS	EFIRRSTT	FRITTERS
EFILMOST	FILEMOTS	EFIMNSTT	FITMENTS	EFIRRSTU	FRITURES
EFILMRSS	FIRMLESS	EFIMOORR	FIREROOM		FRUITERS
EFILMSSS	SELFISMS	EFIMOORT	RETIFORM		FURRIEST
EFILMSST	FILMSETS	EFIMORRW	FIREWORM	EFIRRSZZ	FRIZZERS
	LEFTISMS	EFIMORST	SETIFORM	EFIRRTUY	FRUITERY
EFILMSUY	EMULSIFY	EFIMOSST	SEMISOFT	EFIRSSSU	FISSURES
EFILNNTU	INFLUENT	EFIMOSTT	OFTTIMES	EFIRSSTU	SURFEITS
EFILNOOR	ROOFLINE	EFIMPRRU	FRUMPIER		SURFIEST
EFILNORU	FLUORINE	EFIMRSTU	FREMITUS	EFIRSSTW	SWIFTERS
EFILNOSU	NOISEFUL	EFINNORS	INFERNOS	EFIRSTTU	TURFIEST
EFILNOSX	FLEXIONS	EFINNPSU	FINESPUN		TURFITES
EFILNRTT	FLITTERN	EFINNRST	FERNINST	EFIRSTUX	FIXTURES
EFILNRYZ	FRENZILY	EFINNSTU	FUNNIEST	EFIRSTUZ	FURZIEST
EFILNSUX	INFLUXES	EFINOPRS	FORPINES	EFISSSTU	FUSSIEST

EFISSTTU	FUSTIEST	EFLOORTU	FOOTRULE	EFOOPRTW	WETPROOF
EFISSTTW	SWIFTEST	EFLOORUV	OVERFOUL	EFOOPSTT	FOOTSTEP
EFISTTTU	TUFTIEST	EFLOORVW	OVERFLOW	EFOORRSW	FORSWORE
EFISTUZZ	FUZZIEST	EFLOOSST	FOOTLESS	EFOORSTT	FOOTREST
EFKLLOOR	FOLKLORE	EFLOPPRS	FLOPPERS	EFOORSTV	OVERSOFT
EFKLMNOS	MENFOLKS	EFLOPRUW	POWERFUL	EFOORSTW	WOOFTERS
EFKLMOOT	FOLKMOTE	EFLOPRUX	FOURPLEX	EFOOSTUX	OUTFOXES
EFKLMORS	MERFOLKS	EFLORRUY	RYEFLOUR	EFOPRRSU	PROFUSER
EFKLNRSU	FLUNKERS	EFLORSSS	FLOSSERS	EFOPRSTU	POUFTERS
EFKLNSUY	FLUNKEYS	EFLORSST	FORTLETS	EFORRRUW	FURROWER
EFKLOPSU	POKEFULS	EFLORSTU	FLOUTERS	EFORRSST	FORTRESS
EFKLORSS	FORKLESS	EFLORSTW	FELWORTS	EFORRSTW	FROWSTER
EFKLORUW	FLUEWORK	EFLORSUY	YOURSELF	EFORRSTY	FORESTRY
EFKLPSSU	SKEPFULS	EFLORSVY	FLYOVERS	EFORRSUV	FERVOURS
EFKNOORW	FOREKNOW	EFLOSUUX	FLEXUOUS	EFORRTTU	FROTTEUR
EFKNRSTU	FUNKSTER	EFLPRRSU	PURFLERS	EFORSSST	FOSTRESS
EFKOOPRS	FORSPOKE	EFLPRSSU	PRESSFUL	EGGGIILR	GIGGLIER
EFKORRTW	FRETWORK	EFLPRSUU	PURSEFUL	EGGGILNS	LEGGINGS
EFLLLOOW	WOOLFELL	EFLRSSTU	FLUSTERS	EGGGILOR	GOGGLIER
EFLLLOWY	FELLOWLY		TURFLESS	EGGGILRS	GIGGLERS
EFLLLPSU	SPELLFUL	EFLRSTTU	FLUTTERS	EGGGINPS	PEGGINGS
EFLLNSSU	FULLNESS	EFLRSTUU	FRUSTULE	EGGGIORR	GROGGIER
EFLLNTUY	FLUENTLY		SULFURET	EGGGLORS	GOGGLERS
EFLLOORW	FOLLOWER	EFLRSTUY	FLUSTERY	EGGGNNOR	RONGGENG
EFLLOOTW	FOOTWELL	EFLRTTUY	FLUTTERY	EGGGOOOS	GOOSEGOG
EFLLORSU	FLORULES	EFMNNNUY	FUNNYMEN	EGGGORRY	GROGGERY
EFLLORUV	OVERFULL	EFMNNORT	FRONTMEN	EGGHIINN	NEIGHING
EFLLORUW	WOFULLER	EFMNORTY	FROMENTY	EGGHIINW	WEIGHING
EFLLOSST	LOFTLESS	EFMNRTUY	FRUMENTY	EGGHIKSW	EGGWHISK
EFLLOUWY	WOEFULLY		FURMENTY	EGGHILRS	HIGGLERS
EFLLRUUY	RUEFULLY	EFMOORST	FOREMOST	EGGHINSS	GHESSING
EFLLSUUY	USEFULLY	EFMOORSU	FOURSOME	EGGHIRST	THIGGERS
EFLMMRUY	FLUMMERY	EFMOPRRS	PERFORMS	EGGHISSU	SHUGGIES
EFLMNOOU	MONOFUEL		PREFORMS	EGGHISTU	HUGGIEST
EFLMNOST	LOFTSMEN	EFMOPRST	POMFRETS	EGGHLORU	ROUGHLEG
EFLMNRUU	FRENULUM	EFNNOOOR	FORENOON	EGGHLOSS	SHOGGLES
EFLMORRY	FORMERLY	EFNNORST	FORNENST	EGGHRTUY	THUGGERY
EFLMORSS	FORMLESS	EFNNORSU	FENURONS	EGGIIJLR	JIGGLIER
EFLMORSU	FULSOMER	EFNNORUZ	UNFROZEN	EGGIIJST	JIGGIEST
EFLMOSTT	LEFTMOST	EFNOOOTT	FOOTNOTE	EGGIILLN	GINGELLI
EFLMPRSU	FRUMPLES	EFNOOPRT	PENTROOF	EGGIILNR	NIGGLIER
EFLNOOSU	FELONOUS	EFNOORRW	FOREWORN	EGGIILNS	GINGELIS
EFLNORSU	FLEURONS	EFNOOSST	EFTSOONS	EGGIILRW	WIGGLIER
EFLNORTT	FRONTLET		FESTOONS	EGGIINNN	ENGINING
EFLNORYZ	FROZENLY	EFNOPRST	FORSPENT	EGGIINNR	GREINING
EFLNOSSU	FOULNESS	EFNORRST	REFRONTS		REIGNING
	SULFONES		RENFORST	EGGIINNS	SINGEING
EFLNOSTT	FLETTONS	EFNORRSU	FORERUNS	EGGIINNT	TINGEING
	FONTLETS	EFNORRSW	FROWNERS	EGGIINNW	WINGEING
EFLNOSTY	STONEFLY	EFNORSTU	FORTUNES	EGGIINRV	GRIEVING
EFLNSSTU	NESTFULS	EFNOSSST	SOFTNESS		REGIVING
EFLNSSUY	SYNFUELS	EFNOTUZZ	FUZZTONE	EGGIIPST	PIGGIEST
EFLNSTTU	TENTFULS	EFNRSSTU	FUNSTERS	EGGIIRTW	TWIGGIER
EFLNSUUU	UNUSEFUL	EFOOOPRT	FOOTROPE	EGGIISTW	WIGGIEST
EFLOOPRV	FLOPOVER	EFOOORST	FOOTSORE	EGGIKLNO	GONGLIKE
EFLOORRS	FLOORERS	EFOOPRRS	PROOFERS	EGGIKLNS	KEGLINGS
EFLOORSS	FORSLOES		REPROOFS	EGGIKNOS	GINGKOES
	ROOFLESS	EFOOPRSS	SPOOFERS		GINKGOES
EFLOORST	FOOTLERS	EFOOPRST	FORETOPS	EGGILLNY	GINGELLY
EFLOORSW	FORESLOW		POOFTERS	EGGILMNU	EMULGING
EFLOORSZ	FOOZLERS	EFOOPRSY	SPOOFERY	EGGILMSS	LEGGISMS

EGGILNNO	LONGEING	EGGLORSS	SLOGGERS		HERLINGS
EGGILNNT	GENTLING	EGGLORST	TOGGLERS		SHINGLER
	GLENTLING	EGGLORSV	VLOGGERS	EGHILNSS	SHINGLES
EGGILNNU	LUNGEING	EGGLORUY	GURGOYLE	EGHILNST	ENLIGHTS
EGGILNRS	NIGGLERS	EGGLPRSU	PLUGGERS		LIGHTENS
	SNIGGLER	EGGLRSSU	SLUGGERS	EGHILNSV	SHELVING
EGGILNRU	GRUELING	EGGLRSTU	GURGLETS	EGHILNSW	WELSHING
	REGLUING		STRUGGLE	EGHILNUW	GLUHWEIN
EGGILNRY	GINGERLY	EGGMNTUY	NUTMEGGY	EGHILORT	REGOLITH
EGGILNSS	SNIGGLES	EGGMRSUY	SMUGGERY	EGHILOSU	GHOULIES
EGGILNSU	LUGEINGS	EGGMSSTU	SMUGGEST		OUGHLIES
EGGILNSY	GLEYINGS	EGGNOOST	GEOGNOST		
EGGILOOS	GOOGLIES	EGGNOOSY	GEOGNOSY	EGHILPRT	PLIGHTER
EGGILOST	LOGGIEST	EGGNORST	GONGSTER	EGHILPST	PIGHTLES
EGGILQSU	SQUIGGLE	EGGNRRSU	GRUNGERS	EGHILRST	LIGHTERS
EGGILRRW	WRIGGLER	EGGNRSUY	SNUGGERY		RELIGHTS
EGGILRSW	WIGGLERS	EGGNSSTU	SNUGGEST		SLIGHTER
	WRIGGLES	EGGOORSU	GORGEOUS	EGHILSSS	SIGHLESS
EGGIMNNU	EMUNGING	EGGOPRRS	PROGGERS	EGHILSST	SLEIGHTS
EGGIMNRS	MERGINGS	EGGSSSTU	SUGGESTS	EGHILSTT	LIGHTEST
EGGIMORS	SMOGGIER	EGHHHIST	HEIGHTHS	EGHIMNNS	MENSHING
EGGIMSTU	MUGGIEST	EGHHIIMS	SEMIHIGH	EGHIMNOR	HOMERING
EGGINNNR	GRENNING	EGHHIIRS	HIGHRISE		REHOMING
EGGINNOR	ENGORING	EGHHILTY	EIGHTHLY	EGHIMNSS	MESHINGS
EGGINNSS	GINSENGS	EGHHINSS	HIGHNESS	EGHIMNUX	EXHUMING
EGGINORR	GORGERIN	EGHHIORV	OVERHIGH	EGHIMPRU	GRUMPHIE
	ROGERING	EGHHORUW	ROUGHHEW	EGHIMSTT	MIGHTEST
EGGINORU	ROGUEING	EGHHOSSW	SHOWGHES	EGHINNOY	HONEYING
EGGINOUV	VOGUEING	EGHIIKLS	SIGHLIKE	EGHINNSS	NIGHNESS
EGGINRRU	GRUNGIER	EGHIILLS	GHILLIES	EGHINNST	SENNIGHT
	REURGING	EGHIILNR	HIRELING	EGHINNSU	UNHINGES
EGGINRSS	GRESSING	EGHIILNS	SHEILING	EGHINORT	THROEING
	SERGINGS		SHIELING	EGHINORV	HOVERING
	SNIGGERS	EGHIIMRT	MIGHTIER	EGHINOSS	SHOEINGS
EGGINRSY	GREYINGS	EGHIINNR	INHERING	EGHINOST	HISTOGEN
EGGINSSU	GUESSING	EGHIINRR	REHIRING	EGHINOSU	GINHOUSE
	SNUGGIES	EGHIINRT	THINGIER	EGHINOSY	HOSEYING
EGGINSTT	GETTINGS	EGHIINRW	WHINGIER	EGHINOTZ	GENIZOTH
EGGINSTU	GUESTING	EGHIINST	HEISTING	EGHINPRS	SPHERING
	GUNGIEST		NIGHTIES	EGHINPSS	SPHINGES
EGGIOSST	SOGGIEST		THINGIES	EGHINQTU	QUETHING
EGGIPRRS	PRIGGERS	EGHIINSV	INVEIGHS	EGHINRRS	HERRINGS
	SPRIGGER	EGHIINTV	THIEVING	EGHINRRU	HUNGRIER
EGGIPRRY	PRIGGERY	EGHIIRST	RIGHTIES	EGHINRRY	HERRYING
EGGIPRSU	PUGGRIES		TIGERISH	EGHINRST	RIGHTENS
EGGIPSSU	SPUGGIES	EGHIISTY	HYGIEIST	EGHINRSU	USHERING
EGGIPSTU	PUGGIEST	EGHIKNRS	GHERKINS	EGHINRSW	SHREWING
EGGIRRST	TRIGGERS	EGHIKRSS	SKREIGHS		WHINGERS
EGGIRSSW	SWIGGERS		SKRIEGHS	EGHINRTW	WRETHING
EGGIRSTT	TRIGGEST	EGHILLNO	HELLOING	EGHINSTT	SHETTING
EGGIRSTU	RUGGIEST	EGHILLNS	SHELLING		TIGHTENS
	STUGGIER	EGHILMNW	WHELMING	EGHINTTW	WHETTING
EGGIRSTW	TWIGGERS	EGHILMOR	HOMEGIRL	EGHINTUW	UNWEIGHT
EGGISTUV	VUGGIEST	EGHILMPS	MEGILPHS	EGHIOOSS	SHOOGIES
EGGJLORS	JOGGLERS	EGHILNNU	UNHELING	EGHIOPSS	PISHEOGS
EGGJLRSU	JUGGLERS	EGHILNOT	HOTELING		PISHOGES
EGGJLRUY	JUGGLERY	EGHILNOV	HOVELING	EGHIOPSU	PISHOGUE
EGGLMOOY	GEMOLOGY	EGHILNPS	HELPINGS	EGHIORST	GHOSTIER
EGGLMRSU	SMUGGLER	EGHILNPT	PENLIGHT	EGHIORSU	ROUGHIES
EGGLMSSU	SMUGGLES	EGHILNPW	WHELPING	EGHIOSTT	GOTHITES
EGGLNSSU	SNUGGLES	EGHILNRS	GHRELINS	EGHIOSTU	TOUGHIES
				EGHIOSTV	EIGHTVOS

EGHIOTUW	OUTWEIGH	EGIIKNNS	SKEINING		STEINING
EGHIQRTU	REQUIGHT	EGIILMMN	IMMINGLE	EGIINNSV	VEININGS
EGHIRRST	RIGHTERS	EGIILMST	LEGITIMS	EGIINNSW	SINEWING
EGHIRRUY	HIERURGY	EGIILNNO	ELOINING	EGIINNTU	UNTIEING
EGHIRSST	RESIGHTS	EGIILNNR	RELINING	EGIINNVW	VINEWING
	SIGHTERS	EGIILNNS	ENISLING	EGIINNWZ	WIZENING
EGHIRSTT	RIGHTEST		ENSILING	EGIINOPR	PEIGNOIR
	STREIGHT	EGIILNNT	LENITING	EGIINORS	SEIGNIOR
EGHISSTU	GUSHIEST	EGIILNNU	LINGUINE	EGIINPRS	SPEIRING
EGHISSTY	HYGEISTS	EGIILNNV	LIVENING		SPIERING
EGHISTTT	TIGHTEST	EGIILNOR	LIGROINE		PRIEVING
EGHISTUV	VUGHIEST		RELIGION	EGIINPRV	EXPIRING
EGHKLNOU	GUNKHOLE		REOILING	EGIINPRX	PIGSNIES
EGHLLOPU	PLUGHOLE	EGIILNPR	PERILING	EGIINPSS	QUIETING
EGHLLOSU	LUGHOLES	EGIILNPS	SPEILING	EGIINQTU	RERISING
EGHLMNOP	PHLEGMON		SPIELING	EGIINRRS	RETIRING
EGHLNORS	LEGHORNS	EGIILNRS	RESILING	EGIINRRT	REWIRING
EGHLNPSU	ENGULPHS		RIESLING	EGIINRRW	GIRNIEST
EGHLNRUY	HUNGERLY	EGIILNRT	GIRTLINE	EGIINRST	IGNITERS
EGHLOOOR	HOROLOGE		GLINTIER		REISTING
EGHLOORY	RHEOLOGY		RETILING		RESITING
EGHLOOSS	GOLOSHES		TINGLIER		STINGIER
	SHOOGLES		TIRELING		STRIGINE
EGHLOOST	THEOLOGS	EGIILNRV	LIVERING	EGIINRSU	SIGNIEUR
EGHLOOTY	ETHOLOGY		RELIVING	EGIINRSV	REVISING
	THEOLOGY		REVILING	EGIINRSW	RINGWISE
EGHLOPRU	PLOUGHER	EGIILNST	LIGNITES		SWEIRING
EGHLOPRY	HYPERGOL		LINGIEST		SWINGIER
EGHMNOOY	HOMOGENY	EGIILNSV	VEILINGS	EGIINRSZ	RESIZING
EGHMNORS	GEMSHORN	EGIILNSW	WISELING	EGIINRTU	INTRIGUE
EGHMNOSU	HUMOGENS	EGIILRRS	GRISLIER	EGIINRTV	RIVETING
EGHMOPUY	HYPOGEUM	EGIILRSS	GRISLIES	EGIINRTX	GENITRIX
EGHMOSSU	GUMSHOES	EGIILRST	GIRLIEST	EGIINRVV	REVIVING
EGHNOOPT	PHOTOGEN	EGIILRTU	GUILTIER	EGIINSSS	SEISINGS
EGHNOOSS	HOGNOSES	EGIILRTZ	GLITZIER	EGIINSST	STINGIES
EGHNOOTY	THEOGONY	EGIIMMNO	MIMEOING	EGIINSSZ	SEIZINGS
EGHNORSU	ENROUGHS	EGIIMMNW	IMMEWING	EGIINSTW	WINGIEST
	ROUGHENS	EGIIMMNU	INGENIUM	EGIINSTX	EXISTING
EGHNORUV	HUNGOVER	EGIIMNOS	IGNOMIES	EGIINSTZ	ZINGIEST
	OVERHUNG	EGIIMNPR	IMPINGER	EGIINSVW	VIEWINGS
EGHNOSTU	TOUGHENS	EGIIMNPS	IMPINGES	EGIIOPRS	PIROGIES
EGHNOSUU	GUNHOUSE	EGIIMNRS	REMISING	EGIIPPRR	GRIPPIER
EGHNRSTT	STRENGTH	EGIIMNRT	MERITING	EGIIPRST	GRIPIEST
EGHOOOSW	HOOSEGOW		MITERING	EGIIPRSW	PERIWIGS
EGHORRSU	ROUGHERS		RETIMING	EGIIPSST	PIGSTIES
EGHORRTW	REGROWTH	EGIIMNRX	REMIXING	EGIIRRTT	GRITTIER
EGHORSTU	RESOUGHT	EGIIMNST	MINGIEST	EGIITUXY	EXIGUITY
	ROUGHEST	EGIIMNSV	MISGIVEN	EGIJKNOS	JINGKOES
EGHOSTTU	TOUGHEST	EGIIMNTT	EMITTING	EGIJKNRS	JERKINGS
EGHPSSUU	UPGUSHES	EGIIMOPT	IMPETIGO	EGIJLLNY	JELLYING
EGIIINSV	VISIEING	EGIIMORR	GRIMOIRE	EGIJLNRS	JINGLERS
EGIIJLNR	JINGLIER	EGIIMPST	GIMPIEST	EGIJLNRU	JUNGLIER
EGIIKKLN	KINGLIKE	EGIIMRST	GRIMIEST	EGIJLNST	JINGLETS
EGIIKLLO	KILLOGIE		TIGERISM	EGIJMMNY	JEMMYING
EGIIKLNN	LIKENING	EGIIMSSV	MISGIVES	EGIJNNOS	JONESING
EGIIKLNR	KINGLIER	EGIINNPR	REPINING	EGIJNNOY	ENJOYING
	RINGLIKE		RIPENING	EGIJNQRU	JERQUING
EGIIKLNW	WINGLIKE	EGIINNRS	RESINING	EGIJNSST	JESTINGS
EGIIKLTW	TWIGLIKE	EGIINNRT	INTEGRIN	EGIJNTTY	JETTYING
EGIIKMNS	SMEIKING	EGIINNSS	SEININGS	EGIKKLNS	LEKKINGS
EGIIKNNR	REINKING	EGIINNST	GINNIEST	EGIKKNRT	TREKKING

EGIKLLNN	KNELLING	EGILMOUU	EULOGIUM	EGILOOTY	ETIOLOGY
EGIKLLNV	KVELLING	EGILMPRS	GLIMPSER	EGILOPPR	GLOPPIER
EGIKLNOS	SONGLIKE	EGILMPRU	GLUMPIER	EGILORRW	GROWLIER
EGIKLNPS	SKELPING	EGILMPSS	GLIMPSES	EGILORSS	GLOSSIER
EGIKLNRS	ERLKINGS	EGILNNST	NESTLING	EGILORTV	OVERGILT
EGIKLNSS	KINGLESS	EGILNNTT	NETTLING	EGILORTY	GYROLITE
EGIKLNST	KINGLETS	EGILNNTU	GLUTENIN	EGILOSSS	GLOSSIES
EGIKMNPS	KEMPINGS	EGILNOPP	PEOPLING	EGILOSST	ELOGISTS
EGIKMNRS	SMERKING		POPELING	EGILOSTU	EULOGIST
EGIKNNNS	KENNINGS	EGILNORS	RESOLING	EGILPPRS	GRIPPLES
	SKENNING	EGILNORU	LOUNGIER	EGILPSTU	GULPIEST
EGIKNNOT	TOKENING	EGILNORW	LOWERING	EGILRRZZ	GRIZZLER
EGIKNNRS	KERNINGS		ROWELING	EGILRSST	GLISTERS
EGIKNNSY	ENSKYING	EGILNOSS	LIGNOSES		GRISTLES
EGIKNORV	OVERKING		LOGINESS		GRITLESS
	REVOKING	EGILNOSU	LIGNEOUS	EGILRSTT	GLITTERS
EGIKNORY	YOKERING	EGILNOSW	LONGWISE	EGILRSTU	GURLIEST
EGIKNPPS	SKEPPING	EGILNOTW	TOWELING	EGILRSTY	GREYLIST
EGIKNRRS	SKERRING	EGILNOVV	EVOLVING	EGILRSUV	VIRGULES
EGIKNRSU	RESKUING	EGILNPRS	PINGLERS	EGILRSZZ	GRIZZLES
EGIKNSTT	SKETTING		SPERLING	EGILRTTY	GLITTERY
EGIKNSTU	GUNKIEST		SPRINGLE	EGILSSTW	TWIGLESS
EGILLMNS	SMELLING	EGILNPRY	REPLYING	EGILSTTW	TWIGLETS
EGILLNNO	LONGLINE	EGILNPSS	SPIGNELS	EGIMMNOV	EMMOVING
EGILLNNS	SNELLING	EGILNPST	PELTINGS	EGIMMNST	STEMMING
EGILLNOS	LOGLINES		PESTLING	EGIMMRST	GRIMMEST
EGILLNOV	LIVELONG	EGILNPSY	YELPINGS	EGIMMSTU	GUMMIEST
EGILLNPS	SPELLING	EGILNPTT	PETTLING		GUMMITES
EGILLNQU	QUELLING	EGILNRRU	RULERING	EGIMNNNO	MIGNONNE
EGILLNSS	SELLINGS	EGILNRRY	ERRINGLY	EGIMNNOV	ENMOVING
EGILLNST	GILLNETS	EGILNRSS	RINGLESS		VENOMING
	STELLING		SLINGERS	EGIMNNSW	SWINGMEN
	TELLINGS	EGILNRST	LINGSTER	EGIMNNUW	UNMEWING
EGILLNSW	SWELLING		RINGLETS	EGIMNOOR	GERONIMO
	WELLINGS		STERLING	EGIMNORS	NEGROISM
EGILLNSY	YELLINGS		TINGLERS	EGIMNORV	REMOVING
EGILLNTU	GLUTELIN		TRINGLES	EGIMNOST	MITOGENS
EGILLOOR	GLORIOLE	EGILNRSW	NEWSGIRL	EGIMNOSU	GEMINOUS
EGILLORS	GIROLLES	EGILNRUV	VELURING	EGIMNOSY	MOSEYING
EGILLRRS	GRILLERS	EGILNRUY	GUYLINER	EGIMNPRS	IMPREGNS
EGILLRRY	GRILLERY	EGILNSSS	SIGNLESS	EGIMNPRU	IMPUGNER
EGILMMNS	LEMMINGS	EGILNSST	GLISTENS	EGIMNPST	EMPTINGS
EGILMMRS	GLIMMERS		SINGLETS		PIGMENTS
EGILMMRY	GLIMMERY		SNIGLETS	EGIMNPTT	TEMPTING
EGILMNNO	LEMONING	EGILNSSU	GLUINESS	EGIMNPTY	EMPTYING
EGILMNNU	UNMINGLE		UGLINESS	EGIMNRSS	GRIMNESS
EGILMNOT	LONGTIME	EGILNSSW	SWINGLES	EGIMNRSU	RESUMING
EGILMNPU	IMPLUNGE		WINGLESS	EGIMNRUY	ERYNGIUM
EGILMNRS	GREMLINS	EGILNSTT	LETTINGS	EGIMORSS	OGREISMS
	MERLINGS		SETTLING	EGIMORST	ERGOTISM
	MINGLERS	EGILNSTW	SWELTING		GORMIEST
EGILMNRU	RELUMING		WELTINGS	EGIMOSST	EGOTISMS
EGILMNST	MELTINGS		WINGLETS	EGIMOSTW	TWIGSOME
	SMELTING	EGILNSUV	EVULSING	EGIMPRRU	GRUMPIER
EGILMNSU	GUMLINES	EGILNSUY	GUYLINES	EGIMSSSU	MISGUESS
	LEGUMINS	EGILNTUX	EXULTING	EGINNNOT	TENONING
	MULESING	EGILNVXY	VEXINGLY	EGINNNOZ	ENZONING
EGILMOOR	GLOOMIER	EGILOOOS	OOLOGIES	EGINNNRS	RENNINGS
	OLIGOMER	EGILOOPR	GLOOPIER	EGINNNRU	ENURNING
EGILMORS	GOMERILS	EGILOORR	GROOLIER	EGINNNST	STENNING
EGILMOSU	ELOGIUMS	EGILOOSU	ISOLOGUE	EGINNNUY	ENNUYING

EGINNOOR	RONEOING	**EGINOSTT**	TENTIGOS	**EGIOPRSU**	GROUPIES
EGINNOOS	IONOGENS	**EGINOTUV**	OUTGIVEN		PIROGUES
EGINNOPR	REPONING	**EGINPPPR**	PREPPING	**EGIOPRTU**	PORTIGUE
EGINNOPS	OPENINGS	**EGINPPRS**	REPPINGS	**EGIORRTT**	GROTTIER
EGINNORS	NEGRONIS	**EGINPPST**	STEPPING	**EGIORRTU**	GROUTIER
EGINNORT	NITROGEN	**EGINPRRS**	RESPRING	**EGIORRTV**	OVERGIRT
	RINGTONE		SPERRING	**EGIORSST**	GORSIEST
EGINNORV	VIGNERON		SPRINGER		STRIGOSE
EGINNORZ	REZONING	**EGINPRRU**	REPURING	**EGIORSSU**	GRISEOUS
EGINNOSU	ENGINOUS	**EGINPRSS**	PRESSING	**EGIORSTU**	GOUSTIER
EGINNPRT	PRENTING		SPERSING	**EGIORSTV**	VERTIGOS
EGINNPSU	PENGUINS		SPRINGES	**EGIORSTY**	OYSTRIGE
EGINNRRS	GRINNERS	**EGINPRST**	PRESTING	**EGIORSTZ**	ZORGITES
EGINNRRU	UNERRING	**EGINPRSU**	PERSUING	**EGIORSUV**	GRIEVOUS
EGINNRST	RENTINGS		PERUSING	**EGIOSSTT**	EGOTISTS
	STERNING		SUPERING	**EGIOSTTU**	GOUTIEST
EGINNRSU	ENSURING	**EGINPRTU**	ERUPTING	**EGIOSTUV**	OUTGIVES
EGINNRSV	NERVINGS		REPUTING		VOGUIEST
EGINNRTU	RETUNING	**EGINPRTY**	RETYPING	**EGIOSUUX**	EXIGUOUS
	TENURING	**EGINPRUV**	PREVUING	**EGIPPRRS**	GRIPPERS
EGINNRTV	VENTRING	**EGINPRYY**	PERIGYNY	**EGIPRSUU**	GUIPURES
EGINNSSS	SENSINGS	**EGINPSSY**	PIGSNEYS	**EGIRRRSU**	GURRIERS
EGINNSST	NESTINGS	**EGINPSTT**	PETTINGS	**EGIRRSST**	GRISTERS
EGINNSTT	NETTINGS		SPETTING	**EGIRRSTT**	GRITTERS
	STENTING	**EGINQRUY**	QUERYING	**EGIRRSTY**	REGISTRY
	TENTINGS	**EGINQSTU**	QUESTING	**EGIRSSTU**	SURGIEST
EGINNSTV	VENTINGS	**EGINQSUU**	QUEUINGS	**EGIRSTTT**	GRITTEST
EGINNSUW	UNSEWING	**EGINRRST**	RESTRING	**EGIRSTTU**	TURGITES
EGINNSUX	UNSEXING		RINGSTER	**EGISSTTU**	GUSTIEST
EGINNSVY	ENVYINGS		STRINGER		GUTSIEST
EGINOORV	INGROOVE	**EGINRRSW**	WRINGERS	**EGISSUWY**	WISEGUYS
EGINOOSS	GOOINESS	**EGINRRSY**	SERRYING	**EGISSYYZ**	SYZYGIES
	ISOGONES	**EGINRRTY**	RETRYING	**EGISTTTU**	GUTTIEST
EGINOOST	GOONIEST	**EGINRRST**	RESTINGS	**EGJLNORU**	JONGLEUR
EGINOPRS	PERIGONS		STINGERS	**EGJLNOTU**	JELUTONG
	REPOSING		TRESSING	**EGJOSSTT**	GJETOSTS
	SPONGIER		TRIGNESS	**EGKLORSW**	LEGWORKS
EGINOPRW	POWERING	**EGINRSSV**	SERVINGS	**EGLLMORW**	GROMWELL
EGINOPRY	PIGEONRY		VERSINGS	**EGLLNSSU**	LUNGLESS
EGINOPST	PONGIEST	**EGINRSSW**	SWINGERS	**EGLLOOPR**	GOLLOPER
EGINOPSU	EPIGONUS	**EGINRSSY**	SYRINGES	**EGLLOOPY**	PELOLOGY
EGINOPSX	EXPOSING	**EGINRSTT**	GITTERNS	**EGLLOPSY**	GOSPELLY
EGINOPSY	POESYING	**EGINRSTV**	STERVING	**EGLLOSSY**	SYLLOGES
EGINOPXY	EPOXYING	**EGINRSTW**	STREWING	**EGLLPSSU**	PLUGLESS
EGINORRS	IGNORERS		WRESTING	**EGLMMSTU**	GLUMMEST
EGINORSS	GORINESS	**EGINRSVW**	SWERVING	**EGLMNOOS**	ENGLOOMS
	SIGNORES	**EGINRTTU**	UTTERING		LONGSOME
EGINORST	GENITORS	**EGINSSTT**	SETTINGS	**EGLMNOOY**	MENOLOGY
	ROSETING		TESTINGS	**EGLMNORS**	MONGRELS
EGINORSW	RESOWING	**EGINSSTV**	VESTINGS	**EGLMNSSU**	GLUMNESS
EGINORSY	SEIGNORY	**EGINSSTW**	STEWINGS	**EGLMOORS**	LEGROOMS
EGINORTT	OTTERING		WESTINGS	**EGLMOPRU**	PROMULGE
EGINORTU	OUTREIGN	**EGINSTTT**	STETTING	**EGLMORSS**	GORMLESS
	ROUTEING	**EGINSTTV**	VETTINGS	**EGLMOSSS**	SMOGLESS
EGINORTV	REVOTING	**EGINSTTW**	WETTINGS	**EGLNNOOR**	LONGERON
EGINORTW	TOWERING	**EGINSTTX**	TEXTINGS	**EGLNNOSS**	LONGNESS
EGINORTX	OXTERING	**EGIOOPST**	GOOPIEST	**EGLNNTUY**	UNGENTLY
EGINORTZ	ROZETING	**EGIOORRV**	GROOVIER	**EGLNOOOY**	OENOLOGY
EGINORVW	OVERWING	**EGIOOSST**	GOOSIEST	**EGLNOOPR**	PROLONGE
	WINGOVER	**EGIOPRSS**	GOSSIPER	**EGLNOOPY**	PENOLOGY
EGINORXX	XEROXING		SERPIGOS	**EGLNOORV**	OVERLONG

EGLNOOVY	VENOLOGY	**EGNNSTUU**	UNGUENTS	**EHIIIKST**	HEITIKIS
EGLNOPYY	POLYGENY	**EGNOOOOPR**	GONOPORE	**EHIIIPSX**	PIXIEISH
EGLNORSU	LOUNGERS	**EGNOOPRS**	PROGNOSE	**EHIIKLPT**	PITHLIKE
EGLNORUU	LONGUEUR	**EGNOORRV**	GOVERNOR	**EHIIKLPW**	WHIPLIKE
EGLNOSSS	SONGLESS	**EGNOOTUX**	OXTONGUE	**EHIIKNST**	HINKIEST
EGLNOSSY	LYSOGENS	**EGNOPPRU**	OPPUGNER	**EHIIKSSW**	WHISKIES
EGLNOSUV	UNGLOVES	**EGNOPRSS**	SPONGERS	**EHIILLST**	HILLIEST
EGLNOSXY	LOXYGENS	**EGNOPRSY**	PYROGENS	**EHIILLSW**	WHILLIES
	XYLOGENS	**EGNORRST**	STRONGER	**EHIILMOS**	HOMILIES
EGLNOSYY	LYSOGENY	**EGNORRSW**	WRONGERS	**EHIILNPS**	HIPLINES
EGLNPRSU	PLUNGERS	**EGNORSST**	SONGSTER	**EHIILNRS**	LINISHER
EGLNRSSU	RUNGLESS	**EGNORSSU**	SURGEONS	**EHIILNSS**	LINISHES
EGLNRSTU	GRUNTLES	**EGNORSTT**	TONGSTER	**EHIILOSS**	HELIOSIS
EGLNRTUY	URGENTLY	**EGNORSTU**	STURGEON	**EHIILPSU**	HUIPILES
EGLOOORY	OREOLOGY	**EGNORSTW**	WRONGEST	**EHIILRRW**	WHIRLIER
EGLOOPRU	PROLOGUE	**EGNORSUY**	YOUNGERS	**EHIILRSV**	LIVERISH
EGLOOPTY	LOGOTYPE	**EGNOSTUY**	YOUNGEST	**EHIILRSW**	WHIRLIES
EGLOORSS	REGOSOLS	**EGNPRRSU**	RESPRUNG	**EHIILSTT**	LITHITES
EGLOORSY	SEROLOGY	**EGNPRSUU**	SUPERGUN		THELITIS
EGLOOSXY	SEXOLOGY	**EGNRRSTU**	GRUNTERS	**EHIIMMRW**	WHIMMIER
EGLOPRTU	GROUPLET		RESTRUNG	**EHIIMMSS**	SHIMMIES
EGLOPSTU	GLUEPOTS			**EHIIMNNO**	HOMININE
EGLORRSW	GROWLERS	**EGOOPRRU**	PROROGUE	**EHIIMNOS**	HOMINIES
EGLORRWY	GROWLERY	**EGOORRSV**	GROOVERS		HOMINISE
EGLORSSS	GLOSSERS	**EGOORRVW**	OVERGROW	**EHIIMNOZ**	HOMINIZE
EGLORSSU	ROSESLUG	**EGOORSTT**	GROTTOES	**EHIIMNSS**	MINISHES
EGLORSUU	RUGULOSE	**EGOORSTU**	OUTGOERS	**EHIIMPST**	MEPHITIS
EGLORSUY	RUGOSELY	**EGOPRRSS**	PROGRESS	**EHIIMRSW**	WHIMSIER
EGLPRRSU	SPLURGER	**EGOPRRSU**	GROUPERS	**EHIIMSST**	SMITHIES
EGLPRSSU	SPLURGES		REGROUPS	**EHIIMSSW**	WHIMSIES
EGLPRSUY	GYPLURES	**EGOPSSUY**	GYPSEOUS	**EHIINNOS**	INHESION
EGLRSTTU	GUTTLERS	**EGORRSSS**	GROSSERS	**EHIINNOT**	THIONINE
EGLRSUZZ	GUZZLERS	**EGORRSST**	GROSERTS	**EHIINNQU**	HENIQUIN
EGLSSSTU	GUSTLESS	**EGORRSSU**	GROUSERS	**EHIINNRS**	INSHRINE
EGLSSUUV	VULGUSES	**EGORRSTU**	GROUTERS	**EHIINNRW**	WHINNIER
EGMMNOOR	MONOGERM	**EGORSSST**	GROSSEST	**EHIINNSS**	SHINNIES
EGMMORST	GROMMETS	**EGORSSTU**	GROUSEST	**EHIINNSW**	WHINNIES
EGMMOSSU	GUMMOSES	**EGOSSTUU**	OUTGUESS	**EHIINRRT**	HIRRIENT
EGMMRSTU	GRUMMEST	**EGPRSSTY**	GYPSTERS	**EHIINRST**	INHERITS
	GRUMMETS	**EGPRSSUU**	UPSURGES	**EHIINRSZ**	RHIZINES
EGMNNOOY	MONOGENY	**EHHIIPRS**	HEIRSHIP	**EHIINSST**	SHINIEST
	NOMOGENY	**EHHIISTV**	THIEVISH		SHINTIES
EGMNNOSW	GOWNSMEN	**EHHIKSSS**	SHIKSEHS	**EHIINSTW**	WHINIEST
EGMNOOOS	GONOSOME	**EHHILMNT**	HELMINTH	**EHIINSVX**	VIXENISH
	MONGOOSE	**EHHILOPR**	RHEOPHIL	**EHIIPPRW**	WHIPPIER
EGMNOORY	MEROGONY	**EHHILOST**	SHITHOLE	**EHIIPPSS**	SHIPPIES
EGMNOOSU	MUNGOOSE	**EHHINOPT**	THIOPHEN	**EHIIPPST**	HIPPIEST
EGMNORSU	MURGEONS	**EHHIOPRS**	HEROSHIP	**EHIIPRSV**	VIPERISH
EGMNOSYZ	ZYMOGENS	**EHHIORTT**	HITHERTO	**EHIIPSTT**	PITHIEST
EGMNRSSU	GRUMNESS	**EHHIPRSS**	HERSHIPS	**EHIIRRST**	SHIRTIER
EGMNSSSU	SMUGNESS	**EHHIPSST**	PHTHISES	**EHIIRRSW**	WHIRRIES
EGMOORRS	GROOMERS	**EHHIRSSW**	SHREWISH	**EHIIRRTX**	HERITRIX
	REGROOMS	**EHHIRSTW**	WHITHERS	**EHIIRSSU**	HUISSIER
EGMORSTU	GOURMETS	**EHHISSTU**	HUSHIEST	**EHIIRSSW**	SWISHIER
EGNNOOTY	ONTOGENY	**EHHLOOST**	SHOTHOLE	**EHIIRSTT**	SHITTIER
EGNNORST	RONTGENS	**EHHNOORS**	SHOEHORN		THIRTIES
EGNNOSTU	GUNSTONE	**EHHOOPST**	THEOSOPH	**EHIIRWZZ**	WHIZZIER
	NONGUEST	**EHHOOSSW**	WHOOSHES	**EHIISSST**	HISSIEST
EGNNOTTU	UNGOTTEN	**EHHOOSTU**	HOTHOUSE		STISHIES
EGNNSSSU	SNUGNESS	**EHHORSTU**	SHOUTHER	**EHIISSTT**	STITHIES
EGNNSTTU	TUNGSTEN	**EHHRSSSU**	SHUSHERS	**EHIISTTW**	WHITIEST
		EHHRSSTU	THRUSHES		

	WITHIEST	**EHILNOST**	HOLSTEIN	**EHIMNOST**	HOISTMEN
EHIISTTX	SIXTIETH		HOTLINES	**EHIMNOSU**	HEMIONUS
EHIJNNOS	JOHNNIES		NEOLITHS	**EHIMNOTT**	MONTEITH
EHIKKLOO	HOOKLIKE	**EHILNOSV**	NOVELISH	**EHIMNPRS**	NEPHRISM
EHIKKLSU	HUSKLIKE	**EHILNOTX**	XENOLITH		PHRENISM
EHIKKRSS	SHIKKERS	**EHILNPSY**	SYLPHINE	**EHIMNPST**	SHIPMENT
EHIKLMNY	HYMNLIKE	**EHILNSTY**	ETHINYLS	**EHIMNRRU**	MURRHINE
EHIKLMOT	MOTHLIKE	**EHILNSWY**	NEWISHLY	**EHIMNRRY**	MYRRHINE
EHIKLMPU	HUMPLIKE	**EHILOOPZ**	ZOOPHILE	**EHIMNRSU**	INHUMERS
EHIKLNOR	HORNLIKE	**EHILOOST**	HOOLIEST		RHENIUMS
EHIKLNOS	SINKHOLE	**EHILOPRS**	POLISHER	**EHIMNSTY**	THYMINES
EHIKLOOP	HOOPLIKE		REPOLISH	**EHIMOOSS**	HOMEOSIS
EHIKLOSY	YOKELISH	**EHILOPRT**	HELIPORT	**EHIMOOST**	SMOOTHIE
EHIKLOTY	LEKYTHOI	**EHILOPSS**	POLISHES	**EHIMOPRS**	SOPHERIM
EHIKLRSU	RUSHLIKE	**EHILOPST**	HELISTOP	**EHIMOPSS**	PHIMOSES
EHIKLSTU	HULKIEST		HOPLITES	**EHIMORSS**	HEROISMS
EHIKMNST	METHINKS		ISOPLETH		HORMESIS
EHIKNORS	SHONKIER	**EHILOPXY**	OXYPHILE	**EHIMORST**	ISOTHERM
EHIKNOSS	HOKINESS	**EHILORSS**	SLOSHIER		MOITHERS
EHIKNPSU	SHUNPIKE	**EHILORSU**	HOURLIES	**EHIMORSZ**	RHIZOMES
EHIKNRRS	SHRINKER	**EHILORTY**	RHYOLITE	**EHIMORTU**	MOUTHIER
EHIKNRST	RETHINKS	**EHILOSST**	HOSTILES	**EHIMOSTT**	MOTHIEST
	THINKERS	**EHILPRST**	PHILTERS	**EHIMOSTW**	SHOWTIME
EHIKNRSU	SHURIKEN		PHILTRES	**EHIMPPSS**	PSEPHISM
EHIKNSTU	HUNKIEST	**EHILPRSU**	PLUSHIER	**EHIMPRRS**	SHRIMPER
EHIKOOST	HOOKIEST	**EHILPRSY**	SYLPHIER	**EHIMPRSU**	MURPHIES
EHIKOPRS	POKERISH	**EHILPSSS**	SHIPLESS	**EHIMPRSW**	WHIMPERS
EHIKRRSS	SHIRKERS		SPLISHES	**EHIMPSTU**	HUMPIEST
EHIKRSSW	WHISKERS	**EHILPSST**	PITHLESS		HUMPTIES
EHIKRSWY	WHISKERY		THLIPSES		TUMPHIES
EHIKSSTU	HUSKIEST	**EHILPSSW**	WHIPLESS	**EHIMPSUU**	EUPHUISM
EHIKSSTW	WHISKETS	**EHILPSSY**	PHYLESIS	**EHIMPTTU**	UMPTIETH
EHIKSSWY	WHISKEYS	**EHILPSTU**	SULPHITE	**EHIMRRTY**	HERMITRY
EHILLLMO	MOLEHILL	**EHILRRSW**	WHIRLERS	**EHIMRSST**	SMITHERS
EHILLMOP	PHILOMEL	**EHILRSST**	SLITHERS	**EHIMRSSU**	HEURISMS
EHILLMOY	HOMELILY		THRISSEL	**EHIMRSTT**	THERMITS
EHILLNOS	HELLIONS	**EHILRSSU**	SLUSHIER	**EHIMRSTW**	MISTHREW
EHILLNSS	INSHELLS	**EHILRSSV**	SHRIVELS	**EHIMRSTY**	SMITHERY
EHILLOOS	OILHOLES	**EHILRSTT**	THRISTLE	**EHIMRTUU**	HUMITURE
EHILLOPY	LYOPHILE	**EHILRSTU**	LUTHIERS	**EHIMSSTU**	MUSHIEST
EHILLPTY	PHYLLITE	**EHILRSTW**	WHIRTLES		TUMSHIES
EHILLRRS	SHRILLER		WHISTLER	**EHIMSSTY**	METHYSIS
EHILLRRT	THRILLER	**EHILRSTY**	SLITHERY		MYTHISES
EHILLRST	THILLERS	**EHILRTTW**	WHITTLER	**EHIMSSWY**	WHIMSEYS
EHILLRTY	LITHERLY	**EHILRTTY**	TRIETHYL	**EHIMSTTY**	MYTHIEST
EHILLSST	HILTLESS	**EHILSSST**	SHITLESS		THYMIEST
EHILLSSW	SWELLISH	**EHILSSSU**	SLUSHIES	**EHIMSTYZ**	MYTHIZES
EHILLSTU	HULLIEST	**EHILSSSW**	WISHLESS	**EHINNORT**	INTHRONE
EHILLSVY	ELVISHLY	**EHILSSTT**	THISTLES	**EHINNOTW**	NONWHITE
EHILMNOS	LEMONISH	**EHILSSTU**	LUSHIEST	**EHINNRST**	THINNERS
EHILMOOR	HEIRLOOM	**EHILSSTW**	WHISTLES	**EHINNRSY**	SHINNERY
EHILMOST	HELOTISM	**EHILSTTU**	THULITES	**EHINNSST**	THINNESS
EHILMPSW	WHIMPLES	**EHILSTTW**	WHITTLES	**EHINNSSU**	SUNSHINE
EHILMPSY	SYMPHILE	**EHIMMNUY**	HYMENIUM	**EHINNSSY**	SHINNEYS
EHILMQUU	UMQUHILE	**EHIMMRSS**	SHIMMERS	**EHINNSTT**	THINNEST
EHILMSTT	MELTITHS	**EHIMMRSY**	SHIMMERY	**EHINOOPS**	ISOPHONE
EHILNOOP	OENOPHIL	**EHIMMSSY**	SHIMMEYS	**EHINOPPR**	HORNPIPE
EHILNOPS	PINHOLES	**EHIMNOPR**	MORPHINE	**EHINOPRT**	TRIPHONE
EHILNOPT	THOLEPIN	**EHIMNORT**	THERMION	**EHINOPST**	PHONIEST
EHILNORU	UNHOLIER	**EHIMNOSS**	HOMINESS		SIPHONET
EHILNOSS	HOLINESS		MONISHES	**EHINOPSW**	WINESHOP

EHINORRT	THORNIER	**EHIPPSSU**	HIPPUSES	**EHLMOOST**	LOTHSOME
EHINORSS	HERISSON	**EHIPPSTW**	WHIPPETS	**EHLMOPSY**	MESOPHYL
EHINORST	HORNIEST	**EHIPQSUY**	PHYSIQUE	**EHLMORTY**	MOTHERLY
	ORNITHES	**EHIPRSST**	HIPSTERS	**EHLMOTXY**	METHOXYL
EHINORTV	OVERTHIN		THRIPSES	**EHLMPSSU**	HUMPLESS
EHINORZZ	HIZZONER	**EHIPRSSW**	WHISPERS	**EHLNNOPU**	UNHOLPEN
EHINOSST	HISTONES	**EHIPRSTU**	SUPERHIT	**EHLNOPSU**	SULPHONE
EHINOSTU	OUTSHINE	**EHIPRSTW**	WHIPSTER	**EHLNORSS**	HORNLESS
EHINPPRU	UNHIPPER	**EHIPRSWY**	WHISPERY	**EHLNORST**	HORNLETS
EHINPPSS	SHIPPENS	**EHIPSSTU**	PUSHIEST	**EHLNOSST**	LOTHNESS
EHINPRSU	PUNISHER	**EHIPSTUU**	EUPHUIST	**EHLNOSTY**	HONESTLY
EHINPSSU	PUNISHES	**EHIQSSSU**	SQUISHES	**EHLNRSTU**	LUTHERNS
EHINPSSX	SPHINXES	**EHIRRRSU**	HURRIERS	**EHLNSSSU**	LUSHNESS
EHINRSSU	INRUSHES	**EHIRRSSV**	SHRIVERS		SHUNLESS
EHINRSTZ	ZITHERNS	**EHIRRSTT**	THIRSTER	**EHLNSTYY**	ETHYNYLS
EHINSSST	THISNESS	**EHIRRSTV**	THRIVERS	**EHLOOPRT**	PORTHOLE
EHINSSUW	UNWISHES	**EHIRRSTW**	WHERRITS		POTHOLER
EHIOOPST	ISOPHOTE		WRITHERS	**EHLOOPSS**	HOOPLESS
EHIOOPSW	WHOOPIES	**EHIRRTTU**	TRUTHIER	**EHLOOPST**	POSTHOLE
	WHOOPSIE	**EHIRSSSW**	SWISHERS		POTHOLES
EHIOORST	TOOSHIER	**EHIRSSTU**	RUSHIEST	**EHLOOPTY**	HOLOTYPE
EHIOORTT	TOOTHIER	**EHIRSSTW**	SWITHERS	**EHLOORVY**	OVERHOLY
EHIOOSST	STOOSHIE	**EHIRSTTW**	WHITRETS	**EHLOOSSS**	SLOOSHES
EHIOOSTT	HOOTIEST		WHITSTER	**EHLOPPRS**	HOPPLERS
EHIOPPPS	POPESHIP		WHITTERS	**EHLOPPRT**	THROPPLE
EHIOPPRS	SHOPPIER	**EHIRSWZZ**	WHIZZERS	**EHLOPSSS**	SPLOSHES
EHIOPPST	HOPPIEST	**EHIRTTTW**	WHITTRET	**EHLOPSSY**	SPYHOLES
	POETSHIP	**EHISSSTU**	STUSHIES	**EHLORSST**	HOLSTERS
EHIOPPSU	EOHIPPUS	**EHISSSTW**	SWISHEST		HOSTLERS
EHIOPRSS	POSERISH	**EHISSTUW**	THUSWISE	**EHLORSTT**	THROSTLE
	ROSEHIPS	**EHISSUVW**	HUSWIVES	**EHLORSTW**	WHORTLES
	SPOSHIER	**EHKLNOOT**	KNOTHOLE	**EHLORSTY**	HOSTELRY
EHIOPRST	TROPHIES	**EHKLOOSS**	HOOKLESS	**EHLORSUV**	OVERLUSH
EHIOPTTW	WHITEPOT	**EHKLOOST**	HOOKLETS	**EHLORTTT**	THROTTLE
EHIORRST	HERITORS	**EHKLOOSZ**	KOLHOZES	**EHLOSSTT**	SHOTTLES
EHIORRTU	ROUTHIER	**EHKLOSTY**	LEKYTHOS	**EHLOSSTW**	THOWLESS
EHIORRTW	WORTHIER	**EHKLSTUY**	LEKYTHUS	**EHLOSSTY**	THYLOSES
EHIORSST	HOISTERS	**EHKMOORW**	HOMEWORK	**EHLOSTXY**	ETHOXYLS
	HORSIEST	**EHKMOOSS**	SMOKEHOS	**EHLPSSTU**	PLUSHEST
	HOSTRIES	**EHKMORSU**	HUMORESK	**EHLRSSTU**	HURTLESS
	SHORTIES	**EHKMORSW**	MESHWORK		HUSTLERS
EHIORSTT	THEORIST	**EHKMOSSY**	SKYHOMES		RUTHLESS
	THORITES	**EHKNNRSU**	SHRUNKEN	**EHLRSTTU**	SHUTTLER
EHIORSTU	OUTHIRES	**EHKNOOSS**	HOOKNOSE	**EHLSSTTU**	SHUTTLES
	SHOUTIER	**EHKNORSU**	UNKOSHER	**EHMMOOOR**	HOMEROOM
EHIORSTV	OVERHITS	**EHKOOSSS**	SKOOSHES	**EHMMOOSS**	HOMMOSES
EHIORSTW	WORTHIES	**EHKOPSSY**	KYPHOSES	**EHMMRRTU**	THRUMMER
EHIORTUY	YOUTHIER	**EHKRSSTU**	TUSHKERS	**EHMMSSUU**	HUMMUSES
EHIORTWZ	HOWITZER	**EHLLMOPY**	PHYLLOME	**EHMNNOTY**	ETHNONYM
EHIOSSSW	WHOSISES	**EHLLNSSU**	UNSHELLS	**EHMNNSTU**	HUNTSMEN
EHIOSSTT	TOSHIEST	**EHLLNSTU**	NUTSHELL	**EHMNOOPR**	NEOMORPH
EHIOSSTU	HOUSESIT	**EHLLOOOP**	LOOPHOLE	**EHMNOORS**	HORMONES
	HOUSIEST	**EHLLOORW**	HOLLOWER		MOORHENS
	STOUSHIE	**EHLMMOSW**	WHOMMLES	**EHMNOOST**	SMOOTHEN
EHIOSSTW	SHOWIEST	**EHLMMSUW**	WHUMMLES	**EHMNOOTW**	HOMETOWN
EHIOSSTY	ISOHYETS	**EHLMNOST**	MENTHOLS		TOWNHOME
EHIOSTVY	YESHIVOT	**EHLMNOSY**	HOMELYNS	**EHMNOOTY**	THEONOMY
EHIOTTUW	WHITEOUT	**EHLMNOUY**	UNHOMELY	**EHMNOPSU**	HOMESPUN
EHIPPRSS	PRESHIPS	**EHLMNSSY**	HYMNLESS	**EHMNPRYY**	HYPERNYM
	SHIPPERS	**EHLMOORW**	WORMHOLE	**EHMNPSTY**	NYMPHETS
EHIPPRSW	WHIPPERS			**EHMNSTTU**	HUTMENTS

EHMOOOTZ	ZOOTHOME	EHOOPRSW	WHOOPERS	EIIKKLLM	MILKLIKE
EHMOOPRT	HOMEPORT	EHOOPRSX	HORSEPOX	EIIKKLLS	SILKLIKE
EHMOOPTY	HOMOTYPE	EHOOPRTY	ORTHOEPY	EIIKKLLT	KILTLIKE
EHMOORRS	SHROOMER	EHOOPSTT	PHOTOSET	EIIKKLNS	SKINLIKE
EHMOORST	RESMOOTH	EHOOPSTU	HOUSETOP	EIIKKNST	KINKIEST
	SMOOTHER		POTHOUSE	EIIKLLLY	LILYLIKE
EHMOORSZ	SHMOOZER	EHOOPSTY	OOPHYTES	EIIKLLMN	LIMEKILN
EHMOORTU	OUTHOMER	EHOOPTYZ	ZOOPHYTE	EIIKLLNO	LIONLIKE
EHMOOSSS	SHMOOSES	EHOORSST	ORTHOSES	EIIKLLRS	SKILLIER
	SMOOSHES		RESHOOTS	EIIKLLSS	SKILLIES
EHMOOSST	SMOOTHES		SHEROOTS	EIIKLLST	SLITLIKE
EHMOOSSZ	SHMOOZES		SHOOTERS	EIIKLMRS	MISLIKER
EHMOPRSW	MORPHEWS		SOOTHERS	EIIKLMSS	MISLIKES
EHMORSST	SMOTHERS	EHOORSTV	OVERSHOT	EIIKLMST	MILKIEST
EHMORSTU	MOUTHERS	EHOOSSSW	SWOOSHES	EIIKLNOR	IRONLIKE
EHMORSTY	SMOTHERY	EHOOSSTT	SOOTHEST	EIIKLNPR	PLINKIER
EHMORTUV	VERMOUTH	EHOOSTUU	OUTHOUSE	EIIKLNRS	SLINKIER
EHMOSSUU	HOUMUSES	EHOPPRSS	SHOPPERS	EIIKLNRT	TINKLIER
EHMOTUZZ	MEZUZOTH	EHOPPRST	PROPHETS	EIIKLNST	LINKIEST
EHMPRSTU	THUMPERS	EHOPPRSW	WHOPPERS	EIIKLPSS	PLISKIES
EHMRRSTU	MURTHERS	EHOPPRSY	PROPHESY	EIIKLPSW	WISPLIKE
EHMRSTUV	VERMUTHS	EHOPRRSY	ORPHREYS	EIIKLRTT	KITTLIER
EHMRTUYY	EURYTHMY	EHOPRSST	HOTPRESS	EIIKLSST	SILKIEST
EHMSSTUY	THYMUSES		STROPHES	EIIKLSTU	SUITLIKE
EHNNOPRS	NEPHRONS	EHOPRSSW	PRESHOWS	EIIKMPRS	SKIMPIER
EHNNOPSY	HYPNONES	EHOPRSTU	POUTHERS	EIIKMRRS	SMIRKIER
EHNNORRT	NORTHERN		SUPERHOT	EIIKMRST	MIRKIEST
	THRONNER	EHOPRSTY	TROPHESY	EIIKNNOS	NOISENIK
EHNNORTU	UNTHRONE	EHOPRSUV	PUSHOVER	EIIKNNRS	SKINNIER
EHNNOSTU	UNHONEST	EHOPRTUY	EUTROPHY	EIIKNNSS	INKINESS
EHNNRSSU	SHUNNERS	EHOPSSTY	PHYTOSES		SKINNIES
EHNOOPTY	HONEYPOT	EHORRSTW	THROWERS	EIIKNNST	KINETINS
EHNOORRS	HONORERS	EHORRSTY	HERSTORY	EIIKNNSW	WINESKIN
EHNOORRU	HONOURER	EHORSSTT	SHORTEST	EIIKNPST	PINKIEST
EHNOORSS	SOREHONS	EHORSSTU	SHOUTERS	EIIKNRST	STINKIER
EHNOORSW	WHORESON		SOUTHERS	EIIKNSST	SINKIEST
EHNOORTW	HONEWORT	EHORSTUY	OUTHYRES	EIIKNSTW	TWINKIES
EHNOOSSW	SNOWSHOE	EHORTTUW	OUTTHREW	EIIKNSTZ	ZINKIEST
EHNOOSTU	OUTSHONE	EHOSSSTU	STOUSHES	EIIKPPRS	SKIPPIER
EHNOPRSW	PRESHOWN	EHPRSSSU	SPRUSHES	EIIKPSST	SPIKIEST
EHNOPRSY	HYPERONS	EHPRSSUU	UPRUSHES	EIIKQRRU	QUIRKIER
EHNOPSSS	POSHNESS	EHPRSTTU	TURPETHS	EIIKRSST	RISKIEST
EHNOPSSY	HYPNOSES	EHPSSTUY	TYPHUSES	EIIKSSST	KISSIEST
EHNORRRS	SHNORRER	EHQRSSUU	QURUSHES	EIIKSSTV	SKIVIEST
EHNORRST	NORTHERS	EHQSSSUU	SQUUSHES	EIIKSSVV	SKIVVIES
EHNORRTY	ERYTHRON	EHRRSTTU	THRUSTER	EIILLLVY	LIVELILY
EHNORSST	SHORTENS	EHRSSSTY	SHYSTERS	EIILLMMR	MILLIREM
EHNORSSU	ONRUSHES	EHRSSTTU	SHUTTERS	EIILLMMS	MILLIMES
	UNHORSES	EIIILMSS	SIMILISE	EIILLMNR	MILLINER
EHNORSTT	THORNSET	EIIILMSZ	SIMILIZE	EIILLMNS	MILLINES
EHNORSTU	SOUTHERN	EIIILNRV	INVIRILE		SLIMLINE
EHNORTUV	OVERHUNT	EIIILPPR	LIRIPIPE	EIILLMNU	ILLUMINE
EHNOSSUU	UNHOUSES	EIIILRSV	VIRILISE	EIILLMRS	MILLIERS
EHNOSTUU	NUTHOUSE	EIIILRVZ	VIRILIZE	EIILLNST	NIELLIST
EHNOSTUY	YOUTHENS	EIIIMMNS	MINIMISE	EIILLNSU	SUILLINE
EHNPSSXY	SPHYNXES	EIIIMMNZ	MINIMIZE	EIILLNSV	VILLEINS
EHNRSSTU	HUNTRESS	EIIIRRTV	TIRRIVIE	EIILLNTV	VITELLIN
	SHUNTERS	EIIIRSST	IRITISES	EIILLPSS	ELLIPSIS
EHNSSSTU	THUSNESS	EIIJKNRT	JIRKINET	EIILLRST	STILLIER
EHOOPRRT	HOROPTER	EIIJMPST	JIMPIEST	EIILLRVY	VIRILELY
EHOOPRST	HOOPSTER	EIIJNRSU	INJURIES	EIILLSST	SILLIEST

EIILLSTT	LITTLIES	EIILPPRR	RIPPLIER	EIIMOSTY	MOYITIES
	TILLIEST	EIILPPRS	SLIPPIER	EIIMOSUX	EXIMIOUS
	TILLITES	EIILPPST	LIPPIEST	EIIMOTVV	VOMITIVE
EIILLSTW	TWILLIES	EIILPRST	TRIPLIES	EIIMPRRS	PRIMSIER
EIILLSUV	ILLUSIVE	EIILPRSU	PLURISIE	EIIMPRSS	MISPRISE
EIILMMOS	MILESIMO	EIILPRTT	TRIPLITE		PISMIRES
EIILMMOT	IMMOTILE	EIILPSST	PITILESS	EIIMPRSZ	MISPRIZE
EIILMNNT	LINIMENT		SPILITES	EIIMPSST	PIETISMS
EIILMNOT	LIMONITE	EIILPSTY	PYELITIS	EIIMPSTW	WIMPIEST
EIILMNSS	LIMINESS	EIILPSUZ	SPUILZIE	EIIMQSTU	QUIETISM
EIILMNTT	MELITTIN	EIILQSSU	SILIQUES	EIIMRRRS	SMIRRIER
EIILMOPT	IMPOLITE	EIILRRSW	SWIRLIER	EIIMRSTT	METRITIS
EIILMPPR	PIMPLIER	EIILRRTW	TWIRLIER	EIIMRSTW	MISWRITE
EIILMPRS	IMPERILS	EIILRSTT	SLITTIER	EIIMRSTX	TRIMIXES
	LIMPSIER		STILTIER	EIIMSSSS	MISSISES
EIILMPRT	PRELIMIT	EIILRSTU	UTILISER	EIIMSSST	MISSIEST
EIILMPST	LIMEPITS	EIILRTUZ	UTILIZER	EIIMSSSV	MISSIVES
EIILMRSS	SLIMSIER	EIILSSTT	ELITISTS	EIIMSSSZ	SIZEISMS
EIILMRST	LIMITERS		SILTIEST	EIIMSSTT	MISTIEST
	MIRLIEST	EIILSSTU	ULITISES		SEMITIST
EIILMRZZ	MIZZLIER		UTILISES	EIINNNPS	NINEPINS
EIILMSSS	MISSILES	EIILSTUY	TUILYIES	EIINNOOR	ONIONIER
EIILMSST	ELITISMS	EIILSTUZ	TUILZIES	EIINNOSS	INOSINES
	SLIMIEST		UTILIZES	EIINNOSU	UNIONISE
	SMILIEST	EIIMMNNO	MENOMINI	EIINNOSV	ENVISION
EIILMSSV	MISLIVES	EIIMMNNT	IMMINENT	EIINNOUZ	UNIONIZE
EIILMSTT	MILTIEST		MINIMENT	EIINNPSS	SPINNIES
	MISTITLE	EIIMMNSU	IMMUNISE	EIINNQSU	QUININES
EIILMSTY	MYELITIS	EIIMMNTU	IMMINUTE	EIINNRTV	INVERTIN
EIILNNOT	LENITION	EIIMMNUZ	IMMUNIZE	EIINNSST	TININESS
EIILNORS	LIONISER	EIIMMPRU	IMPERIUM	EIINNSSW	INSINEWS
EIILNORT	TRIOLEIN	EIIMMRSW	SWIMMIER	EIINNSTT	TINNIEST
EIILNORZ	LIONIZER	EIIMMSSS	SEISMISM	EIINNSTW	INTWINES
EIILNOSS	ELISIONS	EIIMMSST	MIMSIEST	EIINOPRS	RIPIENOS
	ISOLINES		MISTIMES	EIINOPRT	POINTIER
	LIONISES	EIIMNOPT	PIMIENTO		POITRINE
	OILINESS	EIIMNOSS	EMISSION	EIINOPST	SINOPITE
EIILNOST	ETIOLINS		SIMONIES	EIINOPTT	PETITION
	NOILIEST		SIMONISE	EIINORRT	INTERIOR
EIILNOSV	OLIVINES	EIIMNOSV	VISNOMIE	EIINORSS	IONISERS
EIILNOSZ	LIONIZES	EIIMNOSZ	SIMONIZE		IRONISES
EIILNOTT	TOILINET	EIIMNOTV	MONITIVE		SIRONISE
EIILNQTU	QUINTILE	EIIMNPRS	PRIMINES	EIINORST	IRONIEST
EIILNRSS	RESILINS	EIIMNRSS	MIRINESS	EIINORSV	REVISION
EIILNRST	NIRLIEST		RIMINESS		VISIONER
	NITRILES	EIIMNRST	INTERIMS	EIINORSZ	IONIZERS
EIILNSSW	WILINESS		MINISTER		IRONIZES
EIILNSTT	INTITLES		MISINTER		SIRONIZE
	LINTIEST		MINIVERS	EIINOSST	INOSITES
EIILNSTY	SENILITY	EIIMNRTT	INTERMIT		NOISIEST
EIILNSVY	SYLVIINE	EIIMNRTX	INTERMIX	EIINOSTV	NOVITIES
EIILNTTU	INTITULE	EIIMNSTT	MINTIEST	EIINPPRS	SNIPPIER
EIILNTUV	VITULINE	EIIMNSTU	MUTINIES	EIINPPSS	PIPINESS
EIILOPPT	POPLITEI	EIIMNSTV	MINIVETS	EIINPPST	NIPPIEST
EIILOPRS	LIRIOPES	EIIMOPRX	MIREPOIX	EIINPRRS	INSPIRER
EIILOPST	PISOLITE	EIIMOPSS	MISPOISE	EIINPRSS	INSPIRES
	POLITIES	EIIMOPST	OPTIMISE	EIINPRST	PRISTINE
EIILORST	ROILIEST	EIIMOPSZ	EPIZOISM	EIINPSST	SNIPIEST
EIILORTT	TROILITE	EIIMOPTZ	OPTIMIZE		SPINIEST
EIILOSST	SOILIEST	EIIMOSSS	SEMIOSIS	EIINPSSX	PIXINESS
EIILOTVV	VOLITIVE	EIIMOSSV	OMISSIVE	EIINPSTZ	PINTSIZE

EIINPTUV	PUNITIVE		WISPIEST	EIKLMNRS	KREMLINS
EIINQRRU	INQUIRER	EIIPSTTT	PITTITES	EIKLMORV	OVERMILK
EIINQRSU	INQUIRES	EIIPSTTU	PITUITES	EIKLMORW	WORMLIKE
EIINQSSU	QUINSIES	EIIQSTTU	QUIETIST	EIKLMOSS	MOSSLIKE
	SQUINIES	EIIRRSTW	WRISTIER	EIKLMPPU	PUMPLIKE
EIINQSTU	INQUIETS	EIIRSSTV	REVISITS	EIKLNOOR	OERLIKON
EIINQTUY	EQUINITY		VISITERS	EIKLNOPR	PLONKIER
	INEQUITY	EIIRSTTU	UTERITIS	EIKLNOSW	SNOWLIKE
EIINRRTW	WINTRIER	EIIRSTTW	TWISTIER	EIKLNPRS	PLINKERS
EIINRSST	INSISTER	EIIRSTTZ	RITZIEST		SPRINKLE
	SINISTER	EIISSSST	SISSIEST	EIKLNPRU	PLUNKIER
EIINRSSW	WIRINESS	EIISSSTZ	SIZEISTS	EIKLNRRU	KNURLIER
EIINRSTT	NITRITES	EIISSTTV	STIVIEST	EIKLNRSS	SLINKERS
	STINTIER	EIISTTTW	WITTIEST	EIKLNRST	LINKSTER
EIINRSTU	NEURITIS	EIJJNTUY	JEJUNITY		STRINKLE
	UNITISER	EIJKKSSU	JUKSKEIS		TINKLERS
EIINRSTV	INVITERS	EIJKNOSS	JOKINESS	EIKLNRSW	WINKLERS
	VINTRIES	EIJKNSTU	JUNKIEST		WRINKLES
	VITRINES	EIJKORRS	SKIJORER	EIKLNRTW	TWINKLER
EIINRTUZ	UNITIZER	EIJLLORS	JOLLIERS	EIKLNSSS	SKINLESS
EIINRTVY	INVERITY	EIJLLOST	JOLLIEST	EIKLNSST	LENTISKS
EIINSSSZ	SIZINESS	EIJLMTTU	MULTIJET	EIKLNSSY	SKYLINES
EIINSSTU	UNITISES	EIJLOSTT	JOLTIEST	EIKLNSTT	KNITTLES
EIINSTTT	NITTIEST	EIJLOSTW	JOWLIEST	EIKLNSTW	TWINKLES
	TINTIEST	EIJMNPSS	JIMPNESS	EIKLOOPR	PLOOKIER
EIINSTTW	TWINIEST	EIJMPSTU	JUMPIEST	EIKLOORT	ROOTLIKE
EIINSTUZ	UNITIZES	EIJNORST	JOINTERS	EIKLOPRU	PLOUKIER
EIIOPRRS	PRIORIES	EIJNORTU	JOINTURE	EIKLOPRW	PILEWORK
EIIOPSTV	POSITIVE	EIJNOSTT	JETTISON	EIKLOPSU	SOUPLIKE
EIIORRST	RIOTRIES	EIJNPRSU	JUNIPERS	EIKLORTY	KRYOLITE
EIIORSST	RIOTISES	EIJNRRSU	INJURERS	EIKLOSSU	LEUKOSIS
EIIORSTZ	RIOTIZES	EIJNRRUY	REINJURY	EIKLOSTY	YOLKIEST
EIIOSSTT	OSTEITIS	EIJNSTTW	TWINJETS	EIKLPSSU	PUSSLIKE
	OTITISES	EIJOSTTT	JOTTIEST	EIKLRSSS	RISKLESS
EIIOSSTZ	ZOISITES	EIJRSTUY	JESUITRY	EIKLRSST	KLISTERS
EIIOTTTV	TOTITIVE	EIJSSSUV	JUSSIVES	EIKLRTUZ	KLUTZIER
EIIPPPST	PIPPIEST	EIKKLNOO	NOOKLIKE	EIKLSSTT	SKITTLES
EIIPPQRU	QUIPPIER	EIKKLNOT	KNOTLIKE	EIKLSSTU	SULKIEST
EIIPPRRS	RIPPIERS	EIKKLNRS	KLINKERS	EIKLSTTT	KITTLEST
EIIPPRRT	TRIPPIER	EIKKLSTU	TUSKLIKE	EIKMMRRS	KRIMMERS
EIIPPSTT	TIPPIEST	EIKKNRSS	SKINKERS	EIKMMRSS	SKIMMERS
EIIPPSTZ	ZIPPIEST	EIKKNRSU	SKUNKIER	EIKMNNOO	MONOKINE
EIIPRRSS	PRISSIER	EIKKOOST	KOOKIEST	EIKMNORS	MONIKERS
EIIPRRST	STRIPIER	EIKKSTUY	YUKKIEST	EIKMNOST	TOKENISM
EIIPRRSU	SIRUPIER	EIKLLMOO	KILOMOLE	EIKMNOSU	MOUSEKIN
EIIPRRTW	TRIPWIRE	EIKLLMPU	PLUMLIKE	EIKMOPSS	MISSPOKE
	TWIRPIER	EIKLLMSS	MILKLESS	EIKMORTW	TIMEWORK
EIIPRSSS	PRISSIES	EIKLLNOR	KNOLLIER	EIKMOSST	SMOKIEST
EIIPRSST	SPIRIEST	EIKLLNSW	INKWELLS	EIKMOSSU	KOUMISES
EIIPRSTT	RISPETTI	EIKLLNUY	UNLIKELY	EIKMOSSY	MISYOKES
	TRIPIEST	EIKLLNXY	LYNXLIKE	EIKMPSSU	MUSPIKES
EIIPRSTU	PURITIES	EIKLLOOW	WOOLLIKE	EIKMRRSS	SMIRKERS
EIIPRSTV	PREVISIT	EIKLLORV	OVERKILL	EIKMRSTU	MURKIEST
	PRIVIEST	EIKLLOSS	SKOLLIES	EIKMSSSU	KUMISSES
EIIPRSTY	PYRITISE	EIKLLOSU	SOULLIKE	EIKMSSTU	MUSKIEST
EIIPRSVV	SPIVVIER	EIKLLRSS	RESKILLS	EIKNNORS	EINKORNS
EIIPRTYZ	PYRITIZE	EIKLLSSS	SKILLESS		NONSKIER
EIIPSSTT	PIETISTS	EIKLLSST	SKILLETS	EIKNNOST	INKSTONE
	STIPITES	EIKLMNNS	LINKSMEN	EIKNNPSS	PINKNESS
	TIPSIEST	EIKLMNOO	MOONLIKE	EIKNNRSS	SKINNERS
EIIPSSTW	SWIPIEST	EIKLMNOS	MOLESKIN	EIKNOORS	ROOINEKS

EIKNOOST	NOOKIEST		UNTIMELY
EIKNOPSS	POKINESS	EILLNOTU	LUTEOLIN
EIKNORST	INSTROKE	EILLNPSW	PINSWELL	EILMOOPS	LIPOSOME
EIKNORSV	INVOKERS	EILLNPUU	LUPULINE	EILMOORS	SLOOMIER
EIKNORTT	KNOTTIER	EILLNSST	LINTLESS	EILMOOST	TOILSOME
EIKNOSTW	WONKIEST	EILLNSTY	SILENTLY	EILMOOSV	MOOLVIES
EIKNPRRS	PRINKERS		TINSELLY	EILMOPRR	IMPLORER
EIKNPRSU	SPUNKIER	EILLNSUV	LEVULINS	EILMOPRS	IMPLORES
EIKNPRTU	TURNPIKE	EILLNSVY	SNIVELLY		PELORISM
EIKNPSSU	SPUNKIES	EILLNUVY	UNLIVELY	EILMOPST	MILEPOST
EIKNPSTU	PUNKIEST	EILLOORW	WOOLLIER		POLEMIST
EIKNRRTU	RETURNIK	EILLOOSW	WOOLLIES	EILMORRS	LORIMERS
EIKNRSST	STINKERS	EILLOPSS	SLIPSOLE	EILMORSY	RIMOSELY
EIKNRSSW	SWINKERS	EILLOPTY	POLITELY	EILMOSTT	MOTLIEST
EIKNRSTT	KNITTERS	EILLORST	TRILLOES	EILMOSTU	OUTSMILE
	TRINKETS		TROLLIES	EILMOSUV	VOLUMISE
EIKNSSSU	UNKISSES	EILLORSU	ROUILLES	EILMOUVZ	VOLUMIZE
EIKNSSTT	SKINTEST	EILLORSZ	ZORILLES	EILMPPRU	IMPURPLE
EIKNSTUZ	KUNZITES	EILLORTT	TORTELLI		PLUMPIER
EIKOOPRS	SPOOKIER	EILLORWW	WILLOWER	EILMPRRU	RUMPLIER
EIKOORST	ROOKIEST	EILLOSSS	SOILLESS	EILMPRSS	SIMPLERS
EIKOOSST	STOOKIES	EILLOSST	TOILLESS	EILMPRSU	SLUMPIER
EIKOPPRS	PORKPIES	EILLOSTW	LOWLIEST	EILMPRUY	IMPURELY
EIKOPPRW	PIPEWORK	EILLOSVW	LOWLIVES	EILMPSST	MISSPELT
EIKOPRST	PORKIEST	EILLPRSS	SPILLERS		SIMPLEST
EIKOPRSV	OVERSKIP	EILLPSSS	SLIPLESS	EILMPSSU	IMPULSES
EIKORRWW	WIREWORK	EILLQSTU	QUILLETS	EILMPSTU	LUMPIEST
EIKPPRSS	SKIPPERS	EILLRRST	TRILLERS		PLUMIEST
EIKPPSST	SKIPPETS	EILLRSST	STILLERS	EILMRSSU	MISRULES
EIKPRRSU	SPRUIKER	EILLRSSW	SWILLERS	EILMRSSY	REMISSLY
EIKRRSST	SKIRRETS	EILLRSTT	TESTRILL	EILMRSTU	MURLIEST
	SKIRTERS	EILLRSVY	SILVERLY	EILMRSTY	LYMITERS
	STRIKERS	EILLSSST	LISTLESS	EILMSSTU	LITMUSES
EIKRRSSU	SKURRIES		SLITLESS	EILMSSTY	MISSTYLE
EIKRSSTT	SKITTERS	EILLSSTT	STILLEST	EILMSTUU	MULTIUSE
EIKRSSTU	TURKISES	EILLSTTT	LITTLEST	EILMSUUV	ELUVIUMS
EIKRSTTY	SKITTERY	EILLSTUV	VITELLUS	EILMTTUU	LUTETIUM
EIKRSTWY	SKYWRITE	EILMMNOS	MOLIMENS	EILMTTUY	MULTEITY
EIKSSTTU	TUSKIEST	EILMMPRU	PLUMMIER	EILNNORS	ONLINERS
EILLLNOY	LONELILY	EILMMRSS	SLIMMERS	EILNNOST	INSOLENT
EILLLOVY	LOVELILY	EILMMRSU	SLUMMIER	EILNNOSV	NONLIVES
EILLLPUV	PULVILLE	EILMMSST	SLIMMEST	EILNNOSW	SNOWLINE
EILLMNNO	MONELLIN	EILMMSTU	LUMMIEST	EILNNOTT	NONTITLE
EILLMNOS	SEMILLON	EILMNNOO	MONOLINE	EILNNOTV	VINOLENT
EILLMNOU	LINOLEUM	EILMNOOS	OINOMELS	EILNNPSU	PINNULES
EILLMNQU	QUILLMEN		SIMOLEON	EILNNSSU	LUNINESS
EILLMNST	STILLMEN	EILMNOPT	PILOTMEN	EILNNSTU	UNSILENT
EILLMNSU	MULLEINS	EILMNORS	MISENROL	EILNNTTY	INTENTLY
EILLMOPR	IMPELLOR	EILMNOST	MOLINETS	EILNOOPP	EPIPLOON
EILLMOPS	PLIMSOLE	EILMNOSU	EMULSION	EILNOOPS	POLONIES
EILLMOST	MELILOTS	EILMNOSV	NOVELISM		POLONISE
EILLMPSS	MISSPELL	EILMNOTU	MOULINET	EILNOOPZ	POLONIZE
	PSELLISM	EILMNOTY	MYLONITE	EILNOOST	LOONIEST
EILLMPTU	MULTIPLE	EILMNPSS	LIMPNESS		OILSTONE
EILLMSSS	MISSELLS		PLENISMS	EILNOOSV	VIOLONES
EILLMSST	MISTELLS	EILMNPSU	SPLENIUM	EILNOOPS	PLENIPOS
EILLMSTU	MULLITES	EILMNPTU	TUMPLINE	EILNOPPY	POLYPINE
EILLMUVX	VEXILLUM	EILMNRST	MINSTREL	EILNOPRS	PLERIONS
EILLNOPT	PLOTLINE	EILMNSSS	SLIMNESS		PROLINES
EILLNOPY	EPYLLION	EILMNSSU	EMULSINS	EILNOPRT	TERPINOL
EILLNOST	STELLION	EILMNSTU	MUSLINET		TOPLINER
		EILMNTUY	MINUTELY	EILNOPRU	NEUROPIL

EILNOPSS	EPSILONS	EILOOSTZ	ZOOLITES	EILPPSSW	SWIPPLES
EILNOPST	POINTELS	EILOPPPR	POPPLIER	EILPPSTU	PULPIEST
	PONTILES	EILOPPRS	SLOPPIER	EILPRRSU	SLURPIER
	POTLINES	EILOPPST	LOPPIEST	EILPRSST	RESPLITS
	TOPLINES	EILOPPTY	POLYPITE		SPIRTLES
EILNOPTU	UNPOLITE	EILOPRRT	PORTLIER	EILPRSTT	SPLITTER
EILNOPTY	LINOTYPE	EILOPRSS	SPOILERS		TRIPLETS
EILNORRS	LORINERS	EILOPRST	POITRELS	EILPRSTY	PRIESTLY
EILNORRT	RITORNEL	EILOPRSU	PERILOUS		SPRITELY
EILNORSS	IRONLESS	EILOPRSV	OVERSLIP	EILPRSUU	PURLIEUS
EILNORST	RETINOLS		SLIPOVER	EILPRSUY	PLEURISY
EILNORTT	TROTLINE	EILOPRSY	PYROLISE	EILPRTTY	PRETTILY
EILNORTU	OUTLINER	EILOPRTT	PLOTTIER	EILPSSSU	PUSSLIES
EILNORTW	TOWNLIER	EILOPRTW	PILEWORT	EILPSSTT	SPITTLES
EILNORVV	INVOLVER	EILOPRYZ	PYROLIZE	EILPSSTU	STIPULES
EILNOSSU	ELUSIONS	EILOPSSS	PSILOSES	EILPSSUY	SPULYIES
EILNOSSW	LEWISSON	EILOPSST	PISTOLES	EILPSSUZ	SPULZIES
EILNOSTU	ELUTIONS		PTILOSES	EILQRRSU	SQUIRREL
	OUTLINES		SLOPIEST	EILQRSTU	QUILTERS
EILNOSTV	NOVELIST	EILOPSSV	PLOSIVES	EILQRSUU	LIQUEURS
	VIOLENTS	EILOPSTT	PISTOLET	EILQRSUY	SQUIRELY
EILNOSTW	TOWLINES		PLOTTIES	EILQSTUU	LUSTIQUE
EILNOSUV	EVULSION		POLITEST	EILRRSSU	SLURRIES
EILNOSVV	INVOLVES	EILOPSTU	SOUTPIEL	EILRRSTU	SULTRIER
EILNOTUV	INVOLUTE	EILOPSTX	EXPLOITS	EILRRSTW	TWIRLERS
EILNOTXY	XYLONITE	EILOPSUV	PLUVIOSE	EILRRTWY	WRITERLY
EILNOTYZ	ZYLONITE	EILORRTU	ULTERIOR	EILRSSST	STIRLESS
EILNPRSS	PILSNERS	EILORSSS	RISSOLES	EILRSSTT	SLITTERS
EILNPRST	SPLINTER	EILORSST	ESTRIOLS		STILTERS
EILNPRSU	PURLINES	EILORSSU	SOILURES		TESTRILS
EILNPRUY	UNRIPELY	EILORSTT	TRIOLETS	EILRSSTU	SURLIEST
EILNPSSS	SPINLESS	EILORSTU	LOURIEST	EILRSSTV	LISTSERV
EILNPSST	PLENISTS		OUTLIERS	EILRSSTY	SISTERLY
EILNPSSU	SPINULES	EILORSUV	RIVULOSE		STYLISER
	SPLENIUS	EILORSZZ	SOZZLIER	EILRSSUV	SURVEILS
EILNPSUY	SUPINELY	EILORTTY	TOILETRY	EILRSSZZ	SIZZLERS
EILNQUUY	UNIQUELY	EILORTUV	OUTLIVER	EILRSTTU	SLUTTIER
EILNRRUU	UNRULIER	EILORVWY	OVERWILY		SURTITLE
EILNRSST	SLINTERS	EILOSSST	LOSSIEST	EILRSTTW	WRISTLET
	SNIRTLES	EILOSSTU	LOUSIEST	EILRSTTZ	STRELITZ
EILNRSTU	INSULTER	EILOSTTT	STILETTO	EILRSTUV	RIVULETS
	LUSTRINE	EILOSTUV	OUTLIVES	EILRSTYZ	STYLIZER
EILNRSTY	TINSELRY		SOLUTIVE	EILRSUUX	LUXURIES
EILNRTUV	VIRULENT	EILOSTUW	OUTWILES	EILRSWZZ	SWIZZLER
EILNRTWY	WINTERLY	EILOTVVY	VOTIVELY	EILSSSTY	STYLISES
EILNSSTT	TINTLESS	EILPPPRY	PREPPILY	EILSSTTU	LUSTIEST
EILNSSTU	UTENSILS	EILPPRRS	RIPPLERS	EILSSTTY	STYLIEST
EILNSSTW	WESTLINS	EILPPRRT	TRIPPLER		STYLITES
EILNSSVY	SYLVINES	EILPPRRU	PURLIER	EILSSTUU	LITUUSES
EILNSTTU	LUTENIST	EILPPRSS	SLIPPERS	EILSSTVY	SYLVITES
EILNSUWY	UNWISELY	EILPPRST	PRESPLIT	EILSSTYZ	STYLIZES
EILOOPRR	POORLIER		RIPPLETS	EILSSWZZ	SWIZZLES
EILOOPST	LOOPIEST		STIPPLER	EILSTWZZ	TWIZZLES
EILOOPTZ	ZOPILOTE		TIPPLERS	EIMMMNOT	IMMOMENT
EILOORST	OESTRIOL		TRIPPLES	EIMMMORZ	MOMZERIM
	TROOLIES	EILPPRSU	PERIPLUS	EIMMNNOT	MONIMENT
EILOORTV	OVERTOIL		SUPPLIER	EIMMNNTU	MUNIMENT
EILOOSST	OSTIOLES	EILPPRSY	SLIPPERY	EIMMNORS	MISNOMER
	STOOLIES	EILPPRTU	PULPITER	EIMMOPRU	EMPORIUM
EILOOSTW	WOOLIEST	EILPPSST	STIPPLES	EIMMOPST	METOPISM
EILOOSTY	OTIOSELY	EILPPSSU	SUPPLIES	EIMMOSSV	MISMOVES

EIMMOSTT	TOTEMISM	EIMNRSTY	ENTRYISM	EIMPRSSU	PRIMUSES
EIMMPRRS	PRIMMERS		MISENTRY	EIMPRSTU	IMPUREST
EIMMPRST	PRIMMEST	EIMNSSSS	SENSISMS		IMPUTERS
EIMMPRSU	PREMIUMS	EIMNSSTU	MISTUNES		STUMPIER
EIMMPSSU	PESSIMUM	EIMNSTTU	MINUTEST	EIMPSSST	MISSTEPS
EIMMRRST	TRIMMERS	EIMNSUZZ	MUEZZINS	EIMPSSTU	SPUMIEST
EIMMRSST	MISTERMS	EIMOORST	MOORIEST		STUMPIES
EIMMRSSW	SWIMMERS		MOTORISE	EIMPSSTY	EMPTYSIS
EIMMRSTT	TRIMMEST		ROOMIEST		MISTYPES
EIMMRSTU	RUMMIEST	EIMOORTZ	MOTORIZE	EIMPSTTU	TUMPIEST
EIMMSSTU	MUMSIEST	EIMOOSST	OSTOMIES	EIMQRRSU	SQUIRMER
EIMMSTUY	YUMMIEST	EIMOPPRR	IMPROPER	EIMQSSTU	MESQUITS
EIMNNOOT	NOONTIME	EIMOPPST	MOPPIEST	EIMQSTUY	MYSTIQUE
EIMNNOPT	IMPONENT	EIMOPRRS	PRIMEROS	EIMQSTUZ	MEZQUITS
	PIMENTON		PRIMROSE	EIMRRRSU	SMURRIER
	POINTMEN		PROMISER	EIMRRSSU	SURMISER
EIMNNOST	MENTIONS	EIMOPRRT	IMPORTER	EIMRSSST	MISTRESS
EIMNNOTT	OINTMENT		REIMPORT	EIMRSSSU	MISUSERS
EIMNNOUY	EUONYMIN	EIMOPRRV	IMPROVER		SURMISES
EIMNOOPS	EMPOISON	EIMOPRSS	IMPOSERS	EIMRSSTT	METRISTS
EIMNOORS	IONOMERS		PROMISES	EIMRSSTY	SMYTRIES
	MOONRISE		SEMIPROS	EIMRSSUU	MIURUSES
EIMNOORT	MOTIONER	EIMOPRST	IMPOSTER	EIMRSTTU	SMUTTIER
	REMOTION	EIMOPRSV	IMPROVES	EIMRSTUV	VITREUMS
EIMNOORV	OMNIVORE	EIMOPRSW	IMPOWERS	EIMRSTUX	MIXTURES
EIMNOOSS	ISONOMES	EIMOPRUU	EUROPIUM	EIMSSSSU	MISSUSES
	MONOSIES	EIMOPSST	STOMPIES	EIMSSSTU	MUSSIEST
EIMNOOST	EMOTIONS	EIMOPSTY	PEYOTISM	EIMSSTTU	MUSTIEST
	MOONIEST	EIMOQSTU	MISQUOTE	EIMSTUZZ	MUZZIEST
EIMNOOSX	EXOMIONS	EIMORRSS	MORRISES	EINNNORT	NONINERT
EIMNOPPU	PEPONIUM	EIMORRST	MORTISER	EINNOOTX	NEOTOXIN
EIMNOPRS	PROMINES		STORMIER	EINNOPPT	PENPOINT
EIMNOPRT	ORPIMENT	EIMORRTT	REMITTOR	EINNOPRU	PREUNION
EIMNOPSS	MOPINESS	EIMORRTV	OVERTRIM	EINNOPRY	PYRONINE
	PEONISMS	EIMORRWW	WIREWORM	EINNOPSS	PENSIONS
EIMNOPST	EMPTIONS	EIMORSST	EROTISMS	EINNOQSU	QUINONES
	NEPOTISM		MORTISES	EINNORSS	IRONNESS
	PIMENTOS		TRISOMES	EINNORST	INTONERS
EIMNOPTT	IMPOTENT	EIMORSSV	VERISMOS		NOINTERS
EIMNOPTV	PIVOTMEN	EIMORSTT	OMITTERS		TERNIONS
EIMNORSS	MERSIONS	EIMORSTU	MISROUTE	EINNORSU	REUNIONS
EIMNORSU	INERMOUS		MOISTURE	EINNORSV	ENVIRONS
	MONSIEUR	EIMORSTV	VOMITERS	EINNORTT	TONTINER
EIMNORSW	WINSOMER	EIMORSTW	MISWROTE	EINNORTU	NEUTRINO
EIMNORTW	TIMEWORN		WORMIEST	EINNORTV	INVENTOR
EIMNORTY	ENORMITY	EIMORSTY	ISOMETRY		NOVERINT
EIMNOSST	MESTINOS	EIMORSVW	OVERSWIM	EINNORWW	WINNOWER
	MOISTENS	EIMORTXY	OXIMETRY	EINNOSSS	NOSINESS
	SENTIMOS	EIMOSSST	MOSSIEST	EINNOSST	TENSIONS
EIMNPRSS	PRIMNESS	EIMOSSTT	MOISTEST	EINNOSSU	NONISSUE
EIMNPSST	MISSPENT	EIMOSSTU	MOUSIEST		UNSONSIE
EIMNPSTU	NUMPTIES	EIMOSSTX	EXOTISMS	EINNOSSV	VENISONS
EIMNRRSU	MURRINES	EIMOSSTZ	MESTIZOS	EINNOSTT	TINSTONE
EIMNRSST	ENTRISMS	EIMOSSYZ	ISOZYMES		TONTINES
	MINSTERS	EIMOSTTT	MOTTIEST	EINNOSTU	NOUNIEST
	TRIMNESS		TOTEMIST	EINNPRSS	SPINNERS
EIMNRSSU	NEURISMS	EIMOSTTU	TIMEOUTS	EINNPRST	ENPRINTS
EIMNRSTU	MUNTRIES		TITMOUSE	EINNPRSY	SPINNERY
	TERMINUS	EIMPRRST	PRETRIMS	EINNPSST	SPINNETS
	UNMITERS	EIMPRRSU	PRIMEURS	EINNPSSU	PUNINESS
	UNMITRES	EIMPRSST	IMPRESTS	EINNPSSY	SPINNEYS

EINNPSTU	PUNNIEST	EINORSSV	VERSIONS	EINSSTTU	NUTSIEST
EINNPSXY	SIXPENNY	EINORSTT	SNOTTIER	EINSSTTW	ENTWISTS
EINNRSTU	RUNNIEST		TENORIST		TWINSETS
	STURNINE		TRITONES	EINSSTUW	UNWISEST
EINNRSTV	VINTNERS	EINORSTU	ROUTINES	EINSSTUX	UNSEXIST
EINNRTTU	NUTRIENT		SNOUTIER	EINSSTXY	SYNTEXIS
EINNSSTT	TENNISTS	EINORSTV	INVESTOR	EINSTTTU	NUTTIEST
EINNSSTU	SUNNIEST	EINORSTX	NITROXES	EINSTTTW	TWITTENS
EINNSSUW	UNSINEWS	EINORSTY	SEROTINY	EIOOPPRS	PORPOISE
EINNSSWY	SWINNEYS		TYROSINE	EIOOPPST	OPPOSITE
EINNSTUW	UNTWINES	EINORSTZ	TRIZONES	EIOOPRST	PORTOISE
EINOOPRS	POISONER	EINORSUV	SOUVENIR		ROOPIEST
	SNOOPIER	EINORTTU	RITENUTO	EIOOPRSW	SWOOPIER
	SPOONIER	EINOSSSS	SESSIONS	EIOOPSST	ISOTOPES
EINOOPSS	OPSONISE	EINOSSST	SONSIEST	EIOOPSTV	POOVIEST
	SPOONIES		STENOSIS	EIOOPTYZ	EPIZOOTY
EINOOPSZ	OPSONIZE	EINOSSTT	SNOTTIES	EIOORRSS	SORORISE
EINOORSS	EROSIONS		STONIEST	EIOORRST	ROOTSIER
EINOORST	SNOOTIER	EINOSSTW	SNOWIEST	EIOORRSZ	SORORIZE
EINOORSW	SWOONIER	EINOSTTT	TOTIENTS	EIOORSTT	ROOTIEST
EINOORSZ	OZONISER	EINOSTTW	NOWTIEST		TORTOISE
	SNOOZIER		TOWNIEST	EIOOSSST	OSTEOSIS
EINOORZZ	OZONIZER	EINOSTUU	TENUIOUS	EIOOSSTT	SOOTIEST
EINOOSST	ISOTONES	EINOSTVY	VENOSITY		TOOTSIES
EINOOSSZ	OOZINESS	EINPPRRT	PREPRINT	EIOOSTTZ	ZOOTIEST
	OZONISES	EINPPRSS	SNIPPERS	EIOOSTWZ	WOOZIEST
EINOOSTW	TWOONIES	EINPPSST	SNIPPETS	EIOPPPST	POPPIEST
EINOOSTZ	ZOONITES	EINPPSTY	SNIPPETY	EIOPPRTW	PIPEWORT
EINOOSZZ	OZONIZES	EINPRRST	PRINTERS	EIOPPSST	SOPPIEST
EINOOTXX	EXOTOXIN		REPRINTS	EIOPPSTT	TOPPIEST
EINOPPRS	POPERINS		SPRINTER	EIOPPTTY	TIPPYTOE
	PROPINES	EINPRRTU	PRURIENT	EIOPQRSU	PIROQUES
EINOPRRS	PRISONER	EINPRRTY	PRINTERY	EIOPQSTU	POSTIQUE
EINOPRSS	PORINESS	EINPRSST	SPINSTER	EIOPRRSS	PRIORESS
	PRESSION	EINPRSTU	REPUNITS	EIOPRRST	PIERROTS
	ROPINESS		UNPRIEST		SPORTIER
EINOPRST	POINTERS		UNRIPEST	EIOPRRSU	SUPERIOR
	PORNIEST	EINPRTTU	INPUTTER	EIOPRRSV	PREVISOR
	PROTEINS	EINPSTTX	SPINTEXT	EIOPRRTV	OVERTRIP
	REPOINTS	EINPSTTY	TINTYPES	EIOPRSSS	PROSSIES
	TROPINES	EINQRSTU	SQUINTER	EIOPRSST	PERIOSTS
EINOPRSU	PRUINOSE	EINQRTTU	QUITRENT		PROSIEST
EINOPRSV	OVERSPIN	EINQSSTU	INQUESTS		PROSTIES
	PROVINES	EINQSTTU	QUINTETS		REPOSITS
EINOPRTU	ERUPTION	EINQSTUU	UNIQUEST		RIPOSTES
EINOPSSW	WINESOPS		UNQUIETS		SPORTIES
EINOPSTT	NEPOTIST	EINQTTTU	QUINTETT		TRIPOSES
EINOPSTU	POUTINES	EINRRSSU	INSURERS	EIOPRSTT	PORTIEST
EINOPSWX	SWINEPOX	EINRSSST	INSTRESS		RISPETTO
EINOQSTU	QUESTION	EINRSSSU	SUNRISES		SPOTTIER
EINOQTTU	QUOTIENT	EINRSSTT	ENTRISTS	EIOPRSTU	ROUPIEST
EINORRSS	ROSINERS		STINTERS		SPOUTIER
EINORRST	INTRORSE	EINRSSXY	SYRINXES	EIOPRSTV	OVERTIPS
	SNORTIER	EINRSTTU	RUNTIEST		PIVOTERS
EINORRTV	INVERTOR	EINRSTTW	TWINTERS		SORPTIVE
EINORRTW	INTERROW	EINRSTTY	ENTRYIST		SPORTIVE
EINORSSS	ROSINESS	EINRSTUV	UNRIVETS	EIOPRSUV	PERVIOUS
EINORSST	OESTRINS		VENTURIS		PREVIOUS
	TERSIONS	EINRSTUW	UNWRITES		VIPEROUS
EINORSSU	NEUROSIS	EINRTUUV	UNVIRTUE	EIOPRTTT	TRIPTOTE
	RESINOUS	EINSSSST	SENSISTS	EIOPRTTY	PETITORY

EIOPRTUZ	OUTPRIZE		UPRISERS	EJORSTUV	OVERJUST
EIOPSSST	SEPIOSTS	EIPRRSTZ	SPRITZER	EJOSSTTU	OUTJESTS
EIOPSSSU	POUSSIES	EIPRRSUV	UPRIVERS	EKKLNPRU	KERPLUNK
EIOPSSTT	SPOTTIES	EIPRRSUY	SYRUPIER	EKKLOOSY	OLYKOEKS
EIOPSSTU	SOUPIEST	EIPRRSUZ	SURPRIZE	EKKLOOSZ	KOLKOZES
EIOPSSTX	EXPOSITS	EIPRSSST	PERSISTS	EKKLRSSU	SKULKERS
EIOPSSTY	ISOTYPES	EIPRSSSU	SUSPIRES	EKKMORSY	KROMESKY
EIOPSTTT	POTTIEST	EIPRSSTT	SPITTERS	EKLLMSSU	SKELLUMS
EIOPSTTU	POUTIEST		TIPSTERS	EKLLNORS	KNOLLERS
EIOPSTTY	PEYOTIST	EIPRSSTU	PURSIEST	EKLLOSSY	KYLLOSES
EIOPSTUW	WIPEOUTS	EIPRSSTZ	SPRITZES		YOLKLESS
EIOQRSTU	QUOITERS	EIPRSTTU	PURTIEST	EKLLRSSU	KRULLERS
EIOQSTUX	QUIXOTES		PUTTIERS	EKLNOOOR	ONLOOKER
EIORRRST	ERRORIST	EIPRSUVW	PURVIEWS	EKLNOPRS	PLONKERS
	TERROIRS	EIPRSVVY	SPIVVERY	EKLNORSS	SNORKELS
EIORRRSW	WORRIERS	EIPSSSTU	PUSSIEST	EKLNOSST	KNOTLESS
EIORRRTU	ROTURIER	EIPSSTXY	PTYXISES	EKLNPRSU	PLUNKERS
EIORRSST	RESISTOR	EIQRRSTU	SQUIRTER	EKLNPSSU	SPELUNKS
	ROISTERS	EIQRSSSU	SQUIRESS	EKLOOORV	LOOKOVER
	SORRIEST	EIQRSSTU	QUERISTS		OVERLOOK
EIORRSSV	REVISORS	EIQRSTTU	QUITTERS	EKLOOPSW	SLOWPOKE
EIORRSTT	RORTIEST	EIQRSTUU	SEQUITUR	EKLORSSW	WORKLESS
EIORRSTU	STOURIER	EIQRSUZZ	QUIZZERS	EKLOSSTV	STOKVELS
EIORRSTV	OVERSTIR	EIQRUYZZ	QUIZZERY	EKLSSSTU	TUSKLESS
	SERVITOR	EIQSSUZZ	SQUIZZES	EKLSSTTU	SKUTTLES
EIORRSUV	OUVRIERS	EIRRRSST	STIRRERS	EKMMORSU	MURKSOME
	REOVIRUS	EIRRRSSTV	STRIVERS	EKMMRSSU	SKUMMERS
EIORRSVV	REVIVORS	EIRRRSTTU	TRUSTIER	EKMNOSSU	MUSKONES
EIORRSVY	REVISORY	EIRRRSUVV	SURVIVER	EKMNOSUX	MUSKOXEN
EIORRTTU	TROUTIER	EIRSSSTU	SUITRESS	EKMOOPRR	MOREPORK
EIORSSTT	STOITERS		TSURISES	EKMOOPST	SMOKEPOT
EIORSSTY	SEROSITY	EIRSSTTU	RUSTIEST	EKMOORSW	WORKSOME
EIORSTTU	TOUSTIER		TRUSTIES	EKMOOSSS	KOSMOSES
	TUTORISE	EIRSSTTW	RETWISTS	EKMOOSTU	OUTSMOKE
EIORSTTV	VIRETOTS		TWISTERS	EKMOSSUY	KOUMYSES
EIORSTTW	SWOTTIER	EIRSSTUV	REVUISTS	EKMPRRSU	KRUMPERS
EIORSTUV	VIRTUOSE		STUIVERS	EKMRSTUY	MUSKETRY
	VITREOUS	EIRSSUVV	SURVIVES	EKNNOORT	KENOTRON
	VOITURES	EIRSSUVW	SURVIEWS	EKNNOPSU	UNSPOKEN
EIORTTUW	OUTWRITE	EIRSTTTU	RUTTIEST	EKNOOPRW	OPENWORK
EIORTTUZ	TUTORIZE	EIRSTTTW	TWITTERS	EKNOORSS	SNOOKERS
EIOSSSTT	TOSSIEST	EIRSTTUX	TUTRIXES	EKNOORST	STROOKEN
EIOSSTTT	STOTTIES	EIRTTTWY	TWITTERY	EKNOPPSU	UPSPOKEN
EIOSSTTU	TOUSIEST	EIRTTUWZ	WURTZITE	EKNOPSSY	PYKNOSES
EIOSSTTW	TOWSIEST	EISSSSTU	TUSSISES	EKNORSST	STONKERS
EIOSSTUZ	OUTSIZES	EISSSTUW	WUSSIEST	EKNORSTT	KNOTTERS
EIOSTTTT	TOTTIEST	EISSTTUW	WETSUITS	EKNORSTW	NETWORKS
EIOSTTTU	TOUTIEST	EISTTTUV	VUTTIEST	EKNORSUY	YOUNKERS
EIOSTTUZ	TOUZIEST	EJLLORSY	JOLLYERS	EKNRSTUY	TURNKEYS
EIOSTTWZ	TOWZIEST	EJLOPSTU	PULSOJET	EKOOOPRT	POKEROOT
EIPPQRSU	QUIPPERS	EJLORSST	JOSTLERS	EKOOORTV	OVERTOOK
EIPPRRST	STRIPPER	EJLRSSUY	JURYLESS	EKOOPRRV	PROVOKER
	TRIPPERS	EJMOPRUV	OVERJUMP	EKOOPRRW	ROPEWORK
EIPPRRSY	PERSPIRY	EJNORRSU	REJOURNS	EKOOPRSV	PROVOKES
EIPPRRTY	TRIPPERY	EJNORSUY	JOURNEYS	EKOOPRSY	SPOOKERY
EIPPRSTT	TRIPPETS	EJNRSTUU	UNJUSTER	EKOOPSTU	OUTSPOKE
EIPQRSTU	QUIPSTER	EJNSSSTU	JUSTNESS	EKOORRVW	OVERWORK
EIPRRRSU	SPURRIER	EJOORSVY	OVERJOYS	EKOORRVW	STOOKERS
EIPRRSST	STRIPERS	EJOPPRST	PROPJETS	EKOORSST	STROOKES
EIPRRSSU	SPURRIES	EJOPRSTT	JETPORTS	EKOORSTW	KOTOWERS
	SURPRISE	EJORSSTU	JOUSTERS	EKOORSUU	EUROKOUS

EKOORTWW	KOWTOWER	ELMMNOTY	MOMENTLY	ELNOPRVY	PROVENLY
EKOPRRSW	PREWORKS	ELMMOPSU	PUMMELOS	ELNOPSTU	PLEUSTON
EKOPRSTU	UPSTROKE	ELMMORST	TROMMELS	ELNOPTTY	POTENTLY
EKOPRSUY	KOUPREYS	ELMMOSUX	LUMMOXES	ELNOPTYY	POLYTENY
EKORRSST	STROKERS	ELMMPSTU	PLUMMEST	ELNORSSU	NOURSLES
EKORRUVY	KURVEYOR		PLUMMETS	ELNORSTU	TURNSOLE
EKORSSTU	KURTOSES	ELMMRSSU	SLUMMERS	ELNORSVY	SLOVENRY
EKORSTWY	SKYWROTE	ELMMRSTU	STRUMMEL	ELNORTTY	ROTTENLY
EKPPSSUU	SEPPUKUS		TUMMLERS	ELNOSSST	LOSTNESS
ELLLMOWY	MELLOWLY	ELMMRSUY	SUMMERLY	ELNOSSSW	SLOWNESS
ELLLNSUY	SULLENLY	ELMMSSTU	STUMMELS		SNOWLESS
ELLLORRS	LORRELLS	ELMNNOSU	UNSOLEMN	ELNOSSTV	SOLVENTS
ELLLOWYY	YELLOWLY	ELMNNOTU	UNMOLTEN	ELNOSSTW	TOWNLESS
ELLMNOOS	MOELLONS	ELMNOOOP	MONOPOLE		WONTLESS
ELLMNOSY	SOLEMNLY	ELMNOOSS	MOONLESS	ELNOSTTW	TOWNLETS
ELLMNOTY	MOLTENLY	ELMNOOST	MOONLETS	ELNOSTUZ	ZONULETS
ELLMNOUW	UNMELLOW	ELMNOPSU	PULMONES	ELNOSUUV	VENULOUS
ELLMNPUY	LUMPENLY	ELMNORSS	NORMLESS	ELNOSUVY	VENOUSLY
ELLMOORS	MORELLOS	ELMNOSTW	SNOWMELT	ELNPPSUU	UNSUPPLE
ELLMORRS	MORRELLS	ELMNPPSU	PLUMPENS	ELNPRTUU	PURULENT
ELLMOSTU	OUTSMELL	ELMNPSUU	UNPLUMES	ELNPRUUY	UNPURELY
ELLMPSUU	PLUMULES	ELMNUUZZ	UNMUZZLE	ELNPUUZZ	UNPUZZLE
ELLNNOST	TONNELLS	ELMOOPPS	POMPELOS	ELNRSUUY	UNSURELY
ELLNNSSU	NULLNESS	ELMOOPSY	POLYSOME	ELNRSUZZ	NUZZLERS
ELLNOORV	LOVELORN	ELMOORST	TREMOLOS	ELNSSUZZ	SNUZZLES
ELLNOOSW	WOOLLENS	ELMOORSY	MOROSELY	ELOOPPRY	POLYPORE
ELLNOPRU	PRUNELLO	ELMOOSSY	LYSOSOME	ELOOPRSS	RESPOOLS
ELLNOSST	STOLLENS	ELMOPRSY	POLYMERS		SPOOLERS
ELLNOSSU	NOUSELLS	ELMOPRTY	METOPRYL	ELOOPRSU	SUPERLOO
ELLNOSVY	SLOVENLY	ELMOPRYY	POLYMERY	ELOOPRTV	OVERPLOT
ELLNOSXY	XYLENOLS	ELMOPSYY	POLYSEMY	ELOOPRUW	OWERLOUP
ELLNOUVY	UNLOVELY	ELMORSSU	EMULSORS	ELOOPSSS	SESSPOOL
ELLNPSSU	UNSPELLS	ELMORSTT	MOTTLERS	ELOORSST	ROOTLESS
ELLOORRV	ROLLOVER	ELMORSTU	MOULTERS	ELOORSTT	ROOTLETS
ELLOOSST	TOOLLESS	ELMORUUV	VERMOULU		TOOTLERS
ELLOOSSW	WOOSELLS	ELMOSTTU	OUTSMELT	ELOORSTU	TORULOSE
ELLOOSTU	TOLUOLES	ELMOSTUU	TUMULOSE	ELOORSUV	OVERSOUL
ELLOPRRS	PROLLERS	ELMOSYYZ	LYSOZYME	ELOORSVW	OVERSLOW
ELLOPRST	POLLSTER	ELMPPRSU	PLUMPERS	ELOOSSST	SOOTLESS
ELLOPRTU	POLLUTER	ELMPPSSU	PUMPLESS	ELOOSSTT	TOOLSETS
ELLOPRUV	PULLOVER	ELMPPSTU	PLUMPEST	ELOOSSTU	OUTSOLES
ELLOPSST	PLOTLESS	ELMPRSSU	RUMPLESS	ELOOSSWY	WOOLSEYS
ELLOPSTU	OUTSPELL	ELMRRTUU	MULTURER	ELOOSTUV	OUTLOVES
	POLLUTES	ELMRSTUU	MULTURES	ELOOSVVX	VOLVOXES
ELLORRST	STROLLER	ELMRSUZZ	MUZZLERS	ELOPPRRY	PROPERLY
	TROLLERS	ELNNNOOV	NONNOVEL	ELOPPRST	POPSTREL
ELLORSTY	TROLLEYS	ELNNOOSU	UNLOOSEN	ELOPPSST	STOPPLES
ELLOSSSS	LOSSLESS	ELNNOPSU	NONUPLES	ELOPPTYY	POLYTYPE
ELLOSSSU	SOULLESS	ELNNOPTU	NONUPLET	ELOPRRSU	PROULERS
ELLOSSTU	OUTSELLS	ELNNORSS	LORNNESS	ELOPRRSW	PROWLERS
	SELLOUTS	ELNNOSSU	NOUNLESS	ELOPRRSY	PYRROLES
ELLOSSYY	LYOLYSES	ELNNOSTY	NONSTYLE	ELOPRRTY	PORTERLY
ELLOSTTU	OUTTELLS	ELNNRSTU	TRUNNELS	ELOPRSSS	PLESSORS
ELLOSTUW	OUTSWELL	ELNOOPPR	PROPENOL	ELOPRSST	PORTLESS
	OUTWELLS	ELNOOPST	PELOTONS	ELOPRSSU	SPORULES
ELLOSTUY	OUTYELLS	ELNOOSST	SOLONETS	ELOPRSTT	PLOTTERS
ELLPPSSU	PULPLESS	ELNOOSSU	NEOSOULS	ELOPRSTU	PLOUTERS
ELLPPSUY	SUPPLELY		UNLOOSES		POULTERS
ELLPSSUW	UPSWELLS	ELNOOSSZ	SNOOZLES	ELOPRSTW	PLOWTERS
ELLSSSTU	LUSTLESS	ELNOOSTZ	SOLONETZ	ELOPRSTY	PROSTYLE
ELMMNOTU	LOMENTUM	ELNOPPRY	PROPENYL		PROTYLES

ELOPRSUV	OVERPLUS	EMMRRRUU	MURMURER	EMOPRSST	STOMPERS
ELOPRSYY	PYROLYSE		REMURMUR	EMOPRSSU	SPERMOUS
ELOPRXYY	PYROXYLE	EMMRRSTU	STRUMMER		SUPREMOS
ELOPRYYZ	PYROLYZE	EMMRSTYY	SYMMETRY	EMORRRUU	RUMOURER
ELOPSSST	SPOTLESS	EMNNNOOU	NOUMENON	EMORRSST	STORMERS
	STOPLESS	EMNNNOOY	NONMONEY	EMORRSSU	MORSURES
ELOPSSSU	SOUPLESS	EMNNOOOT	MONOTONE	EMORRSSU	SMOUSERS
ELOPSSTY	STYLOPES	EMNNOORT	NONMETRO	EMORSSTU	OESTRUMS
ELOPSSUU	OPULUSES	EMNNOPTY	NONEMPTY		STRUMOSE
ELOPSTTU	OUTSLEPT	EMNNOSTW	TOWNSMEN	EMORSUVW	OVERSWUM
	OUTSPELT	EMNNOSYY	SYNONYME	EMOSSSTT	MOSTESTS
ELOPSTUY	OUTYELPS	EMNNPSTU	PUNTSMEN	EMOSSTTW	WESTMOST
ELORSSTT	SETTLORS	EMNNSTTU	STUNTMEN	EMOSSTVZ	ZEMSTVOS
	SLOTTERS	EMNOOPST	METOPONS	EMOSTTTU	TETOTUMS
ELORSTUY	ELYTROUS	EMNOOPTY	MONOTYPE	EMPRRTUY	TRUMPERY
	SOUTERLY	EMNOORST	MESOTRON	EMPRSSTU	RESTUMPS
	UROSTYLE		MONTEROS		STUMPERS
ELORTTTU	TROUTLET		MONTEROS		SUMPTERS
ELOSSSTY	SYSTOLES	EMNOORSU	ENORMOUS		SUMPTERS
ELOSSTUU	SETULOUS		NEMOROUS	EMPRSSUU	RUMPUSES
ELOSSWZZ	SWOZZLES	EMNOORSW	NEWSROOM	EMPRSTTU	STRUMPET
ELPPRSTU	PURPLEST	EMNOORTY	NOOMETRY		TRUMPETS
ELPPRSUY	RESUPPLY	EMNOOSST	MOONSETS	EMRRSSTU	STURMERS
ELPPSSTU	SUPPLEST		MOOTNESS	ENNNOORW	NONOWNER
ELPRRSSU	SLURPERS	EMNOOSUV	VENOMOUS	ENNNOOVW	NONWOVEN
ELPRRSSU	SPURLESS	EMNOOTTY	TENOTOMY	ENNNORTY	NONENTRY
ELPRSSTU	SPURTLES	EMNOOTUV	OUTVENOM	ENNOOORT	TENOROON
ELPRSTTU	SPLUTTER	EMNOOTWY	TOYWOMEN	ENNOOOTZ	ENTOZOON
ELPRSTUU	PULTURES	EMNOPSSU	SPUMONES	ENNOOPPT	OPPONENT
ELPRSUZZ	PUZZLERS	EMNORRSU	MOURNERS	ENNOORST	NORTENOS
ELPSSSUY	PUSSLEYS	EMNORRTY	RETRONYM	ENNOORTV	NONVOTER
ELPSSTUU	PUSTULES	EMNORSST	MONSTERS	ENNOOSTT	NONETTOS
ELPSTUXY	SEXTUPLY	EMNORSTT	SORTMENT	ENNOPRSU	UNPERSON
ELRRSSTU	RUSTLERS		TORMENTS	ENNOPRUV	UNPROVEN
ELRRSTTU	TURTLERS	EMNORSTU	MONTURES	ENNOPTWY	TWOPENNY
ELRSSSTU	RUSTLESS		MOUNTERS	ENNORSST	STERNSON
ELRSTTUY	SLUTTERY		REMOUNTS	ENNORSSU	NONUSERS
ELRSTUUV	VULTURES	EMNORSUU	NUMEROUS	ENNORSSW	WORNNESS
ELSSSTUY	STYLUSES	EMNOSSST	STEMSONS	ENNORSTU	NEUTRONS
ELSSSTYY	SYSTYLES	EMNOSUUY	EUONYMUS	ENNORTTU	UNROTTEN
EMMNNOTU	MOMENTUM	EMNOSUVY	EVONYMUS	ENNOSSTU	NEUSTONS
EMMNNOTU	MONUMENT	EMNRSSTU	MUNSTERS		SUNSTONE
EMMNOOOS	MONOSOME		STERNUMS	ENNPPTUY	TUPPENNY
EMMNOORS	MONOMERS	EMOOPRRT	PROMOTER	ENNRSSTU	STUNNERS
EMMNOORT	MOTORMEN	EMOOPRSS	OOSPERMS	ENOOORSV	OVERSOON
EMMNOOST	MOMENTOS	EMOOPRST	PROMOTES	ENOOOSSZ	ZOONOSES
EMMNOOSY	MONOSEMY	EMOOPRSY	POMEROYS	ENOOPPRS	PROPONES
EMMNORSU	RESUMMON		PYROSOME	ENOOPPST	POSTPONE
	SUMMONER	EMOOPRSZ	ZOOSPERM	ENOOPRSS	POORNESS
EMMNORSY	MERONYMS	EMOOPSSU	ESPUMOSO		SNOOPERS
EMMNORYY	MERONYMY	EMOORRST	RESTROOM	ENOOPSSY	SPOONEYS
EMMNOSTU	OMENTUMS	EMOORRST	MOROSEST	ENOOPSTT	POTSTONE
EMMNOSTY	METONYMS	EMOORSSU	UROSOMES		TOPSTONE
EMMNOTTU	TOMENTUM	EMOORTYZ	ZOOMETRY	ENOORRVW	OVERWORN
EMMNOTYY	METONYMY	EMOOSSTW	TWOSOMES	ENOORSSW	SWOONERS
EMMOOORS	ROOMSOME	EMOOSSTY	MYOSOTES	ENOORSSZ	SNOOZERS
EMMOOSTY	MYOTOMES	EMOOSSXY	OXYSOMES	ENOORSTT	NETROOTS
EMMOPRRS	PROMMERS	EMOOSTUV	OUTMOVES	ENOORSTU	OUTSNORE
EMMOPRSU	SUPERMOM	EMOPPRRT	PROMPTER	ENOORSVW	OVERSOWN
EMMOPTTY	POMMETTY	EMOPPRUV	OVERPUMP	ENOOSSTT	TESTOONS
EMMPRSUU	SUPREMUM	EMOPPSTU	UPTEMPOS	ENOOSTXY	OXYTONES
		EMOPRRSU	PROSUMER	ENOPPRRU	UNPROPER

Key	Word(s)
ENOPRRSU	PRONEURS
ENOPRSST	POSTERNS
ENOPRSTT	PORTENTS
ENOPRTUW	UPTOWNER
ENOPSSST	STEPSONS
ENOPSSSY	SYNOPSES
ENOPSTTU	OUTSPENT
ENOQSTUU	UNQUOTES
ENORRSST	SNORTERS
ENORRSTT	TORRENTS
ENORRSUV	OVERRUNS
	RUNOVERS
ENORRTUU	TOURNURE
ENORRTUV	OVERTURN
	TURNOVER
ENORSSSU	SOURNESS
ENORSSTT	SNOTTERS
	STENTORS
ENORSSTU	TONSURES
ENORSTTU	STENTOUR
ENORSTTY	SNOTTERY
ENORSTUV	VENTROUS
ENORSTUY	TOURNEYS
ENOSSSTT	STETSONS
ENOSSSUU	SENSUOUS
ENOSSTTU	STOUTENS
ENPRRSSU	PRESSRUN
	SPURNERS
ENPRSSSY	SPRYNESS
ENPRSSTU	PUNSTERS
ENPRSSUU	PRUNUSES
	UNPURSES
ENPRTTUY	UNPRETTY
ENRRRTUU	NURTURER
ENRRSTUU	NURTURES
ENRSSSTU	UNSTRESS
ENRSSTTU	ENTRUSTS
ENRSSTUU	UNSUREST
ENRSTTUU	UNTRUEST
EOOOPRSS	OOSPORES
	SOPOROSE
EOOOPRSZ	ZOOSPORE
EOOOPRTZ	ZOOTROPE
EOOORRST	ROSEROOT
EOOPPRRS	PROPOSER
EOOPPRSS	OPPOSERS
	PROPOSES
EOOPPRSU	EUROPOPS
EOOPPRSV	POPOVERS
EOOPPSST	POSTPOSE
EOOPPTTY	TOPOTYPE
EOOPRRSS	SPOORERS
EOOPRRST	PROTORES
	TROOPERS
EOOPRRTU	OUTROPER
	UPROOTER
EOOPRSST	STOOPERS
EOOPRSSW	SWOOPERS
EOOPRSTU	OUTROPES
	PORTEOUS
EOOPRSTV	OVERPOST
	OVERTOPS
	STOPOVER
EOOPRSTW	TOWROPES
EOOPRTUW	OUTPOWER
EOOPSTTV	STOVETOP
EOOPSTYZ	ZOOTYPES
EOOQTTUU	OUTQUOTE
EOORRRSW	SORROWER
EOORRSST	ROOSTERS
EOORRSVW	ROWOVERS
EOORSSTU	OESTROUS
EOORSSTZ	STOOZERS
EOORSSVW	OVERSOWS
EOORSTUW	OUTSWORE
EOORTTUV	OUTVOTER
EOORTTUW	OUTTOWER
	OUTWROTE
EOOSTTUV	OUTVOTES
EOPPRRSS	PROSPERS
EOPPRRST	STROPPER
EOPPRRSU	SUPERPRO
EOPPRRTY	PROPERTY
EOPPRSST	POPSTERS
	STOPPERS
EOPPRSSU	PURPOSES
	SUPPOSER
EOPPRSSW	SWOPPERS
EOPPSSSU	SUPPOSES
EOPRRSSS	PRESSORS
EOPRRSST	PORTRESS
	PRESORTS
	SPORTERS
EOPRRSTU	POSTURER
	RESPROUT
	TROUPERS
EOPRRUVY	PURVEYOR
EOPRSSTT	PROTESTS
	SPOTTERS
EOPRSSTU	OUTPRESS
	POSTURES
	SEPTUORS
	SPOUTERS
EOPRSSUU	POURSUES
	UPROUSES
EOPRSSUV	OVERSUPS
EOPRSSUW	POURSEWS
EOPSSSTU	UPTOSSES
EOPSSTTT	POSTTEST
EOPSSTTU	OUTSTEPS
EOPSSTTW	STEWPOTS
EOPSTTUW	OUTSWEPT
EOQRRSTU	TORQUERS
EOQRSSTU	QUESTORS
EORRRTTU	TORTURER
EORRSSST	STRESSOR
	TROSSERS
EORRSSTT	STERTORS
EORRSSTU	ROUSTERS
	TRESSOUR
	TROUSERS
EORRSSTW	STROWERS
	TROWSERS
EORRSSTY	ROYSTERS
	STROYERS
EORRSTTT	TROTTERS
EORRSTTU	TORTURES
	TROUTERS
EORRSUVY	SURVEYOR
EORRTUUV	TROUVEUR
EORSSSTU	TUSSORES
EORSSTTT	STOTTERS
	STRETTOS
EORSSTTU	OUTSERTS
	TUTORESS
EORSSTTW	SWOTTERS
EORSSTUX	SEXTUORS
EORSTTUW	OUTWREST
EORSTTUY	TUTOYERS
EORSTUUV	VERTUOUS
EOSSTTTU	STOUTEST
EPPPRTUY	PUPPETRY
EPPRRSUU	PURPURES
EPPRSSSU	SUPPRESS
EPPRSSUY	SUPERSPY
EPRRRSSU	SPURRERS
EPRRSSTU	SPURTERS
EPRRSSUU	PURSUERS
	USURPERS
EPRRSSUY	SPURREYS
EPRRSTUU	RUPTURES
EPRSSTTU	SPUTTERS
EPRSSTUY	YUPSTERS
EPRSTTUY	SPUTTERY
EQRRTUUU	TRUQUEUR
ERRSSSTU	TRUSSERS
ERRSSTTU	TRUSTERS
ERRSSTTY	TRYSTERS
ERRSTTTU	STRUTTER
ERSSTTTU	STUTTERS
FFFGILNU	FLUFFING
FFFILLUY	FLUFFILY
FFFILOST	LIFTOFFS
FFFMOOTU	FOOTMUFF
FFGGIILN	GLIFFING
FFGGINRU	GRUFFING
FFGHIINW	WHIFFING
FFGHINOU	HOUFFING
FFGHINOW	HOWFFING
FFGHINSU	HUFFINGS
FFGHIORS	FROGFISH
FFGHIRSU	GRUFFISH
FFGIIKNS	SKIFFING
FFGIILNP	PIFFLING
FFGIILNR	RIFFLING
FFGIILNS	SIFFLING
FFGIINNS	SNIFFING
FFGIINPS	SPIFFING
FFGIINRS	GRIFFINS
FFGIINST	STIFFING
	TIFFINGS
FFGIKNOS	SKOFFING
FFGILMNU	MUFFLING

FFGILNPU	PLUFFING	FGGIILNN	FLINGING	FGIINSZZ	FIZZINGS
FFGILNRU	RUFFLING	FGGIINNR	FRINGING	FGIIRSTU	FIGURIST
FFGILNSU	SLUFFING	FGGIINRT	GRIFTING	FGIKLNNU	FLUNKING
FFGILRUY	GRUFFILY	FGGIINRU	FIGURING	FGILLNOW	WOLFLING
FFGINNSU	SNUFFING	FGGIISZZ	FIZZGIGS	FGILLNOY	FOLLYING
FFGINOPU	POUFFING	FGGILNOR	FROGLING	FGILMNPU	FLUMPING
FFGINORS	GRIFFONS	FGGILNOS	GOLFINGS	FGILMNUY	FUMINGLY
FFGINOSW	SOWFFING	FGGINOOR	FORGOING	FGILNNTU	GUNFLINT
	SWOFFING	FGGINORS	FORGINGS	FGILNOOR	FLOORING
FFGINPSU	PUFFINGS	FGHIIKNS	KINGFISH	FGILNOOS	FOOLINGS
FFGINSTU	STUFFING	FGHIILNT	INFLIGHT	FGILNOOT	FOOTLING
FFGIORTU	FOGFRUIT	FGHIINSS	FISHINGS	FGILNOOZ	FOOZLING
FFHIINSS	SNIFFISH	FGHIINST	INFIGHTS	FGILNOPP	FLOPPING
FFHIISST	STIFFISH		SHIFTING	FGILNOPS	FOPLINGS
FFHIISTY	FIFTYISH	FGHILLTU	LIGHTFUL	FGILNORS	ROLFINGS
FFHIKNSU	HUFFKINS	FGHILMTU	MIGHTFUL	FGILNORU	FLOURING
FFHILOOS	FOOLFISH	FGHILNSU	FLUSHING	FGILNOSS	FLOSSING
FFHILOSW	WOLFFISH		LUNGFISH	FGILNOST	SOFTLING
FFHILOSY	OFFISHLY	FGHILRTU	RIGHTFUL	FGILNOSU	FLOUSING
FFHIOPSS	SPOFFISH	FGHINOOW	WHOOFING		FOULINGS
FFHIRSSU	SURFFISH	FGHINORT	FROTHING	FGILNOSW	FOWLINGS
FFHOOOST	OFFSHOOT	FGHINOTU	INFOUGHT		WOLFINGS
FFHOOSSW	SHOWOFFS	FGHINRSU	FRUSHING	FGILNOTU	FLOUTING
FFHOSSTU	SHUTOFFS	FGHIOPST	GIFTSHOP		OUTFLING
FFIILMOR	FILIFORM	FGHIOTTU	OUTFIGHT	FGILNPRU	PURFLING
FFIILNSY	SNIFFILY	FGHLORUU	FURLOUGH	FGILNPSU	UPFLINGS
FFIILNTY	FLINTIFY	FGHNOORS	FOGHORNS	FGILNRRU	FLURRING
FFIILPSY	SPIFFILY	FGHNOTUU	UNFOUGHT	FGILNSTU	FLUTINGS
FFIINOOS	SOFFIONI	FGIIIKNN	FINIKING	FGILNSTY	FLYTINGS
FFIKLORT	FORKLIFT	FGIIINNX	INFIXING	FGILNUZZ	FUZZLING
FFIKLRSU	FRISKFUL	FGIIKLNS	FLISKING	FGIMNORS	FORMINGS
FFILLLSU	FULFILLS	FGIIKNNS	KNIFINGS	FGIMNPRU	FRUMPING
FFILLOPP	FLIPFLOP	FGIIKNRS	FRISKING	FGIMNRSU	SMURFING
FFILLTUY	FITFULLY	FGIILLNR	FRILLING	FGIMORRU	GRUIFORM
FFILNSUY	SNUFFILY	FGIILLNS	FILLINGS	FGIMOSSY	FOGYISMS
FFILRTUU	FRUITFUL	FGIILMNP	FLIMPING	FGINNORT	FRONTING
FFILSSTU	FISTFULS	FGIILNNT	FLINTING	FGINNORW	FROWNING
FFILSTUY	STUFFILY	FGIILNOO	FOLIOING	FGINOOPR	PROOFING
FFIMORSU	FUSIFORM	FGIILNOS	FOILINGS	FGINOOPS	SPOOFING
FFINOOST	FINFOOTS	FGIILNPP	FLIPPING	FGINOORS	ROOFINGS
FFINOPRT	OFFPRINT	FGIILNRS	RIFLINGS	FGINOOST	FOOTINGS
FFINOPSS	SPINOFFS	FGIILNRT	FLIRTING	FGINORST	FROSTING
FFINOPST	PONTIFFS		TRIFLING	FGINORTU	FOUTRING
FFJMOPSU	JUMPOFFS	FGIILNSS	FISSLING	FGINRRSU	FURRINGS
FFKLORSU	FORKFULS	FGIILNST	STIFLING	FGINRSSU	SURFINGS
	FORKSFUL	FGIILNTT	FLITTING	FGINRSTU	TURFINGS
FFLLOOSU	LOOFFULS	FGIILNZZ	FIZZLING	FGINSTTU	TUFTINGS
FFLMNOOU	MOUFFLON	FGIINNST	SNIFTING	FGIORSTW	FIGWORTS
FFLNOTUU	FOUNTFUL	FGIINNSU	INFUSING	FGISSTUU	FUGUISTS
FFLORRUU	FURFUROL	FGIINNUX	UNFIXING	FGKLNOOS	FOLKSONG
FFNORSTU	TURNOFFS	FGIINNUY	UNIFYING	FGLLMOOU	GLOOMFUL
FFNSTUUY	UNSTUFFY	FGIINOQU	QUOIFING	FGLLNSUU	LUNGFULS
FFOOPSST	STOPOFFS	FGIINOST	FOISTING	FGLNORSU	FURLONGS
FFOORRUU	FROUFROU	FGIINRRS	FIRRINGS	FGLNORUW	WRONGFUL
FGGGIINR	FRIGGING	FGIINRST	FRISTING	FGLOOOST	FOOTSLOG
FGGGILNO	FLOGGING	FGIINRTT	FRITTING	FGLORSUU	FULGOURS
FGGGINOR	FROGGING	FGIINRTU	FRUITING	FGLSSTUU	GUTSFULS
FGGGINRU	FRUGGING	FGIINRZZ	FRIZZING	FGNOORSU	FOURGONS
FGGHIINT	FIGHTING	FGIINSST	SIFTINGS	FGNOORTU	UNFORGOT
FGGHIISS	FISHGIGS	FGIINSTT	FITTINGS	FHHIKOOS	FISHHOOK
FGGHINTU	GUNFIGHT	FGIINSTW	SWIFTING	FHHOORST	SHOFROTH

FHIIKLLS	FISHKILL	FIILNOST	TINFOILS	FIMRSTUU	FUTURISM
FHIIKLMS	MILKFISH	FIILRTUY	FRUITILY	FINOOPSY	OPSONIFY
FHIIKNSS	FISHSKIN	FIILRYZZ	FRIZZILY	FINOPRST	FROSTNIP
FHIIILLTY	FILTHILY	FIILTTUY	FUTILITY	FINOPSSS	SOUPFINS
FHIILNOS	LIONFISH	FIIMMNSU	INFIMUMS	FINORSSS	FRISSONS
FHIILRST	FLIRTISH	FIIMOPRR	PIRIFORM	FINORSUY	INFUSORY
FHIILSTY	SHIFTILY	FIIMOPRS	PISIFORM	FIOORSSU	FURIOSOS
FHIKLLLO	HILLFOLK	FIIMOSTY	MOISTIFY	FIORTTUY	FORTUITY
FHIKMNOS	MONKFISH	FIINNOSU	INFUSION	FIOSTTTU	TOFUTTIS
FHIKNORT	FORTHINK	FIINORTU	FRUITION	FIRSTTUU	FUTURIST
FHILLOOT	FOOTHILL	FIINOSSS	FISSIONS	FIRTTUUY	FUTURITY
FHILLORT	HILLFORT	FIINTUXY	UNFIXITY	FJLLOUYY	JOYFULLY
FHILMPSU	LUMPFISH	FIIOPSST	POSITIFS	FJLNOUUY	UNJOYFUL
FHILMRTU	MIRTHFUL	FIIQUYZZ	QUIZZIFY	FKKLOORW	WORKFOLK
FHILOPST	SHOPLIFT	FIKKLNOS	KINFOLKS	FKKOORTW	KOFTWORK
FHILORSU	FLOURISH		KINSFOLK	FKLMOOOT	FOLKMOOT
FHILORTY	FROTHILY	FIKLLLSU	SKILLFUL	FKLMOOST	FOLKMOTS
FHILPSSU	SHIPFULS	FIKLLOSY	FOLKSILY	FKLNOOTW	TOWNFOLK
FHIMNOOS	MOONFISH	FIKLNOSW	WOLFKINS	FKLNRTUU	TRUNKFUL
FHIMORSW	FISHWORM		WOLFSKIN	FKLOORWW	WORKFLOW
FHIMPRSU	FRUMPISH	FIKLNSSU	SKINFULS	FKMOORRW	FORMWORK
FHINOSSU	FUSHIONS	FIKLSSTU	KISTFULS	FKNORSUW	FORSWUNK
FHINRTTU	UNTHRIFT		LUTFISKS	FKOOORTW	FOOTWORK
FHINSSTU	UNSHIFTS	FIKNORSW	FORSWINK	FKRSSSUY	SKYSURFS
FHIOOPTT	PHOTOFIT	FIKNOSSX	FOXSKINS	FLLNOSUY	SULFONYL
FHIOPSSX	FOXSHIPS	FIKRSSTU	TURFSKIS	FLLOOPUW	FOLLOWUP
FHIORSTY	FORTYISH	FILLLUWY	WILFULLY		UPFOLLOW
FHIPSSTU	UPSHIFTS	FILLNSUY	SINFULLY	FLLRSUUY	SULFURYL
FHKORSTU	FUTHORKS		SULFINYL	FLMNOOSU	MOUFLONS
FHLLLOTU	LOTHFULL	FILLNUUW	UNWILFUL	FLMNORUU	MOURNFUL
FHLLOSTU	SLOTHFUL	FILLOPPY	FLOPPILY	FLMOOORW	MOORFOWL
FHLMORUU	HUMORFUL	FILLOPSU	SPOILFUL	FLMOOOST	TOMFOOLS
FHLMOTUU	MOUTHFUL	FILLOSSY	FLOSSILY	FLMOORSU	ROOMFULS
FHLNORSU	HORNFULS	FILMNOOS	MONOFILS	FLMORSTU	STORMFUL
FHLOOSTU	SOOTHFUL	FILMOPRS	SLIPFORM	FLNOOPSU	SPOONFUL
FHLOOTTU	TOOTHFUL	FILMORRY	LYRIFORM	FLNOORRS	FORLORNS
FHLOPSSU	SHOPFULS	FILMOSSU	MOFUSSIL	FLNOOSTU	SNOOTFUL
FHLORTTU	TROTHFUL	FILMOSTU	MOISTFUL	FLNOOTUW	OUTFLOWN
FHLORTUW	WORTHFUL	FILMPRUY	FRUMPILY	FLOOOPTT	POLTFOOT
	WROTHFUL	FILNNSUU	UNSINFUL	FLOOOSTU	OUTFOOLS
FHLORTUY	FOURTHLY	FILNORSU	FLUORINS	FLOOPTTY	TOPLOFTY
FHLOSTUU	OUTFLUSH	FILNOSUX	FLUXIONS	FLOORSSW	FORSLOWS
FHLOTUUY	YOUTHFUL	FILOOOPR	OILPROOF	FLOOSTUW	OUTFLOWS
FHLRTTUU	TRUTHFUL	FILOOSTW	WITLOOFS	FLOPRSTU	SPORTFUL
FHNOSTUX	FOXHUNTS	FILORSST	FLORISTS	FLORTTUU	TROUTFUL
FHOOORST	FORSOOTH	FILORSTU	FLORUITS	FLRSTTUU	TRUSTFUL
	HOOFROTS	FILORSTY	FROSTILY	FMNOOOOR	MOONROOF
FHOOOSTT	HOTFOOTS	FILORWYZ	FROWZILY	FMOOPPTU	FOOTPUMP
FIIIMNST	FINITISM	FILRSTTU	TRISTFUL	FMOOPRST	POSTFORM
FIIINNOX	INFIXION	FILSSTTU	FLUTISTS	FMRSSTUU	FRUSTUMS
FIIINNTY	INFINITY	FILSTTUY	STULTIFY	FNNOOORT	FRONTOON
FIIKLRSY	FRISKILY	FIMMNOOR	OMNIFORM	FNNOORST	FRONTONS
FIILLMOP	PLIOFILM	FIMMORRU	MURIFORM	FNOOORTW	FOOTWORN
FIILLMOS	MILFOILS	FIMMORSS	MISFORMS	FNOOPRSU	SUNPROOF
FIILLMSY	FLIMSILY	FIMNORSU	UNIFORMS	FNOORRSW	FORSWORN
FIILLMTU	MULTIFIL	FIMOORRT	ROTIFORM	FNOORSSU	SUNROOFS
FIILLNTY	FLINTILY	FIMOORSS	ISOFORMS	FNOORTUW	OUTFROWN
FIILLSSU	FUSILLIS	FIMOPRRY	PYRIFORM	FOOOPRST	ROOFTOPS
FIILMNRY	INFIRMLY	FIMORRSU	URSIFORM	FOOOPSTT	FOOTPOST
FIILMOPR	PILIFORM	FIMORTUY	FUMITORY	FOOOSTTU	OUTFOOTS
FIILMPSY	SIMPLIFY	FIMOSTUY	FUMOSITY	FOORSTTX	FOXTROTS

FOPSSSTU	FUSSPOTS	GGHIINST	SIGHTING	GGILMMNO	GLOMMING
GGGGIILN	GIGGLING	GGHIINTW	WIGHTING	GGILMNOO	GLOOMING
GGGGIINR	GRIGGING	GGHIIPRS	PRIGGISH	GGILNNOP	PLONGING
GGGGILNO	GOGGLING	GGHILSSU	SLUGGISH	GGILNNOS	LONGINGS
GGGGILNU	GLUGGING	GGHIMSTU	THUGGISM	GGILNNOU	LOUNGING
	GUGGLING	GGHINORU	ROUGHING	GGILNNPU	PLUNGING
GGGGINOR	GROGGING	GGHINOST	GHOSTING		PUNGLING
GGHGIILN	HIGGLING	GGHINOSU	SOUGHING	GGILNNUU	UNGLUING
GGHGIINT	THIGGING	GGHINOTU	OUGHTING	GGILNOOP	GLOOPING
GGHGIINW	WHIGGING		TOUGHING	GGILNOPP	GLOPPING
GGHGINOS	HOGGINGS	GGHINOTY	HOGTYING	GGILNORW	GROWLING
	SHOGGING	GGHINSTU	GUNSIGHT	GGILNORY	GLORYING
GGGIIJLN	JIGGLING	GGHOOPRS	GROGSHOP	GGILNOSS	GLOSSING
GGGIIJNS	JIGGINGS	GGIIILLN	GINGILLI		GOSLINGS
GGGIILNN	NIGGLING	GGIIILNS	GINGILIS	GGILNOSV	GLOVINGS
GGGIILNS	LIGGINGS	GGIIINNT	IGNITING	GGILNOSZ	GLOZINGS
GGGIILNW	WIGGLING	GGIIJLNN	JINGLING	GGILNOTU	GLOUTING
GGGIINNS	SNIGGING	GGIIKLNN	KINGLING	GGILNRUY	URGINGLY
GGGIINPR	PRIGGING	GGIILLNR	GRILLING	GGILNTTU	GLUTTING
GGGIINPS	PIGGINGS	GGIILLNY	GILLYING		GUTTLING
GGGIINRS	RIGGINGS	GGIILMNN	MINGLING	GGILNUZZ	GUZZLING
GGGIINRT	TRIGGING	GGIILMNY	GINGLYMI	GGILQSUY	SQUIGGLY
GGGIINSW	SWIGGING	GGIILNNP	PINGLING	GGIMMNSU	GUMMINGS
	WIGGINGS	GGIILNNS	SINGLING	GGIMNOOR	GROOMING
GGGIINTW	TWIGGING		SLINGING	GGIMNOOS	SMOOGING
GGGIJLNO	JOGGLING	GGIILNNT	GLINTING	GGIMNPRU	GRUMPING
GGGIJLNU	JUGGLING		TINGLING	GGINNNSU	GUNNINGS
GGGIJNOS	JOGGINGS	GGIILNPS	PIGLINGS	GGINNOOS	ONGOINGS
GGGIJNSU	JUGGINGS	GGIILNRS	RIGLINGS	GGINNOPP	PINGPONG
GGGIKNSU	SKUGGING	GGIILNTZ	GLITZING	GGINNOPR	PRONGING
GGGILNOO	GOOGLING	GGIIMNOS	MISGOING	GGINNOPS	SPONGING
GGGILNOS	LOGGINGS	GGIIMNPU	GUIMPING	GGINNORW	WRONGING
	SLOGGING	GGIIMPRS	PRIGGISM	GGINNOSS	SINGSONG
GGGILNOT	TOGGLING	GGIINNNR	GRINNING	GGINNOTU	TONGUING
GGGILNOV	VLOGGING	GGIINNNS	GINNINGS	GGINNRTU	GRUNTING
GGGILNPU	PLUGGING	GGIINNOR	GROINING	GGINNUVY	UNGYVING
	PUGGLING		IGNORING	GGINOORV	GROOVING
GGGILNRU	GURGLING	GGIINNOS	INGOINGS	GGINOOST	STOOGING
GGGILNSU	SLUGGING	GGIINNOT	INGOTING	GGINOOTU	OUTGOING
GGGILORY	GROGGILY	GGIINNOW	WONGIING	GGINOPRS	PROGGINS
GGGIMNSU	MUGGINGS	GGIINNRS	RINGINGS	GGINOPRU	GROUPING
	SMUGGING	GGIINNRW	WRINGING	GGINOPSU	UPGOINGS
GGGINNOS	NOGGINGS	GGIINNSS	SIGNINGS	GGINORSS	GROSSING
	SNOGGING		SINGINGS	GGINORSU	GROUSING
GGGINNSU	SNUGGING	GGIINNST	STINGING	GGINORSW	GROWINGS
GGGINOPR	PROGGING	GGIINNSW	SWINGING	GGINORTU	GROUTING
GGGINORT	TROGGING	GGIINNTW	TWINGING	GGINOSUV	VOGUINGS
GGGINOSS	SOGGINGS	GGIINNUV	UNGIVING	GGINPRSU	PURGINGS
GGGINPSU	PUGGINGS	GGIINPPR	GRIPPING	GGINPSYY	GYPSYING
GGGINRSU	RUGGINGS	GGIINPSY	GIPSYING	GGINRSSU	SURGINGS
GGGINSSU	SUGGINGS	GGIINRST	RINGGITS	GGINSSUY	GUSSYING
GGGINSTU	TUGGINGS	GGIINRTT	GRITTING	GGLLOOWY	GOLLYWOG
GGHHIINT	HIGHTING	GGIINSSU	GUISINGS	GGLLPUUY	PLUGUGLY
GGHHINOU	HOUGHING	GGIINSTU	GIUSTING	GHHIILST	LIGHTISH
GGHHISTU	THUGGISH	GGIIRRSS	GRISGRIS	GHHIINPS	PHISHING
GGHIILNT	LIGHTING	GGIITTUU	GUITGUIT	GHHIINSW	WHISHING
GGHIINNO	HONGIING	GGIKKNOR	GROKKING	GHHIIRST	RIGHTISH
GGHIINNW	WHINGING	GGILLNOY	GOLLYING	GHHIISTT	TIGHTISH
GGHIINPT	PIGHTING	GGILLNUW	GULLWING	GHHILOSU	GHOULISH
GGHIINRT	GIRTHING	GGILLNUY	GULLYING	GHHIMNPU	HUMPHING
	RIGHTING	GGILLOOW	GOLLIWOG	GHHIMOST	HIGHMOST

GHHINOOS	HOOSHING		WISHINGS	GHINNORS	HORNINGS
GHHINSSU	SHUSHING	GHIINSTT	SHITTING	GHINNORT	NORTHING
GHHIOPST	HIGHSPOT		TITHINGS		THORNING
	HIGHTOPS	GHIINSTW	WHISTING		THRONING
GHHIORSU	ROUGHISH		WHITINGS	GHINNOST	NOTHINGS
GHHIOSTU	TOUGHISH	GHIINSVV	SHIVVING	GHINNSSU	SNUSHING
GHHIRSST	SHRIGHTS	GHIINTTW	TWINIGHT	GHINNSTU	HUNTINGS
GHHOORTU	THOROUGH	GHIINWZZ	WHIZZING		SHUNTING
GHHOSTTU	THOUGHTS	GHIIORSV	VIGORISH	GHINOOPT	PHOTOING
GHIIIKNO	HIKOIING	GHIIPSSY	GIPSYISH	GHINOOPW	WHOOPING
GHIIILNS	SHILINGI	GHIIRSTT	RIGHTIST	GHINOOST	SHOOTING
GHIIJNOS	JINGOISH	GHIKLNTY	KNIGHTLY		SOOTHING
GHIIKNNT	THINKING	GHIKLSTY	SKYLIGHT	GHINOOSW	WOOSHING
GHIIKNPS	KINGSHIP	GHIKNNTU	THUNKING	GHINOOTT	TOOTHING
GHIIKNRS	SHIRKING		UNKNIGHT	GHINOOTW	WHOOTING
	SHRIKING	GHIKNSSU	HUSKINGS	GHINOPPS	HOPPINGS
GHIIKNSW	WHISKING	GHIKRSTU	TUGHRIKS		SHOPPING
GHIILLNO	HILLOING	GHILLNOO	HOLLOING	GHINOPPW	WHOPPING
GHIILLNS	HILLINGS	GHILLNOU	HULLOING	GHINOPSS	GINSHOPS
	SHILLING	GHILLOTW	LOWLIGHT	GHINORSS	HORSINGS
GHIILMST	MISLIGHT	GHILLSTY	SLIGHTLY		SHORINGS
GHIILMTY	MIGHTILY	GHILMNSU	MULSHING	GHINORST	SHORTING
GHIILNOT	LITHOING	GHILMPSU	GLUMPISH	GHINORSV	SHROVING
GHIILNPR	HIRPLING	GHILNOOS	SHOOLING	GHINORSW	SHOWRING
GHIILNRS	HIRLINGS	GHILNOPP	HOPPLING		SHROWING
	HIRSLING	GHILNOPS	LONGSHIP	GHINORTT	TROTHING
GHIILNRT	THIRLING	GHILNOPY	HOPINGLY	GHINORTW	INGROWTH
GHIILNRW	WHIRLING	GHILNOSS	SLOSHING		THROWING
GHIILNST	TINGLISH	GHILNOST	SLOTHING		WORTHING
GHIILNTW	WHITLING	GHILNOSU	HOUSLING	GHINOSST	HOSTINGS
GHIILOTT	OILTIGHT	GHILNOSW	HOWLINGS	GHINOSSU	HOUSINGS
GHIILTTW	TWILIGHT	GHILNPSU	INGULPHS	GHINOSSV	SHOVINGS
GHIIMMNS	SHIMMING	GHILNRSU	HURLINGS	GHINOSSW	SHOWINGS
GHIIMMNW	WHIMMING	GHILNRTU	HURTLING	GHINOSTT	HOTTINGS
GHIIMNNU	INHUMING	GHILNRUY	HUNGRILY		SHOTTING
GHIIMNST	SMITHING	GHILNSSU	SLUSHING		TONIGHTS
GHIIMRST	RIGHTISM	GHILNSTU	HUSTLING	GHINOSTU	HOUTINGS
GHIINNNS	SHINNING		SUNLIGHT		SHOUTING
GHIINNNT	THINNING	GHILOPRS	SHOPGIRL		SOUTHING
GHIINNNY	HINNYING	GHILORSW	SHOWGIRL	GHINOSTW	SOWTHING
GHIINNRS	SHRINING	GHILORSY	OGRISHLY	GHINOSUY	YOUNGISH
GHIINNST	HINTINGS	GHILOSSU	SLOUGHIS	GHINOTTU	OUTNIGHT
	NITHINGS	GHILPRTY	TRIGLYPH	GHINPPUW	WHUPPING
GHIINNSW	WHININGS	GHILPSTU	UPLIGHTS	GHINPSSU	GUNSHIPS
GHIINNUV	UNHIVING	GHIMMNSU	HUMMINGS	GHINPTTU	PHUTTING
GHIINOST	HOISTING	GHIMNOPR	MORPHING	GHINRRUY	HURRYING
GHIINPPS	HIPPINGS	GHIMNOPU	GUMPHION	GHINRSSU	RUSHINGS
	SHIPPING	GHIMNOPW	WHOMPING	GHINRSTU	UNGIRTHS
GHIINPPW	WHIPPING	GHIMNORU	HUMORING		UNRIGHTS
GHIINRRS	SHIRRING	GHIMNOSS	MOSHINGS	GHINSSTU	HUSTINGS
GHIINRRW	WHIRRING	GHIMNOTU	MOUTHING		UNSIGHTS
GHIINRST	SHIRTING	GHIMNPTU	THUMPING	GHINSTTU	HUTTINGS
GHIINRSV	SHRIVING	GHIMNPUW	WHUMPING		SHUTTING
GHIINRTT	TRITHING	GHIMNSSU	SMUSHING	GHIORTTU	OUTRIGHT
GHIINRTV	THRIVING	GHIMNSTU	GUNSMITH	GHIOSTTU	OUTSIGHT
GHIINRTW	WRITHING	GHIMPRSU	GRUMPISH	GHIPRSST	SPRIGHTS
GHIINSSS	HISSINGS	GHIMPSYY	PYGMYISH	GHIPRSTU	UPRIGHTS
GHIINSST	INSIGHTS	GHIMRSSU	SIMURGHS	GHIPRSUU	GURUSHIP
GHIINSSV	VISHINGS	GHINNNSU	SHUNNING	GHIPSSYY	GYPSYISH
GHIINSSW	SWISHING	GHINNOOR	HONORING	GHLMOOOS	HOMOLOGS
	WHISSING	GHINNOPY	PHONYING	GHLMOOOY	HOMOLOGY

GHLNNOOR	LONGHORN	**GIIKNNPR**	PRINKING		WINTLING
GHLNOORU	HOURLONG	**GIIKNNPS**	KINGPINS	**GIILNNUV**	UNLIVING
GHLNOOYY	HOLOGYNY		PINKINGS	**GIILNOPS**	PIGNOLIS
GHLNORSU	SLUGHORN	**GIIKNNSS**	SINKINGS		SPOILING
GHLOOORY	HOROLOGY	**GIIKNNST**	STINKING	**GIILNOPT**	PILOTING
GHLORTUU	TURLOUGH	**GIIKNNSW**	SWINKING	**GIILNORS**	LIGROINS
GHMNOOOY	HOMOGONY		WINKINGS	**GIILNOSS**	SOILINGS
GHMORSSU	SORGHUMS	**GIIKNNTT**	KNITTING	**GIILNOST**	TOILINGS
GHMOSSTU	MUGSHOTS	**GIIKNNTW**	TWINKING	**GIILNPPR**	RIPPLING
GHMPSSUY	SPHYGMUS	**GIIKNORS**	SKIORING	**GIILNPPS**	LIPPINGS
GHNNOOOZ	GOHONZON	**GIIKNPPS**	SKIPPING		SIPPLING
GHNOPRSY	GRYPHONS	**GIIKNPSS**	PIGSKINS		SLIPPING
GHNOPYYY	HYPOGYNY	**GIIKNQRU**	QUIRKING	**GIILNPPT**	TIPPLING
GHNOSSTU	GUNSHOTS	**GIIKNRRS**	SKIRRING	**GIILNPPU**	UPPILING
	SHOTGUNS	**GIIKNRSS**	GRISKINS	**GIILNPPY**	PIPINGLY
GHNOSTUU	UNSOUGHT	**GIIKNRST**	SKIRTING	**GIILNPRS**	SPIRLING
GHNOSTUY	YOUNGTHS		STRIKING	**GIILNPRT**	TRIPLING
GHOOOSSW	HOOSGOWS	**GIIKNSSS**	KISSINGS	**GIILNPSS**	LISPINGS
GHOORTUY	YOGHOURT	**GIIKNSSV**	SKIVINGS		SPILINGS
GHORSTUY	YOGHURTS	**GIILLMNS**	MILLINGS	**GIILNQSU**	QUISLING
GIIILMNT	LIMITING	**GIILLMNU**	ILLUMING	**GIILNQTU**	QUILTING
GIIILNNS	INISLING	**GIILLNOR**	GRILLION	**GIILNRSW**	SWIRLING
GIIILNNU	LINGUINI	**GIILLNOS**	GILLIONS	**GIILNRTW**	TWIRLING
GIIILOTV	VITILIGO	**GIILLNPR**	PRILLING	**GIILNRVY**	VIRGINLY
GIIIMMNX	IMMIXING	**GIILLNPS**	PILLINGS	**GIILNSST**	LISTINGS
GIIINNOS	IONISING		SPILLING	**GIILNSTT**	SLITTING
GIIINNOT	IGNITION	**GIILLNQU**	QUILLING		STILTING
GIIINNOZ	IONIZING	**GIILLNRT**	TRILLING		TILTINGS
GIIINNTV	INVITING	**GIILLNST**	STILLING		TITLINGS
GIIINORS	SIGNIORI		TILLINGS	**GIILNSTU**	LINGUIST
GIIINRSS	GRISSINI	**GIILLNSW**	SWILLING	**GIILNSTW**	WITLINGS
GIIINSTV	VISITING	**GIILLNTT**	LITTLING	**GIILNSTY**	STINGILY
GIIJMMNY	JIMMYING	**GIILLNTW**	TWILLING	**GIILNSZZ**	SIZZLING
GIIJMNOS	JINGOISM	**GIILLNVY**	LIVINGLY	**GIILNTTT**	TITTLING
GIIJNNOS	JOININGS	**GIILLNWY**	WILLYING	**GIILNTTU**	TITULING
GIIJNNOT	JOINTING	**GIILLOPW**	POLLIWIG	**GIILNTTV**	VITTLING
GIIJNNRU	INJURING	**GIILLPSW**	PIGSWILL	**GIILNTTW**	TWILTING
GIIJNOST	JINGOIST	**GIILLTUY**	GUILTILY	**GIILNZZZ**	ZIZZLING
	JOISTING	**GIILLTYZ**	GLITZILY	**GIILOSST**	OLIGISTS
GIIKKLNP	KINGKLIP	**GIILMMNP**	PLIMMING	**GIILPSTU**	PUGILIST
GIIKKNNS	SKINKING	**GIILMMNS**	SLIMMING	**GIILRSST**	STRIGILS
GIIKKNRS	KIRKINGS	**GIILMNNU**	LUMINING	**GIILRTTY**	GRITTILY
	SKRIKING		UNLIMING	**GIIMMNPR**	PRIMMING
GIIKLLNS	KILLINGS	**GIILMNOS**	SMOILING	**GIIMMNRS**	RIMMINGS
	SKILLING	**GIILMNPR**	RIMPLING	**GIIMMNRT**	TRIMMING
GIIKLMNS	MILKINGS	**GIILMNPS**	LIMPINGS	**GIIMMNRU**	IMMURING
GIIKLNNP	PLINKING		SIMPLING	**GIIMMNSW**	SWIMMING
GIIKLNNS	INKLINGS	**GIILMNPW**	WIMPLING	**GIIMMNOP**	IMPONING
	SLINKING	**GIILMNPY**	IMPLYING	**GIIMNNOR**	MINORING
GIIKLNNT	TINKLING	**GIILMNSS**	SMILINGS	**GIIMNNOY**	IGNOMINY
GIIKLNNW	WINKLING	**GIILMNST**	MISTLING	**GIIMNNTU**	MINUTING
GIIKLNRS	SKIRLING	**GIILMNSY**	MISLYING		MUNITING
GIIKLNST	KILTINGS	**GIILMNZZ**	MIZZLING		MUTINING
	KITLINGS	**GIILMPRS**	PILGRIMS	**GIIMNNUX**	UNMIXING
GIIKLNTT	KITTLING	**GIILMPSU**	PUGILISM	**GIIMNOPS**	IMPOSING
GIIKMMNS	SKIMMING	**GIILNNNU**	UNLINING	**GIIMNOST**	MOISTING
GIIKMNPS	SKIMPING	**GIILNNPP**	NIPPLING	**GIIMNOTT**	OMITTING
GIIKMNRS	SMIRKING	**GIILNNPS**	SPLINING	**GIIMNOTV**	MOTIVING
GIIKNNNS	SKINNING	**GIILNNPU**	UNPILING		VOMITING
GIIKNNOV	INVOKING	**GIILNNTU**	UNTILING	**GIIMNPPR**	PRIMPING
		GIILNNTW	TWINLING	**GIIMNPPS**	PIMPINGS

GIIMNPRS	PRIMINGS	GIINPPRT	TRIPPING	GIKNNOSW	KNOWINGS
GIIMNPRU	UMPIRING	GIINPPST	TIPPINGS		SNOWKING
GIIMNPTU	IMPUTING	GIINPRSS	PRISSING	GIKNNOTT	KNOTTING
GIIMNRRS	SMIRRING		RISPINGS	GIKNNOTU	KNOUTING
GIIMNRST	SMIRTING	GIINPRST	SPIRTING	GIKNNOUY	UNYOKING
GIIMNSST	MISTINGS		STRIPING	GIKNNPSU	SPUNKING
GIIMNSSU	MISUSING	GIINPRSU	SIRUPING	GIKNNRTU	TRUNKING
GIIMNSSW	SWINGISM		UPRISING	GIKNOOPS	SPOOKING
GIIMNSTT	SMITTING	GIINPSTT	PITTINGS	GIKNOOST	STOOKING
GIIMNSTU	MUISTING		SPITTING	GIKNOOTW	KOTOWING
GIIMNSTY	STIMYING	GIINPSTW	WINGTIPS	GIKNOPST	KINGPOST
GIIMORRS	RIGORISM	GIINPSUZ	UPSIZING	GIKNORRW	RINGWORK
GIINNNOO	ONIONING	GIINPTTU	TITUPING	GIKNORST	STROKING
GIINNNOT	INTONING	GIINQRSU	SQUIRING	GIKNORSW	WORKINGS
	NOINTING	GIINQRTU	QUIRTING	GIKNSSTU	TUSKINGS
GIINNNPS	PINNINGS	GIINQTTU	QUITTING	GILLMOOY	GLOOMILY
	SPINNING	GIINQUZZ	QUIZZING	GILLMPUY	GLUMPILY
GIINNNRU	INURNING	GIINRRST	STIRRING	GILLNNSU	NULLINGS
GIINNNST	TINNINGS	GIINRRTV	STRIVING	GILLNOPR	PROLLING
GIINNNSW	WINNINGS	GIINRSTW	WRITINGS	GILLNOPS	POLLINGS
GIINNNTW	TWINNING	GIINSSSW	SWISSING	GILLNORS	ROLLINGS
GIINNOPR	PROINING	GIINSSTT	SITTINGS	GILLNORT	TROLLING
GIINNOPS	PIONINGS	GIINSSTU	SUITINGS	GILLNOST	LONGLIST
GIINNOPT	POINTING		TISSUING		TOLLINGS
GIINNOQU	QUOINING	GIINSTTW	TWISTING	GILLNOSY	LOSINGLY
GIINNORS	IRONINGS		WITTINGS	GILLNOVY	LOVINGLY
	NIGROSIN	GIINSTUW	WINGSUIT	GILLNPUY	PULINGLY
	ROSINING	GIINSWZZ	SWIZZING	GILLNPYY	PLYINGLY
GIINNORT	IGNITRON	GIINTTTW	TWITTING	GILLNRUY	LURINGLY
GIINNPPS	SNIPPING	GIIORRST	RIGORIST	GILLNSUY	SULLYING
GIINNPRT	PRINTING	GIIORSSV	ISOGRIVS	GILLOOPW	POLLIWOG
GIINNPSS	SNIPINGS	GIIPRSTZ	SPRITZIG	GILLOPWY	POLLYWIG
GIINNPSU	PINGUINS	GIJKLNOY	JOKINGLY	GILLORVY	GILLYVOR
GIINNRSS	RINSINGS	GIJLLNOY	JOLLYING	GILLOSSY	GLOSSILY
GIINNRSU	INSURING	GIJLNOST	JOSTLING	GILMMNSU	SLUMMING
	RUININGS	GIJLNSTU	JUNGLIST	GILMMTUY	MULTIGYM
GIINNRTU	UNTIRING		JUSTLING	GILMNOOS	SLOOMING
GIINNRUW	UNWIRING	GIJMNPSU	JUMPINGS	GILMNOPY	MOPINGLY
GIINNSSW	INSWINGS	GIJNOSTT	JOTTINGS	GILMNORS	MORLINGS
GIINNSTT	STINTING	GIJNOSTU	JOUSTING		SLORMING
	TINTINGS	GIJNTTUY	JUTTYING	GILMNORT	MORTLING
GIINNSTU	UNITINGS	GIKKLNSU	SKULKING	GILMNOSS	MOSLINGS
GIINNSTW	TWININGS	GIKKNNSU	SKUNKING	GILMNOSU	MOUSLING
GIINNUVW	UNWIVING	GIKLLNNO	KNOLLING	GILMNOSY	SMOYLING
GIINOPST	POSITING	GIKLLNOS	SKOLLING	GILMNOTT	MOTTLING
	SOPITING	GIKLLNSU	SKULLING	GILMNOTU	MOULTING
GIINOPTV	PIVOTING	GIKLNNOP	PLONKING	GILMNOUV	VOLUMING
GIINOQTU	QUOITING	GIKLNNPU	PLUNKING	GILMNOVY	MOVINGLY
GIINORSS	GRISSINO	GIKLNNRU	KNURLING	GILMNPPU	PLUMPING
	SIGNIORS		RUNKLING	GILMNPRU	RUMPLING
GIINORST	IGNITORS	GIKLNNUY	UNKINGLY	GILMNPSU	SLUMPING
	RIOTINGS	GIKLNOPR	PORKLING	GILMNSUY	MUSINGLY
	ROISTING	GIKLNRSU	LURKINGS	GILMNUZZ	MUZZLING
	ROSITING	GIKLORRW	WORKGIRL	GILMOOSY	MISOLOGY
GIINORSV	VISORING	GIKMNOSS	SMOKINGS	GILMOOXY	MIXOLOGY
GIINORSY	SIGNIORY	GIKMNPPU	PUMPKING	GILMPRUY	GRUMPILY
GIINORTZ	ROZITING	GIKMNPRU	KRUMPING	GILMPSSY	GYMSLIPS
GIINORVZ	VIZORING	GIKNNOOS	SNOOKING	GILNNOOS	GLONOINS
GIINOSTT	STOITING	GIKNNOPR	PRONKING		LOONINGS
GIINPPQU	QUIPPING	GIKNNOQU	QUONKING		SNOOLING
GIINPPRS	RIPPINGS	GIKNNOST	STONKING	GILNNOSU	NOUSLING

GILNNOTU	NONGUILT	GILNUWZZ	WUZZLING	GINNNOOS	NOONINGS
GILNNOTW	TOWNLING	GILOOORS	ROSOGLIO	GINNNOST	STONNING
GILNNOUV	UNLOVING	GILOOOST	OOLOGIST	GINNNOSU	NONUSING
GILNNRSU	NURSLING	GILOORSS	GIROSOLS	GINNNOSW	WONNINGS
GILNNSSU	UNSLINGS	GILOORSU	GLORIOUS	GINNNPSU	PUNNINGS
GILNNUZZ	NUZZLING	GILOORVY	GROOVILY	GINNNRSU	RUNNINGS
GILNOOOY	OINOLOGY		VIROLOGY	GINNNSTU	STUNNING
GILNOOPS	LOOPINGS	GILOOSSS	ISOGLOSS		TUNNINGS
	SPOOLING	GILOOSST	OLOGISTS	GINNNTUU	UNTUNING
GILNOOPT	POOTLING	GILOOSTW	TWIGLOOS	GINNOOPS	SNOOPING
GILNOORT	ROOTLING	GILOOSTY	SITOLOGY		SPOONING
GILNOOSS	LOOSINGS	GILORSTT	TRIGLOTS	GINNOOST	SNOOTING
GILNOOST	LOOTINGS	GILOSSST	GLOSSIST	GINNOOSW	SWOONING
	STOOLING	GILOSTUY	GULOSITY	GINNOOSZ	SNOOZING
	TOOLINGS	GIMMMNSU	MUMMINGS	GINNOPPU	UNPOPING
GILNOOSY	SINOLOGY	GIMMMNUY	MUMMYING	GINNOPRU	UNROPING
GILNOOTT	TOOTLING	GIMMNOTY	TOMMYING	GINNOPRY	PROYNING
GILNOOVY	VINOLOGY	GIMMNSSU	SUMMINGS	GINNOPSS	SPONGINS
GILNOOWY	WOOINGLY	GIMMNSTU	STUMMING		SPONSING
GILNOPPP	PLOPPING	GIMMOSSU	GUMMOSIS	GINNOPSY	PYONINGS
	POPPLING	GIMMPSYY	PYGMYISM	GINNOPTU	GUNPOINT
GILNOPPS	LOPPINGS	GIMNNORS	MORNINGS	GINNOPTY	POYNTING
	SLOPPING	GIMNNORU	MOURNING	GINNORSS	SNORINGS
GILNOPPT	TOPPLING	GIMNNOTU	MOUNTING		SORNINGS
GILNOPRU	PROULING	GIMNNOUV	UNMOVING	GINNORST	SNORTING
GILNOPRW	PROWLING	GIMNNSTU	MUNTINGS	GINNORSU	GRUNIONS
GILNOPSU	SOUPLING	GIMNOOOU	OOGONIUM	GINNOSST	STONINGS
GILNOPSY	POSINGLY	GIMNOOPR	PROMOING	GINNOSTT	SNOTTING
	SPONGILY	GIMNOOPS	SPOOMING	GINNOSTU	SNOUTING
GILNOPTT	PLOTTING	GIMNOORS	MOORINGS		STOUNING
GILNOPTZ	PLOTZING		SMOORING	GINNOSTY	STONYING
GILNORSU	LOURINGS	GIMNOORT	MOTORING	GINNOSUW	SWOUNING
GILNORSY	YORLINGS	GIMNOORV	VROOMING	GINNPRSU	PRUNINGS
GILNORTU	TROULING	GIMNOOSS	OSMOSING		SPURNING
GILNORVY	ROVINGLY	GIMNOOST	MOOTINGS	GINNRSSU	NURSINGS
GILNOSSW	SLOWINGS		SMOOTING	GINNRSTU	TURNINGS
GILNOSTT	SLOTTING	GIMNOPRT	TROMPING		UNSTRING
GILNOSTU	TOUSLING	GIMNOPST	STOMPING	GINNSTTU	NUTTINGS
GILNOSVW	WOLVINGS	GIMNOPTU	GUMPTION		STUNTING
GILNOSWY	YOWLINGS	GIMNORRU	RUMORING	GINNSTUY	UNTYINGS
GILNOSZZ	SOZZLING	GIMNORRW	RINGWORM	GINOOPPS	OPPOSING
GILNOTUY	OUTLYING	GIMNORST	STORMING		POGONIPS
GILNOTUZ	TOUZLING	GIMNORSU	ROUMINGS	GINOOPRS	SPOORING
GILNPPRU	PURPLING	GIMNORSW	MISGROWN	GINOOPRT	TROOPING
GILNPPSU	SUPPLING	GIMNOSST	GNOMISTS	GINOOPSS	SOOPINGS
GILNPRSU	PURLINGS	GIMNOSSU	MOUSINGS	GINOOPST	STOOPING
	SLURPING		MOUSSING	GINOOPSW	SWOOPING
	SPURLING		SMOUSING		WOOPSING
GILNPRYY	PRYINGLY		SOUMINGS	GINOORST	ROOSTING
GILNPSSU	PLUSSING	GIMNOSTU	MOUSTING		ROOTINGS
GILNPUZZ	PUZZLING		SMOUTING	GINOORTW	WROOTING
GILNRRSU	SLURRING	GIMNOSYY	MISOGYNY	GINOOSTT	TOOTSING
GILNRSTU	LUSTRING	GIMNPPSU	PUMPINGS	GINOOSTZ	STOOZING
	RUSTLING	GIMNPRTU	TRUMPING	GINOPPPR	PROPPING
GILNRTTU	TURTLING	GIMNPSTU	STUMPING	GINOPPQU	QUOPPING
GILNRTYY	TRYINGLY	GIMNRRSU	SMURRING	GINOPPSS	SOPPINGS
GILNSSTU	SINGULTS	GIMNSTTU	SMUTTING	GINOPPST	STOPPING
	TUSSLING	GIMNSTYY	STYMYING		TOPPINGS
GILNSSTY	STYLINGS	GIMORSSW	MISGROWS	GINOPPSW	SWOPPING
GILNSTTU	SUTTLING	GIMPSSYY	GYPSYISM	GINOPRSS	PROSINGS
GILNTUUY	UNGUILTY	GIMRSSUU	GURUISMS	GINOPRST	SPORTING

GINOPRSU	INGROUPS		TRUSTING	**GMNNOOOY**	MONOGONY
	POURINGS	**GINRSTTY**	TRYSTING	**GMNNOOOY**	MONOGYNY
GINOPRSV	PROVINGS	**GINRSTUU**	SUTURING	**GMNOORSU**	GUNROOMS
GINOPRTU	TROUPING	**GINSTTTU**	TUTTINGS	**GMNOORSW**	MORWONGS
GINOPSST	POSTINGS	**GIOOORSV**	VIGOROSO	**GMORSTUW**	MUGWORTS
	SIGNPOST	**GIOOPRRS**	PORRIGOS	**GNNPRSUU**	UNSPRUNG
	STOPINGS	**GIOORRSU**	RIGOROUS	**GNNRSTUU**	UNSTRUNG
GINOPSSU	SPOUSING	**GIOORSTU**	GOITROUS	**GNOOORSS**	GORSOONS
GINOPSTT	SPOTTING	**GIOORSUV**	VIGOROUS	**GNOOOSSS**	GOSSOONS
GINOPSTU	POUTINGS	**GIOPRRSU**	PRURIGOS	**GNOORSUW**	WRONGOUS
	SPOUTING	**GIOPRSSY**	GOSSIPRY	**GNOORTUW**	OUTGROWN
GINOPTTY	TYPTOING	**GIOPRSTU**	GROUPIST	**GNOPRSTU**	GUNPORTS
GINOQRTU	TORQUING	**GIORSTUY**	RUGOSITY	**GNOPRSUW**	GROWNUPS
GINORRST	RORTINGS	**GIOSTYYZ**	ZYGOSITY	**GNOSTUUW**	OUTSWUNG
GINORRWY	WORRYING	**GJLMNOPU**	LONGJUMP	**GNPPRSUU**	UPSPRUNG
GINORSST	RINGTOSS	**GJOORSTT**	JOGTROTS	**GOOPRSST**	GOSPORTS
	SORTINGS	**GKKNOOSS**	SONGKOKS	**GOOPRTUU**	OUTGROUP
GINORSSU	SOURINGS	**GKLOOOTY**	TOKOLOGY	**GOORSSTU**	OUTGROSS
GINORSTU	OUTGRINS	**GLLLOORS**	LOGROLLS	**GOORSTUW**	OUTGROWS
	OUTRINGS	**GLLOOPTY**	POLYGLOT	**GOORTTUW**	GOUTWORT
	ROUSTING	**GLLOOPWY**	POLLYWOG	**HHIIIOOP**	PIHOIHOI
	ROUTINGS	**GLLOOXYY**	XYLOLOGY	**HHIILOPT**	THIOPHIL
	TOURINGS	**GLMMSSUU**	SLUMGUMS	**HHIINNST**	THINNISH
GINORSTW	STROWING	**GLMNOOOS**	MONOLOGS	**HHIIPSST**	PHTHISIS
	WORSTING	**GLMNOOOT**	MONOGLOT	**HHILMOSS**	SHLOSHIM
GINORSTY	ROYSTING	**GLMNOOOY**	MONOLOGY	**HHILNOPW**	WHOLPHIN
	STORYING		NOMOLOGY	**HHILPSSY**	SYLPHISH
	STROYING	**GLMNOORW**	LONGWORM	**HHIMMOSS**	MISHMOSH
GINORTTT	TROTTING	**GLMNORUW**	LUNGWORM	**HHIMNPSY**	NYMPHISH
GINORTTU	TROUTING	**GLMNRTUU**	NGULTRUM	**HHIMPSSU**	SUMPHISH
	TUTORING	**GLMNSUUU**	UMLUNGUS	**HHINOOSW**	NOHOWISH
GINOSSSS	SOSSINGS	**GLMOOOPY**	POMOLOGY	**HHINOPPS**	PHOSPHIN
GINOSSST	TOSSINGS	**GLMOOORS**	MOORLOGS	**HHIORSST**	SHORTISH
GINOSSSU	SOUSINGS	**GLMOORWW**	GLOWWORM	**HHKKSSUU**	KHUSKHUS
GINOSSSW	SOWSSING	**GLMOOYYZ**	ZYMOLOGY	**HHMRSTUY**	RHYTHMUS
GINOSSTT	SOTTINGS	**GLMORSUW**	LUGWORMS	**HHOOPPRS**	PHOSPHOR
GINOSSTU	OUTSINGS	**GLNNOORS**	LORGNONS	**HHOOSSTT**	HOTSHOTS
	TOUSINGS	**GLNOOOSY**	NOSOLOGY	**HIIILMNS**	NIHILISM
GINOSSTV	STOVINGS	**GLNOOOTY**	ONTOLOGY	**HIIILNST**	NIHILIST
GINOSSTW	STOWINGS	**GLNOOPRS**	PROLONGS	**HIIILNTY**	NIHILITY
GINOSTTT	STOTTING	**GLNOOPSY**	POLYGONS	**HIIINRST**	RHINITIS
	TOTTINGS	**GLNOOPYY**	POLYGONY	**HIIISSTV**	SHIVITIS
GINOSTTW	SWOTTING	**GLNOPRSU**	LONGSPUR	**HIIKMNST**	MISTHINK
GINOSTUW	OUTSWING	**GLNOPYYY**	POLYGYNY	**HIIKMRSS**	SKIRMISH
	OUTWINGS	**GLNORSTY**	STRONGLY	**HIIKNNSS**	SHINKINS
GINOTUVY	OUTVYING		STRONGYL	**HIIKNOSS**	INKHOSIS
GINPPPUY	PUPPYING	**GLNORTUW**	LUNGWORT	**HIIKNPSS**	KINSHIPS
GINPPRSU	UPSPRING	**GLNOSSUW**	SUNGLOWS	**HIIKOPRS**	PIROSHKI
GINPRRSU	PURRINGS	**GLNOSTTU**	GLUTTONS	**HIIKOPRZ**	PIROZHKI
	SPURRING	**GLNOTTUY**	GLUTTONY	**HIIKQRSU**	QUIRKISH
GINPRSTU	SPURTING	**GLOOOPSY**	POSOLOGY	**HIIKSSTT**	SKITTISH
GINPRSUU	PURSUING	**GLOOOPTY**	OPTOLOGY	**HIILLMMO**	MILLIMHO
	USURPING		TOPOLOGY		MILLIOHM
GINPRSUY	SYRUPING	**GLOOORUY**	OUROLOGY	**HIILLSTT**	LITTLISH
GINPSSUW	UPSWINGS	**GLOOPRYY**	PYROLOGY	**HIILMMSS**	SLIMMISH
GINPSTTU	PUTTINGS	**GLOOPSSY**	GOSSYPOL	**HIILMOST**	HOMILIST
GINPTTUY	PUTTYING	**GLOOPTYY**	LOGOTYPY	**HIILMPSU**	SILPHIUM
GINRSSTU	RUSTINGS		TYPOLOGY	**HIILMPSY**	IMPISHLY
	TRUSSING	**GLOORSUU**	ORGULOUS	**HIILMSTU**	LITHIUMS
GINRSTTU	RUTTINGS	**GLOOSTUW**	OUTGLOWS	**HIILMSWY**	WHIMSILY
	STURTING	**GMMPSUUW**	MUGWUMPS	**HIILMTUY**	HUMILITY

HIILOPST	PISOLITH	**HILOOSTT**	OTOLITHS	**HIOPRSSW**	WORSHIPS
HIILPSST	THLIPSIS	**HILOOSTZ**	ZOOLITHS	**HIOPRSUZ**	RHIZOPUS
HIILPSSY	SYPHILIS	**HILOOTTY**	TOOTHILY	**HIOPSSST**	SOPHISTS
HIILRSTT	TRILITHS	**HILOPPSY**	POPISHLY	**HIOPSSTU**	UPHOISTS
HIILRSTY	SHIRTILY	**HILOPSXY**	OXYPHILS	**HIOPSSTY**	PHYTOSIS
HIILSSTT	SHITLIST	**HILORSTU**	UROLITHS	**HIORRSSY**	SORRYISH
	STILTISH	**HILORSUU**	URUSHIOL	**HIOSSTTU**	STOUTISH
HIILSTTY	SHITTILY	**HILORTUW**	OUTWHIRL	**HIOSTTUW**	WITHOUTS
HIIMNNOS	HOMININS	**HILORTWY**	WORTHILY	**HIPPPSUY**	PUPPYISH
HIIMNSTT	TINSMITH	**HILOSSTW**	WHOLISTS	**HIPPSSTU**	PUSHPITS
HIIMOPSS	PHIMOSIS	**HILOSSTY**	HYLOISTS	**HIPSUYZZ**	ZIZYPHUS
HIIMSSTT	SHITTIMS		THYLOSIS	**HJMOPSUW**	SHOWJUMP
HIINNNSY	NINNYISH	**HILOSTWW**	WHITLOWS	**HJNNOOSS**	JOHNSONS
HIINNOST	THIONINS	**HILOSTYY**	TOYISHLY	**HKKLOOSY**	KOLKHOSY
HIINORST	HISTRION	**HILPPRSU**	PURPLISH	**HKKLOOYZ**	KOLKHOZY
HIINPSTW	TWINSHIP	**HILPPSUY**	UPPISHLY	**HKKOOPYY**	HOKYPOKY
HIIOPRSW	POWHIRIS	**HILPRSUW**	UPWHIRLS	**HKKOOSSY**	SKYHOOKS
HIIORSST	HISTRIOS	**HILSSTTU**	SLUTTISH	**HKMNORRU**	KRUMHORN
HIIPPQSU	QUIPPISH	**HIMMOPRU**	PHORMIUM	**HKMOOORW**	HOOKWORM
HIIPRTTU	PUIRTITH	**HIMMSSTY**	MYTHISMS	**HKNNRSUU**	UNSHRUNK
HIIQRSSU	SQUIRISH	**HIMNOPRS**	MORPHINS	**HKNOORRW**	HORNWORK
HIISSSSY	SISSYISH	**HIMNOPRX**	PHORMINX	**HKNOOSWW**	KNOWHOWS
HIISSTTT	TSITSITH	**HIMNOPSY**	PHISNOMY	**HKOOOPST**	POTHOOKS
HIISSTXY	SIXTYISH	**HIMNOSTY**	THYMOSIN	**HKOOPRSW**	WORKSHOP
HIITTTZZ	TZITZITH	**HIMNSSTY**	HYMNISTS	**HKOORRUW**	WORKHOUR
HIKKNSUU	INUKSHUK	**HIMOOPRS**	ISOMORPH	**HKOOSVYZ**	SOVKHOZY
HIKLNOST	HOTLINKS	**HIMOPRRT**	TRIMORPH	**HLLLOOWY**	HOLLOWLY
HIKLORTY	KRYOLITH	**HIMOPRSS**	ORPHISMS	**HLLMNOOU**	MONOHULL
HIKMNSUU	MINSHUKU	**HIMOPRSW**	SHIPWORM	**HLLOPPRY**	PROPHYLL
HIKMOSTZ	SHKOTZIM	**HIMOPRWW**	WHIPWORM	**HLMOOSTY**	SMOOTHLY
HIKNNORS	INKHORNS	**HIMOPSSS**	SOPHISMS	**HLMORRSY**	MYRRHOLS
HIKNNSTU	UNTHINKS	**HIMOPSST**	PHOTISMS	**HLNOOPPY**	POLYPHON
HIKNOOSU	HOKONUIS	**HIMORSST**	RIMSHOTS	**HLOOSTUW**	OUTHOWLS
HIKNOTTU	OUTTHINK	**HIMORSTU**	HUMORIST	**HLOPRSTY**	PROTHYLS
HIKOOPRZ	PIROZHOK		THORIUMS	**HLPRSSUU**	SULPHURS
HIKOOPSS	SPOOKISH	**HIMORSTW**	MISTHROW	**HLPRSUUY**	SULPHURY
HIKOPSSY	KYPHOSIS	**HIMOSTTV**	MITSVOTH	**HMMNOOSY**	HOMONYMS
HILLMSUY	MULISHLY	**HIMOTTVZ**	MITZVOTH	**HMMNOOYY**	HOMONYMY
HILLNOUY	UNHOLILY	**HIMPRSTU**	TRIUMPHS	**HMMOORSU**	MUSHROOM
HILLOOPT	LOPOLITH	**HIMPSTUY**	PYTHIUMS	**HMMRSTUU**	HUMSTRUM
HILLOOST	LITHOSOL	**HIMRSSTY**	RHYMISTS	**HMNOOOST**	MOONSHOT
HILLOPST	HILLTOPS	**HIMRSTTU**	MISTRUTH	**HMNOOOTY**	HOMOTONY
HILLOSWY	OWLISHLY	**HIMSSTTY**	MYTHISTS	**HMNOORRW**	HORNWORM
HILLPSUY	PLUSHILY	**HINNORST**	TINHORNS	**HMNOOSTU**	UNSMOOTH
HILLSSUY	SLUSHILY	**HINNPSSU**	NUNSHIPS	**HMNOPSYY**	HYPONYMS
HILMMOSU	HOLMIUMS	**HINNSSUY**	SUNSHINY		SYMPHONY
HILMNOOT	MONOLITH	**HINOORST**	HORNITOS	**HMNOPYYY**	HYPONYMY
HILMOOPT	PHILOMOT	**HINOORSZ**	HORIZONS	**HMOOOPRZ**	ZOOMORPH
HILMOPSY	MOPISHLY	**HINOPPSS**	SHIPPONS	**HMOOORSW**	SHOWROOM
HILMOPYY	MYOPHILY	**HINOPSSS**	SONSHIPS	**HMOOPTYY**	HOMOTYPY
HILMOSSW	WHOLISMS	**HINOPSSY**	HYPNOSIS	**HMOORSUU**	HUMOROUS
HILMOTUY	MOUTHILY	**HINOPSTW**	TOWNSHIP	**HMOORTUU**	OUTHUMOR
HILMPPSU	PLUMPISH	**HINORSST**	HORNISTS	**HNNORTTU**	NONTRUTH
HILMPRTU	PHILTRUM	**HINORTXY**	THYROXIN	**HNNOSSTY**	SYNTHONS
HILMPSYY	SYMPHILY	**HINOSSTU**	SNOUTISH	**HNOOOOPR**	OOPHORON
HILMSTUU	THULIUMS	**HINPPSSU**	PUSHPINS	**HNOOPPYY**	HYPOPYON
HILNOPSU	UNPOLISH	**HIOOOPRT**	HOROPITO	**HNOOPRSW**	SHOPWORN
HILNORTY	THORNILY	**HIOOOPRZ**	ZOOPHORI	**HNOOPRTU**	HORNPOUT
HILNOSTY	THIONYLS	**HIOOPRTT**	POORTITH	**HNOOPSTY**	TYPHOONS
	TONISHLY	**HIOORSST**	ORTHOSIS	**HNOORRTW**	HORNWORT
HILOOPYZ	ZOOPHILY	**HIOOSSTT**	SHOOTIST	**HNOORSTU**	SOUTHRON

HNOOSSTU	UNSHOOTS	**IIKKLNOS**	KOLINSKI	**IILOSSTV**	VIOLISTS
HNOPPSTY	SYNTHPOP	**IIKKMMUU**	KUMIKUMI	**IILPRSSY**	PRISSILY
HNOPRTUW	UPTHROWN	**IIKKNPSS**	KIPSKINS	**IILRSSTU**	SILURIST
HNORSTUW	UNWORTHS	**IIKLLNOS**	SKILLION	**IILSSTTT**	TITLISTS
HNORTUWY	UNWORTHY	**IIKLLNSY**	SLINKILY	**IILSTUUV**	UVULITIS
HNOSSTUU	UNSHOUTS	**IIKLMNPS**	LIMPKINS	**IILSTUVV**	VULVITIS
HNOSTTUU	OUTHUNTS	**IIKLMPSY**	SKIMPILY	**IIMMMNSU**	MINIMUMS
HNRSTTUU	UNTRUTHS	**IIKLMRSY**	SMIRKILY	**IIMMNOOT**	MINIMOTO
HOOOSTTU	OUTSHOOT	**IIKLNOSS**	OILSKINS	**IIMMNTUY**	IMMUNITY
	SHOOTOUT	**IIKLQRUY**	QUIRKILY	**IIMMOORR**	MIROMIRO
HOOPPSST	POTSHOPS	**IIKMNNOO**	MONOKINI	**IIMMOPST**	OPTIMISM
HOOPPSTY	PHOTOPSY	**IIKMNORS**	KIRIMONS	**IIMMOPSU**	OPIUMISM
HOOPRRST	PORTHORS	**IIKMNPSS**	SIMPKINS	**IIMMSTTU**	MITTIMUS
HOOPSSTT	HOTSPOTS	**IIKNOSTT**	STOTINKI	**IIMNNOOT**	MONITION
	POTSHOTS	**IILLLMUX**	MILLILUX	**IIMNNOSU**	MISUNION
HOOPSSTU	UPSHOOTS	**IILLLPTU**	LILLIPUT		UNIONISM
HOOPSSTW	POSTSHOW	**IILLLPUV**	PULVILLI	**IIMNNOTU**	MUNITION
HOOPSSTY	TOYSHOPS	**IILLMNOS**	MILLIONS	**IIMNOOSS**	OMISSION
HOOQSSUY	SQUOOSHY	**IILLMRTU**	TRILLIUM	**IIMNOPRS**	IMPRISON
HOORTTUW	OUTTHROW	**IILLMUUV**	ILLUVIUM	**IIMNOPST**	MISPOINT
	OUTWORTH	**IILLNOOR**	ORILLION	**IIMNORTT**	INTROMIT
HOOSSTTU	OUTSHOTS	**IILLNOPS**	PILLIONS	**IIMNORTY**	MINORITY
HOOSTTUU	OUTSHOUT	**IILLNORT**	TRILLION	**IIMNOSSS**	MISSIONS
HOPPRRYY	PORPHYRY	**IILLNOST**	STILLION	**IIMNOSST**	SIMONIST
HOPRRSUY	PYRRHOUS	**IILLNOSU**	ILLUSION	**IIMNOSTX**	MIXTIONS
HOPRSSTU	HOTSPURS	**IILLNOSZ**	ZILLIONS	**IIMNPRST**	IMPRINTS
HOPRSTUW	UPTHROWS	**IILLNSST**	INSTILLS		MISPRINT
HORRSTTU	THRUSTOR	**IILLNSTT**	LITTLINS	**IIMNPTUY**	IMPUNITY
HOSSTTUU	SHUTOUTS	**IILLOPQU**	PIQUILLO	**IIMNRSTY**	MINISTRY
HPRSTTUU	THRUPUTS	**IILLOPUV**	PULVILIO	**IIMOPSTT**	OPTIMIST
	UPTHRUST	**IILLPPSY**	SLIPPILY	**IIMORSTY**	RIMOSITY
IIIJJLNS	JINJILIS	**IILMMNSU**	LUMINISM	**IIMOSSTY**	MYOSITIS
IIIKLNPS	SPILIKIN	**IILMMPSS**	SIMPLISM	**IIMOTTVY**	MOTIVITY
IIIKMNNS	MINIKINS	**IILMMSUU**	SIMULIUM	**IIMPRTUY**	IMPURITY
IIIKMNSS	MINISKIS	**IILMMSWY**	SWIMMILY	**IIMRRTUV**	TRIUMVIR
IIIKNPST	PITIKINS	**IILMNORT**	MIRLITON	**IIMRSTTU**	TRITIUMS
IIILLMMN	MINIMILL	**IILMNOSS**	LIONISMS	**IIMRSTUV**	TRIVIUMS
IIILLMNP	MINIPILL	**IILMNSTU**	LUMINIST	**IIMSSSTU**	MISSUITS
IIILLMNU	ILLINIUM	**IILMORSS**	SIMILORS	**IIMSSTUW**	SWIMSUIT
IIILLNOS	ILLISION	**IILMORST**	TROILISM	**IINNOOPS**	OPINIONS
IIILMRSV	VIRILISM	**IILMOTTY**	MOTILITY	**IINNOPPT**	PINPOINT
IIILMUVX	LIXIVIUM	**IILMPSST**	SIMPLIST	**IINNOPTU**	PUNITION
IIILRTVY	VIRILITY	**IILMRSSY**	MISSILRY	**IINNOSTU**	INUSTION
IIIMMMNS	MINIMISM	**IILNNOOT**	NOLITION		UNIONIST
IIIMMNST	INTIMISM	**IILNNOQU**	QUINOLIN		UNITIONS
	MINIMIST	**IILNNOST**	NITINOLS	**IINNPSST**	TINSNIPS
IIIMMPRS	IMPRIMIS	**IILNNSSU**	INSULINS	**IINNQSTU**	QUINTINS
IIIMNSTT	INTIMIST	**IILNOOST**	INOSITOL	**IINNSTTU**	TINNITUS
IIIMNTTY	INTIMITY	**IILNOOTV**	VOLITION	**IINOOPST**	POSITION
IIINORRS	IRRISION	**IILNOPST**	PINITOLS	**IINOPSSS**	ISOSPINS
IIINPRST	INSPIRIT	**IILNORSS**	SIRLOINS	**IINORSST**	IRONISTS
IIINQTUY	INIQUITY	**IILNPPSY**	SNIPPILY	**IINORSTT**	INTROITS
IIINSSTU	SINUITIS	**IILNPSTU**	PILINUTS	**IINOSTTU**	TUITIONS
IIIOSTTU	OUISTITI	**IILNRTWY**	WINTRILY	**IINOSTVY**	VINOSITY
IIISSTTW	WISTITIS	**IILOOPPR**	LIRIPOOP	**IINRSSTU**	SIRTUINS
IIJJSTUU	JIUJITSU	**IILOPRST**	TRIPOLIS	**IINRTTUY**	TRIUNITY
IIJKNPSU	KIPUNJIS	**IILOPSSS**	PSILOSIS	**IINSSTTW**	INTWISTS
IIJLLNOS	JILLIONS	**IILOPSST**	PTILOSIS	**IIOOPSTV**	OVIPOSIT
IIJMNOSS	MISJOINS	**IILOPSTY**	PILOSITY	**IIOORRRR**	RIRORIRO
IIJNNOST	INJOINTS	**IILORSTT**	TROILIST	**IIOOSTTY**	OTIOSITY
IIJNNSTU	NINJITSU	**IILORSTV**	VITRIOLS	**IIOPRRTY**	PRIORITY

IIOPRSSS	PISSOIRS	IKNOPSSY	PYKNOSIS	ILNOOPSY	SNOOPILY
IIORRRSY	IRRISORY	IKNOPSTT	STINKPOT		SPOONILY
IIORRSSU	RISORIUS	IKNOPSTW	TOWNSKIP	ILNOORSS	ROSINOLS
IIORSSTV	IVORISTS	IKNORSTW	TINWORKS	ILNOORTW	TOILWORN
	VISITORS	IKNPSSTU	SPUTNIKS	ILNOOSST	SOLITONS
IIORSTUV	VIRTUOSI	IKOORSTT	ROOTKITS	ILNOOSTU	SOLUTION
IIOSSTTU	OUSTITIS	IKORSSTU	KURTOSIS	ILNOOSTY	SNOOTILY
IIPRSSTU	SPIRITUS	IKORSTTU	OUTSKIRT	ILNOOTUV	VOLUTION
IJJMSSUU	JUJUISMS	ILLLMOPS	PLIMSOLL	ILNOPRSU	PURLOINS
IJJSSTUU	JUJITSUS	ILLLMPPU	PULPMILL	ILNOPSSU	PULSIONS
	JUJUISTS	ILLLOOPP	LOLLIPOP		UPSILONS
IJJSTUUU	JIUJUTSU	ILLLOOWY	WOOLLILY	ILNOPSSW	SNOWSLIP
IJKLLOSY	KILLJOYS	ILLLOPPY	POLYPILL	ILNOPSSY	YPSILONS
IJLNOQSU	JONQUILS	ILLMNOSU	MULLIONS	ILNOPSTU	UNSPOILT
IJMPSTUU	JUMPSUIT	ILLMNRSU	MILLRUNS	ILNORSST	NOSTRILS
IJNNOSTU	UNJOINTS	ILLMOORS	MOORILLS	ILNORSSU	SURLOINS
IJNNSTUU	NINJUTSU	ILLMOOST	TIMOLOLS	ILNORSTU	TORULINS
IKKLNORW	LINKWORK	ILLMOPRW	PILLWORM	ILNORSTY	NITROSYL
IKKLNOSY	KOLINSKY	ILLMOPSS	PLIMSOLS	ILNORTXY	NITROXYL
IKKMNOSU	KIKUMONS	ILLMOSSY	LISSOMLY	ILNOSSTW	STOWLINS
IKKMOOOR	KOROMIKO	ILLMPSUY	PSYLLIUM	ILNOSSTY	TYLOSINS
IKKNORST	KIRKTONS	ILLMPTUY	MULTIPLY	ILNOSTTY	SNOTTILY
IKKORSSY	SIKORSKY	ILLNOORT	TORNILLO	ILNOSTUV	VOLUTINS
IKLLMORW	MILLWORK	ILLNOQSU	QUILLONS	ILNOSUVY	VINOUSLY
IKLLOOTV	KILOVOLT	ILLNORSU	RULLIONS	ILNPSUVU	PULVINUS
IKLLOSSY	KYLLOSIS	ILLNPSUU	LUPULINS	ILOOORSS	ROSOLIOS
IKLLOSTU	OUTKILLS	ILLOOPRW	POORWILL	ILOOPPRS	PROPOLIS
IKLLPSSU	UPSKILLS	ILLOORSZ	ZORILLOS	ILOOPSST	POLOISTS
IKLMNPSU	LUMPKINS	ILLOORTT	ROTOTILL		TOPSOILS
IKLMOOSS	LOOKISMS	ILLOPPSS	SLIPSLOP	ILOORSTU	RISOLUTO
	LOOKSISM	ILLOPPSY	SLOPPILY	ILOOSSST	SOLOISTS
IKLMOPSS	MILKSOPS	ILLOPRTW	PILLWORT	ILOPPSTU	POPULIST
IKLMORSW	SILKWORM	ILLOPRXY	PROLIXLY	ILOPPTUU	OUTPUPIL
IKLMORTW	MILKWORT	ILLOPSST	POLLISTS	ILOPRSTY	SPORTILY
IKLMOSSY	SOYMILKS	ILLORSTU	TROLLIUS	ILOPSSTU	SLIPOUTS
IKLNOOST	KILOTONS	ILLORSUY	ILLUSORY	ILOPSTTY	SPOTTILY
IKLNOOSW	WOOLSKIN	ILLOSSYY	LYOLYSIS	ILOPSUVV	PLUVIOUS
IKLNOPST	SLIPKNOT	ILLOSTUW	OUTWILLS	ILOQRTUU	LOQUITUR
IKLNORST	LINKROTS	ILLOSTXY	XYLITOLS	ILPPRTUY	PULPITRY
IKLNOTTY	KNOTTILY	ILLOTTWY	WITTOLLY	ILRSTTUY	TRUSTILY
IKLNPSSU	SKULPINS	ILLRSTUY	SULTRILY	ILRSTUUX	LUXURIST
IKLNPSUY	SPUNKILY	ILLSTTUY	SLUTTILY	ILSSSTTY	STYLISTS
IKLOOPSY	SPOOKILY	ILMMSSSU	SLUMISMS	IMMNOORS	MORONISM
IKLOOSST	LOOKISTS	ILMNOOPS	POLONISM	IMMNOSSU	MUSIMONS
IKLOOSTT	TOOLKITS	ILMNOOPU	POLONIUM	IMMNOSUU	MUONIUMS
IKLOSSSU	SOUSLIKS	ILMNOSUU	LUMINOUS	IMMOORTU	MOTORIUM
IKMNNOSW	MISKNOWN	ILMNOTTU	MULTITON	IMMOPSTU	OPTIMUMS
IKMNOOOS	OKIMONOS	ILMOPPSU	POPULISM	IMMOSSTU	STOMIUMS
IKMNOORS	OMIKRONS	ILMORSTU	TURMOILS	IMMRSTUY	SUMMITRY
IKMNOOSS	MONOSKIS	ILMORSTY	STORMILY	IMMSSSTU	SUMMISTS
IKMNORSY	SKYRMION	ILMOSTUV	VOLUMIST	IMNNNOSU	MUNNIONS
IKMNOSSW	MISKNOWS	ILMOSTUY	TIMOUSLY	IMNNOORS	NORIMONS
IKMNPPSU	PUMPKINS	ILMPPTUU	PULPITUM	IMNNOOTT	MONOTINT
IKMNRSTU	TRINKUMS	ILMPSSTU	PLUMISTS	IMNNOSUU	NUMINOUS
IKNNOPSY	PONYSKIN	ILMPSTUY	STUMPILY	IMNOOPPS	POMPIONS
IKNNRSTU	TURNSKIN	ILMSSTTU	STIMULUS	IMNOOPST	TOMPIONS
IKNOOPRT	PINKROOT	ILMSTTUY	SMUTTILY	IMNOOPSU	OPSONIUM
IKNOORRW	IRONWORK	ILNNORSU	LINURONS	IMNOORRS	MORRIONS
IKNOOSST	ISOKONTS	ILNOOPRT	PLIOTRON	IMNOORST	MONITORS
IKNOPRSW	PINWORKS	ILNOOPSS	PLOSIONS		TROMINOS
IKNOPSST	INKSPOTS	ILNOOPSV	VOLPINOS	IMNOORTY	MONITORY

	MORONITY
IMNOORVY	OMNIVORY
IMNOOSUX	OXONIUMS
IMNOPPSU	PUMPIONS
IMNOPRSW	PINWORMS
IMNOPSSU	SPUMONIS
IMNORRSU	MURRIONS
IMNORSTY	TRIONYMS
IMNOSTUU	MUTINOUS
IMNRSTUU	UNTRUISM
IMOOPRRS	PROMISOR
IMOOPRST	IMPOSTOR
IMOOPRSU	IMPOROUS
IMOOQSTU	MOSQUITO
IMOORRTT	TRIMOTOR
IMOORSTT	MOTORIST
IMOORSTU	SUMOTORI
	TIMOROUS
IMOORSTY	MOROSITY
IMOORTVY	VOMITORY
IMOOSSTY	MYOSOTIS
IMOOSTUV	VOMITOUS
IMOPPRRU	PROPRIUM
IMOPRRSY	PRIMROSY
IMOPRSST	TROPISMS
IMOPRSTU	PROTIUMS
IMOPSSST	MISSTOPS
IMOPSSTU	UTOPISMS
IMORSSST	MISSORTS
IMORSSTU	TOURISMS
IMORSTTU	MISTUTOR
	TUTORISM
IMOSSSTU	MISSOUTS
	SUMOISTS
IMOSSTUW	OUTSWIMS
IMPPPSUY	PUPPYISM
IMRSSSTU	SISTRUMS
IMRSSTTU	MISTRUST
IMRSSTTY	MISTRYST
IMRSTTUY	YTTRIUMS
INNNNOOU	NONUNION
INNNOOPT	NONPOINT
INNNOPRT	NONPRINT
INNNORSU	RUNNIONS
INNNORTU	TRUNNION
INNNOSTY	SYNTONIN
INNOOPRT	TROPONIN
INNOOPRU	PROUNION
INNOOPSS	OPSONINS
	SPONSION
INNOOPSU	UNPOISON
INNOORST	NOTORNIS
INNOPRSU	UNPRISON
INNORTTU	NOTTURNI
INNOSSTU	NONSUITS
INOOOSSZ	ZOONOSIS
INOOOTXZ	ZOOTOXIN
INOOPRST	PORTIONS
	POSITRON
	SORPTION
INOOPSSS	POISSONS
INOOPSST	POSITONS
INOOPSTT	SPITTOON
INOOPTTU	OUTPOINT
INOORSST	ISOTRONS
	TORSIONS
INOORSSU	ROSINOUS
INOORSTT	TORTONIS
INOORSTY	SONORITY
INOOSTTV	STOTINOV
INOPPSST	TOPSPINS
INOPRTTU	PRINTOUT
INOPRTUY	PUNITORY
INOPSSSU	POUSSINS
INOPSSSY	SYNOPSIS
INOPSSTU	SPINOUTS
INORSSUV	UNVISORS
INOSSTUW	SNOWSUIT
INPPRRUU	PURPURIN
INPRRSTU	SURPRINT
INPRSSTU	UNSTRIPS
INPRSSTY	TRYPSINS
INPRSTTU	TURNSPIT
INRSSTTU	INTRUSTS
INRSTTUU	UNITRUST
INSSSTUU	SUNSUITS
INSSTTUW	UNTWISTS
IOOPRRSV	PROVISOR
IOOPRSSV	PROVISOS
IOOPRSSY	ISOSPORY
IOOPRSTT	POSTRIOT
IOOPRSTY	ISOTROPY
	POROSITY
IOORRSTY	SORORITY
IOORRTTT	TROTTOIR
IOORSSTT	RISOTTOS
IOORSSUV	VOUSSOIR
IOORSTTU	TORTIOUS
IOORSTTY	TOROSITY
IOORSTUV	VIRTUOSO
IOORSUUX	UXORIOUS
IOOSSTTU	STOTIOUS
IOPPPRST	PITPROPS
IOPPRSST	RIPSTOPS
IOPRRSUV	PROVIRUS
IOPRSSTT	PROTISTS
	TROPISTS
IOPRSSUU	SPURIOUS
IOPRSTTU	OUTSTRIP
IOPRSTUU	POURSUIT
IOPRSTUY	PYRITOUS
IOPRSUVX	POXVIRUS
IOPSSTTU	UTOPISTS
IOQRSTTU	QUITTORS
IOQRSTUU	TURQUOIS
IOQRTUXY	QUIXOTRY
IORRSSST	TSORRISS
IORRSUVV	SURVIVOR
IORSSTTU	TOURISTS
IORSSTTW	TWISTORS
IORSSUUU	USURIOUS
IORSTTUY	TOURISTY
	YTTRIOUS
IORSTUUV	VIRTUOUS
IPPTTTUY	TITTUPPY
IPRRSSTU	STIRRUPS
IPRRSTUU	PRURITUS
IPRSSTUU	PURSUITS
JJSSTUUU	JUJUTSUS
JLNSTUUY	UNJUSTLY
JLOOSUYY	JOYOUSLY
JMOPSTUU	OUTJUMPS
JNNOORRU	NONJUROR
JNOORSSU	SOJOURNS
JNOOSUUY	UNJOYOUS
KKMMOOOO	MOKOMOKO
KKNOORTW	KNOTWORK
KKOOOOTT	TOKOTOKO
KKOOSSUU	KOUSKOUS
KLLMNSUU	NUMSKULL
KLLMOSSU	MOLLUSKS
KLNORSTY	KLYSTRON
KLOOORWW	WOOLWORK
KLOOOSTU	LOOKOUTS
	OUTLOOKS
KLOOPRSW	SLOPWORK
KLOSSTUU	OUTSULKS
KMOOORRW	WORKROOM
KMOORSTU	MUSKROOT
KNNNOSUW	UNKNOWNS
KNOOPSTT	TOPKNOTS
KNOPPSTU	POSTPUNK
KNOPRSTY	KRYPTONS
KNORRSTY	KRYTRONS
KOOORSTV	VOORSKOT
KOOPRSTW	TOPWORKS
	WORKTOPS
KOORSTUW	OUTWORKS
	WORKOUTS
KORRSTWY	TRYWORKS
KORSTTUW	TUTWORKS
LLLMMSUU	MULMULLS
LLLOOPPY	LOLLYPOP
LLMOOPRS	ROLLMOPS
LLMOPRUU	PULLORUM
LLOOPRST	TROLLOPS
LLOOPRTY	TROLLOPY
LLOOPSTU	OUTPOLLS
LLOORSTU	OUTROLLS
	ROLLOUTS
LLOPSTUU	OUTPULLS
	PULLOUTS
LLOSUUVV	VOLVULUS
LMNOOOPY	MONOPOLY
LMNOOPYY	POLYONYM
LMOOOOPR	POOLROOM
LMOOOORT	TOOLROOM
LMOOPRTU	PULMOTOR
LMOOPSYY	POLYSOMY
LMOORSWW	SLOWWORM
LMOOSSSU	MOLOSSUS
LMOOTXYY	XYLOTOMY
LMOPPRTY	PROMPTLY

LMOSTUUU	TUMULOUS	**MNOOORXY**	OXYMORON	**NOOPRSSS**	SPONSORS
LMRSSTUU	LUSTRUMS	**MNOOPRTU**	PRONOTUM	**NOORSSTU**	UNROOSTS
LNOOOPRT	POLTROON	**MNOOPSTY**	TOPONYMS	**NOORSTUW**	OUTSWORN
LNOOOPYZ	POLYZOON	**MNOOPTYY**	TOPONYMY	**NOPSSSTU**	SUNSPOTS
LNOOPPRY	PROPYLON	**MNOORSSU**	SUNROOMS	**NORSTTUU**	OUTTURNS
LNOOPSSU	UNSPOOLS	**MNOOSTTW**	TOWMONTS		TURNOUTS
LNOOPSTU	PULTOONS	**MNORSSTU**	NOSTRUMS		
LNOOPSWW	SNOWPLOW	**MNORSTUU**	SURMOUNT	**NOSTTTUU**	OUTSTUNT
LNRSTUUV	VULTURNS	**MOOOPRRT**	PROMOTOR	**NRSSTTUU**	UNTRUSTS
LOOOORSS	OLOROSOS	**MOOORRTW**	MOORWORT	**NRSTTUUY**	UNTRUSTY
LOOPPSUU	POPULOUS		ROOTWORM	**OOOOPRST**	POTOROOS
LOOPPSUY	POLYPOUS		TOMORROW	**OOOPRSSU**	SOPOROUS
LOOPRSTT	STOLPORT		WORMROOT	**OOOPRSTU**	OUTROOPS
LOOPRSUY	POROUSLY	**MOOPSSSU**	OPOSSUMS	**OOOORSTTU**	OUTROOTS
LOOPSTTU	OUTPLOTS	**MOORRSUU**	RUMOROUS	**OOPRSSSU**	SOURSOPS
LORSSTUU	LUSTROUS	**MOORSTUU**	TUMOROUS	**OOPRSSTV**	PROVOSTS
MMNNOOSY	MONONYMS	**MOORSTUY**	UROSTOMY	**OOPRSTTU**	OUTPORTS
MMNOOOSY	MONOSOMY	**MOPRTTUU**	OUTTRUMP		OUTSPORT
MMOORTTY	TOMMYROT	**MORRSSTU**	ROSTRUMS	**OOPRSTUU**	OUTPOURS
MMOPSSTY	SYMPTOMS	**MORSSTUU**	STRUMOUS	**OOPSSSTT**	TOSSPOTS
MNNOOOSS	MONSOONS	**MSSTTUUU**	TSUTSUMU	**OOPSSTTU**	OUTPOSTS
MNNOOOTY	MONOTONY	**NNOOOPST**	PONTOONS	**OORSTTTU**	OUTTROTS
MNNOORSU	MONURONS		SPONTOON	**OORSTTUU**	TORTUOUS
MNNOPRTU	NONTRUMP	**NNOOPRSU**	PRONOUNS	**OPPRRSTU**	PURPORTS
MNNOSSYY	SYNONYMS	**NNOOPSSS**	SPONSONS	**OPPRRSTU**	SUPPORTS
MNNOSTUU	UNMOUNTS	**NNOOPSST**	NONSTOPS	**OPRSSSUU**	SOURPUSS
MNNOSYYY	SYNONYMY	**NNOORSTY**	NONSTORY	**ORRSSTTU**	TRUSTORS
MNOOOPPS	POMPOONS	**NNOORTTU**	NOTTURNO	**ORSSTTUU**	SURTOUTS
MNOOOPRT	MOONPORT	**NOOOPPRS**	PROSOPON	**RRSSSUUU**	SUSURRUS
MNOOORTW	MOONWORT	**NOOORSSU**	SONOROUS		